P9-CKJ-899

CONTENTS

PAC UPDATE

This PAC is involved in nuclear energy issues. See pp. 216–217 for related PACs.

CBS Corp.

*Phone: (212) 975-4321 * Fax: (212) 975-8714*
51 W. 52nd St., New York, NY 10019-6188
Web: www.wec.com

In December 1997, Westinghouse Electric Co. became CBS, moving its headquarters from Pittsburgh to New York. The CBS television network is the second-rated network behind NBC. CBS sold off most of its non-industrial businesses but continues to build nuclear fuel assemblies and core components for nuclear power plants, electric power generators and gas and steam turbines. With 1997 sales of $5.3 billion, the public company employs about 59,000 people.

The company is seeking to sell nuclear equipment to China. It also supports funding for the Department of Energy's Advanced Light Water Reactor program.

The Westinghouse Electric PAC contributed the most money to 1996 congressional campaigns of any electronics manufacturing PAC. Nearly 95 percent of the contributions went to incumbent candidates. The leading recipients were Sens. Pete V. Domenici, R-N.M., and Mitch McConnell, R-Ky.; each received more than $5,000. No Democratic candidate received more than $3,650 from the company.

The company's PAC will continue under the Westinghouse name. The CBS television unit does not have a PAC.

Westinghouse Electric Corp. Employees Political Participation Program (C00035220) *Phone: (202) 945-6400 * Fax: (202) 945-6404 * 600 New Hampshire Ave. N.W., Suite 1200, Washington, DC 20037 * E-mail: zoglmanrr@westinghouse.com * Treasurer: Robert R. Zoglman*

	1993-94	*1995-96*	*1997*	*Totals*
Receipts	$270,415	$261,970	$120,482	$652,867
Disburse	271,600	245,987	114,222	631,809
Cash	24,976	40,965	47,232	n/a
Contributions	225,175	218,855	96,050	540,080
Republicans	75,825	148,155	68,300	292,280
No. of Cand.	*69*	*109*	*54*	*232*
House	51,825	89,800	41,300	182,925
Senate	24,000	58,355	27,000	109,355
Democrats	149,350	70,700	27,750	247,800
No. of Cand.	*108*	*68*	*28*	*204*
House	105,250	59,200	22,250	186,700
Senate	44,100	11,500	5,500	61,100
Incumbents	203,575	206,505	95,800	505,880
Challengers	9,000	1,000	0	10,000
Open Seat	12,100	10,350	250	22,700
Winners	185,525	195,730	n/a	381,255
Losers	39,650	23,125	n/a	62,775

PREFACE

CQ's Federal PACs Directory 1998–99 provides information on political action committees that contributed $5,000 or more to congressional candidates during the 1995–96 election cycle. It also includes smaller PACs affiliated with those that met CQ's criteria.

CQ's team of 10 researchers delved into corporate filings, web sites, news reports and press releases to profile the organizations behind the PACs and to provide added insight into the policy objectives and spending trends of the 200 largest PACs (screened in gray throughout). The directory includes detailed contact information, including corporate and Washington addresses, phone and fax numbers, Internet addresses and the names of key decision-making personnel.

Also included is an exclusive CQ introductory essay examining the history and impact of PACs on the United States election system.

The appendix features charts that provide PAC rankings and invite easy comparisons. Indexes allow readers to search out PACs based on geographical location, name of sponsoring organization or PAC, and name of PAC personnel.

Information used to develop the spending analyses for each PAC comes from Federal Election Commission records. For the 1995–96 election cycle, FEC data was provided by the Center for Responsive Politics, which created the system employed in this book for identifying similar business and ideological interests. For the 1993–94 and 1997–98 election cycles, the data came directly from the FEC. The FEC provides summary figures for receipts, disbursements and cash on hand. From the itemized contributions, CQ calculated other totals.

CQ's analysis was limited to cash or in-kind contributions from PACs to congressional campaigns. Contributions to presidential candidates, independent expenditures, coordinated expenditures and communication costs were excluded from the charts.

Dan Gainor
Peter Roybal
Derek Willis

Dan Gainor is Senior Editor in CQ New Media, in charge of information about members of Congress, candidates and campaign finance. **Peter Roybal** tracks CQ information on members of Congress, candidates and campaign finance for CQ New Media. **Derek Willis** specializes in computer-assisted reporting for CQ New Media.

WHAT THE NUMBERS MEAN

Contributions: Total cash and in-kind contributions to congressional campaigns. This figure excludes money to presidential campaigns and independent expenditures, which may be made with or without a candidate's consent.

Republicans/Democrats: Total amount to Republican/Democratic congressional campaigns. While PACs did contribute to Independent or third-party candidates, the total was insignificant by comparison to the two major political parties.

Number of Candidates: Total number of congressional candidates of each party who received contributions.

House/Senate: Total amount given to House candidates and Senate candidates of each party.

Incumbents/Challengers/Open Seat: Incumbents were defined as members of Congress who received money for use during the current election cycle or future election cycles. Contributions to candidates who lost in a previous cycle were ignored because those candidates were not incumbents, challengers or open seat candidates in the current election cycle. For example, a 1997 contribution given to a candidate who lost in 1996 would be excluded from these totals.

	1993-94	*1995-96*	*1997*	*Totals*
Receipts	$63,657	$72,629	$40,060	$176,346
Disburse	62,400	76,126	26,005	164,531
Cash	25,777	22,279	36,234	n/a
Contributions	61,400	74,950	24,500	160,850
Republicans	48,650	67,700	21,500	137,850
No. of Cand.	*52*	*83*	*37*	*172*
House	26,650	49,000	18,000	93,650
Senate	22,000	18,700	3,500	44,200
Democrats	11,250	7,250	2,500	21,000
No. of Cand.	*16*	*12*	*4*	*32*
House	10,750	5,000	1,500	17,250
Senate	500	2,250	1,000	3,750
Incumbents	35,400	41,250	23,000	99,650
Challengers	5,000	10,700	1,500	17,200
Open Seat	21,000	23,000	0	44,000
Winners	48,900	54,750	n/a	103,650
Losers	12,500	20,200	n/a	32,700

Winners: Total amount given to candidates who actually won a race or were members of Congress during a particular election cycle. For example, a 1996 contribution to a senator not up for election in 1996 was counted in the "Winners" total.

Losers: Total amount given to candidates during the election cycle who did not win or were not members of Congress. Thus, it includes people who dropped out of the race, lost in previous elections or actually lost in that election cycle. Winners and losers for the 1997–98 election cycle were not calculated because those elections had not yet taken place.

INTRODUCTION

By Jonathan D. Salant

Although political action committees (PACs) have been around for more than half a century, only in the last 25 years have they become a major participant in political campaigns. From a total of 608 at the end of 1974, the number of PACs registered at the Federal Election Commission (FEC) exploded during the next 10 years. By the end of 1984, there were 3,954 PACs. As of Dec. 31, 1997, there were 3,844.

As the number of PACs has grown, so has their importance to congressional incumbents. During the 1995–96 election cycle, which covered the period Jan. 1, 1995, through Dec. 31, 1996, PACs gave $217.8 million to federal candidates, two-thirds of it going to officeholders. Almost one-third of the money raised by the average House candidate came from PACs, and six House members reported raising at least $1 million in PAC contributions. During the previous election cycle, 1993–94, PACs gave $189.6 million to federal candidates. Three House members took in more than $1 million each in PAC money. Twelve years earlier, in 1981–82, PACs gave $87.6 million to federal candidates.

Types of PACs

There are two basic types of PACs: connected and non-connected. Corporations, trade associations, and unions can set up what are known as connected PACs. The parent organization can use its own money to pay the expenses of operating and raising money for the PAC, can name the officers of the PAC, and can decide how the PAC will spend its money. Political contributions to the PAC, however, cannot be made with the organization's money. The PAC can only solicit contributions from people connected with the parent organization, such as company employees or union members, and the funds must be kept in a separate bank account. Connected PACs must register with the FEC within 10 days of their creation. They must name a treasurer before they can begin accepting contributions or spending money.

Non-connected PACs are not tied to a corporation, trade association or labor union. The expenses of operating and raising money for the PAC must be paid out of the PAC's funds, although sponsoring organizations can contribute up to $5,000 a year to help pay expenses. While connected PACs are limited as to whom they can ask for contributions, there are no such restrictions for non-connected PACs. Anyone can give. These PACs must register with the FEC within 10 days of raising or spending at least $1,000 in a calendar year. Similar to connected PACs, these committees also must have a treasurer in place before they can begin accepting contributions or spending money.

Contribution Limits and Disclosure Requirements

PACs can accept contributions of $5,000 a year per person. They can give $5,000 to a candidate (five times more than the $1,000 that individuals can contribute) for both the primary and general elections, or $10,000 a year. In states with runoff elections, the PAC can give an additional $5,000. To be eligible for these larger limits, a PAC must have been registered with the FEC for at least six months, have taken in contributions from more than 50 people and have made donations of any amount to at least five federal candidates.

Those contributions and expenditures must be reported regularly to the FEC. A PAC can decide whether to file its disclosure forms monthly or quarterly. Monthly PACs disclose their contributions and expenditures every month, except for election years when they skip their November and December reports in favor of filing forms before and after the general election. Quarterly PACs file every three months during election years, and before and after the general election. They also may have to file before primary elections. In nonelection years, they file only twice.

Congressional candidates must file with the FEC twice a year in off-years, after June 30 and after Dec. 31. In years in which they are running for office, candidates must file on April 15, July 15, Oct. 15, plus 12 days before the primary elections in their states, 12 days before the general election, 30 days after the general election, and at the end of the year. This accelerated filing schedule applies to Senate candidates once every six years, but to House candidates every other year.

Jonathan D. Salant, a reporter in the Washington bureau of the Associated Press, has covered campaign finance issues on the local, state and federal levels for 20 years.

Controversy Over PACs

Ironically, while campaign finance reformers have set their sights on banning or further restricting PACs, the PACs themselves initially were seen as a major reform. Legislation signed into law in 1972 and 1974 not only made it easier to create political action committees but imposed new financial disclosure requirements so that the public would know which interest groups were making campaign contributions and which candidates were receiving them. The 1974 bill also established the FEC.

If there was any doubt about the role that unions and corporations could play in setting up and running their own political action committees, it was alleviated in 1975. That year, the FEC told the Sun Oil Company that it could pay all of the expenses and make all of the decisions regarding its SunPAC, just as long as the contributions made to the PAC were voluntary. The decision made it clear that corporations and labor unions could finance the operations of their PACs and decide which candidates would receive their contributions.

Today, critics charge that PACs distort the system by giving special interests the access to lawmakers that average citizens do not have. And because most PAC money goes to incumbents, lawmakers seeking reelection have a huge fundraising advantage over challengers. Two of every three dollars contributed by PACs during the 1996 congressional elections went to incumbents. Challengers received only 14 percent of the money.

Campaign finance expert Anthony Corrado, a professor of government at Colby College in Waterville, Maine, thinks PACs play an important role on the political stage.

"They allow small donors to contribute to the group they're members of so their voice can be heard in federal election campaigns," Corrado said. "They're one of the ways individuals pursue their desire to be represented in the political process. They serve as a vehicle for amassing a large number of small contributions and exercising the voice of those small contributors in the political process."

The controversy over PACs has colored efforts to change the way congressional campaigns are funded. Indeed, in the early 1990s PACs were Public Enemy No. 1 in the eyes of those trying to overhaul the system. Then came the 1996 campaign finance controversies, which revealed how both major political parties took in millions of dollars in funds directly from corporations and labor unions. These unregulated sums, known as "soft money," were supposed to be used for get-out-the-vote drives and party-building activities such as voter registration, but instead went for issue-oriented commercials to help specific candidates.

After the 1996 elections, the proponents of the major campaign finance overhaul legislation pending on Capitol Hill—Sens. John McCain, R-Ariz., and Russell D. Feingold, D-Wis., in the Senate, and Reps. Christopher Shays, R-Conn., and Martin T. Meehan, D-Mass., in the House—modified their bills to ban soft money rather than PACs.

Despite the new scrutiny of soft money, PACs still receive their share of criticism. Larry Makinson, executive director of the Center for Responsive Politics, a Washington, D.C.-based organization that studies the relationship between money and campaigns, called PACs the "cash constituents" of Congress.

"Most members of Congress have two major sources of money," Makinson said. "Individual contributions overwhelmingly are local. The other source of money is PAC money coming overwhelmingly in Washington."

PAC money has local origins as well. BellSouth's PAC, for example, is funded by its employees through a voluntary checkoff. Much of that money is earmarked for the members of Congress who represent the states in which the regional telephone company operates.

"You want to be able to help employees channel their political contributions in a meaningful way," said Bill McCloskey of BellSouth. "We encourage our employees to participate in the political system. When people get involved, they want to contribute money as well as their time."

PACs actually date to World War II. In 1943, banned by the federal government from using union dues to make political contributions, the Congress of Industrial Organizations (CIO) started a fund to collect voluntary contributions from its members. That fund was then used to make political contributions. Its name: the Political Action Committee. The CIO later merged with the American Federation of Labor (AFL) to form the AFL-CIO, which continues to run a PAC. Now called the Committee on Public Education, or COPE, the AFL-CIO PAC contributed $1.2 million to federal candidates in 1995–96. Only 28 political action committees in the country gave more.

In the 1970s, PACs became the vehicle of choice for organizations that wanted to make their contributions count. They received a boost when President Richard Nixon signed legislation in 1972 (PL 92-225) that revised the campaign finance laws. The bill banned corporations and unions from contributing directly to federal campaigns and instead allowed those groups to pay the expenses of running their own PACs and seeking voluntary contributions.

"The law forbade corporations and trade unions from making direct contributions out of their treasuries," said Frank Sorauf, Regents' professor emeritus of political science at the

University of Minnesota. "If they were going to be active politically, they were going to have to raise money voluntarily and solely for the purpose of making campaign contributions."

Major PAC Contributors

While business political action committees contribute more money than labor PACs overall, 12 of the 20 individual PACs that contributed the most money to federal campaigns in 1995–96 were union committees. The PAC contributions often are part of an overall lobbying effort to pass favorable legislation, or kill an unfavorable bill, in Congress.

In 1995–96, labor unions helped lead the successful fight to raise the minimum wage, and they fought back efforts to allow businesses to offer their employees compensatory time off rather than overtime pay. During the previous election cycle, 1993–94, when 10 of the top 20 PACs were union committees, labor waged an unsuccessful fight to scuttle the North American Free Trade Agreement.

The Teamsters Union's Democratic Republican Independent Voter Education Committee gave more money to congressional candidates during the 1995–96 election cycle than any other PAC, FEC records show. The Teamsters contributed $2.6 million, slightly above the $2.4 million they gave to candidates during 1993–94. High on the Teamsters' agenda, according to the Center for Responsive Politics, was stopping Republican attempts to scale back the Occupational Safety and Health Administration. The Teamsters also weighed in on highway funding and trade issues.

In second place was the American Federation of State, County and Municipal Employees, which gave $2.5 million to federal candidates, about the same as in 1993–94.

The biggest nonunion giver in 1995–96 was the Association of Trial Lawyers PAC, which gave $2.3 million to candidates. The trial lawyers staunchly opposed efforts by the new Republican majorities in the House and Senate to limit punitive damages in product liability cases. The trial lawyers gave $2.1 million in 1993–94.

Other big givers included the National Rifle Association's (NRA) Political Victory Fund, which gave $1.56 million in 1995–96 and $1.8 million in 1993–94. The issue of gun owners rights was atop the congressional agenda during President Bill Clinton's first term in office. Congress in 1993 enacted a five-day waiting period for handgun purchases and a year later passed a crime bill that included a ban on many assault weapons. When the Republicans captured control of Congress after the 1994 elections, they pledged to do away with the assault weapons ban. The House in 1996 voted to repeal it, but the issue never came up in the Senate.

The PAC that gave the most money in 1993–94 was United Parcel Service (UPS). The company PAC gave $2.6 million to federal candidates. According to the Center for Responsive Politics, UPS opposed efforts to allow the U.S. Postal Service more flexibility in setting its rates and asked Congress to block Labor Department efforts to establish ergonomics regulations. In 1995–96, UPS gave $1.8 million to federal candidates.

Overall, corporate PACs gave $78.2 million to federal candidates in 1995–96, as compared to $48.0 million for labor PACs.

Why Do PACs Contribute?

"Cash is what makes campaigns run," said McCloskey of BellSouth, whose telecommunications PAC contributed $545,867 in 1995–96, 14th highest among corporate political action committees. "When you go to a fundraiser, which costs you money to get in, the candidates or member is likely to be there. You're viewed as a friend if you're contributing to the campaign."

In many cases, the pressure to give comes from the lawmakers themselves. "The incumbents are making the most requests," McCloskey said. "For the most part, our donations are made in response to requests."

Especially after the last two elections, which involved high numbers of first-term members of Congress, lawmakers quickly held fundraisers to pay off debts and build up their campaign bank accounts for the next go-round.

"The quid pro quo can run both ways," Sorauf said. "They [PACs] may find themselves making contributions because they feel they have to make contributions. A number of incumbents made it very clear to PACs that they would incur their disfavor if they didn't make contributions."

When Sallie Mae, the giant student loan company, recently became a private corporation, company executives quickly formed a PAC just in time for the big debate over federal higher education programs. "It's more or less a way to control your own fate and play in the political process the way others like you do," Scott Miller, Sallie Mae's director of government relations, told the Associated Press.

PACs make these contributions as part of their overall lobbying strategy. Many times, corporate lobbyists direct the contributions of their company's PAC. Indeed, a PAC often serves as an admission ticket to the political arena.

"I don't think that they [PACs] get a vote," Republican fundraiser Carolyn Machado said. "But I do see they obviously have access. They're coming to the parties and the dinners. They get their opinions heard. They get an opportunity to present their views."

When lobbyists or PAC representatives call later for an appointment to see the lawmaker, it is hard to tell them no. Rep. Amo Houghton, a New York Republican and former chief executive officer of Corning Glass Works, which had its own PAC, said lawmakers certainly are willing to make time to meet with a representative of a company whose PAC is going to make a $10,000 contribution.

"If somebody comes into your office and says, 'I'd like to max out with you,' that person certainly has a greater ear than a person who hasn't given a dime," Houghton told *The Post-Standard* of Syracuse, N.Y. "That's the way these things work."

PAC contributions go up when an issue of particular importance to an industry is ready for action, and subsequently decline when the issue no longer is in the forefront.

"That's when the interests of the PACs are most challenged, so they tend to be the most active," Corrado said.

During the first six months of 1993, as Congress prepared to take up Clinton's proposed health care reform, PAC contributions from the health care industry to members of the House Ways and Means Committee—which would play a major role in writing the bill—rose by 46 percent over the equivalent period in 1991, according to a computer-assisted analysis of campaign contributions done by Newhouse News Service. The contributions increased from $671,742 to $981,279. For the 17 new members of Ways and Means, their health PAC money rose by 316 percent, from $91,304 during the first six months of 1991 to $379,575 during the same time in 1993.

On the Senate side, the new chairman of the Finance Committee, which also would play a major role in the bill, saw his health care PAC money rise 239 percent during the same period. Sen. Daniel Patrick Moynihan, D-N.Y., had taken in $50,500 from health PACs during the first six months of 1991. He raised $171,000 from those PACs during the first six months of 1993, a computer-assisted analysis by *The Post-Standard* found.

Once the bill was defeated, contributions from health care PACs dropped off. Of the 10 PACs reporting the largest decrease in contributions to candidates between 1996 and 1994, three were health-related. Contributions from the American Nurses Association PAC declined 27 percent, from $1.08 million in 1993–94 to $788,508 in 1995–96. Contributions from the American Chiropractic Association PAC declined more sharply, from $576,628 in 1993–94 to $191,410 in 1995–96, a two-thirds drop-off.

In contrast, when the new Republican majorities in the House and Senate pledged to deregulate the telecommunications industry, those industry PACs readily pumped in money to members of Congress. SBC Communications increased its PAC giving by 76 percent from 1993–94 to 1995–96, from $286,850 to $504,333. Ameritech's contributions rose by 47 percent, from $428,957 to $632,285. And Bell Atlantic boosted its PAC donations from $81,250 in 1993–94 to $275,998 in 1995–96, a jump of 239 percent.

While it is illegal for a lawmaker to sell a vote for a campaign contribution, some political observers insist that PACs are getting more for their money than simply an appointment.

"These people wouldn't be giving all this money if it wasn't buying something," Makinson said. "And that something has to be more than getting your foot in the door of the congressman's office."

Others say the PACs simply are giving to lawmakers who already agree with them.

In 1997, both the House and the Senate took up proposals to cut the amount of money the Forest Service was spending to build logging roads in national forests. Proponents of the cuts said the roads were harmful to the environment and questioned whether private industry should be subsidized when Congress was trying to balance the federal budget. Opponents said the roads were important to local economies and were used by visitors in addition to businesses.

In the Senate, the lawmakers who supported the timber industry and voted to keep the federal funding for logging roads received an average of $42,880 from timber companies from 1991 through 1996, according to the Center for Responsive Politics. The lawmakers who voted to cut the funding received an average of $8,565 during the same six-year period.

Likewise, House members who wanted to continue funding construction of logging roads received an average of $3,873 from timber company PACs during the 1995–96 election cycle. Those who wanted to cut the road construction budget received an average of $606.

The power of money was evident during the debate over the North American Free Trade Agreement (NAFTA). Of the 20 lawmakers that received at least 62 percent of their PAC contributions from organized labor between Jan. 1, 1991, and June 30, 1993, 19 voted against NAFTA. Only Rep. Alcee Hastings, D-Fla., supported the trade agreement. Likewise, virtually all of those who received the greatest percentage of their PAC money from business voted for NAFTA, a top priority of the business community.

In reauthorizing the Federal Aviation Administration in 1996, Congress also included a provision that potentially made it harder for Federal Express employees to unionize—a measure the company had sought. In 1995–96, Federal Express' political action committee contributed $948,000 to congressional candidates, the fourth highest among corporate PACs.

Archer-Daniels-Midland Co. (ADM) made $208,976 worth of contributions in 1995–96. ADM is the nation's largest producer of ethanol, a fuel made from corn, and has successfully blocked efforts to eliminate the federal tax break of 5.4 cents a gallon that ethanol receives.

Food industry PACs gave $41 million in campaign contributions between 1987 and 1997, according to the Center for Public Integrity. The center said the industry was able to prevent or weaken legislation that would tighten regulations for meat and other foods. Congress, for example, has been unwilling to give the agriculture secretary the power to recall tainted meat and has refused to levy user fees on meat and poultry companies to pay for government inspections.

Who Gets PAC Money?

PACs tend to favor incumbents over challengers. Even corporate PACs in the 1980s and early 1990s, which had allies in the Republican ranks, preferred Democratic incumbents to Republican challengers. But when the Democrats lost their majorities on Capitol Hill in the 1994 midterm elections, business PACs quickly switched sides.

Lawmakers who sit on a particular committee usually attract PAC money from the corporations and unions whose concerns fall under that panel's jurisdiction. Hence, four committees are known as the money committees in the House: Appropriations, which controls most federal spending; Banking and Financial Services, since the financial community is the largest contributor to federal campaigns; Commerce, with its jurisdiction over health, energy, finance, and communications; and Ways and Means, which handles all tax bills and also has jurisdiction over health, trade and welfare.

Of the 20 people who received the most PAC money during 1997, 10 were members of one of the big four committees, and another five were members of the House Republican or Democratic leadership. Likewise, during the 1996 elections, 19 of the 20 top recipients of PAC contributions either sat on one of the big four committees or were members of leadership.

House members, who run every two years, rely more on PAC money than do senators, who run once every six years. PACs accounted for 31 percent of the money raised by the average House candidate and 16 percent of the money raised by the average Senate candidate in 1995–96.

Freshmen, traditionally the most vulnerable of all incumbents, rely heavily on PAC money when they seek a second term. Take the examples of two Republican first-termers, John Shimkus of Illinois, who ended 14 years of Democratic hegemony in his district when he won election in 1996 by 1,238 votes; and Kenny Hulshof of Missouri, who ousted 10-term Democratic incumbent Harold Volkmer by fewer than 6,000 votes.

Through Jan. 31, 1998, Shimkus, a member of the Commerce Committee, already had taken in more money from PACs—$258,710—than the $225,024 he raised for his 1996 campaign. "Freshmen members have focused on developing that firm foundation to run again," he said.

Hulshof, who sits on the Ways and Means Committee, raised $494,942 through Jan. 31, 1998, just $200,000 less than he spent for his entire 1996 campaign. He raised $236,805 from PACs, double the $117,425 in PAC money he received for his 1996 campaign.

"We've been very aggressive with our fundraising," Hulshof said. "Any potential opponent, that is a factor he or she has to take into account."

The Power of Incumbency

Even if they had not landed a seat on one of the money committees, Shimkus and Hulshof most likely would have been able to raise more PAC money for their reelection campaigns than in their initial contests. The reason is that in 1998, as opposed to 1996, they were the incumbents. Most PAC money goes to those in office, as opposed to those seeking office. During the 1995–96 election cycle, PACs gave 68 percent of their contributions, $145 million, to incumbents. Challengers received $28.5 million or 13 percent. The remainder, $39.3 million, or 18 percent, went to candidates in open seat races.

The percentage of money going to incumbents, even though it was quite high, actually was the lowest share in a decade. In 1985–86, incumbents received 69 percent of PAC money, and their share climbed to 79 percent in 1989–90. That year, challengers received only 10 percent of PAC contributions.

"In the world of PACs, pragmatism rules," Makinson said. "People don't want to spend their money on someone who's not going to win."

The large percentage of PAC contributions going to incumbents is one reason that they routinely outraise their challengers, making it easier for them to win reelection. Further, by building up huge bank accounts early, incumbents sometimes manage to dissuade potentially strong challengers from even entering the race against them.

"Raising a large war chest early on has proven to be a good way to discourage competition," Corrado said. "Potential challengers have to not only face an incumbent but an incumbent with large sums of money."

Political consultants tell their clients to raise money for their reelection early and often. "The date to win the election is on filing date, and a big fat bank account helps do that," Republican consultant Eddie Mahe said.

After the filing deadline for 1998 congressional races in Illinois had come and gone, the Democrats were left without a first-tier challenger for Shimkus. Likewise, the Republicans failed to lure former San Francisco 49ers tight end Brent Jones into the race against freshman Democrat Ellen O. Tauscher of California, who polled 49 percent of the vote in her 1996 win. Tauscher raised $398,385, including $124,669 from PACs, in 1997 alone as she geared up for her 1998 reelection effort. That amount was about two-thirds of the $187,876 in PAC money she received throughout her entire 1996 campaign. "This is all part of being in politics," Tauscher said. "We wanted to show not only our effectiveness but our competitiveness."

Jones cited the costs of campaigning in deciding not to run. "I did not play 12 years of football to buy an election," he said. "And that is part of the problem with the whole process."

Likewise, freshman Rep. Bill Pascrell Jr., D-N.J., raised $416,216 through Dec. 31, 1997, including $156,684 from PACs. "I wanted to send a message to those folks that we were serious about this," he said. "You have to find a private phone and make those [fundraising] calls. If you don't make those calls, that's like saying you're not prepared to go to your committee meeting or go to the floor and vote."

Former Republican Rep. Bill Martini, who lost to Pascrell by just 6,000 votes in 1996, declined a rematch. He, too, mentioned fundraising as a reason for not running. "To raise money, you have to drop everything and go out and spend the next eight months doing it," he said.

Matching PACs and Committees

Rep. Jim Ryun, R-Kan., a member of the House Banking and Financial Services Committee, raised $32,154 from banking and real estate interests during 1997—35 percent of the $92,325 in PAC money he took in. In 1996, he raised just $12,500 from those industries.

Ryun's fundraiser, Machado, said she went after banking PACs to contribute to the lawmaker once he landed a seat on the banking panel. "We spent the first few months talking to those folks, getting them on board, soliciting them for donations," she said.

The Center for Responsive Politics found that in 1995–96, Rep. Bud Shuster, R-Pa., received more transportation money than any other House member. Shuster chaired the House Transportation and Infrastructure Committee. Sen. John Warner, R-Va., led all recipients in receiving money from the defense industry. Warner was a senior member of the Senate Armed Services Committee. And Rep. Charles Stenholm, D-Texas, the top Democrat on the House Agriculture Committee, raised more money from agriculture interests than any other House member.

"PACs are rational actors in the political process," Corrado said. "Overwhelmingly, they tend to give to incumbents. They tend to target their donations to members who sit on committees important to their voting interests."

As keenly as business PACs watch lawmakers on key committees, so do labor PACs. Although the AFL-CIO spent $35 million in issue-oriented advertisements criticizing the voting records of several Republican incumbents in 1996, individual unions continued to give to the same GOP lawmakers on labor's hit list. Transportation unions in particular donated to Republican members of the House Transportation and Infrastructure Committee even as the parent AFL-CIO was running ads against them. Among the targeted Republicans receiving union money were Martini and Bob Franks of New Jersey, and Randy Tate of Washington State.

"Those members voted with us and we felt we should show our support for them," the national legislative director for the United Transportation Union, James Brunkenhoefer, told Congressional Quarterly during the 1996 campaign.

Switching Sides

Though Republicans traditionally are aligned with business, corporate PACs sided with the Democrats throughout the 1980s. After all, the Democrats had a majority of the House (and a majority of the Senate except from 1981 to 1986), and thus controlled the flow of legislation and the congressional agenda. Former Rep. Tony Coelho, D-Calif., then chairman of the Democratic Congressional Campaign Committee, is credited with making the argument to business PACs that they should be giving to Democrats because they were the majority party and otherwise could push through an antibusiness agenda.

The argument was persuasive. With labor also on their side, Democrats raked in close to two-thirds of all PAC contributions given to House candidates during the 10-year period beginning in 1985. Of the $42.9 million given by corporate PACs to House candidates in 1991–92, $23.4 million, or 55 percent, went to Democrats. Republicans received $19.5 million, or 45 percent. Meanwhile, labor PACs gave Democrats 94 percent of the $30.7 million they handed out to House candidates.

All that changed with the Republican takeover of the House in the 1994 midterm elections, the first time the GOP controlled that chamber since 1954. Overnight, business PACs rushed to support the new Republican majority in a marriage of ideology and political pragmatism.

Still, Democrats received a majority of corporate PAC money during 1993–94, since they were in control until the very end. In 1993–94, 54 percent, or $23.6 million, went to Democrats. Republicans received $19.9 million, or 46 percent. Labor PACs gave House Democrats 95 percent of their $33.4 million in contributions.

Machado, the Republican fundraiser, said business PACs were more willing to give to Democratic incumbents who disagreed with them on most issues rather than probusiness GOP challengers.

"They weren't willing to go against the Democrats," she said.

After the election, however, those PACs did a 180-degree flip. AT&T, which had given 61 percent of its PAC money to Democrats before the 1994 elections, gave 80 percent of its PAC contributions to Republicans in the two months following election day. UPS went from a 53–47 Democratic edge to a 98–2 Republican one. Northrop Grumman, which favored the Democrats by a 59–41 percent margin before the election, gave the GOP an 82–18 percent advantage afterwards.

"The winners went on a fundraising spree," McCloskey said. "They had debts to retire. We contributed at that time. The term of art is, 'Getting on the late train.'"

In 1995–96, corporate PACs gave Republicans 70 percent of the $51.4 million they donated to House candidates. Democrats received 30 percent. The pharmaceutical company Merck & Co., which had given 59 percent of its PAC money to Democrats in 1993–94, gave 67 percent of its contributions to Republicans in 1995–96. Bell Atlantic's PAC gave 66 percent of its contributions to Democratic candidates in 1993–94 and 62 percent of its contributions to Republicans in 1995–96. NationsBank, whose PAC gave 62 percent of its contributions in 1993–94 to Democrats, gave 55 percent of its donations to the GOP in 1995–96.

"Money follows power," Makinson said. "If ever there was a textbook case of proving the point, that did it."

The newly powerful Republicans did not hesitate to remind business PACs that they were expected to support the GOP. The National Republican Congressional Committee (NRCC) issued a report of the top 400 PACs and the percentage of contributions going to the Republicans and the Democrats. Republicans could use the report to pressure business groups into contributing more to them and less to the Democrats.

"Our members have felt they were carrying the legislative water for many of these groups who then gave their money to the other side," said the NRCC chairman at the time, Rep. Bill Paxon, R-N.Y. "It's very difficult for me to argue that people should open their arms to those who are embracing their opponents. I certainly am not going to embrace someone who's constantly stabbing me in the back. We're making sure our members know who's wielding the knife."

Only labor unions remained firmly in the Democratic camp after the 1994 switchover in power. Labor PACs gave 93 percent of their contributions to Democratic candidates in 1995–96.

Leadership PACs

House Speaker Newt Gingrich, R-Ga., and House Minority Leader Richard A. Gephardt, D-Mo., as well as some five dozen other senators and representatives, have set up their own political action committees, known as leadership PACs. These committees provide another opportunity for contributing to powerful lawmakers.

Political action committees, which can give $10,000 every two years to the reelection committees of Gingrich or Gephardt, can then give another $10,000 to Gingrich's and Gephardt's leadership PACs.

The NRA contributed $2,500 to House Majority Leader Dick Armey's Majority Leader's Fund in August 1996, five months after the House voted to repeal the ban on certain assault-style weapons. Repealing the ban was a top NRA priority.

Sen. Edward M. Kennedy, D-Mass., targeted the health care industry for a fundraiser at a time when Congress was working on his bill to make it easier for workers changing jobs to keep their health insurance. His PAC took in $81,000 in health-related contributions in 1996.

Senate Majority Leader Trent Lott, R-Miss., took in $10,000 for his PAC from advocates of private property rights a month before he announced he would bring a bill to the floor requiring the government to compensate property owners whose property values declined because of government actions. He raised $15,000 from health care interests at a time when the Senate was considering the Kennedy legislation, and $20,000 from communications companies as Congress was deregulating the telecommunications industry.

"The people who run leadership PACs are people who ask for money from positions of power," Steven F. Stockmeyer of the National Association of Business Political Action Committees told Congressional Quarterly in 1996. "It's much harder for someone to turn them down when they have that kind of clout. We think it's a perversion of the whole PAC idea."

Similar to other PACs, these leadership committees have their own agendas on Capitol Hill, which are helped along by making campaign contributions to congressional candidates. The votes these PACs seek, however, are cast behind closed doors as party caucuses.

From Jan. 1, 1995 through Dec. 31, 1996, Lott's New Republican Majority Fund contributed $410,142 to congressional candidates. In 1996, Lott was elected by his fellow

Senate Republicans to succeed Bob Dole as majority leader. Many of those senators had received contributions from Lott.

Yet contributions from leadership PACs do not necessarily win votes. Sen. Thad Cochran, R-Miss., also had his own leadership PAC in 1996, but he lost to Lott for majority leader. And though Rep. Bill McCollum's Countdown to Majority handed out $265,241 to House Republican candidates in 1994, the Florida Republican still finished third when he ran for majority whip.

Leadership PACs can also enhance the chances of a potential presidential candidate. The leadership PAC that gave the most money to congressional candidates in 1995–96 was Campaign America, which had been headed by Dole as he sought the Republican nomination for president in 1996. Campaign America gave out $829,971. Many members of Congress lined up behind Dole when he ran for president, helping him win the nomination. After Dole had wrapped up the nomination and had resigned from the Senate to run full-time, he turned over the PAC to another possible presidential aspirant, former Vice President Dan Quayle.

In 1995 Gingrich's leadership PAC, GOPAC, was at the center of the ethics complaints filed against him during his first term as House Speaker. Gingrich eventually was reprimanded by the House and fined $300,000. GOPAC had been involved in helping Gingrich set up a college course that was financed through tax-deductible contributions. Critics said GOPAC should not have been involved at all since the group was a Republican organization and the course had to be non-partisan to accept tax-deductible contributions. Later in 1995, Gingrich gave the reins of GOPAC, to Rep. John Shadegg, R-Ariz.

After turning over GOPAC, Gingrich quickly set up another leadership PAC—Monday Morning PAC. His new PAC gave $771,500 to congressional candidates in 1995–96—the second highest amount behind Dole's Campaign America. Armey's Majority Leader's Fund gave $737,558, the third highest amount. In fourth place was Gephardt's Effective Government Committee, which contributed $461,095 to those running for Congress.

Others with leadership PACs include House Majority Whip Tom DeLay, R-Texas; House GOP Conference Chairman John A. Boehner, R-Ohio; Sen. Edward M. Kennedy, D-Mass.; and Rep. Martin Frost, D-Texas, chairman of the Democratic Congressional Campaign Committee.

Some lawmakers do not wait very long before setting up a leadership PAC. Rep. Jerry Weller, R-Ill., established the RE-FORM PAC (Re-Elect Freshmen of the Republican Majority PAC) during his first term in Washington. Rep. Patrick Kennedy, D-R.I., formed his Rhode Island PAC in his second term.

Besides giving money to candidates, some lawmakers use their leadership PACs to pay travel and other expenses. Sen. Kennedy spent 10 times more on his own travel and fundraising than he gave away, DeLay spent $8,884 from his PAC on office furniture, and House Rules Committee Chairman Gerald B. H. Solomon, R-N.Y., billed his PAC for the $4,403 it cost him to attend the 1996 Republican National Convention in San Diego.

Changing the System

For almost four decades, lawmakers have debated, discussed, proposed, rejected and even occasionally passed efforts to change the way political campaigns are financed.

The last attempt came in February 1998, when the Senate refused to shut off debate on legislation on the latest McCain-Feingold bill (S 25) to overhaul the campaign finance system. This bill was silent on PACs but banned soft money.

"This undeserving legislation is dead," declared Sen. Mitch McConnell, R-Ky., a leader of efforts to stop campaign finance legislation.

The House didn't even get to vote on its version of McCain-Feingold. The GOP leadership prevented the bill from even coming to the floor in March.

The modern effort to rewrite the campaign finance laws had its origins in President John F. Kennedy's historic run for the presidency. Kennedy, the first Catholic and the youngest man ever to be elected president, was stung by allegations that his family's wealth bought him the victory. In 1961, he created a campaign finance commission, which a year later recommended limits on contributions, tax credits for givers and public disclosure of contributors.

Kennedy's successor, Lyndon B. Johnson, was embroiled in some campaign finance controversies of his own. Throughout his 1964 campaign, Johnson hosted $1,000-a-plate "President's Club" dinners. The Democratic National Committee (DNC) declined to release the names of the members of the President's Club. The DNC also charged $15,000 a page for advertisements in a political journal. Corporations could deduct the cost of these ads from their federal taxes.

With the controversy over these practices still simmering, Johnson in 1966 proposed overhauling the 1925 Federal Corrupt Practices Act, the law that for more than 40 years governed the financing of federal campaigns. Though Johnson's bill and a weaker congressional proposal went nowhere, they paved the way for Congress to try to change the law.

Congress finally did. Nixon signed campaign finance reform legislation into law in 1972. The new law limited how much money candidates could contribute to their own campaigns and how much money they could spend on advertising.

"We have a crackerjack bill here," said Rep. Morris K. Udall, D-Ariz., a leader of the effort. "It will stop millionaires from buying Senate seats and the presidency. It brings this television monster under control."

The effort advanced with the enactment of a 1974 law, given a push by the Watergate scandal that forced Nixon to resign. The law, signed by Nixon's successor, Gerald R. Ford, limited individuals to contributing to a candidate for each election, and set overall spending limits on campaigns for federal office.

Things did not work out the way Udall and those other early advocates of change envisioned, largely because of a series of Supreme Court decisions. The biggest blow came in 1976, in the case *Buckley v. Valeo,* in which the Court struck down the limits on campaign spending. The court said the limits violated the First Amendment right to free speech.

Since then, lawmakers who want to change the law have tried to get around the Supreme Court decision by offering incentives to candidates to hold down their spending voluntarily.

Over the years, Democrats have called for public financing, while Republicans have tried to restrict the sources of campaign contributions by banning political action committees and by requiring candidates to raise most of the money from their own congressional districts.

Here is a timeline of modern efforts to change the way federal campaigns are financed:

1966: The disclosures following Johnson's 1964 election led Sen. Russell B. Long, D-La., to propose the first public financing of federal elections. He attached a provision to an unrelated tax bill to allow taxpayers to earmark $1 of their federal income taxes ($2 for a married couple filing jointly) to finance presidential campaigns.

A provision in another tax bill enacted a year later suspended the public financing program until rules were put into place governing how the money was to be allocated. The program was not revived until 1972.

1970: After the Citizens Research Foundation—headed by political science professor Herbert Alexander, former executive director of Kennedy's commission—found that the costs of campaigning for all elective offices had risen from $140 million in 1952 to $300 million in 1968, federal lawmakers decided to go after what they believed to be the major cause of the increase: television and radio advertising.

Both houses of Congress passed and sent to Nixon legislation that limited how much money candidates for president, vice president, senator, representative, governor and lieutenant governor could spend on TV and radio commercials. Nixon vetoed the bill, and the Senate failed to muster the two-thirds majority needed to override.

1972: Nixon signed a comprehensive revision of campaign finance laws that had passed both houses of Congress the previous year. The measure limited how much money candidates could contribute to their own campaigns and how much money they could spend on all advertising, not just TV and radio commercials.

This was the bill that encouraged the growth in PACs. The legislation banned corporations and unions from contributing directly to political campaigns and instead authorized them to set up PACs, funded by voluntary contributions from employees and members.

1974: In the wake of Watergate, Ford signed legislation that limited contributions to $1,000 per individual per election, set spending limits for federal campaigns, restricted how much money candidates could give to their own campaigns, provided federal funding for national party conventions and set up a federal income-tax checkoff to create a pool of matching public funds for presidential primary campaigns.

The law also set up new disclosure requirements for campaign contributions, repealed the limits on media expenditures enacted in 1972, and created the Federal Election Commission to oversee the new campaign finance system.

Lawmakers rejected proposals to expand public financing to congressional campaigns. "The promise of clean elections cannot be fulfilled by using public money," said an opponent of the measure, Rep. Bill Frenzel, R-Minn.

1976: The Supreme Court, in *Buckley v. Valeo,* ruled that spending limits for campaigns were unconstitutional, as were restrictions on how much money candidates could contribute to their own efforts. The court upheld the limits on contributions from individuals.

1979: As a sign of how important the House Democratic leadership felt the issue was, a major campaign finance overhaul bill was given the number HR 1. But the measure failed to get out of the House Administration Committee.

The House did try to reduce PAC contributions from $10,000 to $6,000 per election cycle, and limit candidates to no more than $70,000 in PAC money every two years. But the provision, attached to legislation reauthorizing the Federal Election Commission, never got out of the Senate after the Republicans threatened a filibuster.

Congress did pass legislation, signed by President Jimmy Carter, that allowed political parties to raise so-called soft money for get-out-the-vote and voter registration efforts. Just as the 1972 law aided the explosion of PACs and led to later efforts to ban them, lawmakers would later try to undo this law.

Soft money, not subject to federal contribution limits, later would be tapped for millions of dollars in unregulated, issue-oriented advertising aimed at influencing federal campaigns.

1988: Senate Majority Leader Robert C. Byrd, D-W.Va., held a record-setting eighth vote to try to shut off a Republican-led filibuster and bring to the floor legislation to set voluntary spending limits for Senate campaigns, offer public funds to candidates who agreed to abide by the limits and restrict PAC contributions.

He failed to get the 60 votes needed to end debate. The Republicans particularly attacked the public financing provisions. Their efforts were led by McConnell, then a freshman.

1992: Scarred by the House bank and post office scandals, the Democratic-controlled Congress sent to President George Bush a bill to overhaul the campaign finance system. The legislation merged separate House and Senate bills, creating different rules for each chamber. The Senate offered candidates who agreed to voluntary spending limits taxpayer-financed vouchers to buy television commercial time. The House offered candidates who agreed to limit spending federal matching funds.

Objecting to the public financing provisions, Bush vetoed the bill. Democratic presidential candidate Clinton criticized the president, promising to sign such legislation if elected.

1994: With Clinton in the White House and the Democrats still running Congress, each chamber passed its own campaign finance bill.

In working out the differences between the Senate and House versions, congressional negotiators agreed to lower PAC contributions from $10,000 an election cycle to $6,000, offer cut-rate television time to Senate candidates and provide vouchers for advertising and postage to House candidates who agreed to abide by voluntary spending limits, ban soft money and prevent incumbents from sending out taxpayer-financed mass mailings in election years.

Senate Republicans blocked the legislation by filibustering the procedural motion to formally go to conference.

1995: At a joint forum in New Hampshire, Clinton and new Speaker Gingrich shook hands on a deal to name a blue-ribbon commission to look at ways to change the campaign finance system. No commission was formed.

1996: A bipartisan coalition, led by McCain and Feingold, introduced legislation to ban PACs and soft money, and provide free or discounted television time and reduced mailing rates to candidates willing to limit how much they spend on their campaigns.

The bill reached the Senate floor only after Dole resigned from the Senate to concentrate on his presidential campaign against Clinton. Even then, the McCain-Feingold bill failed to get the 60 votes needed to end debate and bring the bill up for a vote.

1997: The McCain-Feingold bill again came up in the Senate, and again the Republicans successfully filibustered the legislation, preventing it from coming up for a vote.

At the same time, the Republicans offered a campaign finance bill of their own. They proposed banning labor unions from using any dues for political purposes unless they received approval from their members. In the 1996 elections, the AFL-CIO spent $35 million to run advertisements criticizing Republican incumbents for their positions on certain issues, such as raising the minimum wage. The Democrats successfully blocked a vote on that measure.

1998: Following Senate hearings into campaign finance abuses during the 1996 elections, McCain and Feingold offered a scaled-back version of their bill, which would ban soft money and curb issue ads. Once again, the GOP successfully waged a filibuster and killed the bill.

Senate Majority Leader Trent Lott, R-Miss., again proposed legislation requiring unions to get permission from their members before using dues for political activities, and he also failed to end debate and bring the bill to the Senate floor for a vote.

The following month, the House Republican leadership prevented that chamber from voting its version of McCain-Feingold, the bill sponsored by Shays and Meehan. Using a parliamentary maneuver, the Republican leaders instead scheduled a series of votes on other campaign finance legislation, each requiring a two-thirds majority for passage. More importantly, the procedure by which the bills were voted on prevented any amendments.

The House GOP leadership's strategy backfired, however. Angered by the fact that they could not vote on the Shays-Meehan proposal, several Republicans joined with House Democrats and signed a petition to force that bill to the floor.

Faced with the threat of losing control of the House agenda, the GOP leadership capitulated and agreed to allow another vote on overhauling the campaign finance system. This time, both the Shays-Meehan proposal, and a bipartisan bill developed by a group of freshmen, led by Reps. Asa Hutchinson, R-Ark., and Tom Allen, D-Maine, were expected to be up for discussion.

Campaign Finance in the 1997–98 Election Cycle

Meanwhile, lawmakers continue to raise millions of dollars for their reelection campaigns. The FEC reported in March 1998 that congressional candidates raised $232.9 million in

1997, a record for off-year fundraising. Just 10 years earlier, in 1987, congressional candidates raised half that, $111.5 million.

PACs accounted for $62.7 million of the money the candidates raised, or 27 percent. Ten years earlier, the candidates raised $42.2 million from PACs.

Makinson of the Center for Responsive Politics noted that most of the lawmakers raising money for their reelection campaigns did not have opponents by the end of the year, as they were asking PACS to help them amass huge campaign bank accounts.

"You build a relationship of mutual dependence," Makinson said. "Neither side wants the relationship to end."

References

Center for Public Integrity. *Safety Last: The Politics of E. Coli and Other Food-Borne Killers.* Washington, D.C: Center for Public Integrity, 1998.

Center for Public Integrity. *Short-Changed: How Congress and Special Interests Benefit at the Expense of the American People.* Washington, D.C: Center for Public Integrity, 1991.

Center for Responsive Politics. *Political Pac-Analia.* Washington, D.C: Center for Responsive Politics, 1996.

Center for Responsive Politics. *Timber Logging Road Program.* Washington, D.C: Center for Responsive Politics, 1997.

Center for Responsive Politics. *Timber Vote.* Washington, D.C: Center for Responsive Politics, 1997.

Center for Responsive Politics. *Tracking the Cash: Candidate Fund-Raising in the '98 Elections.* Washington, D.C.: Center for Responsive Politics, 1998.

Common Cause. *Pocketbook Politics: How Special-Interest Money Hurts the American Consumer.* Washington, D.C: Common Cause, 1998.

Common Cause. *Return on Investment: The Hidden Story of Soft Money, Corporate Welfare and the 1997 Budget and Tax Deal.* Washington, D.C: Common Cause, 1997.

Congressional Quarterly. *Politics in America 1998: The 105th Congress.* Washington, D.C.: Congressional Quarterly, 1997.

Congressional Quarterly. *Politics in America 1996: The 104th Congress.* Washington, D.C.: Congressional Quarterly, 1995.

Doherty, Carroll J. "Votes a Good Indicator of Depth of Feeling on Both Sides." *Congressional Quarterly Weekly Report* (Oct. 11, 1997): 2449.

Federal Election Commission. *Campaign Guide for Corporations and Labor Organizations.* Washington, D.C.: Federal Election Commission, 1997.

Federal Election Commission. *Campaign Guide for Nonconnected Committees.* Washington, D.C.: Federal Election Commission, 1995.

Federal Election Commission. *Congressional Candidates Raise $233 Million.* Washington, D.C.: Federal Election Commission, March 6, 1998.

Federal Election Commission. *Congressional Fundraising and Spending Up Again in 1996.* Washington, D.C.: Federal Election Commission, April 14, 1997.

Federal Election Commission. *FEC Releases Semi-Annual Federal PAC Count.* Washington, D.C.: Federal Election Commission, January 27, 1998.

Federal Election Commission. *1994 Congressional Fundraising Sets New Record.* Washington, D.C.: Federal Election Commission, November 1995.

Federal Election Commission. *1994 PAC Activity Shows Little Growth Over 1992 Level, Final FEC Report Finds.* Washington, D.C.: Federal Election Commission, November 1995.

Federal Election Commission. *PAC Activity Increases in 1995-96 Election Cycle.* Washington, D.C.: Federal Election Commission, April 1997.

Federal Election Commission. *Twenty-Year Report.* Washington, D.C.: Federal Election Commission, April 1995.

Makinson, Larry. *The Big Picture: Money Follows Power Shift on Capitol Hill.* Washington, D.C.: Center for Responsive Politics, 1997.

Salant, Jonathan D. "Committee Post Makes Moynihan a PAC Magnet," *The [Syracuse]Post-Standard* (Aug. 18, 1993): A-1.

Salant, Jonathan D. "Despite Attempts, Loopholes in Law Remain Unplugged." *Congressional Quarterly Weekly Report* (Nov. 16, 1996).

Salant, Jonathan D. "Fat Bank Accounts Help Some Incumbents Avoid Strong Opposition." *The Associated Press* (March 10, 1998).

Salant, Jonathan D. "Finances Take Priority in This Year's Races."*Congressional Quarterly Weekly Report* (Oct. 26, 1996): 3081–3084.

Salant, Jonathan D. "Lawmakers' Committee Assignments Attract Special Interests." *The [Syracuse] Post-Standard* (Dec. 21, 1991): A-1.

Salant, Jonathan D., "Leaders' PERSONAL PACs Sometimes Spend More Than They Give." *The Associated Press* (July 8, 1997).

Salant, Jonathan D. "Leadership PACs: A Matter of Give and Take."*Congressional Quarterly Weekly Report* (May 25, 1996): 144–443.

Salant, Jonathan D. "Major Lenders Gear Up for Student Loan Debate by Forming PACs." *The Associated Press* (Feb. 17, 1998).

Salant, Jonathan D. "PACs Follow Freshman Committee Assignments." *The Associated Press.* August 29, 1997.

Salant, Jonathan D. "Some on Labor's Hit List Get Labor Contributions."*Congressional Quarterly Weekly Report* (Oct. 5, 1996): 288–885.

Salant, Jonathan D., and Jo-Ann Moriarty. "Data Tie PAC Contributions to Votes For, Against NAFTA." *The [Portland] Oregonian* (Nov. 17, 1993): A-10.

Salant, Jonathan D., and Gilbert D. Martinez. "Health-Related PACs Take Out Insurance." *The [Portland] Oregonian* (Sept. 1, 1993): A-3.

Agriculture

Agricultural Services/Products

APASCO

*Phone: (805) 295-8591 * Fax: (805) 295-0430*
25060 Ave. Stanford #200, Valencia, CA 91355

The Agricultural Producers and Affiliates Service Corp. comprises several agricultural organizations, including the Citrus Avocado Insurance Association.

Agricultural Producers & Affiliates Service Corp. PAC (APASCO PAC) (C00281444) *Address: same as sponsor * Treasurer: Jeanne Robbins Flaherty*

	1993-94	1995-96	1997	Totals
Receipts	$73,757	$38,163	$4,854	$116,774
Disburse	59,776	39,624	10	99,410
Cash	13,985	12,527	17,372	n/a
Contributions	6,600	5,849	0	12,449
Republicans	2,500	2,849	0	5,349
No. of Cand.	*3*	*3*	*0*	*6*
House	1,500	2,849	0	4,349
Senate	1,000	0	0	1,000
Democrats	4,100	3,000	0	7,100
No. of Cand.	*4*	*3*	*0*	*7*
House	3,100	2,000	0	5,100
Senate	1,000	1,000	0	2,000
Incumbents	5,100	4,849	0	9,949
Challengers	1,500	1,000	0	2,500
Open Seat	0	0	0	0
Winners	5,600	4,849	n/a	10,449
Losers	1,000	1,000	n/a	2,000

Agway Inc.

*Phone: (315) 449-7061 * Fax: (315) 449-6008*
333 Butternut Dr., Dewitt, NY 13214
Web: www.agway.com

Agway is a farmer-owned cooperative formed in 1964 by the merger of three regional co-ops. Its 80,000 members produce animal feeds, seeds and fertilizer for other farmers from Ohio to Maine, but those operations constituted less than 40 percent of Agway's 1997 total sales of $1.7 billion.

The co-op has five other businesses: Country Products Group, which includes the world's largest sunflower seed processing plant; Agway Retail Services, a collection of stores in the Northeast; Agway Energy Products, which provides natural gas and electricity; Telmark Inc., a farm equipment leasing company; and Agway Insurance Group.

Agway's headquarters are in Syracuse, N.Y.

AGPAC (C00138636) *Address: same as sponsor * Treasurer: Martin P. Frankenfield*

	1993-94	1995-96	1997	Totals
Receipts	$16,230	$7,594	$4,322	$28,146
Disburse	13,468	10,984	1,654	26,106
Cash	11,342	7,952	10,620	n/a
Contributions	8,000	5,400	-1250	12,150
Republicans	3,500	3,900	-250	7,150
No. of Cand.	*6*	*5*	*1*	*12*
House	3,500	3,400	-250	6,650
Senate	0	500	0	500
Democrats	4,500	1,500	-1000	5,000
No. of Cand.	*7*	*3*	*2*	*12*
House	2,500	1,500	-1000	3,000
Senate	2,000	0	0	2,000
Incumbents	8,000	4,900	-750	12,150
Challengers	0	0	0	0
Open Seat	0	500	0	500
Winners	7,000	5,400	n/a	12,400
Losers	1,000	0	n/a	1,000

Alabama Farmers Federation

*Phone: (334) 613-4205 * Fax: (334) 286-1841*
2108 E. South Blvd., P.O. Box 11023, Montgomery, AL 36191-0001
Web: www.alfafarmers.org

Alabama Farmers Federation (Alfa Farmers) is a grassroots organization which represents the agricultural industry and serves the farming community of Alabama. Founded in 1921, the federation has 400,000 farm and non-farm members.

Alfa Farmers has two affiliated companies: Alfa Services, which provides discounts for members, and Alfa Insurance, which provides farm and rural fire protection insurance.

The Alabama Farmers Federation PAC was established in 1980. Its lobbying efforts have helped to defeat numerous proposed property tax increases and secure tax breaks for farmers on livestock feed, seed, fertilizer, diesel fuel and farm equipment. Additional lobbying efforts have included obtaining state funds for agricultural research and conservation programs.

In February 1997, Alfa Farmers supported legislation that would require foreign country-of-origin labeling in a prominent place on the front of individual frozen food packages.

Elect — The Political Action Committee of The Alabama Farmers Federation (C00094573) *Phone: (205) 647-3864 * 2116 Bonedry Dr., Warrior, AL 35180 * Contact: John Morris, Chairman * Treasurer: John H. Dorrill Jr.*

	1993-94	*1995-96*	*1997*	*Totals*
Receipts	$1,537,025	$1,247,720	$622,030	$3,406,775
Disburse	1,852,573	1,066,209	429,104	3,347,886
Cash	17,237	198,749	391,675	n/a
Contributions	129,421	210,311	128,272	468,004
Republicans	41,900	132,001	92,772	266,673
No. of Cand.	*27*	*69*	*45*	*141*
House	22,900	73,051	79,772	175,723
Senate	19,000	58,950	13,000	90,950
Democrats	85,521	78,310	34,000	197,831
No. of Cand.	*75*	*72*	*31*	*178*
House	67,271	68,810	25,000	161,081
Senate	18,250	9,500	9,000	36,750
Incumbents	112,950	136,506	126,272	375,728
Challengers	2,500	3,500	0	6,000
Open Seat	4,500	69,305	1,000	74,805
Winners	101,450	177,506	n/a	278,956
Losers	27,971	32,805	n/a	60,776

American Association of Crop Insurers

*Phone: (202) 789-4100 * Fax: (202) 408-7763*
One Massachusetts Ave. N.W., Suite 800, Washington, DC 20001
E-mail: aaci@erols.com

The American Association of Crop Insurers represents the governmental and legislative interests of more than 20 companies, or 7,000 agents, that sell crop insurance and reinsurance.

The association's reinsured company members write more than 81 percent of the Multiple Peril Crop Insurance sold by private companies in the United States.

American Association of Crop Insurers Political Action Committee (AACI PAC) (C00172833) *Address: same as sponsor * Treasurer: Michael R. McLeod*

	1993-94	*1995-96*	*1997*	*Totals*
Receipts	$71,655	$80,856	$69,325	$221,836
Disburse	103,317	110,086	51,500	264,903
Cash	67,535	38,309	31,265	n/a
Contributions	93,800	99,000	48,535	241,335
Republicans	35,450	68,500	19,737	123,687
No. of Cand.	*28*	*44*	*25*	*97*
House	28,450	45,000	15,237	88,687
Senate	7,000	23,500	4,500	35,000
Democrats	56,850	30,500	27,298	114,648
No. of Cand.	*37*	*25*	*20*	*82*
House	43,100	21,500	15,500	80,100
Senate	13,750	9,000	11,798	34,548
Incumbents	93,800	76,000	45,035	214,835
Challengers	0	7,500	500	8,000
Open Seat	0	15,500	0	15,500
Winners	78,050	92,500	n/a	170,550
Losers	15,750	6,500	n/a	22,250

American Crop Protection Association

*Phone: (202) 296-1585 * Fax: (202) 463-0474*
1156 15th St. N.W., Suite 400, Washington, DC 20005
Web: www.acpa.org

The American Crop Protection Association represents companies that make and distribute pest control products. Its members produce the bulk of active ingredients used in pesticides registered for use in the United States.

The nonprofit association lobbies on issues related to the Food Quality Protection Act of 1996, which increased the regulatory requirements for pesticides. It also follows legislation related to cultural, biological, chemical and genetic techniques to control pests.

American Crop Protection Association Political Action Committee (CPAC) (formerly known as NACAPAC) (C00248849) *Address: same as sponsor * Treasurer: Jay J. Vroom*

	1993-94	*1995-96*	*1997*	*Totals*
Receipts	$23,990	$83,766	$53,875	$161,631
Disburse	20,150	77,750	31,050	128,950
Cash	8,320	14,337	37,162	n/a
Contributions	20,150	76,750	30,050	126,950
Republicans	8,950	51,000	18,850	78,800
No. of Cand.	*20*	*54*	*27*	*101*
House	6,200	29,250	13,350	48,800
Senate	2,750	21,750	5,500	30,000
Democrats	11,200	25,750	10,200	47,150
No. of Cand.	*23*	*30*	*15*	*68*
House	9,200	22,750	7,700	39,650
Senate	2,000	3,000	2,500	7,500
Incumbents	16,800	53,500	27,550	97,850
Challengers	0	5,500	0	5,500
Open Seat	3,350	17,750	2,500	23,600
Winners	14,150	66,750	n/a	80,900
Losers	6,000	10,000	n/a	16,000

American Feed Industry Association

*Phone: (703) 524-0810 * Fax: (703) 524-1921*
1501 Wilson Blvd., Suite 1100, Arlington, VA 22209
Web: www.afia.org

The American Feed Industry Association is a 700-member trade association representing feed manufacturers and their suppliers. AFIA's lobbying efforts have focused on food safety, the Clean Air Act and animal rights.

On the regulatory end, the association has been working with the Food and Drug Administration to create a "reasonable" regulatory plan for enzyme use in feeds. AFIA also participates in various training and industry-help programs.

In 1997, AFIA lobbied Congress to extend "fast-track" trade pact negotiating authority to the president. Fast-track authority allows the president to engage in unilateral and multilateral trade negotiations, bringing the proposed trade pact to Congress for ratification.

Feed Industry Political Action Committee/American Feed Industry Association (C00033944) *Address: same as sponsor * Treasurer: Steven L. Kopperud*

	1993-94	*1995-96*	*1997*	*Totals*
Receipts	$37,091	$26,814	$8,695	$72,600
Disburse	33,200	29,316	5,500	68,016
Cash	6,266	722	3,917	n/a
Contributions	32,700	29,306	5,500	67,506
Republicans	26,800	26,106	3,500	56,406
No. of Cand.	*41*	*43*	*7*	*91*
House	13,600	13,856	2,000	29,456
Senate	13,200	12,250	1,500	26,950
Democrats	5,900	3,200	1,500	10,600
No. of Cand.	*11*	*5*	*2*	*18*
House	5,400	2,450	500	8,350
Senate	500	750	1,000	2,250
Incumbents	17,000	12,406	5,000	34,406
Challengers	4,500	5,750	0	10,250
Open Seat	11,200	10,400	500	22,100
Winners	28,150	23,256	n/a	51,406
Losers	4,550	6,050	n/a	10,600

American Nursery and Landscape Association

*Phone: (202) 789-2900 * Fax: (202) 789-1893*
1250 Eye St. N.W., Suite 500, Washington, DC 20005
Web: www.anla.org

The American Nursery and Landscape Association, formerly the American Association of Nurserymen, tracks labor, small business, tax and environmental issues that affect its 2,100 members, who operate nurseries, landscape firms and retail centers.

AAN-Nursery Industry Political Action Committee (C00022988) *Address: same as sponsor * Treasurer: Benjamin C. Bolusky*

	1993-94	*1995-96*	*1997*	*Totals*
Receipts	$48,264	$57,388	$34,664	$140,316
Disburse	50,618	65,890	29,062	145,570
Cash	33,441	24,939	30,541	n/a
Contributions	46,550	61,950	27,250	135,750
Republicans	31,050	48,450	21,250	100,750
No. of Cand.	*31*	*41*	*29*	*101*
House	26,550	40,250	18,250	85,050
Senate	4,500	8,200	3,000	15,700
Democrats	15,500	13,500	6,000	35,000
No. of Cand.	*17*	*13*	*10*	*40*
House	14,500	11,500	6,000	32,000
Senate	1,000	2,000	0	3,000
Incumbents	40,450	44,250	26,750	111,450
Challengers	2,500	7,700	500	10,700
Open Seat	3,600	10,000	0	13,600
Winners	37,450	51,750	n/a	89,200
Losers	9,100	10,200	n/a	19,300

American Veterinary Medical Association

*Phone: (847) 925-8070 * Fax: (847) 925-1329*
1931 N. Meacham Rd., Suite 100, Schaumburg, IL 60173
Web: www.avma.org

The American Veterinary Medical Association is a nonprofit national association of veterinarians established in 1863. The AVMA has about 62,000 members, representing more than 80 percent of the active veterinarians in the United States. Nearly half of its members treat only small animals, such as cats and dogs, but others work in the military, in research laboratories and in universities.

The group's interests include animal welfare issues, drug and food safety, animal waste management and graduate education in veterinary medicine. It also lobbies on small business issues, since many members run their own practices.

The only major veterinary PAC, the AVMA was one of the more successful groups in spending money on winning candidates. More than 91 percent of the group's contributions went to winners. Republicans received about 65 percent of the overall total, and the AVMA spent little on challengers.

The leading recipients were Rep. John Ensign, R-Nev., and Sen. Wayne Allard, R-Colo., both veterinarians. Sen. Tom Harkin, D-Iowa, was the top Democratic recipient.

American Veterinary Medical Association Political Action Committee (AVMAPAC) (C00114132) *Phone: (202) 789-0007 x614 * Fax: (202) 842-4360 * 1101 Vermont Ave. N.W., Suite 710, Washington, DC 20005 * E-mail: 74232.57@compuserve.com * Contact: Pamela Abney, Interim PAC Coordinator * Treasurer: Dr. Jack O. Walther*

	1993-94	1995-96	1997	Totals
Receipts	$302,143	$370,437	$101,926	$774,506
Disburse	286,267	304,808	98,671	689,746
Cash	57,431	120,654	123,913	n/a
Contributions	267,700	291,500	85,500	644,700
Republicans	137,700	185,500	51,500	374,700
No. of Cand.	*169*	*160*	*40*	*369*
House	94,700	120,500	23,500	238,700
Senate	43,000	65,000	28,000	136,000
Democrats	129,000	106,000	32,500	267,500
No. of Cand.	*159*	*91*	*29*	*279*
House	101,000	87,000	18,500	206,500
Senate	28,000	19,000	14,000	61,000
Incumbents	245,500	216,000	75,500	537,000
Challengers	1,200	18,000	10,000	29,200
Open Seat	22,000	57,500	0	79,500
Winners	241,700	266,000	n/a	507,700
Losers	26,000	25,500	n/a	51,500

Animal Health Institute

*Phone: (703) 684-3404 * Fax: (703) 684-0125*
501 Wythe St., Alexandria, VA 22313
*Web: www.ahi.org * E-mail: jkeeling@ahi.org*

The Animal Health Institute is the umbrella association for manufacturers of animal health products. The 25 member companies manufacture pharmaceuticals, vaccines and feed additives for domestic and farm animals.

The institute is interested in a variety of issues pertaining to the industry, such as pet product marketing, animal testing and prevention of food contamination.

Animal Health Institute Political Action Committee (AHI PAC) (C00203059) *Address: same as sponsor * Treasurer: John Keeling*

	1993-94	1995-96	1997	Totals
Receipts	$1,872	$4,600	$4,935	$11,407
Disburse	800	6,806	1,314	8,920
Cash	1,191	283	3,903	n/a
Contributions	700	5,500	1,000	7,200
Republicans	700	3,250	500	4,450
No. of Cand.	*4*	*8*	*1*	*13*
House	700	1,750	500	2,950
Senate	0	1,500	0	1,500
Democrats	0	2,250	500	2,750
No. of Cand.	*0*	*7*	*1*	*8*
House	0	1,500	500	2,000
Senate	0	750	0	750
Incumbents	700	3,500	1,000	5,200
Challengers	0	750	0	750
Open Seat	0	1,250	0	1,250
Winners	700	5,500	n/a	6,200
Losers	0	0	n/a	0

Archer-Daniels-Midland Co.

*Phone: (217) 424-5200 * Fax: (217) 424-5447*
P. O. Box 1470, Decatur, IL 62525
Web: www.admworld.com

One of the world's largest processors of oilseeds, corn and wheat, Archer-Daniels-Midland Co. procures, stores, processes and sells agricultural commodities and products. The Decatur, Ill. company also processes cocoa beans, milo, oats, barley and peanuts.

A publicly traded company, ADM reported $9.8 billion in sales in 1997 and employs more than 17,000 people worldwide.

According to the FBI, in October 1996, Archer-Daniels-Midland agreed to plead guilty and pay a $100 million criminal fine for its role in two international price-fixing conspiracies.

Archer-Daniels-Midland Co. (ADM PAC) (C00093963) *Address: same as sponsor * Treasurer: Steven R. Mills*

	1993-94	1995-96	1997	Totals
Receipts	$296,856	$329,290	$97,046	$723,192
Disburse	265,807	269,812	130,555	666,174
Cash	136,624	196,104	162,595	n/a
Contributions	227,170	208,976	94,500	530,646
Republicans	72,600	86,476	43,000	202,076
No. of Cand.	*44*	*44*	*34*	*122*
House	19,600	35,776	17,500	72,876
Senate	53,000	50,700	25,500	129,200
Democrats	143,570	122,500	50,500	316,570
No. of Cand.	*67*	*38*	*27*	*132*
House	78,950	60,500	23,500	162,950
Senate	64,620	62,000	27,000	153,620
Incumbents	187,470	122,276	96,500	406,246
Challengers	12,500	21,700	1,000	35,200
Open Seat	27,850	60,000	2,000	89,850
Winners	149,700	146,750	n/a	296,450
Losers	77,470	62,226	n/a	139,696

Association of American Agricultural Insurers

*Phone: (712) 328-3918 * Fax: (712) 325-5878*
P.O. Box 1574, 535 W. Broadway, Suite 300, Council Bluffs, IA 51503
Web: www.amag.com

The Association of American Agricultural Insurers, or American Agrisurance Inc., is a subsidiary of Acceptance Insurance Companies Inc. American Agrisurance is the sole marketer of crop insurance for Redland Insurance Co. and American Growers Insurance Co.

Founded in 1976, the publicly held company is the third-largest crop insurance company in the United States. In 1996, American Agrisurance developed crop revenue coverage, the first crop insurance policy approved by the Federal Crop Insurance Corp.

Association of American Agricultural Insurers PAC (C00259135) *Address: same as sponsor * Treasurer: Beverly Paul*

	1993-94	1995-96	1997	Totals
Receipts	$28,908	$29,598	$27,396	$85,902
Disburse	19,186	44,596	16,500	80,282
Cash	21,583	6,585	17,481	n/a
Contributions	17,686	41,796	16,500	75,982
Republicans	4,250	20,196	6,250	30,696
No. of Cand.	*5*	*18*	*6*	*29*
House	4,250	9,096	4,500	17,846
Senate	0	11,100	1,750	12,850
Democrats	13,436	21,600	10,250	45,286
No. of Cand.	*7*	*7*	*7*	*21*
House	3,450	1,750	3,000	8,200
Senate	9,986	19,850	7,250	37,086
Incumbents	17,686	16,250	15,500	49,436
Challengers	0	6,350	0	6,350
Open Seat	0	19,196	0	19,196
Winners	15,686	32,700	n/a	48,386
Losers	2,000	9,096	n/a	11,096

Association of Floral Importers of Florida

*Phone: (305) 593-2383 * Fax: (305) 593-0309*
8725 N.W. 18th Terrace, Suite 106, Miami, FL 33172
E-mail: afif@colflowers.com

The Association of Floral Importers represents southern Florida's fresh-cut flower importers. Established in 1982, the association has 50 members. It handles regulatory, small business tax and international trade issues. The association also publishes a bi-monthly newsletter for its members.

In lobbying efforts, it joins with other florist organizations like the Society of American Florists in representing the floral industry.

In March 1998, the association lobbied to change a section of the Fair Labor Standards Act to exempt inside sales personnel from overtime.

Association of Floral Importers of Florida Political Action Committee (AFIF PAC) (C00173161) *Address: same as sponsor * Contact: Lin Watts, PAC Dir. * Treasurer: L. James Teper*

	1993-94	1995-96	1997	Totals
Receipts	$42,759	$58,250	$31,632	$132,641
Disburse	35,630	59,978	16,184	111,792
Cash	10,491	8,766	24,215	n/a
Contributions	28,186	58,747	16,000	102,933
Republicans	19,250	25,499	5,000	49,749
No. of Cand.	*7*	*6*	*2*	*15*
House	16,750	23,499	5,000	45,249
Senate	2,500	2,000	0	4,500
Democrats	8,936	33,248	11,000	53,184
No. of Cand.	*8*	*6*	*5*	*19*
House	8,936	23,248	8,500	40,684
Senate	0	10,000	2,500	12,500
Incumbents	28,186	58,247	16,000	102,433
Challengers	0	0	0	0
Open Seat	0	500	0	500
Winners	27,686	58,747	n/a	86,433
Losers	500	0	n/a	500

Blue Seal Feeds

P.O. Box 8000, 15 Buttrick Rd., Londonderry, NH 03053

Blue Seal Feeds Political Action Committee was terminated in 1996.

Blue Seal Feeds Political Action Committee (formerly known as H.K. Webster Co. PAC) (C00081968) *Address: same as sponsor * Treasurer: Arthur N. Graichen*

	1993-94	1995-96	1997	Totals
Receipts	$0	$26,665	$0	$26,665
Disburse	0	27,870	0	27,870
Cash	0	0	0	n/a
Contributions	0	16,800	0	16,800
Republicans	0	16,800	0	16,800
No. of Cand.	*0*	*51*	*0*	*51*
House	0	9,550	0	9,550
Senate	0	7,250	0	7,250
Democrats	0	0	0	0
No. of Cand.	*0*	*0*	*0*	*0*
House	0	0	0	0
Senate	0	0	0	0
Incumbents	0	8,900	0	8,900
Challengers	0	2,750	0	2,750
Open Seat	0	3,150	0	3,150
Winners	0	8,800	n/a	8,800
Losers	0	8,000	n/a	8,000

CF Industries

Phone: (847) 438-9500
One Salem Lake Dr., Long Grove, IL 60047

Agricultural cooperative CF Industries manufactures and markets fertilizers and food products. It is owned by 11 regional co-ops, with members in 46 states and two Canadian provinces. The co-op primarily produces nitrogen, phosphate and potash.

CF Industries Employees' Good Government Fund (C00076588) *Phone: (202) 371-9279 * Fax: (202) 371-9169 * 1401 Eye St. N.W., Suite 340, Washington, DC 20005 * Contact: Rosemary O'Brien, V.P. of Public Affairs * Treasurer: Margaret K. Van Wissink*

	1993-94	1995-96	1997	Totals
Receipts	$65,803	$68,271	$41,070	$175,144
Disburse	74,312	66,040	21,950	162,302
Cash	6,157	8,403	27,531	n/a
Contributions	60,970	49,075	15,500	125,545
Republicans	25,350	34,700	8,000	68,050
No. of Cand.	*35*	*42*	*10*	*87*
House	15,850	19,500	7,000	42,350
Senate	9,500	15,200	1,000	25,700
Democrats	34,120	14,375	7,500	55,995
No. of Cand.	*46*	*23*	*3*	*72*
House	22,000	10,375	500	32,875
Senate	12,120	4,000	7,000	23,120
Incumbents	53,470	33,125	15,500	102,095
Challengers	0	4,700	0	4,700
Open Seat	7,000	11,250	0	18,250
Winners	49,600	41,250	n/a	90,850
Losers	11,370	7,825	n/a	19,195

California Farm Bureau Federation

*Phone: (916) 561-5503 * Fax: (916) 561-5699*
2300 River Plaza Dr., Sacramento, CA 95833
*Web: www.fb.com/cafb * E-mail: jpeace@cfbf.com*

The California Farm Bureau Federation is a voluntary non-government, non-partisan organization of farm and ranch families. Founded in 1919, CFBF is California's largest farm organization with more than 70,000 member families in 53 county farm bureaus.

In February 1998, CFBF opposed a proposal to list Chinook salmon under the federal Endangered Species Act. The bureau stated that the measure would pose a "serious threat" to Central Valley farmers and the state's economy.

CFBF is affiliated with the American Farm Bureau Federation.

California Farm Bureau Federation Political Action Committee (Farm PAC) (C00041954) *Address: same as sponsor * Contact: John Peace, PAC Dir. * Treasurer: Douglas W. Mosebar*

	1993-94	1995-96	1997	Totals
Receipts	$71,677	$77,355	$48,292	$197,324
Disburse	52,825	80,712	13,300	146,837
Cash	24,451	21,095	56,087	n/a
Contributions	50,240	70,712	13,300	134,252
Republicans	31,310	58,402	9,100	98,812
No. of Cand.	*17*	*21*	*8*	*46*
House	29,810	51,902	9,100	90,812
Senate	1,500	6,500	0	8,000
Democrats	18,930	12,310	4,200	35,440
No. of Cand.	*6*	*5*	*3*	*14*
House	9,000	7,310	4,200	20,510
Senate	9,930	5,000	0	14,930
Incumbents	33,240	52,110	13,300	98,650
Challengers	11,000	13,102	0	24,102
Open Seat	6,000	5,500	0	11,500
Winners	43,740	54,612	n/a	98,352
Losers	6,500	16,100	n/a	22,600

California Westside Farmers Inc.

Phone: (209) 698-7221
2433 N. Highland Ave., Fresno, CA 93727

California Westside Farmers is a cooperative of farms that produces seeds for plants and agricultural products.

California Westside Farmers Fed PAC (C00079566) *Address: same as sponsor * Treasurer: Shelley Orth*

	1993-94	1995-96	1997	Totals
Receipts	$14,885	$7,041	$3	$21,929
Disburse	11,057	7,013	1,786	19,856
Cash	6,124	6,182	4,400	n/a
Contributions	9,000	5,204	1,750	15,954
Republicans	1,100	3,704	0	4,804
No. of Cand.	*2*	*4*	*0*	*6*
House	100	2,704	0	2,804
Senate	1,000	1,000	0	2,000
Democrats	7,900	1,500	1,750	11,150
No. of Cand.	*6*	*1*	*1*	*8*
House	4,900	1,500	1,750	8,150
Senate	3,000	0	0	3,000
Incumbents	8,900	5,204	1,750	15,854
Challengers	100	0	0	100
Open Seat	0	0	0	0
Winners	6,200	5,204	n/a	11,404
Losers	2,800	0	n/a	2,800

Case Corp.

Phone: (414) 636-6011
700 State St., Racine, WI 53404
Web: www.casecorp.com

Case Corp. is a publicly owned company that manufactures agricultural and construction equipment. The Wisconsin-based company had 1997 revenues of $6 billion. Case's products are sold through a network of 4,900 independent dealers and distributors in more than 150 countries. Case has 18,000 employees.

Case Credit Corp., a wholly owned subsidiary of the company, services a $5.2 billion portfolio of receivables and leases, consisting primarily of agricultural and construction equipment.

Case has 20 manufacturing locations in: Iowa, Illinois, North Dakota, Wisconsin, Kansas, Minnesota, Australia, Austria, Brazil, Canada, France, Germany and the United Kingdom. It also has five joint ventures located in: Brazil, China, Uzbekistan and the United States.

Case Excellence in Government Committee (formerly known as Case Corp. PAC) (C00303883) *Phone: (202) 737-7575 * Fax: (202) 737-9090 * 1001 G St. N.W., Suite 100 E., Washington, DC 20001 * Contact: Steven G. Lamb, President and COO * Treasurer: Joseph E. Samora Jr.*

	1993-94	1995-96	1997	Totals
Receipts	$0	$29,422	$18,832	$48,254
Disburse	0	15,026	104	15,130
Cash	0	14,408	33,141	n/a
Contributions	0	15,000	0	15,000
Republicans	0	9,000	0	9,000
No. of Cand.	*0*	*5*	*0*	*5*
House	0	7,000	0	7,000
Senate	0	2,000	0	2,000
Democrats	0	6,000	0	6,000
No. of Cand.	*0*	*3*	*0*	*3*
House	0	6,000	0	6,000
Senate	0	0	0	0
Incumbents	0	14,000	0	14,000
Challengers	0	0	0	0
Open Seat	0	1,000	0	1,000
Winners	0	15,000	n/a	15,000
Losers	0	0	n/a	0

Cenex Inc.

*Phone: (612) 451-5151 * Fax: (612) 451-4905*
5500 Cenex Dr., Inver Grove Heights, MN 55077
Web: www.cnxlol.com

Cenex is a Minnesota-based agriculture and petroleum company. Cenex's agricultural coverage area spans 16 states, including Kansas, Oklahoma, Wisconsin, Washington and Oregon. The company employs 2,500 people and operates two oil refineries in Montana and Kansas. Cenex reported 1997 sales of $2.9 billion.

The company also provides farm equipment, petroleum and technical services to help farmers produce environmentally sound products.

In a joint venture with Land O' Lakes, both companies provide feed and seed, and crop protection products for farmers.

Established in 1982, the bipartisan PAC supports candidates who are involved with agricultural issues and represent the western trade region.

Cenex Political Action Committee-CenexPAC (C00149104)
*Address: same as sponsor * Treasurer: Jay Debertin*

	1993-94	1995-96	1997	Totals
Receipts	$26,056	$26,913	$11,744	$64,713
Disburse	8,808	16,826	10,219	35,853
Cash	23,032	33,131	35,419	n/a
Contributions	8,750	11,100	7,250	27,100
Republicans	2,700	5,700	2,250	10,650
No. of Cand.	*5*	*12*	*4*	*21*
House	1,200	2,700	1,250	5,150
Senate	1,500	3,000	1,000	5,500
Democrats	3,050	5,400	4,000	12,450
No. of Cand.	*4*	*8*	*5*	*17*
House	2,050	3,850	1,000	6,900
Senate	1,000	1,550	3,000	5,550
Incumbents	5,500	7,100	7,250	19,850
Challengers	1,000	2,000	0	3,000
Open Seat	2,250	2,000	0	4,250
Winners	7,250	9,350	n/a	16,600
Losers	1,500	1,750	n/a	3,250

Crop Insurance Research Bureau

*Phone: (913) 338-0470 * Fax: (913) 661-1640*
9200 Indian Creek Pkwy., Suite 220, Overland Park, KS 66210-2008
Web: www.cropinsurance.org

Crop Insurance Research Bureau is a national trade association of crop insurers and other organizations that support the crop insurance industry.

The primary activities of CIRB include Washington representation, research and statistics, regulatory liaison, communications, development of educational media, discussion forum and public affairs. CIRB also monitors the Federal Crop Insurance Corp. to ensure that its regulations and policies do not negatively impact the private crop-hail insurance program.

CIRB-PAC contributes to legislators who support the maintenance of an actuarially bound non-intrusive crop insurance program.

Crop Insurance Research Bureau (CIRB-PAC) (C00150805) *Address: same as sponsor * Contact: Roger Swartz, Chairman * Treasurer: Paul L. Horel*

	1993-94	1995-96	1997	Totals
Receipts	$1,366	$5,149	$3,559	$10,074
Disburse	2,008	5,761	3,602	11,371
Cash	2,265	1,652	2,606	n/a
Contributions	2,000	5,750	2,250	10,000
Republicans	500	4,750	1,250	6,500
No. of Cand.	*1*	*5*	*3*	*9*
House	500	3,250	1,250	5,000
Senate	0	1,500	0	1,500
Democrats	1,500	1,000	1,000	3,500
No. of Cand.	*2*	*2*	*1*	*5*
House	1,500	500	0	2,000
Senate	0	500	1,000	1,500
Incumbents	2,000	3,750	2,250	8,000
Challengers	0	500	0	500
Open Seat	0	1,500	0	1,500
Winners	1,500	5,750	n/a	7,250
Losers	500	0	n/a	500

Deere & Co.

*Phone: (309) 765-4345 * Fax: (309) 765-5183*
Government Affairs Dept., John Deere Rd., Moline, IL 61265
Web: www.deere.com

John Deere is the world's leading producer of agricultural equipment and a major producer of industrial equipment for the construction, forestry and public works markets; lawn and grounds care products for homeowners and commercial users; engines and other powertrain components; and replacement parts for its own products and those of other manufacturers. John Deere also provides financial services including credit, insurance and managed health care plans.

In 1997 Deere reported revenues of nearly $12.8 billion. The company employs 34,000 workers.

Deere & Co. was No. 119 on the Fortune 500 list of the largest U.S. industrials in 1996, and has been called the "most admired" company in the industrial and farm equipment category in Fortune magazine's annual survey of corporate reputations.

Deere & Co. has two subsidiary PACs, Deere & Co. - Iowa and Deere & Co. - Illinois.

Deere & Co. Civic Action Fund (C00204099) *Address: same as sponsor * Contact: Dwayne Lemke, Chairman * Treasurer: Joan A. Vogelgesang*

	1993-94	1995-96	1997	Totals
Receipts	$167,059	$209,305	$134,731	$511,095
Disburse	166,055	200,057	39,612	405,724
Cash	13,652	22,908	118,035	n/a
Contributions	85,000	111,500	22,250	218,750
Republicans	75,500	100,250	18,250	194,000
No. of Cand.	*66*	*65*	*19*	*150*
House	42,500	68,250	15,250	126,000
Senate	33,000	32,000	3,000	68,000
Democrats	9,500	11,250	2,500	23,250
No. of Cand.	*10*	*7*	*3*	*20*
House	9,500	11,250	2,500	23,250
Senate	0	0	0	0
Incumbents	34,000	70,000	21,000	125,000
Challengers	10,000	15,500	1,250	26,750
Open Seat	40,500	26,000	0	66,500
Winners	75,500	76,000	n/a	151,500
Losers	9,500	35,500	n/a	45,000

Deere & Co. Political Action Committee - Illinois (Deere PAC - Illinois) (C00024703) *Phone: (309) 765-4497 * Fax: (309) 765-5183 * John Deere Rd., Moline, IL 61265 * Web: www.deere.com * Contact: Taylor Davis, PAC Administrator * Treasurer: Joan A. Vogelgesang*

	1993-94	1995-96	1997	Totals
Receipts	$74,130	$94,321	$51,007	$219,458
Disburse	73,940	93,481	30,777	198,198
Cash	6,301	7,151	27,388	n/a
Contributions	19,900	46,000	15,750	81,650
Republicans	16,400	43,000	13,750	73,150
No. of Cand.	*18*	*25*	*13*	*56*
House	8,400	19,000	7,750	35,150
Senate	8,000	24,000	6,000	38,000
Democrats	3,500	3,000	2,000	8,500
No. of Cand.	*5*	*4*	*2*	*11*
House	3,500	3,000	1,000	7,500
Senate	0	0	. 1,000	1,000
Incumbents	6,500	15,500	12,500	34,500
Challengers	4,400	13,000	3,250	20,650
Open Seat	9,000	17,500	0	26,500
Winners	14,650	19,000	n/a	33,650
Losers	5,250	27,000	n/a	32,250

Contributed less than $5,000 during 1995-96 cycle:

Deere & Co. Political Action Committee - Iowa (Deere PAC-Iowa) (C00082255) *Phone: (515) 244-9377 * Fax: (515) 289-3307 * 601 Locust, Suite 325, Des Moines, IA 50309 * Contact: Samuel R. Allen, Chairman * Treasurer: Joan A. Vogelgesang*

Farm Credit Council

*Phone: (202) 626-8710 * Fax: (202) 626-8718*
50 F St. N.W., Suite 900, Washington, DC 20001
*Web: www.fccouncil.com * E-mail: auer@fccouncil.com*

The Farm Credit Council is the national trade association for the Farm Credit System, the leading agricultural lender in the United States. A collection of private banks, the system provides 25 percent of all loans made to U.S. agriculture producers. The system's value is about $75 billion.

Among its services are real estate, home mortgage and operating loans, as well as crop insurance and leasing services. Created in 1916 by Congress, the system is regulated by the Farm Credit Administration but receives no government funding.

The association supports legislation that would authorize Farm Credit banks to lend to more rural small businesses by removing eligibility requirements for certain borrowers.

The Farm Credit Council PAC gave most of its money during the 1995-96 cycle to candidate committees — just $3,912 of its $248,000 was for non-candidate expenditures. It was the largest agricultural services PAC contributor to congressional campaigns. The organization gave nearly 92 percent to winning candidates.

The leading recipients were Sens. Tim Johnson, D-S.D., Wayne Allard, R-Colo., and Pete V. Domenici, R-N.M.

Farm Credit Council Political Action Committee (C00193631) *Address: same as sponsor * Contact: Ken Auer, Executive V.P. * Treasurer: William Jeffry Shipp*

	1993-94	1995-96	1997	Totals
Receipts	$244,719	$301,978	$171,146	$717,843
Disburse	217,143	248,514	129,503	595,160
Cash	77,142	130,615	172,263	n/a
Contributions	213,185	244,602	128,150	585,937
Republicans	89,520	150,083	78,850	318,453
No. of Cand.	*84*	*117*	*82*	*283*
House	66,020	104,130	61,350	231,500
Senate	23,500	45,953	17,500	86,953
Democrats	120,415	94,519	48,300	263,234
No. of Cand.	*97*	*79*	*56*	*232*
House	94,075	79,194	37,900	211,169
Senate	26,340	15,325	10,400	52,065
Incumbents	194,085	197,249	128,650	519,984
Challengers	3,000	17,750	0	20,750
Open Seat	15,100	29,603	0	44,703
Winners	169,695	223,927	n/a	393,622
Losers	43,490	20,675	n/a	64,165

Tenth District Farm Credit Council Inc. PAC (TDPAC) (C00305573) *Phone: (512) 465-0577 * Fax: (512) 465-0775 * P.O. Box 15919, Austin, TX 78761 * Contact: Kenneth Andrews, Chairman * Treasurer: Stanley L. Ray*

The Tenth District Farm Credit Council represents farm credit institutions in New Mexico, Texas, Mississippi, Louisiana and Alabama. Established in the 1980s, it follows agricultural, environmental and banking legislative issues. It is affiliated with the Farm Credit Council and its PAC.

	1993-94	1995-96	1997	Totals
Receipts	$0	$19,693	$9,766	$29,459
Disburse	0	6,454	11,778	18,232
Cash	0	13,242	11,230	n/a
Contributions	0	5,300	7,250	12,550
Republicans	0	3,250	4,750	8,000
No. of Cand.	*0*	*7*	*9*	*16*
House	0	2,250	2,750	5,000
Senate	0	1,000	2,000	3,000
Democrats	0	2,050	2,500	4,550
No. of Cand.	*0*	*6*	*2*	*8*
House	0	2,050	2,500	4,550
Senate	0	0	0	0
Incumbents	0	4,300	7,250	11,550
Challengers	0	500	0	500
Open Seat	0	500	0	500
Winners	0	4,800	n/a	4,800
Losers	0	500	n/a	500

Farmland Industries

*Phone: (816) 459-6741 * Fax: (816) 459-5110*
P.O. Box 12473, Kansas City, MO 64116
Web: www.farmland.com

Farmland Industries is the largest farmer-owned cooperative in North America. It is composed of more than 1,400 smaller farms, which are operated by a total of more than 500,000 people, as well as 13,000 beef and pork producers, all scattered throughout the United States, Canada and Mexico. Its 1997 sales were $9 billion.

The co-op operates in all 50 states and maintains fertilizer plants, a petroleum refinery, grain elevators, feed mills and railroad cars. It has offices in Missouri, Kansas, Nebraska, Iowa and overseas.

Farmland Industries Political Action Committee (Farmland PAC) (C00117267) *Address: same as sponsor * Treasurer: Gina Bowman-Morrill*

	1993-94	1995-96	1997	Totals
Receipts	$61,965	$74,182	$35,969	$172,116
Disburse	59,125	71,065	16,500	146,690
Cash	9,980	13,102	32,572	n/a
Contributions	56,100	67,625	21,750	145,475
Republicans	27,600	43,500	11,750	82,850
No. of Cand.	*25*	*39*	*18*	*82*
House	19,100	30,250	6,750	56,100
Senate	8,500	13,250	5,000	26,750
Democrats	27,250	24,125	9,000	60,375
No. of Cand.	*23*	*23*	*12*	*58*
House	19,250	17,375	3,500	40,125
Senate	8,000	6,750	5,500	20,250
Incumbents	49,100	45,375	21,750	116,225
Challengers	0	4,500	0	4,500
Open Seat	7,000	16,250	0	23,250
Winners	49,100	58,750	n/a	107,850
Losers	7,000	8,875	n/a	15,875

Federal Agricultural Mortgage Corp.

*Phone: (202) 872-7700 * Fax: (202) 872-7713*
919 18th St. N.W., Suite 200, Washington, DC 20006
Web: www.farmermac.com

Federal Agricultural Mortgage Corp., or Farmer Mac, is America's secondary market for agricultural real estate and rural housing mortgage loans. Farmer Mac was created by Congress to improve the availability of mortgage credit to U.S. farmers. It purchases qualified loans from lenders and replenishes their source of funds to make new loans.

The loans Farmer Mac purchases are then grouped into pools and used to back securities that Farmer Mac sells periodically into the capital markets. Those securities are supported by Farmer Mac's guarantee of timely payment of principal and interest. Although created by Congress, Farmer Mac is a publicly traded corporation.

Based in Washington, Farmer Mac has about $1.3 billion in assets and reported net income of $4.6 million for 1997.

Federal Agricultural Mortgage Corp. Political Action Committee (C00253468) *Address: same as sponsor * Treasurer: Thomas R. Clark*

	1993-94	1995-96	1997	Totals
Receipts	$41	$7,247	$11,930	$19,218
Disburse	525	7,500	11,930	19,955
Cash	281	30	31	n/a
Contributions	500	6,000	0	6,500

Republicans	0	3,250	0	3,250
No. of Cand.	*1*	*7*	*0*	*8*
House	0	3,250	0	3,250
Senate	0	0	0	0
Democrats	500	2,750	0	3,250
No. of Cand.	*1*	*5*	*0*	*6*
House	0	1,250	0	1,250
Senate	500	1,500	0	2,000
Incumbents	500	4,250	0	4,750
Challengers	0	1,000	0	1,000
Open Seat	0	750	0	750
Winners	500	6,000	n/a	6,500
Losers	0	0	n/a	0

Fertilizer Institute

*Phone: (202) 675-8250 * Fax: (202) 544-8123*
501 Second St. N.E., Washington, DC 20002

The Fertilizer Institute is a lobbying group for fertilizer manufacturers in the United States. The fertilizer industry generates an estimated $15 billion in revenue annually. The group opposes restrictions on ingredients in fertilizer, which can include heavy metals such as lead. In 1994, the industry successfully fought a ban on fertilizers with more than 0.1 percent lead.

Fert PAC (The Political Action Committee of The Fertilizer Institute) (C00085910) *Address: same as sponsor * Treasurer: Ford B. West*

	1993-94	*1995-96*	*1997*	*Totals*
Receipts	$11,250	$21,425	$9,650	$42,325
Disburse	14,150	21,500	9,200	44,850
Cash	361	286	736	n/a
Contributions	14,150	20,625	8,700	43,475
Republicans	5,300	16,800	3,700	25,800
No. of Cand.	*12*	*25*	*8*	*45*
House	3,800	10,050	2,700	16,550
Senate	1,500	6,750	1,000	9,250
Democrats	8,850	3,825	5,000	17,675
No. of Cand.	*12*	*7*	*5*	*24*
House	6,850	1,825	3,000	11,675
Senate	2,000	2,000	2,000	6,000
Incumbents	12,200	17,325	8,700	38,225
Challengers	0	1,200	0	1,200
Open Seat	1,950	2,100	0	4,050
Winners	9,500	16,800	n/a	26,300
Losers	4,650	3,825	n/a	8,475

First Mississippi Corp.

P.O. Box 1249, 700 North St., Jackson, MS 39205

First Mississippi Corp.'s PAC was terminated in 1996.

First Mississippi Corp. Political Action Committee (C00121814) *Address: same as sponsor * Treasurer: Mike Summerford*

	1993-94	*1995-96*	*1997*	*Totals*
Receipts	$10,825	$15,611	$0	$26,436
Disburse	9,080	20,365	0	29,445
Cash	4,248	0	0	n/a
Contributions	9,025	11,750	0	20,775
Republicans	7,425	11,500	0	18,925
No. of Cand.	*14*	*20*	*0*	*34*
House	2,800	8,000	0	10,800
Senate	4,625	3,500	0	8,125
Democrats	1,600	250	0	1,850
No. of Cand.	*4*	*1*	*0*	*5*
House	1,600	250	0	1,850
Senate	0	0	0	0
Incumbents	3,675	7,250	0	10,925
Challengers	800	1,000	0	1,800
Open Seat	4,550	3,500	0	8,050
Winners	7,925	9,250	n/a	17,175
Losers	1,100	2,500	n/a	3,600

Florida Farm Bureau Federation

*Phone: (352) 378-1321 * Fax: (352) 374-1501*
5700 S.W. 34th St., Gainesville, FL 32608
Web: www.ffbic.com

Florida Farm Bureau Federation represents 130,000 farm and ranch families. The nonprofit group seeks to help farmers increase their net income.

Established in 1941, the Farm Bureau represents agriculture at the local, state and national levels and works to educate the public about agriculture. The bureau is affiliated with the American Farm Bureau Federation.

Florida Farm Bureau Federation FedPAC (C00283572) *Address: same as sponsor * Contact: Pat Cockrell, Chairman * Treasurer: Robert W. Richardson*

	1993-94	*1995-96*	*1997*	*Totals*
Receipts	$5,561	$19,056	$3,682	$28,299
Disburse	1,800	11,100	2,045	14,945
Cash	3,764	11,724	13,362	n/a
Contributions	1,650	11,100	2,000	14,750
Republicans	950	6,850	1,000	8,800
No. of Cand.	*5*	*8*	*1*	*14*
House	450	6,850	1,000	8,300
Senate	500	0	0	500
Democrats	700	4,250	1,000	5,950
No. of Cand.	*2*	*3*	*2*	*7*
House	700	4,250	1,000	5,950
Senate	0	0	0	0
Incumbents	1,550	6,600	2,000	10,150
Challengers	0	1,000	0	1,000
Open Seat	100	3,500	0	3,600
Winners	1,650	9,350	n/a	11,000
Losers	0	1,750	n/a	1,750

Freeport-McMoRan Inc.

Phone: (504) 582-4000
1615 Poydras St., New Orleans, LA 70112
Web: www.fmi.com

Freeport-McMoRan's PAC was terminated in January 1998 after the company announced a merger with IMC Global Inc.

Freeport-McMoRan, through its joint venture interest in IMC-Agrico Co., is engaged in the mining and sale of phosphate rock, the production, distribution and sale of phosphate fertilizers and the extraction of uranium oxide from phosphoric acid.

The business also includes mining, purchase, transportation and sale of sulfur. The firm has oil reserves at Main Pass in the Gulf of Mexico and owns Culberson mine in Texas.

Freeport-McMoRan Inc. Citizenship Committee (C00056192) *Phone: (202) 737-1400 * 50 F St. N.W., Suite 1050, Washington, DC 20001 * Treasurer: J. Ronald Combs*

	1993-94	*1995-96*	*1997*	*Totals*
Receipts	$130,146	$83,610	$28,628	$242,384
Disburse	126,329	86,188	36,117	248,634
Cash	10,067	7,489	0	n/a
Contributions	121,120	84,600	30,250	235,970
Republicans	60,500	51,100	15,250	126,850
No. of Cand.	*50*	*54*	*20*	*124*
House	21,500	28,000	10,250	59,750
Senate	39,000	23,100	5,000	67,100
Democrats	60,620	33,500	15,000	109,120
No. of Cand.	*51*	*35*	*14*	*100*
House	32,000	22,500	3,000	57,500
Senate	28,620	11,000	12,000	51,620
Incumbents	106,620	71,100	30,250	207,970
Challengers	500	1,000	0	1,500
Open Seat	14,000	12,500	0	26,500
Winners	110,500	69,600	n/a	180,100
Losers	10,620	15,000	n/a	25,620

Contributed less than $5,000 during 1995-96 cycle:

Freeport-McMoRan Copper & Gold Inc. Citizenship Committee (C00320101) *Phone: (202) 737-1400 * Fax: (202) 737-1568 * 50 F St. N.W., Suite 1050, Washington, DC 20001 * Treasurer: Arthur F. D'Aquin*

Friant Water PAC

*Phone: (805) 725-7270 * Fax: (805) 725-7271*
2331 Girard, Suite A, Delano, CA 93215

Friant Water PAC contributes to federal candidates who support legislation related to the water rights of Friant area farmers.

During 1997, the PAC contributed to one Republican and one Democratic candidate in California.

Friant Water PAC (C00244533) *Address: same as sponsor * Treasurer: Michael W. Turnipseed*

	1993-94	1995-96	1997	Totals
Receipts	$25,797	$14,120	$0	$39,917
Disburse	20,537	22,046	2,132	44,715
Cash	20,889	12,960	10,828	n/a
Contributions	13,341	13,548	2,000	28,889
Republicans	4,008	12,548	1,000	17,556
No. of Cand.	*4*	*12*	*1*	*17*
House	3,008	8,959	1,000	12,967
Senate	1,000	3,589	0	4,589
Democrats	9,333	1,000	1,000	11,333
No. of Cand.	*4*	*1*	*1*	*6*
House	4,000	1,000	1,000	6,000
Senate	5,333	0	0	5,333
Incumbents	10,983	12,048	2,000	25,031
Challengers	2,358	500	0	2,858
Open Seat	0	1,000	0	1,000
Winners	11,341	13,548	n/a	24,889
Losers	2,000	0	n/a	2,000

Glenn Colusa PAC

*Phone: (530) 934-2778 * Fax: (530) 934-5177*
P.O. Box 962, Willows, CA 95988

The Glenn Colusa Irrigation District Board of Directors formed the Glenn Colusa PAC to monitor Congress' allocation of money with respect to irrigation.

The Irrigation District of Glenn and Colusa counties in northern California is a quasi-state entity that appropriates and operates water services under the state water code.

The PAC is bipartisan and gives to candidates from all parts of the nation, generally those who have positions that affect water-allocation issues. It also addresses fish and wildlife issues.

Glenn Colusa Political Action Committee (C00218628) *Address: same as sponsor * Treasurer: Sandy Denn*

	1993-94	1995-96	1997	Totals
Receipts	$10,791	$9,074	$613	$20,478
Disburse	16,345	9,440	700	26,485
Cash	896	533	446	n/a
Contributions	7,833	7,750	700	16,283
Republicans	1,100	4,750	200	6,050
No. of Cand.	*2*	*6*	*1*	*9*
House	600	4,750	200	5,550
Senate	500	0	0	500
Democrats	6,733	3,000	500	10,233
No. of Cand.	*3*	*1*	*1*	*5*
House	5,400	3,000	500	8,900
Senate	1,333	0	0	1,333
Incumbents	7,833	7,750	700	16,283
Challengers	0	0	0	0
Open Seat	0	0	0	0
Winners	7,833	7,750	n/a	15,583
Losers	0	0	n/a	0

Harvest States Cooperatives

*Phone: (612) 646-9433 * Fax: (612) 641-6431*
1667 N. Snelling Ave., P.O. Box 64594, St. Paul, MN 55108
Web: www.harveststates.com

Harvest States Cooperatives is a grain and feed organization of nearly 600 farmer co-ops extending from the Upper Midwest to the Pacific Northwest. The group sells grain, processes soybeans and provides semolina and wheat flour to the pasta industry. Harvest States also offers insurance for agribusinesses, feed products and farm supplies for its members. The co-op reported 1997 sales of $7.1 billion. It employs about 2,350 people.

Harvest States and Cenex, another Minnesota-based co-op, announced in November 1997 that they plan to merge. Cenex specializes in petroleum sales and soil research. Land O'Lakes, another co-op, will combine assets with Harvest States in six Midwestern states.

Harvest States Cooperatives Political Action Committee (C00216259) *Address: same as sponsor * Treasurer: Allen J. Anderson*

	1993-94	1995-96	1997	Totals
Receipts	$13,467	$7,145	$149	$20,761
Disburse	7,880	8,001	4,568	20,449
Cash	7,303	6,451	2,033	n/a
Contributions	5,850	7,450	2,750	16,050
Republicans	500	1,200	750	2,450
No. of Cand.	*1*	*3*	*2*	*6*
House	0	500	250	750
Senate	500	700	500	1,700
Democrats	3,650	6,250	1,500	11,400
No. of Cand.	*9*	*6*	*3*	*18*
House	2,300	4,250	500	7,050
Senate	1,350	2,000	1,000	4,350
Incumbents	4,900	5,250	2,750	12,900
Challengers	0	1,200	0	1,200
Open Seat	950	1,000	0	1,950
Winners	5,150	7,250	n/a	12,400
Losers	700	200	n/a	900

IMC Global Operations Inc.

Phone: (847) 272-9200
2100 Sanders Rd., Northbrook, IL 60062
Web: www.imcglobal.com

IMC Global produces chemicals for agriculture and other uses. The publicly traded Illinois company's major products include phosphate, potash and nitrogen for use as crop nutrients and animal feed ingredients. IMC reported $2.9 billion in 1997 sales.

In December 1997, IMC announced that it will enlarge its chemical business with the acquisition of privately held Harris Chemical Group Inc. The acquisition will add about $850 million to the company's revenues. It also will make IMC Global the world's third-largest producer of salt and soda ash. Other Harris products, which along with soda ash comprise the company's industrial chemical business, include sodium bicarbonate, boron chemicals, sulfate of potash and magnesium chloride.

U.S. locations: California, Colorado, Florida, Georgia, Illinois, Louisiana, Michigan, New Mexico, Ohio, Oregon and Wisconsin.

IMC Global Operations Inc. Political Action Committee (C00225367) *Phone: (202) 737-1400 * 50 F St. N.W., Suite 1050, Washington, DC 20001 * Treasurer: James Siemers*
*Contact: Marschall Smith, Senior V.P. * Phone: (847) 272-9200*

	1993-94	1995-96	1997	Totals
Receipts	$37,768	$109,122	$67,270	$214,160
Disburse	41,182	100,785	50,657	192,624
Cash	8,097	16,433	33,045	n/a
Contributions	40,500	79,100	41,200	160,800
Republicans	24,500	54,600	23,700	102,800
No. of Cand.	*27*	*54*	*28*	*109*
House	10,500	25,500	17,500	53,500
Senate	14,000	29,100	6,200	49,300
Democrats	16,000	24,500	16,500	57,000
No. of Cand.	*21*	*27*	*12*	*60*
House	13,000	15,500	3,000	31,500
Senate	3,000	9,000	13,500	25,500
Incumbents	28,500	54,500	38,700	121,700
Challengers	2,000	3,100	0	5,100
Open Seat	10,000	21,500	1,500	33,000
Winners	35,500	62,500	n/a	98,000
Losers	5,000	16,600	n/a	21,600

Illinois Agricultural Association

*Phone: (309) 557-3554 * Fax: (309) 557-2559*
1701 Towanda Ave., P.O. Box 2901, Bloomington, IL 61701-2901
*Web: www.fb.com/ilfb * E-mail: jhawkins@ilfb.org*

The Illinois Agricultural Association, also known as the Illinois Farm Bureau, is a bipartisan committee that gives to candidates who are "friends of agriculture."

The association publishes voter guides twice a year for its 385,000 members.

Illinois Agricultural Association Activator Political Involvement Fund (Activator) (C00193441) *Address: same as sponsor * Contact: Ralph Feebairn, Chairman * Treasurer: Robert Weldon*

	1993-94	1995-96	1997	Totals
Receipts	$31,381	$16,751	$8,379	$56,511
Disburse	31,732	25,654	3,413	60,799
Cash	13,452	4,551	9,517	n/a
Contributions	19,855	19,370	749	39,974
Republicans	18,435	17,412	749	36,596
No. of Cand.	*9*	*10*	*1*	*20*
House	18,435	17,412	749	36,596
Senate	0	0	0	0
Democrats	1,420	1,958	0	3,378
No. of Cand.	*1*	*1*	*0*	*2*
House	1,420	1,958	0	3,378
Senate	0	0	0	0
Incumbents	6,672	14,372	749	21,793

Challengers	0	4,998	0	4,998
Open Seat	13,183	0	0	13,183
Winners	18,435	14,266	n/a	32,701
Losers	1,420	5,104	n/a	6,524

Indiana Farm Bureau

*Phone: (317) 692-7851 * Fax: (317) 692-7854*
225 S. East St., Indianapolis, IN 46202

The Indiana Farm Bureau is the largest farm organization in the state, with more than 270,000 member families. It is affiliated with the American Farm Bureau Federation.

Indiana Farm Bureau Inc. Elect Political Action Committee Inc. (C00169722) *Address: same as sponsor * Contact: Kent Yeager, Secretary * Treasurer: James J. Edwards*

	1993-94	1995-96	1997	Totals
Receipts	$130,879	$118,519	$111,792	$361,190
Disburse	126,858	91,028	40,152	258,038
Cash	79,858	107,349	178,989	n/a
Contributions	49,325	40,100	0	89,425
Republicans	33,325	30,100	0	63,425
No. of Cand.	*6*	*6*	*0*	*12*
House	30,075	30,100	0	60,175
Senate	3,250	0	0	3,250
Democrats	16,000	10,000	0	26,000
No. of Cand.	*3*	*2*	*0*	*5*
House	16,000	10,000	0	26,000
Senate	0	0	0	0
Incumbents	29,325	30,100	0	59,425
Challengers	10,000	0	0	10,000
Open Seat	10,000	10,000	0	20,000
Winners	34,325	35,100	n/a	69,425
Losers	15,000	5,000	n/a	20,000

Iowa Farm Bureau Federation

*Phone: (515) 225-5408 * Fax: (515) 225-5419*
5400 University Ave., West Des Moines, IA 50265
Web: www.ifbf.org

The Iowa Farm Bureau Federation is a coalition of farmers dedicated to improving net farm income and the quality of rural life. IFBF has more than 159,000 Iowa families as members.

IFBF is active in national and state legislative issues, such as regulatory reform and tax relief, that affect a farmer's bottom line.

In 1998, the Iowa Farm Bureau lobbied to remove "unnecessary" regulations on crop products from the EPA's state management plan.

The bureau is affiliated with the American Farm Bureau Federation.

Iowa Farm Bureau Federation Political Action Committee (FB PAC) (C00200329) *Address: same as sponsor * Contact: Dave Hopp, Chairman * Treasurer: Dick Harris*

	1993-94	1995-96	1997	Totals
Receipts	$125,386	$150,466	$65,512	$341,364
Disburse	136,618	139,447	8,160	284,225
Cash	30,875	41,895	99,247	n/a
Contributions	12,464	21,077	0	33,541
Republicans	11,464	12,945	0	24,409
No. of Cand.	*3*	*5*	*0*	*8*
House	11,464	7,948	0	19,412
Senate	0	4,997	0	4,997
Democrats	1,000	8,132	0	9,132
No. of Cand.	*1*	*1*	*0*	*2*
House	1,000	8,132	0	9,132
Senate	0	0	0	0
Incumbents	10,973	7,948	0	18,921
Challengers	0	4,997	0	4,997
Open Seat	1,491	8,132	0	9,623
Winners	11,464	15,580	n/a	27,044
Losers	1,000	5,497	n/a	6,497

Kansas Farm Bureau

*Phone: (785) 587-6000 * Fax: (785) 587-6914*
2627 KFB Plaza, Manhattan, KS 66503-8508
*Web: www.kfb.org * E-mail: waparker@kfbs.com*

The Kansas Farm Bureau is the largest farm organization in the state, with about 130,000 member families and affiliated local bureaus in all 105 Kansas counties.

The organization, established in 1919, supports legislation that promotes agriculture, protects private property rights and helps small businesses and the self-employed. Based in Manhattan, Kan., the bureau is affiliated with the American Farm Bureau Federation.

Kansas Farm Bureau Voters Organization/Elect Farm Bureau Friends Fund (Kansas Farm Bureau Vote Farm Bureau Friends Fund) (C00285783) *Address: same as sponsor * Contact: Warren Baccus, VOTE FBF Dir. * Treasurer: Steve Baccus*

	1993-94	1995-96	1997	Totals
Receipts	$29,363	$38,864	$21,284	$89,511
Disburse	19,232	21,017	0	40,249
Cash	10,131	28,108	49,392	n/a
Contributions	0	5,700	0	5,700
Republicans	0	5,700	0	5,700
No. of Cand.	*0*	*6*	*0*	*6*
House	0	4,000	0	4,000
Senate	0	1,700	0	1,700
Democrats	0	0	0	0
No. of Cand.	*0*	*0*	*0*	*0*
House	0	0	0	0
Senate	0	0	0	0
Incumbents	0	1,000	0	1,000
Challengers	0	1,000	0	1,000
Open Seat	0	3,700	0	3,700
Winners	0	5,700	n/a	5,700
Losers	0	0	n/a	0

Michigan Farm Bureau

*Phone: (517) 323-6588 * Fax: (517) 323-6558*
7373 W. Saginaw Highway, P.O. Box 30960, Lansing, MI 48909
Web: www.fb.com/mifb/home.htm

The Michigan Farm Bureau is the state's largest farm organization, with more than 155,000 members. The organization's 69 county farm bureaus support agriculture, Michigan's second-largest industry.

In addition to its support for farm issues, the bureau works in both Lansing, Mich. and Washington to protect private property rights, the quality of rural environment and the safety of the food supply. The bureau is affiliated with the American Farm Bureau Federation.

Michigan Farm Bureau Political Action Committee (C00096362) *Address: same as sponsor * Contact: Al Almy, Secretary * Treasurer: John Vander Molen*

	1993-94	1995-96	1997	Totals
Receipts	$77,907	$100,887	$55,227	$234,021
Disburse	104,673	94,066	3,767	202,506
Cash	2,882	9,704	61,164	n/a
Contributions	14,880	25,200	550	40,630
Republicans	14,880	23,200	550	38,630
No. of Cand.	*6*	*8*	*2*	*16*
House	14,880	20,200	550	35,630
Senate	0	3,000	0	3,000
Democrats	0	2,000	0	2,000
No. of Cand.	*0*	*2*	*0*	*2*
House	0	2,000	0	2,000
Senate	0	0	0	0
Incumbents	8,880	15,200	550	24,630
Challengers	3,000	10,000	0	13,000
Open Seat	3,000	0	0	3,000
Winners	10,880	5,450	n/a	16,330
Losers	4,000	19,750	n/a	23,750

Mississippi Chemical Corp.

*Phone: (601) 746-4131 * Fax: (601) 746-9158*
Highway 49 E., Box 388, Yazoo City, MS 39194-0388
*Web: www.misschem.com * E-mail: corpcomm@misschem.com*

Mississippi Chemical Corp. produces and markets three primary crop nutrients — nitrogen fertilizer, diammonium phosphate and potash. Publicly traded MCC has 1,700 employees and posted sales of $520 million in 1997.

Nitrogen products include ammonia; fertilizer-grade ammonium nitrate, which is sold under the trade name Amtrate; UAN solutions, which are sold under the trade name N-Sol; and urea. MCC also is the largest manufacturer and marketer of high-density ammonium nitrate fertilizer in the United States. Ammonium nitrate, which is 34 percent nitrogen, is produced by mixing anhydrous ammonia and nitric acid.

Plants are located in: Yazoo City and Pascagoula, Miss., Donaldsonville, La. and Carlsbad, N.M.

Mississippi Chemical Corp. Voluntary Involvement Political Action Committee (C00143289) *Address: same as sponsor * Contact: Trudy Allen, Attorney * Treasurer: Mickey W. Crane*

	1993-94	1995-96	1997	Totals
Receipts	$25,509	$20,372	$11,995	$57,876
Disburse	17,200	11,000	2,500	30,700
Cash	19,167	28,542	38,038	n/a
Contributions	10,700	10,000	2,500	23,200
Republicans	4,000	10,000	0	14,000
No. of Cand.	*3*	*8*	*0*	*11*
House	2,000	7,000	0	9,000
Senate	2,000	3,000	0	5,000
Democrats	6,700	0	2,500	9,200
No. of Cand.	*6*	*0*	*1*	*7*
House	6,200	0	2,500	8,700
Senate	500	0	0	500
Incumbents	6,200	4,500	2,500	13,200
Challengers	1,000	1,000	0	2,000
Open Seat	3,500	4,500	0	8,000
Winners	6,700	8,000	n/a	14,700
Losers	4,000	2,000	n/a	6,000

Missouri Farm Bureau

Phone: (573) 893-1400
P. O. Box 658, Jefferson City, MO 65109
Web: www.fb.com/mofb

The Missouri Farm Bureau is Missouri's largest general agriculture organization, with more than 85,000 members and local offices in 113 counties. The first state farm bureau to organize, the MFB also provides insurance, investment services and discounts for its members.

The group lobbies on farming, environmental and property rights issues. Missouri's farms produce annually about $4.5 billion worth of livestock and crops. The MFB, which is affiliated with the American Farm Bureau Federation, has six federal PACs which represent different geographical districts in the state.

Missouri Farm Bureau Farm PAC, Southeast District (C00089839) *Phone: (573) 238-2654 * Route 2, Box 155, Marble Hill, MO 63764 * Treasurer: Kenneth Englehart*

	1993-94	1995-96	1997	Totals
Receipts	$16,465	$18,302	$9,166	$43,933
Disburse	11,937	16,237	1,920	30,094
Cash	17,523	19,590	26,838	n/a
Contributions	3,333	9,745	0	13,078
Republicans	3,333	9,745	0	13,078
No. of Cand.	*2*	*1*	*0*	*3*
House	2,500	9,745	0	12,245
Senate	833	0	0	833
Democrats	0	0	0	0
No. of Cand.	*0*	*0*	*0*	*0*
House	0	0	0	0
Senate	0	0	0	0
Incumbents	2,500	0	0	2,500
Challengers	0	0	0	0
Open Seat	833	9,745	0	10,578
Winners	3,333	9,745	n/a	13,078
Losers	0	0	n/a	0

Missouri Farm Bureau Farm PAC, West Central District (C00038968) *Route 1, St. Elizabeth, MO 65075 * Treasurer: Fred L. Harris*

	1993-94	1995-96	1997	Totals
Receipts	$18,031	$18,534	$10,053	$46,618
Disburse	16,969	17,485	2,826	37,280
Cash	18,087	19,138	26,365	n/a
Contributions	8,417	7,050	500	15,967
Republicans	3,167	550	0	3,717
No. of Cand.	*2*	*2*	*0*	*4*
House	2,000	0	0	2,000
Senate	1,167	550	0	1,717
Democrats	5,250	6,500	500	12,250
No. of Cand.	*1*	*1*	*1*	*3*
House	5,250	6,500	500	12,250
Senate	0	0	0	0
Incumbents	5,250	7,050	500	12,800
Challengers	0	0	0	0
Open Seat	3,167	0	0	3,167
Winners	6,417	7,050	n/a	13,467
Losers	2,000	0	n/a	2,000

Contributed less than $5,000 during 1995-96 cycle:

Missouri Farm Bureau Farm PAC, Northeast District (C00019489) *34075 Audrain Rd. 708, Martinsburg, MO 65264 * Treasurer: Jeffrey A. Fennewald*

Missouri Farm Bureau Farm PAC, Northwest District (C00040428) *9117 Highway 87, Prairie Home, MO 65068 * Treasurer: Robert Alpers*

Missouri Farm Bureau Farm PAC, Southwest District (C00093898) *Route 1, Carthage, MO 64836 * Treasurer: Mary Taylor*

Missouri Farm Bureau Farm PAC, St. Louis Area (C00170944) *5896 Highway H, St. Charles, MO 63301 * Treasurer: Earl Heitmann*

National Council of Farmer Co-ops

*Phone: (202) 626-8700 * Fax: (202) 626-8722*
50 F St. N.W., Suite 900, Washington, DC 20001

National Council of Farmer Co-ops represents more than 100 farmer-owned cooperative businesses.

National Council of Farmer Cooperatives Political Action Committee (Co-op PAC) (C00002238) *Address: same as sponsor * Treasurer: Joe Smolskis*

	1993-94	1995-96	1997	Totals
Receipts	$126,380	$136,070	$57,585	$320,035
Disburse	128,898	130,114	57,790	316,802
Cash	9,526	15,480	15,274	n/a
Contributions	124,152	119,062	58,274	301,488
Republicans	36,073	63,203	25,609	124,885
No. of Cand.	*44*	*74*	*47*	*165*
House	25,873	46,250	24,109	96,232
Senate	10,200	16,953	1,500	28,653
Democrats	85,579	55,859	32,165	173,603
No. of Cand.	*89*	*62*	*42*	*193*
House	67,581	44,711	22,165	134,457
Senate	17,998	11,148	10,000	39,146
Incumbents	113,829	100,844	57,274	271,947
Challengers	0	3,000	0	3,000
Open Seat	10,323	15,218	0	25,541
Winners	95,228	103,695	n/a	198,923
Losers	28,924	15,367	n/a	44,291

National Farmers Union

Phone: (303) 752-5800
11900 E. Cornell Ave., Aurora, CO 80014
Web: www.nfu.org

The National Farmers Union is a federation of state and regional Farmers Union groups representing 300,000 members located in every state. Members include cattle ranchers, grain producers, fish farmers, fruit and grain growers and special crop producers.

The group maintains that a viable farm economy is the basis for a strong democracy and pursues progressive farm legislation and opposes legislation that would be harmful to rural America. During the National Farmers Union's annual convention, delegates representing each state discuss and formulate the organization's goals for the next year.

Membership in a state or regional Farmers Union automatically constitutes membership in the National Farmers Union.

National Farmers Union Political Action Committee (NatFarmPAC) (C00151019) *Phone: (202) 554-1600 * Fax: (202) 554-1654 * 400 Virginia Ave. S.W., Suite 710, Washington, DC 20024 * E-mail: nfudcco@aol.com * Contact: Christal Ogene, PAC Administrator * Treasurer: David E. Carter*

	1993-94	1995-96	1997	Totals
Receipts	$60,024	$57,794	$25,959	$143,777
Disburse	56,947	61,922	8,250	127,119
Cash	5,154	1,028	18,738	n/a
Contributions	22,580	25,900	5,750	54,230
Republicans	250	500	500	1,250
No. of Cand.	*1*	*2*	*1*	*4*
House	250	500	500	1,250
Senate	0	0	0	0
Democrats	20,580	25,400	5,000	50,980
No. of Cand.	*59*	*75*	*14*	*148*
House	15,780	17,650	3,250	36,680
Senate	4,800	7,750	1,750	14,300
Incumbents	17,280	16,900	5,750	39,930
Challengers	2,050	4,600	0	6,650
Open Seat	3,250	4,400	0	7,650
Winners	13,280	20,350	n/a	33,630
Losers	9,300	5,550	n/a	14,850

National Grain & Feed Association

*Phone: (202) 289-0873 * Fax: (202) 289-5388*
1201 New York Ave. N.W., Suite 830, Washington, DC 20005
Web: www.ngfa.org

The National Grain and Feed Association represents more than 1,000 grain, feed and related processing companies in the United States and around the world.

The association, which was founded in 1896, is interested in agriculture policy and environmental issues.

National Grain & Feed Association's Fund for Better Government Committee (Grain PAC) (C00240226) *Address: same as sponsor * Contact: Kendell Keith, President * Treasurer: Scott Heddrich*

	1993-94	1995-96	1997	Totals
Receipts	$17,746	$19,738	$7,928	$45,412
Disburse	14,908	22,923	1,021	38,852
Cash	16,343	13,162	20,069	n/a
Contributions	14,850	22,000	1,000	37,850
Republicans	9,250	19,500	500	29,250
No. of Cand.	*13*	*26*	*1*	*40*
House	7,250	11,500	0	18,750
Senate	2,000	8,000	500	10,500
Democrats	5,600	2,500	500	8,600
No. of Cand.	*7*	*3*	*1*	*11*
House	4,600	2,000	0	6,600
Senate	1,000	500	500	2,000
Incumbents	13,600	17,000	1,000	31,600
Challengers	750	2,000	0	2,750
Open Seat	500	3,000	0	3,500
Winners	13,250	20,000	n/a	33,250
Losers	1,600	2,000	n/a	3,600

North Carolina Farm Bureau Federation

*Phone: (919) 782-1705 * Fax: (919) 783-3593*
5301 Glenwood Ave., Raleigh, NC 27612

The North Carolina Farm Bureau is affiliated with the American Farm Bureau Federation.

North Carolina Farm Bureau Federation Inc. Political Action Committee Inc. (also known as N.C. Farm Bureau FarmPAC) (C00216754) *Address: same as sponsor * Treasurer: Hubert Julian Philpott Jr.*

	1993-94	1995-96	1997	Totals
Receipts	$17,046	$4,939	$12,386	$34,371
Disburse	41,435	17,997	2,878	62,310
Cash	18,074	5,016	14,524	n/a
Contributions	30,375	14,200	1,700	46,275
Republicans	9,000	8,900	650	18,550
No. of Cand.	*10*	*9*	*2*	*21*
House	8,000	4,600	150	12,750
Senate	1,000	4,300	500	5,800
Democrats	21,375	5,300	1,050	27,725
No. of Cand.	*11*	*8*	*3*	*22*
House	21,375	5,300	1,050	27,725
Senate	0	0	0	0
Incumbents	22,875	12,400	1,700	36,975
Challengers	1,500	1,050	0	2,550
Open Seat	6,000	750	0	6,750
Winners	17,750	13,200	n/a	30,950
Losers	12,625	1,000	n/a	13,625

Ohio Farm Bureau Federation

*Phone: (614) 249-2411 * Fax: (614) 249-2200*
Two Nationwide Plaza, P.O. Box 479, Columbus, OH 43216-0479
Web: www.fb.com/ohfb

The Ohio Farm Bureau Federation represents about 186,000 individual members, including farmers and others associated with the agricultural industry. The organization is affiliated with the American Farm Bureau Federation.

Ohio Farm Bureau Federation Inc. Agriculture Political Education Program (OFBF-APEP) (C00161265) *Address: same as sponsor * Contact: Keith Stimpert, V.P. of Gov. Affairs * Treasurer: C. William Swank*

	1993-94	1995-96	1997	Totals
Receipts	$238,382	$305,156	$169,797	$713,335
Disburse	219,436	276,836	72,372	568,644
Cash	57,079	85,400	182,827	n/a
Contributions	18,095	17,700	3,650	39,445
Republicans	16,450	17,200	3,650	37,300
No. of Cand.	*9*	*8*	*4*	*21*
House	5,950	17,200	2,150	25,300
Senate	10,500	0	1,500	12,000
Democrats	1,645	500	0	2,145
No. of Cand.	*3*	*1*	*0*	*4*
House	1,645	500	0	2,145
Senate	0	0	0	0
Incumbents	4,850	17,700	2,150	24,700
Challengers	100	0	0	100
Open Seat	13,145	0	1,500	14,645
Winners	15,350	12,700	n/a	28,050
Losers	2,745	5,000	n/a	7,745

Rain & Hail Insurance Society

*Phone: (515) 224-3070 * Fax: (515) 224-3089*
1501 50th St., Suite 200, West Des Moines, IA 50266
*Web: www.rainandhail.com * E-mail: publish@rainhail.com*

Rain and Hail Insurance Society is a privately held company that provides crop insurance to 200,000 farmers in the United States. The company is backed by reinsurers CIGNA, State Farm, National Farmers Union P&C and Agri General. It was founded in 1919 and employs 345 people.

Rain & Hail Insurance Society Political Action Committee (C00279505) *Address: same as sponsor * Treasurer: Ryan D. Miller*

	1993-94	1995-96	1997	Totals
Receipts	$89,305	$112,755	$50,521	$252,581
Disburse	37,548	67,652	27,248	132,448
Cash	51,757	96,860	120,133	n/a
Contributions	30,050	48,175	18,350	96,575
Republicans	10,900	35,425	6,050	52,375
No. of Cand.	*12*	*23*	*8*	*43*
House	9,500	19,075	5,550	34,125
Senate	1,400	16,350	500	18,250
Democrats	18,600	12,750	11,800	43,150
No. of Cand.	*12*	*7*	*5*	*24*
House	11,750	4,800	1,000	17,550
Senate	6,850	7,950	10,800	25,600
Incumbents	29,550	26,825	18,350	74,725
Challengers	500	8,500	0	9,000
Open Seat	0	12,850	0	12,850
Winners	24,300	38,925	n/a	63,225
Losers	5,750	9,250	n/a	15,000

Salt River Valley Water Users' Association

*Phone: (602) 236-5900 * Fax: (602) 236-5608*
1521 N. Project Dr., Phoenix, AZ 85281
*Web: www.srp.gov * E-mail: rxhernan@srp.gov*

Salt River Valley Water Users' Association is a privately held corporation that provides irrigation and drinking water to the area centered around Phoenix, Ariz. It maintains and operates dams, groundwater wells and 131 miles of canals. The company had $11.5 million in 1997 revenues.

The association is the smaller of the two operating entities of the Salt River Project. The larger, the Agricultural Improvement and Power District, is part of the state of Arizona and provides electricity to 650,000 customers in the Phoenix area. SRP operates or has an interest in seven power plants in Arizona, including a 17.5 percent interest in Palo Verde nuclear plant, which is located 55 miles west of Phoenix.

The SRP parent organization, which has 4,300 employees, reported $1.4 billion in 1997 revenues.

Salt River Valley Water Users' Association Political Involvement Committee (formerly known as PPIC) (C00048579) *Address: same as sponsor * Treasurer: Rudy Hernandez*

	1993-94	1995-96	1997	Totals
Receipts	$67,314	$101,836	$51,289	$220,439
Disburse	71,143	94,373	55,410	220,926
Cash	5,344	12,811	8,691	n/a
Contributions	28,990	28,300	25,750	83,040
Republicans	22,000	25,300	20,450	67,750
No. of Cand.	*17*	*21*	*13*	*51*
House	14,250	20,300	13,450	48,000
Senate	7,750	5,000	7,000	19,750
Democrats	6,990	3,000	5,300	15,290
No. of Cand.	*11*	*5*	*6*	*22*
House	6,000	2,500	2,000	10,500
Senate	990	500	3,300	4,790
Incumbents	15,240	26,800	24,950	66,990

(Data for Salt River Valley continued)

Challengers	2,500	0	500	3,000
Open Seat	10,250	1,500	300	12,050
Winners	21,250	27,800	n/a	49,050
Losers	7,740	500	n/a	8,240

Sandoz

1300 E. Touhy Ave., Des Plaines, IL 60018

Sandoz Agro Inc. PAC was terminated in October 1996.

Sandoz Agro Inc. Patriot Committee (C00253146) *Address: same as sponsor * Treasurer: Thomas M. Brennan*

	1993-94	1995-96	1997	Totals
Receipts	$32,117	$24,561	$0	$56,678
Disburse	36,700	32,390	0	69,090
Cash	7,571	0	0	n/a
Contributions	32,150	25,750	0	57,900
Republicans	18,150	7,250	0	25,400
No. of Cand.	*16*	*5*	*0*	*21*
House	14,400	2,000	0	16,400
Senate	3,750	5,250	0	9,000
Democrats	14,000	18,500	0	32,500
No. of Cand.	*16*	*5*	*0*	*21*
House	14,000	11,500	0	25,500
Senate	0	7,000	0	7,000
Incumbents	21,650	8,750	0	30,400
Challengers	0	6,000	0	6,000
Open Seat	10,500	11,000	0	21,500
Winners	26,650	25,250	n/a	51,900
Losers	5,500	500	n/a	6,000

Sandoz Pharmaceuticals Corp. Employees Political Action Committee (C00111716) *Phone: (201) 503-8300 * Fax: (201) 503-7727 * 59 Route 10, East Hanover, NJ 07936 * Treasurer: Richard W. Apgar Jr.*

The Sandoz Pharmaceuticals PAC was dissolved in December 1997. Novartis Pharmaceutical Corp. was formed from the merger of Sandoz Ltd. and Ciba-Geigy Ltd. in 1996.

	1993-94	1995-96	1997	Totals
Receipts	$70,257	$56,109	$13,884	$140,250
Disburse	79,150	60,650	18,038	157,838
Cash	8,685	4,151	0	n/a
Contributions	71,700	56,925	-1250	127,375
Republicans	44,500	49,125	-1250	92,375
No. of Cand.	*90*	*65*	*3*	*158*
House	27,400	39,775	-1250	65,925
Senate	17,100	9,350	0	26,450
Democrats	26,200	7,800	0	34,000
No. of Cand.	*46*	*16*	*0*	*62*
House	18,300	6,800	0	25,100
Senate	7,900	1,000	0	8,900
Incumbents	60,000	49,775	-750	109,025
Challengers	4,550	1,700	0	6,250
Open Seat	8,300	5,450	0	13,750
Winners	60,300	47,475	n/a	107,775
Losers	11,400	9,450	n/a	20,850

Contributed less than $5,000 during 1995-96 cycle:

Master Builders Inc. Political Action Committee (C00302992) *Phone: (216) 831-5500 * Fax: (216) 831-6512 * 23700 Chagrin Blvd., Cleveland, OH 44122 * Treasurer: Thomas Douglas*

Society of American Florists

*Phone: (703) 836-8700 * Fax: (703) 836-8705*
1601 Duke St., Alexandria, VA 22314
*Web: www.aboutflowers.com * E-mail: kmaxwell@safnow.org*

The Society of American Florists represents about 19,000 growers, wholesalers and retailers of fresh flowers and plants. The organization's interests include labor, pesticides, the environment and international trade.

Society of American Florists Political Action Committee (SAF-PAC) (C00111302) *Address: same as sponsor * Treasurer: Drew Gruenburg*

	1993-94	1995-96	1997	Totals
Receipts	$71,182	$82,117	$46,040	$199,339
Disburse	66,418	90,395	41,664	198,477
Cash	23,401	15,122	19,148	n/a
Contributions	59,753	89,602	38,377	187,732
Republicans	48,311	80,900	33,415	162,626
No. of Cand.	*89*	*101*	*44*	*234*
House	33,167	62,885	26,254	122,306
Senate	15,144	18,015	7,161	40,320
Democrats	10,818	8,702	4,962	24,482
No. of Cand.	*25*	*12*	*7*	*44*
House	9,723	8,702	4,962	23,387
Senate	1,095	0	0	1,095
Incumbents	42,358	71,902	37,716	151,976
Challengers	4,965	7,500	500	12,965
Open Seat	12,430	10,200	161	22,791
Winners	56,289	79,419	n/a	135,708
Losers	3,464	10,183	n/a	13,647

Terra Industries Inc.

*Phone: (712) 277-7302 * Fax: (712) 279-8719*
600 Fourth St., P.O. Box 6000, Sioux City, IA 51102-6000
Web: www.terraindustries.com

Terra Industries, a publicly held company, distributes crop production products and services, and manufactures nitrogen products and methanol. The company reported $2.5 billion in 1997 sales and employs 4,435 people in the United States, Canada and the United Kingdom.

In December 1997, Terra reached a settlement with Industrial Risk Insurers (IRI) on its insurance claims for property damages and business interruption losses arising from the 1994 explosion at Terra's Port Neal, Iowa, fertilizer plant. Under the settlement, IRI agreed to pay Terra its proportionate share (50 percent of the overall insurance coverage) of a total claim fixed at $321 million.

In January 1998, the company completed the acquisition of two nitrogen fertilizer manufacturing plants in the United Kingdom. With the acquisition, Terra operates seven such facilities: four in the United States, one in Canada and two in England.

The PAC, which has 100 employee members, contributes to candidates supporting business issues in agriculture and manufacturing.

Terra Industries Inc. PAC (TERRAPAC) (C00305102) *Address: same as sponsor * Contact: George Valentine, Chairman * Treasurer: Vaughn M. Klopfenstein*

	1993-94	1995-96	1997	Totals
Receipts	$0	$41,543	$16,015	$57,558
Disburse	0	28,248	6,500	34,748
Cash	0	13,294	22,809	n/a
Contributions	0	18,850	2,500	21,350
Republicans	0	14,250	1,500	15,750
No. of Cand.	*0*	*15*	*2*	*17*
House	0	10,250	500	10,750
Senate	0	4,000	1,000	5,000
Democrats	0	4,600	1,000	5,600
No. of Cand.	*0*	*5*	*2*	*7*
House	0	3,100	500	3,600
Senate	0	1,500	500	2,000
Incumbents	0	14,600	2,500	17,100
Challengers	0	1,500	0	1,500
Open Seat	0	2,750	0	2,750
Winners	0	16,350	n/a	16,350
Losers	0	2,500	n/a	2,500

Texas Farm Bureau

*Phone: (254) 772-3030 * Fax: (254) 772-3628*
7420 Fish Pond Rd., P.O. Box 2689, Waco, TX 76702
Web: www.fb.com/txfb

The Texas Farm Bureau represents about 300,000 member families from across the state. Members include farmers, workers in related industries and anyone with an interest in agriculture. The organization tracks issues related to agriculture, the environment, taxation and property rights. It is affiliated with the American Farm Bureau Federation.

Texas Farm Bureau Friends of Agriculture Fund (Agfund) Inc. (Texas Farm Bureau Agfund) (C00214981) *Address: same as sponsor * Contact: Bob Stallman, President of the PAC Board * Treasurer: Vernie R. Glasson*

	1993-94	1995-96	1997	Totals
Receipts	$197,434	$272,452	$153,079	$622,965
Disburse	222,628	228,742	47,635	499,005
Cash	28,605	72,318	180,266	n/a
Contributions	54,380	93,429	8,750	156,559
Republicans	20,307	70,679	5,000	95,986
No. of Cand.	*10*	*17*	*3*	*30*

House	14,000	64,679	4,000	82,679
Senate	6,307	6,000	1,000	13,307
Democrats	34,073	22,750	3,750	60,573
No. of Cand.	*9*	*8*	*4*	*21*
House	34,073	22,750	3,750	60,573
Senate	0	0	0	0
Incumbents	54,880	62,849	8,750	126,479
Challengers	500	2,500	0	3,000
Open Seat	-1000	28,080	0	27,080
Winners	50,380	66,750	n/a	117,130
Losers	4,000	26,679	n/a	30,679

Tri Valley Growers

*Phone: (510) 327-6400 * Fax: (510) 327-6984*
12667 Alcosta Blvd., San Ramon, CA 94583

Tri Valley Growers is a cooperative owned by more than 500 fruit and vegetable growers. Members grow peaches, apricots, pears, grapes, cherries, olives and tomatoes.

The co-op is responsible for more than 50 percent of canned peaches, 23 percent of olives, and 10 percent of the canned tomatoes sold in American grocery stores.

Tri Valley Growers for Responsible Government (C00040352) *Address: same as sponsor * Contact: Steve Swayze, Dir. of Public Affairs * Treasurer: J. Richard Eichman*

	1993-94	*1995-96*	*1997*	*Totals*
Receipts	$9,460	$31,810	$13,355	$54,625
Disburse	10,224	13,536	4,660	28,420
Cash	2,059	20,339	29,033	n/a
Contributions	8,324	5,650	2,500	16,474
Republicans	500	500	0	1,000
No. of Cand.	*1*	*1*	*0*	*2*
House	500	500	0	1,000
Senate	0	0	0	0
Democrats	7,824	5,150	2,500	15,474
No. of Cand.	*6*	*4*	*5*	*15*
House	4,824	4,150	2,500	11,474
Senate	3,000	1,000	0	4,000
Incumbents	8,324	5,650	1,000	14,974
Challengers	0	0	0	0
Open Seat	0	0	1,000	1,000
Winners	7,824	5,150	n/a	12,974
Losers	500	500	n/a	1,000

Crop Production & Basic Processing

A. Duda & Sons

*Phone: (407) 365-2111 * Fax: (407) 365-2147*
1975 W. State Rd., 426, Oviedo, FL 32765
Web: www.duda.com

One of Florida's largest agribusinesses, A. Duda and Sons grows celery, grapefruit, oranges and other citrus for domestic and international markets. The privately held company also is involved in real estate — it developed the town of Viera, where the Florida Marlins baseball team trains — and produces onions, lettuce, corn, radishes, peppers, sod and sugarcane.

A. Duda and Sons was founded in 1912 by Andrew Duda in Oviedo, Fla., where it is still headquartered. The company is still operated by the Duda family. It also has businesses in Texas, California and Arizona.

A. Duda & Sons Inc. Political Action Committee (C00213231) *Address: same as sponsor * Treasurer: Douglas M. Mann*

	1993-94	*1995-96*	*1997*	*Totals*
Receipts	$44,365	$49,075	$19,157	$112,597
Disburse	39,895	34,200	17,477	91,572
Cash	8,403	23,278	24,958	n/a
Contributions	34,150	26,700	14,000	74,850
Republicans	8,300	17,500	10,500	36,300
No. of Cand.	*11*	*20*	*17*	*48*
House	6,800	17,000	9,500	33,300
Senate	1,500	500	1,000	3,000
Democrats	25,350	9,200	3,500	38,050
No. of Cand.	*23*	*11*	*6*	*40*
House	23,350	8,200	3,500	35,050
Senate	2,000	1,000	0	3,000
Incumbents	25,750	23,700	14,000	63,450
Challengers	0	0	0	0
Open Seat	8,400	3,000	0	11,400
Winners	24,500	25,700	n/a	50,200
Losers	9,650	1,000	n/a	10,650

AG Processing Inc.

*Phone: (402) 496-7809 * Fax: (402) 498-5548*
P.O. Box 2047, Omaha, NE 68103-2047

AG Processing is a cooperative that processes agricultural products from regional farmer cooperatives located mostly in the upper Midwest. AG Processing is owned by its more than 350,000 farmer-members throughout the United States and Canada. The co-op had 1997 sales of $2.9 billion and an estimated 3,000 employees.

AG Processing Inc. Political Action Committee (AGPAC) (C00207308) *Address: same as sponsor * Contact: James Lindsay, CEO * Treasurer: Gordon V. Dorff*

	1993-94	*1995-96*	*1997*	*Totals*
Receipts	$59,645	$55,986	$20,921	$136,552
Disburse	58,865	75,589	10,587	145,041
Cash	25,435	5,833	16,168	n/a
Contributions	43,458	62,498	7,500	113,456
Republicans	31,208	52,498	4,500	88,206
No. of Cand.	*33*	*28*	*6*	*67*
House	20,458	25,500	3,000	48,958
Senate	10,750	26,998	1,500	39,248
Democrats	10,250	10,000	1,500	21,750
No. of Cand.	*11*	*7*	*2*	*20*
House	9,250	5,500	0	14,750
Senate	1,000	4,500	1,500	7,000
Incumbents	30,133	28,000	7,500	65,633
Challengers	6,575	9,700	0	16,275
Open Seat	7,250	24,798	0	32,048
Winners	37,458	42,500	n/a	79,958
Losers	6,000	19,998	n/a	25,998

Alabama Peanut Producers Association

*Phone: (334) 735-2854 * Fax: (334) 735-2854*
P.O. Box 10182, Dothan, AL 36304
E-mail: appa@ala.net

Alabama Peanut Producers Association promotes peanuts and peanut products for 2,500 Alabama growers. APPA provides educational materials to growers, opinion leaders and consumers. It also conducts a broad range of promotional and market development activities on behalf of growers.

APPA is a member of the American Peanut Shellers Association.

Peanut PAC of Alabama, Political Action Committee of Alabama Peanut Producers Association (C00211037) *Address: same as sponsor * Contact: Carl Sanders, President * Treasurer: H. Randall Griggs*

	1993-94	*1995-96*	*1997*	*Totals*
Receipts	$85,787	$75,740	$32,114	$193,641
Disburse	63,674	76,113	20,223	160,010
Cash	26,473	26,103	37,995	n/a
Contributions	32,760	73,250	20,000	126,010
Republicans	9,660	33,250	10,000	52,910
No. of Cand.	*9*	*23*	*4*	*36*
House	8,660	19,250	7,000	34,910
Senate	1,000	14,000	3,000	18,000
Democrats	23,100	40,000	10,000	73,100
No. of Cand.	*24*	*36*	*7*	*67*
House	20,100	35,000	10,000	65,100
Senate	3,000	5,000	0	8,000
Incumbents	31,260	56,750	20,000	108,010
Challengers	0	2,000	0	2,000
Open Seat	1,500	14,000	0	15,500
Winners	26,510	62,750	n/a	89,260
Losers	6,250	10,500	n/a	16,750

American Cotton Shippers Association

*Phone: (901) 937-4500 * Fax: (901) 937-4461*
c/o Hohenberg Bros. Co., P.O. Box 3000, Cordova, TN 38018

American Cotton Shippers Association member firms handle more than 80 percent of the U.S. cotton sold in domestic and foreign markets. The group is comprised of merchants, primary buyers and mill service agents who are members of four federated associations located throughout the Cotton Belt: the Atlantic Cotton Association, the Southern Cotton Association, the Texas Cotton Association and the Western Cotton Shippers Association.

The group works with other cotton trade organizations to develop national and international standards for trade. It also collaborates with producer organizations throughout the Cotton Belt in formulating farm programs.

Committee Organized for The Trading of Cotton - PAC of The American Cotton Shippers Association (C00014019) *Phone: (202) 296-7116 * Fax: (202) 659-5322 * 1725 K St. N.W., Suite 1404, Washington, DC 20006 * E-mail: acsagillen@aol.com * Treasurer: Neal P. Gillen * Contact: Guy W. Taylor, President * Phone: (901) 937-4500*

	1993-94	1995-96	1997	Totals
Receipts	$41,014	$42,750	$19,040	$102,804
Disburse	43,465	37,225	18,017	98,707
Cash	1,480	7,006	8,028	n/a
Contributions	40,350	35,200	16,500	92,050
Republicans	19,050	25,200	10,500	54,750
No. of Cand.	*25*	*24*	*14*	*63*
House	13,650	15,000	9,500	38,150
Senate	5,400	10,200	1,000	16,600
Democrats	20,800	10,000	5,500	36,300
No. of Cand.	*23*	*9*	*7*	*39*
House	17,700	9,500	4,500	31,700
Senate	3,100	500	1,000	4,600
Incumbents	37,900	27,000	16,500	81,400
Challengers	100	1,700	0	1,800
Open Seat	2,350	6,500	0	8,850
Winners	32,300	31,500	n/a	63,800
Losers	8,050	3,700	n/a	11,750

American Crystal Sugar Co.

*Phone: (218) 236-4407 * Fax: (218) 236-4485*
101 N. Third St., Moorhead, MN 56560

American Crystal Sugar Co. is a private cooperative owned and controlled by about 2,300 sugarbeet growers in northwest Minnesota and eastern North Dakota in the valley of the Red River of the North. About two-thirds of these shareholders live and farm in Minnesota. The company's headquarters, research center and one of its five sugar factories are located in Moorhead, Minn. Its other four sugar factories are in Crookston and East Grand Forks, Minn., and near Hillsboro and Drayton, N.D.

American Crystal and its shareholders employ about 4,000 people on a full-time, year-round basis, and another 14,000 on a seasonal basis. It produces 1.5 to 2 billion pounds of sugar per year, providing about 12-14 percent of the nation's total sugar consumption. Its sugar is marketed together with two other beet sugar cooperatives by United Sugars Corp. of Eden Prairie, Minn.

Like other sugar industry groups, American Crystal favors the continuation of federal price supports for sugar.

American Crystal was the leading sugar industry PAC contributor to congressional campaigns during the 1995-96 election cycle. Its contributions were almost evenly split between members of the two parties. The top recipient was Sen. Paul Wellstone, D-Minn., who received $10,000. Sen. Pat Roberts, R-Kan., was the leading Republican recipient.

American Crystal Sugar Political Action Committee (C00110338) *Address: same as sponsor * Contact: Kevin Price * Treasurer: Samuel S. M. Wai*

	1993-94	1995-96	1997	Totals
Receipts	$638,181	$645,987	$342,231	$1,626,399
Disburse	664,540	660,072	279,770	1,604,382
Cash	86,381	72,302	134,769	n/a
Contributions	595,712	553,950	233,000	1,382,662
Republicans	207,825	283,300	105,000	596,125
No. of Cand.	*144*	*190*	*120*	*454*
House	164,575	215,600	90,500	470,675
Senate	43,250	67,700	14,500	125,450
Democrats	365,850	270,650	122,500	759,000
No. of Cand.	*214*	*160*	*131*	*505*
House	305,850	218,150	88,000	612,000
Senate	60,000	52,500	34,500	147,000
Incumbents	544,512	505,450	227,500	1,277,462
Challengers	8,000	14,000	500	22,500
Open Seat	43,000	32,000	3,500	78,500
Winners	486,812	489,100	n/a	975,912
Losers	108,900	64,850	n/a	173,750

American Peanut Shellers Association

*Phone: (912) 888-2508 * Fax: (912) 888-5150*
P.O. Box 70157, Albany, GA 31708-0157
*Web: www.peanut-shellers.org * E-mail: info@peanut-shellers.org*

The American Peanut Shellers Association is a nonprofit trade association, composed of commercial peanut shellers and crushers from Alabama, Florida and Georgia.

Founded in 1919, the association has about 390 members and is the oldest organized group in the peanut industry.

American Peanut Shellers Political Action Committee (C00214148) *Address: same as sponsor * Treasurer: John Taylor Powell*

	1993-94	1995-96	1997	Totals
Receipts	$93,229	$82,755	$15,439	$191,423
Disburse	61,991	86,802	14,619	163,412
Cash	32,168	28,120	28,939	n/a
Contributions	43,916	75,750	11,750	131,416
Republicans	7,000	57,450	10,250	74,700
No. of Cand.	*6*	*26*	*8*	*40*
House	1,500	34,700	9,750	45,950
Senate	5,500	22,750	500	28,750
Democrats	36,416	18,300	1,500	56,216
No. of Cand.	*13*	*10*	*4*	*27*
House	30,916	14,800	1,500	47,216
Senate	5,500	3,500	0	9,000
Incumbents	43,916	51,250	12,250	107,416
Challengers	0	6,250	0	6,250
Open Seat	0	18,250	0	18,250
Winners	39,116	67,750	n/a	106,866
Losers	4,800	8,000	n/a	12,800

American Sugar Cane League

*Phone: (504) 448-3707 * Fax: (504) 448-3722*
206 E. Bayou Rd., Thibodaux, LA 70302

The American Sugar Cane League is a group of sugar growers and processors from the Southeast. There are 17 sugar producers and mills in Louisiana, where the league has its headquarters. Along with other sugar companies, it is a member of the Sugar Association, a Washington group that promotes the industry.

The American Sugar Cane League opposes proposals to phase out the United States' sugar price support program, which it says is necessary for its members to compete with subsidized foreign sugar companies.

The league ranked third among sugar industry PACs in contributions to congressional candidates during the 1995-96 election cycle. Three percent of its contributions went to challengers. The leading recipients were Sens. Pat Roberts, R-Kan., and Mary L. Landrieu, D-La., and Rep. Robert L. Livingston, R-La. They were the only candidates to receive at least $5,000 from this committee.

American Sugar Cane League Political Action Committee (C00081414) *Phone: (202) 331-4331 * Fax: (202) 331-4330 * 1156 15th St. N.W., Suite 1103, Washington, DC 20005 * Contact: Don Wallace, V.P. of Gov. Relations * Treasurer: Charles J. Melancon*

	1993-94	1995-96	1997	Totals
Receipts	$231,127	$288,985	$189,302	$709,414
Disburse	184,395	311,583	232,614	728,592
Cash	121,974	99,387	56,080	n/a
Contributions	168,270	262,485	209,500	640,255
Republicans	60,000	138,485	106,000	304,485
No. of Cand.	*94*	*146*	*113*	*353*
House	47,000	97,000	76,500	220,500
Senate	13,000	41,485	29,500	83,985
Democrats	107,270	124,000	101,500	332,770
No. of Cand.	*159*	*140*	*116*	*415*
House	85,150	88,500	64,500	238,150
Senate	22,120	35,500	37,000	94,620
Incumbents	159,270	202,985	206,000	568,255
Challengers	0	8,000	500	8,500
Open Seat	9,000	51,500	3,000	63,500
Winners	137,950	225,735	n/a	363,685
Losers	30,320	36,750	n/a	67,070

American Sugarbeet Growers Association

*Phone: (202) 833-2398 * Fax: (202) 833-2962*
1156 15th St. N.W., Suite 1101, Washington, DC 20005-1704
*Web: members.aol.com/asga/sugar.htm * E-mail: asga@aol.com*

The American Sugarbeet Growers Association represents more than 12,000 sugarbeet farmers in California, Texas, New Mexico, Michigan, Colorado, Minnesota, Montana, Nebraska, North Dakota, Idaho, Oregon, Washington and Wyoming. More than half of the sugar produced in the United States comes from sugarbeets.

The ASGA supports federal sugar policy, which provides price supports to domestic sugar companies. The policy was last approved in the 1996 Farm Bill. The group advocates the elimination of trade restrictions and barriers as long as it applies to foreign sugar companies as well. The sugar trade has certain import and production standards set by NAFTA and GATT.

The ASGA ranked second among sugar PACs in contributions to 1996 congressional races. More than 93 percent of its contributions went to incumbent candidates, and the total was almost evenly split between members of the two parties. The top recipients were Sens. Larry E. Craig, R-Idaho, and Tom Harkin, D-Iowa, and Reps. Michael D. Crapo, R-Idaho, and Marcy Kaptur, D-Ohio. All are from sugarbeet-producing states or sit on agriculture-related committees.

American Sugarbeet Growers Association Political Action Committee (C00167684) *Address: same as sponsor * Treasurer: Luther A. Markwart*

	1993-94	1995-96	1997	Totals
Receipts	$312,282	$280,131	$107,619	$700,032
Disburse	329,926	337,427	142,966	810,319
Cash	109,387	52,092	16,745	n/a
Contributions	317,140	304,667	137,025	758,832
Republicans	106,527	153,382	67,290	327,199
No. of Cand.	*96*	*126*	*77*	*299*
House	85,650	120,563	39,854	246,067
Senate	20,877	32,819	27,436	81,132
Democrats	205,613	151,285	68,235	425,133
No. of Cand.	*168*	*125*	*85*	*378*
House	158,115	125,231	41,211	324,557
Senate	47,498	26,054	27,024	100,576
Incumbents	297,640	282,917	136,525	717,082
Challengers	3,500	2,500	0	6,000
Open Seat	15,500	19,250	500	35,250
Winners	257,692	268,923	n/a	526,615
Losers	59,448	35,744	n/a	95,192

California Beet Growers Association Ltd. Political Action Committee (California Sugar Beet PAC) (C00129742) *Phone: (209) 477-5596 * Fax: (209) 477-1610 * Two W. Swain Rd., Stockton, CA 95207-4395 * Contact: Ted Page, Chairman * Treasurer: Ben Goodwin*

The California Beet Growers Association represents about 900 beet growers. It helps members negotiate contracts with processors and represents grower interests at the federal level.

CBGA is affiliated with the American Sugarbeet Growers Association.

	1993-94	1995-96	1997	Totals
Receipts	$13,995	$7,486	$6,255	$27,736
Disburse	10,190	10,695	4,200	25,085
Cash	18,089	14,880	16,935	n/a
Contributions	10,690	10,695	4,200	25,585
Republicans	3,750	5,475	1,700	10,925
No. of Cand.	*4*	*8*	*4*	*16*
House	3,750	5,475	1,700	10,925
Senate	0	0	0	0
Democrats	6,940	5,220	2,500	14,660
No. of Cand.	*7*	*5*	*5*	*17*
House	6,100	5,220	2,500	13,820
Senate	840	0	0	840
Incumbents	10,290	9,945	4,200	24,435
Challengers	400	750	0	1,150
Open Seat	0	0	0	0
Winners	9,290	10,445	n/a	19,735
Losers	1,400	250	n/a	1,650

Arizona Cotton Growers Association

*Phone: (602) 437-1344 * Fax: (602) 437-5401*
4139 E. Broadway, Phoenix, AZ 85040
E-mail: acga1@aol.com

Arizona Cotton Growers Association is a nonprofit organization of 1,700 growers. The association advances the cause of the state's cotton growers and provides members with legislative advocacy services.

Arizona Cotton Growers Association Political Action Committee (C00033795) *Address: same as sponsor * Treasurer: Rick C. Lavis*

	1993-94	1995-96	1997	Totals
Receipts	$15,485	$17,410	$5,625	$38,520
Disburse	15,279	15,445	5,573	36,297
Cash	1,100	3,065	3,116	n/a
Contributions	5,228	5,844	3,075	14,147
Republicans	4,403	5,044	2,525	11,972
No. of Cand.	*7*	*7*	*5*	*19*
House	799	5,025	1,525	7,349
Senate	3,604	19	1,000	4,623
Democrats	825	800	550	2,175
No. of Cand.	*4*	*1*	*2*	*7*
House	825	800	550	2,175
Senate	0	0	0	0
Incumbents	2,200	4,994	2,875	10,069
Challengers	149	850	0	999
Open Seat	2,879	0	0	2,879
Winners	4,879	4,994	n/a	9,873
Losers	349	850	n/a	1,199

Blue Diamond Growers

*Phone: (916) 446-8543 * Fax: (916) 325-2880*
P.O. Box 1768, Sacramento, CA 95812
Web: www.healthyreferral.com/sponsors/diamond

Based in California, the 5,000-member Blue Diamond Growers co-operative was established in 1910 and employs thousands of agricultural workers producing almonds nationwide. It is the largest tree nut company in the world.

The co-op has almond-processing plants in Sacramento and Salida, Calif.

Blue Diamond Growers Political Action Committee (formerly known as California Almond Growers Exchange PAC) (C00080135) *1802 C St., Sacramento, CA 95814 * Treasurer: Steven W. Easter*

	1993-94	1995-96	1997	Totals
Receipts	$91,340	$121,699	$54,945	$267,984
Disburse	115,267	97,807	45,245	258,319
Cash	6,320	30,213	39,912	n/a
Contributions	73,498	65,500	32,500	171,498
Republicans	24,500	31,500	18,000	74,000
No. of Cand.	*9*	*17*	*11*	*37*
House	24,500	30,000	18,000	72,500
Senate	0	1,500	0	1,500
Democrats	48,998	34,000	14,500	97,498
No. of Cand.	*14*	*11*	*6*	*31*
House	38,628	31,000	13,500	83,128
Senate	10,370	3,000	1,000	14,370
Incumbents	72,498	62,000	32,500	166,998
Challengers	0	1,000	0	1,000
Open Seat	1,000	2,500	0	3,500
Winners	67,878	62,500	n/a	130,378
Losers	5,620	3,000	n/a	8,620

Calcot Ltd.

*Phone: (805) 327-5961 * Fax: (805) 861-9870*
P.O. Box 259, Bakersfield, CA 93302
*Web: www.calcot.com * E-mail: glundquist@calcot.com*

Calcot is one of the largest cotton marketing cooperatives in the world. The company represents and is owned by the cotton growers of Arizona and California. Sales were $684 million in 1997 and the company employs 375 workers. More than 80 percent of its annual crop is exported to the countries of the Far East, including Japan, Korea, Taiwan and Indonesia.

The California-based company owns the largest cotton warehouse system in the United States, with 230 warehouses throughout the Southwest.

Calcot and three other regional cooperatives comprise Amcot, a group that supplies the world's textile mills with 35 percent of the annual U.S. cotton crop.

Calcot Ltd. Federal Political Action Committee (C00172775) *Address: same as sponsor * Contact: W. Bruce Heiden, Chairperson * Treasurer: Gene A. Lundquist*

	1993-94	1995-96	1997	Totals
Receipts	$62,275	$57,168	$28,296	$147,739
Disburse	61,190	63,211	21,432	145,833
Cash	21,512	15,473	22,337	n/a
Contributions	44,861	45,063	16,750	106,674

(Data for Calcot Ltd. Federal continued)

Republicans	21,004	27,055	10,500	58,559
No. of Cand.	*22*	*18*	*7*	*47*
House	13,354	17,325	9,500	40,179
Senate	7,650	9,730	1,000	18,380
Democrats	23,857	18,008	6,250	48,115
No. of Cand.	*17*	*9*	*6*	*32*
House	17,617	15,408	6,250	39,275
Senate	6,240	2,600	0	8,840
Incumbents	35,111	34,233	16,750	86,094
Challengers	5,000	2,600	0	7,600
Open Seat	5,500	8,230	0	13,730
Winners	38,371	43,563	n/a	81,934
Losers	6,490	1,500	n/a	7,990

California Association of Winegrape Growers

*Phone: (916) 924-5370 * Fax: (916) 924-5374*
555 University Ave., Suite 250, Sacramento, CA 95825
E-mail: cawginfo@sna.com

The California Association of Winegrape Growers is a trade association and cooperative that represents growers responsible for 65 percent of grapes crushed for wine in the United States.

The co-op, which was founded in 1974, is interested in taxes on alcohol, labeling laws and research funding.

California Association of Winegrape Growers Political Action Committee (CAWG-PAC) (C00155366) *Address: same as sponsor * Treasurer: Karen Ross*

	1993-94	*1995-96*	*1997*	*Totals*
Receipts	$7,660	$13,650	$7,275	$28,585
Disburse	8,526	12,745	564	21,835
Cash	64	969	7,680	n/a
Contributions	8,262	12,645	500	21,407
Republicans	2,750	9,295	0	12,045
No. of Cand.	*4*	*10*	*0*	*14*
House	2,750	7,795	0	10,545
Senate	0	1,500	0	1,500
Democrats	5,512	3,350	500	9,362
No. of Cand.	*6*	*6*	*1*	*13*
House	3,512	2,350	500	6,362
Senate	2,000	1,000	0	3,000
Incumbents	7,262	11,645	500	19,407
Challengers	1,000	0	0	1,000
Open Seat	0	1,000	0	1,000
Winners	8,262	12,345	n/a	20,607
Losers	0	300	n/a	300

California Avocado Proponent

*Phone: (760) 745-6632 * Fax: (760) 745-5043*
P.O. Box 300867, Escondido, CA 92030

The California Avocado Proponent gives to candidates who support legislation advantageous to the 6,000 avocado growers who operate in the United States.

California Avocado Proponent (C00111047) *Address: same as sponsor * Contact: Phil Henry, Chairman * Treasurer: Chris Miller*

	1993-94	*1995-96*	*1997*	*Totals*
Receipts	$37,049	$29,237	$472	$66,758
Disburse	24,882	28,025	5,515	58,422
Cash	25,382	26,598	21,555	n/a
Contributions	18,450	23,150	3,415	45,015
Republicans	6,700	14,550	1,415	22,665
No. of Cand.	*14*	*19*	*3*	*36*
House	5,900	11,050	1,415	18,365
Senate	800	3,500	0	4,300
Democrats	11,750	8,600	2,000	22,350
No. of Cand.	*14*	*10*	*3*	*27*
House	8,250	5,800	1,000	15,050
Senate	3,500	2,800	1,000	7,300
Incumbents	18,450	20,350	3,415	42,215
Challengers	0	0	0	0
Open Seat	0	2,800	0	2,800
Winners	17,150	21,850	n/a	39,000
Losers	1,300	1,300	n/a	2,600

California Canning Peach Association

*Phone: (510) 284-9171 * Fax: (510) 284-4217*
3685 Mt. Diablo Blvd., Suite 200, Lafayette, CA 94549
*Web: pom44.ucdavis.edu/ccpa.html * E-mail: RonSchuler@worldnet.att.net*

The California Canning Peach Association is a bargaining and marketing cooperative which represents about 75 percent of the cling peach tonnage produced in California. Founded in 1922, CCPA has 600 peach grower members.

CCPA's purpose is to achieve equitable prices and terms of delivery for its members' production. The association sells peaches used in canning, freezing, baby food and juices.

California Canning Peach Association Political Action Committee (also known as Peach-PAC) (C00019083) *Address: same as sponsor * Contact: Ronald Schuler, Chairman * Treasurer: Richard Hudgins*

	1993-94	*1995-96*	*1997*	*Totals*
Receipts	$31,525	$21,690	$12,421	$65,636
Disburse	33,774	21,802	7,838	63,414
Cash	4,628	4,521	9,104	n/a
Contributions	31,810	19,660	7,300	58,770
Republicans	13,940	10,100	2,900	26,940
No. of Cand.	*12*	*17*	*5*	*34*
House	13,690	9,350	2,900	25,940
Senate	250	750	0	1,000
Democrats	17,870	9,560	4,400	31,830
No. of Cand.	*13*	*8*	*8*	*29*
House	13,770	9,560	4,400	27,730
Senate	4,100	0	0	4,100
Incumbents	28,060	18,260	7,000	53,320
Challengers	2,250	550	0	2,800
Open Seat	1,400	650	300	2,350
Winners	29,410	16,410	n/a	45,820
Losers	2,400	3,250	n/a	5,650

California Citrus Mutual

*Phone: (209) 592-3790 * Fax: (209) 592-3798*
512 N. Kaweah Ave., Exeter, CA 93221
E-mail: citrus@earthlink.net

California Citrus Mutual represents 750 citrus growers in that state. Established in 1977, CCM follows legislation dealing with water use, pesticides, property taxes and other related issues.

California Citrus Mutual Political Action Committee (C00166355) *Address: same as sponsor * Treasurer: Joel Nelsen*

	1993-94	*1995-96*	*1997*	*Totals*
Receipts	$7,760	$18,964	$14,720	$41,444
Disburse	7,262	18,880	3,735	29,877
Cash	1,944	3,818	14,801	n/a
Contributions	5,250	11,250	1,000	17,500
Republicans	1,400	9,000	1,000	11,400
No. of Cand.	*3*	*7*	*1*	*11*
House	900	8,000	1,000	9,900
Senate	500	1,000	0	1,500
Democrats	3,850	2,250	0	6,100
No. of Cand.	*5*	*3*	*0*	*8*
House	3,350	2,250	0	5,600
Senate	500	0	0	500
Incumbents	4,750	9,500	1,000	15,250
Challengers	500	500	0	1,000
Open Seat	0	1,250	0	1,250
Winners	3,050	9,750	n/a	12,800
Losers	2,200	1,500	n/a	3,700

California Grape & Tree Fruit League

*Phone: (209) 226-6330 * Fax: (209) 222-8326*
1540 E. Shaw, Suite 120, Fresno, CA 93710-8000
Web: www.atinet.org/league

The California Grape & Tree Fruit League represents about 300 growers, shippers and marketers, who produce more than 80 percent of the fresh market table grapes and deciduous tree fruit grown in California. The nonprofit's members are located in the region extending from Lake County to southern Coachella Valley in California.

The league follows issues such as farm labor, pesticides, marketing, environmental resources, trade and transportation. It sponsors an annual convention, an operations workshop and a government relations trip to Sacramento.

California Grape & Tree Fruit League Political Action Committee (C00121582) *Address: same as sponsor * Contact: Brian Haddix, PAC Dir. * Treasurer: Herbert Kaprielian*

	1993-94	1995-96	1997	Totals
Receipts	$17,250	$36,291	$18,348	$71,889
Disburse	20,234	33,815	14,814	68,863
Cash	4,689	7,163	10,697	n/a
Contributions	13,250	8,615	3,850	25,715
Republicans	1,750	5,775	2,100	9,625
No. of Cand.	*3*	*7*	*4*	*14*
House	1,750	5,775	2,100	9,625
Senate	0	0	0	0
Democrats	11,500	2,840	1,750	16,090
No. of Cand.	*9*	*3*	*3*	*15*
House	7,500	2,840	1,750	12,090
Senate	4,000	0	0	4,000
Incumbents	13,250	7,515	3,850	24,615
Challengers	0	1,100	0	1,100
Open Seat	0	0	0	0
Winners	12,250	7,515	n/a	19,765
Losers	1,000	1,100	n/a	2,100

Cargill Inc.

*Phone: (612) 742-7575 * Fax: (612) 742-7393*
P.O. Box 9300, Dept. 5, Minneapolis, MN 55440
Web: www.cargill.com

With more than $50 billion in revenues, Cargill is the largest privately held company in the United States, according to Forbes magazine. Cargill is an international marketer and processor of agricultural, financial and industrial commodities.

The company's largest and most important businesses include grain and commodity merchandising, vegetable oilseed and corn processing and refining, flour milling, meat processing, steel manufacturing and financial services. The company and its subsidiaries and affiliates operate from more than 1,000 locations in 72 countries. Cargill employs 79,000 workers around the world.

The company has been privately held since its inception in 1865. Common equity for the company is jointly owned by members of the Cargill and MacMillan families.

Cargill Inc. Political Action Committee (C00067884) *Address: same as sponsor * Contact: Linda Thrane, General Manager * Treasurer: Dennis E. Walters*

	1993-94	1995-96	1997	Totals
Receipts	$90,690	$171,638	$100,120	$362,448
Disburse	89,110	163,680	29,055	281,845
Cash	9,241	17,202	88,268	n/a
Contributions	87,800	162,500	28,000	278,300
Republicans	66,550	142,500	22,500	231,550
No. of Cand.	*50*	*74*	*26*	*150*
House	44,050	74,500	17,000	135,550
Senate	22,500	68,000	5,500	96,000
Democrats	20,250	20,000	5,500	45,750
No. of Cand.	*17*	*16*	*5*	*38*
House	18,250	14,000	4,500	36,750
Senate	2,000	6,000	1,000	9,000
Incumbents	57,250	70,500	26,500	154,250
Challengers	10,550	31,000	1,000	42,550
Open Seat	20,000	62,000	500	82,500
Winners	72,000	118,500	n/a	190,500
Losers	15,800	44,000	n/a	59,800

Continental Grain Co.

*Phone: (212) 207-5100 * Fax: (212) 207-2980*
277 Park Ave., New York, NY 10172

Continental Grain is one of the world's largest grain companies. It also has business in meat and poultry production and processing, and financial services. The privately held company has facilities in 60 countries and generates an estimated $16 billion in sales. It is No. 5 on the 1997 Forbes list of top private companies.

In January 1998, Continental announced plans to purchase hog producer Premium Standard Farms of Missouri. The move would make Continental one of nation's five largest hog producers. The company already has major hog operations in North Carolina.

Continental is controlled by Chairman Paul Fribourg's family.

Subsidiaries include: ContiFinancial Services Corp., ContiMortgage Corp., ContiTrade Services, ContiSecurities Asset Funding Corp., ContiFunding Corp., ContiSecurities Asset Funding Corp. II, ContiAuto Asset Funding Corp., California Lending Group Inc., Triad Financial Corp., ContiWest Corp. and ContiSecurities Asset Funding L.L.C.

Continental Grain Co. Political Action Committee (C00155853)
*Address: same as sponsor * Treasurer: Daryl C. Natz*

	1993-94	1995-96	1997	Totals
Receipts	$16,082	$13,095	$2,421	$31,598
Disburse	17,287	10,213	6,001	33,501
Cash	790	3,673	93	n/a
Contributions	17,247	10,200	1,000	28,447
Republicans	12,147	9,700	1,000	22,847
No. of Cand.	*17*	*10*	*1*	*28*
House	5,000	4,000	0	9,000
Senate	7,147	5,700	1,000	13,847
Democrats	5,100	500	0	5,600
No. of Cand.	*12*	*1*	*0*	*13*
House	5,000	500	0	5,500
Senate	100	0	0	100
Incumbents	13,497	6,000	1,000	20,497
Challengers	250	200	0	450
Open Seat	3,500	4,000	0	7,500
Winners	14,747	9,000	n/a	23,747
Losers	2,500	1,200	n/a	3,700

Cotton Warehouse Association of America

*Phone: (202) 331-4437 * Fax: (202) 331-4330*
1156 15th St. N.W., Suite 1103, Washington, DC 20005

The Cotton Warehouse Association of America is a certified organization of the National Cotton Council.

Cotton Warehouse Government Relations Committee (C00035477) *Address: same as sponsor * Contact: Donald L. Wallace Jr., Executive V.P. * Treasurer: Lulu Sandifer*

	1993-94	1995-96	1997	Totals
Receipts	$11,125	$9,400	$4,350	$24,875
Disburse	8,655	10,839	2,661	22,155
Cash	11,563	10,124	11,812	n/a
Contributions	3,500	6,000	500	10,000
Republicans	1,500	4,500	500	6,500
No. of Cand.	*3*	*6*	*1*	*10*
House	1,500	3,500	500	5,500
Senate	0	1,000	0	1,000
Democrats	2,000	1,500	0	3,500
No. of Cand.	*4*	*3*	*0*	*7*
House	2,000	1,500	0	3,500
Senate	0	0	0	0
Incumbents	3,000	5,500	500	9,000
Challengers	0	0	0	0
Open Seat	500	500	0	1,000
Winners	2,500	5,500	n/a	8,000
Losers	1,000	500	n/a	1,500

Desert Grape Growers League/California

*Phone: (760) 568-0313 * Fax: (760) 568-6175*
74010 El Paseo, Suite 200, Palm Desert, CA 92260

Desert Grape Growers League of California Political Action Committee (C00154641) *Address: same as sponsor * Treasurer: Jay D. Wahlin*

	1993-94	1995-96	1997	Totals
Receipts	$755	$1,521	$72,236	$74,512
Disburse	8,000	5,500	13,470	26,970
Cash	28,824	24,847	83,613	n/a
Contributions	7,500	5,500	8,000	21,000
Republicans	3,000	3,500	7,000	13,500
No. of Cand.	*3*	*3*	*3*	*9*
House	2,000	3,500	7,000	12,500
Senate	1,000	0	0	1,000
Democrats	4,500	2,000	1,000	7,500
No. of Cand.	*4*	*2*	*1*	*7*
House	4,500	2,000	0	6,500
Senate	0	0	1,000	1,000
Incumbents	5,500	5,500	8,000	19,000
Challengers	1,000	0	0	1,000
Open Seat	1,000	0	0	1,000
Winners	6,500	4,000	n/a	10,500
Losers	1,000	1,500	n/a	2,500

Farmers' Rice Cooperative

*Phone: (916) 923-5100 * Fax: (916) 920-3321*
P.O. Box 15223, Sacramento, CA 95851

The Farmers' Rice Cooperative represents rice farmers and exporters and promotes all aspects of rice technology, from grain types and structures to processing and product development.

Farmers' Rice Cooperative Fund (C00146605) *Address: same as sponsor * Contact: Bill Hoffman * Treasurer: James E. Dodson*

	1993-94	1995-96	1997	Totals
Receipts	$57,313	$32,577	$4,550	$94,440
Disburse	46,336	45,900	7,650	99,886
Cash	18,224	4,902	1,802	n/a
Contributions	30,550	32,841	7,650	71,041
Republicans	9,800	15,300	3,000	28,100
No. of Cand.	*9*	*13*	*3*	*25*
House	7,800	11,300	2,000	21,100
Senate	2,000	4,000	1,000	7,000
Democrats	20,750	17,541	4,650	42,941
No. of Cand.	*13*	*8*	*7*	*28*
House	15,450	16,541	4,150	36,141
Senate	5,300	1,000	500	6,800
Incumbents	30,550	29,000	7,150	66,700
Challengers	0	1,000	0	1,000
Open Seat	0	2,841	500	3,341
Winners	27,550	32,341	n/a	59,891
Losers	3,000	500	n/a	3,500

Florida Citrus Mutual

*Phone: (941) 682-1111 * Fax: (941) 682-1074*
302 S. Massachusetts Ave., P.O. Box 89, Lakeland, FL 33802
Web: www.fl-citrus-mutual.com

Founded in 1948, Florida Citrus Mutual has more than 10,000 grower members. The trade association serves as an information center for citrus growers and represents the industry.

Its PAC was established in 1980.

Florida Citrus Mutual Political Action Committee Inc. (C00131607) *Address: same as sponsor * Treasurer: Bobby F. McKown*

	1993-94	1995-96	1997	Totals
Receipts	$44,101	$42,840	$21,768	$108,709
Disburse	38,772	24,709	27,299	90,780
Cash	84,750	102,885	97,353	n/a
Contributions	32,750	23,100	12,100	67,950
Republicans	17,150	9,200	6,100	32,450
No. of Cand.	*15*	*16*	*10*	*41*
House	13,550	8,700	3,600	25,850
Senate	3,600	500	2,500	6,600
Democrats	15,100	13,900	6,000	35,000
No. of Cand.	*16*	*19*	*5*	*40*
House	14,600	10,300	3,000	27,900
Senate	500	3,600	3,000	7,100
Incumbents	28,250	17,500	12,100	57,850
Challengers	0	1,650	0	1,650
Open Seat	4,000	3,950	0	7,950
Winners	28,250	21,100	n/a	49,350
Losers	4,500	2,000	n/a	6,500

Florida Crystals Inc.

Phone: (561) 655-6303
316 Royal Poinciana Plaza, Palm Beach, FL 33480
Web: www.floridacrystals.com

Florida Crystals, formerly known as Flo-Sun, is a privately owned sugar and rice company based in Palm Beach, Fla.

The company is owned by Florida's Fanjul family. Brothers Jose "Pepe" and Alfonso "Alfy" Fanjul serve as the president and C.E.O., respectively.

According to the Center for Responsive Politics, the two men, and their relatives, companies and employees, have contributed more than $3 million to Democratic and Republican candidates since 1979. In addition, Jose Fanjul served as one of Bob Dole's finance vice chairmen during the Republican primaries in 1996, and Alfonso Fanjul serves on President Clinton's finance committee.

The two Cuban-born brothers have lived in the United States for more than 35 years and neither is a citizen, although both have applied for citizenship, according to news reports.

Fanjul family sugar holdings in the United States and the Dominican Republic exceed 400,000 acres. Through the federal government's sugar subsidy program, Florida Crystals receives about $65 million in benefits each year, based on figures from the General Accounting Office.

A PBS report on March 27, 1997 examined the tie between campaign contributions from large sugar corporations and the continuance of the U.S. sugar subsidy program. When PBS correspondent Hedrick Smith questioned Jorge Dominicis, vice president of Florida Crystals, about the connection between the donations and political decisions, Dominicis responded that "what it suggests is that it is important to contribute to people with whom you agree, whose philosophies you think are good for this country."

Florida Crystals was established in 1926 by Alfonso and Jose's father, Alfonso Fanjul Sr. The company employs about 2,300 people.

Florida Crystals Inc. PAC (formerly known as Flo-Sun Inc. PAC) (C00296624) *Phone: (202) 347-2980 * Fax: (202) 347-2992 * 915 15th St. N.W., Suite 800, Washington, DC 20005 * Treasurer: Van R. Boyette*

	1993-94	1995-96	1997	Totals
Receipts	$44,000	$120,650	$38,799	$203,449
Disburse	35,038	114,899	48,001	197,938
Cash	8,961	14,712	5,509	n/a
Contributions	20,037	81,499	40,812	142,348
Republicans	5,500	39,149	13,500	58,149
No. of Cand.	*8*	*44*	*17*	*69*
House	5,500	30,149	5,500	41,149
Senate	0	9,000	8,000	17,000
Democrats	14,537	42,350	27,312	84,199
No. of Cand.	*17*	*46*	*32*	*95*
House	6,000	28,350	13,812	48,162
Senate	8,537	14,000	13,500	36,037
Incumbents	11,000	63,749	40,812	115,561
Challengers	2,537	5,000	0	7,537
Open Seat	6,500	12,750	0	19,250
Winners	13,000	69,687	n/a	82,687
Losers	7,037	11,812	n/a	18,849

Florida Fruit & Vegetable Association

*Phone: (407) 894-1351 * Fax: (407) 894-7840*
P.O. Box 140155, Orlando, FL 32814-0155
*Web: www.ffva.com * E-mail: info@ffva.com*

The Florida Fruit and Vegetable Association represents 3,800 growers and shippers in Florida.

The association holds seminars and conventions, publishes Harvester magazine, puts out a weekly newsletter and advises members on dealing with laws and regulations.

The bipartisan PAC's mission is to enhance the business environment for its members. It is particularly interested in food safety, environmental protection, marketing, labor, pest management and communications.

Florida Fruit & Vegetable Association Political Action Committee (FFVA-PAC) (C00232967) *Address: same as sponsor * Treasurer: Michael J. Stuart*

	1993-94	1995-96	1997	Totals
Receipts	$26,145	$20,475	$7,346	$53,966
Disburse	20,485	25,036	3,061	48,582
Cash	11,194	6,631	10,916	n/a
Contributions	17,932	19,600	1,250	38,782
Republicans	11,000	12,500	750	24,250
No. of Cand.	*11*	*27*	*4*	*42*
House	8,000	10,000	1,000	19,000
Senate	3,000	2,500	-250	5,250
Democrats	6,932	7,100	500	14,532
No. of Cand.	*8*	*14*	*1*	*23*
House	6,932	5,850	500	13,282
Senate	0	1,250	0	1,250
Incumbents	15,932	16,850	1,250	34,032
Challengers	0	500	0	500
Open Seat	2,000	2,250	0	4,250
Winners	18,432	19,350	n/a	37,782
Losers	-500	250	n/a	-250

Florida Sugar Cane League

*Phone: (813) 983-9151 * Fax: (813) 983-2792*
115 S. Lopez, Drawer 1208, Clewiston, FL 33440

Florida Sugar Cane League represents the largest sugar growers in Florida, U.S. Sugar Corp. and the sugar companies owned by the Fanjul family of Palm Beach.

U.S. Sugar Corp. grows cane on about 115,000 acres and the Fanjuls farm about 190,000 acres in Florida.

In 1990, the Belle Glade-based Sugar Cane Growers Cooperative of Florida resigned from the league because it said the association was not representing its interests.

Florida Sugar Cane League PAC (C00012328) *Phone: (202) 785-4070 * Fax: (202) 659-8581 * 1301 Pennsylvania Ave. N.W., #401, Washington, DC 20004 * Contact: Alisa Fell, PAC Dir. * Treasurer: James E. Terrill*

	1993-94	1995-96	1997	Totals
Receipts	$148,502	$178,629	$82,744	$409,875
Disburse	151,726	174,873	88,150	414,749
Cash	3,583	7,341	1,934	n/a
Contributions	145,200	153,873	82,150	381,223
Republicans	53,550	79,369	39,494	172,413
No. of Cand.	*69*	*112*	*69*	*250*
House	43,550	59,869	29,738	133,157
Senate	10,000	19,500	9,756	39,256
Democrats	89,650	74,504	41,656	205,810
No. of Cand.	*116*	*99*	*71*	*286*
House	77,400	60,535	29,767	167,702
Senate	12,250	13,969	11,889	38,108
Incumbents	138,200	139,365	81,650	359,215
Challengers	0	1,535	0	1,535
Open Seat	6,500	12,973	500	19,973
Winners	120,600	136,015	n/a	256,615
Losers	24,600	17,858	n/a	42,458

Georgia Peanut Producers Association

*Phone: (912) 432-9001 * Fax: (912) 432-7447*
1408 Third Ave., Albany, GA 31707
E-mail: peanut_patriot@msn.com

The Georgia Peanut Producers Association has about 3,400 peanut producing members and 200 associate members. Formed in 1981, GPPA provides its members with a quarterly news magazine and market bulletins on industry trends, government regulations, Farm Service Agency rulings and congressional actions affecting the peanut industry.

GPPA's key legislative issues include: the National Check-Off Promotion Program, the Federal Peanut Stabilization Program, international trade policy, environmental regulation, federal feeding programs, agricultural research and export promotion programs.

Georgia Peanut Producers Association Political Action Committee (C00231597) *Address: same as sponsor * Contact: Bob Brooks, Chairman * Treasurer: Jerald Carter*

	1993-94	1995-96	1997	Totals
Receipts	$45,388	$205,120	$19,355	$269,863
Disburse	24,234	207,059	40,702	271,995
Cash	55,022	53,087	31,740	n/a
Contributions	17,500	164,500	26,250	208,250
Republicans	7,500	107,500	12,750	127,750
No. of Cand.	*4*	*51*	*10*	*65*
House	2,500	69,500	11,750	83,750
Senate	5,000	38,000	1,000	44,000
Democrats	10,000	57,000	13,500	80,500
No. of Cand.	*8*	*52*	*13*	*73*
House	7,500	47,250	12,000	66,750
Senate	2,500	9,750	1,500	13,750
Incumbents	17,500	146,000	26,250	189,750
Challengers	0	5,500	0	5,500
Open Seat	0	12,500	0	12,500
Winners	16,500	148,250	n/a	164,750
Losers	1,000	16,250	n/a	17,250

Great Lakes Sugar Beet Growers

*Phone: (517) 792-1531 * Fax: (517) 792-7165*
4800 Fashion Square Blvd., Suite 485 Plaza N., Saginaw, MI 48604
Web: member.aol.com/asga/gl.htm

The Great Lakes Sugar Beet Growers Association represents about 1,500 Michigan farmers with contracts to grow sugar beets for Michigan Sugar Co., a subsidiary of Savannah Foods and Industries Inc. of Savannah, Ga.

Farmers live in five districts: Alma, Caro, Croswell, Saginaw and Sebewaing. Michigan ranks fifth in the nation in sugar beet production.

Established in 1981, Great Lakes Sugar Beet Growers Association is affiliated with the American Sugar Beet Growers Association but the groups maintain separate PACs.

Great Lakes Sugar Beet Growers Political Action Committee (GLSBGPAC) (C00168542) *Address: same as sponsor * Contact: Marty Lewis, Chairman * Treasurer: Richard E. Leach*

	1993-94	1995-96	1997	Totals
Receipts	$82,471	$66,882	$31,648	$181,001
Disburse	82,158	77,495	16,627	176,280
Cash	31,605	20,993	36,014	n/a
Contributions	70,690	65,140	9,975	145,805
Republicans	33,000	35,140	4,470	72,610
No. of Cand.	*51*	*56*	*13*	*120*
House	30,400	31,640	3,970	66,010
Senate	2,600	3,500	500	6,600
Democrats	37,190	30,000	5,505	72,695
No. of Cand.	*51*	*43*	*17*	*111*
House	35,240	27,000	5,005	67,245
Senate	1,950	3,000	500	5,450
Incumbents	68,390	61,390	10,275	140,055
Challengers	0	1,250	0	1,250
Open Seat	2,300	2,500	0	4,800
Winners	59,890	55,240	n/a	115,130
Losers	10,800	9,900	n/a	20,700

Hawaiian Sugar Planters' Association

99-193 Aiea Heights Dr., Suite 300, Aiea, HI 96701

The Hawaiian Sugar Planters' Association PAC was terminated in October 1997.

Hawaiian Sugar Planters' Association Political Action Committee (Hawaiian Sugar-PAC) (C00161133) *Address: same as sponsor * Treasurer: Ruth Yamato*

	1993-94	1995-96	1997	Totals
Receipts	$35,323	$20,450	$37	$55,810
Disburse	27,650	28,850	1,138	57,638
Cash	9,501	1,101	0	n/a
Contributions	27,150	22,650	0	49,800
Republicans	6,650	12,350	0	19,000
No. of Cand.	*16*	*28*	*0*	*44*
House	3,150	9,350	0	12,500
Senate	3,500	3,000	0	6,500
Democrats	20,000	10,300	0	30,300
No. of Cand.	*42*	*23*	*0*	*65*
House	13,250	6,000	0	19,250
Senate	6,750	4,300	0	11,050
Incumbents	26,450	18,350	0	44,800
Challengers	0	300	0	300
Open Seat	700	4,000	0	4,700
Winners	22,350	19,900	n/a	42,250
Losers	4,800	2,750	n/a	7,550

J.G. Boswell Co.

*Phone: (626) 583-3000 * Fax: (626) 583-3090*
101 W. Walnut St., Pasadena, CA 91103
Web: www.jgboswell.com

J.G. Boswell Co. produces cotton in the San Joaquin Valley of California and in New South Wales, Australia. Acala and Pima cotton crops are processed through company gins and marketed directly to textile mills around the world under the "Diamond B" label. Cotton seed and safflower products, processed through its oil mill, are also sold into international markets. The private company grows other rotation crops, including wheat, seed alfalfa, barley and tomatoes.

In January 1998, the company formed a joint venture with Mycogen Corp. to market cotton seeds internationally.

The venture, Phytogen Seed Co., will continue to market cotton seed under the Phytogen brand in California, Arizona and Greece. It also will develop new cotton seed products for the mid-south and southeastern U.S. markets and selected international markets, including Argentina and Australia. Phytogen had cotton seed sales of about $9 million in 1997.

J.G. Boswell Co. Employees' Political Action Committee (C00082677) *Address: same as sponsor * Contact: Edward Giermann, PAC Chairman * Treasurer: James A. Henry*

	1993-94	1995-96	1997	Totals
Receipts	$59,140	$30,119	$5,121	$94,380
Disburse	28,647	55,106	9,444	93,197
Cash	36,904	11,921	7,598	n/a
Contributions	27,100	49,000	9,416	85,516
Republicans	15,600	39,500	7,916	63,016
No. of Cand.	*9*	*28*	*9*	*46*
House	5,100	30,500	7,000	42,600
Senate	10,500	9,000	916	20,416
Democrats	11,500	9,500	1,500	22,500
No. of Cand.	*8*	*3*	*2*	*13*
House	10,500	9,500	1,500	21,500
Senate	1,000	0	0	1,000
Incumbents	17,000	44,500	8,500	70,000
Challengers	9,100	1,500	916	11,516
Open Seat	1,000	3,000	0	4,000
Winners	15,600	42,000	n/a	57,600
Losers	11,500	7,000	n/a	18,500

J.R. Simplot Co.

*Phone: (208) 389-7337 * Fax: (208) 389-7295*
P.O. Box 27, Boise, ID 83707
Web: www.simplot.com

The J.R. Simplot Co. is a privately held agribusiness corporation with headquarters in Boise, Idaho. Annual revenues are about $2.8 billion, derived principally from food processing, fertilizer manufacturing, agriculture and related businesses.

The company produces fruits, cheeses, vegetables, meats and potatoes. It makes more than 2 billion pounds of frozen potato products each year, primarily for restaurants.

Founded in 1920, J.R. Simplot employs about 13,000 people in the United States, Canada, Mexico, Australia and China. It has operations in virtually every state and a growing number of foreign countries. Simplot is organized into five major groups: corporate, food, agriculture, minerals and chemical and diversified products.

J.R. Simplot Co. Political Action Committee (Sim-PAC) (C00120873) *Address: same as sponsor * Contact: Fred Zerza, Chairman * Treasurer: James D. Crawford*

	1993-94	1995-96	1997	Totals
Receipts	$10,051	$24,636	$14,534	$49,221
Disburse	13,830	24,250	650	38,730
Cash	1,539	1,928	15,813	n/a
Contributions	13,830	24,250	650	38,730
Republicans	13,330	23,750	650	37,730
No. of Cand.	*10*	*12*	*1*	*23*
House	11,070	11,000	0	22,070
Senate	2,260	12,750	650	15,660
Democrats	500	500	0	1,000
No. of Cand.	*1*	*1*	*0*	*2*
House	500	500	0	1,000
Senate	0	0	0	0
Incumbents	3,830	15,000	650	19,480
Challengers	6,500	3,750	0	10,250
Open Seat	3,500	5,500	0	9,000
Winners	11,830	23,000	n/a	34,830
Losers	2,000	1,250	n/a	3,250

Minn-Dak Farmers Cooperative

*Phone: (701) 642-8411 * Fax: (701) 642-6814*
7525 Red River Rd., Wahpeton, ND 58075

The Minn-Dak Farmers Cooperative is a collection of more than 450 sugarbeet farmers in seven counties in Minnesota and North Dakota. Formed in 1972, the co-op has 150 full-time and 320 seasonal workers at its processing mill in Wahpeton, N.D.

Minn-Dak Farmers Cooperative Political Action Committee (MDFPAC) (C00164939) *Address: same as sponsor * Contact: Larry D. Steward, President * Treasurer: Steven M. Caspers*

	1993-94	1995-96	1997	Totals
Receipts	$88,557	$90,397	$41,716	$220,670
Disburse	66,931	86,245	54,607	207,783
Cash	71,387	75,539	62,648	n/a
Contributions	46,250	63,500	41,430	151,180
Republicans	19,750	31,250	20,930	71,930
No. of Cand.	*49*	*33*	*28*	*110*
House	15,000	18,750	12,750	46,500
Senate	4,750	12,500	8,180	25,430
Democrats	24,500	32,250	19,500	76,250
No. of Cand.	*54*	*34*	*28*	*116*
House	17,250	25,750	10,500	53,500
Senate	7,250	6,500	9,000	22,750
Incumbents	46,000	56,500	40,930	143,430
Challengers	0	1,500	0	1,500
Open Seat	250	5,500	0	5,750
Winners	40,750	57,500	n/a	98,250
Losers	5,500	6,000	n/a	11,500

National Association of Wheat Growers

*Phone: (202) 547-7800 * Fax: (202) 546-2638*
415 Second St. N.E., Washington, DC 20002
*Web: www.wheatworld.org * E-mail: wheatworld@wheatworld.org*

The National Association of Wheat Growers represents about 25,000 members and 35 associate members, including railroad, food, farm machinery and agricultural chemical companies.

The group's "Wheat Action Plan" calls for the Department of Agriculture to promote export and credit programs "to help offset European export subsidies and to combat discriminatory pricing practices of state trading enterprises."

National Association of Wheat Growers Political Action Committee (WheatPAC) (C00139964) *Address: same as sponsor * Contact: Jim Miller, Vice President of Governmental Affairs * Treasurer: Carl F. Schwensen*

	1993-94	1995-96	1997	Totals
Receipts	$43,664	$63,817	$20,092	$127,573
Disburse	40,550	40,850	21,850	103,250
Cash	4,704	27,672	25,915	n/a
Contributions	40,550	39,850	21,850	102,250
Republicans	8,950	23,700	11,500	44,150
No. of Cand.	*16*	*20*	*12*	*48*
House	6,250	15,350	7,500	29,100
Senate	2,700	8,350	4,000	15,050
Democrats	29,000	16,150	8,850	54,000
No. of Cand.	*20*	*10*	*10*	*40*
House	22,900	9,300	2,850	35,050
Senate	6,100	6,850	6,000	18,950
Incumbents	39,700	30,500	21,850	92,050
Challengers	0	3,350	0	3,350
Open Seat	850	6,000	0	6,850
Winners	27,100	32,650	n/a	59,750
Losers	13,450	7,200	n/a	20,650

National Cotton Council

*Phone: (901) 274-9030 * Fax: (901) 725-0510*
1918 N. Pkwy., P.O. Box 12292, Memphis, TN 38182
Web: www.cotton.org

The National Cotton Council represents all seven cotton industry segments — producers, ginners, crushers, cooperatives, manufacturers, warehousers and merchants. Nearly all cotton producers in the United States pay dues to the council through their gin, creating a national membership of about 30,000 individuals. The council's interests include agricultural, environmental and international trade issues.

National Cotton Council Committee for the Advancement of Cotton (C00023028) *Phone: (202) 745-7805 * Fax: (202) 483-4040 * 1521 New Hampshire Ave. N.W., Washington, DC 20036 * Contact: Craig Brown, Dir. of Producer Affairs * Phone: (901) 274-9030 * Treasurer: Bill Tracy*

	1993-94	1995-96	1997	Totals
Receipts	$189,629	$169,721	$78,560	$437,910
Disburse	211,267	176,574	98,117	485,958
Cash	36,645	29,795	10,240	n/a
Contributions	206,822	159,226	89,476	455,524
Republicans	77,492	107,177	47,826	232,495
No. of Cand.	*71*	*92*	*41*	*204*
House	55,529	75,114	35,303	165,946
Senate	21,963	32,063	12,523	66,549
Democrats	127,830	51,549	41,650	221,029
No. of Cand.	*92*	*54*	*39*	*185*
House	102,460	45,549	31,000	179,009
Senate	25,370	6,000	10,650	42,020
Incumbents	192,745	137,226	87,976	417,947
Challengers	3,000	2,000	0	5,000
Open Seat	11,077	19,500	0	30,577
Winners	164,525	141,226	n/a	305,751
Losers	42,297	18,000	n/a	60,297

National Grape Cooperative Association

*Phone: (716) 326-3131 * Fax: (716) 326-5111*
Two S. Portage St., Westfield, NY 14787
Web: www.welchs.com

The National Grape Cooperative Association is an agriculture cooperative which produces juice, jam and jellies. The $572-million cooperative employs 1,250 workers.

Its headquarters are in Concord, Mass., but growers harvest in New York, Pennsylvania, Ohio, Michigan, Washington state and Ontario, Canada.

In March 1997, The American College of Cardiology released a study highlighting the benefits to the heart from drinking grape juice. Afterward, the sale of Welch's grape juice rose by 40 percent.

The National/Welch's PAC maintains 1,440 grower members.

National Grape Cooperative Association Inc./Welch Foods Inc., A Cooperative PAC (C00133215) *Address: same as sponsor * Treasurer: Patrick J. O'Donnell*

	1993-94	1995-96	1997	Totals
Receipts	$13,509	$11,645	$6,125	$31,279
Disburse	15,000	14,500	3,000	32,500
Cash	11,188	8,333	11,458	n/a
Contributions	7,000	6,500	0	13,500
Republicans	6,000	5,000	0	11,000
No. of Cand.	*8*	*9*	*0*	*17*
House	2,000	3,500	0	5,500
Senate	4,000	1,500	0	5,500
Democrats	1,000	1,500	0	2,500
No. of Cand.	*1*	*3*	*0*	*4*
House	1,000	1,000	0	2,000
Senate	0	500	0	500
Incumbents	3,500	5,000	0	8,500
Challengers	1,000	1,000	0	2,000
Open Seat	2,500	500	0	3,000
Winners	6,000	5,500	n/a	11,500
Losers	1,000	1,000	n/a	2,000

National Potato Council

*Phone: (303) 773-9295 * Fax: (303) 773-9296*
5690 DTC Blvd., Suite 230E, Englewood, CO 80111
*Web: www.npcspud.com * E-mail: npcspud@ix.netcom.com*

The National Potato Council is a nonprofit trade association that represents more than 10,500 commercial potato growers. Commercial potato growers who farm more than five acres are automatic members.

The bipartisan PAC funds candidates from across the nation who support issues important to potato farmers.

PoPAC (C00154104) *Address: same as sponsor * Treasurer: A. R. Middaugh*

	1993-94	1995-96	1997	Totals
Receipts	$14,331	$11,803	$13,003	$39,137
Disburse	14,983	11,285	1,733	28,001
Cash	1,375	1,897	13,166	n/a
Contributions	12,100	10,700	0	22,800
Republicans	5,700	6,550	0	12,250
No. of Cand.	*14*	*12*	*0*	*26*
House	3,350	4,000	0	7,350
Senate	2,350	2,550	0	4,900
Democrats	6,400	4,150	0	10,550
No. of Cand.	*14*	*7*	*0*	*21*
House	6,200	3,400	0	9,600
Senate	200	750	0	950
Incumbents	12,100	8,800	0	20,900
Challengers	0	250	0	250
Open Seat	0	1,650	0	1,650
Winners	9,000	10,200	n/a	19,200
Losers	3,100	500	n/a	3,600

National Sunflower Association

*Phone: (701) 328-5100 * Fax: (701) 328-5101*
4023 State St., Bismarck, ND 58501-0690
E-mail: klngrtnr@sunflowernsa.com

The National Sunflower Association represents sunflower growers, roasters and suppliers nationwide. It has about 75 paying members, most of whom live in the northern Great Plains.

National Sunflower Political Action Committee (SunPAC) (C00239939) *Address: same as sponsor * Contact: Larry Kleingartner, Executive Dir. * Treasurer: John Burritt*

	1993-94	1995-96	1997	Totals
Receipts	$10,036	$11,616	$7,371	$29,023
Disburse	7,549	7,015	505	15,069
Cash	3,018	7,624	14,490	n/a
Contributions	7,500	7,000	500	15,000
Republicans	1,500	3,000	0	4,500
No. of Cand.	*2*	*3*	*0*	*5*
House	1,500	1,500	0	3,000
Senate	0	1,500	0	1,500
Democrats	6,000	4,000	500	10,500
No. of Cand.	*3*	*4*	*1*	*8*
House	6,000	1,500	0	7,500
Senate	0	2,500	500	3,000
Incumbents	7,500	1,500	500	9,500
Challengers	0	1,500	0	1,500
Open Seat	0	4,000	0	4,000
Winners	7,500	7,000	n/a	14,500
Losers	0	0	n/a	0

Ocean Spray Cranberries Inc.

*Phone: (508) 946-1000 * Fax: (508) 946-7304*
One Ocean Spray Dr., Lakeville-Middleboro, MA 02349
Web: www.oceanspray.com

Ocean Spray is a marketing cooperative of more than 900 cranberry and citrus growers in the United States and Canada. The company, which posted fiscal year 1997 sales of nearly $1.5 billion and has about 2,300 employees, is the largest producer of canned and bottled juices in North America. The company handles about 75 percent of the cranberry crop. In addition to supplying blended juices and fresh cranberries, Ocean Spray grows and distributes grapefruit.

In December 1997, Ocean Spray announced that it would be forming a strategic partnership with Nantucket Nectars, a premium juice maker. As part of the deal, Ocean Spray planned to buy an interest in the company, although Nantucket Nectars would continue to operate as an independent company.

Ocean Spray Cranberries Inc. Political Action Committee (C00114702) *Address: same as sponsor * Contact: Jim O'Shaughnessy, Co-Chairperson * Treasurer: Cindy A. Correia*

	1993-94	1995-96	1997	Totals
Receipts	$163,329	$109,395	$60,431	$333,155
Disburse	183,326	144,106	55,576	383,008
Cash	34,734	26	21,137	n/a
Contributions	110,330	65,550	43,750	219,630
Republicans	28,000	35,500	23,750	87,250
No. of Cand.	*23*	*36*	*28*	*87*
House	23,000	23,500	13,750	60,250
Senate	5,000	12,000	10,000	27,000
Democrats	81,830	30,050	19,000	130,880
No. of Cand.	*80*	*40*	*24*	*144*
House	58,350	24,050	12,000	94,400
Senate	23,480	6,000	7,000	36,480
Incumbents	105,830	61,550	43,750	211,130
Challengers	0	1,000	0	1,000
Open Seat	4,500	3,000	0	7,500
Winners	93,000	59,550	n/a	152,550
Losers	17,330	6,000	n/a	23,330

Raisin Bargaining Association

*Phone: (209) 221-1925 * Fax: (209) 221-0725*
3425 N. First St., Suite 209, Fresno, CA 93726

The Raisin Bargaining Association is a California cooperative representing more than 30 growers. The group meets each year and offers a set price for the raisin harvest to the packing industry. The raisin and grape industries combined generate more than $500 million in annual sales in California.

Raisin Bargaining Association Federal Political Action Committee (C00128686) *Address: same as sponsor * Contact: Vaughn Koligian, CEO * Treasurer: Girard Kasparian*

	1993-94	1995-96	1997	Totals
Receipts	$27,036	$23,932	$5,769	$56,737
Disburse	24,050	20,675	2,650	47,375
Cash	22,898	26,155	29,274	n/a
Contributions	9,050	5,675	2,650	17,375

(Data for Raisin Bargaining Association continued)

	1993-94	1995-96	1997	Totals
Republicans	1,700	2,500	1,400	5,600
No. of Cand.	*4*	*3*	*2*	*9*
House	1,700	2,500	1,400	5,600
Senate	0	0	0	0
Democrats	7,350	3,175	1,250	11,775
No. of Cand.	*8*	*3*	*2*	*13*
House	6,350	3,175	1,250	10,775
Senate	1,000	0	0	1,000
Incumbents	7,350	4,175	2,650	14,175
Challengers	1,950	1,500	0	3,450
Open Seat	0	0	0	0
Winners	4,200	4,175	n/a	8,375
Losers	4,850	1,500	n/a	6,350

Riceland Foods

*Phone: (870) 673-5214 * Fax: (870) 673-5667*
P.O. Box 927, Stuttgart, AR 72160
Web: www.riceland.com

Riceland Foods processes and sells rice, soybeans and grain grown by the cooperative's 10,000 farmer-members located in Arkansas, Missouri, Texas, Louisiana and Mississippi. The cooperative has about 1,850 employees.

Riceland Foods Inc. Political Action Committee (Riceland PAC) (C00220053) *Address: same as sponsor * Treasurer: Bill J. Reed*

	1993-94	1995-96	1997	Totals
Receipts	$38,075	$30,069	$11,250	$79,394
Disburse	37,760	27,919	9,500	75,179
Cash	1,150	3,300	5,050	n/a
Contributions	34,010	22,600	8,500	65,110
Republicans	8,510	14,100	2,500	25,110
No. of Cand.	*7*	*15*	*2*	*24*
House	3,500	9,500	2,500	15,500
Senate	5,010	4,600	0	9,610
Democrats	25,000	8,500	6,000	39,500
No. of Cand.	*21*	*8*	*6*	*35*
House	15,500	6,000	2,500	24,000
Senate	9,500	2,500	3,500	15,500
Incumbents	30,510	11,100	6,500	48,110
Challengers	0	2,000	0	2,000
Open Seat	3,500	9,500	1,000	14,000
Winners	25,510	19,100	n/a	44,610
Losers	8,500	3,500	n/a	12,000

Rio Grande Valley Sugar Growers

Phone: (512) 636-1411
2 1/2 Miles West on Highway 107, Santa Rosa, TX 78593

Rio Grande Valley Sugar Growers is a Texas-based raw sugar cane producer. About 40,000 acres of sugar cane are grown in the Rio Grande region of the state.

Rio Grande Valley Sugar Growers Inc. Political Action Committee (C00185686) *Address: same as sponsor * Treasurer: Randy E. Rolando*

	1993-94	1995-96	1997	Totals
Receipts	$28,763	$70,929	$20,693	$120,385
Disburse	28,667	54,873	20,190	103,730
Cash	1,310	7,823	8,326	n/a
Contributions	24,700	36,115	19,500	80,315
Republicans	6,000	17,580	9,500	33,080
No. of Cand.	*8*	*20*	*13*	*41*
House	3,500	16,580	8,000	28,080
Senate	2,500	1,000	1,500	5,000
Democrats	18,700	18,535	10,000	47,235
No. of Cand.	*22*	*22*	*16*	*60*
House	17,200	18,535	9,500	45,235
Senate	1,500	0	500	2,000
Incumbents	22,700	30,540	18,000	71,240
Challengers	0	1,000	0	1,000
Open Seat	2,000	4,575	1,500	8,075
Winners	19,200	29,615	n/a	48,815
Losers	5,500	6,500	n/a	12,000

Savannah Foods & Industries Inc.

*Phone: (912) 234-1261 * Fax: (912) 651-5159*
2 E. Bryan, P.O. Box 553, Savannah, GA 31401
Web: www.dixiecrystals.com

According to PAC Treasurer Robin Bryant, the Savannah PAC is in the process of being terminated.

Savannah Foods & Industries refines and markets sugar and its products as a subsidiary of Imperial Holly Corp. Savannah posted 1997 sales of $1.1 billion and employs 1,900 people.

After being purchased by Imperial Holly in December 1997, Savannah agreed to merge with Florida Crystals, a private Florida sugar producer.

Its products are sold under the Dixie Crystals, Pioneer, Quick 'n Sweet, Sweet Thing and Evercane brands, as well as under private labels. The firm and its subsidiaries operate 13 refining, processing and production plants. Its products are sold throughout the United States.

Savannah Foods & Industries Inc. Nonpartisan Committee for Better Federal Government (C00130203) *Address: same as sponsor * Treasurer: Robin J. Bryant*

	1993-94	1995-96	1997	Totals
Receipts	$18,242	$35,707	$13,858	$67,807
Disburse	15,550	42,569	7,501	65,620
Cash	5,254	3,473	9,837	n/a
Contributions	15,550	39,900	7,500	62,950
Republicans	7,500	26,200	6,000	39,700
No. of Cand.	*7*	*23*	*7*	*37*
House	6,000	20,700	3,500	30,200
Senate	1,500	5,500	2,500	9,500
Democrats	8,050	13,700	1,500	23,250
No. of Cand.	*8*	*12*	*2*	*22*
House	6,850	11,700	500	19,050
Senate	1,200	2,000	1,000	4,200
Incumbents	14,550	34,400	7,500	56,450
Challengers	0	0	0	0
Open Seat	0	5,500	0	5,500
Winners	11,350	36,900	n/a	48,250
Losers	4,200	3,000	n/a	7,200

Scoular Co.

*Phone: (402) 342-3500 * Fax: (402) 342-5568*
2027 Dodge St., Omaha, NE 68102
Web: www.scoular.com

A century-old company, Scoular is No. 67 on the Forbes list of top privately held corporations in the United States. Its operations now extend across North America. The company had estimated revenues of $1.8 billion in 1997.

Scoular's activities are built around agriculture. Scoular's grain marketing division trades more than 400 million bushels of grain throughout North America every year. The commodity marketing division offers options to customers who trade both grain and grain by-products. Last year, this division marketed more than 1.1 million tons of by-products. The county elevator division, with 11 elevators across Nebraska, offers storage capacity of more than 25 million bushels of grain. Subsidiary Vic's Popping Corn Co. makes popcorn for retail sale.

In January 1998, Scoular announced the formation of a new freight division. The division will be named TSC Freight Marketing and will be located at the Scoular headquarters in Omaha, Neb. TSC Freight Marketing will broker truck freight both inside and outside the company.

Scoular Co. Fund for Effective Government (C00293076) *Address: same as sponsor * Treasurer: Roger Lee Barber*

	1993-94	1995-96	1997	Totals
Receipts	$3,401	$7,589	$0	$10,990
Disburse	3,031	7,825	0	10,856
Cash	305	195	195	n/a
Contributions	2,200	7,625	0	9,825
Republicans	2,200	6,625	0	8,825
No. of Cand.	*3*	*8*	*0*	*11*
House	2,200	3,700	0	5,900
Senate	0	2,925	0	2,925
Democrats	0	1,000	0	1,000
No. of Cand.	*0*	*1*	*0*	*1*
House	0	0	0	0
Senate	0	1,000	0	1,000
Incumbents	200	3,775	0	3,975
Challengers	2,000	0	0	2,000
Open Seat	0	3,850	0	3,850
Winners	1,700	6,025	n/a	7,725
Losers	500	1,600	n/a	2,100

Snake River Sugar Co.

*Phone: (801) 399-3431 * Fax: (801) 393-8042*
2427 Lincoln Ave., Ogden, UT 84401

Amalgamated Sugar Co. is a subsidiary of Snake River Sugar, a Utah beet sugar producer. Snake River was formed after growers in Idaho acquired Amalgamated from Valhi Inc. in 1996 for $266 million. Amalgamated, located in Ogden, Utah, is a sugar processor.

Snake River's territory includes about 220,000 acres of sugar beets in Oregon and Idaho grown by hundreds of independent farmers. The company also has a PAC (FEC ID: C00326389), but it was not registered with the FEC during the 1995-96 election cycle.

Amalgamated closed its PAC during a 1997 reorganization, but later started a new committee (FEC ID: C00326868). During the 1995-96 election cycle, Amalgamated ranked 15th of 17 sugar industry PACs.

The Amalgamated Sugar Co. Political Action Committee (C00109926) *Address: Same as sponsor * Treasurer: John R. Lemke*

	1993-94	1995-96	1997	Totals
Receipts	$21,269	$23,057	$3,055	$47,381
Disburse	37,558	30,183	2,000	69,741
Cash	11,780	4,657	5,712	n/a
Contributions	25,000	25,000	2,000	52,000
Republicans	18,000	18,500	2,000	38,500
No. of Cand.	*9*	*17*	*2*	*28*
House	4,500	11,500	0	16,000
Senate	13,500	7,000	2,000	22,500
Democrats	7,000	6,500	0	13,500
No. of Cand.	*6*	*10*	*0*	*16*
House	5,000	5,000	0	10,000
Senate	2,000	1,500	0	3,500
Incumbents	21,000	18,500	2,000	41,500
Challengers	500	3,500	0	4,000
Open Seat	2,500	3,000	0	5,500
Winners	19,500	19,000	n/a	38,500
Losers	5,500	6,000	n/a	11,500

Southern Cotton Growers Inc.

*Phone: (706) 864-0112 * Fax: (706) 864-5919*
109 N. Grove St., P.O. Box 866, Dahlonega, GA 30533

Founded in 1995, Southern Cotton Growers is an association of 10,000 individual cotton farmers in the Southeast.

Committee for the Advancement of Southeastern Cotton (CASC) Southern Cotton Growers Inc./S.E. Cotton Ginners Association (C00300426) *Address: same as sponsor * Treasurer: Robert McLendon*

	1993-94	1995-96	1997	Totals
Receipts	$0	$41,660	$18,681	$60,341
Disburse	0	31,184	21,650	52,834
Cash	0	10,475	7,207	n/a
Contributions	0	20,634	16,375	37,009
Republicans	0	11,034	9,875	20,909
No. of Cand.	*0*	*12*	*9*	*21*
House	0	7,859	4,500	12,359
Senate	0	3,175	5,375	8,550
Democrats	0	9,600	6,500	16,100
No. of Cand.	*0*	*13*	*7*	*20*
House	0	7,500	6,000	13,500
Senate	0	2,100	500	2,600
Incumbents	0	15,409	16,375	31,784
Challengers	0	500	0	500
Open Seat	0	4,725	0	4,725
Winners	0	17,534	n/a	17,534
Losers	0	3,100	n/a	3,100

Southern Minnesota Beet Sugar Cooperative

*Phone: (320) 329-8305 * Fax: (320) 329-3252*
P.O. Box 500, Renville, MN 56284

The Southern Minnesota Beet Sugar Cooperative is a collection of beet sugar farmers and processors in the upper Midwest. It consists of about 490 shareholders and employees (250 year-round and 350 seasonal). The SMBSC is reportedly the only factory in the world to have processed more than 2 million tons of sugarbeets in one season.

Along with American Crystal Sugar Co. and Minn-Dak Farmers Cooperative, the SMBSC sponsors the Sugarbeet Research and Education Board of Minnesota and North Dakota (www.sbreb.org), which promotes research, education and sugar production throughout Minnesota and North Dakota.

As a member of the sugar industry, the SMBSC supports government price subsidies for U.S. sugar companies.

Although it provided almost equal support to Democratic and Republican candidates, this PAC spent 97 percent of its money on incumbents during 1996. Just two candidates received at least $5,000 — Rep. David Minge, D-Minn., who got $10,000, and Sen. Larry E. Craig, R-Idaho, who received $5,000. Both sit on agriculture committees.

Southern Minnesota Sugar Cooperative Political Action Committee (C00166348) *Address: same as sponsor * Contact: Alan Ritacco, President and CEO * Treasurer: Jeffrey L. Plathe*

	1993-94	1995-96	1997	Totals
Receipts	$217,358	$235,074	$123,209	$575,641
Disburse	178,300	275,900	82,000	536,200
Cash	114,778	73,956	115,165	n/a
Contributions	157,975	244,900	65,000	467,875
Republicans	71,500	132,300	35,500	239,300
No. of Cand.	*73*	*135*	*51*	*259*
House	49,650	100,300	24,000	173,950
Senate	21,850	32,000	11,500	65,350
Democrats	76,075	112,600	28,500	217,175
No. of Cand.	*85*	*103*	*44*	*232*
House	61,050	91,600	18,000	170,650
Senate	15,025	21,000	10,500	46,525
Incumbents	146,125	226,400	64,500	437,025
Challengers	3,000	4,500	0	7,500
Open Seat	8,850	14,000	500	23,350
Winners	137,450	220,600	n/a	358,050
Losers	20,525	24,300	n/a	44,825

Southwest Peanut Membership Organization

*Phone: (202) 484-2773 * Fax: (202) 484-0770*
412 First St. S.E., Suite 1, Washington, DC 20003

Southwest Peanut represents peanut growers in Texas, New Mexico and Oklahoma. The average farm that the association represents is about 100 acres.

The association is interested in legislation pertinent to agricultural issues, trade and food safety.

Southwest Peanut Political Action Committee (C00163154) *Address: same as sponsor * Treasurer: Larry D. Meyers*

	1993-94	1995-96	1997	Totals
Receipts	$110,407	$82,598	$34,942	$227,947
Disburse	147,264	165,185	49,375	361,824
Cash	100,058	17,473	3,041	n/a
Contributions	129,911	152,100	46,375	328,386
Republicans	28,731	72,300	24,125	125,156
No. of Cand.	*28*	*65*	*32*	*125*
House	20,231	50,800	15,125	86,156
Senate	8,500	21,500	9,000	39,000
Democrats	100,680	79,800	22,250	202,730
No. of Cand.	*73*	*83*	*34*	*190*
House	78,680	63,800	15,500	157,980
Senate	22,000	16,000	6,750	44,750
Incumbents	119,286	121,550	44,875	285,711
Challengers	907	6,750	0	7,657
Open Seat	9,718	22,200	1,500	33,418
Winners	94,931	127,150	n/a	222,081
Losers	34,980	24,950	n/a	59,930

Sugar Cane Growers Cooperative of Florida

*Phone: (561) 833-7500 * Fax: (561) 996-4747*
P.O. Box 666, Belle Glade, FL 33430

The Sugar Cane Growers Co-op of Florida is headquartered in Belle Glade, Fla., where it employs more than 900 workers.

According to the Center for Responsive Politics, in February 1997 the Sugar Cane Growers Co-op and the Florida Sugar Cane League paid $10,100 for more than a dozen House staffers to travel to Florida for "an educational trip" about sugar cane. The staffers represented 14 members of Congress, five of whom sit on the House Agriculture Committee, including Chairman Bob Smith, R-Ore.

Members of Congress are barred from accepting gifts from private sources — but the ban does not include meetings, speaking engagements and fact-finding trips. House members and staffers must disclose the details of such travel.

Sugar Cane Growers Cooperative of Florida (PAC) (C00254656) *Address: same as sponsor * Treasurer: John W. Gray*

	1993-94	1995-96	1997	Totals
Receipts	$20,626	$30,056	$33,657	$84,339
Disburse	21,200	36,600	0	57,800
Cash	7,261	717	34,375	n/a
Contributions	20,200	36,100	0	56,300
Republicans	4,000	14,600	0	18,600
No. of Cand.	*5*	*19*	*0*	*24*
House	1,000	9,500	0	10,500
Senate	3,000	5,100	0	8,100
Democrats	16,200	21,500	0	37,700
No. of Cand.	*20*	*27*	*2*	*49*
House	8,200	11,500	0	19,700
Senate	8,000	10,000	0	18,000
Incumbents	18,200	25,600	500	44,300
Challengers	0	4,000	0	4,000
Open Seat	2,000	6,500	0	8,500
Winners	15,400	28,600	n/a	44,000
Losers	4,800	7,500	n/a	12,300

Sun-Diamond Growers

*Phone: (510) 463-8200 * Fax: (510) 463-7439*
5568 Gibraltar Dr., Pleasanton, CA 94588

Sun-Diamond Growers is a private West Coast cooperative which produces walnuts, prunes, raisins and figs. The organization has five members: Diamond Walnut Growers Inc., Sun-Maid Growers of California, Sunsweet Growers Inc., Valley Fig Growers and Hazelnut Growers of Oregon. It had sales of nearly $750 million in 1997. The organization, which employs 1,850 people, has three affiliated PACs, one each for Diamond Walnut, Sunsweet and Sun-Maid.

Sun-Diamond uses methyl bromide to grow young fruit trees and to fumigate stored fruits and nuts. Its advocacy for methyl bromide led to controversy when a federal jury found the co-op guilty of making $9,000 in illegal gifts to then-Agriculture Secretary Mike Espy and the congressional campaign of Espy's brother, Henry Espy of Mississippi. The organization is appealing the September 1996 conviction and $2 million fine, and has been banned from participating in federal purchase programs until 1999.

Sun-Maid Growers of California Political Action Committee (C00108001) *Phone: (209) 896-8000 * Fax: (209) 897-2362 * 13525 S. Bethel Ave., Kingsburg, CA 93631 * Web: www.sunmaid.com * Treasurer: Rich Emde*

	1993-94	1995-96	1997	Totals
Receipts	$31,800	$28,040	$10,760	$70,600
Disburse	27,413	22,550	6,427	56,390
Cash	6,422	9,215	13,548	n/a
Contributions	25,918	22,600	6,250	54,768
Republicans	3,418	12,300	2,000	17,718
No. of Cand.	*3*	*16*	*2*	*21*
House	2,168	8,800	2,000	12,968
Senate	1,250	3,500	0	4,750
Democrats	22,500	10,300	4,250	37,050
No. of Cand.	*13*	*7*	*5*	*25*
House	16,000	7,300	4,250	27,550
Senate	6,500	3,000	0	9,500
Incumbents	19,750	19,500	6,250	45,500
Challengers	1,668	1,600	0	3,268
Open Seat	4,500	1,500	0	6,000
Winners	15,218	21,000	n/a	36,218
Losers	10,700	1,600	n/a	12,300

Diamond Walnut Growers Inc. Political Action Committee (C00126466) *Phone: (209) 467-6000 * Fax: (209) 467-6788 * 1050 S. Diamond St., P.O. Box 9024, Stockton, CA 95205 * Web: www.diamondwalnut.com * E-mail: smcbride@diamondwalnut.com * Treasurer: Sandra J. McBride*

	1993-94	1995-96	1997	Totals
Receipts	$28,842	$15,251	$10,611	$54,704
Disburse	25,021	25,062	9,971	60,054
Cash	22,957	13,155	25,129	n/a
Contributions	23,166	23,500	9,000	55,666
Republicans	9,916	13,000	4,500	27,416
No. of Cand.	*7*	*16*	*6*	*29*
House	8,166	9,500	4,500	22,166
Senate	1,750	3,500	0	5,250
Democrats	13,250	10,500	4,500	28,250
No. of Cand.	*10*	*7*	*4*	*21*
House	8,250	8,500	4,500	21,250
Senate	5,000	2,000	0	7,000
Incumbents	18,750	21,000	9,000	48,750
Challengers	2,166	1,000	0	3,166
Open Seat	2,250	1,500	0	3,750
Winners	18,916	22,500	n/a	41,416
Losers	4,250	1,000	n/a	5,250

Sunsweet Growers Inc. PAC (C00138123) *Phone: (916) 674-5010 * 901 Walton Ave., P.O. Box 9024, Yuba City, CA 95993-9370 * Treasurer: Charles H. Bell Jr.*

	1993-94	1995-96	1997	Totals
Receipts	$14,685	$38,548	$20,229	$73,462
Disburse	30,501	13,180	6,800	50,481
Cash	1,185	26,555	39,985	n/a
Contributions	28,166	11,880	6,500	46,546
Republicans	7,416	3,750	4,000	15,166
No. of Cand.	*5*	*5*	*3*	*13*
House	5,666	2,250	4,000	11,916
Senate	1,750	1,500	0	3,250
Democrats	20,750	8,130	2,500	31,380
No. of Cand.	*13*	*6*	*4*	*23*
House	15,500	8,130	2,500	26,130
Senate	5,250	0	0	5,250
Incumbents	21,500	10,380	6,500	38,380
Challengers	2,166	0	0	2,166
Open Seat	4,500	1,500	0	6,000
Winners	22,166	11,130	n/a	33,296
Losers	6,000	750	n/a	6,750

Sunkist Growers

*Phone: (818) 986-4800 * Fax: (818) 379-7405*
14130 Riverside Dr., P.O. Box 5576, Sherman Oaks, CA 91423-2392
Web: www.sunkist.com

Sunkist Growers, a 103-year-old citrus marketing cooperative, is owned by 6,500 citrus farmers in California and Arizona. It markets fresh fruit and processed products such as fruit juices and oils.

Thirty-four percent of fresh fruit sales come from groups that buy the right to use Sunkist's name.

The cooperative's sales rose by 4.4 percent in 1997. It ended the year with more than $1 billion in total sales.

Sunkist Growers Inc. Political Action Committee (C00099002) *Address: same as sponsor * Contact: Ralph E. Bodine, Chairman Emeritus * Treasurer: W. K. Quarles*

	1993-94	1995-96	1997	Totals
Receipts	$121,685	$103,762	$55,055	$280,502
Disburse	125,150	96,551	49,759	271,460
Cash	12,127	19,349	24,645	n/a
Contributions	96,180	70,800	40,250	207,230
Republicans	35,520	40,000	24,000	99,520
No. of Cand.	*26*	*29*	*26*	*81*
House	29,520	35,000	24,000	88,520
Senate	6,000	5,000	0	11,000
Democrats	60,660	30,800	16,250	107,710
No. of Cand.	*30*	*18*	*16*	*64*
House	45,050	24,800	14,250	84,100
Senate	15,610	6,000	2,000	23,610
Incumbents	86,830	55,300	40,250	182,380
Challengers	3,000	3,000	0	6,000
Open Seat	6,350	12,500	0	18,850
Winners	87,820	64,300	n/a	152,120
Losers	8,360	6,500	n/a	14,860

Texas Rice Producers' Legislative Group

Phone: (512) 782-7156
P.O. Box 249, Eagle Lake, TX 77434

Texas Rice Producers is a 3,000-member association affiliated with the U.S. Rice Producers' Group. Established in 1989, the organization maintains 12 district chapters throughout southern Texas, the state's primary region of rice production.

Texas Rice Producers' Legislative Group Political Action Committee (C00240093) *Address: same as sponsor * Contact: Dennis DeLaughter, Chairman * Treasurer: William H. Harrison*

	1993-94	1995-96	1997	Totals
Receipts	$14,711	$17,055	$2,150	$33,916
Disburse	17,575	16,109	2,000	35,684
Cash	316	102	252	n/a
Contributions	17,474	12,609	2,000	32,083
Republicans	5,600	7,309	0	12,909
No. of Cand.	*5*	*6*	*0*	*11*
House	500	1,809	0	2,309
Senate	5,100	5,500	0	10,600
Democrats	11,874	5,300	2,000	19,174
No. of Cand.	*12*	*5*	*3*	*20*
House	10,074	4,800	1,000	15,874
Senate	1,800	500	1,000	3,300
Incumbents	17,224	9,109	1,000	27,333
Challengers	0	500	1,000	1,500

Open Seat	250	3,000	0	3,250
Winners	11,924	10,400	n/a	22,324
Losers	5,550	2,209	n/a	7,759

Texas Sugar Beet Growers Association

*Phone: (806) 384-8402 * Fax: (806) 384-6870*
119 E. Fourth St., Suite 3, Hereford, TX 79045

Texas Sugar Beet Growers Association represents the interests of sugar beet farmers. South Texas generates a small but significant portion of the nation's sugar supply.

Political Action Committee of the Texas Sugar Beet Growers Association Inc. (also known as Texas Ag PAC) (C00174102)
*Address: same as sponsor * Treasurer: Bill Cleavinger*

	1993-94	1995-96	1997	Totals
Receipts	$43,433	$16,676	$6,810	$66,919
Disburse	34,472	45,604	11,720	91,796
Cash	54,046	25,120	20,211	n/a
Contributions	19,000	34,500	6,000	59,500
Republicans	1,500	17,000	2,000	20,500
No. of Cand.	*3*	*17*	*4*	*24*
House	1,000	11,000	1,500	13,500
Senate	500	6,000	500	7,000
Democrats	17,500	17,500	4,000	39,000
No. of Cand.	*15*	*23*	*8*	*46*
House	15,500	14,000	3,500	33,000
Senate	2,000	3,500	500	6,000
Incumbents	17,500	28,000	5,500	51,000
Challengers	500	1,500	0	2,000
Open Seat	1,000	5,000	500	6,500
Winners	15,500	31,000	n/a	46,500
Losers	3,500	3,500	n/a	7,000

United Foods Inc.

*Phone: (901) 422-7600 * Fax: (800) 561-8810*
10 Pictsweet Dr., Bells, TN 38006

United Foods distributes fruit and vegetable products under the brand Pictsweet to the retail market. In 1996, the publicly owned company had sales of $196 million and 2,350 employees.

The company distributes strawberries, okra and other produce to independent food stores and military bases in the United States.

United Foods Inc. Good Government Committee (C00260885)
*Address: same as sponsor * Contact: James I. Tankersley, Chairman * Treasurer: Carl W. Gruenewald II*

	1993-94	1995-96	1997	Totals
Receipts	$65,045	$14,050	$3,750	$82,845
Disburse	76,500	14,000	0	90,500
Cash	65	115	3,865	n/a
Contributions	60,000	14,000	0	74,000
Republicans	46,500	14,000	0	60,500
No. of Cand.	*14*	*3*	*0*	*17*
House	29,500	7,000	0	36,500
Senate	17,000	7,000	0	24,000
Democrats	13,500	0	0	13,500
No. of Cand.	*3*	*0*	*0*	*3*
House	7,500	0	0	7,500
Senate	6,000	0	0	6,000
Incumbents	32,000	0	0	32,000
Challengers	8,500	3,000	0	11,500
Open Seat	19,500	11,000	0	30,500
Winners	48,000	7,000	n/a	55,000
Losers	12,000	7,000	n/a	19,000

United States Beet Sugar Association

*Phone: (202) 296-4820 * Fax: (202) 331-2065*
1156 15th St. N.W., Suite 1019, Washington, DC 20005

The U.S. Beet Sugar Association represents eight beet sugar processing companies. The association was formed by sugar cooperatives, like the Minn-Dak Farmers Cooperative in North Dakota and the Southern Minnesota Sugarbeet Growers Cooperative, to represent the interests of the sugar industry at the federal level.

United States Beet Sugar Association Political Action Committee (C00063586) *Address: same as sponsor * Contact: Van R. Olsen, Chairperson * Treasurer: James Johnson*

	1993-94	1995-96	1997	Totals
Receipts	$45,684	$35,600	$25,000	$106,284
Disburse	54,165	38,233	13,751	106,149
Cash	5,729	3,095	14,344	n/a
Contributions	51,564	37,731	13,751	103,046
Republicans	15,741	14,347	5,000	35,088
No. of Cand.	*24*	*23*	*9*	*56*
House	9,600	10,500	4,000	24,100
Senate	6,141	3,847	1,000	10,988
Democrats	33,073	23,384	8,251	64,708
No. of Cand.	*48*	*33*	*16*	*97*
House	23,550	17,298	6,500	47,348
Senate	9,523	6,086	1,751	17,360
Incumbents	48,264	27,428	13,251	88,943
Challengers	500	1,500	500	2,500
Open Seat	2,000	8,803	0	10,803
Winners	41,764	33,231	n/a	74,995
Losers	9,800	4,500	n/a	14,300

United States Sugar Corp.

Phone: (941) 983-8121
111 Ponce De Leon Ave., Clewiston, FL 33440
Web: www.ussugar.com

United States Sugar, an employee-owned family of agribusiness companies, is one of the largest producers of sugarcane in the nation. Founded in 1931, the company employed 3,500 people as of February 1997.

The corporation, based in Clewiston, Fla., is the largest and oldest producer of sugarcane in the state. In addition to its sugar business, the company also operates several subsidiaries. Its Southern Gardens Citrus is one of the state's leading producers of oranges and orange juice products, and its Corrulite subsidiary produces the corrugated plastic product of the same name.

The company also farms corn and rice and owns the South Central Florida Express, a short-line railroad with 100 miles of track. It connects the agricultural communities near Lake Okeechobee in Florida with mainline railroads elsewhere in the state. The company also produces Suga-Lik, a livestock feed manufactured with sugarcane molasses.

United States Sugar Corp.-Employee Stock Ownership Plan Political Action Committee (C00234120) *Address: same as sponsor * Contact: Malcolm Wade, Chairman * Treasurer: Stephen Coffman*

	1993-94	1995-96	1997	Totals
Receipts	$78,630	$89,641	$50,044	$218,315
Disburse	149,591	124,267	56,424	330,282
Cash	47,757	13,140	6,765	n/a
Contributions	109,670	83,750	37,750	231,170
Republicans	43,170	41,000	18,750	102,920
No. of Cand.	*40*	*49*	*29*	*118*
House	32,670	27,500	8,750	68,920
Senate	10,500	13,500	10,000	34,000
Democrats	65,500	42,750	19,000	127,250
No. of Cand.	*52*	*40*	*23*	*115*
House	49,750	33,250	10,500	93,500
Senate	15,750	9,500	8,500	33,750
Incumbents	84,250	71,750	36,750	192,750
Challengers	5,000	3,500	0	8,500
Open Seat	20,420	8,500	1,000	29,920
Winners	91,420	72,500	n/a	163,920
Losers	18,250	11,250	n/a	29,500

Virginia-Carolinas Peanut Membership Organization

*Phone: (202) 484-2773 * Fax: (202) 484-0770*
412 First St. S.E., Suite 1, Washington, DC 20003

The Virginia-Carolinas Peanut Membership Organization represents peanut growers in Virginia, North Carolina and South Carolina. The average farm that the association represents is about 100 acres.

The association is interested in legislation pertinent to agricultural issues, trade and food safety.

Virginia-Carolinas Peanut Membership Organization Political Action Committee (C00185652) *Address: same as sponsor * Treasurer: Larry D. Meyers*

	1993-94	1995-96	1997	Totals
Receipts	$19,632	$31,497	$11,923	$63,052
Disburse	26,827	32,000	13,925	72,752
Cash	3,496	2,621	620	n/a
Contributions	16,453	28,000	13,925	58,378
Republicans	2,600	19,000	6,125	27,725
No. of Cand.	*7*	*16*	*10*	*33*
House	2,100	9,000	4,125	15,225
Senate	500	10,000	2,000	12,500
Democrats	13,853	9,000	7,800	30,653
No. of Cand.	*21*	*10*	*14*	*45*
House	10,543	9,000	6,550	26,093
Senate	3,310	0	1,250	4,560
Incumbents	14,503	26,500	13,675	54,678
Challengers	350	1,000	0	1,350
Open Seat	1,600	500	250	2,350
Winners	12,950	23,500	n/a	36,450
Losers	3,503	4,500	n/a	8,003

Western Growers Association

*Phone: (714) 863-1000 * Fax: (714) 863-9028*
17620 Fitch St., P.O. Box 2130, Irvine, CA 92614
Web: www.wga.com

The Western Growers Association represents individuals and businesses in the agricultural industry, particularly those who produce fresh fruit, vegetables and nuts. The organization's members live in California and Arizona.

The group lobbies on produce exports and food safety issues. WGA also offers insurance to its members.

Western Growers Association Political Action Committee Federal (C00193979) *Address: same as sponsor * Contact: Jasper Hempel, V.P. of Legislative Affairs * Treasurer: Harvey Labko*

	1993-94	1995-96	1997	Totals
Receipts	$10,550	$147,037	$16,030	$173,617
Disburse	13,117	94,861	11,387	119,365
Cash	6,191	58,363	63,005	n/a
Contributions	8,810	43,402	6,850	59,062
Republicans	3,500	29,902	5,750	39,152
No. of Cand.	*4*	*21*	*8*	*33*
House	3,500	20,100	5,750	29,350
Senate	0	9,802	0	9,802
Democrats	5,310	13,500	1,100	19,910
No. of Cand.	*5*	*7*	*2*	*14*
House	2,500	9,500	1,100	13,100
Senate	2,810	4,000	0	6,810
Incumbents	7,810	38,145	6,850	52,805
Challengers	0	500	0	500
Open Seat	1,000	4,257	0	5,257
Winners	7,500	40,902	n/a	48,402
Losers	1,310	2,500	n/a	3,810

Western Peanut Growers Association

Phone: (915) 758-2050
P.O. Box 309, Seminole, TX 79360

The Western Peanut Growers is a group of about 300 western Texas peanut growers.

Western Peanut Growers Political Action Committee (C00254847) *Address: same as sponsor * Contact: Doyle Fincher, President * Treasurer: Lee Jameson*

	1993-94	1995-96	1997	Totals
Receipts	$47,791	$69,070	$83,984	$200,845
Disburse	25,202	49,019	14,020	88,241
Cash	33,615	53,666	123,631	n/a
Contributions	20,750	44,250	13,500	78,500
Republicans	7,500	31,500	11,000	50,000
No. of Cand.	*3*	*11*	*7*	*21*
House	5,500	24,500	9,000	39,000
Senate	2,000	7,000	2,000	11,000
Democrats	13,250	12,750	2,500	28,500
No. of Cand.	*7*	*6*	*3*	*16*
House	12,250	10,750	1,000	24,000
Senate	1,000	2,000	1,500	4,500
Incumbents	17,500	28,750	13,500	59,750
Challengers	500	3,000	0	3,500
Open Seat	2,750	8,000	0	10,750
Winners	17,000	38,750	n/a	55,750
Losers	3,750	5,500	n/a	9,250

Western Pistachio Association

*Phone: (202) 543-4455 * Fax: (202) 543-4586*
517 C St. N.E., Washington, DC 20002

The Western Pistachio Association represents 2,800 pistachio growers, processors and service companies.

Western Pistachio Association (C00197715) *Address: same as sponsor * Contact: Dr. Mike Wolf, Chairperson * Treasurer: Dr. John Lake*

	1993-94	1995-96	1997	Totals
Receipts	$28,730	$63,412	$39,130	$131,272
Disburse	29,258	32,629	14,607	76,494
Cash	27,201	57,983	82,507	n/a
Contributions	21,000	20,500	6,500	48,000
Republicans	12,500	13,500	4,000	30,000
No. of Cand.	*7*	*17*	*5*	*29*
House	10,500	10,500	3,000	24,000
Senate	2,000	3,000	1,000	6,000
Democrats	8,500	7,000	2,500	18,000
No. of Cand.	*9*	*7*	*3*	*19*
House	8,500	6,500	1,500	16,500
Senate	0	500	1,000	1,500
Incumbents	19,500	16,500	6,500	42,500
Challengers	0	500	0	500
Open Seat	1,500	2,500	0	4,000
Winners	19,500	18,500	n/a	38,000
Losers	1,500	2,000	n/a	3,500

Dairy

Agri-Mark Inc.

*Phone: (978) 689-4442 x247 * Fax: (978) 685-8716*
Milk St. Office Park, Methuen, MA 01844

Agri-Mark is a New England dairy cooperative with about 1,600 farmer members. The co-op markets its members' milk and produces other dairy items sold in New England, such as Cabot Cheese. Agri-Mark's members are from throughout New England and New York.

The co-op produces about 2 billion pounds of milk each year and has annual sales of about $460 million.

Agri-Mark Inc. Legislative and Educational Committee (ALEC) (C00141242) *Address: same as sponsor * Treasurer: Bob Wellington*

	1993-94	1995-96	1997	Totals
Receipts	$18,787	$21,099	$12,627	$52,513
Disburse	21,981	28,540	13,599	64,120
Cash	33,665	26,225	25,252	n/a
Contributions	20,500	24,310	10,420	55,230
Republicans	10,350	17,910	5,920	34,180
No. of Cand.	*14*	*17*	*8*	*39*
House	5,850	16,010	4,920	26,780
Senate	4,500	1,900	1,000	7,400
Democrats	10,150	6,400	4,500	21,050
No. of Cand.	*19*	*13*	*8*	*40*
House	10,150	5,900	4,000	20,050
Senate	0	500	500	1,000
Incumbents	18,000	20,310	10,420	48,730
Challengers	1,000	3,000	0	4,000
Open Seat	1,500	1,000	0	2,500
Winners	17,500	18,560	n/a	36,060
Losers	3,000	5,750	n/a	8,750

California Cooperative Creamery

*Phone: (707) 763-1931 * Fax: (707) 769-1790*
621 Western Ave., Petaluma, CA 94952-2646
Web: www.cal-gold.com

The California Cooperative Creamery is California's third-largest dairy cooperative. It receives its milk supply from more than 330 producers in California and Nevada. The cooperative produces American and Italian cheeses, condensed and skim milk products, nonfat dry milk, whey protein concentrate and other ingredients. It reported 1996 sales of $485 million and employed 285 people.

The cooperative, founded in 1913 by Italian dairy farmer Silvio Gambonini, reports that 18 percent of the milk consumed in California comes from its farmers.

California Cooperative Creamery Federal Political Action Committee (C00248757) *Address: same as sponsor * Treasurer: Joe Duarte*

	1993-94	1995-96	1997	Totals
Receipts	$76,064	$66,661	$28,445	$171,170
Disburse	49,660	47,509	4,022	101,191
Cash	80,862	100,014	124,240	n/a
Contributions	3,660	13,000	3,950	20,610
Republicans	1,310	5,500	1,700	8,510
No. of Cand.	*2*	*6*	*3*	*11*
House	1,310	5,500	1,700	8,510
Senate	0	0	0	0
Democrats	2,350	7,500	2,250	12,100
No. of Cand.	*2*	*6*	*4*	*12*
House	2,350	7,500	2,250	12,100
Senate	0	0	0	0
Incumbents	3,300	11,000	3,950	18,250
Challengers	360	1,000	0	1,360
Open Seat	0	1,000	0	1,000
Winners	3,300	12,000	n/a	15,300
Losers	360	1,000	n/a	1,360

Dairy Farmers of America

*Phone: (417) 865-7100 x1122 * Fax: (417) 831-8145*
3253 E. Chestnut Expressway, Springfield, MO 65802-2584

The Dairy Farmers of America is a dairy marketing cooperative formed in early 1998 with members in 42 states. It markets about 32 billion pounds of milk for 22,000 manufacturing and bottling plants. Based in Missouri, the organization changed its name in 1997 from the Mid-America Dairymen Inc. to DFA.

It is composed of four regional groups: the Associated Milk Producers Inc. Southern Region, Mid-America Dairymen Inc., Milk Marketing Inc., and Western Dairymen Cooperative Inc. The Associated Milk Producers Inc. North Central is not affiliated with the group.

The DFA lobbies on a number of agricultural and environmental issues, including animal waste management. It also is interested in food research and international trade.

Combined, the four committees that comprise the new DFA PAC contributed nearly $1.3 million to congressional candidates during the 1995-96 election cycle. The leading recipients of the four committees were Reps. Martin Frost, D-Texas, Roy Blunt, R-Mo., and Ike Skelton, D-Mo., former Rep. Harold L. Volkmer, D-Mo., and Sen. Tim Johnson, D-S.D.

Associated Milk Producers Inc., which had its own PAC (C00001594), disbanded in 1997 and that committee was folded into the DFA. Two other dairy PACs, sponsored by the Western Dairymen and Milk Marketing, also will be combined into the main DFA committee.

Dairy Farmers of America Inc. Political Action Trust PAC (formerly known as Mid-America Dairymen Inc. Dairy Educational Political Action Committee) (C00001388) *Address: same as sponsor * Contact: Roger Don Eldridge, V.P. of Gov. Relations * Treasurer: Edwin Wiedeman*

	1993-94	1995-96	1997	Totals
Receipts	$543,207	$828,971	$335,851	$1,708,029
Disburse	528,910	820,813	357,935	1,707,658
Cash	27,922	36,080	13,995	n/a
Contributions	374,550	457,500	258,000	1,090,050
Republicans	91,200	263,250	140,500	494,950
No. of Cand.	*65*	*164*	*119*	*348*
House	58,700	197,250	112,500	368,450
Senate	32,500	66,000	28,000	126,500
Democrats	278,850	194,250	110,500	583,600
No. of Cand.	*175*	*128*	*104*	*407*
House	200,850	160,250	84,000	445,100
Senate	78,000	34,000	26,500	138,500
Incumbents	328,050	377,750	249,500	955,300
Challengers	5,000	15,000	500	20,500
Open Seat	41,500	61,750	6,500	109,750
Winners	290,050	412,250	n/a	702,300
Losers	84,500	45,250	n/a	129,750

Committee for Thorough Agricultural Political Education of Dairy Farmers of America Inc. (C-TAPE of DFA) (C00001594) *Phone: (817) 548-6803 * Fax: (817) 548-6809 * P.O. Box 5288, Arlington, TX 76005 * Treasurer: J. S. Stone*

	1993-94	1995-96	1997	Totals
Receipts	$1,157,237	$877,876	$304,086	$2,339,199
Disburse	1,229,050	1,079,069	506,276	2,814,395
Cash	1,041,846	840,656	638,467	n/a
Contributions	778,231	750,000	175,000	1,703,231
Republicans	182,250	395,500	91,800	669,550
No. of Cand.	*92*	*160*	*90*	*342*
House	156,750	346,500	80,000	583,250
Senate	25,500	49,000	11,800	86,300
Democrats	581,981	354,000	75,200	1,011,181
No. of Cand.	*228*	*149*	*79*	*456*
House	488,981	296,000	63,700	848,681
Senate	93,000	58,000	11,500	162,500
Incumbents	702,231	552,500	173,000	1,427,731
Challengers	25,250	52,500	0	77,750
Open Seat	52,750	144,000	2,000	198,750
Winners	618,731	665,000	n/a	1,283,731
Losers	159,500	85,000	n/a	244,500

Milk Marketing Inc. Political Action Committee (C00167692) *Phone: (216) 826-4730 * 8257 Dow Cir., P.O. Box 368017, Strongsville, OH 44136 * Treasurer: William R. Perry*

	1993-94	1995-96	1997	Totals
Receipts	$71,713	$62,152	$26,911	$160,776
Disburse	84,956	58,393	39,935	183,284
Cash	25,148	28,909	15,886	n/a
Contributions	80,670	44,000	29,750	154,420
Republicans	29,250	26,500	19,000	74,750
No. of Cand.	*29*	*34*	*26*	*89*
House	22,250	21,000	16,000	59,250
Senate	7,000	5,500	3,000	15,500
Democrats	51,420	17,500	10,750	79,670
No. of Cand.	*44*	*19*	*15*	*78*
House	39,550	16,750	9,750	66,050
Senate	11,870	750	1,000	13,620
Incumbents	71,270	38,250	29,750	139,270
Challengers	150	2,000	0	2,150
Open Seat	9,250	3,750	0	13,000
Winners	57,200	42,000	n/a	99,200
Losers	23,470	2,000	n/a	25,470

Political Action Trust Political Action Committee (PAT-PAC) (C00137380) *Phone: (303) 451-0422 * Fax: (303) 452-5484 * 12450 N. Washington, Thornton, CO 80241 * Web: www.wdci.com * Treasurer: Edwin Wiedeman*

	1993-94	1995-96	1997	Totals
Receipts	$37,015	$49,864	$24,920	$111,799
Disburse	27,611	40,500	21,000	89,111
Cash	11,653	21,020	24,938	n/a
Contributions	5,200	29,000	11,000	45,200
Republicans	1,700	22,500	11,000	35,200
No. of Cand.	*3*	*7*	*3*	*13*
House	200	12,000	6,000	18,200
Senate	1,500	10,500	5,000	17,000
Democrats	3,500	6,500	0	10,000
No. of Cand.	*5*	*3*	*0*	*8*
House	1,000	6,500	0	7,500
Senate	2,500	0	0	2,500
Incumbents	4,200	13,000	11,000	28,200
Challengers	0	0	0	0
Open Seat	1,000	16,000	0	17,000
Winners	4,200	14,000	n/a	18,200
Losers	1,000	15,000	n/a	16,000

Dairyman's Cooperative Creamery Association

*Phone: (209) 687-8287 * Fax: (209) 685-6947*
400 S. M St., Tulare, CA 93274

Dairyman's Cooperative Creamery Association Political Action Committee (C00225755) *Address: same as sponsor * Contact: Jack Prince, Chairman * Treasurer: Larry Serpa*

	1993-94	1995-96	1997	Totals
Receipts	$37,511	$33,610	$15,493	$86,614
Disburse	21,111	51,684	9,809	82,604
Cash	30,812	12,742	18,427	n/a
Contributions	18,100	47,784	8,100	73,984
Republicans	3,900	31,884	3,700	39,484
No. of Cand.	*3*	*8*	*4*	*15*
House	3,900	28,884	3,500	36,284
Senate	0	3,000	200	3,200
Democrats	14,200	15,900	4,400	34,500
No. of Cand.	*5*	*3*	*3*	*11*
House	9,200	15,900	4,400	29,500
Senate	5,000	0	0	5,000
Incumbents	16,600	36,784	8,100	61,484
Challengers	1,500	10,000	0	11,500

(*Data for Dairyman's Cooperative Creamery continued*)

Open Seat	0	1,000	0	1,000
Winners	13,700	37,784	n/a	51,484
Losers	4,400	10,000	n/a	14,400

Danish Creamery Association

*Phone: (209) 233-5154 * Fax: (209) 268-5101*
P.O. Box 11865, Fresno, CA 93775

The Danish Creamery Association is the oldest dairy cooperative in the United States. It has 118 member companies and is based in Fresno, Calif.

Danish Creamery Association Federal Political Action Committee (C00281105) *Address: same as sponsor * Contact: Manuel Costa, PAC Chairman * Treasurer: James Anthony Gomes*

	1993-94	1995-96	1997	Totals
Receipts	$23,097	$27,088	$11,241	$61,426
Disburse	5,460	11,927	2,583	19,970
Cash	17,641	32,805	41,464	n/a
Contributions	5,450	11,075	2,120	18,645
Republicans	2,250	6,875	1,700	10,825
No. of Cand.	*3*	*7*	*2*	*12*
House	2,250	5,875	1,700	9,825
Senate	0	1,000	0	1,000
Democrats	3,200	4,200	420	7,820
No. of Cand.	*4*	*3*	*2*	*9*
House	3,200	3,950	420	7,570
Senate	0	250	0	250
Incumbents	3,950	9,275	2,120	15,345
Challengers	1,500	800	0	2,300
Open Seat	0	1,000	0	1,000
Winners	3,750	9,775	n/a	13,525
Losers	1,700	1,300	n/a	3,000

Darigold/Northwest Dairymen's Association

*Phone: (206) 284-7220 * Fax: (206) 281-3456*
635 Elliott Ave. W., Box 79007, Seattle, WA 98119
Web: www.darigold.com

Dariqold is a dairy cooperative with members in Washington state, Oregon, Idaho and northern California. It produces 5 billion pounds of milk annually and has about 900 farmer members. Darigold's annual sales are about $1 billion.

The co-op has three operations: Darigold Farms, the milk marketing co-op; Darigold Inc., the milk processing division; and Dairy Export Co. Inc., which operates the organization's retail stores. Darigold also owns most of Olympic Foods, a regional juice company, and the Western Feed Division of Land O' Lakes, a Minnesota co-op.

Darigold Political Action Committee (formerly known as North Pacific Dairymen's Cooperative Trust) (C00022756) *Address: same as sponsor * Treasurer: Douglas C. Marshall*

	1993-94	1995-96	1997	Totals
Receipts	$55,966	$38,792	$15,489	$110,247
Disburse	55,062	39,737	3,341	98,140
Cash	4,591	3,647	15,795	n/a
Contributions	16,370	18,895	2,500	37,765
Republicans	8,120	17,895	1,500	27,515
No. of Cand.	*7*	*12*	*2*	*21*
House	4,600	9,395	500	14,495
Senate	3,520	8,500	1,000	13,020
Democrats	8,250	1,000	1,000	10,250
No. of Cand.	*10*	*1*	*2*	*13*
House	7,250	1,000	500	8,750
Senate	1,000	0	500	1,500
Incumbents	10,770	11,895	2,000	24,665
Challengers	500	1,000	0	1,500
Open Seat	5,000	6,000	0	11,000
Winners	10,020	17,895	n/a	27,915
Losers	6,350	1,000	n/a	7,350

Dean Foods Co.

*Phone: (847) 678-1680 * Fax: (847) 233-5505*
3600 N. River Rd., Franklin Park, IL 60131-2185
Web: www.dfamboy.com/deanfoods.html

Founded in 1925 as a small Midwestern dairy with one plant in Pecatonica, Ill., Dean Foods Co. has grown into a publicly traded, Fortune 500 dairy and specialty foods manufacturer. It has more than 12,000 employees and annual sales of more than $3 billion. The company produces milk, cottage cheese, yogurt, orange juice, ice cream, dips, frozen and canned vegetables and non-dairy creamers. Its best-known brand is probably Bird's Eye.

Dean Foods operates food processing plants throughout Wisconsin.

Dean Foods Co. Good Government Committee (C00143909) *Address: same as sponsor * Contact: Gary Corbett, V.P. of Gov. Relations * Treasurer: Ernie Matheson*

	1993-94	1995-96	1997	Totals
Receipts	$3,909	$3,013	$912	$7,834
Disburse	1,900	6,800	0	8,700
Cash	4,419	632	1,545	n/a
Contributions	400	5,100	0	5,500
Republicans	400	5,100	0	5,500
No. of Cand.	*2*	*6*	*0*	*8*
House	200	1,100	0	1,300
Senate	200	4,000	0	4,200
Democrats	0	0	0	0
No. of Cand.	*0*	*0*	*0*	*0*
House	0	0	0	0
Senate	0	0	0	0
Incumbents	400	1,100	0	1,500
Challengers	0	0	0	0
Open Seat	0	4,000	0	4,000
Winners	400	4,350	n/a	4,750
Losers	0	750	n/a	750

International Dairy Foods Association

*Phone: (202) 737-4332 * Fax: (202) 331-7820*
1250 H St. N.W., Suite 900, Washington, DC 20005
*Web: www.idfa.org * E-mail: pcarroll@idfa.org*

The International Dairy Foods Association represents about 800 companies that process and distribute milk, cheese, ice cream and frozen desserts. An umbrella organization for three industry groups, the foundation represents 85 percent of the $65 billion U.S. dairy foods industry.

The foundation's constituent groups are: the International Ice Cream Association, the Milk Industry Foundation and the National Cheese Institute.

Ice Cream, Milk & Cheese PAC of the International Ice Cream Association, Milk Industry Foundation & National Cheese Institute (C00128231) *Address: same as sponsor * Treasurer: Patrick B. Carroll*

	1993-94	1995-96	1997	Totals
Receipts	$174,474	$205,644	$97,367	$477,485
Disburse	170,763	210,836	100,554	482,153
Cash	10,340	5,151	1,965	n/a
Contributions	144,209	183,800	82,797	410,806
Republicans	103,709	160,550	69,297	333,556
No. of Cand.	*76*	*104*	*73*	*253*
House	45,550	79,350	41,797	166,697
Senate	58,159	81,200	27,500	166,859
Democrats	39,500	23,250	12,500	75,250
No. of Cand.	*32*	*20*	*14*	*66*
House	33,750	19,750	10,000	63,500
Senate	5,750	3,500	2,500	11,750
Incumbents	127,200	152,000	81,297	360,497
Challengers	3,659	6,700	0	10,359
Open Seat	13,350	25,100	1,000	39,450
Winners	131,709	154,850	n/a	286,559
Losers	12,500	28,950	n/a	41,450

Land O'Lakes Inc.

*Phone: (612) 481-2222 * Fax: (612) 481-2022*
4001 Lexington Ave., Minneapolis, MN 55126
*Web: www.landolakes.com * E-mail: skirk@landolakes.com*

Land O'Lakes is a farmer-owned cooperative operated by Land O'Lakes Inc. The company produces butter, cheese, manufactured dairy products, animal feed and seed. Its revenue was $4.2 billion in 1997.

In April 1997, Land O'Lakes merged with Atlantic Dairy Cooperative, an East Coast milk producer.

The bipartisan PAC has 500 cooperative members and supports candidates whose states have agricultural interests.

Land O'Lakes Inc. Political Action Committee (C00009423)
*Address: same as sponsor * Treasurer: Rita Page Reuss*

	1993-94	1995-96	1997	Totals
Receipts	$79,716	$64,313	$36,500	$180,529
Disburse	78,969	66,748	22,101	167,818
Cash	9,364	6,928	21,328	n/a
Contributions	63,900	55,923	17,000	136,823
Republicans	29,650	32,673	7,500	69,823
No. of Cand.	*28*	*31*	*10*	*69*
House	21,650	21,750	6,500	49,900
Senate	8,000	10,923	1,000	19,923
Democrats	30,000	23,250	8,000	61,250
No. of Cand.	*28*	*15*	*10*	*53*
House	21,500	14,250	5,000	40,750
Senate	8,500	9,000	3,000	20,500
Incumbents	56,400	36,500	17,000	109,900
Challengers	0	5,000	0	5,000
Open Seat	7,500	13,423	0	20,923
Winners	55,650	43,673	n/a	99,323
Losers	8,250	12,250	n/a	20,500

Western United Dairymen's Association

*Phone: (209) 527-6453 * Fax: (209) 527-0630*
1315 K St., Modesto, CA 95354
E-mail: Caldairy@aol.com

The Western United Dairymen's Association is a group of 1,300 California dairy owners. California dairies produced 25.7 billion pounds of milk in 1995, the most in the nation. The group is headquartered in the San Joaquin Valley, which generates two-thirds of the state's milk. Western United is interested in the handling of animal waste, access to water and dairy pricing.

Western United Dairymen's Association Federal Political Action Committee (C00186072) *Address: same as sponsor * Contact: Gary Conover, V.P., Gov. Relations * Treasurer: Joe Pimentel Jr.*

	1993-94	1995-96	1997	Totals
Receipts	$30,512	$23,907	$12,500	$66,919
Disburse	39,727	25,212	11,095	76,034
Cash	1,791	500	1,905	n/a
Contributions	26,850	15,650	11,045	53,545
Republicans	4,200	7,650	3,000	14,850
No. of Cand.	*4*	*9*	*4*	*17*
House	4,200	7,150	3,000	14,350
Senate	0	500	0	500
Democrats	22,650	8,000	8,045	38,695
No. of Cand.	*8*	*4*	*6*	*18*
House	14,400	8,000	6,045	28,445
Senate	8,250	0	2,000	10,250
Incumbents	24,850	15,350	9,545	49,745
Challengers	1,500	300	0	1,800
Open Seat	500	0	1,500	2,000
Winners	23,600	15,350	n/a	38,950
Losers	3,250	300	n/a	3,550

Food Processing & Sales

A.E. Staley Manufacturing Co.

*Phone: (217) 421-3020 * Fax: (217) 421-4507*
2200 E. Eldorado St., Decatur, IL 62521
*Web: www.aestaley.com * E-mail: bjclaypool@aestaley.com*

A.E. Staley Manufacturing is one of the largest corn refiners in the United States. Headquartered in Decatur, Ill., the company is a prominent supplier of corn sweeteners, starches, ethanol and animal feeds. Annual sales exceed $1 billion and total employment is about 1,500.

Staley owns four major corn milling facilities. The largest plant, in Decatur, Ill., is part of a 400-acre complex that includes corporate headquarters and a research development center. Two plants are located in Lafayette, Ind., and the fourth is in Loudon, Ark.

In 1988, Staley was acquired by British-based Tate & Lyle, one of the world's leading sugar, cereal sweetener and starch producers with operations in more than 50 countries.

Tate & Lyle has substantial holdings in North America, including its sugar subsidiaries: Domino Sugar, Western Sugar and Redpath Sugars.

Staley Political Action Committee of A.E. Staley Manufacturing Co. (C00056564) *Address: same as sponsor * Contact: Bobbi Claypool, Assistant Treasurer * Treasurer: Mary E. Matiya*

	1993-94	1995-96	1997	Totals
Receipts	$49,540	$37,942	$14,765	$102,247
Disburse	15,166	44,027	7,257	66,450
Cash	92,494	86,412	93,921	n/a
Contributions	14,000	42,500	6,500	63,000
Republicans	12,500	40,500	6,500	59,500
No. of Cand.	*6*	*20*	*7*	*33*
House	6,500	23,500	6,500	36,500
Senate	6,000	17,000	0	23,000
Democrats	1,500	2,000	0	3,500
No. of Cand.	*3*	*2*	*0*	*5*
House	500	0	0	500
Senate	1,000	2,000	0	3,000
Incumbents	8,000	28,000	6,500	42,500
Challengers	0	2,000	0	2,000
Open Seat	6,000	12,500	0	18,500
Winners	14,000	34,500	n/a	48,500
Losers	0	8,000	n/a	8,000

American Bakers Association

*Phone: (202) 789-0300 x103 * Fax: (202) 898-1164*
1350 Eye St. N.W., Suite 1290, Washington, DC 20005-3305
Web: www.sosland.com/aba

The American Bakers Association is a national trade group representing the wholesale baking industry. It offers members newsletters and bulletins on state and federal legislative developments, environmental regulations and nutrition. The association also provides a retirement plan for member bakeries. Among its members are Flowers Industries Inc., Drake Bakeries Inc., Cargill Inc., Mrs. Baird's Bakeries Inc. and Stroehmann Bakeries.

American Bakers Association Bread Political Action Committee (C00016386) *Address: same as sponsor * Contact: Lee Sanders, Dir. of Legislative Affairs * Treasurer: Paul C. Abenante*

	1993-94	1995-96	1997	Totals
Receipts	$110,255	$103,761	$18,491	$232,507
Disburse	104,664	107,946	10,306	222,916
Cash	6,701	2,516	10,701	n/a
Contributions	99,350	91,400	7,050	197,800
Republicans	98,800	90,900	7,050	196,750
No. of Cand.	*69*	*100*	*14*	*183*
House	46,250	46,700	4,550	97,500
Senate	52,550	44,200	2,500	99,250
Democrats	550	500	0	1,050
No. of Cand.	*1*	*1*	*0*	*2*
House	550	500	0	1,050
Senate	0	0	0	0
Incumbents	36,400	46,400	8,550	91,350
Challengers	33,800	13,200	0	47,000
Open Seat	29,150	31,800	0	60,950
Winners	88,350	61,650	n/a	150,000
Losers	11,000	29,750	n/a	40,750

American Frozen Food Institute

*Phone: (703) 821-0770 * Fax: (703) 821-1350*
2000 Corporate Ridge, Suite 1000, McLean, VA 22102
Web: www.affi.com

The American Frozen Food Institute represents 550 corporate members responsible for more than 90 percent of frozen food production in the United States.

AFFI provides several publications to its members. AFFI's magazine, Frozen Food Report, includes articles on major issues affecting the food industry. AFFI Letter, a bi-weekly news source, highlights pertinent legislative and regulatory happenings and current AFFI activities.

American Frozen Food Institute Political Action Committee (FREEPAC) (C00042960) *Address: same as sponsor * Contact: Dina Land, PAC Administrator * Treasurer: Leslie G. Sarasin*

	1993-94	1995-96	1997	Totals
Receipts	$12,292	$27,530	$13,700	$53,522
Disburse	12,500	26,000	8,750	47,250
Cash	3,786	5,316	10,266	n/a
Contributions	12,000	26,000	8,750	46,750
Republicans	8,350	24,500	8,250	41,100
No. of Cand.	*21*	*33*	*17*	*71*
House	5,550	13,500	5,250	24,300
Senate	2,800	11,000	3,000	16,800
Democrats	3,650	1,500	500	5,650
No. of Cand.	*8*	*3*	*1*	*12*
House	3,650	1,500	500	5,650
Senate	0	0	0	0

(Data for American Frozen Food continued)

Incumbents	10,650	17,000	8,250	35,900
Challengers	500	0	0	500
Open Seat	850	9,000	500	10,350
Winners	10,850	25,000	n/a	35,850
Losers	1,150	1,000	n/a	2,150

American Meat Institute

*Phone: (703) 841-2400 * Fax: (703) 527-0938*
1700 N. Moore St., Room 1600, Arlington, VA 22209
Web: www.meatami.org

The American Meat Institute is a national trade association representing packers and processors of 70 percent of the nation's beef, pork, lamb, veal and turkey products and their suppliers throughout America. AMI provides legislative, regulatory and public relations services, conducts scientific and economic research, offers marketing and technical assistance and sponsors education programs.

In February 1998, AMI opposed $573 million in meat and poultry inspection user fees in the Department of Agriculture's fiscal 1999 budget request. Saying that meat and poultry inspection is a public health and safety program required by federal law, AMI President J. Patrick Boyle said the fees would be a "food tax" levied on the consumer.

American Meat Institute Political Action Committee (C00024281) *Address: same as sponsor * Treasurer: Sara L. Clarke*

	1993-94	1995-96	1997	Totals
Receipts	$126,848	$155,159	$93,192	$375,199
Disburse	103,941	177,826	45,556	327,323
Cash	59,994	25,450	73,087	n/a
Contributions	103,605	158,729	37,250	299,584
Republicans	72,255	132,729	30,750	235,734
No. of Cand.	*82*	*107*	*36*	*225*
House	40,650	80,246	18,250	139,146
Senate	31,605	52,483	12,500	96,588
Democrats	30,350	26,000	5,500	61,850
No. of Cand.	*36*	*26*	*7*	*69*
House	24,350	23,000	3,500	50,850
Senate	6,000	3,000	2,000	11,000
Incumbents	79,350	124,480	36,250	240,080
Challengers	8,172	13,999	0	22,171
Open Seat	16,083	20,250	1,000	37,333
Winners	87,294	133,980	n/a	221,274
Losers	16,311	24,749	n/a	41,060

Basic American Inc.

*Phone: (208) 785-3200 * Fax: (208) 785-8776*
415 W. Collins Rd., Blackfoot, ID 83221

Basic American is a privately owned processor and distributor of potato products sold mainly to food service companies. It owns six plants that process potatoes primarily grown near its plants in Washington, Oregon, Idaho, New Mexico and Wisconsin. It also has a plant in Poland.

Basic's sole subsidiary, Sunspice, sells fresh raw potatoes for the retail market. Basic has about 2,500 employees and had 1995 annual sales of $279 million.

Basic American Inc. Political Action Committee (Basic American Foods PAC) (C00093096) *Address: same as sponsor * Contact: Dennis Conley, President of Sunspice subsidiary * Treasurer: DeVaughn Shipley*

	1993-94	1995-96	1997	Totals
Receipts	$8,000	$13,550	$200	$21,750
Disburse	9,400	10,500	3,000	22,900
Cash	30	3,080	280	n/a
Contributions	9,400	10,500	3,000	22,900
Republicans	6,900	9,000	2,500	18,400
No. of Cand.	*9*	*9*	*3*	*21*
House	5,400	6,500	1,500	13,400
Senate	1,500	2,500	1,000	5,000
Democrats	2,500	1,500	500	4,500
No. of Cand.	*3*	*3*	*1*	*7*
House	2,500	1,500	500	4,500
Senate	0	0	0	0
Incumbents	6,000	8,000	3,000	17,000
Challengers	2,000	1,000	0	3,000
Open Seat	1,400	1,500	0	2,900
Winners	5,900	7,500	n/a	13,400
Losers	3,500	3,000	n/a	6,500

Central Soya Co.

Phone: (219) 425-5100
P.O. Box 1400, Ft. Wayne, IN 46801-1400
Web: www.centralsoya.com

Central Soya purchases and processes soybeans and lecithin for resale to agricultural, industrial and food markets. Its parent company, Eridania Beghin-Say, processes commodity-based products and had 1996 sales of $10.6 billion. Founded in 1934 and headquartered in Fort Wayne, Ind., Central Soya now employs 1,200 people and reported net sales of $1.2 billion in 1996.

Central Soya has eight plants, seven of which are in the states of Indiana, Illinois and Ohio. The other plant is in Denmark. Central Soya also operates joint ventures with Stern Lecithin and Soya, in Germany, and with CanAmera Foods of Ontario, Canada.

Central Soya Co. Inc. Political Action Committee (C00012666) *Address: same as sponsor * Contact: Joe Brocklesby, Dir. Business Development - Processing * Treasurer: Jeffrey H. Fritz*

	1993-94	1995-96	1997	Totals
Receipts	$14,146	$11,908	$6,487	$32,541
Disburse	10,971	10,989	5,085	27,045
Cash	8,970	9,894	11,297	n/a
Contributions	9,225	8,400	3,500	21,125
Republicans	7,975	8,300	3,500	19,775
No. of Cand.	*8*	*12*	*4*	*24*
House	2,975	6,800	2,500	12,275
Senate	5,000	1,500	1,000	7,500
Democrats	1,250	100	0	1,350
No. of Cand.	*1*	*1*	*0*	*2*
House	1,250	100	0	1,350
Senate	0	0	0	0
Incumbents	5,850	6,800	3,500	16,150
Challengers	875	600	0	1,475
Open Seat	2,500	1,000	0	3,500
Winners	7,975	7,600	n/a	15,575
Losers	1,250	800	n/a	2,050

ConAgra Inc.

*Phone: (402) 595-4015 * Fax: (402) 595-4560*
One ConAgra Dr., Omaha, NE 68102
Web: www.conagra.com

ConAgra is the second-largest food company in America and the top producer of frozen foods. A public company, ConAgra's brands include Healthy Choice, Hunt's, Butterball, Swiss Miss, La Choy and Armour. Its subsidiaries include Lamb-Weston Inc., Hunt-Wesson Grocery Products Companies, Swift & Co. and Butterball Turkey Co. ConAgra recently acquired Hester Industries, a Virginia poultry company, and Zoll Foods, a Chicago pork producer. The company had $24 billion in sales during 1997.

ConAgra has 82,170 employees, and operations in Nebraska, Colorado, California, Washington, Illinois and several other states, as well as in 31 countries. It is the world's largest exporter of potato products.

ConAgra supports pro-business candidates and lobbies on a range of food issues, including meat safety. It was the biggest donor among food processing companies during the 1995-96 cycle, just ahead of Flowers Industries. ConAgra supported candidates from its home state; five of the top 25 recipients were Nebraskans. It also gave more money to Republican challengers than to Democratic incumbents.

ConAgra Inc. Good Government Association (C00087874) *Phone: (202) 223-5115 * Fax: (202) 223-5118 * 888 17th St. N.W., Washington, DC 20006-3939 * Contact: Dick Gady, V.P. * Phone: (402) 595-4015 * Treasurer: M. E. Lacey*

	1993-94	1995-96	1997	Totals
Receipts	$364,436	$312,546	$176,358	$853,340
Disburse	331,009	325,570	113,859	770,438
Cash	36,254	23,231	85,731	n/a
Contributions	279,674	272,920	100,450	653,044
Republicans	172,104	224,845	81,450	478,399
No. of Cand.	*85*	*104*	*64*	*253*
House	97,104	107,150	53,950	258,204
Senate	75,000	117,695	27,500	220,195
Democrats	105,070	48,075	18,000	171,145
No. of Cand.	*48*	*27*	*14*	*89*
House	82,450	31,000	12,500	125,950
Senate	22,620	17,075	5,500	45,195
Incumbents	242,924	185,725	94,450	523,099

Challengers	15,500	21,200	0	36,700
Open Seat	19,750	65,995	5,500	91,245
Winners	238,054	230,970	n/a	469,024
Losers	41,620	41,950	n/a	83,570

Fleming Companies Inc.

Phone: (405) 840-7200
P.O. Box 26647, Oklahoma City, OK 73126-0647
Web: www.fleming.com

Fleming Companies is an Oklahoma-based food wholesale and distribution company. The publicly owned company serves more than 7,500 stores, including 3,100 supermarkets located in 42 states, the District of Columbia and other countries. The company also maintains a retail operation of about 270 stores, placing Fleming among the top 20 grocery retailers in the country.

Fleming is a distributor for IGA, Piggly-Wiggly and Price Impact stores. The company, which has more than 39,000 employees, reported 1997 sales of $15.3 billion.

Fleming Companies Inc. Committee for Responsible Government (C00239095) *Address: same as sponsor * Contact: Ronald Frost, Dir. of Public Relations * Treasurer: Kevin J. Twomey*

	1993-94	1995-96	1997	Totals
Receipts	$168,048	$134,651	$51,580	$354,279
Disburse	159,621	149,595	26,306	335,522
Cash	48,068	33,121	58,399	n/a
Contributions	110,000	116,750	8,100	234,850
Republicans	94,250	110,750	7,500	212,500
No. of Cand.	*70*	*82*	*6*	*158*
House	46,000	76,500	3,500	126,000
Senate	48,250	34,250	4,000	86,500
Democrats	15,750	6,000	500	22,250
No. of Cand.	*16*	*6*	*1*	*23*
House	12,250	6,000	500	18,750
Senate	3,500	0	0	3,500
Incumbents	56,250	65,750	7,500	129,500
Challengers	17,000	11,000	0	28,000
Open Seat	36,750	40,000	500	77,250
Winners	94,000	96,250	n/a	190,250
Losers	16,000	20,500	n/a	36,500

Flowers Industries

*Phone: (912) 227-2348 * Fax: (912) 225-3816*
P.O. Box 1338, Thomasville, GA 31799-1338
Web: www.flowersindustries.com

Flowers Industries is a publicly held company that produces fresh and frozen baked foods. Headquartered in Thomasville, Ga., the company has three divisions: Flowers Bakeries Inc., Mrs. Smith's Bakeries Inc. and Flowers Investments.

Among its brands are Nature's Own, Cobblestone Mill, BlueBird, Mrs. Smith's and Oregon Farms. The company is a co-owner of Keebler Corp., the second-largest cookie and cracker company in the nation. Flowers Industries operates more than 40 production, distribution and sales companies in 16 states and employs more than 7,000 people. It reported 1997 sales of $1.4 billion.

Flowers ranked second among 18 food processing companies and associations in 1996 congressional contributions. Flowers was the only corporate PAC among the top 200 that gave exclusively to Republican candidates and committees during the 1995-96 cycle, and it especially favored those from Georgia.

The company gave $57,500 to in-state candidates, $25,000 to Texas races plus $15,000 to candidates in Alabama and Arkansas. It spent more than twice as much money on challenger and open-seat candidates than incumbents. The top recipients were Rep. Nathan Deal, R-Ga., and 1996 House candidate Darrel Ealum of Georgia.

Flowers Industries Inc. Political Action Committee (C00033555) *Address: same as sponsor * Contact: Marta Turner, V.P. of Public Affairs * Treasurer: Earl Q. Quigg*

	1993-94	1995-96	1997	Totals
Receipts	$254,071	$417,587	$163,219	$834,877
Disburse	254,819	383,269	189,825	827,913
Cash	6,484	40,808	14,208	n/a
Contributions	161,000	237,500	10,000	408,500
Republicans	156,000	237,500	10,000	403,500
No. of Cand.	*33*	*47*	*2*	*82*
House	76,000	139,500	5,000	220,500
Senate	80,000	98,000	5,000	183,000
Democrats	5,000	0	0	5,000
No. of Cand.	*1*	*0*	*0*	*1*
House	5,000	0	0	5,000
Senate	0	0	0	0
Incumbents	21,000	64,500	10,000	95,500
Challengers	75,000	70,000	0	145,000
Open Seat	65,000	98,000	0	163,000
Winners	121,000	114,500	n/a	235,500
Losers	40,000	123,000	n/a	163,000

Food Lion Inc.

*Phone: (704) 633-8250 x2299 * Fax: (704) 636-5024*
P.O. Box 1330, 2110 Executive Dr., Salisbury, NC 28145
Web: www.foodlion.com

Food Lion operates a chain of 1,100 supermarkets in 11 states, with the bulk of stores located in North and South Carolina, Virginia and Florida. The company's Food Lion and Kash n' Karry stores reported sales of more than $10.2 billion in 1997 and employ 73,100 workers.

The company offers nationally and regionally advertised brand name merchandise as well as products manufactured and packaged under the private label of Food Lion.

Food Lion plans to open 75 new stores in 1998 and to remodel or expand 133 stores. During 1997, Food Lion added 100 stores through the acquisition of Kash n' Karry supermarkets, and opened an additional 64 new stores. In addition, the company closed 94 stores during the year, which included 61 stores it closed as part of the divestiture of its Southwest markets.

Food Lion Inc. Political Action Committee (C00214304) *Address: same as sponsor * Contact: Lester C. Nail, PAC Administrator * Treasurer: Carol M. Herndon*

	1993-94	1995-96	1997	Totals
Receipts	$77,311	$59,764	$44,408	$181,483
Disburse	69,088	61,598	20,382	151,068
Cash	25,652	23,820	47,846	n/a
Contributions	34,163	31,786	7,500	73,449
Republicans	12,822	23,562	6,000	42,384
No. of Cand.	*22*	*20*	*4*	*46*
House	8,322	16,812	2,750	27,884
Senate	4,500	6,750	3,250	14,500
Democrats	21,341	8,224	1,500	31,065
No. of Cand.	*23*	*7*	*2*	*32*
House	20,841	8,224	1,500	30,565
Senate	500	0	0	500
Incumbents	31,163	30,786	7,500	69,449
Challengers	0	0	0	0
Open Seat	2,500	1,000	0	3,500
Winners	29,563	29,786	n/a	59,349
Losers	4,600	2,000	n/a	6,600

Food Marketing Institute

*Phone: (202) 452-8444 * Fax: (202) 429-4549*
800 Connecticut Ave. N.W., Washington, DC 20006-2701
Web: www.fmi.org

The Food Marketing Institute is a nonprofit association representing 1,500 grocery stores and supermarkets in the United States and abroad. FMI's domestic member companies operate about 21,000 retail food stores with annual sales of $220 billion — more than half of all grocery store sales in the United States. FMI's retail membership is composed of large, multi-store chains, small regional firms and independent supermarkets.

The FMI lobbies on a number of food and agriculture issues, including the sale of tobacco. Other interests include electric utility deregulation and labor issues. It opposes a new OSHA compliance program that could lead to mandatory safety inspections for its members. The FMI has filed suit against bank card associations challenging the fixed prices supermarkets pay to accept debit cards.

The FMI was the leading supermarket industry contributor to 1996 congressional campaigns. About 85 percent of its contributions went to Republican candidates. The leading recipient was former Rep. Dick Zimmer, R-N.J., who lost to then-Rep. Robert G. Torricelli, D-N.J. It also gave $7,000 or more to Sen. Pat Roberts, R-Kan., and Senate candidate Rudy Boschwitz of Minnesota, who was defeated. Sen. Tom Harkin, D-Iowa, and Rep. Charles W. Stenholm, D-Texas, were the leading Democratic recipients.

Food Marketing Institute Political Action Committee (Food PAC) (C00014555) *Address: same as sponsor * Contact: Anne Curry, Gov. Relations Representative * Treasurer: George Green*

	1993-94	1995-96	1997	Totals
Receipts	$477,266	$491,241	$221,381	$1,189,888
Disburse	458,098	456,865	201,211	1,116,174
Cash	196,904	231,283	251,454	n/a
Contributions	452,465	447,703	196,152	1,096,320
Republicans	309,661	378,453	158,152	846,266
No. of Cand.	*198*	*259*	*173*	*630*
House	198,770	266,371	120,750	585,891
Senate	110,891	112,082	37,402	260,375
Democrats	142,054	68,250	37,000	247,304
No. of Cand.	*112*	*61*	*43*	*216*
House	117,254	53,250	30,500	201,004
Senate	24,800	15,000	6,500	46,300
Incumbents	365,443	361,774	192,152	919,369
Challengers	24,792	30,596	1,500	56,888
Open Seat	61,730	53,583	2,500	117,813
Winners	390,995	368,032	n/a	759,027
Losers	61,470	79,671	n/a	141,141

General Mills

*Phone: (612) 540-2300 * Fax: (612) 540-4921*
One General Mills Blvd., Minneapolis, MN 55426
Web: www.generalmills.com

General Mills is a leading producer of packaged consumer foods, including cereals (Wheaties, Cheerios, Chex, Kix, Total, Lucky Charms and Trix), desserts and baking mixes (Betty Crocker, Bisquick), convenience foods (Hamburger Helper), bakery flour (Gold Medal), snack products and beverages (Fruit Roll-Ups and Pop Secret), and yogurt (Yoplait and Colombo).

Internationally, the company has alliances with Nestlé, PepsiCo and CPC International.

In 1997, the Department of Agriculture approved yogurt as a meat substitute for school breakfasts and lunches — a fact General Mills even noted in its annual report.

A publicly traded company with about 10,000 employees, General Mills reported $5.6 billion in 1997 revenues.

General Mills Inc. Political Action Committee (GM PAC) (C00062646) *Phone: (202) 737-8200 * Fax: (202) 638-4914 * 601 Pennsylvania Ave. N.W., Suite 420 N., Washington, DC 20004 * Contact: Austin Sullivan, Chairperson * Phone: (612) 540-2300 * Treasurer: Jack Pugh*

	1993-94	1995-96	1997	Totals
Receipts	$104,461	$104,067	$68,892	$277,420
Disburse	100,118	106,297	33,843	240,258
Cash	8,020	5,792	40,841	n/a
Contributions	99,973	106,887	32,750	239,610
Republicans	74,173	86,887	20,250	181,310
No. of Cand.	*61*	*68*	*23*	*152*
House	34,412	45,300	8,000	87,712
Senate	39,761	41,587	12,250	93,598
Democrats	24,500	20,000	11,000	55,500
No. of Cand.	*30*	*24*	*12*	*66*
House	14,000	13,000	3,000	30,000
Senate	10,500	7,000	8,000	25,500
Incumbents	66,762	70,500	32,750	170,012
Challengers	7,000	16,500	0	23,500
Open Seat	26,211	19,887	1,000	47,098
Winners	83,572	80,587	n/a	164,159
Losers	16,401	26,300	n/a	42,701

Grocery Manufacturers of America

*Phone: (202) 337-9400 * Fax: (202) 337-4508*
1010 Wisconsin Ave. N.W., Suite 800, Washington, DC 20007
*Web: www.gmabrands.com * E-mail: gmapac@gmabrands.com*

Grocery Manufacturers of America represents about 300 companies in the 2.5 million-worker, $430 billion retail grocery trade. It monitors legislation and regulations on the state, federal and international levels.

GMA follows farm and pesticide regulations, FDA rules, tax policy, food and nutrition standards and electricity deregulation, among other issues.

Grocery Manufacturers of America Inc. Political Action Committee (GMA PAC) (C00250068) *Address: same as sponsor * Treasurer: Susan M. Stout*

	1993-94	1995-96	1997	Totals
Receipts	$102,725	$108,138	$42,478	$253,341
Disburse	100,650	121,300	39,250	261,200
Cash	28,724	15,566	18,796	n/a
Contributions	99,400	113,500	35,250	248,150
Republicans	65,600	102,000	25,000	192,600
No. of Cand.	*87*	*121*	*29*	*237*
House	40,100	54,750	13,000	107,850
Senate	25,500	47,250	12,000	84,750
Democrats	33,800	11,500	10,250	55,550
No. of Cand.	*39*	*14*	*12*	*65*
House	22,000	11,500	6,250	39,750
Senate	11,800	0	4,000	15,800
Incumbents	73,100	84,000	32,250	189,350
Challengers	5,800	4,000	2,000	11,800
Open Seat	20,500	25,500	1,000	47,000
Winners	88,600	100,500	n/a	189,100
Losers	10,800	13,000	n/a	23,800

Hy-Vee Food Stores

*Phone: (515) 267-2800 * Fax: (515) 267-2817*
5820 Westown Pkwy., West Des Moines, IA 50266
Web: www.hy-vee.com

Hy-Vee Food Stores is an employee-owned supermarket chain in the Midwest. The company has more than 230 stores and 35,000 employees. Hy-Vee generates nearly $3 billion in annual sales, making it one of the top 10 supermarket chains in the United States.

Hy-Vee stores are located in Iowa, Illinois, Missouri, Kansas, Nebraska, South Dakota and Minnesota. The company operates drug stores and convenience stores in its home state of Iowa. It has several subsidiaries, including its own distribution company.

Hy-Vee Food Stores Inc. Employees' Political Action Committee (C00243659) *Address: same as sponsor * Treasurer: John Briggs*

	1993-94	1995-96	1997	Totals
Receipts	$26,155	$33,920	$21,253	$81,328
Disburse	30,689	42,532	5,375	78,596
Cash	14,199	5,589	21,470	n/a
Contributions	2,250	10,700	250	13,200
Republicans	2,250	8,700	-250	10,700
No. of Cand.	*4*	*9*	*3*	*16*
House	2,250	4,500	500	7,250
Senate	0	4,200	-750	3,450
Democrats	0	2,000	500	2,500
No. of Cand.	*0*	*2*	*1*	*3*
House	0	1,000	500	1,500
Senate	0	1,000	0	1,000
Incumbents	1,000	4,700	1,250	6,950
Challengers	750	3,000	0	3,750
Open Seat	500	3,000	0	3,500
Winners	2,250	7,700	n/a	9,950
Losers	0	3,000	n/a	3,000

IBP Inc.

*Phone: (402) 241-2945 * Fax: (402) 241-2068*
P.O. Box 515, U.S. Hwy. 35, Dakota City, NE 68731-0515
Web: www.ibpinc.com

IBP Inc. began as Iowa Beef Packers Inc. in 1961 in Denison, Iowa, and now produces fresh beef and pork products in Dakota City, Neb. IBP is a publicly held company.

Its primary products include boxed beef and fresh pork marketed mainly in the United States. The company reported $13.3 billion in 1997 sales, and processes more than 9 billion pounds of meat per year — 15 percent of the U.S. total.

In 1997, IBP diversified its products by acquiring three new companies. Foodbrands America makes prepared appetizers, deli meats and pizza crusts and toppings for restaurants and cafeterias. The Bruss Co. processes and sells individual cuts of beef and pork to restaurants. A plant purchased from Hudson Foods in Columbus, Neb. serves as a beef patty manufacturing center.

IBP also produces hides, leather, animal feed and pharmaceuticals. It employs 30,000 people.

IBP-PAC IBP Inc. Political Action Committee (C00114223) *Address: same as sponsor * Contact: Don Willoughby, Chairman * Treasurer: Leon O. Trautwein*

	1993-94	1995-96	1997	Totals
Receipts	$49,384	$70,428	$32,459	$152,271
Disburse	40,307	40,617	6,898	87,822
Cash	82,504	112,327	137,893	n/a
Contributions	26,500	29,750	5,000	61,250
Republicans	22,500	18,500	5,000	46,000
No. of Cand.	*30*	*26*	*1*	*57*
House	9,500	8,500	0	18,000
Senate	13,000	10,000	5,000	28,000
Democrats	4,000	11,250	0	15,250
No. of Cand.	*8*	*4*	*0*	*12*
House	3,000	1,250	0	4,250
Senate	1,000	10,000	0	11,000
Incumbents	15,500	12,750	5,000	33,250
Challengers	6,000	4,500	0	10,500
Open Seat	5,000	12,500	0	17,500
Winners	23,000	14,750	n/a	37,750
Losers	3,500	15,000	n/a	18,500

Independent Bakers Association

*Phone: (202) 333-8190 * Fax: (202) 337-3809*
P.O. Box 3731, Washington, DC 20007
*Web: www.mindspring.com/~independentbaker * E-mail: independentbaker@mindspring.com*

The Independent Bakers Association is a national trade group of more than 400 small wholesale bakeries and allied businesses. The association was founded to protect the interests of independent wholesale bakers from antitrust and anticompetitive mergers and acquisitions and to pressure Congress to support market-oriented farm commodity programs.

BakePAC - The Political Action Committee of The Independent Bakers Association (C00099754) *Address: same as sponsor * Treasurer: Robert N. Pyle*

	1993-94	1995-96	1997	Totals
Receipts	$48,737	$66,984	$16,225	$131,946
Disburse	49,299	63,950	7,043	120,292
Cash	492	3,524	12,707	n/a
Contributions	40,595	53,567	7,000	101,162
Republicans	35,595	51,167	6,250	93,012
No. of Cand.	*140*	*170*	*13*	*323*
House	21,675	33,129	4,000	58,804
Senate	13,920	18,038	2,250	34,208
Democrats	5,000	2,400	750	8,150
No. of Cand.	*8*	*8*	*3*	*19*
House	2,500	1,900	750	5,150
Senate	2,500	500	0	3,000
Incumbents	23,545	30,879	7,000	61,424
Challengers	11,050	5,250	0	16,300
Open Seat	5,900	16,938	0	22,838
Winners	34,145	36,611	n/a	70,756
Losers	6,450	16,956	n/a	23,406

Jitney-Jungle Inc.

*Phone: (601) 965-8600 * Fax: (601) 371-2814*
1770 Ellis Ave., Suite 200, Jackson, MS 39204-3613
Web: www.jitneyjungle.com

Jitney-Jungle, headquartered in Mississippi, operates more than 200 grocery stores and 50 Pump and Save gas stations in the southwestern United States. With sales exceeding $2 billion in 1997, Jitney-Jungle is the 39th-largest grocery store chain in the nation. The privately held company owns conventional supermarkets, large discount stores and upscale markets.

After Jitney-Jungle's September 1997 acquisition of Delchamps Inc., a supermarket chain, sales in the second quarter increased 39 percent over the previous year. Jitney-Jungle is now ranked No. 59 among Forbes' Top 500 Private Companies for 1997, compared to No. 143 in 1996.

Jitney-Jungle was founded in 1919 by the McCarty and Holman families but investment firm Bruckman, Rosser, Sherill and Co. acquired a controlling interest in 1996.

Jitney-Jungle Political Action Committee (C00136341) *Address: same as sponsor * Contact: W. H. Holman III, Chairman * Treasurer: Earl D. Walker*

	1993-94	1995-96	1997	Totals
Receipts	$76,364	$52,563	$6,727	$135,654
Disburse	29,505	71,271	18,554	119,330
Cash	94,448	75,743	63,916	n/a
Contributions	9,250	11,200	500	20,950
Republicans	4,000	2,200	500	6,700
No. of Cand.	*4*	*3*	*1*	*8*
House	750	2,200	500	3,450
Senate	3,250	0	0	3,250
Democrats	5,250	9,000	0	14,250
No. of Cand.	*5*	*4*	*0*	*9*
House	5,250	9,000	0	14,250
Senate	0	0	0	0
Incumbents	8,250	7,500	500	16,250
Challengers	500	0	0	500
Open Seat	500	1,700	0	2,200
Winners	8,750	7,700	n/a	16,450
Losers	500	3,500	n/a	4,000

Kellogg Co.

*Phone: (616) 961-2000 * Fax: (616) 961-2871*
One Kellogg Square, P.O. Box 3599, Battle Creek, MI 49016-3599
Web: www.kelloggs.com

Kellogg produces 12 of the top 15 cereals in the world, including Kellogg's All-Bran, Froot Loops, Frosted Flakes, Rice Krispies and Special K. It also produces other grain-based convenience foods including frozen waffles (Eggo), cereal bars (Nutri-Grain Bars), pastries (Pop Tarts), bagels (Lender's) and snacks (Rice Krispies Treats).

Kellogg's had sales of $6.8 billion in 1997. The company employs more than 14,000 workers.

U.S. manufacturing locations: California, Connecticut, Georgia, Illinois, Kentucky, Michigan, Nebraska, New Jersey, New York and Tennessee.

Kellogg Co. Better Government Committee (C00039552) *Phone: (202) 434-8262 * 601 Pennsylvania Ave. N.W., Suite 900, Washington, DC 20004 * Treasurer: Charles E. French*

	1993-94	1995-96	1997	Totals
Receipts	$147,414	$151,194	$63,638	$362,246
Disburse	130,939	160,655	53,210	344,804
Cash	26,825	17,369	25,997	n/a
Contributions	107,479	131,466	45,500	284,445
Republicans	36,729	95,392	27,500	159,621
No. of Cand.	*33*	*57*	*27*	*117*
House	18,729	46,350	15,500	80,579
Senate	18,000	49,042	12,000	79,042
Democrats	70,750	36,074	18,000	124,824
No. of Cand.	*55*	*18*	*16*	*89*
House	52,250	23,500	10,000	85,750
Senate	18,500	12,574	8,000	39,074
Incumbents	90,229	100,424	45,500	236,153
Challengers	3,000	4,792	0	7,792
Open Seat	14,250	26,250	0	40,500
Winners	69,229	115,424	n/a	184,653
Losers	38,250	16,042	n/a	54,292

Kroger Co.

*Phone: (513) 762-4000 * Fax: (513) 762-1160*
1014 Vine St., Cincinnati, OH 45202-1100
*Web: www.kroger.com * E-mail: lmarmer@kroger.com*

More than 2,000 supermarkets and convenience stores generated 1997 revenue of $26.5 billion for publicly held Kroger. Headquartered in Cincinnati, Kroger operates under the names of Kroger and Dillon supermarkets; its 700 convenience stores operate under the Kwik Shop and Turkey Hill names.

Kroger has 212,000 employees and operates 40 food processing facilities, a warehouse and a distribution center.

Kroger Political Action Committee (KroPAC) (C00059238)
*Address: same as sponsor * Contact: Lynn Marmer, V.P. of Public Affairs * Treasurer: Cynthia K. Holmes*

	1993-94	1995-96	1997	Totals
Receipts	$32,852	$54,384	$21,407	$108,643
Disburse	38,422	42,215	15,325	95,962
Cash	1,624	13,794	19,876	n/a
Contributions	23,850	22,200	6,250	52,300
Republicans	16,000	21,200	3,250	40,450
No. of Cand.	*18*	*27*	*4*	*49*
House	6,500	13,500	1,500	21,500
Senate	9,500	7,700	1,750	18,950

(Data for Kroger Political Action Committee continued)

Democrats	7,850	1,000	3,000	11,850
No. of Cand.	*7*	*2*	*1*	*10*
House	6,350	1,000	0	7,350
Senate	1,500	0	3,000	4,500
Incumbents	10,850	15,500	3,250	29,600
Challengers	2,000	2,700	0	4,700
Open Seat	11,000	4,000	3,000	18,000
Winners	16,000	18,000	n/a	34,000
Losers	7,850	4,200	n/a	12,050

McLane Co. Inc.

*Phone: (254) 771-7500 * Fax: (254) 771-7449*
P.O. Box 6115, Temple, TX 76503
E-mail: bharger@mclaneco.com

McLane is a grocery distributor based in Temple, Texas. The Wal-Mart subsidiary holds 50 percent of the retail grocery market in Texas and reported $5.9 billion in 1997 sales. McLane employs 2,200 people.

McLane Co. Inc. Federal Political Action Committee (C00215558) *Address: same as sponsor * Treasurer: Robert D. Harger*

	1993-94	1995-96	1997	Totals
Receipts	$64,484	$21,603	$17,505	$103,592
Disburse	43,800	46,625	7,010	97,435
Cash	52,114	27,103	37,604	n/a
Contributions	10,000	25,625	6,000	41,625
Republicans	10,000	25,500	1,000	36,500
No. of Cand.	*9*	*27*	*1*	*37*
House	6,000	22,000	0	28,000
Senate	4,000	3,500	1,000	8,500
Democrats	0	125	5,000	5,125
No. of Cand.	*0*	*1*	*1*	*2*
House	0	125	5,000	5,125
Senate	0	0	0	0
Incumbents	1,500	12,125	6,000	19,625
Challengers	4,000	7,500	0	11,500
Open Seat	4,500	6,000	0	10,500
Winners	10,000	12,625	n/a	22,625
Losers	0	13,000	n/a	13,000

National Food Processors Association

*Phone: (202) 639-5900 * Fax: (202) 637-8476*
1401 New York Ave. N.W., Washington, DC 20005
*Web: www.nfpa-food.org * E-mail: nfpa@nfpa-food.org*

National Food Processors Association represents 500 companies that package and manufacture processed meat and poultry products, fish, fruit products and fruit juice products.

Both Triple S Inc., a food processing insurance administrator, and The National Food Laboratory, a nonprofit research group, are subsidiaries of the NFPA.

National Food Processors Association Political Action Committee (NFPAC) (C00003756) *Address: same as sponsor * Treasurer: John R. Cady*

	1993-94	1995-96	1997	Totals
Receipts	$47,900	$65,667	$44,439	$158,006
Disburse	48,729	58,733	32,000	139,462
Cash	3,891	10,827	23,266	n/a
Contributions	44,729	45,748	23,500	113,977
Republicans	31,129	38,948	21,000	91,077
No. of Cand.	*40*	*32*	*21*	*93*
House	16,629	15,250	8,000	39,879
Senate	14,500	23,698	13,000	51,198
Democrats	13,600	6,800	2,500	22,900
No. of Cand.	*20*	*7*	*5*	*32*
House	12,600	6,800	1,500	20,900
Senate	1,000	0	1,000	2,000
Incumbents	28,906	30,548	22,500	81,954
Challengers	3,400	2,200	0	5,600
Open Seat	12,423	12,000	1,000	25,423
Winners	38,729	44,048	n/a	82,777
Losers	6,000	1,700	n/a	7,700

National Meat Association

*Phone: (510) 763-1533 * Fax: (510) 763-6186*
1970 Broadway, Suite 825, Oakland, CA 94612
*Web: www.hooked.net/users/nma * E-mail: nma@hooked.net*

The National Meat Association represents about 300 meat packing and processing companies. In addition, the organization's membership includes 400 companies that manufacture and supply equipment for the meat industry.

National Meat Association Inc. PAC (C00301671) *Address: same as sponsor * Contact: Russell Wilcox, Chairman * Treasurer: Henry Meyer*

	1993-94	1995-96	1997	Totals
Receipts	$0	$17,403	$10,069	$27,472
Disburse	0	14,134	3,059	17,193
Cash	0	3,273	10,284	n/a
Contributions	0	13,750	2,500	16,250
Republicans	0	9,250	500	9,750
No. of Cand.	*0*	*12*	*1*	*13*
House	0	7,250	500	7,750
Senate	0	2,000	0	2,000
Democrats	0	4,500	2,000	6,500
No. of Cand.	*0*	*7*	*2*	*9*
House	0	4,500	1,000	5,500
Senate	0	0	1,000	1,000
Incumbents	0	10,000	2,500	12,500
Challengers	0	1,500	0	1,500
Open Seat	0	2,250	0	2,250
Winners	0	13,750	n/a	13,750
Losers	0	0	n/a	0

National Wholesale Grocers Association

*Phone: (703) 532-9400 * Fax: (703) 538-4673*
201 Park Washington Ct., Falls Church, VA 22046-4521
Web: www.fdi.org

The National Wholesale Grocers Association represents about 265 wholesale grocers and food-service distributors located throughout the United States, Canada and about 20 other countries.

It is affiliated with the National-American Wholesale Grocers' Association and the International Foodservice Distributors Association.

Food Distributors Voice in Politics Committee — The Political Action Committee of Food Distributors International (C00201509) *Address: same as sponsor * Contact: Susan Siemietkowski, Dir. of Gov. Relations * Treasurer: Kevin Burke*

	1993-94	1995-96	1997	Totals
Receipts	$202,269	$150,136	$39,710	$392,115
Disburse	198,325	145,061	41,435	384,821
Cash	12,950	18,028	16,303	n/a
Contributions	192,044	122,986	30,202	345,232
Republicans	183,844	120,486	27,702	332,032
No. of Cand.	*186*	*134*	*38*	*358*
House	119,392	79,286	19,202	217,880
Senate	64,452	41,200	8,500	114,152
Democrats	8,200	2,500	2,500	13,200
No. of Cand.	*14*	*5*	*3*	*22*
House	8,200	2,500	2,500	13,200
Senate	0	0	0	0
Incumbents	89,899	77,246	27,702	194,847
Challengers	54,192	15,240	1,500	70,932
Open Seat	47,453	29,500	1,000	77,953
Winners	156,444	89,609	n/a	246,053
Losers	35,600	33,377	n/a	68,977

Nestlé USA Inc.

*Phone: (440) 248-5131 * Fax: (440) 248-3870*
30003 Bainbridge Rd., Solon, OH 44139
Web: www.nestle.com

Best known for its chocolate, Switzerland-based food giant Nestlé also produces baby foods, dairy products, breakfast cereals (through a joint venture with General Mills), desserts, snacks, ice creams, convenience and prepared foods, beverages, mineral water, cosmetics, pet care and ophthalmological products.

With $45 billion in 1996 revenue, Nestlé is the world's largest food company and one of the world's 50 largest public companies. It is not traded on U.S. stock exchanges, however, because of the company's reluctance to meet U.S. disclosure requirements.

U.S. operations account for about 17 percent, or $8 billion, of Nestlé's revenue. The U.S. division has 20,000 employees and is headquartered in Glendale, Calif. About 4,400 employees work in California; the remainder are spread throughout Nestlé USA's 64 domestic locations.

Nearly 1,000 of the company's employees volunteer in selected schools.

Nestlé has an agreement with The Walt Disney Co. that involves joint marketing, tie-in promotions and licensing.

Brands include: Nescafe, Taster's Choice, Hills Bros., Perrier, Carnation, Coffee-Mate, Stouffer's, Dairy Farm, Kit Kat, Baby Ruth, Butterfinger, Rolo, Friskies, Fancy Feast, Alpo, Mighty Dog, Gourmet and L'Oreal (major interest).

Nestlé USA Inc. Political Action Committee (C00087882) *Phone: (202) 296-4100 * Fax: (202) 296-8555 * 1133 Connecticut Ave. N.W., Suite 310, Washington, DC 20036 * Contact: Maxine Champion, V.P. of Corporate Affairs * Treasurer: Kenneth L. Jalen*

	1993-94	1995-96	1997	Totals
Receipts	$95,489	$83,452	$24,749	$203,690
Disburse	74,475	91,000	28,500	193,975
Cash	21,059	13,515	9,766	n/a
Contributions	66,850	85,500	28,000	180,350
Republicans	32,250	59,500	18,500	110,250
No. of Cand.	*33*	*35*	*23*	*91*
House	20,250	38,500	10,000	68,750
Senate	12,000	21,000	8,500	41,500
Democrats	34,100	26,000	9,500	69,600
No. of Cand.	*45*	*24*	*14*	*83*
House	31,600	24,500	7,000	63,100
Senate	2,500	1,500	2,500	6,500
Incumbents	60,350	71,500	26,500	158,350
Challengers	0	1,000	500	1,500
Open Seat	5,500	13,000	1,000	19,500
Winners	55,850	78,500	n/a	134,350
Losers	11,000	7,000	n/a	18,000

PepsiCo Inc.

*Phone: (914) 253-2862 * Fax: (914) 253-3669*
700 Anderson Hill Rd., Purchase, NY 10577-1444
Web: www.pepsico.com

Pepsi-Cola is the nation's second-largest soft drink maker behind Coca-Cola. The $20-billion public company also owns the top maker of snack food, Frito-Lay. Besides its soft drinks, Pepsi's brands include Fritos, Doritos, Rold Gold pretzels and Ruffles potato chips. The company employs about 486,000 people. In 1997, Pepsi spun off its fast-food restaurants, including Taco Bell, Pizza Hut and KFC, as TRICON Global Restaurants.

Pepsi supports pro-business candidates for Congress. It lobbies on taxes, health care policy and issues that will affect its large workforce and sales.

Although second in the soft-drink markets, Pepsi's PAC ranked first among beverage companies in contributions to 1996 congressional races. The company favored Republicans by a wide margin and was one of the top 100 PACs in contributions to open races, with $79,000 in such contributions.

The top recipients were Sens. Gordon H. Smith, R-Ore., and Pat Roberts, R-Kan., along with 1996 Republican Senate candidates William F. Weld of Massachusetts and Bob Kustra of Illinois. One Democrat, Sen. John D. Rockefeller IV, D-W.Va., received at least $5,000.

PepsiCo Concerned Citizens Fund (C00039321) *Address: same as sponsor * Contact: Galen Reser, Dir. of Gov. Affairs * Treasurer: Robert Bossone*

	1993-94	1995-96	1997	Totals
Receipts	$410,856	$409,491	$164,947	$985,294
Disburse	415,017	412,877	138,847	966,741
Cash	61,469	58,093	84,199	n/a
Contributions	310,719	297,489	58,141	666,349
Republicans	227,092	246,910	47,141	521,143
No. of Cand.	*149*	*151*	*36*	*336*
House	151,342	170,350	29,650	351,342
Senate	75,750	76,560	17,491	169,801
Democrats	82,508	50,579	11,000	144,087
No. of Cand.	*52*	*41*	*16*	*109*
House	73,268	41,579	9,000	123,847
Senate	9,240	9,000	2,000	20,240
Incumbents	195,384	180,941	43,150	419,475
Challengers	36,250	38,048	12,991	87,289
Open Seat	79,085	79,000	2,000	160,085
Winners	273,197	234,989	n/a	508,186
Losers	37,522	62,500	n/a	100,022

Pillsbury Co.

*Phone: (612) 330-4966 * Fax: (612) 330-5288*
200 S. Sixth St., Mailstop 39E3, Minneapolis, MN 55402
Web: www.pillsbury.com

The Pillsbury Co. produces brand-name foods such as Green Giant, Old El Paso, Haagen-Dazs and Progresso, as well as breakfast foods, desserts, baking foods, pizza and snack foods. Pillsbury has 18,000 employees and 64 locations, 27 of which are in the United States.

The company reported 1996 sales of $6.1 billion.

Pillsbury is a subsidiary of the London company Diageo, which was created by the merger of Grand Metropolitan and Guinness food and spirits companies. Diageo also owns many other popular brand-name products.

The Pillsbury Co. Political Action Committee (C00301879)
*Address: same as sponsor * Contact: William H. Birtcil, V.P. of Gov. Affairs * Treasurer: Lionell L. Nowell III*

	1993-94	1995-96	1997	Totals
Receipts	$0	$18,947	$17,743	$36,690
Disburse	0	15,750	1,750	17,500
Cash	0	4,197	20,191	n/a
Contributions	0	10,750	1,750	12,500
Republicans	0	8,500	1,750	10,250
No. of Cand.	*0*	*19*	*2*	*21*
House	0	4,500	1,750	6,250
Senate	0	4,000	0	4,000
Democrats	0	2,250	0	2,250
No. of Cand.	*0*	*6*	*0*	*6*
House	0	1,750	0	1,750
Senate	0	500	0	500
Incumbents	0	4,500	1,750	6,250
Challengers	0	1,000	0	1,000
Open Seat	0	5,250	0	5,250
Winners	0	7,250	n/a	7,250
Losers	0	3,500	n/a	3,500

The Quaker Oats Co.

*Phone: (312) 222-7847 * Fax: (312) 222-8315*
321 N. Clark St., Chicago, IL 60610-4714
Web: www.QuakerOats.com

Quaker Oats produces sports beverages, iced teas, single-serve juice drinks and lemonades, hot cereals, pancake mixes, grain-based snacks, cornmeal, hominy grits and rice products. In addition, it is the second-largest manufacturer of syrups and pasta products and is among the five largest manufacturers of ready-to-eat cereals.

The publicly traded company reported 1997 sales of $5 billion and a net loss of $924 million. Much of the loss was due to the unprofitable line of Snapple beverages. Quaker Oats sold Snapple and several smaller businesses during 1997.

Brands include: Gatorade, Quaker, Cap'n Crunch, Life, Rice-A-Roni, Pasta Roni and Aunt Jemima.

About 80 percent of the company's sales come from the United States and Canada.

The Public Interest Committee of The Quaker Oats Co. (C00022996) *Address: same as sponsor * Treasurer: John B. Kavanaugh*

	1993-94	1995-96	1997	Totals
Receipts	$64,427	$97,465	$38,840	$200,732
Disburse	56,799	101,892	15,850	174,541
Cash	26,154	21,732	40,468	n/a
Contributions	56,950	96,875	10,500	164,325
Republicans	40,750	82,875	10,000	133,625
No. of Cand.	*53*	*77*	*13*	*143*
House	24,750	61,375	7,000	93,125
Senate	16,000	21,500	3,000	40,500
Democrats	16,200	14,000	500	30,700
No. of Cand.	*26*	*17*	*1*	*44*
House	13,000	11,000	500	24,500
Senate	3,200	3,000	0	6,200
Incumbents	37,200	65,375	10,500	113,075
Challengers	4,750	16,250	0	21,000
Open Seat	15,000	15,250	0	30,250
Winners	54,450	79,125	n/a	133,575
Losers	2,500	17,750	n/a	20,250

Open Seat	10,250	4,850	1,500	16,600
Winners	27,230	16,689	n/a	43,919
Losers	10,600	6,950	n/a	17,550

Ralph's Grocery Co.

*Phone: (310) 884-9000 * Fax: (310) 884-2569*
1100 W. Artesia Blvd., Compton, CA 90220
*Web: www.ralphs.com * E-mail: aswiller@ralphs.com*

Ralph's Grocery Co. is a privately owned, California-based company which operates retail grocery stores. Ralph's is the largest supermarket chain in California. It reported 1997 sales of $5.5 billion, employs nearly 28,000 people and was ranked No. 28 on the Forbes 1996 list of top private companies.

Ralph's operations include Ralph's, a 260-store conventional supermarket chain in Southern California; Food 4 Less, a 110-store chain of warehouse food stores in Southern California and the Midwest; and 30 Cala, Bell, Falley's and FoodCo stores.

In June 1997, Ralph's announced plans to install four electric vehicle recharging stations at selected Southern California supermarkets.

Investment firm Yucaipa owns 42 percent of Ralph's, and Fred Meyer, also controlled by Yucaipa, has announced plans to purchase the company.

Ralph's Grocery Co. Political Action Committee (C00247114)
*Address: same as sponsor * Treasurer: Ari Swiller*

	1993-94	*1995-96*	*1997*	*Totals*
Receipts	$13,794	$18,541	$4	$32,339
Disburse	11,650	41,584	93	53,327
Cash	23,558	485	398	n/a
Contributions	7,400	28,000	0	35,400
Republicans	3,900	1,750	0	5,650
No. of Cand.	*5*	*3*	*0*	*8*
House	2,900	1,750	0	4,650
Senate	1,000	0	0	1,000
Democrats	3,500	26,250	0	29,750
No. of Cand.	*3*	*15*	*0*	*18*
House	1,500	13,750	0	15,250
Senate	2,000	12,500	0	14,500
Incumbents	5,400	12,500	0	17,900
Challengers	1,000	8,500	0	9,500
Open Seat	1,000	7,000	0	8,000
Winners	4,400	17,500	n/a	21,900
Losers	3,000	10,500	n/a	13,500

Safeway Inc.

*Phone: (510) 467-3000 * Fax: (510) 467-3323*
5918 Stoneridge Mall Rd., Pleasanton, CA 94588-3229
*Web: www.safeway.com * E-mail: jonathan.mayes@safeway.com*

Safeway is a food retailer based in Pleasanton, Ca., operating more than 1,350 stores in the United States and Canada and posting 1997 sales of $17 billion. Combined operations of the company, which was No. 65 in the 1996 Fortune 500, employ 119,000 people. Safeway is publicly held.

In 1997, Safeway forged a multi-year agreement with 1-800-DATABASE to allow its products to be sold and delivered via the Internet.

U.S. operations are located principally in northern California, Oregon, Washington state and the Rocky Mountain, Southwest, and mid-Atlantic regions. Safeway also operates an extensive network of distribution, manufacturing and food processing facilities to support its retail stores and owns almost 50 percent of Casa Ley, which operates food/variety and wholesale stores in western Mexico. Besides its grocery operations, it manufactures and sells private-label merchandise.

Safeway Inc. Political Action Committee (SafePAC) (C00194084)
*Address: same as sponsor * Contact: Jonathan Mayes, Gov. Affairs Dir. * Treasurer: Melissa C. Plaisance*

	1993-94	*1995-96*	*1997*	*Totals*
Receipts	$63,289	$36,939	$22,742	$122,970
Disburse	45,530	45,039	11,860	102,429
Cash	53,616	45,522	56,409	n/a
Contributions	37,830	23,639	2,750	64,219
Republicans	24,400	17,099	1,000	42,499
No. of Cand.	*24*	*18*	*3*	*45*
House	16,900	13,749	0	30,649
Senate	7,500	3,350	1,000	11,850
Democrats	13,430	6,540	1,750	21,720
No. of Cand.	*19*	*9*	*3*	*31*
House	9,430	4,540	1,750	15,720
Senate	4,000	2,000	0	6,000
Incumbents	22,580	15,389	1,250	39,219
Challengers	4,500	3,500	0	8,000

Services Group of America

*Phone: (206) 933-5225 * Fax: (206) 933-5248*
P.O. Box 3627, Seattle, WA 98124-3627

Services Group of America is a private company engaged in the food distribution, insurance and real estate industries.

With about 3,000 employees and estimated 1996 revenues of $1.2 billion, the company ranked No. 140 on the Forbes list of top private companies. Services Group's main subsidiary is Food Services of America, and it also owns Eagle Insurance Group and Development Services of America. The company has several contracts with the Defense Logistics Agency and other government agencies.

Services Group of America agreed to pay a $5 million fine in 1998 for illegally funneling money into two campaigns in Washington state, including the 1992 9th District congressional race. Company chairman and CEO Thomas J. Stewart is described by Washington state newspapers as one of the state Republican Party's major donors.

Services Group of America Political Action Committee (C00224618) *Address: same as sponsor * Treasurer: Dennis Specht*

	1993-94	*1995-96*	*1997*	*Totals*
Receipts	$0	$111,375	$20,325	$131,700
Disburse	84,433	126,779	11,000	222,212
Cash	46,440	31,035	40,360	n/a
Contributions	75,783	104,789	11,000	191,572
Republicans	75,783	104,789	11,000	191,572
No. of Cand.	*14*	*19*	*11*	*44*
House	55,283	71,789	6,500	133,572
Senate	20,500	33,000	4,500	58,000
Democrats	0	0	0	0
No. of Cand.	*0*	*0*	*0*	*0*
House	0	0	0	0
Senate	0	0	0	0
Incumbents	15,283	72,789	11,000	99,072
Challengers	38,000	13,000	0	51,000
Open Seat	22,000	19,000	0	41,000
Winners	70,283	81,789	n/a	152,072
Losers	5,500	23,000	n/a	28,500

Snack Food Association

*Phone: (703) 836-4500 * Fax: (703) 836-8262*
1711 King St., Suite 1, Alexandria, VA 22314
Web: www.snax.com

The Snack Food Association represents more than 1,000 makers of potato chips, pretzels and other snack foods. Its members include Frito-Lay, Pringles and Olean. The group conducts research on potatoes and corn and acts as the industry's voice before Congress and state legislatures.

Snack Food Association Political Action Committee (SnackPAC) (C00118919) *Address: same as sponsor * Treasurer: James W. Shufelt*

	1993-94	*1995-96*	*1997*	*Totals*
Receipts	$14,150	$17,853	$10,189	$42,192
Disburse	16,787	17,596	10,219	44,602
Cash	2,528	2,789	2,660	n/a
Contributions	15,137	16,750	8,750	40,637
Republicans	9,537	14,750	7,750	32,037
No. of Cand.	*13*	*21*	*10*	*44*
House	5,537	9,750	3,750	19,037
Senate	4,000	5,000	4,000	13,000
Democrats	5,600	2,000	1,000	8,600
No. of Cand.	*9*	*4*	*2*	*15*
House	5,600	2,000	1,000	8,600
Senate	0	0	0	0
Incumbents	14,100	12,250	8,750	35,100
Challengers	0	1,500	0	1,500
Open Seat	1,037	3,000	0	4,037
Winners	13,137	12,000	n/a	25,137
Losers	2,000	4,750	n/a	6,750

Sysco Corp.

*Phone: (281) 584-1390 * Fax: (281) 584-2524*
1390 Enclave Pkwy., Houston, TX 77077-2099
Web: www.sysco.com

Sysco Corp. is the largest marketer and distributor of foodservice products in North America. Operating from 70 distribution facilities, the publicly held company provides products and services to about 270,000 restaurants, hotels, schools, hospitals, retirement homes and other foodservice operations.

Sysco's chain restaurant customers include regional pizza and national hamburger, chicken and steak chain operations. Its distribution network extends to Alaska and Canada.

Founded in 1969, Sysco Corp. has more than 32,000 employees and 52 subsidiaries. Sysco reported $14.4 billion in fiscal year 1997 revenues.

Sysco Corp. Good Government Political Action Committee (Sysco PAC) (C00314625) *Address: same as sponsor * Treasurer: Michael C. Nichols*

	1993-94	1995-96	1997	Totals
Receipts	$0	$31,023	$1,000	$32,023
Disburse	0	27,130	6,160	33,290
Cash	0	3,892	561	n/a
Contributions	0	20,000	6,000	26,000
Republicans	0	19,000	6,000	25,000
No. of Cand.	*0*	*26*	*2*	*28*
House	0	13,000	2,000	15,000
Senate	0	6,000	4,000	10,000
Democrats	0	1,000	0	1,000
No. of Cand.	*0*	*1*	*0*	*1*
House	0	1,000	0	1,000
Senate	0	0	0	0
Incumbents	0	12,500	6,000	18,500
Challengers	0	500	0	500
Open Seat	0	6,000	0	6,000
Winners	0	16,500	n/a	16,500
Losers	0	3,500	n/a	3,500

United Fresh Fruit & Vegetable Association

*Phone: (703) 836-3410 * Fax: (703) 836-7745*
727 N. Washington St., Alexandria, VA 22314

The United Fresh Fruit & Vegetable Association, originally founded as the Western Fruit Jobbers Association in 1904, is a national trade group for the produce industry. It offers technical assistance and government updates for fruit and vegetable growers and processors. One of the group's major issues is food safety and contamination. It has about 1,100 members nationwide.

Fresh Political Action Committee (Fresh PAC) (C00040725) *Address: same as sponsor * Treasurer: John J. Aguirre*

	1993-94	1995-96	1997	Totals
Receipts	$11,290	$16,701	$9,724	$37,715
Disburse	8,400	16,779	8,340	33,519
Cash	2,685	1,668	3,052	n/a
Contributions	5,100	16,700	13,150	34,950
Republicans	2,600	13,900	8,800	25,300
No. of Cand.	*7*	*19*	*11*	*37*
House	2,100	11,200	4,800	18,100
Senate	500	2,700	4,000	7,200
Democrats	2,500	2,800	4,350	9,650
No. of Cand.	*7*	*7*	*6*	*20*
House	2,500	2,450	2,850	7,800
Senate	0	350	1,500	1,850
Incumbents	4,500	13,150	13,150	30,800
Challengers	350	950	0	1,300
Open Seat	250	2,600	0	2,850
Winners	4,100	13,700	n/a	17,800
Losers	1,000	3,000	n/a	4,000

Universal Foods Corp.

*Phone: (414) 271-6755 * Fax: (414) 347-3785*
433 E. Michigan St., Milwaukee, WI 53202

Universal Foods engages in the international development, manufacture and distribution of a variety of ingredients in food products and other items. The company had more than $825 million in 1997 sales.

Principal products of Universal Foods include food, beverage and dairy flavors; certified and natural colors for foods, cosmetics and pharmaceuticals; dehydrated vegetable products; a diverse line of yeast products; and flavor enhancers, secondary flavorings and other bio-products.

Universal Foods operates 46 production and technical facilities in 15 countries, employing more than 4,100 workers.

Universal Foods Corp. Good Government Committee (C00283796) *Address: same as sponsor * Treasurer: Michael L. Hennen*

	1993-94	1995-96	1997	Totals
Receipts	$5,752	$10,973	$25	$16,750
Disburse	2,814	7,356	0	10,170
Cash	2,936	6,551	6,578	n/a
Contributions	2,750	5,800	0	8,550
Republicans	1,250	3,200	0	4,450
No. of Cand.	*4*	*10*	*0*	*14*
House	500	3,200	0	3,700
Senate	750	0	0	750
Democrats	1,500	2,600	0	4,100
No. of Cand.	*4*	*6*	*0*	*10*
House	1,000	2,100	0	3,100
Senate	500	500	0	1,000
Incumbents	2,750	5,450	0	8,200
Challengers	0	200	0	200
Open Seat	0	150	0	150
Winners	2,750	5,450	n/a	8,200
Losers	0	350	n/a	350

Winn-Dixie Stores

*Phone: (904) 783-5000 * Fax: (904) 783-5294*
5050 Edgewood Ct., Jacksonville, FL 32205
Web: www.winndixie.com

Ranked the fifth-largest supermarket chain in the United States, the publicly traded, 1,185-store Winn-Dixie has operations in 10 southern states, Ohio, Indiana, Texas, Oklahoma and the Bahamas. The company has pharmacies in about 500 stores. Another 167 stores have banks.

Founded as a country store in 1914, the Florida-based chain now generates $13 billion in revenue and has 136,000 employees. Chairman A. Dano Davis is a descendent of founder William Davis.

The company owns 22 manufacturing facilities, 17 distribution centers and a 1,100 truck fleet. Manufacturing plants are located in Alabama, Florida, Georgia, Louisiana, North and South Carolina and Texas.

Sunbelt Good Government Committee of Winn-Dixie Stores Inc. (C00033092) *Address: same as sponsor * Treasurer: Gordon A. Stickland*

	1993-94	1995-96	1997	Totals
Receipts	$69,401	$78,012	$34,413	$181,826
Disburse	276,498	97,588	7,316	381,402
Cash	602,028	582,456	609,554	n/a
Contributions	201,500	72,750	2,750	277,000
Republicans	126,500	60,750	2,000	189,250
No. of Cand.	*70*	*60*	*2*	*132*
House	78,500	51,750	1,000	131,250
Senate	48,000	9,000	1,000	58,000
Democrats	75,000	12,000	750	87,750
No. of Cand.	*46*	*10*	*2*	*58*
House	57,000	9,000	500	66,500
Senate	18,000	3,000	250	21,250
Incumbents	182,500	60,750	2,000	245,250
Challengers	2,000	1,000	0	3,000
Open Seat	17,000	10,000	0	27,000
Winners	177,500	69,750	n/a	247,250
Losers	24,000	3,000	n/a	27,000

Forestry & Forest Products

American Forest & Paper Association

*Phone: (202) 463-2700 * Fax: (202) 463-2785*
1111 19th St. N.W., Suite 800, Washington, DC 20036
Web: www.afandpa.org

Representing more than 8 percent of U.S. manufacturing output, American Forest & Paper Association members grow, harvest and process wood and paperboard products.

Forest Industries Political Action Committee of AF&PA (C00029348) *Address: same as sponsor * Treasurer: Robert A. Kirshner*

	1993-94	1995-96	1997	Totals
Receipts	$67,871	$139,050	$57,170	$264,091
Disburse	60,899	133,851	38,829	233,579
Cash	8,774	14,478	31,559	n/a
Contributions	64,828	133,800	38,050	236,678

(Data for Forest Industries Political continued)

	1993-94	1995-96	1997	Totals
Republicans	42,712	122,800	34,350	199,862
No. of Cand.	*47*	*89*	*36*	*172*
House	22,250	66,600	22,750	111,600
Senate	20,462	56,200	11,600	88,262
Democrats	21,116	11,000	3,700	35,816
No. of Cand.	*22*	*17*	*5*	*44*
House	19,015	10,000	1,600	30,615
Senate	2,101	1,000	2,100	5,201
Incumbents	33,893	91,000	38,050	162,943
Challengers	10,435	9,200	0	19,635
Open Seat	20,500	33,600	0	54,100
Winners	57,100	109,600	n/a	166,700
Losers	7,728	24,200	n/a	31,928

Boise Cascade

*Phone: (208) 384-7680 * Fax: (208) 384-4841*
1111 W. Jefferson St., P.O. Box 50, Boise, ID 83728
*Web: www.bc.com * E-mail: kirk_sullivan@bc.com*

Boise Cascade Corp. is a paper and forest products company headquartered in Boise, Idaho, with domestic and international operations. The public company manufactures and distributes paper and wood products, distributes office products and building materials, and owns and manages 2.4 million acres of timberland in Idaho, Minnesota, Washington state and the Pacific Northwest. Sales for 1997 were $45.5 billion and the company employs nearly 20,000 workers.

Through its publicly traded subsidiary and biggest revenue generator, Boise Cascade Office Products, the company distributes office and computer supplies and furniture and paper products. BCOP operates more than 60 distribution centers in the United States, Australia, Canada and the United Kingdom.

Boise owns 74 retail outlets in Canada and Hawaii and five pulp and paper mills located in Alabama, Louisiana, Minnesota, Oregon, and Washington state. In addition, Boise has six regional service centers located in California, Georgia, Illinois, New Jersey, Oregon and Texas and seven corrugated container plants located in Idaho, Nevada, Oregon, Utah and Washington.

Boise Cascade Political Fund (C00039131) *Phone: (202) 293-9066 * Fax: (202) 293-9070 * 1615 M St. N.W., Suite 570, Washington, DC 20036-3267 * Contact: Richard Rohrbach, Dir. of National Affairs * Treasurer: J. Kirk Sullivan*

	1993-94	1995-96	1997	Totals
Receipts	$50,481	$51,613	$32,273	$134,367
Disburse	53,500	50,500	19,500	123,500
Cash	6,016	9,416	22,193	n/a
Contributions	53,500	50,500	19,500	123,500
Republicans	43,000	46,500	15,500	105,000
No. of Cand.	*21*	*23*	*10*	*54*
House	24,500	21,500	6,000	52,000
Senate	18,500	25,000	9,500	53,000
Democrats	9,000	4,000	2,000	15,000
No. of Cand.	*8*	*4*	*2*	*14*
House	9,000	4,000	1,000	14,000
Senate	0	0	1,000	1,000
Incumbents	28,500	27,500	19,500	75,500
Challengers	10,000	6,000	0	16,000
Open Seat	15,000	17,000	0	32,000
Winners	41,500	37,500	n/a	79,000
Losers	12,000	13,000	n/a	25,000

Champion International Corp.

*Phone: (203) 358-7000 * Fax: (203) 358-6444*
One Champion Plaza, Stamford, CT 06921
Web: www.championpaper.com

Paper company Champion International is one of the nation's largest private landowners, with 5.3 million acres under its control. The publicly traded company has 24,300 employees and posted 1997 sales of $5.7 billion.

Champion produces paper for business communications, commercial printing, publications and newspapers. In addition, it has pulp, plywood and lumber manufacturing operations. The company's Canadian and Brazilian subsidiaries own or control significant timber resources supporting their operations.

Champion's locations are mainly in the South but it also has large operations in Maine, New Hampshire, New York, Ohio, Wisconsin, Minnesota and Washington state.

Champions for Good Government of Champion International Corp. (formerly known as Champion International Corp. PAC) (C00088864) *Phone: (202) 785-9888 * Fax: (202) 785-3286 * 1875 Eye St. N.W., Suite 540, Washington, DC 20006 * Contact: Sheila Agee, PAC Dir. * Treasurer: Kenwood C. Nichols*

	1993-94	1995-96	1997	Totals
Receipts	$157,529	$338,520	$263,154	$759,203
Disburse	177,504	295,330	127,411	600,245
Cash	48,253	91,443	227,186	n/a
Contributions	104,479	205,235	89,836	399,550
Republicans	50,131	163,985	61,336	275,452
No. of Cand.	*41*	*91*	*53*	*185*
House	19,125	107,367	40,800	167,292
Senate	31,006	56,618	20,536	108,160
Democrats	51,848	41,250	26,000	119,098
No. of Cand.	*50*	*27*	*24*	*101*
House	36,598	35,750	18,500	90,848
Senate	15,250	5,500	7,500	28,250
Incumbents	93,775	159,608	84,836	338,219
Challengers	500	8,579	0	9,079
Open Seat	12,204	37,048	5,000	54,252
Winners	89,481	171,757	n/a	261,238
Losers	14,998	33,478	n/a	48,476

Coastal Lumber Co.

*Phone: (919) 536-4211 * Fax: (919) 536-3102*
P.O. Box 829, Weldon, NC 27890
Web: www.coastallumber.com

Coastal Lumber is one of the largest privately held forest products companies in the United States, with more than 300,000 acres of timberlands. Coastal produces hardwood lumber, hardwood dimension parts, southern yellow pine lumber, southern yellow pine plywood, treated lumber and white pine millwork.

Founded in 1937, Coastal has developed into a diversified wood products company of 2,000 employees. Its Coastal Lumber International operation markets the company's products worldwide and is headquartered in Weldon, N.C.

The company's mills are located in New York, Pennsylvania, West Virginia, Tennessee, North and South Carolina, Florida and Alabama.

Coastal Lumber Co. Political Action Committee (C00281824) *Address: same as sponsor * Contact: Coleman J. Brian, Chairman * Treasurer: R.F. Seay*

	1993-94	1995-96	1997	Totals
Receipts	$15,732	$16,618	$5,289	$37,639
Disburse	8,250	20,800	3,750	32,800
Cash	7,503	3,325	4,865	n/a
Contributions	6,000	14,500	2,000	22,500
Republicans	6,000	14,500	2,000	22,500
No. of Cand.	*4*	*8*	*2*	*14*
House	5,000	10,500	1,000	16,500
Senate	1,000	4,000	1,000	6,000
Democrats	0	0	0	0
No. of Cand.	*0*	*0*	*0*	*0*
House	0	0	0	0
Senate	0	0	0	0
Incumbents	1,000	13,000	2,000	16,000
Challengers	1,000	0	0	1,000
Open Seat	4,000	1,500	0	5,500
Winners	5,000	9,500	n/a	14,500
Losers	1,000	5,000	n/a	6,000

Federal Paper Board Co.

75 Chestnut Ridge Rd., Montvale, NJ 07645

The Federal Paper Board Co. Inc. PAC was terminated in 1996.

Federal Paper Board Co. Inc. Political Action Committee (C00182626) *Address: same as sponsor * Treasurer: Roger L. Sanders II*

	1993-94	1995-96	1997	Totals
Receipts	$36	$0	$0	$36
Disburse	44	6,898	0	6,942
Cash	6,899	0	0	n/a
Contributions	0	6,898	0	6,898
Republicans	0	6,898	0	6,898
No. of Cand.	*0*	*6*	*0*	*6*
House	0	3,898	0	3,898
Senate	0	3,000	0	3,000
Democrats	0	0	0	0
No. of Cand.	*0*	*0*	*0*	*0*
House	0	0	0	0
Senate	0	0	0	0

Incumbents	0	6,898	0	6,898
Challengers	0	0	0	0
Open Seat	0	0	0	0
Winners	0	6,898	n/a	6,898
Losers	0	0	n/a	0

Forest Landowners Association

*Phone: (404) 325-2954 * Fax: (404) 325-2955*
P.O. Box 95385, Atlanta, GA 30347
Web: www.forestland.org

The Forest Landowners Association consists of 7,000 non-industrial, private forest landowners from 17 states. The association's members, who are mostly from the South, own 50 million acres of land.

The organization began as the Forest Farmers Association, but the name changed as members increasingly turned from farming to using their lands for recreational facilities and home building.

The group has a Washington office and tracks and lobbies legislation that affects forestry. Six times a year it publishes a newsletter that details activity on issues such as endangered species, property rights, forest health and clean water.

Forest Landowners Association Inc. Political Action Committee (formerly known as Forest Farmers Association PAC) (C00242040) *Phone: (202) 508-5822 * Fax: (202) 508-5858 * 700 13th St. N.W., Suite 800, Washington, DC 20005 * E-mail: ahenley@kilstock.com * Contact: April Henley, Gov. Affairs Dir. * Treasurer: Steven Newton*

	1993-94	1995-96	1997	Totals
Receipts	$2,436	$10,466	$8,025	$20,927
Disburse	7,275	5,683	4,456	17,414
Cash	4,488	2,250	5,819	n/a
Contributions	6,750	20,950	3,500	31,200
Republicans	4,500	19,450	3,500	27,450
No. of Cand.	*10*	*34*	*1*	*45*
House	2,000	11,250	0	13,250
Senate	2,500	8,200	3,500	14,200
Democrats	2,250	1,500	0	3,750
No. of Cand.	*6*	*4*	*0*	*10*
House	2,250	1,500	0	3,750
Senate	0	0	0	0
Incumbents	5,500	17,250	3,500	26,250
Challengers	0	500	0	500
Open Seat	1,250	3,200	0	4,450
Winners	6,250	19,250	n/a	25,500
Losers	500	1,700	n/a	2,200

Fort James Corp.

*Phone: (804) 343-4823 * Fax: (804) 343-4941*
650 Lake Cook Rd., Deerfield, IL 60015
Web: www.fortjames.com

Papermaker Fort Howard merged with James River Corp. in August 1997, creating Fort James, the largest bathroom and facial tissue maker in North America. Other products include copy paper, packaging containers, paper towels, napkins, cups, plates and plastic utensils. The publicly traded company has 30,000 employees and posted $7.2 billion in 1997 sales.

Fort James is selling off its timberland. In April 1997, it sold 95,000 acres in Alabama and Mississippi for $111 million. Fort James is also closing its two smallest tissue mills, located in Ashland, Wis. and Carthage, N.Y. The company's biggest mills are in Wisconsin, Oklahoma, Georgia and Alabama.

The company has 65 manufacturing sites in the United States, Canada and Europe. It uses 1.4 million tons of recycled paper each year. The EPA has identified Fort James and other companies as potentially responsible for cleanup costs at a Superfund site.

Fort James Corp. Political Action Committee (formerly known as Fort James Good Government PAC) (C00088765) *Address: same as sponsor * Contact: Charles D. Wilson, Chairperson * Treasurer: R. Michael Lempke*

	1993-94	1995-96	1997	Totals
Receipts	$34,104	$40,236	$17,920	$92,260
Disburse	41,582	57,398	9,708	108,688
Cash	29,680	12,525	20,737	n/a
Contributions	16,925	35,700	8,000	60,625
Republicans	14,425	34,700	6,500	55,625
No. of Cand.	*18*	*32*	*6*	*56*
House	8,225	17,200	2,000	27,425
Senate	6,200	17,500	4,500	28,200
Democrats	2,500	1,000	1,500	5,000
No. of Cand.	*5*	*2*	*2*	*9*
House	2,000	1,000	1,500	4,500
Senate	500	0	0	500
Incumbents	10,425	16,700	7,000	34,125
Challengers	2,500	5,000	1,000	8,500
Open Seat	4,000	14,000	0	18,000
Winners	15,425	20,000	n/a	35,425
Losers	1,500	15,700	n/a	17,200

Georgia-Pacific Corp.

*Phone: (404) 652-4000 * Fax: (404) 827-7010*
133 Peachtree St. N.E., Atlanta, GA 30303
Web: www.gp.com

Georgia-Pacific is a building products and pulp and paper company. The publicly traded Atlanta company has 47,000 workers and posted $13 billion in 1997 sales.

Georgia-Pacific owns 6 million acres of forestland in the United States and Canada, 65 percent of which is in the South. The company is one of the world's major distributors of pulp and paper products and is the largest distributor of building products in the United States.

Manufactured products in the building products segment consist primarily of wood panels, lumber, gypsum products and chemicals. The distribution division of this segment sells a wide range of building products manufactured by the corporation or purchased from others. This segment of the business is primarily affected by the level of housing starts; the level of repairs, remodeling and additions; industrial markets; commercial building activity; and the availability and cost of financing.

G-P Employees Fund of Georgia-Pacific Corp. (C00028670) *Phone: (202) 659-3600 * Fax: (202) 223-1398 * 1875 Eye St. N.W., Suite 775, Washington, DC 20006 * Contact: John Turner, V.P. of Gov. Affairs * Treasurer: Denise M. O'Donnell*

	1993-94	1995-96	1997	Totals
Receipts	$136,149	$243,807	$113,674	$493,630
Disburse	105,515	223,592	48,910	378,017
Cash	34,508	54,733	119,501	n/a
Contributions	90,353	187,076	43,838	321,267
Republicans	50,768	163,076	28,253	242,097
No. of Cand.	*39*	*69*	*19*	*127*
House	22,923	77,576	20,253	120,752
Senate	27,845	85,500	8,000	121,345
Democrats	39,585	24,000	15,585	79,170
No. of Cand.	*36*	*20*	*11*	*67*
House	36,985	15,000	6,000	57,985
Senate	2,600	9,000	9,585	21,185
Incumbents	73,653	117,576	43,588	234,817
Challengers	4,000	4,000	0	8,000
Open Seat	12,700	65,500	250	78,450
Winners	78,753	154,576	n/a	233,329
Losers	11,600	32,500	n/a	44,100

Gilman Paper Co.

Phone: (912) 882-0100
P.O. Box 878, St. Mary's, GA 31558

Founded in 1885, Gilman Paper is the nation's largest privately held manufacturer of paper products and lumber. Ranked No. 371 of 500 privately held companies by Forbes, it operates paper and pulp mills primarily in St. Mary's, Ga., with sales offices in Illinois, New Jersey and New York.

Wholly owned by its parent company, Gilman Investment in New York, Gilman Paper Co. employs 2,600 workers and has about $570 million in annual sales. Gilman Investment also maintains small operations in railroad hauling.

Gilman Paper Co./Gilman Good Government Group (C00180919) *Address: same as sponsor * Contact: John Love, Industrial Relations Manager * Treasurer: W. Burford Clark Jr.*

	1993-94	1995-96	1997	Totals
Receipts	$15,383	$10,388	$6,830	$32,601
Disburse	6,550	18,518	3,000	28,068
Cash	8,763	633	4,463	n/a
Contributions	6,450	15,000	3,000	24,450

(*Data for Gilman Paper Co. continued*)

Republicans	3,500	11,000	0	14,500
No. of Cand.	*3*	*4*	*0*	*7*
House	3,500	2,000	0	5,500
Senate	0	9,000	0	9,000
Democrats	2,950	4,000	3,000	9,950
No. of Cand.	*5*	*4*	*1*	*10*
House	2,950	3,000	0	5,950
Senate	0	1,000	3,000	4,000
Incumbents	6,350	3,500	3,000	12,850
Challengers	0	3,000	0	3,000
Open Seat	0	8,500	0	8,500
Winners	4,850	4,000	n/a	8,850
Losers	1,600	11,000	n/a	12,600

International Paper Co.

*Phone: (914) 397-1500 * Fax: (914) 397-1928*
Two Manhattanville Rd., Purchase, NY 10577
Web: www.ipaper.com

International Paper is the world's leading producer of forest and paper products and a top distributor of paper and office supplies. Its brands include Hammermill paper and Osmose lumber. The public company added Weston Paper & Manufacturing Co., based in Indiana, in a 1998 merger.

The company's non-paper offerings include chemicals, nonwoven fabrics, oil and gas and photographic films. It has production facilities in 31 countries and sells its products in more than 130 countries, although the U.S. market accounts for nearly three-fourths of the company's sales. The company has 87,000 employees and posted 1997 sales of $20 billion.

IP lobbies on international trade issues, tax policy and natural resources. The company is the largest forestland owner in the United States and supports a "managed forests" approach to global warming, in which the company plants new trees in the area where it harvests timber. It has many facilities which emit chemicals listed on the EPA's Toxic Release Inventory.

The company was the largest paper industry PAC contributor to congressional races during the 1995-96 election cycle. IP spent as much on open seats as it did on incumbents. The leading recipients were Sens. Gordon H. Smith, R-Ore., Susan M. Collins, R-Maine, and Jeff Sessions, R-Ala.

Lu Hardin of Arkansas, a 1996 Senate candidate, was the leading Democratic recipient.

International Paper PAC (IPPAC) (C00034405) *Phone: (202) 628-1223 * Fax: (202) 628-1368 * 1101 Pennsylvania Ave. N.W., Suite 200, Washington, DC 20004 * Treasurer: John C. Runyan*

	1993-94	1995-96	1997	Totals
Receipts	$338,001	$492,846	$259,482	$1,090,329
Disburse	333,753	477,020	131,871	942,644
Cash	22,194	38,027	165,643	n/a
Contributions	177,640	249,014	69,849	496,503
Republicans	166,540	234,514	60,849	461,903
No. of Cand.	*72*	*110*	*36*	*218*
House	51,000	116,515	32,849	200,364
Senate	115,540	117,999	28,000	261,539
Democrats	11,100	14,500	9,000	34,600
No. of Cand.	*12*	*9*	*5*	*26*
House	11,100	9,500	2,000	22,600
Senate	0	5,000	7,000	12,000
Incumbents	114,140	107,901	62,849	284,890
Challengers	20,500	31,500	1,000	53,000
Open Seat	43,000	109,113	6,000	158,113
Winners	155,140	170,899	n/a	326,039
Losers	22,500	78,115	n/a	100,615

International Wood Products Association

*Phone: (703) 820-6696 * Fax: (703) 820-8550*
4214 King St. W., Alexandria, VA 22302
*Web: www.ihpa.org * E-mail: info@ihpa.org*

International Wood Products Association, known as IHPA, is a trade association representing companies that handle imported wood products. IHPA advances responsible forest management and international trade in wood products through leadership in business, environmental and governmental affairs.

Established in 1956, IHPA provides a forum, including an annual convention, for industry members worldwide. The association develops and disseminates information, establishes standards of quality and service pertaining to wood products and develops programs that increase public acceptance and greater use of such products.

In 1997, IHPA and the Indonesian Wood Panel Association reached a settlement on a trade dispute. The agreement allows for independent inspections of wood and provides a mechanism for resolving trade disputes in excess of $10,000.

International Wood Products InPAC (C00161190) *Address: same as sponsor * Contact: Elizabeth Pease, Dir. of Gov. and Environmental Affairs * Treasurer: Wendy Baer*

	1993-94	1995-96	1997	Totals
Receipts	$3,935	$8,876	$3,218	$16,029
Disburse	3,906	8,781	303	12,990
Cash	51	146	3,061	n/a
Contributions	3,900	8,525	300	12,725
Republicans	2,600	7,525	300	10,425
No. of Cand.	*6*	*12*	*1*	*19*
House	1,400	5,275	300	6,975
Senate	1,200	2,250	0	3,450
Democrats	1,300	1,000	0	2,300
No. of Cand.	*2*	*1*	*0*	*3*
House	1,300	1,000	0	2,300
Senate	0	0	0	0
Incumbents	3,700	5,775	300	9,775
Challengers	200	2,750	0	2,950
Open Seat	0	0	0	0
Winners	3,700	5,775	n/a	9,475
Losers	200	2,750	n/a	2,950

Louisiana-Pacific Corp.

*Phone: (503) 221-0800 * Fax: (503) 796-0204*
111 S.W. Fifth Ave., Portland, OR 97204
Web: www.lpcorp.com

Louisiana-Pacific is a major manufacturer of building materials, industrial wood products and pulp. Formed in 1973, the publicly traded company owns 1.5 million acres of timberland and operates facilities in 29 U.S. states, Canada and Ireland.

The company produces wallboard, insulation, plywood panels and a plywood substitute used in construction. It has two pulp mills in North America. Louisiana-Pacific reported 1997 sales of $2.4 billion. It has about 12,000 employees.

In 1997, managers working for the company pled guilty to tampering with pollution monitoring equipment at the company's Olathe and Kremmling mills in Colorado. In addition, EPA has brought 55 charges against the company alleging that it lied about air emissions from its Western Slope waferboard mill.

The charges go back to the 1980s and early 1990s. Since then, Louisiana-Pacific has reorganized and complied with EPA regulations. When contacted in early 1998, representatives from the company's PAC would not comment about its activities because of management changes.

Louisiana-Pacific Corp. Federal PAC (C00109165) *Address: same as sponsor * Treasurer: Anita Miller-Davis*

	1993-94	1995-96	1997	Totals
Receipts	$27,713	$29,318	$10,070	$67,101
Disburse	31,499	28,270	2,910	62,679
Cash	3,402	4,468	11,630	n/a
Contributions	31,413	25,750	2,150	59,313
Republicans	28,663	25,250	1,500	55,413
No. of Cand.	*19*	*23*	*3*	*45*
House	14,263	13,250	500	28,013
Senate	14,400	12,000	1,000	27,400
Democrats	2,750	500	650	3,900
No. of Cand.	*3*	*1*	*1*	*5*
House	2,750	500	650	3,900
Senate	0	0	0	0
Incumbents	18,013	17,750	1,500	37,263
Challengers	12,000	3,000	0	15,000
Open Seat	1,400	5,000	650	7,050
Winners	20,013	23,000	n/a	43,013
Losers	11,400	2,750	n/a	14,150

Mead Corp.

*Phone: (937) 495-3303 * Fax: (937) 495-4103*
Courthouse Plaza N.E., Dayton, OH 45463
Web: www.mead.com

Mead's three big products are paper, packaging and school and office supplies. The publicly owned Dayton, Ohio company has 16,000 employees and posted $5 billion in 1997 revenues.

Mead is one of the world's largest manufacturers of paper, producing more than 1.7 million tons annually for printing, business and specialty uses; it also manufactures pulp and lumber. Mead produces 1.5 million tons of paperboard annually for use as coated paperboard, containerboard and packaging. School and office products include the Trapper Keeper and Cambridge personal organizers.

Mead owns more than 2 million acres of forest land in Alabama, Georgia, Kentucky, Maine, Michigan, New Hampshire, Ohio, Tennessee and Vermont. In addition, Mead's jointly owned affiliate, Northwood Forest Industries, has timber-harvesting agreements with the provincial government of British Columbia on 3.4 million acres of Canadian forest land.

Additional U.S. locations include: Arkansas, California, Indiana, Massachusetts, Missouri, Ohio, Oregon, Pennsylvania, South Carolina, Texas and Wisconsin.

Mead Corp. Effective Citizenship Fund (C00034538) *Phone: (202) 833-9643 * 1667 K St. N.W., Suite 420, Washington, DC 20006 * Contact: Ronald F. Budzik, Chairperson * Phone: (937) 495-3303 * Treasurer: T. A. "Pete" Dobrozsi*

	1993-94	1995-96	1997	Totals
Receipts	$45,871	$122,221	$76,881	$244,973
Disburse	43,234	103,434	36,378	183,046
Cash	5,310	24,109	64,612	n/a
Contributions	42,175	76,275	23,350	141,800
Republicans	26,325	64,025	16,850	107,200
No. of Cand.	*23*	*62*	*17*	*102*
House	10,325	30,525	8,850	49,700
Senate	16,000	33,500	8,000	57,500
Democrats	15,850	12,250	6,500	34,600
No. of Cand.	*20*	*16*	*9*	*45*
House	10,850	11,250	5,000	27,100
Senate	5,000	1,000	1,500	7,500
Incumbents	29,925	49,775	18,850	98,550
Challengers	1,500	7,500	0	9,000
Open Seat	10,500	20,000	4,500	35,000
Winners	37,925	55,275	n/a	93,200
Losers	4,250	21,000	n/a	25,250

Menasha Corp.

*Phone: (414) 751-1000 * Fax: (414) 751-1236*
1645 Bergstrom Rd., P.O. Box 367, Neenah, WI 54957-0367
Web: www.menasha.com

Menasha is the third-oldest privately held company in America. It makes plastics and paper products and has operations in 19 states and four foreign countries. The company has annual sales of about $915 million and employs about 5,500 people. Its shareholders are senior employees and 140 descendants of founder Elisha Smith.

Menasha also produces timber and packaging products.

Subsidiaries include: Thermotech, Murfin, Orbis, Menasha Transport Inc. and Poly Hi Solidur.

Menasha Corp. Political Action Committee (also known as Menasha PAC) (C00243774) *Address: same as sponsor * Treasurer: William C. Griffith*

	1993-94	1995-96	1997	Totals
Receipts	$20,392	$8,615	$9	$29,016
Disburse	29,052	400	0	29,452
Cash	5,434	13,400	502	n/a
Contributions	21,500	16,700	0	38,200
Republicans	18,000	16,700	0	34,700
No. of Cand.	*26*	*29*	*0*	*55*
House	9,000	9,700	0	18,700
Senate	9,000	7,000	0	16,000
Democrats	3,500	0	0	3,500
No. of Cand.	*5*	*0*	*0*	*5*
House	2,500	0	0	2,500
Senate	1,000	0	0	1,000
Incumbents	12,000	7,200	0	19,200
Challengers	4,000	4,000	0	8,000
Open Seat	5,500	5,500	0	11,000
Winners	16,500	9,700	n/a	26,200
Losers	5,000	7,000	n/a	12,000

National Hardwood Lumber Association

*Phone: (901) 377-1824 * Fax: (901) 382-6419*
P.O. Box 34518, Memphis, TN 38184-0518
Web: www.natlhardwood.org

The National Hardwood Lumber Association represents about 1,200 companies throughout the United States and Canada. The businesses include saw mills and hardwood lumber manufacturers and distributors.

National Hardwood Lumber Association PAC Inc. (C00311159) *Address: same as sponsor * Contact: Wendell Cramer, President * Treasurer: Paul Houghland Jr.*

	1993-94	1995-96	1997	Totals
Receipts	$0	$26,275	$2,350	$28,625
Disburse	0	25,214	73	25,287
Cash	0	1,060	3,335	n/a
Contributions	0	24,000	0	24,000
Republicans	0	24,000	0	24,000
No. of Cand.	*0*	*19*	*0*	*19*
House	0	15,000	0	15,000
Senate	0	9,000	0	9,000
Democrats	0	0	0	0
No. of Cand.	*0*	*0*	*0*	*0*
House	0	0	0	0
Senate	0	0	0	0
Incumbents	0	14,500	0	14,500
Challengers	0	3,500	0	3,500
Open Seat	0	6,000	0	6,000
Winners	0	15,000	n/a	15,000
Losers	0	9,000	n/a	9,000

Plum Creek Management Co.

*Phone: (206) 467-3626 * Fax: (206) 467-3799*
999 Third Ave., Suite 2300, Seattle, WA 98104-4096
*Web: www.plumcreek.com * E-mail: bjirsa@plumcreek.com*

Plum Creek Management is the general partner for its companies: Plum Creek Manufacturing, which buys the company's raw lumber and turns it into fiberboard, plywood and other products, and Plum Creek Marketing, which sells the finished lumber to retail home centers and other lumber retailers.

Plum Creek Timber owns more than 2 million wooded acres in Washington state, Montana, Idaho, Louisiana and Arkansas.

Seattle-based Plum Creek was at the center of a controversy surrounding 419,000 acres of its Washington state land in 1996 when the Clinton administration signed a 50-year plan that allowed more endangered, spotted owl territory to be logged. U.S. Fish and Wildlife officials called the plan "management of an entire ecosystem," while opponents termed it random clear-cutting.

Plum Creek employs about 2,300 people and posted sales of $725.6 million in 1997.

Plum Creek Management Co. LP Good Government Fund (C00255224) *Phone: (202) 289-7400 * Fax: (202) 289-7414 * Nutter and Harris, 927 15th St. N.W., 3rd Floor, Washington, DC 20005 * E-mail: nuthar@aol.com * Contact: Bob Harris * Treasurer: Robert J. Jirsa*

	1993-94	1995-96	1997	Totals
Receipts	$41,261	$45,197	$27,032	$113,490
Disburse	24,600	48,070	18,017	90,687
Cash	21,336	18,472	27,494	n/a
Contributions	21,900	40,000	16,100	78,000
Republicans	14,400	33,000	10,600	58,000
No. of Cand.	*7*	*14*	*10*	*31*
House	4,400	20,500	4,100	29,000
Senate	10,000	12,500	6,500	29,000
Democrats	7,500	7,000	5,500	20,000
No. of Cand.	*7*	*2*	*2*	*11*
House	7,000	2,000	0	9,000
Senate	500	5,000	5,500	11,000
Incumbents	19,900	32,500	15,100	67,500
Challengers	2,000	0	0	2,000
Open Seat	0	7,500	1,000	8,500
Winners	13,900	37,000	n/a	50,900
Losers	8,000	3,000	n/a	11,000

Potlatch Corp.

*Phone: (509) 835-1559 * Fax: (509) 835-1518*
One Maritime Plaza, Clay and Front St., San Francisco, CA 94111

Potlatch grows and harvests timber and sells wood and paper products through retail outlets nationwide. With 1.5 million acres of timberland in Arkansas, Idaho and Minnesota, the company employs more than 6,000 workers. Sales were $1.6 billion in 1997.

In February 1998, Potlatch Corp. and Anderson-Tully Co. announced a plan to combine all of Potlatch's 514,000 acres of primarily softwood timberlands in Arkansas and all of ATCO's 324,000 acres of primarily hardwood timberlands into Timberland Growth Corp. The newly formed real estate investment trust (REIT) would be the first publicly traded REIT focused on owning timberlands.

Potlatch Employees' Political Fund (C00041608) *Address: same as sponsor * Contact: Hubert D. Travaille, Chairperson * Treasurer: Gerald L. Zuehlke*

	1993-94	1995-96	1997	Totals
Receipts	$48,254	$54,020	$27,730	$130,004
Disburse	45,500	59,116	20,494	125,110
Cash	21,679	16,585	23,821	n/a
Contributions	43,500	59,116	20,494	123,110
Republicans	31,500	46,616	19,994	98,110
No. of Cand.	*25*	*27*	*11*	*63*
House	20,500	29,616	5,700	55,816
Senate	11,000	17,000	14,294	42,294
Democrats	6,000	12,500	500	19,000
No. of Cand.	*8*	*3*	*1*	*12*
House	4,000	7,500	500	12,000
Senate	2,000	5,000	0	7,000
Incumbents	20,000	35,016	18,494	73,510
Challengers	16,500	7,000	0	23,500
Open Seat	7,000	17,100	2,000	26,100
Winners	33,000	42,866	n/a	75,866
Losers	10,500	16,250	n/a	26,750

Riverwood International Corp.

Phone: (770) 644-3000
3350 Cumberland Cir., Suite 1600, Atlanta, GA 30339
Web: fury.riverwood.com

Riverwood International makes packaging, paper products and machinery used to package cans and bottles. Based in Atlanta, the company employs 5,500 workers worldwide and has assets of about $2 billion.

Riverwood's cardboard products are used by companies such as Coca-Cola, PepsiCo, Miller Brewing and Anheuser-Busch. Beverage clients account for 70 percent of Riverwood's sales, which totaled $1.1 billion in 1997.

Riverwood International was taken private in a 1996 leveraged buyout by a group of investors led by the firm Clayton, Dubilier & Rice.

Riverwood International Corp. Employee Action Program (REAP) (C00282566) *Address: same as sponsor * Treasurer: Bradford G. Ankerholz*

	1993-94	1995-96	1997	Totals
Receipts	$24,989	$41,045	$10,139	$76,173
Disburse	15,382	53,000	21	68,403
Cash	9,613	16,611	26,733	n/a
Contributions	13,000	51,000	0	64,000
Republicans	7,500	48,000	0	55,500
No. of Cand.	*12*	*24*	*0*	*36*
House	4,000	33,500	0	37,500
Senate	3,500	14,500	0	18,000
Democrats	5,000	3,000	0	8,000
No. of Cand.	*7*	*2*	*0*	*9*
House	4,000	2,000	0	6,000
Senate	1,000	1,000	0	2,000
Incumbents	10,000	39,000	0	49,000
Challengers	500	2,000	0	2,500
Open Seat	2,500	10,000	0	12,500
Winners	11,500	40,000	n/a	51,500
Losers	1,500	11,000	n/a	12,500

Simpson Investment Co.

*Phone: (206) 224-5040 * Fax: (206) 224-5059*
1201 Third Ave., Suite 4900, Seattle, WA 98101-3045
E-mail: jbreed@smpsn.com

Simpson Investment is a holding company for two main subsidiaries, Simpson Timber and Simpson Paper Co. It employs 4,500 people and was founded by Sol Simpson in 1890. Simpson's descendant, Chairman and CEO Colin Moseley, is the fifth generation of the family to run the company.

Ranked No. 85 on Forbes' Private 500, Simpson Investment Co. is privately held and had an estimated $1.5 billion in 1996 sales.

Simpson Timber acquires less-expensive tracts of land, replants them, and operates them for the long term. Simpson Paper makes coated and specialty papers, packaging and market pulp.

Simpson Investment Co. Political Action Committee (also known as Simpson Political Action Committee/SimPAC) (C00034934)
*Address: same as sponsor * Treasurer: Joseph R. Breed*

	1993-94	1995-96	1997	Totals
Receipts	$55,943	$42,650	$12,300	$110,893
Disburse	53,620	41,200	7,100	101,920
Cash	4,333	5,784	10,984	n/a
Contributions	53,500	39,200	7,100	99,800
Republicans	41,250	34,700	6,100	82,050
No. of Cand.	*25*	*18*	*6*	*49*
House	28,500	28,700	2,600	59,800
Senate	12,750	6,000	3,500	22,250
Democrats	12,250	4,500	1,000	17,750
No. of Cand.	*11*	*3*	*2*	*16*
House	11,750	3,500	1,000	16,250
Senate	500	1,000	0	1,500
Incumbents	32,250	31,200	6,100	69,550
Challengers	15,000	3,000	0	18,000
Open Seat	6,250	4,000	500	10,750
Winners	44,000	29,400	n/a	73,400
Losers	9,500	9,800	n/a	19,300

Southeastern Lumber Manufacturers Association

*Phone: (404) 361-1445 * Fax: (404) 361-5963*
P.O. Box 1788, Forest Park, GA 30298
Web: www.slma.org

The Southeastern Lumber Manufacturers Association represents about 300 privately held lumber company members in the southeastern United States.

Southeastern Lumber Manufacturers Association Political Action Committee (C00128678) *Treasurer: Deborah A. Burns*

	1993-94	1995-96	1997	Totals
Receipts	$23,419	$19,605	$3,230	$46,254
Disburse	19,103	23,506	3,086	45,695
Cash	7,257	3,354	3,497	n/a
Contributions	18,500	22,500	3,000	44,000
Republicans	12,850	20,950	2,500	36,300
No. of Cand.	*22*	*35*	*4*	*61*
House	6,850	12,450	1,000	20,300
Senate	6,000	8,500	1,500	16,000
Democrats	5,650	1,550	500	7,700
No. of Cand.	*13*	*4*	*1*	*18*
House	5,650	1,550	500	7,700
Senate	0	0	0	0
Incumbents	15,750	16,450	3,000	35,200
Challengers	1,550	500	0	2,050
Open Seat	1,200	5,550	0	6,750
Winners	17,000	18,250	n/a	35,250
Losers	1,500	4,250	n/a	5,750

Stone Container Corp.

*Phone: (312) 346-6600 * Fax: (312) 580-2272*
150 N. Michigan Ave., Chicago, IL 60601-7568
Web: www.stonecontainer.com

Stone Container is the world's largest maker of paperboard and paper packaging materials. The publicly traded company produces folding cartons, bags, sacks and containerboard. Stone Container has operations in 16 countries and employs 24,200 workers. It reported 1997 sales of $4.8 billion.

The Federal Trade Commission ruled in February 1998 that Stone Container tried to orchestrate an industry-wide price increase for linerboard in 1993. A settlement agreement stipulates that the company cannot urge any competitor to raise or fix a price for linerboard, which is used to make boxes.

A major Republican contributor during the 1995-96 election cycle, Stone Container gave just more than half of its contributions to winning candidates. The company spent nearly the same amount on challengers, incumbents and open races. The top recipients were Sen. Gordon H. Smith, R-Ore., 1996 Senate candidate Dennis Rehberg of Montana and former Rep. Michael Patrick Flanagan, R-Ill. Rep. Gene Taylor, D-Miss., was the leading Democratic recipient.

Stone Container Corp. Political Action Committee (C00117424) *Address: same as sponsor * Contact: Gordon Cooper * Treasurer: Thomas P. Cutilletta*

	1993-94	1995-96	1997	Totals
Receipts	$276,427	$254,926	$105,917	$637,270
Disburse	97,395	290,364	25,071	412,830
Cash	323,805	362,040	442,891	n/a
Contributions	80,000	163,000	3,100	246,100
Republicans	75,000	157,000	1,100	233,100
No. of Cand.	*37*	*62*	*2*	*101*
House	53,500	102,500	600	156,600
Senate	21,500	54,500	500	76,500
Democrats	5,000	6,000	2,000	13,000
No. of Cand.	*7*	*4*	*2*	*13*
House	4,000	3,000	1,000	8,000
Senate	1,000	3,000	1,000	5,000
Incumbents	29,500	60,000	3,100	92,600
Challengers	28,000	44,500	0	72,500
Open Seat	22,500	56,500	0	79,000
Winners	61,500	95,500	n/a	157,000
Losers	18,500	67,500	n/a	86,000

Sun Studs Inc.

*Phone: (541) 673-0141 * Fax: (541) 440-2516*
P.O. Box 1127, Roseburg, OR 97470

Sun Studs is a private company that manufactures veneer and lumber products. It is affiliated with Lone Rock Timber Co., one of its sources of timber.

Sun Studs Inc. Political Action Committee (C00126789) *Address: same as sponsor * Contact: Richard F. Sohn, Lands Manager * Treasurer: Lios J. Trento*

	1993-94	1995-96	1997	Totals
Receipts	$5,048	$9,429	$2,164	$16,641
Disburse	4,542	9,955	1,620	16,117
Cash	620	98	643	n/a
Contributions	4,432	9,769	1,500	15,701
Republicans	500	8,025	1,500	10,025
No. of Cand.	*1*	*5*	*2*	*8*
House	0	2,525	500	3,025
Senate	500	5,500	1,000	7,000
Democrats	3,932	1,744	0	5,676
No. of Cand.	*3*	*3*	*0*	*6*
House	3,932	744	0	4,676
Senate	0	1,000	0	1,000
Incumbents	2,682	3,269	1,500	7,451
Challengers	250	500	0	750
Open Seat	1,500	6,000	0	7,500
Winners	2,682	8,244	n/a	10,926
Losers	1,750	1,525	n/a	3,275

Union Camp Corp.

*Phone: (973) 628-2527 * Fax: (973) 628-2705*
1600 Valley Rd., Wayne, NJ 07470
*Web: www.unioncamp.com * E-mail: tom_lambrix@ucamp.com*

Union Camp, based in Wayne, N.J., manufactures paper, packaging, chemicals and wood products and engages in land development. A member of the Fortune 500, Union Camp has 18,000 employees and reported $4.4 billion in 1997 sales.

The publicly traded company owns about 1.5 million acres of trees in Alabama, Georgia, North and South Carolina and Virginia, which provide the raw material base for most of its products.

Union Camp operates four pulp and paper mills in the southeastern United States. Two mills produce white paper for business forms, printing and direct mail, while the others produce unbleached paper and linerboard primarily for packaging materials. Other domestic manufacturing plants include nine building products operations, four chemical plants and five flavors and fragrances facilities.

The company's Branigar real estate subsidiary has developed communities including: The Landings and Champion Hills near Hendersonville, N.C.; Port Antiqua in the Florida Keys; The Windings of Ferson Creek near St. Charles, Ill.; Lake Redstone in Chicago; Whispering Pines in central Florida; and one of the largest planned communities in the country, The Galena Territory in Galena, Ill.

Subsidiaries: Union Camp Technology, Alling & Cory Co., The Branigar Organization and Bush Boake Allen.

Union Camp Corp. PAC (C00039479) *Phone: (202) 785-0320 * Fax: (202) 659-8169 * 1730 Rhode Island Ave., Suite 206, Washington, DC 20036 * Treasurer: Donald W. Barney*

*Contact: Tom Lambrix, PAC Chairman * Phone: (973) 628-2527*

	1993-94	1995-96	1997	Totals
Receipts	$86,806	$72,678	$33,691	$193,175
Disburse	81,325	78,612	10,642	170,579
Cash	10,536	4,613	27,667	n/a
Contributions	66,175	68,930	8,642	143,747
Republicans	59,625	62,930	7,642	130,197
No. of Cand.	*36*	*55*	*8*	*99*
House	16,625	28,100	3,642	48,367
Senate	43,000	34,830	4,000	81,830
Democrats	6,550	6,000	1,000	13,550
No. of Cand.	*13*	*7*	*1*	*21*
House	6,550	3,000	0	9,550
Senate	0	3,000	1,000	4,000
Incumbents	29,675	38,130	7,642	75,447
Challengers	13,500	2,000	0	15,500
Open Seat	23,000	28,800	1,000	52,800
Winners	52,375	46,680	n/a	99,055
Losers	13,800	22,250	n/a	36,050

Westvaco Corp.

*Phone: (212) 688-5000 * Fax: (212) 318-5055*
299 Park Ave., New York, NY 10171
Web: www.westvaco.com

One of the nation's largest producers of envelopes, Westvaco also makes paper, packaging and specialty chemicals. The publicly traded company posted sales of $2.9 billion in 1997.

The company owns 1.5 million acres of timberlands in the United States and Brazil and has manufacturing facilities there, as well as in the Czech Republic. International business accounts for 25 percent of Westvaco's sales and the company has customers in more than 70 countries.

Headquartered in New York, Westvaco has manufacturing operations in the mid-Atlantic and Southeast.

Westvaco Corp. Political Participation Program (C00065987) *Address: same as sponsor * Treasurer: John F. Blundell*

	1993-94	1995-96	1997	Totals
Receipts	$213,926	$183,914	$80,476	$478,316
Disburse	229,567	209,271	21,439	460,277
Cash	99,568	74,222	133,267	n/a
Contributions	179,500	174,500	5,500	359,500
Republicans	149,000	161,000	5,500	315,500
No. of Cand.	*51*	*68*	*3*	*122*
House	78,000	97,500	5,500	181,000
Senate	71,000	63,500	0	134,500
Democrats	30,500	13,500	0	44,000
No. of Cand.	*12*	*7*	*0*	*19*
House	22,500	11,000	0	33,500
Senate	8,000	2,500	0	10,500
Incumbents	118,000	124,500	5,500	248,000
Challengers	22,000	20,500	0	42,500
Open Seat	39,500	29,500	0	69,000
Winners	167,500	144,500	n/a	312,000
Losers	12,000	30,000	n/a	42,000

Weyerhaeuser Co.

*Phone: (253) 924-3943 * Fax: (253) 924-2685*
33663 Weyerhaeuser Way S., Federal Way, WA 98003
Web: www.weyerhaeuser.com

Weyerhaeuser is the largest private owner of timber in the United States, with about 5.5 million acres of timberland in the western and southern United States and cutting rights to about 23 million acres in Canada. The company's timberland is located primarily in Washington state, Oregon, North Carolina, Mississippi, Alabama, Louisiana, Oklahoma, Arkansas and Georgia.

In addition to managing its timberlands, Weyerhaeuser manufactures pulp, paper and packaging materials and produces such wood products as logs, wood chips and building products. The company also develops residential real estate, including single-family homes and planned communities.

Almost all of Weyerhaeuser's $11.2 billion in 1997 sales came from U.S. markets, but it is working to increase its overseas operations. The public company employs 40,000 people in the United States and Canada.

Weyerhaeuser Co. Political Action Committee (C00007948)
*Phone: (202) 293-7222 * Fax: (202) 293-2955 * 1100 Connecticut Ave. N.W., Suite 530, Washington, DC 20036 * Contact: Mack L. Hogan, V.P. of Gov. Affairs * Phone: (253) 924-3943 * Treasurer: Annis Upshur*

	1993-94	1995-96	1997	Totals
Receipts	$61,134	$107,459	$60,889	$229,482
Disburse	52,972	110,258	23,031	186,261
Cash	18,332	15,533	53,394	n/a
Contributions	42,584	86,054	22,528	151,166
Republicans	21,421	78,554	20,028	120,003
No. of Cand.	*13*	*50*	*19*	*82*
House	12,974	54,455	11,029	78,458
Senate	8,447	24,099	8,999	41,545
Democrats	21,163	7,500	2,500	31,163
No. of Cand.	*9*	*5*	*3*	*17*
House	21,163	6,500	1,500	29,163
Senate	0	1,000	1,000	2,000
Incumbents	34,484	72,554	22,528	129,566
Challengers	5,000	3,000	0	8,000
Open Seat	2,000	10,500	0	12,500
Winners	27,721	69,324	n/a	97,045
Losers	14,863	16,730	n/a	31,593

Weyerhaeuser Co. Special Shareholders Political Action Committee (C00008425) *Phone: (253) 924-3943 * Fax: (253) 924-2685 * 2100 First National Bank Bldg., St. Paul, MN 55101 * Contact: Mack L. Hogan, V.P. of Gov. Affairs * Treasurer: Jeanne Christenson*

Weyerhaeuser Co. Special Shareholders PAC, based in Minnesota, is associated with another Weyerhaeuser PAC located in Washington state.

	1993-94	1995-96	1997	Totals
Receipts	$74,475	$72,936	$24,325	$171,736
Disburse	76,400	71,700	0	148,100
Cash	7,688	8,924	33,249	n/a
Contributions	74,950	69,200	-1500	142,650
Republicans	50,050	65,200	-1500	113,750
No. of Cand.	*49*	*58*	*1*	*108*
House	27,550	29,700	0	57,250
Senate	22,500	35,500	-1500	56,500
Democrats	24,900	4,000	0	28,900
No. of Cand.	*32*	*7*	*0*	*39*
House	23,900	3,500	0	27,400
Senate	1,000	500	0	1,500
Incumbents	44,050	34,500	-1500	77,050
Challengers	2,500	8,500	0	11,000
Open Seat	28,400	26,200	0	54,600
Winners	59,550	57,200	n/a	116,750
Losers	15,400	12,000	n/a	27,400

Willamette Industries Inc.

*Phone: (503) 227-5581 * Fax: (503) 273-5608*
1300 S.W. Fifth Ave., Suite 3800, Portland, OR 97201
Web: www.wii.com

Willamette Industries is an integrated forest products company which operates 103 mills and manufacturing plants in 23 states including Oregon, Louisiana, North Carolina, South Carolina and Kentucky. It has international operations in Mexico and Ireland. The company also owns or controls 1.8 million acres of timberland in the northwestern and southern United States.

Founded in 1906, the public company employed more than 13,000 people as of 1996 and had 1997 sales of $3.4 billion, with net earnings of nearly $73 million.

Willamette manufactures a variety of paper products, as well as building materials such as lumber, plywood and engineered wood products. The company also manufactures its own ink and printing plates for custom-made products.

WilPAC Willamette Industries Inc. Political Action Committee (C00112664) *Address: same as sponsor * Contact: Craig Hanneman, Dir. of Gov. Affairs * Treasurer: Greig Goddard*

	1993-94	1995-96	1997	Totals
Receipts	$136,190	$141,292	$62,914	$340,396
Disburse	139,249	134,692	736	274,677
Cash	6,243	12,843	75,021	n/a
Contributions	106,500	116,000	0	222,500
Republicans	99,750	109,750	0	209,500
No. of Cand.	*61*	*45*	*0*	*106*
House	54,750	60,750	0	115,500
Senate	45,000	49,000	0	94,000
Democrats	6,750	6,250	0	13,000
No. of Cand.	*7*	*6*	*0*	*13*
House	6,750	6,250	0	13,000
Senate	0	0	0	0
Incumbents	29,250	35,500	0	64,750
Challengers	28,750	10,000	0	38,750
Open Seat	47,000	70,500	0	117,500
Winners	96,750	95,500	n/a	192,250
Losers	9,750	20,500	n/a	30,250

Livestock

American Horse Council

*Phone: (202) 296-4031 * Fax: (202) 296-1970*
1700 K St. N.W., Suite 300, Washington, DC 20006
E-mail: ahc@horsecouncil.com

The American Horse Council is a coalition of equestrian and horse racing organizations from throughout the nation. Its members include the American Quarter Horse Association, Palomino Horse Breeders of America, the United States Trotting Association and the American Saddlebred Horse Association. A 1997 AHC study reported that the horse industry contributed more than $25 billion to the United States' gross domestic product in 1996.

American Horse Council Inc. Committee On Legislation And Taxation (COLT) (C00089987) *Address: same as sponsor * Contact: Steve Ralls, Dir. of Legislative Affairs * Treasurer: James J. Hickey Jr.*

	1993-94	1995-96	1997	Totals
Receipts	$890	$14,835	$40,871	$56,596
Disburse	5,800	13,450	10,625	29,875
Cash	746	2,131	32,377	n/a
Contributions	5,210	11,950	8,000	25,160
Republicans	2,400	9,500	4,350	16,250
No. of Cand.	*6*	*11*	*8*	*25*
House	1,100	4,000	2,850	7,950
Senate	1,300	5,500	1,500	8,300
Democrats	2,810	2,450	3,650	8,910
No. of Cand.	*9*	*7*	*8*	*24*
House	1,900	2,100	1,850	5,850
Senate	910	350	1,800	3,060
Incumbents	5,110	11,500	6,750	23,360
Challengers	0	450	0	450
Open Seat	100	0	1,250	1,350
Winners	4,050	11,700	n/a	15,750
Losers	1,160	250	n/a	1,410

American Sheep Industry Association

*Phone: (303) 771-3500 * Fax: (303) 771-8200*
6911 S. Yosemite St., Suite 200, Englewood, CO 80112-1414
Web: www.sheepusa.org

The American Sheep Industry Association is a federation of state organizations dedicated to promoting the well-being and profitability of the sheep industry in the United States. ASI and its members fund projects to expand the international wool market and to create retail promotions that will boost lamb sales.

In 1997, ASI urged the Department of Agriculture and Congress to establish a basic infrastructure of personnel, equipment, facilities and funds to maintain core programs like foreign animal disease preparedness, animal health monitoring and domestic livestock disease eradication and control.

American Sheep Industry Association Inc. Rams PAC (C00043059)
*Phone: (202) 484-2778 * Fax: (202) 484-0770 * 412 First St. S.E., #1, Washington, DC 20003 * Treasurer: Frank Moore*

	1993-94	1995-96	1997	Totals
Receipts	$57,179	$40,784	$9,613	$107,576
Disburse	48,593	79,479	12,553	140,625
Cash	83,377	44,683	41,744	n/a
Contributions	34,300	51,750	8,500	94,550
Republicans	20,150	42,900	8,000	71,050
No. of Cand.	*30*	*36*	*14*	*80*
House	9,300	10,650	3,000	22,950
Senate	10,850	32,250	5,000	48,100
Democrats	14,150	8,850	0	23,000
No. of Cand.	*18*	*11*	*3*	*32*
House	7,650	2,850	1,000	11,500
Senate	6,500	6,000	-1000	11,500
Incumbents	31,900	39,500	7,500	78,900
Challengers	750	3,500	0	4,250
Open Seat	2,400	8,750	0	11,150
Winners	32,300	48,750	n/a	81,050
Losers	2,000	3,000	n/a	5,000

Livestock Marketing Association

*Phone: (816) 891-0502 * Fax: (816) 891-0552*
7509 Tiffany Springs Pkwy., Kansas City, MO 64153

The Livestock Marketing Association insures option marketers that buy and sell cattle. Established in 1947, the association has 1,100 members.

Livestock Insurance Agency is a subsidiary of the LMA.

Livestock Marketing Association Political Action Committee (LMA-PAC) (C00244400) *Address: same as sponsor * Contact: Nancy Robinson, Chairman * Treasurer: Gary S. Smith*

	1993-94	1995-96	1997	Totals
Receipts	$12,310	$9,875	$6,267	$28,452
Disburse	12,801	7,951	518	21,270
Cash	1,585	3,508	9,256	n/a
Contributions	12,650	7,200	500	20,350
Republicans	5,600	5,000	0	10,600
No. of Cand.	*12*	*10*	*0*	*22*
House	2,750	3,200	0	5,950
Senate	2,850	1,800	0	4,650
Democrats	7,050	2,200	500	9,750
No. of Cand.	*12*	*4*	*1*	*17*
House	6,050	1,850	0	7,900
Senate	1,000	350	500	1,850
Incumbents	12,350	5,350	500	18,200
Challengers	0	1,350	0	1,350
Open Seat	300	500	0	800
Winners	10,650	6,850	n/a	17,500
Losers	2,000	350	n/a	2,350

National Cattlemen's Beef Association

*Phone: (303) 694-0305 * Fax: (303) 694-2851*
5420 S. Quebec St., P.O. Box 3469, Englewood, CO 80155
Web: www.beef.org

The National Cattlemen's Beef Association is a marketing and trade group for about 1 million cattle farmers and ranchers in the United States. The group's paying membership has about 40,000 individual members, 46 state associations and 27 national breed organizations. The NCBA promotes the consumption of beef, conducts market research and lobbies for the cattle-ranching industry.

The NCBA supports a federal private property rights bill which would permit landowners to take Fifth Amendment "takings" claims directly to federal court. It also favors continuing federal support for grazing land management and extending a hold on new EPA ozone standards until further research is conducted. The group opposes setting national environmental standards for the handling of animal waste, preferring state regulation. The NCBA supports "fast-track" trade authority.

The NCBA was the top livestock PAC contributor to 1996 congressional candidates. Nearly 85 percent of its contributions went to Republican candidates, and no Democrat received more than $4,125. Sen. Larry Craig, R-Idaho, and Rep. Bob Smith, R-Ore., both members of agriculture committees, were the leading recipients.

National Cattlemen's Beef Association Political Action Committee (NCBA-PAC) (C00028787) *Phone: (202) 347-0228 * Fax: (202) 638-0607 * 1310 Pennsylvania Ave. N.W., Suite 300, Washington, DC 20004-1701 * E-mail: ct@beef.org * Contact: Christine Taylor, PAC Dir. * Treasurer: Lori Pitts*

	1993-94	1995-96	1997	Totals
Receipts	$409,976	$346,324	$189,835	$946,135
Disburse	428,204	442,655	174,989	1,045,848
Cash	118,427	22,100	36,949	n/a
Contributions	363,324	397,660	148,467	909,451
Republicans	246,374	333,007	120,592	699,973
No. of Cand.	*175*	*217*	*115*	*507*
House	174,475	236,982	81,039	492,496
Senate	71,899	96,025	39,553	207,477
Democrats	115,450	64,653	26,875	206,978
No. of Cand.	*92*	*57*	*35*	*184*
House	97,150	49,313	15,875	162,338
Senate	18,300	15,340	11,000	44,640
Incumbents	266,625	296,226	146,967	709,818
Challengers	34,000	25,050	0	59,050
Open Seat	62,199	75,884	1,500	139,583
Winners	305,774	335,027	n/a	640,801
Losers	57,550	62,633	n/a	120,183

Beef PAC (Beef Political Action Committee of Texas Cattle Feeders Association) (C00015552) *Phone: (806) 358-3681 * Fax: (806) 352-6026 * 5501 W. I-40, Amarillo, TX 79106 * Web: www.tcfa.org * E-mail: brenda@tcfa.org * Treasurer: Brenda A. Higley*

Headquartered in Amarillo, Texas Cattle Feeders Association represents cattle feeders in Texas, Oklahoma and New Mexico, the largest cattle-feeding region in the nation. TCFA works on behalf of its members through state and national legislation, seminars and meetings and industry promotion and research. TCFA was formed in 1967.

Total TCFA membership is nearly 8,000. The vast majority are people who feed cattle in TCFA member feedyards; the remainder are the affiliated companies and individuals who provide goods and services required by area feedyards for operation.

In 1997, Texas, Oklahoma and New Mexico produced about 6.5 million fed cattle — 30 percent of the fed cattle produced in the United States — and contributed $14 billion to the regional economy.

	1993-94	1995-96	1997	Totals
Receipts	$202,732	$159,975	$84,875	$447,582
Disburse	212,259	156,878	37,612	406,749
Cash	13,925	17,025	64,289	n/a
Contributions	107,625	86,750	24,225	218,600
Republicans	64,425	69,500	19,225	153,150
No. of Cand.	*67*	*69*	*29*	*165*
House	44,450	50,500	10,975	105,925
Senate	19,975	19,000	8,250	47,225
Democrats	43,200	17,250	5,000	65,450
No. of Cand.	*38*	*19*	*7*	*64*
House	39,200	16,750	4,500	60,450
Senate	4,000	500	500	5,000
Incumbents	95,625	69,250	23,225	188,100
Challengers	6,000	3,000	0	9,000
Open Seat	6,000	14,000	1,000	21,000
Winners	94,325	76,250	n/a	170,575
Losers	13,300	10,500	n/a	23,800

Illinois Beef Association Political Education Committee (C00276618) *Phone: (217) 793-3535 * Fax: (217) 793-3605 * 2060 W. Iles Ave., Suite B, Springfield, IL 62704 * E-mail: ilbeef@aol.com * Contact: Terry Rush, Chairperson * Treasurer: Richard Jurgens*

The Illinois Beef Association represents 27,000 Illinois beef producers.

	1993-94	1995-96	1997	Totals
Receipts	$14,522	$12,411	$4,491	$31,424
Disburse	12,743	14,934	4,414	32,091
Cash	2,609	87	165	n/a
Contributions	8,179	5,650	1,089	14,918
Republicans	4,750	4,250	589	9,589
No. of Cand.	*5*	*9*	*2*	*16*
House	4,750	3,750	589	9,089
Senate	0	500	0	500
Democrats	3,429	1,400	500	5,329
No. of Cand.	*5*	*3*	*1*	*9*
House	3,429	0	500	3,929
Senate	0	1,400	0	1,400
Incumbents	6,079	2,450	589	9,118
Challengers	1,100	1,000	0	2,100
Open Seat	1,000	2,200	500	3,700
Winners	7,079	3,700	n/a	10,779
Losers	1,100	1,950	n/a	3,050

Contributed less than $5,000 during 1995-96 cycle:

California Cattlemen's Association PAC/Federal (C00115071)
*Phone: (916) 444-0845 * 1221 H St., Sacramento, CA 95814-1910 * Treasurer: John L. Braly*

National Pork Producers Council

*Phone: (515) 223-2600 * Fax: (515) 223-2646*
P.O. Box 10383, Des Moines, IA 50306
Web: www.nppc.org

The National Pork Producers Council represents about 85,000 producers through 44 state groups that act as trade associations for the pork industry. Interests include pork production, nutrition, the environment, trade and federal regulations.

The national organization has two affiliated state PACs, representing producers in North Carolina and Illinois.

National Pork Producers Council Pork PAC (C00201871) *Phone: (202) 347-3600 * Fax: (202) 347-5265 * 122 C St. N.W., Suite 875, Washington, DC 20001 * Contact: Kirk Ferrell, PAC Dir. * Treasurer: Jeff A. Smouse*

	1993-94	1995-96	1997	Totals
Receipts	$124,587	$154,349	$84,244	$363,180
Disburse	131,223	150,378	63,284	344,885
Cash	3,416	7,389	28,348	n/a
Contributions	124,858	109,773	44,356	278,987
Republicans	59,044	69,069	29,795	157,908
No. of Cand.	*70*	*69*	*40*	*179*
House	40,180	41,783	20,807	102,770
Senate	18,864	27,286	8,988	55,138
Democrats	63,964	40,704	13,561	118,229
No. of Cand.	*71*	*29*	*14*	*114*
House	51,702	21,789	9,561	83,052
Senate	12,262	18,915	4,000	35,177
Incumbents	110,800	79,102	43,527	233,429
Challengers	1,937	8,521	0	10,458
Open Seat	12,121	22,150	500	34,771
Winners	102,646	96,752	n/a	199,398
Losers	22,212	13,021	n/a	35,233

North Carolina Pork Producers Association Inc. Political Action Committee (NCPPA Pork PAC) (C00235184) *Phone: (919) 781-0361 * 2300 Rexwoods Dr., Suite 340, Raleigh, NC 27607 * Contact: Walter Cherry, Executive Dir. * Treasurer: Jackie G. Whitley*

	1993-94	1995-96	1997	Totals
Receipts	$34,305	$88,588	$38,806	$161,699
Disburse	62,830	70,859	5,596	139,285
Cash	20,536	38,266	71,476	n/a
Contributions	14,094	5,054	0	19,148
Republicans	6,344	3,548	0	9,892
No. of Cand.	*11*	*11*	*0*	*22*
House	4,712	2,194	0	6,906
Senate	1,632	1,354	0	2,986
Democrats	7,750	1,506	0	9,256
No. of Cand.	*11*	*8*	*0*	*19*
House	7,750	1,256	0	9,006
Senate	0	250	0	250
Incumbents	10,844	4,204	0	15,048
Challengers	750	750	0	1,500
Open Seat	2,500	100	0	2,600
Winners	10,079	4,048	n/a	14,127
Losers	4,015	1,006	n/a	5,021

Illinois Pork Producers Association Political Action Committee (C00175976) *Phone: (217) 529-3100 * Fax: (217) 529-1771 * 6411 S. Sixth St., Springfield, IL 62707-8642 * Contact: Roger Brown, Chairperson * Treasurer: Lary Butcher*

	1993-94	1995-96	1997	Totals
Receipts	$36,277	$19,832	$12,106	$68,215
Disburse	21,425	36,506	7,310	65,241
Cash	16,824	0	24,376	n/a
Contributions	5,395	5,950	1,300	12,645
Republicans	2,945	4,700	1,000	8,645
No. of Cand.	*4*	*10*	*2*	*16*
House	2,945	4,050	1,000	7,995
Senate	0	650	0	650
Democrats	2,450	1,250	300	4,000
No. of Cand.	*5*	*1*	*2*	*8*
House	1,350	0	300	1,650
Senate	1,100	1,250	0	2,350
Incumbents	3,770	3,000	1,000	7,770
Challengers	100	650	0	750
Open Seat	1,525	2,300	300	4,125
Winners	5,295	4,450	n/a	9,745
Losers	100	1,500	n/a	1,600

Tennessee Walking Horse Breeders & Exhibitors Association

*Phone: (931) 359-1574 * Fax: (931) 359-7530*
2033 Richard Jones Rd., Nashville, TN 37215
Web: comtch.iea.com/~adlinkex/HP/695articles/twhbea.html

The Tennessee Walking Horse Breeders & Exhibitors Association is dedicated to the promotion of Tennessee walking horses, popular trail and show horses known for their smooth gait and gentle dispositions.

The organization's primary goals are to record the pedigrees of the horses and maintain the purity of the breed. The association has about 15,000 members.

Tennessee Walking Horse Breeders & Exhibitors Association (C00135731) *Address: same as sponsor * Contact: Stephen B. Smith, President * Treasurer: David L. Howard*

	1993-94	1995-96	1997	Totals
Receipts	$105,835	$126,368	$0	$232,203
Disburse	103,465	137,557	36,982	278,004
Cash	70,019	58,827	21,845	n/a
Contributions	34,000	55,000	25,000	114,000
Republicans	12,500	27,000	10,000	49,500
No. of Cand.	*4*	*5*	*2*	*11*
House	3,500	6,000	0	9,500
Senate	9,000	21,000	10,000	40,000
Democrats	21,500	28,000	15,000	64,500
No. of Cand.	*5*	*5*	*3*	*13*
House	20,500	28,000	15,000	63,500
Senate	1,000	0	0	1,000
Incumbents	27,000	54,000	25,000	106,000
Challengers	5,000	0	0	5,000
Open Seat	2,000	1,000	0	3,000
Winners	31,000	54,000	n/a	85,000
Losers	3,000	1,000	n/a	4,000

Texas & Southwestern Cattle Raisers Association

*Phone: (817) 332-7064 * Fax: (817) 338-4813*
1301 W. Seventh St., Fort Worth, TX 76102

Texas & Southwestern Cattle Raisers Association represents about 13,000 ranchers in Texas and, in smaller numbers, Oklahoma and New Mexico.

The association is interested in legislation and regulations affecting the cattle industry, as well as issues like inheritance taxes.

The association was founded in 1877 to protect Texas cattlemen from having their herds stolen.

Texas & Southwestern Cattle Raisers Association PAC (C00211524) *Address: same as sponsor * Contact: C. Coney Burgess, Chairman * Treasurer: Steve Munday*

	1993-94	1995-96	1997	Totals
Receipts	$249,402	$205,356	$66,896	$521,654
Disburse	233,524	215,384	49,226	498,134
Cash	16,962	6,937	24,608	n/a
Contributions	43,199	41,750	5,900	90,849
Republicans	32,499	35,750	3,900	72,149
No. of Cand.	*24*	*44*	*4*	*72*
House	15,500	26,250	2,900	44,650
Senate	16,999	9,500	1,000	27,499
Democrats	10,700	6,000	2,000	18,700
No. of Cand.	*9*	*8*	*4*	*21*
House	10,700	6,000	2,000	18,700
Senate	0	0	0	0
Incumbents	32,949	32,250	4,900	70,099
Challengers	4,500	500	1,000	6,000
Open Seat	5,750	9,000	0	14,750
Winners	34,199	34,750	n/a	68,949
Losers	9,000	7,000	n/a	16,000

True Companies

*Phone: (307) 237-9301 * Fax: (307) 266-0373*
P.O. Box 2360, Casper, WY 82602

True Companies is a 50-year-old, family-owned company operating throughout the Rocky Mountain region in oil and gas exploration, oil field supply, pipelines, trucking, banking and ranching. The Wyoming-based company has about 500 employees.

True Companies Responsible Government Committee (C00034728) *Address: same as sponsor * Contact: Ervin Schroeder, Chief Accountant * Treasurer: Terry Santoni*

	1993-94	1995-96	1997	Totals
Receipts	$13,248	$11,550	$5,015	$29,813
Disburse	11,900	11,500	1,000	24,400
Cash	1,404	1,458	5,474	n/a
Contributions	6,400	7,200	0	13,600
Republicans	6,400	7,200	0	13,600
No. of Cand.	*18*	*19*	*0*	*37*
House	4,500	3,500	0	8,000
Senate	1,900	3,700	0	5,600
Democrats	0	0	0	0
No. of Cand.	*0*	*0*	*0*	*0*
House	0	0	0	0
Senate	0	0	0	0
Incumbents	0	2,700	0	2,700
Challengers	700	1,200	0	1,900
Open Seat	5,700	3,300	0	9,000
Winners	6,000	5,400	n/a	11,400
Losers	400	1,800	n/a	2,200

Poultry & Eggs

California Poultry Industry Federation

*Phone: (209) 576-6355 * Fax: (209) 576-6119*
3117- A McHenry Ave., Modesto, CA 95350
Web: www.cpif.org

California Poultry Industry Federation represents more than 97 percent of the state's turkey and chicken producers and marketers. Formed in 1990, CPIF has about 130 members and is also the representative for the California Squab Producers.

The federation addresses local, state and federal government issues concerning the poultry industry. In 1996, CPIF successfully lobbied to reform the labeling of "fresh" poultry. Poultry must now be 26 degrees Fahrenheit and above to be labeled "fresh." Previously, poultry could be frozen as low as 1 degree Fahrenheit and still carry a "fresh" label.

California Poultry Industry Federation Poultry PAC (CPIF Poultry PAC) (C00296269) *Address: same as sponsor * Treasurer: Bill Mattos*

	1993-94	1995-96	1997	Totals
Receipts	$2,655	$9,891	$6,258	$18,804
Disburse	2,500	8,350	4,500	15,350
Cash	156	1,701	3,460	n/a
Contributions	2,500	8,250	4,500	15,250
Republicans	1,000	2,500	1,000	4,500
No. of Cand.	*1*	*4*	*2*	*7*
House	1,000	2,000	1,000	4,000
Senate	0	500	0	500
Democrats	1,500	5,750	3,500	10,750
No. of Cand.	*2*	*6*	*4*	*12*
House	1,500	2,750	1,500	5,750
Senate	0	3,000	2,000	5,000
Incumbents	1,500	6,250	4,500	12,250
Challengers	1,000	500	0	1,500
Open Seat	0	1,500	0	1,500
Winners	1,500	8,250	n/a	9,750
Losers	1,000	0	n/a	1,000

Foster Poultry Farms

*Phone: (209) 394-7901 * Fax: (209) 394-6362*
P.O. Box 457, Livingston, CA 95334
Web: www.cimaged.com/fosterfarms

Foster Farms is a private, family-owned company founded in 1939. Now the largest poultry company in the western United States, it has annual sales of more than $1 billion and more than 7,000 employees.

It owns and operates hatcheries, grow-out ranches, feed mills, processing plants and delivery systems with operations in California, Oregon, Washington state and Alabama, producing chicken and turkey luncheon meats, prepared entrees and corn dogs. Foster Farms sells 750 different items in the retail and food service markets in the United States and abroad.

Foster Poultry Farms PAC (C00303628) *Address: same as sponsor * Contact: Robert Fox, President and CEO * Treasurer: Randall C. Boyce*

	1993-94	1995-96	1997	Totals
Receipts	$0	$40,081	$264	$40,345
Disburse	0	14,783	1,500	16,283
Cash	0	25,279	24,044	n/a
Contributions	0	13,500	1,500	15,000
Republicans	0	5,500	0	5,500
No. of Cand.	*0*	*4*	*0*	*4*
House	0	5,500	0	5,500
Senate	0	0	0	0
Democrats	0	8,000	1,500	9,500
No. of Cand.	*0*	*4*	*2*	*6*
House	0	5,500	500	6,000
Senate	0	2,500	1,000	3,500
Incumbents	0	12,000	1,500	13,500
Challengers	0	1,500	0	1,500
Open Seat	0	0	0	0
Winners	0	13,500	n/a	13,500
Losers	0	0	n/a	0

Gold Kist

*Phone: (770) 393-5091 * Fax: (770) 353-5347*
P.O. Box 2210, Atlanta, GA 30301
Web: www.goldkist.com

With 1997 sales of $2.3 billion, Gold Kist is the second-largest poultry processor in the United States. The farm cooperative also produces pork, manufactures feed and markets farm supplies.

Gold Kist has 30,000 farmer members. In addition to its headquarters in Atlanta, it operates in 16 states throughout the Southeast and employs about 17,500 people.

Gold Kist Political Action for Farmers Inc. (C00113902) *Address: same as sponsor * Treasurer: Paul G. Brower*

	1993-94	1995-96	1997	Totals
Receipts	$62,697	$77,663	$24,346	$164,706
Disburse	44,750	92,631	22,000	159,381
Cash	32,888	17,921	20,268	n/a
Contributions	31,750	78,581	16,500	126,831
Republicans	17,050	63,581	13,000	93,631
No. of Cand.	*15*	*24*	*13*	*52*
House	15,050	33,350	11,500	59,900
Senate	2,000	30,231	1,500	33,731
Democrats	14,700	15,000	3,500	33,200
No. of Cand.	*14*	*10*	*4*	*28*
House	14,700	5,500	2,500	22,700
Senate	0	9,500	1,000	10,500
Incumbents	25,500	38,581	16,000	80,081
Challengers	3,500	8,500	0	12,000
Open Seat	2,500	31,000	0	33,500
Winners	26,700	51,581	n/a	78,281
Losers	5,050	27,000	n/a	32,050

National Broiler Council

*Phone: (202) 296-2622 * Fax: (202) 293-4005*
1155 15th St. N.W., Suite 614, Washington, DC 20005
Web: www.eatchicken.com

The National Broiler Council is the nonprofit trade association for the broiler chicken industry. Membership includes broiler producer/processors, poultry distributors and allied firms that supply goods and services to the industry. Members of the council produce, process and market about 95 percent of all U.S. broiler chickens.

National Broiler Council Political Action Committee (C00034272) *Address: same as sponsor * Treasurer: George B. Watts*

	1993-94	1995-96	1997	Totals
Receipts	$157,874	$134,432	$69,052	$361,358
Disburse	158,843	144,228	59,907	362,978
Cash	39,217	29,333	38,478	n/a
Contributions	153,750	136,000	55,000	344,750
Republicans	94,100	109,000	38,500	241,600
No. of Cand.	*79*	*84*	*45*	*208*
House	56,100	63,000	24,000	143,100
Senate	38,000	46,000	14,500	98,500
Democrats	57,650	27,000	15,000	99,650
No. of Cand.	*47*	*25*	*18*	*90*
House	51,650	20,000	11,000	82,650
Senate	6,000	7,000	4,000	17,000
Incumbents	131,750	109,500	54,000	295,250
Challengers	6,000	4,000	0	10,000
Open Seat	16,000	22,000	500	38,500
Winners	131,150	118,500	n/a	249,650
Losers	22,600	17,500	n/a	40,100

National Turkey Federation

*Phone: (202) 898-0100 x226 * Fax: (202) 898-0203*
1225 New York Ave. N.W., Suite 400, Washington, DC 20005
Web: www.turkeyfed.org

The National Turkey Federation represents turkey growers, hatcheries, breeders and processors. The group promotes turkey consumption and monitors legislation and regulations that affect the industry. It also develops consumer education and information resources for the public and aids members in their sales and marketing efforts.

The NTF's members include Cargill Inc., Cooper Foods Inc. and Norbest Inc.

National Turkey Federation Political Action Committee (TurPAC) (C00076182) *Address: same as sponsor * Treasurer: Stuart E. Proctor Jr.*

	1993-94	1995-96	1997	Totals
Receipts	$66,410	$67,952	$39,454	$173,816
Disburse	53,401	75,896	34,750	164,047
Cash	36,849	28,909	33,614	n/a
Contributions	52,400	75,250	34,750	162,400
Republicans	25,100	54,750	22,000	101,850
No. of Cand.	*30*	*46*	*30*	*106*
House	18,600	35,250	15,500	69,350
Senate	6,500	19,500	6,500	32,500
Democrats	24,150	20,500	10,550	55,200
No. of Cand.	*29*	*17*	*16*	*62*
House	21,150	17,000	9,550	47,700
Senate	3,000	3,500	1,000	7,500
Incumbents	47,800	66,250	34,750	148,800
Challengers	1,750	4,000	0	5,750
Open Seat	2,850	5,000	0	7,850
Winners	44,850	70,250	n/a	115,100
Losers	7,550	5,000	n/a	12,550

Seaboard Corp.

*Phone: (913) 676-8800 * Fax: (913) 676-8872*
9000 W. 67th St., Shawnee Mission, KS 66201
Web: www.seaboardcorp.com

Headquartered in Shawnee Mission, Kan., Seaboard is ranked among the top 10 U.S. producers of both poultry and hogs. Its poultry plants slaughter more than 230 million birds annually. A public company, Seaboard has about 10,800 employees. It reported 1996 sales of $1.4 billion.

Seaboard's brands include Gold-n-Fresh and Easy Entrees chicken, which is sold mostly in the East and overseas. Seaboard also operates an ocean liner cargo service in the Caribbean and owns a bakery in Puerto Rico.

Overseas, it trades grains and seeds, raises and processes shrimp, brokers fruits and vegetables, makes polypropylene bags, operates power plants and feed mills and grows sugar cane. Seaboard has manufacturing plants in 17 foreign countries.

Seaboard Corp. Political Action Committee (C00246736) *Phone: (202) 452-7960 * Fax: (202) 452-7942 * 1776 K St. N.W., Washington, DC 20006 * Contact: Ralph Moss, Dir. of Gov. Affairs * Treasurer: David M. Dannov*

	1993-94	1995-96	1997	Totals
Receipts	$21,650	$42,056	$20,001	$83,707
Disburse	20,828	35,538	19,802	76,168
Cash	821	7,341	7,540	n/a
Contributions	16,250	24,150	12,100	52,500
Republicans	8,000	18,950	8,600	35,550
No. of Cand.	*7*	*15*	*11*	*33*
House	5,500	10,450	6,350	22,300
Senate	2,500	8,500	2,250	13,250
Democrats	8,250	5,200	3,500	16,950
No. of Cand.	*12*	*6*	*4*	*22*
House	6,250	5,200	3,500	14,950
Senate	2,000	0	0	2,000
Incumbents	10,250	20,350	12,100	42,700
Challengers	500	1,000	0	1,500
Open Seat	5,500	2,800	0	8,300
Winners	10,000	20,650	n/a	30,650
Losers	6,250	3,500	n/a	9,750

Tyson Foods

*Phone: (501) 290-3865 * Fax: (501) 290-4061*
P.O. Box 2020, Springdale, AR 72765
Web: www.tyson.com

Arkansas-based Tyson Foods is the world's largest poultry producer, processing more than 2 billion chickens a year. It bought competitor Hudson Foods in January 1998. The company also sells seafood, animal feed, pet food and Mexican food products, such as flour and corn tortillas and chips, under the Mexican Original line. Tyson has 73,000 employees and reported sales of $8 billion in 1997.

In January 1998, Tyson agreed to pay $6 million in penalties as it pleaded guilty to a charge of giving $12,000 in illegal gifts to former Secretary of Agriculture Mike Espy. Prosecutors charged that Tyson Foods broke the law by giving Espy a series of gifts, including tickets to a football playoff game in Dallas in January 1994, a $1,200 scholarship for Espy's girlfriend and an invitation to a private Tyson Foods party.

Senior chairman Don Tyson, son of the founder, controls the publicly traded company.

Tyson Foods Inc. Political Action Committee (TyPAC) (C00169821) *Address: same as sponsor * Contact: Archie Shaiffer, Chairman * Treasurer: Gary Wilks*

	1993-94	1995-96	1997	Totals
Receipts	$217,420	$126,471	$41,378	$385,269
Disburse	196,352	156,135	25,982	378,469
Cash	37,912	9,294	24,691	n/a
Contributions	158,400	122,700	21,500	302,600
Republicans	30,200	71,450	13,000	114,650
No. of Cand.	*29*	*59*	*15*	*103*
House	13,600	35,750	9,000	58,350
Senate	16,600	35,700	4,000	56,300
Democrats	127,700	51,250	8,500	187,450
No. of Cand.	*100*	*47*	*11*	*158*
House	84,200	26,750	4,000	114,950
Senate	43,500	24,500	4,500	72,500
Incumbents	137,900	72,450	21,500	231,850
Challengers	5,500	4,250	0	9,750
Open Seat	13,500	45,500	0	59,000
Winners	103,300	86,450	n/a	189,750
Losers	55,100	36,250	n/a	91,350

United Egg Association

*Phone: (770) 587-5871 * Fax: (770) 587-0041*
1303 Hightower Trail, Suite 200, Atlanta, GA 30350
E-mail: alpope@mindspring.com

The United Egg Association is a trade association that represents members of the egg industry nationwide. One becomes a member of the association by contributing money to the organization's PAC. Several of the association's members are also members of the United Egg Producers, an egg cooperative. A spokesperson for the United Egg Association was unsure as to how many members the association had.

United Egg Association Political Action Committee (EggPAC) (C00172841) *Address: same as sponsor * Treasurer: Albert E. Pope*

	1993-94	1995-96	1997	Totals
Receipts	$96,713	$109,605	$54,525	$260,843
Disburse	121,802	117,828	59,315	298,945
Cash	55,576	47,357	42,567	n/a
Contributions	113,400	110,900	57,800	282,100
Republicans	48,700	81,850	33,300	163,850
No. of Cand.	*38*	*65*	*32*	*135*
House	33,700	53,750	28,000	115,450
Senate	15,000	28,100	5,300	48,400
Democrats	62,700	29,050	23,500	115,250
No. of Cand.	*37*	*27*	*28*	*92*
House	49,700	24,050	16,000	89,750
Senate	13,000	5,000	7,500	25,500
Incumbents	106,400	88,300	57,800	252,500
Challengers	0	7,100	0	7,100
Open Seat	7,000	15,500	0	22,500
Winners	94,400	104,300	n/a	198,700
Losers	19,000	6,600	n/a	25,600

Tobacco

American Wholesale Marketers Association

*Phone: (202) 463-2124 * Fax: (202) 467-0559*
1128 16th St. N.W., Washington, DC 20036
*Web: www.awmanet.org * E-mail: jackiec@awmanet.org*

The American Wholesale Marketers Association represents more than 3,000 companies that distribute and sell tobacco, candy and other products sold mainly in convenience stores across the United States. Nearly 4,000 different products are sold by AWMA members. The group was formerly known as the National Candy Wholesalers Association and the National Association of Tobacco Distributors.

American Wholesale Marketers Association Whole-PAC (C00174391) *Address: same as sponsor * Treasurer: Jackie A. Cohen*

	1993-94	1995-96	1997	Totals
Receipts	$23,654	$17,727	$14,286	$55,667
Disburse	36,050	11,971	5,648	53,669
Cash	10,927	17,694	26,338	n/a
Contributions	5,550	5,400	2,648	13,598
Republicans	4,100	5,400	2,648	12,148
No. of Cand.	*6*	*4*	*6*	*16*
House	2,100	2,300	2,648	7,048
Senate	2,000	3,100	0	5,100
Democrats	1,450	0	0	1,450
No. of Cand.	*3*	*0*	*0*	*3*
House	1,450	0	0	1,450
Senate	0	0	0	0
Incumbents	4,200	0	2,000	6,200
Challengers	500	2,300	0	2,800
Open Seat	850	3,100	648	4,598
Winners	4,550	0	n/a	4,550
Losers	1,000	5,400	n/a	6,400

Asworth Corp.

813 Ridgelake Blvd., Memphis, TN 38120

The major contributors to Asworth's PAC are employees of Conwood Co. LP, a Tennessee subsidiary of H Group Holding Inc. Conwood produces smokeless tobacco under the Kodiak brand name. PAC Treasurer Edwin S. Roberson is the vice president and chief financial officer of Conwood.

H Group Holding is the private holding company of the Pritzker family, which also controls Hyatt Hotels and Classic Residence assisted living facilities. A 1997 article in Forbes magazine estimated the fortune of brothers Jay and Robert Pritzker at about $6 billion. In addition, Jay Pritzker was named by the National Rifle Association as a corporate executive who has "used the company name while actively supporting anti-gun proposals or organizations."

Asworth Corp. Political Action Committee (CorPAC) (C00317883) *Address: same as sponsor * Treasurer: Edwin S. Roberson*

	1993-94	1995-96	1997	Totals
Receipts	$0	$21,570	$35,892	$57,462
Disburse	0	16,113	19,534	35,647
Cash	0	5,456	21,814	n/a
Contributions	0	14,000	10,500	24,500
Republicans	0	12,000	7,500	19,500
No. of Cand.	*0*	*16*	*9*	*25*
House	0	7,250	6,500	13,750
Senate	0	4,750	1,000	5,750
Democrats	0	2,000	3,000	5,000
No. of Cand.	*0*	*3*	*4*	*7*
House	0	1,000	2,000	3,000
Senate	0	1,000	1,000	2,000
Incumbents	0	7,000	9,500	16,500
Challengers	0	3,000	0	3,000
Open Seat	0	4,000	1,000	5,000
Winners	0	8,250	n/a	8,250
Losers	0	5,750	n/a	5,750

Brown & Williamson Tobacco

*Phone: (502) 568-7269 * Fax: (502) 568-8262*
P.O. Box 35090, Louisville, KY 40232

Brown & Williamson Tobacco Corp. is the nation's third-largest maker and marketer of tobacco products. Headquartered in Louisville, Ky., the company is a subsidiary of B.A.T. Industries Ltd., the No. 2 cigarette maker in the world.

Brown & Williamson produces Viceroy, Lucky Strike and Kool cigarettes and has a 16 percent share of the United States cigarette market. Its parent corporation makes Pall Mall and Benson & Hedges brands. B.A.T., a public company which also offers financial services, is planning to spin off its tobacco interests.

The company opposes a proposed national tobacco settlement and a bill by Sen. Kent Conrad, D-N.D., that would impose higher taxes and marketing restrictions on the tobacco industry.

Brown & Williamson ranked fourth among tobacco companies in PAC contributions to 1996 congressional candidates. It increased its total contributions 91 percent from 1994 to 1996. The company spent most of its money on incumbent and Republican candidates. The top recipient was Sen. Jesse Helms, R-N.C., who received $10,000. Former Rep. Mike Ward, D-Ky., who lost to Rep. Anne M. Northrup, R-Ky., got $9,000 from Brown & Williamson. Fourteen candidates received at least $5,000.

Brown & Williamson Tobacco Corp. Employee Political Action Committee (also known as EmPAC) (C00087791) *Address: same as sponsor * Treasurer: Michael J. Shannon*

	1993-94	1995-96	1997	Totals
Receipts	$170,169	$512,562	$245,962	$928,693
Disburse	224,650	492,012	175,300	891,962
Cash	22,612	43,168	113,831	n/a
Contributions	194,200	375,000	130,500	699,700
Republicans	118,000	303,500	100,000	521,500
No. of Cand.	*131*	*207*	*85*	*423*
House	85,500	219,750	59,000	364,250
Senate	32,500	83,750	41,000	157,250
Democrats	75,700	71,500	30,000	177,200
No. of Cand.	*85*	*47*	*28*	*160*
House	64,700	66,000	23,000	153,700
Senate	11,000	5,500	7,000	23,500
Incumbents	164,200	302,000	116,000	582,200
Challengers	15,000	21,000	4,500	40,500
Open Seat	15,000	51,000	10,000	76,000
Winners	158,200	267,500	n/a	425,700
Losers	36,000	107,500	n/a	143,500

The Cigar Association of America

Phone: (202) 223-8204
1100 17th St. N.W., Suite 504, Washington, DC 20036

The Cigar Association of America is the national trade group for cigar manufacturers and importers in the United States. According to the group, more than 10 million Americans are cigar smokers; most are men.

The group compiles statistics and serves as the industry's spokesperson before the federal government. The Food and Drug Administration's initial regulatory proposals for tobacco products did not cover cigars.

Cigar-PAC of The Cigar Association of America Inc. (C00121350) *Address: same as sponsor * Treasurer: Norman F. Sharp*

	1993-94	1995-96	1997	Totals
Receipts	$16,065	$15,898	$7,425	$39,388
Disburse	16,968	15,077	4,765	36,810
Cash	179	997	3,656	n/a
Contributions	15,400	15,000	4,000	34,400
Republicans	5,350	8,000	1,500	14,850
No. of Cand.	*9*	*11*	*2*	*22*
House	3,850	6,500	1,500	11,850
Senate	1,500	1,500	0	3,000
Democrats	10,050	7,000	2,500	19,550
No. of Cand.	*13*	*10*	*4*	*27*
House	9,050	6,000	2,500	17,550
Senate	1,000	1,000	0	2,000
Incumbents	14,400	12,200	4,000	30,600
Challengers	500	300	0	800
Open Seat	500	2,000	0	2,500
Winners	12,650	9,700	n/a	22,350
Losers	2,750	5,300	n/a	8,050

DIMON Inc.

*Phone: (804) 792-7511 * Fax: (804) 791-0372*
512 Bridge St., Danville, VA 24543

DIMON is an international company engaged in two business segments — purchasing, processing, storing and selling leaf tobacco and importing and distributing fresh cut flowers. DIMON's customers can be found in more than 60 countries and include Philip Morris, Japan Tobacco and RJR Nabisco.

In 1996, DIMON's revenue was $2.2 billion. The company employs more than 11,000 people.

DIMON Inc. PAC (DIMON PAC) (C00310748) *Address: same as sponsor * Contact: Claude Owen, Chairperson * Treasurer: Jeffrey B. Lance*

	1993-94	1995-96	1997	Totals
Receipts	$0	$29,070	$11,290	$40,360
Disburse	0	26,250	3,007	29,257
Cash	0	2,820	11,102	n/a
Contributions	0	26,250	3,000	29,250
Republicans	0	23,250	3,000	26,250
No. of Cand.	*0*	*23*	*3*	*26*
House	0	14,500	500	15,000
Senate	0	8,750	2,500	11,250
Democrats	0	3,000	0	3,000
No. of Cand.	*0*	*6*	*1*	*7*
House	0	3,000	0	3,000
Senate	0	0	0	0
Incumbents	0	24,250	3,000	27,250
Challengers	0	0	0	0
Open Seat	0	2,000	0	2,000
Winners	0	21,250	n/a	21,250
Losers	0	5,000	n/a	5,000

Loews Corp.

*Phone: (336) 335-7451 * Fax: (336) 335-7671*
714 Green Valley Rd., Greensboro, NC 27408

Lorillard Tobacco Co., a North Carolina-based company, manufactures Newport and True cigarette brands. The company is a subsidiary of publicly traded Loews Corp., which sells insurance through its publicly traded subsidiary, CNA Financial Corp. Loews sales in 1997 exceeded $20 billion and the company employed more than 35,000 workers. It is ranked No. 46 in the Fortune 500.

Based in New York, Loews also owns 14 hotels in the United States, Canada and Monaco, watchmaker Bulova, and oil-drilling subsidiary Diamond Offshore Drilling, which operates 46 oil rigs worldwide. Brothers Robert and Larry Tisch own 31 percent of the company.

Lorillard Public Affairs Committee (C00112888) *Address: same as sponsor * Contact: Arthur J. Stevens, Chairperson * Treasurer: Michael L. Diamond*

	1993-94	1995-96	1997	Totals
Receipts	$56,993	$69,397	$38,995	$165,385
Disburse	51,250	62,622	26,000	139,872
Cash	12,485	19,262	32,258	n/a
Contributions	46,250	51,000	20,500	117,750
Republicans	26,250	36,000	11,500	73,750
No. of Cand.	*46*	*51*	*18*	*115*
House	17,750	24,500	9,000	51,250
Senate	8,500	11,500	2,500	22,500
Democrats	19,500	15,000	8,500	43,000
No. of Cand.	*31*	*26*	*18*	*75*
House	18,500	15,000	8,500	42,000
Senate	1,000	0	0	1,000
Incumbents	36,750	48,000	19,500	104,250
Challengers	2,500	500	0	3,000
Open Seat	6,500	3,500	500	10,500
Winners	39,750	43,500	n/a	83,250
Losers	6,500	7,500	n/a	14,000

CNA Financial Corp. Citizens for Good Government (C00078287) *Phone: (312) 822-5000 * Fax: (312) 822-6419 * CNA Plaza - Corporate Tax (24S), Chicago, IL 60685 * Web: www.cna.com*

*Phone: (202) 296-4662 * Fax: (202) 296-5547 * 1776 Eye St. N.W., Suite 770, Washington, DC 20006 * Contact: Tom DeYulia, V.P. of Federal and State Relations * Treasurer: Jim McGinity*

CNA Financial is a holding company for a wide range of insurance companies that provide individual life, long-term care, property and casualty insurance, as well as insurance and risk management services for businesses.

CNA's subsidiaries also offer reinsurance, a closed-end bond fund, marine insurance, information services, insurance fraud investigations and claims administration. Founded in 1897, the company had 1997 revenues of $17 billion. CNA, which employs 24,300 people, has assets of $61 billion.

About 6,000 of CNA's employees work at the company's Chicago headquarters. CNA maintains offices throughout the United States, and in China, Australia, the United Kingdom, the West Indies and Bermuda.

In addition to the CNA-named family of companies, subsidiaries include MOAC, a marine insurance subsidiary, Viaticus Inc. and Hedge Financial Corp.

Loews owns 84 percent of CNA Financial, while the other 16 percent is publicly traded.

	1993-94	1995-96	1997	Totals
Receipts	$108,780	$185,615	$169,141	$463,536
Disburse	70,350	131,954	46,730	249,034
Cash	81,257	134,919	259,354	n/a
Contributions	66,970	128,050	43,800	238,820
Republicans	30,850	105,550	30,000	166,400
No. of Cand.	*34*	*120*	*33*	*187*
House	17,850	72,250	19,500	109,600
Senate	13,000	33,300	10,500	56,800
Democrats	36,120	22,500	13,800	72,420
No. of Cand.	*25*	*23*	*15*	*63*
House	34,500	16,000	4,000	54,500
Senate	1,620	6,500	9,800	17,920
Incumbents	51,370	91,750	39,300	182,420
Challengers	8,750	10,800	3,500	23,050
Open Seat	6,350	25,500	1,000	32,850
Winners	44,600	94,350	n/a	138,950
Losers	22,370	33,700	n/a	56,070

Philip Morris

*Phone: (212) 880-5000 * Fax: (212) 878-2167*
120 Park Ave., New York, NY 10017

Philip Morris is the world's largest tobacco company. It controls nearly 50 percent of the U.S. market and makes cigarette brands Marlboro and Virginia Slims. One-third of the company's profits come from its food and beer subsidiaries, which include Kraft and Miller Brewing. Among the company's products are Oscar Mayer meats, Jell-O, Kool-Aid and Miller beers. The publicly traded company had 1997 sales of $72 billion and more than 154,000 workers.

Philip Morris' tobacco unit has been involved in national settlement talks and litigation in several states. The tobacco industry originally supported a national agreement reached in 1997 but in April 1998 renounced the deal after Congress tightened restrictions on the industry.

Company documents released in January 1998 caused a stir in Congress by suggesting that Philip Morris targeted children in its marketing campaigns. Philip Morris also lobbies on food and beer issues that affect its subsidiaries. The beer industry is seeking to repeal the 1991 beer tax.

The company's PAC contributions increased 20 percent from the 1993-94 election cycle to the 1995-96 cycle, making Philip Morris the largest contributor among tobacco companies. Southern legislators, including House Commerce Committee Chairman Rep. Tom Bliley, R-Va., were among the top recipients of Philip Morris contributions. The committee held several hearings on the tobacco settlement in 1998.

The company favored Republicans over Democrats, but Rep. Scotty Baesler, D-Ky., and former Democratic Rep. Mike Ward of Kentucky were among the top dozen recipients. Baesler opposes regulation of tobacco by the Food and Drug Administration. Ward lost to Rep. Anne M. Northrup, R-Ky., who did not receive any money from Philip Morris.

Philip Morris subsidiary Kraft General Foods Inc. contributed $30,500 to 1996 congressional candidates. Kraft operates about 60 manufacturing and processing facilities and 230 distribution centers throughout the United States. It is headquartered in Northfield, Ill. Miller Brewing's PAC contributed less than $5,000 to 1996 congressional races.

Philip Morris Companies Inc. Political Action Committee (also known as Phil-PAC) (C00089136) *Phone: (202) 637-1552 * Fax: (202) 638-2116 * 1341 G St. N.W., Suite 900, Washington, DC 20005 * Contact: John F. Ostronic, Administrator * Treasurer: Nancy DeLisi*

	1993-94	1995-96	1997	Totals
Receipts	$1,009,362	$1,350,887	$677,783	$3,038,032
Disburse	1,052,792	1,321,849	633,566	3,008,207
Cash	5,991	35,151	79,367	n/a
Contributions	673,666	850,119	408,026	1,931,811
Republicans	268,849	615,921	270,305	1,155,075
No. of Cand.	*177*	*238*	*155*	*570*
House	182,426	459,574	213,105	855,105
Senate	86,423	156,347	57,200	299,970

	1993-94	1995-96	1997	Totals
Democrats	402,317	233,198	135,221	770,736
No. of Cand.	*192*	*122*	*90*	*404*
House	340,338	222,198	113,471	676,007
Senate	61,979	11,000	21,750	94,729
Incumbents	567,996	738,772	386,526	1,693,294
Challengers	30,500	36,250	6,000	72,750
Open Seat	77,650	77,847	16,000	171,497
Winners	523,336	673,980	n/a	1,197,316
Losers	150,330	176,139	n/a	326,469

Kraft Foods Inc. Political Action Committee (KF PAC) (formerly known as Kraft General Foods Inc. PAC) (C00077701) *Phone: (847) 646-2000 * Fax: (847) 646-2922 * Three Lakes Dr., Northfield, IL 60093 * Web: www.kraftfoods.com*

*Phone: (202) 637-1552 * Fax: (202) 638-2116 * 1341 G St. N.W., Suite 900, Washington, DC 20005 * Contact: John F. Ostronic, Administrator * Treasurer: Nancy DeLisi*

	1993-94	*1995-96*	*1997*	*Totals*
Receipts	$57,009	$38,654	$27,179	$122,842
Disburse	67,377	32,835	34,053	134,265
Cash	78	6,920	49	n/a
Contributions	41,275	30,500	20,500	92,275
Republicans	27,250	30,000	19,000	76,250
No. of Cand.	*32*	*14*	*19*	*65*
House	19,250	14,000	17,000	50,250
Senate	8,000	16,000	2,000	26,000
Democrats	13,025	500	1,500	15,025
No. of Cand.	*20*	*2*	*3*	*25*
House	12,775	-500	1,500	13,775
Senate	250	1,000	0	1,250
Incumbents	35,775	8,000	18,500	62,275
Challengers	2,000	9,000	0	11,000
Open Seat	3,500	14,000	0	17,500
Winners	35,500	20,000	n/a	55,500
Losers	5,775	10,500	n/a	16,275

Contributed less than $5,000 during 1995-96 cycle:

Miller Brewing Co. Federal Committee (C00102780) *Phone: (414) 931-2000 * 3939 W. Highland Blvd., Milwaukee, WI 53208 * Contact: Jacqueline Pascual, Coordinator * Treasurer: Nancy DeLisi*

Pinkerton Tobacco

*Phone: (804) 287-3200 * Fax: (804) 287-3208*
P.O. Box 11588, 6630 W. Broad St., Richmond, VA 23230

Pinkerton Tobacco Co. is a medium-sized tobacco producer based in Richmond, Va. The company manufactures, sells and distributes cigarettes, cigars and other tobacco products throughout the world.

Pinkerton is a member of the Smokeless Tobacco Council, a group that was formed in 1969 to conduct, collect and disseminate research regarding smokeless tobacco products. The group is funded mainly by the American Tobacco Co. Inc.

Pinkerton Tobacco Co. Political Action Committee (C00215053)
*Address: same as sponsor * Treasurer: Michael D. Morris*

	1993-94	*1995-96*	*1997*	*Totals*
Receipts	$66,945	$61,367	$29,569	$157,881
Disburse	75,076	71,569	28,115	174,760
Cash	19,956	9,754	11,207	n/a
Contributions	58,700	61,750	20,500	140,950
Republicans	26,950	47,250	11,750	85,950
No. of Cand.	*29*	*39*	*12*	*80*
House	13,450	37,250	6,750	57,450
Senate	13,500	10,000	5,000	28,500
Democrats	31,750	14,500	8,750	55,000
No. of Cand.	*23*	*15*	*8*	*46*
House	28,750	13,500	8,750	51,000
Senate	3,000	1,000	0	4,000
Incumbents	50,950	55,750	17,000	123,700
Challengers	2,500	3,000	0	5,500
Open Seat	5,250	3,000	1,000	9,250
Winners	47,700	49,000	n/a	96,700
Losers	11,000	12,750	n/a	23,750

RJR Nabisco

*Phone: (212) 258-5600 * Fax: (212) 969-9173*
1301 Ave. of the Americas, New York, NY 10019
Web: www.rjrnabisco.com

RJR Nabisco Holdings Corp. is the parent company of R.J. Reynolds, the second-largest cigarette maker in the United States. It also has an 80 percent stake in Nabisco Holdings Corp., a large multinational food company. RJR Nabisco employed 79,700 workers and had $17 billion in sales during 1997.

Sales were split almost evenly between the food and tobacco industries, but most of RJR Nabisco's profits came from tobacco. R.J. Reynolds makes one of every four cigarettes sold in the domestic market. Nabisco's products include Oreo and SnackWell cookies, Ritz crackers, A1 steak sauce and Parkay margarine.

The company's CEO declared a 1997 national tobacco settlement "dead" in April 1998 after a congressional committee made changes to the pact. During the 1995-96 election cycle, RJR spent more than half of its PAC contributions to congressional candidates on Republican incumbents.

It favored candidates from the tobacco unit's home state, North Carolina, and also gave more than $27,000 to Virginia Democratic candidates. The leading recipients were former Rep. David Funderburk, R-N.C., Rep. John M. Spratt Jr., D-S.C., and Sens. Jesse Helms, R-N.C., and John W. Warner, R-Va.

The company's Nabisco Brands PAC contributed $111,000 to 1996 congressional races, ranking fifth among food companies.

RJR Political Action Committee RJR Nabisco Inc. (RJR PAC) (C00042002) *Phone: (202) 626-7235 * Fax: (202) 626-7208 * 1455 Pennsylvania Ave. N.W., Suite 525, Washington, DC 20004 * Contact: Murray Jones, PAC Dir. * Treasurer: Janis M. Krebs*

	1993-94	*1995-96*	*1997*	*Totals*
Receipts	$1,027,773	$994,532	$491,031	$2,513,336
Disburse	1,018,106	963,958	358,726	2,340,790
Cash	121,885	152,472	284,785	n/a
Contributions	784,400	642,150	206,250	1,632,800
Republicans	417,650	468,750	144,750	1,031,150
No. of Cand.	*201*	*249*	*144*	*594*
House	267,900	339,250	115,250	722,400
Senate	149,750	129,500	29,500	308,750
Democrats	366,000	173,400	60,500	599,900
No. of Cand.	*167*	*92*	*53*	*312*
House	311,450	151,400	49,500	512,350
Senate	54,550	22,000	11,000	87,550
Incumbents	564,900	521,650	199,250	1,285,800
Challengers	53,000	40,500	3,500	97,000
Open Seat	165,000	80,500	5,000	250,500
Winners	603,600	500,150	n/a	1,103,750
Losers	180,800	142,000	n/a	322,800

Nabisco Inc. Political Action Committee (C00079947) *Phone: (973) 682-5000 * 7 Campus Dr., P.O. Box 311, Parsippany, NJ 07054-0311 * Web: www.nabisco.com * Treasurer: Anthony Guerra*

	1993-94	*1995-96*	*1997*	*Totals*
Receipts	$124,357	$145,364	$53,689	$323,410
Disburse	128,236	120,782	17,490	266,508
Cash	39,449	64,036	100,236	n/a
Contributions	120,800	111,000	14,000	245,800
Republicans	63,800	86,750	12,500	163,050
No. of Cand.	*66*	*118*	*17*	*201*
House	45,300	57,250	7,500	110,050
Senate	18,500	29,500	5,000	53,000
Democrats	56,000	24,250	1,500	81,750
No. of Cand.	*64*	*57*	*10*	*131*
House	46,500	22,250	3,500	72,250
Senate	9,500	2,000	-2000	9,500
Incumbents	106,800	86,500	13,500	206,800
Challengers	10,500	3,000	0	13,500
Open Seat	3,000	22,500	1,000	26,500
Winners	103,800	94,500	n/a	198,300
Losers	17,000	16,500	n/a	33,500

Smokeless Tobacco Council

*Phone: (202) 452-1252 * Fax: (202) 452-0118*
1627 K St. N.W., Suite 700, Washington, DC 20006

The Smokeless Tobacco Council has traditionally represented the interests of major U.S. tobacco manufacturers. It was created in 1969 to conduct, collect and disseminate research regarding smokeless tobacco products.

In October 1996 the United States Tobacco Co. pulled out of the Smokeless Tobacco Council, of which it had been a founding member. The withdrawal came after other companies refused to go along with a proposal by UST and Philip Morris in May 1996 for federal legislation to target teen tobacco use.

Members of the Smokeless Tobacco Council as of January 1998 included: Conwood Co. LP, Swedish Match Co. North America, Brown & Williamson Co., North Atlantic Trading Co. and Swisher International.

The council is one of several defendants in a lawsuit filed on March 12, 1998 by HealthPartners and Medica Health Plans, part of Allina Health System. According to a press release, the companies are suing to recover health care costs related to tobacco use in light of new evidence against the tobacco industry uncovered in lawsuits and research.

Smokeless Tobacco Council Inc. Political Action Committee (STCPAC) (C00195339) *Address: same as sponsor * Treasurer: Jeffrey L. Schlagenhauf*

	1993-94	1995-96	1997	Totals
Receipts	$42,770	$26,700	$9,000	$78,470
Disburse	42,128	25,263	6,557	73,948
Cash	778	2,212	4,655	n/a
Contributions	42,100	24,750	5,050	71,900
Republicans	17,000	17,250	4,000	38,250
No. of Cand.	*27*	*25*	*7*	*59*
House	12,750	15,750	2,500	31,000
Senate	4,250	1,500	1,500	7,250
Democrats	25,100	7,500	1,050	33,650
No. of Cand.	*28*	*14*	*3*	*45*
House	23,600	6,500	1,050	31,150
Senate	1,500	1,000	0	2,500
Incumbents	36,850	23,750	4,500	65,100
Challengers	1,250	0	550	1,800
Open Seat	4,000	1,000	0	5,000
Winners	29,100	21,750	n/a	50,850
Losers	13,000	3,000	n/a	16,000

Standard Commercial Tobacco Co.

*Phone: (919) 291-5507 * Fax: (919) 237-1109*
2201 Miller Rd., Wilson, NC 27893

Standard Commercial is the world's third-largest leaf tobacco dealer and is also a leading international wool trading company. Standard Commercial had sales of more than $1.35 billion in 1997.

The company employs 2,200 workers, many at its headquarters in Wilson, N.C. Standard Commercial's tobacco is grown in about 30 countries.

In January 1998, Standard Commercial Corp. announced that it had acquired Meridional de Tabacos, the fourth-largest leaf dealer in Brazil.

Standard Commercial Tobacco Co. Inc. Political Action Committee (C00293670) *Address: same as sponsor * Contact: Robert E. Harrison, CEO * Treasurer: Hampton R. Poole*

	1993-94	1995-96	1997	Totals
Receipts	$5,965	$12,596	$5,234	$23,795
Disburse	5,050	9,450	3,000	17,500
Cash	916	4,066	6,302	n/a
Contributions	4,000	8,750	2,500	15,250
Republicans	1,000	7,750	1,000	9,750
No. of Cand.	*1*	*10*	*1*	*12*
House	1,000	5,250	0	6,250
Senate	0	2,500	1,000	3,500
Democrats	3,000	1,000	1,500	5,500
No. of Cand.	*3*	*1*	*2*	*6*
House	3,000	1,000	1,500	5,500
Senate	0	0	0	0
Incumbents	2,000	7,000	2,500	11,500
Challengers	0	1,750	0	1,750
Open Seat	2,000	0	0	2,000
Winners	2,000	6,000	n/a	8,000
Losers	2,000	2,750	n/a	4,750

Swisher International Inc.

*Phone: (904) 353-4311 * Fax: (904) 353-9175*
459 E. 16th St., Jacksonville, FL 32206

Swisher International Group is a major manufacturer and marketer of cigars and smokeless tobacco products, with its primary market in the United States. Founded in 1861, Swisher had 1997 sales of $276 million and employs about 1,200 people.

Swisher owns two manufacturing facilities in Florida and West Virginia; three smokeless tobacco-aging warehouses in Wisconsin, Virginia and Kentucky; and three properties for sale in Pennsylvania, New Jersey and Georgia.

In December 1997, Swisher signed an agreement to purchase a 50 percent interest in SP Holding of the Dominican Republic, the owner of Puros de Villa Gonzales, a major tobacco processor and manufacturer of premium hand-rolled cigars.

Swisher International Inc. PAC Fund (C00312785) *Address: same as sponsor * Contact: Joseph Augustus, V.P. * Treasurer: Gus Amato*

	1993-94	1995-96	1997	Totals
Receipts	$0	$18,234	$35,861	$54,095
Disburse	0	13,500	21,000	34,500
Cash	0	4,734	19,595	n/a
Contributions	0	11,500	11,500	23,000
Republicans	0	8,000	11,000	19,000
No. of Cand.	*0*	*12*	*13*	*25*
House	0	8,000	5,000	13,000
Senate	0	0	6,000	6,000
Democrats	0	3,500	500	4,000
No. of Cand.	*0*	*5*	*1*	*6*
House	0	2,500	500	3,000
Senate	0	1,000	0	1,000
Incumbents	0	9,000	11,500	20,500
Challengers	0	500	0	500
Open Seat	0	2,000	0	2,000
Winners	0	10,000	n/a	10,000
Losers	0	1,500	n/a	1,500

Tobacco Institute

*Phone: (202) 457-4800 * Fax: (202) 457-9350*
1875 Eye St. N.W., Suite 800, Washington, DC 20006
Web: www.tobaccoinstitute.com

The Tobacco Institute is a foundation created by the top tobacco companies in the United States. It serves as a clearinghouse for tobacco information and a lobbying group. Among its members are Philip Morris Cos., R.J. Reynolds, Brown & Williamson, B.A.T. Industries, Lorillard Tobacco Co., Liggett Group Inc. and United States Tobacco Co.

Tobacco Institute Political Action Committee (C00009761) *Address: same as sponsor * Contact: Scott A. Wilson, Chairperson * Treasurer: Susan R. Ruyle*

	1993-94	1995-96	1997	Totals
Receipts	$124,429	$114,078	$42,848	$281,355
Disburse	122,000	116,425	39,752	278,177
Cash	6,732	4,388	7,483	n/a
Contributions	122,000	113,850	38,250	274,100
Republicans	59,900	85,950	26,250	172,100
No. of Cand.	*84*	*97*	*38*	*219*
House	52,650	65,950	18,000	136,600
Senate	7,250	20,000	8,250	35,500
Democrats	61,350	27,900	12,000	101,250
No. of Cand.	*79*	*46*	*19*	*144*
House	56,850	26,000	10,000	92,850
Senate	4,500	1,900	2,000	8,400
Incumbents	115,250	104,950	37,250	257,450
Challengers	1,250	3,000	0	4,250
Open Seat	5,500	6,500	1,000	13,000
Winners	98,250	96,100	n/a	194,350
Losers	23,750	17,750	n/a	41,500

UST Inc.

*Phone: (203) 661-1100 * Fax: (203) 622-3626*
100 W. Putnam Ave., Greenwich, CT 06830
Web: www.ustobacco.com

United States Tobacco is the primary business of UST, located in Greenwich, Conn. The company controls about 80 percent of the domestic smokeless tobacco, or snuff, market with brands Skoal and Copenhagen. In addition to tobacco, UST owns several wineries, a video production company and produces wood products and smoking pipes. UST, which employs about 4,500 people, had 1996 sales of $1.4 billion.

UST opposes a tax increase on tobacco products. It once favored a national settlement that would provide broad liability protection from future lawsuits, but announced its opposition in April 1998. That agreement states that smokeless tobacco usage must decline by at least 45 percent within 10 years of legislation being enacted.

UST ranked third among tobacco industry PACs in contributions to congressional candidates during the 1995-96 election cycle. It increased its total contributions by more than 40 percent from the 1993-94 cycle. More than 80 percent of UST's contributions went to Republican candidates. The company's Stimson Lane Ltd. subsidiary, a California winery, contributed more than $21,000 to congressional candidates during the 1995-96 cycle.

Eight candidates each received $10,000 from UST's PAC. They included Sens. Jesse Helms, R-N.C., and John W. Warner, R-Va., and

House Minority Leader Richard A. Gephardt, D-Mo., who stopped accepting tobacco industry contributions in 1997.

UST Executives Administrators and Managers Political Action Committee (also known as USTEAM PAC) (C00104851) *Phone: (202) 661-4610 * Fax: (202) 661-4747 * 1201 Pennsylvania Ave. N.W., Suite 300, Washington, DC 20006 * Treasurer: Wendy B. Grammas * Contact: Susan Scogna, Gov. Relations Administrator * Phone: (203) 661-1100*

	1993-94	1995-96	1997	Totals
Receipts	$619,912	$843,045	$320,384	$1,783,341
Disburse	620,701	816,725	258,871	1,696,297
Cash	1,351	27,672	89,187	n/a
Contributions	376,050	528,000	147,850	1,051,900
Republicans	207,050	420,500	104,850	732,400
No. of Cand.	*91*	*170*	*90*	*351*
House	89,800	272,000	77,850	439,650
Senate	117,250	148,500	27,000	292,750
Democrats	168,000	107,500	43,000	318,500
No. of Cand.	*71*	*61*	*41*	*173*
House	112,500	99,000	29,500	241,000
Senate	55,500	8,500	13,500	77,500
Incumbents	271,300	426,000	141,350	838,650
Challengers	29,500	30,500	2,500	62,500
Open Seat	70,250	71,000	5,000	146,250
Winners	287,000	383,500	n/a	670,500
Losers	89,050	144,500	n/a	233,550

Stimson Lane Ltd. Political Action Committee (C00270421) *Phone: (203) 622-3612 * Fax: (203) 863-7250 * 100 W. Putnam Ave., Greenwich, CT 06830 * Contact: Susan Scogna, Gov. Relations Administrator * Treasurer: Wendy B. Grammas*

	1993-94	1995-96	1997	Totals
Receipts	$27,000	$21,250	$3,044	$51,294
Disburse	26,000	21,292	3,000	50,292
Cash	1,000	956	1,000	n/a
Contributions	20,000	21,250	3,000	44,250
Republicans	14,000	21,250	3,000	38,250
No. of Cand.	*5*	*6*	*3*	*14*
House	5,000	21,250	3,000	29,250
Senate	9,000	0	0	9,000
Democrats	6,000	0	0	6,000
No. of Cand.	*2*	*0*	*0*	*2*
House	6,000	0	0	6,000
Senate	0	0	0	0
Incumbents	17,000	20,250	3,000	40,250
Challengers	2,000	0	0	2,000
Open Seat	0	1,000	0	1,000
Winners	14,000	20,250	n/a	34,250
Losers	6,000	1,000	n/a	7,000

Universal Leaf Tobacco Co.

*Phone: (804) 359-9311 * Fax: (804) 254-3594*
1501 N. Hamilton St., Richmond, VA 23230

Universal Leaf Tobacco is a $1.5 billion international tobacco wholesaler. The company purchases and processes tobacco from growers worldwide and then sells it to tobacco product manufacturers. Universal Leaf also owns and/or leases 29 properties in North Carolina, Virginia, Kentucky and Pennsylvania.

The company is a subsidiary of the Universal Corp., the world's largest independent leaf tobacco merchant. Universal is a $2 billion, publicly traded company with 25,000 employees worldwide. For the year ended June 30, 1997, Universal had total sales of $4.1 billion. Tobacco sales to Philip Morris accounted for more than 10% of these revenues.

In addition to its tobacco operations, Universal also has businesses in the lumber, building products and agricultural industries. In addition, it owns and/or leases properties in Indonesia, Malawi, Zimbabwe, Poland, Hungary, Italy, the Netherlands, Germany, Turkey, Brazil, the Dominican Republic, Canada and Colombia. Universal also recently acquired a large processing plant in Tanzania from the Tanzanian government.

Subsidiaries include: Universal Leaf North America NC, Universal Eastern Europe Ltd., Latin America Tobacco Co., Orient Leaf Tobacco Co., Tanzania Leaf Tobacco Co. B. V. and European Tobacco Co.

Universal Leaf Tobacco Co. Inc. Political Action Committee (C00214072) *Address: same as sponsor * Treasurer: Karen M. L. Whelan*

	1993-94	1995-96	1997	Totals
Receipts	$9,195	$14,986	$17,304	$41,485
Disburse	5,650	12,800	3,000	21,450
Cash	7,351	11,237	25,542	n/a
Contributions	5,650	10,000	3,000	18,650
Republicans	2,800	8,900	2,100	13,800
No. of Cand.	*7*	*13*	*3*	*23*
House	1,750	4,850	1,100	7,700
Senate	1,050	4,050	1,000	6,100
Democrats	2,850	1,100	900	4,850
No. of Cand.	*10*	*7*	*3*	*20*
House	2,850	1,100	900	4,850
Senate	0	0	0	0
Incumbents	4,800	9,600	3,000	17,400
Challengers	550	200	0	750
Open Seat	300	200	0	500
Winners	4,400	8,800	n/a	13,200
Losers	1,250	1,200	n/a	2,450

Business

Beer, Wine & Liquor

Allied Domecq Spirits & Wine

*Phone: (519) 961-6611 * Fax: (519) 971-5750*
P.O. Box 33006, Detroit, MI 48232
*Web: www.allieddomecq.co.uk * E-mail: adswdc@aol.com*

Allied Domecq is the world's third-largest distiller, behind Diageo and Seagram. The British company employs more than 50,000 people worldwide and reported 1997 sales of $7.2 billion. Its spirits and wine unit — which makes Presidente and Don Pedro brandies, Sauza tequila, Ballantine scotch, Kahlua liqueur, Canadian Club whiskey, Courvoisier cognac and Beefeater Gin —makes up 60 percent of company sales.

Allied also operates pubs, restaurants and nightclubs under such names as Big Steak Pub, Firkin and Mr. Q's; wine and liquor outlets under the name Victoria Wine; and Baskin-Robbins, Dunkin' Donuts and Togo's Eateries franchise interests. Ranked by number of outlets, Allied is the world's No. 4 retailer. It owns 4,000 pubs in the United Kingdom.

Subsidiaries include: Maker's Mark Distillery Inc., The Wine Alliance, Hiram Walker & Sons Inc. and Domecq Importers Inc.

Allied Domecq Spirits & Wine Political Action Committee (formerly known as Hiram Walker PAC) (C00166926) *Address: same as sponsor * Treasurer: John Deboer * Contact: Chris Swonger, PAC Chairman*

	1993-94	1995-96	1997	Totals
Receipts	$39,218	$49,396	$27,160	$115,774
Disburse	54,100	52,889	35,000	141,989
Cash	15,178	11,688	3,849	n/a
Contributions	32,250	30,888	24,000	87,138
Republicans	11,500	26,388	16,500	54,388
No. of Cand.	*13*	*32*	*19*	*64*
House	7,500	18,292	8,500	34,292
Senate	4,000	8,096	8,000	20,096
Democrats	20,750	4,500	7,500	32,750
No. of Cand.	*25*	*9*	*8*	*42*
House	12,250	3,000	500	15,750
Senate	8,500	1,500	7,000	17,000
Incumbents	30,750	28,292	21,000	80,042
Challengers	1,500	500	1,000	3,000
Open Seat	0	2,096	2,000	4,096
Winners	25,750	27,388	n/a	53,138
Losers	6,500	3,500	n/a	10,000

Anheuser-Busch Companies Inc.

*Phone: (314) 577-2329 * Fax: (314) 577-4476*
One Busch Place, St. Louis, MO 63118
Web: www.anheuser-busch.com

Anheuser-Busch Companies is the holding company parent of Anheuser-Busch, the world's largest brewer of beer. The company also is the parent to a number of subsidiaries that work with the production and acquisition of brewing raw materials, the manufacture and recycling of aluminum beverage containers and the operation of theme parks Busch Gardens and Sea World.

Anheuser-Busch's sales in 1997 topped $11 billion. The publicly traded company employs more than 25,000 workers and was ranked No. 127 in the 1997 Fortune 500.

The company makes leading brands Budweiser, Bud Light, Michelob and Busch, as well as specialty beers including ZiegenBock Amber, Red Wolf Lager and O'Doul's. The company has joint ventures in Japan, Mexico, China, several South American countries and throughout Europe.

Anheuser-Busch Companies Inc. Political Action Committee (AB-PAC) (C00034488) *Phone: (202) 293-9494 * Fax: (202) 223-9594 * 1776 Eye St. N.W., Suite 200, Washington, DC 20006 * Treasurer: William J. Kimmins Jr.*

*Contact: Judy Wierciak, Manager * Phone: (314) 577-2329*

	1993-94	1995-96	1997	Totals
Receipts	$219,015	$212,676	$135,324	$567,015
Disburse	309,700	154,700	65,800	530,200
Cash	72,749	130,733	200,266	n/a
Contributions	279,820	126,450	56,500	462,770
Republicans	90,600	75,500	43,450	209,550
No. of Cand.	*77*	*69*	*35*	*181*
House	62,000	54,500	11,450	127,950
Senate	28,600	21,000	32,000	81,600
Democrats	188,720	50,950	13,050	252,720
No. of Cand.	*121*	*52*	*15*	*188*
House	145,100	45,750	6,050	196,900
Senate	43,620	5,200	7,000	55,820
Incumbents	248,620	118,250	49,500	416,370
Challengers	4,950	4,250	1,000	10,200
Open Seat	25,850	5,700	6,000	37,550
Winners	203,300	110,450	n/a	313,750
Losers	76,520	16,000	n/a	92,520

Brown-Forman Corp.

*Phone: (502) 585-1100 * Fax: (502) 774-6908*
850 Dixie Highway, Louisville, KY 40210-1091
*Web: www.brown-forman.com * E-mail: mark_smith@b-f.com*

Brown-Forman is best known for its Jack Daniel's whiskey, the most popular American spirit in the world according to the company, and its Southern Comfort bourbon whiskey. But the Kentucky-based company also produces and markets a variety of other wines and spirits and, through Lenox Inc., manufactures and markets china, crystal, silver and pewter products and leather accessories.

Founded in 1870, the publicly traded company employs 7,500 people in the United States and abroad. It posted sales of $1.8 billion during fiscal year 1997.

Wine and spirit products, which accounted for $1.3 billion of the company's 1997 sales, include Canadian Mist whiskey, Pepe Lopez tequila, Bolla wines and Korbel champagne. The company's 1992 purchase of Fetzer Vineyards made Brown-Forman the fifth-largest domestic wine marketer in the nation. In addition, the company is the U.S. importer of Finlandia vodkas and Bushmills Irish whiskies.

Other brands include: Lenox China and Crystal, Dansk International Designs, Gorham Silver, Stainless and Crystal, Lenox/Kirk Stieff Silver, Stainless and Pewter Products, and Hartmann Luggage, Business Cases and Personal Leather Accessories.

Brown-Forman Corp. Non-Partisan Committee for Responsible Government (C00059733) *Address: same as sponsor * Treasurer: Larry W. Perry * Contact: Mark Smith, PAC Dir.*

	1993-94	1995-96	1997	Totals
Receipts	$144,137	$131,742	$89,799	$365,678
Disburse	154,806	132,500	64,500	351,806
Cash	19,073	18,319	38,418	n/a
Contributions	123,000	83,000	42,500	248,500
Republicans	86,000	70,500	35,500	192,000
No. of Cand.	*63*	*32*	*15*	*110*
House	39,000	44,000	19,500	102,500
Senate	47,000	26,500	16,000	89,500
Democrats	37,000	12,500	7,000	56,500
No. of Cand.	*31*	*8*	*8*	*47*
House	22,000	8,500	2,000	32,500
Senate	15,000	4,000	5,000	24,000
Incumbents	78,500	54,500	31,500	164,500
Challengers	19,000	17,000	1,000	37,000
Open Seat	25,500	11,500	10,000	47,000
Winners	90,250	55,500	n/a	145,750
Losers	32,750	27,500	n/a	60,250

Canandaigua Wine Co.

*Phone: (716) 394-7900 * Fax: (716) 394-4839*
116 Buffalo St., Canandaigua, NY 14424

Canandaigua Wine is the second-largest wine company in the United States. It also produces beer and distilled spirits. Canandaigua sells more than 125 brands including: Paul Masson, Manischewitz, Monte Alban, Almaden, Barton's Gin and Corona. The beverages are distributed by more than 1,400 wholesalers throughout the United States and in selected international markets.

A publicly traded company, Canandaigua has 2,500 employees and reported sales of $1.1 billion in 1997. The company has facilities in California, Illinois, Kentucky, Georgia, Wisconsin and New York.

Canandaigua operates 12 wineries, two distilling and bottling plants, three bottling plants and a brewery.

Canandaigua Wine Co. Inc. Political Action Committee (C00304832) *Address: same as sponsor * Treasurer: Perry Humphrey * Contact: Jim Finkle, Chairperson*

	1993-94	1995-96	1997	Totals
Receipts	$0	$32,215	$21,379	$53,594
Disburse	0	29,197	12,500	41,697
Cash	0	3,017	11,896	n/a
Contributions	0	23,246	12,500	35,746
Republicans	0	19,750	7,000	26,750
No. of Cand.	*0*	*12*	*5*	*17*
House	0	19,750	6,500	26,250
Senate	0	0	500	500
Democrats	0	3,496	5,500	8,996
No. of Cand.	*0*	*3*	*2*	*5*
House	0	3,496	5,500	8,996
Senate	0	0	0	0
Incumbents	0	20,996	12,000	32,996
Challengers	0	750	500	1,250
Open Seat	0	1,500	0	1,500
Winners	0	19,996	n/a	19,996
Losers	0	3,250	n/a	3,250

Coors Brewing Co.

*Phone: (303) 279-6565 * Fax: (303) 277-6517*
Coors Brewing Co. NH 250, Golden, CO 80401
Web: www.coors.com

Adolph Coors Co. is the holding company for its principal subsidiary, Coors Brewing, the nation's third-largest brewer. Based in Golden, Colo., Coors Brewing employs 5,800 workers and reported 1997 sales of $1.8 billion. It paid $386 million in beer excise taxes in 1997.

Adolph Coors is ranked among the 1,000 largest publicly traded corporations in the United States, based on annual sales. Coors' brand portfolio comprises about two dozen different beers. Coors Light accounts for two-thirds of sales. Besides beer, the company also makes Zima, Coors Cutter and Coors Rocky Mountain Lemon Lime Sparkling Water.

Political Action Coors Employees (PACE) (C00032573) *Phone: (202) 737-4444 * Fax: (202) 737-0951 * 801 Pennsylvania Ave. N.W., Suite 252, Washington, DC 20004 * Treasurer: Frances Morgan * Contact: Richard Crawford, Dir. of Fed. Gov. Affairs*

*Contact: Tony Grampsas, Chairman of PAC * Phone: (303) 279-6565*

	1993-94	1995-96	1997	Totals
Receipts	$27,555	$51,643	$26,610	$105,808
Disburse	28,566	50,573	16,003	95,142
Cash	2,057	3,132	13,740	n/a
Contributions	27,950	49,500	15,500	92,950
Republicans	23,200	46,500	14,000	83,700
No. of Cand.	*29*	*54*	*21*	*104*
House	8,500	25,500	11,500	45,500
Senate	14,700	21,000	2,500	38,200
Democrats	4,750	3,000	1,500	9,250
No. of Cand.	*6*	*5*	*2*	*13*
House	1,750	2,000	500	4,250
Senate	3,000	1,000	1,000	5,000
Incumbents	17,450	25,500	13,000	55,950
Challengers	3,750	5,000	1,000	9,750
Open Seat	6,750	19,000	500	26,250
Winners	24,450	39,000	n/a	63,450
Losers	3,500	10,500	n/a	14,000

Distilled Spirits Council

*Phone: (202) 628-3544 * Fax: (202) 682-8888*
1250 Eye St. N.W., Suite 900, Washington, DC 20005
Web: www.discus.health.org

Distilled Spirits Council is a trade association representing producers, marketers and distributors of distilled spirits products sold in the United States. The group says it represents 90 percent of U.S. distillers.

Distilled Spirits Council Political Action Committee (C00030734) *Address: same as sponsor * Treasurer: F. A. Meister*

	1993-94	1995-96	1997	Totals
Receipts	$49,190	$60,529	$25,013	$134,732
Disburse	49,266	60,415	24,623	134,304
Cash	37	150	540	n/a
Contributions	45,633	55,708	23,333	124,674
Republicans	11,550	40,803	14,833	67,186
No. of Cand.	*19*	*41*	*16*	*76*
House	8,800	27,550	10,367	46,717
Senate	2,750	13,253	4,466	20,469
Democrats	34,083	14,905	8,500	57,488
No. of Cand.	*35*	*18*	*9*	*62*
House	20,364	9,905	2,500	32,769
Senate	13,719	5,000	6,000	24,719
Incumbents	43,833	48,955	21,060	113,848
Challengers	0	1,500	1,000	2,500
Open Seat	1,800	5,253	1,273	8,326
Winners	33,852	49,861	n/a	83,713
Losers	11,781	5,847	n/a	17,628

G. Heileman Brewing Co.

100 Harborview Plaza, La Crosse, WI 54601

G. Heileman Brewing, which makes Old Style and Henry Weinhard's Private Reserve brand beer, has been purchased by The Stroh Brewing Co. Its PAC has been terminated.

G. Heileman Brewing Co. Inc. Political Action Committee (C00040931) *Address: same as sponsor * Treasurer: John A. Massa*

	1993-94	1995-96	1997	Totals
Receipts	$7,002	$4,823	$0	$11,825
Disburse	10,098	28,481	0	38,579
Cash	23,656	0	0	n/a
Contributions	490	5,000	0	5,490
Republicans	490	4,000	0	4,490
No. of Cand.	*1*	*4*	*0*	*5*
House	490	3,000	0	3,490
Senate	0	1,000	0	1,000
Democrats	0	1,000	0	1,000
No. of Cand.	*0*	*1*	*0*	*1*
House	0	1,000	0	1,000
Senate	0	0	0	0
Incumbents	490	2,000	0	2,490
Challengers	0	0	0	0
Open Seat	0	3,000	0	3,000
Winners	490	2,000	n/a	2,490
Losers	0	3,000	n/a	3,000

Jim Beam Brands Co.

Phone: (847) 948-8888
510 Lake Cook Rd., Deerfield, IL 60015
Web: www.jimbeam.com

Jim Beam Brands is an operating company of JBB Worldwide Inc., an international distilled spirits company with brands including: Jim Beam, the No. 1 selling bourbon worldwide; Whyte & Mackay Special Reserve, the No. 2 Scotch in Scotland; and DeKuyper, the No. 1 cordial line in the United States. Jim Beam Brands Co. is the second-largest distilled spirits company in the United States. In 1996, Jim Beam Bourbon sold more than 5 million cases worldwide and made more than $300 million in sales. JBB has more than 2,500 employees.

JBB Worldwide is a subsidiary of Fortune Brands Inc., a publicly held company.

The JBB Worldwide group also includes: Alberta Distillers Limited in Canada, JBB (Asia-Pacific) Limited and JBB (Greater Europe) PLC.

Jim Beam Brands Co. Political Action Committee (C00194126) *Address: same as sponsor * Treasurer: Jeffrey J. Buresh*

	1993-94	1995-96	1997	Totals
Receipts	$33,837	$32,056	$8,940	$74,833
Disburse	36,645	23,752	12,500	72,897
Cash	4,946	13,248	9,730	n/a
Contributions	15,950	7,000	7,500	30,450
Republicans	6,750	6,500	4,500	17,750
No. of Cand.	*8*	*8*	*5*	*21*
House	3,750	4,000	2,500	10,250
Senate	3,000	2,500	2,000	7,500
Democrats	9,200	500	3,000	12,700
No. of Cand.	*11*	*1*	*3*	*15*
House	6,200	500	0	6,700
Senate	3,000	0	3,000	6,000
Incumbents	12,950	6,500	7,500	26,950
Challengers	1,500	0	0	1,500
Open Seat	1,500	500	0	2,000
Winners	9,250	6,500	n/a	15,750
Losers	6,700	500	n/a	7,200

Joseph E. Seagram & Sons Inc.

Phone: (212) 572-7000
375 Park Ave., New York, NY 10152
Web: www.seagram.com

Although known for its liquor, wine, beer and Tropicana fruit juice products, Joseph E. Seagram & Sons also has substantial holdings in the entertainment industry through its 80 percent share in Universal Studios. Seagram, a publicly traded Montreal company, employs 30,000 people worldwide and reported 1997 sales in excess of $12.5 billion. International sales accounted for 40 percent of revenue.

In 1996, Seagram broke a decades-old taboo and aired advertisements for hard liquor on television and radio. The Distilled Spirits Council followed Seagram's example and, in November 1997, announced an end to the industry-wide voluntary ban.

Seagram's beverage brands include 7 Crown, Crown Royal, and V.O. whiskeys; Chivas Regal scotch; and Captain Morgan rum. Tropicana is the world's No. 1 juice company.

Joseph E. Seagram & Sons Inc. Political Action Committee (C00141960) *Phone: (202) 898-6400 * Fax: (202) 898-6407 * 1401 Eye St. N.W., Suite 1220, Washington, DC 20005 * Treasurer: Stephen Heller * Contact: Arthur Shapiro, Chairman*

	1993-94	1995-96	1997	Totals
Receipts	$243,184	$190,188	$94,729	$528,101
Disburse	237,521	158,142	75,431	471,094
Cash	27,482	59,529	78,828	n/a
Contributions	155,870	92,500	52,740	301,110
Republicans	71,000	64,750	29,728	165,478
No. of Cand.	*66*	*84*	*34*	*184*
House	34,500	40,750	21,728	96,978
Senate	36,500	24,000	8,000	68,500
Democrats	83,370	27,750	23,012	134,132
No. of Cand.	*66*	*37*	*30*	*133*
House	47,750	20,250	13,012	81,012
Senate	35,620	7,500	10,000	53,120
Incumbents	127,370	81,250	50,240	258,860
Challengers	9,750	3,250	0	13,000
Open Seat	17,750	8,500	2,500	28,750
Winners	128,000	79,750	n/a	207,750
Losers	27,870	12,750	n/a	40,620

Universal Studios Political Action Committee (formerly known as MCA PAC) (C00117408) *100 Universal City Plaza, Universal City, CA 91608 * Treasurer: Karen Randall*

Universal Studios (formerly MCA) produces and distributes films, videos, comedy television shows and music; operates two Universal Studios theme parks; and operates Spencer Gifts (more than 500 retail gift stores). It also distributes television programming to foreign countries. A subsidiary of Seagram, Universal's 1997 sales were $6.5 billion and it employed about 14,000 people.

The company also owns about 40 percent of movie theater chain Cineplex Odeon, which is merging with Sony's theater unit.

	1993-94	1995-96	1997	Totals
Receipts	$231,999	$211,098	$129,520	$572,617
Disburse	213,895	171,372	77,562	462,829
Cash	67,414	107,150	159,113	n/a
Contributions	186,184	150,375	61,500	398,059
Republicans	37,634	54,525	36,500	128,659
No. of Cand.	*28*	*47*	*37*	*112*
House	14,200	42,025	28,500	84,725
Senate	23,434	12,500	8,000	43,934
Democrats	145,550	95,850	25,000	266,400
No. of Cand.	*79*	*60*	*27*	*166*
House	76,450	48,850	10,000	135,300
Senate	69,100	47,000	15,000	131,100
Incumbents	151,184	111,375	60,500	323,059
Challengers	11,000	8,250	1,000	20,250
Open Seat	24,000	30,750	1,000	55,750
Winners	131,584	122,875	n/a	254,459
Losers	54,600	27,500	n/a	82,100

Michigan Beer & Wine Wholesalers Association

*Phone: (517) 482-5555 * Fax: (517) 482-1532*
332 Townsend St., Lansing, MI 48933
*Web: www.mbwwa.org * E-mail: info@mbwwa.org*

The Michigan Beer & Wine Wholesalers Association is a nonprofit, tax-exempt corporation organized to promote and protect the general welfare and interests of wholesale beer and wine distributors in Michigan. Its membership includes 90 beer and wine distribution companies, as well as brewers, vintners and numerous other related businesses and supporters.

MB&WWA has a for-profit subsidiary, MB&WWA Services Inc., that provides programs to help beer and wine wholesalers. MB&WWA also has a quarterly newsletter, Wholesaler.

MB&WWA is supporting two drunken driving initiatives in the Michigan Legislature. Both bills require highly visible stickers to be placed on the license plates of convicted drunken drivers.

Michigan Beer & Wine Wholesalers Federal Political Action Committee (C00159855) *Address: same as sponsor * Treasurer: Michael J. Lashbrook * Contact: Jim Fabiano, Chairperson*

	1993-94	1995-96	1997	Totals
Receipts	$21,292	$8,926	$5,488	$35,706
Disburse	20,066	10,115	1,424	31,605
Cash	1,275	1,532	5,597	n/a
Contributions	19,982	11,575	400	31,957
Republicans	6,230	3,700	400	10,330
No. of Cand.	*5*	*6*	*1*	*12*
House	5,030	2,700	400	8,130
Senate	1,200	1,000	0	2,200
Democrats	13,752	7,875	0	21,627
No. of Cand.	*9*	*5*	*0*	*14*
House	9,700	6,875	0	16,575
Senate	4,052	1,000	0	5,052
Incumbents	15,200	10,075	400	25,675
Challengers	0	1,500	0	1,500
Open Seat	3,782	0	0	3,782
Winners	12,500	10,575	n/a	23,075
Losers	7,482	1,000	n/a	8,482

National Association of Beverage Retailers

*Phone: (301) 656-1494 * Fax: (301) 656-7539*
5101 River Rd., Suite 108, Bethesda, MD 20816-1508

The National Association of Beverage Retailers represents state associations of on- and off-premise beverage licensees. NABR represents the interests of about 13,000 retailers.

NABR lobbied against lowering the legal blood alcohol content level to 0.08 percent, arguing that such a reduction would not reduce drunken driving fatalities.

National Association of Beverage Retailers Political Action Committee (NABRPAC) (C00302703) *Address: same as sponsor * Treasurer: John B. Burcham Jr. * Contact: Suzi Riga, Chairman*

	1993-94	1995-96	1997	Totals
Receipts	$0	$11,801	$16,010	$27,811
Disburse	0	8,896	7,380	16,276
Cash	0	2,902	11,531	n/a
Contributions	0	8,800	5,800	14,600
Republicans	0	6,500	4,800	11,300
No. of Cand.	*0*	*11*	*7*	*18*
House	0	4,500	3,800	8,300
Senate	0	2,000	1,000	3,000
Democrats	0	2,300	1,000	3,300
No. of Cand.	*0*	*5*	*1*	*6*
House	0	1,800	0	1,800
Senate	0	500	1,000	1,500
Incumbents	0	5,800	4,000	9,800
Challengers	0	500	800	1,300
Open Seat	0	2,500	1,000	3,500
Winners	0	7,800	n/a	7,800
Losers	0	1,000	n/a	1,000

National Beer Wholesalers' Association

*Phone: (703) 683-4300 * Fax: (703) 683-8965*
1100 S. Washington St., Alexandria, VA 22314-4494
Web: www.nbwa.org

The National Beer Wholesalers' Association represents about 1,800 beer distributors throughout the United States. Its president is former Rep. Ronald A. Sarasin, R-Conn. The group has been known to target congressional staffers with minor gifts — coffee mugs and computer mousepads among them.

Congressional candidates receive a questionnaire asking for their positions on more than 20 issues before the NBWA decides whether to contribute money to a campaign.

The NBWA lobbies on tax policy, interstate trucking and advertising restrictions. It favors a reduction in the capital gains tax and the repeal of a 1991 beer tax increase. It opposes a national 0.08 percent blood-alcohol content legal limit and a proposed ergonomics rule by the Occupational Safety and Health Administration.

NBWA is seeking to relax commercial driver's license standards, which require drivers to be tested and licensed by a state government. The group says the cost of the standards has caused a shortage of drivers for small companies.

The group supports efforts to enforce state laws against buying beer via direct mail shipments.

More than 80 percent of NBWA's 1995-96 PAC contributions went to Republican candidates. Among beer and liquor wholesalers, the group ranked first by a wide margin in total contributions to congressional candidates. The top recipients were Sen. Gordon H. Smith, R-Ore., Reps. Barbara Cubin, R-Wyo., Robert Wexler, D-Fla., Greg Ganske, R-Iowa, former Rep. David Funderburk, R-N.C., and 1996 Republican House candidate Jim Bunn of Oregon.

National Beer Wholesalers' Association Political Action Committee (NBWA PAC) (C00144766) *Address: same as sponsor * Treasurer: Ronald A. Sarasin * Contact: David K. Rehr, V.P. of Gov. Relations*

	1993-94	1995-96	1997	Totals
Receipts	$1,361,109	$1,479,970	$766,629	$3,607,708
Disburse	1,452,735	1,541,939	422,674	3,417,348
Cash	72,807	10,837	354,792	n/a
Contributions	1,248,224	1,324,992	340,219	2,913,435
Republicans	954,715	1,105,592	271,219	2,331,526
No. of Cand.	*243*	*270*	*110*	*623*
House	781,465	915,092	205,719	1,902,276
Senate	173,250	190,500	65,500	429,250
Democrats	287,509	219,400	68,000	574,909
No. of Cand.	*104*	*84*	*45*	*233*
House	248,769	186,900	62,000	497,669
Senate	38,740	32,500	6,000	77,240
Incumbents	758,474	948,742	318,219	2,025,435
Challengers	211,000	79,250	5,500	295,750
Open Seat	278,750	297,000	16,500	592,250
Winners	1,082,734	1,008,742	n/a	2,091,476
Losers	165,490	316,250	n/a	481,740

National Licensed Beverage Association

*Phone: (703) 671-7575 * Fax: (703) 845-0310*
4214 King St. W., Alexandria, VA 22302-1507
*Web: www.nlba.org * E-mail: nlba@msn.com*

The National Licensed Beverage Association represents more than 16,000 bars, taverns, restaurants, cocktail lounges, stores and hotels that sell alcoholic beverages. The group has more than 30 affiliated state chapters.

In addition to monitoring legislation and providing information about the industry, the organization also sponsors a program that trains bartenders, waiters and waitresses to serve alcohol in a responsible manner.

National Licensed Beverage Association Beverage Alcohol Retailer PAC (NLBA BAR-PAC) (C00200337) *Address: same as sponsor * Treasurer: Donald W. Larson * Contact: Debra A. Leach, Executive Dir.*

	1993-94	1995-96	1997	Totals
Receipts	$1,935	$19,158	$5,831	$26,924
Disburse	4,410	14,896	3,000	22,306
Cash	3,908	8,173	11,006	n/a
Contributions	4,660	11,750	3,000	19,410
Republicans	2,090	10,000	3,000	15,090
No. of Cand.	*4*	*16*	*4*	*24*
House	750	8,000	3,000	11,750
Senate	1,340	2,000	0	3,340
Democrats	2,570	1,750	0	4,320
No. of Cand.	*6*	*4*	*0*	*10*
House	1,950	1,250	0	3,200
Senate	620	500	0	1,120
Incumbents	2,570	8,750	3,000	14,320
Challengers	840	1,000	0	1,840
Open Seat	1,250	2,000	0	3,250
Winners	2,750	9,750	n/a	12,500
Losers	1,910	2,000	n/a	3,910

Robert Mondavi Corp.

Phone: (800) 228-1395 x4520
841 Latour Ct., Napa, CA 94558
Web: www.mondavi.com

The Robert Mondavi Winery is a private company founded in 1966 by Robert Mondavi and his eldest son, R. Michael Mondavi. Robert Mondavi is the largest exporter of premium California wines. The locations of its wineries include California's Napa Valley, North Coast, Monterey County, Santa Barbara County and Central Valley, as well as Tuscany, Italy, Languedoc-Roussillon, France and Chile. The winery popularized dry-fermented, oak-aged Sauvignon Blanc as Fume Blanc in the late 1960s.

In 1995, Marchesi de'Frescobaldi and the Robert Mondavi Winery formed a joint venture to produce ultra premium and super premium wines from Tuscany vineyards. The first wine of the partnership, Luce, was introduced in June 1997.

The Robert Mondavi Corp. Civic Action Committee (C00283259) *Address: same as sponsor * Treasurer: Roxanne M. Young*

	1993-94	1995-96	1997	Totals
Receipts	$26,722	$31,000	$15,000	$72,722
Disburse	24,558	27,452	9,010	61,020
Cash	2,167	5,715	11,705	n/a
Contributions	12,650	21,650	8,000	42,300
Republicans	2,375	15,650	2,500	20,525
No. of Cand.	*3*	*11*	*3*	*17*
House	2,375	8,650	2,500	13,525
Senate	0	7,000	0	7,000
Democrats	10,275	6,000	5,500	21,775
No. of Cand.	*11*	*5*	*5*	*21*
House	4,775	4,000	4,500	13,275
Senate	5,500	2,000	1,000	8,500
Incumbents	10,650	19,150	6,000	35,800
Challengers	1,500	0	0	1,500
Open Seat	500	2,500	2,000	5,000
Winners	8,150	20,650	n/a	28,800
Losers	4,500	1,000	n/a	5,500

Sebastiani Vineyards Inc.

*Phone: (707) 938-5532 * Fax: (707) 935-1218*
389 Fourth St. E., Sonoma, CA 95476
Web: www.sebastiani.com

Sebastiani Vineyards is the fifth-largest winery in California, producing labels such as August Sebastiani, Talus and Vendange. The company posted sales of about $200 million in 1996 and employs more than 250 people.

Today, the third generation of the Sonoma Valley family runs the winery. Under the direction of August Sebastiani's widow, Sylvia, their son Don Sebastiani acts as chairman of the board and chief executive officer. Other family members involved include: August and Sylvia's daughter, Mary Ann Sebastiani Cuneo and her husband, Richard A. Cuneo, who serves as winery president.

Don Sebastiani was formerly a California state legislator.

Sebastiani Vineyards Inc. Political Action Committee (C00301143) *Address: same as sponsor * Treasurer: James Knapp*

	1993-94	1995-96	1997	Totals
Receipts	$0	$30,114	$16,418	$46,532
Disburse	0	6,054	4,335	10,389
Cash	0	24,060	36,144	n/a
Contributions	0	6,000	3,000	9,000
Republicans	0	3,750	2,000	5,750
No. of Cand.	*0*	*7*	*3*	*10*
House	0	2,750	1,000	3,750
Senate	0	1,000	1,000	2,000
Democrats	0	2,250	1,000	3,250
No. of Cand.	*0*	*5*	*1*	*6*
House	0	2,000	1,000	3,000
Senate	0	250	0	250
Incumbents	0	4,500	3,000	7,500
Challengers	0	750	0	750
Open Seat	0	250	0	250
Winners	0	3,500	n/a	3,500
Losers	0	2,500	n/a	2,500

Southern Wine & Spirits

*Phone: (305) 625-4171 * Fax: (305) 624-7735*
1600 N.W. 163rd St., Miami, FL 33169

Southern Wine & Spirits is the nation's largest wine and spirits distributor. It is a privately held company with 4,000 employees and distribution centers in Arizona, California, Florida, Nevada, Pennsylvania and South Carolina. Estimated 1996 sales were $2.2 billion.

Southern Wine & Spirits PAC (C00217877) *Address: same as sponsor * Treasurer: Steven Becker*

	1993-94	1995-96	1997	Totals
Receipts	$15,908	$17,648	$17,060	$50,616
Disburse	10,785	14,800	4,200	29,785
Cash	13,310	17,419	30,281	n/a
Contributions	10,650	14,750	4,200	29,600
Republicans	2,950	1,250	2,200	6,400
No. of Cand.	*3*	*1*	*2*	*6*
House	2,450	1,250	1,200	4,900
Senate	500	0	1,000	1,500
Democrats	7,700	13,500	2,000	23,200
No. of Cand.	*11*	*8*	*2*	*21*
House	2,700	8,500	0	11,200
Senate	5,000	5,000	2,000	12,000
Incumbents	10,400	12,750	3,200	26,350
Challengers	0	1,000	1,000	2,000
Open Seat	250	1,000	0	1,250
Winners	8,150	13,750	n/a	21,900
Losers	2,500	1,000	n/a	3,500

Tennessee Malt Beverage Association

Phone: (615) 242-7656
404 James Robertson Pkwy., Suite 1006, Nashville, TN 37219

The Tennessee Malt Beverage Association represents the beer industry in that state. The group focuses on state politics in Tennessee. According to the Beer Institute, Tennessee's four breweries and 42 wholesalers employ more than 20,000 people and generate annual sales of about $900 million.

Tennessee Malt Beverage Association Federal Political Action Committee (C00250449) *Address: same as sponsor * Treasurer: Bill T. Williams*

	1993-94	1995-96	1997	Totals
Receipts	$7,167	$8,654	$10,486	$26,307
Disburse	18,229	12,150	3,905	34,284
Cash	12,824	9,332	15,913	n/a
Contributions	9,650	6,850	1,750	18,250
Republicans	900	4,500	1,000	6,400
No. of Cand.	*1*	*4*	*1*	*6*
House	0	1,500	0	1,500
Senate	900	3,000	1,000	4,900
Democrats	8,750	2,350	750	11,850
No. of Cand.	*8*	*5*	*2*	*15*
House	6,750	2,250	750	9,750
Senate	2,000	100	0	2,100
Incumbents	5,500	5,000	1,750	12,250
Challengers	900	850	0	1,750
Open Seat	3,250	1,000	0	4,250
Winners	4,400	5,000	n/a	9,400
Losers	5,250	1,850	n/a	7,100

United Distillers and Vintners North America

*Phone: (860) 702-4000 * Fax: (860) 702-4045*
450 Columbus Blvd., P.O. Box 778, Hartford, CT 06142

United Distillers and Vintners (UDV) North America, formerly known as Heublein, makes alcoholic beverages including Smirnoff, Jose Cuervo, Baileys, J&B and TGI Fridays Frozen Drinks. UDV wines include Beaulieu Vineyard, Glen Ellen, M.G. Vallejo, Blossom Hill, Rutherford Estate Cellars and Christian Brothers. The $1.8-billion Hartford, Conn. company is a wholly owned subsidiary of Grand Metropolitan, a British company that owns Burger King, Pillsbury, Pearle Vision and Foster's. In December 1997, Grand Metropolitan merged with Guinness to become Diageo.

The company said in January 1998 that it will be leaving Hartford for Stamford, Conn., probably by the end of 1998. News stories said there could be 125 layoffs. The company had moved 435 employees to Hartford from Farmington, Conn. about two years ago. The whole company has about 7,500 employees.

UDV operates three wine facilities in California: the Beaulieu Vineyard facility in Napa, the Glen Ellen Winery in Sonoma and the Paicines winery on the central coast.

The company recently bought an island in the Bahamas and named it the Republic of Cuervo Gold.

Heublein was previously owned by R.J. Reynolds.

Heublein Employees' Political Participation Committee (C00034470) *Address: same as sponsor * Treasurer: Daria J. Cirish*

	1993-94	1995-96	1997	Totals
Receipts	$17,688	$21,303	$9,307	$48,298
Disburse	112,496	88,412	33,830	234,738
Cash	237,598	170,493	145,971	n/a
Contributions	84,970	50,275	20,000	155,245
Republicans	28,850	25,175	11,000	65,025
No. of Cand.	*35*	*39*	*18*	*92*
House	19,350	23,425	8,000	50,775
Senate	9,500	1,750	3,000	14,250
Democrats	56,120	25,100	8,500	89,720
No. of Cand.	*64*	*33*	*11*	*108*
House	43,000	15,600	4,000	62,600
Senate	13,120	9,500	4,500	27,120

(Data for Heublein Employees' Political continued)

Incumbents	80,120	46,100	20,500	146,720
Challengers	2,100	175	0	2,275
Open Seat	2,250	4,000	0	6,250
Winners	64,000	45,100	n/a	109,100
Losers	20,970	5,175	n/a	26,145

Heublein Distributors' PAC (formerly known as Smirnoff/Inglenook Distributors PAC) (C00212126) *Phone: (860) 702-4000 * Fax: (860) 702-4169 * 450 Columbus Blvd., Hartford, CT 06142 * Treasurer: Richard S. Sarnowski * Contact: Peter Seremet, Chairman*

This PAC represents the distribution division of UDV North America, formerly known as Heublein Distributors.

	1993-94	1995-96	1997	Totals
Receipts	$5,481	$53,156	$0	$58,637
Disburse	84,078	68,043	35,804	187,925
Cash	84,651	69,765	33,961	n/a
Contributions	77,150	61,925	34,750	173,825
Republicans	19,000	30,575	21,000	70,575
No. of Cand.	*23*	*42*	*27*	*92*
House	13,000	25,075	16,500	54,575
Senate	6,000	5,500	4,500	16,000
Democrats	58,150	31,350	13,750	103,250
No. of Cand.	*55*	*37*	*18*	*110*
House	42,150	24,350	10,700	77,200
Senate	16,000	7,000	3,050	26,050
Incumbents	72,150	60,425	33,250	165,825
Challengers	2,500	0	500	3,000
Open Seat	2,500	1,500	1,000	5,000
Winners	62,650	59,925	n/a	122,575
Losers	14,500	2,000	n/a	16,500

United Liquors Ltd.

*Phone: (508) 588-2300 * Fax: (508) 588-2515*
One United Dr., West Bridgewater, MA 02379

United Liquors is a Massachusetts-based beverage distribution company. It distributes alcoholic and non-alcoholic beverages, such as Concord Pale Ale and Clearly Canadian Beverages.

United Liquors Ltd. Good Government Committee (formerly known as Good Government Committee) (C00249078) *Address: same as sponsor * Treasurer: Lewis P. Gack*

	1993-94	1995-96	1997	Totals
Receipts	$2,200	$5,790	$7,000	$14,990
Disburse	0	7,250	7,500	14,750
Cash	2,222	762	262	n/a
Contributions	0	5,250	-2500	2,750
Republicans	0	0	2,000	2,000
No. of Cand.	*0*	*0*	*1*	*1*
House	0	0	0	0
Senate	0	0	2,000	2,000
Democrats	0	5,250	-4500	750
No. of Cand.	*0*	*6*	*1*	*7*
House	0	5,250	-4500	750
Senate	0	0	0	0
Incumbents	0	5,250	-2500	2,750
Challengers	0	0	0	0
Open Seat	0	0	0	0
Winners	0	5,250	n/a	5,250
Losers	0	0	n/a	0

Wine & Spirits Wholesalers of America Inc.

*Phone: (202) 371-9792 * Fax: (202) 789-2405*
805 15th St. N.W., Suite 430, Washington, DC 20005
Web: www.wswa.org

Wine & Spirits Wholesalers of America represents more than 500 wine and spirits wholesaler companies from 42 states, the District of Columbia and Puerto Rico. WSWA members represent businesses that distribute an estimated 90 percent of all wine and spirits sold wholesale in the United States.

Wine & Spirits Wholesalers of America Inc. Political Action Committee (C00147173) *Address: same as sponsor * Treasurer: Douglas W. Metz * Contact: Amy Deso, Coordinator*

	1993-94	1995-96	1997	Totals
Receipts	$298,404	$282,070	$153,461	$733,935
Disburse	371,223	280,038	152,713	803,974
Cash	39,186	41,219	41,967	n/a
Contributions	190,710	160,715	108,137	459,562
Republicans	71,750	104,165	71,154	247,069
No. of Cand.	*63*	*73*	*59*	*195*
House	49,650	77,465	48,207	175,322
Senate	22,100	26,700	22,947	71,747
Democrats	118,960	56,550	36,983	212,493
No. of Cand.	*85*	*49*	*34*	*168*
House	92,100	42,050	19,483	153,633
Senate	26,860	14,500	17,500	58,860
Incumbents	172,210	146,515	98,690	417,415
Challengers	9,250	450	5,947	15,647
Open Seat	9,750	12,750	4,000	26,500
Winners	157,050	139,015	n/a	296,065
Losers	33,660	21,700	n/a	55,360

Wine Institute

*Phone: (415) 512-0151 * Fax: (415) 442-0742*
425 Market St., Suite 1000, San Francisco, CA 94105
Web: www.wineinstitute.org

The Wine Institute represents about 450 California wineries and affiliated businesses. The organization's interests include issues that affect agriculture and the wine industry.

Wine Institute Political Action Committee (C00065219) *Phone: (202) 408-0870 * Fax: (202) 371-0061 * 601 13th St. N.W., Suite 580 S., Washington, DC 20005 * Treasurer: Steven J. Gross*

	1993-94	1995-96	1997	Totals
Receipts	$151,681	$106,018	$35,445	$293,144
Disburse	166,729	104,152	24,082	294,963
Cash	251	2,114	13,476	n/a
Contributions	135,310	89,349	18,248	242,907
Republicans	11,884	30,202	4,064	46,150
No. of Cand.	*12*	*21*	*4*	*37*
House	11,384	27,202	3,064	41,650
Senate	500	3,000	1,000	4,500
Democrats	121,176	59,147	14,184	194,507
No. of Cand.	*60*	*32*	*15*	*107*
House	73,587	30,503	8,203	112,293
Senate	47,589	28,644	5,981	82,214
Incumbents	118,150	73,546	17,248	208,944
Challengers	6,064	1,632	0	7,696
Open Seat	11,096	14,171	1,000	26,267
Winners	100,863	85,762	n/a	186,625
Losers	34,447	3,587	n/a	38,034

Business Associations

Business and Professional Women/USA

*Phone: (202) 293-1100 * Fax: (202) 861-0298*
2012 Massachusetts Ave. N.W., Washington, DC 20036
Web: www.bpwusa.org

Business and Professional Women/USA (formerly known as the National Federation of Business and Professional Women's Clubs) is a nonprofit organization founded in 1919 that works to benefit women in the working world. It has 70,000 members nationwide.

The organization seeks to promote the interests of business and professional women and to extend educational opportunities through industrial, scientific and vocational activities.

Through 2,000 local chapters nationwide, the BPW Federation offers programs on political, economic and social topics to prepare members for leadership roles. Areas of interest include child care and workplace equality.

BPW also provides scholarships and loans to women who are pursuing their undergraduate and graduate degrees.

The National Federation of Business & Professional Women's Clubs Inc. PAC (C00119545) *Address: same as sponsor * Treasurer: Betty J. Hill*

	1993-94	1995-96	1997	Totals
Receipts	$27,805	$32,429	$23,360	$83,594
Disburse	26,249	38,850	3,800	68,899
Cash	41,552	35,135	54,695	n/a
Contributions	19,000	31,250	1,250	51,500
Republicans	1,250	1,750	0	3,000
No. of Cand.	*3*	*5*	*0*	*8*
House	750	250	0	1,000

Senate	500	1,500	0	2,000
Democrats	16,500	29,500	1,250	47,250
No. of Cand.	*46*	*62*	*3*	*111*
House	13,750	19,000	250	33,000
Senate	2,750	10,500	1,000	14,250
Incumbents	10,500	9,250	1,000	20,750
Challengers	3,000	15,500	0	18,500
Open Seat	5,500	6,500	250	12,250
Winners	8,000	14,500	n/a	22,500
Losers	11,000	16,750	n/a	27,750

Business-Industry PAC

*Phone: (202) 833-1880 * Fax: (202) 833-2338*
888 16th St. N.W., Suite 305, Washington, DC 20006
*Web: www.bipac.org * E-mail: info@bipac.org*

The Business-Industry PAC is an independent, bipartisan organization that promotes free enterprise, economic growth and opportunity and a greater participation of the business community in the political process. BIPAC focuses its efforts on creating a majority favorable to its overall goals in both chambers of Congress, rather than lobbying for a specific legislative agenda.

Since 1963, BIPAC's political action fund has supported pro-business congressional candidates. Through its Business Institute for Political Analysis, BIPAC also generates research and analyses of campaigns, candidates and legislation, including a monthly digest, "Elections In-Sight."

The self-proclaimed "leadership PAC" of business, BIPAC has more than 500 member corporations and associations.

Business-Industry Political Action Committee (C00001727) *Address: same as sponsor * Treasurer: Donald E. Meiners * Contact: Charles S. Mack, President and CEO*

	1993-94	1995-96	1997	Totals
Receipts	$331,334	$320,731	$145,949	$798,014
Disburse	338,081	299,252	46,440	683,773
Cash	103,050	124,529	224,037	n/a
Contributions	107,674	143,437	3,531	254,642
Republicans	97,316	134,692	3,531	235,539
No. of Cand.	*91*	*120*	*5*	*216*
House	76,966	103,388	1,301	181,655
Senate	20,350	31,304	2,230	53,884
Democrats	10,358	8,745	0	19,103
No. of Cand.	*10*	*7*	*0*	*17*
House	10,358	8,745	0	19,103
Senate	0	0	0	0
Incumbents	9,049	50,312	1,301	60,662
Challengers	50,570	30,909	0	81,479
Open Seat	48,055	62,216	2,230	112,501
Winners	66,512	83,674	n/a	150,186
Losers	41,162	59,763	n/a	100,925

Greater Washington Board of Trade

*Phone: (202) 857-5900 * Fax: (202) 223-2648*
1129 20th St. N.W., Suite 200, Washington, DC 20036
*Web: www.bot.org * E-mail: info@bot.org*

The Greater Washington Board of Trade is a regional board of commerce for the District of Columbia area, including suburban Maryland and northern Virginia. The board works to promote Washington businesses locally and across the country. It has been involved in developing the Metro system, building convention centers, creating low-income housing and assisting with job training.

In addition to the federal PAC, the board has three other PACs — for northern Virginia, suburban Maryland and Washington proper.

Greater Washington Board of Trade Federal Political Action Committee (C00009795) *Address: same as sponsor * Treasurer: William M. Freeman*

	1993-94	1995-96	1997	Totals
Receipts	$73,633	$79,394	$28,616	$181,643
Disburse	76,820	103,655	7,150	187,625
Cash	49,812	25,552	47,018	n/a
Contributions	61,000	92,500	26,500	180,000
Republicans	15,000	50,500	11,500	77,000
No. of Cand.	*5*	*10*	*4*	*19*
House	15,000	34,500	11,500	61,000
Senate	0	16,000	0	16,000
Democrats	46,000	42,000	15,000	103,000
No. of Cand.	*16*	*9*	*4*	*29*
House	22,500	34,000	15,000	71,500

Senate	23,500	8,000	0	31,500
Incumbents	52,000	92,000	26,500	170,500
Challengers	6,500	0	0	6,500
Open Seat	2,500	500	0	3,000
Winners	56,000	86,500	n/a	142,500
Losers	5,000	6,000	n/a	11,000

Lincoln Club of San Diego County

*Phone: (619) 237-9782 * Fax: (619) 237-9292*
750 B St., Suite 1600, San Diego, CA 92101
E-mail: l_club98@aol.com

The Lincoln Club of San Diego County is a group of about 200 leading civic and business leaders committed to fiscal responsibility, economic growth and conservative political participation. It supports Republican candidates at all levels of government and recruits candidates for open positions.

This chapter was founded in 1986. In addition to its political action activities, the club also organizes regular meetings with elected representatives for its members and offers seminars on campaigning, political appointments and the media.

The Lincoln Club of San Diego County (formerly known as Golden Eagle Club of San Diego County) (C00177766) *681 Encinitas Blvd., Suite 405, Encinitas, CA 92024 * Treasurer: F. Laurence Scott Jr.*

*Contact: Roxana Foxx, Chairperson * Phone: (619) 237-9782*

	1993-94	1995-96	1997	Totals
Receipts	$191,910	$224,327	$201,459	$617,696
Disburse	195,889	227,665	163,536	587,090
Cash	6,211	2,973	40,896	n/a
Contributions	17,500	11,000	0	28,500
Republicans	17,500	11,000	0	28,500
No. of Cand.	*5*	*3*	*0*	*8*
House	17,500	11,000	0	28,500
Senate	0	0	0	0
Democrats	0	0	0	0
No. of Cand.	*0*	*0*	*0*	*0*
House	0	0	0	0
Senate	0	0	0	0
Incumbents	500	10,000	0	10,500
Challengers	17,000	1,000	0	18,000
Open Seat	0	0	0	0
Winners	12,500	10,000	n/a	22,500
Losers	5,000	1,000	n/a	6,000

National Association of Small Business Investment Companies

*Phone: (202) 628-5055 * Fax: (202) 628-5080*
666 11th St. N.W., Suite 750, Washington, DC 20001
Web: www.envista.com/nasbic

The National Association of Small Business Investment Companies represents companies licensed by the Small Business Administration to provide small businesses with advisory services, equity financing and long-term loans.

Among other activities, NASBIC has successfully fought for government policies permitting SBICs to channel more venture capital and long-term loans to new and growing small businesses.

National Association of Small Business Investment Companies Political Action Committee (C00109991) *Address: same as sponsor * Treasurer: Peter F. McNeish * Contact: Harvey Granat, Chairperson*

	1993-94	1995-96	1997	Totals
Receipts	$0	$69,621	$43,591	$113,212
Disburse	5,750	60,180	48,000	113,930
Cash	1,349	10,789	6,381	n/a
Contributions	5,750	56,050	46,000	107,800
Republicans	500	44,800	39,500	84,800
No. of Cand.	*1*	*44*	*31*	*76*
House	500	31,800	21,000	53,300
Senate	0	13,000	18,500	31,500
Democrats	5,250	11,250	6,500	23,000
No. of Cand.	*7*	*12*	*9*	*28*
House	5,250	8,250	5,500	19,000
Senate	0	3,000	1,000	4,000
Incumbents	5,250	49,050	45,500	99,800
Challengers	0	1,000	500	1,500
Open Seat	500	6,000	0	6,500
Winners	4,000	49,800	n/a	53,800
Losers	1,750	6,250	n/a	8,000

National Cooperative Business Association

*Phone: (202) 638-6222 * Fax: (202) 638-1374*
1401 New York Ave. N.W., Suite 1100, Washington, DC 20005
Web: www.cooperative.org

The National Cooperative Business Association is a"cross-industry membership" trade association that represents 47,000 cooperatives. Formerly known as the Cooperative League of the USA, it was founded in 1916 with a mission of advancing and developing cooperative enterprise.

Members range from cooperative businesses in the fields of housing and agricultural marketing to firms that produce consumer goods and services. NCBA provides training and technical assistance, publications and programs for its members.

The group follows issues such as proposed standards for labeling foods "organic."

National Cooperative Business Association Cooperative Action for Congressional Trust (CoAct) (C00151027) *Address: same as sponsor * Treasurer: Richard Jon Dines*

	1993-94	1995-96	1997	Totals
Receipts	$34,123	$15,452	$5,433	$55,008
Disburse	25,510	23,269	4,500	53,279
Cash	9,908	2,093	3,027	n/a
Contributions	25,950	22,750	4,500	53,200
Republicans	4,000	8,250	1,000	13,250
No. of Cand.	*9*	*17*	*2*	*28*
House	2,000	5,750	1,000	8,750
Senate	2,000	2,500	0	4,500
Democrats	20,950	14,500	3,500	38,950
No. of Cand.	*37*	*29*	*8*	*74*
House	18,450	12,500	3,250	34,200
Senate	2,500	2,000	250	4,750
Incumbents	23,200	15,500	4,500	43,200
Challengers	1,250	1,250	0	2,500
Open Seat	1,500	6,000	0	7,500
Winners	19,950	19,500	n/a	39,450
Losers	6,000	3,250	n/a	9,250

National Federation of Independent Business

*Phone: (615) 385-9745 * Fax: (615) 386-9349*
3322 West End Ave., Suite 700, Nashville, TN 37203
Web: www.nfib.org

The premier lobbying organization for small businesses, the 600,000-member National Federation of Independent Business ranked in a recent Fortune magazine survey as Washington's most powerful business lobby. NFIB pushes for tax breaks for small businesses and greater rights under federal workplace regulations.

The NFIB's top issues in 1998 include defeating several bills that would require businesses to provide health insurance for employees. It supports the SAFE Act, which would allow businesses to hire independent personnel to evaluate workplace safety issues and would encourage a cooperative regulatory approach from the Occupational Safety and Health Administration. It opposes increases in the minimum wage. In September 1997, the NFIB began a petition drive to abolish the current federal tax code by 2000.

The group's contributions to congressional elections catapulted from $371,675 during the 1993-94 cycle to more than $1 million during the 1995-96 cycle. It spent 94 percent of its money on congressional candidates.

The NFIB spent half of its money on incumbents and split the rest between challengers and open races, favoring Republicans. The leading recipients were Sen. Gordon H. Smith, R-Ore., Rep. Allen Boyd, D-Fla., and former Rep. Steve Stockman, R-Texas.

National Federation of Independent Business/Save America's Free Enterprise Trust (C00101105) *Phone: (202) 554-9000 * Fax: (202) 484-9267 * 600 Maryland Ave. S.W., Suite 700, Washington, DC 20024 * Treasurer: Fred Holladay*

	1993-94	1995-96	1997	Totals
Receipts	$508,623	$1,139,433	$790,881	$2,438,937
Disburse	384,393	1,111,102	238,544	1,734,039
Cash	125,250	153,583	705,920	n/a
Contributions	371,675	1,070,543	225,630	1,667,848
Republicans	338,525	1,001,851	193,630	1,534,006
No. of Cand.	*205*	*274*	*105*	*584*
House	236,525	800,457	136,630	1,173,612
Senate	102,000	201,394	57,000	360,394
Democrats	31,400	68,692	29,500	129,592
No. of Cand.	*25*	*26*	*15*	*66*
House	31,400	68,692	29,500	129,592
Senate	0	0	0	0
Incumbents	153,675	533,888	196,630	884,193
Challengers	125,000	231,678	17,500	374,178
Open Seat	93,000	306,627	12,500	412,127
Winners	294,425	623,480	n/a	917,905
Losers	77,250	447,063	n/a	524,313

U.S. Federation of Small Businesses

Phone: (800) 637-3331
249 Green St., Schenectady, NY 12305
Web: www.global2000.net/usfsb

The U.S. Federation of Small Businesses, based in Schenectady, N.Y., represents more than 25,000 small businesses in 50 states.

The USFSB follows tax, minimum wage, paperwork reduction, regulatory reduction, Small Business Administration and banking issues.

U.S. Federation of Small Businesses PAC (Small Biz PAC) (C00218982) *Phone: (202) 547-0555 * Fax: (202) 546-8060 * 208 G St. N.E., Second Floor, Washington, DC 20002 * Treasurer: Carla L. Saunders * Contact: Karl Ottosen, Dir. of Gov. Affairs*

	1993-94	1995-96	1997	Totals
Receipts	$15,484	$15,463	$31	$30,978
Disburse	16,223	16,011	1,158	33,392
Cash	2,838	2,290	1,164	n/a
Contributions	15,350	13,500	1,000	29,850
Republicans	15,350	13,000	1,000	29,350
No. of Cand.	*12*	*12*	*2*	*26*
House	3,100	3,000	500	6,600
Senate	12,250	10,000	500	22,750
Democrats	0	500	0	500
No. of Cand.	*0*	*1*	*0*	*1*
House	0	500	0	500
Senate	0	0	0	0
Incumbents	11,750	7,500	0	19,250
Challengers	2,600	2,500	500	5,600
Open Seat	1,000	3,500	500	5,000
Winners	14,000	11,500	n/a	25,500
Losers	1,350	2,000	n/a	3,350

Business Services

ADVO Inc.

*Phone: (860) 285-6126 * Fax: (860) 285-6230*
One Univac Lane, Windsor, CT 06095-0755
Web: www.advo.com

ADVO is the nation's largest full-service, direct-mail marketing company, distributing more than three billion pieces of advertising annually for 23,000 clients.

Established in 1929, the public company had 1997 sales of $1 billion and nearly 5,000 employees. As the company behind both the Mailbox Values brand and the Missing Child Card, ADVO delivers mail to more than 61 million households weekly, making it the U.S. Postal Service's largest commercial customer.

ADVO also offers transportation services in certain areas, and operates 19 mail processing facilities and 70 sales offices nationwide.

ADVO Inc. Political Action Committee (also known as ADVOPAC) (C00196659) *Address: same as sponsor * Treasurer: Vincent Giuliano*

	1993-94	1995-96	1997	Totals
Receipts	$78,023	$73,289	$29,039	$180,351
Disburse	74,652	118,864	42,851	236,367
Cash	73,821	28,247	14,436	n/a
Contributions	47,732	45,000	17,500	110,232
Republicans	5,125	23,500	7,000	35,625
No. of Cand.	*7*	*13*	*3*	*23*
House	2,500	13,500	6,000	22,000
Senate	2,625	10,000	1,000	13,625
Democrats	42,607	21,500	10,500	74,607
No. of Cand.	*21*	*11*	*10*	*42*
House	16,997	16,000	4,500	37,497
Senate	25,610	5,500	6,000	37,110
Incumbents	46,982	39,000	16,500	102,482
Challengers	0	0	0	0

Open Seat	750	6,000	1,000	7,750
Winners	39,125	40,000	n/a	79,125
Losers	8,607	5,000	n/a	13,607

American Council of Highway Advertisers

1650 Cedar Ln., P.O. Box 388, Shadyside, MD 20764

The American Council of Highway Advertisers PAC was terminated in January 1998.

Highway Advertisers Political Action Committee (C00300889) *Address: same as sponsor * Treasurer: Mary Amelia Roberts*

	1993-94	1995-96	1997	Totals
Receipts	$0	$11,505	$44	$11,549
Disburse	0	6,516	5,036	11,552
Cash	0	4,991	0	n/a
Contributions	0	5,500	5,000	10,500
Republicans	0	1,000	1,000	2,000
No. of Cand.	*0*	*1*	*1*	*2*
House	0	1,000	1,000	2,000
Senate	0	0	0	0
Democrats	0	4,500	3,000	7,500
No. of Cand.	*0*	*5*	*3*	*8*
House	0	4,500	3,000	7,500
Senate	0	0	0	0
Incumbents	0	5,500	5,000	10,500
Challengers	0	0	0	0
Open Seat	0	0	0	0
Winners	0	5,500	n/a	5,500
Losers	0	0	n/a	0

Borg-Warner Security Corp.

*Phone: (312) 322-8500 * Fax: (312) 322-8509*
200 S. Michigan Ave., 21st Floor, Chicago, IL 60604
Web: www.borg-warnersecurity.com

Borg-Warner Security provides a broad line of protective services to more than 140,000 customers, including guard, alarm, armored transport and courier services. The company contends that, based on revenues and the variety of services offered, it is the largest and broadest-based supplier in the protective services industry in the United States. Borg-Warner employs 73,000 workers and had sales of more than $1.7 billion in 1997.

Borg-Warner Security is composed of many of the top brand-names in the security industry, including Burns International, Wells Fargo and Globe.

Among other services, Borg-Warner Security provides physical security personnel and patrol services; design, installation, monitoring and maintenance of electronic security systems; closed-circuit television and access control; intrusion and fire detection; and background screening and investigative services.

Borg-Warner Security PAC (formerly known as Baker Industries PAC) (C00227058) *Address: same as sponsor * Treasurer: Carol Bynoe*

	1993-94	1995-96	1997	Totals
Receipts	$12,215	$5,230	$692	$18,137
Disburse	8,169	8,255	2,250	18,674
Cash	24,042	16,526	14,969	n/a
Contributions	12,280	7,250	2,250	21,780
Republicans	5,780	5,750	1,000	12,530
No. of Cand.	*6*	*8*	*1*	*15*
House	3,280	3,600	0	6,880
Senate	2,500	2,150	1,000	5,650
Democrats	6,500	1,500	1,250	9,250
No. of Cand.	*5*	*2*	*2*	*9*
House	6,500	1,500	500	8,500
Senate	0	0	750	750
Incumbents	10,780	5,600	2,250	18,630
Challengers	500	0	0	500
Open Seat	1,000	1,650	0	2,650
Winners	11,280	5,600	n/a	16,880
Losers	1,000	1,650	n/a	2,650

Central Station Alarm Association

*Phone: (703) 242-4670 * Fax: (703) 242-4675*
440 Maple Ave. E., Suite 201, Vienna, VA 22180
*Web: www.csaaul.org * E-mail: admin@csaaul.org.*

The Central Station Alarm Association represents sellers of burglar and fire alarm equipment. The nonprofit group was founded in 1950 as the Central Station Electrical Protection Association.

In 1997, the group lobbied the FCC to restrain Ameritech Corp. from acquiring alarm monitoring companies in violation of the Telecommunications Act of 1996.

The PAC's supporters include officials from Wells Fargo and ADT.

Alarm Industry Communications Committee Political Action Committee (C00248690) *Address: same as sponsor * Treasurer: Pat Egan * Contact: Steve Doyle, Executive V.P.*

	1993-94	1995-96	1997	Totals
Receipts	$36,204	$52,311	$24,985	$113,500
Disburse	73,705	59,421	12,806	145,932
Cash	23,841	21,958	26,376	n/a
Contributions	67,200	54,300	9,000	130,500
Republicans	10,250	30,500	3,500	44,250
No. of Cand.	*12*	*14*	*5*	*31*
House	7,250	20,000	2,500	29,750
Senate	3,000	10,500	1,000	14,500
Democrats	56,950	23,800	5,500	86,250
No. of Cand.	*40*	*17*	*2*	*59*
House	27,350	13,800	500	41,650
Senate	29,600	10,000	5,000	44,600
Incumbents	66,200	53,800	9,000	129,000
Challengers	0	1,000	0	1,000
Open Seat	1,500	0	0	1,500
Winners	49,100	37,550	n/a	86,650
Losers	18,100	16,750	n/a	34,850

Contract Services Association

*Phone: (202) 347-0600 * Fax: (202) 347-0608*
1200 G St. N.W., Suite 750, Washington, DC 20005
Web: www.csa-dc.org

The Contract Services Association is a nonprofit group representing the government services contracting industry. The association monitors regulations and legislation affecting purchases by federal agencies and helps the more than 300 member businesses seek government contracts.

CSA's members include Lockheed Martin Technology Services Group, Wackenhut Services Inc., First Union National Bank and the law firm of Akin, Gump, Strauss, Hauer & Feld.

Contract Services Association Political Action Committee CSA PAC (C00217661) *Address: same as sponsor * Treasurer: Gary D. Engebretson*

	1993-94	1995-96	1997	Totals
Receipts	$28,403	$31,345	$22,089	$81,837
Disburse	25,870	33,555	19,239	78,664
Cash	4,599	2,388	2,437	n/a
Contributions	25,550	31,775	18,500	75,825
Republicans	18,500	24,775	15,000	58,275
No. of Cand.	*16*	*26*	*14*	*56*
House	8,500	19,275	12,000	39,775
Senate	10,000	5,500	3,000	18,500
Democrats	7,050	7,000	3,500	17,550
No. of Cand.	*9*	*5*	*3*	*17*
House	6,050	7,000	3,500	16,550
Senate	1,000	0	0	1,000
Incumbents	23,050	30,750	18,500	72,300
Challengers	500	1,025	0	1,525
Open Seat	2,000	0	0	2,000
Winners	22,950	28,250	n/a	51,200
Losers	2,600	3,525	n/a	6,125

Dun & Bradstreet Corp.

Phone: (908) 665-5000
One Diamond Hill Rd., Murray Hill, NJ 07974-0027
*Web: www.dnb.com * E-mail: cantrellj@mail.dnb.com*

Dun & Bradstreet is a business information company with three units: D&B, which collects and disseminates data on 45 million companies; Moody's Investors Service, a debt rating agency; and Reuben H. Donnelley, a yellow pages publisher. The publicly traded company employs 16,000 people in 40 countries and is headquartered in Murray Hill, N.J. It posted $2.1 billion in 1997 sales.

In December 1997, Dun & Bradstreet announced plans to spin off Reuben H. Donnelley into a separate, publicly traded company by the summer of 1998. With revenues of $378 million, the Purchase, N.Y.

company is the largest independent marketer of yellow pages in the United States. Donnelley would assume $450 million of D&B's debt.

Dun & Bradstreet also recently announced an agreement with Network Solutions Inc., which assigns Internet addresses. The agreement would enable companies to apply for a Dun & Bradstreet business identification number, a D-U-N-S Number, when they apply for an Internet address. D-U-N-S Numbers are widely used to uniquely identify businesses. Executives said the deal will help enable electronic commerce.

Jean Cantrell, director of government affairs and the PAC's treasurer, is a private sector representative on the California Legislature Joint Task Force on Personal Information & Privacy.

Political Action Committee of the Dun & Bradstreet Corp. (C00119669) *Phone: (202) 463-2154 * Fax: (202) 463-2163 * 1200 New Hampshire Ave. N.W., Suite 440, Washington, DC 20036 * Treasurer: Jean Cantrell*

	1993-94	1995-96	1997	Totals
Receipts	$155,757	$90,441	$4,582	$250,780
Disburse	163,651	90,169	7,014	260,834
Cash	3,154	3,427	995	n/a
Contributions	88,750	54,200	4,000	146,950
Republicans	27,800	37,200	1,000	66,000
No. of Cand.	*24*	*32*	*2*	*58*
House	9,300	15,000	1,000	25,300
Senate	18,500	22,200	0	40,700
Democrats	60,950	17,000	3,000	80,950
No. of Cand.	*49*	*19*	*5*	*73*
House	39,700	13,500	2,000	55,200
Senate	21,250	3,500	1,000	25,750
Incumbents	81,000	45,850	3,500	130,350
Challengers	2,250	3,450	0	5,700
Open Seat	5,500	3,900	500	9,900
Winners	69,750	42,000	n/a	111,750
Losers	19,000	12,200	n/a	31,200

Eller Media Co.

*Phone: (602) 957-8116 * Fax: (602) 381-5731*
2850 E. Camelback Rd., Suite 300, Phoenix, AZ 85016
Web: www.clearchannel.com

Eller Media was purchased in April 1997 by Clear Channel Communications Inc., a publicly held broadcasting company that owns and/or programs 175 radio stations and 18 television stations in 39 markets in the United States and reported $790 million in 1997 revenues. Through its ownership of Eller Media, the company has about 54,000 outdoor advertising displays in 16 major metropolitan markets.

Clear Channel owns 32 percent of Heftel Broadcasting Corp., the largest Spanish-language radio broadcaster in the United States. It also has broadcasting operations in Australia, New Zealand and the Czech Republic.

In September 1997, Eller Media signed an agreement to acquire all the existing stock of Metro Display Advertising. The merger gives Eller Media 4,000 transit shelter displays throughout Los Angeles, Orange and Northern San Diego counties in California.

Eller Media Co. Political Action Committee (C00279216) *Address: same as sponsor * Treasurer: Tim Donmoyer * Contact: Michael Porter, Chairman*

	1993-94	1995-96	1997	Totals
Receipts	$40,470	$44,810	$33,836	$119,116
Disburse	23,974	23,498	36,510	83,982
Cash	16,498	37,871	35,198	n/a
Contributions	12,950	20,900	16,100	49,950
Republicans	4,250	13,850	6,500	24,600
No. of Cand.	*6*	*19*	*10*	*35*
House	2,250	7,600	3,500	13,350
Senate	2,000	6,250	3,000	11,250
Democrats	8,700	7,050	9,600	25,350
No. of Cand.	*16*	*13*	*12*	*41*
House	3,900	5,050	1,600	10,550
Senate	4,800	2,000	8,000	14,800
Incumbents	10,450	15,450	14,100	40,000
Challengers	1,500	2,200	0	3,700
Open Seat	1,000	3,250	2,000	6,250
Winners	10,600	17,950	n/a	28,550
Losers	2,350	2,950	n/a	5,300

Express Services Inc.

*Phone: (405) 840-5000 * Fax: (405) 722-6512*
6300 N.W. Expressway, Oklahoma City, OK 73132
Web: www.expresshr.com

Express Services is a wholly franchised operation. Express Personnel Services is a full-service employment firm offering temporary help, flexible staffing, full-time placement, executive recruiting and human resource services to companies worldwide. Based in Oklahoma, the company's 1996 revenue was more than $850 million.

Founded in 1983, Express is one of the top 10 staffing companies in North America. It employs nearly 300,000 people and supports more than 300 franchised offices, including locations in Russia, Canada and the Ukraine.

Express Services Inc. PAC (C00302240) *Address: same as sponsor * Treasurer: Thomas N. Richards*

	1993-94	1995-96	1997	Totals
Receipts	$0	$25,100	$10,000	$35,100
Disburse	0	22,250	100	22,350
Cash	0	1,850	11,750	n/a
Contributions	0	19,500	0	19,500
Republicans	0	17,000	0	17,000
No. of Cand.	*0*	*16*	*0*	*16*
House	0	8,000	0	8,000
Senate	0	9,000	0	9,000
Democrats	0	2,500	0	2,500
No. of Cand.	*0*	*4*	*0*	*4*
House	0	2,500	0	2,500
Senate	0	0	0	0
Incumbents	0	3,750	0	3,750
Challengers	0	5,000	0	5,000
Open Seat	0	10,750	0	10,750
Winners	0	11,500	n/a	11,500
Losers	0	8,000	n/a	8,000

Heritage Media Corp.

13355 Noel Rd., Suite 1500, Dallas, TX 75240

The Heritage Media PAC filed for termination in August 1997.

Heritage Media Corp. Political Action Committee (C00226779) *Address: same as sponsor * Treasurer: Douglas N. Woodrum*

	1993-94	1995-96	1997	Totals
Receipts	$12,509	$27,991	$0	$40,500
Disburse	15,250	27,800	11,219	54,269
Cash	11,465	11,219	0	n/a
Contributions	11,500	20,500	3,000	35,000
Republicans	10,000	19,500	3,000	32,500
No. of Cand.	*17*	*25*	*3*	*45*
House	2,750	13,250	0	16,000
Senate	7,250	6,250	3,000	16,500
Democrats	1,500	1,000	0	2,500
No. of Cand.	*3*	*1*	*0*	*4*
House	1,500	1,000	0	2,500
Senate	0	0	0	0
Incumbents	6,000	10,500	3,000	19,500
Challengers	2,000	4,000	0	6,000
Open Seat	3,500	6,000	0	9,500
Winners	9,750	10,250	n/a	20,000
Losers	1,750	10,250	n/a	12,000

Kelly Services Inc.

*Phone: (248) 244-4874 * Fax: (248) 244-5497*
999 W. Big Beaver Rd., Troy, MI 48084
*Web: www.kellyservices.com * E-mail: juanita _ pierman@kellyservices.com*

Based in Troy, Mich., Kelly Services provides temporary office personnel and services to 215,000 customers in the United States, Canada and Europe. Its more than 1,500 locations offer clerical, marketing, professional, technical, light industrial, home care, management and other business services.

Founded in 1946, publicly traded Kelly Services has annual sales of $3.3 billion, ranking it No. 406 on the Fortune 500. The company has 150,000 temporary employees and 4,000 full-time employees worldwide.

Subsidiaries include: Kelly Temporary Services, Kelly Assisted Living Services, Kelly Staff Leasing TM, The Wallace Law Registry and Kelly PinPoint.

Kelly Services Inc. Political Action Committee (KellyPAC) (C00212522) *Address: same as sponsor * Treasurer: Juanita L. Pierman*

	1993-94	1995-96	1997	Totals
Receipts	$29,140	$37,086	$0	$66,226
Disburse	34,100	18,120	4,450	56,670
Cash	549	19,515	14,843	n/a
Contributions	12,500	5,650	1,750	19,900
Republicans	7,500	2,700	1,750	11,950
No. of Cand.	*10*	*8*	*2*	*20*
House	2,000	1,700	1,750	5,450
Senate	5,500	1,000	0	6,500
Democrats	5,000	2,950	0	7,950
No. of Cand.	*11*	*5*	*0*	*16*
House	3,500	1,950	0	5,450
Senate	1,500	1,000	0	2,500
Incumbents	8,300	3,950	1,750	14,000
Challengers	500	950	0	1,450
Open Seat	3,700	750	0	4,450
Winners	9,500	3,950	n/a	13,450
Losers	3,000	1,700	n/a	4,700

Lamar Corp.

*Phone: (800) 926-1000 * Fax: (504) 928-3400*
P.O. Box 66338, Baton Rouge, LA 70896-6338
*Web: www.lamar.com * E-mail: clamar@lamar.com*

Lamar is the parent company of Lamar Advertising Co., one of the largest outdoor-advertising companies in the United States, with 45,000 billboards in 26 states. The publicly traded Louisiana company has 800 employees and reported 1996 sales of $27.4 million.

Founded in 1902, Lamar Advertising has four divisions. Lamar Outdoor Advertising owns the billboards and operates 69 outdoor-advertising plants. Lamar Transit Advertising has 17 franchises in seven states, posting displays on buses, bus shelters and benches. Interstate Logos Inc. provides 61,000 blue interstate highway services signs in 18 states. Interstate Graphics provides printing services.

Locally based advertising constitutes more than 80 percent of Lamar's outdoor advertising.

Lamar Advertising plans to purchase 4,297 displays from Midwestern outdoor advertising companies Ragan Outdoor, Derby Outdoor, Pioneer, Overland and Superior for $50.2 million.

Lamar Corp. Political Action Committee (LamarPAC) (C00174599) *Address: same as sponsor * Treasurer: Charles W. Lamar III * Contact: Kevin P. Reilly Jr., Chairperson*

	1993-94	1995-96	1997	Totals
Receipts	$20,574	$14,311	$4,092	$38,977
Disburse	13,868	19,201	6,119	39,188
Cash	8,420	3,530	1,503	n/a
Contributions	7,380	10,300	3,500	21,180
Republicans	5,060	8,050	1,500	14,610
No. of Cand.	*8*	*14*	*5*	*27*
House	2,460	4,550	1,500	8,510
Senate	2,600	3,500	0	6,100
Democrats	2,320	2,250	2,000	6,570
No. of Cand.	*6*	*5*	*4*	*15*
House	1,700	1,750	2,000	5,450
Senate	620	500	0	1,120
Incumbents	5,080	7,300	3,000	15,380
Challengers	300	0	0	300
Open Seat	2,000	3,000	0	5,000
Winners	5,460	8,300	n/a	13,760
Losers	1,920	2,000	n/a	3,920

National Association of Temporary & Staffing Services

*Phone: (703) 549-6287 * Fax: (703) 549-5180*
119 S. Saint Asaph St., Alexandria, VA 22314-3119
*Web: www.natss.org * E-mail: elenz@natss.org*

The National Association of Temporary & Staffing Services represents about 1,600 temping companies. The organization has 80 affiliated chapters in 45 states, the District of Columbia and Puerto Rico.

National Association of Temporary & Staffing Services PAC (C00145623) *Address: same as sponsor * Treasurer: Edward A. Lenz * Contact: Kathie Hanratty-Masi, Chairwoman*

	1993-94	1995-96	1997	Totals
Receipts	$172,899	$154,263	$69,564	$396,726
Disburse	157,523	211,704	63,875	433,102
Cash	131,583	71,792	76,775	n/a
Contributions	56,600	82,922	38,750	178,272
Republicans	40,000	73,422	30,250	143,672
No. of Cand.	*24*	*44*	*32*	*100*
House	16,500	37,425	28,250	82,175
Senate	23,500	35,997	2,000	61,497
Democrats	16,600	9,500	8,500	34,600
No. of Cand.	*12*	*6*	*6*	*24*
House	16,600	9,500	5,500	31,600
Senate	0	0	3,000	3,000
Incumbents	46,600	52,925	42,250	141,775
Challengers	2,500	9,500	0	12,000
Open Seat	8,500	20,497	1,000	29,997
Winners	51,500	56,300	n/a	107,800
Losers	5,100	26,622	n/a	31,722

National Auctioneers Association

*Phone: (913) 541-8084 * Fax: (913) 894-5281*
8880 Ballentine St., Overland Park, KS 66214-1985
*Web: www.auctioneers.org * E-mail: naahq@aol.com*

The National Auctioneers Association represents about 5,600 members from across the nation. The organization was founded in 1949.

National Auctioneers Association PAC (Auction PAC) (C00296962) *Address: same as sponsor * Treasurer: Stephen H. Schofield * Contact: Joseph Keefhaver, Executive V.P.*

	1993-94	1995-96	1997	Totals
Receipts	$480	$32,288	$10,516	$43,284
Disburse	56	27,287	8,463	35,806
Cash	422	5,421	7,473	n/a
Contributions	0	8,500	5,500	14,000
Republicans	0	8,500	5,500	14,000
No. of Cand.	*0*	*6*	*4*	*10*
House	0	6,500	1,000	7,500
Senate	0	2,000	4,500	6,500
Democrats	0	0	0	0
No. of Cand.	*0*	*0*	*0*	*0*
House	0	0	0	0
Senate	0	0	0	0
Incumbents	0	7,500	5,500	13,000
Challengers	0	1,000	0	1,000
Open Seat	0	0	0	0
Winners	0	7,000	n/a	7,000
Losers	0	1,500	n/a	1,500

National Court Reporters Association

*Phone: (703) 556-6272 * Fax: (703) 556-6291*
8224 Old Courthouse Rd., Vienna, VA 22182
Web: www.verbatimreporters.com/ncra/reporter

The National Court Reporters Association was established in 1899 as the National Shorthand Reporters Association, a professional association for court reporters. It has more than 34,000 members, including official and freelance shorthand reporters, students and associate members.

Many of the estimated 50,000 court reporters in the United States are employed by court systems to report both civil and criminal trials. Others are freelance reporters who work for themselves or contract their services to freelance reporting firms. Freelance reporters are hired by attorneys, corporations, unions, associations and other individuals and groups that need records of pretrial depositions, arbitrations, board of directors meetings, stockholders meetings and convention business sessions.

National Court Reporters Association Political Action Committee (C00146506) *Address: same as sponsor * Treasurer: Brian E. Cartier * Contact: John J. Prout Jr., President*

	1993-94	1995-96	1997	Totals
Receipts	$33,501	$48,601	$11,156	$93,258
Disburse	14,662	51,453	6,253	72,368
Cash	74,272	71,424	76,328	n/a
Contributions	12,500	36,500	4,500	53,500
Republicans	5,000	23,500	2,500	31,000
No. of Cand.	*9*	*26*	*4*	*39*
House	2,500	16,000	1,500	20,000
Senate	2,500	7,500	1,000	11,000

(Data for National Court Reporters continued)

Democrats	7,500	13,000	2,000	22,500
No. of Cand.	13	15	3	31
House	5,500	9,500	500	15,500
Senate	2,000	3,500	1,500	7,000
Incumbents	12,500	31,000	4,500	48,000
Challengers	0	0	0	0
Open Seat	0	5,500	0	5,500
Winners	11,000	31,500	n/a	42,500
Losers	1,500	5,000	n/a	6,500

National Customs Brokers & Forwarders Association

*Phone: (202) 466-0222 * Fax: (202) 466-0226*
1200 18th St. N.W., #901, Washington, DC 20036
*Web: www.ncbfaa.org/ncbfaa * E-mail: staff@ncbfaa.org*

The National Customs Brokers & Forwarders Association represents workers who advise companies on processing ocean-shipped freight in and out of the United States.

The association is 101 years old and represents about 700 customs brokers and forwarders.

National Customs Brokers & Forwarders Association PAC (C00207969) *Address: same as sponsor * Treasurer: Eric Scharf * Contact: John Kent, Legislative Representative*

	1993-94	1995-96	1997	Totals
Receipts	$20,822	$29,756	$10,816	$61,394
Disburse	27,910	25,154	11,445	64,509
Cash	10,567	15,169	14,541	n/a
Contributions	24,740	23,500	11,000	59,240
Republicans	8,500	14,000	7,500	30,000
No. of Cand.	9	14	10	33
House	5,000	8,000	5,500	18,500
Senate	3,500	6,000	2,000	11,500
Democrats	16,240	9,500	3,500	29,240
No. of Cand.	19	11	5	35
House	12,500	6,500	1,500	20,500
Senate	3,740	3,000	2,000	8,740
Incumbents	24,240	20,500	11,000	55,740
Challengers	0	0	0	0
Open Seat	500	3,000	0	3,500
Winners	19,000	18,500	n/a	37,500
Losers	5,740	5,000	n/a	10,740

Orion Consulting Inc.

*Phone: (216) 687-1480 * Fax: (216) 687-1488*
1301 E. Ninth St., Suite 3000, Cleveland, OH 44144-1800
Web: www.orion-consulting.com

Orion Consulting is a privately owned management consulting firm with about 140 employees in nine offices across the United States. Orion provides technical expertise in the areas of strategic planning, claim auditing, benefit administration, compliance review, management information systems, managed care, payment systems and actuarial analysis.

Its target customers are the health care industry, health insurance companies, health care maintenance organizations and government agencies.

Orion Consulting Inc. Political Trust PAC (also known as OPTPAC) (C00293761) *Address: same as sponsor * Treasurer: Robert E. Paponetti*

	1993-94	1995-96	1997	Totals
Receipts	$7,361	$17,502	$0	$24,863
Disburse	7,204	17,072	42	24,318
Cash	155	583	540	n/a
Contributions	7,150	12,000	0	19,150
Republicans	7,150	10,000	0	17,150
No. of Cand.	5	2	0	7
House	1,150	0	0	1,150
Senate	6,000	10,000	0	16,000
Democrats	0	2,000	0	2,000
No. of Cand.	0	1	0	1
House	0	2,000	0	2,000
Senate	0	0	0	0
Incumbents	250	5,000	0	5,250
Challengers	900	7,000	0	7,900
Open Seat	6,000	0	0	6,000
Winners	6,450	5,000	n/a	11,450
Losers	700	7,000	n/a	7,700

Outdoor Advertising Association of America

*Phone: (202) 833-5566 * Fax: (202) 833-1522*
1850 M St. N.W., Suite 1040, Washington, DC 20036
*Web: www.oaaa.org * E-mail: ruthsegal@oaaa.org*

The Outdoor Advertising Association of America counts more than 600 outdoor advertising companies among its members — about 90 percent of the outdoor advertising industry.

The association follows taxes affecting billboards and tracks regulations by the Federal Highway Administration relating to the Highway Beautification Act.

Members include billboard manufacturers, as well as other types of outdoor advertisers.

Outdoor Advertising Association of America Political Action Committee (C00045781) *Address: same as sponsor * Treasurer: Ruth L. Segal*

	1993-94	1995-96	1997	Totals
Receipts	$151,495	$152,365	$103,936	$407,796
Disburse	147,767	147,533	104,504	399,804
Cash	4,678	9,506	8,937	n/a
Contributions	131,746	144,022	99,036	374,804
Republicans	55,236	92,467	61,504	209,207
No. of Cand.	38	65	35	138
House	26,259	39,372	24,080	89,711
Senate	28,977	53,095	37,424	119,496
Democrats	71,510	51,555	36,532	159,597
No. of Cand.	46	37	30	113
House	26,369	26,881	16,119	69,369
Senate	45,141	24,674	20,413	90,228
Incumbents	104,098	114,582	94,164	312,844
Challengers	10,694	7,510	0	18,204
Open Seat	16,954	21,930	4,872	43,756
Winners	91,119	119,146	n/a	210,265
Losers	40,627	24,876	n/a	65,503

Outdoor Systems Inc.

Phone: (313) 872-6030
88 Custer Ave., Detroit, MI 48202

Outdoor Systems is the largest outdoor advertising company in the United States. The public company has more than 200,000 billboards and displays in 48 states, which it contracts through advertising agencies. The company, which has about 300 employees, reported 1997 sales of $455 million.

Sign/PAC (C00139089) *Address: same as sponsor * Treasurer: Sam Evola*

	1993-94	1995-96	1997	Totals
Receipts	$25,865	$14,454	$7,735	$48,054
Disburse	28,177	14,799	7,828	50,804
Cash	1,081	734	640	n/a
Contributions	7,850	5,800	500	14,150
Republicans	1,000	1,000	0	2,000
No. of Cand.	3	1	0	4
House	850	0	0	850
Senate	150	1,000	0	1,150
Democrats	6,850	4,800	500	12,150
No. of Cand.	9	5	1	15
House	2,550	2,175	500	5,225
Senate	4,300	2,625	0	6,925
Incumbents	4,150	5,450	500	10,100
Challengers	0	350	0	350
Open Seat	3,700	0	0	3,700
Winners	2,050	4,800	n/a	6,850
Losers	5,800	1,000	n/a	6,800

Penn Advertising

R.D. 24, P.O. Box 6157, York, PA 17406

Penn Advertising's PAC was terminated in April 1997 after the company was purchased by Lamar Advertising.

Penn Advertising Political Action Committee Federal (C00208231) *Address: same as sponsor * Treasurer: Christine Martin*

	1993-94	1995-96	1997	Totals
Receipts	$16,883	$14,669	$876	$32,428
Disburse	16,944	14,643	2,110	33,697
Cash	1,210	1,234	0	n/a
Contributions	11,750	11,460	2,070	25,280
Republicans	7,850	6,760	2,070	16,680
No. of Cand.	6	7	5	18
House	4,900	5,510	1,820	12,230

Senate	2,950	1,250	250	4,450
Democrats	3,900	4,700	0	8,600
No. of Cand.	*5*	*6*	*0*	*11*
House	2,900	2,850	0	5,750
Senate	1,000	1,850	0	2,850
Incumbents	8,200	9,110	1,910	19,220
Challengers	2,950	500	160	3,610
Open Seat	600	1,850	0	2,450
Winners	10,750	9,410	n/a	20,160
Losers	1,000	2,050	n/a	3,050

Professionals in Advertising PAC

1675 Broadway, New York, NY 10019

Professionals in Advertising PAC lobbies members of the Ways and Means and Senate Finance committees to preserve the deductibility of advertising as a business expense. It also opposes banning or restricting truthful speech about legal products, a matter handled by the commerce committees.

ProAdPAC Treasurer Harold A. Shoup is director of the American Association of Advertising Agencies. PAC Chairman Roy Bostock is CEO of The McManus Group in New York.

Leading recipients for the 1995-96 election cycle included both the chairman and ranking member of the Senate Commerce Committee, Sens. Larry Pressler, R-S.D., and Ernest F. Hollings, D-S.C., who received $6,000 and $3,500 respectively.

The PAC was founded in 1988, and has had roughly 400 contributors since that time.

Professionals In Advertising Political Action Committee (C00233353) *Phone: (202) 331-7345 * Fax: (202) 857-3675 * 1899 L St. N.W., Suite 700, Washington, DC 20036 * Treasurer: Harold A. Shoup * Contact: Roy Bostock, Chairman*

	1993-94	1995-96	1997	Totals
Receipts	$68,223	$144,750	$43,775	$256,748
Disburse	71,227	129,456	58,854	259,537
Cash	2,267	17,559	2,475	n/a
Contributions	58,550	111,750	49,049	219,349
Republicans	14,750	77,000	35,300	127,050
No. of Cand.	*15*	*60*	*36*	*111*
House	9,500	53,000	26,300	88,800
Senate	5,250	24,000	9,000	38,250
Democrats	43,800	34,750	13,749	92,299
No. of Cand.	*37*	*34*	*16*	*87*
House	31,050	27,750	7,749	66,549
Senate	12,750	7,000	6,000	25,750
Incumbents	54,300	107,550	45,549	207,399
Challengers	1,250	0	500	1,750
Open Seat	3,000	3,700	3,000	9,700
Winners	44,800	102,250	n/a	147,050
Losers	13,750	9,500	n/a	23,250

ServiceMaster Co.

*Phone: (630) 271-1300 * Fax: (630) 271-5753*
One ServiceMaster Way, Downers Grove, IL 60515
Web: www.svm.com

ServiceMaster is a cleaning, lawn care and pest control company located in Illinois. Its consumer division produces Terminix pest control products and ChemLawn lawn care treatments. The publicly traded company, which employs about 40,000 people, reported 1997 sales of just less than $4 billion. One of its stated objectives is to "honor God in all we do."

ServiceMaster is the nation's largest commercial and residential cleaning franchiser. The company also handles plant operations and maintenance and housekeeping and linen services for hospitals and other health care companies.

ServiceMaster Co. LP PAC (C00303206) *Address: same as sponsor * Treasurer: Claire E. Buchan*

	1993-94	1995-96	1997	Totals
Receipts	$0	$55,942	$25,889	$81,831
Disburse	0	42,245	39,643	81,888
Cash	0	13,703	0	n/a
Contributions	0	35,550	15,320	50,870
Republicans	0	24,550	10,570	35,120
No. of Cand.	*0*	*26*	*8*	*34*
House	0	13,050	8,570	21,620
Senate	0	11,500	2,000	13,500
Democrats	0	11,000	4,750	15,750
No. of Cand.	*0*	*10*	*4*	*14*
House	0	9,000	2,500	11,500
Senate	0	2,000	2,250	4,250
Incumbents	0	23,750	15,320	39,070
Challengers	0	1,500	0	1,500
Open Seat	0	10,300	0	10,300
Winners	0	29,050	n/a	29,050
Losers	0	6,500	n/a	6,500

Wackenhut Corp.

*Phone: (561) 622-5656 * Fax: (561) 691-6736*
4200 Wackenhut Dr. #100, Palm Beach Gardens, FL 33140-4243
Web: www.wackenhut.com

Wackenhut is a worldwide provider of security-related services to business, industry and government agencies. With operations throughout the United States and more than 50 countries on six continents, it is a leader in the privatization of public services for municipal, state and federal agencies. The publicly traded company had $906 million in 1996 sales and has 51,000 employees.

The company's security guard division provides armed and unarmed protection of property. Specialized services include executive protection, crash-fire-rescue services and fire protection at governmental installations and pre-departure passenger and luggage screening in airports. Wackenhut also owns 55 percent of Wackenhut Corrections, the second-largest operator of private prisons in the United States.

Wackenhut is headquartered in Palm Beach Gardens, Fla.

Wackenhut Corp. Political Action Committee (Wackenhut PAC) (C00165365) *Address: same as sponsor * Treasurer: Craig T. Stewart * Contact: Richard R. Wackenhut, President and COO*

	1993-94	1995-96	1997	Totals
Receipts	$18,309	$16,835	$4,699	$39,843
Disburse	13,404	9,186	1,383	23,973
Cash	11,002	18,653	20,984	n/a
Contributions	9,700	5,350	1,250	16,300
Republicans	6,700	3,600	250	10,550
No. of Cand.	*9*	*6*	*1*	*16*
House	5,200	1,600	250	7,050
Senate	1,500	2,000	0	3,500
Democrats	3,000	1,750	1,000	5,750
No. of Cand.	*4*	*4*	*1*	*9*
House	1,000	750	1,000	2,750
Senate	2,000	1,000	0	3,000
Incumbents	5,200	2,500	1,000	8,700
Challengers	2,500	0	0	2,500
Open Seat	2,000	2,600	0	4,600
Winners	5,700	3,600	n/a	9,300
Losers	4,000	1,750	n/a	5,750

Casinos/Gambling

American Gaming Association

*Phone: (202) 637-6500 * Fax: (202) 637-6507*
555 13th St. N.W., Suite 1010 E., Washington, DC 20004-1109
Web: www.americangaming.org

The American Gaming Association is a national trade group for casino gambling companies. Headed by Frank J. Fahrenkopf Jr., former chairman of the Republican National Committee, the association lobbies on behalf of its members, which include Caesars, Harrah's Entertainment Inc., MGM Grand Inc., Mirage Resorts Inc. and other gambling-related businesses. Commercial casinos exist in at least 10 states, and AGA says the industry employs more than 1 million people.

American Gaming Association Political Action Committee (C00309146) *Address: same as sponsor * Treasurer: Judy L. Patterson * Contact: Frank J. Fahrenkopf Jr., President and CEO*

	1993-94	1995-96	1997	Totals
Receipts	$0	$23,600	$10,050	$33,650
Disburse	0	22,363	13,316	35,679
Cash	0	1,234	-41.00	n/a
Contributions	0	10,750	9,250	20,000
Republicans	0	6,750	3,750	10,500
No. of Cand.	*0*	*9*	*5*	*14*
House	0	4,250	750	5,000

(Data for American Gaming Association continued)

Senate	0	2,500	3,000	5,500
Democrats	0	4,000	5,500	9,500
No. of Cand.	*0*	*4*	*4*	*8*
House	0	2,000	1,500	3,500
Senate	0	2,000	4,000	6,000
Incumbents	0	10,500	9,000	19,500
Challengers	0	250	0	250
Open Seat	0	0	250	250
Winners	0	9,500	n/a	9,500
Losers	0	1,250	n/a	1,250

Bally's Grand Inc.

*Phone: (702) 739-4111 * Fax: (702) 739-4804*
P.O. Box 96506, Las Vegas, NV 89199
Web: www.ballyslv.com

Bally's Grand terminated its PAC in May 1997.

The company merged with Hilton Hotels after filing for bankruptcy. Bally's Grand owned and operated Bally's Las Vegas casino in Las Vegas.

Bally's Grand Inc. Recreation Enterprise PAC (C00112425) *Address: same as sponsor * Treasurer: Jerry A. Blumenshine*

	1993-94	1995-96	1997	Totals
Receipts	$22,818	$45,949	$2,701	$71,468
Disburse	27,067	19,510	29,467	76,044
Cash	323	26,765	0	n/a
Contributions	20,500	16,500	0	37,000
Republicans	1,000	3,500	0	4,500
No. of Cand.	*1*	*2*	*0*	*3*
House	1,000	3,500	0	4,500
Senate	0	0	0	0
Democrats	19,500	13,000	0	32,500
No. of Cand.	*6*	*5*	*0*	*11*
House	10,000	12,500	0	22,500
Senate	9,500	500	0	10,000
Incumbents	18,500	1,500	0	20,000
Challengers	0	8,500	0	8,500
Open Seat	2,000	6,500	0	8,500
Winners	8,500	5,000	n/a	13,500
Losers	12,000	11,500	n/a	23,500

Boyd Gaming Corp.

*Phone: (702) 792-7200 * Fax: (702) 792-7266*
2950 S. Industrial Rd., Las Vegas, NV 89109-1100

Boyd Gaming owns 12 gaming and hotel facilities in Nevada, Mississippi, Missouri, Louisiana and Illinois. The company, which went public in 1989, employs more than 14,000 people and reported 1997 sales in excess of $800 million. The Boyd family owns 49 percent of the company.

Boyd owns and operates facilities in three distinct markets in Las Vegas: the Stardust on the Las Vegas Strip; Sam's Town Las Vegas, the Eldorado and Jokers Wild on the Boulder Strip; and the California and the Fremont in downtown Las Vegas.

Subsidiaries include: California Hotel and Casino, Eldorado Casino, Fremont Hotel and Casino, Jokers Wild Hotel and Casino, Sam's Town Tunica, Silver Star Resort and Casino, Stardust Resort and Casino and Treasure Chest Casino.

Boyd Gaming Political Action Committee (C00142315) *Address: same as sponsor * Treasurer: Richard Alan Darnold*

	1993-94	1995-96	1997	Totals
Receipts	$47,600	$172,807	$14,701	$235,108
Disburse	50,014	61,500	59,520	171,034
Cash	2,087	113,396	68,577	n/a
Contributions	40,500	55,500	30,000	126,000
Republicans	18,500	29,500	13,000	61,000
No. of Cand.	*4*	*11*	*4*	*19*
House	13,000	26,000	5,000	44,000
Senate	5,500	3,500	8,000	17,000
Democrats	22,000	26,000	17,000	65,000
No. of Cand.	*6*	*11*	*7*	*24*
House	7,000	10,000	10,000	27,000
Senate	15,000	16,000	7,000	38,000
Incumbents	24,000	28,500	20,000	72,500
Challengers	13,000	1,500	5,000	19,500
Open Seat	3,500	25,500	5,000	34,000
Winners	25,000	42,000	n/a	67,000
Losers	15,500	13,500	n/a	29,000

California Indian Nation PAC

*Phone: (213) 489-4792 * Fax: (213) 489-4818*
555 S. Flower St., Suite 4510, Los Angeles, CA 90071

California Indian Nation PAC represents the Sycuan, Barona and Viejas Indians. All three of the small tribes operate casinos in the San Diego area.

The PAC, which was founded in 1993, is bipartisan.

California Indian Nation Political Action Committee (CIN-PAC) (C00282335) *Address: same as sponsor * Treasurer: David L. Gould*

	1993-94	1995-96	1997	Totals
Receipts	$28,550	$26,000	$0	$54,550
Disburse	27,549	25,746	1,176	54,471
Cash	1,000	1,252	76	n/a
Contributions	5,500	10,500	0	16,000
Republicans	2,000	4,500	0	6,500
No. of Cand.	*2*	*4*	*0*	*6*
House	2,000	3,000	0	5,000
Senate	0	1,500	0	1,500
Democrats	3,500	6,000	0	9,500
No. of Cand.	*3*	*2*	*0*	*5*
House	1,500	4,000	0	5,500
Senate	2,000	2,000	0	4,000
Incumbents	3,000	10,500	0	13,500
Challengers	2,000	0	0	2,000
Open Seat	500	0	0	500
Winners	5,000	10,500	n/a	15,500
Losers	500	0	n/a	500

Circus Circus Enterprises Inc.

*Phone: (702) 734-0410 * Fax: (702) 734-5154*
2880 Las Vegas Blvd. S., Las Vegas, NV 89109-1120

Circus Circus Enterprises owns and operates casinos and hotels in Nevada, Illinois and Mississippi, and is headquartered in Las Vegas. Posting 1997 sales of $1.3 billion, Circus employs 20,000 people.

In February 1998, the company announced its newest Las Vegas hotel and casino, to be named Mandalay Bay. The $950-million, 3,700-room luxury destination resort will be located on 60 acres just south of the company's Luxor resort in Las Vegas.

The company's Nevada properties include Circus Circus, Luxor, Excalibur and Slots-A-Fun in Las Vegas; Circus Circus-Reno; the Colorado Belle and Edgewater in Laughlin; the Gold Strike and Nevada Landing in Jean; and Railroad Pass in Henderson. Circus Circus also operates Silver City in Las Vegas; owns a 50 percent interest in Silver Legacy, Reno, Nev.; and owns a 50 percent interest in and operates the Monte Carlo in Las Vegas.

The company owns and operates the Gold Strike, a riverboat casino and hotel in Tunica County, Miss., and owns a 50 percent interest in and operates the Grand Victoria riverboat casino in Elgin, Ill.

Circus Circus Enterprises Inc. Political Action Committee (also known as CC-PAC) (C00218289) *Address: same as sponsor * Treasurer: Mike H. Sloan*

	1993-94	1995-96	1997	Totals
Receipts	$89,947	$40,330	$128	$130,405
Disburse	78,403	34,104	17,028	129,535
Cash	12,848	19,079	1,722	n/a
Contributions	54,000	31,507	17,000	102,507
Republicans	15,000	25,550	5,000	45,550
No. of Cand.	*3*	*10*	*3*	*16*
House	9,000	15,550	4,000	28,550
Senate	6,000	10,000	1,000	17,000
Democrats	39,000	5,957	12,000	56,957
No. of Cand.	*14*	*7*	*6*	*27*
House	14,000	6,457	0	20,457
Senate	25,000	-500	12,000	36,500
Incumbents	34,500	15,550	17,000	67,050
Challengers	11,000	0	0	11,000
Open Seat	3,500	18,457	0	21,957
Winners	33,000	21,550	n/a	54,550
Losers	21,000	9,957	n/a	30,957

Delaware North Companies Inc.

*Phone: (716) 858-5000 * Fax: (716) 858-5479*
One Delaware N. Place, 438 Main St., Buffalo, NY 14202

Delaware North is a holding company for concession operations and greyhound racing tracks. In 1996, the company ranked No. 256 on the Forbes list of top private companies. It posted $1.2 billion in sales and employed more than 25,000 workers in 1997.

Delaware North has two subsidiaries for concessions: Sportservice Corp. and CA1, for sports arenas and airports, respectively. It also has all concession and tour rights for Yosemite National Park and Spaceport USA at Kennedy Space Center.

A Delaware North subsidiary, Sportsystems Corp., owns and operates eight greyhound racing tracks, as well as one horse racing track.

Delaware North owner Jeremy Jacobs also owns the Boston Bruins hockey team. He has a major interest in the new Boston Fleet Sports Center, which replaced Boston Garden, where DNC had all concessions rights.

Delaware North has other interests in Australia, New Zealand and Canada.

Delaware North Companies Inc. Political Action Committee (C00158899) *Address: same as sponsor * Treasurer: David J. G. Chambers * Contact: Richard Stephens, President*

	1993-94	1995-96	1997	Totals
Receipts	$13,810	$20,765	$-250	$34,325
Disburse	3,485	17,045	10,021	30,551
Cash	11,181	14,901	4,630	n/a
Contributions	700	10,550	4,900	16,150
Republicans	500	8,550	3,900	12,950
No. of Cand.	*1*	*13*	*6*	*20*
House	500	8,050	3,000	11,550
Senate	0	500	900	1,400
Democrats	200	2,000	1,000	3,200
No. of Cand.	*1*	*2*	*2*	*5*
House	200	1,000	1,000	2,200
Senate	0	1,000	0	1,000
Incumbents	0	10,550	4,900	15,450
Challengers	0	0	0	0
Open Seat	500	0	0	500
Winners	500	10,550	n/a	11,050
Losers	200	0	n/a	200

Grand Casinos Inc.

*Phone: (320) 626-5825 * Fax: (320) 449-5992*
Hcr 67 Box 194, Onamia, MN 56359
Web: www.grandcasinos.com

Mah Mah Wi No Min II is the PAC for the Minnesota-based Grand Casinos. The public company owns the three largest casinos in Mississippi — in Gulfport, Biloxi and Tunica. It also receives 40 percent of the profits from four other casinos on Indian reservations in Louisiana and Minnesota, according to The Wall Street Journal. The company, which has 7,300 employees, also owns property in Las Vegas. It reported 1997 sales of $607 million.

Mah Mah Wi No Min II (C00279133) *Address: same as sponsor * Treasurer: Christian M. Sande*

	1993-94	1995-96	1997	Totals
Receipts	$16,390	$11,020	$0	$27,410
Disburse	7,750	15,302	3,500	26,552
Cash	8,640	4,356	856	n/a
Contributions	3,250	10,750	3,500	17,500
Republicans	0	1,750	0	1,750
No. of Cand.	*0*	*4*	*2*	*6*
House	0	1,000	0	1,000
Senate	0	750	0	750
Democrats	2,250	9,000	2,500	13,750
No. of Cand.	*4*	*13*	*5*	*22*
House	3,250	7,500	1,500	12,250
Senate	-1000	1,500	1,000	1,500
Incumbents	750	8,500	3,500	12,750
Challengers	0	2,250	0	2,250
Open Seat	2,500	0	0	2,500
Winners	750	9,000	n/a	9,750
Losers	2,500	1,750	n/a	4,250

Harrah's Entertainment Inc.

*Phone: (901) 762-8623 * Fax: (901) 762-8914*
1023 Cherry Rd., Memphis, TN 38117-5423
*Web: www.harrahs.com * E-mail: communicat@harrahs.com*

Harrah's operates 16 casinos and gaming operations from New Jersey to Washington state. A public company, Harrah's also owns hotels and more than 50 restaurants, but most of its revenues come from casinos in Nevada and Atlantic City and riverboat casinos in the Midwest. Harrah's also is the primary partner in a bankrupt New Orleans casino that it is attempting to revive. The company has operations in Illinois, Louisiana, Missouri, Mississippi and on Indian reservations in Kansas, Arizona and Washington state. It employs about 22,000 people.

The pace of consolidation within the gambling industry increased in late 1997, as Harrah's acquired Showboat Inc., which owns casinos in East Chicago, Ind., Atlantic City and Las Vegas, and has a controlling interest in another in Australia. The merger will create the world's largest gaming company. Harrah's will continue to operate Showboat's PAC.

Harrah's ranked first among gambling companies in total 1995-96 congressional contributions. Showboat's PAC ranked fifth but contributed less than one-tenth of Harrah's total. Harrah's tended to favor Republican candidates. House members made up just five of the top 21 recipients in 1996.

Harrah's Entertainment Inc. Employees' Political Action Committee (formerly known as Promus/Harrah's PAC) (C00239947) *Address: same as sponsor * Treasurer: Gary L. Burhop*

	1993-94	1995-96	1997	Totals
Receipts	$254,269	$625,504	$213,474	$1,093,247
Disburse	188,880	584,172	208,753	981,805
Cash	113,061	142,999	147,725	n/a
Contributions	108,131	462,115	145,150	715,396
Republicans	79,388	316,115	126,650	522,153
No. of Cand.	*22*	*98*	*55*	*175*
House	27,200	221,483	86,650	335,333
Senate	52,188	94,632	40,000	186,820
Democrats	28,743	146,000	18,500	193,243
No. of Cand.	*15*	*43*	*12*	*70*
House	5,966	84,500	9,000	99,466
Senate	22,777	61,500	9,500	93,777
Incumbents	39,943	309,983	125,950	475,876
Challengers	29,188	36,500	10,000	75,688
Open Seat	39,000	115,632	8,000	162,632
Winners	69,165	367,983	n/a	437,148
Losers	38,966	94,132	n/a	133,098

Showboat Inc. Political Action Committee (C00143461) *Phone: (702) 650-1200 * Fax: (702) 791-2955 * 3720 Howard Hughes Pkwy., Suite 200, Las Vegas, NV 89109 * Web: www.showboatcasino.com * Treasurer: Randy Taylor*

	1993-94	1995-96	1997	Totals
Receipts	$36,465	$62,094	$32,107	$130,666
Disburse	32,128	48,350	12,000	92,478
Cash	8,346	22,093	42,201	n/a
Contributions	27,000	32,850	7,000	66,850
Republicans	15,000	21,100	2,000	38,100
No. of Cand.	*4*	*8*	*2*	*14*
House	7,500	18,600	1,000	27,100
Senate	7,500	2,500	1,000	11,000
Democrats	12,000	11,750	5,000	28,750
No. of Cand.	*6*	*6*	*5*	*17*
House	2,500	9,250	1,000	12,750
Senate	9,500	2,500	4,000	16,000
Incumbents	12,500	20,600	7,000	40,100
Challengers	8,500	1,250	0	9,750
Open Seat	6,000	11,000	0	17,000
Winners	12,000	27,500	n/a	39,500
Losers	15,000	5,350	n/a	20,350

International Game Technology

*Phone: (702) 448-7777 * Fax: (702) 448-0120*
9295 Prototype Dr., Reno, NV 89511
Web: www.igtgame.com

International Game Technology is a leader in the design, development and manufacture of microprocessor-based slot machines, video gaming machines and software systems.

IGT employs more than 2,600 people worldwide. The publicly traded company's 1997 sales were in excess of $300 million.

IGT's machine product lines include S-Plus, Vision, Player Edge-Plus, Game King and a variety of interactive games. Software system products include MegaJackpot games like Megabucks, Wheel of Fortune, Jeopardy and the IGT Gaming System.

International Game Technology (IGT) Political Action Committee (C00316331) *Address: same as sponsor * Treasurer: J. Kenneth Creighton * Contact: Brian McKay, Chairman*

	1993-94	1995-96	1997	Totals
Receipts	$0	$20,737	$53,558	$74,295
Disburse	0	8,000	22,000	30,000
Cash	0	12,738	49,436	n/a
Contributions	0	7,000	12,000	19,000
Republicans	0	4,500	3,000	7,500
No. of Cand.	*0*	*5*	*3*	*8*
House	0	4,000	0	4,000
Senate	0	500	3,000	3,500
Democrats	0	2,500	9,000	11,500
No. of Cand.	*0*	*3*	*6*	*9*
House	0	2,000	3,000	5,000
Senate	0	500	6,000	6,500
Incumbents	0	4,500	9,000	13,500
Challengers	0	500	1,000	1,500
Open Seat	0	2,000	2,000	4,000
Winners	0	4,500	n/a	4,500
Losers	0	2,500	n/a	2,500

MGM Grand Inc.

*Phone: (702) 891-3333 * Fax: (702) 891-1114*
3799 Las Vegas Blvd. S., Las Vegas, NV 89109
*Web: www.mgmgrand.com * E-mail: info@mgmgrand.com*

MGM Grand's crown attraction is a 5,000-room hotel, casino and theme park in Las Vegas. It also owns an Australian casino, has a 50 percent stake in a New York casino, and manages a casino in South Africa. MGM was one of three successful bidders to develop a $700 million casino in Detroit.

The publicly traded company reported $891 million in 1997 sales, about half of which came from casino operations. It has about 6,200 employees.

MGM Grand Inc. PAC (also known as MGM Fed-PAC) (C00299321) *777 S. Figueroa St., Suite 3700, Los Angeles, CA 90017 * Treasurer: Dana W. Reed*

	1993-94	1995-96	1997	Totals
Receipts	$0	$40,227	$33,567	$73,794
Disburse	0	28,110	16,932	45,042
Cash	0	12,125	28,763	n/a
Contributions	0	21,500	16,931	38,431
Republicans	0	13,500	7,431	20,931
No. of Cand.	*0*	*6*	*6*	*12*
House	0	13,500	4,671	18,171
Senate	0	0	2,760	2,760
Democrats	0	8,000	9,500	17,500
No. of Cand.	*0*	*4*	*4*	*8*
House	0	7,000	7,000	14,000
Senate	0	1,000	2,500	3,500
Incumbents	0	13,000	11,931	24,931
Challengers	0	0	0	0
Open Seat	0	8,500	5,000	13,500
Winners	0	18,000	n/a	18,000
Losers	0	3,500	n/a	3,500

Mirage Resorts Inc.

*Phone: (702) 791-7126 * Fax: (702) 792-7628*
3400 Las Vegas Blvd. S., Las Vegas, NV 89109
Web: www.mirageresorts.com

Publicly traded Mirage Resorts owns four hotel-casinos in the Las Vegas area and has a share in a fifth. The company plans to open two more resorts in 1998: Bellagio, in Las Vegas, and Beau Rivage, in Biloxi, Miss. In a third project, Mirage announced it will double the size of a planned hotel-casino in Atlantic City, N.J. to 4,000 rooms.

Mirage earned $1.5 billion in revenues in 1997 and has about 18,000 employees. The company was added to the S&P 500 index of blue-chip companies in 1997.

In February 1998, a U.S. district judge dismissed a lawsuit seeking to prevent construction of a highway tunnel that would connect an expressway with the marina district in Atlantic City, where Mirage plans its new resort. The lawsuit claimed that construction would require the demolition of a mostly African-American neighborhood. The tunnel was also opposed by competitor Donald Trump.

The company operates The Mirage, a hotel-casino and destination resort on the Las Vegas Strip; Treasure Island, a hotel-casino resort adjacent to The Mirage; the Golden Nugget, a hotel-casino in downtown Las Vegas; and the Golden Nugget-Laughlin, a hotel-casino in Laughlin, Nev. The company also owns a 50 percent share in a Monte Carlo hotel-casino.

Mirage Resorts Inc. Political Action Committee (formerly known as Golden Nugget PAC) (C00222570) *Address: same as sponsor * Treasurer: Daniel Lee * Contact: Bruce Aguliera, General Counsel*

	1993-94	1995-96	1997	Totals
Receipts	$0	$102,859	$148,918	$251,777
Disburse	0	82,000	44,687	126,687
Cash	0	20,861	125,092	n/a
Contributions	0	74,000	32,683	106,683
Republicans	0	46,500	12,000	58,500
No. of Cand.	*0*	*10*	*4*	*14*
House	0	30,500	10,000	40,500
Senate	0	16,000	2,000	18,000
Democrats	0	27,500	20,683	48,183
No. of Cand.	*0*	*8*	*6*	*14*
House	0	19,500	6,683	26,183
Senate	0	8,000	14,000	22,000
Incumbents	0	40,000	32,683	72,683
Challengers	0	5,000	0	5,000
Open Seat	0	29,000	0	29,000
Winners	0	49,500	n/a	49,500
Losers	0	24,500	n/a	24,500

Schee-chu-umsh

*Phone: (208) 686-0400 * Fax: (208) 686-1182*
P.O. Box 429, Plummer, ID 83851

The Schee-chu-umsh make up a tribe of 1,500 Native Americans based on the Coeur d'Alene reservation in Northern Idaho. The bipartisan PAC, founded in 1995, gives to federal, state and local candidates sympathetic to specific Native American issues.

The Coeur d'Alene tribe runs the Coeur d'Alene Casino in Worley, Idaho.

Schee-chu-umsh (C00308148) *Address: same as sponsor * Treasurer: Kathrine M. Lowley*

	1993-94	1995-96	1997	Totals
Receipts	$0	$20,861	$0	$20,861
Disburse	0	15,068	141	15,209
Cash	0	628	168	n/a
Contributions	0	7,699	0	7,699
Republicans	0	400	0	400
No. of Cand.	*0*	*1*	*0*	*1*
House	0	0	0	0
Senate	0	400	0	400
Democrats	0	7,299	0	7,299
No. of Cand.	*0*	*9*	*0*	*9*
House	0	6,299	0	6,299
Senate	0	1,000	0	1,000
Incumbents	0	600	0	600
Challengers	0	5,499	0	5,499
Open Seat	0	1,600	0	1,600
Winners	0	1,200	n/a	1,200
Losers	0	6,499	n/a	6,499

Station Casinos Inc.

*Phone: (702) 367-2458 * Fax: (702) 221-6613*
2411 W. Sahara Ave., Las Vegas, NV 89102

Station Casinos, a publicly traded company, operates hotels and casinos in Las Vegas, gaming facilities in St. Charles, Mo., and slot and vending operations in southern Nevada and Louisiana. It employs 10,000 workers and its 1997 sales were $583 million.

In January 1998, Station Casinos was acquired by Crescent Real Estate Equities, a real estate investment trust, for $1.7 billion.

Station Casinos Inc. Political Action Committee (C00263731) *Address: same as sponsor * Treasurer: Glenn C. Christenson*

	1993-94	1995-96	1997	Totals
Receipts	$63,521	$87,512	$22,588	$173,621
Disburse	50,236	64,563	35,787	150,586
Cash	19,778	42,732	29,634	n/a
Contributions	16,750	28,375	14,700	59,825

Republicans	13,250	12,875	4,700	30,825
No. of Cand.	*11*	*6*	*4*	*21*
House	4,000	13,875	2,700	20,575
Senate	9,250	-1000	2,000	10,250
Democrats	3,500	15,500	10,000	29,000
No. of Cand.	*3*	*6*	*4*	*13*
House	500	6,000	5,000	11,500
Senate	3,000	9,500	5,000	17,500
Incumbents	10,500	20,125	12,700	43,325
Challengers	2,250	0	2,000	4,250
Open Seat	4,000	8,250	0	12,250
Winners	14,500	25,125	n/a	39,625
Losers	2,250	3,250	n/a	5,500

Chemical & Related Manufacturing

Air Products & Chemicals Inc.

Phone: (610) 481-4911
P.O. Box 441, Trexlertown, PA 18087
Web: www.airproducts.com

Air Products & Chemicals, a $7.2 billion, Pennsylvania-based company, is a leading producer of industrial gases and chemicals. Founded in 1940, the company employs 16,000 people worldwide and touts itself as the No. 1 industrial gas supplier to the electronics industry. The publicly traded company had 1997 sales of $4.6 billion.

The company's industrial gases segment recovers and distributes gases such as oxygen, nitrogen, argon and hydrogen and a variety of medical and specialty gases. The chemicals segment produces and markets polymer chemicals, performance chemicals and chemical intermediates. The equipment and services segment supplies cryogenic and other process equipment and related engineering services.

In February 1998, the company began engineering a new $50 million synthesis gas separation plant in Geismar, La. that will serve BASF Corp., Shell Chemical and other local petrochemical and refining companies. The company maintains specialty gas facilities in Chicago; Long Beach, Calif.; La Porte, Texas; Jacksonville, Fla.; Raleigh, N.C.; and the Lehigh Valley in Pennsylvania. The company has operations in 43 states, the District of Columbia, Puerto Rico and 30 countries — nine of which are in Asia.

During 1997 the company sold its landfill gas recovery business and reached an agreement to sell its equity interest in its American Ref-Fuel joint venture, the third largest waste-to-energy firm in the nation.

Air Products & Chemicals Inc. Political Alliance (C00127258)
*Phone: (202) 289-4110 * 805 15th St. N.W., Suite 410, Washington, DC 20005 * Treasurer: George V. Deputy*
*Contact: James Agger, Chairman * Phone: (610) 481-4911*

	1993-94	*1995-96*	*1997*	*Totals*
Receipts	$102,205	$126,685	$61,890	$290,780
Disburse	101,405	130,099	41,600	273,104
Cash	3,413	35,086	53,376	n/a
Contributions	56,095	42,000	17,750	115,845
Republicans	38,000	34,500	15,500	88,000
No. of Cand.	*37*	*37*	*16*	*90*
House	14,000	28,000	10,500	52,500
Senate	24,000	6,500	5,000	35,500
Democrats	18,095	7,500	2,250	27,845
No. of Cand.	*21*	*12*	*5*	*38*
House	9,595	6,500	2,250	18,345
Senate	8,500	1,000	0	9,500
Incumbents	36,345	29,500	17,750	83,595
Challengers	11,500	7,000	0	18,500
Open Seat	9,250	5,000	0	14,250
Winners	43,395	31,000	n/a	74,395
Losers	12,700	11,000	n/a	23,700

American Wood Preservers Institute

*Phone: (703) 204-0500 * Fax: (703) 204-4610*
2750 Prosperity Ave., Suite 550, Fairfax, VA 22031-4312

The American Wood Preservers Institute is the national industry trade association representing the pressure-treated wood industry throughout the United States. AWPI's members include wood preservers, including manufacturers, formulators of word preservatives and wood treating companies.

Established in 1921, the organization monitors legislation and regulations that affect the industry. It acts as a liaison between the industry and federal agencies, including the EPA. In addition, it sponsors an annual environmental seminar and legislative conference.

American Wood Preservers Institute Political Action Committee (C00151332) *Address: same as sponsor * Treasurer: Gene S. Bartlow * Contact: Allan Wilbur*

	1993-94	*1995-96*	*1997*	*Totals*
Receipts	$8,810	$23,447	$1,520	$33,777
Disburse	10,938	8,500	8,500	27,938
Cash	3,103	28,855	20,740	n/a
Contributions	10,250	14,500	4,500	29,250
Republicans	5,700	12,500	4,500	22,700
No. of Cand.	*16*	*17*	*5*	*38*
House	3,350	12,250	1,500	17,100
Senate	2,350	250	3,000	5,600
Democrats	4,550	2,000	0	6,550
No. of Cand.	*12*	*5*	*0*	*17*
House	4,650	2,000	0	6,650
Senate	-100	0	0	-100
Incumbents	8,450	14,250	4,500	27,200
Challengers	650	0	0	650
Open Seat	1,150	250	0	1,400
Winners	7,900	13,000	n/a	20,900
Losers	2,350	1,500	n/a	3,850

BetzDearborn Inc.

*Phone: (215) 355-3300 * Fax: (215) 953-2484*
4636 Somerton Rd., Trevose, PA 19053
Web: www.betzdearborn.com

BetzDearborn, based in Trevose, Pa., makes chemicals to treat water and wastewater for the chemical, petroleum, paper, automotive, electric utility and steel industries. The company's water treatment group accounts for 65 percent of sales, which exceeded $1.2 billion in 1996. BetzDearborn operates in the United States and 34 other countries and has 6,400 employees worldwide.

The company produces and markets a wide range of specialty chemical products. Its chemical treatment programs are developed and marketed for use in boilers, cooling systems, heat exchangers and paper and petroleum processes.

In November 1997, the company acquired Argo Scientific Inc., a privately held membrane support technology company based in San Marco, Calif. It is also in the process of acquiring Index Industries Inc., a privately held fuel performance additives company headquartered in Grand Rapids, Mich.

BetzDearborn was created in June 1996 from the merger of Betz Laboratories and Grace Dearborn, the water treatment division of W.R. Grace and Co.

BetzDearborn Inc. PAC (C00171314) *Address: same as sponsor * Treasurer: George L. James III * Contact: Jack Pounds, Chairman*

	1993-94	*1995-96*	*1997*	*Totals*
Receipts	$81,028	$76,419	$41,036	$198,483
Disburse	86,350	65,520	43,272	195,142
Cash	19,233	30,132	27,896	n/a
Contributions	16,500	13,250	13,500	43,250
Republicans	13,500	13,000	10,500	37,000
No. of Cand.	*6*	*7*	*6*	*19*
House	8,500	12,000	6,500	27,000
Senate	5,000	1,000	4,000	10,000
Democrats	3,000	250	3,000	6,250
No. of Cand.	*2*	*1*	*2*	*5*
House	2,000	250	3,000	5,250
Senate	1,000	0	0	1,000
Incumbents	8,500	10,250	13,500	32,250
Challengers	8,000	0	0	8,000
Open Seat	0	3,000	0	3,000
Winners	15,500	11,250	n/a	26,750
Losers	1,000	2,000	n/a	3,000

Chemical Manufacturers Association

*Phone: (703) 741-5936 * Fax: (703) 741-6097*
1300 Wilson Blvd., Arlington, VA 22209

The Chemical Manufacturers Association is a chemical trade association with 191 member companies.

CMA advocates positions consistent with "responsible care" that affect the chemical industry. CMA handles issues relating to the environment and to intellectual property rights. It lobbied to revise the air toxic rule in the EPA's 1994 wastewater provision and it has urged the EPA to allow private parties to conduct risk assessments at Superfund sites.

Chemical Manufacturers Association Political Action Committee (C00252338) *Address: same as sponsor * Treasurer: Edward L. Murphy*

	1993-94	1995-96	1997	Totals
Receipts	$56,617	$68,605	$47,857	$173,079
Disburse	57,460	68,035	20,409	145,904
Cash	2,502	3,072	31,556	n/a
Contributions	57,556	65,638	17,741	140,935
Republicans	41,200	54,638	10,000	105,838
No. of Cand.	*69*	*82*	*13*	*164*
House	28,700	39,970	6,500	75,170
Senate	12,500	14,668	3,500	30,668
Democrats	15,856	11,000	7,741	34,597
No. of Cand.	*26*	*20*	*9*	*55*
House	15,856	10,000	4,741	30,597
Senate	0	1,000	3,000	4,000
Incumbents	37,106	47,720	17,241	102,067
Challengers	8,250	6,500	0	14,750
Open Seat	12,200	11,418	500	24,118
Winners	51,556	51,470	n/a	103,026
Losers	6,000	14,168	n/a	20,168

Chemical Specialties Manufacturers Association

*Phone: (202) 872-8110 * Fax: (202) 872-8114*
1913 Eye St. N.W., Washington, DC 20006
*Web: www.csma.org * E-mail: pklein@csma.org*

The Chemical Specialties Manufacturers Association represents more than 400 companies that produce aerosols, waxes, cleaning supplies, disinfectants, floor finishes and home pesticides. Among its member companies are S.C. Johnson Wax, Arco Chemical Co., Price-Driscoll Corp., American Gasket and Rubber Co. and Consumer Products Testing Co. The CSMA monitors legislation and provides technical reports to its members.

Chemical Specialties Manufacturers Association Inc. Political Action Committee (ChemPAC) (C00122937) *Address: same as sponsor * Treasurer: Stephen S. Kellner * Contact: Philip Klein, Dir. of Federal Legislative Affairs*

	1993-94	1995-96	1997	Totals
Receipts	$21,186	$24,899	$7,913	$53,998
Disburse	16,840	21,300	9,903	48,043
Cash	8,740	12,344	10,354	n/a
Contributions	14,100	19,300	9,900	43,300
Republicans	6,100	14,550	6,400	27,050
No. of Cand.	*8*	*15*	*6*	*29*
House	3,100	6,550	1,500	11,150
Senate	3,000	8,000	4,900	15,900
Democrats	8,000	4,750	3,500	16,250
No. of Cand.	*9*	*8*	*3*	*20*
House	7,000	3,750	3,500	14,250
Senate	1,000	1,000	0	2,000
Incumbents	13,500	12,800	9,900	36,200
Challengers	250	3,500	0	3,750
Open Seat	350	3,000	0	3,350
Winners	11,350	17,000	n/a	28,350
Losers	2,750	2,300	n/a	5,050

Clorox Co.

*Phone: (510) 271-7291 * Fax: (510) 271-2946*
1221 Broadway, Oakland, CA 94612
Web: www.clorox.com

Clorox, a publicly held firm, produces and markets non-durable consumer products to grocery stores and other retail outlets. Its products include Clorox Liquid Bleach, Formula 409 cleaner, Pine-Sol cleaner, Armor All car cleaner, Black Flag insecticide, Fresh Step cat litter, Hidden Valley dressing and Brita water filters.

Founded in 1913 as the Electro-Alkaline Co., in Oakland, Calif., Clorox has grown and expanded its business to include 5,500 employees worldwide. Its 1997 revenues were $2.5 billion.

In 1997, Clorox and 10 other firms agreed to pay $4.2 million to settle charges that they violated antitrust laws during a Procter and Gamble test in 1996 of whether lower prices were a better sales tactic than cost-saving coupons. New York state Attorney General Dennis Vacco stated that the settlement will be paid to the state, which will pass it along to consumers in western New York by issuing $2 discount coupons.

German conglomerate Henkel owns 30 percent of the company.

The Clorox Co. Employees' Political Action Committee (C00062224) *Address: same as sponsor * Treasurer: Robin M. Gentz * Contact: Dan Danzig, Chairman*

	1993-94	1995-96	1997	Totals
Receipts	$19,241	$42,085	$19,393	$80,719
Disburse	16,026	21,650	24,800	62,476
Cash	5,101	25,541	20,135	n/a
Contributions	14,350	21,650	22,800	58,800
Republicans	2,500	11,500	8,500	22,500
No. of Cand.	*7*	*17*	*10*	*34*
House	2,500	7,500	3,000	13,000
Senate	0	4,000	5,500	9,500
Democrats	11,850	10,150	14,300	36,300
No. of Cand.	*15*	*17*	*18*	*50*
House	6,850	9,650	12,300	28,800
Senate	5,000	500	2,000	7,500
Incumbents	13,850	20,150	19,750	53,750
Challengers	0	0	550	550
Open Seat	500	1,500	2,500	4,500
Winners	13,250	18,400	n/a	31,650
Losers	1,100	3,250	n/a	4,350

Condea Vista Chemical Co.

*Phone: (281) 588-3210 * Fax: (281) 588-3119*
900 Threadneedle, Houston, TX 77079
Web: www.condeavista.com

Condea Vista, formerly Vista Chemical Co., is a subsidiary of Germany's multinational RWE-DEA AG. The company produces chemicals used in consumer and industrial products such as vinyl, household detergents and industrial cleaners. It is headquartered in Houston with locations in Massachusetts, Maryland, Indiana, Kentucky, Mississippi, Louisiana and Oklahoma.

Condea Vista employs about 1,400 people and has annual sales of about $900 million.

Condea Vista Effective Government Fund (formerly known as Vista Chemical Co.) (C00286930) *Address: same as sponsor * Treasurer: Robert R. Whitlow * Contact: Michael Reynolds, Manager of Public Affairs*

	1993-94	1995-96	1997	Totals
Receipts	$6,096	$15,218	$11,647	$32,961
Disburse	2,250	18,271	4,500	25,021
Cash	3,846	793	7,940	n/a
Contributions	2,250	17,250	-4500	15,000
Republicans	750	13,250	-3500	10,500
No. of Cand.	*1*	*12*	*2*	*15*
House	750	9,750	-1500	9,000
Senate	0	3,500	-2000	1,500
Democrats	1,500	4,000	-1000	4,500
No. of Cand.	*2*	*2*	*1*	*5*
House	1,500	4,000	-1000	4,500
Senate	0	0	0	0
Incumbents	1,500	6,000	-2500	5,000
Challengers	0	2,000	0	2,000
Open Seat	750	9,250	0	10,000
Winners	2,250	11,000	n/a	13,250
Losers	0	6,250	n/a	6,250

Contran Corp.

Phone: (972) 233-1700
5430 LBJ Fwy., Suite 1700, Dallas, TX 75240

Contran controls more than 90 percent of Valhi Inc., a $2.2 billion, Dallas-based holding company with subsidiaries operating in the chemical, component products, fast food and waste management industries. Contran, which is owned by Texas billionaire Harold C. Simmons, has annual sales of $1.2 billion and 7,000 employees.

Contran's primary subsidiary, Valhi, owns all of National Cabinet Lock and most of NL Industries Inc., which manufactures titanium dioxide pigments used in paints. Valhi also controls a toxic waste management company called Waste Management Control Specialists, located in Texas.

Contran's Salt Lake City-based subsidiary Amalgamated Sugar Co. was acquired for $266 million by the Snake River Sugar Cooperative, a group of Oregon, Idaho and Washington sugar beet growers.

Contran Corp. Political Action Committee (ConPAC) (C00148783) *Address: same as sponsor * Treasurer: Eugene K. Anderson * Contact: Harold C. Simmons, Chairperson*

	1993-94	1995-96	1997	Totals
Receipts	$18,324	$18,057	$40,510	$76,891
Disburse	17,488	19,007	42,102	78,597
Cash	3,393	2,449	858	n/a
Contributions	14,000	12,500	2,000	28,500
Republicans	14,000	12,500	1,500	28,000
No. of Cand.	*13*	*9*	*2*	*24*
House	2,000	4,000	1,500	7,500
Senate	12,000	8,500	0	20,500
Democrats	0	0	500	500
No. of Cand.	*0*	*0*	*1*	*1*
House	0	0	500	500
Senate	0	0	0	0
Incumbents	3,000	8,000	2,000	13,000
Challengers	1,500	4,500	0	6,000
Open Seat	9,500	0	0	9,500
Winners	12,500	9,000	n/a	21,500
Losers	1,500	3,500	n/a	5,000

NL Industries Inc. Political Action Committee (C00025023) *Phone: (281) 423-3300 * Fax: (281) 423-3236 * 16825 Northchase Dr., Suite 1200, Houston, TX 77060 * Web: www.nl-ind.com * Treasurer: Lisa K. Broomas * Contact: David Garten, General Counsel*

NL Industries is the world's fourth-largest supplier of titanium dioxide, a white pigment used in paints, paper, ceramics and plastics.

The publicly traded Houston company recently sold its Rheox specialty chemical business. Without the Rheox unit, NL Industries reported 1997 sales of $837 million. The company has 3,100 employees, about 400 of whom are stationed in the United States.

The company's Kronos subsidiary, which produces the titanium dioxide, does its manufacturing in Europe, except for a partially owned plant in Lake Charles, La.

Valhi Inc., a $2.2 billion corporation, and Tremont Corp., each affiliates of Contran Corp., hold 56 percent and 18 percent, respectively, of NL Industries' outstanding common stock.

	1993-94	1995-96	1997	Totals
Receipts	$15,207	$15,374	$25,072	$55,653
Disburse	20,677	11,594	30,015	62,286
Cash	4,110	7,895	2,952	n/a
Contributions	18,250	10,200	0	28,450
Republicans	17,250	5,200	0	22,450
No. of Cand.	*11*	*7*	*0*	*18*
House	8,000	4,000	0	12,000
Senate	9,250	1,200	0	10,450
Democrats	1,000	5,000	0	6,000
No. of Cand.	*1*	*1*	*0*	*2*
House	1,000	5,000	0	6,000
Senate	0	0	0	0
Incumbents	7,000	8,000	0	15,000
Challengers	4,250	200	0	4,450
Open Seat	7,000	2,000	0	9,000
Winners	12,000	9,000	n/a	21,000
Losers	6,250	1,200	n/a	7,450

The Dow Chemical Co.

*Phone: (517) 636-6017 * Fax: (517) 636-5459*
2020 Dow Center, Midland, MI 48674
*Web: www.dow.com * E-mail: tbharwada@dow.com*

With 1997 sales of $20 billion, Dow Chemical is the fifth-largest chemical company in the world. Its products include plastics, agricultural, general and specialty chemicals and consumer products including Saran Wrap, Ziploc and Glass Plus. More than half the company's sales are made outside the United States. A publicly traded company, Dow employs more than 40,000 people at 115 manufacturing sites in 37 countries.

Major product lines include Styrofoam brand foam, adhesives, polyurethane products used by the automotive, furniture and construction industries, latex coatings used by the paper industry and herbicides and insecticides. It is the world's largest chlorine and caustic soda maker and is one of the largest independent electricity producers through its Destec Energy subsidiary.

Major U.S. manufacturing sites are located in Midland, Mich.; Freeport, Texas; and Plaquemine, La. The company's primary U.S. research and development operations are located in these cities as well as in Indianapolis; Pittsburg, Calif.; and Granville, Pa.

Subsidiaries include: DowBrands, Dow Corning Corp., DuPont Dow Elastomers, Essex Specialty Products, Filmtec Corp. and Radian International.

In 1997, seven division or subsidiary PACs were condensed into one PAC called the Political Action Committee for Employees of The Dow Chemical Co.

Political Action Committee for the Employees of The Dow Chemical Co. (C00074096) *Address: Same as sponsor * Treasurer: Ridley Nimmo * Contact: John W. Tysse, Chairperson*

	1993-94	1995-96	1997	Totals
Receipts	$53,297	$60,290	$80,100	$193,687
Disburse	61,086	62,000	1,080	124,166
Cash	6,778	5,079	84,100	n/a
Contributions	61,050	47,500	13,000	121,550
Republicans	54,550	40,000	7,000	101,550
No. of Cand.	*59*	*41*	*8*	*108*
House	32,550	30,500	5,000	68,050
Senate	22,000	9,500	2,000	33,500
Democrats	6,500	7,500	6,000	20,000
No. of Cand.	*8*	*9*	*7*	*24*
House	6,500	5,500	3,000	15,000
Senate	0	2,000	3,000	5,000
Incumbents	29,550	43,500	13,000	86,050
Challengers	12,000	3,000	0	15,000
Open Seat	19,500	1,000	0	20,500
Winners	51,050	36,000	n/a	87,050
Losers	10,000	11,500	n/a	21,500

The Dow Chemical Co. Agricultural Executive Political Action Committee (C00247981) *Phone: (317) 337-4790 * Fax: (317) 337-4880 * 9330 Zionsville Rd., Indianapolis, IN 46268 * Web: www.dowagro.com * E-mail: edmiller@dowagro.com * Treasurer: Gary L. Whitlock * Contact: Elin D. Miller, Chairperson*

	1993-94	1995-96	1997	Totals
Receipts	$53,977	$46,564	$19,826	$120,367
Disburse	57,412	51,522	19,851	128,785
Cash	12,997	8,040	8,017	n/a
Contributions	54,150	48,300	18,250	120,700
Republicans	35,450	36,250	9,250	80,950
No. of Cand.	*42*	*41*	*14*	*97*
House	29,950	27,250	7,000	64,200
Senate	5,500	9,000	2,250	16,750
Democrats	18,700	12,050	9,000	39,750
No. of Cand.	*23*	*17*	*10*	*50*
House	18,700	10,750	7,750	37,200
Senate	0	1,300	1,250	2,550
Incumbents	48,150	34,000	18,000	100,150
Challengers	1,750	2,800	0	4,550
Open Seat	4,250	11,500	250	16,000
Winners	45,150	40,000	n/a	85,150
Losers	9,000	8,300	n/a	17,300

Employees' Political Action Committee, Southeast Region, The Dow Chemical Co. (EMPAC) (C00032623) *Building 3302-C, P.O. Box 500, Plaquemine, LA 70765 * Treasurer: B. B. Babin*

	1993-94	1995-96	1997	Totals
Receipts	$43,207	$33,698	$0	$76,905
Disburse	41,803	42,014	0	83,817
Cash	8,308	0	0	n/a
Contributions	40,700	36,000	0	76,700
Republicans	30,200	28,500	0	58,700
No. of Cand.	*36*	*26*	*0*	*62*
House	23,200	19,500	0	42,700
Senate	7,000	9,000	0	16,000
Democrats	10,500	7,500	0	18,000
No. of Cand.	*9*	*8*	*0*	*17*
House	10,500	6,500	0	17,000
Senate	0	1,000	0	1,000
Incumbents	28,200	21,000	0	49,200
Challengers	2,500	0	0	2,500
Open Seat	9,000	15,000	0	24,000
Winners	39,200	30,000	n/a	69,200
Losers	1,500	6,000	n/a	7,500

Western Employees Political Action Committee of The Dow Chemical Co. (WesPAC) (C00021535) *P.O. Box 1398, Pittsburg, CA 94565 * Treasurer: W. Krist Jensen*

	1993-94	1995-96	1997	Totals
Receipts	$28,800	$28,824	$0	$57,624
Disburse	31,800	30,660	2,430	64,890
Cash	4,256	2,430	0	n/a
Contributions	31,800	29,650	0	61,450
Republicans	27,300	26,650	0	53,950
No. of Cand.	*43*	*19*	*0*	*62*
House	23,800	26,650	0	50,450
Senate	3,500	0	0	3,500
Democrats	4,500	3,000	0	7,500
No. of Cand.	*7*	*4*	*0*	*11*
House	4,500	3,000	0	7,500
Senate	0	0	0	0
Incumbents	18,800	25,150	0	43,950
Challengers	6,000	1,000	0	7,000
Open Seat	7,000	4,000	0	11,000
Winners	27,300	17,650	n/a	44,950
Losers	4,500	12,000	n/a	16,500

The Dow Chemical Co. Employees' Political Action Committee (EMPAC) (C00032813) *2301 N. Brazosport Blvd., APB Building, Freeport, TX 77541 * Treasurer: Jerry V. Burney*

	1993-94	1995-96	1997	Totals
Receipts	$173,081	$111,911	$3,025	$288,017
Disburse	193,654	110,468	11,068	315,190
Cash	6,595	8,042	0	n/a
Contributions	58,500	27,750	-1000	85,250
Republicans	37,000	25,250	-1000	61,250
No. of Cand.	*23*	*10*	*1*	*34*
House	23,500	14,250	-1000	36,750
Senate	13,500	11,000	0	24,500
Democrats	21,500	2,500	0	24,000
No. of Cand.	*10*	*2*	*0*	*12*
House	21,500	2,500	0	24,000
Senate	0	0	0	0
Incumbents	45,500	22,750	-1000	67,250
Challengers	8,500	0	0	8,500
Open Seat	4,500	5,000	0	9,500
Winners	50,000	20,750	n/a	70,750
Losers	8,500	7,000	n/a	15,500

Dow Eastern Employees Political Action Committee of The Dow Chemical Co. (DEEPAC) (C00034124) *Phone: (517) 636-1000 * Fax: (517) 636-3518 * 2030 Dow Center, Midland, MI 48674 * Treasurer: Ridley S. Nimmo*

	1993-94	1995-96	1997	Totals
Receipts	$26,121	$17,588	$16	$43,725
Disburse	31,685	17,700	0	49,385
Cash	1,521	1,420	1,445	n/a
Contributions	24,100	16,500	0	40,600
Republicans	20,600	16,000	0	36,600
No. of Cand.	*25*	*20*	*0*	*45*
House	14,100	12,500	0	26,600
Senate	6,500	3,500	0	10,000
Democrats	3,500	500	0	4,000
No. of Cand.	*6*	*1*	*0*	*7*
House	3,000	500	0	3,500
Senate	500	0	0	500
Incumbents	9,100	10,500	0	19,600
Challengers	6,500	3,500	0	10,000
Open Seat	8,500	2,500	0	11,000
Winners	21,100	9,500	n/a	30,600
Losers	3,000	7,000	n/a	10,000

Midwest Area PAC Employees of The Dow Chemical Co. (MAPAC) (C00040873) *47 Building Room 2453, Midland, MI 48667 * Treasurer: John Larkin*

	1993-94	1995-96	1997	Totals
Receipts	$35,866	$37,000	$0	$72,866
Disburse	32,982	46,248	0	79,230
Cash	7,238	0	0	n/a
Contributions	14,000	5,250	0	19,250
Republicans	13,000	2,250	0	15,250
No. of Cand.	*17*	*4*	*0*	*21*
House	8,500	2,000	0	10,500
Senate	4,500	250	0	4,750
Democrats	1,000	3,000	0	4,000
No. of Cand.	*2*	*3*	*0*	*5*
House	1,000	3,000	0	4,000
Senate	0	0	0	0
Incumbents	5,000	5,000	0	10,000
Challengers	1,500	250	0	1,750
Open Seat	7,500	0	0	7,500
Winners	10,500	4,000	n/a	14,500
Losers	3,500	1,250	n/a	4,750

Contributed less than $5,000 during 1995-96 cycle:

Midland Committee for Employees of The Dow Chemical Co. (C00078279) *2030 Willard H. Dow Center, Midland, MI 48674 * Treasurer: Roger L. Kesseler*

Terminated PACs which contributed less than $5,000 during 1995-96 cycle:

Destec Energy Inc. Political Action Committee (C00249599) *2500 City West Blvd., Suite 1700, Houston, TX 77042 * Treasurer: Patricia A. Agnew*

Dow Corning Corp.

*Phone: (517) 496-4044 * Fax: (517) 496-1657*
C02400, P.O. Box 994, Dow Corning Corp., Midland, MI 48686-0994
Web: www.dow.com

Dow Corning is a Michigan corporation with half of its stock owned by Corning Inc. and half owned by The Dow Chemical Co. The company's principal business is the development and production of silicones, chemical materials, polycrystalline silicon and specialty health care products.

Formed in 1943, Dow Corning serves customers in industrialized and developing countries worldwide with 33 manufacturing locations (12 in the United States) on five continents. More than half of the company's total business is outside the United States.

In May 1995, as a result of 19,000 lawsuits brought against the company for producing breast implants that leaked and ruptured, Dow Corning filed for Chapter 11 bankruptcy protection.

In February 1998, Dow Corning submitted a $3 billion settlement to 177,000 women to resolve their claims that breast implants made them ill. The money would be part of the company's $4.4 billion plan to pay its debts.

The Dow Corning Corp. Employees' PAC (DCEPAC) is affiliated with the PAC for Employees of The Dow Chemical Co. (PACE).

Dow Corning Corp. Employees' Political Action Committee (C00040246) *Address: same as sponsor * Treasurer: Debra K. Kettling * Contact: Jim Pollack, Chairman*

	1993-94	1995-96	1997	Totals
Receipts	$18,668	$24,207	$14,011	$56,886
Disburse	21,010	25,224	2,904	49,138
Cash	2,287	3,720	14,832	n/a
Contributions	10,400	7,300	1,200	18,900
Republicans	9,550	6,450	850	16,850
No. of Cand.	*14*	*8*	*3*	*25*
House	6,550	3,450	700	10,700
Senate	3,000	3,000	150	6,150
Democrats	850	850	350	2,050
No. of Cand.	*2*	*2*	*1*	*5*
House	850	850	350	2,050
Senate	0	0	0	0
Incumbents	4,150	4,050	1,050	9,250
Challengers	1,000	3,250	0	4,250
Open Seat	5,250	0	0	5,250
Winners	8,650	4,050	n/a	12,700
Losers	1,750	3,250	n/a	5,000

Dow Corning Corp. Management Political Action Committee (C00133223) *Phone: (517) 496-6365 * P.O. Box 994, Midland, MI 48686-0994 * Treasurer: Paul A. Marcela*

	1993-94	1995-96	1997	Totals
Receipts	$5,822	$18,432	$7,900	$32,154
Disburse	10,361	11,107	7,519	28,987
Cash	1,887	9,716	10,098	n/a
Contributions	9,800	11,070	7,500	28,370
Republicans	7,300	8,500	6,500	22,300
No. of Cand.	*10*	*9*	*8*	*27*
House	6,300	6,500	5,000	17,800
Senate	1,000	2,000	1,500	4,500
Democrats	2,500	2,570	1,000	6,070
No. of Cand.	*4*	*4*	*2*	*10*
House	2,500	2,070	1,000	5,570
Senate	0	500	0	500
Incumbents	9,300	11,070	6,500	26,870
Challengers	0	0	0	0
Open Seat	500	0	1,000	1,500
Winners	8,800	9,570	n/a	18,370
Losers	1,000	1,500	n/a	2,500

E.I. du Pont de Nemours and Co.

*Phone: (302) 773-6306 * Fax: (302) 773-2010*
1007 Market St. N-10539, Wilmington, DE 19898
Web: www.dupont.com

DuPont is the largest U.S. chemical producer and one of the largest chemical producers worldwide. Its largest subsidiary, Conoco, is the nation's seventh-largest oil company. DuPont also makes polymers, pharmaceuticals and fabrics and performs agricultural research. Conoco and other subsidiaries conduct exploration, production, mining, manufacturing and selling activities.

In 1997, DuPont had revenues of $45 billion. Forty-eight percent of the company's sales were outside the United States. Exports from the United States were $4 billion, making the company one of the largest U.S. exporters. In 1996, the company employed about 97,000 people. About 35 percent of the company's employees work outside the United States.

DuPont operates in 70 countries, with about 175 manufacturing and processing facilities, including 140 chemicals and specialties plants, eight petroleum refineries and 27 natural gas processing plants.

DuPont Good Government Fund (C00171926) *Phone: (202) 728-3600 * Fax: (202) 728-3649 * 1701 Pennsylvania Ave. N.W., Suite 900, Washington, DC 20006 * Treasurer: John H. Korenko*

*Contact: Stacey J. Mobley, Chairman * Phone: (302) 773-6306*

	1993-94	1995-96	1997	Totals
Receipts	$103,915	$198,381	$98,441	$400,737
Disburse	94,427	190,145	73,929	358,501
Cash	12,407	20,647	45,160	n/a
Contributions	65,214	133,700	50,000	248,914
Republicans	39,214	114,200	33,000	186,414
No. of Cand.	*51*	*124*	*38*	*213*
House	19,000	80,700	21,000	120,700
Senate	20,214	33,500	12,000	65,714
Democrats	26,000	19,500	17,000	62,500
No. of Cand.	*37*	*34*	*23*	*94*
House	19,500	15,500	13,000	48,000
Senate	6,500	4,000	4,000	14,500
Incumbents	48,000	95,200	50,000	193,200
Challengers	7,214	5,500	0	12,714
Open Seat	10,000	33,500	0	43,500
Winners	56,714	101,200	n/a	157,914
Losers	8,500	32,500	n/a	41,000

DuPont Merck Pharmaceutical Co. Program for Active Citizenship Inc. (C00255067) *Phone: (302) 992-5000 * WR-2066 Centre Rd., Dupont Merck Plaza, Wilmington, DE 19805 * Web: www.dupontmerck.com * Treasurer: Michael R. Miller*

*Phone: (703) 883-0891 * Fax: (703) 883-0892 * 1447 Colleen Ln., McLean, VA 22101 * Contact: Lynne O'Brien*

Formed in 1991 as a partnership between DuPont and Merck & Co., DuPont Merck develops and manufactures pharmaceuticals to treat heart disease, HIV, central nervous system disorders and cancer. The company also has a large radiopharmaceutical business, which focuses on various X-ray imaging tests. In 1996, DuPont Merck reported revenues of $1.4 billion.

The company is headquartered in Delaware and has locations in North Billerica, Mass. and abroad.

Products include Coumadin, for thromboembolic stroke prevention; Sinemet, for treating Parkinson's Disease; and REVIA, which is used in treating alcohol dependence. Radiopharmaceuticals include Cardiolite, a heart-imaging agent, and Miraluma, for breast imaging.

	1993-94	1995-96	1997	Totals
Receipts	$134,125	$119,965	$47,301	$301,391
Disburse	141,700	104,264	58,987	304,951
Cash	9,634	25,338	13,651	n/a
Contributions	123,993	70,000	29,000	222,993
Republicans	83,593	57,500	19,500	160,593
No. of Cand.	*39*	*41*	*17*	*97*
House	30,522	35,500	10,500	76,522
Senate	53,071	22,000	9,000	84,071
Democrats	39,400	12,500	9,500	61,400
No. of Cand.	*30*	*14*	*9*	*53*
House	28,900	8,500	1,000	38,400
Senate	10,500	4,000	8,500	23,000
Incumbents	91,651	58,500	28,500	178,651
Challengers	12,700	2,000	0	14,700
Open Seat	18,942	9,500	500	28,942
Winners	107,243	57,500	n/a	164,743
Losers	16,750	12,500	n/a	29,250

Eastman Chemical Co.

*Phone: (423) 229-2000 * Fax: (423) 229-1351*
P.O. Box 511, Kingsport, TN 37662-5075
Web: www.eastman.com

Eastman Chemical manufactures and sells polyester plastics such as polyethylene terephthalate, which is widely used in soft drink containers; coatings and paint raw materials; industrial and fine chemicals; and acetate tow, used for the production of filter-tipped cigarettes.

Founded in 1920 in Kingsport, Tenn. as a unit of Eastman Kodak Co., Eastman Chemical was spun off in 1994 and is now an independent, publicly held company traded on the New York Stock Exchange. Eastman has more than 7,000 customers worldwide and posted 1997 sales of $4.6 billion.

Eastman employs 17,500 people in more than 30 countries. The company produces more than 400 chemicals, fibers and plastics. Eastman does not sell consumer products, but it supplies many industries with materials, chiefly the packaging and tobacco industries.

EastPAC, Political Action Committee of Eastman Chemical Co. (C00113159) *Phone: (202) 789-5900 * Fax: (202) 789-5901 * 1301 K St. N.W., Suite 715, Washington, DC 20005 * Treasurer: H. V. Stephens * Contact: D. Lynn Johnson, Chairperson*

	1993-94	1995-96	1997	Totals
Receipts	$124,395	$152,983	$87,984	$365,362
Disburse	121,144	155,249	85,355	361,748
Cash	15,723	13,456	16,084	n/a
Contributions	44,050	56,600	26,000	126,650
Republicans	21,050	47,100	18,000	86,150
No. of Cand.	*13*	*23*	*10*	*46*
House	7,250	24,600	12,500	44,350
Senate	13,800	22,500	5,500	41,800
Democrats	23,000	9,500	8,000	40,500
No. of Cand.	*13*	*8*	*8*	*29*
House	13,000	8,500	8,000	29,500
Senate	10,000	1,000	0	11,000
Incumbents	32,050	36,000	25,000	93,050
Challengers	5,250	2,100	0	7,350
Open Seat	6,750	18,500	1,000	26,250
Winners	32,550	44,600	n/a	77,150
Losers	11,500	12,000	n/a	23,500

Ecolab Inc.

*Phone: (612) 293-2233 * Fax: (612) 225-3105*
370 Wabasha St., St. Paul, MN 55102
Web: www.ecolab.com

Ecolab makes cleaning and sanitary products for hospitals, schools, manufacturers and restaurants. It offers products for janitorial work, water treatment, pest removal, laundry and machine washing. Ecolab's products, most of which are made in company-owned plants, are used in more than 150 countries. A public company, with headquarters in Minnesota, Ecolab has 9,500 employees. It reported 1997 sales of $1.6 billion.

Ecolab Inc. Political Action Committee (C00101485) *Address: same as sponsor * Treasurer: Pat Elliott*

	1993-94	1995-96	1997	Totals
Receipts	$36,738	$36,956	$14,919	$88,613
Disburse	34,976	36,650	2,000	73,626
Cash	2,023	2,331	15,251	n/a
Contributions	29,800	31,500	2,000	63,300
Republicans	19,000	24,250	500	43,750
No. of Cand.	*19*	*20*	*1*	*40*
House	9,000	10,250	0	19,250
Senate	10,000	14,000	500	24,500
Democrats	8,000	7,250	1,000	16,250
No. of Cand.	*9*	*4*	*1*	*14*
House	7,000	7,250	1,000	15,250
Senate	1,000	0	0	1,000
Incumbents	15,550	19,000	1,500	36,050
Challengers	2,750	5,000	500	8,250
Open Seat	11,000	7,500	0	18,500
Winners	20,800	22,500	n/a	43,300
Losers	9,000	9,000	n/a	18,000

Elf Atochem North America Inc.

*Phone: (215) 419-7617 * Fax: (215) 419-5229*
2000 Market St., Philadelphia, PA 19103
*Web: www.elf-atochem.com * E-mail: pmccarthy@ato.com*

Headquartered in Philadelphia, Elf Atochem makes agrichemicals, fluorochemicals, fine, industrial and specialty chemicals. The company is a subsidiary of world petroleum and chemical giant Elf Atochem Worldwide, which is part of the Elf Aquitaine Group, headquartered in Paris.

Elf Atochem employs 3,600 workers at 24 U.S. manufacturing sites.

Elf Atochem North America Inc. Political Action Committee (AtoPAC) (C00182980) *Address: same as sponsor * Treasurer: Joseph M. Urbani * Contact: Peter McCarthy, Chairperson*

	1993-94	1995-96	1997	Totals
Receipts	$28,970	$34,764	$17,068	$80,802
Disburse	29,575	35,791	14,900	80,266
Cash	5,122	4,095	6,263	n/a
Contributions	25,900	30,300	12,400	68,600
Republicans	9,000	25,200	8,900	43,100
No. of Cand.	*9*	*23*	*12*	*44*
House	7,000	22,250	6,500	35,750
Senate	2,000	2,950	2,400	7,350
Democrats	16,900	5,100	3,500	25,500
No. of Cand.	*17*	*6*	*5*	*28*
House	13,900	5,100	3,500	22,500
Senate	3,000	0	0	3,000
Incumbents	19,900	29,300	11,400	60,600
Challengers	4,000	500	0	4,500
Open Seat	2,000	500	1,000	3,500
Winners	18,050	28,800	n/a	46,850
Losers	7,850	1,500	n/a	9,350

Ethyl Corp.

*Phone: (804) 788-5000 * Fax: (804) 788-5688*
330 S. Fourth St., Richmond, VA 23219
*Web: www.ethyl.com * E-mail: ethyl@bznet.com*

Ethyl is a publicly traded company and major developer, manufacturer and blender of petroleum additives for gasoline and diesel fuels. It also works with home heating oils and additives for passenger-car and diesel crankcase lubricants, including railroad engine oil additives, automatic transmission fluids and lubricants for gears, hydraulic and industrial equipment.

Ethyl operates facilities in South Carolina, Illinois, Florida, Virginia, Texas and abroad. It has 1,500 employees and reported 1997 sales of $1 billion.

Ethyl has 13 subsidiaries, located in Liberia, Korea, Japan, Germany, the U.S. Virgin Islands and Delaware.

Ethyl Corp. Political Action Committee (C00086991) *Address: same as sponsor * Treasurer: Henry Page*

	1993-94	1995-96	1997	Totals
Receipts	$428	$15,391	$233	$16,052
Disburse	6,221	9,617	195	16,033
Cash	6,781	12,555	12,593	n/a
Contributions	6,000	7,500	0	13,500
Republicans	4,000	6,500	0	10,500
No. of Cand.	*6*	*5*	*0*	*11*
House	3,000	1,500	0	4,500
Senate	1,000	5,000	0	6,000
Democrats	2,000	1,000	0	3,000
No. of Cand.	*3*	*1*	*0*	*4*
House	1,000	0	0	1,000
Senate	1,000	1,000	0	2,000
Incumbents	4,500	6,500	0	11,000
Challengers	500	0	0	500
Open Seat	1,000	1,000	0	2,000
Winners	4,750	6,500	n/a	11,250
Losers	1,250	1,000	n/a	2,250

FMC Corp.

*Phone: (312) 861-6000 * Fax: (312) 861-5913*
200 E. Randolph Dr., Chicago, IL 60601
Web: www.fmc.com

FMC is one of the world's leading producers of chemicals and machinery for industry and agriculture. The company's performance chemicals division produces crop protection and pest control chemicals. FMC's industrial chemicals unit manufactures hydrogen peroxide, alkali and phosphorus products. The company's machinery and equipment group includes oil and gas wellhead equipment and food handling equipment. The company has about 17,000 employees. Its 1997 sales totaled $4.3 billion.

The company is interested in government regulation of the chemical industry and the Superfund program. Several of its manufacturing plants make the EPA's annual Toxic Release Inventory, and the company has current and former plants on the list of Superfund sites.

FMC was the top chemical company contributor to congressional candidates during the 1995-96 election cycle. It favored Republicans and incumbents, including Sens. Larry Craig, R-Idaho, and John W. Warner, R-Va. Other top recipients included Sen. Pat Roberts, R-Kan., and Senate candidate Rudy Boschwitz of Minnesota.

FMC Corp. Good Government Program (C00033704) *Phone: (202) 956-5208 * Fax: (202) 956-5235 * 1627 K St. N.W., Washington, DC 20006 * Treasurer: Daniel N. Schuchardt * Contact: Alice Troester, PAC Administrator*

	1993-94	1995-96	1997	Totals
Receipts	$257,533	$305,791	$161,248	$724,572
Disburse	258,800	282,466	135,331	676,597
Cash	25,410	48,746	74,669	n/a
Contributions	227,770	261,400	122,200	611,370
Republicans	143,050	207,400	92,450	442,900
No. of Cand.	*117*	*139*	*94*	*350*
House	73,300	113,400	61,950	248,650
Senate	69,750	94,000	30,500	194,250
Democrats	84,720	54,000	29,250	167,970
No. of Cand.	*80*	*50*	*36*	*166*
House	70,100	42,000	20,250	132,350
Senate	14,620	12,000	9,000	35,620
Incumbents	175,770	202,900	121,200	499,870
Challengers	12,250	13,500	500	26,250
Open Seat	39,750	45,000	500	85,250
Winners	194,800	213,900	n/a	408,700
Losers	32,970	47,500	n/a	80,470

GAF Corp.

*Phone: (973) 628-3904 * Fax: (973) 628-3326*
1361 Alps Rd., Wayne, NJ 07470
Web: www.gaf.com

GAF makes chemicals, roofing materials, and runs a New York City classical radio station. The privately held company, based in Wayne, N.J., employs more than 5,000 workers and posted estimated 1996 sales of $1.6 billion.

The company was founded in 1929 as American I.G. Chemical and later renamed General Aniline Film. It was seized by the U.S. government during World War II and remained under federal control until the 1960s. In 1968, GAF went private and today it is owned by its employees.

GAF ranked No. 115 in Forbes' list of top private companies in the United States.

Subsidiaries: GAF Materials Corp., GAF Chemicals and GAF Broadcasting.

GAF Political Action Committee (C00205500) *Address: same as sponsor * Treasurer: Pat Gionnone*

	1993-94	1995-96	1997	Totals
Receipts	$46,283	$38,338	$14,767	$99,388
Disburse	30,377	56,687	3,000	90,064
Cash	39,280	20,935	29,079	n/a
Contributions	20,000	32,000	4,250	56,250
Republicans	4,500	21,500	3,250	29,250
No. of Cand.	*6*	*19*	*3*	*28*
House	3,000	12,000	1,250	16,250
Senate	1,500	9,500	2,000	13,000
Democrats	15,500	10,500	1,000	27,000
No. of Cand.	*12*	*10*	*1*	*23*
House	7,500	8,500	1,000	17,000
Senate	8,000	2,000	0	10,000
Incumbents	17,500	25,000	4,250	46,750
Challengers	1,000	2,000	0	3,000
Open Seat	0	4,000	0	4,000
Winners	15,000	26,000	n/a	41,000
Losers	5,000	6,000	n/a	11,000

Geon Co.

*Phone: (440) 930-3825 * Fax: (440) 930-3830*
One Geon Center, Avon Lake, OH 44012
Web: www.geon.com

Geon is one of the nation's largest producers of vinyl. Its resins and compounds have diverse applications including floor tiles, water pipes, heart catheters, residential siding, automobile upholstery and surgical gloves. Spun off from BFGoodrich in 1993, Geon has 2,100 employees and reported $1.25 billion in 1997 revenues.

The publicly traded Ohio company does about 65 percent of its business in the construction market, where end uses include carpet backing, windows and gutters.

In 1997, Geon opened a chlorine plant in McIntosh, Ala. Chlorine is a key ingredient for the company's products. Geon also purchased Synergistics Industries Ltd., a Canadian firm that produces PVC compounds.

U.S. manufacturing locations: California, Illinois, Indiana, Kentucky, Louisiana, New Jersey, Ohio and Texas. Geon also has operations in Canada, Australia, the United Kingdom and Singapore.

Geon Co. Political Action Committee (C00288712) *Address: same as sponsor * Treasurer: Woodrow W. Ban*

	1993-94	1995-96	1997	Totals
Receipts	$30,215	$87,573	$37,645	$155,433
Disburse	19,156	79,450	16,225	114,831
Cash	11,060	19,187	40,608	n/a
Contributions	9,000	38,875	7,300	55,175
Republicans	6,500	32,375	6,300	45,175
No. of Cand.	*9*	*40*	*7*	*56*
House	2,250	14,875	3,300	20,425
Senate	4,250	17,500	3,000	24,750
Democrats	2,500	6,500	1,000	10,000
No. of Cand.	*5*	*8*	*1*	*14*
House	2,000	5,500	1,000	8,500
Senate	500	1,000	0	1,500
Incumbents	4,500	25,875	7,300	37,675
Challengers	1,000	4,000	0	5,000
Open Seat	3,000	9,000	0	12,000
Winners	6,000	31,250	n/a	37,250
Losers	3,000	7,625	n/a	10,625

Hercules Inc.

*Phone: (302) 594-5000 * Fax: (302) 594-5400*
Hercules Plaza, 13th and Market St., Wilmington, DE 19894
Web: www.herc.com

Hercules is a worldwide producer of chemicals and related products. The public company, based in Delaware, operates in two industry segments: chemical specialties and food and functional products. Sales for 1997 were $1.9 billion and the company employs more than 7,000 workers.

The company's specialty chemicals unit makes products used in papermaking, diapers, home furnishings and automobiles. Its businesses include Aqualon water-soluble polymers, paper technology, resins, food gums and a majority interest in FiberVisions L.L.C., a joint venture in polypropylene fiber.

In 1995, Hercules divested its aerospace unit and an electronics and printing division. During 1996, Hercules divested its composite products division. Hercules also consolidated some of its assets in 1997, selling operations such as its solid-fuel systems and graphite powder businesses.

Hercules Inc. Voluntary Nonpartisan Political Contributions Committee (Hercules PCC) (C00059287) *Phone: (202) 223-8590 * Fax: (202) 296-6679 * 1420 New York Ave. N.W., Suite 610, Washington, DC 20005 * Treasurer: Thomas W. Hunsberger*

*Contact: Samuel Mabry, PAC Chairman * Phone: (302) 594-5000*

	1993-94	1995-96	1997	Totals
Receipts	$97,187	$49,134	$6,975	$153,296
Disburse	88,818	53,050	5,016	146,884
Cash	11,569	7,655	9,613	n/a
Contributions	74,000	51,000	4,216	129,216
Republicans	30,000	19,000	0	49,000
No. of Cand.	*23*	*18*	*0*	*41*
House	20,500	18,000	0	38,500
Senate	9,500	1,000	0	10,500
Democrats	42,500	32,000	4,216	78,716
No. of Cand.	*33*	*21*	*4*	*58*
House	35,000	21,500	1,000	57,500
Senate	7,500	10,500	3,216	21,216
Incumbents	66,500	42,000	4,216	112,716
Challengers	2,250	1,000	0	3,250
Open Seat	4,750	8,000	0	12,750
Winners	64,000	44,000	n/a	108,000
Losers	10,000	7,000	n/a	17,000

ICI Americas Inc.

*Phone: (302) 887-3000 * Fax: (302) 887-2972*
3411 Silverside Rd., Concord Plaza, Wilmington, DE 19850
Web: www.icinorthamerica.com

ICI Americas PAC was terminated in February 1998. The company was purchased by Zeneca Inc.

ICI Americas Inc. Political Action Committee (C00185660)
*Address: same as sponsor * Treasurer: Donald S. Goodwin*

	1993-94	1995-96	1997	Totals
Receipts	$38,007	$38,185	$1,138	$77,330
Disburse	48,089	41,864	6,857	96,810
Cash	9,395	5,719	0	n/a
Contributions	31,218	34,500	6,000	71,718
Republicans	10,468	13,500	2,750	26,718
No. of Cand.	*14*	*13*	*4*	*31*
House	4,768	9,500	2,750	17,018
Senate	5,700	4,000	0	9,700
Democrats	20,750	21,000	3,250	45,000
No. of Cand.	*27*	*18*	*5*	*50*
House	13,250	9,000	500	22,750
Senate	7,500	12,000	2,750	22,250
Incumbents	28,268	29,000	6,500	63,768
Challengers	0	0	0	0
Open Seat	2,950	5,500	0	8,450
Winners	22,968	33,000	n/a	55,968
Losers	8,250	1,500	n/a	9,750

Institute of Makers of Explosives

*Phone: (202) 429-9280 * Fax: (202) 293-2420*
1120 19th St. N.W., Suite 310, Washington, DC 20036
*Web: www.ime.org * E-mail: information@ime.org*

The Institute of Makers of Explosives represents about 35 companies in the commercial explosives industry in the United States and Canada.

IME is a nonprofit association that was founded in 1913 to provide technically accurate information and recommendations concerning commercial explosive materials. The institute's purpose is to promote the safety and protection of employees, users, the public and the environment throughout all aspects of the manufacture and use of explosive materials in industrial blasting and other operations.

The IME follows legislation requiring the use of "taggants" in explosives.

Institute of Makers of Explosives Political Action Committee (IMEPAC) (C00135590) *Address: same as sponsor * Treasurer: James Christopher Ronay*

	1993-94	1995-96	1997	Totals
Receipts	$2,423	$16,947	$2,069	$21,439
Disburse	9,650	23,078	3,112	35,840
Cash	10,538	5,402	4,358	n/a
Contributions	10,650	23,078	3,000	36,728
Republicans	4,650	19,078	3,000	26,728
No. of Cand.	*6*	*17*	*5*	*28*
House	1,650	11,078	1,000	13,728
Senate	3,000	8,000	2,000	13,000
Democrats	5,500	4,000	0	9,500
No. of Cand.	*2*	*3*	*0*	*5*
House	5,500	4,000	0	9,500
Senate	0	0	0	0
Incumbents	9,650	21,078	3,000	33,728
Challengers	0	0	0	0
Open Seat	1,000	2,000	0	3,000
Winners	9,650	21,578	n/a	31,228
Losers	1,000	1,500	n/a	2,500

Kerr-McGee Corp.

*Phone: (405) 270-1313 * Fax: (405) 270-3977*
P.O. Box 25861, Oklahoma City, OK 73125

Energy and chemical company Kerr-McGee announced in January 1998 that it will expand its chemical business — already the firm's largest segment, accounting for 44 percent of 1997 sales of $1.7 billion — by purchasing an 80 percent stake in several European titanium dioxide pigment plants. A week later Kerr-McGee revealed that it would jettison its coal business.

The publicly traded Oklahoma City company will continue to operate its oil and gas exploration and production subsidiary. Kerr-McGee drills in the North Sea, Gulf of Mexico, China, Thailand, Indonesia, Brazil, Yemen, Ireland and Denmark.

Titanium dioxide, a white pigment used in products such as paint and paper, is Kerr-McGee's biggest chemical product. A chemical subsidiary produces it in Hamilton, Miss. and Australia. The subsidiary also owns a plant near Las Vegas that makes a rocket fuel ingredient, ammonium perchlorate, which has been found in small amounts in local ground water. In October 1997, the company announced plans to sell its perchlorate business.

Kerr-McGee also operates railroad crosstie treatment plants in The Dalles, Ore., Madison, Ill. and Springfield, Mo. Other Kerr-McGee plants are located in Mobile, Ala.; Soda Springs, Idaho; and Hamilton, Miss.

Kerr-McGee's coal business experienced difficulties in 1997. Its Jacobs Ranch, Wyo. strip mine, one of the largest in the nation, had transportation problems while its Galatia, Ill. mine suffered an underground ignition.

The company was involved in a U.S. Supreme Court case in the early 1980s after an employee at a nuclear fuels plant it owned in Crescent, Okla. was contaminated by plutonium in 1974. Karen Silkwood was killed in an automobile accident on the day she returned to work at the plant. In Silkwood v. Kerr-McGee Corp. the Supreme Court ruled that courts could impose punitive damages on the nuclear power industry for safety violations.

Kerr-McGee eventually settled with Silkwood's family for $1.3 million. Silkwood's story was made into a 1983 movie starring Meryl Streep and Cher.

Kerr-McGee Corp. Political Action Committee (C00034041) *Address: same as sponsor * Treasurer: John M. Rauh*

	1993-94	1995-96	1997	Totals
Receipts	$71,829	$81,390	$37,948	$191,167
Disburse	74,482	78,052	32,000	184,534
Cash	8,048	11,380	17,329	n/a
Contributions	66,350	53,000	27,500	146,850
Republicans	51,750	46,500	22,500	120,750
No. of Cand.	*55*	*57*	*22*	*134*
House	22,250	23,500	10,000	55,750
Senate	29,500	23,000	12,500	65,000
Democrats	14,600	6,500	5,000	26,100
No. of Cand.	*23*	*11*	*7*	*41*
House	10,000	5,500	2,000	17,500
Senate	4,600	1,000	3,000	8,600
Incumbents	37,600	43,500	26,000	107,100
Challengers	7,500	0	1,500	9,000
Open Seat	21,250	9,500	0	30,750
Winners	57,850	44,500	n/a	102,350
Losers	8,500	8,500	n/a	17,000

Lyondell Petrochemical Co.

*Phone: (713) 652-4629 * Fax: (713) 652-4631*
1221 McKinney St., Suite 1600, Houston, TX 77010
Web: www.lyondell.com

Lyondell Petrochemical is a Houston-based chemical and refining company producing plastics, additives and petroleum products. The public company, which employs 2,500 workers, reported 1997 revenues of $2.8 billion. It owns and/or leases more than six facilities, 3,200 railcars and six pipelines with most operations located near Mont Belvieu, Texas.

Lyondell has majority interest in Equistar Chemicals LP, Lyondell-Citgo Refining Co. Ltd., and Lyondell Methanol Co. LP. After a recent joint venture with another petrochemical company, Lyondell is now a holding company for its former operations.

Lyondell Petrochemical Co. Political Action Committee/Lyondell PAC (C00306175) *Address: same as sponsor * Treasurer: Kerry A. Galvin * Contact: Kerry Galvin*

	1993-94	1995-96	1997	Totals
Receipts	$0	$32,900	$1,000	$33,900
Disburse	0	16,350	6,250	22,600
Cash	0	16,550	9,703	n/a
Contributions	0	5,500	2,500	8,000
Republicans	0	3,000	2,000	5,000
No. of Cand.	*0*	*4*	*2*	*6*
House	0	3,000	1,000	4,000
Senate	0	0	1,000	1,000
Democrats	0	2,500	500	3,000
No. of Cand.	*0*	*2*	*1*	*3*
House	0	2,500	500	3,000
Senate	0	0	0	0
Incumbents	0	4,000	2,500	6,500
Challengers	0	1,000	0	1,000
Open Seat	0	500	0	500
Winners	0	5,000	n/a	5,000
Losers	0	500	n/a	500

Monsanto Co.

*Phone: (314) 694-1000 * Fax: (314) 694-6572*
800 N. Lindbergh Blvd., St. Louis, MO 63167
Web: www.monsanto.com

Monsanto's products include Equal and NutraSweet sweeteners; Roundup, a leading herbicide; genetically engineered plants such as cotton and soybeans; fat substitute Simplesse; and drugs used to treat insomnia, arthritis (Daypro and Arthrotec), hypertension and ulcers.

The publicly traded company has 28,000 employees and posted $7.5 billion in 1997 revenues. Agricultural products account for about 40 percent of sales, with nutrition, consumer and pharmaceutical products making up the balance.

U.S. locations include: California, Georgia, Illinois, Iowa, Louisiana, Missouri, North Carolina and Oklahoma.

A related PAC, G. D. Searle & Co. Good Government Fund, was terminated in September 1996. Searle is a Monsanto subsidiary.

Monsanto Co. Citizenship Fund (also known as Monsanto Citizenship Fund) (C00042069) *Phone: (202) 783-2460 * Fax: (202) 782-2468 * 700 14th St. N.W., Suite 1100, Washington, DC 20005 * Treasurer: Lois B. Johnson*

	1993-94	1995-96	1997	Totals
Receipts	$145,254	$192,395	$82,377	$420,026
Disburse	154,959	173,995	57,318	386,272
Cash	25,392	43,796	68,856	n/a
Contributions	89,330	98,275	31,345	218,950
Republicans	41,130	61,575	20,135	122,840
No. of Cand.	*34*	*56*	*21*	*111*
House	19,350	37,825	8,695	65,870
Senate	21,780	23,750	11,440	56,970
Democrats	48,200	36,700	11,210	96,110
No. of Cand.	*39*	*35*	*12*	*86*
House	43,500	26,100	5,000	74,600
Senate	4,700	10,600	6,210	21,510
Incumbents	76,950	83,575	31,135	191,660
Challengers	350	3,250	210	3,810
Open Seat	12,030	11,000	0	23,030
Winners	83,480	90,075	n/a	173,555
Losers	5,850	8,200	n/a	14,050

G. D. Searle & Co. Good Government Fund (Searle Good Government Fund) (C00111484) *Phone: (847) 982-7000 * 5200 Old Orchard Rd., Skokie, IL 60077 * Treasurer: Joseph E. Basciano*

	1993-94	1995-96	1997	Totals
Receipts	$39,936	$34,899	$0	$74,835
Disburse	38,275	39,506	0	77,781
Cash	4,604	0	0	n/a
Contributions	34,375	13,850	0	48,225
Republicans	17,750	10,850	0	28,600
No. of Cand.	*24*	*13*	*0*	*37*
House	9,000	8,850	0	17,850
Senate	8,750	2,000	0	10,750
Democrats	16,625	3,000	0	19,625
No. of Cand.	*22*	*5*	*0*	*27*
House	8,375	1,500	0	9,875
Senate	8,250	1,500	0	9,750
Incumbents	29,125	11,850	0	40,975
Challengers	2,250	500	0	2,750
Open Seat	3,000	1,500	0	4,500
Winners	30,375	11,000	n/a	41,375
Losers	4,000	2,850	n/a	6,850

Nalco Chemical Co.

*Phone: (630) 305-1000 * Fax: (630) 305-2900*
One Nalco Center, Naperville, IL 60563-1198
Web: www.nalco.com

Nalco Chemical is the world's largest producer of specialty chemicals and services for water and industrial process treatment. The company's products are also used for pollution control, to control dust and to improve combustion. Its consumers are industrial operations and governments.

Nalco operates in more than 120 countries with manufacturing facilities located throughout the world. Nalco's headquarters and largest research center are located in Naperville, Ill. The publicly traded company has more than 6,500 employees worldwide with 1997 sales of more than $1.4 billion.

The company is involved in a number of joint ventures, including: Nalco-Chemserv, Nalco/Exxon Energy Chemicals, Nalco Fuel Tech and Treated Water Outsourcing.

Nalco Chemical Co. Political Action Committee (C00144063)
*Address: same as sponsor * Treasurer: Craig J. Holderness*

	1993-94	1995-96	1997	Totals
Receipts	$53,552	$49,470	$23,049	$126,071
Disburse	50,800	48,750	6,375	105,925
Cash	3,431	4,151	20,825	n/a
Contributions	46,050	40,000	6,375	92,425
Republicans	35,550	37,500	6,250	79,300
No. of Cand.	*26*	*35*	*9*	*70*
House	21,050	24,000	4,750	49,800
Senate	14,500	13,500	1,500	29,500
Democrats	10,500	2,500	125	13,125
No. of Cand.	*11*	*4*	*1*	*16*
House	8,500	1,500	125	10,125
Senate	2,000	1,000	0	3,000
Incumbents	25,550	22,000	5,375	52,925
Challengers	7,000	7,500	1,000	15,500
Open Seat	13,500	11,500	0	25,000
Winners	38,050	24,250	n/a	62,300
Losers	8,000	15,750	n/a	23,750

Olin Corp.

*Phone: (203) 750-3808 * Fax: (203) 750-3162*
401 Merritt Seven, P.O. Box 4500, Norwalk, CT 06856
Web: www.olin.com

Olin produces chemicals, metals and ammunition. The publicly traded Connecticut company has 11,000 employees and reported $2.4 billion in 1997 revenues.

The chemicals segment is separated into three divisions: chlor-alkali, chemicals and microelectronic materials. Chlor-alkali includes chlor-alkali products, sodium hydrosulfite and high strength bleach products. Chemicals includes pool chemicals, biocides, hydrazine, polyols, propylene glycols and surfactants and fluids. Microelectronic materials includes image-forming and electronic interconnect materials and services.

The metals segment produces copper alloy sheet, strip, rod and wire. Winchester ammunition makes shotshells, centerfire rifle, centerfire handgun and rimfire ammunition.

U.S. manufacturing locations include: Alabama, Connecticut, Georgia, Illinois, Indiana, New York, Ohio, Rhode Island and Tennessee.

Olin Corp. Good Government Fund (C00002790) *Address: same as sponsor * Treasurer: Edward J. Krygier * Contact: William B. McDaniel, PAC Chairman*

	1993-94	1995-96	1997	Totals
Receipts	$82,883	$80,841	$26,194	$189,918
Disburse	91,721	75,250	17,750	184,721
Cash	5,833	11,433	19,884	n/a
Contributions	54,100	43,000	9,000	106,100
Republicans	28,250	32,500	5,500	66,250
No. of Cand.	*28*	*31*	*8*	*67*
House	16,250	18,500	3,500	38,250
Senate	12,000	14,000	2,000	28,000
Democrats	25,350	10,500	3,500	39,350
No. of Cand.	*23*	*10*	*5*	*38*
House	19,350	9,500	2,500	31,350
Senate	6,000	1,000	1,000	8,000
Incumbents	48,850	34,000	9,500	92,350
Challengers	3,250	1,000	0	4,250
Open Seat	2,000	8,000	0	10,000
Winners	50,000	32,500	n/a	82,500
Losers	4,100	10,500	n/a	14,600

Praxair Inc.

*Phone: (203) 837-2000 * Fax: (203) 837-2450*
39 Old Ridgebury Rd., P.O. Box 2958, Danbury, CT 06810-5113
*Web: www.praxair.com * E-mail: jim_rouse@praxair.com*

Praxair is the largest supplier of industrial gases in the Western hemisphere, and manufactures surface coatings for heavy machinery and engines to protect them from corrosion. Praxair was the first company in the United States to produce oxygen from air cryogenically (using extremely low temperatures). The public company employs 25,000 people and is headquartered in Danbury, Conn.

Praxair was spun off from Union Carbide in 1992 and reported 1997 sales of $4.7 billion.

The company owns 60 worldwide subsidiaries in the related fields of gas production, beverage carbonation and surface technologies. Subsidiaries have locations in North and South America, Europe, Asia and the Pacific. Fifty percent of the company's income comes from non-U.S. sources.

Praxair Inc. Political Action Committee (C00283440) *Address: same as sponsor * Treasurer: James B. Rouse*

	1993-94	1995-96	1997	Totals
Receipts	$20,038	$58,284	$34,322	$112,644
Disburse	17,907	48,962	11,750	78,619
Cash	2,128	11,453	34,026	n/a
Contributions	14,900	44,150	11,750	70,800
Republicans	11,850	37,000	9,250	58,100
No. of Cand.	*19*	*55*	*14*	*88*
House	5,600	26,500	7,500	39,600
Senate	6,250	10,500	1,750	18,500
Democrats	3,050	7,150	2,500	12,700
No. of Cand.	*6*	*10*	*4*	*20*
House	2,300	7,150	2,000	11,450
Senate	750	0	500	1,250
Incumbents	6,950	26,150	10,750	43,850
Challengers	3,300	7,500	0	10,800
Open Seat	4,650	10,000	1,000	15,650
Winners	12,650	29,150	n/a	41,800
Losers	2,250	15,000	n/a	17,250

Procter & Gamble Co.

*Phone: (513) 983-6875 * Fax: (513) 983-8984*
One Procter & Gamble Plaza, Cincinnati, OH 45202
Web: www.pg.com

Consumer products giant Procter & Gamble produces 300 brands in five product areas — laundry and cleaning, paper goods, beauty care, food and beverage and health care. The publicly traded company has 103,000 employees in 70 countries and posted sales of $35.7 billion in 1997. Roughly half of the company's sales come from outside the United States.

Procter & Gamble developed olestra, a controversial fat substitute used in snacks and crackers. The company also produces soap operas "As The World Turns," "Another World" and "Guiding Light." It is one of the world's largest advertisers, spending more than $3 billion a year.

Brands include: Bounce, Cascade, Cheer, Comet, Dawn, Downy, Fairy, Joy, Lenor, Mr. Clean, Spic and Span, Tide, Charmin, Luvs, Pampers, Puffs, Pringles, Cover Girl, Giorgio, Head & Shoulders, Hugo Boss, Oil of Olay and Old Spice.

The Procter & Gamble Co. Good Government Committee (also known as P&G PAC) (C00257329) *Phone: (202) 393-3400 * Fax: (202) 393-4606 * 801 Pennsylvania Ave. N.W., Suite 720, Washington, DC 20004 * Treasurer: Clayton C. Daley Jr.*

*Contact: Marge Bischoff, Administrator * Phone: (513) 983-6875*

	1993-94	1995-96	1997	Totals
Receipts	$285,946	$387,877	$150,523	$824,346
Disburse	249,000	338,119	158,475	745,594
Cash	44,643	94,417	73,468	n/a
Contributions	100,050	136,125	22,000	258,175
Republicans	64,550	108,000	19,000	191,550
No. of Cand.	*58*	*94*	*6*	*158*
House	30,550	72,000	2,000	104,550
Senate	34,000	36,000	17,000	87,000

(Data for Procter & Gamble continued)

Democrats	35,500	28,125	3,000	66,625
No. of Cand.	*34*	*36*	*3*	*73*
House	30,500	24,125	2,000	56,625
Senate	5,000	4,000	1,000	10,000
Incumbents	71,050	106,625	7,000	184,675
Challengers	9,000	7,500	0	16,500
Open Seat	20,000	22,000	15,000	57,000
Winners	78,050	117,125	n/a	195,175
Losers	22,000	19,000	n/a	41,000

Rohm & Haas Co.

Phone: (215) 592-3069
100 Independence Mall W., Philadelphia, PA 19106
Web: www.rohmhaas.com

Specialty polymer and chemical company Rohm & Haas makes products for use in laundry detergents, house paints, industrial coatings, food packaging, computer equipment, cellular phones, window frames, diapers, refined sugar, construction materials, magazines and the agricultural industry.

The publicly traded Philadelphia company reported $3.9 billion in 1997 sales and has about 11,600 employees. About half its sales are made in the United States.

In January 1998, the company announced it would sell its interest in the AtoHaas venture, which produces Plexiglas, and its European counterpart, Altuglas. Rohm and Haas founders are credited with inventing Plexiglas, a plastic used as a glass substitute.

The company's largest business unit produces polymers, resins and monomers. Other large divisions are performance chemicals, agricultural chemicals and plastics. An electronic chemicals unit supplies chemicals needed to produce semiconductor chips and printed wiring boards.

Manufacturing locations: California, Connecticut, Illinois, Kentucky, Massachusetts, North Carolina, Pennsylvania, Tennessee and Texas.

Rohm & Haas Employees Association for Better Government (C00039057) *Phone: (202) 872-0660 * Fax: (202) 872-0663 * 1667 K St. N.W., Suite 210, Washington, DC 20006 * Treasurer: Linda F. Ward * Contact: Geoff Hurwitz*

	1993-94	1995-96	1997	Totals
Receipts	$77,229	$72,784	$37,429	$187,442
Disburse	70,462	79,286	16,933	166,681
Cash	13,978	7,479	27,977	n/a
Contributions	34,126	44,250	9,500	87,876
Republicans	12,800	26,250	4,500	43,550
No. of Cand.	*12*	*22*	*4*	*38*
House	6,800	16,750	2,000	25,550
Senate	6,000	9,500	2,500	18,000
Democrats	21,326	18,000	5,000	44,326
No. of Cand.	*18*	*13*	*6*	*37*
House	14,576	16,000	5,000	35,576
Senate	6,750	2,000	0	8,750
Incumbents	23,300	35,750	9,500	68,550
Challengers	9,076	4,000	0	13,076
Open Seat	1,750	4,500	0	6,250
Winners	25,876	40,250	n/a	66,126
Losers	8,250	4,000	n/a	12,250

Society of the Plastics Industry

*Phone: (202) 974-5204 * Fax: (202) 296-7218*
1801 K St. N.W., Suite 600K, Washington, DC 20006-1301
*Web: www.socplas.org * E-mail: drichard@socplas.org*

The Society of the Plastics Industry represents 2,000 companies in all segments of the plastics industry, including processors, raw material suppliers, machinery manufacturers and moldmakers. In addition to state chapters, SPI has regional offices in Washington, Boston, Chicago, Los Angeles and Greenville, S.C.

SPI is interested in developing standards for product performance and safety and ensuring the marketability of U.S. plastics products overseas. It also maintains a joint initiative with the American Plastics Council. The APC's mission is to promote plastics as a preferred industry material and an answer to some environmental concerns.

Founded in 1937, SPI has a staff of 140 people.

The Society of The Plastics Industry Inc. PAC (PlasticsPAC) (C00309716) *Address: same as sponsor * Treasurer: Harry B. Ussery * Contact: John Witt, Chairperson*

	1993-94	1995-96	1997	Totals
Receipts	$0	$10,858	$374	$11,232
Disburse	0	8,318	0	8,318
Cash	0	2,520	2,915	n/a
Contributions	0	6,250	0	6,250
Republicans	0	6,250	0	6,250
No. of Cand.	*0*	*17*	*0*	*17*
House	0	6,250	0	6,250
Senate	0	0	0	0
Democrats	0	0	0	0
No. of Cand.	*0*	*0*	*0*	*0*
House	0	0	0	0
Senate	0	0	0	0
Incumbents	0	4,500	0	4,500
Challengers	0	1,000	0	1,000
Open Seat	0	750	0	750
Winners	0	4,750	n/a	4,750
Losers	0	1,500	n/a	1,500

Union Carbide Corp.

*Phone: (203) 794-2000 * Fax: (203) 794-6269*
39 Old Ridgebury Rd., Danbury, CT 06817-0001
Web: www.unioncarbide.com

Union Carbide, a major chemical producer, divides its business into two segments: specialties and intermediates and basic chemicals and polymers. The global company's 1997 sales were $6.5 billion and it employs nearly 12,000 people. The Fortune 500 company manufactures solvents, coatings, latex, resins, emulsions and plasticizers. The company's products are used to make antifreeze and polyester.

Union Carbide has expanded its presence in the Asian plastics market. The company has a joint venture with a unit of France's Elf Aquitaine to produce specialty polyethylene resins and products and has a joint venture with Exxon to develop new polyethylene production technologies.

Union Carbide Corp. Political Action Committee (C00035162) *Phone: (202) 393-3211 * Fax: (202) 347-1684 * 801 Pennsylvania Ave. N.W., Suite 230, Washington, DC 20004 * Treasurer: James V. Murray*

	1993-94	1995-96	1997	Totals
Receipts	$24,238	$38,599	$16,905	$79,742
Disburse	34,600	36,600	14,800	86,000
Cash	6,146	8,145	10,250	n/a
Contributions	25,800	28,500	12,000	66,300
Republicans	9,800	23,000	7,500	40,300
No. of Cand.	*10*	*23*	*9*	*42*
House	5,800	17,000	6,500	29,300
Senate	4,000	6,000	1,000	11,000
Democrats	16,000	5,500	4,500	26,000
No. of Cand.	*17*	*6*	*6*	*29*
House	12,000	3,500	2,500	18,000
Senate	4,000	2,000	2,000	8,000
Incumbents	23,800	24,000	12,000	59,800
Challengers	500	500	0	1,000
Open Seat	1,500	4,000	0	5,500
Winners	22,800	17,000	n/a	39,800
Losers	3,000	11,500	n/a	14,500

Viad Corp.

*Phone: (602) 207-5700 * Fax: (602) 207-5806*
Viad Tower, Phoenix, AZ 85077-2316
Web: www.viad.com

Viad is a publicly owned services company with holdings in the airline catering and fueling, convention services and travel and leisure industries. The company was formed in 1996 when The Dial Corp. split in two; the consumer products division retained the Dial name and the service companies became Viad. Headquartered in Phoenix, Viad earns $2.4 billion in revenue annually and has 25,000 employees.

Subsidiaries include: Dobbs International Services, GES Exposition Services, Greyhound Leisure Services, Travelers Express, Brewster Tours and Restaura.

Dobbs International Services, with headquarters in Memphis, Tenn., provides airline catering services to United, Delta, US Airways, Northwest, TWA, British Airways, Continental and American. Dobbs has 14,800 employees.

GES Exposition Services is the general contractor for about 3,000 conventions a year, including major events such as the 1996 Super Bowl. Travelers Express sells 250 million money orders a year. Its headquarters are in St. Louis Park, Minn.

Greyhound Leisure Services is the world's largest operator of duty-free stores on board cruise ships. Its headquarters are in Miami. Brewster Tours conducts tours of the Canadian Rockies. Restaura is a Phoenix-based food service company whose clients include companies and concession stands.

Viad Corp. Good Government Project (C00097238) *Address: same as sponsor * Treasurer: Richard C. Stephan * Contact: Steve Twist, Assistant General Counsel*

	1993-94	1995-96	1997	Totals
Receipts	$100,254	$88,433	$42,399	$231,086
Disburse	109,767	87,316	14,552	211,635
Cash	62,474	63,596	91,443	n/a
Contributions	97,350	74,050	10,600	182,000
Republicans	70,400	66,750	9,200	146,350
No. of Cand.	*55*	*64*	*7*	*126*
House	32,900	40,750	6,200	79,850
Senate	37,500	26,000	3,000	66,500
Democrats	26,450	7,300	1,400	35,150
No. of Cand.	*26*	*8*	*3*	*37*
House	17,950	7,300	400	25,650
Senate	8,500	0	1,000	9,500
Incumbents	57,650	54,850	10,600	123,100
Challengers	10,700	6,700	0	17,400
Open Seat	29,000	12,500	0	41,500
Winners	88,000	62,050	n/a	150,050
Losers	9,350	12,000	n/a	21,350

W.R. Grace & Co.

*Phone: (561) 362-2000 x1010 * Fax: (561) 362-2193*
One Town Center Rd., Boca Raton, FL 33486-1010
Web: www.grace.com

W.R. Grace is a global supplier of flexible packaging and specialty chemical products. Grace's customers include the food, consumer products, petroleum refinery and construction industries. With 17,000 employees serving customers in more than 100 countries worldwide, Grace's businesses focus on packaging, catalysts and silica products, construction products and container products. The publicly traded company reported $3.3 billion in 1997 sales.

In August 1997, Grace entered into an agreement with Sealed Air Corp. to combine Grace's Cryovac packaging business with Sealed Air to create a new publicly owned company. Sealed Air, the combined entity, will be the world's leading protective and specialty packaging company. The Sealed Air transaction is expected to be completed in early 1998.

The W.R. Grace & Co. PAC did not make any contributions during 1997.

W.R. Grace & Co. Political Action Committee (GracePAC) (C00041996) *Phone: (202) 452-6700 * 919 18th St. N.W., Washington, DC 20006 * Treasurer: Jane D. McGuinness*

	1993-94	1995-96	1997	Totals
Receipts	$170,323	$2,534	$15	$172,872
Disburse	159,130	24,718	0	183,848
Cash	22,359	181	198	n/a
Contributions	123,016	25,133	0	148,149
Republicans	55,146	20,500	0	75,646
No. of Cand.	*38*	*27*	*0*	*65*
House	28,896	15,000	0	43,896
Senate	26,250	5,500	0	31,750
Democrats	67,870	4,633	0	72,503
No. of Cand.	*43*	*9*	*0*	*52*
House	44,648	3,533	0	48,181
Senate	23,222	1,100	0	24,322
Incumbents	93,620	21,650	0	115,270
Challengers	1,500	1,983	0	3,483
Open Seat	27,896	1,500	0	29,396
Winners	103,916	22,150	n/a	126,066
Losers	19,100	2,983	n/a	22,083

Zeneca Inc.

*Phone: (302) 886-3985 * Fax: (302) 886-3644*
1800 Concord Pike, Wilmington, DE 19850-5438
Web: www.zeneca.com

Zeneca is an international group of pharmaceuticals, agrochemicals and bioscience specialty businesses. It is the world's second-largest maker of cancer treatments and the third-largest agrochemical producer. The publicly traded British company has 30,000 employees and posted $8.6 billion in 1997 sales.

Products include: Zoladex and Arimidex, the world's largest-selling breast cancer treatment; Diprivanthe, an intravenous anesthetic; the world's second-largest selling agricultural herbicide; and the United Kingdom's leading meat-alternative brand. Recent additions to Zeneca's product line include three new cancer therapies, new treatments for asthma and migraine and a crop protection fungicide.

Zeneca's products are manufactured in 25 countries and sold in more than 100.

Zeneca Inc. Political Action Committee (C00279455) *Address: same as sponsor * Treasurer: Joseph W. Gibson*

	1993-94	1995-96	1997	Totals
Receipts	$98,367	$142,583	$68,900	$309,850
Disburse	66,662	152,703	58,960	278,325
Cash	30,708	20,590	30,531	n/a
Contributions	67,000	140,547	56,750	264,297
Republicans	35,050	110,475	42,750	188,275
No. of Cand.	*42*	*109*	*62*	*213*
House	18,800	67,475	30,750	117,025
Senate	16,250	43,000	12,000	71,250
Democrats	31,950	30,072	13,500	75,522
No. of Cand.	*43*	*40*	*19*	*102*
House	25,350	24,072	7,500	56,922
Senate	6,600	6,000	6,000	18,600
Incumbents	57,150	116,547	56,500	230,197
Challengers	4,500	6,000	0	10,500
Open Seat	5,350	18,000	250	23,600
Winners	58,700	118,975	n/a	177,675
Losers	8,300	21,572	n/a	29,872

Food & Beverage

Aramark Corp.

*Phone: (215) 238-3242 * Fax: (215) 238-3282*
1101 Market St., Aramark Tower, Philadelphia, PA 19107
Web: www.aramark.com

Aramark is a private company that provides businesses with food services, uniforms, child care and magazine and book distribution.

Aramark's 150,000 employees serve college students food, provide refreshments at sporting events and deliver clean uniforms to companies throughout the nation. The company also provides food services, as well as building maintenance and housekeeping services, to companies, health care facilities and prisons.

The company, which had 1997 sales of $6.3 billion, operates at more than 500,000 locations in 11 countries.

Aramark Political Action Committee (Aramark PAC) (formerly known as ARA PAC) (C00157677) *Address: same as sponsor * Treasurer: Michael C. Kelly * Contact: Martin W. Spector, Chairman*

	1993-94	1995-96	1997	Totals
Receipts	$158,235	$138,085	$58,932	$355,252
Disburse	88,168	108,912	37,430	234,510
Cash	150,655	179,829	201,686	n/a
Contributions	34,956	20,550	7,000	62,506
Republicans	8,250	9,300	4,750	22,300
No. of Cand.	*7*	*7*	*3*	*17*
House	4,750	8,800	250	13,800
Senate	3,500	500	4,500	8,500
Democrats	26,706	11,250	2,250	40,206
No. of Cand.	*11*	*8*	*3*	*22*
House	6,350	11,250	1,250	18,850
Senate	20,356	0	1,000	21,356
Incumbents	28,100	19,050	7,000	54,150
Challengers	3,500	250	0	3,750
Open Seat	0	1,250	0	1,250
Winners	21,600	17,050	n/a	38,650
Losers	13,356	3,500	n/a	16,856

Brinker International Inc.

*Phone: (972) 770-4954 * Fax: (972) 770-9479*
6820 LBJ Frwy., Suite 200, Dallas, TX 75240

Brinker International runs restaurant chains — Chili's Grill & Bar, Romano's Macaroni Grill, On The Border Mexican Cafe, Cozymel's Coastal Mexican Grill, Maggio's Little Italy and the Corner Bakery.

Brinker also operates Eatzi's Market and Bakery.

Brinker International's 1997 revenues approached $2 billion. The publicly traded company employs more than 47,000 workers.

Brinker International Inc. Political Action Committee (C00241851) *Address: same as sponsor * Treasurer: Charles Sonsteby * Contact: Tim Doke, Chairman*

	1993-94	*1995-96*	*1997*	*Totals*
Receipts	$200,029	$197,751	$76,655	$474,435
Disburse	184,850	225,000	55,380	465,230
Cash	86,774	59,540	80,820	n/a
Contributions	155,750	158,950	10,500	325,200
Republicans	142,750	147,950	9,500	300,200
No. of Cand.	*54*	*74*	*8*	*136*
House	87,850	85,750	2,500	176,100
Senate	54,900	62,200	7,000	124,100
Democrats	13,000	11,000	1,000	25,000
No. of Cand.	*8*	*12*	*2*	*22*
House	10,000	11,000	1,000	22,000
Senate	3,000	0	0	3,000
Incumbents	37,700	73,500	7,500	118,700
Challengers	77,600	23,200	0	100,800
Open Seat	40,450	62,250	3,000	105,700
Winners	116,200	91,500	n/a	207,700
Losers	39,550	67,450	n/a	107,000

Coca-Cola Co.

*Phone: (404) 676-2121 * Fax: (404) 676-6792*
P.O. Drawer 1734, Atlanta, GA 30301
Web: www.cocacola.com

Coca-Cola is the world's largest soft drink company and the world's leading marketer of juices, through subsidiary The Minute Maid Co. Every day consumers in 195 countries drink about 773 million servings of Coca-Cola, Diet Coke, Sprite, Fanta and other products. A public company, Coca-Cola had sales of more than $18 billion in 1997.

The company makes syrups, concentrates and beverage bases. Bottling plants are, with some exceptions, locally owned and operated by independent business people.

The company's management structure consists of five geographic groups plus Minute Maid. Houston-based Minute Maid was formerly known as Coca-Cola Foods.

Coca-Cola Co. Nonpartisan Committee for Good Government (C00012468) *Address: same as sponsor * Treasurer: Patrick M. Worsham*

	1993-94	*1995-96*	*1997*	*Totals*
Receipts	$273,418	$202,384	$145,642	$621,444
Disburse	277,847	207,271	102,305	587,423
Cash	30,861	25,972	68,071	n/a
Contributions	174,273	153,400	69,874	397,547
Republicans	78,792	104,550	41,700	225,042
No. of Cand.	*78*	*74*	*39*	*191*
House	38,392	51,700	27,200	117,292
Senate	40,400	52,850	14,500	107,750
Democrats	95,481	48,850	28,174	172,505
No. of Cand.	*104*	*57*	*30*	*191*
House	71,831	29,850	14,924	116,605
Senate	23,650	19,000	13,250	55,900
Incumbents	138,875	105,600	65,374	309,849
Challengers	6,050	5,250	0	11,300
Open Seat	28,348	42,050	4,000	74,398
Winners	135,198	117,600	n/a	252,798
Losers	39,075	35,800	n/a	74,875

Coca-Cola Enterprises Inc. Employee Nonpartisan Committee for Good Government (C00250134) *Phone: (770) 989-3000 * Fax: (770) 989-3790 * 2500 Windy Ridge Pkwy., Atlanta, GA 30339 * Web: www.cokecce.com * Treasurer: Laura E. Brightwell*

A subsidiary of Coca-Cola Co., Coca-Cola Enterprises is the largest licensed bottler of Coca-Cola products in the United States. The Coca-Cola Co. owns 44 percent of Coca-Cola Enterprises' stock.

	1993-94	*1995-96*	*1997*	*Totals*
Receipts	$54,312	$188,898	$131,870	$375,080
Disburse	81,815	182,485	140,683	404,983
Cash	897	7,287	40,856	n/a
Contributions	71,315	140,832	27,750	239,897
Republicans	34,290	113,862	23,500	171,652
No. of Cand.	*40*	*94*	*21*	*155*
House	16,040	64,012	11,500	91,552
Senate	18,250	49,850	12,000	80,100
Democrats	37,025	26,970	4,250	68,245
No. of Cand.	*46*	*35*	*7*	*88*
House	33,525	21,970	2,250	57,745
Senate	3,500	5,000	2,000	10,500
Incumbents	51,775	88,282	26,250	166,307
Challengers	3,500	10,500	0	14,000
Open Seat	16,040	42,050	1,000	59,090
Winners	57,165	112,460	n/a	169,625
Losers	14,150	28,372	n/a	42,522

Cracker Barrel Old Country Store Inc.

*Phone: (615) 444-5533 * Fax: (615) 443-9399*
P.O. Box 787, Hartmann Dr., Lebanon, TN 37088-0787
*Web: www.cbrl.com * E-mail: pcarroll@crackerbarrel.com*

Cracker Barrel Old Country Store is a restaurant and gift shop chain with more than 300 stores in 34 states, primarily in the Midwest and the South. The publicly traded Tennessee company posted $1.1 billion in fiscal year 1997 revenues. Cracker Barrel owns and operates all of its stores and does not offer franchises.

Cracker Barrel restaurants offer homemade food on premises and a rustic, log cabin atmosphere. The gift shop sells glassware, toys, woodcrafts and decorations, as well as jellies, bacon and smoked sausage.

Cracker Barrel Old Country Store Inc. Citizens for Political Accountability (C00252791) *Address: same as sponsor * Treasurer: Patrick A. Scruggs * Contact: Penny Carroll, Community and Gov. Relations*

	1993-94	*1995-96*	*1997*	*Totals*
Receipts	$67,368	$90,981	$46,782	$205,131
Disburse	80,680	71,685	22,572	174,937
Cash	3,150	22,455	46,655	n/a
Contributions	65,000	60,250	6,000	131,250
Republicans	63,500	60,250	6,000	129,750
No. of Cand.	*21*	*25*	*2*	*48*
House	30,000	46,750	0	76,750
Senate	33,500	13,500	6,000	53,000
Democrats	1,500	0	0	1,500
No. of Cand.	*1*	*0*	*0*	*1*
House	1,500	0	0	1,500
Senate	0	0	0	0
Incumbents	16,500	15,000	6,000	37,500
Challengers	28,000	29,250	0	57,250
Open Seat	20,000	16,000	0	36,000
Winners	48,500	26,000	n/a	74,500
Losers	16,500	34,250	n/a	50,750

Darden Restaurants Inc.

*Phone: (407) 245-4702 * Fax: (407) 245-4462*
5900 Lake Ellenor Dr., Orlando, FL 32809

With $3.2 billion in 1997 sales, Dardies Restaurants is one of the largest casual dining restaurant companies in the world.

Headquartered in Orlando, Fla., the company owns and operates more than 1,150 restaurants in the United States and Canada, namely the Red Lobster, The Olive Garden and Bahama Breeze restaurants. The publicly traded company employs 115,000 people.

Darden Restaurants Inc. Employees Good Government Fund (formerly known as General Mills Restaurants Inc. Good Government Fund) (C00108282) *Address: same as sponsor * Treasurer: Richard J. Walsh * Contact: Betty Salvas, Corporate Relations Manager*

	1993-94	*1995-96*	*1997*	*Totals*
Receipts	$144,256	$121,654	$52,778	$318,688
Disburse	134,810	111,493	35,589	281,892
Cash	25,204	28,408	52,567	n/a
Contributions	116,131	104,800	20,354	241,285
Republicans	86,631	83,800	17,354	187,785
No. of Cand.	*80*	*93*	*12*	*185*
House	45,282	52,300	7,000	104,582
Senate	41,349	31,500	10,354	83,203

Democrats	29,500	21,000	3,000	53,500
No. of Cand.	*37*	*35*	*4*	*76*
House	19,500	15,000	1,000	35,500
Senate	10,000	6,000	2,000	18,000
Incumbents	77,782	85,800	18,000	181,582
Challengers	14,099	5,500	0	19,599
Open Seat	24,250	15,000	2,354	41,604
Winners	99,631	88,300	n/a	187,931
Losers	16,500	16,500	n/a	33,000

Friday's Hospitality Worldwide Inc.

Phone: (942) 450-5400
7540 L.B.J. Freeway, Suite 100, Dallas, TX 75251
Web: www.tgifridays.com

Friday's Hospitality Worldwide owns more than 500 casual dining establishments, including T.G.I. Friday's, Italianni's, Friday's Front Row, Sports Grill and Friday's American Bar. Based in Dallas, the company employs 17,000 workers worldwide and posted 1997 revenues of more than $1 billion. Friday's is owned by Carlson Companies Inc., a private hospitality, travel and marketing company based in Minneapolis.

The company has restaurants in more than 36 countries. By 2001, revenue is expected to reach $2 billion, with more than 1,000 restaurants in 60 countries. Expansions during 1997 included 15 Italianni's restaurants in Mexico, three T.G.I. Friday's in Pakistan, and one in Stockholm, Sweden.

Friday's Hospitality Worldwide Participation Active Citizens (formerly known as T.G.I. Friday's Participation Citizens) (C00236372) *Address: same as sponsor * Treasurer: Rosalyn Mallet*

	1993-94	*1995-96*	*1997*	*Totals*
Receipts	$63,059	$43,005	$15,860	$121,924
Disburse	30,999	68,634	14,463	114,096
Cash	88,153	61,537	62,938	n/a
Contributions	19,500	45,200	2,500	67,200
Republicans	18,000	44,200	2,500	64,700
No. of Cand.	*15*	*22*	*2*	*39*
House	7,000	26,000	0	33,000
Senate	11,000	18,200	2,500	31,700
Democrats	1,500	1,000	0	2,500
No. of Cand.	*2*	*2*	*0*	*4*
House	1,500	1,000	0	2,500
Senate	0	0	0	0
Incumbents	12,500	18,500	-500	30,500
Challengers	4,000	11,000	0	15,000
Open Seat	2,500	15,700	3,000	21,200
Winners	17,000	25,500	n/a	42,500
Losers	2,500	19,700	n/a	22,200

Hardee's Food Systems Inc.

*Phone: (919) 450-8562 * Fax: (919) 450-8201*
P.O. Box 1619, Rocky Mount, NC 27801-1619
Web: www.hardeesrestaurants.com

Hardee's Food Systems is a wholly owned subsidiary of CKE Restaurants Inc., a publicly traded company. Hardee's owns and operates a system of 3,080 quick-service restaurants in 39 states and 11 foreign countries. CKE, which also owns several regional fast-food chains, posted $1.1 billion in fiscal year 1998 sales.

In early 1998, CKE agreed to purchase 554 franchisee-operated restaurants from Advantica Corp.

Hardee's Food Systems Inc. Good Government Fund (C00083840) *Address: same as sponsor * Treasurer: James Speed*

	1993-94	*1995-96*	*1997*	*Totals*
Receipts	$21,911	$16,639	$4,975	$43,525
Disburse	2,960	32,826	4,308	40,094
Cash	30,646	14,471	15,144	n/a
Contributions	500	31,500	4,000	36,000
Republicans	500	21,500	4,000	26,000
No. of Cand.	*1*	*27*	*2*	*30*
House	500	11,500	0	12,000
Senate	0	10,000	4,000	14,000
Democrats	0	10,000	0	10,000
No. of Cand.	*3*	*17*	*0*	*20*
House	0	10,000	0	10,000
Senate	0	0	0	0
Incumbents	-500	23,500	4,000	27,000
Challengers	0	2,000	0	2,000
Open Seat	1,000	6,000	0	7,000
Winners	0	28,500	n/a	28,500
Losers	500	3,000	n/a	3,500

Hershey Foods Corp.

*Phone: (717) 534-7771 * Fax: (717) 534-6760*
100 Crystal A Dr., Hershey, PA 17033-0810
Web: www.hersheys.com

Hershey Foods, the biggest candy maker in the United States, produces more than chocolate.

Controlled by The Hershey Trust, the public company makes Hershey's Kisses, Reese's peanut butter cups, Jolly Ranchers and other candies. It is also the largest seller of pasta in North America, under the Ronzoni, Skinner and American Beauty brands.

The company, headquartered in Pennsylvania, has 15,300 employees. Hershey's had 1997 sales of $4.3 billion.

Hershey Foods Corp. Citizenship Fund (formerly known as Hershey EPAC) (C00200139) *Address: same as sponsor * Treasurer: Richard L. Uhrich*

	1993-94	*1995-96*	*1997*	*Totals*
Receipts	$55,155	$72,983	$37,057	$165,195
Disburse	56,125	72,662	13,800	142,587
Cash	4,039	4,065	27,323	n/a
Contributions	25,100	23,692	4,500	53,292
Republicans	16,850	20,192	3,500	40,542
No. of Cand.	*14*	*26*	*4*	*44*
House	8,850	10,942	500	20,292
Senate	8,000	9,250	3,000	20,250
Democrats	8,250	3,500	1,000	12,750
No. of Cand.	*10*	*6*	*2*	*18*
House	5,250	3,500	1,000	9,750
Senate	3,000	0	0	3,000
Incumbents	16,600	16,942	4,500	38,042
Challengers	5,000	3,000	0	8,000
Open Seat	3,500	3,750	0	7,250
Winners	21,850	21,392	n/a	43,242
Losers	3,250	2,300	n/a	5,550

Long John Silver's Restaurants Inc.

*Phone: (606) 388-6000 * Fax: (606) 388-6363*
P.O. Box 11988, Lexington, KY 40579
Web: www.ljsilvers.com

Long John Silver's PAC was terminated in January 1998.

Long John Silver's Restaurants Inc. (formerly known as Jerrico Political Action Committee/J-PAC) (C00083733) *Address: same as sponsor * Treasurer: Melanie Judy*

	1993-94	*1995-96*	*1997*	*Totals*
Receipts	$17,094	$10,323	$2,468	$29,885
Disburse	18,778	16,740	3,727	39,245
Cash	7,987	1,564	0	n/a
Contributions	6,000	4,700	1,000	11,700
Republicans	6,000	3,700	500	10,200
No. of Cand.	*11*	*8*	*1*	*20*
House	2,750	1,750	500	5,000
Senate	3,250	1,950	0	5,200
Democrats	0	1,000	500	1,500
No. of Cand.	*0*	*1*	*1*	*2*
House	0	1,000	0	1,000
Senate	0	0	500	500
Incumbents	6,000	4,000	500	10,500
Challengers	0	700	0	700
Open Seat	0	0	500	500
Winners	6,000	3,500	n/a	9,500
Losers	0	1,200	n/a	1,200

McDonald's Corp.

*Phone: (630) 575-3794 * Fax: (630) 575-5027*
One McDonald's Plaza, Oak Brook, IL 60523
Web: www.mcdonalds.com

One of the great brand names of America, McDonald's now relies on its worldwide restaurants to boost lagging domestic sales. The company licenses more than 23,000 fast-food restaurants around the world. It has a 42 percent market share of the nation's fast-food hamburger business, and most of the 12,300 U.S. restaurants are operated by independent franchisees.

McDonald's plans to add more than 2,000 new outlets during 1998, most of them outside the United States. The company, which employs 237,000 people, had $33.6 billion in sales during 1997. McDonald's is interested in labor, tax and food issues.

McDonald's ranked third among restaurant industry PACs in contributions to congressional candidates during the 1995-96 election cycle. Nearly 90 percent of its contributions went to Republican candidates, but most of the Democrats that McDonald's supported won their races.

The leading recipients were Sens. Gordon H. Smith, R-Ore., and Fred Thompson, R-Tenn., and 1996 Republican Senate candidates Rudy Boschwitz of Minnesota and former Rep. Dick Zimmer, R-N.J. Sen. Charles S. Robb, D-Va., was the top Democratic recipient.

McDonald's Corp. Political Action Committee (C00063164) *Phone: (202) 887-8900 * Fax: (202) 887-8907 * 1725 Desales St. N.W., Suite 802, Washington, DC 20036 * E-mail: mcd-dc@cais.com * Treasurer: Michael D. Richard * Contact: Dick Crawford, Department Dir.*

	1993-94	1995-96	1997	Totals
Receipts	$413,613	$445,497	$145,424	$1,004,534
Disburse	431,417	427,175	120,933	979,525
Cash	43,490	61,812	86,303	n/a
Contributions	326,250	295,125	54,250	675,625
Republicans	246,250	265,000	49,750	561,000
No. of Cand.	*145*	*143*	*41*	*329*
House	102,250	125,500	14,250	242,000
Senate	144,000	139,500	35,500	319,000
Democrats	80,500	30,125	4,500	115,125
No. of Cand.	*58*	*29*	*13*	*100*
House	56,500	24,125	4,500	85,125
Senate	24,000	6,000	0	30,000
Incumbents	192,250	178,125	47,750	418,125
Challengers	38,500	33,000	6,000	77,500
Open Seat	95,500	84,000	0	179,500
Winners	291,750	227,000	n/a	518,750
Losers	34,500	68,125	n/a	102,625

National Confectioners Association

*Phone: (703) 790-5750 * Fax: (703) 790-5752*
7900 Westpark Dr., Suite A-320, McLean, VA 22102
Web: www.candyusa.org

The National Confectioners Association is a trade association for candy makers in the United States. It provides technical assistance, research and lobbying for its members, which include companies such as Clark Bar America, Hershey Foods Corp., M&M/Mars, Russell Stover Candies, Tootsie Roll Industries Inc. and The LifeSavers Co.

National Confectioners Association of the United States Inc. Political Action Committee (C00003855) *Address: same as sponsor * Treasurer: Lawrence T. Graham*

	1993-94	1995-96	1997	Totals
Receipts	$10,155	$23,251	$6,249	$39,655
Disburse	11,217	23,249	4,926	39,392
Cash	985	984	2,306	n/a
Contributions	10,500	16,600	4,800	31,900
Republicans	7,750	12,450	2,800	23,000
No. of Cand.	*15*	*22*	*8*	*45*
House	5,750	7,950	550	14,250
Senate	2,000	4,500	2,250	8,750
Democrats	2,750	4,150	2,000	8,900
No. of Cand.	*6*	*8*	*5*	*19*
House	2,750	3,650	1,500	7,900
Senate	0	500	500	1,000
Incumbents	9,500	14,000	3,800	27,300
Challengers	500	400	1,000	1,900
Open Seat	500	2,000	0	2,500
Winners	8,250	14,200	n/a	22,450
Losers	2,250	2,400	n/a	4,650

National Council of Chain Restaurants

*Phone: (202) 626-8183 * Fax: (202) 626-8185*
325 Seventh St. N.W., Suite 1000, Washington, DC 20004

The National Council of Chain Restaurants represents 40 of the largest multi-state restaurant corporations in the United States. The group was formed during the mid-1960s and lobbies on behalf of the chain restaurant industry at the federal and state levels. The NCCR also provides legal counsel on industry-wide issues and is affiliated with the National Retail Federation.

National Council of Chain Restaurants PAC (formerly known as Foodservice and Lodging Institute PAC) (C00175075) *Address: same as sponsor * Treasurer: Terrie M. Dort*

	1993-94	1995-96	1997	Totals
Receipts	$8,128	$8,013	$7,502	$23,643
Disburse	6,437	10,430	6,519	23,386
Cash	2,495	331	1,314	n/a
Contributions	6,250	7,000	4,250	17,500
Republicans	2,250	6,000	2,750	11,000
No. of Cand.	*5*	*12*	*4*	*21*
House	1,750	4,250	500	6,500
Senate	500	1,750	2,250	4,500
Democrats	4,000	1,000	1,500	6,500
No. of Cand.	*7*	*2*	*2*	*11*
House	4,000	1,000	0	5,000
Senate	0	0	1,500	1,500
Incumbents	5,750	6,250	3,000	15,000
Challengers	500	750	0	1,250
Open Seat	0	0	1,250	1,250
Winners	4,250	6,000	n/a	10,250
Losers	2,000	1,000	n/a	3,000

National Restaurant Association

*Phone: (202) 331-5900 * Fax: (202) 331-5946*
1200 17th St. N.W., Washington, DC 20036-3097
*Web: www.restaurant.org * E-mail: eallen@dineout.org*

The National Restaurant Association represents more than 30,000 members who own or operate more than 175,000 restaurants, cafeterias and institutions associated with the industry. The Educational Foundation of the association, located in Chicago, develops and provides educational training programs.

The group opposes lowering the legal blood-alcohol intoxication level to 0.08 percent. It also opposes increasing FICA taxes and expanding the 1993 Family and Medical Leave Act. The association favors eliminating the Alternative Minimum Tax. It supports Medical Savings Accounts and permanently extending the Work Opportunity Tax Credit. The group also supports legislation to expand deductibility for business meals and to change the IRS method of conducting employer audits on unreported tips.

The group's pro-business stance resulted in heavy support for Republican candidates in 1996. It was the leading restaurant industry contributor to congressional races and increased its total contributions by 29 percent from 1994. Nine of the top 15 recipients of this PAC's contributions were challengers.

National Restaurant Association Political Action Committee (C00003764) *Address: same as sponsor * Treasurer: Elaine Z. Graham * Contact: Don Thoren, PAC Dir.*

	1993-94	1995-96	1997	Totals
Receipts	$726,082	$965,501	$547,975	$2,239,558
Disburse	716,183	950,845	303,341	1,970,369
Cash	42,802	57,460	302,096	n/a
Contributions	658,844	880,119	238,222	1,777,185
Republicans	494,722	780,069	183,222	1,458,013
No. of Cand.	*187*	*249*	*114*	*550*
House	354,222	588,480	144,217	1,086,919
Senate	140,500	191,589	39,005	371,094
Democrats	164,122	100,050	54,500	318,672
No. of Cand.	*91*	*46*	*39*	*176*
House	152,122	94,550	44,500	291,172
Senate	12,000	5,500	10,000	27,500
Incumbents	349,788	494,619	223,322	1,067,729
Challengers	144,500	112,500	10,400	267,400
Open Seat	162,556	273,000	8,500	444,056
Winners	516,344	625,720	n/a	1,142,064
Losers	142,500	254,399	n/a	396,899

Texas Restaurant Association Political Action Committee (C00077636) *Phone: (512) 472-3666 * Fax: (512) 472-2777 * P.O. Box 1651, Austin, TX 78767 * Web: www.txrestaurant.org * E-mail: dswift@tramail.org * Treasurer: Glen Garey * Contact: Jose Cuevas*

The Texas Restaurant Association has 6,400 restaurant-members, including national franchises with locations in Texas. Sixty percent of the association's members are independent restaurants.

	1993-94	1995-96	1997	Totals
Receipts	$56,779	$69,905	$17,595	$144,279
Disburse	56,562	65,124	22,034	143,720
Cash	663	4,731	292	n/a
Contributions	50,457	53,515	14,871	118,843
Republicans	25,844	36,966	14,621	77,431
No. of Cand.	*10*	*19*	*4*	*33*
House	9,844	36,466	9,621	55,931
Senate	16,000	500	5,000	21,500

	1993-94	1995-96	1997	Totals
Democrats	24,613	16,549	250	41,412
No. of Cand.	*14*	*11*	*1*	*26*
House	24,613	16,549	250	41,412
Senate	0	0	0	0
Incumbents	35,457	21,582	14,621	71,660
Challengers	11,000	2,799	0	13,799
Open Seat	4,000	29,134	250	33,384
Winners	40,162	44,582	n/a	84,744
Losers	10,295	8,933	n/a	19,228

National Soft Drink Association

*Phone: (202) 463-6740 * Fax: (202) 659-5349*
1101 16th St. N.W., Washington, DC 20036-6396
Web: www.nsda.org

The National Soft Drink Association is the trade group for America's soft drink industry, representing hundreds of soft drink bottling firms, franchise companies and support industries. Founded in 1919 as the American Bottlers of Carbonated Beverages, NSDA members employ more than 130,000 people who produce U.S. sales in excess of $52 billion a year related to the soft drink industry.

The NSDA acts as liaison between the industry, government and the public and provides a unified voice in legislative matters. The association also provides its members with information on science, technology, recycling and the law.

National Soft Drink Association Political Action Committee (also known as Soft Drink PAC) (C00100107) *Address: same as sponsor * Treasurer: Mark N. Hammond*

	1993-94	1995-96	1997	Totals
Receipts	$81,321	$117,736	$77,208	$276,265
Disburse	81,924	114,516	74,819	271,259
Cash	2,690	3,912	6,302	n/a
Contributions	77,813	102,526	72,291	252,630
Republicans	41,677	75,487	49,000	166,164
No. of Cand.	*54*	*83*	*61*	*198*
House	18,977	37,411	32,000	88,388
Senate	22,700	38,076	17,000	77,776
Democrats	36,136	27,039	23,291	86,466
No. of Cand.	*46*	*33*	*34*	*113*
House	27,136	19,728	16,291	63,155
Senate	9,000	7,311	7,000	23,311
Incumbents	60,663	78,145	69,041	207,849
Challengers	3,500	8,000	500	12,000
Open Seat	13,650	15,881	2,750	32,281
Winners	65,147	82,956	n/a	148,103
Losers	12,666	19,570	n/a	32,236

Outback Steakhouse Inc.

*Phone: (813) 282-1225 * Fax: (813) 282-1209*
550 N. Reo St., Suite 204, Tampa, FL 33609
Web: www.outback.com

Outback Steakhouse operates more than 370 Australian-themed steakhouses in the United States, most of which are company-owned. It also runs Carrabba's Italian Grill, a line of 50 Italian restaurants. A public company, Outback employs about 23,000 people and had sales of $1.1 billion during 1997.

Outback contributed more money to 1996 congressional candidates than any single restaurant business, including McDonald's. In the restaurant industry, it was topped only by the National Restaurant Association.

In the 1997-98 election cycle, Outback's leading recipients were House Speaker Newt Gingrich, R-Ga., 1996 Senate candidate William F. Weld, a Massachusetts Republican, and House candidate Mark Sharpe, a Republican from Florida. No Democrat received more than $3,000 — the top recipient in that party was Rep. Charles W. Stenholm, D-Texas.

Outback Steakhouse Inc. Political Action Committee (C00253153) *Address: same as sponsor * Treasurer: Joseph J. Kadow * Contact: Allison Whitesides, Gov. Relations*

	1993-94	1995-96	1997	Totals
Receipts	$230,022	$597,318	$365,530	$1,192,870
Disburse	165,900	606,582	125,971	898,453
Cash	74,482	65,232	312,877	n/a
Contributions	146,400	493,950	49,500	689,850
Republicans	139,900	467,950	31,500	639,350
No. of Cand.	*55*	*120*	*13*	*188*
House	93,900	342,250	13,500	449,650
Senate	46,000	125,700	18,000	189,700
Democrats	6,500	26,000	18,000	50,500
No. of Cand.	*6*	*13*	*5*	*24*
House	4,000	25,000	11,000	40,000
Senate	2,500	1,000	7,000	10,500
Incumbents	25,900	261,750	37,000	324,650
Challengers	78,000	78,700	5,000	161,700
Open Seat	42,500	153,500	7,500	203,500
Winners	105,400	302,750	n/a	408,150
Losers	41,000	191,200	n/a	232,200

Pacific Seafood Processors Association

*Phone: (206) 281-1667 * Fax: (206) 283-2387*
300 Elliott Ave. W., Suite 360, Seattle, WA 98119
E-mail: pspa@wlink.net

The Pacific Seafood Processors Association is a trade association for the on-shore seafood processing industry in Washington state and Alaska. The organization has about 25 corporate members and about 200 associate members, such as vendors or other industry-related businesses.

Pacific Seafood Processors Political Action Committee (PSPAC) (C00193672) *Address: same as sponsor * Treasurer: John F. Roos*

	1993-94	1995-96	1997	Totals
Receipts	$12,110	$1,060	$2,366	$15,536
Disburse	9,152	5,150	538	14,840
Cash	4,673	583	2,410	n/a
Contributions	2,250	5,150	500	7,900
Republicans	-200	4,650	500	4,950
No. of Cand.	*3*	*7*	*1*	*11*
House	1,300	1,250	500	3,050
Senate	-1500	3,400	0	1,900
Democrats	2,450	500	0	2,950
No. of Cand.	*5*	*1*	*0*	*6*
House	2,450	500	0	2,950
Senate	0	0	0	0
Incumbents	1,550	4,650	500	6,700
Challengers	0	0	0	0
Open Seat	0	500	0	500
Winners	-150	4,150	n/a	4,000
Losers	2,400	1,000	n/a	3,400

Pepsi-Cola Bottlers Association

*Phone: (972) 717-1049 * Fax: (972) 717-9031*
251 O'Connor Ridge Blvd., Suite 250, Irving, TX 75038-6516
E-mail: sallyg@gte.net

The Pepsi-Cola Bottlers Association is the trade association for the Pepsi-Cola bottling franchisers. The organization has about 125 members nationwide, although many of these members own several bottling franchises.

Pepsi-Cola Bottlers Association PAC (C00122671) *Address: same as sponsor * Treasurer: Walter Wilkinson * Contact: David Doherty, Chairperson*

	1993-94	1995-96	1997	Totals
Receipts	$52,864	$65,636	$27,428	$145,928
Disburse	64,734	62,638	13,293	140,665
Cash	10,152	13,152	27,288	n/a
Contributions	46,900	44,200	8,000	99,100
Republicans	27,000	20,850	6,500	54,350
No. of Cand.	*32*	*24*	*8*	*64*
House	10,000	10,600	4,000	24,600
Senate	17,000	10,250	2,500	29,750
Democrats	18,900	23,350	1,500	43,750
No. of Cand.	*21*	*19*	*2*	*42*
House	14,900	16,000	500	31,400
Senate	4,000	7,350	1,000	12,350
Incumbents	30,800	25,100	5,000	60,900
Challengers	4,000	10,500	2,500	17,000
Open Seat	12,100	8,600	500	21,200
Winners	31,500	32,500	n/a	64,000
Losers	15,400	11,700	n/a	27,100

Pepsi-Cola General Bottlers

*Phone: (847) 253-1000 * Fax: (847) 397-7231*
3501 Algonquin Rd., Rolling Meadows, IL 60008
Web: www.whitmancorp.com/pcgb

Pepsi-Cola General Bottlers is a beverage bottling company based in Illinois. The company has the exclusive franchise rights to manufacture, market and distribute Pepsi-Cola's soft drinks in a number of regions throughout 12 Midwestern states.

Through this arrangement, the company sells about 12 percent of Pepsi-Cola's total U.S. volume. The company also distributes Pepsi-Cola products in Eastern Europe and Russia. Although 90 percent of the company's products are Pepsi-Cola brands, Pepsi-Cola General Bottlers also markets such products as Dr. Pepper, 7-Up, iced teas and sports drinks.

Despite its name, the company is not majority-owned by PepsiCo, but rather by Whitman Corp., a publicly traded company. Whitman formerly owned Midas International and Hussman Corp., but both spun off in January 1998. Pepsi-Cola General Bottlers is now the sole operating asset of the company.

Whitman has about 4,000 employees worldwide. The company had 1997 sales of $1.5 billion.

Pepsi-Cola General Bottlers PAC (C00223909) *Address: same as sponsor * Treasurer: Malcolm Chester*

	1993-94	*1995-96*	*1997*	*Totals*
Receipts	$117,438	$130,806	$28,926	$277,170
Disburse	126,665	129,825	14,420	270,910
Cash	18,461	19,448	33,955	n/a
Contributions	65,812	78,425	8,950	153,187
Republicans	28,907	57,600	6,750	93,257
No. of Cand.	*27*	*40*	*10*	*77*
House	21,757	45,600	6,250	73,607
Senate	7,150	12,000	500	19,650
Democrats	36,905	20,825	2,200	59,930
No. of Cand.	*25*	*18*	*3*	*46*
House	33,155	17,825	2,200	53,180
Senate	3,750	3,000	0	6,750
Incumbents	48,337	56,525	8,450	113,312
Challengers	2,625	4,850	500	7,975
Open Seat	14,850	17,050	0	31,900
Winners	51,337	58,075	n/a	109,412
Losers	14,475	20,350	n/a	34,825

Peter Pan Seafoods Inc.

*Phone: (206) 728-6000 * Fax: (206) 441-9090*
2200 Sixth Ave., Suite 1000, Seattle, WA 98121-1821

Peter Pan Seafoods is a privately owned wholesale seafood processor headquartered in Seattle, with four plants in Alaska and two plants in Washington state. It employs about 2,000 people seasonally. The company was founded in 1914.

Peter Pan Seafoods Political Action Committee (1220 Associates) (C00100305) *Address: same as sponsor * Treasurer: Deborah L. Jones * Contact: Barry D. Collier, President and CEO*

	1993-94	*1995-96*	*1997*	*Totals*
Receipts	$15,931	$15,887	$4,045	$35,863
Disburse	15,725	15,050	3,500	34,275
Cash	7,477	8,314	9,704	n/a
Contributions	8,725	10,800	1,500	21,025
Republicans	4,300	10,300	1,500	16,100
No. of Cand.	*3*	*10*	*2*	*15*
House	3,300	7,300	1,500	12,100
Senate	1,000	3,000	0	4,000
Democrats	4,425	500	0	4,925
No. of Cand.	*7*	*1*	*0*	*8*
House	4,425	500	0	4,925
Senate	0	0	0	0
Incumbents	7,600	9,300	1,500	18,400
Challengers	1,000	500	0	1,500
Open Seat	125	1,000	0	1,125
Winners	6,800	9,000	n/a	15,800
Losers	1,925	1,800	n/a	3,725

Pizza Hut Franchisees Association

*Phone: (316) 685-1208 * Fax: (316) 685-2591*
101 S. Webb Rd., Suite 101, P.O. Box 782710, Wichita, KS 67278
E-mail: bev@iphfha.com

The Pizza Hut Franchisees Association represents 240 owners of about 3,000 Pizza Hut stores nationwide. The association is opposed to raising the minimum wage, in favor of less regulation of health care and supports utility deregulation.

IPHFHA Inc. Political Action Committee Inc. (C00251447) *Address: same as sponsor * Treasurer: Rod Taylor * Contact: Beverly Jeskie, Manager*

	1993-94	*1995-96*	*1997*	*Totals*
Receipts	$103,194	$135,004	$11,040	$249,238
Disburse	107,179	158,873	1,642	267,694
Cash	26,179	2,312	11,710	n/a
Contributions	87,500	138,250	1,250	227,000
Republicans	84,000	134,750	1,250	220,000
No. of Cand.	*37*	*42*	*2*	*81*
House	24,500	70,750	1,250	96,500
Senate	59,500	64,000	0	123,500
Democrats	3,500	3,500	0	7,000
No. of Cand.	*3*	*3*	*0*	*6*
House	1,500	3,500	0	5,000
Senate	2,000	0	0	2,000
Incumbents	23,000	32,250	1,250	56,500
Challengers	22,500	23,500	0	46,000
Open Seat	42,000	82,500	0	124,500
Winners	77,500	104,750	n/a	182,250
Losers	10,000	33,500	n/a	43,500

Ruby Tuesday Inc.

*Phone: (334) 344-3000 * Fax: (334) 344-9513*
P.O. Box 160266, Mobile, AL 36625

In 1996, Ruby Tuesday split from Morrison Restaurants Inc. to become an independent company.

Ruby Tuesday is a publicly held restaurant chain with more than 380 casual-dining restaurants. Its 325 Ruby Tuesday restaurants offer fajitas, ribs, chicken, sandwiches and salads. The company's chain of 50 Mozzarella's American Cafes offers pasta, pizza and Italian-influenced entrees, while its Tia's chain features Tex-Mex fare such as fajitas, enchiladas and nachos. Its sales in 1996 were $620 million and it employs more than 10,000 people.

The company's restaurants are concentrated in the Southeast and historically have been placed inside shopping malls. However, a new market strategy is shifting the company away from malls toward free-standing restaurants.

Ruby Tuesday Good Government Fund (formerly known as Morrison's Political Action Committee) (C00080713) *Address: same as sponsor * Treasurer: Arthur Robert Outlaw * Contact: Philip G. Hunt, Chairman*

	1993-94	*1995-96*	*1997*	*Totals*
Receipts	$39,537	$14,647	$17,389	$71,573
Disburse	55,618	20,125	3,114	78,857
Cash	8,010	2,541	16,819	n/a
Contributions	53,400	16,750	3,000	73,150
Republicans	50,550	15,750	3,000	69,300
No. of Cand.	*78*	*42*	*5*	*125*
House	28,550	9,250	1,000	38,800
Senate	22,000	6,500	2,000	30,500
Democrats	2,850	1,000	0	3,850
No. of Cand.	*7*	*1*	*0*	*8*
House	2,600	1,000	0	3,600
Senate	250	0	0	250
Incumbents	22,100	4,250	3,000	29,350
Challengers	12,700	2,000	0	14,700
Open Seat	18,600	11,000	0	29,600
Winners	44,100	12,250	n/a	56,350
Losers	9,300	4,500	n/a	13,800

S and A Restaurant Corp.

*Phone: (972) 588-5000 * Fax: (972) 404-5467*
6500 International Pkwy., Plano, TX 75093

S and A Restaurant is a subsidiary of Metromedia Restaurant Group, the Dallas, Texas based holding company for Ponderosa Steakhouse, Bonanza, Steak and Ale and Bennigan's restaurant chains, with more than 1,100 restaurants worldwide. The Metromedia company had estimated sales in 1996 of $1.8 billion. The private company is controlled by billionaire John Kluge.

The company also has interests in a number of telecommunications ventures in Eastern Europe, Russia, Central Asia and China including wireless cable-TV systems, radio stations, paging systems, mobile phone systems and an international toll calling service.

Metromedia also has a substantial investment in Metromedia Fiber Network, which has a fiber-optic network in the New York metropolitan area.

S and A Restaurant Corp. Employees Political Action Committee (C00012021) *Address: same as sponsor * Treasurer: Carolyn Carpenter * Contact: Jean Weber, PAC Administrator*

	1993-94	1995-96	1997	Totals
Receipts	$93,321	$47,841	$16,727	$157,889
Disburse	97,535	52,644	13,623	163,802
Cash	66,354	61,562	64,672	n/a
Contributions	71,400	45,200	13,000	129,600
Republicans	67,150	43,700	10,000	120,850
No. of Cand.	*54*	*32*	*3*	*89*
House	36,150	19,500	7,000	62,650
Senate	31,000	24,200	3,000	58,200
Democrats	4,250	1,500	3,000	8,750
No. of Cand.	*6*	*1*	*1*	*8*
House	4,250	1,500	3,000	8,750
Senate	0	0	0	0
Incumbents	28,900	22,500	10,000	61,400
Challengers	25,500	5,200	0	30,700
Open Seat	17,000	17,500	3,000	37,500
Winners	57,900	30,500	n/a	88,400
Losers	13,500	14,700	n/a	28,200

Schenck Co.

*Phone: (407) 299-4773 x315 * Fax: (407) 296-6649*
4161 N. John Young Pkwy., Orlando, FL 32804

The Schenck Co. is a privately held beer and ale wholesaler serving five counties in central Florida. The Orlando-based company employs 300 workers and distributes such brands as Coors, Miller, Plank Road, Guinness, Corona and Labatts.

Schenck Family (C00209833) *Address: same as sponsor * Treasurer: Kym P. Boney*

	1993-94	1995-96	1997	Totals
Receipts	$10,620	$14,400	$7,307	$32,327
Disburse	13,750	11,550	5,500	30,800
Cash	3,670	0	8,327	n/a
Contributions	4,850	7,000	2,500	14,350
Republicans	4,850	7,000	2,500	14,350
No. of Cand.	*7*	*4*	*4*	*15*
House	4,950	6,000	1,500	12,450
Senate	-100	1,000	1,000	1,900
Democrats	0	0	0	0
No. of Cand.	*0*	*0*	*0*	*0*
House	0	0	0	0
Senate	0	0	0	0
Incumbents	2,600	7,000	2,500	12,100
Challengers	250	0	0	250
Open Seat	2,000	0	0	2,000
Winners	3,100	7,000	n/a	10,100
Losers	1,750	0	n/a	1,750

Shoney's Inc.

*Phone: (615) 391-5201 * Fax: (615) 231-2531*
1727 Elm Hill Pike, Nashville, TN 37210
Web: www.shoneys.com

Shoney's operates 1,400 casual-dining restaurants, which are mostly located in the South. About 900 are company owned and the rest are franchise restaurants. Shoney's also owns more than 80 inns and the Captain D's restaurant chain. A publicly traded company, Shoney's has 33,000 employees. It reported $1.2 billion in sales in 1997.

In 1992, the company settled a class-action racial discrimination suit based on the company's hiring practices. Company founder Ray Danner agreed to personally pay $67 million of a record $134.5 million settlement.

Subsidiaries: Pargos Restaurants, Shoney's Equipment, Shoney Investment, Commissary Services, TPI Entertainment, TPI Investment, TPI Transportation, TPI Properties, Insurex, Insurex Benefits and SHN Properties LLC.

Shoney's Political Action Committee (C00145177) *Address: same as sponsor * Treasurer: Fred E. McDaniel Jr. * Contact: Michael Skelton, Franchise Development Dir.*

	1993-94	1995-96	1997	Totals
Receipts	$36,455	$4,769	$182	$41,406
Disburse	24,813	17,148	640	42,601
Cash	18,596	6,225	5,772	n/a
Contributions	16,700	4,500	0	21,200
Republicans	11,100	4,500	0	15,600
No. of Cand.	*18*	*3*	*0*	*21*
House	4,100	2,000	0	6,100
Senate	7,000	2,500	0	9,500
Democrats	5,600	0	0	5,600
No. of Cand.	*8*	*0*	*0*	*8*
House	3,600	0	0	3,600
Senate	2,000	0	0	2,000
Incumbents	5,600	2,500	0	8,100
Challengers	2,250	2,000	0	4,250
Open Seat	8,850	0	0	8,850
Winners	11,950	2,500	n/a	14,450
Losers	4,750	2,000	n/a	6,750

Sizzler International Inc.

12655 W. Jefferson Blvd., Los Angeles, CA 90066

The Sizzler International PAC was terminated.

Sizzler International Good Government Fund (C00270702) *Address: same as sponsor * Treasurer: Christopher R. Thomas*

	1993-94	1995-96	1997	Totals
Receipts	$24,886	$10,943	$0	$35,829
Disburse	15,000	24,855	0	39,855
Cash	13,910	0	0	n/a
Contributions	15,000	6,855	0	21,855
Republicans	14,000	6,855	0	20,855
No. of Cand.	*8*	*3*	*0*	*11*
House	13,000	5,855	0	18,855
Senate	1,000	1,000	0	2,000
Democrats	1,000	0	0	1,000
No. of Cand.	*1*	*0*	*0*	*1*
House	1,000	0	0	1,000
Senate	0	0	0	0
Incumbents	3,000	3,000	0	6,000
Challengers	11,000	3,855	0	14,855
Open Seat	1,000	0	0	1,000
Winners	8,000	3,000	n/a	11,000
Losers	7,000	3,855	n/a	10,855

White Castle System

*Phone: (614) 228-5781 * Fax: (614) 464-4033*
P.O. Box 1498, Columbus, OH 43216
*Web: www.whitecastle.com * E-mail: zuknick@whitecastle.com*

White Castle is a fast-food restaurant chain known in the eastern half of the United States for its square hamburgers. Founded in 1921, the company, based in Columbus, Ohio, now has 297 restaurants nationwide with combined gross sales of $325 million.

White Castle System Inc. Political Action Committee (C00112623) *Address: same as sponsor * Treasurer: Jennifer Black * Contact: Nicholas Zuk, Chairman*

	1993-94	1995-96	1997	Totals
Receipts	$16,370	$15,695	$5,530	$37,595
Disburse	21,860	18,195	602	40,657
Cash	4,263	2,950	7,878	n/a
Contributions	20,600	17,050	500	38,150
Republicans	19,950	16,450	500	36,900
No. of Cand.	*48*	*41*	*1*	*90*
House	13,200	9,450	0	22,650
Senate	6,750	7,000	500	14,250
Democrats	650	100	0	750
No. of Cand.	*3*	*1*	*0*	*4*
House	650	100	0	750
Senate	0	0	0	0
Incumbents	6,700	7,050	500	14,250
Challengers	6,200	8,250	0	14,450
Open Seat	7,700	1,750	0	9,450
Winners	15,150	6,550	n/a	21,700
Losers	5,450	10,500	n/a	15,950

Lodging/Tourism

American Hotel & Motel Association

*Phone: (202) 289-3100 * Fax: (202) 289-3185*
1201 New York Ave. N.W., Suite 600, Washington, DC 20005
Web: www.ahma.org

The American Hotel & Motel Association represents 11,000 members of the U.S. lodging industry. Headquartered in Washington, it offers governmental affairs services and market strategies to its members and assists with quality assurance programs.

The group's PAC has 3,000 members.

American Hotel & Motel Political Action Committee (C00001198) *Address: same as sponsor * Treasurer: Robert E. Slater Jr. * Contact: Kirk Harris, PAC Dir.*

	1993-94	1995-96	1997	Totals
Receipts	$151,830	$191,376	$163,657	$506,863
Disburse	141,763	196,011	160,980	498,754
Cash	21,940	17,316	19,996	n/a
Contributions	136,890	181,200	161,277	479,367
Republicans	72,100	129,600	133,527	335,227
No. of Cand.	*98*	*190*	*140*	*428*
House	43,050	98,500	106,200	247,750
Senate	29,050	31,100	27,327	87,477
Democrats	62,940	51,600	26,750	141,290
No. of Cand.	*82*	*66*	*40*	*188*
House	46,350	39,900	19,750	106,000
Senate	16,590	11,700	7,000	35,290
Incumbents	119,890	157,600	153,950	431,440
Challengers	3,900	2,600	4,827	11,327
Open Seat	13,100	20,700	2,500	36,300
Winners	121,440	156,400	n/a	277,840
Losers	15,450	24,800	n/a	40,250

American Society of Travel Agents

*Phone: (703) 739-2782 * Fax: (703) 706-0387*
1101 King St., #200, Alexandria, VA 22314-2944
Web: www.astanet.com

The American Society of Travel Agents is the world's largest association of travel professionals. Members of ASTA include travel agencies, airlines, hotels, car rental firms, cruise lines and tour operators. ASTA's 27,000 members are located in 168 countries.

ASTA provides members with education and information resources, monitors the travel industry to identify those who cheat consumers and fights for fair competition throughout the industry.

In 1998, ASTA and the Coalition for Travel Industry Parity announced a joint legislative initiative called the "Consumer Access to Travel Information Act of 1998." The bill would give the Department of Transportation one year to conduct an investigation of airlines whose actions prevent consumer access to travel information. If the investigation shows unfair or deceptive practices, the bill would direct the department to issue an order terminating those practices.

American Society of Travel Agents PAC (C00114108) *Address: same as sponsor * Treasurer: Robert A. Burge * Contact: Barbara O'Hara, PAC Dir.*

	1993-94	1995-96	1997	Totals
Receipts	$79,761	$73,043	$42,407	$195,211
Disburse	73,950	96,232	29,784	199,966
Cash	44,781	21,593	34,216	n/a
Contributions	48,717	67,125	21,175	137,017
Republicans	24,050	51,700	16,550	92,300
No. of Cand.	*90*	*161*	*53*	*304*
House	19,100	41,700	11,550	72,350
Senate	4,950	10,000	5,000	19,950
Democrats	22,417	15,425	4,075	41,917
No. of Cand.	*77*	*42*	*12*	*131*
House	15,350	13,075	2,575	31,000
Senate	7,067	2,350	1,500	10,917
Incumbents	45,467	64,325	20,625	130,417
Challengers	950	700	300	1,950
Open Seat	2,300	2,050	250	4,600
Winners	42,700	57,525	n/a	100,225
Losers	6,017	9,600	n/a	15,617

Automobile Club of Michigan

*Phone: (313) 336-1234 * Fax: (313) 336-1245*
1 Auto Club Dr., Dearborn, MI 48126
*Web: www.aaamich.com * E-mail: info@aaamich.com*

The Automobile Club of Michigan serves American Automobile Association (AAA) members in Michigan and Wisconsin. Established in 1983, the Michigan motor club has 5,000 employees.

AAA is a federation of 98 motor clubs providing its more than 40 million members in the United States and Canada with a full line of travel, financial, insurance and automotive-related services. The federation has lobbied for the legal rights of motorists and travelers and has sought to make car owning and travel a more pleasurable experience through increased services to members.

The Automobile Club of Michigan PAC is involved in issues concerning travel, automobile safety and insurance.

Automobile Club of Michigan Political Action Committee (ACPAC) (C00197103) *Address: same as sponsor * Treasurer: Christine A. Bernhard * Contact: Larry Givens, V.P. of Corp. Relations*

	1993-94	1995-96	1997	Totals
Receipts	$92,686	$122,054	$87,463	$302,203
Disburse	96,767	116,975	63,315	277,057
Cash	29,905	34,988	59,137	n/a
Contributions	4,450	7,795	1,000	13,245
Republicans	1,500	1,700	1,000	4,200
No. of Cand.	*2*	*5*	*1*	*8*
House	500	400	0	900
Senate	1,000	1,300	1,000	3,300
Democrats	2,950	6,095	0	9,045
No. of Cand.	*4*	*7*	*0*	*11*
House	1,450	4,095	0	5,545
Senate	1,500	2,000	0	3,500
Incumbents	1,200	5,245	1,000	7,445
Challengers	500	2,050	0	2,550
Open Seat	2,750	0	0	2,750
Winners	2,200	6,795	n/a	8,995
Losers	2,250	1,000	n/a	3,250

Gaylord Entertainment Co.

*Phone: (615) 316-6000 * Fax: (615) 316-6320*
One Gaylord Dr., Nashville, TN 37214
Web: www.opryhotel.com

Gaylord Entertainment owns the Opryland businesses in Nashville, Tenn., including the Grand Ole Opry, the 2,800 room Opryland Hotel, Springhouse Golf Course, Wild Horse Saloon, Opryland Themepark, Ryman Auditorium and WSM radio.

A publicly traded company, Gaylord reported $820 million in 1997 revenues. It has about 10,800 employees.

The company also operates a broadcasting and music division that owns television and radio stations, music publishing operations and Word Entertainment. Gaylord sold its cable networks, The Nashville Network and Country Music Television, to CBS in 1997.

Gaylord Entertainment Co. Political Action Committee (C00183707) *Address: same as sponsor * Treasurer: Rod Connor*

	1993-94	1995-96	1997	Totals
Receipts	$140,421	$157,441	$76,133	$373,995
Disburse	155,159	194,741	52,167	402,067
Cash	76,296	39,000	62,966	n/a
Contributions	31,210	27,800	6,500	65,510
Republicans	10,700	22,300	5,500	38,500
No. of Cand.	*5*	*5*	*1*	*11*
House	700	4,800	0	5,500
Senate	10,000	17,500	5,500	33,000
Democrats	19,510	5,500	1,000	26,010
No. of Cand.	*14*	*3*	*2*	*19*
House	8,200	3,500	1,000	12,700
Senate	11,310	2,000	0	13,310
Incumbents	17,860	23,500	6,500	47,860
Challengers	7,000	4,300	0	11,300
Open Seat	6,050	0	0	6,050
Winners	16,050	22,500	n/a	38,550
Losers	15,160	5,300	n/a	20,460

Holiday Inns Inc.

Phone: (404) 256-2211
Three Ravinia Dr., Suite 2000, Atlanta, GA 30346

Hotel franchise Holiday Inns became a subsidiary of United Kingdom-based Bass PLC, the second-largest British brewer, following a merger in 1990. Bass operates more than 2,300 Holiday Inn, Crowne Plaza and Inter-Continental hotels worldwide.

Bass, which also operates more than 2,000 pubs, reported 1996 sales of nearly $8 billion. It acquired Inter-Continental in February 1998.

Atlanta-based Holiday Inns is the world's largest hotel brand. Most are operated by independent franchisees.

Subsidiaries include: Holiday Inn Express, Crowne Plaza Hotels and Resorts and SunSpree Resorts.

Inn/PAC International Association of Holiday Inns Inc. Political Action Committee (C00084822) *Phone: (202) 626-8500 * Fax: (202) 626-8593 * 1341 G St. N.W., Suite 1100, Washington, DC 20005 * Treasurer: James P. McCauley * Contact: Thomas R. Donnelly, Gov. Relations*

	1993-94	1995-96	1997	Totals
Receipts	$49,999	$42,694	$27,289	$119,982
Disburse	46,646	60,953	33,679	141,278
Cash	28,942	10,683	4,293	n/a
Contributions	40,000	55,500	30,000	125,500
Republicans	32,000	47,000	24,500	103,500
No. of Cand.	*49*	*70*	*41*	*160*
House	21,500	39,500	19,000	80,000
Senate	10,500	7,500	5,500	23,500
Democrats	8,000	8,500	5,000	21,500
No. of Cand.	*11*	*16*	*8*	*35*
House	6,000	8,500	3,000	17,500
Senate	2,000	0	2,000	4,000
Incumbents	24,500	43,500	28,000	96,000
Challengers	3,000	4,500	1,000	8,500
Open Seat	12,500	7,500	1,000	21,000
Winners	34,500	47,000	n/a	81,500
Losers	5,500	8,500	n/a	14,000

Host Marriott Services Corp.

*Phone: (301) 380-5591 * Fax: (301) 380-4409*
6600 Rockledge Dr., Dept. 928.83, Bethesda, MD 20817-1109
Web: www.hostmarriott.com

Host Marriott Services operates food, beverage and retail concessions at nearly 200 travel and entertainment venues worldwide. With 24,000 employees, the corporation had 1997 sales of $1.3 billion.

The company has concentrated its growth initiatives on international airports and domestic shopping malls.

Host Marriott Services was a part of Host Marriott Corp. until it was spun off as a separate, publicly traded corporation in 1995.

Host Marriott Services Corp. Political Action Committee (C00109413) *Address: same as sponsor * Treasurer: Lori A. Cramp * Contact: Laura Polvinale, Assistant Secretary*

	1993-94	1995-96	1997	Totals
Receipts	$134,180	$18,999	$90	$153,269
Disburse	132,725	26,221	2,500	161,446
Cash	11,837	4,620	2,139	n/a
Contributions	34,700	8,200	500	43,400
Republicans	15,250	5,000	0	20,250
No. of Cand.	*9*	*1*	*0*	*10*
House	3,250	0	0	3,250
Senate	12,000	5,000	0	17,000
Democrats	18,950	3,200	0	22,150
No. of Cand.	*17*	*4*	*0*	*21*
House	17,200	700	0	17,900
Senate	1,750	2,500	0	4,250
Incumbents	20,200	700	500	21,400
Challengers	3,000	2,000	0	5,000
Open Seat	11,500	5,500	0	17,000
Winners	18,200	6,200	n/a	24,400
Losers	16,500	2,000	n/a	18,500

Marriott International Inc.

*Phone: (301) 380-1236 * Fax: (301) 380-8957*
One Marriott Dr., Washington, DC 20058
Web: www.marriott.com

Marriott International is one of the world's largest hotel companies, operating throughout the United States and in more than 50 other countries and territories.

The company operates more than 1,400 hotels worldwide through such franchises as Marriott Hotels, Resorts and Suites, Courtyard, TownePlace Suites, Fairfield Inns and Suites, Residence Inn and the company's partner hotel brand, Ritz-Carlton.

In March 1997, Marriott acquired Renaissance Hotel Group for $1 billion. The acquisition added the Renaissance, Ramada International and New Worlds brands to the company and doubled Marriott's presence overseas. Marriott also operates vacation club resorts and senior living communities.

In October 1997, Marriott and Sodexho Alliance, an international food and management services company headquartered in France, entered a definitive agreement to merge Marriott's food service and facilities management business with Sodexho's North American operations. The combined company, Sodexho Marriott Services Inc., will be the largest provider of food and facilities management services in North America, with annual sales in excess of $4 billion.

Marriott is headquartered in Bethesda, Md., just outside of Washington, and has 195,000 employees. In fiscal year 1997, the public company reported sales of $12 billion, with net income of $335 million. In addition, Marriott was ranked one of the 100 best companies to work for by Fortune magazine in 1997.

Marriott International was a part of Host Marriott Corp. until it was spun off as a separate, publicly traded company in 1993. Many of the hotels that Marriott International operates are owned by Host Marriott.

Marriott International Inc. Political Action Committee (C00284810) *Address: same as sponsor * Treasurer: Thomas E. Ladd*

	1993-94	1995-96	1997	Totals
Receipts	$154,769	$148,963	$73,601	$377,333
Disburse	100,140	127,107	43,894	271,141
Cash	54,632	76,492	106,201	n/a
Contributions	76,500	101,200	18,000	195,700
Republicans	59,000	96,200	13,500	168,700
No. of Cand.	*48*	*81*	*12*	*141*
House	28,000	44,000	5,000	77,000
Senate	31,000	52,200	8,500	91,700
Democrats	17,500	5,000	4,500	27,000
No. of Cand.	*18*	*5*	*5*	*28*
House	14,500	4,000	1,500	20,000
Senate	3,000	1,000	3,000	7,000
Incumbents	44,000	45,200	16,500	105,700
Challengers	11,000	20,500	0	31,500
Open Seat	21,500	35,500	1,500	58,500
Winners	58,500	71,200	n/a	129,700
Losers	18,000	30,000	n/a	48,000

National Park Hospitality Association

*Phone: (202) 682-9507 * Fax: (202) 682-9509*
1225 New York Ave. N.W., Suite 450, Washington, DC 20005

The National Park Hospitality Association is a national trade association representing the providers of lodging, food service, souvenirs, equipment rentals and other visitor services for the National Park System. Founded in 1929, NPHA is governed by a 13-member board of directors. NPHA provides a mechanism for mutual communication between the National Park Service and its concessionaires.

Conference of National Park Concessioners Political Action Committee (ConPAC) (C00163626) *Address: same as sponsor * Treasurer: Mary L. Jones * Contact: Alan T. Howe, Washington Representative*

	1993-94	1995-96	1997	Totals
Receipts	$15,100	$40,000	$11,625	$66,725
Disburse	13,008	26,015	23,085	62,108
Cash	3,758	17,731	10,770	n/a
Contributions	12,850	23,000	17,000	52,850
Republicans	8,000	18,500	15,500	42,000
No. of Cand.	*8*	*13*	*18*	*39*
House	4,500	14,000	9,500	28,000
Senate	3,500	4,500	6,000	14,000
Democrats	4,850	4,500	1,500	10,850
No. of Cand.	*7*	*5*	*2*	*14*
House	4,850	2,500	1,500	8,850
Senate	0	2,000	0	2,000
Incumbents	11,600	21,000	16,000	48,600
Challengers	0	1,500	1,000	2,500

(*Data for Conference of National Park Concessioners continued*)

Open Seat	1,000	500	0	1,500
Winners	10,600	22,000	n/a	32,600
Losers	2,250	1,000	n/a	3,250

National Tour Association

*Phone: (606) 226-4444 * Fax: (606) 226-4404*
546 E. Main St., Lexington, KY 40508
Web: www.ntaonline.com

The National Tour Association represents about 4,000 businesses associated with the travel and tourism industry, including tour operators and suppliers as well as destination marketers. Its members arrange and coordinate all aspects of vacations and tours, including travel and lodging.

National Tour Association Inc. Political Action Committee (TourPAC) (C00138339) *Phone: (703) 684-0755 * 1101 King St., Suite 350, Alexandria, VA 22314 * Treasurer: Mark Hoffmann * Contact: Jim Santini, Washington Representative*

	1993-94	1995-96	1997	Totals
Receipts	$16,149	$35,639	$8,991	$60,779
Disburse	10,450	17,900	10,640	38,990
Cash	9,121	26,863	25,215	n/a
Contributions	9,875	16,900	10,550	37,325
Republicans	5,175	13,650	6,800	25,625
No. of Cand.	*10*	*19*	*14*	*43*
House	2,950	9,500	4,300	16,750
Senate	2,225	4,150	2,500	8,875
Democrats	4,050	3,250	3,250	10,550
No. of Cand.	*9*	*4*	*6*	*19*
House	2,300	2,000	1,500	5,800
Senate	1,750	1,250	1,750	4,750
Incumbents	10,175	15,250	9,550	34,975
Challengers	0	650	500	1,150
Open Seat	250	1,000	500	1,750
Winners	8,700	15,250	n/a	23,950
Losers	1,175	1,650	n/a	2,825

Promus Hotel Corp.

*Phone: (901) 374-5000 * Fax: (901) 375-5490*
755 Crossover Ln., Memphis, TN 38117
Web: www.promus-hotel.com

In late 1997, Promus Hotel — whose franchises include Embassy Suites, Hampton Inn and Homewood Suites — merged with Doubletree to become one of the largest hotel chains in the United States.

Promus, a publicly traded company, retained its name. The Memphis, Tenn. company now claims 40,000 employees, 1,200 hotels and about 177,000 rooms in the United States, Canada, Latin America and Asia. Revenues from the combined corporation are expected to reach $5 billion.

After the merger, Promus opted to close Doubletree's Phoenix, Ariz. headquarters and consolidate corporate operations in Memphis, Tenn.

Before splitting in 1990, Promus owned the Holiday Inn chain. Promus split from Harrah's Entertainment Inc. in 1995.

Promus Hotel Corp. Employees' Political Action Committee (C00302117) *Address: same as sponsor * Treasurer: Vincent C. Ciaramitaro*

	1993-94	1995-96	1997	Totals
Receipts	$0	$110,979	$56,442	$167,421
Disburse	0	96,856	34,500	131,356
Cash	0	14,125	36,070	n/a
Contributions	0	55,000	5,000	60,000
Republicans	0	50,000	5,000	55,000
No. of Cand.	*0*	*23*	*1*	*24*
House	0	36,500	5,000	41,500
Senate	0	13,500	0	13,500
Democrats	0	5,000	0	5,000
No. of Cand.	*0*	*1*	*0*	*1*
House	0	5,000	0	5,000
Senate	0	0	0	0
Incumbents	0	27,500	5,000	32,500
Challengers	0	4,000	0	4,000
Open Seat	0	23,500	0	23,500
Winners	0	42,000	n/a	42,000
Losers	0	13,000	n/a	13,000

Starwood Hotels & Resorts Inc.

*Phone: (617) 367-5266 * Fax: (617) 367-5216*
60 State St., Boston, MA 02109
*Web: www.starwoodlodging.com * E-mail: kraig_couture@ittsheraton.com*

Starwood Hotels & Resorts bought hotel giant ITT Corp. for $14.6 billion in February 1998, creating the world's largest hotel and casino company. It owns or operates hotels such as Sheraton, Doubletree, Marriott, Hilton, Westin and Caesars.

Prior to the merger, ITT operated hotel properties — including Sheraton, CIGA Hotels and Four Points Hotels — along with Caesars casinos. ITT had 461 hotels with 141,000 rooms, 104,000 employees and sales of $4.7 billion in 1997. More than half of the company's hotels were in the United States. Caesars casinos are located in Las Vegas, Atlantic City, N.J., Mississippi and abroad.

ITT also published international phone directories and had an 83 percent interest in a string of technical training schools with locations in 26 states. Starwood acquired all these businesses.

Starwood is actually composed of two companies — an operating company that runs its hotels and a real estate investment trust that owns hotel properties — that are traded as one public company. The dual company arrangement gives Starwood tax advantages that have been outlawed for all but a handful of grandfathered companies. President Clinton's 1999 budget proposal would limit Starwood's tax advantage.

Starwood Hotels & Resorts Worldwide Inc. PAC (SPAC) (formerly known as ITT Corp. Political Action Council) (C00219717)
*Address: same as sponsor * Treasurer: Kraig Couture*

	1993-94	1995-96	1997	Totals
Receipts	$46,699	$94,217	$34,446	$175,362
Disburse	54,407	76,562	63,057	194,026
Cash	45,865	63,522	34,917	n/a
Contributions	43,061	52,500	45,500	141,061
Republicans	23,281	29,500	23,000	75,781
No. of Cand.	*5*	*25*	*11*	*41*
House	15,000	26,000	13,500	54,500
Senate	8,281	3,500	9,500	21,281
Democrats	19,780	23,000	22,500	65,280
No. of Cand.	*6*	*18*	*14*	*38*
House	5,000	21,000	6,500	32,500
Senate	14,780	2,000	16,000	32,780
Incumbents	17,061	45,500	38,500	101,061
Challengers	15,000	2,000	5,000	22,000
Open Seat	6,500	5,000	2,500	14,000
Winners	24,061	44,000	n/a	68,061
Losers	19,000	8,500	n/a	27,500

Misc. Business

Bureau of Wholesale Sales Representatives

*Phone: (404) 870-7600 * Fax: (404) 870-7601*
1100 Spring St. N.W., Suite 700, Atlanta, GA 30309
Web: bwsr.com

The Bureau of Wholesale Sales Representatives offers discounts and insurance products to its members and monitors legislation at the federal and state levels.

Founded in 1945, the bureau encouraged including sales representatives in the Social Security program. It fought to see that commissions were given priority in bankruptcy cases and has been involved in promoting about 35 state laws protecting sales representatives' commissions.

During the 104th Congress, the bureau lobbied for the health insurance premium deductions legislation included in the Contract With America.

Bureau of Wholesale Sales Representatives PAC (C00107409)
*Address: same as sponsor * Treasurer: Michael Blackman*

	1993-94	1995-96	1997	Totals
Receipts	$44,335	$28,761	$7,393	$80,489
Disburse	82,677	119,628	13,452	215,757
Cash	207,116	116,249	110,189	n/a
Contributions	61,800	86,300	2,800	150,900

Republicans	36,250	73,900	4,250	114,400
No. of Cand.	*91*	*95*	*13*	*199*
House	25,900	50,500	-500	75,900
Senate	10,350	23,400	4,750	38,500
Democrats	24,350	12,400	-1450	35,300
No. of Cand.	*69*	*44*	*7*	*120*
House	18,550	6,650	-1200	24,000
Senate	5,800	5,750	-250	11,300
Incumbents	56,550	56,550	3,550	116,650
Challengers	2,300	6,700	0	9,000
Open Seat	2,950	23,650	0	26,600
Winners	54,250	71,000	n/a	125,250
Losers	7,550	15,300	n/a	22,850

International Warehouse Association

*Phone: (847) 292-1891 * Fax: (847) 292-1896*
1300 W. Higgins Rd., Suite 111, Park Ridge, IL 60068-1564
E-mail: logistx@aol.com

The International Warehouse Association provides services for warehouses including legal and technical assistance, marketing, education and industry information, insurance and a group purchasing program.

Established in 1891, the organization has more than 520 member companies and 1,300 satellite members. The group was formerly known as the American Warehouse Association.

American Warehouse Association Political Action Committee (C00303032) *Address: same as sponsor * Treasurer: Michael L. Jenkins*

	1993-94	1995-96	1997	Totals
Receipts	$0	$32,931	$9,864	$42,795
Disburse	0	17,250	2,500	19,750
Cash	0	15,683	21,419	n/a
Contributions	0	15,250	2,500	17,750
Republicans	0	14,250	2,500	16,750
No. of Cand.	*0*	*35*	*2*	*37*
House	0	9,500	0	9,500
Senate	0	4,750	2,500	7,250
Democrats	0	1,000	0	1,000
No. of Cand.	*0*	*4*	*0*	*4*
House	0	1,000	0	1,000
Senate	0	0	0	0
Incumbents	0	11,250	500	11,750
Challengers	0	1,500	0	1,500
Open Seat	0	2,500	2,000	4,500
Winners	0	9,500	n/a	9,500
Losers	0	5,750	n/a	5,750

National Association of Water Companies

*Phone: (202) 833-8383 * Fax: (202) 331-7442*
1725 K St. N.W., Suite 1212, Washington, DC 20006-1401
E-mail: nawc@us.net

The National Association of Water Companies is a trade organization that supports water utilities. Its 360 members provide drinking water to more than 22 million Americans.

National Association of Water Companies Political Action Committee (NAWC-PAC) (C00075275) *Address: same as sponsor * Treasurer: James B. Groff*

	1993-94	1995-96	1997	Totals
Receipts	$103,160	$86,449	$40,681	$230,290
Disburse	94,350	79,500	20,500	194,350
Cash	10,138	22,957	43,048	n/a
Contributions	90,050	60,000	20,000	170,050
Republicans	35,250	45,000	13,000	93,250
No. of Cand.	*43*	*53*	*18*	*114*
House	24,150	28,750	7,500	60,400
Senate	11,100	16,250	5,500	32,850
Democrats	54,800	15,000	7,000	76,800
No. of Cand.	*49*	*20*	*10*	*79*
House	38,200	10,000	5,000	53,200
Senate	16,600	5,000	2,000	23,600
Incumbents	81,500	50,500	19,500	151,500
Challengers	2,250	2,250	500	5,000
Open Seat	6,100	6,750	0	12,850
Winners	79,300	50,750	n/a	130,050
Losers	10,750	9,250	n/a	20,000

National Association of Wholesale-Distributors

*Phone: (202) 872-0885 * Fax: (202) 296-5940*
1725 K St. N.W., Suite 300, Washington, DC 20006

The National Association of Wholesale-Distributors is the trade group for 114 national delivery and distribution businesses. It works to maintain a pro-business majority in Congress and emphasizes challenger and open seat races. It also provides education on races and candidates and voter registration information to its members.

Wholesaler-Distributor PAC of The National Association of Wholesale-Distributors (C00109306) *Address: same as sponsor * Treasurer: Dirk Van Dongen * Contact: Alan M. Kranowitz, Executive Director*

	1993-94	1995-96	1997	Totals
Receipts	$82,825	$107,987	$35,350	$226,162
Disburse	87,325	106,326	24,600	218,251
Cash	2,253	3,912	14,662	n/a
Contributions	84,825	92,722	19,500	197,047
Republicans	77,175	88,472	17,500	183,147
No. of Cand.	*95*	*96*	*24*	*215*
House	42,025	45,524	10,500	98,049
Senate	35,150	42,948	7,000	85,098
Democrats	7,650	4,250	2,000	13,900
No. of Cand.	*10*	*7*	*3*	*20*
House	5,650	3,250	1,000	9,900
Senate	2,000	1,000	1,000	4,000
Incumbents	45,400	41,600	17,000	104,000
Challengers	15,600	14,740	500	30,840
Open Seat	23,825	36,382	2,000	62,207
Winners	74,325	66,774	n/a	141,099
Losers	10,500	25,948	n/a	36,448

National Rural Water Association

*Phone: (405) 252-0629 * Fax: (405) 252-4896*
2915 S. 13th St., Duncan, OK 73533
Web: www.nrwa.org

The National Rural Water Association is a federation of 45 state organizations that represent about 18,000 water and wastewater utilities. The organization was founded in 1976 and provides technical assistance and regulatory guidance to local water and wastewater systems.

WaterPAC - National Rural Water Association Political Committee (C00202184) *Phone: (202) 955-4555 * Fax: (202) 955-1147 * 1200 New Hampshire Ave. N.W., Suite 430, Washington, DC 20036 * E-mail: keegan@ruralwater.org * Treasurer: Rob Johnson*
*Contact: Jim Dunlap, President * Phone: (405) 252-0629*

	1993-94	1995-96	1997	Totals
Receipts	$32,415	$42,253	$20,063	$94,731
Disburse	27,419	39,948	11,305	78,672
Cash	12,372	14,681	23,441	n/a
Contributions	26,500	38,750	10,750	76,000
Republicans	3,000	25,000	6,000	34,000
No. of Cand.	*4*	*20*	*8*	*32*
House	2,500	16,000	2,500	21,000
Senate	500	9,000	3,500	13,000
Democrats	23,500	13,750	4,750	42,000
No. of Cand.	*22*	*17*	*7*	*46*
House	20,750	10,650	4,500	35,900
Senate	2,750	3,100	250	6,100
Incumbents	24,250	32,500	10,000	66,750
Challengers	0	1,500	500	2,000
Open Seat	2,250	4,750	250	7,250
Winners	22,750	34,000	n/a	56,750
Losers	3,750	4,750	n/a	8,500

United Water Resources Inc.

*Phone: (201) 767-9300 * Fax: (201) 767-7142*
200 Old Hook Rd., Harrington Park, NJ 07460-1799
Web: www.unitedwater.com

United Water Resources is based in New Jersey and operates through United Water Services, a joint operation with France's Suez Lyonnaise des Eaux. United's subsidiaries provide water and wastewater services to about 2 million people in 13 states, with more than half of the company's utility operations located in northeastern New Jersey and southeastern New York.

The publicly traded company's 1997 sales were $351 million and it employs 1,400 people.

Subsidiaries include: United Water New Jersey, United Water New York, United Waterworks and United Water Mid-Atlantic. Non-regulated subsidiary United Properties develops real estate projects, including offices and retail outlets, golf courses and other properties in the Northeast.

United Water Resources Employee PAC (C00280156) *Address: same as sponsor * Treasurer: John Turner * Contact: Joe Simunovich, Chairman*

	1993-94	1995-96	1997	Totals
Receipts	$21,680	$38,626	$19,402	$79,708
Disburse	15,371	38,435	21,395	75,201
Cash	6,308	6,501	4,509	n/a
Contributions	4,517	12,875	3,395	20,787
Republicans	1,707	3,325	845	5,877
No. of Cand.	*3*	*6*	*3*	*12*
House	1,095	3,075	845	5,015
Senate	612	250	0	862
Democrats	2,810	9,550	2,550	14,910
No. of Cand.	*2*	*5*	*3*	*10*
House	2,810	6,550	2,550	11,910
Senate	0	3,000	0	3,000
Incumbents	3,905	5,575	2,985	12,465
Challengers	612	2,050	0	2,662
Open Seat	0	5,250	0	5,250
Winners	3,905	11,625	n/a	15,530
Losers	612	1,250	n/a	1,862

Misc. Manufacturing & Distributing

Alcoa

1501 Alcoa Building, Pittsburgh, PA 15219

Alcoa's PAC was terminated on May 24, 1996. Alcoa is a manufacturer of aluminum products.

Alcoa Employees Political Fund (C00039172) *Address: same as sponsor * Treasurer: Diane Marie Whittaker*

	1993-94	1995-96	1997	Totals
Receipts	$32,344	$16,185	$0	$48,529
Disburse	35,261	25,552	0	60,813
Cash	9,363	0	0	n/a
Contributions	32,225	23,000	0	55,225
Republicans	14,350	19,000	0	33,350
No. of Cand.	*17*	*25*	*0*	*42*
House	6,850	11,000	0	17,850
Senate	7,500	8,000	0	15,500
Democrats	17,875	4,000	0	21,875
No. of Cand.	*19*	*6*	*0*	*25*
House	16,375	4,000	0	20,375
Senate	1,500	0	0	1,500
Incumbents	29,475	21,000	0	50,475
Challengers	1,500	0	0	1,500
Open Seat	1,250	2,000	0	3,250
Winners	24,350	20,000	n/a	44,350
Losers	7,875	3,000	n/a	10,875

Aluminum Association

*Phone: (202) 862-5100 * Fax: (202) 862-5164*
900 19th St. N.W., Washington, DC 20006
Web: www.aluminum.org

The Aluminum Association is a trade group for producers and exporters of aluminum and aluminum products, as well as recyclers. Member companies operate more than 300 plants in 40 states. Aluminum is a $37 billion industry in the United States.

The group provides information on aluminum production, industry shipments and end use market estimates. It also conducts surveys on energy and safety statistics and customer inventories. Foreign trade is a large priority, and the organization issues a monthly trade summary and estimates of industry shipments.

Aluminum Association Political Action Committee (C00085308) *Address: same as sponsor * Treasurer: Becky Snedeker*

	1993-94	1995-96	1997	Totals
Receipts	$12,892	$10,764	$1,124	$24,780
Disburse	13,000	9,500	2,523	25,023
Cash	135	1,399	0	n/a
Contributions	12,500	9,500	2,500	24,500
Republicans	4,000	6,500	1,400	11,900
No. of Cand.	*9*	*12*	*10*	*31*
House	2,500	4,500	900	7,900
Senate	1,500	2,000	500	4,000
Democrats	8,500	3,000	1,100	12,600
No. of Cand.	*17*	*6*	*7*	*30*
House	8,500	2,500	600	11,600
Senate	0	500	500	1,000
Incumbents	12,000	9,500	2,500	24,000
Challengers	0	0	0	0
Open Seat	500	0	0	500
Winners	8,500	9,500	n/a	18,000
Losers	4,000	0	n/a	4,000

American Furniture Manufacturers Association

*Phone: (910) 884-5000 * Fax: (910) 884-5303*
P.O. Box HP-7, High Point, NC 27261
Web: www.afmahp.org

The American Furniture Manufacturers Association is the nation's largest trade association for furniture manufacturers. The association is dedicated to fostering the growth and development of the furniture industry and improving the effectiveness and efficiency of furniture manufacturers in the United States. It encourages a working relationship among manufacturers, and provides information on legislative and regulatory initiatives. It also provides technical, statistical and research programs.

The group's bipartisan PAC supports private enterprise candidates seeking election to Congress. It is governed by a board of directors representing furniture manufacturing companies.

American Furniture Manufacturers Association Political Action Committee (C00077362) *Phone: (202) 466-7362 * Fax: (202) 429-4915 * 918 16th St. N.W., Suite 402, Washington, DC 20006 * Treasurer: Douglas Brackett * Contact: Joseph Gerard, V.P. of Gov. Affairs*

	1993-94	1995-96	1997	Totals
Receipts	$168,131	$173,268	$101,065	$442,464
Disburse	158,526	179,677	101,502	439,705
Cash	10,890	4,483	4,046	n/a
Contributions	140,950	137,700	81,000	359,650
Republicans	125,950	126,200	72,500	324,650
No. of Cand.	*69*	*77*	*55*	*201*
House	61,950	73,500	46,500	181,950
Senate	64,000	52,700	26,000	142,700
Democrats	15,000	11,500	8,500	35,000
No. of Cand.	*18*	*14*	*10*	*42*
House	15,000	11,500	7,500	34,000
Senate	0	0	1,000	1,000
Incumbents	85,000	115,000	80,000	280,000
Challengers	17,150	4,700	0	21,850
Open Seat	38,300	15,000	1,000	54,300
Winners	128,300	120,750	n/a	249,050
Losers	12,650	16,950	n/a	29,600

American National Can Co.

*Phone: (773) 399-3244 * Fax: (773) 399-8605*
8770 W. Bryn Mawr Ave., Chicago, IL 60631
Web: www.pechiney.com

American National Can is a subsidiary of the publicly owned, $12 billion, Paris-based company, Pechiney. ANC manufactures containers and plastic materials for the packaging industry, with more than 100 subsidiaries and plants worldwide, primarily in Europe and the Far East.

ANC owns and operates about 25 plants across the United States with customers in all 50 states. The company has 8,700 employees; 6,600 are in the United States.

American National Can Co. Employees' Good Government Committee (C00034504) *Address: same as sponsor * Treasurer: Alan H. Schumacher * Contact: Clifford Klotz, V.P., Gov. and Environmental Affairs*

	1993-94	1995-96	1997	Totals
Receipts	$10,283	$7,070	$2,590	$19,943
Disburse	8,606	13,400	2,700	24,706
Cash	23,509	17,182	17,072	n/a

Contributions	7,600	13,400	2,700	23,700
Republicans	6,400	13,400	2,700	22,500
No. of Cand.	*7*	*5*	*5*	*17*
House	5,900	11,200	1,700	18,800
Senate	500	2,200	1,000	3,700
Democrats	1,200	0	0	1,200
No. of Cand.	*3*	*0*	*0*	*3*
House	1,200	0	0	1,200
Senate	0	0	0	0
Incumbents	6,600	11,400	1,200	19,200
Challengers	500	0	1,000	1,500
Open Seat	500	2,000	0	2,500
Winners	6,600	1,200	n/a	7,800
Losers	1,000	12,200	n/a	13,200

Association for Manufacturing Technology

*Phone: (703) 893-2900 * Fax: (703) 893-1151*
7901 Westpark Dr., McLean, VA 22102-4206
*Web: www.mfgtech.org * E-mail: amt@mfgtech.org*

The Association for Manufacturing Technology, which was founded in 1902 as the National Machine Tool Builders Association, represents about 375 member companies throughout the United States. Its members make welding, grinding and boring machines, as well as process control equipment and laser systems.

AMT - Association for Manufacturing Technology Machine ToolPAC (C00034173) *Address: same as sponsor * Treasurer: James H. Mack * Contact: Don F. Carlson, Chairman*

	1993-94	*1995-96*	*1997*	*Totals*
Receipts	$80,176	$90,284	$48,955	$219,415
Disburse	68,166	89,500	47,100	204,766
Cash	13,585	14,374	16,229	n/a
Contributions	68,166	83,050	45,100	196,316
Republicans	47,316	69,550	33,100	149,966
No. of Cand.	*47*	*68*	*44*	*159*
House	16,316	32,600	21,600	70,516
Senate	31,000	36,950	11,500	79,450
Democrats	20,850	13,500	12,000	46,350
No. of Cand.	*37*	*20*	*16*	*73*
House	14,100	9,500	6,000	29,600
Senate	6,750	4,000	6,000	16,750
Incumbents	48,466	61,600	41,600	151,666
Challengers	3,000	5,900	0	8,900
Open Seat	16,700	15,550	2,500	34,750
Winners	54,916	53,050	n/a	107,966
Losers	13,250	30,000	n/a	43,250

Avon Products Inc.

*Phone: (212) 282-5000 * Fax: (212) 282-6049*
1345 Ave. of the Americas, New York, NY 10105-0196
Web: www.avon.com

Avon Products is the world's largest direct seller of cosmetics and beauty products. The public company has more than 2 million people selling brands such as Far Away, Rare Gold, Josie, Natori and Skin-So-Soft.

In addition, Avon is one of the nation's largest manufacturers of fashion jewelry and women's apparel. Headquartered in New York, Avon employs 33,700 people and had 1997 sales of $5 billion.

Avon Products Inc. Fund for Responsible Government (C00112722) *Address: same as sponsor * Treasurer: Mary Ann Dirzis*

	1993-94	*1995-96*	*1997*	*Totals*
Receipts	$20,977	$43,886	$24,736	$89,599
Disburse	29,687	32,470	11,553	73,710
Cash	15,458	26,878	40,597	n/a
Contributions	15,400	14,900	6,000	36,300
Republicans	2,800	10,650	2,000	15,450
No. of Cand.	*5*	*13*	*2*	*20*
House	1,800	5,650	2,000	9,450
Senate	1,000	5,000	0	6,000
Democrats	12,600	4,250	4,000	20,850
No. of Cand.	*10*	*8*	*2*	*20*
House	7,600	2,750	4,000	14,350
Senate	5,000	1,500	0	6,500
Incumbents	15,400	10,650	6,000	32,050
Challengers	0	2,000	0	2,000
Open Seat	0	2,250	0	2,250
Winners	14,400	11,400	n/a	25,800
Losers	1,000	3,500	n/a	4,500

BFGoodrich Co.

*Phone: (330) 659-7600 * Fax: (330) 659-7949*
P.O. Box 9, Richfield, OH 44286-0009
Web: www.bfgoodrich.com

Having sold its tire-making business in 1986, BFGoodrich now provides aircraft systems and services and manufactures specialty chemicals. Its corporate headquarters as well as several of its manufacturing plants are located in northeastern Ohio.

In December 1997, the public company completed a merger with Rohr Inc., an aircraft parts manufacturer. Following the $1.3 billion transaction, BFGoodrich had about 18,000 employees and 1997 sales of $3.4 billion.

Established in 1870, BFGoodrich manufactures a wide variety of systems and component parts for the aerospace industry and provides aircraft maintenance, repair and overhaul services. The company also manufactures high-performance plastics, specialty chemical additives and sealants, coatings and adhesives products.

BFGoodrich Political Action Committee (C00101725) *Address: same as sponsor * Treasurer: Fredrick D. Zahn*

	1993-94	*1995-96*	*1997*	*Totals*
Receipts	$81,901	$128,126	$48,975	$259,002
Disburse	79,381	117,900	34,400	231,681
Cash	15,668	25,897	40,474	n/a
Contributions	42,500	84,700	15,800	143,000
Republicans	24,500	71,200	14,000	109,700
No. of Cand.	*23*	*35*	*12*	*70*
House	12,500	34,200	8,000	54,700
Senate	12,000	37,000	6,000	55,000
Democrats	18,000	13,500	1,800	33,300
No. of Cand.	*15*	*6*	*2*	*23*
House	14,000	11,500	1,800	27,300
Senate	4,000	2,000	0	6,000
Incumbents	30,000	54,700	14,000	98,700
Challengers	2,000	11,000	800	13,800
Open Seat	10,500	19,000	1,000	30,500
Winners	32,000	66,700	n/a	98,700
Losers	10,500	18,000	n/a	28,500

Ball Corp.

*Phone: (765) 747-6100 x6187 * Fax: (765) 747-6826*
345 S. High St., Muncie, IN 47305-2326
*Web: www.ball.com * E-mail: hsohn@ball.com*

Ball manufactures metal and plastic packaging for beverages and foods. It also operates an aerospace and technologies segment that provides services to the aerospace, defense and telecommunications markets. The publicly held company reported about $2.4 billion in 1997 sales.

Subsidiary Ball Aerospace & Technologies Corp. generates about $362 million of overall sales. Based in Broomfield, Colo., BATC employs about 2,200 people in California, Colorado, Florida, Georgia, Maryland, New Mexico, Ohio, Texas, Virginia and Washington. Customers include NASA, the Department of Defense, Harvard-Smithsonian Astrophysical Observatory and Johns Hopkins University Applied Physics Laboratory.

Ball announced in February 1998 its decision to relocate its corporate headquarters to Colorado from Indiana after selling its two Indiana manufacturing plants. Ball had been headquartered in Muncie, Ind. since 1887. One hundred and eighty of Ball's 7,900 employees work in the corporate headquarters.

Ball Corp. Political Action Committee (BAC PAC) (C00039461) *Phone: (703) 284-5400 * Fax: (703) 284-5449 * 2200 Clarendon Blvd., Suite 1202, Arlington, VA 22201-3302 * Treasurer: David Westerlund * Contact: Amy Stran*

*Contact: Harold Sohn, Chairman * Phone: (765) 747-6100 x6187*

	1993-94	*1995-96*	*1997*	*Totals*
Receipts	$40,648	$33,211	$12,995	$86,854
Disburse	40,121	33,327	605	74,053
Cash	5,509	5,395	17,786	n/a
Contributions	40,000	32,200	500	72,700
Republicans	33,200	29,200	500	62,900
No. of Cand.	*36*	*41*	*1*	*78*
House	15,600	18,500	500	34,600
Senate	17,600	10,700	0	28,300
Democrats	6,800	3,000	0	9,800
No. of Cand.	*11*	*5*	*0*	*16*
House	5,300	3,000	0	8,300

(Data for Ball Corp. Political continued)

Senate	1,500	0	0	1,500
Incumbents	26,500	22,200	500	49,200
Challengers	4,500	1,000	0	5,500
Open Seat	9,000	9,000	0	18,000
Winners	37,500	27,000	n/a	64,500
Losers	2,500	5,200	n/a	7,700

Blount Inc.

*Phone: (334) 244-4000 x4206 * Fax: (334) 271-8140*
4520 Executive Park Dr., Montgomery, AL 36116-1602
*Web: www.blount.com * E-mail: hel@blount.com*

Blount is a publicly traded international manufacturing company with sales of $717 million in 1997. It employs 5,700 people and manufactures home and garden products, timber harvesting and processing equipment, transmissions and other car components and gun parts.

Blount, which is headquartered in Montgomery, Ala., has three manufacturing divisions. Its sporting equipment division is located in Montgomery. Its outdoor products division is located in Portland, Ore. and its industrial and power equipment group is located in Owatonna, Minn.

Blount Inc. Employees' Political Action Committee (BLTPAC) (C00164293) *Address: same as sponsor * Treasurer: Ronald K. Gorland*

	1993-94	1995-96	1997	Totals
Receipts	$15,862	$27,785	$18,258	$61,905
Disburse	20,763	33,332	6,650	60,745
Cash	8,435	2,891	14,499	n/a
Contributions	7,000	18,000	1,000	26,000
Republicans	4,000	18,000	1,000	23,000
No. of Cand.	*4*	*6*	*1*	*11*
House	2,000	8,500	0	10,500
Senate	2,000	9,500	1,000	12,500
Democrats	3,000	0	0	3,000
No. of Cand.	*2*	*0*	*0*	*2*
House	3,000	0	0	3,000
Senate	0	0	0	0
Incumbents	4,000	0	1,000	5,000
Challengers	3,000	4,500	0	7,500
Open Seat	0	12,500	0	12,500
Winners	4,000	12,500	n/a	16,500
Losers	3,000	5,500	n/a	8,500

Brush Wellman Inc.

*Phone: (216) 486-4200 * Fax: (216) 383-4091*
17876 St. Clair Ave., Cleveland, OH 44110
Web: www.brushwellman.com

Brush Wellman, a publicly held company, provides engineered materials and design services to the high technology industry. These materials include beryllium, beryllium-containing alloys and beryllia ceramic that improve conductivity in electronics equipment.

Founded in 1931, the company has more than 1,900 employees. It reported 1997 revenues of $433.8 million. Brush Wellman has extensive mining rights in Utah.

Brush Wellman Good Government Fund (C00216770) *Address: same as sponsor * Treasurer: Vacant * Contact: Tim Reid, Vice Chairperson*

	1993-94	1995-96	1997	Totals
Receipts	$29,159	$33,277	$12,225	$74,661
Disburse	25,789	29,738	8,197	63,724
Cash	6,939	10,480	14,508	n/a
Contributions	20,500	23,500	7,000	51,000
Republicans	18,500	17,000	6,000	41,500
No. of Cand.	*12*	*14*	*6*	*32*
House	9,500	14,500	4,000	28,000
Senate	9,000	2,500	2,000	13,500
Democrats	2,000	6,500	1,000	9,500
No. of Cand.	*2*	*4*	*1*	*7*
House	0	3,500	1,000	4,500
Senate	2,000	3,000	0	5,000
Incumbents	15,500	23,500	7,000	46,000
Challengers	2,000	0	0	2,000
Open Seat	3,000	0	0	3,000
Winners	20,500	19,500	n/a	40,000
Losers	0	4,000	n/a	4,000

Cement Kiln Recycling Coalition

*Phone: (202) 789-1945 * Fax: (202) 408-9392*
1225 Eye St. N.W., Suite 300, Washington, DC 20005
Web: www.ckrc.org

The Cement Kiln Recycling Coalition includes more than 20 member companies representing about 100 facilities throughout the United States. Members include most major cement companies that use hazardous waste-derived fuel as well as companies involved in the collection, processing, management and marketing of such fuel for use in cement kilns.

Cement Kiln Recycling Coalition Political Action Committee (C00287524) *Address: same as sponsor * Treasurer: Richard C. Creighton * Contact: Chris Cooper, Legislative Coordinator*

	1993-94	1995-96	1997	Totals
Receipts	$3,525	$17,450	$14,500	$35,475
Disburse	2,600	9,350	7,750	19,700
Cash	925	9,025	15,775	n/a
Contributions	2,600	9,350	6,750	18,700
Republicans	1,600	5,500	4,750	11,850
No. of Cand.	*4*	*6*	*4*	*14*
House	1,600	4,250	2,500	8,350
Senate	0	1,250	2,250	3,500
Democrats	1,000	3,850	2,000	6,850
No. of Cand.	*4*	*6*	*3*	*13*
House	1,000	2,000	2,000	5,000
Senate	0	1,850	0	1,850
Incumbents	1,250	8,250	6,750	16,250
Challengers	500	100	0	600
Open Seat	850	1,000	0	1,850
Winners	2,100	8,250	n/a	10,350
Losers	500	1,100	n/a	1,600

Cooper Industries Inc.

*Phone: (713) 209-8835 * Fax: (713) 209-8982*
600 Travis St., Suite 5800, Houston, TX 77002
Web: www.cooperindustries.com

Cooper Industries is a public company which manufactures electrical products, tools and hardware and automotive products. Its products include Champion spark plugs, Wagner lighting products, Weller soldering equipment, Moog steering and suspension products and Halo lighting systems, among others. The company employs 44,000 workers, about half of them in the United States. It had 1997 sales of $5.2 billion.

The company is a supporter of free trade issues, including NAFTA, GATT and "fast-track" trade authority. It lobbies on workplace and environmental issues. Cooper Industries favors liability reform and reduced taxes. Almost all of this PAC's contributions go to federal candidates.

Cooper Industries ranked second among industrial equipment manufacturers in PAC spending for the 1996 congressional elections. All but one of the 95 candidates who received contributions were Republicans. The leading recipients were Rep. Kevin Brady, R-Texas, former Rep. Dick Zimmer, R-N.J., and Sen. Gordon Smith, R-Ore. Zimmer and Brady were the only candidates to receive at least $5,000. Rep. Ruben Hinojosa, D-Texas, who received $2,000, was the lone Democratic recipient.

Cooper Industries Inc. Political Action Committee (CIPAC) (C00099937) *Address: same as sponsor * Treasurer: Alan J. Hill * Contact: John Breed, Manager, Media and Gov. Relations*

	1993-94	1995-96	1997	Totals
Receipts	$350,510	$248,409	$109,925	$708,844
Disburse	480,601	253,147	32,346	766,094
Cash	78,475	73,741	151,321	n/a
Contributions	410,000	222,000	29,500	661,500
Republicans	402,000	220,000	29,500	651,500
No. of Cand.	*121*	*94*	*17*	*232*
House	279,500	150,500	9,500	439,500
Senate	122,500	69,500	20,000	212,000
Democrats	8,000	2,000	0	10,000
No. of Cand.	*3*	*1*	*0*	*4*
House	8,000	2,000	0	10,000
Senate	0	0	0	0
Incumbents	129,000	119,500	27,000	275,500
Challengers	138,500	33,000	0	171,500
Open Seat	142,500	67,500	2,500	212,500
Winners	331,500	144,000	n/a	475,500
Losers	78,500	78,000	n/a	156,500

Corning Inc.

Phone: (607) 974-8764
MP HQ E2-20 T-24, Corning, NY 14831
*Web: www.corning.com * E-mail: corepac@corning.com*

Corning, known for its glassware cooking products, concentrates more on making fiber-optic cables and laboratory equipment.

The public company makes products for digital and video communications, including LCD displays and projection video lenses. Its glass products are used in laboratories and its ceramic products help control vehicle emissions. The company has sold all but a small stake in its consumer products line to Borden.

Corning has 41 plants worldwide; 25 in the United States. The company has operations in 20 states from Alaska to Florida. Corning, which has about 20,000 employees, reported 1997 revenues of more than $4 billion.

Corning Employees Political Action Committee (C00033589)
*Phone: (202) 682-3136 * Fax: (202) 682-3130 * 1350 Eye St., Suite 500, Washington, DC 20005-3305 * Treasurer: Richard B. Klein*

*Contact: Tim Regan, Chairman * Phone: (607) 974-8764*

	1993-94	1995-96	1997	Totals
Receipts	$233,362	$198,679	$87,242	$519,283
Disburse	222,464	196,080	36,161	454,705
Cash	38,693	41,296	92,377	n/a
Contributions	192,926	175,209	28,257	396,392
Republicans	101,000	146,922	25,757	273,679
No. of Cand.	*63*	*59*	*14*	*136*
House	61,500	124,000	17,257	202,757
Senate	39,500	22,922	8,500	70,922
Democrats	91,926	28,287	2,500	122,713
No. of Cand.	*44*	*16*	*2*	*62*
House	77,426	20,787	2,500	100,713
Senate	14,500	7,500	0	22,000
Incumbents	156,426	147,709	28,257	332,392
Challengers	19,500	3,000	0	22,500
Open Seat	17,000	23,500	0	40,500
Winners	171,926	137,209	n/a	309,135
Losers	21,000	38,000	n/a	59,000

Cosmetic, Toiletry & Fragrance Association

*Phone: (202) 331-1770 * Fax: (202) 331-1969*
1101 17th St. N.W., Suite 300, Washington, DC 20036-4702
Web: www.ctfa.org

The Cosmetic, Toiletry & Fragrance Association is a trade association for the personal care products industry.

CTFA's 500 member companies include manufacturers and distributors of finished personal care products, as well as suppliers of ingredients, raw materials, and packaging materials and services used in the production and marketing of finished products.

CTFA members market the vast majority of all personal care products sold in the United States. CTFA represents the industry's interests at the local, state, national and international levels.

Cosmetic, Toiletry & Fragrance Association Political Action Committee (C00113845) *Address: same as sponsor * Treasurer: Hans Hiemstra*

	1993-94	1995-96	1997	Totals
Receipts	$32,969	$28,344	$16,117	$77,430
Disburse	37,890	30,707	9,799	78,396
Cash	35,059	32,698	39,017	n/a
Contributions	35,188	29,844	8,750	73,782
Republicans	17,500	19,219	5,250	41,969
No. of Cand.	*21*	*22*	*6*	*49*
House	14,500	14,219	3,250	31,969
Senate	3,000	5,000	2,000	10,000
Democrats	17,688	10,625	3,500	31,813
No. of Cand.	*23*	*18*	*6*	*47*
House	17,688	10,625	3,000	31,313
Senate	0	0	500	500
Incumbents	33,538	26,344	8,750	68,632
Challengers	0	500	0	500
Open Seat	1,650	3,000	0	4,650
Winners	28,000	25,719	n/a	53,719
Losers	7,188	4,125	n/a	11,313

Crown Cork & Seal Co. Inc.

*Phone: (215) 698-5100 * Fax: (215) 698-7050*
One Crown Way, Philadelphia, PA 19154
Web: www.crowncork.com

Crown Cork & Seal makes packaging products for food, beverage, household and other consumer products, as well as manufacturing filling and material handling machinery.

The $12.6 billion public company has purchased 20 companies since 1989. Its 282 plants, located in 59 countries, employ 44,600 people. Crown Cork recently acquired Paris-based CarnaudMetalbox for nearly $4 billion.

Crown Cork reported 1997 sales of $8.4 billion.

Crown Cork & Seal Co. Inc. Political Action Committee (C00254268) *Address: same as sponsor * Treasurer: Keith E. Lucas * Contact: William J. Avery, Chairperson and CEO*

	1993-94	1995-96	1997	Totals
Receipts	$13,975	$20,400	$26,767	$61,142
Disburse	14,368	17,405	12,697	44,470
Cash	156	3,149	18,019	n/a
Contributions	6,325	14,000	1,500	21,825
Republicans	3,500	8,550	2,500	14,550
No. of Cand.	*4*	*10*	*4*	*18*
House	2,000	4,600	2,000	8,600
Senate	1,500	3,950	500	5,950
Democrats	2,825	5,450	-1000	7,275
No. of Cand.	*6*	*5*	*1*	*12*
House	1,825	5,450	-1000	6,275
Senate	1,000	0	0	1,000
Incumbents	3,325	10,750	2,500	16,575
Challengers	3,000	2,850	-1000	4,850
Open Seat	0	400	0	400
Winners	3,875	9,750	n/a	13,625
Losers	2,450	4,250	n/a	6,700

Eastman Kodak Co.

*Phone: (716) 724-4000 * Fax: (716) 781-5819*
343 State St., Rochester, NY 14650-0516
Web: www.kodak.com

Eastman Kodak manufactures and markets cameras, film and other imaging products throughout the world.

While the company is still the industry leader in the U.S. consumer market, it has been losing ground to the Fuji Corp. over the past few years. In November 1997, Kodak announced plans to cut operating costs by $1 billion over two years, a move that company officials said would result in the loss of 10,000 of its 100,000 jobs worldwide. The company also has been focusing on improving and expanding upon its digital imaging products and services. A public company, Kodak had 1996 sales of $16 billion.

Kodak employs about 30,000 people in New York, with about 20,000 in Rochester. The company also employs about 2,500 people in its Windsor, Colo. plant.

Eastman Kodak Co. Employee PAC (C00297085) *Phone: (202) 857-3400 * Fax: (202) 857-3401 * 1250 H St. N.W., Suite 800, Washington, DC 20005 * Treasurer: Chris Lanphear*

*Contact: Sandra Taylor, Chairperson * Phone: (716) 724-4000*

	1993-94	1995-96	1997	Totals
Receipts	$28,559	$113,703	$59,263	$201,525
Disburse	5,000	122,229	24,500	151,729
Cash	23,560	15,043	49,812	n/a
Contributions	5,000	92,721	17,000	114,721
Republicans	1,500	61,600	11,000	74,100
No. of Cand.	*2*	*72*	*16*	*90*
House	1,000	44,850	7,500	53,350
Senate	500	16,750	3,500	20,750
Democrats	3,500	31,121	6,000	40,621
No. of Cand.	*3*	*36*	*11*	*50*
House	1,500	23,121	5,000	29,621
Senate	2,000	8,000	1,000	11,000
Incumbents	5,000	85,221	17,000	107,221
Challengers	0	2,000	0	2,000
Open Seat	0	5,500	0	5,500
Winners	5,000	84,221	n/a	89,221
Losers	0	8,500	n/a	8,500

Emerson Electric Co.

*Phone: (314) 553-2000 * Fax: (314) 553-1607*
8000 W. Florissant Ave., Station 2579, St. Louis, MO 63136
Web: www.emersonelectric.com

Emerson Electric is a publicly traded maker of electrical and electronic products for heating and air conditioning units, generators and hand tools. The company also makes diesel equipment and process control and automation products.

Sales for 1997 totaled $12.3 billion and the Missouri-based public company employs more than 100,000 workers worldwide. About a third of Emerson's sales are from outside the United States.

Subsidiaries include: Appleton Electric Co., Bueler International, Copeland Co., Emerson Electric Motion Controls, Fisher Controls International Inc., Fisher-Rosemount, Fusite and Intellution Inc.

Emerson Electric Co. Political Action Committee (EMPAC) (C00080515) *Address: same as sponsor * Treasurer: Joel David Hackworth*

	1993-94	1995-96	1997	Totals
Receipts	$32,451	$51,229	$32,250	$115,930
Disburse	29,000	51,407	29,015	109,422
Cash	4,534	4,367	7,609	n/a
Contributions	24,000	39,900	26,000	89,900
Republicans	22,000	36,400	24,000	82,400
No. of Cand.	*8*	*30*	*18*	*56*
House	2,500	18,950	10,000	31,450
Senate	19,500	17,450	14,000	50,950
Democrats	2,000	3,500	1,500	7,000
No. of Cand.	*2*	*5*	*2*	*9*
House	1,000	2,000	500	3,500
Senate	1,000	1,500	1,000	3,500
Incumbents	10,500	21,750	25,000	57,250
Challengers	0	10,900	0	10,900
Open Seat	13,500	7,250	1,000	21,750
Winners	23,000	31,000	n/a	54,000
Losers	1,000	8,900	n/a	9,900

Fisher Scientific International Inc.

*Phone: (603) 926-5911 * Fax: (603) 929-2248*
Liberty Lane, Hampton, NH 03842
Web: www.Fisher1.com

Fisher Scientific International, through its principal operating subsidiary, Fisher Scientific Co., is a supplier of more than 180,000 products and services to the scientific, research, health care, industrial, educational and government markets in 145 countries. The publicly traded company employs 2,000 workers worldwide and posted 1997 sales of $2.18 billion.

Fisher Scientific International Inc. Employees Committee for Sensible Government (C00292318) *Address: same as sponsor * Treasurer: Michael J. Farrell*

	1993-94	1995-96	1997	Totals
Receipts	$36,528	$66,729	$22,127	$125,384
Disburse	88	56,033	21,191	77,312
Cash	36,440	47,146	48,087	n/a
Contributions	0	26,500	13,000	39,500
Republicans	0	19,000	3,000	22,000
No. of Cand.	*0*	*6*	*2*	*8*
House	0	13,000	1,000	14,000
Senate	0	6,000	2,000	8,000
Democrats	0	7,500	10,000	17,500
No. of Cand.	*0*	*3*	*2*	*5*
House	0	0	0	0
Senate	0	7,500	10,000	17,500
Incumbents	0	14,000	13,000	27,000
Challengers	0	5,000	0	5,000
Open Seat	0	7,500	0	7,500
Winners	0	18,000	n/a	18,000
Losers	0	8,500	n/a	8,500

Fruit of the Loom Inc.

*Phone: (312) 993-1867 * Fax: (312) 993-1773*
233 S. Wacker Dr., Chicago, IL 60606
Web: www.fruit.com

Fruit of the Loom is a publicly traded manufacturer and marketer of underwear for children and adults, printable activewear, outerwear, casualwear, sportswear and childrenswear. It employs 30,000 people in more than 60 locations worldwide. Sales for 1997 were $2.4 billion.

Brand names include: Fruit of the Loom, BVD, Gitano, Best, Cumberland Bay and Screen Stars. Licensed brands include Munsingwear and Wilson. The company has licensing agreements with all the major U.S. sports leagues, many universities, and Warner Brothers to market apparel with their names, characters and trademarks.

The company has plants in Canada, El Salvador, Honduras, Ireland, Jamaica, Morocco and the United Kingdom, which manufacture about 60 percent of its annual production. To cut costs, in 1997, Fruit of the Loom began closing a number of U.S. plants and increasing operations overseas. In November 1997, the company closed four facilities in Kentucky and Louisiana.

Fruit of the Loom Good Government Committee (C00303461)
*Address: same as sponsor * Treasurer: Brian J. Hanigan*

	1993-94	1995-96	1997	Totals
Receipts	$0	$60,350	$31,550	$91,900
Disburse	0	52,000	23,000	75,000
Cash	0	8,350	16,900	n/a
Contributions	0	45,750	17,000	62,750
Republicans	0	35,750	11,500	47,250
No. of Cand.	*0*	*31*	*14*	*45*
House	0	18,000	7,000	25,000
Senate	0	17,750	4,500	22,250
Democrats	0	10,000	5,500	15,500
No. of Cand.	*0*	*10*	*6*	*16*
House	0	8,000	2,500	10,500
Senate	0	2,000	3,000	5,000
Incumbents	0	33,750	16,500	50,250
Challengers	0	2,000	500	2,500
Open Seat	0	10,000	0	10,000
Winners	0	40,250	n/a	40,250
Losers	0	5,500	n/a	5,500

General Electric Co.

*Phone: (203) 373-2211 * Fax: (203) 373-3447*
3135 Easton Turnpike, Fairfield, CT 06431
Web: www.ge.com

General Electric is the fifth-largest corporation in the United States. The publicly traded company owns the NBC television network and produces nuclear reactors, aircraft engines, appliances and electrical systems. Subsidiary GE Capital Corp. is one of the largest financial services companies in the nation. The corporation has almost 150 manufacturing plants throughout the United States, including Puerto Rico, and more than 100 plants in 25 other countries. GE had 1997 sales of $90.8 billion and about 240,000 employees.

The company is interested in regulation of the broadcast and financial service industries. It supports funding for the Advanced Light Water Reactor program, which focuses on designing commercial nuclear reactors. GE previously lobbied to preserve the U.S. Commerce Department's industrial research and trade programs.

GE was the largest contributor to 1996 congressional races among makers of commercial and industrial equipment. It contributed 88 percent of its PAC money to incumbent candidates and generally supported Republicans. The top recipients were Sens. John W. Warner, R-Va., Mitch McConnell, R-Ky., and Pete V. Domenici, R-N.M.

Rep. Charles B. Rangel, D-N.Y., was the leading Democratic recipient.

GE subsidiary Greenwich Air Services Inc., which repairs gas turbine engines, closed its PAC in September 1997.

General Electric Co. Political Action Committee (C00024869)
Phone: (202) 637-4223 Fax: (202) 637-4400 * 1299 Pennsylvania Ave. N.W., Washington, DC 20004 * Treasurer: Blaine A. Barron * Contact: Anita Pandolfe, PAC Administrator*

	1993-94	1995-96	1997	Totals
Receipts	$792,730	$839,153	$542,791	$2,174,674
Disburse	796,265	841,570	449,898	2,087,733
Cash	79,559	77,141	170,036	n/a
Contributions	559,045	546,550	307,950	1,413,545
Republicans	224,175	349,050	179,050	752,275
No. of Cand.	*148*	*203*	*141*	*492*
House	122,750	223,575	119,950	466,275
Senate	101,425	125,475	59,100	286,000
Democrats	330,870	196,500	126,400	653,770
No. of Cand.	*200*	*124*	*118*	*442*
House	223,345	148,850	81,900	454,095
Senate	107,525	47,650	44,500	199,675
Incumbents	497,775	484,350	296,850	1,278,975

Challengers	11,925	17,650	500	30,075
Open Seat	49,895	44,250	11,600	105,745
Winners	452,060	482,725	n/a	934,785
Losers	106,985	63,825	n/a	170,810

Greenwich Air Services Inc. Political Action Committee (C00232496) *P.O. Box 522187, Miami, FL 33152 * Treasurer: Orlando Machado*

	1993-94	1995-96	1997	Totals
Receipts	$10,903	$20,901	$16,146	$47,950
Disburse	12,450	16,450	34,533	63,433
Cash	13,932	18,386	0	n/a
Contributions	5,700	15,450	28,250	49,400
Republicans	4,950	13,750	23,250	41,950
No. of Cand.	*7*	*12*	*24*	*43*
House	2,450	3,500	15,750	21,700
Senate	2,500	10,250	7,500	20,250
Democrats	750	1,700	5,000	7,450
No. of Cand.	*2*	*2*	*4*	*8*
House	250	1,700	2,000	3,950
Senate	500	0	3,000	3,500
Incumbents	5,700	15,450	26,750	47,900
Challengers	0	0	1,000	1,000
Open Seat	0	0	0	0
Winners	5,700	12,950	n/a	18,650
Losers	0	2,500	n/a	2,500

Guardian Industries Corp.

*Phone: (248) 340-2102 * Fax: (248) 340-2111*
2300 Harmon Rd., Auburn Hills, MI 48326

Guardian Industries is a private company that manufactures flat float glass, patterned glass and fabricated float glass products used in architectural and automotive applications.

Founded in 1932, it now has manufacturing and fabricating plants in the United States, Europe, Canada, South America, the Middle East and Asia. The company posted estimated sales of $1.9 billion in 1996 and has 13,000 employees.

Guardian Industries Corp. Federal Political Action Committee (Guardian Federal PAC) (C00239285) *Address: same as sponsor * Treasurer: Peter S. Walters*

	1993-94	1995-96	1997	Totals
Receipts	$22,135	$27,500	$21,000	$70,635
Disburse	21,989	27,612	11,000	60,601
Cash	170	58	10,058	n/a
Contributions	20,000	24,600	9,000	53,600
Republicans	4,250	10,900	4,000	19,150
No. of Cand.	*9*	*24*	*4*	*37*
House	1,750	6,650	2,000	10,400
Senate	2,500	4,250	2,000	8,750
Democrats	15,750	13,700	5,000	34,450
No. of Cand.	*25*	*23*	*6*	*54*
House	12,250	8,750	4,000	25,000
Senate	3,500	4,950	1,000	9,450
Incumbents	16,500	22,350	9,000	47,850
Challengers	750	1,000	0	1,750
Open Seat	2,750	1,250	0	4,000
Winners	15,000	23,450	n/a	38,450
Losers	5,000	1,150	n/a	6,150

Harsco Corp.

*Phone: (717) 763-7064 * Fax: (717) 763-6424*
P.O. Box 8888, Camp Hill, PA 17001
Web: www.harsco.com

Harsco is a publicly traded manufacturing and industrial services company. It provides railway maintenance and equipment worldwide, offers industrial mill services to steel producers, and manufactures scaffolding and other equipment for highway construction. The company has eight divisions in 31 countries and employs 14,200 workers. Sales for 1997 exceeded $1.6 billion.

In February 1998, Harsco acquired Racal Electronics Co., a composite cylinder company based in California. Harsco also announced plans to buy Chemi-Trol Chemical Co. for $46 million. The Ohio-based Chemi-Trol makes steel pressure tanks.

Harsco Corp. Political Action Committee (C00084145) *Address: same as sponsor * Treasurer: John G. Ferencz * Contact: Russel S. Swanger Jr.*

	1993-94	1995-96	1997	Totals
Receipts	$48,498	$53,590	$30,882	$132,970
Disburse	49,081	59,981	12,991	122,053
Cash	12,141	5,751	23,642	n/a
Contributions	32,900	38,700	1,725	73,325
Republicans	14,900	27,950	1,725	44,575
No. of Cand.	*18*	*35*	*5*	*58*
House	11,400	23,450	975	35,825
Senate	3,500	4,500	750	8,750
Democrats	18,000	10,750	0	28,750
No. of Cand.	*22*	*13*	*0*	*35*
House	16,500	10,750	0	27,250
Senate	1,500	0	0	1,500
Incumbents	30,400	36,200	1,725	68,325
Challengers	1,500	500	0	2,000
Open Seat	1,500	2,000	0	3,500
Winners	31,400	33,950	n/a	65,350
Losers	1,500	4,750	n/a	6,250

Hunter Engineering Co.

*Phone: (314) 731-3020 x2391 * Fax: (314) 731-7143*
11250 Hunter Dr., Bridgeton, MO 63044
Web: www.hunter.com

Hunter Engineering, a privately held company, manufactures and develops computerized automotive diagnosis and repair equipment sold worldwide. It is headquartered in St. Louis and has additional plants located in Mississippi. It has 11 equipment training centers located throughout the United States. Of its 600 employees, 400 are located in the St. Louis area.

Hunter Engineering Co. Political Action Committee (C00214379) *Address: same as sponsor * Treasurer: Joseph A. Staniszewski*

	1993-94	1995-96	1997	Totals
Receipts	$12,193	$12,197	$6,000	$30,390
Disburse	7,070	9,771	8,512	25,353
Cash	9,545	11,973	9,461	n/a
Contributions	6,000	8,250	8,500	22,750
Republicans	6,000	8,250	8,500	22,750
No. of Cand.	*2*	*8*	*3*	*13*
House	2,500	8,250	1,000	11,750
Senate	3,500	0	7,500	11,000
Democrats	0	0	0	0
No. of Cand.	*0*	*0*	*0*	*0*
House	0	0	0	0
Senate	0	0	0	0
Incumbents	2,500	2,250	8,500	13,250
Challengers	0	4,000	0	4,000
Open Seat	3,500	2,000	0	5,500
Winners	6,000	5,000	n/a	11,000
Losers	0	3,250	n/a	3,250

IMO Industries Inc.

Phone: (609) 896-7600
1009 Lenox Dr., Bldg. Four West, Lawrenceville, NJ 08648

The IMO Industries PAC was terminated in November 1997.

IMO Industries Inc. Political Action Committee (C00242255) *Address: same as sponsor * Treasurer: George J. Mangieri*

	1993-94	1995-96	1997	Totals
Receipts	$84,100	$45,700	$6,798	$136,598
Disburse	89,922	45,936	11,599	147,457
Cash	4,763	4,527	888	n/a
Contributions	78,750	37,000	11,500	127,250
Republicans	34,750	28,500	7,500	70,750
No. of Cand.	*26*	*22*	*6*	*54*
House	28,750	21,500	3,500	53,750
Senate	6,000	7,000	4,000	17,000
Democrats	44,000	8,500	3,500	56,000
No. of Cand.	*18*	*4*	*4*	*26*
House	36,500	8,500	3,500	48,500
Senate	7,500	0	0	7,500
Incumbents	69,250	33,500	11,000	113,750
Challengers	4,500	0	0	4,500
Open Seat	4,500	3,500	0	8,000
Winners	70,250	34,500	n/a	104,750
Losers	8,500	2,500	n/a	11,000

Illinois Tool Works Inc.

*Phone: (847) 657-4232 * Fax: (847) 657-4505*
3600 W. Lake Ave., Glenview, IL 60025-5811
Web: www.itwinc.com

Illinois Tool Works is a publicly traded maker of equipment for the automotive, construction and food and beverage industries. The Fortune 300 company reported $5.2 billion in 1997 sales and employs about 24,000 people in 365 operating units.

It produces spray guns, packaging systems, adhesives, polymers and welding equipment. The company also has a leasing and investment business which concentrates on commercial real estate and mortgage securities.

Illinois Tool Works for Better Government Committee (C00000042) *Address: same as sponsor * Treasurer: Michael J. Lynch*

	1993-94	1995-96	1997	Totals
Receipts	$33,133	$38,774	$21,832	$93,739
Disburse	32,623	39,578	4,500	76,701
Cash	4,178	3,377	20,710	n/a
Contributions	29,300	38,800	4,000	72,100
Republicans	28,700	37,800	4,000	70,500
No. of Cand.	*42*	*49*	*5*	*96*
House	18,700	23,800	4,000	46,500
Senate	10,000	14,000	0	24,000
Democrats	600	1,000	0	1,600
No. of Cand.	*2*	*3*	*0*	*5*
House	600	750	0	1,350
Senate	0	250	0	250
Incumbents	12,950	18,000	4,000	34,950
Challengers	6,000	7,300	0	13,300
Open Seat	10,350	13,500	0	23,850
Winners	25,700	18,000	n/a	43,700
Losers	3,600	20,800	n/a	24,400

Institute of Scrap Recycling Industries

*Phone: (202) 737-1770 * Fax: (202) 626-0900*
1325 G St. N.W., Suite 1000, Washington, DC 20005
Web: www.isri.org

The Institute of Scrap Recycling Industries represents about 1,600 companies that recycle and sell scrap materials such as metals, paper, glass, plastics and rubber. It has 23 chapters around the nation.

The U.S. scrap recycling industry handled more than 120 million tons of recyclables during 1997. ISRI estimates the total value of these products at $20 billion.

Institute of Scrap Recycling Industries Political Action Committee (C00046086) *Address: same as sponsor * Treasurer: Dr. Herschel Cutler*

	1993-94	1995-96	1997	Totals
Receipts	$75,087	$122,635	$35,643	$233,365
Disburse	69,530	85,772	74,254	229,556
Cash	37,394	74,256	35,644	n/a
Contributions	64,301	81,923	69,452	215,676
Republicans	20,750	45,383	34,500	100,633
No. of Cand.	*27*	*38*	*41*	*106*
House	15,250	32,683	25,500	73,433
Senate	5,500	12,700	9,000	27,200
Democrats	43,051	36,540	33,952	113,543
No. of Cand.	*33*	*35*	*35*	*103*
House	28,628	24,640	16,500	69,768
Senate	14,423	11,900	17,452	43,775
Incumbents	62,001	75,223	62,453	199,677
Challengers	500	1,450	0	1,950
Open Seat	1,800	5,250	6,499	13,549
Winners	52,808	73,723	n/a	126,531
Losers	11,493	8,200	n/a	19,693

Kaiser Aluminum & Chemical Corp.

*Phone: (713) 975-7600 * Fax: (713) 267-3644*
P.O. Box 572887, Houston, TX 77257-2887
Web: www.kaiseral.com

Kaiser Aluminum & Chemical mines bauxite, processes it into alumina (the intermediary material) and produces aluminum products for the aircraft, aerospace, automotive, beverage can, electronics, communications, construction and industrial markets. The publicly traded company posted $2.37 billion in 1997 sales. It is 63 percent owned by MAXXAM Inc., a public company.

The company operates in 12 states and eight foreign countries. It employs about 9,500 people.

In 1998, Kaiser announced that it had received notice that the Volta River Authority will reduce the electric power allocation to Kaiser's 90-percent-owned Volta Aluminum Co. Limited (Valco) smelter facility in Ghana. As a result, Kaiser expects to operate only two out of five of its smelting pots at Valco in 1998.

Kaiser Aluminum & Chemical Corp. Political Action Committee (C00047415) *Address: same as sponsor * Treasurer: Grover C. Webb*

	1993-94	1995-96	1997	Totals
Receipts	$16,670	$13,262	$5,524	$35,456
Disburse	19,400	21,877	0	41,277
Cash	8,615	11,877	17,400	n/a
Contributions	19,400	9,000	0	28,400
Republicans	8,000	8,000	0	16,000
No. of Cand.	*9*	*8*	*0*	*17*
House	3,000	4,000	0	7,000
Senate	5,000	4,000	0	9,000
Democrats	11,400	1,000	0	12,400
No. of Cand.	*14*	*1*	*0*	*15*
House	8,900	1,000	0	9,900
Senate	2,500	0	0	2,500
Incumbents	15,400	8,000	0	23,400
Challengers	500	0	0	500
Open Seat	3,500	1,000	0	4,500
Winners	13,400	9,000	n/a	22,400
Losers	6,000	0	n/a	6,000

Lane Industries

*Phone: (847) 498-6789 * Fax: (847) 498-2104*
1200 Shermer Rd., Northbrook, IL 60062

Lane Industries is a family-owned private holding company with interests in office product manufacturing and marketing, hotel management, electronic security services, broadcasting and real estate. Subsidiaries include General Binding Corp., Lane Hospitality Inc., Broadcast Alchemy L.P., and Lane Security Inc. Lane Industries had estimated 1996 sales of $700 million and has 6,600 employees.

Lane Industries Political Action Committee (C00195966) *Address: same as sponsor * Treasurer: Forrest M. Schneider * Contact: William N. Lane III, Chairman and President*

	1993-94	1995-96	1997	Totals
Receipts	$17,015	$18,000	$8,750	$43,765
Disburse	18,894	13,500	8,400	40,794
Cash	2	3,502	3,825	n/a
Contributions	15,875	14,000	10,400	40,275
Republicans	5,125	11,250	7,000	23,375
No. of Cand.	*5*	*11*	*4*	*20*
House	5,125	8,750	7,000	20,875
Senate	0	2,500	0	2,500
Democrats	10,750	2,750	3,400	16,900
No. of Cand.	*10*	*7*	*4*	*21*
House	3,650	1,750	1,750	7,150
Senate	7,100	1,000	1,650	9,750
Incumbents	16,125	12,500	10,400	39,025
Challengers	0	0	0	0
Open Seat	0	1,500	0	1,500
Winners	13,625	12,500	n/a	26,125
Losers	2,250	1,500	n/a	3,750

Leggett & Platt Inc.

*Phone: (417) 358-8131 * Fax: (417) 358-5840*
1 Leggett Rd., Carthage, MO 64836
Web: www.leggett.com

Leggett & Platt is a publicly traded manufacturer of components and related products for bedding, furniture and other furnishings. Founded in 1883, the company has about 25,000 employees worldwide. It reported $2.5 billion in 1997 sales.

The company operates five wire drawing mills, three welded steel tubing mills and about 90 major manufacturing facilities and/or subsidiaries in Texas, New Jersey, Pennsylvania, North Carolina, Arkansas, California, Florida, Mississippi, Missouri, New Mexico, Delaware, Canada, Mexico, the West Indies, the United Kingdom, the Netherlands, Germany, Belgium, Switzerland, Spain, Sweden, Korea and Japan.

Leggett & Platt Inc. Political Involvement Fund (C00229435)
*Address: same as sponsor * Treasurer: James M. Crocker * Contact: Dr. Lance Beshore, V.P. of Public Affairs*

	1993-94	1995-96	1997	Totals
Receipts	$0	$33,403	$32,097	$65,500
Disburse	0	28,360	24,161	52,521
Cash	0	5,044	12,980	n/a
Contributions	0	21,500	22,659	44,159
Republicans	0	21,500	22,659	44,159
No. of Cand.	*0*	*20*	*8*	*28*
House	0	17,000	5,659	22,659
Senate	0	4,500	17,000	21,500
Democrats	0	0	0	0
No. of Cand.	*0*	*0*	*0*	*0*
House	0	0	0	0
Senate	0	0	0	0
Incumbents	0	4,250	23,159	27,409
Challengers	0	5,250	0	5,250
Open Seat	0	12,000	0	12,000
Winners	0	11,750	n/a	11,750
Losers	0	9,750	n/a	9,750

Libbey-Owens-Ford Co.

*Phone: (419) 325-2100 * Fax: (419) 325-2117*
811 Madison Ave., Toledo, OH 43695
Web: www.pilkington.com/sites/lof

Libbey-Owens-Ford is a member of Pilkington Worldwide, which makes glass products for the building, transport and electronics markets.

LOF is one of the world's leading manufacturers of float glass for architectural, mirror, automotive and specialty glass products. The company also manufactures laminated and tempered automotive glass, including tinted and coated glass parts, through a seven-plant network. These are sold directly to original equipment manufacturers and fabricators and to automotive aftermarket distributors and installers.

LOF participates in a partnership with Nippon Sheet Glass of Japan, through NSG's 20 percent ownership of LOF.

In 1996, LOF employed 4,150 people and reported sales of $397 million.

Libbey-Owens-Ford Co. Political Action Committee (C00211284)
*Address: same as sponsor * Treasurer: Ken A. Hermes*

	1993-94	1995-96	1997	Totals
Receipts	$24,392	$21,702	$11,984	$58,078
Disburse	27,500	22,500	3,000	53,000
Cash	1,939	1,145	10,130	n/a
Contributions	24,500	22,500	2,000	49,000
Republicans	21,500	19,500	2,000	43,000
No. of Cand.	*18*	*17*	*3*	*38*
House	10,500	14,250	1,000	25,750
Senate	11,000	5,250	1,000	17,250
Democrats	3,000	3,000	0	6,000
No. of Cand.	*2*	*3*	*0*	*5*
House	3,000	2,500	0	5,500
Senate	0	500	0	500
Incumbents	12,500	20,500	1,000	34,000
Challengers	3,000	1,000	0	4,000
Open Seat	9,000	1,000	1,000	11,000
Winners	22,500	17,750	n/a	40,250
Losers	2,000	4,750	n/a	6,750

Maytag Corp.

*Phone: (515) 787-8592 * Fax: (515) 791-6864*
403 W. Fourth St. N., Newton, IA 50208
Web: www.maytagcorp.com

Maytag manufactures, distributes and services home appliances including laundry machines, dishwashers, refrigerators, cooking appliances, vacuum cleaners and extractors.

The company, which employs about 16,000 people, reported record net sales of $3.4 billion and net income of $180.3 million in 1997 after a year of expansion and acquisition. Maytag made 1996's Fortune 500 list at No. 452.

In October 1997, Maytag completed its acquisition of G.S. Blodgett Corp., a commercial cooking equipment company that includes the Blodgett, Pitco Frialator, MagiKitch'n, and Blodgett-Combi brands.

Maytag's home appliance brands include Maytag, Jenn-Air, Magic Chef, Performa and Hoover. Maytag International Inc. has a joint venture with Hefei Rongshida, one of China's leading washing machine companies. Another subsidiary, Dixie-Narco, manufactures and sells commercial vending equipment and is responsible for about 5 percent of Maytag's sales.

Maytag Corp. Employees for Good Government Fund (formerly known as Maytag Good Government Committee) (C00103010)
*Phone: (202) 639-9420 * Fax: (202) 639-9421 * 1310 G St. N.W., Suite 720, Washington, DC 20005 * Treasurer: John H. Lubben * Contact: Douglas Horstman, V.P. of Gov. Affairs*

	1993-94	1995-96	1997	Totals
Receipts	$53,329	$46,882	$21,776	$121,987
Disburse	56,034	44,871	12,517	113,422
Cash	3,801	5,819	15,084	n/a
Contributions	37,875	33,650	9,500	81,025
Republicans	33,125	30,700	9,250	73,075
No. of Cand.	*55*	*47*	*16*	*118*
House	22,075	20,750	5,750	48,575
Senate	11,050	9,950	3,500	24,500
Democrats	4,250	2,950	250	7,450
No. of Cand.	*11*	*5*	*1*	*17*
House	3,750	2,950	250	6,950
Senate	500	0	0	500
Incumbents	19,000	17,750	8,000	44,750
Challengers	6,800	7,450	500	14,750
Open Seat	11,575	8,450	1,000	21,025
Winners	29,350	21,700	n/a	51,050
Losers	8,525	11,950	n/a	20,475

Minnesota Mining & Manufacturing (3M) Co.

*Phone: (612) 733-1449 * Fax: (612) 736-5596*
3M Center Building, 224-5S-29, St. Paul, MN 55144-1000
Web: www.mmm.com

Minnesota Mining & Manufacturing (3M) is a diversified manufacturing firm, best known for its Scotch tape, Post-It Notes and Scotchgard Fabric Protector. The public company had 1997 sales of $15 billion — $7.2 billion in the United States. 3M employs 76,000 workers worldwide.

The company's products include specialty chemicals, tapes, notes, scouring pads and sponges. 3M's life sciences unit produces medical and surgical supplies, health care information systems, pharmaceuticals and drug-delivery systems, as well as reflective materials for traffic safety and respirators for worker protection.

In 1995, the company decided to spin off its data storage and imaging businesses and to discontinue its audio and video business.

Minnesota Mining & Manufacturing Co. Political Action Committee (3M PAC) (C00084475) *Phone: (202) 331-6900 * 1101 15th St. N.W., Suite 1100, Washington, DC 20005 * Treasurer: Peter J. Abts*

*Contact: L. J. Schoenwetter, Chairman * Phone: (612) 733-1449*

	1993-94	1995-96	1997	Totals
Receipts	$98,316	$105,369	$57,761	$261,446
Disburse	99,704	108,032	42,417	250,153
Cash	8,267	5,610	20,956	n/a
Contributions	45,750	50,229	21,300	117,279
Republicans	26,000	31,429	11,300	68,729
No. of Cand.	*36*	*46*	*16*	*98*
House	13,500	19,179	9,300	41,979
Senate	12,500	12,250	2,000	26,750
Democrats	17,250	18,800	8,000	44,050
No. of Cand.	*25*	*27*	*10*	*62*
House	12,250	12,800	4,000	29,050
Senate	5,000	6,000	4,000	15,000
Incumbents	26,750	32,300	21,300	80,350
Challengers	4,500	4,250	0	8,750
Open Seat	14,500	13,679	0	28,179
Winners	36,750	36,800	n/a	73,550
Losers	9,000	13,429	n/a	22,429

National Tooling & Machining Association

*Phone: (301) 248-6200 * Fax: (301) 248-7104*
9300 Livingston Rd., P.O. Box 44162, Ft. Washington, MD 20749
Web: www.ntma.org

The National Tooling & Machining Association represents the contract precision metalworking industry.

According to the association, of the 14,000 companies in the industry, 2,600 are members of the NTMA. Members are organized into 52 local chapters and tool centers throughout the country. Through member companies, NTMA represents more than 125,000 skilled toolmakers, diemakers, moldmakers and machinists.

The organization assists members in developing and expanding their domestic and foreign markets. It also offers training programs, insurance and legal advice, compiles statistical information and monitors legislation and regulations. The group tracks labor, small business, safety and tax issues.

National Tooling & Machining Association (NTMA) Committee for a Strong Economy (C00043091) *Address: same as sponsor * Treasurer: Gary Rogers * Contact: Matthew B. Coffey, President*

	1993-94	1995-96	1997	Totals
Receipts	$54,324	$52,431	$54,883	$161,638
Disburse	75,698	56,021	26,521	158,240
Cash	49,474	45,887	74,252	n/a
Contributions	58,950	22,850	16,700	98,500
Republicans	52,450	21,850	16,000	90,300
No. of Cand.	*53*	*26*	*16*	*95*
House	29,200	18,750	11,500	59,450
Senate	23,250	3,100	4,500	30,850
Democrats	6,500	1,000	700	8,200
No. of Cand.	*7*	*1*	*2*	*10*
House	5,500	1,000	700	7,200
Senate	1,000	0	0	1,000
Incumbents	41,050	15,750	15,200	72,000
Challengers	6,050	4,100	500	10,650
Open Seat	11,850	3,000	1,000	15,850
Winners	53,050	17,750	n/a	70,800
Losers	5,900	5,100	n/a	11,000

Nike Inc.

*Phone: (503) 677-3120 * Fax: (503) 671-6300*
One Bowerman Dr., Beaverton, OR 97005-6453
Web: www.nikebiz.com

Nike makes and markets athletic footwear, apparel and accessory products worldwide. The publicly held company sells its products through about 18,000 retail accounts in the United States and through a mix of independent distributors, licensees and subsidiaries in about 110 countries. Established in 1972, Nike has more than 17,000 employees worldwide. In 1997, revenues grew by 42 percent to $9.2 billion for the year.

Nike also sponsors athletes, including Michael Jordan in basketball, Tiger Woods in golf and Cal Ripken in baseball. In addition, Nike engages kids in sporting events and supports mentoring programs. In 1994, Nike launched PLAY (Participate in the Lives of America's Youth) to provide kids access to inspirational coaches, organized activities and safe places to play.

In 1997, Nike recalled 38,000 pairs of shoes carrying a logo that offended Muslims because it resembled the word "Allah" in Arabic. Nike also apologized to Muslims.

Nike Inc. Federal Political Action Committee (Nike Federal PAC) (C00142786) *Phone: (202) 543-6453 * 507 Second St. N.E., Washington, DC 20002 * Treasurer: Dennis H. Peterson*

	1993-94	1995-96	1997	Totals
Receipts	$30,308	$21,924	$21,745	$73,977
Disburse	26,722	22,317	17,053	66,092
Cash	16,933	16,544	21,237	n/a
Contributions	24,800	21,500	17,000	63,300
Republicans	10,250	11,500	8,000	29,750
No. of Cand.	*13*	*17*	*8*	*38*
House	3,250	7,000	3,000	13,250
Senate	7,000	4,500	5,000	16,500
Democrats	14,550	10,000	9,000	33,550
No. of Cand.	*18*	*11*	*9*	*38*
House	13,550	7,000	6,500	27,050
Senate	1,000	3,000	2,500	6,500
Incumbents	16,750	16,500	15,000	48,250
Challengers	500	1,500	0	2,000
Open Seat	6,550	3,500	2,000	12,050
Winners	17,250	16,500	n/a	33,750
Losers	7,550	5,000	n/a	12,550

Owens-Illinois Inc.

*Phone: (419) 247-5000 * Fax: (419) 247-1132*
One Seagate, Toledo, OH 43666

Owens-Illinois is the largest producer of glass containers in North America, South America and India. The publicly traded company, which also makes plastic containers, posted $4.6 billion in 1997 sales and has 30,800 employees. Its headquarters are in Toledo, Ohio.

The company's products are mainly used by the food and beverage industry. The company also makes plastic closures, plastic prescription containers, labels and multipack plastic carriers for beverage containers. About one of every two glass containers made worldwide is manufactured by Owens-Illinois, its affiliates or its licensees.

U.S. manufacturing locations: California, Colorado, Connecticut, Florida, Georgia, Illinois, Indiana, Kentucky, Maryland, Massachusetts, Michigan, Missouri, New Hampshire, New Jersey, New York, North Carolina, Ohio, Oklahoma, Oregon, Pennsylvania, South Carolina, Tennessee, Texas and Virginia.

Owens-Illinois Inc. Employees Good Citizenship Fund (C00034330) *Address: same as sponsor * Treasurer: John E. Hoff*

	1993-94	1995-96	1997	Totals
Receipts	$63,918	$62,063	$29,391	$155,372
Disburse	72,650	83,240	28,550	184,440
Cash	25,977	4,803	5,646	n/a
Contributions	55,600	50,990	17,500	124,090
Republicans	31,750	37,500	15,000	84,250
No. of Cand.	*27*	*34*	*12*	*73*
House	22,250	24,500	6,000	52,750
Senate	9,500	13,000	9,000	31,500
Democrats	23,850	13,490	2,000	39,340
No. of Cand.	*18*	*10*	*3*	*31*
House	15,850	8,490	1,000	25,340
Senate	8,000	5,000	1,000	14,000
Incumbents	44,400	47,490	12,500	104,390
Challengers	3,500	0	0	3,500
Open Seat	7,700	3,000	5,000	15,700
Winners	48,750	41,990	n/a	90,740
Losers	6,850	9,000	n/a	15,850

PPG Industries

*Phone: (412) 434-3385 * Fax: (412) 434-4416*
One PPG Place, Pittsburgh, PA 15272
*Web: www.ppg.com * E-mail: dgriebling@ppg.com*

PPG Industries comprises three basic segments: coatings and resins, glass and chemicals. The publicly traded company is the world's No. 1 producer of optical resins and a leading producer of chlorine, caustic soda and other industrial chemicals. PPG employs about 31,000 people and posted 1997 sales of $7.3 billion.

PPG Industries was founded in 1883 as the Pittsburgh Plate Glass Co. Its primary products are automotive, industrial and architectural coatings, flat glass, automotive original and replacement glass, aircraft transparencies, continuous strand fiber glass and industrial and specialty chemicals.

Since August 1997, PPG has acquired eight coatings businesses with combined revenues of more than $400 million. PPG's 1996 coatings segment sales were $2.9 billion.

PPG Employees Voluntary Political Campaign Fund (C00034298) *Address: same as sponsor * Treasurer: D. M. Griebling*

	1993-94	1995-96	1997	Totals
Receipts	$27,128	$34,524	$16,887	$78,539
Disburse	25,500	33,950	300	59,750
Cash	10,732	11,313	27,905	n/a
Contributions	25,000	33,950	300	59,250
Republicans	23,500	29,450	-200	52,750
No. of Cand.	*23*	*34*	*3*	*60*
House	8,000	13,450	-200	21,250
Senate	15,500	16,000	0	31,500
Democrats	1,500	4,500	500	6,500
No. of Cand.	*8*	*4*	*2*	*14*
House	2,000	3,500	500	6,000
Senate	-500	1,000	0	500
Incumbents	8,500	15,950	300	24,750
Challengers	6,000	3,500	0	9,500
Open Seat	10,500	14,500	0	25,000
Winners	23,000	22,250	n/a	45,250
Losers	2,000	11,700	n/a	13,700

Parker-Hannifin Corp.

*Phone: (216) 896-3000 * Fax: (216) 896-4057*
6035 Parkland Blvd., Cleveland, OH 44124-4141
Web: www.parker.com

Headquartered in Cleveland, Parker-Hannifin makes a wide variety of small parts for use in the industrial and aerospace industries. The publicly traded company has 34,900 employees and posted 1997 sales of $4 billion.

Aerospace products account for about 17 percent of the company's revenues. Parker-Hannifin makes hydraulic, pneumatic and fuel systems, as well as related components.

Parker-Hannifin built the hydraulic systems used to sink the set in the movie "Titanic."

Parker-Hannifin Corp. Political Action Committee (Parker PAC) (C00135459) *Address: same as sponsor * Treasurer: Timothy K. Pistell * Contact: Patrick Parker, Chairman*

	1993-94	1995-96	1997	Totals
Receipts	$8,200	$5,500	$2,725	$16,425
Disburse	7,386	8,241	2,045	17,672
Cash	3,383	641	1,321	n/a
Contributions	7,250	7,700	2,000	16,950
Republicans	7,250	7,700	2,000	16,950
No. of Cand.	*9*	*8*	*2*	*19*
House	3,250	4,000	2,000	9,250
Senate	4,000	3,700	0	7,700
Democrats	0	0	0	0
No. of Cand.	*0*	*0*	*0*	*0*
House	0	0	0	0
Senate	0	0	0	0
Incumbents	1,250	4,500	2,000	7,750
Challengers	2,500	2,200	0	4,700
Open Seat	3,500	1,000	0	4,500
Winners	6,250	4,500	n/a	10,750
Losers	1,000	3,200	n/a	4,200

ABEX Inc. Employees Good Government Fund (C00032599) *Phone: (616) 384-3400 * 2220 Palmer Ave., Kalamazoo, MI 49001 * Treasurer: Richard E. Halperin*

Parker ABEX, a subsidiary of Parker-Hannifin, is an aerospace defense contractor headquartered in Kalamazoo, Mich. It produces tilt sensors for missiles and rockets and other instruments for airplanes. Its customers include Boeing, General Electric, the U.S. Air Force and U.S. Army.

	1993-94	1995-96	1997	Totals
Receipts	$36,090	$518	$0	$36,608
Disburse	121,457	32,907	4,874	159,238
Cash	37,263	4,874	0	n/a
Contributions	57,000	15,500	4,874	77,374
Republicans	33,000	18,500	0	51,500
No. of Cand.	*9*	*3*	*0*	*12*
House	12,000	3,500	0	15,500
Senate	21,000	15,000	0	36,000
Democrats	24,000	-3,000	4,874	25,874
No. of Cand.	*4*	*2*	*1*	*7*
House	14,000	-500	0	13,500
Senate	10,000	-2,500	4,874	12,374
Incumbents	34,000	15,500	4,874	54,374
Challengers	11,000	0	0	11,000
Open Seat	12,000	0	0	12,000
Winners	50,000	12,000	n/a	62,000
Losers	7,000	3,500	n/a	10,500

Precision Machined Products Association

*Phone: (440) 526-0300 * Fax: (440) 526-5803*
6700 W. Snowville Rd., Brecksville, OH 44141-3292
Web: www.pmpa.org

The Precision Machined Products Association represents about 600 companies in the United States and Canada that manufacture products using screw machines. A screw machine is a type of automated lathe that is used to produce complex, detailed items rapidly and identically. Total annual sales of the industry are about $4.6 billion.

Final products include anti-lock brakes, transmissions, fuel injection systems and air bags on cars and trucks; personal computer hard drives and video recording equipment; appliances, faucets, lawn mowers and power tools. Some of the PMPA's members include Waltec Components, Sperry Automatics Co. Inc., Apex Machine Products Inc. and Marvel Screw Machine Products Inc.

Precision Machined Products Association Political Action Committee (C00110858) *Address: same as sponsor * Treasurer: Jack D. McNaughton * Contact: David Burch, Dir. of Gov. Relations*

	1993-94	1995-96	1997	Totals
Receipts	$61,310	$65,282	$30,674	$157,266
Disburse	72,683	66,591	233	139,507
Cash	16,180	14,824	45,265	n/a
Contributions	72,000	66,000	0	138,000
Republicans	72,000	66,000	0	138,000
No. of Cand.	*41*	*37*	*0*	*78*
House	13,000	12,000	0	25,000
Senate	59,000	54,000	0	113,000
Democrats	0	0	0	0
No. of Cand.	*0*	*0*	*0*	*0*
House	0	0	0	0
Senate	0	0	0	0
Incumbents	15,500	20,000	0	35,500
Challengers	19,000	16,000	0	35,000
Open Seat	37,500	29,000	0	66,500
Winners	61,000	35,000	n/a	96,000
Losers	11,000	31,000	n/a	42,000

Precision Metalforming Association

*Phone: (440) 585-8800 * Fax: (440) 585-3126*
27027 Chardon Rd., Richmond Heights, OH 44143
*Web: www.pma.org * E-mail: chowell@pma.org*

The Precision Metalforming Association represents about 1,500 companies located in the United States and a few foreign countries. These companies primarily produce metal and steel parts for use in the automobile industry. The PMA estimates the value of the industry to be about $32 billion annually.

Precision Metalforming Association Voice of the Industry Committee (PMAVIC) (C00082271) *6363 Oaktree, Independence, OH 44131 * Treasurer: Christopher E. Howell*

	1993-94	1995-96	1997	Totals
Receipts	$34,000	$69,971	$30,216	$134,187
Disburse	26,557	78,428	7,552	112,537
Cash	14,152	5,694	28,359	n/a
Contributions	26,050	67,500	6,500	100,050
Republicans	26,050	67,000	6,500	99,550
No. of Cand.	*14*	*38*	*9*	*61*
House	2,550	37,000	4,500	44,050
Senate	23,500	30,000	2,000	55,500
Democrats	0	500	0	500
No. of Cand.	*0*	*1*	*0*	*1*
House	0	500	0	500
Senate	0	0	0	0
Incumbents	5,800	34,500	4,500	44,800
Challengers	5,000	16,000	1,000	22,000
Open Seat	15,250	17,000	1,000	33,250
Winners	25,800	35,000	n/a	60,800
Losers	250	32,500	n/a	32,750

Premark International Inc.

*Phone: (847) 405-6000 * Fax: (847) 405-6013*
1717 Deerfield Rd., Deerfield, IL 60015
Web: www.premarkintl.com

The Premark International Inc. PAC was terminated.

Premark International, a $2.4 billion multinational company, markets food service equipment, building products and small appliances in more than 100 countries under brand names such as Hobart, Wilsonart, West Bend, Florida Tile and Precor. It employs more than 16,000 workers.

Premark International Inc. Political Action Committee (C00212811) *Address: same as sponsor * Treasurer: Mark H. Bobek*

	1993-94	1995-96	1997	Totals
Receipts	$42,950	$42,966	$0	$85,916
Disburse	47,278	57,878	0	105,156
Cash	14,910	0	0	n/a
Contributions	45,118	35,681	0	80,799
Republicans	34,118	32,581	0	66,699
No. of Cand.	*30*	*16*	*0*	*46*
House	8,125	24,250	0	32,375
Senate	25,993	8,331	0	34,324
Democrats	11,000	3,100	0	14,100
No. of Cand.	*8*	*4*	*0*	*12*
House	9,000	2,100	0	11,100
Senate	2,000	1,000	0	3,000
Incumbents	26,625	26,250	0	52,875

(Data for Premark International continued)

Challengers	7,993	5,000	0	12,993
Open Seat	10,500	4,431	0	14,931
Winners	37,875	27,350	n/a	65,225
Losers	7,243	8,331	n/a	15,574

Reebok International Ltd.

*Phone: (781) 341-5000 * Fax: (781) 341-7402*
100 Technology Center Dr., Stoughton, MA 02072
Web: www.reebok.com

The second-largest athletic shoemaker in the United States behind Nike, Reebok International makes Reebok brand sneakers and Greg Norman brand apparel. It counts The Rockport Co. and AVIA Group among its subsidiaries. The publicly traded company reported $3.6 billion in 1997 sales. It employs about 6,900 people.

Reebok was founded in 1979 and is based in Stoughton, Mass. The company obtains almost all of its products from contracted manufacturers outside the United States.

Since 1988, Reebok has promoted the Reebok Human Rights Award, and since 1992 it has had a worldwide standard for treatment of its workers, in an attempt to deflect criticism of the athletic apparel industry.

Reebok International Ltd. PAC (C00256313) *1201 Pennsylvania Ave. N.W., Suite 647, Washington, DC 20004 * Treasurer: John B. Douglas*

	1993-94	1995-96	1997	Totals
Receipts	$10,000	$5,000	$5,004	$20,004
Disburse	8,135	6,050	3,504	17,689
Cash	6,211	5,161	6,711	n/a
Contributions	7,900	5,750	3,500	17,150
Republicans	1,000	0	0	1,000
No. of Cand.	*1*	*0*	*0*	*1*
House	0	0	0	0
Senate	1,000	0	0	1,000
Democrats	6,900	5,750	3,500	16,150
No. of Cand.	*6*	*6*	*6*	*18*
House	6,900	3,750	2,500	13,150
Senate	0	2,000	1,000	3,000
Incumbents	7,900	3,750	3,500	15,150
Challengers	0	0	0	0
Open Seat	0	2,000	0	2,000
Winners	7,400	5,750	n/a	13,150
Losers	500	0	n/a	500

Remington Arms Co. Inc.

*Phone: (910) 548-8511 * Fax: (910) 548-8629*
870 Remington Dr., P.O. Box 700, Madison, NC 27025
Web: www.remington.com

Remington Arms makes firearms and ammunition, primarily for hunting and sport. It also makes Stren-brand fishline, targets and accessories. Remington sells products to the retail and wholesale distribution markets.

Remington is a privately held company with estimated annual sales of $400 million. It has 2,500 employees at its headquarters in North Carolina and at plants in New York, Arkansas, Kentucky, Ohio and Oklahoma.

Remington Arms Co. Inc. Political Action Committee (RemPAC) (C00300335) *Address: same as sponsor * Treasurer: Fritz Baumgartner * Contact: Samuel G. Grecco, Secretary*

	1993-94	1995-96	1997	Totals
Receipts	$0	$25,464	$20,483	$45,947
Disburse	0	11,769	3,618	15,387
Cash	0	13,698	30,562	n/a
Contributions	0	10,112	1,000	11,112
Republicans	0	9,112	1,000	10,112
No. of Cand.	*0*	*17*	*1*	*18*
House	0	6,700	1,000	7,700
Senate	0	2,412	0	2,412
Democrats	0	1,000	0	1,000
No. of Cand.	*0*	*2*	*0*	*2*
House	0	1,000	0	1,000
Senate	0	0	0	0
Incumbents	0	6,112	1,000	7,112
Challengers	0	0	0	0
Open Seat	0	4,000	0	4,000
Winners	0	7,612	n/a	7,612
Losers	0	2,500	n/a	2,500

Reynolds Metals Co.

*Phone: (804) 281-4968 * Fax: (804) 281-3924*
6601 W. Broad St., P.O. Box 27003, Richmond, VA 23261
Web: www.rmc.com

Reynolds Metals is the No. 2 aluminum producer in the United States, with more than $6.9 billion in 1997 sales and 29,000 employees.

The Virginia-based public company is known for its Reynolds Wrap aluminum foil, but also makes soft drink and beer cans as well as aluminum packaging, materials for the automobile industry, plastic wrap and containers. In addition, Reynolds owns mineral mining operations and metal recycling and distribution businesses.

Subsidiaries include: Reynolds Aluminum Co. of Cans Inc., Reynolds Aluminum Supply Co., Reynolds Foodservice and Reynolds Recycling.

Reynolds Metals Co. Political Participation Program Fund (RAPPP) (C00045849) *Address: same as sponsor * Treasurer: Michael D. Hall * Contact: W. G. Reynolds Jr., Chairperson*

	1993-94	1995-96	1997	Totals
Receipts	$63,636	$58,568	$24,946	$147,150
Disburse	84,026	67,040	14,275	165,341
Cash	17,537	9,068	19,739	n/a
Contributions	62,050	54,350	14,250	130,650
Republicans	46,200	49,350	13,750	109,300
No. of Cand.	*40*	*39*	*15*	*94*
House	25,200	18,850	3,750	47,800
Senate	21,000	30,500	10,000	61,500
Democrats	14,850	4,500	500	19,850
No. of Cand.	*14*	*5*	*1*	*20*
House	12,650	1,000	500	14,150
Senate	2,200	3,500	0	5,700
Incumbents	45,550	41,850	14,250	101,650
Challengers	6,000	4,000	0	10,000
Open Seat	11,500	8,000	0	19,500
Winners	53,550	45,850	n/a	99,400
Losers	8,500	8,500	n/a	17,000

Russell Corp.

*Phone: (205) 329-4000 * Fax: (205) 329-4474*
P.O. Box 272, Alexander City, AL 35011-0272
Web: www.russellcorp.com

Russell is a publicly traded international manufacturer and marketer of activewear, knit shirts and sports apparel. Its 1997 sales were $1.2 billion. The company has more than 35 plants in Alabama, Florida, Georgia, North Carolina, Virginia, Mexico and Honduras. It employs about 17,000 people.

Russell is the official supplier of uniforms for major-league baseball teams. Its manufacturing operations include the entire process of converting raw fibers into finished apparel and fabrics. Russell's products are marketed through five sales divisions — knit apparel, athletic, licensed products, international and fabrics — as well as through Cross Creek Apparel Inc. and DeSoto Mills Inc., both of which are wholly owned subsidiaries.

Russell Corp. Political Action Committee (C00093195) *Address: same as sponsor * Treasurer: Larry E. Workman * Contact: Fred O. Braswell III, Executive*

	1993-94	1995-96	1997	Totals
Receipts	$14,218	$36,970	$15,894	$67,082
Disburse	691	15,473	6,787	22,951
Cash	19,765	41,266	50,373	n/a
Contributions	500	14,325	5,375	20,200
Republicans	250	12,325	4,375	16,950
No. of Cand.	*1*	*8*	*4*	*13*
House	250	6,450	3,500	10,200
Senate	0	5,875	875	6,750
Democrats	250	2,000	1,000	3,250
No. of Cand.	*1*	*1*	*1*	*3*
House	250	0	0	250
Senate	0	2,000	1,000	3,000
Incumbents	500	1,950	5,375	7,825
Challengers	0	0	0	0
Open Seat	0	12,375	0	12,375
Winners	500	12,075	n/a	12,575
Losers	0	2,250	n/a	2,250

The Stanley Works

Phone: (860) 225-5111
1000 Stanley Dr., New Britain, CT 06053
Web: www.stanleyworks.com

The Stanley Works is a worldwide manufacturer and marketer of tools, hardware and specialty hardware for home improvement, consumer, industrial and professional markets. The company's products range from hammers and wrenches to insulated steel and reinforced fiberglass entrance door systems. Stanley had sales of $2.7 billion in 1996 and 19,000 employees worldwide.

The Connecticut company was founded in 1843. Stanley and its subsidiaries now own or lease facilities for manufacturing, distribution and sales in 28 states and 33 foreign countries. Stanley closed numerous facilities and sold off some of its less profitable businesses and product lines under a restructuring program in 1996.

Stanley is the sole shareholder of Farmington River Power Co. in Connecticut.

The Stanley Works Political Action Committee (C00060087) *Address: same as sponsor * Treasurer: Richard Huck * Contact: Theresa F. Yerkes, V.P. and Controller*

	1993-94	1995-96	1997	Totals
Receipts	$14,856	$11,994	$0	$26,850
Disburse	14,950	10,923	0	25,873
Cash	19,685	20,757	20,757	n/a
Contributions	5,500	6,500	0	12,000
Republicans	5,500	6,500	0	12,000
No. of Cand.	*3*	*3*	*0*	*6*
House	5,500	5,500	0	11,000
Senate	0	1,000	0	1,000
Democrats	0	0	0	0
No. of Cand.	*0*	*0*	*0*	*0*
House	0	0	0	0
Senate	0	0	0	0
Incumbents	0	6,500	0	6,500
Challengers	4,500	0	0	4,500
Open Seat	1,000	0	0	1,000
Winners	0	6,000	n/a	6,000
Losers	5,500	500	n/a	6,000

Temple-Inland Inc.

*Phone: (409) 829-5511 * Fax: (409) 829-1737*
P.O. Box 405, Diboll, TX 75941
Web: www.templeinland.com

Temple-Inland is a publicly traded holding company involved in paper manufacturing, timber, real estate and insurance.

Temple-Inland owns plants, mills and manufacturing facilities at about 60 locations, primarily in the southeastern United States, as well as three plants in Mexico and 50-percent joint venture interests in plants in Argentina and Chile. It has about 80 subsidiary companies, 15,600 employees and total annual sales of $3.5 billion.

Subsidiaries include: Inland Paperboard and Packaging Inc., Temple-Inland Forest Products Corp., Temple-Inland Financial Services Inc., Guaranty Federal and Temple-Inland Mortgage Corp.

Its principal subsidiaries manufacture corrugated boxes, bleached paperboard and building products; own about 2.2 million acres of timberland in Texas, Louisiana, Georgia, and Alabama; and operate 113 banking locations. It also has operations in real estate development and insurance brokerage.

Committee for Responsible Government of Temple-Inland Inc. (formerly known as Committee for Good Government of Temple-Inland) (C00080721) *Address: same as sponsor * Treasurer: Ryan R. Sorrell * Contact: Clifford J. Grum, Chairman and CEO*

	1993-94	1995-96	1997	Totals
Receipts	$101,757	$145,815	$124,852	$372,424
Disburse	99,340	9,843	39,000	148,183
Cash	9,504	24,058	109,917	n/a
Contributions	15,500	25,800	9,500	50,800
Republicans	2,500	18,300	7,000	27,800
No. of Cand.	*1*	*12*	*3*	*16*
House	0	11,000	6,000	17,000
Senate	2,500	7,300	1,000	10,800
Democrats	13,000	7,500	2,500	23,000
No. of Cand.	*7*	*7*	*1*	*15*
House	8,000	7,000	2,500	17,500
Senate	5,000	500	0	5,500
Incumbents	14,500	18,300	9,500	42,300
Challengers	0	0	0	0
Open Seat	1,000	7,500	0	8,500
Winners	7,000	22,300	n/a	29,300
Losers	8,500	3,500	n/a	12,000

Tenneco Inc.

*Phone: (203) 863-1073 * Fax: (203) 863-1134*
1275 King St., Greenwich, CT 06831-2946
Web: www.tenneco.com

Tenneco is a $6.6 billion public company that produces automotive parts and packaging. Its products include Monroe shock absorbers, Walker mufflers and Hefty trash bags. In 1996, the company spun off its Newport News Shipbuilding and Tenneco Energy divisions in order to focus on its two main industries. The company, headquartered in Greenwich, Conn., has about 47,000 employees and operations in more than 30 states.

Tenneco supports increased international trade and lobbies on legislation affecting the automotive industry. Most of the company's activities are regulated by federal and state environmental laws.

Tenneco's primary business has changed since the 1995-96 election cycle, when it favored Republican candidates. Six of the top 10 recipients were from Virginia, where the company's former shipbuilding facilities were located. They included Reps. Robert C. Scott, D-Va., Norman Sisisky, D-Va., and Owen B. Pickett, D-Va., and Sen. John W. Warner, R-Va.

Tenneco is no longer affiliated with the Tenneco Energy PAC after Tenneco Energy merged with El Paso Energy Corp. in 1996.

Tenneco Inc. Employees Good Government Fund (also known as Tenneco Employees Good Government Fund) (C00089961) *Phone: (202) 942-0201 * Fax: (202) 638-3306 * 701 Pennsylvania Ave. N.W., Suite 710, Washington, DC 20004 * E-mail: swshelby@aol.com * Treasurer: Robert T. Blakely * Contact: Sheryl Shelby, Manager of Gov. Relations*

	1993-94	1995-96	1997	Totals
Receipts	$407,964	$866,590	$196,075	$1,470,629
Disburse	380,688	860,515	137,201	1,378,404
Cash	64,800	70,887	129,769	n/a
Contributions	310,600	658,725	95,400	1,064,725
Republicans	150,900	458,875	64,400	674,175
No. of Cand.	*113*	*231*	*69*	*413*
House	81,900	305,375	35,400	422,675
Senate	69,000	153,500	29,000	251,500
Democrats	159,700	199,850	30,500	390,050
No. of Cand.	*122*	*101*	*31*	*254*
House	120,700	160,100	16,000	296,800
Senate	39,000	39,750	14,500	93,250
Incumbents	265,600	543,475	93,400	902,475
Challengers	17,000	27,000	0	44,000
Open Seat	28,000	88,500	2,500	119,000
Winners	272,100	577,475	n/a	849,575
Losers	38,500	81,250	n/a	119,750

The Timken Co.

*Phone: (330) 471-3541 * Fax: (330) 471-4275*
1835 Dueber Ave. S.W., Canton, OH 44706
*Web: www.timken.com * E-mail: lapp@timken.com*

Timken, a public company based in Ohio, manufactures bearings that are used in vehicles, machine tools and railcars. Subsidiary MPB Corp. makes precision bearings for computer peripherals, medical instruments, missile guidance systems and printing presses. Timken has operations in 24 countries and reported sales in 1997 totaling $2.6 billion. The Timken family owns about 19 percent of the firm.

The company, which employs more than 19,000 workers, has bearing-manufacturing joint ventures in India and China. About 32 percent of its sales are outside the United States. A third of Timken's sales come from alloy steels and specialty steels, made by subsidiary Latrobe Steels.

Rail Bearing Service Corp. is a third Timken subsidiary.

The Timken Co. Good Government Fund (C00311308) *Address: same as sponsor * Treasurer: Robert J. Lapp * Contact: Larry R. Brown, Chairman of PAC*

	1993-94	1995-96	1997	Totals
Receipts	$0	$79,717	$137,704	$217,421
Disburse	0	54,050	74,750	128,800
Cash	0	25,669	88,624	n/a
Contributions	0	14,500	29,000	43,500
Republicans	0	11,500	27,000	38,500
No. of Cand.	*0*	*10*	*10*	*20*
House	0	11,500	5,000	16,500
Senate	0	0	22,000	22,000
Democrats	0	3,000	2,000	5,000
No. of Cand.	*0*	*3*	*2*	*5*
House	0	3,000	2,000	5,000
Senate	0	0	0	0
Incumbents	0	10,500	19,000	29,500
Challengers	0	2,000	0	2,000
Open Seat	0	2,000	10,000	12,000
Winners	0	9,500	n/a	9,500
Losers	0	5,000	n/a	5,000

Valmont Industries Inc.

*Phone: (402) 359-6073 * Fax: (402) 343-0668*
W. Highway 275, P.O. Box 358, Valley, NE 68064
Web: www.valmont.com

Valmont Industries makes industrial and irrigation products, including agricultural irrigation equipment and poles, towers and other structures for lighting, communication and utility applications.

Valmont's sales in 1996 were about $644 million. The publicly traded company employs 4,800 workers.

Valmont Industries Inc. Political Action Committee (C00152843)
*Address: same as sponsor * Treasurer: Brian C. Stanley*

	1993-94	1995-96	1997	Totals
Receipts	$789	$39,146	$9,977	$49,912
Disburse	13,636	7,387	6,791	27,814
Cash	6,970	38,733	41,919	n/a
Contributions	13,250	7,250	6,500	27,000
Republicans	8,250	7,250	6,500	22,000
No. of Cand.	*5*	*5*	*3*	*13*
House	3,250	5,500	4,000	12,750
Senate	5,000	1,750	2,500	9,250
Democrats	5,000	0	0	5,000
No. of Cand.	*1*	*0*	*0*	*1*
House	0	0	0	0
Senate	5,000	0	0	5,000
Incumbents	7,250	5,500	6,500	19,250
Challengers	6,000	0	0	6,000
Open Seat	0	1,750	0	1,750
Winners	8,250	7,000	n/a	15,250
Losers	5,000	250	n/a	5,250

Water Quality Association

*Phone: (630) 505-0160 * Fax: (630) 505-9637*
4151 Naperville Rd., Lisle, IL 60532
*Web: www.wqa.org * E-mail: info@mail.wqa.org*

The Water Quality Association is the international trade association representing the household, commercial and industrial water quality improvement industry. The organization's 2,200 corporate member companies manufacture and sell point-of-use/point-of-entry equipment, water treatment plants and customized water treatment systems.

Water Quality Association Political Action Committee (Aqua PAC) (C00195834) *Address: same as sponsor * Treasurer: Alesia Davis*

	1993-94	1995-96	1997	Totals
Receipts	$4,035	$745	$625	$5,405
Disburse	7,127	8,301	0	15,428
Cash	19,940	7,385	8,010	n/a
Contributions	6,000	8,250	0	14,250
Republicans	3,500	6,500	0	10,000
No. of Cand.	*5*	*9*	*0*	*14*
House	3,500	6,000	0	9,500
Senate	0	500	0	500
Democrats	2,500	1,750	0	4,250
No. of Cand.	*4*	*4*	*0*	*8*
House	1,500	1,250	0	2,750
Senate	1,000	500	0	1,500
Incumbents	6,000	8,000	0	14,000
Challengers	0	0	0	0
Open Seat	0	250	0	250
Winners	6,000	8,250	n/a	14,250
Losers	0	0	n/a	0

Western Atlas Inc.

*Phone: (713) 972-4000 * Fax: (713) 952-9837*
10205 Westheimer Rd., Houston, TX 77042
Web: www.westatlas.com

Western Atlas provides oilfield services to the oil and gas industries. The public company, based in Houston, sells logging equipment, seismic data analysis and computer modeling for exploration and pipeline companies around the world.

The company, which has 14,000 employees, reported $1.6 billion in 1997 revenues. Western Atlas spun off its industrial automation business, UNOVA Inc., in 1997. UNOVA created its own PAC in late 1997.

Subsidiaries include: Western Atlas International, E&P Services and Western Geophysical. Western Atlas purchased Wedge Dia-log and 30-D Geophysical, two energy services companies, in 1998.

Western Atlas Employees Good Government Fund (C00301416)
*Phone: (310) 888-2500 * Fax: (310) 888-2848 * 360 N. Crescent Dr., Beverly Hills, CA 90210-4867 * Treasurer: Lori J. Segale*

	1993-94	1995-96	1997	Totals
Receipts	$0	$47,585	$11,639	$59,224
Disburse	0	22,546	36,299	58,845
Cash	0	25,048	393	n/a
Contributions	0	22,500	125	22,625
Republicans	0	19,000	125	19,125
No. of Cand.	*0*	*31*	*1*	*32*
House	0	12,000	125	12,125
Senate	0	7,000	0	7,000
Democrats	0	3,500	0	3,500
No. of Cand.	*0*	*6*	*0*	*6*
House	0	3,500	0	3,500
Senate	0	0	0	0
Incumbents	0	17,500	125	17,625
Challengers	0	5,000	0	5,000
Open Seat	0	0	0	0
Winners	0	16,000	n/a	16,000
Losers	0	6,500	n/a	6,500

Whirlpool Corp.

Phone: (616) 923-4647
701 Main St., Maildrop 9025, St. Joseph, MI 49085
Web: www.WhirlpoolCorp.com

Whirlpool makes home appliances and related products for home and commercial use, including laundry machines, cooking appliances and refrigeration and room air conditioning equipment. The publicly traded company has 48,000 employees and posted $8.6 billion in 1997 sales.

In June 1996, Whirlpool and Daiichi Corp. entered into a deal that allowed Whirlpool to sell its products through Daiichi in Japan. In addition, the two companies are developing products specifically for the Japanese market.

Whirlpool Political Action Committee (C00039040) *Address: same as sponsor * Treasurer: Dennis M. Kennedy * Contact: Michael Thompson, Gov. Relations Dir.*

	1993-94	1995-96	1997	Totals
Receipts	$27,732	$25,954	$10,161	$63,847
Disburse	29,327	25,136	1,500	55,963
Cash	5,050	5,873	12,697	n/a
Contributions	25,900	21,000	1,500	48,400
Republicans	25,900	20,500	1,500	47,900
No. of Cand.	*40*	*34*	*1*	*75*
House	9,900	11,000	1,500	22,400
Senate	16,000	9,500	0	25,500
Democrats	0	500	0	500
No. of Cand.	*0*	*1*	*0*	*1*
House	0	500	0	500
Senate	0	0	0	0
Incumbents	9,900	11,700	1,500	23,100
Challengers	6,300	3,400	0	9,700
Open Seat	9,700	5,900	0	15,600
Winners	19,800	15,000	n/a	34,800
Losers	6,100	6,000	n/a	12,100

Wrangler Inc.

Phone: (910) 373-3400
335 Church Ct., Greensboro, NC 27401
Web: www.wrangler.com

Wrangler, formerly Blue Bell Inc., is a subsidiary of VF Corp., a publicly held company that makes jeans and other apparel. In addition to Wrangler, its other brands include: Jansport, Jantzen, Lee, Lee Printwear, Joe Boxer and Vanity Fair.

Established in the 1890s, VFC has more than $5 billion in annual sales. Wrangler's line features the cowboy cut jeans, Rustler, Wrangler Rugged Wear, Wrangler Hero, Wrangler for Women and Timber Creek.

Blue Bell Inc. Employees' Political Action Committee (C00093971) *Address: same as sponsor * Treasurer: Charles B. Conklin*

	1993-94	1995-96	1997	Totals
Receipts	$4,248	$4,489	$810	$9,547
Disburse	3,775	20,032	381	24,188
Cash	29,846	14,311	14,740	n/a
Contributions	3,000	17,000	0	20,000
Republicans	3,000	17,000	0	20,000
No. of Cand.	*2*	*3*	*0*	*5*
House	0	7,000	0	7,000
Senate	3,000	10,000	0	13,000
Democrats	0	0	0	0
No. of Cand.	*0*	*0*	*0*	*0*
House	0	0	0	0
Senate	0	0	0	0
Incumbents	1,000	2,000	0	3,000
Challengers	0	0	0	0
Open Seat	2,000	15,000	0	17,000
Winners	1,000	17,000	n/a	18,000
Losers	2,000	0	n/a	2,000

Xerox Corp.

*Phone: (203) 968-3000 * Fax: (203) 968-4559*
P.O. Box 1600, 800 Long Ridge Rd., Stamford, CT 06904
Web: www.xerox.com

Xerox, No. 51 on the 1996 Fortune 500 list, sells fax machines, printers, scanners and copiers, as well as PC and workstation software. The publicly held company also sells supplies (ink, paper and toner) and provides a document outsourcing service for larger customers. Sales in 1997 were $18 billion. Xerox employs 86,700 people.

Color digital copiers are the company's fastest-growing division, but more than half of Xerox's revenue comes from low-tech analog devices.

Xerox distributes its products in the western hemisphere through divisions and wholly owned subsidiaries. In Europe, Africa, the Middle East and parts of Asia including Hong Kong, India and China, the company distributes through Rank Xerox Limited and related companies in which it has an 80 percent financial interest. In Japan and other areas of Asia, document processing products are distributed by Fuji Xerox Co. Ltd.

Team Xerox Political Action Committee (TXP) (C00207258)
*Phone: (202) 414-1200 * Fax: (202) 414-1217 * 1401 H St. N.W., Suite 200, Washington, DC 20005 * Treasurer: Jeremiah J. Mahoney * Contact: Rita Allen, Administrator*

	1993-94	1995-96	1997	Totals
Receipts	$47,219	$36,609	$22,326	$106,154
Disburse	53,575	34,000	0	87,575
Cash	15,107	17,718	35,271	n/a
Contributions	53,500	34,000	0	87,500
Republicans	13,750	19,500	0	33,250
No. of Cand.	*23*	*33*	*0*	*56*
House	7,750	15,500	0	23,250
Senate	6,000	4,000	0	10,000
Democrats	39,750	14,500	0	54,250
No. of Cand.	*46*	*23*	*0*	*69*
House	30,250	12,500	0	42,750
Senate	9,500	2,000	0	11,500
Incumbents	53,500	34,000	0	87,500
Challengers	0	0	0	0
Open Seat	0	0	0	0
Winners	49,750	32,500	n/a	82,250
Losers	3,750	1,500	n/a	5,250

Misc. Services

American Rental Association

*Phone: (309) 764-2475 * Fax: (309) 764-1533*
1900 19th St., Moline, IL 61265
Web: www.ararental.org

The American Rental Association represents the equipment rental industry. ARA provides educational materials, annual conventions and advertising to its members. In addition, through Ardi Services Inc., the association provides rental insurance.

ARA consists of more than 4,060 member rental businesses and more than 200 associate members. It also has 1,617 branch locations.

In 1997, ARA lobbied Congress to repeal or reduce the inheritance tax and to reduce the capital gains tax rates for individuals and corporations. In addition, it has lobbied to support a uniform product liability law that clearly defines the respective responsibilities of manufacturers, sellers and users of products for product-related injuries.

American Rental Association Political Action Committee (ARAPAC) (C00107615) *Address: same as sponsor * Treasurer: James R. Irish * Contact: Jay Lageschulte, Chairperson*

	1993-94	1995-96	1997	Totals
Receipts	$19,786	$48,213	$8,019	$76,018
Disburse	19,697	37,611	1,717	59,025
Cash	1,105	11,709	18,012	n/a
Contributions	16,367	33,557	1,702	51,626
Republicans	16,367	32,555	1,602	50,524
No. of Cand.	*29*	*54*	*8*	*91*
House	11,362	23,045	1,402	35,809
Senate	5,005	9,510	200	14,715
Democrats	0	1,002	100	1,102
No. of Cand.	*0*	*2*	*1*	*3*
House	0	1,002	100	1,102
Senate	0	0	0	0
Incumbents	4,849	19,536	1,602	25,987
Challengers	7,013	9,515	100	16,628
Open Seat	4,505	4,506	0	9,011
Winners	12,361	19,033	n/a	31,394
Losers	4,006	14,524	n/a	18,530

Association of Progressive Rental Organizations

*Phone: (512) 794-0095 * Fax: (512) 794-0097*
9015 Mountain Ridge Dr., Suite 220, Austin, TX 78759
Web: www.apro-rto.com

The Association of Progressive Rental Organizations is the only national trade association for the rental-purchase industry. Established in 1980, its members include dealers who rent furniture, electronics, major appliances, computers, jewelry and other products with an option to buy.

APRO and its member businesses support federal legislation that would include strong consumer protections in regulations governing the rental-purchase industry. APRO lobbying efforts resulted in an IRS 1995 ruling that defined the rent-to-own transaction as a lease, not a sale, for tax purposes. APRO also supports a regulatory system that legally defines the rent-to-own transaction as a no-obligation consumer lease with an ownership option.

Association of Progressive Rental Organizations Political Action Committee - RentPAC (C00166223) *Address: same as sponsor * Treasurer: Ronald Waters * Contact: Larry Sutton, Chairman*

	1993-94	1995-96	1997	Totals
Receipts	$66,206	$49,244	$12,400	$127,850
Disburse	54,000	54,086	15,000	123,086
Cash	12,243	7,400	4,843	n/a
Contributions	46,500	48,650	15,000	110,150
Republicans	7,000	25,400	10,500	42,900
No. of Cand.	*8*	*26*	*12*	*46*
House	3,000	19,300	7,500	29,800
Senate	4,000	6,100	3,000	13,100
Democrats	39,500	23,250	4,500	67,250
No. of Cand.	*45*	*26*	*7*	*78*
House	29,000	17,250	3,500	49,750
Senate	10,500	6,000	1,000	17,500

(Data for Association of Progressive Rental Organizations continued)

Incumbents	43,500	43,650	15,000	102,150
Challengers	0	1,000	0	1,000
Open Seat	3,000	4,000	0	7,000
Winners	32,000	39,150	n/a	71,150
Losers	14,500	9,500	n/a	24,000

Equipment Leasing Association of America

*Phone: (703) 527-8655 * Fax: (703) 527-2649*
4301 N. Fairfax Dr., Suite 550, Arlington, VA 22201-1607
Web: www.elaonline.com

The Equipment Leasing Association is a nonprofit organization representing the equipment leasing and finance industry to the business community, government and the media.

Established in 1961, ELA has about 750 member companies. The association provides a variety of programs, information and education to its membership and the public. It also publishes various books and statistical materials in addition to the magazine Equipment Leasing Today.

Equipment Leasing Association LeasePAC Committee (C00132282) *Address: same as sponsor * Treasurer: Michael J. Fleming * Contact: Jim Possehl, Chairman*

	1993-94	1995-96	1997	Totals
Receipts	$132,155	$123,200	$90,477	$345,832
Disburse	108,314	163,784	40,440	312,538
Cash	84,041	43,461	93,499	n/a
Contributions	88,100	119,950	31,300	239,350
Republicans	36,500	95,650	23,000	155,150
No. of Cand.	*33*	*38*	*15*	*86*
House	16,500	41,150	13,000	70,650
Senate	20,000	54,500	10,000	84,500
Democrats	50,600	24,300	8,300	83,200
No. of Cand.	*40*	*18*	*7*	*65*
House	36,100	16,800	4,300	57,200
Senate	14,500	7,500	4,000	26,000
Incumbents	74,600	111,450	28,300	214,350
Challengers	5,000	1,500	3,000	9,500
Open Seat	8,500	6,500	0	15,000
Winners	75,850	100,950	n/a	176,800
Losers	12,250	19,000	n/a	31,250

Mail Boxes Etc.

*Phone: (619) 455-8800 * Fax: (619) 625-3160*
6060 Cornerstone Ct. W., San Diego, CA 92121-3795
*Web: www.mbe.com * E-mail: dgreen@mbe.com*

Mail Boxes Etc. operates a 3,500-store postal and office services franchise, making it the largest company of its type in the world.

The company was purchased by U.S. Office Products Co., a public company, in November 1997, but maintains its San Diego headquarters. In 1996, Mail Boxes Etc. reported revenues of $59 million.

Mail Boxes Etc. was founded in California in 1980 as an alternative to retail services provided by the U.S. Post Office. The company's services include packing, shipping, photocopying and faxing. The company also provides 24-hour mailboxes and sells office supplies.

Mail Boxes Etc. Political Action Committee (C00256230) *Address: same as sponsor * Treasurer: Dan Green * Contact: David Bennett, Chairman*

	1993-94	1995-96	1997	Totals
Receipts	$51,519	$84,385	$40,717	$176,621
Disburse	27,886	103,746	20,065	151,697
Cash	24,961	5,598	26,248	n/a
Contributions	4,500	7,650	4,900	17,050
Republicans	3,000	6,650	4,900	14,550
No. of Cand.	*5*	*8*	*5*	*18*
House	3,000	6,650	4,900	14,550
Senate	0	0	0	0
Democrats	1,500	1,000	0	2,500
No. of Cand.	*2*	*2*	*0*	*4*
House	1,500	1,000	0	2,500
Senate	0	0	0	0
Incumbents	4,500	7,650	4,900	17,050
Challengers	0	0	0	0
Open Seat	0	0	0	0
Winners	4,500	7,650	n/a	12,150
Losers	0	0	n/a	0

National Funeral Directors Association

*Phone: (414) 541-2500 * Fax: (414) 541-1909*
11121 W. Oklahoma Ave., Milwaukee, WI 53227
Web: www.nfda.org

The National Funeral Directors Association represents about 15,000 individual funeral home directors — about one-quarter of all licensed funeral service personnel in the United States.

Established in 1882, the NFDA is the largest funeral director association in the country. Its interests include Federal Trade Commission regulations which stipulate the pricing and sales practices of funeral homes. It is also interested in occupational health and safety regulations and many of the issues that affect small businesses.

National Funeral Directors Association of the United States Inc. Political Action Committee (NFDA-PAC) (C00204008) *Phone: (202) 530-5308 * Fax: (202) 530-5309 * 2000 L St. N.W., Suite 200, Washington, DC 20036 * Treasurer: David R. Pearson * Contact: John Fitch Jr., Dir. of Gov. Affairs*

	1993-94	1995-96	1997	Totals
Receipts	$66,867	$96,144	$77,618	$240,629
Disburse	27,900	19,040	55,473	102,413
Cash	46,277	123,382	145,528	n/a
Contributions	27,900	18,300	49,750	95,950
Republicans	13,650	15,300	34,600	63,550
No. of Cand.	*14*	*21*	*42*	*77*
House	6,150	9,800	28,100	44,050
Senate	7,500	5,500	6,500	19,500
Democrats	14,250	3,000	14,150	31,400
No. of Cand.	*14*	*5*	*18*	*37*
House	11,750	3,000	7,650	22,400
Senate	2,500	0	6,500	9,000
Incumbents	18,400	12,300	49,250	79,950
Challengers	500	1,500	500	2,500
Open Seat	9,000	3,500	0	12,500
Winners	18,400	15,800	n/a	34,200
Losers	9,500	2,500	n/a	12,000

National Pest Control Association

*Phone: (703) 573-8330 * Fax: (703) 573-4116*
8100 Oak St., Dunn Loring, VA 22027
Web: www.nationalpest.org

The National Pest Control Association represents about 4,000 pest management businesses located throughout the world. The organization monitors regulations that affect pesticide use and provides members with technical information.

National Pest Control Association Political Action Committee (C00083915) *Address: same as sponsor * Treasurer: Robert M. Rosenberg * Contact: Paul Adams, Chairperson*

	1993-94	1995-96	1997	Totals
Receipts	$80,928	$76,896	$49,032	$206,856
Disburse	54,940	59,725	16,484	131,149
Cash	63,551	80,733	112,337	n/a
Contributions	54,700	59,000	14,905	128,605
Republicans	30,350	37,800	7,250	75,400
No. of Cand.	*31*	*29*	*8*	*68*
House	28,350	29,300	5,750	63,400
Senate	2,000	8,500	1,500	12,000
Democrats	24,350	21,200	7,155	52,705
No. of Cand.	*22*	*15*	*5*	*42*
House	23,850	21,200	7,155	52,205
Senate	500	0	0	500
Incumbents	50,950	48,000	14,905	113,855
Challengers	750	1,000	0	1,750
Open Seat	2,500	10,000	0	12,500
Winners	46,200	54,000	n/a	100,200
Losers	8,500	5,000	n/a	13,500

Orkin Exterminating Co. Inc.

*Phone: (404) 888-2874 * Fax: (404) 888-2732*
2170 Piedmont Rd. N.E., Atlanta, GA 30324
Web: www.orkin.com

Based in Atlanta, Orkin Exterminating provides pest and termite control services. The company has more than 400 branches serving more than 1.6 million customers across the nation.

Orkin, a division of Rollins Inc., has about 10,000 employees and its total revenue in 1997 was $750 million.

Orkin Exterminating Co. Inc. Political Action Committee (C00131219) *Address: same as sponsor * Treasurer: Thomas Diederich*

	1993-94	1995-96	1997	Totals
Receipts	$27,834	$13,645	$0	$41,479
Disburse	23,300	29,183	3,500	55,983
Cash	35,089	19,543	16,043	n/a
Contributions	18,300	24,000	2,000	44,300
Republicans	10,500	7,000	1,000	18,500
No. of Cand.	*9*	*6*	*1*	*16*
House	9,500	5,000	1,000	15,500
Senate	1,000	2,000	0	3,000
Democrats	7,800	17,000	1,000	25,800
No. of Cand.	*7*	*6*	*1*	*14*
House	6,300	16,000	1,000	23,300
Senate	1,500	1,000	0	2,500
Incumbents	12,800	9,500	2,000	24,300
Challengers	2,000	2,500	0	4,500
Open Seat	3,500	12,000	0	15,500
Winners	16,500	10,500	n/a	27,000
Losers	1,800	13,500	n/a	15,300

Service Corp. International

*Phone: (713) 522-5141 * Fax: (713) 525-5217*
1929 Allen Pkwy., Houston, TX 77019
*Web: www.sci-corp.com * E-mail: cfhughes@world.att.net*

Service Corp. International is the largest funeral and cemetery company in the world.

The public company provides funeral and burial services to about 500,000 families each year, more than any other company. During 1997, about half of those services took place in the United States and Canada, although the company also maintains major operations in France, England and Australia. As of December 1997, SCI operated 3,127 funeral service locations, 392 cemeteries and 166 crematoria worldwide.

With about 30,000 employees worldwide, SCI had 1997 revenues of $2.5 billion.

Service Corp. International Political Action Committee (SRV/PAC) (C00173096) *Address: same as sponsor * Treasurer: George Champagne * Contact: Caressa Hughes, Dir. of Gov. Affairs*

	1993-94	1995-96	1997	Totals
Receipts	$108,610	$152,408	$89,467	$350,485
Disburse	135,650	118,860	111,713	366,223
Cash	108,243	141,802	119,559	n/a
Contributions	41,400	33,775	28,000	103,175
Republicans	20,300	23,850	11,000	55,150
No. of Cand.	*9*	*19*	*9*	*37*
House	15,300	17,100	9,000	41,400
Senate	5,000	6,750	2,000	13,750
Democrats	21,100	9,925	17,000	48,025
No. of Cand.	*15*	*14*	*9*	*38*
House	11,600	7,925	3,000	22,525
Senate	9,500	2,000	14,000	25,500
Incumbents	35,100	20,925	27,000	83,025
Challengers	5,500	2,250	0	7,750
Open Seat	800	10,600	1,000	12,400
Winners	33,100	27,275	n/a	60,375
Losers	8,300	6,500	n/a	14,800

Textile Rental Services Association of America

*Phone: (954) 457-7555 * Fax: (954) 457-3890*
1130 E. Hallandale Beach Blvd., P.O. Box 1283, Hallandale, FL 33009
Web: www.trsa.org

Textile Rental Services Association of America represents the textile rental industry. The industry delivers professionally cleaned uniforms, tablecloths, bed linen, floor mats, towels and health care apparel and linen to thousands of businesses and organizations each day with its fleet of more than 17,000 trucks. Textile rental companies provide services to four major markets: hospitality linen supply, uniform rental, health care linen or uniform rental and dust control.

TRSA is the industry's largest trade association, accounting for 75 percent of the uniform rental market and 90 percent of the linen supply market. Serving both textile rental members and their suppliers, TRSA acts as a clearinghouse for industry information.

Textile Rental Services Association of America Political Action Committee (TRSAPAC) (C00279828) *Phone: (202) 833-8395 * Fax: (202) 833-0018 * 1064 21st St. N.W., Washington, DC 20007-4492 * Treasurer: John J. Contney*

	1993-94	1995-96	1997	Totals
Receipts	$48,054	$28,949	$18,454	$95,457
Disburse	41,229	34,258	4,504	79,991
Cash	6,826	2,408	16,360	n/a
Contributions	30,100	32,100	2,750	64,950
Republicans	26,500	26,500	2,500	55,500
No. of Cand.	*42*	*42*	*9*	*93*
House	15,500	16,500	2,500	34,500
Senate	11,000	10,000	0	21,000
Democrats	3,600	5,600	250	9,450
No. of Cand.	*8*	*11*	*2*	*21*
House	3,600	3,100	250	6,950
Senate	0	2,500	0	2,500
Incumbents	12,100	21,100	2,250	35,450
Challengers	8,250	4,000	0	12,250
Open Seat	9,750	7,000	500	17,250
Winners	24,100	27,100	n/a	51,200
Losers	6,000	5,000	n/a	11,000

Recreation/Live Entertainment

Bowling Proprietors Association

*Phone: (817) 649-5105 * Fax: (817) 633-2940*
615 Six Flags Dr. (76011), P.O. Box 5802, Arlington, TX 76005
Web: www.bpaa.com

The Bowling Proprietors Association of America represents about 3,100 bowling center proprietors. Founded in 1932, the nonprofit association offers tournaments, seminars and expositions.

BPAA's PAC contributes to elected officials who are sympathetic to small business issues.

Bowling Proprietors Association of America PAC (C00079855) *Address: same as sponsor * Treasurer: Judith L. King * Contact: Bob Herbolshiemer, Chairman*

	1993-94	1995-96	1997	Totals
Receipts	$57,286	$45,688	$10,568	$113,542
Disburse	57,350	44,431	4,500	106,281
Cash	19,068	20,324	26,816	n/a
Contributions	66,950	44,400	4,500	115,850
Republicans	57,250	41,900	4,500	103,650
No. of Cand.	*81*	*37*	*7*	*125*
House	43,950	35,700	4,500	84,150
Senate	13,300	6,200	0	19,500
Democrats	9,300	2,500	0	11,800
No. of Cand.	*15*	*4*	*0*	*19*
House	7,300	1,000	0	8,300
Senate	2,000	1,500	0	3,500
Incumbents	51,500	38,800	4,500	94,800
Challengers	1,700	2,700	0	4,400
Open Seat	13,750	2,900	0	16,650
Winners	60,950	38,300	n/a	99,250
Losers	6,000	6,100	n/a	12,100

Retail Sales

Amway Corp.

*Phone: (616) 787-6000 * Fax: (616) 787-6177*
7575 E. Fulton St., Ada, MI 49355-0001
Web: www.amway.com

Amway is one of the world's largest direct-sales companies, offering customers more than 400 commercial, home care, nutrition and personal-care products. About 13,000 people sell Amway products, generating an estimated $6 billion in 1997 sales.

Amway is privately owned by the families of founders Richard DeVos and Jay Van Andel and ranked No. 24 on the Forbes list of top private companies in 1996. It was founded in 1959 in Ada, Mich. and is still headquartered there. DeVos is a major contributor to the Republican Party, having contributed at least $1 million in soft money during 1997, according to FEC records.

Amway, short for "American Way," and its affiliates operate in more than 75 countries and territories, and sales in foreign markets — which have grown considerably in the 1990s — comprise about 70 percent of Amway's sales.

Amway Political Action Committee (C00034884) *Address: same as sponsor * Treasurer: Mark Kuper*

	1993-94	1995-96	1997	Totals
Receipts	$22,103	$30,359	$23,714	$76,176
Disburse	21,622	31,000	0	52,622
Cash	1,323	683	24,398	n/a
Contributions	21,600	31,000	0	52,600
Republicans	21,600	31,000	0	52,600
No. of Cand.	*37*	*45*	*0*	*82*
House	13,600	17,000	0	30,600
Senate	8,000	14,000	0	22,000
Democrats	0	0	0	0
No. of Cand.	*0*	*0*	*0*	*0*
House	0	0	0	0
Senate	0	0	0	0
Incumbents	13,350	25,500	0	38,850
Challengers	3,500	3,000	0	6,500
Open Seat	4,750	2,500	0	7,250
Winners	20,600	23,000	n/a	43,600
Losers	1,000	8,000	n/a	9,000

Circuit City Stores Inc.

*Phone: (804) 527-4014 * Fax: (804) 527-4164*
9950 Mayland Dr., Richmond, VA 23233-1464
Web: www.circuitcity.com

Circuit City Stores sells brand-name consumer electronics, major appliances, personal computers and music software. With 500 locations nationwide and more than 40,000 employees, the company is ranked No. 204 on the Fortune 500. A subsidiary, CarMax, operates 17 fixed-price used car sales stores. Circuit City revenues totaled more than $7.6 billion in 1997.

The Richmond, Va.-based company is planning to open 56 new superstores and to upgrade 11 existing stores by the end of 1998. The following year Circuit City plans to open 50 superstores, including a group in the New York metropolitan area.

Circuit City sells a wide range of consumer electronics including: televisions, digital satellite systems, home stereo systems, compact disc players, car stereo and security systems, computers and fax machines.

Circuit City Stores Inc. Political Action Committee (Circuit City PAC) (C00296632) *Address: same as sponsor * Treasurer: Julie M. Mullian * Contact: Richard Sharp, Chairman*

	1993-94	1995-96	1997	Totals
Receipts	$40,185	$50,090	$42,468	$132,743
Disburse	6,944	67,734	26,250	100,928
Cash	33,240	24,427	40,650	n/a
Contributions	5,850	53,544	21,750	81,144
Republicans	4,850	52,044	21,250	78,144
No. of Cand.	*7*	*53*	*26*	*86*
House	3,850	29,545	8,750	42,145
Senate	1,000	22,499	12,500	35,999
Democrats	0	1,500	500	2,000
No. of Cand.	*0*	*2*	*1*	*3*
House	0	1,500	500	2,000
Senate	0	0	0	0
Incumbents	1,600	33,444	20,750	55,794
Challengers	4,000	9,600	0	13,600
Open Seat	250	10,500	1,000	11,750
Winners	2,850	33,944	n/a	36,794
Losers	3,000	19,600	n/a	22,600

Dayton Hudson Corp.

*Phone: (612) 370-6866 * Fax: (612) 370-5500*
777 Nicollet Mall, Minneapolis, MN 55402
*Web: www.dhc.com * E-mail: ngarvis@aol.com*

Dayton Hudson Corp., which owns Target stores, is the fifth-largest general merchandise retailer in the nation, operating more than 1,000 retail stores and employing more than 200,000 people.

The company generated the majority of its $27 billion in 1997 sales from Target discount stores, which are located in 33 states. Dayton Hudson also operates Mervyn's, a middle-market department store with locations in 16 western, southern and midwestern states. The company also runs 64 stores through three upscale department store chains — Dayton's, Hudson's and Marshall Field's.

Dayton Hudson Corp. DHCitizen's Federal Forum (C00098061) *Address: same as sponsor * Treasurer: Nathan Garvis*

	1993-94	1995-96	1997	Totals
Receipts	$68,844	$83,745	$44,819	$197,408
Disburse	67,000	104,840	25,039	196,879
Cash	36,024	14,933	34,715	n/a
Contributions	68,800	94,200	17,038	180,038
Republicans	38,350	66,750	8,500	113,600
No. of Cand.	*38*	*42*	*12*	*92*
House	28,250	34,750	5,500	68,500
Senate	10,100	32,000	3,000	45,100
Democrats	22,700	27,450	6,019	56,169
No. of Cand.	*27*	*19*	*7*	*53*
House	14,700	19,450	5,519	39,669
Senate	8,000	8,000	500	16,500
Incumbents	38,350	62,700	17,038	118,088
Challengers	6,100	21,000	0	27,100
Open Seat	24,350	10,500	0	34,850
Winners	55,200	63,200	n/a	118,400
Losers	13,600	31,000	n/a	44,600

Direct Marketing Association

*Phone: (202) 955-5030 * Fax: (202) 955-0085*
1111 19th St. N.W., Suite 1100, Washington, DC 20036
*Web: www.the-dma.org * E-mail: govaffairs@the-dma.org*

The Direct Marketing Association is one of the largest trade associations for businesses interested in database marketing. DMA has more than 3,600 member companies from the United States and 49 other nations. First Union National Bank and Randstad Staffing Services are among the group's members.

The DMA handles consumer complaints about telephone and mail-order purchases. It also operates a service that allows consumers to remove their names from mailing and telephone sales lists.

The Direct Marketing Educational Foundation provides career information and guidance for people interested in marketing. It also calls for improved direct marketing instruction at the college level.

DMA's PAC merged with the Advertising Mail Marketing Association's PAC in 1996. The new PAC, which operates under the DMA, will be called Direct Voice.

Direct Marketing Association Political Action Committee (C00235309) *Address: same as sponsor * Treasurer: Richard A. Barton * Contact: Mark Micali, V.P. Govt. Affairs*

	1993-94	1995-96	1997	Totals
Receipts	$37,650	$106,308	$80,801	$224,759
Disburse	33,813	93,399	83,554	210,766
Cash	3,968	16,876	14,124	n/a
Contributions	34,192	84,305	69,254	187,751
Republicans	6,850	56,932	33,254	97,036
No. of Cand.	*12*	*54*	*33*	*99*
House	5,850	25,262	14,500	45,612
Senate	1,000	31,670	18,754	51,424
Democrats	27,342	27,373	35,250	89,965
No. of Cand.	*36*	*29*	*40*	*105*
House	16,921	14,375	17,250	48,546
Senate	10,421	12,998	18,000	41,419
Incumbents	33,692	64,887	65,754	164,333
Challengers	0	3,920	1,000	4,920
Open Seat	500	15,498	2,500	18,498
Winners	27,896	66,432	n/a	94,328
Losers	6,296	17,873	n/a	24,169

Advertising Mail Marketing Association Political Action Committee (C00167239) *1333 F St. N.W., Suite 710, Washington, DC 20004 * Treasurer: Burt Stuttman*

The Advertising Mail Marketing Association represents companies that make up the $34.6 billion direct-mail industry.

AMMA's PAC merged with the Direct Marketing Association PAC in 1996. The DMA PAC (C00235309) will be renamed Direct Voice.

	1993-94	1995-96	1997	Totals
Receipts	$17,009	$12,251	$0	$29,260
Disburse	21,814	21,537	512	43,863
Cash	9,797	512	0	n/a
Contributions	25,000	11,000	0	36,000
Republicans	13,750	10,500	0	24,250
No. of Cand.	*8*	*7*	*0*	*15*

House	11,750	6,500	0	18,250
Senate	2,000	4,000	0	6,000
Democrats	11,250	500	0	11,750
No. of Cand.	*11*	*1*	*0*	*12*
House	8,500	500	0	9,000
Senate	2,750	0	0	2,750
Incumbents	23,500	7,250	0	30,750
Challengers	0	2,250	0	2,250
Open Seat	1,500	1,500	0	3,000
Winners	20,750	6,250	n/a	27,000
Losers	4,250	4,750	n/a	9,000

Direct Selling Association

*Phone: (202) 293-5760 * Fax: (202) 463-4569*
1666 K St. N.W., Suite 1010, Washington, DC 20006-2808
*Web: www.dsa.org * E-mail: info@dsa.org*

The Direct Selling Association is a national trade group of businesses which make and distribute products sold directly to the consumer. Full membership in the association is granted after a one-year screening period, and members agree to a code of ethics.

Its members include Avon Products Inc., Golden Pride International, Mary Kay Inc., Nature's Own and Tupperware Corp. Estimated retail sales for the industry in 1996 were $20 billion.

Direct Selling Association Political Action Committee (C00078535) *Address: same as sponsor * Treasurer: Joseph N. Mariano*

	1993-94	1995-96	1997	Totals
Receipts	$30,677	$16,274	$9,002	$55,953
Disburse	29,975	18,950	5,669	54,594
Cash	3,232	560	3,894	n/a
Contributions	26,475	14,100	5,666	46,241
Republicans	7,000	4,500	0	11,500
No. of Cand.	*10*	*5*	*0*	*15*
House	4,000	1,500	0	5,500
Senate	3,000	3,000	0	6,000
Democrats	19,475	9,600	5,666	34,741
No. of Cand.	*24*	*12*	*6*	*42*
House	17,975	6,350	4,666	28,991
Senate	1,500	3,250	1,000	5,750
Incumbents	24,375	10,100	5,666	40,141
Challengers	2,100	2,250	0	4,350
Open Seat	0	1,750	0	1,750
Winners	24,375	11,100	n/a	35,475
Losers	2,100	3,000	n/a	5,100

Federated Department Stores Inc.

*Phone: (513) 579-7000 * Fax: (513) 579-7555*
Seven W. Seventh St., Cincinnati, OH 45202
Web: www.federated-fds.com

Federated Department Stores is the nation's largest operator of department stores with 412 stores in 36 states. Its franchises include: Macy's, Rich's, Bloomingdale's, Stern's, The Bon Marche, Burdines, Goldsmith's, Lazarus, Aeropostale and Charter Club. The publicly traded company has 120,000 employees and posted 1997 sales of $15.6 billion.

Founded in 1930, FDS stores sell a wide range of merchandise, including men's, women's and children's apparel and accessories, cosmetics, home furnishings and other consumer goods.

Federated Department Stores Inc. Political Action Committee (C00091660) *Address: same as sponsor * Treasurer: Joel Belsky * Contact: James M. Zimmerman, Chairperson and CEO*

	1993-94	1995-96	1997	Totals
Receipts	$0	$17,147	$0	$17,147
Disburse	57	19,000	0	19,057
Cash	34,578	32,725	32,725	n/a
Contributions	0	17,000	0	17,000
Republicans	0	17,000	0	17,000
No. of Cand.	*0*	*16*	*0*	*16*
House	0	15,000	0	15,000
Senate	0	2,000	0	2,000
Democrats	0	0	0	0
No. of Cand.	*0*	*0*	*0*	*0*
House	0	0	0	0
Senate	0	0	0	0
Incumbents	0	13,000	0	13,000
Challengers	0	1,000	0	1,000
Open Seat	0	3,000	0	3,000
Winners	0	11,000	n/a	11,000
Losers	0	6,000	n/a	6,000

Footwear Distributors & Retailers of America

*Phone: (202) 737-5660 * Fax: (202) 638-2615*
1319 F St. N.W., Suite 700, Washington, DC 20004
*Web: www.fdra.org * E-mail: fdra@fdra.org*

Footwear Distributors & Retailers of America is a Washington-based trade association whose 100 member companies operate 20,000 shoe retail outlets and account for nearly three-quarters of U.S. shoe sales.

FDRA focuses its efforts on shoe-specific issues not dealt with by other trade associations. The association lobbies on most favored nation trading status for China, U.S. Customs classification of footwear, Federal Trade Commission shoe labeling standards and "Made in USA" issues. It supports free trade efforts in overseas retail markets, including Europe, Mexico, Argentina, Colombia and Brazil.

Footwear Distributors & Retailers of America Inc. Political Action Committee (C00248427) *Address: same as sponsor * Treasurer: Peter T. Mangione * Contact: Peter Mangione*

	1993-94	1995-96	1997	Totals
Receipts	$27,818	$15,050	$7,200	$50,068
Disburse	26,828	13,645	9,889	50,362
Cash	1,818	3,223	533	n/a
Contributions	25,550	8,200	9,800	43,550
Republicans	10,050	4,350	7,000	21,400
No. of Cand.	*14*	*10*	*10*	*34*
House	2,550	4,350	4,500	11,400
Senate	7,500	0	2,500	10,000
Democrats	15,500	3,850	2,800	22,150
No. of Cand.	*19*	*10*	*5*	*34*
House	12,500	3,350	2,800	18,650
Senate	3,000	500	0	3,500
Incumbents	20,050	7,200	9,800	37,050
Challengers	0	0	0	0
Open Seat	5,500	1,000	0	6,500
Winners	20,550	8,200	n/a	28,750
Losers	5,000	0	n/a	5,000

Home Depot Inc.

*Phone: (770) 384-5735 * Fax: (770) 384-4522*
2727 Paces Ferry Rd., P.O. Box 724087, Atlanta, GA 31139-4024
*Web: www.homedepot.com * E-mail: carol_tome@homedepot.com*

With 624 stores in 41 states, Home Depot is the largest home improvement retailer in the United States. The publicly traded company, based in Atlanta, has 118,000 employees and posted $24 billion in sales in 1997.

In 1998, the company will expand into South America, where its first store will open in Chile. The company's stores sell building materials, home improvement supplies and lawn and garden products.

Home Depot is credited with combining the economies of scale inherent in a warehouse format with a high level of customer service. In 1998 it was named America's most admired retailer by Fortune magazine for the fifth consecutive year.

The Home Depot Inc. Better Government Committee (C00284885) *Address: same as sponsor * Treasurer: Carol Tomé*

	1993-94	1995-96	1997	Totals
Receipts	$71,317	$119,105	$47,192	$237,614
Disburse	55,067	76,400	28,000	159,467
Cash	16,250	58,955	78,147	n/a
Contributions	37,050	44,400	7,500	88,950
Republicans	27,550	38,400	5,500	71,450
No. of Cand.	*46*	*63*	*8*	*117*
House	17,550	26,900	3,000	47,450
Senate	10,000	11,500	2,500	24,000
Democrats	9,500	6,000	2,000	17,500
No. of Cand.	*18*	*10*	*3*	*31*
House	8,500	5,000	1,000	14,500
Senate	1,000	1,000	1,000	3,000
Incumbents	23,050	31,900	7,000	61,950
Challengers	7,500	3,000	0	10,500
Open Seat	6,500	9,500	500	16,500
Winners	32,050	34,900	n/a	66,950
Losers	5,000	9,500	n/a	14,500

International Council of Shopping Centers

*Phone: (703) 549-7404 * Fax: (703) 549-8712*
1033 N. Fairfax St., Suite 404, Alexandria, VA 22314
Web: www.icsc.org

The International Council of Shopping Centers is the trade association of the shopping center industry. Founded in 1957, ICSC has 36,000 members in 72 countries.

In 1997, ICSC lobbied against the capital gains tax, stating that it stifles economic growth.

International Council of Shopping Centers Inc. Political Action Committee (ICSC PAC) (C00217638) *Address: same as sponsor * Treasurer: Kemper Freeman Jr. * Contact: Sylvan Cohen, Chairman*

	1993-94	1995-96	1997	Totals
Receipts	$243,244	$218,538	$89,719	$551,501
Disburse	351,792	233,803	42,889	628,484
Cash	108,656	93,401	140,237	n/a
Contributions	326,340	208,303	42,889	577,532
Republicans	215,841	179,803	33,889	429,533
No. of Cand.	*157*	*134*	*43*	*334*
House	139,343	108,803	24,889	273,035
Senate	76,498	71,000	9,000	156,498
Democrats	110,499	28,500	8,500	147,499
No. of Cand.	*79*	*30*	*14*	*123*
House	84,499	18,500	7,500	110,499
Senate	26,000	10,000	1,000	37,000
Incumbents	243,883	141,803	39,889	425,575
Challengers	27,899	20,500	1,000	49,399
Open Seat	54,558	46,000	2,000	102,558
Winners	275,341	150,803	n/a	426,144
Losers	50,999	57,500	n/a	108,499

International Mass Retail Association

*Phone: (703) 841-2300 * Fax: (703) 841-1184*
1700 N. Moore St., Suite 2250, Arlington, VA 22209-1998
Web: www.imra.org

The International Mass Retail Association represents and promotes the mass retail industry and provides various services to its almost 800 members. IMRA programs include conferences, research, government relations, industry development and encouraging productive relations between retail and supplier members.

In 1997, IMRA opposed the Patient Access to Responsible Care Act, saying that its removal of protections in the Employee Retirement Income Security Act would cause multi-state employers to lose the ability to offer nationally uniform benefit plans.

International Mass Retail Association PAC (formerly known as IMRAPAC) (C00112763) *Address: same as sponsor * Treasurer: John Lowenstein*

	1993-94	1995-96	1997	Totals
Receipts	$16,700	$23,875	$0	$40,575
Disburse	17,500	25,000	1,500	44,000
Cash	5,838	4,713	3,213	n/a
Contributions	16,000	21,500	1,500	39,000
Republicans	14,250	20,500	1,500	36,250
No. of Cand.	*28*	*33*	*2*	*63*
House	8,750	12,500	500	21,750
Senate	5,500	8,000	1,000	14,500
Democrats	1,750	1,000	0	2,750
No. of Cand.	*4*	*2*	*0*	*6*
House	1,250	1,000	0	2,250
Senate	500	0	0	500
Incumbents	9,000	13,000	1,500	23,500
Challengers	3,000	3,500	0	6,500
Open Seat	4,000	5,000	0	9,000
Winners	14,500	14,500	n/a	29,000
Losers	1,500	7,000	n/a	8,500

J.C. Penney Co. Inc.

*Phone: (972) 431-1000 * Fax: (972) 431-1977*
6501 Legacy Dr., Plano, TX 75024-3698
Web: www.jcpenney.com

The nation's fourth-leading retailer, J.C. Penney has more than 1,100 department stories throughout the United States, Mexico and Chile. The company brings in about 70 percent of its revenues selling apparel, accessories and home furnishings. J.C. Penney is the largest catalog retailer in the United States and also sells life, accident, health and credit insurance. The company has 250,000 employees, but plans to eliminate about 4,900 jobs during 1998. It posted 1997 sales of $23.6 billion.

In addition to its department store business, the publicly held company owns the fourth-largest drugstore chain in the nation following its 1996 purchase of Eckerd Drugstores. J.C. Penney is combining its Thrift Drug and Fay drugstores under the Eckerd name. In February 1998, Florida's attorney general charged Eckerd with fraudulently billing the state's Medicaid program more than $3 million. The company denied the allegation.

The J.C. Penney PAC has a review committee which determines which candidates to support. J.C. Penney spent more than 90 percent of its overall expenditures during the 1995-96 cycle on congressional races. J.C. Penney contributed to 165 candidates across the nation, most of them Republicans. It concentrated on elections in Texas, where the company's corporate headquarters are located. Sen. Phil Gramm, R-Texas, House Speaker Newt Gingrich, R-Ga., and House Majority Leader Dick Armey, R-Texas, were the top recipients.

J.C. Penney Co. Inc. Political Action Committee (PenneyPAC) (C00042895) *Phone: (202) 862-4811 * Fax: (202) 862-4829 * 1156 15th St. N.W., Suite 1015, Washington, DC 20005 * Treasurer: John Wirtz * Contact: Richard Gill, Gov. Relations Dir.*

	1993-94	1995-96	1997	Totals
Receipts	$277,474	$271,094	$135,169	$683,737
Disburse	271,212	263,250	123,927	658,389
Cash	30,854	38,706	49,954	n/a
Contributions	243,940	243,050	106,400	593,390
Republicans	160,515	210,250	92,600	463,365
No. of Cand.	*170*	*140*	*64*	*374*
House	101,465	136,500	64,600	302,565
Senate	59,050	73,750	28,000	160,800
Democrats	83,425	32,800	13,800	130,025
No. of Cand.	*97*	*25*	*13*	*135*
House	61,925	22,300	6,550	90,775
Senate	21,500	10,500	7,250	39,250
Incumbents	198,015	209,400	102,650	510,065
Challengers	17,925	13,400	2,000	33,325
Open Seat	28,500	20,250	1,500	50,250
Winners	218,890	196,700	n/a	415,590
Losers	25,050	46,350	n/a	71,400

Eckerd Corp. Political Action Committee (EckPAC) (C00041558) *Phone: (813) 395-6000 * Fax: (813) 395-6468 * P.O. Box 4689, Clearwater, FL 34618 * Web: www.eckerd.com * Treasurer: Martin W. Gladysz * Contact: Robert Hannan, Vice Chairperson of Eckerd Corp.*

Eckerd was acquired by J.C. Penney in 1996. Eckerd's PAC has since merged into the J.C. Penney PAC.

	1993-94	1995-96	1997	Totals
Receipts	$33,271	$34,540	$24,947	$92,758
Disburse	41,288	69,083	17,504	127,875
Cash	43,836	9,295	16,739	n/a
Contributions	26,750	42,200	3,250	72,200
Republicans	17,000	23,500	2,000	42,500
No. of Cand.	*26*	*40*	*2*	*68*
House	12,000	17,500	1,000	30,500
Senate	5,000	6,000	1,000	12,000
Democrats	9,750	18,700	1,250	29,700
No. of Cand.	*14*	*18*	*3*	*35*
House	8,250	15,700	500	24,450
Senate	1,500	3,000	750	5,250
Incumbents	21,500	23,000	2,000	46,500
Challengers	2,500	500	0	3,000
Open Seat	2,500	18,700	0	21,200
Winners	20,500	35,000	n/a	55,500
Losers	6,250	7,200	n/a	13,450

Terminated PACs which contributed less than $5,000 during 1995-96 cycle:

Thrift Drug Inc. Political Action Committee (C00252106) *615 Alpha Dr., Pittsburgh, PA 15238-2876 * Treasurer: Beth Dubyak*

Kmart Corp.

*Phone: (248) 643-1000 * Fax: (248) 643-5398*
3100 W. Big Beaver Rd., Troy, MI 48084-3163
*Web: www.kmart.com * E-mail: mviola@kmart.com*

With $31.4 billion in revenue and 2,100 stores throughout 50 states, Kmart is the nation's fifth-largest discount store. The publicly traded Troy, Mich. company has a 9 percent share of the discount retail industry. Kmart also operates 1,558 pharmacies.

Kmart says it is the sixth-largest employer in the United States, with 265,000 employees.

The company is converting many of its stores to the "Big Kmart" format, in which high-frequency, discounted basics and consumables are displayed in the front of the store. Kmart is also promoting its Martha Stewart paint and home collection.

According to the company, there is a Kmart within 15 minutes of 85 percent of homes in the United States.

Kmart has distribution centers in: California, Colorado, Florida, Georgia, Illinois, Kansas, Massachusetts, Michigan, Minnesota, Nevada, New Jersey, North Carolina, Ohio, Pennsylvania and Texas.

Kmart Corp. Political Action Committee (C00085373) *Address: same as sponsor * Treasurer: Michael Viola*

	1993-94	1995-96	1997	Totals
Receipts	$73,162	$56,704	$18,766	$148,632
Disburse	82,694	81,737	18,762	183,193
Cash	32,397	7,367	7,371	n/a
Contributions	55,050	39,150	7,500	101,700
Republicans	41,100	35,500	7,500	84,100
No. of Cand.	*74*	*57*	*10*	*141*
House	16,100	21,500	4,500	42,100
Senate	25,000	14,000	3,000	42,000
Democrats	13,950	3,650	0	17,600
No. of Cand.	*28*	*8*	*0*	*36*
House	8,450	1,900	0	10,350
Senate	5,500	1,750	0	7,250
Incumbents	34,050	18,850	7,500	60,400
Challengers	5,750	10,500	0	16,250
Open Seat	15,250	9,300	0	24,550
Winners	48,050	22,900	n/a	70,950
Losers	7,000	16,250	n/a	23,250

Limited Inc.

*Phone: (614) 479-7070 * Fax: (614) 479-7079*
Three Limited Pkwy., Columbus, OH 43230
Web: www.limited.com

The Limited is a public company that sells and distributes women's apparel, lingerie, men's apparel, personal care products and children's apparel. The Limited employs 123,000 workers at more than 5,600 stores in the United States. The company's net sales in 1997 were $9 billion.

The Limited operates a distribution system which supports the company's retail activities. These activities are conducted under various trade names through the retail stores and catalog divisions of The Limited. The company also is a majority holder or operator of Victoria's Secret, Bath and Body Works and Structure stores, and is spinning off its Abercrombie & Fitch sportswear division.

Limited Inc. Political Action Committee (C00214338) *Address: same as sponsor * Treasurer: Alfred S. Dietzel*

	1993-94	1995-96	1997	Totals
Receipts	$182,359	$205,508	$83,836	$471,703
Disburse	181,115	205,755	100,040	486,910
Cash	19,903	19,665	3,463	n/a
Contributions	58,770	119,500	73,150	251,420
Republicans	37,150	99,000	64,650	200,800
No. of Cand.	*27*	*49*	*32*	*108*
House	14,050	57,500	27,150	98,700
Senate	23,100	41,500	37,500	102,100
Democrats	21,620	20,500	8,500	50,620
No. of Cand.	*16*	*12*	*6*	*34*
House	11,000	12,000	8,500	31,500
Senate	10,620	8,500	0	19,120
Incumbents	38,670	96,000	63,650	198,320
Challengers	600	11,500	3,500	15,600
Open Seat	16,750	12,000	6,000	34,750
Winners	45,550	83,000	n/a	128,550
Losers	13,220	36,500	n/a	49,720

Longs Drugs Stores Inc.

*Phone: (510) 937-1170 * Fax: (510) 210-6886*
141 N. Civic Dr., Walnut Creek, CA 94596
Web: www.longs.com

Longs Drugs Stores operates 345 stores in California, Hawaii, Nevada and Colorado, with sales averaging more than $8 million per store.

Established in the late 1930s, the publicly held company has more than 16,000 employees, 11,000 of whom are members of the company's profit-sharing plan.

Longs' 1997 sales were $2.8 billion with a net income of $58.6 million.

In 1997, Longs Drugs Stores and American Stores Co. announced the merger of their pharmacy benefits management subsidiaries. The joint venture agreement combines the operations of RxAmerica, the PBM subsidiary of American Stores, and Integrated Health Concepts, the PBM subsidiary of Longs. The new PBM joint venture has retained the name RxAmerica.

Longs Drugs Good Government Council (C00106609) *Address: same as sponsor * Treasurer: Clay Selland * Contact: Ronald A. Plomgren, Chairman*

	1993-94	1995-96	1997	Totals
Receipts	$10,132	$15,166	$736	$26,034
Disburse	19,353	20,865	2,816	43,034
Cash	27,799	22,103	20,024	n/a
Contributions	15,975	16,800	500	33,275
Republicans	5,225	10,300	0	15,525
No. of Cand.	*9*	*17*	*0*	*26*
House	5,225	9,300	0	14,525
Senate	0	1,000	0	1,000
Democrats	10,750	6,500	500	17,750
No. of Cand.	*14*	*10*	*1*	*25*
House	7,750	5,500	500	13,750
Senate	3,000	1,000	0	4,000
Incumbents	15,225	12,300	500	28,025
Challengers	750	500	0	1,250
Open Seat	0	4,000	0	4,000
Winners	15,225	13,500	n/a	28,725
Losers	750	3,300	n/a	4,050

Lowe's Companies Inc.

*Phone: (336) 658-4000 * Fax: (336) 658-4766*
P.O. Box 1111 (Highway 268 E.), North Wilkesboro, NC 28656
Web: www.lowes.com

Lowe's Companies is the second-largest home repair and improvement chain in America, with annual sales exceeding $8 billion. It has more than 450 stores in 25 states, mostly in the Southeast and Midwest.

The publicly traded company sells a variety of home improvement products, including plumbing, woodworking, electronics, lawn and garden and home safety items.

Lowe's began as one store in North Wilkesboro, N.C. in 1946. The chain grew because of increased interest in home repair in recent years. Lowe's aims to have 600 stores by 2000.

Lowe's 54,000 employees own 25 percent of the company's stock. It has been selected twice by Doubleday as one of The 100 Best Companies to Work For in America.

Lowe's Companies Inc. Political Action Committee (LowPAC) (C00251751) *Address: same as sponsor * Treasurer: Robert A. Niblock * Contact: Cliff Oxford, Chairman*

	1993-94	1995-96	1997	Totals
Receipts	$11,895	$13,841	$8,524	$34,260
Disburse	7,155	8,500	1,000	16,655
Cash	7,046	12,388	19,913	n/a
Contributions	6,000	7,000	1,000	14,000
Republicans	4,500	3,000	1,000	8,500
No. of Cand.	*10*	*3*	*1*	*14*
House	4,500	3,000	0	7,500
Senate	0	0	1,000	1,000
Democrats	1,500	4,000	0	5,500
No. of Cand.	*3*	*4*	*0*	*7*
House	1,500	3,500	0	5,000
Senate	0	500	0	500
Incumbents	4,500	4,500	1,000	10,000
Challengers	500	2,500	0	3,000
Open Seat	1,000	0	0	1,000
Winners	6,250	3,000	n/a	9,250
Losers	-250	4,000	n/a	3,750

May Department Stores Co.

*Phone: (314) 342-6300 * Fax: (314) 342-3066*
611 Olive St., St. Louis, MO 63101
Web: www.maycompany.com

May Department Stores operates eight regional department store companies nationwide. Holdings include 369 stores in 30 states and the District of Columbia. Founded in 1877, the publicly traded company has grown to 100,000 employees and posted sales of $12.6 billion in 1997.

The department stores are: Lord & Taylor, New York; Hecht's, Washington; Foley's, Houston; Robinsons-May, Los Angeles; Kaufmann's, Pittsburgh; Filene's, Boston; Famous-Barr, St. Louis; and Meier & Frank, Portland, Ore.

In addition, Famous-Barr operates LS Ayres department stores of Indiana, and Hecht's operates Strawbridge stores of Philadelphia, Delaware and New Jersey.

In February 1998, the company announced plans to open 21 new stores during the year.

May Department Stores Co. Political Action Committee (MayPAC) (C00144311) *Address: same as sponsor * Treasurer: Frank J. Williams Jr. * Contact: John Dunham, Chairman*

	1993-94	1995-96	1997	Totals
Receipts	$152,271	$158,151	$89,488	$399,910
Disburse	155,701	140,346	36,820	332,867
Cash	16,019	33,833	86,509	n/a
Contributions	131,500	110,250	22,000	263,750
Republicans	102,000	97,250	20,000	219,250
No. of Cand.	*160*	*137*	*14*	*311*
House	73,500	58,750	10,500	142,750
Senate	28,500	38,500	9,500	76,500
Democrats	29,500	13,000	2,000	44,500
No. of Cand.	*52*	*23*	*3*	*78*
House	24,500	11,000	2,000	37,500
Senate	5,000	2,000	0	7,000
Incumbents	86,500	66,500	22,000	175,000
Challengers	16,500	16,000	0	32,500
Open Seat	29,000	28,750	0	57,750
Winners	117,000	81,250	n/a	198,250
Losers	14,500	29,000	n/a	43,500

Melville Corp.

One Theall Rd., Rye, NY 10580

Melville terminated its PAC on August 15, 1997. The company changed its name to CVS Corp. in 1996. Melville discontinued or closed many of its retail stores: Melville's Meldisco, Footaction, Thom McAn, Linens 'n Things and Bob's.

Melville Corp. Political Action Committee (C00276600) *Address: same as sponsor * Treasurer: Arthur Richards*

	1993-94	1995-96	1997	Totals
Receipts	$5,000	$15,200	$0	$20,200
Disburse	6,515	16,179	2,286	24,980
Cash	3,266	2,286	0	n/a
Contributions	5,500	14,125	0	19,625
Republicans	4,000	9,000	0	13,000
No. of Cand.	*4*	*11*	*0*	*15*
House	3,000	7,500	0	10,500
Senate	1,000	1,500	0	2,500
Democrats	1,500	5,125	0	6,625
No. of Cand.	*2*	*6*	*0*	*8*
House	500	2,375	0	2,875
Senate	1,000	2,750	0	3,750
Incumbents	5,000	9,625	0	14,625
Challengers	500	1,000	0	1,500
Open Seat	0	3,500	0	3,500
Winners	4,000	11,125	n/a	15,125
Losers	1,500	3,000	n/a	4,500

Montgomery Ward & Co. Inc.

*Phone: (312) 467-2000 * Fax: (312) 467-7898*
535 W. Chicago Ave. (24-S), Chicago, IL 60671
Web: www.mward.com

Montgomery Ward & Co. is one of the oldest and largest privately held retailers in the nation.

Its primary business is specialty retailing, focused on apparel, appliances and electronics, jewelry, furniture, housewares and automotive products. Ward's, which has more than 50,000 employees, operates more than 300 stores in 37 states with 15 distribution centers. It also maintains 82 product service centers, making it the second-largest service organization in the nation.

On July 7, 1997, Ward's filed for reorganization under Chapter 11 bankruptcy protection. The company is in the process of reorganizing, while implementing new merchandise and marketing strategies and restructuring its debt.

On July 31, 1997, Ward's received formal approval from U.S. Bankruptcy Court for its full $1-billion Debtor-in-Possession financing. The company also sought approval from the court to exit its "non-core" specialty retail business: Lechmere, Home Image by Lechmere and Electric Avenue & More. It plans to focus on a core group of its best-performing stores, announcing the closing of 46 stores in October 1997.

Ward's is the parent of The Signature Group, the second largest direct marketing company in the United States.

Montgomery Ward & Co. Inc. Political Action Committee (also known as WardPAC) (C00032656) *Address: same as sponsor * Treasurer: Charles H. Knittle * Contact: Spencer Heine, Chairman*

	1993-94	1995-96	1997	Totals
Receipts	$162,721	$138,969	$33,231	$334,921
Disburse	165,704	148,950	28,100	342,754
Cash	30,555	20,578	25,711	n/a
Contributions	107,000	80,250	8,500	195,750
Republicans	54,500	70,000	6,000	130,500
No. of Cand.	*67*	*67*	*13*	*147*
House	26,000	29,500	4,500	60,000
Senate	28,500	40,500	1,500	70,500
Democrats	52,500	10,250	2,500	65,250
No. of Cand.	*66*	*16*	*4*	*86*
House	39,500	8,750	2,500	50,750
Senate	13,000	1,500	0	14,500
Incumbents	72,000	44,000	7,500	123,500
Challengers	7,000	11,250	0	18,250
Open Seat	28,000	25,000	1,000	54,000
Winners	86,000	56,750	n/a	142,750
Losers	21,000	23,500	n/a	44,500

National Association of Chain Drug Stores

*Phone: (703) 549-3001 * Fax: (703) 836-4869*
P.O. Box 1417-D49, Alexandria, VA 22313
Web: www.nacds.org

The National Association of Chain Drug Stores represents the views and policy positions of member chain drug companies. Founded in 1933, NACDS consists of 135 retail chain community pharmacy companies, more than 1,300 members representing manufacturers, wholesalers and service companies and 75 chain pharmacy and supplier companies operating in 20 countries.

NACDS provides forums for retailers to interact with their suppliers and business partners. It also promotes policies and programs aimed at improving merchandise distribution and retail operations efficiency in the retail drug industry.

In February 1998, NACDS reaffirmed its support of payment for pharmacists' care provided in private and public health insurance programs.

National Association of Chain Drug Stores Inc. Political Action Committee (C00022368) *Address: same as sponsor * Treasurer: R. James Huber * Contact: Ronald L. Ziegler, Chairman*

	1993-94	1995-96	1997	Totals
Receipts	$78,330	$79,175	$79,583	$237,088
Disburse	123,693	80,228	27,662	231,583
Cash	3,565	2,015	53,937	n/a
Contributions	100,320	60,500	26,550	187,370
Republicans	21,500	34,000	15,550	71,050
No. of Cand.	*17*	*36*	*21*	*74*
House	7,500	21,500	10,500	39,500
Senate	14,000	12,500	5,050	31,550
Democrats	78,820	26,500	11,000	116,320
No. of Cand.	*52*	*33*	*11*	*96*
House	54,200	19,000	3,500	76,700
Senate	24,620	7,500	7,500	39,620
Incumbents	85,120	41,500	24,550	151,170
Challengers	2,000	3,500	0	5,500
Open Seat	13,200	13,500	2,000	28,700
Winners	68,000	51,000	n/a	119,000
Losers	32,320	9,500	n/a	41,820

National Association of Convenience Stores

*Phone: (703) 684-3000 * Fax: (703) 836-4564*
1605 King St., Alexandria, VA 22314
*Web: www.cstorecentral.com * E-mail: mkatz@cstorecentral.com*

The National Association of Convenience Stores represents more than 3,000 store operators, petroleum marketers and suppliers in the United States. Its members account for 54 percent of all gasoline sold in the nation. The group's retail members operate about 63,000 convenience stores.

The group lobbies on many issues, including gasoline, tobacco sales, labor issues and environmental regulations. NACS does not support the proposed national tobacco settlement because of its restrictions on retailers, including a licensing program.

It supports legislation that would expand the potential uses of underground storage tank trust funds from the EPA. The group also opposes an Occupational Safety and Health Administration plan recommending that stores have two clerks on duty for night shifts.

The NACS PAC contributed more to 1996 congressional candidates than any single department store or drug store. Nearly 80 percent of the group's total went to Republican candidates. The leading recipients were Sen. Max Baucus, D-Mont., and Sen. Gordon Smith, R-Ore., each of whom received $10,000. Most recipients received less than $5,000.

National Association of Convenience Stores Political Action Committee (C00126763) *Address: same as sponsor * Treasurer: Marc N. Katz * Contact: Marc Katz*

	1993-94	1995-96	1997	Totals
Receipts	$287,242	$579,430	$470,030	$1,336,702
Disburse	200,279	451,287	166,036	817,602
Cash	108,068	236,211	540,206	n/a
Contributions	188,170	370,939	120,087	679,196
Republicans	141,550	303,439	78,087	523,076
No. of Cand.	*119*	*165*	*57*	*341*
House	69,550	217,983	61,541	349,074
Senate	72,000	85,456	16,546	174,002
Democrats	46,620	67,500	40,000	154,120
No. of Cand.	*41*	*32*	*32*	*105*
House	41,500	50,000	29,000	120,500
Senate	5,120	17,500	11,000	33,620
Incumbents	102,920	211,099	118,087	432,106
Challengers	26,000	51,346	1,000	78,346
Open Seat	59,250	108,494	1,000	168,744
Winners	161,800	263,945	n/a	425,745
Losers	26,370	106,994	n/a	133,364

National Automatic Merchandising Association

*Phone: (312) 346-0370 * Fax: (312) 704-4140*
20 N. Wacker Dr., Room 3500, Chicago, IL 60606
*Web: www.vending.org * E-mail: ga@vending.org*

The National Automatic Merchandising Association represents the vending machine and food service industries. Founded in 1936, it has about 2,400 member companies nationwide.

National Automatic Merchandising Association Political Action Committee (NAMAPAC) (C00235762) *Address: same as sponsor * Treasurer: Brian B. Allen * Contact: Michael Cronk, Chairman*

	1993-94	1995-96	1997	Totals
Receipts	$9,850	$6,590	$5,950	$22,390
Disburse	11,288	6,765	3,511	21,564
Cash	2,091	1,916	4,354	n/a
Contributions	9,500	5,600	3,500	18,600
Republicans	5,200	3,850	3,500	12,550
No. of Cand.	*13*	*5*	*2*	*20*
House	4,700	3,750	3,500	11,950
Senate	500	100	0	600
Democrats	4,300	1,750	0	6,050
No. of Cand.	*15*	*4*	*0*	*19*
House	3,050	1,750	0	4,800
Senate	1,250	0	0	1,250
Incumbents	10,750	4,600	3,500	18,850
Challengers	-250	0	0	-250
Open Seat	0	1,000	0	1,000
Winners	7,750	5,600	n/a	13,350
Losers	1,750	0	n/a	1,750

National Retail Federation

*Phone: (202) 783-7971 * Fax: (202) 737-2849*
325 Seventh St. N.W., Suite 1000, Washington, DC 20004
Web: www.nrf.com

The National Retail Federation is the trade association for the retail industry in the United States, including direct mail sellers. It represents all types of stores, from mass merchandisers to discount stores, and has 50 state associations.

The NRF also publishes newsletters and journals containing industry statistics and regulatory updates. It does not release lists of its membership, but each year it publishes a list of the Top 100 retailers in the United States, which includes stores such as Wal-Mart, Sears and Kmart among the leaders.

As a matter of policy the NRF's PAC normally does not contribute to primary elections "absent exceptional circumstances," according to a 1997 letter to the FEC.

National Retail Federation RetailPAC (C00040329) *Address: same as sponsor * Treasurer: John J. Motley III*

	1993-94	1995-96	1997	Totals
Receipts	$11,233	$128,518	$58,058	$197,809
Disburse	12,687	114,374	71,772	198,833
Cash	2,404	16,548	2,834	n/a
Contributions	11,624	100,374	53,270	165,268
Republicans	5,279	86,146	43,924	135,349
No. of Cand.	*11*	*80*	*37*	*128*
House	500	45,320	20,155	65,975
Senate	4,779	40,826	23,769	69,374
Democrats	6,345	14,228	9,346	29,919
No. of Cand.	*9*	*14*	*11*	*34*
House	1,449	10,442	5,346	17,237
Senate	4,896	3,786	4,000	12,682
Incumbents	7,731	53,592	48,770	110,093
Challengers	0	16,802	1,500	18,302
Open Seat	3,893	29,980	3,000	36,873
Winners	9,549	71,653	n/a	81,202
Losers	2,075	28,721	n/a	30,796

Parcel Shippers Association

*Phone: (202) 457-6050 * Fax: (202) 457-6315*
1211 Connecticut Ave. N.W., Suite 406, Washington, DC 20036
Web: www.parcelshippers.org

The Parcel Shippers Association represents nearly 100 member business firms that are concerned with the shipment of parcels. Its members include Reader's Digest Association Inc., Land's End, LL Bean Inc., Amway Corp. and Avon Products. These companies use the services of the U.S. Postal Service, United Parcel Service, Federal Express, Roadway and numerous other national and regional private delivery companies.

PSA speaks for parcel shippers on U.S. Postal Service rates and classification regulatory proceedings before the Postal Rate Commission. The commission makes the recommendation for U.S.P.S. prices and service levels.

Parcel Shippers Association Political Action Committee (C00151761) *Address: same as sponsor * Treasurer: Timothy J. May*

	1993-94	1995-96	1997	Totals
Receipts	$11,080	$2,300	$3,126	$16,506
Disburse	10,950	5,300	2,250	18,500
Cash	4,205	1,205	7,081	n/a
Contributions	10,260	5,300	2,250	17,810
Republicans	2,750	4,000	2,250	9,000
No. of Cand.	*8*	*7*	*3*	*18*
House	2,250	2,750	2,000	7,000
Senate	500	1,250	250	2,000
Democrats	7,510	1,300	0	8,810
No. of Cand.	*14*	*4*	*0*	*18*
House	7,000	1,300	0	8,300
Senate	510	0	0	510
Incumbents	10,160	5,300	2,250	17,710
Challengers	0	0	0	0
Open Seat	100	0	0	100
Winners	6,450	5,050	n/a	11,500
Losers	3,810	250	n/a	4,060

Payless ShoeSource Inc.

*Phone: (785) 295-2022 x7260 * Fax: (785) 368-7524*
3231 E. Sixth St., Topeka, KS 66607
*Web: www.paylessshoesource.com * E-mail: infocntr@paylessshoesource.com*

Payless ShoeSource is a lower-cost family footwear retailer with more than 4,200 stores in 50 states, almost all the United States territories and Canada. The publicly traded company has 25,000 employees and posted $2.5 billion in 1997 sales.

The majority of Payless' footwear is purchased from foreign manufacturers. Based in Kansas, Payless also has a regional office in Taiwan. The company was founded in 1956.

Payless ShoeSource Inc. Political Action Committee (C00319368) *Address: same as sponsor * Treasurer: Ullrich Porzig * Contact: William J. Rainey, Senior V.P.*

	1993-94	1995-96	1997	Totals
Receipts	$0	$26,427	$23,372	$49,799
Disburse	0	15,148	5,036	20,184
Cash	0	11,277	29,614	n/a
Contributions	0	15,000	5,000	20,000
Republicans	0	10,000	4,000	14,000
No. of Cand.	*0*	*10*	*4*	*14*
House	0	8,000	3,000	11,000
Senate	0	2,000	1,000	3,000
Democrats	0	5,000	1,000	6,000
No. of Cand.	*0*	*5*	*1*	*6*
House	0	4,000	1,000	5,000
Senate	0	1,000	0	1,000
Incumbents	0	8,000	5,000	13,000
Challengers	0	1,000	0	1,000
Open Seat	0	6,000	0	6,000
Winners	0	12,000	n/a	12,000
Losers	0	3,000	n/a	3,000

Rite Aid Corp.

*Phone: (717) 761-2633 * Fax: (717) 975-5871*
P.O. Box 3165, Harrisburg, PA 17105
Web: www.riteaid.com

Rite Aid operates drugstores in 25 of the top 50 U.S. metropolitan areas, ranking No.1 or No. 2 in 21 of the areas. Based in Pennsylvania, Rite Aid has more than 3,900 locations that extend to 31 states on both the East and West Coasts. The publicly traded company posted $11.3 billion in sales in 1997.

Rite Aid's prototype store features easy access, expanded parking, a full-service and drive-through pharmacy, one-hour photo finishing, express mail service, convenience foods and cosmetics departments.

The company grew with the purchase of the Thrifty PayLess chain and acquisitions of smaller, regional chains. The company also operates Eagle Managed Care, a wholly owned subsidiary designed to market prescription benefit programs.

William J. Bratton, former police commissioner of New York City, is one of Rite Aid's corporate directors.

Rite Aid Political Action Committee (C00104083) *Address: same as sponsor * Treasurer: Joseph Speaker * Contact: William A. K. Titelman, V.P. of Managed Care & Gov. Affairs*

	1993-94	1995-96	1997	Totals
Receipts	$149,775	$211,705	$135,887	$497,367
Disburse	143,507	276,956	62,184	482,647
Cash	173,315	108,068	181,823	n/a
Contributions	35,575	105,625	6,000	147,200
Republicans	20,075	55,000	6,000	81,075
No. of Cand.	*6*	*60*	*2*	*68*
House	75	29,000	0	29,075
Senate	20,000	26,000	6,000	52,000
Democrats	15,500	50,625	0	66,125
No. of Cand.	*5*	*49*	*0*	*54*
House	3,500	26,625	0	30,125
Senate	12,000	24,000	0	36,000
Incumbents	15,500	87,125	6,000	108,625
Challengers	7,500	5,000	0	12,500
Open Seat	12,575	13,500	0	26,075
Winners	19,575	95,625	n/a	115,200
Losers	16,000	10,000	n/a	26,000

Sears, Roebuck and Co.

*Phone: (847) 286-2400 * Fax: (847) 286-3911*
3333 Beverly Rd., Hoffman Estates, IL 60179
Web: www.sears.com

Sears, Roebuck and Co. is a leading U.S. retailer of apparel, home and automotive services, with 1997 revenue of more than $41 billion.

Founded in 1886 as R.W. Sears Watch Co. in Minneapolis, Sears has continued to grow and expand its business. It has about 300,000 employees worldwide. In 1993, the company began a $4-billion, five-year store modernization program.

In 1996, the company added 27 full-line stores and 71 new neighborhood Sears Hardware stores. In addition, Sears operates 65 Orchard Supply Hardware superstores, 107 off-the-mall HomeLife furniture stores, nearly 470 dealer stores serving smaller communities and 1,685 automotive stores. The company plans to operate 5,000 full-line and specialty stores nationwide by 2000.

According to TCPalm, an online news service, in 1986 Sears was accused of getting bankrupt customers to sign repayment agreements, then failing to file the agreements in court. Failure to file the agreements is a violation of federal law. The company settled the class-action suit with about 190,000 cardholders for $273 million.

Sears Political Action Committee (C00038612) *Address: same as sponsor * Treasurer: William K. Phelan * Contact: Richard Rothschild, National Dir. of Gov. Affairs*

	1993-94	1995-96	1997	Totals
Receipts	$27,270	$37,519	$35,281	$100,070
Disburse	16,400	20,650	14,500	51,550
Cash	16,416	34,008	54,790	n/a
Contributions	7,650	7,750	1,500	16,900
Republicans	5,650	5,750	1,000	12,400
No. of Cand.	*13*	*5*	*1*	*19*
House	2,150	1,250	1,000	4,400
Senate	3,500	4,500	0	8,000
Democrats	2,000	2,000	500	4,500
No. of Cand.	*4*	*2*	*1*	*7*
House	0	1,000	500	1,500
Senate	2,000	1,000	0	3,000
Incumbents	6,250	4,250	1,000	11,500
Challengers	600	1,000	0	1,600
Open Seat	800	2,500	500	3,800
Winners	7,650	5,250	n/a	12,900
Losers	0	2,500	n/a	2,500

Southland Corp.

*Phone: (214) 828-7789 * Fax: (214) 828-7690*
2711 N. Haskell Ave., P.O. Box 711, Dallas, TX 75221-0711
Web: www.7-eleven.com

The world's largest operator, franchiser and licenser of convenience stores, Southland is best-known for its 7-Eleven stores. It is also one of the nation's largest independent gasoline retailers.

Founded in 1927, the public company has more than 5,500 7-Eleven and other convenience stores in the United States and Canada serving about 6 million customers every day. In addition to 7-Eleven, the company operates High's Dairy, Quik Mart and SUPER-7 high-volume gasoline outlets with mini-convenience stores.

Southland licensees and affiliates operate an additional 9,500 7-Eleven stores around the world.

IYG Holding Co., a wholly owned subsidiary of Ito-Yokado Co., Ltd. and 7-Eleven Japan Co., Ltd., has owned a majority interest in Southland since 1991. 7-Eleven Japan operates about 6,100 7-Eleven stores under an area license agreement with Southland.

United States Southland Employees' Political Action Committee (U.S. SEPAC) (C00086298) *Address: same as sponsor * Treasurer: Joe R. Williams * Contact: Joe Gomes, Chairperson*

	1993-94	1995-96	1997	Totals
Receipts	$23,465	$22,012	$8,475	$53,952
Disburse	31,139	21,311	200	52,650
Cash	2,974	3,677	11,952	n/a
Contributions	20,467	12,633	0	33,100
Republicans	6,577	6,570	0	13,147
No. of Cand.	*9*	*10*	*2*	*21*
House	4,563	4,556	0	9,119
Senate	2,014	2,014	0	4,028
Democrats	13,383	6,063	0	19,446
No. of Cand.	*16*	*9*	*2*	*27*
House	8,605	4,049	0	12,654
Senate	4,778	2,014	0	6,792
Incumbents	19,710	10,612	0	30,322
Challengers	0	0	0	0
Open Seat	757	2,021	0	2,778
Winners	17,696	12,633	n/a	30,329
Losers	2,771	0	n/a	2,771

Spiegel Inc.

*Phone: (630) 986-8800 * Fax: (630) 769-2122*
3500 Lacey Rd., 12th Floor, Downers Grove, IL 60515-5431
Web: www.spiegel.com

Spiegel markets apparel, home furnishings and electronics through its catalogs, retail stores and company website. In addition to selling its own brands — Spiegel, Eddie Bauer and Newport News — the company markets Nike, Montblanc, Cuisinart, Mattel and RCA products.

Based in Illinois, the public company has more than 13,000 employees worldwide and posted $3.1 billion in revenues in 1997.

In February 1998, Spiegel announced it would add up to 65 new Eddie Bauer stores by the end of the year. At the end of 1997, Eddie Bauer had more than 200 stores throughout the United States, Canada and Japan.

Spiegel Inc. Executive Political Action Committee (SEPAC) (C00166884) *Address: same as sponsor * Treasurer: Michael R. Moran*

	1993-94	1995-96	1997	Totals
Receipts	$103,969	$80,272	$31,024	$215,265
Disburse	96,793	121,672	31,477	249,942
Cash	179,497	138,100	137,647	n/a
Contributions	46,250	49,750	9,500	105,500
Republicans	22,000	38,750	6,000	66,750
No. of Cand.	*19*	*28*	*7*	*54*
House	4,250	22,750	1,500	28,500
Senate	17,750	16,000	4,500	38,250
Democrats	24,250	11,000	3,500	38,750
No. of Cand.	*22*	*11*	*3*	*36*
House	13,500	6,000	2,500	22,000
Senate	10,750	5,000	1,000	16,750
Incumbents	34,750	37,750	7,500	80,000
Challengers	1,000	4,500	0	5,500
Open Seat	10,500	7,500	2,000	20,000
Winners	41,750	36,750	n/a	78,500
Losers	4,500	13,000	n/a	17,500

Tandy Corp.

*Phone: (817) 415-3775 * Fax: (817) 415-2638*
100 Throckmorton, Suite 1800, Fort Worth, TX 76102
Web: www.tandy.com

Tandy sells consumer electronics, including personal computers, primarily in the United States.

Originally founded in 1919 as a family leather business, Tandy has grown into a $1-billion publicly held electronics corporation with more than 40,000 employees.

The company's principal retail operations include the RadioShack and Computer City store chains. The company-owned RadioShack stores carry a broad assortment of primarily private label electronic parts and accessories, audio/video equipment, digital satellite systems, personal computers and cellular and conventional telephones, as well as specialized products such as scanners, electronic toys and hard-to-find batteries.

In January 1998, RadioShack and Compaq Computer Corp. signed a letter of intent for a multi-year retail sales and service agreement in which Compaq Presario PCs will become the exclusive computer line sold through RadioShack.

Tandy Corp. Government Action Fund (C00242263) *Address: same as sponsor * Treasurer: Ronald L. Parrish*

	1993-94	1995-96	1997	Totals
Receipts	$633	$30,655	$338	$31,626
Disburse	6,873	26,455	5,108	38,436
Cash	2,852	7,055	2,286	n/a
Contributions	5,370	12,850	3,000	21,220
Republicans	1,000	12,250	2,000	15,250
No. of Cand.	*4*	*11*	*1*	*16*
House	750	9,250	0	10,000
Senate	250	3,000	2,000	5,250
Democrats	4,120	600	500	5,220
No. of Cand.	*4*	*2*	*1*	*7*
House	3,500	0	500	4,000
Senate	620	600	0	1,220
Incumbents	5,120	9,750	3,000	17,870
Challengers	0	600	0	600
Open Seat	250	2,500	0	2,750
Winners	3,000	10,250	n/a	13,250
Losers	2,370	2,600	n/a	4,970

Wal-Mart Stores Inc.

*Phone: (501) 273-1927 * Fax: (501) 277-2473*
702 S.W. Eighth St., Bentonville, AR 72716
Web: www.wal-mart.com

Wal-Mart Stores is the world's largest retailer and ranked No. 4 on the 1997 Fortune 500. The publicly traded Arkansas company operates about 2,000 Wal-Mart stores, 433 Sam's Clubs and 239 Wal-Mart Supercenters.

The company reported $117 billion in revenues for the fiscal year ended in January 1998. It employs 728,000 workers.

Wal-Mart also runs stores in Argentina, Canada and Puerto Rico and, by franchise, in Brazil, China, Indonesia and Mexico. It is moving into the European market. In the United States, Wal-Mart is upgrading operations primarily by converting older, smaller Wal-Mart outlets into Supercenters.

Wal-Mart Stores Inc. PAC for Responsible Government (C00093054) *Address: same as sponsor * Treasurer: Don Shinkle*

	1993-94	1995-96	1997	Totals
Receipts	$195,579	$217,345	$115,244	$528,168
Disburse	170,276	217,217	48,849	436,342
Cash	48,402	48,535	114,930	n/a
Contributions	102,000	166,100	16,750	284,850
Republicans	97,750	163,350	14,000	275,100
No. of Cand.	*87*	*141*	*8*	*236*
House	39,750	75,350	5,000	120,100
Senate	58,000	88,000	9,000	155,000
Democrats	4,250	2,750	2,750	9,750
No. of Cand.	*9*	*6*	*3*	*18*
House	4,250	2,750	500	7,500
Senate	0	0	2,250	2,250
Incumbents	43,000	53,350	14,500	110,850
Challengers	18,000	39,750	0	57,750
Open Seat	41,000	73,000	0	114,000
Winners	91,500	98,350	n/a	189,850
Losers	10,500	67,750	n/a	78,250

Walgreen Co.

*Phone: (847) 940-2500 * Fax: (847) 914-2804*
200 Wilmot Rd., Mailstop #2255, Deerfield, IL 60015
*Web: www.walgreens.com * E-mail: ed.king@emc.walgreens.com*

Walgreen is a drugstore company that sells prescription and non-prescription drugs, and carries additional product lines such as general merchandise, liquor and beverages, cosmetics, toiletries and tobacco. The company employs 85,000 people and was ranked No. 116 on the 1996 Fortune 500.

Although it has fewer locations — 2,400 — than several of its rivals, Walgreen, headquartered in Deerfield, Ill., is the No. 1 drugstore chain in the United States with sales of $13 billion in 1997.

Walgreen implemented the Fillmaster pharmacy water purification and dispensing system chainwide in November 1997, which allows pharmacists to reconstitute an antibiotic while interacting with a customer. The implementation is designed to improve customer service.

Stores are located in 34 states and Puerto Rico, with the densest concentrations in Florida, Illinois and Texas. Prescription drugs account for more than 45 percent of the company's sales and the rest come from over-the-counter medicines, general merchandise, toiletries and other items.

Walgreen PAC (C00160770) *Address: same as sponsor * Treasurer: Edward H. King*

	1993-94	1995-96	1997	Totals
Receipts	$51,152	$52,441	$25,114	$128,707
Disburse	45,950	43,750	9,950	99,650
Cash	30,082	38,788	53,960	n/a
Contributions	16,600	25,000	5,000	46,600
Republicans	10,100	20,000	4,500	34,600
No. of Cand.	*16*	*24*	*5*	*45*
House	5,000	9,000	1,000	15,000
Senate	5,100	11,000	3,500	19,600
Democrats	6,500	5,000	500	12,000
No. of Cand.	*9*	*7*	*1*	*17*
House	2,500	4,000	500	7,000
Senate	4,000	1,000	0	5,000
Incumbents	9,600	12,500	2,000	24,100
Challengers	1,000	2,000	1,500	4,500
Open Seat	6,000	10,500	1,500	18,000
Winners	11,100	15,000	n/a	26,100
Losers	5,500	10,000	n/a	15,500

Steel Production

AK Steel Corp.

*Phone: (513) 425-2432 * Fax: (513) 425-5683*
703 Curtis St., Middletown, OH 45043
Web: www.aksteel.com

AK Steel produces coated and cold-rolled carbon and stainless steel products, mainly for the automobile and appliance manufacturing industries. It is a subsidiary of the publicly traded AK Steel Holding Corp.

AK Steel also sells to construction and manufacturing markets, distribution and service centers. In 1997, its sales were $2.4 billion, and it shipped 4.65 million tons of steel, nearly half to the automotive industry.

The company, which employs 5,800 people, operates plants in Kentucky and Ohio and is building a plant for finishing flat-rolled carbon and stainless steel near Rockport, Ind.

AK Steel Political Action Committee (formerly known as Armco Inc.) (C00290973) *Address: same as sponsor * Treasurer: James A. Weyers * Contact: Alan McCoy, V.P. of Public Affairs*

	1993-94	1995-96	1997	Totals
Receipts	$22,231	$42,217	$23,875	$88,323
Disburse	15,172	16,818	9,000	40,990
Cash	7,059	32,462	47,339	n/a
Contributions	4,500	7,475	4,700	16,675
Republicans	4,000	7,475	4,700	16,175
No. of Cand.	*3*	*1*	*3*	*7*
House	3,000	7,475	3,200	13,675
Senate	1,000	0	1,500	2,500
Democrats	500	0	0	500
No. of Cand.	*1*	*0*	*0*	*1*
House	500	0	0	500
Senate	0	0	0	0
Incumbents	3,500	7,475	3,200	14,175
Challengers	0	0	0	0
Open Seat	1,000	0	1,500	2,500
Winners	4,500	7,475	n/a	11,975
Losers	0	0	n/a	0

Allegheny Teledyne Inc.

*Phone: (412) 394-3003 * Fax: (412) 394-3010*
1000 Six PPG Place, Pittsburgh, PA 15222
Web: www.alleghenyteledyne.com.

The result of a merger between Teledyne and Allegheny Ludlum Co., Allegheny Teledyne is a group of companies that manufacture specialty metals as well as electronic, industrial, and consumer products. It is the world's largest producer of specialty alloys and steel, which account for 54 percent of its overall sales. The Pennsylvania-based company employs 24,000 people and reported 1997 sales of more than $3 billion.

Allegheny Teledyne Inc. Political Action Committee (AT-PAC) (C00141697) *Address: same as sponsor * Treasurer: Richard R. Roeser * Contact: Jon Walton, Senior V.P.*

	1993-94	1995-96	1997	Totals
Receipts	$52,477	$67,758	$26,019	$146,254
Disburse	59,525	68,655	19,200	147,380
Cash	11,829	10,932	17,751	n/a
Contributions	23,000	22,850	5,750	51,600
Republicans	14,000	11,600	4,750	30,350
No. of Cand.	*4*	*10*	*8*	*22*
House	3,500	5,100	3,750	12,350
Senate	10,500	6,500	1,000	18,000
Democrats	9,000	11,250	1,000	21,250
No. of Cand.	*7*	*5*	*2*	*14*
House	9,000	9,750	1,000	19,750
Senate	0	1,500	0	1,500
Incumbents	9,000	17,250	5,750	32,000
Challengers	9,500	5,600	0	15,100
Open Seat	4,500	0	0	4,500
Winners	17,500	15,750	n/a	33,250
Losers	5,500	7,100	n/a	12,600

American Iron and Steel Institute

*Phone: (202) 452-7100 * Fax: (202) 463-6573*
1101 17th St. N.W., Suite 1300, Washington, DC 20036
Web: www.steel.org

American Iron and Steel Institute is a trade association representing the North American steel industry and its member companies. Its mission is to promote steel as the material of choice and enhance the competitiveness of the North American steel industry and its member companies.

The group's 217 members include Bethlehem Steel Corp., Inland Steel Industries Inc., WCI Steel Inc. and Harsco Corp.

American Iron and Steel Institute Political Action Committee (C00295097) *Address: same as sponsor * Treasurer: Andrew G. Sharkey III * Contact: Thomas Sneeringer, Senior V.P.*

	1993-94	1995-96	1997	Totals
Receipts	$7,125	$23,450	$11,560	$42,135
Disburse	1,500	25,542	12,000	39,042
Cash	5,625	3,532	3,092	n/a
Contributions	1,500	24,500	12,000	38,000
Republicans	500	14,000	6,000	20,500
No. of Cand.	*1*	*24*	*7*	*32*
House	500	10,000	5,000	15,500
Senate	0	4,000	1,000	5,000
Democrats	1,000	10,500	6,000	17,500
No. of Cand.	*2*	*11*	*9*	*22*
House	1,000	9,000	5,000	15,000
Senate	0	1,500	1,000	2,500
Incumbents	1,500	24,000	11,000	36,500
Challengers	0	500	0	500
Open Seat	0	0	1,000	1,000
Winners	1,500	24,000	n/a	25,500
Losers	0	500	n/a	500

Armco Inc.

*Phone: (412) 255-9845 * Fax: (412) 255-9849*
One Oxford Centre, 301 Grant St., Pittsburgh, PA 15219-1415
Web: www.armco.com

Pittsburgh-based Armco makes specialty flat-rolled stainless, electrical and galvanized steels and is the nation's largest snowplow manufacturer. It also manufactures a wide range of steel pipe and tubing products for use in the construction, industrial and plumbing fields. The publicly traded company posted $1.8 billion in 1997 sales.

Founded in 1900, Armco and its subsidiaries employ 6,000 people at plants in Maine, Tennessee, Wisconsin, Pennsylvania and Ohio.

Subsidiaries: Sawhill Tubular, Fisher Engineering, Western Products and Douglas Dynamics LLC.

Armco Employees' Political Action Committee (APAC) (C00092809) *Address: same as sponsor * Treasurer: Colette M. Hucko * Contact: John Bauer, Dir. of Corporate Affairs*

	1993-94	1995-96	1997	Totals
Receipts	$27,226	$26,910	$11,133	$65,269
Disburse	46,417	16,653	11,354	74,424
Cash	1,995	12,251	12,029	n/a
Contributions	40,850	9,300	6,050	56,200
Republicans	21,250	5,300	4,550	31,100
No. of Cand.	*11*	*3*	*5*	*19*
House	10,250	5,300	2,550	18,100
Senate	11,000	0	2,000	13,000
Democrats	19,600	4,000	1,500	25,100
No. of Cand.	*13*	*5*	*2*	*20*
House	12,600	2,500	1,500	16,600
Senate	7,000	1,500	0	8,500
Incumbents	28,950	8,800	6,050	43,800
Challengers	4,000	500	0	4,500
Open Seat	7,900	0	0	7,900
Winners	27,450	8,800	n/a	36,250
Losers	13,400	500	n/a	13,900

Bethlehem Steel Corp.

*Phone: (610) 694-6684 * Fax: (610) 694-1509*
1725 Martin Tower, Bethlehem, PA 18016-7699
*Web: www.bethsteel.com * E-mail: pubaffrs@fast.net*

Bethlehem Steel, headquartered in Pennsylvania, is the second-largest steel producer in the United States. Bethlehem also produces coke, coal and iron ore, repairs ships and manufactures and sells forgings and cast rolls. The publicly traded company reported 1997 sales of $4.6 billion. It employs more than 17,000 workers.

In December 1997, Bethlehem acquired Lukens Inc., giving the combined company about 19 percent of the steel-plate industry in the United States. The Lukens PAC may be merged with the Bethlehem Steel PAC.

Bethlehem Steel Good Government Committee (C00096560)
*Phone: (202) 775-6200 * Fax: (202) 775-6221 * 1667 K St. N.W., Suite 600, Washington, DC 20006 * Treasurer: Thomas M. Mountain * Contact: Stephen G. Donches, Chairperson * Phone: (610) 694-6684*

	1993-94	1995-96	1997	Totals
Receipts	$54,496	$63,535	$28,022	$146,053
Disburse	51,975	59,150	28,725	139,850
Cash	3,837	8,223	7,520	n/a
Contributions	36,850	37,350	19,000	93,200
Republicans	13,000	20,250	11,500	44,750
No. of Cand.	*12*	*19*	*14*	*45*
House	5,750	14,300	7,500	27,550
Senate	7,250	5,950	4,000	17,200
Democrats	23,350	17,100	6,500	46,950
No. of Cand.	*28*	*15*	*8*	*51*
House	16,600	13,400	5,000	35,000
Senate	6,750	3,700	1,500	11,950
Incumbents	30,950	34,650	18,500	84,100
Challengers	2,400	1,200	0	3,600
Open Seat	3,500	1,500	500	5,500
Winners	27,150	35,400	n/a	62,550
Losers	9,700	1,950	n/a	11,650

Lukens Inc. Political Action Committee (C00061028) *Phone: (610) 383-3379 * Fax: (610) 383-2004 * 50 S. First Ave., Coatesville, PA 19320 * Web: www.lukens.com * Treasurer: P. Blaine Clemens*

A subsidiary of Bethlehem Steel, Lukens owns six manufacturing facilities and eight processing and distribution centers. It employs 3,400 workers and reported 1997 sales of $994 million.

	1993-94	1995-96	1997	Totals
Receipts	$44,779	$53,235	$22,458	$120,472
Disburse	40,274	52,446	13,660	106,380
Cash	8,239	9,031	17,830	n/a
Contributions	13,300	14,600	5,050	32,950
Republicans	11,050	11,100	4,050	26,200
No. of Cand.	*8*	*12*	*6*	*26*
House	5,350	9,600	2,050	17,000
Senate	5,700	1,500	2,000	9,200
Democrats	2,250	3,500	1,000	6,750
No. of Cand.	*3*	*3*	*1*	*7*
House	2,000	2,500	1,000	5,500
Senate	250	1,000	0	1,250
Incumbents	5,550	10,950	5,050	21,550
Challengers	4,700	300	0	5,000
Open Seat	3,050	3,350	0	6,400
Winners	12,250	13,000	n/a	25,250
Losers	1,050	1,600	n/a	2,650

Carpenter Technology Corp.

*Phone: (610) 208-2000 * Fax: (610) 208-2663*
P.O. Box 14662, Reading, PA 19612
Web: www.cartech.com

Carpenter Technology is a publicly traded manufacturer of specialty metals, including stainless steel and titanium.

It has annual sales of about $900 million and has more than 5,000 employees. The Pennsylvania-based firm has 11 plants and 19 sales offices in major urban areas in the United States, as well as in Toronto, Mexico, Taiwan, India, Israel, Belgium, England and Germany.

Carpenter recently acquired full ownership of Talley Industries, a metal fabrication and finishing company.

Carpenter Technology Corp. Federal Political Action Committee (Carpenter Fed-PAC) (C00116061) *Address: same as sponsor * Treasurer: Nick J. Morganti * Contact: William Pendleton, Corporate Affairs Dir.*

	1993-94	1995-96	1997	Totals
Receipts	$11,266	$12,796	$6,817	$30,879
Disburse	10,417	13,759	1,750	25,926
Cash	2,827	1,864	6,932	n/a
Contributions	9,150	13,000	1,250	23,400
Republicans	9,150	13,000	1,250	23,400
No. of Cand.	*22*	*20*	*2*	*44*
House	1,700	6,500	250	8,450
Senate	7,450	6,500	1,000	14,950
Democrats	0	0	0	0
No. of Cand.	*0*	*0*	*0*	*0*
House	0	0	0	0
Senate	0	0	0	0
Incumbents	1,450	2,000	1,250	4,700
Challengers	4,600	7,250	0	11,850
Open Seat	3,100	3,750	0	6,850
Winners	7,150	4,250	n/a	11,400
Losers	2,000	8,750	n/a	10,750

Inland Steel Industries

*Phone: (219) 399-8228 * Fax: (219) 399-3003*
30 W. Monroe St., Chicago, IL 60603
Web: www.inland.com

Inland Steel Industries is the publicly owned holding company for the Inland Steel Co., one of the largest steel producers in the United States with $5 billion in 1997 sales and 14,700 employees.

The company mines and transports iron ore, and produces iron, carbon and high-strength, low-alloy steels at a facility in East Chicago, Ind. Its subsidiary, Ryerson Tull, is the nation's largest metal processor and distributor, with 53 locations in the United States. Subsidiary Inland International markets, trades and distributes abroad.

Subsidiaries: Ryerson Tull, Joseph T. Ryerson & Son, J.M. Tull Metals Co., Ryerson Coil Processing, Inland Industries de Mexico SA de CV, Magnetics International and Inland International.

Foreign joint ventures: Ryerson de Mexico, Shanghai Ryerson Limited I.M.F. Steel International Ltd., in Hong Kong, and two joint ventures with Nippon Steel.

Inland Steel Good Government Fund (C00104109) *Address: same as sponsor * Treasurer: T. A. McCue * Contact: Maria Hibbs, Dir. of Public Affairs*

	1993-94	1995-96	1997	Totals
Receipts	$18,521	$17,150	$6,396	$42,067
Disburse	21,500	15,828	4,750	42,078
Cash	3,727	5,049	6,695	n/a
Contributions	16,500	10,800	4,750	32,050
Republicans	9,500	3,300	3,250	16,050
No. of Cand.	*10*	*6*	*4*	*20*
House	3,750	2,800	1,500	8,050
Senate	5,750	500	1,750	8,000
Democrats	7,000	7,500	1,500	16,000
No. of Cand.	*8*	*8*	*2*	*18*
House	5,500	6,000	0	11,500
Senate	1,500	1,500	1,500	4,500
Incumbents	13,000	9,300	2,250	24,550
Challengers	1,500	500	1,000	3,000
Open Seat	2,000	1,000	1,500	4,500
Winners	13,000	9,800	n/a	22,800
Losers	3,500	1,000	n/a	4,500

Keystone Consolidated Industries Inc.

Phone: (309) 697-7020
7000 S. Adams St., Peoria, IL 61641-0002

Keystone Consolidated Industries is involved in steel smelting, refining and manufacturing and wholesaling of wire and wire products. The private company is based in Peoria, Ill.

Keystone Consolidated Industries Inc. Political Action Committee (Keystone PAC) (C00219535) *Address: same as sponsor * Treasurer: Genevieve Lauterbach*

	1993-94	1995-96	1997	Totals
Receipts	$25,504	$32,105	$7,209	$64,818
Disburse	50,291	50,892	4,479	105,662
Cash	18,976	192	2,922	n/a
Contributions	30,250	29,000	0	59,250
Republicans	22,250	29,000	0	51,250
No. of Cand.	*24*	*27*	*0*	*51*
House	4,250	10,500	0	14,750
Senate	18,000	18,500	0	36,500
Democrats	8,000	0	0	8,000
No. of Cand.	*4*	*0*	*0*	*4*
House	2,000	0	0	2,000
Senate	6,000	0	0	6,000
Incumbents	13,000	16,250	0	29,250
Challengers	8,500	7,250	0	15,750
Open Seat	8,750	5,500	0	14,250
Winners	21,500	16,250	n/a	37,750
Losers	8,750	12,750	n/a	21,500

LTV Steel

Phone: (216) 622-5000
200 Public Square, 39th Floor, Suite 410, Cleveland, OH 44114-2308
Web: www.ltvsteel.com

LTV Steel is the third-largest steel producer in the nation, operating more than 20 plants and facilities in nine states throughout the eastern United States. It manufactures steel and steel-related products, including flat-rolled, tubular and electrical steel. LTV is a major supplier to the transportation, appliance, electrical equipment and service center industries.

The public company employs about 15,000 people and had 1997 sales of about $4.4 billion.

In February 1998, the company announced it would close its Pittsburgh Coke Plant, which employed 714 people.

LTV's subsidiary, VP Buildings, is a leading producer of pre-engineered metal buildings for low-rise commercial applications.

LTV Steel Active Citizenship Campaign (C00034181) *Phone: (202) 872-5522 * 1133 Connecticut Ave. N.W., Suite 620, Washington, DC 20036 * Treasurer: Larry Q. Alden*

*Contact: Michael Lawell, Chairman * Phone: (216) 622-5000*

	1993-94	1995-96	1997	Totals
Receipts	$121,710	$131,383	$55,946	$309,039
Disburse	140,799	132,631	51,637	325,067
Cash	10,828	9,581	13,890	n/a
Contributions	64,800	82,350	29,000	176,150
Republicans	21,350	48,700	14,250	84,300
No. of Cand.	*26*	*40*	*19*	*85*
House	9,600	30,500	9,500	49,600
Senate	11,750	18,200	4,750	34,700
Democrats	42,450	33,650	13,750	89,850
No. of Cand.	*42*	*32*	*19*	*93*
House	30,450	31,650	9,750	71,850
Senate	12,000	2,000	4,000	18,000
Incumbents	45,300	70,000	27,000	142,300
Challengers	5,000	8,850	500	14,350
Open Seat	14,500	3,500	1,500	19,500
Winners	49,000	71,000	n/a	120,000
Losers	15,800	11,350	n/a	27,150

National Steel Corp.

*Phone: (219) 273-7414 * Fax: (219) 273-7478*
4100 Edison Lakes Pkwy., Mishawaka, IN 46545-3440
Web: www.nationalsteel.com

National Steel and its consolidated subsidiaries are engaged in the manufacture and sale of a wide variety of flat-rolled carbon steel products, including hot-rolled, cold-rolled, galvanized, tin and chrome plated steels for use in the automotive, metal buildings and building products, containers, pipe and tube, and service center industries.

Incorporated in 1929, the company is controlled by the Japanese company NKK. National Steel produces more than 6.6 million tons of steel annually. The company employs about 9,500 people and posted 1996 sales of $3 billion.

Headquartered in Mishawaka, Ind., National Steel's major manufacturing facilities are in Michigan, Illinois, Indiana and Minnesota.

National Steel Corp. Political Action Fund (C00252239) *Address: same as sponsor * Treasurer: William E. McDonough*

	1993-94	1995-96	1997	Totals
Receipts	$26,838	$1,455	$0	$28,293
Disburse	22,000	18,400	-1,000	39,400
Cash	17,857	912	1,912	n/a
Contributions	16,900	14,400	0	31,300
Republicans	2,500	2,500	0	5,000
No. of Cand.	*3*	*3*	*0*	*6*
House	500	2,500	0	3,000
Senate	2,000	0	0	2,000
Democrats	13,900	11,900	0	25,800
No. of Cand.	*14*	*7*	*2*	*23*
House	9,400	10,500	0	19,900
Senate	4,500	1,400	0	5,900
Incumbents	16,400	14,400	0	30,800
Challengers	0	0	0	0
Open Seat	500	0	0	500
Winners	10,900	14,400	n/a	25,300
Losers	6,000	0	n/a	6,000

Texas Industries Inc.

*Phone: (972) 647-3366 * Fax: (972) 647-3355*
1341 W. Mockingbird Ln., Suite 700 W., Dallas, TX 75247-6913
Web: www.txi.com

Texas Industries, formerly known as TXI Industries, is a public steel, cement and concrete maker for the construction and manufacturing industries. Subsidiary Chaparral Steel, of which Texas Industries owns 85 percent, makes steel beams and other products from recycled steel.

The company also sells construction aggregates (sand, gravel and crushed limestone) to companies in the Southwest and Midwest. Texas Industries, which has 3,400 employees, reported 1997 sales of $973 million.

Texas Industries Inc. Political Action Committee (formerly known as TXI Industries PAC) (C00176388) *Address: same as sponsor * Treasurer: Julia P. Fuller * Contact: Harold Green, Dir. of Communications*

	1993-94	1995-96	1997	Totals
Receipts	$3,527	$15,890	$14,660	$34,077
Disburse	12,750	18,309	11,040	42,099
Cash	4,797	2,392	6,019	n/a
Contributions	7,750	10,800	4,500	23,050
Republicans	6,750	8,800	3,500	19,050
No. of Cand.	*3*	*11*	*3*	*17*
House	4,750	7,300	3,500	15,550
Senate	2,000	1,500	0	3,500
Democrats	1,000	2,000	1,000	4,000
No. of Cand.	*2*	*3*	*1*	*6*
House	500	2,000	0	2,500
Senate	500	0	1,000	1,500
Incumbents	4,000	3,000	4,500	11,500
Challengers	1,750	1,000	0	2,750
Open Seat	2,000	6,800	0	8,800
Winners	4,000	5,000	n/a	9,000
Losers	3,750	5,800	n/a	9,550

Textiles

American Textile Manufacturers Institute

*Phone: (202) 862-0500 * Fax: (202) 862-0537*
1801 K St. N.W., Suite 900, Washington, DC 20006
Web: www.atmi.org

The American Textile Manufacturers Institute is the national trade association for the domestic textile industry. Its members process about 80 percent of all textile fibers used by plants in the United States.

The textile industry employs about 670,000 people in the United States. ATMI members include textile mills, fiber manufacturers, growers, processors and related businesses. The group is concerned with international trade legislation.

American Textile Manufacturers Institute Inc. Committee for Good Government (C00032441) *Address: same as sponsor * Treasurer: Douglas W. Bulcao * Contact: Carlos Moore, Executive V.P.*

	1993-94	1995-96	1997	Totals
Receipts	$140,748	$181,900	$73,400	$396,048
Disburse	163,860	173,685	76,500	414,045
Cash	2,477	5,439	2,339	n/a
Contributions	152,650	160,000	66,500	379,150
Republicans	52,550	112,000	42,500	207,050
No. of Cand.	*41*	*69*	*41*	*151*
House	39,050	66,000	27,500	132,550
Senate	13,500	46,000	15,000	74,500
Democrats	100,100	48,000	24,000	172,100
No. of Cand.	*63*	*30*	*21*	*114*
House	81,100	40,000	16,000	137,100
Senate	19,000	8,000	8,000	35,000
Incumbents	146,500	146,500	66,500	359,500
Challengers	1,100	2,000	0	3,100
Open Seat	5,050	11,500	0	16,550
Winners	118,900	136,500	n/a	255,400
Losers	33,750	23,500	n/a	57,250

American Yarn Spinners Association

*Phone: (704) 824-3522 * Fax: (704) 824-0630*
P.O. Box 99, Gastonia, NC 28053

American Yarn Spinners Association members, located mainly on the East Coast and in the Midwest, produce yarn for sale to other textile manufacturers.

American Yarn Spinners Association Inc. Political Action Committee (C00172866) *Address: same as sponsor * Treasurer: Jim H. Conner * Contact: Bob Holland, General Chairman*

	1993-94	1995-96	1997	Totals
Receipts	$13,295	$18,607	$23,281	$55,183
Disburse	14,382	17,831	1,079	33,292
Cash	2,052	2,826	25,027	n/a

Contributions	13,250	16,750	1,000	31,000
Republicans	5,250	13,000	1,000	19,250
No. of Cand.	*10*	*19*	*1*	*30*
House	5,250	9,500	1,000	15,750
Senate	0	3,500	0	3,500
Democrats	8,000	3,750	0	11,750
No. of Cand.	*13*	*8*	*0*	*21*
House	8,000	3,750	0	11,750
Senate	0	0	0	0
Incumbents	13,250	16,750	1,000	31,000
Challengers	0	0	0	0
Open Seat	0	0	0	0
Winners	8,500	15,500	n/a	24,000
Losers	4,750	1,250	n/a	6,000

Burlington Industries

*Phone: (336) 379-2560 * Fax: (336) 379-2436*
3330 W. Friendly Ave., Greensboro, NC 27410
Web: www.burlington-ind.com

Burlington Industries makes fabrics and other textile products for apparel and interior furnishings. The $1.9 billion public company is one of the nation's largest producers of woven wool-worsted, specialty synthetic blends, specialty denim, jacquard fabrics, carpets, tufted area rugs and printed accent rugs.

The company, which employs more than 20,000 people, had 1997 sales of about $2 billion.

Founded in 1923, Burlington has more than 46 manufacturing facilities in the Southeast. The company's corporate offices are located in Greensboro, N.C., while its merchandising headquarters are in New York City. Burlington also has international operations in India and Mexico.

Burlington Industries Good Government Committee (C00040238) *Phone: (202) 223-3167 * Fax: (202) 785-2790 * 1001 Connecticut Ave. N.W., Suite 701, Washington, DC 20036 * Treasurer: Ronald E. Markle * Contact: Donna Lee McGee, Chairperson*

	1993-94	1995-96	1997	Totals
Receipts	$145,818	$151,699	$84,363	$381,880
Disburse	154,920	146,080	63,566	364,566
Cash	14,039	19,669	40,470	n/a
Contributions	142,200	143,915	63,566	349,681
Republicans	51,100	98,315	43,066	192,481
No. of Cand.	*41*	*51*	*30*	*122*
House	40,600	61,815	26,066	128,481
Senate	10,500	36,500	17,000	64,000
Democrats	90,850	45,600	20,500	156,950
No. of Cand.	*56*	*28*	*17*	*101*
House	71,850	36,600	17,500	125,950
Senate	19,000	9,000	3,000	31,000
Incumbents	131,800	133,915	63,566	329,281
Challengers	2,150	3,000	0	5,150
Open Seat	9,250	7,500	0	16,750
Winners	113,050	128,415	n/a	241,465
Losers	29,150	15,500	n/a	44,650

Inman Mills

*Phone: (864) 472-2121 * Fax: (864) 472-9674*
P.O. Box 207, Inman, SC 29349

Inman Mills is a privately held textile manufacturer with estimated annual sales of $160 million and 1,300 employees. It buys and produces only 100 percent American-made products. Its textiles are made of cotton, polyester, blends, lycra-producing twills, sheeting, oxfords, dobbies, basket weaves, herringbones, poplins and specially ordered fabrics.

Inman Mills Good Government Fund (C00142893) *Address: same as sponsor * Treasurer: James C. Pace Jr. * Contact: J. Lawrence Morrow, Chairperson*

	1993-94	1995-96	1997	Totals
Receipts	$19,452	$15,109	$6,937	$41,498
Disburse	21,635	18,185	6,398	46,218
Cash	10,346	7,268	7,806	n/a
Contributions	3,000	3,500	500	7,000
Republicans	1,500	2,500	0	4,000
No. of Cand.	*2*	*3*	*0*	*5*
House	500	500	0	1,000
Senate	1,000	2,000	0	3,000
Democrats	1,500	1,000	500	3,000
No. of Cand.	*2*	*1*	*1*	*4*
House	1,500	0	0	1,500
Senate	0	1,000	500	1,500

Incumbents	2,500	3,500	500	6,500
Challengers	0	0	0	0
Open Seat	500	0	0	500
Winners	2,000	3,500	n/a	5,500
Losers	1,000	0	n/a	1,000

Northern Textile Association

*Phone: (617) 542-8220 * Fax: (617) 542-2199*
230 Congress St., Boston, MA 02110

The Northern Textile Association represents about 150 businesses in the fabric industry. NTA is a national organization, although its members are primarily located in the Northeast.

Northern Textile Association Members' Political Action Committee (C00123158) *Address: same as sponsor * Treasurer: Karl H. Spilhaus*

	1993-94	1995-96	1997	Totals
Receipts	$7,016	$8,521	$2,331	$17,868
Disburse	5,265	8,885	799	14,949
Cash	4,841	3,778	5,310	n/a
Contributions	5,000	8,700	650	14,350
Republicans	2,625	6,300	500	9,425
No. of Cand.	*4*	*9*	*1*	*14*
House	375	3,200	500	4,075
Senate	2,250	3,100	0	5,350
Democrats	2,375	2,400	150	4,925
No. of Cand.	*4*	*5*	*1*	*10*
House	2,375	1,900	150	4,425
Senate	0	500	0	500
Incumbents	3,000	7,200	650	10,850
Challengers	1,000	500	0	1,500
Open Seat	1,000	1,000	0	2,000
Winners	5,000	6,500	n/a	11,500
Losers	0	2,200	n/a	2,200

Springs Industries Inc.

*Phone: (803) 547-3736 * Fax: (803) 547-3740*
205 N. White St., Fort Mill, SC 29715
Web: www.springs.com

Springs Industries, headquartered in Fort Mill, S.C., is one of the largest manufacturers of home furnishings and specialty fabrics in the United States. It manufactures bed and bath products such as sheets, pillowcases, bedspreads, towels, shower curtains and bath rugs under brand names such as Springmaid, Wamsutta and Dundee.

Sales for 1997 were more than $2.2 billion, and the public company employed about 20,700 workers. The Close family, descendants of co-founder Leroy Springs, controls 70 percent of the company's voting stock.

The company has manufacturing facilities in 10 states, as well as marketing and distribution subsidiaries in Canada and Mexico.

In February 1998, Springs announced plans to close its Rock Hill, S.C. printing and finishing plant, eliminating 480 jobs. Other changes include consolidation of its bed and bath furnishing units into two functional groupings and an expansion and modernization of its towel plants in Georgia.

Springs Industries Inc. Political Action Committee (C00025098) *Address: same as sponsor * Treasurer: Robert L. Thompson Jr.*

	1993-94	1995-96	1997	Totals
Receipts	$52,650	$57,260	$29,812	$139,722
Disburse	72,300	57,564	10,048	139,912
Cash	16,940	16,637	36,401	n/a
Contributions	66,300	51,650	8,000	125,950
Republicans	18,800	36,150	4,000	58,950
No. of Cand.	*17*	*25*	*7*	*49*
House	12,800	25,150	4,000	41,950
Senate	6,000	11,000	0	17,000
Democrats	47,500	15,500	4,000	67,000
No. of Cand.	*9*	*6*	*4*	*19*
House	47,500	13,500	3,000	64,000
Senate	0	2,000	1,000	3,000
Incumbents	63,000	47,650	7,500	118,150
Challengers	1,000	0	0	1,000
Open Seat	2,300	4,000	0	6,300
Winners	51,800	49,650	n/a	101,450
Losers	14,500	2,000	n/a	16,500

Communications/Electronics

Computer Equipment & Services

Compaq Computer Corp.

Phone: (281) 370-0670
20555 State Highway 249, Mail Code 040511, Houston, TX 77070
Web: www.compaq.com

Compaq Computer is the fifth-largest computer company in the world with $24.6 billion in revenue. It announced plans in January 1998 to buy Digital Equipment Corp. for $9.6 billion. The mega-deal would move Compaq up to the industry's No. 2 slot, behind IBM.

Houston-based Compaq would acquire Digital's big-business clients as well as its expertise with advanced network products. Digital, which has been reinventing itself in recent years because of the decline of mainframe computing, would attach itself to Compaq's highly successful personal computer business. The merger, which requires Justice Department approval, would be the largest in the history of the computer industry.

Compaq's largest manufacturing facility is in Houston. It also operates plants in Scotland, Singapore, China and Brazil.

The company's government and education group, formed in 1994, focuses on selling technology to the U.S. government.

A publicly traded Fortune 100 company, Compaq sells computers in more than 100 countries. It has 32,500 employees.

Compaq Computer Corp. Citizenship Fund (Compaq Citizenship Fund) (C00296020) *Phone: (202) 962-3830 * Fax: (202) 962-3838 * 1300 Eye St. N.W., Suite 490E, Washington, DC 20005 * Treasurer: Chase Untermeyer*

	1993-94	1995-96	1997	Totals
Receipts	$25,758	$88,074	$46,965	$160,797
Disburse	13,539	89,140	47,180	149,859
Cash	12,220	13,250	13,036	n/a
Contributions	1,500	13,750	12,250	27,500
Republicans	1,500	13,750	9,750	25,000
No. of Cand.	*2*	*17*	*11*	*30*
House	500	7,850	5,750	14,100
Senate	1,000	5,900	4,000	10,900
Democrats	0	0	2,500	2,500
No. of Cand.	*0*	*0*	*4*	*4*
House	0	0	1,500	1,500
Senate	0	0	1,000	1,000
Incumbents	1,500	7,750	11,750	21,000
Challengers	0	2,000	0	2,000
Open Seat	0	4,000	500	4,500
Winners	1,500	10,000	n/a	11,500
Losers	0	3,750	n/a	3,750

Computer Sciences Corp.

*Phone: (310) 615-0311 * Fax: (310) 322-9805*
2100 E. Grand Ave., El Segundo, CA 90245
Web: www.csc.com

Computer Sciences operates information technology, consulting, systems integration and outsourcing services for global industries and government agencies. Government contracts account for more than 30 percent of CSC's sales, which totaled $6.3 billion in 1997. The public corporation, headquartered in California, has 600 offices worldwide, primarily in Europe, the Pacific Rim and the United States. It employs nearly 44,000 workers.

In February 1998, CSC received an unsolicited offer from Computer Associates Inc. to acquire CSC in a merger. CSC rejected the offer, but CA attempted a forced merger by offering CSC shareholders $108 per share. The board of directors at CSC voted unanimously to reject Computer Associates' tender offer and not to enter into negotiations with CA. After about two weeks, CA agreed to let the offer expire on March 16, 1998.

CSC subsidiaries/divisions include: American Practice Management, CSC Continuum, CSC Healthcare, CSC Index, CSC Logic, CSC Systems Group, Communications Industry Services, Consulting and Systems Integration, Hogan Systems and Technology Management Group.

Computer Sciences Corp. PAC has been in existence since 1978.

Computer Sciences Corp. PAC (CSC PAC) (C00101410) *Address: same as sponsor * Treasurer: Leon J. Level * Contact: Bruce Plowman, PAC Chairman*

	1993-94	1995-96	1997	Totals
Receipts	$74,130	$72,006	$43,567	$189,703
Disburse	79,612	72,652	45,507	197,771
Cash	10,252	9,610	7,670	n/a
Contributions	60,450	70,600	46,500	177,550
Republicans	24,700	60,600	32,000	117,300
No. of Cand.	*32*	*45*	*25*	*102*
House	11,700	31,100	18,000	60,800
Senate	13,000	29,500	14,000	56,500
Democrats	35,750	10,000	14,500	60,250
No. of Cand.	*32*	*11*	*12*	*55*
House	22,750	10,000	9,000	41,750
Senate	13,000	0	5,500	18,500
Incumbents	53,300	65,100	46,000	164,400
Challengers	1,500	4,500	1,000	7,000
Open Seat	6,000	1,000	0	7,000
Winners	52,300	58,500	n/a	110,800
Losers	8,150	12,100	n/a	20,250

Computing Devices International

Phone: (612) 853-8100
8800 Queen Ave. S., Blcs1B, Bloomington, MN 55431

Computing Devices International, a division of publicly traded Ceridian Corp., was acquired by General Dynamics Information Systems Inc. in December 1997. The Computing Devices PAC was dissolved in February 1998.

Computing Devices International A Division of Ceridian Corp. Political Action Committee (C00280883) *Address: same as sponsor * Treasurer: Donald R. Mathieu*

	1993-94	1995-96	1997	Totals
Receipts	$31,688	$60,156	$28,108	$119,952
Disburse	24,743	54,696	33,270	112,709
Cash	6,947	12,409	7,249	n/a
Contributions	24,500	54,669	33,250	112,419
Republicans	10,500	37,460	19,250	67,210
No. of Cand.	*10*	*23*	*13*	*46*
House	4,500	23,460	15,750	43,710
Senate	6,000	14,000	3,500	23,500
Democrats	13,000	17,209	14,000	44,209
No. of Cand.	*10*	*9*	*7*	*26*
House	11,000	17,209	13,000	41,209
Senate	2,000	0	1,000	3,000
Incumbents	23,500	52,669	33,250	109,419
Challengers	0	2,000	0	2,000
Open Seat	1,000	0	0	1,000
Winners	24,500	52,669	n/a	77,169
Losers	0	2,000	n/a	2,000

EDS Corp.

*Phone: (972) 604-6000 * Fax: (972) 605-2643*
5400 Legacy Dr., Plano, TX 75024-3199
Web: www.eds.com

EDS is a publicly traded consulting and computer services firm for companies in many industries. Its clients include energy, manufacturing, finance, insurance, transportation, health care and government services. The company, founded by former presidential candidate Ross Perot, was spun off by General Motors in 1996. Nearly a third of EDS's revenues come from contracts with GM and its affiliates. The company had 1997 sales of $15.2 billion and about 110,000 employees.

Among the company's federal clients are the Department of Education, the Federal Aviation Administration and all branches of the military. It also serves government agencies in South Korea and the United Kingdom. EDS' health care division clients include Blue Cross and Blue Shield, Medicare and Medicaid. It also works on Year 2000 conversion programs and recently formed a new company with drug manufacturer Eli Lilly and Co. that will provide health professionals with a real-time information network.

EDS was the leading computer services contributor to 1996 congressional candidates. The PAC split its contributions almost evenly between the parties, with a small edge to Republicans. Five of the top 10 recipients were from Texas. The leading recipients were Rep. Martin Frost, D-Texas, and Sen. Max Baucus, D-Mont. Frost was the only candidate to receive at least $5,000.

Electronic Data Systems Employees' Political Action Committee (C00111658) *Phone: (202) 393-4716 * Fax: (202) 637-6759 * 1331 Pennsylvania Ave. N.W., Suite 1300, Washington, DC 20004 * Treasurer: Kim McMann * Contact: Carolyn Carson, PAC Manager*

	1993-94	1995-96	1997	Totals
Receipts	$405,227	$428,700	$199,626	$1,033,553
Disburse	444,056	406,865	180,908	1,031,829
Cash	56,936	78,781	98,227	n/a
Contributions	265,163	237,749	101,000	603,912
Republicans	103,802	127,850	52,000	283,652
No. of Cand.	*81*	*104*	*63*	*248*
House	62,802	96,350	37,500	196,652
Senate	41,000	31,500	14,500	87,000
Democrats	160,361	109,899	48,000	318,260
No. of Cand.	*118*	*85*	*67*	*270*
House	121,611	89,100	38,000	248,711
Senate	38,750	20,799	10,000	69,549
Incumbents	246,959	202,039	98,000	546,998
Challengers	3,004	7,000	500	10,504
Open Seat	15,200	27,710	2,500	45,410
Winners	223,163	198,249	n/a	421,412
Losers	42,000	39,500	n/a	81,500

ElectroCom Automation Inc.

*Phone: (817) 640-5690 * Fax: (817) 640-5691*
P.O. Box 95080, Arlington, TX 76005
Web: usa.siemens.com

ElectroCom Automation, now Siemens ElectroCom LP, is an international manufacturer of sorting and recognition systems for mail processing automation, commercial sorting and imaging and data acquisition systems. Siemens Electrocom Automation employs 1,100 workers in Arlington, Texas.

ElectroCom is a subsidiary of the German electronics company Siemens, whose products and services span a wide range of technologies, from health care to industrial automation.

ElectroCom Automation LP Political Action Committee (C00194860) *Address: same as sponsor * Treasurer: J. D. Welch Jr.*

	1993-94	1995-96	1997	Totals
Receipts	$3,626	$1,664	$656	$5,946
Disburse	14,586	6,370	1,400	22,356
Cash	24,398	19,696	18,953	n/a
Contributions	5,200	5,250	1,000	11,450
Republicans	3,500	3,750	1,000	8,250
No. of Cand.	*4*	*4*	*1*	*9*
House	1,500	2,750	1,000	5,250
Senate	2,000	1,000	0	3,000
Democrats	1,700	1,500	0	3,200
No. of Cand.	*3*	*2*	*0*	*5*
House	1,500	1,500	0	3,000
Senate	200	0	0	200
Incumbents	3,700	4,750	1,000	9,450
Challengers	500	500	0	1,000
Open Seat	1,000	0	0	1,000
Winners	3,000	4,750	n/a	7,750
Losers	2,200	500	n/a	2,700

First Financial Management Corp.

5660 New Northside Dr., Suite 1400, Atlanta, GA 30328

The First Financial Management PAC was terminated in October 1996.

First Financial Management Corp. Political Action Committee (C00250076) *Address: same as sponsor * Treasurer: M. Tarlton Pittard*

	1993-94	1995-96	1997	Totals
Receipts	$11,843	$28,612	$0	$40,455
Disburse	10,072	30,383	0	40,455
Cash	1,770	0	0	n/a
Contributions	9,000	12,000	0	21,000
Republicans	9,000	2,000	0	11,000
No. of Cand.	*4*	*3*	*0*	*7*
House	5,000	1,000	0	6,000
Senate	4,000	1,000	0	5,000
Democrats	0	10,000	0	10,000
No. of Cand.	*0*	*1*	*0*	*1*
House	0	0	0	0
Senate	0	10,000	0	10,000
Incumbents	9,000	2,000	0	11,000
Challengers	0	0	0	0
Open Seat	0	10,000	0	10,000
Winners	9,000	12,000	n/a	21,000
Losers	0	0	n/a	0

Hewlett-Packard Co.

*Phone: (650) 857-7292 * Fax: (650) 857-7594*
3000 Hanover St. 20BQ, Palo Alto, CA 94304
*Web: www.hp.com * E-mail: mary_d_beall@hp.com*

Hewlett-Packard, based in Palo Alto, Calif., is the second-largest computer supplier in the world, with computer-related revenue in excess of $35.4 billion in fiscal year 1997, and total revenue for the same year of $42.9 billion. A publicly traded company, HP has 123,300 employees (69,100 in the United States) and is ranked No. 16 in the Fortune 500.

In addition to computers, HP makes printers, calculators, electronic test equipment, medical electronic equipment and chemical analysis instruments. Services such as systems integration, selective outsourcing management, consulting, education, product financing and rentals and customer support and maintenance are also part of the company's offerings.

HP's primary subsidiary, CoCreate, focuses on producing communications systems that will unite manufacturers with customers and improve product quality and efficiency.

Hewlett-Packard Co. Committee for Effective Congress (C00196725) *Phone: (202) 884-7000 * Fax: (202) 884-7070 * 900 17th St. N.W., Suite 1100, Washington, DC 20006 * Treasurer: D. Craig Nordlund*

*Contact: Nick Fowler, Chairperson * Phone: (650) 857-7292*

	1993-94	1995-96	1997	Totals
Receipts	$56,610	$67,036	$31,372	$155,018
Disburse	48,813	67,194	4,548	120,555
Cash	11,790	11,636	40,405	n/a
Contributions	48,450	66,000	2,000	116,450
Republicans	21,200	54,000	2,000	77,200
No. of Cand.	*19*	*40*	*1*	*60*
House	7,700	29,500	0	37,200
Senate	13,500	24,500	2,000	40,000
Democrats	27,250	12,000	0	39,250
No. of Cand.	*25*	*13*	*0*	*38*
House	18,750	6,000	0	24,750
Senate	8,500	6,000	0	14,500
Incumbents	30,150	38,000	2,000	70,150
Challengers	9,000	8,000	0	17,000
Open Seat	9,300	20,000	0	29,300
Winners	39,300	44,500	n/a	83,800
Losers	9,150	21,500	n/a	30,650

Intel Corp.

*Phone: (408) 765-8080 * Fax: (408) 765-6284*
2200 Mission College Blvd., Santa Clara, CA 95052-8119
*Web: www.intel.com * E-mail: support@cs.intel.com*

Intel, a publicly traded, Fortune 500 company based in Santa Clara, Calif., designs, develops, manufactures and markets microcomputer components and related products. The company's microprocessors, including the Pentium and Pentium II, have provided the operating mechanisms for IBM-compatible computers since 1981.

Time magazine called Chairman and CEO Andrew Groves "the person most responsible for the amazing growth in the power and innovative potential of microchips" (transistors that store and transmit information in computers), and dubbed him 1997's "Man of the Year."

Intel's sales hit $25 billion in 1997, thanks in part to a technology breakthrough that doubles the speed at which new computer chips can be produced. In February 1998, the company introduced its new graphics accelerator chip, the Intel740, increasing visual graphic capability for PC users.

The company employs more than 63,000 people and has sales offices in 31 countries. About 60 percent of its sales are from non-U.S. sources.

Intel Corp. Political Action Committee (C00125641) *Phone: (202) 628-4393 * Fax: (202) 628-2525 * 1634 Eye St. N.W., Suite 300, Washington, DC 20006 * Treasurer: Mike Maibach * Contact: Jonathan Williams, Coordinator*

	1993-94	1995-96	1997	Totals
Receipts	$39,389	$41,912	$28,673	$109,974
Disburse	42,248	43,072	15,279	100,599
Cash	4,688	3,530	16,923	n/a
Contributions	41,994	41,950	15,279	99,223
Republicans	21,000	33,850	10,476	65,326
No. of Cand.	*24*	*39*	*9*	*72*
House	9,000	17,850	5,250	32,100
Senate	12,000	16,000	5,226	33,226
Democrats	20,994	8,100	4,803	33,897
No. of Cand.	*23*	*13*	*6*	*42*
House	12,444	6,600	2,803	21,847
Senate	8,550	1,500	2,000	12,050
Incumbents	25,494	36,450	15,279	77,223
Challengers	4,750	500	0	5,250
Open Seat	11,750	5,000	0	16,750
Winners	33,494	33,700	n/a	67,194
Losers	8,500	8,250	n/a	16,750

Intergraph Corp.

*Phone: (703) 264-5600 * Fax: (703) 264-2339*
2051 Mercator Dr., Reston, VA 22091
Web: www.intergraph.com

Intergraph makes software, computers, workstations, imagesetters and 3-D graphics accelerators, primarily for the computer-aided design market. The tools are used for mapping and geographic information systems, as well as architectural work.

The U.S. government accounts for 15 percent of the publicly traded company's sales, which totaled $1.1 billion in 1997. About 43 percent of the company's sales are made outside the United States, and it employs more than 8,000 workers.

In 1997, Intergraph began moving from UNIX-based CAD systems to systems based on Microsoft's Windows NT operating system and Intel Corp.'s Pentium microprocessors.

In November 1997, Intergraph sued Intel for anti-competitive behavior. Intergraph claimed that Intel engaged in a series of wrongful acts to coerce Intergraph into giving certain patent rights to Intel regarding Windows NT-based applications. The suit was still pending as of February 1998.

In February 1998, Intergraph consolidated all of its imaging systems software and hardware departments into one division. The new imaging systems division will include the following products: Photogammetric, GIS and Reprographics Imaging software, ImageStation Z products, PhotoScan TD scanners and ANA Tech scanning systems hardware.

Intergraph Corp. Political Action Committee (C00201491)
*Address: same as sponsor * Treasurer: Edward A. Wilkinson Jr.*

	1993-94	1995-96	1997	Totals
Receipts	$36,064	$29,077	$9,269	$74,410
Disburse	17,067	56,162	12,828	86,057
Cash	84,008	56,924	53,365	n/a
Contributions	19,550	45,750	12,000	77,300
Republicans	5,250	33,750	7,750	46,750
No. of Cand.	*4*	*9*	*10*	*23*
House	3,250	10,500	4,750	18,500
Senate	2,000	23,250	3,000	28,250
Democrats	14,300	12,000	4,250	30,550
No. of Cand.	*5*	*3*	*4*	*12*
House	14,300	12,000	4,250	30,550
Senate	0	0	0	0
Incumbents	19,050	36,750	12,000	67,800
Challengers	500	0	0	500
Open Seat	0	9,000	0	9,000
Winners	18,750	44,750	n/a	63,500
Losers	800	1,000	n/a	1,800

MSE Technology Applications Inc.

*Phone: (406) 723-8213 * Fax: (406) 723-8328*
P.O. Box 4078, Butte, MT 59701
Web: www.mse-ta.com

MSE Technology Applications is a private engineering company specializing in facility operations and waste treatment technologies. The company has offices in Montana, Idaho and New York. MSE is a wholly owned subsidiary of the Montana Energy Research and Development Institute.

MSE operates the Department of Energy's Western Environmental Technology Office, located in Butte, Mont., which has been used as a test center in the development of waste management technology.

Citizens for Responsible Government Employees of MSE Inc. (C00218131) *Address: same as sponsor * Treasurer: Allan Miller*

	1993-94	1995-96	1997	Totals
Receipts	$4,464	$5,278	$2,249	$11,991
Disburse	5,115	5,218	2,000	12,333
Cash	717	777	1,026	n/a
Contributions	5,100	5,000	2,000	12,100
Republicans	2,500	2,000	1,500	6,000
No. of Cand.	*2*	*2*	*3*	*7*
House	500	500	500	1,500
Senate	2,000	1,500	1,000	4,500
Democrats	2,600	3,000	500	6,100
No. of Cand.	*4*	*3*	*1*	*8*
House	2,600	1,000	500	4,100
Senate	0	2,000	0	2,000
Incumbents	5,100	4,000	2,000	11,100
Challengers	0	0	0	0
Open Seat	0	1,000	0	1,000
Winners	4,600	4,000	n/a	8,600
Losers	500	1,000	n/a	1,500

Microsoft Corp.

*Phone: (425) 882-8080 * Fax: (425) 936-7329*
1 Microsoft Way, Redmond, WA 98073
Web: www.microsoft.com

Microsoft is widely considered the world's leading independent software provider, with products available in more than 30 languages and 50 countries. The public company, based near Seattle, employs about 23,000 people worldwide and has enjoyed double-digit revenue and income increases for the past 10 years. Microsoft's 1997 revenues were $11.3 billion.

CEO and co-founder Bill Gates, the richest man in America, owns about 22 percent of Microsoft. His company's cyber-dominance was investigated in 1997 by the Justice Department for its practice of requiring computer manufacturers to include Microsoft's Internet Explorer browser software on the desktop of the ubiquitous Windows software. Microsoft agreed to give manufacturers the option to delete the browser from the software after Attorney General Janet Reno threatened to levy a $1 million a day fine.

Microsoft develops, manufactures, licenses, sells and supports a wide range of computer software products. These include operating systems for personal computers and servers, server applications for client/server environments, business and consumer productivity applications, interactive media programs and Internet platform and development tools.

Microsoft Corp. Political Action Committee (C00227546) *Phone: (202) 364-2485 * Fax: (202) 364-8853 * 5335 Wisconsin Ave., Suite 600, Washington, DC 20015 * Treasurer: Kimberly Ellwanger*

	1993-94	*1995-96*	*1997*	*Totals*
Receipts	$31,700	$59,750	$65,518	$156,968
Disburse	32,441	49,518	29,000	110,959
Cash	2,720	12,951	49,470	n/a
Contributions	31,741	43,500	21,500	96,741
Republicans	6,550	26,000	13,500	46,050
No. of Cand.	*11*	*25*	*15*	*51*
House	4,550	21,000	9,500	35,050
Senate	2,000	5,000	4,000	11,000
Democrats	25,191	17,500	8,000	50,691
No. of Cand.	*30*	*17*	*8*	*55*
House	17,191	12,000	4,000	33,191
Senate	8,000	5,500	4,000	17,500
Incumbents	29,641	41,000	21,500	92,141
Challengers	1,000	1,000	0	2,000
Open Seat	1,000	1,500	0	2,500
Winners	21,016	38,500	n/a	59,516
Losers	10,725	5,000	n/a	15,725

Oracle Corp.

*Phone: (650) 506-7000 * Fax: (650) 506-7200*
500 Oracle Pkwy., MS 659506, Redwood Shores, CA 94065
Web: www.oracle.com

The world's second-largest software company, Oracle concentrates on database and network products. The publicly traded company posted $5.7 billion in fiscal year 1997 revenues and has 31,000 employees, 14,500 of whom are in the United States.

Oracle has contracts with the Coast Guard and the Department of Defense to develop and support databases, including one that is planned to be the world's largest human resource application.

Headquartered in Redwood Shores, Calif., Oracle offers its database, tools and applications products, along with related consulting, education and support services, in more than 140 countries.

Oracle Corp. Political Action Committee (C00323048) *Phone: (202) 721-4815 * Fax: (202) 467-4250 * 1667 K St., Suite 640, Washington, DC 20006-1605 * Treasurer: Deborah Lange * Contact: Kenneth Glueck, PAC Dir.*

	1993-94	*1995-96*	*1997*	*Totals*
Receipts	$0	$26,100	$1,000	$27,100
Disburse	0	5,500	15,000	20,500
Cash	0	20,600	6,600	n/a
Contributions	0	6,000	16,000	22,000
Republicans	0	2,000	5,500	7,500
No. of Cand.	*0*	*2*	*7*	*9*
House	0	0	4,500	4,500
Senate	0	2,000	1,000	3,000
Democrats	0	4,000	10,500	14,500
No. of Cand.	*0*	*4*	*12*	*16*
House	0	0	3,500	3,500
Senate	0	4,000	7,000	11,000
Incumbents	0	3,000	16,000	19,000
Challengers	0	1,000	0	1,000
Open Seat	0	2,000	0	2,000
Winners	0	4,000	n/a	4,000
Losers	0	2,000	n/a	2,000

SCI Systems Inc.

*Phone: (205) 882-4800 * Fax: (205) 480-4804*
2101 W. Clinton Ave., Huntsville, AL 35805

SCI Systems is a multinational electronics manufacturing services provider. The publicly traded company posted $5.8 billion in 1997 sales. It designs, manufactures and distributes products for computer, telecommunication, medical, industrial, consumer, military and aerospace markets. The public company's markets are in North America, South America, Europe and East Asia.

In 1996, SCI was chosen by Ericsson Telecom AB of Sweden as a primary manufacturing partner, and it acquired Apple Computer's Fountain, Colo. plant.

SCI has 18,450 employees, with 10,200 at its facilities in the following states: Alabama, California, Colorado, Maine, New Hampshire, New York, North Carolina, South Dakota. Abroad, employees work in Quebec, France, Ireland, Malaysia, Mexico, Singapore, Thailand and Scotland, as well as in leased facilities in Brazil, Canada and Mexico, and in newly acquired manufacturing plants and operations in Hungary, Mexico, Spain, Mexico and Brazil.

SCI Systems Inc. Political Action Committee (C00202846) *Address: same as sponsor * Treasurer: Ronald G. Sibold Jr. * Contact: Olin B. King, Chairman and CEO*

	1993-94	*1995-96*	*1997*	*Totals*
Receipts	$4,878	$2,875	$2,048	$9,801
Disburse	6,650	11,000	500	18,150
Cash	28,406	20,283	21,833	n/a
Contributions	400	10,000	500	10,900
Republicans	0	10,000	0	10,000
No. of Cand.	*0*	*1*	*0*	*1*
House	0	0	0	0
Senate	0	10,000	0	10,000
Democrats	400	0	500	900
No. of Cand.	*2*	*0*	*1*	*3*
House	200	0	500	700
Senate	200	0	0	200
Incumbents	400	0	500	900
Challengers	0	0	0	0
Open Seat	0	10,000	0	10,000
Winners	200	0	n/a	200
Losers	200	10,000	n/a	10,200

Storage Technology Corp.

*Phone: (303) 673-3000 * Fax: (303) 673-5019*
2270 S. 88th St., Mailstop 4305, Louisville, CO 80028
Web: www.stortek.com

Storage Technology makes products that store, transport and secure information ranging from mainframe data to client/server applications to video images. With 8,300 employees, the public company posted 1997 revenues of $2.1 billion.

StorageTek ranks No. 681 on the Business Week 1,000 list of companies by market value and No. 705 on the Industry Week 1,000 list of the world's top publicly held manufacturing companies.

StorageTek products are installed in more than 35 countries. Its customers are primarily major corporations and government agencies worldwide.

Storage Technology Corp. Political Action Committee Inc. (C00217737) *Phone: (303) 673-5005 * 700 13th St. N.W., Washington, DC 20005 * Treasurer: Lou Rizzo * Contact: Christine A. Owens*

*Contact: Bill Treadwell, President * Phone: (303) 673-3000*

	1993-94	*1995-96*	*1997*	*Totals*
Receipts	$30,765	$23,770	$3,640	$58,175
Disburse	40,940	36,943	90	77,973
Cash	25,134	10,192	14,460	n/a
Contributions	34,100	32,750	0	66,850
Republicans	22,600	27,500	0	50,100
No. of Cand.	*24*	*28*	*0*	*52*
House	11,600	17,000	0	28,600
Senate	11,000	10,500	0	21,500

Democrats	11,500	5,250	0	16,750
No. of Cand.	*10*	*10*	*0*	*20*
House	8,500	5,250	0	13,750
Senate	3,000	0	0	3,000
Incumbents	26,000	24,500	0	50,500
Challengers	2,100	3,000	0	5,100
Open Seat	6,000	5,250	0	11,250
Winners	34,100	28,750	n/a	62,850
Losers	0	4,000	n/a	4,000

Texas Instruments Inc.

Phone: (972) 480-6789
P.O. Box 742496, Dallas, TX 75374
Web: www.ti.com

Texas Instruments is one of the leading high-technology companies in the world, with sales and manufacturing operations in more than 30 countries. The company's products include semiconductors, consumer electronics, electrical controls and metallurgical materials.

TI also is the market leader in digital signal processors, powerful semiconductor devices that convert analog signals into digital form in real time and operate in products ranging from fax machines and anti-lock brakes to cell phones, disc drives, televisions and modems.

Headquartered in Dallas, the public company employs nearly 60,000 employees. It had 1997 revenues of $9.75 billion.

Since June 1996, when Thomas J. Engibous took over as president and CEO, TI has been relinquishing many of its businesses to focus on the production of digital signal processors. As of February 1998, the company had sold its defense systems and electronics business to the Raytheon Co., and had also relinquished its notebook computer business, printer products business, communications and electronic systems business and software business. In addition, in 1996, TI acquired Silicon Systems Inc., a semiconductor production company, for $575 million.

Constructive Citizenship Program of Texas Instruments (C00007070) *Phone: (202) 628-3133 * Fax: (202) 628-2980 * 1455 Pennsylvania Ave. N.W., Suite 375, Washington, DC 20004 * E-mail: akdc@msg.ti.com * Treasurer: Philip J. Ritter*

*Contact: Elwin L. Skiles Jr., Chairman * Phone: (972) 480-6789*

	1993-94	*1995-96*	*1997*	*Totals*
Receipts	$147,799	$166,599	$59,529	$373,927
Disburse	173,581	134,223	54,848	362,652
Cash	6,606	38,995	43,682	n/a
Contributions	115,419	100,500	19,000	234,919
Republicans	56,149	71,000	13,000	140,149
No. of Cand.	*43*	*51*	*8*	*102*
House	28,150	46,500	9,000	83,650
Senate	27,999	24,500	4,000	56,499
Democrats	59,270	29,500	6,000	94,770
No. of Cand.	*35*	*17*	*2*	*54*
House	52,650	28,500	6,000	87,150
Senate	6,620	1,000	0	7,620
Incumbents	101,419	89,750	19,000	210,169
Challengers	4,000	1,750	0	5,750
Open Seat	10,000	7,500	0	17,500
Winners	102,549	84,500	n/a	187,049
Losers	12,870	16,000	n/a	28,870

Wang Government Services Inc.

*Phone: (703) 827-3000 * Fax: (703) 827-3900*
7900 Westpark Dr., McLean, VA 22102
Web: www.wang.com/governmentservices

Wang Government Services provides information technology products and services to federal, state and local governments and government contractors. It is one of the largest federal computer systems integrators, providing network design, installation, operation and maintenance. It develops and provides secure systems and services to protect information in databases, networks and transmissions.

A subsidiary of publicly traded Wang computer company, Wang Government Services is headquartered in McLean, Va. and has 7,900 employees. The company has offices and customers in about 130 countries. The federal government accounted for about 30 percent of parent company Wang's overall $1.2 billion in 1997 sales.

Wang Government Services Inc. PAC (formerly Wang Federal Inc. PAC) (C00255430) *Address: same as sponsor * Treasurer: Randall Cole*

	1993-94	*1995-96*	*1997*	*Totals*
Receipts	$15,302	$10,551	$1,756	$27,609
Disburse	15,521	9,518	3,000	28,039
Cash	6,741	7,778	7,825	n/a
Contributions	15,450	9,500	3,000	27,950
Republicans	5,850	8,500	2,000	16,350
No. of Cand.	*7*	*7*	*2*	*16*
House	2,850	2,500	2,000	7,350
Senate	3,000	6,000	0	9,000
Democrats	9,600	1,000	1,000	11,600
No. of Cand.	*7*	*2*	*1*	*10*
House	6,600	1,000	0	7,600
Senate	3,000	0	1,000	4,000
Incumbents	11,450	8,500	3,000	22,950
Challengers	1,000	0	0	1,000
Open Seat	3,000	1,000	0	4,000
Winners	14,450	9,500	n/a	23,950
Losers	1,000	0	n/a	1,000

Electronics Manufacturing & Services

AIL Systems Inc.

*Phone: (516) 595-5000 * Fax: (516) 595-5754*
455 Commack Rd., Deer Park, NY 11729-4591
Web: www.ail.com

AIL Systems produces electronics for defense and commercial applications. Products include electronic countermeasures, electronic global reconnaissance, portable and modular radar, environmental products, antenna products and satellite electronic packages.

Established in the 1940s, AIL is an employee-owned company with more than 800 staff members. Headquartered in Deer Park, N.Y., AIL also has a division in Lancaster, Calif. and a wholly owned subsidiary, American Nucleonics Corp., in Westlake Village, Calif. The company has field offices across the United States.

In 1997, AIL acquired Dorne & Margolin Inc. of Bohemia, N.Y. D&M produces antennas and related electronics for both commercial and military customers.

Former astronaut Neil Armstrong is chairman of the company's board of directors.

AIL Systems Inc. Political Action Committee (C00292953) *Address: same as sponsor * Treasurer: Darrell L. Reed*

	1993-94	*1995-96*	*1997*	*Totals*
Receipts	$14,387	$31,615	$12,626	$58,628
Disburse	7,514	26,106	6,184	39,804
Cash	6,874	12,387	18,830	n/a
Contributions	7,500	24,500	4,750	36,750
Republicans	3,500	17,500	3,750	24,750
No. of Cand.	*3*	*6*	*3*	*12*
House	3,500	17,000	3,750	24,250
Senate	0	500	0	500
Democrats	4,000	7,000	1,000	12,000
No. of Cand.	*2*	*2*	*1*	*5*
House	4,000	5,000	1,000	10,000
Senate	0	2,000	0	2,000
Incumbents	6,500	22,500	4,750	33,750
Challengers	1,000	0	0	1,000
Open Seat	0	2,000	0	2,000
Winners	5,500	22,500	n/a	28,000
Losers	2,000	2,000	n/a	4,000

AMP Inc.

*Phone: (717) 564-0100 * Fax: (717) 592-3199*
P.O. Box 3608 (176-22), Harrisburg, PA 17105
Web: www.ampincorporated.com

AMP makes electronic connectors and interconnection systems for use in the aerospace, automotive, computer networking, consumer goods, industrial, power utilities and telecommunication industries. More than 55 percent of AMP sales are machine- or tool-applied. The publicly traded company reported $5.7 billion in 1997 sales and employs 45,000 people.

Headquartered in Harrisburg, Pa., AMP has operations in 50 countries around the world. Founded in 1941 as Aero-Marine Products,

AMP is frequently named as one of the top 50 patent-holding corporations worldwide.

AMP products can be found in almost any product that conducts electricity or uses electronics or optical signals, including satellites, aircraft, automobiles, trucks, trains, ships, computers, telephone equipment, switching equipment, consumer electronics and household appliances. AMP is a supplier to most of the world's major manufacturers of electrical and electronic equipment.

AMP Inc. Political Action Committee (AMP-PAC) (C00298562)
*1901 Pennsylvania Ave. N.W., Suite 700, Washington, DC 20006 * Treasurer: Thomas A. Bowen*

	1993-94	1995-96	1997	Totals
Receipts	$32,312	$159,207	$87,920	$279,439
Disburse	19,317	151,900	3,700	174,917
Cash	12,996	20,401	104,622	n/a
Contributions	8,900	92,600	-1000	100,500
Republicans	8,700	90,100	-1000	97,800
No. of Cand.	*10*	*49*	*2*	*61*
House	5,700	41,100	-1000	45,800
Senate	3,000	49,000	0	52,000
Democrats	200	2,500	0	2,700
No. of Cand.	*1*	*5*	*0*	*6*
House	200	2,500	0	2,700
Senate	0	0	0	0
Incumbents	2,000	45,000	-1000	46,000
Challengers	4,000	22,500	0	26,500
Open Seat	2,500	25,100	0	27,600
Winners	7,500	53,300	n/a	60,800
Losers	1,400	39,300	n/a	40,700

Honeywell Inc.

Phone: (612) 951-0128
Honeywell Plaza, P.O. Box 524, Minneapolis, MN 55440
Web: www.honeywell.com

Honeywell is a publicly traded producer of control systems. Based in Minnesota, Honeywell makes automatic thermostat controls, manufacturing controls and electronic systems for commercial airlines and spacecraft. Its home and business heating and cooling systems division accounted for about 45 percent of the company's $8 billion in sales during 1997. Honeywell has about 57,500 employees.

The company is one of a team of contractors replacing and updating energy systems in federal buildings throughout the southeastern United States, Puerto Rico and the Virgin Islands.

Honeywell's space operations are headquartered in Clearwater, Fla., and its satellite systems operations are located in Glendale, Ariz. Other offices are in Houston and Minneapolis.

In addition to the Honeywell Employee Citizenship Fund, the company has two affiliated PACs, one each for its Florida and Arizona units.

Honeywell Employee Citizenship Fund (C00079533) *Address: same as sponsor * Treasurer: Andrew R. Lindberg*

	1993-94	1995-96	1997	Totals
Receipts	$40,928	$40,547	$30,412	$111,887
Disburse	41,777	34,069	9,000	84,846
Cash	1,951	8,439	29,858	n/a
Contributions	35,200	29,650	7,000	71,850
Republicans	19,000	24,650	4,500	48,150
No. of Cand.	*18*	*34*	*10*	*62*
House	8,500	15,650	3,500	27,650
Senate	10,500	9,000	1,000	20,500
Democrats	13,250	5,000	1,500	19,750
No. of Cand.	*12*	*7*	*2*	*21*
House	5,000	5,000	1,500	11,500
Senate	8,250	0	0	8,250
Incumbents	19,950	20,650	6,000	46,600
Challengers	0	5,000	1,000	6,000
Open Seat	15,250	4,000	0	19,250
Winners	30,450	21,150	n/a	51,600
Losers	4,750	8,500	n/a	13,250

Contributed less than $5,000 during 1995-96 cycle:

Honeywell Florida Political Action Committee (C00090423)
*Phone: (813) 539-2353 * Fax: (813) 539-3403 * 13350 U.S. Highway 19 N., Clearwater, FL 34624 * Web: www.honeywell.com/space * Treasurer: Berton Clemons III*

Honeywell PAC/Arizona Honeywell Employee Citizenship Fund PAC (C00230979) *Phone: (602) 436-2311 * 21111 N. 19th Ave., Phoenix, AZ 85027 * Treasurer: Sandra L. Rush*

Philips Electronics North America Corp.

*Phone: (212) 850-5000 * Fax: (212) 850-7314*
100 E. 42nd St., Fourth Floor, New York, NY 10017
Web: www.philips.com

Philips is one of the world's largest electronics companies and makes cassette tapes, VCRs, CD players and electronic devices under the names Philips, Marantz, Magnavox and Norelco. The publicly traded Dutch company has nearly 265,000 employees and reported $39.2 billion in 1997 sales.

The company also makes lighting equipment, personal care products such as shavers and hair dryers, communications infrastructure equipment, medical systems such as diagnostic imaging and radiation therapy equipment, and industrial electronics such as industrial X-ray and automation systems. Its semiconductor division develops chips for consumer electronics.

Philips owns 75 percent of music company PolyGram.

Philips Electronics North America is the U.S. subsidiary of Philips Electronics N.V.

Philips Electronics North America Corp. Political Action Committee (C00239780) *Phone: (202) 962-8550 * Fax: (202) 962-8560 1300 Eye St. N.W., Suite 1070 E., Washington, DC 20005-3314 * Treasurer: Randy B. Moorhead*

	1993-94	1995-96	1997	Totals
Receipts	$73,394	$76,372	$30,692	$180,458
Disburse	75,707	77,180	30,875	183,762
Cash	13,786	12,980	12,802	n/a
Contributions	74,249	76,646	30,875	181,770
Republicans	51,900	70,197	23,875	145,972
No. of Cand.	*54*	*70*	*36*	*160*
House	36,800	47,298	16,875	100,973
Senate	15,100	22,899	7,000	44,999
Democrats	22,349	6,449	7,000	35,798
No. of Cand.	*18*	*9*	*9*	*36*
House	8,850	5,449	2,500	16,799
Senate	13,499	1,000	4,500	18,999
Incumbents	62,849	65,646	29,375	157,870
Challengers	3,350	1,400	0	4,750
Open Seat	7,050	9,600	1,500	18,150
Winners	64,699	64,348	n/a	129,047
Losers	9,550	12,298	n/a	21,848

Varian Associates Inc.

*Phone: (650) 424-5270 * Fax: (650) 856-4351*
3100 Hansen Way, M/S E-029, Palo Alto, CA 94304-1030
*Web: www.varian.com * E-mail: derrel.depasse@corp.varian.com*

Varian Associates is an electronic instruments company. One of the earliest Silicon Valley high technology businesses, Varian develops X-ray tubes, vacuum equipment, parts for semiconductors and radiation therapy equipment for cancer treatments. It has manufacturing facilities in California, Arizona, Massachusetts, Utah, Illinois and South Carolina.

A publicly traded company, Varian has 6,500 employees and reported 1997 sales of $1.4 billion.

Varian Associates Inc. Employees' Political Action Committee (C00224543) *Address: same as sponsor * Treasurer: Gerald T. Mugnolo * Contact: Derrel DePasse, PAC Chairwoman*

	1993-94	1995-96	1997	Totals
Receipts	$6,289	$10,707	$4,602	$21,598
Disburse	6,750	9,750	3,500	20,000
Cash	32	989	2,091	n/a
Contributions	6,750	9,750	2,500	19,000
Republicans	3,000	6,750	0	9,750
No. of Cand.	*4*	*8*	*0*	*12*
House	1,000	4,500	0	5,500
Senate	2,000	2,250	0	4,250
Democrats	3,750	3,000	2,500	9,250
No. of Cand.	*6*	*4*	*3*	*13*
House	2,750	2,000	2,000	6,750
Senate	1,000	1,000	500	2,500
Incumbents	5,000	7,000	2,500	14,500
Challengers	0	1,000	0	1,000
Open Seat	1,750	1,750	0	3,500
Winners	6,500	6,000	n/a	12,500
Losers	250	3,750	n/a	4,000

Zenith Electronics Corp.

*Phone: (847) 391-7286 * Fax: (847) 391-8876*
1000 Milwaukee Ave., Glenview, IL 60025
*Web: www.zenith.com * E-mail: prweb@zenith.com*

Zenith Electronics primarily makes color television sets and related products such as color picture tubes. A public company, Zenith had 1997 sales of $1.3 billion and 15,900 employees, 11,200 of which were based in Mexico. In 1995, 55 percent of Zenith's stock was purchased by the Korean company LG Electronics Inc.

Zenith has six locations near Chicago; five in Texas; one in Arizona; 12 manufacturing and warehouse locations in Mexico; and one purchasing office in Taiwan.

Founded in 1918, Zenith has incurred losses almost every year since 1985 and has sold or downsized its operations in monochrome video monitors, power supplies, high-security electronic equipment and color computer monitors.

Zenith Electronics Corp. Political Participation Fund (C00200253) *Address: same as sponsor * Treasurer: Willard C. McNitt * Contact: John Taylor, V.P. of Public Affairs*

	1993-94	1995-96	1997	Totals
Receipts	$10,108	$6,211	$809	$17,128
Disburse	17,325	11,500	0	28,825
Cash	17,452	11,140	11,949	n/a
Contributions	10,135	5,500	0	15,635
Republicans	1,325	5,000	0	6,325
No. of Cand.	*3*	*5*	*0*	*8*
House	325	1,500	0	1,825
Senate	1,000	3,500	0	4,500
Democrats	8,810	500	0	9,310
No. of Cand.	*7*	*1*	*0*	*8*
House	6,000	0	0	6,000
Senate	2,810	500	0	3,310
Incumbents	9,635	2,000	0	11,635
Challengers	0	0	0	0
Open Seat	500	3,500	0	4,000
Winners	7,325	1,000	n/a	8,325
Losers	2,810	4,500	n/a	7,310

Printing & Publishing

American Business Press

1350 New York Ave. N.W., Suite 1100, Washington, DC 20036

The American Business Press PAC was terminated in 1996.

American Business Press Specialized Periodical Action Committee (C00011874) *Address: same as sponsor * Treasurer: Stephen M. Feldman*

	1993-94	1995-96	1997	Totals
Receipts	$0	$0	$0	$0
Disburse	0	0	0	0
Cash	0	0	0	n/a
Contributions	0	6,037	0	6,037
Republicans	0	5,537	0	5,537
No. of Cand.	*0*	*4*	*0*	*4*
House	0	2,537	0	2,537
Senate	0	3,000	0	3,000
Democrats	0	500	0	500
No. of Cand.	*0*	*1*	*0*	*1*
House	0	500	0	500
Senate	0	0	0	0
Incumbents	0	6,037	0	6,037
Challengers	0	0	0	0
Open Seat	0	0	0	0
Winners	0	6,037	n/a	6,037
Losers	0	0	n/a	0

Association of American Publishers

*Phone: (212) 255-0200 * Fax: (212) 255-7007*
71 Fifth Ave., New York, NY 10003-3004
Web: www.publishers.org

The Association of American Publishers is the main trade group for the U.S. book publishing industry. About 200 AAP members, including Educational Testing Service, HarperCollins Publishers and The McGraw-Hill Companies, publish hardcover and paperback books. Former Rep. Patricia Schroeder, D-Colo., is the group's president and CEO.

The AAP terminated its PAC in August 1997.

Association of American Publishers PAC (C00020206) *Phone: (202) 232-3335 x232 * Fax: (202) 745-0694 * 1718 Connecticut Ave. N.W., Suite 700, Washington, DC 20009-1148 * Treasurer: Arthur Sackler * Contact: Allan Adler, V.P.*

	1993-94	1995-96	1997	Totals
Receipts	$7,600	$7,950	$0	$15,550
Disburse	13,436	6,954	934	21,324
Cash	17	1,486	590	n/a
Contributions	12,950	6,550	750	20,250
Republicans	2,950	4,100	500	7,550
No. of Cand.	*6*	*9*	*2*	*17*
House	1,450	2,000	500	3,950
Senate	1,500	2,100	0	3,600
Democrats	10,000	2,450	250	12,700
No. of Cand.	*19*	*7*	*1*	*27*
House	5,750	2,100	250	8,100
Senate	4,250	350	0	4,600
Incumbents	12,400	6,200	750	19,350
Challengers	0	0	0	0
Open Seat	550	350	0	900
Winners	8,500	5,250	n/a	13,750
Losers	4,450	1,300	n/a	5,750

Hallmark Cards Inc.

*Phone: (816) 274-7457 * Fax: (816) 274-5061*
2501 McGee St., Mail Drop 288, P.O. Box 419580, Kansas City, MO 64141
Web: www.hallmark.com

With annual revenues of $3.6 billion and 20,100 employees, privately held Hallmark is the largest greeting card company in the United States. In addition to cards distributed under the brands Hallmark and Ambassador, the Kansas City, Mo. company produces family movies for television and owns the company that makes Crayola crayons, Easton, Pa.-based Binney & Smith.

Most of the company's cards are made in Kansas. Distribution centers are located in Liberty, Mo. and Enfield, Conn.

In January 1998, Hallmark acquired Irresistible Ink, a Minneapolis, Minn. firm that sends direct mail made to look as if it was hand-addressed. A month earlier Hallmark bought the second-largest greeting card publisher in Japan. Hallmark sells cards in more than 100 countries.

Founder Joyce C. Hall's descendants have a large stake in the company, which opened for business in 1910.

Other subsidiaries include: Revell-Monogram, a Morton Grove, Ill. firm that is the world's-largest manufacturer of plastic model kits; and New-York based Hallmark Entertainment, which produces television movies. The company also has an interest in Golden Books Family Entertainment.

Hallmark Political Action Committee (HallPAC) (C00000059) *Address: same as sponsor * Treasurer: Greg C. Swarens*

	1993-94	1995-96	1997	Totals
Receipts	$105,184	$88,023	$42,761	$235,968
Disburse	106,298	93,107	7,878	207,283
Cash	17,170	12,091	46,981	n/a
Contributions	94,500	80,250	5,000	179,750
Republicans	71,500	63,250	5,000	139,750
No. of Cand.	*33*	*29*	*1*	*63*
House	8,000	14,750	0	22,750
Senate	63,500	48,500	5,000	117,000
Democrats	23,000	17,000	0	40,000
No. of Cand.	*17*	*12*	*0*	*29*
House	15,000	12,000	0	27,000
Senate	8,000	5,000	0	13,000
Incumbents	42,500	38,250	5,000	85,750
Challengers	9,250	14,000	0	23,250
Open Seat	43,750	27,000	0	70,750
Winners	86,000	55,750	n/a	141,750
Losers	8,500	24,500	n/a	33,000

Magazine Publishers of America

*Phone: (202) 296-7277 * Fax: (202) 296-0343*
1211 Connecticut Ave. N.W., Suite 610, Washington, DC 20036
Web: www.magazine.org/menu/mgnet.home.html

The Magazine Publishers of America, formerly the Magazine Publishers Association, represents the interests of magazine producers and publishers across the country.

Magazine Publishers of America PAC (C00035774) *Address: same as sponsor * Treasurer: George Gross * Contact: Donald D. Kummerfeld, President*

	1993-94	1995-96	1997	Totals
Receipts	$15,090	$17,500	$10,500	$43,090
Disburse	12,775	20,000	7,500	40,275
Cash	2,625	625	3,625	n/a
Contributions	10,560	15,750	6,500	32,810
Republicans	2,000	13,000	4,000	19,000
No. of Cand.	*5*	*15*	*7*	*27*
House	1,000	7,500	3,500	12,000
Senate	1,000	5,500	500	7,000
Democrats	8,560	2,750	2,500	13,810
No. of Cand.	*17*	*5*	*5*	*27*
House	6,750	2,250	1,500	10,500
Senate	1,810	500	1,000	3,310
Incumbents	10,560	15,750	6,000	32,310
Challengers	0	0	0	0
Open Seat	0	0	500	500
Winners	5,750	15,000	n/a	20,750
Losers	4,810	750	n/a	5,560

Meredith Corp.

*Phone: (515) 284-2878 * Fax: (515) 284-3806*
1716 Locust St., Des Moines, IA 50309-3023
*Web: www.home-and-family.com * E-mail: larmatis@mdp.com*

Iowa-based Meredith was founded in 1902 as an agricultural publisher. It has since expanded to include mass audience and special interest publications for the home and family market. Meredith operates publishing, broadcasting and real estate segments. Sales in 1997 were $855 million.

The publicly held company, which employs 2,100 people, produces 278 book titles, 41 special-interest publications, and 21 magazines, including Better Homes and Gardens and Ladies' Home Journal. It owns one NBC-, four CBS- and six Fox-affiliated television stations.

Director E.T. Meredith owns about 17 percent of the company.

Meredith Corp. Employees Fund for Better Government (C00010520) *Address: same as sponsor * Treasurer: Phyllis E. Reynolds * Contact: Leo Armatis, Chairman*

	1993-94	1995-96	1997	Totals
Receipts	$19,880	$36,123	$15,016	$71,019
Disburse	26,623	32,278	10,389	69,290
Cash	2,277	5,423	10,049	n/a
Contributions	7,850	16,250	4,000	28,100
Republicans	6,350	14,250	3,500	24,100
No. of Cand.	*8*	*12*	*5*	*25*
House	4,350	10,750	2,000	17,100
Senate	2,000	3,500	1,500	7,000
Democrats	1,500	2,000	500	4,000
No. of Cand.	*2*	*4*	*1*	*7*
House	500	2,000	500	3,000
Senate	1,000	0	0	1,000
Incumbents	5,450	14,250	4,000	23,700
Challengers	0	1,000	0	1,000
Open Seat	2,400	1,000	0	3,400
Winners	7,350	15,250	n/a	22,600
Losers	500	1,000	n/a	1,500

Phillips Publishing International Inc.

*Phone: (301) 340-2100 * Fax: (301) 251-3758*
7811 Montrose Rd., Potomac, MD 20854
Web: www.phillips.com

Phillips Publishing International produces magazines, newsletters and directories for business and consumer markets. The company's 100-plus publications include Oil and Gas Investor, Aviation Maintenance and Wireless Product News, and reportedly reach 2 million subscribers. The privately held company, founded in 1974 by owner, President and CEO Thomas Phillips, is based in Potomac, Md. Sales in 1996 were estimated at $227 million.

Phillips' subsidiaries include: Phillips Publishing Inc., Phillips Business Information, Hart Publications and Eagle Publishing. The company has offices in Washington, California, Virginia, New York, Colorado, Texas, New Jersey, the United Kingdom and Norway.

Phillips was No. 35 in the Washington Business Journal's list of "Top 100 Private Companies" in the D.C. area in 1996.

Phillips Publishing International Inc. Political Action Committee (C00266536) *Address: same as sponsor * Treasurer: Carl A. Paladino Jr.*

	1993-94	1995-96	1997	Totals
Receipts	$26,317	$38,343	$34,690	$99,350
Disburse	26,186	32,100	11,500	69,786
Cash	211	1,137	24,327	n/a
Contributions	23,500	62,250	7,450	93,200
Republicans	23,500	62,250	7,450	93,200
No. of Cand.	*19*	*67*	*13*	*99*
House	13,250	52,750	5,200	71,200
Senate	10,250	9,500	2,250	22,000
Democrats	0	0	0	0
No. of Cand.	*0*	*0*	*0*	*0*
House	0	0	0	0
Senate	0	0	0	0
Incumbents	1,250	36,000	6,350	43,600
Challengers	20,750	10,000	250	31,000
Open Seat	1,500	16,250	0	17,750
Winners	6,250	32,750	n/a	39,000
Losers	17,250	29,500	n/a	46,750

Printing Industries of America

*Phone: (703) 519-8158 * Fax: (703) 548-3227*
100 Daingerfield Rd., Alexandria, VA 22314-2888
*Web: www.printing.org * E-mail: bcooper@printing.org*

Printing Industries of America is the world's largest graphic arts trade association. It has about 14,000 members in 33 regional affiliates throughout the United States and Canada. Its members are commercial printers, electronic imaging companies and equipment manufacturers. PIA estimates that the printing industry generates more than $116 billion in sales annually.

A top priority for the industry is reducing the depreciation schedule for computers from five to two years. PIA supports reducing the capital gains tax and regulatory reform of workplace safety and health laws. It lobbies on several environmental issues, including the EPA's proposed ozone standard. PIA opposes the agency's new clean air standards.

PIA's PAC only accepts donations from PIA member executives. Its PAC donations go to federal candidates, state candidates and grassroots activity. The group was the top printing contributor to 1996 congressional campaigns. It spent more than half of its money on open races and challengers, but only three Democrats received a contribution. The leading recipients were Sen. Gordon Smith, R-Ore., Rep. Jim Gibbons, R-Nev., and Senate candidate Rudy Boschwitz of Minnesota.

Printing Industries of America (C00018028) *Address: same as sponsor * Treasurer: Benjamin Y. Cooper*

	1993-94	1995-96	1997	Totals
Receipts	$172,034	$295,640	$115,997	$583,671
Disburse	174,711	285,291	69,935	529,937
Cash	4,884	15,243	61,310	n/a
Contributions	139,593	221,275	54,000	414,868
Republicans	133,343	219,650	53,000	405,993
No. of Cand.	*122*	*170*	*47*	*339*
House	56,410	119,900	26,000	202,310
Senate	76,933	99,750	27,000	203,683
Democrats	6,250	1,125	1,000	8,375
No. of Cand.	*8*	*3*	*1*	*12*
House	5,250	1,125	0	6,375
Senate	1,000	0	1,000	2,000
Incumbents	71,288	105,875	48,500	225,663
Challengers	25,122	38,850	6,000	69,972
Open Seat	43,183	76,550	0	119,733
Winners	118,163	154,300	n/a	272,463
Losers	21,430	66,975	n/a	88,405

R.R. Donnelley & Sons Co.

*Phone: (312) 326-8417 * Fax: (312) 326-8262*
77 W. Wacker Dr., Chicago, IL 60601-1696
Web: www.rrdonnelley.com

R.R. Donnelley & Sons is North America's No. 1 printer of catalogs and other magazines such as Time, TV Guide and trade publications. Sales for 1997 were $4.9 billion and the company employs 28,000 people worldwide.

Donnelley & Sons also prints telephone directories and books, and reproduces and distributes software through subsidiary Stream

International. The publicly traded company provides online services as well, including a "bulletin board" service which allows publishers to post advertisements online to be instantly downloaded by the printing service, saving both time and money.

R.R. Donnelley & Sons Co. Political Action Committee (C00033977) *Address: same as sponsor * Treasurer: Kevin C. Richardson * Contact: James R. Donnelley, Chairperson*

	1993-94	1995-96	1997	Totals
Receipts	$50,495	$49,161	$28,250	$127,906
Disburse	46,737	54,438	7,517	108,692
Cash	12,998	5,006	25,747	n/a
Contributions	39,600	40,000	7,500	87,100
Republicans	32,500	39,000	7,500	79,000
No. of Cand.	*33*	*39*	*9*	*81*
House	15,000	20,000	3,000	38,000
Senate	17,500	19,000	4,500	41,000
Democrats	7,100	1,000	0	8,100
No. of Cand.	*10*	*2*	*0*	*12*
House	3,750	500	0	4,250
Senate	3,350	500	0	3,850
Incumbents	27,850	24,500	7,500	59,850
Challengers	3,250	2,500	0	5,750
Open Seat	8,000	13,000	0	21,000
Winners	35,350	29,500	n/a	64,850
Losers	4,250	10,500	n/a	14,750

West Publishing Co.

*Phone: (612) 339-6900 * Fax: (612) 339-0961*
100 Washington Ave. S., Suite 2200, Minneapolis, MN 55401
Web: www.westlaw.com

West Publishing is now part of West Group. The private legal publisher, based in Minnesota, employs about 6,000 people. It is a leading publisher of federal court decisions and maintains an online legal research system, WESTLAW, used by attorneys and law students.

The merger of the West Group companies — Bancroft-Whitney, Clark Boardman Callaghan, Lawyers Cooperative Publishing, Westlaw and West Publishing — assembles several legal reference tools into an integrated research system. West Group aims to be the preeminent provider of information to the U.S. legal market.

West Group is a subsidiary of Thomson Corp., a Canadian publishing conglomerate.

West Publishing Co. PAC (West Publishing PAC) (C00229088) *Address: same as sponsor * Treasurer: Christian M. Sande*

	1993-94	1995-96	1997	Totals
Receipts	$249,322	$126,942	$481	$376,745
Disburse	229,408	199,591	5,658	434,657
Cash	118,102	45,452	40,275	n/a
Contributions	172,658	140,928	0	313,586
Republicans	36,000	62,500	0	98,500
No. of Cand.	*21*	*65*	*0*	*86*
House	17,500	41,250	0	58,750
Senate	18,500	21,250	0	39,750
Democrats	112,180	78,428	0	190,608
No. of Cand.	*39*	*25*	*0*	*64*
House	60,500	42,500	0	103,000
Senate	51,680	35,928	0	87,608
Incumbents	125,862	122,178	0	248,040
Challengers	4,000	5,000	0	9,000
Open Seat	42,796	5,750	0	48,546
Winners	118,502	110,928	n/a	229,430
Losers	54,156	30,000	n/a	84,156

TV/Movies/Music

Adelphia Communications Corp.

*Phone: (814) 274-9830 * Fax: (814) 274-7782*
Main at Water St., Coudersport, PA 16915
*Web: www.adelphia.com * E-mail: rfisher@adelphia.net*

Adelphia Communications owns, operates and manages cable television systems in 10 states, primarily in the Midwest and mid-Atlantic areas. Cable systems owned or managed by Adelphia serve about 1.7 million subscribers who subscribe to more than 750,000 premium service units. Sales for 1997 reached $472 million, a 17 percent increase over 1996.

Early 1998 brought a wave of acquisitions and partnerships for the company, strengthening its presence in several key markets. One of its subsidiaries, Hyperion, acquired six new markets in February 1998. Other partnerships ensued with Tele-Communications (TCI), Cablevision Systems Corp., Time Warner and Lenfest Telephony.

Adelphia's 3,100 employees work in suburban areas of large and medium-sized cities within the 50 largest television markets in the United States, including Boston, Cleveland, Philadelphia and Pittsburgh.

The Rigas family, which founded the company in 1952, still owns 95 percent of the company's NASDAQ-traded stock.

Adelphia Communications Political Action Committee (C00321497) *Phone: (202) 776-2911 * Fax: (202) 776-2222 * 1200 New Hampshire Ave. N.W., Ste. 800, Washington, DC 20036 * E-mail: msr@dlalaw.com * Treasurer: Randall D. Fisher * Contact: Marvin Rappaport, Gov. Affairs Contact*

	1993-94	1995-96	1997	Totals
Receipts	$0	$41,000	$29,410	$70,410
Disburse	0	31,012	15,325	46,337
Cash	0	18,742	14,084	n/a
Contributions	0	10,000	6,196	16,196
Republicans	0	10,000	5,196	15,196
No. of Cand.	*0*	*1*	*5*	*6*
House	0	10,000	1,000	11,000
Senate	0	0	4,196	4,196
Democrats	0	0	1,000	1,000
No. of Cand.	*0*	*0*	*1*	*1*
House	0	0	0	0
Senate	0	0	1,000	1,000
Incumbents	0	0	6,196	6,196
Challengers	0	0	0	0
Open Seat	0	10,000	0	10,000
Winners	0	10,000	n/a	10,000
Losers	0	0	n/a	0

American Society of Composers, Authors and Publishers

*Phone: (212) 621-6000 * Fax: (212) 595-3342*
One Lincoln Plaza, New York, NY 10023
*Web: www.ascap.com * E-mail: info@ascap.com*

The American Society of Composers, Authors and Publishers is the oldest performing-rights licensing organization in the United States and the only one owned and run by its members. It is the largest organization of its type in terms of license-fee collections and performance-royalty payments, and in membership, with more than 75,000 members in the United States and 200,000 abroad.

ASCAP's legislative agenda includes mobilizing its membership in opposition to legislation that would limit licensing rights or decrease copyright limits.

ASCAP Legislative Fund for the Arts (C00228296) *Address: same as sponsor * Treasurer: James R. Collins * Contact: Marilyn Bergman, Chairperson*

	1993-94	1995-96	1997	Totals
Receipts	$113,179	$169,056	$78,991	$361,226
Disburse	137,229	169,552	71,072	377,853
Cash	11,429	10,932	18,851	n/a
Contributions	126,210	141,050	66,650	333,910
Republicans	19,250	59,950	28,500	107,700
No. of Cand.	*12*	*37*	*29*	*78*
House	12,000	45,950	23,750	81,700
Senate	7,250	14,000	4,750	26,000
Democrats	106,960	81,100	38,150	226,210
No. of Cand.	*82*	*61*	*40*	*183*
House	69,100	59,600	24,400	153,100
Senate	37,860	21,500	13,750	73,110
Incumbents	114,860	113,300	66,150	294,310
Challengers	2,100	8,800	500	11,400
Open Seat	9,250	18,950	0	28,200
Winners	97,750	122,250	n/a	220,000
Losers	28,460	18,800	n/a	47,260

Broadcast Music Inc.

*Phone: (212) 586-2000 * Fax: (212) 245-8986*
320 W. 57th St., New York, NY 10019-3790
*Web: www.bmi.com * E-mail: govtrel@bmi.com*

Broadcast Music is a nonprofit organization that protects the performing rights of more than 200,000 songwriters, composers and music publishers. Founded in 1940, BMI tracks radio airplay and distributes royalties to its members for the public performance and copying of their works.

In January 1989, BMI became the first performing rights organization to log radio airplay at college stations. BMI supports legislative efforts to guarantee compensation for songwriters, composers and publishers for digital home taping. Also, it led the fight against The Fairness in Musical Licensing Act of 1997, which would exempt some small businesses from paying for using recorded music.

Broadcast Music Inc. Legislative Fund for Authors Composers & Publishers (C00302950) *Address: same as sponsor * Treasurer: Thomas Curry*

	1993-94	*1995-96*	*1997*	*Totals*
Receipts	$0	$68,840	$9,460	$78,300
Disburse	0	43,969	30,632	74,601
Cash	0	24,871	3,699	n/a
Contributions	0	27,400	21,500	48,900
Republicans	0	7,500	14,750	22,250
No. of Cand.	*0*	*9*	*14*	*23*
House	0	3,500	8,750	12,250
Senate	0	4,000	6,000	10,000
Democrats	0	19,900	6,750	26,650
No. of Cand.	*0*	*33*	*10*	*43*
House	0	14,250	4,250	18,500
Senate	0	5,650	2,500	8,150
Incumbents	0	21,000	21,500	42,500
Challengers	0	2,000	0	2,000
Open Seat	0	4,400	0	4,400
Winners	0	21,450	n/a	21,450
Losers	0	5,950	n/a	5,950

Cablevision Systems Corp.

*Phone: (516) 364-8450 * Fax: (516) 393-1780*
One Media Crossways, Woodbury, NY 11797
*Web: www.cablevision.com * E-mail: contact@cablevision.com*

Cablevision Systems is one of the largest cable television operators and telecommunications companies in the United States. The public company's annual sales are about $1.3 billion and it employs more than 7,000 people.

Headquartered in New York, Cablevision serves more than 2.9 million cable customers primarily in the New York, Boston and Cleveland metro areas, but also offers services in Arkansas, Connecticut, Florida, Illinois, Kentucky, Massachusetts, Michigan, Ohio, New Jersey and North Carolina.

Cablevision also provides high-speed Internet access using existing cable, cable modems and local telephone service. It owns a majority interest in New York City's Madison Square Garden Arena, the New York Knicks basketball team, the New York Rangers hockey team and MSG cable sports network.

Representing nearly a half-billion dollars of its revenues annually, its Rainbow Media Holdings subsidiary, jointly owned with NBC, owns several cable channels including American Movie Classics, Bravo and the Independent Film Channel.

Cablevision Lightpath Inc. is one of the company's subsidiaries.

Cablevision Systems Corp. Political Action Committee (C00197863) *Address: same as sponsor * Treasurer: Sheila Mahony*

	1993-94	*1995-96*	*1997*	*Totals*
Receipts	$10,000	$20,000	$15,000	$45,000
Disburse	13,575	18,445	10,250	42,270
Cash	5,465	7,020	11,770	n/a
Contributions	11,575	16,445	8,250	36,270
Republicans	4,500	13,375	3,000	20,875
No. of Cand.	*4*	*10*	*2*	*16*
House	2,500	8,375	3,000	13,875
Senate	2,000	5,000	0	7,000
Democrats	6,075	3,070	5,250	14,395
No. of Cand.	*8*	*7*	*4*	*19*
House	5,075	3,070	2,250	10,395
Senate	1,000	0	3,000	4,000
Incumbents	11,075	11,945	8,250	31,270

Challengers	500	1,500	0	2,000
Open Seat	0	3,000	0	3,000
Winners	10,450	9,945	n/a	20,395
Losers	1,125	6,500	n/a	7,625

Comcast Corp.

*Phone: (215) 665-1700 * Fax: (215) 981-7744*
1500 Market St., 35th Floor, Philadelphia, PA 19102-2148
Web: www.comcast.com

Comcast is an international communications company with businesses in cable television, wireless and wireline telecommunications and satellite video services. In addition, the company has a majority interest in and manages the cable home-shopping channel QVC and holds a controlling interest in E! Entertainment Television.

With 17,000 employees and 1997 revenues of $4.9 billion, Comcast is the fourth-largest domestic cable company. The company's consolidated and affiliated operations serve more than 10 million customers worldwide, with its cable operation providing service to 4.3 million people in 21 states, including California, Colorado and several eastern states.

Comcast is a public corporation, although 82 percent of the company is owned by Sural Corp. This corporation, in turn, is largely controlled by Brian L. Roberts, president of Comcast, who holds a majority of the voting power of Sural.

Subsidiaries include: Comcast Cable Communications and Comcast Cellular Holdings. The company also owns Comcast UK Cable Partners Limited, although as of January 1998, it had plans to sell this business.

Comcast Corp. Political Action Committee (C00248716) *Address: same as sponsor * Treasurer: William A. Dordelman * Contact: John R. Alchin, Chairman*

	1993-94	*1995-96*	*1997*	*Totals*
Receipts	$169,204	$164,038	$98,270	$431,512
Disburse	169,843	114,393	71,883	356,119
Cash	43,563	93,218	119,610	n/a
Contributions	121,363	95,550	30,775	247,688
Republicans	58,400	63,900	13,275	135,575
No. of Cand.	*36*	*28*	*9*	*73*
House	33,900	39,900	6,275	80,075
Senate	24,500	24,000	7,000	55,500
Democrats	62,963	31,650	17,500	112,113
No. of Cand.	*34*	*25*	*13*	*72*
House	39,500	20,650	4,000	64,150
Senate	23,463	11,000	13,500	47,963
Incumbents	106,650	69,550	29,775	205,975
Challengers	2,500	3,500	0	6,000
Open Seat	14,750	23,000	1,000	38,750
Winners	90,650	71,300	n/a	161,950
Losers	30,713	24,250	n/a	54,963

Home Shopping Network Inc.

Phone: (813) 572-8585
P.O. Box 9090, Clearwater, FL 34618
Web: www.internet.net

The Home Shopping Network PAC was terminated in April 1996.

Home Shopping Network Inc. Political Action Committee (HSN PAC) (C00231225) *Address: same as sponsor * Treasurer: Kevin J. McKeon*

	1993-94	*1995-96*	*1997*	*Totals*
Receipts	$24,497	$33,217	$0	$57,714
Disburse	23,321	40,632	0	63,953
Cash	7,407	0	0	n/a
Contributions	16,821	14,000	0	30,821
Republicans	5,921	13,000	0	18,921
No. of Cand.	*4*	*7*	*0*	*11*
House	3,921	7,000	0	10,921
Senate	2,000	6,000	0	8,000
Democrats	10,900	1,000	0	11,900
No. of Cand.	*8*	*3*	*0*	*11*
House	3,900	0	0	3,900
Senate	7,000	1,000	0	8,000
Incumbents	16,821	14,000	0	30,821
Challengers	0	0	0	0
Open Seat	0	0	0	0
Winners	16,821	6,500	n/a	23,321
Losers	0	7,500	n/a	7,500

Jones International Ltd.

*Phone: (303) 784-8460 * Fax: (303) 790-7324*
9697 E. Mineral Ave., Englewood, CO 80112
Web: www.jii.com

Jones International, formed in 1969, is a privately held company which creates, acquires, produces and distributes programming to radio stations and cable television operators. Glenn R. Jones is founder and serves as chairman of the Englewood, Colo.-based company. Sales in 1996 were $12.7 million and the company reported 154 employees in 1995.

Jones' radio programs are broadcast on more than 1,225 radio station affiliates in the United States and Canada. Its television programs are distributed through the Product Information Network and Great American Country network.

The company owns more than 20 subsidiaries in the cable television, radio and film industries.

Jones International Ltd. Political Action Committee (C00197244)
*Address: same as sponsor * Treasurer: Anne Tell * Contact: Tom Anema, Member*

	1993-94	1995-96	1997	Totals
Receipts	$44,523	$42,991	$21,400	$108,914
Disburse	49,301	47,543	11,589	108,433
Cash	8,039	6	29,746	n/a
Contributions	34,825	27,325	8,840	70,990
Republicans	18,475	23,625	7,740	49,840
No. of Cand.	*23*	*30*	*11*	*64*
House	10,725	14,625	3,240	28,590
Senate	7,750	9,000	4,500	21,250
Democrats	16,350	3,700	1,100	21,150
No. of Cand.	*9*	*8*	*3*	*20*
House	5,350	3,700	1,100	10,150
Senate	11,000	0	0	11,000
Incumbents	29,325	21,375	6,840	57,540
Challengers	750	1,050	1,000	2,800
Open Seat	4,000	4,900	0	8,900
Winners	31,725	21,525	n/a	53,250
Losers	3,100	5,800	n/a	8,900

Marcus Cable Properties Inc.

*Phone: (214) 521-7898 * Fax: (214) 526-2154*
2911 Turtle Creek Blvd., Suite 1300, Dallas, TX 75219
Web: www.marcuscable.com

Marcus Cable Properties is the nation's 10th-largest cable operator, serving more than 1.2 million customers in 18 states. The company had 1997 revenues of $479 million and employs 2,000 workers.

Microsoft Corp. co-founder Paul Allen purchased the private company for about $2 billion in April 1998. Allen will become a full partner in the business.

Marcus Cable has grown by acquiring other cable operators such as Star Cablevision in Wisconsin and Minnesota; Simmons Communications in Texas and the Delaware/Maryland area; Crown Cable in Wisconsin and Alabama; and Sammons Communications Inc. in the Northeast.

In March 1998 Marcus announced plans to sell its cable operations in Virginia and Connecticut to TMC Holdings Inc. The sale will total $150 million.

Marcus Cable Properties Inc. PAC (MarcPAC) (C00317289)
*Address: same as sponsor * Treasurer: John P. Klingstedt*

	1993-94	1995-96	1997	Totals
Receipts	$0	$40,150	$42,618	$82,768
Disburse	0	19,000	46,750	65,750
Cash	0	21,131	16,099	n/a
Contributions	0	18,000	23,250	41,250
Republicans	0	10,000	7,000	17,000
No. of Cand.	*0*	*13*	*5*	*18*
House	0	8,000	3,000	11,000
Senate	0	2,000	4,000	6,000
Democrats	0	7,000	16,250	23,250
No. of Cand.	*0*	*7*	*8*	*15*
House	0	4,000	8,250	12,250
Senate	0	3,000	8,000	11,000
Incumbents	0	11,000	23,250	34,250
Challengers	0	2,000	0	2,000
Open Seat	0	5,000	0	5,000
Winners	0	14,000	n/a	14,000
Losers	0	4,000	n/a	4,000

Metro-Goldwyn-Mayer

*Phone: (310) 449-3520 * Fax: (310) 449-8761*
2500 Broadway St., Santa Monica, CA 90404
*Web: www.mgmua.com * E-mail: mangeletti@mgm.com*

Metro-Goldwyn-Mayer produces and distributes entertainment products, including motion pictures, television programming, home video, interactive software, music and licensed merchandise. It has a 1,500-title film library, a 4,500-title home video library and a significant television library. Headquartered in Santa Monica, Calif., MGM's holding company, MGM Holdings Inc., employs 1,020 people. The publicly traded company reported $831 million in 1997 revenues.

Subsidiaries include: MGM Pictures, United Artists Pictures, MGM Worldwide Television, MGM/UA Telecommunications Group, MGM/UA Distribution Co., MGM/UA Home Entertainment, MGM/UA Music, MGM Interactive and MGM/UA Licensing and Merchandising.

Metro-Goldwyn-Mayer Political Action Committee (C00207589)
*Address: same as sponsor * Treasurer: Deborah J. Arvesen * Contact: Maria Angeletti, V.P. of Corporate Affairs*

	1993-94	1995-96	1997	Totals
Receipts	$482	$47,997	$14,067	$62,546
Disburse	4,642	39,576	18,135	62,353
Cash	7,885	16,316	12,253	n/a
Contributions	500	27,900	13,000	41,400
Republicans	0	12,000	6,000	18,000
No. of Cand.	*0*	*8*	*7*	*15*
House	0	3,500	3,500	7,000
Senate	0	8,500	2,500	11,000
Democrats	500	15,900	7,000	23,400
No. of Cand.	*1*	*17*	*7*	*25*
House	0	5,900	1,000	6,900
Senate	500	10,000	6,000	16,500
Incumbents	0	19,900	13,000	32,900
Challengers	0	1,500	0	1,500
Open Seat	500	6,500	0	7,000
Winners	0	23,900	n/a	23,900
Losers	500	4,000	n/a	4,500

Motion Picture Association of America

*Phone: (202) 293-1966 * Fax: (202) 293-7674*
1600 Eye St. N.W., Washington, DC 20006
Web: www.mpaa.org

The Motion Picture Association of America and its international counterpart, the Motion Picture Association, serve as representatives of the American motion picture, home video and television industries.

Founded in 1922 as the trade association of the American film industry, the MPAA has broadened its mandate over the years to reflect the diversity of an expanding industry. The initial task assigned to the association was to stem the waves of criticism of American movies, then silent, while sometimes rambunctious and rowdy, and to restore a more favorable public image for the motion picture business.

The MPAA serves its members from its offices in Los Angeles and Washington. On its board of directors are the chairmen and presidents of the seven major producers and distributors of motion picture and television programs in the United States. These members include the Walt Disney Co., Sony Pictures Entertainment, Metro-Goldwyn-Mayer Inc., Paramount Pictures Corp., Twentieth Century Fox Film Corp., Universal Studios Inc. and Warner Bros.

Motion Picture Association of America Inc. Political Action Committee (C00139519) *Address: same as sponsor * Treasurer: Cristina Giroux*

	1993-94	1995-96	1997	Totals
Receipts	$25,871	$81,478	$57,650	$164,999
Disburse	23,910	80,608	50,557	155,075
Cash	1,983	2,853	9,946	n/a
Contributions	24,857	65,612	47,307	137,776
Republicans	9,000	33,680	23,807	66,487
No. of Cand.	*9*	*38*	*26*	*73*
House	4,000	22,500	15,807	42,307
Senate	5,000	11,180	8,000	24,180
Democrats	15,857	31,932	23,500	71,289
No. of Cand.	*24*	*37*	*25*	*86*
House	12,035	18,196	11,500	41,731
Senate	3,822	13,736	12,000	29,558
Incumbents	18,987	55,612	47,307	121,906

(Data for Motion Picture Association continued)

Challengers	3,500	2,000	0	5,500
Open Seat	2,370	8,000	0	10,370
Winners	16,986	55,932	n/a	72,918
Losers	7,871	9,680	n/a	17,551

National Association of Broadcasters

*Phone: (202) 429-5301 * Fax: (202) 429-5343*
1771 N St. N.W., Washington, DC 20036
Web: www.nab.org

The National Association of Broadcasters represents radio and television stations throughout the United States, including the major networks. The group also has associate members including equipment and program producers. The NAB is the industry's voice before Congress and the Federal Communications Commission and interprets laws and regulations.

NAB lobbies on a number of communications issues. The group opposed President Clinton's call for free air time for political candidates and maintained that it was a congressional matter. The NAB supports local-to-local satellite delivery of broadcast signals only if satellite carriers are required to carry all local television stations and agree to respect exclusive programming rights. Digital television and parental guidelines are other important issues.

The NAB was the leading radio and television broadcast contributor to 1996 congressional campaigns. The group favored Republican candidates by a 2-to-1 margin. Most candidates received less than $5,000.

The top recipients were Reps. Charles "Chip" Pickering, R-Miss., Rick White, R-Wash., and Tom Coburn, R-Okla. Each received more than $10,000. Sen. Jack Reed, D-R.I., and Rep. Rick Boucher, D-Va., a member of a telecommunications subcommittee, were the leading Democratic recipients.

National Association of Broadcasters Television and Radio Political Action Committee (C00009985) *Address: same as sponsor * Treasurer: James May * Contact: Rae Ann Bevington, PAC Manager*

	1993-94	1995-96	1997	Totals
Receipts	$639,614	$739,226	$447,377	$1,826,217
Disburse	588,716	664,204	305,267	1,558,187
Cash	75,571	150,596	292,707	n/a
Contributions	437,990	434,857	185,601	1,058,448
Republicans	186,900	313,160	120,215	620,275
No. of Cand.	*95*	*125*	*79*	*299*
House	110,900	222,187	73,484	406,571
Senate	76,000	90,973	46,731	213,704
Democrats	251,090	117,750	65,386	434,226
No. of Cand.	*107*	*54*	*42*	*203*
House	180,350	87,750	35,000	303,100
Senate	70,740	30,000	30,386	131,126
Incumbents	392,840	371,160	183,101	947,101
Challengers	14,000	6,500	500	21,000
Open Seat	31,150	57,197	2,000	90,347
Winners	345,900	382,660	n/a	728,560
Losers	92,090	52,197	n/a	144,287

National Cable Television Association

*Phone: (202) 775-3650 * Fax: (202) 775-3671*
1724 Massachusetts Ave. N.W., Washington, DC 20036
Web: www.ncta.com

The National Cable Television Association represents cable systems serving more than 80 percent of the nation's estimated 64 million cable subscribers. It also represents more than 100 cable program networks such as CNN, HBO and MTV. In addition, NCTA represents hardware suppliers and providers of other services to the cable industry.

The NCTA lobbies on many communications issues, including the Telecommunications Act of 1996. It favors easier access to local telephone systems for cable companies seeking to provide other services. The group supports "must-carry" and retransmission requirements for Direct Broadcast Satellite companies that compete with cable services. It opposes federal price regulation of the cable industry.

The association's PAC was the top cable industry PAC contributor to 1996 congressional races. Nearly 50 candidates received at least $5,000, including 13 who received $10,000 each. The NCTA spent nothing on challengers, the largest-spending PAC to do so.

The top recipients included Reps. Dennis Hastert, R-Ill., Joe L. Barton, R-Texas, Dan Schaefer, R-Colo., and Thomas J. Manton, D-N.Y., all members of a House telecommunications subcommittee.

National Cable Television Association Political Action Committee (Cable PAC) (C00010082) *Address: same as sponsor * Treasurer: Kenneth A. Gross * Contact: Eleanor Winter, Dir. of Special Projects*

	1993-94	1995-96	1997	Totals
Receipts	$566,615	$618,053	$291,782	$1,476,450
Disburse	557,931	641,640	286,190	1,485,761
Cash	30,057	6,470	12,059	n/a
Contributions	496,900	547,346	224,354	1,268,600
Republicans	282,000	372,976	116,803	771,779
No. of Cand.	*81*	*92*	*29*	*202*
House	190,500	265,980	108,663	565,143
Senate	91,500	106,996	8,140	206,636
Democrats	214,900	174,370	107,551	496,821
No. of Cand.	*59*	*40*	*32*	*131*
House	177,400	144,870	73,395	395,665
Senate	37,500	29,500	34,156	101,156
Incumbents	427,400	493,846	219,354	1,140,600
Challengers	5,000	0	0	5,000
Open Seat	62,000	53,500	2,500	118,000
Winners	432,700	481,351	n/a	914,051
Losers	64,200	65,995	n/a	130,195

News Corp Ltd.

*Phone: (202) 824-6503 * Fax: (202) 824-6510*
444 N. Capitol St. N.W., Suite 722, Washington, DC 20001
*Web: www.newscorp.com * E-mail: svest@dgsys.com*

Rupert Murdoch's News Corp. counts the Fox television network, movie studio Twentieth Century Fox, HarperCollins Publishers, the New York Post, The Times newspaper in London, The Weekly Standard and TV Guide among its media companies. The company also owns 22 television stations in the United States, an Asian satellite television network, a Latin American cable television channel and interests in an Australian TV network.

Although based in Australia, News Corp. derives about 70 percent of its sales from U.S. businesses. The publicly traded company posted $10.7 billion in 1997 sales.

News Corp.'s 1997 acquisition of New World Communications makes the Fox Group the largest in the country with 22 stations that reach more than 40 percent of all television homes. In 1997, News Corp. acquired a controlling interest in International Family Entertainment, which owns the Family Channel. News Corp. plans to acquire the entire company. The company also bought the Los Angeles Dodgers baseball team.

Fox divisions and subsidiaries include: Fox Kids Network, Fox Sports, Fox Searchlight, Fox Interactive, Fox Merchandising Co., Fox 2000, Fox Animation and Fox News.

FoxPAC (Fox Inc. and subsidiaries) (formerly known as Twentieth Century Fox PAC) (C00171421) *Address: same as sponsor * Treasurer: Steven Vest*

	1993-94	1995-96	1997	Totals
Receipts	$31,980	$61,020	$38,194	$131,194
Disburse	61,672	68,159	28,858	158,689
Cash	12,973	5,834	15,431	n/a
Contributions	57,672	60,159	26,858	144,689
Republicans	24,422	41,159	16,500	82,081
No. of Cand.	*15*	*36*	*14*	*65*
House	7,000	31,000	9,500	47,500
Senate	17,422	10,159	7,000	34,581
Democrats	33,250	19,000	10,358	62,608
No. of Cand.	*27*	*17*	*13*	*57*
House	23,750	15,500	6,910	46,160
Senate	9,500	3,500	3,448	16,448
Incumbents	51,250	53,159	26,858	131,267
Challengers	1,000	1,500	0	2,500
Open Seat	5,422	5,500	0	10,922
Winners	44,672	51,659	n/a	96,331
Losers	13,000	8,500	n/a	21,500

Recording Industry Association of America

*Phone: (202) 775-0101 * Fax: (202) 775-7253*
1330 Connecticut Ave. N.W., Suite 300, Washington, DC 20036
Web: www.riaa.com

Representing the sound recording industry is the Recording Industry Association of America, a trade association whose member companies create, manufacture and distribute about 90 percent of all legitimate sound recordings produced and sold in the United States.

The association has more than 250 members including Warner Bros. Records, Columbia, Motown, RCA, Geffen and Capitol, as well as lesser-known labels such as Sparrow, Jim Henson Records, Rabbit Ears and One Little Indian.

The association addresses issues such as trade regulations and copyright problems and is working with other organizations to develop a global copyright management system that encodes copyright information in recorded music. It also operates an anti-piracy unit and conducts consumer and industry research.

Recording Industry Association of America Inc. Political Action Committee (formerly known as Recording Arts PAC) (C00009357) *Address: same as sponsor * Treasurer: Jennifer L. Bendall*

	1993-94	1995-96	1997	Totals
Receipts	$24,360	$117,125	$5,000	$146,485
Disburse	25,195	90,382	31,255	146,832
Cash	141	26,882	627	n/a
Contributions	19,690	73,839	28,252	121,781
Republicans	2,000	26,000	11,700	39,700
No. of Cand.	*2*	*19*	*14*	*35*
House	0	17,000	8,700	25,700
Senate	2,000	9,000	3,000	14,000
Democrats	17,690	47,839	16,552	82,081
No. of Cand.	*22*	*32*	*10*	*64*
House	10,250	24,250	5,257	39,757
Senate	7,440	23,589	11,295	42,324
Incumbents	16,940	49,250	21,651	87,841
Challengers	1,250	5,000	0	6,250
Open Seat	2,000	19,589	6,601	28,190
Winners	16,200	59,750	n/a	75,950
Losers	3,490	14,089	n/a	17,579

Salem Communications Corp.

*Phone: (805) 987-0400 * Fax: (805) 384-4522*
4880 Santa Rosa Rd., Suite 300, Camarillo, CA 93012
Web: www.salemcomm.com

Salem Communications is a $159 million broadcaster of religious programming and talk for a conservative listening audience. Salem operates religious format radio stations and a national radio network, Salem Radio Network, that offers talk programming, news and music to affiliated stations.

The private California company owns or operates 44 radio stations in 28 markets across the United States. It has about $65 million in annual sales.

Salem Communications Corp. Political Action Committee (C00321158) *Address: same as sponsor * Treasurer: Charles A. Merritt III * Contact: Edward Atsinger, President and CEO*

	1993-94	1995-96	1997	Totals
Receipts	$0	$16,996	$7,335	$24,331
Disburse	0	14,500	6,500	21,000
Cash	0	2,496	3,332	n/a
Contributions	0	13,500	5,500	19,000
Republicans	0	13,500	5,500	19,000
No. of Cand.	*0*	*16*	*9*	*25*
House	0	9,500	5,500	15,000
Senate	0	4,000	0	4,000
Democrats	0	0	0	0
No. of Cand.	*0*	*0*	*0*	*0*
House	0	0	0	0
Senate	0	0	0	0
Incumbents	0	8,000	5,500	13,500
Challengers	0	2,000	0	2,000
Open Seat	0	3,500	0	3,500
Winners	0	7,500	n/a	7,500
Losers	0	6,000	n/a	6,000

Sony Pictures

*Phone: (310) 244-6660 * Fax: (310) 244-2467*
10202 W. Washington Blvd., Thalberg, Room 2514, Culver City, CA 90232-3195
Web: www.spe.sony.com

Sony Pictures is the film, television and video production subsidiary of the entertainment business division of Sony. In 1997, Sony Pictures accounted for $3.5 billion of the publicly traded corporation's total sales of $45.7 billion.

Sony Pictures operates primarily through Columbia TriStar Motion Pictures, Television and Home Video Groups. Through these companies, Sony creates about 25 motion pictures yearly. Past projects have included such films as "Men in Black," "Jerry Maguire" and "As Good As It Gets." These companies also produce and distribute television shows ranging from "Mad About You" and "Jeopardy!" to "Days of Our Lives" and "Ricki Lake."

Sony Pictures also maintains two studios — Sony Picture Studios and Culver Studios — and operates an in-house special effects production company, Imageworks, which has produced the effects for such movies as "Starship Troopers" and "Contact."

Sony Pictures Entertainment Inc. Political Action Committee (C00282038) *Address: same as sponsor * Treasurer: Kenneth S. Williams * Contact: Hope Boonshaft, Senior V.P. of External Affairs*

	1993-94	1995-96	1997	Totals
Receipts	$60,850	$144,427	$72,310	$277,587
Disburse	57,450	122,350	65,250	245,050
Cash	3,400	25,478	32,539	n/a
Contributions	54,450	93,850	56,750	205,050
Republicans	10,250	41,300	31,750	83,300
No. of Cand.	*13*	*48*	*33*	*94*
House	4,750	28,300	22,250	55,300
Senate	5,500	13,000	9,500	28,000
Democrats	44,200	52,550	25,000	121,750
No. of Cand.	*50*	*60*	*26*	*136*
House	25,700	34,050	14,500	74,250
Senate	18,500	18,500	10,500	47,500
Incumbents	44,950	71,350	55,000	171,300
Challengers	2,000	6,500	750	9,250
Open Seat	7,500	16,000	1,000	24,500
Winners	39,450	76,600	n/a	116,050
Losers	15,000	17,250	n/a	32,250

Contributed less than $5,000 during 1995-96 cycle:

Sony Music Entertainment Inc. PAC (C00293837) *Phone: (212) 833-5763 * 550 Madison Ave., New York, NY 10022 * Treasurer: Kevin M. Kelleher*

Tele-Communications Inc.

*Phone: (303) 267-5500 * Fax: (303) 779-1228*
5619 DTC Pkwy., Englewood, CO 80111
Web: www.tci.com

Tele-Communications Inc. (TCI) is involved in many aspects of cable and satellite television. Through its two main subsidiaries, Tele-Communications International and Liberty Media Group, the company is engaged in the construction, acquisition, ownership and operation of cable television systems. TCI had sales of $7.5 billion in 1997 and employs 35,000 workers. Based in Colorado, the publicly traded company has operations in Europe, Latin America and Asia.

TCI also provides satellite-delivered video entertainment, information and home shopping programming services to various video distribution media, principally cable television systems.

In addition, TCI has investments in cable and telecommunications operations and television programming in certain international markets as well as investments in companies and joint ventures involved in developing and providing programming.

In the United States, TCI has various telecommunications operations in more than 20 states on the East Coast and in the midwestern and western regions of the country.

Tele-Communications Inc. PAC (TCI PAC) (C00214015) *Phone: (202) 833-4120 * Fax: (202) 833-4122 * 1730 M St. N.W., Suite 900, Washington, DC 20036 * Treasurer: Gary K. Bracken*

	1993-94	1995-96	1997	Totals
Receipts	$98,527	$163,280	$44,487	$306,294
Disburse	99,901	165,554	53,016	318,471
Cash	11,139	8,873	345	n/a
Contributions	93,575	163,650	46,000	303,225
Republicans	50,875	96,150	19,450	166,475
No. of Cand.	*26*	*54*	*18*	*98*
House	21,375	44,550	7,700	73,625
Senate	29,500	51,600	11,750	92,850
Democrats	42,700	67,500	26,550	136,750
No. of Cand.	*23*	*28*	*23*	*74*
House	26,200	49,500	12,300	88,000
Senate	16,500	18,000	14,250	48,750
Incumbents	77,325	120,950	44,500	242,775
Challengers	1,500	2,200	500	4,200

(Data for Tele-Communications Inc. PAC continued)

Open Seat	15,250	40,500	1,000	56,750
Winners	75,325	124,200	n/a	199,525
Losers	18,250	39,450	n/a	57,700

Time Warner Inc.

*Phone: (212) 484-8000 * Fax: (212) 956-2847*
75 Rockefeller Plaza, New York, NY 10019
Web: pathfinder.com/corp

Time Warner is an entertainment and media conglomerate which owns several cable television networks, movie producer and distributor Warner Bros. and is the publisher of Time magazine, among others. It sold its Six Flags theme park chain in February 1998.

The publicly traded company is a product of the merger between Warner Bros. and Time Inc., and counts among its subsidiaries cable networks CNN and Home Box Office, the Atlanta Braves baseball team, the Warner Music Group and the WB television network. It also has the nation's second-largest cable system. The company, which has 73,400 employees, reported 1996 sales of more than $10 billion.

The company's music division has been a source of controversy over its association with artists whose records have sexually explicit or violent lyrics. Time Warner sold its stake in Interscope Records in 1995 following the release of rap music that purportedly promoted gang violence and degradation of women.

Time Warner's PAC was the leading contributor to 1996 congressional candidates among broadcasting and movie companies. Nearly 90 percent of its contributions went to winning candidates. It split its contributions almost equally between the parties and spent about 1 percent on challengers.

The leading recipients, who got $10,000 apiece, were Sens. Fred Thompson, R-Tenn., Jack Reed, D-R.I., Tom Harkin, D-Iowa, Alfonse M. D'Amato, R-N.Y., and Pete V. Domenici, R-N.M.

Time Warner Inc. Political Action Committee (C00150656) *Phone: (202) 457-8582 * Fax: (202) 457-8861 * 800 Connecticut Ave. N.W., Suite 800, Washington, DC 20036 * Treasurer: John Labarca * Contact: Tim Boggs, Senior V.P.*

	1993-94	1995-96	1997	Totals
Receipts	$351,050	$304,422	$340,334	$995,806
Disburse	307,000	346,447	120,000	773,447
Cash	47,651	5,626	225,960	n/a
Contributions	232,000	279,500	91,000	602,500
Republicans	92,000	143,000	39,500	274,500
No. of Cand.	*40*	*49*	*28*	*117*
House	40,000	84,250	29,000	153,250
Senate	52,000	58,750	10,500	121,250
Democrats	135,000	136,500	51,500	323,000
No. of Cand.	*60*	*52*	*27*	*139*
House	81,500	76,000	22,000	179,500
Senate	53,500	60,500	29,500	143,500
Incumbents	172,000	232,750	86,000	490,750
Challengers	19,000	2,000	5,000	26,000
Open Seat	41,000	44,500	0	85,500
Winners	176,000	250,500	n/a	426,500
Losers	56,000	29,000	n/a	85,000

Turner Broadcasting System PAC Inc. (C00157925) *1 CNN Ctr. Box 10536, Suite 1412, North Tower, Atlanta, GA 30348 * Treasurer: William M. Shaw*

The Turner Broadcasting System PAC was terminated in 1996, when the Turner Broadcasting Group merged with Time Warner.

The Turner Broadcasting Group includes the cable networks CNN, TNT, TBS, The Cartoon Network and Turner Classic Movies.

	1993-94	1995-96	1997	Totals
Receipts	$120,798	$201,227	$0	$322,025
Disburse	116,782	216,829	0	333,611
Cash	15,600	0	0	n/a
Contributions	86,281	168,815	0	255,096
Republicans	41,931	94,048	0	135,979
No. of Cand.	*28*	*72*	*0*	*100*
House	15,750	52,548	0	68,298
Senate	26,181	41,500	0	67,681
Democrats	44,350	74,767	0	119,117
No. of Cand.	*40*	*37*	*0*	*77*
House	22,850	34,267	0	57,117
Senate	21,500	40,500	0	62,000
Incumbents	74,600	139,815	0	214,415
Challengers	500	2,500	0	3,000
Open Seat	11,181	25,500	0	36,681
Winners	66,750	143,815	n/a	210,565
Losers	19,531	25,000	n/a	44,531

Viacom Inc.

*Phone: (202) 785-7300 * Fax: (202) 785-6360*
1501 M St. N.W., Suite 1100, Washington, DC 20005
Web: www.viacom.com

Viacom is an entertainment and publishing company with operations in five segments: networks and broadcasting, entertainment, video and music/theme parks, publishing and cable television. Publicly traded Viacom had sales of more than $12 billion in 1996 and employs more than 83,000 workers.

Viacom operates MTV, Showtime, Nickelodeon/Nick at Nite, VH1 Music First, 12 broadcast television stations and 12 radio stations. It also produces and distributes theatrical motion pictures and television programming through Paramount Pictures and the company's 75-percent-owned subsidiary, Spelling Entertainment.

Viacom also owns Blockbuster Video, which has about 6,000 stores in the United States and overseas. The company planned to sell its Simon & Schuster publishing unit in 1998.

Viacom International Inc. Political Action Committee Corp. (C00167759) *Address: same as sponsor * Treasurer: Michael Cruz * Contact: Carol Melton, Chair*

	1993-94	1995-96	1997	Totals
Receipts	$158,197	$245,093	$77,001	$480,291
Disburse	172,274	240,673	87,203	500,150
Cash	7,897	12,318	2,117	n/a
Contributions	120,270	181,757	56,800	358,827
Republicans	22,750	98,300	28,300	149,350
No. of Cand.	*16*	*62*	*30*	*108*
House	14,250	61,300	22,300	97,850
Senate	8,500	37,000	6,000	51,500
Democrats	97,520	83,457	28,500	209,477
No. of Cand.	*49*	*51*	*28*	*128*
House	52,900	62,874	18,500	134,274
Senate	44,620	20,583	10,000	75,203
Incumbents	103,520	166,374	56,800	326,694
Challengers	5,500	0	0	5,500
Open Seat	11,250	15,383	0	26,633
Winners	88,650	161,457	n/a	250,107
Losers	31,620	20,300	n/a	51,920

Terminated PACs which contributed less than $5,000 during 1995-96 cycle:

Paramount Communications Inc. Political Action Committee (C00177998) *15 Columbus Cir., New York, NY 10023 * Treasurer: Elisa M. Rivlin*

Walt Disney Co.

*Phone: (818) 560-1719 * Fax: (818) 846-8406*
500 S. Buena Vista St., Burbank, CA 91521-7773
Web: www.disney.com

Disney is one of the world's largest diversified entertainment companies, with more than $37.8 billion in assets and nearly 110,000 employees. Disney's 1997 sales were nearly $22.5 billion.

Following Disney's 1996 acquisition of Capital Cities/ABC, the public company owns and operates the television stations ABC, ESPN, A&E, The History Channel, Lifetime and the Disney Channel. In addition, the company operates the Disney radio station.

Disney also produces and acquires live-action and animated motion pictures for the film, television and home video markets. It produces live theatrical performances and markets music, books, magazines and computer software.

Disney owns and operates more than 635 Disney Stores worldwide. These stores offer Disney products, including apparel, stuffed animals and novelty items. Many of the store products feature popular Disney characters such as Mickey Mouse, Donald Duck or characters from films such as "The Little Mermaid."

The company operates Disneyland, Walt Disney World Theme Parks, Disneyland Paris and Tokyo Disneyland. Disney Animal Kingdom opened in Florida in April 1998. It also has plans to open several more amusement parks in the next several years, including

Disney's California Adventure. The Disney company also is developing the Disney Cruise Line based out of Port Canaveral, Fla. that would take people to Castaway Cay, a Disney-owned Caribbean island. Disney also owns the 4,900-acre city of Celebration, Fla., which is designed to eventually accommodate about 20,000 people.

Through Anaheim Sports Inc., Disney owns the Mighty Ducks hockey team of Anaheim and a share of the Anaheim Angels Major League Baseball franchise.

Subsidiaries include: Buena Vista Television, Miramax Film Corp., Touchstone Pictures, Hyperion Press and Hollywood Records.

Walt Disney Productions Employees PAC (Disney Employees Political Action Committee) (C00197749) *Phone: (202) 223-8022 * Fax: (202) 223-8029 * 1150 17th St. N.W., Suite 400, Washington, DC 20036 * Treasurer: Jeffrey A. Schwartz*

*Contact: John Cooke, Chairman * Phone: (818) 560-1719*

	1993-94	1995-96	1997	Totals
Receipts	$56,114	$156,563	$93,419	$306,096
Disburse	56,928	144,950	82,684	284,562
Cash	2,466	14,091	24,825	n/a
Contributions	52,928	139,949	86,622	279,499
Republicans	23,028	63,949	27,628	114,605
No. of Cand.	*22*	*34*	*21*	*77*
House	15,028	37,949	17,378	70,355
Senate	8,000	26,000	10,250	44,250
Democrats	29,900	76,000	58,994	164,894
No. of Cand.	*34*	*31*	*27*	*92*
House	21,000	29,000	17,000	67,000
Senate	8,900	47,000	41,994	97,894
Incumbents	51,428	115,449	83,025	249,902
Challengers	500	0	0	500
Open Seat	1,000	23,500	1,750	26,250
Winners	43,428	122,949	n/a	166,377
Losers	9,500	17,000	n/a	26,500

Telecom Services & Equipment

AirTouch Communications Inc.

*Phone: (415) 658-2000 * Fax: (415) 658-2219*
1 California St., Ninth Floor, San Francisco, CA 94111
Web: www.airtouch.com

AirTouch Communications provides wireless communication to 10.7 million customers in the United States and 11 countries in Asia and Europe. According to company information, it is the world's largest wireless company with market capitalization of more than $24 billion and about 1 million shareholders. Its services include cellular telephone service, paging and personal communication service.

On January 29, 1998, AirTouch and US West Media Group announced a new $5.7 billion plan to merge their U.S. wireless interests.

AirTouch also holds a minority stake in the Globalstar satellite system. This worldwide mobile satellite telephone system is a compilation of 48 satellites and 60 ground stations that will allow people around the world to make or receive calls using cellular-sized, hand-held, and fixed-site terminals. Globalstar is scheduled to be completed by 2000.

Net revenue for AirTouch in 1997 was $4.9 billion. The publicly held company employs more than 8,000 workers.

AirTouch subsidiaries include: AirTouch International Businesses, AirTouch Paging Operations and Domestic Cellular and PCS Operations.

AirTouch Communications Political Action Committee (Federal Account) (ATC PAC) (C00285411) *Address: same as sponsor * Treasurer: Jim Wall*

	1993-94	1995-96	1997	Totals
Receipts	$12,606	$77,680	$58,380	$148,666
Disburse	10,143	70,237	45,197	125,577
Cash	2,467	9,932	23,122	n/a
Contributions	5,100	60,131	38,197	103,428
Republicans	2,100	43,845	22,197	68,142
No. of Cand.	*4*	*37*	*24*	*65*
House	600	33,645	17,697	51,942
Senate	1,500	10,200	4,500	16,200
Democrats	3,000	16,286	16,000	35,286
No. of Cand.	*5*	*21*	*23*	*49*
House	3,000	15,036	8,250	26,286
Senate	0	1,250	7,750	9,000
Incumbents	5,100	54,631	37,947	97,678
Challengers	0	2,500	0	2,500
Open Seat	0	3,000	250	3,250
Winners	3,600	48,339	n/a	51,939
Losers	1,500	11,792	n/a	13,292

American Public Communications Council

*Phone: (703) 385-5300 * Fax: (703) 385-5301*
10306 Eaton Place, Suite 520, Fairfax, VA 22030
Web: www.apcc.net

The American Public Communications Council represents about 2,000 owners, operators, suppliers and manufacturers of public communications equipment and services.

Established in 1988, APCC produces a monthly magazine, Perspectives on Public Communications, dedicated to the public communications industry.

American Public Communications Council Inc. PAC (Public Communications PAC) (C00290890) *Address: same as sponsor * Treasurer: Vincent R. Sandusky*

	1993-94	1995-96	1997	Totals
Receipts	$22,650	$52,846	$0	$75,496
Disburse	16,538	55,250	2,250	74,038
Cash	6,111	24,457	21,707	n/a
Contributions	16,000	33,000	2,250	51,250
Republicans	8,500	19,750	1,000	29,250
No. of Cand.	*11*	*15*	*1*	*27*
House	3,500	12,750	1,000	17,250
Senate	5,000	7,000	0	12,000
Democrats	7,500	13,250	1,250	22,000
No. of Cand.	*10*	*15*	*2*	*27*
House	5,500	7,750	250	13,500
Senate	2,000	5,500	1,000	8,500
Incumbents	16,000	32,000	2,250	50,250
Challengers	0	0	0	0
Open Seat	0	1,000	0	1,000
Winners	15,250	31,000	n/a	46,250
Losers	750	2,000	n/a	2,750

Antec Corp.

*Phone: (847) 439-4444 * Fax: (847) 439-8559*
2850 W. Golf Rd., Sixth Floor, Rolling Meadows, IL 60008
Web: www.antec.com

Antec is a publicly held international communications technology company. It specializes in the design and engineering of hybrid fiber/coax broadband networks and the engineering, manufacturing, product development and distribution of products for these networks.

Antec employs 2,000 people in 34 offices and warehouses located worldwide. It posted $480 million in 1997 sales.

In 1994, Antec acquired several companies, including Keptel, a manufacturer of network interface devices; Power Guard, a manufacturer of network powering and security systems; Engineering Technologies Group, a consulting network engineering firm; and Electronic Systems Products, a product design and engineering services firm.

In November 1995, Antec and Nortel formed a joint venture systems integration firm, Integration Technologies and Arris Interactive, a company focusing on product development of Nortel's integrated digital access technology and Antec's digital video technology.

Antec Political Action Committee (formerly Itel Corp. PAC) (C00221986) *Address: same as sponsor * Treasurer: Daniel J. Distell*

	1993-94	1995-96	1997	Totals
Receipts	$15,480	$8,166	$20,283	$43,929
Disburse	26,776	24,353	14,060	65,189
Cash	19,651	3,468	9,693	n/a
Contributions	18,250	23,500	9,000	50,750
Republicans	11,000	15,500	2,000	28,500
No. of Cand.	*3*	*5*	*1*	*9*
House	5,000	4,000	2,000	11,000
Senate	6,000	11,500	0	17,500
Democrats	7,250	8,000	7,000	22,250
No. of Cand.	*3*	*3*	*2*	*8*
House	0	3,000	0	3,000
Senate	7,250	5,000	7,000	19,250
Incumbents	16,000	16,000	9,000	41,000
Challengers	0	5,000	0	5,000

(*Data for Antec Political Action continued*)

Open Seat	250	2,500	0	2,750
Winners	16,000	11,500	n/a	27,500
Losers	2,250	12,000	n/a	14,250

Cellular Telecom Industry Association

*Phone: (202) 785-0081 * Fax: (202) 785-0721*
1250 Connecticut Ave. N.W., Suite 200, Washington, DC 20036
Web: www.wow-com.com

The Cellular Telecom Industry Association represents more than 800 companies in the cellular communications field.

Cellular Telecommunications Industry Association Political Action Committee (C00262295) *Address: same as sponsor * Treasurer: Wallace J. Henderson*

	1993-94	1995-96	1997	Totals
Receipts	$35,784	$105,966	$481,908	$623,658
Disburse	37,063	95,288	63,289	195,640
Cash	14,518	25,194	443,814	n/a
Contributions	33,846	86,387	31,789	152,022
Republicans	13,000	63,118	12,750	88,868
No. of Cand.	*14*	*52*	*19*	*85*
House	5,500	42,103	9,750	57,353
Senate	7,500	21,015	3,000	31,515
Democrats	20,846	23,269	19,039	63,154
No. of Cand.	*31*	*26*	*18*	*75*
House	10,442	11,590	8,843	30,875
Senate	10,404	11,679	10,196	32,279
Incumbents	31,096	64,841	31,289	127,226
Challengers	500	4,500	500	5,500
Open Seat	2,250	17,046	0	19,296
Winners	24,954	62,587	n/a	87,541
Losers	8,892	23,800	n/a	32,692

Communications Satellite Corp.

*Phone: (301) 214-3697 * Fax: (301) 214-7129*
6560 Rock Spring Dr., Bethesda, MD 20817
Web: www.comsat.com

Communications Satellite provides satellite capacity into and out of the United States for such customers such as AT&T, MCI and Sprint; broadcasters; multinational corporations; news-gathering organizations and the U.S. government. It has operations in Asia, Europe, Latin America and the United States with 1996 sales of $243.2 million. The company employs 725 workers.

Comsat, a Bethesda, Md.-based company that was created by Congress but is now publicly traded, is the only U.S. agent for the Intelsat satellite network. Congress has considered privatizing Intelsat, which would allow other companies to access its services. The Federal Communications Commission has said Comsat charged on average in 1996 a 69 percent markup on Intelsat services.

Comsat was established in 1963 under provision of the Communications Satellite Act of 1962. Under the act, Comsat has assembled the world's first commercial international satellite communications system and serves as the U.S. representative in the International Telecommunications Satellite Organization.

Comsat's divisions develop advanced communications technologies as well as telecommunications services in emerging markets.

Communications Satellite Corp. (Comsat) ComsatPAC (C00151043) *Address: same as sponsor * Treasurer: Gregory Kalinyak * Contact: James M. Carroll, Chairperson*

	1993-94	1995-96	1997	Totals
Receipts	$77,930	$62,842	$31,884	$172,656
Disburse	90,945	59,495	44,788	195,228
Cash	9,782	13,145	266	n/a
Contributions	83,950	58,400	36,200	178,550
Republicans	39,250	43,400	15,200	97,850
No. of Cand.	*32*	*34*	*16*	*82*
House	20,750	24,000	8,700	53,450
Senate	18,500	19,400	6,500	44,400
Democrats	44,700	15,000	21,000	80,700
No. of Cand.	*40*	*14*	*21*	*75*
House	25,600	11,000	12,500	49,100
Senate	19,100	4,000	8,500	31,600
Incumbents	77,950	48,700	35,700	162,350
Challengers	1,000	5,200	0	6,200
Open Seat	5,000	4,500	0	9,500
Winners	73,450	50,200	n/a	123,650
Losers	10,500	8,200	n/a	18,700

DSC Communications Corp.

*Phone: (972) 519-3000 x4358 * Fax: (972) 519-4122*
1000 Coit Rd., Mailstop 005, Plano, TX 75075
*Web: www.dsccc.com * E-mail: tadams@ccmail.dsccc.com*

DSC Communications is a designer, developer, manufacturer and marketer of digital switching, transmission, access and private network system products in telecommunications.

Founded in 1976, the publicly held, Plano, Texas-based company employs 6,600 people in more than 60 countries. Its 1997 revenues were $1.6 billion.

DSC Communications Corp. Political Action Committee (DSCPAC) (C00215277) *Address: same as sponsor * Treasurer: Raymond T. Adams*

	1993-94	1995-96	1997	Totals
Receipts	$39,591	$41,792	$19,215	$100,598
Disburse	45,566	38,656	19,500	103,722
Cash	3,056	6,193	5,909	n/a
Contributions	42,500	38,545	16,000	97,045
Republicans	26,250	29,795	11,000	67,045
No. of Cand.	*26*	*25*	*14*	*65*
House	12,250	25,295	9,000	46,545
Senate	14,000	4,500	2,000	20,500
Democrats	16,250	8,750	5,000	30,000
No. of Cand.	*17*	*11*	*5*	*33*
House	11,250	6,250	2,000	19,500
Senate	5,000	2,500	3,000	10,500
Incumbents	32,000	36,545	16,000	84,545
Challengers	2,000	500	0	2,500
Open Seat	8,000	1,500	0	9,500
Winners	34,000	34,545	n/a	68,545
Losers	8,500	4,000	n/a	12,500

General Instrument Corp.

*Phone: (215) 323-1000 * Fax: (215) 443-9454*
101 Tournament Dr., Horsham, PA 19044
Web: www.gi.com

General Instrument, based in Horsham, Penn., supplies products that allow video, voice and data to be distributed over virtually any type of network. It employs 8,600 workers, and is No. 486 among Fortune 500 companies. GI's sales for 1996 totaled $1.8 billion.

In 1997, GI separated into three companies: NextLevel Systems Inc., CommScope Inc. and General Semiconductor Inc. But in early 1998 NextLevel Systems changed its name back to General Instrument.

GI has recently acquired several new business affiliates in addition to its two main customers, cable giants TCI and Time Warner. In January 1998, GI and Sony announced preliminary plans for an alliance to develop digital television technologies for cable TV devices. GI also announced that it would be working with CompUSA, Cisco Systems and Primestar.

During the fourth quarter of 1997, GI cut costs by reducing a substantial number of jobs at its San Diego satellite television operations, closing its Puerto Rico satellite TV manufacturing facility and consolidating its Chicago office into its new corporate headquarters in Horsham, Pa.

General Instrument Corp. Political Action Committee (GIPAC) (C00196311) *Phone: (202) 833-9700 * Fax: (202) 466-3295 * 1133 21st St. N.W., Suite 405, Washington, DC 20036 * E-mail: qrodgers@gi.com * Treasurer: Quincy Rodgers*

	1993-94	1995-96	1997	Totals
Receipts	$43,675	$72,772	$36,274	$152,721
Disburse	39,294	66,905	34,518	140,717
Cash	18,363	24,237	17,736	n/a
Contributions	32,550	54,250	30,500	117,300
Republicans	19,750	47,250	25,500	92,500
No. of Cand.	*11*	*36*	*12*	*59*
House	3,500	24,250	13,500	41,250
Senate	16,250	23,000	12,000	51,250
Democrats	12,800	7,000	5,000	24,800
No. of Cand.	*10*	*8*	*4*	*22*
House	11,500	4,000	2,000	17,500
Senate	1,300	3,000	3,000	7,300
Incumbents	26,800	44,000	28,500	99,300
Challengers	4,000	2,000	0	6,000
Open Seat	1,750	6,250	0	8,000
Winners	24,300	41,500	n/a	65,800
Losers	8,250	12,750	n/a	21,000

ICG Communications Inc.

*Phone: (303) 372-5960 * Fax: (303) 706-1637*
9605 E. Maroon Cir., P.O. Box 6742, Englewood, CO 80155-6742
Web: www.icgcomm.com

ICG Communications, headquartered in Englewood, Colo., provides satellite services to the Navy, commercial ships and oil rigs, and also sells local phone service. The publicly traded company had sales of $273 million in 1997 and employs more than 1,400 workers.

Subsidiary ICG Telecom competes with incumbent local phone companies by offering local phone service in California, Colorado, the Ohio Valley and areas of the Southeast. ICG uses its own networks to provide service but also joins with utility companies to take advantage of their existing fiber-optic networks. ICG Fiber Optic Technologies provides network integration and support services.

In January 1998, ICG completed a merger with Netcom On-Line Communications Services, which supplies direct Internet access, for $283 million. Netcom has 500,000 customers.

ICG Communications Inc. Political Action Committee (ICG PAC) (C00317784) *Address: same as sponsor * Treasurer: Richard Bambach Jr.*

	1993-94	*1995-96*	*1997*	*Totals*
Receipts	$0	$7,250	$9,550	$16,800
Disburse	0	7,071	4,150	11,221
Cash	0	179	5,579	n/a
Contributions	0	6,000	4,150	10,150
Republicans	0	5,000	150	5,150
No. of Cand.	*0*	*5*	*1*	*6*
House	0	5,000	150	5,150
Senate	0	0	0	0
Democrats	0	1,000	4,000	5,000
No. of Cand.	*0*	*1*	*2*	*3*
House	0	1,000	2,000	3,000
Senate	0	0	2,000	2,000
Incumbents	0	5,000	4,150	9,150
Challengers	0	0	0	0
Open Seat	0	1,000	0	1,000
Winners	0	6,000	n/a	6,000
Losers	0	0	n/a	0

Loral Space & Communications Ltd.

*Phone: (212) 697-1105 * Fax: (212) 661-8988*
600 Third Ave., New York, NY 10016
Web: www.loral.com

Loral Space & Communications is the remaining portion of defense giant Loral Corp., which was purchased by Lockheed Martin. Loral SpaceCom now focuses on its satellite manufacturing and communication businesses. The public company has about 3,750 employees. It reported 1997 revenues of $1.3 billion.

The company owns one-third of Globalstar Telecommunications, a consortium that is developing a low-orbiting satellite system to provide worldwide voice, data and fax services. Loral Space also manages and owns Space Systems/Loral, a maker of commercial telecommunications satellites. In addition, Loral Space owns about 20 percent of aircraft brake maker K&F Industries. Loral Skynet, acquired from AT&T in 1997, is a satellite service provider.

The Justice Department has been investigating whether Loral and another company, Hughes Space & Communications, illegally provided restricted ballistic missile technology to the Chinese government in 1996. Loral Chairman Bernard Schwartz was the largest individual contributor to the Democratic National Committee in 1997.

Loral Spacecom Civic Responsibility Fund (C00319582) *Phone: (703) 414-1041 * Fax: (703) 414-1071 * 1755 Jefferson Davis Hwy., Suite 1007, Arlington, VA 22202 * Treasurer: Steven H. Flajser * Contact: Fred Rhodes, V.P. of Legislative Relations*

	1993-94	*1995-96*	*1997*	*Totals*
Receipts	$0	$52,075	$62,075	$114,150
Disburse	0	14,813	65,775	80,588
Cash	0	37,261	33,561	n/a
Contributions	0	11,700	64,750	76,450
Republicans	0	5,700	22,000	27,700
No. of Cand.	*0*	*9*	*26*	*35*
House	0	3,700	14,500	18,200
Senate	0	2,000	7,500	9,500
Democrats	0	6,000	42,750	48,750
No. of Cand.	*0*	*9*	*34*	*43*
House	0	6,000	25,750	31,750
Senate	0	0	17,000	17,000
Incumbents	0	11,700	63,750	75,450
Challengers	0	0	0	0
Open Seat	0	0	1,000	1,000
Winners	0	11,700	n/a	11,700
Losers	0	0	n/a	0

Motorola Inc.

Phone: (847) 576-4967
1303 E. Algonquin Rd., Schaumburg, IL 60196
Web: www.mot.com

Motorola is a one of the leading worldwide providers of electronic equipment, systems, components and services. The public company designs, manufactures and distributes wireless communications devices, semiconductors, two-way radio systems, computer equipment and systems and automotive, defense and space electronics. The product line includes cellular phones, pagers, Macintosh clones and modems. In addition, Motorola is the prime contractor for the IRIDIUM satellite-based, global personal communications system.

Established in 1928, Motorola is now a Fortune Top 25 company. The company had 1997 sales of almost $30 billion. Motorola employs 139,000 people in its manufacturing, sales and service facilities worldwide. Based just outside of Chicago, the company conducts business worldwide.

Motorola Employees Good Government Committee (C00075341) *Phone: (202) 371-6900 * Fax: (202) 842-3578 * 1350 Eye St. N.W., Suite 400, Washington, DC 20005-3306 * Treasurer: Kenneth J. Johnson * Contact: Joann Piccolo, PAC Administrator*

	1993-94	*1995-96*	*1997*	*Totals*
Receipts	$126,049	$153,868	$70,634	$350,551
Disburse	126,192	149,151	59,083	334,426
Cash	13,171	17,892	29,443	n/a
Contributions	101,770	114,508	51,246	267,524
Republicans	51,172	77,235	35,496	163,903
No. of Cand.	*53*	*79*	*43*	*175*
House	26,182	57,170	27,550	110,902
Senate	24,990	20,065	7,946	53,001
Democrats	50,598	37,273	15,750	103,621
No. of Cand.	*56*	*41*	*22*	*119*
House	36,721	29,273	11,250	77,244
Senate	13,877	8,000	4,500	26,377
Incumbents	80,907	104,208	50,746	235,861
Challengers	2,500	2,300	500	5,300
Open Seat	17,363	8,000	0	25,363
Winners	84,272	100,083	n/a	184,355
Losers	17,498	14,425	n/a	31,923

New Bedford Panoramex Corp.

*Phone: (909) 982-9806 x6435 * Fax: (909) 985-6217 * 1037 W. Ninth Ave., Upland, CA 91786*
Web: www.npbcorp.com

New Bedford Panoramex is a private company with $25 million to $50 million in 1996 annual sales, according to Corptech Inc. Formed in 1962, the company makes aircraft communications, guidance and navigation equipment.

New Bedford Panoramex Corp. Political Action Committee (C00279174) *Address: same as sponsor * Treasurer: Bryce L. Nielsen * Contact: Robert Ozuna*

	1993-94	*1995-96*	*1997*	*Totals*
Receipts	$23,152	$12,933	$3,760	$39,845
Disburse	27,600	17,975	6,200	51,775
Cash	10,399	5,357	2,917	n/a
Contributions	12,050	12,225	4,200	28,475
Republicans	3,000	4,750	1,500	9,250
No. of Cand.	*2*	*5*	*3*	*10*
House	3,000	4,750	1,500	9,250
Senate	0	0	0	0
Democrats	9,050	7,475	2,700	19,225
No. of Cand.	*9*	*6*	*5*	*20*
House	7,000	6,475	1,700	15,175
Senate	2,050	1,000	1,000	4,050
Incumbents	12,050	10,475	4,200	26,725
Challengers	0	750	0	750
Open Seat	0	1,000	0	1,000
Winners	12,050	10,475	n/a	22,525
Losers	0	1,750	n/a	1,750

Northern Telecom Inc.

*Phone: (615) 734-4204 * Fax: (615) 734-4733*
Northern Telecom Plaza, 200 Athens Way, Nashville, TN 37228
Web: www.nortel.com

Northern Telecom is a designer and manufacturer of products for digital communication networks of all kinds. Its five main business divisions are enterprise networks and enterprise data networks, as well as broadband, wireless and public carrier networks. Nortel's customers include the regional Bells, plus other local and long-distance companies, cellular mobile radio and personal communications services providers, and a variety of businesses, universities, governments and other network operators around the world.

Nortel is a publicly held company, with 51 percent of its stock owned by Canada's largest telecommunications company, BCE Inc. Nortel has about 73,000 employees and its 1997 revenues were $15.5 billion.

Northern Telecom Inc. Political Action Committee (C00167627) *Address: same as sponsor * Treasurer: Teresa Deneen * Contact: Donal Schuenke, Chairperson*

	1993-94	1995-96	1997	Totals
Receipts	$45,428	$32,603	$48,356	$126,387
Disburse	51,482	29,934	37,773	119,189
Cash	3,975	5,936	16,523	n/a
Contributions	47,282	30,591	33,241	111,114
Republicans	20,850	18,269	17,150	56,269
No. of Cand.	*30*	*27*	*24*	*81*
House	14,350	14,819	12,150	41,319
Senate	6,500	3,450	5,000	14,950
Democrats	26,432	12,322	16,091	54,845
No. of Cand.	*27*	*17*	*22*	*66*
House	21,932	9,822	8,854	40,608
Senate	4,500	2,500	7,237	14,237
Incumbents	39,832	25,891	31,741	97,464
Challengers	1,500	1,200	500	3,200
Open Seat	5,950	3,500	1,000	10,450
Winners	33,350	23,641	n/a	56,991
Losers	13,932	6,950	n/a	20,882

Orbital Sciences Corp.

*Phone: (703) 406-5000 * Fax: (703) 406-3502*
21700 Atlantic Blvd., Dulles, VA 20166
Web: www.orbital.com

Orbital is a space and satellite company in Virginia. It produces launch vehicles and navigation systems for large and small satellites. The company makes systems for satellites used in mobile communications, mass transit operations and ocean imagery.

Orbital acquired space and automation divisions of CTA Inc. and Rockwell International during 1997, helping it become one of the 10 largest satellite businesses in North America. The publicly traded company, which has about 3,000 employees, reported 1997 sales of $606 million. It has operations in Virginia, Maryland, Arizona and California.

OrbPAC (formerly known as Orbital Sciences Corp. Good Government Committee) (C00195263) *Address: same as sponsor * Treasurer: Katherine Keser*

	1993-94	1995-96	1997	Totals
Receipts	$14,329	$58,835	$25,604	$98,768
Disburse	7,347	49,116	31,478	87,941
Cash	7,094	16,814	10,940	n/a
Contributions	6,575	44,100	26,350	77,025
Republicans	2,900	42,100	22,850	67,850
No. of Cand.	*4*	*22*	*19*	*45*
House	1,500	28,975	17,350	47,825
Senate	1,400	13,125	5,500	20,025
Democrats	3,675	2,000	3,500	9,175
No. of Cand.	*5*	*3*	*2*	*10*
House	1,500	1,000	500	3,000
Senate	2,175	1,000	3,000	6,175
Incumbents	3,000	41,100	25,850	69,950
Challengers	0	0	0	0
Open Seat	3,575	3,000	0	6,575
Winners	3,900	42,850	n/a	46,750
Losers	2,675	1,250	n/a	3,925

Personal Communications Industry Association

*Phone: (703) 739-0300 * Fax: (703) 836-1608*
500 Montgomery St., Suite 700, Alexandria, VA 22314
*Web: www.pcia.com * E-mail: goldenm@pcia.com*

The Personal Communications Industry Association represents telecommunications businesses that provide wireless, cellular, paging, cable and networking services. The group is especially active in lobbying Congress and the Federal Communications Commission on legislation and regulations affecting the wireless industry. Its members include Sprint PCS, Cox Communications, AT&T Wireless Services, Primeco and PageNet.

Personal Communications Industry Association (PCIA) PAC (C00156216) *Address: same as sponsor * Treasurer: Robert R. Cohen * Contact: Mark Golden, Senior V.P.*

	1993-94	1995-96	1997	Totals
Receipts	$600	$10,225	$19,475	$30,300
Disburse	1,020	10,127	15,545	26,692
Cash	27	131	4,061	n/a
Contributions	750	9,950	15,500	26,200
Republicans	750	7,250	10,000	18,000
No. of Cand.	*1*	*8*	*4*	*13*
House	0	2,500	2,000	4,500
Senate	750	4,750	8,000	13,500
Democrats	0	2,700	5,500	8,200
No. of Cand.	*0*	*5*	*2*	*7*
House	0	2,700	500	3,200
Senate	0	0	5,000	5,000
Incumbents	0	9,950	15,500	25,450
Challengers	0	0	0	0
Open Seat	750	0	0	750
Winners	0	6,700	n/a	6,700
Losers	750	3,250	n/a	4,000

RCN Corp.

*Phone: (609) 734-3700 * Fax: (609) 734-7551*
105 Carnegie Center, Princeton, NJ 08540-6215
Web: www.rcn.com

RCN offers local telephone, cable television and Internet access to residential customers in New York City, Boston, Washington and Allentown, Pa.

RCN became a public company in October 1997, when it was spun off from the former diversified international telecommunications company, C-TEC Corp. RCN posted sales of $127 million in 1997 and has nearly 1,000 employees.

In 1998, RCN purchased UltraNet Communications and Erols Internet, making it the largest Internet provider in its region.

RCN Employees Good Government Committee (formerly known as C-Tec Federal Political Action Committee) (C00215533) *Phone: (717) 675-5574 * Fax: (717) 675-6128 * 100 Lake St., Dallas, PA 18612 * Treasurer: William A. Shaner * Contact: Scott Burnside, Senior V.P. of Regulatory and Gov. Affairs*

	1993-94	1995-96	1997	Totals
Receipts	$7,160	$12,790	$0	$19,950
Disburse	5,109	11,724	1,500	18,333
Cash	5,216	6,281	4,781	n/a
Contributions	4,650	5,825	1,500	11,975
Republicans	2,025	2,650	1,000	5,675
No. of Cand.	*4*	*4*	*1*	*9*
House	175	650	0	825
Senate	1,850	2,000	1,000	4,850
Democrats	2,625	3,175	500	6,300
No. of Cand.	*2*	*5*	*1*	*8*
House	2,625	1,925	500	5,050
Senate	0	1,250	0	1,250
Incumbents	2,800	3,825	1,500	8,125
Challengers	1,850	0	0	1,850
Open Seat	0	2,000	0	2,000
Winners	3,650	4,325	n/a	7,975
Losers	1,000	1,500	n/a	2,500

Satellite Broadcasting & Communication Association

*Phone: (703) 549-6990 x345 * Fax: (703) 549-7640*
225 Reinekers Ln., Suite 600, Alexandria, VA 22314
Web: www.sbca.com

The Satellite Broadcasting & Communications Association of America is a national trade group for the satellite industry. Its members include satellite manufacturers, operators and retailers as well as encryption vendors and programmers.

SBCA was formed in 1986 by the combination of Satellite Television Industry Association Inc. and the Direct Broadcast Satellite Association. The group has more than 2,500 members.

Link-PAC — The Political Action Committee of the Satellite Broadcasting & Communication Association of America (C00268300) *Address: same as sponsor * Treasurer: Andrew R. Paul * Contact: Cheryl Crate, Dir. of Gov. Affairs*

	1993-94	1995-96	1997	Totals
Receipts	$3,606	$5,164	$1,500	$10,270
Disburse	2,035	7,073	132	9,240
Cash	2,359	452	1,820	n/a
Contributions	1,500	6,750	0	8,250
Republicans	0	4,000	0	4,000
No. of Cand.	*0*	*5*	*0*	*5*
House	0	4,000	0	4,000
Senate	0	0	0	0
Democrats	1,500	2,750	0	4,250
No. of Cand.	*2*	*4*	*0*	*6*
House	1,500	2,750	0	4,250
Senate	0	0	0	0
Incumbents	1,500	6,750	0	8,250
Challengers	0	0	0	0
Open Seat	0	0	0	0
Winners	1,500	5,750	n/a	7,250
Losers	0	1,000	n/a	1,000

Scientific-Atlanta Inc.

*Phone: (770) 903-4629 * Fax: (770) 903-4775*
One Technology Pkwy., S., Norcross, GA 30092-2967
Web: www.sciatl.com

Scientific-Atlanta is a manufacturing company that provides terrestrial and satellite network products and systems to cable operators, broadcasters, telephone and utility companies, governments and corporations. It also makes set-top cable boxes, which account for 30 percent of the company's sales.

Established in the early 1950s, the publicly traded Scientific-Atlanta has more than 6,000 employees worldwide. In 1997 its revenue was $1.2 billion.

In February 1998, Scientific-Atlanta announced that seven more cable television operators would use its new two-way digital interactive television system. The arrangement would mean nine cable companies would use S-A's system, including Time Warner, Cox Communications and Comcast. S-A's equipment functions both as a digital entertainment device and a television web browser or cable modem.

Scientific-Atlanta Political Action Committee (C00231936)
*Address: same as sponsor * Treasurer: Bill Loughrey*

	1993-94	1995-96	1997	Totals
Receipts	$18,437	$21,755	$9,492	$49,684
Disburse	9,450	21,793	15,400	46,643
Cash	9,490	9,452	3,544	n/a
Contributions	6,450	16,750	9,100	32,300
Republicans	5,000	14,750	8,000	27,750
No. of Cand.	*11*	*16*	*7*	*34*
House	3,750	8,000	8,000	19,750
Senate	1,250	6,750	0	8,000
Democrats	1,450	2,000	1,100	4,550
No. of Cand.	*4*	*2*	*2*	*8*
House	950	1,000	100	2,050
Senate	500	1,000	1,000	2,500
Incumbents	4,650	15,000	9,100	28,750
Challengers	700	1,250	0	1,950
Open Seat	1,100	500	0	1,600
Winners	5,000	13,250	n/a	18,250
Losers	1,450	3,500	n/a	4,950

Telephone Utilities

ALLTEL Corp.

*Phone: (501) 661-8000 * Fax: (501) 661-5444*
One Allied Dr., Little Rock, AR 72202
Web: www.alltel.com

In March 1998, ALLTEL announced that it would be merging with 360° Communications Co. The $6 billion transaction will create a communications company that serves 22 states, primarily in the Midwest and Southeast, and that will be one of the largest wireless carriers in the nation.

ALLTEL, a publicly traded, 16,000-person information services and telecommunications company, had 1997 revenues of $3.2 billion. ALLTEL's local wireline and wireless operations serve 2.5 million customers in 14 states, and it has information services customers around the world, with special emphasis on the financial services and telecommunications industries.

In 1996, the company announced plans to become a full-service telephone provider in Charlotte, N.C. and Little Rock, Ark. ALLTEL projects it will have about 960,000 wireless customers, including 205,000 customers in Georgia, by mid-1998.

The company's products include local, wireless and long-distance telephone service, Internet service, computer network design, information technology outsourcing, telephone directories and paging.

ALLTEL Corp. Political Action Committee (APAC) (C00216556)
*Phone: (202) 783-3973 * Fax: (202) 783-3982 * 655 15th St. N.W., Suite 220, Washington, DC 20006 * Treasurer: Jerry M. Green * Contact: Diane Smith, Acting Chairman*

	1993-94	1995-96	1997	Totals
Receipts	$93,099	$141,261	$70,886	$305,246
Disburse	120,507	207,639	64,853	392,999
Cash	80,972	14,596	20,629	n/a
Contributions	106,775	157,506	45,356	309,637
Republicans	57,475	118,414	29,186	205,075
No. of Cand.	*52*	*71*	*34*	*157*
House	34,475	85,214	24,186	143,875
Senate	23,000	33,200	5,000	61,200
Democrats	49,300	39,092	16,170	104,562
No. of Cand.	*50*	*24*	*14*	*88*
House	34,050	24,250	9,170	67,470
Senate	15,250	14,842	7,000	37,092
Incumbents	94,625	125,806	44,356	264,787
Challengers	2,400	1,700	0	4,100
Open Seat	9,750	30,000	500	40,250
Winners	85,025	119,806	n/a	204,831
Losers	21,750	37,700	n/a	59,450

AT&T Corp.

*Phone: (212) 387-5400 * Fax: (212) 226-4935*
32 Ave. of the Americas, New York, NY 10013-2412
Web: www.att.com

AT&T is America's largest long-distance telephone company with 90 million customers. It spun off NCR and Lucent Technologies to focus on its telephone, wireless and Internet services. The publicly traded company, which employs 130,000 workers, also sold its credit card business to Citicorp. AT&T's 1997 sales were $51.3 billion.

AT&T supports the Telecommunications Act of 1996, which will allow the company to compete for local telephone customers. Several regional Bell companies have challenged that law in court. AT&T maintains that long-distance companies should be able to provide universal service and that the regional phone systems have not fully opened their markets to competition.

AT&T dwarfed other long-distance companies in contributions to 1996 congressional candidates, giving more than four times what the second-ranked PAC, Sprint Corp., contributed. AT&T favored Republicans and incumbents. The top recipients were Rep. Chip Pickering, R-Miss., and former Rep. Daniel Frisa, R-N.Y. Most of the 450 recipients got less than $5,000 each.

To identify which campaigns would receive contributions, AT&T's PAC in 1996 developed a "candidate interview" program.

AT&T Wireless Services' PAC ranked second in congressional contributions among cellular telephone businesses and groups. That committee also favored Republicans. Lucent Technologies, the AT&T spin-off which makes communication equipment, formed its own PAC. Neither Lucent's nor NCR's PAC is affiliated with AT&T.

American Telephone & Telegraph Co. Political Action Committee (AT&T PAC) (C00185124) *Phone: (202) 457-3826 * Fax: (202) 457-2267 * 1120 20th St. N.W., Suite 1000, Washington, DC 20036 * Treasurer: Edward Dwyer * Contact: Steven E. Billet, Dir. of Federal Gov. Affairs*

	1993-94	1995-96	1997	Totals
Receipts	$2,566,703	$2,781,256	$1,013,607	$6,361,566
Disburse	2,669,973	2,746,738	1,099,615	6,516,326
Cash	190,302	224,831	138,790	n/a
Contributions	1,290,884	1,239,046	411,137	2,941,067
Republicans	528,631	782,951	217,880	1,529,462
No. of Cand.	*262*	*257*	*123*	*642*
House	402,121	646,411	158,750	1,207,282
Senate	126,510	136,540	59,130	322,180
Democrats	757,003	456,095	190,757	1,403,855
No. of Cand.	*312*	*212*	*99*	*623*
House	630,878	371,295	129,847	1,132,020
Senate	126,125	84,800	60,910	271,835
Incumbents	1,132,474	1,099,181	390,637	2,622,292
Challengers	40,630	42,500	500	83,630
Open Seat	123,260	96,365	19,000	238,625
Winners	1,070,634	1,078,546	n/a	2,149,180
Losers	220,250	160,500	n/a	380,750

AT&T Wireless Services Inc. Political Action Committee (formerly known as McCaw Cellular Communications Inc. PAC) (C00224105) *Phone: (425) 827-4500 * Fax: (425) 828-8616 * 5000 Carillon Point, Kirkland, WA 98033 * Web: www.attws.com * E-mail: paula.timmons@attws.com * Treasurer: John A. C. Kelly*

*Phone: (202) 223-9222 * Fax: (202) 223-9095 * 1150 Connecticut Ave. N.W., Fourth Floor, Washington, DC 20036 * Contact: Paula Timmons, Federal Affairs Dir.*

With 8.2 million cellular phone subscribers and $4 billion in revenue, AT&T Wireless Services is the nation's largest wireless phone company. Its coverage area includes 93 percent of the U.S. population. The company is based in Kirkland, Wash.

In January 1997, AT&T Wireless spent $406.8 million at the Federal Communication Commission's wireless spectrum auction. The 222 licenses it purchased will enable the company to expand its high-frequency, digital cellular coverage.

The company is exploring putting antennas on houses as a way to break into the local phone market.

AT&T Wireless also owns paging, satellite, wireless data transmission, air-to-ground and ground-to-air communication services. A December 1997 Wall Street Journal article reported the company might jettison its less-profitable paging service. AT&T has phone contracts with Southwest, Northwest, American and Delta airlines.

Formed in 1994 when AT&T purchased McCaw Cellular Communications for $11.5 billion, AT&T Wireless has 13,000 employees worldwide. It is a wholly-owned subsidiary of AT&T.

	1993-94	1995-96	1997	Totals
Receipts	$130,558	$44,351	$18,102	$193,011
Disburse	107,821	94,100	22,400	224,321
Cash	74,911	26,162	21,864	n/a
Contributions	77,821	67,098	11,400	156,319
Republicans	24,800	50,098	8,900	83,798
No. of Cand.	*19*	*39*	*11*	*69*
House	6,250	40,398	5,600	52,248
Senate	18,550	9,700	3,300	31,550
Democrats	53,021	17,000	2,500	72,521
No. of Cand.	*49*	*17*	*3*	*69*
House	31,621	12,000	1,500	45,121
Senate	21,400	5,000	1,000	27,400
Incumbents	69,471	57,148	11,400	138,019
Challengers	1,800	1,200	0	3,000
Open Seat	6,550	8,750	0	15,300
Winners	48,021	57,148	n/a	105,169
Losers	29,800	9,950	n/a	39,750

Ameritech Corp.

*Phone: (312) 750-5353 * Fax: (312) 207-0016*
30 S. Wacker Dr., 35th Floor, Chicago, IL 60606
Web: www.ameritech.com

Ameritech is a regional Bell telephone company serving 12 million customers in the Midwest. A publicly traded company, Ameritech also offers cellular, long distance, Internet, cable television and wireless data services in much of the United States and parts of Europe. The company employed 74,000 workers and had nearly $16 billion in sales during 1997.

The company supports legislation which would remove provisions that permit cable companies to restrict competitors' access to certain channels. Ameritech seeks to expand its ability to provide long-distance service nationwide under the Telecommunications Act of 1996. Ameritech and AT&T have been at odds over access to local markets in Michigan and other areas.

Ameritech was the leading PAC contributor to 1996 congressional races among local and regional telephone companies. Republican candidates received the bulk of the company's contributions. The top recipients were former Rep. Michael Patrick Flanagan, R-Ill., and Reps. David E. Bonior, D-Mich., and Dennis Hastert, R-Ill. Most of the recipients received less than $5,000.

Team Ameritech Political Action Committee (C00174763) *Phone: (202) 326-3800 * Fax: (202) 326-3826 * 1401 H St. N.W., Washington, DC 20005 * E-mail: gerald.f.hogan@ameritech.com * Treasurer: Robert J. Kolbe * Contact: Gerald Hogan, Dir. of Federal Affairs*

	1993-94	1995-96	1997	Totals
Receipts	$1,370,945	$1,395,483	$706,444	$3,472,872
Disburse	1,207,881	1,496,159	594,254	3,298,294
Cash	210,722	110,055	222,250	n/a
Contributions	427,957	632,285	234,269	1,294,511
Republicans	201,357	445,752	143,072	790,181
No. of Cand.	*100*	*176*	*94*	*370*
House	139,582	333,051	103,823	576,456
Senate	61,775	112,701	39,249	213,725
Democrats	226,600	186,533	91,197	504,330
No. of Cand.	*109*	*96*	*63*	*268*
House	168,800	145,154	61,447	375,401
Senate	57,800	41,379	29,750	128,929
Incumbents	320,882	480,381	216,969	1,018,232
Challengers	23,300	53,700	6,000	83,000
Open Seat	83,275	99,004	11,100	193,379
Winners	354,387	504,455	n/a	858,842
Losers	73,570	127,830	n/a	201,400

Bell Atlantic Corp.

*Phone: (215) 963-6354 * Fax: (215) 963-6470*
1717 Arch St., 47th Floor S., Philadelphia, PA 19103
Web: www.ba.com

Bell Atlantic is the leading local telephone provider in the eastern United States and is also involved in wireless services, Internet access and directory publishing. With 40 million telephone access lines and 5.5 million wireless customers worldwide, the corporation — formed through the merger of Bell Atlantic and NYNEX — is one of the world's largest investors in high-growth global communications markets, with operations and investments in 21 countries.

The company has 141,600 employees and serves 13 states and the District of Columbia with local telephone service. Bell Atlantic is the world's largest publisher of Yellow Pages directories, with nearly 80 million copies distributed each year of 600 domestic and international books containing ads from nearly 900,000 advertisers.

Bell Atlantic lobbies on several telecommunications issues, especially the local and long-distance provisions of the Telecommunications Act of 1996. The company favors maintaining an exemption from interconnection compensation requirements for Internet service providers. It is also seeking to provide long-distance service in New York.

The Bell Atlantic-NYNEX merger will result in the folding of NYNEX's PAC into the Bell Atlantic PAC. NYNEX spent about $25,000 more than Bell Atlantic in congressional contributions during the 1995-96 election cycle. The two companies ranked sixth and seventh, respectively, among phone utility companies. NYNEX's leading recipients were former Sen. Larry Pressler, R-S.D., former Rep. Daniel Frisa, R-N.Y., and Rep. Bill Paxon, R-N.Y.

Bell Atlantic's PAC contributed about two-thirds of its total PAC money to Republican candidates. Ninety percent went to incumbents. Pressler, Sen. John Warner, R-Va., and Rep. Rick Boucher, D-Va., who sits on a telecommunications subcommittee, were the top recipients.

The company had two subsidiary PACs that contributed at least $5,000 to congressional campaigns during the last cycle. The Pennsylvania PAC gave $16,100, all of it to in-state incumbents. The company's New Jersey subsidiary gave $13,000 to candidates from that state and from Virginia. Both PACs have been terminated. Another affiliated PAC, for Chesapeake & Potomac Telephone Co., also no longer exists.

Bell Atlantic Corp. Political Action Committee (C00186288) *Phone: (202) 392-1312 * Fax: (202) 296-6082 * 1133 20th St. N.W., Suite 800, Washington, DC 20036 * Treasurer: Sherry Hessenthaler*

*Contact: Kevin McLernon, Dir. Gov. Affairs * Phone: (215) 963-6354*

	1993-94	1995-96	1997	Totals
Receipts	$146,949	$432,155	$348,783	$927,887
Disburse	140,809	388,073	326,517	855,399
Cash	13,450	57,531	79,798	n/a
Contributions	81,250	275,998	254,528	611,776
Republicans	27,400	181,121	155,572	364,093
No. of Cand.	*26*	*102*	*105*	*233*
House	12,400	130,330	112,072	254,802
Senate	15,000	50,791	43,500	109,291
Democrats	53,850	94,877	98,956	247,683
No. of Cand.	*39*	*66*	*65*	*170*
House	29,850	81,677	67,456	178,983
Senate	24,000	13,200	31,500	68,700
Incumbents	77,750	249,898	251,528	579,176
Challengers	500	4,500	0	5,000
Open Seat	3,000	22,000	2,000	27,000
Winners	70,000	240,846	n/a	310,846
Losers	11,250	35,152	n/a	46,402

NYNEX Employees' Federal Political Action Committee (C00179762) *Phone: (212) 395-2121 * Fax: (212) 395-1285 * 1095 Ave. of the Americas, 30th Floor, Room 3000, New York, NY 10036 * Treasurer: Jacqueline C. Yancey*

The NYNEX Employees' Federal PAC was terminated on Jan. 26, 1998.

	1993-94	1995-96	1997	Totals
Receipts	$241,420	$346,809	$195,619	$783,848
Disburse	215,650	349,550	126,000	691,200
Cash	29,913	40,302	109,927	n/a
Contributions	193,700	300,550	101,000	595,250
Republicans	118,700	206,550	70,500	395,750
No. of Cand.	*54*	*95*	*51*	*200*
House	77,200	163,550	34,500	275,250
Senate	41,500	43,000	36,000	120,500
Democrats	73,500	94,000	30,500	198,000
No. of Cand.	*46*	*44*	*31*	*121*
House	65,500	84,000	24,500	174,000
Senate	8,000	10,000	6,000	24,000
Incumbents	144,200	240,250	97,000	481,450
Challengers	20,000	20,000	0	40,000
Open Seat	29,500	40,300	5,000	74,800
Winners	158,950	234,750	n/a	393,700
Losers	34,750	65,800	n/a	100,550

Bell Atlantic Pennsylvania Inc. Federal PAC (formerly known as PA Bell PAC) (C00085332) *Strawberry Square, Fourth Floor, Harrisburg, PA 17101 * Treasurer: Robert J. McGonagle*

	1993-94	1995-96	1997	Totals
Receipts	$79,486	$43,436	$0	$122,922
Disburse	81,289	57,729	0	139,018
Cash	14,292	0	0	n/a
Contributions	28,750	16,100	0	44,850
Republicans	15,900	9,500	0	25,400
No. of Cand.	*11*	*8*	*0*	*19*
House	10,900	9,500	0	20,400
Senate	5,000	0	0	5,000
Democrats	12,850	6,600	0	19,450
No. of Cand.	*14*	*11*	*0*	*25*
House	12,850	6,600	0	19,450
Senate	0	0	0	0
Incumbents	22,950	16,100	0	39,050
Challengers	4,750	0	0	4,750
Open Seat	550	0	0	550
Winners	23,500	13,600	n/a	37,100
Losers	5,250	2,500	n/a	7,750

New Jersey Bell Telephone Co. Federal Political Action Committee (NJB PAC) (C00126110) *Phone: (973) 649-2279 * 1717 Arch St. 46W, Philadelphia, PA 19103 * Treasurer: Joseph Milanowycz * Contact: Tim Ireland, Public Relations*

	1993-94	1995-96	1997	Totals
Receipts	$28,978	$18,159	$0	$47,137
Disburse	29,422	19,917	0	49,339
Cash	1,757	0	0	n/a
Contributions	29,056	13,000	0	42,056
Republicans	14,556	7,500	0	22,056
No. of Cand.	*9*	*8*	*0*	*17*
House	14,556	7,500	0	22,056
Senate	0	0	0	0
Democrats	14,500	5,500	0	20,000
No. of Cand.	*8*	*6*	*0*	*14*
House	12,500	3,500	0	16,000
Senate	2,000	2,000	0	4,000
Incumbents	27,456	12,000	0	39,456
Challengers	1,100	0	0	1,100
Open Seat	500	1,000	0	1,500
Winners	23,556	10,000	n/a	33,556
Losers	5,500	3,000	n/a	8,500

Contributed less than $5,000 during 1995-96 cycle:

Bell Atlantic-Delaware Inc. PAC (C00085324) *911 Tatnall St., Wilmington, DE 19801 * Treasurer: Robert J. McGonagle*

Terminated PACs which contributed less than $5,000 during 1995-96 cycle:

Chesapeake & Potomac Telephone Co. Federal Political Action Committee (C00093468) *1710 H St. N.W., Washington, DC 20006 * Treasurer: Edward S. Williams Jr.*

BellSouth Corp.

*Phone: (404) 249-2270 * Fax: (404) 249-5906*
1155 Peachtree St. N.E., Suite 1925, Atlanta, GA 30309
Web: www.bellsouthcorp.com

BellSouth is a $20-billion publicly traded telecommunications company providing local and long-distance telephone, cellular and Internet services. The largest of the Baby Bells, the company offers local telephone service in nine Southeastern states: Kentucky, Tennessee, North Carolina, South Carolina, Georgia, Florida, Alabama, Mississippi and Louisiana. The company has about 92,000 employees and is headquartered in Atlanta.

BellSouth favors a regulatory moratorium on the Internet and high-speed communications networks. It is seeking to enter the long-distance market in the states it serves with local telephone service, a move the company says will create more than 200,000 new jobs in those states.

BellSouth has a second PAC that contributed to federal campaigns. Combined, BellSouth's two PACs contributed more money to 1996 congressional races than any other local and regional telephone utility company. Individually, the company's two committees ranked second and fifth. Both favored Republican candidates.

The top recipients of BellSouth PAC contributions were Reps. Allen Boyd, D-Fla., Mike Parker, R-Miss., and Sen. Fred Thompson, R-Tenn. More than 60 candidates, mostly from the Southeast, received at least $5,000.

BellSouth Telecommunications Inc. Employees Federal Political Action Committee (C00099655) *Phone: (202) 463-4100 * Fax: (202) 463-4149 * 1133 21st St. N.W., Suite 900, Washington, DC 20036 * Treasurer: Gary L. Walton * Contact: David J. Markey, V.P. of Gov. Affairs*

	1993-94	1995-96	1997	Totals
Receipts	$820,445	$1,052,504	$572,188	$2,445,137
Disburse	843,711	892,547	413,026	2,149,284
Cash	122,362	282,325	441,488	n/a
Contributions	426,500	545,867	212,008	1,184,375
Republicans	188,450	332,367	140,458	661,275
No. of Cand.	*61*	*77*	*59*	*197*
House	146,850	243,317	112,958	503,125
Senate	41,600	89,050	27,500	158,150
Democrats	238,050	212,000	71,550	521,600
No. of Cand.	*72*	*54*	*35*	*161*
House	220,950	192,000	59,050	472,000
Senate	17,100	20,000	12,500	49,600
Incumbents	319,950	414,217	199,508	933,675
Challengers	18,000	5,000	0	23,000
Open Seat	88,050	123,400	9,500	220,950
Winners	327,800	454,417	n/a	782,217
Losers	98,700	91,450	n/a	190,150

BellSouth Corp. Employees' Federal Political Action Committee (C00174060) *Phone: (202) 463-4100 * Fax: (202) 463-4196 * 1133 21st St. N.W., Suite 900, Washington, DC 20036 * Web: www.bellsouthcorp.com * Treasurer: Gary L. Walton * Contact: David J. Markey, V.P. of Gov. Affairs*

	1993-94	1995-96	1997	Totals
Receipts	$551,107	$495,093	$299,741	$1,345,941
Disburse	431,474	552,696	265,651	1,249,821
Cash	132,870	75,267	109,357	n/a
Contributions	248,270	308,250	122,250	678,770
Republicans	129,050	233,700	80,250	443,000
No. of Cand.	*86*	*108*	*60*	*254*
House	88,800	144,500	50,250	283,550
Senate	40,250	89,200	30,000	159,450
Democrats	119,220	74,550	42,000	235,770
No. of Cand.	*70*	*38*	*24*	*132*
House	78,600	50,750	27,500	156,850
Senate	40,620	23,800	14,500	78,920
Incumbents	188,520	246,500	118,750	553,770
Challengers	18,750	18,450	1,000	38,200
Open Seat	40,250	43,300	2,500	86,050
Winners	205,350	239,000	n/a	444,350
Losers	42,920	69,250	n/a	112,170

The Berry Co. Employees' Federal Political Action Committee (formerly known as L.M. Berry & Co.) (C00034207) *Phone: (937) 296-2299 * Fax: (937) 296-4987 * P.O. Box 6000, Dayton, OH 45401 * Web: www.lmberry.com * E-mail: berryco@lmberry.com * Treasurer: Steven D. Milano * Contact: William C. Ferguson, Chairman*

Berry & Co. is the largest Yellow Pages advertising sales agent in the United States, publishing more than 800 Yellow Pages directories nationwide. It is headquartered in Dayton, Ohio, with offices in 39 states, and shared operations with ITT World Directories in Belgium, the Netherlands, South Africa, the Virgin Islands, Norway, Ireland, Portugal, Puerto Rico and Japan.

A subsidiary of BellSouth, Berry's assets and sales information are consolidated with the parent company's, and are not published publicly.

Berry's PAC is associated with BellSouth FedPAC.

	1993-94	1995-96	1997	Totals
Receipts	$32,373	$24,151	$12,557	$69,081
Disburse	28,750	17,750	5,300	51,800
Cash	6,942	13,346	20,604	n/a
Contributions	28,750	16,750	3,300	48,800
Republicans	26,350	12,750	2,300	41,400
No. of Cand.	*31*	*16*	*3*	*50*
House	16,100	7,750	2,300	26,150
Senate	10,250	5,000	0	15,250
Democrats	2,400	4,000	1,000	7,400
No. of Cand.	*3*	*1*	*1*	*5*
House	2,400	4,000	1,000	7,400
Senate	0	0	0	0
Incumbents	11,750	11,500	3,300	26,550
Challengers	5,750	1,500	0	7,250
Open Seat	11,250	3,750	0	15,000
Winners	20,500	14,750	n/a	35,250
Losers	8,250	2,000	n/a	10,250

Century Telephone Enterprises Inc.

*Phone: (318) 362-1583 * Fax: (318) 388-9702*
100 Century Park Dr., Monroe, LA 71203
Web: www.centurytel.com

Century Telephone Enterprises provides communication services to more than 2 million customers in 21 states. Its local telephone businesses operate primarily in Wisconsin, Louisiana, Michigan, Ohio and Texas. In addition, its cellular business has more than 368,000 subscribers, primarily in Louisiana, Michigan, Arkansas, Mississippi and Texas.

Local telephone and cellular services provided 60 percent and 33 percent, respectively, of $750 million in 1996 sales. The publicly traded company also provides long distance, operator and Internet access services in certain local and regional markets, as well as some printing and related services.

Century was incorporated in 1968 and employs 3,400 workers.

Century Telephone Enterprises Inc. Federal Political Action Committee (CTE Fed PAC) (C00225524) *Address: same as sponsor * Treasurer: Wallace Lea * Contact: Harvey P. Perry, General Counsel and Sr. V.P.*

	1993-94	1995-96	1997	Totals
Receipts	$0	$18,691	$4,581	$23,272
Disburse	85	12,250	5,500	17,835
Cash	85	7,527	6,608	n/a
Contributions	0	9,250	3,000	12,250
Republicans	0	5,000	1,000	6,000
No. of Cand.	*0*	*7*	*1*	*8*
House	0	3,500	1,000	4,500
Senate	0	1,500	0	1,500
Democrats	0	4,250	2,000	6,250
No. of Cand.	*0*	*5*	*3*	*8*
House	0	2,500	500	3,000
Senate	0	1,750	1,500	3,250
Incumbents	0	2,250	2,500	4,750
Challengers	0	500	0	500
Open Seat	0	6,500	500	7,000
Winners	0	4,750	n/a	4,750
Losers	0	4,500	n/a	4,500

Cincinnati Bell Inc.

*Phone: (513) 397-7858 * Fax: (513) 241-1543*
201 E. Fourth St. (102-732), P.O. Box 2301, Cincinnati, OH 45201
Web: www.cinbellinc.com

Cincinnati Bell is a holding company engaged in operations through its telephone, information systems and telecommunications subsidiaries. Its operations provide services in Ohio, Kentucky and Indiana, and the publicly traded company's 1997 revenues totaled $1.76 billion.

The telephone operations segment, Cincinnati Bell Telephone Co., provides local service, network access and toll telephone services in the greater Cincinnati area. The information systems segment, Cincinnati Bell Information Systems Inc. provides data processing and software development services primarily to the telecommunications industry in the United States. The marketing segment, Matrixx Marketing, provides customer management solutions.

Cincinnati Bell Inc. Federal Political Action Committee (C00087478) *Address: same as sponsor * Treasurer: William H. Zimmer III * Contact: Charles Biery, Administrator*

	1993-94	1995-96	1997	Totals
Receipts	$32,563	$21,682	$9,300	$63,545
Disburse	31,575	27,380	8,500	67,455
Cash	7,456	1,763	2,564	n/a
Contributions	28,075	18,900	7,500	54,475
Republicans	21,300	16,400	6,000	43,700
No. of Cand.	*11*	*12*	*4*	*27*
House	13,525	13,900	3,000	30,425
Senate	7,775	2,500	3,000	13,275
Democrats	6,775	2,500	1,500	10,775
No. of Cand.	*3*	*3*	*2*	*8*
House	6,525	1,000	500	8,025
Senate	250	1,500	1,000	2,750
Incumbents	19,525	17,900	5,500	42,925
Challengers	2,200	1,000	0	3,200
Open Seat	6,350	0	2,000	8,350
Winners	20,300	16,400	n/a	36,700
Losers	7,775	2,500	n/a	10,275

Frontier Corp

*Phone: (716) 777-7317 * Fax: (716) 325-4624*
180 S. Clinton Ave., Rochester, NY 14646-0700
*Web: www.frontiercorp.com * E-mail: lhigley@frontiercorp.com*

Frontier, the fifth-largest U.S. long-distance company, reported $2.4 billion in 1997 revenue. The telecommunications company offers long distance, local, cellular, paging, data and Internet services to 2 million customers in the United States, Canada and England. Its 34 local telephone companies operate in 13 states and make Frontier the eleventh largest local telephone company in the nation.

Frontier, based in Rochester, N.Y., is publicly traded and employs more than 7,000 people.

In 1997 and early 1998, Frontier formed partnerships with several companies, including American Communications Services and State Communications, and acquired Silicon Valley's GlobalCenter, an Internet, data and digital distribution services provider.

Frontier Corp. Political Action Committee (formerly known as Rochester Telephone Committee PAC) (C00258210) *Address: same as sponsor * Treasurer: Kenneth P. Schirmuhly * Contact: Lucy Higley, PAC Dir.*

	1993-94	1995-96	1997	Totals
Receipts	$33,007	$86,909	$34,735	$154,651
Disburse	16,050	48,968	25,300	90,318
Cash	20,803	58,746	68,482	n/a
Contributions	12,050	36,000	22,800	70,850
Republicans	5,450	25,875	13,800	45,125
No. of Cand.	*10*	*25*	*17*	*52*
House	1,950	17,875	10,100	29,925
Senate	3,500	8,000	3,700	15,200
Democrats	6,600	10,125	9,000	25,725
No. of Cand.	*8*	*11*	*11*	*30*
House	3,100	8,125	6,000	17,225
Senate	3,500	2,000	3,000	8,500
Incumbents	11,200	33,750	21,300	66,250
Challengers	500	2,250	500	3,250
Open Seat	350	500	1,000	1,850
Winners	11,200	32,625	n/a	43,825
Losers	850	3,375	n/a	4,225

GTE Corp.

*Phone: (203) 965-2000 * Fax: (203) 965-2277*
One Stamford Forum, Stamford, CT 06904
Web: www.gte.com

With annual revenues and sales exceeding $21 billion, GTE is one of the largest publicly held telecommunications companies in the world. GTE offers local and wireless service in 29 states (third behind Bell Atlantic and SBC) and long-distance service and Internet access in all 50 states.

GTE is also a leader in government defense communications systems and equipment, directories and telecommunications-based information services, and aircraft-passenger telecommunications. GTE has units in Illinois, Texas, Florida, Massachusetts, Connecticut, California and Georgia.

The company lobbies on a number of telecommunications issues, including implementation of the Telecommunications Act of 1996 and wireless and Internet regulation. Candidates who receive contributions often come from states where GTE offers services or sit on committees with jurisdiction over issues in which the company is interested — commerce, finance and judiciary committees in particular.

GTE ranked fourth among local and regional telephone utility PACs in contributions to congressional candidates during the 1995-96 election cycle. The company favored Republicans by a 3-to-1 margin. The top recipients were Rep. Rick White, R-Wash., who sits on the House Commerce Committee, and former Sen. Larry Pressler, R-S.D.

GTE Corp. Political Action Club (GTE PAC) (C00025163) *Phone: (202) 463-5222 * Fax: (202) 463-5256 * 1850 M St. N.W., Suite 1200, Washington, DC 20036 * E-mail: jminarczik@dcoffice.gte.com * Treasurer: Jennifer A. Minarczik*

	1993-94	1995-96	1997	Totals
Receipts	$593,561	$625,330	$392,142	$1,611,033
Disburse	620,555	639,666	277,584	1,537,805
Cash	46,202	31,864	146,422	n/a
Contributions	472,369	435,691	163,018	1,071,078
Republicans	264,482	331,939	110,642	707,063
No. of Cand.	*164*	*202*	*101*	*467*
House	151,379	259,005	70,025	480,409
Senate	113,103	72,934	40,617	226,654
Democrats	207,637	103,752	52,376	363,765
No. of Cand.	*150*	*97*	*65*	*312*
House	163,287	89,875	44,376	297,538
Senate	44,350	13,877	8,000	66,227
Incumbents	356,475	332,029	154,018	842,522
Challengers	46,342	20,578	4,500	71,420
Open Seat	69,052	83,334	4,500	156,886
Winners	366,143	354,757	n/a	720,900
Losers	106,226	80,934	n/a	187,160

LCI International Inc.

*Phone: (703) 848-4476 * Fax: (703) 918-4668*
8180 Greensboro Dr., Suite 800, McLean, VA 22102
*Web: www.lci.com * E-mail: smithl@lci.com*

LCI International, formerly LiTel Telecommunications Corp., is a $1 billion publicly held long-distance company, providing voice and data transmission services throughout the United States and to more than 220 international locations.

Founded in 1983, LCI had 1997 sales of $1.6 billion.

In 1997, LCI began offering local telephone service in major markets across the country. The company is headquartered in McLean, Va., with offices in more than 45 primarily eastern and central U.S. locations and more than 180 million circuit-miles of digital fiber-optic capacity.

LCI International PAC (C00237156) *Address: same as sponsor * Treasurer: Douglas W. Kinkoph*

	1993-94	1995-96	1997	Totals
Receipts	$12,599	$14,939	$9,709	$37,247
Disburse	11,923	16,775	9,000	37,698
Cash	7,497	5,665	6,385	n/a
Contributions	3,750	11,000	8,500	23,250
Republicans	2,250	7,000	2,500	11,750
No. of Cand.	*5*	*6*	*3*	*14*
House	0	5,000	1,500	6,500
Senate	2,250	2,000	1,000	5,250
Democrats	1,500	4,000	6,000	11,500
No. of Cand.	*2*	*5*	*3*	*10*
House	500	1,500	1,000	3,000
Senate	1,000	2,500	5,000	8,500
Incumbents	3,000	8,500	8,500	20,000
Challengers	0	2,000	0	2,000
Open Seat	750	500	0	1,250
Winners	3,500	7,500	n/a	11,000
Losers	250	3,500	n/a	3,750

MCI Communications Corp.

*Phone: (202) 887-2921 * Fax: (202) 887-2921*
1801 Pennsylvania Ave. N.W., Washington, DC 20006
Web: www.mci.com

MCI Communications is the second-largest nationwide carrier of long-distance calls and the third-largest carrier of international long-distance calls in the world. A public company with 55,000 employees, MCI had 1997 sales of $20 billion.

MCI provides a wide spectrum of domestic and international voice and data services, which include long-distance telephone services, data communications services and electronic messaging services.

In November 1997, WorldCom Inc. and MCI announced a merger agreement creating a communications company that plans to provide a complete range of local, long distance, Internet and international communications services. The combined company, MCI WorldCom, would have more than $30 billion in revenues and would employ about 68,000 people.

MCI Telecommunications Political Action Committee (MCI PAC) (C00142836) *Address: same as sponsor * Treasurer: Gerald J. Kovach * Contact: Laurie Christman, Manager*

	1993-94	1995-96	1997	Totals
Receipts	$104,688	$242,809	$191,183	$538,680
Disburse	110,614	216,104	85,953	412,671
Cash	13,238	39,949	145,185	n/a
Contributions	101,220	212,275	84,500	397,995
Republicans	31,000	90,150	41,500	162,650
No. of Cand.	*40*	*72*	*37*	*149*
House	15,500	62,150	32,500	110,150
Senate	15,500	28,000	9,000	52,500
Democrats	70,220	122,125	43,000	235,345
No. of Cand.	*86*	*97*	*35*	*218*
House	40,700	77,875	15,000	133,575
Senate	29,520	44,250	28,000	101,770
Incumbents	90,970	158,775	82,500	332,245
Challengers	0	20,500	1,000	21,500
Open Seat	10,250	33,000	1,000	44,250
Winners	78,850	178,650	n/a	257,500
Losers	22,370	33,625	n/a	55,995

National Telephone Cooperative Association

*Phone: (202) 298-2300 * Fax: (202) 298-2320*
2626 Pennsylvania Ave. N.W., Washington, DC 20037
Web: www.ntca.org

The National Telephone Cooperative Association is a nonprofit group representing nearly 500 small and rural telephone cooperatives and commercial companies. NTCA also represents 42 international telephone companies from Bolivia, Canada, Mexico, Poland and the Philippines; 60 state and regional telecommunications associations, 302 vendors and 94 subsidiary/independent service providers.

In February 1998, the NTCA led an effort to convince Congress to pass the first technical correction to the Telecommunications Act of 1996 to allow several tribally owned telephone companies to seek designation as eligible carriers from the Federal Communication Commission. The association also lobbies for affordable universal service for rural areas.

National Telephone Cooperative Association Telephone Education Committee Organization (C00004473) *Address: same as sponsor * Treasurer: Keith Taylor * Contact: Thomas D. Wacker, Gov. Affairs*

	1993-94	1995-96	1997	Totals
Receipts	$128,831	$126,258	$73,704	$328,793
Disburse	88,982	146,676	66,432	302,090
Cash	110,307	89,890	97,195	n/a
Contributions	84,750	141,848	59,419	286,017
Republicans	23,500	85,300	32,300	141,100
No. of Cand.	*45*	*115*	*51*	*211*
House	19,450	59,650	24,050	103,150
Senate	4,050	25,650	8,250	37,950
Democrats	59,450	56,548	26,119	142,117
No. of Cand.	*104*	*87*	*36*	*227*
House	51,950	47,840	15,600	115,390
Senate	7,500	8,708	10,519	26,727
Incumbents	79,350	113,400	57,619	250,369
Challengers	1,000	4,550	300	5,850
Open Seat	4,400	23,898	1,500	29,798
Winners	66,400	121,588	n/a	187,988
Losers	18,350	20,260	n/a	38,610

SBC Communications Inc.

*Phone: (210) 351-2159 * Fax: (210) 351-2185*
175 E. Houston, Room 7-A-50, San Antonio, TX 78205
Web: www.sbc.com

SBC Communications is the holding company for a number of telephone and communication businesses located mostly in the western United States. Its units include Southwestern Bell, Pacific Bell and Nevada Bell, which provide local telephone service in California, Nevada, Texas, Oklahoma, Missouri, Kansas and Arkansas. Cellular One, a wireless and Internet access company operating in several states, is another SBC unit. The publicly traded company has more than 114,000 employees. It reported 1997 revenues of $24.8 billion.

A federal District Court ruling in December 1997 opened the way for SBC to provide long-distance service in its territory, including California and Texas. In early 1998, SBC merged with Southern New England Telecommunications Corp., which provides local and long-distance telephone, wireless and Internet services in Connecticut and other areas. SBC lobbies on improving access to the long-distance markets in the areas where it operates.

The company ranked third among regional telephone company PACs in contributions to congressional candidates during the 1995-96 election cycle. It favored Republican candidates and was one of 85 PACs to spend more than $100,000 on open seats. The top recipients were House Speaker Newt Gingrich, R-Ga. and Reps. Jo Ann Emerson, R-Mo., Bill Paxon, R-N.Y., and Ken Bentsen, D-Texas.

SBC Communications Inc. Employee Federal Political Action Committee (SBC EmPAC) (C00109017) *Phone: (202) 326-8800 * Fax: (202) 408-4798 * 1401 Eye St. N.W., Suite 1100, Washington, DC 20005 * Treasurer: Donald E. Kiernan * Contact: Lea Joergenson, Political Manager*

	1993-94	1995-96	1997	Totals
Receipts	$394,283	$692,626	$412,108	$1,499,017
Disburse	365,700	674,857	319,539	1,360,096
Cash	42,071	60,255	152,829	n/a
Contributions	286,850	504,333	249,550	1,040,733
Republicans	148,300	359,133	154,200	661,633
No. of Cand.	*89*	*150*	*112*	*351*
House	74,850	260,963	115,100	450,913
Senate	73,450	98,170	39,100	210,720
Democrats	138,550	145,200	95,350	379,100
No. of Cand.	*80*	*75*	*73*	*228*
House	110,800	126,100	75,350	312,250
Senate	27,750	19,100	20,000	66,850
Incumbents	208,500	376,179	238,700	823,379
Challengers	18,000	23,704	1,000	42,704
Open Seat	60,350	104,450	9,350	174,150
Winners	230,300	422,349	n/a	652,649
Losers	56,550	81,984	n/a	138,534

Pacific Telesis Group Political Action Committee (Federal Account) (C00083865) *130 Kearny St., Suite 3374, San Francisco, CA 94108 * Web: www.sbc.com * Treasurer: Margaret Deb Brown*

The Pacific Telesis Group PAC was terminated in April 1998. The company merged with SBC Communications in 1996.

	1993-94	1995-96	1997	Totals
Receipts	$306,863	$301,291	$123,464	$731,618
Disburse	336,005	266,215	82,561	684,781
Cash	8,712	43,797	84,706	n/a
Contributions	239,245	182,259	52,564	474,068
Republicans	81,720	110,813	29,747	222,280
No. of Cand.	*69*	*79*	*38*	*186*
House	61,720	82,313	20,247	164,280
Senate	20,000	28,500	9,500	58,000
Democrats	157,525	71,446	22,817	251,788
No. of Cand.	*84*	*45*	*27*	*156*
House	124,025	64,811	19,427	208,263
Senate	33,500	6,635	3,390	43,525
Incumbents	230,245	168,009	51,064	449,318
Challengers	1,500	5,000	1,500	8,000
Open Seat	7,500	9,250	0	16,750
Winners	191,195	154,634	n/a	345,829
Losers	48,050	27,625	n/a	75,675

Southern New England Telecommunications Corp.

*Phone: (203) 771-2193 * Fax: (203) 787-6817*
227 Church St., Room 1108, New Haven, CT 06510
Web: www.snet.com

Southern New England Telecommunications is a publicly traded New Haven, Conn. company that provides phone service to 1.5 million business and residential customers across Connecticut. The company also publishes SNET Yellow Pages and sells wholesale and wireless service. SNET had $2 billion in 1997 revenue.

In January 1998, SNET announced that it would be purchased by SBC Communications but would retain its name and headquarters. SBC is a San Antonio company with $24.8 billion in revenue. It operates the Southwestern Bell, Pacific Bell, Nevada Bell and Cellular One companies.

SNET has asked for approval from the state utility commission to enter the local cable market in Connecticut. The company would use its network to deliver programming and pay-per-view services.

Southern New England Telecommunications Corp. Political Action Committee (snetPAC) (C00126276) *Address: same as sponsor * Treasurer: John J. Miller*

	1993-94	1995-96	1997	Totals
Receipts	$87,982	$83,680	$41,292	$212,954
Disburse	86,582	85,260	26,745	198,587
Cash	21,776	20,199	34,656	n/a
Contributions	11,400	18,000	1,750	31,150
Republicans	4,850	12,000	1,000	17,850
No. of Cand.	*5*	*5*	*1*	*11*
House	4,850	11,000	1,000	16,850
Senate	0	1,000	0	1,000
Democrats	6,550	6,000	750	13,300
No. of Cand.	*6*	*4*	*2*	*12*
House	5,350	4,000	750	10,100
Senate	1,200	2,000	0	3,200
Incumbents	10,000	18,000	1,750	29,750
Challengers	1,400	0	0	1,400
Open Seat	0	0	0	0
Winners	10,000	14,500	n/a	24,500
Losers	1,400	3,500	n/a	4,900

Sprint Corp.

*Phone: (913) 624-3000 * Fax: (913) 624-3281*
2330 Shawnee Mission Pkwy., Westwood, KS 66205
Web: www.sprint.com

Sprint is the nation's third-largest long-distance company and a local telephone provider for more than 6 million customers in 19 states, including Florida, Pennsylvania, Ohio, Nevada, Kansas and Oregon. A public company, Sprint also publishes directories, provides Internet access and is involved in a wireless communications venture with cable companies Cox, Comcast and TCI. The company has 48,000 employees. Sprint reported $14.8 billion in sales in 1997.

The company supports the Telecommunications Act of 1996, although it would like to see increased subscriber line charges and a reduction in the "interconnection charges" it pays to use other systems' lines. It favors allowing access providers the flexibility to change their rates according to their costs.

Sprint ranked second among long-distance company PACs in congressional contributions during the 1995-96 election cycle. However, the top-ranked PAC, AT&T, contributed more than $1 million more than Sprint gave. Seven candidates received $5,000 from Sprint, including four from Kansas. The only winning candidate in that group was Sen. Pat Roberts, R-Kan.

Sprint has two subsidiary PACs: Sprint Corp. mid-Atlantic Region and Sprint/United Telephone Co. of Ohio. Neither contributed to congressional races in 1996 and both usually focus on state and local races.

SprintPAC (C00089342) *Phone: (202) 857-1030 * Fax: (202) 822-8999 * 1850 M St. N.W., Suite 1100, Washington, DC 20036 * Treasurer: John Quackenbush * Contact: Bill Barloon, Dir. of Gov. Affairs*

	1993-94	1995-96	1997	Totals
Receipts	$338,244	$358,472	$175,561	$872,277
Disburse	365,000	339,175	137,898	842,073
Cash	37,006	56,315	93,984	n/a
Contributions	314,000	229,674	85,898	629,572
Republicans	153,850	123,300	41,250	318,400
No. of Cand.	*112*	*93*	*35*	*240*
House	94,850	80,300	18,250	193,400
Senate	59,000	43,000	23,000	125,000
Democrats	158,150	106,374	44,648	309,172
No. of Cand.	*115*	*96*	*29*	*240*
House	116,150	78,374	11,148	205,672
Senate	42,000	28,000	33,500	103,500
Incumbents	228,000	154,424	80,898	463,322
Challengers	19,000	16,750	1,000	36,750
Open Seat	66,500	58,000	4,000	128,500
Winners	253,000	180,924	n/a	433,924
Losers	61,000	48,750	n/a	109,750

Contributed less than $5,000 during 1995-96 cycle:

Sprint Corp. mid-Atlantic Region Telecom Political Action (C00297754) *Phone: (919) 554-7240 * 225 Hillsborough St., P.O. Box 2829, Raleigh, NC 27602 * Treasurer: Brenda M. Doughterty*

Sprint/United Telephone Co. of Ohio Political Leadership Program PAC (C00304196) *Phone: (614) 224-3833 * Fax: (614) 224-3902 * 665 Lexington Ave., P.O. Box 3555, Mansfield, OH 44907 * Treasurer: Clarence E. Ellis * Contact: Thomas McCullough, PAC Chairman*

Telephone & Data Systems Inc.

*Phone: (608) 845-4160 * Fax: (608) 845-4184*
301 S. Westfield Rd., P.O. Box 5158, Madison, WI 53705-0158
Web: www.teldta.com

Telephone & Data Systems is a publicly held telecommunications company with cellular telephone, local telephone and radio paging operations. The Chicago-based firm provides telecommunications services to 2.4 million customers in 37 states and the District of Columbia.

The company includes several subsidiaries. The United States Cellular Corp. is a cellular telephone subsidiary. It and TDS have the right to acquire cellular interests representing 25.1 million people in 204 markets. United States Cellular's consolidated markets have almost 1.2 million cellular telephones in service.

TDS Telecommunication Corp. is TDS's wholly owned telephone subsidiary. TDS Telecom operates 105 telephone companies. These companies operate in 28 states, with each serving an average of 3,500 households and several hundred businesses.

Aerial Communications Inc. is TDS's 83 percent-owned Personal Communication Services subsidiary. Aerial owns the licenses to provide PCS service in six major trading areas.

American Paging Inc. is TDS's 82 percent-owned radio paging subsidiary. American Paging provides wireless messaging communications services to 767,400 customers through 42 sales and service operating centers.

Founder Roy Carlson and his family own about half of the company's stock.

TDS Telecommunications Corp. Political Action Committee (C00299750) *Address: same as sponsor * E-mail: kevin.hess@teldta.com * Treasurer: Kevin G. Hess*

	1993-94	1995-96	1997	Totals
Receipts	$20,682	$22,251	$19,655	$62,588
Disburse	58	26,351	4,801	31,210
Cash	20,624	16,524	31,378	n/a
Contributions	0	26,200	4,500	30,700
Republicans	0	21,100	2,500	23,600
No. of Cand.	*0*	*20*	*3*	*23*
House	0	13,100	2,500	15,600
Senate	0	8,000	0	8,000
Democrats	0	5,100	2,000	7,100
No. of Cand.	*0*	*6*	*3*	*9*
House	0	4,100	1,000	5,100
Senate	0	1,000	1,000	2,000
Incumbents	0	23,200	4,500	27,700
Challengers	0	1,000	0	1,000
Open Seat	0	2,000	0	2,000
Winners	0	24,200	n/a	24,200
Losers	0	2,000	n/a	2,000

US West Inc.

*Phone: (303) 793-6500 * Fax: (303) 793-6654*
5325 Zuni, Room 630, Denver, CO 80221
Web: www.uswest.com

The US West Communications Group provides telecommunications services to 25 million customers in 14 Western and Midwestern states: Arizona, Colorado, Idaho, Iowa, Nebraska, Minnesota, Montana, New Mexico, North Dakota, Oregon, South Dakota, Utah, Washington and Wyoming. Subsidiary AirTouch Communications, along with BellAtlantic, is a partner in PrimeCo, a wireless and cellular company. Another subsidiary, MediaOne, provides cable in Atlanta and other areas.

In October 1997, the company announced plans to split US West Media Group, its cable and wireless division, and US West Communications Group, which provides telephone and Internet service, into separate public companies by the end of 1998. US West Inc. is headquartered in Englewood, Colo., a suburb of Denver. The company's total annual revenues approach $13 billion. It has 69,000 employees.

The company generally supports the Telecommunications Act of 1996, but says that the former Bell companies operate under too many restrictions. One of the company's goals is entry into the long-distance telephone market.

US West ranked eighth among local and regional telephone utilities in congressional contributions during the 1995-96 election cycle. The company spent nearly 25 percent of its money on open races and generally favored Republicans. The top 15 recipients were candidates in states west of Indiana. Sen. Gordon Smith, R-Ore., Rep. Barbara Cubin, R-Wyo., and Sen. Larry Craig, R-Idaho, were the leading recipients. Sen. Max Baucus, D-Mont., was the top Democrat.

US West Inc. Political Action Committee (U.S. West PAC) (C00184374) *Phone: (202) 429-0303 * Fax: (202) 293-0561 * 1020 19th St. N.W., Suite 700, Washington, DC 20036 * Treasurer: Debra Pestana*

*Contact: Bruce Posey, V.P. of Federal Relations * Phone: (303) 793-6500*

	1993-94	1995-96	1997	Totals
Receipts	$664,584	$489,935	$221,732	$1,376,251
Disburse	686,299	452,396	138,732	1,277,427
Cash	14,303	51,841	134,841	n/a
Contributions	319,110	264,341	72,969	656,420
Republicans	171,193	195,173	45,619	411,985
No. of Cand.	*93*	*93*	*45*	*231*
House	99,625	123,971	28,900	252,496
Senate	71,568	71,202	16,719	159,489
Democrats	141,667	69,168	26,600	237,435
No. of Cand.	*79*	*45*	*20*	*144*
House	105,635	45,318	16,600	167,553
Senate	36,032	23,850	10,000	69,882
Incumbents	238,391	190,341	71,369	500,101
Challengers	21,050	14,250	1,600	36,900
Open Seat	58,569	59,750	0	118,319
Winners	236,480	217,558	n/a	454,038
Losers	82,630	46,783	n/a	129,413

MediaOne PAC (C00280529) *Phone: (303) 754-5440 * 188 Inverness Dr. W., Englewood, CO 80112 * Web: www.mediaone.com * Treasurer: Lorine Card*

*Phone: (202) 429-3128 * Fax: (202) 293-0561 * 1020 19th St. N.W., Washington, DC 20036 * Contact: Lorine Card*

MediaOne Inc., based in Englewood, Colo., is a wholly owned subsidiary of US West Media Group.

MediaOne, which has more than 9,000 employees, was formed in 1996 when US West purchased Boston-based Continental Cablevision. It provides telephone and television services and Internet access to 5 million subscribers in 19 states nationwide.

US West and Media Group announced plans to separate in 1998.

	1993-94	1995-96	1997	Totals
Receipts	$94,275	$78,701	$7,374	$180,350
Disburse	41,629	72,280	37,250	151,159
Cash	52,637	59,057	29,181	n/a
Contributions	42,300	65,495	23,750	131,545
Republicans	17,050	39,195	9,500	65,745
No. of Cand.	*17*	*33*	*11*	*61*
House	12,050	30,495	5,500	48,045
Senate	5,000	8,700	4,000	17,700
Democrats	25,250	26,300	14,250	65,800
No. of Cand.	*19*	*19*	*10*	*48*
House	21,250	19,300	5,750	46,300
Senate	4,000	7,000	8,500	19,500
Incumbents	35,800	57,345	22,750	115,895
Challengers	0	500	0	500
Open Seat	6,000	7,650	1,000	14,650
Winners	35,800	49,195	n/a	84,995
Losers	6,500	16,300	n/a	22,800

United States Telephone Association

*Phone: (202) 326-7300 * Fax: (202) 326-7333*
1401 H St. N.W., Suite 600, Washington, DC 20005
*Web: www.usta.org * E-mail: lcostello@usta.org*

The United States Telephone Association represents 1,200 companies in the telecommunications industry. The group works with its membership to voice industry concerns, coordinate efforts and share information with member companies. USTA participates in proceedings before the Federal Communications Commission, the Rural Utilities Service, the IRS, the National Telecommunications and Information Administration and others.

Issues of importance to USTA include: the Telecommunications Act of 1996 and how the FCC implements it, wiretap and encryption, copyright laws, universal telephone service and Internet access.

United States Telephone Association PAC (formerly known as United States Independent Telephone Association PAC) (C00000984) *Address: same as sponsor * Treasurer: Lisa M. Costello * Contact: Alan Terrell, Chairperson*

	1993-94	1995-96	1997	Totals
Receipts	$173,210	$162,752	$77,544	$413,506
Disburse	147,080	169,265	54,792	371,137
Cash	33,807	27,302	50,059	n/a
Contributions	105,132	134,464	44,265	283,861
Republicans	54,400	100,208	31,265	185,873
No. of Cand.	*53*	*82*	*42*	*177*
House	19,300	67,208	21,776	108,284
Senate	35,100	33,000	9,489	77,589
Democrats	50,732	34,256	13,000	97,988
No. of Cand.	*50*	*27*	*17*	*94*
House	31,450	29,256	8,000	68,706
Senate	19,282	5,000	5,000	29,282
Incumbents	91,582	110,505	43,265	245,352
Challengers	1,000	10,703	0	11,703
Open Seat	12,050	13,256	1,000	26,306
Winners	81,132	109,805	n/a	190,937
Losers	24,000	24,659	n/a	48,659

WorldCom Inc.

*Phone: (601) 360-8600 * Fax: (601) 974-8350*
515 E. Amite St., Jackson, MS 39201-2702
Web: www.wcom.com

If its proposed merger with MCI is approved, WorldCom will become the nation's second-largest long-distance telephone company. As of March 1998, the merger had been approved by both companies' shareholders and was awaiting federal government approval. The combined company, MCI WorldCom, would have more than $30 billion in revenues and would employ about 68,000 people.

Based in Jackson, Miss., publicly traded WorldCom is the first company to offer local and long-distance service over its own network since the breakup of AT&T. It also offers Internet access and networking services. WorldCom, which employs about 13,000 workers, reported 1997 sales of $7.3 billion.

Subsidiaries include: MFS Communications Co. and UUNET Technologies.

WorldCom Inc. Federal Political Action Committee (formerly known as LDDS Communications Inc. Fed PAC) (C00225763) *Address: same as sponsor * Treasurer: Scott D. Sullivan*

	1993-94	1995-96	1997	Totals
Receipts	$63,542	$209,653	$142,557	$415,752
Disburse	61,300	192,495	114,650	368,445
Cash	6,593	23,753	51,661	n/a
Contributions	49,150	132,045	74,300	255,495
Republicans	13,850	69,225	30,000	113,075
No. of Cand.	*17*	*35*	*24*	*76*
House	3,850	39,500	23,000	66,350
Senate	10,000	29,725	7,000	46,725
Democrats	35,300	62,820	44,300	142,420
No. of Cand.	*29*	*58*	*30*	*117*
House	20,800	36,300	18,800	75,900
Senate	14,500	26,520	25,500	66,520
Incumbents	42,750	89,645	72,300	204,695
Challengers	0	9,500	1,000	10,500
Open Seat	5,900	31,900	1,000	38,800
Winners	41,250	110,145	n/a	151,395
Losers	7,900	21,900	n/a	29,800

MFS Communications Co. Inc. Political Action Committee (MFS-PAC) (C00256248) *Phone: (603) 203-7200 * Fax: (603) 218-0072 * One Tower Ln., Suite 1600, Oakbrook Terrace, IL 60181 * Treasurer: Charles A. Rohe*

Metropolitan Fiber Systems Communications Co. Inc. PAC was terminated in July 1997.

	1993-94	1995-96	1997	Totals
Receipts	$43,100	$91,435	$12,558	$147,093
Disburse	41,857	73,268	35,106	150,231
Cash	4,375	22,548	0	n/a
Contributions	33,750	62,562	6,000	102,312
Republicans	13,250	46,262	2,000	61,512
No. of Cand.	*9*	*24*	*2*	*35*
House	8,250	34,490	2,000	44,740
Senate	5,000	11,772	0	16,772
Democrats	20,500	16,300	4,000	40,800
No. of Cand.	*16*	*19*	*5*	*40*
House	12,500	11,800	2,000	26,300
Senate	8,000	4,500	2,000	14,500
Incumbents	32,500	50,612	6,000	89,112
Challengers	0	1,000	0	1,000
Open Seat	1,250	10,950	0	12,200
Winners	28,250	49,290	n/a	77,540
Losers	5,500	13,272	n/a	18,772

Construction

Building Materials & Equipment

American Portland Cement Alliance

*Phone: (202) 408-9494 * Fax: (202) 408-0877*
1225 Eye St., Washington, DC 20005

The American Portland Cement Alliance was created in 1933 to protect and promote the interests of the cement industry.

APCA focuses on construction-related issues and is involved in federal programs that improve highways, build bridges and construct sewers and water-related facilities. The cement industry also is interested in labor, safety and health legislation. APCA works with agencies such as the EPA and the Mine Safety and Health Administration.

American Portland Cement Alliance PAC is a bipartisan committee that follows general business, transportation, infrastructure and labor legislation. It has about 150 members.

American Portland Cement Alliance Political Action Committee (C00237065) *Address: same as sponsor * Treasurer: Richard C. Creighton*

	1993-94	1995-96	1997	Totals
Receipts	$168,314	$169,138	$98,416	$435,868
Disburse	146,000	194,568	92,454	433,022
Cash	24,762	808	6,769	n/a
Contributions	125,000	162,585	75,750	363,335
Republicans	79,400	125,882	53,000	258,282
No. of Cand.	*88*	*127*	*56*	*271*
House	46,400	77,609	30,000	154,009
Senate	33,000	48,273	23,000	104,273
Democrats	45,100	36,703	21,750	103,553
No. of Cand.	*52*	*44*	*27*	*123*
House	34,600	31,160	10,750	76,510
Senate	10,500	5,543	11,000	27,043
Incumbents	97,300	131,688	72,750	301,738
Challengers	8,250	5,543	1,000	14,793
Open Seat	19,450	25,354	2,000	46,804
Winners	103,750	132,188	n/a	235,938
Losers	21,250	30,397	n/a	51,647

American Supply Association

*Phone: (312) 464-0090 * Fax: (312) 464-0091*
222 Merchandise Mart Plaza, Suite 1360, Chicago, IL 60654
Web: www.asa.net

The American Supply Association is a federation of regional and national organizations serving the plumbing, heating and cooling industries. Established in 1970, the association represents 1,050 manufacturing and distribution members.

ASA provides its member with seminars and manuals, business insurance and publication materials.

American Supply Association PAC (C00166074) *Phone: (202) 223-6222 * Fax: (202) 785-0687 * Kent and O'Connor, 1990 M St. N.W., #340, Washington, DC 20036 * Treasurer: Inga Calderon*
*Contact: Mickey Weinstein, Chairman * Phone: (312) 464-0090*

	1993-94	1995-96	1997	Totals
Receipts	$63,657	$72,629	$40,060	$176,346
Disburse	62,400	76,126	26,005	164,531
Cash	25,777	22,279	36,234	n/a
Contributions	61,400	74,950	24,500	160,850
Republicans	48,650	67,700	21,500	137,850
No. of Cand.	*52*	*83*	*37*	*172*
House	26,650	49,000	18,000	93,650
Senate	22,000	18,700	3,500	44,200
Democrats	11,250	7,250	2,500	21,000
No. of Cand.	*16*	*12*	*4*	*32*
House	10,750	5,000	1,500	17,250
Senate	500	2,250	1,000	3,750
Incumbents	35,400	41,250	23,000	99,650
Challengers	5,000	10,700	1,500	17,200
Open Seat	21,000	23,000	0	44,000
Winners	48,900	54,750	n/a	103,650
Losers	12,500	20,200	n/a	32,700

American Traffic Safety Services Association

*Phone: (540) 898-5400 * Fax: (540) 898-5510*
5440 Jefferson Davis Highway, Fredericksburg, VA 22407-2673
Web: www.atssa.com

The American Traffic Safety Services Association is a national trade association representing companies and individuals in the traffic control business. It works to improve the safety of motorists, pedestrians and workers by providing training and advocacy. Full members include suppliers of work zone traffic control products and services, pavement marking contractors and highway sign manufacturers. Associate members manufacture traffic control equipment.

Established in 1972, the association has about 1,500 members.

ATSSA has lobbied for work zone safety programs before roadway reconstruction begins. It also has lobbied to limit government's authority to subsidize tax-supported businesses which engage in direct economic competition with small, private, for-profit enterprises.

American Traffic Safety Services Association Political Action Committee (ATSSA PAC) (C00281717) *Address: same as sponsor * Treasurer: Robert Dingess*

	1993-94	1995-96	1997	Totals
Receipts	$6,892	$15,218	$9,500	$31,610
Disburse	5,376	9,200	1,111	15,687
Cash	1,514	7,532	15,920	n/a
Contributions	3,500	8,000	0	11,500
Republicans	500	4,000	0	4,500
No. of Cand.	*1*	*3*	*0*	*4*
House	500	2,500	0	3,000
Senate	0	1,500	0	1,500
Democrats	3,000	4,000	0	7,000
No. of Cand.	*2*	*4*	*0*	*6*
House	3,000	3,000	0	6,000
Senate	0	1,000	0	1,000
Incumbents	3,500	8,000	0	11,500
Challengers	0	0	0	0
Open Seat	0	0	0	0
Winners	3,500	7,000	n/a	10,500
Losers	0	1,000	n/a	1,000

Ash Grove Cement Co.

*Phone: (913) 451-8900 x244 * Fax: (913) 451-8324*
P.O. Box 25900, Overland Park, KS 66225

Ash Grove Cement produces lime and cement. The publicly traded company's 1997 sales were $350 million and it employs 1,500 people.

In August 1996, Ash Grove Cement, headquartered in Overland Park, Kan., acquired a hazardous waste permit from the EPA to continue storing its hazardous wastes in tanks and containers and burning the wastes for fuel in two cement kilns at its Chanute, Kan., plant.

The company is part of a joint venture, North Texas Cement Company, which has a cement plant in Midlothian, Texas, and is building another 40 miles north of Dallas.

Ash Grove Cement Political Action Committee (C00102517)
*Address: same as sponsor * Treasurer: John Woodfill * Contact: Kent Sunderland, President*

	1993-94	1995-96	1997	Totals
Receipts	$42,835	$53,816	$26,230	$122,881
Disburse	29,731	41,053	9,500	80,284
Cash	13,631	26,392	43,122	n/a
Contributions	16,700	27,250	2,000	45,950
Republicans	14,700	24,250	2,000	40,950
No. of Cand.	*20*	*32*	*2*	*54*
House	7,200	13,500	0	20,700
Senate	7,500	10,750	2,000	20,250
Democrats	2,000	3,000	0	5,000
No. of Cand.	*4*	*3*	*0*	*7*
House	500	1,500	0	2,000
Senate	1,500	1,500	0	3,000
Incumbents	7,300	11,250	2,000	20,550
Challengers	5,000	4,000	0	9,000
Open Seat	4,400	12,000	0	16,400
Winners	13,300	20,500	n/a	33,800
Losers	3,400	6,750	n/a	10,150

Associated Equipment Distributors

*Phone: (703) 739-9513 * Fax: (703) 739-9488*
121 N. Henry St., Alexandria, VA 22314
*Web: www.aednet.org * E-mail: info@aednet.org*

Associated Equipment Distributors is an association of 1,300 independent distributors, manufacturers and other organizations involved in the distribution of construction equipment and related products in North America and throughout the world.

The organization advocates a pro-business, pro-construction industry public policy. Its past legislative measures have involved the support of the balanced budget amendment, the repeal of the capital gains tax and the opposition against the EPA airborne particulate matter and ozone regulations.

The association also provides business and individual education services, and researches, analyzes and publishes information on markets, economic and business trends and performance benchmarks.

Associated Equipment Distributors Political Action Committee (C00010124) *Phone: (630) 574-0650 * Fax: (630) 574-0132 * 615 W. 22nd St., Oak Brook, IL 60521 * Treasurer: Anthony J. Obadal*

	1993-94	1995-96	1997	Totals
Receipts	$13,000	$92,800	$34,450	$140,250
Disburse	10,557	87,795	7,500	105,852
Cash	5,925	10,930	37,880	n/a
Contributions	5,750	73,200	6,500	85,450
Republicans	5,750	63,700	4,000	73,450
No. of Cand.	*6*	*40*	*3*	*49*
House	1,250	50,000	3,000	54,250
Senate	4,500	13,700	1,000	19,200
Democrats	0	9,500	1,500	11,000
No. of Cand.	*0*	*8*	*2*	*10*
House	0	9,500	500	10,000
Senate	0	0	1,000	1,000
Incumbents	1,000	56,250	6,500	63,750
Challengers	1,250	10,700	0	11,950
Open Seat	3,500	3,750	0	7,250
Winners	5,500	58,250	n/a	63,750
Losers	250	14,950	n/a	15,200

Blue Circle America Inc.

*Phone: (770) 423-4761 * Fax: (770) 499-2830*
1800 Parkway Pl., Suite 1200, Marietta, GA 30067
*Web: www.bluecircle.co.uk * E-mail: lpmcclendon@bluecir.com*

Blue Circle, a United Kingdom-based cement manufacturer, expanded into the United States in 1985. Its American corporate headquarters is in Marietta, Ga., just outside of Atlanta. The company's 1997 sales were $600 million and it employs 2,500 people.

Blue Circle's divisions include heavy building materials, bathrooms, heating and property assets.

Blue Circle America Inc. PAC (Blue Circle PAC) (C00285429)
*Address: same as sponsor * Treasurer: James W. Roebuck * Contact: Phil McClendon, Chairman*

	1993-94	1995-96	1997	Totals
Receipts	$19,827	$56,379	$29,604	$105,810
Disburse	14,500	43,019	10,250	67,769
Cash	5,327	18,687	38,041	n/a
Contributions	4,500	32,000	5,250	41,750
Republicans	3,000	29,500	5,000	37,500
No. of Cand.	*3*	*20*	*4*	*27*
House	1,000	15,500	2,000	18,500
Senate	2,000	14,000	3,000	19,000
Democrats	1,500	2,500	250	4,250
No. of Cand.	*2*	*4*	*1*	*7*
House	500	1,000	0	1,500
Senate	1,000	1,500	250	2,750
Incumbents	3,500	20,500	5,250	29,250
Challengers	1,000	3,000	0	4,000
Open Seat	0	8,500	0	8,500
Winners	3,500	21,500	n/a	25,000
Losers	1,000	10,500	n/a	11,500

CSR America Inc.

*Phone: (561) 820-8383 * Fax: (561) 820-8666*
1501 Belvedere Rd., West Palm Beach, FL 33406
*Web: www.csr.com.au * E-mail: jstone@csra.com*

CSR America makes pre-mixed concrete, concrete pipes, concrete blocks and quarry products and is the third-largest producer of polyethylene pipes in the United States. The company also has a major building materials distribution business in Florida and a large, underground pipeline-rehabilitation business.

CSR America is part of CSR Limited of Australia. It employs more than 7,000 workers and has sales of more than $1 billion annually.

Major U.S. holdings include: Rinker Materials, West Palm Beach, Fla.; Hydro Conduit Corp., Houston; American Aggregates, Dayton, Ohio; Southern Aggregates, Augusta, Ga.; WMK Materials, Las Vegas; Associated Sand and Gravel, Everett, Wash.; and Beadex and Synkaloid in Canada. These companies are involved in the manufacture and distribution of building materials with major activities in aggregate and concrete products.

CSR America Inc. Political Action Committee (C00318204)
*Address: same as sponsor * Treasurer: Jon I. Stone*

	1993-94	1995-96	1997	Totals
Receipts	$0	$21,151	$40,336	$61,487
Disburse	0	8,858	12,752	21,610
Cash	0	12,293	39,878	n/a
Contributions	0	8,750	12,250	21,000

Republicans	0	8,000	7,000	15,000
No. of Cand.	*0*	*12*	*8*	*20*
House	0	8,000	3,000	11,000
Senate	0	0	4,000	4,000
Democrats	0	750	5,250	6,000
No. of Cand.	*0*	*1*	*4*	*5*
House	0	750	1,250	2,000
Senate	0	0	4,000	4,000
Incumbents	0	7,000	10,250	17,250
Challengers	0	0	2,000	2,000
Open Seat	0	1,750	0	1,750
Winners	0	8,250	n/a	8,250
Losers	0	500	n/a	500

Caterpillar Inc.

*Phone: (309) 675-5248 * Fax: (309) 675-5588*
100 N.E. Adams St., Peoria, IL 61629
Web: www.cat.com

Caterpillar makes heavy duty machinery and construction equipment. The publicly traded company has 57,000 employees and posted record sales of $16.5 billion in 1996. Caterpillar is one of the 30 Dow Jones Industrial companies.

The company operates in three principal business segments: machinery, engines and financial products. Machinery deals with the design, manufacture and marketing of construction, mining and agricultural machinery. Engines deals with the design, manufacture and marketing of engines for earth-moving and construction machines. Financial products provides financing alternatives for Caterpillar and noncompetitive related equipment, and extends loans to Caterpillar customers and dealers.

Caterpillar products are manufactured in 32 plants in the United States and 29 plants scattered across the globe from Australia to Russia. Caterpillar marketing headquarters are located in Peoria and Mossville, Ill.; San Diego; Irving, Texas; Geneva; Hong Kong; Tokyo; Melbourne, Australia; Piracicaba, Brazil; Gosselies, Belgium; and Singapore.

Caterpillar's parts distribution network features 13 distribution centers in 10 countries and 12 regional distribution centers in North America. Caterpillar's global dealership network is comprised of 65 dealers in the United States and 127 outside the United States, serving customers in nearly 200 countries.

Caterpillar Committee for Effective Government (C00148031) *Address: same as sponsor * Treasurer: Barton C. Rochman * Contact: Douglas P. Crew, Chairman*

	1993-94	*1995-96*	*1997*	*Totals*
Receipts	$278,982	$361,161	$197,426	$837,569
Disburse	269,860	342,737	135,633	748,230
Cash	26,307	44,733	105,156	n/a
Contributions	149,500	197,000	87,000	433,500
Republicans	133,500	190,500	83,500	407,500
No. of Cand.	*52*	*87*	*49*	*188*
House	78,500	150,000	68,000	296,500
Senate	55,000	40,500	15,500	111,000
Democrats	16,000	6,500	3,500	26,000
No. of Cand.	*13*	*6*	*5*	*24*
House	13,500	5,500	3,500	22,500
Senate	2,500	1,000	0	3,500
Incumbents	96,000	136,500	74,500	307,000
Challengers	19,000	29,500	10,500	59,000
Open Seat	34,000	31,000	2,000	67,000
Winners	134,000	148,000	n/a	282,000
Losers	15,500	49,000	n/a	64,500

Celotex Corp.

*Phone: (813) 873-4334 * Fax: (813) 873-4294*
4010 Boy Scout Blvd., Tampa, FL 33607

Celotex produces residential and commercial building materials in 26 manufacturing facilities; it has 11 sales offices throughout the United States. The private company distributes products in 65 countries worldwide and employs 3,000 workers. Sales for 1997 were estimated at $800 million.

Celotex, founded in 1921, manufactures residential roof shingles, roofing installation products, foam installation and mineral ceiling tiles and panels for retail and commercial use. In addition, it provides testing services for its clients including acoustical, analytical chemistry, fire, physical and thermal.

In 1990, the company filed for Chapter 11 bankruptcy protection after it was sued for asbestos liability stemming from a company it had purchased in the 1970s.

During a recent reorganization, Celotex absorbed the Jim Walter Corp. and two of its subsidiaries, Jim Walter International and the Center for Applied Engineering. The Jim Walter Corp. PAC (JWCPAC) became the Celotex PAC.

Celotex PAC (C00226845) *Address: same as sponsor * Treasurer: J. P. Borreca * Contact: R. Blair Kriever, Exec. V.P. of Administration*

	1993-94	*1995-96*	*1997*	*Totals*
Receipts	$69,477	$60,757	$23,103	$153,337
Disburse	58,562	74,100	16,250	148,912
Cash	25,415	12,074	18,928	n/a
Contributions	32,750	53,000	12,750	98,500
Republicans	5,500	19,000	4,750	29,250
No. of Cand.	*7*	*21*	*6*	*34*
House	3,000	11,000	1,750	15,750
Senate	2,500	8,000	3,000	13,500
Democrats	27,250	34,000	8,000	69,250
No. of Cand.	*26*	*25*	*7*	*58*
House	16,250	20,000	1,500	37,750
Senate	11,000	14,000	6,500	31,500
Incumbents	27,250	33,750	12,750	73,750
Challengers	500	1,250	0	1,750
Open Seat	5,000	18,000	0	23,000
Winners	27,250	40,750	n/a	68,000
Losers	5,500	12,250	n/a	17,750

Energy Absorption Systems

*Phone: (312) 467-6755 * Fax: (312) 467-1356*
One E. Wacker Dr., Suite 3000, Chicago, IL 60601

Energy Absorption Systems of Quixote Corp. develops, manufactures and markets energy-absorbing highway crash cushions and related highway safety products. Its products include the patented Triton Barrier and CushionWall systems. The company also makes flexible guideposts and portable sign systems.

Quixote's 1997 sales were about $45 million. It employs 373 workers.

Energy Absorption Systems of Quixote Corp. Political Committee (C00136432) *Address: same as sponsor * Treasurer: Daniel P. Gorey*

	1993-94	*1995-96*	*1997*	*Totals*
Receipts	$0	$13,650	$0	$13,650
Disburse	4,500	8,500	5,500	18,500
Cash	2,670	7,820	2,320	n/a
Contributions	5,000	5,500	5,500	16,000
Republicans	3,000	3,500	2,000	8,500
No. of Cand.	*1*	*2*	*1*	*4*
House	3,000	2,000	2,000	7,000
Senate	0	1,500	0	1,500
Democrats	2,000	2,000	3,500	7,500
No. of Cand.	*2*	*2*	*4*	*8*
House	2,000	2,000	1,500	5,500
Senate	0	0	2,000	2,000
Incumbents	5,000	5,500	3,500	14,000
Challengers	0	0	0	0
Open Seat	0	0	0	0
Winners	4,000	4,500	n/a	8,500
Losers	1,000	1,000	n/a	2,000

Florida Rock Industries Inc.

*Phone: (904) 355-1781 * Fax: (904) 355-0817*
155 E. 21st St., P.O. Box 4667, Jacksonville, FL 32201

Florida Rock Industries is a public company producing concrete block and ready-mixed concrete for customers mainly in the Southeast. Headquartered in Jacksonville, Fla., the company has about 90 sites, mostly located in Florida. It sells crushed stone, gravel and sand for use in construction projects. Florida Rock, which employs about 2,500 people, reported 1997 sales of $456 million.

Construction of the company's new $80 million cement plant, near Gainesville, Fla., was delayed for nearly two years by citizens over environmental concerns and protests about state regulators' approval of work permits. A federal appeals court threw out the last appeal from a homeowners association in early 1998.

Florida Rock Industries Inc. Good Government Committee (C00125716) *Address: same as sponsor * Treasurer: H. B. Horner*

	1993-94	1995-96	1997	Totals
Receipts	$21,876	$32,582	$8,000	$62,458
Disburse	37,616	36,521	13,061	87,198
Cash	27,185	23,251	18,190	n/a
Contributions	35,100	26,000	10,500	71,600
Republicans	19,900	10,250	3,500	33,650
No. of Cand.	*15*	*10*	*4*	*29*
House	11,200	8,250	2,500	21,950
Senate	8,700	2,000	1,000	11,700
Democrats	15,200	15,750	7,000	37,950
No. of Cand.	*8*	*6*	*2*	*16*
House	13,200	14,750	2,000	29,950
Senate	2,000	1,000	5,000	8,000
Incumbents	26,700	24,250	10,500	61,450
Challengers	7,650	500	0	8,150
Open Seat	750	1,250	0	2,000
Winners	29,450	24,750	n/a	54,200
Losers	5,650	1,250	n/a	6,900

Holnam Inc.

*Phone: (313) 529-2411 * Fax: (313) 529-5512*
6211 Ann Arbor Rd., P.O. Box 122, Dundee, MI 48131
*Web: www.holnam.com * E-mail: jwooll@holnam.com*

A wholly owned subsidiary of Swiss company Holderback Financiere Glaris Ltd., Holnam operates 120 cement distribution facilities in 46 states and produces 10 million tons of cement yearly. The company employs 2,400 people and had 1996 sales of $1 billion.

In the early 1990s, Holnam was the first company in Texas to use scrap automobile tires as a fuel source. After a number of environmental tests, the EPA said that with the proper emission controls, "burning tires for their fuel energy can be an environmentally sound method of disposing of a difficult waste."

Holnam Inc. PAC (formerly known as Ideal Basic Industries Inc. PAC) (C00213348) *Address: same as sponsor * Treasurer: James L. Wooll*

	1993-94	1995-96	1997	Totals
Receipts	$31,220	$61,971	$29,861	$123,052
Disburse	20,849	49,722	30,184	100,755
Cash	13,362	21,279	20,956	n/a
Contributions	9,643	33,850	20,784	64,277
Republicans	2,000	24,950	17,284	44,234
No. of Cand.	*2*	*26*	*20*	*48*
House	0	12,000	7;250	19,250
Senate	2,000	12,950	10,034	24,984
Democrats	7,643	8,900	3,000	19,543
No. of Cand.	*9*	*7*	*4*	*20*
House	3,143	7,900	2,000	13,043
Senate	4,500	1,000	1,000	6,500
Incumbents	8,143	25,900	19,784	53,827
Challengers	0	2,000	0	2,000
Open Seat	1,500	5,950	1,000	8,450
Winners	6,143	26,850	n/a	32,993
Losers	3,500	7,000	n/a	10,500

Johns Manville Corp.

*Phone: (303) 978-2000 * Fax: (303) 978-2318*
717 17th St., Denver, CO 80202
Web: www.jm.com

Building product maker Johns Manville (formerly Schuller Corp. and, before that, Manville Corp.) manufactures insulation and building products and reported 1997 sales of $1.65 billion. The Denver-based, publicly traded company employs about 7,500 people and operates 45 manufacturing facilities in North America, Europe and China.

Under a federal court settlement, a liability trust fund owns 80 percent of Johns Manville and is expected to pay millions of dollars in asbestos injury claims in the next few decades.

Schuller Corp. Employee Action Program (SEAP) (C00282558) *Phone: (202) 530-3960 * 1625 K St. N.W., Suite 750, Washington, DC 20006 * Web: www.schuller.com * Treasurer: David E. Pullen*

	1993-94	1995-96	1997	Totals
Receipts	$31,224	$39,284	$16,165	$86,673
Disburse	23,012	31,560	8	54,580
Cash	8,218	15,959	32,124	n/a
Contributions	23,000	31,000	0	54,000

Republicans	15,000	25,500	0	40,500
No. of Cand.	*14*	*27*	*0*	*41*
House	4,000	12,500	0	16,500
Senate	11,000	13,000	0	24,000
Democrats	8,000	5,500	0	13,500
No. of Cand.	*9*	*7*	*0*	*16*
House	4,000	4,500	0	8,500
Senate	4,000	1,000	0	5,000
Incumbents	16,000	22,500	0	38,500
Challengers	0	1,000	0	1,000
Open Seat	7,000	7,500	0	14,500
Winners	22,500	31,000	n/a	53,500
Losers	500	0	n/a	500

Terminated PACs which contributed less than $5,000 during 1995-96 cycle:

Manville Corp. Employee Action Program (MEAP) (C00009530) *1625 K St. N.W., Suite 750, Washington, DC 20006 * Treasurer: David E. Pullen*

LaFarge Corp.

*Phone: (703) 264-3600 * Fax: (703) 264-0632*
11130 Sunrise Valley Dr., Suite 300, Reston, VA 20191
Web: www.lafargecorp.com

LaFarge produces ready-made portland cement primarily for sale to ready-mixed concrete makers. It is the second-largest cement maker in the United States. With 6,800 employees, the publicly owned, Reston, Va.-based company posted 1997 sales of $1.8 billion.

Fourteen LaFarge plants in the United States and Canada produce 11.6 million tons of cement annually. Other products include asphalt, aggregates, concrete pipes and blocks, and pre-stressed concrete components used in road building.

LaFarge is majority-owned by the French company LaFarge S.A.

LaFarge Corp. Political Action Committee (C00246678) *Address: same as sponsor * Treasurer: David W. Carroll*

	1993-94	1995-96	1997	Totals
Receipts	$43,206	$46,946	$29,194	$119,346
Disburse	37,060	37,663	21,225	95,948
Cash	7,289	16,575	24,544	n/a
Contributions	16,570	19,800	6,100	42,470
Republicans	3,100	16,200	3,400	22,700
No. of Cand.	*9*	*22*	*6*	*37*
House	2,100	7,200	1,400	10,700
Senate	1,000	9,000	2,000	12,000
Democrats	13,470	3,600	2,200	19,270
No. of Cand.	*14*	*7*	*3*	*24*
House	3,850	3,100	200	7,150
Senate	9,620	500	2,000	12,120
Incumbents	12,970	14,150	5,900	33,020
Challengers	250	4,150	0	4,400
Open Seat	3,350	1,500	0	4,850
Winners	11,450	16,550	n/a	28,000
Losers	5,120	3,250	n/a	8,370

Lennox International Inc.

*Phone: (972) 497-5000 * Fax: (972) 497-5299*
P.O. Box 799900, Dallas, TX 75379
Web: www.davelennox.com

Lennox International is one of the world's largest privately owned corporations and is the parent company of three major manufacturers of heating, air conditioning and refrigeration equipment and components. Those subsidiaries include: Lennox Industries Inc., Heatcraft Inc. and Armstrong Air Conditioning Inc. In addition, Lennox Global Ltd. was formed in May 1995 to expand Lennox's presence in worldwide markets.

Lennox International employs 14,000 people worldwide. The company had sales of $1.9 billion in 1997.

The corporation moved its corporate headquarters to Dallas in 1978 and today manufactures at three North American sites with distribution and sales offices throughout the United States and Canada. Lennox markets its products via one-step distribution, directly to its network of 5,000 independent dealers.

Lennox Political Action Committee (Len PAC) (C00116996) *Address: same as sponsor * Treasurer: Kathy Minde * Contact: David F. Lewis, President*

	1993-94	1995-96	1997	Totals
Receipts	$9,845	$7,064	$9,430	$26,339
Disburse	13,152	7,011	561	20,724
Cash	685	740	9,609	n/a
Contributions	7,500	6,485	0	13,985
Republicans	7,500	6,485	0	13,985
No. of Cand.	*11*	*13*	*0*	*24*
House	4,000	4,500	0	8,500
Senate	3,500	1,985	0	5,485
Democrats	0	0	0	0
No. of Cand.	*0*	*0*	*0*	*0*
House	0	0	0	0
Senate	0	0	0	0
Incumbents	6,000	1,500	0	7,500
Challengers	500	500	0	1,000
Open Seat	1,000	4,485	0	5,485
Winners	7,000	3,500	n/a	10,500
Losers	500	2,985	n/a	3,485

Lone Star Industries Inc.

*Phone: (203) 969-8600 * Fax: (203) 969-8546*
300 First Stamford Pl., Stamford, CT 06912-0014

Lone Star Industries is a cement, construction materials and ready-mixed concrete company with operations in the Midwest, South and East. The publicly traded company had $378 million in sales in 1996 and 1,450 employees, of which 940 were union members. Lone Star's customers consist primarily of ready-mixed concrete producers, pre-stressed concrete producers, other concrete product producers and highway construction firms.

Lone Star owns five cement plants located in Missouri, Indiana, Oklahoma, Illinois and Texas. It also has a facility in Louisiana. In addition, Lone Star has a 25 percent interest in Kosmos Cement Co., a partnership that operates cement plants in Kentucky and Pennsylvania, two quarries in New York and several facilities in the Memphis, Tenn. area.

Incorporated in 1919 and formerly known as International Cement Corp. and Lone Star Cement Corp., Lone Star Industries is now headquartered in Connecticut. In April 1994, Lone Star Industries was reorganized under Chapter 11 bankruptcy.

Lone Star Industries Inc. PAC (C00277012) *Address: same as sponsor * Treasurer: Richard J. Neville*

	1993-94	1995-96	1997	Totals
Receipts	$3,180	$17,514	$19,586	$40,280
Disburse	2,550	12,062	11,002	25,614
Cash	3,516	8,969	17,553	n/a
Contributions	2,550	6,550	1,500	10,600
Republicans	900	6,100	500	7,500
No. of Cand.	*5*	*14*	*1*	*20*
House	750	3,500	0	4,250
Senate	150	2,600	500	3,250
Democrats	1,650	450	1,000	3,100
No. of Cand.	*3*	*2*	*1*	*6*
House	150	450	0	600
Senate	1,500	0	1,000	2,500
Incumbents	1,550	2,900	1,500	5,950
Challengers	650	750	0	1,400
Open Seat	350	2,900	0	3,250
Winners	900	4,850	n/a	5,750
Losers	1,650	1,700	n/a	3,350

Medusa Corp.

*Phone: (216) 371-4000 * Fax: (216) 371-2912*
P.O. Box 5668, Cleveland, OH 44101

Cleveland-based Medusa mines, processes and sells aggregates, calcium and limestone products and provides guardrail, signals, signs, lighting and pavement markers for highway safety. Medusa, which employs 1,200 people, reported production increases at three of its four cement plants in 1997, and the public company ended the year with $375 million in sales. The 106-year-old company sells its cement to more than 1,500 customers, mainly concrete dealers in the eastern United States.

The acquisition of Lee Lime Corp. in 1997 and Commonwealth Stone in early 1998 helped increase Medusa's production capacity for construction aggregates by 25 percent. Half of Medusa's revenue is from government and other publicly funded projects, including roads, sewers, bridges, highways and prisons.

Medusa's subsidiaries include: The Medusa Aggregates Co., which operates crushed stone, sand and gravel plants and sells aggregates to the construction industry; Thomasville Stone and Lime, which mines limestone; and James H. Drew Corp., a construction services and highway safety business.

Medusa Corp. Political Action Committee (Medusa PAC) (C00301374) *Address: same as sponsor * Treasurer: R. Breck Denny*

	1993-94	1995-96	1997	Totals
Receipts	$0	$63,953	$38,193	$102,146
Disburse	0	48,700	21,300	70,000
Cash	0	15,256	26,012	n/a
Contributions	0	21,500	9,300	30,800
Republicans	0	14,500	6,000	20,500
No. of Cand.	*0*	*15*	*6*	*21*
House	0	10,000	3,000	13,000
Senate	0	4,500	3,000	7,500
Democrats	0	7,000	3,300	10,300
No. of Cand.	*0*	*5*	*2*	*7*
House	0	7,000	3,300	10,300
Senate	0	0	0	0
Incumbents	0	19,000	8,300	27,300
Challengers	0	500	0	500
Open Seat	0	2,000	1,000	3,000
Winners	0	19,000	n/a	19,000
Losers	0	2,500	n/a	2,500

National Aggregates Association

*Phone: (301) 587-1400 * Fax: (301) 587-9419*
900 Spring St., Silver Spring, MD 20910
Web: www.nationalaggregates.org

The National Aggregates Association represents producers of construction aggregates, which include sand, gravel, crushed and broken stone.

Founded in 1916, the association provides its members with education, training, research, technology and representation before Congress and federal regulatory bodies.

National Aggregates Association PAC (SandPAC) (formerly known as National Sand & Gravel PAC) (C00114017) *Address: same as sponsor * Treasurer: Mark R. Riso*

	1993-94	1995-96	1997	Totals
Receipts	$10,375	$15,687	$8,825	$34,887
Disburse	12,125	14,000	2,090	28,215
Cash	4,198	5,885	10,450	n/a
Contributions	12,125	13,000	0	25,125
Republicans	10,875	12,000	0	22,875
No. of Cand.	*33*	*18*	*0*	*51*
House	5,425	5,000	0	10,425
Senate	5,450	7,000	0	12,450
Democrats	1,250	1,000	0	2,250
No. of Cand.	*3*	*2*	*0*	*5*
House	1,250	1,000	0	2,250
Senate	0	0	0	0
Incumbents	5,375	8,000	0	13,375
Challengers	2,750	3,000	0	5,750
Open Seat	4,000	2,000	0	6,000
Winners	10,375	7,750	n/a	18,125
Losers	1,750	5,250	n/a	7,000

National Concrete Masonry Association

*Phone: (703) 713-1900 * Fax: (703) 713-1910*
2302 Horse Pen Rd., Herndon, VA 20171
Web: www.ncma.org

The National Concrete Masonry Association represents producers of concrete masonry products and suppliers of goods and services related to the industry. The organization was established in 1918.

National Concrete Masonry Association Political Action Committee (C00128975) *Address: same as sponsor * Treasurer: Chris Stinebert*

	1993-94	1995-96	1997	Totals
Receipts	$41,236	$44,003	$23,669	$108,908
Disburse	53,290	43,019	13,381	109,690
Cash	45,669	46,656	56,945	n/a
Contributions	46,250	39,100	18,500	103,850
Republicans	35,550	34,650	17,150	87,350
No. of Cand.	*45*	*45*	*20*	*110*
House	16,700	25,800	12,950	55,450
Senate	18,850	8,850	4,200	31,900

(Data for National Concrete Masonry continued)

Democrats	10,350	4,450	1,350	16,150
No. of Cand.	*19*	*8*	*4*	*31*
House	9,850	3,950	1,100	14,900
Senate	500	500	250	1,250
Incumbents	37,650	36,800	18,300	92,750
Challengers	1,300	1,050	0	2,350
Open Seat	7,000	1,250	0	8,250
Winners	43,550	35,050	n/a	78,600
Losers	2,700	4,050	n/a	6,750

National Lumber & Building Material Dealers Association

*Phone: (202) 547-2230 * Fax: (202) 547-7640*
666 Pennsylvania Ave. N.W., Suite 302A, Washington, DC 20003
Web: www.nlbmda.org
E-mail: nlbmda@nlbmda.org

The National Lumber & Building Material Dealers Association represents 8,500 retail lumber dealers. The typical member owns a small business in a rural area.

The association, which was founded in 1916 to represent the interests of timber dealers, is interested in general timber supply, Canadian timber imports and relevant environmental issues.

National Lumber & Building Material Dealers Association Political Action Committee (LUDPAC) (C00039214) *Address: same as sponsor * Treasurer: Gary W. Donnelly*

	1993-94	1995-96	1997	Totals
Receipts	$41,491	$89,197	$37,059	$167,747
Disburse	39,732	89,789	27,037	156,558
Cash	6,332	5,741	16,203	n/a
Contributions	29,315	77,002	22,000	128,317
Republicans	17,575	67,002	12,500	97,077
No. of Cand.	*20*	*62*	*14*	*96*
House	8,075	36,094	8,500	52,669
Senate	9,500	30,908	4,000	44,408
Democrats	11,740	10,000	9,500	31,240
No. of Cand.	*13*	*14*	*11*	*38*
House	11,740	7,500	7,500	26,740
Senate	0	2,500	2,000	4,500
Incumbents	18,065	40,386	21,000	79,451
Challengers	6,750	14,708	1,000	22,458
Open Seat	4,500	21,908	0	26,408
Winners	18,565	50,002	n/a	68,567
Losers	10,750	27,000	n/a	37,750

National Ready Mixed Concrete Association

*Phone: (301) 587-1400 * Fax: (301) 585-4219*
900 Spring St., Silver Spring, MD 20910

The National Ready Mixed Concrete Association represents about 1,300 member companies that manufacture and distribute ready-mixed concrete. The organization was founded in 1930.

National Ready Mixed Concrete Association Political Committee (C00114025) *Address: same as sponsor * Treasurer: Julie Luther*

	1993-94	1995-96	1997	Totals
Receipts	$15,430	$34,035	$50,875	$100,340
Disburse	16,925	34,000	9,000	59,925
Cash	4,811	4,846	46,721	n/a
Contributions	16,925	33,500	9,000	59,425
Republicans	15,325	32,500	4,500	52,325
No. of Cand.	*39*	*49*	*6*	*94*
House	8,625	19,000	1,500	29,125
Senate	6,700	13,500	3,000	23,200
Democrats	1,600	1,000	3,500	6,100
No. of Cand.	*4*	*2*	*4*	*10*
House	1,600	1,000	500	3,100
Senate	0	0	3,000	3,000
Incumbents	6,725	17,000	9,000	32,725
Challengers	4,750	5,500	0	10,250
Open Seat	5,450	11,000	0	16,450
Winners	14,175	23,250	n/a	37,425
Losers	2,750	10,250	n/a	13,000

National Stone Association

*Phone: (202) 342-1100 * Fax: (202) 342-0702*
1415 Elliot Place N.W., Washington, DC 20007
*Web: www.aggregates.org * E-mail: wkelleher@aggregates.org*

The National Stone Association represents the interests of the aggregate and mining industries. Its members include more than 650 companies accounting for more than 80 percent of the annual production of crushed stone and nearly 60 percent of sand and gravel production in the United States.

The association is organized into seven divisions: government affairs; environment, safety and health; market development; operations; public affairs; pulverized minerals; and manufacturing and services.

National Stone Association StonePAC (C00089458) *Address: same as sponsor * Treasurer: Robert G. Bartlett*

	1993-94	1995-96	1997	Totals
Receipts	$100,020	$118,815	$119,567	$338,402
Disburse	94,122	97,428	132,882	324,432
Cash	48,747	70,134	56,819	n/a
Contributions	65,700	80,000	64,725	210,425
Republicans	41,700	71,500	50,725	163,925
No. of Cand.	*36*	*61*	*30*	*127*
House	24,200	51,000	33,225	108,425
Senate	17,500	20,500	17,500	55,500
Democrats	23,500	8,500	12,000	44,000
No. of Cand.	*17*	*6*	*10*	*33*
House	14,500	7,500	3,000	25,000
Senate	9,000	1,000	9,000	19,000
Incumbents	51,550	65,500	62,225	179,275
Challengers	5,750	3,500	0	9,250
Open Seat	8,400	11,000	2,000	21,400
Winners	55,200	58,500	n/a	113,700
Losers	10,500	21,500	n/a	32,000

Owens Corning

*Phone: (419) 248-8000 * Fax: (419) 248-8445*
One Owens Corning Pkwy., Toledo, OH 43659
Web: www.owenscorning.com

Owens Corning is a public company that produces high-performance glass composites and building materials systems. It has more than 21,000 employees and its 1997 sales reached $4.4 billion. The company, incorporated in Delaware in 1938, maintains manufacturing, sales and research facilities — including joint venture and licensee relationships — in more than 30 countries on six continents.

Owens Corning products are used in industries such as home improvement, new construction, transportation, marine, aerospace, energy, appliance, packaging and electronics. Many products are marketed under the brand "Fiberglas."

Owens Corning Better Government Fund (C00200089) *Address: same as sponsor * Treasurer: Kirk Peterson * Contact: Robert G. Pistole, Chairman*

	1993-94	1995-96	1997	Totals
Receipts	$82,100	$204,218	$140,727	$427,045
Disburse	80,452	196,118	103,835	380,405
Cash	7,106	15,209	52,102	n/a
Contributions	55,335	82,975	43,000	181,310
Republicans	38,985	55,475	32,500	126,960
No. of Cand.	*33*	*48*	*22*	*103*
House	12,500	19,275	8,000	39,775
Senate	26,485	36,200	24,500	87,185
Democrats	16,350	27,500	10,500	54,350
No. of Cand.	*22*	*12*	*7*	*41*
House	12,350	12,000	4,500	28,850
Senate	4,000	15,500	6,000	25,500
Incumbents	37,335	53,775	37,000	128,110
Challengers	2,000	6,700	1,000	9,700
Open Seat	16,000	22,500	5,000	43,500
Winners	49,935	68,150	n/a	118,085
Losers	5,400	14,825	n/a	20,225

Southdown Inc.

*Phone: (713) 650-6200 * Fax: (713) 653-6950*
1200 Smith St., Suite 2400, Houston, TX 77002

Southdown is a cement and ready-mixed concrete company, operating eight manufacturing facilities in Southern California, Colorado, Florida, Kentucky, Ohio, Pennsylvania, Tennessee and Texas. It also has seven quarrying sites.

In 1997, Southdown had revenues of $719 million. The company has 2,400 employees.

The publicly owned company uses a network of 19 cement storage and distribution terminals for the production, importation and distribution of portland and masonry cements, primarily in the Ohio Valley and the southwestern and southeastern United States.

Southdown Inc. Political Action Committee (formerly known as Moore McCormack Resources PAC) (C00111880) *Address: same as sponsor * Treasurer: Thomas E. Daman*

	1993-94	1995-96	1997	Totals
Receipts	$23,000	$27,194	$24,674	$74,868
Disburse	27,460	24,000	15,000	66,460
Cash	2,299	5,499	15,174	n/a
Contributions	17,000	11,000	7,500	35,500
Republicans	6,000	4,500	2,500	13,000
No. of Cand.	*2*	*3*	*3*	*8*
House	1,000	4,500	1,500	7,000
Senate	5,000	0	1,000	6,000
Democrats	11,000	6,500	5,000	22,500
No. of Cand.	*7*	*8*	*5*	*20*
House	4,000	4,500	2,000	10,500
Senate	7,000	2,000	3,000	12,000
Incumbents	6,000	8,000	7,500	21,500
Challengers	5,000	1,000	0	6,000
Open Seat	6,000	2,000	0	8,000
Winners	5,000	10,500	n/a	15,500
Losers	12,000	500	n/a	12,500

Vulcan Materials Co.

*Phone: (205) 877-3229 * Fax: (205) 877-3094*
P.O. Box 530187, Birmingham, AL 35253-0187
*Web: www.vulcanmat.com * E-mail: m_russom@vul.com*

Vulcan Materials produces construction materials and basic industrial and specialty chemicals. Employing more than 5,400 people, the public company had 1997 net earnings of $209 million.

The company's construction materials segment accounted for nearly 65 percent of the company's $1.7 billion in 1997 sales. The segment's principal product, crushed stone, accounted for more than 75 percent of the sales in this division. The company markets construction materials throughout 17 southeastern and midwestern states.

Vulcan's chemicals segment, which accounted for $628 million in sales in 1997, produces chlorine, caustic soda, hydrochloric acid, potassium chemicals and chlorinated organic chemicals. This segment also provides process aids for the pulp, paper and textile industries; chemicals and services to the municipal, industrial and environmental water management markets; and the custom manufacture of a variety of specialty chemicals.

The company operates 127 permanent crushed stone plants, three chloralkali chemical plants, eight specialty chemicals facilities and more than 200 other production and distribution facilities. During 1997, significant property additions included the acquisitions of one quarry in Arkansas, one in Georgia and two in Texas.

Subsidiaries include: Vulcan Chemical Technologies and Callaway Chemical Company. Vulcan Materials is also part of a joint venture that supplies limestone from Mexico to the U.S. Gulf Coast.

Vulcan Materials Co. Political Action Committee (C00116020) *Address: same as sponsor * Treasurer: Mary S. Russom * Contact: William F. Denson III, Chairman*

	1993-94	1995-96	1997	Totals
Receipts	$146,178	$176,182	$73,199	$395,559
Disburse	138,184	127,495	57,140	322,819
Cash	103,766	152,458	168,518	n/a
Contributions	49,975	59,500	22,500	131,975
Republicans	17,850	46,300	17,750	81,900
No. of Cand.	*20*	*44*	*19*	*83*
House	10,350	24,250	14,750	49,350
Senate	7,500	22,050	3,000	32,550
Democrats	32,125	13,200	4,750	50,075
No. of Cand.	*38*	*15*	*7*	*60*
House	18,625	9,700	2,750	31,075
Senate	13,500	3,500	2,000	19,000
Incumbents	46,850	47,300	23,000	117,150
Challengers	125	2,650	0	2,775
Open Seat	3,000	9,550	0	12,550
Winners	37,800	49,300	n/a	87,100
Losers	12,175	10,200	n/a	22,375

Construction Services

American Consulting Engineers Council

*Phone: (202) 347-7474 * Fax: (202) 898-0068*
1015 15th St. N.W., Suite 802, Washington, DC 20005
*Web: www.acec.org * E-mail: acec@acec.org*

The American Consulting Engineers Council represents 5,700 engineering firms around the nation. A consulting engineer is an individual who does not work for a specific company but consults for different contractors on a case-by-case basis.

The ACEC helps to educate these firms and represents their interests in Washington. It was founded in 1910.

American Consulting Engineers Political Action Committee (ACE PAC) (C00010868) *Address: same as sponsor * Treasurer: Howard M. Messner*

	1993-94	1995-96	1997	Totals
Receipts	$136,379	$146,438	$89,171	$371,988
Disburse	102,800	156,282	74,999	334,081
Cash	34,554	24,709	38,882	n/a
Contributions	67,299	94,420	43,285	205,004
Republicans	42,101	76,920	29,043	148,064
No. of Cand.	*49*	*84*	*53*	*186*
House	20,044	42,378	23,143	85,565
Senate	22,057	34,542	5,900	62,499
Democrats	24,698	17,500	11,742	53,940
No. of Cand.	*38*	*28*	*22*	*88*
House	18,632	12,500	7,142	38,274
Senate	6,066	5,000	4,600	15,666
Incumbents	51,395	70,670	42,785	164,850
Challengers	5,054	4,250	1,000	10,304
Open Seat	12,350	19,500	0	31,850
Winners	56,886	76,420	n/a	133,306
Losers	10,413	18,000	n/a	28,413

American Institute of Architects

*Phone: (202) 626-7384 * Fax: (202) 626-7421*
1735 New York Ave. N.W., Washington, DC 20006
Web: www.e-architect.com

The American Institute of Architects is a professional society of more than 59,000 architects in the United States. The group offers continuing education, conferences and legislative monitoring.

The AIA has about 300 state and local chapters, and it lobbies on construction issues, including the Americans with Disabilities Act.

ArchiPAC/The American Institute of Architects (C00139071) *Address: same as sponsor * Treasurer: Alexandra Brkic * Contact: Dan Wilson, Dir. of Federal Affairs*

	1993-94	1995-96	1997	Totals
Receipts	$78,667	$75,886	$54,789	$209,342
Disburse	74,900	69,051	20,825	164,776
Cash	3,892	8,654	42,619	n/a
Contributions	71,150	63,625	5,500	140,275
Republicans	12,400	22,875	1,000	36,275
No. of Cand.	*17*	*28*	*2*	*47*
House	8,900	16,675	1,000	26,575
Senate	3,500	6,200	0	9,700
Democrats	57,750	40,750	4,000	102,500
No. of Cand.	*44*	*37*	*5*	*86*
House	41,000	16,750	2,000	59,750
Senate	16,750	24,000	2,000	42,750
Incumbents	60,950	33,625	5,500	100,075
Challengers	2,500	21,000	0	23,500
Open Seat	7,700	9,000	0	16,700
Winners	49,150	41,125	n/a	90,275
Losers	22,000	22,500	n/a	44,500

Bechtel Corp.

*Phone: (415) 768-1234 * Fax: (415) 768-9038*
50 Beale St., P.O. Box 193965, San Francisco, CA 94119
Web: www.bechtel.com

Engineering and construction giant Bechtel has worked on projects including the Hoover Dam, the Trans-Arabian Pipeline, the San Francisco subway, cleanup of contamination at the Hanford Site in Washington state, dismantling missiles in the former Soviet Union, the Department of Energy's Nevada Test Site, postwar restoration of

Kuwait's oil production and Boston's "Big Dig" highway construction project. A private company, Bechtel reported $8.1 billion in 1996 sales.

The company works in industries and fields including: power, petroleum chemicals, mining and metals, pipelines, surface transportation, aviation services, manufacturing, ports and harbors, space and defense, telecommunications, water supply and treatment, commercial buildings, hotels, resorts and theme parks, environmental and pollution control and hazardous waste cleanup.

Bechtel's 21 North American offices generate about $4 billion in revenue. The company is controlled by the Bechtel family and Riley Bechtel is the CEO.

Bechtel Group Inc. Political Action Committee (C00103697) *1015 15th St., Washington, DC 20005-2605 * Treasurer: Georgeanne Proctor * Contact: Robert Ragan, Manager*

	1993-94	1995-96	1997	Totals
Receipts	$172,561	$147,563	$81,834	$401,958
Disburse	111,888	186,002	71,992	369,882
Cash	84,608	46,169	58,511	n/a
Contributions	94,825	161,850	61,500	318,175
Republicans	31,300	95,650	31,000	157,950
No. of Cand.	*33*	*65*	*30*	*128*
House	20,300	65,650	20,500	106,450
Senate	11,000	30,000	10,500	51,500
Democrats	63,525	66,200	30,500	160,225
No. of Cand.	*45*	*37*	*19*	*101*
House	46,525	50,700	9,500	106,725
Senate	17,000	15,500	21,000	53,500
Incumbents	91,100	139,350	59,000	289,450
Challengers	0	1,000	2,500	3,500
Open Seat	3,500	21,500	0	25,000
Winners	80,600	143,350	n/a	223,950
Losers	14,225	18,500	n/a	32,725

Black & Veatch

*Phone: (913) 458-8548 * Fax: (913) 458-2934*
8400 Ward Pkwy., Kansas City, Mo. 64119
Web: www.bv.com

Black & Veatch is an engineering and construction firm. The private partnership specializes in power, infrastructure, process and buildings sectors. It also provides complete engineering, procurement, construction, telecommunications, architectural, financial, information and management consulting services for utilities, commerce, industry and government agencies worldwide.

Established in 1915, the company now has 7,000 employees in more than 90 offices worldwide. Black & Veatch has completed more than 30,000 projects for some 6,100 different clients worldwide and produced $2.1 billion in 1997 revenue.

In 1997, Black & Veatch was selected to head the Provincial Towns Water Supply and Sanitation Project in Vietnam. As part of this project, Black & Veatch provides a public environmental education program, develops water supply systems and improves environmental sanitation.

Black & Veatch Good Government Fund (C00012310) *Address: same as sponsor * Treasurer: George Christian Hedemann*

	1993-94	1995-96	1997	Totals
Receipts	$12,132	$32,796	$28	$44,956
Disburse	16,000	27,284	5,250	48,534
Cash	90	5,604	384	n/a
Contributions	11,000	19,000	3,750	33,750
Republicans	7,750	15,000	3,250	26,000
No. of Cand.	*7*	*14*	*5*	*26*
House	4,000	7,000	2,250	13,250
Senate	3,750	8,000	1,000	12,750
Democrats	3,250	4,000	500	7,750
No. of Cand.	*4*	*4*	*1*	*9*
House	1,250	3,000	500	4,750
Senate	2,000	1,000	0	3,000
Incumbents	3,500	5,500	3,750	12,750
Challengers	1,000	6,000	0	7,000
Open Seat	6,500	7,500	0	14,000
Winners	8,500	12,000	n/a	20,500
Losers	2,500	7,000	n/a	9,500

Burns and Roe Enterprises Inc.

*Phone: (201) 986-4800 * Fax: (201) 986-4831*
800 Kinderkamack Rd., Oradell, NJ 07649
*Web: www.roe.com * E-mail: info@roe.com*

Burns and Roe Enterprises designs and builds power plants, including coal and nuclear plants. A privately held company, it does not disclose sales information. Burns and Roe also designs systems for treating hazardous and radioactive waste, builds pharmaceutical, chemical and petrochemical processing plants and constructs systems for reducing air and water pollution.

Burns and Roe has benefited from substantial government contracts. In 1996, then-Secretary of Energy Hazel R. O'Leary announced that Burns and Roe had been selected to perform demonstration activities at Los Alamos National Laboratory in New Mexico and to design an Accelerator Production of Tritium plant for the Savannah River Site in South Carolina. If the accelerator option is selected in 1998 as the primary technology, the company would support construction of the plant, which would be fully operational by 2007. The nearly $3 billion contract was awarded by the Department of Energy.

Tritium, which activates the fusion stage of a nuclear weapon, decays at a small rate and must be replenished periodically. The United States has not produced this gas since 1988 but has relied on tritium from dismantled weapons to meet U.S. national security requirements. Based on current arms control agreements and on nuclear weapons stockpile plans, a new tritium production source will be required between 2005 and 2007.

Roe Enterprises Inc. Political Action Committee (REIPAC) (C00318519) *Address: same as sponsor * Treasurer: Michael A. Marcopoto*

	1993-94	1995-96	1997	Totals
Receipts	$0	$17,122	$12,281	$29,403
Disburse	0	7,500	5,500	13,000
Cash	0	7,622	14,403	n/a
Contributions	0	9,500	5,500	15,000
Republicans	0	6,750	3,500	10,250
No. of Cand.	*0*	*9*	*3*	*12*
House	0	3,750	3,500	7,250
Senate	0	3,000	0	3,000
Democrats	0	2,750	2,000	4,750
No. of Cand.	*0*	*4*	*2*	*6*
House	0	1,750	1,000	2,750
Senate	0	1,000	1,000	2,000
Incumbents	0	6,500	5,500	12,000
Challengers	0	0	0	0
Open Seat	0	3,000	0	3,000
Winners	0	8,250	n/a	8,250
Losers	0	1,250	n/a	1,250

CH2M Hill

*Phone: (303) 771-0900 * Fax: (303) 843-0759*
6060 S. Willow Dr., Greenwood Village, CO 80111
*Web: www.ch2m.com * E-mail: vnelson@ch2m.com*

CH2M Hill is an engineering company that serves clients worldwide in the fields of water, environmental, transportation, industrial facilities and related infrastructure. Founded in 1946, the firm has more than 7,000 employees working from more than 120 locations on six continents. The employee-owned company had 1996 sales of $937 million.

The name CH2M HILL is derived from the first letter of the last names of the founders of the company — Holly Cornell, James Howland, T. Burke Hayes, Fred Merryfield and Clair A. Hill.

CH2M Hill Companies Ltd. PAC (C00143305) *Address: same as sponsor * Treasurer: L. L. Nelson * Contact: Philip G. Hall, Chairman*

	1993-94	1995-96	1997	Totals
Receipts	$125,010	$156,710	$69,784	$351,504
Disburse	129,532	143,782	61,138	334,452
Cash	17,192	30,131	38,781	n/a
Contributions	124,745	139,185	57,967	321,897
Republicans	62,000	96,350	35,750	194,100
No. of Cand.	*65*	*88*	*39*	*192*
House	38,500	63,100	25,250	126,850
Senate	23,500	33,250	10,500	67,250
Democrats	61,745	42,835	21,717	126,297
No. of Cand.	*63*	*53*	*29*	*145*
House	49,125	35,885	13,717	98,727
Senate	12,620	6,950	8,000	27,570
Incumbents	113,995	125,185	56,967	296,147
Challengers	3,500	3,000	0	6,500
Open Seat	7,750	11,000	0	18,750
Winners	105,300	120,450	n/a	225,750
Losers	19,445	18,735	n/a	38,180

Foster Wheeler Corp.

*Phone: (908) 730-4020 * Fax: (908) 730-5300*
Perryville Corporate Park, Clinton, NJ 08809-4000
*Web: www.fwc.com * E-mail: thomas_obrien@fwc.com*

New Jersey-based Foster Wheeler is a global company which operates three business groups. Foster Wheeler's engineering and construction group designs, engineers and constructs petroleum, chemical and alternative-fuels facilities. Its energy equipment group designs, manufactures and erects steam generating and auxiliary equipment for power stations and industrial markets worldwide. Its power systems group generates revenues from construction and operating activities.

Foster Wheeler, a publicly traded company, had 1997 revenues of $4.1 billion. The company's 12,000 employees are located in branch offices worldwide, including Europe and North and South America.

Foster Wheeler Corp. Political Action Committee (C00194852) *Phone: (202) 296-9703 * Fax: (202) 296-7461 * 1667 K St. N.W., Suite 650, Washington, DC 20006 * E-mail: sherry_peske@fwc.com * Treasurer: David J. Roberts*

*Contact: Tom O'Brien, PAC Dir. * Phone: (908) 730-4020*

	1993-94	1995-96	1997	Totals
Receipts	$19,050	$51,572	$34,760	$105,382
Disburse	8,700	35,500	16,148	60,348
Cash	12,229	28,301	46,912	n/a
Contributions	6,900	31,000	8,500	46,400
Republicans	5,500	28,000	6,000	39,500
No. of Cand.	*3*	*17*	*5*	*25*
House	4,500	15,500	3,000	23,000
Senate	1,000	12,500	3,000	16,500
Democrats	1,400	3,000	2,500	6,900
No. of Cand.	*2*	*3*	*2*	*7*
House	1,400	1,000	2,500	4,900
Senate	0	2,000	0	2,000
Incumbents	6,900	17,500	8,500	32,900
Challengers	0	0	0	0
Open Seat	0	13,500	0	13,500
Winners	5,400	16,000	n/a	21,400
Losers	1,500	15,000	n/a	16,500

HDR Inc.

*Phone: (402) 399-1009 * Fax: (402) 399-1339*
8404 Indian Hills Dr., Omaha, NE 68114-4049
*Web: www.hdrinc.com * E-mail: lpachman@hdrinc.com*

HDR offers a broad range of architectural and engineering services. The company is based in Omaha, Neb., and maintains 42 offices nationwide. HDR was founded in 1917 and is owned by its 1,600 employees. The company generated revenues of $185.3 million in 1995.

HDR is the holding company for Henningson, Durham & Richardson Inc., (architecture), HDR Engineering Inc. and HDR Project Development Services Inc.

The company was ranked No. 35 in the 1995 Engineering News-Record listing of the top 500 U.S. design firms.

Current HDR projects include: private toll road proposals in Phoenix and Poland; a high-speed rail line in Florida; Cook County Hospital in Chicago; Boston Central Artery in Boston; Durham Wastewater Treatment Plant near Portland, Ore.; Clark County Regional Justice Center in Las Vegas; advanced technology laboratories for the National Institute of Standards and Technology in Maryland and Colorado; and health care facilities in Mexico and England.

Professionals Political Action Committee (P-PAC) (HDR Inc.) (C00103903) *Address: same as sponsor * Treasurer: Wendy L. Lacey * Contact: Louis Pachman, Chairman*

	1993-94	1995-96	1997	Totals
Receipts	$36,004	$37,734	$19,511	$93,249
Disburse	37,246	30,409	16,139	83,794
Cash	17,070	24,399	27,772	n/a
Contributions	8,450	7,550	2,300	18,300
Republicans	2,000	4,900	1,800	8,700
No. of Cand.	*5*	*7*	*3*	*15*
House	1,500	2,750	1,000	5,250
Senate	500	2,150	800	3,450
Democrats	6,450	2,650	500	9,600
No. of Cand.	*11*	*7*	*1*	*19*
House	950	2,150	500	3,600
Senate	5,500	500	0	6,000
Incumbents	5,950	3,750	1,000	10,700

Challengers	1,250	1,150	300	2,700
Open Seat	1,250	2,650	0	3,900
Winners	4,200	5,250	n/a	9,450
Losers	4,250	2,300	n/a	6,550

Harza Engineering Co.

*Phone: (312) 831-3000 * Fax: (312) 831-3999*
233 S. Wacker Dr., Chicago, IL 60606
*Web: www.harza.com * E-mail: info@harza.com*

Harza Engineering is an international engineering and environmental consulting firm specializing in the development of land, water and energy resources. Harza has experience in architecture, equipment acquisition, privatization, facilities management, training and technology transfer.

Projects include: the Baldhill Dam Rehabilitation Project in North Dakota, the Cerron Grande Hydroelectric Project in El Salvador and the Seneca Pumped-Storage Project in Pennsylvania.

Founded in 1920, Harza is a private company with more than 800 employees.

In April 1997, Harza started a new affiliate, Harza Trade Finance LLC, which evaluates project financing needs, prepares studies for loan applications and performs other related services.

Harza Engineering Co. PAC (Harza-PAC) (C00236067) *Address: same as sponsor * Treasurer: Vincent J. Zipparro * Contact: R. Banys, Chairperson*

	1993-94	1995-96	1997	Totals
Receipts	$20,850	$29,575	$2,000	$52,425
Disburse	17,700	22,725	10,650	51,075
Cash	9,141	15,991	7,341	n/a
Contributions	5,000	7,100	1,000	13,100
Republicans	0	4,000	0	4,000
No. of Cand.	*0*	*5*	*0*	*5*
House	0	2,500	0	2,500
Senate	0	1,500	0	1,500
Democrats	5,000	3,100	1,000	9,100
No. of Cand.	*1*	*3*	*1*	*5*
House	5,000	2,100	0	7,100
Senate	0	1,000	1,000	2,000
Incumbents	5,000	3,500	1,000	9,500
Challengers	0	1,100	0	1,100
Open Seat	0	2,500	0	2,500
Winners	0	5,600	n/a	5,600
Losers	5,000	1,500	n/a	6,500

ICF Kaiser International Inc.

*Phone: (703) 934-3840 * Fax: (703) 934-3029*
9300 Lee Highway, Fairfax, VA 22031-1207
*Web: www.icfkaiser.com * E-mail: wgolden@icfkaiser.com*

ICF Kaiser International is a public company with business operations in engineering and construction, environmental and facilities management and consulting. It had 1996 sales of $1.25 billion.

The company provides engineering and construction services for the environmental, industrial and refining and petrochemical industries. Many of ICF Kaiser's management contracts are with the U.S. departments of Energy and Defense. The company's consulting includes financial analysis, management advice and the design of information technology systems.

Headquartered in Fairfax, Va., the 5,000-person company has regional offices in Oakland, Calif., Jacksonville, Fla., Pittsburgh and Houston.

ICF Kaiser International Inc. Political Action Committee (C00080069) *Address: same as sponsor * Treasurer: Tim O'Connor * Contact: Wilson Golden, V.P. of Gov. Relations*

	1993-94	1995-96	1997	Totals
Receipts	$56,260	$118,182	$85,973	$260,415
Disburse	54,187	101,375	91,850	247,412
Cash	4,266	20,576	14,702	n/a
Contributions	49,075	90,875	63,350	203,300
Republicans	8,075	68,625	30,100	106,800
No. of Cand.	*12*	*39*	*25*	*76*
House	6,075	33,125	20,100	59,300
Senate	2,000	35,500	10,000	47,500
Democrats	39,000	22,250	33,250	94,500
No. of Cand.	*32*	*25*	*33*	*90*

(Data for ICF Kaiser International continued)

House	25,750	14,250	15,250	55,250
Senate	13,250	8,000	18,000	39,250
Incumbents	41,825	78,125	60,100	180,050
Challengers	3,000	6,250	0	9,250
Open Seat	4,000	6,500	2,250	12,750
Winners	32,225	76,325	n/a	108,550
Losers	16,850	14,550	n/a	31,400

International Federation of Professional & Technical Engineers

*Phone: (301) 565-9016 * Fax: (301) 565-0018*
8630 Fenton St., Suite 400, Silver Spring, MD 20910
Web: www.ifpte.org

The International Federation of Professional & Technical Engineers represents 50,000 scientists, technicians and engineers.

The union represents federal, public and private employees. It is interested in issues such as pensions, downsizing, immigration and utility deregulation.

International Federation/Professional & Technical Engineers Legislative Education Action Program-PAC (LEAP-PAC) (C00164509) *Address: same as sponsor * Treasurer: Gregory J. Junemann * Contact: Paul Almeida, President*

	1993-94	1995-96	1997	Totals
Receipts	$12,874	$24,761	$11,417	$49,052
Disburse	7,642	23,874	13,918	45,434
Cash	6,915	8,664	6,164	n/a
Contributions	1,150	12,410	1,950	15,510
Republicans	0	450	500	950
No. of Cand.	0	3	2	5
House	0	450	500	950
Senate	0	0	0	0
Democrats	1,150	11,860	1,450	14,460
No. of Cand.	8	25	3	36
House	800	10,190	1,450	12,440
Senate	350	1,670	0	2,020
Incumbents	900	3,290	1,700	5,890
Challengers	150	5,900	0	6,050
Open Seat	100	3,220	250	3,570
Winners	700	8,060	n/a	8,760
Losers	450	4,350	n/a	4,800

Jacobs Engineering Group

*Phone: (626) 578-3500 * Fax: (626) 578-6837*
1111 S. Arroyo Pkwy., Pasadena, CA 91105

Jacobs Engineering Group is one of the largest international engineering and construction firms. The company designs and builds manufacturing plants for clients in the petroleum, chemical, biotechnological and mining industries. The company also provides environmental remediation and hazardous waste management consulting services.

JEG is a public company, with founder Joseph Jacobs owning 17 percent of the company's 26 million shares. It reported 1997 sales of $1.8 billion. Founded in 1947, the company employs 16,000 people.

In December 1997, the company announced that Bechtel Jacobs Co., a joint venture of JEG and Bechtel National Inc., was awarded a $2.5 billion contract by the Energy Department to manage and integrate environmental restoration at the department's facilities in Oak Ridge, Tenn., Paducah, Ky., and Portsmouth, Ohio.

JEG Good Government Committee (C00142299) *Address: same as sponsor * Treasurer: William C. Markley III * Contact: Noel G. Watson, Chairman*

	1993-94	1995-96	1997	Totals
Receipts	$82,631	$127,472	$81,468	$291,571
Disburse	97,250	125,072	51,000	273,322
Cash	33,094	35,498	65,967	n/a
Contributions	76,750	84,571	29,000	190,321
Republicans	20,000	38,823	10,500	69,323
No. of Cand.	16	32	13	61
House	15,750	31,823	9,500	57,073
Senate	4,250	7,000	1,000	12,250
Democrats	56,750	45,748	18,500	120,998
No. of Cand.	42	33	18	93
House	39,750	35,482	11,000	86,232
Senate	17,000	10,266	7,500	34,766
Incumbents	69,250	75,305	28,500	173,055
Challengers	0	3,000	0	3,000
Open Seat	7,500	5,766	500	13,766
Winners	66,000	66,305	n/a	132,305
Losers	10,750	18,266	n/a	29,016

Management Association for Private Photogrammetric Surveyors

*Phone: (703) 391-2739 * Fax: (703) 476-2217*
12020 Sunrise Valley Dr., Suite 100, Reston, VA 22091
*Web: www.mapps.org * E-mail: info@mapps.org*

The Management Association for Private Photogrammetric Surveyors represents 120 companies that do mapping from satellite and aerial photography. It is a business association dedicated to improving the profitability of its firms.

The PAC is bipartisan but mostly supports Republicans. It is particularly concerned with free enterprise because the government uses private businesses for only 8 percent of the $1 billion it spends on mapping and surveying.

The PAC was involved in the introduction of S 314/HR 716, the Freedom From Government Competition Act of 1997.

The PAC assists federal candidates who support free enterprise and understand the role of mapping firms.

Management Association for Private Photogrammetric Surveyors PAC (MAPPS PAC) (C00233247) *Address: same as sponsor * Treasurer: John M. Palatiello*

	1993-94	1995-96	1997	Totals
Receipts	$21,469	$27,310	$4,950	$53,729
Disburse	21,000	27,743	5,406	54,149
Cash	1,163	829	372	n/a
Contributions	21,000	22,243	4,000	47,243
Republicans	17,500	21,743	3,000	42,243
No. of Cand.	21	26	4	51
House	8,000	11,000	3,000	22,000
Senate	9,500	10,743	0	20,243
Democrats	3,500	500	1,000	5,000
No. of Cand.	4	1	1	6
House	2,500	500	1,000	4,000
Senate	1,000	0	0	1,000
Incumbents	12,500	16,243	4,000	32,743
Challengers	4,000	2,000	0	6,000
Open Seat	4,500	4,000	0	8,500
Winners	18,000	14,743	n/a	32,743
Losers	3,000	7,500	n/a	10,500

National Society of Professional Engineers

*Phone: (703) 684-2800 * Fax: (703) 836-4875*
1420 King St., Alexandria, VA 22314-2794
*Web: www.nspe.org * E-mail: mmatlack@nspe.org*

The National Society of Professional Engineers represents about 60,000 individual engineers from all disciplines, including civil and chemical engineering. Established in 1934, the organization has interests in issues related to transportation, environment, scientific research and development.

National Society of Professional Engineers - Political Action Committee (NSPE-PAC) (C00090415) *Address: same as sponsor * Treasurer: John L. Hornbach * Contact: Michael P. Matlack, PAC Dir.*

	1993-94	1995-96	1997	Totals
Receipts	$73,087	$103,364	$51,067	$227,518
Disburse	57,008	80,685	24,008	161,701
Cash	27,196	49,877	71,525	n/a
Contributions	55,750	74,800	23,512	154,062
Republicans	29,750	64,300	17,262	111,312
No. of Cand.	34	68	23	125
House	16,750	44,800	12,262	73,812
Senate	13,000	19,500	5,000	37,500
Democrats	24,500	10,500	5,750	40,750
No. of Cand.	27	21	9	57
House	21,000	8,000	5,250	34,250
Senate	3,500	2,500	500	6,500
Incumbents	42,250	58,800	23,512	124,562
Challengers	1,000	6,500	0	7,500
Open Seat	12,500	9,500	0	22,000
Winners	41,250	54,550	n/a	95,800
Losers	14,500	20,250	n/a	34,750

National Society of Professional Surveyors

*Phone: (301) 493-0200 * Fax: (301) 493-8245*
5410 Grosvenor Ln., Suite 100, Bethesda, MD 20814-2144
Web: www.survmap.org

The American Congress on Surveying and Mapping comprises four organizations — The National Society of Professional Surveyors, which accounts for 70 percent of ACSM's membership, The American Association of Geodetic Surveying, The Cartography and Geographic Information Society and The Geographic and Land Information Society. ACSM's members include about 8,000 surveyors, cartographers, geodesists and other spatial data information professionals working in both public and private sectors throughout the world.

American Congress on Surveying & Mapping/National Society of Professional Surveyors PAC (C00152892) *Address: same as sponsor * Treasurer: Joseph A. Kuchler*

	1993-94	*1995-96*	*1997*	*Totals*
Receipts	$11,664	$17,572	$6,990	$36,226
Disburse	10,642	12,768	3,000	26,410
Cash	3,382	8,187	12,177	n/a
Contributions	10,500	12,750	3,000	26,250
Republicans	6,500	10,500	2,000	19,000
No. of Cand.	*8*	*14*	*4*	*26*
House	3,000	6,000	1,500	10,500
Senate	3,500	4,500	500	8,500
Democrats	4,000	2,250	1,000	7,250
No. of Cand.	*5*	*4*	*2*	*11*
House	3,500	1,500	1,000	6,000
Senate	500	750	0	1,250
Incumbents	8,000	12,250	3,000	23,250
Challengers	1,500	0	0	1,500
Open Seat	1,000	500	0	1,500
Winners	7,500	10,750	n/a	18,250
Losers	3,000	2,000	n/a	5,000

Parsons Brinckerhoff Inc.

*Phone: (212) 465-5036 * Fax: (212) 465-5587*
One Penn Plaza, New York, NY 10119
*Web: www.pbworld.com * E-mail: prieto@pbworld.com*

Parsons Brinckerhoff provides planning, engineering, construction management, operations and maintenance services to large public works projects and private clients worldwide. The privately held 5,500-person New York City company was ranked the No. 1 transportation engineering firm in the world by Engineering News-Record.

Current major projects include expanding the San Francisco, Los Angeles and Cairo, Egypt, subway systems and building the Big Dig highway tunnel and New Federal Courthouse in Boston.

The company works on transportation, water, environmental, power, industrial, energy and facilities projects. In 1997 Parsons Brinckerhoff won a bid to implement electronic toll collection in New Jersey. The company calls the project the largest of its type in the United States.

In January 1998, the company announced that it had acquired St. Louis-based engineering, architectural, planning and construction management firm Booker Associates. The 200-person firm works primarily in the Midwest.

Founded in 1885, Parsons Brinckerhoff designed the original New York City subway system.

Subsidiaries include: Parsons Brinckerhoff Quade & Douglas, PB's U.S. infrastructure company; Parsons Brinckerhoff Construction Services; PB Aviation; Parsons Brinckerhoff Energy Services; Parsons Brinckerhoff International; and PB Constructors.

Parsons Brinckerhoff Inc. PAC (C00287003) *Phone: (202) 783-0241 * Fax: (202) 783-0229 * 700 11th St. N.W., Washington, DC 20001 * Treasurer: Robert Prieto * Contact: Cathy Connor, V.P. of Gov. Affairs*

	1993-94	*1995-96*	*1997*	*Totals*
Receipts	$54,135	$97,578	$73,140	$224,853
Disburse	41,588	78,957	47,560	168,105
Cash	12,545	31,166	56,745	n/a
Contributions	41,454	73,847	40,142	155,443
Republicans	8,550	38,675	17,892	65,117
No. of Cand.	*16*	*37*	*14*	*67*
House	7,200	31,375	7,700	46,275
Senate	1,350	7,300	10,192	18,842
Democrats	32,904	35,172	20,250	88,326
No. of Cand.	*38*	*35*	*24*	*97*
House	20,750	27,172	10,250	58,172

Senate	12,154	8,000	10,000	30,154
Incumbents	34,404	57,797	39,392	131,593
Challengers	1,350	2,800	1,000	5,150
Open Seat	5,700	13,250	250	19,200
Winners	30,604	61,100	n/a	91,704
Losers	10,850	12,747	n/a	23,597

Parsons Corp.

*Phone: (626) 440-2000 * Fax: (626) 440-2630*
100 W. Walnut St., Pasadena, CA 91124
Web: www.parsons.com

Parsons, a privately held company based in Pasadena, Calif., is an engineering and construction firm. Its market sectors consist of energy and chemicals, infrastructure and technology and transportation. Sales in 1996 were $1.6 billion and the company employs 10,000 people. Parsons was No. 100 in Forbes' list of top private companies.

Parsons Transportation Group, a Parsons subsidiary, also has a PAC. Parsons Transportation Group builds rail and transit systems, bridges and highways in the United States, Asia, the Middle East and Africa. Its clients include Amtrak, British Petroleum, Exxon, IBM, Nissan, Procter and Gamble, Shell Oil Co., The New York Times Co., The Walt Disney Co. and nations worldwide.

Parsons Corp. Political Action Committee (C00103549) *Phone: (202) 775-6014 * Fax: (202) 775-6005 * 1133 15th St. N.W., Suite 800, Washington, DC 20005 * E-mail: jack_hargett@parsons.com * Treasurer: Graham W. Gosling * Contact: Jack Hargett, Manager of Gov. Relations*

	1993-94	*1995-96*	*1997*	*Totals*
Receipts	$14,091	$33,448	$32,698	$80,237
Disburse	37,083	33,556	27,035	97,674
Cash	4,233	4,128	9,791	n/a
Contributions	32,970	31,800	23,500	88,270
Republicans	9,750	19,900	14,500	44,150
No. of Cand.	*8*	*19*	*14*	*41*
House	7,250	16,900	8,500	32,650
Senate	2,500	3,000	6,000	11,500
Democrats	23,220	11,900	9,000	44,120
No. of Cand.	*18*	*16*	*9*	*43*
House	13,100	6,700	6,000	25,800
Senate	10,120	5,200	3,000	18,320
Incumbents	25,870	27,300	22,500	75,670
Challengers	1,350	500	0	1,850
Open Seat	5,500	4,000	1,000	10,500
Winners	23,600	28,800	n/a	52,400
Losers	9,370	3,000	n/a	12,370

Parsons Transportation Group Federal PAC (C00119784) *Phone: (202) 775-6093 * Fax: (202) 775-3422 * 1133 15th St. N.W., Suite 800, Washington, DC 20005 * Web: www.parsons.com * E-mail: paulthompson@parsons.com * Treasurer: David P. Hansgen*

	1993-94	*1995-96*	*1997*	*Totals*
Receipts	$34,706	$21,025	$16,398	$72,129
Disburse	36,536	43,359	11,067	90,962
Cash	23,427	1,856	6,328	n/a
Contributions	28,200	21,937	720	50,857
Republicans	4,500	4,675	220	9,395
No. of Cand.	*5*	*6*	*2*	*13*
House	3,000	3,675	220	6,895
Senate	1,500	1,000	0	2,500
Democrats	23,700	17,262	500	41,462
No. of Cand.	*20*	*12*	*1*	*33*
House	15,700	9,762	500	25,962
Senate	8,000	7,500	0	15,500
Incumbents	19,200	12,062	720	31,982
Challengers	3,000	3,175	0	6,175
Open Seat	6,000	6,700	0	12,700
Winners	16,200	18,450	n/a	34,650
Losers	12,000	3,487	n/a	15,487

S&B Engineers

*Phone: (713) 645-4141 * Fax: (713) 621-6426*
7825 Park Place Blvd., Houston, TX 77087
Web: www.sbgroupltd.com

S&B Engineers is part of the S&B affiliated group of companies headquartered in Houston. S&B, a privately owned company, provides a full scope of services from feasibility studies to engineering, procurement, construction and project management consulting to the refining, petrochemical, chemical and polymer processing industries, as well as government and public works projects.

S&B was founded in 1967 to serve the process industries in the Texas/Louisiana Gulf Coast and has expanded to a staff of 1,600 engineering and support personnel. S&B is currently performing the engineering services for just under $1 billion per year of capital projects. The group also includes several subsidiaries: Process Services Inc., Infrastructure, International and Ford, and Bacon & Davis.

S&B also is working on the engineering, procurement and construction of Equistar Chemicals' high density polyethylene expansion in Victoria, Texas. The project will increase the capacity of Equistar's Victoria plant by 125 million pounds per year. The project is scheduled for completion in late 1998.

S&B Engineers Inc. PAC (C00236083) *Address: same as sponsor * Treasurer: Raul Romero*

	1993-94	1995-96	1997	Totals
Receipts	$16,400	$21,000	$5,000	$42,400
Disburse	16,350	21,250	1,000	38,600
Cash	91	91	4,091	n/a
Contributions	11,850	9,600	0	21,450
Republicans	4,100	9,600	1,000	14,700
No. of Cand.	*3*	*9*	*1*	*13*
House	3,500	8,100	0	11,600
Senate	600	1,500	1,000	3,100
Democrats	7,750	0	-1000	6,750
No. of Cand.	*5*	*0*	*1*	*6*
House	1,250	0	-1000	250
Senate	6,500	0	0	6,500
Incumbents	9,100	5,000	0	14,100
Challengers	0	3,100	0	3,100
Open Seat	2,750	1,500	0	4,250
Winners	4,100	5,500	n/a	9,600
Losers	7,750	4,100	n/a	11,850

STV Engineers Inc.

*Phone: (610) 385-8200 * Fax: (610) 385-8501*
205 W. Welsh Dr., Douglassville, PA 19518
Web: www.stvinc.com

A division of the STV Group, STV Engineers provides engineering and architectural design services to projects including prisons, airports, bridges, manufacturing systems and military weapons systems. It designs everything from jet catapults on aircraft carriers to layouts of track and terminals for the railroad industry.

State and local governments account for more than half of STV's revenues. Private contracts make up nearly 30 percent and federal contracts account for about 15 percent.

STV Group is a publicly traded company but its 900 employees own about 70 percent of the stock. It posted sales of $94 million in 1997.

STV Engineers Inc. Political Action Committee (C00214866) *Address: same as sponsor * Treasurer: Peter Knipe*

	1993-94	1995-96	1997	Totals
Receipts	$9,856	$7,272	$4,351	$21,479
Disburse	12,900	6,703	1,000	20,603
Cash	786	1,359	4,712	n/a
Contributions	9,900	4,850	1,000	15,750
Republicans	3,900	5,350	500	9,750
No. of Cand.	*4*	*10*	*6*	*20*
House	1,400	3,100	250	4,750
Senate	2,500	2,250	250	5,000
Democrats	6,000	-500	500	6,000
No. of Cand.	*7*	*2*	*1*	*10*
House	2,500	500	500	3,500
Senate	3,500	-1000	0	2,500
Incumbents	6,000	2,850	1,500	10,350
Challengers	3,900	500	0	4,400
Open Seat	0	1,500	0	1,500
Winners	5,650	2,850	n/a	8,500
Losers	4,250	2,000	n/a	6,250

Stone & Webster Inc.

*Phone: (617) 589-5111 * Fax: (617) 589-2156*
245 Summer St., Boston, MA 02210
Web: www.stoneweb.com

Stone & Webster provides engineering, construction, consulting and environmental services to commercial and governmental clients. The company works in industries including: chemical, petroleum, food and beverage, pharmaceutical and pulp and paper. Based in Boston, the public company reported 1997 sales of $1.3 billion and employs more than 5,000 workers.

Stone & Webster is divided into four units, which specialize in power, process, infrastructure and industrial projects. Major clients include the Tennessee Valley Authority and Indianapolis Power and Light.

The company cleans and maintains nuclear power plants in Virginia and Arizona, as well as Canada, Indonesia and the United Arab Emirates. Forty percent of the company's overall power business is overseas, including Asia, Korea, Taiwan and China and Central and South America.

In January 1998, Stone & Webster acquired Belmont Constructors Inc. of Houston. Belmont is a full-service construction firm that serves a diverse group of clients in the hydrocarbon, water, industrial and power markets. It employs 1,300 workers.

Other U.S. locations include: Albuquerque, N.M., Atlanta, Boston, Cherry Hill, N.J., Decatur, Ala., Denver, Houston, Miami, New York, Pleasanton, Calif., Richland, Wash., and Washington.

Stone & Webster Inc. Political Action Committee (C00104885) *Phone: (202) 466-7415 * Fax: (202) 466-2673 * 1201 Connecticut Ave. N.W., Suite 850, Washington, DC 20036-2605 * Treasurer: Stephen M. Marlo*

*Contact: Robert Marrow, Chairman of PAC * Phone: (617) 589-5111*

	1993-94	1995-96	1997	Totals
Receipts	$92,761	$46,379	$22,331	$161,471
Disburse	96,225	50,650	17,560	164,435
Cash	8,128	3,861	8,633	n/a
Contributions	71,200	45,650	13,010	129,860
Republicans	31,300	34,350	6,860	72,510
No. of Cand.	*29*	*29*	*8*	*66*
House	17,300	19,350	4,860	41,510
Senate	14,000	15,000	2,000	31,000
Democrats	39,900	11,300	6,150	57,350
No. of Cand.	*31*	*14*	*8*	*53*
House	23,400	10,050	4,650	38,100
Senate	16,500	1,250	1,500	19,250
Incumbents	64,850	42,800	12,510	120,160
Challengers	100	500	0	600
Open Seat	6,250	2,350	500	9,100
Winners	58,100	42,150	n/a	100,250
Losers	13,100	3,500	n/a	16,600

Sverdrup Corp.

*Phone: (314) 436-7600 * Fax: (314) 770-5105*
13723 Riverport Dr., Maryland Heights, MO 63043
Web: www.sverdrup.com

Engineering firm Sverdrup began in 1928 as a civil/structural firm and is now among the largest engineering firms by business volume. Sverdrup's sales in 1996 were estimated at $750 million. The private company employs more than 5,000 workers.

Sverdrup is made up of three companies: Sverdrup Civil and Sverdrup Facilities, which provide traditional architectural services for capital projects, and Sverdrup Technology, which provides advanced technology services for government and industry.

Sverdrup has played a role in designing projects ranging from Oriole Park Camden Yards in Baltimore to a space shuttle launch facility in California.

SVGGS Fund (C00165084) *Address: same as sponsor * Treasurer: Robert J. Messey * Contact: James C. Uselton, Chairperson*

	1993-94	1995-96	1997	Totals
Receipts	$172,355	$211,337	$91,512	$475,204
Disburse	136,481	194,163	85,032	415,676
Cash	45,528	62,705	69,185	n/a
Contributions	41,850	93,750	50,950	186,550
Republicans	9,800	71,825	36,500	118,125
No. of Cand.	*8*	*59*	*44*	*111*
House	5,800	50,325	28,500	84,625
Senate	4,000	21,500	8,000	33,500
Democrats	30,050	21,925	12,950	64,925
No. of Cand.	*23*	*19*	*13*	*55*
House	15,050	18,425	8,250	41,725
Senate	15,000	3,500	4,700	23,200
Incumbents	25,550	82,550	49,450	157,550
Challengers	1,500	4,950	2,500	8,950
Open Seat	14,800	4,750	500	20,050
Winners	25,050	76,800	n/a	101,850
Losers	16,800	16,950	n/a	33,750

General Contractors

American Road & Transportation Builders Association

*Phone: (202) 289-4434 x101 * Fax: (202) 289-4435*
1010 Massachusetts Ave. N.W., Washington, DC 20001
Web: www.artba-hq.org

The American Road & Transportation Builders Association has about 4,000 members, including contractors, transportation professors, manufacturers, materials and service companies, planning and design firms, traffic safety companies and government officials.

The group's main purpose is to promote federal investment in transportation. It also follows regulatory and tax issues.

American Road & Transportation Builders Association (ARTBA) - 525 PAC (C00118208) *Address: same as sponsor * Treasurer: James E. Black * Contact: Martin Whitmer Jr., Manager of Political Afffairs*

	1993-94	1995-96	1997	Totals
Receipts	$37,595	$50,440	$49,795	$137,830
Disburse	36,577	50,973	30,861	118,411
Cash	1,668	2,327	21,268	n/a
Contributions	33,850	52,100	16,000	101,950
Republicans	10,500	38,750	10,000	59,250
No. of Cand.	*11*	*27*	*10*	*48*
House	7,500	25,000	9,000	41,500
Senate	3,000	13,750	1,000	17,750
Democrats	22,850	13,350	6,000	42,200
No. of Cand.	*25*	*14*	*7*	*46*
House	11,600	7,350	1,500	20,450
Senate	11,250	6,000	4,500	21,750
Incumbents	26,600	48,100	15,500	90,200
Challengers	1,750	250	500	2,500
Open Seat	5,500	3,250	0	8,750
Winners	22,850	38,600	n/a	61,450
Losers	11,000	13,500	n/a	24,500

Associated Builders and Contractors

*Phone: (703) 812-2000 * Fax: (703) 812-8202*
1300 N. 17th St., Eighth Floor, Rosslyn, VA 22209
*Web: www.abc.org * E-mail: hinton@abc.org*

Associated Builders and Contractors is a national trade association representing more than 19,000 contractors, subcontractors, material suppliers and related construction firms. The group advocates the "merit," or open, shop philosophy, which aims to provide the most competitive bidding and work regardless of labor affiliation.

ABC represents members before Congress and federal agencies concerned with the construction industry: the Department of Labor, the Occupational Safety and Health Administration and the EPA. The group supports tax reform for small businesses, including a return to the cash basis of accounting. It favors a simpler method of classifying workers as independent contractors, a proposal that most labor unions oppose. ABC also lobbies on the structure and operations of the National Labor Relations Board.

ABC was the leading builders association contributor to 1996 congressional campaigns. All but $1,000 of its contributions went to Republican candidates. The top recipients were Rep. Kevin Brady, R-Texas, Sen. Gordon Smith, R-Ore., and 1996 House candidate Ed Harrison of Texas. The lone Democrat recipient was Rep. Chris John, D-La.

PAC contributions are determined by a board of trustees, relying on endorsements by local chapters.

Associated Builders and Contractors Political Action Committee (ABC/PAC) (C00010421) *Address: same as sponsor * Treasurer: Charlotte W. Herbert * Contact: Charlotte W. Herbert*

	1993-94	1995-96	1997	Totals
Receipts	$184,537	$597,514	$501,302	$1,283,353
Disburse	187,989	549,746	110,727	848,462
Cash	(3275.00)	64,633	455,207	n/a
Contributions	169,325	524,600	103,800	797,725
Republicans	161,375	523,600	103,800	788,775
No. of Cand.	*150*	*195*	*76*	*421*
House	82,125	395,600	74,300	552,025
Senate	79,250	128,000	29,500	236,750
Democrats	7,950	1,000	0	8,950
No. of Cand.	*10*	*1*	*0*	*11*
House	7,950	1,000	0	8,950
Senate	0	0	0	0
Incumbents	90,600	194,100	98,800	383,500
Challengers	33,425	147,500	1,000	181,925
Open Seat	45,850	183,000	3,000	231,850
Winners	149,050	271,100	n/a	420,150
Losers	20,275	253,500	n/a	273,775

Associated General Contractors

*Phone: (202) 383-2762 * Fax: (202) 347-5412*
1957 E St. N.W., Washington, DC 20006
*Web: www.agc.org * E-mail: shoafj@agc.org*

The Associated General Contractors of America, founded in 1918, is a national trade association of more than 32,500 firms including 8,000 of America's leading general contracting companies. Its members work on residential, commercial and industrial construction projects for governments and private customers.

The group favors increased construction spending to improve the nation's highways, drinking water, schools and flood controls, which it says will produce thousands of construction jobs. It also advocates changes in Superfund and Occupational Safety and Health Administration legislation to protect small contractors.

The AGC supports a proposal to make it more difficult for unions to file unfair labor practice charges against open-shop contractors for refusing to hire union organizers as workers. It is opposed to expanding the Family and Medical Leave Act to contractors with 25 or more employees. The group supports capital gains tax reductions and preserving the right to classify workers as independent contractors.

AGC ranked first among heavy construction PACs in contributions to 1996 congressional races. For the 1995-96 election cycle, the group spent 98 percent of its total expenditures on congressional candidates. This level of giving placed it in the top five of large PACs in terms of percentage given to candidates. Most of the contributions went to Republican incumbents.

The leading recipients were Sens. James M. Inhofe, R-Okla., and Gordon H. Smith, R-Ore. One Democrat, 1996 Senate candidate Winston Bryant of Arkansas, received $5,000.

Associated General Contractors Political Action Committee (C00082917) *Address: same as sponsor * Treasurer: Stephen E. Sandherr * Contact: Jeff Shoaf, Executive Dir.*

	1993-94	1995-96	1997	Totals
Receipts	$696,753	$810,669	$384,592	$1,892,014
Disburse	703,829	804,375	200,218	1,708,422
Cash	671	6,975	191,354	n/a
Contributions	697,697	791,050	192,945	1,681,692
Republicans	563,497	742,550	166,945	1,472,992
No. of Cand.	*259*	*308*	*157*	*724*
House	365,997	511,050	120,445	997,492
Senate	197,500	231,500	46,500	475,500
Democrats	133,200	48,500	25,000	206,700
No. of Cand.	*81*	*44*	*31*	*156*
House	101,700	43,500	21,000	166,200
Senate	31,500	5,000	4,000	40,500
Incumbents	444,697	510,300	187,945	1,142,942
Challengers	95,000	90,000	3,000	188,000
Open Seat	156,500	191,750	2,000	350,250
Winners	595,647	553,050	n/a	1,148,697
Losers	102,050	238,000	n/a	340,050

Nebraska Construction Industry Political Action Committee (C00050872) *Phone: (402) 435-4355 * P.O. Box 80638, Lincoln, NE 68501 * Treasurer: Thomas M. Price*

	1993-94	1995-96	1997	Totals
Receipts	$655	$6,305	$1,186	$8,146
Disburse	2,004	7,000	1,045	10,049
Cash	2,352	1,642	1,928	n/a
Contributions	7,000	7,000	0	14,000
Republicans	7,000	7,000	0	14,000
No. of Cand.	*2*	*4*	*1*	*7*
House	7,000	6,000	0	13,000
Senate	0	1,000	0	1,000
Democrats	0	0	0	0
No. of Cand.	*0*	*0*	*0*	*0*
House	0	0	0	0
Senate	0	0	0	0
Incumbents	7,000	6,000	0	13,000
Challengers	0	0	0	0
Open Seat	0	1,000	0	1,000
Winners	7,000	7,000	n/a	14,000
Losers	0	0	n/a	0

Iowa Construction Industry PAC/Associated General Contractors of Iowa (C00068452) *Phone: (515) 283-2424 * Fax: (515) 244-6289 * 701 E. Court Ave., Suite B, Des Moines, IA 50309-4901 * Web: www.agcia.org * Treasurer: Scott D. Newhard * Contact: Kurt Rasmussen, Chairman*

Associated General Contractors of Iowa represents more than 230 contractor member firms and more than 175 associate members.

	1993-94	1995-96	1997	Totals
Receipts	$4,072	$11,371	$3,446	$18,889
Disburse	3,731	10,745	500	14,976
Cash	(342.00)	1,353	4,304	n/a
Contributions	1,100	7,400	500	9,000
Republicans	0	3,900	0	3,900
No. of Cand.	*0*	*4*	*0*	*4*
House	0	2,650	0	2,650
Senate	0	1,250	0	1,250
Democrats	1,100	3,500	500	5,100
No. of Cand.	*2*	*2*	*1*	*5*
House	1,100	1,000	500	2,600
Senate	0	2,500	0	2,500
Incumbents	1,000	4,650	500	6,150
Challengers	0	1,250	0	1,250
Open Seat	100	1,500	0	1,600
Winners	0	5,650	n/a	5,650
Losers	1,100	1,750	n/a	2,850

Austin Industries

*Phone: (214) 443-5575 * Fax: (214) 443-5516*
P.O. Box 1590, Dallas, TX 75221
Web: www.austin-ind.com

Austin Industries is a private construction company owned by its employees that engages in civil, commercial and industrial construction. Austin also provides in-plant contract maintenance and capital construction services to the refining and petrochemical industries in Georgia, Louisiana, South Carolina and Texas.

Austin Industries evolved from Austin Bridge Co., which was founded in 1918. The company's total workforce numbers about 6,000.

Austin Commercial, a subsidiary, will serve as construction manager/general contractor for Intel Corp.'s $1.3 billion computer chip facility, which will be built on a 532-acre site north of Fort Worth, Texas. Construction began during the third quarter of 1997 and will be completed by early 1999.

Austin Industries Companies Political Action Committee (C00093179) *Address: same as sponsor * Treasurer: Charles E. Hardy*

	1993-94	1995-96	1997	Totals
Receipts	$16,403	$19,180	$10,046	$45,629
Disburse	21,450	20,655	2,000	44,105
Cash	7,981	6,509	14,556	n/a
Contributions	6,700	7,000	0	13,700
Republicans	2,000	5,500	0	7,500
No. of Cand.	*3*	*7*	*0*	*10*
House	1,500	5,500	0	7,000
Senate	500	0	0	500
Democrats	4,700	1,500	0	6,200
No. of Cand.	*6*	*3*	*0*	*9*
House	4,700	1,500	0	6,200
Senate	0	0	0	0
Incumbents	5,200	4,500	0	9,700
Challengers	1,500	0	0	1,500
Open Seat	0	2,500	0	2,500
Winners	6,200	5,750	n/a	11,950
Losers	500	1,250	n/a	1,750

CBI Industries

800 Jorie Blvd., Oak Brook, IL 60521

CBI Industries PAC was terminated in 1996.

CBI Industries Political Action Committee (CBIPAC) (C00122739) *Address: same as sponsor * Treasurer: James L. Howell*

	1993-94	1995-96	1997	Totals
Receipts	$31,206	$7,332	$0	$38,538
Disburse	30,613	8,335	0	38,948
Cash	1,002	0	0	n/a
Contributions	30,500	8,000	0	38,500
Republicans	19,500	8,000	0	27,500
No. of Cand.	*25*	*7*	*0*	*32*
House	7,500	8,000	0	15,500
Senate	12,000	0	0	12,000
Democrats	11,000	0	0	11,000
No. of Cand.	*10*	*0*	*0*	*10*
House	10,500	0	0	10,500
Senate	500	0	0	500
Incumbents	22,000	8,000	0	30,000
Challengers	2,500	0	0	2,500
Open Seat	6,000	0	0	6,000
Winners	23,000	7,000	n/a	30,000
Losers	7,500	1,000	n/a	8,500

Dillingham Construction Holdings Inc.

*Phone: (510) 463-3300 * Fax: (510) 463-1571*
5960 Inglewood Dr., P.O. Box 1089, Pleasanton, CA 94588
Web: www.nanospace.com/dillingham/dcc.html

Dillingham Construction Holdings is a private, employee-owned construction and engineering company with more than 1,500 employees at worldwide locations. The firm has built refineries, port facilities, chemical and pharmaceutical labs, paper and food-processing plants, steel mills and other facilities.

Dillingham also has operations in the public sector developing alternative energy resources, constructing water treatment facilities and generating electricity. The Japanese firm Shimuzu Construction Co. holds 45 percent of the company's stock.

Dillingham Construction Holdings Inc. Political Action Committee (C00222299) *Address: same as sponsor * Treasurer: John T. Capener*

	1993-94	1995-96	1997	Totals
Receipts	$14,852	$8,194	$3,036	$26,082
Disburse	11,893	13,332	4,037	29,262
Cash	18,862	13,730	12,731	n/a
Contributions	10,250	10,250	4,000	24,500
Republicans	5,500	9,750	2,000	17,250
No. of Cand.	*11*	*14*	*2*	*27*
House	3,000	5,750	0	8,750
Senate	2,500	4,000	2,000	8,500
Democrats	4,750	500	2,000	7,250
No. of Cand.	*7*	*1*	*1*	*9*
House	2,250	500	0	2,750
Senate	2,500	0	2,000	4,500
Incumbents	7,250	9,250	3,000	19,500
Challengers	0	500	1,000	1,500
Open Seat	2,000	500	0	2,500
Winners	8,250	7,500	n/a	15,750
Losers	2,000	2,750	n/a	4,750

Fluor Corp.

*Phone: (714) 975-6995 * Fax: (714) 975-4450*
3353 Michelson Dr., Irvine, CA 92698
Web: www.fluor.com

Fluor is a publicly owned company with two main businesses: Fluor Daniel, an engineering and construction firm, and A.T. Massey Coal, one of the top five coal companies in the United States. Fluor has about 60,000 employees on six continents. It has operations in California, Texas, South Carolina, Ohio, Massachusetts, Rhode Island, North Carolina and other states. The company reported 1997 sales of $14.3 billion.

Fluor subsidiaries work on two major federal environmental projects, at the Department of Energy's Fernald site in Ohio and at DOE's Hanford, Wash., location. The company provides maintenance for nuclear power plants and telecommunications services. It also builds automated systems for cigarette production and the food industry.

The company contributed more than 80 percent of its 1995-96 congressional contributions to Republican candidates. It ranked second among heavy construction PACs. The top recipients were Rep. Tom DeLay, R-Texas, Sen. Strom Thurmond, R-S.C., and Sen. Phil Gramm, R-Texas. The leading Democratic recipient was Rep. Norm Dicks, D-Wash.

Fluor Corp. Public Affairs Committee (Fluor PAC) (C00034132) *Phone: (202) 955-9300 * Fax: (202) 833-1630 * 800 Connecticut Ave. N.W., Suite 600, Washington, DC 20006 * Treasurer: Andrew M. Schwartz*

*Contact: Lawrence N. Fisher, Senior V.P. * Phone: (714) 975-6995*

	1993-94	1995-96	1997	Totals
Receipts	$501,141	$595,631	$268,731	$1,365,503
Disburse	557,357	602,873	198,732	1,358,962
Cash	10,803	3,571	73,577	n/a
Contributions	301,000	295,175	98,750	694,925
Republicans	192,550	244,675	72,750	509,975
No. of Cand.	*96*	*113*	*52*	*261*
House	97,050	150,175	48,750	295,975
Senate	95,500	94,500	24,000	214,000
Democrats	108,450	50,500	26,000	184,950
No. of Cand.	*58*	*38*	*19*	*115*
House	87,950	41,000	13,500	142,450
Senate	20,500	9,500	12,500	42,500
Incumbents	256,650	270,575	94,250	621,475
Challengers	13,100	2,000	1,000	16,100
Open Seat	29,500	22,100	3,500	55,100
Winners	253,400	259,325	n/a	512,725
Losers	47,600	35,850	n/a	83,450

Contributed less than $5,000 during 1995-96 cycle:

A.T. Massey Coal Co. Inc. Political Assistance Committee (A.T. Massey Coal Political Assistance Committee) (C00155358) *Phone: (804) 788-1800 * Fax: (804) 788-1870 * 4 N. Fourth St., P.O. Box 26765, Richmond, VA 23261 * Treasurer: Carolyn B. Gero*

Great Lakes Dredge & Dock Co.

*Phone: (630) 574-2947 * Fax: (630) 574-2981*
2122 York Rd., Oak Brook, IL 60523
*Web: www.gldd.com * E-mail: gldom@gldd.com*

Great Lakes Dredge & Dock claims to have the largest dredging fleet in the United States, with 29 vessels valued at more than $700 million. In recent years, Great Lakes performed about 60 percent of all new work projects annually contracted by the Army Corps of Engineers. The company is owned by the New York investment banking firm Blackstone Group.

Great Lakes performs waterway dredging, beach replenishment and marine construction projects in the United States and worldwide. It has been responsible for much of the work called for in the Water Resources Development Act of 1986, including a $152 million project in New York Harbor that was the largest dredging contract ever ordered by the Army Corp of Engineers.

Founded in 1890, the company has about 1,500 employees at locations in California, Florida, New York, Illinois and New Jersey. Sales were estimated at $250 million in 1997.

Great Lakes affiliate Amboy Aggregates Co. dredges sand in offshore New Jersey, and processes it in South Amboy, N.J.

Subsidiaries: North American Trailing Co., Lydon Dredging & Construction Co. Ltd. (Canada).

Great Lakes Dredge & Dock Co. Political Action Committee (C00264937) *Address: same as sponsor * Treasurer: Ellen Parker * Contact: Bruce Biemeck, Senior V.P.*

	1993-94	1995-96	1997	Totals
Receipts	$24,082	$12,597	$0	$36,679
Disburse	16,500	12,200	1,750	30,450
Cash	8,829	9,226	7,476	n/a
Contributions	15,100	12,200	1,000	28,300
Republicans	3,000	7,700	1,000	11,700
No. of Cand.	*4*	*10*	*1*	*15*
House	2,000	6,700	1,000	9,700
Senate	1,000	1,000	0	2,000
Democrats	12,100	4,500	0	16,600
No. of Cand.	*13*	*7*	*0*	*20*
House	8,000	4,500	0	12,500
Senate	4,100	0	0	4,100
Incumbents	15,600	11,700	0	27,300
Challengers	0	0	0	0
Open Seat	0	500	0	500
Winners	13,500	9,700	n/a	23,200
Losers	1,600	2,500	n/a	4,100

H.B. Zachry Co.

*Phone: (210) 475-8000 * Fax: (210) 475-8060*
527 Logwood, San Antonio, TX 78221
*Web: www.zachry.com * E-mail: info@zachry.com*

The H. B. Zachry Co. is a private industrial and commercial construction company that builds power plants, refineries, highways, dams, missile sites and hotels mainly in the southwestern United States. Headquartered in Texas, it is ranked No. 246 on the Forbes list of top private companies and had estimated 1996 sales of $780 million.

The company has worked on the U.S. Embassy in Moscow. Other projects managed by Zachry are the runways at Dallas-Fort Worth International Airport, the Trans-Alaska pipeline, the Navajo Generating Station in Arizona and the J. C. Penney headquarters in Plano, Texas. The company also owns two Hilton Hotels in San Antonio, Texas.

ZacoPAC (C00048165) *Address: same as sponsor * Treasurer: Joe J. Lozano*

	1993-94	1995-96	1997	Totals
Receipts	$57,269	$90,286	$48,606	$196,161
Disburse	54,900	68,678	9,250	132,828
Cash	5,598	27,210	66,568	n/a
Contributions	17,750	29,250	7,000	54,000
Republicans	7,750	20,250	4,000	32,000
No. of Cand.	*13*	*21*	*4*	*38*
House	6,750	19,250	2,000	28,000
Senate	1,000	1,000	2,000	4,000
Democrats	10,000	9,000	3,000	22,000
No. of Cand.	*14*	*10*	*2*	*26*
House	10,000	9,000	3,000	22,000
Senate	0	0	0	0
Incumbents	13,500	16,500	5,000	35,000
Challengers	3,250	1,500	0	4,750
Open Seat	0	11,250	2,000	13,250
Winners	15,500	25,250	n/a	40,750
Losers	2,250	4,000	n/a	6,250

Heavy Constructors Association

*Phone: (816) 753-6443 * Fax: (816) 753-1239*
3101 Broadway, Suite 780, Kansas City, MO 64111
E-mail: hcakc@swbell.net

The Heavy Constructors Association represents companies that build roads, bridges and highways, as well as their suppliers. Founded in 1950, the organization has 150 member companies.

During the 1995-96 election cycle, the group's PAC contributed $26,962 to Missouri and Kansas congressional candidates.

Heavy Constructors Association Federal Political Action Committee (C00112706) *Address: same as sponsor * Treasurer: Edward DeSoignie * Contact: W. E. Clarkson Sr., Chairman*

	1993-94	1995-96	1997	Totals
Receipts	$968	$31,886	$13,653	$46,507
Disburse	27,556	33,787	8,507	69,850
Cash	8,076	6,178	11,324	n/a
Contributions	19,000	33,000	7,750	59,750
Republicans	2,000	10,000	6,500	18,500
No. of Cand.	*2*	*6*	*3*	*11*
House	2,000	3,250	1,500	6,750
Senate	0	6,750	5,000	11,750
Democrats	17,000	23,000	1,250	41,250
No. of Cand.	*7*	*6*	*2*	*15*
House	10,000	20,000	1,250	31,250
Senate	7,000	3,000	0	10,000
Incumbents	5,000	20,000	7,750	32,750
Challengers	0	6,000	0	6,000
Open Seat	14,000	7,000	0	21,000
Winners	7,000	24,000	n/a	31,000
Losers	12,000	9,000	n/a	21,000

Irby Construction Co.

*Phone: (601) 969-1811 * Fax: (601) 960-7380*
P.O. Box 1819, Jackson, MS 39215-1819
*Web: www.irby.com/irby_construction * E-mail: williams@irby.com*

Irby Construction builds electrical transmission and distribution systems and power lines. It is headquartered in Jackson, Miss., and claims to have erected more Rural Electrification Administration power lines than any other U.S. company. It is privately owned, posted 1997 sales of about $43.6 million and employs 308 people.

Irby Construction Co. Political Action Committee (C00104364) *Address: same as sponsor * Treasurer: Charles R. Campbell III * Contact: Liles Williams, Chairman*

	1993-94	1995-96	1997	Totals
Receipts	$32,951	$33,742	$6,600	$73,293
Disburse	46,131	35,010	5,601	86,742
Cash	1,926	656	1,654	n/a

(Data for Irby Construction Co. continued)

Contributions	41,600	24,500	3,600	69,700
Republicans	39,800	24,500	3,600	67,900
No. of Cand.	*30*	*33*	*3*	*66*
House	13,800	13,000	3,600	30,400
Senate	26,000	11,500	0	37,500
Democrats	1,800	0	0	1,800
No. of Cand.	*4*	*0*	*0*	*4*
House	1,800	0	0	1,800
Senate	0	0	0	0
Incumbents	9,200	5,650	2,600	17,450
Challengers	12,600	4,500	0	17,100
Open Seat	17,800	14,350	0	32,150
Winners	27,000	14,500	n/a	41,500
Losers	14,600	10,000	n/a	24,600

Morrison-Knudsen

*Phone: (208) 386-5000 * Fax: (208) 386-7186*
720 Park Blvd., P.O. Box 73, Boise, ID 83729
Web: www.mk.com

Morrison-Knudsen is a publicly traded worldwide engineering and construction firm that does business with the departments of Defense and Energy in areas including: nuclear waste storage, hazardous waste cleanup, military construction and military base closings. Morrison-Knudsen reported $1.7 billion in 1997 revenues.

Known for completing major projects such as the Hoover Dam, the Trans-Alaska pipeline and the vehicle assembly building at the Kennedy Space Center, Morrison-Knudsen regularly wins government contracts for heavy construction projects, many in the western United States.

The 8,500-person firm has built more than 150 power plants and installs equipment to help utilities meet clean air guidelines. It also decommissions and retrofits old power plants. The firm won a contract with the Tennessee Valley Authority after the 1992 Energy Policy Act required public utilities to deregulate and meet competition requirements.

The firm's Centennial division designs and builds highways, bridges and tunnels and operates toll roads for state and local governments. The division is a preferred provider to the Federal Highway Administration. Recent projects include a $230 million underwater tunnel in Boston and rebuilding an earthquake-damaged freeway in Oakland, Calif. The firm also has built prisons, schools and health care facilities.

Morrison-Knudsen's Industrial/Process Division serves Fortune 100 clients in the chemical, petroleum, pharmaceutical, food and beverage, general manufacturing and automotive industries.

The Mining Group operates strip coal mines in Montana, Texas, Wyoming, Colorado and West Virginia. A 30-year contract to provide coal to a major power plant in Indonesia was put on hold in 1998 following the financial crisis in that country.

Internationally, Morrison-Knudsen has worked on projects funded by the United States Agency for International Development (USAID). It supports military base operations in Kuwait, Egypt and Qatar. The firm also has worked on nuclear decontamination and decommissioning and related issues in Russia and the Ukraine.

Morrison-Knudsen filed for bankruptcy protection in 1996 but was rescued by Montana billionaire Dennis Washington, who merged the firm with Washington Construction, which he controlled. A year later Washington tried unsuccessfully to sell his share in Montana Resources Inc. to Morrison-Knudsen.

Washington is now chairman of Morrison-Knudsen and controls about 38 percent of its stock. The firm, with headquarters in Boise, Idaho, and major domestic offices in 12 states, was founded in 1912.

Morrison-Knudsen Political Action Committee (C00097550)
*Phone: (202) 638-6355 * Fax: (202) 638-1419 * 555 13th St. N.W., Suite 410 W. Tower, P.O. Box 73, Washington, DC 20004 * Treasurer: Betty L. Rendin * Contact: Charles W. Simpson, V.P.*

	1993-94	*1995-96*	*1997*	*Totals*
Receipts	$160,324	$92,502	$35,806	$288,632
Disburse	143,053	99,691	34,950	277,694
Cash	28,926	21,776	22,638	n/a
Contributions	105,328	70,441	23,950	199,719
Republicans	37,500	38,500	14,700	90,700
No. of Cand.	*43*	*37*	*18*	*98*
House	22,500	22,500	12,700	57,700
Senate	15,000	16,000	2,000	33,000
Democrats	67,828	31,941	9,250	109,019
No. of Cand.	*62*	*36*	*12*	*110*
House	47,948	22,191	5,750	75,889
Senate	19,880	9,750	3,500	33,130
Incumbents	96,779	56,691	21,450	174,920
Challengers	800	6,250	0	7,050
Open Seat	7,500	7,500	2,500	17,500
Winners	83,450	58,691	n/a	142,141
Losers	21,878	11,750	n/a	33,628

Morton Buildings Inc.

*Phone: (309) 263-7474 * Fax: (309) 266-5123*
252 W. Adams St., Morton, IL 61550
*Web: www.mortonbuildings.com * E-mail: mmorrison@mortonbldgs.com*

Morton Buildings is a privately owned company that designs, engineers and constructs buildings such as churches, municipal buildings, equestrian complexes, retail businesses, aircraft hangars and homes. It has five manufacturing plants located in Illinois, Iowa, Ohio, Kansas and Pennsylvania, and has 121 sales offices throughout the eastern, central and midwestern United States.

Morton Buildings is sole employer of all its salespeople, office personnel, plant workers, engineers, estimators, architects and construction crews.

Morton Buildings Inc. Political Action Committee (C00123109)
*Address: same as sponsor * Treasurer: Michael E. Morrison*

	1993-94	*1995-96*	*1997*	*Totals*
Receipts	$17,135	$23,844	$11,210	$52,189
Disburse	28,379	12,023	0	40,402
Cash	31,109	42,932	54,143	n/a
Contributions	25,500	12,000	0	37,500
Republicans	25,500	12,000	0	37,500
No. of Cand.	*35*	*12*	*0*	*47*
House	15,500	9,000	0	24,500
Senate	10,000	3,000	0	13,000
Democrats	0	0	0	0
No. of Cand.	*0*	*0*	*0*	*0*
House	0	0	0	0
Senate	0	0	0	0
Incumbents	14,000	8,000	0	22,000
Challengers	5,500	2,000	0	7,500
Open Seat	6,000	2,000	0	8,000
Winners	22,000	11,000	n/a	33,000
Losers	3,500	1,000	n/a	4,500

National Utility Contractors Association

*Phone: (703) 358-9300 * Fax: (703) 358-9307*
4301 N. Fairfax Dr., Suite 360, Arlington, VA 22203-1627

The National Utility Contractors Association represents about 1,900 companies nationwide that perform water, sewer and other underground utility construction. The group monitors public works legislation and regulations.

National Utility Contractors Association Legislative Information & Action Committee (C00004101) *Address: same as sponsor * Treasurer: William G. Harley * Contact: A. William Hillman, Dir. of Gov. Relations*

	1993-94	*1995-96*	*1997*	*Totals*
Receipts	$277,292	$255,244	$132,480	$665,016
Disburse	300,943	252,925	85,969	639,837
Cash	62,509	64,826	78,948	n/a
Contributions	244,500	193,580	54,000	492,080
Republicans	166,500	169,830	44,000	380,330
No. of Cand.	*117*	*129*	*43*	*289*
House	88,500	135,830	36,000	260,330
Senate	78,000	34,000	8,000	120,000
Democrats	77,000	23,750	7,500	108,250
No. of Cand.	*56*	*26*	*8*	*90*
House	59,500	19,750	5,500	84,750
Senate	17,500	4,000	2,000	23,500
Incumbents	158,000	144,080	50,000	352,080
Challengers	36,000	18,000	1,000	55,000
Open Seat	50,500	31,500	0	82,000
Winners	214,000	143,750	n/a	357,750
Losers	30,500	49,830	n/a	80,330

Rogers Group Inc.

*Phone: (615) 780-5735 * Fax: (615) 780-5800*
P.O. Box 25250, Nashville, TN 37202
Web: www.rogersgroupinc.com

The Rogers Group is the fifth-largest crushed stone producer in the nation with 1,600 employees in seven states. Founded in 1908, in Bloomington, Ind., the company produces crushed stone, asphalt, sand and gravel, and offers services such as road construction, coal mining, precast concrete, building materials and supplies, construction materials recycling and specialty products.

The Tennessee-based company owns production and distribution sites in Illinois, Indiana, Ohio, Kentucky, Arkansas, Tennessee, Alabama and Virginia.

The company is privately owned by the family of founder Ralph Rogers.

Rogers Group Inc. Political Action Committee (C00277152)
*Address: same as sponsor * Treasurer: Chet Foster*

	1993-94	1995-96	1997	Totals
Receipts	$49,900	$49,844	$28,185	$127,929
Disburse	22,389	69,637	27,750	119,776
Cash	27,605	7,814	8,250	n/a
Contributions	11,200	27,625	11,250	50,075
Republicans	6,300	19,625	8,750	34,675
No. of Cand.	*8*	*20*	*8*	*36*
House	3,300	15,625	7,750	26,675
Senate	3,000	4,000	1,000	8,000
Democrats	4,900	8,000	2,500	15,400
No. of Cand.	*5*	*6*	*3*	*14*
House	3,900	4,000	0	7,900
Senate	1,000	4,000	2,500	7,500
Incumbents	5,000	15,425	9,750	30,175
Challengers	2,800	9,700	0	12,500
Open Seat	3,400	2,500	1,500	7,400
Winners	6,300	16,125	n/a	22,425
Losers	4,900	11,500	n/a	16,400

T.L. James & Co.

*Phone: (504) 582-8194 * Fax: (504) 582-8011*
201 St. Charles Ave., 49th Floor, New Orleans, LA 70170

T. L. James is a privately owned maritime construction and dredging company that has been a dredging contractor for the U.S. Army Corps of Engineers.

T.L. James & Co. Inc. Political Action Committee (C00276030)
*Address: same as sponsor * Treasurer: R. Patrick Vance*

	1993-94	1995-96	1997	Totals
Receipts	$1,000	$15,180	$6,030	$22,210
Disburse	5,568	16,783	4,066	26,417
Cash	7,817	6,214	8,178	n/a
Contributions	4,500	11,750	3,000	19,250
Republicans	1,500	9,000	1,000	11,500
No. of Cand.	*2*	*10*	*1*	*13*
House	500	5,000	1,000	6,500
Senate	1,000	4,000	0	5,000
Democrats	3,000	2,750	2,000	7,750
No. of Cand.	*4*	*3*	*1*	*8*
House	2,000	500	0	2,500
Senate	1,000	2,250	2,000	5,250
Incumbents	3,500	5,500	3,000	12,000
Challengers	0	0	0	0
Open Seat	1,000	6,250	0	7,250
Winners	3,500	5,750	n/a	9,250
Losers	1,000	6,000	n/a	7,000

Tennessee Road Builders Association

*Phone: (615) 255-5751 * Fax: (615) 255-6937*
P.O. Box 190535, Uptown Station, Nashville, TN 37219
Web: www.trba.org

The Tennessee Road Builders Association is a group of about 370 contracting firms and associated members. It was formed by a 1982 merger with the Tennessee Asphalt Pavement Association and the Tennessee Crushed Stone Association.

According to the group, Tennessee's fuel tax money is earmarked for highway construction; none of it enters the state's general fund and it cannot be used for other purposes. Preserving this system is one of the organization's highest priorities, and TRBA's members raise more than $70,000 annually for the organization's state PAC.

Tennessee Road Builders Association Political Action Committee (C00215012) *Address: same as sponsor * Treasurer: Scott T. Price * Contact: W. T. Ratliff Jr., Chairperson*

	1993-94	1995-96	1997	Totals
Receipts	$15,050	$23,284	$7,750	$46,084
Disburse	14,665	24,606	7,250	46,521
Cash	1,797	475	975	n/a
Contributions	14,500	19,556	4,750	38,806
Republicans	5,400	12,306	3,250	20,956
No. of Cand.	*7*	*10*	*6*	*23*
House	3,550	9,700	2,000	15,250
Senate	1,850	2,606	1,250	5,706
Democrats	9,100	7,250	1,500	17,850
No. of Cand.	*7*	*6*	*2*	*15*
House	5,100	7,000	1,500	13,600
Senate	4,000	250	0	4,250
Incumbents	10,850	15,856	4,750	31,456
Challengers	750	1,200	0	1,950
Open Seat	2,900	2,500	0	5,400
Winners	8,700	15,856	n/a	24,556
Losers	5,800	3,700	n/a	9,500

Home Builders

Fleetwood Enterprises Inc.

*Phone: (909) 351-3500 * Fax: (909) 351-3776*
3125 Myers St., Riverside, CA 92503
*Web: www.fleetwood.com * E-mail: blear@fleetwood.com*

Fleetwood Enterprises, a publicly owned Fortune 500 company, is the nation's largest producer of manufactured housing and recreational vehicles (motor homes, travel trailers, folding trailers and slide-in truck campers). Manufacturing plants are located in 18 states and Canada.

According to Hoover's, Fleetwood commands an 18 percent share in the manufactured housing market and a 26 percent share in the recreational vehicles market. Sales in 1997 were $2.8 billion, and the company agreed to acquire HomeUSA in February 1998 in a $162 million transaction. Fleetwood sold more than 65,000 homes in 1997 and employs 18,000 people.

In addition, Fleetwood operates three supply companies which produce components for the primary manufacturing operations, while also generating outside sales. Fleetwood Credit Corp., the company's wholly owned RV finance subsidiary, was sold in 1996.

Fleetwood Enterprises Inc. Political Action Committee (C00125831) *Address: same as sponsor * Treasurer: Lyle N. Larkin * Contact: Bill Lear, PAC Dir.*

	1993-94	1995-96	1997	Totals
Receipts	$34,590	$40,013	$12,692	$87,295
Disburse	29,350	35,950	12,800	78,100
Cash	14,883	18,948	18,842	n/a
Contributions	29,350	35,450	12,300	77,100
Republicans	20,900	30,950	8,800	60,650
No. of Cand.	*31*	*37*	*11*	*79*
House	16,900	24,500	7,300	48,700
Senate	4,000	6,450	1,500	11,950
Democrats	7,450	4,500	3,000	14,950
No. of Cand.	*19*	*8*	*6*	*33*
House	6,700	4,000	2,500	13,200
Senate	750	500	500	1,750
Incumbents	23,100	30,000	12,300	65,400
Challengers	1,600	1,700	0	3,300
Open Seat	4,650	3,750	0	8,400
Winners	27,550	31,750	n/a	59,300
Losers	1,800	3,700	n/a	5,500

J.A. Jones Inc.

*Phone: (704) 553-3000 * Fax: (704) 553-3174*
J.A. Jones Dr., Charlotte, NC 28287
*Web: www.jajones.com * E-mail: egraves@jajones.com*

J.A. Jones is a private family of companies. It operates as a part of the private German company Phillipp Holzmann AG, an international professional services firm with more than 200 holdings in construction and related fields.

Founded in 1890, J.A. Jones has grown to encompass 12 companies offering construction, financial, development, planning, management, contracting and operating services. The company has about 2,000 employees and about 100 construction projects in the United States. J.A. Jones has operations in North America, South America, Europe, the Middle East and Asia.

U.S. locations include: California, Florida, Georgia, Maryland, New Jersey, New York, Nevada, North Carolina, South Carolina, Virginia and Washington.

J.A. Jones Inc. Addison Club (C00128835) *Address: same as sponsor * Treasurer: Maryann McGerity * Contact: Fred Brandt, Technologies Group*

	1993-94	1995-96	1997	Totals
Receipts	$17,621	$16,315	$6,706	$40,642
Disburse	18,900	31,650	4,308	54,858
Cash	5,488	5,640	8,038	n/a
Contributions	18,900	20,150	2,000	41,050
Republicans	14,950	17,650	2,000	34,600
No. of Cand.	*24*	*18*	*3*	*45*
House	12,950	12,150	1,000	26,100
Senate	2,000	5,500	1,000	8,500
Democrats	3,950	2,500	0	6,450
No. of Cand.	*5*	*3*	*0*	*8*
House	2,950	2,000	0	4,950
Senate	1,000	500	0	1,500
Incumbents	5,150	13,650	2,000	20,800
Challengers	3,150	2,000	0	5,150
Open Seat	10,600	4,500	0	15,100
Winners	16,050	13,150	n/a	29,200
Losers	2,850	7,000	n/a	9,850

Kaufman & Broad Home Corp.

P.O. Box 5250, San Antonio, TX 78201

KBSA Political Action Committee (formerly known as Rayco PAC) was terminated in March 1997. The PAC converted to a Texas state and local PAC. Rayco was acquired by Kaufman & Broad, a California-based public home building company.

KBSA Political Action Committee (formerly known as Rayco PAC) (C00140731) *Address: same as sponsor * Treasurer: Walter E. Nielsen*

	1993-94	1995-96	1997	Totals
Receipts	$59,998	$39,706	$1,500	$101,204
Disburse	49,094	44,729	1,500	95,323
Cash	35,098	30,078	30,078	n/a
Contributions	6,700	4,500	0	11,200
Republicans	4,000	2,000	0	6,000
No. of Cand.	*3*	*1*	*0*	*4*
House	3,000	2,000	0	5,000
Senate	1,000	0	0	1,000
Democrats	2,700	2,500	0	5,200
No. of Cand.	*4*	*4*	*0*	*8*
House	2,200	3,000	0	5,200
Senate	500	-500	0	0
Incumbents	5,200	5,000	0	10,200
Challengers	500	0	0	500
Open Seat	0	0	0	0
Winners	5,200	5,000	n/a	10,200
Losers	1,500	-500	n/a	1,000

Manufactured Housing Institute

*Phone: (703) 558-0400 * Fax: (703) 558-0401*
2101 Wilson Blvd., Suite 610, Arlington, VA 22201-3062
Web: www.mfghome.org

The Manufactured Housing Institute is a national trade association for manufactured housing that represents all segments of the industry, including manufacturers, component suppliers, retailers, community owners and operators, state associations and financial institutions involved in the lending and insuring of manufactured homes. The association publishes two quarterly magazines and provides videos, industry brochures and special publications to its members.

MHI has lobbied the Department of Housing and Urban Development to remove barriers to greater availability of manufactured housing. This action, MHI contends, would increase home ownership without federal subsidies.

Manufactured Housing Institute Political Action Committee (MHI PAC) (C00043463) *Address: same as sponsor * Treasurer: Sherri Stone * Contact: Dave Czech, Chairman*

	1993-94	1995-96	1997	Totals
Receipts	$65,296	$275,446	$158,731	$499,473
Disburse	43,238	137,100	157,707	338,045
Cash	34,063	172,458	173,483	n/a
Contributions	38,570	131,000	137,500	307,070
Republicans	14,984	89,400	94,500	198,884
No. of Cand.	*22*	*86*	*74*	*182*
House	10,174	63,200	71,500	144,874
Senate	4,810	26,200	23,000	54,010
Democrats	23,086	41,600	42,000	106,686
No. of Cand.	*33*	*34*	*32*	*99*
House	17,686	27,600	23,000	68,286
Senate	5,400	14,000	19,000	38,400
Incumbents	34,945	109,350	136,000	280,295
Challengers	625	4,200	500	5,325
Open Seat	3,000	17,450	1,000	21,450
Winners	32,820	113,050	n/a	145,870
Losers	5,750	17,950	n/a	23,700

National Association of Home Builders

*Phone: (202) 822-0470 * Fax: (202) 822-0572*
1201 15th St. N.W., Washington, DC 20005-2800
*Web: www.nahb.com * E-mail: printye@nahb.com*

The National Association of Home Builders consists of about 195,000 developers and residential construction businesses in the United States. The group conducts research, offers training and lobbies on behalf of its members. It supports pro-housing, pro-business candidates for Congress.

The group's legislative focus is passage of property rights legislation. It supports the removal of barriers to affordable housing and the retention of the mortgage interest deduction. The group also lobbies on wetlands mitigation and opposes a 1996 trade agreement that restricts the amount of duty-free lumber shipped from Canada to the United States.

The NAHB dwarfs other home building organizations in total spending and is one of the largest-spending PACs overall. It gave more than 80 percent of its 1995-96 congressional contributions to Republican candidates, including former Rep. Frank Cremeans, R-Ohio, and Rep. Jack Metcalf, R-Wash., who were members of a House timber subcommittee. Just three Democratic candidates were among the top 30 recipients: Rep. Ken Bentsen, D-Texas, Rep. Jim Turner, D-Texas, and Rep. Vic Fazio, D-Calif.

Build Political Action Committee of The National Association of Home Builders (C00000901) *Address: same as sponsor * Treasurer: Phillip L. Blair * Contact: Peter Rintye, V.P. of Political Affairs*

	1993-94	1995-96	1997	Totals
Receipts	$1,740,689	$1,944,259	$1,027,999	$4,712,947
Disburse	1,779,659	1,886,424	672,328	4,338,411
Cash	83,080	120,850	496,592	n/a
Contributions	1,329,599	1,442,849	533,250	3,305,698
Republicans	836,800	1,183,849	333,000	2,353,649
No. of Cand.	*219*	*270*	*149*	*638*
House	639,300	986,849	257,500	1,883,649
Senate	197,500	197,000	75,500	470,000
Democrats	488,799	259,000	192,750	940,549
No. of Cand.	*186*	*80*	*82*	*348*
House	399,600	215,000	139,250	753,850
Senate	89,199	44,000	53,500	186,699
Incumbents	954,599	1,087,349	518,750	2,560,698
Challengers	161,500	108,000	7,000	276,500
Open Seat	200,500	245,000	7,500	453,000
Winners	1,089,849	1,133,249	n/a	2,223,098
Losers	239,750	309,600	n/a	549,350

Contributed less than $5,000 during 1995-96 cycle:

Northern Kentucky Housing Industry Political Action Committee of Kentucky (HIPACK) (C00103713) *Phone: (606) 331-9500 * 209 Grandview, Ft. Mitchell, KY 41017 * Treasurer: Thomas Rechtin*

Oregon Building Industry Association Committee To Build A Better Oregon (C00082909) *Phone: (503) 378-9066 * 375 Taylor St. N.E., Salem, OR 97303 * Treasurer: Beth Bauer*

National Multi Housing Council

*Phone: (202) 974-2300 * Fax: (202) 775-0112*
1850 M St. N.W., Suite 540, Washington, DC 20036
*Web: www.nmhc.org * E-mail: info@nmhc.org*

The National Multi Housing Council represents 800 apartment owners, managers and financiers who specialize in the multifamily rental housing industry.

The association was founded in 1978 in response to growing economic constraints on multifamily housing, such as rent control. It is interested in legislative issues such as property rights, property management, building codes, environmental issues and senior citizens issues.

NMHC is affiliated with the American Seniors Housing Association.

National Multi Housing Council Political Action Committee (C00130773) *Address: same as sponsor * Treasurer: Jonathan L. Kempner*

	1993-94	1995-96	1997	Totals
Receipts	$80,939	$158,604	$108,850	$348,393
Disburse	55,793	163,121	85,208	304,122
Cash	28,158	23,642	47,290	n/a
Contributions	53,131	149,400	80,950	283,481
Republicans	19,231	120,600	60,300	200,131
No. of Cand.	*22*	*65*	*36*	*123*
House	10,250	89,600	42,800	142,650
Senate	8,981	31,000	17,500	57,481
Democrats	33,900	28,800	20,650	83,350
No. of Cand.	*32*	*26*	*20*	*78*
House	21,800	23,550	9,000	54,350
Senate	12,100	5,250	11,650	29,000
Incumbents	51,631	146,900	77,950	276,481
Challengers	500	0	0	500
Open Seat	1,000	2,500	3,000	6,500
Winners	41,881	138,100	n/a	179,981
Losers	11,250	11,300	n/a	22,550

Rural Builders of America PAC

P.O. Box 23190, Washington, DC 20026

Rural Builders of America PAC - (RBAPAC) (C00250944) *Address: same as sponsor * Treasurer: Robert M. Arcand*

*Contact: Keith J. Gloeckl and William E. Johnston, Co-Chairpersons * Phone: (813) 461-4801*

	1993-94	1995-96	1997	Totals
Receipts	$124,501	$0	$0	$124,501
Disburse	86,144	46,526	57	132,727
Cash	50,142	3,616	3,559	n/a
Contributions	69,600	30,500	0	100,100
Republicans	2,500	21,000	0	23,500
No. of Cand.	*3*	*12*	*0*	*15*
House	1,000	12,000	0	13,000
Senate	1,500	9,000	0	10,500
Democrats	66,100	9,500	0	75,600
No. of Cand.	*39*	*13*	*0*	*52*
House	43,600	7,500	0	51,100
Senate	22,500	2,000	0	24,500
Incumbents	63,600	28,000	0	91,600
Challengers	0	0	0	0
Open Seat	6,000	2,500	0	8,500
Winners	42,100	26,000	n/a	68,100
Losers	27,500	4,500	n/a	32,000

Toll Brothers Inc.

*Phone: (215) 938-8040 * Fax: (215) 938-8010*
3103 Philmont Ave., Huntingdon Valley, PA 19006
*Web: www.tollbrothers.com * E-mail: info@tollbrothers.com*

Homebuilder Toll Brothers has erected more than 16,000 homes in Arizona, California, Connecticut, Delaware, Florida, Maryland, Massachusetts, New Jersey, New York, North Carolina, Ohio, Pennsylvania, Tennessee, Texas and Virginia. It also operates its own architectural, engineering, mortgage, title, landscaping and manufacturing operations.

Toll Brothers won the National Housing Quality Award in 1997. It also has earned the National Builder of the Year award from Professional Builder Magazine, the Award for Construction Excellence and the Build America Beautiful Award for outstanding achievement in recycling.

A publicly traded company, Toll Brothers posted $972 million in sales in 1997. Brothers Robert and Bruce Toll, CEO and president respectively, own 35 percent of the company.

Toll Brothers Inc. PAC (C00128561) *Address: same as sponsor * Treasurer: Joel H. Rassman*

	1993-94	1995-96	1997	Totals
Receipts	$13,460	$19,620	$13,374	$46,454
Disburse	21,941	5,055	5,568	32,564
Cash	2,643	17,212	25,020	n/a
Contributions	1,000	5,000	5,000	11,000
Republicans	1,000	5,000	5,000	11,000
No. of Cand.	*1*	*1*	*1*	*3*
House	0	5,000	5,000	10,000
Senate	1,000	0	0	1,000
Democrats	0	0	0	0
No. of Cand.	*0*	*0*	*0*	*0*
House	0	0	0	0
Senate	0	0	0	0
Incumbents	0	5,000	5,000	10,000
Challengers	1,000	0	0	1,000
Open Seat	0	0	0	0
Winners	0	5,000	n/a	5,000
Losers	1,000	0	n/a	1,000

Walter Industries Inc.

*Phone: (813) 871-4448 * Fax: (813) 871-4430*
1500 N. Dale Mabry Highway, Tampa, FL 33607
Web: www.walterind.com

Walter Industries operates home building, mining, iron water pipe manufacturing and industrial products subsidiaries, all based in the South. The publicly traded company has 7,800 employees and reported $1.5 billion in 1997 sales.

The company's third largest business after home building and water pipes, subsidiary Jim Walter Resources operates eight underground coal mines in Alabama. It is headquartered in Brookwood, Ala., 55 miles southwest of Birmingham.

Subsidiary Jim Walter Homes has built 320,000 mostly single-family homes in the South since 1946. It provides financing for 95 percent of its homes. Another subsidiary, United States Pipe and Foundry Co., makes iron pipes that are used extensively in residential construction.

Other subsidiaries include: JW Aluminum of Mt. Holley, S.C.; Sloss Industries of Birmingham, Ala.; Southern Precision of Irondale, Ala.; JW Window Components, with plants in Tennessee, Wisconsin and South Dakota; and Vestal Manufacturing in Sweetwater, Tenn.

In January 1998, Walter Industries announced that Lehman Brothers Holding Co. and Asbestos Settlement Trust (Celotex Trust) will sell 12 million shares of their combined 18.8 million share position in the company's common stock in a secondary offering.

Walter Industries Inc. PAC (WaltPAC) (formerly known as Jim Walter Corp. PAC) (C00106971) *Address: same as sponsor * Treasurer: Dean M. Fjelstul * Contact: David L. Townsend, V.P. of Administration, Walter Industries*

	1993-94	1995-96	1997	Totals
Receipts	$50,236	$46,576	$18,297	$115,109
Disburse	48,522	55,509	8,632	112,663
Cash	29,989	21,060	30,724	n/a
Contributions	30,700	43,650	6,750	81,100
Republicans	12,200	25,350	6,250	43,800
No. of Cand.	*14*	*29*	*7*	*50*
House	7,500	17,100	2,750	27,350
Senate	4,700	8,250	3,500	16,450
Democrats	18,500	18,300	500	37,300
No. of Cand.	*18*	*18*	*4*	*40*
House	15,500	16,300	0	31,800
Senate	3,000	2,000	500	5,500
Incumbents	28,700	26,150	7,750	62,600
Challengers	0	-400	0	-400
Open Seat	2,000	17,900	0	19,900
Winners	29,700	31,050	n/a	60,750
Losers	1,000	12,600	n/a	13,600

Special Trade Contractors

Air Conditioning Contractors of America

*Phone: (202) 483-9370 * Fax: (202) 265-9804*
1712 New Hampshire Ave. N.W., Washington, DC 20009
*Web: www.acca.org * E-mail: jherzog@acca.org*

The Air Conditioning Contractors of America represents more than 4,000 heating, ventilation and air conditioning contractors in 65 chapters throughout the United States. The industry is a $150 billion-a-year business. ACCA offers its members training, continuing education on government regulations and representation before Congress. The group is interested in utility deregulation and EPA and Occupational Safety and Health Administration standards.

Air Conditioning Contractors of America PAC (C00100974)
*Address: same as sponsor * Treasurer: Christoper Ingram * Contact: John Herzog, Dir. of Gov. Relations*

	1993-94	1995-96	1997	Totals
Receipts	$0	$20,062	$11,741	$31,803
Disburse	500	15,500	0	16,000
Cash	349	4,912	16,654	n/a
Contributions	500	15,500	0	16,000
Republicans	500	14,500	0	15,000
No. of Cand.	*1*	*25*	*0*	*26*
House	0	11,000	0	11,000
Senate	500	3,500	0	4,000
Democrats	0	1,000	0	1,000
No. of Cand.	*0*	*2*	*0*	*2*
House	0	1,000	0	1,000
Senate	0	0	0	0
Incumbents	0	8,500	0	8,500
Challengers	500	3,500	0	4,000
Open Seat	0	3,500	0	3,500
Winners	0	11,000	n/a	11,000
Losers	500	4,500	n/a	5,000

Mason Contractors Association of America

*Phone: (630) 705-4200 * Fax: (630) 705-4209*
1910 S. Highland Ave., Suite 101, Lombard, IL 60148
*Web: www.masoncontractors.com * E-mail: info@masoncontractors.com*

The Mason Contractors Association of America provides education, training, research and information on safety and the legislative process for its 1,000 members. Established in the late 1940s, MCAA writes industry codes and standards and promotes market expansion. It also provides training manuals to its members.

MCAA lobbies Congress on such issues as estate taxes, employee flex/comp time and the reform of the Occupational Safety and Health Act.

The MCAA PAC contributes to members of Congress who support small businesses.

MCAAPAC (C00291799) *Address: same as sponsor * Treasurer: Liz Fidoruk * Contact: Mike Adelizzi, Chairman*

	1993-94	1995-96	1997	Totals
Receipts	$4,600	$6,900	$6,110	$17,610
Disburse	3,503	7,458	2,873	13,834
Cash	1,096	537	3,773	n/a
Contributions	2,250	6,050	750	9,050
Republicans	2,250	6,050	750	9,050
No. of Cand.	*6*	*15*	*2*	*23*
House	1,250	4,050	250	5,550
Senate	1,000	2,000	500	3,500
Democrats	0	0	0	0
No. of Cand.	*0*	*0*	*0*	*0*
House	0	0	0	0
Senate	0	0	0	0
Incumbents	2,250	4,500	750	7,500
Challengers	0	250	0	250
Open Seat	0	1,300	0	1,300
Winners	2,250	4,750	n/a	7,000
Losers	0	1,300	n/a	1,300

National Electrical Contractors Association

*Phone: (301) 215-4522 * Fax: (301) 215-4500*
Three Bethesda Metro Center, Suite 1100, Bethesda, MD 20814
*Web: www.necanet.org * E-mail: rlw@necanet.org*

The National Electrical Contractors Association represents more than 4,000 electrical contractors from 118 U.S. and foreign chapters. Its members employ unionized electrical workers in the construction industry. NECA contractors work on interior wiring and outside utility lines.

The group tracks legislative issues relating to organized labor and workplace regulation. It opposes the repeal of the Davis-Bacon Act, arguing instead for reforms that protect large federal construction projects from wage-cutting practices. It seeks a clearer definition of independent contractors and reform of the Occupational Safety and Health Administration. NECA advocates protections for small businesses under utility deregulation. It contributes to "pro-business, pro-construction industry" candidates.

NECA favored Republican candidates during the 1995-96 election cycle. Just two of the 145 recipients of this PAC's contributions received $5,000: Rep. Jack Quinn, R-N.Y., and Sen. Ted Stevens, R-Alaska. The top Democratic recipient was Rep. Collin Peterson, D-Minn.

Electrical Construction PAC- National Electrical Contractors Association Inc. (ECPAC) (C00113811) *Address: same as sponsor * Treasurer: J. Michael Thompson * Contact: Robert L. White, Gov. Affairs Dir.*

	1993-94	1995-96	1997	Totals
Receipts	$254,305	$330,501	$199,630	$784,436
Disburse	262,247	324,709	83,935	670,891
Cash	371	6,161	120,857	n/a
Contributions	185,500	220,200	24,000	429,700
Republicans	175,500	201,700	23,500	400,700
No. of Cand.	*112*	*135*	*40*	*287*
House	86,500	125,500	17,500	229,500
Senate	89,000	76,200	6,000	171,200
Democrats	10,000	18,500	1,500	30,000
No. of Cand.	*10*	*14*	*2*	*26*
House	9,000	16,000	1,500	26,500
Senate	1,000	2,500	0	3,500
Incumbents	97,500	152,500	27,000	277,000
Challengers	32,000	24,200	-1000	55,200
Open Seat	56,000	41,500	0	97,500
Winners	159,500	170,500	n/a	330,000
Losers	26,000	49,700	n/a	75,700

National Roofing Contractors Association

*Phone: (202) 546-7584 * Fax: (202) 546-9289*
324 Fourth St. N.E., Washington, DC 20002

The National Roofing Contractors Association represents roofers, roof, deck and waterproofing contractors and industry-related associates in the United States, with affiliates in Europe, South America and the Caribbean. The group works to lessen federal regulations on roof contractors, educate the industry on waste management and recycling, address the shortage of workers in the industry and provide relief for natural disasters.

RoofPAC is administered by an advisory committee. Its funding sources include member donations, annual golf and tennis tournaments and auctions.

National Roofing Contractors Association RoofPAC (C00244863)
*Address: same as sponsor * Treasurer: Craig S. Brightup*

	1993-94	1995-96	1997	Totals
Receipts	$65,019	$164,017	$55,106	$284,142
Disburse	62,654	157,000	46,600	266,254
Cash	5,426	12,444	20,950	n/a
Contributions	62,400	129,000	39,500	230,900
Republicans	58,400	127,500	39,500	225,400
No. of Cand.	*70*	*134*	*40*	*244*
House	34,150	81,750	22,500	138,400
Senate	24,250	45,750	17,000	87,000
Democrats	4,000	1,500	0	5,500
No. of Cand.	*5*	*3*	*0*	*8*
House	2,000	1,500	0	3,500
Senate	2,000	0	0	2,000
Incumbents	38,250	85,750	33,500	157,500
Challengers	10,300	10,000	500	20,800
Open Seat	13,850	32,750	5,000	51,600
Winners	54,800	97,250	n/a	152,050
Losers	7,600	31,750	n/a	39,350

Sheet Metal and Air Conditioning Contractors National Association

Phone: (703) 803-2980

4201 Lafayette Center Dr., Chantilly, VA 22021

Web: www.smacna.org

The Sheet Metal and Air Conditioning Contractors National Association represents about 2,000 members located throughout the United States, Canada, Australia, Brazil and Japan. Members include contractors in commercial, industrial and residential heating, ventilating and air conditioning, as well as those involved in architectural and industrial sheet metal manufacturing, testing and balancing.

Sheet Metal and Air Conditioning Contractors' Political Action Committee (C00013961) *Phone: (202) 547-8202 * Fax: (202) 547-8810 * 305 Fourth St. N.E., Washington, DC 20002 * E-mail: dthompson@smacna.org * Treasurer: Dana Thompson*

	1993-94	*1995-96*	*1997*	*Totals*
Receipts	$187,745	$201,682	$101,022	$490,449
Disburse	205,457	166,068	43,786	415,311
Cash	11,738	47,355	104,593	n/a
Contributions	185,490	136,800	27,675	349,965
Republicans	172,690	115,550	24,175	312,415
No. of Cand.	*75*	*73*	*12*	*160*
House	72,690	76,650	12,675	162,015
Senate	100,000	38,900	11,500	150,400
Democrats	12,800	21,250	3,500	37,550
No. of Cand.	*10*	*14*	*2*	*26*
House	12,800	12,750	3,500	29,050
Senate	0	8,500	0	8,500
Incumbents	84,490	87,300	27,675	199,465
Challengers	30,500	27,500	0	58,000
Open Seat	71,250	22,000	0	93,250
Winners	164,240	96,700	n/a	260,940
Losers	21,250	40,100	n/a	61,350

Defense

Defense Aerospace

AlliedSignal Inc.

*Phone: (973) 662-2657 * Fax: (973) 662-2674*
101 Columbia Rd., Box 2093, Morristown, NJ 07962-2497
Web: www.alliedsignal.com

AlliedSignal is a worldwide transportation, defense and manufacturing company with interests in the aerospace, automotive and chemical industries.

The public company produces brakes and engines for cars and trucks, aircraft equipment and landing systems and plastics and specialty films used in the pharmaceutical industry. It is a major parts supplier for military aircraft.

With $14.5 billion in 1997 revenues, AlliedSignal ranks among the Fortune 100 and is one of the 30 companies comprising the Dow Jones Industrial Average. AlliedSignal has more than 76,000 employees.

The company's other products include aircraft engines, anti-lock braking system components and packaging resins. In addition, AlliedSignal is the only manufacturer licensed by the Federal Aviation Administration to make an enhanced ground collision warning system for passenger aircraft. The FAA announced regulations in April 1998 requiring the systems on domestic passenger planes.

AlliedSignal Political Action Committee (C00096156) *Phone: (202) 662-2650 * 1001 Pennsylvania Ave., Suite 700, Washington, DC 20004 * Treasurer: Joseph M. McGuire*

*Contact: Ken Cole, Chairman * Phone: (973) 662-2657*

	1993-94	1995-96	1997	Totals
Receipts	$261,521	$267,279	$115,871	$644,671
Disburse	264,702	263,682	131,341	659,725
Cash	28,579	32,182	16,712	n/a
Contributions	196,530	199,700	70,000	466,230
Republicans	85,550	151,200	38,500	275,250
No. of Cand.	*89*	*142*	*50*	*281*
House	48,550	97,200	23,000	168,750
Senate	37,000	54,000	15,500	106,500
Democrats	110,480	48,500	31,500	190,480
No. of Cand.	*106*	*48*	*24*	*178*
House	70,000	33,500	9,500	113,000
Senate	40,480	15,000	22,000	77,480
Incumbents	163,530	168,700	67,000	399,230
Challengers	2,000	5,500	0	7,500
Open Seat	31,500	26,000	3,000	60,500
Winners	160,050	174,000	n/a	334,050
Losers	36,480	25,700	n/a	62,180

DynCorp

*Phone: (703) 264-8726 * Fax: (703) 715-4450*
2000 Edmund Halley Dr., Fourth Floor, Reston, VA 20191
*Web: www.dyncorp.com * E-mail: whitesd@dyncorp.com*

Headquartered in Reston, Va., DynCorp provides technology and management solutions to government and industry. With a global network of more than 17,500 employees and more than $1 billion in annual revenues, it is among the largest employee-owned high-tech companies in the country.

The company, which was founded in 1946 and became private in 1988, is ranked No. 204 on the Forbes list of top 500 private companies and has 31 federal clients.

In February 1998, DynCorp acquired FMAS Corp., a health care outcome performance measurement firm based in Maryland. It also secured a $22.7 million contract to work with the Department of State in bringing increased accuracy to the enforcement of U.S.-Mexico border-crossing procedures with computerized identification cards and other devices.

DynCorp Federal Political Action Committee (formerly known as Dynalectron Corp. Fed PAC) (C00131383) *Address: same as sponsor * Treasurer: Susan Drake White * Contact: Richard E. Stephenson, PAC Chairman*

	1993-94	1995-96	1997	Totals
Receipts	$48,854	$61,069	$40,038	$149,961
Disburse	54,900	65,843	24,600	145,343
Cash	17,863	13,092	28,531	n/a
Contributions	51,520	50,950	13,100	115,570
Republicans	18,400	41,750	11,100	71,250
No. of Cand.	*20*	*26*	*9*	*55*
House	14,900	20,750	8,100	43,750
Senate	3,500	21,000	3,000	27,500
Democrats	32,120	9,200	2,000	43,320
No. of Cand.	*22*	*8*	*4*	*34*
House	18,000	8,000	1,750	27,750
Senate	14,120	1,200	250	15,570
Incumbents	46,520	49,950	12,600	109,070
Challengers	3,500	0	0	3,500
Open Seat	1,000	1,000	500	2,500
Winners	41,900	48,950	n/a	90,850
Losers	9,620	2,000	n/a	11,620

GenCorp Inc.

*Phone: (330) 869-4494 * Fax: (330) 869-4288*
175 Ghent Rd., Fairlawn, OH 44333-3300
*Web: www.gencorp.com * E-mail: ryounts@gencorp.com*

GenCorp targeted its smart munitions and space surveillance businesses as avenues for expansion in 1998. Aerospace and defense products, sold through subsidiary Aerojet, generated 37 percent of GenCorp's $1.5 billion in 1997 sales.

The 10,000-employee publicly traded Ohio company also produces polymers, automotive materials and tennis balls.

In addition to munitions and space surveillance equipment, Aerojet produces propulsion systems for space launch vehicles, strategic and tactical missiles, intercept weapons and specialized chemicals. Aerojet has made the Stage 2 solid rocket motor for the Minuteman Intercontinental Ballistic Missile weapon system for 40 years. The Sacramento, Calif. subsidiary sells its products to the Department of Defense and NASA.

GenCorp's largest business, polymer products makes latex for paper coating, carpet backing and other applications. GenCorp purchased an 80-employee Calhoun, Ga. latex plant from The Goodyear Tire & Rubber Co. in March 1998.

A decorative and building products subsidiary makes wallpaper and coated fabrics. A vehicle sealings subsidiary outfits vehicles built by Ford, General Motors and Mercedes-Benz.

GenCorp also owns Penn Racquet Sports, which makes tennis balls and racquetballs.

U.S. manufacturing locations: Arizona, Arkansas, California, Indiana, Mississippi, Missouri, New Mexico, North Carolina, Ohio, Pennsylvania, Tennessee and Wisconsin.

GenCorp Inc. Political Action Committee (GenPAC) (C00129122) *Phone: (202) 828-6800 * Fax: (202) 828-6849 * 1025 Connecticut Ave. N.W., Suite 1107, Washington, DC 20036 * Treasurer: Christine G. Rasor Contact: Rosemary Younts, Senior V.P. of Communications * Phone: (330) 869-4494*

	1993-94	1995-96	1997	Totals
Receipts	$81,961	$74,230	$46,575	$202,766
Disburse	80,941	77,302	42,687	200,930
Cash	14,936	11,866	15,754	n/a
Contributions	79,100	73,650	40,100	192,850
Republicans	26,650	49,450	25,000	101,100
No. of Cand.	*18*	*29*	*19*	*66*
House	21,900	30,450	19,500	71,850
Senate	4,750	19,000	5,500	29,250
Democrats	52,450	24,200	15,100	91,750
No. of Cand.	*36*	*17*	*13*	*66*
House	29,950	20,200	12,100	62,250
Senate	22,500	4,000	3,000	29,500
Incumbents	79,100	70,150	39,600	188,850
Challengers	0	1,000	0	1,000
Open Seat	0	2,500	500	3,000
Winners	69,100	68,150	n/a	137,250
Losers	10,000	5,500	n/a	15,500

Lockheed Martin

*Phone: (301) 897-6000 * Fax: (301) 897-6252*
6801 Rockledge Dr., Bethesda, MD 20817
*Web: www.lmco.com * E-mail: Mona.Coan@lmco.com*

Lockheed Martin is the largest defense contractor in the United States — and plans on getting bigger. The public company plans to expand its defense electronics and systems integration operations by acquiring Northrop Grumman, but the federal government objected to the merger in early 1998.

Lockheed employs 190,000 workers and reported 1997 sales of $30 billion. It has operations in Tennessee, Florida, Texas, Maryland, California, New Mexico, New Jersey, New York and nearly a dozen other states.

The product of a merger between Lockheed and Martin Marietta Corp., the company is concentrating on obtaining contracts from the Middle East and Asia. The company's government aerospace products include the Trident II submarine-launched ballistic missile, external fuel tanks for the space shuttle and the Titan IV space launch vehicle. It also makes spacecraft for Motorola's satellite communication network.

Subsidiaries include: KAPL Inc., FORMTEK Inc., Sanders, PRICE Systems, Perry Technologies and MountainGate. Lockheed's energy systems division manages several facilities and programs for the Department of Energy. Other subsidiaries manage multi-billion-dollar government projects, low-level and high-level waste tank farms, including those at the Hanford site near Richland, Wash. and seven national and 31 government and private labs.

Lockheed Martin's PAC gave the most money of any aviation defense company to 1996 congressional campaigns and was the only such PAC to top $1 million in donations. Northrop Grumman ranked a distant second. Lockheed favored Republicans and incumbents. Another Lockheed-affiliated PAC contributed more than $100,000 to candidates during the same cycle. Among the leading recipients: Reps. Randy "Duke" Cunningham, R-Calif., Martin Frost, D-Texas, and Saxby Chambliss, R-Ga. Cunningham and Chambliss sit on House committees dealing with military and national security issues.

In 1996, Lockheed acquired most of Loral Corp., which had been the second-largest PAC contributor to 1996 congressional candidates among defense electronics companies. The Loral Systems PAC was terminated in March 1998.

The Martin Marietta PAC was terminated in January 1997, and the original Lockheed PAC has also been terminated.

Lockheed Martin Employees Political Action Committee (C00303024) *Phone: (703) 413-5996 * Fax: (703) 413-5932 * 1725 Jefferson Davis Highway, Suite 300, Arlington, VA 22202 * E-mail: ken.phelps@lmco.com * Treasurer: Kenneth D. Phelps III * Contact: Stephen E. Chaudet, V.P.*

	1993-94	1995-96	1997	Totals
Receipts	$0	$1,567,998	$547,582	$2,115,580
Disburse	0	1,222,149	611,242	1,833,391
Cash	0	345,848	282,187	n/a
Contributions	0	1,013,850	515,650	1,529,500
Republicans	0	709,850	345,400	1,055,250
No. of Cand.	*0*	*231*	*169*	*400*
House	0	514,200	278,400	792,600
Senate	0	195,650	67,000	262,650
Democrats	0	304,000	167,250	471,250
No. of Cand.	*0*	*127*	*108*	*235*
House	0	271,250	124,400	395,650
Senate	0	32,750	42,850	75,600
Incumbents	0	869,050	510,650	1,379,700
Challengers	0	44,300	3,000	47,300
Open Seat	0	100,500	1,000	101,500
Winners	0	899,950	n/a	899,950
Losers	0	113,900	n/a	113,900

Civic Action Fund - Loral Systems Group (formerly known as Goodyear Aerospace Corp. PAC) (C00205443) *Phone: (330) 796-2800 * Fax: (330) 796-9693 * 1210 Massillon Rd., Akron, OH 44315 * Treasurer: C. J. Schafer*

	1993-94	1995-96	1997	Totals
Receipts	$358,895	$236,002	$0	$594,897
Disburse	312,913	322,181	5,060	640,154
Cash	93,542	7,365	2,304	n/a
Contributions	270,759	299,600	0	570,359
Republicans	66,660	148,750	0	215,410
No. of Cand.	*57*	*100*	*0*	*157*
House	44,040	104,750	0	148,790
Senate	22,620	44,000	0	66,620
Democrats	202,099	150,850	0	352,949
No. of Cand.	*116*	*90*	*0*	*206*
House	125,400	116,000	0	241,400
Senate	76,699	34,850	0	111,549
Incumbents	239,795	292,600	0	532,395
Challengers	1,015	0	0	1,015
Open Seat	28,949	7,000	0	35,949
Winners	209,610	276,600	n/a	486,210
Losers	61,149	23,000	n/a	84,149

Lockheed Employees' Political Action Committee (C00030783) *Phone: (703) 413-5947 * Fax: (703) 413-5932 * 1725 Jefferson Davis Highway, Arlington, VA 22202 * Treasurer: Stephen E. Chaudet * Contact: David S. Osterhout, Chairman*

	1993-94	1995-96	1997	Totals
Receipts	$965,467	$184,135	$0	$1,149,602
Disburse	708,346	486,548	0	1,194,894
Cash	302,410	0	0	n/a
Contributions	592,611	59,400	0	652,011
Republicans	254,401	58,900	0	313,301
No. of Cand.	*120*	*38*	*0*	*158*
House	164,576	26,700	0	191,276
Senate	89,825	32,200	0	122,025

Democrats	337,160	500	0	337,660
No. of Cand.	*126*	*4*	*0*	*130*
House	261,610	1,500	0	263,110
Senate	75,550	-1000	0	74,550
Incumbents	519,319	59,000	0	578,319
Challengers	16,592	200	0	16,792
Open Seat	56,800	200	0	57,000
Winners	488,169	45,500	n/a	533,669
Losers	104,442	13,900	n/a	118,342

Martin Marietta Corp. Political Action Committee (C00119651)
*6801 Rockledge Dr., Bethesda, MD 20817 * Treasurer: James M. Desmond*

	1993-94	1995-96	1997	Totals
Receipts	$518,017	$121,543	$0	$639,560
Disburse	529,709	122,349	0	652,058
Cash	805	0	0	n/a
Contributions	530,310	54,000	0	584,310
Republicans	254,250	51,500	0	305,750
No. of Cand.	*158*	*59*	*0*	*217*
House	148,750	31,500	0	180,250
Senate	105,500	20,000	0	125,500
Democrats	274,560	2,500	0	277,060
No. of Cand.	*152*	*5*	*0*	*157*
House	200,300	2,500	0	202,800
Senate	74,260	0	0	74,260
Incumbents	478,560	53,000	0	531,560
Challengers	14,750	0	0	14,750
Open Seat	36,500	0	0	36,500
Winners	441,400	47,500	n/a	488,900
Losers	88,910	6,500	n/a	95,410

Northrop Grumman Corp.

*Phone: (310) 553-6262 * Fax: (310) 201-3023*
1840 Century Park E., Los Angeles, CA 90067
Web: www.northgrum.com

Northrop Grumman, headquartered in Los Angeles, is a leading defense and aerospace company. The company had 52,000 employees and sales of $8.1 billion during 1996. In July 1997, Lockheed Martin Corp. and Northrop Grumman announced an agreement to combine the companies, creating a leading technology company with revenues of about $37 billion and nearly 230,000 employees. The federal government has opposed the merger as anti-competitive.

Northrop Grumman was formed in 1994 when Northrop Corp. acquired Grumman Corp. The combined company has since purchased Vought Aircraft, a major producer of military and commercial airplanes, and the defense and electronics systems business of Westinghouse Electric Corp. In 1997, it completed a merger with Logicon Inc., a leading defense information technology company. Northrop Grumman is a prime contractor for the U.S. Air Force's B-2 stealth bomber, a long-range, heavy bomber touted for its ability to penetrate sophisticated radar defenses undetected.

Northrop Grumman ranked second among aviation defense PACs in contributions to 1996 congressional campaigns, behind Lockheed Martin. But the more than $681,000 the company gave represented a 100 percent increase from the combined total of the 1993-94 cycle.

Northrop gave incumbents 92 percent of its money during the 1995-96 election cycle. Republicans received nearly three quarters of the company's total contributions. The top recipients were Reps. Martin Frost, D-Texas, and Randy "Duke" Cunningham, R-Calif.

Vought Aircraft's PAC, which contributed less than $5,000 to congressional campaigns during the 1995-96 cycle, has been terminated.

Employees of Northrop Grumman Corp. Political Action Committee (ENGPAC) (C00088591) *Phone: (703) 875-8460 * Fax: (703) 875-8521 * 1000 Wilson Blvd., Suite 2800, Arlington, VA 22209 * Treasurer: Daralyn E. Reed*

*Contact: Robert W. Helm, V.P. of Gov. Relations * Phone: (310) 553-6262*

	1993-94	1995-96	1997	Totals
Receipts	$493,395	$766,618	$306,949	$1,566,962
Disburse	422,969	794,880	344,263	1,562,112
Cash	77,898	49,647	12,341	n/a
Contributions	335,439	681,675	278,575	1,295,689
Republicans	147,499	492,325	178,225	818,049
No. of Cand.	*82*	*203*	*136*	*421*
House	64,600	370,350	141,000	575,950
Senate	82,899	121,975	37,225	242,099
Democrats	187,440	189,350	100,350	477,140
No. of Cand.	*79*	*88*	*66*	*233*
House	118,322	161,500	77,750	357,572
Senate	69,118	27,850	22,600	119,568
Incumbents	307,790	622,275	275,075	1,205,140
Challengers	6,500	6,875	2,000	15,375
Open Seat	21,149	47,025	500	68,674
Winners	305,197	603,100	n/a	908,297
Losers	30,242	78,575	n/a	108,817

Terminated PACs which contributed less than $5,000 during 1995-96 cycle:

Vought Aircraft Co. Political Action Committee (C00277517)
*9314 W. Jefferson Blvd., M/S 49L-09, Dallas, TX 75211 * Treasurer: H.F. "Pat" Johnson*

Rockwell International Corp.

*Phone: (714) 424-4200 * Fax: (714) 424-4251*
600 Anton Blvd., Suite 700, Costa Mesa, CA 92626-7147
Web: www.rockwell.com

Rockwell International, a former defense giant, is a leading automation and electronics company. It is the top supplier of automation products in North America and produces flight control and management systems under the Collins brand name.

The company's systems are used for about 70 percent of all U.S. military airborne communications. A public company, Rockwell also makes semiconductors for telephones, modems and other devices.

Rockwell, which has corporate offices in Pittsburgh and its world headquarters in Costa Mesa, Calif., has annual revenues of about $7.7 billion and about 45,000 employees. Rockwell sold its aerospace and defense businesses to Boeing in December 1996 and spun off its automotive unit as Meritor Automotive Inc.

The company lobbies on international trade issues, the Superfund program and product liability reform.

Rockwell terminated its PAC after selling its defense and aerospace units. In January 1997, the company created another PAC (FEC ID: C00324996), which had collected about $24,000 by the end of 1997.

The former PAC ranked fourth among aviation defense contributors to 1996 congressional races. It tended to favor Republicans and incumbents. The top recipients were Sen. James M. Inhofe, R-Okla., Rep. Jerry Lewis, R-Calif., and Sen. Ted Stevens, R-Alaska.

Rockwell International Corp. Good Government Committee (also known as Rockwell Good Government Committee) (C00038471)
*Phone: (703) 412-6900 * Fax: (703) 412-6811 * 1745 Jefferson Davis Highway, Arlington, VA 22202-3402 * E-mail: rgarcia@corp.rockwell.com * Treasurer: W. E. Sanders * Contact: Ray Garcia, V.P. of Public Policy & Gov. Affairs*

	1993-94	1995-96	1997	Totals
Receipts	$348,026	$306,125	$0	$654,151
Disburse	317,421	356,755	6,130	680,306
Cash	56,760	6,130	0	n/a
Contributions	282,969	321,700	0	604,669
Republicans	128,149	237,750	0	365,899
No. of Cand.	*95*	*131*	*0*	*226*
House	73,250	168,250	0	241,500
Senate	54,899	69,500	0	124,399
Democrats	154,820	83,950	0	238,770
No. of Cand.	*97*	*56*	*0*	*153*
House	124,300	72,850	0	197,150
Senate	30,520	11,100	0	41,620
Incumbents	251,070	293,900	0	544,970
Challengers	8,000	8,500	0	16,500
Open Seat	23,399	19,300	0	42,699
Winners	240,649	292,200	n/a	532,849
Losers	42,320	29,500	n/a	71,820

Contributed less than $5,000 during 1995-96 cycle:

Rockwell International Corp. Good Government Committee (C00324996) *Phone: (412) 565-7202 * 625 Liberty Ave., Pittsburgh, PA 15222-3123 * Treasurer: George W. Pritts Jr.*

Textron Inc.

*Phone: (401) 421-2800 * Fax: (401) 457-3598*
P.O. Box 878, Providence, RI 02901
Web: www.textron.com

Textron is a major producer of helicopters, airplanes and automotive parts. A Fortune 500 member with 1997 revenues of $10.5 billion, the public company has its headquarters in Providence, R.I. It employs about 57,000 people and has operations in 13 states.

Subsidiary Bell Helicopter is the world's leading maker of commercial and military helicopters. In early 1998, it purchased most of Boeing's helicopter division. Another subsidiary, Cessna Aircraft, has produced nearly half of the general aviation airplanes in the world. Textron also builds golf carts and plastic parts for cars and provides financial services.

The company has a wide range of lobbying interests, including aviation and automotive issues. It is developing the Bell Boeing V-22 Osprey tiltrotor aircraft for the U.S. Marine Corps and U.S. Navy and upgrading 280 Marine helicopters to increase the speed and range of the aircraft.

Textron ranked fifth among aviation defense contractor PACs in 1995-96 election cycle congressional contributions. It was one of 13 PACs that contributed at least 90 percent of their contributions to winning candidates. Textron favored Republicans and spent nothing on challengers.

Seven candidates received $10,000 from this PAC; three were from Texas, where Bell Helicopter has its headquarters. Rep. John P. Murtha, R-Pa., and Sen. Ted Stevens, R-Alaska, also were among the leading recipients. Both sit on defense-related panels.

Textron Inc. Political Action Committee (C00123612) *Phone: (202) 637-3821 * Fax: (202) 637-3860 * 1101 Pennsylvania Ave. N.W., Suite 400, Washington, DC 20004 * Treasurer: William P. Janovitz * Contact: Gordon Thomas, Gov. Affairs Dir.*

	1993-94	1995-96	1997	Totals
Receipts	$420,277	$356,609	$150,030	$926,916
Disburse	420,393	361,886	154,050	936,329
Cash	24,369	19,094	15,076	n/a
Contributions	356,810	295,800	128,050	780,660
Republicans	121,150	189,300	87,300	397,750
No. of Cand.	*56*	*80*	*51*	*187*
House	63,650	114,300	73,300	251,250
Senate	57,500	75,000	14,000	146,500
Democrats	232,160	106,500	40,250	378,910
No. of Cand.	*96*	*53*	*26*	*175*
House	183,000	95,250	36,750	315,000
Senate	49,160	11,250	3,500	63,910
Incumbents	328,310	276,800	126,550	731,660
Challengers	0	0	0	0
Open Seat	28,500	18,500	1,500	48,500
Winners	294,450	269,300	n/a	563,750
Losers	62,360	26,500	n/a	88,860

Thiokol Corp.

*Phone: (801) 629-2270 * Fax: (801) 629-2420*
2475 Washington Blvd., P.O. Box 9260, Ogden, UT 84409
Web: www.thiokol.com

Thiokol, a Utah-based company, manufactures solid rocket propulsion systems, gas generators and actuators. The firm provides services for the aerospace and defense markets and specialty fastening systems for aerospace and industrial applications. The publicly traded company reported sales of $890 million in 1997, with $606 million coming from the propulsion group. The company employs 5,300 people.

Thiokol is the sole manufacturer of the reusable solid rocket boosters used on NASA's space shuttle. Its propulsion systems are also used for the Trident II missile system and commercial launch vehicles. Thiokol's Huck International subsidiary makes specialty fasteners and other parts for the transportation and construction industries. Thiokol has a 62 percent interest in Howmet Corp., which makes castings for aircraft turbine engines.

Thiokol Political Action Committee (C00143206) *Address: same as sponsor * Treasurer: Michael R. Ayers * Contact: Gil Barley, Chairperson*

	1993-94	1995-96	1997	Totals
Receipts	$65,742	$55,028	$21,829	$142,599
Disburse	72,147	56,433	17,897	146,477
Cash	11,027	9,625	13,559	n/a
Contributions	71,120	53,800	17,850	142,770
Republicans	35,250	36,200	13,250	84,700
No. of Cand.	*33*	*41*	*15*	*89*
House	20,750	25,200	9,250	55,200
Senate	14,500	11,000	4,000	29,500
Democrats	35,870	17,600	4,600	58,070
No. of Cand.	*37*	*19*	*8*	*64*
House	30,600	14,750	3,000	48,350
Senate	5,270	2,850	1,600	9,720
Incumbents	67,770	50,550	17,600	135,920
Challengers	250	1,000	0	1,250
Open Seat	3,100	2,250	250	5,600
Winners	64,650	47,050	n/a	111,700
Losers	6,470	6,750	n/a	13,220

United Technologies Corp.

*Phone: (860) 728-7000 * Fax: (860) 728-7979*
One Financial Plaza, Hartford, CT 06101
Web: www.utc.com

United Technologies is a $24.7 billion public corporation involved in the aerospace, construction and automotive industries worldwide. UTC's best known products include Pratt & Whitney aircraft engines, Otis elevators and escalators, Carrier heating and air conditioning systems, Sikorsky helicopters, Hamilton Standard aerospace systems and UT Automotive components and systems.

The corporation also supplies equipment and services to the United States space program. UTC employs 173,800 workers, including 104,000 outside the United States. Pratt & Whitney and flight systems make up 37 percent of UTC's business. The remaining portion is split among Otis, Carrier and UT Automotive operations. The company has its headquarters in Hartford, Conn., and has significant operations in Florida and Michigan.

As a major government contractor, UT has several lobbying interests. The company supports "fast-track" authority on trade agreements. Pratt & Whitney is actively involved in building new engines for Air Force planes and missiles. UT's automotive group built the electrical distribution system for a new electric truck.

UT ranked sixth among aviation defense companies in congressional contributions during the 1995-96 election cycle. Ninety percent of its contributions went to incumbent candidates, mostly Republicans. It was one of 13 PACs in the top 200 that gave more than 90 percent of its money to winning candidates. The leading recipients were Rep. Nancy Johnson, R-Conn., Sen. Ted Stevens, R-Alaska, Sen. Mitch McConnell, R-Ky, Rep. Robert Livingston, R-La., and Sen. Fred Thompson, R-Tenn. The top Democratic recipient was Rep. Sam Gejdenson, D-Conn.

United Technologies Corp. Political Action Committee (C00035683) *Phone: (202) 336-7425 * Fax: (202) 336-7515 * 1401 Eye St. N.W., Suite 600, Washington, DC 20005 * Treasurer: John Humphries * Contact: Wade Robert, Chairman*

	1993-94	1995-96	1997	Totals
Receipts	$252,427	$483,087	$165,072	$900,586
Disburse	263,300	450,078	152,880	866,258
Cash	8,317	12,815	25,013	n/a
Contributions	218,252	266,874	125,600	610,726
Republicans	82,700	186,674	76,600	345,974
No. of Cand.	*75*	*88*	*60*	*223*
House	49,400	105,174	40,350	194,924
Senate	33,300	81,500	36,250	151,050
Democrats	135,552	80,200	49,000	264,752
No. of Cand.	*78*	*39*	*28*	*145*
House	98,100	59,700	36,500	194,300
Senate	37,452	20,500	12,500	70,452
Incumbents	188,952	239,874	125,100	553,926
Challengers	1,750	13,500	0	15,250
Open Seat	24,300	13,500	500	38,300
Winners	175,700	243,224	n/a	418,924
Losers	42,552	23,650	n/a	66,202

Defense Electronics

AEL Industries Inc.

305 Richardson Rd., Lansdale, PA 19446

AEL Industries PAC was terminated in June 1997.

AEL Industries Inc. Political Action Committee (AEL PAC) (C00184549) *Address: same as sponsor * Treasurer: Jesse H. Riebman*

	1993-94	1995-96	1997	Totals
Receipts	$27,204	$20,906	$0	$48,110
Disburse	21,560	30,486	0	52,046
Cash	9,578	0	0	n/a
Contributions	20,850	23,500	0	44,350
Republicans	4,250	13,250	0	17,500
No. of Cand.	*4*	*8*	*0*	*12*
House	4,000	11,250	0	15,250
Senate	250	2,000	0	2,250
Democrats	16,600	10,250	0	26,850
No. of Cand.	*13*	*7*	*0*	*20*
House	15,600	7,250	0	22,850
Senate	1,000	3,000	0	4,000
Incumbents	20,350	20,500	0	40,850
Challengers	500	0	0	500
Open Seat	0	3,000	0	3,000
Winners	18,350	23,500	n/a	41,850
Losers	2,500	0	n/a	2,500

American Systems Corp.

*Phone: (703) 968-6300 * Fax: (703) 968-5151*
14200 Park Meadow Dr., Chantilly, VA 20151-2219
*Web: www.ascacc.com * E-mail: john.baker@ascacc.com*

American Systems provides systems engineering, systems and network integration, cable plant installation and related services to clients in government, defense, telecommunications, health care and commercial markets. It also provides training devices and simulation systems and technical and specialized information services to the defense and intelligence community. A private company, American Systems has 700 employees and estimated annual revenues of $69 million.

Established in 1975, American Systems is headquartered in Chantilly, Va. with locations in Newport, R.I.; Palm Coast, Fla.; Arlington, Va.; Groton, Ct.; Norfolk, Va.; Philadelphia; Dahlgren, Va.; Charleston, S.C.; Orlando, Fla.; Kingsland, Ga.; San Diego; and Bremerton, Wash.

American Systems Corp. Political Action Committee (ASC-PAC) (C00215590) *Address: same as sponsor * Treasurer: Jack Baker * Contact: Elliot Needleman, President*

	1993-94	1995-96	1997	Totals
Receipts	$14,115	$11,122	$3,772	$29,009
Disburse	8,749	16,166	15,010	39,925
Cash	54,962	49,920	38,683	n/a
Contributions	7,200	10,300	5,500	23,000
Republicans	4,600	11,050	4,500	20,150
No. of Cand.	*4*	*8*	*4*	*16*
House	4,000	9,550	4,000	17,550
Senate	600	1,500	500	2,600
Democrats	2,600	-750	1,000	2,850
No. of Cand.	*3*	*2*	*1*	*6*
House	2,600	250	1,000	3,850
Senate	0	-1000	0	-1000
Incumbents	5,600	11,800	5,500	22,900
Challengers	1,600	-1000	0	600
Open Seat	0	0	0	0
Winners	6,300	11,800	n/a	18,100
Losers	900	-1500	n/a	-600

Cubic Corp.

*Phone: (619) 277-6780 * Fax: (619) 277-1878*
9333 Balboa Ave., San Diego, CA 92123
Web: www.cubic.com

Cubic makes combat training systems that simulate live military action for field exercises. It also produces instruments and surveillance equipment for sale to the Department of Defense. About 52 percent of Cubic's revenues come from defense products, although defense generates only 33 percent of the company's operating profit. The other half of Cubic's revenues comes from its devices for mass transit fare collection, which are used in New York, Washington, Chicago and London.

A publicly traded company, Cubic reported sales of $388 million in 1997.

A subsidiary, Cubic VideoComm Inc., has produced a program that enables computer users to attach video clips to electronic mail messages. The software is an outgrowth of technology for high-speed data compression that Cubic originally developed for its defense-related business.

U.S. locations: California, Florida, Kansas, New Jersey, New York, Tennessee, Virginia and Washington state.

Subsidiaries include: Cubic Applications, Cubic Transportation Systems, Cubic Communications, Cubic Defense Systems, Cubic VideoComm and Cubic Worldwide Technical Services.

Cubic Corp. Employees' Political Action Committee (C00151787) *Phone: (703) 415-1600 * Fax: (703) 415-1608 * Crystal Gateway One, Suite 1102, 1235 Jefferson Davis Hwy., Arlington, VA 22202 * Treasurer: Victor R. Pitcock * Contact: Jack Liddle, Congressional Liaison*

	1993-94	1995-96	1997	Totals
Receipts	$23,371	$31,945	$33,729	$89,045
Disburse	50,844	29,892	30,883	111,619
Cash	11,451	13,518	16,370	n/a
Contributions	43,750	26,000	22,600	92,350
Republicans	31,750	25,500	18,100	75,350
No. of Cand.	*15*	*13*	*13*	*41*
House	29,750	14,250	8,850	52,850
Senate	2,000	11,250	9,250	22,500
Democrats	12,000	500	4,500	17,000
No. of Cand.	*7*	*1*	*3*	*11*
House	10,500	500	3,500	14,500
Senate	1,500	0	1,000	2,500
Incumbents	35,250	24,750	22,600	82,600
Challengers	6,000	500	0	6,500
Open Seat	500	0	0	500
Winners	33,750	24,750	n/a	58,500
Losers	10,000	1,250	n/a	11,250

DRS Technologies

*Phone: (973) 898-1500 * Fax: (973) 898-4730*
5 Sylvan Way, Parsippany, NJ 07054
Web: www.drs.com

DRS Technologies, formerly known as Diagnostic/Retrieval Systems, primarily builds electronic systems that process, display and store data for military applications. Major products include combat display systems, flight data recorders and navigation-related equipment. The publicly traded Parsippany, N.J. company does 82 percent of its business with governments. DRS reported revenues of $143 million for fiscal year 1997.

Notable contracts include a $14.2 million order from the U.S. Navy to build ship radar systems, a $2.7 million contract with China for helicopter flight data recorders and a $2 million order to manufacture cable and wire harnesses for the U.S. Army's new Bradley M2A3 Infantry Fighting Vehicle. Lockheed Martin also recently ordered $64 million worth of tactical workstations for use by the U.S. Navy.

The company also has a commercial product line that includes magnetic heads used in products such as computer disk drives and videocassette recorders. DRS's commercial and industrial products are used mainly by the airline, banking, computer disk drive, security, transportation, retail sales and broadcast industries.

DRS has U.S. operations in: California, Florida, Illinois, Maryland, Minnesota, New Jersey, Pennsylvania, Virginia and Wisconsin.

DRS Technologies Good Government Fund (formerly known as Diagnostic/Retrieval Systems Inc. Good Government Fund) (C00275123) *Phone: (202) 337-3371 * Fax: (202) 337-0240 * 2600 Virginia Ave. N.W., Suite 210, Washington, DC 20037 * E-mail: coronadogp@aol.com * Treasurer: Cynthia L. Martin*

	1993-94	1995-96	1997	Totals
Receipts	$60,333	$65,910	$33,558	$159,801
Disburse	42,756	78,673	28,784	150,213
Cash	17,676	4,911	9,686	n/a
Contributions	37,700	64,250	23,150	125,100
Republicans	6,000	35,300	13,150	54,450
No. of Cand.	*6*	*18*	*10*	*34*
House	6,000	31,050	11,150	48,200
Senate	0	4,250	2,000	6,250
Democrats	31,700	28,950	10,000	70,650
No. of Cand.	*17*	*15*	*8*	*40*
House	20,700	15,750	9,000	45,450
Senate	11,000	13,200	1,000	25,200
Incumbents	37,200	54,300	23,150	114,650
Challengers	0	200	0	200
Open Seat	500	9,750	0	10,250
Winners	32,700	58,300	n/a	91,000
Losers	5,000	5,950	n/a	10,950

ESCO Electronics Corp.

*Phone: (314) 213-7200 * Fax: (314) 213-7250*
8888 Ladue Rd., Suite 200, St. Louis, MO 63124-2090
*Web: www.obatadesign.com/esco * E-mail: mmainer@seistl.com*

ESCO Electronics, a publicly traded holding company, has subsidiaries engaged in the research, development, manufacture, sale and support of a wide variety of defense and commercial systems. Products include: aircraft cargo loaders, weapons systems, tactical wheeled vehicles, naval gun mounts, microwave antennas and radar and electronic warfare systems.

The company, which was spun off from Emerson Electric in 1990, makes most of its money from the U.S. government, including the Army, Navy and Air Force. However, the military has cut back on its purchases from ESCO in the last few years. ESCO also sells defense products to foreign companies.

ESCO reported $378 million in 1997 sales and employs 3,400 people. Its main sales office is in Washington.

ESCO Electronics Corp. Political Action Committee (C00253609)
*Phone: (703) 416-7600 * Fax: (703) 416-7606 * 1235 Jefferson Davis Highway, Suite 305, Arlington, VA 22202 * Treasurer: Donald Nonnenkamp * Contact: Matt Hey, Manager of Legislative Affairs*
*Contact: Matt Mainer, Assistant Treasurer * Phone: (314) 213-7200*

	1993-94	1995-96	1997	Totals
Receipts	$40,718	$36,550	$35,572	$112,840
Disburse	32,032	31,832	17,230	81,094
Cash	10,647	15,364	33,706	n/a
Contributions	31,600	23,450	19,750	74,800
Republicans	12,500	20,450	17,250	50,200
No. of Cand.	*7*	*22*	*8*	*37*
House	5,500	14,700	8,500	28,700
Senate	7,000	5,750	8,750	21,500
Democrats	19,100	3,000	2,500	24,600
No. of Cand.	*19*	*5*	*3*	*27*
House	17,850	3,000	2,500	23,350
Senate	1,250	0	0	1,250
Incumbents	22,000	18,950	19,750	60,700
Challengers	100	1,000	0	1,100
Open Seat	9,500	3,500	0	13,000
Winners	27,500	19,450	n/a	46,950
Losers	4,100	4,000	n/a	8,100

FEL Corp.

Phone: (732) 919-2400
One Central Ave., Farmingdale, NJ 07727
E-mail: felbus@felcorp.com

FEL is a 35-year-old privately owned defense contractor that develops and manufactures radar and countermeasures electronics primarily for the U.S. Navy. FEL is based in Farmingdale, N.J., with a sales office in Arlington, Va. It has 200 employees.

FEL Corp. Political Action Committee (FELPAC) (C00287300)
*Address: same as sponsor * Treasurer: Stacey E. Petitt*

	1993-94	1995-96	1997	Totals
Receipts	$6,554	$10,732	$5,572	$22,858
Disburse	4,792	10,698	4,098	19,588
Cash	1,763	1,857	3,371	n/a
Contributions	4,750	10,193	4,000	18,943
Republicans	500	7,693	4,000	12,193
No. of Cand.	*1*	*9*	*5*	*15*
House	500	6,000	4,000	10,500
Senate	0	1,693	0	1,693
Democrats	4,250	2,500	0	6,750
No. of Cand.	*6*	*3*	*0*	*9*
House	2,000	1,500	0	3,500
Senate	2,250	1,000	0	3,250
Incumbents	3,750	10,193	4,000	17,943
Challengers	0	0	0	0
Open Seat	1,000	0	0	1,000
Winners	3,500	10,193	n/a	13,693
Losers	1,250	0	n/a	1,250

GEC-Marconi Electronic Systems Corp.

*Phone: (973) 633-6300 * Fax: (973) 633-4318*
164 Totowa Rd., CN-975, Wayne, NJ 07474
Web: www.gec.com

GEC-Marconi is a defense contractor and maker of radar absorbing materials, textiles, radomes, fiber reinforced composites and radar absorbing structures. Materials with these properties give the Stealth Bomber its stealth.

The company is a subsidiary of the British electronics firm General Electric Co., one of the largest defense electronics suppliers in Europe. It has operations in Wayne, N.J., Braintree, Mass. and Greenlawn, N.Y.

GEC-Marconi Electronic Systems Corp. Political Action Committee (G-PAC) (C00245555) *Address: same as sponsor * Treasurer: William G. Douma * Contact: John Currier, President*

	1993-94	1995-96	1997	Totals
Receipts	$31,859	$36,416	$19,003	$87,278
Disburse	25,000	22,550	10,800	58,350
Cash	34,073	47,955	56,164	n/a
Contributions	24,000	22,550	10,800	57,350
Republicans	8,000	19,050	8,000	35,050
No. of Cand.	*8*	*14*	*12*	*34*
House	4,000	13,050	8,000	25,050
Senate	4,000	6,000	0	10,000
Democrats	16,000	3,500	2,800	22,300
No. of Cand.	*12*	*5*	*5*	*22*
House	11,000	3,000	2,800	16,800
Senate	5,000	500	0	5,500
Incumbents	23,500	20,550	10,800	54,850
Challengers	0	0	0	0
Open Seat	500	2,000	0	2,500
Winners	19,300	16,550	n/a	35,850
Losers	4,700	6,000	n/a	10,700

Harris Corp.

*Phone: (407) 727-9100 * Fax: (407) 727-9636*
1205 W. Nasa Blvd., Melbourne, FL 32919
*Web: www.harris.com * E-mail: glane01@harris.com*

Harris is a worldwide company focused on four core businesses: communications, semiconductors, office equipment and advanced electronic systems. In 1997, the publicly traded company had sales of more than $3.7 billion. It employs 29,000 people.

The U.S. government accounts for more than 20 percent of the company's sales. In 1998, the company, along with Motorola Inc., won a contract to provide the FBI with 500 secure radios.

Products include air traffic control systems, energy management systems, radiation-hardened circuits for the military, mobile radio networks, Lanier color digital copiers, integrated circuits, two-way pagers and newspaper publishing software and information systems.

Harris Corp. Federal Political Action Committee (C00100321)
*Address: same as sponsor * Treasurer: George E. Lane * Contact: Phillip W. Farmer, Chairman*

	1993-94	1995-96	1997	Totals
Receipts	$233,523	$201,715	$97,363	$532,601
Disburse	222,293	201,415	35,205	458,913
Cash	87,768	88,068	150,225	n/a
Contributions	182,500	156,133	8,650	347,283
Republicans	181,000	155,633	8,750	345,383
No. of Cand.	*95*	*46*	*12*	*153*
House	85,000	119,533	7,750	212,283
Senate	96,000	36,100	1,000	133,100
Democrats	1,500	500	-100	1,900
No. of Cand.	*3*	*1*	*1*	*5*
House	1,500	500	0	2,000
Senate	0	0	-100	-100
Incumbents	70,500	102,433	8,750	181,683
Challengers	21,500	19,700	0	41,200
Open Seat	91,000	34,000	0	125,000
Winners	171,000	107,433	n/a	278,433
Losers	11,500	48,700	n/a	60,200

ITT Industries

Phone: (914) 641-2000
4 W. Red Oak Ln., White Plains, NY 10604
Web: www.ittind.com

A supplier of defense-related electronics and services to the U.S. government, ITT Industries also has businesses in automotive and fluid technology products. The publicly traded White Plains, N.Y., company has 60,000 employees and had $8.7 billion in 1997 sales, about half of which came from outside the United States.

ITT's PAC was formerly known as the Corporate Citizenship Committee (ITT).

The company's ITT Defense & Electronics subsidiary, headquartered in McLean, Va., does major business in the tactical communication, operations and maintenance and connectors markets. Smaller businesses include night vision, radar and space. In 1996, the subsidiary was awarded 100 percent of the U.S. Army's contracts for night vision goggles. The subsidiary says it is the world's largest manufacturer of frequency-hopping combat net radio systems and one of the largest U.S.-based technical and support services contractors in the world.

Customers include the departments of Defense, Labor and State and NASA. About 65 percent of the subsidiary's business is with governments — and almost all of that is with the U.S. government. The subsidiary, which posts about $1.5 billion in sales and has 13,000 employees, also has operations in Europe, the Middle East and Asia.

ITT's largest subsidiary, ITT Automotive, accounts for about 60 percent of the company's overall sales. Headquartered in Auburn Hills, Mich., the company is the world's second largest producer of anti-lock braking systems and traction control systems. ITT Automotive also makes shocks, fluid handling systems and components for chassis and electrical systems. Sales to General Motors and Ford accounted for about 40 percent of the subsidiary's revenue.

A third subsidiary, ITT Fluid Technology, calls itself the world's leading pump manufacturer. Headquartered in Midland Park, N.J., the subsidiary's business units include: Goulds Pumps, ITT Aerospace Controls, ITT Bell & Gossett and ITT Richter Chemie-Technik.

ITT Industries PAC (C00141002) *Phone: (202) 842-9830 * Fax: (202) 842-9838 * 1650 Tysons Blvd., Suite 1700, McLean, VA 22102 * E-mail: wooleyiin@aol.com * Treasurer: Charles Wurst * Contact: Linda Wooley, Dir. of Public Affairs*

	1993-94	1995-96	1997	Totals
Receipts	$86,038	$79,765	$22,309	$188,112
Disburse	56,408	78,913	11,769	147,090
Cash	38,551	39,414	49,960	n/a
Contributions	56,000	40,250	10,700	106,950
Republicans	24,500	29,750	6,200	60,450
No. of Cand.	*37*	*29*	*12*	*78*
House	13,500	17,750	6,200	37,450
Senate	11,000	12,000	0	23,000
Democrats	31,500	10,500	4,500	46,500
No. of Cand.	*44*	*10*	*6*	*60*
House	22,000	5,000	1,500	28,500
Senate	9,500	5,500	3,000	18,000
Incumbents	52,000	34,750	10,700	97,450
Challengers	0	1,500	0	1,500
Open Seat	4,000	4,000	0	8,000
Winners	47,000	34,750	n/a	81,750
Losers	9,000	5,500	n/a	14,500

Kaman Corp.

*Phone: (860) 243-6307 * Fax: (860) 243-6365*
1332 Blue Hills Ave., P.O. Box 1, Bloomfield, CT 06002
*Web: www.kaman.com * E-mail: rhj-corp@kaman.com*

Kaman serves government and commercial markets with industrial products, aircraft manufacturing and design, music products and manufacture of advanced technology products and systems. A publicly traded company, Kaman employs about 5,400 people and reported 1996 sales of $953.7 million.

Kaman's products include helicopters for military units in the United States, Australia, New Zealand and Egypt. The company also supplies parts for all Boeing aircraft.

In 1997, Kaman sold two of its divisions. ITT Industries bought Kaman Sciences Corp. for $135 million. Trace Elliott Limited, Kaman Music's amplifier manufacturing business, was purchased by three members of the Trace Elliott management team for an undisclosed amount.

Kaman, headquartered in Bloomfield, Conn., supplies its industrial manufacturing equipment through 175 locations in 35 states and Canada. Its musical production business accounts for more than 60 percent of the company's revenues.

Kaman Corp. Good Government Fund (C00126847) *Phone: (703) 416-2500 * 1111 Jefferson Davis Highway, Suite 700, Arlington, VA 22202 * Treasurer: Russell H. Jones*

	1993-94	1995-96	1997	Totals
Receipts	$39,835	$33,645	$17,475	$90,955
Disburse	32,075	34,500	17,500	84,075
Cash	7,763	6,908	6,883	n/a
Contributions	22,635	27,000	11,500	61,135
Republicans	10,425	19,500	8,500	38,425
No. of Cand.	*9*	*14*	*11*	*34*
House	9,425	17,500	7,500	34,425
Senate	1,000	2,000	1,000	4,000
Democrats	12,210	7,500	3,000	22,710
No. of Cand.	*13*	*12*	*4*	*29*
House	7,600	5,000	3,000	15,600
Senate	4,610	2,500	0	7,110
Incumbents	21,135	25,500	11,500	58,135
Challengers	1,000	500	0	1,500
Open Seat	500	1,000	0	1,500
Winners	19,775	25,000	n/a	44,775
Losers	2,860	2,000	n/a	4,860

Litton Industries Inc.

*Phone: (818) 598-5000 * Fax: (818) 598-3366*
21240 Burbank Blvd., Woodland Hills, CA 91367-6675
Web: www.littoncorp.com

Litton Industries is an international company operating in the commercial electronics, defense, shipbuilding and information technology industries.

Litton Industries, a publicly held company, had 1997 sales of $4.2 billion, with net earnings of $162 million. The company has operations in the United States, Canada, Germany and Italy.

Founded in 1953 as a small electronics company, it now has 31,500 employees. The company specializes in navigation, guidance and control systems, as well as electronic warfare systems and electronic components and materials. The company also is a major designer and builder of large, surface-combatant ships for the U.S. Navy and a major provider of overhaul, repair, ship design and engineering services.

Subsidiaries include Ingall's Shipbuilding and Planning Research Corp.

Litton Industries Inc. Employees Political Assistance Committee (LEPAC) (C00035667) *Phone: (703) 413-3904 * Fax: (703) 413-7061 * 1725 Jefferson Davis Highway, Suite 601, Arlington, VA 22202 * Treasurer: Nancy Gaymon*

*Contact: Timothy Paulson, Chairman * Phone: (818) 598-5000*

	1993-94	1995-96	1997	Totals
Receipts	$117,412	$139,342	$43,261	$300,015
Disburse	123,913	137,914	34,932	296,759
Cash	19,796	21,233	29,565	n/a
Contributions	113,200	126,299	29,600	269,099
Republicans	60,500	96,799	22,350	179,649
No. of Cand.	*43*	*59*	*25*	*127*
House	30,900	68,799	18,350	118,049
Senate	29,600	28,000	4,000	61,600
Democrats	52,700	29,500	7,250	89,450
No. of Cand.	*40*	*20*	*11*	*71*
House	40,080	28,000	6,250	74,330
Senate	12,620	1,500	1,000	15,120
Incumbents	107,050	109,049	29,600	245,699
Challengers	650	2,500	0	3,150
Open Seat	5,500	14,750	0	20,250
Winners	101,930	108,049	n/a	209,979
Losers	11,270	18,250	n/a	29,520

PRC Inc. Political Action Committee (C00216853) *Phone: (703) 556-1000 * Fax: (703) 556-1174 * c/o Caroline Cho, 1500 PRC Dr., Mailstop 4E6, McLean, VA 22102-5050 * Web: www.prc.com * E-mail: becka_john@prc.com * Treasurer: Clive Blackwell * Contact: John Becka, Senior V.P.*

Planning Research, a subsidiary of Litton Industries, provides information systems and services to government and commercial clients. PRC holds hundreds of contracts with U.S. governmental agencies, such as the departments of Defense and Justice and the National Weather Service. PRC reported 1997 net revenue of $712 million and employs 5,800 people.

PRC computer systems support warning systems for the U.S. Air Force, aid 911 dispatchers, aid forecasters at the National Weather

Service and have helped the FBI to create an automatic fingerprint identification system.

PRC headquarters are in McLean, Va., just outside Washington.

	1993-94	1995-96	1997	Totals
Receipts	$50,534	$43,158	$18,388	$112,080
Disburse	67,138	48,432	12,250	127,820
Cash	9,732	4,460	10,599	n/a
Contributions	56,200	32,833	9,250	98,283
Republicans	21,700	30,833	6,000	58,533
No. of Cand.	*15*	*16*	*3*	*34*
House	16,950	17,850	6,000	40,800
Senate	4,750	12,983	0	17,733
Democrats	34,500	2,000	1,500	38,000
No. of Cand.	*29*	*2*	*2*	*33*
House	25,000	1,000	500	26,500
Senate	9,500	1,000	1,000	11,500
Incumbents	41,700	28,333	9,250	79,283
Challengers	7,500	3,500	0	11,000
Open Seat	7,000	1,000	0	8,000
Winners	48,700	22,983	n/a	71,683
Losers	7,500	9,850	n/a	17,350

Nichols Research Corp.

*Phone: (205) 883-1140 * Fax: (205) 880-0367*
4040 Memorial Pkwy. S., Huntsville, AL 35802
*Web: www.nichols.com * E-mail: info@nichols.com*

Nichols Research, headquartered in Huntsville, Ala., provides information technology and technical services for the Department of Defense, federal civilian agencies, state governments and commercial clients. Ninety percent of Nichols' sales come from government contracts.

The publicly traded company operates 28 locations in the United States and employs 2,400 workers. Sales for the 1997 fiscal year, ended in August, were $379 million. Nichols' extensive contracts with the military and government include installing computing systems at Wright-Patterson Air Force Base in Ohio and providing microprocessor and network systems for the Centers for Disease Control (CDC) in Atlanta.

Nichols was established in 1976 to perform research involving optics and sensors for military and space programs.

Nichols Research Corp. Political Action Committee (C00302174) *Address: same as sponsor * Treasurer: Allen E. Dillard * Contact: Michael J. Mruz, CEO*

	1993-94	1995-96	1997	Totals
Receipts	$0	$35,686	$24,854	$60,540
Disburse	0	9,127	7,500	16,627
Cash	0	26,259	43,614	n/a
Contributions	0	9,125	7,500	16,625
Republicans	0	7,625	7,500	15,125
No. of Cand.	*0*	*6*	*4*	*10*
House	0	3,500	2,000	5,500
Senate	0	4,125	5,500	9,625
Democrats	0	1,500	0	1,500
No. of Cand.	*0*	*2*	*0*	*2*
House	0	500	0	500
Senate	0	1,000	0	1,000
Incumbents	0	6,125	7,500	13,625
Challengers	0	0	0	0
Open Seat	0	3,000	0	3,000
Winners	0	8,125	n/a	8,125
Losers	0	1,000	n/a	1,000

Raytheon Co.

*Phone: (781) 862-2525 * Fax: (781) 862-2520*
141 Spring St., Lexington, MA 02173-7899
Web: www.raytheon.com

Raytheon is one of the largest companies in the United States, with units in defense electronics, aviation and engineering. The company's recent $9.5-billion merger with Hughes Aircraft created the Raytheon Systems Co., which has more than $14 billion in defense and government sales worldwide.

Raytheon has 120,000 employees and its Raytheon Systems division is the third-largest military contractor after a 1995 merger with E-Systems. The company also has commercial electronics, engineering and general aviation operations and locations in Massachusetts, California, Texas, Florida, Pennsylvania, Kansas, Alabama and other states. It produces air traffic control systems, "fishfinder" radar devices and Beech aircraft.

Raytheon's defense business works on several projects for the U.S. military, including the Joint Primary Aircraft Training System for the Navy and Air Force, a program worth an estimated $4 billion to $7 billion. In early 1998, it won contracts for a guided artillery round and an infrared night vision equipment for police officers. It lobbies on defense and electronics issues.

The main Raytheon PAC ranked third among defense electronics PACs in contributions to 1996 congressional candidates. Hughes Electronics, most of which was merged into Raytheon, was the top PAC in that category. In addition, four Raytheon E-Systems subsidiary PACs each contributed at least $5,000 to congressional races. The combined total for those four topped $100,000, which would have ranked ninth among defense electronics PACs. Most of those PACs have since been terminated.

Raytheon favored Republican candidates. The leading recipients were Sens. Al D'Amato, R-N.Y.,Ted Stevens, R-Alaska, Tom Harkin, D-Iowa, and Rep. John Murtha, D-Pa. All but D'Amato are members of defense or security appropriations subcommittees.

Raytheon Co. Political Action Committee (C00097568) *Phone: (703) 416-5829 * Fax: (703) 416-5902 * 1215 Jefferson Davis Highway, Suite 1500, Arlington, VA 22202 * Treasurer: Robert A. Skelly * Contact: Judy Paultich*

	1993-94	1995-96	1997	Totals
Receipts	$325,736	$474,633	$278,528	$1,078,897
Disburse	355,007	385,863	238,445	979,315
Cash	68,532	157,305	197,388	n/a
Contributions	279,655	275,108	177,600	732,363
Republicans	104,545	193,100	114,250	411,895
No. of Cand.	*68*	*123*	*89*	*280*
House	59,200	111,850	80,575	251,625
Senate	45,345	81,250	33,675	160,270
Democrats	175,110	82,008	61,850	318,968
No. of Cand.	*91*	*58*	*53*	*202*
House	125,550	62,508	41,350	229,408
Senate	49,560	19,500	20,500	89,560
Incumbents	244,905	241,262	176,600	662,767
Challengers	9,400	6,450	0	15,850
Open Seat	24,850	26,396	500	51,746
Winners	221,545	239,183	n/a	460,728
Losers	58,110	35,925	n/a	94,035

Hughes Electronics Corp. Active Citizenship Fund (C00002162) *Phone: (310) 568-6652 * Fax: (310) 568-6942 * 7200 Hughes Terrace, P.O. Box 80028 C-129, Los Angeles, CA 90080 * Web: www.hughes.com * Treasurer: Daralyn E. Reed * Contact: Joe Dooling, Manager of Gov. Relations*

The Hughes Electronics PAC was terminated in 1998.

	1993-94	1995-96	1997	Totals
Receipts	$251,429	$355,504	$233,154	$840,087
Disburse	279,721	416,624	276,686	973,031
Cash	104,830	43,720	192	n/a
Contributions	181,780	314,250	131,000	627,030
Republicans	65,150	218,750	79,000	362,900
No. of Cand.	*52*	*143*	*76*	*271*
House	53,650	178,750	67,000	299,400
Senate	11,500	40,000	12,000	63,500
Democrats	115,130	95,500	51,000	261,630
No. of Cand.	*85*	*61*	*39*	*185*
House	91,250	87,500	41,000	219,750
Senate	23,880	8,000	10,000	41,880
Incumbents	170,280	304,750	130,500	605,530
Challengers	1,000	500	0	1,500
Open Seat	8,500	9,000	500	18,000
Winners	159,800	279,750	n/a	439,550
Losers	21,980	34,500	n/a	56,480

E-Systems Corporate Division PAC (C00039032) *P.O. Box 660248, Dallas, TX 75266 * Treasurer: Loyd R. Cunningham*

This PAC has been terminated.

	1993-94	1995-96	1997	Totals
Receipts	$108,852	$61,234	$0	$170,086
Disburse	100,324	83,885	0	184,209
Cash	22,647	0	0	n/a
Contributions	94,649	75,232	0	169,881
Republicans	33,000	50,070	0	83,070
No. of Cand.	*41*	*54*	*0*	*95*
House	25,000	41,820	0	66,820
Senate	8,000	8,250	0	16,250
Democrats	61,649	25,162	0	86,811
No. of Cand.	*49*	*23*	*0*	*72*

House	55,084	25,162	0	80,246
Senate	6,565	0	0	6,565
Incumbents	87,149	73,232	0	160,381
Challengers	2,500	250	0	2,750
Open Seat	3,500	1,250	0	4,750
Winners	77,834	62,632	n/a	140,466
Losers	16,815	12,600	n/a	29,415

E-Systems (Greenville Division) Political Action Committee (C00066613) *Phone: (903) 457-4855 * Fax: (903) 457-7700 * P.O. Box 6056, Greenville, TX 75403-6056 * Treasurer: Sharon R. Rife * Contact: John Murray, Chairman*

The Greenville, Texas, division of Raytheon (formerly known as E-Systems), is a worldwide developer and producer of electronics systems in the areas of intelligence, reconnaissance and surveillance systems and communications and data systems.

The division employs more than 16,000 people at locations in Texas, Florida, California, Pennsylvania, Virginia, Kentucky, Maryland and Colorado. This PAC is still active.

	1993-94	1995-96	1997	Totals
Receipts	$38,923	$36,424	$16,065	$91,412
Disburse	47,356	36,762	14,014	98,132
Cash	13,328	13,000	15,054	n/a
Contributions	18,604	13,279	3,682	35,565
Republicans	10,651	6,913	1,350	18,914
No. of Cand.	*11*	*9*	*5*	*25*
House	5,086	3,795	1,298	10,179
Senate	5,565	3,118	52	8,735
Democrats	7,953	6,366	2,332	16,651
No. of Cand.	*9*	*6*	*2*	*17*
House	7,203	5,984	2,332	15,519
Senate	750	382	0	1,132
Incumbents	16,871	12,012	3,682	32,565
Challengers	636	382	0	1,018
Open Seat	1,017	745	0	1,762
Winners	16,838	10,612	n/a	27,450
Losers	1,766	2,667	n/a	4,433

E-Systems Garland Division Political Action Committee (C00038810) *Phone: (972) 272-0515 * P.O Box 660023, Dallas, TX 75266 * Web: www.raytheon.com/e-sys * Treasurer: Chana Wilson * Contact: Ralph Conjou, Chairman*

Raytheon E-Systems Garland Division announced its PAC to be dissolved as of February 1998.

	1993-94	1995-96	1997	Totals
Receipts	$8,938	$10,293	$4,640	$23,871
Disburse	1,250	18,015	2,205	21,470
Cash	14,393	6,680	8,486	n/a
Contributions	1,500	11,550	500	13,550
Republicans	1,500	5,300	500	7,300
No. of Cand.	*2*	*6*	*2*	*10*
House	750	4,800	500	6,050
Senate	750	500	0	1,250
Democrats	0	6,250	0	6,250
No. of Cand.	*0*	*8*	*0*	*8*
House	0	4,750	0	4,750
Senate	0	1,500	0	1,500
Incumbents	1,500	9,650	500	11,650
Challengers	0	1,500	0	1,500
Open Seat	0	400	0	400
Winners	1,500	7,800	n/a	9,300
Losers	0	3,750	n/a	3,750

E-Systems Inc. Melpar Division PAC (C00043166) *Phone: (703) 560-5000 * Fax: (703) 280-4627 * 7700 Arlington Blvd., Falls Church, VA 22046 * Web: www.raytheon.com/e-sys/asd/flschrch/falls.htm * Treasurer: Barbara Lynn Quantrille*

A spokesperson for E-Systems Melpar Division PAC said that the PAC is disbanding, and plans to file with the FEC for termination in 1998.

	1993-94	1995-96	1997	Totals
Receipts	$6,088	$4,768	$1,481	$12,337
Disburse	13,009	8,300	2,196	23,505
Cash	4,246	715	0	n/a
Contributions	8,250	7,300	1,971	17,521
Republicans	3,500	7,050	1,471	12,021
No. of Cand.	*3*	*3*	*1*	*7*
House	3,500	3,550	1,471	8,521
Senate	0	3,500	0	3,500
Democrats	4,750	250	500	5,500
No. of Cand.	*5*	*1*	*1*	*7*
House	3,250	250	500	4,000
Senate	1,500	0	0	1,500
Incumbents	8,250	7,300	1,971	17,521
Challengers	0	0	0	0
Open Seat	0	0	0	0
Winners	6,750	7,300	n/a	14,050
Losers	1,500	0	n/a	1,500

Terminated PACs which contributed less than $5,000 during 1995-96 cycle:

E-Systems ECI Division Political Action Committee (C00108597) *1501 72nd St. N., P.O. Box 12248, St. Petersburg, FL 33733 * Treasurer: Larry A. Cottrell*

E-Systems Montek PAC (C00038802) *2268 S. 3270 W., Salt Lake City, UT 84119 * Treasurer: Mary Lou Young*

SPD Technologies Inc.

*Phone: (215) 677-4900 * Fax: (215) 677-1504*
13500 Roosevelt Blvd., Philadelphia, PA 19116
Web: www.spdtech.com

SPD Technologies designs and makes electrical and electronic products such as shock-hardened circuit breakers, switchgears and utility monitoring systems for military and commercial maritime use. The company's products are aboard nearly all U.S. Navy vessels.

In July 1997, SPD Technologies acquired Power Paragon Inc., based in Anaheim, Calif., with operations in Germany and Phoenix. The addition will allow SPD to further pursue the Navy, marine, rail transportation and utilities markets. The acquisition boosted the private company from 700 employees to 1,200.

SPD Technologies was founded in 1888 as Cutter Electrical Mfg., and later known as I-T-E Circuit Breaker Co., then I-T-E Imperial Corp.

Subsidiaries: Henschel and PacOrd.

SPD Technologies Inc. Political Action Committee (C00225037) *Address: same as sponsor * Treasurer: John C. Fleury*

	1993-94	1995-96	1997	Totals
Receipts	$5,554	$16,550	$7,943	$30,047
Disburse	6,700	14,140	6,229	27,069
Cash	0	15,145	14,106	n/a
Contributions	6,700	18,750	5,000	30,450
Republicans	1,000	11,500	2,000	14,500
No. of Cand.	*1*	*5*	*3*	*9*
House	1,000	4,500	1,000	6,500
Senate	0	7,000	1,000	8,000
Democrats	5,700	7,250	3,000	15,950
No. of Cand.	*8*	*4*	*3*	*15*
House	4,200	7,250	3,000	14,450
Senate	1,500	0	0	1,500
Incumbents	6,700	18,750	5,000	30,450
Challengers	0	0	0	0
Open Seat	0	0	0	0
Winners	6,000	18,750	n/a	24,750
Losers	700	0	n/a	700

Science Applications International Corp.

*Phone: (619) 546-6338 * Fax: (619) 546-6191*
10010 Campus Point Dr., F2, San Diego, CA 92121-1578
Web: www.saic.com

Science Applications International, based in San Diego, provides technology services and computer products to many United States military agencies, including the Defense Nuclear Agency and the Ballistic Missile Defense Organization.

The private company also provides automated services to the space program and health care providers.

Founded by Dr. J. R. Beyster and a small group of scientists in 1969, SAIC now ranks as the largest employee-owned high-tech firm in the nation. SAIC and its subsidiaries have offices in more than 150 cities worldwide. SAIC also owns BellCore, the research arm of the regional Bells.

SAIC's 1997 sales were $2.4 billion. It has more than 30,000 employees.

Science Applications International Corp. Voluntary Political Action Committee (C00300418) *Address: same as sponsor * Treasurer: Daniel Baldwin*

	1993-94	1995-96	1997	Totals
Receipts	$100	$170,310	$48,130	$218,540
Disburse	0	150,342	56,527	206,869
Cash	100	20,070	11,674	n/a
Contributions	0	141,750	56,500	198,250
Republicans	0	95,250	37,750	133,000
No. of Cand.	*0*	*48*	*25*	*73*
House	0	68,750	34,750	103,500
Senate	0	26,500	3,000	29,500
Democrats	0	46,500	18,750	65,250
No. of Cand.	*0*	*28*	*15*	*43*
House	0	39,500	17,750	57,250
Senate	0	7,000	1,000	8,000
Incumbents	0	130,750	56,500	187,250
Challengers	0	0	0	0
Open Seat	0	10,000	0	10,000
Winners	0	133,500	n/a	133,500
Losers	0	8,250	n/a	8,250

TRW Inc.

*Phone: (216) 291-7000 * Fax: (216) 291-7629*
1900 Richmond Rd., Cleveland, OH 44124
Web: www.trw.com

TRW is a public automotive parts and information technology company with headquarters in Cleveland.

TRW's automotive operations, which include supplying manufacturers with air bags, seat belts and steering columns, account for two-thirds of its business. The remaining portion comes from TRW's growing space, defense and information businesses, which have contracts with more than 10 federal agencies, including the IRS and the Census Bureau. The company employs about 65,000 people in 24 countries. It reported 1997 sales of $10.8 billion.

The company is interested in legislation affecting the automotive industry and trade issues in general. It supports global trade agreements and "fast-track" negotiating authority. It has lobbied for standardized product liability laws. Its other issues include nuclear waste storage and funding for defense satellite and information technology programs.

Most of TRW's 1995-96 contributions went to Republican candidates, but it spent more than $5,000 on Democrats in Washington state, Texas and California. In its home state of Ohio, TRW's spending favored GOP candidates by a nine-to-one margin. The top recipients included Reps. Steven LaTourette, R-Ohio, Jane Harman, D-Calif., C.W. "Bill" Young, R-Fla., Norm Dicks, D-Wash., and the 1998 Senate campaign of Ohio Gov. George Voinovich, a Republican.

TRW Good Government Fund (C00025536) *Phone: (703) 276-5100 * Fax: (703) 276-5057 * 1001 19th St. N., Suite 800, Arlington, VA 22209 * Treasurer: Joseph E. Durk*

	1993-94	1995-96	1997	Totals
Receipts	$242,482	$306,148	$157,537	$706,167
Disburse	240,160	306,547	109,925	656,632
Cash	30,942	30,554	78,171	n/a
Contributions	162,130	241,061	88,245	491,436
Republicans	70,450	193,311	62,286	326,047
No. of Cand.	*67*	*134*	*52*	*253*
House	44,450	128,804	39,636	212,890
Senate	26,000	64,507	22,650	113,157
Democrats	91,680	47,750	25,959	165,389
No. of Cand.	*71*	*39*	*24*	*134*
House	72,415	44,200	20,959	137,574
Senate	19,265	3,550	5,000	27,815
Incumbents	129,000	212,761	88,995	430,756
Challengers	9,150	14,000	-250	22,900
Open Seat	26,480	14,300	0	40,780
Winners	147,465	205,354	n/a	352,819
Losers	14,665	35,707	n/a	50,372

BDM International Inc. Political Action Committee (BDM-PAC) (C00074310) *Phone: (703) 848-5000 * 1501 BDM Way, McLean, VA 22102 * Treasurer: Judith N. Huntzinger*

BDM International, a software development and information technology company, was acquired by TRW in December 1997. A spokesperson for BDM said the PAC would either be terminated or absorbed into TRW's PAC during 1998.

	1993-94	1995-96	1997	Totals
Receipts	$135,613	$115,140	$54,749	$305,502
Disburse	134,911	104,838	22,242	261,991
Cash	29,922	40,229	72,737	n/a
Contributions	105,874	94,434	16,505	216,813
Republicans	41,874	73,484	13,750	129,108
No. of Cand.	*26*	*36*	*9*	*71*
House	18,975	31,675	9,000	59,650
Senate	22,899	41,809	4,750	69,458
Democrats	63,500	20,950	2,755	87,205
No. of Cand.	*29*	*13*	*4*	*46*
House	36,000	18,950	2,755	57,705
Senate	27,500	2,000	0	29,500
Incumbents	82,600	86,284	16,505	185,389
Challengers	3,500	200	0	3,700
Open Seat	19,774	7,950	0	27,724
Winners	92,374	87,735	n/a	180,109
Losers	13,500	6,699	n/a	20,199

Talley Industries Inc.

7929 Westpark Dr., Suite 400, P.O. Box 849, McLean, VA 22102
Web: www.talleyind.com

Talley Industries was acquired by Carpenter Technology Corp. in January 1998. As a result, the company's PAC is scheduled to be terminated in 1998.

Talley Industries Inc. Political Action Committee (Talley-PAC) (C00107219) *Address: same as sponsor * Treasurer: Charles E. Raley*

	1993-94	1995-96	1997	Totals
Receipts	$19,654	$23,414	$7,690	$50,758
Disburse	18,101	21,149	12,511	51,761
Cash	5,651	7,919	3,097	n/a
Contributions	17,090	21,050	12,400	50,540
Republicans	11,300	15,700	10,900	37,900
No. of Cand.	*8*	*18*	*13*	*39*
House	5,800	13,200	8,900	27,900
Senate	5,500	2,500	2,000	10,000
Democrats	5,790	5,350	1,500	12,640
No. of Cand.	*7*	*5*	*2*	*14*
House	5,300	5,350	1,500	12,150
Senate	490	0	0	490
Incumbents	12,340	20,800	12,400	45,540
Challengers	0	250	0	250
Open Seat	4,750	0	0	4,750
Winners	16,100	20,800	n/a	36,900
Losers	990	250	n/a	1,240

Tracor Inc.

*Phone: (703) 418-6208 * Fax: (703) 415-1459*
1215 Jefferson Davis Highway, Suite 1109, Arlington, VA 22202
Web: www.tracor.com

Tracor provides electronic and information technology products, systems and services to the Department of Defense, other U.S. government agencies, foreign governments and commercial customers.

The public company provides operations and maintenance support for U.S. Air Force missile test centers, collects case information from all federal bankruptcy courts and provides logistical support for the U.S. Navy's Undersea Warfare Center.

Tracor's sales in 1997 were $1.2 billion and the company employs more than 10,000 workers.

The company's business units operate in the defense electronics, information technology and systems engineering and integration markets. Tracor's products and services largely support high-priority DOD weapons, platforms and systems that enable defense customers to enhance the operational performance and readiness of existing systems and platforms.

Tracor Inc. Political Action Committee (Tracor PAC) (formerly known as GDE Systems Inc.) (C00281212) *Address: same as sponsor * Treasurer: Sydelle Lyon * Contact: Robert Fitch, Chairperson*

	1993-94	1995-96	1997	Totals
Receipts	$99,998	$242,094	$139,585	$481,677
Disburse	60,298	209,101	182,450	451,849
Cash	39,705	72,710	29,851	n/a
Contributions	58,220	167,865	152,950	379,035
Republicans	26,900	120,750	108,450	256,100
No. of Cand.	*28*	*67*	*61*	*156*
House	20,900	84,500	83,450	188,850
Senate	6,000	36,250	25,000	67,250
Democrats	30,820	47,115	44,500	122,435
No. of Cand.	*29*	*34*	*35*	*98*
House	26,200	39,300	40,000	105,500
Senate	4,620	7,815	4,500	16,935
Incumbents	56,170	154,500	152,950	363,620
Challengers	1,050	2,250	0	3,300

Open Seat	1,000	10,815	0	11,815
Winners	49,920	154,565	n/a	204,485
Losers	8,300	13,300	n/a	21,600

Veda Inc.

*Phone: (703) 575-3170 * Fax: (703) 575-3240*
2001 N. Beauregard St., Suite 1200, Alexandria, VA 22311
Web: www.veda.com

Based in Alexandria, Va., Veda provides defense engineering services to the Department of Defense, other government agencies and the commercial sector. The company reported $97 million in 1997 sales and employs 1,240 people.

Veda is a subsidiary of the privately held U.S. company Veridian, an aeronautics and space industries firm. Its ultimate parent is Veda International Inc.

Veda operates 18 offices, concentrated mainly on the East and West Coasts.

Veda Inc. Employees Political Action Committee (C00206052) *Address: same as sponsor * Treasurer: Katherine Snavely * Contact: Phyllis Seidler, Secretary*

	1993-94	1995-96	1997	Totals
Receipts	$26,847	$23,342	$11,821	$62,010
Disburse	17,650	31,000	1,750	50,400
Cash	11,183	3,540	13,619	n/a
Contributions	15,450	26,000	1,750	43,200
Republicans	10,250	25,000	1,250	36,500
No. of Cand.	*15*	*28*	*2*	*45*
House	6,750	21,000	250	28,000
Senate	3,500	4,000	1,000	8,500
Democrats	5,200	1,000	500	6,700
No. of Cand.	*7*	*1*	*1*	*9*
House	5,200	1,000	500	6,700
Senate	0	0	0	0
Incumbents	11,700	24,000	1,750	37,450
Challengers	1,250	0	0	1,250
Open Seat	2,500	2,000	0	4,500
Winners	13,700	20,000	n/a	33,700
Losers	1,750	6,000	n/a	7,750

Whittaker Corp.

*Phone: (806) 526-5700 * Fax: (806) 526-4869*
1955 N. Surveyor Ave., Simi Valley, CA 93063

The Whittaker PAC was terminated in January 1998.

Whittaker Political Action Committee (C00134775) *Address: same as sponsor * Treasurer: Steve Wilder*

	1993-94	1995-96	1997	Totals
Receipts	$0	$2,124	$1,647	$3,771
Disburse	3,120	5,900	2,500	11,520
Cash	4,132	357	0	n/a
Contributions	3,120	5,550	2,500	11,170
Republicans	1,870	5,550	2,500	9,920
No. of Cand.	*1*	*3*	*2*	*6*
House	1,870	5,550	2,500	9,920
Senate	0	0	0	0
Democrats	1,250	0	0	1,250
No. of Cand.	*1*	*0*	*0*	*1*
House	1,250	0	0	1,250
Senate	0	0	0	0
Incumbents	3,120	5,550	2,500	11,170
Challengers	0	0	0	0
Open Seat	0	0	0	0
Winners	1,870	5,550	n/a	7,420
Losers	1,250	0	n/a	1,250

Misc. Defense

AAI Corp.

Phone: (410) 628-3386
P.O. Box 8006, Hunt Valley, MD 21030-8006
Web: www.aaicorp.com

AAI manufactures mechanical and electronic systems for government and industry. A subsidiary of United Industrial Corp., the private company employs 1,200 people and posts annual sales of more than $170 million. It is headquartered in Hunt Valley, Md.

AAI is divided into four business units: defense systems, fluid test systems, transportation systems and engineering and maintenance services. Among its products are radar systems, simulators and microwave transmitters.

AAI Corp. Political Action Committee (C00169508) *Address: same as sponsor * Treasurer: William Lowe*

	1993-94	1995-96	1997	Totals
Receipts	$22,994	$42,197	$21,659	$86,850
Disburse	25,547	37,156	27,183	89,886
Cash	1,521	6,567	1,043	n/a
Contributions	24,003	35,371	26,388	85,762
Republicans	13,203	26,271	20,888	60,362
No. of Cand.	*13*	*22*	*14*	*49*
House	10,203	23,271	20,638	54,112
Senate	3,000	3,000	250	6,250
Democrats	10,800	9,100	4,500	24,400
No. of Cand.	*12*	*5*	*5*	*22*
House	8,000	7,500	3,500	19,000
Senate	2,800	1,600	1,000	5,400
Incumbents	23,003	34,271	26,388	83,662
Challengers	0	600	0	600
Open Seat	1,000	500	0	1,500
Winners	19,003	33,021	n/a	52,024
Losers	5,000	2,350	n/a	7,350

Alliant Techsystems Inc.

*Phone: (612) 931-6000 * Fax: (612) 931-5433*
600 Second St. N.E., MN 11-2443, Hopkins, MN 55343
Web: www.atk.com

Alliant Techsystems is an aerospace and defense company with 6,400 employees and operations in 23 states. Primary clients include the U.S. government and its allies. Headquartered in Hopkins, Minn., Alliant does business in conventional munitions and space, defense and emerging systems. The publicly traded company reported $1.1 billion in 1997 sales.

Alliant's conventional munitions division is the U.S. Army's largest supplier of 120mm tank ammunition and also produces military and commercial gunpowder, tactical missile propulsion systems and flares. It has operations in Illinois, Kansas, Minnesota, New Jersey, New Mexico, Tennessee, Virginia and West Virginia.

The company's space division produces solid rocket motors for expendable space launch vehicles, including the Titan IV, Delta II and Delta III. It also supplies solid rocket propulsion systems for the U.S. Navy's Trident II Intercontinental Ballistic Missile. A composites division, based in Utah, makes satellite assemblies, space-based antennae, aircraft components and space launch vehicle structures. The space group employs 1,800 people in California, Florida and Utah.

Alliant's defense systems division, with about 925 employees, enhances the capability of guns, ammunition, electronic warfare systems, and reconnaissance and surveillance systems. It is building a remotely piloted surveillance aircraft for the Department of Defense.

Alliant Techsystems Inc. Employee Citizenship Fund (C00250209) *Address: same as sponsor * Treasurer: Wayne E. Gilbert * Contact: David Nicpomski, Chairman*

	1993-94	1995-96	1997	Totals
Receipts	$76,428	$105,406	$71,576	$253,410
Disburse	39,098	107,262	82,196	228,556
Cash	56,077	54,222	43,602	n/a
Contributions	37,800	93,450	60,500	191,750
Republicans	15,000	64,150	45,500	124,650
No. of Cand.	*12*	*40*	*34*	*86*
House	11,000	38,350	26,500	75,850
Senate	4,000	25,800	19,000	48,800
Democrats	21,800	29,300	13,000	64,100
No. of Cand.	*16*	*21*	*15*	*52*
House	16,800	29,300	12,000	58,100
Senate	5,000	0	1,000	6,000
Incumbents	32,300	88,650	59,000	179,950
Challengers	0	3,000	1,500	4,500
Open Seat	5,500	500	0	6,000
Winners	29,700	85,150	n/a	114,850
Losers	8,100	8,300	n/a	16,400

Avondale Industries

*Phone: (504) 436-5237 * Fax: (504) 436-5304*
P.O. Box 50280, New Orleans, LA 70150-0280
Web: www.avondale.com

Avondale Industries manufactures oceangoing vessels for military and commercial markets. Vessel classifications include U.S. Navy amphibious assault ships, fleet support ships and surface combatants, Coast Guard icebreakers and cutters, product and chemical carriers, lighter aboard ships and dredges. In addition to manufacturing military and commercial vessels, Avondale undertakes repairs and modernizations.

The publicly traded company employs more than 5,000 people and reported 1997 sales of $613 million.

In 1997, Congress allocated $100 million to Avondale Industries to begin work on an amphibious ship.

Avondale Industries Political Action Fund (C00199158) *Address: same as sponsor * Treasurer: Mel Adams * Contact: Thomas M. Kitchen, Chairman*

	1993-94	1995-96	1997	Totals
Receipts	$20,047	$25,638	$11,597	$57,282
Disburse	22,750	23,425	13,000	59,175
Cash	1,130	3,346	1,944	n/a
Contributions	22,750	23,425	13,000	59,175
Republicans	11,000	18,925	10,500	40,425
No. of Cand.	*9*	*18*	*13*	*40*
House	9,000	14,175	8,000	31,175
Senate	2,000	4,750	2,500	9,250
Democrats	11,750	4,500	2,500	18,750
No. of Cand.	*11*	*2*	*3*	*16*
House	7,750	4,500	2,000	14,250
Senate	4,000	0	500	4,500
Incumbents	21,250	21,300	11,500	54,050
Challengers	500	0	500	1,000
Open Seat	1,000	2,125	1,000	4,125
Winners	21,250	21,550	n/a	42,800
Losers	1,500	1,875	n/a	3,375

Bird-Johnson Co.

*Phone: (508) 668-9610 * Fax: (508) 660-6210*
110 Norfolk St., Walpole, MA 02081

Bird-Johnson makes propeller systems and water jet systems for marine vehicles, as well as suspension devices used in earth-moving vehicles. The company also offers maritime design engineering services. A subsidiary of the privately held Axel Johnson Inc., Bird-Johnson generates an estimated $50 to $100 million in annual sales.

In 1994, Bird-Johnson was one of 16 companies selected for MARITECH, the Clinton administration's program to improve the international competitiveness of the U.S. shipbuilding industry. The MARITECH program awards matching federal funds to develop technologies for the competitive design, marketing, production and support of commercial ships. Bird-Johnson was awarded in the categories of penetrating the international market for small ships and developing high technology tanker vessels.

Bird-Johnson is certified by the Naval Sea Systems Command, U.S. Coast Guard and Det Norske Veritas, an international maritime foundation.

Bird-Johnson Co. PAC (C00301259) *Phone: (206) 782-9190 * Fax: (206) 752-0176 * 4451 14th Ave. N.W., Seattle, WA 98107-4617 * Treasurer: Joseph J. Riley*

*Contact: Peter J. Gwyn, President and CEO * Phone: (508) 668-9610*

	1993-94	1995-96	1997	Totals
Receipts	$0	$18,116	$0	$18,116
Disburse	0	9,419	3,650	13,069
Cash	0	8,698	5,048	n/a
Contributions	0	8,300	3,650	11,950
Republicans	0	5,000	1,000	6,000
No. of Cand.	*0*	*5*	*2*	*7*
House	0	4,000	1,000	5,000
Senate	0	1,000	0	1,000
Democrats	0	3,300	2,650	5,950
No. of Cand.	*0*	*3*	*3*	*6*
House	0	3,300	2,650	5,950
Senate	0	0	0	0
Incumbents	0	7,800	3,650	11,450
Challengers	0	0	0	0
Open Seat	0	500	0	500
Winners	0	8,300	n/a	8,300
Losers	0	0	n/a	0

General Dynamics Corp.

*Phone: (703) 876-3305 * Fax: (703) 876-3125*
3190 Fairview Park Dr., Falls Church, VA 22042-4523

General Dynamics is a publicly traded defense contractor which produces nuclear submarines and weapons systems, focusing on tanks. Its two main divisions are Electric Boat, which makes Seawolf and Trident class submarines, and Land Systems, which produces the Abrams battle tank.

The company employs 23,100 people and has acquired several defense electronics businesses from Lockheed Martin, Teledyne and Ceridian Corp. General Dynamics had revenues of $3.58 billion in 1996. The company recently named former Pentagon acquisition chief Paul G. Kaminsky to its board. Kaminsky was a supporter of the consolidation of the defense industry.

Among the company's units are Bath Iron Works, which will share in the building of the Navy's next generation of destroyers, and Electric Boat Corp., which produces Seawolf-class submarines. Electric Boat also has the preliminary design contract for a new attack class of submarines. General Dynamics Land Systems operates the nation's only heavy main battle tank production facility in Lima, Ohio.

General Dynamics has facilities in California, Virginia, Maine, Pennsylvania, Florida and Michigan.

General Dynamics gave more money to Republican candidates than Democrats during the 1995-96 election cycle, but didn't leave out key Democrats from states where the company operates — Michigan and Connecticut, for example. The company also concentrated on members of defense and national security committees and subcommittees.

Bath Iron Works, the largest private employer in Maine, terminated its PAC.

General Dynamics Corp. Voluntary Political Contribution Plan (C00078451) *Address: same as sponsor * Treasurer: Diane L. Mossler*

	1993-94	1995-96	1997	Totals
Receipts	$606,332	$395,171	$270,462	$1,271,965
Disburse	686,372	396,926	199,550	1,282,848
Cash	61,434	59,689	130,607	n/a
Contributions	385,112	306,062	152,550	843,724
Republicans	149,250	196,712	88,100	434,062
No. of Cand.	*74*	*79*	*50*	*203*
House	76,750	107,512	60,600	244,862
Senate	72,500	89,200	27,500	189,200
Democrats	235,362	109,350	64,450	409,162
No. of Cand.	*104*	*44*	*39*	*187*
House	183,262	83,350	48,950	315,562
Senate	52,100	26,000	15,500	93,600
Incumbents	326,112	269,612	152,550	748,274
Challengers	5,250	9,700	0	14,950
Open Seat	52,750	26,750	0	79,500
Winners	323,162	267,862	n/a	591,024
Losers	61,950	38,200	n/a	100,150

Bath Iron Works Corp. Political Action Committee (formerly known as Congoleum Corp. PAC) (C00120816) *700 Washington St., Bath, ME 04530 * Treasurer: Gerard F. Lamb*

	1993-94	1995-96	1997	Totals
Receipts	$24,940	$11,560	$0	$36,500
Disburse	26,840	11,875	0	38,715
Cash	308	0	0	n/a
Contributions	25,350	8,250	0	33,600
Republicans	7,050	6,750	0	13,800
No. of Cand.	*7*	*8*	*0*	*15*
House	5,050	3,250	0	8,300
Senate	2,000	3,500	0	5,500
Democrats	18,300	1,500	0	19,800
No. of Cand.	*23*	*3*	*0*	*26*
House	17,250	1,500	0	18,750
Senate	1,050	0	0	1,050
Incumbents	25,350	8,250	0	33,600
Challengers	0	0	0	0
Open Seat	0	0	0	0
Winners	22,050	5,500	n/a	27,550
Losers	3,300	2,750	n/a	6,050

ManTech International Corp.

*Phone: (703) 218-6000 * Fax: (703) 218-6301*
12015 Lee Jackson Highway, Suite 128, Fairfax, VA 22033
Web: www.mantech.com

ManTech International specializes in aerospace and aeronautics technology and weapons system support. Based in Fairfax, Va., the company has more than 3,000 employees at 100 locations around the world, including Australia, Germany, Korea, Sweden, Taiwan and Turkey.

In addition to its defense work, the public company designs databases, performs environmental testing and research and offers telecommunication service. ManTech has average annual sales of about $300 million.

Subsidiaries include: ManTech Systems Engineering Corp., ManTech Environmental Technology Inc., ManTech Environmental Corp. and ManTech Advanced Systems International Inc.

ManTech International Corp. Political Action Committee (C00208983) *Address: same as sponsor * Treasurer: Terry G. Myers * Contact: George J. Pederson, Chairperson*

	1993-94	1995-96	1997	Totals
Receipts	$49,070	$63,207	$35,458	$147,735
Disburse	55,510	63,218	31,171	149,899
Cash	5,345	5,337	9,624	n/a
Contributions	47,510	58,675	20,750	126,935
Republicans	11,460	39,975	12,000	63,435
No. of Cand.	*12*	*18*	*6*	*36*
House	6,425	13,175	7,000	26,600
Senate	5,035	26,800	5,000	36,835
Democrats	36,050	18,700	8,750	63,500
No. of Cand.	*20*	*6*	*6*	*32*
House	27,750	18,700	8,750	55,200
Senate	8,300	0	0	8,300
Incumbents	45,085	57,175	20,750	123,010
Challengers	1,000	500	0	1,500
Open Seat	1,500	1,000	0	2,500
Winners	45,085	55,000	n/a	100,085
Losers	2,425	3,675	n/a	6,100

Marinette Marine Corp.

*Phone: (715) 735-9341 x260 * Fax: (715) 735-3516*
P.O. Box 1101, Marinette, WI 54143

Marinette Marine, a privately owned shipbuilding company founded in 1942, employs 600 people. It is based in Marinette, Wis. and posts annual sales of about $80 million.

The company builds tugboats, ferries, buoy tenders, research vessels, torpedo weapon retrievers, mine counter measure ships, yard patrol craft and a variety of landing craft.

Marinette Marine Political Action Committee (MMPAC) (C00287847) *Phone: (202) 371-5732 * Fax: (202) 371-5950 * Winston and Strawn, 1401 L St. N.W., Washington, DC 20005 * Treasurer: David J. Roland * Contact: Charlie Papavizus, Lobbyist*

*Contact: Dan Gulling, Chairman * Phone: (715) 735-9341 x260*

	1993-94	1995-96	1997	Totals
Receipts	$19,058	$33,505	$12,748	$65,311
Disburse	15,862	36,298	8,040	60,200
Cash	3,196	403	5,111	n/a
Contributions	11,350	31,200	7,500	50,050
Republicans	1,650	18,450	3,000	23,100
No. of Cand.	*2*	*17*	*4*	*23*
House	650	12,950	1,000	14,600
Senate	1,000	5,500	2,000	8,500
Democrats	9,700	12,750	4,500	26,950
No. of Cand.	*9*	*12*	*6*	*27*
House	5,700	8,250	3,000	16,950
Senate	4,000	4,500	1,500	10,000
Incumbents	7,350	24,700	7,500	39,550
Challengers	0	0	0	0
Open Seat	4,000	6,500	0	10,500
Winners	7,850	27,000	n/a	34,850
Losers	3,500	4,200	n/a	7,700

Mason & Hanger Corp.

*Phone: (606) 223-2277 * Fax: (606) 223-1846*
2355 Harrodsburg Rd., Lexington, KY 40504
Web: www.masonhanger.com

Mason & Hanger has operated the nation's nuclear weapons production and modification plants since 1947.

A subsidiary of the privately held Mason Co., Mason & Hanger also provides secure storage and surveillance for America's largest stockpile of plutonium and is the nation's sole source contractor for producing high-explosive components for nuclear weapons.

Estimated 1996 sales were $450 million. The company has about 5,000 employees.

Company locations include: the Pantex Plant in the Texas Panhandle, the nation's only nuclear weapons assembly and disassembly facility; and the Iowa Army Ammunition Plant in Middletown, Iowa, where the company demilitarizes conventional weapons and assembles missiles, mines and other weapons. Other munitions plants are located in Indiana, Mississippi and Ohio. Mason & Hanger says it is the only company experienced in the production and demilitarization of the three major weapons types: nuclear, conventional and chemical.

Through subsidiaries, Mason provides facilities management services for the departments of Defense and Energy and NASA at locations including Langley Research Center, Goddard Space Flight Center and the U.S. Navy base in Puerto Rico. The company has hazardous materials handling contracts with the EPA.

Formed in 1827, Mason is the oldest engineering and construction contractor in the United States. It built the Lincoln Tunnel in New York, Old Hickory Powder Plant during World War I, and designed the first hardened, underground ICBM complexes. During the Vietnam and Korean Wars, Mason & Hanger ran the Iowa and Cornhusker Army Ammunition Plants that produced more than 80 different munitions products.

Mason & Hanger Corp. PAC (C00316513) *Address: same as sponsor * Treasurer: William R. Lickert*

	1993-94	1995-96	1997	Totals
Receipts	$0	$9,635	$4,405	$14,040
Disburse	0	8,500	1,000	9,500
Cash	0	1,135	4,540	n/a
Contributions	0	8,500	1,000	9,500
Republicans	0	6,750	500	7,250
No. of Cand.	*0*	*19*	*1*	*20*
House	0	3,500	500	4,000
Senate	0	3,250	0	3,250
Democrats	0	1,750	500	2,250
No. of Cand.	*0*	*5*	*1*	*6*
House	0	1,250	500	1,750
Senate	0	500	0	500
Incumbents	0	8,000	500	8,500
Challengers	0	500	0	500
Open Seat	0	0	500	500
Winners	0	8,000	n/a	8,000
Losers	0	500	n/a	500

Norfolk Shipbuilding & Drydock Corp.

*Phone: (757) 494-4000 * Fax: (757) 494-4307*
P.O. Box 2100, Norfolk, VA 23501-2100
Web: www.norshipco.com

Norfolk Shipbuilding & Drydock is a privately held company that has served the port of Hampton Roads, Va. since 1915. Norshipco is a full-service shipyard and repair facility contractor and is one of the largest ship repair facilities on the East Coast.

Norshipco is the largest shipyard in the United States devoted exclusively to ship maintenance and repair. The company has 20 agents on five continents.

Subsidiaries: DMI-Norshipco and Norshipco Marine Sales.

Norfolk Shipbuilding & Drydock Corp. Political Action Committee (Norshipco PAC) (C00193490) *Address: same as sponsor * Treasurer: Fred Shafer*

	1993-94	1995-96	1997	Totals
Receipts	$22,289	$13,748	$6,268	$42,305
Disburse	17,133	13,164	6,623	36,920
Cash	12,712	13,297	12,941	n/a
Contributions	17,000	11,725	6,000	34,725
Republicans	1,500	4,100	0	5,600
No. of Cand.	*2*	*2*	*0*	*4*
House	1,500	500	0	2,000
Senate	0	3,600	0	3,600
Democrats	15,500	7,625	6,000	29,125
No. of Cand.	*10*	*3*	*1*	*14*
House	10,500	7,125	6,000	23,625
Senate	5,000	500	0	5,500
Incumbents	17,000	11,725	6,000	34,725
Challengers	0	0	0	0
Open Seat	0	0	0	0
Winners	15,000	11,725	n/a	26,725
Losers	2,000	0	n/a	2,000

Rotary Power International Inc.

*Phone: (201) 777-7979 * Fax: (201) 778-5595*
22 Passaic St., Gate 2, Woodridge, NJ 07075
Web: www.rotarypower.com

Rotary Power International builds rotary engines for military vehicles and boats. The public company had announced in 1997 a plan to merge with PowerCold Corp., but the merger was never consummated and, according to SEC filings, Rotary Power fired all of its remaining employees in May 1997.

Rotary Power is seeking financing and has elected to maintain its federal PAC, which contributed a total of $500 during 1997.

Rotary Power International Inc. PAC (RPI PAC) (C00274035)
*Address: same as sponsor * Treasurer: Ken L. Brody*

	1993-94	1995-96	1997	Totals
Receipts	$9,089	$7,207	$23	$16,319
Disburse	7,000	7,500	557	15,057
Cash	3,163	2,873	2,345	n/a
Contributions	6,500	7,000	500	14,000
Republicans	2,000	2,500	500	5,000
No. of Cand.	*2*	*2*	*1*	*5*
House	2,000	2,500	500	5,000
Senate	0	0	0	0
Democrats	4,500	4,500	0	9,000
No. of Cand.	*3*	*3*	*0*	*6*
House	3,500	2,500	0	6,000
Senate	1,000	2,000	0	3,000
Incumbents	6,500	5,000	500	12,000
Challengers	0	0	0	0
Open Seat	0	2,000	0	2,000
Winners	6,500	7,000	n/a	13,500
Losers	0	0	n/a	0

Sequa Corp.

*Phone: (212) 986-5500 * Fax: (212) 370-1969*
200 Park Ave., New York, NY 10166

Atlantic Research Corp., a wholly owned subsidiary of Sequa, makes tactical rocket motors for the Department of Defense and airbags for automobiles. Sequa is a public company that also makes coatings for steel and aluminum coil used in building products. Sequa reported 1996 sales of $1.4 billion and is based in New York. The company employs 9,350 people nationwide.

Another Sequa subsidiary, Chromalloy Gas Turbine Corp., also has a federal PAC. Chromalloy makes engines for helicopters and airplanes.

Atlantic Research Corp. Political Action Committee (ARC-PAC) (C00196709) *Phone: (703) 754-5619 * Fax: (703) 754-5214 * 5945 Wellington Rd., Gainesville, VA 20155-1633 * Web: www.arcmaterials.com * E-mail: lparkinson@arc-ag.com * Treasurer: Thomas D. Haggerty * Contact: Leonard Parkinson, Gov. Relations Dir.*

	1993-94	1995-96	1997	Totals
Receipts	$41,251	$29,135	$13,377	$83,763
Disburse	40,993	30,686	4,815	76,494
Cash	37,799	36,248	44,810	n/a
Contributions	36,155	30,465	4,500	71,120
Republicans	12,035	22,965	2,500	37,500
No. of Cand.	*11*	*12*	*4*	*27*
House	8,000	12,000	2,500	22,500
Senate	4,035	10,965	0	15,000
Democrats	24,120	7,500	2,000	33,620
No. of Cand.	*26*	*8*	*4*	*38*
House	16,000	5,500	1,500	23,000
Senate	8,120	2,000	500	10,620
Incumbents	33,155	29,965	4,500	67,620
Challengers	1,000	0	0	1,000
Open Seat	2,000	0	0	2,000
Winners	29,535	28,465	n/a	58,000
Losers	6,620	2,000	n/a	8,620

Contributed less than $5,000 during 1995-96 cycle:

Chromalloy Gas Turbine Corp. Political Action Committee (C00235911) *Phone: (210) 333-6010 * Fax: (210) 359-5570 * 4430 Director Dr., P.O. Box 200150, San Antonio, TX 78220 * Treasurer: Stephen N. Chapman*

Energy & Natural Resources

Commercial Fishing

American Sportfishing Association

*Phone: (703) 519-9691 * Fax: (703) 519-1872*
1033 N. Fairfax St., Suite 200, Alexandria, VA 22314
E-mail: amsportfish@delphi.com

The American Sportfishing Association works to ensure healthy and sustainable fishery resources, increase sportfishing participation and provide services to make its members more profitable. The non-profit group is involved in education, conservation, promotion and marketing on behalf of the sportfishing industry and America's more than 50 million anglers.

ASA's efforts have resulted in the banning of gill nets off the coast of Florida. The group has secured federal funds to improve fishery management on the Atlantic Coast. In addition, ASA has completed economic studies for each state that include specific dollars in tourism revenue and jobs created from sportfishing.

In January 1998, ASA urged the commercial fishing industry to do more to avoid killing sea animals not intended for catch.

American Sportfishing Association Political Action Committee (C00249532) *Address: same as sponsor * Treasurer: Steven F. Knell*

	1993-94	1995-96	1997	Totals
Receipts	$2,507	$30,160	$5,500	$38,167
Disburse	2,009	14,643	7,000	23,652
Cash	498	16,017	14,519	n/a
Contributions	0	14,500	6,500	21,000
Republicans	0	10,000	5,500	15,500
No. of Cand.	*0*	*12*	*7*	*19*
House	0	5,500	3,500	9,000
Senate	0	4,500	2,000	6,500
Democrats	0	4,500	1,000	5,500
No. of Cand.	*0*	*5*	*1*	*6*
House	0	2,500	0	2,500
Senate	0	2,000	1,000	3,000
Incumbents	0	14,000	6,500	20,500
Challengers	0	0	0	0
Open Seat	0	500	0	500
Winners	0	12,500	n/a	12,500
Losers	0	2,000	n/a	2,000

National Fisheries Institute

*Phone: (703) 524-8880 * Fax: (703) 524-4619*
1901 N. Fort Meyer Dr., Suite 700, Arlington, VA 22209
*Web: www.nfi.org * E-mail: office@nfi.org*

The National Fisheries Institute represents about 1,000 members involved in the fishing industry, including individual fishermen, vessel owners and distributors, processors, wholesalers, importers, traders and brokers of fish and shellfish. The organization monitors legislation and regulations on fisheries.

National Fisheries Institute Fisheries Political Action Committee (FishPAC) (C00101204) *Address: same as sponsor * Treasurer: William Wright*

	1993-94	1995-96	1997	Totals
Receipts	$37,550	$51,482	$29,564	$118,596
Disburse	44,031	71,121	14,709	129,861
Cash	36,192	32,739	47,597	n/a
Contributions	45,713	59,062	13,500	118,275
Republicans	30,550	51,562	9,000	91,112
No. of Cand.	*15*	*28*	*11*	*54*
House	12,550	29,362	6,000	47,912
Senate	18,000	22,200	3,000	43,200
Democrats	15,163	7,500	4,500	27,163
No. of Cand.	*10*	*8*	*2*	*20*
House	13,163	4,500	500	18,163
Senate	2,000	3,000	4,000	9,000
Incumbents	44,213	46,162	12,500	102,875
Challengers	0	6,900	0	6,900
Open Seat	1,500	6,000	1,000	8,500
Winners	43,713	46,662	n/a	90,375
Losers	2,000	12,400	n/a	14,400

Purse Seine Vessel Owners Association

Phone: (206) 283-7733
4209 21st Ave. W., Suite 301, Seattle, WA 98199
E-mail: psvoa@aol.com

The Purse Seine Vessel Owners Association represents about 500 West Coast commercial fishing vessel owners.

The group takes its name from a large net, called a purse seine, often used to catch fish such as tuna, that can be closed like a drawstring purse once it has been set.

Purse Seine Vessel Owners Association - Political Action Committee (C00317305) *Address: same as sponsor * Treasurer: Robert Plenkovich * Contact: Robert Zuanich, Executive Dir.*

	1993-94	1995-96	1997	Totals
Receipts	$0	$10,000	$0	$10,000
Disburse	0	6,419	1,308	7,727
Cash	0	3,580	1,048	n/a
Contributions	0	7,598	1,250	8,848
Republicans	0	2,998	0	2,998
No. of Cand.	*0*	*4*	*0*	*4*
House	0	2,498	0	2,498
Senate	0	500	0	500
Democrats	0	4,600	1,250	5,850
No. of Cand.	*0*	*3*	*2*	*5*
House	0	4,500	1,000	5,500
Senate	0	100	250	350
Incumbents	0	3,598	250	3,848
Challengers	0	4,000	0	4,000
Open Seat	0	0	1,000	1,000
Winners	0	3,598	n/a	3,598
Losers	0	4,000	n/a	4,000

Electric Utilities

Action Committee for Rural Electrification

*Phone: (703) 907-5826 * Fax: (703) 907-5516*
4301 Wilson Blvd., Arlington, VA 22203
Web: www.nreca.org

Most ACRE PACs are sponsored by the National Rural Electric Cooperative Association, which represents the interests of cooperative electric utilities, located mostly in rural areas. NRECA's 1,000 member cooperatives serve 30 million people in 46 states.

Of the about 1,000 rural electric systems, more than 60 are generation and transmission cooperatives, which produce 7 percent of the nation's coal-fired generation. Most of the more than 900 distribution systems are consumer-owned cooperatives; some are public power districts. The chief spokesman for the nation's electric cooperatives is NRECA Chief Executive Officer and former Rep. Glenn English, D-Okla.

NRECA opposes the consolidation of the utility industry and the repeal of the Public Utility Holding Company Act. The group will be heavily involved in the utility deregulation discussion and revisions of the Clean Air Act.

In 1996, NRECA spent more on federal elections than any single utility or energy PAC, including the multinational oil and gas producers, and gave 85 percent of its contributions to winning candidates. NRECA also has affiliated state PACs in Missouri, Indiana, Mississippi and Oklahoma which contributed smaller amounts (totaling nearly $80,000) to federal campaigns.

Action Committee for Rural Electrification (ACRE) (C00002972) *Address: same as sponsor * Treasurer: Patrick E. Gioffre * Contact: Robert Dawson, PAC Dir.*

	1993-94	1995-96	1997	Totals
Receipts	$1,055,794	$1,207,449	$686,069	$2,949,312
Disburse	1,048,884	1,168,748	529,463	2,747,095
Cash	111,463	150,169	306,779	n/a
Contributions	501,200	651,866	269,321	1,422,387
Republicans	129,350	297,250	138,446	565,046
No. of Cand.	*101*	*171*	*122*	*394*
House	85,950	187,750	101,946	375,646
Senate	43,400	109,500	36,500	189,400
Democrats	366,100	354,616	127,973	848,689
No. of Cand.	*227*	*209*	*128*	*564*
House	276,100	264,438	93,654	634,192
Senate	90,000	90,178	34,319	214,497
Incumbents	420,700	487,966	267,321	1,175,987
Challengers	22,400	31,500	0	53,900
Open Seat	58,100	132,400	2,000	192,500
Winners	368,250	556,116	n/a	924,366
Losers	132,950	95,750	n/a	228,700

Action Committee for Rural Electrification/Missouri Cooperatives (formerly known as Missouri ACRE) (C00008169) *Phone: (573) 659-3409 * Fax: (573) 659-3411 * 2722 E. McCarty, Jefferson City, MO 65101 * Treasurer: Linda Bolten*

	1993-94	1995-96	1997	Totals
Receipts	$21,203	$21,903	$11,930	$55,036
Disburse	17,935	40,657	18,130	76,722
Cash	37,670	18,916	12,717	n/a
Contributions	15,000	35,000	15,312	65,312
Republicans	2,350	11,250	14,312	27,912
No. of Cand.	*4*	*4*	*4*	*12*
House	2,100	10,000	7,000	19,100
Senate	250	1,250	7,312	8,812
Democrats	12,650	23,750	1,000	37,400
No. of Cand.	*5*	*4*	*2*	*11*
House	12,650	23,750	1,000	37,400
Senate	0	0	0	0
Incumbents	11,500	25,000	15,312	51,812
Challengers	0	500	0	500
Open Seat	3,500	9,500	0	13,000
Winners	15,000	29,000	n/a	44,000
Losers	0	6,000	n/a	6,000

Mississippi ACRE Committee (C00004952) *P.O. Box 8101, Jackson, MS 39284 * Treasurer: Hobson Waits*

	1993-94	1995-96	1997	Totals
Receipts	$93,599	$85,328	$60,957	$239,884
Disburse	29,372	124,018	16,622	170,012
Cash	70,674	31,986	76,322	n/a
Contributions	23,400	17,100	6,000	46,500
Republicans	7,200	13,100	4,000	24,300
No. of Cand.	*3*	*7*	*4*	*14*
House	3,200	9,100	3,000	15,300
Senate	4,000	4,000	1,000	9,000
Democrats	16,200	3,000	2,000	21,200
No. of Cand.	*8*	*2*	*2*	*12*
House	16,200	3,000	2,000	21,200
Senate	0	0	0	0
Incumbents	17,000	12,000	6,000	35,000
Challengers	0	1,000	0	1,000
Open Seat	6,400	3,100	0	9,500
Winners	19,200	14,100	n/a	33,300
Losers	4,200	3,000	n/a	7,200

Indiana ACRE/Indiana Statewide Association of Rural Electric Cooperatives Inc. (C00103978) *Phone: (317) 487-2220 * Fax: (317) 247-5220 * 720 N. High School Rd., Indianapolis, IN 46214 * Web: www.indremcs.org * Treasurer: Ron Hale*

	1993-94	1995-96	1997	Totals
Receipts	$17,344	$19,845	$8,376	$45,565
Disburse	14,484	20,200	10,100	44,784
Cash	3,324	2,793	1,070	n/a
Contributions	14,479	17,200	10,100	41,779
Republicans	8,729	7,900	5,600	22,229
No. of Cand.	*6*	*6*	*4*	*16*
House	4,730	7,900	4,600	17,230
Senate	3,999	0	1,000	4,999
Democrats	5,750	9,300	4,500	19,550
No. of Cand.	*5*	*4*	*4*	*13*
House	5,750	9,300	2,500	17,550
Senate	0	0	2,000	2,000
Incumbents	12,249	13,900	7,100	33,249
Challengers	0	0	0	0
Open Seat	1,750	3,300	3,000	8,050
Winners	11,249	14,500	n/a	25,749
Losers	3,230	2,700	n/a	5,930

Oklahoma ACRE (C00133561) *Phone: (580) 667-5281 * P.O. Box 542, Tipton, OK 73570 * Web: www.oaec.com * Treasurer: Wayne Loafman*

	1993-94	1995-96	1997	Totals
Receipts	$3,177	$7,575	$4,762	$15,514
Disburse	8,350	7,517	2,002	17,869
Cash	4,366	4,424	6,184	n/a
Contributions	8,350	8,500	0	16,850
Republicans	3,350	7,000	0	10,350
No. of Cand.	*4*	*5*	*0*	*9*
House	3,000	6,000	0	9,000
Senate	350	1,000	0	1,350
Democrats	5,000	1,500	0	6,500
No. of Cand.	*4*	*2*	*0*	*6*
House	5,000	1,000	0	6,000
Senate	0	500	0	500
Incumbents	4,500	6,500	0	11,000
Challengers	0	0	0	0
Open Seat	3,850	2,000	0	5,850
Winners	4,850	7,500	n/a	12,350
Losers	3,500	1,000	n/a	4,500

Speak Up for Rural Electrification (SURE) (C00007849) *Phone: (502) 451-2430 * Fax: (502) 459-3209 * P.O. Box 32170, 4515 Bishop Lane, Louisville, KY 40232 * Treasurer: William Nelson Curry*

Speak Up for Rural Electrification is sponsored and supported by Action Committee for Rural Electrification.

	1993-94	1995-96	1997	Totals
Receipts	$34,382	$44,927	$21,505	$100,814
Disburse	31,153	49,550	6,703	87,406
Cash	25,213	20,591	35,393	n/a
Contributions	3,800	6,000	1,500	11,300
Republicans	1,750	4,000	1,000	6,750
No. of Cand.	*3*	*4*	*2*	*9*
House	1,750	4,000	1,000	6,750
Senate	0	0	0	0
Democrats	2,050	2,000	500	4,550
No. of Cand.	*3*	*2*	*1*	*6*
House	2,050	2,000	500	4,550
Senate	0	0	0	0
Incumbents	3,300	6,000	1,000	10,300
Challengers	500	0	0	500
Open Seat	0	0	500	500
Winners	2,550	5,000	n/a	7,550
Losers	1,250	1,000	n/a	2,250

Contributed less than $5,000 during 1995-96 cycle:

Colorado Advocates for Rural Electrification (C00011387) *Phone: (303) 455-2700 * 1313 W. 46th Ave., Denver, CO 80211 * Treasurer: Ray E. Clifton*

Kansas Action Committee for Rural Electrification (C00010561) *Phone: (785) 478-4554 * P.O. Box 740, Meade, KS 67864 * Web: www.kec.org * Treasurer: Kirk A. Thompson*

Louisiana Action Committee for Rural Electrification (C00083337) *10725 Airline Highway, Baton Rouge, LA 70816 * Treasurer: A. Paul Wood*

Montana Action Committee for Rural Electrification (C00139360) *P.O. Box 1306, Great Falls, MT 59403 * Treasurer: Jay T. Downen*

Ohio Action Committee for Rural Electrification (C00040881) *6677 Busch Blvd., P.O. Box 26036, Columbus, OH 43226 * Web: www.buckeyepower.com/buckeye * Treasurer: David A. Berger*

South Dakota Action Committee for Rural Electrification (C00129205) *Phone: (605) 224-8823 * Fax: (605) 224-4430 * P.O. Box 1138, 222 W. Pleasant Ave., Pierre, SD 57501 * Web: www.sdrea.com * Treasurer: Ronald D. Holsteen*

Ameren Corp.

*Phone: (314) 554-4673 * Fax: (314) 554-4014*
1901 Chouteau Ave., P.O. Box 66149, St. Louis, MO 63166-6149
Web: www.ameren.com

Ameren is a publicly held company that provides energy services to 1.5 million customers in Missouri and Illinois. More than 93 percent of its $3 billion in revenue comes from electricity sales, with the remainder from natural gas sales. Ameren employs about 8,000 people.

The company has a 26 percent share in a nuclear plant in Callaway County, Mo.

Ameren is the parent of Union Electric Co., now known as AmerenUE, and Central Illinois Public Service Co., now known as AmerenCIPS. At the close of 1997, Union Electric and Cipsco Inc. merged to create Ameren Corp.

Other subsidiaries include: Ameren Energy, an energy marketing and trading affiliate; CIPSCO Investment Co., which manages non-utility investments, including leveraged leases, marketable securities and energy projects; and Ameren Services, which provides support services to the corporation and its subsidiaries.

Union Electric Co. Employees Federal Political Action Committee (UEFedPAC) (C00206136) *Phone: (573) 681-7202 * Fax: (573) 681-7296 * P.O. Box 780, Jefferson City, MO 65102 * Treasurer: Donald L. Hollingsworth * Contact: Kathy Hale, Chairman*

*Contact: Dave Hennen * Phone: (314) 554-4673*

	1993-94	1995-96	1997	Totals
Receipts	$25,063	$33,238	$19,249	$77,550
Disburse	22,167	26,150	18,250	66,567
Cash	3,581	10,672	11,672	n/a
Contributions	21,150	26,650	17,750	65,550
Republicans	9,250	15,850	11,500	36,600
No. of Cand.	*7*	*19*	*10*	*36*
House	4,250	10,550	6,000	20,800
Senate	5,000	5,300	5,500	15,800
Democrats	11,900	10,800	6,250	28,950
No. of Cand.	*12*	*7*	*8*	*27*
House	9,550	10,800	6,250	26,600
Senate	2,350	0	0	2,350
Incumbents	13,800	20,600	17,750	52,150
Challengers	500	1,000	0	1,500
Open Seat	6,850	5,050	0	11,900
Winners	17,800	21,650	n/a	39,450
Losers	3,350	5,000	n/a	8,350

Central Illinois Public Service Co. PAC (CIPS-PAC) (C00118935) *Phone: (217) 523-3600 * Fax: (217) 535-5555 * 607 E. Adams St., Springfield, IL 62701 * Web: www.ameren.com * Treasurer: Bob Mill * Contact: Bruce Fritz, Regional Manager*

Central Illinois Public Service merged in 1997 with the $6.9 billion public utility Union Electric, which has operations in Missouri and Illinois, to form the new holding company, Ameren.

CIPS is an electric and gas public utility that sells electricity and natural gas to 322,000 and 169,000 customers, respectively, in portions of central and southern Illinois. The utility has 13 power plants at five locations, with four underground gas storage fields and one propane-air gas plant.

	1993-94	1995-96	1997	Totals
Receipts	$9,107	$15,296	$9,030	$33,433
Disburse	8,500	12,550	4,500	25,550
Cash	2,310	5,057	9,587	n/a
Contributions	7,500	9,000	500	17,000
Republicans	6,500	7,000	500	14,000
No. of Cand.	*6*	*6*	*1*	*13*
House	6,500	7,000	500	14,000
Senate	0	0	0	0
Democrats	1,000	2,000	0	3,000
No. of Cand.	*1*	*2*	*0*	*3*
House	0	1,000	0	1,000
Senate	1,000	1,000	0	2,000
Incumbents	5,500	7,000	500	13,000
Challengers	0	1,000	0	1,000
Open Seat	2,000	1,000	0	3,000
Winners	6,500	8,000	n/a	14,500
Losers	1,000	1,000	n/a	2,000

American Electric Power

*Phone: (614) 223-1000 * Fax: (614) 223-1823*
One Riverside Plaza, Columbus, OH 43216
Web: www.aep.com

American Electric Power is a public energy company that provides electricity to 2.9 million customers in Ohio, Indiana, Michigan, West Virginia, Virginia, Tennessee and Kentucky. With 18,000 employees, the company had 1997 revenues of $6.1 billion.

In December 1997, AEP announced plans to merge with Central and South West Corp., an electric utility holding company based in Dallas that serves parts of Texas, Louisiana, Oklahoma and Arkansas.

AEP operates 38 power plants, most of which are coal-fired, with one nuclear, and has holdings in Great Britain and China.

AEP has several affiliated PACs, including Columbus Southern Power Co. and American Electric Power Fuel Supply.

The American Electric Power Committee for Responsible Government (C00096842) *Phone: (202) 628-1645 * 801 Pennsylvania Ave. N.W., Suite 214, Washington, DC 20004-2615 * Treasurer: Doreen W. Hohl * Contact: Bruce Beam, V.P. of Gov. Affairs*

	1993-94	1995-96	1997	Totals
Receipts	$90,883	$106,155	$51,124	$248,162
Disburse	86,900	100,250	51,500	238,650
Cash	9,181	15,087	14,713	n/a
Contributions	84,020	87,000	48,500	219,520
Republicans	39,350	66,000	38,000	143,350
No. of Cand.	*52*	*75*	*46*	*173*
House	29,850	44,000	21,500	95,350
Senate	9,500	22,000	16,500	48,000
Democrats	43,670	21,000	10,500	75,170
No. of Cand.	*52*	*28*	*17*	*97*
House	30,800	18,000	9,500	58,300
Senate	12,870	3,000	1,000	16,870
Incumbents	76,270	79,500	44,000	199,770
Challengers	1,000	2,000	0	3,000
Open Seat	7,250	4,500	3,000	14,750
Winners	68,550	74,500	n/a	143,050
Losers	15,470	12,500	n/a	27,970

Columbus Southern Power Co. Political Action Committee (also known as C&SOE PAC) (C00158113) *Phone: (614) 223-1000 * Fax: (614) 223-1823 * 301 Cleveland Ave. S.W., Canton, OH 44701 * Treasurer: Gerald F. Clifton*

	1993-94	1995-96	1997	Totals
Receipts	$11,852	$7,181	$1,840	$20,873
Disburse	11,445	7,200	3,600	22,245
Cash	2,643	2,626	866	n/a
Contributions	7,625	6,950	1,500	16,075
Republicans	6,750	6,950	1,500	15,200
No. of Cand.	*9*	*8*	*2*	*19*
House	5,750	6,950	1,500	14,200
Senate	1,000	0	0	1,000
Democrats	875	0	0	875
No. of Cand.	*3*	*0*	*0*	*3*
House	875	0	0	875
Senate	0	0	0	0
Incumbents	4,875	6,950	1,500	13,325
Challengers	750	0	0	750
Open Seat	2,000	0	0	2,000
Winners	6,500	6,700	n/a	13,200
Losers	1,125	250	n/a	1,375

American Electric Power Fuel Supply Political Action Committee (C00234963) *Phone: (614) 681-2009 * Fax: (614) 687-3175 * One Memorial Dr., P.O. Box 700, Lancaster, OH 43130 * Treasurer: David M. Cohen*

	1993-94	1995-96	1997	Totals
Receipts	$29,876	$30,738	$14,687	$75,301
Disburse	29,687	31,304	18,285	79,276
Cash	17,232	16,666	13,069	n/a
Contributions	5,262	5,543	3,680	14,485
Republicans	3,742	4,893	2,200	10,835
No. of Cand.	*3*	*5*	*3*	*11*
House	3,242	5,393	2,200	10,835
Senate	500	-500	0	0
Democrats	1,520	650	1,480	3,650
No. of Cand.	*2*	*1*	*2*	*5*
House	1,520	650	1,480	3,650
Senate	0	0	0	0
Incumbents	2,762	4,893	3,480	11,135
Challengers	0	650	200	850
Open Seat	2,500	0	0	2,500
Winners	3,742	4,893	n/a	8,635
Losers	1,520	650	n/a	2,170

Contributed less than $5,000 during 1995-96 cycle:

Indiana Michigan Power Co. Civic Action Program (C00139642) *Phone: (219) 425-2111 * Fax: (219) 425-2112 * One Summit Square, P.O. Box 60, Fort Wayne, IN 46801 * Treasurer: Maurice C. McIntyre*

Ohio Power Political Action Committee (C00145540) *Phone: (330) 456-8173 * Fax: (330) 438-7330 * 301 Cleveland Ave. S.W., P.O. Box 24400, Canton, OH 44701 * Treasurer: Gerald F. Clifton*

The Appalachian Power Committee for Responsible Government (C00235986) *Phone: (540) 985-2900 * Fax: (540) 985-2596 * 40 Franklin Rd., P.O. Box 2021, Roanoke, VA 24022 * Treasurer: Thomas E. Mitchell*

American Public Power Association

*Phone: (202) 467-2900 * Fax: (202) 467-2910*
2301 M St. N.W., Washington, DC 20037
*Web: www.appanet.org * E-mail: kwalls@appanet.org*

The American Public Power Association represents 2,000 local and state nonprofit electric utilities. Community-owned utility systems provide electricity for 35 million Americans, according to the group.

The APPA represents members before Congress and federal agencies. It generally opposes many proposals from investor-owned utility companies, such as the repeal of the Public Utility Holding Company Act.

American Public Power Association Public Ownership of Electric Resources PAC (POWER PAC) (C00161570) *Address: same as sponsor * Treasurer: Betsy Oilman * Contact: Karen Walls*

	1993-94	1995-96	1997	Totals
Receipts	$29,172	$12,954	$0	$42,126
Disburse	25,693	15,700	15,500	56,893
Cash	6,632	0	2,375	n/a
Contributions	25,200	15,700	16,091	56,991
Republicans	3,750	10,750	5,500	20,000
No. of Cand.	*6*	*25*	*13*	*44*
House	1,750	7,250	4,000	13,000
Senate	2,000	3,500	1,500	7,000
Democrats	21,450	4,950	10,091	36,491
No. of Cand.	*39*	*14*	*17*	*70*
House	16,200	4,450	7,091	27,741
Senate	5,250	500	3,000	8,750
Incumbents	24,700	14,200	15,091	53,991
Challengers	0	0	0	0
Open Seat	500	500	1,000	2,000
Winners	19,250	11,750	n/a	31,000
Losers	5,950	3,950	n/a	9,900

Arizona Public Service Co.

*Phone: (602) 379-2670 * Fax: (602) 379-2640*
P.O. Box 53999, M.S. 8104, Phoenix, AZ 85072-3999
*Web: www.apsc.com * E-mail: wekstr01@apsc.com*

Arizona Public Service is the principal electricity supplier in Arizona, serving 11 of the state's 15 counties. The company, which also serves parts of California, employs about 6,500 people.

APS operates and co-owns the Palo Verde Nuclear Generating Station, the largest nuclear facility in the nation. It also operates two coal-fired power plants — Cholla, in northeastern Arizona, and Four Corners, in northwestern New Mexico — and is a part-owner of the Navajo Generating Station near Page, Ariz. Additionally, the company owns five gas and oil and two hydroelectric power plants.

APS is the largest subsidiary of Pinnacle West Capital Corp., a public company which reported 1997 revenues of $444 million.

Arizona Public Service Co. Political Action Committee (APSPAC) (C00015933) *Address: same as sponsor * Treasurer: Bob Ekstrom * Contact: Bonnie Kabin, Chairwoman*

	1993-94	1995-96	1997	Totals
Receipts	$47,553	$134,800	$68,680	$251,033
Disburse	48,495	110,314	79,057	237,866
Cash	7,517	32,004	21,628	n/a
Contributions	26,275	74,777	47,750	148,802
Republicans	17,525	64,277	42,750	124,552
No. of Cand.	*35*	*58*	*36*	*129*
House	11,325	42,027	17,250	70,602
Senate	6,200	22,250	25,500	53,950
Democrats	8,750	10,500	5,000	24,250
No. of Cand.	*16*	*13*	*8*	*37*
House	7,250	10,500	3,500	21,250
Senate	1,500	0	1,500	3,000
Incumbents	18,075	67,200	45,250	130,525
Challengers	2,000	2,500	0	4,500
Open Seat	6,200	5,577	2,500	14,277
Winners	19,125	67,700	n/a	86,825
Losers	7,150	7,077	n/a	14,227

Baltimore Gas & Electric Co.

*Phone: (410) 234-6581 * Fax: (410) 234-7426*
1000 Gas and Electric Building, P.O. Box 1475, Baltimore, MD 21203
*Web: www.bge.com * E-mail: corpcomm@bge.com*

Baltimore Gas & Electric is a publicly traded power company that serves Baltimore City and 10 Maryland counties. The $8 billion company employs 8,000 workers and serves more than 1 million electric customers and 547,000 gas customers. It operates Calvert Cliffs Nuclear Power Plant in Maryland.

BGE announced in late December 1997 that it was canceling its proposed merger with another utility company, PEPCO, which serves the Washington area. The proposed merger would have made the resulting utility one of the 10 largest in the United States. Instead, the company in March 1998 reorganized into three divisions to prepare for state-mandated utility competition in 2002.

BGE subsidiaries include: Constellation Holdings Inc., Constellation Investments Inc., Constellation Real Estate Group, BGE Energy Projects & Services Inc., BGE Home Products and Services Inc., BGE Commercial Building Systems and Constellation Energy Source.

Baltimore Gas & Electric Co. Political Action Committee (BG&E PAC) (C00041376) *Address: same as sponsor * Treasurer: Haskell N. Arnold * Contact: Florence Kerdle, Chairperson*

	1993-94	1995-96	1997	Totals
Receipts	$83,077	$65,759	$45,490	$194,326
Disburse	81,792	66,886	39,180	187,858
Cash	7,469	6,347	12,658	n/a

Contributions	67,150	55,700	31,180	154,030
Republicans	37,500	45,450	23,180	106,130
No. of Cand.	*38*	*54*	*30*	*122*
House	25,500	32,950	15,680	74,130
Senate	12,000	12,500	7,500	32,000
Democrats	29,150	10,250	8,000	47,400
No. of Cand.	*33*	*8*	*10*	*51*
House	22,650	9,000	7,000	38,650
Senate	6,500	1,250	1,000	8,750
Incumbents	49,400	50,200	31,180	130,780
Challengers	1,500	2,500	0	4,000
Open Seat	15,750	3,000	0	18,750
Winners	55,150	49,200	n/a	104,350
Losers	12,000	6,500	n/a	18,500

Basin Electric Power Cooperative

*Phone: (701) 223-0441 * Fax: (701) 224-5315*
1717 E. Interstate Ave., Bismarck, ND 58501

The Basin Electric Power Cooperative is a wholesale electric generating operation that has power plant facilities in North Dakota and Wyoming. The co-op serves 1.5 million customers in North Dakota, South Dakota, Montana, Wyoming, Colorado, Nebraska, Minnesota and Iowa.

The co-op has 128 members that buy and distribute power in the eight-state area. It has one of the largest geographic bases of any utility in the United States.

The cooperative is interested in legislative issues such as electric industry deregulation and environmental issues related to air emissions.

Basin Electric Power Cooperative Political Action Committee (Basin Electric PAC) (C00220269) *Address: same as sponsor * Treasurer: Sheryl Massey * Contact: Bob McPhail, President*

	1993-94	*1995-96*	*1997*	*Totals*
Receipts	$18,263	$16,986	$10,723	$45,972
Disburse	14,216	17,234	7,786	39,236
Cash	6,505	6,257	9,194	n/a
Contributions	5,500	9,250	3,600	18,350
Republicans	2,000	6,000	0	8,000
No. of Cand.	*1*	*5*	*0*	*6*
House	0	1,000	0	1,000
Senate	2,000	5,000	0	7,000
Democrats	3,000	3,250	3,500	9,750
No. of Cand.	*2*	*4*	*4*	*10*
House	1,000	2,000	500	3,500
Senate	2,000	1,250	3,000	6,250
Incumbents	3,500	7,250	3,600	14,350
Challengers	0	0	0	0
Open Seat	2,000	2,000	0	4,000
Winners	5,500	8,250	n/a	13,750
Losers	0	1,000	n/a	1,000

Black Hills Power & Light Co.

*Phone: (605) 348-1700 * Fax: (605) 348-9749*
P.O. Box 1400, Rapid City, SD 57709
Web: www.blackhillspower.com

Black Hills Power & Light is a subsidiary of the publicly traded Black Hills Corp. The corporation's Wyoming operations include mining, processing and selling coal; marketing and wholesaling electric power; and exploring, developing and operating more than 277 oil and gas wells in Wyoming. The company also deals in software and owns utility, oil and gas properties. It provides power to 54,000 customers in 9,300 square miles of South Dakota, Wyoming and Montana.

BHP&L has annual sales of about $163 million. Electricity accounts for 73 percent of sales, while coal mining and oil/gas sales represent 19 percent and 8 percent, respectively. Black Hills Power has 400 employees with more than 350 people in its 12 district offices and five electric power plants. Almost all of Black Hills' power is generated from its own coal.

Subsidiaries include: Clovis Point Mine Properties, Wyodak Resources, Western Production, Enserco Energy Inc., Wickford Energy Marketing and Daksoft.

Black Hills Power & Light Co. Political Action Committee (C00125732) *Address: same as sponsor * Treasurer: Gail L. Madler * Contact: Mutch Usera, Manager of Marketing and Economic Development*

	1993-94	*1995-96*	*1997*	*Totals*
Receipts	$12,110	$14,334	$7,905	$34,349
Disburse	14,425	13,400	100	27,925
Cash	888	1,824	9,629	n/a
Contributions	1,500	7,800	0	9,300
Republicans	900	6,800	0	7,700
No. of Cand.	*3*	*5*	*0*	*8*
House	600	1,300	0	1,900
Senate	300	5,500	0	5,800
Democrats	600	1,000	0	1,600
No. of Cand.	*2*	*1*	*0*	*3*
House	300	0	0	300
Senate	300	1,000	0	1,300
Incumbents	300	1,000	0	1,300
Challengers	300	1,000	0	1,300
Open Seat	900	5,800	0	6,700
Winners	900	7,050	n/a	7,950
Losers	600	750	n/a	1,350

CMS Energy Corp.

Phone: (313) 436-9200
Fairlake Plaza S., 330 Town Center Dr., Dearborn, MI 48126
Web: www.cmsenergy.com

CMS Energy is an international energy company with businesses in electric and natural gas utility operations; oil and gas exploration and development; independent power production; and natural gas transmission, storage and marketing. The company's primary subsidiary is Consumers Energy, which serves more than 6 million residents of the Michigan Lower Peninsula, making it the largest natural gas and electric utility in the state and fourth-largest in the nation.

In addition to its Michigan utility business, CMS Energy operates energy facilities throughout the United States and in 18 other countries.

CMS Energy, a public company with 9,600 employees, had 1997 revenues of $5.7 billion.

CMS Energy is also the parent company of Consumers Gas Group and CMS Enterprises.

CMS Energy Corp. Employees for Better Government - Federal (C00075473) *Phone: (517) 788-1623 * Fax: (517) 788-1315 * 212 W. Michigan Ave., M-809, Jackson, MI 49201-2277 * Treasurer: Thomas William Heikkinen * Contact: Jennifer Bertram, Administrator*

	1993-94	*1995-96*	*1997*	*Totals*
Receipts	$114,198	$133,136	$72,950	$320,284
Disburse	117,455	128,981	68,401	314,837
Cash	3,385	7,550	12,104	n/a
Contributions	111,455	114,963	61,392	287,810
Republicans	45,050	68,588	32,267	145,905
No. of Cand.	*34*	*48*	*28*	*110*
House	40,800	50,088	20,267	111,155
Senate	4,250	18,500	12,000	34,750
Democrats	66,155	46,375	29,125	141,655
No. of Cand.	*49*	*20*	*25*	*94*
House	48,095	37,125	26,125	111,345
Senate	18,060	9,250	3,000	30,310
Incumbents	94,205	106,825	61,392	262,422
Challengers	500	6,638	0	7,138
Open Seat	16,750	1,000	0	17,750
Winners	83,145	95,325	n/a	178,470
Losers	28,310	19,638	n/a	47,948

Carolina Power & Light Co.

*Phone: (919) 546-6444 * Fax: (919) 546-7448*
P.O. Box 1510, Raleigh, NC 27602
Web: www.cplc.com

Carolina Power & Light is a public utility that generates and distributes electricity to more than 1.1 million customers in North and South Carolina. The company, which has 6,700 employees, reported 1997 revenues of $3 billion.

Carolina Power & Light operates the Harris Nuclear Plant in Wake County, the Brunswick Nuclear Plant near Southport, N.C., and the Robinson Nuclear Plant near Hartsville, S.C. About one-third of the company's electricity is from nuclear sources.

In December 1997, Carolina Power & Light subsidiary CaroNet acquired Capitol Information Services Inc., an Internet service provider selling access under the brand name Interpath. The organizations will be merged, and the new company will be called Interpath Communications.

Employees Federal PAC - Carolina Power & Light Co. (C00091884) *Address: same as sponsor * Treasurer: Joan R. Stutts * Contact: John Robinson, Chairman*

	1993-94	1995-96	1997	Totals
Receipts	$189,511	$192,441	$90,531	$472,483
Disburse	134,112	233,865	104,589	472,566
Cash	136,491	95,079	81,196	n/a
Contributions	118,200	200,750	79,000	397,950
Republicans	62,850	152,000	49,000	263,850
No. of Cand.	*57*	*93*	*42*	*192*
House	44,350	101,500	34,000	179,850
Senate	18,500	50,500	15,000	84,000
Democrats	55,100	48,750	30,000	133,850
No. of Cand.	*44*	*24*	*27*	*95*
House	52,100	46,750	25,000	123,850
Senate	3,000	2,000	5,000	10,000
Incumbents	83,350	168,250	78,500	330,100
Challengers	8,000	15,000	0	23,000
Open Seat	26,100	18,000	500	44,600
Winners	87,100	169,750	n/a	256,850
Losers	31,100	31,000	n/a	62,100

Central and South West Corp.

*Phone: (214) 777-1491 * Fax: (214) 777-3926*
1616 Woodall Rogers Fwy., P.O. Box 660164, Dallas, TX 75266
Web: www.csw.com

Central and South West is a publicly traded holding company whose subsidiaries serve about 1.7 million customers in one of the largest service territories in the United States, covering 152,000 square miles in portions of Texas, Oklahoma, Louisiana and Arkansas. Utility subsidiaries include: Southwestern Electric Power Co., Central Power & Light Co., West Texas Utilities Co. and Public Service Co. of Oklahoma. The company posted $5.2 billion in 1997 sales.

CSW also owns SEEBOARD, a utilities company in the United Kingdom that serves 2 million customers.

In 1997, CSW and American Electric Power announced plans to merge. The combined company would serve 4.6 million customers in the United States, and 4 million customers overseas.

In January 1998, CSW created CSW Electric Vehicles, an unregulated business that will seek to take advantage of opportunities within the electric vehicle industry.

Four CSW subsidiaries have PACs — Central Power & Light, Southwestern Electric Power Co., West Texas Utilities, and Public Service Co. of Oklahoma, located in Tulsa, Okla. Other subsidiaries include CSW Energy and International.

Central and South West Services Inc. Political Action Committee (C00083089) *Phone: (202) 628-0886 * Fax: (202) 628-1038 * 801 Pennsylvania Ave. N.W., Suite 352, Washington, DC 20004 * Treasurer: Roger Murphree*

	1993-94	1995-96	1997	Totals
Receipts	$57,841	$142,106	$110,373	$310,320
Disburse	56,785	69,800	52,954	179,539
Cash	5,556	77,799	129,123	n/a
Contributions	23,750	44,750	44,499	112,999
Republicans	5,000	34,500	24,499	63,999
No. of Cand.	*7*	*27*	*28*	*62*
House	3,000	24,000	14,999	41,999
Senate	2,000	10,500	9,500	22,000
Democrats	18,750	10,250	20,000	49,000
No. of Cand.	*24*	*15*	*18*	*57*
House	13,500	10,500	12,000	36,000
Senate	5,250	-250	8,000	13,000
Incumbents	21,750	31,750	43,499	96,999
Challengers	0	500	0	500
Open Seat	1,500	12,000	2,000	15,500
Winners	18,250	39,250	n/a	57,500
Losers	5,500	5,500	n/a	11,000

Southwestern Electric Power Co. Political Action Committee (C00084988) *Phone: (318) 673-3646 * Fax: (318) 227-2147 * 428 Travis St., Shreveport, LA 71101 * E-mail: jballard@csw.com * Treasurer: David B. Camp * Contact: Jack Ballard, Chairman*

Southwestern Electric Power serves more than 400,000 customers in a 25,000-square mile service territory in northwest Louisiana, northeast Texas and western Arkansas.

SWEPCO is headquartered in Shreveport, La. and has operations in Longview and Texarkana, Texas; and Fayetteville, Ark. It is a wholly owned subsidiary of Central and South West Corp., headquartered in Dallas.

	1993-94	1995-96	1997	Totals
Receipts	$29,898	$38,816	$29,642	$98,356
Disburse	27,150	42,963	25,150	95,263
Cash	9,221	5,080	9,573	n/a
Contributions	8,500	10,500	5,000	24,000
Republicans	2,500	7,000	500	10,000
No. of Cand.	*3*	*8*	*1*	*12*
House	2,000	4,000	0	6,000
Senate	500	3,000	500	4,000
Democrats	6,000	3,500	4,500	14,000
No. of Cand.	*6*	*4*	*4*	*14*
House	4,500	3,000	1,000	8,500
Senate	1,500	500	3,500	5,500
Incumbents	8,000	6,000	4,500	18,500
Challengers	0	500	0	500
Open Seat	500	4,000	500	5,000
Winners	7,000	8,500	n/a	15,500
Losers	1,500	2,000	n/a	3,500

Central Power & Light Co. Political Action Committee (C00082248) *Phone: (512) 881-5300 * 539 N. Carancahua, Corpus Christi, TX 78401 * Treasurer: Grady O'Shields*

Central Power & Light provides electric power to more than 600,000 south Texas customers. CPL's 44,000-square mile service territory is headquartered in Corpus Christi, with divisions in Laredo and San Benito.

	1993-94	1995-96	1997	Totals
Receipts	$11,907	$18,500	$11,242	$41,649
Disburse	10,120	12,000	7,512	29,632
Cash	13,075	19,579	23,312	n/a
Contributions	10,100	10,500	6,500	27,100
Republicans	500	3,500	500	4,500
No. of Cand.	*1*	*3*	*1*	*5*
House	0	2,500	0	2,500
Senate	500	1,000	500	2,000
Democrats	9,600	7,000	6,000	22,600
No. of Cand.	*8*	*5*	*3*	*16*
House	8,100	7,000	6,000	21,100
Senate	1,500	0	0	1,500
Incumbents	9,600	7,500	2,500	19,600
Challengers	0	0	0	0
Open Seat	500	3,000	4,000	7,500
Winners	8,600	7,500	n/a	16,100
Losers	1,500	3,000	n/a	4,500

West Texas Utilities Co. Political Action Committee (C00082420) *Phone: (915) 674-7000 * P.O. Box 841, Abilene, TX 79604 * Treasurer: Ray Woodard * Contact: Bill Holley*

West Texas Utilities is owned by CSW. It serves 184,000 customers in an area that spans 52 counties and 53,000 square miles of west Texas, from the Red River to the Rio Grande. WTU is headquartered in Abilene and also has operating divisions based in San Angelo, Childress and Marfa, Texas.

	1993-94	1995-96	1997	Totals
Receipts	$34,638	$20,071	$6,458	$61,167
Disburse	36,850	16,600	3,000	56,450
Cash	5,761	9,236	12,695	n/a
Contributions	7,500	4,000	2,000	13,500
Republicans	2,000	2,000	1,000	5,000
No. of Cand.	*2*	*4*	*2*	*8*
House	0	2,000	500	2,500
Senate	2,000	0	500	2,500
Democrats	5,500	2,000	1,000	8,500
No. of Cand.	*5*	*1*	*2*	*8*
House	4,500	2,000	1,000	7,500
Senate	1,000	0	0	1,000
Incumbents	7,500	4,000	1,500	13,000
Challengers	0	0	0	0
Open Seat	0	0	500	500
Winners	5,500	4,000	n/a	9,500
Losers	2,000	0	n/a	2,000

Contributed less than $5,000 during 1995-96 cycle:

Public Service Co. of Oklahoma Political Action Committee (C00056572) *Phone: (918) 599-2995 * Fax: (918) 599-3007 * P.O. Box 201, Tulsa, OK 74102-0201 * E-mail: vconrad@csw.com * Treasurer: Vaughn L. Conrad*

Cinergy Corp.

*Phone: (513) 381-2000 * Fax: (513) 287-4212*
139 E. Fourth St., Cincinnati, OH 45202
Web: www.cinergy.com

Cinergy is a public energy company that serves more than 1.3 million electric customers and 450,000 gas customers through its primary subsidiaries, The Cincinnati Gas & Electric Co. and PSI Energy Inc. The company's 25,000-square mile service territory spans Indiana, southwest Ohio and northern Kentucky.

The company, which has about 8,000 employees, had 1997 sales of almost $4.4 billion.

In September 1997, Cinergy, along with Florida Progress Corp. of St. Petersburg and New Century Energies of Denver, announced the formation of a joint venture. The new company, named Cadence, will provide single source energy management services and products designed to lower energy costs for national companies that operate in multiple locations throughout the United States.

Other subsidiaries include: Lawrenceburg Gas and Union Light, Heat and Power. Cinergy also holds a 50 percent interest in Midlands Electricity, which serves 2.2 million customers in the United Kingdom.

Cinergy Corp. Political Action Committee (C00304964) *Phone: (202) 824-0400 * 1301 Pennsylvania Ave. N.W., Suite 1030, Washington, DC 20004 * Treasurer: Jon Johnston * Contact: Julia Blankenship, Manager of Federal Gov. Affairs*

	1993-94	1995-96	1997	Totals
Receipts	$0	$173,329	$115,134	$288,463
Disburse	0	145,106	112,541	257,647
Cash	0	28,226	30,820	n/a
Contributions	0	31,825	25,350	57,175
Republicans	0	25,325	17,100	42,425
No. of Cand.	*0*	*29*	*21*	*50*
House	0	23,325	10,600	33,925
Senate	0	2,000	6,500	8,500
Democrats	0	6,500	8,250	14,750
No. of Cand.	*0*	*9*	*11*	*20*
House	0	6,500	7,750	14,250
Senate	0	0	500	500
Incumbents	0	28,650	22,350	51,000
Challengers	0	1,000	0	1,000
Open Seat	0	2,175	3,000	5,175
Winners	0	27,825	n/a	27,825
Losers	0	4,000	n/a	4,000

PSI Energy Inc. Political Action Committee (C00096859) *1000 E. Main St., Plainfield, IN 46168 * Treasurer: Jon Johnston*

PSI Energy, the Indiana subsidiary of Cinergy, dissolved its PAC in September 1997.

	1993-94	1995-96	1997	Totals
Receipts	$119,390	$31,160	$0	$150,550
Disburse	111,192	73,043	63	184,298
Cash	41,945	63	0	n/a
Contributions	31,850	15,050	0	46,900
Republicans	18,600	12,700	0	31,300
No. of Cand.	*13*	*17*	*0*	*30*
House	12,850	11,000	0	23,850
Senate	5,750	1,700	0	7,450
Democrats	13,250	2,350	0	15,600
No. of Cand.	*14*	*3*	*0*	*17*
House	10,250	2,350	0	12,600
Senate	3,000	0	0	3,000
Incumbents	24,100	13,850	0	37,950
Challengers	0	200	0	200
Open Seat	5,250	0	0	5,250
Winners	23,850	13,350	n/a	37,200
Losers	8,000	1,700	n/a	9,700

Terminated PACs which contributed less than $5,000 during 1995-96 cycle:

The Cincinnati Gas & Electric Co. Employee PAC (C00193185) *139 E. Fourth St., Cincinnati, OH 45202 * Treasurer: William L. Sheafer*

Commonwealth Edison Co.

*Phone: (312) 394-7399 * Fax: (312) 394-7251*
P.O. Box 767, Chicago, IL 60690-0767
Web: www.ceco.com:80/ucm/info/comed.htm

Publicly traded Commonwealth Edison provides electricity to 3.4 million customers in northern Illinois. The company serves about 70 percent of the state's population, including Chicago. It posted $7 billion in 1997 sales and employs about 16,000 workers. A subsidiary of Unicom Corp., ComEd gets some of its energy from five nuclear plants in Illinois and Wisconsin.

In February 1998, Commonwealth Edison agreed to terminate a controversial marketing program, designed to give the utility's affiliate companies an edge in the coming competitive market, as part of a settlement reached between the company and the Citizens Utility Board.

Commonwealth Edison Co. Political Action Committee (C00141218) *Address: same as sponsor * Treasurer: John T. Costello*

	1993-94	1995-96	1997	Totals
Receipts	$169,989	$210,152	$117,780	$497,921
Disburse	185,838	208,454	110,700	504,992
Cash	45,652	47,360	54,445	n/a
Contributions	20,750	81,480	49,450	151,680
Republicans	11,800	59,355	26,950	98,105
No. of Cand.	*21*	*47*	*27*	*95*
House	8,800	32,800	12,950	54,550
Senate	3,000	26,555	14,000	43,555
Democrats	8,950	22,125	22,500	53,575
No. of Cand.	*23*	*22*	*16*	*61*
House	8,700	15,875	7,500	32,075
Senate	250	6,250	15,000	21,500
Incumbents	21,900	55,455	43,950	121,305
Challengers	0	2,325	0	2,325
Open Seat	1,850	23,700	5,500	31,050
Winners	20,250	51,930	n/a	72,180
Losers	500	29,550	n/a	30,050

Commonwealth Energy System

*Phone: (617) 225-4000 * Fax: (617) 225-4831*
One Main St., P.O. Box 9150, Cambridge, MA 02142
Web: www.comenergy.com

Commonwealth Energy System serves 367,000 electric customers and 237,000 gas customers in central, eastern and southeastern Massachusetts, including the cities of Boston and Cambridge. The public company, which has about 2,000 employees, reported $1 billion in 1997 revenues.

About 13 percent of the company's electricity is produced by nuclear sources.

COM/Energy also owns a steam company that serves Harvard University, the Museum of Science, Massachusetts General Hospital, Genzyme and Polaroid, among other customers.

Subsidiaries: Commonwealth Electric, Cambridge Electric Light, Canal Electric and Commonwealth Gas. The company also owns five real estate trusts.

COM/Energy Services Co. Employees for a Responsible Congress (C00140277) *Address: same as sponsor * Treasurer: James W. Cardella*

	1993-94	1995-96	1997	Totals
Receipts	$10,391	$11,161	$4,490	$26,042
Disburse	8,668	5,750	1,149	15,567
Cash	5,081	10,503	13,849	n/a
Contributions	8,200	5,250	1,100	14,550
Republicans	6,400	4,950	0	11,350
No. of Cand.	*9*	*6*	*0*	*15*
House	5,600	1,650	0	7,250
Senate	800	3,300	0	4,100
Democrats	1,800	300	1,100	3,200
No. of Cand.	*3*	*1*	*2*	*6*
House	1,800	300	1,100	3,200
Senate	0	0	0	0
Incumbents	7,600	2,750	1,100	11,450
Challengers	300	2,500	0	2,800
Open Seat	300	0	0	300
Winners	7,700	1,400	n/a	9,100
Losers	500	3,850	n/a	4,350

Consolidated Edison Co. of New York

*Phone: (212) 460-1327 * Fax: (212) 777-4351*
4 Irving Pl., New York, NY 10003
*Web: www.coned.com * E-mail: webbh@coned.com*

Consolidated Edison supplies electric service in all of New York City (except part of Queens) and most of Westchester County. This region encompasses an about 660-square mile service area with a population of more than 8 million people and 122,000 miles of electric cable.

CONED also supplies gas in Manhattan, the Bronx and parts of Queens and Westchester County through its 4,000 miles of gas mains.

The company also supplies steam in part of Manhattan via 100 miles of steam mains. Publicly traded Consolidated Edison employs 16,600 people and posted $7.1 billion in 1997 sales.

The company operates two nuclear units in Buchanan, N.Y.

Consolidated Edison Co. of New York Inc. Employees Political Action Committee (C00055616) *Address: same as sponsor * Treasurer: Hyman Schoenblum * Contact: Horace Webb, Chairperson of Executive Committee*

	1993-94	1995-96	1997	Totals
Receipts	$39,918	$46,953	$28,680	$115,551
Disburse	39,225	44,251	31,580	115,056
Cash	2,956	5,663	2,764	n/a
Contributions	8,250	8,936	7,400	24,586
Republicans	1,300	3,950	3,800	9,050
No. of Cand.	*3*	*6*	*7*	*16*
House	1,300	3,450	2,000	6,750
Senate	0	500	1,800	2,300
Democrats	6,950	4,986	3,600	15,536
No. of Cand.	*11*	*7*	*7*	*25*
House	5,350	4,486	3,600	13,436
Senate	1,600	500	0	2,100
Incumbents	8,250	8,936	6,900	24,086
Challengers	0	0	0	0
Open Seat	0	0	500	500
Winners	8,250	8,936	n/a	17,186
Losers	0	0	n/a	0

Dayton Power and Light Co.

*Phone: (937) 259-7665 * Fax: (937) 259-7813*
P.O. Box 8825, Dayton, OH 45401
Web: www.waytogo.com

Dayton Power and Light, the principal subsidiary of DPL Inc., sells electricity and natural gas in a 6,000-square mile area of west-central Ohio.

Electricity for DP&L's 24-county service area is generated at eight plants and is distributed to more than 476,000 customers. Natural gas service is provided to 294,000 customers in 16 counties. DP&L has 2,700 employees and annual sales of more than $1.1 billion.

Dayton Power and Light Co. Employees' Fund for Responsible Citizenship (C00102947) *Address: same as sponsor * Treasurer: Thomas Studevant*

	1993-94	1995-96	1997	Totals
Receipts	$26,194	$25,548	$11,917	$63,659
Disburse	33,167	24,413	7,660	65,240
Cash	5,755	5,893	10,151	n/a
Contributions	19,255	11,500	3,435	34,190
Republicans	17,200	9,500	1,955	28,655
No. of Cand.	*9*	*7*	*4*	*20*
House	12,150	8,500	1,680	22,330
Senate	5,050	1,000	275	6,325
Democrats	2,055	2,000	1,480	5,535
No. of Cand.	*2*	*1*	*2*	*5*
House	1,055	2,000	1,480	4,535
Senate	1,000	0	0	1,000
Incumbents	10,315	11,500	2,935	24,750
Challengers	1,890	0	500	2,390
Open Seat	7,050	0	0	7,050
Winners	14,865	9,500	n/a	24,365
Losers	4,390	2,000	n/a	6,390

Detroit Edison

*Phone: (313) 235-4000 * Fax: (313) 235-0223*
2000 Second Ave., Room 1069 WCB, Detroit, MI 48226
Web: www.dteenergy.com

DTE Energy Co.'s principal operating subsidiary, Detroit Edison, provides electricity to 2 million customers in southeast Michigan.

The company also provides energy-related services through non-utility subsidiaries such as Biomass Energy Systems, landfill gas-to-energy operations; EdVenture Capital Corp., energy-related investments; Echelon Corp., a building automation technology provider; Edison Energy Services, which provides energy cost-reduction services for industrial and institutional customers; and UTS Systems, which provides specialty engineering services for industrial and utility clients.

Detroit Edison also operates a nuclear power plant in Newport, Mich.

Detroit Edison Political Action Committee - State (C00081547)
*Address: same as sponsor * Treasurer: Marie E. Wayman*

	1993-94	1995-96	1997	Totals
Receipts	$176,233	$192,782	$107,128	$476,143
Disburse	197,226	184,557	91,112	472,895
Cash	5,393	13,622	29,638	n/a
Contributions	151,535	147,815	72,300	371,650
Republicans	65,960	76,550	34,100	176,610
No. of Cand.	*54*	*55*	*39*	*148*
House	44,710	57,800	27,100	129,610
Senate	21,250	18,750	7,000	47,000
Democrats	84,825	71,265	38,200	194,290
No. of Cand.	*52*	*32*	*31*	*115*
House	70,125	60,665	33,200	163,990
Senate	14,700	10,600	5,000	30,300
Incumbents	117,835	138,115	72,300	328,250
Challengers	2,000	8,500	0	10,500
Open Seat	31,700	1,200	0	32,900
Winners	117,985	129,565	n/a	247,550
Losers	33,550	18,250	n/a	51,800

Dominion Resources Inc.

*Phone: (804) 771-4442 * Fax: (804) 771-3643*
One James River Plaza, P.O. Box 26666, Richmond, VA 23261
Web: www.domres.com

Dominion Resources is a holding company with businesses in electricity, natural gas, oil, real estate and financial services. The publicly traded Richmond company has 15,000 employees and generated 1997 revenues of $4.8 billion.

Dominion's primary subsidiary, Virginia Electric and Power Co., generates, transmits and sells electricity within a 30,000-square mile area in Virginia and northeastern North Carolina. It transacts business under the names Virginia Power and North Carolina Power.

The company has two nuclear plants in Virginia — North Anna Power Station and Surry Power Station. An energy efficiency unit, Evantage, has contracts with the U.S. Navy.

Another subsidiary, Dominion Energy, is an independent power production and natural gas and oil company. It has ownership and operating interests in 27 generating facilities in six U.S. states, Argentina, Belize, Bolivia and Peru. Dominion's financial services subsidiary, Dominion Capital, provides business financing, runs a mortgage company, develops real estate and operates a hydroelectric power plant in Louisiana. In 1997, Dominion acquired East Midlands Electricity, which serves customers in the United Kingdom. Dominion has $20 billion in assets.

Committee for Responsible Government - Dominion Resources Inc. (C00108209) *Address: same as sponsor * Treasurer: William C. Hall Jr. * Contact: Hiram Johnson, Chairperson*

	1993-94	1995-96	1997	Totals
Receipts	$153,219	$138,602	$63,581	$355,402
Disburse	140,963	165,722	59,546	366,231
Cash	60,215	33,093	37,129	n/a
Contributions	75,645	83,600	44,750	203,995
Republicans	32,785	66,250	25,250	124,285
No. of Cand.	*30*	*48*	*23*	*101*
House	20,335	41,650	19,250	81,235
Senate	12,450	24,600	6,000	43,050
Democrats	41,860	17,350	19,500	78,710
No. of Cand.	*35*	*15*	*15*	*65*
House	32,050	16,350	14,500	62,900
Senate	9,810	1,000	5,000	15,810
Incumbents	60,085	80,950	44,750	185,785
Challengers	7,860	0	0	7,860
Open Seat	7,450	3,650	0	11,100
Winners	54,925	74,800	n/a	129,725
Losers	20,720	8,800	n/a	29,520

Duke Energy Corp.

*Phone: (704) 382-8034 * Fax: (704) 382-3588*
422 S. Church St. PBO 5D, Charlotte, NC 28242-1244
Web: www.duke-energy.com

Duke Energy is a global energy company formed in 1997 by the merger of electric utility company Duke Power Co. and natural gas pipeline operator PanEnergy Corp. Duke Energy now provides electricity to 2 million customers and accounts for 12 percent of all natural gas consumed in the United States. The publicly traded company reported $16 billion in 1997 sales.

Duke Power serves a 200,000-square mile service territory in North and South Carolina. The energy is provided by three nuclear power plants, eight coal-fired stations, and hydroelectric and combustion turbine plants.

PanEnergy's pipeline subsidiaries move natural gas primarily from Texas to customers in the Northwest, Midwest and Gulf Coast states.

Additionally, Duke Energy participates in energy development projects around the world, imports natural gas, markets power and gas services, deals in wireless telecommunications, provides real estate services and operates hydroelectric, co-generation and chemical plants.

Employees Federal PAC - Duke Power Co. (C00083535) *Address: same as sponsor * Treasurer: Phyllis T. Simpson * Contact: Larry Griffin, Administrator*

	1993-94	*1995-96*	*1997*	*Totals*
Receipts	$67,043	$69,970	$33,550	$170,563
Disburse	75,049	73,775	26,750	175,574
Cash	16,529	12,724	19,524	n/a
Contributions	67,500	61,775	24,750	154,025
Republicans	45,050	50,025	18,000	113,075
No. of Cand.	*25*	*22*	*15*	*62*
House	35,550	30,025	12,500	78,075
Senate	9,500	20,000	5,500	35,000
Democrats	22,450	11,750	6,750	40,950
No. of Cand.	*17*	*13*	*11*	*41*
House	22,450	10,750	5,500	38,700
Senate	0	1,000	1,250	2,250
Incumbents	33,200	56,775	23,750	113,725
Challengers	3,500	3,000	0	6,500
Open Seat	30,500	1,500	0	32,000
Winners	48,500	52,275	n/a	100,775
Losers	19,000	9,500	n/a	28,500

PanEnergy Corp. Political Action Committee (C00040907) *Phone: (713) 627-4900 * Fax: (713) 627-4652 * 5400 Westheimer Ct., Houston, TX 77251-1642 * Treasurer: James W. Hart Jr.*

PanEnergy merged with Duke Power to form Duke Energy on June 18, 1997. The two companies retained their separate PACs.

	1993-94	*1995-96*	*1997*	*Totals*
Receipts	$154,463	$155,343	$75,391	$385,197
Disburse	144,234	183,196	87,334	414,764
Cash	54,943	32,228	12,391	n/a
Contributions	96,400	115,551	46,000	257,951
Republicans	48,500	91,376	32,000	171,876
No. of Cand.	*63*	*96*	*48*	*207*
House	28,500	55,162	19,000	102,662
Senate	20,000	36,214	13,000	69,214
Democrats	47,400	24,175	14,000	85,575
No. of Cand.	*54*	*38*	*23*	*115*
House	29,400	23,175	11,000	63,575
Senate	18,000	1,000	3,000	22,000
Incumbents	68,900	84,837	44,500	198,237
Challengers	11,500	7,500	0	19,000
Open Seat	16,000	22,714	1,500	40,214
Winners	73,400	90,676	n/a	164,076
Losers	23,000	24,875	n/a	47,875

Duquesne Light Co.

*Phone: (412) 393-6091 * Fax: (412) 393-6645*
411 Seventh Ave. 16-015, c/o Kim C. Kennedy, Pittsburgh, PA 15230-1930
Web: www.dqe.com

Energy holding company Duquesne supplies electricity to 580,000 customers in an 817-square mile area in western Pennsylvania that includes Allegheny and Beaver counties. It employs more than 3,000 workers and reported sales of $1.2 billion in 1997.

Duquesne has a stake in two nuclear plants, including Beaver Valley Power Station.

In January 1998, Duquesne announced it was in the first stages of a merger with Allegheny Energy, also based in Pennsylvania. The merger is expected to be completed in mid-1998.

Subsidiaries: Duquesne Light Co., Duquesne Enterprises, DQE Energy Services and Montauk.

Federal Duquesne Light Political Action Committee (FEDUPAC) (C00164244) *Address: same as sponsor * Treasurer: Donald J. Clayton * Contact: Ernest M. Varhola, PAC Chairman*

	1993-94	*1995-96*	*1997*	*Totals*
Receipts	$59,158	$68,571	$34,535	$162,264
Disburse	64,296	65,592	26,579	156,467
Cash	6,609	9,589	17,545	n/a
Contributions	53,670	54,900	15,200	123,770
Republicans	26,800	29,100	5,800	61,700
No. of Cand.	*23*	*33*	*6*	*62*
House	13,800	23,550	2,750	40,100
Senate	13,000	5,550	3,050	21,600
Democrats	26,870	25,800	9,400	62,070
No. of Cand.	*31*	*17*	*12*	*60*
House	17,300	25,550	9,150	52,000
Senate	9,570	250	250	10,070
Incumbents	37,020	54,000	15,200	106,220
Challengers	9,750	550	0	10,300
Open Seat	6,900	350	0	7,250
Winners	38,650	49,850	n/a	88,500
Losers	15,020	5,050	n/a	20,070

Edison Electric Institute

*Phone: (202) 508-5000 * Fax: (202) 508-5759*
701 Pennsylvania Ave. N.W., Washington, DC 20004-2696
Web: www.eei.org

The Edison Electric Institute is a national trade association of about 200 shareholder-owned electric companies, including large utilties such as Northern States, Southern Co. and American Electric Power. The group's members distribute about 75 percent of the nation's electricity.

Power PAC of the Edison Electric Institute (C00095869) *Address: same as sponsor * Treasurer: Frederick G. Davis*

	1993-94	*1995-96*	*1997*	*Totals*
Receipts	$85,095	$100,804	$112,837	$298,736
Disburse	85,029	81,000	59,018	225,047
Cash	7,573	26,879	74,480	n/a
Contributions	84,750	81,000	58,994	224,744
Republicans	49,000	66,500	34,248	149,748
No. of Cand.	*75*	*85*	*43*	*203*
House	37,250	41,500	24,750	103,500
Senate	11,750	25,000	9,498	46,248
Democrats	35,750	14,500	24,746	74,996
No. of Cand.	*55*	*20*	*26*	*101*
House	31,500	14,500	18,246	64,246
Senate	4,250	0	6,500	10,750
Incumbents	68,500	68,500	57,994	194,994
Challengers	5,500	4,500	0	10,000
Open Seat	10,750	7,000	1,000	18,750
Winners	72,000	66,000	n/a	138,000
Losers	12,750	15,000	n/a	27,750

Entergy Corp.

*Phone: (504) 529-5262 * Fax: (504) 569-4001*
639 Loyola Ave., New Orleans, LA 70113
Web: www.entergy.com

Entergy is a U.S.-based global energy company with power production and distribution operations on five continents. Entergy distributes energy to 4.8 million customers, about half of whom reside in the United States (portions of Arkansas, Louisiana, Mississippi and Texas) and half in international markets (London; Melbourne, Australia; and Buenos Aires, Argentina).

Entergy also owns, manages or invests in power plants generating nearly 30,000 megawatts of electricity, provides power marketing services, sells electricity wholesale, and offers a broad range of energy management, security monitoring and telecommunications services.

Headquartered in New Orleans, the publicly traded Entergy ranks among the largest U.S. utility companies. Entergy's 1997 revenues were $9.5 billion, and the company employs 17,000 workers worldwide. Among U.S. electric and gas companies in 1996, Entergy was third in megawatt-hour sales, third in electric generation capacity, fourth in total revenues and fifth in assets.

Entergy has five wholly owned domestic retail electric utility subsidiaries: Entergy Arkansas, Entergy Gulf States, Entergy Louisiana, Entergy Mississippi and Entergy New Orleans.

Entergy has six subsidiary PACs: one each for its Arkansas, Mississippi and Gulf States utilities, Entergy Services Inc. and two for Entergy Operations.

ENPAC-Louisiana, Political Action Committee for the Louisiana Employees of Entergy Services Inc., Entergy Gulf States Inc., Entergy Louisiana Inc., Entergy New Orleans Inc. (C00300368) *Address: same as sponsor * Treasurer: John F. Shepherd*

	1993-94	1995-96	1997	Totals
Receipts	$0	$200,739	$125,537	$326,276
Disburse	0	154,708	121,278	275,986
Cash	0	46,031	41,034	n/a
Contributions	0	44,950	31,500	76,450
Republicans	0	28,200	13,000	41,200
No. of Cand.	*0*	*31*	*10*	*41*
House	0	19,200	10,000	29,200
Senate	0	9,000	3,000	12,000
Democrats	0	16,750	18,500	35,250
No. of Cand.	*0*	*15*	*12*	*27*
House	0	12,250	7,000	19,250
Senate	0	4,500	11,500	16,000
Incumbents	0	29,500	31,500	61,000
Challengers	0	500	0	500
Open Seat	0	14,450	0	14,450
Winners	0	34,500	n/a	34,500
Losers	0	10,450	n/a	10,450

Employees of Entergy Operations Inc. Political Action Committee (EMPAC) (C00246033) *Phone: (601) 368-5684 * Fax: (601) 368-5694 * 1340 Echelon Pkwy., Jackson, MS 39213 * Treasurer: Amy A. Blaylock*

	1993-94	1995-96	1997	Totals
Receipts	$64,650	$82,229	$80,225	$227,104
Disburse	58,789	68,886	60,708	188,383
Cash	49,978	63,322	82,840	n/a
Contributions	41,100	25,750	45,050	111,900
Republicans	17,500	20,750	26,300	64,550
No. of Cand.	*16*	*26*	*29*	*71*
House	10,000	14,750	17,800	42,550
Senate	7,500	6,000	8,500	22,000
Democrats	23,250	5,000	18,750	47,000
No. of Cand.	*25*	*5*	*19*	*49*
House	21,250	5,000	8,750	35,000
Senate	2,000	0	10,000	12,000
Incumbents	30,500	22,500	45,050	98,050
Challengers	3,350	500	0	3,850
Open Seat	5,250	2,750	0	8,000
Winners	30,000	19,000	n/a	49,000
Losers	11,100	6,750	n/a	17,850

ENPAC-Arkansas, PAC for the Arkansas Employees of Entergy Ark. Inc. and Entergy Service Inc. (C00113035) *Phone: (501) 377-4474 * Fax: (501) 377-3599 * P.O. Box 551, Little Rock, AR 72203 * Treasurer: Shirley Rose * Contact: Mike Maulden, Chairman*

	1993-94	1995-96	1997	Totals
Receipts	$22,170	$23,220	$27,841	$73,231
Disburse	16,162	27,254	14,019	57,435
Cash	8,980	4,699	20,521	n/a
Contributions	9,500	17,000	8,500	35,000
Republicans	2,500	5,750	2,500	10,750
No. of Cand.	*2*	*8*	*2*	*12*
House	2,500	3,750	1,500	7,750
Senate	0	2,000	1,000	3,000
Democrats	7,000	11,250	6,000	24,250
No. of Cand.	*7*	*9*	*6*	*22*
House	5,750	8,750	4,000	18,500
Senate	1,250	2,500	2,000	5,750
Incumbents	6,750	2,750	9,500	19,000
Challengers	2,000	0	0	2,000
Open Seat	750	14,250	-1000	14,000
Winners	5,750	7,500	n/a	13,250
Losers	3,750	9,500	n/a	13,250

Entergy Services Inc. Good Government Action Committee (C00100727) *639 Loyola Ave., P.O. Box 61000, New Orleans, LA 70113 * Treasurer: John F. Shepherd*

	1993-94	1995-96	1997	Totals
Receipts	$87,599	$19,208	$0	$106,807
Disburse	101,042	27,547	0	128,589
Cash	8,338	0	0	n/a
Contributions	83,300	17,250	0	100,550
Republicans	33,850	13,750	0	47,600
No. of Cand.	*34*	*22*	*0*	*56*
House	20,600	10,250	0	30,850
Senate	13,250	3,500	0	16,750
Democrats	49,450	3,500	0	52,950
No. of Cand.	*50*	*7*	*0*	*57*
House	37,950	3,500	0	41,450
Senate	11,500	0	0	11,500
Incumbents	73,550	16,000	0	89,550
Challengers	1,500	-250	0	1,250
Open Seat	8,250	500	0	8,750
Winners	70,200	11,500	n/a	81,700
Losers	13,100	5,750	n/a	18,850

ENPAC-Texas PAC for the Texas Employees of Entergy Gulf States Inc. & Entergy Services Inc. (C00103788) *Phone: (409) 981-3442 * P.O. Box 2951, Beaumont, TX 77704 * Treasurer: Danny M. Taylor Phone: (409) 760-7016 * Fax: (281) 362-4060 * 919 Congress, Suite 740, Austin, TX 78701 * Contact: Doug McCormick, Chairperson*

	1993-94	1995-96	1997	Totals
Receipts	$10,871	$24,594	$38,294	$73,759
Disburse	11,759	22,921	28,838	63,518
Cash	2,381	4,054	13,509	n/a
Contributions	11,250	9,500	8,000	28,750
Republicans	5,250	7,500	1,500	14,250
No. of Cand.	*11*	*6*	*2*	*19*
House	2,250	7,000	1,500	10,750
Senate	3,000	500	0	3,500
Democrats	6,000	2,000	6,500	14,500
No. of Cand.	*13*	*4*	*8*	*25*
House	6,000	2,000	6,500	14,500
Senate	0	0	0	0
Incumbents	11,250	6,000	6,500	23,750
Challengers	0	0	0	0
Open Seat	0	3,500	1,500	5,000
Winners	10,000	7,500	n/a	17,500
Losers	1,250	2,000	n/a	3,250

ENPAC-Mississippi PAC/Mississippi Employees Entergy Mississippi Inc. & Entergy Services Inc. (C00100347) *Phone: (601) 368-1660 * Fax: (601) 969-2402 * P.O. Box 1640, Jackson, MS 39215 * E-mail: cbryan@entergy.com * Treasurer: Charles Bryan * Contact: Bill Howell, Chairperson*

	1993-94	1995-96	1997	Totals
Receipts	$64,793	$63,626	$38,719	$167,138
Disburse	31,071	67,959	18,039	117,069
Cash	63,144	58,813	79,493	n/a
Contributions	11,050	7,100	4,950	23,100
Republicans	6,550	6,300	2,700	15,550
No. of Cand.	*7*	*7*	*4*	*18*
House	2,800	4,300	2,700	9,800
Senate	3,750	2,000	0	5,750
Democrats	4,500	800	2,250	7,550
No. of Cand.	*8*	*2*	*4*	*14*
House	4,500	800	1,750	7,050
Senate	0	0	500	500
Incumbents	5,700	4,000	4,950	14,650
Challengers	1,000	0	0	1,000
Open Seat	4,350	3,100	0	7,450
Winners	6,700	5,000	n/a	11,700
Losers	4,350	2,100	n/a	6,450

ANO Employees of Entergy Operations Inc. Political Action Committee (ANOPAC) (C00258335) *Phone: (601) 368-5684 * Fax: (601) 368-5694 * 1340 Echelon Pkwy., Jackson, MS 39213 * Treasurer: Amy A. Blaylock*

	1993-94	1995-96	1997	Totals
Receipts	$25,617	$5,627	$4,598	$35,842
Disburse	7,497	6,533	4,090	18,120
Cash	33,713	32,806	33,314	n/a
Contributions	0	5,000	1,000	6,000
Republicans	0	0	1,000	1,000
No. of Cand.	*0*	*0*	*1*	*1*
House	0	0	0	0
Senate	0	0	1,000	1,000
Democrats	0	5,000	0	5,000
No. of Cand.	*0*	*1*	*0*	*1*
House	0	0	0	0
Senate	0	5,000	0	5,000
Incumbents	0	0	1,000	1,000
Challengers	0	0	0	0
Open Seat	0	5,000	0	5,000
Winners	0	0	n/a	0
Losers	0	5,000	n/a	5,000

Terminated PACs which contributed less than $5,000 during 1995-96 cycle:

Employees of Louisiana Power & Light Co./New Orleans Public Serv Inc. PAC-La. Power PAC (C00260463) *Phone: (504) 529-5262 * P.O. Box 60340, New Orleans, LA 70160 * Treasurer: Vincent W. Peperone*

FirstEnergy Corp.

*Phone: (330) 384-5100 * Fax: (330) 761-4204*
76 S. Main St., Akron, OH 44308-1890
Web: www.firstenergycorp.com

FirstEnergy is a public electric utility that, through its four operating companies, provides electric service to 2.2 million customers in central and northern Ohio and western Pennsylvania.

FirstEnergy was formed by the November 1997 merger of Ohio Edison and Centerior Energy. The merger created a company with more than 10,000 employees, estimated annual sales of $5 billion and total assets of $19 billion.

The four principal operating utilities of FirstEnergy are Ohio Edison, Pennsylvania Power, The Illuminating Co. and The Toledo Edison Co.

FirstEnergy Political Action Committee (formerly known as Ohio Edison Political Action Committee) (C00140855) *Address: same as sponsor * Treasurer: Theodore F. Struck III * Contact: David C. Luff, Chairperson*

	1993-94	1995-96	1997	Totals
Receipts	$15,547	$152,971	$116,802	$285,320
Disburse	19,200	141,885	85,225	246,310
Cash	884	11,974	43,552	n/a
Contributions	18,200	52,030	39,900	110,130
Republicans	9,800	41,700	28,900	80,400
No. of Cand.	*7*	*27*	*26*	*60*
House	6,800	33,700	16,900	57,400
Senate	3,000	8,000	12,000	23,000
Democrats	8,400	10,330	11,000	29,730
No. of Cand.	*10*	*6*	*12*	*28*
House	8,400	10,330	10,000	28,730
Senate	0	0	1,000	1,000
Incumbents	13,450	48,030	38,400	99,880
Challengers	500	4,000	0	4,500
Open Seat	4,250	0	1,500	5,750
Winners	15,200	46,530	n/a	61,730
Losers	3,000	5,500	n/a	8,500

Centerior Fund — A Political Action Committee of the Centerior Energy Corp. (C00214429) *Phone: (216) 447-3100 * P.O. Box 94661, Independence, OH 44101 * Treasurer: Douglas J. Hogan*

The Centerior Fund PAC was terminated in March 1998 after the 1997 merger of Centerior Energy and Ohio Edison.

	1993-94	1995-96	1997	Totals
Receipts	$105,268	$155,618	$97,525	$358,411
Disburse	92,845	158,533	124,571	375,949
Cash	13,974	11,058	-877	n/a
Contributions	20,881	26,968	14,980	62,829
Republicans	11,674	19,298	7,980	38,952
No. of Cand.	*18*	*18*	*8*	*44*
House	8,624	13,798	4,980	27,402
Senate	3,050	5,500	3,000	11,550
Democrats	9,207	7,670	7,000	23,877
No. of Cand.	*20*	*10*	*8*	*38*
House	7,407	7,170	6,000	20,577
Senate	1,800	500	1,000	3,300
Incumbents	13,581	21,568	12,980	48,129
Challengers	1,750	5,150	0	6,900
Open Seat	4,850	250	2,000	7,100
Winners	16,781	19,443	n/a	36,224
Losers	4,100	7,525	n/a	11,625

Florida Power & Light Co.

*Phone: (561) 694-4000 * Fax: (561) 694-4999*
700 Universe Blvd., P.O. Box 14000, Juno Beach, FL 33408
Web: www.fplgroup.com

The principal subsidiary of FPL Group Inc., Florida Power & Light provides electricity to about half of the Florida population — 7 million people — in an area covering almost the entire eastern seaboard of Florida and the southern third of the state. The publicly traded parent company generates annual revenues of $6 billion. FPL Group employs about 10,000 people.

The company operates two nuclear power plants in Florida, which provide about 25 percent of the company's power.

FPL Group was selected as America's "most admired" electric and gas utility in a 1998 national survey of companies conducted by Fortune magazine. Its subsidiaries include ESI Energy, Turner Foods and FPL Group International. Turner Foods is one of the largest land developers and citrus grove operators in the state.

FPL PAC, Florida Power & Light Co. Employees' Political Action Committee (C00064774) *Phone: (202) 347-7082 * Fax: (202) 347-7076 * 801 Pennsylvania Ave. N.W., Suite 640, Washington, DC 20004-2604 * Treasurer: D. N. Johnson*

	1993-94	1995-96	1997	Totals
Receipts	$204,907	$219,820	$119,873	$544,600
Disburse	193,109	218,795	111,211	523,115
Cash	35,034	36,071	44,735	n/a
Contributions	78,760	143,250	70,500	292,510
Republicans	53,750	118,750	53,000	225,500
No. of Cand.	*51*	*76*	*42*	*169*
House	34,500	68,250	31,000	133,750
Senate	19,250	50,500	22,000	91,750
Democrats	24,760	24,500	17,500	66,760
No. of Cand.	*28*	*13*	*13*	*54*
House	22,950	22,500	13,500	58,950
Senate	1,810	2,000	4,000	7,810
Incumbents	56,410	103,750	69,500	229,660
Challengers	3,500	6,000	0	9,500
Open Seat	18,350	33,500	1,000	52,850
Winners	68,750	120,250	n/a	189,000
Losers	10,010	23,000	n/a	33,010

Florida Power Corp.

*Phone: (813) 866-4442 * Fax: (813) 866-4986*
P.O. Box 14042 AC3, St. Petersburg, FL 33733
Web: www.fpc.com/flpower

Florida Power serves 1.3 million customers in a 20,000-square mile area of west-central Florida. The company's service includes St. Petersburg and Clearwater, as well as the areas surrounding Orlando, Ocala and Tallahassee.

The company, which employs 4,600 people, maintains 57 generating units and uses a variety of fuels to generate power. In 1995, coal accounted for 39 percent of the power generated, while 19 percent came from nuclear, 12 percent from oil, 4 percent from gas and 26 percent from purchased power.

Florida Power operates Crystal River Nuclear Power Plant in northwestern Citrus County, Fla.

The company is the principal subsidiary of St. Petersburg-based Florida Progress Corp., a publicly traded, Fortune 500 electric utility holding company with assets of $5.8 billion.

Founded in 1899, Florida Power is the second-largest investor-owned electric utility in Florida.

Political Action Committee of Florida Power Corp. Employees (Power PAC) (C00149484) *Address: same as sponsor * Treasurer: Greg Beuris * Contact: William Micklon, Chairperson*

	1993-94	1995-96	1997	Totals
Receipts	$96,430	$172,333	$105,979	$374,742
Disburse	85,190	146,581	38,208	269,979
Cash	35,730	61,484	129,255	n/a
Contributions	28,580	44,188	31,037	103,805
Republicans	17,830	29,688	16,500	64,018
No. of Cand.	*23*	*39*	*26*	*88*
House	13,330	24,688	12,500	50,518
Senate	4,500	5,000	4,000	13,500
Democrats	10,750	14,500	14,537	39,787
No. of Cand.	*16*	*16*	*19*	*51*
House	10,250	13,500	9,500	33,250
Senate	500	1,000	5,037	6,537
Incumbents	24,330	37,188	31,037	92,555
Challengers	1,000	1,000	0	2,000
Open Seat	2,750	6,000	0	8,750
Winners	24,080	38,688	n/a	62,768
Losers	4,500	5,500	n/a	10,000

GPU Inc.

Phone: (973) 455-8200
300 Madison Ave., Morristown, NJ 07054-1149
Web: www.gpu.com

GPU, formerly General Public Utilities Corp., is a publicly traded holding company that operates three wholly owned electric utility companies and several other energy-related subsidiaries.

The three electric utilities are Jersey Central Power & Light, Metropolitan Edison Co. and Pennsylvania Electric Co. This group's 9,200 employees supply energy to about 2 million customers in a service territory covering about half of Pennsylvania and New Jersey. The companies' revenues for 1997 exceeded $4 billion.

In October 1997, GPU announced that it was trying to divest its generation assets by selling its nuclear and non-nuclear generation businesses to focus the company on its transmission and distribution businesses. The main assets to be sold include Genco, which operates about 100 generating units in New Jersey, Pennsylvania and Maryland, and GPU Nuclear, which operates two nuclear power plants — Three Mile Island, near Harrisburg, Pa., and Oyster Creek Nuclear Generating Station, in Forked River, N.J.

GPU Corp. Power Political Action Committee (GPU Power PAC) (C00130575) *Phone: (202) 434-8140 * Fax: (202) 434-8156 * 801 Pennsylvania Ave. N.W., Suite 310, Washington, DC 20004 * Treasurer: Joel L. Brubaker*

	1993-94	1995-96	1997	Totals
Receipts	$103,257	$113,248	$59,056	$275,561
Disburse	97,896	119,004	59,420	276,320
Cash	25,689	19,937	18,574	n/a
Contributions	81,795	94,043	50,981	226,819
Republicans	34,991	62,990	33,281	131,262
No. of Cand.	*37*	*53*	*37*	*127*
House	27,991	47,227	22,350	97,568
Senate	7,000	15,763	10,931	33,694
Democrats	46,804	31,053	17,700	95,557
No. of Cand.	*45*	*25*	*20*	*90*
House	32,373	28,553	12,700	73,626
Senate	14,431	2,500	5,000	21,931
Incumbents	71,953	83,650	50,981	206,584
Challengers	3,900	1,000	0	4,900
Open Seat	5,942	8,893	0	14,835
Winners	63,066	76,400	n/a	139,466
Losers	18,729	17,643	n/a	36,372

Houston Industries Inc.

*Phone: (713) 207-3000 * Fax: (713) 207-0206*
P.O. Box 4567, Houston, TX 77210
Web: www.houind.com

Houston Industries is a public electric and gas utility serving about 3.6 million customers, mostly in Texas. The company also distributes natural gas to Arkansas, Louisiana, Mississippi, Oklahoma and Texas, and has investments in several South American utilities.

Subsidiary Houston Lighting & Power Co. is the nation's tenth-largest electric utility in kilowatt-hour sales. HL&P provides electric service to a 5,000-square mile area which includes Houston and its surrounding suburbs. Houston Industries, which employs about 15,000 people, has annual revenues of about $9 billion.

With the 1997 acquisition of NorAm Energy Corp., Houston Industries has become one of the largest combination electric and gas utilities in the United States. About 9 percent of the company's electricity comes from nuclear power plants.

Subsidiaries: HI Trading and Transportation and HI Power Generation.

NorAm Energy, which operates in Arkansas and Texas, has two affiliated PACs.

Houston Industries Inc. Political Action Committee (C00081455) *Address: same as sponsor * Treasurer: Dan Cromack*

	1993-94	1995-96	1997	Totals
Receipts	$341,439	$518,959	$379,259	$1,239,657
Disburse	334,482	470,646	365,536	1,170,664
Cash	12,804	61,124	74,850	n/a
Contributions	79,036	119,490	98,728	297,254
Republicans	43,536	75,048	61,500	180,084
No. of Cand.	*12*	*21*	*36*	*69*
House	18,536	74,048	45,500	138,084
Senate	25,000	1,000	16,000	42,000
Democrats	35,500	44,442	37,228	117,170
No. of Cand.	*21*	*14*	*19*	*54*
House	34,500	43,442	36,228	114,170
Senate	1,000	1,000	1,000	3,000
Incumbents	65,036	91,926	88,500	245,462
Challengers	5,000	500	1,000	6,500
Open Seat	9,000	27,064	9,228	45,292
Winners	64,036	101,265	n/a	165,301
Losers	15,000	18,225	n/a	33,225

Entex (NorAm Energy Corp.) Better Government Committee (C00082818) *Phone: (713) 654-5532 * Fax: (713) 654-5549 * P.O. Box 2628, 1600 Smith St., Houston, TX 77252 * Treasurer: Robert W. Claude*

NorAm Energy was acquired by Houston Industries in August 1997. NorAm is a Houston-based natural gas distribution company that serves about 2.7 million households in six southern states.

	1993-94	1995-96	1997	Totals
Receipts	$33,265	$22,972	$7,460	$63,697
Disburse	20,257	43,250	1,750	65,257
Cash	25,863	4,020	9,730	n/a
Contributions	6,750	8,250	1,750	16,750
Republicans	500	7,500	1,500	9,500
No. of Cand.	*1*	*3*	*2*	*6*
House	0	2,500	500	3,000
Senate	500	5,000	1,000	6,500
Democrats	6,250	750	250	7,250
No. of Cand.	*6*	*2*	*1*	*9*
House	6,250	750	250	7,250
Senate	0	0	0	0
Incumbents	3,250	5,000	1,750	10,000
Challengers	2,500	1,000	0	3,500
Open Seat	1,000	2,250	0	3,250
Winners	5,750	7,250	n/a	13,000
Losers	1,000	1,000	n/a	2,000

NorAm Energy Corp. PAC (formerly known as Arkla Inc. PAC) (C00197855) *Phone: (501) 377-4876 * Fax: (501) 337-4880 * P.O. Box 751, Little Rock, AR 72203 * Treasurer: Robert W. Claude*

ArklaPAC was renamed the NorAm Energy PAC.

Arkla Inc. is now a subsidiary of NorAm, which merged with Houston Industries in August 1997. Established in 1905, Arkla distributes natural gas to 740,000 customers throughout Arkansas, northern Louisiana, eastern Texas and Oklahoma. The company employs about 1,500 workers.

	1993-94	1995-96	1997	Totals
Receipts	$10,037	$6,059	$2,523	$18,619
Disburse	7,455	7,750	1,000	16,205
Cash	5,749	4,336	5,860	n/a
Contributions	5,950	1,750	1,000	8,700
Republicans	750	0	0	750
No. of Cand.	*2*	*0*	*0*	*2*
House	750	0	0	750
Senate	0	0	0	0
Democrats	5,200	1,750	1,000	7,950
No. of Cand.	*7*	*5*	*2*	*14*
House	3,450	1,250	500	5,200
Senate	1,750	500	500	2,750
Incumbents	3,500	0	0	3,500
Challengers	1,200	500	0	1,700
Open Seat	1,250	1,500	500	3,250
Winners	3,500	500	n/a	4,000
Losers	2,450	1,250	n/a	3,700

IPALCO Enterprises

*Phone: (317) 261-8995 * Fax: (317) 630-5763*
1 Monument Cir., Indianapolis, IN 46204
*Web: www.ipalco.com * E-mail: smeyer@ipalco.com*

Indiana Power & Light is the principal subsidiary of publicly traded IPALCO Enterprises.

Indiana Power provides electricity to 420,000 customers in Indianapolis and neighboring communities. It also produces, distributes and sells steam within a limited area in Indianapolis.

The company reported that 1996 was its steam operations division's most profitable year in history, with $3 million in net income — surpassing the previous 12 years' net income combined.

In late 1997, IPALCO retired a power plant and sold the property to be used as the headquarters for the NCAA when it moves to Indianapolis from Kansas City in 2000.

Subsidiaries include: Mid-America Capital Resources, Mid-America Energy Resources and Shape Energy Resources.

IPALCO Enterprises Political Action Committee (formerly known as Indianapolis Power & Light Co. PAC) (C00115030) *Address: same as sponsor * Treasurer: Steven L. Meyer*

	1993-94	1995-96	1997	Totals
Receipts	$22,663	$50,201	$28,297	$101,161
Disburse	24,921	46,066	28,225	99,212
Cash	1,256	7,395	7,468	n/a
Contributions	200	8,750	5,500	14,450
Republicans	0	7,250	4,500	11,750
No. of Cand.	*0*	*8*	*5*	*13*
House	0	7,250	4,500	11,750
Senate	0	0	0	0
Democrats	200	1,500	1,000	2,700
No. of Cand.	*1*	*1*	*2*	*4*
House	200	0	1,000	1,200
Senate	0	1,500	0	1,500

Incumbents	200	6,300	5,000	11,500
Challengers	0	1,500	0	1,500
Open Seat	0	950	500	1,450
Winners	200	7,250	n/a	7,450
Losers	0	1,500	n/a	1,500

Idaho Power Co.

*Phone: (208) 388-2261 * Fax: (208) 388-6903*
P.O. Box 70, Boise, ID 83707
Web: www.idahopower.com

Idaho Power is a publicly traded utility with 17 hydroelectric plants and part ownership in three coal-fired generating plants. It provides solar, hydroelectric and coal-burning power to more than 350,000 customers in southern Idaho, eastern Oregon and northern Nevada.

In 1997 Applied Power Corp., the largest solar electric system supplier to the federal government and a subsidiary of Idaho Power, agreed to join President Clinton's proposal to place "solar energy systems on 1 million American roofs by 2010."

The PAC supports the right of customers to choose their electricity provider.

Ida-PAC Political Action Committee (C00083832) *Address: same as sponsor * Treasurer: Linda Franks Nelson * Contact: Larry B. Taylor, Chairperson*

	1993-94	1995-96	1997	Totals
Receipts	$13,858	$14,384	$4,146	$32,388
Disburse	11,262	29,302	2,000	42,564
Cash	7,464	4,637	6,784	n/a
Contributions	10,762	14,801	2,000	27,563
Republicans	10,762	14,801	2,000	27,563
No. of Cand.	*10*	*10*	*2*	*22*
House	7,262	7,893	1,000	16,155
Senate	3,500	6,908	1,000	11,408
Democrats	0	0	0	0
No. of Cand.	*0*	*0*	*0*	*0*
House	0	0	0	0
Senate	0	0	0	0
Incumbents	5,062	12,301	2,000	19,363
Challengers	2,000	500	0	2,500
Open Seat	3,700	2,000	0	5,700
Winners	10,762	13,301	n/a	24,063
Losers	0	1,500	n/a	1,500

Illinois Power Co.

*Phone: (217) 424-8243 * Fax: (217) 425-4161*
500 S. 27th St., Decatur, IL 62525-1805
*Web: www.illinova.com * E-mail: jay_henry@illinova.com*

Illinois Power is a gas and electric power utility with 3,600 employees. It is a subsidiary of Illinova Corp. and had 1997 revenues of $1.6 billion. The company serves about 650,000 customers across a 15,000-square mile area of Illinois and has electric generating capability of more than 4,100 megawatts.

Illinova subsidiaries include: Illinova Energy Partners and Illinova Generating Co.

Illinois Power Employees' Federal Political Action Committee (C00157107) *Address: same as sponsor * Treasurer: Kathy A. Baker * Contact: Jay Henry, Chairperson*

	1993-94	1995-96	1997	Totals
Receipts	$50,000	$41,465	$18,300	$109,765
Disburse	48,284	42,901	5,682	96,867
Cash	28,704	27,272	39,891	n/a
Contributions	36,746	34,504	11,220	82,470
Republicans	25,946	28,250	7,870	62,066
No. of Cand.	*18*	*13*	*8*	*39*
House	22,100	20,250	7,870	50,220
Senate	3,846	8,000	0	11,846
Democrats	10,800	6,254	3,350	20,404
No. of Cand.	*11*	*4*	*4*	*19*
House	8,800	5,000	850	14,650
Senate	2,000	1,254	2,500	5,754
Incumbents	27,700	19,850	9,370	56,920
Challengers	700	1,200	1,500	3,400
Open Seat	7,250	13,454	350	21,054
Winners	33,700	22,954	n/a	56,654
Losers	3,046	11,550	n/a	14,596

Iowa Association of Electric Cooperatives

*Phone: (515) 276-5350 * Fax: (515) 276-7946*
8525 Douglas Ave., Suite 48, Des Moines, IA 50322-2992
*Web: www.iowarec.org * E-mail: iowarec@netins.net*

The Iowa Association of Electric Cooperatives represents the state's rural electric cooperatives.

Formed in 1942, IAEC provides legislative representation at the state and national levels and creates safety programs, demonstrations and campaigns to encourage the use of electricity. It also studies electric rates and reviews utility regulations.

IAEC publishes an industry newsletter for its members.

Iowa Friends of Rural Electrification - IAEC PAC (C00076703) *Address: same as sponsor * Treasurer: Dawn Vance * Contact: Roger Arthur, Chairperson*

	1993-94	1995-96	1997	Totals
Receipts	$18,214	$26,156	$29,858	$74,228
Disburse	22,035	26,809	20,168	69,012
Cash	821	168	9,858	n/a
Contributions	4,100	6,750	0	10,850
Republicans	3,000	4,250	0	7,250
No. of Cand.	*3*	*5*	*0*	*8*
House	3,000	3,250	0	6,250
Senate	0	1,000	0	1,000
Democrats	1,100	2,500	0	3,600
No. of Cand.	*2*	*2*	*0*	*4*
House	1,100	1,000	0	2,100
Senate	0	1,500	0	1,500
Incumbents	3,000	4,750	0	7,750
Challengers	100	1,000	0	1,100
Open Seat	1,000	1,000	0	2,000
Winners	3,000	5,500	n/a	8,500
Losers	1,100	1,250	n/a	2,350

Kansas City Power & Light Co.

*Phone: (816) 556-2653 * Fax: (816) 556-2975*
1201 Walnut, Kansas City, MO 64106

Kansas City Power & Light provides electricity to more than 435,000 customers in a 4,700-square mile area of western Missouri and eastern Kansas. Seventy-five percent of its energy is generated by coal, and the remaining 25 percent comes from nuclear sources.

Retail revenues in Missouri and Kansas accounted for about 91 percent of publicly traded KCPL's total revenues in 1996. Wholesale firm power, bulk power sales and miscellaneous electric revenues accounted for the remainder of revenues. Sales for 1996 were roughly $900 million.

KCPL's main subsidiary, KLT Inc., pursues other ventures, including real estate, energy management services, industrial power and co-generation projects, oil and gas exploration and telecommunications.

In early 1998, discussions began between KCPL and Western Resources Inc., of Topeka, Kan., regarding a possible merger of the two companies. Western Resources supplies electric energy to 600,000 customers in Kansas and northeastern Oklahoma.

K.C. Power PAC - Federal - Kansas City Power & Light Co. (C00111310) *Address: same as sponsor * Treasurer: Joe Werner * Contact: Michael Messer, Administrator*

	1993-94	1995-96	1997	Totals
Receipts	$20,882	$92,667	$63,408	$176,957
Disburse	21,213	73,680	41,500	136,393
Cash	1,786	20,776	42,685	n/a
Contributions	6,350	19,680	12,500	38,530
Republicans	3,100	13,180	8,000	24,280
No. of Cand.	*6*	*12*	*8*	*26*
House	2,600	9,680	5,000	17,280
Senate	500	3,500	3,000	7,000
Democrats	3,250	6,500	4,500	14,250
No. of Cand.	*8*	*6*	*7*	*21*
House	2,750	6,500	4,000	13,250
Senate	500	0	500	1,000
Incumbents	4,750	10,180	12,500	27,430
Challengers	0	1,000	0	1,000
Open Seat	1,600	8,500	0	10,100
Winners	4,850	16,430	n/a	21,280
Losers	1,500	3,250	n/a	4,750

Kentucky Utilities Co.

*Phone: (606) 255-2100 * Fax: (606) 367-5782*
One Quality St., Lexington, KY 40507
*Web: www.kuenergy.com * E-mail: jeff.rhoads@kuenergy.com*

Kentucky Utilities serves 470,000 customers in 77 Kentucky counties and five counties in southwestern Virginia. It had revenues of $712 million in 1997.

KU and non-utility KU Capital Corp. are wholly owned subsidiaries of the investor-owned holding company KU Energy Corp. When completed, the pending merger between KU Energy and LG&E Energy Corp., parent of Louisville Gas & Electric, will create one of the nation's largest energy services holding companies.

Kentucky Utilities Co. Political Action Committee (KY EPAC) (C00208520) *Address: same as sponsor * Treasurer: Michael D. Robinson * Contact: Michael R. Whitley, Chairperson and President*

	1993-94	1995-96	1997	Totals
Receipts	$16,193	$12,151	$4,498	$32,842
Disburse	13,547	17,458	5,413	36,418
Cash	8,773	3,466	2,552	n/a
Contributions	11,300	16,800	4,800	32,900
Republicans	7,300	13,300	2,800	23,400
No. of Cand.	*11*	*12*	*4*	*27*
House	6,050	9,300	1,800	17,150
Senate	1,250	4,000	1,000	6,250
Democrats	4,000	3,500	2,000	9,500
No. of Cand.	*4*	*4*	*3*	*11*
House	4,000	3,000	2,000	9,000
Senate	0	500	0	500
Incumbents	9,300	15,050	3,300	27,650
Challengers	0	1,500	0	1,500
Open Seat	2,000	250	1,500	3,750
Winners	9,300	15,000	n/a	24,300
Losers	2,000	1,800	n/a	3,800

Louisville Gas & Electric Co.

*Phone: (502) 627-2202 * Fax: (502) 627-2930*
P.O. Box 32010, Louisville, KY 40232
Web: www.lgeenergy.com

Louisville Gas & Electric is a Kentucky utility and subsidiary of the publicly traded holding company LG&E Energy Corp. The company has agreed to acquire KU Energy Corp. of Lexington, Ky.

LG&E Energy Systems and LG&E Gas Systems supply electricity and gas to 351,000 and 277,000 customers, respectively, in a 17-county area around Louisville, Ky. The area includes the military base at Fort Knox.

The corporation has three coal-fired power plants, all operated in Kentucky, a hydroelectric power plant, and underground natural gas storage fields. LG&E Energy has about 3,000 employees. The holding company reported 1997 sales of $4.2 billion.

Operations of Energy Systems' subsidiaries are located throughout the United States and also include investments in Spain and Argentina. LG&E Natural is involved in the marketing and storage of natural gas.

Federal Louisville Gas & Electric Co. Political Action Committee (FedLouPAC) (C00247775) *Address: same as sponsor * Treasurer: Sharon Weston * Contact: Jim Pearl, Senior H.R. Generalist*

	1993-94	1995-96	1997	Totals
Receipts	$9,660	$7,539	$3,328	$20,527
Disburse	7,223	11,530	6,500	25,253
Cash	12,720	8,730	5,558	n/a
Contributions	7,000	11,500	6,500	25,000
Republicans	3,000	7,000	5,000	15,000
No. of Cand.	*3*	*6*	*4*	*13*
House	3,000	6,000	4,000	13,000
Senate	0	1,000	1,000	2,000
Democrats	4,000	4,500	1,500	10,000
No. of Cand.	*4*	*3*	*2*	*9*
House	4,000	4,500	1,500	10,000
Senate	0	0	0	0
Incumbents	4,000	10,500	5,000	19,500
Challengers	0	1,000	0	1,000
Open Seat	3,000	0	1,500	4,500
Winners	4,000	9,000	n/a	13,000
Losers	3,000	2,500	n/a	5,500

MidAmerican Energy Co.

*Phone: (515) 281-2288 * Fax: (515) 242-4395*
666 Grand Ave., P.O. Box 657, Des Moines, IA 50303-0657
*Web: www.midamerican.com * E-mail: dccaris@midamerican.com*

MidAmerican Energy, owned by holding company MidAmerican Energy Holdings Co., provides electric and natural gas service to 1.25 million customers in a 10,000-square mile area from Sioux Falls, S.D. to the Quad Cities area of Iowa and Illinois. The company posted $1.87 billion in 1996 revenue and employs 3,300 people. The Des Moines, Iowa company is publicly traded.

The company owns a nuclear plant, Cooper Nuclear Station, near Brownville, Neb., and has a 25 percent stake in the Quad Cities Nuclear Power Station.

MidAmerican has 4,321 megawatts of electrical generating capacity. Sixty-five percent of that capacity is fueled by coal, 18 percent by nuclear power and 17 percent by natural gas and oil. More than 4,100 miles of transmission lines connect the company's generation facilities with distribution substations and provide interconnections with five surrounding states.

MidAmerican also owns five liquefied natural gas and liquefied propane facilities.

MidAmerican Energy Co. Employee Government Committee (formerly known as Midwest Resources Inc.) (C00081273) *Phone: (202) 824-0410 * Fax: (202) 347-7752 * 1301 Pennsylvania Ave. N.W., Suite 1030, Washington, DC 20004 * Treasurer: Rick R. Tunning*

*Contact: David Caris, Manager of Legislative Afffairs * Phone: (515) 281-2288*

	1993-94	1995-96	1997	Totals
Receipts	$38,697	$43,756	$26,400	$108,853
Disburse	40,016	40,270	7,739	88,025
Cash	2,827	6,316	24,977	n/a
Contributions	11,900	13,750	500	26,150
Republicans	8,400	11,250	250	19,900
No. of Cand.	*4*	*7*	*1*	*12*
House	8,400	6,750	250	15,400
Senate	0	4,500	0	4,500
Democrats	3,500	2,500	250	6,250
No. of Cand.	*2*	*2*	*1*	*5*
House	3,500	1,500	250	5,250
Senate	0	1,000	0	1,000
Incumbents	8,900	4,750	500	14,150
Challengers	0	4,500	0	4,500
Open Seat	3,000	4,500	0	7,500
Winners	9,400	7,250	n/a	16,650
Losers	2,500	6,500	n/a	9,000

Contributed less than $5,000 during 1995-96 cycle:

MidAmerican Energy Co. Executive PAC (C00324483) *Phone: (515) 242-4300 * Fax: (515) 281-2981 * 666 Grand Ave., P.O. Box 657, Des Moines, IA 50303-0657 * Treasurer: Rick R. Tunning*

Terminated PACs which contributed less than $5,000 during 1995-96 cycle:

MidAmerican Energy Co. PAC - Federal (formerly known as Iowa-Illinois Gas & Electric) (C00109264) *106 E. Second St., P.O. Box 4350, Davenport, IA 52808 * Treasurer: David M. Blomquist*

Minnesota Power

*Phone: (218) 722-2641 * Fax: (218) 723-3944*
30 W. Superior St., Duluth, MN 55802
Web: www.mnpower.com

Minnesota Power is a $2.2 billion operating public utility incorporated in 1906. Minnesota Power's operations, which include electricity, natural gas and auto auctions, are in 28 states and Canada. The company had $953 million in 1997 annual sales and 6,800 employees.

The company provides electricity and natural gas to customers in Minnesota and Wisconsin, but also provides water and wastewater treatment services in Florida, North Carolina and South Carolina. Most of its electricity comes from a company-owned coal mine in North Dakota. Subsidiary ADESA Corp. is an auto auction and financial services business in the United States and Canada.

Subsidiaries: Instrumentation Services Inc., Florida Gas Service Corp., Heater Utilities, ADESA and Lehigh Acquisition Corp.

Minnesota Power Active Citizens Team (C00142489) *Address: same as sponsor * Treasurer: Steven C. Leino * Contact: Paul B. Johnson, Strategy and Growth Consultant*

	1993-94	1995-96	1997	Totals
Receipts	$8,178	$10,671	$8,275	$27,124
Disburse	9,183	10,450	5,700	25,333
Cash	504	1,045	3,625	n/a
Contributions	8,100	9,700	6,400	24,200
Republicans	3,000	4,950	3,400	11,350
No. of Cand.	*7*	*9*	*3*	*19*
House	1,750	3,250	3,000	8,000
Senate	1,250	1,700	400	3,350
Democrats	3,850	4,750	2,000	10,600
No. of Cand.	*7*	*7*	*2*	*16*
House	1,850	4,750	1,000	7,600
Senate	2,000	0	1,000	3,000
Incumbents	6,600	7,450	6,400	20,450
Challengers	0	2,250	0	2,250
Open Seat	1,500	0	0	1,500
Winners	7,600	7,450	n/a	15,050
Losers	500	2,250	n/a	2,750

Montana Power Co.

*Phone: (406) 542-5932 * Fax: (406) 542-5906*
P.O. Box 624, Butte, MT 59703
*Web: www.mtpower.com * E-mail: events@mtpower.com*

Montana Power is a publicly owned power company involved in electric and natural gas power production. It serves about 600,000 customers in Montana. The company's 1997 revenues were $1 billion and it has 2,900 employees.

All of its electric generation facilities in Montana have been offered for sale. This includes 13 dams, four coal-fired plants, and interest in other power facilities worth about $600 million. MPC also owns 50 percent of North American Energy Services through its subsidiary Continental Energy Services.

MPC also owns Entech, one of the largest coal mining companies in the nation, and develops gas-powered projects in China and Europe. Touch America Inc., another subsidiary, provides telephone and Internet communications in 13 Western states.

Subsidiaries: Montana Power Trading and Marketing Co., Continental Energy Services, Touch America, FTV Communications LLC and Tetragenics.

Citizens for Responsible Government - Employees of the Montana Power Co. (C00068056) *Address: same as sponsor * Treasurer: Karen Lee Simpson * Contact: Vickie Judd, Chairperson*

	1993-94	1995-96	1997	Totals
Receipts	$23,624	$22,630	$10,130	$56,384
Disburse	21,771	19,970	2,711	44,452
Cash	4,870	7,539	14,964	n/a
Contributions	3,750	5,000	1,000	9,750
Republicans	3,250	3,500	1,000	7,750
No. of Cand.	*5*	*4*	*1*	*10*
House	1,250	1,500	1,000	3,750
Senate	2,000	2,000	0	4,000
Democrats	500	1,500	0	2,000
No. of Cand.	*1*	*2*	*0*	*3*
House	500	0	0	500
Senate	0	1,500	0	1,500
Incumbents	2,250	2,500	1,000	5,750
Challengers	500	500	0	1,000
Open Seat	1,000	2,000	0	3,000
Winners	3,250	4,500	n/a	7,750
Losers	500	500	n/a	1,000

NIPSCO Industries Inc.

*Phone: (219) 647-6237 * Fax: (219) 647-6240*
5265 Hohman Ave., Hammond, IN 46320
Web: www.nipsco.com

NIPSCO Industries is an energy-based holding company with annual sales of $1.8 billion. The company has five regulated businesses: Northern Indiana Public Service Co., Kokomo Gas and Fuel Co., Northern Indiana Fuel and Light Co., Crossroads Pipeline Co. and IWC Resources Corp. The company is publicly owned and employs nearly 4,200 people.

In January 1998, the company was the first in the United States to pass environmental certification under the International Standardization Organization for its entire electric generation operations. Certification means the facilities have demonstrated business activities that efficiently incorporate and improve environmental performance in day-to-day work practices.

NIPSCO Industries Inc. PAC (also known as NI-PAC) (C00298596) *Address: same as sponsor * Treasurer: Fran Girot * Contact: Ray Arredondo, Dir. of Legislative Affairs*

	1993-94	1995-96	1997	Totals
Receipts	$9,370	$43,562	$28,748	$81,680
Disburse	1,071	40,260	25,050	66,381
Cash	8,298	11,604	15,303	n/a
Contributions	0	6,075	2,750	8,825
Republicans	0	3,225	1,250	4,475
No. of Cand.	*0*	*6*	*3*	*9*
House	0	2,225	750	2,975
Senate	0	1,000	500	1,500
Democrats	0	2,850	1,500	4,350
No. of Cand.	*0*	*3*	*3*	*6*
House	0	2,850	1,500	4,350
Senate	0	0	0	0
Incumbents	0	5,950	2,000	7,950
Challengers	0	0	500	500
Open Seat	0	125	250	375
Winners	0	5,950	n/a	5,950
Losers	0	125	n/a	125

National Independent Energy Producers

601 13th St. N.W., Suite 320 S., Washington, DC 20005

The National Independent Energy Producers PAC filed for termination in 1997.

National Independent Energy Producers PAC NIEPAC (C00230821) *Address: same as sponsor * Treasurer: Merribel Ayres*

	1993-94	1995-96	1997	Totals
Receipts	$15,282	$11,913	$0	$27,195
Disburse	12,972	14,793	0	27,765
Cash	4,698	1,821	0	n/a
Contributions	12,969	14,210	0	27,179
Republicans	4,490	9,460	0	13,950
No. of Cand.	*6*	*11*	*0*	*17*
House	1,500	5,209	0	6,709
Senate	2,990	4,251	0	7,241
Democrats	8,479	4,750	0	13,229
No. of Cand.	*15*	*6*	*0*	*21*
House	5,100	3,000	0	8,100
Senate	3,379	1,750	0	5,129
Incumbents	12,469	14,210	0	26,679
Challengers	0	0	0	0
Open Seat	500	0	0	500
Winners	9,042	13,210	n/a	22,252
Losers	3,927	1,000	n/a	4,927

New Century Energies Inc.

Phone: (303) 571-7511
1225 17th St., Suite 900, P.O. Box 840, Denver, CO 80201
Web: www.psco.com/nce/

New Century Energies is the result of a 1997 merger between the Public Service Co. of Colorado and Southwestern Public Service Co., two public utilities providing electricity and natural gas to about 3.8 million customers in Colorado, Wyoming, New Mexico, Texas, Oklahoma and Kansas.

Headquartered in Denver, NCE also provides non-utility power generation and engineering services for projects in the United States and worldwide. NCE also owns Yorkshire Electricity Group, an electricity and natural gas supplier in England. The new company has about 6,300 employees and reported 1997 revenues of $883 million.

The Public Service Co. of Colorado PAC filed for termination in December 1997. NCE created its own PAC in 1998 and Southwestern Public Service maintained its PAC.

Public Service Co. of Colorado Political Action Committee (C00131235) *Address: same as sponsor * Treasurer: W. Wayne Brown*

	1993-94	1995-96	1997	Totals
Receipts	$24,142	$16,023	$5,808	$45,973
Disburse	26,332	6,805	420	33,557
Cash	1,985	2,084	7,573	n/a
Contributions	7,225	5,050	350	12,625
Republicans	5,125	4,550	100	9,775
No. of Cand.	*5*	*6*	*1*	*12*

(Data for Public Service Co. continued)

House	5,125	3,550	0	8,675
Senate	0	1,000	100	1,100
Democrats	2,100	500	250	2,850
No. of Cand.	*3*	*1*	*1*	*5*
House	1,100	500	250	1,850
Senate	1,000	0	0	1,000
Incumbents	7,225	3,550	350	11,125
Challengers	0	0	0	0
Open Seat	0	1,500	0	1,500
Winners	6,475	5,050	n/a	11,525
Losers	750	0	n/a	750

Southwestern Committee on Political Education for Southwestern Public Service Co. (C00059477) *Phone: (806) 378-2812 * Fax: (806) 378-2995 * P.O. Box 1261, Amarillo, TX 79170 * Treasurer: Kurt Shaughnessy * Contact: Gary Gibson, Chairperson*

	1993-94	1995-96	1997	Totals
Receipts	$87,998	$94,443	$42,938	$225,379
Disburse	97,223	70,618	10,883	178,724
Cash	20,049	43,878	75,933	n/a
Contributions	23,400	20,200	5,000	48,600
Republicans	18,000	18,700	3,000	39,700
No. of Cand.	*14*	*13*	*3*	*30*
House	9,500	16,500	2,000	28,000
Senate	8,500	2,200	1,000	11,700
Democrats	5,400	1,500	2,000	8,900
No. of Cand.	*9*	*3*	*1*	*13*
House	4,400	1,000	2,000	7,400
Senate	1,000	500	0	1,500
Incumbents	20,900	18,200	3,000	42,100
Challengers	2,000	500	0	2,500
Open Seat	500	1,500	2,000	4,000
Winners	21,000	19,200	n/a	40,200
Losers	2,400	1,000	n/a	3,400

New England Electric System

*Phone: (508) 389-2097 * Fax: (508) 389-2327*
25 Research Dr., Westborough, MA 01582
*Web: www.nees.com/pro/subsid.htm * E-mail: benned@neesnet.com*

New England Electric System is a public utility serving more than 1.3 million customers in Massachusetts, Rhode Island and New Hampshire. The utility posted 1997 sales of $2.5 billion and employs 4,790 people.

Sale of the company's 18 power plants located in New England was pending in March 1998, in conjunction with utility deregulation in the region. The proposed purchaser was U.S. Generating, a subsidiary of San Francisco-based Pacific Gas and Electric.

Subsidiaries: NEES Global Transmission, AllEnergy Marketing and NEES Communications.

New England Electric PAC Established by New England Power Service Co. (NEEPAC) (C00048702) *Phone: (202) 783-7959 * 633 Pennsylvania Ave. N.W., Sixth Floor, Washington, DC 20004 * Treasurer: David M. Bennett * Contact: Ralph Loomis, V.P. of Federal Affairs*

	1993-94	1995-96	1997	Totals
Receipts	$31,034	$45,204	$24,784	$101,022
Disburse	43,744	40,409	23,750	107,903
Cash	18,360	23,161	24,195	n/a
Contributions	42,700	34,900	23,050	100,650
Republicans	18,300	22,250	11,500	52,050
No. of Cand.	*20*	*29*	*15*	*64*
House	10,550	14,750	7,500	32,800
Senate	7,750	7,500	4,000	19,250
Democrats	24,400	12,650	11,550	48,600
No. of Cand.	*28*	*12*	*16*	*56*
House	18,400	10,150	9,300	37,850
Senate	6,000	2,500	2,250	10,750
Incumbents	40,650	29,150	22,050	91,850
Challengers	300	1,250	1,000	2,550
Open Seat	1,750	4,500	0	6,250
Winners	36,950	25,650	n/a	62,600
Losers	5,750	9,250	n/a	15,000

New York State Electric & Gas Corp.

*Phone: (607) 762-7307 * Fax: (607) 762-8751*
Corporate Dr., Kirkwood Industrial Park, P.O. Box 5224, Binghamton, NY 13902-5224
Web: www.nyseg.com

New York State Electric & Gas provides electricity to 800,000 customers and natural gas to 238,000 customers spread across the state. The publicly traded company has 4,100 employees.

Subsidiaries include: NGE Enterprises, NYSEG's wholly owned subsidiary, and its two unregulated businesses, XENERGY and NGE EnergyPoints.

New York State Electric & Gas Corp. Political Action Committee (NYSEGPAC) (C00156471) *Address: same as sponsor * Treasurer: Norma J. O'Connor * Contact: Angela Sparks, Chairperson*

	1993-94	1995-96	1997	Totals
Receipts	$23,524	$18,148	$12,869	$54,541
Disburse	21,060	23,275	10,011	54,346
Cash	8,954	3,827	6,686	n/a
Contributions	19,060	21,170	9,000	49,230
Republicans	13,685	16,620	7,250	37,555
No. of Cand.	*12*	*19*	*9*	*40*
House	13,185	15,620	4,250	33,055
Senate	500	1,000	3,000	4,500
Democrats	4,875	4,550	1,750	11,175
No. of Cand.	*9*	*8*	*4*	*21*
House	2,625	4,550	1,500	8,675
Senate	2,250	0	250	2,500
Incumbents	19,060	20,920	9,000	48,980
Challengers	0	0	0	0
Open Seat	0	250	0	250
Winners	17,560	20,420	n/a	37,980
Losers	1,500	750	n/a	2,250

Niagara Mohawk Power Corp.

*Phone: (315) 428-6941 * Fax: (315) 428-6149*
P.O. Box 7102, Federal Station, Syracuse, NY 13261
*Web: www.nimo.com * E-mail: murphym@nimo.com*

Niagara Mohawk Power provides electricity to 1.5 million customers throughout a 24,000 square-mile area of upstate New York. The company's 7,700-mile natural gas system serves 525,000 residential and business customers.

The company, which has 8,500 employees, reported 1997 revenues of nearly $4 billion.

In October 1997, Niagara Mohawk created its PowerChoice program, a comprehensive rate reduction and restructuring settlement. According to a study by ICF Resources of Fairfax, Va., the settlement calls for residential and commercial customers to see average electricity prices drop by 3.2 percent and industrial price reductions of up to 25 percent from 1995 tariff levels.

Niagara Mohawk Power Corp. Management Voluntary Federal Political Action Committee (C00125658) *Address: same as sponsor * Treasurer: David R. Dzwonkowski * Contact: Michael Murphy, Chairperson*

	1993-94	1995-96	1997	Totals
Receipts	$22,360	$26,677	$22,418	$71,455
Disburse	23,632	28,142	19,458	71,232
Cash	4,449	2,987	5,947	n/a
Contributions	22,160	26,515	16,640	65,315
Republicans	12,410	21,265	11,140	44,815
No. of Cand.	*12*	*18*	*10*	*40*
House	11,410	17,765	8,215	37,390
Senate	1,000	3,500	2,925	7,425
Democrats	9,000	5,250	5,500	19,750
No. of Cand.	*10*	*7*	*7*	*24*
House	5,500	5,250	4,500	15,250
Senate	3,500	0	1,000	4,500
Incumbents	22,160	25,765	16,640	64,565
Challengers	0	250	0	250
Open Seat	0	500	0	500
Winners	19,910	23,815	n/a	43,725
Losers	2,250	2,700	n/a	4,950

Northeast Utilities Service Co.

*Phone: (860) 665-5166 * Fax: (860) 665-3177*
P.O. Box 270, Hartford, CT 06141
*Web: www.nu.com * E-mail: finnujj@nu.com*

Northeast Utilities is a holding company for the largest electric utility system in New England, and one of the 20 largest in the United States. Its four main subsidiaries comprise the Northeast Utilities System, which provides electricity to 1.7 million customers in Connecticut, New Hampshire and western Massachusetts. With assets of more than $10 billion, NU employs 8,000 workers.

The company owns 34 hydroelectric plants as well as several coal, oil, and gas-generated plants. In addition, the company owns two nuclear power plants in Connecticut and New Hampshire, and has controlling shares in two additional plants in Maine and Vermont. One other nuclear power plant in Connecticut was closed in 1996 for financial reasons.

In addition to retail electric service, the subsidiaries furnish wholesale electric service to five municipal electric systems and one investor-owned utility. The companies also supply other wholesale electric services to municipalities and utilities.

Subsidiaries include: Connecticut Light and Power Co., Holyoke Water Power Co., Northeast Nuclear Energy Co., Rocky River Realty Co., Charter Oak Energy Inc., HEC Inc., Public Service Co. of New Hampshire, North Atlantic Energy Co., North Atlantic Energy Service Corp., and Northeast Utilities Service Co.

Northeast Utilities Political Action Committee (C00102160)
*Address: same as sponsor * Treasurer: James J. Finnucan * Contact: Gregory B. Butler, Chairperson*

	1993-94	1995-96	1997	Totals
Receipts	$17,922	$80,295	$40,012	$138,229
Disburse	5,550	63,314	29,950	98,814
Cash	12,677	29,660	39,723	n/a
Contributions	5,050	58,822	25,450	89,322
Republicans	4,300	45,122	14,450	63,872
No. of Cand.	*6*	*28*	*11*	*45*
House	3,650	33,500	13,450	50,600
Senate	650	11,622	1,000	13,272
Democrats	750	13,700	11,000	25,450
No. of Cand.	*2*	*15*	*14*	*31*
House	750	10,200	9,000	19,950
Senate	0	3,500	2,000	5,500
Incumbents	4,250	50,422	23,700	78,372
Challengers	800	4,400	1,250	6,450
Open Seat	0	4,000	500	4,500
Winners	4,550	43,422	n/a	47,972
Losers	500	15,400	n/a	15,900

Northern States Power Co.

*Phone: (612) 229-2566 * Fax: (612) 229-2596*
414 Nicollet Mall, Minneapolis, MN 55401
Web: www.nspco.com

Northern States Power, based in Minnesota, is a public utility holding company that provides electricity to 1.4 million customers and natural gas to 400,000 customers throughout the Dakotas, Michigan, Minnesota and Wisconsin. Sales totaled $2.7 billion in 1997.

NSP called off a merger with Wisconsin Energy Corp. because of regulatory objections. But in December 1997, NSP announced plans to merge with Black Mountain Gas Co. of Cave Creek, Ariz. Black Mountain Gas serves 6,500 customers and had 1997 revenues of $46 million.

Northern States is ranked No. 489 in the Fortune 500 and has 7,147 employees. It owns and operates the Monticello nuclear unit near Minneapolis.

Subsidiaries include: Cenerprise, Viking Gas Transmission, NRG Energy and Seren.

Northern States Power Employee Political Interest Committee (C00107771) *Address: same as sponsor * Treasurer: Andrea Schmidt*

	1993-94	1995-96	1997	Totals
Receipts	$59,261	$62,455	$27,398	$149,114
Disburse	48,268	73,921	46,115	168,304
Cash	43,714	32,248	13,531	n/a
Contributions	40,340	66,444	36,037	142,821
Republicans	17,290	42,094	17,500	76,884
No. of Cand.	*26*	*46*	*24*	*96*
House	7,700	21,944	10,000	39,644
Senate	9,590	20,150	7,500	37,240
Democrats	20,150	24,350	15,937	60,437
No. of Cand.	*33*	*23*	*21*	*77*
House	13,400	18,600	8,550	40,550
Senate	6,750	5,750	7,387	19,887
Incumbents	29,500	50,244	35,287	115,031
Challengers	3,150	13,450	250	16,850
Open Seat	7,690	2,750	500	10,940
Winners	30,940	47,294	n/a	78,234
Losers	9,400	19,150	n/a	28,550

Northwestern Public Service Co.

*Phone: (605) 226-4164 * Fax: (605) 225-5503*
33 Third St. S.E., Huron, SD 57350-1605
Web: www.nwps.com

Northwestern Public Service sells electricity, natural gas and propane. About 80 percent of the company's sales come from propane. Northwestern reported $918 million in 1997 revenues, a 167 percent increase over the previous year.

Northwestern generates and distributes electricity to 55,000 customers in eastern South Dakota. The company also purchases, distributes, sells and transports natural gas to 76,400 customers in four communities in Nebraska and more than 50 communities in eastern South Dakota.

Northwestern owns and manages 34 percent of Cornerstone Propane Partners, a publicly traded retail propane marketer. Cornerstone is the fifth largest retail propane marketer in the United States. Other subsidiaries include Northwestern Energy Corp., Northwestern Growth Corp. and ServiCenter USA.

Northwestern's electric and natural gas industries employ 430 people.

Northwestern Public Service Co. PAC (NWPS Employees' PAC) (C00187799) *Address: same as sponsor * Treasurer: Garlyn R. Grosse * Contact: Larry Frost, Chairperson*

	1993-94	1995-96	1997	Totals
Receipts	$23,013	$32,517	$15,516	$71,046
Disburse	18,957	20,233	7,100	46,290
Cash	10,782	23,069	31,485	n/a
Contributions	50	7,500	4,000	11,550
Republicans	50	5,000	4,000	9,050
No. of Cand.	*1*	*2*	*1*	*4*
House	0	2,000	4,000	6,000
Senate	50	3,000	0	3,050
Democrats	0	2,500	0	2,500
No. of Cand.	*0*	*2*	*0*	*2*
House	0	500	0	500
Senate	0	2,000	0	2,000
Incumbents	50	3,000	4,000	7,050
Challengers	0	2,000	0	2,000
Open Seat	0	2,500	0	2,500
Winners	50	4,000	n/a	4,050
Losers	0	3,500	n/a	3,500

Oklahoma Gas and Electric Co.

*Phone: (405) 553-3651 * Fax: (405) 553-3743*
321 N. Harvey, Oklahoma City, OK 73102
*Web: www.oge.com * E-mail: kroppwa@oge.com*

Oklahoma Gas and Electric is the largest electric utility in Oklahoma, providing electric service to 274 communities in a 30,000 square-mile area. Its parent company, OGE, posted 1997 revenues of $1.4 billion and employs 2,700 workers.

The public company serves about 685,000 customers and generates electricity from coal and natural gas. Subsidiary Enogex is the company's natural gas business.

OGE was recognized in 1996 and 1997 by Resource Data International, an independent research company which analyzes energy industries, for operating two of the country's most cost-efficient power plants. The company's Sooner and Muskogee power plants were ranked as No. 2 and No. 10, respectively, in the nation.

Oklahoma Gas and Electric Co. OG&E Employees PAC (C00066985) *Address: same as sponsor * Treasurer: Wendell A. Kropp*

	1993-94	1995-96	1997	Totals
Receipts	$31,024	$41,086	$24,713	$96,823
Disburse	33,250	36,500	21,100	90,850
Cash	7,754	12,343	15,957	n/a
Contributions	12,550	13,000	8,000	33,550
Republicans	8,300	12,500	8,000	28,800
No. of Cand.	*8*	*9*	*6*	*23*
House	6,750	9,500	5,000	21,250
Senate	1,550	3,000	3,000	7,550
Democrats	4,000	500	0	4,500
No. of Cand.	*2*	*1*	*0*	*3*
House	4,000	500	0	4,500
Senate	0	0	0	0
Incumbents	8,750	12,000	8,000	28,750
Challengers	1,000	0	0	1,000
Open Seat	2,550	1,000	0	3,550
Winners	10,300	12,500	n/a	22,800
Losers	2,250	500	n/a	2,750

PECO Energy Co.

*Phone: (215) 841-4166 * Fax: (215) 841-4083*
2301 Market St., Philadelphia, PA 19103
*Web: www.peco.com * E-mail: truch@peco-energy.com*

PECO Energy is a publicly owned utility that provides electric and gas service to 1.5 million customers in southeastern Pennsylvania, including Philadelphia. The company has 7,000 employees and reported $4.6 billion in 1997 revenue.

PECO has two local nuclear plants, Peach Bottom and Limerick, and a 42 percent share in a plant in Salem, N.J. In addition, PECO recently won a three-year contract to manage a Clinton, Ill. nuclear facility, which has been shut down since September 1996.

The firm is also returning a Northeast Utilities nuclear plant to service in Connecticut. In September 1997, PECO announced a joint venture, AmerGen Energy Co., with British Energy of Scotland to acquire and operate U.S. nuclear plants.

The company faces new competition in its electricity business now that the Public Utility Commission has begun a 14-month pilot program allowing other utilities to sell electricity in PECO's area.

PECO operates nine electric generating plants, a gas storage plant, a liquefied natural gas storage plant and maintains nearly 540 electric substations, 12,588 miles of aerial lines and 20,748 miles of underground cable.

PECO Energy Co. Political Action Committee (formerly known as Philadelphia Electric Co. PAC) (C00160101) *Address: same as sponsor * Treasurer: Theresa M. Ruch*

	1993-94	1995-96	1997	Totals
Receipts	$85,219	$93,057	$53,803	$232,079
Disburse	78,788	85,300	50,443	214,531
Cash	11,533	19,300	22,663	n/a
Contributions	59,500	64,600	41,350	165,450
Republicans	29,150	51,600	30,250	111,000
No. of Cand.	*25*	*43*	*27*	*95*
House	16,650	37,100	16,250	70,000
Senate	12,500	14,500	14,000	41,000
Democrats	30,350	13,000	11,100	54,450
No. of Cand.	*30*	*11*	*18*	*59*
House	19,850	13,000	8,600	41,450
Senate	10,500	0	2,500	13,000
Incumbents	40,750	55,350	40,750	136,850
Challengers	14,500	1,500	0	16,000
Open Seat	4,250	7,250	600	12,100
Winners	42,950	55,600	n/a	98,550
Losers	16,550	9,000	n/a	25,550

PacifiCorp

*Phone: (503) 464-5768 * Fax: (503) 275-2650*
825 N.E. Multnomah, Suite 410, Portland, OR 97232-2155
*Web: www.pacificorp.com * E-mail: lucious.hicks@pacificorp.com*

Through its Pacific Power & Light and Utah Power & Light subsidiaries, PacifiCorp sells electricity to 1.4 million customers in seven western states.

PacifiCorp is now the third-largest electric utility west of the Mississippi River and the largest bulk power trader in the West. It also sells electricity to Australia and sells natural gas through subsidiary TPC. The public company, which has 12,000 employees, reported 1997 revenues of $6.2 billion.

The company has offered to buy Energy Group, a diversified energy company in the United Kingdom, the United States and Australia.

PacifiCorp Federal Political Action Committee (C00082800) *Address: same as sponsor * Treasurer: Kevin A. Lynch * Contact: Lucious Hicks, Public Policy Manager*

	1993-94	1995-96	1997	Totals
Receipts	$12,317	$23,821	$11,635	$47,773
Disburse	10,707	24,179	6,366	41,252
Cash	3,420	3,915	9,190	n/a
Contributions	10,000	22,808	6,356	39,164
Republicans	4,500	13,501	3,796	21,797
No. of Cand.	*6*	*17*	*5*	*28*
House	2,000	7,838	1,250	11,088
Senate	2,500	5,663	2,546	10,709
Democrats	5,500	9,307	2,560	17,367
No. of Cand.	*11*	*11*	*4*	*26*
House	4,500	5,057	2,500	12,057
Senate	1,000	4,250	60	5,310
Incumbents	7,000	15,308	6,356	28,664
Challengers	0	1,250	0	1,250
Open Seat	3,000	6,250	0	9,250
Winners	5,500	17,808	n/a	23,308
Losers	4,500	5,000	n/a	9,500

Pacific Gas & Electric Co.

*Phone: (415) 973-7000 * Fax: (415) 973-0585*
P.O. Box 770000, San Francisco, CA 94177
Web: www.pge.com

PG&E is the public utility holding company for Pacific Gas & Electric, which serves more than 8 million customers in northern and central California with electricity and natural gas. The second-largest public utility in the nation, PG&E reported $15 billion in revenues during 1997. The company has 23,500 employees.

In 1997, PG&E picked up several lucrative contracts to provide electric services to Blockbuster Video stores, Safeway's California stores, Smucker's West Coast facilities, McDonald's California restaurants and several community colleges in California.

Because of utility deregulation in California, the company is shifting its focus from being a power supplier to distributing power and gas. PG&E has purchased extensive U.S. natural gas operations as well as a 389-mile pipeline in Queensland, Australia. It is selling its fossil-fuel power plants.

Pacific Gas & Electric Co. Employees' Federal Political Action Committee (C00177469) *Address: same as sponsor * Treasurer: Eric Pressler*

	1993-94	1995-96	1997	Totals
Receipts	$138,904	$141,037	$115,725	$395,666
Disburse	167,703	154,143	89,593	411,439
Cash	30,034	16,934	43,071	n/a
Contributions	157,067	143,402	86,057	386,526
Republicans	47,850	96,782	51,377	196,009
No. of Cand.	*49*	*70*	*42*	*161*
House	31,450	74,400	30,759	136,609
Senate	16,400	22,382	20,618	59,400
Democrats	109,217	46,620	34,680	190,517
No. of Cand.	*60*	*29*	*33*	*122*
House	89,717	41,620	29,780	161,117
Senate	19,500	5,000	4,900	29,400
Incumbents	144,217	140,402	85,057	369,676
Challengers	3,550	1,250	1,000	5,800
Open Seat	9,550	1,750	0	11,300
Winners	129,967	121,202	n/a	251,169
Losers	27,100	22,200	n/a	49,300

Contributed less than $5,000 during 1995-96 cycle:

PG&E Gas Transmission Texas Corp. Political Action Committee (PG&E Texas PAC) (C00326603) *Phone: (210) 246-2903 * Fax: (210) 246-2484 * P.O. Box 400, San Antonio, TX 78292 * Treasurer: Mark Stavinoha*

Pennsylvania Power & Light Co.

*Phone: (610) 774-5529 * Fax: (610) 774-5884*
2 N. Ninth St., Allentown, PA 18101-1179
*Web: www.papl.com * E-mail: flzingone@papl.com*

PP&L Resources is a publicly held, electric utility holding company which serves 1.2 million customers in the eastern United States and around the world. The company owns a nuclear power plant in Susquehanna, Pa.

Pennsylvania Power & Light is PP&L Resources' major subsidiary and is engaged in the business of generating, transmitting and distributing electric energy at retail and wholesale. PP&L Resources' 1997 sales were $3 billion. The company employs 6,400 people.

Other subsidiaries include: PP&L Global, PP&L Spectrum and PP&L Access.

Pennsylvania Power & Light Co. People for Good Government (C00228106) *Phone: (202) 662-8750 * Fax: (202) 662-8749 * 1331 Pennsylvania Ave. N.W., Suite 512, Washington, DC 20004 * E-mail: jssparkman@papl.com * Treasurer: John P. Kierzkowski*

*Contact: Frank Zingone, Constituency Development Manager * Phone: (610) 774-5529*

	1993-94	1995-96	1997	Totals
Receipts	$26,755	$44,400	$41,293	$112,448
Disburse	25,530	40,991	35,607	102,128
Cash	1,296	4,709	10,396	n/a
Contributions	25,100	33,555	33,810	92,465
Republicans	8,850	20,380	19,700	48,930
No. of Cand.	*10*	*20*	*15*	*45*
House	4,750	16,130	14,500	35,380
Senate	4,100	4,250	5,200	13,550
Democrats	16,250	13,175	14,110	43,535
No. of Cand.	*12*	*10*	*13*	*35*
House	13,750	13,175	11,610	38,535
Senate	2,500	0	2,500	5,000
Incumbents	21,800	29,525	33,810	85,135
Challengers	2,600	0	0	2,600
Open Seat	700	4,030	0	4,730
Winners	19,900	29,555	n/a	49,455
Losers	5,200	4,000	n/a	9,200

Potomac Electric Power Co.

*Phone: (202) 872-2089 * Fax: (202) 872-7967*
1900 Pennsylvania Ave. N.W., Room 804, Washington, DC 20068
*Web: www.pepco.com * E-mail: jacool@pepco.com*

Potomac Electric Power is a public electric utility providing service to the Washington area and parts of southern Maryland. The company produces, distributes and sells electricity. Most of the company's sales come from commercial and government customers.

PEPCO serves roughly 1.9 million customers in a 640-square mile area. Its sales in 1997 were $1.9 billion and PEPCO employs more than 5,000 workers.

Subsidiary Potomac Capital Investment derives revenue from leasing aircraft, aircraft engines, and power plants and from its real estate holdings.

In December 1997, PEPCO and Baltimore Gas and Electric Co. canceled their merger plans, citing regulatory setbacks.

Potomac Electric Power Co. Political Action Committee (PEPCO PAC) (C00118885) *Address: same as sponsor * Treasurer: Nathaniel E. Dove Jr. * Contact: James S. Potts, Chairperson*

	1993-94	1995-96	1997	Totals
Receipts	$50,127	$48,550	$22,769	$121,446
Disburse	72,310	54,702	24,784	151,796
Cash	13,216	7,069	5,055	n/a
Contributions	32,250	30,750	13,500	76,500
Republicans	6,250	15,000	7,000	28,250
No. of Cand.	*9*	*12*	*8*	*29*
House	6,250	11,000	4,000	21,250
Senate	0	4,000	3,000	7,000
Democrats	26,000	15,750	6,500	48,250
No. of Cand.	*27*	*19*	*9*	*55*
House	23,000	13,250	5,500	41,750
Senate	3,000	2,500	1,000	6,500
Incumbents	29,750	30,000	13,500	73,250
Challengers	0	0	0	0
Open Seat	1,500	750	0	2,250
Winners	28,000	29,750	n/a	57,750
Losers	4,250	1,000	n/a	5,250

Public Service Co. of New Mexico

*Phone: (505) 241-2759 * Fax: (505) 241-4386*
Alvarado Sq. MS1110, Albuquerque, NM 87158
Web: www.pnm.com

The Public Service Co. of New Mexico is a publicly owned electric utility. It also operates Santa Fe's water system. The company's new non-utility activities operate through its energy services business unit.

PNM had revenues of $1.1 billion in 1997. The company owns and operates two coal burning and two gas and oil burning power plants in New Mexico, and one nuclear plant in Arizona. PNM employs about 2,800 people.

The company sells electricity to about 349,000 customers in a large area of north central and parts of southwestern and northeastern New Mexico. It provides natural gas to most of the major communities in New Mexico, including Albuquerque and Santa Fe, serving about 410,000 customers.

PNM Responsible Citizens Group (C00025395) *Address: same as sponsor * Treasurer: Donna M. Burnett * Contact: Arthur Hull, Gov. Affairs Office*

	1993-94	1995-96	1997	Totals
Receipts	$10,337	$12,973	$6,176	$29,486
Disburse	10,700	11,096	4,003	25,799
Cash	5,332	7,212	9,385	n/a
Contributions	7,200	9,450	1,980	18,630
Republicans	1,600	6,200	1,000	8,800
No. of Cand.	*3*	*3*	*1*	*7*
House	1,100	1,200	1,000	3,300
Senate	500	5,000	0	5,500
Democrats	5,600	3,250	980	9,830
No. of Cand.	*1*	*2*	*2*	*5*
House	0	1,000	980	1,980
Senate	5,600	2,250	0	7,850
Incumbents	6,700	9,450	1,000	17,150
Challengers	0	0	500	500
Open Seat	500	0	480	980
Winners	7,200	9,450	n/a	16,650
Losers	0	0	n/a	0

Public Service Electric & Gas Co.

*Phone: (973) 430-7000 * Fax: (973) 623-8711*
80 Park Plaza - T4A, Newark, NJ 07101
Web: www.pseg.com

Public Service Electric & Gas is among the 10 largest combined electric and gas companies in the nation. The public utility provides electric and gas service to parts of New Jersey.

It is the state's oldest and largest utility and serves nearly three-quarters of the state's population, about 2.2 million people. The company's service area consists of a 2,600-square mile diagonal corridor across the state from Bergen to Camden counties that includes 300 communities and New Jersey's six largest cities.

The company operates nuclear units at Salem and Hope Creek, N.J., and owns part of Peach Bottom Generating Station near Lancaster, Pa.

PSE&G is a wholly owned subsidiary of Public Service Enterprise Group Inc. The corporation is a publicly traded, diversified energy company which ranked 234 on the Fortune 500 list in 1996, and employs 11,000 people. Public Service Enterprise Group had 1997 revenues of more than $6 billion, with more than 90 percent of the revenues generated by Public Service Electric & Gas Co.

Public Service Electric & Gas Co. Political Action Committee (PEGPAC) (C00214940) *Address: same as sponsor * Treasurer: Mark G. Kahrer * Contact: Roger Schwarz, Chairperson*

	1993-94	1995-96	1997	Totals
Receipts	$136,324	$131,680	$65,538	$333,542
Disburse	130,275	137,456	45,897	313,628
Cash	13,617	7,848	27,490	n/a
Contributions	110,037	99,432	38,223	247,692
Republicans	56,733	65,316	19,680	141,729
No. of Cand.	*41*	*51*	*18*	*110*
House	36,924	55,316	17,180	109,420
Senate	19,809	10,000	2,500	32,309
Democrats	53,304	34,116	18,543	105,963
No. of Cand.	*47*	*17*	*15*	*79*
House	41,806	27,539	14,300	83,645
Senate	11,498	6,577	4,243	22,318
Incumbents	86,528	84,155	38,223	208,906
Challengers	16,498	6,650	0	23,148
Open Seat	6,511	8,127	0	14,638
Winners	83,978	75,966	n/a	159,944
Losers	26,059	23,466	n/a	49,525

Puget Sound Energy

*Phone: (425) 454-6363 * Fax: (425) 462-3214*
Puget Power Building, Bellevue, WA 98009
Web: www.psechoice.com

Puget Sound Energy is a public utility company in Washington state furnishing electric and gas service in a territory covering about 6,000 square miles. As of 1996, the company had about 857,000 electric customers, consisting of 761,000 residential, 90,500 commercial, 4,100 industrial and 1,400 other customers.

Formed in a February 1997 merger between Washington Energy Co. and Puget Sound Power & Light Co., PSE has established three areas of business focused on the emerging, competitive energy industry: energy delivery, energy commodity sales and energy-related services.

In December 1997, Tenaska Washington Partners of Omaha, Neb. and Puget Sound Energy of Bellevue, Wash. reached a preliminary agreement that will lower the price the utility pays for power from Tenaska's facility located at Ferndale, Wash. The agreement states that Puget Sound Energy will buy out the final 14 years of Tenaska's underlying fixed-price gas supply. In addition, Puget Sound Energy will become the principal natural gas supplier to the Ferndale facility and will supply Tenaska with natural gas.

Puget Power Energy Inc. Good Government Committee - Federal (C00101592) *Address: same as sponsor * Treasurer: William E. Enger * Contact: Gary Nonensen, Chairperson*

	1993-94	1995-96	1997	Totals
Receipts	$20,339	$17,784	$8,056	$46,179
Disburse	23,777	24,194	7,890	55,861
Cash	8,677	2,270	2,436	n/a
Contributions	23,775	23,150	6,350	53,275
Republicans	16,050	22,400	6,350	44,800
No. of Cand.	10	12	6	28
House	10,450	18,150	3,850	32,450
Senate	5,600	4,250	2,500	12,350
Democrats	7,725	750	0	8,475
No. of Cand.	6	3	0	9
House	7,725	750	0	8,475
Senate	0	0	0	0
Incumbents	14,325	23,150	6,350	43,825
Challengers	8,250	0	0	8,250
Open Seat	1,000	0	0	1,000
Winners	19,500	16,750	n/a	36,250
Losers	4,275	6,400	n/a	10,675

SCANA Corp.

*Phone: (803) 748-3693 * Fax: (803) 748-3336*
1426 Main St., Columbia, SC 29218
*Web: www.scana.com * E-mail: wtimmerman@scana.com*

SCANA is a publicly traded holding company with 13 wholly owned subsidiaries engaged in regulated electric and natural gas utility businesses. In addition, its business includes the telecommunications sector and a marketing division. The company, which has 4,500 employees, reported 1997 revenues of $1.5 billion.

The company's principal subsidiary, South Carolina Electric & Gas, provides electricity to about 475,000 customers in a 15,000-square mile area of South Carolina. It also provides natural gas to about 240,000 customers over a 20,000-square mile area. The company operates a nuclear power plant near Jenkinsville, S.C.

In addition, SCE&G operates the Columbia and Charleston, S.C. urban bus services. Subsidiary MPX Systems provides fiber-optic telecommunications, videoconferencing and mobile radio services in the southeastern United States.

SCANA Corp. Federal Political Action Committee (C00200907) *Address: same as sponsor * Treasurer: Mark R. Cannon * Contact: William B. Timmerman, Chairperson*

	1993-94	1995-96	1997	Totals
Receipts	$23,233	$25,140	$11,363	$59,736
Disburse	15,725	26,125	2,000	43,850
Cash	12,810	11,828	21,193	n/a
Contributions	14,725	17,625	2,000	34,350
Republicans	5,875	14,625	1,500	22,000
No. of Cand.	6	6	2	14
House	5,375	4,125	1,500	11,000
Senate	500	10,500	0	11,000
Democrats	8,850	3,000	500	12,350
No. of Cand.	10	4	1	15
House	7,350	2,000	500	9,850
Senate	1,500	1,000	0	2,500
Incumbents	7,225	17,625	2,000	26,850
Challengers	0	0	0	0
Open Seat	7,500	0	0	7,500
Winners	8,975	17,625	n/a	26,600
Losers	5,750	0	n/a	5,750

San Diego Gas & Electric Co.

*Phone: (619) 654-1127 * Fax: (619) 654-0349*
P.O. Box 1831, San Diego, CA 92112
Web: www.sdge.com

Established in 1881, San Diego Gas & Electric is the chief subsidiary of the Enova Corp. It provides electric service to 1.2 million customers in San Diego and Orange counties, and regulated gas service to 710,000 customers in San Diego County.

In November 1997, as a further step in its conversion from an electrical-generating to electrical-transmitting facility, San Diego Gas & Electric announced plans to auction its fossil power plants in Chula Vista and Carlsbad, Calif.

The PAC contributes to state and federal candidates who support the free enterprise system and who affect utility issues. It was founded in the mid-1970s.

San Diego Gas & Electric Co. Citizens for Good Government Committee (C00063131) *Address: same as sponsor * Treasurer: Gail Bennett*

	1993-94	1995-96	1997	Totals
Receipts	$32,522	$32,593	$15,410	$80,525
Disburse	36,408	29,552	8,535	74,495
Cash	3,964	7,010	13,885	n/a
Contributions	35,800	29,000	8,500	73,300
Republicans	13,450	22,500	5,000	40,950
No. of Cand.	16	21	6	43
House	11,450	17,500	5,000	33,950
Senate	2,000	5,000	0	7,000
Democrats	22,350	6,500	3,500	32,350
No. of Cand.	21	8	6	35
House	18,100	6,500	3,000	27,600
Senate	4,250	0	500	4,750
Incumbents	33,600	26,500	6,500	66,600
Challengers	1,200	1,000	1,500	3,700
Open Seat	1,000	1,500	500	3,000
Winners	30,100	26,500	n/a	56,600
Losers	5,700	2,500	n/a	8,200

Sierra Pacific Resources

*Phone: (702) 834-3979 * Fax: (702) 834-4202*
P.O. Box 7724, 6100 Neil Rd., Reno, NV 89510
Web: www.sierrapacific.com

Sierra Pacific Resources is the holding company for a public gas and electric utility in Nevada. It has three primary subsidiaries: Sierra Pacific Power Co., Tuscarora Gas Pipeline Co. and Lands of Sierra Inc.

SPR, which has about 1,500 employees, reported 1997 revenues of $663 million.

The company provides electricity for about 286,000 customers in a 50,000 square-mile area of northern Nevada and northeastern California, including the Lake Tahoe region. It also provides natural gas and water to customers in Reno, Nev.

A second company PAC was terminated in 1996.

Sierra Pacific Employees Political Action Committee (C00153379) *Address: same as sponsor * Treasurer: Jack McElwee * Contact: Susan Miller, Gov. Affairs Representative*

	1993-94	1995-96	1997	Totals
Receipts	$11,452	$11,895	$16,496	$39,843
Disburse	13,288	14,220	5,873	33,381
Cash	4,325	2,005	12,628	n/a
Contributions	7,450	10,200	4,500	22,150
Republicans	5,200	5,450	3,500	14,150
No. of Cand.	4	6	4	14
House	5,200	2,950	1,000	9,150
Senate	0	2,500	2,500	5,000
Democrats	2,250	4,750	1,000	8,000
No. of Cand.	3	3	1	7
House	1,250	750	0	2,000
Senate	1,000	4,000	1,000	6,000
Incumbents	5,450	8,600	3,000	17,050
Challengers	1,000	500	1,500	3,000
Open Seat	0	1,100	0	1,100
Winners	6,200	7,850	n/a	14,050
Losers	1,250	2,350	n/a	3,600

Sierra Pacific Resources Committee for Good Government Political Action Committee (C00207878) *P.O. Box 30023, Reno, NV 89520 * Treasurer: Richard E. Hughs*

	1993-94	1995-96	1997	Totals
Receipts	$8,963	$4,694	$1,860	$15,517
Disburse	7,785	5,210	3,259	16,254
Cash	1,913	1,399	0	n/a
Contributions	7,285	5,200	0	12,485
Republicans	4,000	5,000	0	9,000
No. of Cand.	4	5	0	9

House	1,000	4,000	0	5,000
Senate	3,000	1,000	0	4,000
Democrats	3,285	200	0	3,485
No. of Cand.	*2*	*1*	*0*	*3*
House	500	200	0	700
Senate	2,785	0	0	2,785
Incumbents	6,285	4,500	0	10,785
Challengers	1,000	0	0	1,000
Open Seat	0	700	0	700
Winners	5,785	2,500	n/a	8,285
Losers	1,500	2,700	n/a	4,200

Southern California Edison

*Phone: (626) 302-2823 * Fax: (626) 302-6315*
2244 Walnut Grove Ave., Rosemead, CA 91770
Web: www.edisonx.com

Southern California Edison is the nation's second-largest electric utility in number of customers, serving more than 11 million people. Its service territory exceeds 50,000 square miles within central, coastal and Southern California. The publicly held SCE is planning to sell several of its plants in 1998 in the wake of utility competition in California. The company had $9.2 billion in sales during 1997 and employs more than 13,000 workers.

The company is majority owner of the San Onofre Nuclear Generating Station in northern San Diego County.

SCE is a subsidiary of Edison International, which also manages industrial parks and invests in power projects. SCE's subsidiaries include Edison ESI, which specializes in large electrical and mechanical equipment repair and maintenance. Another subsidiary, Edison Mission Energy, has several power plants in the United States.

SCE's top legislative issue at the state and federal levels is how to implement electric utility deregulation, which was mandated by the California Assembly. SCE proposes that all electric providers maintain the right to measure electricity used and bill customers. It opposes separate line-item charges on utility bills, which it says could lead to different energy rates for different areas and billing inaccuracies.

SCE was the leading contributor to 1996 congressional campaigns among electric utilities, although it gave less than it did in 1994. Republican candidates received nearly 56 percent of the money, and nine of the top 20 recipients were from California. Rep. Frank Pallone Jr., D-N.J., a member of the House Energy & Power Subcommittee, was the top recipient outside California.

Edison International Companies Federal PAC (formerly known as Southern California Edison Co.) (C00019653) *Address: same as sponsor * Treasurer: Kenneth S. Stewart * Contact: Padget Kaiser, Deputy Dir. of External Affairs*

	1993-94	*1995-96*	*1997*	*Totals*
Receipts	$367,591	$348,199	$163,767	$879,557
Disburse	353,675	355,629	165,479	874,783
Cash	23,617	16,192	14,485	n/a
Contributions	283,620	233,583	140,057	657,260
Republicans	68,300	130,483	75,793	274,576
No. of Cand.	*55*	*81*	*62*	*198*
House	54,800	103,949	52,828	211,577
Senate	13,500	26,534	22,965	62,999
Democrats	215,320	103,100	63,764	382,184
No. of Cand.	*91*	*57*	*50*	*198*
House	159,200	90,600	45,800	295,600
Senate	56,120	12,500	17,964	86,584
Incumbents	244,520	206,583	137,557	588,660
Challengers	7,500	4,000	0	11,500
Open Seat	21,600	20,000	500	42,100
Winners	193,400	215,333	n/a	408,733
Losers	90,220	18,250	n/a	108,470

Southern Co.

*Phone: (404) 506-6926 * Fax: (404) 506-2894*
241 Ralph McGill Blvd., Bin 10111, Atlanta, GA 30308-3374
Web: www.southernco.com

One of the largest publicly traded utilities in the United States, Southern provides electricity to more than 3.6 million people in the Southeast. The 30,000-employee company reported $12.7 billion in 1997 sales.

The company operates through its five primary subsidiaries — Alabama Power, Georgia Power, Gulf Power, Mississippi Power and Savannah Electric — each of which also has a separate PAC. The utility companies provide electricity throughout their respective states, with Gulf serving Florida and Savannah serving southeast Georgia. The company also owns the Birmingham, Ala.-based Southern Nuclear Operating Co., which has its own PAC.

Nuclear power accounts for 17 percent of the company's output. Southern operates three nuclear plants — near Dothan, Ala., near Baxley, Ga. and near the Georgia and South Carolina border. Southern relies on coal for 77 percent of its power output.

Southern Energy Inc., the company's energy generation subsidiary, helps make Southern the largest generator of electricity in the nation.

Southern Co. Services PAC (C00144774) *Address: same as sponsor * Treasurer: James A. Mason Jr. * Contact: Jerry Stewart, Chairman*

	1993-94	*1995-96*	*1997*	*Totals*
Receipts	$98,619	$125,656	$60,876	$285,151
Disburse	107,304	106,929	49,000	263,233
Cash	8,825	27,559	39,442	n/a
Contributions	100,650	95,800	40,250	236,700
Republicans	66,000	86,050	35,000	187,050
No. of Cand.	*108*	*122*	*48*	*278*
House	37,500	49,600	23,500	110,600
Senate	28,500	36,450	11,500	76,450
Democrats	34,650	9,750	5,250	49,650
No. of Cand.	*60*	*21*	*9*	*90*
House	27,150	10,500	4,750	42,400
Senate	7,500	-750	500	7,250
Incumbents	66,500	71,100	35,750	173,350
Challengers	7,250	3,200	0	10,450
Open Seat	26,400	20,500	5,000	51,900
Winners	85,950	79,600	n/a	165,550
Losers	14,700	16,200	n/a	30,900

Alabama Power Co. Employees Federal Political Action Committee (APC Employees Federal PAC) (C00077305) *Phone: (205) 257-1000 * 600 N. 18th St., P.O. Box 2641, Birmingham, AL 35291 * Treasurer: R. Neil Boyd * Contact: Julian H. Smith Jr., Chairperson*

	1993-94	*1995-96*	*1997*	*Totals*
Receipts	$117,869	$104,386	$41,524	$263,779
Disburse	123,595	143,659	41,794	309,048
Cash	43,081	3,819	3,554	n/a
Contributions	94,300	86,950	33,000	214,250
Republicans	45,300	54,450	19,250	119,000
No. of Cand.	*69*	*82*	*18*	*169*
House	29,050	32,750	12,750	74,550
Senate	16,250	21,700	6,500	44,450
Democrats	48,500	32,500	13,750	94,750
No. of Cand.	*66*	*33*	*11*	*110*
House	38,500	30,500	5,000	74,000
Senate	10,000	2,000	8,750	20,750
Incumbents	84,700	60,250	24,500	169,450
Challengers	2,000	2,200	0	4,200
Open Seat	7,600	23,500	1,000	32,100
Winners	82,200	64,000	n/a	146,200
Losers	12,100	22,950	n/a	35,050

Georgia Power Co. Federal PAC Inc. (C00119776) *Phone: (404) 506-2406 * Fax: (404) 506-2488 * 241 Ralph McGill Blvd. N.E., Atlanta, GA 30308-3374 * Web: www.southernco.com * Treasurer: Jimmy A. Wilson*

	1993-94	*1995-96*	*1997*	*Totals*
Receipts	$91,575	$90,526	$53,835	$235,936
Disburse	100,280	89,462	56,298	246,040
Cash	8,447	9,513	7,054	n/a
Contributions	74,050	67,200	41,000	182,250
Republicans	44,750	61,700	32,750	139,200
No. of Cand.	*59*	*72*	*29*	*160*
House	23,500	48,750	29,750	102,000
Senate	21,250	12,950	3,000	37,200
Democrats	29,300	5,500	8,250	43,050
No. of Cand.	*42*	*9*	*10*	*61*
House	25,800	4,500	3,500	33,800
Senate	3,500	1,000	4,750	9,250
Incumbents	58,900	58,000	40,000	156,900
Challengers	4,000	1,950	0	5,950
Open Seat	10,700	6,250	1,500	18,450
Winners	60,250	61,250	n/a	121,500
Losers	13,800	5,950	n/a	19,750

Southern Nuclear Operating Co. Inc. Employees PAC (Southern Nuclear PAC) (C00250407) *Phone: (205) 992-5523 * Fax: (205) 992-6165 * P.O. Box 1295 (Bin B022), Birmingham, AL 35201 * Web: www.southernco.com/site/southernnuclear * Treasurer: E. F. Cobb * Contact: J. H. Miller III, Chairperson*

	1993-94	1995-96	1997	Totals
Receipts	$47,439	$70,943	$33,880	$152,262
Disburse	43,974	67,450	37,500	148,924
Cash	7,601	11,104	7,490	n/a
Contributions	41,600	59,700	32,250	133,550
Republicans	32,100	55,200	27,750	115,050
No. of Cand.	*56*	*75*	*33*	*164*
House	15,600	29,000	17,750	62,350
Senate	16,500	26,200	10,000	52,700
Democrats	9,500	4,500	4,500	18,500
No. of Cand.	*27*	*12*	*6*	*45*
House	8,750	4,250	500	13,500
Senate	750	250	4,000	5,000
Incumbents	31,350	45,250	29,750	106,350
Challengers	2,750	1,200	0	3,950
Open Seat	7,750	12,750	2,500	23,000
Winners	36,500	52,250	n/a	88,750
Losers	5,100	7,450	n/a	12,550

Responsible Government Committee of Gulf Employees Inc. (C00120519) *Phone: (850) 444-6467 * Fax: (850) 444-6026 * One Energy Pl., Bin 733, P.O. Box 1151, Pensacola, FL 32520 * Web: www.gulfpower.com * Treasurer: C. A. Punyko * Contact: Carl A. Punyko*

	1993-94	1995-96	1997	Totals
Receipts	$57,834	$66,373	$38,460	$162,667
Disburse	61,772	62,096	19,919	143,787
Cash	6,754	11,046	29,595	n/a
Contributions	24,700	22,400	8,850	55,950
Republicans	17,250	19,650	6,500	43,400
No. of Cand.	*50*	*56*	*21*	*127*
House	11,250	16,450	6,250	33,950
Senate	6,000	3,200	250	9,450
Democrats	7,450	2,750	2,350	12,550
No. of Cand.	*22*	*9*	*4*	*35*
House	6,950	2,750	1,600	11,300
Senate	500	0	750	1,250
Incumbents	17,450	18,700	8,850	45,000
Challengers	1,000	450	0	1,450
Open Seat	6,250	3,000	0	9,250
Winners	19,500	19,950	n/a	39,450
Losers	5,200	2,450	n/a	7,650

Mississippi Power Co. Federal PAC (also known as Mississippi Power Co. Employees' Committee for Responsible Federal Government) (C00144147) *Phone: (228) 864-1211 * Fax: (228) 865-5616 * P.O. Box 4079, Gulfport, MS 39502-4079 * Treasurer: Walter L. Smitherman * Contact: Don Mason, Chairperson*

	1993-94	1995-96	1997	Totals
Receipts	$24,913	$28,652	$14,793	$68,358
Disburse	26,579	27,059	10,352	63,990
Cash	3,200	4,803	9,247	n/a
Contributions	25,050	21,250	7,850	54,150
Republicans	13,950	18,250	5,850	38,050
No. of Cand.	*30*	*32*	*8*	*70*
House	4,950	12,050	5,350	22,350
Senate	9,000	6,200	500	15,700
Democrats	11,100	3,000	2,000	16,100
No. of Cand.	*14*	*6*	*1*	*21*
House	10,600	3,000	2,000	15,600
Senate	500	0	0	500
Incumbents	14,850	13,800	7,850	36,500
Challengers	1,000	200	0	1,200
Open Seat	9,200	7,000	0	16,200
Winners	19,350	16,300	n/a	35,650
Losers	5,700	4,950	n/a	10,650

Savannah Electric and Power Co. Employees Federal PAC (SEEPAC) (C00296533) *Phone: (912) 231-2514 * P.O. Box 968, 600 E. Bay St., Savannah, GA 31402 * Web: www.southernco.com/site/savannah * Treasurer: Cathy Easterling*

	1993-94	1995-96	1997	Totals
Receipts	$950	$32,183	$15,771	$48,904
Disburse	0	20,250	8,750	29,000
Cash	950	12,883	19,904	n/a
Contributions	0	20,250	8,250	28,500
Republicans	0	14,500	5,750	20,250
No. of Cand.	*0*	*28*	*10*	*38*
House	0	9,500	3,750	13,250
Senate	0	5,000	2,000	7,000
Democrats	0	5,750	2,500	8,250
No. of Cand.	*0*	*15*	*5*	*20*
House	0	5,250	2,500	7,750
Senate	0	500	0	500
Incumbents	0	14,750	6,750	21,500
Challengers	0	500	0	500
Open Seat	0	4,500	1,500	6,000
Winners	0	18,250	n/a	18,250
Losers	0	2,000	n/a	2,000

Southern Indiana Gas and Electric Co.

*Phone: (812) 464-4621 * Fax: (812) 464-4554*
20 N.W. Fourth St., Evansville, IN 47741
*Web: www.sigcorpinc.com * E-mail: gmcmanus@sigeco.com*

Southern Indiana Gas and Electric is a gas and electric utility company serving more than 120,000 electric customers and 104,000 natural gas customers in a 10-county area of southwest Indiana. The company's 1997 revenues were $359.2 million.

As the chief subsidiary of Sigcorp Inc., it also provides wholesale electric power service to five municipal electric systems in southwest Indiana and sells energy to a growing number of power marketers and other utilities in the region.

Southern Indiana Gas and Electric Co. Employees' Federal Political Action Committee (C00240069) *Address: same as sponsor * Treasurer: Andrew E. Goebel * Contact: Greg McManus, Chairperson*

	1993-94	1995-96	1997	Totals
Receipts	$16,963	$16,926	$9,269	$43,158
Disburse	10,000	29,000	0	39,000
Cash	20,490	8,420	17,690	n/a
Contributions	10,000	29,000	0	39,000
Republicans	10,000	26,000	0	36,000
No. of Cand.	*5*	*8*	*0*	*13*
House	9,000	26,000	0	35,000
Senate	1,000	0	0	1,000
Democrats	0	3,000	0	3,000
No. of Cand.	*0*	*1*	*0*	*1*
House	0	3,000	0	3,000
Senate	0	0	0	0
Incumbents	8,000	18,000	0	26,000
Challengers	0	2,000	0	2,000
Open Seat	2,000	9,000	0	11,000
Winners	10,000	22,000	n/a	32,000
Losers	0	7,000	n/a	7,000

TECO Energy Inc.

*Phone: (813) 228-4111 * Fax: (813) 228-1670*
P.O. Box 111, Tampa, FL 33601-0111
Web: www.teco.net

TECO is an energy holding company providing electrical and gas service in Florida. The company's largest subsidiary, Tampa Electric Co., serves 500,000 customers in west central Florida. Subsidiary Peoples Gas System serves 230,000 customers from Tampa to Jacksonville, making it the state's largest natural gas distribution company.

Publicly owned TECO reported 1997 revenues of $1.8 billion. The company has 4,350 employees and generates almost all of its electricity from burning coal.

Other subsidiaries include: TECO Coal, which has mines in eastern Kentucky and Tennessee; Bosek, Gibson and Associates, an energy efficiency consulting practice; TECO Coalbed Methane, which produces natural gas in Alabama; TECO Power Services, which has built power plants in Florida and Guatemala; TECO Properties; TECO Transport; and TeCom.

The company also had an oil and gas exploration unit, which it sold to American Resources of Delaware Inc. in March 1998.

TECO Energy Inc. Employees' PAC (C00161422) *Address: same as sponsor * Treasurer: Robin Hastings * Contact: Rod Burkhardt, President*

	1993-94	1995-96	1997	Totals
Receipts	$112,295	$102,627	$49,230	$264,152
Disburse	117,634	103,420	33,861	254,915
Cash	10,983	10,192	25,560	n/a
Contributions	27,050	45,130	22,500	94,680
Republicans	18,050	35,130	11,500	64,680
No. of Cand.	*20*	*28*	*13*	*61*
House	6,550	23,630	7,500	37,680
Senate	11,500	11,500	4,000	27,000
Democrats	9,000	10,000	11,000	30,000
No. of Cand.	*11*	*7*	*7*	*25*
House	5,500	7,500	2,500	15,500
Senate	3,500	2,500	8,500	14,500
Incumbents	22,300	39,880	21,500	83,680
Challengers	1,000	0	0	1,000
Open Seat	3,250	5,250	1,000	9,500
Winners	25,200	43,630	n/a	68,830
Losers	1,850	1,500	n/a	3,350

Texas Utilities Co.

*Phone: (214) 812-4600 * Fax: (214) 812-4002*
1601 Bryan St., Suite 27-100, Dallas, TX 75201
Web: www.tu.com

Texas Utilities is a publicly traded holding company whose principal subsidiary, TU Electric, serves 2.4 million customers — or about one-third of the Texas population — including Dallas, Fort Worth, Midland and surrounding areas. Together, Texas Utility's 11 subsidiaries have 12,000 employees and reported 1996 revenues of $6.6 billion.

TU Electric has 24 generating plants, including the Comanche Peak nuclear facility located 80 miles southwest of Dallas. The nuclear facility's two units, located in Glen Rose, Texas, began operating in 1990 and 1993. Many of the company's other plants are fueled with natural gas. The company also transmits, distributes and sells electricity.

In 1997, Texas Utilities purchased ENSERCH Corp., a natural gas distribution company. The transaction included two large pipeline and distribution companies, Lone Star Gas Co. and Lone Star Pipeline Co.

The company also purchased the fourth-largest telephone company in Texas for $328 million. Lufkin-Conroe Communications Co. provides local phone service to part of Southeast Texas.

Other subsidiaries include: Southwestern Electric Service Co., which serves 126,000 people in East and Central Texas; TU Australia, which holds stock in an electric utility in that country; Texas Utilities Fuel Co.; Texas Utilities Mining Co.; Texas Utilities Properties; and Chaco Energy Co.

Texas Utilities Co. Political Action Committee (C00226548) *Address: same as sponsor * Treasurer: Marc D. Moseley * Contact: Patti Richards, Chairperson*

	1993-94	1995-96	1997	Totals
Receipts	$101,594	$145,549	$81,992	$329,135
Disburse	104,219	136,209	76,075	316,503
Cash	4,194	13,545	19,469	n/a
Contributions	47,750	75,000	39,000	161,750
Republicans	21,700	55,000	24,500	101,200
No. of Cand.	*20*	*44*	*21*	*85*
House	12,900	41,000	12,500	66,400
Senate	8,800	14,000	12,000	34,800
Democrats	26,050	20,000	14,000	60,050
No. of Cand.	*22*	*12*	*10*	*44*
House	22,750	20,000	13,500	56,250
Senate	3,300	0	500	3,800
Incumbents	45,250	68,500	38,000	151,750
Challengers	0	1,000	0	1,000
Open Seat	2,500	5,500	1,000	9,000
Winners	38,950	58,000	n/a	96,950
Losers	8,800	17,000	n/a	25,800

Transmission & Pipeline PAC of Texas Utilities Co. (formerly known as ENSERCH Corp. Employees Political Support Association) (C00035709) *Phone: (214) 573-5227 * Fax: (214) 573-5134 * 300 S. St. Paul St., Suite 270EC, Dallas, TX 75201 * Treasurer: Nancy Blackburn * Contact: Ron Hewlett, Chairman*

The Transmission and Pipeline PAC of Texas Utilities represents the transmission and pipeline business units of the company. The committee was formerly known as the ENSERCH Employees Political Support Association.

	1993-94	1995-96	1997	Totals
Receipts	$201,508	$146,912	$73,289	$421,709
Disburse	207,744	146,877	59,200	413,821
Cash	4,930	4,979	19,075	n/a
Contributions	110,020	64,650	23,000	197,670
Republicans	32,950	46,100	15,500	94,550
No. of Cand.	*37*	*43*	*14*	*94*
House	13,350	36,600	9,000	58,950
Senate	19,600	9,500	6,500	35,600
Democrats	77,070	18,550	7,500	103,120
No. of Cand.	*59*	*20*	*9*	*88*
House	54,700	18,050	5,500	78,250
Senate	22,370	500	2,000	24,870
Incumbents	101,270	52,800	23,000	177,070
Challengers	800	500	0	1,300
Open Seat	6,950	11,350	0	18,300
Winners	84,250	51,600	n/a	135,850
Losers	25,770	13,050	n/a	38,820

Electric Service Political Action Committee of Texas Utilities Co. (C00255992) *Phone: (214) 812-2858 * Fax: (214) 812-5456 * 1601 Bryan St., Suite 21052, Dallas, TX 75201 * Treasurer: Edward M. Shivers * Contact: John Self, Chairperson*

The Electric Service PAC of Texas Utilities represents the distribution and customer service business units of the company.

	1993-94	1995-96	1997	Totals
Receipts	$171,492	$166,834	$77,271	$415,597
Disburse	173,651	159,020	74,600	407,271
Cash	4,677	12,471	15,150	n/a
Contributions	52,120	55,500	29,000	136,620
Republicans	21,150	30,500	17,000	68,650
No. of Cand.	*12*	*14*	*7*	*33*
House	8,800	28,500	12,000	49,300
Senate	12,350	2,000	5,000	19,350
Democrats	30,970	25,000	12,000	67,970
No. of Cand.	*17*	*8*	*5*	*30*
House	27,250	25,000	12,000	64,250
Senate	3,720	0	0	3,720
Incumbents	45,370	49,500	29,000	123,870
Challengers	1,500	0	0	1,500
Open Seat	3,250	6,000	0	9,250
Winners	42,400	45,000	n/a	87,400
Losers	9,720	10,500	n/a	20,220

Power Political Action Committee of Texas Utilities Co. (C00255950) *Phone: (214) 812-8345 * Fax: (214) 812-5651 * 1601 Bryan St., Suite 18002, Dallas, TX 75201-3411 * Treasurer: Jimmy Estes * Contact: Larry Williford, Chairperson*

The Power PAC of Texas Utilities represents the generation and mining business units of the company.

	1993-94	1995-96	1997	Totals
Receipts	$66,104	$99,848	$53,435	$219,387
Disburse	68,100	95,550	46,750	210,400
Cash	3,113	7,419	14,112	n/a
Contributions	29,000	31,500	18,000	78,500
Republicans	15,650	11,500	6,500	33,650
No. of Cand.	*12*	*8*	*6*	*26*
House	8,800	8,500	5,500	22,800
Senate	6,850	3,000	1,000	10,850
Democrats	13,350	20,000	11,500	44,850
No. of Cand.	*9*	*6*	*4*	*19*
House	11,500	20,000	11,500	43,000
Senate	1,850	0	0	1,850
Incumbents	25,750	23,000	18,000	66,750
Challengers	1,000	500	0	1,500
Open Seat	2,250	8,000	0	10,250
Winners	25,150	28,500	n/a	53,650
Losers	3,850	3,000	n/a	6,850

Texas-New Mexico Power Co.

*Phone: (817) 737-1304 * Fax: (817) 377-5521*
P.O. Box 2943, Fort Worth, TX 76113
*Web: www.tnpe.com/tnp.htm * E-mail: sforbes@tnpe.com*

Texas-New Mexico Power is a wholly owned subsidiary of TNP Enterprises, a publicly held company. Texas-New Mexico Power provides electric service to more than 222,000 customers in Texas and New Mexico.

The company filed a transition-to-competition plan in July 1997 to prepare for May 2000, when the company's customers will be able to choose their electric supplier.

Texas-New Mexico Power is organized into three operating areas: the Mountain Region, which serves nine communities in southwestern and south-central New Mexico; the North-Central Region, which serves 55 communities in northeastern and central Texas; and the Gulf Coast Region, which serves 20 communities in western and southeastern Texas.

Texas-New Mexico Power Co. Responsible Government Association (C00102798) *Address: same as sponsor * Treasurer: Scott Forbes*

	1993-94	1995-96	1997	Totals
Receipts	$56,936	$33,455	$28,289	$118,680
Disburse	71,478	47,450	18,800	137,728
Cash	15,168	1,176	10,667	n/a
Contributions	17,000	10,800	7,000	34,800
Republicans	6,500	10,000	5,500	22,000
No. of Cand.	*6*	*10*	*5*	*21*
House	2,000	10,000	5,500	17,500
Senate	4,500	0	0	4,500
Democrats	10,000	800	1,500	12,300
No. of Cand.	*11*	*2*	*2*	*15*
House	7,750	800	1,500	10,050
Senate	2,250	0	0	2,250
Incumbents	14,750	6,800	7,000	28,550
Challengers	500	1,500	0	2,000

(Data for Texas-New Mexico Power continued)

Open Seat	1,750	2,500	0	4,250
Winners	13,250	10,300	n/a	23,550
Losers	3,750	500	n/a	4,250

United Illuminating Co.

*Phone: (203) 499-2000 * Fax: (203) 499-2414*
157 Church St., P.O. Box 1564, New Haven, CT 06506-0901
Web: www.uinet.com

United Illuminating is a public utility that provides electricity to 17 southern Connecticut towns in a 335 square-mile service area. The electricity is generated from coal, oil, gas and nuclear sources. The company reported $710 million in 1997 revenues.

Subsidiaries include: American Payment Systems, Precision Power and Thermal Energies. The company operates two nuclear units, one in Connecticut and the other in New Hampshire.

In fall 1997, United Illuminating and NEES Global Transmission Inc. agreed to collaborate on a proposal to develop an electric power cable under Long Island Sound. The cable would allow for the transfer of energy between New England and Long Island, New York.

The company has 1,200 employees.

Electric Employees Committee of The United Illuminating Co. (C00216341) *Address: same as sponsor * Treasurer: James L. Benjamin * Contact: Bill Murphy, Chairperson*

	1993-94	1995-96	1997	Totals
Receipts	$31,742	$27,337	$13,751	$72,830
Disburse	31,499	21,576	4,750	57,825
Cash	3,375	10,412	19,415	n/a
Contributions	20,250	17,800	3,250	41,300
Republicans	10,600	11,500	1,250	23,350
No. of Cand.	18	15	3	36
House	7,100	9,000	500	16,600
Senate	3,500	2,500	750	6,750
Democrats	9,650	6,300	2,000	17,950
No. of Cand.	12	7	5	24
House	5,650	3,300	1,500	10,450
Senate	4,000	3,000	500	7,500
Incumbents	17,300	16,800	3,250	37,350
Challengers	1,400	0	0	1,400
Open Seat	1,550	1,000	0	2,550
Winners	17,100	12,800	n/a	29,900
Losers	3,150	5,000	n/a	8,150

UtiliCorp United Inc.

*Phone: (402) 221-2091 * Fax: (402) 221-2501*
1815 Capitol Ave., Omaha, NE 68102
Web: www.utilicorp.com

UtiliCorp United provides electricity and gas to more than 1 million customers in Missouri, Kansas, Colorado, West Virginia, Nebraska, Iowa, Michigan and Minnesota. The publicly traded company also distributes electricity to parts of British Columbia, Canada and Australia.

The company also owns interests in two electric utilities in New Zealand and markets natural gas to wholesale and industrial customers in the United Kingdom.

In 1997, UtiliCorp's total sales were more than $8.9 billion. The company employs 4,700 people.

UtiliCorp has three subsidiaries: Aquila Energy, Aquila Power and UtilCo Group.

UtiliCorp United Inc. Employee PAC (also known as UtiliCorp United Employee PAC) (C00211615) *Address: same as sponsor * Treasurer: Douglas R. Clark*

	1993-94	1995-96	1997	Totals
Receipts	$40,556	$19,338	$16,369	$76,263
Disburse	49,841	21,122	1,500	72,463
Cash	4,085	4,548	19,320	n/a
Contributions	44,822	20,550	1,500	66,872
Republicans	23,119	14,000	1,500	38,619
No. of Cand.	18	21	1	40
House	8,869	8,000	1,500	18,369
Senate	14,250	6,000	0	20,250
Democrats	21,453	6,550	0	28,003
No. of Cand.	16	6	0	22
House	12,353	4,050	0	16,403
Senate	9,100	2,500	0	11,600
Incumbents	21,319	12,800	1,500	35,619
Challengers	5,250	1,000	0	6,250
Open Seat	18,253	6,750	0	25,003
Winners	33,972	17,550	n/a	51,522
Losers	10,850	3,000	n/a	13,850

Washington Water Power Co.

*Phone: (509) 482-4576 * Fax: (509) 482-4823*
P.O. Box 3727, Spokane, WA 99220
*Web: www.wwpco.com * E-mail: sbarry@wwpco.com*

Washington Water Power is a public utility company supplying nearly 300,000 electric customers in eastern Washington state and northern Idaho, and nearly 250,000 natural gas customers in Washington state, Idaho, Oregon and California.

WWP, which has about 3,200 employees, reported $1.3 billion in revenues during 1997.

Washington Water Power is also involved in non-regulated businesses: Avista Energy, an energy-trading and marketing company; Avista Advantage, a firm engaged in energy services and new product development; and Pentzer Corp., a wholly owned private investment firm.

Water Power Federal Political Action Committee (C00041038) *Address: same as sponsor * Treasurer: Susan Barry * Contact: Thomas Paine, Chairperson*

	1993-94	1995-96	1997	Totals
Receipts	$21,653	$18,896	$8,658	$49,207
Disburse	26,509	17,817	6,030	50,356
Cash	1,575	2,658	5,286	n/a
Contributions	26,498	17,817	6,030	50,345
Republicans	13,437	17,317	3,280	34,034
No. of Cand.	9	11	4	24
House	6,237	11,317	1,780	19,334
Senate	7,200	6,000	1,500	14,700
Democrats	13,061	500	2,750	16,311
No. of Cand.	5	1	3	9
House	13,061	500	500	14,061
Senate	0	0	2,250	2,250
Incumbents	20,998	14,317	6,030	41,345
Challengers	5,000	1,500	0	6,500
Open Seat	500	2,000	0	2,500
Winners	14,437	16,317	n/a	30,754
Losers	12,061	1,500	n/a	13,561

Western Resources Inc.

*Phone: (785) 575-8369 * Fax: (785) 575-8119*
P.O. Box 889, Topeka, KS 66601-0889
Web: www.wstnres.com

Western Resources is a security and energy holding company with 600,000 electric customers in Kansas. The company also operates a natural gas business in Kansas and Oklahoma. A publicly traded company, Western Resources has nearly 6,000 employees and reported $2.1 billion in 1997 sales.

Western's utility subsidiary has a 47 percent share in a nuclear plant, Wolf Creek Generating Station, located about 50 miles south of Topeka. Western also has a 45 percent interest in Tulsa-based natural gas company ONEOK Inc., which serves more than 1 million customers. Western's Wing Group has power plant projects in China, Turkey and Colombia.

The company owns 82 percent of security company Protection One, which provides alarm services to nearly 1 million customers across the nation.

Subsidiaries: Westar Security, Westar Energy, Westar Capital, Westar Gas Marketing, Protection One and The Wing Group

Western Resources Employee Political Action Committee (C00218040) *Address: same as sponsor * Treasurer: Nancy J. Sumpter * Contact: T. A. Mindrup, Public and Work Force Safety Dir.*

	1993-94	1995-96	1997	Totals
Receipts	$12,436	$15,696	$4,592	$32,724
Disburse	20,995	14,133	3,500	38,628
Cash	1,281	2,848	3,941	n/a
Contributions	15,950	13,250	3,500	32,700
Republicans	11,850	12,750	3,000	27,600
No. of Cand.	12	14	6	32
House	9,100	6,750	2,500	18,350
Senate	2,750	6,000	500	9,250

Democrats	4,100	500	500	5,100
No. of Cand.	*7*	*1*	*1*	*9*
House	3,600	500	500	4,600
Senate	500	0	0	500
Incumbents	8,350	5,000	3,500	16,850
Challengers	2,000	2,000	0	4,000
Open Seat	5,600	6,250	0	11,850
Winners	14,450	11,250	n/a	25,700
Losers	1,500	2,000	n/a	3,500

Wisconsin Electric Power Co.

*Phone: (414) 221-2114 * Fax: (414) 221-3814*
231 W. Michigan St., Milwaukee, WI 53203
Web: www.wisenergy.com

Wisconsin Electric is a subsidiary of the $4.8 billion publicly owned Wisconsin Energy Corp. Wisconsin Electric provides electricity and gas to 2.3 million and 1.1 million customers, respectively, in 12,500 square miles in southeastern Wisconsin, portions of northeastern Wisconsin and Michigan's Upper Peninsula.

The company owns and operates two nuclear power units at Point Beach, Wis.

Headquartered in Milwaukee, Wisconsin Electric's annual sales are $1.8 billion and it has 4,500 employees. Parent company Wisconsin Energy also has non-utility businesses, including coal ash and transmission services.

Wisconsin Energy's planned merger with Northern States Power was abandoned because of regulatory objections.

Wisconsin Electric Political Action Committee (WEPAC) (C00099945) *Address: same as sponsor * Treasurer: Christopher P. Schoenherr * Contact: Larry Salustro, V.P. of Legal, Regulatory and Gov. Affairs*

	1993-94	*1995-96*	*1997*	*Totals*
Receipts	$15,360	$21,169	$17,126	$53,655
Disburse	14,724	13,979	8,350	37,053
Cash	2,586	9,809	22,616	n/a
Contributions	14,274	12,478	4,750	31,502
Republicans	5,056	9,028	4,250	18,334
No. of Cand.	*7*	*8*	*4*	*19*
House	4,556	5,125	500	10,181
Senate	500	3,903	3,750	8,153
Democrats	9,218	3,450	500	13,168
No. of Cand.	*9*	*5*	*1*	*15*
House	8,218	3,450	500	12,168
Senate	1,000	0	0	1,000
Incumbents	12,774	11,728	4,250	28,752
Challengers	500	500	0	1,000
Open Seat	1,000	250	500	1,750
Winners	10,774	11,978	n/a	22,752
Losers	3,500	500	n/a	4,000

Wisconsin Power & Light Co.

*Phone: (608) 252-3311 * Fax: (608) 252-3481*
P.O. Box 192, Madison, WI 53701
Web: www.wpl.com

WPL Holdings' primary subsidiary, Wisconsin Power & Light, provides electricity and natural gas service to about 400,000 customers in south-central Wisconsin. Another subsidiary, Heartland Development Corp., runs 14 affordable housing projects, primarily in Wisconsin. The publicly traded holding company reported $919 million in 1997 sales.

During 1998, WPL plans to merge with IES Industries Inc. and Interstate Power Co., both of Iowa, to form a $4.5 billion holding company that will be known as Interstate Energy Corp. The new company will be headquartered in Madison, Wis.

WP&L generates about 17 percent of its electricity from a nuclear plant it partially owns in Kewaunee, Wis. Most of its power comes from coal.

WPL has 2,339 employees, of whom 1,617 are union members.

WPL Holdings Inc. Employees' Political Action Committee (C00132092) *Address: same as sponsor * Treasurer: Brandon R. Scholz * Contact: Nino Amato, Senior V.P. of External Affairs*

	1993-94	*1995-96*	*1997*	*Totals*
Receipts	$11,692	$10,018	$4,716	$26,426
Disburse	12,650	9,552	3,150	25,352
Cash	1,457	1,925	3,491	n/a
Contributions	12,150	6,750	2,900	21,800

Republicans	8,850	5,100	1,200	15,150
No. of Cand.	*10*	*10*	*3*	*23*
House	7,500	4,800	700	13,000
Senate	1,350	300	500	2,150
Democrats	3,300	1,650	1,700	6,650
No. of Cand.	*5*	*5*	*4*	*14*
House	2,500	1,550	1,700	5,750
Senate	800	100	0	900
Incumbents	9,700	5,600	2,150	17,450
Challengers	2,150	0	0	2,150
Open Seat	300	1,050	250	1,600
Winners	9,500	5,650	n/a	15,150
Losers	2,650	1,100	n/a	3,750

Environmental Services/Equipment

Battelle Memorial Institute

Phone: (614) 855-1420
24 Wiveliscombe, New Albany, OH 43054
Web: www.battelle.org

The Battelle Memorial Institute is an Ohio nonprofit corporation that assists companies, government organizations and trade associations with commercial research, product development and technological services.

Battelle Memorial Institute, founded in 1925, has 7,000 employees who work for clients in more than 30 countries. The institute was instrumental in developing the compact disc, copier, hologram and protective coatings for golf balls. It derives much of its annual revenue, almost $100 million, from government contracts.

The Institute was formed through the will of Gordon Battelle, who founded it in tribute to his family. Although nonprofit, it pays taxes.

The PAC is bipartisan and gives to federal, state and occasionally local candidates. It is most concerned with candidate positions on research, development and science and technology. It was founded in 1986.

Battelle Memorial Institute Good Government Committee (also known as Battelle Good Government Committee) (C00208462) *Address: same as sponsor * Treasurer: J. R. Bahlmann*

	1993-94	*1995-96*	*1997*	*Totals*
Receipts	$15,178	$41,454	$16,505	$73,137
Disburse	20,475	27,044	11,731	59,250
Cash	476	14,136	18,911	n/a
Contributions	15,750	21,450	9,400	46,600
Republicans	3,750	16,200	4,750	24,700
No. of Cand.	*7*	*23*	*8*	*38*
House	2,000	9,200	3,750	14,950
Senate	1,750	7,000	1,000	9,750
Democrats	12,000	5,250	4,650	21,900
No. of Cand.	*14*	*8*	*6*	*28*
House	8,000	4,750	2,000	14,750
Senate	4,000	500	2,650	7,150
Incumbents	14,000	20,700	8,650	43,350
Challengers	0	500	-250	250
Open Seat	1,750	250	1,000	3,000
Winners	10,750	19,450	n/a	30,200
Losers	5,000	2,000	n/a	7,000

Montgomery Watson Americas Inc.

*Phone: (626) 796-9141 * Fax: (626) 568-6619*
300 N. Lake Ave., Suite 1200, Pasadena, CA 91101
Web: www.mw.com

Environmental engineering company Montgomery Watson Americas designs projects in areas including water and wastewater treatment, air quality control and solid waste management. It also provides construction and environmental program management and laboratory services. The company is a division of the privately held California firm Montgomery Watson, which was formed in 1992 by the merger of Watson Hawksley and James M. Montgomery Co.

Montgomery Watson has a staff of more than 3,200 worldwide including more than 2,000 employees in the Americas. It had estimated 1997 sales of $442 million. The company has operations in 26 states.

In 1997, Terramatrix of Steamboat Springs, Colo., merged into Montgomery Watson Americas. The merger expanded the company's presence in civil, geotechnical and mining engineering.

Montgomery Watson's two other divisions are: MW Asia, the Pacific and Asian offices of both Watson Hawksley and JMM, and MW Ltd., the U.K., European and Near East offices of Watson Hawksley.

Montgomery Watson Americas Inc. Employee PAC (C00242370) *Address: same as sponsor * Treasurer: David J. D. Harper*

	1993-94	1995-96	1997	Totals
Receipts	$52,459	$69,644	$35,463	$157,566
Disburse	42,739	54,502	20,348	117,589
Cash	27,860	40,472	55,586	n/a
Contributions	39,600	43,550	14,750	97,900
Republicans	12,750	26,750	8,750	48,250
No. of Cand.	*18*	*26*	*9*	*53*
House	9,250	17,750	6,250	33,250
Senate	3,500	9,000	2,500	15,000
Democrats	26,850	16,800	6,000	49,650
No. of Cand.	*25*	*13*	*6*	*44*
House	22,750	13,300	5,000	41,050
Senate	4,100	3,500	1,000	8,600
Incumbents	29,750	36,750	13,750	80,250
Challengers	6,500	300	1,000	7,800
Open Seat	3,100	6,500	0	9,600
Winners	31,750	39,550	n/a	71,300
Losers	7,850	4,000	n/a	11,850

Ogden Corp.

*Phone: (212) 868-6040 * Fax: (212) 868-5714*
Two Pennsylvania Plaza, 26th Floor, New York, NY 10121
*Web: www.ogdencorp.com * E-mail: phil_husby@ogden.com*

The publicly held Ogden Energy Group develops power sources, provides water and wastewater services, energy-related design and engineering and develops and manages waste-to-energy projects.

Ogden, which reported 1997 revenues of $1.7 billion, is the parent company of Ogden Energy Group, Ogden Aviation and Ogden Entertainment.

Ogden Aviation provides airport services such as ground and cargo handling, catering, and fueling around the world.

Ogden Entertainment is one of the world's top providers of concessions and facilities management to entertainment and sports venues. The company has interests in theme parks, concerts and gaming. About 12 percent of Ogden's sales are outside the United States, primarily in Europe and Latin America.

In February 1998, Ogden announced that it will form a new joint venture with The Mills Corp. to operate food and beverage and retail and entertainment venues. The joint venture will create and operate in new food court, restaurant, pushcart and kiosk concepts.

Ogden Corp. Political Action Fund (C00142158) *Phone: (202) 371-5144 * Fax: (202) 371-9236 * 1212 New York Ave., Suite 300, Washington, DC 20005 * Treasurer: Philip G. Husby * Contact: Irene Hollerback, Gov. Relations Specialist*

	1993-94	1995-96	1997	Totals
Receipts	$30,140	$26,877	$12,830	$69,847
Disburse	34,610	26,890	11,550	73,050
Cash	3,794	3,781	5,061	n/a
Contributions	26,000	15,350	2,950	44,300
Republicans	5,950	7,850	1,750	15,550
No. of Cand.	*10*	*11*	*6*	*27*
House	4,500	6,300	1,250	12,050
Senate	1,450	1,550	500	3,500
Democrats	20,050	7,500	1,200	28,750
No. of Cand.	*19*	*12*	*2*	*33*
House	11,425	7,500	0	18,925
Senate	8,625	0	1,200	9,825
Incumbents	23,700	14,850	2,950	41,500
Challengers	450	250	0	700
Open Seat	1,775	250	0	2,025
Winners	20,050	14,100	n/a	34,150
Losers	5,950	1,250	n/a	7,200

Roy F. Weston Inc.

*Phone: (610) 701-3000 * Fax: (610) 610-3186*
One Weston Way, West Chester, PA 19380-1499
Web: www.rfweston.com

Roy F. Weston is a public environmental services company. It creates occupational safety and health plans, inspects facilities to identify potential hazards and assists in designing landfills for corporations and government agencies. The company also works on air and water quality systems. Weston has 2,250 employees in 22 states and three foreign countries. It reported 1997 sales of $142 million.

Weston's federal government work includes restoring Department of Defense bases, Department of Energy facilities and Superfund site remediation. The company's PAC contributed nearly $15,000 to congressional candidates during the 1995-96 election cycle. It also contributes to state and local races in Pennsylvania.

Weston Political Action Committee (C00251843) *Phone: (202) 434-8290 * Fax: (202) 639-8238 * 601 Pennsylvania Ave. N.W., Suite 900 S., Washington, DC 20004 * Treasurer: Wayne F. Hosking Jr.*

	1993-94	1995-96	1997	Totals
Receipts	$14,995	$68,694	$38,689	$122,378
Disburse	18,739	31,596	28,084	78,419
Cash	1,105	38,204	48,810	n/a
Contributions	6,600	14,700	5,000	26,300
Republicans	0	5,500	1,250	6,750
No. of Cand.	*0*	*9*	*2*	*11*
House	0	2,750	250	3,000
Senate	0	2,750	1,000	3,750
Democrats	6,600	9,200	3,750	19,550
No. of Cand.	*11*	*18*	*4*	*33*
House	3,850	8,000	2,750	14,600
Senate	2,750	1,200	1,000	4,950
Incumbents	5,100	8,650	3,500	17,250
Challengers	500	800	0	1,300
Open Seat	1,000	5,000	1,500	7,500
Winners	3,350	8,700	n/a	12,050
Losers	3,250	6,000	n/a	9,250

Mining

Amvest Corp.

Phone: (804) 977-3350
One Boar's Head Place, P.O. Box 5347, Charlottesville, VA 22905

Amvest is a private coal mining company based in Charlottesville, Va.

As of March 1998, the Amvest PAC was in existence, but not active.

Amvest Corp. Political Action Committee (Amvest PAC) (C00266551) *Address: same as sponsor * Treasurer: Randolph H. Huffman*

	1993-94	1995-96	1997	Totals
Receipts	$1,822	$21,652	$1,847	$25,321
Disburse	21,683	21,962	3,000	46,645
Cash	2,366	2,057	904	n/a
Contributions	14,500	18,250	3,000	35,750
Republicans	10,000	14,250	0	24,250
No. of Cand.	*15*	*20*	*0*	*35*
House	2,250	9,750	0	12,000
Senate	7,750	4,500	0	12,250
Democrats	4,500	4,000	3,000	11,500
No. of Cand.	*3*	*2*	*2*	*7*
House	3,500	4,000	3,000	10,500
Senate	1,000	0	0	1,000
Incumbents	6,500	14,250	3,000	23,750
Challengers	4,000	1,000	0	5,000
Open Seat	4,000	3,000	0	7,000
Winners	12,500	16,500	n/a	29,000
Losers	2,000	1,750	n/a	3,750

Asarco Inc.

*Phone: (212) 510-1810 * Fax: (212) 510-1835*
180 Maiden Ln., New York, NY 10038-4991
Web: www.asarco.com

Asarco is a publicly owned producer of nonferrous metals, primarily copper. The company also mines zinc, lead and molybdenum and makes specialty chemicals and aggregates. It has more than 20 facilities in states including Texas, Montana, Nebraska, Tennessee and Arizona.

The company also owns 54 percent of the Southern Peru Copper Corp., in which it plans to invest more than $1 billion for upgrades and improvements. Asarco, which employs about 12,000 people, reported 1997 sales of $2.7 billion. It was the fourth-leading mining PAC contributor to 1996 congressional races.

Asarco Employees Political Action Committee (AsarcoPAC) (C00034553) *Phone: (202) 857-1028 * Fax: (202) 463-7581 * 2121 K St. N.W., Washington, DC 20037 * Treasurer: Emil A. Romagnoli*

	1993-94	1995-96	1997	Totals
Receipts	$27,392	$37,590	$22,593	$87,575
Disburse	27,771	38,875	21,445	88,091
Cash	3,555	3,031	4,166	n/a
Contributions	25,125	34,850	15,300	75,275
Republicans	15,875	30,850	14,800	61,525
No. of Cand.	*22*	*30*	*19*	*71*
House	8,875	24,100	10,800	43,775
Senate	7,000	6,750	4,000	17,750
Democrats	9,250	4,000	500	13,750
No. of Cand.	*11*	*3*	*1*	*15*
House	6,250	1,000	500	7,750
Senate	3,000	3,000	0	6,000
Incumbents	18,125	33,350	15,300	66,775
Challengers	2,000	0	0	2,000
Open Seat	5,000	1,500	0	6,500
Winners	18,375	32,350	n/a	50,725
Losers	6,750	2,500	n/a	9,250

BHP Co.

*Phone: (415) 981-1515 * Fax: (415) 774-2028*
550 California St., San Francisco, CA 94104
Web: www.bhp.com.au/minerals

BHP is a $29 billion, publicly held Australian company. BHP has four major businesses: minerals, copper, petroleum and steel. The 112-year-old company has operations, offices and more than 60,000 employees in 70 countries.

BHP Minerals is one of the world's largest and most diverse minerals resource enterprises. It owns, operates and develops mining properties throughout the world. BHP Minerals also maintains worldwide minerals exploration, production, marketing and business development activities. The company reported $425 million in fiscal 1997 profits.

BHP Minerals employs people in more than 20 countries and sells its products to customers in more than 40 countries. About 20 percent of BHP Minerals' profit is earned from operations outside Australia.

The company has four operating divisions: BHP Manganese; BHP Coal; BHP Iron Ore; and BHP World Minerals. In addition, BHP Exploration is charged with identifying new growth opportunities and BHP Minerals Marketing provides support for the operating divisions and assists in assessing business possibilities. The World Minerals and Exploration divisions are based in San Francisco.

BHP Minerals is currently developing the Cannington silver, lead and zinc deposit located near McKinlay in Northwest Queensland, Australia.

BHP Minerals is represented by the BHP Utah International PAC.

BHP Utah International Inc. Political Action Committee (C00040469) *Address: same as sponsor * Treasurer: Pierre L. Hirsch * Contact: Roger Nelson, Chairperson*

	1993-94	1995-96	1997	Totals
Receipts	$17,725	$19,575	$9,900	$47,200
Disburse	13,186	24,920	1,277	39,383
Cash	6,222	877	9,500	n/a
Contributions	8,750	20,000	1,250	30,000
Republicans	7,250	18,000	750	26,000
No. of Cand.	*12*	*21*	*2*	*35*
House	3,250	10,000	750	14,000
Senate	4,000	8,000	0	12,000
Democrats	1,500	2,000	500	4,000
No. of Cand.	*1*	*4*	*1*	*6*
House	0	1,500	500	2,000
Senate	1,500	500	0	2,000
Incumbents	6,750	17,500	750	25,000
Challengers	0	0	0	0
Open Seat	2,000	2,500	500	5,000
Winners	8,750	19,500	n/a	28,250
Losers	0	500	n/a	500

BHP Copper Concerned Citizens PAC (C00319046) *Phone: (520) 575-5600 * Fax: (520) 575-5639 * 7400 N. Oracle Rd., Suite 252, Tucson, AZ 85704 * Web: www.bhp.com.au/copper * Treasurer: Patricia Peraza*

BHP Copper is one of the world's largest commercial copper mining companies. It produces 10 percent of the global supply of copper metal, and more than 40 percent of the world's supply of copper concentrates. The 8,500-employee company is headquartered in San Francisco and has a significant corporate presence in Tucson, Ariz.

Among its worldwide mines, BHP Copper has four mining operations in Nevada and Arizona and had one in British Columbia, Canada. BHP Copper is proposing a full scale in situ leaching operation in Florence, Ariz.

BHP Copper consists primarily of Magma Copper Co., of Tucson, Ariz., acquired in 1996, and the existing BHP mines in Chile and Papua New Guinea. BHP Copper's sales come from world markets in Asia (48 percent), the Americas (32 percent) and Europe (20 percent). It owns the Escondida open pit mine in Chile — the world's largest copper mine.

	1993-94	1995-96	1997	Totals
Receipts	$0	$13,611	$10,023	$23,634
Disburse	0	12,411	4,564	16,975
Cash	0	1,201	6,661	n/a
Contributions	0	6,270	4,500	10,770
Republicans	0	4,000	3,500	7,500
No. of Cand.	*0*	*5*	*5*	*10*
House	0	4,000	2,000	6,000
Senate	0	0	1,500	1,500
Democrats	0	2,270	1,000	3,270
No. of Cand.	*0*	*3*	*1*	*4*
House	0	500	1,000	1,500
Senate	0	1,770	0	1,770
Incumbents	0	5,500	4,000	9,500
Challengers	0	270	500	770
Open Seat	0	500	0	500
Winners	0	5,500	n/a	5,500
Losers	0	770	n/a	770

Contributed less than $5,000 during 1995-96 cycle:

BHP Hawaii PAC (C00077370) *Phone: (808) 547-3111 * Fax: (808) 547-3145 * P.O. Box 3379, 733 Bishop St., Honolulu, HI 96842 * Web: www.energypeople.com * Treasurer: Karin Y. Fujiwara * Contact: Ruth Chu, Chairperson*

Barrick Goldstrike Mines Inc.

Phone: (702) 738-8043
P.O. Box 29, Elko, NV 89803
Web: www.barrick.com

Barrick Goldstrike Mines is a subsidiary of Toronto-based Barrick Gold Corp., with assets of $4.5 billion and 1997 sales of $1.3 billion. Barrick Gold employs 6,000 workers, who produced 2.3 million ounces of gold from five U.S. mines and 500,000 ounces from four Canadian mines in 1996. Barrick also is developing two mines in Chile.

Barrick Gold says it has the largest proven and probable reserves in North and South America and is the lowest cost major producer, at $193 an ounce versus the western world average of $269.

Barrick's financial board of advisers includes former President George Bush, former Canadian Prime Minister Brian Mulroney and former Sen. Howard H. Baker, R-Tenn.

Barrick Goldstrike Mines Inc. Political Action Committee (Barrick Goldstrike PAC) (C00320580) *Address: same as sponsor * Treasurer: Michael J. Brown * Contact: Rodney Sled, Manager of Human Resources*

	1993-94	1995-96	1997	Totals
Receipts	$0	$26,469	$41,481	$67,950
Disburse	0	17,107	13,000	30,107
Cash	0	9,364	37,847	n/a
Contributions	0	17,000	12,000	29,000
Republicans	0	9,000	3,500	12,500
No. of Cand.	*0*	*10*	*2*	*12*
House	0	5,000	1,500	6,500
Senate	0	4,000	2,000	6,000
Democrats	0	8,000	8,500	16,500
No. of Cand.	*0*	*8*	*5*	*13*
House	0	2,000	500	2,500
Senate	0	6,000	8,000	14,000

(Data for Barrick Goldstrike Mines continued)

Incumbents	0	9,000	9,500	18,500
Challengers	0	3,000	2,000	5,000
Open Seat	0	5,000	500	5,500
Winners	0	12,000	n/a	12,000
Losers	0	5,000	n/a	5,000

China Clay Producers Association

*Phone: (770) 961-7680 * Fax: (770) 961-7767*
7183 Jonesboro Rd., Suite 101, Morrow, GA 30260
*Web: www.mindspring.com/~gamining/ccpa.htm * E-mail: kwj@kaolin.com*

The Georgia-based China Clay Producers Association advances and encourages the development and production of kaolin-based products. The greatest demand for kaolin-based pigments comes from the paper industry, which uses them to coat and fill papers and boards. Kaolin is a $500 million, 4,200-employee industry in Georgia, according to the association.

The association works with the people of Georgia in the communities where the mineral is mined and products are manufactured. Founded in 1978, the association has five member companies: Dry Branch Kaolin Co., ECC International, Engelhard Corp., J.M. Huber Corp. and Thiele Kaolin Co.

The group informs members about proposed legislation, regulatory actions and other matters affecting the kaolin industry.

China Clay Producers Association Inc. Political Action Committee (C00100289) *Address: same as sponsor * Treasurer: Kenneth W. Jackman*

	1993-94	1995-96	1997	Totals
Receipts	$13,180	$11,435	$5,090	$29,705
Disburse	6,651	15,550	1,311	23,512
Cash	6,851	2,736	6,515	n/a
Contributions	6,850	15,550	1,200	23,600
Republicans	4,850	12,800	1,200	18,850
No. of Cand.	*10*	*12*	*2*	*24*
House	4,100	11,200	1,000	16,300
Senate	750	1,600	200	2,550
Democrats	2,000	2,750	0	4,750
No. of Cand.	*5*	*3*	*0*	*8*
House	2,000	750	0	2,750
Senate	0	2,000	0	2,000
Incumbents	5,000	12,750	1,200	18,950
Challengers	1,350	200	0	1,550
Open Seat	500	2,600	0	3,100
Winners	5,750	14,250	n/a	20,000
Losers	1,100	1,300	n/a	2,400

Cleveland-Cliffs Iron Co.

*Phone: (216) 694-5537 * Fax: (216) 694-4880*
1100 Superior Ave., Room 1800, Cleveland, OH 44114-2589
E-mail: dwbyrne@worldnet.att.net

Cleveland-Cliffs, which operates mines in upper Michigan and northern Minnesota, produces and sells iron ore pellets and reportedly supplies almost all integrated steel producers in North America.

Employing 5,200 workers, the 151-year-old publicly held company reported 1997 income of about $50 million.

Cleveland-Cliffs controls, develops, and leases reserves to mine owners; manages and owns interests in mines; sells iron ore; and owns interests in ancillary companies providing services to the mines. Iron ore production takes place at seven mines in the United States, Canada and Australia.

Along with two other steel-producing firms, Cleveland-Cliffs owns Minnesota Power, a manufacturer of taconite pellets used for making steel.

Cleveland-Cliffs Inc. Political Action Committee (Cliffs PAC) (C00039016) *Address: same as sponsor * Treasurer: Dana W. Byrne*

	1993-94	1995-96	1997	Totals
Receipts	$44,652	$43,336	$21,986	$109,974
Disburse	44,714	43,380	18,375	106,469
Cash	6,025	5,991	9,607	n/a
Contributions	38,400	40,050	18,125	96,575
Republicans	22,300	32,700	12,625	67,625
No. of Cand.	*25*	*45*	*15*	*85*
House	10,000	18,000	5,125	33,125
Senate	12,300	14,700	7,500	34,500
Democrats	14,100	7,350	4,500	25,950
No. of Cand.	*15*	*9*	*5*	*29*
House	8,000	6,850	3,500	18,350
Senate	6,100	500	1,000	7,600
Incumbents	25,200	33,100	13,625	71,925
Challengers	1,300	3,700	0	5,000
Open Seat	11,900	3,250	4,500	19,650
Winners	33,300	32,850	n/a	66,150
Losers	5,100	7,200	n/a	12,300

Consol Inc.

*Phone: (412) 831-4000 * Fax: (412) 831-4916*
1800 Washington Rd., Pittsburgh, PA 15241

Consol is a coal mining company that operates in Kentucky, West Virginia, Virginia, Illinois, Pennsylvania and Alberta, Canada. It is a subsidiary of Consol Energy Inc., a 50-50 joint venture between DuPont and Rheinbraun, a German company.

Consol Inc. Coal Group PAC (C00279331) *Address: same as sponsor * Treasurer: Eugene H. Dioguardi * Contact: Steve Young, V.P. of Gov. Affairs*

	1993-94	1995-96	1997	Totals
Receipts	$33,430	$40,705	$19,662	$93,797
Disburse	30,456	42,358	15,881	88,695
Cash	2,975	1,327	5,114	n/a
Contributions	16,900	24,350	15,125	56,375
Republicans	9,600	14,250	8,000	31,850
No. of Cand.	*12*	*13*	*6*	*31*
House	4,100	7,750	6,000	17,850
Senate	5,500	6,500	2,000	14,000
Democrats	7,300	10,100	7,125	24,525
No. of Cand.	*7*	*7*	*6*	*20*
House	4,300	7,100	7,125	18,525
Senate	3,000	3,000	0	6,000
Incumbents	8,400	22,100	15,125	45,625
Challengers	2,750	1,000	0	3,750
Open Seat	5,750	1,250	0	7,000
Winners	14,650	22,350	n/a	37,000
Losers	2,250	2,000	n/a	4,250

Cyprus Amax Minerals Co.

*Phone: (303) 643-5000 * Fax: (303) 643-5049*
P.O. Box 3299, 9100 E. Mineral Cir., Englewood, CO 80155
Web: www.cyprusamax.com

Cyprus Amax is the world's largest producer of molybdenum and lithium. It also mines for copper, coal and gold. The publicly traded Colorado company, which has about 10,000 employees worldwide, reported 1997 earnings of $69 million on $3.3 billion of sales.

In February 1998, Cyprus announced plans to sell its coal properties to AEI Holding Co. Inc. of Ashland, Ky.

The company has extensive reserves of copper, molybdenum, coal, gold and lithium and is exploring for base and precious metals throughout the world. Cyprus manages operations across the United States and on six continents around the globe.

Although most of Cyprus' mines are located abroad, the company has manufacturing plants in Miami; Chicago; Fort Madison, Iowa; Silver Peak, Nev.; Kings Mountain, N.C.; and Fairbanks, Alaska.

Cymax PAC Cyprus Amax Minerals Political Action Committee (C00200204) *Address: same as sponsor * Treasurer: Lola A. Ball*

	1993-94	1995-96	1997	Totals
Receipts	$134,283	$297,773	$169,065	$601,121
Disburse	136,244	262,433	146,819	545,496
Cash	8,580	43,925	66,173	n/a
Contributions	120,428	222,595	129,650	472,673
Republicans	79,288	195,195	110,150	384,633
No. of Cand.	*32*	*62*	*43*	*137*
House	22,600	83,750	46,250	152,600
Senate	56,688	111,445	63,900	232,033
Democrats	41,140	27,400	19,500	88,040
No. of Cand.	*20*	*14*	*13*	*47*
House	10,400	17,000	8,500	35,900
Senate	30,740	10,400	11,000	52,140
Incumbents	97,278	150,400	122,150	369,828
Challengers	1,000	5,700	2,500	9,200
Open Seat	21,000	66,495	5,000	92,495
Winners	111,638	185,395	n/a	297,033
Losers	8,790	37,200	n/a	45,990

Dravo Corp.

*Phone: (412) 995-5500 * Fax: (412) 995-5594*
11 Stanwix St., 11th Floor, Pittsburgh, PA 15222
Web: www.dravo.com

Dravo is a publicly traded natural resources company with 1997 sales of $162 million and more than 750 employees. Operating principally in the United States, its activities include the production of aggregates for construction and industrial uses and lime for industrial, utility, municipal, environmental and construction applications. Dravo's operations are principally carried on by two wholly owned subsidiaries: Dravo Basic Materials Co. Inc. and Dravo Lime Co.

Its primary operation, Dravo Lime, processes lime for use in reducing acid rain-causing sulfur dioxide, particularly in coal-fired power plants. Most of the lime is sold to customers in the central and southern United States. Dravo Lime, headquartered in Pittsburgh, with two plants in Kentucky and one in Alabama, is one of the largest producers of lime in the United States.

Dravo Employees for Better Government Fund (C00038794)
*Address: same as sponsor * Treasurer: Larry J. Walker * Contact: Carl A. Gilbert, Interim Chairman*

	1993-94	1995-96	1997	Totals
Receipts	$34,135	$10,645	$4,124	$48,904
Disburse	35,504	17,836	0	53,340
Cash	9,487	2,300	6,426	n/a
Contributions	29,500	11,750	0	41,250
Republicans	20,000	10,750	0	30,750
No. of Cand.	*18*	*16*	*0*	*34*
House	9,000	3,750	0	12,750
Senate	11,000	7,000	0	18,000
Democrats	9,500	1,000	0	10,500
No. of Cand.	*12*	*2*	*0*	*14*
House	6,000	1,000	0	7,000
Senate	3,500	0	0	3,500
Incumbents	27,000	8,250	0	35,250
Challengers	500	1,000	0	1,500
Open Seat	1,500	2,500	0	4,000
Winners	26,000	7,750	n/a	33,750
Losers	3,500	4,000	n/a	7,500

Drummond Co.

*Phone: (205) 945-6500 * Fax: (205) 945-4254*
P.O. Box 10246, Birmingham, AL 35202-0246

Drummond is an Alabama-based private company with coal mining and real estate operations.

Drummond operates mines in Alabama and the country of Colombia. It sold its former Wyoming site to RTZ-CRA, now Rio Tinto, the largest mining company in the world, in January 1997 for $99 million. Drummond also manufactures coke, a by-product of coal processing that is used as an industrial fuel. Its coke plant in Tarrant, Ala. is the largest in the United States.

Employing more than 33,000 people, the company ranked No. 268 on Forbes' list of top private companies in 1996. Founded as a small coal-mining company in 1935, Drummond had 1996 revenues of $725 million.

The company's real estate division finances, develops, builds and manages planned housing communities. Drummond currently operates Liberty Park in Birmingham, Ala., Rancho LaQuinta in LaQuinta, Calif., and Oakbridge in Lakeland, Fla.

Drummond Co. Inc. Political Action Committee (DPAC) (formerly known as Alabama By-Products PAC) (C00160630) *Address: same as sponsor * Treasurer: Thomas W. Walters * Contact: Jerry C. Byars, Chairperson*

	1993-94	1995-96	1997	Totals
Receipts	$95,624	$134,760	$42,344	$272,728
Disburse	96,965	130,100	20,600	247,665
Cash	2,059	6,719	28,464	n/a
Contributions	45,750	111,500	19,600	176,850
Republicans	27,750	52,000	9,600	89,350
No. of Cand.	*12*	*18*	*6*	*36*
House	11,250	23,500	8,000	42,750
Senate	16,500	28,500	1,600	46,600
Democrats	18,000	59,500	10,000	87,500
No. of Cand.	*10*	*14*	*7*	*31*
House	11,000	41,500	3,000	55,500
Senate	7,000	18,000	7,000	32,000
Incumbents	36,250	34,000	13,600	83,850
Challengers	0	500	0	500
Open Seat	8,000	71,000	0	79,000
Winners	44,250	49,000	n/a	93,250
Losers	1,500	62,500	n/a	64,000

Echo Bay Inc.

6400 S. Fiddlers Green Cir., Suite 1000, Englewood, CO 80111

The Echo Bay Employees Good Government Fund was terminated in December 1997.

Echo Bay Inc. Employees Good Government Fund (C00319020)
*Address: same as sponsor * Treasurer: Gary Scherping*

	1993-94	1995-96	1997	Totals
Receipts	$0	$5,297	$80	$5,377
Disburse	0	5,047	181	5,228
Cash	0	250	148	n/a
Contributions	0	5,000	0	5,000
Republicans	0	4,000	0	4,000
No. of Cand.	*0*	*5*	*0*	*5*
House	0	1,000	0	1,000
Senate	0	3,000	0	3,000
Democrats	0	1,000	0	1,000
No. of Cand.	*0*	*1*	*0*	*1*
House	0	0	0	0
Senate	0	1,000	0	1,000
Incumbents	0	4,000	0	4,000
Challengers	0	0	0	0
Open Seat	0	1,000	0	1,000
Winners	0	5,000	n/a	5,000
Losers	0	0	n/a	0

Georgia Marble Co.

*Phone: (770) 421-6500 * Fax: (770) 421-6506*
1201 Roberts Blvd., Bldg. 100, Kennesaw, GA 30144
*Web: www.georgiamarble.com * E-mail: info@georgiamarble.com*

Georgia Marble is the largest producer of marble and calcium carbonate products in the world. It is an operating company of DBK Minerals Inc., a wholly owned subsidiary of Paris-based IMETAL S.A., which had sales of $1.6 billion in 1996.

Georgia Marble is composed of three product groups: industrial, consumer and dimension stone. Headquartered in Atlanta, the dimension stone group, consisting of the structural and memorial products plants, has facilities in Georgia. Georgia Marble also owns properties and plants in Alabama, South Carolina, New York, Wyoming, Arizona, Florida, Tennessee and California.

Georgia Marble's PAC is in the process of being dissolved.

Georgia Marble Co. Political Action Committee (GMCPAC) (C00238576) *Address: same as sponsor * Treasurer: Eugene G. Hartleb * Contact: Eugene G. Hartleb*

	1993-94	1995-96	1997	Totals
Receipts	$12,693	$9,673	$6,032	$28,398
Disburse	7,948	14,204	31,237	53,389
Cash	29,797	25,269	65	n/a
Contributions	7,700	12,150	2,104	21,954
Republicans	3,500	9,650	2,104	15,254
No. of Cand.	*4*	*6*	*2*	*12*
House	3,000	3,650	2,104	8,754
Senate	500	6,000	0	6,500
Democrats	4,200	2,500	0	6,700
No. of Cand.	*2*	*1*	*0*	*3*
House	4,200	0	0	4,200
Senate	0	2,500	0	2,500
Incumbents	4,700	5,400	2,104	12,204
Challengers	2,000	0	0	2,000
Open Seat	1,000	6,750	0	7,750
Winners	6,200	8,150	n/a	14,350
Losers	1,500	4,000	n/a	5,500

Kennecott Corp.

Phone: (801) 252-3000
8315 W. 3595 S., P.O. Box 6001, Magna, UT 84044

Kennecott, based in Magna, Utah, mines copper, gold, silver and coal. It is a subsidiary of Rio Tinto, a British firm. Annual sales average $2.2 billion and the company employs 3,500 people.

In 1998, Kennecott forged agreements with other mining companies to explore areas in Canada and Mexico.

Kennecott Corp. Political Action Committee (also known as Kennecott PAC) (C00243675) *Phone: (202) 393-0266 * Fax: (202) 393-0232 * 1325 Pennsylvania Ave. N.W., Seventh Floor, Washington, DC 20004 * E-mail: michael@kennecott-borax.com * Treasurer: Roger P. Johnson*

	1993-94	1995-96	1997	Totals
Receipts	$67,433	$44,807	$19,552	$131,792
Disburse	52,137	44,258	12,925	109,320
Cash	19,220	19,767	26,394	n/a
Contributions	41,905	33,000	7,500	82,405
Republicans	28,250	24,000	5,000	57,250
No. of Cand.	*23*	*23*	*5*	*51*
House	9,750	11,500	1,500	22,750
Senate	18,500	12,500	3,500	34,500
Democrats	13,655	9,000	2,500	25,155
No. of Cand.	*12*	*4*	*3*	*19*
House	7,500	6,000	1,000	14,500
Senate	6,155	3,000	1,500	10,655
Incumbents	32,655	28,000	8,000	68,655
Challengers	3,500	500	0	4,000
Open Seat	5,750	4,500	0	10,250
Winners	35,000	27,500	n/a	62,500
Losers	6,905	5,500	n/a	12,405

National Council of Coal Lessors

Phone: (304) 346-0569
1050 One Valley Square, Charleston, WV 25301

The National Council of Coal Lessors is an organization that represents businesses and individuals who lease coal.

National Council of Coal Lessors Inc. PAC (C00009597) *Phone: (202) 628-5093 * Fax: (202) 628-5932 * 1616 H St. N.W., Suite 902, Washington, DC 20006 * Treasurer: Chiswell D. Langhorne Jr.*

	1993-94	1995-96	1997	Totals
Receipts	$13,220	$6,650	$1,800	$21,670
Disburse	8,519	7,056	7,101	22,676
Cash	7,655	7,249	1,947	n/a
Contributions	6,500	7,200	7,000	20,700
Republicans	0	3,000	1,500	4,500
No. of Cand.	*0*	*4*	*2*	*6*
House	0	3,000	1,500	4,500
Senate	0	0	0	0
Democrats	6,500	4,200	5,500	16,200
No. of Cand.	*10*	*7*	*6*	*23*
House	3,500	3,000	3,500	10,000
Senate	3,000	1,200	2,000	6,200
Incumbents	5,500	7,200	7,000	19,700
Challengers	1,000	0	0	1,000
Open Seat	0	0	0	0
Winners	5,000	7,200	n/a	12,200
Losers	1,500	0	n/a	1,500

National Mining Association

*Phone: (202) 463-2625 * Fax: (202) 833-1965*
1130 17th St. N.W., Washington, DC 20036-4677
Web: www.nma.org

The National Mining Association was created in 1995 as a result of the merger of two major groups representing the mining industry at the national level: the National Coal Association and the American Mining Congress. NMA members represent coal, metal and mineral hardrock mining operators, mineral processors, bulk transporters, mining equipment manufacturers, financial and engineering firms and other businesses related to the mining industry. The association has about 400 member companies.

CoalPAC A Political Action Committee of The National Mining Association (C00109819) *Address: same as sponsor * Treasurer: Andrea L. Innes*

	1993-94	1995-96	1997	Totals
Receipts	$202,534	$206,610	$86,128	$495,272
Disburse	226,196	213,266	65,491	504,953
Cash	9,828	3,174	23,814	n/a
Contributions	223,200	207,017	62,778	492,995
Republicans	181,200	193,517	54,278	428,995
No. of Cand.	*115*	*130*	*63*	*308*
House	86,950	114,517	35,278	236,745
Senate	94,250	79,000	19,000	192,250
Democrats	42,000	13,500	8,000	63,500
No. of Cand.	*31*	*16*	*7*	*54*
House	24,000	13,500	8,000	45,500
Senate	18,000	0	0	18,000
Incumbents	138,100	153,017	59,778	350,895
Challengers	25,000	10,500	1,000	36,500
Open Seat	59,100	43,500	2,000	104,600
Winners	207,850	166,686	n/a	374,536
Losers	15,350	40,331	n/a	55,681

MinePAC A Political Action Committee of The National Mining Association (C00304634) *Phone: (202) 463-2621 * Fax: (202) 833-9636 * 1130 17th St. N.W., Washington, DC 20036 * Web: www.nma.org * Treasurer: M. Darrell Williams * Contact: Richard L. Lawson, President and CEO*

	1993-94	1995-96	1997	Totals
Receipts	$0	$39,125	$67,003	$106,128
Disburse	0	37,002	31,465	68,467
Cash	0	2,126	37,667	n/a
Contributions	0	36,750	29,028	65,778
Republicans	0	32,750	26,028	58,778
No. of Cand.	*0*	*36*	*37*	*73*
House	0	17,250	16,528	33,778
Senate	0	15,500	9,500	25,000
Democrats	0	4,000	3,000	7,000
No. of Cand.	*0*	*5*	*4*	*9*
House	0	2,000	2,000	4,000
Senate	0	2,000	1,000	3,000
Incumbents	0	24,250	28,528	52,778
Challengers	0	2,500	500	3,000
Open Seat	0	10,000	0	10,000
Winners	0	31,000	n/a	31,000
Losers	0	5,750	n/a	5,750

Newmont Mining Corp.

*Phone: (303) 863-7414 * Fax: (303) 837-5837*
1700 Lincoln St., Denver, CO 80203
Web: www.newmont.com

Newmont Mining became the largest gold company in North America after its 1997 acquisition of Santa Fe Pacific Gold Corp. The public company's American operations, located near Carlin, Nev., produce more than 1.5 million ounces of gold each year. The company reported 1997 revenues of $412 million.

Newmont laid off about 11 percent of its U.S. workforce in early 1998 because of tumbling gold prices, leaving its total number of employees at about 11,000 worldwide. About 3,400 employees work in the United States.

The company owns a majority stake in Peru's Yanacocha mine. Newmont Mining also produces gold through operations in Uzbekistan and Indonesia. It conducts worldwide exploration, with an emphasis on Mexico, Asia and South America.

Newmont Mining Corp. Political Action Committee (C00206672) *Phone: (202) 628-0005 * Fax: (202) 628-0934 * 801 Pennsylvania Ave. N.W., Suite 740, Washington, DC 20004 * Treasurer: Scott E. Earnest * Contact: Mary Beth Donnelly, V.P. of Gov. Relations*

	1993-94	1995-96	1997	Totals
Receipts	$12,835	$26,432	$23,372	$62,639
Disburse	14,250	20,250	11,000	45,500
Cash	5,276	11,458	23,830	n/a
Contributions	11,250	13,250	8,500	33,000
Republicans	2,000	7,000	5,500	14,500
No. of Cand.	*5*	*11*	*6*	*22*
House	1,500	4,000	3,500	9,000
Senate	500	3,000	2,000	5,500
Democrats	9,250	6,250	3,000	18,500
No. of Cand.	*11*	*12*	*2*	*25*
House	3,750	-1,750	0	2,000
Senate	5,500	8,000	3,000	16,500
Incumbents	9,250	7,750	7,500	24,500
Challengers	0	1,000	1,000	2,000
Open Seat	2,000	6,500	0	8,500
Winners	6,750	10,750	n/a	17,500
Losers	4,500	2,500	n/a	7,000

North American Coal Corp.

*Phone: (972) 239-2625 * Fax: (972) 387-1051*
14785 Preston Rd., Suite 1100, Dallas, TX 75240-7891

North American Coal is a wholly owned subsidiary of the publicly traded, $951 million NACCO Industries of Cleveland. NACCO is a holding company whose other subsidiaries make forklifts and kitchen appliances.

NACC mines and markets lignite for use primarily as fuel for power generation by electric utilities. Eighty-two percent of NACC's coal is mined in North Dakota. NACC also owns or operates mines in Texas and Louisiana and has three additional undeveloped mines. It also provides mining services for a limerock quarry near Miami. NACC's principal customers are electric utilities and synthetic fuels plants. The company earns royalty income from the lease of various coal and gas properties.

In December 1996, NACC was the successful bidder for two long-term coal mining projects, the San Miguel Lignite Project in south Texas and Phillips Coal Co.'s Lignite Project in Mississippi. In addition, North American Coal was chosen by Phillips Coal Co. to be its 25 percent joint venture partner to develop a new lignite mine.

Subsidiaries: Coteau Properties Co., Falkirk Mining Co., Sabine Mining Co. and Red River Mining Co.

NACC terminated one PAC (FEC ID: C00115576) on July 26, 1996, but later replaced it with another with a similar name — The North American Coal Corp. PAC (FEC ID: C00303685).

North American Coal Political Action Committee (NACPAC) (C00115576) *Address: same as sponsor * Treasurer: K. Donald Grischow*

	1993-94	1995-96	1997	Totals
Receipts	$7,218	$8,728	$0	$15,946
Disburse	16,250	13,440	0	29,690
Cash	4,713	0	0	n/a
Contributions	11,750	6,000	0	17,750
Republicans	1,750	4,250	0	6,000
No. of Cand.	*4*	*6*	*0*	*10*
House	750	3,250	0	4,000
Senate	1,000	1,000	0	2,000
Democrats	9,500	1,750	0	11,250
No. of Cand.	*4*	*2*	*0*	*6*
House	3,000	1,750	0	4,750
Senate	6,500	0	0	6,500
Incumbents	10,250	6,000	0	16,250
Challengers	0	0	0	0
Open Seat	1,500	0	0	1,500
Winners	11,250	4,500	n/a	15,750
Losers	500	1,500	n/a	2,000

Contributed less than $5,000 during 1995-96 cycle:

The North American Coal Corp. Political Action Committee (NACPAC) (C00303685) *Phone: (972) 239-2625 * Fax: (972) 387-1051 * 14785 Preston Rd., Suite 1100, Dallas, TX 75240-7891 * Treasurer: K. Donald Grischow * Contact: Herschell Cashion, Senior V.P.*

Ohio Valley Coal Co.

*Phone: (740) 926-1351 * Fax: (740) 686-2160*
56854 Pleasant Ridge Rd., Alledonia, OH 43902

Privately held Ohio Valley Coal operates two mines — in Belmont County, Ohio and Washington County, Pa. — and has corporate offices near Cleveland. The company sells coal to utilities.

The company is a subsidiary of Ohio Valley Resources, which Robert Murray wholly owns. Murray, who is the president and CEO of the parent company, also owns Coal Resources along with two other Ohio Valley companies.

In 1997, the company won preliminary state approval of a controversial Ohio Valley Coal application to extend its Belmont County mine within 2 miles of a stand of 500-year-old trees in Dysart Woods, which is located about 100 miles east of Columbus. Over the protests of environmental groups, the state determined the mining would not damage the trees.

A December 1997 Lexington Herald-Leader report chronicled the decline of coal production in Ohio since the Clear Air Act went on the books in 1970. Only half as much coal was mined in Ohio in 1996 as in 1970, the article stated.

The story described Murray as an opponent of the global warming treaty.

"I am very threatened for my business and I am frightened for my employees. They only want to work," he said. "I have nothing but contempt for Al Gore and Bill Clinton."

The Ohio Valley Coal Co. PAC (C00255315) *Address: same as sponsor * Treasurer: Paul B. Piccolini*

	1993-94	1995-96	1997	Totals
Receipts	$34,818	$104,544	$109,098	$248,460
Disburse	32,907	81,366	45,006	159,279
Cash	2,922	26,100	90,194	n/a
Contributions	4,700	27,900	22,000	54,600
Republicans	4,300	27,600	21,000	52,900
No. of Cand.	*10*	*9*	*6*	*25*
House	4,800	20,600	15,000	40,400
Senate	-500	7,000	6,000	12,500
Democrats	400	300	1,000	1,700
No. of Cand.	*2*	*1*	*1*	*4*
House	400	300	1,000	1,700
Senate	0	0	0	0
Incumbents	2,400	22,900	16,000	41,300
Challengers	2,900	5,000	5,000	12,900
Open Seat	-600	0	1,000	400
Winners	3,100	20,900	n/a	24,000
Losers	1,600	7,000	n/a	8,600

Peabody Coal

*Phone: (314) 342-3400 * Fax: (314) 342-3449*
701 Market St., Suite 700, St. Louis, MO 63101
*Web: www.PeabodyGroup.com * E-mail: rbruch@peabodygroup.com*

Peabody Coal's parent company, Peabody Holding Co., bills itself as the world's largest private coal producer. The St. Louis holding company operates 29 mines in the United States and Australia and had $2 billion in 1996 revenues. The company's subsidiaries supply about 17 percent of the coal used by U.S. electric utilities.

With headquarters in Charleston, W.Va., the 2,000-employee company operates eight mines — four of which are strip mines — in Illinois, Indiana and western Kentucky.

The bulk of the company's coal is used by 18 electric power plants, most of which are in the Midwest.

Founded in 1883, Peabody Coal also owns three barge loading facilities and ships about half of its products by barges. The remainder is transported by rail.

Peabody Political Action Committee (C00110478) *Address: same as sponsor * Treasurer: Thomas S. Hilton * Contact: Rebecca Bruch, Administrative Assistant*

	1993-94	1995-96	1997	Totals
Receipts	$102,036	$89,830	$44,737	$236,603
Disburse	114,243	94,615	28,670	237,528
Cash	13,938	9,157	24,696	n/a
Contributions	96,220	69,350	26,250	191,820
Republicans	60,800	59,850	20,750	141,400
No. of Cand.	*44*	*58*	*21*	*123*
House	24,800	32,250	9,500	66,550
Senate	36,000	27,600	11,250	74,850
Democrats	35,420	9,500	5,500	50,420
No. of Cand.	*33*	*10*	*5*	*48*
House	16,800	3,500	3,500	23,800
Senate	18,620	6,000	2,000	26,620
Incumbents	72,720	59,850	26,250	158,820
Challengers	5,000	500	0	5,500
Open Seat	18,500	9,500	0	28,000
Winners	81,100	63,850	n/a	144,950
Losers	15,120	5,500	n/a	20,620

Phelps Dodge Corp.

*Phone: (602) 234-8100 * Fax: (602) 234-4814*
2600 N. Central Ave., Phoenix, AZ 85004
*Web: www.phelpsdodge.com * E-mail: kkinsall@phelpsd.com*

Phelps Dodge is the world's largest producer of copper rod and is among the top producers of copper in general. The Phoenix, Ariz. company also has a manufacturing arm to help it weather fluctuations in the copper market. A publicly traded company, Phelps Dodge had $3.9 billion in 1997 revenues and 16,000 employees.

The company runs the largest copper producing operation in North America, operates an open pit mine in Morenci, Ariz., and also has mines in Tyrone, Hurley, Santa Rita and Playas, N.M. International locations include Mexico, China, Chile and South Africa. Phelps Dodge manufactures copper rod in its El Paso, Texas and Norwich, Conn. plants.

Phelps Dodge also is one of the world's largest producers of carbon black, the world's largest manufacturer of magnet wire and has operations in mines and wire and cable manufacturing facilities around the world. The company is the leading North American fabricator of wheels and rims for medium and heavy trucks through its Accuride unit. However, the company announced in November 1996 that it would sell Accuride.

Subsidiaries include: Phelps Dodge Mining Co., Phelps Dodge Industries, Columbian Chemicals Co., Accuride Corp., Phelps Dodge Magnet Wire Co. and Chino Mines Co.

U.S. locations of subsidiaries include: Arkansas, Georgia, Indiana, Kansas, Kentucky, Louisiana, New Jersey, North Carolina, South Carolina, Texas and West Virginia.

Phelps Dodge was founded in 1834.

Phelps Dodge Employees Fund for Good Government (C00033456) *Phone: (202) 789-1745 * Fax: (202) 371-1731 * 1420 New York Ave. N.W., Suite 210, Washington, DC 20005 * Treasurer: Kevin R. Kinsall * Contact: Linda Findlay, Chairperson*

	1993-94	1995-96	1997	Totals
Receipts	$72,345	$66,761	$54,121	$193,227
Disburse	72,750	81,660	44,500	198,910
Cash	28,761	13,870	23,469	n/a
Contributions	72,750	79,740	42,000	194,490
Republicans	53,900	73,490	36,000	163,390
No. of Cand.	*41*	*46*	*28*	*115*
House	33,800	50,490	22,500	106,790
Senate	20,100	23,000	13,500	56,600
Democrats	18,850	6,250	6,000	31,100
No. of Cand.	*15*	*5*	*6*	*26*
House	11,850	4,250	4,000	20,100
Senate	7,000	2,000	2,000	11,000
Incumbents	53,900	72,990	40,500	167,390
Challengers	6,500	2,000	500	9,000
Open Seat	11,850	4,750	1,000	17,600
Winners	62,250	69,600	n/a	131,850
Losers	10,500	10,140	n/a	20,640

Pittston Co.

*Phone: (804) 553-3600 * Fax: (804) 553-3770*
P.O. Box 4229, Richmond, VA 23058-4229

Pittston has three main divisions: Pittston Minerals Group, Pittston Burlington and Pittston Brink's Group. Pittston Minerals is primarily engaged in gold and coal mining, and had 1997 sales of $630 million. Pittston Burlington is a global freight transportation company with 1997 sales of $1.7 billion. Pittston Brink's Group produces and markets home security systems and secure transportation. Brink's reported 1997 sales of $921 million.

Overall, the publicly traded company employs 24,500 workers, 17,000 of whom work for the Brink's Group.

The minerals segment operates 30 surface and deep coal mines in Virginia, West Virginia and Kentucky. It mines for gold through the Pittston Mineral Ventures Co., a gold production and exploration company, which operates gold mines in Australia and Nevada.

Pittston also controls about 100,000 acres of timber-producing surface property overlaying coal reserves in Virginia and West Virginia.

Pittston Co. Political Action Committee (C00207472) *Address: same as sponsor * Treasurer: Gary R. Rogliano*

	1993-94	1995-96	1997	Totals
Receipts	$55,008	$68,531	$32,352	$155,891
Disburse	39,302	58,389	12,070	109,761
Cash	26,154	36,295	56,577	n/a
Contributions	35,270	52,000	9,750	97,020
Republicans	19,900	43,000	6,750	69,650
No. of Cand.	*25*	*44*	*5*	*74*
House	6,150	22,000	1,750	29,900
Senate	13,750	21,000	5,000	39,750
Democrats	15,370	9,000	2,000	26,370
No. of Cand.	*15*	*11*	*2*	*28*
House	6,750	6,500	0	13,250
Senate	8,620	2,500	2,000	13,120
Incumbents	25,270	42,000	6,750	74,020
Challengers	4,000	1,000	1,000	6,000
Open Seat	6,000	8,500	2,000	16,500
Winners	32,250	48,000	n/a	80,250
Losers	3,020	4,000	n/a	7,020

Thompson Creek Metals Co.

*Phone: (303) 757-2020 * Fax: (303) 761-7420*
945 W. Kenyon Ave., Englewood, CO 80110

Thompson Creek Metals is a privately held mining company based in Englewood, Colo. It owns the Thompson Creek Mining Co., which mines molybdenum in Challis, Colo.

The company also owns a molybdenum mine in British Columbia, Canada.

Molybdenum is a metal that is used mainly in electric heaters, but is also used in nuclear energy applications and for missile and aircraft parts. It is also a catalyst in the refining of petroleum.

The company was founded in 1993. Langeloth Metallurgical Co. in Langeloth, Pa. is its only subsidiary.

Thompson Creek PAC (C00298232) *Address: same as sponsor * Treasurer: Margaret W. Pereira*

	1993-94	1995-96	1997	Totals
Receipts	$10,000	$25,820	$10,000	$45,820
Disburse	0	33,203	6,950	40,153
Cash	10,000	2,613	5,663	n/a
Contributions	0	32,450	6,500	38,950
Republicans	0	32,350	6,500	38,850
No. of Cand.	*0*	*10*	*4*	*14*
House	0	8,600	2,500	11,100
Senate	0	23,750	4,000	27,750
Democrats	0	100	0	100
No. of Cand.	*0*	*1*	*0*	*1*
House	0	100	0	100
Senate	0	0	0	0
Incumbents	0	26,700	6,500	33,200
Challengers	0	250	0	250
Open Seat	0	5,500	0	5,500
Winners	0	32,200	n/a	32,200
Losers	0	250	n/a	250

Zeigler Coal Holding Co.

*Phone: (618) 394-2400 * Fax: (618) 394-2479*
50 Jerome Ln., Fairview Heights, IL 62208

Zeigler Coal is a publicly owned $1.1 billion company with annual sales of $732 million and 2,000 employees. It has operations in coal mining and sales, coal conversion technology, power generation, asset management and emerging environmental and international divisions. It is the parent company of utility company Zeigler Power.

Zeigler's coal mining operations are primarily in the Appalachian region. Because of electric utility deregulation, Zeigler established the subsidiary EnerZ Corp., to provide energy marketing, trading and risk management products and services. Zeigler also operates ship terminal companies in Charleston, S.C., and Newport News, Va. and owns land in nine states. Zeigler is expected to acquire Cajun Electric Power Cooperative Inc. of Baton Rouge, La.

Subsidiaries include: Zeigler Energy, EnerZ, Zenergy Inc., Zeigler Property Development Co., Zeigler Environmental Services Co., ENCOAL Corp./TEK-KOL Partnership, Pier IX Terminal Company, Shipyard River Terminal Co., Phoenix Land Co., Old Ben Coal Co., Mountaineer Coal Development Co., Bluegrass Coal Development Co., Triton Coal Co., Franklin Coal Sales Co. and Americoal Development Corp.

Zeigler Coal Holding Co. (C00267039) *Address: same as sponsor * Treasurer: Francis Canavan * Contact: Francis Barkofske, Senior V.P. and CFO*

	1993-94	1995-96	1997	Totals
Receipts	$11,672	$19,321	$11,207	$42,200
Disburse	11,672	13,377	7,750	32,799
Cash	4,230	10,176	13,634	n/a
Contributions	9,000	12,250	8,250	29,500
Republicans	4,500	9,250	6,250	20,000
No. of Cand.	*6*	*10*	*8*	*24*
House	1,500	3,750	4,250	9,500
Senate	3,000	5,500	2,000	10,500
Democrats	4,500	3,000	2,000	9,500
No. of Cand.	*6*	*3*	*2*	*11*
House	2,500	0	0	2,500
Senate	2,000	3,000	2,000	7,000
Incumbents	3,500	9,250	8,250	21,000
Challengers	0	250	0	250
Open Seat	4,500	2,750	0	7,250
Winners	6,500	11,500	n/a	18,000
Losers	2,500	750	n/a	3,250

Misc. Energy

American Wind Energy Association

*Phone: (202) 383-2500 * Fax: (202) 383-2505*
122 C St. N.W., Suite 400, Washington, DC 20001
*Web: www.igc.org/awea * E-mail: windmail@mcimail.com*

The American Wind Energy Association is a trade and advocacy organization based in Washington.

AWEA represents the U.S. wind energy industry and individuals who support clean energy. Its annual windpower meeting is the only national conference devoted solely to wind energy and features technical papers from experts in the field.

American Wind Energy Association Political Action Committee (WINDPAC) (C00259572) *Address: same as sponsor * Treasurer: Michael L. Marvin*

	1993-94	1995-96	1997	Totals
Receipts	$26,290	$3,550	$13,650	$43,490
Disburse	24,137	8,049	5,285	37,471
Cash	5,035	535	8,900	n/a
Contributions	23,319	8,049	4,785	36,153
Republicans	6,444	4,074	2,250	12,768
No. of Cand.	*11*	*6*	*4*	*21*
House	2,300	1,954	1,750	6,004
Senate	4,144	2,120	500	6,764
Democrats	16,375	3,975	1,785	22,135
No. of Cand.	*24*	*7*	*5*	*36*
House	13,125	3,950	650	17,725
Senate	3,250	25	1,135	4,410
Incumbents	21,719	7,724	4,250	33,693
Challengers	0	325	0	325
Open Seat	1,100	0	535	1,635
Winners	20,094	7,749	n/a	27,843
Losers	3,225	300	n/a	3,525

Asea Brown Boveri Inc.

Phone: (203) 750-2200
501 Merritt 7, Norwalk, CT 06856
Web: www.abb.com/americas/usa

Electrical engineering company Asea Brown Boveri produces technical equipment for industrial, power transmission and power generation applications. Its products include nuclear power plant equipment, robots, manufacturing automation equipment and electric power transformers. Headquartered in Norwalk, Conn., ABB and its affiliates employ 22,000 people in 41 states and posted $5.8 billion in 1997 revenues. The company sold its ABB Environmental Services unit to Harding Lawson Associates Group Inc. in 1998.

The company has supplied about 40 percent of the utility boilers in the United States. ABB is part of ABB Group, which had 215,000 employees worldwide in 1996 and revenues of $35 billion. ABB Group is a public company and is owned by ABB AB, of Sweden, and ABB AG, of Switzerland.

Employees' Fund for Effective Government (C00041947) *Phone: (202) 429-9180 * Fax: (202) 429-9199 * 1401 H St. N.W., Suite 1060, Washington, DC 20005 * Web: www.abb.com * Treasurer: Bruce B. Talley*

	1993-94	1995-96	1997	Totals
Receipts	$61,048	$76,077	$38,926	$176,051
Disburse	56,926	67,564	43,893	168,383
Cash	8,165	16,678	11,712	n/a
Contributions	39,000	31,650	32,750	103,400
Republicans	10,850	18,750	21,250	50,850
No. of Cand.	*13*	*18*	*25*	*56*
House	8,100	10,750	10,750	29,600
Senate	2,750	8,000	10,500	21,250
Democrats	28,150	12,900	11,500	52,550
No. of Cand.	*24*	*11*	*15*	*50*
House	14,900	12,650	9,500	37,050
Senate	13,250	250	2,000	15,500
Incumbents	36,750	30,400	32,750	99,900
Challengers	0	0	0	0
Open Seat	2,250	1,000	0	3,250
Winners	29,900	27,400	n/a	57,300
Losers	9,100	4,250	n/a	13,350

CalEnergy Co.

*Phone: (402) 341-4500 * Fax: (402) 345-9318*
302 S. 36th St., Suite 400, Omaha, NE 68131-3845
Web: www.calenergy.com

CalEnergy owns and operates about 20 independent power production facilities worldwide with an emphasis on environmentally responsible energy production. The company uses natural gas and hydroelectric energy, and is the world's largest independent producer of geothermal power. The publicly traded CalEnergy has 4,400 employees and reported $2.3 billion in 1997 sales.

CalEnergy has a long-term contract with the Navy to develop geothermal resources at the Naval Air Weapons Station in the Mojave Desert at China Lake, Calif. The company supplies electricity in the United States, the United Kingdom, the Philippines, Indonesia, Bermuda and the Netherlands. It also operates a natural gas exploration subsidiary.

Founded in 1971, CalEnergy has more than 100 subsidiary corporations and about 20 domestic and foreign joint ventures and partnerships.

U.S. locations include: Arizona, California, Nebraska, Nevada, New York, Pennsylvania, Texas and Utah.

CalEnergy Co. PAC (C00271361) *Phone: (202) 828-1378 * Fax: (202) 828-1380 * 2101 L St. N.W., Washington, DC 20037 * Treasurer: Jonathan Michael Weisgall * Contact: David L. Sokol*

	1993-94	1995-96	1997	Totals
Receipts	$1,500	$24,315	$228	$26,043
Disburse	620	9,900	228	10,748
Cash	979	15,394	15,394	n/a
Contributions	1,200	9,900	0	11,100
Republicans	1,200	8,900	0	10,100
No. of Cand.	*2*	*9*	*0*	*11*
House	600	3,400	0	4,000
Senate	600	5,500	0	6,100
Democrats	0	1,000	0	1,000
No. of Cand.	*0*	*2*	*0*	*2*
House	0	1,000	0	1,000
Senate	0	0	0	0
Incumbents	0	5,900	0	5,900
Challengers	1,200	0	0	1,200
Open Seat	0	4,000	0	4,000
Winners	600	6,900	n/a	7,500
Losers	600	3,000	n/a	3,600

Energy Research Corp.

*Phone: (203) 825-6000 * Fax: (203) 825-6100*
3 Great Pasture Rd., Danbury, CT 06813
Web: www.ercc.com

Energy Research is a publicly owned developer of fuel cells and batteries for various industrial and government uses. Its customers include the Department of Energy and National Institutes of Health, among others.

ERC produces nickel-zinc batteries and carbonate fuel cells, two alternative energy sources.

Its assets are $23.5 million, with annual revenues of $29.5 million and more than 150 employees. Government agencies account for about 95 percent of the company's revenues.

Subsidiaries include: Fuel Cell Manufacturing Corp. and Fuel Cell Engineering Corp.

Energy Research Corp. PAC (C00204180) *Phone: (202) 737-1372 * Fax: (202) 737-7337 * 1634 Eye St. N.W., Suite 900, Washington, DC 20006 * Treasurer: Donald R. Glenn * Contact: Eric L. Simpkins, Dir. of Business Development - Eastern Region*

	1993-94	1995-96	1997	Totals
Receipts	$10,407	$8,924	$6,595	$25,926
Disburse	8,450	14,633	6,300	29,383
Cash	7,273	3,809	4,410	n/a
Contributions	8,450	11,350	6,300	26,100
Republicans	2,450	6,100	2,300	10,850
No. of Cand.	*3*	*4*	*2*	*9*
House	2,450	4,100	2,300	8,850
Senate	0	2,000	0	2,000
Democrats	6,000	5,250	4,000	15,250
No. of Cand.	*5*	*4*	*5*	*14*
House	6,000	5,250	3,500	14,750
Senate	0	0	500	500

(Data for Energy Research Corp. continued)

Incumbents	8,450	11,350	6,300	26,100
Challengers	0	0	0	0
Open Seat	0	0	0	0
Winners	8,450	9,250	n/a	17,700
Losers	0	2,100	n/a	2,100

McDermott Inc.

*Phone: (504) 587-4411 * Fax: (504) 587-6153*
P.O. Box 60035, New Orleans, LA 70160
Web: www.mcdermott.com

McDermott International, based in New Orleans, is a publicly owned energy systems and marine construction company. Its 1997 sales were $3.1 billion.

McDermott's companies provide nuclear reactor components to the Navy. They also provide fossil fuels and nuclear steam generating systems and equipment to the electric industry.

McDermott, which employs about 24,000 people, owns a majority stake in J. Ray McDermott, a marine construction firm which supplies services to offshore oil and gas exploration industries. Its units have secured recent million-dollar contracts with Shell Offshore and Fluor Chemical.

The company's nuclear power subsidiary, Babcock & Wilcox, has its own PAC.

Better Government Fund of McDermott Inc. (C00136317) *Phone: (703) 528-6237 * Fax: (703) 351-6418 * 1525 Wilson Blvd., Suite 100, Arlington, VA 22209 * Treasurer: Tony Hymel * Contact: Bruce Hatton, Committee Member*

	1993-94	1995-96	1997	Totals
Receipts	$46,716	$37,513	$20,691	$104,920
Disburse	46,100	37,500	17,500	101,100
Cash	5,038	5,061	8,256	n/a
Contributions	43,600	31,000	17,500	92,100
Republicans	16,500	22,500	9,500	48,500
No. of Cand.	*14*	*20*	*12*	*46*
House	10,500	16,000	8,500	35,000
Senate	6,000	6,500	1,000	13,500
Democrats	27,100	8,500	8,000	43,600
No. of Cand.	*23*	*8*	*8*	*39*
House	22,100	6,500	3,500	32,100
Senate	5,000	2,000	4,500	11,500
Incumbents	41,600	25,500	17,500	84,600
Challengers	0	500	0	500
Open Seat	1,500	5,000	0	6,500
Winners	38,100	25,500	n/a	63,600
Losers	5,500	5,500	n/a	11,000

The Babcock & Wilcox Co. Good Government Fund (C00063461) *Phone: (504) 587-4411 * Fax: (504) 587-4872 * P.O. Box 61038, New Orleans, LA 70161 * Web: www.babcock.com * Treasurer: Tony Hymel*

Babcock & Wilcox is known as the single supplier of nuclear fuel and reactor components for the Navy's nuclear-powered submarines and aircraft carriers. In addition, the company has contracts with the Department of Energy for nuclear cleanup and storage and management of the Strategic Petroleum Reserve in Texas and Louisiana.

Babcock says it is the only remaining designer and manufacturer of nuclear steam generators in North America. Major equipment customers include electric utilities and waste-to-energy, chemical, steel, oil and paper plants.

The company is headquartered in Baberton, Ohio and has manufacturing plants in Texas and Mississippi. Major international offices are located in Mexico, China, Indonesia, Egypt, India and Turkey.

Babcock has 5,500 employees in North America and 11,000 worldwide.

	1993-94	1995-96	1997	Totals
Receipts	$108,980	$93,772	$38,264	$241,016
Disburse	104,100	97,120	31,500	232,720
Cash	11,743	8,407	15,178	n/a
Contributions	104,100	99,600	31,500	235,200
Republicans	35,500	76,350	21,500	133,350
No. of Cand.	*28*	*56*	*27*	*111*
House	19,000	44,250	14,000	77,250
Senate	16,500	32,100	7,500	56,100
Democrats	68,600	23,250	10,000	101,850
No. of Cand.	*51*	*26*	*13*	*90*
House	45,600	20,750	6,500	72,850
Senate	23,000	2,500	3,500	29,000
Incumbents	94,600	89,600	28,500	212,700
Challengers	0	500	0	500
Open Seat	9,500	9,000	3,000	21,500
Winners	93,000	86,600	n/a	179,600
Losers	11,100	13,000	n/a	24,100

Stewart & Stevenson Services Inc.

*Phone: (713) 868-7676 * Fax: (713) 868-2130*
P.O. Box 1637, Houston, TX 77251
Web: www.ssss.com

Stewart & Stevenson Services markets industrial equipment, engineered power systems and tactical vehicles. Its 1997 sales were $1.2 billion.

The publicly held company distributes industrial equipment such as Detroit Diesel engines, Waukesha natural gas engines, Hyster material handling equipment and Thermo King refrigeration systems. It also makes snow removal equipment and wheelchair lifts. The Tactical Vehicle Systems segment makes troop carriers, wreckers, cargo trucks and vans for the Army.

Subsidiaries include: Machinery Acceptance Corp., a wholly owned subsidiary established as a financial tool to assist the sales staff and its customers with financing Stewart & Stevenson equipment.

Stewart & Stevenson Services Inc. Good Government Committee (C00199653) *Address: same as sponsor * Treasurer: Lawrence E. Wilson*

	1993-94	1995-96	1997	Totals
Receipts	$16,100	$27,463	$32,175	$75,738
Disburse	11,500	24,787	19,000	55,287
Cash	5,460	8,137	21,313	n/a
Contributions	10,500	23,250	18,500	52,250
Republicans	2,000	17,750	12,500	32,250
No. of Cand.	*2*	*15*	*11*	*28*
House	0	12,500	11,000	23,500
Senate	2,000	5,250	1,500	8,750
Democrats	8,500	5,500	6,000	20,000
No. of Cand.	*10*	*6*	*5*	*21*
House	8,000	5,500	5,000	18,500
Senate	500	0	1,000	1,500
Incumbents	9,500	21,250	18,500	49,250
Challengers	0	500	0	500
Open Seat	1,000	1,500	0	2,500
Winners	8,500	20,750	n/a	29,250
Losers	2,000	2,500	n/a	4,500

Nuclear Energy*

*Please see CBS Corp. on p. *iv*.

General Atomics

*Phone: (619) 455-3000 * Fax: (619) 455-2232*
P.O. Box 85608, San Diego, CA 92138
Web: www.ga.com

General Atomics is a privately owned nuclear technology company. Founded as a division of defense contractor General Dynamics, the company is the primary developer of gas-cooled nuclear power reactor technology in the United States. For 40 years, GA has been qualified by the Department of Energy, Department of Defense and the National Science Foundation as a government contractor and facilities operator.

General Atomics has built 65 nuclear research reactors located in 23 countries worldwide and carries out the largest and most successful fusion program in private industry. It also develops unmanned aircraft for the Air Force and NASA for use in military and scientific operations.

The company's main facility is located in San Diego and it has other sites around the world. It employs about 1,200 people.

Nine of the top 12 recipients of GA's PAC in 1996 came from California. House Appropriations Committee member Rep. John P. Murtha, D-Pa., was the only top recipient from east of New Mexico. The company spent 97 percent of its money on incumbent candidates and favored Republicans over Democrats 3-to-1.

General Atomics Political Action Committee (C00215285) *Phone: (202) 496-8200 * Fax: (202) 659-1110 * 1100 17th St. N.W., Suite 1200, Washington, DC 20036 * Treasurer: Anthony G. Navarra * Contact: Wayne Willis, V.P.*

*Contact: Brenda Dawson, Chairperson * Phone: (619) 455-3000*

	1993-94	1995-96	1997	Totals
Receipts	$245,909	$295,122	$165,096	$706,127
Disburse	242,588	264,048	132,984	639,620
Cash	33,615	64,587	96,840	n/a
Contributions	204,070	244,250	131,400	579,720
Republicans	70,100	180,750	84,500	335,350
No. of Cand.	*36*	*64*	*51*	*151*
House	54,600	140,750	73,500	268,850
Senate	15,500	40,000	11,000	66,500
Democrats	133,970	63,000	46,900	243,870
No. of Cand.	*52*	*31*	*33*	*116*
House	101,350	58,000	36,400	195,750
Senate	32,620	5,000	10,500	48,120
Incumbents	198,070	235,250	129,900	563,220
Challengers	5,000	1,500	1,000	7,500
Open Seat	5,000	7,000	500	12,500
Winners	164,950	218,750	n/a	383,700
Losers	39,120	25,500	n/a	64,620

Nuclear Energy Institute

*Phone: (202) 739-8000 * Fax: (202) 785-4019*
1776 Eye St. N.W., Suite 400, Washington, DC 20006-3708
Web: www.nei.org

The Nuclear Energy Institute represents the nuclear power industry. Its members include utilities, industries, labor, service and research organizations, law firms, universities and government agencies interested in peaceful uses of nuclear energy, mainly for the generation of electricity.

The Institute acts as a voice for the nuclear power industry, provides information on licensing and plant siting, research and development, safety and security, waste disposal, and legislative issues.

NEI addresses such issues as the management of used fuel from nuclear power plants, the safe transportation of used nuclear fuel, China's nuclear energy outlook, non-proliferation issues and the restructuring of the U.S. electric power industry.

Nuclear Energy Institute Fed Political Action Committee (C00239848) *Address: same as sponsor * Treasurer: J. Scott Peterson*

	1993-94	1995-96	1997	Totals
Receipts	$24,352	$44,797	$54,342	$123,491
Disburse	25,593	40,473	17,148	83,214
Cash	724	2,795	39,298	n/a
Contributions	24,691	39,550	15,500	79,741
Republicans	8,634	29,800	8,500	46,934
No. of Cand.	*16*	*35*	*14*	*65*
House	4,634	12,300	4,500	21,434
Senate	4,000	17,500	4,000	25,500
Democrats	16,057	9,750	7,000	32,807
No. of Cand.	*19*	*15*	*10*	*44*
House	9,557	7,750	3,000	20,307
Senate	6,500	2,000	4,000	12,500
Incumbents	22,384	36,050	15,500	73,934
Challengers	0	2,000	0	2,000
Open Seat	2,307	1,500	0	3,807
Winners	17,534	33,550	n/a	51,084
Losers	7,157	6,000	n/a	13,157

Nuclear Fuel Services Inc.

*Phone: (423) 743-1751 * Fax: (423) 743-1780*
1205 Banner Hill Rd., Erwin, TN 37650
*Web: www.atnfs.com * E-mail: nfsnbg@usit.net*

Nuclear Fuel Services is a nuclear fuel production company with extensive federal and state government contracts. The private Tennessee company has produced research missiles for NASA and fuel for the Navy.

NFS converts nuclear warhead material into fuel for commercial power reactors. The company has developed technologies to eliminate mixed waste (waste containing both radioactive and hazardous material) and to decontaminate and decommission radioactively contaminated buildings and equipment.

NFS is a partner in America's largest environmental clean-up project at Fernald, Ohio.

Nuclear Fuel Services Inc. PAC (NFS PAC) (C00282053) *Address: same as sponsor * Treasurer: C. Glenn Jones*

	1993-94	1995-96	1997	Totals
Receipts	$5,254	$6,596	$2,617	$14,467
Disburse	2,100	6,650	500	9,250
Cash	3,154	3,100	5,221	n/a
Contributions	1,100	6,650	500	8,250
Republicans	1,100	6,650	500	8,250
No. of Cand.	*4*	*12*	*1*	*17*
House	600	4,250	500	5,350
Senate	500	2,400	0	2,900
Democrats	0	0	0	0
No. of Cand.	*0*	*0*	*0*	*0*
House	0	0	0	0
Senate	0	0	0	0
Incumbents	500	5,250	500	6,250
Challengers	350	0	0	350
Open Seat	250	1,400	0	1,650
Winners	1,100	5,250	n/a	6,350
Losers	0	1,400	n/a	1,400

Yankee Atomic Electric Co.

580 Main St., Bolton, MA 01740
Web: www.yankee.com

Yankee Atomic Electric maintains an inactive nuclear power plant in Rowe, Mass. The company ceased power generation there in 1992 and plans to close the site after the plant is fully decommissioned.

In October 1997, the company sold its Nuclear Services Division, which provides consulting and management for governments and the nuclear industry, to Duke Engineering & Services, a subsidiary of North Carolina-based Duke Energy Corp. The Yankee Atomic Electric PAC will be dissolved.

Yankee Atomic Electric Co. Political Action Committee (Yankee PAC) (C00240440) *Address: same as sponsor * Treasurer: Thomas W. Bennet Jr.*

	1993-94	1995-96	1997	Totals
Receipts	$21,612	$16,216	$3,918	$41,746
Disburse	11,811	17,790	10,933	40,534
Cash	23,650	22,087	15,078	n/a
Contributions	10,750	16,350	10,800	37,900
Republicans	8,950	13,000	7,500	29,450
No. of Cand.	*13*	*16*	*9*	*38*
House	6,150	8,500	4,500	19,150
Senate	2,800	4,500	3,000	10,300
Democrats	1,800	3,350	3,300	8,450
No. of Cand.	*4*	*7*	*6*	*17*
House	1,300	3,050	3,300	7,650
Senate	500	300	0	800
Incumbents	9,450	13,050	10,800	33,300
Challengers	500	3,000	0	3,500
Open Seat	800	300	0	1,100
Winners	9,900	10,350	n/a	20,250
Losers	850	6,000	n/a	6,850

Oil & Gas

American Gas Association

*Phone: (703) 841-8400 * Fax: (703) 841-8406*
1515 Wilson Blvd., 12th Floor, Arlington, VA 22209
Web: www.aga.com

The American Gas Association represents about 300 natural gas distribution, transmission, gathering and marketing companies in North America. In addition, 30 natural gas organizations from countries around the world participate in AGA's international programs.

AGA's primary role is to serve as an advocate for natural gas local distribution companies in the federal legislative and regulatory arena. AGA's budget is about $29 million per year, of which about $20 million comes from dues.

Gas Employees Political Action Committee (C00007450) *Address: same as sponsor * Treasurer: Joseph L. Martin * Contact: Jeff Murray, PAC Executive Dir.*

	1993-94	1995-96	1997	Totals
Receipts	$82,609	$62,965	$26,962	$172,536
Disburse	81,151	52,844	19,275	153,270
Cash	5,136	15,267	22,958	n/a
Contributions	65,645	51,777	14,775	132,197
Republicans	27,850	39,777	10,775	78,402
No. of Cand.	*37*	*66*	*11*	*114*
House	10,850	27,579	5,000	43,429
Senate	17,000	12,198	5,775	34,973
Democrats	37,795	12,000	4,000	53,795
No. of Cand.	*50*	*29*	*6*	*85*
House	26,295	9,000	2,000	37,295
Senate	11,500	3,000	2,000	16,500
Incumbents	58,295	38,277	14,275	110,847
Challengers	1,000	2,000	0	3,000
Open Seat	6,350	11,500	500	18,350
Winners	57,145	44,777	n/a	101,922
Losers	8,500	7,000	n/a	15,500

Amoco Corp.

*Phone: (312) 856-6133 * Fax: (312) 856-4883*
200 E. Randolph Dr., Mail Code 2306, Chicago, IL 60601-7126
*Web: www.amoco.com * E-mail: info@amoco.com*

Amoco is one of the largest publicly traded producers of crude oil and natural gas in the world, with assets exceeding $32 billion and 1997 revenues of $36 billion.

The company is the largest private holder and producer of natural gas reserves in the United States and Canada. It also owns more than 16,000 domestic wells and has exploratory operations in 19 countries. Amoco markets its gasoline in 30 states through more than 9,000 service stations.

The company was founded in 1889 and employs about 42,000 people worldwide.

Amoco Political Action Committee (AMOCO PAC) (C00060103) *Phone: (202) 857-5300 * Fax: (202) 857-1608 * 1615 M St. N.W., Suite 200, Washington, DC 20036-3260 * Treasurer: Thomas J. Medaglia III*

*Contact: Robert D. Jones, Chairman * Phone: (312) 856-6133*

	1993-94	1995-96	1997	Totals
Receipts	$443,908	$380,428	$179,101	$1,003,437
Disburse	463,816	395,905	87,009	946,730
Cash	45,591	30,125	122,224	n/a
Contributions	225,250	202,550	56,000	483,800
Republicans	169,600	168,050	36,500	374,150
No. of Cand.	*147*	*164*	*34*	*345*
House	102,600	107,550	13,500	223,650
Senate	67,000	60,500	23,000	150,500
Democrats	55,650	34,500	19,000	109,150
No. of Cand.	*59*	*44*	*20*	*123*
House	37,150	30,500	9,000	76,650
Senate	18,500	4,000	10,000	32,500
Incumbents	116,350	134,050	45,500	295,900
Challengers	33,900	8,000	6,000	47,900
Open Seat	75,000	60,500	4,500	140,000
Winners	182,950	158,250	n/a	341,200
Losers	42,300	44,300	n/a	86,600

Apache Corp.

*Phone: (713) 296-6000 * Fax: (713) 296-6979*
2000 Post Oak Blvd., Suite 100, Houston, TX 77056-4400
*Web: www.apachecorp.com * E-mail: obie.o'brien@apachecorp.com*

Apache explores for and produces crude oil and natural gas. The publicly held company reported $1.2 billion in 1997 revenue, a 20 percent increase over 1996.

Apache's exploration and production interests are located in the Gulf of Mexico, the Gulf Coast, the western Sedimentary Basin of Canada, western Australia, Egypt, Indonesia, offshore China and offshore of the Ivory Coast.

Apache sells its natural gas through ProEnergy and sells its crude oil to refiners, traders and transporters. The company employs about 1,300 people.

Apache Corp. PAC (ApachePAC) (C00279224) *Address: same as sponsor * Treasurer: Urban F. O'Brien III*

	1993-94	1995-96	1997	Totals
Receipts	$20,905	$30,453	$17,792	$69,150
Disburse	19,750	30,499	8,500	58,749
Cash	1,155	6,255	15,554	n/a
Contributions	6,000	14,250	2,000	22,250
Republicans	4,500	8,500	1,000	14,000
No. of Cand.	*6*	*6*	*1*	*13*
House	3,000	7,500	1,000	11,500
Senate	1,500	1,000	0	2,500
Democrats	1,500	5,750	1,000	8,250
No. of Cand.	*3*	*5*	*1*	*9*
House	1,500	5,500	1,000	8,000
Senate	0	250	0	250
Incumbents	3,500	5,000	2,000	10,500
Challengers	0	1,000	0	1,000
Open Seat	2,000	8,000	0	10,000
Winners	5,000	12,500	n/a	17,500
Losers	1,000	1,750	n/a	2,750

Ashland Inc.

*Phone: (606) 324-3600 * Fax: (606) 329-4786*
1000 Ashland Dr., Russell, KY 41114
*Web: www.ashland.com * E-mail: srwalker@ashland.com*

Maker of Valvoline products, Ashland also manufactures petrochemicals and constructs highways. The company's oil refining operations are now part of Marathon Ashland Petroleum, a joint venture between Ashland and the USX Corp.'s Marathon Oil Co. The combined oil company is one of the leading oil refiners and marketers in the nation. Ashland, which owns a 38 percent share in the joint venture, is a publicly traded company with 20,000 employees and 1997 sales of $13 billion.

Ashland manufactures and markets automotive oils and chemicals. Its product line includes Valvoline, Zerex and Pyroil brand products. The company also owns and operates about 400 Valvoline Instant Oil Change service centers in 15 states.

Through subsidiary Ashland Chemical, the company claims to be the largest distributor of chemicals and plastics in North America. The company distributes industrial chemicals, solvents, thermoplastics, resins and fiberglass materials, and manufactures a variety of specialty chemicals.

Through APAC, the company's construction division, Ashland is the nation's largest highway contractor, with operations in 13 Southern and Midwestern states. It also sells construction materials.

In July 1997, Ashland Coal Inc. merged with Arch Mineral Corp. to form Arch Coal Inc. Ashland owns about 54 percent of the company.

Ashland Refining Co. was organized as a Kentucky corporation in 1924 by Swiss Oil Corp., an oil and gas exploration and production company based in Lexington, Ky.

Ashland Inc. Political Action Committee for Employees (PACE) (C00075994) *Address: same as sponsor * Treasurer: Sharon R. Walker * Contact: Harry Zachem, Chairman of Contributions Committee*

	1993-94	1995-96	1997	Totals
Receipts	$163,988	$172,293	$124,771	$461,052
Disburse	171,473	174,790	66,560	412,823
Cash	12,421	9,937	62,360	n/a
Contributions	160,700	165,475	62,550	388,725
Republicans	87,100	137,850	50,800	275,750
No. of Cand.	*75*	*113*	*42*	*230*
House	64,600	102,850	26,800	194,250
Senate	22,500	35,000	24,000	81,500
Democrats	68,850	27,625	7,000	103,475
No. of Cand.	*43*	*27*	*10*	*80*
House	40,850	21,125	5,000	66,975
Senate	28,000	6,500	2,000	36,500
Incumbents	105,900	112,350	48,550	266,800
Challengers	19,500	26,625	1,000	47,125
Open Seat	35,300	26,500	13,000	74,800
Winners	118,800	122,350	n/a	241,150
Losers	41,900	43,125	n/a	85,025

Arch Coal Political Action Committee (ArchPAC) (C00167668) *Phone: (314) 994-2725 * Fax: (314) 994-2734 * One Cityplace Dr., Suite 300, St. Louis, MO 63141 * Web: www.archcoal.com * Treasurer: Patrick A. Kriegshauser * Contact: Blair Gardner, Senior Counsel, Gov. Affairs*

Arch Coal, headquartered in St. Louis, was formed in 1997 with the combination of Arch Mineral and Ashland Coal. The new company, which produces and markets steam and metallurgical coal, is now one of the largest in the industry. In 1997, it sold 40 million tons of coal and had revenues of more than $1 billion.

Through its subsidiaries, Arch Coal produces, processes and markets bituminous coal from Illinois, Kentucky, Virginia, West Virginia and Wyoming. Arch Coal concentrates primarily on acquiring and developing low-sulfur steam coal reserves for sale to electric utility customers in the United States, Europe, the Far East and South Africa.

In November 1997, Arch Coal purchased low-sulfur coal reserves in Boone County, W.Va. for $6 million.

Subsidiaries: Catenary Coal Holdings, Hobet Mining, Ark Land Co. and Arch Coal Sales Company.

The Arch Coal PAC was formerly known as the Arch Mineral PAC.

	1993-94	1995-96	1997	Totals
Receipts	$19,132	$32,435	$16,659	$68,226
Disburse	17,515	29,045	15,114	61,674
Cash	6,674	10,067	11,612	n/a
Contributions	13,000	14,425	9,750	37,175
Republicans	11,000	12,175	6,000	29,175
No. of Cand.	*7*	*15*	*6*	*28*
House	4,500	8,575	5,500	18,575
Senate	6,500	3,600	500	10,600
Democrats	2,000	2,250	3,750	8,000
No. of Cand.	*3*	*2*	*4*	*9*
House	1,000	250	3,750	5,000
Senate	1,000	2,000	0	3,000
Incumbents	7,500	10,550	7,250	25,300
Challengers	500	500	0	1,000
Open Seat	5,000	3,375	0	8,375
Winners	12,250	14,425	n/a	26,675
Losers	750	0	n/a	750

Atlanta Gas Light Co.

*Phone: (404) 584-3876 * Fax: (404) 584-3711*
P.O. Box 4569, Atlanta, GA 30302

Atlanta Gas Light is the largest natural gas distribution company in the southeastern United States, serving more than 1.4 million customers in Georgia and southern Tennessee. Atlanta Gas Light is the primary subsidiary of AGL Resources Inc., a publicly traded company with 3,000 employees and 1997 sales of $1.3 billion.

In accordance with the industry shift toward deregulation of public utilities, Atlanta Gas Light filed a plan in November 1997 with the Georgia Public Service Commission that will allow independent marketers to sell natural gas directly to their customers.

Atlanta Gas Light Co. for Good Government Committee Inc. (C00145037) *Address: same as sponsor * Treasurer: J. S. Thomas*

	1993-94	1995-96	1997	Totals
Receipts	$24,053	$13,205	$15,974	$53,232
Disburse	35,792	36,528	16,137	88,457
Cash	52,464	27,873	27,710	n/a
Contributions	13,700	17,075	7,250	38,025
Republicans	5,750	14,075	7,250	27,075
No. of Cand.	*6*	*13*	*7*	*26*
House	4,750	8,575	5,250	18,575
Senate	1,000	5,500	2,000	8,500
Democrats	7,950	3,000	0	10,950
No. of Cand.	*8*	*3*	*0*	*11*
House	7,950	1,000	0	8,950
Senate	0	2,000	0	2,000
Incumbents	12,050	11,075	7,250	30,375
Challengers	500	1,500	0	2,000
Open Seat	1,050	4,500	0	5,550
Winners	8,750	13,075	n/a	21,825
Losers	4,950	4,000	n/a	8,950

Atlantic Richfield Co.

*Phone: (213) 486-0273 * Fax: (213) 486-2063*
515 S. Flower St., Suite 4639, Los Angeles, CA 90071
Web: www.arco.com

Atlantic Richfield, the seventh largest oil company in the United States, also produces natural gas and chemicals. The publicly traded company had 1997 net income of $1.8 billion on revenues of $19.3 billion. It employs 24,000 workers.

ARCO explores for and produces oil and natural gas throughout the world. It operates two U.S. petroleum refineries: the Los Angeles Refinery in Carson, Calif. and the Cherry Point Refinery near Ferndale, Wash. ARCO is a leading retailer of gasoline on the West Coast, with more than 1,500 retail outlets in California, Oregon, Washington, Arizona and Nevada. In addition, the company has ancillary businesses, including retail convenience stores, steam cogeneration plants and electronic payment systems.

In March 1998, the company agreed to sell its domestic coal operations to Arch Coal for $1.14 billion.

ARCO has an 82.5 percent interest in ARCO Chemical Co. and a 20 percent interest in Zhenhai Refining and Chemical Co., China's third largest oil refiner.

Atlantic Richfield Co., ARCO PAC (C00032805) *Address: same as sponsor * Treasurer: Margaret M. McCallister*

	1993-94	1995-96	1997	Totals
Receipts	$423,834	$374,931	$192,075	$990,840
Disburse	445,612	358,155	105,649	909,416
Cash	114,961	131,745	218,178	n/a
Contributions	222,480	176,650	52,804	451,934
Republicans	117,350	153,750	41,804	312,904
No. of Cand.	*87*	*115*	*45*	*247*
House	68,050	114,250	29,700	212,000
Senate	49,300	39,500	12,104	100,904
Democrats	105,130	22,900	10,500	138,530
No. of Cand.	*98*	*29*	*14*	*141*
House	83,250	21,900	7,500	112,650
Senate	21,880	1,000	3,000	25,880
Incumbents	176,430	135,750	52,304	364,484
Challengers	11,300	6,500	500	18,300
Open Seat	35,000	34,500	0	69,500
Winners	167,890	150,750	n/a	318,640
Losers	54,590	25,900	n/a	80,490

BP America

*Phone: (202) 457-6578 * Fax: (202) 457-6597*
1776 Eye St. N.W., Suite 1000, Washington, DC 20006
Web: www.bp.com

BP America is the U.S. subsidiary of British Petroleum Co., one of Britain's biggest companies and the world's third largest oil and petrochemical group. The company explores for, produces, refines and markets petroleum and makes chemicals. It operates a chain of gas stations in the East. BP has more than 53,000 employees and posted $71 billion in 1997 sales.

Holdings in Alaska produce more than half of the company's annual oil output; North Sea holdings account for nearly a third. BP's chemicals operation markets petrochemicals, polymers and specialty chemicals.

BP has operations in more than 70 countries.

BP America PAC (C00033530) *Address: same as sponsor * Treasurer: Mary Jane Klocke * Contact: Paul Basham, V.P. of Chemicals*

	1993-94	1995-96	1997	Totals
Receipts	$198,806	$204,004	$107,544	$510,354
Disburse	204,506	194,301	91,450	490,257
Cash	9,910	19,622	35,719	n/a
Contributions	75,950	81,100	36,250	193,300
Republicans	40,100	68,350	27,500	135,950
No. of Cand.	*40*	*66*	*21*	*127*
House	16,100	38,850	5,750	60,700
Senate	24,000	29,500	21,750	75,250
Democrats	35,850	12,750	8,750	57,350
No. of Cand.	*45*	*23*	*13*	*81*
House	31,850	12,750	6,750	51,350
Senate	4,000	0	2,000	6,000
Incumbents	63,450	78,450	27,250	169,150
Challengers	4,000	1,200	0	5,200
Open Seat	8,000	1,200	9,000	18,200
Winners	62,200	72,450	n/a	134,650
Losers	13,750	8,650	n/a	22,400

Bay State Gas Co.

*Phone: (508) 836-7355 * Fax: (508) 836-7073*
300 Friberg Pkwy., Westborough, MA 01581-5039
Web: www.bgc.com

Bay State Gas provides natural gas to more than 306,000 customers in Massachusetts, New Hampshire and Maine. The publicly traded utility has 1,100 employees and reported 1997 sales of $474 million.

Bay State's nonregulated energy products and services business serves about 90,000 residential, commercial and industrial customers throughout the United States. It markets products and services through its subsidiaries, EnergyUSA, Savage-Alert Inc. and EnergyEXPRESS.

Bay State plans to merge with energy and utility holding company NIPSCO Industries of Hammond, Ind.

Bay State Gas Co. Political Action Committee (C00147819) *Address: same as sponsor * Treasurer: William D. MacGillivray * Contact: Barbara McKay, V.P.*

	1993-94	1995-96	1997	Totals
Receipts	$8,169	$6,750	$2,126	$17,045
Disburse	3,490	10,800	500	14,790
Cash	7,658	3,611	5,239	n/a
Contributions	3,450	10,300	500	14,250
Republicans	1,300	5,450	500	7,250
No. of Cand.	*4*	*9*	*1*	*14*
House	800	2,950	0	3,750
Senate	500	2,500	500	3,500
Democrats	2,150	4,850	0	7,000
No. of Cand.	*8*	*8*	*0*	*16*
House	1,650	3,850	0	5,500
Senate	500	1,000	0	1,500
Incumbents	2,700	6,600	500	9,800
Challengers	0	1,700	0	1,700
Open Seat	1,250	2,000	0	3,250
Winners	2,700	5,600	n/a	8,300
Losers	750	4,700	n/a	5,450

Brooklyn Union Gas Co.

*Phone: (718) 403-2983 * Fax: (718) 488-1778*
One Metro Tech Center, Brooklyn, NY 11201
*Web: www.bug.com * E-mail: bdolan@bug.com*

Brooklyn Union Gas claims to be the fifth largest natural gas distribution company in the country, serving 1.1 million residential, commercial, industrial and governmental customers in the New York City boroughs of Brooklyn, Queens and Staten Island. The company, a subsidiary of Keyspan Energy Corp., reported 1997 earnings of $195 million.

Brooklyn Union Gas Co. Federal PAC (C00141150) *1225 19th St. N.W., Suite 320, Washington, DC 20036 * Treasurer: Vincent D. Enright Contact: Brian Dolan, Dir. of Federal Gov. Relations * Phone: (718) 403-2983*

	1993-94	1995-96	1997	Totals
Receipts	$32,785	$39,568	$20,072	$92,425
Disburse	33,058	40,138	20,650	93,846
Cash	4,276	3,711	3,134	n/a
Contributions	14,600	20,149	9,250	43,999
Republicans	3,600	10,100	5,250	18,950
No. of Cand.	*4*	*11*	*8*	*23*
House	2,100	6,100	2,750	10,950
Senate	1,500	4,000	2,500	8,000
Democrats	11,000	10,049	4,000	25,049
No. of Cand.	*17*	*11*	*7*	*35*
House	9,250	9,549	4,000	22,799
Senate	1,750	500	0	2,250
Incumbents	14,600	20,149	8,750	43,499
Challengers	0	0	500	500
Open Seat	0	0	0	0
Winners	14,350	19,549	n/a	33,899
Losers	250	600	n/a	850

Burlington Resources

*Phone: (717) 624-9000 * Fax: (717) 624-9640*
5051 Westheimer, Suite 1400, Houston, TX 77056
*Web: www.br-inc.com * E-mail: gsmith@br-inc.com*

Burlington Resources is the second-largest independent oil and gas exploration and production company in the United States. It owns and operates natural gas gathering systems and intrastate natural gas pipelines and has an interest in crude oil pipelines. The company also markets oil and gas, including the acquisition and resale of third-party oil and gas.

A publicly traded company, Burlington Resources had sales of more than $500 million in 1997. It employs 1,800 workers.

The company's principal subsidiary is Burlington Resources Oil & Gas. The company purchased Louisiana Land and Exploration Co. in October 1997.

Burlington Resources/Meridian Oil Political Action Committee (C00004960) *Address: same as sponsor * Treasurer: Gavin H. Smith * Contact: Bobby S. Shackouls, Chairman of Advisory Board*

	1993-94	1995-96	1997	Totals
Receipts	$139,777	$174,117	$79,194	$393,088
Disburse	144,971	153,283	36,477	334,731
Cash	79,257	100,105	142,828	n/a
Contributions	92,800	91,400	13,850	198,050
Republicans	42,250	72,900	11,850	127,000
No. of Cand.	*44*	*83*	*17*	*144*
House	25,250	39,000	7,750	72,000
Senate	17,000	33,900	4,100	55,000
Democrats	50,550	18,500	2,000	71,050
No. of Cand.	*56*	*28*	*5*	*89*
House	36,050	15,500	1,000	52,550
Senate	14,500	3,000	1,000	18,500
Incumbents	80,500	69,500	12,350	162,350
Challengers	3,800	5,500	0	9,300
Open Seat	8,000	16,400	1,500	25,900
Winners	77,050	76,400	n/a	153,450
Losers	15,750	15,000	n/a	30,750

The Louisiana Land and Exploration Co. Political Action Committee (LL&E-PAC) (C00216564) *Phone: (504) 566-6500 * Fax: (504) 566-6860 * 909 Poydras St., New Orleans, LA 70112 * Treasurer: Donna Walther Fiorella * Contact: Robert Armstrong, Executive Assistant*

Louisiana Land and Exploration terminated its PAC on March 11, 1998.

	1993-94	1995-96	1997	Totals
Receipts	$33,839	$26,673	$8,546	$69,058
Disburse	36,776	29,404	12,171	78,351
Cash	7,910	5,180	1,556	n/a
Contributions	31,700	28,500	11,000	71,200
Republicans	18,700	26,500	1,500	46,700
No. of Cand.	*18*	*20*	*2*	*40*
House	5,200	7,500	1,500	14,200
Senate	13,500	19,000	0	32,500
Democrats	13,000	2,000	9,500	24,500
No. of Cand.	*12*	*3*	*7*	*22*
House	7,500	2,000	500	10,000
Senate	5,500	0	9,000	14,500
Incumbents	22,200	18,500	11,000	51,700
Challengers	1,000	0	0	1,000
Open Seat	6,500	10,000	0	16,500
Winners	26,700	20,000	n/a	46,700
Losers	5,000	8,500	n/a	13,500

California Independent Petroleum Association

*Phone: (916) 447-1177 * Fax: (916) 447-1144*
1112 I St., Suite 350, Sacramento, CA
*Web: www.cipa.org * E-mail: cipa@cipa.org*

California Independent Petroleum Association represents 400 independent producers, royalty owners and service and supply companies in California.

The nonprofit group supports legislation that would reform idle well management practices. It also opposes exchanging federal oil and gas leases for surface rights in the Headwaters forest in California.

California Independent Petroleum Association/CIPA Political Action Committee (C00318766) *Phone: (714) 540-7234 x234 * Fax: (714) 850-0830 * 1251 E. Dyer Rd., #100, Santa Ana, CA 92705 * Treasurer: Betty Presley*

	1993-94	1995-96	1997	Totals
Receipts	$0	$14,194	$9,763	$23,957
Disburse	0	13,903	5,785	19,688
Cash	0	290	4,267	n/a
Contributions	0	10,500	3,750	14,250
Republicans	0	10,000	1,750	11,750
No. of Cand.	*0*	*17*	*5*	*22*
House	0	9,000	750	9,750
Senate	0	1,000	1,000	2,000
Democrats	0	500	2,000	2,500
No. of Cand.	*0*	*1*	*1*	*2*
House	0	500	2,000	2,500
Senate	0	0	0	0
Incumbents	0	9,000	2,750	11,750
Challengers	0	500	1,000	1,500
Open Seat	0	1,000	0	1,000
Winners	0	9,000	n/a	9,000
Losers	0	1,500	n/a	1,500

Chevron Corp.

*Phone: (415) 894-3976 * Fax: (415) 894-3583*
575 Market St., Room 908, San Francisco, CA 94105-2856
Web: www.chevron.com

Chevron is an international public company involved in the fuel process from the well to the pump. Headquartered in San Francisco, the company has interests in natural gas and fuel refining and marketing. It has extensive operations in the Caspian Sea, offshore Angola, near Newfoundland and in the Gulf of Mexico. The company holds a 25 percent stake in NGC Corp., the largest wholesaler of natural gas in North America, and half of Caltex, a worldwide fuel refiner and marketer.

The company is working to develop a stake in the European gas market and recently joined with Royal Dutch Shell to explore for fuel in the Caspian Sea. It lobbies on Superfund reform, greenhouse gas emissions and other energy issues. Former Sen. J. Bennett Johnston, D-La., now a registered utility lobbyist, was elected to Chevron's board of directors in 1997.

Chevron ranked second in PAC contributions to 1996 congressional candidates among oil and gas producers, behind Exxon Corp. More than 90 percent went to Republican candidates. Sen. Gordon Smith, R-Ore., was the leading recipient. Of the 20 candidates who received at least $5,000, all were Republicans and all but three were Senate candidates.

Chevron Employees Political Action Committee (C00035006)
*Phone: (202) 408-5800 * Fax: (202) 408-5845 * 1401 Eye St. N.W., Washington, DC 20005 * Treasurer: Carol Lottice*

*Contact: Bill May, Manager * Phone: (415) 894-3976*

	1993-94	1995-96	1997	Totals
Receipts	$420,467	$407,863	$202,098	$1,030,428
Disburse	400,402	424,515	107,604	932,521
Cash	38,095	21,457	115,957	n/a
Contributions	337,498	372,952	83,949	794,399
Republicans	254,049	338,952	59,749	652,750
No. of Cand.	*135*	*147*	*52*	*334*
House	138,560	187,450	27,750	353,760
Senate	115,489	151,502	31,999	298,990
Democrats	83,449	34,000	24,200	141,649
No. of Cand.	*60*	*35*	*16*	*111*
House	53,450	31,000	9,200	93,650
Senate	29,999	3,000	15,000	47,999
Incumbents	194,898	219,702	75,449	490,049
Challengers	54,078	33,000	500	87,578
Open Seat	88,032	117,250	8,000	213,282
Winners	295,112	293,202	n/a	588,314
Losers	42,386	79,750	n/a	122,136

Coastal Corp.

*Phone: (713) 877-7502 * Fax: (713) 877-3299*
9 Greenway Plaza, Houston, TX 77046-0995
Web: www.coastalcorp.com

Coastal operates the nation's fourth largest natural gas pipeline, with most locations in the Midwest and Rocky Mountains. It also explores for, produces and processes oil and gas and builds and runs power plants. Coastal sold most of its coal operations in 1996, but continues to mine in West Virginia, Virginia and Kentucky. The publicly traded company reported 1997 sales of $9.6 billion and employs 14,700 workers.

Sixty-one percent of profit comes from natural gas. Coastal operates refineries in New Jersey, Texas, Alabama and Aruba. It also has a small chemical business; four plants in Wyoming and Nevada produce anhydrous ammonia, ammonium nitrate, nitric acid, liquid carbon dioxide and urea.

Subsidiaries include: ANR Pipeline, Colorado Interstate Gas, Engage Energy, Great Lakes Gas, HIOS-UTOS and Coastal Power.

Coastal Corp. Employee Action Fund (C00091702) *Phone: (202) 466-7430 * Fax: (202) 331-4694 * 2000 M St. N.W., Suite 300, Washington, DC 20036 * Treasurer: Ronald D. Matthews*

*Contact: M. Frank Powell, Chairperson * Phone: (713) 877-7502*

	1993-94	1995-96	1997	Totals
Receipts	$626,145	$542,076	$228,553	$1,396,774
Disburse	634,112	623,842	219,217	1,477,171
Cash	158,300	76,541	85,882	n/a
Contributions	292,369	190,700	73,771	556,840
Republicans	89,975	126,200	49,500	265,675
No. of Cand.	*51*	*78*	*27*	*156*
House	52,975	67,700	21,000	141,675
Senate	37,000	58,500	28,500	124,000
Democrats	201,394	64,500	24,271	290,165
No. of Cand.	*90*	*37*	*11*	*138*
House	143,600	38,000	9,771	191,371
Senate	57,794	26,500	14,500	98,794
Incumbents	245,869	133,700	70,771	450,340
Challengers	14,500	10,500	1,000	26,000
Open Seat	30,000	47,500	2,000	79,500
Winners	214,869	160,700	n/a	375,569
Losers	77,500	30,000	n/a	107,500

Columbia Energy Group

*Phone: (703) 295-0300 * Fax: (703) 758-8796*
12355 Sunrise Valley Dr., Suite 300, Reston, VA 20191-3420
Web: www.columbiaenergy.com

Columbia Energy Group, formerly known as Columbia Gas System, is one of the nation's leading energy groups with assets of about $6 billion. The group is a holding company for 18 subsidiaries operating in all phases of the natural gas business, including marketing and fuel management services, and in electric power generation, sales and trading. Columbia companies serve more than 7 million natural gas customers — 12 percent of the nation's total — in 15 eastern states and the District of Columbia.

Employing more than 9,000 people, the publicly traded company had 1997 sales of $5 billion.

The company's primary PAC represents the employees of Columbia Energy Group, Columbia Energy Group Service Corp., Columbia Energy Services Corp., Columbia Gulf Transmission Co., Columbia LNG Corp., Columbia Network Services, Columbia Propane Corp. and Columbia Electric Corp.

Columbia Energy Employees Political Action Fund (C00051979)
*Address: same as sponsor * Treasurer: Jeffrey W. Grossman * Contact: Richard Casali, Chairman*

	1993-94	1995-96	1997	Totals
Receipts	$122,665	$119,484	$54,236	$296,385
Disburse	112,619	129,882	55,066	297,567
Cash	29,962	19,565	18,736	n/a
Contributions	98,350	100,800	39,350	238,500
Republicans	56,150	75,300	26,100	157,550
No. of Cand.	*45*	*67*	*22*	*134*
House	24,000	47,700	13,600	85,300
Senate	32,150	27,600	12,500	72,250
Democrats	42,200	25,500	13,250	80,950
No. of Cand.	*36*	*25*	*11*	*72*
House	31,700	21,500	3,750	56,950
Senate	10,500	4,000	9,500	24,000
Incumbents	81,150	81,300	39,350	201,800
Challengers	4,700	4,000	0	8,700
Open Seat	13,500	15,500	0	29,000
Winners	90,750	78,800	n/a	169,550
Losers	7,600	22,000	n/a	29,600

Columbia Employees Political Action Fund (C00055236) *Phone: (304) 357-2000 * Fax: (304) 357-2150 * 1700 MacCorkle Ave. S.E., Charleston, WV 25314 * Treasurer: Nazzi Zola*

*Phone: (703) 227-3266 * 12801 Fair Lakes Pkwy., Fairfax, VA 22030 * Contact: Kathleen O'Leary, Chairwoman*

This PAC represents Columbia Gas Transmission Corp. and Columbia Natural Resources Inc. — two subsidiaries of Columbia Energy Group.

Columbia Gas Transmission, one of the group's two transmission companies, operates a 19,000 mile pipeline network in the Northeast, as well as one of the nation's largest underground storage systems. Headquartered in Charleston, W.Va., and spread across 10 states, Columbia Gas Transmission provides gas transportation and storage services to more than 70 local distribution companies serving more than 7 million businesses and homes, as well as to hundreds of large-volume customers in the East. The company employs about 3,000 people.

Columbia Natural Resources is the exploration and production subsidiary of Columbia Energy Group. The company, with about 400 employees, explores for, develops and produces natural gas and oil throughout the Appalachian Basin. The company also owns and operates more than 3,500 miles of natural gas gathering facilities.

	1993-94	1995-96	1997	Totals
Receipts	$178,403	$180,088	$75,047	$433,538
Disburse	158,000	211,356	38,024	407,380
Cash	72,157	40,891	77,915	n/a
Contributions	81,700	97,191	12,740	191,631
Republicans	36,800	64,000	4,000	104,800
No. of Cand.	*45*	*65*	*3*	*113*

(Data for Columbia Employees Political continued)

House	26,800	44,000	2,000	72,800
Senate	10,000	20,000	2,000	32,000
Democrats	44,900	33,191	8,740	86,831
No. of Cand.	*41*	*35*	*5*	*81*
House	34,000	28,100	7,740	69,840
Senate	10,900	5,091	1,000	16,991
Incumbents	66,950	82,400	8,740	158,090
Challengers	4,750	2,291	0	7,041
Open Seat	10,000	12,500	4,000	26,500
Winners	73,200	79,900	n/a	153,100
Losers	8,500	17,291	n/a	25,791

Columbia Gas Distribution Employees Political Action Fund (C00054890) *Phone: (614) 460-5933 * Fax: (614) 460-4206 * 200 Civic Center Dr., Columbus, OH 43215-0117 * Treasurer: Robert M. Smith * Contact: John W. Partridge Jr., Chairman*

This PAC represents Columbia Energy Group's five distribution companies, which provide gas service to 2 million homes, businesses and industries in Ohio, Pennsylvania, Virginia, Kentucky and Maryland.

	1993-94	*1995-96*	*1997*	*Totals*
Receipts	$204,048	$277,948	$138,105	$620,101
Disburse	195,685	235,943	119,388	551,016
Cash	60,601	102,606	121,324	n/a
Contributions	34,060	40,830	13,550	88,440
Republicans	24,694	31,730	12,650	69,074
No. of Cand.	*24*	*30*	*10*	*64*
House	17,844	26,710	5,600	50,154
Senate	6,850	5,020	7,050	18,920
Democrats	9,366	9,100	900	19,366
No. of Cand.	*15*	*14*	*3*	*32*
House	8,616	8,600	900	18,116
Senate	750	500	0	1,250
Incumbents	21,140	36,330	7,250	64,720
Challengers	5,175	1,500	500	7,175
Open Seat	7,745	3,000	5,800	16,545
Winners	31,644	34,430	n/a	66,074
Losers	2,416	6,400	n/a	8,816

Consolidated Natural Gas Co.

*Phone: (412) 690-1245 * Fax: (412) 690-7633*
CNG Tower, 625 Liberty Ave., 21st Floor, Pittsburgh, PA 15222-3199
Web: www.cng.com

Consolidated Natural Gas is one of the largest natural gas systems in the United States. Through its subsidiaries, it engages in all phases of the natural gas business including exploration, production, transmission, distribution and marketing. It serves 1.8 million customers in Ohio, Pennsylvania, Virginia and West Virginia. Sales for 1997 were $5.7 billion, and CNG employed more than 6,000 workers. The public company is ranked No. 360 among Fortune 500 companies.

Other company activities include gas storage, the extraction and sale of oil, condensate, natural gas, butane, propane and ethane and electric power marketing throughout the four-state region.

Subsidiaries include: Consolidated Natural Gas Service Co., CNG Transmission Corp., CNG Producing Co., CNG Energy Services Corp., CNG Power Services Corp., CNG Research Co., East Ohio Gas Co., Hope Gas Inc., Virginia Natural Gas Inc. and Peoples Natural Gas.

CNG also has four subsidiary PACs representing CNG Transmission, East Ohio Gas, Peoples Natural Gas and CNG Producing.

Consolidated Natural Gas Service Co. Inc. Executives' Political Fund (ConPAC) (C00040824) *Address: same as sponsor * Treasurer: Donna M. Pirollo * Contact: George Taaffe, PAC Chairman*

	1993-94	*1995-96*	*1997*	*Totals*
Receipts	$71,416	$55,533	$42,143	$169,092
Disburse	64,965	59,383	48,442	172,790
Cash	15,768	11,928	5,630	n/a
Contributions	52,150	51,383	34,270	137,803
Republicans	14,850	28,983	18,483	62,316
No. of Cand.	*16*	*33*	*25*	*74*
House	4,350	20,483	11,483	36,316
Senate	10,500	8,500	7,000	26,000
Democrats	37,050	22,400	15,787	75,237
No. of Cand.	*34*	*31*	*16*	*81*
House	18,550	15,400	8,787	42,737
Senate	18,500	7,000	7,000	32,500
Incumbents	47,150	37,133	32,770	117,053
Challengers	0	3,000	1,500	4,500
Open Seat	5,000	10,250	0	15,250
Winners	43,650	40,383	n/a	84,033
Losers	8,500	11,000	n/a	19,500

CNG Transmission Corp. Concerned Employees Political Team (CONCEPT) (C00010967) *Phone: (304) 623-8000 * Fax: (304) 623-8323 * P.O. Box 2450, Clarksburg, WV 26301-2450 * Web: www.cng.com/cngt * Treasurer: Donna M. Pirollo * Contact: Michael D. Greer, V.P. of External. Affairs*

CNG Transmission transports natural gas to markets in the Midwest, mid-Atlantic and Northeast.

CNG Transmission maintains 10,000 miles of pipelines and operates 74 compressor stations in Ohio, West Virginia, Pennsylvania, New York, Maryland and Virginia. It claims to operate the world's largest underground natural gas storage system.

	1993-94	*1995-96*	*1997*	*Totals*
Receipts	$92,565	$74,203	$32,052	$198,820
Disburse	100,949	80,729	23,923	205,601
Cash	26,612	20,092	28,225	n/a
Contributions	19,250	18,633	3,750	41,633
Republicans	3,750	11,883	1,750	17,383
No. of Cand.	*8*	*18*	*3*	*29*
House	3,000	9,883	1,750	14,633
Senate	750	2,000	0	2,750
Democrats	15,500	6,750	2,000	24,250
No. of Cand.	*17*	*14*	*2*	*33*
House	9,000	7,250	2,000	18,250
Senate	6,500	-500	0	6,000
Incumbents	18,000	17,383	3,750	39,133
Challengers	250	250	0	500
Open Seat	1,000	1,000	0	2,000
Winners	17,250	18,383	n/a	35,633
Losers	2,000	250	n/a	2,250

East Ohio Gas Employees Voluntary Good Government Association (C00014472) *Phone: (216) 736-6221 * Fax: (216) 736-5385 * 1717 E. Ninth St., #804, Cleveland, OH 44114 * Web: www.cng.com/eog * Treasurer: Franklin C. Lewis * Contact: Michael Bartels, Chairman*

East Ohio Gas serves more than 1 million residential, commercial and industrial customers in 270 eastern Ohio communities. Based in Cleveland, it is the largest subsidiary of Consolidated Natural Gas and employs about 2,200 people.

In December 1997, East Ohio Gas launched the 14th year of the People-Helping-People Fuel Fund, a joint program with the Salvation Army. The program provides needy customers last-resort assistance to avoid utility service shut off.

Formed in the early 1970s, the East Ohio Gas Employees Voluntary Good Government Association is a nonpartisan PAC providing contributions to Ohio campaigns. The PAC's issues are energy and the environment.

	1993-94	*1995-96*	*1997*	*Totals*
Receipts	$75,105	$53,778	$21,881	$150,764
Disburse	81,388	60,373	14,309	156,070
Cash	13,811	7,219	14,791	n/a
Contributions	9,575	10,450	2,625	22,650
Republicans	6,800	10,250	2,250	19,300
No. of Cand.	*8*	*10*	*7*	*25*
House	3,800	7,250	2,000	13,050
Senate	3,000	3,000	250	6,250
Democrats	2,775	200	375	3,350
No. of Cand.	*6*	*1*	*2*	*9*
House	2,275	200	375	2,850
Senate	500	0	0	500
Incumbents	4,625	7,750	2,525	14,900
Challengers	750	2,700	100	3,550
Open Seat	4,200	0	0	4,200
Winners	7,775	7,100	n/a	14,875
Losers	1,800	3,350	n/a	5,150

Peoples Natural Gas Co. Employees Political Involvement Committee (PEPIC) (C00033167) *Phone: (412) 497-6887 * Fax: (412) 497-6838 * 625 Liberty Ave., Pittsburgh, PA 15222 * Web: www.cng.com/png * E-mail: WBoswell@png.cng.com * Treasurer: Abby Jo Corbin * Contact: William P. Boswell, Chairman*

Peoples Natural Gas provides natural gas to 337,000 residential and commercial customers in southwestern Pennsylvania. The company employs 900 people.

	1993-94	*1995-96*	*1997*	*Totals*
Receipts	$58,108	$45,607	$22,217	$125,932
Disburse	67,499	45,712	14,280	127,491
Cash	12,199	12,096	20,035	n/a
Contributions	8,250	6,100	1,500	15,850
Republicans	3,950	4,000	1,000	8,950
No. of Cand.	*8*	*6*	*2*	*16*
House	2,950	3,750	1,000	7,700

Senate	1,000	250	0	1,250
Democrats	4,300	2,100	500	6,900
No. of Cand.	*7*	*6*	*2*	*15*
House	4,300	1,850	500	6,650
Senate	0	250	0	250
Incumbents	5,600	5,600	1,500	12,700
Challengers	1,000	0	0	1,000
Open Seat	1,150	500	0	1,650
Winners	6,700	6,100	n/a	12,800
Losers	1,550	0	n/a	1,550

Contributed less than $5,000 during 1995-96 cycle:

CNGPAC A Political Action Committee of CNG Producing Co. (C00160085) *Phone: (504) 593-7301 * CNG Tower, 1450 Poydras St., New Orleans, LA 70112-8000 * Web: www.cng.com/cngp * Treasurer: Aline Wyman*

Crown Central Petroleum Corp.

*Phone: (410) 539-7400 * Fax: (410) 659-4747*
One N. Charles St., Baltimore, MD 21201

Crown Central Petroleum refines and markets gasoline, highway diesel and jet fuel as well as home heating oil. The publicly traded company has 2,800 employees and reported sales of $1.6 billion in 1997.

Founded in 1917, Crown markets its refined petroleum products and merchandise through a network of 348 gasoline stations and convenience stores (Fast Fare and Zippy Mart). The stores are located in the mid-Atlantic and Southeast, with core retail market areas in Maryland, Virginia and North Carolina.

Headquartered in Baltimore, Crown Central Petroleum operates two Texas refineries and 17 product terminals.

In February 1996, Crown started a lockout of its union employees at its Pasadena, Texas refinery. In January 1998, the National Labor Relations Board found in favor of the company, dismissing the Oil, Chemical and Atomic Workers Union claims that the company had engaged in unfair labor practices. As of March 1998, negotiations continued.

Subsidiaries in Maryland: Crown Central Holding Corp., Crown Gold Inc., The Crown Oil and Gas Co., F Z Corp., Health Plan Administrators Inc., Crown Stations Inc., Locot Inc., Tiara Properties Inc. and T.B. & Co. Inc.

Subsidiaries in Delaware: Continental American Corp., Coronet Security Systems Inc., Coronet Software Inc., Fast Fare Inc., La Gloria Oil and Gas Co.; in Texas: Crown Central Pipe Line Co., Crown-Rancho Pipe Line Corp., McMurrey Pipe Line Co.; in Vermont: Tiara Insurance Co.; Crowncen International N.V. in the Netherlands Antilles; and Crown Central International (U.K.) in the United Kingdom.

Crown Central Petroleum Federal Political Action Committee (C00202911) *Address: same as sponsor * Treasurer: John E. Wheeler Jr.*

	1993-94	*1995-96*	*1997*	*Totals*
Receipts	$5,733	$4,881	$2,775	$13,389
Disburse	9,771	10,150	0	19,921
Cash	6,489	1,231	4,013	n/a
Contributions	10,571	4,900	0	15,471
Republicans	5,721	1,750	0	7,471
No. of Cand.	*5*	*4*	*0*	*9*
House	1,200	1,000	0	2,200
Senate	4,521	750	0	5,271
Democrats	4,850	3,150	0	8,000
No. of Cand.	*9*	*7*	*0*	*16*
House	1,650	2,800	0	4,450
Senate	3,200	350	0	3,550
Incumbents	5,150	3,100	0	8,250
Challengers	4,321	700	0	5,021
Open Seat	800	1,100	0	1,900
Winners	4,900	4,200	n/a	9,100
Losers	5,671	700	n/a	6,371

Dresser Industries Inc.

*Phone: (214) 740-6000 * Fax: (214) 740-6584*
1600 Pacific, P.O. Box 774, Dallas, TX 75221
Web: www.dresser.com

Dallas-based Dresser Industries provides highly engineered products, technical services and project management for hydrocarbon energy-related activities. The firm's products are primarily used in oil and gas drilling, production and transmission; power generation; gas processing; petroleum refining and marketing; and petrochemical production.

The publicly owned company had 1997 revenues of $7.5 billion, 66 percent of which came from customers outside the United States.

In February 1998, the company agreed to be purchased by Halliburton Co. for $7.7 billion.

Subsidiaries include: Baroid Drilling Fluids; Sperry-Sun Drilling Services; Security DBS; Dresser Kellogg Energy Services; Granherne; Paragon Engineering Services; Dresser Oil Tools; Fann Instrument Co.; Sub Sea International; The M.W. Kellogg Co; Wayne; Dresser Instrument; Waukesha Engine; and Roots.

Dresser Industries Political Action Committee (DIPAC) (C00066449) *Address: same as sponsor * Treasurer: William Bradle*

	1993-94	*1995-96*	*1997*	*Totals*
Receipts	$112,466	$89,290	$43,748	$245,504
Disburse	122,113	94,395	34,475	250,983
Cash	9,652	4,555	13,833	n/a
Contributions	110,850	70,068	31,500	212,418
Republicans	81,450	64,568	26,500	172,518
No. of Cand.	*65*	*69*	*32*	*166*
House	41,950	44,068	17,500	103,518
Senate	39,500	20,500	9,000	69,000
Democrats	29,400	5,500	5,000	39,900
No. of Cand.	*22*	*7*	*9*	*38*
House	21,400	5,500	4,000	30,900
Senate	8,000	0	1,000	9,000
Incumbents	81,150	61,000	31,500	173,650
Challengers	10,200	1,000	0	11,200
Open Seat	19,500	8,068	0	27,568
Winners	100,350	57,068	n/a	157,418
Losers	10,500	13,000	n/a	23,500

El Paso Energy Corp.

Phone: (713) 757-2131
1001 Louisiana St., Houston, TX 77252
Web: www.epng.com

El Paso Energy is a public company whose 26,000-mile natural gas pipeline spans from coast to coast, making it one of the largest pipeline networks in the country.

The 1,500-employee Houston company owns five distinct pipeline systems — El Paso Natural Gas and Mojave in the West, and Tennessee Gas Pipeline, East Tennessee Natural Gas and Midwestern Gas Transmission in the East. It also has an interest in the TransColorado pipeline under construction in Colorado.

A subsidiary, El Paso Field Service Co., has interests in 21 gas treatment and processing plants in Texas, Louisiana and New Mexico. A global unit, El Paso Energy International, has 11 projects under construction or in service.

Founded in 1929, the firm grew dramatically in 1996 when it acquired Tenneco Energy's network of pipelines in the East for $4 billion. Tenneco Energy's PAC has been terminated.

The El Paso Energy Corp. Political Action Committee (C00093948) *Phone: (202) 662-4300 * Fax: (202) 662-4315 * 601 13th St. N.W., Suite 850 S., Washington, DC 20005 * Treasurer: Nancy Whorton George*

	1993-94	*1995-96*	*1997*	*Totals*
Receipts	$74,169	$75,920	$128,938	$279,027
Disburse	118,550	99,585	91,852	309,987
Cash	74,713	51,061	88,154	n/a
Contributions	68,300	67,850	59,500	195,650
Republicans	40,800	59,350	49,250	149,400
No. of Cand.	*25*	*41*	*45*	*111*
House	15,300	37,350	32,250	84,900
Senate	25,500	22,000	17,000	64,500
Democrats	27,500	8,500	10,250	46,250
No. of Cand.	*20*	*8*	*11*	*39*
House	10,750	7,000	8,250	26,000
Senate	16,750	1,500	2,000	20,250
Incumbents	56,550	59,850	56,750	173,150
Challengers	3,000	500	1,750	5,250
Open Seat	7,750	7,500	1,000	16,250
Winners	53,050	61,350	n/a	114,400
Losers	15,250	6,500	n/a	21,750

Contributed less than $5,000 during 1995-96 cycle:

Tenneco Energy Employees Good Government Fund (also known as TEEGGF) (C00325183) *701 Pennsylvania Ave., Suite 710, Washington, DC 20004 * Treasurer: Wayne Allred*

Energen Corp.

*Phone: (205) 326-8100 * Fax: (205) 326-2704*
2101 Sixth Ave. N., Birmingham, AL 35203
Web: www.energen.com

Energen is a natural gas distribution company based in Alabama. The company also explores for and produces natural gas and oil. A publicly traded company, Energen had 1997 sales of $448 million and employs more than 1,400 workers.

Its Alabama gas subsidiary, Alagasco, is a regulated gas utility with 19,000 miles of service lines. It supplies natural gas to 460,000 homes, businesses and industries in central and northern Alabama.

Taurus Exploration acquires and develops oil and gas wells in Alabama, New Mexico, Louisiana and Mississippi. In January 1998 Taurus purchased $17 million of Gulf of Mexico properties from Chateau Oil and Gas Inc.

Energen Corp. Political Action Committee (formerly known as Alagasco Inc. PAC) (C00135855) *Address: same as sponsor * Treasurer: Dudley C. Reynolds * Contact: Roy Etheridge, Chairperson*

	1993-94	1995-96	1997	Totals
Receipts	$66,537	$61,725	$29,825	$158,087
Disburse	73,172	57,800	16,600	147,572
Cash	31,438	35,366	48,593	n/a
Contributions	9,000	9,000	5,600	23,600
Republicans	4,000	7,500	5,600	17,100
No. of Cand.	*1*	*6*	*3*	*10*
House	4,000	6,500	600	11,100
Senate	0	1,000	5,000	6,000
Democrats	5,000	1,500	0	6,500
No. of Cand.	*3*	*2*	*0*	*5*
House	5,000	1,500	0	6,500
Senate	0	0	0	0
Incumbents	9,000	5,000	5,600	19,600
Challengers	0	0	0	0
Open Seat	0	4,000	0	4,000
Winners	9,000	8,000	n/a	17,000
Losers	0	1,000	n/a	1,000

Enron Corp.

*Phone: (713) 853-6710 * Fax: (713) 646-4995*
P.O. Box 1188 EB 4520, Houston, TX 77251
Web: www.enron.com

Enron explores for, produces and distributes natural gas and crude oil in the United States, Canada, Trinidad and India and, to a lesser extent, other international areas. It reported $20 billion in 1997 revenues. The publicly traded company employs more than 15,000 workers.

Enron also builds and manages worldwide natural gas transportation, power generation, liquids and clean fuels facilities. It operates a natural gas pipeline in Argentina and markets gas in Europe.

The company has been seeking to enter the electricity market in several states, but backed away from offering residential service in California because of regulatory concerns.

Subsidiaries include: Enron Oil and Gas Co., Portland General Electric, which serves 45 percent of Oregon's population; Enron Gas Pipeline Group, with 32,000 miles of pipeline; and Enron Renewable Energy Corp., which works with solar and wind energy.

Enron Corp. Political Action Committee (C00104810) *Address: same as sponsor * Treasurer: Robert H. Butts * Contact: Terence Thorn, Chairman*

	1993-94	1995-96	1997	Totals
Receipts	$486,580	$507,275	$247,326	$1,241,181
Disburse	467,079	462,892	237,818	1,167,789
Cash	80,079	124,463	133,972	n/a
Contributions	189,565	154,171	116,262	459,998
Republicans	90,100	126,421	85,381	301,902
No. of Cand.	*78*	*115*	*79*	*272*
House	48,850	77,618	45,500	171,968
Senate	41,250	48,803	39,881	129,934
Democrats	99,465	27,750	30,881	158,096
No. of Cand.	*74*	*32*	*36*	*142*
House	74,600	19,750	16,625	110,975
Senate	24,865	8,000	14,256	47,121
Incumbents	154,415	124,271	109,262	387,948
Challengers	15,800	7,500	4,500	27,800
Open Seat	19,350	22,400	2,500	44,250
Winners	149,450	127,171	n/a	276,621
Losers	40,115	27,000	n/a	67,115

Portland General Electric Bi-PAC Bipartisan Committee for Effective Government (PGE BiPAC Federal) (C00082008) *Phone: (503) 464-8820 * Fax: (503) 464-2676 * 121 S.W. Salmon 1WTC0901, Portland, OR 97204 * Web: www.pge-online.com * Treasurer: Randy Oliver*

Portland General Electric's PAC was terminated in December 1997. Its activities have been merged with Enron's PAC.

	1993-94	1995-96	1997	Totals
Receipts	$8,279	$10,088	$2,946	$21,313
Disburse	3,639	14,056	5,026	22,721
Cash	6,065	2,074	0	n/a
Contributions	3,175	12,075	2,750	18,000
Republicans	850	8,350	1,000	10,200
No. of Cand.	*3*	*9*	*1*	*13*
House	350	3,600	0	3,950
Senate	500	4,750	1,000	6,250
Democrats	2,325	3,725	1,750	7,800
No. of Cand.	*3*	*6*	*2*	*11*
House	2,325	1,375	1,750	5,450
Senate	0	2,350	0	2,350
Incumbents	2,700	6,975	2,750	12,425
Challengers	0	500	0	500
Open Seat	475	4,600	0	5,075
Winners	3,050	7,125	n/a	10,175
Losers	125	4,950	n/a	5,075

Exxon Corp.

*Phone: (713) 656-6379 * Fax: (713) 656-7492*
P.O. Box 2180, Houston, TX 77252-2180
Web: www.exxon.com

Exxon is the world's second-largest oil company behind Royal Dutch/Shell. The public company sells about 65 million gallons of gasoline every day. It also produces and sells other petroleum chemicals, mines coal and owns part of a Hong Kong electric power generation plant. Its affiliates operate or market products in more than 100 countries on six continents and employ 79,000 workers. The company had 1997 sales of $136.6 billion.

The company lobbies on environmental and fuel issues. It actively tracks legislation affecting alternative fuels, global climate issues and international trade. Exxon supports reform of OSHA workplace regulations. It opposes new EPA ozone regulations as too costly and unnecessary. Exxon is one of several major oil companies participating in an international consortium with the government of Azerbaijan to drill for oil in the Caspian Sea.

Exxon was the leading oil and gas industry PAC contributor to congressional campaigns during the 1995-96 election cycle. Republican candidates received more than 97 percent of the PAC's contributions. The top recipients were former Sen. Larry Pressler, R-S.D., and Sens. Michael B. Enzi, R-Wyo., Gordon H. Smith, R-Ore., Larry Craig, R-Idaho, and 1996 Republican Senate candidates Louis "Woody" Jenkins of Louisiana and Rudy Boschwitz of Minnesota.

Exxon Corp. Political Action Committee (ExPAC) (C00121368) *Phone: (202) 862-0200 * Fax: (202) 862-0267 * 2001 Pennsylvania Ave. N.W., Suite 300, Washington, DC 20006 * Treasurer: Karen M. Kresta Contact: Mike Quinn, Administrator * Phone: (713) 656-6379*

	1993-94	1995-96	1997	Totals
Receipts	$537,406	$619,212	$334,915	$1,491,533
Disburse	547,962	621,886	85,505	1,255,353
Cash	17,659	14,998	264,413	n/a
Contributions	496,275	556,950	37,600	1,090,825
Republicans	465,425	540,450	35,100	1,040,975
No. of Cand.	*224*	*242*	*45*	*511*
House	298,825	369,800	22,100	690,725
Senate	166,600	170,650	13,000	350,250
Democrats	30,350	16,500	2,500	49,350
No. of Cand.	*41*	*22*	*6*	*69*
House	28,300	16,850	1,500	46,650
Senate	2,050	-350	1,000	2,700
Incumbents	204,275	314,850	36,600	555,725
Challengers	136,200	65,600	1,000	202,800
Open Seat	155,900	172,500	0	328,400
Winners	403,550	363,550	n/a	767,100
Losers	92,725	193,400	n/a	286,125

Fina Inc.

*Phone: (214) 750-2816 * Fax: (214) 706-4262*
8350 N. Central Expressway, Dallas, TX 75206
Web: www.fina.com

Fina is an oil and natural gas exploration and production company. With 1997 sales of $4.4 billion, it is the publicly traded U.S. subsidiary of Belgian oil, gas and chemical conglomerate PetroFina S.A.

Fina employs about 2,660 people and owns and operates two refineries in Port Arthur and Big Spring, Texas. It also sells motor fuel through nearly 2,600 fuel stations located in 13 southeastern and southwestern states. The company's headquarters are in Dallas.

The company's primary subsidiary is Fina Oil and Chemical Co.

Fina Inc. & Fina Oil and Chemical Co. Political Action Committee (C00109793) *Address: same as sponsor * Treasurer: Brendan M. O'Connor * Contact: Linda Middleton, Assistant Treasurer*

	1993-94	1995-96	1997	Totals
Receipts	$47,074	$44,861	$31,986	$123,921
Disburse	50,200	34,700	36,350	121,250
Cash	15,398	25,564	21,202	n/a
Contributions	21,300	12,500	6,300	40,100
Republicans	11,200	10,500	3,300	25,000
No. of Cand.	*5*	*11*	*4*	*20*
House	5,500	6,500	2,300	14,300
Senate	5,700	4,000	1,000	10,700
Democrats	10,100	2,000	3,000	15,100
No. of Cand.	*11*	*2*	*3*	*16*
House	7,600	2,000	2,000	11,600
Senate	2,500	0	1,000	3,500
Incumbents	17,800	8,000	6,300	32,100
Challengers	3,000	500	0	3,500
Open Seat	500	4,000	0	4,500
Winners	18,300	9,500	n/a	27,800
Losers	3,000	3,000	n/a	6,000

Halliburton Co.

*Phone: (214) 978-2600 * Fax: (214) 978-2611*
1700 S. Highway 81, Duncan, OK 73536-0250
Web: www.halliburton.com

Halliburton provides engineering, maintenance and construction services to the oil and gas exploration and production industry. The company's capabilities range from the initial evaluation of formations to drilling, production and well maintenance. Halliburton runs 300 service centers in more than 60 countries.

A public company with 70,000 employees worldwide, Halliburton had 1997 revenues of $8.8 billion. Its subsidiaries include Brown & Root Energy Services.

In February 1998, the company announced that it had agreed to buy Dresser Industries Inc. for $7.7 billion.

Halliburton Energy Services PAC (C00035691) *Address: same as sponsor * Treasurer: Joe C. Graham * Contact: Don Deline, Gov. Relations Manager*

	1993-94	1995-96	1997	Totals
Receipts	$111,788	$164,089	$129,903	$405,780
Disburse	165,256	175,979	40,699	381,934
Cash	20,921	9,037	98,341	n/a
Contributions	148,500	150,500	37,000	336,000
Republicans	111,000	142,500	35,500	289,000
No. of Cand.	*69*	*84*	*36*	*189*
House	51,000	78,500	19,500	149,000
Senate	60,000	64,000	16,000	140,000
Democrats	37,500	8,000	1,500	47,000
No. of Cand.	*28*	*12*	*3*	*43*
House	26,500	9,000	1,500	37,000
Senate	11,000	-1000	0	10,000
Incumbents	99,500	85,500	36,000	221,000
Challengers	17,500	20,500	0	38,000
Open Seat	32,500	45,500	1,000	79,000
Winners	130,000	110,500	n/a	240,500
Losers	18,500	40,000	n/a	58,500

Brownbuilders Political Action Committee of Brown & Root Inc. Employees (C00030478) *Phone: (713) 676-5149 * Fax: (713) 676-3560 * 4100 Clinton Dr., P.O. Box 3, 03-1006, Houston, TX 77001 * Web: www.halliburton.com/bres * Treasurer: M. Steve Bender * Contact: Dave Lesar, Chairperson*

Brown & Root supplies engineering and construction services to the upstream oil and gas industry worldwide. Brown & Root Energy Services currently employs more than 7,000 people worldwide.

The company's primary role is the engineering, project management, construction and operation of facilities needed to produce and transport oil and gas.

	1993-94	1995-96	1997	Totals
Receipts	$280,538	$241,660	$125,469	$647,667
Disburse	271,675	248,605	56,585	576,865
Cash	36,291	29,358	98,247	n/a
Contributions	162,000	164,139	18,700	344,839
Republicans	133,000	156,639	16,500	306,139
No. of Cand.	*100*	*109*	*18*	*227*
House	82,500	111,939	9,500	203,939
Senate	50,500	44,700	7,000	102,200
Democrats	29,000	7,500	2,200	38,700
No. of Cand.	*28*	*9*	*4*	*41*
House	25,000	7,000	1,200	33,200
Senate	4,000	500	1,000	5,500
Incumbents	116,000	103,499	18,700	238,199
Challengers	11,000	14,700	0	25,700
Open Seat	35,000	44,440	0	79,440
Winners	149,000	129,440	n/a	278,440
Losers	13,000	34,699	n/a	47,699

Hunt Oil Co.

*Phone: (214) 978-8000 * Fax: (214) 978-8888*
1445 Ross At Field, Dallas, TX 75202-2785

Hunt Oil is a privately held global oil and gas exploration and production company. Founded in 1934, the bulk of the firm's foreign operations are in Yemen.

In 1996, Hunt Oil had estimated revenues of $600 million and employed 1,300 workers.

According to Alabama Live, an online news service, Hunt Oil Co. paid $250,000 in fines to the state of Alabama for failing to comply with royalty provisions in off-shore natural-gas leases signed in the early 1980s.

Hunt Oil Co. Political Action Committee (C00141945) *Address: same as sponsor * Treasurer: Ben Golding * Contact: Carl Boetticher, Chairman*

	1993-94	1995-96	1997	Totals
Receipts	$12,803	$23,315	$20,984	$57,102
Disburse	19,910	26,268	0	46,178
Cash	4,126	1,170	22,154	n/a
Contributions	19,120	20,500	0	39,620
Republicans	18,750	19,000	0	37,750
No. of Cand.	*21*	*19*	*0*	*40*
House	3,750	6,000	0	9,750
Senate	15,000	13,000	0	28,000
Democrats	370	500	0	870
No. of Cand.	*3*	*1*	*0*	*4*
House	750	500	0	1,250
Senate	-380	0	0	-380
Incumbents	11,620	6,500	0	18,120
Challengers	3,000	4,000	0	7,000
Open Seat	4,500	9,000	0	13,500
Winners	18,000	12,250	n/a	30,250
Losers	1,120	8,250	n/a	9,370

Independent Petroleum Association of America

*Phone: (202) 857-4722 * Fax: (202) 857-4799*
1101 16th St. N.W., Suite 200, Washington, DC 20036
Web: www.ipaa.org

The Independent Petroleum Association of America represents 8,000 independent oil and natural gas explorers/producers in the United States. It also operates in close cooperation with 44 independent national, state and regional associations.

The IPAA works to ensure a strong, viable domestic oil and natural gas industry, based on the belief that an adequate and secure supply of energy is essential to the national economy.

Independent Petroleum Association of America Wildcatters Fund (IPAA Wildcatters Fund) (C00246306) *Address: same as sponsor * Treasurer: Cindy Grisso * Contact: George Yates, Chairperson*

	1993-94	1995-96	1997	Totals
Receipts	$91,835	$112,181	$24,518	$228,534
Disburse	86,107	125,596	26,996	238,699
Cash	16,630	3,214	735	n/a
Contributions	53,250	86,020	17,038	156,308

(Data for Independent Petroleum Association continued)

Republicans	30,000	70,770	10,538	111,308
No. of Cand.	41	62	13	116
House	15,000	52,770	6,038	73,808
Senate	15,000	18,000	4,500	37,500
Democrats	23,250	15,250	6,500	45,000
No. of Cand.	29	22	7	58
House	17,250	13,250	3,500	34,000
Senate	6,000	2,000	3,000	11,000
Incumbents	32,250	60,520	16,038	108,808
Challengers	4,000	3,000	500	7,500
Open Seat	17,000	22,500	0	39,500
Winners	45,750	79,020	n/a	124,770
Losers	7,500	7,000	n/a	14,500

International Association of Drilling Contractors

*Phone: (281) 578-7171 * Fax: (281) 578-0589*
P.O. Box 4287, 15810 Park Ten Place, Suite 242, Houston, TX 77084-5139
Web: www.iadc.org

The International Association of Drilling Contractors represents about 1,000 members of the worldwide oil and gas drilling industry. Its goal is to promote commitment to safety, preservation of the environment and advances in drilling technology.

Established in 1940, its members include companies involved in oil and gas exploration and production, well servicing, oil field manufacturing and other rig site services. IADC also operates in Europe, South America, Africa, Asia, Australia and the Middle East.

In 1998, IADC and the offshore operators committee established a deep water well control task force to develop and publish guidelines on well control issues and practices in deep water drilling operations. The task force also will identify and comment on actions that could further advance deep water well control operations.

International Association of Drilling Contractors Political Action Committee (C00059329) *Phone: (202) 293-0670 * Fax: (202) 872-0047 * 1901 L St. N.W., Suite 702, Washington, DC 20036-3506 * E-mail: brian.petty@iadc.org * Treasurer: A. Lee Hunt Jr. * Contact: Brian T. Petty, Chairman*

	1993-94	1995-96	1997	Totals
Receipts	$11,791	$17,691	$8,602	$38,084
Disburse	11,620	20,040	3,571	35,231
Cash	18,218	15,870	20,902	n/a
Contributions	11,000	16,750	2,500	30,250
Republicans	7,000	16,750	1,500	25,250
No. of Cand.	12	26	2	40
House	5,500	10,750	500	16,750
Senate	1,500	6,000	1,000	8,500
Democrats	4,000	0	1,000	5,000
No. of Cand.	7	0	1	8
House	2,500	0	0	2,500
Senate	1,500	0	1,000	2,500
Incumbents	8,000	12,750	2,500	23,250
Challengers	1,000	1,000	0	2,000
Open Seat	2,000	3,000	0	5,000
Winners	7,500	16,250	n/a	23,750
Losers	3,500	500	n/a	4,000

Interstate Natural Gas Association of America

*Phone: (202) 216-5900 * Fax: (202) 216-0877*
10 G St. N.E., Suite 700, Washington, DC 20002
Web: www.ingaa.org

Interstate Natural Gas Association of America represents about 50 members of the natural gas pipeline industry.

Members include 30 U.S interstate pipelines, six Canadian interprovincial pipelines and 13 international pipeline companies.

Interstate Natural Gas Association of America Political Action Committee (C00116145) *Address: same as sponsor * Treasurer: Gay H. Friedmann*

	1993-94	1995-96	1997	Totals
Receipts	$119,874	$107,586	$51,719	$279,179
Disburse	115,081	114,159	49,502	278,742
Cash	12,039	5,464	7,600	n/a
Contributions	97,700	94,317	37,318	229,335
Republicans	42,666	70,628	21,609	134,903
No. of Cand.	56	84	27	167
House	22,650	41,401	15,609	79,660
Senate	20,016	29,227	6,000	55,243
Democrats	55,034	23,689	15,709	94,432
No. of Cand.	56	32	16	104
House	31,645	16,950	5,058	53,653
Senate	23,389	6,739	10,651	40,779
Incumbents	82,176	77,821	35,968	195,965
Challengers	3,500	3,250	0	6,750
Open Seat	12,024	12,946	1,350	26,320
Winners	77,088	75,924	n/a	153,012
Losers	20,612	18,393	n/a	39,005

KN Energy Inc.

Phone: (303) 989-1740
370 Van Gordon St., P.O. Box 281304, Lakewood, CO 80228
*Web: www.knenergy.com * E-mail: kne_web@kne.com*

KN Energy provides natural gas to more than 210,000 customers in Colorado, Nebraska and Wyoming. It also operates more than 8,800 miles of pipelines in the western and mid-continent United States. In addition, KN runs 19 natural gas processing plants and seven storage facilities. The publicly traded company posted 1997 sales of $2.2 billion.

In October 1997, the company announced that it planned to sell its Kansas retail gas distribution properties to MidWest Energy Inc. during the first half of 1998. Then, in January 1998, KN purchased MidCon Corp. from Occidental Petroleum for $3.5 billion.

Locations of KN's 62 subsidiary operations include: Wyoming, Texas, Illinois, Colorado, Nebraska and Mexico.

EN PAC, The KN Energy Inc. Political Action Committee (C00103028) *Address: Same as sponsor * Treasurer: Stuart L. Wheeler * Contact: Larry D. Hall, Chairman, President & CEO*

	1993-94	1995-96	1997	Totals
Receipts	$27,491	$37,452	$20,281	$85,224
Disburse	28,916	33,667	14,000	76,583
Cash	276	4,070	10,356	n/a
Contributions	10,116	21,970	13,000	45,086
Republicans	7,266	19,054	11,000	37,320
No. of Cand.	9	18	6	33
House	6,266	12,000	6,000	24,266
Senate	1,000	7,054	5,000	13,054
Democrats	2,850	2,916	2,000	7,766
No. of Cand.	2	2	3	7
House	0	250	1,000	1,250
Senate	2,850	2,666	1,000	6,516
Incumbents	4,766	9,750	13,000	27,516
Challengers	0	1,000	0	1,000
Open Seat	5,350	11,220	0	16,570
Winners	8,266	16,804	n/a	25,070
Losers	1,850	5,166	n/a	7,016

MidCon Corp. PAC (C00147256) *Phone: (713) 963-3100 * Fax: (713) 963-3087 * 3100 Southwest Fwy., Houston, TX 77027-7523 * Treasurer: James J. McElligott * Contact: John F. Riordan, Chairman*

*Phone: (202) 857-3000 * Fax: (202) 857-3040 * 1717 Pennsylvania Ave. N.W., Suite 400, Washington, DC 20006-4603*

	1993-94	1995-96	1997	Totals
Receipts	$32,584	$29,643	$13,999	$76,226
Disburse	40,965	37,774	13,000	91,739
Cash	14,649	6,525	7,525	n/a
Contributions	27,750	25,250	8,500	61,500
Republicans	16,000	21,750	6,500	44,250
No. of Cand.	19	24	9	52
House	9,000	18,750	6,500	34,250
Senate	7,000	3,000	0	10,000
Democrats	11,750	3,500	2,000	17,250
No. of Cand.	15	5	3	23
House	5,750	1,500	2,000	9,250
Senate	6,000	2,000	0	8,000
Incumbents	23,750	21,250	8,500	53,500
Challengers	2,000	0	0	2,000
Open Seat	2,000	4,000	0	6,000
Winners	23,250	21,250	n/a	44,500
Losers	4,500	4,000	n/a	8,500

Koch Industries Inc.

*Phone: (316) 828-8053 * Fax: (316) 828-7976*
4111 E. 37th St. N., Wichita, KS 67220

Koch Industries of Wichita, Kan., is the second largest privately held corporation in the U.S., with more than 13,000 employees worldwide. It is run by Charles Koch, a billionaire GOP fundraiser, and his brother David, who provides money for The Cato Institute. Koch refines about 4 percent of the gasoline produced in the U.S. at its two refineries. The company also owns 40,000 miles of pipeline and 450,000 acres of cattle-ranching land. Forbes magazine estimated Koch's 1997 revenues at $30 billion.

Koch produces crude oil and natural gas, high-performance plastics and benzene. Its mining division makes cement and other construction products, and its agricultural division includes cattle ranching and feed processing. Koch is a co-owner of ExSeed Genetics, a developer of genetic agricultural products.

Koch supported only a handful of Democratic candidates in 1996. Kansas Republicans received more than $50,000 from this PAC, which tended to give the most to candidates from around the Midwest. Koch ranked third among oil and gas producers in congressional contributions in 1995-96, ahead of industry giants Texaco and Mobil.

Koch Industries Inc. Political Action Committee (KochPAC) (C00236489) *Phone: (202) 737-1977 * Fax: (202) 737-8111 * 1450 G St. N.W., Suite 445, Washington, DC 20005-2001 * Web: www.kochind.com * Treasurer: Kimberlyrenee Kehoe*

	1993-94	1995-96	1997	Totals
Receipts	$202,392	$428,074	$389,764	$1,020,230
Disburse	191,055	428,664	129,222	748,941
Cash	27,252	26,663	287,158	n/a
Contributions	133,449	294,500	73,000	500,949
Republicans	115,199	281,500	62,000	458,699
No. of Cand.	*41*	*92*	*43*	*176*
House	52,599	170,000	50,500	273,099
Senate	62,600	111,500	11,500	185,600
Democrats	16,750	13,000	9,500	39,250
No. of Cand.	*18*	*15*	*6*	*39*
House	15,500	12,000	4,500	32,000
Senate	1,250	1,000	5,000	7,250
Incumbents	35,599	142,000	70,000	247,599
Challengers	34,500	26,500	500	61,500
Open Seat	63,350	125,000	2,500	190,850
Winners	114,199	248,500	n/a	362,699
Losers	19,250	46,000	n/a	65,250

Contributed less than $5,000 during 1995-96 cycle:

Delhi Gas Pipeline Corp. PAC (formerly known as Texas Oil & Gas Corp. PAC) (C00115345) *Phone: (214) 954-2000 * Fax: (214) 954-2032 * 1700 Pacific Ave., Dallas, TX 75201-4696 * Treasurer: Kimberlyrenee Kehoe * Contact: Gene Gradick, Chairman*

MCN Energy Group

*Phone: (313) 256-5108 * Fax: (313) 965-6128*
500 Griswold St., 11th Floor, Detroit, MI 48226
Web: www.mcnenergy.com

MCN Energy Group's subsidiary, Michigan Consolidated Gas Co., distributes natural gas to 1.2 million customers in more than 500 communities throughout Michigan.

The publicly traded MCN Energy Group's other principal subsidiary, MCN Investment Corp., is involved in oil and gas exploration and production, gas gathering, transmission, processing and storage, energy marketing and electric power generation and distribution.

MCN Energy Group posted 1997 sales of $2.2 billion and employs about 3,200 people.

MCN Energy Group Federal Political Action Committee (C00159418) *Address: same as sponsor * Treasurer: William K. McCrackin * Contact: Renze Hoeksema, Dir. of Public Policy*

	1993-94	1995-96	1997	Totals
Receipts	$96,889	$128,070	$68,660	$293,619
Disburse	128,038	118,491	52,583	299,112
Cash	24,600	34,181	50,261	n/a
Contributions	97,016	89,035	37,000	223,051
Republicans	17,325	36,435	21,100	74,860
No. of Cand.	*12*	*21*	*21*	*54*
House	10,825	26,435	13,100	50,360
Senate	6,500	10,000	8,000	24,500
Democrats	78,691	52,600	15,900	147,191
No. of Cand.	*36*	*28*	*10*	*74*
House	55,941	42,600	15,900	114,441
Senate	22,750	10,000	0	32,750
Incumbents	72,816	81,985	36,500	191,301
Challengers	1,500	5,050	500	7,050
Open Seat	22,700	2,000	0	24,700
Winners	65,366	79,235	n/a	144,601
Losers	31,650	9,800	n/a	41,450

Mid-Continent Oil & Gas Association

*Phone: (202) 638-4400 * Fax: (202) 638-5967*
801 Pennsylvania Ave. N.W., Suite 840, Washington, DC 20004

The Mid-Continent Oil & Gas Association represents about 3,500 oil and gas companies of all sizes. Members include Mobil, Exxon, Texaco, Kerr-McGee, Conoco and small, independent producers.

Mid-Continent Oil & Gas Association Political Action Committee (Mid PAC) (C00111427) *Address: same as sponsor * Treasurer: Albert L. Modiano*

	1993-94	1995-96	1997	Totals
Receipts	$16,443	$32,865	$18,475	$67,783
Disburse	16,313	20,358	10,492	47,163
Cash	6,543	19,048	27,030	n/a
Contributions	9,750	13,750	6,000	29,500
Republicans	3,750	10,750	1,500	16,000
No. of Cand.	*5*	*14*	*2*	*21*
House	1,750	5,750	500	8,000
Senate	2,000	5,000	1,000	8,000
Democrats	6,000	3,000	4,500	13,500
No. of Cand.	*9*	*4*	*6*	*19*
House	6,000	2,500	1,500	10,000
Senate	0	500	3,000	3,500
Incumbents	9,250	10,250	6,000	25,500
Challengers	0	0	0	0
Open Seat	500	3,500	0	4,000
Winners	9,750	12,750	n/a	22,500
Losers	0	1,000	n/a	1,000

Contributed less than $5,000 during 1995-96 cycle:

Mid-Continent Oil & Gas Association MS/AL Division PAC (MidCon PAC) (formerly known as Dix PAC) (C00120808) *Phone: (601) 948-8903 * 210 E. Capitol St., Suite 1156, Jackson, MS 39201-2301 * Treasurer: Joseph K. Sims*

Mitchell Energy & Development Corp.

*Phone: (713) 377-6170 * Fax: (713) 377-7138*
2001 Timberloch, The Woodlands, TX 77380
Web: www.mitchellenergy.com

Mitchell Energy & Development is an oil and gas producer and a real estate developer in the Houston-Galveston area. Its energy-related operations include exploration and production of natural gas and crude oil, production of natural gas liquids and the operation of gas gathering systems. The company has substantial real estate holdings, mostly within a 50-mile radius of Houston.

Founded in 1946, Mitchell Energy's largest, most important producing area is the Fort Worth Basin in north Texas, accounting for nearly half its production and reserves. A public company with 1,100 employees, Mitchell had 1997 revenues of $800 million.

In February 1998, Mitchell Energy announced that it had significantly expanded its 3-D seismic survey program. Seismic expenditures will increase almost 50 percent in 1998 compared with the previous year. A computer survey tool has increased drilling success by 60 to 80 percent in north Texas and Louisiana.

Mitchell Energy & Development Corp. Political Action Committee (C00087965) *Address: same as sponsor * Treasurer: Koy L. Kragh * Contact: Bob Stout, Chairman*

	1993-94	1995-96	1997	Totals
Receipts	$24,738	$21,266	$10,100	$56,104
Disburse	22,135	23,366	10,548	56,049
Cash	3,132	1,032	585	n/a
Contributions	9,000	8,500	2,000	19,500
Republicans	7,500	8,500	2,000	18,000
No. of Cand.	*8*	*7*	*2*	*17*
House	4,500	8,500	1,000	14,000
Senate	3,000	0	1,000	4,000
Democrats	1,500	0	0	1,500
No. of Cand.	*3*	*0*	*0*	*3*
House	1,500	0	0	1,500
Senate	0	0	0	0
Incumbents	6,500	5,000	2,000	13,500
Challengers	1,000	0	0	1,000
Open Seat	1,500	3,500	0	5,000
Winners	7,500	6,500	n/a	14,000
Losers	1,500	2,000	n/a	3,500

Mobil Corp.

*Phone: (703) 846-3000 * Fax: (703) 846-4669*
3225 Gallows Rd., Fairfax, VA 22037
Web: www.mobil.com

One of the world's preeminent oil companies, Mobil has energy and chemical operations in more than 125 countries. The publicly traded company has 43,000 employees and posted 1997 sales of $65 billion.

Mobil finds and produces crude oil and natural gas, manufactures liquefied natural gas and markets all three. It produces crude oil in North America, Europe, Nigeria and Indonesia and is expanding into West Africa, Eastern Canada, Central Asia, Qatar, the Asia-Pacific region and South America.

The company operates five U.S. oil refineries located in Beaumont, Texas; Chalmette, La.; Joliet, Ill.; Paulsboro, N.J.; and Torrance, Calif. It also markets gasoline in 28 states and Washington, D.C.

Mobil also makes basic petrochemicals that form the building blocks of thousands of consumer products, such as plastic bags, milk bottles, toys and synthetic lubricants. Mobil has plans to expand its core chemical businesses, particularly aromatics products, such as paraxylene, and ethylene derivatives, such as polyethylene.

Mobil Corp. Political Action Committee (also known as Mobil PAC) (C00095406) *Address: same as sponsor * Treasurer: Mary Ellen Reardon*

	1993-94	1995-96	1997	Totals
Receipts	$226,918	$238,682	$125,246	$590,846
Disburse	248,789	205,948	32,894	487,631
Cash	25,341	58,075	150,426	n/a
Contributions	210,000	134,250	27,000	371,250
Republicans	181,500	130,750	18,000	330,250
No. of Cand.	*143*	*141*	*12*	*296*
House	92,000	69,250	8,000	169,250
Senate	89,500	61,500	10,000	161,000
Democrats	27,750	3,500	9,000	40,250
No. of Cand.	*33*	*5*	*3*	*41*
House	26,750	3,500	1,000	31,250
Senate	1,000	0	8,000	9,000
Incumbents	113,250	86,250	27,000	226,500
Challengers	32,250	16,500	0	48,750
Open Seat	64,500	31,500	0	96,000
Winners	185,750	102,500	n/a	288,250
Losers	24,250	31,750	n/a	56,000

Murphy Oil Corp.

*Phone: (870) 862-6411 * Fax: (870) 864-6220*
P.O. Box 602, El Dorado, AR 71731-0602
Web: www.murphyoilcorp.com

Murphy Oil operates oil refineries and explores for natural gas and oil worldwide. The publicly held company reported $2.1 billion in 1997 revenues.

In the United States, the company owns and operates a refinery on the Mississippi River at Meraux, La., which produces refined petroleum products for distribution over an 11-state area in the Gulf Coast market. It also owns and operates a refinery in Superior, Wis., which serves a five-state area in the upper Midwest. The company employs 1,340 people.

Murphy explores for and produces oil and natural gas in Canada, the United Kingdom sector of the North Sea, Spain and Ecuador. In addition, Murphy conducts an ongoing worldwide exploration program, which is currently concentrating on Peru and Pakistan.

Murphy Oil is drilling in Bo Hai Bay, off the coast of China and, in mid-1998, will begin drilling in the North Falklands Basin in the South Atlantic.

Murphy Oil Corp. PAC (formerly known as Murphy Oil USA PAC (MurPAC)) (C00145722) *Address: same as sponsor * Treasurer: Kevin G. Fitzgerald * Contact: Claiborne P. Deming, Chairman*

	1993-94	1995-96	1997	Totals
Receipts	$1,458	$34,026	$291	$35,775
Disburse	2,035	22,580	6,240	30,855
Cash	9,406	20,855	14,906	n/a
Contributions	2,000	11,000	5,000	18,000
Republicans	2,000	1,500	0	3,500
No. of Cand.	*2*	*2*	*0*	*4*
House	1,000	500	0	1,500
Senate	1,000	1,000	0	2,000
Democrats	0	9,500	5,000	14,500
No. of Cand.	*0*	*4*	*1*	*5*
House	0	1,000	0	1,000
Senate	0	8,500	5,000	13,500
Incumbents	0	0	5,000	5,000
Challengers	1,000	0	0	1,000
Open Seat	1,000	11,000	0	12,000
Winners	0	6,000	n/a	6,000
Losers	2,000	5,000	n/a	7,000

NATSO Inc.

Phone: (703) 549-2100
1199 N. Fairfax St., Suite 801, Alexandria, VA 22314
Web: www.natso.com

NATSO, formerly the National Association of Truck Stop Operators, is a professional association representing the $35 billion travel plaza and truck stop industry.

Founded in 1960 by truck stop operators as a way to manage credit information on their customers, the association now acts as the representative body of the entire truck stop and travel plaza industry. The organization provides information about the industry, holds an annual convention attended by about 2,000 industry members and represents the industry in Washington on legislative and regulatory matters.

NATSO tracks issues such as transportation spending, fuel tax evasion and Native American tax compliance.

NATSO/PAC (C00097865) *Phone: (202) 554-2510 * Fax: (202) 554-2520 * 499 S. Capitol St. S.W., Suite 502, Washington, DC 20003 * E-mail: seimus@natso.com * Treasurer: W. Dewey Clower * Contact: Scot Imus, V.P. of Gov. Affairs*

	1993-94	1995-96	1997	Totals
Receipts	$49,356	$71,640	$42,868	$163,864
Disburse	47,678	82,323	15,406	145,407
Cash	16,572	5,890	33,353	n/a
Contributions	40,000	74,500	12,500	127,000
Republicans	22,000	50,500	8,000	80,500
No. of Cand.	*30*	*52*	*13*	*95*
House	14,500	43,500	7,500	65,500
Senate	7,500	7,000	500	15,000
Democrats	17,000	24,000	3,500	44,500
No. of Cand.	*23*	*21*	*5*	*49*
House	14,500	18,000	3,500	36,000
Senate	2,500	6,000	0	8,500
Incumbents	38,000	69,500	13,000	120,500
Challengers	0	0	0	0
Open Seat	2,000	5,000	0	7,000
Winners	36,000	67,500	n/a	103,500
Losers	4,000	7,000	n/a	11,000

NICOR Inc.

*Phone: (630) 983-8676 * Fax: (630) 548-3574*
1844 Ferry Rd., Naperville, IL 60563-9600
Web: www.nicorinc.com

NICOR's primary subsidiary, Northern Illinois Gas, is the fifth-largest natural gas distribution company in the United States. NICOR also owns Tropical Shipping, which transports containerized freight between West Palm Beach, Fla. and 26 ports in the Caribbean.

NICOR PAC deals mostly with state legislatures and has little activity at the federal level.

Northern Illinois Gas distributes natural gas to about 1.9 million customers in northern Illinois, excluding Chicago. The utility earned 91 percent of NICOR's operating income in 1996. Operating revenues for 1997 were about $2 billion.

In July 1997, NICOR announced agreement on a letter of intent to join Calgary-based TransCanada PipeLines Limited and Minneapolis-based Northern States Power Co. as a 20 percent partner in the Viking Voyageur Gas Transmission project, a $1 billion pipeline designed to transport natural gas from the Canadian border to the Midwest.

NICOR Inc. Political Action Committee (C00164970) *Address: same as sponsor * Treasurer: D. Scott Lewis*

	1993-94	1995-96	1997	Totals
Receipts	$6,491	$9,264	$4,852	$20,607
Disburse	9,425	9,250	4,179	22,854
Cash	2,072	2,090	2,763	n/a
Contributions	8,175	6,250	3,000	17,425

Republicans	5,425	5,750	2,500	13,675
No. of Cand.	*8*	*10*	*5*	*23*
House	5,425	5,050	2,000	12,475
Senate	0	700	500	1,200
Democrats	2,750	500	500	3,750
No. of Cand.	*5*	*2*	*1*	*8*
House	1,250	500	500	2,250
Senate	1,500	0	0	1,500
Incumbents	7,925	5,550	3,000	16,475
Challengers	0	0	0	0
Open Seat	250	700	0	950
Winners	8,175	5,300	n/a	13,475
Losers	0	950	n/a	950

National Fuel Gas Co.

*Phone: (716) 857-7705 * Fax: (716) 857-7413*
10 Lafayette Sq., Room 900, Buffalo, NY 14203
Web: www.natfuel.com

National Fuel Gas transports and markets natural gas to 700,000 customers in northwestern Pennsylvania and western New York. Headquartered in Buffalo, N.Y., the publicly traded company had 1997 sales of $1.3 billion and employs more than 2,500 workers.

The company's $2.1 billion in assets is distributed among four major business segments: utility, pipeline and storage, exploration and production and other nonregulated activities. Unregulated activities include pipeline construction, sawmill and dry kiln operations and natural gas marketing and brokerage.

National Fuel Gas Supply, a major subsidiary, stores and transports gas. Subsidiary Senneca Resources explores, develops and buys oil in California, Texas, Louisiana and the Appalachian area.

National Fuel Gas Federal Political Action Committee (NFG FedPAC) (C00083758) *Address: same as sponsor * Treasurer: Richard C. Fiorello * Contact: Nancy J. Cantoni, Chairwoman*

	1993-94	1995-96	1997	Totals
Receipts	$51,191	$55,241	$30,843	$137,275
Disburse	47,267	58,467	25,935	131,669
Cash	8,740	5,600	10,507	n/a
Contributions	38,350	49,882	22,275	110,507
Republicans	23,950	40,882	16,275	81,107
No. of Cand.	*14*	*30*	*17*	*61*
House	17,950	31,882	11,775	61,607
Senate	6,000	9,000	4,500	19,500
Democrats	14,400	9,000	6,000	29,400
No. of Cand.	*15*	*10*	*11*	*36*
House	9,500	6,000	3,000	18,500
Senate	4,900	3,000	3,000	10,900
Incumbents	33,790	47,075	22,275	103,140
Challengers	3,000	0	0	3,000
Open Seat	1,560	2,807	0	4,367
Winners	36,700	46,382	n/a	83,082
Losers	1,650	3,500	n/a	5,150

National Propane Gas Association

Phone: (630) 515-0600
1600 Eisenhower Ln., Suite 100, Lisle, IL 60532
Web: www.propanegas.com

The National Propane Gas Association represents 3,600 members of the U.S. liquefied petroleum industry. It also has 200 international members from 26 countries.

The group represents all businesses associated with the industry, including retail marketers, producers, wholesale distributors, appliance and equipment manufacturers, equipment fabricators and distributors and transporters of liquefied petroleum gas. NPGA provides its members with representation in Washington, conventions, trade shows, seminars, training, consumer safety programs and a voice in the national standards-setting process.

National Propane Gas Association Political Action Committee (PropanePAC) (C00079681) *Phone: (202) 466-7200 * Fax: (202) 466-7205 * 1101 17th St. N.W., Suite 1004, Washington, DC 20036 * Treasurer: Daniel N. Myers * Contact: Wilfred Otero, Political Affairs Coordinator*

	1993-94	1995-96	1997	Totals
Receipts	$32,910	$37,620	$23,726	$94,256
Disburse	24,863	46,935	15,461	87,259
Cash	18,223	8,908	17,172	n/a
Contributions	24,700	46,632	15,461	86,793

Republicans	14,050	40,282	14,961	69,293
No. of Cand.	*24*	*50*	*15*	*89*
House	5,200	26,527	6,250	37,977
Senate	8,850	13,755	8,711	31,316
Democrats	10,650	6,350	500	17,500
No. of Cand.	*14*	*11*	*1*	*26*
House	9,000	5,850	500	15,350
Senate	1,650	500	0	2,150
Incumbents	17,350	38,432	8,250	64,032
Challengers	0	2,000	7,211	9,211
Open Seat	7,350	6,200	0	13,550
Winners	22,000	42,632	n/a	64,632
Losers	2,700	4,000	n/a	6,700

Northwest Natural Gas

*Phone: (503) 226-4211 * Fax: (503) 721-2506*
220 N.W. Second Ave., Portland, OR 97209

Northwest Natural Gas serves more than 433,000 customers in northwest Oregon and southwest Washington, including the Portland-Vancouver metropolitan area. The publicly owned company employs 1,300 workers and had $380 million in 1996 sales.

Northwest Natural Gas is seeking to expand investment in non-regulated activities, including the production, gathering and marketing of natural gas and the development of other energy-related businesses.

In July 1997, Northwest Natural Gas formed an alliance with another major Northwest energy company, PacifiCorp, to market gas and electricity in Oregon and Washington. Customers can already choose their gas supplier and many will soon be able to choose among electric companies.

Northwest Natural Gas Political Action Committee (NWNGPAC) (C00174367) *Address: same as sponsor * Treasurer: George E. Richardson Jr. * Contact: Richard Reiten, CEO*

	1993-94	1995-96	1997	Totals
Receipts	$4,948	$9,633	$7,296	$21,877
Disburse	4,541	8,970	4,860	18,371
Cash	706	1,373	3,810	n/a
Contributions	3,350	8,500	4,550	16,400
Republicans	250	3,500	0	3,750
No. of Cand.	*4*	*3*	*0*	*7*
House	1,000	750	0	1,750
Senate	-750	2,750	0	2,000
Democrats	3,100	5,000	4,550	12,650
No. of Cand.	*7*	*5*	*4*	*16*
House	3,100	2,250	4,550	9,900
Senate	0	2,750	0	2,750
Incumbents	950	3,250	4,550	8,750
Challengers	0	0	0	0
Open Seat	2,400	5,250	0	7,650
Winners	1,450	6,500	n/a	7,950
Losers	1,900	2,000	n/a	3,900

ONEOK Inc.

*Phone: (918) 588-7162 * Fax: (918) 588-7114*
100 W. Fifth St., Tulsa, OK 74103
*Web: www.oneok.com * E-mail: cvandiver@oneok.com*

ONEOK provides natural gas to about 1.4 million customers in Oklahoma and Kansas through Oklahoma Natural Gas and Kansas Gas Service. The publicly traded Tulsa, Okla. company reported sales of $1.1 billion in 1997. It employs 1,800 people.

The company owns more than 18,000 miles of pipeline and transmission lines in Oklahoma and holds interests in 15 gas processing plants.

About 80 percent of ONEOK's profits come from its gas utilities. Other subsidiaries buy, sell, produce and process natural gas in the central United States.

ONEOK Inc. Employee Political Action Committee (C00215384) *Address: same as sponsor * Treasurer: Claudia Vandiver*

	1993-94	1995-96	1997	Totals
Receipts	$40,622	$42,981	$24,483	$108,086
Disburse	40,358	41,817	11,170	93,345
Cash	4,561	5,729	19,043	n/a
Contributions	13,600	12,350	2,500	28,450
Republicans	3,250	10,650	2,500	16,400
No. of Cand.	*4*	*12*	*5*	*21*
House	3,250	6,900	2,000	12,150
Senate	0	3,750	500	4,250

(Data for ONEOK Inc. Employee continued)

Democrats	10,350	1,700	0	12,050
No. of Cand.	*14*	*2*	*0*	*16*
House	7,850	1,700	0	9,550
Senate	2,500	0	0	2,500
Incumbents	8,600	10,150	2,500	21,250
Challengers	0	1,200	0	1,200
Open Seat	5,000	1,000	0	6,000
Winners	7,000	9,150	n/a	16,150
Losers	6,600	3,200	n/a	9,800

Occidental Petroleum Corp.

*Phone: (310) 208-8800 * Fax: (310) 443-6690*
10889 Wilshire Blvd., Suite 600, Los Angeles, CA 90024
Web: www.oxy.com

Occidental Petroleum manufactures chemicals and explores for and produces oil and gas. The publicly traded Los Angeles company has 14,300 employees worldwide and reported $8 billion in 1997 revenues.

The company sold its MidCon natural gas transmission and marketing subsidiary in early 1998.

Subsidiary OxyChem produces chloro/vinyls and petrochemicals and provides custom chemical manufacturing in 3,000 categories. OxyChem is headquartered in Dallas. The oil and gas subsidiary, headquartered in Bakersfield, Calif., does most of its U.S. work in California, Kansas, Oklahoma, Louisiana, Mississippi and Texas.

Occidental Petroleum Corp. Political Action Committee (C00083857) *Address: same as sponsor * Treasurer: C. Thomas Oliver * Contact: Gerald T. McPhee, V.P. of Federal Relations*

	1993-94	1995-96	1997	Totals
Receipts	$208,547	$211,834	$149,033	$569,414
Disburse	215,190	212,259	75,962	503,411
Cash	28,370	27,953	101,025	n/a
Contributions	131,550	164,500	48,500	344,550
Republicans	43,000	109,000	29,500	181,500
No. of Cand.	*41*	*96*	*41*	*178*
House	21,500	71,000	21,500	114,000
Senate	21,500	38,000	8,000	67,500
Democrats	88,550	55,500	19,000	163,050
No. of Cand.	*53*	*43*	*19*	*115*
House	62,550	35,000	9,000	106,550
Senate	26,000	20,500	10,000	56,500
Incumbents	118,550	140,000	46,000	304,550
Challengers	1,750	4,000	500	6,250
Open Seat	11,250	20,500	2,000	33,750
Winners	96,550	141,500	n/a	238,050
Losers	35,000	23,000	n/a	58,000

Occidental Oil & Gas Corp. PAC (OOGPAC) (also known as Cities Service Oil & Gas Corp. PAC) (C00035527) *Phone: (918) 561-2211 * 110 W. Seventh St., Tulsa, OK 74119 * Treasurer: Christopher R. Jolley*

Occidental Oil and Gas Corp. PAC was terminated in October 1997.

	1993-94	1995-96	1997	Totals
Receipts	$59,924	$57,996	$18,495	$136,415
Disburse	57,841	37,817	44,462	140,120
Cash	5,771	25,962	0	n/a
Contributions	34,850	17,250	500	52,600
Republicans	29,350	17,250	500	47,100
No. of Cand.	*45*	*25*	*1*	*71*
House	15,850	13,750	500	30,100
Senate	13,500	3,500	0	17,000
Democrats	5,500	0	0	5,500
No. of Cand.	*8*	*2*	*0*	*10*
House	5,500	0	0	5,500
Senate	0	0	0	0
Incumbents	15,000	12,750	500	28,250
Challengers	9,000	1,000	0	10,000
Open Seat	10,850	3,500	0	14,350
Winners	29,850	17,250	n/a	47,100
Losers	5,000	0	n/a	5,000

Oryx Energy Co.

*Phone: (972) 715-8942 * Fax: (972) 715-3311*
P.O. Box 2880, Dallas, TX 75221
Web: www.oryx.com

Oryx Energy is a global oil and natural gas exploration, production and marketing company. Based in Dallas, the publicly traded company has operations in Oklahoma and the Gulf of Mexico. Oryx had 1997 revenues of $1.2 billion and employs about 1,000 workers.

Oryx Energy entered into a five-year contract with Noble Drilling for deep water exploration and drilling. The program involves the use of a deep water semi-submersible drilling rig capable of drilling in water depths of up to 6,000 feet.

Oryx Energy conducts its domestic business under the name Sun Energy Partners.

Oryx Energy Co. Political Action Committee (Oryx Energy PAC) (C00234773) *Address: same as sponsor * Treasurer: J. Sharon Russell * Contact: William Lemmer, Chairman*

	1993-94	1995-96	1997	Totals
Receipts	$38,615	$31,795	$17,370	$87,780
Disburse	42,437	29,649	600	72,686
Cash	3,142	5,291	22,062	n/a
Contributions	33,750	25,000	500	59,250
Republicans	24,000	23,000	500	47,500
No. of Cand.	*30*	*29*	*1*	*60*
House	12,500	14,000	500	27,000
Senate	11,500	9,000	0	20,500
Democrats	9,750	2,000	0	11,750
No. of Cand.	*18*	*4*	*0*	*22*
House	7,750	2,000	0	9,750
Senate	2,000	0	0	2,000
Incumbents	19,000	13,000	500	32,500
Challengers	5,500	1,000	0	6,500
Open Seat	8,750	11,000	0	19,750
Winners	29,500	22,000	n/a	51,500
Losers	4,250	3,000	n/a	7,250

Pacific Enterprises Companies

*Phone: (213) 244-2530 * Fax: (213) 244-4997*
555 W. Fifth St., ML 28H5, Los Angeles, CA 90013-1011
Web: www.pacent.com

Pacific Enterprises' subsidiary, Southern California Gas Co., is the nation's largest natural gas distribution utility. SCGC supplies natural gas to 17 million customers throughout most of southern and part of central California.

Through other subsidiaries, Pacific Enterprises is engaged in interstate and offshore natural gas transmission to serve its utility operations; alternate energy development; centralized heating and cooling for large building complexes; and natural gas distribution operations in Latin America.

In October 1997, Pacific Enterprises announced that it would be merging with the Enova Corp. As of March 1998, the company expected the transaction to be finished by the summer. The resulting company will be named Sempra Energy.

Pacific Enterprises Companies Political Action Team (C00008748) *Phone: (202) 662-1705 * 1001 G St. N.W., Sixth Floor East, Washington, DC 20001 * Treasurer: Carolyn R. Williams*

*Contact: Jan Porush, PAC Administrator * Phone: (213) 244-2530*

	1993-94	1995-96	1997	Totals
Receipts	$92,486	$109,207	$60,295	$261,988
Disburse	141,900	108,175	48,625	298,700
Cash	35,687	35,821	47,492	n/a
Contributions	120,000	69,600	41,500	231,100
Republicans	33,600	45,800	18,300	97,700
No. of Cand.	*28*	*40*	*17*	*85*
House	19,600	31,800	9,300	60,700
Senate	14,000	14,000	9,000	37,000
Democrats	86,400	23,800	23,200	133,400
No. of Cand.	*50*	*23*	*17*	*90*
House	56,400	24,800	14,700	95,900
Senate	30,000	-1,000	8,500	37,500
Incumbents	112,000	63,875	37,500	213,375
Challengers	1,000	1,475	3,000	5,475
Open Seat	7,000	4,250	1,000	12,250
Winners	106,000	67,600	n/a	173,600
Losers	14,000	2,000	n/a	16,000

Pennzoil Co.

*Phone: (713) 546-4000 * Fax: (713) 546-6247*
Pennzoil Place, 700 Milam St., Houston, TX 77002
Web: www.pzl.com

Pennzoil makes the No. 1 brand of oil in the United States and owns Jiffy Lube, the largest chain of oil change centers nationwide. The publicly traded company also explores for and produces oil and gas. Sales for 1996 were $2.3 billion and the company employed more than 10,000 workers.

Pennzoil Exploration and Production Co. conducts the majority of Pennzoil's oil and gas exploration and production operations. In 1997, the company acquired a fifth oil exploration site in Egypt.

In February 1998, the Department of Justice sued four major oil companies for failure to pay the full amount of tax on the oil they extracted from federal or Native American land. An additional group of 10 companies, including Pennzoil, are under investigation, but no charges had been filed as of February 1998.

Pennzoil Political Action Committee (C00060079) *Address: same as sponsor * Treasurer: Robert L. Springfield * Contact: James Shaddix, PAC Chairman*

	1993-94	1995-96	1997	Totals
Receipts	$70,935	$19,235	$24,227	$114,397
Disburse	68,924	63,359	23,722	156,005
Cash	52,100	17,809	18,314	n/a
Contributions	49,300	27,000	19,500	95,800
Republicans	20,400	19,500	10,500	50,400
No. of Cand.	*23*	*30*	*14*	*67*
House	13,400	12,000	5,500	30,900
Senate	7,000	7,500	5,000	19,500
Democrats	28,900	7,500	9,000	45,400
No. of Cand.	*30*	*11*	*9*	*50*
House	15,400	5,500	2,000	22,900
Senate	13,500	2,000	7,000	22,500
Incumbents	46,000	24,500	18,500	89,000
Challengers	1,800	0	0	1,800
Open Seat	1,500	1,500	1,000	4,000
Winners	41,800	21,000	n/a	62,800
Losers	7,500	6,000	n/a	13,500

Petroleum Marketers Association of America

*Phone: (703) 351-8000 * Fax: (703) 351-9160*
1901 N. Fort Myer Dr., Suite 1200, Arlington, VA 22209-1604
*Web: www.pmaa.org * E-mail: srdodge@pmaa.org*

The Petroleum Marketers Association of America is a federation of 41 state and regional trade associations representing about 10,000 gas stations and convenience stores nationwide. Collectively, these businesses sell about half the gasoline, 60 percent of the diesel fuel and 80 percent of the home heating oil consumed in America annually. The association's members employ about 300,000 workers nationwide.

The PMAA lobbies on fuel storage tanks, gasoline tax policy, workplace safety and transportation issues. It supports a proposal that would transfer most of the money for the Leaking Underground Storage Tank program to the states and give states more flexibility in spending it. The group favors a four-year moratorium on new ozone/particulate matter standards from the EPA. The group backs the formation of the National Oilheat Research Alliance, an industry organization, and opposes restrictions on tobacco sales by convenience stores.

The top PAC contributor to 1996 congressional campaigns among gas station organizations, the PMAA spent nearly 88 percent of its money on Republican candidates. The top recipients were Sen. Gordon Smith, R-Ore., and Reps. Rick White, R-Wash., and David McIntosh, R-Ind. Each received at least $7,000. Rep. Barbara Kennelly, D-Conn., was the top Democratic recipient.

The PMAA has two affiliated state PACs, in Illinois and Alabama.

Petroleum Marketers Association of America/Small Business Committee (C00035204) *Address: same as sponsor * Treasurer: Phillip R. Chisholm * Contact: Sarah Ryan Dodge, Dir. of Legislative Affairs*

	1993-94	1995-96	1997	Totals
Receipts	$272,077	$261,331	$136,740	$670,148
Disburse	210,276	343,765	113,659	667,700
Cash	86,627	4,191	27,271	n/a
Contributions	189,725	275,888	79,331	544,944
Republicans	115,255	240,188	69,581	425,024
No. of Cand.	*120*	*177*	*66*	*363*
House	82,355	184,438	45,681	312,474
Senate	32,900	55,750	23,900	112,550
Democrats	74,470	35,700	9,500	119,670
No. of Cand.	*91*	*53*	*19*	*163*
House	63,600	35,400	10,000	109,000
Senate	10,870	300	-500	10,670
Incumbents	132,670	231,892	71,831	436,393
Challengers	30,105	7,500	1,000	38,605
Open Seat	32,150	35,996	6,500	74,646
Winners	147,594	245,242	n/a	392,836
Losers	42,131	30,646	n/a	72,777

Illinois Marketers Political Action Committee (C00096743) *Phone: (217) 544-4609 * P.O. Box 3662, Springfield, IL 62708 * Treasurer: Carl Adams Jr.*

	1993-94	1995-96	1997	Totals
Receipts	$10,558	$13,128	$4,265	$27,951
Disburse	4,127	16,153	2,978	23,258
Cash	6,522	3,491	4,778	n/a
Contributions	3,800	15,900	2,900	22,600
Republicans	2,500	12,700	2,900	18,100
No. of Cand.	*8*	*13*	*6*	*27*
House	2,500	10,200	3,400	16,100
Senate	0	2,500	-500	2,000
Democrats	1,300	3,200	0	4,500
No. of Cand.	*3*	*4*	*0*	*7*
House	1,300	1,700	0	3,000
Senate	0	1,500	0	1,500
Incumbents	2,750	8,700	3,400	14,850
Challengers	0	1,200	0	1,200
Open Seat	1,050	6,000	0	7,050
Winners	3,800	10,550	n/a	14,350
Losers	0	5,350	n/a	5,350

Contributed less than $5,000 during 1995-96 cycle:

Alabama Oilmen's Association Inc. FEDPAC (AOA FEDPAC) (C00326447) *Phone: (334) 834-1044 * 400 S. Union St., Suite 395, Montgomery, AL 36104 * Treasurer: James B. Fletcher II*

Phillips Petroleum Co.

*Phone: (918) 661-5060 * Fax: (918) 661-1525*
Phillips Building, Bartlesville, OK 74004
*Web: www.phillips66.com * E-mail: mdgarbe@ppco.com*

Phillips Petroleum is a major producer of oil and gas products. The company has three U.S. oil refineries and sells Phillips 66 gasoline through 6,900 outlets in 26 states. It also owns about 300 Phillips 66 convenience stores.

The publicly traded company had sales of more than $15 billion in 1997, and employs 17,000 workers.

The company's operations include oil and natural gas exploration and production; gas gathering, processing and marketing; oil refining, transporting and marketing; and the manufacture of natural gas and petroleum-based chemicals. The chemicals unit produces petrochemicals and plastics such as ethylene, polyethylene, polypropylene and K-Resin copolymers.

Phillips has oil and gas properties in 20 countries and conducts exploration and production activities in six: Canada, China, Nigeria, Norway, the United Kingdom and the United States.

Phillips Petroleum Co. Political Action Committee (C00112896) *Address: same as sponsor * Treasurer: Michael A. Pregler * Contact: Martin Garber, Chairman*

	1993-94	1995-96	1997	Totals
Receipts	$282,649	$256,669	$119,531	$658,849
Disburse	277,683	269,399	47,777	594,859
Cash	105,489	92,756	164,509	n/a
Contributions	165,046	168,600	30,500	364,146
Republicans	120,748	158,000	27,500	306,248
No. of Cand.	*102*	*121*	*24*	*247*
House	79,250	107,000	9,500	195,750
Senate	41,498	51,000	18,000	110,498
Democrats	44,298	10,600	3,000	57,898
No. of Cand.	*40*	*12*	*4*	*56*
House	30,299	10,600	2,000	42,899
Senate	13,999	0	1,000	14,999
Incumbents	82,049	77,600	29,500	189,149
Challengers	32,000	21,000	0	53,000
Open Seat	50,997	69,000	1,000	120,997
Winners	130,548	125,100	n/a	255,648
Losers	34,498	43,500	n/a	77,998

Popham Haik

3300 Piper Jaffray Tower, 222 9th St. S., Minneapolis, MN 55402

Popham Haik Independent Federal PAC was terminated in November 1997.

Popham Haik Independent Federal PAC (C00218636) *Address: same as sponsor * Treasurer: Robert C. Moilanen*

	1993-94	1995-96	1997	Totals
Receipts	$34,586	$21,649	$116	$56,351
Disburse	9,371	7,565	41,793	58,729
Cash	28,805	40,526	0	n/a
Contributions	8,993	4,592	2,100	15,685
Republicans	728	500	700	1,928
No. of Cand.	*2*	*1*	*2*	*5*
House	628	500	700	1,828
Senate	100	0	0	100
Democrats	6,765	4,092	750	11,607
No. of Cand.	*7*	*4*	*3*	*14*
House	3,127	4,092	750	7,969
Senate	3,638	0	0	3,638
Incumbents	2,186	4,342	2,100	8,628
Challengers	500	250	0	750
Open Seat	6,307	0	0	6,307
Winners	2,981	4,342	n/a	7,323
Losers	6,012	250	n/a	6,262

Santa Fe International Corp.

*Phone: (972) 701-7300 * Fax: (972) 701-7600*
5420 LBJ Freeway, Suite 1100, Two Lincoln Centre, Dallas, TX 75240
Web: www.sfdrill.com

Santa Fe Communications is a subsidiary of Santa Fe International, an international offshore and land contract driller. In 1997, the publicly traded company had sales of $578 million and 5,500 employees.

Santa Fe International explores for oil worldwide, with its primary focus on the Middle East, South America and North Africa. It owns and operates a fleet of 26 marine drilling rigs and 28 land drilling rigs located in 16 countries.

Santa Fe Communications Inc. Political Action Committee (C00092304) *Address: same as sponsor * Treasurer: Donald G. Barber * Contact: Sted Garber, President and CEO*

	1993-94	1995-96	1997	Totals
Receipts	$18,922	$24,580	$2,797	$46,299
Disburse	19,146	18,700	300	38,146
Cash	775	2,459	4,958	n/a
Contributions	19,100	17,200	300	36,600
Republicans	17,100	17,200	300	34,600
No. of Cand.	*16*	*20*	*1*	*37*
House	8,400	1,400	300	10,100
Senate	8,700	15,800	0	24,500
Democrats	2,000	0	0	2,000
No. of Cand.	*3*	*0*	*0*	*3*
House	1,000	0	0	1,000
Senate	1,000	0	0	1,000
Incumbents	5,900	4,200	300	10,400
Challengers	6,000	3,000	0	9,000
Open Seat	7,200	10,000	0	17,200
Winners	14,600	9,600	n/a	24,200
Losers	4,500	7,600	n/a	12,100

Shell Oil Co.

Phone: (713) 241-1015
P.O. Box 2846, Houston, TX 77252-2846
Web: www.countonshell.com

With 1997 revenues of $7.1 billion, Shell Oil is the largest gasoline marketer in the United States and a leading producer of oil, natural gas and chemical products.

Shell Oil, which employs more than 20,000 workers, maintains four principal businesses. Shell Exploration and Production Co. focuses its oil and natural gas development activities in the Gulf of Mexico and along the Gulf Coast. Shell Oil Products Co. is a leading U.S. marketer of gasoline and a supplier of aviation fuel, lubricants and asphalt. It operates six refineries in the United States, including one in partnership with Pemex, the Mexican National Oil Co. Shell Chemical Co. makes base and value-added chemicals. Shell Services International provides business services related to the oil industry.

Shell Oil is the U.S. operating company of the Royal Dutch/Shell Group, the most profitable company in the world in 1996, according to Fortune magazine. Sixty percent of the Royal Dutch/Shell Group is owned by Royal Dutch Petroleum Co., while the other 40 percent is held by Shell Transport & Trading Co.

Shell purchased Transok, a Texas, Oklahoma and Louisiana pipeline company, from Central and South West Corp. in 1998. The Transok PAC will file for termination in 1998, according to the company.

Shell Oil Co. Employees' Political Awareness Committee (C00039503) *Phone: (202) 466-1405 * 1401 Eye St. N.W., Suite 1050, Washington, DC 20005 * Treasurer: George E. Meany*

	1993-94	1995-96	1997	Totals
Receipts	$124,140	$139,398	$74,097	$337,635
Disburse	123,900	135,480	73,100	332,480
Cash	11,680	15,604	16,605	n/a
Contributions	107,500	109,600	62,500	279,600
Republicans	65,250	98,600	42,500	206,350
No. of Cand.	*51*	*94*	*46*	*191*
House	32,750	67,600	27,500	127,850
Senate	32,500	31,000	15,000	78,500
Democrats	42,250	11,000	20,000	73,250
No. of Cand.	*38*	*13*	*15*	*66*
House	29,750	9,000	6,500	45,250
Senate	12,500	2,000	13,500	28,000
Incumbents	92,500	93,600	62,500	248,600
Challengers	2,000	500	0	2,500
Open Seat	12,500	15,500	0	28,000
Winners	89,500	95,800	n/a	185,300
Losers	18,000	13,800	n/a	31,800

Contributed less than $5,000 during 1995-96 cycle:

Tejas/Transok Political Action Committee (C00296616) *Phone: (918) 591-2000 * P.O. Box 3008, Tulsa, OK 74101-3008 * Treasurer: Debbie Dawson*

Society of Independent Gasoline Marketers of America

*Phone: (703) 709-7000 * Fax: (703) 709-7007*
11911 Freedom Dr., Suite 590, Reston, VA 20190

The Society of Independent Gasoline Marketers of America represents about 340 companies that market gasoline.

The organization seeks to ensure adequate supplies of gasoline at competitive prices. It also monitors legislation and regulations affecting gasoline supply and price.

Society of Independent Gasoline Marketers of America (C00120030) *Address: same as sponsor * Treasurer: Millicent Hurlbut*

	1993-94	1995-96	1997	Totals
Receipts	$42,199	$100,413	$64,895	$207,507
Disburse	37,750	48,626	39,419	125,795
Cash	7,102	58,888	84,364	n/a
Contributions	36,500	44,000	38,500	119,000
Republicans	16,500	29,750	27,500	73,750
No. of Cand.	*20*	*32*	*32*	*84*
House	15,500	27,750	23,500	66,750
Senate	1,000	2,000	4,000	7,000
Democrats	20,000	14,250	11,000	45,250
No. of Cand.	*26*	*15*	*15*	*56*
House	16,500	13,250	9,000	38,750
Senate	3,500	1,000	2,000	6,500
Incumbents	34,000	42,000	38,500	114,500
Challengers	1,000	0	0	1,000
Open Seat	1,500	2,000	0	3,500
Winners	28,000	40,500	n/a	68,500
Losers	8,500	3,500	n/a	12,000

Sonat Inc.

*Phone: (205) 325-7410 * Fax: (205) 326-2048*
1900 Fifth Ave. N., Birmingham, AL 35203
Web: www.sonat.com

Fortune 500 energy holding company Sonat reported $4.1 billion in 1997 revenue. The company's operations include domestic oil and natural gas exploration and production; natural gas transmission and storage; and natural gas and electric power marketing.

About half the firm's revenue comes from oil and gas exploration. Its subsidiary, Sonat Exploration, is the ninth-largest independent oil and gas producer in the United States and operates primarily in Texas, Oklahoma, Louisiana, Arkansas and the Gulf of Mexico.

The other half of Sonat's revenue comes mostly from its role in transporting natural gas to the Southeast through its subsidiary, Southern Natural Gas, which owns and operates 9,055 miles of pipeline. Sonat also has a 50 percent share in Citrus Corp., which owns Florida Gas.

Sonat is headquartered in Birmingham, Ala. and has major subsidiary offices in Houston.

Sonat Inc. Political Action Committee (C00050310) *Phone: (202) 347-8890 * Fax: (202) 347-1684 * 801 Pennsylvania Ave. N.W., Suite 230, Washington, DC 20004 * Treasurer: Norman G. Holmes*

	1993-94	*1995-96*	*1997*	*Totals*
Receipts	$74,555	$164,541	$76,176	$315,272
Disburse	116,521	89,752	75,521	281,794
Cash	13,284	88,075	88,734	n/a
Contributions	45,850	49,500	50,750	146,100
Republicans	22,200	43,500	40,750	106,450
No. of Cand.	*19*	*39*	*26*	*84*
House	7,700	25,500	21,750	54,950
Senate	14,500	18,000	19,000	51,500
Democrats	23,650	6,000	10,000	39,650
No. of Cand.	*24*	*7*	*12*	*43*
House	14,250	5,000	3,000	22,250
Senate	9,400	1,000	7,000	17,400
Incumbents	36,200	47,000	51,250	134,450
Challengers	1,000	1,000	0	2,000
Open Seat	9,000	1,500	-500	10,000
Winners	39,100	42,500	n/a	81,600
Losers	6,750	7,000	n/a	13,750

Southwest Gas Corp.

*Phone: (702) 876-7237 * Fax: (702) 873-3820*
P.O. Box 98510, Las Vegas, NV 89193
Web: www.swgas.com

Southwest Gas is a public natural gas utility located in Nevada. It provides natural gas to about 1.1 million customers in Nevada, Arizona and California. Southwest Gas, which has 2,400 employees, reported 1997 sales of $732 million.

Southwest Gas' subsidiary, Paiute Pipeline Co., transports natural gas to the company and its industrial customers.

Along with three other gas companies and the Department of Energy, Southwest Gas is working to develop gas-fired heating and cooling units that will lower installation and operating costs.

Southwest Gas Corp. Political Action Committee (C00076737) *Address: same as sponsor * Treasurer: Charles A. Silvestri*

	1993-94	*1995-96*	*1997*	*Totals*
Receipts	$33,890	$38,609	$22,219	$94,718
Disburse	33,300	21,455	8,300	63,055
Cash	28,203	45,358	59,277	n/a
Contributions	27,020	17,325	6,500	50,845
Republicans	15,650	14,575	5,500	35,725
No. of Cand.	*14*	*10*	*4*	*28*
House	10,150	13,575	3,000	26,725
Senate	5,500	1,000	2,500	9,000
Democrats	11,370	2,750	1,000	15,120
No. of Cand.	*8*	*5*	*1*	*14*
House	7,750	1,250	1,000	10,000
Senate	3,620	1,500	0	5,120
Incumbents	16,370	14,325	5,000	35,695
Challengers	1,200	500	500	2,200
Open Seat	8,700	2,500	1,000	12,200
Winners	17,600	15,825	n/a	33,425
Losers	9,420	1,500	n/a	10,920

Texaco Inc.

*Phone: (914) 253-4000 * Fax: (914) 253-7753*
2000 Westchester Ave., White Plains, NY 10650
Web: www.texaco.com

Texaco is the No. 3 U.S. oil and gas producer and operates 25 refineries worldwide. In 1997, the publicly traded company posted sales of $46 billion and was ranked No. 11 in the Fortune 500. Texaco employs more than 28,000 workers.

As of year-end 1996, Texaco owned or had interests in seven U.S. refineries and 18 plants abroad. The company markets Texaco-branded motor fuels through 13,550 retail outlets in the United States and about 8,500 retail outlets in Europe, Central and South America, the Caribbean and West Africa.

Texaco and its subsidiaries had an average daily net production worldwide of 787,000 barrels of crude oil and natural gas liquids and more than 2 billion cubic feet of salable natural gas in 1996.

Texaco Political Involvement Committee (C00041178) *Phone: (202) 331-1427 * 1050 17th St. N.W., Suite 500, Washington, DC 20036 * Treasurer: Barbara E. Stanley*

*Contact: Carl B. Davidson, Chairperson * Phone (914) 253-4000*

	1993-94	*1995-96*	*1997*	*Totals*
Receipts	$234,912	$255,037	$135,686	$625,635
Disburse	274,800	234,985	78,350	588,135
Cash	15,016	35,080	92,421	n/a
Contributions	200,300	188,135	70,450	458,885
Republicans	142,600	171,635	53,000	367,235
No. of Cand.	*136*	*163*	*62*	*361*
House	82,100	118,385	35,000	235,485
Senate	60,500	53,250	18,000	131,750
Democrats	56,950	16,500	17,450	90,900
No. of Cand.	*53*	*22*	*22*	*97*
House	41,700	15,500	12,450	69,650
Senate	15,250	1,000	5,000	21,250
Incumbents	164,500	162,635	68,450	395,585
Challengers	9,650	8,000	1,000	18,650
Open Seat	26,150	17,000	1,000	44,150
Winners	177,800	153,385	n/a	331,185
Losers	22,500	34,750	n/a	57,250

Tidewater Inc.

*Phone: (504) 568-1010 * Fax: (504) 566-4582*
1440 Canal St., Suite 2100, New Orleans, LA 70112
Web: www.tdw.com

Tidewater is the world's largest provider of offshore supply ships and services. It supplies tugboats and other ships, along with natural gas compressors, to marine gas and oil exploration projects worldwide.

The public company has about 8,400 employees and operations in most areas of the world where gas and oil drilling projects exist. Tidewater's 1997 sales were $803 million.

Tidewater Inc. Political Action Committee (TidePAC) (C00199471) *Address: same as sponsor * Treasurer: Michael A. Coscino*

	1993-94	*1995-96*	*1997*	*Totals*
Receipts	$33,083	$32,898	$14,951	$80,932
Disburse	32,605	38,130	1,200	71,935
Cash	18,340	13,112	26,863	n/a
Contributions	10,550	23,250	200	34,000
Republicans	7,050	18,750	200	26,000
No. of Cand.	*12*	*12*	*2*	*26*
House	3,900	4,750	700	9,350
Senate	3,150	14,000	-500	16,650
Democrats	3,500	4,500	0	8,000
No. of Cand.	*6*	*3*	*1*	*10*
House	2,500	3,500	0	6,000
Senate	1,000	1,000	0	2,000
Incumbents	9,550	8,750	200	18,500
Challengers	500	0	0	500
Open Seat	500	14,500	0	15,000
Winners	9,550	9,750	n/a	19,300
Losers	1,000	13,500	n/a	14,500

Tosco Corp.

*Phone: (203) 977-1000 * Fax: (203) 326-3144*
72 Cummings Point Rd., Stamford, CT 06902

Tosco is one of the largest independent refiners and marketers of petroleum products in the United States, operating principally on the East and West Coasts. The publicly traded company posted $9.9 billion in 1996 sales.

Tosco has refineries in the San Francisco Bay area, Puget Sound north of Seattle, Linden, N.J. and near Philadelphia. It has 44 subsidiaries located in Colorado, California, Arizona, Texas, Massachusetts, Connecticut, Florida, the United Kingdom and Bermuda.

In December 1996, Tosco acquired Unocal's West Coast petroleum assets for about $1.4 billion. With the acquisition of The Circle K Corp. in May 1996, Tosco is the nation's largest operator of company-controlled convenience stores.

Incorporated in 1955, Tosco has 24,300 employees, about 4,200 of whom are part-time.

Tosco Corp. Political Action Committee (C00116400) *Address: same as sponsor * Treasurer: Robert I. Santo * Contact: Ann Farner Miller, V.P. of Gov. Relations*

	1993-94	*1995-96*	*1997*	*Totals*
Receipts	$17,560	$0	$5,500	$23,060
Disburse	11,120	11,650	4,600	27,370
Cash	14,447	2,967	3,867	n/a
Contributions	10,100	6,850	4,600	21,550
Republicans	4,000	4,850	1,600	10,450
No. of Cand.	*6*	*10*	*3*	*19*
House	1,750	3,350	600	5,700

(Data for Tosco Corp. Political continued)

Senate	2,250	1,500	1,000	4,750
Democrats	6,100	2,000	3,000	11,100
No. of Cand.	*8*	*2*	*4*	*14*
House	5,100	2,000	2,000	9,100
Senate	1,000	0	1,000	2,000
Incumbents	8,850	4,850	4,100	17,800
Challengers	250	500	0	750
Open Seat	1,000	1,500	500	3,000
Winners	8,250	4,050	n/a	12,300
Losers	1,850	2,800	n/a	4,650

Total Petroleum Inc.

Total Tower, 900 19th St., Denver, CO 80202

The Total Petroleum PAC filed for termination in September 1997.

Total Petroleum Inc. PAC (Total PAC) (C00281618) *Address: same as sponsor * Treasurer: Melanie Kelley*

	1993-94	1995-96	1997	Totals
Receipts	$8,266	$26,540	$3,673	$38,479
Disburse	7,223	22,020	7,725	36,968
Cash	749	5,270	1,218	n/a
Contributions	4,600	12,300	6,702	23,602
Republicans	3,000	10,300	6,202	19,502
No. of Cand.	*3*	*9*	*7*	*19*
House	500	5,500	5,202	11,202
Senate	2,500	4,800	1,000	8,300
Democrats	1,600	2,000	500	4,100
No. of Cand.	*2*	*3*	*1*	*6*
House	1,600	2,000	500	4,100
Senate	0	0	0	0
Incumbents	2,100	5,500	5,702	13,302
Challengers	0	500	0	500
Open Seat	2,500	6,300	0	8,800
Winners	4,600	8,800	n/a	13,400
Losers	0	3,500	n/a	3,500

USX Corp.

Phone: (412) 433-1121
600 Grant St., Pittsburgh, PA 15219
Web: www.usx.com

Although it is known as the nation's largest steel maker, USX's oil and natural gas operations generate twice as much revenue as steel. The publicly traded Pittsburgh company employs 40,000 workers and posted $22.6 billion in 1997 sales.

Subsidiary Marathon Oil Co., with headquarters in Houston, has major holdings in Yates Field in west Texas. Other U.S. drilling locations include the Rocky Mountains, Alaska and states in the southwest and central regions. Manufacturing plants are located in Detroit; Garyville, La.; Robinson, Ill.; and Texas City, Texas. The company has 2,300 independent Marathon brand service stations in 11 states and more than 1,600 gasoline and convenience store outlets in 15 states. Brand names include Speedway, Starvin' Marvin, Bonded and Gastown.

USX's steel subsidiary, U.S. Steel, has plants in Pittsburgh; Philadelphia; Gary, Ind.; Fairfield, Ala.; and northern Minnesota.

In 1997, USX sold Delhi Gas Pipeline Corp. to Koch Industries. Delhi's PAC is no longer affiliated with USX.

USX Corp. PAC (C00030676) *Phone: (202) 783-6333 * Fax: (202) 783-6309 * 1101 Pennsylvania Ave. N.W., Suite 510, Washington, DC 20004 * Treasurer: Marilyn A. Harris * Contact: Terrence Straub, Chairman*

	1993-94	1995-96	1997	Totals
Receipts	$163,082	$192,252	$116,224	$471,558
Disburse	162,970	195,140	104,454	462,564
Cash	9,524	6,645	18,421	n/a
Contributions	74,270	83,669	55,378	213,317
Republicans	20,920	50,084	26,207	97,211
No. of Cand.	*20*	*51*	*31*	*102*
House	11,420	34,999	18,708	65,127
Senate	9,500	15,085	7,499	32,084
Democrats	51,850	33,585	28,171	113,606
No. of Cand.	*52*	*32*	*25*	*109*
House	43,850	27,850	18,500	90,200
Senate	8,000	5,735	9,671	23,406
Incumbents	65,120	75,434	49,879	190,433
Challengers	4,000	4,735	999	9,734
Open Seat	5,150	3,500	4,000	12,650
Winners	54,770	77,934	n/a	132,704
Losers	19,500	5,735	n/a	25,235

Marathon Oil Co. Employees Political Action Committee (MEPAC) (C00040568) *Phone: (419) 422-2121 * Fax: (419) 422-2129 * 539 S. Main St., Findlay, OH 45840 * Web: www.marathon.com * Treasurer: John A. Evans*

*Phone: (713) 829-8600 * Fax: (713) 296-2952 * P.O. Box 3128, Houston, TX 77253 * Contact: R. G. Becker, Chairman*

	1993-94	1995-96	1997	Totals
Receipts	$194,431	$237,214	$135,614	$567,259
Disburse	197,056	218,569	63,164	478,789
Cash	11,789	30,443	102,899	n/a
Contributions	82,950	97,250	40,750	220,950
Republicans	47,100	84,250	31,250	162,600
No. of Cand.	*32*	*74*	*29*	*135*
House	30,100	53,250	17,250	100,600
Senate	17,000	31,000	14,000	62,000
Democrats	35,850	13,000	9,500	58,350
No. of Cand.	*30*	*21*	*12*	*63*
House	24,850	11,000	4,500	40,350
Senate	11,000	2,000	5,000	18,000
Incumbents	57,600	80,400	35,000	173,000
Challengers	7,000	500	250	7,750
Open Seat	18,350	16,350	5,500	40,200
Winners	71,100	80,250	n/a	151,350
Losers	11,850	17,000	n/a	28,850

Ultramar Diamond Shamrock Inc.

*Phone: (210) 592-2000 * Fax: (210) 370-4070*
P.O. Box 696000, San Antonio, TX 78269-6000
*Web: www.udscorp.com * E-mail: carolyn_green@udscorp.com*

Ultramar Diamond Shamrock is the third largest independent oil refining and marketing company in the United States, operating primarily in the Southwest and Northeast.

The publicly traded corporation was formed by the 1996 merger of Ultramar Corp. and Diamond Shamrock Inc. It has 23,000 employees throughout 19 states and reported 1997 sales of $11 billion.

UDS owns seven refineries in the United States and Canada, two of which are in Texas, with the others in California, Colorado, Michigan, Oklahoma and Quebec.

UDS also has a network of about 6,400 retail gasoline/convenience merchandise stores in 19 states and eastern Canada. These stores operate under the names Diamond Shamrock, Corner Store, Stop N Go, Ultramar, Beacon, Sergaz and Total. UDS is the largest retail marketer of gasoline in the state of Texas.

The company also has growing petrochemical and home heating oil businesses.

Ultramar Diamond Shamrock Employees' Political Action Committee (C00215939) *Address: same as sponsor * Treasurer: Mary Hartman * Contact: Robbin Hahns, Chairwoman*

	1993-94	1995-96	1997	Totals
Receipts	$91,540	$95,646	$50,436	$237,622
Disburse	89,859	102,338	34,320	226,517
Cash	13,557	7,581	23,699	n/a
Contributions	30,500	35,500	6,500	72,500
Republicans	28,000	24,750	3,750	56,500
No. of Cand.	*11*	*29*	*4*	*44*
House	12,000	21,000	1,750	34,750
Senate	16,000	3,750	2,000	21,750
Democrats	2,500	10,750	2,750	16,000
No. of Cand.	*3*	*11*	*4*	*18*
House	2,500	10,500	2,750	15,750
Senate	0	250	0	250
Incumbents	25,000	24,000	5,000	54,000
Challengers	5,000	2,500	0	7,500
Open Seat	500	9,000	1,500	11,000
Winners	27,000	29,000	n/a	56,000
Losers	3,500	6,500	n/a	10,000

United Co.

*Phone: (540) 466-3322 * Fax: (540) 645-1431*
P.O. Box 1280, Bristol, VA 24203

United is a private company that operates, through its subsidiaries, throughout the United States and Canada in the oil and gas, leisure, golf course, financial and manufacturing industries. The company has between 500 and 1,000 employees.

In 1997, United sold its coal-mining division to A.T. Massey Coal, a subsidiary of the Fluor Corp.

The United Co. Political Action Committee (C00256461) *Address: same as sponsor * Treasurer: Willard W. Owens*

	1993-94	1995-96	1997	Totals
Receipts	$23,750	$16,256	$0	$40,006
Disburse	20,844	17,100	400	38,344
Cash	7,327	6,483	6,083	n/a
Contributions	18,144	14,250	400	32,794
Republicans	15,194	12,750	400	28,344
No. of Cand.	*26*	*6*	*1*	*33*
House	4,400	3,750	400	8,550
Senate	10,794	9,000	0	19,794
Democrats	2,950	1,500	0	4,450
No. of Cand.	*7*	*2*	*0*	*9*
House	1,450	1,500	0	2,950
Senate	1,500	0	0	1,500
Incumbents	8,550	10,750	400	19,700
Challengers	6,544	0	0	6,544
Open Seat	3,050	3,500	0	6,550
Winners	14,300	11,750	n/a	26,050
Losers	3,844	2,500	n/a	6,344

Unocal Corp.

*Phone: (805) 595-7657 * Fax: (805) 595-7611*
2141 Rosecrans Ave., Suite 4153, El Segundo, CA 90245
Web: www.unocal.com

One of the biggest oil exploration companies in the United States, Unocal primarily develops crude oil and natural gas properties in the Gulf of Mexico and Asia. The publicly traded company reported $6 billion in 1997 revenue.

Unocal has sold its California-based refining and marketing operations, including its refineries and its "76" brand gas stations. It remains the world's No. 1 producer of geothermal energy. Other products include chemicals for the agricultural and industrial markets.

The company has geothermal electricity projects at The Geysers in northern California and three foreign locations. It has fertilizer plants in Kenai, Alaska; Finley and Kennewick, Wash.; and West Sacramento, Calif.

Subsidiary Molycorp produces lanthanide products, which are used in many high-technology applications, and molybdenum, a key alloying element for high-strength steel. Molycorp has mines in Mountain Pass, Calif., about 55 miles south of Las Vegas, and Questa, N.M.

Unocal has oil-related operations in: Texas, Oklahoma, Michigan, Utah, New Mexico, Alabama and Louisiana.

Union Oil (Unocal) Political Awareness Fund (C00001289) *Phone: (202) 639-9712 * Fax: (202) 639-0356 * 1401 New York Ave. N.W., Suite 1250, Washington, DC 20005 * Treasurer: Dennis W. Lamb * Contact: John L. Rafuse, Washington Office Dir.*

	1993-94	1995-96	1997	Totals
Receipts	$112,241	$72,389	$32,247	$216,877
Disburse	108,739	76,444	15,207	200,390
Cash	10,148	6,103	23,145	n/a
Contributions	108,274	75,000	15,000	198,274
Republicans	89,206	66,500	11,500	167,206
No. of Cand.	*83*	*54*	*9*	*146*
House	44,670	36,500	3,500	84,670
Senate	44,536	30,000	8,000	82,536
Democrats	19,068	8,500	3,500	31,068
No. of Cand.	*22*	*10*	*4*	*36*
House	17,068	7,500	1,500	26,068
Senate	2,000	1,000	2,000	5,000
Incumbents	57,588	52,000	15,000	124,588
Challengers	19,700	4,000	0	23,700
Open Seat	30,986	19,000	0	49,986
Winners	96,224	59,000	n/a	155,224
Losers	12,050	16,000	n/a	28,050

Valero Energy Corp.

*Phone: (210) 370-2000 * Fax: (210) 370-2234*
P.O. Box 500, San Antonio, TX 78292-0500
Web: www.valero.com

Valero Energy is one of the five largest independent oil refiners and marketers in the United States and the largest on the Gulf Coast. With the 1997 acquisition of Basis Petroleum Inc., the company now owns and operates four refineries in Texas and Louisiana. A public company, Valero reported 1997 revenue of $5.8 billion.

The four refineries are located in Corpus Christi, Texas; Texas City, Texas; Houston; and Krotz Springs, La. Valero is a leading producer of such products as reformulated gasoline, CARB Phase II gasoline, low-sulfur diesel and oxygenates. The company also produces a substantial slate of petrochemicals and jet fuel. Valero markets its products to wholesale customers in more than 30 states and selected export markets.

Valero sold off its natural gas operations to utility company PG&E during 1997.

Valero Energy Corp. Political Action Committee (ValPAC) (C00109546) *Address: same as sponsor * Treasurer: John D. Gibbons * Contact: James A. Greenwood, Chairman*

	1993-94	1995-96	1997	Totals
Receipts	$251,323	$249,021	$105,335	$605,679
Disburse	277,256	213,696	88,710	579,662
Cash	13,864	49,192	65,817	n/a
Contributions	66,750	52,500	18,000	137,250
Republicans	21,000	31,000	10,500	62,500
No. of Cand.	*7*	*13*	*7*	*27*
House	13,000	25,000	5,500	43,500
Senate	8,000	6,000	5,000	19,000
Democrats	45,750	21,500	7,500	74,750
No. of Cand.	*24*	*15*	*8*	*47*
House	31,500	15,000	2,500	49,000
Senate	14,250	6,500	5,000	25,750
Incumbents	55,250	43,000	17,000	115,250
Challengers	4,500	1,000	0	5,500
Open Seat	7,000	7,500	1,000	15,500
Winners	48,750	46,500	n/a	95,250
Losers	18,000	6,000	n/a	24,000

Washington Gas Light Co.

*Phone: (202) 624-6266 * Fax: (202) 624-6699*
1100 H St. N.W., Washington, DC 20080
Web: www.washgas.com

Washington Gas Light services 770,000 natural gas meters in metropolitan Washington, D.C. The publicly traded company posted $1 billion in 1997 sales.

Established in 1948, Washington Gas employs more than 2,200 workers. It has business divisions in Washington, Maryland and Virginia. Portions of West Virginia are served by one of the company's distribution subsidiaries.

In November 1997, Washington Gas Energy Services and Columbia Energy Services announced an agreement with the state of Maryland to provide natural gas to more than 100 state facilities.

Washington Gas Light Co. Federal Political Action Committee (C00102152) *Address: same as sponsor * Treasurer: Douglas A. Campbell * Contact: Debbie Homburger, Federal Relations Specialist*

	1993-94	1995-96	1997	Totals
Receipts	$21,676	$15,482	$10,214	$47,372
Disburse	21,150	26,180	10,250	57,580
Cash	17,005	6,308	6,272	n/a
Contributions	16,100	19,880	8,250	44,230
Republicans	5,950	12,580	5,500	24,030
No. of Cand.	*7*	*11*	*4*	*22*
House	5,950	9,580	5,500	21,030
Senate	0	3,000	0	3,000
Democrats	10,150	7,300	2,750	20,200
No. of Cand.	*11*	*8*	*2*	*21*
House	8,900	6,300	2,750	17,950
Senate	1,250	1,000	0	2,250
Incumbents	13,350	19,880	8,250	41,480
Challengers	2,200	0	0	2,200
Open Seat	550	0	0	550
Winners	15,900	17,880	n/a	33,780
Losers	200	2,000	n/a	2,200

Wickland Oil Co.

*Phone: (916) 978-2500 * Fax: (916) 978-2410*
3640 American River Dr., Sacramento, CA 95864

Wickland Oil operates chemical bulk-storage stations and petroleum terminals in the United States, the Caribbean and Asia. Although it was formed in 1954 as chain of gas stations, Wickland has changed by moving from the retail side of the industry through wholesale operations to pure handling. The private company also manages several real estate operations.

The business is still owned and managed by members of the Wickland family. Wickland reported 1996 sales of more than $850 million. The company employs 250 workers.

Wickland Oil Co. Political Committee (C00148411) *Address: same as sponsor * Treasurer: John A. Wickland III*

	1993-94	1995-96	1997	Totals
Receipts	$6,850	$6,243	$5,600	$18,693
Disburse	7,153	6,284	5,644	19,081
Cash	163	123	79	n/a
Contributions	6,900	6,000	3,500	16,400
Republicans	2,000	3,000	1,000	6,000
No. of Cand.	*1*	*3*	*1*	*5*
House	2,000	3,000	1,000	6,000
Senate	0	0	0	0
Democrats	4,900	3,000	2,500	10,400
No. of Cand.	*3*	*3*	*3*	*9*
House	4,900	3,000	2,500	10,400
Senate	0	0	0	0
Incumbents	6,900	6,000	3,500	16,400
Challengers	0	0	0	0
Open Seat	0	0	0	0
Winners	6,900	5,000	n/a	11,900
Losers	0	1,000	n/a	1,000

The Williams Companies

*Phone: (918) 588-2000 * Fax: (918) 588-4503*
One Williams Center, MD 48-8, P.O. Box 2400, Tulsa, OK 74172-2400
Web: www.twc.com

The Williams Companies is an energy and telecommunications firm. A publicly held company with 14,400 employees, Williams posted 1997 revenues of $4.4 billion.

Through subsidiary Williams Energy, the company operates five interstate natural gas pipelines that make it the nation's largest-volume transporter of natural gas. Williams Energy also provides a range of other energy-related services, including the sale, storage and distribution of natural gas, electricity and petroleum products. It also is involved in energy exploration, production, marketing and trading.

Another primary subsidiary, Williams Communications, provides business communications services worldwide, including telecommunications equipment and integration services, international satellite and fiber-optic transmission services, and multi-point video- and audio-conferencing.

In November 1997, the company entered into a definitive agreement to acquire MAPCO Inc., an oil refining and gas marketing company. MAPCO subsequently terminated its PAC.

The Williams Companies Political Action Committee (Willco PAC) (C00040394) *Address: same as sponsor * Treasurer: David M. Higbee * Contact: Keith Bailey, Chairman*

	1993-94	1995-96	1997	Totals
Receipts	$103,594	$130,908	$117,321	$351,823
Disburse	92,429	134,195	88,430	315,054
Cash	47,466	44,418	73,309	n/a
Contributions	74,300	124,940	76,850	276,090
Republicans	41,100	103,250	64,750	209,100
No. of Cand.	*44*	*85*	*75*	*204*
House	20,600	73,250	46,250	140,100
Senate	20,500	30,000	18,500	69,000
Democrats	33,200	21,690	11,600	66,490
No. of Cand.	*37*	*29*	*17*	*83*
House	24,700	18,190	7,500	50,390
Senate	8,500	3,500	4,100	16,100
Incumbents	63,550	106,750	75,850	246,150
Challengers	1,500	4,500	500	6,500
Open Seat	9,250	13,690	500	23,440
Winners	55,800	103,250	n/a	159,050
Losers	18,500	21,690	n/a	40,190

MAPCO Employees Political Action Committee (C00041616) *1800 S. Baltimore Ave., P.O. Box 645, Tulsa, OK 74119 * Treasurer: Donald R. Wellendorf*

MAPCO Employees PAC filed for termination in March 1998. MAPCO refines petroleum, markets propane and operates a chain of convenience stores. A publicly traded company with 5,000 employees, MAPCO had 1997 sales of $3.8 billion.

In addition to operating refineries in Alaska and Tennessee, MAPCO also manages the Mid-America pipeline, which transports natural gas liquids 10,000 miles through 15 states, including Utah, Texas and Illinois. The company's convenience store chain, MAPCO Express, operates in eight southeastern states, Texas and Alaska.

	1993-94	1995-96	1997	Totals
Receipts	$132,597	$118,353	$49,037	$299,987
Disburse	135,188	116,972	35,601	287,761
Cash	6,585	7,978	21,420	n/a
Contributions	90,250	82,450	28,000	200,700
Republicans	82,750	79,950	25,500	188,200
No. of Cand.	*67*	*58*	*19*	*144*
House	35,200	34,450	4,500	74,150
Senate	47,550	45,500	21,000	114,050
Democrats	7,500	2,500	2,500	12,500
No. of Cand.	*10*	*4*	*4*	*18*
House	7,500	2,500	1,500	11,500
Senate	0	0	1,000	1,000
Incumbents	36,200	60,700	27,000	123,900
Challengers	19,500	5,500	1,000	26,000
Open Seat	34,550	16,250	0	50,800
Winners	80,750	73,450	n/a	154,200
Losers	9,500	9,000	n/a	18,500

Terminated PACs which contributed less than $5,000 during 1995-96 cycle:

Texas Gas Transmission Corp. PAC (C00032771) *3800 Frederica St., P.O. Box 1160, Owensboro, KY 42301 * Treasurer: Louis D. Bellamy*

Transco Energy Co. Political Action Committee (formerly known as TransPAC) (C00092254) *2800 Post Oak Blvd., P.O. Box 1396, Houston, TX 77056 * Treasurer: Jack D. McCarthy*

Waste Management

Allwaste Inc.

3301 Millcorss Ct., Oakton, VA 22124

The Allwaste PAC was terminated in 1997.

Allwaste Inc. Political Action Committee (C00239301) *Address: same as sponsor * Treasurer: Albert B. Rosenbaum III*

	1993-94	1995-96	1997	Totals
Receipts	$20,259	$6,133	$0	$26,392
Disburse	12,695	7,200	9,641	29,536
Cash	10,270	9,641	0	n/a
Contributions	2,250	5,000	9,641	16,891
Republicans	3,250	2,000	2,750	8,000
No. of Cand.	*4*	*4*	*2*	*10*
House	2,500	1,500	2,750	6,750
Senate	750	500	0	1,250
Democrats	-1000	3,000	6,891	8,891
No. of Cand.	*7*	*6*	*6*	*19*
House	3,500	3,000	4,891	11,391
Senate	-4500	0	2,000	-2500
Incumbents	500	4,500	9,641	14,641
Challengers	0	0	0	0
Open Seat	1,750	500	0	2,250
Winners	0	3,500	n/a	3,500
Losers	2,250	1,500	n/a	3,750

Browning-Ferris Industries

*Phone: (281) 870-8100 * Fax: (281) 870-7844*
757 N. Eldridge Rd., Houston, TX 77079
*Web: www.bfi.com * E-mail: bob.price@bfi.com*

Browning-Ferris Industries provides waste disposal services. The publicly owned company collects, transports, treats and/or processes, recycles and disposes of commercial, residential and municipal solid waste and industrial wastes. BFI also is involved in waste-to-energy conversion, medical waste services, portable restroom services and municipal and commercial sweeping operations.

BFI's 14,400 trucks collect solid waste in 45 states, Puerto Rico, and 13 foreign countries.

The company employs 40,000 workers and had sales of more than $5 billion in 1997.

Browning-Ferris Industries Political Action Committee (BFI PAC) (C00193474) *Address: same as sponsor * Treasurer: Suzanne Walstad * Contact: Robert Price, Executive Dir.*

	1993-94	1995-96	1997	Totals
Receipts	$251,626	$209,102	$126,830	$587,558
Disburse	251,964	203,344	98,665	553,973
Cash	14,867	20,631	48,803	n/a
Contributions	139,589	108,969	54,475	303,033
Republicans	77,800	84,944	38,625	201,369
No. of Cand.	*59*	*79*	*39*	*177*
House	29,200	65,594	22,650	117,444
Senate	48,600	19,350	15,975	83,925
Democrats	60,789	24,025	15,850	100,664
No. of Cand.	*60*	*38*	*24*	*122*
House	36,550	18,825	10,850	66,225
Senate	24,239	5,200	5,000	34,439
Incumbents	117,489	98,019	48,725	264,233
Challengers	10,500	2,100	2,750	15,350
Open Seat	11,600	8,100	2,000	21,700
Winners	118,889	94,419	n/a	213,308
Losers	20,700	14,550	n/a	35,250

City Management Corp.

*Phone: (313) 567-4700 * Fax: (313) 567-8934*
3400 E. Lafayette, Detroit, MI 48207
*Web: www.citymanagement.com * E-mail: cmcwm@citymanagement.com*

City Management, headquartered in Detroit, is the fourth-largest waste disposal company in the United States. City Management provides residential and commercial solid waste collection to most of Michigan's lower peninsula and portions of Ohio, Florida and Alabama.

City Management employs more than 2,000 workers in the Midwest and Southeast. The company was formed in 1968 as Hamlin Development Co., located in Utica, Mich. In 1974, the company acquired the refuse collection, transfer and disposal system that became known as City Disposal Systems and City Sand & Landfill.

City Management Corp. Political Action Committee (C00225078) *Address: same as sponsor * Treasurer: Richard P. Manczak*

	1993-94	1995-96	1997	Totals
Receipts	$15,000	$16,000	$0	$31,000
Disburse	15,800	8,640	3,225	27,665
Cash	-321	7,038	3,813	n/a
Contributions	9,300	8,500	1,225	19,025
Republicans	1,000	4,000	0	5,000
No. of Cand.	*2*	*4*	*0*	*6*
House	500	3,000	0	3,500
Senate	500	1,000	0	1,500
Democrats	8,300	4,500	725	13,525
No. of Cand.	*11*	*5*	*2*	*18*
House	5,000	3,500	725	9,225
Senate	3,300	1,000	0	4,300
Incumbents	5,850	5,500	1,225	12,575
Challengers	850	3,000	0	3,850
Open Seat	2,800	0	0	2,800
Winners	5,750	5,500	n/a	11,250
Losers	3,550	3,000	n/a	6,550

EnviroSource Inc.

*Phone: (215) 956-5500 * Fax: (215) 956-5588*
1155 Business Center Dr., Horsham, PA 19044-3454

EnviroSource is a publicly owned environmental services company in the business of recycling, handling, treatment and disposal of hazardous wastes. It has more than 50 locations in the United States and Canada among its 25 wholly owned subsidiaries.

In 1996, EnviroSource had sales of $213 million and 1,800 employees.

Subsidiaries operate commercial hazardous waste landfills in Idaho and Ohio.

EnviroSource Inc. Political Action Committee (C00276782) *Address: same as sponsor * Treasurer: James C. Hull * Contact: Leon Z. Heller, General Counsel and Secretary*

	1993-94	1995-96	1997	Totals
Receipts	$10,285	$52,002	$22,180	$84,467
Disburse	7,838	16,179	14,121	38,138
Cash	4,385	40,210	48,269	n/a
Contributions	3,250	4,600	0	7,850
Republicans	3,250	1,100	0	4,350
No. of Cand.	*5*	*4*	*0*	*9*
House	1,750	100	0	1,850
Senate	1,500	1,000	0	2,500
Democrats	0	3,500	0	3,500
No. of Cand.	*0*	*3*	*0*	*3*
House	0	3,000	0	3,000
Senate	0	500	0	500
Incumbents	1,500	4,000	0	5,500
Challengers	1,750	500	0	2,250
Open Seat	0	500	0	500
Winners	3,250	4,500	n/a	7,750
Losers	0	100	n/a	100

Environmental Industry Associations

*Phone: (202) 244-4700 * Fax: (202) 966-4818*
4301 Connecticut Ave. N.W., Suite 300, Washington, DC 20008
Web: www.envasns.org

The Environmental Industry Associations represents about 2,000 companies that manage solid, hazardous and medical wastes and sell waste equipment. It is an umbrella organization for The National Solid Wastes Management Association and The Waste Equipment Technology Association.

Environmental Industry Associations PAC (EIA Waste PAC) (C00120642) *Address: same as sponsor * Treasurer: Allen R. Frischkorn*

	1993-94	1995-96	1997	Totals
Receipts	$27,725	$76,014	$9,975	$113,714
Disburse	61,681	76,725	7,785	146,191
Cash	2,349	1,638	3,828	n/a
Contributions	48,600	47,725	7,500	103,825
Republicans	19,100	36,725	5,000	60,825
No. of Cand.	*26*	*32*	*7*	*65*
House	12,100	25,625	5,000	42,725
Senate	7,000	11,100	0	18,100
Democrats	29,000	11,000	2,500	42,500
No. of Cand.	*25*	*14*	*5*	*44*
House	18,500	10,000	2,500	31,000
Senate	10,500	1,000	0	11,500
Incumbents	45,500	47,225	7,500	100,225
Challengers	0	0	0	0
Open Seat	3,100	0	0	3,100
Winners	43,000	45,225	n/a	88,225
Losers	5,600	2,500	n/a	8,100

OHM Corp.

*Phone: (202) 452-1540 * Fax: (202) 785-0529*
816 Connecticut Ave. N.W., Suite 900, Washington, DC 20006
Web: www.ohm.com

OHM is an environmental consulting and remediation firm with 1996 revenues of $551 million. The company's clients have included several branches of the military, the Department of Energy and the EPA. The public company employs about 3,000 people throughout the United States.

In January 1998, OHM announced that it had entered into a definitive agreement to merge with Information Technology Corp., an environmental infrastructure solutions firm that provides consulting, engineering and construction services. According to the terms of the merger, which was expected to be completed in April 1998, IT would acquire OHM for about $365 million. IT does not have a PAC, and a spokesperson for OHM said that it was uncertain whether OHM's PAC would be transferred to IT or would be terminated.

OHM Corp. Clean PAC (OHM Clean PAC) (C00287508) *Address: same as sponsor * Treasurer: Robert J. Blackwell * Contact: Zelda Shute, Manager*

	1993-94	1995-96	1997	Totals
Receipts	$39,691	$140,726	$87,466	$267,883
Disburse	28,440	131,941	42,056	202,437
Cash	11,253	20,046	65,461	n/a
Contributions	23,441	98,645	33,000	155,086
Republicans	2,300	75,095	22,000	99,395
No. of Cand.	*3*	*46*	*17*	*66*
House	1,300	45,095	20,000	66,395
Senate	1,000	30,000	2,000	33,000
Democrats	21,141	23,550	11,000	55,691
No. of Cand.	*11*	*18*	*10*	*39*
House	9,141	21,050	8,000	38,191
Senate	12,000	2,500	3,000	17,500
Incumbents	13,441	91,360	33,000	137,801
Challengers	0	1,000	0	1,000
Open Seat	10,000	5,000	0	15,000
Winners	13,191	91,075	n/a	104,266
Losers	10,250	7,570	n/a	17,820

Safety-Kleen Corp.

*Phone: (847) 697-8460 * Fax: (847) 468-8535*
1000 N. Randall Rd., Elgin, IL 60123
Web: www.safetykleen.com

Safety-Kleen provides industrial waste recycling and disposal, tool and parts cleaning, used oil recycling and other waste disposal services in North America and Europe. It removes and disposes of a variety of industrial waste such as solvents, acids and metals.

Safety-Kleen has annual revenues of $923 million and 7,300 employees. Founded in 1968, it is the second-largest oil collector in the United States with operations in nearly every state. Among its facilities are 13 recycling centers, two oil re-refineries and three fuel-blending facilities.

In February 1998, Safety-Kleen agreed to be purchased for more than $1.94 billion by Philip Services, The Blackstone Group and Apollo Advisors, while rejecting an ongoing bid by Laidlaw Environmental.

Safety-Kleen Corp. Political Action Committee (C00313312) *Address: same as sponsor * Treasurer: Laurence Rudnick * Contact: Bill Constantelos, Chairman*

	1993-94	1995-96	1997	Totals
Receipts	$0	$21,604	$22,321	$43,925
Disburse	0	19,165	2,049	21,214
Cash	0	2,447	22,721	n/a
Contributions	0	12,000	2,000	14,000
Republicans	0	6,000	2,000	8,000
No. of Cand.	*0*	*9*	*5*	*14*
House	0	4,500	1,000	5,500
Senate	0	1,500	1,000	2,500
Democrats	0	6,000	0	6,000
No. of Cand.	*0*	*10*	*0*	*10*
House	0	4,000	0	4,000
Senate	0	2,000	0	2,000
Incumbents	0	11,000	2,000	13,000
Challengers	0	0	0	0
Open Seat	0	1,000	0	1,000
Winners	0	11,500	n/a	11,500
Losers	0	500	n/a	500

Waste Management Inc.

*Phone: (630) 572-8800 * Fax: (630) 572-0355*
3003 Butterfield Rd., Oak Brook, IL 60521
Web: www.wmx.com

Waste Management is the world's largest provider of waste management services. Its revenues in 1996 were $9.2 billion. The public company handles solid and hazardous waste collection in 23 countries. In 1996, it sold its water and wastewater treatment facilities and other operations not related to garbage.

Waste Management announced a merger with USA Waste Services Inc., a non-hazardous solid waste management company, in March 1998. The combined company will have more than 77,000 employees and annual sales of nearly $13 billion. The new company will be called Waste Management Inc. and will be based in Houston.

The company is interested in EPA waste management and landfill regulations, as well as trucking and hauling laws. It also is a large contributor at the state and local levels.

Waste Management was the leading garbage industry PAC in contributions to congressional candidates during the 1995-96 election cycle. It favored Republican candidates by a more than two-to-one margin. The leading recipients were House Minority Leader Richard A. Gephardt, D-Mo., and Rep. Bill Paxon, R-N.Y. Most recipients got less than $5,000 from this PAC.

Subsidiary Wheelabrator Technologies ranked second among garbage industry PACs in contributions to 1996 congressional races. The top recipient was Sen. Richard C. Shelby, R-Ala. USA Waste Services' PAC contributed $12,000 to congressional campaigns during the 1995-96 cycle.

Waste Management Employees' Better Government Fund (Waste Management PAC) (C00119008) *Phone: (202) 628-3500 * Fax: (202) 628-0400 * 601 Pennsylvania Ave. N.W., Suite 300, Washington, DC 20004 * Treasurer: James L. Elitzak * Contact: Kimberley W. Engle, Manager of Gov. Affairs*

	1993-94	1995-96	1997	Totals
Receipts	$925,015	$786,406	$315,884	$2,027,305
Disburse	886,508	775,394	262,913	1,924,815
Cash	121,600	102,159	155,128	n/a
Contributions	386,846	315,200	79,600	781,646
Republicans	125,214	219,100	46,650	390,964
No. of Cand.	*120*	*131*	*29*	*280*
House	67,500	135,850	33,100	236,450
Senate	57,714	83,250	13,550	154,514
Democrats	258,132	96,100	30,950	385,182
No. of Cand.	*183*	*83*	*28*	*294*
House	184,376	66,600	13,700	264,676
Senate	73,756	29,500	17,250	120,506
Incumbents	298,020	245,850	69,700	613,570
Challengers	25,350	12,500	0	37,850
Open Seat	63,576	52,350	10,300	126,226
Winners	268,840	259,050	n/a	527,890
Losers	118,006	56,150	n/a	174,156

Rust Environment & Infrastructure Inc./Wheelabrator Technologies Inc. Sensible Government Fund (C00249904) *Phone: (202) 628-3500 * Fax: (202) 628-0400 * 601 Pennsylvania Ave. N.W., Suite 300 N., Washington, DC 20004 * Treasurer: Robert J. Gagalis * Contact: Kimberley W. Engle, Manager of Gov. Affairs*

	1993-94	1995-96	1997	Totals
Receipts	$144,344	$167,202	$57,312	$368,858
Disburse	169,592	184,577	27,233	381,402
Cash	77,392	60,018	90,099	n/a
Contributions	91,700	112,975	12,750	217,425
Republicans	48,250	86,075	10,500	144,825
No. of Cand.	*41*	*70*	*8*	*119*
House	26,250	47,075	7,000	80,325
Senate	22,000	39,000	3,500	64,500
Democrats	43,450	26,900	2,250	72,600
No. of Cand.	*35*	*24*	*2*	*61*
House	24,250	21,200	250	45,700
Senate	19,200	5,700	2,000	26,900
Incumbents	82,900	94,225	12,000	189,125
Challengers	6,700	5,500	500	12,700
Open Seat	2,600	12,750	250	15,600
Winners	73,900	91,925	n/a	165,825
Losers	17,800	21,050	n/a	38,850

USA Waste Services Inc. Employees for Good Government (C00211623) *Phone: (713) 512-6200 * Fax: (713) 512-6299 * 1001 Fannin St., Suite 4000, Houston, TX 77002 * Treasurer: Lawrence Yatch*

	1993-94	1995-96	1997	Totals
Receipts	$45,646	$31,501	$3,200	$80,347
Disburse	46,640	37,800	3,700	88,140
Cash	6,717	1,419	19	n/a
Contributions	34,040	10,000	0	44,040
Republicans	5,240	6,600	0	11,840
No. of Cand.	*6*	*8*	*0*	*14*
House	1,240	3,600	0	4,840
Senate	4,000	3,000	0	7,000
Democrats	28,800	3,400	0	32,200
No. of Cand.	*19*	*4*	*0*	*23*
House	13,050	3,400	0	16,450
Senate	15,750	0	0	15,750
Incumbents	28,490	9,000	0	37,490
Challengers	4,000	0	0	4,000
Open Seat	1,550	1,000	0	2,550
Winners	27,540	10,000	n/a	37,540
Losers	6,500	0	n/a	6,500

Finance, Insurance & Real Estate

Accountants

American Institute of Certified Public Accountants

*Phone: (201) 938-3000 * Fax: (201) 938-3329*
Harborside Financial Center, 201 Plaza 3, Jersey City, NJ 07311-3861
Web: www.aicpa.org

The American Institute of CPAs is the largest professional association for accountants in the United States. It has about 330,000 members working in public practice or for private industry. A small percentage of its members work in education, government or are retired. Its total membership has increased by nearly 100,000 since 1985.

A top legislative issue for AICPA is reforming the IRS. The group favors increased taxpayer confidentiality and an oversight board for the IRS. It also supports a proposal requiring that securities class action suits be heard in federal court instead of state courts. The AICPA opposes attempts to have the federal government set accounting standards. The Financial Accounting Standards Board, which sets policy, is partially funded by AICPA. The group also opposes allowing non-licensed persons perform external audits of federally insured credit unions.

The AICPA was the leading contributor to 1996 congressional campaigns among accountant groups and businesses. Republican candidates received more than twice as much money as Democratic candidates. Two percent of the group's total contributions went to challengers. The leading recipients were Rep. Martin Frost, D-Texas, and Senate candidate Guy Millner of Georgia, who lost to Sen. Max Cleland, D-Ga. More than half of the candidates AICPA contributed to received at least $5,000.

American Institute of Certified Public Accountants Effective Legislation Committee (AICPA) (C00077321) *Phone: (202) 434-9205 * Fax: (202) 638-4512 * 1455 Pennsylvania Ave. N.W., Washington, DC 20004-1081 * E-mail: thigginbotham@aicpa.org * Treasurer: Donna G. Borowicz * Contact: J. Thomas Higginbotham, V.P.*

	1993-94	1995-96	1997	Totals
Receipts	$1,266,506	$1,542,807	$689,685	$3,498,998
Disburse	1,890,052	1,848,826	280,069	4,018,947
Cash	370,931	64,922	474,540	n/a
Contributions	1,737,520	1,690,925	212,986	3,641,431
Republicans	870,021	1,145,425	131,846	2,147,292
No. of Cand.	*206*	*247*	*93*	*546*
House	665,700	887,425	98,838	1,651,963
Senate	204,321	258,000	33,008	495,329
Democrats	852,499	540,500	73,854	1,466,853
No. of Cand.	*222*	*119*	*51*	*392*
House	756,931	447,550	56,372	1,260,853
Senate	95,568	92,950	17,482	206,000
Incumbents	1,520,449	1,404,725	197,925	3,123,099
Challengers	39,221	34,000	4,000	77,221
Open Seat	175,350	248,700	11,061	435,111
Winners	1,499,770	1,475,925	n/a	2,975,695
Losers	237,750	215,000	n/a	452,750

Arthur Andersen LLP

*Phone: (312) 580-0033 * Fax: (312) 507-4758*
33 W. Monroe, Chicago, IL 60603
Web: www.arthurandersen.com

Arthur Andersen is an accounting and professional services business employing more than 52,000 people in 78 countries. The company earned $5.2 billion in 1997 revenues. The private firm is part of Andersen Worldwide, the world's largest accounting and consulting firm. Andersen Consulting, the San Francisco-based unit of the company, filed a complaint in a New York court in December 1997 seeking to split the company into two parts.

The company follows legislation affecting tax and finance policy.

Arthur Andersen ranked fourth among accounting industry PACs in total contributions to 1996 congressional races. Andersen Consulting's PAC ranked eighth but gave less than one-tenth of what the accounting unit did. The accounting unit's PAC contributed about 1 percent to challengers.

The top recipients were Sen. Pete V. Domenici, R-N.M.; Reps. Martin Frost, D-Texas, Vic Fazio, D-Calif. and Billy Tauzin, R-La.; and 1996 Senate candidate Guy Millner, a Georgia Republican.

Arthur Andersen PAC (formerly known as Arthur Andersen/ Andersen Consulting PAC) (C00221168) *Phone: (202) 862-6560 * Fax: (202) 785-4689 * 1666 K St. N.W., Washington, DC 20006 * E-mail: washington/vienna@ArthurAndersen.com * Treasurer: Jeffrey J. Peck*

	1993-94	1995-96	1997	Totals
Receipts	$560,253	$641,937	$303,143	$1,505,333
Disburse	479,288	713,678	227,145	1,420,111
Cash	99,744	27,999	103,998	n/a
Contributions	344,010	480,301	151,238	975,549
Republicans	142,450	276,816	85,306	504,572
No. of Cand.	*101*	*160*	*62*	*323*

(Data for Arthur Andersen PAC continued)

House	73,750	166,824	53,806	294,380
Senate	68,700	109,992	31,500	210,192
Democrats	193,810	203,485	64,932	462,227
No. of Cand.	*110*	*89*	*46*	*245*
House	109,950	132,399	43,432	285,781
Senate	83,860	71,086	21,500	176,446
Incumbents	274,060	404,551	142,738	821,349
Challengers	11,200	6,500	1,000	18,700
Open Seat	58,750	70,250	6,500	135,500
Winners	282,200	418,301	n/a	700,501
Losers	61,810	62,000	n/a	123,810

Andersen Consulting PAC (C00300707) *Phone: (202) 862-6449 * Fax: (202) 862-7098 * 1666 K St. N.W., Washington, DC 20006 * Treasurer: Jeffrey J. Peck*

	1993-94	1995-96	1997	Totals
Receipts	$0	$132,795	$3,052	$135,847
Disburse	0	39,045	4,838	43,883
Cash	0	93,756	91,973	n/a
Contributions	0	34,363	3,500	37,863
Republicans	0	34,363	3,500	37,863
No. of Cand.	*0*	*17*	*3*	*20*
House	0	23,863	1,500	25,363
Senate	0	10,500	2,000	12,500
Democrats	0	0	0	0
No. of Cand.	*0*	*0*	*0*	*0*
House	0	0	0	0
Senate	0	0	0	0
Incumbents	0	32,363	3,500	35,863
Challengers	0	1,000	0	1,000
Open Seat	0	1,000	0	1,000
Winners	0	26,363	n/a	26,363
Losers	0	8,000	n/a	8,000

Coopers & Lybrand LLP

*Phone: (212) 259-1000 * Fax: (212) 259-1301*
1301 Ave. of the Americas, New York, NY 10019-6013
Web: www.colybrand.com

Coopers & Lybrand is a privately owned accounting and professional services firm headquartered in New York. It employs more than 74,000 people worldwide, including 16,000 in the United States. One of the Big Six accounting firms, it announced in 1997 a merger with Price Waterhouse, an accounting company. The combined firm would have annual revenues exceeding $13 billion, if the merger receives regulatory approvals.

The firm tracks legislation affecting taxes and a number of industries that affect its clients, including energy, health care and telecommunications. Coopers & Lybrand employees frequently appear before congressional committees to testify on tax policy and other financial issues.

Coopers & Lybrand ranked fifth among accounting industry PAC contributors to congressional candidates during the 1995-96 election cycle. Nearly 90 percent of the firm's contributions went to incumbents. The leading recipients were Sen. Christopher J. Dodd, D-Conn., and Reps. Martin Frost, D-Texas, Vic Fazio, D-Calif., W.J. "Billy" Tauzin, R-La., and Sherrod Brown, D-Ohio.

Coopers & Lybrand PAC (C00107235) *Phone: (202) 822-4000 * Fax: (202) 822-5800 * 1900 K St. N.W., Washington, DC 20006 * Treasurer: Allen J. Weltmann*

	1993-94	1995-96	1997	Totals
Receipts	$362,838	$587,964	$379,509	$1,330,311
Disburse	381,003	575,690	326,213	1,282,906
Cash	27,724	40,001	93,299	n/a
Contributions	285,697	397,058	233,321	916,076
Republicans	126,649	226,201	138,982	491,832
No. of Cand.	*82*	*131*	*106*	*319*
House	59,449	144,987	108,267	312,703
Senate	67,200	81,214	30,715	179,129
Democrats	153,548	170,857	92,339	416,744
No. of Cand.	*125*	*87*	*67*	*279*
House	111,526	129,357	73,839	314,722
Senate	42,022	41,500	18,500	102,022
Incumbents	238,497	350,019	224,106	812,622
Challengers	13,500	4,000	1,715	19,215
Open Seat	34,200	45,039	7,500	86,739
Winners	239,887	356,019	n/a	595,906
Losers	45,810	41,039	n/a	86,849

Deloitte & Touche LLP

*Phone: (212) 489-1600 * Fax: (212) 489-1687*
1633 Broadway, New York, NY 10019-6754
Web: www.us.deloitte.com

Deloitte & Touche is a privately owned accounting and professional services firm with about 23,000 employees. One of the Big Six accounting firms, Deloitte & Touche is a member of Deloitte Touche Tohmatsu International, which reported 1997 revenues of $7.4 billion.

The firm is interested in business laws generally and especially in changes to securities and tax laws. It has opposed mergers of the large accounting firms, which are subject to government approval.

Deloitte & Touche ranked third among accounting industry PACs in contributions to congressional candidates during the 1995-96 election cycle. It gave twice as much money to Republican candidates as it did to Democrats. More than 85 percent of the overall total went to incumbents.

The leading recipients were Sens. Max Baucus, D-Mont., Phil Gramm, R-Texas, Pete V. Domenici, R-N.M., and Alfonse M. D'Amato, R-N.Y., along with Rep. E. Clay Shaw Jr., R-Fla.

Deloitte & Touche LLP Federal Political Action Committee (C00211318) *Phone: (202) 879-4973 * Fax: (202) 879-5309 * 1001 Pennsylvania Ave. N.W., Suite 350 N., Washington, DC 20004 * Treasurer: Wade S. Williams*

	1993-94	1995-96	1997	Totals
Receipts	$335,694	$802,543	$460,064	$1,598,301
Disburse	307,859	754,684	326,635	1,389,178
Cash	31,854	79,689	213,420	n/a
Contributions	227,003	588,402	244,041	1,059,446
Republicans	124,496	399,089	148,300	671,885
No. of Cand.	*86*	*294*	*107*	*487*
House	65,046	238,050	90,075	393,171
Senate	59,450	161,039	58,225	278,714
Democrats	98,007	189,313	91,241	378,561
No. of Cand.	*69*	*124*	*80*	*273*
House	64,898	128,707	73,741	267,346
Senate	33,109	60,606	17,500	111,215
Incumbents	165,253	501,973	236,816	904,042
Challengers	11,500	18,929	2,500	32,929
Open Seat	49,750	66,500	4,725	120,975
Winners	192,753	496,473	n/a	689,226
Losers	34,250	91,929	n/a	126,179

Ernst & Young LLP

*Phone: (212) 773-3000 * Fax: (212) 773-2821*
787 Seventh Ave., New York, NY 10019
Web: www.ey.com

Ernst & Young is a Big Six accounting and professional services firm with revenues of $4.4 billion and 27,000 employees. E&Y provides auditing, consulting and tax services to 115 Fortune 500 companies and three professional sports leagues.

E&Y and KPMG Peat Marwick, another Big Six firm, called off a merger in early 1998, several months after it had been announced. The move would have produced a combined firm with $18 billion in annual revenue and more than 163,000 employees. Both firms cited a lengthy regulatory approval process as a main reason for the cancellation.

The company is primarily interested in tax issues which affect its business and clients, such as capital gains and estate taxes. It favors tighter standards for securities lawsuits. The PAC has a board that decides which candidates will receive contributions.

E&Y's PAC contributed the most money of any accounting firm to 1996 congressional races and trailed the American Institute of CPAs among all accounting groups and businesses. E&Y also gave more money to Democratic candidates — just more than half of its total — than any other Big Six firm. The leading recipients included Rep. Martin Frost, D-Texas, and Sen. Pete V. Domenici, R-N.M.

Ernst & Young Political Action Committee (C00227744) *Phone: (202) 327-7584 * Fax: (202) 327-8863 * 1225 Connecticut Ave. N.W., Suite 200, Washington, DC 20036 * Treasurer: George H. McCallum * Contact: K. C. Tominovich, Political and Legislative Dir.*

	1993-94	1995-96	1997	Totals
Receipts	$784,826	$1,096,512	$542,375	$2,423,713
Disburse	657,547	1,068,091	398,042	2,123,680
Cash	250,920	279,151	423,477	n/a
Contributions	510,510	883,115	299,498	1,693,123

Republicans	205,450	438,075	153,499	797,024
No. of Cand.	*160*	*249*	*109*	*518*
House	127,450	241,675	95,499	464,624
Senate	78,000	196,400	58,000	332,400
Democrats	291,060	445,040	144,999	881,099
No. of Cand.	*187*	*188*	*83*	*458*
House	181,550	259,040	75,999	516,589
Senate	109,510	186,000	69,000	364,510
Incumbents	420,410	610,815	277,498	1,308,723
Challengers	23,050	77,300	8,000	108,350
Open Seat	66,750	195,000	13,500	275,250
Winners	405,850	709,315	n/a	1,115,165
Losers	104,660	173,800	n/a	278,460

Terminated PACs which contributed less than $5,000 during 1995-96 cycle:

Kenneth Leventhal & Co. PAC (also known as KL&Co. PAC) (C00224071) *Phone: (310) 284-0880 * Fax: (310) 284-7970 * 2049 Century Park E., Suite 1700, Los Angeles, CA 90067 * Treasurer: Paul L. Kester*

KPMG Peat Marwick LLP

Phone: (201) 307-7000
Three Chestnut Ridge Rd., Montvale, NJ 07645
Web: www.us.kpmg.com

KPMG Peat Marwick is the U.S. member firm of KPMG International, the worldwide accounting and professional services firm. KPMG International has more than 1,100 offices in 837 cities in 134 countries. The private company offers consulting and services in the tax, health care, manufacturing and entertainment industries. Its American clients include Citicorp, Travelers, Apple Computer, Aetna U.S. Healthcare and Federal Express. The firm has 78,000 employees, with some 22,000 in the United States, and reported $9 billion in revenues during 1997.

KPMG and fellow Big Six accounting firm Ernst & Young in February 1998 called off a proposed merger, citing a lengthy approval process. The deal would have created a company with 163,000 employees around the world.

KPMG lobbies on tax and securities issues that could affect its clients.

For the 1995-96 election cycle, KPMG ranked seventh among accounting firms and associations in total contributions to congressional races. Ernst & Young ranked second.

Senate Banking Committee Chairman Sen. Alfonse M. D'Amato, R-N.Y., and ranking member Sen. Christopher J. Dodd, D-Conn., were the top two congressional recipients.

Peat Marwick Partners/Principals & Employees Political Action Committee (Peat Marwick/PAC) (C00280222) *Phone: (202) 296-6495 * Fax: (202) 467-3974 * P.O. Box 18254, Washington, DC 20036-9998 * Treasurer: Stephen E. Allis*

	1993-94	*1995-96*	*1997*	*Totals*
Receipts	$419,555	$452,357	$353,132	$1,225,044
Disburse	364,014	494,160	245,239	1,103,413
Cash	55,539	11,233	119,125	n/a
Contributions	212,508	314,750	140,989	668,247
Republicans	80,750	196,000	99,225	375,975
No. of Cand.	*68*	*125*	*67*	*260*
House	47,350	114,000	70,225	231,575
Senate	33,400	82,000	29,000	144,400
Democrats	130,058	118,750	41,264	290,072
No. of Cand.	*87*	*68*	*31*	*186*
House	78,988	82,250	23,500	184,738
Senate	51,070	36,500	17,764	105,334
Incumbents	171,908	272,500	136,989	581,397
Challengers	13,500	6,500	1,000	21,000
Open Seat	26,100	36,750	3,000	65,850
Winners	165,638	267,750	n/a	433,388
Losers	46,870	47,000	n/a	93,870

National Society of Public Accountants

*Phone: (703) 549-6400 * Fax: (703) 549-2984*
1010 N. Fairfax St., Alexandria, VA 22314
Web: www.nsacct.org

The National Society of Public Accountants represents about 30,000 individual certified public accountants through its national organization and state affiliate organizations.

National Society of Public Accountants Political Action Committee (C00129189) *Address: same as sponsor * Treasurer: Robert Grille * Contact: Elizabeth Ellis, Chairwoman*

	1993-94	*1995-96*	*1997*	*Totals*
Receipts	$49,421	$57,187	$17,648	$124,256
Disburse	26,425	35,094	14,438	75,957
Cash	87,701	109,794	113,004	n/a
Contributions	11,250	8,250	7,000	26,500
Republicans	5,750	5,250	5,500	16,500
No. of Cand.	*8*	*9*	*7*	*24*
House	4,750	5,250	3,000	13,000
Senate	1,000	0	2,500	3,500
Democrats	5,500	3,000	1,500	10,000
No. of Cand.	*6*	*4*	*2*	*12*
House	5,500	3,000	500	9,000
Senate	0	0	1,000	1,000
Incumbents	8,750	7,750	7,000	23,500
Challengers	1,500	0	0	1,500
Open Seat	1,000	500	0	1,500
Winners	8,000	7,250	n/a	15,250
Losers	3,250	1,000	n/a	4,250

Price Waterhouse

*Phone: (212) 596-7000 * Fax: (212) 596-8880*
1177 Ave. of the Americas, New York, NY 10036
Web: www.pw.com

Price Waterhouse is a Big Six accounting and professional services firm employing 56,000 people in 119 countries, including 16,000 in the United States. The private company reported $5.7 billion in revenue for 1997.

Its partners approved in late 1997 a merger with Coopers & Lybrand, another of the Big Six firms. The resulting company's revenue would surpass $13 billion, if the merger receives U.S. and European regulatory approvals.

In January 1998, the firm announced that Kenneth Kies, former chief of staff of the Joint Taxation Committee, would join Price Waterhouse's Washington national tax services office. Among its other services, Price Waterhouse tracks tax policy and regulation and lobbies on tax and securities issues.

Price Waterhouse ranked sixth among accounting PACs in 1996 congressional contributions. It favored Republican candidates and spent 1 percent of its money on challengers. The leading recipients were Rep. Vic Fazio, D-Calif., former Sen. Larry Pressler, R-S.D., Sen. Alfonse M. D'Amato, R-N.Y., and Rep. Martin Frost, D-Texas. D'Amato chairs the Senate Banking Committee.

Price Waterhouse Partners' Political Action Committee (C00232173) *Phone: (202) 414-1375 * Fax: (202) 414-1301 * 1301 K St. N.W., Suite 800 W., Washington, DC 20005-3333 * E-mail: Thomas_Craren@notes.pw.com * Treasurer: Thomas J. Craren*

	1993-94	*1995-96*	*1997*	*Totals*
Receipts	$462,309	$483,918	$246,302	$1,192,529
Disburse	343,197	474,555	233,501	1,051,253
Cash	124,926	134,290	147,092	n/a
Contributions	293,638	331,855	162,662	788,155
Republicans	136,147	193,630	107,162	436,939
No. of Cand.	*124*	*124*	*72*	*320*
House	89,452	116,300	77,775	283,527
Senate	46,695	77,330	29,387	153,412
Democrats	150,991	138,225	53,500	342,716
No. of Cand.	*115*	*82*	*38*	*235*
House	110,631	102,725	30,500	243,856
Senate	40,360	35,500	23,000	98,860
Incumbents	256,138	291,525	156,162	703,825
Challengers	9,000	5,000	2,000	16,000
Open Seat	28,500	36,330	4,500	69,330
Winners	253,778	285,980	n/a	539,758
Losers	39,860	45,875	n/a	85,735

Commercial Banks

1st Source Corp.

*Phone: (219) 235-2459 * Fax: (219) 235-2719*
P.O. Box 1602, South Bend, IN 46634
Web: www.1stsource.com

Indiana-based bank holding company 1st Source has about $1.8 billion in assets and 900 employees. Through 1st Source Bank, it operates about 35 branches in northern Indiana. The bank has been operating since 1872.

The bank offers a range of commercial banking, personal banking and trust services. In addition, 1st Source provides transportation, equipment and lease financing through a diversified group of commercial and industrial firms, including truck and automobile leasing companies.

1st Source Corp. Political Action Committee (C00181529)
*Address: same as sponsor * Treasurer: Charles H. Krueger * Contact: Duke Jones, Chairman*

	1993-94	1995-96	1997	Totals
Receipts	$13,161	$18,053	$8,253	$39,467
Disburse	3,580	8,734	408	12,722
Cash	18,585	27,907	35,753	n/a
Contributions	2,500	4,500	0	7,000
Republicans	1,500	3,500	0	5,000
No. of Cand.	*2*	*5*	*0*	*7*
House	500	2,000	0	2,500
Senate	1,000	1,500	0	2,500
Democrats	1,000	1,000	0	2,000
No. of Cand.	*1*	*1*	*0*	*2*
House	1,000	1,000	0	2,000
Senate	0	0	0	0
Incumbents	2,500	3,500	0	6,000
Challengers	0	1,000	0	1,000
Open Seat	0	0	0	0
Winners	2,500	3,500	n/a	6,000
Losers	0	1,000	n/a	1,000

AMCORE Financial Inc.

*Phone: (815) 961-7006 * Fax: (815) 961-7728*
501 Seventh St., Rockford, IL 61104
Web: www.amcore.com

AMCORE Financial is a publicly held, Illinois-based multi-bank holding company with assets of more than $3 billion. The company has 1,400 employees.

Incorporated in 1982, AMCORE has grown to include five primary subsidiaries. AMCORE Insurance Group Inc. is a full service insurance agency that writes all forms of personal, business and agricultural insurance. It serves customers in northern Illinois and southern Wisconsin. AMCORE Investment Group NA provides trust services. Other subsidiaries include AMCORE Mortgage Inc., AMCORE Consumer Finance Co. and Rockford Mercantile Agency Inc., a collection service.

In February 1998, AMCORE Financial completed its acquisition of Investors Management Group, the largest independent asset management firm in Des Moines, Iowa. IMG will become an investment subsidiary of AMCORE Investment Group.

AMCORE Financial Inc. (AMCORE-PAC) (Federal Fund) (C00236430) *Address: same as sponsor * Treasurer: Charles E. Gagnier * Contact: Robert J. Meuleman, Chairman*

	1993-94	1995-96	1997	Totals
Receipts	$17,861	$18,570	$8,050	$44,481
Disburse	13,000	21,350	12,000	46,350
Cash	15,122	12,345	8,395	n/a
Contributions	1,000	7,350	0	8,350
Republicans	1,000	7,350	0	8,350
No. of Cand.	*1*	*4*	*0*	*5*
House	1,000	6,350	0	7,350
Senate	0	1,000	0	1,000
Democrats	0	0	0	0
No. of Cand.	*0*	*0*	*0*	*0*
House	0	0	0	0
Senate	0	0	0	0
Incumbents	1,000	5,850	0	6,850
Challengers	0	500	0	500
Open Seat	0	1,000	0	1,000
Winners	1,000	5,850	n/a	6,850
Losers	0	1,500	n/a	1,500

AmSouth Bancorp

*Phone: (205) 320-7151 * Fax: (205) 581-7755*
P.O. Box Drawer 431, Montgomery, AL 36101
Web: www.amsouth.com

AmSouth Bancorp is a bank holding company with major operations in Alabama, Florida and Tennessee.

The company has assets of $18.6 billion, ranking it among the top 50 financial service institutions in the United States. AmSouth operates 273 branches and more than 600 ATMs in Alabama, Florida, Tennessee and Georgia. Company services include investment management, consumer and commercial banking, mortgages and trust services. AmSouth has 6,400 employees.

Publicly owned AmSouth has alliances with three investment management companies: Rockhaven Asset Management in Pittsburgh, Sawgrass Asset Management in Jacksonville, Fla., and Chicago-based OakBrook Investments.

AmSouth Political Action Committee (C00168575) *Address: same as sponsor * Treasurer: Lynda Kern*

	1993-94	1995-96	1997	Totals
Receipts	$305,517	$332,493	$106,898	$744,908
Disburse	447,344	359,665	91,410	898,419
Cash	41,137	33,017	47,336	n/a
Contributions	27,800	109,400	48,500	185,700
Republicans	17,700	77,400	40,500	135,600
No. of Cand.	*7*	*25*	*17*	*49*
House	9,500	52,000	25,500	87,000
Senate	8,200	25,400	15,000	48,600
Democrats	10,100	32,000	8,000	50,100
No. of Cand.	*10*	*11*	*4*	*25*
House	9,100	16,000	5,500	30,600
Senate	1,000	16,000	2,500	19,500
Incumbents	25,050	29,400	47,500	101,950
Challengers	250	10,000	0	10,250
Open Seat	2,500	69,750	0	72,250
Winners	21,550	53,900	n/a	75,450
Losers	6,250	55,500	n/a	61,750

American Bankers Association

*Phone: (202) 663-5113 * Fax: (202) 828-4547*
1120 Connecticut Ave. N.W., Suite 851, Washington, DC 20036
*Web: www.aba.com * E-mail: gfields@aba.com*

The American Bankers Association is the largest banking trade group in the United States. Its members, covering 90 percent of the nation's commercial bank assets, include local and regional banks, savings associations and trust companies. It has been named as one of the most influential lobbying organizations in Washington by Fortune magazine.

The bankers' group lobbies for changes in bankruptcy law that would reduce the number of people who declare bankruptcy. It prefers a system in which debtors would receive only as much relief as they need, not a total erasure of debt. The group supports the use of digital signatures in financial transactions and a proposal to raise the limit from six to 24 on the number of monthly transfers between demand deposit and interest-bearing accounts. The ABA opposes the expansion of the credit union industry to include unrelated groups of employees.

The leading congressional contributor among commercial banks and banking organizations, the ABA fields input from its 50 state associations in deciding which candidates should receive PAC money. In 1996, it gave more than $900,000 to Republicans, ranking among the top 12 givers to GOP candidates. The leading recipients were Sen. Gordon H. Smith, R-Ore., Sen. James M. Inhofe, R-Okla., and Rep. Peter T. King, R-N.Y. Most of the top recipients were Republicans, but former Rep. Bill Orton, D-Utah, and Rep. John J. LaFalce, D-N.Y., both of whom sat on banking committees, received $10,000 during that cycle.

Nine state affiliates contributed at least $5,000 each to congressional candidates. State PACs in Virginia, Ohio and Florida were the top three.

American Bankers Association BankPAC (C00004275) *Address: same as sponsor * Treasurer: Gary W. Fields*

	1993-94	1995-96	1997	Totals
Receipts	$1,563,312	$1,638,301	$788,691	$3,990,304
Disburse	1,591,197	1,529,576	587,990	3,708,763
Cash	147,101	255,827	455,527	n/a
Contributions	1,343,150	1,299,850	472,100	3,115,100
Republicans	704,100	937,650	264,350	1,906,100
No. of Cand.	*204*	*265*	*145*	*614*
House	499,250	658,650	194,850	1,352,750
Senate	204,850	279,000	69,500	553,350

Democrats	632,050	362,200	206,750	1,201,000
No. of Cand.	*209*	*127*	*99*	*435*
House	509,150	296,500	135,250	940,900
Senate	122,900	65,700	71,500	260,100
Incumbents	1,168,300	1,027,850	442,100	2,638,250
Challengers	36,500	72,500	5,500	114,500
Open Seat	136,350	197,500	23,500	357,350
Winners	1,145,400	1,106,350	n/a	2,251,750
Losers	197,750	193,500	n/a	391,250

Virginia BankPAC (C00101626) *Phone: (804) 643-7469 * Fax: (804) 643-6308 * 700 E. Main St., Suite 1411, Richmond, VA 23219 * Web: www.vabankers.org * E-mail: wayers@vabankers.org * Treasurer: Walter C. Ayers*

The Virginia Bankers Association represents about 190 commercial banks and savings and loans.

	1993-94	1995-96	1997	Totals
Receipts	$139,483	$176,943	$100,208	$416,634
Disburse	133,810	96,075	29,472	259,357
Cash	34,041	114,913	185,650	n/a
Contributions	34,850	45,750	3,750	84,350
Republicans	22,600	23,000	2,750	48,350
No. of Cand.	*7*	*5*	*2*	*14*
House	22,600	22,500	2,750	47,850
Senate	0	500	0	500
Democrats	12,250	22,750	1,000	36,000
No. of Cand.	*4*	*6*	*1*	*11*
House	12,250	22,750	1,000	36,000
Senate	0	0	0	0
Incumbents	25,350	40,750	3,750	69,850
Challengers	7,000	0	0	7,000
Open Seat	0	5,000	0	5,000
Winners	30,350	45,750	n/a	76,100
Losers	4,500	0	n/a	4,500

Ohio Bankers Political Campaign Committee (Ohio BankPAC-Federal) (C00074799) *Phone: (614) 221-5121 * Fax: (614) 221-3421 * 37 W. Broad St., Suite 1001, Columbus, OH 43215-4162 * Web: www.obanet.com * Treasurer: William N. Morgan * Contact: Dan Conklin, Gov. Affairs Specialist*

The Ohio Bankers Association represents about 285 commercial and savings banks in Ohio.

	1993-94	1995-96	1997	Totals
Receipts	$89,045	$135,238	$71,037	$295,320
Disburse	126,327	182,036	53,089	361,452
Cash	71,677	24,876	42,823	n/a
Contributions	16,000	40,500	9,000	65,500
Republicans	10,500	35,500	8,000	54,000
No. of Cand.	*5*	*7*	*5*	*17*
House	10,500	35,500	4,500	50,500
Senate	0	0	3,500	3,500
Democrats	5,500	5,000	1,000	11,500
No. of Cand.	*5*	*2*	*2*	*9*
House	5,500	5,000	1,000	11,500
Senate	0	0	0	0
Incumbents	14,000	40,500	8,000	62,500
Challengers	0	0	0	0
Open Seat	4,500	0	1,000	5,500
Winners	15,500	29,750	n/a	45,250
Losers	500	10,750	n/a	11,250

Florida Bankers Association Political Action Committee (also known as Florida Bank PAC) (C00012484) *Phone: (850) 224-2265 * Fax: (850) 224-2423 * 1001 Thomasville Rd., Suite 201, Box 1360, Tallahassee, FL 32303 * Web: www.webbanker.com * E-mail: fba!asanchez@fbamail.attmail.com * Treasurer: Christine Follmar * Contact: Alejandro (Alex) Sanchez, CEO*

The Florida Bankers Association represents 14,000 banks and individuals in Florida. The PAC's main issues are credit union regulations, banking modernization and electronic banking.

	1993-94	1995-96	1997	Totals
Receipts	$56,909	$152,405	$40,142	$249,456
Disburse	57,034	103,294	42,120	202,448
Cash	1,309	50,591	48,618	n/a
Contributions	6,000	27,200	2,000	35,200
Republicans	3,000	6,500	1,000	10,500
No. of Cand.	*5*	*5*	*3*	*13*
House	3,000	6,500	1,000	10,500
Senate	0	0	0	0
Democrats	3,000	20,700	1,000	24,700
No. of Cand.	*4*	*7*	*1*	*12*
House	3,000	20,700	1,000	24,700
Senate	0	0	0	0
Incumbents	2,500	8,200	2,000	12,700
Challengers	0	0	0	0
Open Seat	3,500	19,000	0	22,500
Winners	4,000	26,000	n/a	30,000
Losers	2,000	1,200	n/a	3,200

Nebraska Bankers Association Federal Political Action Committee (C00083790) *233 S. 13th St., Suite 1100, Lincoln, NE 68508 * Web: www.nebankers.org * Treasurer: Claudia Russell*

	1993-94	1995-96	1997	Totals
Receipts	$45,876	$48,607	$24,954	$119,437
Disburse	40,608	42,790	14,651	98,049
Cash	38,484	44,305	54,609	n/a
Contributions	14,500	15,000	1,000	30,500
Republicans	14,500	15,000	1,000	30,500
No. of Cand.	*3*	*3*	*1*	*7*
House	7,500	5,000	0	12,500
Senate	7,000	10,000	1,000	18,000
Democrats	0	0	0	0
No. of Cand.	*0*	*0*	*0*	*0*
House	0	0	0	0
Senate	0	0	0	0
Incumbents	2,500	5,000	1,000	8,500
Challengers	12,000	0	0	12,000
Open Seat	0	10,000	0	10,000
Winners	7,500	12,500	n/a	20,000
Losers	7,000	2,500	n/a	9,500

Illinois BankPAC (C00139568) *111 N. Canal, Suite 1111, Chicago, IL 60606 * Web: www.ilbanker.com * Treasurer: Stephen W. Lind*

	1993-94	1995-96	1997	Totals
Receipts	$204,282	$219,625	$105,946	$529,853
Disburse	223,105	234,033	124,293	581,431
Cash	118,160	103,751	83,876	n/a
Contributions	20,600	9,000	0	29,600
Republicans	8,500	4,000	0	12,500
No. of Cand.	*4*	*3*	*0*	*7*
House	8,500	4,000	0	12,500
Senate	0	0	0	0
Democrats	12,100	5,000	0	17,100
No. of Cand.	*7*	*5*	*0*	*12*
House	12,000	5,000	0	17,000
Senate	100	0	0	100
Incumbents	8,100	5,000	0	13,100
Challengers	6,000	1,000	0	7,000
Open Seat	6,500	3,000	0	9,500
Winners	10,600	4,000	n/a	14,600
Losers	10,000	5,000	n/a	15,000

Kansas Bankers Association BankPAC (C00086611) *1500 Merchants National Building, Topeka, KS 66612 * Web: www.ink.org/public/kbank * Treasurer: Donna L. Adams*

	1993-94	1995-96	1997	Totals
Receipts	$31,524	$33,897	$13,293	$78,714
Disburse	27,767	33,603	13,486	74,856
Cash	4,557	4,853	4,661	n/a
Contributions	1,500	6,200	250	7,950
Republicans	500	1,200	250	1,950
No. of Cand.	*1*	*2*	*1*	*4*
House	500	200	250	950
Senate	0	1,000	0	1,000
Democrats	1,000	5,000	0	6,000
No. of Cand.	*1*	*2*	*0*	*3*
House	1,000	1,000	0	2,000
Senate	0	4,000	0	4,000
Incumbents	0	1,200	250	1,450
Challengers	500	4,000	0	4,500
Open Seat	1,000	1,000	0	2,000
Winners	500	200	n/a	700
Losers	1,000	6,000	n/a	7,000

Jersey Bankers Political Action Committee-Federal Fund (JEBPAC) (C00086355) *499 N. Harrison St., P.O. Box 573, Princeton, NJ 08540 * Treasurer: W. Stuart Cameron*

	1993-94	1995-96	1997	Totals
Receipts	$42,454	$33,457	$13,500	$89,411
Disburse	41,590	38,038	9,150	88,778
Cash	5,207	627	4,977	n/a
Contributions	4,000	5,500	1,150	10,650
Republicans	500	1,500	0	2,000
No. of Cand.	*1*	*2*	*0*	*3*
House	0	1,500	0	1,500
Senate	500	0	0	500
Democrats	3,500	4,000	1,150	8,650
No. of Cand.	*2*	*3*	*2*	*7*
House	1,000	500	150	1,650
Senate	2,500	3,500	1,000	7,000
Incumbents	3,500	2,000	1,150	6,650
Challengers	500	500	0	1,000

(Data for Jersey Bankers Political continued)

Open Seat	0	3,000	0	3,000
Winners	2,500	5,000	n/a	7,500
Losers	1,500	500	n/a	2,000

Connecticut Bankers Association Political Action Committee (CBA Fed PAC) (C00108605) *Phone: (860) 527-5161 * Fax: (860) 527-5161 * 450 Church St., Hartford, CT 06103 * Web: www.ctbank.com/home.asp * Treasurer: Gerald M. Noonan*

	1993-94	1995-96	1997	Totals
Receipts	$9,992	$16,762	$9,916	$36,670
Disburse	6,479	15,176	7,361	29,016
Cash	3,513	5,097	7,651	n/a
Contributions	2,250	5,200	2,150	9,600
Republicans	1,750	1,500	0	3,250
No. of Cand.	*4*	*3*	*0*	*7*
House	1,750	1,000	0	2,750
Senate	0	500	0	500
Democrats	500	3,700	2,150	6,350
No. of Cand.	*2*	*5*	*3*	*10*
House	250	2,700	2,150	5,100
Senate	250	1,000	0	1,250
Incumbents	1,750	5,200	1,150	8,100
Challengers	500	0	0	500
Open Seat	0	0	1,000	1,000
Winners	1,750	4,700	n/a	6,450
Losers	500	500	n/a	1,000

Tennessee Bankers Association Federal Political Action Committee (C00114447) *Phone: (615) 244-4871 * Fax: (615) 244-0995 * 201 Venture Cir., Nashville, TN 37228-1603 * Web: www.tnbankers.org * Treasurer: Ed C. Loughry Jr.*

	1993-94	1995-96	1997	Totals
Receipts	$84,083	$70,461	$15,297	$169,841
Disburse	45,610	51,520	20,894	118,024
Cash	39,872	58,815	53,219	n/a
Contributions	2,000	2,000	1,000	5,000
Republicans	0	1,000	1,000	2,000
No. of Cand.	*0*	*1*	*1*	*2*
House	0	1,000	1,000	2,000
Senate	0	0	0	0
Democrats	2,000	1,000	0	3,000
No. of Cand.	*2*	*1*	*0*	*3*
House	1,000	1,000	0	2,000
Senate	1,000	0	0	1,000
Incumbents	1,000	1,000	1,000	3,000
Challengers	0	0	0	0
Open Seat	1,000	1,000	0	2,000
Winners	0	2,000	n/a	2,000
Losers	2,000	0	n/a	2,000

Contributed less than $5,000 during 1995-96 cycle:

Arizona Bankers Association Political Action Committee (C00039941) *2700 N. Central Ave., Suite 620, Phoenix, AZ 85004 * Treasurer: Edwin H. Jelliff*

Bankers Unite in Legislative Decisions (also known as BUILD) (formerly known as Iowa Bankers Association) (C00085977) *Phone: (515) 286-4399 * Fax: (515) 280-4140 * 418 Sixth Ave., Suite 430, Des Moines, IA 50309 * Web: www.iabankers.com * Treasurer: John Sorensen*

California Bankers Association Federal PAC (also known as CalBankPAC) (C00082834) *Phone: (415) 284-6999 * Fax: (415) 284-6998 * 201 Mission St., Suite 2400, San Francisco, CA 94105 * Web: www.calbankers.com * Treasurer: Katy Taylor*

Colorado Bankers Political Action Committee (ColBankPAC) (C00102731) *1099 18th St., Suite 500, Denver, CO 80202 * Web: www.capcon.com/cba * Treasurer: Don Childears*

Georgia Bankers Political Action Committee (C00092841) *50 Hurt Plaza, Suite 1050, Atlanta, GA 30303 * Web: www.gabankers.com * Treasurer: J. Joseph Brannen*

Idaho Bankers Political Action Committee (C00056523) *P.O. Box 638, Boise, ID 83701 * Treasurer: Barbara Strickfaden*

Indiana BankPAC - Federal (C00115832) *Phone: (317) 921-3135 * Fax: (317) 921-3131 * 3135 N. Meridian St., Indianapolis, IN 46208 * Web: www.inbankers.org * Treasurer: Kerry B. Spradlin*

Kentucky Bankers Political Action Committee (C00062836) *325 Main St., Suite 1000, One Riverfront Plaza, Louisville, KY 40202 * Web: www.kybanks.com * Treasurer: Judy Blain*

Louisiana Bankers Association FEDPAC (C00140707) *666 North St., P.O. Box 2871, Baton Rouge, LA 70821 * Web: www.lba.org * Treasurer: Robert T. Taylor*

Maine Bankers Associaton Political Action Committee (Maine BankPAC) (C00108456) *132 State St., P.O. Box 745, Augusta, ME 04330-0745 * Web: www.mainebankers.com * Treasurer: Joseph J. Pietroski Jr.*

Massachusetts Bankers PAC-Federal Fund (C00221507) *73 Tremont St., Third Floor, Boston, MA 02108 * Web: www.massbankers.org * Treasurer: David E. Floreen*

Michigan Bankers Association - MiBankPAC - Federal (C00080648) *Phone: (517) 485-3600 * Fax: (517) 485-3672 * 222 N. Washington Sq., Suite 320, Lansing, MI 48933 * Web: www.mibankers.com * Treasurer: Terry Greisinger*

Mississippi Bankers Association PAC Federal Fund (Miss. BankPAC-Federal Fund) (C00106716) *640 N. State St., P.O. Box 1091, Jackson, MS 39205 * Treasurer: L. Chad Driskell*

Missouri Bankers Association Federal Political Action Committee (C00172494) *Phone: (573) 636-8151 * Fax: (573) 634-2754 * 207 E. Capitol Ave., Jefferson City, MO 65101 * Web: www.mobankers.com * Treasurer: William O. Ratliff*

New Hampshire Bankers Association BankPAC (C00109678) *P.O. Box 2586, 122 N. Main St., Concord, NH 03302 * Web: www.nh.com/banking/nhbank.html * Treasurer: Gerald H. Little*

New Mexico Bankers Political Action Committee (C00147645) *7770 Jefferson N.E., Suite 300, Albuquerque, NM 87109 * Treasurer: John W. Anderson*

New York State Bankers Political Action Committee- Federal Fund (C00081422) *99 Park Ave., New York, NY 10016 * Treasurer: William J. Bosies Jr.*

Oklahoma Bankers Association Fed Elect (C00139477) *643 N.E. 41st St., Oklahoma City, OK 73105 * Web: www.oba.com * Treasurer: Roger M. Beverage*

Oregon Bankers Political Action Committee (C00035253) *P.O. Box 13429, 777 13th St. S.E., Suite 130, Salem, OR 97309 * Web: www.oregonbankers.com * Treasurer: Frank E. Brawner*

Pennsylvania Bankers Public Affairs Committee (Federal) (C00094896) *Phone: (717) 255-6900 * 3897 N. Front St., Harrisburg, PA 17110 * Web: www.pabanker.com * Treasurer: Daniel J. Reisteter*

Texas Bankers Association Bankers Legislative League of Texas (TBA BALLOT) (C00196444) *203 W. 10th St., Austin, TX 78701 * Web: www.txbanc.com * Treasurer: John M. Heasley*

Washington Bankers Association Political Action Committee (C00114090) *1601 Fifth Ave., Suite 1400, Seattle, WA 98101 * Treasurer: Meara G. Nisbet*

Wisconsin Bankers Association Political Action Committee Inc. (C00048181) *P.O. Box 1667, Madison, WI 53701 * Web: www.wisbank.com * Treasurer: Jodi Reinke*

Banc One Corp.

*Phone: (614) 248-9376 * Fax: (614) 248-5624*
100 E. Broad St., Columbus, OH 43215
Web: www.bankone.com

Banc One is the nation's seventh-largest bank holding company with total managed assets of $142.9 billion and total assets of $113 billion.

The company operates more than 1,200 branches in 12 states including: Ohio, West Virginia, Kentucky, Wisconsin, Texas, Oklahoma, Louisiana, Illinois, Indiana, Arizona, Utah and Colorado. In 1997, the company announced plans to acquire First Commerce Corp., making Banc One the largest bank in Louisiana.

In April 1998, the company announced plans to acquire First Chicago NBD Corp., the nation's seventh-largest bank.

The company is interested in legislation affecting the financial services industry. It opposes limits on bank-owned life insurance, which it buys for its officers and high-ranking employees. Banc One spent 35 percent of its 1995-96 PAC money on congressional candidates, the lowest percentage for a corporation in the top 200 PACs. The top recipients were former Rep. Frank A. Cremeans, R-Ohio, Rep. Martin Frost, D-Texas, Rep. Bob Ney, R-Ohio, and the late Rep. Sonny Bono, R-Calif.

First Commerce Corp.'s PAC contributed $26,400 to congressional candidates during the 1995-96 election cycle, mostly from Louisiana.

Banc One PAC (C00128512) *Address: same as sponsor * Treasurer: Robert E. Wahlman * Contact: Richard McGivern, PAC Administrator*

	1993-94	1995-96	1997	Totals
Receipts	$1,037,361	$1,473,818	$837,697	$3,348,876
Disburse	934,434	1,330,484	746,343	3,011,261
Cash	341,377	484,708	576,064	n/a
Contributions	211,465	467,917	265,211	944,593
Republicans	121,750	323,347	171,211	616,308
No. of Cand.	*69*	*98*	*62*	*229*
House	70,300	273,597	128,211	472,108
Senate	51,450	49,750	43,000	144,200
Democrats	89,715	144,570	94,000	328,285
No. of Cand.	*64*	*58*	*46*	*168*
House	78,215	119,820	69,500	267,535
Senate	11,500	24,750	24,500	60,750
Incumbents	169,615	395,167	247,711	812,493
Challengers	8,600	13,400	2,000	24,000
Open Seat	33,250	59,450	15,000	107,700
Winners	164,365	398,018	n/a	562,383
Losers	47,100	69,899	n/a	116,999

First Commerce Corp. Political Action Committee (C00129262) *Phone: (504) 623-1371 * 201 St. Charles Ave., 49th Floor, New Orleans, LA 70170 * Treasurer: R. Patrick Vance*

	1993-94	1995-96	1997	Totals
Receipts	$30,550	$19,550	$66,750	$116,850
Disburse	24,060	31,900	20,250	76,210
Cash	15,769	3,419	49,919	n/a
Contributions	17,450	26,400	18,750	62,600
Republicans	6,450	13,900	12,250	32,600
No. of Cand.	*5*	*10*	*4*	*19*
House	5,950	9,900	10,250	26,100
Senate	500	4,000	2,000	6,500
Democrats	11,000	12,500	6,500	30,000
No. of Cand.	*5*	*7*	*3*	*15*
House	7,500	6,500	2,000	16,000
Senate	3,500	6,000	4,500	14,000
Incumbents	16,700	15,500	18,750	50,950
Challengers	250	0	0	250
Open Seat	500	10,900	0	11,400
Winners	17,200	22,200	n/a	39,400
Losers	250	4,200	n/a	4,450

Contributed less than $5,000 during 1995-96 cycle:

Liberty National Bank and Trust Co. of Oklahoma City and Affiliates PAC (C00100859) *100 Broadway Liberty Tower, Oklahoma City, OK 73125 * Treasurer: Marcia Matthews*

Terminated PACs which contributed less than $5,000 during 1995-96 cycle:

Liberty Bank & Trust of Tulsa PAC (C00093062) *100 N. Broadway, Oklahoma City, OK 73102 * Treasurer: Marcia Matthews*

Bank South Corp.

55 Marietta St. N.W., Atlanta, GA 30303

Bank South, an Atlanta-based bank company, terminated its PAC in 1996.

Bank South Corp. Committee on Public Affairs (formerly known as BSCPA) (C00166934) *Address: same as sponsor * Treasurer: Barry R. Anderson*

	1993-94	1995-96	1997	Totals
Receipts	$113,730	$62,228	$0	$175,958
Disburse	108,887	70,445	0	179,332
Cash	8,466	0	0	n/a
Contributions	16,050	17,500	0	33,550
Republicans	12,100	13,000	0	25,100
No. of Cand.	*9*	*7*	*0*	*16*
House	8,600	7,500	0	16,100
Senate	3,500	5,500	0	9,000
Democrats	3,950	4,500	0	8,450
No. of Cand.	*10*	*5*	*0*	*15*
House	3,950	3,000	0	6,950
Senate	0	1,500	0	1,500
Incumbents	12,000	9,000	0	21,000
Challengers	2,350	3,000	0	5,350
Open Seat	1,950	5,500	0	7,450
Winners	13,550	10,000	n/a	23,550
Losers	2,500	7,500	n/a	10,000

Bank of Mississippi

*Phone: (601) 680-2330 * Fax: (601) 680-2382*
One Mississippi Plaza, Tupelo, MS 38802
*Web: www.bancorpsouth.com * E-mail: nash.allen@bxs.com*

The Bank of Mississippi is a state trust company which accepts commercial accounts. It is part of holding company BancorpSouth, which also owns Volunteer Bank of Jackson, Tenn. The publicly traded BancorpSouth has $4.2 billion in assets.

Bank of Mississippi employs 1,380 people and is headquartered in Tupelo, Miss.

Bank of Mississippi Officers' Voluntary Political Committee (C00183962) *P.O. Box 789, Tupelo, MS 38802-0789 * Treasurer: L. Nash Allen Jr.*

	1993-94	1995-96	1997	Totals
Receipts	$28,197	$29,726	$14,526	$72,449
Disburse	22,750	36,500	6,000	65,250
Cash	19,073	12,304	20,832	n/a
Contributions	17,750	14,750	2,500	35,000
Republicans	10,750	12,500	2,500	25,750
No. of Cand.	*4*	*5*	*2*	*11*
House	9,500	11,500	1,500	22,500
Senate	1,250	1,000	1,000	3,250
Democrats	7,000	2,250	0	9,250
No. of Cand.	*5*	*2*	*0*	*7*
House	7,000	2,250	0	9,250
Senate	0	0	0	0
Incumbents	3,000	8,750	2,500	14,250
Challengers	0	2,000	0	2,000
Open Seat	14,750	4,000	0	18,750
Winners	9,500	12,750	n/a	22,250
Losers	8,250	2,000	n/a	10,250

Bank of New York Co.

*Phone: (212) 495-1480 * Fax: (212) 495-2546*
48 Wall St., 10th Floor, New York, NY 10286
Web: www.bankofny.com

A publicly traded bank holding company, Bank of New York has assets of $60 billion and reported 1997 net income of $1.1 billion. It is one of the largest U.S. bank holding companies, employing more than 16,000 people.

Founded in 1784, the Bank of New York provides a range of banking and other financial services to corporations, businesses and individuals worldwide through its major businesses: securities, trust, investment and private banking, corporate banking, retail banking and financial market services.

Bank of New York Co. Political Action Committee-BNY PAC (C00185884) *Phone: (212) 635-1057 * Fax: (212) 635-1121 * One Wall St., 10th Floor, New York, NY 10286 * Treasurer: Robert E. Keilman * Contact: Newton P. S. Merrill, Senior Executive V.P.*

	1993-94	1995-96	1997	Totals
Receipts	$15,181	$29,720	$431	$45,332
Disburse	19,632	21,794	7,713	49,139
Cash	13,797	21,726	14,445	n/a
Contributions	10,175	12,950	3,000	26,125
Republicans	6,675	8,700	0	15,375
No. of Cand.	*5*	*6*	*0*	*11*
House	5,925	6,500	0	12,425
Senate	750	2,200	0	2,950
Democrats	3,000	4,250	3,000	10,250
No. of Cand.	*7*	*2*	*2*	*11*
House	1,500	3,250	500	5,250
Senate	1,500	1,000	2,500	5,000
Incumbents	8,675	10,450	500	19,625
Challengers	850	1,500	2,500	4,850
Open Seat	650	1,000	0	1,650
Winners	8,175	10,450	n/a	18,625
Losers	2,000	2,500	n/a	4,500

Bank of Stockton

*Phone: (209) 464-8781 * Fax: (209) 465-5483*
P.O. Box 1110, Stockton, CA 95201
*Web: www.bankofstockton.com * E-mail: BankofStockton@netmktg.com*

Bank of Stockton is a private, family-owned bank and one of the largest independent trusts and banks in northern California, with nine offices, more than 350 employees and more than $902 million in assets.

Bank of Stockton Political Action Committee (C00165829)
*Address: same as sponsor * Treasurer: Ray Robinson * Contact: Douglass M. Eberhardt, President*

	1993-94	1995-96	1997	Totals
Receipts	$29,618	$27,228	$20,000	$76,846
Disburse	29,600	15,500	2,500	47,600
Cash	9,280	21,010	38,511	n/a
Contributions	23,500	6,000	0	29,500
Republicans	18,000	6,000	0	24,000
No. of Cand.	*6*	*1*	*0*	*7*
House	15,000	6,000	0	21,000
Senate	3,000	0	0	3,000
Democrats	5,500	0	0	5,500
No. of Cand.	*1*	*0*	*0*	*1*
House	5,500	0	0	5,500
Senate	0	0	0	0
Incumbents	19,500	6,000	0	25,500
Challengers	500	0	0	500
Open Seat	500	0	0	500
Winners	20,000	6,000	n/a	26,000
Losers	3,500	0	n/a	3,500

BankAmerica Corp.

*Phone: (415) 622-8558 * Fax: (415) 622-1142*
Box 37000, Unit 13117, San Francisco, CA 94137
*Web: www.bankamerica.com * E-mail: greg.swanson@bankamerica.com*

BankAmerica is the fifth-largest bank holding company in the United States based on total assets. Bank of America NT&SA, the corporation's principal banking subsidiary, ranked third among U.S. banks in total assets as of September 30, 1997. BankAmerica has assets of $571 billion.

In April 1998, the company announced a merger with NationsBank, a deal that would form the nation's first coast-to-coast bank.

BankAmerica's subsidiaries operate branches in California, Washington, Texas, Arizona, Illinois, Oregon, Nevada, New Mexico, Idaho and Alaska. It employs 90,500 people and is a public company. In October 1997, it acquired Robertson Stephens & Company, a San Francisco investment banking firm.

BankAmerica supports the modernization of the nation's financial system and changes to bankruptcy laws. It lobbies to preserve flexibility in ATM fees and the types of financial services it can offer. The company also seeks to limit certain types of lawsuits against the banking industries and to reduce regulatory requirements.

BankAmerica ranked seventh among commercial banking PACs in 1996 congressional contributions. Its 1996 total represented an 87 percent increase over its 1993-94 election cycle contributions. The company favored Republican candidates. The top recipients were Sen. Alfonse D'Amato, R-N.Y., chairman of the Senate Banking Committee; and Reps. Richard Baker, R-La., and John LaFalce, D-N.Y. The latter two sit on the House Banking Committee.

SeaFirst Bank, a BankAmerica subsidiary, contributed more than $34,000 to 1996 congressional candidates, most from Washington state.

BankAmerica Corp. Political Action Committee (BACPAC) (formerly known as BankAmerica Election Fund) (C00147702)
*Phone: (202) 383-3430 * Fax: (202) 383-3475 * 1401 New York Ave. N.W., Suite 1110, Washington, DC 20005 * Treasurer: Gregory E. Swanson * Contact: Rex Wackerle, Senior V.P.*

	1993-94	1995-96	1997	Totals
Receipts	$345,778	$467,559	$347,737	$1,161,074
Disburse	311,633	535,516	319,312	1,166,461
Cash	129,639	61,689	90,115	n/a
Contributions	191,446	362,651	223,208	777,305
Republicans	94,511	229,248	155,563	479,322
No. of Cand.	*69*	*109*	*83*	*261*
House	44,475	164,948	95,063	304,486
Senate	50,036	64,300	60,500	174,836
Democrats	96,935	133,403	67,645	297,983
No. of Cand.	*68*	*67*	*46*	*181*
House	65,835	94,600	35,395	195,830
Senate	31,100	38,803	32,250	102,153
Incumbents	155,996	300,151	211,144	667,291
Challengers	13,500	9,500	5,000	28,000
Open Seat	21,450	53,000	7,000	81,450
Winners	164,246	317,451	n/a	481,697
Losers	27,200	45,200	n/a	72,400

Bank of America NW NA-SeaFirst Bank Political Action Committee (C00007427) *Phone: (206) 358-3433 * Fax: (206) 358-6800 * 701 Fifth Ave., Suite 3130, Seattle, WA 98104 * Web: www.bankamerica.com * Treasurer: Douglas G. Rogers*

	1993-94	1995-96	1997	Totals
Receipts	$29,374	$38,448	$0	$67,822
Disburse	38,380	34,771	5	73,156
Cash	2,349	6,026	6,021	n/a
Contributions	33,960	34,549	0	68,509
Republicans	12,535	24,949	0	37,484
No. of Cand.	*8*	*8*	*0*	*16*
House	6,500	23,549	0	30,049
Senate	6,035	1,400	0	7,435
Democrats	21,425	9,600	0	31,025
No. of Cand.	*11*	*4*	*0*	*15*
House	15,825	5,500	0	21,325
Senate	5,600	4,100	0	9,700
Incumbents	22,460	34,549	0	57,009
Challengers	5,500	0	0	5,500
Open Seat	5,500	0	0	5,500
Winners	16,935	31,849	n/a	48,784
Losers	17,025	2,700	n/a	19,725

BankBoston Corp.

*Phone: (617) 434-2200 * Fax: (617) 434-7547*
100 Federal St. 01-20-02, Boston, MA 02110
Web: www.bankboston.com

BankBoston, formed in 1996 from the merger between Bank of Boston Corp. and BayBanks Inc., is a bank holding company with national and international operations. Assets in 1997 totaled more than $69 billion. The company operates more than 100 offices in 23 countries in Latin America, Europe and Asia.

Services include personal banking, consumer finance, private banking, trust, mortgage origination and servicing, domestic corporate and investment banking, leasing, global banking and commercial real estate.

Rhode Island Hospital Trust National Bank operates an affiliated PAC.

BankBoston Federal Political Action Committee (C00102293)
*Address: same as sponsor * Treasurer: John A. Kahwaty * Contact: Peter Manning, Chairperson*

	1993-94	1995-96	1997	Totals
Receipts	$50,925	$69,321	$43,997	$164,243
Disburse	43,700	71,555	52,414	167,669
Cash	70,130	67,898	59,482	n/a
Contributions	23,450	39,150	29,450	92,050
Republicans	8,200	14,300	6,100	28,600
No. of Cand.	*9*	*15*	*12*	*36*
House	5,700	8,300	6,100	20,100
Senate	2,500	6,000	0	8,500
Democrats	15,250	24,850	23,350	63,450
No. of Cand.	*18*	*21*	*15*	*54*
House	11,000	16,850	7,850	35,700
Senate	4,250	8,000	15,500	27,750
Incumbents	21,950	28,650	27,450	78,050
Challengers	250	3,000	0	3,250
Open Seat	1,250	7,500	2,500	11,250
Winners	20,950	31,900	n/a	52,850
Losers	2,500	7,250	n/a	9,750

Rhode Island Hospital Trust National Bank Governmental Fund (C00144949) *Phone: (401) 278-8564 * Fax: (401) 278-8006 * One Hospital Trust Plaza, Providence, RI 02903 * Web: www.bkb.com * Treasurer: James H. Waterman Jr. * Contact: Mike Lee, Chairperson*

	1993-94	1995-96	1997	Totals
Receipts	$13,520	$11,680	$6,786	$31,986
Disburse	15,727	25,415	7,042	48,184
Cash	21,204	7,468	7,828	n/a
Contributions	3,225	18,525	4,350	26,100
Republicans	1,725	1,700	0	3,425
No. of Cand.	*2*	*1*	*0*	*3*
House	750	0	0	750
Senate	975	1,700	0	2,675
Democrats	1,500	16,825	4,350	22,675
No. of Cand.	*2*	*6*	*3*	*11*
House	1,400	11,325	4,350	17,075
Senate	100	5,500	0	5,600
Incumbents	2,375	1,500	3,350	7,225
Challengers	100	0	0	100
Open Seat	750	17,025	0	17,775
Winners	2,375	13,500	n/a	15,875
Losers	850	5,025	n/a	5,875

Bankers Roundtable

*Phone: (202) 289-4322 * Fax: (202) 289-1903*
805 15th St. N.W., Suite 600, Washington, DC 20005
Web: www.bankersround.org

Bankers Roundtable promotes the business of banking and encourages the development of sound banking and financial policies and practices. Membership is reserved for the 125 largest banking companies in the United States.

Bankers Roundtable - Political Action Committee (C00193177)
*Address: same as sponsor * Treasurer: Richard Whiting*

	1993-94	1995-96	1997	Totals
Receipts	$50,433	$48,397	$33,892	$132,722
Disburse	63,977	57,868	8,657	130,502
Cash	18,216	8,747	33,982	n/a
Contributions	42,450	31,500	5,500	79,450
Republicans	14,800	19,000	3,500	37,300
No. of Cand.	*18*	*20*	*6*	*44*
House	9,800	7,000	2,500	19,300
Senate	5,000	12,000	1,000	18,000
Democrats	27,650	12,500	2,000	42,150
No. of Cand.	*34*	*16*	*3*	*53*
House	23,150	8,500	1,000	32,650
Senate	4,500	4,000	1,000	9,500
Incumbents	41,450	30,500	5,500	77,450
Challengers	500	0	0	500
Open Seat	500	1,000	0	1,500
Winners	33,950	29,500	n/a	63,450
Losers	8,500	2,000	n/a	10,500

Bankers Trust New York Corp.

*Phone: (212) 250-7297 * Fax: (212) 669-1681*
130 Liberty St., 27th Floor, New York, NY 10006
Web: www.bankerstrust.com

Bankers Trust New York is a holding company for Bankers Trust Co. and Alex. Brown, which it acquired in 1997. The publicly traded company posted sales of $6.2 billion in 1997, up 20 percent from the previous year.

Through its subsidiaries, the company provides investment banking, trading, corporate and institutional finance, loans and international merchant banking.

Based in New York, the company employs more than 15,000 workers worldwide, and ranks No. 155 in the Fortune 500.

Bankers Trust Co., the corporation's primary subsidiary, also engages in capital markets underwriting and trading activities.

Bankers Trust New York Corp. Political Action Committee (C00097089) *Address: same as sponsor * Treasurer: Douglas B. Kidd * Contact: Rhonda Pohl, V.P. of Gov. Relations*

	1993-94	1995-96	1997	Totals
Receipts	$43,477	$84,594	$139,276	$267,347
Disburse	48,000	61,500	24,500	134,000
Cash	36,514	59,609	174,386	n/a
Contributions	37,000	46,000	22,000	105,000
Republicans	14,500	20,500	12,000	47,000
No. of Cand.	*9*	*16*	*9*	*34*
House	11,000	11,500	7,000	29,500
Senate	3,500	9,000	5,000	17,500
Democrats	22,500	25,500	10,000	58,000
No. of Cand.	*19*	*15*	*9*	*43*
House	21,500	19,500	6,000	47,000
Senate	1,000	6,000	4,000	11,000
Incumbents	36,500	39,500	21,000	97,000
Challengers	0	4,500	0	4,500
Open Seat	500	2,000	1,000	3,500
Winners	28,000	41,000	n/a	69,000
Losers	9,000	5,000	n/a	14,000

Alex. Brown Inc. Political Action Committee (C00208967) *135 E. Baltimore St., Baltimore, MD 21202 * Treasurer: Robert F. Price*

The Alex. Brown Inc. PAC was dissolved in January 1998. Alex. Brown Inc. became BT Alex. Brown in 1997 when the company merged with Bankers Trust New York.

	1993-94	1995-96	1997	Totals
Receipts	$97,283	$76,000	$30	$173,313
Disburse	37,750	53,105	82,650	173,505
Cash	59,731	82,625	0	n/a
Contributions	3,500	28,000	10,000	41,500
Republicans	1,500	27,000	10,000	38,500
No. of Cand.	*2*	*5*	*1*	*8*
House	1,500	20,000	10,000	31,500
Senate	0	7,000	0	7,000

Democrats	2,000	1,000	0	3,000
No. of Cand.	*3*	*1*	*0*	*4*
House	1,000	0	0	1,000
Senate	1,000	1,000	0	2,000
Incumbents	3,500	26,000	10,000	39,500
Challengers	0	0	0	0
Open Seat	0	2,000	0	2,000
Winners	1,500	26,000	n/a	27,500
Losers	2,000	2,000	n/a	4,000

Branch Banking & Trust Co.

*Phone: (336) 733-3004 * Fax: (336) 733-7118*
150 S. Stratford Rd., Winston-Salem, NC 27104
*Web: www.bbandt.com * E-mail: 71111.3225@compuserve.com*

Branch Banking & Trust is the principal banking subsidiary of BB&T Corp., the sixth-largest bank holding company in the Southeast with $27.2 billion in assets. BB&T is the oldest bank in North Carolina and has branches in South Carolina and Virginia.

The public company's banking subsidiaries also provide trust, insurance, leasing, international, investment and travel services.

In 1997, the company announced that it will acquire Franklin Bancorp of Washington. The acquisition will give BB&T its first entry into the metropolitan Washington area market.

Branch Banking & Trust Co. PAC (C00075291) *Address: same as sponsor * Treasurer: Ed Simpson*

	1993-94	1995-96	1997	Totals
Receipts	$6,444	$33,599	$24,027	$64,070
Disburse	15,109	27,199	16,000	58,308
Cash	1,015	7,420	15,448	n/a
Contributions	11,600	18,650	10,500	40,750
Republicans	10,750	16,600	9,500	36,850
No. of Cand.	*7*	*14*	*4*	*25*
House	7,250	9,100	5,000	21,350
Senate	3,500	7,500	4,500	15,500
Democrats	850	2,050	1,000	3,900
No. of Cand.	*3*	*3*	*1*	*7*
House	850	2,050	1,000	3,900
Senate	0	0	0	0
Incumbents	4,600	17,900	10,500	33,000
Challengers	2,000	0	0	2,000
Open Seat	5,000	750	0	5,750
Winners	11,500	15,050	n/a	26,550
Losers	100	3,600	n/a	3,700

Central Carolina Bank & Trust Co.

*Phone: (919) 683-7777 * Fax: (919) 682-1191*
P. O. Box 931, Durham, NC 27702

Central Carolina Bank & Trust is a privately owned bank with $7 billion in assets and 200 branches in North and South Carolina. It offers consumer banking and issues bank cards.

Central Carolina Bank & Trust Co. Free Enterprise Fund (C00087502) *Address: same as sponsor * Treasurer: David P. Shaw * Contact: William L. Burns Jr., Chairman*

	1993-94	1995-96	1997	Totals
Receipts	$5,953	$11,888	$4,083	$21,924
Disburse	6,686	11,864	3,471	22,021
Cash	1,932	1,906	2,517	n/a
Contributions	4,900	7,100	2,000	14,000
Republicans	3,100	5,800	1,000	9,900
No. of Cand.	*4*	*5*	*2*	*11*
House	1,600	1,800	500	3,900
Senate	1,500	4,000	500	6,000
Democrats	1,800	1,300	1,000	4,100
No. of Cand.	*3*	*3*	*2*	*8*
House	1,800	800	1,000	3,600
Senate	0	500	0	500
Incumbents	3,000	6,300	2,000	11,300
Challengers	300	800	0	1,100
Open Seat	1,600	0	0	1,600
Winners	3,800	5,100	n/a	8,900
Losers	1,100	2,000	n/a	3,100

Centura Banks Inc.

*Phone: (919) 977-4768 * Fax: (919) 977-8283*
P.O. Box 1220, Rocky Mount, NC 27802-1220
*Web: www.centura.com * E-mail: jedmundson@centura.com*

Centura Banks operates 180 branches in North Carolina and Virginia. The publicly traded Rocky Mount, N.C. company has assets of $7 billion.

The company owns Centura Securities Inc., a brokerage company, and Centura Insurance Services, an independent insurance agency for individuals and businesses.

In January 1998, Centura agreed to acquire Pee Dee State Bank, headquartered in Timmonsville, S.C., for stock valued at $40 million.

Centura Banks Inc. Good Government Committee (Federal) (C00250431) *Address: same as sponsor * Treasurer: James J. Edmundson*

	1993-94	*1995-96*	*1997*	*Totals*
Receipts	$9,579	$23,558	$9,992	$43,129
Disburse	14,791	21,800	5,300	41,891
Cash	1,578	3,337	8,030	n/a
Contributions	12,250	19,050	5,300	36,600
Republicans	8,750	18,800	4,300	31,850
No. of Cand.	*8*	*9*	*3*	*20*
House	5,850	13,800	3,300	22,950
Senate	2,900	5,000	1,000	8,900
Democrats	3,500	250	1,000	4,750
No. of Cand.	*4*	*1*	*1*	*6*
House	3,500	250	1,000	4,750
Senate	0	0	0	0
Incumbents	5,400	18,300	5,300	29,000
Challengers	1,850	0	0	1,850
Open Seat	5,000	750	0	5,750
Winners	9,250	10,250	n/a	19,500
Losers	3,000	8,800	n/a	11,800

Chase Manhattan Corp.

*Phone: (212) 270-7133 * Fax: (212) 270-5158*
270 Park Ave., 44th Floor, New York, NY 10017
Web: www.chase.com

Chase Manhattan is America's largest bank and the product of the 1995 merger of Chase and Chemical Banking. Chase offers banking services to corporations, governments and consumers worldwide and is expanding its investment banking and credit card services. In addition, the public company provides mortgage banking and mutual fund services. Headquartered in New York, the company has about 68,000 employees. It reported 1996 sales of $27.4 billion.

The company supports many New York candidates and contributes to state and local campaigns and committees. Chase also supports other federal banking and securities PACs. It lobbies on banking industry regulation and the modernization of the nation's financial services system.

Chase Manhattan spent almost half of what second-largest bank Citicorp spent on 1996 congressional races and ranked tenth overall among commercial banks. The company increased its contributions to candidates by 68 percent compared to the 1994 elections. Chase favored Republican incumbents in 1996. House Banking Committee members Reps. Ken Bentsen, D-Tex., Rick Lazio, R-N.Y., and Steve Stockman, R-Tex., were among the top recipients in 1996.

Prior to the merger with Chemical Bank, Chase had another PAC which contributed more than $94,000 to congressional candidates in 1996. That committee, ChasePAC, was terminated. Chase Bank of Texas, a subsidiary formerly known as Texas Commerce Bank, gave almost exclusively to Texas candidates in 1996. It has switched to nonfederal status and will contribute to state and local candidates in the future.

Chase Manhattan Corp. Fund for Good Government (C00003830) *Address: same as sponsor * Treasurer: Bridget A. Filippon*

	1993-94	*1995-96*	*1997*	*Totals*
Receipts	$602,484	$702,719	$426,046	$1,731,249
Disburse	576,369	682,116	424,321	1,682,806
Cash	44,632	65,240	66,966	n/a
Contributions	146,850	247,625	132,450	526,925
Republicans	67,600	177,250	92,900	337,750
No. of Cand.	*55*	*104*	*68*	*227*
House	34,850	112,500	57,900	205,250
Senate	32,750	64,750	35,000	132,500
Democrats	79,250	70,375	39,550	189,175
No. of Cand.	*66*	*51*	*38*	*155*
House	61,750	59,875	24,550	146,175
Senate	17,500	10,500	15,000	43,000
Incumbents	129,750	189,125	123,950	442,825
Challengers	5,800	24,000	1,000	30,800
Open Seat	11,300	34,500	7,500	53,300
Winners	121,600	200,125	n/a	321,725
Losers	25,250	47,500	n/a	72,750

Chase Manhattan Corp. Political Action Committee - (ChasePAC) (C00113043) *Address: same as sponsor * Treasurer: Bridget A. Filippon*

	1993-94	*1995-96*	*1997*	*Totals*
Receipts	$471,439	$315,328	$0	$786,767
Disburse	445,855	376,167	0	822,022
Cash	60,837	0	0	n/a
Contributions	181,341	94,087	0	275,428
Republicans	110,012	77,087	0	187,099
No. of Cand.	*66*	*55*	*0*	*121*
House	60,012	55,132	0	115,144
Senate	50,000	21,955	0	71,955
Democrats	70,329	17,000	0	87,329
No. of Cand.	*41*	*14*	*0*	*55*
House	47,302	16,000	0	63,302
Senate	23,027	1,000	0	24,027
Incumbents	150,591	88,587	0	239,178
Challengers	15,500	0	0	15,500
Open Seat	14,750	5,500	0	20,250
Winners	155,841	80,087	n/a	235,928
Losers	25,500	14,000	n/a	39,500

Texas Commerce Bank National Association Fund for Good Government (C00043570) *712 Main St., Houston, TX 77002 * Treasurer: Jeffrey B. Reitman*

The Texas Commerce Bank PAC filed for termination in January 1998.

	1993-94	*1995-96*	*1997*	*Totals*
Receipts	$53,034	$204,516	$103,273	$360,823
Disburse	61,719	119,876	92,681	274,276
Cash	1,152	85,795	91,863	n/a
Contributions	20,000	22,600	7,200	49,800
Republicans	9,000	12,150	4,200	25,350
No. of Cand.	*4*	*11*	*4*	*19*
House	4,000	9,900	1,200	15,100
Senate	5,000	2,250	3,000	10,250
Democrats	11,000	10,450	3,000	24,450
No. of Cand.	*11*	*11*	*4*	*26*
House	8,000	9,950	3,000	20,950
Senate	3,000	500	0	3,500
Incumbents	16,000	12,850	7,200	36,050
Challengers	3,000	250	0	3,250
Open Seat	1,000	9,500	0	10,500
Winners	18,500	20,250	n/a	38,750
Losers	1,500	2,350	n/a	3,850

Citicorp

*Phone: (212) 559-1000 * Fax: (212) 559-5138*
399 Park Ave., New York, NY 10043
Web: www.citibank.com

Citicorp is the United States' second-largest bank and the world's top issuer of credit cards. The publicly traded company has 3,200 locations in 98 countries and territories around the world. Its main subsidiary is Citibank, and consumer banking accounts for half the company's sales. Citicorp reported 1996 net income of $3.8 billion.

Citibank agreed in late 1997 to purchase AT&T Universal Card Services for $3.5 billion in cash. In April 1998, Citicorp and Travelers Group Inc. announced plans for an $82 billion merger. The deal is contingent on congressional action to remove regulatory barriers between the banking and financial services industries. In addition, Citibank is one of 13 commercial banks that agreed in January 1998 to extend South Korea's short-term debt to prevent further economic problems. Those banks hold more than $24 billion in South Korean foreign debt.

Citicorp ranked fifth among commercial banks in contributions to congressional races during 1995-96. The company gave more to Republicans and was a heavy supporter of incumbent candidates, who received nine of every 10 dollars Citicorp spent. Rep. Bill McCollum, R-Fla., the No. 2 Republican on the Banking Committee, topped the list of Citicorp PAC recipients, with fellow committee member Rep. Ken Bentsen, D-Texas, right behind. Citicorp spent the most on elections in New York, where it is headquartered, and Texas.

Citicorp Voluntary Political Fund Federal (C00088088) *Phone: (202) 879-6800 * Fax: (202) 879-6823 * 1101 Pennsylvania Ave. N.W., Suite 1000, Washington, DC 20004 * Treasurer: Martha A. Golden*

	1993-94	1995-96	1997	Totals
Receipts	$493,431	$496,457	$287,753	$1,277,641
Disburse	452,814	521,079	245,949	1,219,842
Cash	50,438	26,650	68,457	n/a
Contributions	333,168	418,800	186,143	938,111
Republicans	169,946	262,126	117,495	549,567
No. of Cand.	*99*	*135*	*79*	*313*
House	113,947	208,146	90,495	412,588
Senate	55,999	53,980	27,000	136,979
Democrats	161,222	156,674	68,648	386,544
No. of Cand.	*100*	*78*	*61*	*239*
House	141,652	138,525	49,648	329,825
Senate	19,570	18,149	19,000	56,719
Incumbents	285,769	365,320	178,143	829,232
Challengers	18,000	14,500	2,000	34,500
Open Seat	28,899	38,480	6,000	73,379
Winners	267,688	352,820	n/a	620,508
Losers	65,480	65,980	n/a	131,460

Contributed less than $5,000 during 1995-96 cycle:

Citicorp Voluntary Political Fund - State/Local (C00316976)
*Phone: (202) 879-6830 * Fax: (202) 783-4462 * 1101 Pennsylvania Ave. N.W., Suite 1000, Washington, DC 20004 * Treasurer: Martha A. Golden*

Colonial BancGroup Inc.

*Phone: (334) 240-5000 * Fax: (334) 240-5345*
One Commerce St., Montgomery, AL 36104
Web: www.colonialbank.com

Colonial BancGroup operates 228 branches in Alabama, Tennessee, Georgia and Florida. The bank began 1998 with a buying spree, purchasing four southern banks with $735 million in assets at the beginning of the year. In February Colonial struck a deal to buy Commercial Bank of Nevada, which has $120 million in assets. A month later it announced plans to buy Commercial National Bank of Daytona, Fla., which has $83 million in assets.

Before the mergers, the publicly traded Colonial had $7.6 billion in assets.

Banks include: Ashville Savings Bank, United American Bank, First Central Bank of St. Petersburg and South Florida Banking Corp.

Colonial BancGroup Inc. Federal Political Action Committee (Colonial Fed PAC) (C00309526) *Address: same as sponsor * Treasurer: Donna R. Piel*

	1993-94	1995-96	1997	Totals
Receipts	$0	$28,832	$7,339	$36,171
Disburse	0	12,950	5,381	18,331
Cash	0	15,882	17,841	n/a
Contributions	0	11,250	750	12,000
Republicans	0	2,250	500	2,750
No. of Cand.	*0*	*2*	*1*	*3*
House	0	2,250	500	2,750
Senate	0	0	0	0
Democrats	0	9,000	250	9,250
No. of Cand.	*0*	*6*	*1*	*7*
House	0	6,000	0	6,000
Senate	0	3,000	250	3,250
Incumbents	0	3,250	750	4,000
Challengers	0	0	0	0
Open Seat	0	8,000	0	8,000
Winners	0	3,250	n/a	3,250
Losers	0	8,000	n/a	8,000

Comerica Inc.

*Phone: (313) 222-7496 * Fax: (313) 222-8720*
c/o PAC Services, Mail Code 2250, Detroit, MI 48275
Web: www.comerica.com

With operating groups assigned to business, individual and investment banking, Comerica is a diverse bank holding company with $36 billion in assets, making it the 26th-largest holding bank in the nation. The publicly traded Detroit company has subsidiaries in Michigan, Texas, California and Florida. The bulk of its branches are in Michigan.

Formed out of The Detroit Bank, Comerica offers personal and corporate banking, commercial loans and mortgages, life, disability and long-term care insurance.

The 12,000-employee company is the nation's 14th-largest commercial business lender and the 16th-largest small business lender.

Subsidiaries include: Comerica Bank, Comerica Trust Co. of Bermuda, Comerica Acceptance Corp., Comerica Community Development Corp., Comerica Leasing Corp., Comerica Insurance Group, W.Y. Campbell & Co., Comerica Securities and Wilson, Kemp & Associates.

Comerica Inc. Committee for Responsible Political Action (Comerica PAC) (C00035501) *Address: same as sponsor * Treasurer: James M. Garavaglia * Contact: Mike McLauchlan, V.P. of Gov. Affairs*

	1993-94	1995-96	1997	Totals
Receipts	$76,614	$38,483	$8,557	$123,654
Disburse	95,193	85,075	4,250	184,518
Cash	47,801	1,213	5,521	n/a
Contributions	43,675	40,825	1,000	85,500
Republicans	24,825	34,175	250	59,250
No. of Cand.	*12*	*16*	*1*	*29*
House	16,950	22,275	250	39,475
Senate	7,875	11,900	0	19,775
Democrats	18,850	6,650	750	26,250
No. of Cand.	*13*	*9*	*1*	*23*
House	14,100	6,450	750	21,300
Senate	4,750	200	0	4,950
Incumbents	27,450	28,825	1,000	57,275
Challengers	1,000	11,500	0	12,500
Open Seat	14,525	500	0	15,025
Winners	35,225	17,825	n/a	53,050
Losers	8,450	23,000	n/a	31,450

Commerce Bancorp Inc.

*Phone: (609) 751-9000 * Fax: (609) 751-9260*
1701 Route 70 E., Cherry Hill, NJ 08034-5400
Web: www.yesbank.com

Commerce Bancorp operates New Jersey- and Pennsylvania-based Commerce Bank, which touts itself as "America's Most Convenient Bank" and offers regular hours on weekends. The publicly traded company has $3.9 billion in assets and 75 branches.

Commerce Bank plans to open 18 to 20 new branches during 1998.

Commerce Bancorp Inc. - Political Action Committee FED (C00303156) *Address: same as sponsor * Treasurer: C. Edward Jordan Jr.*

	1993-94	1995-96	1997	Totals
Receipts	$0	$29,136	$46,591	$75,727
Disburse	0	7,109	59,902	67,011
Cash	0	22,025	8,714	n/a
Contributions	0	7,000	14,000	21,000
Republicans	0	7,000	8,000	15,000
No. of Cand.	*0*	*2*	*3*	*5*
House	0	7,000	8,000	15,000
Senate	0	0	0	0
Democrats	0	0	6,000	6,000
No. of Cand.	*0*	*0*	*2*	*2*
House	0	0	1,000	1,000
Senate	0	0	5,000	5,000
Incumbents	0	7,000	14,000	21,000
Challengers	0	0	0	0
Open Seat	0	0	0	0
Winners	0	7,000	n/a	7,000
Losers	0	0	n/a	0

Commerce Bancshares Inc.

*Phone: (314) 746-7381 * Fax: (314) 746-8513*
8000 Forsyth Blvd., Clayton, MO 63105
*Web: www.commercebank.com * E-mail: tomn@commercebank.com*

Commerce Bancshares is a holding company that operates 270 branches in Missouri, Illinois and Kansas. It employs 4,200 people and has assets of $10 billion. The publicly traded company also operates a credit card bank in Nebraska.

The company announced plans in 1997 to acquire City National Bank of Pittsburg, Kan., with assets of $120 million.

Commerce Bancshares' subsidiary banks provide business, retail, trust, leasing, insurance, mortgage banking and investment services to individual and commercial customers. The banks also offer checking, savings, loans, MasterCard, Visa and money market deposit accounts.

A 1997 Dean Witter report named Commerce as one of the top 10 banks in the nation technologically.

Commerce Bancs PAC (C00072967) *Phone: (816) 234-2000 * Fax: (816) 234-2369 * 922 Walnut, Suite 930, P.O. Box 13686, Kansas City, MO 64199-3686 * Treasurer: William F. Durham Jr. * Contact: Tom Noonan, Chairman * Phone: (314) 746-7381*

	1993-94	1995-96	1997	Totals
Receipts	$46,821	$52,766	$25,793	$125,380
Disburse	47,120	31,635	10,325	89,080
Cash	9,380	30,519	45,994	n/a
Contributions	17,948	17,800	4,475	40,223
Republicans	9,798	12,450	4,475	26,723
No. of Cand.	*11*	*18*	*6*	*35*
House	5,000	7,450	1,500	13,950
Senate	4,798	5,000	2,975	12,773
Democrats	8,150	5,350	0	13,500
No. of Cand.	*13*	*9*	*0*	*22*
House	6,650	3,600	0	10,250
Senate	1,500	1,750	0	3,250
Incumbents	9,550	6,850	4,475	20,875
Challengers	500	3,350	0	3,850
Open Seat	7,498	7,600	0	15,098
Winners	15,098	13,750	n/a	28,848
Losers	2,850	4,050	n/a	6,900

Community Bankers Association of Illinois

*Phone: (217) 529-2265 * Fax: (217) 529-9484*
901 Community Dr., Springfield, IL 62703-5184
Web: www.cbai.com

The Community Bankers Association of Illinois represents more than 500 Illinois financial institutions and 130 associate members. CBAI is an advocate for community banking, both in the state capitol at Springfield, Ill. and in Washington.

CBAI has lobbied against unitary thrift charters by the Office of Thrift Supervision and against President Clinton's new federal examination fee on state-chartered banks and bank holding companies.

Community Bankers Association of Illinois FedPAC (C00291914) *Address: same as sponsor * Treasurer: Robert J. Wingert*

	1993-94	1995-96	1997	Totals
Receipts	$5,002	$9,037	$6,832	$20,871
Disburse	2,651	9,835	3,430	15,916
Cash	2,350	1,553	4,954	n/a
Contributions	2,500	8,050	3,200	13,750
Republicans	2,500	4,050	1,250	7,800
No. of Cand.	*3*	*7*	*2*	*12*
House	2,500	3,050	250	5,800
Senate	0	1,000	1,000	2,000
Democrats	0	4,000	1,950	5,950
No. of Cand.	*0*	*4*	*3*	*7*
House	0	1,500	1,750	3,250
Senate	0	2,500	200	2,700
Incumbents	0	2,950	1,450	4,400
Challengers	1,000	500	0	1,500
Open Seat	1,500	4,600	1,750	7,850
Winners	2,500	4,700	n/a	7,200
Losers	0	3,350	n/a	3,350

Compass Bancshares Inc.

*Phone: (205) 933-3000 * Fax: (205) 715-7812*
P.O. Box 10566, Birmingham, AL 35296
Web: www.compassweb.com

Compass Bancshares is a $13.5 billion bank holding company headquartered in Birmingham, Ala. with 250 branches and 5,500 employees in Alabama, Houston, Dallas, and Pensacola and Jacksonville, Fla.

Subsidiary Compass Bank provides business, retail, trust, correspondent, leasing, insurance, mortgage banking, real estate and investment services to individual and commercial customers. It also offers checking, savings, loans, MasterCard, Visa and money market deposit accounts.

Compass continues to acquire other banks, including 1st Performance National Bank (Florida), Spring National Bank (Texas), Horizon Bank (Texas) and Security Bank (Texas). In February 1998, Compass announced that it had acquired Fidelity Resources Co. and its subsidiary, Fidelity Bank, with 13 branches in Dallas.

Compass Bancshares Inc. Political Action Committee (Compass BancPAC) (C00142596) *Address: same as sponsor * Treasurer: Sue L. Brewis*

	1993-94	1995-96	1997	Totals
Receipts	$790,103	$857,507	$509,248	$2,156,858
Disburse	974,893	729,612	587,515	2,292,020
Cash	391,764	519,663	441,396	n/a
Contributions	36,000	91,750	27,500	155,250
Republicans	30,500	57,750	27,500	115,750
No. of Cand.	*12*	*19*	*5*	*36*
House	24,500	30,500	17,500	72,500
Senate	6,000	27,250	10,000	43,250
Democrats	5,500	34,000	0	39,500
No. of Cand.	*5*	*10*	*0*	*15*
House	2,500	19,500	0	22,000
Senate	3,000	14,500	0	17,500
Incumbents	30,500	40,000	25,000	95,500
Challengers	3,000	500	0	3,500
Open Seat	2,500	51,250	0	53,750
Winners	30,500	58,500	n/a	89,000
Losers	5,500	33,250	n/a	38,750

Consumer Bankers Association

*Phone: (703) 276-1750 * Fax: (703) 528-1290*
1000 Wilson Blvd., Suite 3012, Arlington, VA 22209-3908
Web: www.cbanet.org

The Consumer Bankers Association represents about 700 retail banks with assets of more than $2.9 trillion. Founded in 1919, its member institutions are involved in all types of banking including: consumer, auto, home equity and education finance, bank sales of investment products and community development.

CBA has lobbied to defend ATM convenience fees and against creating an unreasonable cost burden on banks as the federal government moves to mandatory disbursement of benefit payments. CBA also lobbied for the continuing role of private capital in making student loans.

The Consumer Bankers Association Political Action Committee (C00035535) *Address: same as sponsor * Treasurer: Jayne E. Hunt*

	1993-94	1995-96	1997	Totals
Receipts	$30,966	$40,264	$16,403	$87,633
Disburse	39,716	33,157	27,363	100,236
Cash	38,548	42,382	31,423	n/a
Contributions	36,600	27,550	24,040	88,190
Republicans	9,500	17,500	16,000	43,000
No. of Cand.	*12*	*17*	*18*	*47*
House	7,500	14,500	10,000	32,000
Senate	2,000	3,000	6,000	11,000
Democrats	27,100	10,050	8,040	45,190
No. of Cand.	*37*	*10*	*13*	*60*
House	23,250	9,300	5,500	38,050
Senate	3,850	750	2,540	7,140
Incumbents	35,600	25,550	23,540	84,690
Challengers	0	1,000	0	1,000
Open Seat	1,000	0	500	1,500
Winners	30,600	25,550	n/a	56,150
Losers	6,000	2,000	n/a	8,000

CoreStates Financial Corp.

*Phone: (215) 786-7643 * Fax: (215) 973-2073*
1500 Market St., (SC1-3-20-13), Philadelphia, PA 19102-7618
Web: www.corestates.com

CoreStates Financial is a Philadelphia-based bank holding company. Through its primary subsidiary, CoreStates Bank, the corporation provides personal, business and international banking services at its 600-plus branches located throughout Pennsylvania, New Jersey and Delaware. The $46.8 billion publicly traded company employs about 16,000 people.

In November 1997, CoreStates Financial and Charlotte, N.C.-based First Union Corp. announced plans to merge the two companies. Combining the two would create an entity with more than $200 billion in assets, nearly 3,000 branches and the largest share of deposits on the East Coast. The merger is expected to be completed in the second quarter of 1998, pending CoreStates and First Union shareholder approval, regulatory approvals and other conditions of closing.

CoreStates Financial Corp. Political Action Committee (CorePAC) (C00249441) *Address: same as sponsor * Treasurer: Richard J. Welsh*

	1993-94	1995-96	1997	Totals
Receipts	$141,478	$134,025	$70,664	$346,167
Disburse	140,363	137,280	77,444	355,087
Cash	10,714	7,461	681	n/a
Contributions	12,800	11,400	8,500	32,700
Republicans	8,550	7,750	8,500	24,800
No. of Cand.	*7*	*9*	*5*	*21*
House	2,050	5,500	1,000	8,550
Senate	6,500	2,250	7,500	16,250

Democrats	4,250	3,650	0	7,900
No. of Cand.	*5*	*4*	*0*	*9*
House	1,250	2,650	0	3,900
Senate	3,000	1,000	0	4,000
Incumbents	4,500	10,000	8,500	23,000
Challengers	6,800	900	0	7,700
Open Seat	500	500	0	1,000
Winners	8,750	10,500	n/a	19,250
Losers	4,050	900	n/a	4,950

Crestar Financial Corp.

*Phone: (804) 782-7816 * Fax: (804) 782-5191*
919 E. Main St., 12th Floor, Richmond, VA 23219
*Web: www.crestar.com * E-mail: brenda.skidmore@crestar.com*

Crestar Financial is a holding company for Crestar Bank, the largest independent bank headquartered in Virginia.

The bank employs 9,000 workers and operates more than 550 branches located throughout Virginia, Maryland and Washington. Crestar has assets of $25 billion. It offers traditional checking and savings services, as well as business loans, credit cards and Internet banking.

Crestar's other subsidiaries include Crestar Mortgage Corp., Crestar Securities Corp., Capitoline Investment Services and Crestar Insurance Agency.

Crestar Financial Corp. Responsible Government Fund (C00214965) *Address: same as sponsor * Treasurer: J. Thomas Vaughan*

	1993-94	1995-96	1997	Totals
Receipts	$121,663	$115,646	$66,001	$303,310
Disburse	124,709	109,575	46,200	280,484
Cash	20,078	26,152	45,254	n/a
Contributions	31,625	22,650	14,350	68,625
Republicans	16,575	16,550	4,850	37,975
No. of Cand.	*20*	*19*	*8*	*47*
House	9,975	11,300	3,850	25,125
Senate	6,600	5,250	1,000	12,850
Democrats	15,050	6,100	9,500	30,650
No. of Cand.	*21*	*7*	*8*	*36*
House	11,750	5,800	3,000	20,550
Senate	3,300	300	6,500	10,100
Incumbents	23,550	20,900	14,350	58,800
Challengers	7,275	250	0	7,525
Open Seat	800	1,500	0	2,300
Winners	23,850	21,350	n/a	45,200
Losers	7,775	1,300	n/a	9,075

Fifth Third Bancorp

*Phone: (513) 579-5300 * Fax: (513) 744-8621*
38 Fountain Square Plaza, Cincinnati, OH 45263
Web: www.fifththird.com

Headquartered in Cincinnati, Fifth Third Bancorp owns 11 banks with locations in Ohio, Kentucky, Indiana and the Naples, Fla. region. The publicly traded company has $21.4 billion in assets.

Affiliate banks, which all use the Fifth Third name, operate 886 ATMs and 414 branches.

Subsidiaries include: Midwest Payment Systems, an electronic funds transfer and data processing company; Fifth Third Securities Inc., which provides brokerage and financial services; and Fifth Third Leasing Co., which offers financing for business equipment leasing.

Fifth Third Bancorp Political Action Committee (C00290502) *Address: same as sponsor * Treasurer: John P. Wallace*

	1993-94	1995-96	1997	Totals
Receipts	$98,576	$226,147	$127,146	$451,869
Disburse	67,595	151,486	82,476	301,557
Cash	30,980	105,641	150,311	n/a
Contributions	8,440	7,800	11,750	27,990
Republicans	7,100	7,300	10,750	25,150
No. of Cand.	*6*	*8*	*6*	*20*
House	2,800	4,550	2,500	9,850
Senate	4,300	2,750	8,250	15,300
Democrats	1,340	500	1,000	2,840
No. of Cand.	*4*	*1*	*2*	*7*
House	1,340	0	500	1,840
Senate	0	500	500	1,000
Incumbents	1,650	5,300	2,500	9,450
Challengers	1,650	1,500	0	3,150
Open Seat	5,140	1,000	9,250	15,390
Winners	8,400	5,800	n/a	14,200
Losers	40	2,000	n/a	2,040

First American Corp.

*Phone: (615) 770-4074 * Fax: (615) 748-8949*
712 First American Center, Nashville, TN 37237
*Web: www.fanb.com * E-mail: jeff.gish@fanb.com*

Based in Nashville, Tenn., First American is the third-largest bank holding company in Tennessee, with 4,200 employees and $10.6 billion in assets. The company does business in Tennessee, Kentucky and Virginia.

First American plans to merge with Deposit Guaranty, a $6.9 billion Jackson, Miss. bank, during 1998. The combined company is expected to be headquartered in Nashville. It will be the fourth-largest financial services institution in its six-state region, based on total assets. The deal is scheduled to eliminate 500 to 900 jobs.

Subsidiaries: First American National Bank, First American National Bank of Kentucky, First American Federal Savings Bank and First American Enterprises.

First American Corp. PAC (C00175091) *Address: same as sponsor * Treasurer: John D. Gilbert Jr. * Contact: Jeff Gish, PAC Administrator*

	1993-94	1995-96	1997	Totals
Receipts	$70,411	$122,876	$71,251	$264,538
Disburse	77,996	81,900	15,487	175,383
Cash	29,259	70,236	126,001	n/a
Contributions	30,050	19,850	4,800	54,700
Republicans	15,900	17,650	3,500	37,050
No. of Cand.	*9*	*10*	*1*	*20*
House	3,400	8,600	0	12,000
Senate	12,500	9,050	3,500	25,050
Democrats	14,150	2,200	1,300	17,650
No. of Cand.	*7*	*5*	*2*	*14*
House	5,150	2,200	1,300	8,650
Senate	9,000	0	0	9,000
Incumbents	13,700	15,250	4,800	33,750
Challengers	7,500	1,850	0	9,350
Open Seat	8,850	2,500	0	11,350
Winners	16,950	17,250	n/a	34,200
Losers	13,100	2,600	n/a	15,700

Deposit Guaranty Corp. Employees' Voluntary Political Committee (C00016550) *Phone: (601) 354-8401 * Fax: (601) 354-8192 * P.O. Box 1200, Jackson, MS 39205 * Web: www.dgb.com * Treasurer: James L. Moore*

Deposit Guaranty is a publicly traded $6.9 billion bank holding company with 3,500 employees and banking locations in Mississippi, Louisiana and Arkansas. The company has mortgage offices in Oklahoma, Nebraska, Texas, Indiana and Iowa. It is scheduled to merge with First American during 1998.

Deposit Guaranty also has announced plans to purchase Memphis, Tenn.-based Victory Bancshares in 1998. For now, though, the company's business is focused in Mississippi.

	1993-94	1995-96	1997	Totals
Receipts	$61,161	$86,621	$50,875	$198,657
Disburse	43,514	82,124	33,643	159,281
Cash	30,904	30,018	52,634	n/a
Contributions	8,250	19,000	5,250	32,500
Republicans	3,050	16,000	3,750	22,800
No. of Cand.	*4*	*7*	*3*	*14*
House	1,550	11,000	3,500	16,050
Senate	1,500	5,000	250	6,750
Democrats	5,200	3,000	1,500	9,700
No. of Cand.	*6*	*2*	*1*	*9*
House	5,200	3,000	1,500	9,700
Senate	0	0	0	0
Incumbents	4,500	14,000	5,250	23,750
Challengers	1,250	2,000	0	3,250
Open Seat	2,500	2,000	0	4,500
Winners	5,000	16,000	n/a	21,000
Losers	3,250	3,000	n/a	6,250

First Chicago NBD Corp.

Phone: (312) 732-4000
1 First National Plaza, Mail Suite 0303, Chicago, IL 60670
Web: www.fcnbd.com

First Chicago NBD terminated all of its PACs in 1997.

In November 1997, First Chicago and NBD Bancorp merged in a stock swap valued at $5.14 billion, the second-largest bank merger ever. The combined entity is the nation's seventh-largest bank with assets of about $120 billion.

The company will merge with Ohio-based Banc One in 1998.

First Chicago NBD Corp. Political Action Committee/FCC (formerly known as First Chicago Corp. PAC) (C00077347)
*Address: same as sponsor * Treasurer: Dennis P. Carroll*

	1993-94	1995-96	1997	Totals
Receipts	$198,655	$170,672	$24,202	$393,529
Disburse	115,550	250,450	76,079	442,079
Cash	131,650	51,877	0	n/a
Contributions	102,550	189,650	23,500	315,700
Republicans	41,550	113,950	9,500	165,000
No. of Cand.	*42*	*65*	*15*	*122*
House	26,550	74,250	6,500	107,300
Senate	15,000	39,700	3,000	57,700
Democrats	60,750	75,700	14,000	150,450
No. of Cand.	*53*	*40*	*14*	*107*
House	45,700	50,500	8,000	104,200
Senate	15,050	25,200	6,000	46,250
Incumbents	92,650	143,750	22,500	258,900
Challengers	1,000	10,900	0	11,900
Open Seat	8,900	32,500	1,000	42,400
Winners	84,600	151,250	n/a	235,850
Losers	17,950	38,400	n/a	56,350

NBD Good Citizenship Committee (NBD Bank, N.A.) (C00040006)
*611 Woodward Ave., Detroit, MI 48226 * Treasurer: Daniel T. Lis*

	1993-94	1995-96	1997	Totals
Receipts	$234,924	$218,356	$113,544	$566,824
Disburse	294,667	256,730	67,064	618,461
Cash	57,218	18,845	65,326	n/a
Contributions	34,700	43,650	0	78,350
Republicans	20,000	31,600	0	51,600
No. of Cand.	*13*	*27*	*0*	*40*
House	12,000	24,150	0	36,150
Senate	8,000	7,450	0	15,450
Democrats	14,700	12,050	0	26,750
No. of Cand.	*13*	*18*	*0*	*31*
House	10,700	10,800	0	21,500
Senate	4,000	1,250	0	5,250
Incumbents	20,450	35,950	0	56,400
Challengers	750	7,700	0	8,450
Open Seat	13,500	0	0	13,500
Winners	29,450	28,700	n/a	58,150
Losers	5,250	14,950	n/a	20,200

First Chicago NBD Corp. Political Action Committee - NBD (formerly known as NBD Bancorp Inc. PAC) (C00198077) *611 Woodward Ave., Detroit, MI 48226 * Treasurer: Daniel T. Lis*

	1993-94	1995-96	1997	Totals
Receipts	$110,737	$117,465	$20,294	$248,496
Disburse	107,087	140,682	25,446	273,215
Cash	28,366	5,153	0	n/a
Contributions	24,370	19,450	-500	43,320
Republicans	13,800	14,200	0	28,000
No. of Cand.	*15*	*12*	*0*	*27*
House	7,350	12,200	0	19,550
Senate	6,450	2,000	0	8,450
Democrats	10,570	5,250	-500	15,320
No. of Cand.	*18*	*10*	*1*	*29*
House	7,570	4,750	-500	11,820
Senate	3,000	500	0	3,500
Incumbents	18,920	6,400	-500	24,820
Challengers	450	10,650	0	11,100
Open Seat	5,000	2,400	0	7,400
Winners	16,170	9,600	n/a	25,770
Losers	8,200	9,850	n/a	18,050

Contributed less than $5,000 during 1995-96 cycle:

First Chicago NBD Corp. Political Action Committee (C00326165)
*Phone: (312) 407-8110 * One National Plaza, Suite 0303/1ND-14, Chicago, IL 60670 * Treasurer: Dennis P. Carroll*

First Citizens Bank & Trust Co.

*Phone: (919) 716-7424 * Fax: (919) 716-2844*
P.O. Box 27131, Raleigh, NC 27611-7131
Web: www.firstcitizens.com

First Citizens Bank & Trust has 300 branches in North Carolina, Virginia and West Virginia. The publicly traded Raleigh, N.C. company has about $9 billion in assets, making it among the 100 largest banks in the United States.

First Citizens serves 170 communities and offers consumer and commercial banking, as well as mutual funds, leasing, annuities, discount brokerage and trust services. It has 4,300 employees.

First Citizens Bank & Trust Co. Political Action Committee (C00168914) *Address: same as sponsor * Treasurer: Alexander G. MacFadyen Jr.*

	1993-94	1995-96	1997	Totals
Receipts	$18,359	$29,032	$15,609	$63,000
Disburse	26,700	38,851	11,350	76,901
Cash	16,479	7,396	11,655	n/a
Contributions	25,400	31,351	6,350	63,101
Republicans	19,850	28,351	4,500	52,701
No. of Cand.	*13*	*11*	*3*	*27*
House	13,100	16,851	2,500	32,451
Senate	6,750	11,500	2,000	20,250
Democrats	5,550	3,000	1,850	10,400
No. of Cand.	*6*	*4*	*2*	*12*
House	5,550	3,000	1,850	10,400
Senate	0	0	0	0
Incumbents	13,150	28,851	6,350	48,351
Challengers	4,500	1,500	0	6,000
Open Seat	7,750	1,000	0	8,750
Winners	19,750	22,500	n/a	42,250
Losers	5,650	8,851	n/a	14,501

First Commercial Corp.

*Phone: (501) 371-7000 * Fax: (501) 371-7413*
P.O. Box 1471, Little Rock, AR 72203
*Web: www.firstcommercial.com * E-mail: bankinfo@firstcommercial.com*

First Commercial is a publicly owned $6.9 billion bank holding company and the largest bank based in Arkansas. Founded in 1983, the company has more than 3,300 employees and branches in Arkansas, Texas, Tennessee and Louisiana. It also has a 50 percent interest in two banks in Oklahoma.

Subsidiaries: First Commercial Mortgage Co., First Commercial Trust Co., First Commercial Investment Inc., First Commercial Capital Management and Financial Fleet Services Inc.

First PAC First Commercial Bank N.A. Political Action Committee (C00080283) *Address: same as sponsor * Treasurer: Bill Matthews * Contact: Charles Stewart, Senior V.P. and Manager of Public Affairs*

	1993-94	1995-96	1997	Totals
Receipts	$12,743	$13,081	$4,869	$30,693
Disburse	3,626	15,950	329	19,905
Cash	10,871	8,009	12,459	n/a
Contributions	3,200	9,950	800	13,950
Republicans	500	4,000	100	4,600
No. of Cand.	*2*	*4*	*1*	*7*
House	0	1,000	0	1,000
Senate	500	3,000	100	3,600
Democrats	2,700	5,950	700	9,350
No. of Cand.	*4*	*6*	*2*	*12*
House	2,700	2,750	500	5,950
Senate	0	3,200	200	3,400
Incumbents	2,000	0	600	2,600
Challengers	1,200	0	0	1,200
Open Seat	0	9,950	200	10,150
Winners	2,000	3,500	n/a	5,500
Losers	1,200	6,450	n/a	7,650

First Interstate Bancorp

633 W. Fifth St., Los Angeles, CA 90071

The First Interstate Bank of California PAC was terminated in August 1996. The company had affiliated PACs in Texas, Arizona, Nevada, Washington, Oregon and Utah. They were terminated shortly after the 1996 election.

First Interstate Bancorp was acquired by Wells Fargo & Co. in April 1996.

First Interstate Bank of California Political Action Committee (C00102590) *Address: same as sponsor * Treasurer: Lawrence B. Gotlieb*

	1993-94	1995-96	1997	Totals
Receipts	$36,295	$41,183	$0	$77,478
Disburse	37,655	90,782	0	128,437
Cash	49,650	0	0	n/a
Contributions	32,270	28,350	0	60,620
Republicans	19,020	17,500	0	36,520
No. of Cand.	*14*	*14*	*0*	*28*
House	5,450	15,500	0	20,950
Senate	13,570	2,000	0	15,570
Democrats	13,250	10,850	0	24,100
No. of Cand.	*13*	*13*	*0*	*26*
House	7,250	6,850	0	14,100
Senate	6,000	4,000	0	10,000

Incumbents	28,270	26,350	0	54,620
Challengers	0	0	0	0
Open Seat	3,000	2,000	0	5,000
Winners	28,520	26,900	n/a	55,420
Losers	3,750	1,450	n/a	5,200

Terminated PACs which contributed less than $5,000 during 1995-96 cycle:

First Interstate Bank of Arizona Good Government Committee (C00033415) *P.O. Box 53456, Phoenix, AZ 85072 * Treasurer: Leo L. Miller*

First Interstate Bank of Nevada Employee PAC - Federal (C00149997) *420 Montgomery St., 12th Floor, San Francisco, CA 94163 * Treasurer: Mendy Cavanagh*

First Interstate Bank of Oregon N.A. Employees Federal Political Action Committee (C00170308) *1300 S.W. Fifth Ave., Portland, OR 97201 * Treasurer: Catherine Holland*

First Interstate Bank of Utah Employee Political Action Committee (C00251975) *180 S. Main St., Suite 1600, 16th Floor, Salt Lake City, UT 84101 * Treasurer: Stephanie Harpst*

First Interstate Bank of Washington Political Action Committee (C00038679) *P.O. Box 1997, Mailstop 241, Tacoma, WA 98401 * Treasurer: Michael C. Worthy*

First Interstate Texas Leadership Funds/Federal (C00118984) *808 Travis, Suite 210, P.O. Box 3326, Houston, TX 77002 * Treasurer: Mary Gibbs*

First Maryland Bancorp

Phone: (410) 244-4000
25 S. Charles St., Baltimore, MD 21201

Bank holding company First Maryland Bancorp operates about 300 branches in the mid-Atlantic region. Subsidiaries include First National Bank of Maryland, Dauphin Deposit Corp., First Omni Bank and The York Bank and Trust Co.

First Maryland Bancorp is itself a subsidiary of Allied Irish Banks.

First National Bank of Maryland has 4,800 employees and operates 216 branches in Maryland, Washington and Virginia, with one office in Pennsylvania. Its international activities are operated out of its Baltimore headquarters, the Cayman Islands and London. It maintains correspondent accounts with about 55 foreign banks.

Other subsidiaries: First National Mortgage Corp., with 20 offices in Maryland, Virginia, Delaware, Pennsylvania, North Carolina, Kentucky, Tennessee and Mississippi; First Maryland Leasecorp; First Maryland Mortgage Corp. and First Omni.

First Maryland Bancorp Federal Political Action Committee (C00190785) *Address: same as sponsor * Treasurer: Howard L. Millard * Contact: Ronald C. McGuirk, Senior V.P.*

	1993-94	1995-96	1997	Totals
Receipts	$17,810	$13,349	$18,357	$49,516
Disburse	25,118	12,218	7,111	44,447
Cash	7,048	8,180	19,426	n/a
Contributions	13,050	10,175	4,475	27,700
Republicans	7,150	6,575	2,750	16,475
No. of Cand.	*14*	*8*	*5*	*27*
House	5,150	5,575	1,450	12,175
Senate	2,000	1,000	1,300	4,300
Democrats	5,900	3,600	1,725	11,225
No. of Cand.	*8*	*5*	*4*	*17*
House	1,900	3,600	725	6,225
Senate	4,000	0	1,000	5,000
Incumbents	6,200	8,825	3,975	19,000
Challengers	2,950	350	0	3,300
Open Seat	2,800	1,000	500	4,300
Winners	7,000	8,825	n/a	15,825
Losers	6,050	1,350	n/a	7,400

First National Bank of Omaha

*Phone: (402) 571-0100 * Fax: (402) 633-7426*
1620 Dodge St., Omaha, NE 68102
Web: www.fnbomaha.com

The First National Bank of Omaha operates the largest locally owned bank in Nebraska, but much of its business is generated from Visa and MasterCard sales to customers across the nation. The publicly traded bank is one of the top-25 issuers of Visa and MasterCard and a top-10 processor of the cards. It has $7 billion in assets and 5,000 employees.

First National Bank was the first bank in the Midwest and the seventh in the country to offer credit cards to its customers. The company has 3.5 million credit card customers.

Subsidiaries include: Laser One, which personalizes direct mail pieces, and First Integrated Systems, a data processing service for banks.

First National Bank of Omaha PAC (First National PAC) (C00300863) *Address: same as sponsor * Treasurer: Christopher O. Howard*

	1993-94	1995-96	1997	Totals
Receipts	$0	$103,932	$41,118	$145,050
Disburse	0	102,521	35,850	138,371
Cash	0	1,412	6,681	n/a
Contributions	0	52,370	8,500	60,870
Republicans	0	39,770	5,500	45,270
No. of Cand.	*0*	*16*	*8*	*24*
House	0	14,144	3,000	17,144
Senate	0	25,626	2,500	28,126
Democrats	0	12,600	3,000	15,600
No. of Cand.	*0*	*7*	*3*	*10*
House	0	2,500	1,000	3,500
Senate	0	10,100	2,000	12,100
Incumbents	0	13,144	6,000	19,144
Challengers	0	5,100	0	5,100
Open Seat	0	34,126	3,000	37,126
Winners	0	36,520	n/a	36,520
Losers	0	15,850	n/a	15,850

First Tennessee National Corp.

*Phone: (901) 523-4444 x4380 * Fax: (901) 523-4945*
165 Madison Ave., Memphis, TN 38103
Web: www.ftb.com

First Tennessee National is a regional bank holding company — Tennessee's largest — and through its subsidiaries provides banking services for businesses, corporations, financial institutions and governments. The corporation employs 7,700 people. The company was designated one of the top 100 companies to work for in America in January 1998's Fortune magazine.

First Tennessee Bank, the corporation's principal subsidiary, has $13.5 billion in assets and more than 175 locations throughout the state. The company's other banking subsidiaries serve parts of northern Mississippi and northwest Arkansas and have total combined assets of nearly $1 billion. The company also provides mortgage banking, bond broker/agency, merchant credit card processing, trust, venture capital and credit life services in 28 states.

First Tennessee National Corp. Federal PAC (First Tennessee Banks Federal PAC) (C00008151) *Address: same as sponsor * Treasurer: J. Terrence Lee*

	1993-94	1995-96	1997	Totals
Receipts	$35,316	$32,625	$24,665	$92,606
Disburse	55,358	39,517	7,831	102,706
Cash	13,552	6,662	23,496	n/a
Contributions	39,199	31,700	6,750	77,649
Republicans	19,999	26,350	4,000	50,349
No. of Cand.	*14*	*9*	*3*	*26*
House	11,450	8,650	2,000	22,100
Senate	8,549	17,700	2,000	28,249
Democrats	19,200	5,350	2,750	27,300
No. of Cand.	*10*	*8*	*3*	*21*
House	7,950	5,350	750	14,050
Senate	11,250	0	2,000	13,250
Incumbents	28,599	26,450	6,750	61,799
Challengers	100	0	0	100
Open Seat	10,500	5,250	0	15,750
Winners	19,749	28,800	n/a	48,549
Losers	19,450	2,900	n/a	22,350

First Union Corp.

*Phone: (704) 374-6611 * Fax: (704) 374-3105*
One First Union Center, Charlotte, NC 28288-0630
Web: www.firstunion.com

First Union, with headquarters in Charlotte, N.C., is the nation's sixth-largest banking company, with assets of $143 billion as of June 1997.

The company has about 1,900 full-service branches on the East Coast (the nation's third-largest branch network) providing retail banking, retail investment and commercial banking services. It also runs the nation's sixth largest ATM network. First Union employs 44,000 workers serving a customer base of 12 million people.

Through more than 200 additional diversified offices, First Union also provides other financial services nationwide, including mortgage banking, home equity lending, leasing, insurance, securities brokerage and capital markets services.

The company announced in November 1997 that it would purchase CoreStates Financial Corp., a Philadelphia-based bank, and the Money Store, a home equity lender.

First Union Corp. Employees Good Government "F" Fund (C00012518) *Address: same as sponsor * Treasurer: Rufus Beaty*

	1993-94	1995-96	1997	Totals
Receipts	$92,764	$119,980	$48,695	$261,439
Disburse	142,160	160,916	65,941	369,017
Cash	107,837	66,914	49,672	n/a
Contributions	96,950	114,270	51,620	262,840
Republicans	51,850	73,500	32,750	158,100
No. of Cand.	*35*	*49*	*27*	*111*
House	30,850	46,000	19,500	96,350
Senate	21,000	27,500	13,250	61,750
Democrats	44,600	40,770	18,870	104,240
No. of Cand.	*38*	*41*	*18*	*97*
House	38,100	29,270	8,120	75,490
Senate	6,500	11,500	10,750	28,750
Incumbents	60,300	80,470	45,370	186,140
Challengers	10,200	16,800	250	27,250
Open Seat	25,250	16,000	5,500	46,750
Winners	70,550	80,670	n/a	151,220
Losers	26,400	33,600	n/a	60,000

Wheat First Butcher Singer Inc. Responsible Government Fund (C00238386) *Phone: (804) 782-3392 * Fax: (804) 782-6698 * 901 E. Byrd St., Richmond, VA 23219 * Web: www.wheatfirst.com * Treasurer: Jolene Carter*

Wheat First Butcher Singer was purchased by First Union Corp. in February 1998. As of March 1998, the company did not know whether it would retain its PAC.

Based in Richmond, Va., the merged company will be known as Wheat First Union. In addition to traditional banking, it provides securities brokerage, investment banking, asset management and financial advising services to individual and institutional investors. Wheat First Union has 3,000 employees and $30 billion in assets.

The bank's branches are clustered on the East Coast, although it also has offices in California, Texas, Idaho, Michigan and Missouri.

With the merger, Wheat First Union became part of the sixth-largest commercial bank in the United States.

	1993-94	1995-96	1997	Totals
Receipts	$116,100	$141,374	$69,908	$327,382
Disburse	99,755	88,260	38,180	226,195
Cash	33,654	86,772	118,500	n/a
Contributions	11,050	21,800	11,500	44,350
Republicans	6,550	15,800	9,000	31,350
No. of Cand.	*10*	*12*	*9*	*31*
House	3,050	8,300	6,000	17,350
Senate	3,500	7,500	3,000	14,000
Democrats	4,500	6,000	2,500	13,000
No. of Cand.	*8*	*5*	*2*	*15*
House	3,250	3,000	500	6,750
Senate	1,250	3,000	2,000	6,250
Incumbents	7,200	19,000	11,000	37,200
Challengers	2,850	1,300	500	4,650
Open Seat	0	1,500	0	1,500
Winners	7,700	19,000	n/a	26,700
Losers	3,350	2,800	n/a	6,150

First Fidelity PAC N.J. (C00104182) *Phone: (973) 565-3200 * 550 Broad St., 18th Floor, Newark, NJ 07102 * Treasurer: Michael Balbirnie*

The First Fidelity PAC N.J. was terminated in May 1996. The company has since merged with First Union.

	1993-94	1995-96	1997	Totals
Receipts	$73,141	$47,243	$0	$120,384
Disburse	79,239	48,940	0	128,179
Cash	1,747	51	0	n/a
Contributions	17,450	6,650	0	24,100
Republicans	6,450	1,500	0	7,950
No. of Cand.	*5*	*2*	*0*	*7*
House	1,450	1,500	0	2,950
Senate	5,000	0	0	5,000
Democrats	11,000	5,150	0	16,150
No. of Cand.	*4*	*2*	*0*	*6*
House	1,000	150	0	1,150
Senate	10,000	5,000	0	15,000
Incumbents	12,250	6,650	0	18,900
Challengers	5,200	0	0	5,200
Open Seat	0	0	0	0
Winners	11,450	6,150	n/a	17,600
Losers	6,000	500	n/a	6,500

Firstar Corp.

*Phone: (414) 765-5221 * Fax: (414) 765-6111*
777 E. Wisconsin Ave., Legal Dept., Milwaukee, WI 53202
*Web: www.firstar.com * E-mail: yingljohn@aol.com*

Firstar is a $20-billion bank holding company with 240 branches in Illinois, Wisconsin, Minnesota and Iowa. The publicly traded company has 8,000 employees and reported $1.9 billion in 1997 sales.

Firstar's non-bank subsidiaries provide residential mortgages, title insurance, business and consumer insurance and brokerage and investment services.

The company serves about 1.2 million households in the United States.

Subsidiaries: Firstar Investment Services, Elan Investment Services Inc., Firstar Insurance Services, Elan MasterCard and Visa, Firstar Investment Research & Management Co. and Firstar Trust Affiliates.

Firstar Corp. Civic Affairs Committee (formerly known as First Wisconsin Civic Affairs Committee) (C00041301) *Address: same as sponsor * Treasurer: William H. Risch * Contact: John Yingling, V.P. of Gov. Relations*

	1993-94	1995-96	1997	Totals
Receipts	$54,823	$59,437	$26,307	$140,567
Disburse	79,918	57,907	23,950	161,775
Cash	6,387	7,921	10,279	n/a
Contributions	19,750	29,500	13,500	62,750
Republicans	11,250	18,000	6,000	35,250
No. of Cand.	*11*	*12*	*9*	*32*
House	9,650	18,000	4,500	32,150
Senate	1,600	0	1,500	3,100
Democrats	8,500	11,500	7,500	27,500
No. of Cand.	*7*	*7*	*6*	*20*
House	8,000	10,500	6,500	25,000
Senate	500	1,000	1,000	2,500
Incumbents	17,150	22,500	8,000	47,650
Challengers	1,600	0	1,500	3,100
Open Seat	1,000	7,000	4,000	12,000
Winners	16,100	22,500	n/a	38,600
Losers	3,650	7,000	n/a	10,650

Firstar Corp. of Iowa Political Action Committee (C00262972) *Phone: (515) 245-6100 * Fax: (515) 247-4911 * P.O. Box 10317, Des Moines, IA 50306 * Treasurer: Steven L. Caves*

	1993-94	1995-96	1997	Totals
Receipts	$26,250	$14,911	$0	$41,161
Disburse	23,375	17,580	650	41,605
Cash	9,143	6,475	5,825	n/a
Contributions	5,000	6,250	0	11,250
Republicans	4,000	5,250	0	9,250
No. of Cand.	*3*	*4*	*0*	*7*
House	4,000	3,750	0	7,750
Senate	0	1,500	0	1,500
Democrats	1,000	1,000	0	2,000
No. of Cand.	*1*	*1*	*0*	*2*
House	1,000	1,000	0	2,000
Senate	0	0	0	0
Incumbents	4,000	3,750	0	7,750
Challengers	1,000	1,500	0	2,500
Open Seat	0	1,000	0	1,000
Winners	4,000	4,750	n/a	8,750
Losers	1,000	1,500	n/a	2,500

Fleet Financial Group Inc.

*Phone: (617) 346-4000 * Fax: (617) 346-5765*
One Federal St., Boston, MA 02110
Web: www.fleet.com

Fleet Financial Group is an $83 billion general commercial banking and trust business. Its primary subsidiary, Fleet Bank, has branches in Rhode Island, New York, Connecticut, Massachusetts, Maine, New Hampshire and Florida.

The company also owns 11 financial services companies involved in mortgage banking, asset-based lending, equipment leasing, consumer finance, real estate financing, securities brokerage services, investment banking, investment advice and management, data processing and student loan servicing.

The publicly traded Fleet Financial Group is headquartered in Boston.

Subsidiaries include: AFSA Data, Quick & Reilly, Fleet Capital, Fleet Investment Advisors, Fleet Securities and Option One Mortgage Corp., a discount brokerage.

Fleet Financial Group Inc. Federal Political Action Committee (C00128140) *Address: same as sponsor * Treasurer: James F. X. Doherty*

	1993-94	1995-96	1997	Totals
Receipts	$95,775	$76,540	$100	$172,415
Disburse	79,832	90,014	17,232	187,078
Cash	30,759	17,284	151	n/a
Contributions	62,582	64,753	16,674	144,009
Republicans	15,250	40,853	5,000	61,103
No. of Cand.	*19*	*25*	*5*	*49*
House	9,150	16,850	2,000	28,000
Senate	6,100	24,003	3,000	33,103
Democrats	47,332	23,900	11,674	82,906
No. of Cand.	*38*	*17*	*13*	*68*
House	35,532	13,020	7,174	55,726
Senate	11,800	10,880	4,500	27,180
Incumbents	52,832	39,970	16,674	109,476
Challengers	2,200	5,403	0	7,603
Open Seat	7,250	19,380	0	26,630
Winners	51,582	47,650	n/a	99,232
Losers	11,000	17,103	n/a	28,103

Shawmut National Corp. Political Action Committee (formerly known as Hartford National Corp. PAC) (C00159848) *777 Main St., Hartford, CT 06115 * Treasurer: Kyle L. Ballou*

Shawmut National, a banking company in the Northeast, merged with Fleet Financial in November 1995. Shawmut's PAC was terminated after the merger.

	1993-94	1995-96	1997	Totals
Receipts	$38,643	$9,423	$0	$48,066
Disburse	38,325	13,143	0	51,468
Cash	1,709	0	0	n/a
Contributions	23,075	9,150	0	32,225
Republicans	7,000	4,500	0	11,500
No. of Cand.	*9*	*6*	*0*	*15*
House	6,000	2,000	0	8,000
Senate	1,000	2,500	0	3,500
Democrats	15,825	4,650	0	20,475
No. of Cand.	*23*	*9*	*0*	*32*
House	12,225	2,850	0	15,075
Senate	3,600	1,800	0	5,400
Incumbents	19,925	8,850	0	28,775
Challengers	1,850	0	0	1,850
Open Seat	1,300	300	0	1,600
Winners	19,725	7,900	n/a	27,625
Losers	3,350	1,250	n/a	4,600

Contributed less than $5,000 during 1995-96 cycle:

Fleet Bank National Association Political Action Committee (formerly known as National Westminster PAC) (C00265041)
*Phone: (201) 547-7571 * 10 Exchange Place, Jersey City, NJ 07302 * Treasurer: Christian M. Abeel*

HSBC Americas Inc.

Phone: (716) 841-2424
One Marine Midland Center, Buffalo, NY 14203
Web: www.marinemidland.com

Headquartered in Buffalo, N.Y., Marine Midland Bank is a New York state regional banking institution with 400 offices and more than $32 billion in assets.

The company is the principal subsidiary of HSBC Americas, which is an indirectly held, wholly owned subsidiary of HSBC Holdings, a London bank holding company. With more than 5,500 offices in 79 countries and territories and assets of $458 billion as of June 1997, the HSBC Group is among the world's largest banking and financial services organizations.

In 1996, Marine Midland completed a series of acquisitions: two New York City Hang Seng Bank branches, 11 metropolitan New York area East River Savings Bank branches and J.P. Morgan's U.S. dollar clearing operations. The company also acquired First Federal Savings and Loan Association of Rochester in March 1997.

HSBC Americas Inc. Bipartisan Political Action Committee (also known as Marine BiPAC) (C00139774) *Address: same as sponsor * Treasurer: Mary B. Sommer*

	1993-94	1995-96	1997	Totals
Receipts	$80,000	$63,584	$31,845	$175,429
Disburse	76,181	62,190	25,790	164,161
Cash	108,321	109,717	115,773	n/a
Contributions	12,650	8,790	2,540	23,980
Republicans	6,275	5,790	2,540	14,605
No. of Cand.	*14*	*11*	*3*	*28*
House	4,275	3,040	290	7,605
Senate	2,000	2,750	2,250	7,000
Democrats	6,375	3,000	0	9,375
No. of Cand.	*12*	*4*	*0*	*16*
House	5,625	3,000	0	8,625
Senate	750	0	0	750
Incumbents	12,650	8,290	2,540	23,480
Challengers	250	500	0	750
Open Seat	250	0	0	250
Winners	11,775	8,040	n/a	19,815
Losers	875	750	n/a	1,625

Hibernia Corp.

*Phone: (504) 533-2545 * Fax: (504) 533-2199*
313 Carondelet St., Internal Control Department, New Orleans, LA 70130
Web: www.hiberniabank.com

Hibernia is the holding company for Hibernia National Bank, which operates more than 200 banking offices throughout Louisiana and in east Texas, where it is acquiring more banks. Hibernia, a publicly traded company, had $11 billion in assets and posted sales of $895 million in 1997. The company is based in New Orleans and employs 4,500 people.

Hibernia is a full-service bank, offering checking, savings, money market and individual retirement accounts. It also offers a wide range of lending options, including automobile, residential real estate and construction loans.

Hibernia People for Good Government Inc. - Federal A PAC of Hibernia Corp. (C00149583) *Address: same as sponsor * Treasurer: Faith Mascot * Contact: Ann Schiffman, Manager of Gov. Relations*

	1993-94	1995-96	1997	Totals
Receipts	$19,792	$71,585	$42,114	$133,491
Disburse	11,200	40,000	10,500	61,700
Cash	8,594	40,182	71,798	n/a
Contributions	11,200	40,000	8,500	59,700
Republicans	6,100	30,500	5,500	42,100
No. of Cand.	*18*	*43*	*3*	*64*
House	4,600	20,500	5,500	30,600
Senate	1,500	10,000	0	11,500
Democrats	5,100	9,500	3,000	17,600
No. of Cand.	*19*	*14*	*2*	*35*
House	3,600	4,000	0	7,600
Senate	1,500	5,500	3,000	10,000
Incumbents	11,200	32,000	8,500	51,700
Challengers	0	250	0	250
Open Seat	0	7,250	0	7,250
Winners	10,350	31,250	n/a	41,600
Losers	850	8,750	n/a	9,600

Huntington Bancshares Inc.

*Phone: (614) 480-4718 * Fax: (614) 480-5485*
41 S. High St., 34th Floor, Columbus, OH 43215-6101
*Web: www.huntington.com * E-mail: jon.baesman@huntington.com*

Huntington Bancshares operates Ohio-based Huntington Bank, which has $25 billion in assets and 645 branch offices throughout Florida, Indiana, Kentucky, Michigan, Ohio and West Virginia.

The bank offers personal and business banking services, including traditional checking and savings accounts, as well as loans, investment services and Internet banking. Based in Columbus, Ohio, the bank was founded in 1866 and employs nearly 10,000 people.

The corporation also owns the Huntington State Bank, with a single office in Alexandria, Ohio, and about $67 million in assets.

Huntington Bancshares Inc. Political Action Committee (HBI-PAC) (C00165589) *Address: same as sponsor * Treasurer: Jon Baesman * Contact: Rick Zarnoch, Chairman*

	1993-94	1995-96	1997	Totals
Receipts	$130,454	$154,210	$92,666	$377,330
Disburse	136,715	122,170	75,020	333,905
Cash	6,893	38,936	56,583	n/a
Contributions	19,064	29,971	14,184	63,219
Republicans	16,764	29,321	14,134	60,219
No. of Cand.	*13*	*9*	*7*	*29*
House	9,054	21,101	9,000	39,155
Senate	7,710	8,220	5,134	21,064
Democrats	2,300	650	50	3,000
No. of Cand.	*5*	*3*	*1*	*9*
House	800	400	50	1,250
Senate	1,500	250	0	1,750
Incumbents	8,474	26,001	8,550	43,025
Challengers	2,350	3,970	1,000	7,320
Open Seat	8,240	0	4,634	12,874
Winners	11,844	21,418	n/a	33,262
Losers	7,220	8,553	n/a	15,773

Contributed less than $5,000 during 1995-96 cycle:

Huntington Banks of Michigan Political Action Fund (formerly known as Macomb Warren Bank) (C00091272) *Phone: (810) 469-6900 * Fax: (810) 244-9480 * 1 N. Main St., Mount Clemens, MI 48043 * Treasurer: Gordon K. Brown*

Independent Bankers Association of America

*Phone: (800) 422-7285 * Fax: (320) 352-5766*
518 Lincoln Rd., P.O. Box 267, Sauk Centre, MN 56378
*Web: www.ibaa.org * E-mail: info@ibaa.org*

The Independent Bankers Association of America represents about 5,500 independent community banks with 15,000 locations nationwide. Member banks hold nearly $375 billion in insured deposits, $445 billion in assets, and more than $240 billion in loans for consumers, small businesses and farms. IBAA members employ more than 200,000 people. The majority of the nation's commercial banks are community banks.

The IBAA opposes ATM "interchange fees," which require banks to charge a price for using the machines. It is the only banking association opposed to allowing banks to offer insurance and other financial services. It supports bankruptcy reform legislation which would give filers the exact amount of debt relief they need and not more. The IBAA also works on consumer privacy issues and the legislative definition of credit unions.

Nearly 90 percent of the IBAA's PAC contributions during the 1995-96 election cycle went to winning candidates. The group favored Republicans and ranked eighth among commercial banks in total congressional contributions. The leading recipients were Sen. John W. Warner, R-Va., and Rep. Doug Bereuter, R-Neb. Bereuter sits on the House Banking Committee. Five candidates received at least $5,000 from IBAA.

Independent Bankers Association of America Political Action Committee (IBAA PAC) (C00032698) *Phone: (800) 422-8439 * Fax: (202) 659-9216 * One Thomas Circle N.W., Suite 950, Washington, DC 20005-5802 * Treasurer: Ronald K. Ence * Contact: Ronald K. Ence*

	1993-94	1995-96	1997	Totals
Receipts	$466,875	$575,489	$323,369	$1,365,733
Disburse	455,704	519,707	278,786	1,254,197
Cash	84,739	140,542	184,887	n/a
Contributions	366,890	358,500	185,790	911,180
Republicans	152,450	239,950	102,350	494,750
No. of Cand.	*134*	*165*	*100*	*399*
House	108,450	170,950	70,850	350,250
Senate	44,000	69,000	31,500	144,500
Democrats	210,440	118,050	82,940	411,430
No. of Cand.	*178*	*108*	*74*	*360*
House	158,700	92,050	48,520	299,270
Senate	51,740	26,000	34,420	112,160
Incumbents	323,340	293,950	178,470	795,760
Challengers	8,700	13,250	1,000	22,950
Open Seat	34,850	50,800	6,320	91,970
Winners	300,950	322,000	n/a	622,950
Losers	65,940	36,500	n/a	102,440

Integra Financial Corp.

300 Fourth Ave., 1-181, Pittsburgh, PA 15278

Integra PAC, formerly known as the PennBancorp PAC, was terminated in 1996.

Integra Political Action Committee (formerly known as PennBancorp PAC) (C00193094) *Address: same as sponsor * Treasurer: Donald E. Warner*

	1993-94	1995-96	1997	Totals
Receipts	$184,165	$132,896	$0	$317,061
Disburse	183,659	183,098	0	366,757
Cash	50,201	0	0	n/a
Contributions	27,159	13,785	0	40,944
Republicans	17,515	13,235	0	30,750
No. of Cand.	*11*	*6*	*0*	*17*
House	8,315	11,400	0	19,715
Senate	9,200	1,835	0	11,035
Democrats	9,644	550	0	10,194
No. of Cand.	*10*	*2*	*0*	*12*
House	9,494	550	0	10,044
Senate	150	0	0	150
Incumbents	7,494	12,485	0	19,979
Challengers	9,400	1,300	0	10,700
Open Seat	9,765	0	0	9,765
Winners	19,309	10,385	n/a	29,694
Losers	7,850	3,400	n/a	11,250

International Bank of Commerce

*Phone: (956) 722-7611 * Fax: (956) 722-2556*
1200 San Bernardo, Laredo, TX 78042
*Web: www.iboc.com * E-mail: jorgeb_haynes@iboc.com*

International Bancshares Corp. is a publicly traded bank holding company with about $4 billion in total assets, 1,200 employees and 55 branch offices throughout southern Texas. The corporation's banks offer personal and business checking and savings accounts, credit cards, international trade services, mortgage loans and annuities.

The corporation's largest bank is the International Bank of Commerce of Laredo, Texas, with more than $3.3 billion in assets and nearly $2.3 billion in total deposits. Established in 1966, this bank operates 42 branch offices located primarily in the Texas counties of Bexar, Hidalgo and Webb.

International Bancshares also operates the International Banks of Commerce of Brownsville and Zapata County, as well as Commerce Bank of Laredo. Collectively, these banks operate 13 branches and have total assets of more than $660 million.

The company is the largest minority-owned bank holding company in the United States.

International Bank of Commerce Committee for Improvement and Betterment of the Country (C00276592) *Address: same as sponsor * Treasurer: Jorge Haynes * Contact: Dennis Nixon, Chairman and CEO of IBC*

	1993-94	1995-96	1997	Totals
Receipts	$112,652	$125,832	$60,981	$299,465
Disburse	108,611	127,100	62,192	297,903
Cash	19,185	28,565	17,481	n/a
Contributions	12,620	8,750	7,500	28,870
Republicans	2,000	3,750	1,500	7,250
No. of Cand.	*2*	*4*	*2*	*8*
House	1,000	3,750	1,500	6,250
Senate	1,000	0	0	1,000
Democrats	10,620	5,000	6,000	21,620
No. of Cand.	*9*	*2*	*4*	*15*
House	5,000	5,000	6,000	16,000
Senate	5,620	0	0	5,620
Incumbents	14,120	4,750	5,000	23,870
Challengers	0	0	1,000	1,000
Open Seat	0	3,000	1,500	4,500
Winners	8,500	7,750	n/a	16,250
Losers	4,120	1,000	n/a	5,120

J.P. Morgan & Co. Inc.

*Phone: (212) 648-3407 * Fax: (212) 648-5446*
60 Wall St., New York, NY 10260
Web: www.jpmorgan.com

J.P. Morgan is a $17.7 billion international banking company with offices in 23 countries. It provides investment banking, brokerage and asset management services. A public company, its largest subsidiary is

Morgan Guaranty; other subsidiaries are J.P. Morgan Securities Inc. in New York, J.P. Morgan Securities Ltd. in London, and J.P. Morgan Securities Asia Ltd. The company employs about 15,500 people.

The company is interested in legislation affecting the financial services business, including modernization efforts and International Monetary Fund financing. J.P. Morgan is one of a group of U.S. banks that created a loan guarantee plan for South Korean banks in early 1998. The company also follows other international trade issues.

J.P. Morgan was one of the most successful PAC contributors during the 1995-96 election cycle. Nine of every 10 dollars spent went to winning candidates, 13th best among the top 200 PACs. The company gave 93 percent of its contributions to incumbents.

The top six recipients were all members of congressional banking or commerce committees. All received $10,000 each. Five were House members; the sixth was Sen. John D. Rockefeller IV, D-W.Va.

J.P. Morgan & Co. Inc. Political Action Committee (MorganPAC) (C00104299) *Address: same as sponsor * Treasurer: Cory N. Strupp*

	1993-94	1995-96	1997	Totals
Receipts	$783,329	$652,813	$305,077	$1,741,219
Disburse	717,554	754,237	252,950	1,724,741
Cash	171,249	69,828	121,956	n/a
Contributions	531,550	522,000	168,350	1,221,900
Republicans	260,000	302,000	102,300	664,300
No. of Cand.	*87*	*107*	*61*	*255*
House	145,500	219,500	77,800	442,800
Senate	114,500	82,500	24,500	221,500
Democrats	271,550	220,000	66,050	557,600
No. of Cand.	*92*	*63*	*52*	*207*
House	206,000	182,500	58,050	446,550
Senate	65,550	37,500	8,000	111,050
Incumbents	461,050	484,000	163,350	1,108,400
Challengers	6,500	10,000	1,000	17,500
Open Seat	64,000	27,000	4,000	95,000
Winners	459,000	470,000	n/a	929,000
Losers	72,550	52,000	n/a	124,550

KeyCorp

*Phone: (216) 689-6300 * Fax: (216) 689-7009*
127 Public Square, Seventh Floor, Cleveland, OH 44114-1306
Web: www.keybank.com

Headquartered in Cleveland, KeyCorp operates about 1,000 branches in 15 states. The publicly traded company had $64.8 billion in assets at the close of 1997.

KeyCorp provides a wide range of banking, fiduciary and other financial services to its corporate, individual and institutional customers. KeyCorp provides trust services, mutual funds, investment banking services, international banking services and investment management.

The company posted 1997 sales of $6 billion. It employs more than 26,000 workers.

Locations include: Alaska, Colorado, Idaho, Indiana, Maine, Michigan, New Hampshire, New York, Ohio, Oregon, Utah, Vermont and Washington state.

KeyCorp Political Action Committee (formerly known as Society Corp. PAC) (C00073155) *Address: same as sponsor * Treasurer: Peter E. Brereton*

	1993-94	1995-96	1997	Totals
Receipts	$289,233	$433,236	$319,469	$1,041,938
Disburse	289,115	376,200	241,460	906,775
Cash	7,536	64,577	142,588	n/a
Contributions	58,115	98,100	81,450	237,665
Republicans	28,115	75,150	60,850	164,115
No. of Cand.	*27*	*53*	*43*	*123*
House	10,090	54,250	30,850	95,190
Senate	18,025	20,900	30,000	68,925
Democrats	30,000	22,950	20,600	73,550
No. of Cand.	*31*	*27*	*24*	*82*
House	22,750	19,450	13,850	56,050
Senate	7,250	3,500	6,750	17,500
Incumbents	27,990	81,450	75,500	184,940
Challengers	10,600	11,100	1,000	22,700
Open Seat	18,525	5,350	5,250	29,125
Winners	28,390	72,000	n/a	100,390
Losers	29,725	26,100	n/a	55,825

Klein Bank

*Phone: (281) 320-1416 * Fax: (281) 320-1487*
P.O. Box 73249, Houston, TX 77273
*Web: www.kleinbank.com * E-mail: kleinonline@kleinbank.com*

Klein Bank is a $3-billion locally owned and operated community bank with 260 employees at 21 branches in the Houston area. It offers bank cards, consumer loans, certificates of deposit, IRAs, trust services, mortgage loans and other business services.

Klein Bank Political Action Committee (C00284596) *Address: same as sponsor * Treasurer: Jeanette Cobb*

	1993-94	1995-96	1997	Totals
Receipts	$15,000	$15,000	$10,000	$40,000
Disburse	11,799	18,200	6,650	36,649
Cash	3,201	1	3,351	n/a
Contributions	1,500	4,000	0	5,500
Republicans	1,500	4,000	0	5,500
No. of Cand.	*2*	*3*	*0*	*5*
House	1,000	4,000	0	5,000
Senate	500	0	0	500
Democrats	0	0	0	0
No. of Cand.	*0*	*0*	*0*	*0*
House	0	0	0	0
Senate	0	0	0	0
Incumbents	1,500	1,000	0	2,500
Challengers	0	500	0	500
Open Seat	0	2,500	0	2,500
Winners	1,500	2,500	n/a	4,000
Losers	0	1,500	n/a	1,500

LaSalle National Corp.

*Phone: (312) 904-8629 * Fax: (312) 904-4949*
130 S. LaSalle, P.O. Box 1182, Chicago, IL 60690
Web: www.lasallebanks.com

Headquartered in Chicago with more than $15 billion in assets, LaSalle National Bank is one of the Midwest's largest commercial banks. The bank is a subsidiary of LaSalle National and its parent organization, ABN AMRO North America Inc.

ABN AMRO N.A. is owned by ABN AMRO Bank N.V., the world's 15th largest bank, with assets of $398 billion and more than 1,800 locations in 71 countries.

LaSalle owns other banks, including LaSalle Bank N.A. and LaSalle Bank F.S.B. LaSalle Bank N.A. provides consumer and commercial deposit and loan services and has $5.6 billion in assets. LaSalle Bank F.S.B. is one of the largest banks in Illinois, with more than 70 branches and $10.8 billion in assets.

LaSalle National Corp. Community Action Committee (formerly known as LaSalle National Bancorp Inc.) (C00135186) *Address: same as sponsor * Treasurer: Mark A. Nystuen * Contact: Mark Hoppe, Chairperson*

	1993-94	1995-96	1997	Totals
Receipts	$56,129	$85,935	$45,745	$187,809
Disburse	56,550	66,919	22,250	145,719
Cash	11,083	30,103	53,600	n/a
Contributions	31,550	36,600	9,250	77,400
Republicans	17,550	28,950	4,000	50,500
No. of Cand.	*9*	*13*	*4*	*26*
House	17,300	18,950	500	36,750
Senate	250	10,000	3,500	13,750
Democrats	14,000	7,650	5,250	26,900
No. of Cand.	*8*	*8*	*5*	*21*
House	6,500	4,650	1,250	12,400
Senate	7,500	3,000	4,000	14,500
Incumbents	27,550	27,400	6,500	61,450
Challengers	1,500	650	2,500	4,650
Open Seat	2,500	8,550	250	11,300
Winners	32,550	28,200	n/a	60,750
Losers	-1000	8,400	n/a	7,400

MBNA Corp.

*Phone: (302) 432-0716 * Fax: (302) 432-3614*
1100 King St., Wilmington, DE 19884-0515
Web: www.mbnainternational.com

MBNA is the world's second-largest credit card company. Its main U.S. business is MBNA America Bank, N.A., which had $43.1 billion in managed loans in 1997 and also offers savings and investment accounts. The company has about 15,000 employees.

MBNA ranked sixth among the 110 commercial banks that gave to 1996 congressional campaigns. The company increased its total contributions from 1994 to 1996 by 90 percent. MBNA contributed 86 percent of its money to Republican candidates in 1996.

Top recipients included banking committee members Reps. Jon D. Fox, R-Pa., Richard H. Baker, R-La., and John J. LaFalce, D-N.Y., and Sens. Richard C. Shelby, R-Ala., and Pete Domenici, R-N.M.

The public bank holding company that controls MBNA America also issues credit cards in the United Kingdom. Its subsidiaries include MBNA Consumer Services, which provides home equity loans, and MBNA Insurance Services, which sells mostly auto insurance. The company has plans for expanding its home equity loan business in 1998.

MBNA Corp. Federal Political Committee (C00252866) *Phone: (202) 833-5405 * Fax: (202) 833-5414 * 800 Connecticut Ave. N.W., Washington, DC 20006 * Treasurer: John W. Scheflen * Contact: Joe Crouse, Executive V.P.*

	1993-94	1995-96	1997	Totals
Receipts	$393,256	$903,599	$506,460	$1,803,315
Disburse	403,796	825,974	481,500	1,711,270
Cash	50,386	128,020	152,986	n/a
Contributions	193,132	367,904	227,500	788,536
Republicans	146,382	317,404	180,500	644,286
No. of Cand.	*36*	*77*	*54*	*167*
House	68,500	166,850	119,500	354,850
Senate	77,882	150,554	61,000	289,436
Democrats	46,750	50,500	47,000	144,250
No. of Cand.	*21*	*12*	*22*	*55*
House	29,750	50,500	35,000	115,250
Senate	17,000	0	12,000	29,000
Incumbents	123,386	269,350	225,500	618,236
Challengers	18,000	32,500	0	50,500
Open Seat	50,996	66,054	0	117,050
Winners	146,386	255,904	n/a	402,290
Losers	46,746	112,000	n/a	158,746

Mellon Bank Corp.

*Phone: (412) 234-5000 * Fax: (412) 234-9495*
One Mellon Bank Center, Room 1905, Pittsburgh, PA 15258
Web: www.mellon.com

Mellon Bank ranks among the nation's largest bank holding companies in market capitalization. The company operates Mellon Bank through 450 branch offices, more than 400 of which are located in Pennsylvania, with the others in Delaware, New Jersey and Maryland. These banks have combined assets of $41 billion.

Employing more than 24,000 workers, the corporation provides a full range of banking, investment and trust products and services to individuals and businesses and institutions. Mellon Bank's services include investment assistance, loans, credit cards, checking and savings accounts, insurance, securitizations and network services. Its mutual fund company, The Dreyfus Corp., places Mellon as the leading bank manager of mutual funds.

Mellon also operates the $4.4 billion Boston Safe Deposit and Trust Co.

Bipartisan Political Action Committee, Mellon Bank Corp. (BiPAC/MBC) (C00017558) *Address: same as sponsor * Treasurer: Howard S. Fahnestock*

	1993-94	1995-96	1997	Totals
Receipts	$264,358	$332,366	$203,962	$800,686
Disburse	265,188	319,298	151,668	736,154
Cash	17,262	30,330	82,625	n/a
Contributions	52,544	63,325	33,284	149,153
Republicans	23,140	43,675	22,534	89,349
No. of Cand.	*23*	*44*	*22*	*89*
House	11,765	28,725	11,000	51,490
Senate	11,375	14,950	11,534	37,859
Democrats	29,404	19,300	10,750	59,454
No. of Cand.	*37*	*22*	*13*	*72*
House	20,414	17,600	9,000	47,014
Senate	8,990	1,700	1,750	12,440
Incumbents	36,994	56,775	32,784	126,553
Challengers	9,675	2,950	500	13,125
Open Seat	5,475	3,500	0	8,975
Winners	36,729	55,350	n/a	92,079
Losers	15,815	7,975	n/a	23,790

Mercantile Bancorp

*Phone: (314) 425-2525 * Fax: (314) 425-1286*
P.O. Box 524, Mercantile Tower, St. Louis, MO 63166
Web: www.mercantile.com

With assets of $30 billion, Mercantile Bancorp is a locally managed and independently owned financial services organization based in the lower Midwest. It is the 26th-largest bank holding company in the United States. Mercantile currently has acquisitions pending with CBT Corp., headquartered in Paducah, Ky., and Firstbank of Illinois Co., headquartered in Springfield, Ill.

Mercantile operates banks in more than 500 locations in Missouri, Iowa, Kansas, Illinois and Arkansas. Mercantile's non-banking subsidiaries include companies providing brokerage services, asset-based lending, investment advisory services, leasing services and credit life and other insurance products.

Mercantile employs more than 7,800 people.

Mercantile Bancorp. Inc. (Federal) Political Action Committee (C00150680) *Address: same as sponsor * Treasurer: Michael T. Normile*

	1993-94	1995-96	1997	Totals
Receipts	$170,494	$207,642	$94,847	$472,983
Disburse	62,399	180,051	45,984	288,434
Cash	184,951	212,550	261,417	n/a
Contributions	30,150	92,150	20,350	142,650
Republicans	19,050	63,050	16,500	98,600
No. of Cand.	*9*	*20*	*12*	*41*
House	13,300	43,100	9,500	65,900
Senate	5,750	19,950	7,000	32,700
Democrats	11,100	29,100	3,850	44,050
No. of Cand.	*11*	*14*	*4*	*29*
House	5,850	17,650	350	23,850
Senate	5,250	11,450	3,500	20,200
Incumbents	15,700	26,100	16,750	58,550
Challengers	700	14,750	3,000	18,450
Open Seat	13,500	51,300	600	65,400
Winners	22,450	60,600	n/a	83,050
Losers	7,700	31,550	n/a	39,250

Hawkeye Bancorp Political Action Committee (Hawkeye Ban/PAC) (C00113209) *One Washington St., P.O. Box 709, Mt. Pleasant, IA 52641 * Treasurer: Sharyl Van Dorin*

Hawkeye Bancorp was taken over by Mercantile Bancorp. As a result, according to an official of Hawkeye, Hawkeye's PAC will be folded into Mercantile's PAC.

	1993-94	1995-96	1997	Totals
Receipts	$31,719	$13,177	$12,239	$57,135
Disburse	19,059	28,427	500	47,986
Cash	35,114	19,869	31,609	n/a
Contributions	12,500	25,250	500	38,250
Republicans	10,000	25,250	500	35,750
No. of Cand.	*4*	*5*	*1*	*10*
House	10,000	20,250	500	30,750
Senate	0	5,000	0	5,000
Democrats	2,500	0	0	2,500
No. of Cand.	*1*	*0*	*0*	*1*
House	2,500	0	0	2,500
Senate	0	0	0	0
Incumbents	7,500	15,250	500	23,250
Challengers	2,500	5,000	0	7,500
Open Seat	2,500	5,000	0	7,500
Winners	10,000	15,250	n/a	25,250
Losers	2,500	10,000	n/a	12,500

Mercantile Bankshares Corp.

*Phone: (410) 237-5252 * Fax: (410) 237-5427*
2 Hopkins Plaza, P.O. Box 1477, Baltimore, MD 21203
Web: www.mercantile.net

Mercantile Bankshares is a public, multi-bank holding company with assets in excess of $7 billion. Services include personal and commercial banking. The company's largest bank is Mercantile Safe Deposit & Trust Co., with $2.7 billion in assets and 19 Maryland offices.

Established in 1969, the holding company also owns 20 other locally managed and directed financial institutions. Combined, these businesses have about 140 offices located throughout Maryland, Virginia and Delaware, and total assets of $4.3 billion. Mortgage banking services are provided by Mercantile Mortgage Corp.

In 1997, Marshall National Bank and Trust Co., a Virginia bank with $81 million in assets, became an affiliate of Mercantile Bankshares.

Mercantile Bankshares Corp. Political Action Committee (MBC PAC) (C00186064) *Address: same as sponsor * Treasurer: William T. Skinner Jr. * Contact: H. Furlong Baldwin, Chairman*

	1993-94	1995-96	1997	Totals
Receipts	$23,984	$27,615	$15,360	$66,959
Disburse	25,250	22,500	10,000	57,750
Cash	28,519	33,634	38,994	n/a
Contributions	14,250	9,500	4,000	27,750
Republicans	8,500	2,500	1,000	12,000
No. of Cand.	*4*	*3*	*1*	*8*
House	5,000	2,500	1,000	8,500
Senate	3,500	0	0	3,500
Democrats	5,750	7,000	3,000	15,750
No. of Cand.	*6*	*5*	*3*	*14*
House	4,750	6,000	2,000	12,750
Senate	1,000	1,000	1,000	3,000
Incumbents	7,000	6,000	4,000	17,000
Challengers	3,750	500	0	4,250
Open Seat	3,500	3,000	0	6,500
Winners	8,000	9,000	n/a	17,000
Losers	6,250	500	n/a	6,750

Michigan National Corp.

Phone: (248) 473-3000
27777 Inkster Rd., P.O. Box 9065, Farmington Hills, MI 48333-9065
Web: www.michigannational.com

Michigan National Bank, the principal subsidiary of Michigan National, has nearly 200 offices statewide and $9.6 billion in assets. Employing 3,600 people, the bank offers checking and savings accounts, mortgage loans and computer and telephone banking.

Michigan National is a member of the National Australia Bank Group, an international financial services group. Michigan National serves as the flagship for the group's North American expansion.

Michigan Citizens' Political Action Committee (C00152298) *Address: same as sponsor * Treasurer: Lawrence L. Gladchun*

	1993-94	1995-96	1997	Totals
Receipts	$25,834	$23,412	$11,517	$60,763
Disburse	26,073	36,173	15,879	78,125
Cash	19,761	7,003	2,641	n/a
Contributions	4,747	5,650	1,600	11,997
Republicans	3,597	4,350	1,000	8,947
No. of Cand.	*4*	*7*	*1*	*12*
House	1,100	1,850	1,000	3,950
Senate	2,497	2,500	0	4,997
Democrats	1,150	1,300	600	3,050
No. of Cand.	*2*	*2*	*2*	*6*
House	650	300	600	1,550
Senate	500	1,000	0	1,500
Incumbents	1,150	3,250	1,600	6,000
Challengers	0	1,900	0	1,900
Open Seat	3,597	0	0	3,597
Winners	4,147	3,300	n/a	7,447
Losers	600	2,350	n/a	2,950

National Association of Government Guaranteed Lenders

*Phone: (405) 377-4022 * Fax: (405) 377-3931*
P.O. Box 332, Stillwater, OK 74076-0332
E-mail: naggl@aol.com

The National Association of Government Guaranteed Lenders represents about 650 financial institutions that provide Small Business Administration loans. About 90 percent of the nation's highest-volume lenders are NAGGL members.

In addition, the member institutions account for more than 75 percent of all the SBA 7(a) loans approved annually. An SBA 7(a) loan is a loan in which up to 90 percent of the loan made by a private lender is guaranteed by the Small Business Administration.

National Association of Government Guaranteed Lenders Inc. PAC (C00241000) *Address: same as sponsor * Treasurer: Anthony Robert Wilkinson*

	1993-94	1995-96	1997	Totals
Receipts	$3,216	$16,053	$856	$20,125
Disburse	5,175	9,775	1,500	16,450
Cash	295	6,576	5,933	n/a
Contributions	5,175	7,750	1,500	14,425
Republicans	825	7,750	1,500	10,075
No. of Cand.	*2*	*7*	*2*	*11*
House	825	5,500	500	6,825
Senate	0	2,250	1,000	3,250
Democrats	4,350	0	0	4,350
No. of Cand.	*6*	*0*	*0*	*6*
House	1,350	0	0	1,350
Senate	3,000	0	0	3,000
Incumbents	4,675	7,500	1,500	13,675
Challengers	500	0	0	500
Open Seat	0	250	0	250
Winners	3,325	5,750	n/a	9,075
Losers	1,850	2,000	n/a	3,850

National Bank of Commerce

*Phone: (901) 523-3371 * Fax: (901) 523-3303*
One Commerce Square, Suite 850, Memphis, TN 38150
Web: www.ncbccorp.com

National Bank of Commerce in Memphis, Tenn. is a commercial bank and a subsidiary of National Commerce Bancorp. With more than 30 offices throughout the state and assets of $3.3 billion, National Bank of Commerce offers in-store and supermarket banking, ATM services and personal and commercial lending.

National Commerce Bancorp is a $5 billion sales and marketing organization that provides financial services and consulting activities through a national network of banking affiliates and non-banking subsidiaries. In addition to its Tennessee operations, it has banking offices in Virginia, North Carolina, Georgia and Mississippi.

National Bank of Commerce Committee on Political Affairs (C00095786) *Address: same as sponsor * Treasurer: Charles A. Neale * Contact: Gus Denton, Chairman*

	1993-94	1995-96	1997	Totals
Receipts	$48,567	$52,524	$24,833	$125,924
Disburse	70,656	44,556	17,925	133,137
Cash	8,206	16,180	23,090	n/a
Contributions	30,554	11,953	3,144	45,651
Republicans	18,584	11,453	2,144	32,181
No. of Cand.	*9*	*5*	*1*	*15*
House	6,250	4,100	0	10,350
Senate	12,334	7,353	2,144	21,831
Democrats	11,970	500	1,000	13,470
No. of Cand.	*3*	*1*	*1*	*5*
House	4,970	500	0	5,470
Senate	7,000	0	1,000	8,000
Incumbents	8,500	10,953	3,144	22,597
Challengers	8,384	0	0	8,384
Open Seat	13,670	1,000	0	14,670
Winners	14,434	9,953	n/a	24,387
Losers	16,120	2,000	n/a	18,120

National City Corp.

*Phone: (216) 575-3367 * Fax: (216) 575-2620*
1900 E. Ninth St., National City Center, Cleveland, OH 44114
Web: www.national-city.com

National City is a $54.7 billion diversified financial services company based in Cleveland. National City operates banks and other financial services subsidiaries principally in Ohio, Indiana, Kentucky and Pennsylvania.

On Dec. 1, 1997, National City announced a definitive agreement to merge with First of America Bank Corp., a $21.1 billion bank holding company headquartered in Kalamazoo, Mich. On Jan. 12, 1998, National City announced a definitive agreement to acquire Fort Wayne National Corp., a $3.4 billion bank holding company based in Fort Wayne, Ind. This transaction is expected to close in the second quarter of 1998, subject to regulatory and stockholder approval.

National City's acquisition of Fort Wayne National Corp. will significantly expand National City's presence in northern Indiana, and the company will become the second-largest bank in Indiana.

National City's agreement with First of America will create the 13th-largest banking organization in the United States in terms of total assets. The new organization plans to serve more than 8 million households in six states.

National City Corp. PAC (also known as National City PAC or NC PAC) (C00141036) *Address: same as sponsor * Treasurer: Allen C. Waddle*

	1993-94	1995-96	1997	Totals
Receipts	$457,571	$531,279	$326,616	$1,315,466
Disburse	473,401	464,083	260,564	1,198,048
Cash	87,036	154,234	220,286	n/a
Contributions	95,873	110,375	57,775	264,023
Republicans	58,523	82,825	47,375	188,723
No. of Cand.	*42*	*43*	*31*	*116*
House	39,873	66,975	24,000	130,848
Senate	18,650	15,850	23,375	57,875
Democrats	37,350	27,550	10,400	75,300
No. of Cand.	*40*	*21*	*12*	*73*
House	32,600	23,550	6,400	62,550
Senate	4,750	4,000	4,000	12,750
Incumbents	62,473	91,425	51,525	205,423
Challengers	14,100	14,450	150	28,700
Open Seat	18,700	4,500	6,100	29,300
Winners	62,473	82,925	n/a	145,398
Losers	33,400	27,450	n/a	60,850

First of America Bank Corp. Federal/States PAC (FOABC Federal/States PAC) (C00308072) *Phone: (616) 376-9170 * Fax: (616) 376-9172 * 225 N. Rose St., Kalamazoo, MI 49007 * Web: www.foa.com * Treasurer: Patty L. Taylor * Contact: John Schreuder, Chairperson*

First of America Bank is a bank holding company with $21 billion in assets and 613 offices in Michigan, Illinois and Indiana. The bank sold its Florida operations in late 1997.

	1993-94	1995-96	1997	Totals
Receipts	$0	$28,408	$23,637	$52,045
Disburse	0	20,016	14,695	34,711
Cash	0	8,394	17,337	n/a
Contributions	0	7,200	3,695	10,895
Republicans	0	6,200	1,320	7,520
No. of Cand.	*0*	*8*	*3*	*11*
House	0	5,100	70	5,170
Senate	0	1,100	1,250	2,350
Democrats	0	1,000	2,375	3,375
No. of Cand.	*0*	*1*	*4*	*5*
House	0	1,000	2,375	3,375
Senate	0	0	0	0
Incumbents	0	2,100	3,445	5,545
Challengers	0	5,100	250	5,350
Open Seat	0	0	0	0
Winners	0	1,100	n/a	1,100
Losers	0	6,100	n/a	6,100

NationsBank Corp.

*Phone: (704) 386-5000 * Fax: (704) 386-6699*
100 N. Tryon St., 23rd Floor, Charlotte, NC 28202
Web: www.nationsbank.com

NationsBank is the country's third-largest banking company, with offices in 16 Southern states and the District of Columbia. Its January 1998 merger with Barnett Banks created the largest bank in Florida, serving more than 3.9 million households in that state. That acquisition is expected to result in 6,000 jobs permanently lost in Florida during 1998.

In April 1998, the company announced a merger with BankAmerica Corp., a move which would create the nation's first coast-to-coast bank.

The company also has expanded into investment banking through its NationsBanc Montgomery Securities subsidiary. It acquired Boatmen's Bancshares, based in St. Louis, in January 1997. NationsBank has nearly 63,000 employees and, as of January 1998, assets of $310.6 billion, just behind Citicorp.

NationsBank split its 1996 congressional contributions between the two parties, with a slight edge to Republican candidates. It ranked fourth among commercial banks in contributions, but its contribution total represented a 30 percent decrease from the 1993-94 election cycle.

NationsBank gave the most to candidates in Texas, North Carolina, Georgia and Florida — where the company has operations. Sen. Alfonse M. D'Amato, R-N.Y., and Reps. Rick A. Lazio, R-N.Y., and John J. LaFalce, D-N.Y., who sit on banking committees, were among the top 15 recipients of this PAC's money.

The Barnett merger, announced in August 1997, will result in the eventual termination of Barnett Banks' PAC, according to FEC filings. Barnett's PAC gave 75 percent of its money to Republican candidates during that cycle, and ranked ninth among banks. Taken together, the two PACs gave $775,000 to candidates. NationsBank also has affiliated state PACs in each of the 16 states where it operates.

NationsBank Corp. PAC (C00043489) *Phone: (404) 607-5249 * Fax: (404) 607-6422 * 600 Peachtree St. N.E., Suite 1500, Atlanta, GA 30308 * Treasurer: J. Mark Leggett*

	1993-94	1995-96	1997	Totals
Receipts	$635,424	$535,045	$315,418	$1,485,887
Disburse	875,890	700,663	310,203	1,886,756
Cash	326,812	161,207	166,427	n/a
Contributions	626,800	442,285	223,950	1,293,035
Republicans	235,950	226,300	108,700	570,950
No. of Cand.	*89*	*103*	*85*	*277*
House	156,450	151,050	83,700	391,200
Senate	79,500	75,250	25,000	179,750
Democrats	390,850	214,985	115,250	721,085
No. of Cand.	*133*	*105*	*91*	*329*
House	339,850	174,885	89,750	604,485
Senate	51,000	40,100	25,500	116,600
Incumbents	541,150	364,285	218,250	1,123,685
Challengers	22,750	24,250	1,000	48,000
Open Seat	61,400	54,000	2,700	118,100
Winners	491,200	381,535	n/a	872,735
Losers	135,600	60,750	n/a	196,350

Barnett People for Better Government Inc. Federal - A PAC oı **Barnett Banks Inc. (C00094656)** *50 N. Laura St., Jacksonville, FL 32202-3664 * Web: www.barnett.com * Treasurer: Brian A. Babcock*

Barnett Banks merged with NationsBank in 1997. Barnett's PAC was scheduled be terminated in March 1998 and rolled into NationsBank's PAC.

	1993-94	1995-96	1997	Totals
Receipts	$629,917	$560,701	$292,986	$1,483,604
Disburse	682,178	588,399	344,330	1,614,907
Cash	256,930	229,236	177,895	n/a
Contributions	397,581	333,625	181,900	913,106
Republicans	208,281	251,075	117,350	576,706
No. of Cand.	*133*	*134*	*95*	*362*
House	127,350	164,875	77,350	369,575
Senate	80,931	86,200	40,000	207,131
Democrats	188,300	82,550	64,550	335,400
No. of Cand.	*117*	*57*	*47*	*221*
House	144,800	64,450	35,550	244,800
Senate	43,500	18,100	29,000	90,600
Incumbents	330,081	298,475	168,400	796,956
Challengers	11,750	2,950	0	14,700
Open Seat	55,750	32,200	14,000	101,950
Winners	319,081	295,475	n/a	614,556
Losers	78,500	38,150	n/a	116,650

BoBancPAC, A Political Action Committee of Boatmen's Bancshares Inc. (C00159103) *P.O. Box 236, St. Louis, MO 63166 * Treasurer: Douglas B. Woodruff*

Boatmen's Bancshares PAC filed for termination in July 1997. The corporation was bought by NationsBank in January 1997.

	1993-94	1995-96	1997	Totals
Receipts	$151,069	$129,624	$6,344	$287,037
Disburse	139,832	116,218	44,374	300,424
Cash	24,621	38,029	0	n/a
Contributions	70,085	39,750	0	109,835
Republicans	26,175	23,500	0	49,675
No. of Cand.	*20*	*21*	*0*	*41*
House	14,175	16,250	0	30,425
Senate	12,000	7,250	0	19,250
Democrats	43,910	16,250	0	60,160
No. of Cand.	*19*	*19*	*0*	*38*
House	34,660	11,250	0	45,910
Senate	9,250	5,000	0	14,250
Incumbents	38,460	20,500	0	58,960
Challengers	4,250	2,000	0	6,250
Open Seat	26,375	17,250	0	43,625
Winners	53,410	31,000	n/a	84,410
Losers	16,675	8,750	n/a	25,425

Terminated PACs which contributed less than $5,000 during 1995-96 cycle:

Boatmen's Arkansas Inc. Federal Political Action Committee (C00237487) *200 W. Capitol, P.O. Box 1681, Little Rock, AR 72203 * Treasurer: Susan F. Smith*

North Carolina Bankers Association

*Phone: (919) 781-7979 * Fax: (919) 881-9909*
P.O. Box 19999, Raleigh, NC 27619-1999
Web: www.ncba.com

The North Carolina Bankers Association has 126 members across the state, including banks, trust companies and savings institutions. Affiliate members include firms, companies and individuals whose business or profession brings them in contact with community banks.

In 1997, the North Carolina Bankers Association and the American Bankers Association brought a case against the AT&T Federal Credit Union in North Carolina. The case charged that a 1980s interpretation of the Credit Union Act that allows credit unions to market to more than one group should be struck down. In February 1998, the Supreme Court ruled that individual credit unions cannot broadly draw members from a variety of occupations.

North Carolina Bankers Association PAC (also known as Community Bank PAC) (C00249995) *Address: same as sponsor * Treasurer: Vera K. Edmonds * Contact: Thad Woodard, Chairman*

	1993-94	1995-96	1997	Totals
Receipts	$40,127	$36,774	$36,202	$113,103
Disburse	25,941	45,153	48,220	119,314
Cash	39,839	31,461	19,444	n/a
Contributions	10,800	35,000	13,250	59,050
Republicans	3,500	25,000	3,000	31,500
No. of Cand.	*6*	*14*	*1*	*21*
House	2,500	22,000	3,000	27,500
Senate	1,000	3,000	0	4,000
Democrats	7,300	10,000	10,250	27,550
No. of Cand.	*7*	*7*	*5*	*19*
House	7,300	10,000	10,250	27,550
Senate	0	0	0	0
Incumbents	8,300	31,000	13,250	52,550
Challengers	0	2,000	0	2,000
Open Seat	2,500	2,000	0	4,500
Winners	8,500	26,500	n/a	35,000
Losers	2,300	8,500	n/a	10,800

Northern Trust Corp.

*Phone: (312) 444-7015 * Fax: (312) 630-1512*
50 S. LaSalle St. - M-9, Chicago, IL 60675
Web: www.northerntrust.com

Northern Trust is a publicly traded bank holding company with operations in Arizona, California, Colorado, Florida, Georgia, Illinois, New York, Texas and Washington state. The company, which has about 7,000 employees, has $25.3 billion in assets and reported 1997 sales of $1.4 billion.

The company's principal subsidiary, The Northern Trust Co., provides banking, investment management and pension services for businesses and governments. The company acquired Trust Bank of Colorado in February 1998.

Northern Trust Corp. also operates in five foreign countries.

Northern Trust Co. Good Government Committee (C00024935) *Address: same as sponsor * Treasurer: Marilyn J. Steben*

	1993-94	1995-96	1997	Totals
Receipts	$66,646	$41,799	$28,185	$136,630
Disburse	65,180	33,240	17,955	116,375
Cash	2,905	11,465	21,696	n/a
Contributions	16,350	9,850	5,825	32,025
Republicans	10,600	7,450	1,600	19,650
No. of Cand.	*11*	*18*	*6*	*35*
House	6,600	4,450	1,350	12,400
Senate	4,000	3,000	250	7,250
Democrats	5,750	2,400	4,225	12,375
No. of Cand.	*10*	*7*	*5*	*22*
House	4,250	900	225	5,375
Senate	1,500	1,500	4,000	7,000
Incumbents	14,100	8,150	2,825	25,075
Challengers	0	250	0	250
Open Seat	2,250	1,450	2,500	6,200
Winners	14,600	8,650	n/a	23,250
Losers	1,750	1,200	n/a	2,950

Norwest Corp.

*Phone: (612) 667-9406 * Fax: (612) 667-9403*
Norwest Center, Sixth and Marquette, Minneapolis, MN 55479
Web: www.norwest.com

Norwest is an $88 billion financial services company providing banking, insurance, investments, mortgage and consumer finance products. It offers these services through 4,087 stores in all 50 states, Canada, the Caribbean, Latin America and elsewhere internationally.

In February 1998, Fortune ranked Norwest the nation's "most admired" super-regional bank in its 16th annual corporate reputation survey. The company employs more than 53,000 workers.

Subsidiaries of the corporation provide retail, commercial, and corporate banking services to customers through banks located in Arizona, Colorado, Illinois, Indiana, Iowa, Minnesota, Montana, Nebraska, Nevada, New Mexico, North Dakota, South Dakota, Texas, Wisconsin and Wyoming.

Norwest Corp. PAC (Norwest PAC) (C00034595) *Address: same as sponsor * Treasurer: William N. Kelly*

	1993-94	1995-96	1997	Totals
Receipts	$142,738	$206,227	$130,342	$479,307
Disburse	117,489	176,675	82,470	376,634
Cash	89,913	119,469	167,342	n/a
Contributions	112,150	138,125	59,425	309,700
Republicans	45,150	87,375	37,225	169,750
No. of Cand.	*43*	*65*	*30*	*138*
House	35,150	68,375	17,225	120,750
Senate	10,000	19,000	20,000	49,000
Democrats	61,500	50,750	21,200	133,450
No. of Cand.	*41*	*30*	*17*	*88*
House	32,500	33,250	7,700	73,450
Senate	29,000	17,500	13,500	60,000
Incumbents	97,650	97,125	53,425	248,200
Challengers	3,000	8,500	1,000	12,500
Open Seat	11,500	32,500	5,000	49,000
Winners	92,350	130,125	n/a	222,475
Losers	19,800	8,000	n/a	27,800

Norwest Bank New Mexico Political Action Committee (formerly known as United New Mexico Financial Corp. PAC) (C00142844) *Phone: (505) 765-5086 * Fax: (505) 765-5281 * 200 Lomas Blvd. N.W., P.O. Box 1081, Albuquerque, NM 87102 * Treasurer: Kim Ronquillo * Contact: Larry D. Willard, Chairperson*

	1993-94	1995-96	1997	Totals
Receipts	$97,279	$68,133	$40,058	$205,470
Disburse	94,655	66,458	13,802	174,915
Cash	60,507	62,184	88,441	n/a
Contributions	21,312	15,250	5,000	41,562
Republicans	10,812	9,250	5,000	25,062
No. of Cand.	*4*	*3*	*2*	*9*
House	2,562	7,500	5,000	15,062
Senate	8,250	1,750	0	10,000
Democrats	10,500	6,000	0	16,500
No. of Cand.	*3*	*2*	*0*	*5*
House	2,000	4,000	0	6,000
Senate	8,500	2,000	0	10,500
Incumbents	21,312	15,250	5,000	41,562
Challengers	0	0	0	0
Open Seat	0	0	0	0
Winners	18,812	15,250	n/a	34,062
Losers	2,500	0	n/a	2,500

Contributed less than $5,000 during 1995-96 cycle:

Norwest Financial Services Inc. Political Action Committee (C00205401) *Phone: (515) 243-2131 * Fax: (515) 557-7666 * 206 Eighth St., Des Moines, IA 50309 * Web: www.norwestfinancial.com * Treasurer: Dennis E. Young * Contact: David Wood, Chairperson*

Terminated PACs which contributed less than $5,000 during 1995-96 cycle:

Norwest State PAC — Texas Inc. (C00238832) *16414 San Pedro Ave., Suite 100, San Antonio, TX 78232 * Treasurer: Larry Wilson*

PNC Bank Corp.

*Phone: (412) 762-1553 * Fax: (412) 762-6238*
Two PNC Plaza, 620 Liberty Ave., Pittsburgh, PA 15222
Web: www.pncbank.com

PNC Bank is among the 20 largest financial institutions in the nation, with assets of more than $71 billion as of September 1997. Headquartered in Pittsburgh, and with more than 800 branches throughout Pennsylvania, the company also operates in Delaware, Illinois, Indiana, Kentucky, Nebraska, New Jersey and Ohio. In 1996, PNC Bank employed more than 25,000 people.

The bank handles corporate, consumer, private and real estate banking, as well as mortgage loans and asset management. It was created by the 1983 merger of Pittsburgh National Corp., which began business in 1852, and Provident National Corp.

One of PNC Bank's subsidiaries is BlackRock Inc., one of the 25 largest asset management companies in the nation, with more than $108 billion under management.

Bipartisan Voluntary Public Affairs Committee of PNC Bank National Association (PNCBankPAC) (C00035519) *Address: same as sponsor * Treasurer: Thomas E. McGuire*

	1993-94	1995-96	1997	Totals
Receipts	$361,183	$329,590	$152,491	$843,264
Disburse	299,853	345,917	172,673	818,443
Cash	131,996	115,670	95,488	n/a
Contributions	49,695	52,590	22,650	124,935
Republicans	17,195	28,925	10,350	56,470
No. of Cand.	*26*	*29*	*9*	*64*
House	7,475	23,325	3,750	34,550
Senate	9,720	5,600	6,600	21,920
Democrats	32,500	23,665	12,300	68,465
No. of Cand.	*37*	*20*	*11*	*68*
House	24,950	21,865	11,050	57,865
Senate	7,550	1,800	1,250	10,600
Incumbents	34,200	43,040	22,650	99,890
Challengers	7,070	5,300	0	12,370
Open Seat	8,675	4,250	0	12,925
Winners	28,720	42,415	n/a	71,135
Losers	20,975	10,175	n/a	31,150

Midlantic Political Action Committee (C00088062) *Metro Park Plaza, P.O. Box 600, Edison, NJ 08818 * Treasurer: John M. Sperger*

Midlantic National Bank's PAC was terminated in 1996. Midlantic became a subsidiary of PNC Bank following a 1995 merger.

	1993-94	1995-96	1997	Totals
Receipts	$11,409	$20,494	$0	$31,903
Disburse	19,674	20,869	0	40,543
Cash	374	0	0	n/a
Contributions	19,574	9,520	0	29,094
Republicans	14,274	6,520	0	20,794
No. of Cand.	*8*	*6*	*0*	*14*
House	9,950	6,270	0	16,220
Senate	4,324	250	0	4,574
Democrats	5,300	3,000	0	8,300
No. of Cand.	*5*	*2*	*0*	*7*
House	3,500	2,000	0	5,500
Senate	1,800	1,000	0	2,800
Incumbents	7,750	9,270	0	17,020
Challengers	8,324	0	0	8,324
Open Seat	3,500	250	0	3,750
Winners	8,200	4,270	n/a	12,470
Losers	11,374	5,250	n/a	16,624

Contributed less than $5,000 during 1995-96 cycle:

PNC Bancorp Inc. PAC (Ohio/Northern Kentucky) (C00226175) *201 E. Fifth St., PNC Center, Central Trust Center, Cincinnati, OH 45202 * Treasurer: Craig M. Johnson*

PNCBankPAC - Delaware (C00194340) *Phone: (302) 429-1011 * Fax: (302) 427-5810 * 222 Delaware Ave., P.O. Box 791, Wilmington, DE 19899 * Treasurer: Maria C. Schaffer * Contact: George Forbes, Chairman*

Pacific Century Financial Corp.

*Phone: (808) 537-8263 * Fax: (808) 537-8180*
P.O. Box 2900, Honolulu, HI 96846

Pacific Century Financial operates Hawaii's largest commercial bank, the Bank of Hawaii, with 86 branches and $12.4 billion in assets. It has operations elsewhere in the Pacific and in Asia and the U.S. mainland. The publicly traded company has 5,000 employees.

Pacific Century also operates the First Federal Savings and Loan Association of America, California United Bank and Pacific Century Bank. These banks operate throughout Hawaii, California and Arizona and have combined assets of about $2.5 billion. The company also runs the Guam-based First Savings and Loan Association of America and the Hawaiian Trust Co.

Pacific Century Financial Corp. Special Political Education Committee (formerly known as Bancorp Hawaii Special Political Education Committee) (C00025668) *Address: same as sponsor * Treasurer: Robert I. Crowell * Contact: Alton Kuioka, Chairman*

	1993-94	1995-96	1997	Totals
Receipts	$151,050	$148,750	$94,004	$393,804
Disburse	171,124	121,265	46,350	338,739
Cash	58,920	86,405	134,059	n/a
Contributions	8,000	11,100	11,000	30,100
Republicans	600	600	2,500	3,700
No. of Cand.	*3*	*1*	*1*	*5*
House	400	600	2,500	3,500
Senate	200	0	0	200
Democrats	7,400	10,500	8,500	26,400
No. of Cand.	*5*	*3*	*3*	*11*
House	4,200	10,500	3,500	18,200
Senate	3,200	0	5,000	8,200
Incumbents	7,000	6,500	7,500	21,000
Challengers	400	4,600	2,500	7,500
Open Seat	600	0	0	600
Winners	7,600	6,500	n/a	14,100
Losers	400	4,600	n/a	5,000

Regions Financial Corp.

*Phone: (205) 326-7860 * Fax: (205) 326-7751*
417 20th St. N., Birmingham, AL 35203
Web: www.regionsbank.com

Regions Financial is a publicly traded bank holding company with $22 billion in assets and 430 offices in Alabama, Florida, Georgia, Louisiana and Tennessee. The company's flagship subsidiary operates under the name Regions Bank.

Regions has announced plans to acquire banks in South Carolina, a new market for the company. Regions grew rapidly in 1996, acquiring 28 companies. The company now has 9,000 employees.

The company is engaged in mortgage banking, credit life insurance, leasing, commercial accounts receivable factoring and securities brokerage activities.

Regions was formed in 1971 as First Alabama Bancshares, Alabama's first multi-bank holding company.

Regions Financial Corp. Political Action Committee (C00179473) *Address: same as sponsor * Treasurer: Samuel E. Upchurch Jr.*

	1993-94	1995-96	1997	Totals
Receipts	$158,033	$147,306	$67,506	$372,845
Disburse	209,750	84,850	80,200	374,800
Cash	63,306	125,315	112,623	n/a
Contributions	9,250	32,350	16,200	57,800
Republicans	3,500	23,250	15,700	42,450
No. of Cand.	*2*	*15*	*6*	*23*
House	2,500	13,250	6,700	22,450
Senate	1,000	10,000	9,000	20,000
Democrats	5,750	9,100	500	15,350
No. of Cand.	*6*	*6*	*1*	*13*
House	5,750	6,100	0	11,850
Senate	0	3,000	500	3,500
Incumbents	8,000	14,850	16,200	39,050
Challengers	0	1,500	0	1,500
Open Seat	1,000	13,000	0	14,000
Winners	7,000	21,750	n/a	28,750
Losers	2,250	10,600	n/a	12,850

SouthTrust Corp.

*Phone: (205) 254-5291 * Fax: (205) 254-5404*
420 20th St. N., P.O. Box 2554, Birmingham, AL 35290
Web: www.southtrust.com

SouthTrust is a $30.9 billion bank headquartered in Birmingham, Ala. SouthTrust serves customers through more than 540 offices in Alabama, Florida, Georgia, Mississippi, North Carolina, South Carolina and Tennessee. The company's basic strategy focuses on Southern high-growth markets, establishing a presence and then growing internally.

SouthTrust has 10 banking subsidiaries. The banks offer checking, savings, individual retirement and money market accounts as well as bank credit cards and various types of loans to both individual and business customers. SouthTrust's non-banking subsidiaries provide insurance, investment management, computer services and trust services.

SouthTrust Corp. Committee for Good Government (C00077024) *Address: same as sponsor * Treasurer: Paul Gourley Jr. * Contact: Charles Whitfield, Chairman*

	1993-94	1995-96	1997	Totals
Receipts	$276,375	$302,190	$209,997	$788,562
Disburse	443,968	266,593	156,152	866,713
Cash	37,393	72,992	126,837	n/a
Contributions	21,700	82,175	22,350	126,225
Republicans	16,800	59,250	21,250	97,300
No. of Cand.	*13*	*26*	*13*	*52*
House	10,550	22,000	14,500	47,050
Senate	6,250	37,250	6,750	50,250
Democrats	4,900	22,925	1,100	28,925
No. of Cand.	*6*	*16*	*3*	*25*
House	4,900	14,050	1,100	20,050
Senate	0	8,875	0	8,875
Incumbents	18,700	20,800	21,350	60,850
Challengers	750	5,000	750	6,500
Open Seat	250	56,375	250	56,875
Winners	19,200	42,800	n/a	62,000
Losers	2,500	39,375	n/a	41,875

Southwest Bank of Texas

*Phone: (713) 235-8800 x1101 * Fax: (713) 439-5905*
4400 Post Oak Pkwy., Houston, TX 77027
Web: www.swbanktx.com

Southwest Bank of Texas is the wholly owned subsidiary of Southwest Bancorp of Texas, a publicly owned company. The bank is Houston's major independent bank with more than $1.2 billion in assets.

The commercial bank specializes in lending to middle market companies in the Houston area. It also offers treasury management, private and international banking, investment services and foreign exchange.

In February 1998, Southwest Bancorp of Texas purchased First Republic Capital Corp. and City Financial Services in Houston, both firms that help young start-up businesses obtain capital. Southwest officials said the deal will enable the bank to offer its customers an alternative to conventional financing.

Southwest Bank of Texas National Political Action Committee (C00283069) *Address: same as sponsor * Treasurer: Richard J. McWhorter * Contact: Walter Johnson, Chairman*

	1993-94	1995-96	1997	Totals
Receipts	$17,244	$21,546	$10,444	$49,234
Disburse	5,194	23,650	15,000	43,844
Cash	12,054	8,954	3,399	n/a
Contributions	2,575	15,750	1,500	19,825
Republicans	1,950	12,250	1,500	15,700
No. of Cand.	*5*	*8*	*2*	*15*
House	250	11,250	500	12,000
Senate	1,700	1,000	1,000	3,700
Democrats	625	3,500	0	4,125
No. of Cand.	*1*	*1*	*0*	*2*
House	625	3,500	0	4,125
Senate	0	0	0	0
Incumbents	1,300	13,750	1,500	16,550
Challengers	775	2,000	0	2,775
Open Seat	500	0	0	500
Winners	2,075	8,500	n/a	10,575
Losers	500	7,250	n/a	7,750

Star Banc Corp.

*Phone: (513) 632-4132 * Fax: (513) 632-4279*
425 Walnut St., Cincinnati, OH 45202-1038
Web: www.starbank.com

Star Banc is a publicly traded $14 billion bank holding company with 325 branch offices in Ohio, Kentucky and Indiana. The company's banks operate under the name Star Bank. It has about 4,000 employees.

In February 1998, the company announced a $5.15 billion, five-year community development initiative in low- and moderate-income neighborhoods throughout its market. The bank expects to use the money for home mortgages, home improvement loans, mortgage refinancing, small business loans, community development loans and small farm loans. It also will offer some community grants.

Star Bank provides consumer, commercial and trust financial services and products, including a line of mutual funds known as Star Funds. It claims to have been the first bank in the United States to offer a fully integrated 24-hour banking system. Today the system includes Internet banking, voice-activated phone banking, PC banking, ATMs, screen phone banking and video kiosk banking.

Founded in 1863, the company previously operated as The First National Bank of Cincinnati.

Star Banc Corp. Political Action Committee (C00256396) *Address: same as sponsor * Treasurer: Vacant * Contact: Richard J. Hidy, V.P.*

	1993-94	1995-96	1997	Totals
Receipts	$36,592	$79,210	$72,448	$188,250
Disburse	30,882	80,520	48,119	159,521
Cash	6,252	4,945	27,275	n/a
Contributions	12,950	19,600	22,400	54,950
Republicans	4,250	18,600	18,900	41,750
No. of Cand.	*5*	*9*	*9*	*23*
House	3,250	16,600	9,400	29,250
Senate	1,000	2,000	9,500	12,500
Democrats	8,700	1,000	3,500	13,200
No. of Cand.	*3*	*1*	*2*	*6*
House	8,700	1,000	500	10,200
Senate	0	0	3,000	3,000
Incumbents	9,450	19,600	11,400	40,450
Challengers	2,500	0	0	2,500
Open Seat	1,000	0	11,000	12,000
Winners	4,200	16,900	n/a	21,100
Losers	8,750	2,700	n/a	11,450

Summit Bancorp

*Phone: (609) 987-3647 * Fax: (609) 695-2428*
P.O. Box 2066, Princeton, NJ 08543
*Web: www.summitbank.com * E-mail: call_center@summitbank.com*

Summit Bancorp is a $30 billion financial services organization with more than 450 locations throughout New Jersey and eastern Pennsylvania.

Summit Bancorp's major lines of business include commercial, retail and mortgage banking, investment management and private banking. It has 9,000 employees and annual sales of $1.4 billion.

Subsidiaries: Summit Bank, Summit Discount Brokerage Co., Summit Venture Capital, Summit Commercial/Gibraltar Corp.

Summit Bancorp Political Action Committee (Summit FedPAC) (C00173559) *Address: same as sponsor * Treasurer: Deborah Finaldi * Contact: John Custodio, V.P. of Gov. Relations*

	1993-94	1995-96	1997	Totals
Receipts	$19,200	$17,450	$7,400	$44,050
Disburse	20,064	16,527	8,350	44,941
Cash	162	1,085	135	n/a
Contributions	11,936	11,500	3,350	26,786
Republicans	7,936	9,250	2,850	20,036
No. of Cand.	*11*	*11*	*5*	*27*
House	6,350	8,100	3,000	17,450
Senate	1,586	1,150	-150	2,586
Democrats	4,000	2,250	500	6,750
No. of Cand.	*3*	*5*	*1*	*9*
House	2,500	1,250	500	4,250
Senate	1,500	1,000	0	2,500
Incumbents	7,600	6,800	3,500	17,900
Challengers	2,836	750	0	3,586
Open Seat	1,250	3,950	0	5,200
Winners	7,000	8,350	n/a	15,350
Losers	4,936	3,150	n/a	8,086

Terminated PACs which contributed less than $5,000 during 1995-96 cycle:

Summit Bancorp Political Action Committee (C00194688) *Phone: (609) 987-3647 * Fax: (609) 695-2428 * P.O. Box 2066, Princeton, NJ 08543 * Treasurer: Karen A. Curry*

SunTrust Banks

*Phone: (404) 588-8265 * Fax: (404) 230-5550*
25 Park Pl. N.E., P.O. Box 4418, Atlanta, GA 30302
Web: www.suntrust.com

SunTrust Banks is a $58 billion bank holding company with operations in Alabama, Florida, Georgia and Tennessee.

The publicly traded company has 30 subsidiaries and more than 700 full-service branches. SunTrust continues to grow through the acquisition of banks in the affluent retirement markets of Florida, where it does more business than in its home state of Georgia.

Through its subsidiaries, SunTrust conducts a broad range of commercial banking activities, including handling deposits, making both secured and unsecured business and consumer loans and leases, extending commercial lines of credit and issuing and servicing credit cards.

SunTrust Banks of Georgia Inc. Good Government Group (C00009639) *Address: same as sponsor * Treasurer: James C. Armstrong * Contact: James Adams, Chairperson*

	1993-94	1995-96	1997	Totals
Receipts	$108,147	$121,900	$52,386	$282,433
Disburse	144,040	170,478	43,975	358,493
Cash	126,139	83,917	92,331	n/a
Contributions	22,720	58,350	3,150	84,220
Republicans	17,050	47,150	3,150	67,350
No. of Cand.	*12*	*14*	*7*	*33*
House	13,050	15,400	1,650	30,100
Senate	4,000	31,750	1,500	37,250
Democrats	5,670	11,200	0	16,870
No. of Cand.	*12*	*9*	*0*	*21*
House	5,320	4,100	0	9,420
Senate	350	7,100	0	7,450
Incumbents	15,570	17,900	3,750	37,220
Challengers	5,000	3,350	250	8,600
Open Seat	1,950	37,100	0	39,050
Winners	18,100	25,250	n/a	43,350
Losers	4,620	33,100	n/a	37,720

SunTrust Banks of Florida Inc. Political Action Committee (C00111567) *Phone: (904) 222-2231 * Fax: (904) 222-1922 * 215 S. Monroe St., Suite 125, Tallahassee, FL 32301 * Treasurer: Linda T. Brinkley * Contact: Ronald Spencer, Senior V.P. of Gov. Relations*

	1993-94	1995-96	1997	Totals
Receipts	$64,059	$92,391	$38,934	$195,384
Disburse	103,408	120,264	44,288	267,960
Cash	407,049	379,184	373,835	n/a
Contributions	33,750	40,000	20,250	94,000
Republicans	19,750	29,500	13,750	63,000
No. of Cand.	*22*	*40*	*18*	*80*
House	10,750	19,000	6,000	35,750
Senate	9,000	10,500	7,750	27,250
Democrats	14,000	10,500	6,500	31,000
No. of Cand.	*22*	*10*	*11*	*43*
House	13,500	9,500	3,000	26,000
Senate	500	1,000	3,500	5,000
Incumbents	29,750	27,500	19,500	76,750
Challengers	0	1,000	250	1,250
Open Seat	4,000	11,500	500	16,000
Winners	24,750	34,500	n/a	59,250
Losers	9,000	5,500	n/a	14,500

SunTrust Banks of Tennessee Inc. Good Government Fund (formerly known as Third National Corp. Good Government Fund) (C00043265) *Phone: (615) 748-4407 * P.O. Box 305110, Nashville, TN 37230 * Treasurer: Gale B. Haddock * Contact: Tom VanEtten, PAC Chairman*

	1993-94	1995-96	1997	Totals
Receipts	$91,124	$93,349	$34,438	$218,911
Disburse	83,168	85,319	23,360	191,847
Cash	113,502	121,537	132,617	n/a
Contributions	25,500	25,000	4,000	54,500
Republicans	17,000	19,500	2,500	39,000
No. of Cand.	*6*	*7*	*1*	*14*
House	4,500	5,500	0	10,000
Senate	12,500	14,000	2,500	29,000
Democrats	8,500	5,500	1,500	15,500
No. of Cand.	*4*	*4*	*1*	*9*
House	5,500	4,500	1,500	11,500
Senate	3,000	1,000	0	4,000
Incumbents	11,500	21,500	4,000	37,000
Challengers	10,000	2,500	0	12,500
Open Seat	4,000	1,000	0	5,000
Winners	21,000	21,500	n/a	42,500
Losers	4,500	3,500	n/a	8,000

Contributed less than $5,000 during 1995-96 cycle:

SunTrust Bank Alabama N.A. PAC (formerly known as First National Bank of Florence PAC) (C00241315) *Phone: (205) 767-8400 * Fax: (205) 767-8476 * P.O. Box 758, Florence, AL 35631 * Treasurer: Charles Doss*

Synovus Financial Corp.

*Phone: (706) 649-2267 * Fax: (706) 649-2342*
P.O. Box 120, Columbus, GA 31902
Web: www.synovus.com

Synovus Financial is a $9.3 billion holding company that provides a variety of financial services. It owns 34 banking companies in Alabama, Florida, Georgia and South Carolina. Synovus employs nearly 6,700 workers.

In February 1998, Synovus announced the reorganization of its bank data processing operations into a new affiliate company, Synovus Technologies Inc.

Synovus also has 80 percent ownership of Total System Services. The company provides online bank card, data processing systems, related computer equipment sales and leasing, direct mail and telemarketing services and commercial bank card printing. Total System handles nearly 80 million accounts including AT&T Universal Card Services and NationsBank.

Other subsidiaries include: Synovus Mortgage Co., Synovus Securities Inc. and Synovus Trust Co.

Synovus Financial Corp. Fund for Effective Leadership (C00032607) *Address: same as sponsor * Treasurer: G. Sanders Griffith III * Contact: Rebecca W. Rumer, Chairperson of PAC*

	1993-94	1995-96	1997	Totals
Receipts	$19,925	$103,731	$84,529	$208,185
Disburse	34,550	52,759	12,156	99,465
Cash	3,928	54,478	126,852	n/a
Contributions	33,550	47,250	10,100	90,900
Republicans	7,750	30,750	8,600	47,100
No. of Cand.	*5*	*8*	*7*	*20*
House	7,750	8,750	2,100	18,600
Senate	0	22,000	6,500	28,500
Democrats	25,800	16,500	1,500	43,800
No. of Cand.	*12*	*4*	*2*	*18*
House	25,800	11,500	0	37,300
Senate	0	5,000	1,500	6,500
Incumbents	19,550	25,750	10,100	55,400
Challengers	10,500	1,500	0	12,000
Open Seat	3,500	20,000	0	23,500
Winners	19,750	30,750	n/a	50,500
Losers	13,800	16,500	n/a	30,300

National Bank of South Carolina PAC (NBSC PAC) (C00194191) *Phone: (803) 929-2049 * Fax: (803) 929-2064 * P.O. Box 1457, Columbia, SC 29202 * Treasurer: Fred Green*

The National Bank of South Carolina is a subsidiary of Synovus, which purchased the bank in 1995.

	1993-94	1995-96	1997	Totals
Receipts	$39,735	$46,574	$25,431	$111,740
Disburse	28,810	33,146	8,983	70,939
Cash	14,160	27,592	44,041	n/a
Contributions	3,750	12,000	1,500	17,250
Republicans	500	7,000	500	8,000
No. of Cand.	*1*	*2*	*1*	*4*
House	500	2,000	500	3,000
Senate	0	5,000	0	5,000
Democrats	3,250	5,000	1,000	9,250
No. of Cand.	*5*	*3*	*1*	*9*
House	3,250	4,000	0	7,250
Senate	0	1,000	1,000	2,000
Incumbents	2,000	12,000	1,000	15,000
Challengers	0	0	0	0
Open Seat	1,750	0	500	2,250
Winners	2,000	12,000	n/a	14,000
Losers	1,750	0	n/a	1,750

U.S. Bancorp

*Phone: (612) 973-2097 * Fax: (612) 973-4584*
601 Second Ave. S., Minneapolis, MN 55402-4302
*Web: www.usbank.com * E-mail: pagunn@visi.com*

U.S. Bancorp was formed in August 1997 when Minneapolis-based First Bank System bought Portland, Ore.-based U.S. Bancorp. The company is the 14th largest bank holding company in the nation, with assets of $70 billion. It serves 17 Western and Midwestern states through more than 1,000 locations. The publicly traded, Fortune 500 company employs almost 13,000 people.

U.S. Bancorp provides commercial and retail banking, asset management, leasing, insurance, mortgage banking and investment services to individual and commercial customers.

The bank agreed in December 1997 to purchase Piper Jaffray Companies, allowing it to offer retail brokerage and investment banking services.

U.S. Bancorp Political Participation Program (formerly known as First Bank System Political Participation Program) (C00018036)
*Address: same as sponsor * Treasurer: Peggy A. Gunn*

	1993-94	1995-96	1997	Totals
Receipts	$35,440	$85,349	$66,901	$187,690
Disburse	27,951	46,091	20,154	94,196
Cash	11,796	51,058	97,805	n/a
Contributions	11,866	14,025	11,400	37,291
Republicans	4,450	7,450	5,300	17,200
No. of Cand.	*6*	*10*	*6*	*22*
House	3,700	2,200	1,800	7,700
Senate	750	5,250	3,500	9,500
Democrats	6,216	6,575	6,100	18,891
No. of Cand.	*11*	*13*	*8*	*32*
House	5,716	4,075	2,100	11,891
Senate	500	2,500	4,000	7,000
Incumbents	7,716	6,925	10,600	25,241
Challengers	1,000	2,500	500	4,000
Open Seat	3,150	4,600	300	8,050
Winners	8,516	10,425	n/a	18,941
Losers	3,350	3,600	n/a	6,950

U.S. Bancorp PAC-Northwest (C00106955) *Phone: (503) 275-5793 * P.O. Box 8837, Portland, OR 97208-8837 * Treasurer: Don Fordyce*

	1993-94	1995-96	1997	Totals
Receipts	$46,532	$56,559	$31,700	$134,791
Disburse	50,524	43,600	5,500	99,624
Cash	3,883	16,846	43,050	n/a
Contributions	36,000	35,100	5,500	76,600
Republicans	14,800	24,350	3,000	42,150
No. of Cand.	*10*	*14*	*3*	*27*
House	8,200	21,850	3,000	33,050
Senate	6,600	2,500	0	9,100
Democrats	21,200	10,750	2,500	34,450
No. of Cand.	*12*	*6*	*1*	*19*
House	16,750	3,000	0	19,750
Senate	4,450	7,750	2,500	14,700
Incumbents	31,350	29,100	5,500	65,950
Challengers	3,900	1,000	0	4,900
Open Seat	750	5,000	0	5,750
Winners	20,300	33,600	n/a	53,900
Losers	15,700	1,500	n/a	17,200

U.S. Bancorp PAC-Oregon (C00225946) *Phone: (503) 275-5793 * P.O. Box 8837, Portland, OR 97208 * Treasurer: Don Fordyce*

	1993-94	1995-96	1997	Totals
Receipts	$22,719	$22,889	$15,858	$61,466
Disburse	12,938	32,827	4,250	50,015
Cash	17,309	7,374	19,089	n/a
Contributions	10,622	28,799	4,250	43,671
Republicans	1,500	16,799	2,000	20,299
No. of Cand.	*2*	*4*	*1*	*7*
House	1,500	5,500	0	7,000
Senate	0	11,299	2,000	13,299
Democrats	9,122	12,000	2,250	23,372
No. of Cand.	*3*	*5*	*1*	*9*
House	9,122	10,000	2,250	21,372
Senate	0	2,000	0	2,000
Incumbents	9,122	12,300	4,250	25,672
Challengers	0	3,500	0	3,500
Open Seat	1,500	12,999	0	14,499
Winners	10,622	25,999	n/a	36,621
Losers	0	2,800	n/a	2,800

FirsTier Financial Inc. Political Action Committee (also known as FirsTier-PAC) (C00236877) *Phone: (402) 348-6000 * 1700 Farnam St., Omaha, NE 68102 * Treasurer: Alan J. Rausch*

The FirsTier Financial PAC was terminated in March 1996. The company merged with First Bank System Inc., which is now known as U.S. Bancorp, in February 1996.

	1993-94	1995-96	1997	Totals
Receipts	$19,984	$8,592	$0	$28,576
Disburse	38,225	16,963	0	55,188
Cash	8,370	0	0	n/a
Contributions	36,475	15,500	0	51,975
Republicans	27,750	14,500	0	42,250
No. of Cand.	*21*	*6*	*0*	*27*
House	14,500	7,000	0	21,500
Senate	13,250	7,500	0	20,750
Democrats	8,725	1,000	0	9,725
No. of Cand.	*3*	*1*	*0*	*4*
House	4,250	0	0	4,250
Senate	4,475	1,000	0	5,475
Incumbents	23,975	7,500	0	31,475
Challengers	11,000	0	0	11,000
Open Seat	1,500	8,000	0	9,500
Winners	23,975	11,500	n/a	35,475
Losers	12,500	4,000	n/a	16,500

Piper Jaffray Companies Inc. Employee Fund for Responsible Government (C00121301) *Phone: (612) 342-6000 * Fax: (612) 342-6085 * 222 S. Ninth St., Minneapolis, MN 55402 * Web: www.piperjaffray.com * Treasurer: David Evans Rosedahl*

In December 1997, U.S. Bancorp announced plans to acquire Piper Jaffray Companies.

Piper Jaffray is a diversified financial services company operating 89 branch offices in 17 Midwestern, Rocky Mountain, Southwestern and Pacific states. It offers customers a broad array of investment products and services, including brokerage and asset management. Piper Jaffray's sales in 1997 were about $600 million. The company employs more than 3,000 workers.

	1993-94	1995-96	1997	Totals
Receipts	$2,000	$12,829	$13,780	$28,609
Disburse	4,280	5,872	6,689	16,841
Cash	399	6,999	14,090	n/a
Contributions	3,250	5,050	1,000	9,300
Republicans	850	2,150	500	3,500
No. of Cand.	*4*	*9*	*1*	*14*
House	850	1,150	0	2,000
Senate	0	1,000	500	1,500
Democrats	1,950	2,900	500	5,350
No. of Cand.	*8*	*9*	*1*	*18*
House	1,250	1,750	0	3,000
Senate	700	1,150	500	2,350
Incumbents	2,550	3,900	1,000	7,450
Challengers	350	450	0	800
Open Seat	200	450	0	650
Winners	2,350	4,300	n/a	6,650
Losers	900	750	n/a	1,650

Contributed less than $5,000 during 1995-96 cycle:

U.S. Bancorp Inc. Political Action Committee (C00320002) *Phone: (814) 533-5300 * Fax: (814) 533-5427 * Main & Franklin Streets, Johnstown, PA 15901 * Treasurer: W. Harrison Vail*

Union Planters Corp.

*Phone: (901) 580-6656 * Fax: (901) 580-6687*
7130 Goodlett Farms Pkwy., Cordova, TN 38018
Web: www.unionplanters.com

Union Planters is a publicly traded bank holding company that operates primarily in the South. With $18 billion in assets, it is the largest bank holding company headquartered in Tennessee and is one of the 50 largest bank holding companies in the United States.

The company's largest subsidiary, Union Planters National Bank, is headquartered in Memphis, Tenn. and mainly does business in Tennessee, Mississippi, Missouri, Arkansas, Louisiana, Alabama and Kentucky.

Subsidiaries are engaged in mortgage origination and servicing; investment management and trust services; credit and debit cards; loans; full-service and discount brokerage services; and the sale of bank-eligible insurance products.

Subsidiaries include: First National Bank of Shelbyville, The First National Bank of Crossville, Bank of Goodlettsville, The First State Bank, First Financial Bank of Mississippi County and Simpson County Bank.

Union Planters Corp. Committee on Government Affairs (C00044024) *Address: same as sponsor * Treasurer: Kirk Walters*

	1993-94	1995-96	1997	Totals
Receipts	$75,688	$151,902	$52,473	$280,063
Disburse	68,325	83,595	50,584	202,504
Cash	9,088	77,399	79,289	n/a
Contributions	14,550	20,800	10,700	46,050
Republicans	8,100	16,550	7,350	32,000
No. of Cand.	*8*	*12*	*6*	*26*
House	2,550	8,250	5,000	15,800
Senate	5,550	8,300	2,350	16,200
Democrats	6,450	4,250	3,350	14,050
No. of Cand.	*4*	*5*	*4*	*13*
House	1,450	3,750	1,350	6,550
Senate	5,000	500	2,000	7,500
Incumbents	6,450	15,300	10,700	32,450
Challengers	3,000	1,250	0	4,250
Open Seat	5,100	4,250	0	9,350
Winners	7,000	13,800	n/a	20,800
Losers	7,550	7,000	n/a	14,550

Magna Group Inc. Magna-PAC (Federal) (C00243071) *Phone: (314) 963-3007 * Fax: (314) 963-2570 * 1401 S. Brentwood Blvd., 10th Floor, St. Louis, MO 63144-1401 * Web: www.magnabank.com * Treasurer: Julia Roberts*

On Feb. 23, 1998, Magna Group agreed to be acquired by Memphis-based Union Planters National Bank. Their PACs will merge in 1998.

Magna Group is a publicly traded bank holding company for Magna Bank of Illinois, Magna Bank of Iowa and Magna Bank of Missouri. Magna operates more than 140 banking centers in more than 60 communities, and 90 Magna Carta ATMs. The company employs about 2,100 people.

	1993-94	*1995-96*	*1997*	*Totals*
Receipts	$14,170	$44,394	$33,973	$92,537
Disburse	14,133	38,490	28,300	80,923
Cash	53	5,957	11,630	n/a
Contributions	8,133	8,390	4,800	21,323
Republicans	200	4,840	3,000	8,040
No. of Cand.	*1*	*6*	*3*	*10*
House	0	4,090	2,750	6,840
Senate	200	750	250	1,200
Democrats	7,933	3,550	1,800	13,283
No. of Cand.	*6*	*3*	*1*	*10*
House	4,300	3,250	1,800	9,350
Senate	3,633	300	0	3,933
Incumbents	4,200	6,240	4,800	15,240
Challengers	0	0	0	0
Open Seat	3,933	2,150	0	6,083
Winners	4,400	7,390	n/a	11,790
Losers	3,733	1,000	n/a	4,733

First Magnolia Federal Savings & Loan Association Voluntary PAC for Federal Elections (C00142737) *100 W. Front St., Hattiesburg, MS 39401 * Treasurer: Minnie Boutwell*

First Magnolia Federal Savings & Loan is a subsidiary of Magna Group which merged with Union Planters in 1997. A spokesperson said that PACs associated with Magna Group were to be transferred in name to Union Planters in the first half of 1998.

	1993-94	*1995-96*	*1997*	*Totals*
Receipts	$23,401	$47,081	$13,566	$84,048
Disburse	29,278	42,450	16,000	87,728
Cash	3,482	8,116	5,682	n/a
Contributions	12,650	32,450	11,000	56,100
Republicans	9,500	31,950	11,000	52,450
No. of Cand.	*6*	*17*	*7*	*30*
House	5,700	23,450	5,000	34,150
Senate	3,800	8,500	6,000	18,300
Democrats	3,150	500	0	3,650
No. of Cand.	*4*	*1*	*0*	*5*
House	2,950	500	0	3,450
Senate	200	0	0	200
Incumbents	5,900	14,450	11,000	31,350
Challengers	2,000	10,000	0	12,000
Open Seat	4,750	8,000	0	12,750
Winners	8,900	21,950	n/a	30,850
Losers	3,750	10,500	n/a	14,250

UnionBanCal Corp.

*Phone: (415) 445-0211 * Fax: (415) 445-0508*
350 California St. H-800, P.O. Box 7104, San Francisco, CA 94104

Bank holding company UnionBanCal's primary subsidiary is Union Bank of California, the state's third-largest commercial bank with assets of $30 billion. The bank has 240 branches in California, five in Oregon and Washington state and 17 international facilities, located primarily along the Pacific Rim.

Formed by the 1996 merger of Union Bank with BanCal Tri-State Corp. and its banking subsidiary, Bank of California, UNBC is 81 percent owned by the Bank of Tokyo-Mitsubishi Ltd.

UNBC employs more than 9,500 people.

UnionBanCal Corp. Political Action Committee (C00172205) *Address: same as sponsor * Treasurer: J. K. Sasaki * Contact: Richard Hartnack, Chairperson*

	1993-94	*1995-96*	*1997*	*Totals*
Receipts	$24,781	$25,432	$10,032	$60,245
Disburse	21,500	20,492	6,000	47,992
Cash	8,215	13,158	17,182	n/a
Contributions	11,500	9,000	1,000	21,500
Republicans	3,000	5,200	0	8,200
No. of Cand.	*6*	*9*	*0*	*15*
House	3,000	4,200	0	7,200
Senate	0	1,000	0	1,000
Democrats	8,500	3,800	1,000	13,300
No. of Cand.	*8*	*6*	*1*	*15*
House	8,000	3,800	1,000	12,800
Senate	500	0	0	500
Incumbents	9,000	8,000	1,000	18,000
Challengers	2,000	0	0	2,000
Open Seat	500	1,000	0	1,500
Winners	9,000	8,500	n/a	17,500
Losers	2,500	500	n/a	3,000

Wachovia Corp.

*Phone: (910) 770-5000 * Fax: (910) 732-2281*
100 N. Main St., Winston-Salem, NC 27150
Web: www.wachovia.com

Wachovia is a public bank holding company. Its primary subsidiary, Wachovia Bank, has $52 billion in total assets and operates more than 470 branches throughout North Carolina, South Carolina and Georgia.

The corporation's other subsidiaries include the First National Bank of Atlanta, which oversees Wachovia's credit card business, and Wachovia Trust Services.

The corporation has no overall PAC; instead, it has three PACs that represent its different state operations.

The Wachovia Bank of North Carolina N.A. Employees for Good Government PAC represents the bank's North Carolina operations. Wachovia Bank is headquartered in Winston-Salem, N.C., and it has 210 branches in the state and $13.6 billion in deposits.

Wachovia Bank of North Carolina N.A. Employees for Good Government (Wachovia Bank of N.C. Employees for Good Government) (C00282103) *Address: same as sponsor * Treasurer: William C. Baggett*

	1993-94	*1995-96*	*1997*	*Totals*
Receipts	$168,767	$231,471	$124,513	$524,751
Disburse	116,130	201,681	62,711	380,522
Cash	52,642	82,437	144,251	n/a
Contributions	37,925	50,925	23,250	112,100
Republicans	22,285	39,025	14,250	75,560
No. of Cand.	*11*	*12*	*10*	*33*
House	17,285	28,025	10,250	55,560
Senate	5,000	11,000	4,000	20,000
Democrats	15,640	11,900	9,000	36,540
No. of Cand.	*10*	*11*	*4*	*25*
House	15,640	6,900	7,000	29,540
Senate	0	5,000	2,000	7,000
Incumbents	18,200	41,250	22,000	81,450
Challengers	2,035	7,300	250	9,585
Open Seat	17,690	2,675	1,000	21,365
Winners	27,185	33,100	n/a	60,285
Losers	10,740	17,825	n/a	28,565

Wachovia Bank of Georgia N.A. Fund for Better Government (C00011718) *Phone: (404) 332-5483 * Fax: (404) 332-5919 * 191 Peachtree St. N.E., c/o Government Division, MC GA 700, Atlanta, GA 30303 * Treasurer: John O'Connor * Contact: Thomas D. Hills, Chairman*

This PAC represents Wachovia's Georgia operations, which include 129 branches and deposits of $8.6 billion.

	1993-94	*1995-96*	*1997*	*Totals*
Receipts	$140,333	$145,328	$68,274	$353,935
Disburse	141,113	102,361	58,750	302,224
Cash	11,416	54,388	63,912	n/a
Contributions	18,800	32,361	7,250	58,411
Republicans	11,000	26,061	4,750	41,811
No. of Cand.	*10*	*10*	*3*	*23*
House	8,000	15,561	2,000	25,561
Senate	3,000	10,500	2,750	16,250
Democrats	7,800	6,300	2,500	16,600
No. of Cand.	*11*	*6*	*1*	*18*
House	7,550	3,300	0	10,850
Senate	250	3,000	2,500	5,750
Incumbents	15,700	20,211	7,250	43,161
Challengers	2,150	2,300	0	4,450
Open Seat	700	9,850	0	10,550
Winners	14,100	23,211	n/a	37,311
Losers	4,700	9,150	n/a	13,850

Wachovia Bank N.A. South Carolina Political Action Committee (C00110593) *Phone: (803) 765-3359 * Fax: (803) 765-4333 * 1426 Main St., Columbia, SC 29226 * Treasurer: Charles D. Bryant Jr. * Contact: Charlton E. Law, Chairperson*

This PAC represents Wachovia's South Carolina operations, which include 133 branches and deposits of $5.6 billion.

	1993-94	1995-96	1997	Totals
Receipts	$67,867	$66,440	$31,144	$165,451
Disburse	72,025	62,953	24,340	159,318
Cash	50,972	54,463	61,268	n/a
Contributions	10,800	11,250	2,800	24,850
Republicans	3,750	7,750	1,550	13,050
No. of Cand.	*7*	*5*	*2*	*14*
House	3,550	2,350	1,550	7,450
Senate	200	5,400	0	5,600
Democrats	7,050	3,500	1,250	11,800
No. of Cand.	*6*	*5*	*3*	*14*
House	7,050	2,500	1,250	10,800
Senate	0	1,000	0	1,000
Incumbents	4,500	11,350	2,050	17,900
Challengers	0	0	0	0
Open Seat	6,200	0	0	6,200
Winners	4,500	11,350	n/a	15,850
Losers	6,300	-100	n/a	6,200

Wells Fargo & Co.

*Phone: (415) 396-6327 * Fax: (415) 421-2121*
420 Montgomery St., Public and Governmental Affairs Dept., San Francisco, CA 94163
Web: www.wellsfargo.com

Wells Fargo & Co. is a public bank holding company that operates primarily in California, Arizona, Texas, Oregon and Washington. In April 1996, Wells Fargo merged with Los Angeles-based First Interstate Bancorp, which had $54.6 billion in assets. As of December 1997, Wells Fargo had total assets $97.5 billion, making it the tenth-largest bank holding company in the nation.

Its primary subsidiary, Wells Fargo Bank, N.A., provides personal banking and investment services, as well as small business, commercial and international banking services. The bank maintained total deposits of $72.2 billion and loans of $65.7 billion as of December 1997.

Wells Fargo was founded in 1852 as a banking and express firm that provided various services, including the operation of a stagecoach service, the protection and transportation of gold and the delivery of mail. The company employs about 33,100 people throughout its 2,000 branches.

Wells Fargo & Co. Impact Fund (C00033753) *Address: same as sponsor * Treasurer: Craig G. Wolfson * Contact: Paul Hazen, Chairman*

	1993-94	1995-96	1997	Totals
Receipts	$65,161	$185,168	$26,929	$277,258
Disburse	85,923	136,103	37,676	259,702
Cash	49,201	98,266	87,527	n/a
Contributions	68,500	78,249	13,400	160,149
Republicans	29,500	53,999	6,300	89,799
No. of Cand.	*24*	*37*	*6*	*67*
House	21,500	42,999	2,300	66,799
Senate	8,000	11,000	4,000	23,000
Democrats	39,000	24,250	7,100	70,350
No. of Cand.	*21*	*23*	*7*	*51*
House	26,000	18,750	6,100	50,850
Senate	13,000	5,500	1,000	19,500
Incumbents	54,500	66,499	13,400	134,399
Challengers	9,500	1,500	0	11,000
Open Seat	4,500	10,250	0	14,750
Winners	59,500	66,999	n/a	126,499
Losers	9,000	11,250	n/a	20,250

Credit Unions

Credit Union National Association

*Phone: (800) 356-9655 * Fax: (608) 231-4263*
5710 Mineral Point Rd., Madison, WI 53705
Web: www.cuna.org

The Credit Union National Association represents member-owned credit unions nationwide. About 72 million Americans belong to credit unions, which provide loans and other financial services. The group's president is former Rep. Daniel A. Mica, R-Fla. CUNA tracks legislation and regulation on the state and federal levels.

The group's main goal is to amend the Federal Credit Union Act of 1934 to allow credit unions to reach a wider audience. In February 1998, the U.S. Supreme Court ruled that credit unions had exceeded their congressional mandate by offering membership to customers who did not share a common occupation or employer. CUNA has said the ruling could affect between 10 and 20 million customers.

CUNA was, by far, the leading credit union PAC contributor to congressional candidates during the 1995-96 election cycle. The group favored Republican candidates and spent about 20 percent of its contributions on open races.

The leading recipients were Speaker Newt Gingrich, R-Ga., Rep. Bob Barr, R-Ga., and Sen. Mitch McConnell, R-Ky. Gingrich voiced support for a bill that would enable credit unions to attract members without a common employer. The top Democratic recipient was Sen. Max Baucus, D-Mont.

Credit Union Legislative Action Council (C00007880) *Phone: (202) 682-4200 * Fax: (202) 682-9054 * 805 15th St. N.W., Suite 300, Washington, DC 20005 * E-mail: dorothy@cuna.org * Treasurer: Thomas J. Griffiths * Contact: Sonja S. Simmons, Assistant Treasurer*

	1993-94	1995-96	1997	Totals
Receipts	$688,652	$757,219	$462,566	$1,908,437
Disburse	673,199	778,647	339,176	1,791,022
Cash	82,083	60,656	184,045	n/a
Contributions	526,096	642,688	274,979	1,443,763
Republicans	213,423	370,672	141,335	725,430
No. of Cand.	*121*	*175*	*88*	*384*
House	134,423	259,772	101,435	495,630
Senate	79,000	110,900	39,900	229,800
Democrats	308,173	271,016	133,144	712,333
No. of Cand.	*166*	*146*	*111*	*423*
House	223,814	215,781	112,644	552,239
Senate	84,359	55,235	20,500	160,094
Incumbents	414,396	498,075	265,979	1,178,450
Challengers	17,500	15,986	2,000	35,486
Open Seat	100,500	128,627	6,000	235,127
Winners	432,986	548,011	n/a	980,997
Losers	93,110	94,677	n/a	187,787

Alabama Credit Union Legislative Action Council (C00139600) *Phone: (205) 991-9710 * 22 Inverness Center Pkwy., Suite 200, Birmingham, AL 35242 * Treasurer: A. Dale Dalbey*

	1993-94	1995-96	1997	Totals
Receipts	$34,898	$38,080	$20,037	$93,015
Disburse	31,366	41,088	25,852	98,306
Cash	135,339	132,332	126,517	n/a
Contributions	4,000	15,000	11,500	30,500
Republicans	1,000	9,500	8,500	19,000
No. of Cand.	*1*	*5*	*5*	*11*
House	1,000	8,500	4,500	14,000
Senate	0	1,000	4,000	5,000
Democrats	3,000	5,500	3,000	11,500
No. of Cand.	*2*	*3*	*2*	*7*
House	3,000	3,500	3,000	9,500
Senate	0	2,000	0	2,000
Incumbents	4,000	9,500	11,500	25,000
Challengers	0	1,500	0	1,500
Open Seat	0	4,000	0	4,000
Winners	4,000	12,500	n/a	16,500
Losers	0	2,500	n/a	2,500

Michigan Credit Union League Legislative Action Fund (C00139279) *Phone: (248) 352-1250 * 20800 Civic Center Dr., Southfield, MI 48076 * Web: www.mcul.org * Treasurer: Lonnie L. Bone*

	1993-94	1995-96	1997	Totals
Receipts	$85,063	$67,147	$114,470	$266,680
Disburse	84,169	54,802	64,910	203,881
Cash	4,746	17,094	66,653	n/a
Contributions	29,185	13,940	4,020	47,145
Republicans	10,310	5,500	600	16,410
No. of Cand.	*7*	*7*	*1*	*15*
House	10,250	5,500	600	16,350
Senate	60	0	0	60
Democrats	18,875	8,440	3,420	30,735
No. of Cand.	*8*	*9*	*7*	*24*
House	16,745	7,440	3,420	27,605
Senate	2,130	1,000	0	3,130
Incumbents	25,245	11,540	4,020	40,805
Challengers	0	2,400	0	2,400
Open Seat	3,940	0	0	3,940
Winners	25,805	13,340	n/a	39,145
Losers	3,380	600	n/a	3,980

Contributed less than $5,000 during 1995-96 cycle:

California Credit Union League Political Action Committee (C00235929) *Phone: (909) 628-5167 * Fax: (909) 628-6044 * 2350 S. Garey Ave., Suite 402, Pomona, CA 91766 * Web: www.ccul.org * E-mail: league@ccul.org * Treasurer: Paul Bonell*

Kentucky Credit Union League Members Political Action Committee (C00130831) *Phone: (502) 459-6110 * Fax: (502) 459-8027 * 3615 Newburg Rd., Louisville, KY 40218 * Web: www.kycul.org * E-mail: kycul@kycul.org * Treasurer: Norman D. Asher*

Pennsylvania Credit Union Legislative Action Committee of the Penn Credit Union League (C00109397) *Phone: (717) 234-3156 * 4309 N. Front St., Box 60007, Harrisburg, PA 17106 * Web: www.pacul.org * Treasurer: Georgeann D. Lawson*

National Association of Federal Credit Unions

*Phone: (703) 522-4770 * Fax: (703) 524-1082*
3138 N. 10th St., Arlington, VA 22201-2149
Web: www.nafcunet.org

The National Association of Federal Credit Unions represents 1,100 federal credit unions. Founded in 1967, NAFCU provides its members with representation, information, education and assistance.

NAFCU has successfully lobbied with other groups to create a separate federal regulator, the National Credit Union Administration, and a central bank for liquidity purposes. It also worked to expand the powers of credit unions and to lessen the regulatory burden on credit unions. The NAFCU PAC contributed an average of about $950 per candidate during the 1995-1996 election cycle.

National Association of Federal Credit Unions Political Action Committee (NAFCUPAC) (C00040659) *Address: same as sponsor * Treasurer: William J. Donovan * Contact: Michael Vadala, Chairman*

	1993-94	1995-96	1997	Totals
Receipts	$75,241	$65,697	$83,330	$224,268
Disburse	72,543	70,501	62,892	205,936
Cash	64,343	59,543	79,981	n/a
Contributions	70,090	66,700	56,666	193,456
Republicans	21,500	32,700	29,056	83,256
No. of Cand.	*23*	*40*	*31*	*94*
House	16,500	26,200	23,056	65,756
Senate	5,000	6,500	6,000	17,500
Democrats	48,590	34,000	27,110	109,700
No. of Cand.	*51*	*32*	*34*	*117*
House	37,590	30,500	25,110	93,200
Senate	11,000	3,500	2,000	16,500
Incumbents	64,090	63,400	56,666	184,156
Challengers	1,000	0	0	1,000
Open Seat	5,000	3,300	0	8,300
Winners	55,875	57,700	n/a	113,575
Losers	14,215	9,000	n/a	23,215

Finance/Credit Companies

Advanta Corp.

*Phone: (302) 266-5265 * Fax: (302) 266-5250*
P.O. Box 15170, Wilmington, DE 19850-5170
Web: www.advanta.com

In February 1998, Advanta sold its consumer credit card business, one of the 10 largest in the nation, to Fleet Financial Group Inc. Following the $1.3 billion transaction, Advanta provides mortgages, home equity loans and other business services to consumers and small businesses. The publicly traded company retained its banking subsidiaries — Advanta Financial Corp. and Advanta National Bank.

After the sale, Advanta had about 2,200 employees, about $6.6 billion in managed assets and an additional $9.2 billion in assets serviced for third parties.

Advanta Mortgage, with about 1,300 employees, services $9 billion in mortgages and provides home equity loans to consumers.

The company's other primary business unit, Advanta Business Services, with about 600 employees, provides financial services to small businesses through equipment leasing and flexible lease financing programs.

Advanta Partners is a venture capital affiliate of Advanta. Formed in 1994, the company is a $100-million private equity firm. It invests in companies in the information and financial services industries that require growth capital or are candidates for restructurings or management buyouts.

Advanta Corp. Employees' Political Involvement Fund (C00279604) *Address: same as sponsor * Treasurer: John Calamari * Contact: Frank Salinger, V.P. of Gov. Relations*

	1993-94	1995-96	1997	Totals
Receipts	$126,188	$138,835	$57,659	$322,682
Disburse	118,070	138,157	62,301	318,528
Cash	8,122	8,802	4,160	n/a
Contributions	103,070	106,657	54,301	264,028
Republicans	43,000	78,357	41,000	162,357
No. of Cand.	*16*	*42*	*27*	*85*
House	17,000	54,357	27,000	98,357
Senate	26,000	24,000	14,000	64,000
Democrats	60,070	28,300	13,301	101,671
No. of Cand.	*26*	*17*	*14*	*57*
House	37,320	25,800	9,801	72,921
Senate	22,750	2,500	3,500	28,750
Incumbents	99,820	101,157	54,301	255,278
Challengers	3,250	1,500	0	4,750
Open Seat	0	4,000	0	4,000
Winners	84,250	92,657	n/a	176,907
Losers	18,820	14,000	n/a	32,820

American Express Co.

Phone: (212) 640-2000
American Express Tower, World Financial Center, New York, NY 10285
Web: www.americanexpress.com

American Express is one of the United States' largest financial services companies and is the largest corporate travel agency. In addition to financial products such as American Express cards and Travelers Cheques, the publicly traded company also publishes magazines (Food & Wine, Departures, Travel & Leisure) and provides financial advisory services.

American Express is continuing the aggressive makeover that began with its spinoff of stockbroker Lehman Brothers and is focusing on its corporate-travel and credit card businesses. Investor Warren Buffett owns about 10 percent of American Express. American Express reported 1997 sales of $17.7 billion.

Vernon Jordan,. a longtime friend and associate of President Clinton, is on the board of directors.

Advisers to the board include former President Gerald Ford and Former Secretary of State Henry Kissinger.

American Express Co. Political Action Committee (C00040535) *Phone: (202) 434-0154 * Fax: (202) 624-0775 * 801 Pennsylvania Ave. N.W., Suite 650, Washington, DC 20004 * Treasurer: Timothy S. Davis * Contact: Tom Schick, Chairman, PAC Steering Committee*

	1993-94	1995-96	1997	Totals
Receipts	$110,549	$232,756	$120,782	$464,087
Disburse	132,793	226,911	101,768	461,472
Cash	17,725	23,573	42,587	n/a
Contributions	100,550	155,400	73,500	329,450
Republicans	31,550	91,000	43,000	165,550
No. of Cand.	*45*	*73*	*54*	*172*
House	18,550	62,000	33,500	114,050
Senate	13,000	29,000	9,500	51,500
Democrats	68,000	64,400	30,000	162,400
No. of Cand.	*78*	*50*	*35*	*163*
House	45,500	46,400	17,500	109,400
Senate	22,500	18,000	12,500	53,000
Incumbents	94,650	133,700	72,000	300,350
Challengers	250	7,750	1,500	9,500
Open Seat	5,650	13,950	1,000	20,600
Winners	78,850	127,850	n/a	206,700
Losers	21,700	27,550	n/a	49,250

Terminated PACs which contributed less than $5,000 during 1995-96 cycle:

American Express Financial Advisors Political Action Committee (C00142356) *Tax Department - Unit #156, IDS Tower 10, Minneapolis, MN 55440 * Treasurer: Douglas R. Jordal*

American Financial Services Association

*Phone: (202) 296-5544 * Fax: (202) 223-0321*
919 18th St. N.W., Washington, DC 20006
Web: www.americanfinsvcs.com

The American Financial Services Association is the national trade group for consumer and small business lenders. It represents more than 500 companies which provide personal and automobile loans, home equity loans and credit cards.

Among the association's members are Beneficial Corp., American Express Co., Avco Financial Services and auto finance companies such as Ford Motor Credit Co.

American Financial Services Association PAC (formerly known as National Consumer Finance Association PAC) (C00038604) *Address: same as sponsor * Treasurer: Thomas L. Thomas * Contact: Tom Rosenkoetter*

	1993-94	1995-96	1997	Totals
Receipts	$156,612	$224,352	$109,042	$490,006
Disburse	165,160	234,629	100,868	500,657
Cash	18,770	10,744	18,914	n/a
Contributions	142,150	183,653	92,642	418,445
Republicans	68,800	165,315	73,781	307,896
No. of Cand.	*55*	*104*	*52*	*211*
House	50,100	122,687	60,716	233,503
Senate	18,700	42,628	13,065	74,393
Democrats	73,350	18,338	18,861	110,549
No. of Cand.	*53*	*30*	*22*	*105*
House	59,550	17,488	13,361	90,399
Senate	13,800	850	5,500	20,150
Incumbents	121,525	160,775	88,426	370,726
Challengers	8,125	7,550	0	15,675
Open Seat	12,500	14,878	3,250	30,628
Winners	107,625	155,019	n/a	262,644
Losers	34,525	28,634	n/a	63,159

Associated Credit Bureaus

*Phone: (202) 371-0910 * Fax: (202) 371-0134*
1090 Vermont Ave. N.W., Suite 200, Washington, DC 20005-4905
Web: www.acb-credit.com

Associated Credit Bureaus is an international trade association representing more than 1,450 consumer credit, mortgage reporting and collection service companies.

Associated Credit Bureaus Inc. Political Action Committee (C00030593) *Address: same as sponsor * Treasurer: D. Barry Connelly*

	1993-94	1995-96	1997	Totals
Receipts	$66,761	$52,243	$34,245	$153,249
Disburse	50,822	56,700	28,500	136,022
Cash	37,530	33,073	38,818	n/a
Contributions	48,850	56,200	28,500	133,550
Republicans	27,300	42,600	21,000	90,900
No. of Cand.	*30*	*42*	*23*	*95*
House	20,300	32,100	11,000	63,400
Senate	7,000	10,500	10,000	27,500
Democrats	21,550	13,600	7,500	42,650
No. of Cand.	*27*	*22*	*9*	*58*
House	18,050	13,100	4,500	35,650
Senate	3,500	500	3,000	7,000
Incumbents	46,200	54,700	28,250	129,150
Challengers	200	500	0	700
Open Seat	2,450	1,000	250	3,700
Winners	42,550	50,000	n/a	92,550
Losers	6,300	6,200	n/a	12,500

Beneficial Management Corp.

*Phone: (302) 425-2500 * Fax: (302) 425-2518*
301 N. Walnut St., Wilmington, DE 19801
Web: www.beneficial.com

Beneficial Management, a subsidiary of Beneficial Corp., is a $17-billion, Delaware-based public consumer loan and insurance company. It is the third-largest consumer finance company in the United States and employs about 9,700 people.

Its main products are home mortgages and equity lines of credit. In addition, the company owns a commercial bank and a credit card bank, Beneficial National Bank USA. Since late 1997, the company has sold off Canadian and German subsidiaries and real estate holdings in Florida and New Jersey. The company put itself up for sale in February 1998.

Beneficial lobbies on banking and finance issues. It supports the modernization of the U.S. financial services industry, which would permit banks to affiliate themselves with businesses providing insurance and securities management.

Beneficial was the leading credit and loan PAC contributor to 1996 congressional races. Nearly 70 percent of its contributions went to Republican candidates. The leading recipients were Rep. Steny H. Hoyer, D-Md., who received $10,000, and Sen. Alfonse M. D'Amato, R-N.Y., and former Rep. Dick Zimmer, R-N.J. All but 11 of the recipients received less than $5,000.

Beneficial Management Corp. and Affiliated Corps. Political Action Committee (C00043711) *Phone: (202) 646-1260 * Fax: (202) 646-0351 * 453 New Jersey Ave. S.E., Washington, DC 20003 * E-mail: lperez@beneficial.com * Treasurer: Lisa M. Perez*

	1993-94	1995-96	1997	Totals
Receipts	$451,505	$420,845	$212,391	$1,084,741
Disburse	384,557	459,832	210,046	1,054,435
Cash	104,979	66,000	68,354	n/a
Contributions	234,843	299,819	107,012	641,674
Republicans	81,190	203,319	57,751	342,260
No. of Cand.	*65*	*121*	*52*	*238*
House	44,990	144,926	44,251	234,167
Senate	36,200	58,393	13,500	108,093
Democrats	153,153	96,500	49,261	298,914
No. of Cand.	*102*	*61*	*43*	*206*
House	122,403	82,400	33,111	237,914
Senate	30,750	14,100	16,150	61,000
Incumbents	212,243	250,666	103,262	566,171
Challengers	2,050	8,193	1,000	11,243
Open Seat	20,550	40,960	2,750	64,260
Winners	178,693	238,510	n/a	417,203
Losers	56,150	61,309	n/a	117,459

Household International Inc.

*Phone: (708) 564-5000 * Fax: (708) 205-7403*
2700 Sanders Rd., Prospect Heights, IL 60070
Web: www.household.com

Household International provides consumer loans and credit cards in the United States, Canada and the United Kingdom. Credit cards include the GM Card and the AFL-CIO's Union Privilege Card. One of the company's largest businesses, Household Finance Corp., is the nation's oldest consumer finance company. A publicly traded company, Household has $51 billion in assets.

Headquartered in Prospect Heights, Ill., a suburb of Chicago, Household also has facilities in Elmhurst and Wood Dale, Ill.; Salinas and Pomona, Calif.; Las Vegas; Chesapeake and Virginia Beach, Va.; Canada; and the United Kingdom.

Household International Inc. & Subsidiary Companies Political Action Committee (HousePAC) (C00033423) *Address: same as sponsor * Treasurer: Paul R. Shay*

	1993-94	1995-96	1997	Totals
Receipts	$555,399	$507,634	$241,992	$1,305,025
Disburse	524,150	545,626	238,977	1,308,753
Cash	103,454	65,473	68,492	n/a
Contributions	236,095	198,625	98,250	532,970
Republicans	108,125	141,025	62,000	311,150
No. of Cand.	*88*	*99*	*59*	*246*
House	66,125	92,525	44,500	203,150
Senate	42,000	48,500	17,500	108,000
Democrats	127,970	57,600	36,250	221,820
No. of Cand.	*96*	*45*	*33*	*174*
House	96,850	45,100	15,750	157,700
Senate	31,120	12,500	20,500	64,120
Incumbents	209,895	174,125	92,500	476,520
Challengers	8,000	2,250	750	11,000
Open Seat	16,950	21,000	5,000	42,950
Winners	198,725	173,125	n/a	371,850
Losers	37,370	25,500	n/a	62,870

Insurance

AFLAC Inc.

*Phone: (706) 596-3264 * Fax: (706) 596-3577*
Worldwide Headquarters, Columbus, GA 31999
Web: www.aflac.com

American Family Life Assurance Co. is the largest seller of supplemental medical insurance in the United States. It is also the top cancer insurance company in Japan, which accounts for about 80 percent of annual revenue. The company, which employs about 4,000 workers, had 1997 sales of $7.2 billion.

A public company, AFLAC provides benefits for intensive care and nursing home care or as a Medicare supplement. Its sales come primarily through employers. Local government employees are a large market.

AFLAC's insurance subsidiary paid an $80,000 civil fine in January 1998 for campaign contributions to the brother of former Agriculture Secretary Mike Espy. American Family Life Insurance Co. reimbursed several employees for contributions they made to the 1993 congressional campaign of Henry Espy of Mississippi.

The company lobbies on health care and Medicare policy, taxes and trade relations with Japan.

AFLAC was the top health insurance PAC contributor to 1996 congressional races. The company contributed more than 89 percent to winning candidates. The leading recipients were Reps. Charlie Norwood, R-Ga., and Bob Barr, R-Ga., and Sen. Gordon H. Smith, R-Ore. Most recipients got less than $5,000.

AFLAC Inc. Political Action Committee (AFLACPAC) (C00034157) *Phone: (202) 628-6074 * Fax: (202) 628-6076 * 801 Pennsylvania Ave. N.W., Suite 850, Washington, DC 20004 * E-mail: dpringle@aflac.com * Treasurer: Joey M. Loudermilk * Contact: David Pringle, V.P. of Federal Relations*

	1993-94	1995-96	1997	Totals
Receipts	$681,566	$731,084	$404,283	$1,816,933
Disburse	653,265	697,559	345,131	1,695,955
Cash	89,141	122,679	181,835	n/a
Contributions	499,550	510,450	253,500	1,263,500
Republicans	220,200	324,950	150,000	695,150
No. of Cand.	*84*	*103*	*76*	*263*
House	114,700	222,500	113,000	450,200
Senate	105,500	102,450	37,000	244,950
Democrats	277,350	185,500	103,500	566,350
No. of Cand.	*94*	*64*	*52*	*210*
House	222,850	151,000	66,000	439,850
Senate	54,500	34,500	37,500	126,500
Incumbents	439,550	449,250	249,000	1,137,800
Challengers	19,500	6,200	1,500	27,200
Open Seat	39,500	55,000	3,000	97,500
Winners	398,550	460,250	n/a	858,800
Losers	101,000	50,200	n/a	151,200

Acacia Mutual Life Insurance Co.

*Phone: (301) 280-1000 * Fax: (301) 280-1031*
7315 Wisconsin Ave., Bethesda, MD 20814-3202
Web: www.acaciagroup.com

Acacia Mutual Life Insurance is a private insurance company, as well as the parent company of a variety of financial companies that provide insurance, banking and investment services under the name of the Acacia Group.

These companies include Acacia National Insurance Co., which provides insurance, and Acacia Federal Savings Bank, which provides loans, mortgages and lines of credit. The Calvert Groups Ltd. and The Advisors Group Inc. offer investment services, including mutual funds and retirement accounts.

The group, which is owned by its policyholders, has total assets of more than $7.3 billion.

In 1869, Acacia Mutual's predecessor company, Masonic Mutual Relief Association, was established by an act of Congress. Acacia Mutual claims it is the only life insurance company currently operating under a congressional charter.

Acacia Mutual Political Action Committee (C00169789) *Address: same as sponsor * Treasurer: Tracy Dowis * Contact: Ellen Jane Abromson, Associate Counsel*

	1993-94	1995-96	1997	Totals
Receipts	$23,272	$14,281	$2,943	$40,496
Disburse	15,893	15,000	8,150	39,043
Cash	17,901	17,185	11,979	n/a
Contributions	7,500	8,500	3,500	19,500
Republicans	2,000	7,000	3,000	12,000
No. of Cand.	*3*	*7*	*2*	*12*
House	500	3,500	0	4,000
Senate	1,500	3,500	3,000	8,000
Democrats	5,500	1,500	500	7,500
No. of Cand.	*8*	*2*	*1*	*11*
House	4,500	1,500	500	6,500
Senate	1,000	0	0	1,000
Incumbents	7,000	8,500	3,500	19,000
Challengers	500	0	0	500
Open Seat	0	0	0	0
Winners	4,500	8,500	n/a	13,000
Losers	3,000	0	n/a	3,000

Aegon USA Inc.

Phone: (319) 363-5400
4333 Edgewood Rd. N.E., Cedar Rapids, IA 52499

Aegon USA is a holding company with subsidiaries marketing life and health insurance, as well as investment and retirement products. Based in Cedar Rapids, Iowa, Aegon USA employs 10,000 workers and has total assets of $32 billion. Annual sales average $4.5 billion.

It is a wholly owned subsidiary of Aegon, N.V., a $94 billion public international insurance group and financial services firm headquartered in The Hague, Netherlands. Aegon, N.V. is one of the 10 largest insurance organizations worldwide.

Aegon USA Inc. Political Action Committee (C00236414) *Phone: (410) 576-4529 * Fax: (410) 347-8685 * 1111 N. Charles St., Baltimore, MD 21201 * Treasurer: Katherine A. Schulze*

	1993-94	1995-96	1997	Totals
Receipts	$22,794	$26,010	$16,052	$64,856
Disburse	30,002	19,283	7,392	56,677
Cash	610	7,338	15,999	n/a
Contributions	17,650	9,550	2,450	29,650
Republicans	15,200	7,150	1,100	23,450
No. of Cand.	*28*	*23*	*5*	*56*
House	2,100	3,150	650	5,900
Senate	13,100	4,000	450	17,550
Democrats	2,450	2,400	1,350	6,200
No. of Cand.	*9*	*7*	*2*	*18*
House	1,700	2,150	350	4,200
Senate	750	250	1,000	2,000
Incumbents	8,950	6,100	2,100	17,150
Challengers	3,250	2,000	0	5,250
Open Seat	5,450	1,450	350	7,250
Winners	16,050	5,550	n/a	21,600
Losers	1,600	4,000	n/a	5,600

Aetna Inc.

*Phone: (860) 273-0123 * Fax: (860) 275-2677*
151 Farmington Ave., Hartford, CT 06156
Web: www.aetna.com

Aetna is the nation's largest health benefits company, based on membership, and one of the largest insurance and financial services organizations.

Aetna U.S. Healthcare provides health care benefits, specialty health and group life and disability products and services to 11.1 million managed care members. Aetna Retirement Services markets retirement, investment and life insurance products to individuals, businesses and nonprofit institutions. The subsidiaries of Aetna Retirement Services serve more than 2 million customers directly and through 30,000 plan sponsors. Aetna International offers a variety of insurance and financial services to people and businesses outside the United States.

The public company had $18.5 billion in revenues in 1997. Seventy percent of revenues came from Aetna U.S. Healthcare, 21 percent came from Retirement Services and 9 percent came from Aetna International. Aetna employs 38,600 workers.

The company announced plans in 1998 to acquire a health insurance subsidiary from New York Life Insurance Co. The deal will add about 2.2 million members to Aetna U.S. Healthcare.

Aetna Inc. Political Action Committee (formerly known as Aetna Life and Casualty) (C00181826) *Phone: (202) 463-4023 * Fax: (202) 331-4205 * 1501 M St. N.W., Suite 400, Washington, DC 20005 * Treasurer: Jonathan M. Topodas*

*Contact: Vin McMurtry, Chairman * Phone: (860) 273-0123*

	1993-94	1995-96	1997	Totals
Receipts	$214,379	$168,859	$93,598	$476,836
Disburse	227,165	178,231	71,646	477,042
Cash	18,293	8,926	30,878	n/a
Contributions	125,080	70,575	39,500	235,155
Republicans	53,450	48,325	25,000	126,775
No. of Cand.	*46*	*52*	*15*	*113*
House	25,200	31,325	8,000	64,525
Senate	28,250	17,000	17,000	62,250
Democrats	71,630	22,250	14,500	108,380
No. of Cand.	*53*	*27*	*9*	*89*
House	35,750	15,250	4,000	55,000
Senate	35,880	7,000	10,500	53,380
Incumbents	112,580	64,200	39,500	216,280
Challengers	5,750	1,375	0	7,125
Open Seat	6,750	3,500	0	10,250
Winners	96,950	57,950	n/a	154,900
Losers	28,130	12,625	n/a	40,755

Agents for Good Government

Route 2, Box 118A2, Emory, TX 75440

Agents for Good Government (C00274464) *Address: same as sponsor * Treasurer: Karen Gore*

	1993-94	1995-96	1997	Totals
Receipts	$161,370	$66,760	$275	$228,405
Disburse	158,207	88,410	-750	245,867
Cash	24,715	3,058	4,083	n/a
Contributions	97,500	44,750	-2,500	139,750
Republicans	78,500	34,750	-2,500	110,750
No. of Cand.	*21*	*30*	*2*	*53*
House	33,500	27,000	-2,500	58,000
Senate	45,000	7,750	0	52,750
Democrats	19,000	10,000	0	29,000
No. of Cand.	*9*	*1*	*0*	*10*
House	19,000	0	0	19,000
Senate	0	10,000	0	10,000
Incumbents	30,000	28,750	-2,500	56,250
Challengers	35,500	500	0	36,000
Open Seat	32,000	15,500	0	47,500
Winners	62,500	32,250	n/a	94,750
Losers	35,000	12,500	n/a	47,500

Aid Association for Lutherans

*Phone: (920) 730-3753 * Fax: (920) 730-3711*
P.O. Box 1892, Appleton, WI 54913
*Web: www.aal.org * E-mail: mary_beth_leib@aal.org*

Aid Association for Lutherans is a nonprofit company that offers insurance and financial services, as well as charitable and educational opportunities, to its members.

AAL is the largest fraternal benefit society in the United States, providing services to nearly 1.7 million people nationwide. The organization was established in 1902 and has since grown to more than 1,500 employees and 1996 sales of nearly $3 billion.

In addition to the financial services the association offers to its members, AAL provides opportunities for volunteer and community-building activities. The organization maintains a network of more than 9,700 volunteer groups nationwide that contribute more than 3 million volunteer hours each year.

Aid Association for Lutherans Political Action Committee (C00121319) *Address: same as sponsor * Treasurer: Cheryl Jawort * Contact: Mary Beth Leib, Chairperson*

	1993-94	1995-96	1997	Totals
Receipts	$41,157	$34,009	$13,584	$88,750
Disburse	42,661	39,185	10,070	91,916
Cash	7,386	2,213	5,729	n/a
Contributions	11,750	14,600	2,195	28,545
Republicans	10,500	12,600	2,195	25,295
No. of Cand.	*8*	*9*	*4*	*21*
House	9,250	11,800	695	21,745
Senate	1,250	800	1,500	3,550
Democrats	1,250	2,000	0	3,250
No. of Cand.	*3*	*3*	*0*	*6*
House	1,250	1,500	0	2,750
Senate	0	500	0	500
Incumbents	9,150	7,000	195	16,345
Challengers	2,100	800	2,000	4,900
Open Seat	500	6,800	0	7,300
Winners	9,750	6,700	n/a	16,450
Losers	2,000	7,900	n/a	9,900

Alliance of American Insurers

*Phone: (847) 330-8500 * Fax: (847) 330-8602*
1501 Woodfield Rd., Suite 400 W., Schaumburg, IL 60173-4980
Web: www.allianceai.org

The Alliance of American Insurers is a national trade association of more than 260 property and casualty insurance companies.

Founded in 1922, the alliance represents its members in regulatory and legislative matters covering all aspects of insurance operations at the state and federal level. The alliance maintains regional offices in Washington; Atlanta; Austin, Texas; Boston; New York; San Francisco; Sacramento, Calif.; and Tallahassee, Fla.

Alliance of American Insurers Political Action Committee (C00131045) *Phone: (202) 822-8811 * Fax: (202) 872-1885 * 1211 Connecticut Ave. N.W., Suite 400, Washington, DC 20036 * Treasurer: Gregory W. Heidrich * Contact: Dave Farmer, Senior V.P. of Federal Affairs*

	1993-94	1995-96	1997	Totals
Receipts	$10,548	$33,209	$13,588	$57,345
Disburse	7,500	31,450	14,750	53,700
Cash	3,418	5,189	4,032	n/a
Contributions	7,500	25,850	15,000	48,350
Republicans	4,500	19,350	12,500	36,350
No. of Cand.	*8*	*23*	*25*	*56*
House	3,500	12,350	10,750	26,600
Senate	1,000	7,000	1,750	9,750
Democrats	3,000	6,500	2,500	12,000
No. of Cand.	*5*	*9*	*5*	*19*
House	2,000	4,500	2,500	9,000
Senate	1,000	2,000	0	3,000
Incumbents	6,500	14,750	14,250	35,500
Challengers	500	4,000	0	4,500
Open Seat	500	7,000	750	8,250
Winners	6,000	14,750	n/a	20,750
Losers	1,500	11,100	n/a	12,600

Allstate Insurance Co.

*Phone: (847) 502-5000 * Fax: (847) 836-3998*
2775 Sanders Rd., Suite A4, Northbrook, IL 60062
Web: www.allstate.com

Allstate is the nation's second largest personal insurer, behind State Farm. The public company sells property and casualty and life insurance in the United States and Canada.

Allstate's life insurance and annuity operations are conducted through Allstate Life Insurance Co. and through various subsidiaries. Its primary business is the sale of private passenger automobile and homeowners insurance through its personal property and casualty unit.

Allstate offers life, homeowner's, business, motorcycle, boat, motor home and recreational vehicle insurance. Allstate has 250 claim service offices and 680 drive-in centers in North America.

Allstate employs more than 48,000 workers and had sales of more than $24 billion in 1997.

Allstate Insurance Co. Political Action Committee (C00040253) *Address: same as sponsor * Treasurer: James Zils * Contact: Robert W. Gary, Chairman*

	1993-94	1995-96	1997	Totals
Receipts	$309,072	$300,345	$232,925	$842,342
Disburse	287,227	353,057	153,169	793,453
Cash	75,105	22,398	102,155	n/a
Contributions	83,480	117,950	49,500	250,930
Republicans	58,900	110,450	42,000	211,350
No. of Cand.	*55*	*72*	*41*	*168*
House	32,900	63,500	30,000	126,400
Senate	26,000	46,950	12,000	84,950
Democrats	24,580	7,500	7,500	39,580
No. of Cand.	*23*	*8*	*8*	*39*

(Data for Allstate Insurance Co. continued)

House	16,350	3,500	1,500	21,350
Senate	8,230	4,000	6,000	18,230
Incumbents	71,930	84,500	46,500	202,930
Challengers	2,500	3,950	1,000	7,450
Open Seat	9,050	29,250	2,000	40,300
Winners	76,250	82,000	n/a	158,250
Losers	7,230	35,950	n/a	43,180

AmerUs Life Holdings Inc.

*Phone: (515) 283-2371 * Fax: (515) 362-3652*
699 Walnut St., Suite 2000, Des Moines, IA 50309
Web: www.amerus.com

AmerUs Life Holdings markets, underwrites and distributes a range of life insurance and annuity products to individuals and businesses. The publicly held company, with about 400 employees, offers whole life, universal life and term life insurance policies and fixed annuities in 45 states and the District of Columbia.

AmerUs had 1996 sales of $500,000 and, following its December 1997 acquisition of AmVestors Financial, had about $10 billion in assets.

Subsidiaries include: AmerUs Life and AmVestors Financial. The company also holds a 34 percent share in Ameritas, a variable life insurance and annuity company.

AmerUs Group Political Action Committee (C00180901) *Address: same as sponsor * Treasurer: James A. Smallenberger * Contact: Roger K. Brooks, Chairman*

	1993-94	1995-96	1997	Totals
Receipts	$13,291	$22,578	$16,872	$52,741
Disburse	17,900	14,141	5,500	37,541
Cash	3,151	11,590	22,963	n/a
Contributions	2,400	6,850	2,500	11,750
Republicans	1,500	5,150	2,500	9,150
No. of Cand.	*3*	*7*	*3*	*13*
House	1,500	4,650	1,500	7,650
Senate	0	500	1,000	1,500
Democrats	900	1,700	0	2,600
No. of Cand.	*2*	*3*	*0*	*5*
House	900	700	0	1,600
Senate	0	1,000	0	1,000
Incumbents	1,900	5,850	2,500	10,250
Challengers	0	0	0	0
Open Seat	500	1,000	0	1,500
Winners	1,900	6,350	n/a	8,250
Losers	500	500	n/a	1,000

American Council of Life Insurance

*Phone: (202) 624-2159 * Fax: (202) 624-2093*
1001 Pennsylvania Ave. N.W., Washington, DC 20004-2599

The American Council of Life Insurance is a national trade organization with 580 member life insurance companies. Its members represent about 90 percent of the life insurance policies issued in the United States. Many members also sell disability income and long-term care insurance.

The group strongly supports state, not federal, regulation of the insurance industry. But it does favor federal patient confidentiality laws that do not curb companies' ability to collect and use patient information. The ACLI supports reform of the nation's financial services regulations, which would permit banks to align themselves with companies offering investment and insurance services.

The ACLI ranked second among life insurance industry PACs in contributions to congressional candidates during the 1995-96 election cycle. The group contributed nearly 85 percent of its money to Republican candidates. The top recipients were Sens. Jesse Helms, R-N.C., and Gordon H. Smith, R-Ore., and 1996 Senate candidate William F. Weld of Massachusetts.

American Council of Life Insurance, Life Insurance PAC (C00147066) *Address: same as sponsor * Treasurer: Richard Gunderson * Contact: Robert Arensberg, Dir. of Political Affairs*

	1993-94	1995-96	1997	Totals
Receipts	$741,854	$655,228	$333,834	$1,730,916
Disburse	693,666	760,936	205,200	1,659,802
Cash	149,275	43,575	172,215	n/a
Contributions	595,415	600,531	164,966	1,360,912
Republicans	317,152	507,531	117,316	941,999
No. of Cand.	*153*	*233*	*99*	*485*
House	160,349	308,217	94,000	562,566
Senate	156,803	199,314	23,316	379,433
Democrats	278,263	93,000	47,150	418,413
No. of Cand.	*138*	*62*	*54*	*254*
House	195,496	78,000	30,150	303,646
Senate	82,767	15,000	17,000	114,767
Incumbents	503,612	416,031	153,466	1,073,109
Challengers	21,304	46,000	1,500	68,804
Open Seat	70,999	138,500	11,000	220,499
Winners	517,092	459,900	n/a	976,992
Losers	78,323	140,631	n/a	218,954

American Fidelity Corp.

*Phone: (405) 523-2000 * Fax: (405) 523-5411*
P.O. Box 25523, Oklahoma City, OK 73125-0523
Web: www.af-group.com

American Fidelity is a privately owned network of companies that provide insurance products and services, including disability income insurance, group and individual life insurance, cancer insurance, hospital indemnity insurance, tax-deferred annuities and flexible spending programs.

The company is based in Oklahoma City and employs 1,800 people.

Subsidiaries include: American Fidelity Insurance Co., American Fidelity Life Insurance Co. and American Fidelity Property Co.

American Fidelity Corp. PAC (C00210526) *Address: same as sponsor * Treasurer: Kenneth Dean Klehm * Contact: Stephen Garrett, Senior V.P.*

	1993-94	1995-96	1997	Totals
Receipts	$45,563	$55,294	$24,845	$125,702
Disburse	38,915	32,562	10,624	82,101
Cash	48,409	71,144	85,367	n/a
Contributions	3,450	7,750	500	11,700
Republicans	2,650	6,250	500	9,400
No. of Cand.	*3*	*5*	*1*	*9*
House	1,650	5,000	500	7,150
Senate	1,000	1,250	0	2,250
Democrats	800	1,500	0	2,300
No. of Cand.	*2*	*2*	*0*	*4*
House	800	500	0	1,300
Senate	0	1,000	0	1,000
Incumbents	2,250	5,750	500	8,500
Challengers	0	0	0	0
Open Seat	1,200	2,000	0	3,200
Winners	3,250	6,250	n/a	9,500
Losers	200	1,500	n/a	1,700

American General Corp.

*Phone: (713) 522-1111 * Fax: (713) 831-3104*
2929 Allen Pkwy., Houston, TX 77019
Web: www.agc.com

American General provides retirement services, consumer loans and life insurance to 12 million customers. The publicly traded Houston company reported $868 million in 1997 sales. It has about 15,000 employees.

In 1998, the company purchased Western National Corp., a fixed annuities provider. American General's 1997 acquisition of U.S. Life Corp. made it the third-largest writer of individual annuities in the nation.

American General offers traditional life insurance through six companies, including American General Life Insurance, Franklin Life Insurance and American General Life and Accident Insurance.

Subsidiary Variable Annuity Life Insurance Co. provides a variety of retirement products, including investment products, tax-deferred retirement plans and retirement counseling services to individuals and businesses. American General Finance, another division, offers consumer loans.

American General Corp. Political Action Committee (C00024299) *Address: same as sponsor * Treasurer: Pamela J. Penny*

	1993-94	1995-96	1997	Totals
Receipts	$153,493	$182,254	$142,899	$478,646
Disburse	169,239	174,530	117,644	461,413
Cash	19,428	27,161	52,416	n/a
Contributions	64,340	62,040	48,050	174,430

Republicans	43,000	44,850	35,250	123,100
No. of Cand.	*21*	*32*	*24*	*77*
House	9,000	31,750	14,750	55,500
Senate	34,000	13,100	20,500	67,600
Democrats	21,340	17,190	12,800	51,330
No. of Cand.	*17*	*10*	*10*	*37*
House	13,340	13,190	8,800	35,330
Senate	8,000	4,000	4,000	16,000
Incumbents	48,340	44,440	47,050	139,830
Challengers	3,500	10,000	0	13,500
Open Seat	12,500	7,600	1,000	21,100
Winners	53,340	40,440	n/a	93,780
Losers	11,000	21,600	n/a	32,600

American General Finance Inc. Political Action Committee (formerly known as Credithrift of America PAC) (C00139030) *Phone: (812) 461-2573 * Fax: (812) 468-5396 * 601 N.W. Second St., Evansville, IN 47708 * Web: www.agfinance.com * E-mail: phitz@agfinance.com * Treasurer: David McManigal * Contact: Phil Hitz, Chairperson*

	1993-94	1995-96	1997	Totals
Receipts	$117,352	$151,969	$77,794	$347,115
Disburse	109,402	100,294	43,561	253,257
Cash	41,418	93,093	127,326	n/a
Contributions	14,950	16,319	3,500	34,769
Republicans	8,850	12,069	2,000	22,919
No. of Cand.	*8*	*13*	*2*	*23*
House	1,850	5,700	2,000	9,550
Senate	7,000	6,369	0	13,369
Democrats	6,100	4,250	1,500	11,850
No. of Cand.	*10*	*5*	*2*	*17*
House	4,600	4,250	500	9,350
Senate	1,500	0	1,000	2,500
Incumbents	10,350	10,700	1,000	22,050
Challengers	500	4,869	1,000	6,369
Open Seat	4,100	750	1,500	6,350
Winners	10,850	9,450	n/a	20,300
Losers	4,100	6,869	n/a	10,969

American Insurance Association

*Phone: (202) 828-7100 * Fax: (202) 293-1219*
1130 Connecticut Ave. N.W., Suite 1000, Washington, DC 20036
Web: www.aiadc.org

The American Insurance Association represents more than 300 property and casualty insurers.

Property and casualty insurers provide personal insurance, commercial auto insurance, commercial property and liability coverage, workers' compensation, homeowners' insurance, medical malpractice insurance and product liability insurance.

The AIA is focused on financial services modernization, workers' compensation, regulatory reform, tort issues, automobile insurance and international insurance issues.

American Insurance Association Political Action Committee (C00103143) *Address: same as sponsor * Treasurer: Betty Vodra McElroy*

	1993-94	1995-96	1997	Totals
Receipts	$130,893	$129,492	$79,167	$339,552
Disburse	129,263	131,598	70,045	330,906
Cash	3,002	907	10,032	n/a
Contributions	126,980	114,200	44,014	285,194
Republicans	36,500	97,200	35,764	169,464
No. of Cand.	*55*	*119*	*44*	*218*
House	24,500	67,564	25,996	118,060
Senate	12,000	29,636	9,768	51,404
Democrats	90,480	17,000	8,250	115,730
No. of Cand.	*81*	*23*	*12*	*116*
House	59,560	14,000	4,250	77,810
Senate	30,920	3,000	4,000	37,920
Incumbents	103,850	80,700	43,764	228,314
Challengers	4,250	8,750	500	13,500
Open Seat	18,770	24,750	250	43,770
Winners	103,280	88,450	n/a	191,730
Losers	23,700	25,750	n/a	49,450

American International Group Inc.

*Phone: (212) 770-7000 * Fax: (212) 509-9705*
70 Pine St., New York, NY 10270
Web: www.aig.com

American International Group's member companies write property, casualty, marine, life and financial services insurance in about 130 countries and jurisdictions, and are engaged in a range of financial services businesses.

The publicly traded company reported $30.6 billion in 1997 sales. AIG has $165 billion in assets and about 36,600 employees.

AIG's domestic strengths are business and auto insurance. The company concentrates on life insurance overseas and more than half of its revenues comes from foreign business.

American International Group Inc. Employee Political Action Committee (C00097725) *Address: same as sponsor * Treasurer: Vincent E. Cantwell * Contact: John J. Roberts, PAC Dir.*

	1993-94	1995-96	1997	Totals
Receipts	$209,806	$196,725	$80,427	$486,958
Disburse	211,553	196,634	65,529	473,716
Cash	2,337	2,437	17,334	n/a
Contributions	163,402	148,230	57,500	369,132
Republicans	74,885	87,940	20,000	182,825
No. of Cand.	*51*	*61*	*14*	*126*
House	38,100	58,240	7,000	103,340
Senate	36,785	29,700	13,000	79,485
Democrats	88,017	61,290	37,500	186,807
No. of Cand.	*54*	*29*	*15*	*98*
House	52,542	36,790	13,500	102,832
Senate	35,475	24,500	24,000	83,975
Incumbents	153,274	119,740	47,500	320,514
Challengers	4,128	12,500	10,000	26,628
Open Seat	4,000	17,700	0	21,700
Winners	141,164	119,040	n/a	260,204
Losers	22,238	29,190	n/a	51,428

American National Insurance Co.

*Phone: (409) 766-6537 * Fax: (409) 766-6803*
One Moody Plaza, Galveston, TX 77550
Web: www.anico.com

American National Insurance provides life, personal property and casualty and credit insurance. Based in Galveston, Texas, the public company employs 4,300 people. It posted 1996 sales of $1.5 billion.

The company has operations in the United States and Europe, and is reportedly among the three largest home service life insurance companies in the United States. American National has more than 3.5 million policyholders in the United States.

Subsidiaries include: Standard Life and Accident Insurance, American National Life Insurance Co. of Texas, American National Property and Casualty Co., and Garden State Life Insurance.

American National Insurance Co. Good Government Committee (C00135525) *Address: same as sponsor * Treasurer: Vincent Emile Soler Jr.*

	1993-94	1995-96	1997	Totals
Receipts	$36,934	$36,988	$21,295	$95,217
Disburse	43,081	35,718	7,123	85,922
Cash	6,354	7,625	21,798	n/a
Contributions	12,000	7,000	0	19,000
Republicans	12,000	7,000	0	19,000
No. of Cand.	*5*	*6*	*0*	*11*
House	5,000	6,000	0	11,000
Senate	7,000	1,000	0	8,000
Democrats	0	0	0	0
No. of Cand.	*0*	*0*	*0*	*0*
House	0	0	0	0
Senate	0	0	0	0
Incumbents	12,000	7,000	0	19,000
Challengers	0	0	0	0
Open Seat	0	0	0	0
Winners	12,000	5,000	n/a	17,000
Losers	0	2,000	n/a	2,000

Ameritas Financial Services

*Phone: (402) 467-7176 * Fax: (402) 467-7956*
5900 O St., Lincoln, NE 68510
Web: www.ameritas.com

Ameritas Financial Services is a private insurance and annuity company headquartered in Nebraska. Ameritas has accumulated more than $3 billion in assets and has more than $10 billion of insurance coverage in force.

Ameritas, its subsidiaries and affiliates market products in all 50 states and the District of Columbia. The company offers products and services in four key lines of business: individual, group, pensions and investments.

AmerUs Life Holdings Co. holds a 34 percent share in Ameritas.

Ameritas Financial Services Political Action Committee (formerly known as Bankers Life Nebraska PAC) (C00187138) *Address: same as sponsor * Treasurer: Craig Mahal * Contact: Norman Krivosha, Chairman*

	1993-94	1995-96	1997	Totals
Receipts	$40,491	$41,545	$21,582	$103,618
Disburse	51,250	33,560	10,997	95,807
Cash	5,888	13,877	24,462	n/a
Contributions	4,550	15,200	2,450	22,200
Republicans	3,550	10,000	2,200	15,750
No. of Cand.	*3*	*3*	*3*	*9*
House	2,550	3,000	200	5,750
Senate	1,000	7,000	2,000	10,000
Democrats	1,000	5,200	250	6,450
No. of Cand.	*1*	*2*	*1*	*4*
House	1,000	200	0	1,200
Senate	0	5,000	250	5,250
Incumbents	2,550	3,000	2,450	8,000
Challengers	2,000	200	0	2,200
Open Seat	0	12,000	0	12,000
Winners	2,550	10,000	n/a	12,550
Losers	2,000	5,200	n/a	7,200

Amica Mutual Insurance Co

*Phone: (401) 334-6000 * Fax: (401) 334-4241*
P.O. Box 6008, Providence, RI 02940-6008
Web: www.amica.com

Amica Mutual Insurance provides automobile insurance plans, homeowner protection, marine insurance, personal excess liability and life insurance to nearly 500,000 insured households around the United States. Amica employs 3,300 workers in 40 offices.

Amica's assets at the end of 1996 exceeded $2.2 billion. In 1997, Amica moved its headquarters from downtown Providence, R.I., where it had been since 1907, to Lincoln, a northern suburb.

Amica Mutual Insurance Co. Federal Political Action Committee (C00268987) *Address: same as sponsor * Treasurer: Robert A. Dimuccio * Contact: Kenneth Nails, Chairman*

	1993-94	1995-96	1997	Totals
Receipts	$8,802	$9,294	$7,113	$25,209
Disburse	9,700	9,450	1,000	20,150
Cash	1,201	1,045	7,158	n/a
Contributions	6,200	5,450	500	12,150
Republicans	5,400	3,700	0	9,100
No. of Cand.	*6*	*2*	*0*	*8*
House	2,900	0	0	2,900
Senate	2,500	3,700	0	6,200
Democrats	800	1,750	500	3,050
No. of Cand.	*4*	*2*	*1*	*7*
House	800	1,750	500	3,050
Senate	0	0	0	0
Incumbents	3,600	250	500	4,350
Challengers	100	500	0	600
Open Seat	2,500	4,700	0	7,200
Winners	3,400	1,750	n/a	5,150
Losers	2,800	3,700	n/a	6,500

Anthem Insurance Companies Inc.

*Phone: (317) 488-6044 * Fax: (317) 488-6306*
120 Monument Circle, Indianapolis, IN 46204-4903
*Web: www.anthem-inc.com * E-mail: john_willey@aici.com*

Anthem Insurance, formerly known as Associated Insurance Companies, provides health insurance and services to nearly 10 million people nationwide. In Connecticut, Indiana, Kentucky and Ohio, the company operates under the Blue Cross and Blue Shield name as Anthem Blue Cross and Blue Shield.

Anthem was created in 1944 and today employs more than 17,000 people. Based in Indianapolis, the private company had 1996 sales of nearly $6.3 billion.

Subsidiaries include: AdminaStar Federal Inc., American Health Network, Anthem Casualty, Anthem Health - US, Anthem Prescription and SpecialMed.

Anthem Insurance Companies Inc. Good Government Program PAC (C00198069) *Address: same as sponsor * Treasurer: Richard J. Cockrum * Contact: John Willey, Manager*

	1993-94	1995-96	1997	Totals
Receipts	$40,181	$53,508	$152,135	$245,824
Disburse	42,968	52,342	57,625	152,935
Cash	5,566	9,463	103,974	n/a
Contributions	10,600	1,750	4,000	16,350
Republicans	9,300	1,250	1,500	12,050
No. of Cand.	*2*	*3*	*4*	*9*
House	1,800	1,250	1,000	4,050
Senate	7,500	0	500	8,000
Democrats	1,300	500	2,500	4,300
No. of Cand.	*3*	*2*	*3*	*8*
House	800	500	1,500	2,800
Senate	500	0	1,000	1,500
Incumbents	9,600	750	1,000	11,350
Challengers	0	700	0	700
Open Seat	500	300	3,000	3,800
Winners	9,300	1,050	n/a	10,350
Losers	1,300	700	n/a	2,000

Contributed less than $5,000 during 1995-96 cycle:

Blue Cross & Blue Shield of Connecticut Inc. PAC (C00152660) *Phone: (203) 239-4911 * 370 Bassett Rd., North Haven, CT 06473 * Treasurer: Frank J. Duzy*

Aon Corp.

*Phone: (312) 701-4000 x3602 * Fax: (312) 701-3785*
123 N. Wacker Dr., Chicago, IL 60606
Web: www.aon.com

Aon, which had 1997 sales of $5.8 billion, is a public holding company with subsidiaries engaged in insurance and financial services, life insurance brokerage and consulting, accidental and health insurance and extended warranties. It employs 28,000 people and has headquarters in Chicago.

Aon's brokerage and consulting services are provided through 550 offices in more than 100 countries.

In 1997 and early 1998, Aon had a wave of acquisitions, including Rath & Strong, a management consulting firm with offices in the United States, England and Germany, and Gil y Carvajal, Spain's largest reinsurance group.

Aon Corp. Political Action Committee (Aon PAC) (C00211250) *Address: same as sponsor * Treasurer: Arlene H. Hardy*

	1993-94	1995-96	1997	Totals
Receipts	$31,961	$40,527	$27,309	$99,797
Disburse	28,350	47,201	20,828	96,379
Cash	38,056	31,385	37,867	n/a
Contributions	2,550	13,000	8,109	23,659
Republicans	750	11,000	6,909	18,659
No. of Cand.	*2*	*6*	*3*	*11*
House	250	1,000	1,909	3,159
Senate	500	10,000	5,000	15,500
Democrats	1,800	2,000	1,200	5,000
No. of Cand.	*2*	*3*	*2*	*7*
House	1,800	0	1,000	2,800
Senate	0	2,000	200	2,200
Incumbents	2,550	1,000	2,109	5,659
Challengers	0	4,500	5,000	9,500
Open Seat	0	7,500	1,000	8,500
Winners	2,550	1,000	n/a	3,550
Losers	0	12,000	n/a	12,000

Blue Cross and Blue Shield

*Phone: (202) 626-4780 * Fax: (202) 626-4833*
1330 G St. N.W., 12th Floor, Washington, DC 20005
Web: www.bluecares.com

The Blue Cross and Blue Shield system comprises 55 independent member plans which provide health care coverage for more than 68.7 million people. The member plans have 150,000 employees nationwide, making the Blue Cross and Blue Shield System the 19th largest employer in the United States. Member plans provide most types of health insurance coverage, including Medicare HMOs.

More than 3.6 million federal employees and retirees enrolled in the Federal Health Benefits Program are Blue Cross and Blue Shield members, making legislation affecting federal employees a priority. The association also is interested in changes to Medicare and advocates full funding for Medicaid. Along with small business groups, it opposes a patients' rights proposal as unnecessary.

The Blue Cross and Blue Shield Association ranked second among health insurance PACs in contributions to 1996 congressional candidates. It favored Republican candidates by a greater than two-to-one margin and more than 86 percent of its contributions were spent on winning candidates. The leading recipients were Speaker Newt Gingrich, R-Ga., Sen. Paul Coverdell, R-Ga., and Rep. Richard M. Burr, R-N.C.

Minority Leader Richard A. Gephardt, D-Mo., and Rep. Earl Pomeroy, D-N.D., were the top Democratic recipients.

Eleven Blue Cross and Blue Shield state and regional associations contributed at least $5,000 to congressional campaigns during the 1995-96 election cycle. Most concentrated on candidates in their areas. Together, the 11 regional PACs spent $243,611 on congressional races. In addition, four other state association PACs were registered with the FEC but did not contribute $5,000.

CarePAC, The Blue Cross and Blue Shield Association Political Action Committee (C00194746) *Address: same as sponsor * Treasurer: Brenda Larsen Becker * Contact: Sharon L. Cohen, Congressional Relations Dir.*

	1993-94	*1995-96*	*1997*	*Totals*
Receipts	$335,073	$396,783	$221,928	$953,784
Disburse	350,032	373,575	211,977	935,584
Cash	25,099	48,312	59,264	n/a
Contributions	304,126	322,221	156,062	782,409
Republicans	112,345	222,446	101,562	436,353
No. of Cand.	*98*	*167*	*82*	*347*
House	65,745	154,332	67,062	287,139
Senate	46,600	68,114	34,500	149,214
Democrats	191,081	99,775	53,500	344,356
No. of Cand.	*136*	*89*	*50*	*275*
House	143,581	74,525	35,000	253,106
Senate	47,500	25,250	18,500	91,250
Incumbents	262,176	269,321	149,812	681,309
Challengers	13,750	10,100	2,500	26,350
Open Seat	27,200	42,800	3,750	73,750
Winners	247,676	279,621	n/a	527,297
Losers	56,450	42,600	n/a	99,050

WellPoint Health Networks (WellPAC) (C00197228) *Phone: (818) 712-6888 * Fax: (818) 703-4351 * 21555 Oxnard St., Woodland Hills, CA 91367 * Web: www.wellpoint.com * E-mail: cal.lockett@wellpoint.com * Treasurer: Susan Nagy * Contact: Callen M. Lockett, Chairperson*

WellPoint Health Networks is a publicly traded insurance company that operates under the Blue Cross Blue Shield name in California. Although the company operates outside of California under the name UNICARE, it is still considered an affiliate of Blue Cross Blue Shield's national PAC.

The company provides health insurance and related services to more than 6.1 million people nationwide. With 9,500 employees in 115 offices throughout the country, WellPoint had 1997 sales of $5.8 billion.

	1993-94	*1995-96*	*1997*	*Totals*
Receipts	$77,280	$106,583	$76,057	$259,920
Disburse	73,947	100,371	49,000	223,318
Cash	10,579	16,793	43,851	n/a
Contributions	56,950	67,850	34,000	158,800
Republicans	22,400	41,250	21,500	85,150
No. of Cand.	*17*	*20*	*22*	*59*
House	20,650	41,250	15,000	76,900
Senate	1,750	0	6,500	8,250
Democrats	34,550	26,600	12,500	73,650
No. of Cand.	*21*	*18*	*16*	*55*
House	31,050	25,600	11,000	67,650
Senate	3,500	1,000	1,500	6,000
Incumbents	55,700	64,600	29,000	149,300
Challengers	1,500	0	2,500	4,000
Open Seat	0	3,250	2,500	5,750
Winners	50,950	65,350	n/a	116,300
Losers	6,000	2,500	n/a	8,500

Blue Cross and Blue Shield of Michigan Political Action Committee (BCBSM PAC) (C00084061) *Phone: (313) 225-7828 * Fax: (313) 225-8667 * 600 Lafayette E., Suite 1920, Detroit, MI 48226 * Web: www.bcbsm.com * Treasurer: Dale Robertson * Contact: Robert Naftaly, Executive V.P. and COO*

	1993-94	*1995-96*	*1997*	*Totals*
Receipts	$264,997	$307,310	$172,776	$745,083
Disburse	251,390	240,500	120,717	612,607
Cash	54,221	121,033	173,093	n/a
Contributions	28,300	49,699	11,400	89,399
Republicans	7,600	11,500	500	19,600
No. of Cand.	*6*	*6*	*1*	*13*
House	2,600	7,500	500	10,600
Senate	5,000	4,000	0	9,000
Democrats	20,700	38,199	10,900	69,799
No. of Cand.	*16*	*13*	*7*	*36*
House	14,950	29,700	10,900	55,550
Senate	5,750	8,499	0	14,249
Incumbents	16,800	44,699	11,400	72,899
Challengers	0	5,000	0	5,000
Open Seat	11,500	0	0	11,500
Winners	23,300	48,699	n/a	71,999
Losers	5,000	1,000	n/a	6,000

Florida Health Political Action Committee (The PAC of Blue Cross & Blue Shield of Florida) (C00161141) *Phone: (904) 905-4561 * Fax: (904) 905-4593 * P.O. Box 6936, Jacksonville, FL 32236 * Web: www.bcbsfl.com * Treasurer: Kenneth L. Thurston * Contact: Anthony Benevento, Chairperson*

Blue Cross Blue Shield of Florida is one of the largest private employers in Florida. The company's net income for 1996 was $69.2 million. The company owns the largest and fastest-growing HMO in the state.

	1993-94	*1995-96*	*1997*	*Totals*
Receipts	$68,757	$81,667	$43,468	$193,892
Disburse	69,661	69,761	42,006	181,428
Cash	5,759	17,669	19,132	n/a
Contributions	25,150	21,750	19,000	65,900
Republicans	16,400	11,250	6,500	34,150
No. of Cand.	*19*	*13*	*10*	*42*
House	9,800	9,250	5,500	24,550
Senate	6,600	2,000	1,000	9,600
Democrats	8,750	10,500	12,500	31,750
No. of Cand.	*13*	*10*	*7*	*30*
House	8,750	9,000	6,500	24,250
Senate	0	1,500	6,000	7,500
Incumbents	19,900	16,750	19,000	55,650
Challengers	1,500	0	0	1,500
Open Seat	3,750	5,000	0	8,750
Winners	19,400	20,250	n/a	39,650
Losers	5,750	1,500	n/a	7,250

Blue PAC (Capital Independence Northeastern & Western Pennsylvania Blue Cross Plans PAC) (C00270967) *Phone: (717) 541-6135 * Fax: (717) 541-6696 * 2500 Elmerton Ave., Harrisburg, PA 17177-2531 * Treasurer: Vincent Carocci*

	1993-94	*1995-96*	*1997*	*Totals*
Receipts	$171,445	$226,342	$106,188	$503,975
Disburse	165,847	218,145	108,794	492,786
Cash	14,148	22,348	19,743	n/a
Contributions	23,559	17,550	2,000	43,109
Republicans	10,859	7,850	2,000	20,709
No. of Cand.	*8*	*10*	*3*	*21*
House	4,050	5,750	-500	9,300
Senate	6,809	2,100	2,500	11,409
Democrats	12,700	9,700	0	22,400
No. of Cand.	*14*	*9*	*0*	*23*
House	6,700	9,700	0	16,400
Senate	6,000	0	0	6,000
Incumbents	9,450	15,650	2,000	27,100
Challengers	8,059	350	0	8,409
Open Seat	2,550	1,550	0	4,100
Winners	13,109	16,700	n/a	29,809
Losers	10,450	850	n/a	11,300

Blue Cross and Blue Shield of Missouri Federal Government Affairs Committee (C00220608) *Phone: (314) 923-5039 * 1831 Chestnut St., St. Louis, MO 63103 * Web: www.abcbs.com * Treasurer: Mark Johnston*

	1993-94	*1995-96*	*1997*	*Totals*
Receipts	$36,794	$33,362	$6,416	$76,572
Disburse	36,460	35,920	6,050	78,430
Cash	4,724	2,168	2,534	n/a
Contributions	22,675	16,850	6,550	46,075
Republicans	7,900	5,750	4,550	18,200
No. of Cand.	*5*	*9*	*4*	*18*
House	3,100	5,000	4,300	12,400
Senate	4,800	750	250	5,800
Democrats	14,775	11,100	2,000	27,875
No. of Cand.	*12*	*7*	*1*	*20*
House	11,425	11,100	2,000	24,525
Senate	3,350	0	0	3,350

(Data for Blue Cross continued)

Incumbents	11,325	13,600	6,550	31,475
Challengers	0	0	0	0
Open Seat	10,750	3,000	0	13,750
Winners	18,725	15,000	n/a	33,725
Losers	3,950	1,850	n/a	5,800

Blue Cross and Blue Shield of Nebraska PAC (C00276311) *Phone: (402) 390-1819 * Fax: (402) 398-3737 * 7261 Mercy Rd., P.O. Box 3248, Omaha, NE 68180 * Treasurer: David V. Realph * Contact: G. Randy Boldt, PAC Dir.*

	1993-94	1995-96	1997	Totals
Receipts	$21,075	$25,594	$12,244	$58,913
Disburse	16,354	28,078	9,500	53,932
Cash	6,102	3,621	6,366	n/a
Contributions	6,625	15,562	3,000	25,187
Republicans	4,375	10,062	3,000	17,437
No. of Cand.	*4*	*4*	*2*	*10*
House	3,350	5,562	3,000	11,912
Senate	1,025	4,500	0	5,525
Democrats	2,250	5,500	0	7,750
No. of Cand.	*3*	*2*	*0*	*5*
House	1,200	500	0	1,700
Senate	1,050	5,000	0	6,050
Incumbents	3,600	5,562	500	9,662
Challengers	3,025	500	0	3,525
Open Seat	0	9,500	2,500	12,000
Winners	4,600	10,062	n/a	14,662
Losers	2,025	5,500	n/a	7,525

Blue Cross and Blue Shield of North Carolina Employee Political Action Committee - Federal (C00312223) *Phone: (919) 765-4119 * Fax: (919) 765-2432 * P.O. Box 2291, Durham, NC 27702 * Treasurer: Bradley T. Adcock * Contact: Beth Milchuck, PAC Dir.*

	1993-94	1995-96	1997	Totals
Receipts	$0	$76,042	$85,363	$161,405
Disburse	0	60,876	63,543	124,419
Cash	0	15,168	36,989	n/a
Contributions	0	11,500	8,000	19,500
Republicans	0	2,500	2,500	5,000
No. of Cand.	*0*	*3*	*2*	*5*
House	0	1,500	500	2,000
Senate	0	1,000	2,000	3,000
Democrats	0	9,000	5,500	14,500
No. of Cand.	*0*	*4*	*3*	*7*
House	0	9,000	5,500	14,500
Senate	0	0	0	0
Incumbents	0	3,500	8,000	11,500
Challengers	0	6,000	0	6,000
Open Seat	0	2,000	0	2,000
Winners	0	11,500	n/a	11,500
Losers	0	0	n/a	0

Blue Cross and Blue Shield of Maryland Employees' PAC (C00286922) *Phone: (410) 581-3000 * 10455 Mill Run Circle, Owings Mills, MD 21117 * Web: www.bcbsmd.com * Treasurer: Jeanne Kennedy*

	1993-94	1995-96	1997	Totals
Receipts	$8,952	$18,512	$10,221	$37,685
Disburse	8,058	17,500	11,675	37,233
Cash	895	1,910	457	n/a
Contributions	2,500	9,000	4,875	16,375
Republicans	250	2,000	500	2,750
No. of Cand.	*1*	*1*	*1*	*3*
House	250	2,000	500	2,750
Senate	0	0	0	0
Democrats	2,250	7,000	4,375	13,625
No. of Cand.	*4*	*6*	*3*	*13*
House	1,750	3,800	1,375	6,925
Senate	500	3,200	3,000	6,700
Incumbents	2,250	7,700	4,875	14,825
Challengers	0	300	0	300
Open Seat	250	1,000	0	1,250
Winners	2,500	8,700	n/a	11,200
Losers	0	300	n/a	300

Federal Health PAC of Pennsylvania Blue Shield (formerly known as Blue Health PAC) (C00302844) *Phone: (717) 763-3151 * 1800 Center St., Camp Hill, PA 17089 * Web: www.highmark.com * Treasurer: Donald L. Fisher*

	1993-94	1995-96	1997	Totals
Receipts	$0	$31,484	$85,938	$117,422
Disburse	0	23,790	54,403	78,193
Cash	0	7,697	39,232	n/a
Contributions	0	8,000	4,750	12,750
Republicans	0	7,250	2,500	9,750
No. of Cand.	*0*	*5*	*4*	*9*
House	0	6,000	1,500	7,500
Senate	0	1,250	1,000	2,250
Democrats	0	750	2,250	3,000
No. of Cand.	*0*	*1*	*3*	*4*
House	0	750	2,250	3,000
Senate	0	0	0	0
Incumbents	0	3,500	4,750	8,250
Challengers	0	0	0	0
Open Seat	0	4,500	0	4,500
Winners	0	8,000	n/a	8,000
Losers	0	0	n/a	0

Trigon Blue Cross Blue Shield Federal Political Action Committee (Trigon BCBS Federal PAC) (C00211375) *Phone: (804) 354-7000 * Fax: (804) 354-3399 * 2015 Staples Mill Rd., Richmond, VA 23230 * Web: www.trigon.com * Treasurer: Leonard L. Hopkins Jr.*

Trigon Healthcare Inc. changed its name from Blue Cross Blue Shield of Virginia because it plans to offer managed care services outside the state. The company went public in 1997 and is the largest managed care company in Virginia, serving about 1.9 million clients.

	1993-94	1995-96	1997	Totals
Receipts	$29,305	$30,261	$9,471	$69,037
Disburse	32,401	21,131	7,520	61,052
Cash	2,513	11,644	13,596	n/a
Contributions	11,700	7,450	4,000	23,150
Republicans	5,700	6,950	3,000	15,650
No. of Cand.	*6*	*5*	*3*	*14*
House	3,700	5,700	3,000	12,400
Senate	2,000	1,250	0	3,250
Democrats	6,000	500	1,000	7,500
No. of Cand.	*9*	*4*	*3*	*16*
House	4,000	1,500	1,000	6,500
Senate	2,000	-1000	0	1,000
Incumbents	8,450	7,950	4,000	20,400
Challengers	2,000	0	0	2,000
Open Seat	1,000	500	0	1,500
Winners	8,200	7,950	n/a	16,150
Losers	3,500	-500	n/a	3,000

Blue Cross and Blue Shield of Kansas City Federal PAC (C00301358) *Phone: (816) 395-2086 * Fax: (816) 395-2379 * One Pershing Square, 2301 Main St., Kansas City, MO 64108-2428 * Treasurer: B. Jeannie Brocato*

	1993-94	1995-96	1997	Totals
Receipts	$0	$13,685	$1,944	$15,629
Disburse	0	8,283	250	8,533
Cash	0	5,405	7,100	n/a
Contributions	0	5,250	250	5,500
Republicans	0	1,250	0	1,250
No. of Cand.	*0*	*3*	*0*	*3*
House	0	750	0	750
Senate	0	500	0	500
Democrats	0	4,000	250	4,250
No. of Cand.	*0*	*3*	*1*	*4*
House	0	4,000	250	4,250
Senate	0	0	0	0
Incumbents	0	4,500	250	4,750
Challengers	0	0	0	0
Open Seat	0	750	0	750
Winners	0	4,750	n/a	4,750
Losers	0	500	n/a	500

Contributed less than $5,000 during 1995-96 cycle:

Blue Cross & Blue Shield United of Wisconsin Political Action Committee (C00135202) *Phone: (414) 226-6201 * Fax: (414) 226-6229 * 401 W. Michigan St., C-10, Milwaukee, WI 53203 * Web: www.bcbsuw.org * Treasurer: Gail Hanson * Contact: Timothy Cullen, President of Gov. Programs*

Blue Cross and Blue Shield of Texas Inc. Federal Political Action Committee (C00236323) *Phone: (972) 766-6191 * Fax: (972) 766-6234 * 901 S. Central Expressway, Richardson, TX 75080 * Treasurer: Vernon Walker * Contact: John Comola, V.P. of Gov. Relations*

Blue Cross and Blue Shield of Utah Federal Political Action Committee (C00252684) *Phone: (801) 487-6441 * 2455 Parley's Way, Salt Lake City, UT 84109-0270 * Web: www.BCBSUtah.com * E-mail: bcbsuweb@regence.com * Treasurer: R. Paul Warburton*

Healthy Government Committee The Political Action Committee/Blue Cross & Blue Shield of Arizona (C00215202) *Phone: (602) 864-4676 * Fax: (602) 864-4242 * P.O. Box 13466, Phoenix, AZ 85002-3466 * Web: www.bcbsaz.com * E-mail: dhannon@phx1.bcbsaz.com * Treasurer: Tony A. Astorga * Contact: Richard Hannon, Chairman*

Brooke Holdings Inc.

*Phone: (517) 394-3400 * Fax: (517) 394-3505*
5901 Executive Dr., Lansing, MI 48911
Web: www.jacksonnational.com

Brooke Holdings' primary subsidiary, Jackson National Life Insurance Co., sells individual annuity products, including immediate and deferred annuities, variable annuities, guaranteed investment contracts, and individual life insurance products in 49 states and the District of Columbia. Total 1996 income for Jackson was $6.5 billion. Brooke Holdings is owned by Prudential Corp. of London, a public company.

Subsidiaries include: First Jackson National Life Insurance Company, Chrissy Corp., Jackson National Financial Services Inc. and Jackson National Life Distributors Inc. The company also owns 90 percent of the common stock for Jackson National Compania De Seguros De Vida S.A., a life insurance company in Argentina.

Brooke Holdings Inc. and Jackson National Life Insurance Co. Separate Segregated Fund (C00254953) *Address: same as sponsor * Treasurer: Robert A. Fritz*

	1993-94	1995-96	1997	Totals
Receipts	$43,108	$51,113	$31,760	$125,981
Disburse	36,616	60,934	18,271	115,821
Cash	24,251	14,435	27,580	n/a
Contributions	29,601	37,849	16,850	84,300
Republicans	13,351	32,949	12,850	59,150
No. of Cand.	*13*	*16*	*12*	*41*
House	9,101	25,449	10,850	45,400
Senate	4,250	7,500	2,000	13,750
Democrats	16,250	4,900	4,000	25,150
No. of Cand.	*15*	*7*	*6*	*28*
House	10,250	3,900	3,000	17,150
Senate	6,000	1,000	1,000	8,000
Incumbents	19,350	32,249	15,550	67,149
Challengers	3,501	5,500	0	9,001
Open Seat	6,750	100	1,000	7,850
Winners	18,850	21,250	n/a	40,100
Losers	10,751	16,599	n/a	27,350

Business Men's Assurance Co. of America

*Phone: (816) 753-8000 * Fax: (816) 751-5561*
P.O. Box 419458, Kansas City, MO 64141

Business Men's Assurance is a private company that provides life and health insurance through 20 locations throughout the United States, excluding New York. The company has about 600 employees and had total sales of $756 million in 1997.

Business Men's Assurance Co. of America PAC-Federal (BMA-PAC Federal) (C00120089) *Address: same as sponsor * Treasurer: Susan A. Sweeney*

	1993-94	1995-96	1997	Totals
Receipts	$24,388	$16,272	$5,835	$46,495
Disburse	31,475	13,950	3,500	48,925
Cash	12,600	14,926	17,262	n/a
Contributions	19,375	7,950	500	27,825
Republicans	10,375	4,250	500	15,125
No. of Cand.	*7*	*5*	*1*	*13*
House	6,375	3,250	500	10,125
Senate	4,000	1,000	0	5,000
Democrats	9,000	3,700	0	12,700
No. of Cand.	*5*	*2*	*0*	*7*
House	6,000	3,700	0	9,700
Senate	3,000	0	0	3,000
Incumbents	8,000	5,700	500	14,200
Challengers	1,750	250	0	2,000
Open Seat	9,625	2,000	0	11,625
Winners	14,750	6,700	n/a	21,450
Losers	4,625	1,250	n/a	5,875

CIGNA Corp.

*Phone: (215) 761-6223 * Fax: (215) 761-5522*
One Liberty Place, P.O. Box 7716, Philadelphia, PA 19192
Web: www.cigna.com

CIGNA is a public company that provides health, life and accident insurance and investment services worldwide. Its eight groups include CIGNA Group Insurance, CIGNA HealthCare, CIGNA Property & Casualty and CIGNA Retirement & Investment Services.

The company ranks among the largest investor-owned insurance organizations in the United States, with shareholders' equity of $7.2 billion. It also is one of the largest U.S.-based insurers active in international markets, as measured by international revenues of $3.1 billion in 1996.

CIGNA's principal subsidiaries are Connecticut General Life Insurance Co. and Insurance Co. of North America in Philadelphia. The CIGNA HealthCare unit has 5.4 million HMO members in 30 states; the firm's indemnity business includes coverage of 6.6 million people for medical indemnity and 10.5 million for dental indemnity. The company has 42,800 employees and reported 1996 sales of $18.9 billion.

CIGNA opposes insurance-specific taxes and restrictions on managed care programs. It will lobby for changes in U.S. taxes on its foreign operations. The company supports Medical Savings Accounts and changes in Medicare that would allow seniors to enroll in competing plans. As an insurer, CIGNA supports Superfund reform.

CIGNA ranked third in 1996 among insurance businesses and associations in total contributions to congressional candidates. Of the 162 candidates it gave to, only five received $5,000 or more, and four of those were Senate candidates. Ninety percent of CIGNA's money went to Republicans.

Cigna Corp. Political Action Committee (C00085316) *Phone: (202) 296-7174 * Fax: (202) 296-2521 * 2001 Pennsylvania Ave. N.W., Suite 350, Washington, DC 20006-1825 * Treasurer: Paul Rohrkemper * Contact: A. J. Harris, V.P. of Federal Affairs*

	1993-94	1995-96	1997	Totals
Receipts	$350,099	$369,054	$219,615	$938,768
Disburse	371,931	382,171	144,377	898,479
Cash	38,171	25,062	100,306	n/a
Contributions	211,575	230,300	89,300	531,175
Republicans	140,075	207,300	75,500	422,875
No. of Cand.	*115*	*139*	*68*	*322*
House	82,075	129,300	44,000	255,375
Senate	58,000	78,000	31,500	167,500
Democrats	71,500	23,000	13,800	108,300
No. of Cand.	*41*	*23*	*14*	*78*
House	51,000	21,000	8,800	80,800
Senate	20,500	2,000	5,000	27,500
Incumbents	153,475	162,250	85,000	400,725
Challengers	31,500	18,250	1,000	50,750
Open Seat	26,600	49,800	3,300	79,700
Winners	170,325	162,750	n/a	333,075
Losers	41,250	67,550	n/a	108,800

Chubb Corp.

*Phone: (908) 903-3556 * Fax: (908) 903-2955*
15 Mountain View Rd., P.O. Box 1615, Warren, NJ 07061-1615
Web: www.chubb.com

Chubb is a public holding company that sells property and casualty insurance to companies and personal insurance policies. It also offers specialized business insurance. The company sold its health and life insurance businesses in 1997.

The company provides insurance coverage principally in the United States, Canada, Europe, Australia and the Far East. Chubb reported $6.6 billion in revenues during 1997. The company has about 11,500 employees.

Its subsidiaries are Chubb & Son, which offers management services, and Bellemead Development Corp., a real estate developer.

Chubb Corp. Political Action Committee (ChubbPAC) (C00229203) *Address: same as sponsor * Treasurer: Henry G. Gulick * Contact: Robert Rufis, President*

	1993-94	1995-96	1997	Totals
Receipts	$245,480	$267,047	$121,029	$633,556
Disburse	209,909	302,531	121,156	633,596
Cash	42,451	6,968	6,842	n/a
Contributions	116,600	186,099	84,100	386,799
Republicans	55,650	140,849	49,600	246,099
No. of Cand.	*43*	*95*	*48*	*186*
House	28,650	84,100	28,100	140,850
Senate	27,000	56,749	21,500	105,249
Democrats	60,950	45,250	34,500	140,700
No. of Cand.	*43*	*34*	*23*	*100*
House	38,950	32,000	15,500	86,450
Senate	22,000	13,250	19,000	54,250
Incumbents	106,100	155,349	83,600	345,049
Challengers	6,000	3,200	0	9,200

(Data for Chubb Corp. Political continued)

Open Seat	4,500	27,550	1,500	33,550
Winners	101,100	153,849	n/a	254,949
Losers	15,500	32,250	n/a	47,750

Community Mutual Insurance Co.

37 W. Broad St., Suite 980, Columbus, OH 43215

The Community Insurance PAC filed for termination in January 1998.

Community Insurance Co. Good Government Program (C00294645) *Address: same as sponsor * Treasurer: James T. Parker*

	1993-94	1995-96	1997	Totals
Receipts	$28,167	$108,055	$2,470	$138,692
Disburse	12,825	112,805	13,438	139,068
Cash	15,341	10,543	0	n/a
Contributions	2,000	5,050	1,400	8,450
Republicans	1,500	5,050	1,400	7,950
No. of Cand.	*2*	*9*	*3*	*14*
House	500	3,050	400	3,950
Senate	1,000	2,000	1,000	4,000
Democrats	500	0	0	500
No. of Cand.	*1*	*0*	*0*	*1*
House	500	0	0	500
Senate	0	0	0	0
Incumbents	500	3,000	650	4,150
Challengers	0	2,000	0	2,000
Open Seat	1,500	0	750	2,250
Winners	1,500	3,000	n/a	4,500
Losers	500	2,050	n/a	2,550

Conseco Inc.

*Phone: (317) 817-6100 * Fax: (317) 817-2246*
11825 N. Pennsylvania St., Carmel, IN 46032
Web: www.conseco.com

Conseco, through its subsidiaries, is one of the nation's leading providers of supplemental health insurance, retirement annuities and universal life insurance.

With more than 9 million policyholders nationwide, the company had 1997 annual revenues of $5.6 billion, and nearly $36 billion in assets. A public company, Conseco's 7,000 officers, directors and employees own about 25 percent of the company's stock.

Founded in Carmel, Ind., in 1979, the company now maintains additional corporate offices in Chicago, Rockford, Ill., and Philadelphia.

From July 1996 to February 1998, Conseco grew dramatically, acquiring more than seven companies worth more than $4 billion. Among the companies acquired were American Travelers Corp., a leading provider of long-term care insurance, and Transport Holdings Inc., a leading provider of cancer insurance.

Other subsidiaries include: Bankers Life and Casualty, Great American Reserve, National Fidelity Life Insurance, American Life and Casualty Insurance, and Lincoln American Life Insurance. Conseco Risk Management, a property and casualty insurance agency, became, in 1996, the largest insurance company of its kind in Indiana and among the 50 largest in the nation. The company also owns and operates Conseco Fund Group, a mutual fund company, and Conseco Capital Management, an investment management firm.

Conseco Inc.-Bankers Life Concerned Citizens PAC (also known as Conseco Inc.-Bankers Life Concerned Citizen PAC) (C00303503) *Address: same as sponsor * Treasurer: Rollin M. Dick * Contact: Steve Robertson, V.P. of Gov. Relations*

	1993-94	1995-96	1997	Totals
Receipts	$0	$146,686	$77,661	$224,347
Disburse	0	122,520	15,600	138,120
Cash	0	24,174	86,240	n/a
Contributions	0	70,000	5,000	75,000
Republicans	0	53,000	0	53,000
No. of Cand.	*0*	*18*	*0*	*18*
House	0	42,000	0	42,000
Senate	0	11,000	0	11,000
Democrats	0	17,000	5,000	22,000
No. of Cand.	*0*	*4*	*1*	*5*
House	0	6,000	0	6,000
Senate	0	11,000	5,000	16,000
Incumbents	0	34,000	0	34,000
Challengers	0	5,000	0	5,000
Open Seat	0	31,000	5,000	36,000
Winners	0	47,000	n/a	47,000
Losers	0	23,000	n/a	23,000

Council of Insurance Agents & Brokers

*Phone: (202) 783-4400 x222 * Fax: (202) 783-4410*
701 Pennsylvania Ave. N.W., Suite 750, Washington, DC 20004
*Web: www.ciab.com * E-mail: kcrerar@ciab.com*

The Council of Insurance Agents & Brokers represents more than 3,000 property and casualty insurance agencies and 260 brokerage firms in the United States.

Members of the council place 75 percent of U.S. commercial property and casualty premiums annually. The group is exploring a merger with the National Association of Insurance Brokers.

The CIAB is interested in Superfund, financial services modernization and legislation affecting the managed care industry.

The Council of Insurance Agents & Brokers Political Action Committee (C00039578) *Address: same as sponsor * Treasurer: Ken A. Crerar*

	1993-94	1995-96	1997	Totals
Receipts	$209,863	$228,684	$103,592	$542,139
Disburse	196,611	258,320	106,553	561,484
Cash	81,789	52,155	45,634	n/a
Contributions	169,623	211,865	103,885	485,373
Republicans	100,329	164,462	78,935	343,726
No. of Cand.	*89*	*120*	*72*	*281*
House	68,054	125,862	64,435	258,351
Senate	32,275	38,600	14,500	85,375
Democrats	69,294	47,403	24,450	141,147
No. of Cand.	*57*	*30*	*24*	*111*
House	48,674	29,657	18,450	96,781
Senate	20,620	17,746	6,000	44,366
Incumbents	116,805	159,425	97,385	373,615
Challengers	22,768	10,643	500	33,911
Open Seat	29,550	41,797	6,000	77,347
Winners	126,205	175,655	n/a	301,860
Losers	43,418	36,210	n/a	79,628

Delta Dental Plans Association

*Phone: (630) 574-6001 * Fax: (630) 574-6999*
1515 W. 22nd St., Suite 1200, Oak Brook, IL 60521
Web: www.deltadental.com

Delta Dental Plans Association is a national organization made up of local plans that provide groups and businesses with dental benefits coverage.

Founded in 1954, the organization is the largest dental benefits carrier in the nation. Its members provide dental coverage to nearly one of every four Americans with dental insurance through more than 31,000 client groups. Delta Dental pays about 25 percent of total claims paid annually by all dental carriers.

Delta Dental's clients include Lockheed Martin, Toyota, Boeing, the Screen Actors Guild and many state and local governments.

Delta Dental Plans Association PAC (DeltaPAC) (C00213819) *Address: same as sponsor * Treasurer: Stephen E. White*

	1993-94	1995-96	1997	Totals
Receipts	$65,766	$78,188	$34,316	$178,270
Disburse	76,159	40,547	23,440	140,146
Cash	15,672	53,314	64,190	n/a
Contributions	64,350	33,500	23,100	120,950
Republicans	8,600	20,200	17,100	45,900
No. of Cand.	*9*	*21*	*13*	*43*
House	2,600	11,200	9,100	22,900
Senate	6,000	9,000	8,000	23,000
Democrats	55,750	13,300	6,000	75,050
No. of Cand.	*46*	*21*	*6*	*73*
House	42,250	10,300	3,000	55,550
Senate	13,500	3,000	3,000	19,500
Incumbents	58,350	31,500	23,100	112,950
Challengers	2,000	1,500	0	3,500
Open Seat	4,000	500	0	4,500
Winners	55,350	28,500	n/a	83,850
Losers	9,000	5,000	n/a	14,000

The Doctors' Co.

*Phone: (707) 226-0357 * Fax: (707) 226-0153*
185 Greenwood Rd., Napa, CA 94558
Web: www.thedoctors.com

The Doctors' Co. is the nation's largest professional liability insurer owned by physicians. It provides coverage to more than 20,000 doctors across the nation.

The private company supports a governmental relations program designed to monitor liability and insurance legislation on the state and federal levels.

Formed in 1976, the company has several publications including the Risk Management quarterly newsletter, The Doctors' Advocate and special bulletins on topics of vital interest to physicians.

In January 1998, TDC entered into a partnership with California Advantage Inc., a physician-owned managed care organization. Under the agreement, TDC will provide financial backing to California Advantage, which will in turn work with TDC to market TDC coverage to California Advantage doctors.

The Doctors' Co. Federal PAC (DocPAC) (C00300376) *Address: same as sponsor * Treasurer: James Cathcart*

	1993-94	1995-96	1997	Totals
Receipts	$0	$30,375	$2,293	$32,668
Disburse	0	26,426	3,500	29,926
Cash	0	3,950	2,758	n/a
Contributions	0	19,100	1,000	20,100
Republicans	0	16,850	1,000	17,850
No. of Cand.	*0*	*20*	*1*	*21*
House	0	10,350	1,000	11,350
Senate	0	6,500	0	6,500
Democrats	0	2,250	0	2,250
No. of Cand.	*0*	*3*	*0*	*3*
House	0	2,250	0	2,250
Senate	0	0	0	0
Incumbents	0	12,500	1,000	13,500
Challengers	0	2,250	0	2,250
Open Seat	0	4,350	0	4,350
Winners	0	13,100	n/a	13,100
Losers	0	6,000	n/a	6,000

The Equitable Companies

*Phone: (212) 314-3185 * Fax: (212) 707-1755*
1290 Ave. of the Americas, 17th Floor, New York, NY 10104
Web: www.equitable.com

The Equitable is a publicly held international financial services corporation operating in the insurance and investment management and banking industries.

The New York-based corporation employed nearly 15,000 people and reported $8.3 billion in revenues during 1996. The primary operation of the corporation is the Equitable Life Assurance Society of the United States, which provides financial planning, life insurance and annuities. At the end of 1996, the society had more than $230 billion worth of life insurance contracts.

Subsidiaries include the Equitable Life Assurance Society of the United States; Alliance Capital Management; and Donaldson, Lufkin & Jenrette. The Equitable is a part of AXA, a French insurance and financial services company.

Equitable Companies Inc. Political Action Committee (C00161901) *Address: same as sponsor * Treasurer: Paul J. Flora * Contact: Derry Bishop, Chairman*

	1993-94	1995-96	1997	Totals
Receipts	$93,069	$138,077	$91,959	$323,105
Disburse	53,030	169,700	78,000	300,730
Cash	71,591	39,974	53,935	n/a
Contributions	34,000	138,500	56,000	228,500
Republicans	6,000	101,500	26,000	133,500
No. of Cand.	*7*	*61*	*20*	*88*
House	3,000	67,500	12,000	82,500
Senate	3,000	34,000	14,000	51,000
Democrats	28,000	37,000	30,000	95,000
No. of Cand.	*19*	*18*	*16*	*53*
House	14,000	29,500	18,000	61,500
Senate	14,000	7,500	12,000	33,500
Incumbents	30,500	108,000	53,000	191,500
Challengers	3,500	8,500	0	12,000
Open Seat	0	22,000	3,000	25,000
Winners	31,500	111,500	n/a	143,000
Losers	2,500	27,000	n/a	29,500

Donaldson, Lufkin & Jenrette Inc. Better Government Fund (C00103325) *Phone: (212) 892-4730 * Fax: (212) 892-2608 * 277 Park Ave., New York, NY 10172 * Web: www.dlj.com * Treasurer: Anthony F. Daddino * Contact: John S. Chalsty, Chairman*

Donaldson, Lufkin & Jenrette, a subsidiary of the Equitable Companies, is a publicly held investment and merchant bank that serves institutional, corporate, governmental and individual clients. Based in New York City, DL&J has total capital of more than $4.5 billion.

The company functions as a holding company conducting its business through its principal broker-dealer subsidiary, Donaldson, Lufkin & Jenrette Securities Corp. Its businesses include: securities underwriting, sales and trading, merchant banking, financial advisory services, investment research, correspondent brokerage services and asset management.

	1993-94	1995-96	1997	Totals
Receipts	$64,460	$93,208	$8,960	$166,628
Disburse	67,171	68,064	9,250	144,485
Cash	1,716	26,859	26,569	n/a
Contributions	6,500	21,227	4,000	31,727
Republicans	3,000	15,727	2,000	20,727
No. of Cand.	*2*	*4*	*1*	*7*
House	2,000	0	0	2,000
Senate	1,000	15,727	2,000	18,727
Democrats	3,500	5,500	2,000	11,000
No. of Cand.	*5*	*3*	*1*	*9*
House	2,000	4,500	0	6,500
Senate	1,500	1,000	2,000	4,500
Incumbents	5,000	17,500	2,000	24,500
Challengers	2,000	0	2,000	4,000
Open Seat	0	3,727	0	3,727
Winners	1,000	17,500	n/a	18,500
Losers	5,500	3,727	n/a	9,227

Farmers Mutual Hail Insurance Co. of Iowa

Phone: (515) 282-9104
2323 Grand Ave., Des Moines, IA 50312
Web: www.fmh.com

Farmers Mutual Hail Insurance Co. of Iowa insures farmers against hail damage to crops in Arkansas, Missouri, Nebraska, Kansas, Colorado, North and South Dakota, Minnesota, Michigan, Wisconsin, Illinois, Indiana, Iowa and Ohio.

Founded in 1893 and owned by its policy holders, Farmers Mutual is the largest strictly crop hail insurance company in the United States, with $178 million in assets. A minority of its business is providing reinsurance to other insurance companies. It also operates Farmers Union Cooperative of Nebraska.

Farmers Mutual Hail Insurance Co. of Iowa Political Action Committee (FMH PAC) (C00117614) *Address: same as sponsor * Treasurer: Ken Felton * Contact: William A. Rutledge, President*

	1993-94	1995-96	1997	Totals
Receipts	$13,084	$17,349	$8,375	$38,808
Disburse	9,973	15,227	7,505	32,705
Cash	22,731	24,857	25,728	n/a
Contributions	5,200	8,600	3,000	16,800
Republicans	4,000	6,400	2,500	12,900
No. of Cand.	*5*	*8*	*4*	*17*
House	3,500	3,900	1,500	8,900
Senate	500	2,500	1,000	4,000
Democrats	1,200	2,200	500	3,900
No. of Cand.	*3*	*3*	*1*	*7*
House	700	200	0	900
Senate	500	2,000	500	3,000
Incumbents	4,700	5,600	3,000	13,300
Challengers	500	1,500	0	2,000
Open Seat	0	1,500	0	1,500
Winners	4,200	6,850	n/a	11,050
Losers	1,000	1,750	n/a	2,750

Fireman's Fund Insurance Co.

*Phone: (415) 899-2000 * Fax: (415) 899-3263*
777 San Marin Dr., Novato, CA 94998
*Web: www.the-fund.com * E-mail: the-fund@ffic.com*

Fireman's Fund Insurance provides both business and personal insurance services. The $12 billion company employs 8,000 workers, with an additional 6,000 independent agents nationwide.

Fireman's Fund, founded in 1863, was a publicly owned company until it was purchased in 1991 by Alianz A.G. of Munich, Germany. Alianz is one of the largest property and casualty insurers in the world.

With more than $12 billion in invested assets, including $10 billion in liabilities and $2 billion in policy surplus, Fireman's Fund handled more than 15,000 catastrophe claims in 1997.

Fireman's Fund Insurance Co. Employees Committee for Responsible Government (FundPAC) (C00095109) *Phone: (202) 785-3575 * Fax: (202) 785-3023 * 1101 Connecticut Ave. N.W., Suite 950, Washington, DC 20036 * Treasurer: Deborah J. Nosowsky * Contact: Peter Leskin, Senior V.P.*

	1993-94	1995-96	1997	Totals
Receipts	$75,512	$69,504	$30,511	$175,527
Disburse	89,418	74,993	28,965	193,376
Cash	17,155	11,673	13,220	n/a
Contributions	69,900	64,100	23,125	157,125
Republicans	36,050	45,650	14,350	96,050
No. of Cand.	*47*	*63*	*25*	*135*
House	24,800	38,050	11,650	74,500
Senate	11,250	7,600	2,700	21,550
Democrats	33,850	18,450	8,775	61,075
No. of Cand.	*36*	*22*	*14*	*72*
House	27,350	15,950	7,050	50,350
Senate	6,500	2,500	1,725	10,725
Incumbents	55,100	50,500	22,725	128,325
Challengers	2,850	3,300	400	6,550
Open Seat	10,950	10,050	0	21,000
Winners	58,850	49,550	n/a	108,400
Losers	11,050	14,550	n/a	25,600

First Allmerica Financial Life Insurance Co.

*Phone: (508) 855-2664 * Fax: (508) 852-7588*
440 Lincoln St., Worcester, MA 01653
Web: www.allmerica.com

First Allmerica Financial Life Insurance, through its many subsidiaries, offers a variety of insurance products and financial services.

Based in Massachusetts, First Allmerica is a public company with more than 7,000 agents throughout the United States. The company, which was established in 1844 under the name State Mutual Life Assurance Co. of Worcester, now has total assets of more than $19 billion. The company reported 1997 revenues of $3.4 billion.

Subsidiaries include The Hanover Insurance Company; AMGRO Inc.; Sterling Risk Management Services Inc.; Citizens Corp.; Citizens Insurance Co. of America; and Citizens Management Inc.

First Allmerica Financial Life Insurance Co. Federal PAC (Allmerica Federal PAC) (C00169516) *Address: same as sponsor * Treasurer: Richard J. Baker * Contact: John F. O'Brien, Chairman*

	1993-94	1995-96	1997	Totals
Receipts	$21,457	$29,182	$9,185	$59,824
Disburse	17,934	24,388	10,377	52,699
Cash	4,141	8,938	7,747	n/a
Contributions	8,100	14,375	5,350	27,825
Republicans	5,300	13,275	3,750	22,325
No. of Cand.	*7*	*21*	*5*	*33*
House	3,850	6,125	3,750	13,725
Senate	1,450	7,150	0	8,600
Democrats	2,800	1,100	1,600	5,500
No. of Cand.	*5*	*2*	*3*	*10*
House	2,800	100	1,600	4,500
Senate	0	1,000	0	1,000
Incumbents	6,650	5,850	4,350	16,850
Challengers	0	3,750	1,000	4,750
Open Seat	1,450	4,775	0	6,225
Winners	8,000	6,100	n/a	14,100
Losers	100	8,275	n/a	8,375

First Health Group Corp.

*Phone: (630) 241-7511 * Fax: (630) 719-0093*
3200 S. Highland Ave., Downers Grove, IL 60515-1282
Web: www.firsthealth.com

First Health Group, formerly known as HealthCare COMPARE, is a national managed care organization that claims to have the largest integrated Preferred Provider Organization in the country.

With 1,500 employees nationwide, the company had almost $390 million in revenues in 1997.

The company specializes in offering national, integrated health care cost-management products to companies that operate in numerous sites throughout the country. First Health also offers stand-alone managed care products to employers, government employee groups, unions and group health and workers' compensation insurance carriers.

Through its medical networks, the company serves customers in 49 states, with 2,100 hospitals and 181,000 outpatient care providers under direct contract. This represents about 40 percent of all inpatient beds in the country and 30 percent of all physicians in private practice, according to the company.

First Health Group Corp. PAC (FHGPAC) (C00217216) *Address: same as sponsor * Treasurer: Joseph E. Whitters*

	1993-94	1995-96	1997	Totals
Receipts	$149,900	$192,810	$108,130	$450,840
Disburse	54,058	119,579	81,346	254,983
Cash	129,829	203,088	229,871	n/a
Contributions	39,058	90,046	53,998	183,102
Republicans	16,500	53,552	33,995	104,047
No. of Cand.	*16*	*41*	*26*	*83*
House	8,500	40,552	25,495	74,547
Senate	8,000	13,000	8,500	29,500
Democrats	22,558	36,494	20,003	79,055
No. of Cand.	*27*	*29*	*19*	*75*
House	20,558	27,994	11,003	59,555
Senate	2,000	8,500	9,000	19,500
Incumbents	33,058	77,046	51,498	161,602
Challengers	500	2,500	1,500	4,500
Open Seat	5,500	10,000	1,000	16,500
Winners	30,058	77,546	n/a	107,604
Losers	9,000	12,500	n/a	21,500

Franklin Life

Franklin Square, Springfield, IL 62713

Franklin Life Employees' Campaign Fund filed for termination in June 1997.

Franklin Life Employees' Campaign Fund (C00182246) *Address: same as sponsor * Treasurer: Earl W. Baucom*

	1993-94	1995-96	1997	Totals
Receipts	$12,520	$12,229	$0	$24,749
Disburse	15,156	19,271	0	34,427
Cash	4,039	0	0	n/a
Contributions	1,550	5,500	0	7,050
Republicans	550	4,500	0	5,050
No. of Cand.	*2*	*2*	*0*	*4*
House	550	1,500	0	2,050
Senate	0	3,000	0	3,000
Democrats	1,000	1,000	0	2,000
No. of Cand.	*1*	*1*	*0*	*2*
House	1,000	0	0	1,000
Senate	0	1,000	0	1,000
Incumbents	1,350	0	0	1,350
Challengers	200	0	0	200
Open Seat	0	5,500	0	5,500
Winners	1,000	2,500	n/a	3,500
Losers	550	3,000	n/a	3,550

GEICO Corp.

*Phone: (301) 986-2757 * Fax: (301) 986-3225*
One Geico Plaza, Washington, DC 20076
*Web: www.geico.com * E-mail: smithw@ibm.net*

GEICO is one of the largest U.S. auto insurers, and one of the few companies that relies on auto insurance for its primary revenues. The company is owned by billionaire Warren Buffett's investment firm, Berkshire Hathaway.

GEICO also offers motorcycle and overseas insurance, as well as emergency road services. Its 1997 revenues were $2.7 billion. The company employs 9,700 people and is the holding company for Government Employees Insurance Co.

In January 1998, GEICO announced its plans to invest $36.5 million in a new call center in Macon, Ga., and add about 2,000 new jobs to its current work force.

GEICO PAC (C00142828) *Address: same as sponsor * Treasurer: Michael Campbell * Contact: Walter Smith, Chairman*

	1993-94	1995-96	1997	Totals
Receipts	$29,129	$49,495	$21,756	$100,380
Disburse	45,850	42,931	14,150	102,931
Cash	5,594	12,158	19,764	n/a
Contributions	3,700	22,000	7,250	32,950
Republicans	3,200	20,000	6,750	29,950
No. of Cand.	*5*	*31*	*9*	*45*
House	3,200	12,050	2,750	18,000
Senate	0	7,950	4,000	11,950
Democrats	500	2,000	500	3,000
No. of Cand.	*1*	*1*	*1*	*3*
House	500	2,000	500	3,000
Senate	0	0	0	0
Incumbents	2,750	11,650	6,250	20,650
Challengers	500	4,850	0	5,350
Open Seat	450	5,500	1,000	6,950
Winners	2,950	14,700	n/a	17,650
Losers	750	7,300	n/a	8,050

General American Life Insurance Co.

*Phone: (314) 444-0634 * Fax: (314) 444-0510*
700 Market St., St. Louis, MO 63101
*Web: www.genam.com * E-mail: bbanstetter@genam.com*

General American Life Insurance provides individual and group life and health, as well as retirement plans and investment services. The company is one of the nation's 50 largest life insurers.

The private company has about 425,000 life insurance and annuities customers. Founded in 1933, the company had about $300 billion worth of life insurance policies as of June 1997, and total assets of $20 billion as of May 1997. General American Life employs about 4,300 people.

The largest life insurance company in Missouri, General American operates through a network of general agencies and group sales offices as well as through some 50 affiliated companies. General American and its subsidiaries are licensed in 50 states, Puerto Rico, the District of Columbia and 10 Canadian provinces.

General American Life Insurance is a wholly owned subsidiary of General American Mutual Holding Company, which is owned by its policyholders.

The company's subsidiaries include Reinsurance Group of America, one of the largest providers of life reinsurance in the nation, GenMark Inc., Walnut Street Securities, Cova Corp., Conning Corp., Paragon Life Insurance Co., Security Equity Life Insurance Co. and Consultec Inc., which aids in the administration of state and federal government welfare programs, including Medicaid. The company also owns Genelco, a 23-year-old company that provides services and software to businesses.

General American Life Insurance Co. Associates Federal Political Action Committee (C00111773) *Address: same as sponsor * Treasurer: Milton F. Svetanics * Contact: Robert J. Banstetter, President*

	1993-94	1995-96	1997	Totals
Receipts	$118,936	$130,592	$70,450	$319,978
Disburse	110,800	132,250	50,500	293,550
Cash	23,582	21,929	41,880	n/a
Contributions	78,800	64,450	24,500	167,750
Republicans	57,500	48,200	24,000	129,700
No. of Cand.	*33*	*34*	*16*	*83*
House	14,500	19,500	13,500	47,500
Senate	43,000	28,700	10,500	82,200
Democrats	21,300	16,250	500	38,050
No. of Cand.	*15*	*14*	*1*	*30*
House	16,800	15,750	500	33,050
Senate	4,500	500	0	5,000
Incumbents	46,800	55,950	24,500	127,250
Challengers	6,500	3,500	0	10,000
Open Seat	25,000	5,000	0	30,000
Winners	70,300	50,450	n/a	120,750
Losers	8,500	14,000	n/a	22,500

Golden Rule Financial Corp.

*Phone: (317) 297-4123 * Fax: (317) 297-0908*
7440 Woodland Dr., Indianapolis, IN 46278
Web: www.goldenrule.com

Golden Rule Financial is a private insurer offering life and health insurance to individuals and groups. The company has become one of the nation's most profitable insurers of individuals — especially those who are self-employed or work for companies without insurance plans.

More than 750,000 Americans own Golden Rule life insurance, group and individual health insurance, or annuities. The company had profits of $663 million in 1996 and employs 1,125 workers.

Golden Rule has been a proponent of Medical Savings Accounts, which would permit individuals to withdraw from Medicare and contribute money to pay for their own health care. Opponents have argued that allowing MSAs would remove healthy seniors from the insurance pool, driving up rates for those who remained.

Golden Rule and its chairman, J. Patrick Rooney, have been consistent contributors to House Speaker Newt Gingrich, R-Ga., and other Republican candidates and committees. The company has contributed more than $130,000 in "soft money" to Republican Party committees since 1995.

A Nov. 1995 Dallas Morning News article quoted a Golden Rule Life Insurance spokesman as saying, "The only way you get heard in D.C. is making political contributions."

Golden Rule Financial Corp. - Political Action Committee (C00231407) *Address: same as sponsor * Treasurer: Patrick F. Carr*

	1993-94	1995-96	1997	Totals
Receipts	$191,043	$174,312	$87,644	$452,999
Disburse	189,865	181,166	51,895	422,926
Cash	10,429	3,788	39,538	n/a
Contributions	126,000	94,560	7,400	227,960
Republicans	97,000	90,560	4,900	192,460
No. of Cand.	*81*	*48*	*7*	*136*
House	45,000	65,560	2,900	113,460
Senate	52,000	25,000	2,000	79,000
Democrats	29,000	4,000	2,500	35,500
No. of Cand.	*39*	*3*	*3*	*45*
House	19,500	1,000	1,500	22,000
Senate	9,500	3,000	1,000	13,500
Incumbents	76,500	74,560	6,650	157,710
Challengers	14,500	8,000	750	23,250
Open Seat	35,000	11,500	0	46,500
Winners	116,000	68,560	n/a	184,560
Losers	10,000	26,000	n/a	36,000

Grange Mutual Casualty Co.

*Phone: (614) 445-2698 * Fax: (614) 445-2428*
650 S. Front St., Columbus, OH 43206
Web: www.grangeinsurance.com

Grange Mutual Casualty is an insurance company based in Columbus, Ohio. It is owned and run by the Grange Mutual Family of Companies, which also includes Grange Life Insurance and Grange Guardian.

The company offers life, property and casualty insurance in Ohio, Indiana, Illinois, Kentucky, Tennessee and Georgia. Grange is a member of the National Association of Mutual Insurance Companies.

Grange Mutual Casualty Co. PAC (C00302695) *Address: same as sponsor * Treasurer: Larry Wolpert*

	1993-94	1995-96	1997	Totals
Receipts	$0	$11,558	$6,963	$18,521
Disburse	0	7,277	5,250	12,527
Cash	0	4,283	5,997	n/a
Contributions	0	5,250	2,000	7,250
Republicans	0	5,250	2,000	7,250
No. of Cand.	*0*	*7*	*2*	*9*
House	0	3,750	2,000	5,750
Senate	0	1,500	0	1,500
Democrats	0	0	0	0
No. of Cand.	*0*	*0*	*0*	*0*
House	0	0	0	0
Senate	0	0	0	0
Incumbents	0	5,250	2,000	7,250
Challengers	0	0	0	0
Open Seat	0	0	0	0
Winners	0	4,250	n/a	4,250
Losers	0	1,000	n/a	1,000

Great-West Life Assurance Co.

*Phone: (800) 537-2033 * Fax: (303) 689-5997*
8515 E. Orchard Rd., Englewood, CO 80111
Web: www.gwla.com

The $19.4 billion Great-West Life & Annuity Insurance is a wholly owned subsidiary of Canadian insurance giant The Great-West Life Assurance Co. That company is part of the Power Financial group.

GWL&A provides managed care, life and disability insurance, 401(k) and IRA plans to 9,000 companies and is licensed in every state except New York. Its HMO, One Health Plan, is active in Colorado, Georgia, Illinois, Texas and California.

The 5,000-person, Colorado-based company has offices throughout the United States. Its programs are also distributed through The New England, The Guardian and Trustmark.

Subsidiaries include: FASCorp, Benefits Communication Corp, One Corp., GWL Properties and Maxim Series Fund Inc.

Great-West Life & Annuity Insurance Co. Political Action Committee (C00263723) *Address: same as sponsor * Treasurer: John N. Clayton*

	1993-94	1995-96	1997	Totals
Receipts	$114,043	$99,146	$28,807	$241,996
Disburse	103,132	98,189	18,360	219,681
Cash	11,416	12,376	22,823	n/a
Contributions	80,850	76,500	11,950	169,300
Republicans	60,250	71,000	10,950	142,200
No. of Cand.	*25*	*27*	*9*	*61*
House	18,750	19,500	5,000	43,250
Senate	41,500	51,500	5,950	98,950
Democrats	20,600	5,500	1,000	27,100
No. of Cand.	*13*	*4*	*1*	*18*
House	6,100	2,000	1,000	9,100
Senate	14,500	3,500	0	18,000
Incumbents	48,350	22,500	8,500	79,350
Challengers	6,000	10,000	2,450	18,450
Open Seat	26,500	44,000	0	70,500
Winners	76,350	59,500	n/a	135,850
Losers	4,500	17,000	n/a	21,500

Guarantee Life Companies Inc.

*Phone: (402) 361-7300 * Fax: (402) 361-7571*
8801 Indian Hills Dr., Omaha, NE 68114-4066
Web: www.guar.com

Guarantee Life Insurance provides health and life insurance to 1.8 million customers across the United States. The Nebraska company reported that 1997 revenues rose to $349 million, a 19 percent increase over the previous year.

The company is a wholly owned subsidiary of the publicly traded Guarantee Life Companies.

Guarantee Life provides insurance in the following areas: accidental death and dismemberment, short and long term disability, dental, universal life, interest-sensitive whole life and term life coverage and annuities.

In October 1997, Guarantee Life acquired Philadelphia Financial Group Inc., the parent company of AGL Life Assurance Co.

Guarantee Life Insurance Companies Political Action Committee (C00192526) *Address: same as sponsor * Treasurer: Richard A. Spellman*

	1993-94	1995-96	1997	Totals
Receipts	$24,793	$23,549	$13,872	$62,214
Disburse	20,960	28,864	5,000	54,824
Cash	8,895	3,584	12,457	n/a
Contributions	15,460	22,200	1,500	39,160
Republicans	7,460	16,700	1,000	25,160
No. of Cand.	*5*	*7*	*2*	*14*
House	5,000	10,150	500	15,650
Senate	2,460	6,550	500	9,510
Democrats	8,000	5,500	500	14,000
No. of Cand.	*2*	*2*	*1*	*5*
House	6,000	1,000	0	7,000
Senate	2,000	4,500	500	7,000
Incumbents	9,000	10,150	1,500	20,650
Challengers	6,460	1,500	0	7,960
Open Seat	0	10,550	0	10,550
Winners	7,000	15,200	n/a	22,200
Losers	8,460	7,000	n/a	15,460

Harleysville Group Inc.

*Phone: (215) 256-5000 * Fax: (215) 256-5008*
355 Maple Ave., Harleysville, PA 19438
Web: www.harleysvillegroup.com

Harleysville Group is a public holding company for nine regional property and casualty insurance companies. Harleysville provides a variety of insurance-related products and services, including property, casualty and life insurance. Harleysville Mutual Insurance Co. owns 55 percent of Harleysville Group.

Founded in 1917, the Harleysville network has more than 2,650 employees and more than 22,000 independent insurance agents in 31 states.

In 1997, the company posted revenues of $724.2 million. Its subsidiaries include Minnesota Fire and Casualty, Great Oaks Insurance, Huron Insurance, Lake States Insurance, New York Casualty Insurance and Mid-America Insurance.

Harleysville Insurance Political Action Committee (C00123950) *Address: same as sponsor * Treasurer: Joseph P. Craugh Jr. * Contact: Walter R. Bateman, Chairman*

	1993-94	1995-96	1997	Totals
Receipts	$28,802	$32,281	$18,221	$79,304
Disburse	22,400	30,355	9,750	62,505
Cash	18,283	16,812	21,284	n/a
Contributions	10,900	22,205	8,250	41,355
Republicans	9,900	22,205	8,250	40,355
No. of Cand.	*10*	*19*	*9*	*38*
House	2,650	9,555	4,100	16,305
Senate	7,250	12,650	4,150	24,050
Democrats	1,000	0	0	1,000
No. of Cand.	*1*	*0*	*0*	*1*
House	1,000	0	0	1,000
Senate	0	0	0	0
Incumbents	2,050	13,505	8,250	23,805
Challengers	6,900	5,000	0	11,900
Open Seat	1,950	3,700	0	5,650
Winners	9,150	11,455	n/a	20,605
Losers	1,750	10,750	n/a	12,500

The Hartford Financial Services Group

*Phone: (860) 547-5000 * Fax: (860) 547-2680*
Controller Operations, Hartford Plaza, Hartford, CT 06115
Web: www.thehartford.com

The Hartford is one of the largest stock-owned insurance companies in the United States and a major insurer of home and automobiles. The company's 1997 net written premiums provided $1.89 billion for its personal lines operations.

The Hartford is one of the nation's oldest and largest international insurance and financial services operations, with 1997 revenues of $13.3 billion. About 60 percent of its business comes from commercial and life insurance policies.

The company is a leading provider of commercial property and casualty insurance, automobile and homeowners coverage, and a variety of life insurance, annuities, employee benefits, and asset management plans. It purchased Omni Insurance Group Inc., an Atlanta auto insurer, in 1998.

The Hartford employs 22,000 workers.

Hartford Financial Services Group Inc. Advocates Fund (formerly known as Hartford Advocates Fund) (C00168864) *Phone: (202) 296-7513 * 1101 Connecticut Ave. N.W., Washington, D.C. 20036 * Treasurer: Richard Benson*

	1993-94	1995-96	1997	Totals
Receipts	$250,566	$261,811	$156,475	$668,852
Disburse	283,042	275,760	114,185	672,987
Cash	58,055	44,103	86,394	n/a
Contributions	120,650	118,400	49,975	289,025
Republicans	40,800	85,250	36,975	163,025
No. of Cand.	*39*	*72*	*34*	*145*
House	35,800	70,750	30,975	137,525
Senate	5,000	14,500	6,000	25,500
Democrats	79,850	33,150	13,000	126,000
No. of Cand.	*50*	*29*	*12*	*91*
House	55,350	22,150	6,500	84,000
Senate	24,500	11,000	6,500	42,000
Incumbents	117,750	101,400	49,975	269,125
Challengers	1,600	4,500	0	6,100
Open Seat	1,300	12,500	0	13,800
Winners	102,550	93,900	n/a	196,450
Losers	18,100	24,500	n/a	42,600

Health Insurance Association of America

*Phone: (202) 824-1600 * Fax: (202) 824-1722*
555 13th St. N.W., Suite 600 E., Washington, DC 20004
Web: www.hiaa.org

The Health Insurance Association of America is a national trade group of more than 250 insurance and managed care companies. Its members include AFLAC, State Farm Insurance, Blue Cross Blue Shield plans, HMOs and businesses that provide services to the health insurance industry. HIAA represents the industry before Congress and state legislatures, where it argues against most federal oversight proposals.

Health Insurance Political Action Committee of The Health Insurance Association of America (C00110494) *Address: same as sponsor * Treasurer: Joanne M. Duncan * Contact: Ron Souders, V.P. of Gov. Affairs*

	1993-94	1995-96	1997	Totals
Receipts	$277,362	$218,025	$103,556	$598,943
Disburse	269,335	228,831	78,441	576,607
Cash	45,528	34,720	59,833	n/a
Contributions	209,855	164,590	56,665	431,110
Republicans	76,175	109,951	38,677	224,803
No. of Cand.	*71*	*91*	*34*	*196*
House	44,479	80,246	19,843	144,568
Senate	31,696	29,705	18,834	80,235
Democrats	133,680	54,639	17,988	206,307
No. of Cand.	*97*	*48*	*18*	*163*
House	101,725	40,639	7,656	150,020
Senate	31,955	14,000	10,332	56,287
Incumbents	172,295	130,489	51,665	354,449
Challengers	9,335	11,000	2,500	22,835
Open Seat	28,225	23,101	2,500	53,826
Winners	161,315	133,296	n/a	294,611
Losers	48,540	31,294	n/a	79,834

Humana Inc.

*Phone: (920) 337-5618 * Fax: (920) 337-7661*
500 W. Main St., Sixth Floor, Louisville, KY 40202
Web: www.humana.com

Louisville, Ky.-based Humana operates health plans that serve 6.2 million people in 16 states, with the largest membership in Florida, Illinois and Wisconsin.

The publicly held company runs HMOs, preferred provider organizations, point-of-service plans, medical savings accounts and health plan administrative services for businesses, governments and individuals. In 1996, Humana signed a contract with the Department of Defense to provide HMO service to 1.1 million employees in the Southeast. The contract is renewable yearly for five years.

Humana has 7,000 employees and posted revenues of a record $7.9 billion in 1997, an 18 percent increase over the previous year.

In March 1997, Advocate Health Care of Oak Brook, Ill. assumed operation of 13 Humana health centers in the Chicago area and will provide health care services under a long-term provider agreement.

Humana Inc. Political Action Committee (C00271007) *Phone: (202) 429-2015 * 1825 Eye St. N.W., Suite 400, Washington, D.C. 20006 * Treasurer: Allan Patek*

	1993-94	1995-96	1997	Totals
Receipts	$25,556	$31,673	$10,735	$67,964
Disburse	23,780	27,715	10,875	62,370
Cash	4,266	8,234	8,099	n/a
Contributions	15,950	12,650	2,500	31,100
Republicans	8,700	9,150	1,000	18,850
No. of Cand.	*9*	*5*	*1*	*15*
House	4,700	9,150	0	13,850
Senate	4,000	0	1,000	5,000
Democrats	7,250	3,500	1,500	12,250
No. of Cand.	*10*	*3*	*2*	*15*
House	4,750	3,500	500	8,750
Senate	2,500	0	1,000	3,500
Incumbents	13,950	4,650	2,500	21,100
Challengers	1,000	0	0	1,000
Open Seat	1,000	8,000	0	9,000
Winners	12,450	3,900	n/a	16,350
Losers	3,500	8,750	n/a	12,250

Independent Insurance Agents of America

*Phone: (202) 863-7000 * Fax: (202) 863-7015*
412 First St. S.E., Suite 300, Washington, DC 20003
*Web: www.iiaa.org * E-mail: lleger@iiaa.org*

The Independent Insurance Agents of America is the nation's largest association of independent insurance agents, representing a network of more than 300,000 agents and agency employees. Its members are mostly small businesses that offer many lines of insurance — property, casualty, life and health.

The group lobbies on financial services reform, which it first opposed because of provisions allowing banks to offer insurance. The insurance and banking industries reached a compromise on proposed legislation in March 1998. The IIAA opposes cuts in the federal crop insurance program. It favors a measure that would provide reinsurance to states prone to natural disasters.

The IIAA was the leading general (non-life) insurance PAC contributor to congressional candidates during the 1995-96 election cycle. More than 88 percent of its contributions went to winning candidates, and the group favored Republican candidates by a more than two-to-one margin.

The leading recipients were Rep. Gerald B.H. Solomon, R-N.Y., Sen. Carl Levin, D-Mich., Speaker Newt Gingrich, R-Ga., Minority Leader Richard A. Gephardt, D-Mo., and 1996 Senate candidate Ben Nelson, a Republican from Nebraska. Solomon was an insurance company executive.

Independent Insurance Agents of America Inc. Political Action Committee (InsurPAC) (C00022343) *Address: same as sponsor * Treasurer: Paul A. Equale * Contact: Liz Leger, Political Dir.*

	1993-94	1995-96	1997	Totals
Receipts	$685,381	$734,032	$332,258	$1,751,671
Disburse	680,501	722,850	315,859	1,719,210
Cash	56,027	67,212	83,611	n/a
Contributions	538,992	570,467	231,744	1,341,203
Republicans	255,247	403,999	145,917	805,163
No. of Cand.	*136*	*187*	*101*	*424*
House	190,139	325,353	117,473	632,965
Senate	65,108	78,646	28,444	172,198
Democrats	282,745	166,468	84,327	533,540
No. of Cand.	*116*	*75*	*56*	*247*
House	202,285	106,272	51,476	360,033
Senate	80,460	60,196	32,851	173,507
Incumbents	441,400	470,633	215,750	1,127,783
Challengers	27,035	7,000	0	34,035
Open Seat	70,557	92,834	15,994	179,385
Winners	446,142	503,797	n/a	949,939
Losers	92,850	66,670	n/a	159,520

Jefferson-Pilot Corp.

*Phone: (910) 691-3000 * Fax: (910) 691-3938*
100 N. Greene St., P.O. Box 21008, Greensboro, NC 27420
Web: www.jpc.com

Jefferson-Pilot is a public insurance and media company located in the Southeast. Its insurance offerings, which account for about 90 percent of the company's annual revenues, include life, health, accident and annuities.

Its principal subsidiaries, which are wholly owned, are Jefferson-Pilot Life Insurance Co., Jefferson-Pilot Communications Co., of Greensboro, N.C., and Alexander Hamilton Life Insurance Co. of America, of Farmington Hills, Mich. Through these and other subsidiaries, Jefferson-Pilot reported sales of $2.6 billion in 1997, and employs 4,200 people.

Jefferson-Pilot operates TV stations in Charlotte, N.C., and Richmond, Va., and radio stations in Atlanta, Denver, Miami, San Diego and Charlotte, N.C. The company also produces collegiate sports programming.

The company also acquired Chubb Life Insurance Co. of America, which offers property and casualty insurance.

Jefferson-Pilot Corp. Federal Good Government Committee (Jefferson-Pilot FedPAC) (C00148528) *Address: same as sponsor * Treasurer: Dennis R. Glass*

	1993-94	1995-96	1997	Totals
Receipts	$33,541	$33,415	$18,444	$85,400
Disburse	55,922	57,416	15,069	128,407
Cash	29,233	5,232	8,608	n/a
Contributions	29,450	37,507	4,000	70,957
Republicans	13,500	28,000	4,000	45,500
No. of Cand.	*9*	*15*	*8*	*32*
House	12,500	16,350	3,000	31,850
Senate	1,000	11,650	1,000	13,650
Democrats	15,950	9,507	0	25,457
No. of Cand.	*11*	*10*	*0*	*21*
House	15,950	2,850	0	18,800
Senate	0	6,657	0	6,657
Incumbents	21,450	27,600	4,000	53,050
Challengers	1,000	7,657	0	8,657
Open Seat	7,000	2,250	0	9,250
Winners	18,950	23,450	n/a	42,400
Losers	10,500	14,057	n/a	24,557

	1993-94	1995-96	1997	Totals
Receipts	$8,266	$8,610	$3,414	$20,290
Disburse	8,200	8,523	1,000	17,723
Cash	871	960	3,374	n/a
Contributions	7,200	8,500	1,000	16,700
Republicans	2,700	2,500	500	5,700
No. of Cand.	*3*	*2*	*1*	*6*
House	1,200	2,500	500	4,200
Senate	1,500	0	0	1,500
Democrats	4,500	6,000	500	11,000
No. of Cand.	*3*	*5*	*1*	*9*
House	3,500	6,000	500	10,000
Senate	1,000	0	0	1,000
Incumbents	2,500	6,000	1,000	9,500
Challengers	0	0	0	0
Open Seat	4,700	2,500	0	7,200
Winners	6,000	7,250	n/a	13,250
Losers	1,200	1,250	n/a	2,450

John Hancock Mutual Life Insurance Co.

*Phone: (617) 572-6612 * Fax: (617) 572-1545*
200 Clarendon St., Boston, MA 02117
*Web: www.jhancock.com * E-mail: bburgess@jhancock.com*

John Hancock Mutual Life Insurance offers insurance, investment and other financial services.

Established in 1862, the Boston-based private company employs more than 9,000 people worldwide and had 1996 net revenues of more than $300 million. The company's products include life insurance, annuities, mutual funds, long-term care coverage and managed care services. In addition, the company is one of the largest managers of timber, agriculture, energy and real estate investments. At the end of 1996, the business had more than $100 billion under management.

Subsidiaries include: Maritime Life Assurance Co., First Signature Bank & Trust Co., Independence Investment Associates Inc., ENERGY Investors Management Inc., Sovereign Asset Management Corp., Patriot Group Inc., and NM Capital Management Inc.

John Hancock Mutual Life Insurance Co. Federal Political Action Committee (C00137265) *Phone: (202) 638-6612 * Fax: (202) 638-5331 * 801 Pennsylvania Ave. N.W., Suite 730, Washington, DC 20004 * Treasurer: Barbara A. Burgess*

	1993-94	1995-96	1997	Totals
Receipts	$82,433	$82,928	$55,309	$220,670
Disburse	77,143	98,611	49,035	224,789
Cash	22,842	7,168	13,447	n/a
Contributions	47,000	52,000	29,000	128,000
Republicans	11,500	31,750	15,000	58,250
No. of Cand.	*11*	*28*	*17*	*56*
House	2,500	15,750	8,500	26,750
Senate	9,000	16,000	6,500	31,500
Democrats	35,500	20,250	14,000	69,750
No. of Cand.	*29*	*10*	*10*	*49*
House	22,500	19,750	8,000	50,250
Senate	13,000	500	6,000	19,500
Incumbents	40,500	38,000	28,000	106,500
Challengers	1,500	10,250	0	11,750
Open Seat	5,000	3,750	1,000	9,750
Winners	35,000	36,750	n/a	71,750
Losers	12,000	15,250	n/a	27,250

Liberty Corp.

*Phone: (864) 609-3496 * Fax: (864) 609-4390*
2000 Wade Hampton Blvd., Greenville, SC 29602

Liberty is a $3.1-billion publicly owned insurance and broadcasting company. The company employed 2,754 people and reported sales of $660 million in 1997.

Headquartered in Greenville, S.C., Liberty Life Insurance Co. leases about 50 branch offices primarily located in North Carolina, South Carolina and Louisiana. Liberty's insurance subsidiaries also provide insurance company support services, investment advisory services, property development and management.

Liberty subsidiary Cosmos Broadcasting Corp. owns and operates eight network affiliated television stations in Columbia, S.C.; Montgomery, Ala.; Toledo, Ohio; Louisville, Ky.; Evansville, Ind.; Jonesboro, Ariz.; Lake Charles, La.; and Biloxi, Miss. The stations account for about 20 percent of the company's revenues.

Other subsidiaries: Liberty Life Insurance, Pierce National Life Insurance Co. and Liberty Insurance Services Corp.

Liberty Corp. Federal Political Action Committee (C00116384) *Address: same as sponsor * Treasurer: Kenneth Jones * Contact: W. Hayne Hipp, CEO*

	1993-94	1995-96	1997	Totals
Receipts	$13,687	$2,313	$3,978	$19,978
Disburse	12,250	12,000	5,019	29,269
Cash	19,483	9,796	8,755	n/a
Contributions	5,250	3,500	750	9,500
Republicans	2,000	3,500	0	5,500
No. of Cand.	*2*	*2*	*0*	*4*
House	2,000	1,000	0	3,000
Senate	0	2,500	0	2,500
Democrats	3,250	0	750	4,000
No. of Cand.	*4*	*0*	*2*	*6*
House	3,250	0	750	4,000
Senate	0	0	0	0
Incumbents	1,500	3,500	0	5,000
Challengers	0	0	0	0
Open Seat	3,750	0	0	3,750
Winners	3,000	3,500	n/a	6,500
Losers	2,250	0	n/a	2,250

Kansas City Life Insurance Co.

*Phone: (816) 753-7000 * Fax: (816) 753-1354*
3520 Broadway, Kansas City, MO 64111-2565
*Web: www.kclife.com * E-mail: kclife@kclife.com*

Kansas City Life Insurance has nearly $14 billion of life insurance in force serving more than 500,000 policy owners across the nation. The public company reported $462 million in 1997 revenues.

The company, formed in 1895, has grown to include two life insurance subsidiaries. Sunset Life, based in Olympia, Wash., offers the same policies as Kansas City Life. The other subsidiary, Old American Insurance, focuses on burial and other final needs insurance. The company has about 1,500 agents.

Kansas City Life Insurance Co. Employees' Political Action Committee (Fund LI) (C00042663) *Address: same as sponsor * Treasurer: Dallas Pollin*

Liberty Mutual Insurance Co.

*Phone: (617) 357-9500 * Fax: (617) 350-7648*
175 Berkeley St., Boston, MA 02117
Web: www.libertymutual.com

Liberty Mutual Insurance is the largest workers' compensation insurer in the United States. In addition to providing homeowners, auto, group life and disability insurance, the private company performs workplace safety analysis.

Liberty Mutual also operates rehabilitation facilities and has a number of alliances with health care providers to manage disability care. Liberty Mutual's financial services companies, grouped under the Liberty Financial umbrella, provide investment management services and sell fixed and variable annuities and mutual funds. The company operates in 12 countries, including Canada, Japan, Mexico, the United Kingdom and the United States.

Liberty Mutual posted 1996 sales of $8.7 billion. Liberty Mutual employs 23,000 employees at more than 500 offices worldwide.

Liberty Mutual Insurance Co. Political Action Committee (C00171843) *Address: same as sponsor * Treasurer: Elliot J. Williams*

	1993-94	1995-96	1997	Totals
Receipts	$140,168	$182,692	$134,508	$457,368
Disburse	137,888	171,037	63,958	372,883
Cash	15,152	43,511	131,799	n/a
Contributions	94,649	111,000	39,000	244,649
Republicans	76,200	94,500	26,000	196,700
No. of Cand.	*73*	*51*	*12*	*136*
House	46,100	48,500	17,500	112,100
Senate	30,100	46,000	8,500	84,600
Democrats	18,449	16,500	13,000	47,949
No. of Cand.	*18*	*10*	*10*	*38*
House	16,449	12,000	11,000	39,449
Senate	2,000	4,500	2,000	8,500
Incumbents	67,049	56,000	39,000	162,049
Challengers	12,500	16,500	0	29,000
Open Seat	15,100	38,500	0	53,600
Winners	91,149	63,500	n/a	154,649
Losers	3,500	47,500	n/a	51,000

Lincoln National Corp.

*Phone: (219) 455-2128 * Fax: (219) 455-1550*
200 E. Berry St., P.O. Box 7813, Fort Wayne, IN 46802
Web: www.lnc.com

Lincoln National is a public insurance holding company and the leading writer of individual annuities in the nation. Through subsidiary companies, LNC operates multiple insurance and investment management businesses. LNC, which has more than 10,000 employees, reported $4.9 billion in revenues in 1997.

The company's operations are divided into four business segments: life insurance and annuities, reinsurance, property-casualty and investment management. The investment management segment was added in April of 1995 following the acquisition of Delaware Management Holdings Inc. LNC's reinsurance division is one of the world's largest.

LNC's subsidiaries include: Lincoln National Life Insurance Co., First Penn-Pacific Life Insurance Co., Lincoln UK, Lincoln National Investment Companies and Lincoln National Reinsurance Companies.

Lincoln National Corp. Political Action Committee (C00110577) *Address: same as sponsor * Treasurer: Janet Whitney * Contact: Mark Pope, V.P. and Dir. of Gov. Relations*

	1993-94	1995-96	1997	Totals
Receipts	$67,148	$73,861	$66,986	$207,995
Disburse	60,305	63,553	42,268	166,126
Cash	15,057	25,367	50,085	n/a
Contributions	35,800	44,700	30,354	110,854
Republicans	10,350	34,650	20,354	65,354
No. of Cand.	*12*	*48*	*27*	*87*
House	2,950	23,150	16,354	42,454
Senate	7,400	11,500	4,000	22,900
Democrats	25,450	10,050	10,000	45,500
No. of Cand.	*23*	*13*	*13*	*49*
House	20,950	7,050	7,500	35,500
Senate	4,500	3,000	2,500	10,000
Incumbents	31,300	34,200	28,354	93,854
Challengers	2,000	3,500	0	5,500
Open Seat	2,500	7,000	2,000	11,500
Winners	22,050	38,200	n/a	60,250
Losers	13,750	6,500	n/a	20,250

Terminated PACs which contributed less than $5,000 during 1995-96 cycle:

American States Insurance Co. Political Action Committee (ASPAC) (C00192617) *500 N. Meridian St., P.O. Box 1636, Indianapolis, IN 46207 * Treasurer: Thomas M. Ober*

MMI Companies Inc.

*Phone: (847) 940-7550 * Fax: (847) 374-1334*
540 Lake Cook Rd., Deerfield, IL 60015
Web: www.mmicompanies.com

MMI is a public health care insurance and services network. Based in Deerfield, Ill., MMI writes insurance products such as primary, umbrella and excess-liability insurance for hospitals, clinics and their employees.

The company has about 8,000 employees and posted revenues of $407 million in 1997. The company has offices throughout the United States and overseas, including Ireland, the United Kingdom and Australia.

Subsidiary UnionAmerica offers indemnity insurance and specialty casualty and property reinsurance.

Other subsidiaries include: American Continental Life Insurance Co., MMI Agency Inc., Healthcare Risk Underwriters, Professional Risk Management Inc., McMannis Associates Inc., Management Science Associates Inc., The Profile Group, and Healthcare Credentials Management Services Inc.

MMI Companies Inc. Political Action Committee (C00214924) *Phone: (202) 728-0269 * Fax: (202) 728-0271 * 1900 K St. N.W., Washington, DC 20006 * Treasurer: Wayne A. Sinclair*

	1993-94	1995-96	1997	Totals
Receipts	$36,792	$72,648	$30,682	$140,122
Disburse	39,744	59,410	28,270	127,424
Cash	2,224	15,465	17,878	n/a
Contributions	27,500	43,857	19,500	90,857
Republicans	2,500	27,857	11,000	41,357
No. of Cand.	*3*	*21*	*11*	*35*
House	500	9,857	7,000	17,357
Senate	2,000	18,000	4,000	24,000
Democrats	24,000	16,000	8,500	48,500
No. of Cand.	*23*	*13*	*7*	*43*
House	14,500	4,000	2,500	21,000
Senate	9,500	12,000	6,000	27,500
Incumbents	24,000	30,857	19,500	74,357
Challengers	1,000	6,000	0	7,000
Open Seat	2,500	7,000	0	9,500
Winners	20,500	33,357	n/a	53,857
Losers	7,000	10,500	n/a	17,500

Massachusetts Mutual Life Insurance Co.

*Phone: (413) 744-6250 * Fax: (413) 744-4949*
1295 State St., Springfield, MA 01111-0001
*Web: www.massmutual.com * E-mail: eellis@massmutual.com*

Massachusetts Mutual Life Insurance is the seventh-largest life insurance company in the United States. The private company offers insurance, money management and investment counseling. Its subsidiaries include mutual fund manager OppenheimerFunds Inc., David Babson & Co., and Cornerstone Real Estate Advisers. The company manages assets in excess of $130 billion and has offices in every state.

The company tracks legislative issues concerning annuities and life insurance. It supports the reform of the financial services industry, which would allow banks to affiliate themselves with insurance and investment companies.

MassMutual ranked third among life insurance PACs in total contributions to 1996 congressional candidates. The company spent most of its PAC money on Republican candidates. Incumbents received nearly 75 percent of the total. The top recipients were Rep. Richard Neal, D-Mass., who represents the district where the company is headquartered; and Senate candidates William Weld, a Republican from Massachusetts, and Democrat Ben Nelson of Nebraska. Most recipients got less than $5,000.

Massachusetts Mutual Life Insurance Co. Political Action Committee (C00118943) *Phone: (202) 737-0440 * Fax: (202) 628-2313 * 701 Pennsylvania Ave. N.W., Suite 750, Washington, DC 20004 * Treasurer: Allan B. Bixby*

*Contact: Ellen Watkins Ellis, V.P. * Phone: (413) 744-6250*

	1993-94	1995-96	1997	Totals
Receipts	$456,243	$520,744	$251,142	$1,228,129
Disburse	456,051	511,628	259,991	1,227,670
Cash	7,590	16,714	7,869	n/a
Contributions	272,800	267,178	141,500	681,478
Republicans	95,700	188,378	85,000	369,078
No. of Cand.	*65*	*124*	*76*	*265*
House	41,600	122,878	51,500	215,978
Senate	54,100	65,500	33,500	153,100
Democrats	177,100	78,800	56,500	312,400
No. of Cand.	*84*	*42*	*46*	*172*
House	134,100	56,700	40,500	231,300
Senate	43,000	22,100	16,000	81,100
Incumbents	232,600	203,960	133,000	569,560
Challengers	10,000	20,768	4,000	34,768
Open Seat	29,700	42,450	4,500	76,650
Winners	211,850	212,410	n/a	424,260
Losers	60,950	54,768	n/a	115,718

Connecticut Mutual Life Insurance Co.-Political Action Committee (CM-PAC/CM PAC/CML PAC) (C00164780) *140 Garden St., Hartford, CT 06154 * Treasurer: Charles H. Dyer*

The Connecticut Mutual Life Insurance PAC was terminated in 1996. The company merged with Massachusetts Mutual Life Insurance Co. in March 1996.

	1993-94	1995-96	1997	Totals
Receipts	$44,646	$10,253	$0	$54,899
Disburse	32,473	62,613	0	95,086
Cash	52,359	0	0	n/a
Contributions	23,050	17,000	0	40,050
Republicans	8,050	7,000	0	15,050
No. of Cand.	*11*	*2*	*0*	*13*
House	4,550	7,000	0	11,550
Senate	3,500	0	0	3,500
Democrats	15,000	10,000	0	25,000
No. of Cand.	*17*	*5*	*0*	*22*
House	11,000	6,000	0	17,000
Senate	4,000	4,000	0	8,000
Incumbents	16,300	17,500	0	33,800
Challengers	5,000	0	0	5,000
Open Seat	3,250	-500	0	2,750
Winners	18,800	16,000	n/a	34,800
Losers	4,250	1,000	n/a	5,250

Metrahealth Associates

1620 L St. N.W., Suite 800, Washington, DC 20036

The Metrahealth Associates' Political Participation Fund was terminated in 1996.

Metrahealth Associates' Political Participation Fund (Metrahealth PAC) (C00302604) *Address: same as sponsor * Treasurer: Gail Marcus*

	1993-94	1995-96	1997	Totals
Receipts	$0	$8,700	$0	$8,700
Disburse	0	8,699	0	8,699
Cash	0	0	0	n/a
Contributions	0	6,500	0	6,500
Republicans	0	5,000	0	5,000
No. of Cand.	*0*	*6*	*0*	*6*
House	0	3,000	0	3,000
Senate	0	2,000	0	2,000
Democrats	0	1,500	0	1,500
No. of Cand.	*0*	*2*	*0*	*2*
House	0	1,500	0	1,500
Senate	0	0	0	0
Incumbents	0	5,500	0	5,500
Challengers	0	0	0	0
Open Seat	0	1,000	0	1,000
Winners	0	5,500	n/a	5,500
Losers	0	1,000	n/a	1,000

Metropolitan Life Insurance Co.

*Phone: (212) 578-2211 * Fax: (212) 578-3320*
One Madison Ave., New York, NY 10010-3690
Web: www.metlife.com

Metropolitan Life Insurance is a mutually owned insurance company headquartered in New York and the nation's second-largest life insurance company. Its private stock is owned by policyholders. The company's subsidiaries include New England Financial, Farmers National and Metropolitan Property and Casualty. In 1996, it employed 43,500 people and reported sales of $23.2 billion.

About 15 states and the District of Columbia have passed legislation that would allow companies like MetLife to sell some stock publicly. A coalition of 10 publicly traded insurers has formed a lobbying group to oppose such laws. MetLife lobbies on many insurance and tax issues. Several states, including Connecticut, Florida, Texas and Massachusetts, have investigated whether the company misled some policyholders into buying expensive life insurance through a process known as churning.

MetLife ranked fourth among life insurance PACs in total contributions to 1996 congressional candidates. It split its contributions almost evenly between Democrats and Republicans, with a slight edge to the GOP candidates. The leading recipients were Reps. Charles Schumer, D-N.Y., and Charles Rangel, D-N.Y., and Sen. Richard Durbin, D-Ill.

Rep. Jon Christensen, R-Neb., an insurance agent, also was among the leaders.

Metropolitan Life Insurance Co. (MetLife) Employees' Political Participation Fund A (C00040923) *Phone: (202) 659-3575 * Fax: (202) 659-1026 * 1620 L St. N.W., Suite 800, Washington, DC 20036 * Treasurer: Robert C. Tarnok * Contact: Kathleen Mellody, PAC Dir.*

	1993-94	1995-96	1997	Totals
Receipts	$362,982	$355,136	$162,051	$880,169
Disburse	356,016	360,938	148,805	865,759
Cash	36,035	30,246	43,496	n/a
Contributions	224,715	234,147	104,800	563,662
Republicans	65,230	125,525	52,523	243,278
No. of Cand.	*66*	*90*	*44*	*200*
House	39,151	88,608	42,000	169,759
Senate	26,079	36,917	10,523	73,519
Democrats	159,485	108,622	52,277	320,384
No. of Cand.	*90*	*58*	*44*	*192*
House	116,995	72,420	37,740	227,155
Senate	42,490	36,202	14,537	93,229
Incumbents	198,765	190,376	102,050	491,191
Challengers	7,100	9,369	1,500	17,969
Open Seat	18,850	34,402	1,250	54,502
Winners	195,385	202,158	n/a	397,543
Losers	29,330	31,989	n/a	61,319

New England Life Insurance Co. Political Action Committee (C00113464) *Phone: (617) 578-2000 * Fax: (617) 536-5566 * 501 Boylston St., Boston, MA 02116 * Web: www.tne.com * Treasurer: Frances A. O'Keefe * Contact: Kathryn Plazak, Chairwoman*

New England Life Insurance (known as New England Financial) provides insurance, investment and retirement services to individuals and small business owners throughout the United States.

Headquartered in Boston, the company has offices in every major U.S. city and is licensed to do business in all 50 states and the District of Columbia. Owned by its policyholders, the company has been in business for 160 years and employs about 2,500 people nationwide.

Until January 1998, New England Financial was known as The New England.

	1993-94	1995-96	1997	Totals
Receipts	$82,672	$82,813	$39,345	$204,830
Disburse	86,178	80,241	38,201	204,620
Cash	7,246	9,818	10,962	n/a
Contributions	74,100	76,500	37,500	188,100
Republicans	36,500	52,500	23,000	112,000
No. of Cand.	*35*	*42*	*29*	*106*
House	22,000	40,000	16,500	78,500
Senate	14,500	12,500	6,500	33,500
Democrats	37,600	24,000	14,500	76,100
No. of Cand.	*31*	*22*	*19*	*72*
House	31,100	21,500	11,000	63,600
Senate	6,500	2,500	3,500	12,500
Incumbents	63,100	72,000	36,500	171,600
Challengers	4,000	1,500	0	5,500
Open Seat	7,000	3,000	1,000	11,000
Winners	59,600	66,500	n/a	126,100
Losers	14,500	10,000	n/a	24,500

Minnesota Mutual Life Insurance Co.

*Phone: (612) 665-3747 * Fax: (612) 665-7938*
400 Robert St. N., St. Paul, MN 55101
Web: www.minnesotamutual.com

Minnesota Mutual Life Insurance provides insurance and investment products for individuals and businesses. Founded in 1880, the company employs more than 4,000 associates throughout the nation. It provides $136 billion of life insurance protection and manages more than $14 billion in assets.

In October 1997 the private company sold its Minnesota Fire and Casualty Insurance Co. to Harleysville Group for about $35 million.

Minnesota Mutual Life Insurance Co. PAC (Minnesota Mutual Life PAC) (C00120006) *Address: same as sponsor * Treasurer: Vacant * Contact: Dwayne Radel, PAC Administrator*

	1993-94	1995-96	1997	Totals
Receipts	$6,784	$32,930	$25,910	$65,624
Disburse	7,288	27,354	10,007	44,649
Cash	33	5,609	21,512	n/a
Contributions	3,575	18,850	5,000	27,425
Republicans	2,375	15,850	5,000	23,225
No. of Cand.	*4*	*7*	*1*	*12*
House	1,425	8,950	5,000	15,375
Senate	950	6,900	0	7,850
Democrats	1,050	3,000	0	4,050
No. of Cand.	*4*	*4*	*0*	*8*

	1993-94	1995-96	1997	Totals
House	1,050	3,000	0	4,050
Senate	0	0	0	0
Incumbents	1,500	13,200	0	14,700
Challengers	300	5,650	5,000	10,950
Open Seat	1,775	0	0	1,775
Winners	2,450	13,200	n/a	15,650
Losers	1,125	5,650	n/a	6,775

Mortgage Insurance Companies of America

*Phone: (202) 393-5566 * Fax: (202) 393-5557*
727 15th St. N.W., #110, Washington, DC 20005

The Mortgage Insurance Companies of America is the trade association for the private mortgage insurance industry.

MICA provides information on legislative and regulatory issues and represents the industry's positions before Congress. The association also promotes mortgage insurance nationwide.

Mortgage Insurance Companies of America Political Action Committee (C00113258) *Address: same as sponsor * Treasurer: Suzanne C. Hutchinson*

	1993-94	1995-96	1997	Totals
Receipts	$51,243	$115,256	$64,680	$231,179
Disburse	59,385	107,555	43,407	210,347
Cash	5,634	13,333	34,470	n/a
Contributions	55,650	93,619	37,250	186,519
Republicans	20,500	79,119	26,750	126,369
No. of Cand.	*20*	*53*	*29*	*102*
House	13,500	41,819	16,250	71,569
Senate	7,000	37,300	10,500	54,800
Democrats	35,150	14,500	10,500	60,150
No. of Cand.	*37*	*14*	*12*	*63*
House	23,150	8,500	4,500	36,150
Senate	12,000	6,000	6,000	24,000
Incumbents	53,800	87,619	36,250	177,669
Challengers	0	5,000	500	5,500
Open Seat	1,850	1,500	500	3,850
Winners	50,350	84,554	n/a	134,904
Losers	5,300	9,065	n/a	14,365

Mutual Life Insurance Co. of New York

*Phone: (212) 708-2225 * Fax: (212) 708-2278*
1740 Broadway, Suite 7-28, New York, NY 10019
Web: www.mony.com

The Mutual Life Insurance Co. of New York offers traditional life insurance and annuities, although in the past several years it has branched out to develop subsidiaries in the financial services industry.

The company, which has been in business more than 150 years, had 1996 net revenues of almost $65 million and total sales of $2.76 billion. As the ninth largest mutual life insurance company in the United States, MONY employs more than 4,000 people nationwide.

Over the last several years, the company has diversified into such areas as mutual funds, securities brokerage and investment management.

In September 1997, the company announced plans to convert from a mutual life insurance company, in which the company is owned by its policyholders, to a stock-ownership based firm to increase the company's access to capital.

The company's subsidiaries include Enterprise Capital Management, MONY Brokerage, MONY Securities, and 1740 Advisers Inc.

Mutual Life Insurance Co. of New York MONY Political Action Committee (C00129437) *Address: same as sponsor * Treasurer: Lee M. Smith*

	1993-94	1995-96	1997	Totals
Receipts	$96,224	$91,671	$33,056	$220,951
Disburse	66,301	119,624	43,000	228,925
Cash	56,303	28,353	18,410	n/a
Contributions	29,750	48,500	18,000	96,250
Republicans	9,000	36,000	8,500	53,500
No. of Cand.	*11*	*36*	*9*	*56*
House	2,000	23,000	4,500	29,500
Senate	7,000	13,000	4,000	24,000
Democrats	20,750	12,500	9,500	42,750
No. of Cand.	*16*	*13*	*9*	*38*
House	13,250	11,000	4,500	28,750
Senate	7,500	1,500	5,000	14,000
Incumbents	25,250	44,000	18,000	87,250
Challengers	2,000	1,500	0	3,500
Open Seat	2,500	3,000	0	5,500
Winners	26,250	35,000	n/a	61,250
Losers	3,500	13,500	n/a	17,000

Mutual of Omaha Companies

*Phone: (402) 342-7600 * Fax: (402) 351-2775*
Mutual of Omaha Plaza, Omaha, NE 68175
Web: www.mutualofomaha.com

One of the nation's largest providers of managed health care, Mutual of Omaha is a privately held insurance and financial services company with assets of $12.5 billion. It has 6.3 million customers, 7,000 employees and reported sales of $3.8 billion in 1996.

The company's eight subsidiaries have offices across the country that offer brokerage, investment, foreign currency and investment banking services, and sell travel, auto, homeowners, residential fire, boat owners, health and accident insurance.

Subsidiaries: United of Omaha Life Insurance Co., Companion Life Insurance Co. of New York, Mutual of Omaha Investor Service Inc., Kirkpatrick Pettis, Tele-Trip Co. Inc., Omaha Property and Casualty Insurance Co., and United World Life Insurance Co.

Mutual of Omaha Companies PAC (ImPAC) (C00094581) *Phone: (202) 393-6200 * Fax: (202) 639-8808 * 1700 Pennsylvania Ave. N.W., Suite 500, Washington, DC 20006 * Treasurer: Galen F. Ullstrom*

	1993-94	1995-96	1997	Totals
Receipts	$319,846	$332,785	$147,812	$800,443
Disburse	304,049	295,170	138,879	738,098
Cash	39,653	77,275	86,207	n/a
Contributions	205,030	170,029	93,353	468,412
Republicans	107,347	123,580	76,853	307,780
No. of Cand.	*70*	*92*	*65*	*227*
House	74,348	94,080	48,354	216,782
Senate	32,999	29,500	28,499	90,998
Democrats	96,683	45,949	16,500	159,132
No. of Cand.	*57*	*31*	*18*	*106*
House	73,933	30,699	10,500	115,132
Senate	22,750	15,250	6,000	44,000
Incumbents	176,781	143,529	89,853	410,163
Challengers	18,000	7,000	2,500	27,500
Open Seat	10,249	19,500	1,000	30,749
Winners	167,445	147,029	n/a	314,474
Losers	37,585	23,000	n/a	60,585

General Agents and Managers Association of The Mutual of Omaha Companies PAC (ComPAC) (C00103572) *Phone: (202) 393-6200 * Fax: (202) 639-8808 * 1700 Pennsylvania Ave. N.W., Suite 500, Washington, DC 20006 * Treasurer: Conan Grace * Contact: Bill Maddox, Executive V.P.*

	1993-94	1995-96	1997	Totals
Receipts	$65,741	$54,132	$25,661	$145,534
Disburse	80,482	57,285	12,500	150,267
Cash	11,467	8,322	21,485	n/a
Contributions	78,597	56,000	12,500	147,097
Republicans	55,097	52,000	11,500	118,597
No. of Cand.	*53*	*59*	*16*	*128*
House	34,597	35,500	8,500	78,597
Senate	20,500	16,500	3,000	40,000
Democrats	23,500	4,000	1,000	28,500
No. of Cand.	*18*	*6*	*2*	*26*
House	19,500	4,000	1,000	24,500
Senate	4,000	0	0	4,000
Incumbents	60,999	44,000	12,500	117,499
Challengers	8,599	2,500	0	11,099
Open Seat	8,999	9,500	0	18,499
Winners	74,497	47,500	n/a	121,997
Losers	4,100	8,500	n/a	12,600

National Association of Independent Insurers

*Phone: (847) 297-7800 * Fax: (847) 297-5064*
2600 River Rd., Des Plaines, IL 60018
Web: www.naii.org

The National Association of Independent Insurers is the nation's largest property-casualty trade association with more than 560 members in the United States. NAII members write more than $63 billion in annual premiums representing automobile, homeowners and business insurance, as well as workers' compensation and surplus lines.

The organization supports the modernization of the nation's financial services, which would allow insurance companies to affiliate themselves with banks and other financial institutions. It also favors legislation increasing the availability of insurance to people living in areas where natural disasters are more common. It opposes new taxes on the insurance industry and is concerned with national highway funding and roadway safety issues.

The NAII ranked second among general insurance PACs in contributions to 1996 congressional campaigns. More than 95 percent of its contributions went to Republican candidates. The leading recipients were 1996 Senate candidate Dennis Rehberg of Montana, and Sens. Robert C. Smith, R-N.H., and Strom Thurmond, R-S.C. Ben Nelson, who lost a Senate race to Sen. Chuck Hagel, R-Neb., was the top Democratic recipient.

National Association of Independent Insurers Political Action Committee (C00066472) *Phone: (202) 639-0490 * Fax: (202) 639-0494 * 499 S. Capitol St. S.W., Suite 401, Washington, DC 20003 * E-mail: jlobert@naii.org * Treasurer: June Holmes * Contact: John Lobert, Senior V.P.*

	1993-94	1995-96	1997	Totals
Receipts	$283,324	$223,380	$151,542	$658,246
Disburse	279,020	225,205	115,267	619,492
Cash	17,624	9,849	46,125	n/a
Contributions	271,570	244,215	110,157	625,942
Republicans	242,070	233,091	106,082	581,243
No. of Cand.	*157*	*148*	*81*	*386*
House	109,070	118,474	51,478	279,022
Senate	133,000	114,617	54,604	302,221
Democrats	29,500	11,124	4,075	44,699
No. of Cand.	*29*	*10*	*6*	*45*
House	19,400	7,124	4,000	30,524
Senate	10,100	4,000	75	14,175
Incumbents	184,370	185,885	105,179	475,434
Challengers	26,500	26,333	1,000	53,833
Open Seat	60,700	31,997	4,000	96,697
Winners	249,520	183,009	n/a	432,529
Losers	22,050	61,206	n/a	83,256

National Association of Insurance Brokers

*Phone: (202) 628-6700 * Fax: (202) 628-6707*
1300 Eye St. N.W., Suite 900E, Washington, DC 20009
Web: www.naib.org

National Association of Insurance Brokers is an association of commercial insurance brokers and specialty brokers. It provides risk management and promotes the establishment of brokerage systems across the world.

Former Rep. Guy Vander Jagt, R-Mich., who served from 1966 to 1992, lobbies for the NAIB. The NAIB and the Council of Insurance Agents & Brokers announced merger discussions.

National Association of Insurance Brokers Political Action Committee (NAIBPAC) (C00162529) *Address: same as sponsor * Treasurer: Graham S. Anderson * Contact: Carl A. Modecki, President*

	1993-94	1995-96	1997	Totals
Receipts	$75,275	$56,034	$12,701	$144,010
Disburse	58,200	68,550	26,000	152,750
Cash	47,052	34,538	25,639	n/a
Contributions	54,250	57,800	20,295	132,345
Republicans	24,400	39,400	12,295	76,095
No. of Cand.	*34*	*46*	*13*	*93*
House	16,900	31,900	11,795	60,595
Senate	7,500	7,500	500	15,500
Democrats	29,850	18,400	8,000	56,250
No. of Cand.	*32*	*22*	*11*	*65*
House	21,350	13,600	4,000	38,950
Senate	8,500	4,800	4,000	17,300
Incumbents	49,350	48,700	19,795	117,845
Challengers	2,600	2,800	0	5,400
Open Seat	2,300	6,300	500	9,100
Winners	41,450	48,000	n/a	89,450
Losers	12,800	9,800	n/a	22,600

National Association of Life Underwriters

*Phone: (202) 331-6022 * Fax: (202) 835-9603*
1922 F St. N.W., Washington, DC 20006
*Web: www.agents-online.com/nalu/naluhome.html * E-mail: sharvey@nalu.org*

The National Association of Life Underwriters is a federation of nearly 1,000 state and local life insurance associations. NALU's local associations have a membership of 108,000 sales professionals in life and health insurance and other financial fields. The group has affiliates in every state and about 950 local organizations.

NALU supports banking and financial services reform proposals that keep intact state regulation of insurance and permit banks to affiliate themselves with insurance and securities companies. The group opposes a budget tax plan that would raise about $8 billion over five years from life insurance and annuities. It has lobbied for legislation expanding insurance protection for victims of natural disasters.

NALU contributed nearly $1 million — 69 percent of its contributions — to Republican candidates during 1996 and ranked first among life insurance PACs in total contributions. Of the 429 candidates who received contributions from NALU, more than 120 received $5,000 or more. Speaker Newt Gingrich, R-Ga., and Minority Leader Richard A. Gephardt, D-Mo., were among the 32 candidates who received $10,000 from this PAC.

National Association of Life Underwriters Political Action Committee (C00005249) *Address: same as sponsor * Treasurer: Paul M. Smith Sr. * Contact: Michael L. Kerley, Senior V.P.*

	1993-94	1995-96	1997	Totals
Receipts	$2,097,172	$2,117,658	$981,351	$5,196,181
Disburse	1,891,351	1,894,532	816,517	4,602,400
Cash	410,734	633,863	798,698	n/a
Contributions	1,338,890	1,426,750	341,000	3,106,640
Republicans	696,750	984,750	203,000	1,884,500
No. of Cand.	*272*	*288*	*125*	*685*
House	523,000	776,500	168,000	1,467,500
Senate	173,750	208,250	35,000	417,000
Democrats	636,140	442,000	137,500	1,215,640
No. of Cand.	*223*	*149*	*91*	*463*
House	538,900	355,000	109,500	1,003,400
Senate	97,240	87,000	28,000	212,240
Incumbents	1,034,890	1,087,750	323,500	2,446,140
Challengers	104,500	58,500	2,500	165,500
Open Seat	199,000	280,500	15,000	494,500
Winners	1,129,750	1,223,250	n/a	2,353,000
Losers	209,140	203,500	n/a	412,640

National Association of Mutual Insurance Companies

*Phone: (317) 875-5250 * Fax: (317) 879-8408*
3601 Vincennes Rd., Indianapolis, IN 46268
Web: www.namic.org

The National Association of Mutual Insurance Companies is the casualty insurance industry's largest trade association. Established in the mid-1890s, the association has nearly 1,200 members from 41 states and Canada and Europe.

NAMIC's legislative issues include Superfund reform, Department of Housing and Urban Development regulation of property insurance, natural disaster legislation, financial services reform and tort reform.

NAMIC PAC contributes to federal candidates who agree with the group's positions on insurance regulation and a free-market business environment.

National Association of Mutual Insurance Companies (NAMIC) PAC (C00170258) *Phone: (202) 628-1558 * Fax: (202) 628-1601 * 122 C St. N.W., Suite 540, Washington, DC 20001 * E-mail: pallen@namic.org * Treasurer: Pamela J. Allen*

	1993-94	1995-96	1997	Totals
Receipts	$19,499	$38,072	$18,623	$76,194
Disburse	30,570	50,075	14,812	95,457
Cash	17,483	4,985	8,795	n/a
Contributions	29,418	48,201	13,250	90,869
Republicans	21,550	45,101	11,250	77,901
No. of Cand.	*35*	*65*	*17*	*117*
House	18,050	37,151	8,250	63,451
Senate	3,500	7,950	3,000	14,450
Democrats	7,868	3,100	2,000	12,968
No. of Cand.	*14*	*5*	*3*	*22*
House	6,248	2,600	500	9,348
Senate	1,620	500	1,500	3,620
Incumbents	28,168	39,751	13,250	81,169
Challengers	500	2,700	0	3,200
Open Seat	1,250	5,750	0	7,000
Winners	26,918	37,150	n/a	64,068
Losers	2,500	11,051	n/a	13,551

National Association of Professional Insurance Agents

*Phone: (703) 836-9340 * Fax: (703) 836-4933*
400 N. Washington St., Alexandria, VA 22314-2353
*Web: www.pianet.com * E-mail: meghanbr@pianet.com*

The National Association of Professional Insurance Agents represents 180,000 independent, professional agents and brokers located throughout the United States and its territories.

The organization operates schools to provide agents with basic training, offers seminars and provides educational materials, and monitors legislation and regulations related to the insurance industry.

Professional Insurance Agents Political Action Committee (C00004994) *Address: same as sponsor * Treasurer: Dean R. Sackett III * Contact: Meghan Brady, PAC Dir.*

	1993-94	1995-96	1997	Totals
Receipts	$192,775	$205,983	$103,110	$501,868
Disburse	194,840	291,144	103,890	589,874
Cash	86,279	5,035	4,304	n/a
Contributions	161,667	205,050	84,495	451,212
Republicans	99,170	177,950	66,396	343,516
No. of Cand.	105	148	59	312
House	67,670	107,450	52,396	227,516
Senate	31,500	70,500	14,000	116,000
Democrats	61,922	27,100	18,099	107,121
No. of Cand.	56	30	20	106
House	43,802	21,600	14,099	79,501
Senate	18,120	5,500	4,000	27,620
Incumbents	130,292	162,550	82,495	375,337
Challengers	12,575	14,000	1,000	27,575
Open Seat	18,800	28,500	1,000	48,300
Winners	136,972	157,800	n/a	294,772
Losers	24,695	47,250	n/a	71,945

National Association of Surety Bond Producers

*Phone: (202) 686-3700 * Fax: (202) 686-3656*
5301 Wisconsin Ave. N.W., Suite 450, Washington, DC 20015-2014
*Web: www.nasbp.org * E-mail: tpierce@nasbp.org*

The National Association of Surety Bond Producers is a nonprofit group of 600 insurance agencies and brokerage firms which provide bonding for construction contractors.

NASBP provides educational programs on surety bonding and construction and maintains liaison committees with the major construction industry organizations. It also represents the surety bond industry before Congress and federal agencies.

National Association of Surety Bond Producers PAC (SuretyPAC) (C00300525) *Address: same as sponsor * Treasurer: J. Martin Huber * Contact: Ted Pierce, V.P. of Gov. Affairs*

	1993-94	1995-96	1997	Totals
Receipts	$0	$37,650	$21,875	$59,525
Disburse	0	22,500	3,000	25,500
Cash	0	15,150	34,025	n/a
Contributions	0	21,500	2,000	23,500
Republicans	0	18,000	1,000	19,000
No. of Cand.	0	26	2	28
House	0	8,000	1,000	9,000
Senate	0	10,000	0	10,000
Democrats	0	3,500	500	4,000
No. of Cand.	0	6	1	7
House	0	2,500	500	3,000
Senate	0	1,000	0	1,000
Incumbents	0	20,000	2,000	22,000
Challengers	0	0	0	0
Open Seat	0	1,500	0	1,500
Winners	0	20,500	n/a	20,500
Losers	0	1,000	n/a	1,000

National Structured Settlements Trade Association

*Phone: (202) 797-5108 * Fax: (202) 332-2301*
1420 16th St. N.W., Washington, DC 20036
*Web: www.nssta.com * E-mail: nssta@aol.com*

The National Structured Settlements Trade Association is an organization of insurance companies and individuals who negotiate and implement structured settlements in physical injury cases.

In a structured settlement, at least a portion of the financial claim is due at a later date. These settlements are usually used in cases involving serious, long-term physical injuries. The settlement is paid out over a period of time, throughout the duration of the injury or the life of the person. Often the defendant will purchase an annuity contract to fund the settlement, although trust funds have also been used.

Founded in 1986, the 500-member association promotes the use of structured settlements as a means of resolving personal injury, workers' compensation and other claims.

National Structured Settlements Trade Association Political Action Committee (C00219444) *Address: same as sponsor * Treasurer: William R. Dyer * Contact: Jerry Lothrop, Chairman*

	1993-94	1995-96	1997	Totals
Receipts	$76,435	$157,924	$79,670	$314,029
Disburse	75,095	105,316	84,250	264,661
Cash	18,487	71,197	66,618	n/a
Contributions	36,804	54,250	59,500	150,554
Republicans	7,500	22,500	34,500	64,500
No. of Cand.	7	9	10	26
House	7,500	22,500	31,000	61,000
Senate	0	0	3,500	3,500
Democrats	29,304	31,750	25,000	86,054
No. of Cand.	26	17	5	48
House	29,304	23,250	20,000	72,554
Senate	0	8,500	5,000	13,500
Incumbents	35,804	49,250	57,000	142,054
Challengers	500	0	2,500	3,000
Open Seat	500	5,000	0	5,500
Winners	31,304	52,250	n/a	83,554
Losers	5,500	2,000	n/a	7,500

Nationwide Insurance Enterprise

Phone: (614) 249-7811
One Nationwide Plaza, Columbus, OH 43216
Web: www.nationwide.com

Nationwide Insurance is the fifth-largest U.S. property and casualty insurer with $60 billion in assets. Its auto, homeowner and life insurance practices rank among the largest in the country. The company also sells health and commercial insurance and financial products including mutual funds and annuities. Nationwide does business in every state. A subsidiary sells insurance in Germany.

The company also administers the Medicare Part B (outpatient) program for 1.9 million residents in Ohio and West Virginia.

Founded in 1925, the mutual company has more than 28,000 employees and services 13 million policies.

Subsidiaries include: Wausau Insurance, Nationwide Direct, Nationwide Health Plans, Public Employees Benefit Services Corp. (PEBSCO), Scottsdale Insurance, Gates McDonald, Nationwide Advisory Services and Farmland Insurance.

Nationwide Political Participation Committee (C00076174) *Address: same as sponsor * Treasurer: James Benney*

	1993-94	1995-96	1997	Totals
Receipts	$110,473	$110,819	$47,446	$268,738
Disburse	113,512	94,930	49,003	257,445
Cash	23,630	39,530	37,396	n/a
Contributions	71,883	47,200	28,250	147,333
Republicans	52,235	41,950	23,750	117,935
No. of Cand.	24	23	16	63
House	39,235	35,700	20,250	95,185
Senate	13,000	6,250	3,500	22,750
Democrats	19,648	5,250	4,500	29,398
No. of Cand.	17	6	7	30
House	14,648	4,750	3,000	22,398
Senate	5,000	500	1,500	7,000
Incumbents	54,583	40,950	26,750	122,283
Challengers	2,450	5,000	500	7,950
Open Seat	14,850	1,500	1,000	17,350
Winners	62,583	37,450	n/a	100,033
Losers	9,300	9,750	n/a	19,050

Wausau Insurance Companies Political Action Committee-Federal (WICPAC-Federal) (C00148502) *Phone: (715) 842-6583 * Fax: (715) 847-8168 * 2000 Westwood (54401), P.O. Box 8017, Wausau, WI 54402-8017 * Web: www.wausau.com * Treasurer: Patrick G. Gosz * Contact: Gay Baumgart, Gov. Affairs Political Coordinator*

Wausau Insurance is a private international insurer offering a broad range of commercial property and casualty coverage, loss management service, employee benefits products and underwriting throughout the United States and foreign countries.

Founded in 1911 as The Employers Mutual Liability Insurance Co., Wausau includes several companies and divisions, including workers' compensation, integrated disability management, risk management accounts, standard accounts and Wausau Insurance Companies UK Ltd.

Wausau offers community-based health care plans in Wisconsin, Michigan, Indiana and California and HMO and PPO coverage throughout the country under the Wausau and Nationwide brands.

	1993-94	1995-96	1997	Totals
Receipts	$19,831	$17,339	$8,573	$45,743
Disburse	32,569	27,089	8,104	67,762
Cash	16,006	6,259	6,728	n/a
Contributions	27,610	18,350	5,200	51,160
Republicans	16,410	14,850	1,750	33,010
No. of Cand.	*25*	*27*	*5*	*57*
House	6,760	11,600	1,500	19,860
Senate	9,650	3,250	250	13,150
Democrats	11,200	3,500	3,450	18,150
No. of Cand.	*16*	*5*	*6*	*27*
House	9,100	3,000	3,200	15,300
Senate	2,100	500	250	2,850
Incumbents	17,860	13,400	3,450	34,710
Challengers	3,500	1,750	750	6,000
Open Seat	6,250	3,200	1,000	10,450
Winners	25,360	12,700	n/a	38,060
Losers	2,250	5,650	n/a	7,900

New York Life Insurance Co.

*Phone: (212) 576-7790 * Fax: (212) 576-4473*
51 Madison Ave., Suite 910, New York, NY 10010
Web: www.newyorklife.com

New York Life Insurance offers a variety of insurance and financial services.

Owned by its policyholders, the $75 billion private company's clients include General Motors, the National Basketball Association, the Air Line Pilots Association and The American Institute of Architects. Founded in 1845, it has grown to employ more than 11,000 agents in nearly 150 offices worldwide.

On the insurance side, New York Life and its affiliates offer traditional life and group health insurance, annuities and managed health care plans. On the financial side, New York Life and its affiliates provide institutional investment management, trust services and 401(k) services.

New York Life Insurance Company's subsidiaries include NYLCare, NYLIFE Securities Inc., and New York Life Worldwide Holding Inc.

New York Life Insurance Co. Political Action Committee (C00158881) *Address: same as sponsor * Treasurer: Maura McLaughlin * Contact: Jeannine Dowling, PAC Dir.*

	1993-94	1995-96	1997	Totals
Receipts	$332,002	$387,644	$218,030	$937,676
Disburse	265,319	330,320	192,804	788,443
Cash	76,985	134,314	159,541	n/a
Contributions	162,667	180,300	115,770	458,737
Republicans	46,166	111,350	67,200	224,716
No. of Cand.	*52*	*92*	*63*	*207*
House	30,166	82,150	48,200	160,516
Senate	16,000	29,200	19,000	64,200
Democrats	114,501	68,950	48,570	232,021
No. of Cand.	*67*	*41*	*32*	*140*
House	62,665	53,450	32,570	148,685
Senate	51,836	15,500	16,000	83,336
Incumbents	141,306	165,300	112,270	418,876
Challengers	8,465	3,700	2,000	14,165
Open Seat	13,896	11,300	1,500	26,696
Winners	136,866	162,600	n/a	299,466
Losers	25,801	17,700	n/a	43,501

Northwestern Mutual Life Insurance Co.

*Phone: (414) 299-2508 * Fax: (414) 299-7016*
720 E. Wisconsin Ave., Room 647, Milwaukee, WI 53202-4797
Web: www.northwesternmutual.com

Northwestern Mutual Life Insurance is a Milwaukee-based private life insurance company. One of the nation's 10 largest life insurers, the company sells more individual life insurance than any other company in the nation. It also sells health and retirement products, fixed and variable annuities and mutual funds.

Northwestern is the fifth-largest of all U.S. life insurance firms in assets. It has about 2.8 million policyholders who have more than 5 million life, disability and annuity policies.

Northwestern has annual revenues of $13 billion. The company employs more than 3,500 workers.

Northwestern Mutual Life Insurance Co. Federal Political Action Committee (NML FedPAC) (C00197095) *Address: same as sponsor * Treasurer: Wilson D. Perry * Contact: Peter W. Bruce, Chairman*

	1993-94	1995-96	1997	Totals
Receipts	$248,641	$264,349	$141,190	$654,180
Disburse	233,574	251,137	84,626	569,337
Cash	54,691	67,906	124,470	n/a
Contributions	184,850	191,785	53,500	430,135
Republicans	94,000	128,785	28,000	250,785
No. of Cand.	*41*	*59*	*28*	*128*
House	46,000	75,785	17,000	138,785
Senate	48,000	53,000	11,000	112,000
Democrats	90,850	63,000	25,500	179,350
No. of Cand.	*40*	*25*	*21*	*86*
House	64,600	48,000	17,500	130,100
Senate	26,250	15,000	8,000	49,250
Incumbents	160,000	147,785	50,500	358,285
Challengers	1,500	3,500	500	5,500
Open Seat	22,100	40,000	2,500	64,600
Winners	157,000	149,785	n/a	306,785
Losers	27,850	42,000	n/a	69,850

Ohio National Financial Services

*Phone: (513) 794-6294 * Fax: (513) 794-4506*
One Financial Way, Cincinnati, OH 45242
Web: www.ohionatl.com

Ohio National Financial Services, formerly known as Ohio National Life Insurance Co., is a Cincinnati-based mutual insurance company with $6.5 billion in consolidated assets.

Founded in 1909, the company employs more than 4,500 people in offices throughout 47 states, the District of Columbia and Puerto Rico. The company offers individual and group life and disability insurance, as well as annuities and pension plans.

At the end of 1996, Ohio National held life insurance policies worth almost $30 billion.

Ohio National Life Insurance Co. Political Action Committee (also known as ONLI-PAC) (C00296657) *Address: same as sponsor * Treasurer: Roylene Broadwell * Contact: David B. O'Maley, PAC Dir.*

	1993-94	1995-96	1997	Totals
Receipts	$10,288	$27,642	$13,753	$51,683
Disburse	13,800	27,710	13,760	55,270
Cash	751	686	681	n/a
Contributions	3,000	8,375	1,500	12,875
Republicans	2,000	8,375	1,500	11,875
No. of Cand.	*1*	*6*	*2*	*9*
House	0	6,375	500	6,875
Senate	2,000	2,000	1,000	5,000
Democrats	1,000	0	0	1,000
No. of Cand.	*1*	*0*	*0*	*1*
House	1,000	0	0	1,000
Senate	0	0	0	0
Incumbents	1,000	7,125	500	8,625
Challengers	0	1,000	0	1,000
Open Seat	2,000	250	1,000	3,250
Winners	2,000	6,125	n/a	8,125
Losers	1,000	2,250	n/a	3,250

Pacific Mutual Life Insurance Co.

*Phone: (714) 640-3280 * Fax: (714) 640-7614*
700 Newport Center Dr., Newport Beach, CA 92660
Web: www.pacificlife.com

Pacific Mutual Life Insurance's family of companies forms one of America's largest financial institutions, managing more than $150 billion in assets. Pacific Life offers life insurance, annuities, pension fund investments, group employee benefits, mutual funds and other investment-related products to individuals and businesses.

Through its Pacific Life Insurance unit, Pacific Mutual is the largest life and health insurer in California. Pacific Life's sales in 1996 were more than $2 billion. The private company employs 2,750 workers.

Pacific Mutual Life Insurance Co. Political Action Committee (PMPAC) (C00068528) *Address: same as sponsor * Treasurer: Robert G. Haskell * Contact: Lynn C. Miller, Chairman*

	1993-94	1995-96	1997	Totals
Receipts	$142,505	$157,962	$91,661	$392,128
Disburse	147,961	153,481	70,920	372,362
Cash	5,771	10,260	31,002	n/a
Contributions	116,925	117,800	49,000	283,725
Republicans	47,875	67,800	19,500	135,175
No. of Cand.	*27*	*38*	*19*	*84*
House	28,375	62,300	18,500	109,175
Senate	19,500	5,500	1,000	26,000
Democrats	69,050	50,000	29,500	148,550
No. of Cand.	*42*	*34*	*26*	*102*
House	43,050	38,500	17,000	98,550
Senate	26,000	11,500	12,500	50,000
Incumbents	95,925	96,300	49,000	241,225
Challengers	10,500	8,000	0	18,500
Open Seat	10,500	14,000	0	24,500
Winners	92,425	103,800	n/a	196,225
Losers	24,500	14,000	n/a	38,500

Pan-American Life Insurance Co.

*Phone: (504) 566-3774 * Fax: (504) 566-3799*
601 Poydras St., Legal Department, New Orleans, LA 70130
Web: www.palic.com

Pan-American Life Insurance has more than $15 billion of life insurance in force and $2 billion in assets. Pan-American Life is licensed to sell insurance in 41 states, the District of Columbia, eight countries in Central and South America, Puerto Rico and the Virgin Islands.

Established in 1912, the private company has expanded into four major divisions: U.S. Life, U.S. Health Group Operations, International Life & Health and Retirement Services.

In September 1997, United Wisconsin Services acquired all of the small group health insurance business of Pan-American Life Insurance Co.

Pan-American Life Insurance Co. PAC (PALIC PAC) (C00232272) *Address: same as sponsor * Treasurer: William T. Steen * Contact: Peter F. Maunoir, Chairman*

	1993-94	1995-96	1997	Totals
Receipts	$22,999	$18,118	$10,829	$51,946
Disburse	24,070	22,380	11,400	57,850
Cash	8,675	4,415	3,845	n/a
Contributions	9,000	6,750	4,250	20,000
Republicans	6,000	5,000	3,750	14,750
No. of Cand.	*7*	*8*	*6*	*21*
House	0	3,500	1,750	5,250
Senate	6,000	1,500	2,000	9,500
Democrats	3,000	1,750	500	5,250
No. of Cand.	*4*	*3*	*2*	*9*
House	3,000	750	500	4,250
Senate	0	1,000	0	1,000
Incumbents	7,000	4,000	2,750	13,750
Challengers	1,250	0	0	1,250
Open Seat	750	2,750	1,500	5,000
Winners	7,750	4,500	n/a	12,250
Losers	1,250	2,250	n/a	3,500

	1993-94	1995-96	1997	Totals
Receipts	$76,673	$59,547	$25,276	$161,496
Disburse	77,584	48,956	8,035	134,575
Cash	7,152	17,746	34,990	n/a
Contributions	30,900	15,750	0	46,650
Republicans	19,500	12,900	0	32,400
No. of Cand.	*11*	*14*	*0*	*25*
House	8,500	7,500	0	16,000
Senate	11,000	5,400	0	16,400
Democrats	11,400	2,850	0	14,250
No. of Cand.	*14*	*5*	*0*	*19*
House	7,900	2,850	0	10,750
Senate	3,500	0	0	3,500
Incumbents	18,650	12,850	0	31,500
Challengers	10,150	2,650	0	12,800
Open Seat	1,600	250	0	1,850
Winners	26,400	11,100	n/a	37,500
Losers	4,500	4,650	n/a	9,150

Phoenix Home Life Mutual Insurance Co.

*Phone: (860) 403-5025 * Fax: (860) 403-5755*
One American Row, 12th Floor, Hartford, CT 06102-5056
Web: www.phl.com

Phoenix Home Life Mutual Insurance is an insurance and investment management company based in Hartford, Conn.

The 146-year-old private company employs nearly 4,000 people nationwide and has more than $50 billion in assets under management, making it the nation's ninth-largest mutual life insurer. The company provides insurance and financial services to 2.5 million people.

Phoenix Home Life Mutual Insurance was formed in 1992 with the merger of Phoenix Mutual Insurance and Home Life Mutual of New York.

The company's subsidiaries include Phoenix Duff & Phelps, Phoenix Charter Oak Trust Co., Phoenix Realty Group Inc., and PHL Associates Inc.

Phoenix Home Life Political Action Committee (C00168203) *Address: same as sponsor * Treasurer: Maura L. Melley * Contact: Dona Young, Member of the Board of Dir.*

	1993-94	1995-96	1997	Totals
Receipts	$61,571	$73,710	$40,879	$176,160
Disburse	78,888	68,842	37,613	185,343
Cash	12,450	17,322	20,589	n/a
Contributions	37,825	29,125	16,000	82,950
Republicans	12,000	10,000	5,500	27,500
No. of Cand.	*13*	*9*	*6*	*28*
House	9,000	9,000	4,500	22,500
Senate	3,000	1,000	1,000	5,000
Democrats	25,825	19,125	10,500	55,450
No. of Cand.	*24*	*20*	*11*	*55*
House	13,825	10,125	6,000	29,950
Senate	12,000	9,000	4,500	25,500
Incumbents	34,625	24,875	16,000	75,500
Challengers	1,700	1,000	0	2,700
Open Seat	1,500	3,250	0	4,750
Winners	28,625	26,375	n/a	55,000
Losers	9,200	2,750	n/a	11,950

Penn Mutual Life Insurance Co.

*Phone: (215) 956-8411 * Fax: (215) 956-8749*
600 Dresher Rd., Horsham, PA 19044
Web: www.pennmutual.com

Penn Mutual Life Insurance, based in Philadelphia, offers insurance and financial planning services, including annuities, pension products and single and survivorship life insurance. The $7.8 billion private company employs about 2,700 people, and according to Hoover's, targets "already affluent" customers, such as business owners, entrepreneurs, executives and professionals.

Penn Mutual's main subsidiaries include the Penn Insurance and Annuity Company, Janney Montgomery Scott Inc., and Hornor, Townsend & Kent Inc.

Penn Mutual Political Action Committee (C00142372) *Address: same as sponsor * Treasurer: Steven Herzberg * Contact: Michael Biondolillo, Chairman*

Principal Mutual Life Insurance Co.

*Phone: (515) 235-6031 * Fax: (515) 246-5475*
711 High St., Tax Dept., Des Moines, IA 50392
Web: www.principal.com

Principal Mutual Life Insurance is a branch of the Principal Financial Group, a diversified family of private financial services companies headquartered in Des Moines, Iowa. Principal provides customers with financial protection through a variety of products and services.

Principal serves more than 9 million customers and is continuing to expand its range of products. For individuals, Principal provides basic financial protection against death or disability and for retirement. Principal's products and services for employee benefit plans include life, disability, comprehensive medical, Health Maintenance Organizations, Preferred Provider Organizations, dental, vision, prescription drug and pension coverage.

Principal's sales in 1997 exceeded $8.6 billion. The company employs more than 17,000 people.

Principal Mutual Life Insurance Co. - Federal Political Action Committee (PrinPAC) (C00128918) *Address: same as sponsor * Treasurer: Luanne Inderski * Contact: Jack Stewart, Chairman*

	1993-94	1995-96	1997	Totals
Receipts	$167,705	$207,142	$113,807	$488,654
Disburse	157,265	218,065	102,120	477,450
Cash	19,456	8,538	20,225	n/a
Contributions	114,500	135,692	64,745	314,937
Republicans	49,890	79,100	37,935	166,925
No. of Cand.	*48*	*71*	*40*	*159*
House	37,640	65,600	27,100	130,340
Senate	12,250	13,500	10,835	36,585
Democrats	64,610	56,592	26,810	148,012
No. of Cand.	*58*	*51*	*31*	*140*
House	43,611	37,842	16,500	97,953
Senate	20,999	18,750	10,310	50,059
Incumbents	104,180	120,092	61,745	286,017
Challengers	4,070	3,500	1,000	8,570
Open Seat	6,250	12,100	2,000	20,350
Winners	94,000	119,592	n/a	213,592
Losers	20,500	16,100	n/a	36,600

Protective Life Corp.

*Phone: (205) 879-9230 * Fax: (205) 868-3597*
P.O. Box 2606, Birmingham, AL 35202
Web: www.protective.com

Protective Life is a publicly held company providing life and health insurance products. It has about 1,300 employees and reported 1996 revenues of $1 billion.

The company includes six divisions: Acquisitions, Financial Institutions, Dental and Consumer Benefits, Guaranteed Investment Contracts, Individual Life and Investment Products.

Founded in 1907, the company's principal operating subsidiary is Protective Life Insurance Co.

Its products are distributed nationally through independent agents and brokers; through broker-dealers and financial institutions to their customers; through full-time sales representatives; and through other insurance companies. The company also seeks to acquire blocks of insurance policies from other insurers.

Protective Life Corp. Federal Political Action Committee (C00161414) *Address: same as sponsor * Treasurer: A. S. Williams III * Contact: Deborah J. Long, Chairman*

	1993-94	1995-96	1997	Totals
Receipts	$18,994	$23,692	$17,660	$60,346
Disburse	16,252	28,565	12,014	56,831
Cash	8,621	3,748	9,394	n/a
Contributions	1,250	14,250	12,000	27,500
Republicans	1,000	13,750	12,000	26,750
No. of Cand.	*1*	*8*	*4*	*13*
House	1,000	3,000	3,000	7,000
Senate	0	10,750	9,000	19,750
Democrats	250	500	0	750
No. of Cand.	*1*	*1*	*0*	*2*
House	0	500	0	500
Senate	250	0	0	250
Incumbents	1,250	3,500	12,000	16,750
Challengers	0	0	0	0
Open Seat	0	10,750	0	10,750
Winners	1,250	12,500	n/a	13,750
Losers	0	1,750	n/a	1,750

Provident Life & Accident Insurance Co.

*Phone: (423) 755-1011 * Fax: (423) 755-8503*
One Fountain Sq., Seventh Floor, Chattanooga, TN 37402

Provident Life & Accident Insurance is a public insurance holding company that sells life and disability insurance products in the United States, Puerto Rico and Canada. Based in Chattanooga, Tenn., the company reported 1997 sales of $3.5 billion. It employs nearly 2,000 people.

Provident merged with Paul Revere Corp. in 1997, resulting in a company with combined sales of $4 billion and $23 billion in assets. In late 1997, Provident's individual and tax-sheltered annuity business was acquired by American General Corp.

Through its seven subsidiaries, Provident offers accident and accidental death insurance, as well as dental, dismemberment and life insurance to individuals and groups.

Provident Life & Accident Insurance Co. Political Action Committee (ProPAC) (C00177436) *Phone: (615) 255-3973 * Fax: (615) 255-8026 * The Tower, Suite 3109, 611 Commerce St., Nashville, TN 37203 * E-mail: roybess_@providentcompanies.com * Treasurer: Henry T. Hardin * Contact: Roy Bess Jr., Chairman*

	1993-94	1995-96	1997	Totals
Receipts	$47,116	$27,713	$12,567	$87,396
Disburse	50,919	35,459	12,388	98,766
Cash	10,297	2,555	2,734	n/a
Contributions	14,175	5,350	2,000	21,525
Republicans	4,300	4,350	2,000	10,650
No. of Cand.	*7*	*6*	*3*	*16*
House	3,300	2,850	1,000	7,150
Senate	1,000	1,500	1,000	3,500
Democrats	9,875	1,000	0	10,875
No. of Cand.	*7*	*2*	*0*	*9*
House	4,875	1,000	0	5,875
Senate	5,000	0	0	5,000
Incumbents	11,875	5,250	2,000	19,125
Challengers	750	100	0	850
Open Seat	1,550	0	0	1,550
Winners	7,875	4,250	n/a	12,125
Losers	6,300	1,100	n/a	7,400

Providian Corp.

*Phone: (415) 543-0404 * Fax: (415) 278-6013*
201 Mission St., 28th Floor, San Francisco, CA 94105
Web: www.providian.com

The Providian PAC was terminated in September 1997, after Providian sold its insurance business and spun off a financial services unit. Providian is now known as Providian Financial and has its own PAC (FEC ID: C00327908).

Providian Corp. Political Action Committee (formerly known as Capital Holding PAC) (C00200550) *1155 Connecticut Ave. N.W., Suite 500, Washington, DC 20036 * Treasurer: Colleen Lyons*

	1993-94	1995-96	1997	Totals
Receipts	$138,325	$169,961	$30,340	$338,626
Disburse	112,054	162,367	120,338	394,759
Cash	83,947	91,554	0	n/a
Contributions	76,475	105,475	32,900	214,850
Republicans	40,625	77,975	32,700	151,300
No. of Cand.	*32*	*58*	*36*	*126*
House	22,000	57,600	18,700	98,300
Senate	18,625	20,375	14,000	53,000
Democrats	35,850	27,500	200	63,550
No. of Cand.	*39*	*26*	*12*	*77*
House	25,850	22,000	-800	47,050
Senate	10,000	5,500	1,000	16,500
Incumbents	67,475	96,975	26,900	191,350
Challengers	0	5,500	0	5,500
Open Seat	9,000	3,000	6,500	18,500
Winners	61,475	97,875	n/a	159,350
Losers	15,000	7,600	n/a	22,600

Prudential Insurance Co. of America

*Phone: (973) 802-6000 * Fax: (973) 802-2812*
751 Broad St. 13th Floor, Prudential Plaza, Newark, NJ 07102
Web: www.prudential.com

Prudential Insurance Co. of America is the largest insurer in the country. In addition to the company's traditional efforts in insurance and health care, Prudential has expanded its services in investments, banking and real estate.

Prudential reported revenues of $37.1 billion for the year ending Dec. 31, 1997. The private company has announced plans to convert to stock ownership by 2000.

Prudential also provides asset management, as well as health care management and other benefit programs for employees and group members. Other businesses include relocation, human resources, and real estate services to the business community. Other subsidiaries offer credit cards, group life and health, and individual life insurance overseas.

The company is paying more than $2 billion to policyholders after a class-action lawsuit was filed charging that Prudential engaged in improper sales tactics and destroyed documents.

Prudential Insurance Co. of America Federal PAC (Prudential PAC) (C00127779) *Phone: (202) 463-0060 * 1140 Connecticut Ave. N.W., Washington, DC 20036 * Treasurer: Peter B. Sayre*

	1993-94	1995-96	1997	Totals
Receipts	$355,347	$324,328	$145,554	$825,229
Disburse	343,718	343,173	148,545	835,436
Cash	34,995	16,151	13,161	n/a
Contributions	214,841	214,592	98,250	527,683
Republicans	64,600	131,000	53,250	248,850
No. of Cand.	*61*	*91*	*58*	*210*
House	37,600	82,250	34,250	154,100
Senate	27,000	48,750	19,000	94,750
Democrats	149,741	83,592	45,000	278,333
No. of Cand.	*92*	*57*	*33*	*182*
House	83,400	58,547	27,000	168,947
Senate	66,341	25,045	18,000	109,386
Incumbents	170,091	174,092	94,750	438,933
Challengers	6,500	12,500	2,000	21,000
Open Seat	37,750	28,000	1,500	67,250
Winners	153,841	174,592	n/a	328,433
Losers	61,000	40,000	n/a	101,000

Prudential Securities Inc. Political Action Committee (C00117051) *Phone: (212) 214-5750 * 1 Seaport Plaza, New York, NY 10292 * Web: www.prusec.com * Treasurer: Bruno G. Bissetta * Contact: Phillip T. Smith, President*

Prudential Securities is a global securities firm based in New York City. The fifth-largest brokerage firm in the United States, Prudential Securities is a subsidiary of the Prudential Insurance Co. of America.

The company's retail sales force has about 6,000 financial advisers in 300 offices in 18 countries.

Prudential Securities is successor to the 100-year-old firm founded as J.S. Bache & Co. In 1981 the company was acquired by The Prudential, and was renamed Prudential Securities Inc. in 1991.

Prudential's services include investment advice, asset management, investment banking, retirement planning and securities brokerage. The company services more than 2.3 million accounts, and as of June 1995, client assets totaled about $164 billion.

	1993-94	1995-96	1997	Totals
Receipts	$136,511	$145,479	$65,870	$347,860
Disburse	128,294	159,170	71,515	358,979
Cash	37,340	23,656	18,016	n/a
Contributions	90,650	114,675	44,000	249,325
Republicans	57,250	74,925	28,000	160,175
No. of Cand.	*62*	*76*	*31*	*169*
House	37,000	55,925	20,000	112,925
Senate	20,250	19,000	8,000	47,250
Democrats	32,400	39,750	16,000	88,150
No. of Cand.	*35*	*47*	*16*	*98*
House	23,400	29,250	9,000	61,650
Senate	9,000	10,500	7,000	26,500
Incumbents	76,150	92,750	41,500	210,400
Challengers	4,750	5,675	1,500	11,925
Open Seat	9,250	18,000	1,000	28,250
Winners	71,400	90,000	n/a	161,400
Losers	19,250	24,675	n/a	43,925

	1993-94	1995-96	1997	Totals
Receipts	$20,406	$24,563	$18,370	$63,339
Disburse	20,300	28,100	16,820	65,220
Cash	4,336	800	2,600	n/a
Contributions	19,100	21,100	16,320	56,520
Republicans	10,600	15,000	10,750	36,350
No. of Cand.	*15*	*19*	*14*	*48*
House	8,600	9,750	7,250	25,600
Senate	2,000	5,250	3,500	10,750
Democrats	8,500	6,100	5,570	20,170
No. of Cand.	*9*	*6*	*3*	*18*
House	4,000	3,750	1,000	8,750
Senate	4,500	2,350	4,570	11,420
Incumbents	15,300	11,500	15,320	42,120
Challengers	1,250	2,000	0	3,250
Open Seat	2,550	7,600	1,000	11,150
Winners	18,600	10,750	n/a	29,350
Losers	500	10,350	n/a	10,850

Reliance Group Holdings Inc.

*Phone: (212) 909-1278 * Fax: (212) 308-0484*
Park Ave. Plaza, 55 E. 52nd St., 29th Floor, New York, NY 10055
Web: www.rgh.com

Reliance Group Holdings is a holding company for insurance firms that serve mainly commercial customers. Its units are located throughout North America and in Europe, Latin America and the Pacific Rim.

The 9,300-employee company reported 1997 sales of $3.4 billion.

Subsidiaries Reliance Insurance, Reliance National, Reliance Reinsurance Corp. and Reliance Surety provide a wide range of property and casualty coverage for corporations. The company also offers reinsurance services mainly to small and mid-sized specialty insurers and provides surety bonds for contractors and financial institutions. It sold its title insurance businesses.

Reliance Group Holdings Inc. Political Action Committee (ReliancePAC) (C00157842) *Address: same as sponsor * Treasurer: Philip S. Sherman*

	1993-94	1995-96	1997	Totals
Receipts	$6,894	$3,823	$22,445	$33,162
Disburse	89,250	45,750	15,000	150,000
Cash	84,286	42,361	49,807	n/a
Contributions	9,500	26,250	4,000	39,750
Republicans	4,500	16,000	4,000	24,500
No. of Cand.	*4*	*4*	*2*	*10*
House	1,000	4,000	0	5,000
Senate	3,500	12,000	4,000	19,500
Democrats	5,000	10,250	0	15,250
No. of Cand.	*5*	*2*	*0*	*7*
House	3,000	10,250	0	13,250
Senate	2,000	0	0	2,000
Incumbents	5,500	22,250	4,000	31,750
Challengers	3,000	4,000	0	7,000
Open Seat	1,000	0	0	1,000
Winners	6,500	22,250	n/a	28,750
Losers	3,000	4,000	n/a	7,000

Reinsurance Association of America

*Phone: (202) 638-3690 * Fax: (202) 638-0936*
1301 Pennsylvania Ave. N.W., Suite 900, Washington, DC 20004
Web: www.raanet.org

The Reinsurance Association of America is a nonprofit trade association of property and casualty reinsurers in the United States. Reinsurance protects against unforeseen or substantial losses. Established in 1968, the association is headquartered in Washington.

The primary purpose of the group is to advance the interests of the U.S. property and casualty reinsurance industry through effective government relations with state and federal regulatory agencies, legislators and other elected officials. The RAA is active on insurance regulatory issues and others such as environmental liability, Superfund, and natural disasters.

Conferences and publications for RAA members cover reinsurance legal developments, tax, claims, accounting and environmental issues.

Reinsurance Association of America Political Action Committee Inc. (RePAC) (C00256453) *Address: same as sponsor * Treasurer: Francis D. Bouchard*

Reliastar Financial Corp.

*Phone: (612) 342-3732 * Fax: (612) 342-3966*
Reliastar-Route 5010, 20 Washington Ave. S., Minneapolis, MN 55401
*Web: www.reliastar.com * E-mail: don.stiles@reliastar.com*

Reliastar Life Insurance Co., formerly known as Northwestern National Life Insurance Co., is the oldest and largest subsidiary of Reliastar Financial.

Reliastar Financial is the twelfth-largest publicly held life insurance holding company in the United States, serving 4 million customers in all 50 states. Its 14 subsidiaries offer individual insurance and annuities, employee benefits, retirement plans, health and life reinsurance, educational seminars, mutual funds, fund management and residential mortgages.

The company's 1997 revenues were $2.2 billion. The company, which employs more than 3,000 workers, collects 25 percent of its premiums in both the Southeast and Pacific regions of the United States. It also has reinsurance operations in Europe, South America and the Far East.

Major subsidiaries include: Reliastar Life Insurance, Security-Connecticut Life, Washington Square Securities, and PrimeVest Financial Services.

Reliastar Federal Political Action Committee (formerly known as NWNL Federal PAC) (C00151357) *Address: same as sponsor * Treasurer: Don Stiles*

	1993-94	1995-96	1997	Totals
Receipts	$44,122	$70,412	$36,522	$151,056
Disburse	54,975	70,407	39,623	165,005
Cash	6,766	6,775	3,675	n/a
Contributions	35,243	44,972	34,750	114,965
Republicans	23,202	33,222	25,500	81,924
No. of Cand.	*26*	*39*	*30*	*95*
House	8,202	24,722	17,500	50,424
Senate	15,000	8,500	8,000	31,500
Democrats	8,341	11,750	7,750	27,841
No. of Cand.	*10*	*16*	*10*	*36*
House	6,841	9,250	3,250	19,341
Senate	1,500	2,500	4,500	8,500
Incumbents	22,091	36,472	34,250	92,813
Challengers	2,850	4,750	500	8,100
Open Seat	10,302	3,250	0	13,552
Winners	25,441	35,722	n/a	61,163
Losers	9,802	9,250	n/a	19,052

SAFECO Corp.

*Phone: (206) 545-5537 * Fax: (206) 545-5500*
Safeco Plaza, Seattle, WA 98185
Web: www.safeco.com

SAFECO sells property and casualty insurance, life and health insurance, commercial credit and mutual funds. The publicly owned Seattle company had $4.7 billion in 1997 revenues. Offices are primarily located in the Pacific Northwest and Midwest, with major offices in Indiana, Kansas and Washington state.

In October 1997, SAFECO purchased insurance-writer American States Financial Corp. for $2.8 billion. The deal makes SAFECO the 15th largest property and casualty insurer in the United States and expands the firm's presence east of the Rocky Mountains. Many of SAFECO's insurance contracts are with small businesses.

SAFECO, which has 11,000 employees, offers a variety of stock, bond and money market mutual funds under its name.

Founded in 1923 as General Insurance Co. of America, SAFECO also owns more than 20 real estate companies.

SAFECO PAC (C00034876) *Address: same as sponsor * Treasurer: George P. Yonker*

	1993-94	1995-96	1997	Totals
Receipts	$79,306	$94,437	$58,528	$232,271
Disburse	80,489	86,252	21,308	188,049
Cash	5,525	13,718	50,939	n/a
Contributions	67,150	72,000	13,238	152,388
Republicans	62,000	71,000	13,238	146,238
No. of Cand.	*20*	*23*	*9*	*52*
House	33,000	44,500	6,238	83,738
Senate	29,000	26,500	7,000	62,500
Democrats	5,150	0	0	5,150
No. of Cand.	*2*	*0*	*0*	*2*
House	5,150	0	0	5,150
Senate	0	0	0	0
Incumbents	26,150	43,500	13,238	82,888
Challengers	28,000	8,500	0	36,500
Open Seat	13,000	20,000	0	33,000
Winners	66,150	49,500	n/a	115,650
Losers	1,000	22,500	n/a	23,500

Security Benefit Group Inc.

*Phone: (785) 431-3000 * Fax: (785) 431-3080*
700 S.W. Harrison St., Topeka, KS 66636-0001
Web: www.sbl.com

Security Benefit Group is an international insurance and financial support company that offers annuities, mutual funds, life insurance and asset management through a network of 16,500 sales representatives serving a half million customers. Security Benefit is a $7 billion private financial organization.

Security Benefit Group Inc. Federal Political Action Committee (C00216358) *Address: same as sponsor * Treasurer: Roger K. Viola * Contact: Howard Fricke, Chairman*

	1993-94	1995-96	1997	Totals
Receipts	$8,578	$6,001	$2,512	$17,091
Disburse	6,802	8,400	4,037	19,239
Cash	5,901	3,503	1,977	n/a
Contributions	800	4,400	0	5,200
Republicans	450	3,400	0	3,850
No. of Cand.	*3*	*7*	*0*	*10*
House	450	500	0	950
Senate	0	2,900	0	2,900
Democrats	350	1,000	0	1,350
No. of Cand.	*2*	*2*	*0*	*4*
House	350	500	0	850
Senate	0	500	0	500
Incumbents	300	500	0	800
Challengers	0	1,950	0	1,950
Open Seat	500	1,950	0	2,450
Winners	450	3,100	n/a	3,550
Losers	350	1,300	n/a	1,650

Security Life of Denver Insurance Co.

*Phone: (303) 860-1290 * Fax: (303) 860-2134*
1290 Broadway, Denver, CO 80203
Web: www.sldenver.com

Security Life of Denver, a member of the ING Group, is a private company that primarily markets life insurance products. Its product portfolio provides wealth transfer, asset protection, retirement planning, business continuity and investment management options in general account and variable product lines.

Established in 1928, Security Life has more than 500 employees. The company manages total assets of more than $6.1 billion and during 1996 generated sales of more $116 million in total first year premiums.

In 1994, Security Life established ING America Equities Inc. as its broker-dealer. Security Life and ING America Equities jointly contract with retail broker-dealers to distribute life and annuity products.

Security Life of Denver Insurance Co. Political Action Committee (Security Life PAC) (C00163113) *Address: same as sponsor * Treasurer: Thomas F. Conroy*

	1993-94	1995-96	1997	Totals
Receipts	$26,731	$29,453	$12,844	$69,028
Disburse	24,525	29,542	13,000	67,067
Cash	2,595	3,470	3,315	n/a
Contributions	23,025	28,275	12,000	63,300
Republicans	8,025	22,200	9,500	39,725
No. of Cand.	*8*	*14*	*11*	*33*
House	7,525	10,600	6,000	24,125
Senate	500	11,600	3,500	15,600
Democrats	15,000	6,075	2,500	23,575
No. of Cand.	*12*	*7*	*3*	*22*
House	6,000	6,075	1,500	13,575
Senate	9,000	0	1,000	10,000
Incumbents	20,525	14,925	11,500	46,950
Challengers	1,000	500	500	2,000
Open Seat	1,500	12,850	0	14,350
Winners	21,025	26,025	n/a	47,050
Losers	2,000	2,250	n/a	4,250

Shelter Mutual Insurance Co.

*Phone: (573) 874-4293 * Fax: (573) 445-9319*
1817 W. Broadway, Columbia, MO 65218
Web: www.shelterins.com

Shelter Mutual Insurance is a subsidiary of Shelter Insurance, a private regional insurance group and an international reinsurance operation. The Shelter Insurance group includes Shelter General Insurance Co., Shelter Life Insurance Co. and Shelter Reinsurance Co.

Shelter provides life, home, car, farm and business insurance.

Established in 1946, the company has grown from a single-line, single-state insurer into a multiple-line company with 1,300 agents in 13 Midwestern states. The company employs 1,600 people to staff its Columbia, Mo. headquarters. Shelter also has 25 claims-service facilities throughout the Midwest and a network of independent adjusters nationwide.

Shelter Mutual Insurance Co. Federal PAC (C00140384) *Address: same as sponsor * Treasurer: R. T. Cox * Contact: John Lenox, Chairman*

	1993-94	1995-96	1997	Totals
Receipts	$27,254	$20,687	$11,658	$59,599
Disburse	30,800	21,313	10,500	62,613
Cash	1,726	1,103	2,262	n/a
Contributions	20,727	7,300	3,500	31,527
Republicans	11,954	0	3,500	15,454
No. of Cand.	*5*	*0*	*3*	*8*
House	5,200	0	1,500	6,700
Senate	6,754	0	2,000	8,754
Democrats	8,773	7,300	0	16,073
No. of Cand.	*4*	*3*	*0*	*7*
House	8,773	7,300	0	16,073
Senate	0	0	0	0
Incumbents	12,973	7,300	3,500	23,773
Challengers	0	0	0	0
Open Seat	6,754	0	0	6,754
Winners	19,727	6,000	n/a	25,727
Losers	1,000	1,300	n/a	2,300

Southland Life Insurance Co.

Phone: (770) 850-7784
5780 Powers Ferry Rd. N.W., Atlanta, GA 30327
Web: www.southlandlife.com

Southland Life Insurance, based in Atlanta, offers life insurance and other services. The private company holds about $1.3 billion in assets and generated more than $239.7 million in premiums in 1996. Southland has more than 5,000 agents and 230 home office employees.

The company's three operating units are: Southland Life general agency, ING medical risk solutions and emerging markets. Southland Life is a unit of ING Group, a Netherlands-based financial services company that operates in more than 50 countries worldwide.

Life Insurance Co. of Georgia/Southland Life Insurance Co. PAC (C00184028) *Address: same as sponsor * Treasurer: John Schellack * Contact: Jeff McClellan, Public Relations Officer*

	1993-94	1995-96	1997	Totals
Receipts	$38,656	$19,549	$10,494	$68,699
Disburse	20,054	37,105	12,617	69,776
Cash	19,025	2,942	821	n/a
Contributions	14,450	27,750	13,000	55,200
Republicans	7,000	22,250	11,000	40,250
No. of Cand.	*5*	*20*	*10*	*35*
House	4,500	18,250	6,500	29,250
Senate	2,500	4,000	4,500	11,000
Democrats	7,450	5,000	2,000	14,450
No. of Cand.	*8*	*7*	*2*	*17*
House	6,950	2,750	2,000	11,700
Senate	500	2,250	0	2,750
Incumbents	14,450	23,500	13,000	50,950
Challengers	0	500	0	500
Open Seat	0	3,250	0	3,250
Winners	12,450	24,000	n/a	36,450
Losers	2,000	3,750	n/a	5,750

St. Paul Companies Inc.

*Phone: (612) 310-3865 * Fax: (612) 310-6942*
P.O. Box 2209, St. Paul, MN 55102
*Web: www.stpaul.com * E-mail: pete.thrane@spcmail.stpaul.com*

St. Paul Companies is Minnesota's largest insurer, offering property and casualty insurance, reinsurance and investment services through its subsidiaries. The public company, headquartered in St. Paul, Minn., reported 1997 sales of $6.2 billion and employs 10,200 people.

In April 1998, St. Paul acquired USF&G Corp. in a move that made it the eighth-largest U.S. property and casualty insurer.

Its subsidiaries include St. Paul Fire and Marine, which sells commercial insurance and personal coverage; St. Paul Re, which offers reinsurance for property/liability insurers; and the John Nuveen Co., which offers tax-free investment products. The company's products are sold through independent U.S. agents and brokers.

St. Paul Companies Inc. Volunteer Committee for Good Federal Government (C00042424) *Address: same as sponsor * Treasurer: Peter Thrane*

	1993-94	1995-96	1997	Totals
Receipts	$55,368	$39,876	$17,676	$112,920
Disburse	54,396	38,610	14,372	107,378
Cash	5,655	6,921	10,227	n/a
Contributions	37,950	17,000	5,650	60,600
Republicans	25,450	13,000	4,500	42,950
No. of Cand.	*22*	*12*	*5*	*39*
House	16,700	7,000	2,500	26,200
Senate	8,750	6,000	2,000	16,750
Democrats	12,500	4,000	1,150	17,650
No. of Cand.	*12*	*6*	*2*	*20*
House	11,500	4,000	150	15,650
Senate	1,000	0	1,000	2,000
Incumbents	19,950	10,500	5,150	35,600
Challengers	7,000	5,000	500	12,500
Open Seat	11,000	1,000	0	12,000
Winners	28,950	10,500	n/a	39,450
Losers	9,000	6,500	n/a	15,500

Standard Insurance Co.

*Phone: (503) 321-8447 * Fax: (503) 321-6776*
P.O. Box 711, Portland, OR 97207-0711
Web: www.standard.com

Standard Insurance is one of the 25 largest mutual insurance companies in the nation. The Oregon company offers life and disability insurance, retirement plans for groups and individuals and dental insurance for groups.

The $4 billion company serves more than 4 million people nationwide. Through its 64 sales offices, the company offers insurance in all 50 states and the District of Columbia, although in New York it is licensed only to provide reinsurance. The company, with 1,750 employees, had 1996 sales of more than $1 billion.

Founded in 1906 as Oregon Life Insurance Company, the company changed to its present name in 1946.

The company, which is owned by its policyholders, announced in December 1997 that it was planning to convert to a publicly traded company within the next two years.

The PAC is directed by a committee of four company managers.

Standard Insurance Co. Political Action Committee (Stan-PAC) (C00193169) *Address: same as sponsor * Treasurer: John W. Mangan*

	1993-94	1995-96	1997	Totals
Receipts	$31,480	$9,506	$9,725	$50,711
Disburse	32,200	12,250	4,000	48,450
Cash	3,981	1,241	6,968	n/a
Contributions	4,700	6,500	1,000	12,200
Republicans	3,750	4,750	0	8,500
No. of Cand.	*9*	*4*	*0*	*13*
House	2,750	2,000	0	4,750
Senate	1,000	2,750	0	3,750
Democrats	950	1,750	1,000	3,700
No. of Cand.	*4*	*2*	*1*	*7*
House	950	750	0	1,700
Senate	0	1,000	1,000	2,000
Incumbents	1,150	1,750	1,000	3,900
Challengers	1,500	1,000	0	2,500
Open Seat	2,050	3,750	0	5,800
Winners	2,900	4,500	n/a	7,400
Losers	1,800	2,000	n/a	3,800

Torchmark Corp.

*Phone: (205) 325-4200 * Fax: (205) 325-4230*
2001 Third Ave. S., Birmingham, AL 35233
Web: www.torchmarkcorp.com

Torchmark is a diversified insurance and financial services company. Through such subsidiaries as Liberty National Life Insurance Co., United American Insurance Co., Globe Life & Accident Insurance Co., American Income Insurance Co., United Investors Life Insurance Co. and Family Service Life Insurance Co., it offers complete lines of individual life and health insurance products.

Torchmark is a publicly traded insurance and financial services holding company. It posted $2 billion in 1997 revenues. Torchmark employs more than 4,800 workers.

Torchmark Corp. Political Action Committee (Torch-PAC) (C00167460) *Address: same as sponsor * Treasurer: Stephen W. Still*

	1993-94	1995-96	1997	Totals
Receipts	$213,625	$198,488	$82,760	$494,873
Disburse	258,308	218,005	79,355	555,668
Cash	48,104	28,586	31,991	n/a
Contributions	185,250	128,750	63,000	377,000
Republicans	117,500	116,250	61,000	294,750
No. of Cand.	*54*	*81*	*35*	*170*
House	24,000	41,750	22,500	88,250
Senate	93,500	74,500	38,500	206,500
Democrats	67,750	12,500	2,000	82,250
No. of Cand.	*55*	*10*	*3*	*68*
House	53,750	-2,500	500	51,750
Senate	14,000	15,000	1,500	30,500
Incumbents	117,250	82,000	62,500	261,750
Challengers	21,000	11,000	0	32,000
Open Seat	41,500	49,250	500	91,250
Winners	143,500	101,000	n/a	244,500
Losers	41,750	27,750	n/a	69,500

TransAmerica Corp.

*Phone: (415) 983-4160 * Fax: (415) 983-4234*
600 Montgomery St., San Francisco, CA 94111
*Web: www.transamerica.com * E-mail: james.lockhart@transamerica.com*

TransAmerica is one of the largest U.S. financial service companies. Its primary business is life insurance, but other divisions offer lending services, real estate services, data-management software, home mortgaging and intermodal transportation. TransAmerica is a Fortune 500 company.

Headquartered in San Francisco, the publicly traded company posted $6.2 billion in 1997 revenue and employs 10,400 people.

A subsidiary, TransAmerica Life, dissolved its PAC in February 1998.

TransAmerica Corp. Political Action Committee (TransPAC) (C00122614) *Address: same as sponsor * Treasurer: James B. Lockhart*

	1993-94	1995-96	1997	Totals
Receipts	$34,371	$45,678	$30,004	$110,053
Disburse	38,192	39,460	6,351	84,003
Cash	52,186	58,409	82,063	n/a
Contributions	26,499	33,750	4,500	64,749
Republicans	7,999	17,250	3,000	28,249
No. of Cand.	*2*	*12*	*2*	*16*
House	1,000	9,750	0	10,750
Senate	6,999	7,500	3,000	17,499
Democrats	18,500	16,500	1,500	36,500
No. of Cand.	*7*	*9*	*5*	*21*
House	9,000	9,000	4,500	22,500
Senate	9,500	7,500	-3000	14,000
Incumbents	26,499	29,250	3,000	58,749
Challengers	0	0	1,000	1,000
Open Seat	0	4,500	500	5,000
Winners	26,499	29,750	n/a	56,249
Losers	0	4,000	n/a	4,000

TransAmerica Life Companies Political Action Committee (TALCPAC) (C00112144) *Phone: (213) 742-2111 * 1150 S. Olive St., Suite 2500, Los Angeles, CA 90015 * Treasurer: James M. Jackson*

	1993-94	1995-96	1997	Totals
Receipts	$56,810	$62,442	$25,023	$144,275
Disburse	56,359	66,702	28,582	151,643
Cash	7,812	3,557	0	n/a
Contributions	42,150	37,950	6,500	86,600
Republicans	4,850	16,100	4,500	25,450
No. of Cand.	*12*	*14*	*4*	*30*
House	5,850	13,350	3,500	22,700
Senate	-1,000	2,750	1,000	2,750
Democrats	36,800	21,850	2,000	60,650
No. of Cand.	*43*	*17*	*1*	*61*
House	34,300	17,350	2,000	53,650
Senate	2,500	4,500	0	7,000
Incumbents	39,650	28,600	6,500	74,750
Challengers	0	3,750	0	3,750
Open Seat	3,000	5,600	0	8,600
Winners	39,900	29,700	n/a	69,600
Losers	2,250	8,250	n/a	10,500

Travelers Group Inc.

*Phone: (212) 816-6000 * Fax: (212) 816-8915*
388 Greenwich St., New York, NY 10013
Web: www.travelers.com

Travelers Group is a financial services firm whose products include life, property and casualty insurance, credit cards, investment banking, mutual funds and asset management. The public company has 58,000 employees and reported more than $37 billion in 1997 revenues.

In April 1998, Citicorp and Travelers Group announced plans for an $82 billion merger. The deal is contingent on congressional action to remove regulatory barriers between the banking and financial services industries. In October 1997, the Travelers Group acquired Salomon Inc., parent of the Salomon Brothers investment banking firm, in a stock swap valued at about $9 billion. The unit, combined under the name Salomon Smith Barney Holdings Inc., formed the heart of a multiservice financial behemoth with a total stock market value of $55 billion.

Subsidiaries include: Commercial Credit Co., Travelers Property Casualty Corp. and The Travelers Insurance Co.

Travelers Group Inc. Political Action Committee (formerly known as The Travelers Inc. PAC) (C00039305) *Phone: (202) 789-1380 * Fax: (202) 739-0776 * 901 15th St. N.W., Washington, DC 20005 * Treasurer: Daniel E. Rubenstein*

	1993-94	1995-96	1997	Totals
Receipts	$26,993	$391,216	$260,662	$678,871
Disburse	8,880	392,053	238,997	639,930
Cash	36,494	35,667	57,337	n/a
Contributions	8,500	177,400	75,026	260,926
Republicans	0	133,150	46,926	180,076
No. of Cand.	*0*	*105*	*50*	*155*
House	0	89,150	33,500	122,650
Senate	0	44,000	13,426	57,426
Democrats	8,500	44,250	28,100	80,850
No. of Cand.	*3*	*31*	*28*	*62*
House	3,500	28,750	20,100	52,350
Senate	5,000	15,500	8,000	28,500
Incumbents	8,500	150,000	71,026	229,526
Challengers	0	5,500	1,000	6,500
Open Seat	0	21,900	3,000	24,900
Winners	8,500	144,750	n/a	153,250
Losers	0	32,650	n/a	32,650

Salomon Brothers Inc. Political Action Committee (C00148734) *Phone: (212) 816-6000 * Fax: (212) 816-8915 * 388 Greenwich St., New York, NY 10013 * Web: www.salomon.com*

*Phone: (202) 879-4100 * Fax: (202) 638-4811 * 1455 Pennsylvania Ave. N.W., Suite 500, Washington, DC 20004 * Treasurer: William J. Jennings*

Located in New York, Salomon Brothers is a leading investment banking firm and one of the largest bond traders in the world. The company provides a range of underwriting, research, financial advisory and investment management services to governments, corporations and institutional investors. Acquired by Travelers Group in 1997, the company now operates under Salomon Smith Barney Holdings.

	1993-94	1995-96	1997	Totals
Receipts	$320,250	$193,250	$157,250	$670,750
Disburse	363,500	171,000	191,691	726,191
Cash	26,332	48,582	14,141	n/a
Contributions	219,000	87,400	131,691	438,091
Republicans	114,000	43,400	60,000	217,400
No. of Cand.	*71*	*34*	*47*	*152*
House	48,000	23,000	35,000	106,000
Senate	66,000	20,400	25,000	111,400
Democrats	104,500	44,000	71,691	220,191
No. of Cand.	*48*	*33*	*47*	*128*
House	43,500	20,500	31,691	95,691
Senate	61,000	23,500	40,000	124,500
Incumbents	183,500	79,900	131,691	395,091
Challengers	4,000	0	0	4,000
Open Seat	26,500	7,500	0	34,000
Winners	184,500	83,900	n/a	268,400
Losers	34,500	3,500	n/a	38,000

Smith Barney Inc. Better Government Committee (Smith Barney Better Government Committee) (C00008474) *Phone: (212) 816-4965 * Fax: (212) 816-8996 * 388 Greenwich St., New York, NY 10013 * Web: www.smithbarney.com * Treasurer: Timothy R. Campbell*

Smith Barney is one of Wall Street's leading brokerage firms. The company provides research and trading of stocks, options and mutual funds. It also offers fixed-income securities and financial management accounts.

Smith Barney now operates under Salomon Smith Barney Holdings, the company created by the Travelers Group's October 1997 acquisition of Salomon Inc. Salomon Smith Barney Holdings is a global securities firm. The company, which employs 7,000 workers, also provides asset management and financial research and advice. It operates more than 500 offices in the United States, Canada, Asia, Australia, Europe and South America. Total estimated sales for Salomon Smith Barney for 1996 were $9 billion.

	1993-94	1995-96	1997	Totals
Receipts	$5,542	$128,843	$127,709	$262,094
Disburse	5,213	64,685	178,915	248,813
Cash	474	64,637	13,431	n/a
Contributions	-5000	36,000	142,725	173,725
Republicans	0	24,000	105,100	129,100
No. of Cand.	*0*	*21*	*100*	*121*
House	0	12,000	79,100	91,100
Senate	0	12,000	26,000	38,000
Democrats	-5000	12,000	37,625	44,625
No. of Cand.	*1*	*12*	*39*	*52*
House	0	9,000	27,625	36,625
Senate	-5000	3,000	10,000	8,000
Incumbents	0	21,500	141,225	162,725
Challengers	0	2,000	500	2,500
Open Seat	0	12,500	1,000	13,500
Winners	0	23,500	n/a	23,500
Losers	-5000	12,500	n/a	7,500

Terminated PACs which contributed less than $5,000 during 1995-96 cycle:

The Travelers Insurance Group Inc. Political Action Committee (TIGI-PAC) (C00167593) *Phone: (860) 277-0111 * One Tower Square, Hartford, CT 06183 * Treasurer: Christine B. Mead*

UNUM Corp.

*Phone: (207) 770-4493 * Fax: (207) 770-4375*
2211 Congress St., Portland, ME 04122
Web: www.unum.com

UNUM is a publicly held disability and special risk insurance company based in Portland, Maine.

The company, established in 1848, is the largest provider of long-term disability insurance in the United States. UNUM employs nearly 7,000 people in offices throughout the United States and most of the world. The $15.5 billion, Fortune 500 company had 1997 revenues of $4 billion.

In 1997, Business Week magazine rated UNUM fifth on its list of the top 30 family-friendly companies in the United States, and Working Mother magazine has included the corporation on its "100 Best Companies for Working Mothers" for the last nine years.

UNUM's affiliates include: Duncanson & Holt Inc., Colonial Life & Accident Insurance Co., UNUM Life Insurance Co. of America and First UNUM Life Insurance Co.

UNUM Political Action Committee (C00155770) *Address: same as sponsor * Treasurer: Donna T. Mundy * Contact: Jean C. Hasch, Secretary*

	1993-94	1995-96	1997	Totals
Receipts	$64,020	$70,909	$37,240	$172,169
Disburse	56,213	73,146	23,617	152,976
Cash	35,145	32,602	45,547	n/a
Contributions	44,250	46,642	16,500	107,392
Republicans	18,500	29,092	10,500	58,092
No. of Cand.	*18*	*32*	*14*	*64*
House	5,500	16,092	4,500	26,092
Senate	13,000	13,000	6,000	32,000
Democrats	25,750	17,550	6,000	49,300
No. of Cand.	*23*	*21*	*8*	*52*
House	19,250	11,050	4,000	34,300
Senate	6,500	6,500	2,000	15,000
Incumbents	27,250	28,892	15,500	71,642
Challengers	1,250	4,500	0	5,750
Open Seat	15,750	13,000	1,000	29,750
Winners	32,750	35,550	n/a	68,300
Losers	11,500	11,092	n/a	22,592

ColPAC - The Political Action Committee of Colonial Life & Accident Insurance Co. (C00111898) *Phone: (803) 798-7000 * Fax: (803) 798-7564 * P.O. Box 1365, Columbia, SC 29202-1365 * Web: www.unum.com/Colonial * Treasurer: Jacqueline B. Winston*

Colonial Life & Accident Insurance is a business unit of UNUM. Colonial specializes in payroll-deducted, voluntary benefits offered to employees at the worksite. Based in Columbia, S.C., and operating in 49 states, Colonial underwrites a broad line of insurance coverages, including personal, accident and sickness, disability, life and cancer insurance policies.

	1993-94	1995-96	1997	Totals
Receipts	$39,072	$39,097	$14,637	$92,806
Disburse	34,049	33,014	11,300	78,363
Cash	13,122	19,209	22,546	n/a
Contributions	25,099	29,000	9,300	63,399
Republicans	15,950	24,750	8,800	49,500
No. of Cand.	*26*	*23*	*10*	*59*
House	9,450	11,250	5,800	26,500
Senate	6,500	13,500	3,000	23,000
Democrats	9,149	4,250	500	13,899
No. of Cand.	*14*	*6*	*1*	*21*
House	8,149	3,250	500	11,899
Senate	1,000	1,000	0	2,000
Incumbents	19,899	28,750	8,300	56,949
Challengers	500	0	0	500
Open Seat	4,700	250	1,000	5,950
Winners	21,399	25,750	n/a	47,149
Losers	3,700	3,250	n/a	6,950

United Services Automobile Association Group

*Phone: (210) 498-5381 * Fax: (210) 498-0608*
9800 Fredericksburg Rd., San Antonio, TX 78288
Web: www.usaa.com

United Services Automobile Association, a member-owned company in San Antonio, is the nation's fifth-biggest car insurer. Its policyholders are primarily members of the United States military and their families. The company offers a wide range of financial services, including banking, mutual funds, life and health insurance and discount brokers. The company has property and casualty insurance policies in all 50 states and is also the largest mail-order company in the nation.

Most of USAA's regulatory oversight comes from state governments and it concentrates its legislative tracking on state issues.

USAA was the leading property insurance PAC contributor to 1996 congressional candidates. The company favored Republican candidates and spent about 25 percent of its contributions on challengers and open races. Of the six candidates who received at least $5,000 from USAA, five were from Texas. The top recipients were former Rep. Steve Stockman, R-Texas, Sen. Phil Gramm, R-Texas, Rep. Ken Bentsen, D-Texas, and Sen. Wayne Allard, R-Colo.

United Services Automobile Association Group Political Action Committee (USAA Group PAC) (C00164145) *Address: same as sponsor * Treasurer: Josue Robles Jr. * Contact: Fred Bosse, V.P.*

	1993-94	1995-96	1997	Totals
Receipts	$372,366	$424,816	$245,702	$1,042,884
Disburse	335,931	470,868	220,369	1,027,168
Cash	127,604	41,313	72,634	n/a
Contributions	127,500	299,000	103,750	530,250
Republicans	98,500	264,500	93,250	456,250
No. of Cand.	*97*	*196*	*104*	*397*
House	55,000	181,900	63,250	300,150
Senate	43,500	82,600	30,000	156,100
Democrats	29,000	34,500	10,500	74,000
No. of Cand.	*33*	*29*	*16*	*78*
House	24,000	29,000	9,000	62,000
Senate	5,000	5,500	1,500	12,000
Incumbents	101,150	223,900	99,750	424,800
Challengers	6,350	20,500	500	27,350
Open Seat	20,000	54,100	3,500	77,600
Winners	109,400	237,650	n/a	347,050
Losers	18,100	61,350	n/a	79,450

Vesta Insurance Group Inc.

*Phone: (205) 970-7138 * Fax: (205) 970-7007*
3760 River Run Dr., Birmingham, AL 35243

Vesta Insurance Group, headquartered in Birmingham, Ala., is the public holding company for several insurance and reinsurance companies. It reported $563 million in 1997 revenues. The company employed 220 people in 1996.

Vesta Insurance offers commercial, homeowners and nonstandard personal auto insurance, primarily in the southern United States. The company also offers commercial transportation and commercial property insurance, and insurance for property used to secure mortgages. The company has a branch office in Copenhagen, Denmark.

Vesta Insurance Group Inc. FedPAC (VestPAC) (C00297473) *Address: same as sponsor * Treasurer: Donald W. Thornton * Contact: Rob McLaughlin, Administrator*

	1993-94	1995-96	1997	Totals
Receipts	$20,669	$65,422	$61,617	$147,708
Disburse	2,100	32,750	22,000	56,850
Cash	18,514	51,191	90,808	n/a
Contributions	0	10,000	12,000	22,000
Republicans	0	7,500	12,000	19,500
No. of Cand.	*0*	*7*	*4*	*11*
House	0	4,000	5,000	9,000
Senate	0	3,500	7,000	10,500
Democrats	0	2,500	0	2,500
No. of Cand.	*0*	*3*	*0*	*3*
House	0	500	0	500
Senate	0	2,000	0	2,000
Incumbents	0	3,000	12,000	15,000
Challengers	0	500	0	500
Open Seat	0	6,500	0	6,500
Winners	0	5,000	n/a	5,000
Losers	0	5,000	n/a	5,000

Western and Southern Life Insurance Co.

*Phone: (513) 629-1464 * Fax: (513) 629-1050*
400 Broadway, Cincinnati, OH 45202
Web: www.westernsouthernlife.com

Western and Southern Life Insurance offers life, health and business insurance.

The private company, headquartered in Cincinnati, has more than 200 offices in 20 states and the District of Columbia. Through these offices, Western and Southern Life employs more than 3,000 licensed insurance personnel. The company is owned by its policyholders.

Western and Southern Life is one of nine subsidiaries of Western-Southern Enterprises, a group of financial services companies with more than $11 billion in assets at the end of 1997.

Western and Southern Life Insurance Co. Political Action Committee (Western-Southern PAC) (C00258228) *Address: same as sponsor * Treasurer: Edward J. Babbitt*

	1993-94	1995-96	1997	Totals
Receipts	$24,966	$27,572	$15,275	$67,813
Disburse	24,166	29,920	14,800	68,886
Cash	3,687	2,143	2,619	n/a
Contributions	3,075	5,900	1,500	10,475
Republicans	1,875	5,650	1,500	9,025
No. of Cand.	*4*	*6*	*3*	*13*
House	875	3,650	0	4,525
Senate	1,000	2,000	1,500	4,500
Democrats	1,200	250	0	1,450
No. of Cand.	*1*	*1*	*0*	*2*
House	1,200	0	0	1,200
Senate	0	250	0	250
Incumbents	1,375	4,650	500	6,525
Challengers	0	1,000	0	1,000
Open Seat	1,700	250	1,000	2,950
Winners	1,375	3,650	n/a	5,025
Losers	1,700	2,250	n/a	3,950

Zurich Holding Co. of America Inc.

*Phone: (847) 550-5500 * Fax: (847) 550-5530*
One Kemper Dr. T-1, Long Grove, IL 60049
Web: www.zurichkemper.com

Zurich Holding Co. of America is a publicly owned holding company for the $10 billion Zurich Kemper Life Insurance Co. and other subsidiaries.

Its parent company is the $97.5 billion, 125-year-old Zurich Group, which has operations in 49 countries and more than 40,000 employees. The Kemper Corp. was acquired by the Zurich Group for more than $2 billion, creating Zurich Kemper Life. Zurich Group also acquired B.A.T. Industries' financial services units in 1998.

Kemper provides property and casualty insurance, reinsurance and risk management services in all 50 states.

Subsidiaries: Federal Kemper Life Assurance Company, Kemper Investors Life Insurance Company, Zurich Life Insurance Co. of America and Fidelity Life Association.

Kemper Insurance maintains a separate PAC. Another committee, The Kemper Corp. PAC, was terminated in 1996.

Zurich Holding Co. of America Inc. Committee for Good Government (Zurich-Kemper PAC) (C00235036) *Address: same as sponsor * Treasurer: Robert Daniel * Contact: Deborah Rezabek, General Counsel*

	1993-94	1995-96	1997	Totals
Receipts	$2,625	$24,550	$13,970	$41,145
Disburse	9,688	14,350	26,550	50,588
Cash	6,503	16,704	4,124	n/a
Contributions	1,250	12,350	26,550	40,150
Republicans	750	11,000	20,000	31,750
No. of Cand.	*1*	*20*	*30*	*51*
House	750	8,000	18,000	26,750
Senate	0	3,000	2,000	5,000
Democrats	500	1,350	6,550	8,400
No. of Cand.	*1*	*4*	*10*	*15*
House	0	600	3,550	4,150
Senate	500	750	3,000	4,250
Incumbents	1,250	8,850	26,050	36,150
Challengers	0	1,500	0	1,500
Open Seat	0	2,000	500	2,500
Winners	1,250	8,850	n/a	10,100
Losers	0	3,500	n/a	3,500

Kemper Insurance Campaign Fund (formerly known as Kemper Group Campaign Fund) (C00009035) *Phone: (847) 320-2000 * Fax: (847) 320-2494 * One Kemper Dr., Long Grove, IL 60049 * Web: www.kemperinsurance.com * Treasurer: Raymond Jilek * Contact: Steve Schneider, Chairman*

	1993-94	1995-96	1997	Totals
Receipts	$38,930	$48,598	$38,453	$125,981
Disburse	38,555	48,162	25,550	112,267
Cash	8,213	8,651	21,554	n/a
Contributions	30,500	39,900	20,800	91,200
Republicans	23,550	37,150	17,850	78,550
No. of Cand.	*42*	*43*	*31*	*116*
House	23,050	32,150	14,850	70,050
Senate	500	5,000	3,000	8,500
Democrats	6,950	2,750	2,950	12,650
No. of Cand.	*13*	*6*	*5*	*24*
House	6,250	1,250	1,200	8,700
Senate	700	1,500	1,750	3,950
Incumbents	28,000	33,650	19,300	80,950
Challengers	250	1,500	1,000	2,750
Open Seat	2,250	4,750	500	7,500
Winners	27,650	32,900	n/a	60,550
Losers	2,850	7,000	n/a	9,850

Farmers Group Inc. Political Action Committee (C00135681) *Phone: (213) 964-8020 * Fax: (213) 964-8095 * 4680 Wilshire Blvd., Los Angeles, CA 90010 * Web: www.farmersinsurance.com * Treasurer: Ronald J. Bassolino * Contact: Jeanie Sauder, Dir. of Political Action*

Farmers Insurance Group is the nation's third-largest writer of homeowner and private passenger auto insurance. The company, which posted 1996 sales of $2 billion, operates in 29 U.S. states on the West Coast, in the Midwest and Southeast. Farmers' parent company, B.A.T., announced a merger with Zurich Holding in late 1997.

	1993-94	1995-96	1997	Totals
Receipts	$56,219	$57,233	$21,455	$134,907
Disburse	53,508	39,330	11,119	103,957
Cash	7,202	25,106	35,443	n/a
Contributions	51,300	36,703	5,100	93,103
Republicans	42,000	34,703	4,600	81,303
No. of Cand.	*36*	*32*	*5*	*73*
House	25,750	29,258	3,600	58,608
Senate	16,250	5,445	1,000	22,695
Democrats	9,300	2,000	500	11,800
No. of Cand.	*12*	*3*	*1*	*16*
House	7,800	1,000	500	9,300
Senate	1,500	1,000	0	2,500
Incumbents	39,300	28,345	5,100	72,745
Challengers	5,500	400	0	5,900
Open Seat	6,500	7,708	0	14,208
Winners	47,300	27,645	n/a	74,945
Losers	4,000	9,058	n/a	13,058

Kemper Corp. Political Action Fund (C00258616) *Phone: (847) 320-4700 * Fax: (847) 320-2494 * One Kemper Dr., Long Grove, IL 60049 * Treasurer: John W. Burns*

	1993-94	1995-96	1997	Totals
Receipts	$68,957	$20,843	$0	$89,800
Disburse	58,335	45,900	0	104,235
Cash	29,634	9,298	0	n/a
Contributions	43,350	29,750	0	73,100
Republicans	22,800	21,250	0	44,050
No. of Cand.	*32*	*32*	*0*	*64*

House	10,800	18,250	0	29,050
Senate	12,000	3,000	0	15,000
Democrats	20,550	8,500	0	29,050
No. of Cand.	*26*	*12*	*0*	*38*
House	15,050	4,500	0	19,550
Senate	5,500	4,000	0	9,500
Incumbents	37,600	28,250	0	65,850
Challengers	1,750	0	0	1,750
Open Seat	4,000	500	0	4,500
Winners	38,600	25,250	n/a	63,850
Losers	4,750	4,500	n/a	9,250

Misc. Finance

American Collectors Association

*Phone: (612) 926-6547 * Fax: (612) 926-1624*
4040 W. 70th St., Minneapolis, MN 55435
Web: www.collector.com

The American Collectors Association is an international trade organization of third-party debt collection businesses. Its 3,700 member agencies provide receivable management services to more than 1 million credit grantors. Headquartered in Minneapolis, ACA serves members in the United States, Canada and 55 other countries.

In 1997, ACA lobbied successfully for the repeal of a garnishment policy initiated in 1996 by the Department of Defense. The policy had imposed a $75 processing fee to be paid by the creditor on all garnishment applications and renewals for garnishments on DoD civilian employees.

American Collectors Association Inc. ACPAC (C00034785) *Address: same as sponsor * Treasurer: Paul Williams*

	1993-94	1995-96	1997	Totals
Receipts	$56,214	$144,527	$86,526	$287,267
Disburse	48,050	143,412	29,857	221,319
Cash	9,213	10,325	66,993	n/a
Contributions	41,050	117,500	13,500	172,050
Republicans	27,550	110,500	12,500	150,550
No. of Cand.	*27*	*79*	*16*	*122*
House	17,550	65,500	7,000	90,050
Senate	10,000	45,000	5,500	60,500
Democrats	13,500	7,000	1,000	21,500
No. of Cand.	*15*	*7*	*1*	*23*
House	11,500	6,000	1,000	18,500
Senate	2,000	1,000	0	3,000
Incumbents	39,050	86,500	11,000	136,550
Challengers	500	16,500	500	17,500
Open Seat	2,000	14,500	2,000	18,500
Winners	38,050	84,500	n/a	122,550
Losers	3,000	33,000	n/a	36,000

Bass Brothers Enterprises

*Phone: (817) 332-2500 * Fax: (817) 870-0371*
201 Main St., Suite 2500, Fort Worth, TX 76102

Bass Brothers Enterprises is a land investment, farming and livestock pasturing company owned by brothers Lee and Sid Bass of Texas. The Associated Press reported the family's fortune was worth an estimated $5 billion in 1991.

The Bass brothers are investors in several public companies, including Disney, Freeport McMoRan Copper Co. Inc., La Quinta Inns Inc., Fisher Scientific International Inc., and Universal Health Services Inc., according to SEC records.

Bass Brothers Enterprises Inc. Political Action Committee (C00172635) *Address: same as sponsor * Treasurer: Dee J. Kelly*

	1993-94	1995-96	1997	Totals
Receipts	$58,625	$74,056	$42,513	$175,194
Disburse	59,083	49,186	33,308	141,577
Cash	80,100	104,980	114,191	n/a
Contributions	47,810	38,000	31,500	117,310
Republicans	14,000	37,000	20,000	71,000
No. of Cand.	*4*	*12*	*3*	*19*
House	3,000	20,000	20,000	43,000
Senate	11,000	17,000	0	28,000
Democrats	33,310	1,000	11,500	45,810
No. of Cand.	*11*	*1*	*4*	*16*
House	13,500	1,000	5,500	20,000
Senate	19,810	0	6,000	25,810
Incumbents	32,810	25,000	26,500	84,310
Challengers	6,000	0	5,000	11,000
Open Seat	9,000	13,000	0	22,000
Winners	31,500	36,000	n/a	67,500
Losers	16,310	2,000	n/a	18,310

Employee Stock Ownership Association

*Phone: (202) 293-2971 * Fax: (202) 293-7568*
1726 M St. N.W., Suite 501, Washington, DC 20036
Web: www.the-esop-emplowner.org

The Employee Stock Ownership Association is a national nonprofit group of companies with employee stock ownership plans. It has 2,155 members.

Founded in 1979, the group's purpose is to spread the philosophy of ESOP via regular conferences and newsletters and by lobbying Congress to increase the number of companies with ESOP.

ESOP Association PAC (C00196089) *Address: same as sponsor * Treasurer: J. Michael Keeling*

	1993-94	1995-96	1997	Totals
Receipts	$63,365	$75,829	$31,511	$170,705
Disburse	63,272	74,713	30,000	167,985
Cash	917	6,080	7,591	n/a
Contributions	62,800	68,200	27,500	158,500
Republicans	49,650	54,550	19,000	123,200
No. of Cand.	*73*	*76*	*30*	*179*
House	47,150	46,050	16,750	109,950
Senate	2,500	8,500	2,250	13,250
Democrats	13,150	13,650	8,500	35,300
No. of Cand.	*22*	*19*	*8*	*49*
House	10,650	7,250	3,500	21,400
Senate	2,500	6,400	5,000	13,900
Incumbents	56,900	64,950	26,500	148,350
Challengers	3,500	500	250	4,250
Open Seat	2,400	2,500	750	5,650
Winners	55,800	64,250	n/a	120,050
Losers	7,000	3,950	n/a	10,950

Equifax Inc.

*Phone: (404) 885-8974 * Fax: (404) 885-8215*
P.O. Box 4081, Atlanta, GA 30302-4081
Web: www.equifax.com

Equifax is a holding company for the largest credit reporting agency in the United States. Equifax provides information services to businesses that help them grant credit, authorize and process credit card and check transactions, insure lives and property and manage and control health care costs. The principal lines of business are credit services, payment services and health care information services.

Founded in 1899, Equifax is a publicly held company with $1.3 billion in 1997 sales and 14,100 employees. It operates in 17 countries with sales in 40 countries.

Equifax Inc. Political Action Committee (EquiPAC) (C00143867) *Address: same as sponsor * Treasurer: Marietta Edmunds Zakas * Contact: Bruce Richards, Corporate V.P. and General Counsel*

	1993-94	1995-96	1997	Totals
Receipts	$15,860	$15,450	$4,189	$35,499
Disburse	30,216	16,209	4,219	50,644
Cash	7,774	7,018	6,522	n/a
Contributions	15,300	11,950	0	27,250
Republicans	9,750	11,200	0	20,950
No. of Cand.	*12*	*21*	*0*	*33*
House	6,250	6,450	0	12,700
Senate	3,500	4,750	0	8,250
Democrats	5,550	750	0	6,300
No. of Cand.	*12*	*3*	*0*	*15*
House	5,050	750	0	5,800
Senate	500	0	0	500
Incumbents	12,800	11,950	0	24,750
Challengers	2,000	0	0	2,000
Open Seat	500	0	0	500
Winners	13,100	11,200	n/a	24,300
Losers	2,200	750	n/a	2,950

H&R Block

*Phone: (816) 753-6900 * Fax: (816) 753-8628*
4410 Main St., Kansas City, MO 64111
Web: www.hrblock.com

In addition to providing tax preparation services for 18 million people, H&R Block operates financial services subsidiaries focused on mortgages and online banking. The company sold its 80 percent interest in CompuServe in February 1998 after the online service reported a $119 million loss in 1997.

H&R Block prepared about one in seven 1996 tax returns and 51 percent of electronic returns. The publicly traded Kansas City, Mo. company has 10,000 offices in the United States, Canada and Australia and posted $1.1 billion in fiscal year 1997 revenue.

Subsidiary Block Financial Corp. offers credit card and online financial services and sells software including Kiplinger TaxCut, Kiplinger's Small Business Attorney and Kiplinger's Home Legal Advisor. The company also sells mortgages through Option One Mortgage.

H&R Block Political Action Committee (BlockPAC) (C00188177) *Phone: (202) 508-6363 * Fax: (202) 508-6330 * 700 13th St. N.W., Suite 700, Washington, DC 20005 * Treasurer: Carol Hall * Contact: Robert Weinberger*

	1993-94	1995-96	1997	Totals
Receipts	$70,219	$75,356	$24,683	$170,258
Disburse	75,074	78,935	21,171	175,180
Cash	52,258	48,689	52,201	n/a
Contributions	51,940	57,750	19,500	129,190
Republicans	10,650	22,750	10,500	43,900
No. of Cand.	*11*	*30*	*14*	*55*
House	6,650	15,750	7,500	29,900
Senate	4,000	7,000	3,000	14,000
Democrats	41,290	35,000	9,000	85,290
No. of Cand.	*42*	*31*	*13*	*86*
House	29,050	21,750	5,000	55,800
Senate	12,240	13,250	4,000	29,490
Incumbents	42,840	49,250	19,500	111,590
Challengers	0	2,000	0	2,000
Open Seat	9,100	6,250	0	15,350
Winners	42,100	52,500	n/a	94,600
Losers	9,840	5,250	n/a	15,090

International Association for Financial Planning

*Phone: (404) 845-0011 * Fax: (404) 845-3660*
5775 Glenridge Dr. N.E., Suite B-300, Atlanta, GA 30328-5364
Web: www.iafp.org

International Association for Financial Planning represents 17,000 financial advisers and financial companies.

IAFP supports tax and economic policies that promote savings, investment, capital formation and a vigorous free enterprise system. It also supports a regulatory policy that fosters an environment in which consumers can achieve their financial objectives.

The group has more than 100 local chapters that offer members educational programs and networking opportunities.

International Association for Financial Planning Political Action Committee Inc. (IAFP-PAC) (C00170910) *Address: same as sponsor * Treasurer: Dale E. Brown*

	1993-94	1995-96	1997	Totals
Receipts	$3,087	$1,785	$2,623	$7,495
Disburse	7,900	6,015	1,830	15,745
Cash	17,214	13,084	13,877	n/a
Contributions	7,100	5,700	1,500	14,300
Republicans	4,600	5,700	1,000	11,300
No. of Cand.	*5*	*9*	*1*	*15*
House	1,600	2,250	1,000	4,850
Senate	3,000	3,450	0	6,450
Democrats	2,500	0	500	3,000
No. of Cand.	*3*	*0*	*1*	*4*
House	1,500	0	500	2,000
Senate	1,000	0	0	1,000
Incumbents	6,100	5,500	1,500	13,100
Challengers	0	200	0	200
Open Seat	1,000	0	0	1,000
Winners	7,100	5,500	n/a	12,600
Losers	0	200	n/a	200

National Check Cashers Association

*Phone: (201) 487-0412 * Fax: (201) 487-3954*
Court Plaza N. 25 Main St., P.O. Box 647, Hackensack, NJ 07602
Web: www.nacca.org

The National Check Cashers Association represents 3,600 check-cashing facilities nationwide.

The group is monitoring plans for all federal employees to receive payment electronically by 1999 because the policy would have an effect on the check-cashing industry. It also follows action in congressional banking committees, at the Treasury Department and the IRS.

National Check Cashers Association Inc. Political Action Committee (C00232843) *Address: same as sponsor * Treasurer: William Siegel * Contact: Henry F. Shyne, Executive Dir.*

	1993-94	1995-96	1997	Totals
Receipts	$38,825	$47,075	$19,250	$105,150
Disburse	46,500	37,748	10,550	94,798
Cash	19,097	28,423	36,773	n/a
Contributions	46,500	28,350	10,550	85,400
Republicans	20,000	16,250	8,300	44,550
No. of Cand.	*23*	*22*	*5*	*50*
House	15,000	14,550	2,300	31,850
Senate	5,000	1,700	6,000	12,700
Democrats	26,500	12,100	2,250	40,850
No. of Cand.	*29*	*15*	*4*	*48*
House	20,500	11,100	2,250	33,850
Senate	6,000	1,000	0	7,000
Incumbents	40,500	23,350	10,550	74,400
Challengers	1,500	1,000	0	2,500
Open Seat	4,500	4,000	0	8,500
Winners	40,000	21,600	n/a	61,600
Losers	6,500	6,750	n/a	13,250

State Street Bank & Trust

*Phone: (617) 664-3866 * Fax: (617) 451-6315*
225 Franklin St., Boston, MA 02110
*Web: www.statestreet.com * E-mail: garussell@statestreet.com*

State Street Bank & Trust provides asset management services to institutional investors around the globe. Services include: accounting, foreign exchange, cash management, securities lending, performance and analytic measurement, daily pricing and decision support tools. A publicly traded company, State Street manages $458 billion in assets.

The company has offices in the United States, Canada, Chile, China, Cayman Islands, Netherlands Antilles, the United Kingdom, France, Belgium, Luxembourg, Denmark, Germany, United Arab Emirates, Taiwan, Japan, Singapore, Australia and New Zealand.

State Street Bank & Trust Co. Voluntary Political Action (C00072751) *Address: same as sponsor * Treasurer: George A. Russell Jr.*

	1993-94	1995-96	1997	Totals
Receipts	$25,150	$32,170	$26,431	$83,751
Disburse	19,914	40,238	18,200	78,352
Cash	12,935	4,871	13,102	n/a
Contributions	7,000	20,750	10,700	38,450
Republicans	0	10,450	5,700	16,150
No. of Cand.	*0*	*8*	*6*	*14*
House	0	4,250	3,200	7,450
Senate	0	6,200	2,500	8,700
Democrats	7,000	10,300	5,000	22,300
No. of Cand.	*8*	*11*	*6*	*25*
House	5,000	5,300	3,000	13,300
Senate	2,000	5,000	2,000	9,000
Incumbents	5,500	13,550	8,700	27,750
Challengers	500	2,000	0	2,500
Open Seat	1,000	5,200	1,000	7,200
Winners	4,000	12,800	n/a	16,800
Losers	3,000	7,950	n/a	10,950

Stephens Inc.

*Phone: (501) 377-2218 * Fax: (501) 377-3498*
111 Center St., Little Rock, AR 72201
E-mail: bschulte@stephens.com

Stephens is a publicly held brokerage and investment banking firm that provides debt management and stock and bond brokerage, and handles mergers and acquisitions. In 1970, it was involved in the emergence of Wal Mart. Since then, it has overseen many large acquisitions and mergers, including Tyson Foods' $1.5 billion takeover of Holly Farms.

The company is headquartered in Little Rock, Ark., with offices in Atlanta, Dallas, Houston, Boston, New Orleans, Tampa, Fla. and London.

In January 1998, Stephens became financial adviser to Aquagenix Inc., the largest public company to provide landscaping services for utility, government, commercial, golf course and private customers.

The company's PAC used to be associated with an office in Washington that no longer exists. After the Washington office was closed, the Stephens Overseas Services PAC was renamed Stephens Inc. Federal PAC.

Stephens Inc. Federal PAC (C00166553) *Address: same as sponsor * Treasurer: Robert L. Schulte*

	1993-94	1995-96	1997	Totals
Receipts	$66,796	$56,241	$40,270	$163,307
Disburse	52,750	73,833	9,030	135,613
Cash	23,119	5,531	36,771	n/a
Contributions	39,500	54,500	9,000	103,000
Republicans	5,500	26,000	1,500	33,000
No. of Cand.	*3*	*10*	*2*	*15*
House	3,500	13,000	1,500	18,000
Senate	2,000	13,000	0	15,000
Democrats	34,000	28,500	7,500	70,000
No. of Cand.	*11*	*11*	*7*	*29*
House	19,000	11,000	4,500	34,500
Senate	15,000	17,500	3,000	35,500
Incumbents	38,000	13,000	9,000	60,000
Challengers	0	0	0	0
Open Seat	1,500	41,500	0	43,000
Winners	24,000	29,500	n/a	53,500
Losers	15,500	25,000	n/a	40,500

Trans Union Corp.

Phone: (312) 466-7764
555 W. Adams St., Chicago, IL 60661
Web: www.tuc.com

Trans Union is a private credit information company located in Chicago. It provides personal credit information to banks, insurers, retailers and communications companies, among others. The company has a national data center, plus regional offices in Springfield, Pa., and Fullerton, Calif. Trans Union has 200 independent credit bureaus as members of its network.

Trans Union Corp. Political Action Committee (C00313700) *Address: same as sponsor * Treasurer: David Emery * Contact: Chuck Golly*

	1993-94	1995-96	1997	Totals
Receipts	$0	$15,105	$0	$15,105
Disburse	0	5,600	4,500	10,100
Cash	0	9,505	5,005	n/a
Contributions	0	5,100	4,500	9,600
Republicans	0	2,500	2,500	5,000
No. of Cand.	*0*	*4*	*4*	*8*
House	0	1,500	1,500	3,000
Senate	0	1,000	1,000	2,000
Democrats	0	2,600	2,000	4,600
No. of Cand.	*0*	*5*	*4*	*9*
House	0	2,600	1,000	3,600
Senate	0	0	1,000	1,000
Incumbents	0	5,100	4,500	9,600
Challengers	0	0	0	0
Open Seat	0	0	0	0
Winners	0	5,100	n/a	5,100
Losers	0	0	n/a	0

Real Estate

American Land Title Association

*Phone: (202) 296-3671 * Fax: (202) 223-5843*
1828 L St. N.W., Suite 705, Washington, DC 20036
Web: www.alta.org

The American Land Title Association represents land title insurance underwriting companies, abstracters and title insurance agents. The association searches and insures land titles to protect real estate investors, including home buyers and mortgage lenders.

Title Industry Political Action Committee (C00012914) *Address: same as sponsor * Treasurer: James R. Maher*

	1993-94	1995-96	1997	Totals
Receipts	$191,933	$163,659	$108,616	$464,208
Disburse	122,613	202,124	97,254	421,991
Cash	192,603	154,139	165,503	n/a
Contributions	110,868	172,995	95,078	378,941
Republicans	37,368	127,495	67,078	231,941
No. of Cand.	*38*	*74*	*51*	*163*
House	19,650	81,995	50,578	152,223
Senate	17,718	45,500	16,500	79,718
Democrats	73,500	45,500	28,000	147,000
No. of Cand.	*43*	*39*	*29*	*111*
House	41,000	29,500	14,500	85,000
Senate	32,500	16,000	13,500	62,000
Incumbents	103,818	151,995	91,578	347,391
Challengers	4,500	5,000	1,500	11,000
Open Seat	2,900	16,000	2,000	20,900
Winners	89,718	152,805	n/a	242,523
Losers	21,150	20,190	n/a	41,340

American Resort Development Association

*Phone: (202) 371-6700 * Fax: (202) 289-8544*
1220 L St. N.W., Fifth Floor, Washington, DC 20005
Web: www.arda.org

The American Resort Development Association represents about 1,000 companies in the vacation and resort industries. Its members are involved in timeshares, community development, camping resorts, lot sales and resort communities throughout the nation and concentrated in Florida. Its members include Shell Vacations, Four Seasons U.S.A., Vacation Resorts International, Hilton Grand Vacations Co. and Marriott Leisure.

American Resort Development Association Political Action Committee (ARDA-PAC) (C00129932) *Address: same as sponsor * Treasurer: Michael F. Hussey * Contact: Karen Valanzano, Dir. of Federal Relations*

	1993-94	1995-96	1997	Totals
Receipts	$38,414	$61,599	$34,221	$134,234
Disburse	50,745	64,512	20,677	135,934
Cash	6,591	4,598	18,141	n/a
Contributions	22,050	40,768	9,250	72,068
Republicans	8,800	23,768	3,750	36,318
No. of Cand.	*18*	*15*	*3*	*36*
House	3,550	13,268	3,750	20,568
Senate	5,250	10,500	0	15,750
Democrats	13,250	17,000	5,500	35,750
No. of Cand.	*23*	*10*	*3*	*36*
House	11,250	9,500	1,500	22,250
Senate	2,000	7,500	4,000	13,500
Incumbents	17,250	26,768	9,250	53,268
Challengers	0	0	0	0
Open Seat	4,800	14,000	0	18,800
Winners	17,200	33,268	n/a	50,468
Losers	4,850	7,500	n/a	12,350

Apartment and Office Building Association of Metropolitan Washington, D.C.

*Phone: (202) 296-3390 * Fax: (202) 296-3399*
1050 17th St. N.W., Suite 300, Washington, DC 20036

The Apartment and Office Building Association represents 450 commercial and residential real estate companies.

Apartment and Office Building Association of Metropolitan Washington, D.C. Inc. Metro PAC-FED (C00295642) *Address: same as sponsor * Treasurer: Thomas R. Hyland * Contact: Margaret Jeffers, PAC Chairwoman*

	1993-94	1995-96	1997	Totals
Receipts	$8,458	$8,571	$2,782	$19,811
Disburse	6,807	10,225	2,290	19,322
Cash	1,652	0	492	n/a
Contributions	5,000	8,750	1,000	14,750
Republicans	4,500	3,650	1,000	9,150
No. of Cand.	*2*	*3*	*1*	*6*
House	4,500	3,650	1,000	9,150
Senate	0	0	0	0
Democrats	500	5,100	0	5,600
No. of Cand.	*1*	*5*	*0*	*6*

(Data for Apartment and Office continued)

House	500	2,100	0	2,600
Senate	0	3,000	0	3,000
Incumbents	1,000	6,250	1,000	8,250
Challengers	4,000	0	0	4,000
Open Seat	0	1,500	0	1,500
Winners	5,000	7,750	n/a	12,750
Losers	0	1,000	n/a	1,000

Appraisal Institute

*Phone: (312) 335-4100 * Fax: (312) 335-4400*
875 N. Michigan Ave., Suite 2400, Chicago, IL 60611-1980
Web: www.appraisalinstitute.org

Headquartered in Chicago, the Appraisal Institute has 12,000 members and 130 chapters across the country. It works on residential and commercial appraisal education, research, publishing and professional membership designation programs.

Appraisal Institute members must adhere to a Code of Professional Ethics and Standards of Professional Appraisal Practice.

Appraisal Institute Political Action Committee (C00144261)
*Phone: (202) 296-4447 * Fax: (202) 296-9464 * 2600 Virginia Ave. N.W., Suite 200, Washington, DC 20037 * Treasurer: William D. Park*
*Contact: Joseph R. Stanfield Jr., President * Phone: (312) 335-4100*

	1993-94	1995-96	1997	Totals
Receipts	$39,211	$23,962	$10,135	$73,308
Disburse	28,422	20,969	13,900	63,291
Cash	17,212	20,204	16,439	n/a
Contributions	28,275	19,469	12,900	60,644
Republicans	7,550	16,019	9,600	33,169
No. of Cand.	*10*	*22*	*13*	*45*
House	7,550	11,781	7,600	26,931
Senate	0	4,238	2,000	6,238
Democrats	20,725	3,450	3,300	27,475
No. of Cand.	*14*	*5*	*8*	*27*
House	18,225	2,950	3,300	24,475
Senate	2,500	500	0	3,000
Incumbents	13,275	14,931	12,900	41,106
Challengers	5,000	3,538	0	8,538
Open Seat	10,000	1,000	0	11,000
Winners	11,325	18,169	n/a	29,494
Losers	16,950	1,300	n/a	18,250

Association for Commercial Real Estate

2201 Cooperative Way, Third Floor, Herndon, VA 20171

Association for Commercial Real Estate American Development PAC (C00233304) *Address: same as sponsor * Treasurer: John T. Abbott*

	1993-94	1995-96	1997	Totals
Receipts	$20,675	$82,595	$60,510	$163,780
Disburse	17,085	42,094	21,050	80,229
Cash	5,013	45,515	84,975	n/a
Contributions	14,000	42,065	15,850	71,915
Republicans	7,000	40,065	14,850	61,915
No. of Cand.	*14*	*47*	*21*	*82*
House	7,000	24,065	11,850	42,915
Senate	0	16,000	3,000	19,000
Democrats	7,000	2,000	1,000	10,000
No. of Cand.	*14*	*4*	*2*	*20*
House	7,000	2,000	1,000	10,000
Senate	0	0	0	0
Incumbents	13,500	27,815	15,850	57,165
Challengers	500	1,750	0	2,250
Open Seat	0	12,500	0	12,500
Winners	13,000	25,315	n/a	38,315
Losers	1,000	16,750	n/a	17,750

CMAC Investment Corp.

*Phone: (215) 564-6600 x3374 * Fax: (215) 405-9160*
1601 Market St., Philadelphia, PA 19103

CMAC Investment is a publicly owned company that provides private mortgage insurance coverage and risk management services to residential mortgage lenders. CMAC Investment has assets of $593 million. It had 1997 revenue of $275 million and has 512 employees.

Commonwealth Mortgage Assurance Co. is one of its subsidiaries.

CMAC Investment Corp. Employees PAC (CMAC - PAC) (C00302166) *Address: same as sponsor * Treasurer: C. Robert Quint * Contact: Thomas J. Shelley Jr.*

	1993-94	1995-96	1997	Totals
Receipts	$0	$42,272	$22,003	$64,275
Disburse	0	15,550	15,000	30,550
Cash	0	26,729	33,740	n/a
Contributions	0	5,250	2,500	7,750
Republicans	0	5,250	2,500	7,750
No. of Cand.	*0*	*7*	*3*	*10*
House	0	3,250	500	3,750
Senate	0	2,000	2,000	4,000
Democrats	0	0	0	0
No. of Cand.	*0*	*0*	*0*	*0*
House	0	0	0	0
Senate	0	0	0	0
Incumbents	0	4,250	2,500	6,750
Challengers	0	1,000	0	1,000
Open Seat	0	0	0	0
Winners	0	4,250	n/a	4,250
Losers	0	1,000	n/a	1,000

Century 21 Real Estate Corp.

*Phone: (973) 952-1593 * Fax: (973) 496-5331*
6 Sylvan Way, Parsippany, NJ 07054
Web: www.century21.com

Century 21 Real Estate is the world's largest franchiser of residential real estate brokerage offices.

The Century 21 network involves more than 6,200 independently owned and operated offices with 110,000 brokers and agents throughout the United States and the world. The company provides comprehensive training, management, administrative and marketing support to its network offices.

Century 21 is owned by the Cendant Corp., a public company that provides consumer and business services. Cendant was formed by the December 1997, $14 billion merger of CUC International Inc. and HFS Inc. Based on the two companies' individual performances, Cendant would have had 1997 revenues of $4.5 billion.

Century 21 Political Action Committee (CEN-PAC) (C00141226)
*Address: same as sponsor * Treasurer: Paul McNicol * Contact: Samuel Wright, Chairman*

	1993-94	1995-96	1997	Totals
Receipts	$144,070	$81,955	$1,060	$227,085
Disburse	129,525	126,498	43	256,066
Cash	101,572	57,038	58,061	n/a
Contributions	118,000	94,000	-1,000	211,000
Republicans	76,500	65,500	-1,000	141,000
No. of Cand.	*39*	*37*	*1*	*77*
House	29,000	52,000	-1,000	80,000
Senate	47,500	13,500	0	61,000
Democrats	41,500	28,500	0	70,000
No. of Cand.	*29*	*23*	*0*	*52*
House	31,500	21,500	0	53,000
Senate	10,000	7,000	0	17,000
Incumbents	82,000	93,500	-1,000	174,500
Challengers	6,500	500	0	7,000
Open Seat	29,500	0	0	29,500
Winners	105,000	88,500	n/a	193,500
Losers	13,000	5,500	n/a	18,500

Countrywide Credit Industries Inc.

Phone: (818) 225-3000
4500 Park Grenada, Calabasas, CA 91302
Web: www.countrywide.com

Countrywide Credit Industries is a publicly owned mortgage banking business with 6,000 workers and more than 300 branch offices nationwide.

Its principal subsidiary, Countrywide Home Loans (formerly Countrywide Funding Corp.), originates, purchases, sells and services mortgage loans. The company reported net income of $257 million in 1997. The company's mortgage loans are principally prime credit quality first-lien mortgage loans secured on single-family residences.

Countrywide Credit Industries also offers a variety of financial products, including insurance, loan closing services, mutual funds and financial planning.

Subsidiaries include: Countrywide Agency, Countrywide Capital Markets, Countrywide Financial Planning Services, Countrywide Investments, Countrywide Title Corp. and LandSafe.

Countrywide Credit Industries Inc. PAC (Countrywide PAC) (C00282731) *Phone: (202) 624-3928 * Fax: (202) 737-2645 * 1001 Pennsylvania Ave. N.W., #600-s, Washington, DC 20004 * E-mail: kirk_willison@countrywide.com * Treasurer: Kirk G. Willison*

	1993-94	1995-96	1997	Totals
Receipts	$56,510	$81,157	$40,807	$178,474
Disburse	29,380	72,258	40,750	142,388
Cash	27,131	28,334	28,392	n/a
Contributions	23,380	58,758	35,750	117,888
Republicans	8,500	44,258	26,000	78,758
No. of Cand.	*4*	*25*	*30*	*59*
House	0	39,258	22,500	61,758
Senate	8,500	5,000	3,500	17,000
Democrats	14,880	14,500	9,750	39,130
No. of Cand.	*14*	*12*	*9*	*35*
House	5,380	8,500	7,750	21,630
Senate	9,500	6,000	2,000	17,500
Incumbents	15,880	42,964	31,250	90,094
Challengers	0	0	3,000	3,000
Open Seat	7,500	15,794	1,500	24,794
Winners	20,880	46,464	n/a	67,344
Losers	2,500	12,294	n/a	14,794

Del Webb Corp.

*Phone: (602) 808-8000 * Fax: (602) 808-8097*
6001 N. 24th St., Phoenix, AZ 85016
Web: www.delwebb.com

Del Webb, a Phoenix-based real estate company, is the nation's leading developer and operator of active-adult communities for people 55 and older.

Established in 1928 as a home-building company, Del Webb is now the sixth largest builder of single-family homes in the United States. The public company, which employs about 2,500 people, had 1997 sales of nearly $1.2 billion, with a net income of nearly $40 million.

Since 1960, the company has built and sold more than 60,000 homes in the active-adult market. In addition to its construction business, Del Webb also owns Fairmont Mortgage, a mortgage brokerage.

The company operates about 15 communities in Arizona, Nevada, South Carolina, Texas and California, and in January 1998, acquired Spruce Creek Golf & Country Club near Ocala, Fla. Future communities are planned in Illinois and Virginia. These communities are operated under such names as Sun Cities, Bellasera, Sunflower and Clover Springs.

Del Webb Employees' Fund for Better Government (formerly known as Del Webb Corp. Employees PAC) (C00170480) *Address: same as sponsor * Treasurer: Donald V. Mickus * Contact: Rob Jones, Chairman*

	1993-94	1995-96	1997	Totals
Receipts	$108,338	$138,349	$92,341	$339,028
Disburse	100,157	126,744	63,230	290,131
Cash	13,142	24,746	53,856	n/a
Contributions	51,358	54,022	24,220	129,600
Republicans	34,350	36,022	22,220	92,592
No. of Cand.	*16*	*15*	*11*	*42*
House	24,000	33,022	15,520	72,542
Senate	10,350	3,000	6,700	20,050
Democrats	17,008	18,000	2,000	37,008
No. of Cand.	*10*	*3*	*1*	*14*
House	10,958	8,000	2,000	20,958
Senate	6,050	10,000	0	16,050
Incumbents	19,008	48,022	23,970	91,000
Challengers	3,750	500	250	4,500
Open Seat	27,600	5,000	0	32,600
Winners	36,798	48,022	n/a	84,820
Losers	14,560	6,000	n/a	20,560

Howard Hughes Corp.

*Phone: (702) 791-4266 * Fax: (702) 791-4476*
3800 Howard Hughes Pkwy., One Maritime Plaza, Las Vegas, NV 89109
Web: www.therousecompany.com

Howard Hughes is a real estate developer and subsidiary of Maryland-based Rouse Co., a publicly traded company which had 1997 revenue of $935 million. Rouse engages in "build-to-suit" commercial real estate, primarily in Nevada, and employs 4,000 people.

Howard Hughes owns properties in Las Vegas and Los Angeles, including shopping centers and planned communities.

The Howard Hughes Corp. Employees Public Affairs Committee (C00076919) *Phone: (410) 992-6000 * 10275 Little Patuxent Parkway, Columbia, MD 21044 * Treasurer: John Ramirez*

*Contact: Mark Brown, Senior V.P. of Corp. and Gov. Relations * Phone: (702) 791-4266*

	1993-94	1995-96	1997	Totals
Receipts	$23,841	$39,960	$20,144	$83,945
Disburse	47,439	33,297	7,066	87,802
Cash	16,191	22,859	35,938	n/a
Contributions	43,620	31,670	7,000	82,290
Republicans	20,500	22,000	3,500	46,000
No. of Cand.	*5*	*9*	*4*	*18*
House	19,500	21,000	2,500	43,000
Senate	1,000	1,000	1,000	3,000
Democrats	23,120	9,670	3,500	36,290
No. of Cand.	*10*	*4*	*2*	*16*
House	12,500	1,670	2,500	16,670
Senate	10,620	8,000	1,000	19,620
Incumbents	37,620	24,670	3,500	65,790
Challengers	6,000	0	1,000	7,000
Open Seat	0	7,000	2,500	9,500
Winners	32,000	23,170	n/a	55,170
Losers	11,620	8,500	n/a	20,120

Irvine Co.

*Phone: (714) 720-3463 * Fax: (714) 759-9328*
550 Newport Center Dr., Newport Beach, CA 92660
*Web: www.irvineco.com * E-mail: wisner@irvineco.com*

Based in Newport Beach, Calif., Irvine is a private land development company. It posted $29.6 million in 1997 sales and employs 200 people.

Irvine plans and designs residential communities and then sells land to residential builders, who construct large-scale residential villages according to the company's architectural design standards. The company also owns a growing portfolio of income-producing properties that totals about 20 million square feet of office, industrial and retail space. Also included in its holdings are two hotels, five marinas and three public golf courses.

Irvine operates real estate management services, rental agents, general farms and cable television services, primarily in Orange County, Calif.

The Irvine Co. Employees' Political Action Committee (C00131615) *Address: same as sponsor * Treasurer: Franz Wisner*

	1993-94	1995-96	1997	Totals
Receipts	$23,333	$28,649	$18,942	$70,924
Disburse	29,150	37,809	16,750	83,709
Cash	9,405	245	2,438	n/a
Contributions	26,150	23,900	14,750	64,800
Republicans	9,050	20,400	13,750	43,200
No. of Cand.	*10*	*17*	*11*	*38*
House	6,050	10,400	6,250	22,700
Senate	3,000	10,000	7,500	20,500
Democrats	17,100	3,500	1,000	21,600
No. of Cand.	*12*	*5*	*2*	*19*
House	3,600	2,500	500	6,600
Senate	13,500	1,000	500	15,000
Incumbents	17,150	15,900	5,250	38,300
Challengers	2,500	5,500	9,500	17,500
Open Seat	4,500	2,000	0	6,500
Winners	17,650	13,400	n/a	31,050
Losers	8,500	10,500	n/a	19,000

JPI Texas Development Inc.

Phone: (512) 322-5510
Land Financial Corporation POL, 100 Congress Ave., Suite 1300, Austin, TX 78701

JPI Texas Development is an Austin-based real estate developer active in the local apartment building industry. The PAC's contributors are company employees and it gives to state and federal candidates and to housing PACs.

JPI Good Government (formerly known as Southland Financial Corp. Political Action Committee) (C00115774) *Address: same as sponsor * Treasurer: David B. Armbrust*

	1993-94	1995-96	1997	Totals
Receipts	$9,163	$386	$15,182	$24,731
Disburse	8	6,000	3,061	9,069
Cash	9,852	2,242	14,364	n/a
Contributions	0	1,000	1,000	2,000
Republicans	0	1,000	0	1,000
No. of Cand.	*0*	*1*	*0*	*1*
House	0	1,000	0	1,000
Senate	0	0	0	0
Democrats	0	0	1,000	1,000
No. of Cand.	*0*	*0*	*1*	*1*
House	0	0	1,000	1,000
Senate	0	0	0	0
Incumbents	0	0	0	0
Challengers	0	0	0	0
Open Seat	0	1,000	0	1,000
Winners	0	0	n/a	0
Losers	0	1,000	n/a	1,000

Mortgage Bankers Association of America

*Phone: (202) 861-6505 * Fax: (202) 452-8785*
1125 15th St. N.W., Suite 700, Washington, DC 20005-2766
*Web: www.mbaa.org * E-mail: royal_roth@mbaa.org*

The Mortgage Bankers Association of America represents nearly 2,700 businesses in the real estate finance industry. The MBAA sponsors programs and research on mortgage banking, brokers and other lenders.

The group favors the increased Federal Housing Administration loan limit contained in the Clinton administration's 1999 budget proposal. The MBAA says a limit of $227,150 will increase home ownership. It supports a strengthened Mutual Mortgage Insurance Fund, which will enable the FHA to better support riskier loans.

The MBAA's PAC contributions were split almost evenly between Democratic and Republican candidates in 1996, with a slight edge to Republicans. The group far outranked other mortgage banking organizations and companies in total congressional contributions. The top recipients — Sen. Alfonse M. D'Amato, R-N.Y., Rep. Jerry Weller, R-Ill., and Rep. Sue W. Kelly, R-N.Y. — sit on Senate and House banking committees. All received more than $5,000 from the MBAA.

Mortgage Bankers Association of America Political Action Committee (C00004812) *Address: same as sponsor * Treasurer: William E. Cumberland * Contact: Royal Roth, Political Dir.*

	1993-94	1995-96	1997	Totals
Receipts	$491,495	$354,184	$217,724	$1,063,403
Disburse	359,438	379,634	265,608	1,004,680
Cash	193,813	168,367	120,485	n/a
Contributions	242,458	251,100	191,180	684,738
Republicans	88,598	135,450	132,147	356,195
No. of Cand.	*70*	*80*	*86*	*236*
House	50,850	101,450	102,165	254,465
Senate	37,748	34,000	29,982	101,730
Democrats	153,860	115,650	59,033	328,543
No. of Cand.	*107*	*80*	*48*	*235*
House	104,860	80,650	33,400	218,910
Senate	49,000	35,000	25,633	109,633
Incumbents	198,708	205,800	178,741	583,249
Challengers	5,500	4,800	500	10,800
Open Seat	38,250	40,500	11,439	90,189
Winners	198,708	207,800	n/a	406,508
Losers	43,750	43,300	n/a	87,050

National Apartment Association

*Phone: (703) 518-6141 * Fax: (703) 518-6191*
201 N. Union St., Suite 200, Alexandria, VA 22314
Web: www.naahq.org

The National Apartment Association is a nonprofit trade association representing the multi-family housing industry. Founded in the late 1940s, the association includes about 150 state and local associations across the country.

The NAA monitors legislative and regulatory activity in all 50 states. It distributes issue briefs highlighting various issues of interest to NAA members and acts as a clearinghouse for information and statistical analysis concerning the multi-family housing industry.

National Apartment Association PAC (NAA PAC) (C00113241) *Address: same as sponsor * Treasurer: Amy Dozier * Contact: Barbara Bassallo, Chairwoman*

	1993-94	1995-96	1997	Totals
Receipts	$18,670	$38,159	$33,053	$89,882
Disburse	14,566	38,396	11,917	64,879
Cash	8,832	8,596	29,732	n/a
Contributions	13,750	18,650	9,500	41,900
Republicans	3,750	13,950	8,000	25,700
No. of Cand.	*6*	*16*	*8*	*30*
House	750	11,200	4,000	15,950
Senate	3,000	2,750	4,000	9,750
Democrats	10,000	4,700	1,500	16,200
No. of Cand.	*15*	*4*	*2*	*21*
House	8,100	4,200	1,500	13,800
Senate	1,900	500	0	2,400
Incumbents	13,750	13,650	8,500	35,900
Challengers	0	0	0	0
Open Seat	0	5,000	1,000	6,000
Winners	10,250	16,650	n/a	26,900
Losers	3,500	2,000	n/a	5,500

National Association of Mortgage Brokers

*Phone: (703) 610-9009 x260 * Fax: (703) 610-9005*
8201 Greensboro Dr., Suite 300, McLean, VA 22102
*Web: www.namb.org * E-mail: cfrohman@namb.org*

The National Association of Mortgage Brokers is a nonprofit group with more than 6,000 members whose collective goal is to improve regulations governing the home buying and financing process.

NAMB has developed a certification program to recognize brokers who have attained the highest levels of professional expertise. Developed through research by mortgage industry experts, NAMB certification is given if the candidate has met certain requirements of mortgage brokerage experience and knowledge and has passed a written examination.

National Association of Mortgage Brokers Political Action Committee (NAMB PAC) (C00254201) *Address: same as sponsor * Treasurer: Brian Kinsella * Contact: Charlie Frohman, Congressional Affairs Dir.*

	1993-94	1995-96	1997	Totals
Receipts	$14,055	$42,307	$71,765	$128,127
Disburse	10,696	44,287	36,498	91,481
Cash	4,266	2,282	37,548	n/a
Contributions	16,900	29,825	32,500	79,225
Republicans	1,400	26,325	25,500	53,225
No. of Cand.	*2*	*30*	*29*	*61*
House	1,000	20,325	18,000	39,325
Senate	400	6,000	7,500	13,900
Democrats	15,500	3,500	7,000	26,000
No. of Cand.	*5*	*7*	*11*	*23*
House	13,500	3,000	4,500	21,000
Senate	2,000	500	2,500	5,000
Incumbents	15,500	28,325	32,000	75,825
Challengers	1,000	500	500	2,000
Open Seat	400	1,000	0	1,400
Winners	14,900	26,075	n/a	40,975
Losers	2,000	3,750	n/a	5,750

Illinois Association of Mortgage Brokers Inc. FedPAC (IAMB FedPAC) (C00308163) *Phone: (630) 916-7720 * Fax: (630) 916-7862 350 W. 22nd St., Suite 104, Lombard, IL 60148 * Web: www.iamb.org * E-mail: office@iamb.org * Treasurer: Angelo Cusinato*

The Illinois Association of Mortgage Brokers was founded in 1987. The group closed its PAC in 1997 and started another one with the same name (FEC ID: C00327460).

	1993-94	1995-96	1997	Totals
Receipts	$0	$50,029	$0	$50,029
Disburse	0	50,027	0	50,027
Cash	0	2	0	n/a
Contributions	0	10,450	0	10,450
Republicans	0	5,800	0	5,800
No. of Cand.	*0*	*17*	*0*	*17*
House	0	5,000	0	5,000
Senate	0	800	0	800
Democrats	0	4,650	0	4,650
No. of Cand.	*0*	*14*	*0*	*14*
House	0	2,950	0	2,950
Senate	0	1,700	0	1,700

Incumbents	0	8,950	0	8,950
Challengers	0	0	0	0
Open Seat	0	1,500	0	1,500
Winners	0	8,200	n/a	8,200
Losers	0	2,250	n/a	2,250

National Association of Real Estate Investment Trusts

*Phone: (202) 785-8717 * Fax: (202) 785-8723*
1129 20th St. N.W., Suite 305, Washington, DC 20036-3482
*Web: www.nareit.com * E-mail: mdepoy@nareit.com*

The National Association of Real Estate Investment Trusts supports the legislative, capital and educational needs of the REIT industry, which produced more than $15 billion in deals during the first six months of 1997. It has more than 2,000 members, including business trusts, real estate corporations and other associations that are qualified as REITs under Internal Revenue Code guidelines.

NAREIT has been in existence since President Eisenhower signed the real estate investment trust tax provisions into law in 1960. Today NAREIT lobbies Congress to enact favorable REIT legislation and works with the IRS and the Securities and Exchange Commission to seek more flexible regulatory rules affecting REITs.

It also provides its members and the public with investor information on the REIT industry, including current tax structures and updates on publicly traded real estate operations in the United States.

National Association of Real Estate Investment Trusts Political Action Committee (NAREIT PAC) (C00303339) *Address: same as sponsor * Treasurer: Martin L. DePoy*

	1993-94	*1995-96*	*1997*	*Totals*
Receipts	$0	$70,471	$35,516	$105,987
Disburse	0	32,592	32,159	64,751
Cash	0	37,877	41,233	n/a
Contributions	0	28,507	32,157	60,664
Republicans	0	23,135	29,157	52,292
No. of Cand.	*0*	*18*	*18*	*36*
House	0	11,635	15,652	27,287
Senate	0	11,500	13,505	25,005
Democrats	0	5,372	3,000	8,372
No. of Cand.	*0*	*6*	*3*	*9*
House	0	3,872	1,500	5,372
Senate	0	1,500	1,500	3,000
Incumbents	0	26,307	32,157	58,464
Challengers	0	500	0	500
Open Seat	0	1,700	0	1,700
Winners	0	27,257	n/a	27,257
Losers	0	1,250	n/a	1,250

National Association of Realtors

*Phone: (312) 329-8200 * Fax: (312) 329-8576*
430 N. Michigan Ave., Chicago, IL 60611
Web: nar.realtor.com

The National Association of Realtors has 720,000 members nationwide who are brokers, property managers, appraisers and salespeople in the real estate industry. It is the world's largest professional association.

The NAR supports policies and legislative proposals that promote home ownership. Its top congressional priorities include reforming the Real Estate Settlement Procedures Act to allow realtors to provide a wider range of real estate services than home sales alone.

The group supports strengthened private property rights and the increased availability of disaster insurance in states prone to natural disasters. The NAR also works to preserve the mortgage interest tax deduction and advocates raising the limits on loans insured by the Federal Housing Administration.

The NAR's committee, RPAC, spent 92 percent of its 1995-96 disbursements on candidate committees, contributing more than $2 million. It gave the second-highest total of any PAC — nearly $1.8 million — to winning candidates. More than 500 candidates, mostly Republican incumbents, received contributions from this group, and nearly 200 received at least $5,000. The leading recipients were Rep. Kevin Brady, R-Texas, Sen. James M. Inhofe, R-Okla., and Rep. Ken Bentsen, D-Texas.

RPAC's 1997 fundraising efforts surpassed the previous year by nearly 30 percent.

Realtors Political Action Committee (C00030718) *Phone: (202) 383-1238 * Fax: (202) 383-7580 * 700 11th St. N.W., Washington, DC 20004-4907 * E-mail: sdriesler@realtors.org * Treasurer: Martin Edwards Jr. * Contact: Stephen D. Driesler, Senior V.P.*

	1993-94	*1995-96*	*1997*	*Totals*
Receipts	$3,554,354	$1,358,829	$1,325,657	$6,238,840
Disburse	2,572,473	2,269,891	654,080	5,496,444
Cash	1,100,275	192,216	863,793	n/a
Contributions	1,851,478	2,099,683	491,238	4,442,399
Republicans	856,845	1,441,448	277,738	2,576,031
No. of Cand.	*230*	*302*	*193*	*725*
House	691,218	1,207,053	218,390	2,116,661
Senate	165,627	234,395	59,348	459,370
Democrats	970,633	655,235	212,500	1,838,368
No. of Cand.	*286*	*210*	*159*	*655*
House	840,974	600,735	176,100	1,617,809
Senate	129,659	54,500	36,400	220,559
Incumbents	1,483,500	1,656,183	461,738	3,601,421
Challengers	64,000	64,500	3,000	131,500
Open Seat	302,478	377,000	26,500	705,978
Winners	1,532,318	1,798,940	n/a	3,331,258
Losers	319,160	300,743	n/a	619,903

National Realty Committee

*Phone: (202) 639-8400 * Fax: (202) 639-8442*
1420 New York Ave. N.W., Suite 1100, Washington, DC 20005

National Realty Committee members are real estate owners, advisers, builders, investors, lenders and managers. The group lobbies on federal policy on real estate.

The NRC's goals include comprehensive tax system reform that would treat real estate comparably with other business activities and assets; the enactment of policies that will promote prudent real estate investment; and environmental regulation reform.

National Realty Political Action Committee (RealPAC) (C00033779) *Address: same as sponsor * Treasurer: Steven A. Wechsler * Contact: James J. Didion, Chairman*

	1993-94	*1995-96*	*1997*	*Totals*
Receipts	$44,071	$37,091	$25,568	$106,730
Disburse	89,883	79,919	11,393	181,195
Cash	60,534	17,711	31,891	n/a
Contributions	53,660	33,589	11,000	98,249
Republicans	12,250	18,500	6,500	37,250
No. of Cand.	*12*	*20*	*5*	*37*
House	5,750	10,000	4,500	20,250
Senate	6,500	8,500	2,000	17,000
Democrats	41,410	15,089	4,500	60,999
No. of Cand.	*34*	*12*	*6*	*52*
House	26,350	8,000	0	34,350
Senate	15,060	7,089	4,500	26,649
Incumbents	47,410	26,000	11,000	84,410
Challengers	3,000	0	0	3,000
Open Seat	3,250	7,589	0	10,839
Winners	37,160	28,089	n/a	65,249
Losers	16,500	5,500	n/a	22,000

Newhall Land and Farming Co.

*Phone: (805) 255-4000 * Fax: (805) 255-3960*
23823 Valencia Blvd., Valencia, CA 91355
*Web: www.newhall.com * E-mail: jbacker@newhall.com*

Newhall Land and Farming develops residential, industrial and commercial real estate. Its 1997 sales were $208 million and it employed 233 people. Newhall is publicly traded.

Newhall's primary business is developing master-planned communities containing homes and businesses, primarily on the company's 36,000 acres located about 30 miles north of downtown Los Angeles. The company's Valencia community is located in the region, as is its newest development, Newhall Ranch.

The company also operates farms and leases land for cattle grazing.

Newhall Land and Farming Co. Political Action Committee (NewPAC) (C00111104) *Address: same as sponsor * Treasurer: David E. Peterson * Contact: Jim Backer, Chairman*

	1993-94	*1995-96*	*1997*	*Totals*
Receipts	$23,809	$28,503	$13,698	$66,010
Disburse	19,283	34,338	7,845	61,466
Cash	8,534	2,704	8,558	n/a
Contributions	16,100	24,250	6,750	47,100
Republicans	12,600	23,500	6,000	42,100
No. of Cand.	*15*	*21*	*6*	*42*

(Data for Newhall Land continued)

	1993-94	1995-96	1997	Totals
House	9,600	19,500	5,000	34,100
Senate	3,000	4,000	1,000	8,000
Democrats	3,500	750	750	5,000
No. of Cand.	*3*	*2*	*2*	*7*
House	3,500	250	500	4,250
Senate	0	500	250	750
Incumbents	11,600	16,500	5,750	33,850
Challengers	1,000	1,000	1,000	3,000
Open Seat	0	6,750	0	6,750
Winners	11,350	18,500	n/a	29,850
Losers	4,750	5,750	n/a	10,500

Ohio Association of Mortgage Brokers

Phone: (216) 287-2595
3424 RUF Dr., Brunswick, OH 44212
Web: www.oamb.org

The Ohio Association of Mortgage Brokers has about 500 member companies. Its PAC is not affiliated with the National Association of Mortgage Brokers, according to FEC filings.

Ohio Association of Mortgage Brokers PAC (OAMB PAC) (C00300939) *Address: same as sponsor * Treasurer: James L. Nabors II*

	1993-94	1995-96	1997	Totals
Receipts	$0	$28,361	$33,193	$61,554
Disburse	0	19,900	18,810	38,710
Cash	0	8,461	22,844	n/a
Contributions	0	13,440	13,275	26,715
Republicans	0	10,000	8,775	18,775
No. of Cand.	*0*	*10*	*5*	*15*
House	0	9,900	8,775	18,675
Senate	0	100	0	100
Democrats	0	3,440	4,500	7,940
No. of Cand.	*0*	*6*	*3*	*9*
House	0	3,190	3,500	6,690
Senate	0	250	1,000	1,250
Incumbents	0	10,190	12,275	22,465
Challengers	0	3,000	0	3,000
Open Seat	0	0	1,000	1,000
Winners	0	8,790	n/a	8,790
Losers	0	4,650	n/a	4,650

Stewart Title Guaranty Co.

*Phone: (713) 625-8100 * Fax: (713) 552-9523*
1980 Post Oak Blvd., Suite 800, Houston, TX 77056
Web: www.stewart.com

Stewart Title Guaranty offers products and services geared toward automating title offices and accelerating growth in the real estate information business. Stewart develops technology, such as computing and digital imaging, to increase productivity in real estate transactions. It also markets and outsources real estate information services and products to the real estate and mortgage industries.

Founded in 1893, Stewart employs 4,500 associates around the world. Sales in 1997 exceeded $365 million.

Stewart Title Guaranty Co. PAC (StewPAC) (C00226712) *Phone: (202) 857-0213 * Fax: (202) 331-9306 * 1818 N St. N.W., Suite 200, Washington, DC 20036 * Treasurer: Malcolm Morris*

*Contact: Carloss Morris, Chairman and Co-CEO * Phone: (713) 625-8100*

	1993-94	1995-96	1997	Totals
Receipts	$6,551	$8,305	$1,300	$16,156
Disburse	10,000	9,050	1,000	20,050
Cash	2,105	1,360	1,660	n/a
Contributions	8,850	7,050	500	16,400
Republicans	7,350	6,050	500	13,900
No. of Cand.	*8*	*9*	*1*	*18*
House	5,600	6,050	500	12,150
Senate	1,750	0	0	1,750
Democrats	1,500	1,000	0	2,500
No. of Cand.	*1*	*2*	*0*	*3*
House	1,500	1,000	0	2,500
Senate	0	0	0	0
Incumbents	3,850	5,050	500	9,400
Challengers	2,250	750	0	3,000
Open Seat	2,750	1,250	0	4,000
Winners	7,850	5,050	n/a	12,900
Losers	1,000	2,000	n/a	3,000

Watson Land Co.

*Phone: (310) 952-6400 * Fax: (310) 522-8788*
22010 S. Wilmington Ave., Suite 400, Carson, CA 90745
*Web: www.watsonlandcompany.com * E-mail: rvonting@watsonlandcompany.com*

Watson Land is the largest developer of industrial centers in Los Angeles County and among the largest industrial developers in the nation.

In the past 25 years, the privately owned company has developed more than 1,000 acres of property for industrial and office facilities, as well as multi-tenant business centers. The company owns and maintains more than 9.6 million square feet of buildings and a wide array of land available for "build-to-suit" constructions.

Watson primarily builds industrial facilities for warehousing, distribution, assembly and manufacturing. The company also develops corporate headquarters, administrative and general offices as well as computer operations, data processing and technology.

Watson Employees Political Action Committee (formerly known as Watson Land Co. PAC) (C00107680) *Address: same as sponsor * Treasurer: Bruce A. Choate*

	1993-94	1995-96	1997	Totals
Receipts	$12,382	$7,427	$2,593	$22,402
Disburse	11,520	6,700	500	18,720
Cash	1,171	1,241	3,336	n/a
Contributions	9,500	6,700	500	16,700
Republicans	9,000	6,700	500	16,200
No. of Cand.	*17*	*11*	*1*	*29*
House	9,500	6,700	500	16,700
Senate	-500	0	0	-500
Democrats	500	0	0	500
No. of Cand.	*1*	*0*	*0*	*1*
House	500	0	0	500
Senate	0	0	0	0
Incumbents	7,000	2,700	500	10,200
Challengers	3,500	1,500	0	5,000
Open Seat	1,000	2,500	0	3,500
Winners	9,500	2,450	n/a	11,950
Losers	0	4,250	n/a	4,250

Wing Group Limited Co.

*Phone: (281) 362-9966 * Fax: (281) 364-7325*
1610 Woodstead Ct., Suite 220, The Woodlands, TX 77380
Web: www.wstnres.com/wing

The Wing Group develops gas- and coal-fired power generation plants around the globe, with major business in China, Thailand, the Philippines, Turkey, Colombia and the United States. Wing has a joint venture with China Power International, a private development arm of China's Ministry of Electric Power. It also built the world's largest independent power plant at Teeside in the United Kingdom.

Wing is a subsidiary of Western Resources, a publicly traded consumer services company with interests in security and energy. Western Resources posted $2.1 billion in 1997 revenues.

The Wing Group Limited Co. PAC (C00317123) *Address: same as sponsor * Treasurer: Kimberly E. Fox*

	1993-94	1995-96	1997	Totals
Receipts	$0	$22,500	$0	$22,500
Disburse	0	22,186	120	22,306
Cash	0	312	192	n/a
Contributions	0	22,018	0	22,018
Republicans	0	15,618	0	15,618
No. of Cand.	*0*	*5*	*0*	*5*
House	0	14,991	0	14,991
Senate	0	627	0	627
Democrats	0	6,400	0	6,400
No. of Cand.	*0*	*2*	*0*	*2*
House	0	6,400	0	6,400
Senate	0	0	0	0
Incumbents	0	19,518	0	19,518
Challengers	0	0	0	0
Open Seat	0	2,500	0	2,500
Winners	0	20,518	n/a	20,518
Losers	0	1,500	n/a	1,500

Savings & Loans

America's Community Bankers

*Phone: (202) 857-3100 * Fax: (202) 296-8716*
900 19th St. N.W., Suite 400, Washington, DC 20006
Web: www.acbankers.org

America's Community Bankers is a national trade group representing 2,000 savings and loans and related businesses. Most of these banks are home lenders, but some offer consumer and other types of loans. The community banking industry has more than $1 trillion in assets and 250,000 employees nationwide. The ACB is a major supporter of a federal plan to increase home ownership rates by the end of 2000.

The organization supports an expansion of banks' ability to offer more financial services, including insurance. It also lobbies to change government benefit payments from paper to electronic format and to create a single deposit insurance fund for banks. ACB is trying to end federal tax exemptions for certain credit unions that offer full banking services, arguing that the credit union industry has grown beyond the original intent of Congress.

ACB ranked first among savings and loan PACs in total contributions to congressional candidates during the 1995-96 election cycle. The group contributed more than two-thirds of its PAC spending total to Republican candidates.

Among the largest PACs overall, ACB was one of the top 20 supporters of incumbent candidates during the 1996 cycle. The top four recipients — Sen. Pete V. Domenici, R-N.M., Sen. Phil Gramm, R-Tex., Rep. Jon D. Fox, R-Pa., and Rep. Rick A. Lazio, R-N.Y. — all sit on banking committees.

America's Community Bankers Community Campaign Committee (formerly known as Savings & Community Bankers) (C00001875) *Address: same as sponsor * Treasurer: Steven D. Hailer * Contact: Robert R. Davis, Gov. Relations Dir.*

	1993-94	1995-96	1997	Totals
Receipts	$198,989	$205,844	$137,579	$542,412
Disburse	276,021	344,079	126,760	746,860
Cash	145,224	6,957	43,045	n/a
Contributions	241,972	283,337	92,903	618,212
Republicans	73,580	190,642	55,779	320,001
No. of Cand.	*74*	*107*	*67*	*248*
House	50,430	121,427	44,314	216,171
Senate	23,150	69,215	11,465	103,830
Democrats	168,392	92,695	37,124	298,211
No. of Cand.	*116*	*73*	*42*	*231*
House	128,726	63,786	24,524	217,036
Senate	39,666	28,909	12,600	81,175
Incumbents	212,779	257,008	90,001	559,788
Challengers	7,750	6,900	730	15,380
Open Seat	21,793	19,429	3,000	44,222
Winners	189,362	245,339	n/a	434,701
Losers	52,610	37,998	n/a	90,608

Western League of Savings Institutions (formerly known as California League Savings Institutions FEDPAC) (C00003459) *Phone: (310) 670-6300 * Fax: (310) 410-0372 * 1960 E. Grand Ave., Suite 1000, El Segundo, CA 90245 * Treasurer: Kathleen A. Wedeking*

	1993-94	1995-96	1997	Totals
Receipts	$27,816	$28,240	$10,732	$66,788
Disburse	41,438	38,819	17,270	97,527
Cash	26,621	16,044	9,507	n/a
Contributions	29,080	38,395	15,000	82,475
Republicans	8,250	27,367	8,000	43,617
No. of Cand.	*10*	*27*	*12*	*49*
House	6,750	23,517	7,000	37,267
Senate	1,500	3,850	1,000	6,350
Democrats	20,830	11,028	7,000	38,858
No. of Cand.	*22*	*11*	*13*	*46*
House	17,830	11,028	6,000	34,858
Senate	3,000	0	1,000	4,000
Incumbents	27,580	36,045	14,250	77,875
Challengers	500	350	0	850
Open Seat	500	2,000	750	3,250
Winners	24,580	35,145	n/a	59,725
Losers	4,500	3,250	n/a	7,750

Heartland Community Bankers Association Political Action Committee (HCBA-PAC) (C00160978) *700 Kansas Ave., Suite 512, Topeka, KS 66603 * Treasurer: John C. Dicus * Contact: Larry Schugart, Chairman*

	1993-94	1995-96	1997	Totals
Receipts	$17,530	$18,875	$13,317	$49,722
Disburse	13,865	23,282	3,421	40,568
Cash	4,706	298	10,195	n/a
Contributions	7,500	18,250	3,000	28,750
Republicans	6,000	16,750	3,000	25,750
No. of Cand.	*8*	*20*	*5*	*33*
House	6,000	10,600	2,000	18,600
Senate	0	6,150	1,000	7,150
Democrats	1,500	1,500	0	3,000
No. of Cand.	*2*	*2*	*0*	*4*
House	1,500	500	0	2,000
Senate	0	1,000	0	1,000
Incumbents	4,500	10,150	3,000	17,650
Challengers	1,000	2,400	0	3,400
Open Seat	2,000	5,700	0	7,700
Winners	6,000	16,750	n/a	22,750
Losers	1,500	1,500	n/a	3,000

Indiana League of Savings Institutions Committee on Public Affairs (C00074252) *Phone: (317) 632-2353 * 3135 N. Meridian St., Indianapolis, IN 46204 * Treasurer: James H. Cousins*

	1993-94	1995-96	1997	Totals
Receipts	$106,237	$114,086	$27,796	$248,119
Disburse	44,640	80,364	32,674	157,678
Cash	71,993	105,503	100,626	n/a
Contributions	4,050	18,100	5,225	27,375
Republicans	2,250	13,100	2,725	18,075
No. of Cand.	*4*	*9*	*4*	*17*
House	2,000	11,100	2,725	15,825
Senate	250	2,000	0	2,250
Democrats	1,800	5,000	2,500	9,300
No. of Cand.	*3*	*4*	*2*	*9*
House	1,800	5,000	2,500	9,300
Senate	0	0	0	0
Incumbents	3,050	12,600	4,725	20,375
Challengers	0	4,000	500	4,500
Open Seat	1,000	1,500	0	2,500
Winners	3,250	15,600	n/a	18,850
Losers	800	2,500	n/a	3,300

Michigan League of Savings Institutions Political Action Committee (Federal Fund) (C00001156) *Phone: (517) 371-2200 * 200 Washington Sq. N., Suite 300, Lansing, MI 48933 * Treasurer: Robert G. Howell * Contact: Michael Green, Dir. of Gov. Affairs*

	1993-94	1995-96	1997	Totals
Receipts	$40,226	$34,713	$10,252	$85,191
Disburse	28,053	26,395	5,808	60,256
Cash	21,355	29,676	34,120	n/a
Contributions	13,700	15,800	400	29,900
Republicans	8,700	10,800	150	19,650
No. of Cand.	*9*	*9*	*2*	*20*
House	7,700	9,800	150	17,650
Senate	1,000	1,000	0	2,000
Democrats	5,000	5,000	250	10,250
No. of Cand.	*5*	*8*	*2*	*15*
House	4,000	4,000	250	8,250
Senate	1,000	1,000	0	2,000
Incumbents	7,200	15,550	400	23,150
Challengers	2,000	250	0	2,250
Open Seat	4,500	0	0	4,500
Winners	8,200	10,500	n/a	18,700
Losers	5,500	5,300	n/a	10,800

Savings Associations Voluntary Political Action Committee Washington Savings League (C00116988) *Phone: (360) 943-2731 * 1501 S. Capitol Way, Suite 203, Olympia, WA 98501 * Treasurer: M. Scott Gaspard*

	1993-94	1995-96	1997	Totals
Receipts	$22,566	$15,659	$10,775	$49,000
Disburse	18,403	18,845	9,885	47,133
Cash	15,479	12,296	13,186	n/a
Contributions	13,020	13,000	6,250	32,270
Republicans	5,170	9,250	4,750	19,170
No. of Cand.	*6*	*7*	*4*	*17*
House	3,120	7,250	3,500	13,870
Senate	2,050	2,000	1,250	5,300
Democrats	7,850	3,750	1,500	13,100
No. of Cand.	*11*	*4*	*1*	*16*
House	7,650	3,000	1,500	12,150
Senate	200	750	0	950
Incumbents	9,900	12,000	6,250	28,150
Challengers	2,320	1,000	0	3,320
Open Seat	800	0	0	800
Winners	6,920	12,500	n/a	19,420
Losers	6,100	500	n/a	6,600

Minnesota League of Savings & Community Bankers Community Campaign Committee (MN-COMPAC) (C00145201) *Phone: (612) 332-4555 * 19000 St. Edwards Ct., Eden Prairie, MN 55346 * Treasurer: Diana L. Lee*

	1993-94	1995-96	1997	Totals
Receipts	$5,790	$11,514	$3,525	$20,829
Disburse	12,226	17,546	4,677	34,449
Cash	10,765	4,733	3,580	n/a
Contributions	8,400	12,450	600	21,450
Republicans	3,000	5,400	0	8,400
No. of Cand.	*7*	*5*	*0*	*12*
House	1,400	3,600	0	5,000
Senate	1,600	1,800	0	3,400
Democrats	3,400	7,050	600	11,050
No. of Cand.	*4*	*7*	*1*	*12*
House	3,400	6,550	600	10,550
Senate	0	500	0	500
Incumbents	3,950	11,650	600	16,200
Challengers	0	800	0	800
Open Seat	4,450	0	0	4,450
Winners	5,750	11,650	n/a	17,400
Losers	2,650	800	n/a	3,450

N.J. Savings League - SAPEC-NJ - Savings Association Political Election Committee - New Jersey (C00011221) *Phone: (908) 272-8500 * Fax: (908) 272-6626 * 411 North Ave. E., Cranford, NJ 07016 * Treasurer: James R. Silkensen*

	1993-94	1995-96	1997	Totals
Receipts	$58,645	$60,946	$26,930	$146,521
Disburse	82,854	56,283	25,899	165,036
Cash	30,574	35,239	36,270	n/a
Contributions	15,650	11,700	4,324	31,674
Republicans	9,000	8,200	2,574	19,774
No. of Cand.	*7*	*11*	*6*	*24*
House	8,000	6,700	2,074	16,774
Senate	1,000	1,500	500	3,000
Democrats	6,650	3,500	1,750	11,900
No. of Cand.	*8*	*7*	*4*	*19*
House	5,650	2,500	750	8,900
Senate	1,000	1,000	1,000	3,000
Incumbents	13,650	7,900	4,324	25,874
Challengers	2,000	500	0	2,500
Open Seat	0	3,300	0	3,300
Winners	12,000	8,650	n/a	20,650
Losers	3,650	3,050	n/a	6,700

Savings Association Public Affairs Committee of Kentucky (C00106849) *P.O. Box 559, Frankfort, KY 40602 * Treasurer: Tony W. Whitaker*

The Kentucky League of Savings Institutions PAC was terminated in April 1997.

	1993-94	1995-96	1997	Totals
Receipts	$19,661	$3,214	$286	$23,161
Disburse	24,938	26,565	41,553	93,056
Cash	64,615	41,267	0	n/a
Contributions	9,000	10,500	0	19,500
Republicans	4,000	9,500	0	13,500
No. of Cand.	*3*	*6*	*0*	*9*
House	4,000	7,500	0	11,500
Senate	0	2,000	0	2,000
Democrats	5,000	1,000	0	6,000
No. of Cand.	*2*	*1*	*0*	*3*
House	5,000	1,000	0	6,000
Senate	0	0	0	0
Incumbents	5,500	9,500	0	15,000
Challengers	0	1,000	0	1,000
Open Seat	3,500	0	0	3,500
Winners	8,000	10,500	n/a	18,500
Losers	1,000	0	n/a	1,000

Savings and Loan Political Action Committee II (SAL PAC II) (C00116756) *Phone: (515) 282-8168 * Fax: (515) 282-9117 * 206 Sixth Ave., Suite 900, Des Moines, IA 50309 * Treasurer: Sam Deaver * Contact: Richard Goodson Jr., President*

	1993-94	1995-96	1997	Totals
Receipts	$3,759	$12,092	$1,907	$17,758
Disburse	5,685	11,500	2,150	19,335
Cash	1,578	1,512	1,271	n/a
Contributions	5,125	10,000	2,150	17,275
Republicans	3,000	8,000	2,150	13,150
No. of Cand.	*3*	*5*	*4*	*12*
House	3,000	6,000	1,900	10,900
Senate	0	2,000	250	2,250
Democrats	2,125	2,000	0	4,125
No. of Cand.	*2*	*2*	*0*	*4*
House	2,000	1,000	0	3,000
Senate	125	1,000	0	1,125
Incumbents	3,625	8,000	1,900	13,525
Challengers	0	1,000	0	1,000
Open Seat	1,500	1,000	0	2,500
Winners	3,125	9,000	n/a	12,125
Losers	2,000	1,000	n/a	3,000

Savings Associations' League Political Action Committee Ohio (C00004010) *88 E. Broad St., Suite 1850, Columbus, OH 43215 * Treasurer: Mark K. Milligan*

	1993-94	1995-96	1997	Totals
Receipts	$79,178	$70,326	$36,112	$185,616
Disburse	74,143	72,170	20,417	166,730
Cash	12,056	10,214	25,910	n/a
Contributions	11,500	9,450	-500	20,450
Republicans	6,250	8,350	-500	14,100
No. of Cand.	*8*	*10*	*1*	*19*
House	2,750	8,350	-500	10,600
Senate	3,500	0	0	3,500
Democrats	5,250	1,100	0	6,350
No. of Cand.	*7*	*3*	*0*	*10*
House	5,250	1,100	0	6,350
Senate	0	0	0	0
Incumbents	8,750	9,450	-500	17,700
Challengers	250	0	0	250
Open Seat	2,500	0	0	2,500
Winners	10,250	6,950	n/a	17,200
Losers	1,250	2,500	n/a	3,750

Texas Savings and Community Bankers Association Political Action Committee (C00196634) *Phone: (512) 476-6131 * 910 Congress Ave., Second Floor, Austin, TX 78701 * Treasurer: J. Eric T. Sandberg Jr.*

	1993-94	1995-96	1997	Totals
Receipts	$250	$9,900	$4,265	$14,415
Disburse	500	7,250	2,500	10,250
Cash	250	2,900	4,665	n/a
Contributions	500	7,250	2,500	10,250
Republicans	500	7,000	2,250	9,750
No. of Cand.	*2*	*7*	*4*	*13*
House	0	1,500	1,500	3,000
Senate	500	5,500	750	6,750
Democrats	0	250	250	500
No. of Cand.	*0*	*1*	*1*	*2*
House	0	250	250	500
Senate	0	0	0	0
Incumbents	250	7,250	2,500	10,000
Challengers	0	0	0	0
Open Seat	250	0	0	250
Winners	250	6,750	n/a	7,000
Losers	250	500	n/a	750

Alabama Savings Association Public Affairs Committee (ASAPAC) (C00065391) *P.O. Box 11628, Montgomery, AL 36111 * Treasurer: Larry A. Vinson*

	1993-94	1995-96	1997	Totals
Receipts	$19,976	$11,663	$5,872	$37,511
Disburse	25,071	8,230	2,000	35,301
Cash	3,782	7,329	7,285	n/a
Contributions	2,314	5,250	500	8,064
Republicans	1,564	4,500	500	6,564
No. of Cand.	*2*	*5*	*1*	*8*
House	1,564	3,000	500	5,064
Senate	0	1,500	0	1,500
Democrats	750	750	0	1,500
No. of Cand.	*3*	*2*	*0*	*5*
House	750	750	0	1,500
Senate	0	0	0	0
Incumbents	2,064	1,500	500	4,064
Challengers	0	0	0	0
Open Seat	0	3,750	0	3,750
Winners	2,064	4,500	n/a	6,564
Losers	250	750	n/a	1,000

Contributed less than $5,000 during 1995-96 cycle:

New England League of Savings Institutions Political Action Committee (NELPAC) (C00196469) *40 Broad St., Suite 205, Boston, MA 02109 * Treasurer: Donald S. Glass*

Savings Associations of Louisiana Federal Political Action Committee (C00147538) *P.O. Box 80311, 4825 Jamestown Ave., Baton Rouge, LA 70898 * Treasurer: Daniel P. Digby*

Terminated PACs which contributed less than $5,000 during 1995-96 cycle:

Savings Association Public Affairs Committee of South Carolina (C00125526) *P.O. Box 1740, Conway, SC 29526 * Treasurer: Teresa D. Jones*

Associated Bank

*Phone: (715) 341-0400 * Fax: (715) 345-4139*
1305 Main St., Stevens Point, WI 54481
*Web: www.assocbank.com * E-mail: info@assocbank.com*

Associated Bank, formerly First Financial Bank, serves Wisconsin and Illinois through more than 100 branches. A subsidiary of Associated Banc-Corp., it manages assets of $4.4 billion.

Headquartered in Green Bay, parent company Associated Banc-Corp. also operates 128 First Financial banking offices and more than 180 ATMs in Wisconsin and Illinois. The $10.7-billion company has 2,000 employees. It is the third largest Wisconsin-based bank holding company.

First Financial Political Action Committee - Federal (C00079061)
*Address: same as sponsor * Treasurer: Wanda C. Lay*

	1993-94	1995-96	1997	Totals
Receipts	$7,171	$8,918	$1,090	$17,179
Disburse	7,500	10,000	0	17,500
Cash	3,996	2,919	5,641	n/a
Contributions	6,500	9,500	0	16,000
Republicans	4,500	8,000	0	12,500
No. of Cand.	*8*	*12*	*0*	*20*
House	4,000	7,000	0	11,000
Senate	500	1,000	0	1,500
Democrats	2,000	1,500	0	3,500
No. of Cand.	*2*	*3*	*0*	*5*
House	2,000	1,500	0	3,500
Senate	0	0	0	0
Incumbents	3,000	5,000	0	8,000
Challengers	3,500	3,000	0	6,500
Open Seat	0	1,500	0	1,500
Winners	3,500	4,500	n/a	8,000
Losers	3,000	5,000	n/a	8,000

CenFed Financial Corp.

Phone: (626) 585-2400
199 N. Lake Ave., Pasadena, CA 91101

CenFed Financial terminated its PAC in February 1998 after the company was purchased by Glendale Federal Corp.

CenFed was a $2.2-billion publicly owned savings and loan holding company operating 19 branches in Southern California. It had acquired United California Savings Bank in 1994.

CenFed Bank FSB PAC (C00300723) *Address: same as sponsor * Treasurer: William D. Nichol*

	1993-94	1995-96	1997	Totals
Receipts	$0	$14,104	$4,932	$19,036
Disburse	0	12,076	7,999	20,075
Cash	0	3,067	0	n/a
Contributions	0	7,500	2,650	10,150
Republicans	0	6,000	2,650	8,650
No. of Cand.	*0*	*8*	*5*	*13*
House	0	3,500	1,150	4,650
Senate	0	2,500	1,500	4,000
Democrats	0	1,500	0	1,500
No. of Cand.	*0*	*2*	*0*	*2*
House	0	1,500	0	1,500
Senate	0	0	0	0
Incumbents	0	7,500	1,650	9,150
Challengers	0	0	1,000	1,000
Open Seat	0	0	0	0
Winners	0	7,500	n/a	7,500
Losers	0	0	n/a	0

Chevy Chase Savings Bank

*Phone: (301) 986-6874 * Fax: (301) 968-7401*
8401 Connecticut Ave., Chevy Chase, MD 20815
Web: www.chevychasebank.com

The largest bank headquartered in the Washington area, Chevy Chase Savings Bank operates 135 full-service branches and 615 ATMs in Maryland, Northern Virginia and Washington. The publicly held company is expanding into the Baltimore market.

Chevy Chase had $6 billion in assets at the close of fiscal year 1997. The company is giving new attention to business banking and was able to double commercial deposits during fiscal year 1997. Chevy Chase also has been opening full-service branches in supermarkets.

To broaden its institutional client base, Chevy Chase purchased ASB Capital Management in 1997. ASB had about $3 billion of assets under management.

Chevy Chase Bank FSB Political Action Committee (C00283986)
*Address: same as sponsor * Treasurer: Stephen R. Halpin * Contact: Jessica Parker, V.P.*

	1993-94	1995-96	1997	Totals
Receipts	$7,291	$108,531	$68,174	$183,996
Disburse	6,700	85,061	51,580	143,341
Cash	593	24,068	40,665	n/a
Contributions	4,700	20,250	22,000	46,950
Republicans	0	13,500	17,000	30,500
No. of Cand.	*0*	*8*	*11*	*19*
House	0	8,500	7,500	16,000
Senate	0	5,000	9,500	14,500
Democrats	4,700	6,750	5,000	16,450
No. of Cand.	*5*	*8*	*6*	*19*
House	2,200	4,750	3,000	9,950
Senate	2,500	2,000	2,000	6,500
Incumbents	3,700	19,000	22,000	44,700
Challengers	0	0	0	0
Open Seat	1,000	1,000	0	2,000
Winners	3,700	19,000	n/a	22,700
Losers	1,000	1,250	n/a	2,250

Commercial Federal Corp.

*Phone: (402) 390-5336 * Fax: (402) 390-5328*
2120 S. 72nd St., Suite 1300, Omaha, NE 68124
Web: www.comfedbank.com

Commercial Federal is the holding company for Commercial Federal Bank, one of the largest savings banks in the Midwest and the 19th-largest thrift in the nation.

Based in Omaha, Neb., the company operates 115 branches throughout Nebraska, Kansas, Colorado, Oklahoma and Iowa. Commercial Federal, which began in 1887, employs more than 1,500 people. The company had sales of more than $560 million in 1997 and its assets total about $7 billion.

Commercial Federal, a public company, offers traditional thrift products as well as mortgage financing, consumer lending, insurance and stock brokerage services.

In January 1998, Commercial Federal purchased First National Bank Shares, the parent company of First Union National Bank and Trust Co. Then in February 1998, the company agreed to purchase AmerUs Bank, a wholly owned subsidiary of AmerUs Group Co.

Commercial Federal Savings & Loan Association Political Action Committee (C00127274) *Address: same as sponsor * Treasurer: James R. May Jr. * Contact: John J. Griffith, Chairman*

	1993-94	1995-96	1997	Totals
Receipts	$3,914	$19,339	$12,918	$36,171
Disburse	13,459	20,046	10,596	44,101
Cash	18,484	17,780	20,102	n/a
Contributions	1,750	11,250	3,500	16,500
Republicans	1,750	10,250	3,500	15,500
No. of Cand.	*3*	*13*	*3*	*19*
House	750	3,250	500	4,500
Senate	1,000	7,000	3,000	11,000
Democrats	0	1,000	0	1,000
No. of Cand.	*0*	*1*	*0*	*1*
House	0	0	0	0
Senate	0	1,000	0	1,000
Incumbents	250	4,750	3,500	8,500
Challengers	1,500	1,000	0	2,500
Open Seat	0	5,500	0	5,500
Winners	750	9,250	n/a	10,000
Losers	1,000	2,000	n/a	3,000

Community Bankers Association of N.Y. State

Phone: (212) 573-5500
200 Park Ave., New York, NY 10166

The Savings Banks Association of N.Y. State changed its name to Community Bankers Association of New York State. The organization is a New York City-based trade group for thrifts.

Community Bankers Association of N.Y. State Political Action Committee (C00098301) *Address: same as sponsor * Treasurer: Philip S. Messina * Contact: Paul E. Proske, Chairperson*

	1993-94	1995-96	1997	Totals
Receipts	$77,905	$61,795	$33,458	$173,158
Disburse	39,336	50,645	15,250	105,231
Cash	62,831	73,986	92,195	n/a
Contributions	26,265	38,635	14,250	79,150
Republicans	8,540	23,600	7,000	39,140
No. of Cand.	*12*	*21*	*13*	*46*
House	7,790	20,100	6,500	34,390
Senate	750	3,500	500	4,750
Democrats	17,225	15,035	7,250	39,510
No. of Cand.	*17*	*14*	*13*	*44*
House	13,225	14,535	7,250	35,010
Senate	4,000	500	0	4,500
Incumbents	25,015	38,135	13,000	76,150
Challengers	1,250	0	1,000	2,250
Open Seat	0	500	250	750
Winners	24,265	38,635	n/a	62,900
Losers	2,000	0	n/a	2,000

Dime Savings Bank of New York

*Phone: (212) 326-6152 * Fax: (212) 326-6163*
589 Fifth Ave., New York, NY 10017
Web: www.dime.com

Dime Savings Bank of New York is the fifth largest thrift in the nation, with total deposits of $12.9 billion. It is owned by the publicly traded holding company Dime Bancorp of New York City, which merged with Anchor Bancorp Inc. in 1995.

Founded in 1859, Dime Savings has about 3,160 employees and 90 branches in the greater New York metropolitan area.

Dime Savings Bank of N.Y. Political Action Committee (DimePAC) (C00184838) *Address: same as sponsor * Treasurer: Franklin L. Wright Jr.*

	1993-94	1995-96	1997	Totals
Receipts	$14,529	$13,948	$5,975	$34,452
Disburse	12,475	12,341	7,250	32,066
Cash	5,282	6,891	5,616	n/a
Contributions	11,125	11,325	7,250	29,700
Republicans	4,200	8,825	5,500	18,525
No. of Cand.	*6*	*9*	*6*	*21*
House	1,200	3,325	2,000	6,525
Senate	3,000	5,500	3,500	12,000
Democrats	6,925	2,500	1,750	11,175
No. of Cand.	*7*	*3*	*3*	*13*
House	4,425	2,500	1,750	8,675
Senate	2,500	0	0	2,500
Incumbents	9,925	11,325	7,250	28,500
Challengers	1,200	0	0	1,200
Open Seat	0	0	0	0
Winners	9,925	11,325	n/a	21,250
Losers	1,200	0	n/a	1,200

Dollar Savings Bank

*Phone: (412) 261-8852 * Fax: (412) 261-8273*
Three Gateway Center, 7 South, Pittsburgh, PA 15222
Web: www.dollarbank.com

Dollar Savings Bank is a Pittsburgh-based savings bank with more than $2.6 billion in assets. It has 46 offices located in Pittsburgh and Cleveland and their surrounding counties. Established in 1855, the bank has nearly 1,100 employees and more than $2 billion in deposits.

Dollar Savings Bank Political Action Committee (DolPAC) (C00151563) *Address: same as sponsor * Treasurer: Robert J. Cromer*

	1993-94	1995-96	1997	Totals
Receipts	$5,109	$15,105	$11,266	$31,480
Disburse	5,660	14,775	9,785	30,220
Cash	613	949	2,431	n/a
Contributions	1,750	10,150	4,300	16,200
Republicans	0	7,075	3,300	10,375
No. of Cand.	*0*	*8*	*3*	*11*
House	0	1,750	500	2,250
Senate	0	5,325	2,800	8,125
Democrats	1,750	3,075	1,000	5,825
No. of Cand.	*3*	*3*	*1*	*7*
House	750	3,075	1,000	4,825
Senate	1,000	0	0	1,000
Incumbents	1,750	9,400	4,300	15,450
Challengers	0	500	0	500
Open Seat	0	0	0	0
Winners	500	8,900	n/a	9,400
Losers	1,250	1,250	n/a	2,500

First Federal Bank of California

*Phone: (310) 319-6041 * Fax: (310) 319-6046*
401 Wilshire Blvd., Suite 1200, Santa Monica, CA 90401

First Federal Bank of California has 25 branches in Southern California and assets of $4.2 billion. It is a wholly owned subsidiary of the publicly traded savings and loan holding company FirstFed Financial Corp.

Subsidiaries: Seaside Financial Corp., Oceanside Insurance Agency and Santa Monica Capital Group.

First Federal Bank of California Federal Political Action Committee (C00137158) *Address: same as sponsor * Treasurer: Colleen C. McAndrews*

	1993-94	1995-96	1997	Totals
Receipts	$17,327	$9,326	$2,843	$29,496
Disburse	9,789	16,362	1,526	27,677
Cash	23,078	16,046	17,363	n/a
Contributions	2,250	7,100	500	9,850
Republicans	750	6,100	500	7,350
No. of Cand.	*2*	*10*	*1*	*13*
House	750	5,100	500	6,350
Senate	0	1,000	0	1,000
Democrats	1,500	1,000	0	2,500
No. of Cand.	*2*	*1*	*0*	*3*
House	500	1,000	0	1,500
Senate	1,000	0	0	1,000
Incumbents	2,000	6,100	500	8,600
Challengers	250	0	0	250
Open Seat	0	1,000	0	1,000
Winners	2,000	6,100	n/a	8,100
Losers	250	1,000	n/a	1,250

Great Western Financial Corp.

9200 Oakdale Ave., Chatsworth, CA 91311

The Great Western Financial PAC was terminated in November 1997. The company merged with Washington Mutual in July 1997.

Great Western Financial Corp. Good Government Committee (C00076075) *Address: same as sponsor * Treasurer: Linda J. Gwyn*

	1993-94	1995-96	1997	Totals
Receipts	$85,115	$103,529	$23,523	$212,167
Disburse	104,419	104,600	32,903	241,922
Cash	10,432	9,374	0	n/a
Contributions	74,960	85,650	16,900	177,510
Republicans	31,210	62,650	9,400	103,260
No. of Cand.	*38*	*55*	*15*	*108*
House	24,460	47,150	6,400	78,010
Senate	6,750	15,500	3,000	25,250
Democrats	43,750	23,000	7,500	74,250
No. of Cand.	*47*	*29*	*12*	*88*
House	32,250	17,500	5,500	55,250
Senate	11,500	5,500	2,000	19,000
Incumbents	69,960	79,650	16,900	166,510
Challengers	1,000	3,750	0	4,750
Open Seat	3,500	1,750	0	5,250
Winners	63,710	75,650	n/a	139,360
Losers	11,250	10,000	n/a	21,250

GreenPoint Bank

*Phone: (212) 834-1000 * Fax: (212) 834-1407*
90 Park Ave., Fourth Floor, New York, NY 10016
Web: www.greenpoint.com

GreenPoint Bank is one of the largest no-documentation residential mortgage lenders in the New York metropolitan area. It has 74 branches in Manhattan, Brooklyn, Queens, Nassau, Suffolk and Westchester counties. GreenPoint reported deposits of $11 billion at the close of 1997.

The bank is a subsidiary of GreenPoint Financial Corp., a publicly traded New York holding company with assets of $13.1 billion. The parent company's other principal subsidiary, GreenPoint Mortgage Corp., offers mortgage lending nationally. It is headquartered in Charlotte, N.C.

GreenPoint Bank Federal Political Action Committee (C00212613) *Address: same as sponsor * Treasurer: Walter Steunenberg*

	1993-94	1995-96	1997	Totals
Receipts	$290	$24,396	$297	$24,983
Disburse	1,400	8,900	2,700	13,000
Cash	3,829	19,327	16,925	n/a
Contributions	1,300	8,750	2,700	12,750
Republicans	700	6,000	1,700	8,400
No. of Cand.	*2*	*6*	*2*	*10*
House	700	3,000	700	4,400
Senate	0	3,000	1,000	4,000
Democrats	600	2,750	1,000	4,350
No. of Cand.	*2*	*4*	*1*	*7*
House	100	2,750	0	2,850
Senate	500	0	1,000	1,500
Incumbents	800	8,750	2,700	12,250
Challengers	500	0	0	500
Open Seat	0	0	0	0
Winners	800	8,250	n/a	9,050
Losers	500	500	n/a	1,000

H.F. Ahmanson & Co.

*Phone: (415) 389-6800 * Fax: (415) 388-6874*
591 Redwood Hwy., #4000, Mill Valley, CA 94941
Web: www.homesavings.com

H.F. Ahmanson & Co. is a holding company for Home Savings of America, a consumer and small business bank. The publicly traded company has $56 billion in assets and employs 9,000 workers.

In February 1998, Ahmanson acquired Coast Savings Financial Inc., a parent of Coast Federal Bank, in a merger valued at $900 million. The combined company serves more than 2 million households in California, Florida, Arizona and Texas. It plans to close 52 Coast Federal and Home Savings branches, leaving 407 branches.

Another major Ahmanson subsidiary, Griffin Financial Services, provides investment services and insurance, as well as its own mutual fund family.

H.F. Ahmanson & Co. Federal Political Action Committee (C00166983) *Address: same as sponsor * Treasurer: James R. Sutton*

	1993-94	1995-96	1997	Totals
Receipts	$52,824	$103,934	$37,226	$193,984
Disburse	89,162	74,256	42,057	205,475
Cash	5,206	34,892	30,061	n/a
Contributions	55,500	45,250	41,500	142,250
Republicans	10,300	32,250	16,000	58,550
No. of Cand.	*6*	*20*	*11*	*37*
House	3,300	23,250	15,000	41,550
Senate	7,000	9,000	1,000	17,000
Democrats	45,200	13,000	25,500	83,700
No. of Cand.	*18*	*11*	*8*	*37*
House	15,450	10,500	19,500	45,450
Senate	29,750	2,500	6,000	38,250
Incumbents	53,750	42,050	41,500	137,300
Challengers	250	1,500	0	1,750
Open Seat	1,500	1,700	0	3,200
Winners	45,750	42,750	n/a	88,500
Losers	9,750	2,500	n/a	12,250

Coast FedPAC - A Political Action Committee of Coast Federal Bank (C00099572) *1000 Wilshire Blvd., Main Floor, Los Angeles, CA 90017 * Web: www.coastfederal.com * Treasurer: David Porges*

Coast Federal Bank's PAC was terminated in February 1998.

	1993-94	1995-96	1997	Totals
Receipts	$29,012	$39,282	$9,201	$77,495
Disburse	22,281	35,286	11,145	68,712
Cash	9,938	13,937	11,993	n/a
Contributions	15,030	24,002	4,900	43,932
Republicans	8,230	23,002	4,900	36,132
No. of Cand.	*5*	*16*	*4*	*25*
House	8,230	19,502	4,900	32,632
Senate	0	3,500	0	3,500
Democrats	6,800	1,000	0	7,800
No. of Cand.	*9*	*1*	*0*	*10*
House	4,800	1,000	0	5,800
Senate	2,000	0	0	2,000
Incumbents	9,700	16,100	4,900	30,700
Challengers	5,330	6,102	0	11,432
Open Seat	0	1,500	0	1,500
Winners	8,200	17,100	n/a	25,300
Losers	6,830	6,902	n/a	13,732

Harris Trust & Savings Bank

Phone: (312) 361-2121
111 W. Monroe (60603), P.O. Box 755, Chicago, IL 60690-0755
*Web: www.harrisbank.com * E-mail: webinfo@harrisbank.com*

Harris Trust & Savings Bank provides banking, trust and investment services in the Chicago area. It is a leading provider of corporate banking services in the Midwest. Harris Trust has 140 locations, 6,700 employees and assets of $21.5 billion.

The bank also offers credit card services throughout the United States. It will open six full-service branches in Florida in spring 1998.

Harris Trust is a wholly owned subsidiary of Harris Bankcorp Inc., which itself is a wholly owned subsidiary of the Bank of Montreal. In January 1998, the Bank of Montreal and Royal Bank of Canada announced plans to merge into a new bank as equal partners.

Harris Government Affairs Fund (Harris Trust & Savings Bank) (C00086256) *Address: same as sponsor * Treasurer: Donna Streibich Curtis*

	1993-94	1995-96	1997	Totals
Receipts	$22,209	$10,537	$4,111	$36,857
Disburse	6,265	20,400	9,150	35,815
Cash	26,005	16,146	11,108	n/a
Contributions	0	7,400	3,500	10,900
Republicans	0	5,100	1,500	6,600
No. of Cand.	*0*	*3*	*2*	*5*
House	0	100	0	100
Senate	0	5,000	1,500	6,500
Democrats	0	2,300	2,000	4,300
No. of Cand.	*0*	*6*	*2*	*8*
House	0	1,550	1,000	2,550
Senate	0	750	1,000	1,750
Incumbents	0	5,700	3,500	9,200
Challengers	0	100	0	100
Open Seat	0	1,600	0	1,600
Winners	0	6,550	n/a	6,550
Losers	0	850	n/a	850

Leader Federal Bank for Savings

1730 Goodlett Farms Pkwy., Cordova, TN 38108

The Leader Federal Bank for Savings PAC was terminated.

Leader Federal Bank for Savings Political Action Committee (C00078014) *Address: same as sponsor * Treasurer: Morris Fair*

	1993-94	1995-96	1997	Totals
Receipts	$16,139	$19,110	$0	$35,249
Disburse	20,654	35,099	0	55,753
Cash	15,986	0	0	n/a
Contributions	14,150	8,950	0	23,100
Republicans	7,950	7,150	0	15,100
No. of Cand.	*12*	*8*	*0*	*20*
House	5,200	3,150	0	8,350
Senate	2,750	4,000	0	6,750
Democrats	6,200	1,800	0	8,000
No. of Cand.	*5*	*6*	*0*	*11*
House	4,600	1,800	0	6,400
Senate	1,600	0	0	1,600
Incumbents	6,650	6,950	0	13,600
Challengers	3,000	600	0	3,600
Open Seat	4,500	1,400	0	5,900
Winners	7,050	7,950	n/a	15,000
Losers	7,100	1,000	n/a	8,100

Long Island Savings Bank

Phone: (516) 547-2000
201 Old Country Rd., Melville, NY 11747
Web: www.lisb.com

Long Island Savings Bank operates 35 branches in the New York metropolitan area and 25 mortgage offices in eight eastern states. Outside of New York, the mortgage business operates under the name Entrust.

The bank is the principal subsidiary of Long Island Bancorp Inc., which completed its second full year as a publicly traded company in 1997 by posting sales of $436 million. The 120-year-old bank has assets of $5.9 billion and employs 1,500 people.

Long Island Savings Bank FSB Political Action Committee (LISB PAC) (C00234245) *Address: same as sponsor * Treasurer: Christine Quigley * Contact: Pamela Agnone, President*

	1993-94	1995-96	1997	Totals
Receipts	$0	$29,128	$13,636	$42,764
Disburse	0	11,350	4,700	16,050
Cash	0	17,778	26,714	n/a
Contributions	0	9,350	3,200	12,550
Republicans	0	6,100	1,200	7,300
No. of Cand.	*0*	*7*	*3*	*10*
House	0	4,100	1,100	5,200
Senate	0	2,000	100	2,100
Democrats	0	3,250	2,000	5,250
No. of Cand.	*0*	*4*	*2*	*6*
House	0	3,250	2,000	5,250
Senate	0	0	0	0
Incumbents	0	9,250	3,200	12,450
Challengers	0	100	0	100
Open Seat	0	0	0	0
Winners	0	8,250	n/a	8,250
Losers	0	1,100	n/a	1,100

North Side Savings Bank

Phone: (516) 437-4201
170 Tulip Ave., Floral Park, NY 11001

North Side Savings Bank was bought in 1997 by North Fork Bancorp. Its PAC was dissolved in June 1997.

North Side Savings Bank Political Action Committee (C00294058) *Address: same as sponsor * Treasurer: Judith A. MacGregor*

	1993-94	1995-96	1997	Totals
Receipts	$12,000	$12,065	$0	$24,065
Disburse	4,606	18,500	959	24,065
Cash	7,394	959	0	n/a
Contributions	2,500	14,600	0	17,100
Republicans	750	9,600	0	10,350
No. of Cand.	*1*	*13*	*0*	*14*
House	0	5,350	0	5,350
Senate	750	4,250	0	5,000
Democrats	1,750	5,000	0	6,750
No. of Cand.	*3*	*6*	*0*	*9*
House	1,750	4,000	0	5,750
Senate	0	1,000	0	1,000
Incumbents	2,500	12,100	0	14,600
Challengers	0	0	0	0
Open Seat	0	2,500	0	2,500
Winners	2,500	13,100	n/a	15,600
Losers	0	1,500	n/a	1,500

People's Bank

*Phone: (203) 338-3667 * Fax: (860) 280-2884*
850 Main St., P.O. Box 1580, Bridgeport, CT 06604-4913
Web: www.peoples.com

People's Bank is the largest independently owned bank in Connecticut, with assets of $10.8 billion. It is also the 24th-largest Visa and MasterCard issuer in the nation. The publicly traded company acquired Norwich Financial Corp. in February 1998, boosting its size to 128 branches and about 3,000 employees.

In December 1997, the company announced plans to purchase Independent Resources Inc., an equipment leasing firm, and form a new subsidiary named People's Capital and Leasing Corp. In addition, in November 1997, the bank announced the acquisition of Olson Mobeck & Associates, an asset management company.

People's offers investment services through its wholly owned subsidiary, People's Securities Inc.

People's Bank Federal Political Action Committee (C00178012) *Address: same as sponsor * Treasurer: Claude Bouvier * Contact: William Kosturko, Chairperson*

	1993-94	1995-96	1997	Totals
Receipts	$13,944	$20,407	$0	$34,351
Disburse	8,740	9,400	3,800	21,940
Cash	5,254	16,261	12,461	n/a
Contributions	6,850	8,400	3,800	19,050
Republicans	3,600	4,550	1,300	9,450
No. of Cand.	*5*	*7*	*3*	*15*
House	2,600	3,050	800	6,450
Senate	1,000	1,500	500	3,000
Democrats	3,250	3,850	2,500	9,600
No. of Cand.	*5*	*4*	*3*	*12*
House	2,250	1,850	2,000	6,100
Senate	1,000	2,000	500	3,500
Incumbents	6,250	7,900	2,800	16,950
Challengers	600	500	0	1,100
Open Seat	0	0	1,000	1,000
Winners	6,250	7,300	n/a	13,550
Losers	600	1,100	n/a	1,700

Rochester Community Savings Bank

235 E. Main St., Rochester, NY 14604

Rochester Community Savings Bank PAC filed for termination in November 1997.

Rochester Community Savings Bank Political Action Committee (C00162883) *Address: same as sponsor * Treasurer: Stephen G. Rumery*

	1993-94	1995-96	1997	Totals
Receipts	$23,613	$29,038	$5,988	$58,639
Disburse	20,729	22,524	17,609	60,862
Cash	5,103	11,621	0	n/a
Contributions	7,150	11,850	3,850	22,850
Republicans	2,150	7,400	3,350	12,900
No. of Cand.	*6*	*10*	*7*	*23*
House	1,150	3,400	500	5,050
Senate	1,000	4,000	2,850	7,850
Democrats	5,000	3,450	500	8,950
No. of Cand.	*11*	*4*	*1*	*16*
House	2,750	3,250	0	6,000
Senate	2,250	200	500	2,950
Incumbents	6,150	10,650	3,850	20,650
Challengers	500	0	0	500
Open Seat	500	200	0	700
Winners	6,650	10,850	n/a	17,500
Losers	500	1,000	n/a	1,500

Roosevelt Savings Bank

Phone: (516) 742-9300
1122 Franklin Ave., Garden City, NY 11530
Web: www.rooseveltsb.com

Roosevelt Savings Bank, through its 15 branch offices, serves the New York City boroughs of Brooklyn and Queens and the counties of Nassau and Suffolk.

The bank offers traditional savings and loan services, primarily investing in residential real estate loans. Established in 1895 as a mutual savings bank, it had 1996 net income of about $30 million and total assets of more than $3 billion. Roosevelt Savings Bank is held by TR Financial Corp., a publicly traded company.

Roosevelt Savings Bank Federal Political Action Committee (C00170928) *Address: same as sponsor * Treasurer: Dennis E. Henchy*

	1993-94	1995-96	1997	Totals
Receipts	$9,060	$8,925	$6,060	$24,045
Disburse	4,030	12,550	1,840	18,420
Cash	14,463	10,838	15,058	n/a
Contributions	3,500	8,050	1,000	12,550
Republicans	750	4,800	0	5,550
No. of Cand.	*2*	*7*	*0*	*9*
House	250	3,300	0	3,550
Senate	500	1,500	0	2,000
Democrats	2,750	3,250	1,000	7,000
No. of Cand.	*3*	*7*	*1*	*11*
House	2,500	3,250	1,000	6,750
Senate	250	0	0	250
Incumbents	3,250	7,550	1,000	11,800
Challengers	250	500	0	750
Open Seat	0	0	0	0
Winners	3,250	6,800	n/a	10,050
Losers	250	1,250	n/a	1,500

TCF Financial Corp.

Phone: (612) 661-8720
801 Marquette Ave., Minneapolis, MN 55402
Web: www.tcfbank.com

TCF Financial is a publicly held $9.8 billion national bank holding company based in Minneapolis. Subsidiary TCF National Bank has branches in Minnesota, Illinois, Wisconsin and Colorado. Subsidiary Great Lakes National Bank has a branch in Michigan. TCF also provides services in business equipment leasing, consumer finance, mortgage banking, title insurance, annuity and mutual fund sales.

TCF Financial recently acquired 76 branches in the greater Chicago area, bringing its total in Illinois to 125 branches. The deal makes TCF the fourth-largest retail bank in that market, according to William A. Cooper, TCF chairman and CEO.

TCF PAC (C00218263) *Address: same as sponsor * Treasurer: Douglas L. Young * Contact: Hank Fisher, Chairman*

	1993-94	1995-96	1997	Totals
Receipts	$7,076	$27,273	$9,698	$44,047
Disburse	8,035	29,400	5,300	42,735
Cash	5,204	3,080	7,478	n/a
Contributions	8,025	16,300	3,000	27,325
Republicans	7,000	11,700	2,500	21,200
No. of Cand.	*9*	*9*	*2*	*20*
House	5,000	4,700	500	10,200
Senate	2,000	7,000	2,000	11,000
Democrats	900	4,600	500	6,000
No. of Cand.	*2*	*3*	*1*	*6*
House	900	4,600	500	6,000
Senate	0	0	0	0
Incumbents	2,900	7,600	3,000	13,500
Challengers	500	8,200	0	8,700
Open Seat	4,625	500	0	5,125
Winners	3,700	7,600	n/a	11,300
Losers	4,325	8,700	n/a	13,025

Washington Mutual Inc.

*Phone: (206) 461-8854 * Fax: (206) 554-2790*
1201 Third Ave., Suite 1500, Seattle, WA 98101
Web: www.wamu.com

Following its 1996 purchase of American Savings and 1997 purchase of Great Western Financial, Washington Mutual is the largest thrift in the United States. The savings and loan provides financial services to more than 4 million households in the West and Florida. A publicly traded company, Washington Mutual has $96 billion in assets and posted 1997 sales of $7.5 billion.

The Seattle-based company employs more than 8,000 people in 1,700 offices.

Washington Mutual Political Action Committee (WMPAC) (C00129833) *Address: same as sponsor * Treasurer: Paul Bonde * Contact: Benson Porter, V.P. of Gov. Relations*

	1993-94	1995-96	1997	Totals
Receipts	$44,858	$81,620	$68,101	$194,579
Disburse	42,779	74,163	27,859	144,801
Cash	24,039	27,497	67,741	n/a
Contributions	9,950	16,949	14,302	41,201
Republicans	2,200	12,649	9,552	24,401
No. of Cand.	*4*	*12*	*9*	*25*
House	350	7,149	5,700	13,199
Senate	1,850	5,500	3,852	11,202
Democrats	7,750	4,300	4,750	16,800
No. of Cand.	*13*	*6*	*5*	*24*
House	6,250	3,800	3,750	13,800
Senate	1,500	500	1,000	3,000
Incumbents	8,900	12,949	13,302	35,151
Challengers	600	2,000	0	2,600
Open Seat	700	2,000	1,000	3,700
Winners	5,450	15,449	n/a	20,899
Losers	4,500	1,500	n/a	6,000

American Savings Bank Political Action Committee (C00237628) *Phone: (206) 461-8854 * Fax: (206) 554-2790 * 1201 Third Ave., Suite 1500, Seattle, WA 98101 * Treasurer: Jimmy D. Holland * Contact: Benson Porter, V.P. of Gov. Relations*

American Savings Bank was purchased by Washington Mutual in 1996. A spokesperson for Washington Mutual said in February 1998 that the American Savings Bank PAC was in the process of being terminated.

	1993-94	1995-96	1997	Totals
Receipts	$22,106	$12,999	$2,579	$37,684
Disburse	37,972	28,603	-2,916	63,659
Cash	20,526	4,928	10,429	n/a
Contributions	10,750	17,500	-3,000	25,250
Republicans	1,750	8,500	-1,000	9,250
No. of Cand.	*4*	*10*	*1*	*15*
House	1,500	7,500	-1,000	8,000
Senate	250	1,000	0	1,250
Democrats	9,000	9,000	-2,000	16,000
No. of Cand.	*11*	*7*	*1*	*19*
House	5,000	3,000	0	8,000
Senate	4,000	6,000	-2,000	8,000
Incumbents	8,750	16,500	-3,000	22,250
Challengers	1,000	0	0	1,000
Open Seat	1,000	1,000	0	2,000
Winners	7,750	17,500	n/a	25,250
Losers	3,000	0	n/a	3,000

Western Financial Savings Bank

*Phone: (714) 727-1000 * Fax: (714) 727-1644*
23 Pasteur Rd., Irvine, CA 92618

Western Financial Savings Bank operates 26 branches in California, but its main business is residential mortgage loans, which, at $6.4 billion, account for 80 percent of the bank's total loan portfolio. The bank is a subsidiary of the publicly traded financial services holding company Westcorp, which also has major business in automobile loans.

Westcorp employs more than 2,000 people through all of its subsidiaries, and has assets of $3.7 billion.

Western Financial Savings Bank Political Action Committee (C00199059) *Address: same as sponsor * Treasurer: Dave E. Haggard * Contact: Joan VanWinkle, legal counsel*

	1993-94	1995-96	1997	Totals
Receipts	$9,638	$3,700	$1,033	$14,371
Disburse	5,070	14,978	2,238	22,286
Cash	32,593	21,318	20,113	n/a
Contributions	2,100	5,750	1,250	9,100
Republicans	800	5,750	1,250	7,800
No. of Cand.	*2*	*6*	*3*	*11*
House	800	3,750	500	5,050
Senate	0	2,000	750	2,750
Democrats	1,300	0	0	1,300
No. of Cand.	*2*	*0*	*0*	*2*
House	300	0	0	300
Senate	1,000	0	0	1,000
Incumbents	2,100	5,750	750	8,600
Challengers	0	0	500	500
Open Seat	0	0	0	0
Winners	2,100	5,750	n/a	7,850
Losers	0	0	n/a	0

World Savings & Loan Association

*Phone: (510) 446-3420 * Fax: (510) 446-4259*
1901 Harrison St., Second Floor, Oakland, CA 94612

The World Savings & Loan Association is the primary banking subsidiary of Golden West Financial Corp., a $37.7-billion holding company. Based on assets, it was the seventh-largest, California-based bank and thrift in 1997, according to the Los Angeles Times. It has more than 250 branch locations in seven states, primarily in California and Colorado. The corporation's sales for 1996 were $2.7 billion. It has 4,028 employees.

World Savings & Loan Association Political Action Committee (WorldPAC) (C00193144) *Address: same as sponsor * Treasurer: J. L. Helvey * Contact: Dan R. Dixon, Senior V.P.*

	1993-94	1995-96	1997	Totals
Receipts	$9,712	$9,817	$4,476	$24,005
Disburse	12,200	11,250	4,082	27,532
Cash	7,959	6,526	6,919	n/a
Contributions	9,200	6,500	1,500	17,200
Republicans	0	5,000	1,500	6,500
No. of Cand.	*0*	*3*	*2*	*5*
House	0	5,000	1,500	6,500
Senate	0	0	0	0
Democrats	9,200	1,500	0	10,700
No. of Cand.	*5*	*1*	*0*	*6*
House	3,200	1,500	0	4,700
Senate	6,000	0	0	6,000
Incumbents	9,200	6,500	1,500	17,200
Challengers	0	0	0	0
Open Seat	0	0	0	0
Winners	7,200	6,500	n/a	13,700
Losers	2,000	0	n/a	2,000

Securities & Investment

AIM Management Group

*Phone: (713) 214-1453 * Fax: (713) 993-9890*
11 Greenway Plaza, Suite 100, Houston, TX 77046
*Web: www.aimfunds.com * E-mail: jeff_horne@aimfunds.com*

AIM Management Group, based in Houston, is a mutual fund manager that employs 1,500 people. Its distribution system of advisers, brokers and bankers includes 120,000 financial advisers and more than 500 banks and brokerage houses, such as Merrill Lynch and Co. The company's combined managed assets total $83 billion.

London-based Invesco purchased AIM for $1.6 billion in February 1997. The resulting company, renamed Amvesco PLC, now oversees more than $150 billion in client assets. AIM Management Group became a subsidiary of Amvesco.

AIM was No. 96 in the Houston Chronicle's 1997 list of the area's top 100 employers.

AIM Management Inc. for A Better America (also known as AIM for A Better America) (AIM PAC) (C00253369) *Address: same as sponsor * Treasurer: Jeff Horne*

	1993-94	1995-96	1997	Totals
Receipts	$35,236	$41,368	$28,103	$104,707
Disburse	39,600	45,288	18,950	103,838
Cash	14,477	10,557	19,710	n/a
Contributions	22,750	26,285	11,750	60,785
Republicans	13,500	25,035	9,500	48,035
No. of Cand.	*9*	*25*	*14*	*48*
House	5,000	17,675	6,750	29,425
Senate	8,500	7,360	2,750	18,610
Democrats	9,250	1,250	2,250	12,750
No. of Cand.	*9*	*3*	*3*	*15*
House	1,750	1,250	1,250	4,250
Senate	7,500	0	1,000	8,500
Incumbents	18,500	21,635	11,750	51,885
Challengers	0	1,400	0	1,400
Open Seat	3,750	3,250	0	7,000
Winners	17,000	21,185	n/a	38,185
Losers	5,750	5,100	n/a	10,850

American Stock Exchange

*Phone: (212) 306-1000 * Fax: (212) 306-2139*
86 Trinity Pl., New York, NY 10006-1881
Web: www.amex.com

The American Stock Exchange provides programs for its listed companies designed to enhance visibility and provide access to the investment community. AMEX provides analysis and tools for its 800 companies to manage their institutional shareholder base. It organizes forums, hosts conferences and holds communications meetings.

In 1996, AMEX share volume was more than 5.6 billion and its market value was more than $135 billion.

American Stock Exchange Federal PAC (AMEX FED PAC) (C00180000) *Address: same as sponsor * Treasurer: J. Bruce Ferguson * Contact: Geraldine Brindisi, Chairwoman*

	1993-94	1995-96	1997	Totals
Receipts	$18,576	$28,682	$10,966	$58,224
Disburse	19,720	22,012	16,315	58,047
Cash	12,503	19,171	13,823	n/a
Contributions	15,225	19,000	16,000	50,225
Republicans	4,800	13,000	11,000	28,800
No. of Cand.	*7*	*15*	*13*	*35*
House	3,800	6,500	5,000	15,300
Senate	1,000	6,500	6,000	13,500
Democrats	10,425	6,000	5,000	21,425
No. of Cand.	*17*	*8*	*8*	*33*
House	6,850	3,000	5,000	14,850
Senate	3,575	3,000	0	6,575
Incumbents	15,225	15,000	16,000	46,225
Challengers	0	2,000	0	2,000
Open Seat	0	2,000	0	2,000
Winners	13,675	14,500	n/a	28,175
Losers	1,550	4,500	n/a	6,050

Association of Private Pension & Welfare Plans

*Phone: (202) 289-6700 * Fax: (202) 289-4582*
1212 New York Ave. N.W., Suite 1250, Washington, DC 20005
Web: www.appwp.org/appwp

The Association of Private Pension & Welfare Plans is a group of large corporations and smaller businesses that administer employee corporate benefit plans. It is the main lobbying organization representing private sector benefits interests.

The group's members include some of the largest companies in the nation, such as Georgia-Pacific Corp., Amoco Corp., Citibank, Sprint Corp., Prudential Investments, New York Life Insurance Co. and McDonald's Corp. APPWP works on Medicare proposals and other legislative plans that would affect employee benefits.

Association of Private Pension & Welfare Plans (C00153171)
*Address: same as sponsor * Treasurer: James A. Klein*

	1993-94	1995-96	1997	Totals
Receipts	$13,024	$9,911	$8,419	$31,354
Disburse	16,648	15,319	2,654	34,621
Cash	11,387	5,981	11,746	n/a
Contributions	15,270	15,127	2,567	32,964
Republicans	5,445	12,113	2,067	19,625
No. of Cand.	*8*	*14*	*4*	*26*
House	2,500	9,613	1,600	13,713
Senate	2,945	2,500	467	5,912
Democrats	9,825	3,014	500	13,339
No. of Cand.	*15*	*4*	*1*	*20*
House	7,325	2,514	0	9,839
Senate	2,500	500	500	3,500
Incumbents	15,270	14,127	2,567	31,964
Challengers	0	500	0	500
Open Seat	0	500	0	500
Winners	13,270	12,877	n/a	26,147
Losers	2,000	2,250	n/a	4,250

Bear, Stearns & Co.

*Phone: (212) 272-2000 * Fax: (212) 272-8239*
245 Park Ave., New York, NY 10167
Web: www.bearstearns.com

Bear, Stearns & Co., a worldwide investment banking and securities trading and brokerage firm, is the major subsidiary of The Bear, Stearns Companies Inc. The publicly traded company has $141 billion in assets and posted sales of $6 billion in 1997.

The company provides services including corporate finance, mergers and acquisitions, equity and fixed income sales and trading, private client services, derivatives, securities research, asset management, foreign exchange, futures sales and trading, clearing and securities lending and custody.

Headquartered in New York City, the company has about 8,900 employees located in domestic offices in Atlanta, Boston, Chicago, Dallas, Los Angeles, and San Francisco; and an international presence in Beijing; Buenos Aires, Argentina; Dublin, Ireland; Geneva; Hong Kong; London; Lugano, Switzerland; Paris; Sao Paulo, Brazil; Shanghai, China; Singapore; and Tokyo.

Bear, Stearns & Co. Political Campaign Committee (C00127357)
*Address: same as sponsor * Treasurer: Michael Abatemarco * Contact: Mary Lynn O'Neill, PAC Dir.*

	1993-94	1995-96	1997	Totals
Receipts	$347,348	$126,750	$114,250	$588,348
Disburse	302,327	162,055	61,750	526,132
Cash	199,063	163,758	216,258	n/a
Contributions	59,000	104,100	41,750	204,850
Republicans	8,500	53,100	20,700	82,300
No. of Cand.	*8*	*35*	*22*	*65*
House	4,500	31,500	14,700	50,700
Senate	4,000	21,600	6,000	31,600
Democrats	50,500	51,000	20,550	122,050
No. of Cand.	*35*	*37*	*20*	*92*
House	32,000	33,000	14,550	79,550
Senate	18,500	18,000	6,000	42,500
Incumbents	53,500	89,500	39,750	182,750
Challengers	3,500	2,500	2,000	8,000
Open Seat	2,000	12,100	0	14,100
Winners	40,000	87,100	n/a	127,100
Losers	19,000	17,000	n/a	36,000

The Bond Market Association

*Phone: (212) 440-9400 * Fax: (212) 440-5260*
40 Broad St., New York, NY 10004-2373
*Web: www.bondmarkets.com * E-mail: bondpac@bondmarkets.com*

The Public Securities Association changed its name to The Bond Market Association in September 1997. The Bond Market Association represents securities firms and banks that underwrite, trade and sell debt securities both domestically and internationally. Headquartered in New York, The Bond Market Association has about 264 member and associate member firms and 21 affiliates.

At least 20 percent of its member firms are substantially owned by foreign institutions. Consequently, one of the association's main objectives is endorsement of the goal of "open and free access to the public securities markets throughout the world," with participation of multinational financial institutions not restricted by questions of nationality.

Other areas of interest include municipal securities market issues, corporate bond market issues, government securities market issues and mortgage and asset-backed securities issues.

The association wants to standardize market practices and commonly used documents to promote efficiency and reduce costs.

The Bond Market Association Political Action Committee (C00158980) *Phone: (202) 434-8400 * Fax: (202) 434-8456 * 1445 New York Ave. N.W., Suite 800, Washington, DC 20005-2158 * E-mail: kkern@bondmarkets.com * Treasurer: Micah Green * Contact: Kathleen Kern, Dir. of Political Affairs*

	1993-94	1995-96	1997	Totals
Receipts	$130,211	$145,613	$126,367	$402,191
Disburse	136,086	145,313	126,376	407,775
Cash	332	636	727	n/a
Contributions	124,695	137,508	106,816	369,019
Republicans	38,652	92,475	63,918	195,045
No. of Cand.	*46*	*81*	*51*	*178*
House	25,152	65,475	39,441	130,068
Senate	13,500	27,000	24,477	64,977
Democrats	85,793	45,033	42,398	173,224
No. of Cand.	*78*	*42*	*37*	*157*
House	62,179	35,297	23,043	120,519
Senate	23,614	9,736	19,355	52,705
Incumbents	116,745	131,226	101,741	349,712
Challengers	3,250	32	1,043	4,325
Open Seat	4,700	6,250	4,032	14,982
Winners	93,426	119,226	n/a	212,652
Losers	31,269	18,282	n/a	49,551

Brinson Partners Inc.

*Phone: (312) 220-7100 * Fax: (312) 220-7199*
209 S. Lasalle St., Chicago, IL 60604-1295
E-mail: gallagherp@brinson.com

Brinson Partners is a private company and wholly owned subsidiary of SBC Brinson, which is responsible for global institutional asset management within one of the four divisions of Swiss Bank Corp. It manages assets of $108.5 billion with additional SBC Private Banking mutual fund assets totaling $67.4 billion.

Parent company SBC Brinson has more than 590 employees with headquarters in Chicago and offices in New York and 10 other worldwide locations.

Brinson Partners Inc. PAC (C00249375) *Address: same as sponsor * Treasurer: Barbara L. Alger * Contact: Samuel W. Anderson, V.P.*

	1993-94	1995-96	1997	Totals
Receipts	$14,500	$15,500	$0	$30,000
Disburse	12,489	17,205	1,250	30,944
Cash	4,461	3,606	2,356	n/a
Contributions	1,500	5,000	0	6,500
Republicans	1,000	2,000	0	3,000
No. of Cand.	*1*	*2*	*0*	*3*
House	1,000	0	0	1,000
Senate	0	2,000	0	2,000
Democrats	500	3,000	0	3,500
No. of Cand.	*1*	*2*	*0*	*3*
House	500	1,000	0	1,500
Senate	0	2,000	0	2,000
Incumbents	500	0	0	500
Challengers	1,000	1,000	0	2,000
Open Seat	0	4,000	0	4,000
Winners	0	1,000	n/a	1,000
Losers	1,500	4,000	n/a	5,500

CIBC Oppenheimer Corp.

*Phone: (212) 667-6105 * Fax: (212) 667-4472*
Oppenheimer Tower, World Financial Center, New York, NY 10281
Web: www.oppenheimer.com

CIBC Oppenheimer is a full-service, publicly owned securities brokerage, investment banking and asset management firm offering a broad range of financial services to corporations, institutions and a substantial number of private investors worldwide.

The company was formed when Oppenheimer & Co. Inc. was acquired by CIBC Wood Gundy Securities Corp. CIBC Wood Gundy is the corporate and investment banking arm of Canadian Imperial Bank of Commerce. The new company is part of CIBC's World Markets division.

CIBC Oppenheimer Corp. Political Committee (C00185298)
*Address: same as sponsor * Treasurer: Melvin S. Herman*

	1993-94	1995-96	1997	Totals
Receipts	$1,574	$1,832	$572	$3,978
Disburse	4,500	20,201	175	24,876
Cash	30,543	12,115	12,575	n/a
Contributions	4,000	12,500	0	16,500
Republicans	0	8,500	0	8,500
No. of Cand.	*0*	*4*	*0*	*4*
House	0	2,500	0	2,500
Senate	0	6,000	0	6,000
Democrats	3,000	4,000	0	7,000
No. of Cand.	*3*	*2*	*0*	*5*
House	1,000	0	0	1,000
Senate	2,000	4,000	0	6,000
Incumbents	3,000	7,000	0	10,000
Challengers	1,000	500	0	1,500
Open Seat	0	5,000	0	5,000
Winners	3,000	9,000	n/a	12,000
Losers	1,000	3,500	n/a	4,500

Chicago Board Options Exchange

*Phone: (312) 786-7182 * Fax: (312) 786-7407*
400 S. Lasalle St., Chicago, IL 60605
Web: www.cboe.com

The Chicago Board Options Exchange is the world's largest options exchange and the second largest securities exchange in the United States.

In fiscal 1997, the exchange, which employs about 900 people, garnered net revenues of nearly $10 billion, with a total exchange-wide volume of 187.2 million contracts. The CBOE, which began in 1973, now lists options on the stock of more than 1,120 companies and maintains a 92 percent share of the U.S. index option market.

Chicago Board Options Exchange Inc. PAC (C00100693) *Address: same as sponsor * Treasurer: Alan J. Dean * Contact: Amy Zisook, Gov. Affairs Dir.*

	1993-94	1995-96	1997	Totals
Receipts	$39,750	$51,085	$256,525	$347,360
Disburse	67,000	85,000	41,000	193,000
Cash	46,336	12,421	227,946	n/a
Contributions	34,500	67,500	34,000	136,000
Republicans	11,500	39,000	14,500	65,000
No. of Cand.	*10*	*17*	*7*	*34*
House	6,000	27,000	5,500	38,500
Senate	5,500	12,000	9,000	26,500
Democrats	23,000	28,500	19,500	71,000
No. of Cand.	*15*	*26*	*15*	*56*
House	17,500	25,500	4,500	47,500
Senate	5,500	3,000	15,000	23,500
Incumbents	34,500	60,500	34,000	129,000
Challengers	0	0	0	0
Open Seat	0	7,000	0	7,000
Winners	29,500	52,000	n/a	81,500
Losers	5,000	15,500	n/a	20,500

Chicago Board of Trade

*Phone: (312) 435-3602 * Fax: (312) 435-7150*
141 W. Jackson Blvd., Chicago, IL 60604
Web: www.cbot.com

The Chicago Board of Trade, established in 1848, is the world's oldest and largest futures and options exchange. Its members trade contracts based on U.S. Treasury Bond futures, agricultural commodities, insurance and the Dow Jones Industrial Average. A record 242.7 million contracts were traded in 1997. The CBOT is a self-governing, membership association that serves as an umbrella organization for the 3,600 member firms.

The CBOT tracks issues that affect the futures industry, financial markets and agriculture. The PAC is funded largely by executives, brokers and traders from around the Chicago area.

The CBOT ranked second among commodity investment PACs in contributions to congressional candidates during the 1995-96 election cycle. The organization supports mostly incumbents and Republicans. The top recipients were Sens. Pat Roberts, R-Kan., and Richard J. Durbin, D-Ill., and Minority Leader Richard A. Gephardt, D-Mo.

Auction Markets Political Action Committee of the Chicago Board of Trade (also known as AMPAC/CBT) (C00059832) *Phone: (202) 783-1190 * Fax: (202) 347-5835 * 1455 Pennsylvania Ave. N.W., Suite 1225, Washington, DC 20004 * Treasurer: Glen M. Johnson * Contact: Julie Bower, Senior Coordinator for Gov. Relations*

	1993-94	1995-96	1997	Totals
Receipts	$236,278	$423,659	$364,057	$1,023,994
Disburse	299,210	379,658	217,786	896,654
Cash	109,084	153,092	299,364	n/a
Contributions	246,964	308,893	153,804	709,661
Republicans	64,600	185,643	79,750	329,993
No. of Cand.	*59*	*100*	*61*	*220*
House	33,850	94,750	39,250	167,850
Senate	30,750	90,893	40,500	162,143
Democrats	179,364	123,250	73,054	375,668
No. of Cand.	*100*	*71*	*53*	*224*
House	112,624	76,250	32,500	221,374
Senate	66,740	47,000	40,554	154,294
Incumbents	219,464	241,643	150,804	611,911
Challengers	8,000	13,000	0	21,000
Open Seat	19,500	54,250	3,000	76,750
Winners	181,350	270,643	n/a	451,993
Losers	65,614	38,250	n/a	103,864

Chicago Mercantile Exchange

*Phone: (312) 930-3434 * Fax: (312) 930-3439*
30 S. Wacker Dr., Chicago, IL 60606
Web: www.cme.com

The Chicago Mercantile Exchange, known as the Merc, is a futures and options trading facility. The Merc is a nonprofit corporation owned by the 2,725 members who have bought seats on the Exchange. Members include the world's largest banks and investment houses. The Merc serves as a trading place for futures and options in agricultural commodities, foreign currencies, interest rates and stock indexes.

The Merc was the top commodity investment industry PAC in contributions to congressional candidates during the 1995-96 election cycle. The exchange favored Republican and incumbent candidates.

The top recipients were Sens. Phil Gramm, R-Texas, Richard J. Durbin, D-Ill., and Pat Roberts, R-Kan., along with Rep. David E. Bonior, D-Mich., former Rep. Michael Patrick Flanagan, R-Ill., and 1996 Senate candidate Rudy Boschwitz, a Minnesota Republican.

Commodity Futures Political Fund of the Chicago Mercantile Exchange (C00076299) *Phone: (202) 638-3838 * 1299 Pennsylvania Ave. N.W., Suite 1275, Washington, DC 20004 * Treasurer: M. Scott Gordon * Contact: Lyda Schilling*

	1993-94	1995-96	1997	Totals
Receipts	$306,995	$606,054	$234,182	$1,147,231
Disburse	611,371	560,082	218,107	1,389,560
Cash	772,416	818,399	832,479	n/a
Contributions	419,800	377,000	164,500	961,300
Republicans	138,350	218,500	85,500	442,350
No. of Cand.	*82*	*127*	*60*	*269*
House	59,850	129,500	39,000	228,350
Senate	78,500	89,000	46,500	214,000
Democrats	279,450	158,500	78,000	515,950
No. of Cand.	*139*	*86*	*52*	*277*
House	167,350	93,500	37,000	297,850
Senate	112,100	65,000	41,000	218,100
Incumbents	374,300	299,000	159,500	832,800
Challengers	6,500	20,000	2,000	28,500
Open Seat	41,500	58,000	3,000	102,500
Winners	340,450	322,500	n/a	662,950
Losers	79,350	54,500	n/a	133,850

Chicago Stock Exchange Inc.

*Phone: (312) 663-2222 * Fax: (312) 663-2231*
440 S. Lasalle St., Chicago, IL 60605-1070
Web: www.chicagostockex.com

The Chicago Stock Exchange is the second-largest stock exchange in the nation, and the fastest growing. The CHX trades more than 4,000 NYSE, AMEX, NASDAQ and CHX-exclusive issues. In 1997, 5.5 billion shares were traded on the market.

In 1998, the Chicago Stock Exchange announced that it is the first U.S. stock exchange to use an independent auditor to analyze trades. The CHX will use the Transaction Auditing Group to conduct audits on a quarterly basis.

Chicago Stock Exchange Inc. Political Action Committee (formerly known as Midwest Stock Exchange PAC) (C00176628) *Address: same as sponsor * Treasurer: J. Montville Henige * Contact: David Fox, Chairman*

	1993-94	1995-96	1997	Totals
Receipts	$13,000	$8,600	$0	$21,600
Disburse	8,000	11,950	3,500	23,450
Cash	7,000	3,650	150	n/a
Contributions	8,000	4,450	3,500	15,950
Republicans	1,000	5,250	0	6,250
No. of Cand.	*1*	*4*	*0*	*5*
House	0	3,250	0	3,250
Senate	1,000	2,000	0	3,000
Democrats	7,000	-800	3,500	9,700
No. of Cand.	*4*	*8*	*2*	*14*
House	5,500	-2000	0	3,500
Senate	1,500	1,200	3,500	6,200
Incumbents	8,000	250	3,500	11,750
Challengers	0	1,500	0	1,500
Open Seat	0	2,700	0	2,700
Winners	7,500	1,450	n/a	8,950
Losers	500	3,000	n/a	3,500

Credit Suisse First Boston

*Phone: (212) 325-2000 * Fax: (212) 325-8058*
11 Madison Ave., New York, NY 10010-3629
Web: www.csfb.com

Credit Suisse First Boston is a global corporate and investment banking firm, providing financial advisory, capital raising, sales and trading and financial products for users and suppliers of capital around the world. As of January 1997, Credit Suisse First Boston operated in 50 offices across 30 countries and six continents, and had more than 10,000 employees.

Credit Suisse First Boston is the principal business unit of a Swiss bank of the same name. The Swiss bank had $7.2 billion of equity capital as of January 1, 1997 and is 99 percent owned by the Zurich-based financial services organization Credit Suisse Group.

CS First Boston Government Action Fund (C00111559) *Address: same as sponsor * Treasurer: Mary Whalen*

	1993-94	1995-96	1997	Totals
Receipts	$275,296	$279,353	$178,559	$733,208
Disburse	222,864	309,202	89,500	621,566
Cash	71,386	41,545	130,604	n/a
Contributions	186,000	195,500	48,000	429,500
Republicans	65,500	132,500	22,000	220,000
No. of Cand.	*34*	*69*	*20*	*123*
House	36,500	83,500	20,000	140,000
Senate	29,000	49,000	2,000	80,000
Democrats	120,500	63,000	26,000	209,500
No. of Cand.	*58*	*31*	*18*	*107*
House	81,000	55,500	14,000	150,500
Senate	39,500	7,500	12,000	59,000
Incumbents	172,000	182,000	48,000	402,000
Challengers	1,000	4,000	0	5,000
Open Seat	13,000	9,500	0	22,500
Winners	136,500	175,500	n/a	312,000
Losers	49,500	20,000	n/a	69,500

Dillon, Read & Co.

535 Madison Ave., New York, NY 10022

The Dillon, Read & Co. PAC was terminated in December 1997.

Dillon, Read & Co. Political Action Committee (C00202788) *Address: same as sponsor * Treasurer: Richard R. Macek*

	1993-94	1995-96	1997	Totals
Receipts	$70,666	$0	$0	$70,666
Disburse	67,200	29,500	10,140	106,840
Cash	39,640	10,140	9,140	n/a
Contributions	4,600	13,000	0	17,600
Republicans	2,100	12,000	0	14,100
No. of Cand.	*3*	*3*	*0*	*6*
House	1,600	0	0	1,600
Senate	500	12,000	0	12,500
Democrats	2,500	1,000	0	3,500
No. of Cand.	*2*	*1*	*0*	*3*
House	0	1,000	0	1,000
Senate	2,500	0	0	2,500
Incumbents	4,000	13,000	0	17,000
Challengers	0	0	0	0
Open Seat	0	0	0	0
Winners	4,000	11,000	n/a	15,000
Losers	600	2,000	n/a	2,600

FMR Corp.

*Phone: (617) 563-6272 * Fax: (617) 476-0932*
82 Devonshire St., Boston, MA 02109
Web: www.fidelity.com

FMR is the privately held parent company of Fidelity Investments. FMR is a diversified financial services conglomerate with interests in mutual funds, life insurance and banking and retirement services. FMR also is involved in publishing, telecommunications, art, limousines, real estate and job placement.

Formed in 1946, Fidelity is the No. 1 mutual fund company in the world, managing more than $596 billion in 200 funds for 11 million customers. In 1996, the company reported sales of $5 billion and net income of $423 million.

Founder Edward Johnson II's family controls FMR.

FMR Corp. Federal Political Action Committee (C00215046)
*Address: same as sponsor * Treasurer: Kenneth J. McDonald * Contact: David C. Weinstein, Chairman*

	1993-94	1995-96	1997	Totals
Receipts	$32,869	$52,459	$15,103	$100,431
Disburse	24,100	25,450	31,930	81,480
Cash	31,812	58,827	42,001	n/a
Contributions	21,100	19,950	25,900	66,950
Republicans	4,500	12,200	13,250	29,950
No. of Cand.	*4*	*11*	*11*	*26*
House	2,500	6,450	2,500	11,450
Senate	2,000	5,750	10,750	18,500
Democrats	16,600	7,750	12,650	37,000
No. of Cand.	*13*	*5*	*10*	*28*
House	8,600	7,750	4,650	21,000
Senate	8,000	0	8,000	16,000
Incumbents	21,100	16,200	25,900	63,200
Challengers	0	750	0	750
Open Seat	0	3,000	0	3,000
Winners	19,100	13,500	n/a	32,600
Losers	2,000	6,450	n/a	8,450

Federated Investors Inc.

Phone: (800) 341-7400
Liberty Center, 27th Floor, Pittsburgh, PA 15222
Web: www.federatedinvestors.com

Financial Services Political Committee is supported by employees of Federated Investors, one of the 10 largest mutual fund managers in the nation. Through its subsidiaries, the private company manages more than $130 billion in assets.

The PAC supports candidates at all levels of government and is bipartisan in its giving.

Financial Services Political Committee (C00162735) *Address: same as sponsor * Treasurer: J. Christopher Donahue*

	1993-94	1995-96	1997	Totals
Receipts	$97,280	$121,313	$48,638	$267,231
Disburse	99,938	118,487	42,011	260,436
Cash	358	3,196	9,829	n/a
Contributions	31,750	19,650	11,500	62,900
Republicans	8,750	4,000	2,500	15,250
No. of Cand.	*11*	*3*	*3*	*17*
House	5,500	3,000	1,500	10,000
Senate	3,250	1,000	1,000	5,250
Democrats	22,500	15,650	9,000	47,150
No. of Cand.	*20*	*13*	*9*	*42*
House	13,500	12,650	9,000	35,150
Senate	9,000	3,000	0	12,000
Incumbents	23,750	18,650	11,500	53,900
Challengers	2,500	0	0	2,500
Open Seat	5,500	1,000	0	6,500
Winners	18,750	18,650	n/a	37,400
Losers	13,000	1,000	n/a	14,000

Futures Industry Association

*Phone: (202) 466-5460 * Fax: (202) 296-3184*
2001 Pennsylvania Ave. N.W., Suite 600, Washington, DC 20006
Web: www.fiafii.org

The Futures Industry Association is a U.S.-based international association that acts as a principal spokesman for the futures and options industry. The association represents all facets of the futures industry, including many international exchanges. FIA actively works to preserve the system of free and competitive markets by representing the interests of the industry in connection with legislative and regulatory issues.

Founded in 1955 as the Association of Commodity Exchange Firms, the FIA has more than 200 corporate members, reaching thousands of industry participants. Members include futures commissions merchants, banks, legal and accounting firms, brokers, trading advisers and commodity pool operators.

Futures Industry Political Action Committee (C00133389)
*Address: same as sponsor * Treasurer: John M. Damgard*

	1993-94	1995-96	1997	Totals
Receipts	$23,500	$31,750	$10,500	$65,750
Disburse	25,600	30,500	12,500	68,600
Cash	900	2,150	150	n/a
Contributions	24,600	28,000	11,500	64,100
Republicans	13,250	26,000	7,500	46,750
No. of Cand.	*13*	*20*	*9*	*42*
House	4,000	8,000	3,500	15,500
Senate	9,250	18,000	4,000	31,250
Democrats	11,350	2,000	4,000	17,350
No. of Cand.	*14*	*3*	*4*	*21*
House	7,350	500	0	7,850
Senate	4,000	1,500	4,000	9,500
Incumbents	21,100	21,000	11,500	53,600
Challengers	1,750	1,500	0	3,250
Open Seat	1,750	5,500	0	7,250
Winners	19,600	25,500	n/a	45,100
Losers	5,000	2,500	n/a	7,500

Goldman Sachs Group

Phone: (202) 637-3700
1101 Pennsylvania Ave. N.W., Suite 900, Washington, DC 20004
Web: www.goldman.com

The Goldman Sachs Group is an international investment banking and brokerage firm. The firm is among the oldest and largest U.S.-based investment banks.

Founded in 1869, the privately held firm has grown to nearly 9,000 employees in more than 30 offices worldwide. In 1997, it posted more than $17 billion in sales. The partnership, which is based in New York, focuses on research, investment and financing services, mergers and acquisitions, foreign exchange and commodities, real estate and operations technology. It provides these services to governments, corporations, institutions and individuals around the globe.

Treasury Secretary Robert E. Rubin is former co-chairman of the firm.

Goldman Sachs maintains offices in San Francisco, Houston, Chicago, Washington, Los Angeles, Boston, Atlanta, Miami, Dallas, Philadelphia, Tampa, Fla., and Memphis, Tenn.

Subsidiaries include: Archon Group, Grupo Archon (Mexico) and Goldman, Sachs & Co.

Goldman Sachs Partners PAC (C00265124) *Address: same as sponsor * Treasurer: Judah C. Sommer * Contact: Robin Neustein, Chairman*

	1993-94	1995-96	1997	Totals
Receipts	$405,515	$348,648	$209,678	$963,841
Disburse	394,562	359,206	208,971	962,739
Cash	13,528	2,964	3,669	n/a
Contributions	168,500	138,250	99,813	406,563
Republicans	34,750	87,250	47,813	169,813
No. of Cand.	*25*	*57*	*43*	*125*
House	17,250	47,250	34,313	98,813
Senate	17,500	40,000	13,500	71,000
Democrats	133,250	51,000	51,000	235,250
No. of Cand.	*80*	*41*	*38*	*159*
House	83,750	37,500	25,000	146,250
Senate	49,500	13,500	26,000	89,000
Incumbents	150,750	123,750	89,813	364,313
Challengers	4,750	3,500	0	8,250
Open Seat	11,000	11,000	7,000	29,000
Winners	124,750	126,250	n/a	251,000
Losers	43,750	12,000	n/a	55,750

The Investment Company Institute

*Phone: (202) 326-5800 * Fax: (202) 326-5806*
1401 H St. N.W., Suite 1200, Washington, DC 20005-2146
Web: www.ici.org

The Investment Company Institute is the national association of the investment company industry. Founded in 1940, its membership includes 6,725 mutual funds, 447 closed-end funds and 10 sponsors of unit investment trusts. Its mutual fund members represent more than 62 million individual shareholders and manage more than $4.4 trillion.

The Institute supports legislation that would remove mutual fund companies and securities subsidiaries from regulation by the Federal Reserve Board. ICI also supports a Securities and Exchange Commission proposal to allow companies to send a single copy of investment documents to investors at a single address, a process called "householding." The group supports granting banks the power to sponsor and underwrite mutual funds and permitting banks' affiliation with other financial services businesses.

The ICI was the leading stock investment contributor to 1996 congressional campaigns, ahead of Merrill Lynch. Former Rep. Dick Zimmer, R-N.J., who lost a race for the seat occupied by former Sen. Bill Bradley, D-N.J., was the leading recipient. Sen. Max Baucus, D-Mont., who sits on the Senate Finance and Joint Taxation committees, was the leading Democratic recipient.

Investment Management Political Action Committee of The Investment Company Institute (ImPAC) (C00105981) *Address: same as sponsor * Treasurer: C. Richard Pogue * Contact: Shannon M. Billings, Dir. of Political Affairs*

	1993-94	*1995-96*	*1997*	*Totals*
Receipts	$393,598	$585,023	$331,546	$1,310,167
Disburse	469,607	582,245	266,456	1,318,308
Cash	95,495	99,016	164,109	n/a
Contributions	359,668	444,014	203,847	1,007,529
Republicans	97,250	271,014	133,902	502,166
No. of Cand.	*46*	*103*	*102*	*251*
House	45,250	190,514	103,904	339,668
Senate	52,000	80,500	29,998	162,498
Democrats	261,918	173,000	69,945	504,863
No. of Cand.	*79*	*67*	*60*	*206*
House	192,918	113,500	45,949	352,367
Senate	69,000	59,500	23,996	152,496
Incumbents	344,668	385,514	200,347	930,529
Challengers	1,000	5,000	2,500	8,500
Open Seat	14,000	53,500	1,000	68,500
Winners	281,668	379,514	n/a	661,182
Losers	78,000	64,500	n/a	142,500

Lehman Brothers Holdings Inc.

*Phone: (212) 526-7000 * Fax: (212) 526-3738*
200 Vesey St., 27th Floor, World Financial Center, New York, NY 10285
Web: www.lehman.com

Global investment banking company Lehman Brothers Holdings serves institutional, corporate, government and wealthy individual clients through its subsidiaries.

Founded in 1850, Lehman Brothers employs more than 8,000 workers. In 1997, the publicly traded company posted $6.8 billion in revenues.

Action Fund of Lehman Brothers Holdings Inc. (C00127670) *Phone: (202) 452-4700 * 800 Connecticut Ave. N.W., Suite 1200, Washington, DC 20006 * Treasurer: Edward Grieb * Contact: Judith Winchester*

	1993-94	*1995-96*	*1997*	*Totals*
Receipts	$402,202	$333,416	$132,397	$868,015
Disburse	296,738	321,611	129,014	747,363
Cash	118,885	130,699	134,083	n/a
Contributions	109,075	153,625	68,650	331,350
Republicans	30,050	91,500	29,600	151,150
No. of Cand.	*28*	*57*	*25*	*110*
House	14,800	46,500	18,100	79,400
Senate	15,250	45,000	11,500	71,750
Democrats	79,025	62,125	39,050	180,200
No. of Cand.	*62*	*42*	*25*	*129*
House	43,525	36,125	11,550	91,200
Senate	35,500	26,000	27,500	89,000
Incumbents	98,950	131,125	54,150	284,225
Challengers	3,000	6,500	10,500	20,000
Open Seat	7,125	16,000	4,000	27,125
Winners	82,950	134,000	n/a	216,950
Losers	26,125	19,625	n/a	45,750

Massachusetts Financial Services Co.

*Phone: (617) 954-5410 * Fax: (617) 954-7845*
500 Boylston St., Boston, MA 02116
*Web: www.mfs.com * E-mail: jrussell@mfs.com*

Massachusetts Financial Services is the investment adviser for the Massachusetts Investors Trust, a mutual fund company and a subsidiary of Sun Life Assurance Co. of Canada. The company is an investment firm that aims to provide long-term growth of capital and income.

Established in 1924, the company had 296,992 shareholders in 1997 and $6 billion in assets.

Massachusetts Financial Services Co. Political Action Committee (MFS PAC) (C00229534) *Address: same as sponsor * Treasurer: James E. Russell*

	1993-94	*1995-96*	*1997*	*Totals*
Receipts	$46,144	$4,801	$1,329	$52,274
Disburse	13,230	20,216	14,340	47,786
Cash	48,211	32,799	19,788	n/a
Contributions	13,100	5,000	8,500	26,600
Republicans	0	4,000	6,000	10,000
No. of Cand.	*0*	*2*	*6*	*8*
House	0	2,000	1,000	3,000
Senate	0	2,000	5,000	7,000
Democrats	13,100	1,000	2,500	16,600
No. of Cand.	*9*	*1*	*5*	*15*
House	3,100	1,000	1,000	5,100
Senate	10,000	0	1,500	11,500
Incumbents	13,100	5,000	8,500	26,600
Challengers	0	0	0	0
Open Seat	0	0	0	0
Winners	11,100	5,000	n/a	16,100
Losers	2,000	0	n/a	2,000

Merrill Lynch & Co. Inc.

*Phone: (212) 449-1000 * Fax: (212) 236-4384*
World Financial Center, 250 Vesey St., New York, NY 10281-1332
Web: www.ml.com

Merrill Lynch is the nation's leading brokerage firm and a leader in domestic and foreign equities underwriting. The public company combines retail brokerage and cash management with investment banking. It also offers clearing services, retail banking and insurance. Its combined asset-management companies make it one of the largest mutual fund managers in the world. Merrill Lynch also deals in government bonds and derivatives and provides insurance services. The company has 54,200 employees and reported 1997 sales of $31.7 billion.

Merrill Lynch is one of the major financial services companies pushing for reform and modernization of securities laws. It favors expanding the activities that financial services companies, including banks, can offer. A House proposal would also allow subsidiaries of national banks to offer investment services.

The company ranked second among stock investment firms in contributions to 1996 congressional candidates. Republicans, including Speaker Newt Gingrich, R-Ga., who got $7,000, received about 75 percent of the money. Former Rep. Dick Zimmer, R-N.J., who lost a 1996 Senate race, was the top recipient. Reps. Charles Schumer, D-N.Y., and Charles Rangel, D-N.Y., and Sen. Max Baucus, D-Mont., were the top Democratic recipients.

Merrill Lynch & Co. Inc. Political Action Committee (C00040550) *Phone: (202) 661-7100 * Fax: (202) 661-7110 * 1455 Pennsylvania Ave. N.W., Suite 950, Washington, DC 20004-1087 * Treasurer: William R. Dereuter * Contact: Bruce E. Thompson Jr., Chairman*

	1993-94	*1995-96*	*1997*	*Totals*
Receipts	$386,833	$308,833	$128,359	$824,025
Disburse	418,410	412,962	99,450	930,822
Cash	162,049	57,931	86,844	n/a
Contributions	276,000	254,427	59,050	589,477
Republicans	144,350	189,677	35,000	369,027
No. of Cand.	*97*	*116*	*33*	*246*
House	68,350	125,677	23,000	217,027
Senate	76,000	64,000	12,000	152,000
Democrats	131,150	64,750	24,050	219,950
No. of Cand.	*77*	*48*	*17*	*142*
House	69,150	48,750	8,550	126,450
Senate	62,000	16,000	15,500	93,500
Incumbents	248,250	238,427	54,050	540,727
Challengers	7,250	1,500	2,000	10,750
Open Seat	21,500	14,000	3,000	38,500
Winners	240,950	206,927	n/a	447,877
Losers	35,050	47,500	n/a	82,550

Morgan Stanley Dean Witter & Co.

*Phone: (212) 761-4000 * Fax: (212) 761-0086*
1221 Ave. of the Americas, 34th Floor, New York, NY 10020
Web: www.ms.com

Morgan Stanley Dean Witter & Co. is the result of the 1997 merger between investment bank Morgan Stanley and retail brokerage and consumer financial services firm Dean Witter, Discover & Co. The company operates a global network of more than 46,000 employees in 435 offices worldwide and has more than $330 billion in assets under management. Both companies continue to maintain their respective PACs.

Morgan Stanley is a worldwide institutional investment banking, trading and asset management firm with headquarters in New York. The company was the top worldwide mergers and acquisitions adviser in 1996, according to Securities Data Co.

It reported 1996 revenues of $13 billion. Morgan Stanley has more than 11,000 employees. Employees and directors hold about 39 percent of the publicly traded firm's common stock.

Morgan Stanley gave more of its money to winning candidates — nearly 96 percent — than any other top 200 PAC. It also gave almost every dollar to incumbents, spending just $4,000 on challengers and open races. However, the company's contributions along party lines were more even; 40 percent went to Democrats.

Speaker Newt Gingrich, R-Ga., was the top recipient, while Sen. Max Baucus, D-Mont., and Minority Leader Richard A. Gephardt, D-Mo., were the leading Democrats.

Morgan Stanley & Co. Inc. Better Government Fund (C00067215) *Phone: (202) 326-3993 * Fax: (202) 326-3981 * 1300 Eye St. N.W., 12th Floor West, Washington, DC 20005 * Treasurer: James A. Runde * Contact: Kelly McNamara, Gov. Relations Dir.*

	1993-94	1995-96	1997	Totals
Receipts	$381,700	$701,737	$35,050	$1,118,487
Disburse	577,878	543,809	123,724	1,245,411
Cash	285,189	443,127	354,453	n/a
Contributions	330,740	384,000	35,500	750,240
Republicans	118,500	224,000	19,500	362,000
No. of Cand.	*59*	*138*	*22*	*219*
House	73,500	188,500	18,500	280,500
Senate	45,000	35,500	1,000	81,500
Democrats	210,240	160,000	15,000	385,240
No. of Cand.	*108*	*79*	*21*	*208*
House	161,000	117,000	16,500	294,500
Senate	49,240	43,000	-1500	90,740
Incumbents	325,240	380,000	34,500	739,740
Challengers	0	1,000	1,000	2,000
Open Seat	4,000	3,000	0	7,000
Winners	279,000	367,000	n/a	646,000
Losers	51,740	17,000	n/a	68,740

Morgan Stanley Dean Witter & Co. Political Action Committee (C00214445) *Phone: (212) 761-4000 * Fax: (212) 761-0086 * Two World Trade Center, 45th Floor, New York, NY 10048 * Web: www.deanwitterdiscover.com * Treasurer: Lee Horwitz*

The Morgan Stanley Dean Witter & Co. PAC was formerly known as the Dean Witter, Discover & Co. PAC.

Dean Witter provides financial services to individuals. The company's retail brokerage operation is the third largest in the United States, with more than 370 offices nationwide. It also is a leading credit card issuer, with more than 39 million customers.

	1993-94	1995-96	1997	Totals
Receipts	$170,468	$179,175	$81,251	$430,894
Disburse	170,869	183,599	82,500	436,968
Cash	23,511	19,097	17,854	n/a
Contributions	162,500	167,825	80,000	410,325
Republicans	67,400	119,725	46,500	233,625
No. of Cand.	*52*	*80*	*38*	*170*
House	38,400	85,225	27,000	150,625
Senate	29,000	34,500	19,500	83,000
Democrats	95,100	48,100	33,500	176,700
No. of Cand.	*68*	*38*	*30*	*136*
House	67,600	39,600	16,500	123,700
Senate	27,500	8,500	17,000	53,000
Incumbents	147,000	153,075	79,500	379,575
Challengers	6,250	1,500	-1000	6,750
Open Seat	9,250	13,250	1,500	24,000
Winners	130,250	141,200	n/a	271,450
Losers	32,250	26,625	n/a	58,875

National Venture Capital Association

*Phone: (703) 524-2549 * Fax: (703) 524-3940*
1655 N. Fort Myer Dr., Suite 850, Arlington, VA 22209
*Web: www.nvca.org * E-mail: mmyers@nvca.org*

The National Venture Capital Association is the public policy advocate for the venture capital and private equity industries. It represents 240 member firms which invest in innovative or rapidly expanding businesses. The NVCA supports American Entrepreneurs for Economic Growth, an organization of nearly 10,000 emerging growth company executives.

The NVCA focuses on public policy issues that affect the flow of private equity to developing and growing companies. Such issues include: reducing the capital gains tax, intellectual property protection and Internet taxation. The group supports reform of the Food and Drug Administration and seeks to limit the number of securities lawsuits in states such as California, where many of the NVCA's members are located.

The only venture capital PAC contributing more than $5,000 to 1996 congressional candidates, the NVCA supported Republicans and incumbents. The group contributed nearly 25 percent of its PAC money to open races. Sen. Alfonse M. D'Amato, R-N.Y., Rep. Vic Fazio, D-Calif., and Sen. Bob Smith, R-N.H., were the leading recipients. Twenty other candidates each received $5,000.

National Venture Capital Association Political Action Committee (NVCAPAC) (C00150367) *Address: same as sponsor * Treasurer: Daniel Kingsley * Contact: Mark G. Heesen, Legislative Dir.*

	1993-94	1995-96	1997	Totals
Receipts	$322,530	$541,063	$372,380	$1,235,973
Disburse	278,923	396,088	175,325	850,336
Cash	67,948	166,775	363,830	n/a
Contributions	219,500	224,000	100,000	543,500
Republicans	90,000	176,000	61,500	327,500
No. of Cand.	*21*	*53*	*32*	*106*
House	23,500	76,000	44,500	144,000
Senate	66,500	100,000	17,000	183,500
Democrats	129,500	48,000	38,500	216,000
No. of Cand.	*30*	*21*	*23*	*74*
House	89,000	35,000	26,000	150,000
Senate	40,500	13,000	12,500	66,000
Incumbents	186,500	152,000	96,000	434,500
Challengers	7,000	19,000	2,000	28,000
Open Seat	27,000	53,000	2,000	82,000
Winners	186,500	189,000	n/a	375,500
Losers	33,000	35,000	n/a	68,000

New York Mercantile Exchange

*Phone: (212) 299-2380 * Fax: (212) 301-4615*
One North End Ave., 15th Floor, World Financial Center, New York, NY 10282-1101
Web: www.nymex.com

The New York Mercantile Exchange is the world's largest physical commodity futures exchange and the nation's third largest futures exchange.

The Exchange is the premier trading forum for energy, precious metals, and, in North America, copper. It also handled the world's first electricity futures contracts, launched in March 1996. In early 1998, the company applied for three more electricity futures and options contracts and had plans to apply for new aluminum and coal contracts as well. The Exchange is also working with the International Petroleum Exchange to create an electronic trading system.

The exchange, which employs about 500 people, traded nearly 84 million contracts in 1997.

The New York Mercantile Exchange, which recently celebrated its 125th anniversary, became the world's largest commodity futures exchange following its 1994 merger with the Commodity Exchange Inc.

New York Mercantile Exchange Political Action Committee Inc. (C00230185) *Address: same as sponsor * Treasurer: Bernard Purta * Contact: Kenneth Piasio, Chairman*

	1993-94	1995-96	1997	Totals
Receipts	$86,576	$166,510	$78,877	$331,963
Disburse	72,200	142,943	41,500	256,643
Cash	20,879	44,445	81,822	n/a
Contributions	45,700	110,700	31,500	187,900
Republicans	13,700	65,700	11,500	90,900
No. of Cand.	*20*	*37*	*12*	*69*

(Data for New York Mercantile continued)

House	8,200	32,000	9,500	49,700
Senate	5,500	33,700	2,000	41,200
Democrats	32,000	45,000	20,000	97,000
No. of Cand.	28	29	11	68
House	25,500	39,500	8,000	73,000
Senate	6,500	5,500	12,000	24,000
Incumbents	42,500	96,500	21,500	160,500
Challengers	1,700	7,700	10,000	19,400
Open Seat	1,000	4,500	0	5,500
Winners	40,500	102,500	n/a	143,000
Losers	5,200	8,200	n/a	13,400

New York Stock Exchange

*Phone: (202) 293-5740 * Fax: (202) 331-4158*
1800 K St. N.W., Suite 1100, Washington, DC 20006
Web: www.nyse.com

The New York Stock Exchange is the world's largest equities market, with a total market capitalization of more than $12 trillion. It provides a visible forum for the trading of securities worldwide, as well as open pricing through its competitive agency-auction market. For 1997, total member firm revenues were $145 billion, a 20.6 percent increase over 1996 total revenue of $120.25 billion. The NYSE, sometimes called "The Big Board," is located in New York City.

In February 1998, there were 3,044 companies listed on the NYSE. Its roster of listed companies is continually expanding to include large, mid-sized and small enterprises in all business sectors, based both in the United States and throughout the world.

New York Stock Exchange Inc. Political Action Committee (NYSE PAC) (C00200188) *Address: same as sponsor * Treasurer: Gerald Clark * Contact: Sheila Bair, PAC Dir.*

	1993-94	1995-96	1997	Totals
Receipts	$46,700	$136,900	$101,000	$284,600
Disburse	45,752	137,500	100,500	283,752
Cash	10,674	10,074	10,574	n/a
Contributions	25,000	58,000	51,750	134,750
Republicans	14,200	34,000	29,750	77,950
No. of Cand.	13	26	20	59
House	7,000	22,500	13,750	43,250
Senate	7,200	11,500	16,000	34,700
Democrats	10,800	24,000	22,000	56,800
No. of Cand.	14	22	17	53
House	4,300	15,500	16,000	35,800
Senate	6,500	8,500	6,000	21,000
Incumbents	23,800	55,000	51,750	130,550
Challengers	0	0	0	0
Open Seat	1,200	3,000	0	4,200
Winners	21,500	52,000	n/a	73,500
Losers	3,500	6,000	n/a	9,500

PIMCO Advisors Holdings

Phone: (212) 504-1611
200 Liberty St., New York, NY 10281

PIMCO Advisors Holdings purchased investment management firm Oppenheimer Capital in November 1997. Prior to the sale, Oppenheimer was a private company and managed $60 billion in assets, primarily for corporate and public pension funds, endowments and foundations. The combined companies have assets of $200 billion.

As part of the sale, Oppenheimer Capital will be renamed PIMCO Advisors Holdings L.P. and will operate as a subsidiary of PIMCO.

Oppenheimer Capital Political Action Committee (C00258897) *Address: same as sponsor * Treasurer: Lawrence K. Becker*

	1993-94	1995-96	1997	Totals
Receipts	$24,200	$0	$27,700	$51,900
Disburse	9,200	10,650	2,050	21,900
Cash	17,110	6,460	32,110	n/a
Contributions	8,000	5,500	500	14,000
Republicans	0	3,500	500	4,000
No. of Cand.	0	4	1	5
House	0	1,500	500	2,000
Senate	0	2,000	0	2,000
Democrats	8,000	2,000	0	10,000
No. of Cand.	6	5	0	11
House	2,000	2,500	0	4,500
Senate	6,000	-500	0	5,500
Incumbents	7,000	3,500	500	11,000
Challengers	500	2,000	0	2,500
Open Seat	500	500	0	1,000
Winners	6,500	3,500	n/a	10,000
Losers	1,500	2,000	n/a	3,500

Paine Webber Group Inc.

*Phone: (212) 713-2000 * Fax: (212) 713-4889*
1285 Ave. of the Americas, New York, NY 10019
Web: www.painewebber.com

Paine Webber Group is a holding company which, together with its operating subsidiaries, forms one of the largest full-service securities and commodities firms in the industry. A portion of its revenues is generated from commissions or fees earned as a broker for individual and institutional clients in the purchase and sale of securities, mutual funds, insurance products and other financial instruments. It also earns commissions or fees for services provided in the areas of employee benefits, managed accounts and personal trusts.

Paine Webber reported profits of $6.6 billion in 1997 and employed more than 15,000 workers, including 6,000 investment executives, in more than 300 offices around the world.

Founded in 1879, Paine Webber serves the investment and capital needs of more than 2 million clients worldwide, including individuals, institutions, state and local governments and public agencies.

Paine Webber Fund for Better Government (C00012245) *Address: same as sponsor * Treasurer: Terry L. Atkinson*

	1993-94	1995-96	1997	Totals
Receipts	$186,788	$128,596	$58,046	$373,430
Disburse	208,637	165,517	27,094	401,248
Cash	66,764	29,856	60,813	n/a
Contributions	80,922	82,000	15,050	177,972
Republicans	31,523	49,500	8,550	89,573
No. of Cand.	13	32	11	56
House	2,750	20,500	6,550	29,800
Senate	28,773	29,000	2,000	59,773
Democrats	46,899	32,500	6,500	85,899
No. of Cand.	34	23	8	65
House	15,400	8,000	2,500	25,900
Senate	31,499	24,500	4,000	59,999
Incumbents	77,172	58,000	14,050	149,222
Challengers	3,000	7,000	500	10,500
Open Seat	5,750	17,000	500	23,250
Winners	67,872	61,500	n/a	129,372
Losers	13,050	20,500	n/a	33,550

Putnam Investments Inc.

*Phone: (617) 760-8296 * Fax: (617) 760-7167*
One Post Office Sq., Mailstop A11, Boston, MA 02109
Web: www.putnaminv.com

Putnam Investments, a subsidiary of Marsh & McLennan Companies Inc., is a global money manager of $181 billion in mutual funds and $53 billion in institutional accounts. Putnam offers customers institutional portfolios, retirement plans, mutual funds, variable annuities and variable life insurance services. The Boston-based company employs 4,862 people.

In 1997, Putnam Investments formed an alliance with Nippon Life Group for the management of Japanese pension fund assets. Nippon Life, a life insurance company based in Osaka, has about 17.5 million policyholders and $355 billion in assets.

Putnam Investments Inc. Public Affairs Committee (C00289595) *Address: same as sponsor * Treasurer: Timothy P. Moran*

	1993-94	1995-96	1997	Totals
Receipts	$31,300	$50,824	$83,053	$165,177
Disburse	11,089	48,518	20,500	80,107
Cash	20,210	22,515	85,068	n/a
Contributions	6,000	23,000	16,500	45,500
Republicans	500	5,000	10,500	16,000
No. of Cand.	1	3	9	13
House	500	0	3,500	4,000
Senate	0	5,000	7,000	12,000
Democrats	5,500	18,000	6,000	29,500
No. of Cand.	3	11	6	20
House	2,000	8,000	3,000	13,000
Senate	3,500	10,000	3,000	16,500
Incumbents	5,500	18,500	16,500	40,500

Challengers	500	500	0	1,000
Open Seat	0	4,000	0	4,000
Winners	4,000	20,500	n/a	24,500
Losers	2,000	2,500	n/a	4,500

Russell, Rea, Zappala & Gomulka Holdings Inc.

CNG Tower, Suite 3100, Pittsburgh, PA 15222

The Russell, Rea, Zappala & Gomulka Holdings PAC was terminated in November 1996.

Russell, Rea, Zappala & Gomulka Holdings Inc. Political Action Committee (also known as RRZG PAC) (C00197020) *Address: same as sponsor * Treasurer: Thomas M. Lechner*

	1993-94	1995-96	1997	Totals
Receipts	$19,500	$1,000	$0	$20,500
Disburse	20,210	9,441	0	29,651
Cash	8,457	13	0	n/a
Contributions	13,210	6,500	0	19,710
Republicans	1,210	0	0	1,210
No. of Cand.	*1*	*0*	*0*	*1*
House	0	0	0	0
Senate	1,210	0	0	1,210
Democrats	12,000	6,500	0	18,500
No. of Cand.	*7*	*3*	*0*	*10*
House	7,500	6,500	0	14,000
Senate	4,500	0	0	4,500
Incumbents	8,000	6,500	0	14,500
Challengers	1,210	0	0	1,210
Open Seat	4,000	0	0	4,000
Winners	7,210	6,500	n/a	13,710
Losers	6,000	0	n/a	6,000

Securities Industry Association

*Phone: (202) 296-9410 * Fax: (202) 296-9775*
1401 Eye St. N.W., Suite 1000, Washington, DC 20005-2225
*Web: www.sia.com * E-mail: hkaufman@sia.com*

The Securities Industry Association represents nearly 800 investment banks, broker-dealers and mutual fund companies.

In the United States, SIA members collectively account for about 90 percent, or $100 billion, of security firm revenues and employ about 350,000 people. The group supports policies that "contribute to the financial well-being of investors and the economic strength of the nation and its capital markets."

Issues of importance to the group include tax proposals, financial services modernization and uniform standards. SIA also works with the IRS on financial issues such as global trade regulations and tax procedures.

Securities Industry Political Action Committee (C00067504) *Address: same as sponsor * Treasurer: J. Steven Judge * Contact: Hope Kaufman, Chairwoman*

	1993-94	1995-96	1997	Totals
Receipts	$163,135	$144,401	$78,605	$386,141
Disburse	153,518	147,119	78,383	379,020
Cash	16,942	14,221	13,823	n/a
Contributions	145,988	134,245	78,708	358,941
Republicans	50,397	81,744	45,115	177,256
No. of Cand.	*51*	*80*	*52*	*183*
House	36,103	70,745	38,615	145,463
Senate	14,294	10,999	6,500	31,793
Democrats	94,591	52,501	33,593	180,685
No. of Cand.	*89*	*50*	*41*	*180*
House	73,144	40,516	22,593	136,253
Senate	21,447	11,985	11,000	44,432
Incumbents	141,388	129,584	77,091	348,063
Challengers	1,500	1,000	0	2,500
Open Seat	4,000	4,161	1,617	9,778
Winners	121,039	121,996	n/a	243,035
Losers	24,949	12,249	n/a	37,198

Spear, Leeds & Kellogg

Phone: (212) 433-7140
120 Broadway, New York, NY 10271
Web: www.slk.com

Spear, Leeds & Kellogg is among the largest clearing firms in the nation, clearing the trading of market professionals in all domestic stock, options and futures markets. Established in 1931, the company has more than 2,000 employees.

The Justice Department accused Spear and 23 other firms of fixing transaction costs for investors who buy and sell stocks on the Nasdaq market. In 1996, the firm settled the dispute out of court. As a result, each firm will install taping systems to monitor and record at least 3.5 percent, or a maximum of 70 hours per week, of all trader telephone conversations on its over-the-counter desk.

Spear, Leeds & Kellogg Good Government Fund Committee (C00074328) *Address: same as sponsor * Treasurer: John Cutillo*

	1993-94	1995-96	1997	Totals
Receipts	$101,996	$74,981	$35,665	$212,642
Disburse	96,193	76,917	41,909	215,019
Cash	58,796	56,860	50,616	n/a
Contributions	7,500	11,000	2,000	20,500
Republicans	2,000	8,000	0	10,000
No. of Cand.	*2*	*3*	*0*	*5*
House	1,000	2,000	0	3,000
Senate	1,000	6,000	0	7,000
Democrats	5,500	3,000	2,000	10,500
No. of Cand.	*5*	*2*	*2*	*9*
House	500	2,000	0	2,500
Senate	5,000	1,000	2,000	8,000
Incumbents	5,000	10,000	2,000	17,000
Challengers	2,500	1,000	0	3,500
Open Seat	0	0	0	0
Winners	5,000	10,000	n/a	15,000
Losers	2,500	1,000	n/a	3,500

Health

Health Professionals

American Academy of Audiology

8201 Greensboro Dr., Suite 300, McLean, VA 22102

The American Academy of Audiology PAC was terminated in July 1997.

American Academy of Audiology PAC (AAA-PAC) (C00300491)
*Address: same as sponsor * Treasurer: John Bruce Wardle*

	1993-94	1995-96	1997	Totals
Receipts	$0	$19,353	$0	$19,353
Disburse	0	15,018	4,332	19,350
Cash	0	4,332	0	n/a
Contributions	0	5,600	0	5,600
Republicans	0	3,100	0	3,100
No. of Cand.	*0*	*2*	*0*	*2*
House	0	3,100	0	3,100
Senate	0	0	0	0
Democrats	0	2,500	0	2,500
No. of Cand.	*0*	*4*	*0*	*4*
House	0	1,500	0	1,500
Senate	0	1,000	0	1,000
Incumbents	0	5,600	0	5,600
Challengers	0	0	0	0
Open Seat	0	0	0	0
Winners	0	5,600	n/a	5,600
Losers	0	0	n/a	0

American Academy of Ophthalmology

*Phone: (415) 561-8500 * Fax: (415) 561-8575*
655 Beach St., San Francisco, CA 94120-7424
Web: www.aao.org

The American Academy of Ophthalmology represents about 25,000 eye doctors nationwide. Ophthalmologists are medical doctors who provide optical and surgical care. More than 90 percent of practicing ophthalmologists are members of the organization.

The AAO's biggest issue is maintaining support for Medicare and eye programs. It also favors legislation that would provide patients with certain rights and protections within the managed care system. The group supports private contracting under the Medicare system.

The AAO ranked second among eye care PACs in contributions to congressional candidates during the 1995-96 election cycle. The group gave slightly more to Democratic candidates than to Republicans. The top recipients were Rep. Nick Lampson, D-Texas, and Sen. Richard J. Durbin, D-Ill. Six other candidates received $10,000 each, but most recipients got less than $5,000.

American Academy of Ophthalmology Inc. Political Committee (OPHTHPAC) (C00196246) *Phone: (202) 737-6662 * Fax: (202) 737-7061 * 1101 Vermont Ave. N.W., Suite 700, Washington, DC 20005-3570 * E-mail: smiller@aao.org * Treasurer: Paula E. Lent * Contact: Steve Miller, PAC Dir.*

	1993-94	1995-96	1997	Totals
Receipts	$1,485,968	$877,902	$407,592	$2,771,462
Disburse	1,404,724	942,958	231,710	2,579,392
Cash	254,693	189,632	365,468	n/a
Contributions	877,155	606,975	150,409	1,634,539
Republicans	352,890	276,600	62,409	691,899
No. of Cand.	*129*	*138*	*58*	*325*
House	228,390	204,600	46,909	479,899
Senate	124,500	72,000	15,500	212,000
Democrats	521,265	330,375	88,000	939,640
No. of Cand.	*169*	*128*	*69*	*366*
House	405,797	257,000	60,500	723,297
Senate	115,468	73,375	27,500	216,343
Incumbents	573,683	375,600	133,250	1,082,533
Challengers	71,437	62,875	1,659	135,971
Open Seat	231,535	164,500	16,500	412,535
Winners	624,033	519,975	n/a	1,144,008
Losers	253,122	87,000	n/a	340,122

American Academy of Otolaryngology

*Phone: (703) 836-4444 * Fax: (703) 683-5100*
One Prince St., Alexandria, VA 22314-3357
Web: www.entnet.org

The American Academy of Otolaryngology-Head and Neck Surgery is the world's largest society of physicians who treat disorders of the ear, nose and throat, and head and neck injuries. AAO-HNS coordinates research, provides continuing education, monitors legislation and establishes regulations. Related interests include plastic and reconstructive surgery and medical problems resulting from the use of tobacco.

Established in 1896, AAO-HNS has more than 10,000 member physicians. Its efforts to strengthen the specialty's biomedical research activities are facilitated through leadership and staff activities, and the AAO-HNSF Research Endowment Fund.

American Academy of Otolaryngology - Head and Neck Surgery Inc. (ENT PAC) (C00306449) *Address: same as sponsor * Treasurer: Michael D. Maves * Contact: Beverly Nessenbaum, Health Policy and Gov. Affairs Dir.*

	1993-94	1995-96	1997	Totals
Receipts	$0	$45,697	$52,096	$97,793
Disburse	0	14,815	22,605	37,420
Cash	0	30,864	60,354	n/a
Contributions	0	13,550	21,434	34,984
Republicans	0	7,050	10,684	17,734
No. of Cand.	*0*	*10*	*10*	*20*
House	0	5,550	10,684	16,234
Senate	0	1,500	0	1,500
Democrats	0	6,500	10,750	17,250
No. of Cand.	*0*	*9*	*17*	*26*
House	0	5,000	8,250	13,250
Senate	0	1,500	2,500	4,000
Incumbents	0	10,550	19,934	30,484
Challengers	0	500	500	1,000
Open Seat	0	2,500	0	2,500
Winners	0	13,050	n/a	13,050
Losers	0	500	n/a	500

American Academy of Physician Assistants

*Phone: (703) 836-2272 * Fax: (703) 684-1924*
950 N. Washington St., Alexandria, VA 22314-1552
*Web: www.aapa.org * E-mail: aapa@aapa.org*

The American Academy of Physician Assistants sponsors continuing medical education programs for recertification of physician assistants. It also offers malpractice insurance and monitors legislation and regulations.

Its interests include federal support for physician assistants, education programs, health issues related to underserved populations, Medicare coverage of physician assistants services and state law regulating practices. AAPA has more than 27,000 members.

American Academy of Physician Assistants Political Action Committee (C00122499) *Address: same as sponsor * Treasurer: Robert Alpheas Johnston Jr. * Contact: Justine Strand, Chair of the Board Trust*

	1993-94	1995-96	1997	Totals
Receipts	$29,273	$17,161	$796	$47,230
Disburse	27,675	15,293	7,868	50,836
Cash	29,282	31,149	24,076	n/a
Contributions	22,650	12,257	6,000	40,907
Republicans	4,500	6,757	4,500	15,757
No. of Cand.	*7*	*10*	*7*	*24*
House	2,000	5,757	2,500	10,257
Senate	2,500	1,000	2,000	5,500
Democrats	18,150	5,500	1,500	25,150
No. of Cand.	*27*	*6*	*2*	*35*
House	11,650	1,500	0	13,150
Senate	6,500	4,000	1,500	12,000
Incumbents	20,650	9,350	5,500	35,500
Challengers	500	300	500	1,300
Open Seat	1,500	2,607	0	4,107
Winners	18,150	9,850	n/a	28,000
Losers	4,500	2,407	n/a	6,907

American Association for Marriage and Family Therapy

*Phone: (202) 452-0109 * Fax: (202) 223-2329*
1133 15th St. N.W., Suite 300, Washington, DC 20005
*Web: www.aamft.org * E-mail: jambrose@aamft.org*

The American Association for Marriage and Family Therapy represents more than 23,000 marriage and family therapists in the United States, Canada and worldwide. The group develops standards for graduate and continuing education and ethical guidelines. It also produces a research journal, newsletters and videotapes for its members.

American Association for Marriage and Family Therapy (C00198259) *Address: same as sponsor * Treasurer: Dr. Anna Beth Benningfield * Contact: John Ambrose, Dir. of Gov. Affairs*

	1993-94	1995-96	1997	Totals
Receipts	$41,272	$1,453	$8,641	$51,366
Disburse	33,613	28,110	10,055	71,778
Cash	37,980	11,325	10,912	n/a
Contributions	14,600	10,500	1,000	26,100
Republicans	2,500	2,500	0	5,000
No. of Cand.	*5*	*3*	*0*	*8*

House	2,000	2,500	0	4,500
Senate	500	0	0	500
Democrats	12,100	8,000	1,000	21,100
No. of Cand.	*14*	*8*	*1*	*23*
House	5,600	6,000	1,000	12,600
Senate	6,500	2,000	0	8,500
Incumbents	14,100	7,000	1,000	22,100
Challengers	500	2,000	0	2,500
Open Seat	0	1,500	0	1,500
Winners	13,100	8,500	n/a	21,600
Losers	1,500	2,000	n/a	3,500

American Association for Respiratory Care

*Phone: (972) 243-2272 * Fax: (972) 484-2720*
11030 Ables Ln., Dallas, TX 75229
Web: www.aarc.org

The American Association for Respiratory Care is the only professional society for respiratory care practitioners in hospitals and with home care companies. Its members include managers of respiratory and cardiopulmonary services and educators who provide respiratory care training. Established in 1947, the association has more than 37,000 members.

AARC advocates Medicare coverage of respiratory care professional services as a Medicare benefit across all care sites. It supports bills that strengthen Food and Drug Administration authority to regulate tobacco products and the EPA's authority to support Clean Indoor Air Act regulations. It fights against reductions in Medicare HMO payments, which may prevent them from offering non-hospital-based RCPs to their Medicare participants.

In addition, AARC participates in congressionally mandated studies assessing home oxygen quality and access to services.

American Association for Respiratory Care Political Action Committee (AARCPAC) (C00150201) *Phone: (703) 548-8506 * 1225 King St., Second Floor, Alexandria, VA 22314 * Treasurer: Richard P. Larson*

*Contact: Sheryl West, Gov. Affairs Dir. * Phone: (972) 243-2272*

	1993-94	1995-96	1997	Totals
Receipts	$19,662	$20,134	$10,479	$50,275
Disburse	10,180	16,199	8,314	34,693
Cash	60,329	64,263	66,428	n/a
Contributions	7,300	11,500	6,750	25,550
Republicans	1,900	4,850	2,150	8,900
No. of Cand.	*4*	*9*	*5*	*18*
House	900	3,850	1,000	5,750
Senate	1,000	1,000	1,150	3,150
Democrats	5,400	6,350	4,600	16,350
No. of Cand.	*12*	*10*	*8*	*30*
House	3,800	3,950	2,100	9,850
Senate	1,600	2,400	2,500	6,500
Incumbents	6,200	9,300	5,850	21,350
Challengers	1,100	500	400	2,000
Open Seat	0	1,400	500	1,900
Winners	5,600	9,900	n/a	15,500
Losers	1,700	1,600	n/a	3,300

American Association of Clinical Urologists

*Phone: (847) 517-1050 * Fax: (847) 517-7229*
1111 N. Plaza Dr., Suite 550, Schaumburg, IL 60173

The American Association of Clinical Urologists' mission is to stimulate interest in the science and practice of urology. It promotes understanding of socioeconomic and political affairs affecting medical practice among members of the American Urological Association and the American Medical Association.

AACU represents about 3,800 members.

American Association of Clinical Urologists Political Action Committee (UROPAC) (C00273003) *Address: same as sponsor * Treasurer: Dr. Harry C. Miller Jr. * Contact: Dr. Anthony Middleton Jr., Chairman*

	1993-94	1995-96	1997	Totals
Receipts	$56,820	$85,780	$54,515	$197,115
Disburse	44,914	75,574	37,500	157,988
Cash	14,198	24,403	41,418	n/a
Contributions	42,400	74,000	36,500	152,900
Republicans	16,050	56,500	22,500	95,050
No. of Cand.	*19*	*41*	*17*	*77*
House	10,500	42,500	16,500	69,500
Senate	5,550	14,000	6,000	25,550

Democrats	26,350	17,500	14,000	57,850
No. of Cand.	*27*	*14*	*16*	*57*
House	20,350	16,500	10,000	46,850
Senate	6,000	1,000	4,000	11,000
Incumbents	37,350	56,500	35,500	129,350
Challengers	4,000	3,500	0	7,500
Open Seat	1,050	14,000	1,000	16,050
Winners	36,350	58,500	n/a	94,850
Losers	6,050	15,500	n/a	21,550

American Association of Nurse Anesthetists

*Phone: (847) 692-7050 * Fax: (847) 692-6968*
222 S. Prospect Ave., Park Ridge, IL 60068-4001
Web: www.aana.com

Founded in 1931, the American Association of Nurse Anesthetists is a professional association representing 27,000 certified members nationwide. Its members are the sole anesthesia providers in more than 70 percent of rural hospitals and administer more than half of the anesthetics delivered each year in the United States.

The group's top priority has been to eliminate the requirement that certified nurse anesthetists be supervised in order for hospitals to be reimbursed by Medicare. The Health Care Financing Administration in late 1997 proposed to abolish the federal standard and defer to state law.

The AANA ranked second among nursing groups in PAC contributions to 1996 congressional candidates. Nearly 85 percent of the group's total went to winning candidates. The top recipients were former Sen. Larry Pressler, R-S.D., Sen. Jeff Sessions, R-Ala., and Rep. Dan Schaefer, R-Colo. Rep. Charles Rangel, D-N.Y., was the leading Democratic recipient.

American Association of Nurse Anesthetists Separate Segregated Fund (CRNA-PAC) (C00173153) *Phone: (202) 484-8400 * Fax: (202) 484-8408 * 412 First St. S.E., Suite 12, Washington, DC 20003 * E-mail: dhebert@aanadc.com * Treasurer: William E. Yeo * Contact: David Hebert, Gov. Affairs Dir.*

	1993-94	1995-96	1997	Totals
Receipts	$189,255	$705,153	$497,645	$1,392,053
Disburse	117,114	785,958	365,694	1,268,766
Cash	209,410	128,607	260,558	n/a
Contributions	81,641	426,760	135,396	643,797
Republicans	17,500	269,425	85,572	372,497
No. of Cand.	*24*	*155*	*76*	*255*
House	10,500	182,175	60,776	253,451
Senate	7,000	87,250	24,796	119,046
Democrats	63,141	157,335	49,824	270,300
No. of Cand.	*48*	*103*	*49*	*200*
House	40,141	97,586	33,324	171,051
Senate	23,000	59,749	16,500	99,249
Incumbents	75,141	289,599	128,896	493,636
Challengers	2,000	29,662	3,500	35,162
Open Seat	4,500	107,499	3,000	114,999
Winners	57,210	362,599	n/a	419,809
Losers	24,431	64,161	n/a	88,592

American Association of Oral & Maxillofacial Surgeons

*Phone: (847) 678-6200 x5701 * Fax: (847) 678-6286*
9700 W. Bryn Mawr Ave., Rosemont, IL 60018
Web: www.aaoms.org

The American Association of Oral & Maxillofacial Surgeons is a professional association of dental specialists who treat conditions, defects, injuries, and aesthetic aspects of the mouth, teeth, jaws and face. Their training includes a four-year graduate degree in dentistry and the completion of a minimum four-year hospital surgical residency program.

Established in 1918, AAOMS is dedicated to promoting the highest quality of patient care and education, maintaining high professional standards of practice through continuing education, and fostering and supporting specialty research.

In 1993, AAOMS created the State Technical Assistance Program to more effectively service OMS societies in a legislative capacity. As a result, it has supported many states in developing legislative strategies, strengthening relationships with the American Dental Association and identifying legislative trends.

Oral & Maxillofacial Surgery Political Action Committee (OMSPAC) (C00005660) *Address: same as sponsor * Treasurer: Dr. Thomas Weil * Contact: Philip B. Peters, Chairman*

	1993-94	1995-96	1997	Totals
Receipts	$394,138	$375,294	$187,021	$956,453
Disburse	337,826	290,797	77,873	706,496
Cash	193,908	278,402	387,551	n/a
Contributions	176,950	107,700	-1,000	283,650
Republicans	70,750	75,200	2,500	148,450
No. of Cand.	*36*	*48*	*6*	*90*
House	28,250	57,200	0	85,450
Senate	42,500	18,000	2,500	63,000
Democrats	106,200	32,500	-3,500	135,200
No. of Cand.	*48*	*25*	*4*	*77*
House	74,000	22,500	-4,000	92,500
Senate	32,200	10,000	500	42,700
Incumbents	153,950	78,950	-1,500	231,400
Challengers	10,500	10,000	0	20,500
Open Seat	12,500	18,750	500	31,750
Winners	155,450	90,450	n/a	245,900
Losers	21,500	17,250	n/a	38,750

American Association of Orthodontists

*Phone: (314) 993-1700 * Fax: (314) 997-1745*
401 N. Lindbergh Blvd., St. Louis, MO 63141-7816
Web: www.aaortho.org

American Association of Orthodontists advances the art and science of orthodontics and dentofacial orthopedics, promotes quality orthodontic care and supports the successful practice of orthodontics. AAO's members must meet the educational requirements of the Council on Dental Education of the American Dental Association for a specialist.

Established in 1901, the organization includes 13,200 members worldwide, 7,800 of which are from the United States and Canada.

American Association of Orthodontists Political Action Committee (C00293910) *Address: same as sponsor * Treasurer: Ronald S. Moen * Contact: Dr. Peter Knudson, Chairman*

	1993-94	1995-96	1997	Totals
Receipts	$18,782	$173,887	$87,960	$280,629
Disburse	0	120,235	37,138	157,373
Cash	18,782	72,433	123,255	n/a
Contributions	0	107,000	21,500	128,500
Republicans	0	85,000	18,500	103,500
No. of Cand.	*0*	*29*	*11*	*40*
House	0	64,000	9,500	73,500
Senate	0	21,000	9,000	30,000
Democrats	0	22,000	3,000	25,000
No. of Cand.	*0*	*11*	*3*	*14*
House	0	16,000	1,000	17,000
Senate	0	6,000	2,000	8,000
Incumbents	0	94,000	21,500	115,500
Challengers	0	6,000	0	6,000
Open Seat	0	7,000	0	7,000
Winners	0	96,000	n/a	96,000
Losers	0	11,000	n/a	11,000

American Association of Physicians from India

*Phone: (630) 530-2277 * Fax: (630) 530-2475*
17 W. 22nd St., Suite 250, Oak Brook, IL 60181-4490

The American Association of Physicians from India represents about 9,000 doctors of Indian heritage in the United States. Headquartered in Chicago, it is the largest ethnic medical association in the nation. The AAPI estimates that about 26,000 U.S. physicians and about 10-12 percent of medical students in the United States are from India.

AAPI was created to address obstacles facing international medical graduate students. The AAPI's Legislative Office maintains a database of about 23,000 Indian physicians and lobbies on graduate medical education and other issues affecting doctors and health care.

American Association of Physicians from India Political Action Committee (C00199935) *Phone: (202) 452-2182 * 236 Massachusetts Ave. N.W., Suite 206A, Washington, DC 20002 * Treasurer: Krishna Prasad Vallabhaneni*

	1993-94	1995-96	1997	Totals
Receipts	$3,835	$50,806	$13,552	$68,193
Disburse	8,436	60,393	9,815	78,644
Cash	0	823	4,559	n/a
Contributions	2,000	14,725	1,500	18,225
Republicans	0	7,725	0	7,725
No. of Cand.	*0*	*4*	*0*	*4*
House	0	2,500	0	2,500
Senate	0	5,225	0	5,225
Democrats	2,000	7,000	1,500	10,500
No. of Cand.	*2*	*5*	*2*	*9*
House	2,000	2,500	1,500	6,000
Senate	0	4,500	0	4,500
Incumbents	1,000	14,725	1,500	17,225
Challengers	1,000	0	0	1,000
Open Seat	0	0	0	0
Winners	1,000	11,500	n/a	12,500
Losers	1,000	3,225	n/a	4,225

American Chiropractic Association

*Phone: (703) 276-8800 * Fax: (703) 243-2593*
1701 Clarendon Blvd., Arlington, VA 22209
*Web: www.jamesedwards.com/pac * E-mail: memberinfo@amerchiro.org*

The American Chiropractic Association is a national professional association for chiropractors with 12,000 members and 7,000 student members. A spokesperson said it was the largest chiropractic association in the United States.

The association produces two publications, ACA Today and JACA (Journal of American Chiropractic Association). The association was founded in 1963.

American Chiropractic Association Political Action Committee (C00102764) *Address: same as sponsor * Treasurer: Joe Martin, D.C. * Contact: Steve LaPierre, PAC Dir.*

	1993-94	1995-96	1997	Totals
Receipts	$1,123,057	$420,992	$185,919	$1,729,968
Disburse	1,269,718	476,843	171,733	1,918,294
Cash	89,557	33,714	47,900	n/a
Contributions	571,628	191,410	125,385	888,423
Republicans	124,300	97,750	63,091	285,141
No. of Cand.	*62*	*57*	*40*	*159*
House	79,800	70,250	48,091	198,141
Senate	44,500	27,500	15,000	87,000
Democrats	441,328	93,660	62,294	597,282
No. of Cand.	*163*	*72*	*48*	*283*
House	354,480	75,160	46,794	476,434
Senate	86,848	18,500	15,500	120,848
Incumbents	455,128	147,410	120,885	723,423
Challengers	23,500	8,000	2,000	33,500
Open Seat	93,000	33,500	2,000	128,500
Winners	383,598	146,410	n/a	530,008
Losers	188,030	45,000	n/a	233,030

Ohio State Chiropractic Association Inc. Federal Political Action Committee (C00225300) *Phone: (614) 442-2610 * Fax: (614) 442-2617 * 1115 Bethel Rd., Second Floor, Columbus, OH 43220 * Treasurer: Robert Sheely, D.C.*

	1993-94	1995-96	1997	Totals
Receipts	$23,490	$9,420	$2,662	$35,572
Disburse	23,079	12,256	1,238	36,573
Cash	4,798	1,960	3,384	n/a
Contributions	13,245	6,025	300	19,570
Republicans	10,625	4,225	300	15,150
No. of Cand.	*11*	*7*	*2*	*20*
House	5,525	4,225	300	10,050
Senate	5,100	0	0	5,100
Democrats	2,620	1,800	0	4,420
No. of Cand.	*5*	*3*	*0*	*8*
House	2,620	1,800	0	4,420
Senate	0	0	0	0
Incumbents	4,975	5,725	300	11,000
Challengers	3,200	300	0	3,500
Open Seat	5,070	0	0	5,070
Winners	8,125	4,925	n/a	13,050
Losers	5,120	1,100	n/a	6,220

Contributed less than $5,000 during 1995-96 cycle:

Connecticut Chiropractic Association Inc. Political Action Committee (C00246371) *Phone: (203) 257-0404 * Fax: (203) 257-0406 * 2257 Silas Deane Highway, Suite 5, Rocky Hill, CT 06067 * Treasurer: Linda A. Kowalski*

American College of Emergency Physicians

*Phone: (972) 550-0911 * Fax: (972) 580-2816*
1125 Executive Circle, Irving, TX 75038-2522
Web: www.acep.org

The American College of Emergency Physicians represents about 19,000 physicians who specialize in emergency medicine. ACEP offers continuing education, research and public education to its members. The American Board of Emergency Medicine is the independent certifying body for the specialty.

The organization supports legislation which would guarantee that consumers be covered for legitimate emergency room visits. It favors giving patients the right to appeal managed care decisions and greater access to their medical information. The group advocates alcohol testing by law enforcement officials for all drivers in accidents involving a fatality or serious injury, but objects to legislation that would require doctors to report results of alcohol tests to police.

ACEP ranked a distant second (behind the AMA) among doctors' organizations in contributions to 1996 congressional races. Nearly two-thirds of the group's contributions went to Democratic candidates. ACEP was one of 13 PACs that gave at least 90 percent of its contributions to winning candidates.

The top recipients were Sens. Jack Reed, D-R.I., and Tim Johnson, D-S.D.

Rep Greg Ganske, R-Iowa, a plastic surgeon, was the leading Republican recipient.

National Emergency Medicine PAC of The American College of Emergency Physicians (C00140061) *Phone: (202) 728-0610 * Fax: (202) 728-0617 * 1111 19th St. N.W., Suite 650, Washington, DC 20036-3603 * E-mail: fedgovtaffairs.ctte@acep.org * Treasurer: Colin C. Rorrie Jr. * Contact: Randy Dwyer, Manager*

	1993-94	1995-96	1997	Totals
Receipts	$395,999	$371,722	$178,156	$945,877
Disburse	537,812	389,451	86,859	1,014,122
Cash	64,800	47,065	138,362	n/a
Contributions	468,650	303,956	56,175	828,781
Republicans	157,750	101,998	25,925	285,673
No. of Cand.	*74*	*67*	*39*	*180*
House	121,750	89,248	26,675	237,673
Senate	36,000	12,750	-750	48,000
Democrats	309,900	201,458	29,750	541,108
No. of Cand.	*130*	*141*	*43*	*314*
House	250,900	156,458	23,750	431,108
Senate	59,000	45,000	6,000	110,000
Incumbents	372,650	245,206	57,175	675,031
Challengers	24,000	10,000	0	34,000
Open Seat	72,500	48,750	0	121,250
Winners	344,650	274,706	n/a	619,356
Losers	124,000	29,250	n/a	153,250

American Dental Association

*Phone: (312) 440-2500 * Fax: (312) 440-2800*
211 E. Chicago Ave., Chicago, IL 60611
Web: www.ada.org

The American Dental Association is the nation's largest and oldest dentist group. It has more than 141,000 members and affiliates in every state. The ADA's Council on Dental Education/Commission on Dental Accreditation is the nationally recognized accrediting agency for 1,242 dental educational and dental auxiliary educational programs in the United States.

The ADA supports legislation that would enable patients to choose their own doctors and create greater accountability for managed care providers. The group favors increased federal funding for dental education and research, especially in the area of child oral health care. The ADA is interested in ergonomics legislation and dental benefits under Medicaid.

The ADA spent more on congressional races in 1996 than all but one health-related PAC — the American Medical Association. Most of the organization's money went to Republicans. It was one of 18 PACs to contribute more than $1 million to incumbent candidates.

The top recipients were Sens. Larry E. Craig, R-Idaho, and John W. Warner, R-Va. Seventy-nine candidates received at least $5,000.

American Dental Political Action Committee (C00000729) *Phone: (202) 898-2424 * Fax: (202) 898-2437 * 1111 14th St. N.W., Washington, DC 20005 * E-mail: mclaughlinf@ada.org * Treasurer: Dr. Michael Donohoo * Contact: Frank McLaughlin, Dir. of Political Education*

	1993-94	1995-96	1997	Totals
Receipts	$1,423,530	$1,410,481	$749,458	$3,583,469
Disburse	1,397,328	1,488,290	466,706	3,352,324
Cash	105,640	36,911	312,845	n/a
Contributions	1,177,197	1,283,425	365,836	2,826,458
Republicans	569,584	841,800	191,633	1,603,017
No. of Cand.	*214*	*280*	*139*	*633*
House	414,929	645,550	154,133	1,214,612
Senate	154,655	196,250	37,500	388,405
Democrats	604,613	441,625	174,203	1,220,441
No. of Cand.	*241*	*184*	*133*	*558*
House	516,313	399,425	150,703	1,066,441
Senate	88,300	42,200	23,500	154,000
Incumbents	929,093	1,018,225	348,836	2,296,154
Challengers	68,654	59,750	500	128,904
Open Seat	183,550	203,950	16,500	404,000
Winners	979,969	1,075,075	n/a	2,055,044
Losers	197,228	208,350	n/a	405,578

Florida Dental Political Action Committee (C00013672) *Phone: (904) 681-3629 * Fax: (904) 561-0504 * 1111 E. Tennessee St., Suite 102, Tallahassee, FL 32308 * Web: www.floridadental.org * E-mail: fda@floridadental.org * Treasurer: Dr. James F. Walton III*

	1993-94	1995-96	1997	Totals
Receipts	$328,653	$344,755	$308,159	$981,567
Disburse	315,273	389,216	166,121	870,610
Cash	101,398	56,935	198,973	n/a
Contributions	3,000	6,500	0	9,500
Republicans	3,000	2,500	0	5,500
No. of Cand.	*1*	*1*	*0*	*2*
House	3,000	2,500	0	5,500
Senate	0	0	0	0
Democrats	0	4,000	0	4,000
No. of Cand.	*0*	*4*	*0*	*4*
House	0	4,000	0	4,000
Senate	0	0	0	0
Incumbents	0	2,500	0	2,500
Challengers	0	0	0	0
Open Seat	3,000	4,000	0	7,000
Winners	3,000	4,500	n/a	7,500
Losers	0	2,000	n/a	2,000

California Dental PAC - Federal (C00005751) *Phone: (916) 443-0505 * Fax: (916) 443-2943 * 1201 K St., Sacramento, CA 95814 * Web: www.cda.org * Treasurer: R. Kent Farnsworth*

	1993-94	1995-96	1997	Totals
Receipts	$96,002	$344,582	$84,054	$524,638
Disburse	234,060	357,491	80,037	671,588
Cash	13,752	846	4,863	n/a
Contributions	4,000	3,445	5,000	12,445
Republicans	0	500	0	500
No. of Cand.	*0*	*1*	*0*	*1*
House	0	500	0	500
Senate	0	0	0	0
Democrats	4,000	2,945	5,000	11,945
No. of Cand.	*4*	*1*	*1*	*6*
House	3,000	2,945	5,000	10,945
Senate	1,000	0	0	1,000
Incumbents	3,000	3,445	0	6,445
Challengers	1,000	0	0	1,000
Open Seat	0	0	5,000	5,000
Winners	3,000	2,945	n/a	5,945
Losers	1,000	500	n/a	1,500

Contributed less than $5,000 during 1995-96 cycle:

Empire Dental Political Action Committee (C00006296) *7 Fifth Ave., Fairport, NY 14450 * Treasurer: Dr. Warren M. Shaddock*

Indiana Dental PAC (C00082636) *Phone: (317) 634-2610 * Fax: (317) 634-2612 * 1200 N. Walnut St., Hartford City, IN 47348 * E-mail: idadmb@indy.net * Treasurer: Raymond M. Maddox*

Kentucky Dental Political Action Committee (C00008334) *Phone: (502) 459-5373 * Fax: (502) 458-5915 * 1940 Princeton Dr., Louisville, KY 40205 * Treasurer: Dr. Todd Stephenson*

New Jersey Dental Association Federal PAC (C00326918) *Phone: (732) 821-9400 * Fax: (732) 821-1082 * One Dental Plaza, P.O. Box 6020, North Brunswick, NJ 08902 * Web: www.njda.org * Treasurer: Dr. Frederic C. Sterritt*

Tennessee Dental Political Action Committee (C00044818) *Phone: (615) 383-8962 * Fax: (615) 383-0214 * P.O. Box 120188, 2104 Sunset Place, Nashville, TN 37212 * Web: members.aol.com/TennDental * E-mail: TennDental@aol.com * Treasurer: Dr. Stephen A. Brooks*

American Dietetic Association

*Phone: (202) 371-0500 * Fax: (202) 371-0840*
1225 Eye St. N.W., Suite 1250, Washington, DC 20005-3914
Web: www.eatright.org

With nearly 70,000 members, the American Dietetic Association is the largest organization of food and nutrition professionals in the world. The association is open to those who meet the academic and experience requirements. About 75 percent are registered dietitians and 4 percent are registered dietetic technicians. Members also include clinical and community dietetic professionals, food service managers, educators, researchers and students.

The group's members represent a wide range of practice areas and special interests, including public health, sports nutrition, medical nutrition therapy, diet counseling, cholesterol reduction, diabetes, vegetarianism and food service management.

To promote sound nutrition information for the public, the association sponsors publications, national events and media and marketing programs. The association establishes and enforces standards of quality for academic training and professional practice in clinical nutrition food service systems management and community dietetics. It lobbies for federal legislation that will contribute to the nutritional well-being of the public through its government affairs office.

The American Dietetic Association Political Action Committee (C00143560) *Address: same as sponsor * Treasurer: Jeff Taylor * Contact: Mary Hager, Chairperson*

	1993-94	1995-96	1997	Totals
Receipts	$55,118	$76,712	$183,760	$315,590
Disburse	69,800	53,960	118,074	241,834
Cash	30,601	53,354	119,041	n/a
Contributions	70,050	51,950	55,900	177,900
Republicans	13,200	29,000	37,300	79,500
No. of Cand.	*20*	*29*	*27*	*76*
House	8,700	24,000	25,050	57,750
Senate	4,500	5,000	12,250	21,750
Democrats	56,850	22,950	18,600	98,400
No. of Cand.	*65*	*34*	*24*	*123*
House	46,600	20,450	9,600	76,650
Senate	10,250	2,500	9,000	21,750
Incumbents	66,750	47,450	50,400	164,600
Challengers	0	1,250	5,000	6,250
Open Seat	2,800	3,250	0	6,050
Winners	59,250	48,950	n/a	108,200
Losers	10,800	3,000	n/a	13,800

American Medical Association

*Phone: (312) 464-5000 * Fax: (312) 464-4184*
515 N. State St., Chicago, IL 60610
Web: www.ama-assn.org

The American Medical Association is the nation's largest physicians organization. It has a membership of about 300,000, which includes doctors, residents and medical students. It publishes a leading medical journal and lobbies on many aspects of health care. State affiliates endorse congressional candidates and forward those choices to the national organization for PAC contributions.

The AMA has lobbied for greater patient privacy standards, and it supports safe zones for hospitals and clinics providing abortion procedures. It favors medical savings accounts to reduce the number of people who require Medicare coverage. The AMA also supports federal regulation of tobacco manufacturing, advertising and sales. The group's proposal for Medicare reform includes a fixed federal benefit plus the choice to go outside Medicare to receive medical treatment.

The AMA gave more than $2 million to federal candidates and committees during the last election cycle, the most of any doctors organization. The PAC gave money to more than 400 candidates, most of them Republicans. It ranked third in the total amount contributed to incumbent candidates. Eight state AMA affiliates each contributed more than $5,000 to congressional campaigns. The AMA's New Jersey state PAC ranked fourth among doctors' organizations.

The leading recipients were Reps. Kevin Brady, R-Texas, Allen Boyd, D-Fla., and Sen. Gordon H. Smith, R-Ore. Nearly 250 candidates received at least $5,000 from the AMA. Of the seven physicians in Congress, six received contributions in 1996, including Reps. Vic Snyder, D-Ark., and Dave Weldon, R-Fla., who each received at least $10,000. The seventh doctor, Sen. Bill Frist, R-Tenn., was not up for election in 1996.

American Medical Association Political Action Committee (C00000422) *Phone: (202) 789-7467 * Fax: (202) 789-7469 * 1101 Vermont Ave. N.W., Washington, DC 20005 * E-mail: kevin_walker@ama-assn.org * Treasurer: Kevin Walker*

	1993-94	*1995-96*	*1997*	*Totals*
Receipts	$4,465,815	$4,344,254	$2,256,215	$11,066,284
Disburse	3,924,057	4,133,528	739,229	8,796,814
Cash	829,101	1,039,826	2,556,813	n/a
Contributions	2,386,947	2,321,197	367,650	5,075,794
Republicans	1,361,395	1,879,154	252,650	3,493,199
No. of Cand.	*253*	*295*	*123*	*671*
House	1,146,009	1,647,219	197,400	2,990,628
Senate	215,386	231,935	55,250	502,571
Democrats	1,005,552	442,043	114,000	1,561,595
No. of Cand.	*236*	*125*	*53*	*414*
House	956,702	399,043	97,000	1,452,745
Senate	48,850	43,000	17,000	108,850
Incumbents	1,737,827	1,572,358	315,650	3,625,835
Challengers	229,670	207,400	8,000	445,070
Open Seat	414,950	541,439	42,000	998,389
Winners	1,951,097	1,864,626	n/a	3,815,723
Losers	435,850	456,571	n/a	892,421

New Jersey Medical PAC (C00039123) *Phone: (609) 896-1766 * Fax: (609) 896-1368 * Two Princess Rd., Lawrenceville, NJ 08648 * Web: www.msnj.org * E-mail: info@msnj.org * Treasurer: Dr. Walter J. Kahn * Contact: Barbara S. Mihalik, Executive Dir.*

The Medical Society of New Jersey is a professional trade association with about 9,500 physician members throughout the state. Established in 1766, it is the oldest state medical society in the nation.

	1993-94	*1995-96*	*1997*	*Totals*
Receipts	$103,500	$71,284	$8,045	$182,829
Disburse	124,984	83,421	14,107	222,512
Cash	28,448	16,312	10,250	n/a
Contributions	62,803	46,000	10,000	118,803
Republicans	49,303	27,000	7,500	83,803
No. of Cand.	*13*	*9*	*2*	*24*
House	39,303	26,000	7,500	72,803
Senate	10,000	1,000	0	11,000
Democrats	13,500	19,000	2,500	35,000
No. of Cand.	*5*	*5*	*1*	*11*
House	8,500	14,000	2,500	25,000
Senate	5,000	5,000	0	10,000
Incumbents	32,303	31,000	10,000	73,303
Challengers	17,500	5,000	0	22,500
Open Seat	12,500	10,000	0	22,500
Winners	43,553	41,500	n/a	85,053
Losers	19,250	4,500	n/a	23,750

Kentucky Educational Medical Political Action Committee (C00016444) *Phone: (502) 426-6200 * Fax: (502) 426-6877 * 4965 U.S. Highway 42, Suite 2000, Louisville, KY 40222-6301 * Treasurer: Michael W. Dee * Contact: William B. Monnig, Chairperson*

	1993-94	*1995-96*	*1997*	*Totals*
Receipts	$208,585	$223,777	$102,713	$535,075
Disburse	142,185	219,135	93,567	454,887
Cash	106,322	110,965	120,111	n/a
Contributions	0	16,000	0	16,000
Republicans	0	10,000	0	10,000
No. of Cand.	*0*	*1*	*0*	*1*
House	0	10,000	0	10,000
Senate	0	0	0	0
Democrats	0	6,000	0	6,000
No. of Cand.	*0*	*1*	*0*	*1*
House	0	6,000	0	6,000
Senate	0	0	0	0
Incumbents	0	6,000	0	6,000
Challengers	0	10,000	0	10,000
Open Seat	0	0	0	0
Winners	0	6,000	n/a	6,000
Losers	0	10,000	n/a	10,000

Texas Medical Association Political Action Committee (C00001214) *Phone: (512) 370-1300 * Fax: (512) 370-1632 * 401 W. 15th St., Austin, TX 78701-1680 * Web: www.texmed.org * Treasurer: David A. Marwitz*

	1993-94	*1995-96*	*1997*	*Totals*
Receipts	$1,578,299	$1,425,804	$733,101	$3,737,204
Disburse	1,567,542	1,360,707	568,890	3,497,139
Cash	111,487	176,585	340,797	n/a
Contributions	7,291	10,666	3,110	21,067
Republicans	3,267	8,166	1,110	12,543
No. of Cand.	*3*	*3*	*2*	*8*
House	17	8,166	110	8,293
Senate	3,250	0	1,000	4,250
Democrats	4,024	2,500	2,000	8,524
No. of Cand.	*5*	*1*	*1*	*7*
House	4,024	2,500	2,000	8,524
Senate	0	0	0	0
Incumbents	7,291	11,666	1,110	20,067
Challengers	0	0	0	0
Open Seat	0	-1,000	2,000	1,000
Winners	6,291	7,500	n/a	13,791
Losers	1,000	3,166	n/a	4,166

Missouri Medical Political Action Committee (C00001420) *Phone: (573) 636-5151 * Fax: (573) 636-8552 * P.O. Box 1402, Jefferson City, MO 65102 * Web: www.msma.org * Treasurer: C. C. Swarens*

	1993-94	*1995-96*	*1997*	*Totals*
Receipts	$177,105	$166,265	$140,165	$483,535
Disburse	190,021	156,135	71,860	418,016
Cash	17,251	27,400	95,705	n/a
Contributions	6,450	7,600	0	14,050
Republicans	4,000	4,450	0	8,450
No. of Cand.	*5*	*7*	*0*	*12*
House	3,000	3,600	0	6,600
Senate	1,000	850	0	1,850
Democrats	2,450	3,150	0	5,600
No. of Cand.	*5*	*4*	*0*	*9*
House	2,300	3,150	0	5,450
Senate	150	0	0	150
Incumbents	2,800	4,000	0	6,800
Challengers	1,000	3,500	0	4,500
Open Seat	2,150	1,100	0	3,250
Winners	4,800	6,100	n/a	10,900
Losers	1,650	1,500	n/a	3,150

Illinois State Medical Society Political Action Committee (IMPAC) (C00005488) *Phone: (312) 782-1654 * Fax: (312) 782-2023 * 20 N. Michigan Ave., Suite 700, Chicago, IL 60602 * Web: www.isms.org * Treasurer: Dr. Paul F. Mahon*

	1993-94	*1995-96*	*1997*	*Totals*
Receipts	$599,976	$524,334	$305,666	$1,429,976
Disburse	653,307	512,424	260,068	1,425,799
Cash	12,116	24,027	69,625	n/a
Contributions	7,000	7,000	0	14,000
Republicans	6,500	6,000	0	12,500
No. of Cand.	*2*	*2*	*0*	*4*
House	6,500	6,000	0	12,500
Senate	0	0	0	0
Democrats	500	1,000	0	1,500
No. of Cand.	*2*	*1*	*0*	*3*
House	500	1,000	0	1,500
Senate	0	0	0	0
Incumbents	2,000	7,000	0	9,000
Challengers	5,000	0	0	5,000
Open Seat	0	0	0	0
Winners	2,000	2,000	n/a	4,000
Losers	5,000	5,000	n/a	10,000

California Medical Political Action Committee (C00003194) *Phone: (415) 882-5100 * Fax: (415) 882-3349 * 221 Main St., Second Floor, San Francisco, CA 94105 * Treasurer: Ben Schwachman*

	1993-94	*1995-96*	*1997*	*Totals*
Receipts	$734,564	$680,673	$103,421	$1,518,658
Disburse	710,780	701,810	80,076	1,492,666
Cash	123,716	102,579	125,925	n/a
Contributions	5,600	6,750	0	12,350
Republicans	5,600	1,500	0	7,100
No. of Cand.	*3*	*2*	*0*	*5*
House	5,600	1,500	0	7,100
Senate	0	0	0	0
Democrats	0	5,250	0	5,250
No. of Cand.	*0*	*2*	*0*	*2*
House	0	5,250	0	5,250
Senate	0	0	0	0
Incumbents	5,100	5,250	0	10,350
Challengers	500	1,500	0	2,000
Open Seat	0	0	0	0
Winners	5,100	5,250	n/a	10,350
Losers	500	1,500	n/a	2,000

Oklahoma Medical Political Action Committee (C00030007) *Phone: (405) 843-9571 * Fax: (405) 842-1834 * P.O. Box 54520, Oklahoma City, OK 73154 * Web: www.osmaonline.org * Treasurer: Sherry Strebel * Contact: Judy Lake, PAC Dir.*

	1993-94	1995-96	1997	Totals
Receipts	$116,210	$143,727	$47,349	$307,286
Disburse	118,621	124,540	69,561	312,722
Cash	17,094	36,281	14,069	n/a
Contributions	13,700	6,250	0	19,950
Republicans	11,500	1,000	0	12,500
No. of Cand.	*6*	*2*	*0*	*8*
House	9,000	1,000	0	10,000
Senate	2,500	0	0	2,500
Democrats	2,200	5,250	0	7,450
No. of Cand.	*3*	*2*	*0*	*5*
House	2,000	250	0	2,250
Senate	200	5,000	0	5,200
Incumbents	6,500	1,250	0	7,750
Challengers	2,500	5,000	0	7,500
Open Seat	4,700	0	0	4,700
Winners	11,500	1,000	n/a	12,500
Losers	2,200	5,250	n/a	7,450

Arkansas Medical Society Political Action Committee (C00002907) *Phone: (501) 224-8967 * Fax: (501) 224-6489 * P.O. Box 55088, Little Rock, AR 72215-5088 * Treasurer: Barbara Moody*

	1993-94	1995-96	1997	Totals
Receipts	$32,496	$34,630	$20,867	$87,993
Disburse	36,881	43,594	24,239	104,714
Cash	19,985	11,023	7,653	n/a
Contributions	0	5,500	3,500	9,000
Republicans	0	1,000	2,500	3,500
No. of Cand.	*0*	*1*	*1*	*2*
House	0	1,000	2,500	3,500
Senate	0	0	0	0
Democrats	0	4,500	1,000	5,500
No. of Cand.	*0*	*2*	*1*	*3*
House	0	2,500	1,000	3,500
Senate	0	2,000	0	2,000
Incumbents	0	1,000	2,500	3,500
Challengers	0	0	0	0
Open Seat	0	4,500	0	4,500
Winners	0	1,000	n/a	1,000
Losers	0	4,500	n/a	4,500

Contributed less than $5,000 during 1995-96 cycle:

Alabama Medical PAC (C00004911) *Phone: (334) 263-6441 * Fax: (334) 269-5200 * P.O. Box 22, Montgomery, AL 36101 * Web: www.masalink.org * Treasurer: Richard Carlton Whitaker*

Alaska Medical Political Action Committee (C00001461) *Phone: (907) 562-2662 * Fax: (907) 561-2063 * 4107 Laurel St., Anchorage, AK 99508-5334 * Treasurer: Dr. Jerry Coles * Contact: Kevin M. Tomer, President*

Arizona Medical Association Inc. Political Action Committee (C00004499) *Phone: (602) 246-8901 * Fax: (602) 242-6283 * 810 W. Bethany Home Rd., Phoenix, AZ 85013 * Treasurer: Chic Older*

Connecticut Medical Political Action Committee (C00003020) *Phone: (203) 865-0587 * Fax: (203) 865-4997 * P.O. Box 266, Middlefield, CT 06455 * Treasurer: Dr. Roger Beck*

District of Columbia PAC of The Medical Society of The District of Columbia (C00003921) *Phone: (202) 466-1800 * Fax: (202) 452-1542 * 2215 M St. N.W., Washington, DC 20037 * Treasurer: Carlos A. Silva*

Florida Medical Political Action Committee (C00007484) *Phone: (850) 224-6496 * Fax: (850) 224-6627 * P.O. Box 10269, Tallahassee, FL 32302 * Treasurer: Steven R. West * Contact: Karl M. Altenburger, President*

Hawaii Medical Political Action Committee (C00001347) *Phone: (808) 536-7702 * Fax: (808) 528-2376 * 1360 S. Beretania St., Second Floor, Honolulu, HI 96814 * Treasurer: Susan Wong*

Idaho Medical Political Action Committee (C00009449) *Phone: (208) 344-7888 * Fax: (208) 344-7903 * 305 W. Jefferson, P.O. Box 2668, Boise, ID 83701 * Treasurer: Robert K. Seehusen*

Independent Medicine's Political Action Committee-TN (IMPACT) (C00001354) *2301 21st Ave. S., P.O. Box 120909, Nashville, TN 37212-0909 * Treasurer: Dr. Ralph E. Wesley*

Indiana Medical Political Action Committee (C00000638) *Phone: (317) 261-2060 * Fax: (317) 261-2076 * 322 Canal Walk, Canal Level, Indianapolis, IN 46202-3252 * Web: www.ismanet.org * Treasurer: Dr. Regino Urgena*

Kansas Medical Political Action Committee (C00000547) *Phone: (913) 235-2383 * Fax: (913) 235-5114 * 623 S.W. 10th Ave., Topeka, KS 66612-1627 * Treasurer: C. Richard Bonebrake*

Maryland Medical Political Action Committee (C00002501) *Phone: (410) 539-0872 * Fax: (410) 547-0915 * 1211 Cathedral St., Baltimore, MD 21201 * Treasurer: George Malouf*

Mississippi Medical Political Action Committee (C00004804) *Phone: (601) 354-5433 * Fax: (601) 352-4834 * P.O. Box 5229, Jackson, MS 39296-5229 * Treasurer: William F. Roberts*

Montana Medical Political Action Committee (C00003293) *2021 11th Ave., Suite 12, Helena, MT 59601 * Treasurer: Jean L. Crellin*

Nebraska Medical Political Action Committee (C00002147) *Phone: (402) 474-4472 * Fax: (402) 474-2198 * 233 S. 13th St., Suite 1512, Lincoln, NE 68508-2091 * Web: www.nebmed.org * Treasurer: Dr. James A. Fosnaugh*

Nevada Medical Political Action Committee (NEMPAC) (C00039248) *Phone: (702) 825-6788 * Fax: (702) 825-3202 * 3660 Baker Ln., Suite 101, Reno, NV 89509 * Treasurer: Joseph A. Reinkemeyer*

New Hampshire Medical Society Physicians' Political Action Committee (C00206417) *Phone: (603) 224-1909 * Fax: (603) 226-2432 * 7 N. State St., Concord, NH 03301-6389 * Web: www.mednexus.com/nhms * Treasurer: Dr. Henry A. Lewis*

New Mexico Medical Political Action Committee (also known as NEMPAC) (C00001776) *Phone: (505) 828-0237 * Fax: (505) 828-0336 * 7770 Jefferson N.E., Suite 400, Albuquerque, NM 87109 * Web: www.nmms.org/nmms * Treasurer: Dr. Steven Komadina*

North Carolina Medical Society Political Education and Action Committee (C00003152) *Phone: (919) 833-3836 * Fax: (919) 833-2023 * 222 N. Person St., P.O. Box 25834, Raleigh, NC 27611 * Treasurer: Michael R. Towarnicky*

North Dakota Committee On Medical Political Action (C00003061) *Phone: (701) 223-9475 * Fax: (701) 223-9476 * P.O. Box 1198, Bismarck, ND 58502-1198 * Treasurer: Brad R. Buell*

Ohio Medical Political Action Committee (OMPAC) (C00003327) *Phone: (614) 486-2401 * Fax: (614) 486-3130 * 1500 Lake Shore Dr., Columbus, OH 43204-3891 * Treasurer: Tim Maglione*

Oregon Medical Political Action Committee (C00035766) *Phone: (503) 226-1555 * Fax: (503) 241-7148 * 5210 S.W. Corbett Ave., Portland, OR 97201 * Treasurer: Dr. Martin D. Skinner*

Pennsylvania Medical Political Action Committee (C00004929) *Phone: (717) 558-7750 * Fax: (717) 558-7840 * P.O. Box 8820, Harrisburg, PA 17105-8820 * Web: www.pamedsoc.org * Treasurer: Jerry L. Rothenberger*

South Carolina Political Action Committee South Carolina Medical Association (C00003475) *Phone: (803) 798-6207 * P.O. Box 11188, 3210 Fernandina Rd., Columbia, SC 29211 * Treasurer: Benjamin E. Nicholson * Contact: William F. Mahon, CEO*

South Dakota State Medical Association Political Action Committee (C00005132) *Phone: (605) 336-1965 * Fax: (605) 336-0270 * 1323 S. Minnesota Ave., Sioux Falls, SD 57105 * Treasurer: Robert D. Johnson*

Utah Medical PAC (C00003210) *Phone: (801) 355-7477 * Fax: (801) 532-1550 * 540 E. 500 S., Salt Lake City, UT 84102-2784 * Web: www.utahmed.org * E-mail: uma@utahmed.org * Treasurer: Val J. Bateman*

Washington Medical Political Action Committee (C00001818) *Phone: (206) 441-9762 * Fax: (206) 441-5863 * 2033 Sixth Ave., UAL Bldg., Suite 1100, Seattle, WA 98121 * Web: www.wsma.org * Treasurer: Mark C. Adams*

Wyoming Political Action Committee (c/o Wyoming State Medical Society) (C00028415) *Phone: (307) 635-2424 * Fax: (307) 632-1973 * P.O. Drawer 4009, Cheyenne, WY 82003-4009 * Treasurer: Wendy P. Curran*

American Medical Group Association

*Phone: (703) 838-0033 * Fax: (703) 548-1890*
1422 Duke St., Alexandria, VA 22314
Web: www.amga.org

The American Medical Group Association, formerly known as the American Group Practice Association, is a national organization of more than 200 physician-led groups. Developed through the 1996 merger of AGPA and the Unified Medical Group Association, the association provides three main services: reimbursement practices, legislative advocacy and advancement of quality patient care.

Founded in 1949, AMGA is a national trade association of more than 25,000 physicians and administrators. AMGA promotes the group medical practice mode of ambulatory health care delivery. AMGA's customers include group practices, organized medicine, the public, government and its staff.

Founded in 1975, UMGA provided support for service providers in prepaid health care. UMGA membership included more than 90 medical groups.

Group Practice Political Action Committee (C00022178) *Address: same as sponsor * Treasurer: Donald Fisher * Contact: Dr. Arthur R. Traugott, Chairman*

	1993-94	*1995-96*	*1997*	*Totals*
Receipts	$33,708	$27,873	$8,385	$69,966
Disburse	36,709	27,375	9,230	73,314
Cash	1,033	1,529	684	n/a
Contributions	27,700	19,338	8,500	55,538
Republicans	8,500	8,634	7,000	24,134
No. of Cand.	*9*	*7*	*5*	*21*
House	3,000	7,134	4,000	14,134
Senate	5,500	1,500	3,000	10,000
Democrats	18,700	10,704	1,500	30,904
No. of Cand.	*20*	*8*	*2*	*30*
House	13,200	6,750	1,500	21,450
Senate	5,500	3,954	0	9,454
Incumbents	22,200	15,884	8,500	46,584
Challengers	2,500	3,204	0	5,704
Open Seat	3,000	250	0	3,250
Winners	16,950	16,134	n/a	33,084
Losers	10,750	3,204	n/a	13,954

American Nurses Association

*Phone: (202) 651-7096 * Fax: (202) 554-0189*
600 Maryland Ave. S.W., Suite 100 W., Washington, DC 20024-2571
*Web: www.nursingworld.org * E-mail: aberry@ana.org*

The American Nurses Association represents about 2.2 million registered nurses through its 53 state and territorial associations. More than 25 of the ANA's constituent associations serve as the collective bargaining agents for nurses.

Among the group's priorities are a restructured health care system that delivers primary health care in community-based settings and an expanded role for registered nurses and advanced practice nurses in the delivery of basic and primary health care. The organization opposes cuts in federal nursing training programs funded by the Nurse Education Act.

The ANA was the leading nursing PAC contributor to 1996 congressional elections. More than 88 percent of its contributions went to Democratic candidates. Its contributions dropped more than 25 percent from the 1993-94 election cycle, when it contributed more than $1 million to congressional candidates.

The top recipients during the 1995-96 cycle were Reps. Jim Turner, D-Texas, Maurice D. Hinchey, D-N.Y., and Debbie Stabenow, D-Mich., and Sens. Paul Wellstone, D-Minn., John D. Rockefeller IV, D-W.Va., and Tim Johnson, D-S.D. The leading Republican recipient was 1996 House candidate Kathleen A. Donovan of New Jersey.

American Nurses Association PAC (ANA-PAC) (formerly known as N-CAP) (C00017525) *Address: same as sponsor * Treasurer: Rebecca M. Patton * Contact: Anne Berry, Coordinator*

	1993-94	*1995-96*	*1997*	*Totals*
Receipts	$1,230,907	$1,004,132	$452,155	$2,687,194
Disburse	1,215,485	967,707	147,671	2,330,863
Cash	43,559	85,562	390,045	n/a
Contributions	1,084,508	788,508	87,470	1,960,486
Republicans	92,025	82,695	8,700	183,420
No. of Cand.	*32*	*33*	*10*	*75*
House	68,525	74,695	7,500	150,720
Senate	23,500	8,000	1,200	32,700
Democrats	973,483	700,259	78,770	1,752,512
No. of Cand.	*246*	*224*	*46*	*516*
House	874,977	592,065	63,420	1,530,462
Senate	98,506	108,194	15,350	222,050
Incumbents	851,925	405,684	57,300	1,314,909
Challengers	71,399	251,256	0	322,655
Open Seat	162,684	131,025	30,170	323,879
Winners	717,682	560,231	n/a	1,277,913
Losers	366,826	228,277	n/a	595,103

American Occupational Therapy Association

*Phone: (301) 652-2682 * Fax: (301) 652-7711*
4720 Montgomery Lane, Bethesda, MD 20814-3425
*Web: www.aota.org * E-mail: govtrel@aota.org*

The American Occupational Therapy Association represents about 60,000 registered occupational therapists, certified assistants and students. The organization also accredits colleges and universities and certifies therapists. Its members work in hospitals and private settings.

AOTA's legislative priorities include a patient's rights bill sponsored by Rep. Charlie Norwood, R-Ga., and Sen. Alfonse M. D'Amato, R-N.Y., which would guarantee patient access to medical information, the right to appeal decisions by a managed care network and greater provider responsibility. The group also comments on Health Care Financing Administration regulations and proposals involving Medicaid, Medicare and hospitals.

AOTA ranked second among non-physician health practitioner PACs in contributions to 1996 congressional candidates. More than 60 percent of its contributions went to Democratic candidates. Twelve of the top 13 recipients were Senate candidates.

The leading recipients were Sens. Max Cleland, D-Ga., Richard J. Durbin, D-Ill., Tim Johnson, D-S.D., and Ron Wyden, D-Ore. The top Republican recipient was Sen. Bill Frist, R-Tenn., a surgeon.

American Occupational Therapy Association Inc. Political Action Committee (C00089086) *Address: same as sponsor * Treasurer: Chris Bluhm * Contact: Frederick P. Somers, Associate Executive Dir.*

	1993-94	*1995-96*	*1997*	*Totals*
Receipts	$349,301	$774,087	$182,708	$1,306,096
Disburse	302,219	678,341	269,361	1,249,921
Cash	57,936	153,685	67,034	n/a
Contributions	247,150	352,834	78,825	678,809
Republicans	57,250	140,868	33,823	231,941
No. of Cand.	*45*	*83*	*35*	*163*
House	33,750	100,583	23,320	157,653
Senate	23,500	40,285	10,503	74,288
Democrats	186,900	211,966	45,002	443,868
No. of Cand.	*104*	*114*	*50*	*268*
House	114,898	119,964	28,002	262,864
Senate	72,002	92,002	17,000	181,004
Incumbents	202,648	255,333	74,825	532,806
Challengers	11,500	25,500	1,500	38,500
Open Seat	29,502	72,001	3,000	104,503
Winners	181,648	310,084	n/a	491,732
Losers	65,502	42,750	n/a	108,252

American Optometric Association

*Phone: (314) 991-4100 * Fax: (314) 991-4101*
243 N. Lindbergh Blvd., St. Louis, MO 63141
Web: www.aoanet.org

The American Optometric Association represents more than 32,000 eye doctors, optometry students and paraoptometric assistants and technicians throughout the United States and abroad. It has associations in all 50 states. The organization's goal is to improve the quality and availability of eye care in America.

The AOA supports a patient's rights bill that would spell out patient notification requirements for managed care companies and give patients the option to appeal decisions. It supports increased funding for health education and eye research. The group also advocates adding regular eye exams to the coverage provided by public health plans.

The AOA was the leading eye doctor PAC contributor to congressional candidates during the 1995-96 election cycle. It favored Democrats over Republicans and spent 25 percent of its contributions on open races. The leading recipients were Sen. Jack Reed, D-R.I., Rep. Gary L. Ackerman, D-N.Y., and 1996 Democratic Senate candidate

Ben Nelson of Nebraska. The top Republican recipients were Rep. John E. Peterson, R-Pa., and Sen. Pete V. Domenici, R-N.M.

American Optometric Association Political Action Committee (C00024968) *Phone: (703) 739-9200 * Fax: (703) 739-9497 * 1505 Prince St., Suite 300, Alexandria, VA 22314 * E-mail: pacaoa@aol.com * Treasurer: Robert Easton, O.D. * Contact: Noel Brazil, PAC Manager*

	1993-94	1995-96	1997	Totals
Receipts	$1,101,699	$930,146	$379,352	$2,411,197
Disburse	948,904	968,683	268,057	2,185,644
Cash	468,252	441,109	552,404	n/a
Contributions	659,130	644,323	156,500	1,459,953
Republicans	194,750	297,973	69,500	562,223
No. of Cand.	*106*	*147*	*58*	*311*
House	141,750	225,973	45,750	413,473
Senate	53,000	72,000	23,750	148,750
Democrats	457,380	346,350	87,000	890,730
No. of Cand.	*181*	*143*	*73*	*397*
House	342,880	277,250	64,000	684,130
Senate	114,500	69,100	23,000	206,600
Incumbents	508,580	441,073	147,500	1,097,153
Challengers	25,500	44,000	2,000	71,500
Open Seat	123,550	159,250	7,000	289,800
Winners	473,630	545,073	n/a	1,018,703
Losers	185,500	99,250	n/a	284,750

American Osteopathic Association

*Phone: (312) 280-5800 * Fax: (312) 280-3860*
142 E. Ontario St., Chicago, IL 60611
Web: www.am-osteo-assn.org

The American Osteopathic Association was established to "promote public health and encourage scientific research." AOA also sets the standards for and accredits osteopathic medical colleges and hospitals, as well as board certification programs.

Osteopathic physicians, known as D.O.s instead of the more traditional M.D.s, focus on the body's ability to heal itself and stress preventive medicine, eating properly and keeping fit.

The AOA's governmental interests include the Grassroots Osteopathic Action on Legislation (GOAL) Program, and it has lobbied to get a D.O. onto the "Baby Boom Commission," the bipartisan group appointed to look at future Social Security options. It also pushes for the consideration of D.O.s during debates on managed care and post-graduate educational funding.

The Osteopathic PAC's largest contribution during the 1995-96 election cycle was to Ways and Means Health Subcommittee Chairman Rep. Bill Thomas, R-Calif., totaling $6,000. Other top recipients included House Commerce Chairman Tom Bliley, R-Va., Health and Environment Subcommittee Chairman Michael Bilirakis, R-Fla., and House Speaker Newt Gingrich, R-Ga. Each received $5,000.

Osteopathic Political Action Committee (C00113803) *Phone: (202) 414-0140 * Fax: (202) 544-3525 * 1090 Vermont Ave. N.W., Suite 510, Washington, DC 20005 * Treasurer: Robert George * Contact: Dr. Marcelino Oliva, Chairman*

	1993-94	1995-96	1997	Totals
Receipts	$98,541	$60,332	$50,382	$209,255
Disburse	95,139	121,262	54,957	271,358
Cash	64,968	46,961	42,386	n/a
Contributions	54,896	86,950	10,500	152,346
Republicans	13,510	54,450	6,750	74,710
No. of Cand.	*17*	*30*	*6*	*53*
House	8,950	39,950	6,750	55,650
Senate	4,560	14,500	0	19,060
Democrats	41,386	32,500	3,750	77,636
No. of Cand.	*42*	*35*	*4*	*81*
House	36,386	26,500	3,250	66,136
Senate	5,000	6,000	500	11,500
Incumbents	48,396	83,950	8,500	140,846
Challengers	1,500	0	0	1,500
Open Seat	5,000	3,000	2,000	10,000
Winners	41,360	81,950	n/a	123,310
Losers	13,536	5,000	n/a	18,536

American Osteopathic Healthcare Association

*Phone: (301) 968-2642 * Fax: (301) 968-4195*
5550 Friendship Blvd., Suite 300, Chevy Chase, MD 20815
Web: www.aoha.org

The American Osteopathic Healthcare Association is dedicated to the interests of osteopathic hospitals and health care systems.

Since 1934, the association has promoted the health and welfare of the American public and the promotion of osteopathic health care. It also educates its members about developments in osteopathic medicine.

Political Action Committee of The American Osteopathic Healthcare Association (C00101493) *Address: same as sponsor * Treasurer: Robert Dixon*

	1993-94	1995-96	1997	Totals
Receipts	$22,628	$19,132	$5,405	$47,165
Disburse	31,503	12,568	7,700	51,771
Cash	38,215	44,779	42,484	n/a
Contributions	28,800	12,500	1,000	42,300
Republicans	13,000	7,000	500	20,500
No. of Cand.	*18*	*9*	*1*	*28*
House	6,000	7,000	500	13,500
Senate	7,000	0	0	7,000
Democrats	15,800	5,500	500	21,800
No. of Cand.	*21*	*7*	*1*	*29*
House	11,800	4,500	500	16,800
Senate	4,000	1,000	0	5,000
Incumbents	26,300	12,000	1,000	39,300
Challengers	500	0	0	500
Open Seat	1,500	500	0	2,000
Winners	24,800	12,000	n/a	36,800
Losers	4,000	500	n/a	4,500

American Pharmaceutical Association

*Phone: (202) 628-4410 * Fax: (202) 783-2351*
2215 Constitution Ave. N.W., Washington, DC 20037
Web: www.aphanet.org

The American Pharmaceutical Association handles issues concerning health care, confidentiality with medical records, Medicare and Medicaid. It is the professional society for all licensed pharmacists. The association promotes communication between pharmacists and physicians to ensure excellent patient care.

American Pharmaceutical Association Political Action Committee (C00193854) *Address: same as sponsor * Treasurer: Charles Dobis*

	1993-94	1995-96	1997	Totals
Receipts	$229,993	$202,197	$80,538	$512,728
Disburse	190,342	274,586	74,138	539,066
Cash	122,430	50,042	56,442	n/a
Contributions	130,600	172,550	28,100	331,250
Republicans	32,150	77,300	14,400	123,850
No. of Cand.	*29*	*51*	*26*	*106*
House	18,150	43,050	12,400	73,600
Senate	14,000	34,250	2,000	50,250
Democrats	95,950	95,250	13,700	204,900
No. of Cand.	*67*	*53*	*24*	*144*
House	65,950	49,000	10,200	125,150
Senate	30,000	46,250	3,500	79,750
Incumbents	97,750	128,550	27,600	253,900
Challengers	9,000	11,500	500	21,000
Open Seat	23,750	32,500	0	56,250
Winners	84,250	138,300	n/a	222,550
Losers	46,350	34,250	n/a	80,600

American Physical Therapy Association

*Phone: (703) 706-3163 * Fax: (703) 684-7343*
1111 N. Fairfax St., Alexandria, VA 22314
*Web: www.apta.org * E-mail: govtaffair@apta.org*

The American Physical Therapy Association is a national organization representing more than 75,000 physical therapists and PT assistants. Physical therapists treat patients with health problems resulting from injury or disease. More than 70 percent practice in non-hospital settings.

The group supports a patient bill of rights and legislation that would allow health care providers to discuss alternative treatment options, including physical therapy, with patients. It advocates holding managed care organizations accountable for consumer choice and quality of care.

APTA comments on a wide range of regulations issued by various agencies, especially the Health Care Financing Administration. The organization also supports the conclusions of a federal study that found abuses in Medicare reimbursements for physical therapy treatments in physicians' offices and recommends that general guidelines covering other PT treatment locations be applied to doctors' offices.

APTA was the leading non-physician health practitioner PAC in contributions to 1996 congressional candidates. It contributed slightly more to Democrats than to Republicans. The leading recipients were Reps. Scott Klug, R-Wis., Bill Thomas, R-Calif., and Greg Ganske, R-Iowa.

Physical Therapy Political Action Committee (PT-PAC) (C00012880) *Address: same as sponsor * Treasurer: Pamela Phillips * Contact: Nancy Garland, Gov. Affairs Dir.*

	1993-94	1995-96	1997	Totals
Receipts	$762,151	$1,030,468	$298,890	$2,091,509
Disburse	321,447	1,306,049	217,408	1,844,904
Cash	483,964	205,388	289,873	n/a
Contributions	252,097	593,737	107,957	953,791
Republicans	65,647	282,944	55,957	404,548
No. of Cand.	*53*	*130*	*52*	*235*
House	40,647	217,700	40,202	298,549
Senate	25,000	65,244	15,755	105,999
Democrats	182,450	310,793	52,000	545,243
No. of Cand.	*138*	*132*	*51*	*321*
House	140,150	243,709	32,500	416,359
Senate	42,300	67,084	19,500	128,884
Incumbents	212,097	458,212	103,957	774,266
Challengers	12,350	64,000	1,500	77,850
Open Seat	27,650	71,525	2,500	101,675
Winners	185,497	517,487	n/a	702,984
Losers	66,600	76,250	n/a	142,850

American Podiatric Medical Association

*Phone: (301) 571-9200 * Fax: (301) 530-2752*
9312 Old Georgetown Rd., Bethesda, MD 20814-1698
Web: www.apma.org

The American Podiatric Medical Association is the leading professional society for foot and ankle specialists in the United States. It has more than 9,000 active members and 50 locations throughout the nation. APMA represents about 80 percent of the podiatrists in the country. The group's Council on Podiatric Medical Education is the body designated by the Department of Education to accredit the nation's podiatric medical schools.

The group lobbies on health care reform issues and specifically on proposed changes to Medicaid and Medicare. Its top legislative priority is supporting a bill that would define patient protection standards for managed care companies. It has lobbied in the past on graduate medical education issues.

The APMA ranked second among specialist physician PACs in total congressional contributions during the 1995-96 cycle. Nearly 80 percent of its contributions went to incumbent candidates of both major parties. It gave more than 90 percent to winning candidates, placing it tenth among the top 200 PACs in percentage given to winners. Rep. Greg Ganske, R-Iowa, a plastic surgeon, and Sen. Jeff Sessions, R-Ala., were the top two recipients. Of the more than 250 candidates who received money from APMA, just seven received more than $5,000.

Podiatry Political Action Committee (C00008839) *Address: same as sponsor * Treasurer: Gerald D. Peterson, D.P.M. * Contact: John R. Carson, Gov. Affairs Dir.*

	1993-94	1995-96	1997	Totals
Receipts	$427,444	$514,172	$276,625	$1,218,241
Disburse	554,310	527,363	188,048	1,269,721
Cash	112,556	99,361	187,943	n/a
Contributions	445,770	450,691	164,000	1,060,461
Republicans	142,500	232,500	77,000	452,000
No. of Cand.	*81*	*130*	*57*	*268*
House	92,500	176,500	56,000	325,000
Senate	50,000	56,000	21,000	127,000
Democrats	300,770	217,191	85,000	602,961
No. of Cand.	*151*	*126*	*89*	*366*
House	245,650	175,691	65,000	486,341
Senate	55,120	41,500	20,000	116,620
Incumbents	368,770	356,691	149,500	874,961
Challengers	17,500	25,000	5,500	48,000
Open Seat	56,500	70,000	8,500	135,000
Winners	344,200	409,403	n/a	753,603
Losers	101,570	41,288	n/a	142,858

Alabama Podiatry Federal Political Action Committee (APFPAC) (C00304402) *Phone: (205) 933-9595 * Fax: (205) 933-5250 * 1717 11th Ave., Suite 402, Birmingham, AL 35205 * Treasurer: Robert I. Russell*

	1993-94	1995-96	1997	Totals
Receipts	$0	$5,000	$0	$5,000
Disburse	0	5,000	0	5,000
Cash	0	0	0	n/a
Contributions	0	5,000	0	5,000
Republicans	0	5,000	0	5,000
No. of Cand.	*0*	*1*	*0*	*1*
House	0	0	0	0
Senate	0	5,000	0	5,000
Democrats	0	0	0	0
No. of Cand.	*0*	*0*	*0*	*0*
House	0	0	0	0
Senate	0	0	0	0
Incumbents	0	0	0	0
Challengers	0	0	0	0
Open Seat	0	5,000	0	5,000
Winners	0	0	n/a	0
Losers	0	5,000	n/a	5,000

American Psychiatric Association

*Phone: (202) 682-6320 * Fax: (202) 682-6287*
1400 K St. N.W., Washington, DC 20005
Web: www.psych.org

The Corporation for the Advancement of Psychiatry works to bring the needs and concerns of the mentally ill to the attention of the political community.

Founded in 1981 by the American Psychiatric Association, the 1,000-member corporation works to reach its aims by politically educating its members. The organization provides its members with a newsletter that offers information on congressional legislation and activities that affect the psychiatric community. CAP also encourages its members to represent the corporation at meetings and events with congressional leaders.

Corporation for the Advancement of Psychiatry Political Action Committee (CAPPAC) (C00147736) *Address: same as sponsor * Treasurer: Dr. Gerald Flamm * Contact: Jay B. Cutler, Executive Dir.*

	1993-94	1995-96	1997	Totals
Receipts	$109,305	$137,339	$45,991	$292,635
Disburse	113,625	113,847	40,550	268,022
Cash	51,783	75,274	80,714	n/a
Contributions	95,295	108,944	39,050	243,289
Republicans	21,700	43,685	9,555	74,940
No. of Cand.	*27*	*45*	*11*	*83*
House	13,400	30,433	9,555	53,388
Senate	8,300	13,252	0	21,552
Democrats	72,595	65,259	29,495	167,349
No. of Cand.	*96*	*71*	*37*	*204*
House	59,975	51,607	23,495	135,077
Senate	12,620	13,652	6,000	32,272
Incumbents	69,495	91,632	38,550	199,677
Challengers	7,000	5,660	0	12,660
Open Seat	18,500	11,652	500	30,652
Winners	63,875	100,377	n/a	164,252
Losers	31,420	8,567	n/a	39,987

American Society for Clinical Lab Science

*Phone: (301) 657-2768 * Fax: (301) 657-2909*
7910 Woodmont Ave., Suite 530, Bethesda, MD 20814-3015
*Web: www.ascls.org * E-mail: ascls@ascls.org*

The American Society for Clinical Laboratory Science promotes the profession of clinical laboratory science and provides services to those who practice it. Its mission is to promote high standards of practice in the workplace, advocate professional autonomy, ensure professional competence, support educational efforts and encourage laboratory research.

In a published position paper in 1995, ASCLS urged Congress and state legislative bodies to take incremental actions to deal with inequitable access to health care and to reduce health care costs. ASCLS stated that it supports access to accurate and reliable laboratory testing, reimbursement at appropriate levels for quality services and the efficient and cost-effective delivery of laboratory services.

American Society for Clinical Laboratory Science Political Action Committee (formerly known as ASMT/PAC) (C00034645) *Address: same as sponsor * Treasurer: Wayne Ketchersid*

	1993-94	1995-96	1997	Totals
Receipts	$49,460	$38,029	$40,055	$127,544
Disburse	24,150	55,050	12,880	92,080
Cash	45,613	34,240	61,416	n/a
Contributions	7,050	17,500	1,500	26,050
Republicans	600	6,000	1,000	7,600
No. of Cand.	*2*	*6*	*1*	*9*
House	600	1,500	0	2,100
Senate	0	4,500	1,000	5,500
Democrats	6,450	11,500	500	18,450
No. of Cand.	*10*	*12*	*1*	*23*
House	5,450	7,000	500	12,950
Senate	1,000	4,500	0	5,500
Incumbents	6,550	9,500	500	16,550
Challengers	0	2,500	1,000	3,500
Open Seat	500	5,500	0	6,000
Winners	4,800	15,000	n/a	19,800
Losers	2,250	2,500	n/a	4,750

American Society of Anesthesiologists

*Phone: (847) 825-6586 * Fax: (847) 825-1692*
520 N. Northwest Highway, Park Ridge, IL 60068-2573
Web: www.asahq.org

The American Society of Anesthesiologists represents more than 34,000 physicians specializing in anesthesiology. It publishes a monthly medical journal and provides continuing education and training. Its members must be licensed doctors who have successfully completed an accredited training program in anesthesiology.

The ASA supports a patients' rights proposal that would provide greater access to medical information and the right to appeal managed care providers' decisions. That support, however, is contingent on allowing managed care companies to discriminate among physicians on the basis of training and experience, a position the American Medical Association supports.

It opposes a federal proposal that nurse anesthetists no longer be required to be supervised by a physician. The ASA favors permitting physicians and Medicare beneficiaries to contract for medical services outside the Medicare program.

The ASA was the leading contributor among physician specialists to congressional candidates during the 1995-96 election cycle. The group favored Republicans over Democrats. The top recipients were Reps. Greg Ganske, R-Iowa, Tom Coburn, R-Okla., and Vic Fazio, D-Calif., and Sen. Jesse Helms, R-N.C. Ganske is a plastic surgeon and Coburn is a physician.

American Society of Anethesiologists Inc. Political Action Committee (ASAPAC) (C00255752) *Phone: (202) 289-2222 * Fax: (202) 371-0384 * 1101 Vermont Ave. N.W., Washington, DC 20090 * E-mail: m.scott@asawash.org * Treasurer: Dr. Roger A. Moore * Contact: Michael Scott, Gov. Affairs Dir.*

	1993-94	1995-96	1997	Totals
Receipts	$702,793	$738,034	$521,972	$1,962,799
Disburse	626,636	779,655	357,014	1,763,305
Cash	282,335	240,712	405,669	n/a
Contributions	484,000	538,172	241,469	1,263,641
Republicans	209,000	346,312	122,750	678,062
No. of Cand.	*91*	*152*	*76*	*319*
House	133,000	241,204	100,250	474,454
Senate	76,000	105,108	22,500	203,608
Democrats	275,000	191,860	116,219	583,079
No. of Cand.	*103*	*78*	*62*	*243*
House	231,500	164,560	88,719	484,779
Senate	43,500	27,300	27,500	98,300
Incumbents	364,500	416,584	217,969	999,053
Challengers	40,000	31,588	7,500	79,088
Open Seat	79,500	91,000	16,000	186,500
Winners	380,500	463,134	n/a	843,634
Losers	103,500	75,038	n/a	178,538

American Society of Cataract & Refractive Surgery

*Phone: (703) 591-2220 * Fax: (703) 591-0614*
4000 Legato Rd., Suite 850, Fairfax, VA 22033
*Web: www.ascrs.org * E-mail: ascrs@ascrs.org*

The American Society of Cataract & Refractive Surgery aims to improve the skills of anterior segment eye surgeons and promote quality eye care.

Founded in 1974, the 7,000-member, nonprofit organization hosts a yearly symposium and publishes a monthly journal. In addition, the society provides members with a monthly Washington newsletter that discusses congressional legislation and regulatory issues that affect members of the eye-care industry.

American Society of Cataract & Refractive Surgery Political Action Committee (also known as EYEPAC) (C00171504) *Address: same as sponsor * Treasurer: Dr. Douglas D. Koch * Contact: Nancey McCann, Gov. Relations Dir.*

	1993-94	1995-96	1997	Totals
Receipts	$81,581	$55,835	$26,544	$163,960
Disburse	198,374	134,083	37,071	369,528
Cash	169,660	91,420	80,900	n/a
Contributions	80,094	67,430	22,040	169,564
Republicans	24,575	36,930	7,543	69,048
No. of Cand.	*22*	*17*	*6*	*45*
House	8,075	30,920	7,543	46,538
Senate	16,500	6,010	0	22,510
Democrats	55,519	30,500	14,497	100,516
No. of Cand.	*34*	*14*	*10*	*58*
House	36,019	17,000	11,997	65,016
Senate	19,500	13,500	2,500	35,500
Incumbents	45,969	53,130	21,540	120,639
Challengers	7,000	3,000	500	10,500
Open Seat	27,125	11,300	0	38,425
Winners	45,269	64,930	n/a	110,199
Losers	34,825	2,500	n/a	37,325

American Society of Consultant Pharmacists

*Phone: (703) 739-1300 * Fax: (703) 739-1321*
1321 Duke St., Fourth Floor, Alexandria, VA 22314-3563
Web: www.ascp.com

The American Society of Consultant Pharmacists promotes safe and effective medication therapy for the nation's long-term care residents. ASCP represents more than 6,500 pharmacists who provide medication distribution and consultant services to manage and improve drug therapy outcomes of individuals residing in long-term care environments.

Founded in 1969, ASCP members serve the full spectrum of long-term care settings, including nursing homes, subacute care and assisted living facilities, psychiatric hospitals, facilities for the mentally retarded, correctional institutions, hospices and home care.

ASCP is lobbying to retain federal laws governing the provision of consultant pharmacy services that protect and improve nursing home patient health.

American Society of Consultant Pharmacists Political Action Committee (ASCP PAC) (C00199547) *Address: same as sponsor * Treasurer: Bill Green * Contact: Dean Pedalino, Chairperson*

	1993-94	1995-96	1997	Totals
Receipts	$79,567	$43,584	$10,821	$133,972
Disburse	71,070	54,071	26,886	152,027
Cash	67,001	56,513	40,449	n/a
Contributions	30,000	37,900	24,050	91,950
Republicans	2,500	20,300	13,050	35,850
No. of Cand.	*3*	*14*	*16*	*33*
House	0	12,500	10,050	22,550
Senate	2,500	7,800	3,000	13,300
Democrats	27,500	17,600	11,000	56,100
No. of Cand.	*14*	*20*	*12*	*46*
House	19,500	13,100	5,000	37,600
Senate	8,000	4,500	6,000	18,500
Incumbents	29,000	33,800	24,050	86,850
Challengers	1,000	2,100	0	3,100
Open Seat	0	2,000	0	2,000
Winners	29,000	29,900	n/a	58,900
Losers	1,000	8,000	n/a	9,000

American Society of Internal Medicine

*Phone: (202) 835-2746 x280 * Fax: (202) 835-0442*
2011 Pennsylvania Ave. N.W., Suite 800, Washington, DC 20006-1808
*Web: www.asim.org * E-mail: anelson@asim.org*

The American Society of Internal Medicine is a national medical group representing internists and internist-subspecialists. Its members diagnose and treat injuries and illnesses among internal organs and serve as consultants to other physicians.

The ASIM has more than 20,000 members and chapters in all 50 states and Puerto Rico. The group sponsors a research and education foundation and announced a planned merger with the American College of Physicians.

American Society of Internal Medicine PAC (ASIMPAC) (C00280578) *Address: same as sponsor * Treasurer: Alan R. Nelson*

	1993-94	1995-96	1997	Totals
Receipts	$42,740	$70,015	$37,920	$150,675
Disburse	37,667	69,000	29,000	135,667
Cash	5,073	6,089	15,009	n/a
Contributions	36,500	68,100	27,000	131,600
Republicans	12,000	40,600	16,500	69,100
No. of Cand.	*15*	*34*	*15*	*64*
House	9,000	32,500	14,500	56,000
Senate	3,000	8,100	2,000	13,100
Democrats	24,500	27,500	10,500	62,500
No. of Cand.	*27*	*27*	*14*	*68*
House	17,500	22,000	9,500	49,000
Senate	7,000	5,500	1,000	13,500
Incumbents	32,500	50,000	24,500	107,000
Challengers	2,000	4,000	1,000	7,000
Open Seat	2,000	14,100	1,500	17,600
Winners	29,000	57,000	n/a	86,000
Losers	7,500	11,100	n/a	18,600

American Society of Plastic & Reconstructive Surgeons

*Phone: (847) 228-9900 * Fax: (847) 228-9131*
444 E. Algonquin Rd., Arlington Heights, IL 60005
Web: www.plasticsurgery.org

The American Society of Plastic & Reconstruction Surgeons, which has about 5,000 members, promotes high-quality patient care and professional and ethical standards through education, research and advocacy.

ASPRS wants coverage for reconstructive procedures to be part of new health care proposals and lobbies for patient choice and access to specialists.

In June 1997, ASPRS supported the Breast Reconstruction Surgery Benefits Act of 1997. The legislation would require insurance companies to cover breast reconstruction following a mastectomy.

Political Action Committee of The American Society of Plastic & Reconstructive Surgeons Inc. (ASPRS) PlastyPAC (C00249342) *Address: same as sponsor * Treasurer: Dr. William B. Riley Jr. * Contact: Michael Vincent, Chairperson*

	1993-94	1995-96	1997	Totals
Receipts	$24,339	$41,107	$28,925	$94,371
Disburse	50,250	51,000	23,148	124,398
Cash	126,586	116,696	122,474	n/a
Contributions	49,490	51,000	23,000	123,490
Republicans	33,750	39,500	15,000	88,250
No. of Cand.	*33*	*36*	*16*	*85*
House	21,500	29,500	11,000	62,000
Senate	12,250	10,000	4,000	26,250
Democrats	15,740	11,500	8,000	35,240
No. of Cand.	*23*	*16*	*13*	*52*
House	14,000	7,500	6,500	28,000
Senate	1,740	4,000	1,500	7,240
Incumbents	26,990	37,500	22,500	86,990
Challengers	18,000	2,500	0	20,500
Open Seat	4,500	10,500	500	15,500
Winners	43,250	46,000	n/a	89,250
Losers	6,240	5,000	n/a	11,240

American Speech-Language-Hearing Association

*Phone: (301) 897-5700 * Fax: (301) 571-0457*
10801 Rockville Pike, Rockville, MD 20852
Web: ns3-v1.btg.com

The American Speech-Language-Hearing Association is the professional, scientific and credentialing association for more than 91,000 audiologists, speech-language pathologists, and speech, language and hearing scientists. ASHA's purpose is to promote the interests of and provide services for professionals in audiology, speech-language pathology and speech and hearing science, and to advocate for people with communication disabilities.

Founded in 1986, the PAC of the American Speech-Language-Hearing Association contributes to congressional candidates who "recognize the importance of speech-language pathology and audiology services and who demonstrate concern for the rights of all citizens to receive these services."

American Speech-Language-Hearing Association Political Action Committee (C00210666) *Address: same as sponsor * Treasurer: Frederick T. Spahr * Contact: Susan Friedman, Dir. Cong. Constituent Relations*

	1993-94	1995-96	1997	Totals
Receipts	$119,872	$222,536	$173,461	$515,869
Disburse	75,648	239,038	121,871	436,557
Cash	57,194	40,693	91,877	n/a
Contributions	72,243	213,249	113,100	398,592
Republicans	10,250	55,349	20,300	85,899
No. of Cand.	*12*	*47*	*23*	*82*
House	4,000	34,849	15,800	54,649
Senate	6,250	20,500	4,500	31,250
Democrats	59,993	157,900	92,300	310,193
No. of Cand.	*59*	*110*	*98*	*267*
House	32,393	107,400	70,300	210,093
Senate	27,600	50,500	22,000	100,100
Incumbents	61,693	154,499	105,600	321,792
Challengers	0	22,900	1,000	23,900
Open Seat	10,550	34,850	6,500	51,900
Winners	49,743	187,149	n/a	236,892
Losers	22,500	26,100	n/a	48,600

Anesthesia Service Medical Group

Phone: (619) 493-0498
3626 Ruffin Rd., P.O. Box 82807, San Diego, CA 92138

Anesthesia Service Medical Group Good Government Fund is a PAC composed of 100 physicians who contribute to candidates involved in health legislation.

Founded in 1988 by Dr. Robert Hertzka and several other physicians to bring greater attention to anesthesia service issues, the PAC contributes only to individuals it has personally met.

Anesthesia Service Medical Group Inc. Good Government Fund (C00216184) *Address: same as sponsor * Treasurer: Dr. Robert E. Hertzka*

	1993-94	1995-96	1997	Totals
Receipts	$26,040	$25,381	$10,800	$62,221
Disburse	30,077	29,215	14,090	73,382
Cash	11,032	7,198	3,907	n/a
Contributions	12,000	15,250	9,685	36,935
Republicans	5,000	12,000	8,685	25,685
No. of Cand.	*3*	*5*	*4*	*12*
House	5,000	12,000	7,000	24,000
Senate	0	0	1,685	1,685
Democrats	7,000	3,250	1,000	11,250
No. of Cand.	*3*	*2*	*1*	*6*
House	7,000	3,250	1,000	11,250
Senate	0	0	0	0
Incumbents	9,000	15,250	8,000	32,250
Challengers	3,000	0	1,685	4,685
Open Seat	0	0	0	0
Winners	9,000	15,250	n/a	24,250
Losers	3,000	0	n/a	3,000

Association for the Advancement of Psychology

*Phone: (800) 869-6595 * Fax: (719) 520-7375*
P.O. Box 38129, Colorado Springs, CO 80937
E-mail: smpfeiffer@aol.com

The Association for the Advancement of Psychology advances and promotes sciences in the field of psychology. Established in 1974, the organization has 5,000 members.

AAP publishes a quarterly newsletter for its members called Advance.

Association for The Advancement of Psychology Inc. Psychologists for Legislative Action Now (PLAN) (C00002956) *Address: same as sponsor * Treasurer: Elizabeth Fulford * Contact: Stephen M. Pfeiffer, Executive Dir.*

	1993-94	1995-96	1997	Totals
Receipts	$230,407	$227,781	$109,296	$567,484
Disburse	246,694	218,442	67,268	532,404
Cash	39,916	49,256	86,752	n/a
Contributions	222,683	190,789	49,190	462,662
Republicans	29,000	83,569	19,605	132,174
No. of Cand.	*26*	*55*	*25*	*106*
House	19,000	57,484	12,605	89,089
Senate	10,000	26,085	7,000	43,085
Democrats	190,683	107,220	29,585	327,488
No. of Cand.	*100*	*90*	*28*	*218*
House	152,395	77,626	22,663	252,684
Senate	38,288	29,594	6,922	74,804
Incumbents	191,733	147,113	46,425	385,271
Challengers	10,750	20,110	0	30,860
Open Seat	20,200	23,566	2,765	46,531
Winners	159,848	163,774	n/a	323,622
Losers	62,835	27,015	n/a	89,850

Association of American Physicians and Surgeons

*Phone: (520) 325-2689 x3450 * Fax: (520) 325-4230*
1601 N. Tucson Blvd., Suite 9, Tucson, AZ 85716
Web: www.aapsonline.org

The Association of American Physicians and Surgeons is a national association of physicians dedicated to preserving freedom in the one-on-one, patient-physician relationship. AAPS members endeavor to protect the patient-physician relationship from all forms of third-party intervention.

Founded in 1943, AAPS has defended the right of patients in various court cases, including protecting physicians against threats of Health and Human Services sanctions for unassigned laboratory test billing, establishing the right of physicians to be heard in federal court in a challenge to a fee freeze, and challenging the Health Care Financing Administration's attempt to abrogate the freedom of patients and physicians to contract privately if no Medicare benefits are claimed.

On Dec. 18, 1997, AAPS won its case against Hillary Rodham Clinton in (AAPA v. Clinton). A federal judge ruled that the White House, the Justice Department and the "highest levels of government," allowed the President's Task Force on Health Care Reform to operate illegally, relying on private advisers and meeting in secret. A misconduct sanction of more than $285,000 was fined against the government to be paid to AAPS.

Association of American Physicians and Surgeons Political Action Committee (AAPS-PAC) (C00041590) *Address: same as sponsor * Treasurer: Dr. R. Lowell Campbell * Contact: Dr. Jane Orient, Executive Dir.*

	1993-94	1995-96	1997	Totals
Receipts	$17,694	$42,876	$0	$60,570
Disburse	31,357	41,440	0	72,797
Cash	881	2,316	2,316	n/a
Contributions	25,500	36,250	0	61,750
Republicans	25,500	36,250	0	61,750
No. of Cand.	*13*	*19*	*0*	*32*
House	23,500	32,250	0	55,750
Senate	2,000	4,000	0	6,000
Democrats	0	0	0	0
No. of Cand.	*0*	*0*	*0*	*0*
House	0	0	0	0
Senate	0	0	0	0
Incumbents	4,000	17,000	0	21,000
Challengers	19,500	14,000	0	33,500
Open Seat	2,000	5,250	0	7,250
Winners	20,000	19,250	n/a	39,250
Losers	5,500	17,000	n/a	22,500

College of American Pathologists

*Phone: (847) 446-8800 * Fax: (847) 446-3563*
325 Waukegan Rd., Northfield, IL 60093-2750
Web: www.cap.org

The College of American Pathologists is the world's largest organization of pathologists. Headquartered in Illinois, it has more than 15,000 members who specialize in laboratory medicine and provide analysis and advice to patients and other doctors. The CAP provides educational programs and support for its members.

The group supports legislation requiring health plans that restrict access to outside physicians to permit doctors to seek out-of-network treatments for all covered benefits. It advocates patient privacy standards for health care providers and all pathology departments. The CAP supports medical liability reform that includes a $250,000 limit on non-economic damages and a sliding scale contingency fee for attorneys.

The CAP ranked third among physician specialist PACs in total contributions to 1996 congressional races. It favored Republican candidates and spent more than 20 percent of its contributions on open races. The top recipients were Rep. Greg Ganske, R-Iowa, and Rep. Tom Coburn, R-Okla., both physicians. The leading Democratic recipient was Sen. Richard Durbin, D-Ill.

College of American Pathologists Political Action Committee (C00274944) *Phone: (202) 371-6617 x109 * Fax: (202) 371-0028 * 1350 Eye St. N.W., Suite 590, Washington, DC 20005-3305 * E-mail: jchambe@cap.org * Treasurer: Gordon Johnson * Contact: Jayne Hart Chambers, V.P.*

	1993-94	1995-96	1997	Totals
Receipts	$195,207	$238,942	$147,034	$581,183
Disburse	248,284	225,496	25,883	499,663
Cash	5,371	18,804	139,949	n/a
Contributions	247,000	224,500	24,000	495,500
Republicans	144,000	168,000	15,500	327,500
No. of Cand.	*66*	*81*	*12*	*159*
House	95,000	121,000	9,500	225,500
Senate	49,000	47,000	6,000	102,000
Democrats	103,000	56,500	8,500	168,000
No. of Cand.	*49*	*36*	*13*	*98*
House	70,000	48,500	4,500	123,000
Senate	33,000	8,000	4,000	45,000
Incumbents	179,500	165,000	24,000	368,500
Challengers	19,500	9,500	0	29,000
Open Seat	48,000	50,000	0	98,000
Winners	229,000	193,500	n/a	422,500
Losers	18,000	31,000	n/a	49,000

Committee for Quality Orthopaedic Health Care

*Phone: (202) 546-4732 * Fax: (202) 546-5051*
317 Massachusetts Ave. N.E., #100, Washington, DC 20002

The Committee for Quality Orthopaedic Health Care is "dedicated to protecting the interests of orthopaedic surgeons by developing ongoing relationships with federal elected officials." Some of the organization's legislative concerns include assuring freedom of choice and access to specialists within health care plans, Food and Drug Administration reforms for faster approval of medical technologies, and increased funding for the National Institute of Arthritis and Musculoskeletal and Skin Diseases.

The nonpartisan PAC was founded in 1986 as a freestanding, independent committee by members of the American Academy of Orthopaedic Surgeons Board of Councillors. To further its goal of increasing interaction with elected officials, the PAC arranges for its members to deliver contribution checks in person, preferably in a mutual home state or district.

Committee for Quality Orthopaedic Health Care Inc. (C00210542) *Address: same as sponsor * Treasurer: Charles M. Younger * Contact: Nicholas G. Cavarocchi, Assistant Treasurer*

	1993-94	1995-96	1997	Totals
Receipts	$318,062	$217,378	$193,991	$729,431
Disburse	332,570	221,947	104,183	658,700
Cash	43,503	38,933	129,248	n/a
Contributions	175,653	102,578	52,182	330,413
Republicans	113,364	71,950	28,763	214,077
No. of Cand.	*70*	*55*	*25*	*150*
House	58,945	47,686	24,263	130,894
Senate	54,419	24,264	4,500	83,183
Democrats	62,289	30,628	23,419	116,336
No. of Cand.	*61*	*31*	*18*	*110*
House	55,789	26,128	20,235	102,152
Senate	6,500	4,500	3,184	14,184
Incumbents	120,734	76,188	42,063	238,985
Challengers	28,919	5,500	6,435	40,854
Open Seat	26,000	22,140	3,684	51,824
Winners	137,986	80,188	n/a	218,174
Losers	37,667	22,390	n/a	60,057

Cooperative of American Physicians

*Phone: (213) 473-8600 * Fax: (213) 473-8773*
333 S. Hope St., Eighth Floor, Los Angeles, CA 90078
Web: www.cap-mpt.org

The Cooperative of American Physicians and the Mutual Protection Trust were founded in the 1970s to protect liability coverage for physicians and surgeons in California. The association has more than 4,500 active member physicians.

The Mutual Protection Trust provides professional liability protection services for qualified member physicians, groups and affiliated entities. CAP was formed in 1975, and it paved the way for the formation of MPT. MPT was founded in 1977 with 469 members who contributed the $10 million in trust contributions required. CAP/MPT now has more than $119 million in assets, including more than $71 million in the Trust Corpus.

The association is based in Los Angeles but also has California offices in Palo Alto and Orange County.

Cooperative of American Physicians Federal Action Committee (CAP/FAC) (C00161604) *Address: same as sponsor * Treasurer: Dr. Alfred V. Budris*

	1993-94	1995-96	1997	Totals
Receipts	$107,161	$103,620	$35,645	$246,426
Disburse	143,910	116,939	40,250	301,099
Cash	58,928	36,559	31,951	n/a
Contributions	130,460	120,239	33,125	283,824
Republicans	47,110	83,589	25,025	155,724
No. of Cand.	*38*	*54*	*33*	*125*
House	41,110	76,089	22,025	139,224
Senate	6,000	7,500	3,000	16,500
Democrats	83,350	36,650	8,100	128,100
No. of Cand.	*51*	*30*	*14*	*95*
House	63,850	31,150	7,600	102,600
Senate	19,500	5,500	500	25,500
Incumbents	115,790	106,814	31,375	253,979
Challengers	5,850	4,000	1,250	11,100
Open Seat	6,500	9,425	500	16,425
Winners	111,890	107,739	n/a	219,629
Losers	18,570	12,500	n/a	31,070

DermPAC

*Phone: (847) 433-1501 * Fax: (415) 564-1967*
750 Homewood Ave., Suite 130, Highland Park, IL 60035

DermPAC (C00297614) *Address: same as sponsor * Treasurer: Andrew P. Lazar * Contact: Dr. Richard G. Glogau, Chairman*

	1993-94	1995-96	1997	Totals
Receipts	$114,312	$70,091	$38,755	$223,158
Disburse	31,621	109,884	42,910	184,415
Cash	82,689	46,757	42,601	n/a
Contributions	5,000	26,000	6,500	37,500
Republicans	5,000	16,500	3,000	24,500
No. of Cand.	*8*	*20*	*4*	*32*
House	1,000	9,000	2,000	12,000
Senate	4,000	7,500	1,000	12,500
Democrats	0	9,500	3,500	13,000
No. of Cand.	*1*	*8*	*4*	*13*
House	0	7,500	3,500	11,000
Senate	0	2,000	0	2,000
Incumbents	1,000	21,000	6,500	28,500
Challengers	2,000	3,000	0	5,000
Open Seat	2,000	2,000	0	4,000
Winners	5,000	19,500	n/a	24,500
Losers	0	6,500	n/a	6,500

National Community Pharmacists Association

*Phone: (703) 683-8200 * Fax: (703) 683-3619*
205 Daingerfield Rd., Alexandria, VA 22314-2885
Web: www.ncpanet.org

The National Community Pharmacists Association, formerly known as the National Association of Retail Druggists, is a trade association that serves pharmacy owners, managers, and employees of nearly 30,000 independent pharmacies across the nation.

National Association of Retail Druggists Political Action Committee (NARDPAC) (C00030809) *Address: same as sponsor * Treasurer: John M. Rector * Contact: Salvatore D'Angelo, Chairperson*

	1993-94	1995-96	1997	Totals
Receipts	$215,321	$169,547	$73,180	$458,048
Disburse	220,630	180,163	83,040	483,833
Cash	41,145	30,537	20,675	n/a
Contributions	148,750	146,000	71,750	366,500
Republicans	16,000	70,000	29,250	115,250
No. of Cand.	*10*	*58*	*30*	*98*
House	11,500	55,000	22,250	88,750
Senate	4,500	15,000	7,000	26,500
Democrats	132,750	76,000	42,500	251,250
No. of Cand.	*90*	*61*	*45*	*196*
House	86,750	56,500	27,500	170,750
Senate	46,000	19,500	15,000	80,500
Incumbents	123,750	120,000	68,250	312,000
Challengers	6,500	4,500	0	11,000
Open Seat	18,500	20,000	3,500	42,000
Winners	106,500	119,000	n/a	225,500
Losers	42,250	27,000	n/a	69,250

National Medical Association

*Phone: (202) 806-6300 * Fax: (202) 806-4898*
1012 10th St. N.W., Washington, DC 20001
Web: www.natmed.org

The National Medical Association represents 22,000 African-American physicians.

The association was founded in Atlanta during the Cotton States Exposition in 1895. It was then known as the National Association of Colored Physicians, Dentists and Pharmacists.

The NMA focuses on health issues related to blacks and "medically underserved" populations.

National Medical Political Action Committee (C00168856) *Address: same as sponsor * Treasurer: Dr. Henry W. Williams*

	1993-94	1995-96	1997	Totals
Receipts	$31,805	$9,680	$0	$41,485
Disburse	31,143	12,563	0	43,706
Cash	3,105	219	0	n/a
Contributions	6,250	6,743	0	12,993
Republicans	0	0	0	0
No. of Cand.	*0*	*0*	*0*	*0*
House	0	0	0	0
Senate	0	0	0	0
Democrats	6,250	6,743	0	12,993
No. of Cand.	*3*	*1*	*0*	*4*
House	1,250	0	0	1,250
Senate	5,000	6,743	0	11,743
Incumbents	6,000	6,743	0	12,743
Challengers	250	0	0	250
Open Seat	0	0	0	0
Winners	6,250	6,743	n/a	12,993
Losers	0	0	n/a	0

Physicians Interindemnity Trust

Phone: (818) 241-5119
541 W. Colorado Blvd., Glendale, CA 91204

The Physicians Interindemnity Trust is a group offering medical malpractice insurance coverage to doctors in California. The co-op terminated its PAC in 1996.

Physicians Interindemnity/Federal PAC (C00228817) *Address: same as sponsor * Treasurer: Sabri M. El Farra*

	1993-94	1995-96	1997	Totals
Receipts	$45,600	$20,450	$0	$66,050
Disburse	21,815	61,694	0	83,509
Cash	41,245	0	0	n/a
Contributions	17,325	5,150	0	22,475
Republicans	7,075	1,500	0	8,575
No. of Cand.	*14*	*3*	*0*	*17*
House	4,075	1,000	0	5,075
Senate	3,000	500	0	3,500
Democrats	10,250	3,650	0	13,900
No. of Cand.	*7*	*3*	*0*	*10*
House	8,750	3,650	0	12,400
Senate	1,500	0	0	1,500
Incumbents	8,400	4,150	0	12,550
Challengers	4,300	500	0	4,800
Open Seat	2,250	500	0	2,750
Winners	10,650	4,650	n/a	15,300
Losers	6,675	500	n/a	7,175

Southeast Anesthesia Associates

Phone: (704) 355-2372
P.O. Box 36351, Charlotte, NC 28236

Southeast Anesthesia Associates is a private organization of 22 anesthesiologists from the Charlotte, N.C., area.

Southeast Anesthesia Associates Political Action Committee (C00306878) *Address: same as sponsor * Treasurer: Dr. H. Arthur McCulloch*

	1993-94	1995-96	1997	Totals
Receipts	$0	$21,000	$10,600	$31,600
Disburse	0	31,776	7,600	39,376
Cash	0	6,024	9,024	n/a
Contributions	0	14,250	-6,000	8,250
Republicans	0	14,250	-6,000	8,250
No. of Cand.	*0*	*3*	*3*	*6*
House	0	250	1,000	1,250
Senate	0	14,000	-7,000	7,000
Democrats	0	0	0	0
No. of Cand.	*0*	*0*	*0*	*0*
House	0	0	0	0
Senate	0	0	0	0
Incumbents	0	14,250	-6,000	8,250
Challengers	0	0	0	0
Open Seat	0	0	0	0
Winners	0	14,250	n/a	14,250
Losers	0	0	n/a	0

Women in Psychology for Legislative Action

*Phone: (602) 912-5300 * Fax: (602) 957-4828*
3900 E. Camelback, Suite 200, Phoenix, AZ 85018

Women in Psychology for Legislative Action is a bipartisan group of about 1,000 women that raises funds for female federal candidates.

Once or twice a year the group holds a fundraiser to which one candidate is invited. It then donates all of the year's proceeds to that person.

The group also holds occasional functions in Washington.

Women in Psychology for Legislative Action (C00237404) *Address: same as sponsor * Treasurer: Dr. Mathilda Canter * Contact: Loretta Kroin, Chairperson*

	1993-94	1995-96	1997	Totals
Receipts	$35,693	$26,745	$12,020	$74,458
Disburse	34,905	26,943	11,511	73,359
Cash	3,631	3,430	3,938	n/a
Contributions	8,650	5,500	0	14,150
Republicans	0	5,000	0	5,000
No. of Cand.	*0*	*1*	*0*	*1*
House	0	5,000	0	5,000
Senate	0	0	0	0
Democrats	8,650	500	0	9,150
No. of Cand.	*4*	*1*	*0*	*5*
House	5,650	500	0	6,150
Senate	3,000	0	0	3,000
Incumbents	5,650	5,500	0	11,150
Challengers	0	0	0	0
Open Seat	3,000	0	0	3,000
Winners	5,000	5,500	n/a	10,500
Losers	3,650	0	n/a	3,650

Health Services

Aetna U.S. Healthcare Inc.

*Phone: (215) 775-6690 * Fax: (215) 775-5664*
980 Jolly Rd., P.O. Box 1109, Blue Bell, PA 19422
Web: www.aetnaushc.com

Aetna U.S. Healthcare serves 23 million customers in 50 states, including 10.3 million in managed care plans. The company, which had $18.5 billion in 1997 revenues, contracts with 2,300 hospitals and 250,000 physicians.

Aetna U.S. Healthcare was formed by the 1996 merger of U.S. Healthcare and insurance giant Aetna. The company offers medical and dental plans, along with group insurance and supplemental benefit programs.

Subsidiaries include: U.S. Quality Algorithms, which measures health care performance; WCA, a managed care program for worker's compensation; Health Care Administrators, which contracts with self-insured employers to provide administrative services; Managed Care Coordinators, which assists multi-state employers with benefits administration; and Criterion Communications, a marketing and public relations firm.

Although U.S. Healthcare's PAC will continue to distribute money during the 1998 election cycle, officials are no longer accepting contributions and plan to fold the PAC into that of its new parent company, Aetna, following the election.

U.S. Healthcare Inc. Political Action Committee (USHC-PAC) (C00238659) *Address: same as sponsor * Treasurer: Kylius J. Jones*

	1993-94	1995-96	1997	Totals
Receipts	$108,095	$97,671	$0	$205,766
Disburse	109,811	95,954	6,002	211,767
Cash	4,987	6,707	705	n/a
Contributions	32,338	9,650	0	41,988
Republicans	12,815	7,650	0	20,465
No. of Cand.	*10*	*9*	*0*	*19*
House	4,180	5,000	0	9,180
Senate	8,635	2,650	0	11,285
Democrats	19,523	2,000	0	21,523
No. of Cand.	*17*	*2*	*0*	*19*
House	9,023	2,000	0	11,023
Senate	10,500	0	0	10,500
Incumbents	20,253	5,750	0	26,003
Challengers	9,585	500	0	10,085
Open Seat	2,000	3,000	0	5,000
Winners	14,065	7,750	n/a	21,815
Losers	18,273	1,900	n/a	20,173

American Ambulance Association

*Phone: (202) 296-8390 * Fax: (202) 223-8199*
1615 L. St. N.W., Suite 1000, Washington, DC 20036

The American Ambulance Association represents about 800 companies, most of which are private-sector ambulance providers. It has state chapters in California, Pennsylvania, New York and Minnesota.

The group lobbies on issues related to the ambulance and health care industries, such as Medicare reimbursement of emergency medical services.

American Ambulance Association Federal PAC (also known as AMBU-PAC) (C00168070) *Address: same as sponsor * Treasurer: Royce L. Rollins*

	1993-94	1995-96	1997	Totals
Receipts	$89,858	$75,394	$49,754	$215,006
Disburse	100,941	68,396	31,011	200,348
Cash	3,835	10,833	29,576	n/a
Contributions	69,970	45,000	23,000	137,970
Republicans	16,900	27,250	14,000	58,150
No. of Cand.	*18*	*25*	*10*	*53*
House	11,000	24,250	10,000	45,250
Senate	5,900	3,000	4,000	12,900
Democrats	52,820	17,750	9,000	79,570
No. of Cand.	*38*	*19*	*9*	*66*
House	36,100	11,250	4,000	51,350
Senate	16,720	6,500	5,000	28,220
Incumbents	55,320	36,750	21,500	113,570
Challengers	2,000	2,000	1,000	5,000
Open Seat	12,650	6,250	500	19,400
Winners	51,600	40,000	n/a	91,600
Losers	18,370	5,000	n/a	23,370

American Association of Health Plans

*Phone: (202) 778-3200 * Fax: (202) 778-8479*
1129 20th St. N.W., Suite 600, Washington, DC 20036
Web: www.aahp.org

The American Association of Health Plans is a trade association that represents more than 1,000 HMOs, PPOs and other similar health plans that provide health care for more than 140 million Americans nationwide.

The association provides legal counsel and conducts educational programs. It also conducts research and analysis of managed care issues and monitors legislation and regulations.

In February 1998, the association's board of directors voted to support principles for reducing tobacco use and protecting public health.

AAHP was created in 1996 by the merger of the Group Health Association of America and the American Managed Care and Review Association.

Health Plan PAC of the American Association of Health Plans (formerly known as Group Health Associations of America PAC) (C00106740) *Address: same as sponsor * Treasurer: Robert Borchardt * Contact: Julie L. Goon, V.P. of Gov. Affairs*

	1993-94	1995-96	1997	Totals
Receipts	$23,450	$84,605	$32,784	$140,839
Disburse	22,308	65,066	39,603	126,977
Cash	3,298	22,833	16,014	n/a
Contributions	20,200	46,358	26,780	93,338
Republicans	6,500	25,845	20,192	52,537
No. of Cand.	7	27	21	55
House	1,500	23,345	14,192	39,037
Senate	5,000	2,500	6,000	13,500
Democrats	13,700	20,513	6,588	40,801
No. of Cand.	17	22	8	47
House	8,000	17,013	5,088	30,101
Senate	5,700	3,500	1,500	10,700
Incumbents	19,200	43,858	25,780	88,838
Challengers	1,000	0	500	1,500
Open Seat	0	2,500	500	3,000
Winners	16,200	43,358	n/a	59,558
Losers	4,000	3,000	n/a	7,000

American HomePatient Inc.

*Phone: (615) 221-8884 * Fax: (615) 373-8357*
5200 Maryland Way, Suite 400, Brentwood, TN 37027-5018

American HomePatient is a publicly owned home health care provider of primarily respiratory and intravenous (IV) services, home medical equipment and supplies. It is based in Tennessee with 330 locations in 35 states, mostly in mid-size and smaller cities.

The company has 4,100 employees and reported 1997 sales of $387 million.

American HomePatient PAC (C00302547) *Address: same as sponsor * Treasurer: Robert L. Fringer*

	1993-94	1995-96	1997	Totals
Receipts	$0	$14,272	$4,689	$18,961
Disburse	0	13,630	3,979	17,609
Cash	0	257	967	n/a
Contributions	0	6,600	3,500	10,100
Republicans	0	5,000	1,000	6,000
No. of Cand.	0	3	1	4
House	0	4,000	0	4,000
Senate	0	1,000	1,000	2,000
Democrats	0	1,600	2,500	4,100
No. of Cand.	0	3	2	5
House	0	600	1,000	1,600
Senate	0	1,000	1,500	2,500
Incumbents	0	6,600	2,500	9,100
Challengers	0	0	1,000	1,000
Open Seat	0	0	0	0
Winners	0	6,600	n/a	6,600
Losers	0	0	n/a	0

American Medical Security Inc.

*Phone: (920) 661-1353 * Fax: (920) 661-3270*
3100 AMS Blvd., Green Bay, WI 54313
*Web: www.amschoices.com * E-mail: amcgeepo@amschoices.com*

American Medical Security offers health care insurance to employers and other insurance products, such as employee and dependent term life, short-term disability, dental and accidental death and dismemberment. The company covered 624,000 members during 1997. Headquartered in Green Bay, Wis., the company reported 1997 sales of $981 million and employs 2,300 people.

The company is a wholly owned subsidiary of United Wisconsin Services Inc., a public company and Wisconsin's largest HMO. In September 1997, the company acquired the majority of the small group health insurance business of Pan-American Life Insurance Co.

American Medical Security Inc. PAC (C00283457) *Address: same as sponsor * Treasurer: Mary Jane Rintelman*

	1993-94	1995-96	1997	Totals
Receipts	$67,888	$73,272	$4,821	$145,981
Disburse	46,375	36,963	17,250	100,588
Cash	21,516	57,833	45,405	n/a
Contributions	30,850	18,813	13,100	62,763
Republicans	14,350	11,213	9,000	34,563
No. of Cand.	19	15	6	40
House	4,350	9,713	6,000	20,063
Senate	10,000	1,500	3,000	14,500
Democrats	16,500	7,600	3,600	27,700
No. of Cand.	22	12	5	39
House	11,500	4,000	3,600	19,100
Senate	5,000	3,600	0	8,600
Incumbents	27,100	11,213	7,100	45,413
Challengers	1,000	600	6,000	7,600
Open Seat	2,750	6,500	0	9,250
Winners	27,850	12,713	n/a	40,563
Losers	3,000	6,100	n/a	9,100

Apria Healthcare Group Inc.

*Phone: (714) 427-4937 * Fax: (714) 540-9475*
3560 Hyland Ave., Costa Mesa, CA 92626
E-mail: 110257.2760@compuserve.com

Apria Healthcare Group is one of the U.S.'s largest home health care companies. Sales in 1997 were $1.2 billion, and the company, formed in 1995 when Homedco Group and Abbey Healthcare merged, is publicly traded. Apria employs 9,500 people in 50 states.

Apria provides or manages comprehensive homecare services including home infusion, respiratory therapy, home medical equipment, women's health care, nursing and coordinated care through more than 350 branches.

The company plans to jettison its women's health care, nursing and medical supply businesses.

Apria Healthcare Inc. Political Action Committee (formerly known as Homedco Inc. PAC) (C00240218) *Phone: (412) 873-7804 * Fax: (412) 873-0718 * 250 Technology Dr., Canonsburg, PA 15317-9564 * Treasurer: John A. Fioretto Jr. * Contact: Kimberly Rogers-Bowers, V.P. of Regulatory Compliance*

	1993-94	1995-96	1997	Totals
Receipts	$37,828	$47,373	$52,888	$138,089
Disburse	25,450	44,650	16,000	86,100
Cash	27,411	30,137	67,026	n/a
Contributions	22,200	36,950	16,000	75,150
Republicans	2,700	16,150	5,000	23,850
No. of Cand.	6	14	4	24
House	1,700	13,650	2,500	17,850
Senate	1,000	2,500	2,500	6,000
Democrats	19,500	20,800	11,000	51,300
No. of Cand.	22	16	8	46
House	11,500	16,000	8,500	36,000
Senate	8,000	4,800	2,500	15,300
Incumbents	19,700	34,950	12,500	67,150
Challengers	1,000	0	2,500	3,500
Open Seat	1,500	2,000	1,000	4,500
Winners	16,200	35,950	n/a	52,150
Losers	6,000	1,000	n/a	7,000

Foundation Health Corp.

*Phone: (916) 631-5504 * Fax: (916) 631-5335*
3400 Data Dr., Rancho Cordova, CA 95670
*Web: www.fhs.com * E-mail: cynthia_k_suzuki@notes.fh.com*

Foundation Health is a managed health care provider for more than 6 million people in 18 states, mainly in the West. It is the fourth-largest managed health care provider in the United States. The publicly held company's 1997 sales were $7.2 billion and it employs 3,800 people.

In January 1998, Foundation Health acquired Physicians Health Services of New Jersey for $271 million. It also announced the formation of its Northeast Region, comprised of three health plans with more than 1 million members in the New York tri-state area, making it the third-largest operator of health plans in the region.

Foundation Health Corp. PAC (C00230789) *Address: same as sponsor * Treasurer: Cynthia Suzuki*

	1993-94	1995-96	1997	Totals
Receipts	$66,861	$74,414	$33,890	$175,165
Disburse	24,289	35,826	52,037	112,152
Cash	66,939	105,529	87,382	n/a
Contributions	16,152	18,000	39,000	73,152
Republicans	600	3,000	22,000	25,600
No. of Cand.	1	3	5	9
House	600	3,000	17,000	20,600
Senate	0	0	5,000	5,000

Democrats	15,552	15,000	17,000	47,552
No. of Cand.	*6*	*4*	*5*	*15*
House	10,552	15,000	16,000	41,552
Senate	5,000	0	1,000	6,000
Incumbents	16,152	18,000	34,000	68,152
Challengers	0	0	5,000	5,000
Open Seat	0	0	0	0
Winners	16,152	18,000	n/a	34,152
Losers	0	0	n/a	0

Group Health Inc.

*Phone: (212) 615-0891 * Fax: (212) 563-8569*
441 Ninth Ave., New York, NY 10001
Web: www.ghi.com

Group Health is a nonprofit health insurance provider in New York, serving more than 2.9 million people through a network of 44,364 practitioners.

Services include hospital, medical and dental insurance for 1.9 million people and third-party administrative services for more than 980,000 people. In operation since 1937, Group Health is headquartered in New York City and has four regional offices in New York.

Group Health Inc. Federal Political Action Committee (C00250613) *Address: same as sponsor * Treasurer: Jeffrey L. Goodwin * Contact: Frank Branchini, President and CEO*

	1993-94	*1995-96*	*1997*	*Totals*
Receipts	$9,942	$10,113	$10,170	$30,225
Disburse	12,110	10,000	4,800	26,910
Cash	2,717	2,833	8,204	n/a
Contributions	6,610	7,500	4,800	18,910
Republicans	310	6,000	3,000	9,310
No. of Cand.	*1*	*2*	*1*	*4*
House	310	1,000	0	1,310
Senate	0	5,000	3,000	8,000
Democrats	6,300	1,500	1,800	9,600
No. of Cand.	*4*	*3*	*2*	*9*
House	3,550	1,000	1,800	6,350
Senate	2,750	500	0	3,250
Incumbents	6,610	7,000	4,600	18,210
Challengers	0	0	0	0
Open Seat	0	500	200	700
Winners	6,610	7,500	n/a	14,110
Losers	0	0	n/a	0

HealthSouth Corp.

*Phone: (205) 967-7116 * Fax: (205) 969-4729*
One Health South Pkwy., Birmingham, AL 35243
Web: www.healthsouth.com

HealthSouth is the nation's largest provider of outpatient and rehabilitative health care services. HealthSouth provides services through its national network of outpatient and inpatient rehabilitation facilities, outpatient surgery centers, medical centers and other health care facilities.

HealthSouth operates in all 50 states and has more than 2,000 contracts with insurance and managed care plans. The company owns 73 of its facilities and leases the remainder. HealthSouth had 1997 sales of $3 billion. HealthSouth has about 36,400 workers, of whom 20,930 are full-time.

HealthSouth Rehabilitation Corp. PAC (C00257048) *Address: same as sponsor * Treasurer: Richard M. Scrushy * Contact: Jabo Waggoner, Chairperson*

	1993-94	*1995-96*	*1997*	*Totals*
Receipts	$61,632	$118,271	$52,199	$232,102
Disburse	44,024	94,177	79,255	217,456
Cash	23,208	47,306	20,252	n/a
Contributions	7,500	25,350	33,505	66,355
Republicans	7,500	22,350	23,505	53,355
No. of Cand.	*9*	*16*	*10*	*35*
House	3,000	16,850	10,750	30,600
Senate	4,500	5,500	12,755	22,755
Democrats	0	3,000	10,000	13,000
No. of Cand.	*0*	*2*	*1*	*3*
House	0	3,000	0	3,000
Senate	0	0	10,000	10,000
Incumbents	4,500	12,850	32,505	49,855
Challengers	1,500	1,500	1,000	4,000
Open Seat	1,500	11,000	0	12,500
Winners	7,000	23,850	n/a	30,850
Losers	500	1,500	n/a	2,000

Mid Atlantic Medical Services Inc.

*Phone: (301) 762-8205 * Fax: (301) 762-5728*
Four Taft Ct., Rockville, MD 20850
Web: www.mamsi.com

Mid Atlantic Medical Services is a holding company for subsidiaries active in managed health care. MAMSI subsidiaries provide health insurance to more than 1.7 million people in Delaware, Washington, Maryland, North Carolina, Pennsylvania, Virginia and West Virginia.

Subsidiaries include: Alliance PPO Inc., HomeCall Inc., MD-Individual Practice Association Inc., MAMSI Life & Health Insurance Co., Mid Atlantic Psychiatric Services Inc., Optimum Choice Inc., Optimum Choice of the Carolinas Inc. and Optimum Choice Inc. of Pennsylvania.

Mid Atlantic Medical Service PAC contributes to candidates with interests in health care regulations, Medicare issues and HMOs.

Mid Atlantic Medical Services Inc. Political Action Committee (C00267245) *Address: same as sponsor * Treasurer: Daniel D. Willoth * Contact: Joseph Guarriello, President*

	1993-94	*1995-96*	*1997*	*Totals*
Receipts	$52,489	$40,157	$13,095	$105,741
Disburse	44,609	27,920	18,750	91,279
Cash	23,251	35,498	29,856	n/a
Contributions	35,600	25,400	16,000	77,000
Republicans	12,000	14,450	7,500	33,950
No. of Cand.	*10*	*9*	*7*	*26*
House	7,600	8,450	6,500	22,550
Senate	4,400	6,000	1,000	11,400
Democrats	23,600	10,950	8,500	43,050
No. of Cand.	*18*	*9*	*6*	*33*
House	18,100	7,500	6,500	32,100
Senate	5,500	3,450	2,000	10,950
Incumbents	32,100	21,650	16,000	69,750
Challengers	400	1,250	0	1,650
Open Seat	3,100	2,500	0	5,600
Winners	30,700	23,650	n/a	54,350
Losers	4,900	1,750	n/a	6,650

National Association for Home Care

*Phone: (202) 547-7424 * Fax: (202) 547-3540*
519 C St. N.E., Stanton Park, Washington, DC 20002-5089
Web: www.nahc.org

The National Association for Home Care represents more than 6,000 home health care agencies, hospices and home health aide groups. Its members also include individual social workers and nurses.

The group advocates home health care as an alternative to nursing homes and hospitals. It promotes reform of the Medicare reimbursement process and a reduction in paperwork for nursing homes and hospices.

National Association for Home Care Congressional Action Committee (C00188987) *Address: same as sponsor * Treasurer: Michaele N. Woods*

	1993-94	*1995-96*	*1997*	*Totals*
Receipts	$75,480	$88,475	$27,078	$191,033
Disburse	43,754	125,980	16,098	185,832
Cash	39,598	2,090	13,070	n/a
Contributions	32,225	106,500	14,500	153,225
Republicans	7,500	36,250	6,000	49,750
No. of Cand.	*5*	*30*	*8*	*43*
House	1,500	28,250	5,500	35,250
Senate	6,000	8,000	500	14,500
Democrats	24,725	70,250	8,500	103,475
No. of Cand.	*39*	*53*	*11*	*103*
House	20,975	48,150	6,500	75,625
Senate	3,750	22,100	2,000	27,850
Incumbents	29,475	72,500	14,000	115,975
Challengers	-250	8,000	500	8,250
Open Seat	3,000	26,000	0	29,000
Winners	26,925	93,000	n/a	119,925
Losers	5,300	13,500	n/a	18,800

National Association of Rehabilitation Agencies

*Phone: (703) 437-4377 * Fax: (703) 435-4390*
11250 Roger Bacon Dr., Suite 8, Reston, VA 20190
*Web: www.naranet.org/nara * E-mail: nara@naranet.org*

The National Association of Rehabilitation Agencies was founded in 1978 to serve as the trade association representing the interests of Medicare-certified rehabilitation agencies and businesses that treat Medicare patients.

The majority of its 250 members are Medicare Part B providers that contract with long-term care facilities for one or more of the three primary rehabilitation services — physical therapy, occupational therapy and speech pathology.

The typical NARA member is a small-to-medium sized company with fewer than 100 employees, whose owner has a therapy background. NARA promotes the growth and welfare of Medicare certified rehabilitation agencies and multidisciplinary rehabilitation businesses that treat Medicare patients. It also supports those agencies in their efforts to enhance patient care, services and business success.

NARA PAC contributes to candidates for national office and elected officials who support the rehabilitation industry and its patients.

National Association of Rehabilitation Agencies Inc. Political Action Committee (C00192153) *Address: same as sponsor * Treasurer: Ernest A. Burch Jr.*

	1993-94	1995-96	1997	Totals
Receipts	$15,160	$9,447	$3,240	$27,847
Disburse	11,157	7,200	2,000	20,357
Cash	7,602	9,849	11,089	n/a
Contributions	9,100	7,200	2,000	18,300
Republicans	1,500	4,950	0	6,450
No. of Cand.	*2*	*8*	*0*	*10*
House	500	2,950	0	3,450
Senate	1,000	2,000	0	3,000
Democrats	7,600	2,250	2,000	11,850
No. of Cand.	*12*	*4*	*3*	*19*
House	4,100	1,250	1,500	6,850
Senate	3,500	1,000	500	5,000
Incumbents	8,600	6,700	2,000	17,300
Challengers	0	0	0	0
Open Seat	500	500	0	1,000
Winners	7,100	7,200	n/a	14,300
Losers	2,000	0	n/a	2,000

National Renal Administrators Association

*Phone: (703) 437-4377 * Fax: (703) 435-4390*
11250 Roger Bacon Dr., Suite 8, Reston, VA 20190
*Web: www.nraa.org/renal * E-mail: nraa@nraa.org*

The National Renal Administrators Association represents about 800 administrators and managers of dialysis facilities nationwide. Dialysis is used to remove impurities from the blood of patients with kidney failure or malfunction.

National Renal Administrators Association Political Action Committee (NRAA-PAC) (C00255091) *Address: same as sponsor * Treasurer: Terry Bahr * Contact: Ann Stivers, Chairwoman*

	1993-94	1995-96	1997	Totals
Receipts	$9,338	$15,128	$14,021	$38,487
Disburse	12,228	25,987	15,028	53,243
Cash	13,036	2,617	2,861	n/a
Contributions	11,700	20,500	15,000	47,200
Republicans	200	6,500	10,500	17,200
No. of Cand.	*1*	*7*	*6*	*14*
House	200	6,500	6,500	13,200
Senate	0	0	4,000	4,000
Democrats	11,500	14,000	4,500	30,000
No. of Cand.	*13*	*12*	*6*	*31*
House	10,500	13,000	3,500	27,000
Senate	1,000	1,000	1,000	3,000
Incumbents	11,500	20,500	12,000	44,000
Challengers	200	0	3,000	3,200
Open Seat	0	0	0	0
Winners	10,000	20,000	n/a	30,000
Losers	1,700	500	n/a	2,200

NovaCare Inc.

*Phone: (610) 992-7200 * Fax: (610) 992-3328*
1016 W. Ninth Ave., King of Prussia, PA 19406
Web: www.novacare.com

NovaCare is the second-largest rehabilitation company in the United States, with operations in 43 states. More than half of the company's business comes from providing physical and speech therapy to patients in nursing homes. It also offers outpatient rehabilitation, prosthetic devices and human resource management.

In 1997, the public company acquired more than 20 outpatient facilities. NovaCare, which has 39,800 employees, reported 1997 sales of $1 billion.

NovaCare Inc. Political Action Committee (C00263558) *Address: same as sponsor * Treasurer: Laurence F. Lane*

	1993-94	1995-96	1997	Totals
Receipts	$54,689	$39,365	$22,611	$116,665
Disburse	39,931	32,950	6,650	79,531
Cash	31,352	37,771	53,733	n/a
Contributions	28,700	21,950	6,500	57,150
Republicans	16,600	9,950	3,000	29,550
No. of Cand.	*10*	*15*	*2*	*27*
House	2,000	4,000	1,000	7,000
Senate	14,600	5,950	2,000	22,550
Democrats	12,100	12,000	3,500	27,600
No. of Cand.	*12*	*11*	*5*	*28*
House	4,600	9,000	1,000	14,600
Senate	7,500	3,000	2,500	13,000
Incumbents	17,700	13,250	6,500	37,450
Challengers	2,000	2,200	0	4,200
Open Seat	6,500	6,500	0	13,000
Winners	25,200	15,500	n/a	40,700
Losers	3,500	6,450	n/a	9,950

Oxford Health Plans Inc.

*Phone: (203) 851-2713 * Fax: (203) 851-1530*
800 Connecticut Ave., Norwalk, CT 06854
Web: www.oxhp.com

Oxford Health Plans is a publicly owned health care company with 1997 revenues of $4.2 billion. The firm provides health benefit plans through subsidiaries in New York, New Jersey, Pennsylvania, Connecticut and New Hampshire.

The company's product line includes POS plans, traditional HMOs, the Freedom Plan and the Liberty Plan, Medicare and Medicaid plans, third-party administration of employer-funded benefit plans and dental plans. Oxford became publicly owned in 1991. Since then membership has increased from 91,000 in 1992 to 1.9 million in 1997. The company has a provider network of 340 hospitals and more than 36,000 physicians.

Subsidiaries: OakTree Health Plan and Oxford Health Insurance.

Oxford Health Plans Inc. Committee for Quality Health Care (C00305177) *Address: same as sponsor * Treasurer: Robert J. Murphy Jr. * Contact: Scott Schwartz, Assistant General Counsel*

	1993-94	1995-96	1997	Totals
Receipts	$0	$50,750	$42,490	$93,240
Disburse	0	15,425	52,124	67,549
Cash	0	35,326	25,693	n/a
Contributions	0	6,350	18,500	24,850
Republicans	0	4,000	16,500	20,500
No. of Cand.	*0*	*5*	*9*	*14*
House	0	4,000	6,500	10,500
Senate	0	0	10,000	10,000
Democrats	0	2,350	2,000	4,350
No. of Cand.	*0*	*4*	*4*	*8*
House	0	1,350	1,500	2,850
Senate	0	1,000	500	1,500
Incumbents	0	4,850	17,000	21,850
Challengers	0	0	1,500	1,500
Open Seat	0	1,500	0	1,500
Winners	0	4,850	n/a	4,850
Losers	0	1,500	n/a	1,500

PacifiCare Health Systems

*Phone: (714) 825-5116 * Fax: (714) 825-5032*
P.O. Box 25186, Santa Ana, CA 92799-5186
*Web: www.phs.com * E-mail: douglass_ps@exchange.phs.com*

PacifiCare Health Systems is a health maintenance organization with 3.8 million members in 11 states and Guam. The company, which employs about 5,000 people, reported 1997 revenues of $4.6 billion. The publicly held company is based in Santa Ana, Calif.

In addition to Medicare services, the company offers dental and vision care, laboratory and radiology services, pharmacy services, psychological counseling and traditional indemnity insurance plans.

The acquisition of California rival FHP International Corp. in February 1997 nearly doubled PacifiCare's membership.

UniHealth, a not-for-profit health care company also based in California, controls 48 percent of PacifiCare's stock.

CarePAC: The Political Action Committee of Pacificare Health Systems Inc. (C00240903) *Address: same as sponsor * Treasurer: Nick Franklin * Contact: Pat Douglass, Dir. of Gov. Relations*

	1993-94	1995-96	1997	Totals
Receipts	$24,680	$61,948	$31,251	$117,879
Disburse	27,150	48,311	24,600	100,061
Cash	4,230	17,866	24,518	n/a
Contributions	16,770	40,622	16,500	73,892
Republicans	10,150	23,622	9,500	43,272
No. of Cand.	*10*	*27*	*12*	*49*
House	6,150	21,122	7,000	34,272
Senate	4,000	2,500	2,500	9,000
Democrats	6,620	17,000	7,000	30,620
No. of Cand.	*8*	*18*	*7*	*33*
House	2,500	15,000	3,000	20,500
Senate	4,120	2,000	4,000	10,120
Incumbents	13,120	32,622	14,000	59,742
Challengers	650	1,500	1,500	3,650
Open Seat	3,000	6,000	1,000	10,000
Winners	12,500	35,122	n/a	47,622
Losers	4,270	5,500	n/a	9,770

FHP Inc. Health Services Political Action Committee (C00120550) *3120 Lake Center Dr., Santa Ana, CA 92799 * Treasurer: Nick Franklin*

FHP Inc. Health Services PAC filed a termination report in July 1997. FHP International was purchased by PacifiCare Health Systems in February 1997.

	1993-94	1995-96	1997	Totals
Receipts	$170,363	$152,014	$6,157	$328,534
Disburse	167,640	131,724	37,458	336,822
Cash	59,666	13,411	0	n/a
Contributions	78,154	85,919	1,000	165,073
Republicans	23,904	52,919	0	76,823
No. of Cand.	*31*	*37*	*0*	*68*
House	19,404	45,669	0	65,073
Senate	4,500	7,250	0	11,750
Democrats	54,250	33,000	1,000	88,250
No. of Cand.	*40*	*23*	*1*	*64*
House	25,000	30,000	1,000	56,000
Senate	29,250	3,000	0	32,250
Incumbents	69,654	75,669	0	145,323
Challengers	4,000	4,000	0	8,000
Open Seat	4,500	6,250	1,000	11,750
Winners	66,154	80,169	n/a	146,323
Losers	12,000	5,750	n/a	17,750

Sierra Health Services Inc.

*Phone: (702) 242-7190 * Fax: (702) 242-7931*
P.O. Box 15645, Las Vegas, NV 89114-5645
Web: www.sierrahealth.com

Sierra Health Services, a publicly held company headquartered in Las Vegas, is Nevada's largest managed care company. It provides home and hospice care, health insurance and HMO coverage. Sierra has 2,600 employees.

In September 1997, Sierra Military Health Services Inc., a subsidiary of Sierra Health Services, was awarded a multi-year, $1.5 billion contract to serve about 600,000 beneficiaries of the Civilian Health and Medical Program of the Uniformed Services (CHAMPUS) in 13 northeastern and mid-Atlantic states and the District of Columbia.

Subsidiaries include: Health Plan of Nevada, Southwest Medical Associates, Sierra Health and Life, Behavioral Healthcare Options, CII Insurance Group, Family Healthcare Services, HMO Texas, Sierra Healthcare Options, Sierra Military Health and Family Home Hospice.

Sierra Health Services Political Action Committee (SHSPAC) (C00295360) *Address: same as sponsor * Treasurer: Marie H. Soldo*

	1993-94	1995-96	1997	Totals
Receipts	$12,898	$27,147	$9,528	$49,573
Disburse	2,182	26,150	8,612	36,944
Cash	10,716	11,739	12,656	n/a
Contributions	1,035	25,000	8,000	34,035
Republicans	1,035	8,750	1,000	10,785
No. of Cand.	*1*	*4*	*1*	*6*
House	1,035	8,750	0	9,785
Senate	0	0	1,000	1,000
Democrats	0	16,250	7,000	23,250
No. of Cand.	*0*	*7*	*3*	*10*
House	0	6,500	1,000	7,500
Senate	0	9,750	6,000	15,750
Incumbents	0	9,750	7,000	16,750
Challengers	1,035	5,000	0	6,035
Open Seat	0	10,250	1,000	11,250
Winners	1,035	16,750	n/a	17,785
Losers	0	8,250	n/a	8,250

United HealthCare Corp.

*Phone: (612) 936-3693 * Fax: (612) 935-1471*
900 Bren Rd. E., Route MN008-W212, Minnetonka, MN 55440
*Web: www.unitedhealthcare.com * E-mail: tmahowa@ccmail.uhc.com*

Minnesota-based United HealthCare offers health care coverage and related services through 16 HMOs and PPOs. It is a publicly held company.

United serves about 13 million patients in all 50 U.S. states, and serves millions more through workers' compensation programs, Medicare and Medicaid groups and other plans. The company employs 27,000 people.

Sales in 1997 were $11.8 billion, making United the No. 3 managed care corporation in the United States in sales, after competitors Aetna U.S. Healthcare and Kaiser Foundation.

United formed a joint venture with insurer AIG in January 1998 to provide health care services in Asia. The joint venture's first health care services organization, AIA United HealthCare Limited, has been established in Hong Kong and is expected to begin enrolling members in the first quarter of 1998.

United Healthcare Corp. Political Fund (C00274431) *Phone: (202) 659-3059 * Fax: (202) 659-1169 * 1620 L St. N.W., Suite 800, Washington, DC 20036 * Treasurer: David Koppe*

*Contact: Tom Mahowald, V.P. of Public Affairs * Phone: (612) 936-3693 * P.O. Box 1459, Minneapolis, MN 55440-1459*

	1993-94	1995-96	1997	Totals
Receipts	$34,537	$89,376	$79,859	$203,772
Disburse	24,850	43,105	34,000	101,955
Cash	12,987	59,262	105,122	n/a
Contributions	20,850	41,700	27,000	89,550
Republicans	10,100	26,500	18,000	54,600
No. of Cand.	*10*	*24*	*20*	*54*
House	3,600	18,500	10,500	32,600
Senate	6,500	8,000	7,500	22,000
Democrats	10,250	15,200	8,500	33,950
No. of Cand.	*13*	*19*	*9*	*41*
House	6,250	10,200	2,500	18,950
Senate	4,000	5,000	6,000	15,000
Incumbents	15,250	28,200	25,000	68,450
Challengers	1,100	4,000	0	5,100
Open Seat	4,500	9,500	2,000	16,000
Winners	15,750	32,700	n/a	48,450
Losers	5,100	9,000	n/a	14,100

Vivra Inc.

Phone: (650) 577-5700
1850 Gateway Dr., Fifth Floor, San Mateo, CA 94404

Vivra is a publicly traded specialized medical care company with 1996 annual sales of $517 million. It is one of the largest providers of dialysis in the United States.

Vivra coordinates care in multiple specialties, including asthma/allergy, cardiology, diabetes, dialysis/nephrology, and orthopedics through Vivra Renal Care and Vivra Specialty Partners. It has about 5,600 employees.

The company, which is being purchased by Swedish conglomerate Incentive AB, did not file a report with the FEC during 1997 and plans to terminate its PAC.

Vivra PAC (C00302091) *Address: same as sponsor * Treasurer: Leanne Zumwalt*

	1993-94	1995-96	1997	Totals
Receipts	$0	$34,150	$0	$34,150
Disburse	0	11,620	0	11,620
Cash	0	14,690	0	n/a
Contributions	0	8,000	0	8,000
Republicans	0	3,000	0	3,000
No. of Cand.	*0*	*2*	*0*	*2*
House	0	1,000	0	1,000
Senate	0	2,000	0	2,000

(*Data for Vivra PAC continued*)

Democrats	0	5,000	0	5,000
No. of Cand.	*0*	*5*	*0*	*5*
House	0	3,000	0	3,000
Senate	0	2,000	0	2,000
Incumbents	0	6,000	0	6,000
Challengers	0	1,000	0	1,000
Open Seat	0	1,000	0	1,000
Winners	0	8,000	n/a	8,000
Losers	0	0	n/a	0

Hospitals/Nursing Homes

American Health Care Association

*Phone: (202) 898-2858 * Fax: (202) 842-3860*
1201 L St. N.W., Washington, DC 20005
*Web: www.ahca.org * E-mail: byarwood@ahca.org*

The American Health Care Association represents the long-term care community — nearly 12,000 nonprofit and for-profit assisted-living, nursing home, long-term care, and subacute care providers that care for more than 1 million elderly and disabled individuals nationally. It has chapters in all 50 states.

The group supports replacing the Medicaid long-term care financing system with a Medicare system in which coverage would be based on an individual's income and assets. It lobbies for a change in the Medicare prospective payment system so that skilled nursing facilities can immediately switch to the national reimbursement rate instead of phasing it in over time.

AHCA was the leading nursing home contributor to 1996 congressional races. It favored Republicans and contributed just 5 percent of its PAC money to challengers. The top recipients were Sens. John D. Rockefeller IV, D-W.Va., Jesse Helms, R-N.C., and Max Baucus, D-Mont., Minority Leader Richard A. Gephardt, D-Mo., and Rep. Bill Thomas, R-Calif.

American Health Care Association Political Action Committee (AHCA-PAC) (C00006080) *Address: same as sponsor * Treasurer: Gerald L. Baker * Contact: Bruce Yarwood, Legislative Counsel*

	1993-94	1995-96	1997	Totals
Receipts	$638,609	$789,333	$394,942	$1,822,884
Disburse	671,304	754,401	364,228	1,789,933
Cash	38,132	73,064	103,776	n/a
Contributions	475,080	560,171	289,798	1,325,049
Republicans	170,550	309,499	149,448	629,497
No. of Cand.	*121*	*156*	*92*	*369*
House	104,650	216,615	94,448	415,713
Senate	65,900	92,884	55,000	213,784
Democrats	298,030	250,672	139,350	688,052
No. of Cand.	*175*	*132*	*80*	*387*
House	222,530	168,972	87,950	479,452
Senate	75,500	81,700	51,400	208,600
Incumbents	368,780	424,362	274,298	1,067,440
Challengers	28,100	29,059	6,500	63,659
Open Seat	76,550	95,250	8,000	179,800
Winners	369,350	481,887	n/a	851,237
Losers	105,730	78,284	n/a	184,014

American Hospital Association

*Phone: (312) 422-3000 * Fax: (312) 422-4796*
One N. Franklin, Chicago, IL 60606
Web: www.aha.org

The American Hospital Association is a nonprofit association of hospitals and health care networks. The group has 5,000 institutional and 40,000 personal members. Founded in 1898, AHA provides education for health care leaders and is a source of information on health care issues and trends.

The group supports a permanent independent commission on Medicare and entitlement reforms that do not penalize hospitals. It recommends a standard set of Medicare managed care payments that is not linked to variations in fee-for-service payments. The AHA supports graduate medical education funding for facilities other than teaching hospitals and advocates separating GME payments from Medicare funding. It supports all proposals to reduce the number of uninsured children.

The AHA was the third-leading contributor among health PACs during the 1995-96 cycle, behind the American Medical Association and the American Dental Association. More than 87 percent of its money went to winning candidates, including members of the congressional leadership. Of the 359 candidates who received money from this group, a slight majority were Republicans.

The top recipient was Rep. Nathan Deal, R-Ga. Ten other candidates received $10,000. The majority of candidates received less than $5,000.

American Hospital Association Political Action Committee (AHAPAC) (C00106146) *Phone: (202) 626-4625 * Fax: (202) 626-2355 * 325 Seventh St. N.W., Washington, DC 20004-2802 * E-mail: pollack@aha.org * Treasurer: Al Jackson * Contact: Rick Pollack, Executive V.P.*

	1993-94	1995-96	1997	Totals
Receipts	$1,082,356	$1,256,055	$693,901	$3,032,312
Disburse	1,354,303	1,129,589	394,343	2,878,235
Cash	71,118	199,590	510,304	n/a
Contributions	1,037,896	879,863	321,557	2,239,316
Republicans	351,476	451,799	164,640	967,915
No. of Cand.	*129*	*195*	*101*	*425*
House	267,776	359,799	94,640	722,215
Senate	83,700	92,000	70,000	245,700
Democrats	674,720	427,564	156,417	1,258,701
No. of Cand.	*208*	*171*	*88*	*467*
House	585,870	342,400	89,767	1,018,037
Senate	88,850	85,164	66,650	240,664
Incumbents	874,792	642,506	291,057	1,808,355
Challengers	28,750	50,000	2,000	80,750
Open Seat	132,854	186,857	28,500	348,211
Winners	789,842	769,489	n/a	1,559,331
Losers	248,054	110,374	n/a	358,428

Hospital Association Political Action Committee - Federal (HAPAC-Federal) (C00128082) *Phone: (717) 564-9200 * 4750 Lindle Rd., P.O. Box 8600, Harrisburg, PA 17105 * Treasurer: James M. Redmond*

	1993-94	1995-96	1997	Totals
Receipts	$85,001	$67,965	$39,874	$192,840
Disburse	71,866	80,971	36,368	189,205
Cash	14,799	1,797	5,304	n/a
Contributions	11,300	5,800	2,000	19,100
Republicans	2,500	3,200	2,000	7,700
No. of Cand.	*1*	*5*	*1*	*7*
House	0	2,850	0	2,850
Senate	2,500	350	2,000	4,850
Democrats	8,800	2,600	0	11,400
No. of Cand.	*7*	*4*	*0*	*11*
House	2,300	2,600	0	4,900
Senate	6,500	0	0	6,500
Incumbents	4,300	3,300	2,000	9,600
Challengers	2,500	0	0	2,500
Open Seat	2,000	2,500	0	4,500
Winners	3,800	5,800	n/a	9,600
Losers	7,500	0	n/a	7,500

Contributed less than $5,000 during 1995-96 cycle:

AZHHA Political Action Committee (formerly known as PAC of The Arizona Hospital Association) (C00217687) *Phone: (602) 968-1083 * 1501 W. Fountainhead Pkwy., Suite 650, Tempe, AZ 85282 * Web: www.azhha.org * Treasurer: Laurie Lange * Contact: Sheri Farr, Senior Dir. of Regulatory Affairs*

Healthcare Association of New York State PAC-Federal (HANYS PAC-Federal) (C00160259) *Phone: (518) 431-7600 * Fax: (518) 431-7915 * 74 N. Pearl St., Albany, NY 12207 * Web: www.hanys.org * Treasurer: Steven Kroll*

Political Action Committee of the Missouri Hospital Association (C00289777) *Phone: (573) 893-3700 * 4712 Country Club Dr., P.O. Box 60, Jefferson City, MO 65102-0060 * Treasurer: Dwight L. Fine*

California Healthcare Association

*Phone: (916) 443-7401 * Fax: (916) 552-7588*
1201 K St., Suite 800, Sacramento, CA 95814
Web: www.calhealth.org

California Healthcare Association is a nonprofit organization representing the interests of hospitals, health systems, physician organizations and other health care providers in California. Established in 1935, CHA has more than 630 members.

CHA provides members with state and federal representation and advocacy in the legislative and regulatory arenas. It advocates managed care reforms, protecting funding for Medi-Cal and other state health programs, preventing arbitrary Medicare and Medicaid funding reductions, and defeating anti-provider/employer laws and regulations.

California Healthcare Association PAC - Federal (CHPAC Federal) (C00237495) *Address: same as sponsor * Treasurer: Richard Eichman*

	1993-94	1995-96	1997	Totals
Receipts	$197,246	$189,752	$80,731	$467,729
Disburse	199,707	201,331	69,784	470,822
Cash	16,592	5,014	15,961	n/a
Contributions	54,467	56,525	13,820	124,812
Republicans	8,450	18,315	3,750	30,515
No. of Cand.	*12*	*13*	*5*	*30*
House	8,450	18,315	3,750	30,515
Senate	0	0	0	0
Democrats	46,017	38,210	10,070	94,297
No. of Cand.	*31*	*18*	*9*	*58*
House	40,517	38,210	6,070	84,797
Senate	5,500	0	4,000	9,500
Incumbents	46,717	54,275	12,820	113,812
Challengers	750	0	0	750
Open Seat	7,250	2,500	1,000	10,750
Winners	41,217	56,275	n/a	97,492
Losers	13,250	250	n/a	13,500

Columbia/HCA Healthcare Corp.

*Phone: (615) 344-9551 * Fax: (615) 320-2222*
P.O. Box 550, One Park Plaza, Nashville, TN 37202
Web: www.columbia-hca.com

Columbia/HCA Healthcare is the largest hospital company in the United States. The public company owns and operates more than 330 hospitals and other health care facilities with about 60,000 licensed beds in 36 states, England, Spain and Switzerland.

Columbia is the subject of a federal investigation for alleged Medicare fraud at several locations, which has caused several company executives to step down. Three mid-level Columbia employees in Florida were indicted in 1997. An accompanying investigation by the Securities and Exchange Commission was disclosed in March 1998.

The hospital giant began selling several assets in 1998. Columbia agreed to sell its pharmacy benefit management company to Express Scripts Inc. for $445 million in cash and sold 34 surgery centers to HealthSouth Corp.

The publicly traded company posted $18.8 billion in revenues in 1997. It has about 285,000 employees. CEO Dr. Thomas F. Frist Jr. is the brother of Sen. Bill Frist, R-Tenn.

Columbia/HCA Healthcare Corp. Good Government Fund (C00067231) *Address: same as sponsor * Treasurer: David G. Anderson * Contact: Victor L. Campbell, Chairman*

	1993-94	1995-96	1997	Totals
Receipts	$163,657	$153,121	$20,273	$337,051
Disburse	130,260	174,936	29,250	334,446
Cash	41,688	19,875	10,898	n/a
Contributions	39,625	99,700	24,550	163,875
Republicans	25,625	61,100	8,200	94,925
No. of Cand.	*18*	*75*	*6*	*99*
House	22,000	47,000	3,200	72,200
Senate	3,625	14,100	5,000	22,725
Democrats	14,000	38,600	16,250	68,850
No. of Cand.	*15*	*43*	*7*	*65*
House	10,000	25,100	3,250	38,350
Senate	4,000	13,500	13,000	30,500
Incumbents	24,725	64,400	19,950	109,075
Challengers	10,900	8,350	2,000	21,250
Open Seat	4,000	28,950	1,500	34,450
Winners	28,825	83,100	n/a	111,925
Losers	10,800	16,600	n/a	27,400

Columbia/HCA Healthcare Corp. Columbia/HCA Texas Good Government Fund (C00307033) *Phone: (615) 344-9551 * Fax: (615) 320-2222 * 1 Park Plaza, Nashville, TN 37203 * Treasurer: Christopher A. Holden*

*Phone: (972) 789-2716 * Fax: (972) 385-3183 * 13455 Noel Rd., 20th Floor, Dallas, TX 75240*

	1993-94	1995-96	1997	Totals
Receipts	$0	$110,322	$82,729	$193,051
Disburse	0	72,824	61,250	134,074
Cash	0	37,498	58,978	n/a
Contributions	0	59,514	36,250	95,764
Republicans	0	31,164	18,750	49,914
No. of Cand.	*0*	*21*	*12*	*33*
House	0	24,664	11,000	35,664
Senate	0	6,500	7,750	14,250
Democrats	0	23,350	17,500	40,850
No. of Cand.	*0*	*18*	*9*	*27*
House	0	17,850	12,500	30,350
Senate	0	5,500	5,000	10,500
Incumbents	0	23,950	32,250	56,200
Challengers	0	2,750	0	2,750
Open Seat	0	27,814	4,000	31,814
Winners	0	36,264	n/a	36,264
Losers	0	23,250	n/a	23,250

Federation of American Health Systems

*Phone: (202) 836-3090 * Fax: (202) 861-0063*
1111 19th St. N.W., Suite 402, Washington, DC 20036
*Web: www.fahs.com * E-mail: aberdahl@fahs.com*

The Federation of American Health Systems represents about 1,700 investor-owned hospitals and health systems that provide psychiatric, ambulatory and rehabilitative care. The group's members include Columbia/HCA Healthcare Corp., Tenet Healthcare Corp., and HealthSouth Corp.

FAHS represents its members' interests before Congress and federal agencies, and conducts research on the investor-owned health care industry. The group's PAC supports candidates who "support a market driven approach to the nation's health care delivery system."

Federation of American Health Systems Political Action Committee (C00002261) *Address: same as sponsor * Treasurer: Sylvia Urlich * Contact: Anne E. Berdahl, Federal Legislative Representative*

	1993-94	1995-96	1997	Totals
Receipts	$203,496	$219,652	$82,029	$505,177
Disburse	220,495	229,162	90,523	540,180
Cash	112,610	103,102	94,612	n/a
Contributions	151,000	182,526	70,271	403,797
Republicans	59,000	109,826	49,771	218,597
No. of Cand.	*44*	*88*	*38*	*170*
House	16,500	66,626	28,500	111,626
Senate	42,500	43,200	21,271	106,971
Democrats	92,000	72,700	20,000	184,700
No. of Cand.	*62*	*47*	*14*	*123*
House	52,500	30,000	6,500	89,000
Senate	39,500	42,700	13,500	95,700
Incumbents	119,000	144,976	62,691	326,667
Challengers	17,500	9,200	4,080	30,780
Open Seat	14,500	27,850	3,500	45,850
Winners	110,000	157,326	n/a	267,326
Losers	41,000	25,200	n/a	66,200

Genesis Health Ventures Inc.

*Phone: (610) 444-6350 * Fax: (610) 444-3365*
148 W. State St., Kennett Square, PA 19348
Web: www.ghv.com

Genesis Health Ventures provides basic and specialty health care services to the elderly in four eastern regions of the United States under the brand name Genesis ElderCare. Its 1997 sales exceeded $1 billion and the company employs 43,400 workers.

Genesis, a public company based in Pennsylvania, owns and manages 340 geriatric care facilities that provide services such as skilled, intermediate and personal nursing, rehabilitation, nutrition management and respiratory therapy. In addition, the company's extended network includes primary care clinics, institutional and community-based pharmacies, medical supply distribution centers and home health care agencies.

Genesis Health Ventures Inc. Political Action Committee (C00292094) *Address: same as sponsor * Treasurer: Bruce D. Thevenot*

	1993-94	1995-96	1997	Totals
Receipts	$58,962	$148,785	$75,304	$283,051
Disburse	26,250	63,100	57,394	146,744
Cash	32,713	118,401	136,127	n/a
Contributions	7,000	37,500	16,000	60,500
Republicans	3,000	21,750	6,000	30,750

(*Data for Genesis Health Ventures continued*)

No. of Cand.	*1*	*21*	*4*	*26*
House	0	19,750	2,500	22,250
Senate	3,000	2,000	3,500	8,500
Democrats	4,000	15,750	10,000	29,750
No. of Cand.	*4*	*18*	*9*	*31*
House	2,000	10,750	4,500	17,250
Senate	2,000	5,000	5,500	12,500
Incumbents	1,500	26,000	16,000	43,500
Challengers	5,500	2,000	0	7,500
Open Seat	0	9,500	0	9,500
Winners	4,500	32,500	n/a	37,000
Losers	2,500	5,000	n/a	7,500

Health Care and Retirement Corp.

*Phone: (419) 252-6010 * Fax: (419) 252-6013*
One Seagate, Toledo, OH 43604-2616

Health Care and Retirement is a long-term health care provider with services including subacute medical care, rehabilitation therapy, Alzheimer's care and home health care. The publicly traded Toledo company has 18,500 employees and reported 1997 sales of $891 million.

HCR operates 129 nursing centers in 16 states. The company owns 121 of the centers, with 93 operating under the Heartland name. In 1997, HCR operated 63 medical specialty units within its nursing centers.

HCR has two wholly owned subsidiaries: MileStone Healthcare Inc., which provides program management services for subacute care and acute rehabilitation programs; and Heartland Rehabilitation Services Inc., a provider of rehabilitation therapy.

Health Care and Retirement Corp. (HCR) Employees Good Citizenship Fund (C00260141) *Address: same as sponsor * Treasurer: Frank A. Jannazo*

	1993-94	*1995-96*	*1997*	*Totals*
Receipts	$33,418	$42,458	$13,435	$89,311
Disburse	31,725	28,750	9,878	70,353
Cash	14,941	28,659	32,224	n/a
Contributions	13,900	5,400	1,500	20,800
Republicans	300	100	1,000	1,400
No. of Cand.	*2*	*1*	*1*	*4*
House	300	100	0	400
Senate	0	0	1,000	1,000
Democrats	13,600	5,300	500	19,400
No. of Cand.	*6*	*6*	*1*	*13*
House	2,100	2,100	0	4,200
Senate	11,500	3,200	500	15,200
Incumbents	13,650	3,900	500	18,050
Challengers	0	0	0	0
Open Seat	0	1,500	1,000	2,500
Winners	13,650	4,300	n/a	17,950
Losers	250	1,100	n/a	1,350

Living Centers of America

*Phone: (281) 578-4650 * Fax: (281) 578-4786*
15415 Katy Fwy., Suite 800, Houston, TX 77094
E-mail: mchatelle@livingcenters.com

Living Centers of America and GranCare merged in 1997 to form AmeriHealth Services. Living Center of America's PAC will continue, according to a PAC spokesperson.

Living Centers of America Federal Political Action Committee (C00294371) *Address: same as sponsor * Treasurer: Charles W. Frank * Contact: Melody Chatelle, V.P. of Gov. Relations*

	1993-94	*1995-96*	*1997*	*Totals*
Receipts	$21,057	$97,005	$50,801	$168,863
Disburse	10,313	39,802	52,981	103,096
Cash	10,745	67,957	65,781	n/a
Contributions	1,750	13,525	11,000	26,275
Republicans	0	2,875	7,000	9,875
No. of Cand.	*0*	*5*	*5*	*10*
House	0	2,875	2,000	4,875
Senate	0	0	5,000	5,000
Democrats	1,750	10,650	4,000	16,400
No. of Cand.	*3*	*16*	*9*	*28*
House	750	7,150	3,250	11,150
Senate	1,000	3,500	750	5,250
Incumbents	1,750	8,225	10,750	20,725
Challengers	0	500	0	500
Open Seat	0	4,800	500	5,300
Winners	1,750	7,925	n/a	9,675
Losers	0	5,600	n/a	5,600

Magellan Health Services Inc.

*Phone: (800) 342-9660 * Fax: (404) 814-5794*
3414 Peachtree Rd. N.E., Suite 1400, Atlanta, GA 30326
Web: www.magellanhealth.com

Once the largest operator of psychiatric hospitals in the United States, Magellan Health Services sold most of its hospitals during 1997 to focus on providing substance abuse treatment and to help employees suffering from mild mental health problems.

Serving about 55 million people covered by health plans such as Blue Cross and Aetna, Magellan is nearly twice the size of its closest competitor, Value Health Inc. Magellan has 5,000 employees and posted 1997 sales of $1.2 billion.

The company also offers nonbehavioral specialty managed care, franchising and therapeutic foster care. Magellan sold 50 percent of its subsidiary, Charter Behavioral Health Systems, which offers residential treatment, acute inpatient hospitalization and outpatient care.

Other subsidiaries include: National Mentor, Green Spring Health Services and Magellan Public Solutions.

Magellan Health Services Employee Committee for Good Government (C00247262) *Address: same as sponsor * Treasurer: James R. Bedenbaugh*

	1993-94	*1995-96*	*1997*	*Totals*
Receipts	$26,266	$51,764	$29,419	$107,449
Disburse	38,224	51,188	23,920	113,332
Cash	1,412	1,995	7,492	n/a
Contributions	7,000	30,926	15,500	53,426
Republicans	4,150	16,150	10,000	30,300
No. of Cand.	*8*	*11*	*7*	*26*
House	1,650	3,650	4,000	9,300
Senate	2,500	12,500	6,000	21,000
Democrats	2,850	14,776	5,500	23,126
No. of Cand.	*5*	*7*	*3*	*15*
House	2,350	4,500	0	6,850
Senate	500	10,276	5,500	16,276
Incumbents	4,650	13,926	15,500	34,076
Challengers	600	5,000	0	5,600
Open Seat	1,750	12,000	0	13,750
Winners	4,250	21,926	n/a	26,176
Losers	2,750	9,000	n/a	11,750

Manor Care Inc.

*Phone: (301) 979-4000 * Fax: (301) 979-4002*
11555 Darnestown Rd., Fourth Floor, Gaithersburg, MD 20878-3200
*Web: www.manorcare.com * E-mail: ann_mcdermott@manorcare.com*

With $1.5 billion in 1997 sales and more than 27,000 employees, Manor Care is one of the largest nursing and assisted living care companies in the nation.

A public company, Manor Care provides long-term senior living care through 200 facilities located in 29 states. It provides these services under the name ManorCare Health Services.

In September 1997 Manor Care announced its intention to split its business operations into two distinct companies — Manor Care Health Services Inc., which will own and operate nursing homes and assisted-living facilities; and Manor Care Realty Inc., which will develop the company's properties.

Manor Care plans to sell its 51 percent stake in Vitalink Pharmacy Services and holds a controlling interest of In Home Health Inc.

Manor Healthcare Corp. Federal Political Action Committee (C00156851) *Address: same as sponsor * Treasurer: Leigh C. Comas * Contact: Ann McDermott, PAC Dir.*

	1993-94	*1995-96*	*1997*	*Totals*
Receipts	$125,956	$143,316	$97,827	$367,099
Disburse	136,866	149,639	74,315	360,820
Cash	14,198	7,877	31,389	n/a
Contributions	90,300	105,600	41,999	237,899
Republicans	25,800	42,000	15,999	83,799
No. of Cand.	*19*	*34*	*13*	*66*
House	5,800	31,500	9,000	46,300
Senate	20,000	10,500	6,999	37,499
Democrats	63,500	63,600	26,000	153,100
No. of Cand.	*30*	*34*	*18*	*82*
House	41,500	38,100	10,000	89,600
Senate	22,000	25,500	16,000	63,500
Incumbents	70,000	70,100	40,999	181,099
Challengers	9,800	9,000	1,000	19,800
Open Seat	8,000	26,500	0	34,500
Winners	71,500	93,600	n/a	165,100
Losers	18,800	12,000	n/a	30,800

National Association of Psychiatric Health Systems

*Phone: (202) 393-6700 * Fax: (202) 783-6041*
1317 F St. N.W., Suite 301, Washington, DC 20004-1105
*Web: www.naphs.org * E-mail: naphs@naphs.org*

The National Association of Psychiatric Health Systems represents psychiatric hospitals, psychiatric health units in general hospitals, partial hospitalization programs, community mental health centers, residential treatment centers and behavioral group practices. It represents more than 300 individual organizations, some groups of which are owned by larger companies.

It is concerned with legislation that deals with psychiatric care and substance abuse, more specifically mental health and substance abuse funding parity, Medicare, Medicaid and budget issues.

The association was founded in 1933.

National Association of Psychiatric Health Systems Political Action Committee (NAPHS/PAC) (C00107136) *Address: same as sponsor * Treasurer: Cidette Perrin*

	1993-94	1995-96	1997	Totals
Receipts	$46,351	$34,633	$19,061	$100,045
Disburse	58,095	44,535	22,664	125,294
Cash	33,472	23,569	19,966	n/a
Contributions	50,600	32,500	15,500	98,600
Republicans	24,000	19,500	9,500	53,000
No. of Cand.	*20*	*21*	*12*	*53*
House	10,000	15,000	8,000	33,000
Senate	14,000	4,500	1,500	20,000
Democrats	26,600	13,000	6,000	45,600
No. of Cand.	*31*	*14*	*5*	*50*
House	21,100	3,500	1,000	25,600
Senate	5,500	9,500	5,000	20,000
Incumbents	45,350	26,750	15,000	87,100
Challengers	2,500	500	500	3,500
Open Seat	2,750	5,250	0	8,000
Winners	34,350	31,500	n/a	65,850
Losers	16,250	1,000	n/a	17,250

National HealthCare Corp.

*Phone: (615) 890-2020 * Fax: (615) 890-0123*
100 Vine St., P.O. Box 1398, Murfreesboro, TN 37130-1398

National HealthCare is a public company that operates about 110 long-term health care centers throughout the South. The company reported 1997 sales of $465 million.

NHC's 14,000 employees operate long-term health care centers throughout Tennessee, Florida, Alabama, Missouri, Indiana, North Carolina, South Carolina, Virginia, Kentucky and Georgia. NHC also operates 36 home-care programs, as well as several independent and assisted living centers. NHC's other services include managed care specialty medical units, Alzheimer's disease units and a rehabilitation services company.

In December 1997, the company sold off its real estate assets and created a separate company called National Health Realty Inc., a real estate investment trust.

National Health Corp. Political Action Committee (C00153445) *Address: same as sponsor * Treasurer: Doran Johnson * Contact: Gerald Coggin, PAC Dir.*

	1993-94	1995-96	1997	Totals
Receipts	$107,048	$140,665	$72,816	$320,529
Disburse	74,600	125,450	19,250	219,300
Cash	158,864	174,083	227,650	n/a
Contributions	63,600	58,450	16,750	138,800
Republicans	27,600	24,700	2,000	54,300
No. of Cand.	*6*	*13*	*3*	*22*
House	16,600	22,500	2,000	41,100
Senate	11,000	2,200	0	13,200
Democrats	36,000	33,750	14,750	84,500
No. of Cand.	*9*	*12*	*5*	*26*
House	22,500	30,750	13,750	67,000
Senate	13,500	3,000	1,000	17,500
Incumbents	24,100	31,000	16,500	71,600
Challengers	21,000	4,500	0	25,500
Open Seat	18,500	20,950	250	39,700
Winners	30,100	45,750	n/a	75,850
Losers	33,500	12,700	n/a	46,200

Tenet Healthcare Corp.

*Phone: (805) 563-6864 * Fax: (805) 682-5462*
3820 State St., Santa Barbara, CA 93105
Web: www.tenethealth.com

Tenet Healthcare is the second-largest investor-owned hospital company in the United States, behind Columbia/HCA.

Tenet's sales in 1997 were $8.6 billion. The company employs 105,000 workers.

As of May 1997, it owned or operated 128 general hospitals with 27,959 licensed beds. It also owned or managed related health care facilities serving urban and rural communities in 22 states and held investments in other health care companies.

Tenet's subsidiaries also owned or operated a small number of rehabilitation hospitals, specialty hospitals, long-term care facilities, psychiatric facilities and medical office buildings located on the same campus as, or near, its hospitals.

Tenet Healthcare Corp. Political Action Committee (formely known as National Medical Entrepreneurs Inc.) (C00119354) *Address: same as sponsor * Treasurer: Susan Limon * Contact: Christie Sulzbach, Chair*

	1993-94	1995-96	1997	Totals
Receipts	$110,981	$213,036	$75,478	$399,495
Disburse	89,944	233,557	101,050	424,551
Cash	83,837	63,321	37,742	n/a
Contributions	19,799	66,446	26,100	112,345
Republicans	6,304	37,196	13,700	57,200
No. of Cand.	*8*	*32*	*12*	*52*
House	4,304	30,196	5,200	39,700
Senate	2,000	7,000	8,500	17,500
Democrats	13,495	29,250	12,400	55,145
No. of Cand.	*10*	*20*	*8*	*38*
House	8,745	14,500	5,400	28,645
Senate	4,750	14,750	7,000	26,500
Incumbents	17,745	40,696	24,100	82,541
Challengers	250	1,000	2,000	3,250
Open Seat	1,804	24,750	0	26,554
Winners	17,845	56,946	n/a	74,791
Losers	1,954	9,500	n/a	11,454

Transitional Hospitals Corp.

5110 W. Sahara Ave., Las Vegas, NV 89102

Transitional Hospitals Corp. PAC filed a termination report with the FEC in July 1997.

It was bought by Vencor Inc. in June 1997.

Transitional Hospitals Corp. - PAC (C00286609) *Address: same as sponsor * Treasurer: Julia Kopta*

	1993-94	1995-96	1997	Totals
Receipts	$16,994	$59,826	$14,854	$91,674
Disburse	9,041	51,033	31,603	91,677
Cash	7,953	16,749	0	n/a
Contributions	9,000	50,000	0	59,000
Republicans	2,500	24,000	0	26,500
No. of Cand.	*3*	*11*	*0*	*14*
House	500	16,000	0	16,500
Senate	2,000	8,000	0	10,000
Democrats	6,500	26,000	0	32,500
No. of Cand.	*5*	*16*	*0*	*21*
House	3,500	14,000	0	17,500
Senate	3,000	12,000	0	15,000
Incumbents	9,000	49,500	0	58,500
Challengers	0	0	0	0
Open Seat	0	500	0	500
Winners	8,500	45,500	n/a	54,000
Losers	500	4,500	n/a	5,000

THC II Federal PAC (formerly known as Community Psychiatric Centers Federal PAC) (C00249409) *Address: same as sponsor * Treasurer: Julia Kopta*

THC II PAC, formerly known as Community Psychiatric Centers PAC, was terminated in July 1997.

	1993-94	1995-96	1997	Totals
Receipts	$18,386	$23,364	$106	$41,856
Disburse	27,500	27,000	8,860	63,360
Cash	12,388	8,754	0	n/a
Contributions	7,500	16,000	0	23,500
Republicans	1,500	9,500	0	11,000
No. of Cand.	*2*	*7*	*0*	*9*
House	500	4,500	0	5,000
Senate	1,000	5,000	0	6,000

(Data for THC II Federal PAC continued)

Democrats	6,000	6,500	0	12,500
No. of Cand.	*7*	*3*	*0*	*10*
House	2,500	500	0	3,000
Senate	3,500	6,000	0	9,500
Incumbents	6,500	16,000	0	22,500
Challengers	500	0	0	500
Open Seat	500	0	0	500
Winners	6,500	16,000	n/a	22,500
Losers	1,000	0	n/a	1,000

Universal Health Services Inc.

*Phone: (610) 768-3300 * Fax: (610) 768-3336*
367 S. Gulph Rd., King Of Prussia, PA 19406
Web: www.uhsinc.com

Universal Health Services is the third-largest hospital management company in the United States, employing 14,500 people. Founded in 1978, UHS now operates 69 health care facilities with 4,583 beds in 21 states. UHS's headquarters are in Pennsylvania, with offices in Delaware, Texas and Nevada. The company's annual sales are about $2.3 billion.

UHS also provides lab services, MRI and CT scan imaging, managed care and HMO services.

Continuing its ongoing acquisition of medical facilities, UHS has formed a three-hospital joint venture with Quorum Health Group Inc. in Nevada, which encompasses net sales of more than $300 million. UHS has also acquired three hospitals and an ambulatory surgery center from Hospital San Pablo Inc. of Puerto Rico. UHS has formed a joint venture ownership in George Washington University Hospital in Washington. UHS also purchased the 357-bed Northwest Texas Hospital in Amarillo, Texas.

Subsidiaries: Universal Health Realty Income Trust and UHS of Delaware Inc.

Universal Health Services Inc. Employees' Good Government Fund (C00185520) *Address: same as sponsor * Treasurer: Cheryl K. Ramagano * Contact: Bruce R. Gilbert, PAC Dir.*

	1993-94	1995-96	1997	Totals
Receipts	$19,569	$20,179	$13,470	$53,218
Disburse	11,542	18,925	5,561	36,028
Cash	14,704	15,958	23,868	n/a
Contributions	4,000	12,875	3,500	20,375
Republicans	1,500	4,625	1,000	7,125
No. of Cand.	*3*	*7*	*1*	*11*
House	1,000	4,125	0	5,125
Senate	500	500	1,000	2,000
Democrats	2,500	8,250	2,500	13,250
No. of Cand.	*3*	*5*	*3*	*11*
House	2,000	2,000	1,000	5,000
Senate	500	6,250	1,500	8,250
Incumbents	3,000	10,125	2,500	15,625
Challengers	1,000	500	1,000	2,500
Open Seat	0	2,250	0	2,250
Winners	1,000	11,375	n/a	12,375
Losers	3,000	1,500	n/a	4,500

Vencor Inc.

*Phone: (502) 596-7463 * Fax: (502) 596-4055*
3300 Aegon Center, 400 W. Market St., Louisville, KY 40202
*Web: www.vencor.com * E-mail: patricia_deutsche@vencor.com*

Focused on the long-term health care needs of the elderly, Vencor owns and operates a network of 60 hospitals and 309 nursing centers in 46 states. The Louisville, Ky., company also operates a contract services business that provides respiratory therapy and medical services to about 2,900 facilities, most of them nursing centers.

In February 1998, Vencor announced plans to separate into two companies in the second quarter of 1998. VenTrust would control Vencor's land and buildings, including long-term acute care hospitals and nursing centers. The other company would retain the Vencor name and continue to operate its businesses, leasing facilities from VenTrust. The firm would divide its $2 billion debt evenly between the two new companies.

Founded in 1985, the company says it is the largest long-term care hospital group in the United States and has more than 64,000 employees. A publicly traded company, Vencor reported 1997 sales of $3.1 billion.

Vencor Inc. Political Action Committee (formerly known as HillHavenPAC) (C00242271) *Address: same as sponsor * Treasurer: Richard A. Lechleiter * Contact: Patricia A. Deutsche, Manager of Gov. Affairs*

	1993-94	1995-96	1997	Totals
Receipts	$59,875	$77,743	$84,710	$222,328
Disburse	48,900	94,994	42,982	186,876
Cash	60,041	42,794	84,452	n/a
Contributions	23,950	24,750	15,100	63,800
Republicans	5,500	16,750	8,500	30,750
No. of Cand.	*7*	*26*	*6*	*39*
House	1,500	15,250	2,500	19,250
Senate	4,000	1,500	6,000	11,500
Democrats	18,450	8,000	6,600	33,050
No. of Cand.	*17*	*17*	*8*	*42*
House	12,750	6,500	2,600	21,850
Senate	5,700	1,500	4,000	11,200
Incumbents	18,750	19,000	6,100	43,850
Challengers	100	4,000	1,000	5,100
Open Seat	5,100	1,750	8,000	14,850
Winners	17,000	21,000	n/a	38,000
Losers	6,950	3,750	n/a	10,700

Voluntary Hospitals of America

Phone: (202) 822-9750
1200 New Hampshire Ave. N.W., Suite 410, Washington, DC 20036

Voluntary Hospitals of America is a national cooperative of more than 1,500 nonprofit hospitals and health care providers.

Voluntary Hospitals of America Inc. PAC (C00199497) *Address: same as sponsor * Treasurer: Daniel P. Bourque*

	1993-94	1995-96	1997	Totals
Receipts	$1,474	$1,070	$313	$2,857
Disburse	10,727	14,861	127	25,715
Cash	24,980	11,190	11,377	n/a
Contributions	9,500	14,500	0	24,000
Republicans	3,000	9,000	0	12,000
No. of Cand.	*5*	*12*	*0*	*17*
House	1,500	6,000	0	7,500
Senate	1,500	3,000	0	4,500
Democrats	6,500	5,500	0	12,000
No. of Cand.	*7*	*7*	*0*	*14*
House	3,500	1,500	0	5,000
Senate	3,000	4,000	0	7,000
Incumbents	7,500	12,500	0	20,000
Challengers	2,000	1,000	0	3,000
Open Seat	0	1,000	0	1,000
Winners	7,500	11,500	n/a	19,000
Losers	2,000	3,000	n/a	5,000

Pharmaceuticals/Health Products

Abbott Laboratories

*Phone: (847) 937-6645 * Fax: (847) 937-1511*
100 Abbott Park Rd., Abbott Park, IL 60064-3500
Web: www.abbott.com

Abbott Laboratories is an Illinois corporation that makes pharmaceuticals, medical equipment and nutritional products. The public company's brands include Selsun Blue shampoo, Murine eye care products and Ensure, a nutritional drink for seniors.

Abbott also makes antibiotics, diagnostic systems and treatments for HIV and AIDS. The company was incorporated in 1900. Abbott had sales of $11.8 billion in 1997 and employs more than 54,000 workers.

Abbott Laboratories Better Government Fund (ALBGF) (C00040279) *Address: same as sponsor * Treasurer: Carol A. Sebesta*

	1993-94	1995-96	1997	Totals
Receipts	$193,891	$222,274	$110,852	$527,017
Disburse	204,239	215,640	114,834	534,713
Cash	9,776	16,417	12,439	n/a
Contributions	146,169	156,579	91,121	393,869
Republicans	79,825	123,679	63,499	267,003
No. of Cand.	*79*	*112*	*64*	*255*
House	37,075	79,060	39,499	155,634

Senate	42,750	44,619	24,000	111,369
Democrats	65,594	32,900	27,622	126,116
No. of Cand.	*72*	*42*	*30*	*144*
House	46,857	28,800	15,122	90,779
Senate	18,737	4,100	12,500	35,337
Incumbents	114,319	119,610	87,121	321,050
Challengers	4,300	7,869	2,000	14,169
Open Seat	29,550	29,100	2,000	60,650
Winners	124,029	122,860	n/a	246,889
Losers	22,140	33,719	n/a	55,859

Allergan Inc.

*Phone: (714) 246-4656 * Fax: (714) 246-6525*
2525 Dupont Dr., Irvine, CA 92715
Web: www.allergan.com

Allergan makes eye and skin care products including surgical equipment, contact lens cleaners and medications for acne and psoriasis. Sales exceeded $1 billion in 1997 and the company employs 6,100 workers. Allergan's products are marketed in more than 100 countries outside the United States, accounting for 60 percent of total sales.

In 1998 the company is expected to acquire Allergan Ligand Retinoid Therapeutics, an independent company collaborating with Allergan to develop Panretin, a treatment for certain types of cancer.

Founded in 1948, Allergan went public in 1970. It merged with SmithKline Beecham in 1980 and was reestablished as an independent entity in 1989.

Allergan Inc. Political Action Comm for Employees (APACE) (C00292102) *Address: same as sponsor * Treasurer: Terry Nielenga * Contact: George Lasezkay, Chairperson*

	1993-94	*1995-96*	*1997*	*Totals*
Receipts	$17,214	$61,932	$24,038	$103,184
Disburse	13,077	59,310	26,861	99,248
Cash	4,137	6,762	2,940	n/a
Contributions	12,000	40,450	21,825	74,275
Republicans	7,000	27,450	16,450	50,900
No. of Cand.	*10*	*22*	*15*	*47*
House	3,000	25,950	14,950	43,900
Senate	4,000	1,500	1,500	7,000
Democrats	5,000	13,000	5,375	23,375
No. of Cand.	*6*	*11*	*6*	*23*
House	3,000	7,000	3,375	13,375
Senate	2,000	6,000	2,000	10,000
Incumbents	10,500	35,950	21,825	68,275
Challengers	1,000	1,500	0	2,500
Open Seat	500	3,000	0	3,500
Winners	11,000	37,450	n/a	48,450
Losers	1,000	3,000	n/a	4,000

American Home Products Corp.

*Phone: (973) 660-5000 * Fax: (973) 660-7156*
Five Giralda Farms, Madison, NJ 07940
Web: www.ahp.com

American Home Products is one of the world's largest pharmaceutical and health care companies. AHP develops, manufactures and markets a diversified line of products, including prescription and over-the-counter medicines, vaccines and animal health care and agricultural products.

The company, which makes such products as Advil, Chap Stick and Robitussin, is the sixth-largest pharmaceutical company in the world in terms of sales. AHP also manufactures Premarin, one of the most commonly prescribed estrogen replacements for post-menopausal women. The company also made Redux and Pondimin, two anti-obesity drugs, although it withdrew them from the market in 1997 following adverse medical testing results.

In December 1997, AHP agreed to sell Sherwood, Davis & Geck, a manufacturer and marketer of medical devices, to Tyco International for $1.77 billion. In October of the same year, the company sold Storz Instrument Co., a similar company.

Based in Madison, N.J., the publicly traded company employs 60,000 people and operates in 145 countries. AHP, which was established in 1926, had 1997 sales of more than $14 billion, with net income of $2 billion. In that same year, the company spent $1.5 billion on research and development.

In 1997, AHP acquired the international animal health company, Solvay. The company's other subsidiaries include Wyeth Ayerst, Whitehall Robins, Genetics Institute, Cyanimid, Fort Dodge and Eurand. The company also owns a majority share in Immunex.

American Cyanimid and Immunex each had PACs during the 1995-96 election cycle, but neither contributed at least $5,000 to congressional campaigns.

American Home Products Corp.-AHP Good Government Fund (C00115303) *Phone: (202) 659-8320 * Fax: (202) 659-2158 * 1726 M St. N.W., Washington, DC 20036 * Treasurer: Robert G. Blount*
*Contact: John R. Stafford, Chairman * Phone: (973) 660-5000*

	1993-94	*1995-96*	*1997*	*Totals*
Receipts	$124,513	$157,497	$14,095	$296,105
Disburse	75,432	144,512	78,283	298,227
Cash	82,538	95,526	31,340	n/a
Contributions	51,000	70,000	36,500	157,500
Republicans	29,750	48,500	25,000	103,250
No. of Cand.	*38*	*59*	*37*	*134*
House	11,250	30,500	12,500	54,250
Senate	18,500	18,000	12,500	49,000
Democrats	21,250	21,500	11,500	54,250
No. of Cand.	*31*	*35*	*15*	*81*
House	14,250	18,000	3,500	35,750
Senate	7,000	3,500	8,000	18,500
Incumbents	43,750	56,000	36,000	135,750
Challengers	1,500	3,500	500	5,500
Open Seat	6,750	10,500	0	17,250
Winners	46,250	59,000	n/a	105,250
Losers	4,750	11,000	n/a	15,750

Contributed less than $5,000 during 1995-96 cycle:

Immunex Corp. Political Action Committee (C00255323) *Phone: (206) 587-0430 * Fax: (206) 587-0606 * 51 University St., Seattle, WA 98101 * Web: www.immunex.com * Treasurer: Valoree E. Dowell*

Terminated PACs which contributed less than $5,000 during 1995-96 cycle:

American Cyanamid Co. Good Government Fund (C00175000) *1575 Eye St. N.W., Suite 200, Washington, DC 20005 * Treasurer: Stephen J. Robbins*

American Orthotic & Prosthetic Association

*Phone: (703) 836-7116 * Fax: (703) 836-0838*
1650 King St., Suite 500, Alexandria, VA 22314
Web: www.theaopa.org

The American Orthotic & Prosthetic Association is a trade association serving the interests of orthotic and prosthetic facilities, manufacturers and suppliers.

Established in 1917, AOPA monitors developments in the field and keeps members informed of new technologies and services. It also fights for reimbursement policies that enable the physically challenged population to receive orthotic and prosthetic care.

AOPA has several publications available to members. O&P Almanac, AOPA's Capitol Express and President's Report, all contain information on AOPA's activities on Capitol Hill as well as news from federal regulatory agencies.

American Orthotic & Prosthetic Association Political Action Committee (AOPAPAC) (C00118430) *Address: same as sponsor * Treasurer: Martha L. Rinker*

	1993-94	*1995-96*	*1997*	*Totals*
Receipts	$18,784	$12,756	$16,227	$47,767
Disburse	32,179	26,030	8,493	66,702
Cash	17,719	4,447	12,182	n/a
Contributions	32,000	26,000	6,000	64,000
Republicans	9,000	16,500	6,000	31,500
No. of Cand.	*6*	*10*	*4*	*20*
House	2,000	7,000	1,000	10,000
Senate	7,000	9,500	5,000	21,500
Democrats	22,500	9,500	0	32,000
No. of Cand.	*17*	*11*	*2*	*30*
House	17,000	7,000	0	24,000
Senate	5,500	2,500	0	8,000
Incumbents	31,000	24,000	6,000	61,000
Challengers	0	0	0	0
Open Seat	1,000	2,000	0	3,000
Winners	28,000	21,000	n/a	49,000
Losers	4,000	5,000	n/a	9,000

Amgen Inc.

*Phone: (805) 447-8520 * Fax: (805) 498-1075*
One Amgen Center Dr., Thousand Oaks, CA 91320-1789
Web: www.amgen.com

Amgen is a publicly held global biotechnology company that develops, manufactures and markets human therapeutics based on advanced cellular and molecular biology. The company manufactures and markets two human therapeutic products, Filgrastim and Epoetin alfa, which stimulate the production of neutrophils, one type of white blood cell. The company markets in the United States, the European Union, Canada and Australia.

Incorporated in 1980 as AMGen (Applied Molecular Genetics Inc.), the company has 4,650 employees worldwide. Its total revenues for 1997 were $2.4 billion.

In October 1997, Amgen's newest product, INFERGEN, a bioengineered drug for the treatment of chronic hepatitis C viral infection, was approved by the Food and Drug Administration.

Amgen Inc. Political Action Committee (C00251876) *Phone: (202) 289-7447 * Fax: (202) 289-7448 * 1300 Eye St. N.W., Suite 207W, Washington, DC 20005 * Treasurer: Michael E. Yurosko * Contact: Pete Teeley*

	1993-94	1995-96	1997	Totals
Receipts*	$29,364	$24,765	$21,549	$75,678
Disburse	29,550	23,248	18,342	71,140
Cash	3,784	5,302	8,508	n/a
Contributions	22,170	21,247	17,542	60,959
Republicans	11,000	16,747	13,037	40,784
No. of Cand.	*11*	*24*	*17*	*52*
House	3,000	8,091	7,037	18,128
Senate	8,000	8,656	6,000	22,656
Democrats	11,170	4,500	4,505	20,175
No. of Cand.	*8*	*7*	*5*	*20*
House	7,550	2,500	1,505	11,555
Senate	3,620	2,000	3,000	8,620
Incumbents	20,170	17,247	17,042	54,459
Challengers	2,000	2,500	500	5,000
Open Seat	0	1,500	0	1,500
Winners	16,050	17,747	n/a	33,797
Losers	6,120	3,500	n/a	9,620

Ares-Serono Inc.

*Phone: (781) 982-9000 * Fax: (781) 982-1369*
100 Longwater Circle, Norwell, MA 02061

Ares-Serono is the U.S. subsidiary of the Ares-Serono Group, a Swiss developer and marketer of pharmaceutical products with headquarters in Geneva, Switzerland. Ares-Serono develops drugs to treat infertility and is active in the fields of growth and immunology/oncology.

Ares-Serono operates subsidiaries and manufacturing facilities in 30 countries and its products are sold under the trademark Serono in more than 90 countries. Shares of Ares-Serono S.A., the holding company of the group, are traded on the Swiss stock exchange.

The company is the leading marketer of infertility products in the United States, including Fertinex, Profasi, Serophene and Pergonal. Its parent company reported 1997 sales of $864 million.

Ares-Serono Inc. Political Action Committee (C00258236) *Address: same as sponsor * Treasurer: Peter Zarrella*

	1993-94	1995-96	1997	Totals
Receipts	$4,950	$4,750	$7,600	$17,300
Disburse	3,950	5,000	5,857	14,807
Cash	1,315	1,065	2,808	n/a
Contributions	3,950	4,500	5,857	14,307
Republicans	250	1,500	500	2,250
No. of Cand.	*1*	*1*	*1*	*3*
House	250	1,500	0	1,750
Senate	0	0	500	500
Democrats	3,700	3,000	5,357	12,057
No. of Cand.	*6*	*6*	*3*	*15*
House	3,700	3,000	857	7,557
Senate	0	0	4,500	4,500
Incumbents	3,750	4,500	5,857	14,107
Challengers	0	0	0	0
Open Seat	200	0	0	200
Winners	3,950	2,500	n/a	6,450
Losers	0	2,000	n/a	2,000

Baxter Healthcare Corp.

*Phone: (847) 948-2000 * Fax: (847) 948-3948*
One Baxter Pkwy., DF3-1E, Deerfield, IL 60015
*Web: www.baxter.com * E-mail: kanes@baxter.com*

Baxter Healthcare makes cardiovascular, kidney dialysis, biotechnical and intravenous systems, treatments for hemophilia and heart surgery equipment. The publicly traded company employs about 41,000 workers and its 1997 revenues were $6.1 billion. Foreign markets account for more than half of its sales.

In January 1998, Baxter acquired the pharmaceutical products division of Ohmeda Healthcare from The BOC Group, a British industrial gases firm, for about $104 million. According to Baxter, Ohmeda's pharmaceutical division is the North American leader in production of gases and drugs used for general and local anesthesia.

Additional subsidiaries include: Baxter Biotechnology, Baxter Cardiovascular Medicine, Baxter I.V. Systems/Medical Products and Baxter Renal Therapy.

Baxter Healthcare Corp. Political Action Committee (C00117838) *Phone: (202) 223-4016 * Fax: (202) 296-7177 * 800 Connecticut Ave. N.W., Washington, DC 20006 * Treasurer: Steven E. Kane*

	1993-94	1995-96	1997	Totals
Receipts	$56,158	$66,463	$17,392	$140,013
Disburse	41,764	74,887	18,871	135,522
Cash	22,598	14,176	12,697	n/a
Contributions	41,750	67,849	15,355	124,954
Republicans	22,750	45,349	11,000	79,099
No. of Cand.	*26*	*37*	*16*	*79*
House	13,750	28,049	5,500	47,299
Senate	9,000	17,300	5,500	31,800
Democrats	19,000	22,500	4,355	45,855
No. of Cand.	*22*	*18*	*7*	*47*
House	12,000	9,000	1,355	22,355
Senate	7,000	13,500	3,000	23,500
Incumbents	39,250	51,099	14,355	104,704
Challengers	0	5,250	1,000	6,250
Open Seat	2,500	11,500	0	14,000
Winners	38,250	55,849	n/a	94,099
Losers	3,500	12,000	n/a	15,500

Bayer Corp.

*Phone: (412) 777-7817 * Fax: (412) 777-5590*
100 Bayer Rd., Building 14, Pittsburgh, PA 15205-9741
Web: www.bayerus.com

Best known for its aspirin, Bayer produces more than 8,000 chemical, health care and imaging technology products.

The $9-billion company, with 24,000 employees at more than 50 locations across the United States, is the largest subsidiary of the Bayer Group, a publicly traded German chemical company with 1997 sales of $30.5 billion.

Bayer's businesses are concentrated in three major areas: health care and life sciences (Bayer aspirin, Alka-Seltzer and Advantage flea control), chemicals (pigments, fibers and industrial chemicals) and imaging technologies (Agfa Division).

Some of Bayer's major U.S. research and production facilities are located in Baytown and Orange, Texas; Berkeley, Calif.; West Haven, Conn.; Bushy Park, S.C.; Clayton, N.C.; Kansas City, Mo.; Elkhart, Ind.; Tarrytown, N.Y.; Worthington, Minn.; Omaha, Neb.; and New Martinsville, W.V.

Bayer Corp. Political Action Committee (C00281162) *Address: same as sponsor * Treasurer: W. Michael Weaber * Contact: Dr. Richard L. White, Chairman*

	1993-94	1995-96	1997	Totals
Receipts	$47,481	$126,955	$92,410	$266,846
Disburse	29,596	104,100	68,445	202,141
Cash	17,885	40,743	64,710	n/a
Contributions	29,550	104,000	68,000	201,550
Republicans	20,550	86,500	53,000	160,050
No. of Cand.	*26*	*51*	*47*	*124*
House	9,550	44,500	29,000	83,050
Senate	11,000	42,000	24,000	77,000
Democrats	9,000	17,500	15,000	41,500
No. of Cand.	*11*	*9*	*17*	*37*
House	7,000	13,500	9,000	29,500
Senate	2,000	4,000	6,000	12,000

Incumbents	18,500	81,000	64,500	164,000
Challengers	4,000	4,000	500	8,500
Open Seat	7,050	19,000	3,000	29,050
Winners	28,000	84,500	n/a	112,500
Losers	1,550	19,500	n/a	21,050

Bristol-Myers Squibb Co.

*Phone: (212) 546-4000 * Fax: (212) 546-4020*
345 Park Ave., Suite 43-17, New York, NY 10154
Web: www.bms.com

Bristol-Myers Squibb makes prescription and over-the-counter drugs, medical equipment, nutrition products and beauty care supplies. The publicly traded company has 51,000 employees and reported sales of more than $16 billion in 1997.

Bristol-Myers Squibb is comprised of four industry segments: pharmaceuticals, which includes sales of prescription medicines, mainly cardiovascular, anti-infective and anti-cancer drugs; medical devices and equipment; nonprescription health products, including infant formulas and other nutritional products; and toiletries and beauty aids.

Products include: Bufferin, Excedrin, Ban deodorant, the heart disease drug Pravachol (the company's largest product, with $1.4 billion in 1997 sales), Keri skin care products, Clairol hair products and Herbal Essences products.

Bristol-Myers Squibb Co. Employee Political Action Committee (C00035675) *Phone: (202) 783-0900 * Fax: (202) 783-2308 * 655 15th St. N.W., Suite 410, Washington, DC 20005 * Treasurer: Francis I. Perier Jr.*

	1993-94	1995-96	1997	Totals
Receipts	$130,319	$202,302	$128,759	$461,380
Disburse	134,616	200,269	132,660	467,545
Cash	14,780	16,822	12,928	n/a
Contributions	97,000	164,100	117,250	378,350
Republicans	55,900	115,500	77,250	248,650
No. of Cand.	*54*	*112*	*79*	*245*
House	21,400	63,500	45,250	130,150
Senate	34,500	52,000	32,000	118,500
Democrats	41,100	48,600	40,000	129,700
No. of Cand.	*42*	*54*	*45*	*141*
House	24,600	37,000	24,500	86,100
Senate	16,500	11,600	15,500	43,600
Incumbents	84,150	135,650	113,500	333,300
Challengers	2,750	4,200	1,000	7,950
Open Seat	9,100	24,750	2,250	36,100
Winners	86,000	141,150	n/a	227,150
Losers	11,000	22,950	n/a	33,950

Centocor Inc.

*Phone: (610) 889-4422 * Fax: (610) 889-4701*
200 Great Valley Pkwy., Malvern, PA 19355-1307
*Web: www.centocor.com * E-mail: wulfing@centocor.com*

Centocor manufactures biopharmaceutical products to treat cardiovascular, inflammatory and infectious diseases and cancer. The publicly traded company's 1997 sales were $200 million and it employs 640 people.

Centocor's two FDA-approved products, ReoPro and Panorex, are used to increase the size of blood vessels during angioplasty surgery and to treat cancer, respectively. ReoPro, which accounts for nearly 80 percent of the company's sales, is used in nearly half of all angioplasty procedures in the United States. Centocor also develops in vitro products, including ovarian, breast, and gastric cancer tests.

The firm has distribution agreements with U.S., Japanese, French and German companies. Centocor is acquiring the U.S. and Canadian marketing rights for an anticlotting drug, Retavase, from Roche Holding.

Centocor Inc. Employee Action Fund (C00297481) *Address: same as sponsor * Treasurer: Paul G. Wulfing*

	1993-94	1995-96	1997	Totals
Receipts	$17,272	$41,333	$19,115	$77,720
Disburse	11,300	30,091	16,125	57,516
Cash	5,973	17,218	20,210	n/a
Contributions	9,000	16,800	9,500	35,300
Republicans	4,000	13,300	9,500	26,800
No. of Cand.	*5*	*13*	*10*	*28*
House	1,500	11,750	7,500	20,750
Senate	2,500	1,550	2,000	6,050
Democrats	5,000	3,500	0	8,500
No. of Cand.	*4*	*4*	*0*	*8*
House	3,000	500	0	3,500
Senate	2,000	3,000	0	5,000
Incumbents	7,500	15,300	9,500	32,300
Challengers	1,500	0	0	1,500
Open Seat	0	1,500	0	1,500
Winners	4,500	16,300	n/a	20,800
Losers	4,500	500	n/a	5,000

Eli Lilly and Co.

*Phone: (317) 276-2000 * Fax: (317) 276-2095*
Lilly Corporate Center, Indianapolis, IN 46285
Web: www.lilly.com

Eli Lilly is a top American drug company and the maker of Prozac, the world's No. 1 antidepressant. The public company employs 31,000 people worldwide and markets its products in 156 countries. In 1997, Lilly's worldwide sales were $8.5 billion.

Lilly's other pharmaceutical products include antibiotics, chemotherapy treatments and vitamins. The company markets blood clot inhibitors and antiulcer drugs. Subsidiaries PCS Health Systems and Integrated Medical Systems specialize in health care management services.

Eli Lilly and Co. Political Action Committee (C00082792) *Address: same as sponsor * Treasurer: Edwin W. Miller * Contact: Ronald F. Stowe, Chairman*

	1993-94	1995-96	1997	Totals
Receipts	$340,532	$400,306	$345,730	$1,086,568
Disburse	330,763	375,583	159,145	865,491
Cash	21,010	45,736	232,323	n/a
Contributions	115,400	182,156	58,800	356,356
Republicans	74,900	128,656	39,300	242,856
No. of Cand.	*56*	*95*	*47*	*198*
House	29,150	72,300	23,050	124,500
Senate	45,750	56,356	16,250	118,356
Democrats	40,500	53,500	19,000	113,000
No. of Cand.	*47*	*58*	*20*	*125*
House	31,500	38,500	5,500	75,500
Senate	9,000	15,000	13,500	37,500
Incumbents	83,000	128,156	56,050	267,206
Challengers	6,500	13,700	250	20,450
Open Seat	25,700	40,500	3,000	69,200
Winners	103,200	149,156	n/a	252,356
Losers	12,200	33,000	n/a	45,200

Genentech Inc.

*Phone: (650) 225-1000 * Fax: (650) 225-5024*
1 DNA Way, South San Francisco, CA 94080-4990
Web: www.gene.com

Biotechnology company Genentech develops, manufactures and sells pharmaceuticals for use in cardiovascular, oncology and endocrinology applications. The publicly traded company is one of the few biotech firms to turn a profit — $129 million in 1997 on revenues of $1 billion.

Vice President Al Gore visited Genentech's San Francisco headquarters in January 1998. Almost all of the company's operations are in San Francisco, although it is building a new manufacturing facility in nearby Vacaville, Calif.

In 1997, Genentech received FDA approval for four drugs, including Rituxan, which is used to treat non-Hodgkins lymphoma. Despite its Dec. 16 launch date, Rituxan produced $5.5 million in 1997 sales for the company.

The company's uninsured patients program has provided $200 million worth of drugs to qualified patients.

Founded in 1976 by venture capitalist Robert A. Swanson and biochemist Herbert W. Boyer, Genentech is one of the nation's oldest biotechnology companies. Switzerland-based Roche Holdings now controls more than 60 percent of the company.

Genentech Inc. Political Action Committee (GenenPAC) (C00199257) *Phone: (202) 296-7272 * Fax: (202) 296-7290 * 808 17th St. N.W., Suite 250, Washington, DC 20006 * E-mail: dbeier@gene.com * Treasurer: Bradford S. Goodwin * Contact: David Beier, V.P. of Gov. Affairs*

	1993-94	1995-96	1997	Totals
Receipts	$55,773	$111,306	$54,924	$222,003
Disburse	57,722	104,500	60,000	222,222
Cash	1,307	8,127	3,056	n/a
Contributions	50,064	87,500	52,000	189,564
Republicans	10,500	49,500	23,000	83,000
No. of Cand.	*12*	*54*	*28*	*94*
House	3,000	37,500	17,000	57,500
Senate	7,500	12,000	6,000	25,500
Democrats	39,564	38,000	29,000	106,564
No. of Cand.	*38*	*34*	*31*	*103*
House	22,704	27,000	19,000	68,704
Senate	16,860	11,000	10,000	37,860
Incumbents	45,314	74,000	52,000	171,314
Challengers	3,250	1,500	0	4,750
Open Seat	1,500	12,000	0	13,500
Winners	44,954	74,500	n/a	119,454
Losers	5,110	13,000	n/a	18,110

Glaxo Wellcome Inc.

*Phone: (919) 483-2100 * Fax: (919) 549-7459*
Five Moore Dr., Research Triangle Park, NC 27709
Web: www.glaxowellcome.com

Glaxo Wellcome is one of the nation's biggest pharmaceutical researchers and manufacturers. Based in North Carolina, the company is a subsidiary of Glaxo Wellcome plc, a London company formed in a 1995 merger.

Its products include Zantac, neuromuscular blocking agents, the anti-depression drug Wellbutrin, and Imuran, which aids in kidney transplants. The company employs 8,300 people across the United States and operates manufacturing facilities in Zebulon and Greenville, N.C., and in West Greenwich, R.I. Glaxo's 1997 sales were $13 billion.

Glaxo and SmithKline Beecham announced in early 1998 that the two companies were discussing a merger that would create the world's largest pharmaceutical company, but talks collapsed. Glaxo lobbies on drug regulation and access to medical records, among other health issues.

Glaxo was the leading pharmaceutical company contributor to 1996 congressional campaigns. More than 80 percent of the company's contributions went to Republicans. The leading recipient was Sen. Gordon Smith, R-Ore. Sens. Jesse Helms, R-N.C., Phil Gramm, R-Texas, and Fred Thompson, R-Tenn., each received $10,000.

Sen. Ernest "Fritz" Hollings, D-S.C., Rep. Eva Clayton, D-N.C., and Senate candidate and former Glaxo CEO Charles Sanders of North Carolina were the leading Democratic recipients.

Glaxo Wellcome Inc. Political Action Committee (C00199703) *Phone: (202) 783-1277 * Fax: (202) 783-1740 * 1500 K St. N.W., Suite 650, Washington, DC 20005 * Treasurer: Thomas A. Ginsler * Contact: Sara Froelich, Dir. of Federal Gov. Relations*

	1993-94	1995-96	1997	Totals
Receipts	$607,224	$674,808	$338,478	$1,620,510
Disburse	608,710	651,979	304,136	1,564,825
Cash	23,672	46,506	80,847	n/a
Contributions	441,319	411,454	192,752	1,045,525
Republicans	266,291	333,129	125,627	725,047
No. of Cand.	*110*	*170*	*86*	*366*
House	116,150	169,919	67,927	353,996
Senate	150,141	163,210	57,700	371,051
Democrats	175,028	78,325	67,125	320,478
No. of Cand.	*88*	*62*	*35*	*185*
House	126,913	57,325	45,125	229,363
Senate	48,115	21,000	22,000	91,115
Incumbents	316,221	333,504	189,252	838,977
Challengers	32,000	23,500	2,500	58,000
Open Seat	93,098	52,950	2,000	148,048
Winners	365,100	336,603	n/a	701,703
Losers	76,219	74,851	n/a	151,070

Terminated PACs which contributed less than $5,000 during 1995-96 cycle:

Burroughs Wellcome Co. Good Government Fund (C00177477) *3030 Cornwallis Rd., Research Triangle, NC 27709 * Treasurer: A. W. Ludlam Jr.*

Guidant Corp.

*Phone: (317) 971-2012 * Fax: (317) 971-2050*
111 Monument Cir., 29th Floor, Indianapolis, IN 46204
Web: www.guidant.com

Guidant designs cardiovascular products. Formed in 1994 with headquarters in Indianapolis, Guidant is a publicly held company with nearly 5,000 employees. It reported 1997 sales of $1.3 billion.

The company consists of three business groups: cardiac rhythm management, cardiac and vascular surgery, and vascular intervention.

The cardiar rhythm management group, based in St. Paul, Minn., was responsible for launching the world's first implantable defibrillator in 1985 and produces cardioverter defibrillator systems which treat life-threatening rapid heart rhythms. The cardiac and vascular surgery group, based in Menlo Park, Calif., develops medical instruments that help surgeons perform minimally invasive surgical procedures. The vascular intervention group, based in Santa Clara, Calif., develops products that help clear blocked arteries.

Guidant Corp. Political Action Committee (C00307769) *Address: same as sponsor * Treasurer: Keith E. Brauer * Contact: Kathy Ranucci, Tax Dir.*

	1993-94	1995-96	1997	Totals
Receipts	$0	$52,243	$43,202	$95,445
Disburse	0	26,500	9,453	35,953
Cash	0	25,746	59,495	n/a
Contributions	0	21,000	3,500	24,500
Republicans	0	16,000	2,500	18,500
No. of Cand.	*0*	*22*	*3*	*25*
House	0	12,000	2,500	14,500
Senate	0	4,000	0	4,000
Democrats	0	5,000	1,000	6,000
No. of Cand.	*0*	*9*	*1*	*10*
House	0	5,000	1,000	6,000
Senate	0	0	0	0
Incumbents	0	18,000	3,500	21,500
Challengers	0	2,000	0	2,000
Open Seat	0	1,000	0	1,000
Winners	0	17,500	n/a	17,500
Losers	0	3,500	n/a	3,500

Health Industry Distributors Association

*Phone: (703) 549-4432 * Fax: (703) 549-6495*
66 Canal Center Plaza, Suite 520, Alexandria, VA 22314-1591
*Web: www.hida.org * E-mail: hida@hida.org*

The Health Industry Distributors Association is a nonprofit trade association representing medical products distributors and home care companies. Established in 1902, HIDA provides its members with products and services in several areas: industry information and data, industry-specific education and training, federal and state government relations, and an annual trade show and education forum.

In the 1997 Balanced Budget Act, HIDA successfully lobbied Congress to create a "dispensing fee" to be paid to "licensed pharmacies approved to dispense drugs or biologicals."

Health Industry Distributors PAC (C00130161) *Address: same as sponsor * Treasurer: Cara Conway Bachenheimer * Contact: Erin Bush, Chairperson*

	1993-94	1995-96	1997	Totals
Receipts	$8,401	$11,345	$3,550	$23,296
Disburse	18,563	12,239	3,150	33,952
Cash	1,594	700	1,100	n/a
Contributions	14,100	11,200	2,650	27,950
Republicans	8,750	8,500	1,200	18,450
No. of Cand.	*11*	*15*	*3*	*29*
House	4,250	7,500	800	12,550
Senate	4,500	1,000	400	5,900
Democrats	5,350	2,700	1,450	9,500
No. of Cand.	*10*	*5*	*2*	*17*
House	3,850	1,700	500	6,050
Senate	1,500	1,000	950	3,450
Incumbents	12,350	8,250	2,650	23,250
Challengers	250	500	0	750
Open Seat	1,500	1,750	0	3,250
Winners	13,050	9,250	n/a	22,300
Losers	1,050	1,950	n/a	3,000

Hoechst Marion Roussel Inc.

*Phone: (816) 966-5000 * Fax: (816) 966-3805*
10236 Marion Park Dr., P.O. Box 9627, Kansas City, MO 64134-0627
Web: www.hmri.com

Hoechst Marion Roussel is the pharmaceutical company of Hoechst Group, a German company. HMR makes drugs that treat cardiovascular diseases, allergies, infections, cancer and diabetes. Products include Cardizem and Allegra.

Established in 1995, HMR is a publicly held company with about 2,100 employees in the United States.

HMR has one subsidiary, Hoechst Celanese Corp. It manufactures and markets petrochemicals and acetate products throughout the world.

The Hoechst Group, based in Frankfurt, Germany, is an international network of independently operating companies that are suppliers in the fields of life sciences and industrial chemicals.

Hoechst Marion Roussel Inc. Political Action Committee (HMRPAC) (formerly known as Marion Merrell Dow) (C00144345) *Phone: (202) 383-5427 * Fax: (202) 639-0446 * 325 Seventh St. N.W., Suite 1100, Washington, DC 20004 * Treasurer: Sue G. Bowlen * Contact: Eddie Evans, V.P. of Federal Gov. Relations*

	1993-94	1995-96	1997	Totals
Receipts	$33,470	$31,757	$23,555	$88,782
Disburse	34,455	29,466	14,364	78,285
Cash	11,842	14,644	23,842	n/a
Contributions	26,700	24,525	11,656	62,881
Republicans	19,050	18,275	8,656	45,981
No. of Cand.	*19*	*24*	*11*	*54*
House	8,550	11,975	5,656	26,181
Senate	10,500	6,300	3,000	19,800
Democrats	7,650	6,250	3,000	16,900
No. of Cand.	*13*	*11*	*4*	*28*
House	6,400	5,250	3,000	14,650
Senate	1,250	1,000	0	2,250
Incumbents	15,700	16,425	11,656	43,781
Challengers	3,250	2,500	0	5,750
Open Seat	7,750	5,600	0	13,350
Winners	22,450	19,725	n/a	42,175
Losers	4,250	4,800	n/a	9,050

Hoechst Celanese Corp. Political Action Committee (C00084871) *Phone: (908) 231-2371 * Fax: (908) 231-2379 * 30 Independence Blvd., P.O. Box 4915, Warren, NJ 07060-4915 * Treasurer: John M. Kacani*

	1993-94	1995-96	1997	Totals
Receipts	$175,078	$148,518	$43,629	$367,225
Disburse	172,000	158,000	26,000	356,000
Cash	17,188	9,977	27,606	n/a
Contributions	171,600	143,500	26,000	341,100
Republicans	93,700	97,000	16,500	207,200
No. of Cand.	*65*	*65*	*20*	*150*
House	50,300	62,500	12,500	125,300
Senate	43,400	34,500	4,000	81,900
Democrats	77,400	46,500	9,500	133,400
No. of Cand.	*64*	*37*	*13*	*114*
House	65,300	39,500	7,500	112,300
Senate	12,100	7,000	2,000	21,100
Incumbents	153,400	120,500	25,000	298,900
Challengers	8,000	4,000	0	12,000
Open Seat	10,200	19,000	1,000	30,200
Winners	147,600	118,500	n/a	266,100
Losers	24,000	25,000	n/a	49,000

Invacare Corp.

*Phone: (216) 329-6102 * Fax: (216) 366-9672*
One Invacare Way, Elyria, OH 44036
Web: www.invacare.com

Invacare is the world's largest manufacturer of home medical equipment with $652 million in revenue. The publicly owned company has 4,200 employees and is headquartered outside of Cleveland.

Company products include wheelchairs, beds and other equipment used by people recovering from accident or sickness at home and by people with long-term disabilities.

The company has U.S. plants in: Sacramento, Calif.; San Diego; Pinellas Park, Fla; Sanford, Fla; Sarasota, Fla; Northbrook, Ill; Wright City, Mo; Beltsville, Md; Elyria, Ohio; and North Ridgeville, Ohio.

Brand names include: Action, Pin-Dot, The Aftermarket Group, Dynamic Touch, Aurora, Kitschall Design and Opale.

Invacare Corp. Political Action Committee (also known as Inva PAC) (C00249896) *Address: same as sponsor * Treasurer: Jerome E. Fox Jr.*

	1993-94	1995-96	1997	Totals
Receipts	$76,546	$87,772	$47,216	$211,534
Disburse	91,000	85,276	40,500	216,776
Cash	7,050	9,548	16,265	n/a
Contributions	42,750	66,276	36,500	145,526
Republicans	11,500	32,750	23,500	67,750
No. of Cand.	*6*	*27*	*13*	*46*
House	1,500	23,750	7,000	32,250
Senate	10,000	9,000	16,500	35,500
Democrats	31,250	33,526	13,000	77,776
No. of Cand.	*18*	*21*	*14*	*53*
House	22,250	21,026	2,500	45,776
Senate	9,000	12,500	10,500	32,000
Incumbents	32,750	59,776	32,500	125,026
Challengers	1,000	3,000	1,000	5,000
Open Seat	6,000	3,500	4,000	13,500
Winners	32,000	56,526	n/a	88,526
Losers	10,750	9,750	n/a	20,500

Johnson & Johnson

*Phone: (732) 524-0400 * Fax: (732) 524-3300*
One Johnson & Johnson Plaza, New Brunswick, NJ 08933-7204
Web: www.johnsonandjohnson.com

Johnson & Johnson is the world's largest and most comprehensive manufacturer of health care products, serving the consumer, pharmaceutical, diagnostics and professional markets.

Johnson & Johnson reported 1997 sales of $22.6 billion. The public company employs more than 90,500 workers.

The Johnson & Johnson family includes 180 companies in more than 51 countries around the world, selling products in more than 175 countries. The consumer products include many familiar names, such as Band-Aid brand adhesive bandages, Tylenol Acetaminophen products, Johnson's baby products, Neutrogena brand shampoos and skin products, and Stayfree sanitary products.

Johnson & Johnson Employees' Good Government Fund (C00010983) *Address: same as sponsor * Treasurer: Jose F. Sosa*

	1993-94	1995-96	1997	Totals
Receipts	$240,594	$359,979	$230,649	$831,222
Disburse	289,776	342,237	199,750	831,763
Cash	35,069	52,814	83,716	n/a
Contributions	148,100	117,350	87,000	352,450
Republicans	83,500	80,250	50,500	214,250
No. of Cand.	*65*	*74*	*60*	*199*
House	43,500	52,750	37,500	133,750
Senate	40,000	27,500	13,000	80,500
Democrats	64,600	37,100	36,500	138,200
No. of Cand.	*60*	*40*	*38*	*138*
House	48,100	30,100	21,500	99,700
Senate	16,500	7,000	15,000	38,500
Incumbents	112,600	91,350	86,000	289,950
Challengers	8,000	8,500	1,000	17,500
Open Seat	27,000	17,500	0	44,500
Winners	119,250	89,850	n/a	209,100
Losers	28,850	27,500	n/a	56,350

Kinetic Concepts Inc.

*Phone: (210) 524-9000 * Fax: (210) 255-6554*
P.O. Box 659508, San Antonio, TX 78265-9508
*Web: www.kci1.com * E-mail: olsonl@kci1.com*

Kinetic Concepts manufactures therapeutic equipment that treats complications associated with patient immobility and helps reduce pain suffered by cancer and burn patients. In 1996 the publicly held, San Antonio company reported sales of nearly $270 million and employed about 2,000 people.

KCI International markets the company's products in the Middle East, Asia, Africa and Europe.

Richard C. Blum & Associates and equity fund Fremont Partners purchased the company in November 1997. Blum is married to Sen. Dianne Feinstein, D-Calif.

Kinetic Concepts Inc. Political Action Committee (KCIPAC) (C00235176) *Address: same as sponsor * Treasurer: Lulu P. Olson*

	1993-94	1995-96	1997	Totals
Receipts	$43,519	$30,958	$11,562	$86,039
Disburse	43,018	30,733	3,400	77,151
Cash	3,063	3,292	11,459	n/a
Contributions	29,050	13,100	-1,650	40,500
Republicans	16,000	9,600	100	25,700
No. of Cand.	*9*	*10*	*1*	*20*
House	6,750	8,600	100	15,450
Senate	9,250	1,000	0	10,250
Democrats	13,050	3,500	-1,750	14,800
No. of Cand.	*16*	*5*	*3*	*24*
House	13,050	2,500	-750	14,800
Senate	0	1,000	-1,000	0
Incumbents	29,050	11,600	-1,650	39,000
Challengers	0	0	0	0
Open Seat	0	1,000	0	1,000
Winners	28,050	10,350	n/a	38,400
Losers	1,000	2,750	n/a	3,750

Mallinckrodt Inc.

*Phone: (314) 854-5270 * Fax: (314) 654-5315*
675 McDonnell Blvd., Hazelwood, MO 63042
*Web: www.mallinckrodt.com * E-mail: mjcaldw@mkg.com*

Mallinckrodt is a publicly traded global health care and chemical company with locations in North, Central and South America, Europe, Asia, Australia, New Zealand and the Pacific. Mallinckrodt had 7,870 employees in 1997, with 5,000 U.S.-based workers. It posted 1997 sales of $1.8 billion.

A majority of Mallinckrodt's services involve health care, including pharmaceuticals, nuclear imaging, medical imaging and critical care. Additional company products and services include coatings, plastics, microelectronics and specialty chemicals.

In February 1998, Mallinckrodt purchased Trigate Ltd., a South African medical supply distributor with annual sales of $9 million.

Mallinckrodt Inc. Political Action Committee (MPAC) (C00113753) *Address: same as sponsor * Treasurer: Sandra M. Shaffer*

	1993-94	1995-96	1997	Totals
Receipts	$21,878	$119,744	$62,422	$204,044
Disburse	15,034	45,136	30,560	90,730
Cash	8,970	83,583	115,445	n/a
Contributions	12,300	37,000	21,300	70,600
Republicans	8,800	21,000	15,300	45,100
No. of Cand.	*10*	*28*	*16*	*54*
House	5,000	13,000	7,300	25,300
Senate	3,800	8,000	8,000	19,800
Democrats	3,500	16,000	6,000	25,500
No. of Cand.	*5*	*14*	*9*	*28*
House	3,500	11,500	4,500	19,500
Senate	0	4,500	1,500	6,000
Incumbents	10,500	30,500	20,100	61,100
Challengers	0	1,000	0	1,000
Open Seat	1,800	5,500	1,200	8,500
Winners	11,800	35,500	n/a	47,300
Losers	500	1,500	n/a	2,000

Mallinckrodt Medical Inc. Political Action Committee (C00119313) *675 McDonnell Blvd., P.O. Box 5840, St. Louis, MO 63134 * Treasurer: Bruce A. Beeler*

The Mallinckrodt Medical Inc. PAC was terminated in July 1996.

	1993-94	1995-96	1997	Totals
Receipts	$27,708	$23,521	$0	$51,229
Disburse	24,721	37,534	0	62,255
Cash	14,012	0	0	n/a
Contributions	17,150	14,500	0	31,650
Republicans	7,650	10,000	0	17,650
No. of Cand.	*9*	*7*	*0*	*16*
House	5,050	10,000	0	15,050
Senate	2,600	0	0	2,600
Democrats	9,500	4,500	0	14,000
No. of Cand.	*14*	*5*	*0*	*19*
House	7,500	3,500	0	11,000
Senate	2,000	1,000	0	3,000
Incumbents	14,800	13,500	0	28,300
Challengers	0	0	0	0
Open Seat	2,350	1,000	0	3,350
Winners	15,650	14,000	n/a	29,650
Losers	1,500	500	n/a	2,000

Mallinckrodt Chemical Inc. Federal Political Action Committee (C00280479) *675 McDonnell Blvd., St. Louis, MO 63134 * Treasurer: Michael J. Caldwell*

The Mallinckrodt Chemical PAC was terminated in 1996.

	1993-94	1995-96	1997	Totals
Receipts	$22,271	$15,225	$0	$37,496
Disburse	13,950	23,547	0	37,497
Cash	8,322	0	0	n/a
Contributions	13,850	6,500	0	20,350
Republicans	8,100	5,000	0	13,100
No. of Cand.	*7*	*6*	*0*	*13*
House	3,500	4,000	0	7,500
Senate	4,600	1,000	0	5,600
Democrats	5,750	1,500	0	7,250
No. of Cand.	*5*	*1*	*0*	*6*
House	5,750	1,500	0	7,250
Senate	0	0	0	0
Incumbents	8,500	6,500	0	15,000
Challengers	2,500	0	0	2,500
Open Seat	2,850	0	0	2,850
Winners	12,600	6,000	n/a	18,600
Losers	1,250	500	n/a	1,750

McKesson Corp.

*Phone: (415) 983-8629 * Fax: (415) 983-9075*
One Post St., 12th Floor, San Francisco, CA 94104
Web: www.mckesson.com

Founded in 1833, McKesson provides health care products and services to retail pharmacies, hospitals and health care networks. McKesson is the largest health care supply management company in North America through its U.S. HealthCare businesses, its Canadian subsidiary, Medis Health and Pharmaceutical Services Inc., and its minority interest in Mexico's Nadro, S.A. The publicly traded San Francisco company posted $12.9 billion in 1997 sales and has more than 13,000 employees.

With its acquisition of General Medical Corp., the largest multimarket distributor of medical-surgical supplies, McKesson has further expanded its health care supply management business. The company also owns McKesson Water Products Co., one of the nation's largest distributors of bottled drinking water.

Subsidiaries include: McKesson General Medical, McKesson Pharmaceutical Systems, McKesson Water Products Co. and Medis.

McKesson Corp. Employees Political Fund (C00108035) *Address: same as sponsor * Treasurer: Claudia Newbold * Contact: Shayron Barnes-Selby, Chairperson*

	1993-94	1995-96	1997	Totals
Receipts	$43,832	$53,770	$40,881	$138,483
Disburse	37,890	57,525	2,387	97,802
Cash	11,320	7,569	46,064	n/a
Contributions	37,500	57,000	2,000	96,500
Republicans	22,500	45,500	1,500	69,500
No. of Cand.	*20*	*33*	*2*	*55*
House	9,000	27,500	1,500	38,000
Senate	13,500	18,000	0	31,500
Democrats	15,000	11,500	500	27,000
No. of Cand.	*11*	*13*	*1*	*25*
House	7,500	10,500	500	18,500
Senate	7,500	1,000	0	8,500
Incumbents	20,500	20,000	2,000	42,500
Challengers	1,000	9,000	0	10,000
Open Seat	16,000	28,000	0	44,000
Winners	29,000	37,500	n/a	66,500
Losers	8,500	19,500	n/a	28,000

Merck & Co.

Phone: (908) 423-1000
1 Merck Dr., Whitehouse Station, N.J. 08889
Web: www.merck.com

One of the world's largest pharmaceutical companies, Merck develops, manufactures and markets a broad range of human and animal health products and services. Merck had sales of $22 billion in 1997. The publicly traded company employs more than 49,000 workers.

The company's industry focus is human and animal health products and services, which includes Merck-Medco Managed Care. Human health products include therapeutic and preventive agents, generally sold by prescription, for the treatment of human disorders. Animal health/crop protection products include medicines used to control and alleviate disease in livestock, small animals and poultry.

Merck & Co. Inc. Political Action Committee (Merck PAC) (C00097485) *Phone: (202) 638-4170 * Fax: (202) 638-3670 * 601 Pennsylvania Ave. N.W., North Building, Suite 1200, Washington, DC 20004 * Treasurer: Michael G. Atieh * Contact: Teel Oliver, V.P. of Gov. Relations*

	1993-94	1995-96	1997	Totals
Receipts	$240,171	$327,476	$235,251	$802,898
Disburse	253,505	302,666	171,070	727,241
Cash	12,921	37,731	103,858	n/a
Contributions	160,800	213,687	114,115	488,602
Republicans	65,900	150,400	75,454	291,754
No. of Cand.	*62*	*102*	*66*	*230*
House	36,900	101,200	39,954	178,054
Senate	29,000	49,200	35,500	113,700
Democrats	94,400	63,287	38,161	195,848
No. of Cand.	*87*	*47*	*39*	*173*
House	66,900	43,787	22,161	132,848
Senate	27,500	19,500	16,000	63,000
Incumbents	135,800	180,537	111,115	427,452
Challengers	4,500	5,700	2,000	12,200
Open Seat	20,500	27,950	1,000	49,450
Winners	128,800	185,037	n/a	313,837
Losers	32,000	28,650	n/a	60,650

National Association for Medical Equipment Services

*Phone: (703) 836-6263 * Fax: (703) 836-6730*
625 Slaters Lane, Suite 200, Alexandria, VA 22314-1171
*Web: www.names.org * E-mail: info@names.org*

The National Association for Medical Equipment Services promotes access to quality home-based health services. Founded in 1982, NAMES represents more than 1,200 home medical equipment manufacturers and services providers, rehabilitation technology suppliers, and regional associations.

NAMES provides its members with industry communications, legislative/regulatory advocacy, educational opportunities, Medicare reimbursement assistance, national conferences and numerous products and services.

In 1998, NAMES urged Congress to encourage Medicare plans to work with home medical equipment providers to provide greater access to home care and services.

National Association for Medical Equipment Services Political Action Committee (NAMESPAC) (C00213520) *Address: same as sponsor * Treasurer: James T. Kelly * Contact: Brian Rasmussen, Chairman*

	1993-94	1995-96	1997	Totals
Receipts	$33,675	$37,145	$50,060	$120,880
Disburse	40,258	37,299	30,194	107,751
Cash	12,448	12,292	22,402	n/a
Contributions	33,174	34,173	30,195	97,542
Republicans	9,820	22,504	14,195	46,519
No. of Cand.	*15*	*23*	*6*	*44*
House	5,320	15,891	6,195	27,406
Senate	4,500	6,613	8,000	19,113
Democrats	23,354	11,669	16,000	51,023
No. of Cand.	*28*	*14*	*11*	*53*
House	19,004	8,669	2,500	30,173
Senate	4,350	3,000	13,500	20,850
Incumbents	31,354	32,423	30,195	93,972
Challengers	500	500	0	1,000
Open Seat	1,320	750	0	2,070
Winners	28,138	30,252	n/a	58,390
Losers	5,036	3,921	n/a	8,957

National Wholesale Druggists Association

*Phone: (703) 787-0000 * Fax: (703) 787-6930*
1821 Michael Faraday Dr., Suite 400, Reston, VA 20190-5348
Web: www.nwda.org

The National Wholesale Druggists Association is a group of full-service drug wholesalers.

The association's membership includes 82 pharmaceutical distributors, operating about 245 distribution centers, as well as 270 manufacturers of pharmaceuticals and over-the-counter drugs and health products. The organization also represents providers of industry-related services and about 30 related international companies.

The organization works to improve relations among suppliers and customer industries, serves as a forum on major industry issues, researches and disseminates information on management practices for drug wholesalers, and monitors legislation and regulations.

National Wholesale Druggists Association Political Action Committee (C00247569) *Address: same as sponsor * Treasurer: Nancy Hanagan * Contact: Ronald J. Streck, President*

	1993-94	1995-96	1997	Totals
Receipts	$11,343	$11,185	$3,040	$25,568
Disburse	12,137	13,152	575	25,864
Cash	20,806	18,841	21,306	n/a
Contributions	6,175	8,200	250	14,625
Republicans	2,450	6,550	250	9,250
No. of Cand.	*4*	*11*	*1*	*16*
House	1,450	4,050	250	5,750
Senate	1,000	2,500	0	3,500
Democrats	3,725	1,650	0	5,375
No. of Cand.	*6*	*4*	*0*	*10*
House	2,925	1,650	0	4,575
Senate	800	0	0	800
Incumbents	4,925	5,900	250	11,075
Challengers	700	750	0	1,450
Open Seat	550	1,550	0	2,100
Winners	4,625	5,650	n/a	10,275
Losers	1,550	2,550	n/a	4,100

Nonprescription Drug Manufacturers Association

*Phone: (202) 429-9260 * Fax: (202) 223-6835*
1150 Connecticut Ave. N.W., Washington, DC 20036
Web: ndmainfo.org

Known as the Proprietary Association until 1989, the Nonprescription Drug Manufacturers Association represents U.S. manufacturers and distributors of nonprescription, over-the-counter medicines.

It has more than 70 active members and 175 associate members marketing close to 95 percent of the OTC medicines on U.S. store shelves. Associate members include testing laboratories, advertising media and manufacturers of bulk chemicals and packaging.

The association is active on issues such as industry codes and guidelines for packaging, labeling and advertising, and promotes a unified national regulation of the industry.

Nonprescription Drug Manufacturers Association's Political Action Committee (C00040584) *Address: same as sponsor * Treasurer: J. Robert Brouse*

	1993-94	1995-96	1997	Totals
Receipts	$51,300	$35,401	$39,075	$125,776
Disburse	54,046	39,739	29,128	122,913
Cash	4,627	289	10,236	n/a
Contributions	52,135	35,650	25,600	113,385
Republicans	29,366	28,150	14,100	71,616
No. of Cand.	*23*	*34*	*23*	*80*
House	18,988	21,550	11,500	52,038
Senate	10,378	6,600	2,600	19,578
Democrats	22,769	7,500	10,500	40,769
No. of Cand.	*21*	*10*	*16*	*47*
House	21,769	7,000	7,500	36,269
Senate	1,000	500	3,000	4,500
Incumbents	49,935	33,550	25,600	109,085
Challengers	1,100	1,000	0	2,100
Open Seat	1,100	1,100	0	2,200
Winners	44,385	32,550	n/a	76,935
Losers	7,750	3,100	n/a	10,850

Novartis AG

Phone: (908) 277-5000
564 Morris Ave., Summit, NJ 07901
Web: www.novartis.com

Novartis AG is a public company formed by the January 1997, $27 billion merger of Ciba-Geigy Limited and Sandoz, which the company claims is the largest corporate merger in history.

The new company, based in Switzerland, works in the health care, nutrition and agricultural industries. Novartis employs about 87,000 people in more than 100 countries. In 1997, the company had group sales of about $21.2 billion and invested nearly $2.4 billion in research and development.

Through its health care division, the company produces pharmaceuticals, consumer health products, generic drugs and ophthalmic products. The division's product line includes Triaminic, Theraflu, Tavist, Maalox, Gas-X and ExLax, as well as treatments for central nervous system disorders; cancer; cardiovascular, metabolic and respiratory diseases; rheumatism and bone diseases; hormone replacement; and dermatological problems.

Novartis says its nutrition division is the largest health food marketer in Europe. In addition, the company says it is second in the world in the medical nutrition industry and, through Gerber, one of the Novartis Group companies, is the world's leader in jarred infant and baby food.

The company's agribusiness division focuses on crop protection, animal health and seeds. Novartis says it has the largest research and development budget in the crop protection industry. In addition, in May 1997, the company agreed to acquire Merck and Co.'s crop protection business for $910 million.

Novartis Employee Good Government Fund (formerly known as Ciba Employee Good Government Fund) (C00033969) *Phone: (202) 293-3019 * Fax: (202) 659-0249 * 2001 Pennsylvania Ave. N.W., Suite 925, Washington, DC 20006 * Treasurer: Lisa Bentley*

*Contact: Paul Sartori, Chairman * Phone: (908) 277-5000*

	1993-94	1995-96	1997	Totals
Receipts	$150,233	$143,062	$74,892	$368,187
Disburse	149,542	139,721	73,117	362,380
Cash	12,122	15,477	17,258	n/a
Contributions	126,713	132,746	62,000	321,459
Republicans	79,463	105,246	45,000	229,709
No. of Cand.	*75*	*108*	*71*	*254*
House	52,963	69,746	30,500	153,209
Senate	26,500	35,500	14,500	76,500
Democrats	46,250	27,500	16,500	90,250
No. of Cand.	*50*	*35*	*22*	*107*
House	42,250	25,500	8,000	75,750
Senate	4,000	2,000	8,500	14,500
Incumbents	114,713	111,746	60,500	286,959
Challengers	2,500	6,500	500	9,500
Open Seat	9,500	14,500	1,000	25,000
Winners	108,213	114,246	n/a	222,459
Losers	18,500	18,500	n/a	37,000

Pfizer Inc.

*Phone: (212) 573-2323 * Fax: (212) 573-7851*
235 E. 42nd St., New York, NY 10017
Web: www.pfizer.com

Pfizer is an international pharmaceutical researcher and producer. It makes consumer products, prescription drugs and health care equipment. The public company is the world's largest producer of veterinary medicine for farm and domestic animals. Pfizer's health care products account for 85 percent of sales. The company had 46,500 employees and $12.5 billion in sales during 1997. Pfizer's products include Ben-Gay, Visine, the antidepressant Zoloft and Bain de Soleil sunscreen.

Chief among Pfizer's policy priorities is preventing health care reform legislation that is damaging to its business. It supports changes that do not target drug makers specifically but distribute costs among providers, consumers and pharmaceutical companies.

Pfizer ranked second among drug company PACs in contributions to 1996 congressional campaigns. The company supported Republicans by nearly a three-to-one margin. The leading recipients were Sens. Gordon H. Smith, R-Ore., Wayne Allard, R-Colo., and former Rep. Dick Zimmer, R-N.J., who lost a Senate race in 1996. Sen. Max Baucus, D-Mont., was the top Democratic recipient.

Pfizer Inc. PAC (C00016683) *Phone: (202) 783-7070 * Fax: (202) 347-2044 * 325 Seventh St. N.W., Suite 1200, Washington, DC 20004 * Treasurer: Alan G. Levin * Contact: Margie Finkelnburg, Assistant Dir. of Gov. Relations*

	1993-94	1995-96	1997	Totals
Receipts	*$427,366*	*$492,429*	*$237,578*	*$1,157,373*
Disburse	424,242	457,531	188,275	1,070,048
Cash	13,352	48,255	97,559	n/a
Contributions	248,042	263,100	139,500	650,642
Republicans	107,342	195,670	96,000	399,012
No. of Cand.	*86*	*136*	*88*	*310*
House	43,950	110,170	58,000	212,120
Senate	63,392	85,500	38,000	186,892
Democrats	140,450	67,430	43,500	251,380
No. of Cand.	103	54	46	203
House	91,900	48,430	27,000	167,330
Senate	48,550	19,000	16,500	84,050
Incumbents	201,650	194,980	129,000	525,630
Challengers	12,000	19,520	2,000	33,520
Open Seat	32,500	48,100	6,500	87,100
Winners	203,900	213,980	n/a	417,880
Losers	44,142	49,120	n/a	93,262

Pharmaceutical Research & Manufacturers of America

*Phone: (202) 835-3400 * Fax: (202) 835-3488*
1100 15th St. N.W., Washington, DC 20005

Pharmaceutical Research & Manufacturers of America represents the views and interests of the pharmaceutical industry. It is active on issues involving health regulations and has a research and development program.

Pharmaceutical Research & Manufacturers of America Better Government Committee (C00021972) *Address: same as sponsor * Treasurer: Joy A. Garrish * Contact: Rich Buckley, PAC Secretary*

	1993-94	1995-96	1997	Totals
Receipts	$34,742	$45,712	$22,927	$103,381
Disburse	38,788	47,222	23,613	109,623
Cash	2,091	686	1,939	n/a
Contributions	36,993	43,152	21,550	101,695
Republicans	17,687	25,002	13,250	55,939
No. of Cand.	*22*	*39*	*16*	*77*
House	8,763	16,157	9,250	34,170
Senate	8,924	8,845	4,000	21,769
Democrats	19,306	18,150	8,300	45,756
No. of Cand.	*28*	*17*	*11*	*56*
House	12,556	7,400	4,300	24,256
Senate	6,750	10,750	4,000	21,500
Incumbents	30,945	38,602	21,550	91,097
Challengers	2,892	500	0	3,392
Open Seat	3,156	4,050	0	7,206
Winners	33,727	38,902	n/a	72,629
Losers	3,266	4,250	n/a	7,516

Pharmacia & Upjohn Inc.

Phone: (616) 833-4000
7000 Portage Rd., 9810-88-19, Kalamazoo, MI 49001-0102
Web: www.pharmacia.se

With 1997 sales of $6.3 billion and 30,000 employees worldwide, Pharmacia & Upjohn is one of the largest pharmaceutical companies in the world. The publicly traded company manufactures and sells prescription pharmaceuticals and over-the-counter products.

The company's focus areas include: incontinence, cancer, AIDS/HIV, impotence, hereditary hair loss, clinical anxiety, glaucoma and smoking cessation. Pharmacia & Upjohn invests about $1 billion annually on research and development.

Pharmacia & Upjohn's products include Rogaine, a hair-growth product; the contraceptive Depo-Provera; Nicotrol and Nicorette, two treatments for smoking-cessation; Genotropin, a growth hormone; and Xanax, which is used for the relief of anxiety and panic attacks.

The company also has businesses in animal health, diagnostics and pharmaceutical commercial services.

The company's principal markets are the United States, Western Europe, Japan, the Pacific Region, Latin America, the Middle East and Canada. Smaller markets are in Eastern Europe, Russia, India, China and South America.

Pharmacia & Upjohn Legislative Support Exchange (C00091942) *Phone: (202) 393-6040 * Fax: (202) 393-6050 * 1455 F St. N.W., Suite 450, Washington, DC 20004 * Treasurer: Robert T. McDonough*

*Contact: Phillip C. Carra, Chairman * Phone: (616) 833-4000*

	1993-94	1995-96	1997	Totals
Receipts	$138,803	$105,919	$41,551	$286,273
Disburse	137,905	140,562	54,033	332,500
Cash	59,071	24,433	11,951	n/a
Contributions	119,480	106,000	44,000	269,480
Republicans	59,500	78,000	31,500	169,000
No. of Cand.	*64*	*81*	*39*	*184*
House	32,000	45,000	17,500	94,500
Senate	27,500	33,000	14,000	74,500
Democrats	59,480	28,000	12,500	99,980

No. of Cand.	*68*	*37*	*17*	*122*
House	41,500	17,500	6,500	65,500
Senate	17,980	10,500	6,000	34,480
Incumbents	91,980	89,500	42,000	223,480
Challengers	7,500	7,000	1,000	15,500
Open Seat	20,000	9,500	1,000	30,500
Winners	102,500	90,500	n/a	193,000
Losers	16,980	15,500	n/a	32,480

Rhone-Poulenc Inc.

Phone: (919) 549-2000

2 T.W. Alexander Dr., Research Triangle Park, NC 27709

Paris-based Rhone-Poulenc manufactures chemicals, polymers, fibers, pharmaceuticals and agricultural chemicals. The company has sales offices and manufacturing facilities, mainly in France, the United States and Canada. With 1997 sales of $15 billion, the publicly traded company employs 68,000 people in 160 countries.

In March 1998, the company was cleared to market Taxatere in 19 countries. The drug is used to treat advanced metastatic breast cancer. In the same month, the company sold two pharmaceutical plants to SPI Polyols Inc. for $20 million. The plants were located in France and Delaware.

The company's main subsidiary is Pennsylvania-based Rhone-Poulenc Rorer.

Rhone-Poulenc Inc. Political Action Committee (RPAC) (C00232330) *Phone: (202) 628-0500 * Fax: (202) 628-6622 * 801 Pennsylvania Ave. N.W., Suite 725, Washington, DC 20004 * Treasurer: Karen B. Glasser*

*Contact: Rick Rountree * Phone: (919) 549-2000*

	1993-94	1995-96	1997	Totals
Receipts	$64,430	$46,042	$18,131	$128,603
Disburse	60,500	50,032	21,045	131,577
Cash	11,434	7,456	4,549	n/a
Contributions	54,500	44,500	20,500	119,500
Republicans	34,500	39,500	11,500	85,500
No. of Cand.	*29*	*43*	*15*	*87*
House	23,000	26,000	7,000	56,000
Senate	11,500	13,500	4,500	29,500
Democrats	20,000	5,000	9,000	34,000
No. of Cand.	*21*	*7*	*11*	*39*
House	13,000	3,000	6,000	22,000
Senate	7,000	2,000	3,000	12,000
Incumbents	51,000	36,500	18,500	106,000
Challengers	2,000	2,000	0	4,000
Open Seat	1,500	6,000	2,000	9,500
Winners	52,000	35,000	n/a	87,000
Losers	2,500	9,500	n/a	12,000

Connaught Laboratories Inc. A Pasteur Merieux Connaught Co. Political Action Committee (C00215236) *Phone: (717) 839-7187 Route 611, Box 187, Swiftwater, PA 18370*

*Phone: (202) 898-3193 * Fax: (202) 371-1107 * 801 Pennsylvania Ave. N.W., Suite 725, Washington, DC 20004 * Treasurer: Damian A. Braga * Contact: Jeff Peterson, Gov. Affairs Dir.*

Pasteur Merieux Connaught North America, formerly Connaught Laboratories Inc., is now a division of Pasteur Merieux Connaught. The company is part of the Rhone-Poulenc Group, a French pharmaceutical company.

Based in Pennsylvania, Pasteur Merieux Connaught North America manufactures and distributes vaccines throughout the United States, Canada and Europe. The company employs about 1,000 people.

Pasteur Merieux Connaught North America, along with the Canadian and European divisions, is the world's largest vaccine manufacturer, producing more than 1 billion doses each year to immunize about 400 million people. Currently, the company produces vaccines for 18 different diseases — more than any other company.

	1993-94	1995-96	1997	Totals
Receipts	$50,897	$73,930	$48,707	$173,534
Disburse	50,250	85,170	38,628	174,048
Cash	23,648	12,412	22,492	n/a
Contributions	32,000	69,750	38,000	139,750
Republicans	24,000	39,250	16,500	79,750
No. of Cand.	*29*	*51*	*22*	*102*
House	12,500	25,750	10,000	48,250
Senate	11,500	13,500	6,500	31,500
Democrats	8,000	30,500	21,500	60,000

No. of Cand.	*9*	*41*	*24*	*74*
House	3,000	16,000	10,000	29,000
Senate	5,000	14,500	11,500	31,000
Incumbents	26,000	54,250	36,500	116,750
Challengers	3,500	3,000	0	6,500
Open Seat	2,000	12,500	1,500	16,000
Winners	28,500	60,750	n/a	89,250
Losers	3,500	9,000	n/a	12,500

Rhone-Poulenc Rorer Inc. PAC (C00113639) *Phone: (610) 454-8366 * Fax: (610) 454-3674 * 500 Arcola Rd., Collegeville, PA 19426 * Web: www.rp-rorer.com * E-mail: paul.baldwin@rp-rorer.com * Treasurer: Paul Baldwin*

*Phone: (202) 682-2442 * Fax: (202) 682-0538 * 801 Pennsylvania Ave. N.W., Suite 725, Washington, DC 20004 * E-mail: mary.mcgrane@rp-rorer.com*

Rhone-Poulenc Rorer is a subsidiary of Rhone-Poulenc. Pennsylvania-based Rhone-Poulenc Rorer, which posted 1997 sales of $5.5 billion, specializes in the manufacture of respiratory, allergy, oncology, thrombosis (blood clotting), cardiology and anti-infective drugs.

Formed in 1990 when the U.S.-based Rorer group merged with Rhone Poulenc's human pharmaceuticals division, the company employs 26,000 people worldwide.

	1993-94	1995-96	1997	Totals
Receipts	$62,928	$45,894	$51,046	$159,868
Disburse	66,989	49,850	16,925	133,764
Cash	8,773	4,822	38,943	n/a
Contributions	51,250	30,900	9,500	91,650
Republicans	46,250	29,650	8,500	84,400
No. of Cand.	*59*	*28*	*9*	*96*
House	27,000	21,650	3,500	52,150
Senate	19,250	8,000	5,000	32,250
Democrats	5,000	1,250	1,000	7,250
No. of Cand.	*6*	*3*	*1*	*10*
House	4,500	500	1,000	6,000
Senate	500	750	0	1,250
Incumbents	7,900	26,650	9,000	43,550
Challengers	20,250	500	500	21,250
Open Seat	20,600	3,750	0	24,350
Winners	38,450	27,400	n/a	65,850
Losers	12,800	3,500	n/a	16,300

Roche Holding AG

*Phone: (650) 855-5567 * Fax: (650) 852-1966*

3401 Hillview Ave., Mailstop A2-225, Palo Alto, CA 94304

Web: www.roche.com/bioscience

Headquartered in Basel, Switzerland, Roche Holding makes pharmaceuticals, diagnostics, vitamins, fine chemicals, fragrances and flavors. The company reported 1997 sales of $12.8 billion and employs about 50,000 people worldwide.

Subsidiary Syntex, a pharmaceutical manufacturer, was purchased by Roche Bioscience in January 1995. The company is headquartered in Palo Alto, Calif. Syntex researches AIDS, tumor metastasis, cardiovascular disease and inflammation.

Roche controls more than 60 percent of the biotechnology company Genentech.

Syntex (USA) Inc. Employee Political Action Committee (C00219790) *Address: same as sponsor * Treasurer: Dennis Kreuser * Contact: Nancy Peterson, Chairperson*

	1993-94	1995-96	1997	Totals
Receipts	$284,022	$27,870	$4,902	$316,794
Disburse	200,598	35,503	33,669	269,770
Cash	158,417	150,796	122,031	n/a
Contributions	163,101	9,500	2,000	174,601
Republicans	55,841	6,000	0	61,841
No. of Cand.	*34*	*6*	*0*	*40*
House	38,350	3,000	0	41,350
Senate	17,491	3,000	0	20,491
Democrats	107,260	3,500	2,000	112,760
No. of Cand.	*48*	*4*	*1*	*53*
House	84,300	3,500	0	87,800
Senate	22,960	0	2,000	24,960
Incumbents	136,652	8,500	2,000	147,152
Challengers	1,000	0	0	1,000
Open Seat	25,449	1,500	0	26,949
Winners	140,141	9,500	n/a	149,641
Losers	22,960	0	n/a	22,960

Hoffmann-La Roche Inc. Good Government Committee (C00072769) *Phone: (201) 235-5000 * Fax: (201) 562-2208 * 340 Kingsland St., Nutley, NJ 07110-1199 * Web: www.roche.com * Treasurer: David P. McDede*

A subsidiary of Roche Holding, Hoffmann-LaRoche has developed several drugs to treat HIV. Products include: Hivid, Invirase, Cytovene, Vitrasert, Roferon-A and Bactrim. Roche also develops HIV-related diagnostic tests.

	1993-94	*1995-96*	*1997*	*Totals*
Receipts	$154,226	$125,426	$72,587	$352,239
Disburse	119,505	161,668	71,681	352,854
Cash	63,411	27,171	28,077	n/a
Contributions	98,850	127,393	56,049	282,292
Republicans	54,850	96,893	36,050	187,793
No. of Cand.	*51*	*68*	*34*	*153*
House	37,950	57,393	20,550	115,893
Senate	16,900	39,500	15,500	71,900
Democrats	44,000	30,500	19,999	94,499
No. of Cand.	*39*	*29*	*17*	*85*
House	28,450	13,750	6,999	49,199
Senate	15,550	16,750	13,000	45,300
Incumbents	85,300	100,143	55,849	241,292
Challengers	7,900	9,000	200	17,100
Open Seat	5,650	18,250	0	23,900
Winners	77,450	105,393	n/a	182,843
Losers	21,400	22,000	n/a	43,400

Schering-Plough Corp.

*Phone: (201) 822-7000 * Fax: (201) 822-7048*
1 Giralda Farm, Madison, NJ 07940-1000
Web: www.sch-plough.com

Schering-Plough develops products for allergic and inflammatory disorders, infectious diseases, oncology and central nervous system diseases. In 1997, Schering-Plough had sales of $6.7 billion. The publicly traded company employs more than 20,000 workers.

Schering-Plough's top-selling products include the Claritin, Proventil, Eulexin, Nitro-Dur (nitroglycerin) and Vancenase product lines. The company's consumer products include Coppertone sun care and Dr. Scholl's foot care products, as well as more than 30 over-the-counter medications, including Tinactin, Drixoral, Afrin, Coricidin and Gyne-Lotrimin.

Schering-Plough Corp. Better Government Fund (C00108290) *Phone: (202) 463-7372 * Fax: (202) 463-8809 * 1850 K St. N.W., Washington, DC 20006 * Treasurer: E. Kevin Moore*

*Contact: Joseph Roth, Dir. of Gov. Affairs * Phone: (201) 822-7000*

	1993-94	*1995-96*	*1997*	*Totals*
Receipts	$194,129	$189,083	$98,420	$481,632
Disburse	206,250	183,775	113,000	503,025
Cash	16,433	21,746	7,168	n/a
Contributions	152,750	134,500	82,000	369,250
Republicans	109,000	101,500	57,000	267,500
No. of Cand.	*42*	*48*	*21*	*111*
House	52,000	52,000	27,000	131,000
Senate	57,000	49,500	30,000	136,500
Democrats	43,750	33,000	25,000	101,750
No. of Cand.	*24*	*17*	*9*	*50*
House	25,000	16,500	9,000	50,500
Senate	18,750	16,500	16,000	51,250
Incumbents	122,000	104,500	81,000	307,500
Challengers	14,750	6,000	0	20,750
Open Seat	15,750	23,500	1,000	40,250
Winners	120,000	94,000	n/a	214,000
Losers	32,750	40,500	n/a	73,250

Shaklee Corp.

Phone: (415) 954-3000
444 Market St., San Francisco, CA 94111
*Web: www.shaklee.com * E-mail: shaklead@slip.net*

Shaklee is a privately owned direct selling company that manufactures and distributes nutritional supplements, personal care and household products and water treatment devices.

Shaklee Corp. Federal Good Government Fund (C00126805) *Address: same as sponsor * Treasurer: Evelyn Jarvis-Ferris*

	1993-94	*1995-96*	*1997*	*Totals*
Receipts	$19,496	$20,364	$8,892	$48,752
Disburse	24,764	16,700	3,000	44,464
Cash	7,134	10,802	16,695	n/a
Contributions	21,750	14,500	1,500	37,750
Republicans	14,500	9,500	1,000	25,000
No. of Cand.	*10*	*13*	*1*	*24*
House	2,000	4,500	0	6,500
Senate	12,500	5,000	1,000	18,500
Democrats	7,250	5,000	500	12,750
No. of Cand.	*10*	*7*	*1*	*18*
House	3,750	2,500	500	6,750
Senate	3,500	2,500	0	6,000
Incumbents	16,250	8,500	1,500	26,250
Challengers	1,500	2,500	0	4,000
Open Seat	4,000	3,500	0	7,500
Winners	20,750	11,000	n/a	31,750
Losers	1,000	3,500	n/a	4,500

Contributed less than $5,000 during 1995-96 cycle:

Bear Creek Corp. Political Action Committee (C00298885) *Phone: (541) 776-2362 * Fax: (541) 776-2194 * 2518 S. Pacific Highway, Medford, OR 97501 * Web: www.harryanddavid.com * Treasurer: John C. Dailey*

SmithKline Beecham

*Phone: (215) 751-5046 * Fax: (215) 751-5355*
One Franklin Plaza, P.O. Box 7929, Philadelphia, PA 19101
Web: www.sb.com

SmithKline Beecham develops, manufactures and markets pharmaceuticals, vaccines, over-the-counter medicines and health-related consumer products. It also provides health care services including disease management, clinical laboratory testing and pharmaceutical benefit management. The publicly held company reported more than $12.7 billion in 1997 sales.

SmithKline Beecham is a core pharmaceutical company with two central businesses — consumer health care and health care services. SB markets more than 400 branded products, including Seroxat/Paxil, the fastest-growing antidepressant in its class; Augmentin, an antibiotic; and Aquafresh, which makes toothbrushes and toothpaste.

The company announced in February 1998 that a proposed merger with Glaxo Wellcome would not take place.

SmithKline Beecham employs 53,000 people worldwide and has operations in 160 countries.

SmithKline Beecham Political Action Committee (SB-PAC) (C00009928) *Phone: (202) 452-8495 * 1020 19th St. N.W., Washington, DC 20036 * Treasurer: Norman J. Vojir*

	1993-94	*1995-96*	*1997*	*Totals*
Receipts	$131,849	$174,960	$89,146	$395,955
Disburse	137,970	176,022	81,375	395,367
Cash	10,668	9,605	17,377	n/a
Contributions	120,920	134,400	104,750	360,070
Republicans	56,250	94,750	68,750	219,750
No. of Cand.	*54*	*87*	*54*	*195*
House	24,250	54,750	43,000	122,000
Senate	32,000	40,000	25,750	97,750
Democrats	64,670	39,650	36,000	140,320
No. of Cand.	*63*	*39*	*30*	*132*
House	37,550	26,150	22,500	86,200
Senate	27,120	13,500	13,500	54,120
Incumbents	91,170	93,800	101,250	286,220
Challengers	4,250	9,850	2,000	16,100
Open Seat	24,500	29,750	1,500	55,750
Winners	90,050	110,050	n/a	200,100
Losers	30,870	24,350	n/a	55,220

St. Jude Medical Inc.

*Phone: (612) 483-2000 * Fax: (612) 490-4344*
One Lillehei Plaza, St. Paul, MN 55117-9983
Web: www.sjm.com

St. Jude Medical develops and sells medical devices for people with heart ailments. The publicly traded company makes mechanical heart valves, pacemaker components and exploratory devices. With 1997 sales of $994 million and 3,600 employees, St. Jude Medical's products are sold in more than 100 countries.

In recent years St. Jude Medical has merged with Daig and acquired Pacesetter, Ventritex, Telectronics and Medtel.

St. Jude Medical Inc. Political Action Committee (C00305029)
*Address: same as sponsor * Treasurer: Peter L. Gove*

	1993-94	1995-96	1997	Totals
Receipts	$0	$24,569	$90	$24,659
Disburse	0	17,911	4,000	21,911
Cash	0	6,657	2,747	n/a
Contributions	0	14,811	2,000	16,811
Republicans	0	10,711	2,000	12,711
No. of Cand.	*0*	*10*	*3*	*13*
House	0	7,211	2,000	9,211
Senate	0	3,500	0	3,500
Democrats	0	4,100	0	4,100
No. of Cand.	*0*	*5*	*0*	*5*
House	0	2,100	0	2,100
Senate	0	2,000	0	2,000
Incumbents	0	10,811	2,000	12,811
Challengers	0	3,500	0	3,500
Open Seat	0	500	0	500
Winners	0	10,811	n/a	10,811
Losers	0	4,000	n/a	4,000

United States Surgical Corp.

*Phone: (203) 845-1000 * Fax: (203) 845-5988*
150 Glover Ave., Norwalk, CT 06856
Web: www.ussurg.com

United States Surgical is the largest maker of minimally invasive surgical stapling products and a leading maker of laparoscopic products and breast biopsy instruments. It posted 1997 sales of $1.2 billion, and the publicly traded company employs more than 5,500 people worldwide.

The company's products include single-use and reusable surgical staplers and staples, absorbable ligation clips and trocars used in laparoscopic surgery.

In January 1998, USSC acquired Valleylab from Pfizer Inc. for $425 million. Valleylab manufactures electrosurgical and ultrasonic equipment.

Also in 1998, the company's vascular therapies division signed a worldwide product development, sales and distribution agreement with Chase Medical for cannulae and ancillary products used in cardiovascular surgery. USSC also is developing technology such as AngioRad Radiation to treat coronary artery disease.

United States Surgical Corp. Health PAC (C00302257) *Address: same as sponsor * Treasurer: Scott Spitzer * Contact: Thomas Bremer, General Counsel*

	1993-94	1995-96	1997	Totals
Receipts	$0	$64,109	$62,496	$126,605
Disburse	0	54,720	52,165	106,885
Cash	0	9,391	19,723	n/a
Contributions	0	22,000	31,500	53,500
Republicans	0	12,500	19,500	32,000
No. of Cand.	*0*	*10*	*14*	*24*
House	0	3,000	7,500	10,500
Senate	0	9,500	12,000	21,500
Democrats	0	9,500	12,000	21,500
No. of Cand.	*0*	*12*	*8*	*20*
House	0	5,000	3,000	8,000
Senate	0	4,500	9,000	13,500
Incumbents	0	12,500	31,500	44,000
Challengers	0	7,000	0	7,000
Open Seat	0	2,500	0	2,500
Winners	0	14,000	n/a	14,000
Losers	0	8,000	n/a	8,000

Warner-Lambert Co.

*Phone: (973) 540-3822 * Fax: (973) 540-3930*
201 Tabor Rd., Morris Plains, NJ 07950
*Web: www.warner-lambert.com * E-mail: wwodsow@mops.wl.com*

Maker of well-known brands such as Listerine, Clorets and Sudafed, publicly traded Warner-Lambert is engaged in three primary areas of business — pharmaceutical products, consumer health care products and confectionery goods. The New Jersey company has a large international presence with 55 percent of its revenue coming from abroad. Only 35 percent of the company's 38,000 employees work in the United States. Warner-Lambert posted 1997 sales of $8.1 billion.

The company makes over-the-counter health care, shaving and pet care products. The confectionery products unit makes chewing gums, breath mints and hard candies. Pharmaceutical products, which represent Warner-Lambert's biggest business, include heartburn remedy Zantac 75, which is made in a joint venture with Glaxo-Wellcome. Warner-Lambert also has an alliance with Pfizer drug company.

The company's cholesterol-lowering medication, Lipitor, produced by subsidiary Parke-Davis, was recently noted as the first pharmaceutical product ever to achieve $1 billion in worldwide sales in its first year on the market.

Product names include: Schick and Wilkinson Sword wet-shave products, Halls, Bubbaloo, Lipitor, Listerine, Trident, Dentyne, Clorets, Sudafed, oral contraceptive Loestrin, Certs, Lubriderm, Tetra aquarium products and Benadryl.

U.S. plant locations include: Greenwood, S.C.; Lititz, Pa.; Vega Baja, Puerto Rico; Rockford, Ill.; Milford, Conn.; and Blacksburg, Va.

Warner-Lambert Co. Political Action Committee (WALPAC) (C00198184) *Phone: (202) 862-3840 * Fax: (202) 296-0623 * 1667 K St. N.W., Suite 1270, Washington, DC 20006 * Treasurer: William S. Woodson*

	1993-94	1995-96	1997	Totals
Receipts	$92,710	$106,656	$51,769	$251,135
Disburse	111,356	81,950	33,510	226,816
Cash	9,747	34,453	52,710	n/a
Contributions	70,668	64,783	32,500	167,951
Republicans	30,978	33,165	15,500	79,643
No. of Cand.	*25*	*28*	*19*	*72*
House	14,525	20,015	11,500	46,040
Senate	16,453	13,150	4,000	33,603
Democrats	39,690	31,618	17,000	88,308
No. of Cand.	*35*	*22*	*15*	*72*
House	25,830	9,250	6,000	41,080
Senate	13,860	22,368	11,000	47,228
Incumbents	58,147	46,883	32,000	137,030
Challengers	3,000	8,750	0	11,750
Open Seat	9,021	9,150	500	18,671
Winners	59,208	45,883	n/a	105,091
Losers	11,460	18,900	n/a	30,360

Ideological/Single-Issue

Abortion Policy/Pro-Choice

Minnesota Women's Campaign Fund

*Phone: (612) 904-6723 * Fax: (612) 397-9725*
112 N. Third St., #203, Minneapolis, MN 55401-1650

The Minnesota Women's Campaign Fund supports the election of qualified pro-choice women to public office, regardless of party affiliation. Almost all of the candidates the group has supported hail from Minnesota.

Founded in 1982, the campaign fund now has more than 650 contributors.

Minnesota Women's Campaign Fund (C00282327) *Address: same as sponsor * Treasurer: Sharon R. Frank * Contact: Karla Ekdahl, President*

	1993-94	1995-96	1997	Totals
Receipts	$144,845	$242,015	$120,082	$506,942
Disburse	141,251	216,084	117,344	474,679
Cash	3,594	29,524	32,262	n/a
Contributions	28,500	15,000	5,000	48,500
Republicans	14,500	5,000	0	19,500
No. of Cand.	*3*	*1*	*0*	*4*
House	9,500	0	0	9,500
Senate	5,000	5,000	0	10,000
Democrats	1,000	10,000	5,000	16,000
No. of Cand.	*1*	*1*	*1*	*3*
House	0	10,000	5,000	15,000
Senate	1,000	0	0	1,000
Incumbents	0	5,000	0	5,000
Challengers	4,500	10,000	5,000	19,500
Open Seat	24,000	0	0	24,000
Winners	0	0	n/a	0
Losers	28,500	15,000	n/a	43,500

National Abortion and Reproductive Rights Action League (NARAL)

*Phone: (202) 973-3050 * Fax: (202) 973-3097*
1156 15th St. N.W., Suite 700, Washington, DC 20005
*Web: www.naral.org * E-mail: kregula@naral.org*

NARAL is an abortion-rights organization with about 500,000 members and 35 state affiliates. It contributes to political campaigns and provides a range of candidate services, including polling, advertising and organizing. Founded in 1969, the group is headed by Kate Michelman.

The group supports increased federal funding for family planning programs and public education campaigns. It advocates wider access to contraceptives and full coverage from private health insurance plans for contraceptives. It opposes measures that would require women to notify their spouses before getting an abortion. NARAL also opposes a ban on "partial-birth" abortions.

NARAL was the leading abortion-rights PAC contributor to 1996 congressional races. Democrats received almost 97 percent of the group's contributions. The leading recipients were Rep. Ken Bentsen, D-Texas, Sen. Paul Wellstone, D-Minn., and Rep. Elizabeth Furse, D-Ore. The top Republican recipient was Rep. Sue W. Kelly, R-N.Y.

National Abortion and Reproductive Rights Action League PAC (C00079541) *Address: same as sponsor * Treasurer: Gloria A. Totten * Contact: Kristin Regula, Manager*

	1993-94	1995-96	1997	Totals
Receipts	$711,661	$548,698	$151,704	$1,412,063
Disburse	772,903	589,302	154,977	1,517,182
Cash	128,966	108,823	105,552	n/a
Contributions	461,941	302,027	64,834	828,802
Republicans	34,921	8,250	2,000	45,171
No. of Cand.	*14*	*4*	*3*	*21*
House	23,000	8,250	2,000	33,250
Senate	11,921	0	0	11,921
Democrats	421,520	292,777	62,834	777,131
No. of Cand.	*180*	*141*	*73*	*394*
House	331,417	228,224	51,917	611,558
Senate	90,103	64,553	10,917	165,573
Incumbents	297,071	123,764	58,561	479,396
Challengers	62,548	102,738	4,217	169,503
Open Seat	104,822	71,579	2,000	178,401
Winners	236,825	192,669	n/a	429,494
Losers	225,116	109,358	n/a	334,474

Contributed less than $5,000 during 1995-96 cycle:

National Abortion Rights Action League of North Carolina PAC (NARAL-NC PAC) (C00167361) *Phone: (919) 687-4959 * P.O. Box 0908, 327 W. Main St., Durham, NC 27702 * Treasurer: Kathryn Wellman*

New York Choice PAC II

Phone: (212) 517-3522
1202 Lexington Ave., Box 246, New York, NY 10028

New York Choice PAC II, formerly Citizens for Family Planning II, is a bipartisan federal PAC that supports pro-abortion rights candidates from the state of New York.

New York Choice PAC I is the group's state PAC.

New York Choice PAC II (formerly known as Citizens for Family Planning II) (C00146472) *Address: same as sponsor * Treasurer: Shelby White * Contact: Jane Havemeyer, PAC Dir.*

	1993-94	1995-96	1997	Totals
Receipts	$14,825	$31,220	$11,075	$57,120
Disburse	19,466	31,500	9	50,975
Cash	2,518	2,238	13,304	n/a
Contributions	8,750	31,000	0	39,750
Republicans	1,000	4,000	0	5,000
No. of Cand.	*1*	*4*	*0*	*5*
House	1,000	4,000	0	5,000
Senate	0	0	0	0
Democrats	7,750	27,000	0	34,750
No. of Cand.	*6*	*8*	*0*	*14*
House	7,750	27,000	0	34,750
Senate	0	0	0	0
Incumbents	6,250	11,500	0	17,750
Challengers	1,500	19,500	0	21,000
Open Seat	1,000	0	0	1,000
Winners	5,250	19,500	n/a	24,750
Losers	3,500	11,500	n/a	15,000

Our Choice II

Phone: (313) 663-7025
P.O. Box 7710, Ann Arbor, MI 48107

Our Choice II is a federal PAC that gives to pro-abortion rights candidates with good environmental records.

The PAC generally gives to Democratic contenders.

Our Choice II (C00267096) *Address: same as sponsor * Treasurer: Naomi Gottlieb * Contact: Lena Pollack, Chairperson*

	1993-94	1995-96	1997	Totals
Receipts	$6,133	$35,505	$0	$41,638
Disburse	4,044	35,217	758	40,019
Cash	2,473	2,760	2,002	n/a
Contributions	3,530	24,280	0	27,810
Republicans	0	0	0	0
No. of Cand.	*0*	*0*	*0*	*0*
House	0	0	0	0
Senate	0	0	0	0
Democrats	3,500	24,280	0	27,780
No. of Cand.	*8*	*12*	*0*	*20*
House	2,500	21,300	0	23,800
Senate	1,000	2,980	0	3,980
Incumbents	1,500	10,000	0	11,500
Challengers	0	11,800	0	11,800
Open Seat	2,030	3,500	0	5,530
Winners	1,750	23,300	n/a	25,050
Losers	1,780	980	n/a	2,760

Republican Pro-Choice PAC

*Phone: (212) 207-8266 * Fax: (212) 207-8629*
57 W. 57th St., Suite 712, New York, NY 10019
E-mail: rpcn@aol.com

The Republican Pro-Choice PAC supports pro-abortion rights Republican candidates in federal elections and some state elections. Candidates are chosen for their viability as well as for their support of abortion rights.

The PAC is a new organization, founded in late 1995, but has already made an impact. Because it "bundles" contributions, acting as a conduit through which individuals contribute directly to campaigns, it is difficult to determine the full amount raised for candidates. The PAC's political director estimated that more than $250,000 was distributed by the organization during the 1995-96 election cycle.

Besides using direct mailings and telemarketing to contact and mobilize supporters, the PAC also holds private fundraising events for individual candidates. In February 1998, Sen. Olympia Snowe, R-Maine, was the beneficiary of one such event that brought in more than $60,000.

RPC-PAC was part of a coalition that in January 1998 helped defeat the passage of an anti-abortion plank in the Republican Party platform. The proposed rule would have kept party members who supported abortion rights from receiving any party money. RPC-PAC, along with Republicans for Choice and other like-minded groups, staged a successful grassroots mobilization and media blitz to prevent the plank's adoption.

Republican Pro-Choice Political Action Committee (C00307272) *Address: same as sponsor * Treasurer: Jeffrey E. Livingston * Contact: Lynn Grefe, Political Dir.*

	1993-94	1995-96	1997	Totals
Receipts	$0	$143,780	$53,900	$197,680
Disburse	0	137,935	43,787	181,722
Cash	0	5,844	15,956	n/a
Contributions	0	28,000	2,433	30,433
Republicans	0	28,000	2,433	30,433
No. of Cand.	*0*	*49*	*7*	*56*
House	0	20,500	2,433	22,933
Senate	0	7,500	0	7,500
Democrats	0	0	0	0
No. of Cand.	*0*	*0*	*0*	*0*
House	0	0	0	0
Senate	0	0	0	0
Incumbents	0	6,750	2,433	9,183
Challengers	0	11,650	0	11,650
Open Seat	0	9,600	0	9,600
Winners	0	7,750	n/a	7,750
Losers	0	20,250	n/a	20,250

Republicans for Choice

*Phone: (703) 960-9882 * Fax: (703) 960-9885*
2760 Eisenhower Ave., Suite 260, Alexandria, VA 22314
*Web: www.rfc-pac.org * E-mail: GOP4Choice@aol.com*

Republicans for Choice aims to be a "big tent political action committee" that supports and unites all party members who are for abortion rights. RFC opposes any attempt by Republicans to amend the Constitution to prohibit abortion or to limit the freedoms set forth in Roe v. Wade.

RFC's other stated goals are to build an abortion-rights majority in the party through grassroots support and to raise money to back candidates who share its views. RFC supports candidates running for all levels of government on the basis of their proven commitment to abortion rights, their viability and support of the GOP.

At the January 1998 party convention, Republicans faced a vote on a measure that would have required candidates to pledge to oppose abortion rights in order to receive party money. RFC led the charge to defeat the measure by sponsoring radio ads and working with other abortion-rights organizations.

RFC was founded in the late 1980s by Chairman Ann Stone, then-Rep. Susan Molinari, R-N.Y., and Harriet Stinson. It now claims almost 200,000 members nationwide.

Republicans for Choice (C00241083) *Address: same as sponsor * Treasurer: Ann E. W. Stone*

	1993-94	1995-96	1997	Totals
Receipts	$240,534	$990,475	$1,013,639	$2,244,648
Disburse	242,120	992,863	257,505	1,492,488
Cash	1,052	88	783,861	n/a
Contributions	4,440	63,951	1,059	69,450
Republicans	4,440	63,951	1,059	69,450
No. of Cand.	*15*	*46*	*3*	*64*
House	1,624	40,855	939	43,418
Senate	2,816	23,096	120	26,032
Democrats	0	0	0	0
No. of Cand.	*0*	*0*	*0*	*0*
House	0	0	0	0
Senate	0	0	0	0
Incumbents	2,212	13,464	1,059	16,735
Challengers	1,476	14,054	0	15,530
Open Seat	257	36,433	0	36,690
Winners	2,562	17,772	n/a	20,334
Losers	1,878	46,179	n/a	48,057

Voters for Choice/Friends of Family Planning

*Phone: (202) 588-5200 * Fax: (202) 588-0600*
P.O. Box 53301, Suite 201, Washington, DC 20009-9301
*Web: www.voters4choice.org * E-mail: vfc@ibm.net*

Voters for Choice is an independent, pro-abortion rights organization founded in 1979 by Gloria Steinem and members of Planned Parenthood. Its purpose is to defend "reproductive freedom" and support like-minded candidates nationwide.

In addition to direct contributions, the group offers candidates guides on talking about abortion rights, as well as in-kind and independent expenditures. It spent more than $100,000 in indirect contributions in support of Democratic candidates in 1995-96. Steinem, the group's president, also campaigns for selected candidates during a six-week period leading up to an election.

While Voters for Choice spent more than $1 million during the 1995-96 cycle, just 20 percent of that total went to candidates for federal office. When it did give directly to congressional candidates, this committee usually backed winning Democrats. Its top recipients were Sen. Paul Wellstone, D-Minn., Sen. Mary Landrieu, D-La., Rep. Elizabeth Furse, D-Ore., and the late Rep. Walter Capps, D-Calif.

Voters for Choice/Friends of Family Planning (C00109355) *Address: same as sponsor * Treasurer: Mary Jean Collins * Contact: Julie Burton, Executive Dir.*

	1993-94	1995-96	1997	Totals
Receipts	$1,050,182	$1,230,575	$331,098	$2,611,855
Disburse	1,036,229	1,178,929	251,524	2,466,682
Cash	41,042	24,277	103,762	n/a
Contributions	180,420	240,432	18,040	438,892
Republicans	2,500	6,000	0	8,500
No. of Cand.	*5*	*4*	*0*	*9*
House	2,500	4,500	0	7,000
Senate	0	1,500	0	1,500
Democrats	173,920	231,403	18,040	423,363
No. of Cand.	*106*	*116*	*8*	*230*
House	129,250	160,040	7,000	296,290
Senate	44,670	71,363	11,040	127,073
Incumbents	109,420	72,744	13,040	195,204
Challengers	26,000	92,133	0	118,133
Open Seat	45,000	75,055	5,000	125,055
Winners	58,250	149,236	n/a	207,486
Losers	122,170	91,196	n/a	213,366

WISH List

*Phone: (800) 756-9474 * Fax: (202) 342-9190*
3205 N St. N.W., Washington, DC 20007
*Web: www.thewishlist.org * E-mail: thewishlist@aol.com*

The WISH List, which stands for "Women in the Senate and House," is a donor network created to support Republican women candidates who support abortion rights. In particular, the organization chooses women in strategic races, who have strong campaign organizations and who have a previously demonstrated ability to raise money. Some recent beneficiaries are New Jersey Gov. Christine Todd Whitman and Sens. Kay Bailey Hutchison, R-Texas, and Olympia Snowe, R-Maine.

WISH List is similar in structure to EMILY's List; members contribute a minimum $100 membership fee to the organization and are then asked to contribute to at least two recommended candidates. The network has swelled to more than 3,000 members since its founding in 1992.

WISH List (C00258277) *Address: same as sponsor * Treasurer: Kendall Wilson * Contact: Karen Raye, Executive Dir.*

	1993-94	1995-96	1997	Totals
Receipts	$462,658	$504,512	$261,997	$1,229,167
Disburse	438,815	505,812	204,587	1,149,214
Cash	28,700	27,396	84,804	n/a
Contributions	131,416	75,140	12,415	218,971
Republicans	128,116	75,140	12,415	215,671
No. of Cand.	*33*	*21*	*11*	*65*
House	97,059	48,743	8,077	153,879
Senate	31,057	26,397	4,338	61,792
Democrats	3,300	0	0	3,300
No. of Cand.	*1*	*0*	*0*	*1*
House	3,300	0	0	3,300
Senate	0	0	0	0
Incumbents	19,950	12,686	5,000	37,636
Challengers	41,007	20,201	4,838	66,046
Open Seat	70,459	42,253	2,577	115,289
Winners	32,464	17,601	n/a	50,065
Losers	98,952	57,539	n/a	156,491

Women in Leadership

*Phone: (714) 451-3800 * Fax: (714) 475-4628*
4 Park Plaza, Suite 1700, Irvine, CA 92614
E-mail: kclark@gdclaw.com

Women in Leadership is a pro-abortion rights PAC that supports "moderate" women who run for office at the local, state or federal level. It is a bipartisan group with 124 members.

The group is based in Orange County, Calif., a traditionally conservative area.

Women In Leadership (C00283432) *Address: same as sponsor * Treasurer: Jinx Hack Ring * Contact: Karen Clark, Chairperson*

	1993-94	1995-96	1997	Totals
Receipts	$24,457	$34,404	$21,047	$79,908
Disburse	20,699	34,429	14,365	69,493
Cash	3,755	3,725	10,406	n/a
Contributions	0	5,599	1,000	6,599
Republicans	0	0	1,000	1,000
No. of Cand.	*0*	*0*	*1*	*1*
House	0	0	1,000	1,000
Senate	0	0	0	0
Democrats	0	5,599	0	5,599
No. of Cand.	*0*	*1*	*0*	*1*
House	0	5,599	0	5,599
Senate	0	0	0	0
Incumbents	0	0	0	0
Challengers	0	5,599	1,000	6,599
Open Seat	0	0	0	0
Winners	0	5,599	n/a	5,599
Losers	0	0	n/a	0

Abortion Policy/Pro-Life

California Right to Life

*Phone: (805) 685-5721 * Fax: (805) 685-5721*
450 A St., Second Floor, San Diego, CA 92101
E-mail: right2life@grid.net

California Right to Life, an independent PAC not associated with National Right to Life, is an anti-abortion, anti-euthanasia PAC that funds candidates running in California races.

The bipartisan committee publishes endorsement sheets and solicits its funding through direct mail.

California Right to Life Political Action Committee (C00117440) *Address: same as sponsor * Treasurer: Mimi Streett * Contact: Susan Peters, Executive Dir.*

	1993-94	1995-96	1997	Totals
Receipts	$5,735	$25,312	$20,211	$51,258
Disburse	12,247	22,758	23,288	58,293
Cash	747	3,301	224	n/a
Contributions	3,000	8,000	1,500	12,500
Republicans	3,000	8,000	1,500	12,500
No. of Cand.	*3*	*3*	*1*	*7*
House	2,500	8,000	1,500	12,000
Senate	500	0	0	500
Democrats	0	0	0	0
No. of Cand.	*0*	*0*	*0*	*0*
House	0	0	0	0
Senate	0	0	0	0
Incumbents	0	6,000	0	6,000
Challengers	1,500	2,000	0	3,500
Open Seat	1,500	0	1,500	3,000
Winners	1,500	0	n/a	1,500
Losers	1,500	8,000	n/a	9,500

National Right to Life Committee

*Phone: (202) 626-8800 * Fax: (202) 984-4256*
419 Seventh St. N.W., Suite 500, Washington, DC 20004
*Web: www.nrlc.org * E-mail: nrlc@nrlc.org*

Since its founding in 1973, after the landmark Roe v. Wade decision, the National Right to Life Committee has grown to incorporate more than 3,000 state and local chapters. Many affiliated chapters support their own associated PACs.

NRLC is dedicated to the protection of life from fertilization to natural death. It advocates legislation banning abortion and euthanasia and providing alternatives to abortion. The group works to support these causes through legislation and education.

NRLC has also taken a position against recent attempts at campaign reform, including proposed restrictions on issue advocacy. The organization claims the limitations would be in violation of the First Amendment and would be crippling to the anti-abortion effort.

National Right to Life Political Action Committee (C00111278)
*Address: same as sponsor * Treasurer: Amarie Natividad * Contact: David N. O'Steen, Executive Dir.*

	1993-94	1995-96	1997	Totals
Receipts	$1,407,973	$2,491,583	$471,154	$4,370,710
Disburse	1,399,624	2,230,796	262,267	3,892,687
Cash	117,519	378,305	587,192	n/a
Contributions	202,509	155,577	28,219	386,305
Republicans	170,981	142,425	23,719	337,125
No. of Cand.	*210*	*329*	*28*	*567*
House	121,456	71,687	19,719	212,862
Senate	49,525	70,738	4,000	124,263
Democrats	25,528	13,152	4,500	43,180
No. of Cand.	*27*	*17*	*3*	*47*
House	24,528	13,152	3,500	41,180
Senate	1,000	0	1,000	2,000
Incumbents	75,086	83,072	16,516	174,674
Challengers	54,139	41,096	2,703	97,938
Open Seat	76,159	27,393	8,000	111,552
Winners	131,635	83,052	n/a	214,687
Losers	70,874	72,525	n/a	143,399

Right to Life of Michigan Political Action Committee (C00101212) *Phone: (616) 532-2300 * Fax: (616) 532-3461 * 2340 Porter S.W., P.O. Box 901, Grand Rapids, MI 49509 * Web: www.rtl.org * E-mail: info@rtl.org * Treasurer: Judith Lachniet * Contact: Jane Muldoon, Chairperson*

The Right to Life of Michigan PAC is the political arm of the Right to Life of Michigan organization. RLM PAC supports anti-abortion candidates at all levels of government. It has a policy to support any Michigan incumbent who opposes abortion, but will also give money to like-minded challengers or open-seat candidates who answer its questionnaire and go through an interview process.

RLM is the parent group to more than 100 statewide affiliates. Originally founded in 1972 as "Voice of the Unborn," RLM is now affiliated with the National Right to Life organization but sets its own policy guidelines. RLM also opposes euthanasia and infanticide. Unlike the national committee, RLM has not taken a position on campaign reform.

	1993-94	1995-96	1997	Totals
Receipts	$106,196	$251,745	$146	$358,087
Disburse	106,108	251,222	525	357,855
Cash	468	991	612	n/a
Contributions	7,000	24,165	0	31,165
Republicans	4,000	20,901	0	24,901
No. of Cand.	*3*	*5*	*0*	*8*
House	4,000	11,276	0	15,276
Senate	0	9,625	0	9,625
Democrats	3,000	3,264	0	6,264
No. of Cand.	*2*	*3*	*0*	*5*
House	3,000	3,264	0	6,264
Senate	0	0	0	0
Incumbents	3,000	5,264	0	8,264
Challengers	2,000	18,901	0	20,901
Open Seat	2,000	0	0	2,000
Winners	3,000	3,264	n/a	6,264
Losers	4,000	20,901	n/a	24,901

New York State Right to Life Political Action Committee (C00105080) *Phone: (518) 434-1293 * Fax: (518) 426-1200 * 41 State St., Suite M-108, Albany, NY 12207 * Treasurer: Warren G. Sweeney * Contact: William J. Doyle, Chairperson*

The N.Y. State Right to Life Committee is the New York chapter of the 3,000-affiliate National Right to Life Committee, the nation's largest anti-abortion organization.

The group has spoken out against President Clinton's 1997 veto of the partial-birth abortion bill.

	1993-94	1995-96	1997	Totals
Receipts	$13,214	$64,398	$1,977	$79,589
Disburse	32,304	64,865	371	97,540
Cash	6,704	6,237	7,843	n/a
Contributions	0	17,489	350	17,839
Republicans	0	17,489	350	17,839
No. of Cand.	*0*	*4*	*2*	*6*
House	0	17,489	350	17,839
Senate	0	0	0	0
Democrats	0	0	0	0
No. of Cand.	*0*	*0*	*0*	*0*
House	0	0	0	0
Senate	0	0	0	0
Incumbents	0	7,904	350	8,254
Challengers	0	9,585	0	9,585
Open Seat	0	0	0	0
Winners	0	3,250	n/a	3,250
Losers	0	14,239	n/a	14,239

Right to Life/Oregon PAC (RTL/O PAC) (C00141572) *Phone: (503) 463-8563 * Fax: (503) 463-8564 * 4335 River Rd. N., Salem, OR 97303 * Web: www.ortl.org * E-mail: ortl@ortl.org * Treasurer: Sharon I. Rueda * Contact: Nedora Counts, Chairperson*

The Right to Life/Oregon PAC is one of two PACs supported by the Oregon Right to Life organization. The RTL/O PAC gives money and grassroots help to candidates at all levels of government who support anti-abortion legislation.

Oregon Right to Life was founded in 1970, and is affiliated with the National Right to Life committee. There are at least 35 local affiliates in the state.

	1993-94	1995-96	1997	Totals
Receipts	$541,073	$164,817	$3,782	$709,672
Disburse	544,406	246,115	4,746	795,267
Cash	97,678	16,381	15,417	n/a
Contributions	23,693	16,800	0	40,493
Republicans	22,693	16,800	0	39,493
No. of Cand.	*4*	*5*	*0*	*9*
House	22,693	10,800	0	33,493
Senate	0	6,000	0	6,000
Democrats	1,000	0	0	1,000
No. of Cand.	*1*	*0*	*0*	*1*
House	1,000	0	0	1,000
Senate	0	0	0	0
Incumbents	0	5,300	0	5,300
Challengers	9,577	5,500	0	15,077
Open Seat	14,116	6,000	0	20,116
Winners	13,116	6,500	n/a	19,616
Losers	10,577	10,300	n/a	20,877

Minnesota Citizens Concerned for Life Committee for a Pro-Life Congress (C00129171) *Phone: (612) 825-6831 * Fax: (612) 825-5527 * 4249 Nicollet Ave. S., Minneapolis, MN 55409 * Web: www.mccl-inc.org * E-mail: mccl@juno.com * Treasurer: Jacqueline A. Schweitz*

The Minnesota Citizens Concerned for Life Committee for a Pro-Life Congress is the federal PAC of Minnesota's anti-abortion organization.

MCCL claims 176 chapters statewide and 50,000 member families who are dedicated to ending legalized abortion and euthanasia through education and grassroots mobilization and action. MCCL also has taken a stance against campaign finance limitations.

The MCCL PAC was formed in 1980 and backs candidates who support an anti-abortion rights agenda.

	1993-94	1995-96	1997	Totals
Receipts	$204,698	$193,989	$10	$398,697
Disburse	228,236	202,396	6,206	436,838
Cash	16,098	7,686	1,488	n/a
Contributions	17,600	13,915	0	31,515
Republicans	10,500	13,915	0	24,415
No. of Cand.	*8*	*3*	*0*	*11*
House	10,200	8,915	0	19,115
Senate	300	5,000	0	5,300
Democrats	7,100	0	0	7,100
No. of Cand.	*2*	*0*	*0*	*2*
House	7,100	0	0	7,100
Senate	0	0	0	0
Incumbents	0	2,935	0	2,935
Challengers	5,000	10,980	0	15,980
Open Seat	12,600	0	0	12,600
Winners	3,600	2,935	n/a	6,535
Losers	14,000	10,980	n/a	24,980

Kansans for Life Political Action Committee (C00175521) *Phone: (316) 687-5433 * Fax: (316) 687-0303 * P.O. Box 40223, Wichita, KS 66212 * Web: www.kfl.org * E-mail: Kans4life@aol.com * Treasurer: Roy Heinbach * Contact: Tim Golba, PAC Dir.*

*Phone: (800) 928-5433 * 2501 E. Central, Wichita, KS 67214*

Kansans for Life is the largest anti-abortion organization in Kansas, with more than 10,000 members. The PAC supports candidates endorsed by the National Right to Life Committee.

It distributes a monthly newsletter to members, gives free presentations and shows a movie on statewide television that features women describing their personal experiences with abortion.

Though it focuses most of its energy on abortion issues, the organization is also anti-euthanasia. It has chapters in Wichita, Topeka and Kansas City.

	1993-94	1995-96	1997	Totals
Receipts	$8,955	$37,962	$0	$46,917
Disburse	8,332	35,334	3,225	46,891
Cash	847	3,475	249	n/a
Contributions	300	13,699	0	13,999
Republicans	300	13,699	0	13,999
No. of Cand.	*6*	*5*	*1*	*12*
House	275	8,786	0	9,061
Senate	25	4,913	0	4,938
Democrats	0	0	0	0
No. of Cand.	*0*	*0*	*0*	*0*
House	0	0	0	0
Senate	0	0	0	0
Incumbents	25	30	0	55
Challengers	1,000	4,876	0	5,876
Open Seat	775	8,793	0	9,568
Winners	1,550	13,699	n/a	15,249
Losers	-1250	0	n/a	-1250

California Pro-Life Council Inc. Political Action Committee (C00228122) *Phone: (916) 442-8315 * Fax: (916) 441-7508 * 2306 J St., Suite 200, Sacramento, CA 95816 * Web: www.californiaprolife.org * E-mail: prolife@californiaprolife.org * Treasurer: James Mathwig * Contact: Brian Johnston, PAC Dir.*

The California Pro-Life Council is National Right to Life's California affiliate. The anti-abortion organization has 60,000 members in five offices around the state.

The PAC is nonpartisan but generally gives to California Republicans. It is also concerned with euthanasia and health care.

The council has an educational foundation that sends out information, broadcasts radio advertisements and publishes voter guides.

	1993-94	1995-96	1997	Totals
Receipts	$12,807	$54,641	$394	$67,842
Disburse	15,438	19,203	3,646	38,287
Cash	4,616	40,411	965	n/a
Contributions	11,960	6,057	0	18,017
Republicans	11,960	6,057	0	18,017
No. of Cand.	*5*	*7*	*0*	*12*
House	11,960	6,057	0	18,017
Senate	0	0	0	0
Democrats	0	0	0	0
No. of Cand.	*0*	*0*	*0*	*0*
House	0	0	0	0
Senate	0	0	0	0
Incumbents	1,610	3,344	0	4,954
Challengers	10,350	1,125	0	11,475
Open Seat	0	1,288	0	1,288
Winners	6,610	2,288	n/a	8,898
Losers	5,350	3,769	n/a	9,119

Illinois Federation for Right to Life Inc. PAC (C00141341) *Phone: (618) 465-3211 * Fax: (618) 465-3268 * 412 Langdon, Alton, IL 62002 * Treasurer: James M. Quirke * Contact: Felicia Goekem, Chairperson*

	1993-94	1995-96	1997	Totals
Receipts	$19,926	$96,421	$2,357	$118,704
Disburse	20,876	91,608	3,562	116,046
Cash	710	5,520	4,315	n/a
Contributions	1,992	5,863	0	7,855
Republicans	1,992	4,303	0	6,295
No. of Cand.	*4*	*13*	*0*	*17*
House	1,992	4,178	0	6,170
Senate	0	125	0	125
Democrats	0	1,560	0	1,560
No. of Cand.	*0*	*3*	*0*	*3*
House	0	1,560	0	1,560
Senate	0	0	0	0
Incumbents	831	3,115	0	3,946
Challengers	527	807	0	1,334
Open Seat	634	1,941	0	2,575
Winners	1,465	3,863	n/a	5,328
Losers	527	2,000	n/a	2,527

Contributed less than $5,000 during 1995-96 cycle:

Allen County Right to Life Inc. Political Action Committee (C00235861) *Phone: (219) 471-1849 * 3409 Conestoga Dr., Suite A, Fort Wayne, IN 46808 * Treasurer: Anne Wall*

Arizona Right to Life PAC (C00186486) *Phone: (602) 285-0063 * Fax: (602) 285-0082 * 77 E. Columbus Ave., Suite 209, Phoenix, AZ 85012 * Treasurer: Patti Rosset * Contact: Laureen Tetzlaff, President*

Arkansas Right to Life Political Action Committee (C00208439) *Phone: (501) 663-4237 * P.O. Box 1697, Little Rock, AR 72203 * Treasurer: Robert Burr*

Florida Right to Life Political Action Committee (C00155564) *Phone: (407) 422-7111 * Fax: (407) 422-1144 * 3336 Edgewater Dr., Orlando, FL 32804 * Treasurer: Robin Hoffman * Contact: Lynda Bell, President*

Georgia Right to Life National PAC (C00172601) *P.O. Box 81474, Atlanta, GA 30366 * Treasurer: Nancy J. Stith*

Indiana Right to Life Political Action Committee Inc. (C00248898) *Phone: (765) 868-8068 * Fax: (765) 455-9821 * 608 E Blvd., P.O. Box 6487, Kokomo, IN 46904 * Treasurer: Gerri Fernandez * Contact: Mark Lantz, President*

Iowa Right to Life PAC (C00213355) *Phone: (515) 244-1012 * Fax: (515) 244-1018 * 1500 Illinois St., Des Moines, IA 50314 * Treasurer: Sandy De Jong * Contact: Deb Taylor, President*

Maine State Right to Life Political Action Committee (C00141754) *Phone: (207) 622-3837 * Fax: (207) 621-9812 * Eight Green St., Augusta, ME 04330 * Web: www.mint.net/life4me * Treasurer: Ray Delorme*

Metro Right to Life Political Action Committee (C00268649) *Phone: (402) 399-0299 * 9001 Arbor St., Suite 104, Omaha, NE 68124 * Treasurer: Elaine T. Heaston*

Mississippi Right to Life Political Action Committee (C00264036) *Phone: (601) 693-5433 * 117 Fox Meadow Dr., Brandon, MS 39042 * Treasurer: Jim Partin*

Missouri Right to Life Federal Political Action Committee (C00157958) *Phone: (573) 635-5110 * Fax: (573) 635-9285 * P.O. Box 651, Jefferson City, MO 65102 * E-mail: missourilife@mail.ultraweb.net * Treasurer: Linda Bell*

Montana Right to Life Political Action Committee (C00171413) *Phone: (406) 443-0827 * Fax: (406) 443-0840 * 1900 N. Last Chance Gulch, Suite C, Helena, MT 59601 * Treasurer: Richard A. Tappe * Contact: Julie Daffin, President*

North Carolina Right to Life Inc. PAC (C00117200) *Phone: (910) 274-5433 * Fax: (910) 274-4361 * 3926 Gracemont Dr., Winston-Salem, NC 27106 * Treasurer: W. C. Pearson * Contact: Barbara Holt, President*

Ohio Right to Life Society PAC (C00097196) *Phone: (614) 241-5200 * Eight E. Broad St., Columbus, OH 43215 * Web: www.ohiolife.org * Treasurer: Robert Knodel*

The Rhode Island State Right to Life Political Action Committee (C00154112) *27 Marcy St., Cranston, RI 02905 * Treasurer: Donald Silva*

Wisconsin Right to Life Political Action Committee (C00173278) *Phone: (414) 778-5780 * 10625 W. North Ave., Suite LL, Milwaukee, WI 53226-2331 * Web: www.wrtl.org * Treasurer: Susan M. Armacost*

Terminated PACs which contributed less than $5,000 during 1995-96 cycle:

Delaware Right to Life Political Action Committee (C00163675) *P.O. Box 205, Dover, DE 19901 * Treasurer: Ann Thomas*

New Jersey Right to Life

*Phone: (908) 276-6620 * Fax: (908) 276-5516*
49 Alden St., Cranford, NJ 07016
*Web: www.njrtl.org * E-mail: njrtl@njrtl.org*

New Jersey Right to Life PAC is a bipartisan anti-abortion committee affiliated with the independent organization New Jersey Right to Life.

The PAC generally gives to federal candidates from New Jersey.

Founded in 1972, NJRTL has 110,000 members. The group publishes a newsletter five times a year and holds an annual convention. The organization is not affiliated with National Right to Life.

New Jersey Right to Life PAC (C00260331) *Address: same as sponsor * Treasurer: Faith Willis * Contact: Daniel Clark, Executive Dir.*

	1993-94	1995-96	1997	Totals
Receipts	$75	$24,905	$0	$24,980
Disburse	2,571	23,084	4,525	30,180
Cash	2,340	8,796	1,661	n/a
Contributions	1,612	8,750	1,000	11,362
Republicans	1,612	8,750	1,000	11,362
No. of Cand.	*3*	*4*	*1*	*8*
House	1,012	8,250	1,000	10,262

(Data for New Jersey Right to Life continued)

Senate	600	500	0	1,100
Democrats	0	0	0	0
No. of Cand.	*0*	*0*	*0*	*0*
House	0	0	0	0
Senate	0	0	0	0
Incumbents	1,012	1,000	1,000	3,012
Challengers	600	500	0	1,100
Open Seat	0	7,250	0	7,250
Winners	1,012	7,750	n/a	8,762
Losers	600	1,000	n/a	1,600

Republican National Coalition for Life

*Phone: (972) 387-4160 * Fax: (972) 387-3830*
5009 Harvest Hill Rd., Dallas, TX 75244
*Web: www.rnclife.org * E-mail: cp.rnclife@ibm.net*

The Republican National Coalition for Life works to support the election of Republican congressional candidates unconditionally dedicated to stopping all forms of abortion.

The 30,000-member coalition was created in November 1990 by Phyllis Schlafly, founder of the conservative Eagle Forum; Gary Bauer, president of the Family Research Council; and Beverly LaHaye of Concerned Women for America. They created the group as a grassroots effort to keep the "pro-life" position an integral part of the Republican Party platform.

The PAC supports conservative candidates who oppose abortion, assisted suicide and euthanasia.

Republican National Coalition for Life Political Action Committee (RNC/Life PAC) (C00255406) *P.O. Box 618, Alton, IL 62002 * Treasurer: John Schlafly*

*Contact: Colleen Parro, Executive Dir. * Phone: (972) 387-4160*

	1993-94	*1995-96*	*1997*	*Totals*
Receipts	$85,701	$169,594	$46,282	$301,577
Disburse	87,329	166,097	6,000	259,426
Cash	17,310	20,813	61,096	n/a
Contributions	67,954	151,570	5,000	224,524
Republicans	67,954	151,570	5,000	224,524
No. of Cand.	*31*	*61*	*4*	*96*
House	56,954	115,570	3,000	175,524
Senate	11,000	36,000	2,000	49,000
Democrats	0	0	0	0
No. of Cand.	*0*	*0*	*0*	*0*
House	0	0	0	0
Senate	0	0	0	0
Incumbents	15,500	41,975	2,000	59,475
Challengers	26,500	59,900	0	86,400
Open Seat	24,954	49,695	1,000	75,649
Winners	42,954	45,470	n/a	88,424
Losers	25,000	106,100	n/a	131,100

Spring Lake Pro-Life

1401 Third Ave., Spring Lake, NJ 07762

Spring Lake Pro-Life Friends of Federal Election Candidates (C00278481) *Address: same as sponsor * Treasurer: John S. MacGowan*

	1993-94	*1995-96*	*1997*	*Totals*
Receipts	$10,966	$18,822	$9,133	$38,921
Disburse	12,864	20,474	8,371	41,709
Cash	1,638	1,588	2,351	n/a
Contributions	6,435	5,500	5,100	17,035
Republicans	6,435	5,500	5,100	17,035
No. of Cand.	*10*	*6*	*2*	*18*
House	6,335	5,400	100	11,835
Senate	100	100	5,000	5,200
Democrats	0	0	0	0
No. of Cand.	*0*	*0*	*0*	*0*
House	0	0	0	0
Senate	0	0	0	0
Incumbents	5,435	3,200	0	8,635
Challengers	900	100	100	1,100
Open Seat	100	2,200	0	2,300
Winners	5,535	5,100	n/a	10,635
Losers	900	400	n/a	1,300

Susan B. Anthony List

P.O. Box 19136, Alexandria, VA 22320

The Susan B. Anthony List PAC filed for termination on Jan. 6, 1998.

Susan B. Anthony List PAC Inc. (C00280057) *Address: same as sponsor * Treasurer: Maura K. Dunne*

	1993-94	*1995-96*	*1997*	*Totals*
Receipts	$38,632	$229,414	$118,891	$386,937
Disburse	38,108	229,039	119,981	387,128
Cash	1,412	1,785	694	n/a
Contributions	3,610	16,846	100	20,556
Republicans	3,610	16,596	100	20,306
No. of Cand.	*4*	*13*	*1*	*18*
House	3,610	15,831	100	19,541
Senate	0	765	0	765
Democrats	0	250	0	250
No. of Cand.	*0*	*1*	*0*	*1*
House	0	0	0	0
Senate	0	250	0	250
Incumbents	500	5,446	100	6,046
Challengers	360	9,714	0	10,074
Open Seat	2,750	1,686	0	4,436
Winners	3,250	7,670	n/a	10,920
Losers	360	9,176	n/a	9,536

Democratic/Liberal

Agenda for the 90's

Phone: (415) 772-7000
555 California St., Suite 4900, San Francisco, CA 94104

Agenda for the 90's PAC is chaired by Walter H. Shorenstein, founder and chairman of the Shorenstein Co., a privately owned real estate development and management firm. The PAC is based out of the company's corporate office in San Francisco.

Shorenstein Co. ranked No. 350 on the Forbes list of top private companies. Shorenstein owns and manages about 25 million square feet of office space, 10 million of which is located in San Francisco.

Shorenstein served as senior adviser to Presidents Lyndon B. Johnson and Jimmy Carter. In 1983 he received the Democratic National Committee's highest honor, "The Distinguished Service Award," according to the John F. Kennedy School of Government at Harvard University.

Agenda for the 90's (C00235069) *Address: same as sponsor * Treasurer: Barbara Koch*

	1993-94	*1995-96*	*1997*	*Totals*
Receipts	$18,857	$53,449	$320	$72,626
Disburse	19,845	33,385	11,604	64,834
Cash	29	20,093	8,809	n/a
Contributions	10,000	16,500	9,000	35,500
Republicans	0	0	0	0
No. of Cand.	*0*	*0*	*0*	*0*
House	0	0	0	0
Senate	0	0	0	0
Democrats	10,000	16,500	9,000	35,500
No. of Cand.	*5*	*8*	*5*	*18*
House	2,000	8,500	5,000	15,500
Senate	8,000	8,000	4,000	20,000
Incumbents	7,000	8,000	9,000	24,000
Challengers	1,000	7,500	0	8,500
Open Seat	2,000	1,000	0	3,000
Winners	7,000	10,500	n/a	17,500
Losers	3,000	6,000	n/a	9,000

American Democratic PAC

P.O. Box 70646, Washington, DC 20024

The Washington-based PAC listed debts of more than $40,000 at the beginning of 1998.

American Democratic Political Action Committee (C00148577) *Address: same as sponsor * Treasurer: Eric A. White*

	1993-94	*1995-96*	*1997*	*Totals*
Receipts	$13,602	$7,875	$500	$21,977
Disburse	12,538	8,657	500	21,695
Cash	1,614	832	832	n/a
Contributions	4,350	7,800	500	12,650
Republicans	0	0	0	0
No. of Cand.	*0*	*0*	*0*	*0*
House	0	0	0	0
Senate	0	0	0	0

Democrats	4,350	7,800	500	12,650
No. of Cand.	*7*	*10*	*1*	*18*
House	2,350	4,600	500	7,450
Senate	2,000	3,200	0	5,200
Incumbents	3,100	4,700	500	8,300
Challengers	0	1,100	0	1,100
Open Seat	1,250	2,000	0	3,250
Winners	3,100	4,700	n/a	7,800
Losers	1,250	3,100	n/a	4,350

Americans for Democratic Action

Phone: (202) 785-5980
1625 K St. N.W., Suite 210, Washington, DC 20006
Web: adaction.org

Americans for Democratic Action is an independent, liberal political organization dedicated to "promoting individual liberty and economic justice for all Americans." It was founded in 1947 by prominent political figures including Eleanor Roosevelt, labor leader Walter Reuther, economist John Kenneth Galbraith, historian Arthur Schlesinger Jr., theologian Reinhold Niebuhr and former Vice President Hubert Humphrey.

Since 1948, when ADA's efforts led to the adoption of a civil rights plank in the Democratic Party platform, the organization has taken early and influential stands on civil rights and civil liberties issues, as well as against the Vietnam War and apartheid in South Africa. ADA also lobbies for other traditional liberal policies such as workers' rights, women's issues and abortion rights, increases in the minimum wage, reduced military spending and a progressive tax structure. ADA uses "sustained political and legislative action to help formulate and achieve significant social change through government action."

ADA campaigns at national and local levels, working for the passage of legislation and the election of liberal candidates. During the 1995-96 election cycle, the PAC's leading recipients were Sen. Paul Wellstone, D-Minn., who gathered $6,500, and North Carolina Senate challenger Harvey Gantt, who received $4,000.

Americans for Democratic Action Inc. Political Action Committee (C00112680) *Address: same as sponsor * Treasurer: Leon Shull*

	1993-94	*1995-96*	*1997*	*Totals*
Receipts	$47,658	$103,132	$14,447	$165,237
Disburse	51,300	102,392	3,104	156,796
Cash	2,539	3,280	14,624	n/a
Contributions	42,250	88,287	1,500	132,037
Republicans	0	0	0	0
No. of Cand.	*0*	*0*	*0*	*0*
House	0	0	0	0
Senate	0	0	0	0
Democrats	41,250	87,287	1,500	130,037
No. of Cand.	*59*	*100*	*3*	*162*
House	30,250	64,287	1,500	96,037
Senate	11,000	23,000	0	34,000
Incumbents	16,500	33,000	0	49,500
Challengers	10,750	41,287	500	52,537
Open Seat	15,000	14,000	1,000	30,000
Winners	8,750	60,500	n/a	69,250
Losers	33,500	27,787	n/a	61,287

Archer's Arrows PAC

*Phone: (313) 568-6880 * Fax: (313) 568-6635*
400 Renaissance Center, Suite 3600, Detroit, MI 48243

Archer's Arrows was formed in 1995 by Detroit Mayor Dennis Archer, to support like-minded Michigan Democrats running for federal office.

Archer's Arrows PAC (C00304642) *Address: same as sponsor * Treasurer: Nicole Y. Lamb-Hale * Contact: Dennis W. Archer, Mayor of Detroit*

	1993-94	*1995-96*	*1997*	*Totals*
Receipts	$0	$21,800	$102,580	$124,380
Disburse	0	19,125	10,749	29,874
Cash	0	2,672	94,503	n/a
Contributions	0	10,950	0	10,950
Republicans	0	0	0	0
No. of Cand.	*0*	*0*	*0*	*0*
House	0	0	0	0
Senate	0	0	0	0
Democrats	0	10,950	0	10,950
No. of Cand.	*0*	*13*	*0*	*13*
House	0	10,700	0	10,700
Senate	0	250	0	250
Incumbents	0	8,250	0	8,250
Challengers	0	2,200	0	2,200
Open Seat	0	500	0	500
Winners	0	10,250	n/a	10,250
Losers	0	700	n/a	700

Blue Dog PAC

*Phone: (202) 225-2165 * Fax: (202) 225-1593*
1001 Pennsylvania Ave. N.W., Suite 350N, Washington, DC 20004
Web: www.house.gov/collinpeterson/bluedog/bluedog.htm

The Blue Dog PAC supports the conservative Democratic House caucus known as the Blue Dog Coalition.

The coalition is a group of about 25 conservative House Democrats, independent of the leadership of either party. It seeks to define the center of the spectrum in the House and to develop substantive proposals and positions distinct from those advocated by the extremes of both parties. The group has become an influential swing bloc, often working with Republicans to modify legislation in exchange for support on a close vote.

The Blue Dog Coalition was founded in February 1995 by Louisiana Reps. Jimmy Hayes and Billy Tauzin (both became Republicans). The name comes from the artwork of Cajun painter George Rodrigue, but is also an allusion to the old, fiercely partisan "yellow dog" Democrats of the South. Rep. John Tanner, D-Tenn., maintains that Blue Dogs are simply "yellow dogs who have been choked by the extremes in both parties to the point they have turned blue." Current members hail from all regions of the nation.

Blue Dog Political Action Committee (C00305318) *P.O. Box 7668, Washington, DC 20044-7668 * Web: www.house.gov/tanner/blue.htm * Treasurer: Collin C. Peterson*

	1993-94	*1995-96*	*1997*	*Totals*
Receipts	$0	$170,367	$95,291	$265,658
Disburse	0	167,100	40,117	207,217
Cash	0	3,267	58,439	n/a
Contributions	0	102,000	5,500	107,500
Republicans	0	5,000	0	5,000
No. of Cand.	*0*	*2*	*0*	*2*
House	0	0	0	0
Senate	0	5,000	0	5,000
Democrats	0	97,000	5,500	102,500
No. of Cand.	*0*	*27*	*2*	*29*
House	0	87,000	5,500	92,500
Senate	0	10,000	0	10,000
Incumbents	0	67,500	4,500	72,000
Challengers	0	5,000	0	5,000
Open Seat	0	29,500	1,000	30,500
Winners	0	70,500	n/a	70,500
Losers	0	31,500	n/a	31,500

Clinton Township Democratic Club

Phone: (810) 790-2477
36700 Barr St., Clinton Township, MI 48035

The Clinton Township Democratic Club is a Democratic Party organization in Macomb County, Mich. Clinton Township is the state's largest township with about 90,000 residents. The chairman of the Michigan Democratic Party, Mark Brewer, is a former president of the Clinton Township group.

Clinton Township Democratic Club Federal Election Account (C00148635) *Address: same as sponsor * Treasurer: Yolanda Kahler*

	1993-94	*1995-96*	*1997*	*Totals*
Receipts	$9,970	$12,150	$6,000	$28,120
Disburse	10,000	12,149	5,889	28,038
Cash	250	250	360	n/a
Contributions	5,000	8,887	0	13,887
Republicans	0	0	0	0
No. of Cand.	*0*	*0*	*0*	*0*
House	0	0	0	0
Senate	0	0	0	0
Democrats	5,000	8,887	0	13,887
No. of Cand.	*1*	*2*	*0*	*3*
House	5,000	8,787	0	13,787
Senate	0	100	0	100
Incumbents	5,000	8,887	0	13,887
Challengers	0	0	0	0
Open Seat	0	0	0	0
Winners	5,000	8,887	n/a	13,887
Losers	0	0	n/a	0

Congressional Agenda: 90's

Phone: (202) 342-9192
3220 N St. N.W., Suite 178, Washington, DC 20007

Congressional Agenda: 90's has updated its name every decade since its formation in 1969. The PAC was started to support opponents of the Vietnam War. The group promotes "a sensible defense budget, the environment and civil rights," as well as abortion rights and gun control.

The PAC contributes mainly to federal Democratic candidates and tries to focus on close races in smaller states, particularly ones designated by the Democratic Congressional Campaign Committee as being in need of support. Founder and Treasurer John R. Wagley says he maintains close contact with a group of 800 core contributors through direct telephone contact and monthly newsletters.

Congressional Agenda: 90's (C00151282) *Address: same as sponsor * Treasurer: John R. Wagley*

	1993-94	*1995-96*	*1997*	*Totals*
Receipts	$220,335	$191,176	$38,797	$450,308
Disburse	213,503	193,242	39,338	446,083
Cash	30,413	28,347	27,806	n/a
Contributions	5,600	12,000	0	17,600
Republicans	0	300	0	300
No. of Cand.	*0*	*1*	*0*	*1*
House	0	300	0	300
Senate	0	0	0	0
Democrats	5,600	11,700	0	17,300
No. of Cand.	*21*	*28*	*0*	*49*
House	5,000	7,700	0	12,700
Senate	600	4,000	0	4,600
Incumbents	4,850	5,350	0	10,200
Challengers	0	4,100	0	4,100
Open Seat	750	2,550	0	3,300
Winners	4,650	9,650	n/a	14,300
Losers	950	2,350	n/a	3,300

Democratic Candidate Fund

*Phone: (202) 466-6596 * Fax: (202) 466-6555*
1310 19th St. N.W., Washington, DC 20036

The Democratic Candidate Fund was founded by Rep. Thomas P. "Tip" O'Neill Jr., D-Mass., in the early 1970s. At the time he served as House majority leader and chairman of the Democratic Congressional Campaign Committee.

O'Neill went on to become the speaker of the House, a position he held for 10 years (1977-1987). He retired from Congress at the end of that tenure.

Since O'Neill's death in 1994, the fund is managed by his son, Washington lawyer Christopher O'Neill. The fund is mostly inactive, but it occasionally donates to federal Democratic candidates whom Tip O'Neill would have supported.

Democratic Candidate Fund (also known as Thomas P. O'Neill Jr. Congress Fund) (C00018135) *Address: same as sponsor * Treasurer: Christopher O'Neill*

	1993-94	*1995-96*	*1997*	*Totals*
Receipts	$12,358	$16,250	$200	$28,808
Disburse	12,586	14,493	1,896	28,975
Cash	2	1,755	58	n/a
Contributions	9,750	14,250	1,500	25,500
Republicans	0	0	0	0
No. of Cand.	*0*	*0*	*0*	*0*
House	0	0	0	0
Senate	0	0	0	0
Democrats	9,750	14,250	1,500	25,500
No. of Cand.	*19*	*14*	*2*	*35*
House	8,750	13,750	500	23,000
Senate	1,000	500	1,000	2,500
Incumbents	9,250	6,000	1,500	16,750
Challengers	0	5,750	0	5,750
Open Seat	0	2,500	0	2,500
Winners	6,500	10,750	n/a	17,250
Losers	3,250	3,500	n/a	6,750

Democrats for the House 1996

7435 Watson Rd., Suite 107, St. Louis, MO 63119

Democrats for the House 1996 was a joint fundraising committee sponsored by the Democratic Congressional Campaign Committee, created solely for that year's election cycle. It has been terminated, with no activity in 1997.

Democrats for the House 1996 (C00321752) *Address: same as sponsor * Treasurer: John D. Ryan*

	1993-94	*1995-96*	*1997*	*Totals*
Receipts	$0	$134,950	$0	$134,950
Disburse	0	134,949	0	134,949
Cash	0	0	0	n/a
Contributions	0	7,224	0	7,224
Republicans	0	0	0	0
No. of Cand.	*0*	*0*	*0*	*0*
House	0	0	0	0
Senate	0	0	0	0
Democrats	0	7,224	0	7,224
No. of Cand.	*0*	*2*	*0*	*2*
House	0	7,224	0	7,224
Senate	0	0	0	0
Incumbents	0	2,238	0	2,238
Challengers	0	4,986	0	4,986
Open Seat	0	0	0	0
Winners	0	0	n/a	0
Losers	0	7,224	n/a	7,224

Democratic Foundation of Orange County

Phone: (714) 979-4436
Three Imperial Promenade, #800, Santa Ana, CA 92707

The Democratic Foundation of Orange County is a membership-driven PAC whose purpose is to revitalize the Democratic Party in the area. It supports "moderate" local candidates, but contributes to Democratic campaigns at all levels.

The organization holds various programs for its members to meet and discuss issues with politicians and candidates. Founded in 1987, the foundation has roughly 110 members, most of whom are local business people.

Democratic Foundation of Orange County (C00176420) *9531 Via Ricardo, Los Angeles, CA 91504 * Treasurer: Susan Naples*
*Contact: Wylie Aitken, Chairperson * Phone: (714) 979-4436*

	1993-94	*1995-96*	*1997*	*Totals*
Receipts	$139,472	$130,015	$63,516	$333,003
Disburse	140,554	133,954	70,835	345,343
Cash	357	8,572	1,253	n/a
Contributions	8,000	10,250	5,000	23,250
Republicans	0	0	0	0
No. of Cand.	*0*	*0*	*0*	*0*
House	0	0	0	0
Senate	0	0	0	0
Democrats	8,000	10,250	5,000	23,250
No. of Cand.	*2*	*3*	*1*	*6*
House	3,000	5,250	5,000	13,250
Senate	5,000	5,000	0	10,000
Incumbents	5,000	5,000	5,000	15,000
Challengers	3,000	5,250	0	8,250
Open Seat	0	0	0	0
Winners	5,000	10,000	n/a	15,000
Losers	3,000	250	n/a	3,250

Democratic Study Group Campaign Fund

Phone: (202) 225-5231
P.O. Box 2884, Washington, DC 20013

The Democratic Study Group is an in-house research and strategy group for the Democratic Caucus. It studies legislative policy and institutional matters and prepares materials on those subjects for the use of caucus members, according to caucus by-laws. The group began to play a larger role for Democrats after the party lost the majority in 1994 and was subject to large staff cuts.

According to Mary Anne Walsh, the DSG executive committee contact, the DSG Campaign Fund was supposed to be disbanded several years ago. The PAC has not taken contributions since 1996, and candidate donations from both the 1995-96 and 1997-98 election cycles are listed as loan write-offs for polling services.

Democratic Study Group Campaign Fund (C00042382) *Address: same as sponsor * Treasurer: Dick Warden*

	1993-94	*1995-96*	*1997*	*Totals*
Receipts	$128,885	$16,545	$15	$145,445
Disburse	136,552	41,727	148	178,427
Cash	21,413	399	253	n/a
Contributions	4,000	83,850	39,000	126,850
Republicans	0	0	0	0
No. of Cand.	*0*	*0*	*0*	*0*
House	0	0	0	0
Senate	0	0	0	0

Democrats	4,000	83,850	39,000	126,850
No. of Cand.	*2*	*47*	*14*	*63*
House	4,000	78,850	39,000	121,850
Senate	0	5,000	0	5,000
Incumbents	0	1,000	25,000	26,000
Challengers	3,000	4,000	0	7,000
Open Seat	1,000	1,000	0	2,000
Winners	0	2,000	n/a	2,000
Losers	4,000	81,850	n/a	85,850

EDGE-Electing a Democratic Generation

Phone: (202) 638-3778 x4

2020 Pennsylvania Ave. N.W., Suite 364, Washington, DC 20006

*Web: www.demscalendar.com/edge * E-mail: edgepac@aol.com*

Electing a Democratic Generation was founded to support young Democratic congressional candidates through a nationwide donor network. EDGE supports House candidates under age 40 and Senate candidates under age 45. It aims to provide crucial "early money" to build a successful campaign.

Founded in 1993, the organization serves as a bundling conduit through which individuals may contribute directly to candidate campaigns. Members pay $50 to join and to receive information on candidates chosen by EDGE through its screening process. They are then expected to contribute at least $50 to one other campaign during the election cycle.

In 1995-96, EDGE supported 15 House and one Senate candidate, 11 of whom were elected. Leading recipients, with $2,000 each, were Reps. Ron Kind, D-Wis., Loretta Sanchez, D-Calif., and Ken Bentsen, D-Texas.

EDGE - Electing a Democratic Generation (formerly known as Youth National Organization for Tomorrow) (C00281220) *Address: same as sponsor * Treasurer: Gregory T. Karmazan*

	1993-94	*1995-96*	*1997*	*Totals*
Receipts	$25,983	$45,391	$7,241	$78,615
Disburse	25,980	43,182	5,319	74,481
Cash	4	2,261	4,133	n/a
Contributions	12,050	17,880	0	29,930
Republicans	0	0	0	0
No. of Cand.	*0*	*0*	*0*	*0*
House	0	0	0	0
Senate	0	0	0	0
Democrats	12,050	17,880	0	29,930
No. of Cand.	*10*	*16*	*0*	*26*
House	11,219	16,880	0	28,099
Senate	831	1,000	0	1,831
Incumbents	331	4,130	0	4,461
Challengers	2,081	8,000	0	10,081
Open Seat	9,638	5,750	0	15,388
Winners	2,412	13,380	n/a	15,792
Losers	9,638	4,500	n/a	14,138

Fifth Horseman PAC

Phone: (312) 876-1575

250 S. Wacker, Suite 650, Chicago, IL 60606

Fifth Horseman PAC gives to socially liberal candidates who support a free-market economy.

Founded in 1986, the bipartisan PAC supports federal candidates from all parts of the nation.

Fifth Horseman Political Action Committee (C00212902) *Address: same as sponsor * Treasurer: Craig Kennedy*

	1993-94	*1995-96*	*1997*	*Totals*
Receipts	$5,600	$0	$0	$5,600
Disburse	75,019	23,851	7,596	106,466
Cash	40,534	16,683	5,087	n/a
Contributions	50,000	26,000	6,000	82,000
Republicans	0	8,000	0	8,000
No. of Cand.	*0*	*2*	*0*	*2*
House	0	0	0	0
Senate	0	8,000	0	8,000
Democrats	50,000	18,000	6,000	74,000
No. of Cand.	*13*	*5*	*2*	*20*
House	19,500	6,000	1,000	26,500
Senate	30,500	12,000	5,000	47,500
Incumbents	24,500	8,000	6,000	38,500
Challengers	6,000	13,000	0	19,000
Open Seat	19,500	5,000	0	24,500
Winners	20,500	13,000	n/a	33,500
Losers	29,500	13,000	n/a	42,500

Frank J. Kelley Independent PAC

*Phone: (517) 487-2070 * Fax: (517) 374-6304*

One Michigan Ave., Suite 900, Lansing, MI 48933

The Frank J. Kelley Independent PAC supports Democratic candidates from Michigan. Kelley has been Michigan's attorney general since 1962.

Kelley, who founded the committee in 1995, is an active supporter of anti-lobbying legislation. He also opposes term limits.

Frank J. Kelley Independent Political Action Committee (C00314849) *Address: same as sponsor * Treasurer: Michael J. Hodge*

	1993-94	*1995-96*	*1997*	*Totals*
Receipts	$0	$19,025	$0	$19,025
Disburse	0	14,810	2,099	16,909
Cash	0	4,213	2,113	n/a
Contributions	0	8,000	0	8,000
Republicans	0	0	0	0
No. of Cand.	*0*	*0*	*0*	*0*
House	0	0	0	0
Senate	0	0	0	0
Democrats	0	8,000	0	8,000
No. of Cand.	*0*	*8*	*0*	*8*
House	0	8,000	0	8,000
Senate	0	0	0	0
Incumbents	0	7,000	0	7,000
Challengers	0	1,000	0	1,000
Open Seat	0	0	0	0
Winners	0	8,000	n/a	8,000
Losers	0	0	n/a	0

Harry S Truman Club

*Phone: (916) 924-6774 * Fax: (916) 925-2307*

100 Commerce Cir., Sacramento, CA 95815

E-mail: lindatoch@aol.com

The Harry S Truman Club supports Democratic candidates. The Sacramento, Calif. based club has 125 members, primarily individuals and locally elected officials.

The Truman Club was organized in 1981 by former Rep. John Moss, D-Calif., who served from 1953-78, and several other people.

Harry S Truman Club (C00140970) *Address: same as sponsor * Treasurer: Julie A. Green * Contact: Beverly Hunter*

	1993-94	*1995-96*	*1997*	*Totals*
Receipts	$146,230	$65,101	$41,825	$253,156
Disburse	149,914	70,307	33,099	253,320
Cash	10,436	15,034	9,059	n/a
Contributions	10,400	5,000	300	15,700
Republicans	0	0	0	0
No. of Cand.	*0*	*0*	*0*	*0*
House	0	0	0	0
Senate	0	0	0	0
Democrats	10,400	5,000	300	15,700
No. of Cand.	*4*	*1*	*2*	*7*
House	10,400	5,000	300	15,700
Senate	0	0	0	0
Incumbents	7,350	5,000	300	12,650
Challengers	3,050	0	0	3,050
Open Seat	0	0	0	0
Winners	7,350	5,000	n/a	12,350
Losers	3,050	0	n/a	3,050

Hollywood Women's Political Committee

444 S. Occidental Blvd., #421, Los Angeles, CA 90057

*Web: www.raygun.com/hwpc * E-mail: www.raygun.com/hwpc/touch.html*

Hollywood Women's Political Committee closed in June 1997, stating it no longer wanted to be a part of "a system that promotes the buying and selling of political office." HWPC said that it would be hypocritical to continue to raise money while it advocated reducing the role of money in elections.

Before its termination, HWPC supported the Democratic party at the state and national level. Founded in 1984, the organization supported a progressive agenda including abortion rights, civil rights and affirmative action and environmental conservation.

HWPC members included more than 200 women involved in the entertainment industry and was a major Hollywood fundraising source.

Hollywood Women's Political Committee (C00188979) *Address: same as sponsor * Treasurer: Judith Dornstein*

	1993-94	1995-96	1997	Totals
Receipts	$1,070,303	$1,417,457	$184,030	$2,671,790
Disburse	1,195,168	1,402,269	201,329	2,798,766
Cash	3,960	19,149	1,850	n/a
Contributions	189,500	197,500	0	387,000
Republicans	0	0	0	0
No. of Cand.	*0*	*0*	*0*	*0*
House	0	0	0	0
Senate	0	0	0	0
Democrats	179,500	195,000	0	374,500
No. of Cand.	*56*	*66*	*0*	*122*
House	118,500	147,000	0	265,500
Senate	61,000	48,000	0	109,000
Incumbents	102,500	68,500	0	171,000
Challengers	26,000	88,500	0	114,500
Open Seat	61,000	40,500	0	101,500
Winners	54,000	136,000	n/a	190,000
Losers	135,500	61,500	n/a	197,000

Independent Action Inc.

Phone: (202) 543-2500
645 Pennsylvania Ave. S.E., Second Floor, Washington, DC 20003

Independent Action supports Democratic challengers or candidates in open or marginal races in an effort to increase party strength in the House and Senate. The organization looks for candidates who promote traditional progressive aims, including handgun control, affirmative action and abortion rights.

Independent Action makes headlines with its annual "roast" of a major Democratic figure of the year. Former Texas Gov. Ann Richards and former White House Chief of Staff Leon Panetta have both been honored in recent years.

One-time presidential candidate and retired Rep. Morris K. Udall, D-Ariz., helped form the PAC in 1981. Sen. Tom Harkin, D-Iowa, also has been associated with the group. It now claims more than 5,000 supporters.

Independent Action Inc. (C00139741) *Address: same as sponsor * Treasurer: Mark Ingram * Contact: Ralph Santora, Executive Dir.*

	1993-94	1995-96	1997	Totals
Receipts	$627,725	$478,898	$200,324	$1,306,947
Disburse	630,313	478,605	200,990	1,309,908
Cash	511	803	138	n/a
Contributions	104,000	57,595	726	162,321
Republicans	0	0	0	0
No. of Cand.	*0*	*0*	*0*	*0*
House	0	0	0	0
Senate	0	0	0	0
Democrats	99,000	57,595	726	157,321
No. of Cand.	*24*	*32*	*1*	*57*
House	65,500	54,095	726	120,321
Senate	33,500	3,500	0	37,000
Incumbents	20,500	10,000	0	30,500
Challengers	32,500	35,060	0	67,560
Open Seat	51,000	12,535	0	63,535
Winners	10,000	27,500	n/a	37,500
Losers	94,000	30,095	n/a	124,095

Labor for America PAC

*Phone: (202) 861-9700 * Fax: (202) 861-9711*
P.O. Box 18206, Washington, DC 20036

Labor for America, founded in 1996, gives to candidates who support labor issues. The PAC, which generally gives to Democrats, backs federal, state and local candidates from all parts of the nation.

Labor for America Political Action Committee (C00309286) *Address: same as sponsor * Treasurer: Carey R. Butsavage*

	1993-94	1995-96	1997	Totals
Receipts	$0	$15,850	$3,750	$19,600
Disburse	0	14,767	1,758	16,525
Cash	0	1,082	3,073	n/a
Contributions	0	6,500	-1000	5,500
Republicans	0	0	0	0
No. of Cand.	*0*	*0*	*0*	*0*
House	0	0	0	0
Senate	0	0	0	0
Democrats	0	6,500	-1000	5,500
No. of Cand.	*0*	*8*	*3*	*11*
House	0	5,250	-1500	3,750
Senate	0	1,250	500	1,750
Incumbents	0	2,000	-500	1,500
Challengers	0	3,000	-500	2,500
Open Seat	0	1,500	0	1,500
Winners	0	2,250	n/a	2,250
Losers	0	4,250	n/a	4,250

Majority '96

*Phone: (202) 966-7988 * Fax: (202) 362-6656*
3811 Yuma St., Washington, DC 20016
E-mail: kwasch@aol.com

Majority '96 funds Democratic challengers in close congressional races.

Founded in 1995 to help restore a Democratic majority in Congress, the PAC only gives to federal candidates. During election periods the group uses e-mail mailing lists to send out information about candidates it supports.

Majority '96 (C00301614) *Address: same as sponsor * Treasurer: Ken Wasch*

	1993-94	1995-96	1997	Totals
Receipts	$0	$29,475	$0	$29,475
Disburse	0	27,763	0	27,763
Cash	0	1,709	0	n/a
Contributions	0	5,350	0	5,350
Republicans	0	0	0	0
No. of Cand.	*0*	*0*	*0*	*0*
House	0	0	0	0
Senate	0	0	0	0
Democrats	0	5,350	0	5,350
No. of Cand.	*0*	*26*	*0*	*26*
House	0	4,850	0	4,850
Senate	0	500	0	500
Incumbents	0	0	0	0
Challengers	0	4,450	0	4,450
Open Seat	0	900	0	900
Winners	0	2,700	n/a	2,700
Losers	0	2,650	n/a	2,650

National Committee for an Effective Congress

*Phone: (202) 547-1151 * Fax: (202) 547-3191*
122 C St. N.W., Suite 650, Washington, DC 20001-2109
*Web: www.ncec.org * E-mail: info@ncec.org*

The National Committee for an Effective Congress, the oldest PAC in the country, says it favors "progressive" candidates who support civil rights, environmental protection and gun control, among other issues. Founded in 1948 by former First Lady Eleanor Roosevelt, NCEC offers candidates get-out-the-vote planning, voter profile analysis and precinct targeting. The group tries to identify and support candidates that meet its standards and have the best chance of winning.

NCEC produces an "ideological index" to rate voting records on whether legislators agree with NCEC's positions. The leading recipients of the group's 1995-96 PAC contributions often had ratings of more than 90 percent agreement, but some members of both parties had ratings of 10 percent or lower.

NCEC contributed nothing to Republicans running for Congress in 1996. The group ranked second behind the National Rifle Association in total contributions among unaffiliated PACs. NCEC also ranked eighth among PACs having the highest percentage of money given to challengers. Slightly more than half of the NCEC's contributions went to winning candidates.

National Committee for an Effective Congress (C00003558) *Address: same as sponsor * Treasurer: James E. Byron * Contact: Russell Hemenway, PAC Dir.*

	1993-94	1995-96	1997	Totals
Receipts	$1,818,422	$2,403,101	$723,713	$4,945,236
Disburse	1,716,606	2,341,074	817,531	4,875,211
Cash	437,226	499,257	479,319	n/a
Contributions	780,499	1,118,475	98,500	1,997,474
Republicans	0	0	0	0
No. of Cand.	*0*	*0*	*0*	*0*
House	0	0	0	0
Senate	0	0	0	0
Democrats	765,999	1,113,475	96,000	1,975,474
No. of Cand.	*261*	*293*	*38*	*592*
House	623,499	977,975	95,000	1,696,474
Senate	142,500	135,500	1,000	279,000
Incumbents	430,499	390,175	61,000	881,674
Challengers	168,450	513,000	12,500	693,950

Open Seat	179,050	212,475	17,500	409,025
Winners	333,674	592,150	n/a	925,824
Losers	446,825	526,325	n/a	973,150

New Democrat Network

*Phone: (202) 544-9000 * Fax: (202) 547-2929*
501 Capitol Ct. N.E., Suite 200, Washington, DC 20002
*Web: www.newdem.org * E-mail: info@newdem.org*

The New Democrat Network is a new and growing organization dedicated to making the Democratic Party the majority party in the 21st Century. NDN seeks to recruit, train, promote and fund promising Democrats at all levels of elected office.

NDN was founded in 1996 by Sens. Joe Lieberman, D-Conn., and John Breaux, D-La., to strengthen and increase numbers of Clintonite "New Democrats." Ideologically, the New Democrats endorse an economic agenda of growth and fiscal responsibility, a decentralized government that empowers instead of abandons and an inclusive, responsible community.

NDN uses mass faxings, e-mail and its web site to support endorsed candidates, but its "bundling" method of campaign contributions is its most successful enterprise. With this method, members write checks to individual campaigns but send them to NDN for distribution. In its first year, NDN raised more than $600,000. NDN set a goal to raise $1.4 million for the 1998 cycle, with $150,000 earmarked for freshmen members of Congress facing difficult reelection races.

The main beneficiary of the NDN's immediate fundraising prowess is the New Democrat Coalition, a House caucus of about 43 members co-chaired by Reps. Jim Moran, D-Va., Tim Roemer, D-Ind., and Calvin Dooley, D-Calif.

New Democrat Network (C00319772) *Address: same as sponsor * Treasurer: Simon Rosenberg*

	1993-94	1995-96	1997	Totals
Receipts	$0	$206,399	$489,533	$695,932
Disburse	0	201,052	457,401	658,453
Cash	0	5,348	37,480	n/a
Contributions	0	34,512	16,278	50,790
Republicans	0	0	0	0
No. of Cand.	*0*	*0*	*0*	*0*
House	0	0	0	0
Senate	0	0	0	0
Democrats	0	34,512	16,278	50,790
No. of Cand.	*0*	*43*	*19*	*62*
House	0	26,936	13,119	40,055
Senate	0	7,576	3,159	10,735
Incumbents	0	2,500	11,619	14,119
Challengers	0	17,411	0	17,411
Open Seat	0	14,577	4,659	19,236
Winners	0	16,579	n/a	16,579
Losers	0	17,933	n/a	17,933

Ohio Democratic Congressional PAC

1019 Langley Hill Dr., McLean, VA 22101

The Ohio Democratic Congressional PAC filed for termination in 1997.

Ohio Democratic Congressional Political Action Committee (C00146639) *Address: same as sponsor * Treasurer: Marcy Kaptur*

	1993-94	1995-96	1997	Totals
Receipts	$16	$15,473	$33	$15,522
Disburse	0	14,200	4,037	18,237
Cash	356	1,632	0	n/a
Contributions	0	31,850	4,037	35,887
Republicans	0	0	0	0
No. of Cand.	*0*	*0*	*0*	*0*
House	0	0	0	0
Senate	0	0	0	0
Democrats	0	31,850	4,037	35,887
No. of Cand.	*0*	*13*	*1*	*14*
House	0	31,850	4,037	35,887
Senate	0	0	0	0
Incumbents	0	0	4,037	4,037
Challengers	0	31,850	0	31,850
Open Seat	0	0	0	0
Winners	0	10,000	n/a	10,000
Losers	0	21,850	n/a	21,850

People! Peace! Progress!

*Phone: (704) 375-7361 * Fax: (704) 375-7362*
715 E. Fifth St., Suite 216, Charlotte, NC 28202

People! Peace! Progress! was formed by Harvey Gantt, the Democratic senatorial candidate who challenged Sen. Jesse Helms, R-N.C., in 1990 and 1996. The PAC gives to Gantt as well as to other candidates and causes in which Gantt believes. Gantt was a two-term mayor of Charlotte, N.C.

The PAC is scheduled to be terminated.

People! Peace! Progress! (C00277897) *Address: same as sponsor * Treasurer: Bobby T. Martin*

	1993-94	1995-96	1997	Totals
Receipts	$18,460	$9,675	$0	$28,135
Disburse	5,811	15,202	5,560	26,573
Cash	14,853	9,322	3,761	n/a
Contributions	1,800	5,000	500	7,300
Republicans	0	0	0	0
No. of Cand.	*0*	*0*	*0*	*0*
House	0	0	0	0
Senate	0	0	0	0
Democrats	1,800	5,000	500	7,300
No. of Cand.	*7*	*1*	*1*	*9*
House	1,800	0	0	1,800
Senate	0	5,000	500	5,500
Incumbents	850	0	500	1,350
Challengers	300	5,000	0	5,300
Open Seat	650	0	0	650
Winners	650	0	n/a	650
Losers	1,150	5,000	n/a	6,150

Philip A. Hart Democratic Club

31119 Rothbury Way, Chesterfield Township, MI 48047

The Philip A. Hart Democratic Club is a local Democratic Party organization in Michigan. Hart was a Democratic senator from Michigan from 1959 to 1976. The Hart Senate Office Building is named after him.

Philip A. Hart Democratic Club (C00224717) *Address: same as sponsor * Treasurer: Brian A. Brdak*

	1993-94	1995-96	1997	Totals
Receipts	$5,380	$2,125	$0	$7,505
Disburse	2,830	11,050	1,000	14,880
Cash	10,074	1,149	149	n/a
Contributions	2,080	8,985	0	11,065
Republicans	0	0	0	0
No. of Cand.	*0*	*0*	*0*	*0*
House	0	0	0	0
Senate	0	0	0	0
Democrats	2,080	8,985	0	11,065
No. of Cand.	*6*	*3*	*0*	*9*
House	1,080	8,885	0	9,965
Senate	1,000	100	0	1,100
Incumbents	680	8,985	0	9,665
Challengers	0	0	0	0
Open Seat	1,400	0	0	1,400
Winners	905	8,985	n/a	9,890
Losers	1,175	0	n/a	1,175

Shelby-Utica Democratic Club

P.O. Box 182071, Shelby, MI 48318

As of January 1997, the Shelby Independent Committee, which was associated with the Shelby-Utica Democratic Club, had been terminated.

Shelby Independent Committee/Political Action Committee (SIC/PAC-Federal) (C00237990) *Address: same as sponsor * Treasurer: Alfreda Kemp*

	1993-94	1995-96	1997	Totals
Receipts	$30,660	$6,101	$0	$36,761
Disburse	30,931	6,777	0	37,708
Cash	678	0	0	n/a
Contributions	26,160	6,540	0	32,700
Republicans	0	0	0	0
No. of Cand.	*0*	*0*	*0*	*0*
House	0	0	0	0
Senate	0	0	0	0
Democrats	26,160	6,540	0	32,700
No. of Cand.	*5*	*3*	*0*	*8*
House	19,660	5,340	0	25,000
Senate	6,500	1,200	0	7,700

(Data for Shelby Independent Committee continued)

	1993-94	1995-96	1997	Totals
Incumbents	19,160	6,540	0	25,700
Challengers	500	0	0	500
Open Seat	6,500	0	0	6,500
Winners	19,160	6,540	n/a	25,700
Losers	7,000	0	n/a	7,000

Take Back the House

74 Massasoit St., Northampton, MA 01060

Take Back the House filed for termination in November 1996.

Take Back the House (C00305581) *Address: same as sponsor * Treasurer: Paul Spector*

	1993-94	1995-96	1997	Totals
Receipts	$0	$32,088	$0	$32,088
Disburse	0	32,004	0	32,004
Cash	0	79	0	n/a
Contributions	0	28,000	0	28,000
Republicans	0	200	0	200
No. of Cand.	*0*	*1*	*0*	*1*
House	0	200	0	200
Senate	0	0	0	0
Democrats	0	27,800	0	27,800
No. of Cand.	*0*	*11*	*0*	*11*
House	0	27,800	0	27,800
Senate	0	0	0	0
Incumbents	0	0	0	0
Challengers	0	25,800	0	25,800
Open Seat	0	2,000	0	2,000
Winners	0	15,600	n/a	15,600
Losers	0	12,400	n/a	12,400

Teamwork America

1050 Connecticut Ave. N.W., Suite 900, Washington, DC 20036

Teamwork America has closed its accounts and will file for termination in 1998.

Teamwork America (C00233106) *Address: same as sponsor * Treasurer: Peter L. Baumbusch*

	1993-94	1995-96	1997	Totals
Receipts	$830	$566	$0	$1,396
Disburse	6,801	10,395	5,019	22,215
Cash	15,729	5,901	882	n/a
Contributions	2,750	7,677	0	10,427
Republicans	0	0	0	0
No. of Cand.	*0*	*0*	*0*	*0*
House	0	0	0	0
Senate	0	0	0	0
Democrats	2,750	7,677	0	10,427
No. of Cand.	*4*	*9*	*0*	*13*
House	1,750	6,077	0	7,827
Senate	1,000	1,600	0	2,600
Incumbents	2,000	2,000	0	4,000
Challengers	250	3,077	0	3,327
Open Seat	500	2,600	0	3,100
Winners	0	3,900	n/a	3,900
Losers	2,750	3,777	n/a	6,527

Environment

Forest & Nature Protection PAC

Six Library Ct. SE, Washington, DC 20003

Forest & Nature Protection Political Action Committee (also known as Forest & Nature Protection PAC) (C00320507) *Address: same as sponsor * Treasurer: Carl Ross*

	1993-94	1995-96	1997	Totals
Receipts	$0	$15,801	$614	$16,415
Disburse	0	12,510	3,854	16,364
Cash	0	3,291	50	n/a
Contributions	0	6,725	2,350	9,075
Republicans	0	250	0	250
No. of Cand.	*0*	*1*	*0*	*1*
House	0	250	0	250
Senate	0	0	0	0
Democrats	0	6,475	2,350	8,825
No. of Cand.	*0*	*40*	*13*	*53*
House	0	5,225	1,650	6,875
Senate	0	1,250	700	1,950
Incumbents	0	4,675	2,350	7,025
Challengers	0	650	0	650
Open Seat	0	1,400	0	1,400
Winners	0	5,575	n/a	5,575
Losers	0	1,150	n/a	1,150

Friends of the Earth

*Phone: (206) 633-1661 * Fax: (206) 633-1935*
4512 University Way N.E., Seattle, WA 98105
*Web: www.foe.org * E-mail: foe@foe.org*

Friends of the Earth addresses a full range of environmental issues including the prevention of environmental catastrophes. One of its campaigns, Economics for the Earth, focuses on eliminating government subsidies that damage the environment and on promoting economic policies that encourage sustainable development. Its annual "Green Scissors Report" details what the group believes is wasteful spending.

Other FOE campaigns focus on corporate accountability, shareholder action, preventing urban sprawl, industrial cleanup and healing the atmosphere.

Friends of the Earth, which is based in Washington, has more than 30,000 members. The U.S. organization also has an office in Seattle. Friends of the Earth International, based in Amsterdam, has more than 1 million members in 58 countries.

In 1990, Friends of the Earth, the Oceanic Society and the Environmental Policy Institute merged.

Friends of the Earth PAC is bipartisan and gives to candidates who support environment-friendly policies.

Friends of the Earth Political Action Committee (C00141044) *Phone: (202) 783-7400 * Fax: (202) 783-0444 * 1025 Vermont Ave. N.W., Suite 300, Washington, DC 20005-6303 * Treasurer: Brent Blackwelder*

	1993-94	1995-96	1997	Totals
Receipts	$0	$26,000	$6,400	$32,400
Disburse	0	25,846	584	26,430
Cash	0	295	6,110	n/a
Contributions	0	20,881	0	20,881
Republicans	0	1,185	0	1,185
No. of Cand.	*0*	*2*	*0*	*2*
House	0	1,185	0	1,185
Senate	0	0	0	0
Democrats	0	19,696	0	19,696
No. of Cand.	*0*	*17*	*0*	*17*
House	0	17,553	0	17,553
Senate	0	2,143	0	2,143
Incumbents	0	2,335	0	2,335
Challengers	0	16,153	0	16,153
Open Seat	0	2,393	0	2,393
Winners	0	14,556	n/a	14,556
Losers	0	6,325	n/a	6,325

Greenvote

160 Second St., Second Floor, Cambridge, MA 02142

Greenvote filed for termination in February 1998. Its final disbursement was to Future Strategies Inc., located at the same address, for "office overhead and secretarial" purposes.

Greenvote was the second-largest contributor among environmental PACs during the 1995-96 election cycle.

Leading recipients included Reps. Jim McGovern, D-Mass., Nick Lampson, D-Texas, and Walter Capps, D-Calif., as well as Sen. Paul Wellstone, D-Minn. Challengers Harvey Gantt of North Carolina and Deborah Arnesen of New Hampshire each received roughly $5,000 in contributions, as did others in Washington and California.

Greenvote (C00243691) *Address: same as sponsor * Treasurer: Francis Smith*

	1993-94	1995-96	1997	Totals
Receipts	$117,200	$197,125	$8,000	$322,325
Disburse	135,212	185,121	27,142	347,475
Cash	7,143	19,143	0	n/a
Contributions	67,150	129,400	4,000	200,550
Republicans	0	0	0	0
No. of Cand.	*0*	*0*	*0*	*0*
House	0	0	0	0

Senate	0	0	0	0
Democrats	62,150	129,400	4,000	195,550
No. of Cand.	*77*	*97*	*8*	*182*
House	33,650	91,900	4,000	129,550
Senate	28,500	37,500	0	66,000
Incumbents	21,500	24,850	3,500	49,850
Challengers	16,650	80,200	0	96,850
Open Seat	29,000	24,350	500	53,850
Winners	11,650	69,100	n/a	80,750
Losers	55,500	60,300	n/a	115,800

Idahoans for the Outdoors

Phone: (208) 726-1023
P.O. Box 6855, Boise, ID 83707
E-mail: jhormel@micron.net

Idahoans for the Outdoors is an independent PAC that assists federal candidates who support protection of natural resources, wilderness and wildlife. It is particularly interested in conserving Idaho public lands.

The PAC, which was founded in 1995, is bipartisan. It has about 80 members.

Idahoans for the Outdoors (C00308635) *Address: same as sponsor * Treasurer: Jay C. Hormel*

	1993-94	1995-96	1997	Totals
Receipts	$0	$20,041	$140	$20,181
Disburse	0	17,162	61	17,223
Cash	0	2,878	2,957	n/a
Contributions	0	12,000	0	12,000
Republicans	0	250	0	250
No. of Cand.	*0*	*1*	*0*	*1*
House	0	250	0	250
Senate	0	0	0	0
Democrats	0	11,750	0	11,750
No. of Cand.	*0*	*4*	*0*	*4*
House	0	5,500	0	5,500
Senate	0	6,250	0	6,250
Incumbents	0	250	0	250
Challengers	0	11,500	0	11,500
Open Seat	0	250	0	250
Winners	0	500	n/a	500
Losers	0	11,500	n/a	11,500

Keep Tahoe Blue PAC

*Phone: (916) 329-7901 * Fax: (916) 329-4900*
400 Capitol Mall, Suite 3000, Sacramento, CA 95814
E-mail: jwbruner@orrick.com

Keep Tahoe Blue assists candidates who regard the preservation of northern California's Lake Tahoe as a high priority.

The PAC, which was founded in 1980, gives to federal, state and local candidates. It generally gives to candidates from California or bordering states.

Keep Tahoe Blue Political Action Committee (C00311597) *Address: same as sponsor * Treasurer: James W. Bruner Jr.*

	1993-94	1995-96	1997	Totals
Receipts	$0	$15,983	$8,434	$24,417
Disburse	0	17,335	3,796	21,131
Cash	0	6,531	11,168	n/a
Contributions	0	6,000	1,000	7,000
Republicans	0	0	0	0
No. of Cand.	*0*	*0*	*0*	*0*
House	0	0	0	0
Senate	0	0	0	0
Democrats	0	6,000	1,000	7,000
No. of Cand.	*0*	*4*	*1*	*5*
House	0	6,000	1,000	7,000
Senate	0	0	0	0
Incumbents	0	3,500	1,000	4,500
Challengers	0	2,250	0	2,250
Open Seat	0	250	0	250
Winners	0	3,750	n/a	3,750
Losers	0	2,250	n/a	2,250

League of Conservation Voters

*Phone: (202) 785-8683 * Fax: (202) 835-0491*
1707 L St. N.W., Suite 750, Washington, DC 20036
*Web: www.lcv.org * E-mail: betsy_loyless@lcv.org*

The League of Conservation Voters was founded in 1970 and claims 30,000 members nationwide. Members support environmentally friendly candidates for Congress.

The association targets 12 anti-environmental candidates each election cycle. It funds campaigns against anti-environmental candidates without supporting their opponents.

League of Conservation Voters Inc. Political Action Committee (LCV Earth Fund) (C00252940) *Address: same as sponsor * Treasurer: Sydney Butler * Contact: Betsy Loyless, Political Dir.*

	1993-94	1995-96	1997	Totals
Receipts	$841,505	$1,279,179	$470,277	$2,590,961
Disburse	839,460	1,289,716	4,909	2,134,085
Cash	16,231	5,696	471,067	n/a
Contributions	776,559	66,090	3,192	845,841
Republicans	34,949	17,511	0	52,460
No. of Cand.	*9*	*7*	*0*	*16*
House	23,233	17,362	0	40,595
Senate	11,716	149	0	11,865
Democrats	725,301	46,579	3,192	775,072
No. of Cand.	*153*	*25*	*3*	*181*
House	584,014	27,613	2,128	613,755
Senate	141,287	18,966	1,064	161,317
Incumbents	401,319	39,427	3,192	443,938
Challengers	121,037	11,684	0	132,721
Open Seat	248,613	15,483	0	264,096
Winners	308,415	52,545	n/a	360,960
Losers	468,144	13,545	n/a	481,689

California League of Conservation Voters (C00012401) *Phone: (415) 896-5550 * Fax: (415) 896-5580 * 965 Mission St., Suite 625, San Francisco, CA 94103 * Web: www.igc.org/ecovote * Treasurer: Fredric D. Woocher * Contact: Sam Schuchat, Executive Dir.*

	1993-94	1995-96	1997	Totals
Receipts	$69,235	$114,856	$11,500	$195,591
Disburse	68,927	113,122	283	182,332
Cash	304	1,937	13,153	n/a
Contributions	20,490	49,110	250	69,850
Republicans	0	0	0	0
No. of Cand.	*0*	*0*	*0*	*0*
House	0	0	0	0
Senate	0	0	0	0
Democrats	20,490	49,110	250	69,850
No. of Cand.	*8*	*14*	*1*	*23*
House	20,490	48,710	250	69,450
Senate	0	400	0	400
Incumbents	12,389	14,650	250	27,289
Challengers	4,800	26,830	0	31,630
Open Seat	3,301	7,930	0	11,231
Winners	2,299	28,880	n/a	31,179
Losers	18,191	20,230	n/a	38,421

Contributed less than $5,000 during 1995-96 cycle:

New York League of Conservation Voters (NYLCV) Education Fund Inc. - Federal Fund (C00278424) *Phone: (212) 766-0014 * Fax: (212) 766-0071 * 130 Williams St., Suite 801, New York, NY 10038 * Web: www.nylcv.org * E-mail: voters@pipeline.com * Treasurer: Rosalind Walrath * Contact: Paul J. Elston, Chairperson*

Oregon League of Conservation Voters PAC/OLCV PAC (C00035154) *Phone: (503) 224-4011 * 111 S.W. Front Ave., Portland, OR 97204 * Treasurer: Jonathan Poisner*

The New West Network Inc.

*Phone: (970) 748-1174 * Fax: (970) 748-1619*
P.O. Box 18494, Avon, CO 81620
E-mail: budall@indra.com

The New West Network assists candidates from the western United States who will work to preserve public lands in that part of the nation. The PAC, founded in 1995, is bipartisan and generally supports federal candidates running in close races.

The New West Network Inc. (C00310078) *Address: same as sponsor * Treasurer: Bradley H. Udall*

	1993-94	1995-96	1997	Totals
Receipts	$0	$16,948	$25	$16,973
Disburse	0	15,802	1,157	16,959
Cash	0	1,142	9	n/a
Contributions	0	8,364	0	8,364
Republicans	0	62	0	62
No. of Cand.	*0*	*1*	*0*	*1*
House	0	62	0	62
Senate	0	0	0	0

(Data for The New West continued)

Democrats	0	8,302	0	8,302
No. of Cand.	*0*	*10*	*0*	*10*
House	0	3,792	0	3,792
Senate	0	4,510	0	4,510
Incumbents	0	62	0	62
Challengers	0	5,530	0	5,530
Open Seat	0	2,772	0	2,772
Winners	0	696	n/a	696
Losers	0	7,668	n/a	7,668

Oregon Natural Resources Council

*Phone: (503) 283-6343 * Fax: (503) 283-0756*
5825 N. Greeley Ave., Portland, OR 97217-4145
*Web: www.onrc.org * E-mail: ms@onrc.org*

The Oregon Natural Resources Council is an environmental advocacy organization of about 3,000 individuals living in Oregon. The organization's interests include wilderness and wildlife preservation and restoration.

Oregon Natural Resources Council Action Federal PAC (ONRC Action Federal PAC) (C00306613) *Address: same as sponsor * Treasurer: Marc Smiley*

	1993-94	1995-96	1997	Totals
Receipts	$0	$30,724	$745	$31,469
Disburse	0	28,988	1,025	30,013
Cash	0	1,730	1,444	n/a
Contributions	0	14,764	625	15,389
Republicans	0	100	0	100
No. of Cand.	*0*	*1*	*0*	*1*
House	0	100	0	100
Senate	0	0	0	0
Democrats	0	14,664	625	15,289
No. of Cand.	*0*	*6*	*1*	*7*
House	0	8,401	625	9,026
Senate	0	6,263	0	6,263
Incumbents	0	7,469	625	8,094
Challengers	0	1,182	0	1,182
Open Seat	0	6,113	0	6,113
Winners	0	8,801	n/a	8,801
Losers	0	5,963	n/a	5,963

Sierra Club

*Phone: (415) 977-3500 * Fax: (415) 977-5799*
85 Second St., Second Floor, San Francisco, CA 94105-3441
Web: www.sierraclub.org

The Sierra Club is a nonprofit environmental group based in San Francisco with 65 chapters throughout North America. It promotes conservation through publications, lobbying and grass-roots campaigns. The group claims more than 600,000 members.

The Sierra Club supports fuel-efficiency standards for automakers and reduced emissions from vehicles and industrial facilities. It favors a moratorium on new road construction in national forests. The organization opposes legislation that would remove zoning and planning authority from local agencies. It also opposes weaker protections for endangered species.

The Sierra Club was the top environmental policy PAC in contributions to 1996 congressional elections. It spent more of its money on challengers than incumbents, and backed Democrats with nearly 95 percent of its contributions.

The top recipients were Reps. George E. Brown Jr., D-Calif., and Nick Lampson, D-Texas, and Sen. Paul Wellstone, D-Minn. Karen L. Martynick, a 1996 House candidate from Pennsylvania, was the top Republican recipient.

Sierra Club Political Committee (C00135368) *Phone: (202) 675-6275 * Fax: (202) 547-6009 * 408 C St. N.E., Washington, DC 20002-5818 * E-mail: dan.weiss@sierraclub.org * Treasurer: Daniel Weiss*

	1993-94	1995-96	1997	Totals
Receipts	$354,251	$736,685	$37,244	$1,128,180
Disburse	431,725	677,883	19,257	1,128,865
Cash	1,929	60,730	78,717	n/a
Contributions	406,631	371,710	13,342	791,683
Republicans	6,755	15,757	500	23,012
No. of Cand.	*6*	*10*	*1*	*17*
House	6,158	15,257	500	21,915
Senate	597	500	0	1,097
Democrats	391,176	350,225	12,842	754,243
No. of Cand.	*150*	*121*	*11*	*282*
House	319,147	307,776	7,842	634,765
Senate	72,029	42,449	5,000	119,478
Incumbents	208,624	134,449	8,872	351,945
Challengers	74,166	162,429	0	236,595
Open Seat	123,841	74,753	4,470	203,064
Winners	138,500	223,196	n/a	361,696
Losers	268,131	148,514	n/a	416,645

Foreign & Defense Policy

Aerospace and Defense PAC

*Phone: (609) 273-8115 * Fax: (609) 273-8084*
133-N Gaither Dr., Mt. Laurel, NJ 08054
*Web: www.voicenet.com/~aspep * E-mail: aspep@voicenet.com*

The Aerospace and Defense PAC is affiliated with the Association of Scientists and Professional Engineers, the labor union representing employees of Lockheed Martin and L-3 Communications, a company that split from Lockheed Martin in 1996.

Lockheed Martin is the largest defense contractor in the United States.

ASPEP represents the 15,000 scientists and engineers who work for the two companies in the New Jersey cities of Camden, Cherry Hill and Moorestown.

The association was founded in 1948 as the union for RCA, which was sold to GE Aerospace Division in 1989. The company then became Martin Marietta, which merged with Lockheed in 1995 to form Lockheed Martin.

The PAC is interested in general NASA issues (the space station in particular), defense contracting, radar technology and naval combat.

Aerospace and Defense Political Action Committee (C00251728) *Address: same as sponsor * Treasurer: Bill Mays * Contact: Harold Ammond, PAC Dir.*

	1993-94	1995-96	1997	Totals
Receipts	$7,755	$7,904	$6,649	$22,308
Disburse	1,200	9,160	2,720	13,080
Cash	8,601	3,977	7,907	n/a
Contributions	7,600	6,250	1,720	15,570
Republicans	1,350	4,650	720	6,720
No. of Cand.	*1*	*4*	*1*	*6*
House	1,350	4,150	720	6,220
Senate	0	500	0	500
Democrats	6,250	1,600	1,000	8,850
No. of Cand.	*3*	*3*	*1*	*7*
House	5,500	1,000	0	6,500
Senate	750	600	1,000	2,350
Incumbents	7,600	5,250	1,720	14,570
Challengers	0	0	0	0
Open Seat	0	1,000	0	1,000
Winners	7,600	5,750	n/a	13,350
Losers	0	500	n/a	500

American Task Force for Lebanon

*Phone: (202) 223-9292 * Fax: (202) 223-1399*
2213 M St. N.W., Third Floor, Washington, DC 20037
Web: www.atfl.org

The American Task Force for Lebanon was established as an independent organization, with the objective: "to marshal whatever resources possible to assist, direct, and persuade the various United States government entities to provide much needed assistance to Lebanon."

The organization consists of more than 100 Lebanese Americans from around the United States who are professionals in the fields of politics, business, law, medicine, arts and sciences. The goal of ATFL is to work towards reestablishing a "secure, stable, independent, and sovereign Lebanon with full control over all its territory."

According to ATFL, some of its specific goals include: to secure the departure of all non-Lebanese forces from Lebanese territory, to disarm all militias on Lebanese soil, to reestablish the historic military relationship between the United States and Lebanon, to increase U.S. monetary support, to foster schools and hospitals in Lebanon and to encourage Lebanese Americans to fully engage in the political process by communicating directly and frequently with their elected representatives.

American Task Force for Lebanon Policy Council PAC (C00246827) *Address: same as sponsor * Treasurer: David J. Sadd*

	1993-94	1995-96	1997	Totals
Receipts	$21,396	$32,755	$1,212	$55,363
Disburse	19,089	50,296	2,162	71,547
Cash	4,094	1,278	63	n/a
Contributions	18,350	22,800	1,000	42,150
Republicans	6,850	7,200	1,000	15,050
No. of Cand.	*8*	*6*	*1*	*15*
House	3,600	6,200	0	9,800
Senate	3,250	1,000	1,000	5,250
Democrats	11,500	15,600	0	27,100
No. of Cand.	*9*	*11*	*0*	*20*
House	10,500	15,600	0	26,100
Senate	1,000	0	0	1,000
Incumbents	12,500	19,150	1,000	32,650
Challengers	750	650	0	1,400
Open Seat	5,100	3,000	0	8,100
Winners	15,600	22,150	n/a	37,750
Losers	2,750	650	n/a	3,400

Arab American Leadership PAC

*Phone: (202) 429-9210 * Fax: (202) 429-9214*
918 16th St. N.W., Suite 501, Washington, DC 20006

The Arab American Leadership PAC gives money to federal and local candidates who are Arab Americans.

James Zogby, treasurer and founder of the committee, is president of the Arab American Institute in Washington. The PAC is not affiliated with the institute.

Arab American Leadership Political Action Committee (C00194225) *Address: same as sponsor * Treasurer: James Joseph Zogby*

	1993-94	1995-96	1997	Totals
Receipts	$0	$28,969	$0	$28,969
Disburse	0	26,890	1,182	28,072
Cash	0	2,077	895	n/a
Contributions	0	17,000	1,050	18,050
Republicans	0	5,500	350	5,850
No. of Cand.	*0*	*2*	*2*	*4*
House	0	5,500	350	5,850
Senate	0	0	0	0
Democrats	0	11,500	700	12,200
No. of Cand.	*0*	*5*	*2*	*7*
House	0	10,500	700	11,200
Senate	0	1,000	0	1,000
Incumbents	0	7,500	500	8,000
Challengers	0	3,000	100	3,100
Open Seat	0	6,500	450	6,950
Winners	0	13,000	n/a	13,000
Losers	0	4,000	n/a	4,000

Council for a Livable World

*Phone: (202) 543-4100 * Fax: (202) 543-6297*
110 Maryland Ave. N.E., Suite 409, Washington, DC 20002
*Web: www.clark.net/pub/clw * E-mail: clw@clw.org*

The Council for a Livable World advocates the elimination and non-proliferation of nuclear weapons and other weapons of mass destruction. It seeks to strengthen and promote multi-lateral conflict resolution and international peace-keeping efforts, and to reduce overall military spending. Programs include drafting arms control bills, holding seminars for members of Congress and publishing fact sheets and voting records regarding national security measures.

The council also acts as a bundling PAC for Senate candidates, supporting both incumbents and challengers. The PAC concentrates on races where there is a clear difference between the views of the candidates on arms-control issues, smaller races where money goes further, and close races where money could be crucial.

The council, founded in 1962 by nuclear physicist Leo Szilard, claims more than 25,000 supporters. In 1982, it spawned an affiliate organization, PeacePAC, to support House candidates.

Council for a Livable World (C00029165) *Address: same as sponsor * Treasurer: Philip Schrag * Contact: John Isaacs, President and Executive Dir.*

	1993-94	1995-96	1997	Totals
Receipts	$738,458	$651,223	$326,883	$1,716,564
Disburse	776,635	657,086	301,090	1,734,811
Cash	47,888	42,025	67,818	n/a
Contributions	55,067	75,328	12,990	143,385
Republicans	799	190	0	989
No. of Cand.	*1*	*1*	*0*	*2*
House	0	190	0	190
Senate	799	0	0	799
Democrats	48,729	75,138	12,990	136,857
No. of Cand.	*20*	*21*	*5*	*46*
House	0	0	0	0
Senate	48,729	75,138	12,990	136,857
Incumbents	17,147	21,028	10,407	48,582
Challengers	11,495	16,782	2,583	30,860
Open Seat	26,425	38,518	0	64,943
Winners	8,361	43,832	n/a	52,193
Losers	46,706	31,496	n/a	78,202

Peace Political Action Committee (C00155119) *Phone: (202) 543-4100 * Fax: (202) 543-6297 * 110 Maryland Ave. N.E., Washington, DC 20002 * Web: www.clw.org/pub/clw/pp/ppinfo.html * Treasurer: Jerome Grossman * Contact: Robert Drinan, Chairperson*

PeacePAC was formed in 1982 to support House candidates.

PeacePAC, like Council for a Livable World's Senate PAC, uses the bundling method in sending its campaign contributions. The organization selects viable candidates through a questionnaire and interview process, then recommends its choices to its members.

	1993-94	1995-96	1997	Totals
Receipts	$116,437	$143,147	$52,682	$312,266
Disburse	109,150	148,847	49,295	307,292
Cash	12,074	6,374	9,762	n/a
Contributions	33,252	54,337	0	87,589
Republicans	0	0	0	0
No. of Cand.	*0*	*0*	*0*	*0*
House	0	0	0	0
Senate	0	0	0	0
Democrats	32,661	54,337	0	86,998
No. of Cand.	*34*	*46*	*0*	*80*
House	32,661	54,337	0	86,998
Senate	0	0	0	0
Incumbents	15,273	8,043	0	23,316
Challengers	6,455	31,487	0	37,942
Open Seat	11,524	14,807	0	26,331
Winners	9,714	37,605	n/a	47,319
Losers	23,538	16,732	n/a	40,270

Free Cuba PAC

Phone: (305) 551-3511
3075 N.W. 107th Ave., Miami, FL 33166

The Free Cuba PAC supports candidates who take a "hard line against Fidel Castro," according to PAC Administrator Cristina Otero. It is associated with the Cuban American National Foundation, which has contributed more than three-fourths of Cuba-related campaign contributions, according to the Center for Public Integrity.

A CPI study titled "Squeeze Play: The United States, Cuba and the Helms-Burton Act," found that of $4.4 million spent to influence Cuba policy since 1979, $3.2 million came from CANF trustees and directors, or the PAC. The study concluded that "dollar for dollar [CANF] is arguably the most effective lobbying force in Washington."

Lawmakers identified as receiving the largest donations from CANF's Free Cuba PAC include Reps. Ileana Ros-Lehtinen, R-Fla.; Lincoln Diaz-Balart, R-Fla.; and Robert Menendez, D-N.J. Senators receiving PAC donations include Robert G. Torricelli, D-N.J.; Jesse Helms, R-N.C.; Connie Mack, R-Fla.; Ernest F. Hollings, D-S.C.; and Bob Graham, D-Fla. During the 1995-96 election cycle, Torricelli and Helms each received $10,000.

Free Cuba PAC Inc. (C00142117) *Address: same as sponsor * Treasurer: Mario L. del Valle * Contact: Carlos de Cespedes, President*

	1993-94	1995-96	1997	Totals
Receipts	$217,291	$127,145	$6,550	$350,986
Disburse	220,959	129,706	10,912	361,577
Cash	7,089	4,525	1,948	n/a
Contributions	133,000	126,550	8,000	267,550
Republicans	36,000	66,850	1,000	103,850
No. of Cand.	*17*	*20*	*1*	*38*
House	11,000	21,850	0	32,850
Senate	25,000	45,000	1,000	71,000
Democrats	97,000	59,700	7,000	163,700
No. of Cand.	*33*	*17*	*2*	*52*
House	65,700	28,500	0	94,200
Senate	31,300	31,200	7,000	69,500
Incumbents	109,300	89,050	8,000	206,350
Challengers	7,200	6,500	0	13,700
Open Seat	16,500	31,000	0	47,500
Winners	100,700	110,050	n/a	210,750
Losers	32,300	16,500	n/a	48,800

Neighbor to Neighbor PAC

*Phone: (510) 419-0101 * Fax: (510) 419-0202*
1611 Telegraph Ave., Suite 1111, Oakland, CA 94612

Neighbor to Neighbor Political Action Committee (C00211235) *Phone: (202) 543-2429 * Fax: (202) 543-8198 * 236 Massachusetts Ave. N.E., Washington, DC 20002 * Treasurer: Sherri Chiesa*

	1993-94	1995-96	1997	Totals
Receipts	$1,673	$305,503	$52,069	$359,245
Disburse	3,153	294,016	60,587	357,756
Cash	1,025	13,133	2,162	n/a
Contributions	0	32,272	0	32,272
Republicans	0	0	0	0
No. of Cand.	*0*	*0*	*0*	*0*
House	0	0	0	0
Senate	0	0	0	0
Democrats	0	32,272	0	32,272
No. of Cand.	*0*	*7*	*0*	*7*
House	0	32,272	0	32,272
Senate	0	0	0	0
Incumbents	0	0	0	0
Challengers	0	27,441	0	27,441
Open Seat	0	4,831	0	4,831
Winners	0	18,473	n/a	18,473
Losers	0	13,799	n/a	13,799

Veterans of Foreign Wars

*Phone: (202) 544-5868 * Fax: (202) 544-8495*
200 Maryland Ave. N.E., Suite 506, Washington, DC 20002
*Web: www.vfw.org * E-mail: vfw@vfw.org*

Veterans of Foreign Wars is a national organization of more than 2.1 million members. All members served in the U.S. military overseas in some capacity. The majority of VFW members served in WWII, Vietnam or the Korean War. The remainder served in Haiti, Somalia, the Persian Gulf War, Grenada, Panama, Lebanon, WWI and other campaigns.

The VFW supports the enactment of legislation "that reflects the VFW's pro-veteran, pro-national defense and pro-America goals and protects veterans." The organization supports employment opportunities, training and educational programs for all veterans.

The VFW also favors a strong U.S. military that promotes "democratic ideals and interests abroad and seeks the fullest possible accounting of our comrades missing from all wars."

In addition to government activity, the VFW promotes community and educational programs to increase awareness about foreign service and to promote patriotism. It also provides assistance to veterans regarding discharge upgrades, records corrections, disability compensation and more. The VFW awards educational scholarships to children every year amounting to more than $15,000 per child.

Veterans of Foreign Wars Political Action Committee Inc. (C00113001) *Address: same as sponsor * Treasurer: Gerald E. Jonas * Contact: Kelly Goddard, PAC Dir.*

	1993-94	1995-96	1997	Totals
Receipts	$670,129	$565,624	$250,994	$1,486,747
Disburse	739,783	545,161	291,436	1,576,380
Cash	87,120	107,585	67,143	n/a
Contributions	12,550	14,700	0	27,250
Republicans	10,600	6,200	0	16,800
No. of Cand.	*14*	*12*	*0*	*26*
House	8,100	5,200	0	13,300
Senate	2,500	1,000	0	3,500
Democrats	1,950	8,500	0	10,450
No. of Cand.	*5*	*16*	*0*	*21*
House	1,750	8,000	0	9,750
Senate	200	500	0	700
Incumbents	8,550	14,200	0	22,750
Challengers	2,000	500	0	2,500
Open Seat	2,000	0	0	2,000
Winners	10,050	14,200	n/a	24,250
Losers	2,500	500	n/a	3,000

Women's Action for New Directions

*Phone: (781) 643-6740 * Fax: (781) 643-6744*
691 Massachusetts Ave., Arlington, MA 02174
*Web: www.wand.org * E-mail: wand@world.std.com*

Women's Action for New Directions is a bipartisan PAC designed to encourage women legislators to become involved in the issue of military spending. The organization's 15,000 members support cuts in military spending.

All candidates who receive money from the PAC automatically become members of the Women Legislators Lobby, a group formed by WAND.

The group, founded in 1981, was formerly called Women's Action for Nuclear Disarmament. It primarily gives to federal candidates.

Women's Action for New Directions Inc. (WAND) (C00170316) *Phone: (202) 543-8505 * Fax: (202) 675-6469 * 110 Maryland Ave. N.E., Suite 205, Washington, DC 20002 * Treasurer: Edith W. Allen * Contact: Kimberly Robson, PAC Dir.*

*Contact: Susan Schaer, Executive Dir. * Phone: (781) 643-6740*

	1993-94	1995-96	1997	Totals
Receipts	$10,781	$19,941	$239	$30,961
Disburse	11,222	19,982	0	31,204
Cash	1,118	1,084	1,324	n/a
Contributions	7,048	15,270	0	22,318
Republicans	0	250	0	250
No. of Cand.	*0*	*1*	*0*	*1*
House	0	250	0	250
Senate	0	0	0	0
Democrats	7,048	15,020	0	22,068
No. of Cand.	*13*	*15*	*0*	*28*
House	6,470	14,520	0	20,990
Senate	578	500	0	1,078
Incumbents	1,750	6,770	0	8,520
Challengers	1,296	7,250	0	8,546
Open Seat	4,002	1,250	0	5,252
Winners	3,252	9,020	n/a	12,272
Losers	3,796	6,250	n/a	10,046

Gun Control

Handgun Control Inc.

*Phone: (202) 898-0792 * Fax: (202) 371-9615*
1225 Eye St. N.W., Suite 1100, Washington, DC 20005
Web: www.handguncontrol.org

Handgun Control is a nonpartisan, nonprofit, gun control group based in Washington. The 380,000-member organization lobbies for government restrictions on the manufacture, importation, sale, transfer and civilian possession of handguns. Originally, the organization supported a handgun ban through gradual steps, but in 1991 it altered its objectives to support restrictions on rifles and shotguns as well.

HCI has supported both the Brady Law, which required criminal background checks of firearms purchasers, and the Violent Crime Control and Law Enforcement Act, which included an assault weapons ban.

Dr. Mark Borinsky, a victim of gun violence, founded the organization in 1974 as the National Council to Control Handguns. The organization is now chaired by Sarah Brady, the wife of James Brady, a former press secretary to President Ronald Reagan. James Brady was shot and paralyzed during an assassination attempt on Reagan in 1981.

An affiliated arm of the organization is the Center for the Prevention of Handgun Violence, also chaired by Sarah Brady. Created in 1983, it serves as an education, legal advocacy and research affiliate.

Handgun Control Voter Education Fund (C00113449) *Address: same as sponsor * Treasurer: Mark A. Ingram * Contact: Robert J. Walker, President*

	1993-94	1995-96	1997	Totals
Receipts	$531,904	$379,170	$5,682	$916,756
Disburse	627,730	364,249	43,130	1,035,109
Cash	88,232	103,156	64,708	n/a
Contributions	213,691	213,984	28,750	456,425
Republicans	10,500	13,820	1,500	25,820
No. of Cand.	*9*	*9*	*2*	*20*
House	7,500	11,820	1,500	20,820
Senate	3,000	2,000	0	5,000
Democrats	199,191	200,164	27,250	426,605
No. of Cand.	*84*	*88*	*35*	*207*
House	153,345	149,965	20,250	323,560
Senate	45,846	50,199	7,000	103,045
Incumbents	104,642	84,287	24,750	213,679
Challengers	58,238	70,399	3,500	132,137
Open Seat	50,811	59,298	500	110,609
Winners	56,342	137,816	n/a	194,158
Losers	157,349	76,168	n/a	233,517

Gun Rights

Gun Owners of America

*Phone: (703) 321-8585 * Fax: (703) 321-8408*
8001 Forbes Place, Suite 102, Springfield, VA 22151
*Web: www.gunowners.org * E-mail: goamail@gunowners.org*

Gun Owners of America is a nonprofit lobbying group that seeks to protect the Second Amendment rights of gun owners. The group, formed in 1975, has fought federal and state legislation that would restrict the use of guns, including the anti-terrorism bill brought up after the Oklahoma City bombing in 1995, and has supported candidates who share its views. The group has 150,000 members.

Executive Director Larry Pratt resigned as co-chairman of Patrick J. Buchanan's 1996 presidential campaign after controversy surfaced over his alleged links to white supremacist and militia organizations. A report released by the nonpartisan Center for Public Integrity claimed that Pratt had attended and spoken at meetings of the groups. According to a Feb. 16, 1996 Washington Post article, Pratt acknowledged attending the meetings but said he was not a member of a militia and had never discussed his racial views with white supremacists.

Later in the year, an opponent of Rep. Roscoe G. Bartlett, R-Md., attacked his campaign for accepting $6,700 from the GOA. When Bartlett tried to return the money, the GOA announced that his check would not be accepted. Bartlett later donated the money to nonprofit groups.

Gun Owners of America Inc. Political Victory Fund (C00278101)
*Address: same as sponsor * Treasurer: Walter J. Olson*

	1993-94	1995-96	1997	Totals
Receipts	$101,369	$93,086	$28,454	$222,909
Disburse	94,202	94,851	24,914	213,967
Cash	7,165	5,394	8,933	n/a
Contributions	47,990	78,211	1,673	127,874
Republicans	41,958	76,671	1,673	120,302
No. of Cand.	*47*	*49*	*5*	*101*
House	38,270	63,034	1,240	102,544
Senate	3,688	13,637	433	17,758
Democrats	5,769	1,540	0	7,309
No. of Cand.	*4*	*3*	*0*	*7*
House	520	1,540	0	2,060
Senate	5,249	0	0	5,249
Incumbents	8,610	16,995	2,240	27,845
Challengers	33,442	34,332	0	67,774
Open Seat	5,438	26,644	0	32,082
Winners	21,547	22,486	n/a	44,033
Losers	26,443	55,725	n/a	82,168

National Rifle Association

*Phone: (703) 267-3820 * Fax: (703) 267-3976*
11250 Waples Mill Rd., Fairfax, VA 22030
*Web: www.nra.org * E-mail: tm@nra.org*

The National Rifle Association is the leading gun rights lobby in the United States. It promotes recreational hunting, personal gun use and a strong law enforcement presence. The group claims more than 3 million members from all 50 states and lists its annual budget as about $80 million.

The group's Institute for Legislative Action tracks gun and crime issues at the national and state levels. The NRA supports right-to-carry, hunter protection and range protection laws. It opposes any legislation that would ban most types of firearms or make them more difficult to obtain. It has sought, both in Congress and federal courts, to overturn a 1994 gun and magazine ban enacted by Congress.

The NRA has been involved in preserving shooting ranges and other gun activities on U.S. Forest Service land after an Arizona club was closed by federal officials. At the state level, it contributed to the defeat of a 1997 handgun licensing ballot initiative in Washington state.

The NRA was among the 20 biggest PAC contributors to 1996 congressional candidates. That total was 16 percent less than its contributions during the 1993-94 election cycle, but the spending pattern remained much the same. Republican candidates accounted for 83 percent of the NRA's contributions.

The top recipients were Reps. Ed Bryant, R-Tenn., Barbara Cubin, R-Wyo., Helen Chenoweth, R-Idaho, and former Reps. Frank A. Cremeans, R-Ohio, and Steve Stockman, R-Texas. The top Democratic recipient was Rep. Tim Holden, D-Pa.

NRA Political Victory Fund (C00053553) *Phone: (202) 651-2560 * Fax: (202) 651-2577 * 410 First St. S.E., Second Floor, Washington, DC 20003 * Treasurer: Mary Rose Jennison*

*Contact: Tanya K. Metaksa, Executive Dir. * Phone: (703) 267-3820*

	1993-94	1995-96	1997	Totals
Receipts	$6,831,712	$6,650,678	$3,444,491	$16,926,881
Disburse	5,948,803	6,642,888	1,888,213	14,479,904
Cash	1,416,678	1,424,467	2,980,744	n/a
Contributions	1,853,038	1,560,871	497,711	3,911,620
Republicans	1,442,519	1,301,771	379,211	3,123,501
No. of Cand.	*254*	*245*	*145*	*644*
House	1,212,919	1,101,621	318,711	2,633,251
Senate	229,600	200,150	60,500	490,250
Democrats	409,019	259,100	116,500	784,619
No. of Cand.	*79*	*47*	*32*	*158*
House	393,169	243,200	116,500	752,869
Senate	15,850	15,900	0	31,750
Incumbents	991,796	1,053,675	473,811	2,519,282
Challengers	466,350	222,659	14,900	703,909
Open Seat	392,892	288,487	8,000	689,379
Winners	1,375,318	1,084,840	n/a	2,460,158
Losers	477,720	476,031	n/a	953,751

Safari Club International

Phone: (509) 877-3280
P.O. Box 159, Wapato, WA 98951
Web: www.safariclub.org

Safari Club International is a national big-game hunters' rights organization. The group is dedicated to conservation of wildlife, education of the public and protection of hunters' rights.

Safari Club International promotes hunters' rights to the media, aims to reshape regulatory direction both on domestic and foreign issues and monitors the activities of federal and state agencies.

SCI has former Rep. Bill Brewster, D-Okla., on its executive committee. Former Rep. Ron Marlenee, R-Mont., is the organization's legislative director.

Safari Club International Political Action Committee (C00122101) *1001 26th St. N.W., Suite 902, Washington, DC 20037 * E-mail: mhogan1@compuserve.com * Treasurer: Glen Rasmussen*

	1993-94	1995-96	1997	Totals
Receipts	$94,149	$545,915	$130,792	$770,856
Disburse	96,850	337,551	223,807	658,208
Cash	4,329	212,694	119,680	n/a
Contributions	48,650	135,500	60,500	244,650
Republicans	37,450	116,000	48,000	201,450
No. of Cand.	*34*	*78*	*60*	*172*
House	29,700	88,500	38,000	156,200
Senate	7,750	27,500	10,000	45,250
Democrats	9,200	19,500	11,500	40,200
No. of Cand.	*11*	*20*	*17*	*48*
House	9,200	18,500	8,500	36,200
Senate	0	1,000	3,000	4,000
Incumbents	29,450	79,000	58,000	166,450
Challengers	9,950	29,500	1,500	40,950
Open Seat	8,250	24,500	0	32,750
Winners	38,200	90,000	n/a	128,200
Losers	10,450	45,500	n/a	55,950

Human Rights

Albanian American PAC

*Phone: (914) 762-5530 * Fax: (914) 762-5102*
5 Old Rd., Elmsford, NY 10523

The Albanian American PAC focuses on current issues involving Albania. PAC Chairman and former Rep. Joseph J. DioGuardi, R-N.Y., said the New York-based group would be actively raising funds in 1998 in response to tensions between Serbs and Albanians.

Albanian American Public Affairs Committee (C00278689)
*Address: same as sponsor * Treasurer: Jessie Sadiku * Contact: Hon. Joseph J. DioGuardi*

	1993-94	1995-96	1997	Totals
Receipts	$25,435	$7,200	$13,424	$46,059
Disburse	17,441	7,895	13,032	38,368
Cash	7,991	55	446	n/a
Contributions	4,500	7,820	10,650	22,970
Republicans	3,500	7,820	6,050	17,370
No. of Cand.	*5*	*2*	*1*	*8*
House	3,500	7,820	6,050	17,370
Senate	0	0	0	0
Democrats	0	0	2,600	2,600
No. of Cand.	*0*	*0*	*1*	*1*
House	0	0	2,600	2,600
Senate	0	0	0	0
Incumbents	3,250	320	8,650	12,220
Challengers	0	7,500	0	7,500
Open Seat	1,250	0	0	1,250
Winners	3,500	320	n/a	3,820
Losers	1,000	7,500	n/a	8,500

American AIDS PAC

*Phone: (202) 462-8061 * Fax: (202) 483-1964*
1808 Swann St. N.W., Washington, DC 20009

The American AIDS PAC's stated mission is to inform the public about challenges created by the HIV/AIDS epidemic and to endorse and support federal office seekers who will face those challenges. In agreement with recommendations made by the National Commission on AIDS, American AIDS PAC urges a comprehensive, coordinated national plan to respond to the problems posed by HIV/AIDS.

The nonpartisan group was formed in 1993 and has about 300 contributors. Although the Sheridan Group was previously contracted to manage the PAC, it now is supported in-house.

American AIDS Political Action Committee (C00283101) *Address: same as sponsor * Treasurer: Thomas F. Sheridan * Contact: Ellen Globokar, Chairperson*

	1993-94	1995-96	1997	Totals
Receipts	$846,380	$565,249	$163,873	$1,575,502
Disburse	807,346	601,786	149,412	1,558,544
Cash	39,035	2,498	16,958	n/a
Contributions	44,000	39,500	14,717	98,217
Republicans	1,000	4,000	0	5,000
No. of Cand.	*2*	*2*	*0*	*4*
House	1,000	4,000	0	5,000
Senate	0	0	0	0
Democrats	41,000	35,500	14,717	91,217
No. of Cand.	*50*	*34*	*4*	*88*
House	30,000	28,000	3,517	61,517
Senate	11,000	7,500	11,200	29,700
Incumbents	19,000	9,000	14,717	42,717
Challengers	12,000	20,500	0	32,500
Open Seat	13,000	6,500	0	19,500
Winners	17,750	22,000	n/a	39,750
Losers	26,250	17,500	n/a	43,750

Armenian National Committee

*Phone: (818) 500-1918 * Fax: (818) 246-7353*
104 N. Belmont, Glendale, CA 91206
Web: www.cwire.com/orgs/anc

Armenian National Committee of Glendale, Calif. is the western U.S. chapter of the Armenian National Committee of America. The regional organization is composed of 14 chapters and has 2,500 members.

Established in 1921, ANCA, working with a network of offices, chapters and supporters, advances the concerns of the Armenian American community on a broad range of issues.

Armenian National Committee PAC (C00146969) *Phone: (202) 775-1918 * Fax: (202) 775-5648 * 888 17th St. N.W., Suite 904, Washington, DC 20006 * Treasurer: Karo Khanjian*

*Contact: Armand Keosian, Chairperson * Phone: (818) 500-1918*

	1993-94	1995-96	1997	Totals
Receipts	$49,930	$16,480	$550	$66,960
Disburse	48,731	17,655	700	67,086
Cash	1,345	170	5,200	n/a
Contributions	33,025	30,655	700	64,380
Republicans	8,375	8,805	200	17,380
No. of Cand.	*8*	*5*	*1*	*14*
House	7,750	7,805	200	15,755
Senate	625	1,000	0	1,625
Democrats	24,650	21,850	500	47,000
No. of Cand.	*12*	*9*	*1*	*22*
House	20,400	17,150	500	38,050
Senate	4,250	4,700	0	8,950
Incumbents	29,775	19,455	700	49,930
Challengers	3,250	0	0	3,250
Open Seat	0	11,200	0	11,200
Winners	24,075	30,655	n/a	54,730
Losers	8,950	0	n/a	8,950

Bay Area Non-Partisan Alliance

584 Castro St., #324, San Francisco, CA 94414

Bay Area Non-Partisan Alliance Political Action Committee (C00265561) *Address: same as sponsor * Treasurer: Jeff Bryant*

	1993-94	1995-96	1997	Totals
Receipts	$7,357	$10,350	$125	$17,832
Disburse	7,393	10,505	2,615	20,513
Cash	1,013	858	613	n/a
Contributions	7,250	11,515	0	18,765
Republicans	0	0	0	0
No. of Cand.	*0*	*0*	*0*	*0*
House	0	0	0	0
Senate	0	0	0	0
Democrats	7,250	11,515	0	18,765
No. of Cand.	*5*	*5*	*0*	*10*
House	3,250	11,515	0	14,765
Senate	4,000	0	0	4,000
Incumbents	7,000	2,500	0	9,500
Challengers	250	9,015	0	9,265
Open Seat	0	0	0	0
Winners	6,000	4,279	n/a	10,279
Losers	1,250	7,236	n/a	8,486

Democracy and Human Rights PAC

614 W. Brown Deer Dr., Suite 221, Bayside, WI 53217

The Democracy and Human Rights PAC did not report any receipts or expenditures during 1997, according to FEC records.

Democracy and Human Rights Political Action Committee (C00281154) *Address: same as sponsor * Treasurer: Gulshad P. Bhatti*

	1993-94	1995-96	1997	Totals
Receipts	$34,432	$36	$0	$34,468
Disburse	29,080	5,242	0	34,322
Cash	5,204	0	0	n/a
Contributions	21,765	5,000	0	26,765
Republicans	0	3,000	0	3,000
No. of Cand.	*0*	*3*	*0*	*3*
House	0	1,000	0	1,000
Senate	0	2,000	0	2,000
Democrats	21,765	2,000	0	23,765
No. of Cand.	*14*	*4*	*0*	*18*
House	2,965	500	0	3,465
Senate	18,800	1,500	0	20,300
Incumbents	10,765	4,000	0	14,765
Challengers	250	1,000	0	1,250
Open Seat	10,750	0	0	10,750
Winners	10,765	2,500	n/a	13,265
Losers	11,000	2,500	n/a	13,500

Elections Committee of the County of Orange

*Phone: (714) 975-0866 * Fax: (714) 975-0865*
1700 E. Garry St., Suite 108, P.O. Box 1028, Santa Ana, CA 92705

The Elections Committee of the County of Orange is a lesbian/gay PAC which contributes to California candidates. Rep. Steve Horn, R-Calif., was the only incumbent to receive a contribution during the 1995-96 election cycle, which was for $50. Rep. Loretta Sanchez, D-Calif., received $2,500.

Elections Committee of the County of Orange (C00192302) *Address: same as sponsor * Treasurer: Jeff Letourneau*

	1993-94	1995-96	1997	Totals
Receipts	$86,033	$115,724	$53,073	$254,830
Disburse	86,794	114,736	47,188	248,718
Cash	905	1,893	7,778	n/a
Contributions	4,800	5,100	500	10,400
Republicans	300	350	0	650
No. of Cand.	*1*	*2*	*0*	*3*
House	300	350	0	650
Senate	0	0	0	0

Democrats	4,500	4,750	500	9,750
No. of Cand.	*3*	*2*	*1*	*6*
House	2,250	4,750	0	7,000
Senate	2,250	0	500	2,750
Incumbents	2,250	50	500	2,800
Challengers	2,250	5,050	0	7,300
Open Seat	0	0	0	0
Winners	2,250	2,550	n/a	4,800
Losers	2,550	2,550	n/a	5,100

Five Civilized Tribes PAC

Phone: (405) 436-7204

P.O. Box 948, Tahlequah, OK 74465

Five Civilized Tribes PAC represents several Native American tribes in Oklahoma, including the Muskogee Creek Nation and the Chickasaw Nation.

Five Civilized Tribes Political Action Committee (C00321703)
*Address: same as sponsor * Treasurer: Jerry Haney*

	1993-94	1995-96	1997	Totals
Receipts	$0	$0	$0	$0
Disburse	0	0	5,500	5,500
Cash	0	0	0	n/a
Contributions	0	11,000	0	11,000
Republicans	0	0	0	0
No. of Cand.	*0*	*0*	*0*	*0*
House	0	0	0	0
Senate	0	0	0	0
Democrats	0	11,000	0	11,000
No. of Cand.	*0*	*3*	*0*	*3*
House	0	11,000	0	11,000
Senate	0	0	0	0
Incumbents	0	0	0	0
Challengers	0	6,000	0	6,000
Open Seat	0	5,000	0	5,000
Winners	0	0	n/a	0
Losers	0	11,000	n/a	11,000

Gay and Lesbian Victory Fund

*Phone: (202) 842-8679 * Fax: (202) 289-3863*

1012 14th St. N.W., Suite 1000, Washington, DC 20005

*Web: www.victoryfund.org * E-mail: victoryf@aol.com*

The Gay and Lesbian Victory Fund's goal is to increase the number of openly gay and lesbian public officeholders nationwide. Its hope is that by 2000, all 50 states will have at least one openly gay elected official. It supports candidates with referrals to campaign professionals and access to the group's donor network of more than 3,000 members, as well as direct contributions.

Since its founding in May 1991, the fund has donated more than $1.5 million to local, state and national office seekers. The Victory Fund serves as a "bundling" agency and recommends candidates to its members, who are then expected to donate $100 to at least two candidates per election cycle.

Gay and Lesbian Victory Fund (C00251835) *Address: same as sponsor * Treasurer: Brian K. Bond*

	1993-94	1995-96	1997	Totals
Receipts	$1,128,363	$1,062,857	$628,353	$2,819,573
Disburse	1,188,556	1,053,979	637,544	2,880,079
Cash	2,039	10,916	1,717	n/a
Contributions	0	6,080	6,614	12,694
Republicans	0	0	0	0
No. of Cand.	*0*	*0*	*0*	*0*
House	0	0	0	0
Senate	0	0	0	0
Democrats	0	6,080	6,614	12,694
No. of Cand.	*0*	*2*	*2*	*4*
House	0	6,080	6,614	12,694
Senate	0	0	0	0
Incumbents	0	0	0	0
Challengers	0	6,080	2,832	8,912
Open Seat	0	0	3,782	3,782
Winners	0	0	n/a	0
Losers	0	6,080	n/a	6,080

Health Care Concerns PAC

Phone: (816) 942-5495

P.O. Box 37063, Kansas City, MO 64138

Health Care Concerns Political Action Committee (C00183376)
*Address: same as sponsor * Treasurer: Barry L. Seward*

	1993-94	1995-96	1997	Totals
Receipts	$32,380	$38,350	$17,050	$87,780
Disburse	30,500	35,737	11,555	77,792
Cash	1,992	4,603	10,097	n/a
Contributions	11,125	6,700	4,250	22,075
Republicans	4,125	2,250	3,750	10,125
No. of Cand.	*3*	*6*	*4*	*13*
House	1,125	2,100	750	3,975
Senate	3,000	150	3,000	6,150
Democrats	7,000	4,450	500	11,950
No. of Cand.	*4*	*4*	*1*	*9*
House	3,000	4,450	500	7,950
Senate	4,000	0	0	4,000
Incumbents	2,500	4,125	4,250	10,875
Challengers	0	0	0	0
Open Seat	8,625	2,575	0	11,200
Winners	6,500	4,950	n/a	11,450
Losers	4,625	1,750	n/a	6,375

Hellenic American Council

*Phone: (213) 651-3507 * Fax: (213) 658-6306*

8124 W. Third St., Second Floor, Los Angeles, CA 90048

*Web: www.starone.com/~hellenic * E-mail: hellenic@starone.com*

The Hellenic American Council of Southern California lobbies Congress for the protection and promotion of Hellenic-American interests. Members communicate with Congress through letters, faxes, e-mails and telephone calls. In addition, the council urges representatives to join the Congressional Caucus on Hellenic Issues.

Founded in 1974, HAC advocates peace, justice and stability in Greece, Cyprus and the surrounding region.

Hellenic American Council Inc. Political Action Committee (C00212456) *Address: same as sponsor * Treasurer: Jacob Suzmeyan*

	1993-94	1995-96	1997	Totals
Receipts	$14,385	$13,025	$2,000	$29,410
Disburse	10,587	7,250	8,600	26,437
Cash	3,881	9,656	3,056	n/a
Contributions	7,900	7,250	4,600	19,750
Republicans	1,000	500	0	1,500
No. of Cand.	*1*	*1*	*0*	*2*
House	0	0	0	0
Senate	1,000	500	0	1,500
Democrats	6,900	6,750	4,600	18,250
No. of Cand.	*5*	*6*	*2*	*13*
House	5,900	6,750	3,100	15,750
Senate	1,000	0	1,500	2,500
Incumbents	6,900	5,250	4,600	16,750
Challengers	0	2,000	0	2,000
Open Seat	1,000	0	0	1,000
Winners	7,900	6,250	n/a	14,150
Losers	0	1,000	n/a	1,000

Hispanic PAC USA

*Phone: (202) 467-8029 * Fax: (202) 785-1944*

1215 17th St. N.W., Washington, DC 20036

Hispanic PAC USA is associated with Rep. Esteban E. Torres, D-Calif.

Hispanic PAC USA Inc. (C00250217) *Phone: (202) 835-1556 * Fax: (202) 363-3411 * 4201 Linnean Ave. N.W., Washington, DC 20008-3808 * Treasurer: Mari Carmen Aponte*

	1993-94	1995-96	1997	Totals
Receipts	$39,687	$208,403	$10,353	$258,443
Disburse	38,545	210,321	11,713	260,579
Cash	5,022	3,104	2,164	n/a
Contributions	23,000	27,000	1,000	51,000
Republicans	0	0	0	0
No. of Cand.	*0*	*0*	*0*	*0*
House	0	0	0	0
Senate	0	0	0	0
Democrats	23,000	27,000	1,000	51,000
No. of Cand.	*16*	*9*	*1*	*26*
House	23,000	22,000	1,000	46,000
Senate	0	5,000	0	5,000
Incumbents	13,500	0	0	13,500

(Data for Hispanic PAC USA continued)

Challengers	9,500	21,000	0	30,500
Open Seat	0	6,000	1,000	7,000
Winners	8,500	7,000	n/a	15,500
Losers	14,500	20,000	n/a	34,500

Human Rights Campaign

*Phone: (202) 628-4160 * Fax: (202) 347-5323*
1101 14th St. N.W., Suite 200, Washington, DC 20005
*Web: www.hrc.org * E-mail: susanne.salkind@hrc.org*

The Human Rights Campaign is the largest national lesbian and gay political organization. Founded in 1980, HRC maintains the largest nonpartisan, full-time lobbying team in the nation devoted to issues of fairness for lesbian and gay Americans. In addition to contributing money to congressional campaigns, HRC's political efforts include voter organizing, training and fundraising within the gay community. It also works on issues and ballot initiatives in the states.

Among the group's goals is enacting legislation that would prevent job discrimination on the basis of sexual orientation. Its other priorities are expanding hate-crime laws to include attacks on gay people and increasing funding for AIDS research. HRC maintains profiles on members of Congress and tracks voting records on gay and lesbian issues.

HRC was by far the largest contributor to 1995-96 congressional candidates among gay and lesbian issue PACs. More than 88 percent of its contributions went to Democratic candidates, and it mostly favored incumbents. The top recipients included Rep. Jane Harman, D-Calif., former Rep. Mike Ward, D-Ky., and Rep. Sam Gejdenson, D-Conn.

Rep. Sue W. Kelly, R-N.Y., was the leading Republican recipient.

Human Rights Campaign Fund Political Action Committee (C00235853) *Address: same as sponsor * Treasurer: Elizabeth Birch * Contact: Susanne Salkind, Senior Manager*

	1993-94	1995-96	1997	Totals
Receipts	$758,727	$1,165,143	$448,068	$2,371,938
Disburse	762,873	1,137,121	242,050	2,142,044
Cash	39,604	67,630	267,118	n/a
Contributions	625,424	688,766	201,775	1,515,965
Republicans	35,500	68,127	21,000	124,627
No. of Cand.	*9*	*14*	*7*	*30*
House	17,000	58,127	20,000	95,127
Senate	18,500	10,000	1,000	29,500
Democrats	579,924	610,639	180,775	1,371,338
No. of Cand.	*132*	*165*	*77*	*374*
House	465,495	494,639	149,775	1,109,909
Senate	114,429	116,000	31,000	261,429
Incumbents	447,068	432,065	185,775	1,064,908
Challengers	37,500	135,701	2,000	175,201
Open Seat	140,500	122,500	14,000	277,000
Winners	362,746	555,423	n/a	918,169
Losers	262,678	133,343	n/a	396,021

Indo American PAC

*Phone: (713) 464-4765 * Fax: (713) 464-0389*
P.O. Box 924367, Houston, TX 77292

The Indo American PAC works to promote voter involvement within the Indian-American community.

The PAC, which is bipartisan, gives to federal, state and local candidates.

Indo American Political Action Committee (C00315812) *Address: same as sponsor * Treasurer: Randhir Sahni * Contact: Jagat Kamdar, President*

	1993-94	1995-96	1997	Totals
Receipts	$0	$9,000	$19,306	$28,306
Disburse	0	8,060	9,892	17,952
Cash	0	938	10,352	n/a
Contributions	0	6,000	-3000	3,000
Republicans	0	5,000	-4000	1,000
No. of Cand.	*0*	*1*	*1*	*2*
House	0	0	0	0
Senate	0	5,000	-4000	1,000
Democrats	0	1,000	1,000	2,000
No. of Cand.	*0*	*1*	*1*	*2*
House	0	1,000	1,000	2,000
Senate	0	0	0	0
Incumbents	0	6,000	1,000	7,000
Challengers	0	0	0	0
Open Seat	0	0	0	0
Winners	0	1,000	n/a	1,000
Losers	0	5,000	n/a	5,000

Italian American Democratic Leadership Council

*Phone: (202) 296-8016 * Fax: (202) 682-3984*
1275 K St. N.W., Suite 602, Washington, DC 20005
E-mail: iadlc@erols.com

Former New York Gov. Mario Cuomo and 1998 senatorial candidate Geraldine Ferraro are honorary co-chairs of the Italian American Democratic Leadership Council. The IADLC was founded in 1992 to promote Democratic Italian Americans running for Congress and seeking high administrative positions, as well as to win support within the Italian American community for current Democratic leaders.

Italian American Democratic Leadership Council (C00299396) *Address: same as sponsor * Treasurer: Charles A. Gueli * Contact: Robert Blancato*

	1993-94	1995-96	1997	Totals
Receipts	$38,777	$87,637	$54,913	$181,327
Disburse	34,580	85,381	60,859	180,820
Cash	4,196	6,452	505	n/a
Contributions	21,000	27,325	5,000	53,325
Republicans	0	0	0	0
No. of Cand.	*0*	*0*	*0*	*0*
House	0	0	0	0
Senate	0	0	0	0
Democrats	20,500	27,325	5,000	52,825
No. of Cand.	*22*	*29*	*5*	*56*
House	20,500	17,000	5,000	42,500
Senate	0	10,325	0	10,325
Incumbents	13,500	7,000	2,000	22,500
Challengers	1,500	14,500	0	16,000
Open Seat	6,000	11,825	5,000	22,825
Winners	9,000	21,325	n/a	30,325
Losers	12,000	6,000	n/a	18,000

KidsPAC

Phone: (617) 492-2229
80 Trowbridge St., Cambridge, MA 02138

KidsPAC contributes to candidates who support federal funding for children's programs like Head Start and Early Head Start. The organization's main interest is children ages 0 to 5, but it is interested in kids of all ages. KidsPAC was the only committee devoted to children's issues among the top 200 PACs.

The PAC was founded by William W. Harris, a Massachusetts businessman and college professor. Harris heads an investment firm with offices in Cambridge, Mass. and Chicago.

Although the organization says it generally supports incumbents, it gave almost as much to challengers during the 1995-96 election cycle. More than 99 percent of its contributions went to Democratic candidates.

The top recipients were Sens. Carl Levin, D-Mich., Paul Wellstone, D-Minn., Jack Reed, D-R.I., Ron Wyden, D-Ore., Tim Johnson, D-S.D., and Rep. David E. Bonior, D-Mich. The only Republican to receive a contribution was Rep. John Edward Porter, R-Ill.

KidsPAC (C00147975) *Phone: (202) 728-1100 * 2100 Pennsylvania Ave. N.W., Suite 500, Washington, DC 20037 * Treasurer: William W. Harris*

	1993-94	1995-96	1997	Totals
Receipts	$367,639	$428,073	$190,050	$985,762
Disburse	460,116	423,817	78,415	962,348
Cash	18,849	23,105	134,740	n/a
Contributions	399,000	372,000	53,000	824,000
Republicans	3,500	2,000	0	5,500
No. of Cand.	*2*	*1*	*0*	*3*
House	1,000	2,000	0	3,000
Senate	2,500	0	0	2,500
Democrats	383,500	369,000	52,000	804,500
No. of Cand.	*131*	*109*	*19*	*259*
House	264,000	269,500	31,500	565,000
Senate	119,500	99,500	20,500	239,500
Incumbents	307,000	139,000	51,000	497,000
Challengers	38,500	125,000	0	163,500
Open Seat	52,500	108,000	2,000	162,500
Winners	206,500	243,500	n/a	450,000
Losers	192,500	128,500	n/a	321,000

Log Cabin Republicans PAC

*Phone: (202) 347-5306 * Fax: (202) 347-5224*
1633 Q St. N.W., Suite 210, Washington, DC 20009
Web: www.lcr.org

Founded in the heat of battle over the nation's first anti-gay ballot measure, Log Cabin Republicans is the largest gay and lesbian Republican organization.

Since 1978, LCR has sought to educate Republicans about issues facing the gay and lesbian community. Although based in Washington, the group has more than 50 chapters across the nation.

Log Cabin Republicans Political Action Committee (LCR PAC) (C00301655) *Address: same as sponsor * Treasurer: Richard Leonard Tafel*

	1993-94	1995-96	1997	Totals
Receipts	$0	$56,245	$2,550	$58,795
Disburse	0	53,039	3,207	56,246
Cash	0	4,203	2,546	n/a
Contributions	0	21,981	1,500	23,481
Republicans	0	21,981	1,500	23,481
No. of Cand.	*0*	*25*	*3*	*28*
House	0	17,246	1,500	18,746
Senate	0	4,735	0	4,735
Democrats	0	0	0	0
No. of Cand.	*0*	*0*	*0*	*0*
House	0	0	0	0
Senate	0	0	0	0
Incumbents	0	12,246	1,500	13,746
Challengers	0	4,735	0	4,735
Open Seat	0	5,000	0	5,000
Winners	0	11,850	n/a	11,850
Losers	0	10,131	n/a	10,131

Mobilization for Economic Opportunities PAC

*Phone: (919) 688-0620 * Fax: (919) 688-5333*
103 W. Main St., c/o Sloan Financial Group Inc., Durham, NC 27701

The Mobilization for Economic Opportunities PAC was formed in 1995 by leading African-American business executives, mainly members of the Black Enterprise 100, to "fight efforts to eliminate or modify affirmative action programs," according to the New York Times.

During the 1995-96 election cycle, the PAC contributed mainly to minority Democratic candidates. Of the 19 beneficiaries, only three were Caucasian and two were Republican. None of the contributions were smaller than $1,000 and eight candidates, including North Carolina Senate challenger Harvey Gantt and House Budget Committee Ranking Member John M. Spratt Jr., D-S.C., received $5,000.

The PAC is run by Treasurer Maceo K. Sloan, of the Sloan Financial Group. Sloan Financial is an umbrella organization for such groups as North Carolina Mutual Capital, as well as PCS Development, New Africa Advisers and Capstone Capital Group.

Mobilization for Economic Opportunities PAC (C00303420) *Address: same as sponsor * Treasurer: Maceo K. Sloan*

	1993-94	1995-96	1997	Totals
Receipts	$0	$241,454	$20,711	$262,165
Disburse	0	216,220	9,970	226,190
Cash	0	20,234	31,435	n/a
Contributions	0	56,500	-1500	55,000
Republicans	0	3,500	0	3,500
No. of Cand.	*0*	*2*	*0*	*2*
House	0	3,500	0	3,500
Senate	0	0	0	0
Democrats	0	53,000	-1500	51,500
No. of Cand.	*0*	*17*	*3*	*20*
House	0	40,500	-2500	38,000
Senate	0	12,500	1,000	13,500
Incumbents	0	43,000	-1500	41,500
Challengers	0	5,000	0	5,000
Open Seat	0	8,500	0	8,500
Winners	0	46,500	n/a	46,500
Losers	0	10,000	n/a	10,000

Montana Indian PAC

P.O. Box 130, Pablo, MT 59855

Montana Indian PAC supports candidates with a good understanding of Indian issues, particularly treaty rights and reservation governments. The PAC is not affiliated with any organization — instead, it relies on independent contributions.

Montana Indian Political Action Committee (C00299677) *Address: same as sponsor * Treasurer: Michael T. Pablo*

	1993-94	1995-96	1997	Totals
Receipts	$1,885	$5,299	$0	$7,184
Disburse	1,455	5,790	0	7,245
Cash	430	74	0	n/a
Contributions	1,400	5,300	0	6,700
Republicans	100	0	0	100
No. of Cand.	*1*	*0*	*0*	*1*
House	0	0	0	0
Senate	100	0	0	100
Democrats	1,300	5,300	0	6,600
No. of Cand.	*5*	*4*	*0*	*9*
House	800	5,200	0	6,000
Senate	500	100	0	600
Incumbents	900	200	0	1,100
Challengers	500	100	0	600
Open Seat	0	5,000	0	5,000
Winners	900	200	n/a	1,100
Losers	500	5,100	n/a	5,600

National Community Action Foundation

*Phone: (202) 775-0223 * Fax: (202) 775-0225*
2100 M St. N.W., Suite 604, Washington, DC 20037
*Web: www.ncaf.org * E-mail: dbradley@ncaf.com*

The National Community Action Foundation is a nonprofit lobbying organization for low-income programs. Its PAC receives contributions from about 957 community action agencies. NCAF follows issues such as the community services block grant, welfare reform, low-income energy assistance and weatherization, employment and job training, housing and shelter for the homeless and tax and income policy.

Community Action Program PAC (SSF of National Community Action Foundation Inc.) (C00163048) *Address: same as sponsor * Treasurer: Charles Braithwait*

	1993-94	1995-96	1997	Totals
Receipts	$120,280	$203,195	$103,729	$427,204
Disburse	111,750	192,650	104,463	408,863
Cash	11,091	21,639	4,981	n/a
Contributions	95,250	140,150	74,500	309,900
Republicans	8,500	23,400	21,500	53,400
No. of Cand.	*3*	*18*	*13*	*34*
House	1,500	18,400	18,500	38,400
Senate	7,000	5,000	3,000	15,000
Democrats	85,000	116,750	53,000	254,750
No. of Cand.	*35*	*41*	*20*	*96*
House	40,500	56,750	23,500	120,750
Senate	44,500	60,000	29,500	134,000
Incumbents	85,500	96,900	68,500	250,900
Challengers	2,500	14,750	5,000	22,250
Open Seat	7,250	28,500	1,000	36,750
Winners	69,500	117,400	n/a	186,900
Losers	25,750	22,750	n/a	48,500

National Lesbian PAC

Phone: (202) 467-6408
1718 M St. N.W., Suite 141, Washington, DC 20036
*Web: www.lesbian.org/nlpac * E-mail: nlpac@lesbian.org*

The National Lesbian PAC gives to candidates who support lesbian issues.

The PAC, which claims to be the only PAC that focuses exclusively on lesbian issues, was founded in January 1996 to strengthen lesbian visibility in national politics. It wants to shape a lesbian agenda and encourage lesbians to become more involved in national politics.

NLPAC is particularly interested in the Employment Non-Discrimination Act, adoption and custody issues affecting lesbians, lesbian health issues, inclusion of sexual orientation in hate crimes legislation, domestic partnership and same-sex marriage, HIV status and military service and abortion rights.

National Lesbian Political Action Committee (NLPAC) (C00313304) *Address: same as sponsor * Treasurer: Karen A. Armagost * Contact: Mindy A. Daniels, Executive Dir.*

	1993-94	1995-96	1997	Totals
Receipts	$0	$16,504	$6,153	$22,657
Disburse	0	15,590	5,700	21,290
Cash	0	912	1,364	n/a
Contributions	0	6,200	250	6,450
Republicans	0	0	0	0
No. of Cand.	*0*	*0*	*0*	*0*
House	0	0	0	0
Senate	0	0	0	0
Democrats	0	6,200	250	6,450
No. of Cand.	*0*	*10*	*1*	*11*
House	0	6,200	0	6,200
Senate	0	0	250	250
Incumbents	0	4,600	250	4,850
Challengers	0	1,600	0	1,600
Open Seat	0	0	0	0
Winners	0	5,600	n/a	5,600
Losers	0	600	n/a	600

National Muslims for a Better America

*Phone: (703) 521-1155 * Fax: (703) 521-1156*
1212 New York Ave. N.W., Suite 400, Washington, DC 20005

National Muslims for a Better America was founded to give to candidates with views similar to those of the American Muslim Council.

The council, which is not directly associated with the PAC, was founded to serve the interests of the Muslim community. PAC Treasurer Khalid Saffuri was deputy director of the organization until January 1998.

In addition to Muslim issues, the PAC is also interested in campaign finance, immigration and the war in Bosnia.

National Muslims for a Better America (C00278036) *Address: same as sponsor * Treasurer: Khalid Saffuri*

	1993-94	1995-96	1997	Totals
Receipts	$18,303	$18,816	$6,010	$43,129
Disburse	18,823	8,340	6,123	33,286
Cash	45	10,520	4,310	n/a
Contributions	11,250	10,947	5,500	27,697
Republicans	3,000	2,500	3,500	9,000
No. of Cand.	*4*	*2*	*2*	*8*
House	1,250	2,500	2,500	6,250
Senate	1,750	0	1,000	2,750
Democrats	8,250	8,447	2,000	18,697
No. of Cand.	*7*	*9*	*2*	*18*
House	8,250	7,447	2,000	17,697
Senate	0	1,000	0	1,000
Incumbents	7,250	9,947	5,500	22,697
Challengers	2,500	0	0	2,500
Open Seat	1,500	1,000	0	2,500
Winners	5,000	10,947	n/a	15,947
Losers	6,250	0	n/a	6,250

National Unity Caucus

*Phone: (320) 532-4181 * Fax: (320) 532-5800*
HCR 67, Box 194, Onamia, MN 56359

The National Unity Caucus is a PAC funded by Indian tribes and their leaders from around the nation. The PAC's mailing address is located on the reservation of the Mille Lacs Band of Chippewa in Minnesota.

According to PAC political consultant Scott Dacey, of the PACE lobbying firm, the group assists candidates who support tribal rights of governance and minimal federal interference, among other issues. Some of the contributing tribes have gambling interests, but that is not necessarily the main issue for the PAC.

During the 1995-96 election cycle, about 60 percent of the PAC's money went to candidates from midwestern or western states. The PAC was established in 1996. Since then, more than 45 tribes have made contributions.

National Unity Caucus (C00311761) *Phone: (703) 518-8600 * Fax: (703) 518-8611 * 44 Canal Plaza, Suite 400, Alexandria, VA 22314 * Treasurer: Marge Anderson * Contact: Scott Dacey, Political Consultant*

	1993-94	1995-96	1997	Totals
Receipts	$0	$217,820	$43,345	$261,165
Disburse	0	207,430	35,836	243,266
Cash	0	10,387	17,896	n/a
Contributions	0	45,000	15,000	60,000
Republicans	0	10,000	5,000	15,000
No. of Cand.	*0*	*14*	*1*	*15*
House	0	8,000	5,000	13,000
Senate	0	2,000	0	2,000
Democrats	0	35,000	10,000	45,000
No. of Cand.	*0*	*30*	*5*	*35*
House	0	31,000	9,000	40,000
Senate	0	4,000	1,000	5,000
Incumbents	0	28,000	9,000	37,000
Challengers	0	11,000	0	11,000
Open Seat	0	6,000	5,000	11,000
Winners	0	29,000	n/a	29,000
Losers	0	16,000	n/a	16,000

Pakistani Physicians PAC

*Phone: (203) 639-3134 * Fax: (203) 639-3018*
Southridge Lane, Cromwell, CT 06416

The Pakistani Physicians PAC had 95 contributors during 1997. During that period, no contributions were made to campaigns. PAC contributions were mostly spent on bookkeeping, phone and consulting fees, and to pay a $9,000 fine to the FEC for submitting reports late.

Pakistani Physicians Public Affairs Committee (C00238204)
*Address: same as sponsor * Treasurer: Arif Toor*

	1993-94	1995-96	1997	Totals
Receipts	$51,562	$82,184	$49,468	$183,214
Disburse	46,187	76,768	40,602	163,557
Cash	7,406	12,819	21,684	n/a
Contributions	22,500	22,000	0	44,500
Republicans	2,000	2,000	0	4,000
No. of Cand.	*2*	*1*	*0*	*3*
House	2,000	2,000	0	4,000
Senate	0	0	0	0
Democrats	20,500	20,000	0	40,500
No. of Cand.	*10*	*3*	*0*	*13*
House	11,500	0	0	11,500
Senate	9,000	20,000	0	29,000
Incumbents	18,500	7,000	0	25,500
Challengers	2,000	10,000	0	12,000
Open Seat	2,000	5,000	0	7,000
Winners	17,000	22,000	n/a	39,000
Losers	5,500	0	n/a	5,500

West Los Angeles Health PAC

*Phone: (916) 442-2280 * Fax: (916) 442-1693*
1127 11th St., Suite 300, Sacramento, CA 95814

West Los Angeles Health PAC is interested in federal heath care funding and regulation. It wants to make sure that quality health care survives and access is ensured.

The PAC, which is bipartisan, gives to federal, state and local candidates.

West Los Angeles Health Political Action Committee (C00198861) *Address: same as sponsor * Treasurer: J. Richard Eichman*

	1993-94	1995-96	1997	Totals
Receipts	$14,050	$12,900	$5,500	$32,450
Disburse	15,601	10,583	6,000	32,184
Cash	4,794	7,111	6,611	n/a
Contributions	6,900	9,000	4,000	19,900
Republicans	500	3,000	1,000	4,500
No. of Cand.	*1*	*3*	*1*	*5*
House	0	1,000	0	1,000
Senate	500	2,000	1,000	3,500
Democrats	6,400	6,000	3,000	15,400
No. of Cand.	*9*	*8*	*2*	*19*
House	4,650	5,750	3,000	13,400
Senate	1,750	250	0	2,000
Incumbents	5,650	8,500	4,000	18,150
Challengers	500	0	0	500
Open Seat	750	750	0	1,500
Winners	5,150	7,750	n/a	12,900
Losers	1,750	1,250	n/a	3,000

Women For:

*Phone: (310) 657-7411 * Fax: (310) 289-0719*
8913 W. Olympic Blvd., Suite 103, Beverly Hills, CA 90211
E-mail: womenfor@lafn.org

Women For: is a self-described "liberal" support group. It promotes peace, civil rights, environmental protections and abortion rights. Besides congressional candidates, the group supports community organizations such as the Rural Legal Assistance Fund, Women Against Gun Violence and the Committee to Bridge the Gap.

Most of the PAC's 2,000 members are women from the west side of Los Angeles, so the organization focuses on candidates from that area. Actress Joanne Woodward is a contributor.

Women For: (C00010488) *Address: same as sponsor * Treasurer: Jeanette Bello * Contact: Lucie Bava, Coordinator*

	1993-94	1995-96	1997	Totals
Receipts	$191,582	$137,096	$54,613	$383,291
Disburse	158,983	141,542	65,867	366,392
Cash	52,912	48,467	37,213	n/a
Contributions	1,250	8,050	2,125	11,425
Republicans	0	0	0	0
No. of Cand.	*0*	*0*	*0*	*0*
House	0	0	0	0
Senate	0	0	0	0
Democrats	1,250	8,050	2,125	11,425
No. of Cand.	*3*	*12*	*2*	*17*
House	1,250	7,550	125	8,925
Senate	0	500	2,000	2,500
Incumbents	200	1,250	2,125	3,575
Challengers	1,050	6,000	0	7,050
Open Seat	0	800	0	800
Winners	200	4,450	n/a	4,650
Losers	1,050	3,600	n/a	4,650

Leadership PACs

'98 Leadership PAC

Phone: (703) 548-8621

515 King St., #420, Alexandria, VA 22314

The '98 Leadership PAC, formerly known as the '96 Leadership PAC, is associated with Rep. Michael G. Oxley, R-Ohio. Oxley, who is serving his eighth term in the 105th Congress, is chairman of the House Commerce Subcommittee on Finance and Hazardous Materials, which has jurisdiction over the securities markets, as well as Superfund issues.

'98 Leadership PAC (formerly known as '96 Leadership PAC) (C00314641) *Address: same as sponsor * Treasurer: Pam Sederholm*

	1993-94	1995-96	1997	Totals
Receipts	$0	$127,512	$143,555	$271,067
Disburse	0	89,073	83,616	172,689
Cash	0	38,440	98,380	n/a
Contributions	0	57,000	8,000	65,000
Republicans	0	57,000	8,000	65,000
No. of Cand.	*0*	*12*	*5*	*17*
House	0	57,000	8,000	65,000
Senate	0	0	0	0
Democrats	0	0	0	0
No. of Cand.	*0*	*0*	*0*	*0*
House	0	0	0	0
Senate	0	0	0	0
Incumbents	0	57,000	8,000	65,000
Challengers	0	0	0	0
Open Seat	0	0	0	0
Winners	0	47,000	n/a	47,000
Losers	0	10,000	n/a	10,000

29th Congressional District of California PAC

Phone: (310) 652-7831

8665 Wilshire Blvd., Suite 220, Beverly Hills, CA 90211

The 29th Congressional District of California PAC is a leadership PAC affiliated with Rep. Henry A. Waxman, D-Calif. The PAC was inactive during 1997, but a spokesman said in early 1998 that the PAC does not plan to terminate.

29th Congressional District of California PAC (C00095059) *Address: same as sponsor * Treasurer: Irwin Levin*

	1993-94	1995-96	1997	Totals
Receipts	$14,030	$47,000	$0	$61,030
Disburse	18,025	61,604	2,129	81,758
Cash	9,168	2,564	434	n/a
Contributions	14,000	40,500	0	54,500
Republicans	0	0	0	0
No. of Cand.	*0*	*0*	*0*	*0*
House	0	0	0	0
Senate	0	0	0	0
Democrats	14,000	40,500	0	54,500
No. of Cand.	*6*	*12*	*0*	*18*
House	14,000	38,500	0	52,500
Senate	0	2,000	0	2,000
Incumbents	9,000	3,500	0	12,500
Challengers	5,000	28,000	0	33,000
Open Seat	0	9,000	0	9,000
Winners	3,000	13,500	n/a	16,500
Losers	11,000	27,000	n/a	38,000

Acorn PAC

Phone: (248) 693-8097

320 Shady Oaks, Lake Orion, MI 48362

Acorn PAC was formed with the remaining $300,000 in campaign funds of former Rep. William S. Broomfield, R-Mich. It gives to Republicans whom Broomfield supports. Broomfield represented a region of southeastern Michigan for 36 years and retired in 1992.

The PAC generally supports federal candidates from Michigan and collects money from investments.

Acorn Political Action Committee (C00281089) *Address: same as sponsor * Treasurer: William S. Broomfield*

	1993-94	1995-96	1997	Totals
Receipts	$329,746	$43,043	$29,010	$401,799
Disburse	17,853	34,111	13,709	65,673
Cash	311,892	320,825	336,125	n/a
Contributions	6,120	6,250	0	12,370
Republicans	6,120	6,250	0	12,370
No. of Cand.	*8*	*7*	*0*	*15*
House	5,620	4,750	0	10,370
Senate	500	1,500	0	2,000
Democrats	0	0	0	0
No. of Cand.	*0*	*0*	*0*	*0*
House	0	0	0	0
Senate	0	0	0	0
Incumbents	2,120	1,750	0	3,870
Challengers	3,500	2,500	0	6,000
Open Seat	500	2,000	0	2,500
Winners	2,620	3,750	n/a	6,370
Losers	3,500	2,500	n/a	6,000

Adam Smith PAC

*Phone: (813) 254-4918 * Fax: (813) 253-0283*

P.O. Box 2392, Tampa, FL 33601-2392

E-mail: nhwatkins@aol.com

The Adam Smith PAC is the leadership committee of Sen. Connie Mack, R-Fla., the junior senator from that state. The committee supports Republican candidates for Congress (mostly Senate) from every region of the nation who share Mack's free-market ideals.

The committee contributed almost as much to open races as it did to incumbents during the 1995-96 election cycle. The Adam Smith PAC ranked fifth among Republican leadership committees in congressional contributions.

The leading recipients were Sen. Gordon H. Smith, R-Ore., and 1996 Senate candidate Guy Millner of Georgia. All but two of the recipients received at least $5,000, and four House candidates also received a contribution.

The Adam Smith Political Action Committee (C00301457) *Address: same as sponsor * Treasurer: Nancy H. Watkins*

	1993-94	1995-96	1997	Totals
Receipts	$0	$433,557	$199,290	$632,847
Disburse	0	420,731	150,103	570,834
Cash	0	12,824	62,010	n/a
Contributions	0	320,000	110,000	430,000
Republicans	0	320,000	105,000	425,000
No. of Cand.	*0*	*37*	*18*	*55*
House	0	17,000	0	17,000
Senate	0	303,000	105,000	408,000
Democrats	0	0	5,000	5,000
No. of Cand.	*0*	*0*	*1*	*1*
House	0	0	0	0
Senate	0	0	5,000	5,000
Incumbents	0	130,000	80,000	210,000
Challengers	0	65,000	15,000	80,000
Open Seat	0	125,000	15,000	140,000
Winners	0	194,000	n/a	194,000
Losers	0	126,000	n/a	126,000

Alliance for American Leadership

103 W. Maple St., c/o Terrence O'Donnell, Alexandria, VA 22301

The Alliance for American Leadership, formerly known as Cheney for Congress, was terminated after the 1996 election cycle. The PAC, associated with former Defense Secretary and Rep. Dick Cheney, R-Wyo., contributed nearly $92,000 to Republican candidates in 1995-96.

Alliance for American Leadership (formerly known as Cheney for Congress) (C00084863) *Address: same as sponsor * Treasurer: David S. Addington*

	1993-94	1995-96	1997	Totals
Receipts	$1,374,127	$70,527	$0	$1,444,654
Disburse	1,294,356	226,702	0	1,521,058
Cash	156,174	0	0	n/a
Contributions	178,250	91,900	0	270,150
Republicans	178,250	91,900	0	270,150
No. of Cand.	*92*	*30*	*0*	*122*
House	82,000	64,400	0	146,400
Senate	96,250	27,500	0	123,750
Democrats	0	0	0	0
No. of Cand.	*0*	*0*	*0*	*0*
House	0	0	0	0
Senate	0	0	0	0
Incumbents	41,000	71,400	0	112,400
Challengers	67,000	3,000	0	70,000
Open Seat	70,000	17,500	0	87,500
Winners	131,000	69,000	n/a	200,000
Losers	47,250	22,900	n/a	70,150

AmeriPAC: The Fund for a Greater America

*Phone: (202) 347-5990 * Fax: (202) 347-5941*
1341 G St. N.W., Suite 200, Washington, DC 20005

AmeriPAC: The Fund for a Greater America is the leadership PAC of Rep. Steny H. Hoyer, D-Md. Hoyer is serving his eighth full term during the 105th Congress, and sits on the House Appropriations, House Oversight and Joint Printing committees. He also was the sole Democrat appointed by the House Oversight Committee to the task force that investigated vote fraud charges in the 1996 election of Rep. Loretta Sanchez, D-Calif.

In the 1995-96 election cycle, AmeriPAC gave $10,000 to New Hampshire Senate candidate Dick Swett and $6,000 to fellow Marylander Connie Galiazzo DeJuliis, who ran unsuccessfully in the 2nd District.

AmeriPAC: The Fund for a Greater America (C00271338) *Address: same as sponsor * Treasurer: Jim Copeland*

	1993-94	1995-96	1997	Totals
Receipts	$50,705	$99,500	$39,914	$190,119
Disburse	53,826	99,917	6,513	160,256
Cash	906	486	33,887	n/a
Contributions	40,800	93,000	4,000	137,800
Republicans	0	0	0	0
No. of Cand.	*0*	*0*	*0*	*0*
House	0	0	0	0
Senate	0	0	0	0
Democrats	40,800	93,000	4,000	137,800
No. of Cand.	*38*	*60*	*3*	*101*
House	38,800	81,000	4,000	123,800
Senate	2,000	12,000	0	14,000
Incumbents	26,300	12,500	0	38,800
Challengers	6,000	58,000	0	64,000
Open Seat	7,500	22,500	3,000	33,000
Winners	14,300	35,500	n/a	49,800
Losers	26,500	57,500	n/a	84,000

America 2000 Fund

188 W. Randolph St., Suite 2127, Chicago, IL 60601

The America 2000 Fund is a committee associated with former Illinois Gov. James R. Thompson, R. All of the PAC's 1997 receipts were transfers from Thompson's former campaign committee. Thompson is now chairman of the Chicago-based law firm Winston & Strawn.

America 2000 Fund (C00247395) *Address: same as sponsor * Treasurer: John A. Janicik*

	1993-94	1995-96	1997	Totals
Receipts	$76,601	$124,712	$11,154	$212,467
Disburse	89,936	105,391	18,329	213,656
Cash	8,683	28,004	20,829	n/a
Contributions	9,500	14,250	2,500	26,250
Republicans	9,000	12,250	2,500	23,750
No. of Cand.	*13*	*9*	*3*	*25*
House	2,000	3,500	0	5,500
Senate	7,000	8,750	2,500	18,250
Democrats	500	2,000	0	2,500
No. of Cand.	*1*	*2*	*0*	*3*
House	500	1,000	0	1,500
Senate	0	1,000	0	1,000
Incumbents	6,250	6,000	2,000	14,250
Challengers	750	1,000	0	1,750
Open Seat	2,500	7,250	500	10,250
Winners	8,250	4,500	n/a	12,750
Losers	1,250	9,750	n/a	11,000

America First PAC

*Phone: (650) 692-8456 * Fax: (650) 401-5530*
851 Burlway Rd., Burlingame, CA 94010

America First was created in the early 1990s to support Republican Pat Buchanan's bid for president and his opposition to the Gulf War. Buchanan is not directly involved with the organization.

The group calls itself a supporter of "the classical old right," which it describes as non-interventionist.

America First Political Action Committee (C00254540) *Address: same as sponsor * Treasurer: Burton S. Blumert*

	1993-94	1995-96	1997	Totals
Receipts	$750	$18,265	$0	$19,015
Disburse	4,833	38,044	0	42,877
Cash	19,800	4,285	4,285	n/a
Contributions	100	7,500	0	7,600
Republicans	100	7,500	0	7,600
No. of Cand.	*1*	*6*	*0*	*7*
House	100	7,500	0	7,600
Senate	0	0	0	0
Democrats	0	0	0	0
No. of Cand.	*0*	*0*	*0*	*0*
House	0	0	0	0
Senate	0	0	0	0
Incumbents	0	200	0	200
Challengers	100	7,300	0	7,400
Open Seat	0	0	0	0
Winners	0	7,100	n/a	7,100
Losers	100	400	n/a	500

Americans for a Republican Majority

Phone: (202) 547-9320
1155 21st St. N.W., Suite 300, Washington, DC 20036
E-mail: armpac@msn.com

Americans for a Republican Majority is the leadership PAC of House Majority Whip Tom DeLay, R-Texas. The PAC supports Republican candidates, seeking to maintain and increase the party's hold in both the Senate and House.

ARMPAC is becoming one of the larger House leadership PACs. It made more contributions to congressional candidates during 1997 than House Speaker Newt Gingrich's Monday Morning PAC or House Minority Leader Richard A. Gephardt's Effective Government Committee.

Americans for a Republican Majority (ARMPAC) (C00292946) *Address: same as sponsor * Treasurer: Corwin Teltschik * Contact: Rep. Tom DeLay, Chairman*

	1993-94	1995-96	1997	Totals
Receipts	$312,178	$681,895	$368,454	$1,362,527
Disburse	292,703	701,335	366,820	1,360,858
Cash	19,470	18	1,649	n/a
Contributions	227,627	222,059	93,080	542,766
Republicans	227,601	222,059	93,080	542,740
No. of Cand.	*430*	*116*	*31*	*577*
House	227,531	221,065	93,080	541,676
Senate	70	994	0	1,064
Democrats	20	0	0	20
No. of Cand.	*2*	*0*	*0*	*2*
House	20	0	0	20
Senate	0	0	0	0
Incumbents	4,092	139,596	92,607	236,295
Challengers	108,853	42,020	500	151,373
Open Seat	114,612	39,587	0	154,199
Winners	197,088	112,360	n/a	309,448
Losers	30,539	109,699	n/a	140,238

Campaign America

*Phone: (602) 607-9000 * Fax: (602) 607-9436*
6263 N. Scottsdale Rd., Suite 292, Scottsdale, AZ 85250
*Web: www.quayle.org * E-mail: jp@quayle.org*

Founded by former Sen. Bob Dole, R-Kan., Campaign America is now chaired by former Vice President Dan Quayle. The organization's goals are to preserve and extend the Republican majority in Congress and to strengthen the Republican Party.

Campaign America offers campaign contributions, consulting and campaign visits by Quayle, who made more than 90 such appearances between Labor Day and the November election during 1996. The PAC identifies as potential recipients candidates who support lower taxes and less government regulation.

Campaign America contributed to 250 Republican candidates during the 1995-96 election cycle. The leading recipients were Rep. Michael P. Forbes, R-N.Y., former Rep. Frank A. Cremeans, R-Ohio, and Senate candidate Ronna Romney of Michigan. Slightly more than 40 percent of the PAC's contributions went to candidates who eventually lost their races.

Campaign America (C00088369) *Address: same as sponsor * Treasurer: William R. Neale*

	1993-94	*1995-96*	*1997*	*Totals*
Receipts	$8,642,680	$2,923,397	$2,258,377	$13,824,454
Disburse	6,701,622	4,859,674	2,141,617	13,702,913
Cash	2,473,035	536,759	653,519	n/a
Contributions	605,759	829,971	21,685	1,457,415
Republicans	598,910	825,971	21,685	1,446,566
No. of Cand.	*164*	*258*	*13*	*435*
House	310,739	581,851	11,163	903,753
Senate	288,171	244,120	10,522	542,813
Democrats	1,000	4,000	0	5,000
No. of Cand.	*1*	*1*	*0*	*2*
House	1,000	4,000	0	5,000
Senate	0	0	0	0
Incumbents	183,461	440,175	19,438	643,074
Challengers	243,783	171,515	2,247	417,545
Open Seat	174,040	220,471	0	394,511
Winners	408,441	491,147	n/a	899,588
Losers	197,318	338,824	n/a	536,142

Campaign for a New American Century

*Phone: (615) 329-1932 * Fax: (615) 329-3078*
1922 West End Ave., Nashville, TN 37203
E-mail: cnac@usa.net

Campaign for a New American Century is the federal PAC of Lamar Alexander, former Tennessee governor and U.S. Secretary of Education. It contributes to Republican congressional candidates who, like Alexander, support a "common sense, conservative national agenda."

Alexander ran for president in 1996, but dropped out due in part to a lack of financial support. Not wanting to make the same mistake in 2000, Alexander has used the PAC to help him gain recognition and support, particularly in the early primary states of Iowa and New Hampshire. In November 1997, it was announced that retiring Gov. Terry Branstad of Iowa would become the PAC's national chairman. Branstad's 1994 campaign director and former Iowa GOP Chairman Brian Kennedy was brought on as political director.

Campaign for a New American Century was formerly known as Republican Fund for the Nineties. It was founded in 1993.

Campaign for a New American Century (formerly known as Republican Fund for the Nineties) (C00281923) *Address: same as sponsor * Treasurer: Stacey R. Lukens * Contact: Terry Branstad, Chairman*

	1993-94	*1995-96*	*1997*	*Totals*
Receipts	$402,519	$748,831	$1,502,483	$2,653,833
Disburse	400,306	683,844	1,554,529	2,638,679
Cash	2,211	67,198	15,150	n/a
Contributions	78,649	79,250	9,500	167,399
Republicans	78,649	79,250	9,500	167,399
No. of Cand.	*51*	*32*	*4*	*87*
House	42,149	45,500	3,500	91,149
Senate	36,500	33,750	6,000	76,250
Democrats	0	0	0	0
No. of Cand.	*0*	*0*	*0*	*0*
House	0	0	0	0
Senate	0	0	0	0

Incumbents	22,000	32,750	7,000	61,750
Challengers	29,500	22,250	2,500	54,250
Open Seat	27,149	24,250	0	51,399
Winners	62,899	48,750	n/a	111,649
Losers	15,750	30,500	n/a	46,250

Capitol Committee

Phone: (801) 328-8173
257 E. 200 S., Suite 950, Salt Lake City, UT 84111

The Capitol Committee is the leadership PAC of Sen. Orrin G. Hatch, R-Utah, chairman of the Senate Judiciary Committee. First elected to the Senate in 1976, Hatch presides over judicial nominations and strongly supports a balanced budget amendment. The PAC supports Republican candidates, mostly those seeking Senate seats.

The committee ranked sixth among Republican leadership PACs in contributions to congressional candidates during the 1995-96 election cycle. One-third of the total amount went to candidates in open races.

A dozen Senate candidates received $10,000 from the Capitol Committee, along with Reps. Christopher B. Cannon, R-Utah, and James V. Hansen, R-Utah. Most of the candidates who received contributions got at least $5,000.

The Capitol Committee (C00235572) *Address: same as sponsor * Treasurer: Stanley R. De Waal*

	1993-94	*1995-96*	*1997*	*Totals*
Receipts	$0	$471,293	$120,650	$591,943
Disburse	59	440,749	61,875	502,683
Cash	0	30,544	88,818	n/a
Contributions	0	292,000	19,000	311,000
Republicans	0	292,000	19,000	311,000
No. of Cand.	*0*	*46*	*11*	*57*
House	0	36,000	2,000	38,000
Senate	0	256,000	17,000	273,000
Democrats	0	0	0	0
No. of Cand.	*0*	*0*	*0*	*0*
House	0	0	0	0
Senate	0	0	0	0
Incumbents	0	141,000	13,000	154,000
Challengers	0	52,000	1,000	53,000
Open Seat	0	99,000	5,000	104,000
Winners	0	196,000	n/a	196,000
Losers	0	96,000	n/a	96,000

Chief Deputy Whip's Fund

1310 19th St. N.W., Washington, DC 20036

The Chief Deputy Whip's Fund was terminated in December 1996.

Chief Deputy Whip's Fund (C00292995) *Address: same as sponsor * Treasurer: Andrew Athy Jr.*

	1993-94	*1995-96*	*1997*	*Totals*
Receipts	$90,025	$60,571	$0	$150,596
Disburse	84,232	66,355	0	150,587
Cash	5,789	0	0	n/a
Contributions	75,250	52,864	0	128,114
Republicans	0	0	0	0
No. of Cand.	*0*	*0*	*0*	*0*
House	0	0	0	0
Senate	0	0	0	0
Democrats	74,250	52,864	0	127,114
No. of Cand.	*143*	*72*	*0*	*215*
House	73,250	42,364	0	115,614
Senate	1,000	10,500	0	11,500
Incumbents	61,500	16,500	0	78,000
Challengers	3,000	24,364	0	27,364
Open Seat	10,750	11,500	0	22,250
Winners	47,250	30,500	n/a	77,750
Losers	28,000	22,364	n/a	50,364

Citizens for Gary J. LaPaille

*Phone: (312) 960-2215 * Fax: (312) 960-2220*
P.O. Box 3800, Chicago, IL 60654

Citizens for Gary J. LaPaille was founded by Gary J. LaPaille, chairman of the Democratic Party of Illinois and a vice chairman of the Democratic National Committee. He founded the committee when he ran for the Illinois party chairmanship in 1990.

The committee gives to Democratic federal candidates whom LaPaille supports.

Citizens for Gary J. LaPaille (C00253484) *Address: same as sponsor * Treasurer: Anne Knibbs * Contact: Gary J. LaPaille, PAC Dir.*

	1993-94	1995-96	1997	Totals
Receipts	$21,309	$12,138	$791	$34,238
Disburse	21,589	25,164	3,975	50,728
Cash	25,080	12,055	8,872	n/a
Contributions	6,600	19,000	2,875	28,475
Republicans	0	0	0	0
No. of Cand.	*0*	*0*	*0*	*0*
House	0	0	0	0
Senate	0	0	0	0
Democrats	6,600	19,000	2,875	28,475
No. of Cand.	*10*	*12*	*4*	*26*
House	5,600	11,550	250	17,400
Senate	1,000	7,450	2,625	11,075
Incumbents	2,000	3,250	1,875	7,125
Challengers	0	750	0	750
Open Seat	4,600	15,000	1,000	20,600
Winners	1,500	9,750	n/a	11,250
Losers	5,100	9,250	n/a	14,350

Committee for Democratic Action

*Phone: (703) 978-6718 * Fax: (202) 797-9093*
1424 16th St. N.W., Suite 504, Washington, DC 20036

The Committee for Democratic Action was formed from the remaining funds of former Sen. Howard M. Metzenbaum's leadership PAC, Metzenbaum for Senate - 1988. Metzenbaum, a Democrat from Ohio, retired from the Senate in 1994. When he retired, the fund had about $40,000.

The PAC gives to Democratic candidates and charitable organizations. It is particularly interested in children's rights.

Committee for Democratic Action (formerly known as Metzenbaum for Senate - 1988) (C00167478) *Address: same as sponsor * Treasurer: Juanita Powe * Contact: Howard Metzenbaum, President*

	1993-94	1995-96	1997	Totals
Receipts	$41,690	$7,875	$3,202	$52,767
Disburse	49,191	31,474	5,962	86,627
Cash	71,940	39,234	36,474	n/a
Contributions	11,500	13,650	2,750	27,900
Republicans	0	0	0	0
No. of Cand.	*0*	*0*	*0*	*0*
House	0	0	0	0
Senate	0	0	0	0
Democrats	11,500	13,650	2,750	27,900
No. of Cand.	*10*	*13*	*4*	*27*
House	2,500	3,150	1,000	6,650
Senate	9,000	10,500	1,750	21,250
Incumbents	0	7,800	2,500	10,300
Challengers	500	4,850	0	5,350
Open Seat	11,000	1,000	250	12,250
Winners	3,000	10,550	n/a	13,550
Losers	8,500	3,100	n/a	11,600

Committee for a Democratic Consensus

P.O. Box 11217, Washington, DC 20008

The Committee for a Democratic Consensus is a leadership PAC affiliated with former Sen. Alan Cranston, D-Calif. During 1997, the PAC made one contribution for $1,000 to Sen. Russell D. Feingold, D-Wis.

The Committee for a Democratic Consensus (C00195305) *Address: same as sponsor * Treasurer: Daniel P. Perry*

	1993-94	1995-96	1997	Totals
Receipts	$129,337	$61,069	$5,937	$196,343
Disburse	136,964	57,408	4,419	198,791
Cash	11,901	15,561	17,079	n/a
Contributions	30,000	33,750	1,000	64,750
Republicans	0	0	0	0
No. of Cand.	*0*	*0*	*0*	*0*
House	0	0	0	0
Senate	0	0	0	0
Democrats	30,000	33,750	1,000	64,750
No. of Cand.	*17*	*22*	*1*	*40*
House	5,000	13,250	0	18,250
Senate	25,000	20,500	1,000	46,500
Incumbents	25,000	10,000	1,000	36,000
Challengers	2,000	14,500	0	16,500
Open Seat	3,000	9,250	0	12,250
Winners	12,000	24,500	n/a	36,500
Losers	18,000	9,250	n/a	27,250

Committee for a Democratic Majority

*Phone: (202) 544-4889 * Fax: (202) 546-2285*
426 C St. N.E., Rear Building, Washington, DC 20002

The Committee for a Democratic Majority, the leadership PAC of Sen. Edward M. Kennedy, D-Mass., is one of the three largest of the party and the only one in the Senate. The organization supports both challenger and incumbent Democratic candidates for House and Senate.

In 1994, the Boston Herald reported that the committee financed more than 90 percent of Sen. Kennedy's travel, meals and consultants. The PAC also accepted contributions from other PACs, something Kennedy does not allow his reelection committee to do. Kennedy answered that the PAC money was going toward his activities on behalf of other Democratic candidates.

Committee for a Democratic Majority (C00302067) *Address: same as sponsor * Treasurer: William C. Oldaker * Contact: Jill Gimmel, Executive Dir.*

	1993-94	1995-96	1997	Totals
Receipts	$0	$710,342	$268,613	$978,955
Disburse	0	686,883	284,233	971,116
Cash	0	23,453	7,833	n/a
Contributions	0	50,500	39,000	89,500
Republicans	0	0	0	0
No. of Cand.	*0*	*0*	*0*	*0*
House	0	0	0	0
Senate	0	0	0	0
Democrats	0	50,500	39,000	89,500
No. of Cand.	*0*	*22*	*15*	*37*
House	0	11,000	6,500	17,500
Senate	0	39,500	32,500	72,000
Incumbents	0	20,000	36,500	56,500
Challengers	0	12,000	500	12,500
Open Seat	0	18,500	2,000	20,500
Winners	0	38,500	n/a	38,500
Losers	0	12,000	n/a	12,000

Committee for a Livable Future

*Phone: (503) 228-9692 * Fax: (503) 228-9477*
P.O. Box 6496, Portland, OR 97228

The Committee for a Livable Future is advised by Rep. Earl Blumenauer, D-Ore., but gives no money to him. It supports Democratic nominees who members believe work for federal policies that improve the quality of city life.

Its mission is to build grassroots support for policies that work against urban sprawl, improve transportation and work toward sustainable development. The committee has 160 members.

Committee for a Livable Future (C00323352) *Address: same as sponsor * Treasurer: Robert Stacey * Contact: T. Austin Raglione, Executive Dir.*

	1993-94	1995-96	1997	Totals
Receipts	$0	$42,750	$47,277	$90,027
Disburse	0	36,752	37,530	74,282
Cash	0	5,997	20,742	n/a
Contributions	0	35,000	10,000	45,000
Republicans	0	0	0	0
No. of Cand.	*0*	*0*	*0*	*0*
House	0	0	0	0
Senate	0	0	0	0
Democrats	0	35,000	10,000	45,000
No. of Cand.	*0*	*34*	*2*	*36*
House	0	35,000	10,000	45,000
Senate	0	0	0	0
Incumbents	0	10,000	10,000	20,000
Challengers	0	20,000	0	20,000
Open Seat	0	5,000	0	5,000
Winners	0	23,000	n/a	23,000
Losers	0	12,000	n/a	12,000

Committee for a Progressive Congress

Phone: (703) 435-6391
2201 Wisconsin Ave. N.W., Suite 320, Washington, DC 20007

The Committee for a Progressive Congress is a leadership PAC for Rep. David R. Obey, D-Wis. The committee gives to labor unions, associations and Democratic candidates. It was founded in 1985.

Obey, who is an influential member of the House Democratic Caucus, chaired the House Appropriations Committee when the

Democrats had the majority. He received publicity for an April 1997 shoving match with House Majority Whip Tom DeLay, R-Texas, on the House floor.

Committee for a Progressive Congress Inc. (C00196824) *Address: same as sponsor * Treasurer: Jay Myerson * Contact: Rep. David Obey, Congressman*

	1993-94	*1995-96*	*1997*	*Totals*
Receipts	$97,451	$21,985	$30,742	$150,178
Disburse	87,018	32,970	13,221	133,209
Cash	16,563	5,579	23,101	n/a
Contributions	62,693	25,500	10,000	98,193
Republicans	0	0	0	0
No. of Cand.	*0*	*0*	*0*	*0*
House	0	0	0	0
Senate	0	0	0	0
Democrats	62,693	25,500	10,000	98,193
No. of Cand.	*84*	*46*	*2*	*132*
House	62,693	25,500	10,000	98,193
Senate	0	0	0	0
Incumbents	44,500	6,000	0	50,500
Challengers	4,693	12,000	0	16,693
Open Seat	13,500	7,500	10,000	31,000
Winners	28,500	16,500	n/a	45,000
Losers	34,193	9,000	n/a	43,193

Congressional Black Caucus PAC

Phone: (202) 737-1593
1311 L St. N.W., Washington, DC 20005

The Congressional Black Caucus PAC contributes mostly to "progressive" African-American candidates.

Formed in the early 1980s, this small PAC is chaired by Rep. Chaka Fattah, D-Pa. Its members consist of other PACs and private individuals. PAC contributors include the AFL-CIO and United Mine Workers of America.

Congressional Black Caucus Political Action Committee (CBC-PAC) (C00147512) *Address: same as sponsor * Treasurer: Jeanice M. Salter * Contact: Rep. Chaka Fattah, Chairperson*

	1993-94	*1995-96*	*1997*	*Totals*
Receipts	$15,594	$66,035	$28,200	$109,829
Disburse	17,665	67,286	28,489	113,440
Cash	7,343	5,516	5,225	n/a
Contributions	17,500	30,500	0	48,000
Republicans	0	0	0	0
No. of Cand.	*0*	*0*	*0*	*0*
House	0	0	0	0
Senate	0	0	0	0
Democrats	17,500	30,500	0	48,000
No. of Cand.	*6*	*10*	*0*	*16*
House	11,000	30,500	0	41,500
Senate	6,500	0	0	6,500
Incumbents	8,000	29,500	0	37,500
Challengers	1,000	0	0	1,000
Open Seat	5,500	1,000	0	6,500
Winners	7,000	23,500	n/a	30,500
Losers	10,500	7,000	n/a	17,500

Continue The Majority

*Phone: (407) 649-4321 * Fax: (407) 648-2771*
P.O. Box 533971, Orlando, FL 32853

Continue The Majority is the leadership PAC of Rep. Bill McCollum, R-Fla. McCollum, in his ninth term, is chairman of the House Judiciary Subcommittee on Crime as well as the No. 2 member on the House Banking and Financial Services Committee.

Continue The Majority (C00285387) *Address: same as sponsor * Treasurer: Nancy C. Barth * Contact: Ted Hoepner, General Chairperson*

	1993-94	*1995-96*	*1997*	*Totals*
Receipts	$546,159	$160,793	$72,859	$779,811
Disburse	534,495	171,733	27,429	733,657
Cash	11,665	723	46,153	n/a
Contributions	299,238	55,042	0	354,280
Republicans	295,653	55,042	0	350,695
No. of Cand.	*158*	*45*	*0*	*203*
House	295,653	55,042	0	350,695
Senate	0	0	0	0
Democrats	2,585	0	0	2,585
No. of Cand.	*4*	*0*	*0*	*4*
House	2,585	0	0	2,585
Senate	0	0	0	0
Incumbents	45,585	17,768	0	63,353
Challengers	148,160	10,500	0	158,660
Open Seat	105,493	26,774	0	132,267
Winners	218,126	27,000	n/a	245,126
Losers	81,112	28,042	n/a	109,154

DiFrancesco '93

70 Ormont Rd., Chatham Township, NJ 07928

DiFrancesco '93 filed a termination report on June 1, 1997.

DiFrancesco '93 (C00269258) *Address: same as sponsor * Treasurer: Carol Caprarola*

	1993-94	*1995-96*	*1997*	*Totals*
Receipts	$3,991	$1,800	$163	$5,954
Disburse	33,970	34,290	2,974	71,234
Cash	35,297	2,810	0	n/a
Contributions	19,304	27,000	0	46,304
Republicans	19,304	27,000	0	46,304
No. of Cand.	*7*	*9*	*0*	*16*
House	14,152	19,000	0	33,152
Senate	5,152	8,000	0	13,152
Democrats	0	0	0	0
No. of Cand.	*0*	*0*	*0*	*0*
House	0	0	0	0
Senate	0	0	0	0
Incumbents	6,152	6,000	0	12,152
Challengers	7,152	2,500	0	9,652
Open Seat	6,000	13,500	0	19,500
Winners	9,152	7,000	n/a	16,152
Losers	10,152	20,000	n/a	30,152

Effective Government Committee

*Phone: (202) 347-6112 * Fax: (202) 544-8612*
607 14th St. N.W., Suite 800, Washington, DC 20005

The Effective Government Committee is the leadership PAC of House Minority Leader Richard A. Gephardt, D-Mo. The committee contributes to Democratic candidates, mostly those seeking House seats. In 1997, EGC received about $15,000 from a joint fundraising committee called the New Democratic Majority. EGC got half of the money; the Democratic Congressional Campaign Committee got the other half. The New Democratic Majority committee was terminated in 1997.

EGC serves as a fundraising tool for House Democrats, providing offices from which members can solicit donations. It also contributes in-kind services and focuses on assisting freshman Democrats win re-election.

EGC contributed more to 1996 congressional races than any other Democratic leadership committee. It gave more than half of its contributions to challengers. The top three recipients were all from New Hampshire. The leading recipients — none of whom won — were Senate candidate Dick Swett and House candidates Joe Keefe and Deborah "Arnie" Arnesen.

Effective Government Committee (C00190876) *Address: same as sponsor * Treasurer: Melissa Feld*

	1993-94	*1995-96*	*1997*	*Totals*
Receipts	$1,627,209	$1,164,024	$416,243	$3,207,476
Disburse	1,632,415	1,152,356	423,009	3,207,780
Cash	2,915	14,580	7,814	n/a
Contributions	704,596	461,095	11,500	1,177,191
Republicans	1,000	2,190	0	3,190
No. of Cand.	*1*	*1*	*0*	*2*
House	1,000	2,190	0	3,190
Senate	0	0	0	0
Democrats	690,576	458,905	11,500	1,160,981
No. of Cand.	*187*	*130*	*12*	*329*
House	674,134	422,905	11,500	1,108,539
Senate	16,442	36,000	0	52,442
Incumbents	426,317	74,571	-4000	496,888
Challengers	73,166	259,393	0	332,559
Open Seat	205,113	126,131	15,000	346,244
Winners	289,908	181,763	n/a	471,671
Losers	414,688	279,332	n/a	694,020

Empire Majority Leadership Fund

Phone: (202) 842-3340
P.O. Box 456, Washington, DC 20044

Empire Majority Leadership Fund was the leadership PAC of husband and wife Reps. Bill Paxon, R-N.Y., and Susan Molinari, R-N.Y.

Molinari, former vice chairman of the House Republican Conference, resigned from Congress in the summer of 1997. Paxon was chairman of the National Republican Congressional Committee from 1993 to 1996, and after the Republicans gained the majority, chaired House Republican leadership planning meetings.

Paxon later resigned from that position, after a failed coup to replace Speaker Newt Gingrich in July 1997. Despite that fall from favor, Paxon again rose in popularity with newer Republican members and helped with fundraisers for many candidates, especially those who became freshmen when he ran the NRCC. On Feb. 25, 1998, Paxon announced that he would not seek reelection. He cited wanting to spend time with his family as the main reason for his departure.

As of March 1998, the future of the PAC had yet to be determined, according to Marilyn Abel of Epiphany Productions, the fund's manager. Possible options are to terminate, continue operations for another member of Congress or restructure as more of an ideological organization.

The Empire Majority Leadership Fund was founded in 1996. That year, it gave $92,500 to House Republican candidates.

Empire Majority Leadership Fund (C00312710) *Address: same as sponsor * Treasurer: Maria Cino*

	1993-94	*1995-96*	*1997*	*Totals*
Receipts	$0	$163,992	$60,311	$224,303
Disburse	0	135,122	79,319	214,441
Cash	0	28,868	9,860	n/a
Contributions	0	92,500	65,558	158,058
Republicans	0	92,500	65,558	158,058
No. of Cand.	*0*	*46*	*28*	*74*
House	0	92,500	54,745	147,245
Senate	0	0	10,813	10,813
Democrats	0	0	0	0
No. of Cand.	*0*	*0*	*0*	*0*
House	0	0	0	0
Senate	0	0	0	0
Incumbents	0	48,500	62,121	110,621
Challengers	0	19,000	1,000	20,000
Open Seat	0	20,000	813	20,813
Winners	0	39,500	n/a	39,500
Losers	0	53,000	n/a	53,000

Faith, Family & Freedom PAC

Phone: (317) 259-8918
321 E. Westfield Blvd., Indianapolis, IN 46220
E-mail: devin_daniel@msn.com

Faith, Family & Freedom is the leadership PAC of Rep. David M. McIntosh, R-Ind., who came to Congress with the Republican wave in 1994. McIntosh is chairman of the Government Reform and Oversight's Subcommittee on National Economic Growth, Natural Resources and Regulatory Affairs.

The FFF PAC primarily supports conservative candidates, according to PAC Treasurer Devin Anderson. Founded in 1995, the PAC has had roughly 150 contributors. Top recipients for 1996 were Sen. Sam Brownback, R-Kan., who collected $5,000, and former Rep. Randy Tate, R-Wash., who accepted $6,000 for his failed reelection attempt.

The Center for Responsive Politics alleged that during the 1995-96 election cycle, the PAC "received and disbursed money in a way that could have let donations circumvent federal giving limits." There were 41 instances when a donor who had reached the $1,000 maximum in giving to an individual campaign also gave to Faith, Family & Freedom. The PAC then contributed to that same candidate, usually within a week.

The PAC and Rep. McIntosh were involved with Triad Management Services, as were several of the donors in question. Triad, which matches donors with conservative PACs and candidates, was subpoenaed by the Senate Governmental Affairs Committee as part of its investigation of campaign fundraising during the 1996 elections.

McIntosh denied that the PAC had done anything wrong and said that he personally decided which candidates the PAC would support.

Faith, Family & Freedom PAC (C00309088) *Address: same as sponsor * Treasurer: Devin Anderson * Contact: Rep. David McIntosh, Chairman*

	1993-94	*1995-96*	*1997*	*Totals*
Receipts	$0	$99,173	$0	$99,173
Disburse	0	83,976	1,300	85,276
Cash	0	15,195	7,213	n/a
Contributions	0	85,250	5,500	90,750
Republicans	0	85,250	5,500	90,750
No. of Cand.	*0*	*52*	*4*	*56*
House	0	80,250	2,000	82,250
Senate	0	5,000	3,500	8,500
Democrats	0	0	0	0
No. of Cand.	*0*	*0*	*0*	*0*
House	0	0	0	0
Senate	0	0	0	0
Incumbents	0	58,000	1,000	59,000
Challengers	0	11,000	3,500	14,500
Open Seat	0	16,250	1,000	17,250
Winners	0	53,250	n/a	53,250
Losers	0	32,000	n/a	32,000

Fight-PAC

*Phone: (202) 682-5390 * Fax: (202) 682-5395*
900 Second St. N.E., Suite 114, Washington, DC 20002

Fight-PAC is the leadership committee of Sen. Rick Santorum, R-Pa. Elected to the Senate in 1994, Santorum is an outspoken opponent of partial-birth abortion and one of the youngest members of the Senate. He is a supporter of trimming welfare benefits and a balanced-budget constitutional amendment.

Fight-PAC ranked eighth among Republican leadership PACs in total contributions to 1996 congressional campaigns. The PAC contributes to Republican candidates for the House and Senate. About 40 percent of its contributions went to candidates in open races. Winning candidates accounted for about 45 percent of the PAC's contributions. Eight recipients were from Pennsylvania.

Six of the top seven recipients were Senate candidates; of those, three won their races: Sens. Gordon H. Smith, R-Ore., Sam Brownback, R-Kan., and Chuck Hagel, R-Neb.

Christian Leinbach, who lost to Rep. Tim Holden, D-Pa., was the top House candidate recipient.

Fight-PAC (C00305797) *Address: same as sponsor * Treasurer: Mark D. Rodgers * Contact: Susan Nelson, Administrator*

	1993-94	*1995-96*	*1997*	*Totals*
Receipts	$0	$338,002	$108,906	$446,908
Disburse	0	322,467	58,058	380,525
Cash	0	14,531	60,149	n/a
Contributions	0	227,500	5,000	232,500
Republicans	0	227,500	5,000	232,500
No. of Cand.	*0*	*58*	*4*	*62*
House	0	95,000	1,000	96,000
Senate	0	132,500	4,000	136,500
Democrats	0	0	0	0
No. of Cand.	*0*	*0*	*0*	*0*
House	0	0	0	0
Senate	0	0	0	0
Incumbents	0	51,500	4,000	55,500
Challengers	0	86,000	0	86,000
Open Seat	0	90,000	1,000	91,000
Winners	0	103,000	n/a	103,000
Losers	0	124,500	n/a	124,500

Freedom Project

Phone: (513) 755-6293
8862 Cincinnati Dayton Rd., West Chester, OH 45069

The Freedom Project is the leadership PAC of House Republican Conference Chairman John A. Boehner, R-Ohio. According to its literature, it is "committed to a better America based upon individual freedoms and opportunities, empowered citizens and personal responsibility."

In 1997, the organization led all other House leadership PACs in giving to candidates, distributing more than $135,000. During the previous election cycle, the PAC gave more than $200,000 to House candidates, with roughly half going to challenger and open seat races.

The Freedom Project (C00305805) *Phone: (202) 546-6335 * 111 C St. S.E., Lower Unit, Washington, DC 20003 * Treasurer: Dick Alderson*

	1993-94	*1995-96*	*1997*	*Totals*
Receipts	$0	$319,681	$352,020	$671,701
Disburse	0	315,656	309,400	625,056
Cash	0	4,019	46,041	n/a
Contributions	0	210,221	136,886	347,107
Republicans	0	210,221	136,886	347,107
No. of Cand.	*0*	*77*	*34*	*111*
House	0	210,221	136,146	346,367
Senate	0	0	740	740

Democrats	0	0	0	0
No. of Cand.	*0*	*0*	*0*	*0*
House	0	0	0	0
Senate	0	0	0	0
Incumbents	0	104,578	125,146	229,724
Challengers	0	49,273	10,740	60,013
Open Seat	0	56,370	1,000	57,370
Winners	0	102,160	n/a	102,160
Losers	0	108,061	n/a	108,061

Fund for Democratic Leadership

555 Capitol Mall, Suite 1425, Sacramento, CA 95814

The Fund for Democratic Leadership did not contribute any money to candidates during 1997. But the PAC, set up for Rep. Robert T. Matsui, D-Calif., was a big giver through the 1995-96 election cycle, distributing $120,000 to Matsui's fellow Democratic candidates for Congress.

The third-ranking Democrat on the Ways and Means Committee and the ranking member of the Trade Subcommittee, Matsui is popular with corporate PACs, which gave the Fund for Democratic Leadership $63,500 in 1996.

Fund for Democratic Leadership (formerly known as SAC PAC) (C00165548) *Phone: (703) 916-1700 * 5501 Cherokee Ave., Alexandria, VA 22312 * Treasurer: Warren P. Kashiwagi*

	1993-94	*1995-96*	*1997*	*Totals*
Receipts	$231,049	$143,167	$4,774	$378,990
Disburse	189,019	171,738	17,899	378,656
Cash	42,031	13,453	326	n/a
Contributions	126,000	113,000	0	239,000
Republicans	0	1,000	0	1,000
No. of Cand.	*0*	*1*	*0*	*1*
House	0	1,000	0	1,000
Senate	0	0	0	0
Democrats	125,000	112,000	0	237,000
No. of Cand.	*81*	*83*	*0*	*164*
House	125,000	110,000	0	235,000
Senate	0	2,000	0	2,000
Incumbents	102,000	54,000	0	156,000
Challengers	6,000	30,000	0	36,000
Open Seat	18,000	28,000	0	46,000
Winners	50,000	86,000	n/a	136,000
Losers	76,000	27,000	n/a	103,000

Fund for a Responsible Future

P.O. Box 529, Washington, DC 20044

Rep. Thomas J. Bliley Jr., R-Va., is honorary chairman of his leadership PAC, Fund for a Responsible Future. It was founded in 1995 to "get like-minded conservative Republicans elected to Congress by helping them get their message to voters," according to Linda Pedigo, then treasurer of the PAC, as quoted in the Richmond Times-Dispatch.

Bliley, House Commerce Committee chairman, was a popular target for corporate and law firm PAC contributions; they gave almost $100,000 during the 1995-96 election cycle.

Fund for a Responsible Future (C00301887) *Phone: (703) 379-0978 * 3001 Park Center Dr., Suite 1105, Alexandria, VA 22302 * Treasurer: Janet Bain*

	1993-94	*1995-96*	*1997*	*Totals*
Receipts	$0	$172,676	$137,301	$309,977
Disburse	0	145,723	56,639	202,362
Cash	0	26,950	107,612	n/a
Contributions	0	97,224	8,000	105,224
Republicans	0	97,224	8,000	105,224
No. of Cand.	*0*	*74*	*3*	*77*
House	0	92,224	8,000	100,224
Senate	0	5,000	0	5,000
Democrats	0	0	0	0
No. of Cand.	*0*	*0*	*0*	*0*
House	0	0	0	0
Senate	0	0	0	0
Incumbents	0	46,224	8,000	54,224
Challengers	0	16,000	0	16,000
Open Seat	0	35,000	0	35,000
Winners	0	50,088	n/a	50,088
Losers	0	47,136	n/a	47,136

Fund to Keep America #1

One Fawcett Pl., Suite 130, Greenwich, CT 06831

The Fund to Keep America #1 made just one contribution during 1997 — to Florida Republican gubernatorial candidate Jeb Bush.

Fund to Keep America #1 (C00167007) *Address: same as sponsor * Treasurer: Stephen S. Szymanski*

	1993-94	*1995-96*	*1997*	*Totals*
Receipts	$20,000	$10,000	$0	$30,000
Disburse	-987	12,070	500	11,583
Cash	31,038	28,967	28,467	n/a
Contributions	0	5,000	0	5,000
Republicans	0	5,000	0	5,000
No. of Cand.	*0*	*2*	*0*	*2*
House	0	0	0	0
Senate	0	5,000	0	5,000
Democrats	0	0	0	0
No. of Cand.	*0*	*0*	*0*	*0*
House	0	0	0	0
Senate	0	0	0	0
Incumbents	0	1,000	0	1,000
Challengers	0	4,000	0	4,000
Open Seat	0	0	0	0
Winners	0	1,000	n/a	1,000
Losers	0	4,000	n/a	4,000

GOPAC

*Phone: (202) 484-2282 * Fax: (202) 783-3306*
122 C St. N.W., Suite 505, Washington, DC 20001
*Web: gopac.com * E-mail: gopac.com/email/index.htm*

GOPAC is a Republican organization dedicated to promoting the ideas of limited government, individual responsibility and free enterprise by training and supporting Republican candidates for state and federal elections.

Pete du Pont, then-governor of Delaware, founded GOPAC in 1979 to further Republican aims and build a strong Republican base in state governments. House Speaker Newt Gingrich, R-Ga., took over as general chairperson in 1986 but resigned from the position in 1995 amid allegations of campaign finance and ethics violations. Rep. John Shadegg, R-Ariz., is the current chairperson.

In 1994, GOPAC was sued by the FEC for violating federal campaign disclosure laws. The FEC alleged that GOPAC attempted to influence federal elections between 1989 and 1991 — before it was registered as a federal PAC. The FEC sought to compel GOPAC, through the lawsuit, to disclose the sources and dispensation of more than $500,000 in that time period.

The case was thrown out of federal court in 1996. The judge found in GOPAC's favor, ruling that the group had not directly assisted any federal candidates. The judge rejected the FEC's claim that GOPAC also had spent more than $250,000 on consultants' fees and travel expenses related to Gingrich's reelection.

GOPAC registered as a federal PAC in 1991, and recently opened its records to the public at its offices.

GOPAC Inc. (C00251801) *Address: same as sponsor * Treasurer: Lisa B. Nelson * Contact: Rep. John Shadegg, General Chairperson*

	1993-94	*1995-96*	*1997*	*Totals*
Receipts	$3,955,375	$4,664,569	$1,536,880	$10,156,824
Disburse	3,954,645	4,654,338	1,541,687	10,150,670
Cash	15,072	25,301	20,491	n/a
Contributions	20,059	39,739	6,306	66,104
Republicans	20,059	39,739	6,306	66,104
No. of Cand.	*41*	*68*	*3*	*112*
House	20,059	39,739	6,306	66,104
Senate	0	0	0	0
Democrats	0	0	0	0
No. of Cand.	*0*	*0*	*0*	*0*
House	0	0	0	0
Senate	0	0	0	0
Incumbents	59	24,930	6,806	31,795
Challengers	13,500	7,559	0	21,059
Open Seat	6,500	7,250	0	13,750
Winners	9,559	15,731	n/a	25,290
Losers	10,500	24,008	n/a	34,508

Good Government for America

Phone: (202) 675-6081
P.O. Box 11666, Atlanta, GA 30355

The leadership PAC of Sen. Paul Coverdell, R-Ga., is Good Government for America. Coverdell, elected in 1992, rose to the party's No. 4 leadership job, GOP conference secretary, for the 105th Congress.

Good Government for America supports Republican candidates for Congress.

Good Government for America (C00317479) *Address: same as sponsor * Treasurer: John A. Stabler * Contact: Liz Murray, Executive Dir.*

	1993-94	1995-96	1997	Totals
Receipts	$0	$66,646	$10,000	$76,646
Disburse	0	52,894	10,625	63,519
Cash	0	13,749	13,122	n/a
Contributions	0	36,050	0	36,050
Republicans	0	36,050	0	36,050
No. of Cand.	*0*	*26*	*0*	*26*
House	0	3,000	0	3,000
Senate	0	33,050	0	33,050
Democrats	0	0	0	0
No. of Cand.	*0*	*0*	*0*	*0*
House	0	0	0	0
Senate	0	0	0	0
Incumbents	0	4,000	0	4,000
Challengers	0	9,750	0	9,750
Open Seat	0	22,300	0	22,300
Winners	0	18,800	n/a	18,800
Losers	0	17,250	n/a	17,250

Grassroots Victory Fund

*Phone: (202) 887-0981 * Fax: (202) 293-4693*
P.O. Box 1775, Washington, DC 20013

The Grassroots Victory Fund uses money remaining from former Republican Sen. Larry Pressler's 1996 campaign. Sen. Tim Johnson, D-S.D., defeated Pressler in a highly publicized race. The Grassroots Victory Fund was founded before Pressler lost the 1996 election. It gives to federal, state and local candidates he supports.

Pressler spent more than $4 million on his last campaign — $1.4 million of which came from PACs. He received more money from PACs than any other candidate in 1995.

In February 1998, the FEC threw out complaints against both Pressler and Johnson citing a heavy caseload. The Democratic Senatorial Campaign Committee had filed a complaint in October 1996 after a newspaper reported Pressler had reimbursed himself for more than $125,000 without explaining the purpose of the expenses. Three days later, the National Republican Senatorial Committee alleged that Johnson had $71,000 in unexplained expenses.

Grassroots Victory Fund (C00298695) *Address: same as sponsor * Treasurer: Daniel A. Nelson * Contact: Larry Pressler*

	1993-94	1995-96	1997	Totals
Receipts	$31,925	$41,100	$0	$73,025
Disburse	28,110	35,589	3,444	67,143
Cash	3,813	9,322	5,878	n/a
Contributions	2,300	10,960	1,000	14,260
Republicans	2,300	10,960	1,000	14,260
No. of Cand.	*3*	*5*	*1*	*9*
House	0	3,960	1,000	4,960
Senate	2,300	7,000	0	9,300
Democrats	0	0	0	0
No. of Cand.	*0*	*0*	*0*	*0*
House	0	0	0	0
Senate	0	0	0	0
Incumbents	1,300	0	1,000	2,300
Challengers	0	2,000	0	2,000
Open Seat	1,000	8,960	0	9,960
Winners	2,300	7,960	n/a	10,260
Losers	0	3,000	n/a	3,000

House Majority Fund

*Phone: (301) 622-9250 * Fax: (301) 622-9251*
12329 Needlepine Ter., Silver Spring, MD 20904

The House Majority Fund is the leadership PAC for Rep. John Lewis, D-Ga. The treasurer, Butler C. Derrick Jr., was a Democratic representative from South Carolina from 1975 to 1995.

House Majority Fund (C00321596) *Address: same as sponsor * Treasurer: Butler C. Derrick Jr.*

	1993-94	1995-96	1997	Totals
Receipts	$0	$44,885	$0	$44,885
Disburse	0	44,102	120	44,222
Cash	0	782	662	n/a
Contributions	0	43,000	0	43,000
Republicans	0	0	0	0
No. of Cand.	*0*	*0*	*0*	*0*
House	0	0	0	0
Senate	0	0	0	0
Democrats	0	43,000	0	43,000
No. of Cand.	*0*	*71*	*0*	*71*
House	0	43,000	0	43,000
Senate	0	0	0	0
Incumbents	0	4,000	0	4,000
Challengers	0	29,000	0	29,000
Open Seat	0	10,000	0	10,000
Winners	0	22,000	n/a	22,000
Losers	0	21,000	n/a	21,000

Leadership Council PAC

*Phone: (202) 659-6623 * Fax: (202) 659-6699*
P.O. Box 457, Haverford, PA 19041

The Leadership Council is the PAC for former Rep. Lawrence Coughlin, R-Pa. Coughlin, who represented the suburbs of Philadelphia in the 13th District, retired from the House in 1992. He founded the PAC in 1993 with remaining campaign funds.

Coughlin uses the fund to give to Republican candidates he supports. He gives to federal, state and local candidates.

Leadership Council PAC (formerly known as Coughlin for Congress) (C00001248) *Address: same as sponsor * Treasurer: Elizabeth Dunn * Contact: Lawrence Coughlin, Chairman*

	1993-94	1995-96	1997	Totals
Receipts	$6,913	$3,420	$765	$11,098
Disburse	230,759	24,752	3,840	259,351
Cash	35,272	13,944	10,869	n/a
Contributions	5,000	15,000	250	20,250
Republicans	5,000	15,000	250	20,250
No. of Cand.	*11*	*25*	*1*	*37*
House	4,000	14,000	250	18,250
Senate	1,000	1,000	0	2,000
Democrats	0	0	0	0
No. of Cand.	*0*	*0*	*0*	*0*
House	0	0	0	0
Senate	0	0	0	0
Incumbents	2,750	10,500	250	13,500
Challengers	1,750	2,000	0	3,750
Open Seat	1,000	2,500	0	3,500
Winners	4,750	10,500	n/a	15,250
Losers	250	4,500	n/a	4,750

Leadership for America

*Phone: (214) 706-9164 * Fax: (214) 706-9165*
P.O. Box 565087, Dallas, TX 75356-5087

Leadership for America is a leadership PAC for Sen. Phil Gramm, R-Texas. The PAC was inactive during much of 1997.

Leadership for America (C00281188) *Address: same as sponsor * Treasurer: D. R. White*

	1993-94	1995-96	1997	Totals
Receipts	$283,669	$0	$10,004	$293,673
Disburse	226,350	56,710	1,691	284,751
Cash	57,316	604	8,917	n/a
Contributions	33,166	39,500	918	73,584
Republicans	33,166	39,500	918	73,584
No. of Cand.	*26*	*13*	*2*	*41*
House	31,936	18,500	0	50,436
Senate	1,230	21,000	918	23,148
Democrats	0	0	0	0
No. of Cand.	*0*	*0*	*0*	*0*
House	0	0	0	0
Senate	0	0	0	0
Incumbents	16,162	19,500	918	36,580
Challengers	13,847	13,000	0	26,847
Open Seat	3,157	7,000	0	10,157
Winners	27,373	17,000	n/a	44,373
Losers	5,793	22,500	n/a	28,293

Leadership for America Committee

Phone: (518) 584-3260
P.O. Box 459, Saratoga Springs, NY 12866

Leadership for America Committee is the leadership PAC of Rep. Gerald B.H. Solomon, R-N.Y. The chairman of the Rules Committee, now in his tenth term, has not faced a serious challenge to his seat since he was elected in 1978. Solomon announced in April 1998 that he would retire at the end of the 105th Congress.

During the 1996 election cycle, the group brought in more than $130,000, of which roughly $120,000 was from other PACs. Of that, $22,500 went to the National Republican Congressional Committee, and another $20,000 went directly to candidates' campaign funds.

Leadership for America Committee (C00282632) *Address: same as sponsor * Treasurer: J. Ronald Williams*

	1993-94	1995-96	1997	Totals
Receipts	$0	$137,541	$64,220	$201,761
Disburse	0	170,207	10,676	180,883
Cash	0	24,134	77,678	n/a
Contributions	0	20,250	3,000	23,250
Republicans	0	20,250	3,000	23,250
No. of Cand.	*0*	*28*	*3*	*31*
House	0	19,250	2,000	21,250
Senate	0	1,000	1,000	2,000
Democrats	0	0	0	0
No. of Cand.	*0*	*0*	*0*	*0*
House	0	0	0	0
Senate	0	0	0	0
Incumbents	0	15,250	1,000	16,250
Challengers	0	3,500	0	3,500
Open Seat	0	1,500	2,000	3,500
Winners	0	11,000	n/a	11,000
Losers	0	9,250	n/a	9,250

Leadership for the Future

Phone: (202) 736-8000
1722 Eye St. N.W., Washington, DC 20006

Leadership for the Future is a mostly inactive PAC that supported former Sen. Jim Sasser, D-Tenn., as well as his Democratic colleagues, while he was in the Senate.

Sasser had been in the Senate for three terms and was chairman of the Senate Budget Committee when he was defeated by Republican Bill Frist in 1994. Sasser was widely expected to become the Democratic leader in his fourth term.

The PAC was founded in 1993. Since Sasser's defeat it has donated a small amount to Democrats running for the Senate.

Leadership for the Future (C00294363) *Address: same as sponsor * Treasurer: Michael Nemeroff * Contact: Jim Sasser, Former Senator*

	1993-94	1995-96	1997	Totals
Receipts	$93,849	$1,819	$146	$95,814
Disburse	77,907	10,420	95	88,422
Cash	15,941	7,339	7,390	n/a
Contributions	24,000	5,000	0	29,000
Republicans	0	0	0	0
No. of Cand.	*0*	*0*	*0*	*0*
House	0	0	0	0
Senate	0	0	0	0
Democrats	22,000	5,000	0	27,000
No. of Cand.	*18*	*3*	*0*	*21*
House	4,000	0	0	4,000
Senate	18,000	5,000	0	23,000
Incumbents	8,000	1,000	0	9,000
Challengers	4,000	0	0	4,000
Open Seat	12,000	0	0	12,000
Winners	8,000	1,000	n/a	9,000
Losers	16,000	4,000	n/a	20,000

Lone Star Fund

*Phone: (214) 943-5581 * Fax: (214) 948-6030*
P.O. Box 4219, Dallas, TX 75208

The Lone Star Fund was formed to support Rep. Martin Frost, D-Texas, and other Democrats running for federal office. The PAC has given a nominal amount to Republicans.

Frost has represented the 24th District, which includes parts of Dallas and Fort Worth, since 1978. He chaired the Democratic Congressional Campaign Committee during the 105th Congress.

Lone Star Fund (C00269779) *Address: same as sponsor * Treasurer: Bonnie Breazeale * Contact: Rep. Martin Frost*

	1993-94	1995-96	1997	Totals
Receipts	$17,000	$25,100	$25,985	$68,085
Disburse	17,186	20,500	27,531	65,217
Cash	393	4,993	3,446	n/a
Contributions	2,000	18,000	10,250	30,250
Republicans	0	1,000	0	1,000
No. of Cand.	*0*	*1*	*0*	*1*
House	0	0	0	0
Senate	0	1,000	0	1,000
Democrats	2,000	17,000	10,250	29,250
No. of Cand.	*2*	*5*	*7*	*14*
House	500	15,000	9,000	24,500
Senate	1,500	2,000	1,250	4,750
Incumbents	500	5,000	3,000	8,500
Challengers	0	7,000	0	7,000
Open Seat	1,500	5,000	6,250	12,750
Winners	500	10,000	n/a	10,500
Losers	1,500	8,000	n/a	9,500

MODRN PAC

*Phone: (212) 755-6528 * Fax: (212) 755-0021*
14 E. 60th St., Suite 702, New York, NY 10022

The MODRN PAC supports progressive Republican candidates. According to its chairman and treasurer, former Rep. Bill Green, R-N.Y., that includes candidates who "agree with the ideals of Presidents Lincoln and Teddy Roosevelt." The PAC raises money through a direct-mail operation, receiving donations from "several thousand people" nationwide.

The PAC was founded in 1983 by former Rep. Carl D. Pursell, R-Mich., after his party suffered major defeats in the 1982 election. The chairman of the Northern Republican "Gypsy Moths" Caucus wanted to help the moderates of his party. MODRN PAC mainly supports federal candidates but has contributed to gubernatorial races in previous years. During the 1996 election, the average contribution was roughly $1,000 per race, with the largest contributions of $4,500 going to unsuccessful challengers Susy Heintz, who ran in Michigan's 10th District, and Karen Martynick from Pennsylvania's 16th.

MODRN Political Action Committee (C00165159) *Address: same as sponsor * Treasurer: S. William Green*

	1993-94	1995-96	1997	Totals
Receipts	$66,813	$91,975	$24,971	$183,759
Disburse	64,803	90,724	12,205	167,732
Cash	6,909	8,129	20,895	n/a
Contributions	28,000	47,500	4,500	80,000
Republicans	28,000	47,000	4,500	79,500
No. of Cand.	*31*	*49*	*9*	*89*
House	20,000	37,500	4,000	61,500
Senate	8,000	9,500	500	18,000
Democrats	0	500	0	500
No. of Cand.	*0*	*1*	*0*	*1*
House	0	500	0	500
Senate	0	0	0	0
Incumbents	7,500	16,000	4,500	28,000
Challengers	8,500	14,000	0	22,500
Open Seat	12,000	17,000	0	29,000
Winners	15,500	16,000	n/a	31,500
Losers	12,500	31,500	n/a	44,000

Majority Leader's Fund

*Phone: (703) 802-3218 * Fax: (703) 802-3219*
4451 Brookfield Corporate Dr., Suite 200, Chantilly, VA 20151

The Majority Leader's Fund is the leadership PAC of House Majority Leader Dick Armey, R-Texas. Armey is a proponent of a flat income tax. He opposes a minimum wage and federal funding for the National Endowment for the Arts. The PAC supports House Republican candidates. It contributed to one Senate candidate in 1996, Sen. Tim Hutchinson, R-Ark.

Armey's PAC ranked second among Republican leadership committees in contributions to 1996 congressional races. Less than 50 percent of its contributions went to winning candidates, and it ranked among the top 35 PACs in total money contributed to challengers.

The top recipients were former Reps. Martin R. Hoke, R-Ohio, and Steve Stockman, R-Texas. Nearly 70 candidates received at least $5,000 from this PAC.

Majority Leader's Fund (C00301366) *Address: same as sponsor * Treasurer: Dan Morgan*

	1993-94	1995-96	1997	Totals
Receipts	$0	$1,659,947	$636,265	$2,296,212
Disburse	0	1,574,332	486,127	2,060,459
Cash	0	86,614	235,752	n/a
Contributions	0	737,558	10,500	748,058
Republicans	0	737,558	10,500	748,058
No. of Cand.	*0*	*149*	*5*	*154*
House	0	735,558	10,500	746,058
Senate	0	2,000	0	2,000
Democrats	0	0	0	0
No. of Cand.	*0*	*0*	*0*	*0*
House	0	0	0	0
Senate	0	0	0	0
Incumbents	0	384,363	9,500	393,863
Challengers	0	168,503	1,000	169,503
Open Seat	0	182,692	0	182,692
Winners	0	359,611	n/a	359,611
Losers	0	377,947	n/a	377,947

Monday Morning PAC

*Phone: (202) 296-0570 * Fax: (202) 296-6140*
P.O. Box 10097, Arlington, VA 22210

The Monday Morning PAC is the leadership PAC of House Speaker Newt Gingrich, R-Ga. The PAC, founded prior to the 1996 congressional elections, donates to Republican candidates, mostly those seeking House seats. It also gave $5,000 to Jack Kemp's 1996 presidential campaign committee.

The committee was the top Republican leadership PAC contributor to 1996 congressional elections. All but nine recipients received at least $5,000. The leading recipients were Rep. Jo Ann Emerson, R-Mo., and former Rep. Steve Stockman, R-Texas. Nearly 40 other House Republican candidates received $10,000 from this PAC.

The PAC split its contributions almost evenly between winning and losing candidates. Incumbent candidates received just more than half of its contributions.

Monday Morning Political Action Committee (C00304022) *Address: same as sponsor * Treasurer: Trudy Matthes Barksdale * Contact: Tim Crawford, Executive Dir.*

	1993-94	1995-96	1997	Totals
Receipts	$0	$1,354,897	$334,893	$1,689,790
Disburse	0	1,297,721	310,988	1,608,709
Cash	0	57,175	81,077	n/a
Contributions	0	766,500	10,000	776,500
Republicans	0	766,500	10,000	776,500
No. of Cand.	*0*	*113*	*4*	*117*
House	0	762,500	10,000	772,500
Senate	0	4,000	0	4,000
Democrats	0	0	0	0
No. of Cand.	*0*	*0*	*0*	*0*
House	0	0	0	0
Senate	0	0	0	0
Incumbents	0	392,000	10,000	402,000
Challengers	0	178,500	0	178,500
Open Seat	0	196,000	0	196,000
Winners	0	394,000	n/a	394,000
Losers	0	372,500	n/a	372,500

New Republican Majority Fund

*Phone: (202) 347-1233 * Fax: (202) 347-1238*
1301 Pennsylvania Ave. N.W., Suite 500, Washington, DC 20004
E-mail: nrmf@msn.com

The New Republican Majority Fund is the leadership PAC for Senate Majority Leader Trent Lott, R-Miss. Lott assumed a leadership role in 1994 by defeating former Sen. Alan K. Simpson, R-Wyo., for the post of majority whip; he then became majority leader in 1996.

The PAC began 1998 with more than $1 million in cash, even though it spent more than $2 million during 1997 on contributions and other expenses. During the 1995-96 election cycle, the committee ranked third in congressional contributions among Republican leadership PACs. Twenty-three candidates received $10,000 from the fund; all but two sought Senate seats. The PAC contributed more to open races than it did to incumbents.

The leading recipients included Sen. Gordon H. Smith, R-Ore., and Rep. Charles "Chip" Pickering Jr., R-Miss. More than half of the recipients got at least $5,000.

New Republican Majority Fund (C00300483) *Address: same as sponsor * Treasurer: J. Stanley Huckaby * Contact: John Green, Executive Dir.*

	1993-94	1995-96	1997	Totals
Receipts	$0	$1,799,550	$2,937,381	$4,736,931
Disburse	0	1,386,087	2,150,768	3,536,855
Cash	0	413,459	1,200,074	n/a
Contributions	0	410,142	107,499	517,641
Republicans	0	410,142	107,499	517,641
No. of Cand.	*0*	*81*	*22*	*103*
House	0	112,335	23,000	135,335
Senate	0	297,807	84,499	382,306
Democrats	0	0	0	0
No. of Cand.	*0*	*0*	*0*	*0*
House	0	0	0	0
Senate	0	0	0	0
Incumbents	0	159,368	91,499	250,867
Challengers	0	79,275	6,000	85,275
Open Seat	0	171,499	10,000	181,499
Winners	0	237,367	n/a	237,367
Losers	0	172,775	n/a	172,775

Northwest Leadership PAC

Phone: (703) 379-4453
1075 Bellevue Way N.E., Suite 401, Bellevue, WA 98004

The Northwest Leadership PAC is the leadership PAC for Sen. Slade Gorton, R-Wash.

It has held events in conjunction with the New Republican Majority Fund, the PAC for Senate Majority Leader Trent Lott, R-Miss. The committee declined to disclose any further information.

Northwest Leadership Political Action Committee (C00323360) *Address: same as sponsor * Treasurer: Jeffrey J. Rich*

	1993-94	1995-96	1997	Totals
Receipts	$0	$45,448	$97,839	$143,287
Disburse	0	33,651	73,464	107,115
Cash	0	11,797	36,173	n/a
Contributions	0	16,000	0	16,000
Republicans	0	16,000	0	16,000
No. of Cand.	*0*	*12*	*0*	*12*
House	0	12,000	0	12,000
Senate	0	4,000	0	4,000
Democrats	0	0	0	0
No. of Cand.	*0*	*0*	*0*	*0*
House	0	0	0	0
Senate	0	0	0	0
Incumbents	0	10,000	0	10,000
Challengers	0	2,500	0	2,500
Open Seat	0	3,000	0	3,000
Winners	0	11,000	n/a	11,000
Losers	0	5,000	n/a	5,000

Oregon Smith Fund

Phone: (541) 535-4524
3431 S. Pacific Highway, #135B, Medford, OR 97501

The Oregon Smith Fund, formerly known as the Bob Smith for Congress Committee, is a leadership PAC. The PAC has no members; its money comes from a trust account and a corporate bond fund.

The PAC contributes to state and federal Republican candidates and to candidate recruitment programs.

Oregon Smith Fund (formerly known as Bob Smith for Congress Committee) (C00146886) *Address: same as sponsor * Treasurer: Catherine Aurand*

	1993-94	1995-96	1997	Totals
Receipts	$0	$56,637	$33,666	$90,303
Disburse	0	67,997	23,978	91,975
Cash	0	219,473	228,703	n/a
Contributions	30,258	31,000	0	61,258
Republicans	30,258	30,500	0	60,758
No. of Cand.	*5*	*24*	*0*	*29*
House	30,258	23,500	0	53,758
Senate	0	7,000	0	7,000
Democrats	0	0	0	0
No. of Cand.	*0*	*0*	*0*	*0*
House	0	0	0	0
Senate	0	0	0	0
Incumbents	27,850	20,500	0	48,350
Challengers	2,000	2,000	0	4,000
Open Seat	408	8,500	0	8,908
Winners	1,408	26,000	n/a	27,408
Losers	28,850	5,000	n/a	33,850

Participation 2000

*Phone: (202) 543-5540 * Fax: (202) 543-5547*
236 Massachusetts Ave. N.E., Suite 206, Washington, DC 20002
E-mail: partic2000@aol.com

Participation 2000 provides campaigns with trained political staffers rather than direct cash payments. Each June, "Part 2" selects, trains and pays recent college graduates to work on "progressive" Democratic campaigns nationwide, placing an emphasis on women and minority candidates. For the 1998 campaigns, the group hopes to provide support staffers to 35 campaigns.

Participation 2000 claims an overall success rate of slightly more than 50 percent. A majority of the program's graduates stay in the political sphere, and "Part 2" hopes they will prove to be valuable resources for the Democratic party.

In 1988, Ohio Governor Richard Celeste founded Participation 2000 in Columbus, Ohio. The organization moved to Washington in 1991, the same year former Sen. Bill Bradley, D-N.J., became honorary co-chairman. "Part 2" is supported by about 500 contributors.

Participation 2000 Inc. (C00221887) *Address: same as sponsor * Treasurer: James Zazzali * Contact: Joyce Gresko, Executive Dir.*

	1993-94	1995-96	1997	Totals
Receipts	$220,470	$299,110	$156,001	$675,581
Disburse	220,704	301,536	152,487	674,727
Cash	19	352	3,867	n/a
Contributions	23,949	39,650	2,811	66,410
Republicans	307	0	0	307
No. of Cand.	*1*	*0*	*0*	*1*
House	307	0	0	307
Senate	0	0	0	0
Democrats	23,642	39,650	2,811	66,103
No. of Cand.	*25*	*22*	*11*	*58*
House	19,945	38,150	2,811	60,906
Senate	3,697	1,500	0	5,197
Incumbents	12,726	3,796	1,520	18,042
Challengers	3,608	24,745	0	28,353
Open Seat	7,015	11,109	0	18,124
Winners	6,309	25,438	n/a	31,747
Losers	17,640	14,212	n/a	31,852

People Helping People

Phone: (213) 489-4792
555 S. Flower St., Suite 4510, Los Angeles, CA 90071

People Helping People is a leadership PAC affiliated with Rep. Maxine Waters, D-Calif. The PAC contributes to Democratic congressional candidates as well as other groups like the AFL-CIO and the American Federation of State, County & Municipal Employees.

People Helping People (C00248948) *Address: same as sponsor * Treasurer: David L. Gould*

	1993-94	1995-96	1997	Totals
Receipts	$46,417	$61,710	$25,508	$133,635
Disburse	47,180	61,824	16,221	125,225
Cash	192	74	9,361	n/a
Contributions	11,500	25,000	0	36,500
Republicans	0	0	0	0
No. of Cand.	*0*	*0*	*0*	*0*
House	0	0	0	0
Senate	0	0	0	0
Democrats	11,500	25,000	0	36,500
No. of Cand.	*11*	*8*	*0*	*19*
House	10,000	25,000	0	35,000
Senate	1,500	0	0	1,500
Incumbents	8,000	18,000	0	26,000
Challengers	1,000	0	0	1,000
Open Seat	2,500	7,000	0	9,500
Winners	7,000	19,000	n/a	26,000
Losers	4,500	6,000	n/a	10,500

Posthumus Victory Fund USA

*Phone: (517) 373-0797 * Fax: (517) 373-5236*
P.O. Box 14212, Lansing, MI 48901

The Posthumus Victory Fund was set up by Michigan Republican state Sen. Dick Posthumus. It gives to Republican candidates, primarily those from Michigan. The fund is largely inactive and is scheduled to be terminated in 1998.

Posthumus Victory Fund USA (C00276774) *Address: same as sponsor * Treasurer: Saul Anuzis * Contact: State Sen. Dick Posthumus, Chairman*

	1993-94	1995-96	1997	Totals
Receipts	$9,195	$24,075	$0	$33,270
Disburse	7,106	22,134	0	29,240
Cash	2,088	4,026	4,026	n/a
Contributions	7,000	17,000	0	24,000
Republicans	7,000	17,000	0	24,000
No. of Cand.	*4*	*6*	*0*	*10*
House	2,000	11,000	0	13,000
Senate	5,000	6,000	0	11,000
Democrats	0	0	0	0
No. of Cand.	*0*	*0*	*0*	*0*
House	0	0	0	0
Senate	0	0	0	0
Incumbents	500	4,000	0	4,500
Challengers	1,500	13,000	0	14,500
Open Seat	5,000	0	0	5,000
Winners	5,500	0	n/a	5,500
Losers	1,500	17,000	n/a	18,500

Rangel National Leadership PAC

Phone: (202) 955-3000
2100 Pennsylvania Ave. N.W., Suite 400, Washington, DC 20037

The Rangel National Leadership PAC was terminated in February 1998.

Rangel National Leadership PAC (formerly known as National Leadership PAC) (C00302588) *Address: same as sponsor * Treasurer: George A. Dalley*

	1993-94	1995-96	1997	Totals
Receipts	$0	$133,351	$20,992	$154,343
Disburse	0	68,320	19,000	87,320
Cash	0	65,030	67,272	n/a
Contributions	0	62,805	2,000	64,805
Republicans	0	1,000	0	1,000
No. of Cand.	*0*	*1*	*0*	*1*
House	0	1,000	0	1,000
Senate	0	0	0	0
Democrats	0	61,805	2,000	63,805
No. of Cand.	*0*	*44*	*1*	*45*
House	0	60,805	2,000	62,805
Senate	0	1,000	0	1,000
Incumbents	0	26,305	0	26,305
Challengers	0	24,000	0	24,000
Open Seat	0	12,500	2,000	14,500
Winners	0	43,305	n/a	43,305
Losers	0	19,500	n/a	19,500

Re-Elect Freshmen of the Republican Majority

Phone: (703) 931-9747
4520 King St., Suite 807, Alexandria, VA 22302

Re-Elect Freshmen of the Republican Majority is the leadership PAC of Rep. Jerry Weller, R-Ill. Weller was elected in the 1994 Republican takeover of Congress and became sophomore class president for the 105th Congress.

Weller was quickly moved into influential places, with seats on the Republican Steering Committee and the House Ways and Means panel. In July 1997, he made a bid to move even higher up the leadership ladder, to secretary of the Republican Conference, but came in last out of four candidates.

REFORM-PAC has earned Weller praise for his fundraising prowess, and also criticism for using his committee positions to draw in corporate PAC donations. At a June 1997 breakfast for GOP freshmen, Weller handed out $500 contribution checks from his PAC as well as from the National Association of Realtors and the Mortgage Bankers Association.

During the 1995-96 election cycle, REFORM-PAC gave $118,000 to Republican incumbents elected in 1994.

Re-Elect Freshmen of the Republican Majority (REFORM-PAC) (C00315275) *Address: same as sponsor * Treasurer: Carol L. Lindamood * Contact: Rep. Jerry Weller, Chairman*

	1993-94	1995-96	1997	Totals
Receipts	$0	$153,528	$51,900	$205,428
Disburse	0	153,243	43,562	196,805
Cash	0	283	8,621	n/a
Contributions	0	118,000	33,500	151,500
Republicans	0	118,000	33,000	151,000
No. of Cand.	*0*	*41*	*46*	*87*
House	0	118,000	33,000	151,000
Senate	0	0	0	0

(Data for Re-Elect Freshmen continued)

Democrats	0	0	500	500
No. of Cand.	*0*	*0*	*1*	*1*
House	0	0	500	500
Senate	0	0	0	0
Incumbents	0	118,000	31,500	149,500
Challengers	0	0	1,000	1,000
Open Seat	0	0	0	0
Winners	0	76,500	n/a	76,500
Losers	0	41,500	n/a	41,500

Renew America PAC

Phone: (202) 224-8375
P.O. Box 77824, Washington, DC 20013

Renew America, the leadership PAC of Sen. Alfonse M. D'Amato, R-N.Y., was one of the top five Senate leadership PACs in contributions to congressional candidates for 1997. D'Amato also chaired the National Republican Senatorial Committee, which helped the GOP pick up two seats in 1996.

During the 1995-96 election cycle, Renew America gave most heavily to challengers and candidates seeking open seats, including Al Salvi, who lost a bid for a Senate seat to Sen. Richard J. Durbin, D-Ill. Salvi received $10,000.

D'Amato has good reason to cultivate a strong network of support in the Senate. He faces a tough and costly reelection campaign in 1998, and his challengers had already raised more than $10 million by the start of that year.

Renew America PAC (C00290098) *Address: same as sponsor * Treasurer: Michael Giuliani*

	1993-94	*1995-96*	*1997*	*Totals*
Receipts	$101,060	$193,216	$59,500	$353,776
Disburse	81,970	181,799	19,579	283,348
Cash	19,090	30,504	70,423	n/a
Contributions	48,500	125,500	17,500	191,500
Republicans	47,500	125,500	17,500	190,500
No. of Cand.	*16*	*24*	*4*	*44*
House	22,000	32,000	7,500	61,500
Senate	25,500	93,500	10,000	129,000
Democrats	0	0	0	0
No. of Cand.	*0*	*0*	*0*	*0*
House	0	0	0	0
Senate	0	0	0	0
Incumbents	11,500	49,500	17,500	78,500
Challengers	30,000	25,000	0	55,000
Open Seat	7,000	51,000	0	58,000
Winners	23,500	64,500	n/a	88,000
Losers	25,000	61,000	n/a	86,000

Republican Leadership Council

*Phone: (202) 547-1700 * Fax: (202) 547-4228*
236 Massachusetts Ave. N.E., Suite 503, Washington, DC 20002
E-mail: therlcpac@aol.com

In 1992, the Republican Leadership Council, formerly known as the Committee for Responsible Government, was created in the image of its successful opposite, the Democratic Leadership Council, to unite and expand the GOP.

RLC founders New Jersey Gov. Christine Todd Whitman, then-Rep. Susan Molinari, R-N.Y., and New Jersey State Rep. Richard Zimmer recognized after the 1992 convention that moderate GOP members were beginning to feel excluded from the party. RLC was their attempt to counter the party's perceived move toward the far right and instead promote an "inclusive, common sense conservative" message. The group would still emphasize the traditional Republican aims of lower taxes and a smaller, smarter government but would avoid taking a stance on divisive issues such as abortion.

Although formed by northeastern politicians, RLC has board members from across the nation, including Govs. John Engler, R-Mich., and Pete Wilson, R-Calif., as well as Sens. Jon Kyl, R-Ariz., and Pete Domenici, R-N.M.

N.Y./N.J. Port Authority Chairman Lewis Eisenberg is the current RLC chairman.

Republican Leadership Council (formerly known as Committee for Responsible Government) (C00282004) *Address: same as sponsor * Treasurer: Ron Gravino * Contact: Mark L. Miller, Executive Dir.*

	1993-94	*1995-96*	*1997*	*Totals*
Receipts	$39,400	$416,234	$270,358	$725,992
Disburse	34,114	390,217	212,968	637,299
Cash	4,190	30,807	94,089	n/a
Contributions	10,000	84,500	42,000	136,500
Republicans	10,000	84,500	42,000	136,500
No. of Cand.	*11*	*19*	*12*	*42*
House	9,000	46,500	7,000	62,500
Senate	1,000	38,000	35,000	74,000
Democrats	0	0	0	0
No. of Cand.	*0*	*0*	*0*	*0*
House	0	0	0	0
Senate	0	0	0	0
Incumbents	2,000	36,000	37,000	75,000
Challengers	5,000	20,500	0	25,500
Open Seat	3,000	28,000	5,000	36,000
Winners	5,500	28,000	n/a	33,500
Losers	4,500	56,500	n/a	61,000

Republican Majority Fund

*Phone: (580) 234-1737 * Fax: (580) 234-8460*
201 N. Grand, Mezzanine, Enid, OK 73701

The Republican Majority Fund is the leadership PAC of Sen. Don Nickles, R-Okla., the majority whip. Nickles chaired the National Republican Senatorial Committee in 1990 and was Policy Committee chairman. He is known as a staunch conservative who supports tax cuts, regulatory reform and consistent military funding.

This PAC supports Republican candidates for federal office. Most of its contributions have gone to Senate and House candidates, but the group has contributed to presidential campaigns. The RMF has also contributed to other PACs.

Twenty Republican candidates in 1996 received at least $10,000 from the Republican Majority Fund. Those included Sens. Strom Thurmond, R-S.C., and Mitch McConnell, R-Ky., and successful candidate Gordon H. Smith, R-Ore. The lone House candidate to receive $10,000 was Rep. Tom Coburn, R-Okla. The PAC spent a greater percentage of its money on open races than any other PAC that contributed more than $200,000 to congressional races.

Republican Majority Fund (C00296640) *Phone: (202) 659-8201 * 1155 21st St. N.W., Suite 300, Washington, DC 20036 * Treasurer: Mike Wright*

	1993-94	*1995-96*	*1997*	*Totals*
Receipts	$81,662	$789,324	$320,708	$1,191,694
Disburse	49,212	646,208	232,751	928,171
Cash	32,449	175,562	263,518	n/a
Contributions	21,500	390,676	55,997	468,173
Republicans	21,500	390,676	55,997	468,173
No. of Cand.	*24*	*82*	*13*	*119*
House	3,500	80,743	2,000	86,243
Senate	18,000	309,933	53,997	381,930
Democrats	0	0	0	0
No. of Cand.	*0*	*0*	*0*	*0*
House	0	0	0	0
Senate	0	0	0	0
Incumbents	4,000	147,243	30,110	181,353
Challengers	6,000	59,936	15,887	81,823
Open Seat	11,500	183,497	10,000	204,997
Winners	18,500	259,742	n/a	278,242
Losers	3,000	130,934	n/a	133,934

Rhode Island PAC

750 Elmgrove Ave., Providence, RI 02906

The Rhode Island PAC is affiliated with Seventh Street PAC, a joint fundraising committee. Its chairman is Rep. Patrick J. Kennedy, D-R.I.

Rhode Island Political Action Committee (RI PAC) (C00307991) *Phone: (202) 544-2636 * 530 Seventh St. S.E., Washington, DC 20003 * Treasurer: John J. McConnell Jr. * Contact: Rep. Patrick J. Kennedy, Chairman*

	1993-94	*1995-96*	*1997*	*Totals*
Receipts	$0	$106,246	$85,750	$191,996
Disburse	0	103,676	81,350	185,026
Cash	0	2,567	6,960	n/a
Contributions	0	31,000	0	31,000
Republicans	0	0	0	0
No. of Cand.	*0*	*0*	*0*	*0*
House	0	0	0	0
Senate	0	0	0	0

Democrats	0	31,000	0	31,000
No. of Cand.	*0*	*33*	*2*	*35*
House	0	22,500	0	22,500
Senate	0	8,500	0	8,500
Incumbents	0	7,000	-1000	6,000
Challengers	0	13,000	0	13,000
Open Seat	0	11,000	1,000	12,000
Winners	0	21,500	n/a	21,500
Losers	0	9,500	n/a	9,500

Senate Victory Fund

*Phone: (601) 842-6475 * Fax: (601) 842-4531*
P.O. Box 7274, Tupelo, MS 38802-7274

The Senate Victory Fund is a leadership PAC of Sen. Thad Cochran, R-Miss. It formerly was known as the Cochran Committee. Cochran, the senior senator from Mississippi, is chairman of the Appropriations Agriculture Subcommittee and a member of the Senate Governmental Affairs Committee. He previously was chairman of the Senate Republican Conference.

The Senate Victory Fund ranked seventh among Republican leadership PACs in contributions to 1996 congressional races. The committee supported Republican candidates for Senate, although it gave a small amount to House and presidential candidates during the 1995-96 election cycle.

Seventeen Senate candidates received at least $10,000 from the PAC, including Sens. Gordon H. Smith, R-Ore., Jeff Sessions, R-Ala., and Bob Smith, R-N.H. The House candidates who received a contribution were mostly from Mississippi.

Senate Victory Fund PAC (formerly known as Cochran Committee) (C00202861) *Address: same as sponsor * Treasurer: John M. Robinson*

	1993-94	1995-96	1997	Totals
Receipts	$154,991	$477,178	$9,063	$641,232
Disburse	144,204	354,771	15,230	514,205
Cash	14,662	137,068	130,902	n/a
Contributions	98,655	283,711	5,000	387,366
Republicans	98,655	283,711	5,000	387,366
No. of Cand.	*32*	*40*	*3*	*75*
House	5,174	18,500	1,000	24,674
Senate	93,481	265,211	4,000	362,692
Democrats	0	0	0	0
No. of Cand.	*0*	*0*	*0*	*0*
House	0	0	0	0
Senate	0	0	0	0
Incumbents	43,481	102,000	4,000	149,481
Challengers	24,000	56,000	1,000	81,000
Open Seat	31,174	125,711	0	156,885
Winners	79,655	173,711	n/a	253,366
Losers	19,000	110,000	n/a	129,000

Spirit of America

*Phone: (202) 547-5270 * Fax: (202) 547-5785*
505 Capitol Ct. N.E., Washington, DC 20002

Spirit of America was created by Sen. John Ashcroft, R-Mo., to assist candidates who share his conservative ideals. The PAC does not give money to Ashcroft but supports some of his travel expenses.

Sen. Ashcroft is a possible candidate for the Republican nomination for president in 2000. He has been endorsed by the Christian Coalition.

Spirit of America (C00320291) *Address: same as sponsor * Treasurer: Marise Stewart * Contact: Sen. John Ashcroft, Chairperson*

	1993-94	1995-96	1997	Totals
Receipts	$0	$39,190	$235,500	$274,690
Disburse	0	25,157	105,900	131,057
Cash	0	14,031	143,630	n/a
Contributions	0	15,000	322	15,322
Republicans	0	15,000	322	15,322
No. of Cand.	*0*	*15*	*1*	*16*
House	0	2,000	322	2,322
Senate	0	13,000	0	13,000
Democrats	0	0	0	0
No. of Cand.	*0*	*0*	*0*	*0*
House	0	0	0	0
Senate	0	0	0	0
Incumbents	0	0	0	0
Challengers	0	5,000	322	5,322
Open Seat	0	10,000	0	10,000
Winners	0	9,000	n/a	9,000
Losers	0	6,000	n/a	6,000

TR Fund

*Phone: (202) 408-1100 * Fax: (202) 408-1100*
P.O. Box 889, Washington, DC 20044-0889

Sen. John H. Chafee, R-R.I., and Rep. Sherwood Boehlert, R-N.Y., formed the TR Fund to assist Republicans interested in environmental issues. It supports Republicans with moderate to conservative viewpoints.

The committee also gives to environmental and leadership PACs associated with Chafee and Boehlert.

Chafee is chairman of the Senate Environment and Public Works Committee and Boehlert is chairman of the Transportation and Infrastructure panel's Water Resources and Environment Subcommittee in the House.

TR Fund (C00316414) *Address: same as sponsor * Treasurer: Robert F. Hurley * Contact: Sen. John Chafee, Chairperson*

	1993-94	1995-96	1997	Totals
Receipts	$0	$30,458	$25,100	$55,558
Disburse	0	24,711	3,782	28,493
Cash	0	5,744	10,211	n/a
Contributions	0	15,650	625	16,275
Republicans	0	15,650	625	16,275
No. of Cand.	*0*	*23*	*2*	*25*
House	0	8,000	625	8,625
Senate	0	7,650	0	7,650
Democrats	0	0	0	0
No. of Cand.	*0*	*0*	*0*	*0*
House	0	0	0	0
Senate	0	0	0	0
Incumbents	0	10,150	625	10,775
Challengers	0	1,500	0	1,500
Open Seat	0	4,000	0	4,000
Winners	0	10,650	n/a	10,650
Losers	0	5,000	n/a	5,000

Time Future Inc.

Phone: (609) 252-0120
4 Hawthorne Ave., Princeton, NJ 08540

Time Future was established after former Sen. Bill Bradley, D-N.J, announced he would not run for reelection in 1996. Bradley contributed the remaining funds of his Senate reelection PAC, $174,000, to the new organization. In late 1997, the Washington Post speculated that Time Future would be poised to become Bradley's presidential committee, should he decide to run in 2000.

Time Future Inc. (formerly known as Bill Bradley for U.S. Senate) (C00270736) *Address: same as sponsor * Treasurer: John V. Roos * Contact: Betty Sapoch, Executive Dir.*

	1993-94	1995-96	1997	Totals
Receipts	$0	$735,085	$2,283	$737,368
Disburse	0	878,251	72,213	950,464
Cash	0	105,638	35,209	n/a
Contributions	-330	19,450	-500	18,620
Republicans	0	0	0	0
No. of Cand.	*0*	*0*	*0*	*0*
House	0	0	0	0
Senate	0	0	0	0
Democrats	-330	19,450	-500	18,620
No. of Cand.	*1*	*10*	*1*	*12*
House	0	4,000	-500	3,500
Senate	-330	15,450	0	15,120
Incumbents	-330	11,450	-500	10,620
Challengers	0	7,000	0	7,000
Open Seat	0	1,000	0	1,000
Winners	-330	7,000	n/a	6,670
Losers	0	12,450	n/a	12,450

Victory America

P.O. Box 11771, Columbia, SC 29211

Victory America, formerly known as the Fund for Southern Progress, is chaired by Carroll A. Campbell Jr., the former Republican governor and representative from South Carolina.

Victory America (formerly known as Fund for Southern Progress) (C00216077) *Address: same as sponsor * Treasurer: Mark R. Elam*

	1993-94	1995-96	1997	Totals
Receipts	$294,267	$1,924	$457	$296,648
Disburse	250,204	15,257	817	266,278
Cash	46,934	32,870	32,510	n/a
Contributions	98,250	7,000	250	105,500

(Data for Victory America continued)				
Republicans	98,250	7,000	250	105,500
No. of Cand.	*113*	*12*	*1*	*126*
House	63,000	3,000	250	66,250
Senate	35,250	4,000	0	39,250
Democrats	0	0	0	0
No. of Cand.	*0*	*0*	*0*	*0*
House	0	0	0	0
Senate	0	0	0	0
Incumbents	8,000	-1000	0	7,000
Challengers	45,000	2,000	250	47,250
Open Seat	45,250	6,000	0	51,250
Winners	75,750	4,500	n/a	80,250
Losers	22,500	2,500	n/a	25,000

Victory USA

*Phone: (916) 442-2952 * Fax: (916) 442-1280*
555 Capitol Mall, Suite 1425, Sacramento, CA 95814

Victory USA is the leadership PAC of Democratic Caucus Chairman Rep. Vic Fazio, D-Calif. Besides serving as the No. 3 House Democratic leader, Fazio was chairman of the Democratic Congressional Campaign Committee for the 1992 and 1994 elections.

In November 1997, Fazio announced that he would retire at the end of the 105th Congress. Spokesperson Steve Maviglio said the PAC has been disbanded, but as of March 1998, it had not filed a termination report.

The PAC was an active supporter of Democratic House candidates. In the 1993-94 and 1995-96 election cycles, it was one of the top four Democratic leadership PACs.

Victory USA (C00254318) *Address: same as sponsor * Treasurer: Lance H. Olson*

	1993-94	1995-96	1997	Totals
Receipts	$196,350	$203,900	$6,000	$406,250
Disburse	173,599	216,778	18,156	408,533
Cash	25,981	13,095	938	n/a
Contributions	134,000	166,550	13,500	314,050
Republicans	0	1,000	0	1,000
No. of Cand.	*0*	*1*	*0*	*1*
House	0	1,000	0	1,000
Senate	0	0	0	0
Democrats	133,000	165,550	13,500	312,050
No. of Cand.	*111*	*112*	*6*	*229*
House	128,000	147,550	13,500	289,050
Senate	5,000	18,000	0	23,000
Incumbents	60,500	44,000	500	105,000
Challengers	19,000	78,550	0	97,550
Open Seat	50,500	44,000	13,000	107,500
Winners	42,500	95,550	n/a	138,050
Losers	91,500	71,000	n/a	162,500

Washington Fund

*Phone: (425) 957-1567 * Fax: (425) 957-1452*
P.O. Box 53393, Bellevue, WA 98015

The Washington Fund strives to maintain a Republican majority in the legislature at both the state and federal level.

Established in 1996, the fund is chaired by Rep. Jennifer Dunn, R-Wash., and has about 500 contributors.

The Washington Fund (C00312579) *Address: same as sponsor * Treasurer: John W. Meyers*

	1993-94	1995-96	1997	Totals
Receipts	$0	$67,582	$7,498	$75,080
Disburse	0	63,501	8,060	71,561
Cash	0	1,277	927	n/a
Contributions	0	47,000	500	47,500
Republicans	0	47,000	500	47,500
No. of Cand.	*0*	*28*	*1*	*29*
House	0	47,000	500	47,500
Senate	0	0	0	0
Democrats	0	0	0	0
No. of Cand.	*0*	*0*	*0*	*0*
House	0	0	0	0
Senate	0	0	0	0
Incumbents	0	43,500	500	44,000
Challengers	0	2,000	0	2,000
Open Seat	0	1,500	0	1,500
Winners	0	25,000	n/a	25,000
Losers	0	22,000	n/a	22,000

Misc. Issues

Anti-Tax PAC

Phone: (703) 908-0298
1812 N. Quinn, Suite 128, Alexandria, VA 22304
*Web: www.atr.org * E-mail: dbansel@aol.com*

The Anti-Tax PAC is affiliated with Americans for Tax Reform, an Alexandria, Va.-based umbrella organization that represents 70,000 individuals and 2,000 anti-tax groups throughout the nation.

ATR created the Taxpayer Protection Pledge, an oath taken by members of Congress stating that they will not raise any taxes. Forty-one senators and 203 representatives have taken the pledge. The majority of those are Republicans but a few are Democrats. Many congressional and presidential candidates also have taken the oath.

The organization was founded in 1986 to give President Reagan's fiscal policies an active, long-lasting legacy.

Grover Norquist, ATR's director, is a Washington lobbyist who previously served as chief speechwriter and economist for the U.S. Chamber of Commerce and as executive director of the National Taxpayers Union. He also was an adviser to the 1988 Bush-Quayle campaign.

Founded in 1996, the Anti-Tax PAC gives to candidates who have signed the pledge.

Anti-Tax Political Action Committee (C00316786) *Address: same as sponsor * Treasurer: Damon Ansell*

	1993-94	1995-96	1997	Totals
Receipts	$0	$9,958	$590	$10,548
Disburse	0	8,687	1,746	10,433
Cash	0	1,273	23	n/a
Contributions	0	6,425	250	6,675
Republicans	0	6,425	250	6,675
No. of Cand.	*0*	*9*	*1*	*10*
House	0	5,825	250	6,075
Senate	0	600	0	600
Democrats	0	0	0	0
No. of Cand.	*0*	*0*	*0*	*0*
House	0	0	0	0
Senate	0	0	0	0
Incumbents	0	325	250	575
Challengers	0	5,000	0	5,000
Open Seat	0	1,100	0	1,100
Winners	0	1,125	n/a	1,125
Losers	0	5,300	n/a	5,300

Arts and Humanities for America PAC

*Phone: (212) 223-2787 * Fax: (212) 753-1325*
1 E. 53rd St., Third Floor, New York, NY 10022

Arts and Humanities for America PAC is a single-issue, bipartisan PAC that gives money to candidates dedicated to promoting arts and humanities funding.

The group is based in Washington but also has an office in New York City.

Arts and Humanities for America Political Action Committee (C00303321) *Phone: (202) 289-8981 * Fax: (202) 289-8983 * P.O. Box 27994, Washington, DC 20038-7994 * Treasurer: Robert L. Lynch * Contact: Martha Chowning, PAC Dir.*

	1993-94	1995-96	1997	Totals
Receipts	$0	$45,915	$13,205	$59,120
Disburse	0	33,370	14,714	48,084
Cash	0	12,544	13,456	n/a
Contributions	0	33,000	500	33,500
Republicans	0	20,750	0	20,750
No. of Cand.	*0*	*27*	*0*	*27*
House	0	17,250	0	17,250
Senate	0	3,500	0	3,500
Democrats	0	12,250	500	12,750
No. of Cand.	*0*	*25*	*1*	*26*
House	0	9,750	500	10,250
Senate	0	2,500	0	2,500
Incumbents	0	28,250	500	28,750
Challengers	0	3,250	0	3,250
Open Seat	0	1,500	0	1,500
Winners	0	31,250	n/a	31,250
Losers	0	1,750	n/a	1,750

California Senior Citizen Voter Guide

1015 Gayley Ave., Suite 320, Los Angeles, CA 90024

California Senior Citizen Voter Guide filed for termination in 1996.

California Senior Citizen Voter Guide (C00313593) *Address: same as sponsor * Treasurer: Jeffrey Joya*

	1993-94	1995-96	1997	Totals
Receipts	$0	$14,601	$0	$14,601
Disburse	0	12,954	0	12,954
Cash	0	0	0	n/a
Contributions	0	6,000	0	6,000
Republicans	0	4,000	0	4,000
No. of Cand.	*0*	*1*	*0*	*1*
House	0	4,000	0	4,000
Senate	0	0	0	0
Democrats	0	2,000	0	2,000
No. of Cand.	*0*	*1*	*0*	*1*
House	0	2,000	0	2,000
Senate	0	0	0	0
Incumbents	0	0	0	0
Challengers	0	0	0	0
Open Seat	0	2,000	0	2,000
Winners	0	2,000	n/a	2,000
Losers	0	4,000	n/a	4,000

Citizen Action

*Phone: (518) 465-4600 x112 * Fax: (518) 465-2890*
94 Central Ave., Albany, NY 12206
E-mail: canyalb@aol.com

Citizen Action of New York is a nonprofit dedicated to "organizing New Yorkers for progressive political change." The group has its headquarters in Albany, N.Y. and offices in four other cities. It claims a membership of about 60,000.

Citizen Action is interested in universal access to health care, recycling programs and workplace safety. According to the organization, its annual budget is about $800,000 and it employs 35 people.

Citizen Action of New York Inc. PAC (Citizen Action of N.Y. PAC) (C00275297) *Address: same as sponsor * Treasurer: Karen Scharff*

	1993-94	1995-96	1997	Totals
Receipts	$7,415	$5,173	$227	$12,815
Disburse	7,244	5,637	227	13,108
Cash	480	12	11	n/a
Contributions	4,860	5,367	0	10,227
Republicans	0	0	0	0
No. of Cand.	*0*	*0*	*0*	*0*
House	0	0	0	0
Senate	0	0	0	0
Democrats	4,860	5,367	0	10,227
No. of Cand.	*2*	*4*	*0*	*6*
House	4,860	5,367	0	10,227
Senate	0	0	0	0
Incumbents	40	214	0	254
Challengers	4,820	5,153	0	9,973
Open Seat	0	0	0	0
Winners	40	214	n/a	254
Losers	4,820	5,153	n/a	9,973

Contributed less than $5,000 during 1995-96 cycle:

Connecticut Citizen Action Group Fed PAC (C00158998) *Phone: (860) 561-6006 * Fax: (860) 561-6018 * 45 S. Main St., West Hartford, CT 06107 * Treasurer: Steven Derby*

Corridor 67 Inc.

*Phone: (501) 525-2944 * Fax: (501) 525-6083*
155 W. Morton Ave., Jacksonville, IL 62650

Corridor 67 wants Interstate Highway 67 expanded from two lanes to four on the 210 miles between St. Louis and the Quad Cities — Rock Island and Moline, Ill., and Davenport and Bettendorf, Iowa.

The committee's 30-member board of directors includes politicians, journalists and business people from Illinois. Corridor 67 was founded in 1989.

Corridor PAC Chairman Barney Elias said the project is expected to cost $1 billion. As of February 1998, $350 million had been acquired through state and federal government funds. Elias said he anticipated another $152 million through the federal government's ISTEA highway bill.

Corridor 67 Inc. Political Action Committee - PAC 67 (C00238691) *Address: same as sponsor * Treasurer: M. Blanchette * Contact: Barney Elias, Chairman*

	1993-94	1995-96	1997	Totals
Receipts	$7,360	$13,276	$1,725	$22,361
Disburse	6,690	9,409	4,900	20,999
Cash	817	4,683	1,508	n/a
Contributions	2,650	6,950	4,600	14,200
Republicans	1,650	5,000	2,100	8,750
No. of Cand.	*3*	*7*	*3*	*13*
House	1,650	4,650	2,100	8,400
Senate	0	350	0	350
Democrats	1,000	1,950	2,500	5,450
No. of Cand.	*6*	*3*	*3*	*12*
House	3,200	950	2,000	6,150
Senate	-2200	1,000	500	-700
Incumbents	4,050	4,850	4,600	13,500
Challengers	0	750	0	750
Open Seat	1,000	1,350	0	2,350
Winners	4,350	6,100	n/a	10,450
Losers	-1700	850	n/a	-850

English First

*Phone: (703) 321-8818 * Fax: (703) 321-8408*
8001 Forbes Pl., Suite 102, Springfield, VA 22151
*Web: www.englishfirst.org * E-mail: jboulet@englishfirst.org*

English First is a national, nonprofit, grassroots lobbying organization that promotes English as the official language of the United States. Founded in 1986, the organization is based in Springfield, Va. and claims more than 170,000 members.

English First Political Victory Fund (C00245720) *Address: same as sponsor * Treasurer: Walter J. Olson*

	1993-94	1995-96	1997	Totals
Receipts	$272	$14,118	$2,350	$16,740
Disburse	2,445	12,629	1,130	16,204
Cash	1,826	3,314	4,535	n/a
Contributions	300	10,900	0	11,200
Republicans	300	10,900	0	11,200
No. of Cand.	*9*	*15*	*0*	*24*
House	600	6,900	0	7,500
Senate	-300	4,000	0	3,700
Democrats	0	0	0	0
No. of Cand.	*0*	*0*	*0*	*0*
House	0	0	0	0
Senate	0	0	0	0
Incumbents	600	3,679	0	4,279
Challengers	200	2,721	0	2,921
Open Seat	500	4,500	0	5,000
Winners	1,100	5,892	n/a	6,992
Losers	-800	5,008	n/a	4,208

English Language PAC

*Phone: (202) 775-1307 * Fax: (202) 775-1307*
P.O. Box 9558, Washington, DC 20016
Web: www.workings.com/elpac.htm

The English Language PAC is an independent organization that supports candidates who favor declaring English the official language of the United States.

Established in 1986, ELPAC says it protects the common language of the United States by supporting teachers who teach English without including other languages or cultural interests.

In addition, ELPAC promotes its mission through media advertisements and by hiring campaign activists.

English Language Political Action Committee (C00199802) *Address: same as sponsor * Treasurer: Jan C. Zall * Contact: Steven Workings, Executive Dir.*

	1993-94	1995-96	1997	Totals
Receipts	$515,290	$465,450	$166,850	$1,147,590
Disburse	524,073	471,636	197,322	1,193,031
Cash	110,030	103,845	73,373	n/a
Contributions	17,100	23,500	9,500	50,100
Republicans	13,600	22,500	8,500	44,600
No. of Cand.	*23*	*34*	*13*	*70*
House	8,600	15,000	5,000	28,600
Senate	5,000	7,500	3,500	16,000
Democrats	3,500	1,000	1,000	5,500
No. of Cand.	*7*	*2*	*1*	*10*
House	2,500	1,000	1,000	4,500

(Data for English Language Political continued)

Senate	1,000	0	0	1,000
Incumbents	13,100	16,500	9,000	38,600
Challengers	250	3,500	0	3,750
Open Seat	3,750	3,500	500	7,750
Winners	14,600	16,500	n/a	31,100
Losers	2,500	7,000	n/a	9,500

Free America PAC

*Phone: (303) 751-2900 * Fax: (303) 751-1081*
10020 E. Girard Ave., Suite 300, Denver, CO 80231

The Free America PAC, based out of Denver, is an organization of people interested in educational issues.

Free America PAC (C00303230) *Address: same as sponsor * Treasurer: Omar Duwaik*

	1993-94	1995-96	1997	Totals
Receipts	$0	$38,160	$0	$38,160
Disburse	0	26,531	0	26,531
Cash	0	11,629	11,629	n/a
Contributions	0	11,500	0	11,500
Republicans	0	11,500	0	11,500
No. of Cand.	*0*	*3*	*0*	*3*
House	0	7,500	0	7,500
Senate	0	4,000	0	4,000
Democrats	0	0	0	0
No. of Cand.	*0*	*0*	*0*	*0*
House	0	0	0	0
Senate	0	0	0	0
Incumbents	0	0	0	0
Challengers	0	3,500	0	3,500
Open Seat	0	8,000	0	8,000
Winners	0	8,000	n/a	8,000
Losers	0	3,500	n/a	3,500

Howard Jarvis Taxpayers Association

*Phone: (213) 384-9656 * Fax: (213) 384-9870*
621 S. Westmoreland Ave., Suite 202, Los Angeles, CA 90005-3971

The Howard Jarvis Taxpayers Association says it represents the taxpayers of California. Established in 1978, the organization has about 250,000 members.

In July 1997, the association sued the city of Los Angeles for violating Proposition 218. The proposition allows citizens to vote on new tax increases. The organization claims that the government violated the provision when it began collecting taxes from businesses inside the Pacific Beach Business Improvement District.

Howard Jarvis Taxpayers Association Political Action Committee (C00255232) *Address: same as sponsor * Treasurer: Joseph Ransom * Contact: Joel Fox, President*

	1993-94	1995-96	1997	Totals
Receipts	$429,948	$20,656	$0	$450,604
Disburse	406,191	86,036	1,500	493,727
Cash	85,777	20,397	18,897	n/a
Contributions	28,950	25,650	1,500	56,100
Republicans	28,950	25,650	1,500	56,100
No. of Cand.	*21*	*16*	*1*	*38*
House	28,950	23,650	0	52,600
Senate	0	2,000	1,500	3,500
Democrats	0	0	0	0
No. of Cand.	*0*	*0*	*0*	*0*
House	0	0	0	0
Senate	0	0	0	0
Incumbents	9,600	11,650	0	21,250
Challengers	18,350	8,500	1,500	28,350
Open Seat	1,000	5,500	0	6,500
Winners	15,850	8,150	n/a	24,000
Losers	13,100	17,500	n/a	30,600

International Fund for Animal Welfare

*Phone: (508) 362-5180 * Fax: (508) 362-8964*
411 Main St., P.O. Box 193, Yarmouth Port, MA 02675
Web: www.ifaw.org

Based in the United Kingdom, the International Fund for Animal Welfare says it is the world's largest animal welfare organization. It has 660,000 members in the United States and more than 1.4 million supporters around the globe.

Brian Davies founded the organization in 1969 to protest what he considered the cruel practice of hunting and clubbing seals in Canada. It has expanded its goals to include the promotion of animal welfare, prevention of animal cruelty and the improvement of the quality of animals' lives and their environment.

IFAW Animal Action Committee Inc. (C00178517) *Address: same as sponsor * Treasurer: T. H. Brennan * Contact: Mary I. Govoni, Chairperson*

	1993-94	1995-96	1997	Totals
Receipts	$130,579	$494,729	$136,327	$761,635
Disburse	54,716	429,317	266,057	750,090
Cash	76,249	141,670	11,940	n/a
Contributions	0	33,000	0	33,000
Republicans	0	5,000	0	5,000
No. of Cand.	*0*	*1*	*0*	*1*
House	0	5,000	0	5,000
Senate	0	0	0	0
Democrats	0	28,000	0	28,000
No. of Cand.	*0*	*6*	*0*	*6*
House	0	4,500	0	4,500
Senate	0	23,500	0	23,500
Incumbents	0	13,500	0	13,500
Challengers	0	8,500	0	8,500
Open Seat	0	11,000	0	11,000
Winners	0	17,000	n/a	17,000
Losers	0	16,000	n/a	16,000

Law Enforcement Alliance of America

*Phone: (703) 847-2677 * Fax: (703) 556-6485*
7700 Leesburg Pike, Suite 421, Falls Church, VA 22043

The Law Enforcement Alliance of America is a nonprofit organization of law enforcement officers, citizens and crime victims. It is concerned with victims' rights, gun control, juvenile justice reform and police use-of-force policies.

Law Enforcement Alliance of America Inc. Fund for Responsible Government (LEAA) (C00291393) *Address: same as sponsor * Treasurer: James J. Fotis*

	1993-94	1995-96	1997	Totals
Receipts	$25,742	$18,250	$31,191	$75,183
Disburse	22,123	20,299	6,447	48,869
Cash	3,617	1,730	26,474	n/a
Contributions	8,310	17,870	1,500	27,680
Republicans	6,460	17,370	1,500	25,330
No. of Cand.	*36*	*30*	*2*	*68*
House	5,200	10,092	1,500	16,792
Senate	1,260	7,278	0	8,538
Democrats	1,850	500	0	2,350
No. of Cand.	*8*	*3*	*0*	*11*
House	1,850	500	0	2,350
Senate	0	0	0	0
Incumbents	2,700	4,325	500	7,525
Challengers	4,750	5,940	1,000	11,690
Open Seat	860	7,605	0	8,465
Winners	4,710	8,232	n/a	12,942
Losers	3,600	9,638	n/a	13,238

National Association for Uniformed Services

*Phone: (703) 750-1342 * Fax: (703) 354-4380*
5535 Hempstead Way, Springfield, VA 22151-3004
Web: www.naus.org

The National Association for Uniformed Services is the only military-affiliated association that represents the entire military/veteran community. NAUS represents its members on issues of universal concern such as Medicare, Social Security and other earned federal entitlements.

The association supports a strong national defense and promotes and protects the interests of all members of the uniformed services, their families and survivors.

NAUS-PAC is a nonpartisan PAC. Established in 1978, it encourages candidates to support legislation important to a strong national defense.

National Association for Uniformed Services PAC (C00086348) *Address: same as sponsor * Treasurer: James W. Bradbury * Contact: Chuck Partridge, Chairperson*

	1993-94	1995-96	1997	Totals
Receipts	$187,841	$156,929	$8,405	$353,175
Disburse	91,049	151,843	54,219	297,111
Cash	160,545	165,632	119,818	n/a
Contributions	36,069	50,820	10,550	97,439

Republicans	21,069	38,320	9,050	68,439
No. of Cand.	*24*	*23*	*10*	*57*
House	17,969	33,070	10,050	61,089
Senate	3,100	5,250	-1000	7,350
Democrats	15,000	12,500	1,500	29,000
No. of Cand.	*14*	*11*	*2*	*27*
House	13,000	8,500	1,500	23,000
Senate	2,000	4,000	0	6,000
Incumbents	25,000	41,320	10,550	76,870
Challengers	3,600	4,500	0	8,100
Open Seat	7,469	5,000	0	12,469
Winners	28,000	40,320	n/a	68,320
Losers	8,069	10,500	n/a	18,569

National Committee to Preserve Social Security and Medicare

*Phone: (202) 216-0420 * Fax: (202) 216-0446*
2000 K St. N.W., Suite 800, Washington, DC 20005
Web: www.ncpssm.org

The National Committee to Preserve Social Security and Medicare is the second-largest seniors lobbying group in the United States. It has about 6 million members and supporters dedicated to protecting government entitlements. The group produces brochures, a bi-monthly magazine and periodic newsletters. The president is Martha McSteen, a former acting commissioner of the Social Security Administration.

The group's legislative agenda includes removing Social Security from federal budget calculations and eliminating the earnings limitation for Social Security benefit recipients between the ages of 65 and 69. It also supports protecting Medicare from cuts in the program's spending growth.

It favors increasing the limit on assets a person can have and still be eligible to receive Supplemental Security Income. While the committee opposes the wholesale privatization of Social Security, it recommends investing a portion of the trust fund reserves in a "broad selection of stocks."

The National Committee was the leading contributor to 1996 congressional candidates among seniors PACs. Democratic candidates received more than 78 percent of the group's contributions. The top recipients were Sens. Tim Johnson, D-S.D., and Tom Harkin, D-Iowa, and 1996 Senate candidate Ben Nelson, who lost to Sen. Chuck Hagel, R-Neb. Rep. Bill Paxon, R-N.Y., was the top Republican recipient.

National Committee to Preserve Social Security and Medicare PAC (C00172296) *Address: same as sponsor * Treasurer: Shelly Shapiro * Contact: Max Richtman, Executive V.P.*

	1993-94	1995-96	1997	Totals
Receipts	$1,430,516	$2,314,060	$522,354	$4,266,930
Disburse	2,208,721	2,277,182	588,520	5,074,423
Cash	321,028	357,908	291,742	n/a
Contributions	543,511	709,426	189,389	1,442,326
Republicans	90,806	151,382	47,000	289,188
No. of Cand.	*58*	*105*	*41*	*204*
House	63,806	135,882	39,000	238,688
Senate	27,000	15,500	8,000	50,500
Democrats	441,705	555,044	139,389	1,136,138
No. of Cand.	*247*	*250*	*132*	*629*
House	353,605	427,102	112,116	892,823
Senate	88,100	127,942	27,273	243,315
Incumbents	395,911	468,724	182,019	1,046,654
Challengers	49,850	112,243	500	162,593
Open Seat	89,250	128,959	7,000	225,209
Winners	354,256	558,774	n/a	913,030
Losers	189,255	150,652	n/a	339,907

National Council of Senior Citizens

*Phone: (301) 578-8800 * Fax: (301) 578-8911*
8403 Colesville Rd., Suite 1200, Silver Spring, MD 20910
Web: www.ncscinc.org

The National Council of Senior Citizens is one of the oldest and largest groups for older Americans. It represents more than 500,000 members in about 2,000 senior clubs across the nation.

The NCSC is also a sponsor of housing for the elderly, with more than 3,500 tenants in 32 buildings in the United States. With the Department of Labor, the group operates a jobs program for low-income seniors. The NCSC was one of the leading proponents of the original Medicare law in 1965.

National Council of Senior Citizens Political Action Committee (C00166322) *Address: same as sponsor * Treasurer: Michael A. Ingrao * Contact: Harry Guenther, President*

	1993-94	1995-96	1997	Totals
Receipts	$201,352	$183,642	$1,693	$386,687
Disburse	198,984	290,610	10,764	500,358
Cash	21,374	6,322	0	n/a
Contributions	81,500	14,300	7,348	103,148
Republicans	0	0	0	0
No. of Cand.	*0*	*0*	*0*	*0*
House	0	0	0	0
Senate	0	0	0	0
Democrats	80,500	14,300	7,348	102,148
No. of Cand.	*62*	*11*	*11*	*84*
House	51,000	12,300	7,098	70,398
Senate	29,500	2,000	250	31,750
Incumbents	48,000	4,500	4,850	57,350
Challengers	22,000	7,500	0	29,500
Open Seat	10,500	2,300	2,498	15,298
Winners	18,500	6,000	n/a	24,500
Losers	63,000	8,300	n/a	71,300

National Right to Work Committee

Phone: (703) 321-8075
5240 Port Royal Rd., Suite 211, Springfield, VA 22151

The National Right to Work Committee is composed largely of independent entrepreneurs and employers who oppose mandatory worker unionization and support "right to work" legislation.

Founded in 1955, NRWC now claims 1.7 million contributors. According to the Center for Civil Society International, the nonprofit, nonpartisan organization is "one of the largest public-interest groups in America."

The affiliated National Right to Work Legal Defense Foundation is a charitable foundation providing free legal aid to employees who "feel their rights have been violated by compulsory unionism abuses."

Reed Larson, president of both the foundation and the committee, is also the treasurer of the Right to Work PAC and the National Right to Work PAC.

Right to Work Political Action Committee (C00164392) *Address: same as sponsor * Treasurer: Reed E. Larson*

	1993-94	1995-96	1997	Totals
Receipts	$228,471	$312,933	$43,401	$584,805
Disburse	230,474	298,444	47,613	576,531
Cash	4,384	18,872	14,661	n/a
Contributions	114,800	142,080	16,835	273,715
Republicans	113,800	142,080	16,835	272,715
No. of Cand.	*59*	*65*	*16*	*140*
House	62,300	63,103	11,000	136,403
Senate	51,500	78,977	5,835	136,312
Democrats	0	0	0	0
No. of Cand.	*0*	*0*	*0*	*0*
House	0	0	0	0
Senate	0	0	0	0
Incumbents	27,000	69,737	17,000	113,737
Challengers	61,050	28,698	0	89,748
Open Seat	27,500	43,645	0	71,145
Winners	67,300	101,790	n/a	169,090
Losers	47,500	40,290	n/a	87,790

Contributed less than $5,000 during 1995-96 cycle:

The National Right to Work Political Action Committee (C00164384) *Address: Same as sponsor*

National Taxpayers Union

*Phone: (703) 683-5700 * Fax: (703) 683-5722*
108 N. Alfred St., Alexandria, VA 22314
*Web: www.townhall.com/NTU * E-mail: alcors@ntu.org*

The National Taxpayers Union is a nonprofit organization founded in 1969. It lobbies Congress and state legislatures on tax issues and seeks to reduce government spending. The NTU has more than 300,000 members. The National Taxpayers Union Foundation is the organization's educational research arm. It compiles studies of congressional bills and votes pertaining to tax and fiscal issues and congressional pensions.

National Taxpayers Union Campaign Fund (C00298141) *Address: same as sponsor * Treasurer: Al Cors Jr.*

	1993-94	1995-96	1997	Totals
Receipts	$82,378	$74,186	$11,250	$167,814
Disburse	81,448	74,833	640	156,921
Cash	929	282	10,892	n/a
Contributions	9,489	8,876	0	18,365
Republicans	8,659	8,072	0	16,731
No. of Cand.	*97*	*7*	*0*	*104*
House	5,035	0	0	5,035
Senate	3,624	8,072	0	11,696
Democrats	830	804	0	1,634
No. of Cand.	*10*	*4*	*0*	*14*
House	830	804	0	1,634
Senate	0	0	0	0
Incumbents	3,039	898	0	3,937
Challengers	3,659	3,034	0	6,693
Open Seat	2,791	4,944	0	7,735
Winners	6,908	2,592	n/a	9,500
Losers	2,581	6,284	n/a	8,865

Ruff PAC

*Phone: (703) 257-7861 * Fax: (703) 257-4758*
7526-B Diplomat Dr., Manassas, VA 22110

The Ruff PAC contributes to Republican candidates from across the nation. Most of its 1995-96 election cycle contributions were in $250 increments, but three unsuccessful candidates received more than $1,000 each: Steve Gill and former Rep. Dick Zimmer of New Jersey and Raymond J. Clatworthy, a Senate candidate from Delaware.

Ruff Political Action Committee (Ruff-PAC) (C00124040) *Address: same as sponsor * Treasurer: Tammy J. Lyles * Contact: Howard J. Ruff, Chairman*

	1993-94	1995-96	1997	Totals
Receipts	$370,851	$152,643	$25,911	$549,405
Disburse	382,996	160,264	27,561	570,821
Cash	10,207	2,585	862	n/a
Contributions	5,067	17,420	500	22,987
Republicans	5,067	17,420	500	22,987
No. of Cand.	*10*	*44*	*2*	*56*
House	5,067	13,000	250	18,317
Senate	0	4,420	250	4,670
Democrats	0	0	0	0
No. of Cand.	*0*	*0*	*0*	*0*
House	0	0	0	0
Senate	0	0	0	0
Incumbents	1,850	500	250	2,600
Challengers	3,217	11,085	250	14,552
Open Seat	0	5,835	0	5,835
Winners	4,067	3,750	n/a	7,817
Losers	1,000	13,670	n/a	14,670

Term Limits America

Phone: (501) 754-9023
4 Fairway Dr., Maumelle, AR 72114

Term Limits America contributed to mostly Republican candidates during the 1995-96 cycle. The PAC moved from Virginia to Arkansas in late 1997.

Term Limits America (C00286880) *Address: same as sponsor * Treasurer: Kathleen J. Richman*

	1993-94	1995-96	1997	Totals
Receipts	$6,721	$73,286	$75,825	$155,832
Disburse	8,872	53,299	36,837	99,008
Cash	-60	19,924	58,911	n/a
Contributions	0	26,500	1,250	27,750
Republicans	0	24,000	0	24,000
No. of Cand.	*0*	*13*	*0*	*13*
House	0	23,750	0	23,750
Senate	0	250	0	250
Democrats	0	2,500	1,250	3,750
No. of Cand.	*0*	*1*	*1*	*2*
House	0	2,500	1,250	3,750
Senate	0	0	0	0
Incumbents	0	3,250	0	3,250
Challengers	0	7,500	0	7,500
Open Seat	0	15,750	1,250	17,000
Winners	0	11,000	n/a	11,000
Losers	0	15,500	n/a	15,500

U.S. Immigration Reform PAC

Phone: (212) 869-4250
1450 Broadway, 17th Floor, New York, NY 10018

The U.S. Immigration Reform PAC, which contributed mostly to House Republican candidates during the 1995-96 election cycle, did not make a contribution to a federal candidate during 1997.

U.S. Immigration Reform PAC (C00253906) *Address: same as sponsor * Treasurer: James Barnes*

	1993-94	1995-96	1997	Totals
Receipts	$62,202	$44,560	$1,232	$107,994
Disburse	39,535	80,021	4,287	123,843
Cash	32,333	12,268	9,717	n/a
Contributions	6,500	26,500	0	33,000
Republicans	3,500	25,000	0	28,500
No. of Cand.	*6*	*19*	*0*	*25*
House	1,000	17,000	0	18,000
Senate	2,500	8,000	0	10,500
Democrats	3,000	1,500	0	4,500
No. of Cand.	*4*	*2*	*0*	*6*
House	1,500	1,000	0	2,500
Senate	1,500	500	0	2,000
Incumbents	6,000	25,000	0	31,000
Challengers	500	0	0	500
Open Seat	0	1,500	0	1,500
Winners	5,000	25,500	n/a	30,500
Losers	1,500	1,000	n/a	2,500

Pro-Israel

Americans for Good Government Inc.

Phone: (205) 221-4000
P.O. Box 3128, Jasper, AL 35502

Americans for Good Government is a pro-Israel PAC, with most of its members living in Alabama.

Leading recipients during the 1995-96 election cycle include Rep. Robert E. "Bud" Cramer, R-Ala., and two Alabama Democratic challengers, Ted Little and Bob Wilson. The group also contributed $5,000 to competing Senate candidates in the state, giving to Democrat Roger Bedford as well as to the Republican winner, Sen. Jeff Sessions. Sen. Carl Levin, D-Mich., also received $5,000.

Americans for Good Government Inc. (C00138701) *Address: same as sponsor * Treasurer: Alan Z. Engel*

	1993-94	1995-96	1997	Totals
Receipts	$130,884	$126,046	$63,224	$320,154
Disburse	107,459	127,207	60,202	294,868
Cash	42,520	41,358	44,379	n/a
Contributions	93,250	107,000	52,850	253,100
Republicans	42,000	58,100	32,750	132,850
No. of Cand.	*31*	*47*	*20*	*98*
House	11,500	26,100	10,750	48,350
Senate	30,500	32,000	22,000	84,500
Democrats	51,250	48,900	20,100	120,250
No. of Cand.	*45*	*31*	*19*	*95*
House	28,750	26,800	7,100	62,650
Senate	22,500	22,100	13,000	57,600
Incumbents	79,250	66,200	49,350	194,800
Challengers	1,000	2,600	2,000	5,600
Open Seat	13,000	38,200	1,000	52,200
Winners	80,500	79,200	n/a	159,700
Losers	12,750	27,800	n/a	40,550

BAYPAC

Phone: (813) 961-8709
Box 271082, Tampa, FL 33688

BAYPAC supports strong relations between the United States and Israel. The organization is based in Tampa, Fla. Unlike many other pro-Israel groups, BAYPAC has contributed most of its money to Republican candidates.

BAYPAC (C00155713) *Address: same as sponsor * Treasurer: Herb Swarzman*

	1993-94	1995-96	1997	Totals
Receipts	$6,485	$7,370	$3,125	$16,980
Disburse	6,413	6,062	3,150	15,625
Cash	102	1,410	1,385	n/a
Contributions	6,052	5,562	2,800	14,414
Republicans	4,262	5,362	2,200	11,824
No. of Cand.	*6*	*10*	*4*	*20*
House	1,862	3,512	0	5,374
Senate	2,400	1,850	2,200	6,450
Democrats	1,790	200	600	2,590
No. of Cand.	*8*	*1*	*2*	*11*
House	1,300	200	600	2,100
Senate	490	0	0	490
Incumbents	5,352	3,312	2,700	11,364
Challengers	0	550	0	550
Open Seat	700	1,700	0	2,400
Winners	5,362	3,312	n/a	8,674
Losers	690	2,250	n/a	2,940

Bi-County PAC

Phone: (516) 747-0300
28 Elm St., Huntington, NY 11743

The Bi-County PAC, formerly known as Suffolk PAC, is supported by members from Long Island, N.Y. The bipartisan organization supports House and Senate candidates "committed to positive U.S.-Israel relations."

BiCPAC conducts training seminars for its members, as well as public education programs about the area's candidates.

Bi-County Political Action Committee (formerly known as Suffolk PAC) (C00204388) *Address: same as sponsor * Treasurer: Ira Lamel * Contact: Lewis Meltzer, President*

	1993-94	1995-96	1997	Totals
Receipts	$49,751	$38,657	$32,464	$120,872
Disburse	48,375	46,208	12,133	106,716
Cash	9,560	2,010	24,511	n/a
Contributions	18,500	25,500	2,000	46,000
Republicans	2,000	8,000	2,000	12,000
No. of Cand.	*2*	*5*	*1*	*8*
House	1,000	3,000	2,000	6,000
Senate	1,000	5,000	0	6,000
Democrats	16,500	17,500	0	34,000
No. of Cand.	*11*	*11*	*0*	*22*
House	6,500	9,000	0	15,500
Senate	10,000	8,500	0	18,500
Incumbents	17,500	11,500	2,000	31,000
Challengers	0	8,000	0	8,000
Open Seat	1,000	2,500	0	3,500
Winners	16,500	10,000	n/a	26,500
Losers	2,000	15,500	n/a	17,500

California PAC

*Phone: (818) 954-6323 * Fax: (818) 954-6607*
8665 Wilshire Blvd., #220, Beverly Hills, CA 90211

California PAC is a pro-abortion rights and pro-Israel organization. It gives only to Democratic federal candidates from all parts of the nation.

The PAC was founded in 1993.

California PAC (C00291922) *Address: same as sponsor * Treasurer: Howard Welinsky * Contact: Mel Levine, Chairperson*

	1993-94	1995-96	1997	Totals
Receipts	$30,626	$15,000	$22,000	$67,626
Disburse	8,000	26,847	7,319	42,166
Cash	22,626	10,778	25,458	n/a
Contributions	8,000	19,780	5,256	33,036
Republicans	0	0	0	0
No. of Cand.	*0*	*0*	*0*	*0*
House	0	0	0	0
Senate	0	0	0	0
Democrats	8,000	19,780	5,256	33,036
No. of Cand.	*8*	*14*	*6*	*28*
House	7,000	4,500	1,256	12,756
Senate	1,000	15,280	4,000	20,280
Incumbents	7,000	7,500	4,256	18,756
Challengers	1,000	6,500	0	7,500
Open Seat	0	5,780	1,000	6,780
Winners	4,000	12,280	n/a	16,280
Losers	4,000	7,500	n/a	11,500

Citizens Concerned for the National Interest

Phone: (312) 951-8957
211 E. Chicago Ave., #1020, Chicago, IL 60611

Citizens Concerned for the National Interest is a pro-Israel PAC, based in Chicago. During 1997, the PAC had 12 contributors who gave a total of $55,000.

Citizens Concerned for the National Interest (C00113019)
*Address: same as sponsor * Treasurer: Robert C. Gebert * Contact: Debbie Capocci, Secretary*

	1993-94	1995-96	1997	Totals
Receipts	$51,000	$72,000	$55,000	$178,000
Disburse	51,500	72,500	54,013	178,013
Cash	666	166	1,152	n/a
Contributions	49,000	62,500	54,000	165,500
Republicans	29,000	51,500	34,000	114,500
No. of Cand.	*10*	*11*	*4*	*25*
House	3,500	6,000	0	9,500
Senate	25,500	45,500	34,000	105,000
Democrats	20,000	11,000	20,000	51,000
No. of Cand.	*3*	*4*	*2*	*9*
House	0	1,000	0	1,000
Senate	20,000	10,000	20,000	50,000
Incumbents	43,000	33,000	54,000	130,000
Challengers	0	10,000	0	10,000
Open Seat	6,000	19,500	0	25,500
Winners	49,000	34,000	n/a	83,000
Losers	0	28,500	n/a	28,500

Citizens Organized PAC

*Phone: (310) 277-1010 * Fax: (310) 203-7199*
1800 Avenue of the Stars, Suite 900, Los Angeles, CA 90067

The Citizens Organized PAC, an "informal" pro-Israel organization, is administratively based out of the office of Treasurer Marvin S. Shapiro's Los Angeles law firm, Irell & Manella. The PAC is supported by a small core of contributors from Los Angeles and Beverly Hills. From only 52 donations of more than $200 made to the PAC in 1995-96, the total amount received was nearly $117,000, for an average of $2,250 per contribution.

Citizens Organized favored Senate races. Five incumbents received the maximum allowable contribution of $10,000 — Sens. Mitch McConnell, R-Ky., Tom Harkin, D-Iowa, Ron Wyden, D-Ore., Carl Levin, D-Mich., and Max Baucus, D-Mont.

Citizens Organized Political Action Committee (C00110585)
*Address: same as sponsor * Treasurer: Marvin S. Shapiro*

	1993-94	1995-96	1997	Totals
Receipts	$129,479	$118,560	$51,311	$299,350
Disburse	145,212	95,323	31,929	272,464
Cash	5,894	29,135	48,518	n/a
Contributions	140,000	93,000	31,000	264,000
Republicans	35,000	29,500	17,500	82,000
No. of Cand.	*7*	*12*	*4*	*23*
House	5,000	5,000	0	10,000
Senate	30,000	24,500	17,500	72,000
Democrats	100,000	63,500	13,500	177,000
No. of Cand.	*15*	*15*	*4*	*34*
House	0	2,000	0	2,000
Senate	100,000	61,500	13,500	175,000
Incumbents	110,000	53,500	31,000	194,500
Challengers	5,000	5,000	0	10,000
Open Seat	25,000	33,500	0	58,500
Winners	92,500	74,000	n/a	166,500
Losers	47,500	19,000	n/a	66,500

City Political Action Committee

Phone: (312) 464-9396
440 N. Wabash #2606, Chicago, IL 60611

City Political Action Committee is a pro-Israel group with a membership base in the Chicago metropolitan area. The leading recipient was Rep. Rod Blagojevich, D-Ill., who received $2,750 in 1996. Eight other candidates from Illinois also received contributions, including Republican Reps. Ray LaHood and Jerry Weller, as well as Democratic Sen. Richard J. Durbin.

City Political Action Committee (City PAC) (C00187526) *Address: same as sponsor * Treasurer: Matt Mitzen*

	1993-94	1995-96	1997	Totals
Receipts	$202,843	$130,957	$11,579	$345,379
Disburse	187,241	118,323	24,945	330,509
Cash	22,472	35,103	21,737	n/a
Contributions	46,525	46,500	4,000	97,025
Republicans	7,500	16,000	0	23,500
No. of Cand.	*5*	*13*	*0*	*18*
House	4,500	12,000	0	16,500
Senate	3,000	4,000	0	7,000
Democrats	38,025	30,500	4,000	72,525
No. of Cand.	*23*	*20*	*3*	*46*
House	28,025	19,500	3,000	50,525
Senate	10,000	11,000	1,000	22,000
Incumbents	35,025	29,000	3,000	67,025
Challengers	7,000	10,500	0	17,500
Open Seat	4,500	7,000	1,000	12,500
Winners	25,250	35,000	n/a	60,250
Losers	21,275	11,500	n/a	32,775

Congressional Action Committee of Texas

Phone: (713) 238-6775
10035 Cedar Creek Dr., Houston, TX 77042

The Congressional Action Committee of Texas is a pro-Israel PAC based in Houston. It gives to federal candidates from all areas of the United States.

Congressional Action Committee of Texas (C00142422) *Address: same as sponsor * Treasurer: Charles Silverman*

	1993-94	1995-96	1997	Totals
Receipts	$1,900	$11,100	$0	$13,000
Disburse	4,260	9,585	0	13,845
Cash	85	1,600	1,600	n/a
Contributions	0	9,500	0	9,500
Republicans	0	3,500	0	3,500
No. of Cand.	*0*	*5*	*0*	*5*
House	0	2,000	0	2,000
Senate	0	1,500	0	1,500
Democrats	0	6,000	0	6,000
No. of Cand.	*0*	*7*	*0*	*7*
House	0	4,000	0	4,000
Senate	0	2,000	0	2,000
Incumbents	0	5,000	0	5,000
Challengers	0	0	0	0
Open Seat	0	4,500	0	4,500
Winners	0	7,000	n/a	7,000
Losers	0	2,500	n/a	2,500

Delaware Valley PAC

*Phone: (215) 735-5955 * Fax: (215) 735-9733*
121 S. Broad St., Suite 500, Philadelphia, PA 19107

The Delaware Valley PAC gives to federal candidates who support continued foreign aid for Israel. The 350-person group, whose members are mainly from the Philadelphia area, is bipartisan.

Delaware Valley Political Action Committee (C00152579) *Address: same as sponsor * Treasurer: Laurence Spector * Contact: Howard Silverman, PAC Dir.*

	1993-94	1995-96	1997	Totals
Receipts	$46,017	$35,097	$15,559	$96,673
Disburse	50,239	30,445	14,911	95,595
Cash	3,219	7,872	8,519	n/a
Contributions	46,000	27,800	12,900	86,700
Republicans	12,750	5,750	5,500	24,000
No. of Cand.	*10*	*5*	*7*	*22*
House	2,500	250	0	2,750
Senate	10,250	5,500	5,500	21,250
Democrats	33,150	22,050	7,400	62,600
No. of Cand.	*34*	*29*	*8*	*71*
House	11,300	6,550	1,400	19,250
Senate	21,850	15,500	6,000	43,350
Incumbents	41,800	15,800	11,400	69,000
Challengers	250	5,150	0	5,400
Open Seat	3,700	6,850	1,500	12,050
Winners	35,700	19,800	n/a	55,500
Losers	10,300	8,000	n/a	18,300

Desert Caucus

Phone: (520) 886-9224
P.O. Box 31564, Tucson, AZ 85751

The Desert Caucus labels itself as a "single-issue organization — pro-Israel." The group has about 110 members, mostly from the Tucson, Ariz. area. It was founded in 1977.

Eleven senators received the maximum allowable contribution of $10,000 during 1995-96.

Desert Caucus (C00102368) *Address: same as sponsor * Treasurer: James R. Wezelman*

	1993-94	1995-96	1997	Totals
Receipts	$272,930	$201,919	$151,673	$626,522
Disburse	252,333	225,845	139,488	617,666
Cash	24,260	334	12,520	n/a
Contributions	167,000	147,750	98,300	413,050
Republicans	44,500	58,750	48,300	151,550
No. of Cand.	*10*	*16*	*6*	*32*
House	2,000	2,750	0	4,750
Senate	42,500	56,000	48,300	146,800
Democrats	122,500	89,000	50,000	261,500
No. of Cand.	*37*	*25*	*5*	*67*
House	29,500	18,000	0	47,500
Senate	93,000	71,000	50,000	214,000
Incumbents	154,000	113,250	98,300	365,550
Challengers	0	2,000	0	2,000
Open Seat	14,000	33,000	0	47,000
Winners	137,500	119,750	n/a	257,250
Losers	29,500	28,000	n/a	57,500

Florida Congressional Committee

*Phone: (305) 949-6445 * Fax: (305) 949-6316*
1380 N.E. Miami Gardens Dr., #207, Miami, FL 33179

The Florida Congressional Committee is a pro-Israel PAC. Its major contributors are from the Miami area. A spokesperson would not comment on its activities or goals.

Florida Congressional Committee (C00127811) *Address: same as sponsor * Treasurer: Forrest B. Raffel * Contact: Leroy Raffel*

	1993-94	1995-96	1997	Totals
Receipts	$146,750	$89,125	$30,625	$266,500
Disburse	143,855	77,456	30,025	251,336
Cash	4,917	16,584	17,183	n/a
Contributions	125,350	57,250	26,800	209,400
Republicans	48,250	24,500	11,000	83,750
No. of Cand.	*20*	*17*	*3*	*40*
House	10,750	4,800	0	15,550
Senate	37,500	19,700	11,000	68,200
Democrats	77,100	32,750	15,800	125,650
No. of Cand.	*31*	*16*	*5*	*52*
House	21,500	5,750	800	28,050
Senate	55,600	27,000	15,000	97,600
Incumbents	121,100	46,750	26,000	193,850
Challengers	1,750	2,200	0	3,950
Open Seat	7,500	8,300	500	16,300
Winners	110,250	49,550	n/a	159,800
Losers	15,100	7,700	n/a	22,800

Garden State PAC

P.O. Box 3433, Union, NJ 07083

The Garden State PAC, a pro-Israel organization, informed the FEC in 1997 that it was "defunct," although the FEC had not received a termination report from the group by early 1998.

Garden State Political Action Committee (C00169136) *Address: same as sponsor * Treasurer: Philip J. Solondz*

	1993-94	1995-96	1997	Totals
Receipts	$37,572	$15,693	$0	$53,265
Disburse	46,450	8,568	0	55,018
Cash	156	7,303	0	n/a
Contributions	40,000	6,500	0	46,500
Republicans	16,250	1,500	0	17,750
No. of Cand.	*19*	*2*	*0*	*21*
House	4,500	0	0	4,500
Senate	11,750	1,500	0	13,250
Democrats	23,250	5,000	0	28,250
No. of Cand.	*28*	*6*	*0*	*34*
House	11,750	1,000	0	12,750
Senate	11,500	4,000	0	15,500
Incumbents	27,750	5,500	0	33,250
Challengers	1,000	0	0	1,000
Open Seat	10,750	1,000	0	11,750
Winners	26,500	6,500	n/a	33,000
Losers	13,500	0	n/a	13,500

Heartland PAC

*Phone: (216) 514-4994 * Fax: (216) 514-5154*
23875 Commerce Park Rd., Suite 140, Beechwood, OH 44122

Heartland PAC is a pro-Israel volunteer organization in Ohio. Its donors mostly come from Cleveland and surrounding areas.

Heartland PAC (formerly known as Youngstown Political Action Committee) (C00131557) *Address: same as sponsor * Treasurer: David B. Orlean*

	1993-94	1995-96	1997	Totals
Receipts	$100,748	$99,389	$41,588	$241,725
Disburse	101,119	93,079	19,206	213,404
Cash	1,657	7,967	30,347	n/a
Contributions	85,500	75,000	18,000	178,500
Republicans	15,500	31,000	3,000	49,500
No. of Cand.	*7*	*18*	*2*	*27*
House	4,000	7,500	1,000	12,500
Senate	11,500	23,500	2,000	37,000
Democrats	70,000	44,000	15,000	129,000
No. of Cand.	*28*	*29*	*6*	*63*
House	26,000	21,000	0	47,000
Senate	44,000	23,000	15,000	82,000
Incumbents	70,500	53,000	15,500	139,000
Challengers	4,000	7,000	0	11,000
Open Seat	11,000	15,000	2,500	28,500
Winners	55,000	64,000	n/a	119,000
Losers	30,500	11,000	n/a	41,500

Joint Action Committee for Political Affairs

*Phone: (847) 433-5999 * Fax: (847) 433-6194*
1724 First St., P.O. Box 105, Highland Park, IL 60035
*Web: www.jacpac.org * E-mail: jacpac123@aol.com*

The Joint Action Committee for Political Affairs is a bipartisan PAC that supports candidates who endorse strong U.S.-Israel relations, abortion rights and separation of church and state, and who oppose the intrusion of "right-wing ideology into national priorities."

The nationwide network was founded after the 1980 elections by an activist group of Jewish women in response to the defeat of many pro-Israel members of Congress and the perceived rise of Christian conservative activism in national politics. Men were not invited to join JAC until 1993. It now claims about 3,000 members. Activities include publishing candidate profiles and newsletters with issue and political analyses.

The group became a conduit PAC in 1993, sending "bundles" of checks from its members written specifically to candidates' campaigns. JAC also makes direct contributions to candidates.

Joint Action Committee for Political Affairs (C00139659) *Address: same as sponsor * Treasurer: Joan Canel * Contact: Claire Levenberg, President*

	1993-94	1995-96	1997	Totals
Receipts	$454,754	$459,926	$259,909	$1,174,589
Disburse	458,851	468,396	241,529	1,168,776
Cash	28,442	19,970	38,352	n/a
Contributions	79,208	70,745	27,414	177,367
Republicans	1,000	3,699	0	4,699
No. of Cand.	*3*	*4*	*0*	*7*
House	1,000	3,230	0	4,230
Senate	0	469	0	469
Democrats	76,916	67,046	27,414	171,376
No. of Cand.	*74*	*68*	*24*	*166*
House	40,458	31,852	9,829	82,139
Senate	36,458	35,194	17,585	89,237
Incumbents	57,051	35,274	25,097	117,422
Challengers	4,890	14,846	0	19,736
Open Seat	17,267	20,625	2,317	40,209
Winners	41,353	57,664	n/a	99,017
Losers	37,855	13,081	n/a	50,936

Louisiana for American Security

Phone: (504) 522-7791
P.O. Box 80395, Baton Rouge, LA 70898

Louisiana for American Security PAC supports candidates who promote strong U.S.-Israel relations. Founded in 1981, it consists of 200 members statewide.

Louisiana for American Security Political Action Committee (C00144170) *Address: same as sponsor * Treasurer: Charles G. Glaser * Contact: Richard Katz, Chairperson*

	1993-94	1995-96	1997	Totals
Receipts	$35,980	$46,561	$28,870	$111,411
Disburse	29,637	46,074	19,528	95,239
Cash	7,932	8,417	17,758	n/a
Contributions	16,500	29,250	9,500	55,250
Republicans	8,000	10,500	5,500	24,000
No. of Cand.	*4*	*12*	*5*	*21*
House	7,000	8,000	4,500	19,500
Senate	1,000	2,500	1,000	4,500
Democrats	8,500	18,750	4,000	31,250
No. of Cand.	*9*	*10*	*3*	*22*
House	7,500	6,250	0	13,750
Senate	1,000	12,500	4,000	17,500
Incumbents	16,000	6,750	9,000	31,750
Challengers	0	0	0	0
Open Seat	500	22,500	0	23,000
Winners	15,500	23,750	n/a	39,250
Losers	1,000	5,500	n/a	6,500

MOPAC

*Phone: (248) 642-0500 * Fax: (248) 642-5241*
1533 N. Woodward Ave., Suite 250, Bloomfield Hills, MI 48304

MOPAC is a pro-Israel PAC whose contributions come mainly from the Detroit area. The PAC receives mail at the law offices of Treasurer Nathan Upfal of Jackier, Gould, Bean, Upfal, Eizelman & Goldman.

MOPAC contributed solely to Democratic campaigns during the 1995-96 election cycle. Michigan candidates received the largest contributions — Sen. Carl Levin received $5,000, as did Rep. Sander M. Levin. Rep. Debbie Stabenow received $4,500.

MOPAC (C00199950) *Address: same as sponsor * Treasurer: Nathan Upfal*

	1993-94	1995-96	1997	Totals
Receipts	$50,500	$81,769	$36,526	$168,795
Disburse	52,262	81,243	-88	133,417
Cash	71	846	37,461	n/a
Contributions	50,000	79,750	-250	129,500
Republicans	500	0	0	500
No. of Cand.	*1*	*0*	*0*	*1*
House	500	0	0	500
Senate	0	0	0	0
Democrats	49,500	79,750	-250	129,000
No. of Cand.	*49*	*59*	*1*	*109*
House	23,500	42,750	-250	66,000
Senate	26,000	37,000	0	63,000
Incumbents	35,000	35,000	-250	69,750
Challengers	4,250	16,250	0	20,500
Open Seat	10,750	28,500	0	39,250
Winners	28,000	53,000	n/a	81,000
Losers	22,000	26,750	n/a	48,750

Maryland Association for Concerned Citizens

Phone: (410) 486-9050
P.O. Box 32196, Pikesville, MD 21282-2196

The Maryland Association for Concerned Citizens PAC is a bipartisan pro-Israel PAC. It contributes to federal candidates who support a strong U.S.-Israel relationship.

The PAC was established in 1985, and its board is composed of 18 members. Its contributors are mostly Maryland residents.

Maryland Association for Concerned Citizens Political Action Committee (C00195024) *Address: same as sponsor * Treasurer: Jimmy Berg * Contact: Michael F. Klein, President*

	1993-94	1995-96	1997	Totals
Receipts	$81,645	$75,021	$31,800	$188,466
Disburse	81,063	76,709	20,549	178,321
Cash	5,581	3,888	15,139	n/a
Contributions	73,000	56,000	16,500	145,500
Republicans	16,000	20,000	10,500	46,500
No. of Cand.	*11*	*13*	*5*	*29*
House	3,000	5,000	0	8,000
Senate	13,000	15,000	10,500	38,500
Democrats	55,500	36,000	6,000	97,500
No. of Cand.	*32*	*26*	*2*	*60*
House	20,500	9,000	0	29,500
Senate	35,000	27,000	6,000	68,000
Incumbents	53,500	36,500	16,500	106,500
Challengers	4,000	7,000	0	11,000
Open Seat	15,500	12,500	0	28,000
Winners	43,000	49,500	n/a	92,500
Losers	30,000	6,500	n/a	36,500

Mid Manhattan PAC

Phone: (212) 787-4153
450 Seventh Ave., Suite 1100, New York, NY 10123

The Mid Manhattan PAC supports a strong relationship between the United States and Israel. Established in the early 1980s, the bipartisan group has 500 members.

Mid Manhattan Political Action Committee (Mid PAC) (C00165944) *Address: same as sponsor * Treasurer: Anton A. Weiss * Contact: Jean Lindenvaum, Chairperson*

	1993-94	1995-96	1997	Totals
Receipts	$111,739	$62,902	$9,322	$183,963
Disburse	111,082	64,043	8,448	183,573
Cash	2,125	984	1,858	n/a
Contributions	59,650	39,750	3,500	102,900
Republicans	10,150	4,500	0	14,650
No. of Cand.	*10*	*9*	*0*	*19*
House	3,400	750	0	4,150
Senate	6,750	3,750	0	10,500
Democrats	49,000	35,250	3,500	87,750
No. of Cand.	*29*	*19*	*3*	*51*
House	10,500	5,250	500	16,250
Senate	38,500	30,000	3,000	71,500
Incumbents	37,150	19,750	3,000	59,900
Challengers	7,250	3,000	0	10,250
Open Seat	15,250	17,000	500	32,750
Winners	29,150	33,750	n/a	62,900
Losers	30,500	6,000	n/a	36,500

NORPAC

*Phone: (212) 605-3132 * Fax: (212) 605-3128*
P.O. Box 5595, Englewood, NJ 07631

NORPAC, formerly known as the North Jersey Political Action Committee, is a pro-Israel organization whose contributors come from the North Jersey area, including Englewood and Teaneck.

During the 1995-96 cycle, House Minority Leader Richard Gephardt was the leading recipient, receiving $5,000 apiece for his campaign committee and his Democratic Leader's Victory Fund.

NORPAC (formerly known as North Jersey PAC) (C00247403) *Address: same as sponsor * Treasurer: Mitchell J. Eichen*

	1993-94	1995-96	1997	Totals
Receipts	$141,999	$95,372	$67,270	$304,641
Disburse	113,425	98,946	46,117	258,488
Cash	54,355	50,779	71,932	n/a
Contributions	57,750	68,250	29,750	155,750
Republicans	12,500	20,500	8,000	41,000
No. of Cand.	*10*	*25*	*10*	*45*
House	6,000	11,000	4,000	21,000
Senate	6,500	9,500	4,000	20,000
Democrats	45,250	47,750	21,750	114,750
No. of Cand.	*39*	*42*	*24*	*105*
House	19,750	28,250	9,750	57,750
Senate	25,500	19,500	12,000	57,000
Incumbents	48,000	54,250	28,750	131,000
Challengers	1,000	3,000	-500	3,500
Open Seat	8,750	11,000	1,500	21,250
Winners	38,750	63,250	n/a	102,000
Losers	19,000	5,000	n/a	24,000

National Action Committee

*Phone: (305) 358-9207 * Fax: (305) 358-1618*
700 Brickell Ave., Suite 3260, Miami, FL 33131

The National Action Committee supports "members of Congress, or their challengers, who support a strong U.S.-Israel alliance."

NACPAC has more than 350 members, most of whom are from the greater Miami area. It was founded in 1981.

National Action Committee - NACPAC (C00147983) *Address: same as sponsor * Treasurer: Judy Ellenbogen * Contact: Mark R. Vogel, Chairperson*

	1993-94	1995-96	1997	Totals
Receipts	$208,827	$140,801	$83,762	$433,390
Disburse	202,932	148,461	69,530	420,923
Cash	8,882	1,222	15,454	n/a
Contributions	150,550	101,050	51,750	303,350
Republicans	49,500	34,600	19,750	103,850
No. of Cand.	*23*	*19*	*7*	*49*
House	14,500	10,100	1,750	26,350
Senate	35,000	24,500	18,000	77,500
Democrats	101,050	66,450	32,000	199,500
No. of Cand.	*59*	*38*	*16*	*113*
House	53,950	27,450	9,500	90,900
Senate	47,100	39,000	22,500	108,600
Incumbents	126,800	81,950	50,250	259,000
Challengers	2,250	0	0	2,250
Open Seat	20,750	16,600	1,000	38,350
Winners	98,750	87,700	n/a	186,450
Losers	51,800	13,350	n/a	65,150

National Jewish Democratic Council

*Phone: (202) 544-7636 * Fax: (202) 544-7645*
503 Capitol Court N.E., Suite 300, Washington, DC 20002
Web: www.webcom.com/~digitals/njdc

The National Jewish Democratic Council is a partisan organization that advocates the separation of church and state, supports Israel and promotes abortion rights. Established in 1996 by the National Jewish Democratic Council, the NJDC PAC provides a pro-Israel voter guide for selected congressional candidates.

The National Jewish Democratic Council also lobbies against any constitutional amendments to protect school prayer, establish term limits or require a balanced budget. The council supports campaign finance reform.

National Jewish Democratic Council Political Action Committee (C00306670) *Address: same as sponsor * Treasurer: Ken Gross * Contact: Steve Erd, PAC Dir.*

	1993-94	1995-96	1997	Totals
Receipts	$0	$70,273	$40,815	$111,088
Disburse	0	70,143	37,513	107,656
Cash	0	127	3,428	n/a
Contributions	0	56,254	25,776	82,030
Republicans	0	0	0	0
No. of Cand.	*0*	*0*	*0*	*0*
House	0	0	0	0
Senate	0	0	0	0
Democrats	0	56,254	25,776	82,030
No. of Cand.	*0*	*36*	*30*	*66*
House	0	34,155	13,807	47,962
Senate	0	22,099	11,969	34,068
Incumbents	0	8,304	15,284	23,588
Challengers	0	28,448	3,883	32,331
Open Seat	0	19,502	6,609	26,111
Winners	0	30,405	n/a	30,405
Losers	0	25,849	n/a	25,849

National PAC

*Phone: (202) 879-7710 * Fax: (202) 879-7728*
600 Pennsylvania Ave. S.E., Suite 207, Washington, DC 20003
E-mail: lbrent@clark.net

National PAC is a Washington-based pro-Israel committee that supports consistent foreign and anti-terrorist aid to Israel. Candidates are selected for contributions depending on their friendliness to Israel, through a review of position papers and by analyzing their voting records.

National PAC was the top pro-Israel PAC in terms of contributions to congressional candidates during the 1995-96 election cycle. The $560,000 it spent on congressional campaigns was more than three times the next-largest pro-Israel PAC. About 75 percent of its contributions went to incumbents.

The leading recipients were Sens. Richard J. Durbin, D-Ill.; Tom Harkin, D-Iowa; Max Baucus, D-Mont.; former Sen. Larry Pressler, R-S.D.; and former Rep. Gary Franks, R-Conn. National PAC gave slightly more to Republican candidates.

National PAC (C00150995) *Address: same as sponsor * Treasurer: Marvin Josephson * Contact: Lane Brent Forsythe, Political Dir.*

	1993-94	1995-96	1997	Totals
Receipts	$1,394,443	$1,375,183	$615,873	$3,385,499
Disburse	1,310,308	1,441,207	562,497	3,314,012
Cash	104,646	38,621	92,000	n/a
Contributions	219,000	560,000	141,000	920,000
Republicans	87,000	301,500	91,000	479,500
No. of Cand.	*44*	*92*	*19*	*155*
House	51,500	199,000	41,000	291,500
Senate	35,500	102,500	50,000	188,000
Democrats	132,000	258,500	50,000	440,500
No. of Cand.	*65*	*87*	*11*	*163*
House	84,000	181,000	12,500	277,500

Senate	48,000	77,500	37,500	163,000
Incumbents	180,500	423,500	138,500	742,500
Challengers	2,000	27,000	0	29,000
Open Seat	36,500	109,500	2,500	148,500
Winners	188,500	457,000	n/a	645,500
Losers	30,500	103,000	n/a	133,500

Northern Californians for Good Government

*Phone: (415) 441-6335 * Fax: (415) 441-6335*
601 Van Ness Ave., #28, San Francisco, CA 94102

Northern Californians for Good Government calls itself a "political action committee for strong U.S.-Israel relations." It supports federal candidates who "seek out campaign assistance in the Bay Area," as "recognition for their efforts" in working for a strong Israeli partnership.

During the 1995-96 election cycle, Sens. Tom Harkin, D-Iowa, Max Baucus, D-Mont., and Carl Levin, D-Mich., were the three top beneficiaries, each receiving about $6,500.

The PAC was founded in 1981 and has about 300 members who hail from San Francisco and the surrounding area.

Northern Californians for Good Government (C00141747) *55 Francisco St., San Francisco, CA 94133 * Treasurer: Russell S. Holdstein Contact: Andrea Rouah Spiegel, Executive Dir. * Phone: (415) 441-6335*

	1993-94	1995-96	1997	Totals
Receipts	$158,937	$151,890	$80,276	$391,103
Disburse	150,857	155,876	72,721	379,454
Cash	9,229	5,240	12,793	n/a
Contributions	81,500	77,400	29,000	187,900
Republicans	8,000	21,000	8,000	37,000
No. of Cand.	*5*	*13*	*4*	*22*
House	1,500	5,000	0	6,500
Senate	6,500	16,000	8,000	30,500
Democrats	72,500	56,400	21,000	149,900
No. of Cand.	*29*	*25*	*10*	*64*
House	18,500	12,000	6,000	36,500
Senate	54,000	44,400	15,000	113,400
Incumbents	63,500	52,400	28,000	143,900
Challengers	0	7,500	0	7,500
Open Seat	18,000	17,500	1,000	36,500
Winners	49,500	61,400	n/a	110,900
Losers	32,000	16,000	n/a	48,000

San Diego Community PAC

*Phone: (619) 236-1000 x2 * Fax: (619) 238-4208*
111 Elm St., Suite 415, San Diego, CA 92101

The San Diego Community PAC gives to pro-Israel federal candidates who are not from the state of California. The PAC, which is bipartisan, solicits funds in the San Diego area.

San Diego Community Political Action Committee Inc. (also known as SanCPAC) (C00177055) *Address: same as sponsor * Treasurer: Kenneth L. Weiss * Contact: Lawrence Sherman, Chairperson*

	1993-94	1995-96	1997	Totals
Receipts	$16,676	$13,398	$5,001	$35,075
Disburse	16,804	14,070	2,500	33,374
Cash	1,497	828	3,330	n/a
Contributions	16,000	11,500	2,500	30,000
Republicans	9,000	9,500	2,500	21,000
No. of Cand.	*9*	*9*	*2*	*20*
House	1,500	500	0	2,000
Senate	7,500	9,000	2,500	19,000
Democrats	7,000	2,000	0	9,000
No. of Cand.	*9*	*2*	*0*	*11*
House	3,500	0	0	3,500
Senate	3,500	2,000	0	5,500
Incumbents	13,500	8,500	2,500	24,500
Challengers	0	2,000	0	2,000
Open Seat	2,500	1,000	0	3,500
Winners	15,500	8,000	n/a	23,500
Losers	500	3,500	n/a	4,000

St. Louisians for Better Government

*Phone: (314) 721-0577 * Fax: (314) 721-6205*
801 S. Skinker, #10C, St. Louis, MO 63105

St. Louisians for Better Government is a pro-Israel PAC with donors in St. Louis and nearby areas of Missouri. The group's members elect officers who organize meetings with political candidates.

The committee does not have an office; most of its business is conducted at members' homes. It was one of the top 10 pro-Israel PACs in total contributions to congressional candidates during the 1995-96 election cycle.

St. Louisians for Better Government (C00148155) *Address: same as sponsor * Treasurer: Bernard Pasternak*

	1993-94	1995-96	1997	Totals
Receipts	$113,785	$108,502	$45,899	$268,186
Disburse	112,757	107,384	36,334	256,475
Cash	4,444	5,565	15,130	n/a
Contributions	98,000	93,000	26,500	217,500
Republicans	9,500	19,000	11,500	40,000
No. of Cand.	*6*	*7*	*3*	*16*
House	2,000	2,000	1,500	5,500
Senate	7,500	17,000	10,000	34,500
Democrats	88,500	74,000	15,000	177,500
No. of Cand.	*28*	*25*	*3*	*56*
House	27,000	13,500	0	40,500
Senate	61,500	60,500	15,000	137,000
Incumbents	92,500	57,500	26,500	176,500
Challengers	3,500	6,000	0	9,500
Open Seat	2,000	29,500	0	31,500
Winners	82,000	73,000	n/a	155,000
Losers	16,000	20,000	n/a	36,000

To Protect Our Heritage PAC

*Phone: (312) 540-4421 * Fax: (312) 946-9818*
2421 W. Pratt, Chicago, IL 60645

To Protect Our Heritage PAC is a bipartisan pro-Israel group, based in Chicago.

Founded in 1990, the committee has 400 members who organize letter writing campaigns, produce occasional advertisements and hold community forums.

To Protect Our Heritage Political Action Committee (C00135541) *Address: same as sponsor * Treasurer: Alan E. Molotsky*

	1993-94	1995-96	1997	Totals
Receipts	$12,888	$13,535	$13,013	$39,436
Disburse	10,623	15,901	7,976	34,500
Cash	3,833	2,567	7,603	n/a
Contributions	6,625	7,084	3,000	16,709
Republicans	500	250	1,200	1,950
No. of Cand.	*1*	*2*	*1*	*4*
House	500	0	0	500
Senate	0	250	1,200	1,450
Democrats	6,125	6,834	1,800	14,759
No. of Cand.	*9*	*10*	*3*	*22*
House	3,375	2,800	250	6,425
Senate	2,750	4,034	1,550	8,334
Incumbents	6,225	1,250	2,750	10,225
Challengers	0	650	0	650
Open Seat	400	5,184	250	5,834
Winners	4,125	5,759	n/a	9,884
Losers	2,500	1,325	n/a	3,825

Washington PAC

*Phone: (202) 347-6613 * Fax: (202) 393-7006*
444 N. Capitol St. N.W., Suite 712, Washington, DC 20001

Washington PAC's core belief is that a "secure Israel is in the best interest of the United States." This nonpartisan group supports incumbent candidates who have a record of supporting Israeli interests, but also gives money to challenger or open seat candidates if they pass a screening process.

Washington PAC publishes a quarterly newsletter about upcoming Senate races and holds bi-weekly lunches for about 20 of its 600 members to meet with Senate candidates.

The PAC was founded in December 1980 by its treasurer, Washington lawyer Morris J. Amitay, and is operated out of his office.

Washington Political Action Committee (C00138560) *Address: same as sponsor * Treasurer: Morris J. Amitay*

	1993-94	1995-96	1997	Totals
Receipts	$202,537	$203,750	$101,592	$507,879
Disburse	206,150	205,743	92,322	504,215
Cash	6,503	4,510	13,780	n/a
Contributions	151,950	144,225	68,850	365,025
Republicans	24,500	56,675	22,000	103,175
No. of Cand.	*22*	*41*	*19*	*82*
House	10,000	20,500	9,000	39,500
Senate	14,500	36,175	13,000	63,675

(Data for Washington Political Action continued)

Democrats	126,450	87,550	46,850	260,850
No. of Cand.	*90*	*68*	*43*	*201*
House	62,250	35,050	19,850	117,150
Senate	64,200	52,500	27,000	143,700
Incumbents	142,350	109,600	67,350	319,300
Challengers	2,500	10,875	0	13,375
Open Seat	7,000	23,250	1,500	31,750
Winners	111,750	123,600	n/a	235,350
Losers	40,200	20,625	n/a	60,825

Women's Alliance for Israel

Phone: (818) 281-3120
8306 Wilshire Blvd., #1579, Beverly Hills, CA 90211

The Women's Alliance for Israel is a bipartisan organization that supports strong U.S.-Israel relations. Founded in 1988, WAI-PAC has about 600 members, most of whom are from California.

Women's Alliance for Israel (C00236596) *Address: same as sponsor * Treasurer: Helen Pollak * Contact: Elaine Robinson, President*

	1993-94	1995-96	1997	Totals
Receipts	$157,805	$154,351	$105,957	$418,113
Disburse	150,363	153,545	63,493	367,401
Cash	30,373	31,181	73,645	n/a
Contributions	127,000	113,000	41,000	281,000
Republicans	34,000	45,500	15,000	94,500
No. of Cand.	*21*	*23*	*4*	*48*
House	14,000	23,000	0	37,000
Senate	20,000	22,500	15,000	57,500
Democrats	93,000	67,500	26,000	186,500
No. of Cand.	*36*	*19*	*7*	*62*
House	30,500	23,000	3,000	56,500
Senate	62,500	44,500	23,000	130,000
Incumbents	112,500	94,000	41,000	247,500
Challengers	2,000	4,500	0	6,500
Open Seat	12,500	15,500	0	28,000
Winners	101,250	97,500	n/a	198,750
Losers	25,750	15,500	n/a	41,250

Women's Pro-Israel National PAC

Phone: (202) 296-2946
2020 Pennsylvania Ave. N.W., #275, Washington, DC 20006

The Women's Pro-Israel National PAC is a nonpartisan group with a nationwide support network. It supports federal candidates who are for strong U.S.-Israel relations.

Women's Pro-Israel National Political Action Committee (WIN PAC) (C00203182) *Address: same as sponsor * Treasurer: Joyce Ullman*

	1993-94	1995-96	1997	Totals
Receipts	$288,985	$191,558	$81,746	$562,289
Disburse	293,661	194,481	75,679	563,821
Cash	22,067	19,142	25,208	n/a
Contributions	118,250	88,700	45,500	252,450
Republicans	56,250	41,950	25,000	123,200
No. of Cand.	*27*	*29*	*14*	*70*
House	16,000	16,250	4,000	36,250
Senate	40,250	25,700	21,000	86,950
Democrats	62,000	46,750	20,500	129,250
No. of Cand.	*35*	*30*	*13*	*78*
House	23,000	6,250	500	29,750
Senate	39,000	40,500	20,000	99,500
Incumbents	105,750	60,450	44,500	210,700
Challengers	0	2,500	0	2,500
Open Seat	12,000	25,750	1,000	38,750
Winners	99,750	78,950	n/a	178,700
Losers	18,500	9,750	n/a	28,250

Young Jewish Leadership PAC

*Phone: (212) 806-5244 * Fax: (212) 806-6006*
240 E. 27th St., Room 20C, New York, NY 10016
E-mail: djavdan@strook.com

The Young Jewish Leadership PAC, which has affiliates in eight states, works to help develop a relationship between the pro-Israel community and the Republican Party. It gives to federal candidates.

The group often invites politicians to come speak to its 125 members.

Young Jewish Leadership PAC (C00305607) *Address: same as sponsor * Treasurer: Fredric Danishefsky * Contact: David Javdan, Chairperson*

	1993-94	1995-96	1997	Totals
Receipts	$0	$23,566	$11,149	$34,715
Disburse	0	20,080	6,908	26,988
Cash	0	3,486	7,727	n/a
Contributions	0	16,450	1,500	17,950
Republicans	0	16,450	1,500	17,950
No. of Cand.	*0*	*24*	*3*	*27*
House	0	8,450	1,250	9,700
Senate	0	8,000	250	8,250
Democrats	0	0	0	0
No. of Cand.	*0*	*0*	*0*	*0*
House	0	0	0	0
Senate	0	0	0	0
Incumbents	0	8,250	1,500	9,750
Challengers	0	2,700	0	2,700
Open Seat	0	5,500	0	5,500
Winners	0	9,250	n/a	9,250
Losers	0	7,200	n/a	7,200

Republican/Conservative

ARENA PAC

1155 21st St. N.W., Suite 300, Washington, DC 20036

Charlton Heston's ARENA PAC was founded to support the travel of the actor, who campaigns on behalf of federal candidates. It was named in reference to Teddy Roosevelt's oratorio on "the man who is actually in the arena, whose face is marred with sweat ... who strives valiantly."

Heston's organization, commonly referred to as the Moses PAC, is dedicated to helping candidates who support the Bill of Rights, especially the Second Amendment and gun owners' rights. During 1996, Heston, also a vice president of the National Rifle Association, traveled around the country to speak on behalf of 56 House and Senate hopefuls, accounting for roughly $36,000 of in-kind contributions to the candidates.

ARENA Political Action Committee (ARENA PAC) (C00305532) *Phone: (703) 299-1098 * Fax: (703) 299-9478 * 201 N. Union St., Alexandria, VA 22314-2642 * Treasurer: Barbara E. Wixon-Bonfiglio Contact: Tony Makris, Executive Dir.*

	1993-94	1995-96	1997	Totals
Receipts	$0	$162,512	$171,414	$333,926
Disburse	0	154,901	84,058	238,959
Cash	0	7,606	88,955	n/a
Contributions	0	49,949	-632	49,317
Republicans	0	48,949	-632	48,317
No. of Cand.	*0*	*65*	*3*	*68*
House	0	28,014	790	28,804
Senate	0	20,935	-1422	19,513
Democrats	0	1,000	0	1,000
No. of Cand.	*0*	*1*	*0*	*1*
House	0	1,000	0	1,000
Senate	0	0	0	0
Incumbents	0	26,826	-632	26,194
Challengers	0	7,648	0	7,648
Open Seat	0	15,475	0	15,475
Winners	0	34,433	n/a	34,433
Losers	0	15,516	n/a	15,516

America's PAC

*Phone: (703) 481-5712 * Fax: (703) 318-9122*
710 Pine St., Herndon, VA 22070

America's PAC supports conservative candidates, mostly on the federal level, although the PAC has given in local and state races. According to PAC Chairman James B. Taylor, such issues as "taxation, smaller government and crime" are the most important when the organization decides to contribute to a candidate.

Taylor is executive director of the Young America's Foundation, a college-oriented conservative group. Before joining YAF, he was public relations director of the National Right to Work Legal Defense Foundation.

Founded in 1983, America's PAC now has a donor base of roughly 1,600 people, contacted mainly through direct mail. Rep. Ron Paul, R-Texas, was the leading recipient during the 1995-96 election cycle with $5,000.

America's Political Action Committee (C00184143) *Address: same as sponsor * Treasurer: Michael Boos * Contact: James B. Taylor, Chairman*

	1993-94	1995-96	1997	Totals
Receipts	$106,960	$114,482	$39,247	$260,689
Disburse	109,863	108,446	37,293	255,602
Cash	3,386	9,418	11,371	n/a
Contributions	10,350	12,300	1,000	23,650
Republicans	10,350	12,300	1,000	23,650
No. of Cand.	*6*	*19*	*1*	*26*
House	1,850	10,300	1,000	13,150
Senate	8,500	2,000	0	10,500
Democrats	0	0	0	0
No. of Cand.	*0*	*0*	*0*	*0*
House	0	0	0	0
Senate	0	0	0	0
Incumbents	500	4,350	0	4,850
Challengers	9,250	6,950	1,000	17,200
Open Seat	600	1,000	0	1,600
Winners	1,100	8,350	n/a	9,450
Losers	9,250	3,950	n/a	13,200

American Conservative Union

*Phone: (703) 836-8602 * Fax: (703) 836-8606*
1007 Cameron St., Alexandria, VA 22314
Web: www.townhall.com/conservative

The American Conservative Union is the nation's oldest conservative lobbying organization, working to advance the goals of conservatism since 1964.

The group, which has about 1 million members, acts as a multi-issue, umbrella organization that supports capitalism, a strong national defense and "traditional moral values." The organization, in addition to lobbying, produces ratings of all members of Congress, assessing their voting record on certain conservative issues. The ACU also publishes several books and guides to conservative politics and hosts the annual Conservative Political Action Conference.

American Conservative Union Political Action Committee (ACU-PAC) (C00130658) *Address: same as sponsor * Treasurer: D. Jeffrey Hollingsworth * Contact: Tom Katina, PAC Dir.*

	1993-94	1995-96	1997	Totals
Receipts	$37,026	$13,450	$6,996	$57,472
Disburse	29,551	19,879	6,980	56,410
Cash	7,473	1,043	1,059	n/a
Contributions	30,758	15,650	1,600	48,008
Republicans	30,758	15,650	1,600	48,008
No. of Cand.	*67*	*27*	*3*	*97*
House	22,308	5,800	600	28,708
Senate	8,450	9,850	1,000	19,300
Democrats	0	0	0	0
No. of Cand.	*0*	*0*	*0*	*0*
House	0	0	0	0
Senate	0	0	0	0
Incumbents	5,700	4,800	1,600	12,100
Challengers	18,458	750	0	19,208
Open Seat	6,600	9,850	0	16,450
Winners	19,800	6,550	n/a	26,350
Losers	10,958	9,100	n/a	20,058

California 2000

7111 Bettola Place, Alta Loma, CA 91701

Since 1995, California 2000 has contributed exclusively to in-state Republican House candidates.

California 2000 (C00315747) *Address: same as sponsor * Treasurer: Ravelle Lyn Greene*

	1993-94	1995-96	1997	Totals
Receipts	$0	$32,672	$1,000	$33,672
Disburse	0	29,504	1,000	30,504
Cash	0	3,167	3,167	n/a
Contributions	0	16,750	0	16,750
Republicans	0	16,750	0	16,750
No. of Cand.	*0*	*9*	*1*	*10*
House	0	16,750	0	16,750
Senate	0	0	0	0
Democrats	0	0	0	0
No. of Cand.	*0*	*0*	*0*	*0*
House	0	0	0	0
Senate	0	0	0	0
Incumbents	0	4,000	0	4,000
Challengers	0	10,750	0	10,750
Open Seat	0	2,000	0	2,000
Winners	0	3,000	n/a	3,000
Losers	0	13,750	n/a	13,750

California Lincoln Clubs

343 N. Citrus Ave., Los Angeles, CA 90036
Web: www.cohq.com/LincolnClub/LCIndex.html

California Lincoln Clubs is dedicated to the election of Republican candidates to partisan and nonpartisan offices. The PAC works through seven local chapters in Los Angeles County: the Downtown Chapter, the Fernando Valley Chapter, the San Gabriel Valley Chapter, the South Bay Chapter, the South County Chapter, the West Los Angeles Chapter and the Tri-Cities Chapter.

California Lincoln Clubs Fed PAC (C00248658) *Address: same as sponsor * Treasurer: Douglas R. Boyd Sr. * Contact: William T. Huston, Chairperson*

	1993-94	1995-96	1997	Totals
Receipts	$16,674	$42,310	$28,572	$87,556
Disburse	15,432	42,768	9,101	67,301
Cash	1,242	784	20,255	n/a
Contributions	10,500	27,425	1,500	39,425
Republicans	10,500	27,425	1,500	39,425
No. of Cand.	*8*	*6*	*3*	*17*
House	11,000	27,425	1,000	39,425
Senate	-500	0	500	0
Democrats	0	0	0	0
No. of Cand.	*0*	*0*	*0*	*0*
House	0	0	0	0
Senate	0	0	0	0
Incumbents	800	150	1,250	2,200
Challengers	10,450	8,275	250	18,975
Open Seat	250	19,000	0	19,250
Winners	1,050	9,150	n/a	10,200
Losers	9,450	18,275	n/a	27,725

California Republican Heritage Groups Council

*Phone: (818) 962-0124 * Fax: (818) 962-1423*
P.O. Box 506, Pasadena, CA 91102-0506
E-mail: leloed@aol.com

The California Republican Heritage Groups Council publicizes Republican issues in ethnic communities around the state to ensure all nationalities are properly represented and recruited by the Republican Party.

The council focuses on 12 major ethnic groups, most of which are Asian or European. It organizes demonstrations and places ads in ethnic publications.

The organization is chartered by the California Republican Party and the National Republican Heritage Groups Council.

California Republican Heritage Groups Council (C00175489) *Address: same as sponsor * Treasurer: Leslie Eloed * Contact: Ilona Reksz, PAC Dir.*

	1993-94	1995-96	1997	Totals
Receipts	$8,007	$20,641	$940	$29,588
Disburse	9,462	20,418	1,081	30,961
Cash	715	938	797	n/a
Contributions	45	8,212	0	8,257
Republicans	45	8,212	0	8,257
No. of Cand.	*1*	*1*	*0*	*2*
House	45	8,212	0	8,257
Senate	0	0	0	0
Democrats	0	0	0	0
No. of Cand.	*0*	*0*	*0*	*0*
House	0	0	0	0
Senate	0	0	0	0
Incumbents	45	8,212	0	8,257
Challengers	0	0	0	0
Open Seat	0	0	0	0
Winners	45	8,212	n/a	8,257
Losers	0	0	n/a	0

Citizens Allied for Free Enterprise

Phone: (714) 385-8191
921 11th St., Suite 600, Sacramento, CA 95814-2845

Citizens Allied for Free Enterprise is a conservative, anti-big government PAC that calls for reduced government spending.

The group rates candidates on their tendency to vote against big-spending measures and sends the information about the ratings to those who request it.

Citizens Allied for Free Enterprise (C00307371) *Address: same as sponsor * Treasurer: Laura Mahan Cunningham*

	1993-94	*1995-96*	*1997*	*Totals*
Receipts	$0	$38,575	$5,500	$44,075
Disburse	0	33,250	4,624	37,874
Cash	0	5,325	6,201	n/a
Contributions	0	29,500	0	29,500
Republicans	0	29,500	0	29,500
No. of Cand.	*0*	*23*	*0*	*23*
House	0	27,500	0	27,500
Senate	0	2,000	0	2,000
Democrats	0	0	0	0
No. of Cand.	*0*	*0*	*0*	*0*
House	0	0	0	0
Senate	0	0	0	0
Incumbents	0	6,000	0	6,000
Challengers	0	11,000	0	11,000
Open Seat	0	12,500	0	12,500
Winners	0	14,000	n/a	14,000
Losers	0	15,500	n/a	15,500

Citizens for Reform and Fiscal Responsibility

124 Argyle Rd., Langhorne, PA 19047

Citizens for Reform and Fiscal Responsibility said it planned to file for termination with the FEC in March 1998, but as of April 1998 no such filing had been made with the FEC.

Citizens for Reform and Fiscal Responsibility Inc. (C00316505) *Address: same as sponsor * Treasurer: Jo Farley*

	1993-94	*1995-96*	*1997*	*Totals*
Receipts	$0	$42,250	$0	$42,250
Disburse	0	30,951	625	31,576
Cash	0	11,202	14,131	n/a
Contributions	0	12,000	0	12,000
Republicans	0	12,000	0	12,000
No. of Cand.	*0*	*4*	*0*	*4*
House	0	7,000	0	7,000
Senate	0	5,000	0	5,000
Democrats	0	0	0	0
No. of Cand.	*0*	*0*	*0*	*0*
House	0	0	0	0
Senate	0	0	0	0
Incumbents	0	6,000	0	6,000
Challengers	0	0	0	0
Open Seat	0	6,000	0	6,000
Winners	0	1,000	n/a	1,000
Losers	0	11,000	n/a	11,000

Citizens United

*Phone: (703) 352-4788 * Fax: (703) 591-2505*
11094-D Lee Highway, #200, Fairfax, VA 22030
Web: www.citizensunited.org

Citizens United is a conservative grassroots organization. Established in 1988, the group says it has more than 100,000 members. It supports limited government, freedom of enterprise, strong families and national sovereignty and security.

In 1992, the organization established the Citizens United Foundation. CUF is organized and operated exclusively as a nonprofit, educational organization that conducts research and educates the public on issues such as the Constitution, national defense, the free enterprise system, freedom of religion and the family as the basic unit of society.

Citizens United Political Victory Fund (C00295527) *Address: same as sponsor * Treasurer: Kevin Allen * Contact: Michael Boos, V.P.*

	1993-94	*1995-96*	*1997*	*Totals*
Receipts	$49,306	$47,612	$250	$97,168
Disburse	37,857	52,125	1,250	91,232
Cash	11,449	6,929	5,929	n/a
Contributions	15,938	38,500	250	54,688
Republicans	15,938	38,500	250	54,688
No. of Cand.	*12*	*15*	*1*	*28*
House	11,940	31,500	250	43,690
Senate	3,998	7,000	0	10,998
Democrats	0	0	0	0
No. of Cand.	*0*	*0*	*0*	*0*
House	0	0	0	0
Senate	0	0	0	0
Incumbents	0	23,500	0	23,500
Challengers	13,962	8,000	250	22,212
Open Seat	1,976	7,000	0	8,976
Winners	5,976	10,500	n/a	16,476
Losers	9,962	28,000	n/a	37,962

Cleo Bohls Fund

Phone: (830) 625-0872
422 Saddle Tree, New Braunfels, TX 78130

Established in the early 1970s, the Cleo Bohls Fund is affiliated with the Texas Federation of Republican Women. It is a multipurpose fund that provides political contributions to conservative candidates within Texas.

The Texas Federation of Republican Women was founded in 1945 and has a membership of 10,000 people.

Cleo Bohls Fund (C00248799) *Address: same as sponsor * Treasurer: Dona C. Bruns*

	1993-94	*1995-96*	*1997*	*Totals*
Receipts	$44,628	$72,321	$42,207	$159,156
Disburse	44,411	63,159	18,886	126,456
Cash	2,816	11,973	35,294	n/a
Contributions	6,500	5,800	0	12,300
Republicans	6,500	5,800	0	12,300
No. of Cand.	*3*	*13*	*0*	*16*
House	1,500	4,800	0	6,300
Senate	5,000	1,000	0	6,000
Democrats	0	0	0	0
No. of Cand.	*0*	*0*	*0*	*0*
House	0	0	0	0
Senate	0	0	0	0
Incumbents	5,000	2,950	0	7,950
Challengers	500	1,450	0	1,950
Open Seat	1,000	1,400	0	2,400
Winners	5,500	2,800	n/a	8,300
Losers	1,000	3,000	n/a	4,000

Conservative Campaign Fund

Phone: (703) 448-0360
1309 Vincent Pl., Suite 2000, McLean, VA 22101

The Conservative Campaign Fund, formerly known as the Honest Elections PAC, supports mostly federal-level Republican candidates. During the 1995-96 election cycle, recipients included Reps. David McIntosh, R-Ind., and J.C. Watts, R-Okla., as well as Louisiana Senate challenger Louis "Woody" Jenkins.

Conservative Campaign Fund (formerly known as Honest Elections PAC) (C00116715) *Address: same as sponsor * Treasurer: Peter T. Flaherty*

	1993-94	*1995-96*	*1997*	*Totals*
Receipts	$447,283	$197,595	$30	$644,908
Disburse	500,879	196,417	5,080	702,376
Cash	7,417	8,593	4,601	n/a
Contributions	26,401	62,132	0	88,533
Republicans	24,401	60,932	0	85,333
No. of Cand.	*15*	*37*	*0*	*52*
House	14,735	37,601	0	52,336
Senate	9,666	23,331	0	32,997
Democrats	0	0	0	0
No. of Cand.	*0*	*0*	*0*	*0*
House	0	0	0	0
Senate	0	0	0	0
Incumbents	3,000	13,156	0	16,156
Challengers	10,601	22,975	0	33,576
Open Seat	12,800	26,001	0	38,801
Winners	14,400	20,450	n/a	34,850
Losers	12,001	41,682	n/a	53,683

Conservative Leadership PAC

3128 N. 17th St., Arlington, VA 22201

The Conservative Leadership PAC contributed to 14 Republican congressional candidates during the 1995-96 cycle. Four of them won their races. The Arlington, Va., based PAC is not associated with any organization.

Conservative Leadership Political Action Committee (C00010363) *Address: same as sponsor * Treasurer: Howard P. Estes Jr.*

	1993-94	1995-96	1997	Totals
Receipts	$44,845	$95,823	$22,064	$162,732
Disburse	50,072	85,640	10,048	145,760
Cash	479	10,656	22,672	n/a
Contributions	8,692	29,675	2,202	40,569
Republicans	7,992	29,675	2,202	39,869
No. of Cand.	*7*	*14*	*2*	*23*
House	6,242	18,559	2,202	27,003
Senate	1,750	11,116	0	12,866
Democrats	700	0	0	700
No. of Cand.	*1*	*0*	*0*	*1*
House	700	0	0	700
Senate	0	0	0	0
Incumbents	700	5,200	0	5,900
Challengers	5,617	12,226	0	17,843
Open Seat	2,375	12,249	0	14,624
Winners	3,375	5,200	n/a	8,575
Losers	5,317	24,475	n/a	29,792

Conservative Order of Good Guys

450 A St., Second Floor, San Diego, CA 92101

The Conservative Order of Good Guys PAC contributed $5,000 to Republican House candidates from California during the 1995-96 cycle. Rep. Randy "Duke" Cunningham was the leading recipient.

Conservative Order of Good Guys (C00138107) *Address: same as sponsor * Treasurer: Chris Miller*

	1993-94	1995-96	1997	Totals
Receipts	$48,232	$20,210	$2,600	$71,042
Disburse	51,564	19,018	4,262	74,844
Cash	4,312	5,503	3,841	n/a
Contributions	9,700	5,000	250	14,950
Republicans	9,700	5,000	250	14,950
No. of Cand.	*5*	*5*	*1*	*11*
House	9,700	5,000	250	14,950
Senate	0	0	0	0
Democrats	0	0	0	0
No. of Cand.	*0*	*0*	*0*	*0*
House	0	0	0	0
Senate	0	0	0	0
Incumbents	3,700	4,000	250	7,950
Challengers	6,000	1,000	0	7,000
Open Seat	0	0	0	0
Winners	7,700	4,000	n/a	11,700
Losers	2,000	1,000	n/a	3,000

Conservative Victory Committee

Phone: (703) 683-5004

113 S. West St., Suite 200, Alexandria, VA 22314

The Conservative Victory Committee is an independent PAC "dedicated to electing conservative candidates at every level of public office."

CVC has been causing controversy over negative advertisements since its founding in 1988. That year, it put out print and TV ads against presidential candidate Michael Dukakis, including a couple dealing with his support for the Massachusetts prison furlough program. Former Speaker of the House Jim Wright was another target, as were Sens. Edward Kennedy, D-Mass., Joseph Biden, D-Del., and Alan Cranston, D-Calif., for their support of Anita Hill during the 1991 confirmation hearings for Supreme Court nominee Clarence Thomas.

L. Brent Bozell, current president of the Media Research Center, founded CVC. In 1992, Bozell served as national finance chairman for the Buchanan for President campaign. He was also finance director and later president of the National Conservative PAC.

Conservative Victory Committee (C00218172) *Address: same as sponsor * Treasurer: Leif E. Noren * Contact: Brent Bozell, President*

	1993-94	1995-96	1997	Totals
Receipts	$166,364	$215,004	$5,598	$386,966
Disburse	201,931	195,833	23,237	421,001
Cash	7,824	26,994	9,356	n/a
Contributions	32,800	73,000	0	105,800
Republicans	32,800	72,000	0	104,800
No. of Cand.	*19*	*49*	*0*	*68*
House	22,550	46,000	0	68,550
Senate	10,250	26,000	0	36,250
Democrats	0	1,000	0	1,000
No. of Cand.	*0*	*1*	*0*	*1*
House	0	1,000	0	1,000
Senate	0	0	0	0
Incumbents	3,000	31,000	0	34,000
Challengers	22,050	17,000	0	39,050
Open Seat	7,750	24,500	0	32,250
Winners	9,250	37,000	n/a	46,250
Losers	23,550	36,000	n/a	59,550

Conservative Victory Fund

*Phone: (202) 546-5833 * Fax: (202) 546-3091*

104 North Carolina Ave. S.E., Washington, DC 20003

The Conservative Victory Fund was founded in 1969 by former Rep. John Ashbrook, R-Ohio, to support conservative candidates for congressional office. CVF's treasurer is Thomas Winter, editor-in-chief of "Human Events," a conservative weekly publication.

Conservative Victory Fund (C00009704) *Address: same as sponsor * Treasurer: Thomas Winter * Contact: Ronald Pearson, Executive Dir.*

	1993-94	1995-96	1997	Totals
Receipts	$201,595	$269,408	$100,929	$571,932
Disburse	204,505	245,036	95,300	544,841
Cash	13,095	37,470	43,099	n/a
Contributions	36,385	123,979	40,222	200,586
Republicans	35,885	123,458	40,222	199,565
No. of Cand.	*55*	*110*	*47*	*212*
House	21,677	93,880	36,185	151,742
Senate	14,208	29,578	4,037	47,823
Democrats	500	521	0	1,021
No. of Cand.	*1*	*1*	*0*	*2*
House	500	0	0	500
Senate	0	521	0	521
Incumbents	7,805	75,930	37,003	120,738
Challengers	14,479	15,486	2,969	32,934
Open Seat	14,101	32,018	0	46,119
Winners	26,057	78,880	n/a	104,937
Losers	10,328	45,099	n/a	55,427

DALENPAC

Phone: (972) 298-4211

1701 N. Hampton, Desoto, TX 75115

Founded in 1977 by Arthur J. Wessly, the Dallas Entrepreneurial PAC (DALENPAC) is a small conservative organization that contributes federal funds mostly to Republican candidates outside of Texas. The group focuses its efforts on high-risk races.

DALENPAC (C00283523) *Address: same as sponsor * Treasurer: Fran Sauls * Contact: Richard Collins, Chairperson*

	1993-94	1995-96	1997	Totals
Receipts	$28,500	$71,165	$27,200	$126,865
Disburse	25,573	74,032	6,407	106,012
Cash	2,926	57	20,849	n/a
Contributions	23,000	64,850	6,000	93,850
Republicans	23,000	64,850	6,000	93,850
No. of Cand.	*17*	*28*	*8*	*53*
House	1,000	16,350	-1000	16,350
Senate	22,000	48,500	7,000	77,500
Democrats	0	0	0	0
No. of Cand.	*0*	*0*	*0*	*0*
House	0	0	0	0
Senate	0	0	0	0
Incumbents	3,000	10,850	8,000	21,850
Challengers	6,000	20,000	0	26,000
Open Seat	14,000	34,000	0	48,000
Winners	21,000	30,850	n/a	51,850
Losers	2,000	34,000	n/a	36,000

Eagle Forum

*Phone: (618) 462-5415 * Fax: (618) 462-8909*

P.O. Box 618, Alton, IL 62002

*Web: www.eagleforum.org * E-mail: eagle@eagleforum.org*

The Eagle Forum is a conservative organization headed by Phyllis Schlafly, a Republican activist and author. Based in Illinois, the group has 80,000 members nationwide and participates in elections at all levels of government, promoting school choice, tax cuts, stronger national defense and an end to legal abortion. It also has an organization for college students.

Specifically, the group supports major cuts in federal spending, the development of a strong ballistic missile defense system and the designation of English as the official language for the nation. It opposes federal funding for the National Endowment for the Arts, payment of back assessments to the United Nations and statehood for Puerto Rico and the District of Columbia. It also opposes NATO expansion and funding for the International Monetary Fund.

The Eagle Forum spent the most on 1996 congressional candidates of any conservative PAC not associated with a member of Congress. It gave all but $500 of its candidate contributions to Republicans, but 62 percent of that money went to candidates who lost in 1996, the second-lowest success ratio among the top 200 PACs. The leading recipients were 1996 Senate candidate Woody Jenkins of Louisiana, Rep. Ron Paul, R-Texas, and former Rep. Steve Stockman, R-Texas.

Eagle Forum PAC (C00103937) *Phone: (202) 544-0353 * Fax: (202) 547-6996 * 316 Pennsylvania Ave. S.E., Suite 203, Washington, DC 20003 * Treasurer: Margaret Gaul * Contact: Megan Owens, Legislative Assistant*

	1993-94	*1995-96*	*1997*	*Totals*
Receipts	$243,797	$327,174	$33,116	$604,087
Disburse	282,899	309,045	19,340	611,284
Cash	50,219	68,351	82,128	n/a
Contributions	178,757	242,735	16,500	437,992
Republicans	176,957	242,235	16,500	435,692
No. of Cand.	*124*	*112*	*18*	*254*
House	150,257	190,450	13,000	353,707
Senate	26,700	51,785	3,500	81,985
Democrats	1,800	500	0	2,300
No. of Cand.	*3*	*1*	*0*	*4*
House	1,800	500	0	2,300
Senate	0	0	0	0
Incumbents	26,850	71,100	11,500	109,450
Challengers	63,970	92,500	1,000	157,470
Open Seat	86,437	78,635	5,000	170,072
Winners	127,057	92,935	n/a	219,992
Losers	51,700	149,800	n/a	201,500

Family Values PAC

9001 Glenbrook Ct., Fairfax, VA 22031

Family Values PAC was terminated on July 25, 1997. Its treasurer was Gary Bauer, head of the Family Research Council.

Family Values PAC (C00260729) *Address: same as sponsor * Treasurer: Gary Bauer*

	1993-94	*1995-96*	*1997*	*Totals*
Receipts	$21,000	$500	$0	$21,500
Disburse	17,137	9,759	4,541	31,437
Cash	13,801	4,541	0	n/a
Contributions	15,100	7,000	0	22,100
Republicans	15,100	7,000	0	22,100
No. of Cand.	*22*	*7*	*0*	*29*
House	13,100	6,000	0	19,100
Senate	2,000	1,000	0	3,000
Democrats	0	0	0	0
No. of Cand.	*0*	*0*	*0*	*0*
House	0	0	0	0
Senate	0	0	0	0
Incumbents	100	1,500	0	1,600
Challengers	4,800	3,000	0	7,800
Open Seat	10,200	2,500	0	12,700
Winners	11,500	2,500	n/a	14,000
Losers	3,600	4,500	n/a	8,100

Forum

Phone: (313) 396-4200

300 Talon Centre, Detroit, MI 48207

Forum contributed only to Michigan Republican candidates during the 1995-96 election cycle. It did not contribute to a winning federal candidate.

Forum (C00224568) *Address: same as sponsor * Treasurer: Shannon M. Nichols*

	1993-94	*1995-96*	*1997*	*Totals*
Receipts	$5,000	$22,000	$0	$27,000
Disburse	13,044	17,267	123	30,434
Cash	566	5,297	5,159	n/a
Contributions	13,000	6,000	0	19,000
Republicans	12,000	6,000	0	18,000
No. of Cand.	*8*	*6*	*0*	*14*
House	8,000	5,000	0	13,000
Senate	4,000	1,000	0	5,000
Democrats	1,000	0	0	1,000
No. of Cand.	*1*	*0*	*0*	*1*
House	1,000	0	0	1,000
Senate	0	0	0	0

	1993-94	*1995-96*	*1997*	*Totals*
Incumbents	0	0	0	0
Challengers	7,000	6,000	0	13,000
Open Seat	6,000	0	0	6,000
Winners	5,000	0	n/a	5,000
Losers	8,000	6,000	n/a	14,000

Free Congress PAC

Phone: (202) 546-3000

717 Second St. N.E., Washington, DC 20002

Free Congress PAC, formerly known as the Committee for the Survival of a Free Congress, is operated out of the offices of Coalition for America. The PAC contributed almost exclusively to Republican challenger and open seat federal races during the 1995-96 election cycle. Rep. Tom Campbell, R-Calif., and Sen. Sam Brownback, R-Kan., were the leading recipients.

Free Congress PAC (formerly known as Committee for the Survival of a Free Congress) (C00019976) *Address: same as sponsor * Treasurer: Keri Pendleton * Contact: Lisa Dean, President*

	1993-94	*1995-96*	*1997*	*Totals*
Receipts	$22,981	$40,602	$10,035	$73,618
Disburse	31,944	38,367	14,804	85,115
Cash	12,396	14,628	9,858	n/a
Contributions	6,017	27,460	107	33,584
Republicans	6,017	27,460	107	33,584
No. of Cand.	*3*	*16*	*1*	*20*
House	6,017	17,200	107	23,324
Senate	0	10,260	0	10,260
Democrats	0	0	0	0
No. of Cand.	*0*	*0*	*0*	*0*
House	0	0	0	0
Senate	0	0	0	0
Incumbents	0	5,500	107	5,607
Challengers	5,867	11,370	0	17,237
Open Seat	150	10,590	0	10,740
Winners	5,150	15,920	n/a	21,070
Losers	867	11,540	n/a	12,407

Freedom Club

*Phone: (612) 941-9470 * Fax: (612) 941-1838*

7901 Flying Cloud Dr., Eden Prairie, MN 55344

The Freedom Club contributed more than $55,000 to registered candidates during the 1995-96 election cycle. All the money went to seven Minnesota Republicans, including five House challengers as well as Rep. Gil Gutknecht and Sen. Rod Grams.

Freedom Club Federal PAC (C00307777) *Address: same as sponsor * Treasurer: Jodi Neuharth * Contact: Midge Dean, Executive Dir.*

	1993-94	*1995-96*	*1997*	*Totals*
Receipts	$0	$84,502	$36,000	$120,502
Disburse	0	84,477	11,875	96,352
Cash	0	25	24,149	n/a
Contributions	0	57,145	5,000	62,145
Republicans	0	57,145	5,000	62,145
No. of Cand.	*0*	*7*	*1*	*8*
House	0	49,995	5,000	54,995
Senate	0	7,150	0	7,150
Democrats	0	0	0	0
No. of Cand.	*0*	*0*	*0*	*0*
House	0	0	0	0
Senate	0	0	0	0
Incumbents	0	10,249	0	10,249
Challengers	0	46,896	5,000	51,896
Open Seat	0	0	0	0
Winners	0	10,249	n/a	10,249
Losers	0	46,896	n/a	46,896

GOP-5 Committee

Phone: (203) 888-9988

14 Edward Rd., Seymour, CT 06483

The GOP-5 Committee is located in Connecticut's 5th District. The PAC's largest contribution in 1996 was to former Rep. Gary A. Franks, R-Conn., who previously represented the 5th but lost to Democrat Jim Maloney.

GOP-5 Committee (C00181230) *Address: same as sponsor * Treasurer: Lucy McConologue*

	1993-94	1995-96	1997	Totals
Receipts	$38,208	$14,720	$10,840	$63,768
Disburse	38,146	14,791	424	53,361
Cash	693	619	11,035	n/a
Contributions	7,500	6,400	0	13,900
Republicans	7,500	6,400	0	13,900
No. of Cand.	*3*	*6*	*0*	*9*
House	7,250	6,400	0	13,650
Senate	250	0	0	250
Democrats	0	0	0	0
No. of Cand.	*0*	*0*	*0*	*0*
House	0	0	0	0
Senate	0	0	0	0
Incumbents	7,000	5,750	0	12,750
Challengers	500	400	0	900
Open Seat	0	250	0	250
Winners	7,000	500	n/a	7,500
Losers	500	5,900	n/a	6,400

Gold Circle Federal Committee

*Phone: (501) 782-3670 * Fax: (501) 782-7569*
First National Bank Bldg., Suite 600, Fort Smith, AR 72901

Gold Circle Federal Committee is based in northwestern Arkansas and gives to federal Republican candidates from all parts of the nation.

It was founded in 1994.

Gold Circle Federal Committee (C00289728) *Address: same as sponsor * Treasurer: John Langham*

	1993-94	1995-96	1997	Totals
Receipts	$1,100	$11,800	$10,355	$23,255
Disburse	300	12,358	9,250	21,908
Cash	800	241	1,346	n/a
Contributions	300	12,358	-250	12,408
Republicans	300	12,358	-1250	11,408
No. of Cand.	*1*	*4*	*4*	*9*
House	300	12,000	-1250	11,050
Senate	0	358	0	358
Democrats	0	0	1,000	1,000
No. of Cand.	*0*	*0*	*1*	*1*
House	0	0	1,000	1,000
Senate	0	0	0	0
Incumbents	300	0	750	1,050
Challengers	0	0	0	0
Open Seat	0	12,000	0	12,000
Winners	300	5,358	n/a	5,658
Losers	0	7,000	n/a	7,000

HOUPAC

Phone: (713) 960-8806
P.O. Box 27497, Houston, TX 77027

HOUPAC is made up of Houston professionals with conservative economic philosophies. The PAC, which is fairly inactive, gives mostly to Republican candidates. It was founded in 1978.

HOUPAC (C00039610) *Address: same as sponsor * Treasurer: John E. Kehn Jr. * Contact: Jack M. Webb, PAC Dir.*

	1993-94	1995-96	1997	Totals
Receipts	$11,456	$3,262	$144	$14,862
Disburse	20,576	18,920	1,518	41,014
Cash	25,693	10,037	8,663	n/a
Contributions	16,050	16,000	0	32,050
Republicans	15,300	15,750	0	31,050
No. of Cand.	*31*	*26*	*0*	*57*
House	3,750	4,750	0	8,500
Senate	11,550	11,000	0	22,550
Democrats	750	0	0	750
No. of Cand.	*3*	*0*	*0*	*3*
House	750	0	0	750
Senate	0	0	0	0
Incumbents	5,050	3,750	0	8,800
Challengers	4,750	4,500	0	9,250
Open Seat	6,250	7,500	0	13,750
Winners	13,550	7,000	n/a	20,550
Losers	2,500	9,000	n/a	11,500

Justice-PAC

Phone: (714) 730-1761
2091 E. Valley Pkwy., Suite 1C, Escondido, CA 92027

Justice-PAC is a conservative organization concerned with "justice-related issues." The PAC is run from the same offices as the United States Justice Foundation, a nonprofit public interest, legal action organization.

Randy Goodwin, the PAC treasurer, denied any direct connection between the two organizations, but the executive director of USJF is Gary Kreep, the president of Justice-PAC. USJF has been involved in "fighting reverse discrimination and the racism involved in so-called 'affirmative action' programs."

Justice-PAC was founded in 1986 to support both state and federal candidates. During the 1995-96 election cycle, it posted total receipts of $544,752 but gave only $12,700 to campaign committees. For 1997, the PAC spent $484,867 with $6,500 going to candidates.

According to its 1997 year-end filings with the FEC, the majority of the PAC's expenses go toward mailing list rental, maintenance and direct-mailing companies. It also posted a debt of $42,000 to these same companies.

Justice-PAC (C00159319) *Address: same as sponsor * Treasurer: Randy J. Goodwin * Contact: Gary Kreep, President*

	1993-94	1995-96	1997	Totals
Receipts	$416,362	$544,752	$477,688	$1,438,802
Disburse	411,044	534,254	484,867	1,430,165
Cash	5,344	15,843	8,663	n/a
Contributions	4,150	12,700	6,500	23,350
Republicans	4,150	12,700	6,500	23,350
No. of Cand.	*29*	*64*	*4*	*97*
House	2,550	11,200	6,250	20,000
Senate	1,600	1,500	250	3,350
Democrats	0	0	0	0
No. of Cand.	*0*	*0*	*0*	*0*
House	0	0	0	0
Senate	0	0	0	0
Incumbents	1,350	5,100	1,250	7,700
Challengers	1,800	6,100	250	8,150
Open Seat	1,000	1,500	5,000	7,500
Winners	3,050	8,500	n/a	11,550
Losers	1,100	4,200	n/a	5,300

Keep Our Majority PAC

*Phone: (703) 256-6744 * Fax: (703) 256-5883*
6344 Cavalier Corridor, Falls Church, VA 22044

Keep Our Majority PAC's honorary chairman is Rep. J. Dennis Hastert, R-Ill.

Keep Our Majority Political Action Committee (KOMPAC) (C00307405) *Address: same as sponsor * Treasurer: Jane G. Mattoon * Contact: Hon. Samuel K. Skinner, General Chairman*

	1993-94	1995-96	1997	Totals
Receipts	$0	$100,172	$45,477	$145,649
Disburse	0	95,466	23,454	118,920
Cash	0	4,711	26,742	n/a
Contributions	0	53,252	16,000	69,252
Republicans	0	53,252	16,000	69,252
No. of Cand.	*0*	*50*	*13*	*63*
House	0	53,252	16,000	69,252
Senate	0	0	0	0
Democrats	0	0	0	0
No. of Cand.	*0*	*0*	*0*	*0*
House	0	0	0	0
Senate	0	0	0	0
Incumbents	0	36,252	13,500	49,752
Challengers	0	7,500	2,500	10,000
Open Seat	0	9,500	0	9,500
Winners	0	29,252	n/a	29,252
Losers	0	24,000	n/a	24,000

Lincoln Club of Northern California

*Phone: (415) 854-2321 * Fax: (415) 854-3170*
3000 Sand Hill Rd., Building 3, Suite 140, Menlo Park, CA 94025

The Lincoln Club of Northern California is a group of nearly 200 business and civic leaders in the greater San Francisco Bay area whose purpose is to promote and foster excellence in Republican candidates. This particular chapter begins to support its favored candidates before the primary elections.

According to the San Francisco Chronicle, the Lincoln Club of Northern California "represents the largest source of Republican campaign money in the region," and is "dominated by moderate GOPers." Founded in 1982, the club has a membership that includes David Packard, founder of computer company Hewlett-Packard, and Charles Schwab, of Charles Schwab & Co.

Lincoln Club of Northern California (C00148882) *Address: same as sponsor * Treasurer: Thomas W. Ford * Contact: Frederick K. Lowell, Chairperson*

	1993-94	1995-96	1997	Totals
Receipts	$332,839	$344,636	$173,568	$851,043
Disburse	323,984	335,408	151,231	810,623
Cash	31,687	40,916	63,253	n/a
Contributions	17,000	25,000	6,000	48,000
Republicans	17,000	25,000	6,000	48,000
No. of Cand.	*4*	*3*	*2*	*9*
House	17,000	25,000	1,000	43,000
Senate	0	0	5,000	5,000
Democrats	0	0	0	0
No. of Cand.	*0*	*0*	*0*	*0*
House	0	0	0	0
Senate	0	0	0	0
Incumbents	0	15,000	0	15,000
Challengers	12,000	10,000	6,000	28,000
Open Seat	5,000	0	0	5,000
Winners	5,000	15,000	n/a	20,000
Losers	12,000	10,000	n/a	22,000

Lincoln Club of Orange County

950 S. Coast Dr., #195, Costa Mesa, CA 92626

The Lincoln Club of Orange County PAC was terminated in May 1997. A new committee, the Lincoln Club of Orange County Federal PAC, was organized in July 1997. Its FEC identification number is C00328401. The new PAC had raised nearly $47,000 by the end of 1997, but its lone congressional contribution was $1,000 to Rep. J.C. Watts, R-Okla.

Lincoln Club of Orange County (C00035246) *Address: same as sponsor * Treasurer: Frank H. Greinke*

	1993-94	1995-96	1997	Totals
Receipts	$418,437	$480,828	$6,102	$905,367
Disburse	411,057	492,156	18,215	921,428
Cash	23,442	12,113	0	n/a
Contributions	29,800	28,750	0	58,550
Republicans	29,800	28,750	0	58,550
No. of Cand.	*7*	*13*	*0*	*20*
House	20,800	26,250	0	47,050
Senate	9,000	2,500	0	11,500
Democrats	0	0	0	0
No. of Cand.	*0*	*0*	*0*	*0*
House	0	0	0	0
Senate	0	0	0	0
Incumbents	11,000	13,750	0	24,750
Challengers	9,800	8,000	0	17,800
Open Seat	9,000	7,000	0	16,000
Winners	25,000	9,750	n/a	34,750
Losers	4,800	19,000	n/a	23,800

Lincoln Club of Sacramento Valley

*Phone: (916) 783-7508 * Fax: (916) 783-7508*
5098 Foothills Blvd., Suite 3-333, Roseville, CA 95747

The Lincoln Club of Sacramento Valley is a group of about 200 civic and business leaders committed to fiscal responsibility, economic growth and conservative political participation. It supports California Republican candidates.

The Sacramento chapter was founded in 1978.

Lincoln Club of Sacramento Valley PAC (C00304485) *Address: same as sponsor * Treasurer: Tom O'Neil * Contact: Ross Relles, President*

	1993-94	1995-96	1997	Totals
Receipts	$0	$23,422	$2,414	$25,836
Disburse	0	15,441	1,000	16,441
Cash	0	7,981	9,395	n/a
Contributions	0	8,200	1,000	9,200
Republicans	0	8,200	1,000	9,200
No. of Cand.	*0*	*4*	*1*	*5*
House	0	8,200	1,000	9,200
Senate	0	0	0	0
Democrats	0	0	0	0
No. of Cand.	*0*	*0*	*0*	*0*
House	0	0	0	0
Senate	0	0	0	0
Incumbents	0	3,200	1,000	4,200
Challengers	0	5,000	0	5,000
Open Seat	0	0	0	0
Winners	0	3,200	n/a	3,200
Losers	0	5,000	n/a	5,000

Loose Group

Phone: (404) 355-5054
3165 Brandy Station, Atlanta, GA 30339

The Loose Group is, as the name might suggest, a casual consortium of Georgia businessmen interested in promoting "traditional conservative political values." According to Chairman Robert Redfearn, these include "less government, fewer regulations and a strong defense."

The PAC supports candidates on all political levels and makes a point to encourage younger candidates to run, particularly those who are venturing into public office for the first time. On the federal level, it contributed mainly to Georgia Republicans, giving $5,000 to Sen. Paul Coverdell, as well as to six of the state's GOP representatives.

The Loose Group was founded in 1964. Its small size, roughly 65 members total, is conducive to members becoming acquainted with the politicians it backs, and the PAC holds frequent events for such interaction.

The Loose Group (C00010793) *Address: same as sponsor * Treasurer: Frank G. Stevenson Jr. * Contact: Robert Redfearn, Chairman*

	1993-94	1995-96	1997	Totals
Receipts	$86,730	$135,904	$80,589	$303,223
Disburse	85,785	123,786	49,463	259,034
Cash	1,098	13,216	46,747	n/a
Contributions	25,000	70,000	15,000	110,000
Republicans	25,000	70,000	15,000	110,000
No. of Cand.	*8*	*15*	*3*	*26*
House	24,000	48,000	10,000	82,000
Senate	1,000	22,000	5,000	28,000
Democrats	0	0	0	0
No. of Cand.	*0*	*0*	*0*	*0*
House	0	0	0	0
Senate	0	0	0	0
Incumbents	8,000	37,000	15,000	60,000
Challengers	11,000	16,000	0	27,000
Open Seat	5,000	17,000	0	22,000
Winners	23,000	37,000	n/a	60,000
Losers	2,000	33,000	n/a	35,000

MADISON Project Inc.

*Phone: (540) 338-7575 * Fax: (540) 338-1998*
P.O. Box 479, Hamilton, VA 20159
E-mail: TimTeepell@msn.com

The MADISON Project is a nonprofit organization with about 6,000 members that works to elect conservatives to Congress.

Established in 1993, the organization's name stands for "Make A Difference In Saving Our Nation." It was founded by Michael Farris, an ordained minister, who is vice president of the Executive Board of Christian Solidarity International and the president of the Home School Legal Defense Association.

The organization states that it supports the election of principled conservatives dedicated to economic common sense and traditional values.

Recently the group has advocated "parental rights" legislation similar to that of the "Parental Rights and Responsibilities Act," introduced in the House and Senate in 1995. This legislation, a part of the Christian Coalition's "Contract with the American Family," would give parents the legal right to control their children's education, health care, discipline and religious instruction. The act states that no federal, state or local government "shall interfere with or usurp the right of a parent to direct the upbringing" of his or her child.

The MADISON Project Inc. Fund (C00298000) *Address: same as sponsor * Treasurer: David Edward Pearson * Contact: Timmy Teepell, Executive Dir.*

	1993-94	1995-96	1997	Totals
Receipts	$8,467	$201,701	$48,558	$258,726
Disburse	8,010	200,292	47,404	255,706
Cash	455	1,791	2,945	n/a
Contributions	5,170	25,891	10,289	41,350
Republicans	4,920	25,891	10,289	41,100
No. of Cand.	*10*	*25*	*23*	*58*
House	4,920	15,996	8,159	29,075
Senate	0	9,895	2,130	12,025
Democrats	250	0	0	250
No. of Cand.	*1*	*0*	*0*	*1*
House	250	0	0	250
Senate	0	0	0	0

Incumbents	250	3,011	3,134	6,395
Challengers	3,741	14,778	1,729	20,248
Open Seat	1,179	8,096	4,326	13,601
Winners	3,057	9,404	n/a	12,461
Losers	2,113	16,487	n/a	18,600

Massachusetts Congressional Victory Fund

*Phone: (617) 426-3070 * Fax: (617) 426-3078*
P.O. Box 180240, Boston, MA 02118

The Massachusetts Congressional Victory Fund is a partisan organization that contributes to the campaigns of Republican political candidates.

Established in 1984, the organization advocates conservative policies and has more than 1,000 members.

Massachusetts Congressional Victory Fund (C00282319) *Address: same as sponsor * Treasurer: Nancy S. Clapp * Contact: Steven Myers, Financial Dir.*

	1993-94	*1995-96*	*1997*	*Totals*
Receipts	$62,104	$86,707	$7,480	$156,291
Disburse	62,011	78,899	15,304	156,214
Cash	90	7,895	71	n/a
Contributions	11,450	28,050	250	39,750
Republicans	11,450	28,050	250	39,750
No. of Cand.	*14*	*14*	*1*	*29*
House	8,450	14,150	250	22,850
Senate	3,000	13,900	0	16,900
Democrats	0	0	0	0
No. of Cand.	*0*	*0*	*0*	*0*
House	0	0	0	0
Senate	0	0	0	0
Incumbents	4,300	2,500	250	7,050
Challengers	6,650	9,550	0	16,200
Open Seat	250	16,000	0	16,250
Winners	4,550	850	n/a	5,400
Losers	6,900	27,200	n/a	34,100

Minnesota Republican Congressional Committee

Phone: (612) 373-0638
P.O. Box 201506, Bloomington, MN 55420

The Minnesota Republican Congressional Committee was formed in 1994 to support the state's Republican candidates for federal office. The PAC claims more than 1,500 contributors, about 97 percent of which are in-state. Former Rep. Vin Weber is the group's honorary chairman.

Minnesota Republican Congressional Committee (C00286583) *Address: same as sponsor * Treasurer: Tim A. Berkness * Contact: State Rep. Greg Davids, Chairperson*

	1993-94	*1995-96*	*1997*	*Totals*
Receipts	$132,804	$313,626	$45,802	$492,232
Disburse	111,745	329,813	49,209	490,767
Cash	21,056	4,866	1,458	n/a
Contributions	28,506	36,250	484	65,240
Republicans	28,506	36,250	484	65,240
No. of Cand.	*9*	*9*	*1*	*19*
House	24,387	31,250	0	55,637
Senate	4,119	5,000	484	9,603
Democrats	0	0	0	0
No. of Cand.	*0*	*0*	*0*	*0*
House	0	0	0	0
Senate	0	0	0	0
Incumbents	1,000	5,000	484	6,484
Challengers	14,062	31,250	0	45,312
Open Seat	13,444	0	0	13,444
Winners	8,447	5,000	n/a	13,447
Losers	20,059	31,250	n/a	51,309

Public Affairs PAC

Phone: (703) 536-7880
6734 Westcott Rd., Falls Church, VA 22042

The Public Affairs PAC supported national Republican candidates in the 1996 election cycle, contributing a total of $9,150. According to FEC records, the PAC took in more than $550,000 in the same time period, almost all from people who listed their occupation as retired.

In a 1997 FEC filing, Public Affairs PAC lists outstanding debt of about $72,000 from 1988 for "printing and services for independent expenditure against Jesse Jackson for President" and "printing and mail services to defend Dan Quayle as a victim of the News Media."

Public Affairs PAC (C00224493) *Address: same as sponsor * Treasurer: Eugene A. DelGaudio*

	1993-94	*1995-96*	*1997*	*Totals*
Receipts	$47,198	$586,825	$19,542	$653,565
Disburse	55,163	569,548	29,916	654,627
Cash	118	17,395	7,021	n/a
Contributions	25	9,150	50	9,225
Republicans	25	9,150	50	9,225
No. of Cand.	*1*	*8*	*1*	*10*
House	25	3,150	50	3,225
Senate	0	6,000	0	6,000
Democrats	0	0	0	0
No. of Cand.	*0*	*0*	*0*	*0*
House	0	0	0	0
Senate	0	0	0	0
Incumbents	25	1,100	0	1,125
Challengers	0	2,450	0	2,450
Open Seat	0	5,600	50	5,650
Winners	25	500	n/a	525
Losers	0	8,650	n/a	8,650

Republican Liberty Federal Campaign Fund

*Phone: (713) 867-9060 * Fax: (281) 492-7195*
10878 Westheimer, Suite 395, Houston, TX 77042

The Republican Liberty Federal Campaign Fund is the PAC for the Republican Liberty Caucus, an independent organization that supports Republicans who are focused on limited government and agree with libertarian positions. The group has more than 1,000 members from all areas of the United States.

The group sends out a member newsletter six times a year. In the first issue, the newsletter rated the previous year's members of Congress according to their libertarian positions.

Republican Liberty Federal Campaign Fund (C00269241) *Address: same as sponsor * Treasurer: Michael E. Holmes*

	1993-94	*1995-96*	*1997*	*Totals*
Receipts	$11,035	$24,134	$4,565	$39,734
Disburse	10,686	24,427	3,787	38,900
Cash	389	92	870	n/a
Contributions	3,500	16,625	1,000	21,125
Republicans	3,250	16,625	1,000	20,875
No. of Cand.	*10*	*17*	*1*	*28*
House	2,500	14,725	1,000	18,225
Senate	750	1,900	0	2,650
Democrats	250	0	0	250
No. of Cand.	*1*	*0*	*0*	*1*
House	250	0	0	250
Senate	0	0	0	0
Incumbents	950	3,250	1,000	5,200
Challengers	700	11,400	0	12,100
Open Seat	1,850	1,975	0	3,825
Winners	2,700	12,250	n/a	14,950
Losers	800	4,375	n/a	5,175

Republican Primary PAC

*Phone: (202) 986-3453 * Fax: (202) 588-5876*
2127 California St. N.W., Suite 507, Washington, DC 20008

The Republican Primary PAC mostly supports young, non-incumbent candidates in Republican primaries who they see as "up-and-coming," with leadership potential.

The PAC, which was founded in 1995, gives to federal candidates from all areas of the nation.

Republican Primary PAC (C00309195) *Address: same as sponsor * Treasurer: Bruce P. Jackson*

	1993-94	*1995-96*	*1997*	*Totals*
Receipts	$0	$30,125	$5,497	$35,622
Disburse	0	30,103	500	30,603
Cash	0	20	5,017	n/a
Contributions	0	29,000	500	29,500
Republicans	0	29,000	500	29,500
No. of Cand.	*0*	*22*	*1*	*23*
House	0	14,500	500	15,000
Senate	0	14,500	0	14,500
Democrats	0	0	0	0
No. of Cand.	*0*	*0*	*0*	*0*
House	0	0	0	0
Senate	0	0	0	0
Incumbents	0	4,000	500	4,500

(Data for Republican Primary PAC continued)

Challengers	0	9,500	0	9,500
Open Seat	0	15,500	0	15,500
Winners	0	12,000	n/a	12,000
Losers	0	17,000	n/a	17,000

USCA Federal PAC

*Phone: (503) 463-0653 * Fax: (503) 463-8745*
P.O. Box 9127, Brooks, OR 97305

USCA Federal (United States Citizens Alliance) is a conservative PAC operated by the Oregon Citizens Alliance in Brooks, Ore. The group opposes abortion, NAFTA, same-sex marriages and giving homosexuals minority status.

The PAC was created to support former Republican Rep. Jim Bunn's campaign for Oregon's 5th District seat. Bunn was elected to the House in 1994 and defeated in 1996 by Rep. Darlene Hooley, D-Ore.

USCA Federal PAC (C00290536) *Address: same as sponsor * Treasurer: Bonnie J. Mabon * Contact: Lon Mabon, Chairperson*

	1993-94	1995-96	1997	Totals
Receipts	$14,198	$36,485	$237	$50,920
Disburse	14,211	36,419	239	50,869
Cash	-16	46	44	n/a
Contributions	2,971	159	0	3,130
Republicans	1,971	159	0	2,130
No. of Cand.	*3*	*1*	*0*	*4*
House	1,971	0	0	1,971
Senate	0	159	0	159
Democrats	0	0	0	0
No. of Cand.	*0*	*0*	*0*	*0*
House	0	0	0	0
Senate	0	0	0	0
Incumbents	0	0	0	0
Challengers	2,221	0	0	2,221
Open Seat	750	159	0	909
Winners	750	159	n/a	909
Losers	2,221	0	n/a	2,221

United Republican Fund of Illinois

*Phone: (312) 606-0953 * Fax: (312) 606-0879*
100 W. Monroe St., Suite 1600, c/o Morris, Rathnau & Dela Rosa, Chicago, IL 60603
Web: redtape.uchicago.edu/users/goparris
E-mail: goparris@midway.uchicago.edu

The United Republican Fund of Illinois is a 65-year-old fund that contributes to state and federal Republican candidates. Formed before the creation of the FEC in 1975, the fund registered as a PAC upon the creation of the commission. URF supports free enterprise and individual liberty. It also supports limiting taxation that would harm entrepreneurs.

United Republican Fund of Illinois Inc. Federal Election Committee (C00005819) *Address: same as sponsor * Treasurer: Deborah D. Dietz * Contact: Gordon Parrish, Executive Dir.*

	1993-94	1995-96	1997	Totals
Receipts	$3,702	$60,887	$67,130	$131,719
Disburse	4,025	57,830	69,329	131,184
Cash	0	3,054	1,993	n/a
Contributions	0	12,300	1,950	14,250
Republicans	0	12,300	1,950	14,250
No. of Cand.	*0*	*8*	*3*	*11*
House	0	6,300	1,950	8,250
Senate	0	6,000	0	6,000
Democrats	0	0	0	0
No. of Cand.	*0*	*0*	*0*	*0*
House	0	0	0	0
Senate	0	0	0	0
Incumbents	0	3,500	1,000	4,500
Challengers	0	2,300	500	2,800
Open Seat	0	6,500	0	6,500
Winners	0	2,500	n/a	2,500
Losers	0	9,800	n/a	9,800

United Seniors PAC

*Phone: (703) 533-5858 * Fax: (703) 533-5858*
6932 N. Fairfax Dr., Suite 204, Arlington, VA 22213

United Seniors PAC is associated with the United Seniors Association, which describes itself as a conservative seniors' organization with more than 540,000 members nationwide.

The group states that it supports retirement security through strong Medicare and Social Security programs. The organization was founded in 1991 by Richard A. Viguerie, a pioneer of direct-mail fundraising who has raised millions of dollars for conservative causes.

A Nov. 15, 1992 article in the Orange County Register alleged that Viguerie and several of his associates used the United Seniors Association to turn a profit for themselves. The article stated that USA solicited from the elderly millions of dollars in donations which then financed Viguerie's personal companies. The article claimed that the nonprofit association would rent mailing lists from the for-profit companies, and then many of the donations that came in to USA would be spent paying the debts owed to the private companies. The New York state attorney general investigated these allegations in 1992 and 1993, but no charges were filed.

While the organization and PAC are not technically affiliated, the president of the organization is also the chairman of the PAC, and the PAC, according to 1997 FEC documents, has rented mailing lists from the association.

United Seniors PAC Inc. (C00077354) *Address: same as sponsor * Treasurer: Rosemary Boulter * Contact: Sandra L. Butler, Chairperson*

	1993-94	1995-96	1997	Totals
Receipts	$821,299	$276,362	$167,730	$1,265,391
Disburse	808,977	286,127	138,233	1,233,337
Cash	12,678	2,910	32,408	n/a
Contributions	62,942	23,300	2,500	88,742
Republicans	62,942	23,300	2,500	88,742
No. of Cand.	*52*	*22*	*3*	*77*
House	53,236	18,350	1,500	73,086
Senate	9,706	4,950	1,000	15,656
Democrats	0	0	0	0
No. of Cand.	*0*	*0*	*0*	*0*
House	0	0	0	0
Senate	0	0	0	0
Incumbents	1,285	19,100	1,500	21,885
Challengers	49,541	700	0	50,241
Open Seat	12,116	3,500	1,000	16,616
Winners	38,936	15,500	n/a	54,436
Losers	24,006	7,800	n/a	31,806

United States Republican Committee

Phone: (202) 298-8630
3220 N St. N.W., Suite 276, Washington, DC 20007

The United States Republican Committee contributed solely to Republican candidates for the 1996 election. The PAC is run by volunteers and has no central office. According to a letter to the FEC, USRC maintains a voicemail account and a post office box in Washington, but has no other administrative expenses.

United States Republican Committee (USRC) (C00305409) *Address: same as sponsor * Treasurer: Timothy B. Schmidt*

	1993-94	1995-96	1997	Totals
Receipts	$0	$279,118	$38,528	$317,646
Disburse	0	278,679	38,812	317,491
Cash	0	435	151	n/a
Contributions	0	6,000	0	6,000
Republicans	0	6,000	0	6,000
No. of Cand.	*0*	*51*	*0*	*51*
House	0	5,200	0	5,200
Senate	0	800	0	800
Democrats	0	0	0	0
No. of Cand.	*0*	*0*	*0*	*0*
House	0	0	0	0
Senate	0	0	0	0
Incumbents	0	5,400	0	5,400
Challengers	0	200	0	200
Open Seat	0	400	0	400
Winners	0	4,400	n/a	4,400
Losers	0	1,600	n/a	1,600

Women's Issues

Alabama Solution

*Phone: (205) 250-0205 * Fax: (205) 250-0205*
P.O. Box 370821, Birmingham, AL 35237

Alabama Solution raises money to support women running for office in Alabama. Established in 1994, the organization has 2,000 members.

Alabama Solution (formerly known as Women's PAC) (C00274274) *Address: same as sponsor * Treasurer: Cameron Vowell*

	1993-94	1995-96	1997	Totals
Receipts	$137,657	$110,340	$64,061	$312,058
Disburse	120,242	104,648	56,470	281,360
Cash	24,268	29,959	37,549	n/a
Contributions	0	6,500	0	6,500
Republicans	0	0	0	0
No. of Cand.	*0*	*0*	*0*	*0*
House	0	0	0	0
Senate	0	0	0	0
Democrats	0	6,500	0	6,500
No. of Cand.	*0*	*2*	*0*	*2*
House	0	1,500	0	1,500
Senate	0	5,000	0	5,000
Incumbents	0	0	0	0
Challengers	0	1,500	0	1,500
Open Seat	0	5,000	0	5,000
Winners	0	0	n/a	0
Losers	0	6,500	n/a	6,500

EMILY's List

*Phone: (202) 326-1400 * Fax: (202) 326-1415*
805 15th St. N.W., Suite 400, Washington, DC 20005
Web: www.emilyslist.org

EMILY's List supports pro-abortion rights Democratic women candidates for key federal and statewide elections. The organization selects a number of "viable" candidates who meet its qualifications, and then recommends a list of women for its members to support.

EMILY is an acronym for "Early Money is Like Yeast (it makes the dough rise.)" Founded in 1986 by Ellen R. Malcolm, the intent behind EMILY's List was to provide directed, early support to candidates from a large, grassroots network of women in the form of campaign funds, elections expertise and research, and voter mobilization.

There are more than 45,000 members in the organization. Each member is expected to contribute $100 or more to at least two campaigns per election cycle, and the checks are made out to the individual candidates. Under current federal law, individuals may contribute up to $1,000 per candidate per election up to $25,000.

Although it is a PAC and subject to the federal law limiting contributions to $5,000 per candidate per election, EMILY's List is able to generate more money for its candidates by this indirect "bundling" contribution method. There is no limit on the amount a PAC can send in "bundles," but candidates are required to disclose that they received the money via a conduit.

EMILY's List (C00193433) *Address: same as sponsor * Treasurer: Ellen R. Malcolm*

	1993-94	1995-96	1997	Totals
Receipts	$7,422,835	$13,619,906	$7,235,744	$28,278,485
Disburse	7,945,905	13,660,696	6,767,815	28,374,416
Cash	469,437	428,646	896,574	n/a
Contributions	227,689	253,218	17,272	498,179
Republicans	0	0	0	0
No. of Cand.	*0*	*0*	*0*	*0*
House	0	0	0	0
Senate	0	0	0	0
Democrats	216,749	253,218	17,272	487,239
No. of Cand.	*42*	*49*	*14*	*105*
House	202,266	233,218	17,272	452,756
Senate	14,483	20,000	0	34,483
Incumbents	59,415	46,881	5,000	111,296
Challengers	50,883	129,721	6,472	187,076
Open Seat	112,276	77,259	5,800	195,335
Winners	40,960	108,247	n/a	149,207
Losers	186,729	144,971	n/a	331,700

National Organization for Women (NOW)

*Phone: (202) 331-0066 * Fax: (202) 785-8576*
1000 16th St. N.W., Suite 700, Washington, DC 20036
Web: www.now.org/now

The National Organization for Women (NOW) is a feminist activist organization that advocates equality for women and organizes mass marches and rallies. NOW has 250,000 members and 600 chapters in the United States.

Issues such as reproductive freedom, gay rights and ending violence against women rank high with NOW PAC. The group endorsed nearly 900 candidates in 1994, supporting some of them with donations and organizing assistance.

In addition to contributing to candidates, NOW PAC follows up after elections to ensure candidates support reproductive freedom and civil rights for all.

National Organization for Women Political Action Committee (NOW PAC) (C00092247) *Address: same as sponsor * Treasurer: Karen Johnson*

	1993-94	1995-96	1997	Totals
Receipts	$328,611	$185,071	$70,782	$584,464
Disburse	286,202	206,879	60,735	553,816
Cash	81,670	34,905	44,052	n/a
Contributions	98,812	73,768	7,960	180,540
Republicans	2,500	0	0	2,500
No. of Cand.	*4*	*0*	*0*	*4*
House	1,500	0	0	1,500
Senate	1,000	0	0	1,000
Democrats	90,184	73,768	7,960	171,912
No. of Cand.	*79*	*84*	*7*	*170*
House	80,031	60,295	6,408	146,734
Senate	10,153	13,473	1,552	25,178
Incumbents	47,632	23,198	6,408	77,238
Challengers	12,690	30,895	0	43,585
Open Seat	36,490	19,675	1,552	57,717
Winners	35,717	40,216	n/a	75,933
Losers	63,095	33,552	n/a	96,647

National Women's Political Caucus

*Phone: (202) 785-1100 * Fax: (202) 785-3605*
1211 Connecticut Ave., Suite 425, Washington, DC 20036
*Web: feminist.com/nwpc.htm * E-mail: MailNWPC@aol.com*

The National Women's Political Caucus is dedicated to increasing the number of women in elected or appointed government offices, regardless of political affiliation.

More than 50,000 people participate in NWPC activities each year, although NWPC's actual membership is about 10,000 to 15,000 people. The organization, which was founded in 1971, is aided by hundreds of state and local chapters in identifying, recruiting, training and supporting women who run for political office.

NWPC conducts numerous training camps for women interested in entering politics, publishes a quarterly newsletter, and hosts several conferences and awards ceremonies throughout the year.

The National Women's Political Caucus Victory Fund is the larger of two PACs related to the NWPC. It is funded by people who are not official members of the NWPC.

National Women's Political Caucus Victory Fund (NWPC) (C00133504) *Address: same as sponsor * Treasurer: Elisa Sanchez*

	1993-94	1995-96	1997	Totals
Receipts	$161,100	$73,111	$8,113	$242,324
Disburse	157,485	79,424	3,101	240,010
Cash	6,499	185	5,198	n/a
Contributions	83,500	31,900	0	115,400
Republicans	15,000	5,000	0	20,000
No. of Cand.	*5*	*3*	*0*	*8*
House	5,000	1,500	0	6,500
Senate	10,000	3,500	0	13,500
Democrats	63,500	26,900	0	90,400
No. of Cand.	*32*	*22*	*0*	*54*
House	50,000	25,900	0	75,900
Senate	13,500	1,000	0	14,500
Incumbents	23,500	5,000	0	28,500
Challengers	9,000	11,000	0	20,000
Open Seat	51,000	15,900	0	66,900
Winners	15,500	10,500	n/a	26,000
Losers	68,000	21,400	n/a	89,400

National Women's Political Caucus Campaign Support Committee (C00034256) *Address: Same as sponsor * Treasurer: Anita Perez Ferguson*

The National Women's Political Caucus Campaign Support Committee is the second of two PACs affiliated with the NWPC. It is the group's "internal" PAC, for contributions made by members of the organization.

	1993-94	*1995-96*	*1997*	*Totals*
Receipts	$58,007	$18,855	$18,528	$95,390
Disburse	58,145	18,721	7,932	84,798
Cash	606	746	11,343	n/a
Contributions	35,750	16,500	5,900	58,150
Republicans	4,500	5,500	0	10,000
No. of Cand.	*4*	*4*	*0*	*8*
House	3,000	1,000	0	4,000
Senate	1,500	4,500	0	6,000
Democrats	29,750	11,000	5,900	46,650
No. of Cand.	*17*	*12*	*6*	*35*
House	22,250	9,000	3,500	34,750
Senate	7,500	2,000	2,400	11,900
Incumbents	11,000	0	1,400	12,400
Challengers	2,750	3,500	0	6,250
Open Seat	19,500	12,000	4,500	36,000
Winners	13,000	2,000	n/a	15,000
Losers	22,750	14,500	n/a	37,250

Women's Campaign Fund

*Phone: (202) 393-8164 * Fax: (202) 393-0649*
734 15th St. N.W., Suite 500, Washington, DC 20005
E-mail: womenscampaignfund@erols.com

The Women's Campaign Fund trains and promotes abortion rights candidates of all parties. It is not a lobbying organization but aids candidates at the local, state and national levels. From 1996 to early 1998, it was headed by former Rep. Marjorie Margolies-Mezvinsky, D-Pa., who left the organization to run for statewide office in Pennsylvania.

The WCF sends out questionnaires to candidates to identify their positions on women's issues and federal funding for abortion.

The WCF devoted just 11 percent of its 1995-96 expenditures to candidates, the lowest percentage in the top 200. Some $2.4 million of the group's money went toward independent expenditures and other expenses. The top-ranked women's issues PAC in 1995-96 contributions, it donated the lowest percentage of its money to winning candidates — 34 percent.

Of the top 10 recipients of WCF PAC contributions, just three won their 1996 races: Sens. Susan Collins, R-Maine, and Mary L. Landrieu, D-La., and Rep. Sue W. Kelly, R-N.Y. More than half of the recipients received at least $5,000. Most recipients were female.

Women's Campaign Fund Inc. (C00015024) *Address: same as sponsor * Treasurer: Doreen Frasca * Contact: Charlie Carter, Managing Dir.*

	1993-94	*1995-96*	*1997*	*Totals*
Receipts	$1,815,052	$2,778,428	$1,345,164	$5,938,644
Disburse	1,823,221	2,771,841	1,281,524	5,876,586
Cash	43,881	50,469	114,106	n/a
Contributions	262,038	307,185	30,500	599,723
Republicans	77,100	93,000	5,000	175,100
No. of Cand.	*23*	*18*	*2*	*43*
House	54,750	67,500	5,000	127,250
Senate	22,350	25,500	0	47,850
Democrats	173,438	214,185	25,500	413,123
No. of Cand.	*51*	*52*	*16*	*119*
House	149,938	189,433	15,000	354,371
Senate	23,500	24,752	10,500	58,752
Incumbents	57,500	44,170	12,500	114,170
Challengers	37,600	132,680	2,000	172,280
Open Seat	165,438	130,335	16,000	311,773
Winners	65,952	104,360	n/a	170,312
Losers	196,086	202,825	n/a	398,911

Women's Political Committee

Phone: (213) 954-3100
5670 Wilshire Blvd., Suite 1450, Los Angeles, CA 90036

The Women's Political Committee contributes to "women seeking elected office," according to the group. Based in Los Angeles, the organization has contributed exclusively to California candidates since 1995.

Women's Political Committee (C00188193) *Address: same as sponsor * Treasurer: Nancy S. Brakensiek * Contact: Georgia Merce, Co-Chair*

	1993-94	*1995-96*	*1997*	*Totals*
Receipts	$261,555	$215,118	$95,901	$572,574
Disburse	263,661	208,664	66,019	538,344
Cash	2,320	8,876	38,758	n/a
Contributions	55,000	30,000	30,000	115,000
Republicans	2,500	0	0	2,500
No. of Cand.	*1*	*0*	*0*	*1*
House	0	0	0	0
Senate	2,500	0	0	2,500
Democrats	50,000	30,000	30,000	110,000
No. of Cand.	*10*	*5*	*6*	*21*
House	33,500	25,000	20,000	78,500
Senate	16,500	5,000	10,000	31,500
Incumbents	33,000	15,000	25,000	73,000
Challengers	6,000	10,000	0	16,000
Open Seat	13,500	5,000	5,000	23,500
Winners	29,500	25,000	n/a	54,500
Losers	25,500	5,000	n/a	30,500

Labor

Building Trade Unions

Asbestos Workers Union

*Phone: (202) 785-2388 * Fax: (202) 429-0568*
1776 Massachusetts Ave. N.W., Suite 301, Washington, DC 20036

The International Association of Heat and Frost Insulators and Asbestos Workers represents about 20,000 pipe coverers in the United States and Canada.

The union, which was founded in the early 1900s, has 107 locals.

International Association of Heat & Frost Insulators and Asbestos Workers PAC (C00115527) *Address: same as sponsor * Treasurer: James A. Grogan*

	1993-94	*1995-96*	*1997*	*Totals*
Receipts	$84,274	$81,296	$36,670	$202,240
Disburse	136,587	100,415	41,348	278,350
Cash	63,619	44,503	39,826	n/a
Contributions	45,350	51,350	10,600	107,300
Republicans	1,000	0	0	1,000
No. of Cand.	*1*	*0*	*0*	*1*
House	0	0	0	0
Senate	1,000	0	0	1,000
Democrats	42,850	51,350	10,600	104,800
No. of Cand.	*37*	*50*	*11*	*98*
House	27,700	37,850	9,050	74,600
Senate	15,150	13,500	1,550	30,200
Incumbents	23,050	24,750	8,800	56,600
Challengers	10,850	10,800	1,000	22,650
Open Seat	11,450	15,800	800	28,050
Winners	15,500	37,350	n/a	52,850
Losers	29,850	14,000	n/a	43,850

Contributed less than $5,000 during 1995-96 cycle:

Asbestos Workers Local 27 PAC (C00286203) *Phone: (816) 252-0588 * 400 S. Main St., Independence, MO 64050 * Treasurer: Mike Sandnes*

Asbestos Workers Local 60 PAC (C00152223) *Phone: (305) 681-0679 * 13000 N.W. 47th Ave., Miami, FL 33054 * Treasurer: Bryon Stevens*

Terminated PACs which contributed less than $5,000 during 1995-96 cycle:

International Association of Heat & Frost Insulators and Asbestos Workers Local #14 Political Action Fund (C00251884) *Phone: (215) 289-4303 * Fax: (215) 289-8655 * 6513 Bustleton Ave., Philadelphia, PA 19149 * Treasurer: Patrick J. Eiding*

Baltimore Building & Construction Trades Council

*Phone: (410) 426-9415 * Fax: (410) 426-4438*
5913 Harford Rd., Baltimore, MD 21214

The Baltimore Building & Construction Trades Council is an umbrella organization for 19 Maryland building and construction affiliates. The council represents about 15,000 workers.

The council has lobbyists in Annapolis but not in Washington. B.U.I.L.D. stands for "Building Unions Individual Labor Donations."

B.U.I.L.D. Fund: Baltimore Building & Construction Trades Council, AFL-CIO (C00086264) *Address: same as sponsor * Treasurer: Jack L. Johns*

	1993-94	*1995-96*	*1997*	*Totals*
Receipts	$48,430	$49,034	$23,086	$120,550
Disburse	52,802	50,877	23,012	126,691
Cash	2,860	1,019	1,092	n/a
Contributions	1,300	9,500	1,500	12,300
Republicans	0	0	0	0
No. of Cand.	*0*	*0*	*0*	*0*
House	0	0	0	0
Senate	0	0	0	0
Democrats	1,300	9,500	1,500	12,300
No. of Cand.	*3*	*5*	*1*	*9*
House	1,100	9,000	0	10,100
Senate	200	500	1,500	2,200
Incumbents	300	1,000	1,500	2,800
Challengers	0	7,000	0	7,000
Open Seat	1,000	1,500	0	2,500
Winners	300	2,500	n/a	2,800
Losers	1,000	7,000	n/a	8,000

Bricklayers Union

*Phone: (202) 783-3788 * Fax: (202) 393-0219*
815 15th St. N.W., Suite 300, Washington, DC 20005
Web: www.bacweb.org

The International Union of Bricklayers and Allied Craftsmen represents about 84,000 masonry, tile and stone workers in the United States and Canada. It is affiliated with the International Masonry Institute, which offers training and technical assistance to the trowel trades.

Like many other unions, the union gave an overwhelming percentage of its money — 98 percent — to Democrats during the 1995-96 election cycle. Unlike some of the larger unions, however, it contributed more than three-fourths of its total contributions to winning candidates, mostly because it gave more to incumbents.

The top recipients were Reps. Maurice D. Hinchey, D-N.Y., Patrick J. Kennedy, D-R.I., and House Minority Leader Richard A. Gephardt, D-Mo. The leading Republican recipient was Sen. Arlen Specter, R-Pa.

One Bricklayers' local, in Rhode Island, has a federal PAC, but it contributed less than $5,000 to congressional candidates during the 1995-96 election cycle.

International Union of Bricklayers and Allied Craftsmen Political Action Committee (C00003632) *Address: same as sponsor * Treasurer: John J. Flynn * Contact: Joanna Reagan*

	1993-94	1995-96	1997	Totals
Receipts	$333,853	$405,058	$233,252	$972,163
Disburse	328,819	388,078	122,784	839,681
Cash	29,843	46,824	157,292	n/a
Contributions	229,100	252,300	66,125	547,525
Republicans	6,500	5,000	0	11,500
No. of Cand.	*3*	*5*	*0*	*8*
House	1,500	3,000	0	4,500
Senate	5,000	2,000	0	7,000
Democrats	220,100	247,300	66,125	533,525
No. of Cand.	*137*	*116*	*30*	*283*
House	143,050	163,800	40,125	346,975
Senate	77,050	83,500	26,000	186,550
Incumbents	189,600	136,450	66,625	392,675
Challengers	16,500	45,100	0	61,600
Open Seat	23,000	70,750	500	94,250
Winners	150,350	193,950	n/a	344,300
Losers	78,750	58,350	n/a	137,100

Contributed less than $5,000 during 1995-96 cycle:

R.I. Bricklayers Political Action Committee (C00151837) *Phone: (401) 946-9940 * Fax: (401) 946-5060 * 150 Midway Rd., Suite 153, Cranston, RI 02920-5743 * Treasurer: Raymond F. Rigney Jr.*

California State Pipe Trades Council

*Phone: (916) 446-7311 * Fax: (916) 446-3520*
915 L St., Suite 1240, Sacramento, CA 95814

The California State Pipe Trades Council is an umbrella union representing 28,000 plumbers and pipe fitters in the state. Twenty-six local organizations are members of the union, which was founded in 1943.

The union's PAC gives to federal candidates.

California State Pipe Trades Council Voluntary Federal Political Action Fund (C00265033) *Address: same as sponsor * Treasurer: Joe Winstead*

	1993-94	1995-96	1997	Totals
Receipts	$16,552	$25,700	$22,960	$65,212
Disburse	14,582	36,871	17,530	68,983
Cash	5,730	478	5,908	n/a
Contributions	10,039	26,960	11,500	48,499
Republicans	0	0	0	0
No. of Cand.	*0*	*0*	*0*	*0*
House	0	0	0	0
Senate	0	0	0	0
Democrats	10,039	26,960	11,500	48,499
No. of Cand.	*8*	*18*	*6*	*32*
House	8,039	21,460	11,500	40,999
Senate	2,000	5,500	0	7,500
Incumbents	7,000	15,960	4,000	26,960
Challengers	2,039	6,000	0	8,039
Open Seat	1,000	5,000	7,500	13,500
Winners	3,000	21,960	n/a	24,960
Losers	7,039	5,000	n/a	12,039

Carpenters Union

*Phone: (202) 546-6206 x269 * Fax: (202) 546-3873*
101 Constitution Ave. N.W., Washington, DC 20001

The United Brotherhood of Carpenters & Joiners of America has about 500,000 members in the United States and Canada. The union represents the traditional carpentry trades in construction as well as a large and diversified membership in the industrial sector.

Contributions to candidates come at the request of the union's local organizations. The union supports increased funding for construction projects, legislation including ISTEA, and work on roads in national forests. It opposes a plan to make it easier for employers to classify workers as independent contractors.

The union gave heavily to Democrats during the 1995-96 cycle and ranked second in 1995-96 congressional contributions among construction unions. Candidates in California, Illinois, Pennsylvania and Texas received the most money.

The top individual recipients were Rep. John F. Tierney, D-Mass., 1996 Senate candidate Winston Bryant of Arkansas, Reps. Nick Lampson, D-Texas, and Ken Bentsen, D-Texas. More than 55 candidates received $10,000 from this union. Rep. Frank A. LoBiondo, R-N.J., was the top Republican recipient.

Carpenters Legislative Improvement Committee, United Brotherhood of Carpenters & Joiners of America (C00001016) *Address: same as sponsor * Treasurer: William Luddy*

	1993-94	1995-96	1997	Totals
Receipts	$1,651,585	$1,823,548	$863,420	$4,338,553
Disburse	1,723,095	1,774,193	527,652	4,024,940
Cash	48,229	97,646	433,417	n/a
Contributions	1,423,200	1,464,606	471,068	3,358,874
Republicans	49,750	66,500	31,318	147,568
No. of Cand.	*14*	*22*	*12*	*48*
House	49,750	61,500	23,818	135,068
Senate	0	5,000	7,500	12,500
Democrats	1,344,450	1,390,606	437,750	3,172,806
No. of Cand.	*280*	*259*	*140*	*679*
House	1,125,450	1,174,106	354,750	2,654,306
Senate	219,000	216,500	83,000	518,500
Incumbents	995,250	721,756	396,568	2,113,574
Challengers	201,450	448,850	36,500	686,800
Open Seat	219,000	287,000	32,000	538,000
Winners	813,250	948,500	n/a	1,761,750
Losers	609,950	516,106	n/a	1,126,056

Southern California District Council of Carpenters Carpenters Legislative Improvement Committee (C00285593) *Phone: (213) 385-1457 * Fax: (213) 385-3759 * 520 S. Virgil Ave., Suite 300, Los Angeles, CA 90020 * Treasurer: James Bernsen * Contact: Mike McCarron, President*

	1993-94	1995-96	1997	Totals
Receipts	$337,639	$336,457	$176,003	$850,099
Disburse	141,897	339,690	16,651	498,238
Cash	195,745	192,519	351,875	n/a
Contributions	14,500	56,910	0	71,410
Republicans	0	0	0	0
No. of Cand.	*0*	*0*	*0*	*0*
House	0	0	0	0
Senate	0	0	0	0
Democrats	14,500	56,910	0	71,410
No. of Cand.	*9*	*13*	*0*	*22*
House	14,500	33,000	0	47,500
Senate	0	23,910	0	23,910
Incumbents	14,500	13,000	0	27,500
Challengers	0	25,000	0	25,000
Open Seat	0	18,910	0	18,910
Winners	7,000	26,910	n/a	33,910
Losers	7,500	30,000	n/a	37,500

Connecticut Carpenters Legislative Improvement Committee (C00150045) *Phone: (203) 846-2003 * Fax: (203) 846-2027 * P.O. Box 562, Norwalk, CT 06852 * Treasurer: James Gleason*

	1993-94	1995-96	1997	Totals
Receipts	$24,109	$44,633	$12,027	$80,769
Disburse	27,516	39,089	5,410	72,015
Cash	316	5,862	12,481	n/a
Contributions	18,500	29,000	5,000	52,500
Republicans	0	0	0	0
No. of Cand.	*0*	*0*	*0*	*0*
House	0	0	0	0
Senate	0	0	0	0
Democrats	18,500	29,000	5,000	52,500
No. of Cand.	*3*	*7*	*2*	*12*
House	18,500	25,000	5,000	48,500
Senate	0	4,000	0	4,000
Incumbents	3,500	8,500	2,500	14,500
Challengers	15,000	20,500	2,500	38,000
Open Seat	0	0	0	0
Winners	3,500	18,500	n/a	22,000
Losers	15,000	10,500	n/a	25,500

Nassau County District Council of Carpenters and Joiners of America AFL-CIO PAF-FED (C00208819) *Phone: (416) 454-9525 * Fax: (416) 454-9558 * 91 Carolyn Blvd., Farmingdale, NY 11735 * Web: www.licarpenters.org * Treasurer: John J. Fuchs*

	1993-94	1995-96	1997	Totals
Receipts	$1,010	$12,592	$4,682	$18,284
Disburse	7,958	19,314	1,774	29,046
Cash	16,549	9,832	12,742	n/a
Contributions	1,750	13,500	1,000	16,250
Republicans	0	4,800	1,000	5,800
No. of Cand.	*0*	*1*	*1*	*2*

House	0	4,800	1,000	5,800
Senate	0	0	0	0
Democrats	1,750	8,700	0	10,450
No. of Cand.	*3*	*3*	*0*	*6*
House	1,750	8,700	0	10,450
Senate	0	0	0	0
Incumbents	1,000	5,800	1,000	7,800
Challengers	750	7,700	0	8,450
Open Seat	0	0	0	0
Winners	1,000	11,100	n/a	12,100
Losers	750	2,400	n/a	3,150

Contributed less than $5,000 during 1995-96 cycle:

Carpenters Federal Political Action Committee of Philadelphia and Vicinity (C00260893) *Phone: (215) 569-1634 * 1803 Spring Garden St., Philadelphia, PA 19130 * Treasurer: Edward Coryell*

South Jersey Carpenters Nonpartisan Political Education Committee (C00108027) *Phone: (609) 456-4816 * 430 S. Broadway, Gloucester City, NJ 08030 * Treasurer: John S. Robinson*

Southern California District Council of Carpenters, Carpenters Committee on Political Action (C00007328) *Phone: (213) 385-3510 * 520 S. Virgil Ave., Suite 300, Los Angeles, CA 90020 * Treasurer: Robert Milewsky*

Terminated PACs which contributed less than $5,000 during 1995-96 cycle:

Westchester District Council of Carpenters Political Action Committee (C00159350) *Road 8, Box 326, Middletown, NY 10940 * Treasurer: Salvatore Pelliccio*

International Union of Operating Engineers (IUOE)

*Phone: (202) 429-9100 * Fax: (202) 778-2680*
1125 17th St. N.W., Washington, DC 20036
Web: www.iuoe.org

The International Union of Operating Engineers represents heavy equipment operators, mechanics and surveyors in the construction industry, and stationary engineers, who operate refrigeration and heating systems and generators. It has 400,000 members in about 200 local unions throughout the United States and Canada. The IUOE is the 12th largest union in the AFL-CIO.

The union opposes the reclassification of workers as independent contractors. It continues to oppose "fast-track" trade authority and efforts to alter the Davis-Bacon Act, which preserves a "prevailing wage" for union workers on federal projects.

The IUOE ranked sixth among building trade unions in contributions to congressional candidates during the 1995-96 election cycle. It raised the total amount spent on congressional races by more than 19 percent from the 1993-94 election period. The overwhelming majority of contributions went to Democratic candidates.

The leading recipients were 1996 House candidate Emily Firebaugh of Missouri, Rep. Mike Doyle, D-Pa., Rep. Ron Klink, D-Pa., Rep. Frank Mascara, D-Pa., Sen. Tom Harkin, D-Iowa, and Sen. Mary Landrieu, D-La. Rep. Jerry Weller, R-Ill., was the top Republican recipient.

Engineers Political Education Committee (EPEC)/International Union of Operating Engineers (C00029504) *Address: same as sponsor * Treasurer: Michael J. Murphy * Contact: Tim James, Dir. of Politics and Legislation*

	1993-94	*1995-96*	*1997*	*Totals*
Receipts	$814,371	$1,139,936	$568,278	$2,522,585
Disburse	614,020	1,420,967	374,286	2,409,273
Cash	883,145	602,116	796,106	n/a
Contributions	422,139	506,450	217,550	1,146,139
Republicans	25,864	27,750	51,750	105,364
No. of Cand.	*45*	*19*	*31*	*95*
House	22,864	25,750	48,750	97,364
Senate	3,000	2,000	3,000	8,000
Democrats	386,775	476,200	161,300	1,024,275
No. of Cand.	*271*	*232*	*159*	*662*
House	300,775	396,200	140,800	837,775
Senate	86,000	80,000	20,500	186,500
Incumbents	298,839	219,100	203,550	721,489
Challengers	53,750	170,100	500	224,350
Open Seat	66,550	119,250	8,000	193,800
Winners	245,089	307,350	n/a	552,439
Losers	177,050	199,100	n/a	376,150

Hoisting & Portable Engineers Local Union 101 Political Fund (C00114850) *Phone: (816) 361-0880 * Fax: (816) 361-1698 * 6301 Rockhill Rd., Suite 101, Kansas City, MO 64131 * Treasurer: Raymond Moore*

	1993-94	*1995-96*	*1997*	*Totals*
Receipts	$57,823	$108,529	$94,930	$261,282
Disburse	37,673	105,522	47,630	190,825
Cash	24,396	27,408	72,860	n/a
Contributions	7,400	51,500	0	58,900
Republicans	0	0	0	0
No. of Cand.	*0*	*0*	*0*	*0*
House	0	0	0	0
Senate	0	0	0	0
Democrats	7,400	51,500	0	58,900
No. of Cand.	*7*	*8*	*0*	*15*
House	5,400	38,500	0	43,900
Senate	2,000	13,000	0	15,000
Incumbents	1,650	11,000	0	12,650
Challengers	1,500	13,000	0	14,500
Open Seat	4,250	27,500	0	31,750
Winners	2,500	11,000	n/a	13,500
Losers	4,900	40,500	n/a	45,400

International Union of Operating Engineers Local 68 Political Action Committee (C00138966) *Phone: (973) 244-5800 * Fax: (973) 575-2512 * 11 Fairfield Pl., West Caldwell, NJ 07006 * Web: www.iuoe-68.org * E-mail: webinfo@iuoe-68.org * Treasurer: Vincent J. Giblin*

	1993-94	*1995-96*	*1997*	*Totals*
Receipts	$75,126	$72,030	$38,954	$186,110
Disburse	105,706	91,679	37,317	234,702
Cash	27,388	7,738	9,375	n/a
Contributions	27,625	49,150	6,130	82,905
Republicans	0	0	0	0
No. of Cand.	*0*	*0*	*0*	*0*
House	0	0	0	0
Senate	0	0	0	0
Democrats	27,625	49,150	6,130	82,905
No. of Cand.	*7*	*15*	*5*	*27*
House	25,125	41,650	4,130	70,905
Senate	2,500	7,500	2,000	12,000
Incumbents	26,625	23,600	6,130	56,355
Challengers	1,000	15,550	0	16,550
Open Seat	0	10,000	0	10,000
Winners	17,625	35,750	n/a	53,375
Losers	10,000	13,400	n/a	23,400

Operating Engineers Local 324 National Political Activities Committee (C00093989) *Phone: (313) 462-3660 * Fax: (313) 462-4830 * 37450 Schoolcraft Rd., Suite 110, Livonia, MI 48150 * Treasurer: John Hamilton*

	1993-94	*1995-96*	*1997*	*Totals*
Receipts	$260,402	$272,909	$158,520	$691,831
Disburse	313,604	237,800	107,578	658,982
Cash	30,552	65,659	116,600	n/a
Contributions	26,420	37,050	7,850	71,320
Republicans	0	0	0	0
No. of Cand.	*0*	*0*	*0*	*0*
House	0	0	0	0
Senate	0	0	0	0
Democrats	26,420	37,050	7,850	71,320
No. of Cand.	*14*	*8*	*5*	*27*
House	16,920	28,150	7,850	52,920
Senate	9,500	8,900	0	18,400
Incumbents	14,720	31,550	7,850	54,120
Challengers	0	5,500	0	5,500
Open Seat	11,700	0	0	11,700
Winners	13,820	37,550	n/a	51,370
Losers	12,600	-500	n/a	12,100

International Union of Operating Engineers Local 150 Political Action Committee (C00142851) *Phone: (708) 482-8800 * Fax: (708) 482-7186 * 6200 Joliet Rd., Countryside, IL 60525 * Treasurer: Jim Sullivan*

	1993-94	*1995-96*	*1997*	*Totals*
Receipts	$23,876	$29,648	$14,829	$68,353
Disburse	26,060	33,838	4,694	64,592
Cash	7,078	2,885	13,020	n/a
Contributions	22,670	27,110	2,650	52,430
Republicans	12,250	14,500	1,000	27,750
No. of Cand.	*5*	*4*	*1*	*10*
House	10,750	5,500	1,000	17,250
Senate	1,500	9,000	0	10,500
Democrats	10,420	12,610	1,650	24,680
No. of Cand.	*6*	*9*	*4*	*19*
House	10,420	12,610	1,650	24,680
Senate	0	0	0	0
Incumbents	5,170	6,020	850	12,040
Challengers	0	1,090	0	1,090

(Data for International Union continued)

Open Seat	17,500	16,500	500	34,500
Winners	10,170	7,020	n/a	17,190
Losers	12,500	20,090	n/a	32,590

International Union of Operating Engineers Local 825 Political Action and Education Committee (C00017194) *Phone: (973) 785-0500 * Fax: (973) 785-3061 * 535 U.S. Route 46 E., Little Falls, NJ 07424 * Treasurer: Joseph Whittles*

	1993-94	*1995-96*	*1997*	*Totals*
Receipts	$65,889	$139,455	$21,982	$227,326
Disburse	64,705	81,422	30,721	176,848
Cash	55,689	112,723	103,984	n/a
Contributions	18,755	25,020	8,050	51,825
Republicans	9,075	7,500	4,700	21,275
No. of Cand.	*6*	*4*	*4*	*14*
House	9,075	7,500	4,700	21,275
Senate	0	0	0	0
Democrats	9,680	17,520	3,350	30,550
No. of Cand.	*7*	*8*	*2*	*17*
House	9,680	15,020	350	25,050
Senate	0	2,500	3,000	5,500
Incumbents	14,775	18,020	6,550	39,345
Challengers	1,000	0	0	1,000
Open Seat	2,980	7,000	0	9,980
Winners	10,350	23,020	n/a	33,370
Losers	8,405	2,000	n/a	10,405

International Union of Operating Engineers Voluntary Political Action Fund - Local 832 (C00111674) *Phone: (716) 272-9890 * Fax: (716) 272-7785 * P.O. Box 93310, Town Line Rd., Rochester, NY 14692 * Treasurer: William Murphy*

	1993-94	*1995-96*	*1997*	*Totals*
Receipts	$19,603	$18,484	$952	$39,039
Disburse	13,005	28,000	300	41,305
Cash	17,572	8,059	8,713	n/a
Contributions	13,000	25,000	0	38,000
Republicans	0	0	0	0
No. of Cand.	*0*	*0*	*0*	*0*
House	0	0	0	0
Senate	0	0	0	0
Democrats	13,000	25,000	0	38,000
No. of Cand.	*3*	*7*	*0*	*10*
House	11,000	17,000	0	28,000
Senate	2,000	8,000	0	10,000
Incumbents	13,000	13,000	0	26,000
Challengers	0	6,000	0	6,000
Open Seat	0	6,000	0	6,000
Winners	13,000	15,000	n/a	28,000
Losers	0	10,000	n/a	10,000

Operating Engineers Local 12 Voluntary Legislative Fund (C00219568) *Phone: (626) 792-8900 * Fax: (626) 792-9039 * 150 E. Corson St., Pasadena, CA 91103 * Treasurer: Steve Billy*

	1993-94	*1995-96*	*1997*	*Totals*
Receipts	$56,749	$64,124	$49,700	$170,573
Disburse	58,072	51,876	50,990	160,938
Cash	17,767	30,020	30,261	n/a
Contributions	29,000	20,250	30,250	79,500
Republicans	0	0	0	0
No. of Cand.	*0*	*0*	*0*	*0*
House	0	0	0	0
Senate	0	0	0	0
Democrats	29,000	20,250	30,250	79,500
No. of Cand.	*12*	*12*	*10*	*34*
House	17,000	20,250	18,250	55,500
Senate	12,000	0	12,000	24,000
Incumbents	24,000	15,250	28,250	67,500
Challengers	3,000	3,000	1,000	7,000
Open Seat	2,000	1,000	1,000	4,000
Winners	23,000	16,750	n/a	39,750
Losers	6,000	3,500	n/a	9,500

Supporters of Engineers Local 3 Endorsed Candidates (SELEC) (C00024422) *Phone: (510) 748-7400 * Fax: (510) 748-7471 * 1620 S. Loop Rd., Alameda, CA 94501 * Treasurer: Garland Rosauro*

	1993-94	*1995-96*	*1997*	*Totals*
Receipts	$72,944	$71,637	$38,505	$183,086
Disburse	86,296	73,509	34,385	194,190
Cash	11,198	9,023	13,142	n/a
Contributions	28,845	20,812	5,150	54,807
Republicans	0	0	0	0
No. of Cand.	*0*	*0*	*0*	*0*
House	0	0	0	0
Senate	0	0	0	0
Democrats	28,845	20,812	5,150	54,807
No. of Cand.	*21*	*14*	*5*	*40*
House	23,245	21,812	3,150	48,207
Senate	5,600	-1000	2,000	6,600
Incumbents	19,575	14,765	4,000	38,340
Challengers	9,270	4,772	0	14,042
Open Seat	0	1,250	1,150	2,400
Winners	13,825	12,585	n/a	26,410
Losers	15,020	8,227	n/a	23,247

Operating Engineers Local 649 Political Action Committee (C00225573) *Phone: (309) 697-0070 * Fax: (309) 697-0025 * 6408 W. Plank Rd., Peoria, IL 61604 * Treasurer: G. Kent Bobell*

	1993-94	*1995-96*	*1997*	*Totals*
Receipts	$60,537	$63,434	$30,798	$154,769
Disburse	63,854	56,364	23,468	143,686
Cash	100	7,174	14,505	n/a
Contributions	12,000	18,600	5,500	36,100
Republicans	0	0	0	0
No. of Cand.	*0*	*0*	*0*	*0*
House	0	0	0	0
Senate	0	0	0	0
Democrats	12,000	18,600	5,500	36,100
No. of Cand.	*3*	*4*	*2*	*9*
House	12,000	14,600	4,500	31,100
Senate	0	4,000	1,000	5,000
Incumbents	2,000	8,500	5,500	16,000
Challengers	0	6,100	0	6,100
Open Seat	10,000	4,000	0	14,000
Winners	2,000	12,500	n/a	14,500
Losers	10,000	6,100	n/a	16,100

International Union of Operating Engineers Locals 545, 545C and 545D Voluntary PAC (C00111591) *Phone: (315) 492-1752 * Fax: (315) 469-7870 * 4325 S. Salina St., Syracuse, NY 13205 * Treasurer: Jack M. Webb*

	1993-94	*1995-96*	*1997*	*Totals*
Receipts	$99,028	$57,473	$29,442	$185,943
Disburse	82,212	73,949	21,106	177,267
Cash	18,054	1,580	9,918	n/a
Contributions	2,000	17,000	0	19,000
Republicans	0	0	0	0
No. of Cand.	*0*	*0*	*0*	*0*
House	0	0	0	0
Senate	0	0	0	0
Democrats	2,000	17,000	0	19,000
No. of Cand.	*2*	*3*	*0*	*5*
House	2,000	17,000	0	19,000
Senate	0	0	0	0
Incumbents	2,000	7,000	0	9,000
Challengers	0	10,000	0	10,000
Open Seat	0	0	0	0
Winners	2,000	7,000	n/a	9,000
Losers	0	10,000	n/a	10,000

Local 138, 138A and 138B International Union of Operating Engineers Political Action Fund Federal (C00247197) *Phone: (516) 694-2480 * Fax: (516) 694-6932 * P.O. Box 206, Gazza Blvd., Farmingdale, NY 11735 * Treasurer: James J. Duffy Jr.*

	1993-94	*1995-96*	*1997*	*Totals*
Receipts	$15,000	$15,500	$5,000	$35,500
Disburse	13,300	15,150	5,286	33,736
Cash	3,800	4,150	3,863	n/a
Contributions	13,300	12,400	4,750	30,450
Republicans	4,100	10,800	3,250	18,150
No. of Cand.	*4*	*6*	*2*	*12*
House	1,100	6,800	3,250	11,150
Senate	3,000	4,000	0	7,000
Democrats	9,200	1,600	1,500	12,300
No. of Cand.	*6*	*3*	*2*	*11*
House	9,200	1,600	1,500	12,300
Senate	0	0	0	0
Incumbents	8,600	11,600	4,750	24,950
Challengers	4,200	300	0	4,500
Open Seat	500	0	0	500
Winners	5,600	10,100	n/a	15,700
Losers	7,700	2,300	n/a	10,000

International Union of Operating Engineers Local 17 Political Action Committee (C00104455) *Phone: (716) 675-4544 * Fax: (716) 675-0801 * 150 N. America Dr., West Seneca, NY 14224 * Treasurer: Mark N. Kirsch*

	1993-94	*1995-96*	*1997*	*Totals*
Receipts	$50,754	$41,671	$17,923	$110,348
Disburse	65,513	21,016	277	86,806
Cash	9,272	29,927	47,573	n/a
Contributions	2,225	12,200	0	14,425
Republicans	0	0	0	0
No. of Cand.	*0*	*0*	*0*	*0*

House	0	0	0	0
Senate	0	0	0	0
Democrats	2,225	12,200	0	14,425
No. of Cand.	*4*	*3*	*0*	*7*
House	2,225	12,200	0	14,425
Senate	0	0	0	0
Incumbents	1,000	2,000	0	3,000
Challengers	225	10,200	0	10,425
Open Seat	0	0	0	0
Winners	1,000	2,000	n/a	3,000
Losers	1,225	10,200	n/a	11,425

International Union of Operating Engineers Local 302 Voluntary Political Fund (C00008409) *Phone: (425) 806-0302 * Fax: (425) 806-0300 * 18701 120th Ave. N.E., Bothell, WA 98011 * Treasurer: Jack Jakubiec*

	1993-94	*1995-96*	*1997*	*Totals*
Receipts	$30,368	$26,260	$14,212	$70,840
Disburse	33,131	25,698	4,461	63,290
Cash	4,818	5,388	15,144	n/a
Contributions	9,950	12,750	600	23,300
Republicans	3,000	4,000	0	7,000
No. of Cand.	*2*	*2*	*0*	*4*
House	2,000	2,000	0	4,000
Senate	1,000	2,000	0	3,000
Democrats	6,950	8,750	600	16,300
No. of Cand.	*10*	*3*	*2*	*15*
House	4,950	8,750	250	13,950
Senate	2,000	0	350	2,350
Incumbents	7,500	4,000	350	11,850
Challengers	1,500	8,750	0	10,250
Open Seat	950	0	250	1,200
Winners	4,450	7,250	n/a	11,700
Losers	5,500	5,500	n/a	11,000

IUOE Local 542 Operating Engineers Political Action Fund (C00136739) *Phone: (610) 825-6595 * Fax: (610) 825-6378 * 3031 Walton Rd., First Floor, Norristown, PA 19403 * Treasurer: Robert T. Heenan*

	1993-94	*1995-96*	*1997*	*Totals*
Receipts	$90,174	$92,242	$46,079	$228,495
Disburse	101,156	90,497	38,864	230,517
Cash	3,530	5,276	12,491	n/a
Contributions	14,160	10,700	150	25,010
Republicans	0	0	0	0
No. of Cand.	*0*	*0*	*0*	*0*
House	0	0	0	0
Senate	0	0	0	0
Democrats	14,160	10,700	150	25,010
No. of Cand.	*8*	*6*	*1*	*15*
House	12,160	10,700	150	23,010
Senate	2,000	0	0	2,000
Incumbents	12,160	7,200	150	19,510
Challengers	2,000	3,500	0	5,500
Open Seat	0	0	0	0
Winners	10,910	7,200	n/a	18,110
Losers	3,250	3,500	n/a	6,750

International Union of Operating Engineers Local 15 Political Action Committee (C00163956) *Phone: (212) 929-5327 * Fax: (212) 206-0357 * 265 W. 14th St., New York, NY 10011 * Treasurer: Robert Shaw * Contact: Thomas P. Maguire, President*

	1993-94	*1995-96*	*1997*	*Totals*
Receipts	$37,595	$28,039	$54,879	$120,513
Disburse	42,949	36,756	34,191	113,896
Cash	38,485	29,773	50,461	n/a
Contributions	9,500	9,600	7,700	26,800
Republicans	1,000	4,100	4,400	9,500
No. of Cand.	*1*	*2*	*4*	*7*
House	0	500	3,750	4,250
Senate	1,000	3,600	650	5,250
Democrats	8,500	5,500	3,300	17,300
No. of Cand.	*8*	*7*	*7*	*22*
House	7,500	5,500	3,300	16,300
Senate	1,000	0	0	1,000
Incumbents	9,500	6,350	5,700	21,550
Challengers	0	3,000	0	3,000
Open Seat	0	0	2,000	2,000
Winners	9,500	6,850	n/a	16,350
Losers	0	2,750	n/a	2,750

Local 106 Voluntary Political Action Fund (C00112995) *Phone: (518) 453-6518 * Fax: (518) 453-6549 * 1284 Central Ave., Albany, NY 12205 * Treasurer: Daniel J. McGraw II*

	1993-94	*1995-96*	*1997*	*Totals*
Receipts	$61,117	$47,886	$21,247	$130,250
Disburse	81,685	59,940	19,815	161,440
Cash	35,154	23,102	24,534	n/a
Contributions	3,115	5,610	1,000	9,725
Republicans	2,240	500	0	2,740
No. of Cand.	*2*	*1*	*0*	*3*
House	1,990	500	0	2,490
Senate	250	0	0	250
Democrats	875	5,110	1,000	6,985
No. of Cand.	*2*	*1*	*1*	*4*
House	875	5,110	1,000	6,985
Senate	0	0	0	0
Incumbents	3,115	5,610	1,000	9,725
Challengers	0	0	0	0
Open Seat	0	0	0	0
Winners	3,115	5,610	n/a	8,725
Losers	0	0	n/a	0

International Union of Operating Engineers Local 103 Voluntary Political Education Fund (C00162545) *Phone: (317) 849-0163 * Fax: (317) 849-3590 * 9501 Corporation Dr., Indianapolis, IN 46256 * Treasurer: Keith Frey * Contact: Ken Johnson, Manager*

	1993-94	*1995-96*	*1997*	*Totals*
Receipts	$31,649	$34,323	$19,674	$85,646
Disburse	28,443	40,146	7,920	76,509
Cash	9,277	3,455	13,960	n/a
Contributions	16,010	5,000	2,000	23,010
Republicans	0	0	0	0
No. of Cand.	*0*	*0*	*0*	*0*
House	0	0	0	0
Senate	0	0	0	0
Democrats	16,010	5,000	2,000	23,010
No. of Cand.	*6*	*3*	*2*	*11*
House	14,510	3,000	2,000	19,510
Senate	1,500	2,000	0	3,500
Incumbents	1,150	0	1,000	2,150
Challengers	6,860	4,000	0	10,860
Open Seat	8,000	1,000	1,000	10,000
Winners	0	1,000	n/a	1,000
Losers	16,010	4,000	n/a	20,010

International Union of Operating Engineers Local 137 PAC (C00114371) *Phone: (914) 762-0600 * Fax: (914) 762-0524 * 1360 Pleasantville Rd., Briarcliff Manor, NY 10510 * Treasurer: Salvatore Santamorena*

	1993-94	*1995-96*	*1997*	*Totals*
Receipts	$87,306	$81,124	$44,269	$212,699
Disburse	92,200	84,621	54,125	230,946
Cash	19,434	15,939	6,084	n/a
Contributions	1,200	4,620	2,125	7,945
Republicans	450	3,070	2,000	5,520
No. of Cand.	*2*	*3*	*1*	*6*
House	450	2,070	2,000	4,520
Senate	0	1,000	0	1,000
Democrats	750	1,550	125	2,425
No. of Cand.	*3*	*2*	*1*	*6*
House	750	1,550	125	2,425
Senate	0	0	0	0
Incumbents	500	4,620	2,125	7,245
Challengers	0	0	0	0
Open Seat	700	0	0	700
Winners	750	4,620	n/a	5,370
Losers	450	0	n/a	450

International Union of Operating Engineers Local 14-14B Voluntary Political Action Committee (C00134726) *Phone: (718) 939-0600 * Fax: (718) 939-3131 * 141-57 Northern Blvd., Flushing, NY 11354 * E-mail: L14fund@aol.com * Treasurer: Joseph M. Rizzuto * Contact: Joyce Cassano, Fund Manager*

	1993-94	*1995-96*	*1997*	*Totals*
Receipts	$123,065	$144,752	$62,644	$330,461
Disburse	61,828	146,802	61,097	269,727
Cash	99,815	97,767	99,315	n/a
Contributions	750	2,700	500	3,950
Republicans	0	1,000	0	1,000
No. of Cand.	*0*	*1*	*0*	*1*
House	0	0	0	0
Senate	0	1,000	0	1,000
Democrats	750	1,700	500	2,950
No. of Cand.	*3*	*4*	*1*	*8*
House	750	1,700	500	2,950
Senate	0	0	0	0
Incumbents	750	1,700	0	2,450
Challengers	0	1,000	0	1,000
Open Seat	0	0	500	500
Winners	750	1,700	n/a	2,450
Losers	0	1,000	n/a	1,000

Contributed less than $5,000 during 1995-96 cycle:

IUOE Local 4 Social Action Committee-federal (C00115568) *Phone: (617) 323-9300 * Fax: (617) 323-7821 * 120 Mt. Hope St., Roslindale, MA 02131 * Treasurer: Paul J. Hayes*

IUOE Local 463 Federal PAC (C00121673) *Phone: (716) 434-3327 * Fax: (716) 434-2160 * 3365 Ridge Rd., Ransomville, NY 14131 * Treasurer: Paul McCollum*

International Union of Operating Engineers Local 37 Political Action Committee (C00239434) *Phone: (410) 254-2030 * Fax: (410) 319-9197 * 5901 Harford Rd., Suite A, Baltimore, MD 21214 * Treasurer: Joseph Anthony DeJuliis*

International Union of Operating Engineers Local 487 PAC (C00133611) *Phone: (305) 634-3419 * Fax: (305) 633-0698 * 1425 N.W. 36th St., Miami, FL 33142 * Treasurer: Scott Singer*

Operating Engineers Local 98 Social Action Fund (C00142083) *Phone: (413) 525-4291 * Fax: (413) 525-7553 * Two Center Sq., P.O. Box 217, East Longmeadow, MA 01028 * Treasurer: Thomas Young*

Political Education Patterns, Political Arm International Union Operating Engineers Local 18 (C00065870) *Phone: (216) 432-3138 * Fax: (216) 432-0370 * 3515 Prospect Ave., Cleveland, OH 44115 * Treasurer: James H. Gardner*

Ironworkers Union

*Phone: (202) 383-4880 * Fax: (202) 347-3569*
1750 New York Ave. N.W., Suite 400, Washington, DC 20006
Web: www.diro.com/iabsoiw.htm

The International Association of Bridge, Structural, Ornamental and Reinforcing Ironworkers represents about 82,000 workers nationwide. Its members construct highways, bridges, large buildings and power transmission stations. Most work in metropolitan areas.

The ironworkers union opposes changing Occupational Safety and Health Administration regulations to allow third parties to certify workplaces as safe. It seeks to preserve the Davis-Bacon Act, which provides a minimum pay rate for federal construction jobs, and supports raising the threshold where Davis-Bacon applies and eliminating several paperwork requirements. The union opposes reductions in Medicare benefits for its retired members.

The ironworkers union ranked fifth among construction unions in contributions to 1996 congressional candidates. It spent nearly a third of its contributions on challengers. Democrats received nearly 95 percent of the union's contributions. The top recipient was Rep. Joseph P. Kennedy II, D-Mass.; eight other candidates received $10,000. Rep. Frank A. LoBiondo, R-N.J., was the leading Republican recipient.

Ironworkers Political Action League (C00027359) *Address: same as sponsor * Treasurer: James E. Cole * Contact: Frank Voyack*

	1993-94	1995-96	1997	Totals
Receipts	$1,102,275	$1,445,200	$750,980	$3,298,455
Disburse	1,078,496	1,458,226	481,603	3,018,325
Cash	100,918	87,896	357,075	n/a
Contributions	526,126	828,615	341,450	1,696,191
Republicans	33,200	42,070	27,000	102,270
No. of Cand.	*14*	*23*	*19*	*56*
House	31,200	39,070	22,000	92,270
Senate	2,000	3,000	5,000	10,000
Democrats	479,426	783,045	308,950	1,571,421
No. of Cand.	*221*	*259*	*141*	*621*
House	416,926	649,495	233,950	1,300,371
Senate	62,500	133,550	75,000	271,050
Incumbents	374,330	399,315	292,450	1,066,095
Challengers	66,100	267,950	17,000	351,050
Open Seat	85,696	161,350	22,000	269,046
Winners	294,880	530,315	n/a	825,195
Losers	231,246	298,300	n/a	529,546

International Association of Bridge Structural & Ornamental Iron Workers Local 67 PAC (C00156554) *Phone: (515) 262-9366 * Fax: (515) 262-2197 * 1501 E. Aurora, Des Moines, IA 50313 * Treasurer: Michael Alitz*

	1993-94	1995-96	1997	Totals
Receipts	$14,102	$19,293	$6,719	$40,114
Disburse	7,623	17,350	2,875	27,848
Cash	17,957	19,902	23,747	n/a
Contributions	450	11,500	1,750	13,700
Republicans	0	0	0	0
No. of Cand.	*0*	*0*	*0*	*0*
House	0	0	0	0
Senate	0	0	0	0
Democrats	450	11,500	1,750	13,700
No. of Cand.	*2*	*4*	*1*	*7*
House	300	8,000	1,750	10,050
Senate	150	3,500	0	3,650
Incumbents	150	3,500	1,750	5,400
Challengers	300	5,500	0	5,800
Open Seat	0	2,500	0	2,500
Winners	150	6,000	n/a	6,150
Losers	300	5,500	n/a	5,800

Local 401 Iron Workers Political Action Fund (C00163535) *Phone: (215) 676-3000 * 11600 Norcom Rd., Philadelphia, PA 19154 * Treasurer: Joseph J. Dougherty*

	1993-94	1995-96	1997	Totals
Receipts	$1,978	$54,904	$38,120	$95,002
Disburse	25,110	50,490	22,517	98,117
Cash	13,890	18,311	33,917	n/a
Contributions	7,350	7,000	1,000	15,350
Republicans	500	0	0	500
No. of Cand.	*1*	*0*	*0*	*1*
House	500	0	0	500
Senate	0	0	0	0
Democrats	6,850	7,000	1,000	14,850
No. of Cand.	*5*	*6*	*1*	*12*
House	4,350	7,000	1,000	12,350
Senate	2,500	0	0	2,500
Incumbents	4,350	4,000	1,000	9,350
Challengers	500	2,750	0	3,250
Open Seat	0	0	0	0
Winners	4,000	4,000	n/a	8,000
Losers	3,350	3,000	n/a	6,350

Contributed less than $5,000 during 1995-96 cycle:

Iron Workers Local 167 Political Action League (C00272468) *Phone: (901) 367-1676 * Fax: (901) 367-9696 * 2574 Lindawood Cove, Memphis, TN 38118 * Treasurer: Edward G. Panis*

Laborers' International Union of North America (LIUNA)

*Phone: (202) 737-8320 * Fax: (202) 737-2754*
905 16th St. N.W., Washington, DC 20006
Web: www.liuna.org

The Laborers' International Union of North America comprises nearly 750,000 members nationwide. Its members work in construction, government, health care, custodial services, shipbuilding and hazardous waste handling. The union is affiliated with the AFL-CIO and has about 650 locals.

The Department of Justice reached an agreement with the union in February 1995 to remove corruption from the organization. The union's President Arthur Coia has been investigated for ties to organized crime, but has not been convicted of any wrongdoing.

LIUNA supports greater federal funding for new and current transportation projects that would benefit union members. It opposes a proposal that would enable employers to reclassify workers as independent contractors and another that would have removed "prevailing wage" rates on Washington school construction projects. LIUNA advocates the preservation of the Davis-Bacon Act, which protects unionized contractors on federal projects from low-wage outside competition.

LIUNA was the leading congressional contributor among construction unions during the 1995-96 election cycle. Two of its western regional affiliates were among the top 11. LIUNA was one of 19 PACs that gave more than $1 million to Democratic candidates, and it gave a greater percentage to incumbent candidates than either of the next two largest construction unions. Of the 351 candidates who received a contribution from LIUNA, 208 received $5,000 or more during the full cycle.

Coia, union president since 1993, gave $50,000 to the Democratic National Committee in 1994 and the union was one of the top three contributors to President Clinton's 1996 inauguration.

Laborers' Political League (C00007922) *Address: same as sponsor * Treasurer: R. P. Vinall * Contact: Don Kaniewski, PAC Dir.*

	1993-94	1995-96	1997	Totals
Receipts	$1,411,267	$2,448,991	$846,318	$4,706,576
Disburse	1,451,138	2,392,101	631,079	4,474,318
Cash	170,979	227,879	444,621	n/a
Contributions	1,201,367	1,917,800	524,250	3,643,417
Republicans	60,750	166,000	57,500	284,250
No. of Cand.	*25*	*41*	*31*	*97*
House	56,250	150,000	48,000	254,250
Senate	4,500	16,000	9,500	30,000
Democrats	1,114,617	1,743,800	458,750	3,317,167
No. of Cand.	*300*	*310*	*176*	*786*
House	921,117	1,485,300	380,250	2,786,667
Senate	193,500	258,500	78,500	530,500
Incumbents	848,167	1,154,800	482,750	2,485,717
Challengers	162,200	425,250	1,500	588,950
Open Seat	188,500	328,250	37,000	553,750
Winners	710,600	1,370,800	n/a	2,081,400
Losers	490,767	547,000	n/a	1,037,767

Laborers International Union of North America Western Political League (C00169201) *Phone: (916) 446-3622 * Fax: (916) 446-6655 * 620 Sunbeam Ave., Sacramento, CA 95814 * Treasurer: Ken Casarez * Contact: Mason Warren, V.P.*

	1993-94	1995-96	1997	Totals
Receipts	$238,857	$191,898	$94,844	$525,599
Disburse	246,327	186,060	62,426	494,813
Cash	4,726	10,567	44,897	n/a
Contributions	194,000	136,500	46,000	376,500
Republicans	0	0	0	0
No. of Cand.	*0*	*0*	*0*	*0*
House	0	0	0	0
Senate	0	0	0	0
Democrats	194,000	136,500	46,000	376,500
No. of Cand.	*49*	*38*	*31*	*118*
House	164,000	136,500	46,000	346,500
Senate	30,000	0	0	30,000
Incumbents	153,500	91,500	39,000	284,000
Challengers	28,500	28,000	0	56,500
Open Seat	12,000	17,000	7,000	36,000
Winners	131,500	109,500	n/a	241,000
Losers	62,500	27,000	n/a	89,500

Laborers' International Union of North America PAC (Laborers Political League - Seattle Account) (C00270413) *Address: Same as sponsor * Treasurer: R. P. Vinall*

	1993-94	1995-96	1997	Totals
Receipts	$49,388	$54,121	$43,433	$146,942
Disburse	43,008	63,291	27,466	133,765
Cash	16,342	7,178	23,150	n/a
Contributions	42,000	64,250	24,250	130,500
Republicans	0	1,000	5,000	6,000
No. of Cand.	*0*	*1*	*2*	*3*
House	0	1,000	5,000	6,000
Senate	0	0	0	0
Democrats	42,000	63,250	19,250	124,500
No. of Cand.	*12*	*23*	*8*	*43*
House	32,000	52,500	8,000	92,500
Senate	10,000	10,750	11,250	32,000
Incumbents	25,500	15,750	21,750	63,000
Challengers	11,000	35,500	0	46,500
Open Seat	5,500	12,500	2,500	20,500
Winners	5,000	20,250	n/a	25,250
Losers	37,000	44,000	n/a	81,000

New Jersey State Laborers' Political Action Committee/Laborers Political League (NJSLPAC) (C00214643) *Phone: (609) 860-2887 * Fax: (609) 860-2845 * 104 Interchange Plaza, Suite 301, P.O. Box 554, Cranbury, NJ 08512 * Treasurer: Frank Sorge*

	1993-94	1995-96	1997	Totals
Receipts	$1,171,852	$1,235,040	$625,031	$3,031,923
Disburse	1,208,890	1,459,125	784,703	3,452,718
Cash	672,156	448,071	288,399	n/a
Contributions	1,125	24,250	2,500	27,875
Republicans	1,125	11,500	2,000	14,625
No. of Cand.	*2*	*2*	*2*	*6*
House	125	5,500	2,000	7,625
Senate	1,000	6,000	0	7,000
Democrats	0	12,750	500	13,250
No. of Cand.	*0*	*7*	*1*	*8*
House	0	12,750	500	13,250
Senate	0	0	0	0
Incumbents	0	4,750	2,500	7,250
Challengers	1,000	3,000	0	4,000
Open Seat	0	16,500	0	16,500
Winners	0	7,750	n/a	7,750
Losers	1,125	16,500	n/a	17,625

Labor Political League of Laborers Local 113 (C00249086) *Phone: (414) 873-4520 * Fax: (414) 873-5155 * 6310 W. Appleton Ave., Milwaukee, WI 53210 * Treasurer: Alex Jordan*

	1993-94	1995-96	1997	Totals
Receipts	$22,244	$19,692	$5,710	$47,646
Disburse	23,450	20,400	500	44,350
Cash	6,629	5,963	11,174	n/a
Contributions	22,200	15,400	500	38,100
Republicans	0	0	0	0
No. of Cand.	*0*	*0*	*0*	*0*
House	0	0	0	0
Senate	0	0	0	0
Democrats	22,200	15,400	500	38,100
No. of Cand.	*7*	*7*	*1*	*15*
House	21,200	15,400	500	37,100
Senate	1,000	0	0	1,000
Incumbents	14,200	5,900	500	20,600
Challengers	8,000	5,500	0	13,500
Open Seat	0	4,000	0	4,000
Winners	8,200	6,900	n/a	15,100
Losers	14,000	8,500	n/a	22,500

Contributed less than $5,000 during 1995-96 cycle:

Laborers' District Council of the Metro Area of Philadelphia and Vicinity PAC (C00253294) *Phone: (215) 684-2090 * 665 N. Broad St., Philadelphia, PA 19123 * Treasurer: Samuel Staten Sr.*

Laborer's International Union of North America Local 17 Political League (C00233049) *Phone: (914) 565-2737 * 305A Little Britain Rd., Newburgh, NY 12550 * Treasurer: Joseph R. Libonati*

Laborers' Local 66 Political Action Committee (C00218644) *Phone: (516) 249-1110 * Box 666, 1600 Walt Whitman Rd., Melville, NY 11747 * Treasurer: Michael R. LaBarbara*

Laborers' Local 91 Political Action Fund (C00155069) *Phone: (716) 297-6441 * 2556 Seneca Ave., Niagara Falls, NY 14305 * Treasurer: Dominick J. Dellacio*

Laborers' Local 1184 Political Campaign Fund (C00164228) *Phone: (909) 684-1484 * 1128 E. Cadena Dr., Riverside, CA 92501 * Treasurer: John L. Smith*

New York State Laborers Political Action Committee (C00220566) *Phone: (212) 722-4280 * 1828 Second Ave., New York, NY 10128 * Treasurer: Samuel Fresina*

Painters & Allied Trades Union

*Phone: (202) 637-0738 * Fax: (202) 637-0771*
1750 New York Ave. N.W., Eighth Floor, Washington, DC 20006
Web: www.ibpat.org

The International Brotherhood of Painters and Allied Trades represents more than 130,000 painters, paint makers, drywall finishers, decorators, carpet and soft tile layers, sign painters, scenic artists and metal polishers. It is affiliated with the AFL-CIO.

The union lobbies on many labor issues, including the Davis-Bacon law that preserves a "prevailing wage" for workers on federal jobs. It opposes several proposals to alter Occupational Safety and Health Administration workplace safety regulations. The IBPAT seeks to defeat changes to regulations governing unions' political activity. The union supports legislation calling for mandatory safety certification for workers in its trades. Other top issues include preserving Social Security, Medicaid and Medicare.

International Brotherhood of Painters & Allied Trades Political Action Together Political Committee (C00000885) *Address: same as sponsor * Treasurer: James A. Williams * Contact: Bill Anderson, Political Action Representative*

	1993-94	1995-96	1997	Totals
Receipts	$220,825	$339,197	$445,543	$1,005,565
Disburse	185,788	584,027	146,057	915,872
Cash	121,570	(214178.00)	425,940	n/a
Contributions	72,800	185,620	65,200	323,620
Republicans	2,000	5,500	2,000	9,500
No. of Cand.	*2*	*2*	*1*	*5*
House	2,000	5,500	2,000	9,500
Senate	0	0	0	0
Democrats	68,900	180,120	63,050	312,070
No. of Cand.	*58*	*91*	*25*	*174*
House	55,900	157,820	39,300	253,020
Senate	13,000	22,300	23,750	59,050
Incumbents	42,550	68,500	49,900	160,950

(Data for International Brotherhood continued)

Challengers	10,350	87,120	5,000	102,470
Open Seat	19,400	29,500	8,300	57,200
Winners	25,900	94,820	n/a	120,720
Losers	46,900	90,800	n/a	137,700

Contributed less than $5,000 during 1995-96 cycle:

International Brotherhood of Painters & Allied Trades District Council 21 PAC (C00276253) *Phone: (215) 677-7980 * Fax: (215) 677-3877 * 2980 Southampton Rd., Philadelphia, PA 19154 * Treasurer: Joseph Ashdale*

Southern California Painters & Allied Trades District Council 36 Federal Voluntary Account (C00191916) *Phone: (626) 584-9925 * Fax: (626) 584-1949 * 297 N. Marengo Ave., Suite 120, Pasadena, CA 91101 * Treasurer: Grant Mitchell*

Plasterers' and Cement Masons' Union

*Phone: (301) 470-4200 * Fax: (301) 470-2502*
14405 Laurel Pl., Suite 300, Laurel, MD 20707

The Operative Plasterers' and Cement Masons' International Association of the United States and Canada represents about 29,000 workers in the construction industry who specialize in working with concrete and building terrazzo floors and walkways.

Plasterers' and Cement Masons' Action Committee (C00134742)
*Address: same as sponsor * Treasurer: Patrick D. Finley * Contact: John Dougherty, President*

	1993-94	1995-96	1997	Totals
Receipts	$31,026	$13,629	$5,234	$49,889
Disburse	23,182	25,211	6,808	55,201
Cash	26,874	15,292	13,717	n/a
Contributions	14,050	15,050	4,700	33,800
Republicans	1,500	0	0	1,500
No. of Cand.	*2*	*0*	*0*	*2*
House	1,500	0	0	1,500
Senate	0	0	0	0
Democrats	11,750	15,050	4,200	31,000
No. of Cand.	*15*	*27*	*9*	*51*
House	11,750	14,550	3,600	29,900
Senate	0	500	600	1,100
Incumbents	9,600	4,150	3,500	17,250
Challengers	2,350	8,400	800	11,550
Open Seat	2,100	2,500	400	5,000
Winners	5,600	8,150	n/a	13,750
Losers	8,450	6,900	n/a	15,350

Plumbers & Pipefitters Union (UA)

*Phone: (202) 628-5823 * Fax: (202) 628-5024*
901 Massachusetts Ave. N.W., Washington, DC 20001
Web: www.ua.org

The United Association of Journeymen and Apprentices of the Plumbing and Pipe Fitting Industry of the United States and Canada represents about 291,000 workers who build, install and repair pipes. UA members are involved in just about every aspect of construction involving piping from the space program to nuclear power housing to refineries to shipbuilding.

Known as the plumbers and pipe fitters union, the UA opposes new clean air standards proposed by the EPA because it says ozone level restrictions could hurt the construction industry. The union also lobbies against allowing employers to classify some workers as independent contractors. It favors publicly funded elections and a ban on "soft money" political contributions.

The UA ranked fourth in 1996 congressional contributions among building trades unions. More than 95 percent of its money went to Democratic candidates, and incumbents received more than challengers. No GOP candidates were among the top 100 recipients, and five of the top six recipients were Democratic House challengers. Rep. Martin Frost, D-Texas, was the exception in that group.

United Association Political Education Committee (C00012476)
*Address: same as sponsor * Treasurer: Martin J. Maddaloni * Contact: Luckie McClintock, Dir. of Political Affairs*

	1993-94	1995-96	1997	Totals
Receipts	$861,630	$1,384,215	$577,755	$2,823,600
Disburse	853,802	1,209,040	357,727	2,420,569
Cash	69,175	244,359	464,392	n/a
Contributions	636,350	958,000	249,000	1,843,350
Republicans	18,500	38,500	20,500	77,500
No. of Cand.	*10*	*23*	*10*	*43*
House	11,500	36,500	14,500	62,500
Senate	7,000	2,000	6,000	15,000
Democrats	603,850	916,500	225,500	1,745,850
No. of Cand.	*275*	*314*	*156*	*745*
House	509,000	765,000	190,000	1,464,000
Senate	94,850	151,500	35,500	281,850
Incumbents	483,850	482,000	225,000	1,190,850
Challengers	77,500	327,500	9,000	414,000
Open Seat	75,000	147,500	14,500	237,000
Winners	366,350	567,000	n/a	933,350
Losers	270,000	391,000	n/a	661,000

Pipefitters Local 533 Volunteer Political Fund (C00206177)
*Phone: (816) 523-1533 * Fax: (816) 523-1536 * 8600 Hillcrest Rd., Kansas City, MO 64138 * Treasurer: Francis A. Quinn*

	1993-94	1995-96	1997	Totals
Receipts	$140,197	$175,338	$87,945	$403,480
Disburse	135,929	180,691	78,777	395,397
Cash	16,293	17,223	26,391	n/a
Contributions	9,890	29,700	6,000	45,590
Republicans	0	0	0	0
No. of Cand.	*0*	*0*	*0*	*0*
House	0	0	0	0
Senate	0	0	0	0
Democrats	9,890	29,700	6,000	45,590
No. of Cand.	*8*	*9*	*3*	*20*
House	8,890	21,700	1,000	31,590
Senate	1,000	8,000	5,000	14,000
Incumbents	3,390	8,500	1,000	12,890
Challengers	1,500	2,250	5,000	8,750
Open Seat	5,000	18,950	0	23,950
Winners	4,990	8,500	n/a	13,490
Losers	4,900	21,200	n/a	26,100

Plumbers & Pipefitters Local 9 Political Action Committee (C00155440) *Phone: (908) 792-0999 * Fax: (908) 792-1999 * Two Iron Ore Rd. at Route 33, Englishtown, NJ 07726 * Treasurer: Michael F. Cantwell*

	1993-94	1995-96	1997	Totals
Receipts	$168,734	$379,816	$208,954	$757,504
Disburse	173,616	334,918	289,490	798,024
Cash	50,762	95,660	116,088	n/a
Contributions	22,819	25,200	1,000	49,019
Republicans	10,619	4,000	0	14,619
No. of Cand.	*4*	*3*	*0*	*7*
House	7,719	2,500	0	10,219
Senate	2,900	1,500	0	4,400
Democrats	12,200	21,200	1,000	34,400
No. of Cand.	*3*	*5*	*1*	*9*
House	8,200	17,850	1,000	27,050
Senate	4,000	3,350	0	7,350
Incumbents	17,024	14,650	1,000	32,674
Challengers	2,900	2,200	0	5,100
Open Seat	0	8,350	0	8,350
Winners	17,024	16,000	n/a	33,024
Losers	5,795	9,200	n/a	14,995

UA Local 85 Political Action Committee (C00281303) *Phone: (517) 799-5261 * Fax: (517) 791-3468 * P.O. Box 6547, Saginaw, MI 48608 * Treasurer: Thomas J. Boensch*

	1993-94	1995-96	1997	Totals
Receipts	$82,802	$51,746	$15,570	$150,118
Disburse	66,345	47,475	14,921	128,741
Cash	16,452	20,726	21,374	n/a
Contributions	12,850	20,600	7,450	40,900
Republicans	0	0	0	0
No. of Cand.	*0*	*0*	*0*	*0*
House	0	0	0	0
Senate	0	0	0	0
Democrats	12,850	20,600	7,450	40,900
No. of Cand.	*6*	*8*	*5*	*19*
House	11,700	19,850	7,250	38,800
Senate	1,150	750	200	2,100
Incumbents	5,150	13,200	7,450	25,800
Challengers	5,200	7,400	0	12,600
Open Seat	2,500	0	0	2,500
Winners	5,000	18,100	n/a	23,100
Losers	7,850	2,500	n/a	10,350

United Association of Journeymen & Apprentices/Plumbing & Pipe Fitting Industry Local Union 335 (C00232835) *Phone: (616) 968-0993 * Fax: (616) 968-0025 * 5906 E. Morgan Rd., Battle Creek, MI 49017 * Treasurer: Richard D. Frantz*

	1993-94	1995-96	1997	Totals
Receipts	$16,135	$21,341	$6,453	$43,929
Disburse	9,646	15,796	7,040	32,482
Cash	9,518	15,067	20,045	n/a
Contributions	8,400	14,225	7,000	29,625
Republicans	0	0	0	0
No. of Cand.	*0*	*0*	*0*	*0*
House	0	0	0	0
Senate	0	0	0	0
Democrats	8,400	14,225	7,000	29,625
No. of Cand.	*6*	*9*	*2*	*17*
House	3,900	11,475	7,000	22,375
Senate	4,500	2,750	0	7,250
Incumbents	4,000	7,975	0	11,975
Challengers	0	6,250	5,000	11,250
Open Seat	3,500	0	0	3,500
Winners	3,000	9,225	n/a	12,225
Losers	5,400	5,000	n/a	10,400

Pipefitters Political Action Committee (C00129627) *Phone: (313) 345-8550 * Fax: (313) 345-6660 * 16856 Meyers Rd., Detroit, MI 48235 * Treasurer: Nick Stefanich * Contact: Tom Devlin, Chairman*

	1993-94	1995-96	1997	Totals
Receipts	$13,677	$23,893	$15,273	$52,843
Disburse	13,685	22,794	7,934	44,413
Cash	724	1,827	9,165	n/a
Contributions	11,250	13,475	3,850	28,575
Republicans	0	0	0	0
No. of Cand.	*0*	*0*	*0*	*0*
House	0	0	0	0
Senate	0	0	0	0
Democrats	11,250	13,475	3,850	28,575
No. of Cand.	*13*	*11*	*4*	*28*
House	9,000	11,725	3,850	24,575
Senate	2,250	1,750	0	4,000
Incumbents	6,500	10,975	3,850	21,325
Challengers	0	2,500	0	2,500
Open Seat	4,750	0	0	4,750
Winners	7,000	12,975	n/a	19,975
Losers	4,250	500	n/a	4,750

United Association Journeymen & Apprentices of Plumbing & Pipefitting Industry Local 322 Committee for Political Education (C00173419) *Phone: (609) 567-3322 * Fax: (609) 567-9695 * 534 S. Route 73, P.O. Box 73, Winslow, NJ 08095 * Treasurer: James Reed*

	1993-94	1995-96	1997	Totals
Receipts	$112,148	$118,321	$80,922	$311,391
Disburse	147,206	136,277	68,666	352,149
Cash	81,020	63,064	75,321	n/a
Contributions	4,500	12,750	0	17,250
Republicans	1,000	5,000	0	6,000
No. of Cand.	*2*	*2*	*0*	*4*
House	1,000	5,000	0	6,000
Senate	0	0	0	0
Democrats	3,500	7,750	0	11,250
No. of Cand.	*2*	*3*	*0*	*5*
House	1,500	3,250	0	4,750
Senate	2,000	4,500	0	6,500
Incumbents	3,500	9,250	0	12,750
Challengers	0	0	0	0
Open Seat	1,000	3,500	0	4,500
Winners	4,000	12,750	n/a	16,750
Losers	500	0	n/a	500

Plumbers Union Local 690 Plumbing & Pipe Fitting Industry Local Election Political Action Fund (C00252825) *Phone: (215) 677-6900 * Fax: (215) 677-7102 * 2791 Southampton Rd., Philadelphia, PA 19154 * Treasurer: Edward C. Keenan*

	1993-94	1995-96	1997	Totals
Receipts	$96,143	$148,188	$87,394	$331,725
Disburse	68,376	153,613	48,433	270,422
Cash	38,281	32,857	71,819	n/a
Contributions	4,150	11,500	0	15,650
Republicans	0	0	0	0
No. of Cand.	*0*	*0*	*0*	*0*
House	0	0	0	0
Senate	0	0	0	0
Democrats	4,150	11,500	0	15,650
No. of Cand.	*3*	*5*	*0*	*8*
House	2,150	11,500	0	13,650
Senate	2,000	0	0	2,000
Incumbents	4,150	9,500	0	13,650
Challengers	0	2,000	0	2,000
Open Seat	0	0	0	0
Winners	2,150	9,500	n/a	11,650
Losers	2,000	2,000	n/a	4,000

United Association of Journeymen & Apprentices/Plumbing & Pipefitting Industry Local Union 337 (C00243790) *Phone: (616) 381-6180 * Fax: (616) 381-6266 * 5070 E. Main, Kalamazoo, MI 49004 * Treasurer: Douglas J. Lemmer*

	1993-94	1995-96	1997	Totals
Receipts	$26,240	$2,820	$495	$29,555
Disburse	23,500	10,750	2,500	36,750
Cash	18,151	10,223	8,220	n/a
Contributions	22,500	9,750	2,500	34,750
Republicans	0	0	0	0
No. of Cand.	*0*	*0*	*0*	*0*
House	0	0	0	0
Senate	0	0	0	0
Democrats	22,500	9,750	2,500	34,750
No. of Cand.	*9*	*7*	*1*	*17*
House	16,000	8,500	2,500	27,000
Senate	6,500	1,250	0	7,750
Incumbents	11,000	6,250	0	17,250
Challengers	4,000	4,500	2,500	11,000
Open Seat	7,500	0	0	7,500
Winners	9,000	6,250	n/a	15,250
Losers	13,500	3,500	n/a	17,000

Plumbers & Fitters Union Local 675 AFL-CIO Political Action Committee Fund (C00225151) *Phone: (808) 536-5454 * Fax: (808) 528-2629 * 1109 Bethel St., Basement Level, Honolulu, HI 96813 * Treasurer: Herbert S. K. Kaopua Sr.*

	1993-94	1995-96	1997	Totals
Receipts	$67,322	$88,484	$55,746	$211,552
Disburse	65,034	38,723	18,350	122,107
Cash	52,024	101,786	139,183	n/a
Contributions	10,500	9,000	6,000	25,500
Republicans	0	0	0	0
No. of Cand.	*0*	*0*	*0*	*0*
House	0	0	0	0
Senate	0	0	0	0
Democrats	10,500	9,000	6,000	25,500
No. of Cand.	*4*	*2*	*1*	*7*
House	6,500	9,000	6,000	21,500
Senate	4,000	0	0	4,000
Incumbents	10,500	9,000	6,000	25,500
Challengers	0	0	0	0
Open Seat	0	0	0	0
Winners	10,500	9,000	n/a	19,500
Losers	0	0	n/a	0

United Association of Journeymen & Apprentices/Plumbing & Pipe Fitting Industry Local 447 Federal Political Action Fund (C00320218) *Phone: (916) 457-6595 * Fax: (916) 454-6151 * 5841 Newman Ct., Sacramento, CA 95819 * Treasurer: Harry M. Rotz*

	1993-94	1995-96	1997	Totals
Receipts	$0	$36,322	$48,110	$84,432
Disburse	0	34,533	17,066	51,599
Cash	0	1,788	32,833	n/a
Contributions	0	8,000	2,000	10,000
Republicans	0	0	0	0
No. of Cand.	*0*	*0*	*0*	*0*
House	0	0	0	0
Senate	0	0	0	0
Democrats	0	8,000	2,000	10,000
No. of Cand.	*0*	*2*	*3*	*5*
House	0	8,000	2,000	10,000
Senate	0	0	0	0
Incumbents	0	3,000	1,000	4,000
Challengers	0	5,000	0	5,000
Open Seat	0	0	1,000	1,000
Winners	0	3,000	n/a	3,000
Losers	0	5,000	n/a	5,000

United Association of Steam/Pipefitters Local Union 524 Political Action Fund (C00131706) *Phone: (717) 347-9214 * Fax: (717) 347-5451 * 711 Corey St., Scranton, PA 18505 * Treasurer: Anthony Galenas*

	1993-94	1995-96	1997	Totals
Receipts	$24,813	$27,566	$14,536	$66,915
Disburse	58,560	36,356	12,615	107,531
Cash	87,488	78,702	80,623	n/a
Contributions	8,750	5,150	110	14,010
Republicans	0	450	0	450
No. of Cand.	*0*	*1*	*0*	*1*
House	0	450	0	450
Senate	0	0	0	0

(Data for United Association continued)

Democrats	8,750	4,700	110	13,560
No. of Cand.	*6*	*3*	*1*	*10*
House	6,000	4,700	110	10,810
Senate	2,750	0	0	2,750
Incumbents	6,250	5,150	110	11,510
Challengers	1,500	0	0	1,500
Open Seat	500	0	0	500
Winners	6,000	5,150	n/a	11,150
Losers	2,750	0	n/a	2,750

Plumbers & Steamfitters Local 467 Voluntary Federal Political Action Fund (C00209296) *Phone: (650) 692-4730 * 1519 Rollins Rd., Burlingame, CA 94010 * Treasurer: Gary J. Saunders*

	1993-94	1995-96	1997	Totals
Receipts	$17,019	$31,514	$13,816	$62,349
Disburse	13,185	21,514	11,500	46,199
Cash	8,650	18,650	20,966	n/a
Contributions	8,750	5,000	7,500	21,250
Republicans	0	0	0	0
No. of Cand.	*0*	*0*	*0*	*0*
House	0	0	0	0
Senate	0	0	0	0
Democrats	8,750	5,000	7,500	21,250
No. of Cand.	*5*	*3*	*3*	*11*
House	3,750	4,000	3,500	11,250
Senate	5,000	1,000	4,000	10,000
Incumbents	9,000	5,000	5,000	19,000
Challengers	0	0	0	0
Open Seat	0	0	2,500	2,500
Winners	7,500	5,000	n/a	12,500
Losers	1,250	0	n/a	1,250

Contributed less than $5,000 during 1995-96 cycle:

Pipefitters Local Union 274 Political Action Committee (C00190991) *Phone: (201) 943-4700 * Fax: (201) 943-0878 * 1000 Hendricks Causeway, Ridgefield, NJ 07657 * Treasurer: John Wende*

Plumbers & Gas Fitters Local Union 59 Political Action Committee (C00242024) *Phone: (513) 821-7124 * Fax: (513) 821-0932 * 19 Knollcrest Dr., Suite A, Cincinnati, OH 45237 * Treasurer: Robert J. Jump*

Plumbers & Pipefitters Local Union 25 Political Action Committee (C00137794) *Phone: (309) 788-4569 * Fax: (309) 788-3226 * 1228 Third Ave., Rock Island, IL 61201 * Treasurer: Patrick J. Verschoore*

Plumbers & Pipefitters Local Union 619 Political Action Committee (C00165233) *Phone: (601) 638-2546 * Fax: (601) 638-2692 * P.O. Box 261, Vicksburg, MS 39180 * Treasurer: Grady Edwards Jr.*

Plumbers & Steamfitters Local 486 Federal PAC (formerly known as Steamfitters Local Union #438 STMPAC) (C00228585) *Phone: (410) 866-4380 * Fax: (410) 866-1995 * 7830 Philadelphia Rd., Baltimore, MD 21237 * Treasurer: Robert A. Beck * Contact: Bud Schuler, President*

Plumbers & Steamfitters Local 589 Political Action Committee (C00308502) *Phone: (218) 741-2482 * Fax: (218) 741-2493 * 107 S. 15th Ave. W., Virginia, MN 55792 * Treasurer: John Grahek*

Plumbers Local 14 PAC Fund (C00191213) *Phone: (973) 473-5544 * Fax: (973) 473-6303 * 150 Main St., Lodi, NJ 07644 * Treasurer: Charles Iverson * Contact: Tom Siefert, PAC Dir.*

Plumbers Local 24 Political Action Committee (C00252056) *Phone: (973) 912-0092 * Fax: (973) 912-0464 * 986 S. Springfield Ave., Springfield, NJ 07081 * Treasurer: Richard Blunt * Contact: Owen Sharkey, Co-Chairperson*

Plumbers Local 519 Political Action Committee (C00143362) *Phone: (305) 362-0519 * Fax: (305) 826-9792 * 14105 N.W. 58th Ct., Miami Lakes, FL 33014 * Treasurer: Phil Trucks Jr.*

Plumbers Local Union 1 Political Action Committee (C00327478) *Phone: (718) 738-7500 * Fax: (718) 835-0896 * 158-29 Cross Bay Blvd., Howard Beach, NY 11414 * Treasurer: Jimmy Hart*

Steamfitters Local 475 Political Action Committee (C00252395) *Phone: (908) 754-1030 * Fax: (908) 754-4819 * 136 Mt. Bethel Rd., Warren, NJ 07059 * Treasurer: Gerard D. Higgins*

Steamfitters Local 602 COPE Committee (C00149773) *Phone: (202) 544-6100 * Fax: (202) 546-1383 * 809 Maryland Ave. N.E., Washington, DC 20002 * Treasurer: William C. Lamm*

Steamfitters Union Local 476 Political Action Committee (C00318832) *Phone: (401) 943-3033 * Fax: (401) 943-8027 * 55 Stamp Farm Rd., Cranston, RI 02921 * Treasurer: Kenneth Aurecchia*

United Association of Plumbers & Pipefitters Local 816 Political Action Committee (C00235101) *Phone: (517) 684-7981 * Fax: (517) 684-4336 * 1300 W. Thomas St., Bay City, MI 48706 * Treasurer: Clifford J. Pflueger*

United Association of Plumbers & Steamfitters Local Union 47 Political Action Committee (C00163477) *Phone: (412) 775-2578 * Fax: (412) 775-0223 * 186 Wagner Rd., Monaca, PA 15061 * Treasurer: Donald A. Bonomo*

Sheet Metal Workers International Association

*Phone: (202) 783-5880 * Fax: (202) 662-0889*
1750 New York Ave. N.W., Washington, DC 20006
*Web: www.smwia.org * E-mail: smwia@compuserve.com*

The Sheet Metal Workers International Association represents about 134,000 members in the construction, manufacturing and freight industries. Along with a national sheet metal contractors association, it jointly administers a national training program for sheet metal workers.

The SMWIA raised its total congressional contributions by more than 30 percent from the 1993-94 cycle to 1995-96, joining the ranks of PACs that contributed more than $1 million to candidates. It ranked third among construction-trade unions in total contributions. The SMWIA spent 35 percent of its money on challengers and another 21 percent on open races.

The union contributed more than $1 million to Democratic congressional candidates during the 1995-96 election cycle. House Minority Leader Richard A. Gephardt, D-Mo., and Rep. David E. Bonior, D-Mich., were among the top recipients. Twenty-eight Democrats each received $10,000, and just two Republicans received more than $5,000: Reps. Peter T. King, R-N.Y., and Jack Quinn, R-N.Y.

Sheet Metal Workers International Association Political Action League (PAL) (C00007542) *Address: same as sponsor * Treasurer: Michael J. Sullivan * Contact: Jackie Gallodoro*

	1993-94	1995-96	1997	Totals
Receipts	$1,216,032	$1,497,050	$826,955	$3,540,037
Disburse	1,214,349	1,477,632	452,913	3,144,894
Cash	143,900	163,321	537,363	n/a
Contributions	781,050	1,064,500	319,900	2,165,450
Republicans	10,000	28,500	21,500	60,000
No. of Cand.	*4*	*9*	*5*	*18*
House	5,000	24,000	21,500	50,500
Senate	5,000	4,500	0	9,500
Democrats	744,050	1,030,500	298,400	2,072,950
No. of Cand.	*226*	*249*	*81*	*556*
House	589,550	829,500	220,900	1,639,950
Senate	154,500	201,000	77,500	433,000
Incumbents	481,050	473,750	260,500	1,215,300
Challengers	164,000	368,750	22,000	554,750
Open Seat	134,000	221,000	22,900	377,900
Winners	380,050	636,750	n/a	1,016,800
Losers	401,000	427,750	n/a	828,750

Contributed less than $5,000 during 1995-96 cycle:

COPE 65 (Sheet Metal Workers COPE 65) (C00211987) *Phone: (216) 391-1645 * Fax: (216) 391-4335 * 3666 Carnegie Ave., Cleveland, OH 44115 * Treasurer: William Gambatese*

Sheet Metal Workers International Association Local 28 Political Action Committee (C00169490) *Phone: (212) 941-7700 * Fax: (212) 226-0603 * 500 Greenwich St., New York, NY 10013 * Treasurer: John Harrington*

Sheet Metal Workers Local 100 Political Action Committee (100 PAC) (C00189266) *Phone: (310) 568-8655 * Fax: (310) 967-1683 * 4725 Silver Hill Rd., Suitland, MD 20746 * Treasurer: Charles Henson*

Sheet Metal Workers Local Union 19 League for Political Education (C00119289) *Phone: (215) 952-1999 * Fax: (215) 952-0250 * 1301 S. Columbus Ave., Philadelphia, PA 19147 * Treasurer: Dennis L. Valerino*

Sheet Metal Workers, Local Union 19, Delaware League for Political Education (C00197848) *Phone: (215) 952-1999 * Fax: (215) 952-0250 * 1301 S. Columbus Ave., Philadelphia, PA 19147 * Treasurer: Dennis L. Valerino*

Terminated PACs which contributed less than $5,000 during 1995-96 cycle:

Sheet Metal Workers Local 25 Political Action League (C00282665) *Phone: (201) 507-0330 * 440 Barell Ave., Carlstadt, NJ 07072 * Treasurer: Michael F. Wymes Sr.*

Industrial Unions

American Radio Association

*Phone: (212) 809-0600 * Fax: (212) 990-8400*
17 Battery Pl., Suite 1443, New York, NY 10004-1101
*Web: ourworld.compuserve.com/homepages/ara_az * E-mail: arany@juno.com*

The American Radio Association represents 200 radio and electronics officers aboard United States Merchant Marine flagships. The association, which was founded in 1948, is affiliated with the International Longshoremen's Association. The ARA has three locals around the nation.

American Radio Association AFL-CIO (C00028720) *Address: same as sponsor * Treasurer: Philip Clegg*

	1993-94	1995-96	1997	Totals
Receipts	$35,000	$10,000	$0	$45,000
Disburse	32,500	11,000	0	43,500
Cash	5,918	8,917	8,917	n/a
Contributions	23,000	10,500	0	33,500
Republicans	500	5,000	0	5,500
No. of Cand.	*1*	*1*	*0*	*2*
House	0	0	0	0
Senate	500	5,000	0	5,500
Democrats	22,500	5,500	0	28,000
No. of Cand.	*20*	*3*	*0*	*23*
House	16,500	3,500	0	20,000
Senate	6,000	2,000	0	8,000
Incumbents	20,000	10,500	0	30,500
Challengers	0	0	0	0
Open Seat	3,000	0	0	3,000
Winners	15,000	5,500	n/a	20,500
Losers	8,000	5,000	n/a	13,000

Boilermakers Union

*Phone: (913) 371-2640 * Fax: (913) 281-8102*
753 State Ave., Suite 565, Kansas City, KS 66101
Web: www.boilermakers.org

The International Brotherhood of Boilermakers, Iron Ship Builders, Blacksmiths, Forgers and Helpers represents about 90,000 workers throughout the United States and Canada in construction, repair, maintenance, manufacturing, professional emergency medical services and related industries. Union members work on a variety of projects, including the new attack submarines for the Navy.

The union supports a moratorium on 1996 Clean Air Act ozone standards issues by the EPA. It opposes deregulation of the electric utility industry and proposed changes to make the Occupational Safety and Health Administration more efficient. The Boilermakers Union also supports maintaining strict definitions of employees and independent contractors.

The Boilermakers Union's 1995-96 congressional contributions ranked fourth among manufacturing unions but were $1.1 million less than the third-ranked organization, the steelworkers. The Boilermakers Union spent more of its money on winning candidates than did many other labor groups during the 1996 election cycle. It also favored incumbents more than other union PACs. The leading recipients were Rep. Neil Abercrombie, D-Hawaii, Rep. William O. Lipinski, D-Ill., and House candidate Judy Hancock of Kansas. Although the union gave most of its contributions to Democratic candidates, two Republicans — Sen. Arlen Specter, R-Pa., and Rep. Don Young, R-Alaska. — both received more than $1,000.

International Brotherhood of Boilermakers, Iron Ship Builders, Blacksmiths, Forgers & Helpers-Legislative Education Fund (C00005157) *Phone: (703) 560-1493 * Fax: (703) 560-2584 * 2722 Merrilee Dr., Suite 360, Fairfax, VA 22031 * E-mail: andea@erols.com * Treasurer: Jerry Willburn * Contact: Ande Abbott, Legislative Department Dir.*

	1993-94	1995-96	1997	Totals
Receipts	$326,423	$455,924	$230,017	$1,012,364
Disburse	323,689	446,060	239,850	1,009,599
Cash	18,619	28,490	18,662	n/a
Contributions	305,250	422,350	235,750	963,350
Republicans	8,500	14,250	14,500	37,250
No. of Cand.	*7*	*13*	*11*	*31*
House	5,500	9,250	9,500	24,250
Senate	3,000	5,000	5,000	13,000
Democrats	294,250	404,600	219,250	918,100
No. of Cand.	*175*	*228*	*137*	*540*
House	242,000	339,600	190,750	772,350
Senate	52,250	65,000	28,500	145,750
Incumbents	246,000	280,000	211,250	737,250
Challengers	25,750	79,350	11,500	116,600
Open Seat	33,500	60,000	12,000	105,500
Winners	190,750	306,000	n/a	496,750
Losers	114,500	116,350	n/a	230,850

International Brotherhood of Boilermakers, Blacksmiths, Forgers & Helpers of America Local 169 (C00040949) *Phone: (313) 584-8520 * Fax: (313) 584-8777 * 5936 Chase, Dearborn, MI 48126 * Treasurer: Anthony N. Jacobs*

	1993-94	1995-96	1997	Totals
Receipts	$47,592	$49,635	$21,056	$118,283
Disburse	46,194	49,252	11,712	107,158
Cash	3,532	3,815	13,158	n/a
Contributions	25,415	27,915	5,370	58,700
Republicans	0	0	0	0
No. of Cand.	*0*	*0*	*0*	*0*
House	0	0	0	0
Senate	0	0	0	0
Democrats	25,415	27,915	5,370	58,700
No. of Cand.	*14*	*10*	*6*	*30*
House	19,585	26,915	5,170	51,670
Senate	5,830	1,000	200	7,030
Incumbents	15,185	20,635	5,370	41,190
Challengers	200	7,280	0	7,480
Open Seat	10,030	0	0	10,030
Winners	16,585	27,735	n/a	44,320
Losers	8,830	180	n/a	9,010

Contributed less than $5,000 during 1995-96 cycle:

Boilermakers Local 85 Federal Political Action Committee (C00118828) *Phone: (419) 666-9724 * Fax: (419) 666-8605 * 319 Glenwood Rd., P.O. Box 35, Rossford, OH 43460 * Treasurer: Robert E. Nagy*

Central States Joint Board

*Phone: (312) 738-0822 * Fax: (312) 738-3553*
1950 W. Erie St., Chicago, IL 60622

The Central States Joint Board represents workers who make ladders.

Central States Joint Board Federal Political Action Committee (C00246017) *Address: same as sponsor * Treasurer: Maria Busillo * Contact: John Serpico, Chair*

	1993-94	1995-96	1997	Totals
Receipts	$42,498	$39,735	$33,492	$115,725
Disburse	19,145	29,857	6,281	55,283
Cash	66,123	76,002	95,239	n/a
Contributions	2,600	5,200	0	7,800
Republicans	0	5,000	0	5,000
No. of Cand.	*0*	*1*	*0*	*1*
House	0	0	0	0
Senate	0	5,000	0	5,000
Democrats	2,600	200	0	2,800
No. of Cand.	*3*	*1*	*0*	*4*
House	2,600	200	0	2,800
Senate	0	0	0	0
Incumbents	2,400	0	0	2,400
Challengers	0	0	0	0
Open Seat	200	5,200	0	5,400
Winners	2,600	0	n/a	2,600
Losers	0	5,200	n/a	5,200

Communications Workers of America

*Phone: (202) 434-1320 * Fax: (202) 434-1318*
501 Third St. N.W., Washington, DC 20001-2797
*Web: www.cwa-union.org * E-mail: hssison@cwa-union.org*

The largest telecommunications union in North America, the Communications Workers of America represents 600,000 workers in the broadcasting, print and news media industries. Some of the largest employers of its members include AT&T, the regional Bell telephone companies, GTE and television networks ABC and NBC. Most of its members work in production and customer service jobs. CWA also represents health care and prison industry employees.

The CWA has a wide range of interests, from control over the Internet to consolidation among the regional Bell companies. It opposes the MCI-WorldCom Inc. merger on the grounds that the combined company would be anti-competitive. CWA has argued against the privatization of prisons and helped defeat the "fast-track" trade authority proposal.

The CWA is a major supporter of Democratic candidates — less than 1 percent of its total 1995-96 contributions went to Republican candidates. It ranked first among communications unions by a wide margin and spent more than half of its contributions on challengers. The union's total contribution to congressional races grew by 20 percent between 1994 and 1996, and the CWA has a goal of increasing membership donations to $2 million by 2000.

A Philadelphia union local contributed $93,400 to congressional candidates; all but one were Pennsylvania Democrats. The top five recipients received $10,000 each.

CWA-COPE Political Contributions Committee (C00002089)
*Address: same as sponsor * Treasurer: Barbara J. Easterling * Contact: Loretta Bowen, Dir. of Political Affairs*

	1993-94	1995-96	1997	Totals
Receipts	$2,180,004	$2,505,909	$1,412,207	$6,098,120
Disburse	2,131,112	2,321,469	654,703	5,107,284
Cash	246,694	431,133	1,188,638	n/a
Contributions	1,059,073	1,297,286	322,160	2,678,519
Republicans	4,600	1,250	3,500	9,350
No. of Cand.	*6*	*4*	*3*	*13*
House	4,600	1,250	3,500	9,350
Senate	0	0	0	0
Democrats	1,032,573	1,288,536	317,660	2,638,769
No. of Cand.	*277*	*285*	*121*	*683*
House	829,493	1,042,146	238,160	2,109,799
Senate	203,080	246,390	79,500	528,970
Incumbents	628,711	506,020	240,660	1,375,391
Challengers	199,162	444,113	17,500	660,775
Open Seat	218,000	343,563	62,000	623,563
Winners	493,480	752,483	n/a	1,245,963
Losers	565,593	544,803	n/a	1,110,396

Local 13000 CWA AFL-CIO (C00109595) *Phone: (514) 564-6169 * Fax: (514) 564-2520 * 2124 Race St., Philadelphia, PA 19103 * Web: www.cwalocal13000.com * E-mail: unity@cwalocal13000.com * Treasurer: Patricia A. Maisano * Contact: Joseph Clinton, President*

	1993-94	1995-96	1997	Totals
Receipts	$178,554	$187,924	$106,093	$472,571
Disburse	117,583	175,942	41,020	334,545
Cash	73,912	85,896	150,969	n/a
Contributions	35,500	93,400	9,500	138,400
Republicans	0	0	0	0
No. of Cand.	*0*	*0*	*0*	*0*
House	0	0	0	0
Senate	0	0	0	0
Democrats	35,500	93,400	9,500	138,400
No. of Cand.	*10*	*17*	*3*	*30*
House	23,500	91,400	9,500	124,400
Senate	12,000	2,000	0	14,000
Incumbents	26,000	61,400	9,500	96,900
Challengers	500	30,000	0	30,500
Open Seat	7,000	2,000	0	9,000
Winners	19,000	61,400	n/a	80,400
Losers	16,500	32,000	n/a	48,500

Connecticut Union of Telephone Workers

Phone: (203) 288-5271
3055 Dixwell Ave., Hamden, CT 06518

The Connecticut Union of Telephone Workers serves telephone employees in Connecticut.

Political Action Committee for Education - Connecticut Union of Telephone Workers (C00055590) *Address: same as sponsor * Treasurer: Thomas E. Chausse*

	1993-94	1995-96	1997	Totals
Receipts	$6,037	$2,019	$243	$8,299
Disburse	36,351	15,166	1,377	52,894
Cash	44,003	30,857	29,724	n/a
Contributions	32,250	12,300	0	44,550
Republicans	7,000	0	0	7,000
No. of Cand.	*2*	*0*	*0*	*2*
House	7,000	0	0	7,000
Senate	0	0	0	0
Democrats	25,250	12,300	0	37,550
No. of Cand.	*5*	*5*	*0*	*10*
House	20,250	12,300	0	32,550
Senate	5,000	0	0	5,000
Incumbents	27,250	5,300	0	32,550
Challengers	5,000	7,000	0	12,000
Open Seat	0	0	0	0
Winners	27,250	10,300	n/a	37,550
Losers	5,000	2,000	n/a	7,000

Electronic, Machine and Furniture Workers

*Phone: (202) 785-7200 * Fax: (202) 785-4563*
1126 16th St. N.W., Washington, DC 20036-4866
Web: www.iue.org

The International Union of Electronic, Electrical, Salaried, Machine and Furniture Workers represents about 122,000 people who work in industrial electronics, beer breweries, donut bakeries and furniture factories. The group is affiliated with the AFL-CIO.

Major employers of union members include General Electric, General Motors and La-Z-Boy. More than 30 percent of the members are women. The union has been losing members during the past few years and President Edward Fire has said it could merge with another AFL-CIO affiliate.

The IUE opposes "fast-track" trade authority and the expansion of NAFTA. About 50,000 IUE members work at either GE or GM. The union tracks legislation that could affect its members' companies. It opposes restrictions on the political use of union dues and attempts to reclassify workers as independent contractors.

The IUE ranked 39th among labor unions in total congressional contributions during the 1995-96 election cycle. It gave more money to challengers than to incumbents, and contributed nothing to Republican candidates. The leading recipients were Reps. John F. Tierney, D-Mass., David E. Bonior, D-Mich., and 1996 House candidate Thomas M. Fricano of New York and Senate candidate Winston Bryant of Arkansas.

IUE Committee on Political Education, International Union of Electronic, Electrical, Salaried and Furniture Workers, AFL-CIO (C00006247) *Address: same as sponsor * Treasurer: Edward L. Fire*

	1993-94	1995-96	1997	Totals
Receipts	$441,180	$532,028	$253,814	$1,227,022
Disburse	460,346	502,896	161,370	1,124,612
Cash	36,303	65,442	157,892	n/a
Contributions	298,551	356,280	68,900	723,731
Republicans	0	0	0	0
No. of Cand.	*2*	*0*	*0*	*2*
House	0	0	0	0
Senate	0	0	0	0
Democrats	288,751	353,280	67,900	709,931
No. of Cand.	*117*	*130*	*34*	*281*
House	198,250	291,980	47,400	537,630
Senate	90,501	61,300	20,500	172,301
Incumbents	173,150	132,550	33,900	339,600
Challengers	62,000	148,480	10,500	220,980
Open Seat	57,001	75,250	22,500	154,751
Winners	108,900	201,280	n/a	310,180
Losers	189,651	155,000	n/a	344,651

International Union of Electronic Electrical Salaried Machine Furniture Workers AFL-CIO (C00122374) *Phone: (201) 933-9494 * Fax: (201) 933-6468 * 355 Murray Hill Pkwy., East Rutherford, NJ 07073 * Treasurer: Harold Morrison * Contact: Sal Ingrassia, President*

	1993-94	1995-96	1997	Totals
Receipts	$60,053	$29,457	$19,370	$108,880
Disburse	56,017	32,072	15,352	103,441
Cash	4,580	1,964	5,981	n/a
Contributions	24,100	19,700	6,334	50,134
Republicans	100	0	574	674
No. of Cand.	*1*	*0*	*2*	*3*
House	100	0	574	674
Senate	0	0	0	0
Democrats	24,000	19,700	5,760	49,460
No. of Cand.	*12*	*10*	*5*	*27*
House	23,500	14,700	5,760	43,960
Senate	500	5,000	0	5,500
Incumbents	19,100	9,400	6,334	34,834

Challengers	5,000	4,800	0	9,800
Open Seat	0	5,500	0	5,500
Winners	8,100	17,400	n/a	25,500
Losers	16,000	2,300	n/a	18,300

Glass, Molders, Pottery, Plastics & Allied Workers

*Phone: (610) 565-5051 * Fax: (610) 565-0983*
608 E. Baltimore Pike, P.O. Box 607, Media, PA 19063

The Glass, Molders, Pottery, Plastics and Allied Trades International represents 65,700 workers from those industries. It also represents workers in the fiberglass industry.

The association, which was founded in the 1970s, was the Glass Bottle Blowers Association before it joined with pottery workers in 1984 and molders in 1988.

The union represents workers for Owens Corning, Anchor Glass, Continental Can and others.

Glass, Molders, Pottery, Plastics & Allied Workers International Union - Political Education League (C00011189) *Address: same as sponsor * Treasurer: Frank Trojan*

	1993-94	1995-96	1997	Totals
Receipts	$61,765	$131,927	$29,998	$223,690
Disburse	72,295	128,716	23,492	224,503
Cash	6,581	9,796	16,303	n/a
Contributions	38,500	66,300	14,000	118,800
Republicans	0	0	0	0
No. of Cand.	*0*	*0*	*0*	*0*
House	0	0	0	0
Senate	0	0	0	0
Democrats	38,500	66,300	14,000	118,800
No. of Cand.	*22*	*41*	*9*	*72*
House	17,000	52,800	7,000	76,800
Senate	21,500	13,500	7,000	42,000
Incumbents	17,500	26,800	7,000	51,300
Challengers	12,500	28,500	1,000	42,000
Open Seat	7,500	11,000	6,000	24,500
Winners	4,500	35,300	n/a	39,800
Losers	34,000	31,000	n/a	65,000

Graphic Communications International Union

*Phone: (202) 462-1400 * Fax: (202) 721-0600*
1900 L St. N.W., Washington, DC 20036

The Graphic Communications International Union represents 200,000 printing industry workers. Members of the union's 300 locals include lithographers, photo engravers and people who run newspaper presses.

Graphic Communications International Union Political Contributions Committee (C00027144) *Address: same as sponsor * Treasurer: Gerald Deneau * Contact: Lawrence Martinez, Chair*

	1993-94	1995-96	1997	Totals
Receipts	$30,410	$76,112	$12,997	$119,519
Disburse	50,700	90,500	24,675	165,875
Cash	53,531	39,143	27,465	n/a
Contributions	36,000	62,950	9,275	108,225
Republicans	0	500	500	1,000
No. of Cand.	*0*	*1*	*1*	*2*
House	0	500	500	1,000
Senate	0	0	0	0
Democrats	33,000	62,450	8,775	104,225
No. of Cand.	*49*	*60*	*9*	*118*
House	22,000	42,650	8,775	73,425
Senate	11,000	19,800	0	30,800
Incumbents	26,700	34,150	8,275	69,125
Challengers	4,800	15,500	0	20,300
Open Seat	3,500	13,300	1,000	17,800
Winners	18,500	45,150	n/a	63,650
Losers	17,500	17,800	n/a	35,300

International Brotherhood of Electrical Workers (IBEW)

*Phone: (202) 833-7000 * Fax: (202) 467-6316*
1125 15th St. N.W., Washington, DC 20005
*Web: ourworld.compuserve.com/homepages/ibewnet * E-mail: journalmedia@compuserve.com*

The International Brotherhood of Electrical Workers represents about 679,000 electric utility and contract workers throughout North America. Many of the union's members work for electric power supply companies, but the IBEW also represents broadcast engineers and clerical workers. The union is affiliated with the AFL-CIO.

Electric utility deregulation is the top legislative issue for the IBEW. It opposes the creation of regional utility companies as anti-competitive. The union has said that current deregulation proposals would weaken worker training rules and electricity reliability. The IBEW, along with the AFL-CIO, also opposes any restrictions on utility companies providing services in former franchise areas.

Other issues include NAFTA and a proposal to restrict the political use of union dues. The IBEW opposes both.

The IBEW's main PAC contributed more than $2 million to congressional candidates during the 1995-96 cycle. Five union locals each contributed more than $5,000. The main PAC contributed the third-highest total to challengers. The leading recipients included Reps. Loretta Sanchez, D-Calif., and Max Sandlin, D-Texas, and House candidate Brian Baird of Washington, who lost to Rep. Linda Smith, R-Wash., in 1996.

International Brotherhood of Electrical Workers Committee on Political Education (C00027342) *Address: same as sponsor * Treasurer: Edwin D. Hill*

	1993-94	1995-96	1997	Totals
Receipts	$2,418,884	$3,388,825	$2,096,454	$7,904,163
Disburse	2,376,812	3,413,113	1,589,498	7,379,423
Cash	203,445	179,167	686,127	n/a
Contributions	1,607,425	2,070,587	692,335	4,370,347
Republicans	20,700	43,637	15,160	79,497
No. of Cand.	*18*	*23*	*13*	*54*
House	20,700	40,637	13,160	74,497
Senate	0	3,000	2,000	5,000
Democrats	1,562,325	2,020,450	670,175	4,252,950
No. of Cand.	*364*	*387*	*191*	*942*
House	1,287,825	1,753,260	566,300	3,607,385
Senate	274,500	267,190	103,875	645,565
Incumbents	1,043,825	880,737	551,235	2,475,797
Challengers	264,250	730,600	48,750	1,043,600
Open Seat	279,900	445,500	65,450	790,850
Winners	809,025	1,165,027	n/a	1,974,052
Losers	798,400	905,560	n/a	1,703,960

ElectroPAC 728 IBEW (International Brotherhood of Electrical Workers Local 728) (C00113225) *Phone: (954) 525-3106 * Fax: (954) 525-5742 * 201 S.E. 24th St., Ft. Lauderdale, FL 33316 * Treasurer: David Svetlick * Contact: Jim Weldon, PAC Dir.*

	1993-94	1995-96	1997	Totals
Receipts	$95,349	$117,288	$53,546	$266,183
Disburse	63,574	106,808	28,978	199,360
Cash	38,431	48,915	73,482	n/a
Contributions	9,000	18,700	500	28,200
Republicans	0	0	0	0
No. of Cand.	*0*	*0*	*0*	*0*
House	0	0	0	0
Senate	0	0	0	0
Democrats	9,000	18,700	500	28,200
No. of Cand.	*4*	*8*	*1*	*13*
House	9,000	18,700	500	28,200
Senate	0	0	0	0
Incumbents	4,000	4,000	500	8,500
Challengers	2,000	8,000	0	10,000
Open Seat	3,000	6,700	0	9,700
Winners	4,000	9,700	n/a	13,700
Losers	5,000	9,000	n/a	14,000

Electrical Workers Voluntary, Political, Educational & Legislative Fund (IBEW Local 1) (C00041939) *Phone: (314) 647-5900 * Fax: (314) 647-1358 * 5850 Elizabeth Ave., St. Louis, MO 63110 * Treasurer: Frances Telle*

	1993-94	1995-96	1997	Totals
Receipts	$103,725	$112,886	$60,249	$276,860
Disburse	74,100	162,298	60,266	296,664
Cash	86,150	36,737	36,720	n/a
Contributions	1,500	12,950	3,000	17,450
Republicans	0	0	0	0
No. of Cand.	*0*	*0*	*0*	*0*
House	0	0	0	0
Senate	0	0	0	0
Democrats	1,500	12,950	3,000	17,450
No. of Cand.	*2*	*4*	*1*	*7*
House	1,500	12,950	0	14,450
Senate	0	0	3,000	3,000
Incumbents	0	1,950	0	1,950

(Data for Electrical Workers Voluntary continued)

Challengers	500	5,500	3,000	9,000
Open Seat	1,000	5,500	0	6,500
Winners	1,000	1,950	n/a	2,950
Losers	500	11,000	n/a	11,500

Political Action Committee of Local Union 915, IBEW (C00140749) *Phone: (813) 621-6451 * Fax: (813) 623-1623 * 5621 Harney Rd., Tampa, FL 33610 * Treasurer: Larry Campbell * Contact: Larry B. Jenkins, Chairperson*

	1993-94	1995-96	1997	Totals
Receipts	$39,777	$58,453	$31,083	$129,313
Disburse	29,697	40,973	6,209	76,879
Cash	17,655	35,139	63,736	n/a
Contributions	500	12,000	0	12,500
Republicans	0	0	0	0
No. of Cand.	*0*	*0*	*0*	*0*
House	0	0	0	0
Senate	0	0	0	0
Democrats	500	12,000	0	12,500
No. of Cand.	*1*	*3*	*0*	*4*
House	500	12,000	0	12,500
Senate	0	0	0	0
Incumbents	0	0	0	0
Challengers	0	2,000	0	2,000
Open Seat	0	10,000	0	10,000
Winners	0	10,000	n/a	10,000
Losers	500	2,000	n/a	2,500

Consolidated Local Union 177 of the IBEW Outside-Inside PAC Fund (C00139683) *Phone: (904) 355-4560 * Fax: (904) 353-8064 * 966 Liberty St., Jacksonville, FL 32206 * Treasurer: Thomas M. Gibbons * Contact: Mike Williams, Business Manager*

	1993-94	1995-96	1997	Totals
Receipts	$67,175	$104,388	$41,668	$213,231
Disburse	78,042	116,407	45,150	239,599
Cash	158,819	146,802	100,429	n/a
Contributions	2,500	7,875	500	10,875
Republicans	0	0	0	0
No. of Cand.	*0*	*0*	*0*	*0*
House	0	0	0	0
Senate	0	0	0	0
Democrats	2,500	7,875	500	10,875
No. of Cand.	*1*	*5*	*1*	*7*
House	2,500	7,875	500	10,875
Senate	0	0	0	0
Incumbents	2,500	3,000	500	6,000
Challengers	0	2,750	0	2,750
Open Seat	0	2,125	0	2,125
Winners	2,500	3,000	n/a	5,500
Losers	0	4,875	n/a	4,875

International Brotherhood of Electrical Workers Local 98 Committee on Political Education (C00162818) *Phone: (215) 563-2274 * Fax: (215) 561-2168 * 1719 Spring Garden St., Philadelphia, PA 19130 * Treasurer: James Mackin*

	1993-94	1995-96	1997	Totals
Receipts	$47,023	$264,004	$139,015	$450,042
Disburse	44,468	201,032	136,732	382,232
Cash	3,068	66,039	68,322	n/a
Contributions	2,735	6,900	12,500	22,135
Republicans	0	1,000	4,000	5,000
No. of Cand.	*0*	*1*	*2*	*3*
House	0	0	2,500	2,500
Senate	0	1,000	1,500	2,500
Democrats	2,735	5,900	8,500	17,135
No. of Cand.	*4*	*4*	*4*	*12*
House	2,000	5,900	8,000	15,900
Senate	735	0	500	1,235
Incumbents	2,735	4,900	12,000	19,635
Challengers	0	2,000	0	2,000
Open Seat	0	0	500	500
Winners	300	4,900	n/a	5,200
Losers	2,435	2,000	n/a	4,435

Contributed less than $5,000 during 1995-96 cycle:

IBEW 349 Electro - PAC (C00136689) *Phone: (305) 325-1330 * Fax: (305) 325-1521 * 1657 N.W. 17th Ave., Miami, FL 33125 * Treasurer: Brian Rappaport*

IBEW Local 112 Political Action Committee (C00143081) *Phone: (509) 735-0512 * 2637 W. Albany, Kennewick, WA 99336 * Treasurer: Lori T. Johnson*

IBEW Local 480 Political Action Committee (C00151423) *Phone: (601) 373-8434 * Fax: (601) 371-2191 * P.O. Box 6467, Jackson, MS 39282 * Treasurer: Wayne Divine*

IBEW Local 1464 COPE Committee (C00166959) *Phone: (816) 231-1464 * 6300 Enterprise Rd., Suite 105, Kansas City, MO 64120 * Treasurer: Mark G. Johnson*

IBEW Local 6 Committee on Political Education (COPE) (C00250324) *Phone: (415) 861-5752 * 55 Fillmore St., San Francisco, CA 94117 * Treasurer: James M. Reed*

IBEW Local Union 716 PAC (C00137513) *Phone: (713) 869-8900 * Fax: (713) 868-6342 * 1475 N. Loop W., Houston, TX 77008 * Treasurer: Danny O'Tilley*

IBEW Local Union 756 Political Action Committee (C00127282) *Phone: (904) 756-2756 * Fax: (904) 756-2785 * 5901 Airport Rd., Daytona Beach, FL 32124 * Treasurer: Loomis R. Hart Jr.*

IBEW Local Union 1191 Electro PAC (C00140830) *Phone: (561) 820-9000 * Fax: (561) 820-9260 * 1942 Derby Trail, West Palm Beach, FL 33414 * Treasurer: Mark H. Wilson*

International Brotherhood of Electrical Workers (IBEW) Local Union 237 Community Action Program (C00236893) *Phone: (716) 297-3650 * Fax: (716) 297-8471 * 8803 Niagara Falls Blvd., P.O. Box 120, Niagara Falls, NY 14304 * Treasurer: Timothy J. Reed*

International Brotherhood of Electrical Workers Local 606 PAC (C00131508) *Phone: (407) 896-7271 * Fax: (407) 896-7274 * 820 Virginia Dr., Orlando, FL 32803 * Treasurer: Wade Lewis*

International Brotherhood of Electrical Workers Local Union 313 PAC (C00143396) *Phone: (302) 328-0773 * Fax: (302) 322-5083 * 7 E. Skippack Pike, Suite 275, Ambler, PA 19002 * Treasurer: Thomas Hazewski*

Local 41 International Brotherhood of Electrical Workers - Political Action Committee (C00155374) *Phone: (716) 662-6111 * S-3546 California Rd., Orchard Park, NY 14127 * Treasurer: James Voye*

Local Union 8 IBEW Federal Political Action Committee (C00080994) *Phone: (419) 666-8920 * 807 Lime City Rd., Rossford, OH 43460 * Treasurer: James J. Kozlowski*

Terminated PACs which contributed less than $5,000 during 1995-96 cycle:

IBEW Local 359 Electro-PAC (C00136770) *7811 Coral Way, Suite 101, Miami, FL 33156 * Treasurer: William B. Jacobs*

International Brotherhood of Electrical Workers, Local 292 Voluntary Political Education Fund (C00170951) *312 Central Ave., Suite 292, Minneapolis, MN 55414 * Treasurer: Steve Claypatch*

International Chemical Workers Union

*Phone: (330) 867-2444 * Fax: (330) 867-0544*
1655 W. Market St., Akron, OH 44313

The International Chemical Workers Union, which merged with United Food and Chemical Workers union in July 1996, represents 35,000 people who work in chemical processing. The ICWU was founded in 1944.

International Chemical Workers Union Labor's Investment In Voter Education (C00005835) *Address: same as sponsor * Treasurer: Frank Martino*

	1993-94	1995-96	1997	Totals
Receipts	$44,035	$38,193	$19,063	$101,291
Disburse	36,960	80,610	3,843	121,413
Cash	50,704	8,286	23,509	n/a
Contributions	35,310	64,400	500	100,210
Republicans	0	0	0	0
No. of Cand.	*0*	*0*	*0*	*0*
House	0	0	0	0
Senate	0	0	0	0
Democrats	34,110	64,400	500	99,010
No. of Cand.	*78*	*60*	*1*	*139*
House	20,600	37,900	500	59,000
Senate	13,510	26,500	0	40,010
Incumbents	19,410	22,800	500	42,710
Challengers	7,700	25,100	0	32,800
Open Seat	7,900	16,500	0	24,400
Winners	13,500	34,300	n/a	47,800
Losers	21,810	30,100	n/a	51,910

Machinists and Aerospace Workers Union (IAM)

*Phone: (301) 967-4500 * Fax: (301) 967-4586*
9000 Machinists Place, Upper Marlboro, MD 20772-2687
Web: www.iamaw.org

The International Association of Machinists and Aerospace Workers is a union of more than 500,000 active members in the United States and Canada. It represents nearly 120,000 commercial airline employees at Northwest, Trans World Airlines, Continental and US Airways. The IAM also represents 100,000 employees of defense and space contractors such as Boeing, Raytheon, Lockheed-Martin and Pratt & Whitney.

The union plans to combine with the auto workers and steelworkers unions to create a 2-million member organization by the year 2000. Those three groups spent a total of $6 million on 1996 congressional races.

The IAM opposes a series of bills introduced in late 1997 that change Occupational Safety and Health Administration worker safety regulations. The union is collecting accident statistics in support of greater workplace safety measures. Its other top issues include ensuring that U.S. airplanes are repaired by American workers, not foreign employees, and preventing changes to rules governing political activity by unions.

The machinists union donated nearly $2 million to federal campaigns in 1995-96, of which 99 percent went to Democrats. The union's total contributions during that cycle represented a 16 percent increase over 1994 donations, and placed them seventh among all labor unions and second among manufacturing unions. More than 90 candidates received at least $10,000; Democrats in Texas, Ohio, North Carolina and California were among the leading recipients.

Rep. Lincoln Diaz-Balart, R-Fla., Rep. Benjamin A. Gilman, R-N.Y., Rep. Jack Quinn, R-N.Y., and 1996 Senate candidate Larry Rockefeller of New York were the only Republicans to receive contributions. One machinists' local, in Missouri, contributed $21,500 to congressional candidates, mostly from Missouri and Illinois.

Machinists Non-Partisan Political League (C00002469) *Address: same as sponsor * Treasurer: Donald E. Wharton * Contact: Rich Michalski, Legislative and Political Action Dir.*

	1993-94	*1995-96*	*1997*	*Totals*
Receipts	$3,508,238	$3,671,387	$1,811,708	$8,991,333
Disburse	3,684,825	3,615,292	1,120,731	8,420,848
Cash	404,604	460,705	1,151,681	n/a
Contributions	1,697,081	1,999,675	405,150	4,101,906
Republicans	11,000	7,750	0	18,750
No. of Cand.	*9*	*4*	*0*	*13*
House	11,000	2,750	0	13,750
Senate	0	5,000	0	5,000
Democrats	1,639,581	1,981,925	397,150	4,018,656
No. of Cand.	*313*	*337*	*146*	*796*
House	1,414,081	1,732,925	347,400	3,494,406
Senate	225,500	249,000	49,750	524,250
Incumbents	1,148,181	884,225	335,900	2,368,306
Challengers	264,800	715,450	19,000	999,250
Open Seat	282,600	395,000	45,000	722,600
Winners	929,631	1,165,725	n/a	2,095,356
Losers	767,450	833,950	n/a	1,601,400

Aerospace District Lodge 837 IAMAW PAC (C00169151) *Phone: (314) 731-0603 * Fax: (314) 731-5833 * 212 Utz Ln., Hazelwood, MO 63042 * Treasurer: Larry Meadows * Contact: Gerald Ide, Co-Chairpersons*

Aerospace District Lodge 837 is the union for 7,000 Boeing Corp. workers in the St. Louis area. The union is a part of the Washington-based International Association of Machinists and Aerospace Workers.

Boeing is the world's leading maker of commercial jet aircraft. In 1997, it bought McDonnell Douglas, the world's leading maker of military aircraft.

The Aerospace District Lodge 837 PAC is particularly interested in labor and defense issues.

	1993-94	*1995-96*	*1997*	*Totals*
Receipts	$31,555	$26,322	$12,261	$70,138
Disburse	31,205	29,200	1,800	62,205
Cash	5,461	7,277	17,739	n/a
Contributions	15,800	21,500	1,800	39,100
Republicans	0	0	0	0
No. of Cand.	*0*	*0*	*0*	*0*
House	0	0	0	0
Senate	0	0	0	0
Democrats	15,800	21,500	1,800	39,100
No. of Cand.	*4*	*8*	*1*	*13*
House	15,800	21,500	1,800	39,100
Senate	0	0	0	0
Incumbents	15,800	13,000	1,800	30,600
Challengers	0	2,500	0	2,500
Open Seat	0	6,000	0	6,000
Winners	15,800	12,000	n/a	27,800
Losers	0	9,500	n/a	9,500

Contributed less than $5,000 during 1995-96 cycle:

Texas State Council of Machinists and Aerospace Workers Non-Partisan Political League (C00012575) *Phone: (817) 448-9328 * Fax: (817) 246-2909 * 555 N. Grants Ln., Ft. Worth, TX 76108 * Treasurer: David Hardison*

Oil, Chemical and Atomic Workers International Union

*Phone: (303) 987-2229 * Fax: (303) 987-1967*
P.O. Box 281200, 255 Union Blvd., Lakewood, CO 80228
*Web: www.ocaw.org * E-mail: ocawiure@aol.com*

The Oil, Chemical and Atomic Workers International Union represents more than 100,000 workers and is affiliated with the AFL-CIO. OCAW was formed in 1955 from the merger of the Oil Workers International Union and the United Gas, Coke & Chemical Workers Union. The union includes workers in a wide range of energy, chemical, pharmaceutical and allied industries. There are 370 local unions in 45 states and about 1,100 contracts in force with about 600 employers.

OCAW's Committee on Political Education Fund, OCAW-COPE, is the union's main PAC and operates out of its international headquarters in Lakewood, Colo.

Candidates who benefited most from OCAW-COPE include two challengers, now-Rep. Nick Lampson, D-Texas, and Jeffrey Gray, who ran against Rep. Robert Goodlatte, R-Va. Each received $10,000. Sen. Paul Wellstone, D-Minn., received $7,000, the maximum contributed to any Senate candidate.

Oil, Chemical and Atomic Workers International Union Committee on Political Education Fund (OCAW-COPE) (C00030635) *Phone: (303) 987-2229 * 255 Union Blvd., Lakewood, CO 80228 * Treasurer: Ernest J. Rousselle*

*Contact: Paula R. Littles, Legislative Dir. * Phone: (303) 987-2229*

	1993-94	*1995-96*	*1997*	*Totals*
Receipts	$191,705	$170,190	$90,173	$452,068
Disburse	181,913	219,417	67,381	468,711
Cash	61,153	11,933	34,725	n/a
Contributions	99,164	164,200	42,200	305,564
Republicans	1,000	0	0	1,000
No. of Cand.	*1*	*0*	*0*	*1*
House	0	0	0	0
Senate	1,000	0	0	1,000
Democrats	93,164	159,200	41,700	294,064
No. of Cand.	*71*	*127*	*56*	*254*
House	72,164	128,400	37,200	237,764
Senate	21,000	30,800	4,500	56,300
Incumbents	73,664	84,500	31,000	189,164
Challengers	11,500	49,300	1,500	62,300
Open Seat	12,000	30,900	9,700	52,600
Winners	49,964	117,900	n/a	167,864
Losers	49,200	46,300	n/a	95,500

Oil, Chemical and Atomic Workers Local 1-369 National PAC (OCAW Local 1-369) (C00307686) *Phone: (509) 943-8441 * Fax: (509) 943-8443 * P.O. Box 524, 1305 Knight St., Richland, WA 99352 * Treasurer: Terry A. Klute*

	1993-94	*1995-96*	*1997*	*Totals*
Receipts	$0	$19,163	$13,907	$33,070
Disburse	0	16,669	6,107	22,776
Cash	0	2,932	10,735	n/a
Contributions	0	12,500	650	13,150
Republicans	0	0	0	0
No. of Cand.	*0*	*0*	*0*	*0*
House	0	0	0	0
Senate	0	0	0	0
Democrats	0	12,500	650	13,150
No. of Cand.	*0*	*6*	*1*	*7*
House	0	11,000	0	11,000
Senate	0	1,500	650	2,150
Incumbents	0	3,200	650	3,850

(Data for Oil, Chemical continued)

	1993-94	1995-96	1997	Totals
Challengers	0	9,300	0	9,300
Open Seat	0	0	0	0
Winners	0	3,200	n/a	3,200
Losers	0	9,300	n/a	9,300

Contributed less than $5,000 during 1995-96 cycle:

Gas Workers Local 5-6 Voluntary Political Action Committee (C00136176) *Phone: (314) 721-8448 * Fax: (314) 721-8789 * 7750 Olive Blvd., St. Louis, MO 63130 * Treasurer: Joseph L. Schulte*

Rubber Cork Linoleum & Plastic Workers

570 White Pond Dr., Attn: Political Education Dept., Akron, OH 44320

The COPE Committee of the United Rubber Cork Linoleum and Plastic Workers of America filed for termination with the FEC in 1996.

COPE Committee of the United Rubber Cork Linoleum & Plastic Workers of America AFL-CIO (C00004283) *Address: same as sponsor * Treasurer: Glenn Ellison*

	1993-94	1995-96	1997	Totals
Receipts	$529,252	$187,081	$0	$716,333
Disburse	556,545	221,326	0	777,871
Cash	34,240	0	0	n/a
Contributions	317,550	23,000	0	340,550
Republicans	0	0	0	0
No. of Cand.	*0*	*0*	*0*	*0*
House	0	0	0	0
Senate	0	0	0	0
Democrats	308,550	23,000	0	331,550
No. of Cand.	*94*	*7*	*0*	*101*
House	227,550	22,500	0	250,050
Senate	81,000	500	0	81,500
Incumbents	211,000	22,000	0	233,000
Challengers	71,500	1,000	0	72,500
Open Seat	34,000	0	0	34,000
Winners	131,000	17,500	n/a	148,500
Losers	186,550	5,500	n/a	192,050

UNITE

*Phone: (212) 265-7000 * Fax: (212) 265-3415*
1710 Broadway, New York, NY 10019-5299
*Web: www.uniteunion.org * E-mail: kkonef@uniteunion.org*

Union of Needletrades, Industrial & Textile Employees was formed in 1995 by the merger of two of the nation's oldest unions, the International Ladies' Garment Workers' Union and the Amalgamated Clothing and Textile Workers Union. It represents about 285,000 workers.

UNITE members work in the basic apparel and textile industries. The union also represents workers in the auto parts and auto supply industries, millinery, shoe, laundry, glove and tanning, bag and packaging and retail industries. In 1994, the apparel and textile industries employed about 1.8-million manufacturing workers in the United States and Canada, a larger number than either the steel or automobile industries.

UNITE aims to eliminate sweatshops in the United States and abroad. It also supports a higher minimum wage.

All but five recipients of UNITE's 1996 contributions were Democrats. Sen. Max Cleland, D-Ga., Sen. Carl Levin, D-Mich., and Senate candidate Harvey Gantt of North Carolina received the most money. The Republicans included Rep. Gerald B.H. Solomon, R-N.Y., and Rep. Sherwood Boehlert, R-N.Y., and Rep. Lincoln Diaz-Balart, R-Fla.

UNITE ranked fifth among manufacturing unions in total contributions.

Union of Needletrades Industrial & Textile Employees Campaign Committee (UNITE Campaign Committee) (C00004861) *Phone: (202) 347-7417 * Fax: (202) 347-0708 * 888 16th St. N.W., Suite 303, Washington, DC 20006 * E-mail: unite@bellatlantic.net * Treasurer: Bruce Raynor * Contact: Ann F. Hoffman*

	1993-94	1995-96	1997	Totals
Receipts	$773,000	$906,798	$319,459	$1,999,257
Disburse	523,801	879,467	341,282	1,744,550
Cash	1,786,947	1,814,283	1,793,457	n/a
Contributions	315,842	324,629	122,996	763,467
Republicans	8,070	4,500	8,000	20,570
No. of Cand.	*13*	*4*	*4*	*21*
House	8,070	2,000	8,000	18,070
Senate	0	2,500	0	2,500
Democrats	303,772	319,629	114,496	737,897
No. of Cand.	*236*	*196*	*107*	*539*
House	226,672	240,129	108,996	575,797
Senate	77,100	79,500	5,500	162,100
Incumbents	243,528	136,779	111,996	492,303
Challengers	35,100	98,850	1,500	135,450
Open Seat	36,450	86,500	9,500	132,450
Winners	194,878	209,179	n/a	404,057
Losers	120,964	115,450	n/a	236,414

Chicago & Central States PEC of the Amalgamated Clothing & Textile Workers Union AFL-CIO (C00026096) *Phone: (312) 738-6100 * Fax: (312) 738-0784 * 333 S. Ashland Ave., Chicago, IL 60607 * Treasurer: James E. Skonicki*

	1993-94	1995-96	1997	Totals
Receipts	$46,244	$77,052	$97,500	$220,796
Disburse	53,143	50,616	54,341	158,100
Cash	12,227	38,667	81,826	n/a
Contributions	21,700	29,250	7,500	58,450
Republicans	0	0	0	0
No. of Cand.	*0*	*0*	*0*	*0*
House	0	0	0	0
Senate	0	0	0	0
Democrats	21,700	29,250	7,500	58,450
No. of Cand.	*17*	*14*	*2*	*33*
House	19,100	25,750	7,500	52,350
Senate	2,600	3,500	0	6,100
Incumbents	11,600	9,250	2,500	23,350
Challengers	8,600	11,000	0	19,600
Open Seat	1,500	9,000	5,000	15,500
Winners	10,600	20,250	n/a	30,850
Losers	11,100	9,000	n/a	20,100

Baltimore Regional Joint Board Amalgamated Clothing & Textile Workers Union Political Education Committee (C00007104) *Phone: (410) 669-8300 * Fax: (410) 728-8842 * 1505 Eutaw Pl., Baltimore, MD 21217 * Treasurer: Robert Gasior*

	1993-94	1995-96	1997	Totals
Receipts	$19,880	$9,205	$3,816	$32,901
Disburse	13,800	11,440	5,000	30,240
Cash	22,891	20,659	19,475	n/a
Contributions	5,800	10,440	5,000	21,240
Republicans	0	0	0	0
No. of Cand.	*0*	*0*	*0*	*0*
House	0	0	0	0
Senate	0	0	0	0
Democrats	5,800	10,440	5,000	21,240
No. of Cand.	*6*	*4*	*1*	*11*
House	3,800	10,440	0	14,240
Senate	2,000	0	5,000	7,000
Incumbents	2,800	1,000	5,000	8,800
Challengers	250	9,240	0	9,490
Open Seat	2,750	200	0	2,950
Winners	2,800	1,000	n/a	3,800
Losers	3,000	9,440	n/a	12,440

Philadelphia Joint Board UNITE (C00165324) *Phone: (215) 751-9770 * Fax: (215) 751-0513 * 22 S. 22nd St., Philadelphia, PA 19103 * Treasurer: Mildred Saldana*

	1993-94	1995-96	1997	Totals
Receipts	$62,851	$31,648	$15,340	$109,839
Disburse	62,966	29,179	8,261	100,406
Cash	111,810	114,284	121,364	n/a
Contributions	10,100	7,500	0	17,600
Republicans	0	5,000	0	5,000
No. of Cand.	*0*	*1*	*0*	*1*
House	0	0	0	0
Senate	0	5,000	0	5,000
Democrats	10,100	2,500	0	12,600
No. of Cand.	*8*	*3*	*0*	*11*
House	7,500	2,500	0	10,000
Senate	2,600	0	0	2,600
Incumbents	9,500	7,000	0	16,500
Challengers	500	500	0	1,000
Open Seat	0	0	0	0
Winners	4,000	7,000	n/a	11,000
Losers	6,100	500	n/a	6,600

Rochester Joint Board Political Education Committee (C00011239) *Phone: (716) 473-3280 * Fax: (716) 473-2109 * 750 East Ave., Rochester, NY 14607 * Treasurer: Christopher T. Ferriter*

	1993-94	1995-96	1997	Totals
Receipts	$7,808	$6,204	$2,852	$16,864
Disburse	7,000	9,442	1,000	17,442
Cash	12,037	8,802	10,655	n/a
Contributions	1,000	6,250	1,000	8,250

Republicans	0	0	0	0
No. of Cand.	*0*	*0*	*0*	*0*
House	0	0	0	0
Senate	0	0	0	0
Democrats	1,000	6,250	1,000	8,250
No. of Cand.	*1*	*2*	*1*	*4*
House	0	6,250	1,000	7,250
Senate	1,000	0	0	1,000
Incumbents	1,000	5,250	1,000	7,250
Challengers	0	1,000	0	1,000
Open Seat	0	0	0	0
Winners	1,000	5,250	n/a	6,250
Losers	0	1,000	n/a	1,000

Terminated PACs which contributed less than $5,000 during 1995-96 cycle:

Amalgamated Clothing and Textile Workers Union - Political Action Committee (ACTWU-PAC) (C00005728) *15 Union Square, New York, NY 10003 * Treasurer: Arthur R. Loevy*

United Auto Workers

*Phone: (313) 926-5505 * Fax: (313) 824-5750*
8000 E. Jefferson, Detroit, MI 48214
Web: www.uaw.org

The United Auto Workers represents about 775,000 active employees of the auto and truck assembly, auto parts, defense and heavy equipment industries throughout North America. The UAW plans to combine with the Steelworkers Union and the Machinists & Aerospace Workers Union by 2000, creating a 2-million member organization that spent a combined $6 million on congressional races during the 1995-96 election cycle.

The union lobbies on trade issues — NAFTA and expanded trade authority chief among them — and opposes a ban on affirmative action. It favors tightening corporate tax regulations and the retention of the capital gains tax.

The UAW gave $2.4 million to candidates during the 1995-96 election cycle, ranking third among all PACs and first among manufacturing unions in total contributions. Only $20,000 of that went to non-Democrats. More than half of the nearly 400 candidates who received a contribution from the UAW received more than $5,000. The leading recipients included Rep. Nick Lampson, D-Texas, Rep. Gene Green, D-Texas, and Rep. Ken Bentsen, D-Texas.

The UAW has a second PAC, which gave $8,500 to 1996 congressional races. It is used primarily for state and local races. The states with the largest UAW memberships are Michigan, Ohio, Indiana, Illinois, New York, Wisconsin, Pennsylvania, California, Missouri, Iowa, New Jersey, Tennessee, Kentucky and Texas.

UAW - V - Cap (UAW Voluntary Community Action Program) (C00002840) *Phone: (202) 828-8500 * Fax: (202) 293-3457 * 1757 N St. N.W., Washington, DC 20036 * Treasurer: Roy O. Wyse * Contact: Tim Foley*

	1993-94	*1995-96*	*1997*	*Totals*
Receipts	$4,335,563	$5,117,604	$2,636,365	$12,089,532
Disburse	3,595,504	3,955,068	1,086,247	8,636,819
Cash	2,946,023	4,108,561	5,658,685	n/a
Contributions	2,147,190	2,467,319	493,710	5,108,219
Republicans	14,455	10,975	1,500	26,930
No. of Cand.	*8*	*6*	*2*	*16*
House	14,455	10,475	1,500	26,430
Senate	0	500	0	500
Democrats	2,087,735	2,446,344	489,210	5,023,289
No. of Cand.	*369*	*394*	*187*	*950*
House	1,863,376	2,177,344	416,210	4,456,930
Senate	224,359	269,000	73,000	566,359
Incumbents	1,377,997	1,049,269	386,210	2,813,476
Challengers	392,359	876,000	51,500	1,319,859
Open Seat	365,250	535,500	44,500	945,250
Winners	1,180,997	1,402,769	n/a	2,583,766
Losers	966,193	1,064,550	n/a	2,030,743

Committee for Good Government International Union UAW (C00002832) *Phone: (313) 926-5000 * Fax: (313) 823-6016 * 8000 E. Jefferson Ave., Detroit, MI 48214 * Treasurer: Larry M. Smith*

	1993-94	*1995-96*	*1997*	*Totals*
Receipts	$249,834	$299,139	$154,390	$703,363
Disburse	139,291	253,629	4,669	397,589
Cash	280,562	326,072	475,798	n/a
Contributions	15,000	8,500	0	23,500
Republicans	0	0	0	0
No. of Cand.	*0*	*0*	*0*	*0*
House	0	0	0	0
Senate	0	0	0	0
Democrats	15,000	8,500	0	23,500
No. of Cand.	*3*	*1*	*0*	*4*
House	5,000	8,500	0	13,500
Senate	10,000	0	0	10,000
Incumbents	0	0	0	0
Challengers	15,000	8,500	0	23,500
Open Seat	0	0	0	0
Winners	0	0	n/a	0
Losers	15,000	8,500	n/a	23,500

United Mine Workers of America

*Phone: (202) 842-7206 * Fax: (202) 842-7264*
900 15th St. N.W., Washington, DC 20005
Web: www.access.digex.net/~miner

The United Mine Workers of America represents nearly 100,000 workers and retirees from the coal, copper, gold and mineral mining industries. Wyoming, West Virginia, Kentucky, Alabama and Pennsylvania are among the leading coal-producing states, according to the Department of Energy. More than half of the electricity produced in the United States is made by burning coal.

The union supports strong workplace health and safety regulations and monitors federal mine safety efforts. It favors further study of the health and economic impacts of ozone and some air quality standards before new rules are enacted. In a rare alliance with the coal industry, the UMWA will lobby against emission limits set forth in the Kyoto Protocol.

The UMWA was the only mine workers PAC to contribute at least $5,000 to congressional campaigns during the 1995-96 election cycle. The union contributed nearly 98 percent to Democratic candidates. The leading recipients were three Alabama Democrats who all lost their respective races: Senate candidate Roger Bedford and House candidates T.D. "Ted" Little and Robert T. "Bob" Wilson. Sen. Arlen Specter, R-Pa., was the top Republican recipient.

United Mine Workers of America - Coal Miners Political Action Committee (C00013342) *Address: same as sponsor * Treasurer: Carlo Tarley * Contact: William Banig, PAC Coordinator*

	1993-94	*1995-96*	*1997*	*Totals*
Receipts	$944,089	$948,499	$459,045	$2,351,633
Disburse	908,572	952,986	229,120	2,090,678
Cash	42,415	37,935	267,865	n/a
Contributions	519,170	414,200	122,250	1,055,620
Republicans	8,500	4,000	1,500	14,000
No. of Cand.	*6*	*5*	*2*	*13*
House	8,500	4,000	500	13,000
Senate	0	0	1,000	1,000
Democrats	505,670	409,700	119,750	1,035,120
No. of Cand.	*220*	*181*	*99*	*500*
House	366,270	314,200	91,250	771,720
Senate	139,400	95,500	28,500	263,400
Incumbents	337,770	200,000	101,750	639,520
Challengers	75,400	105,200	3,000	183,600
Open Seat	98,500	108,000	17,000	223,500
Winners	259,270	235,000	n/a	494,270
Losers	259,900	179,200	n/a	439,100

United Paperworkers International

*Phone: (615) 333-9891 * Fax: (615) 834-7741*
3340 Perimeter Hill Dr., Nashville, TN 37211

United Paperworkers International represents 250,000 workers from different industries. In addition to paper plant workers, it represents nurses, tire company employees and auto parts workers.

The union was created from a merger between the Pulp and Papermakers Union and the Sulfite Workers Union.

United Paperworkers International Union Political Education Program (C00002394) *Address: same as sponsor * Treasurer: James H. Dunn*

	1993-94	*1995-96*	*1997*	*Totals*
Receipts	$121,321	$251,908	$55,980	$429,209
Disburse	107,108	200,894	25,850	333,852
Cash	15,969	66,986	97,117	n/a
Contributions	97,050	162,400	20,000	279,450

(Data for United Paperworkers International continued)

Republicans	1,000	0	0	1,000
No. of Cand.	*1*	*0*	*0*	*1*
House	1,000	0	0	1,000
Senate	0	0	0	0
Democrats	92,550	159,000	19,000	270,550
No. of Cand.	*63*	*91*	*14*	*168*
House	63,350	105,000	12,000	180,350
Senate	29,200	54,000	7,000	90,200
Incumbents	61,950	41,850	14,000	117,800
Challengers	18,100	48,350	3,000	69,450
Open Seat	16,000	71,700	3,000	90,700
Winners	34,450	75,750	n/a	110,200
Losers	62,600	86,650	n/a	149,250

United Steelworkers of America

*Phone: (412) 562-2442 * Fax: (412) 562-2445*
5 Gateway Center, Pittsburgh, PA 15222
Web: www.uswa.org

The USWA represents more than 700,000 steelworkers, utility and aluminum workers in the United States and Canada. It is planning to combine with unions representing auto workers, machinists and aerospace workers to create a 2 million member organization by 2000.

The steelworkers union restructured its divisions in 1996, halving the number of districts nationwide to nine. The states with the largest union membership include Pennsylvania, Ohio, Michigan and Indiana.

The union opposed financial support to Asian economies through the International Monetary Fund and helped defeat the "fast-track" trade authority proposal. The USWA supports a higher minimum wage and changes in labor laws that permit greater union organization.

The only PAC among the top 200 to contribute exclusively to Democrats, the steelworkers union spent more on challengers than incumbents during the 1995-96 cycle. It ranked third among manufacturing unions in total contributions and increased its 1996 total by 45 percent over 1994. More than 180 candidates received $5,000 or more from this PAC, and five of the top seven recipients were from Texas, where many aluminum and electrical workers are union members.

United Steelworkers of America Political Action Fund (C00003590) *Phone: (202) 778-4384 * Fax: (202) 293-5308 * 1150 17th St. N.W., Suite 300, Washington, DC 20036 * Treasurer: Leo W. Gerard * Contact: William Klinefelter, Legislative and Political Dir.*

	1993-94	1995-96	1997	Totals
Receipts	$1,371,848	$1,953,741	$733,046	$4,058,635
Disburse	1,458,622	1,915,676	651,537	4,025,835
Cash	59,488	97,562	179,074	n/a
Contributions	1,039,762	1,523,650	129,437	2,692,849
Republicans	2,000	0	0	2,000
No. of Cand.	*2*	*0*	*0*	*2*
House	2,000	0	0	2,000
Senate	0	0	0	0
Democrats	1,004,262	1,523,650	129,437	2,657,349
No. of Cand.	*230*	*258*	*37*	*525*
House	822,762	1,304,150	98,437	2,225,349
Senate	181,500	219,500	31,000	432,000
Incumbents	600,950	575,150	105,437	1,281,537
Challengers	198,500	590,000	13,000	801,500
Open Seat	243,550	350,500	11,000	605,050
Winners	485,750	843,650	n/a	1,329,400
Losers	554,012	680,000	n/a	1,234,012

Aluminum Brick & Glass Workers International Union Local 105 Federal COPE Account (C00226860) *Phone: (319) 355-1181 * Fax: (319) 359-3529 * 880 Devils Glen Rd., Bettendorf, IA 52722 * Treasurer: Vacant*

	1993-94	1995-96	1997	Totals
Receipts	$5,159	$5,609	$6	$10,774
Disburse	5,200	5,302	3	10,505
Cash	51	360	364	n/a
Contributions	5,000	5,300	0	10,300
Republicans	0	0	0	0
No. of Cand.	*0*	*0*	*0*	*0*
House	0	0	0	0
Senate	0	0	0	0
Democrats	5,000	5,300	0	10,300
No. of Cand.	*2*	*3*	*0*	*5*
House	5,000	5,000	0	10,000
Senate	0	300	0	300
Incumbents	0	2,800	0	2,800
Challengers	4,000	2,500	0	6,500
Open Seat	1,000	0	0	1,000
Winners	0	2,800	n/a	2,800
Losers	5,000	2,500	n/a	7,500

Aluminum Brick & Glass Workers International Union Federal PAC Local 104 (C00297838) *P.O. Box 247, Newburgh, IN 47629 * Treasurer: Charles R. Wyatt*

	1993-94	1995-96	1997	Totals
Receipts	$516	$14,719	$0	$15,235
Disburse	508	9,230	561	10,299
Cash	7	561	0	n/a
Contributions	500	5,000	561	6,061
Republicans	0	0	0	0
No. of Cand.	*0*	*0*	*0*	*0*
House	0	0	0	0
Senate	0	0	0	0
Democrats	500	5,000	561	6,061
No. of Cand.	*1*	*4*	*1*	*6*
House	500	3,000	0	3,500
Senate	0	2,000	561	2,561
Incumbents	500	1,000	0	1,500
Challengers	0	4,000	0	4,000
Open Seat	0	0	561	561
Winners	0	1,000	n/a	1,000
Losers	500	4,000	n/a	4,500

Contributed less than $5,000 during 1995-96 cycle:

ABG 169 PAC - Aluminum Brick & Glass Workers Local 169 (C00297945) *Phone: (573) 883-2509 * P.O. Box 147, 950 S. Gabouri St., St. Genevieve, MO 63670 * Treasurer: Robert W. Thomure*

Aluminum Brick & Glass Workers International Union Local 105 COPE Fund (C00161703) *Phone: (319) 355-1181 * Fax: (319) 358-3529 * 880 Devils Glen Rd., Bettendorf, IA 52722 * Treasurer: Vacant*

Aluminum Brick & Glass Workers International Union Local 119A Federal PAC (C00315283) *R.R. #18, Box 198-1, Bedford, IN 47421 * Treasurer: Sofia M. Boling*

Aluminum Brick & Glass Workers International Union Local 420 PAC (C00299867) *Phone: (315) 764-0531 * 24 Woodlawn Ave., Massena, NY 13662 * Treasurer: David G. Rabideau*

Buffalo Local 222 Aluminum Brick & Glass Workers International Union AFL-CIO (Local 222 ABG-PAC) (C00276287) *P.O. Box 64, Cheektowaga, NY 14225 * Treasurer: Richard L. King*

Local 450 of the United Steelworkers of America (also known as USWA Local 450 APAC) (C00193680) *Phone: (315) 679-7510 * Fax: (315) 764-7558 * 24 Woodlawn Ave., Massena, NY 13662 * Treasurer: Bernard F. Leatherland*

Local 88 Aluminum Brick & Glass Workers International PAC (Local 88 ABG PAC) (C00215293) *Phone: (215) 788-3393 * 1014 Wood St., Bristol, PA 19007 * Treasurer: Michael Horan*

Terminated PACs which contributed less than $5,000 during 1995-96 cycle:

Aluminum Brick & Glass Workers International Union Local 188A PAC (C00296905) *Phone: (219) 462-1138 * P.O. Box 177, Wanatah, IN 46390 * Treasurer: Steven Charles Beresford*

Aluminum Brick & Glass Workers International Union PAC (C00244301) *3362 Hollenberg Dr., Bridgeton, MO 63044 * Treasurer: Harvey G. Martin*

Utility Workers Union of America

*Phone: (202) 347-8105 * Fax: (202) 347-4872*
815 16th St. N.W., Washington, DC 20006

The Utility Workers Union of America represents production, transmission and distribution workers for large electric companies. The union has 43,000 members and 250 locals.

The union represents workers for Detroit Edison, Southern California Edison, St. Louis Water, Pacific Gas & Electric, Consolidated Edison (New York), Toledo Edison, West Penn Power, Pennsylvania Electric and United Illuminated, among others.

The union, which was founded in 1938, is a competitor of International Brotherhood of Electrical Workers.

Utility Workers Union of America Political Contributions Committee (C00040741) *Address: same as sponsor * Treasurer: John M. Walsh Jr. * Contact: Donald Wightman, President*

	1993-94	1995-96	1997	Totals
Receipts	$47,443	$62,093	$44,422	$153,958
Disburse	75,176	84,942	26,258	186,376
Cash	26,189	3,342	21,507	n/a
Contributions	45,900	37,950	19,000	102,850

	1993-94	1995-96	1997	Totals
Republicans	500	0	0	500
No. of Cand.	*1*	*0*	*0*	*1*
House	500	0	0	500
Senate	0	0	0	0
Democrats	44,900	37,950	19,000	101,850
No. of Cand.	*64*	*32*	*19*	*115*
House	32,200	33,200	17,000	82,400
Senate	12,700	4,750	2,000	19,450
Incumbents	32,150	23,200	16,500	71,850
Challengers	3,000	7,500	1,500	12,000
Open Seat	10,750	6,500	1,000	18,250
Winners	29,450	28,700	n/a	58,150
Losers	16,450	9,250	n/a	25,700

Misc. Unions

AFL-CIO

*Phone: (202) 637-5000 * Fax: (202) 508-6961*
815 16th St. N.W, Washington, DC 20006
Web: www.aflcio.org

The AFL-CIO is the umbrella labor organization for some 13 million American workers in a variety of industries. It lobbies on nearly every labor-related issue. More than 75 unions are affiliated with the AFL-CIO.

The organization opposes "fast-track" trade authority and restrictions on the political use of union dues. It has voiced support for allowing people aged 62 to 64 to buy into the Medicare program and other health care expansions. The organization seeks to protect Social Security and to make pensions simpler and more portable. The AFL-CIO opposes attempts to reclassify certain workers as independent contractors and the proposed merger of telecommunications companies MCI and WorldCom. It endorses a workplace ergonomics standard. John Sweeney is the organization's president.

The AFL-CIO spent all but $13,000 of its nearly $1.2 million in 1995-96 congressional contributions on Democratic candidates. It backed challengers with nearly 41 percent of its contributions — second-most among PACs that contributed $1 million or more. But the union's biggest political strategy was a series of advertisements run during the 1996 elections that cost organized labor $35 million. Many of the ads attacked Republican proposals on Medicare and education spending.

The leading recipient of AFL-CIO contributions was Rep. John F. Tierney, D-Mass., who received $12,250, including in-kind expenditures. More than 120 candidates received at least $5,000 from the AFL-CIO PAC. The top Republican recipients included Reps. Christopher H. Smith, R-N.J., and Sherwood Boehlert, R-N.Y.

AFL-CIO Committee on Political Education/Political Contributions Committee (C00003806) *Address: same as sponsor * Treasurer: Richard L. Trumka * Contact: Steve Rosenthal*

	1993-94	1995-96	1997	Totals
Receipts	$1,337,807	$1,720,105	$469,286	$3,527,198
Disburse	1,330,716	1,720,161	362,423	3,413,300
Cash	94,894	94,839	201,699	n/a
Contributions	981,439	1,190,514	270,745	2,442,698
Republicans	6,880	9,000	5,500	21,380
No. of Cand.	*7*	*5*	*3*	*15*
House	6,880	9,000	5,500	21,380
Senate	0	0	0	0
Democrats	949,759	1,177,514	264,745	2,392,018
No. of Cand.	*286*	*257*	*99*	*642*
House	791,909	973,873	209,695	1,975,477
Senate	157,850	203,641	55,050	416,541
Incumbents	565,449	366,220	218,745	1,150,414
Challengers	160,210	486,044	6,000	652,254
Open Seat	251,500	341,500	47,000	640,000
Winners	391,326	636,040	n/a	1,027,366
Losers	590,113	554,474	n/a	1,144,587

Political Educational Fund of the Building and Construction Trades Department (C00003160) *Phone: (202) 347-1461 * Fax: (202) 737-1275 * 815 16th St. N.W., Suite 603, Washington, DC 20006 * Treasurer: Robert A. Georgine*

	1993-94	1995-96	1997	Totals
Receipts	$213,062	$198,924	$169,949	$581,935
Disburse	217,583	184,859	32,123	434,565
Cash	2,935	17,005	154,833	n/a
Contributions	209,768	156,892	21,150	387,810
Republicans	13,764	13,750	500	28,014
No. of Cand.	*14*	*14*	*3*	*31*
House	11,764	9,750	500	22,014
Senate	2,000	4,000	0	6,000
Democrats	194,004	142,525	20,650	357,179
No. of Cand.	*177*	*144*	*36*	*357*
House	159,454	124,275	16,650	300,379
Senate	34,550	18,250	4,000	56,800
Incumbents	186,868	140,142	20,650	347,660
Challengers	10,000	6,750	0	16,750
Open Seat	12,800	10,000	500	23,300
Winners	161,891	145,212	n/a	307,103
Losers	47,877	11,680	n/a	59,557

Transportation Trades Department AFL-CIO Political Action Committee (TTD/PAC) (C00280909) *Phone: (202) 628-9262 * Fax: (202) 628-0391 * 1000 Vermont Ave. N.W., Suite 900, Washington, DC 20005 * Treasurer: Sonny Hall*

	1993-94	1995-96	1997	Totals
Receipts	$21,325	$52,800	$26,900	$101,025
Disburse	18,354	43,397	22,026	83,777
Cash	2,970	12,371	17,244	n/a
Contributions	17,750	42,850	21,750	82,350
Republicans	0	3,000	3,000	6,000
No. of Cand.	*0*	*5*	*6*	*11*
House	0	3,000	2,500	5,500
Senate	0	0	500	500
Democrats	16,250	39,850	17,750	73,850
No. of Cand.	*35*	*59*	*32*	*126*
House	13,750	30,350	17,000	61,100
Senate	2,500	9,500	750	12,750
Incumbents	16,000	26,850	21,750	64,600
Challengers	750	3,500	0	4,250
Open Seat	1,000	12,500	0	13,500
Winners	11,750	31,850	n/a	43,600
Losers	6,000	11,000	n/a	17,000

Contributed less than $5,000 during 1995-96 cycle:

Industrial Union Department AFL-CIO Voluntary Fund (C00117937) *Phone: (202) 842-7800 * 815 16th St. N.W., Suite 301, Washington, DC 20006 * Treasurer: Joseph B. Uehlein*

American Federation of Musicians

*Phone: (212) 869-1330 * Fax: (212) 764-6134*
1501 Broadway, Suite 600, New York, NY 10036

The American Federation of Musicians represents 110,000 musicians in the United States and Canada. It is the only union representing musicians.

The federation has 300 chapters in the United States and Canada. The Washington office lobbies Congress about labor issues as well as copyright law, patent law and National Endowment for the Arts funding. AFM also works with the Occupational Safety and Health Administration to ensure workplace safety.

The bipartisan PAC gives to federal candidates.

American Federation of Musicians - TEMPO Political Contributions Committee (C00073627) *Phone: (202) 338-0469 * Fax: (202) 338-0474 * 4400 MacArthur Blvd., Washington, DC 20007 * Treasurer: Stephen R. Sprague * Contact: Alfonso Pollard, Gov. Affairs Dir.*

*Contact: Steve Young, President * Phone: (212) 869-1330*

	1993-94	1995-96	1997	Totals
Receipts	$40,269	$61,807	$32,167	$134,243
Disburse	38,426	42,893	14,770	96,089
Cash	3,268	22,184	39,581	n/a
Contributions	21,500	35,152	11,700	68,352
Republicans	350	162	0	512
No. of Cand.	*1*	*2*	*0*	*3*
House	350	662	0	1,012
Senate	0	-500	0	-500
Democrats	20,550	34,740	11,700	66,990
No. of Cand.	*82*	*94*	*22*	*198*
House	15,450	24,890	6,100	46,440
Senate	5,100	9,850	5,600	20,550
Incumbents	18,900	18,787	9,450	47,137
Challengers	1,500	8,015	500	10,015
Open Seat	1,100	8,350	1,750	11,200
Winners	16,450	23,325	n/a	39,775
Losers	5,050	11,827	n/a	16,877

Bakery, Confectionery & Tobacco Workers International Union

Phone: (301) 933-8600 * Fax: (301) 946-8452
10401 Connecticut Ave., Kensington, MD 20895

The Bakery, Confectionery & Tobacco Workers International Union represents 105,000 people working in food processing. Sixty-three percent of the members bake bread, cookies, crackers and cakes; 25 percent make candy and 12 percent process tobacco.

The union, which was founded in 1886, has 160 local affiliates around the nation.

Bakery, Confectionery & Tobacco Workers International Union Political Action Committee (C00127621) *Address: same as sponsor * Treasurer: Gene McDonald*

	1993-94	1995-96	1997	Totals
Receipts	$249,061	$233,654	$112,749	$595,464
Disburse	267,328	242,928	62,059	572,315
Cash	27,409	18,146	68,841	n/a
Contributions	183,615	117,100	16,250	316,965
Republicans	1,000	1,000	0	2,000
No. of Cand.	*2*	*1*	*0*	*3*
House	1,000	1,000	0	2,000
Senate	0	0	0	0
Democrats	178,615	116,100	15,750	310,465
No. of Cand.	*127*	*121*	*28*	*276*
House	125,915	96,150	12,250	234,315
Senate	52,700	19,950	3,500	76,150
Incumbents	121,915	51,950	16,250	190,115
Challengers	27,200	41,500	-1000	67,700
Open Seat	34,000	23,650	1,000	58,650
Winners	83,300	66,650	n/a	149,950
Losers	100,315	50,450	n/a	150,765

Bakery & Confectionery Workers International Union Local No. 19 Political Organization (C00249359) *Phone: (216) 771-5386 * Fax: (216) 771-8232 * 1870 E. 19th St., Cleveland, OH 44114 * Treasurer: Bill Jurevicius*

	1993-94	1995-96	1997	Totals
Receipts	$63,173	$61,558	$33,403	$158,134
Disburse	66,100	105,387	45,284	216,771
Cash	132,966	89,139	77,259	n/a
Contributions	29,000	46,500	16,000	91,500
Republicans	0	0	0	0
No. of Cand.	*0*	*0*	*0*	*0*
House	0	0	0	0
Senate	0	0	0	0
Democrats	29,000	46,500	16,000	91,500
No. of Cand.	*4*	*10*	*4*	*18*
House	29,000	44,000	11,000	84,000
Senate	0	2,500	5,000	7,500
Incumbents	10,000	13,500	11,000	34,500
Challengers	14,000	33,000	0	47,000
Open Seat	5,000	0	5,000	10,000
Winners	0	23,500	n/a	23,500
Losers	29,000	23,000	n/a	52,000

Directors Guild of America

Phone: (310) 289-2000 * Fax: (310) 289-2029
7920 Sunset Blvd., Los Angeles, CA 90046
Web: www.dga.org

The Directors Guild of America represents more than 10,000 directors who work on theatrical and educational films, television, video and commercials.

The Political Action Committee of the Directors Guild of America Inc. (DGA-PAC) (C00311944) *Address: same as sponsor * Treasurer: Sheldon Leonard*

	1993-94	1995-96	1997	Totals
Receipts	$0	$14,460	$10,006	$24,466
Disburse	0	7,550	2,567	10,117
Cash	0	6,910	14,349	n/a
Contributions	0	6,500	2,000	8,500
Republicans	0	2,500	0	2,500
No. of Cand.	*0*	*3*	*0*	*3*
House	0	500	0	500
Senate	0	2,000	0	2,000
Democrats	0	4,000	2,000	6,000
No. of Cand.	*0*	*5*	*2*	*7*
House	0	2,500	1,000	3,500
Senate	0	1,500	1,000	2,500
Incumbents	0	6,000	2,000	8,000
Challengers	0	0	0	0
Open Seat	0	500	0	500
Winners	0	6,500	n/a	6,500
Losers	0	0	n/a	0

Hotel Employees & Restaurant Employees International Union

Phone: (202) 393-4373 * Fax: (202) 333-0468
1219 28th St. N.W., Washington, DC 20007
Web: www.erols.com/hereiu * E-mail: hereiu@erols.com

The Hotel Employees & Restaurant Employees International Union represents about 241,000 workers in the tourism, restaurant and lodging industries. In addition to collective bargaining, it provides its members with notices on hotel boycotts and other union activities.

The union ranked first among food service worker PACs in contributions to congressional campaigns during the 1995-96 election cycle. It favored Democratic candidates, but five Republicans were among the top 25 recipients.

The leading recipients were Sens. Robert G. Torricelli, D-N.J., Richard J. Durbin, D-Ill., and Max Baucus, D-Mont. Rep. John Ensign, R-Nev., was the top Republican recipient.

Hotel Employees & Restaurant Employees International Union TIP (To Insure Progress) (C00004515) *Address: same as sponsor * Treasurer: Herman Leavitt * Contact: Robert Juliano, Legislative Representative*

	1993-94	1995-96	1997	Totals
Receipts	$301,733	$257,268	$207,306	$766,307
Disburse	300,139	263,383	165,950	729,472
Cash	19,267	13,160	54,521	n/a
Contributions	278,259	215,915	130,850	625,024
Republicans	16,950	33,849	21,800	72,599
No. of Cand.	*14*	*30*	*21*	*65*
House	8,950	22,849	14,300	46,099
Senate	8,000	11,000	7,500	26,500
Democrats	258,509	182,066	108,050	548,625
No. of Cand.	*199*	*165*	*75*	*439*
House	203,588	138,166	76,550	418,304
Senate	54,921	43,900	31,500	130,321
Incumbents	228,781	147,154	115,350	491,285
Challengers	10,600	26,861	2,000	39,461
Open Seat	38,378	41,600	8,500	88,478
Winners	175,961	177,154	n/a	353,115
Losers	102,298	38,761	n/a	141,059

National Council of Field Labor Locals

Phone: (415) 975-4088
71 Stevenson St., Suite 432, San Francisco, CA 94105
Web: www.ncfll.org * E-mail: jgreene@sj.bigger.net

The National Council of Field Labor Locals represents more than 10,000 regional and field personnel, including office support staff, investigators, compliance officers and safety and health inspectors in both the Occupational Safety and Health Administration and the Mine Safety and Health Administration.

Affiliated with the American Federation of Government Employees, the union also represents economists, auditors, employment and training personnel and other professionals and specialists in the Department of Labor's 14 agencies.

The organization lobbies on Department of Labor appropriations bills and federal employee benefit programs. It also is interested in OSHA reform legislation. The NCFFL did not file a report with the FEC during 1997 and was named in an FEC complaint in October 1997, but no action was taken at the time.

National Council of Field Labor Locals PAC (NCFLL PAC) (C00301564) *Address: same as sponsor * Treasurer: James S. Greene*

	1993-94	1995-96	1997	Totals
Receipts	$0	$23,278	$0	$23,278
Disburse	0	24,538	0	24,538
Cash	0	(1258.00)	0	n/a
Contributions	0	7,000	0	7,000
Republicans	0	0	0	0
No. of Cand.	*0*	*0*	*0*	*0*
House	0	0	0	0
Senate	0	0	0	0
Democrats	0	7,000	0	7,000
No. of Cand.	*0*	*5*	*0*	*5*

House	0	0	0	0
Senate	0	7,000	0	7,000
Incumbents	0	5,000	0	5,000
Challengers	0	1,000	0	1,000
Open Seat	0	1,000	0	1,000
Winners	0	7,000	n/a	7,000
Losers	0	0	n/a	0

National Health and Human Services Employees Union

*Phone: (212) 582-1890 * Fax: (212) 262-4985*
310 W. 43rd St., New York, NY 10036

The Local 1199 Federal Political Action Fund is sponsored by the AFL-CIO-affiliated National Health and Human Services Employees Union. The PAC contributed only to Democrats, including $30,000 to the Democratic Congressional Campaign Committee, during the 1995-96 election cycle.

Five of the six top recipients, each receiving $10,000, were from New York, including three challengers. The other was House Minority Leader Richard A. Gephardt, D-Mo.

Local 1199 Federal Political Action Fund (C00022400) *Address: same as sponsor * Treasurer: Phyllis Harris * Contact: Dennis Rivera, President*

	1993-94	1995-96	1997	Totals
Receipts	$35,500	$427,900	$185,600	$649,000
Disburse	35,500	427,900	185,600	649,000
Cash	0	0	0	n/a
Contributions	30,500	156,400	51,600	238,500
Republicans	5,000	0	0	5,000
No. of Cand.	*1*	*0*	*0*	*1*
House	5,000	0	0	5,000
Senate	0	0	0	0
Democrats	24,500	156,400	51,600	232,500
No. of Cand.	*7*	*28*	*11*	*46*
House	24,500	149,400	43,500	217,400
Senate	0	7,000	8,100	15,100
Incumbents	19,500	96,400	44,100	160,000
Challengers	6,000	60,000	0	66,000
Open Seat	5,000	0	5,000	10,000
Winners	18,000	116,400	n/a	134,400
Losers	12,500	40,000	n/a	52,500

New England Health Care Employees Union

Phone: (860) 728-1100
77 Huyshope Ave., Hartford, CT 06106

New England Health Care Employees Union Political Action Fund (C00129965) *Address: same as sponsor * Treasurer: David Zevin*

	1993-94	1995-96	1997	Totals
Receipts	$20,534	$16,786	$1,000	$38,320
Disburse	21,280	11,052	1,000	33,332
Cash	4,421	10,156	846	n/a
Contributions	6,000	6,625	1,000	13,625
Republicans	0	0	0	0
No. of Cand.	*0*	*0*	*0*	*0*
House	0	0	0	0
Senate	0	0	0	0
Democrats	6,000	6,625	1,000	13,625
No. of Cand.	*4*	*6*	*1*	*11*
House	5,000	4,625	1,000	10,625
Senate	1,000	2,000	0	3,000
Incumbents	2,250	1,625	1,000	4,875
Challengers	3,750	1,000	0	4,750
Open Seat	0	4,000	0	4,000
Winners	2,250	5,625	n/a	7,875
Losers	3,750	1,000	n/a	4,750

Office & Professional Employees International Union (OPEIU)

Phone: (800) 346-7348
265 W. 14th St., Sixth Floor, New York, NY 10011
Web: www.opeiu.org

The Office & Professional Employees International Union represents more than 140,000 workers in the United States and Canada, including computer analysts, programmers, data entry operators, copywriters, nurses and other health care personnel, attorneys, artists, engineers, law enforcement operators and security guards, accountants, secretaries, bank employees, insurance agents and models. Members work in the public and private sectors.

The OPEIU was chartered by the AFL in 1945, and is affiliated with the AFL-CIO as well as the Canadian Labour Congress. It seeks to help members negotiate pay, benefits and better working conditions and conducts training programs. The union monitors and lobbies for favored legislation, such as the Americans with Disabilities Act and the Family and Medical Leave Act.

During the 1995-96 election cycle, the union's PAC, OPEIU-Voice of the Electorate, contributed almost exclusively to Democratic congressional candidates, with the exception of $2,000 to Independent Texas House candidate Janet Carroll Richardson. The Democratic Congressional Campaign Committee received $30,000, and other affiliated union committees were transferred more than $38,000.

Office & Professional Employees International Union Voice of the Electorate (C00007898) *Phone: (202) 393-4464 * Fax: (202) 347-0649 * 1660 C St. N.W., Suite 801, Washington, DC 20036 * Treasurer: Gilles Beauregard*

	1993-94	1995-96	1997	Totals
Receipts	$262,929	$337,784	$179,163	$779,876
Disburse	268,312	336,407	149,590	754,309
Cash	15,457	16,842	46,416	n/a
Contributions	132,150	212,825	83,100	428,075
Republicans	1,000	0	0	1,000
No. of Cand.	*1*	*0*	*0*	*1*
House	1,000	0	0	1,000
Senate	0	0	0	0
Democrats	130,150	212,825	83,100	426,075
No. of Cand.	*63*	*93*	*25*	*181*
House	64,150	117,700	37,100	218,950
Senate	66,000	95,125	46,000	207,125
Incumbents	103,450	99,575	71,600	274,625
Challengers	15,700	46,750	1,000	63,450
Open Seat	10,300	69,500	10,000	89,800
Winners	51,750	149,075	n/a	200,825
Losers	80,400	63,750	n/a	144,150

OPEIU Local 153 VOTE (Voice of the Electorate) Committee (C00008896) *Phone: (212) 741-8282 * Fax: (212) 463-9479 * 265 W. 14th St., New York, NY 10011 * Web: www.opeiu-153.org * E-mail: 4info@opeiu-153.org * Treasurer: Richard J. Lanigan*

	1993-94	1995-96	1997	Totals
Receipts	$39,286	$37,588	$16,853	$93,727
Disburse	42,633	37,307	19,118	99,058
Cash	5,557	5,838	3,572	n/a
Contributions	3,200	5,750	0	8,950
Republicans	500	0	0	500
No. of Cand.	*1*	*0*	*0*	*1*
House	500	0	0	500
Senate	0	0	0	0
Democrats	2,700	5,750	0	8,450
No. of Cand.	*4*	*3*	*0*	*7*
House	700	5,750	0	6,450
Senate	2,000	0	0	2,000
Incumbents	3,000	0	0	3,000
Challengers	200	5,250	0	5,450
Open Seat	0	500	0	500
Winners	3,000	5,750	n/a	8,750
Losers	200	0	n/a	200

Contributed less than $5,000 during 1995-96 cycle:

Office & Professional Employees International Union (OPEIU) Local 2 COPE (C00135707) *Phone: (301) 608-8080 * Fax: (301) 608-2586 * 8455 Colesville Rd., Suite 1250, Silver Spring, MD 20910-3320 * Treasurer: Michael W. Cowan*

Retail, Wholesale & Department Store Union

*Phone: (212) 684-5300 * Fax: (212) 779-2809*
30 E. 29th St., New York, NY 10016

The Retail, Wholesale & Department Store Union represents department store workers, poultry workers and manufacturers.

Retail, Wholesale & Department Store Union Committee on Political Education (RWDSU COPE) (C00174011) *Address: same as sponsor * Treasurer: Stewart Applebaum*

	1993-94	1995-96	1997	Totals
Receipts	$40,097	$37,198	$20,051	$97,346
Disburse	28,434	25,405	11,925	65,764
Cash	69,888	81,683	89,810	n/a
Contributions	19,600	14,600	9,500	43,700
Republicans	0	0	0	0
No. of Cand.	*0*	*0*	*0*	*0*
House	0	0	0	0
Senate	0	0	0	0
Democrats	19,600	14,600	9,500	43,700
No. of Cand.	*13*	*13*	*4*	*30*
House	18,600	10,600	9,000	38,200
Senate	1,000	4,000	500	5,500
Incumbents	15,000	4,800	9,500	29,300
Challengers	4,600	4,500	0	9,100
Open Seat	0	5,300	1,500	6,800
Winners	9,500	7,800	n/a	17,300
Losers	10,100	6,800	n/a	16,900

Contributed less than $5,000 during 1995-96 cycle:

District 1199C National Union of Hospital & Health Care Employees Political Action Fund (C00034066) *Phone: (215) 735-1300 * Fax: (215) 735-9878 * 1319 Locust St., Philadelphia, PA 19107 * Treasurer: Marguerite Morrison * Contact: Henry Nicholas, President*

Service Employees International Union

*Phone: (202) 898-3333 * Fax: (202) 898-3491*
1313 L St. N.W., Washington, DC 20005
*Web: www.seiu.org * E-mail: carterc@seiu.org*

Service Employees International Union is the largest union of health care workers in the United States. The 1.1 million members include hospital and nursing home employees, school bus drivers and nearly 200,000 janitors.

SEIU lobbies to preserve federal funding for hospitals that treat the poor and uninsured. It opposes the spread of managed care and seeks to maintain local hospital ownership. The union is waging a protest, led by its Las Vegas chapter, against hospital giant Columbia/HCA. SEIU's pension fund owns nearly 27,500 Columbia shares. The union seeks to stop Columbia from buying hospitals.

SEIU also opposes "sweatshop" working conditions in the garment industry.

SEIU dropped its contributions to congressional races by $75,000 from the 1994 cycle to 1996, but continued its pattern of giving almost exclusively to Democrats. The top sixteen recipients, who each received $10,000, were all Democrats. Rep. Sherwood Boehlert, R-N.Y., and former Rep. Bill Martini, R-N.J., were the only Republicans to receive contributions.

Service Employees International Union Political Campaign Committee (C00004036) *Address: same as sponsor * Treasurer: Betty Bednarczyk * Contact: Daniel Lucas*

	1993-94	1995-96	1997	Totals
Receipts	$1,184,377	$1,335,503	$775,844	$3,295,724
Disburse	1,187,151	1,291,615	312,932	2,791,698
Cash	120,716	164,613	627,525	n/a
Contributions	896,194	820,950	248,250	1,965,394
Republicans	14,000	2,500	16,500	33,000
No. of Cand.	*3*	*2*	*21*	*26*
House	13,000	2,500	16,500	32,000
Senate	1,000	0	0	1,000
Democrats	866,694	817,450	229,750	1,913,894
No. of Cand.	*290*	*211*	*157*	*658*
House	688,194	704,800	203,750	1,596,744
Senate	178,500	112,650	26,000	317,150
Incumbents	567,944	351,950	219,750	1,139,644
Challengers	149,500	303,000	5,000	457,500
Open Seat	170,750	165,000	23,000	358,750
Winners	473,694	545,450	n/a	1,019,144
Losers	422,500	275,500	n/a	698,000

Contributed less than $5,000 during 1995-96 cycle:

Local 617 COPE Committee (C00305227) *Phone: (201) 643-8080 * 51 Central Ave, Newark, NJ 07102 * Treasurer: Minnie McElroy*

Service Employees International Union Local 99 Federal Political Action Committee (C00323451) *Phone: (213) 387-8393 * 2724 W. Eighth St., Los Angeles, CA 90005 * Treasurer: Janett Humphries*

United Food & Commercial Workers Union

*Phone: (202) 223-3111 * Fax: (202) 466-1562*
1775 K St. N.W., Washington, DC 20006-1598
Web: www.ufcw.org

The United Food & Commercial Workers Union represents 1.4 million workers who work in food processing, retailing and health care industries. Four of every five UFCW members work in food-related businesses.

Major employers of members include Macy's and Bloomingdale's department stores, Pathmark and A&P supermarkets and Heinz, Frito-Lay and Kraft. UFCW's health care members work at nursing homes and hospitals owned by Beverly Enterprises and Kaiser-Permanente.

The union lobbies extensively for workplace safety and rights, especially for its members working on high-speed production lines at food processing plants. Along with other unions, it worked to defeat the "fast-track" trade authority.

The UFCW ranked sixth among labor unions in total contributions to federal candidates during the 1995-96 cycle. The group gave a greater percentage of its money to winning candidates than several other larger unions, including the Teamsters and United Auto Workers. UFCW was one of eight PACs to give more than $1 million to challengers during the 1995-96 cycle. More than 200 candidates received at least $5,000 from this PAC.

United Food & Commercial Workers Active Ballot Club (C00002766) *Address: same as sponsor * Treasurer: Joseph T. Hansen * Contact: Greg Sauter, PAC Dir.*

	1993-94	1995-96	1997	Totals
Receipts	$2,279,950	$3,058,977	$1,504,908	$6,843,835
Disburse	2,152,055	3,167,640	869,323	6,189,018
Cash	235,165	126,506	762,089	n/a
Contributions	1,456,139	2,030,795	523,941	4,010,875
Republicans	24,500	23,050	15,300	62,850
No. of Cand.	*10*	*11*	*9*	*30*
House	24,500	13,050	12,300	49,850
Senate	0	10,000	3,000	13,000
Democrats	1,397,139	1,998,745	500,141	3,896,025
No. of Cand.	*324*	*368*	*176*	*868*
House	1,175,222	1,778,095	432,641	3,385,958
Senate	221,917	220,650	67,500	510,067
Incumbents	960,671	948,351	426,691	2,335,713
Challengers	193,600	662,094	37,250	892,944
Open Seat	305,867	421,350	58,000	785,217
Winners	763,275	1,277,635	n/a	2,040,910
Losers	692,864	753,160	n/a	1,446,024

Contributed less than $5,000 during 1995-96 cycle:

United Food & Commercial Workers Union Local 1428 Federal PAC (C00297796) *705 W. Arrow Highway, Claremont, CA 91711 * Treasurer: Joe F. Barragan*

Public Sector Unions

AFSCME

*Phone: (202) 429-5020 * Fax: (202) 223-3413*
1625 L St. N.W., Washington, DC 20036
*Web: www.afscme.org * E-mail: dgouin@afscme.org*

One of the largest public-sector unions, the American Federation of State, County & Municipal Employees represents government and health care workers throughout the United States. Its membership totals about 1.3 million.

White collar employees account for one-third of the membership, while health and hospital workers constitute the largest industry with more than 325,000 members. Clerical and secretarial employees make up more than 300,000 of AFSCME's members, making it the largest union of office workers. AFSCME also is the largest union for correctional officers.

AFSCME is active in health care legislation, pushing for guarantees that managed care plans do not discriminate against teaching hospitals, among other issues. The union lobbies on state unemployment insurance reform and opposes weakening workplace safety regulations. The union also opposes removing collective bargaining rights for District of Columbia workers.

The union contributed more than $2.5 million to congressional races in 1996, second only to the Teamsters Union among labor committees. Two percent of AFSCME's PAC money went to Republican candidates. Sen. Alfonse M. D'Amato, R-N.Y., was the only Republican to receive more than $3,500. Among the 134 Democrats who received at least $10,000, Rep. Nick Lampson, D-Texas, and Rep. Ken Bentsen, D-Texas, were the top two recipients.

American Federation of State County & Municipal Employees - P E O P L E (C00011114) *Address: same as sponsor * Treasurer: William Lucy * Contact: Charles M. Loveless, Dir. of Legislation*

	1993-94	1995-96	1997	Totals
Receipts	$5,694,792	$7,052,002	$3,589,992	$16,336,786
Disburse	6,414,368	4,307,997	1,180,587	11,902,952
Cash	182,763	2,926,770	5,336,175	n/a
Contributions	2,514,682	2,504,021	925,350	5,944,053
Republicans	40,120	40,925	31,000	112,045
No. of Cand.	*16*	*22*	*20*	*58*
House	29,120	27,925	22,000	79,045
Senate	11,000	13,000	9,000	33,000
Democrats	2,426,062	2,453,096	880,350	5,759,508
No. of Cand.	*373*	*376*	*224*	*973*
House	2,144,512	2,191,301	774,100	5,109,913
Senate	281,550	261,795	106,250	649,595
Incumbents	1,706,760	1,245,074	808,250	3,760,084
Challengers	350,525	731,826	36,500	1,118,851
Open Seat	451,897	523,371	71,000	1,046,268
Winners	1,434,460	1,635,574	n/a	3,070,034
Losers	1,080,222	868,447	n/a	1,948,669

Contributed less than $5,000 during 1995-96 cycle:

American Federation of State, County and Municipal Employees Local 752 PAC (C00189415) *Phone: (215) 546-9880 * 1606 Walnut St., Philadelphia, PA 19103 * Treasurer: Bessie M. Carter*

District 1199J N.U.H.H.C.E. AFSCME AFL-CIO Political Action Committee (C00079327) *Phone: (973) 624-1199 * Fax: (973) 622-0801 * 9-25 Alling St., Third Floor, Newark, NJ 07102 * Treasurer: Joseph Franklin * Contact: Victor Garcia, President*

District Council 37, AFSCME Public Employees Organized for Political & Legislative Equality (DC37PEOPLE) (C00149211) *Phone: (212) 815-1000 * Fax: (212) 815-1218 * P.O. Box 2882, Church St. Station, New York, NY 10008 * Treasurer: Robert F. Myers Jr.*

American Federation of Government Employees

*Phone: (202) 737-8700 * Fax: (202) 639-6490*
80 F St. N.W., Washington, DC 20001
Web: www.afge.org

The American Federation of Government Employees is the largest federal employee union, representing about 700,000 federal and District of Columbia government workers. Agencies with the highest concentration of union membership include the departments of Defense, Veterans Affairs, Justice and the Social Security Administration.

The AFGE's primary objective is seeking pay raises of at least 6 percent for its members in 1999 and 2000. Other issues include preventing the repeal of a law barring the Pentagon from hiring outside contractors if money is budgeted to pay federal employees to do the same work. The group also wants to ensure a role for its members in the reform of D.C. government. Some 5,000 members are district employees. In general, the union lobbies against further government privatization.

The AFGE ranked second among unions of current or former federal government employees, but its total contributions were more than $1 million less than the top-ranked union, the National Association of Retired Federal Employees. Just four candidates received $5,000 or more from AFGE, and only one Republican, Sen. Pete Domenici, R-N.M., received more than $1,000. Reps. Steny H. Hoyer, D-Md., and Martin Frost, D-Texas, were the leading recipients.

American Federation of Government Employees' Political Action Committee (C00009936) *Address: same as sponsor * Treasurer: Bobby L. Harnage * Contact: Peggy C. Kans, PAC Dir.*

	1993-94	1995-96	1997	Totals
Receipts	$326,350	$340,675	$197,956	$864,981
Disburse	308,322	335,449	122,107	765,878
Cash	24,179	29,392	105,246	n/a
Contributions	260,070	241,200	87,950	589,220
Republicans	7,500	5,700	8,250	21,450
No. of Cand.	*7*	*8*	*12*	*27*
House	4,500	2,700	7,250	14,450
Senate	3,000	3,000	1,000	7,000
Democrats	249,570	235,000	78,200	562,770
No. of Cand.	*172*	*248*	*85*	*505*
House	163,650	197,900	63,800	425,350
Senate	85,920	37,100	14,400	137,420
Incumbents	209,020	141,850	77,450	428,320
Challengers	23,850	61,100	0	84,950
Open Seat	27,200	39,050	10,000	76,250
Winners	162,450	174,900	n/a	337,350
Losers	97,620	66,300	n/a	163,920

Terminated PACs which contributed less than $5,000 during 1995-96 cycle:

AFGE Local 2391 PAC (C00301572) *2788 Bush St., San Francisco, CA 94115 * Treasurer: James S. Greene*

American Federation of Teachers (AFT)

*Phone: (202) 879-4436 * Fax: (202) 393-6375*
555 New Jersey Ave. N.W., Washington, DC 20001
*Web: www.aft.org * E-mail: lsmith@aft.org*

The American Federation of Teachers represents about 950,000 teachers, health care employees and local government workers in the United States. It is the second-largest teachers union and has been discussing a merger with its larger counterpart, the National Education Association, that would create an organization with about 2 million members.

The two unions recently proposed a 10-year, $30-billion federal effort to modernize public school buildings in the United States. The AFT supports increased funding for the pre-school Head Start program and Pell Grants. It opposes public funding for religious and private schools and fights against the deterioration of the academic tenure system in higher education.

The AFT ranked second among teachers groups in total contributions to 1996 congressional races. The union spent just more than half of its contributions on challengers. Of the 64 candidates who received at least $10,000 from the AFT, all but one were Democrats. Rep. Sherwood Boehlert, R-N.Y., was the lone exception. Reps. Ken Bentsen, D-Texas, Martin Frost, D-Texas, and Nick Lampson, D-Texas, were the leading overall recipients.

American Federation of Teachers Committee on Political Education (C00028860) *Address: same as sponsor * Treasurer: Edward J. McElroy * Contact: Elizabeth Smith, Political Dir.*

	1993-94	1995-96	1997	Totals
Receipts	$2,320,690	$2,754,381	$1,320,407	$6,395,478
Disburse	1,839,479	2,655,527	470,644	4,965,650
Cash	922,250	1,021,105	1,870,869	n/a
Contributions	1,290,690	1,614,833	362,550	3,268,073
Republicans	11,000	19,750	7,200	37,950
No. of Cand.	*6*	*4*	*4*	*14*
House	7,000	19,750	4,450	31,200
Senate	4,000	0	2,750	6,750
Democrats	1,256,190	1,590,466	351,850	3,198,506
No. of Cand.	*240*	*305*	*137*	*682*
House	1,037,190	1,391,419	301,600	2,730,209
Senate	219,000	199,047	50,250	468,297
Incumbents	821,190	750,436	317,050	1,888,676
Challengers	187,500	526,397	4,500	718,397
Open Seat	274,000	332,000	37,500	643,500
Winners	689,090	1,024,936	n/a	1,714,026
Losers	601,600	589,897	n/a	1,191,497

American Federation of Teachers Staff Union Committee on Political Education (C00157545) *Address: same as sponsor * Treasurer: Yvonne P. Freeman*

	1993-94	1995-96	1997	Totals
Receipts	$7,016	$12,474	$7,505	$26,995
Disburse	47	27,000	12	27,059
Cash	16,994	2,469	9,962	n/a
Contributions	0	16,500	0	16,500
Republicans	0	0	0	0
No. of Cand.	*0*	*0*	*0*	*0*
House	0	0	0	0

(Data for American Federation continued)

Senate	0	0	0	0
Democrats	0	16,500	0	16,500
No. of Cand.	*0*	*5*	*0*	*5*
House	0	0	0	0
Senate	0	16,500	0	16,500
Incumbents	0	4,000	0	4,000
Challengers	0	4,000	0	4,000
Open Seat	0	8,500	0	8,500
Winners	0	10,000	n/a	10,000
Losers	0	6,500	n/a	6,500

Contributed less than $5,000 during 1995-96 cycle:

Political Action Council of Educators (United Teachers-Los Angeles) (C00023754) *Phone: (213) 487-5560 * Fax: (213) 487-3319 * 3303 Wilshire Blvd., 10th Floor, Los Angeles, CA 90010 * Web: www.gse.ucla.edu/turn/utla/utla.html * Treasurer: Patricia Stanyo * Contact: Inola Henry, Chairperson*

Voice of Teachers for Education/Committee on Political Education of N.Y. State United Teachers (VOTE/COPE) of NYSUT (C00021121) *Phone: (518) 459-7740 * 159 Wolf Rd., Box 15008, Albany, NY 12212-5008 * Web: www.nysut.org * Treasurer: Alan B. Lubin * Contact: Thomas Y. Hobart Jr., Chairman*

American Postal Workers Union

*Phone: (202) 842-4210 * Fax: (202) 682-2528*
1300 L St. N.W., Washington, DC 20005
*Web: www.apwu.org * E-mail: usb01461@interramp.com*

The American Postal Workers Union represents 366,000 employees of the U.S. Postal Service who are clerks, maintenance employees, motor vehicle operators, special delivery messengers and non-mail processing professional employees. The world's largest postal union, APWU is also the 15th largest union in the AFL-CIO.

Any legislation affecting the U.S. Postal Service is the union's top lobbying priority. It opposes privatization efforts and price caps on certain types of mail, as well as a proposal to end time spent on union activities at federal agencies. The AWPU also called on its members to support the nomination of Bill Lann Lee as Assistant Attorney General for Civil Rights.

The APWU ranked second among postal unions in total contributions to 1996 congressional races. The organization contributed a greater percentage of its money to winning candidates than all but two other unions. The leading recipients included Rep. Joseph P. Kennedy II, D-Mass., Rep. Patrick J. Kennedy, D-R.I., Sen. Carl Levin, D-Mich., and Rep. Jesse L. Jackson Jr., D-Ill. All but two of the top 50 recipients were Democrats, the exceptions being Rep. John M. McHugh, R-N.Y., and Sen. Ted Stevens, R-Alaska, both of whom chaired postal service subcommittees.

Committee on Political Action of the American Postal Workers Union, AFL-CIO (C00010322) *Address: same as sponsor * Treasurer: Douglas C. Holbrook * Contact: Roy Braunstein, Legislative Department Dir.*

	1993-94	1995-96	1997	Totals
Receipts	$1,224,082	$1,093,235	$358,216	$2,675,533
Disburse	1,247,262	1,179,368	361,562	2,788,192
Cash	145,871	59,743	56,399	n/a
Contributions	744,235	657,110	185,670	1,587,015
Republicans	28,500	24,500	6,200	59,200
No. of Cand.	*19*	*9*	*6*	*34*
House	24,500	20,500	6,200	51,200
Senate	4,000	4,000	0	8,000
Democrats	702,235	629,410	177,470	1,509,115
No. of Cand.	*262*	*238*	*131*	*631*
House	557,875	514,500	153,970	1,226,345
Senate	144,360	114,910	23,500	282,770
Incumbents	608,235	468,700	179,670	1,256,605
Challengers	49,000	105,910	1,000	155,910
Open Seat	86,000	82,500	6,000	174,500
Winners	500,175	534,700	n/a	1,034,875
Losers	244,060	122,410	n/a	366,470

Contributed less than $5,000 during 1995-96 cycle:

The PAF Committee (St. Paul, Minn. Area Local, American Postal Workers Union AFL-CIO) (C00162891) *Phone: (612) 778-1637 * Box 65065, St. Paul, MN 55165 * Treasurer: James C. Bryan*

Pittsburgh Metro Area Political Action Fund (C00097204) *Phone: (412) 321-4700 * 1414 Brighton Rd., 400 Epicenter, Pittsburgh, PA 15212 * Treasurer: Christian D. Schwemm*

Federal Managers' Association

*Phone: (703) 683-8700 * Fax: (703) 683-8707*
1641 Prince St., Alexandria, VA 22314
*Web: www.fpmi.com/fma * E-mail: fma@ix.netcom.com*

The Federal Managers' Association is a nonprofit advocacy association that represents 15,000 managers and supervisors in 25 federal departments.

FMA, which was founded in 1913, has two lobbyists in Washington.

The association's PAC is particularly interested in civil service issues, government contracting and government worker benefits. It is bipartisan and gives to federal candidates.

Federal Managers' Association Political Action Committee (C00164848) *Address: same as sponsor * Treasurer: R. Mark Gable*

	1993-94	1995-96	1997	Totals
Receipts	$60,690	$62,889	$23,220	$146,799
Disburse	71,890	53,303	16,619	141,812
Cash	3,464	14,744	21,348	n/a
Contributions	58,450	46,950	14,000	119,400
Republicans	8,450	20,550	6,400	35,400
No. of Cand.	*14*	*17*	*8*	*39*
House	6,950	13,050	5,400	25,400
Senate	1,500	7,500	1,000	10,000
Democrats	48,500	26,400	7,600	82,500
No. of Cand.	*50*	*29*	*12*	*91*
House	31,400	22,400	7,100	60,900
Senate	17,100	4,000	500	21,600
Incumbents	52,950	43,350	13,000	109,300
Challengers	2,000	1,600	0	3,600
Open Seat	3,500	2,000	1,000	6,500
Winners	45,950	45,350	n/a	91,300
Losers	12,500	1,600	n/a	14,100

International Association of Fire Fighters (IAFF)

*Phone: (202) 737-8484 * Fax: (202) 783-4570*
1750 New York Ave. N.W., Washington, DC 20006
Web: www.iaff.org

The International Association of Fire Fighters represents more than 225,000 professional firefighters and emergency medical personnel in the United States and Canada.

The IAFF is concerned with firefighter pay, collective bargaining rights for public safety officers and federal pension issues. It opposes restrictions on the political use of union dues. The IAFF also opposes two proposed changes to the Fair Labor Standards Act that would allow firefighters to volunteer for no pay and would extend the 53-hour work-week standard to emergency medical personnel who are not cross-trained as firefighters. It is against contracting government services to private employers.

The IAFF's PAC spent nearly 90 percent of its disbursements on congressional races in 1996, ranking fifth among unions. It rates incumbent candidates' voting records and asks challengers to fill out questionnaires on issues important to the union.

The IAFF spent the most on congressional races of any public safety PAC. More than 70 percent of its contributions went to winning candidates, a better percentage than many larger unions. No Republicans received more than $5,000 from this PAC, while 11 Democrats received at least $10,000. Those included Rep. Nick Lampson, D-Texas, Rep. Dale E. Kildee, D-Mich., and Charles P. Jones, who lost to Rep. Henry Bonilla, R-Texas.

International Association of Fire Fighters Interested in Registration and Education PAC (C00029447) *Address: same as sponsor * Treasurer: Vincent J. Bollon * Contact: Frederick H. Nesbitt, Gov. Affairs Dir.*

	1993-94	1995-96	1997	Totals
Receipts	$759,645	$787,849	$434,153	$1,981,647
Disburse	736,318	791,393	337,309	1,865,020
Cash	68,732	65,198	162,049	n/a
Contributions	684,467	703,875	312,450	1,700,792
Republicans	33,200	71,075	64,800	169,075
No. of Cand.	*27*	*40*	*42*	*109*
House	30,200	60,075	60,300	150,575
Senate	3,000	11,000	4,500	18,500
Democrats	642,267	631,800	244,150	1,518,217
No. of Cand.	*266*	*207*	*143*	*616*
House	518,352	518,300	215,150	1,251,802
Senate	123,915	113,500	29,000	266,415
Incumbents	457,275	333,425	286,950	1,077,650
Challengers	91,327	190,650	2,000	283,977
Open Seat	131,450	177,300	23,500	332,250
Winners	357,975	498,375	n/a	856,350
Losers	326,492	205,500	n/a	531,992

Phoenix Fire Fighters Local 493 Fire PAC Committee (C00134676) *Phone: (602) 277-1500 * Fax: (602) 277-0003 * 61 E. Columbus Ave., #200, Phoenix, AZ 85012 * Treasurer: Brian P. Tobin*

	1993-94	1995-96	1997	Totals
Receipts	$142,583	$172,525	$92,994	$408,102
Disburse	147,943	168,149	77,241	393,333
Cash	4,129	8,205	23,959	n/a
Contributions	3,841	8,000	5,000	16,841
Republicans	1,000	0	0	1,000
No. of Cand.	*1*	*0*	*0*	*1*
House	1,000	0	0	1,000
Senate	0	0	0	0
Democrats	2,841	8,000	5,000	15,841
No. of Cand.	*4*	*3*	*4*	*11*
House	4,000	5,000	4,500	13,500
Senate	-1,159	3,000	500	2,341
Incumbents	2,000	3,000	3,000	8,000
Challengers	0	5,000	1,000	6,000
Open Seat	1,841	0	1,000	2,841
Winners	2,000	3,000	n/a	5,000
Losers	1,841	5,000	n/a	6,841

Contributed less than $5,000 during 1995-96 cycle:

Dade County Fire Fighters Local 1403 PAC (C00130187) *Phone: (305) 593-6100 * Fax: (305) 591-9654 * 8000 N.W. 21st St., Suite 222, Miami, FL 33122 * Treasurer: Steven D. Lowe*

Houston Fire Fighters Political Action Fund, International Association of Fire Fighters (C00203497) *Phone: (713) 223-9166 * Fax: (713) 237-0912 * 1907 Freeman St., Houston, TX 77009 * Treasurer: Robert Britt*

Miami FirePAC - IAFF Local 587 (C00139014) *Phone: (305) 633-3442 * 2980 N.W. S. River Dr., Miami, FL 33125 * Treasurer: Joe D. Burns*

International Union of Police Association

*Phone: (703) 549-7473 * Fax: (703) 673-9048*
1421 Prince St., Suite 330, Alexandria, VA 22314
*Web: www.sddi.com/iupa * E-mail: iupa@iupa.org*

The International Union of Police Association represents all levels of government law enforcement officers, as well as deputy sheriffs, corrections officers and law enforcement support employees nationwide. The association was chartered by the AFL-CIO in February 1979 as the only federation union exclusively designed for law enforcement personnel. Its focus is to provide its member community with "improved working conditions, wages and benefits through legislative initiatives."

International Union of Police Association AFL-CIO Law Enforcement Political Action Committee (IUPA LEPAC) (C00264382) *Address: same as sponsor * Treasurer: Sam A. Cabral*

	1993-94	1995-96	1997	Totals
Receipts	$28,911	$10,321	$2,366	$41,598
Disburse	30,653	5,833	2,000	38,486
Cash	872	4,918	7,785	n/a
Contributions	26,575	5,200	250	32,025
Republicans	0	1,950	0	1,950
No. of Cand.	*0*	*3*	*0*	*3*
House	0	1,950	0	1,950
Senate	0	0	0	0
Democrats	25,575	3,250	250	29,075
No. of Cand.	*36*	*9*	*5*	*50*
House	21,075	3,000	750	24,825
Senate	4,500	250	-500	4,250
Incumbents	15,975	2,200	1,250	19,425
Challengers	3,000	550	0	3,550
Open Seat	7,600	2,450	0	10,050
Winners	12,750	4,400	n/a	17,150
Losers	13,825	800	n/a	14,625

National Association of Letter Carriers

*Phone: (202) 393-4695 * Fax: (202) 737-1540*
100 Indiana Ave. N.W., Washington, DC 20001-2144
*Web: www.nalc.org * E-mail: nalcinf@access.digex.net*

The National Association of Letter Carriers represents about 315,000 city letter carriers in the United States. Its counterpart, the National Rural Letter Carriers' Association, is a separate union for rural postal carriers. The NALC has 49 state associations and about 3,000 local branches.

The union lobbies on any legislation affecting the U.S. Postal Service and especially postal carrier pay and retirement funding. Keeping the USPS from privatizing and protecting its favorable first class delivery rates are among the union's top priorities.

The NALC opposes medical savings accounts and a fixed federal contribution to the Federal Employees Health Benefits Program. It opposes attempts to restrict the use of union money in the political process and generally supports most positions of the AFL-CIO.

Members' donations to the union's PAC in 1997 were 18 percent less than those in either one of the prior two years. In 1996, the NALC contributed more than $1.7 million to congressional campaigns, the most of any postal union. It ranked sixth among all unions in the total amount given to incumbent candidates. The leading recipients were Reps. Ken Bentsen, D-Texas, and Nick Lampson, D-Texas. Fifty-eight candidates, mostly Democrats, each received $10,000.

Three affiliated union PACs, in Illinois, Missouri and Minnesota, contributed at least $5,000 to congressional races. Each gave exclusively to Democratic candidates.

Committee on Letter Carriers Political Education (Letter Carriers Political Action Fund) (C00023580) *Address: same as sponsor * Treasurer: Florence M. Johnson * Contact: Tom Nagle, Special Assistant*

	1993-94	1995-96	1997	Totals
Receipts	$1,600,399	$2,284,350	$893,544	$4,778,293
Disburse	1,669,554	1,689,071	392,510	3,751,135
Cash	80,401	150,214	689,517	n/a
Contributions	1,428,290	1,706,564	307,646	3,442,500
Republicans	96,275	205,750	42,000	344,025
No. of Cand.	*34*	*52*	*27*	*113*
House	88,775	168,250	36,500	293,525
Senate	7,500	37,500	5,500	50,500
Democrats	1,308,515	1,491,314	263,646	3,063,475
No. of Cand.	*316*	*299*	*169*	*784*
House	1,090,525	1,261,914	206,646	2,559,085
Senate	217,990	229,400	57,000	504,390
Incumbents	1,087,750	989,464	284,646	2,361,860
Challengers	113,290	382,850	0	496,140
Open Seat	225,750	340,450	23,000	589,200
Winners	877,410	1,240,264	n/a	2,117,674
Losers	550,880	466,300	n/a	1,017,180

Illinois Political Active Letter Carriers (C00264689) *Phone: (309) 674-0408 * Fax: (309) 674-0404 * P.O. Box 561, 4820 22nd Ave., Orland Park, IL 60462 * Treasurer: Jack Heniff * Contact: Jesse Johnson*

	1993-94	1995-96	1997	Totals
Receipts	$18,076	$42,526	$25,992	$86,594
Disburse	15,600	44,706	14,496	74,802
Cash	12,037	9,855	21,351	n/a
Contributions	8,000	20,150	1,650	29,800
Republicans	0	0	0	0
No. of Cand.	*0*	*0*	*0*	*0*
House	0	0	0	0
Senate	0	0	0	0
Democrats	8,000	20,150	1,650	29,800
No. of Cand.	*9*	*12*	*3*	*24*
House	8,000	20,000	1,650	29,650
Senate	0	150	0	150
Incumbents	4,500	9,100	1,300	14,900
Challengers	1,000	7,650	0	8,650
Open Seat	2,500	3,400	0	5,900
Winners	4,500	10,750	n/a	15,250
Losers	3,500	9,400	n/a	12,900

Branch 343 National Association of Letter Carriers Political Action Fund (C00140772) *Phone: (314) 645-1086 * 2225 Blendon Pl., St. Louis, MO 63143 * Treasurer: Tom Harman*

	1993-94	1995-96	1997	Totals
Receipts	$24,282	$24,873	$9,491	$58,646
Disburse	17,753	23,931	7,374	49,058
Cash	10,965	11,910	14,028	n/a
Contributions	7,150	7,250	0	14,400
Republicans	0	0	0	0
No. of Cand.	*0*	*0*	*0*	*0*
House	0	0	0	0
Senate	0	0	0	0
Democrats	7,150	7,250	0	14,400
No. of Cand.	*5*	*4*	*0*	*9*
House	4,650	7,250	0	11,900
Senate	2,500	0	0	2,500
Incumbents	4,400	3,000	0	7,400
Challengers	250	4,000	0	4,250
Open Seat	2,500	250	0	2,750
Winners	4,400	1,450	n/a	5,850
Losers	2,750	5,800	n/a	8,550

National Association of Letter Carriers of United States of America Branch 9 Political Action League (C00114314) *Phone: (612) 781-9858 * Fax: (612) 781-9849 * 2408 Central Ave. N.E., Minneapolis, MN 55418 * Treasurer: Ron Lawrence*

11581 Ilex St. N.W., Coon Rapids, MN 55448

	1993-94	1995-96	1997	Totals
Receipts	$13,943	$17,039	$9,458	$40,440
Disburse	15,822	15,976	2,870	34,668
Cash	1,901	2,966	9,554	n/a
Contributions	2,000	6,500	-1000	7,500
Republicans	0	0	0	0
No. of Cand.	*0*	*0*	*0*	*0*
House	0	0	0	0
Senate	0	0	0	0
Democrats	2,000	6,500	0	8,500
No. of Cand.	*1*	*7*	*0*	*8*
House	2,000	6,500	0	8,500
Senate	0	0	0	0
Incumbents	0	4,500	-1000	3,500
Challengers	0	2,000	0	2,000
Open Seat	2,000	0	0	2,000
Winners	2,000	4,500	n/a	6,500
Losers	0	2,000	n/a	2,000

Contributed less than $5,000 during 1995-96 cycle:

Branch 28 National Association of Letter Carriers Political Action Committee (C00142935) *Phone: (612) 771-0533 * 1390 Charles Ave., St. Paul, MN 55104 * Treasurer: James E. Hannah*

Branch 193 National Association of Letter Carriers Political Action Committee (C00213645) *Phone: (408) 288-8138 * Fax: (408) 288-8172 * 1715 Mt. Pleasant Rd., San Jose, CA 95148 * Treasurer: George Katai*

National Association of Postal Supervisors

*Phone: (703) 836-9660 * Fax: (703) 836-9665*
1727 King St., Suite 400, Alexandria, VA 22314
Web: www.naps.org

The National Association of Postal Supervisors represents more than 35,000 active and retired U.S. Postal Service supervisors and managers. It is a management association, not a union, although the FEC considers NAPS a labor organization for PAC purposes.

NAPS members are supervisors who do not work at the Postal Service's Washington headquarters. Other members include managers in human resource, maintenance and marketing departments. The group is governed by a 24-member executive board, which has representatives from across the nation.

National Association of Postal Supervisors Political Action Committee (C00092957) *Address: same as sponsor * Treasurer: Timothy J. May*

	1993-94	1995-96	1997	Totals
Receipts	$88,561	$85,457	$20,590	$194,608
Disburse	86,466	58,881	19,243	164,590
Cash	40,378	66,963	68,314	n/a
Contributions	83,517	56,575	18,550	158,642
Republicans	11,500	20,775	6,300	38,575
No. of Cand.	*15*	*28*	*10*	*53*
House	11,500	17,275	6,300	35,075
Senate	0	3,500	0	3,500
Democrats	72,017	35,800	12,250	120,067
No. of Cand.	*91*	*53*	*18*	*162*
House	50,350	30,550	7,250	88,150
Senate	21,667	5,250	5,000	31,917
Incumbents	82,017	52,725	18,550	153,292
Challengers	0	1,000	0	1,000
Open Seat	2,500	2,850	0	5,350
Winners	70,167	52,075	n/a	122,242
Losers	13,350	4,500	n/a	17,850

National Association of Postmasters of the United States

*Phone: (703) 683-9027 * Fax: (703) 683-6820*
8 Herbert St., Alexandria, VA 22305-2600
*Web: www.napus.org * E-mail: napus8@napus.org*

The National Association of Postmasters of the United States represents more than 40,000 current and retired postmasters. The group has chapters in all 50 states, Puerto Rico and the Virgin Islands. NAPUS offers its members insurance and travel benefits and represents postmasters in disciplinary proceedings. It is not a labor union, because its members are considered executive personnel of the U.S. Postal Service.

NAPUS' chief legislative issue is maintaining benefits and pay for postmasters. The group supports postal service reform legislation which keeps the price of universal service consistent. It strongly opposes the privatization of the Postal Service. NAPUS was removed from the Federal Employees' Health Benefit Program in 1996 and is seeking to re-enter in 1999. It also opposes the consolidation of small rural post offices.

NAPUS ranked fourth among postal employee PACs in 1996 congressional campaign contributions. Nearly three-quarters of its contributions went to Democratic candidates, although the top three recipients were Republicans: Rep. Benjamin Gilman, R-N.Y., Sen. Ted Stevens, R-Alaska, and Rep. John McHugh, R-N.Y. McHugh chairs a postal service subcommittee which Gilman also sits on. Rep. David Bonior, D-Mich., and Sen. Richard Durbin, D-Ill., were the top Democratic recipients.

NAPUS PAC for Postmasters (formerly known as Political Education for Postmasters) (C00100404) *Address: same as sponsor * Treasurer: Teena Cregan * Contact: Nick Lewis, Gov. Relations Dir.*

	1993-94	1995-96	1997	Totals
Receipts	$421,113	$542,192	$269,382	$1,232,687
Disburse	434,127	540,003	150,764	1,124,894
Cash	115,145	117,336	240,136	n/a
Contributions	312,096	400,188	85,825	798,109
Republicans	45,705	105,179	36,275	187,159
No. of Cand.	*38*	*67*	*43*	*148*
House	38,955	76,479	26,275	141,709
Senate	6,750	28,700	10,000	45,450
Democrats	261,091	294,009	48,550	603,650
No. of Cand.	*199*	*191*	*61*	*451*
House	198,421	233,509	34,350	466,280
Senate	62,670	60,500	14,200	137,370
Incumbents	270,880	313,289	82,975	667,144
Challengers	9,466	32,199	0	41,665
Open Seat	29,550	54,200	1,850	85,600
Winners	224,980	347,588	n/a	572,568
Losers	87,116	52,600	n/a	139,716

National Association of Retired Federal Employees

*Phone: (703) 838-7760 * Fax: (703) 838-7782*
606 N. Washington St., Alexandria, VA 22314-1914
*Web: www.narfe.org * E-mail: narfelegis@aol.com*

The National Association of Retired Federal Employees has about 500,000 members and 1,700 chapters throughout the United States and its territories. Membership is open to civilians with at least five years of service in any federal or District of Columbia government agency. Members do not have to be retired.

NARFE is primarily concerned with legislation that would affect the pensions or retirement benefits of federal government employees. It opposes indexed flat payments by the government to the Federal Employees Health Benefits Program and proposals to end nursing home benefit guarantees for Medicaid-eligible patients. It also lobbies against medical savings accounts in the FEHBP. NARFE supports a managed care bill of rights for patients and, in general, legislation which maintains or boosts pay for federal employees.

NARFE was the leading contributor among federal employees' groups to 1996 congressional elections. Most of its PAC contributions went to Democratic candidates, and NARFE spent more than $400,000 on challengers and open seats. Reps. Martin Frost, D-Texas, Ken Bentsen, D-Texas, and Sam Gejdenson, D-Conn., were the top recipients. Two Republicans, Sens. John W. Warner, R-Va., and Ted Stevens, R-Alaska, each received $10,000.

National Association of Retired Federal Employees Political Action Committee (NARFE-PAC) (C00091561) *Address: same as sponsor * Treasurer: Frank G. Atwater * Contact: Charles R. Jackson, President*

	1993-94	1995-96	1997	Totals
Receipts	$1,933,619	$1,513,971	$128,350	$3,575,940
Disburse	1,373,956	1,673,758	361,743	3,409,457
Cash	1,346,158	1,186,369	952,978	n/a
Contributions	996,500	1,243,350	245,750	2,485,600
Republicans	101,450	205,400	36,750	343,600
No. of Cand.	*49*	*98*	*24*	*171*
House	74,450	163,900	32,250	270,600
Senate	27,000	41,500	4,500	73,000
Democrats	882,050	1,035,950	208,000	2,126,000
No. of Cand.	*252*	*258*	*102*	*612*
House	785,050	898,950	183,000	1,867,000
Senate	97,000	137,000	25,000	259,000
Incumbents	742,900	799,850	239,750	1,782,500
Challengers	126,100	236,500	0	362,600
Open Seat	127,500	206,000	6,000	339,500
Winners	648,900	959,800	n/a	1,608,700
Losers	347,600	283,550	n/a	631,150

National Education Association (NEA)

*Phone: (202) 833-4000 * Fax: (202) 822-7292*
1201 16th St. N.W., Washington, DC 20036
Web: www.nea.org

The largest teachers union in the United States, the National Education Association has more than 2.3 million members at all levels of education. The group has an affiliate in every state and more than 13,000 local organizations. It was ranked by *Fortune* magazine in 1997 as one of the top 10 most influential groups in Washington.

The NEA and the American Federation of Teachers, the second-largest teachers union, are negotiating a merger that could take place over the next few years. The AFT has about 950,000 members, including state and municipal employees. Together, the two unions contributed more than $3.9 million to congressional candidates in 1996.

The NEA supports increasing federal spending for education, including the Head Start program and school modernization efforts. Both teachers unions proposed a $30 billion, 10 year federal effort to upgrade school buildings. The NEA lobbies on education standards and supports equal requirements for charter schools and public schools.

The NEA has been a stalwart booster of Democratic candidates; during the 1995-96 cycle more than 99 percent of its contributions went to members of that party. The top recipients included Rep. Ken Bentsen, D-Texas, and Rep. Robert Wexler, D-Fla. More than 140 Democrats received at least $10,000. The GOP candidates who received $1,000 or more were Kathleen Donovan, who lost to Rep. Steven R. Rothman, D-N.J.; Rep. Sherwood Boehlert, R-N.Y., and Maggie Tinsman, who lost to Sen. Tom Harkin, D-Iowa. Seven other Republicans each received less than $1,000.

In total contributions to federal races, the NEA ranked fourth among unions. It also spent nearly $500,000 on independent expenditures for and against candidates and was among the top three contributors to challengers. Two NEA state affiliates — in Oregon and Michigan — spent more than $5,000 on congressional races in 1996.

National Education Association Political Action Committee (C00003251) *Address: same as sponsor * Treasurer: Don Cameron * Contact: Mary Elizabeth Teasley, PAC Dir.*

	1993-94	1995-96	1997	Totals
Receipts	$4,500,796	$4,896,927	$2,752,365	$12,150,088
Disburse	4,434,084	5,031,657	735,308	10,201,049
Cash	368,102	233,376	2,250,434	n/a
Contributions	2,260,850	2,326,830	345,695	4,933,375
Republicans	25,800	11,850	13,600	51,250
No. of Cand.	*13*	*13*	*12*	*38*

House	19,800	10,350	8,500	38,650
Senate	6,000	1,500	5,100	12,600
Democrats	2,196,050	2,304,980	329,595	4,830,625
No. of Cand.	*362*	*383*	*195*	*940*
House	1,934,750	2,051,680	286,645	4,273,075
Senate	261,300	253,300	42,950	557,550
Incumbents	1,410,350	1,035,380	279,195	2,724,925
Challengers	405,000	745,500	21,000	1,171,500
Open Seat	438,500	545,450	45,500	1,029,450
Winners	1,144,300	1,384,330	n/a	2,528,630
Losers	1,116,550	942,500	n/a	2,059,050

Oregon Education Association People for Improvement of Education (C00017343) *Phone: (503) 684-3300 * 6900 S.W. Haines Rd., Tigard, OR 97223 * Treasurer: Roger Gray*

The Oregon Education Association People for Improvement of Education was terminated on Feb. 12, 1998.

	1993-94	1995-96	1997	Totals
Receipts	$812,473	$935,161	$426,151	$2,173,785
Disburse	843,795	902,590	47,330	1,793,715
Cash	53,776	86,350	465,172	n/a
Contributions	9,900	17,700	100	27,700
Republicans	0	5,000	0	5,000
No. of Cand.	*0*	*1*	*0*	*1*
House	0	0	0	0
Senate	0	5,000	0	5,000
Democrats	9,900	12,700	100	22,700
No. of Cand.	*6*	*4*	*1*	*11*
House	9,900	2,200	100	12,200
Senate	0	10,500	0	10,500
Incumbents	2,400	200	100	2,700
Challengers	0	2,000	0	2,000
Open Seat	7,500	15,500	0	23,000
Winners	2,400	10,700	n/a	13,100
Losers	7,500	7,000	n/a	14,500

Citizens for Public Education (C/PAC) (C00255778) *Phone: (313) 259-1500 * 2237 E. Maple Rapids Rd., St. Johns, MI 48879 * Treasurer: Sharon Morford*

	1993-94	1995-96	1997	Totals
Receipts	$95,331	$65,666	$23,296	$184,293
Disburse	93,215	49,795	7,587	150,597
Cash	15,661	31,732	47,441	n/a
Contributions	350	5,026	300	5,676
Republicans	0	500	0	500
No. of Cand.	*0*	*1*	*0*	*1*
House	0	500	0	500
Senate	0	0	0	0
Democrats	350	4,526	300	5,176
No. of Cand.	*2*	*5*	*1*	*8*
House	350	1,905	300	2,555
Senate	0	2,621	0	2,621
Incumbents	150	3,221	300	3,671
Challengers	0	1,305	0	1,305
Open Seat	200	0	0	200
Winners	150	4,476	n/a	4,626
Losers	200	550	n/a	750

Contributed less than $5,000 during 1995-96 cycle:

Kansas National Education Association Pacesetter PAC (Pacesetter-PAC) (C00167536) *Phone: (913) 232-8271 * Fax: (913) 232-6012 * 715 S.W. Tenth Ave., Topeka, KS 66612 * Treasurer: Bruce T. Goeden*

National League of Postmasters

*Phone: (703) 548-5922 * Fax: (703) 683-0549*
1023 N. Royal St., Alexandria, VA 22314

The National League of Postmasters represents more than 10,000 postmasters with its state and area associations throughout the United States. The organization promotes effective postal management and monitors legislation and regulations.

National League of Postmasters Political Action Committee (C00164152) *Address: same as sponsor * Treasurer: Richard A. Weinberg * Contact: Penny Dimler, Dir. of Gov. Relations*

	1993-94	1995-96	1997	Totals
Receipts	$228,234	$304,292	$148,210	$680,736
Disburse	200,944	221,130	83,905	505,979
Cash	384,103	469,091	533,396	n/a
Contributions	189,650	171,800	60,550	422,000
Republicans	23,000	65,300	23,800	112,100
No. of Cand.	*32*	*85*	*28*	*145*
House	16,500	49,300	15,300	81,100
Senate	6,500	16,000	8,500	31,000

(*Data for National League continued*)

Democrats	164,150	106,000	36,250	306,400
No. of Cand.	*214*	*156*	*47*	*417*
House	131,150	91,000	28,250	250,400
Senate	33,000	15,000	8,000	56,000
Incumbents	187,950	158,300	59,050	405,300
Challengers	1,600	4,000	500	6,100
Open Seat	3,350	9,000	1,000	13,350
Winners	149,300	159,000	n/a	308,300
Losers	40,350	12,800	n/a	53,150

National Rural Letter Carriers' Association

*Phone: (703) 684-5545 * Fax: (703) 548-8735*
1630 Duke St., Fourth Floor, Alexandria, VA 22314-3465
Web: www.nrlca.org

The National Rural Letter Carriers' Association represents more than 95,000 postal workers in rural areas of the nation. The states with the largest membership are Texas, Pennsylvania and Illinois. The NRLCA is the bargaining unit for its members. The National Association of Letter Carriers represents postal workers in cities and suburbs.

The NRLCA is concerned with federal retirement and benefits issues and any legislation affecting the U.S. Postal Service. Since most rural postal carriers own the vehicles they use to deliver mail, the organization lobbies on tax issues relating to work use of vehicles.

The rural letter carriers' PAC ranked third among postal unions in contributions to 1996 congressional races. Nearly 75 percent of the group's contributions went to Democratic candidates. Challengers and open races accounted for more than 40 percent of the overall total. The leading recipients were Sens. Jack Reed, D-R.I., Tim Johnson, D-S.D., and Carl Levin, D-Mich. The top Republican recipients were Sens. Pete V. Domenici, R-N.M., and Ted Stevens, R-Alaska.

National Rural Letter Carriers' Association Political Action Committee (C00072025) *Address: same as sponsor * Treasurer: Ruth C. Pugh * Contact: Ken Parmalee, V.P. of Gov. Affairs*

	1993-94	*1995-96*	*1997*	*Totals*
Receipts	$560,830	$684,183	$319,117	$1,564,130
Disburse	567,662	693,806	212,739	1,474,207
Cash	84,298	74,676	181,053	n/a
Contributions	455,300	541,800	174,150	1,171,250
Republicans	77,600	131,250	45,500	254,350
No. of Cand.	*76*	*93*	*37*	*206*
House	62,100	91,250	27,500	180,850
Senate	15,500	40,000	18,000	73,500
Democrats	367,450	406,050	128,650	902,150
No. of Cand.	*241*	*182*	*107*	*530*
House	258,400	271,300	82,900	612,600
Senate	109,050	134,750	45,750	289,550
Incumbents	368,300	315,300	159,650	843,250
Challengers	17,000	91,500	1,000	109,500
Open Seat	72,500	134,500	12,500	219,500
Winners	301,150	407,200	n/a	708,350
Losers	154,150	134,600	n/a	288,750

National Star Route Mail Contractors Association

324 E. Capitol St., Washington, DC 20003

National Star Route Mail Contractors Political Action Committee (StarPAC) (C00163311) *Address: same as sponsor * Treasurer: Dale Foreman*

	1993-94	*1995-96*	*1997*	*Totals*
Receipts	$34,670	$63,512	$0	$98,182
Disburse	28,904	56,244	16,405	101,553
Cash	41,761	49,028	32,622	n/a
Contributions	16,500	31,300	12,000	59,800
Republicans	2,500	29,300	12,000	43,800
No. of Cand.	*3*	*19*	*11*	*33*
House	2,500	20,800	9,000	32,300
Senate	0	8,500	3,000	11,500
Democrats	14,000	2,000	0	16,000
No. of Cand.	*9*	*3*	*0*	*12*
House	13,000	2,000	0	15,000
Senate	1,000	0	0	1,000
Incumbents	16,000	30,800	12,000	58,800
Challengers	0	0	0	0
Open Seat	500	500	0	1,000
Winners	8,500	29,800	n/a	38,300
Losers	8,000	1,500	n/a	9,500

National Treasury Employees Union

*Phone: (202) 783-4444 * Fax: (202) 783-4085*
901 E St. N.W., Suite 600, Washington, DC 20004-2037
*Web: www.nteu.org * E-mail: nmill@nteuhq1.nteu.org*

The National Treasury Employees Union represents about 150,000 workers in 18 government agencies — including more than 97,000 in the Internal Revenue Service — making it the largest independent non-postal federal employees union. The union has local chapters in every state and represents non-supervisory civilian employees.

The NTEU supports legislation that would help close the pay gap between private and public employees. It opposes federal agencies, such as the IRS, who seek to contract work to non-federal employees. NTEU advocates for consistent funding for federal agencies and the restructuring of the IRS. The group opposes the line-item veto as unconstitutional.

The NTEU ranked third among federal employee unions in contributions to 1996 congressional candidates. Most of that money went to Democrats and incumbents. The top recipient was Rep. Steny H. Hoyer, D-Md., who sponsored a 1998 bill to make federal workers' salaries comparable to those in the private sector. The other leading recipients included Sens. Tim Johnson, D-S.D., Paul Wellstone, D-Minn., and Ted Stevens, R-Alaska.

National Treasury Employees Union Political Action Committee (TEPAC) (C00107128) *Address: same as sponsor * Treasurer: Nancy Marcus Miller*

	1993-94	*1995-96*	*1997*	*Totals*
Receipts	$208,168	$326,670	$232,425	$767,263
Disburse	221,561	289,925	112,061	623,547
Cash	12,512	49,264	163,207	n/a
Contributions	180,178	229,429	78,000	487,607
Republicans	7,100	22,740	4,000	33,840
No. of Cand.	*11*	*19*	*5*	*35*
House	5,850	10,740	3,000	19,590
Senate	1,250	12,000	1,000	14,250
Democrats	167,728	205,989	73,500	447,217
No. of Cand.	*130*	*180*	*77*	*387*
House	91,528	155,689	48,250	295,467
Senate	76,200	50,300	25,250	151,750
Incumbents	144,103	139,690	75,500	359,293
Challengers	10,225	47,789	0	58,014
Open Seat	25,600	41,950	2,000	69,550
Winners	113,158	178,290	n/a	291,448
Losers	67,020	51,139	n/a	118,159

Southern States Police Benevolence Association

*Phone: (770) 960-0092 * Fax: (770) 961-4814*
1517 Southlake Pkwy., Morrow, GA 30260
Web: www.sspba.org

Founded in 1990, the Southern States Police Benevolence Association represents more than 15,000 law enforcement officers in Alabama, Arkansas, Georgia, Mississippi, North Carolina, South Carolina, Tennessee and Virginia. Funded by member dues and private donations, the organization provides legal aid and advocates changes to improve the working conditions of people in all areas and levels of the criminal justice system. The group also states that it prohibits its members from engaging in or condoning any law enforcement strike, but that it will represent its members through aggressive political activity.

Southern States PBA Inc. PAC Fund (C00265546) *Address: same as sponsor * Treasurer: Joe Stiles * Contact: Jack L. Roberts, President*

	1993-94	*1995-96*	*1997*	*Totals*
Receipts	$130,201	$136,102	$77,507	$343,810
Disburse	118,388	142,446	51,136	311,970
Cash	17,386	11,041	37,412	n/a
Contributions	12,687	14,726	5,222	32,635
Republicans	6,462	12,894	3,043	22,399
No. of Cand.	*5*	*15*	*3*	*23*
House	5,462	6,165	3,043	14,670
Senate	1,000	6,729	0	7,729
Democrats	6,225	1,832	2,179	10,236
No. of Cand.	*8*	*8*	*1*	*17*
House	6,225	832	2,179	9,236
Senate	0	1,000	0	1,000
Incumbents	2,000	11,574	5,222	18,796
Challengers	4,500	144	0	4,644
Open Seat	6,187	3,008	0	9,195
Winners	6,462	11,394	n/a	17,856
Losers	6,225	3,332	n/a	9,557

Transportation Unions

Air Line Pilots Association

*Phone: (202) 797-4033 * Fax: (202) 797-4052*
1625 Massachusetts Ave. N.W., Washington, DC 20036
Web: www.alpa.org

The Air Line Pilots Association represents about 49,000 commercial pilots from 48 airlines in the United States and Canada. The union has about 8,000 members at Delta Airlines and 5,000 at U.S. Airways. It lobbies on aviation issues and uses about 20 percent of its dues to support aviation safety programs. The organization is divided into pilot groups, which represent members at each airline. ALPA is associated with the AFL-CIO.

ALPA supports adequate funding for the Federal Aviation Administration's service and safety divisions. It also supports a bill that would confirm that U.S. pilots working overseas are covered by the same collective bargaining agreements that cover their airlines' U.S. operations. The union's pilot groups lobby on issues specific to the airlines they are associated with, such as changes in takeoff and landing rights at specific airports.

ALPA was the leading aviation union contributor to 1996 congressional campaigns. More than 75 percent of its contributions went to Democratic candidates, but one Republican, Rep. Jack Quinn, R-N.Y., was among the top recipients. The leading recipient was Rep. Peter A. DeFazio, D-Ore. A dozen other Democratic candidates each received $10,000.

Air Line Pilots Association Political Action Committee (C00035451) *Address: same as sponsor * Treasurer: Duane E. Woerth * Contact: Jerry Baker, Senior Legislative Representative*

	1993-94	1995-96	1997	Totals
Receipts	$1,254,938	$1,146,911	$529,801	$2,931,650
Disburse	1,210,520	1,089,607	478,680	2,778,807
Cash	212,387	269,694	320,815	n/a
Contributions	1,001,186	822,000	376,500	2,199,686
Republicans	139,500	190,000	103,500	433,000
No. of Cand.	*60*	*70*	*51*	*181*
House	102,000	163,000	86,500	351,500
Senate	37,500	27,000	17,000	81,500
Democrats	832,186	632,000	264,500	1,728,686
No. of Cand.	*227*	*202*	*136*	*565*
House	675,000	482,000	210,000	1,367,000
Senate	157,186	150,000	54,500	361,686
Incumbents	843,500	625,000	370,000	1,838,500
Challengers	56,500	66,500	0	123,000
Open Seat	103,000	129,500	6,500	239,000
Winners	724,000	659,500	n/a	1,383,500
Losers	277,186	162,500	n/a	439,686

United Pilots Political Action Committee (UAL-MEC) (C00251009) *Phone: (847) 292-1700 * Fax: (847) 292-1760 * 6400 Shafer Ct., Suite 700, Rosemont, IL 60018 * Treasurer: Mark Bathurst * Contact: Michael Glawe, Chair*

The United Pilots PAC is sponsored by the United Airlines Master Executive Council of the Air Line Pilots Association, a union affiliate of the Air Line Pilots Association.

This affiliate represents more than 9,000 United Airlines pilots.

	1993-94	1995-96	1997	Totals
Receipts	$304,603	$287,056	$134,048	$725,707
Disburse	197,401	300,300	77,774	575,475
Cash	161,322	148,093	204,371	n/a
Contributions	13,100	53,000	27,250	93,350
Republicans	6,000	500	0	6,500
No. of Cand.	*3*	*1*	*0*	*4*
House	6,000	500	0	6,500
Senate	0	0	0	0
Democrats	7,100	52,500	27,250	86,850
No. of Cand.	*3*	*30*	*14*	*47*
House	4,500	42,500	12,250	59,250
Senate	2,600	10,000	15,000	27,600
Incumbents	5,500	4,000	22,250	31,750
Challengers	0	26,500	0	26,500
Open Seat	7,600	20,000	5,000	32,600
Winners	6,000	29,500	n/a	35,500
Losers	7,100	23,500	n/a	30,600

Allied Pilots Association

*Phone: (972) 988-3188 * Fax: (972) 606-5612*
P.O. Box 5524, Arlington, TX 76005
Web: www.alliedpilots.org

The Allied Pilots Association is the union for 9,000 American Airlines pilots. It is based in Arlington, Texas, near the airline's headquarters at the Dallas/Fort Worth Airport.

The union split from the Air Line Pilots Association in 1963 following a dispute over working hours. American's sister airline, American Eagle, is represented by ALPA.

APA has had well-publicized problems with American, often threatening to strike and disagreeing with many the company's decisions. In 1997, President Clinton intervened to end a lengthy pilots strike.

APA, which was founded in 1931, has locations in Boston, Chicago, Los Angeles, Miami, New York and San Francisco.

Allied Pilots Association Political Action Committee (also known as APA PAC) (C00267849) *Address: same as sponsor * Treasurer: Michael Cronin * Contact: Richard T. LaVoy, Chairman*

	1993-94	1995-96	1997	Totals
Receipts	$126,564	$176,362	$104,286	$407,212
Disburse	52,146	141,115	77,090	270,351
Cash	78,465	113,713	140,910	n/a
Contributions	50,100	123,100	76,000	249,200
Republicans	20,000	77,500	43,500	141,000
No. of Cand.	*18*	*51*	*27*	*96*
House	15,000	42,000	30,500	87,500
Senate	5,000	35,500	13,000	53,500
Democrats	29,100	45,600	29,500	104,200
No. of Cand.	*19*	*34*	*14*	*67*
House	25,100	28,600	17,000	70,700
Senate	4,000	17,000	12,500	33,500
Incumbents	49,100	114,000	76,000	239,100
Challengers	0	3,100	0	3,100
Open Seat	1,000	6,000	0	7,000
Winners	43,100	114,100	n/a	157,200
Losers	7,000	9,000	n/a	16,000

Amalgamated Transit Union

*Phone: (202) 537-1645 * Fax: (202) 244-7824*
5025 Wisconsin Ave. N.W., Washington, DC 20016-4139
Web: www.cais.net/atu

The Amalgamated Transit Union is the largest labor organization representing transit workers in the United States and Canada. Founded in 1892, the union represents 160,000 members in 46 states and nine provinces. Its members operate school buses, subway cars, vans and ambulances. Others are baggage handlers, maintenance employees and municipal government workers.

Greyhound Lines Inc. is a major employer of ATU members, as are bus systems in many major cities with the notable exception of New York, where the Transport Workers Union dominates.

ATU supports increased federal funding for mass transit projects through the Building Efficient Surface Transportation and Equity Act. It opposes privatizing public transportation. ATU is a member of The Campaign for Efficient Passenger Transportation, an industry group that lobbies on transportation spending legislation and public mass transit issues.

During the 1995-96 election cycle, ATU ranked second in congressional contributions among transportation unions drawing from more than one industry. Almost 75 percent of the union's contributions went to winning candidates, a relatively high percentage among labor PACs.

The leading recipients were Minority Leader Richard A. Gephardt, D-Mo., Rep. Jack Quinn, R-N.Y., Sen. Richard J. Durbin, D-Ill., and 1996 House candidate Michael Coles, a Georgia Democrat.

Amalgamated Transit Union - COPE (C00032995) *Address: same as sponsor * Treasurer: Oliver W. Green * Contact: John Remark, Legislative Representative*

	1993-94	1995-96	1997	Totals
Receipts	$696,455	$949,408	$422,853	$2,068,716
Disburse	692,176	957,981	332,362	1,982,519
Cash	63,267	54,702	145,195	n/a
Contributions	409,825	567,350	213,200	1,190,375
Republicans	2,500	64,500	37,250	104,250
No. of Cand.	*4*	*36*	*30*	*70*
House	2,000	61,000	30,500	93,500
Senate	500	3,500	6,750	10,750
Democrats	396,425	501,350	170,950	1,068,725
No. of Cand.	*224*	*239*	*124*	*587*
House	270,175	375,950	143,800	789,925
Senate	126,250	125,400	27,150	278,800
Incumbents	302,425	371,650	196,250	870,325
Challengers	45,200	86,450	4,500	136,150
Open Seat	61,700	108,250	13,450	183,400
Winners	231,675	422,450	n/a	654,125
Losers	178,150	144,900	n/a	323,050

Association of Flight Attendants

*Phone: (202) 712-9738 * Fax: (202) 712-9798*
1275 K St. N.W., Washington, DC 20036

The Association of Flight Attendants represents 42,000 flight attendants who work for 27 airlines. It is the largest flight attendants union. The association represents flight attendants for US Airways, United, America West, Alaska, Hawaiian, and American Eagle, in addition to other airlines.

In 1996 the union challenged ValuJet Airlines, questioning its ability to "run a safe airline." The union asked the Department of Transportation to remove ValuJet's management team before allowing it to resume operations. In late 1997, the association led a movement to limit carry-on luggage.

The association has 70 locals around the nation. It is affiliated with the AFL-CIO, as well as the International Transport Workers Federation.

Association of Flight Attendants Political Action Committee (Flight PAC) (C00151811) *Address: same as sponsor * Treasurer: Sharon E. Madigan*

	1993-94	1995-96	1997	Totals
Receipts	$267,597	$314,591	$157,305	$739,493
Disburse	269,017	368,028	24,854	661,899
Cash	166,945	113,510	245,963	n/a
Contributions	223,250	201,980	0	425,230
Republicans	2,250	15,750	0	18,000
No. of Cand.	*6*	*19*	*0*	*25*
House	2,250	11,750	0	14,000
Senate	0	4,000	0	4,000
Democrats	207,500	183,730	0	391,230
No. of Cand.	*160*	*178*	*0*	*338*
House	125,000	126,730	0	251,730
Senate	82,500	57,000	0	139,500
Incumbents	174,250	140,080	0	314,330
Challengers	22,000	25,350	0	47,350
Open Seat	27,500	36,550	0	64,050
Winners	128,000	165,550	n/a	293,550
Losers	95,250	36,430	n/a	131,680

Association of Professional Flight Attendants

*Phone: (817) 540-0108 x8131 * Fax: (817) 540-2077*
1004 W. Euless Blvd., Euless, TX 76040
Web: www.apfa.org

The Association of Professional Flight Attendants represents 20,000 American Airlines flight attendants.

The union, which was founded in 1977 after a break with the Transport Workers Union, has offices in 11 U.S. cities.

APFA spearheaded a flight attendant strike in November 1993, forcing American Airlines into binding arbitration.

Association of Professional Flight Attendants (APFA PAC) Political Action Committee (C00246421) *Address: same as sponsor * Treasurer: Michael L. Parker*

	1993-94	1995-96	1997	Totals
Receipts	$38,089	$34,172	$17,443	$89,704
Disburse	37,845	37,149	13,924	88,918
Cash	6,369	3,395	6,915	n/a
Contributions	31,250	21,700	8,800	61,750
Republicans	550	1,250	500	2,300
No. of Cand.	*2*	*4*	*1*	*7*
House	550	1,250	500	2,300
Senate	0	0	0	0
Democrats	29,700	20,450	7,300	57,450
No. of Cand.	*83*	*61*	*24*	*168*
House	17,150	14,250	4,800	36,200
Senate	12,550	6,200	2,500	21,250
Incumbents	27,650	16,850	8,800	53,300
Challengers	1,600	1,200	0	2,800
Open Seat	2,000	3,650	0	5,650
Winners	22,600	18,550	n/a	41,150
Losers	8,650	3,150	n/a	11,800

Brotherhood of Locomotive Engineers

*Phone: (216) 241-2630 * Fax: (216) 241-6516*
1370 Ontario St., Mezzanine, Cleveland, OH 44113-1702
Web: www.ble.org

The Brotherhood of Locomotive Engineers is North America's oldest railroad union. It represents 55,000 active and retired engineers and associated rail employees. In 1993, the 2,000-member American Train Dispatchers Association merged into BLE. Locomotive engineers in the United States must be federally certified.

BLE has been resisting a proposal from the United Transportation Union, a larger railroad organization, to consolidate the two unions by creating a single class of railroad employees. BLE supports continued funding for Amtrak. Of the $344 million federal subsidy Amtrak received in 1997 for operating expenses, $142 million pays for railroad retirement pension benefits.

BLE ranked second among railroad unions in 1995-96 congressional contributions; it spent nearly $1 million less than the UTU. Most of its contributions went to Democrats — the 16 candidates who received more than $3,500 came from that party.

The leaders included Rep. David E. Bonior, D-Mich., and Senate candidates Winston Bryant of Arkansas and Ben Nelson of Nebraska. Each received at least $10,000. The two Republicans who received at least $3,000 were Sen. Alfonse M. D'Amato, R-N.Y., and former Rep. Bill Martini, R-N.J.

Brotherhood of Locomotive Engineers PAC Fund (C00099234) *Phone: (202) 347-7936 * Fax: (202) 347-5237 * 10 G. St. N.E., Suite 480, Washington, DC 20002 * E-mail: bledc@aol.com * Treasurer: Russell W. Bennett * Contact: Leroy D. Jones, V.P.*

	1993-94	1995-96	1997	Totals
Receipts	$464,463	$615,097	$350,193	$1,429,753
Disburse	428,133	630,197	215,940	1,274,270
Cash	108,948	93,851	228,108	n/a
Contributions	247,260	365,615	120,515	733,390
Republicans	6,310	23,200	11,915	41,425
No. of Cand.	*7*	*18*	*14*	*39*
House	4,910	18,000	10,315	33,225
Senate	1,400	5,200	1,600	8,200
Democrats	233,450	341,915	106,300	681,665
No. of Cand.	*186*	*202*	*112*	*500*
House	173,000	251,900	75,500	500,400
Senate	60,450	90,015	30,800	181,265
Incumbents	135,910	178,200	98,415	412,525
Challengers	54,750	70,965	5,500	131,215
Open Seat	56,350	116,450	15,600	188,400
Winners	106,310	217,500	n/a	323,810
Losers	140,950	148,115	n/a	289,065

Contributed less than $5,000 during 1995-96 cycle:

Brotherhood of Locomotive Engineers/Texas State Legislative Board, Engineers Political Education League (C00166645) *Phone: (903) 569-3818 * P.O. Box 990, Mineola, TX 75773 * Treasurer: Raymond A. Holmes*

Political League of the American Train Dispatchers Department/Brotherhood of Locomotive Engineers (Train Dispatchers Political League) (C00287748) *Phone: (216) 241-2630 * 1370 Ontario St., Suite 1040, Cleveland, OH 44113-1701 * Treasurer: F. Leo McCann*

Brotherhood of Maintenance of Way Employees (BMWE)

*Phone: (248) 948-1010 * Fax: (248) 948-9140*
26555 Evergreen Rd., Suite 200, Southfield, MI 48076
Web: www.bmwe.org

The Brotherhood of Maintenance of Way Employees represents rail workers in the United States and Canada. Once a union with more than 350,000 members, BMWE has shrunk to 52,000 railroad track and bridge construction and maintenance workers. The union has opposed a consolidated railroad workers union proposed by the United Transportation Union, a larger railroad workers union with about 150,000 members.

The union's chief legislative issues include Amtrak authorization and worker safety. It opposes "fast-track" trade authority. BMWE also weighed in against a bill to establish a central nuclear waste repository, citing a lack of money to train railway workers to handle waste as the chief reason. It also opposes any changes to the Railroad Retirement Act that would limit benefits to federal railroad employees.

BMWE ranked third among five railroad unions in total contributions to 1996 congressional races. It gave heavily to Democrats during that cycle, but also spent $30,500 on Republican candidates, including $5,000 apiece to Sen. Arlen Specter, R-Pa., and Rep. Bud Shuster, R-Pa.

Maintenance of Way Political League (C00000372) *Phone: (202) 638-2135 * Fax: (202) 737-3085 * 10 G. St. N.E., Suite 460, Washington, DC 20002 * E-mail: 71363.1767@compuserve.com * Treasurer: William E. LaRue * Contact: Andrew T. Malleck, National Legislative Representative*

	1993-94	1995-96	1997	Totals
Receipts	$238,816	$298,550	$158,716	$696,082
Disburse	217,355	287,552	114,991	619,898
Cash	52,689	31,005	74,738	n/a
Contributions	193,600	254,057	103,491	551,148
Republicans	2,500	25,500	16,800	44,800
No. of Cand.	*3*	*25*	*17*	*45*
House	2,500	24,500	12,800	39,800
Senate	0	1,000	4,000	5,000
Democrats	185,150	226,557	84,691	496,398
No. of Cand.	*155*	*165*	*83*	*403*
House	125,650	177,807	69,950	373,407
Senate	59,500	48,750	14,741	122,991
Incumbents	161,250	186,557	96,991	444,798
Challengers	11,850	29,250	2,000	43,100
Open Seat	18,000	37,750	4,500	60,250
Winners	130,050	212,557	n/a	342,607
Losers	63,550	41,500	n/a	105,050

Brotherhood of Railroad Signalmen

*Phone: (847) 439-3732 * Fax: (847) 439-3743*
P.O. Box U, Mt. Prospect, IL 60056
*Web: www.brs.org * E-mail: signal@brs.org*

The Brotherhood of Railroad Signalmen represents 14,000 signalmen around the nation. The union, which was founded in 1901, has 180 local chapters.

Brotherhood of Railroad Signalmen Political Action Committee (C00011262) *Address: same as sponsor * Treasurer: R. R. Foley*

	1993-94	1995-96	1997	Totals
Receipts	$115,248	$179,050	$79,748	$374,046
Disburse	108,323	187,470	79,417	375,210
Cash	13,294	9,685	10,017	n/a
Contributions	89,200	76,250	42,231	207,681
Republicans	2,100	3,500	0	5,600
No. of Cand.	*6*	*5*	*0*	*11*
House	2,100	3,000	0	5,100
Senate	0	500	0	500
Democrats	83,600	70,300	41,231	195,131
No. of Cand.	*112*	*78*	*54*	*244*
House	52,050	44,300	26,731	123,081
Senate	31,550	26,000	14,500	72,050
Incumbents	67,700	46,400	37,731	151,831
Challengers	8,850	8,800	2,000	19,650
Open Seat	12,650	20,100	2,000	34,750
Winners	57,350	61,200	n/a	118,550
Losers	31,850	15,050	n/a	46,900

Independent Federation of Flight Attendants

*Phone: (314) 621-1177 * Fax: (314) 621-3722*
720 Olive St., Suite 1700, St. Louis, MO 63101

The Independent Federation of Flight Attendants was founded to represent flight attendants who work for St. Louis-based Trans World Airlines. However, in early 1997, 5,000 TWA flight attendants voted to switch to the International Association of Machinists.

As of early 1998, IFFA has no right to represent TWA flight attendants. A court case is pending.

After the summer 1997 explosion of TWA Flight 800, IFFA started the Friends of Flight 800 Fund to assist the 19 children of flight attendants who were killed.

Independent Federation of Flight Attendants Jet PAC (C00241307) *Address: same as sponsor * Treasurer: James Gordon Tuller * Contact: Flip Becker, President*

	1993-94	1995-96	1997	Totals
Receipts	$26,712	$23,329	$3,317	$53,358
Disburse	27,088	26,690	600	54,378
Cash	6,783	3,424	6,141	n/a
Contributions	21,660	15,400	0	37,060
Republicans	850	750	0	1,600
No. of Cand.	*2*	*2*	*0*	*4*
House	850	750	0	1,600
Senate	0	0	0	0
Democrats	20,060	14,650	0	34,710
No. of Cand.	*55*	*46*	*0*	*101*
House	13,810	10,350	0	24,160
Senate	6,250	4,300	0	10,550
Incumbents	19,860	12,650	0	32,510
Challengers	350	850	0	1,200
Open Seat	1,450	1,900	0	3,350
Winners	16,460	13,650	n/a	30,110
Losers	5,200	1,750	n/a	6,950

International Longshore and Warehouse Union

*Phone: (415) 775-0533 * Fax: (415) 775-1302*
1188 Franklin St., San Francisco, CA 94109

The International Longshore and Warehouse Union represents 60,000 longshoremen, marine clerks and warehouse workers in California, Oregon, Alaska, Hawaii, Washington state and British Columbia. It also represents X-ray technicians and Hawaiian agricultural workers.

The union split from the International Longshoremen's Association in 1937 after a general strike in San Francisco. The strike was part of an international strike of marine workers.

International Longshore and Warehouse Union - Political Action Fund (C00176214) *Address: same as sponsor * Treasurer: Joe Ibarra * Contact: Bryan McWilliams, President*

	1993-94	1995-96	1997	Totals
Receipts	$162,589	$112,655	$25,705	$300,949
Disburse	170,456	110,994	23,314	304,764
Cash	9,873	11,534	13,925	n/a
Contributions	124,038	74,600	13,745	212,383
Republicans	1,000	2,500	0	3,500
No. of Cand.	*1*	*3*	*0*	*4*
House	1,000	1,500	0	2,500
Senate	0	1,000	0	1,000
Democrats	122,538	71,500	13,745	207,783
No. of Cand.	*53*	*40*	*11*	*104*
House	97,538	57,500	11,745	166,783
Senate	25,000	14,000	2,000	41,000
Incumbents	99,038	44,600	12,445	156,083
Challengers	16,000	20,500	0	36,500
Open Seat	9,000	10,500	1,300	20,800
Winners	76,438	60,100	n/a	136,538
Losers	47,600	14,500	n/a	62,100

Contributed less than $5,000 during 1995-96 cycle:

Inlandboatmen's Union Political Action Committee (IBU-PAC) (C00074393) *Phone: (206) 448-9736 * Fax: (206) 448-9738 * 500 John St., Seattle, WA 98109 * Web: www.ibu.org * E-mail: 71363.510@compuserve.com * Treasurer: Terri Mast*

International Longshoremen's Association

*Phone: (212) 425-1200 * Fax: (212) 425-2928*
17 Battery Pl., Suite 1530, New York, NY 10004

The International Longshoremen's Association represents about 61,000 dock, port and warehouse workers, along with various equipment operators and mechanics. The union's division of Masters, Mates

& Pilots represents about 6,800 vessel pilots and other personnel on U.S.-flag commercial ships and has a separate, non-affiliated PAC.

Unlike most other unions affiliated with the AFL-CIO, the longshoremen support increased international trade, since their work depends on the shipping industry.

ILA ranked third among ocean transportation unions in congressional contributions during the 1995-96 election cycle. Nearly 96 percent of its contributions went to Democrats. The top recipients were Texas Democrat Reps. Martin Frost, Nick Lampson and Ken Bentsen. Sen. Alfonse M. D'Amato, R-N.Y., was the leading Republican recipient.

International Longshoremen's Association AFL-CIO Committee on Political Education ILA-COPE (C00158576) *Phone: (202) 955-6304 * Fax: (202) 955-6048 * 1101 17th St. N.W., Washington, DC 20036 * Treasurer: Robert E. Gleason * Contact: John Bowers Jr., Legislative Dir.*

	1993-94	1995-96	1997	Totals
Receipts	$1,248,148	$1,163,159	$573,896	$2,985,203
Disburse	891,923	1,396,226	496,913	2,785,062
Cash	4,868,646	4,635,579	4,712,564	n/a
Contributions	371,475	559,550	179,450	1,110,475
Republicans	11,350	22,950	8,050	42,350
No. of Cand.	*6*	*6*	*4*	*16*
House	10,350	10,950	8,050	29,350
Senate	1,000	12,000	0	13,000
Democrats	353,125	536,600	171,400	1,061,125
No. of Cand.	*120*	*134*	*58*	*312*
House	295,625	466,100	133,400	895,125
Senate	57,500	70,500	38,000	166,000
Incumbents	256,475	306,200	155,950	718,625
Challengers	57,500	142,100	5,500	205,100
Open Seat	56,500	111,250	14,500	182,250
Winners	227,125	424,450	n/a	651,575
Losers	144,350	135,100	n/a	279,450

Contributed less than $5,000 during 1995-96 cycle:

International Longshoremen's Association District Council of Philadelphia/Wilmington PAC (ILA District Council PAC) (C00327353) *Phone: (215) 426-9898 * Fax: (215) 426-9978 * P.O. Box 43557, Philadelphia, PA 19106 * Treasurer: Louis Carberry * Contact: John McCann, Chairman of PAC*

International Longshoremen's Association Local 1402 PAC (C00133769) *Phone: (813) 229-1192 * Fax: (813) 228-9205 * 703 E. Harrison St., Tampa, FL 33602 * Treasurer: Theodore Myles*

Local 1814 International Longshoremen's Association AFL-CIO Political Action and Education Fund (C00001743) *Phone: (718) 499-9600 * 70 20th St., Brooklyn, NY 11232 * Treasurer: Anthony Graffino*

PAC/CT Longshoremen/ILA Local 1398 New Haven/Bridgeport (C00322065) *65 Townsend Ave., New Haven, CT 06513 * Treasurer: Joseph T. Russo Jr.*

International Organization of Masters, Mates & Pilots

*Phone: (410) 850-8700 * Fax: (410) 850-0973*
700 Maritime Blvd., Suite 500, Linthicum Heights, MD 21090
Web: www.bridgedeck.com

The International Organization of Masters, Mates & Pilots is the International Marine Division of the International Longshoremen's Association. It is also a member of the AFL-CIO's Maritime Trades Department and is active with the International Transport Workers' Federation.

MM&P consists of six membership groups — offshore, inland Atlantic and Gulf, Pacific maritime, Great Lakes and rivers, pilotage and government employees. MM&P represents 6,800 licensed deck officers, state pilots and other marine personnel on U.S.-flagged commercial vessels sailing in the inland waterways and Great Lakes of the United States, the Panama Canal and Caribbean, as well as crews sailing civilian-crewed military vessels of the United States.

MM&P is interested in maintaining the Jones Act, which supports "an American owned, built and crewed domestic fleet," as well as promotion of the Maritime Security Act. The act is intended to assist development of a more competitive, cost-effective and efficient fleet of militarily useful U.S.-flag and U.S.-citizen crewed commercial vessels.

The union's PAC bucked the trend of most AFL-CIO unions, and gave more than 50 percent of its overall contributions during the 1995-96 election cycle to Republican candidates. The two leading recipients, with $8,000 each, were San Diego area Reps. Randy "Duke" Cunningham, R-Calif., who served in the Navy for 20 years, and Duncan Hunter, R-Calif., chairman of the National Security Military Procurement Subcommittee.

Masters, Mates & Pilots Political Contribution Fund (C00073056)
*Address: same as sponsor * Treasurer: John A. Gorman*

	1993-94	1995-96	1997	Totals
Receipts	$184,544	$228,137	$93,994	$506,675
Disburse	180,388	230,954	81,628	492,970
Cash	16,475	13,659	26,026	n/a
Contributions	150,432	190,770	66,500	407,702
Republicans	28,932	98,270	20,500	147,702
No. of Cand.	*17*	*50*	*20*	*87*
House	14,932	75,750	16,500	107,182
Senate	14,000	22,520	4,000	40,520
Democrats	121,500	92,500	45,000	259,000
No. of Cand.	*78*	*64*	*42*	*184*
House	71,800	66,000	29,500	167,300
Senate	49,700	26,500	15,500	91,700
Incumbents	131,932	149,770	65,000	346,702
Challengers	1,500	7,500	500	9,500
Open Seat	17,000	33,500	1,000	51,500
Winners	107,832	160,270	n/a	268,102
Losers	42,600	30,500	n/a	73,100

Marine Engineers' Beneficial Association (MEBA)

*Phone: (202) 638-5355 * Fax: (202) 638-5369*
444 N. Capitol St. N.W., Suite 800, Washington, DC 20001
E-mail: mebahq@aol.com

The Marine Engineers' Beneficial Association is the oldest union for merchant mariners in the United States. It represents licensed engine, radio and deck officers of U.S.-flag oceangoing ships. It is affiliated with five district PACs and the New York-based American Maritime Officers, which spent the most of any MEBA PAC during the 1995-96 election cycle.

MEBA is committed to a strong merchant marine. It supports the Jones Act, which ensures that ships used to transport cargo between American ports are built, staffed and owned by U.S. citizens.

The American Maritime Officers ranked first among sea transport unions in 1995-96 congressional contributions. MEBA's District 1 PAC, representing the Pacific Coast, ranked fourth. The remaining four PACs contributed a total of $203,500 to congressional candidates. Unlike many other unions, MEBA often split its contributions evenly between the parties, and some district PACs favored Republican candidates. The American Maritime Officers' PAC spent 95 percent of its contributions on incumbent candidates.

The top recipients of contributions from all MEBA PACs combined were Reps. Ken Calvert, R-Calif., David E. Bonior, D-Mich., Sens. Max Baucus, D-Mont., James M. Inhofe, R-Okla., former Sen. Larry Pressler, R-S.D., Rep. Tom DeLay, R-Texas, and former Democratic House candidate Jeffrey Coopersmith of Washington.

American Maritime Officers AFL-CIO Voluntary Political Action Fund (C00027532) *Phone: (718) 965-6700 * Fax: (718) 965-1766 * 650 Fourth Ave., Brooklyn, NY 11232 * Treasurer: Edward V. Kelly Contact: Thomas Bethel, Chairman * Phone: (202) 638-5355*

	1993-94	1995-96	1997	Totals
Receipts	$1,209,636	$1,078,329	$575,615	$2,863,580
Disburse	1,156,862	1,176,327	552,942	2,886,131
Cash	119,365	21,364	44,038	n/a
Contributions	926,120	973,960	470,000	2,370,080
Republicans	320,150	553,250	276,000	1,149,400
No. of Cand.	*138*	*196*	*152*	*486*
House	278,200	439,750	238,500	956,450
Senate	41,950	113,500	37,500	192,950
Democrats	597,470	420,210	190,500	1,208,180
No. of Cand.	*237*	*191*	*166*	*594*
House	487,350	361,710	150,500	999,560
Senate	110,120	58,500	40,000	208,620
Incumbents	876,220	924,960	463,500	2,264,680
Challengers	10,200	9,500	2,000	21,700
Open Seat	37,700	39,500	4,500	81,700
Winners	756,800	872,210	n/a	1,629,010
Losers	169,320	101,750	n/a	271,070

District 1-PCD MEBA Political Action Fund (MEBA-PAF) (C00279380) *Address: same as sponsor * Treasurer: Paul Krupa * Contact: Richard Herring, Legislative Dir.*

	1993-94	1995-96	1997	Totals
Receipts	$1,261,160	$522,883	$298,027	$2,082,070
Disburse	439,421	700,303	276,011	1,415,735
Cash	821,743	644,325	666,343	n/a
Contributions	305,835	411,905	172,835	890,575
Republicans	40,000	185,750	66,200	291,950
No. of Cand.	*20*	*83*	*66*	*169*
House	22,500	156,250	63,200	241,950
Senate	17,500	29,500	3,000	50,000
Democrats	261,835	226,155	104,635	592,625
No. of Cand.	*132*	*142*	*114*	*388*
House	160,075	177,580	81,000	418,655
Senate	101,760	48,575	23,635	173,970
Incumbents	235,160	325,105	168,835	729,100
Challengers	31,925	43,700	0	75,625
Open Seat	38,750	46,600	6,000	91,350
Winners	182,400	335,555	n/a	517,955
Losers	123,435	76,350	n/a	199,785

District 4-MNU/MEBA AFL-CIO Political & Legislative Organization On Watch (NMU PLOW) (C00286401) *Phone: (202) 446-7060 * Fax: (202) 872-0912 * 1150 17th St. N.W., Suite 700, Washington, DC 20036 * Treasurer: Rene Lioeanjie*

	1993-94	1995-96	1997	Totals
Receipts	$101,511	$50,954	$14,954	$167,419
Disburse	50,637	94,034	18,800	163,471
Cash	50,874	7,794	3,948	n/a
Contributions	40,000	80,500	11,750	132,250
Republicans	5,000	21,000	500	26,500
No. of Cand.	*7*	*18*	*4*	*29*
House	3,000	11,000	2,500	16,500
Senate	2,000	10,000	-2000	10,000
Democrats	34,000	59,500	11,250	104,750
No. of Cand.	*49*	*74*	*19*	*142*
House	24,000	45,000	7,750	76,750
Senate	10,000	14,500	3,500	28,000
Incumbents	31,000	61,500	11,750	104,250
Challengers	3,500	3,500	0	7,000
Open Seat	5,500	16,500	500	22,500
Winners	26,500	67,000	n/a	93,500
Losers	13,500	13,500	n/a	27,000

American Maritime Officers AFL-CIO Retirees Association Voluntary Political Action Fund (C00089557) *Phone: (718) 965-6700 * Fax: (718) 369-0710 * 635 Fourth Ave., Brooklyn, NY 11232 * Treasurer: Gordon W. Spencer*

The American Maritime Officers Retirees Association is a labor union that represents retired marine engineers, captains and other officers. It has about 5,000 members.

	1993-94	1995-96	1997	Totals
Receipts	$94,704	$92,996	$45,303	$233,003
Disburse	91,416	98,088	52,790	242,294
Cash	17,744	12,660	4,678	n/a
Contributions	51,500	70,000	50,000	171,500
Republicans	32,000	49,000	35,000	116,000
No. of Cand.	*25*	*41*	*33*	*99*
House	26,000	24,500	30,000	80,500
Senate	6,000	24,500	5,000	35,500
Democrats	17,500	21,000	15,000	53,500
No. of Cand.	*12*	*20*	*18*	*50*
House	11,500	16,500	12,000	40,000
Senate	6,000	4,500	3,000	13,500
Incumbents	34,000	61,500	49,000	144,500
Challengers	12,500	2,500	0	15,000
Open Seat	5,000	6,000	1,000	12,000
Winners	35,500	63,500	n/a	99,000
Losers	16,000	6,500	n/a	22,500

District 6-PASS/NMEBA (AFL-CIO) Political Action Committee (PASS PAC) (C00286807) *Phone: (202) 293-7277 * Fax: (202) 293-7727 * 1150 17th St. N.W., Suite 702, Washington, DC 20036 * Web: www.passnational.org * E-mail: 75173.3341@compuserve.com * Treasurer: Abby Bernstein * Contact: Michael D. Fanfalone, President*

	1993-94	1995-96	1997	Totals
Receipts	$4,549	$52,294	$34,808	$91,651
Disburse	1,574	45,532	17,500	64,606
Cash	2,973	9,738	27,046	n/a
Contributions	1,400	44,000	15,500	60,900
Republicans	200	14,000	5,500	19,700
No. of Cand.	*1*	*17*	*9*	*27*
House	200	10,750	4,500	15,450
Senate	0	3,250	1,000	4,250
Democrats	1,200	30,000	9,000	40,200
No. of Cand.	*5*	*48*	*14*	*67*
House	700	17,500	7,000	25,200
Senate	500	12,500	2,000	15,000
Incumbents	900	26,500	15,500	42,900
Challengers	0	8,000	0	8,000
Open Seat	500	9,500	0	10,000
Winners	200	33,000	n/a	33,200
Losers	1,200	11,000	n/a	12,200

District 5 ITPE-NMU/MEBA Political Action Committee (ITPE PAC) (C00286419) *Phone: (912) 232-6181 * Fax: (912) 232-5982 * 1150 17th St. N.W., Suite 700, Washington, DC 20036 * Treasurer: John Conley*

	1993-94	1995-96	1997	Totals
Receipts	$5,627	$10,576	$4,420	$20,623
Disburse	134	12,075	4,250	16,459
Cash	5,492	3,995	4,165	n/a
Contributions	0	9,000	2,500	11,500
Republicans	0	1,000	500	1,500
No. of Cand.	*0*	*1*	*1*	*2*
House	0	1,000	500	1,500
Senate	0	0	0	0
Democrats	0	8,000	2,000	10,000
No. of Cand.	*0*	*15*	*3*	*18*
House	0	6,000	2,000	8,000
Senate	0	2,000	0	2,000
Incumbents	0	5,000	2,500	7,500
Challengers	0	2,000	0	2,000
Open Seat	0	2,000	0	2,000
Winners	0	5,500	n/a	5,500
Losers	0	3,500	n/a	3,500

Contributed less than $5,000 during 1995-96 cycle:

Marine Engineers' Beneficial Association Retirees Group Fund (also known as MEBA Retirees Group Fund) (C00003863) *Phone: (202) 638-5355 * 444 N. Capitol St. N.W., Suite 800, Washington, DC 20001 * Treasurer: Gilbert Ladana*

National Air Traffic Controllers Association

*Phone: (202) 223-2900 * Fax: (202) 659-3991*
1150 17th St. N.W., Suite 701, Washington, DC 20036
*Web: www.natca.org * E-mail: kmontoya@natcadc.org*

The National Air Traffic Controllers Association is the collective bargaining unit for the more than 14,000 air traffic controllers serving the Federal Aviation Administration, Department of Defense and private aviation industry. It lobbies primarily on aviation safety issues.

NATCA opposes restrictions on the political use of union dues. The union also opposes the establishment of a new air traffic control system known as STARS, arguing that it did not address human factors. It advocates hiring more than 3,000 new controllers and additional inspectors and technicians. It generally supports the concept of "free flight," which would provide unrestricted access to all U.S. air space and allow pilots to select a path and speed in real time. NATCA opposes the privatization of air traffic controllers.

NATCA was the No. 2 aviation union in 1995-96 congressional contributors, behind the Air Line Pilots Association. Most of the group's contributions went to Democratic candidates. It spent more than $100,000 on challengers and candidates in open races. The leading recipients were Sens. James M. Inhofe, R-Okla., Richard J. Durbin, D-Ill., and Rep. Frank R. Wolf, R-Va. Wolf is chairman of a transportation appropriations subcommittee.

National Air Traffic Controllers Association Political Action Committee (also known as NATCA PAC) (C00238725) *Address: same as sponsor * Treasurer: Barry Krasner * Contact: Ken Montoya, Legislative Dir.*

	1993-94	1995-96	1997	Totals
Receipts	$331,683	$468,422	$288,946	$1,089,051
Disburse	316,286	439,594	212,938	968,818
Cash	35,155	44,157	118,027	n/a
Contributions	281,645	356,990	187,150	825,785
Republicans	33,750	84,700	34,650	153,100
No. of Cand.	*30*	*51*	*34*	*115*
House	23,750	64,700	29,525	117,975
Senate	10,000	20,000	5,125	35,125
Democrats	239,395	272,290	151,000	662,685
No. of Cand.	*173*	*199*	*114*	*486*
House	189,175	220,290	115,500	524,965
Senate	50,220	52,000	35,500	137,720
Incumbents	235,820	228,635	171,150	635,605
Challengers	13,125	72,855	7,500	93,480
Open Seat	32,200	55,500	7,500	95,200
Winners	195,750	263,040	n/a	458,790
Losers	85,895	93,950	n/a	179,845

National Association of Air Traffic Specialists

*Phone: (301) 933-6228 * Fax: (301) 933-3902*
11303 Amherst Ave., Suite 4, Wheaton, MD 20902
Web: www.naats.org

The National Association of Air Traffic Specialists represents the Federal Aviation Administration's flight service station controllers. Its purpose is to promote the welfare and stature of its members, as well as to improve their wages and working conditions.

The association's PAC was bipartisan in its giving during the 1995-96 election cycle, with the largest contributions going to members in relevant committees. House Transportation Committee Chairman Bud Shuster, R-Pa., and Ranking Member James L. Oberstar, D-Minn., received two of the largest contributions, with $2,000 and $1,750 respectively. Aviation Subcommittee Chairman John Duncan, R-Tenn., also received $2,000, as did Sen. Ted Stevens, R-Alaska, chairman of the Senate Appropriations Committee.

National Association of Air Traffic Specialists Political Action Fund (C00075358) *Address: same as sponsor * Treasurer: Harold M. Gross*

	1993-94	*1995-96*	*1997*	*Totals*
Receipts	$13,766	$34,401	$17,850	$66,017
Disburse	6,063	32,059	18,640	56,762
Cash	8,879	11,224	10,435	n/a
Contributions	6,000	31,550	18,500	56,050
Republicans	1,500	12,500	8,500	22,500
No. of Cand.	*2*	*10*	*8*	*20*
House	1,500	8,000	7,500	17,000
Senate	0	4,500	1,000	5,500
Democrats	3,500	19,050	8,000	30,550
No. of Cand.	*3*	*25*	*10*	*38*
House	0	12,200	7,500	19,700
Senate	3,500	6,850	500	10,850
Incumbents	3,500	19,800	18,500	41,800
Challengers	0	6,250	0	6,250
Open Seat	2,500	5,500	0	8,000
Winners	3,500	23,550	n/a	27,050
Losers	2,500	8,000	n/a	10,500

Seafarers International Union

*Phone: (301) 899-0675 * Fax: (301) 899-7355*
5201 Auth Way, Camp Springs, MD 20746
Web: www.seafarers.org

The Seafarers International Union, Atlantic, Gulf, Lakes and Inland Waters District, is the largest union representing unlicensed U.S. merchant mariners sailing aboard U.S.-flag vessels in the deep sea, Great Lakes and inland trades. Its members work on commercial ships and tankers, military support ships, tugboats and barges and passenger ships.

The Seafarers' main issue is maintaining federal spending for the U.S. fleet of ships. The union opposes changes that would undermine the Jones Act, which requires that cargo moved between U.S. ports must be transported aboard ships built and staffed by U.S. workers. It helped defeat "fast-track" trade authority and lobbied to extend the cutoff date for veterans' benefits for World War II merchant mariners.

The PAC spent 75 percent of its money on Democratic candidates in 1996. It ranked second among sea transport unions in total spending. Rep. Martin Frost, D-Texas, was the top recipient, and 14 other Democrats each received $10,000. Three Republican candidates, Rep. Don Young, R-Alaska, former Sen. Larry Pressler, R-S.D., and Rep. Randy "Duke" Cunningham, R-Calif., each received at least $10,000. Young sits on a transportation committee, while Cunningham serves on a military readiness panel.

Seafarers Political Activity Donation-Seafarers International Union of North America-AGLIWD District (SPAD) (C00004325) *Address: same as sponsor * Treasurer: Michael Neuman * Contact: Terry Turner*

	1993-94	*1995-96*	*1997*	*Totals*
Receipts	$1,352,414	$1,648,781	$697,434	$3,698,629
Disburse	1,387,034	1,608,582	614,517	3,610,133
Cash	79,006	59,204	142,122	n/a
Contributions	709,544	735,399	322,750	1,767,693
Republicans	75,100	179,099	73,000	327,199
No. of Cand.	*19*	*52*	*29*	*100*
House	51,100	132,599	55,000	238,699
Senate	24,000	46,500	18,000	88,500
Democrats	633,444	556,300	248,750	1,438,494
No. of Cand.	*168*	*158*	*128*	*454*
House	477,285	434,700	140,850	1,052,835
Senate	156,159	121,600	107,900	385,659
Incumbents	602,844	497,599	292,250	1,392,693
Challengers	50,900	86,800	13,000	150,700
Open Seat	55,800	145,500	16,000	217,300
Winners	486,184	555,999	n/a	1,042,183
Losers	223,360	179,400	n/a	402,760

Marine Fireman's Union Political Action Fund (C00017244) *Phone: (415) 362-4592 * Fax: (415) 546-7340 * 240 Second St., San Francisco, CA 94105 * Treasurer: Henry Disley*

	1993-94	*1995-96*	*1997*	*Totals*
Receipts	$36,371	$38,180	$17,240	$91,791
Disburse	32,719	27,126	15,396	75,241
Cash	78,098	89,154	90,999	n/a
Contributions	16,200	14,600	7,500	38,300
Republicans	0	1,500	1,500	3,000
No. of Cand.	*0*	*2*	*3*	*5*
House	0	0	1,000	1,000
Senate	0	1,500	500	2,000
Democrats	16,200	13,100	6,000	35,300
No. of Cand.	*11*	*10*	*5*	*26*
House	5,700	12,100	2,000	19,800
Senate	10,500	1,000	4,000	15,500
Incumbents	15,700	13,100	7,500	36,300
Challengers	500	1,500	0	2,000
Open Seat	0	0	0	0
Winners	14,700	13,100	n/a	27,800
Losers	1,500	1,500	n/a	3,000

Sailor's Union of the Pacific Political Fund (C00011338) *Phone: (415) 777-3400 * Fax: (415) 777-5088 * 450 Harrison St., San Francisco, CA 94105 * Treasurer: Gunnar Lundeberg*

	1993-94	*1995-96*	*1997*	*Totals*
Receipts	$13,944	$14,640	$7,062	$35,646
Disburse	29,103	21,261	12,961	63,325
Cash	18,833	12,215	6,317	n/a
Contributions	18,550	13,250	11,000	42,800
Republicans	0	1,500	0	1,500
No. of Cand.	*0*	*2*	*0*	*2*
House	0	1,500	0	1,500
Senate	0	0	0	0
Democrats	18,550	11,750	11,000	41,300
No. of Cand.	*15*	*13*	*8*	*36*
House	8,550	10,250	5,000	23,800
Senate	10,000	1,500	6,000	17,500
Incumbents	17,250	10,750	11,000	39,000
Challengers	1,000	1,000	0	2,000
Open Seat	300	1,500	0	1,800
Winners	16,800	11,750	n/a	28,550
Losers	1,750	1,500	n/a	3,250

Teamsters Union

*Phone: (202) 624-6800 * Fax: (202) 624-8973*
25 Louisiana Ave. N.W., Washington, DC 20001
Web: www.teamster.org

One of the nation's largest private-sector unions, the International Brotherhood of Teamsters has been plagued by leadership and political controversy for several years. The union's membership also has changed radically since its heyday during the 1970s.

The union now has more members in the warehouse and food industries and at United Parcel Service than in its freight division. More than 300,000 Teamsters are women and the union includes employees of Gatorade, Northwest Airlines and state correctional officers. The union's membership includes about 1.4 million workers and 400,000 retirees.

Former UPS driver Ron Carey was elected president in 1991 and narrowly defeated James P. Hoffa, son of the legendary former union chief, in 1996. But that election was later overturned by a federal monitor and Carey has been barred from running for re-election.

Federal investigators are examining whether, under Carey's leadership, the union diverted Teamster money to advocacy groups, who then donated the money to Carey's 1996 campaign. A recent Teamsters report showed that the union was steadily losing money and risked bankruptcy during 1998; however, the union's final 1997 FEC report showed its PAC collected nearly $4 million during the year.

The Teamsters played a leading role in defeating the "fast-track" trade authority sought by President Clinton during 1997 and also went on strike against UPS, one of the largest Teamster employers. Among the union's 1998 goals are maintaining Occupational Safety and Health Administration safety regulations, defeating the proposed $18 billion IMF Asian bailout and renegotiating NAFTA's trucking provisions.

The Teamsters have spent more than any other PAC during the past two election cycles, but much of that money went to issue advertising and indirect contributions. In the 1993-94 cycle, the Teamsters gave 28 percent of its $8.8 million to candidates. That figure dropped to 26 percent during the 1995-96 cycle, although the group's total spending rose to $9.9 million. Still, the Teamsters ranked first in candidate contributions during the most recent cycle and second in 1993-94. The leading recipients in 1996 included Rep. Robert Wexler, D-Fla., Rep. Ken Bentsen, D-Texas, and Rep. Nick Lampson, D-Texas.

The Teamsters Union has more than 20 affiliated local PACs, but just two spent more than $5,000 on congressional races in 1996. Most devoted their funds to local and state races.

Democratic Republican Independent Voter Education Committee (C00032979) *Address: same as sponsor * Treasurer: Tom Sever * Contact: Bob Nicklas, Acting Dir.*

	1993-94	1995-96	1997	Totals
Receipts	$9,190,610	$9,605,690	$3,935,089	$22,731,389
Disburse	8,844,525	9,931,244	3,420,843	22,196,612
Cash	639,535	313,981	828,227	n/a
Contributions	2,482,152	2,606,140	657,150	5,745,442
Republicans	59,475	100,810	50,000	210,285
No. of Cand.	*16*	*35*	*28*	*79*
House	47,475	90,110	39,000	176,585
Senate	12,000	10,700	11,000	33,700
Democrats	2,367,677	2,495,330	597,350	5,460,357
No. of Cand.	*352*	*385*	*199*	*936*
House	2,086,517	2,233,080	534,600	4,854,197
Senate	281,160	262,250	62,750	606,160
Incumbents	1,523,035	1,192,140	560,850	3,276,025
Challengers	455,900	843,500	25,500	1,324,900
Open Seat	485,667	559,000	62,500	1,107,167
Winners	1,309,442	1,572,805	n/a	2,882,247
Losers	1,172,710	1,033,335	n/a	2,206,045

Local 745 DRIVE (C00004440) *Phone: (214) 398-0661 * 1007 Jonelle St., Dallas, TX 75217 * Treasurer: Tom Sever * Contact: Cliff Bauerly*

	1993-94	1995-96	1997	Totals
Receipts	$257,983	$214,472	$47,124	$519,579
Disburse	177,579	111,449	15,250	304,278
Cash	343,065	449,090	480,965	n/a
Contributions	32,250	20,000	10,000	62,250
Republicans	14,250	5,000	0	19,250
No. of Cand.	*3*	*1*	*0*	*4*
House	3,000	5,000	0	8,000
Senate	11,250	0	0	11,250
Democrats	18,000	15,000	10,000	43,000
No. of Cand.	*4*	*2*	*2*	*8*
House	13,000	15,000	10,000	38,000
Senate	5,000	0	0	5,000
Incumbents	32,250	10,000	10,000	52,250
Challengers	0	0	0	0
Open Seat	0	10,000	0	10,000
Winners	27,250	20,000	n/a	47,250
Losers	5,000	0	n/a	5,000

Teamsters Local 1150 Federal PAC (C00297630) *Phone: (203) 381-9240 * Fax: (203) 381-9314 * 150 Garfield Ave., Stratford, CT 06497 * Treasurer: John B. Santamaria*

	1993-94	1995-96	1997	Totals
Receipts	$1,702	$14,820	$5,947	$22,469
Disburse	278	14,322	2,160	16,760
Cash	1,424	1,923	5,710	n/a
Contributions	0	10,500	0	10,500
Republicans	0	0	0	0
No. of Cand.	*0*	*0*	*0*	*0*
House	0	0	0	0
Senate	0	0	0	0
Democrats	0	10,500	0	10,500
No. of Cand.	*0*	*4*	*0*	*4*
House	0	10,500	0	10,500
Senate	0	0	0	0
Incumbents	0	5,000	0	5,000
Challengers	0	5,500	0	5,500
Open Seat	0	0	0	0
Winners	0	6,000	n/a	6,000
Losers	0	4,500	n/a	4,500

Contributed less than $5,000 during 1995-96 cycle:

Brewery Soft Drink Beer Distributors, Optical, Dental, Miscellaneous Workers, Warehouseman Help Local 830 PAC (C00174847) *Phone: (215) 671-9850 * Fax: (215) 676-1324 * 12298 Townsend Rd., Philadelphia, PA 19154 * Treasurer: Gerard Zaccagni*

DRIVE 42 (C00001099) *Phone: (213) 383-4242 * Fax: (213) 383-5242 * 1616 W. Ninth St., Room 500, Los Angeles, CA 90015 * Treasurer: Hugo Morris * Contact: Jim Santangelo, President*

DRIVE Political Fund, Chapter 886 (C00000489) *Phone: (405) 947-2333 * Fax: (405) 943-1026 * P.O. Box 25556, Oklahoma City, OK 73125-0556 * Treasurer: Shirley A. Russell*

Democratic Republican Independent Voter Education - Chapter 557 (Teamster) (C00007161) *Phone: (410) 485-9200 * 6000 Erdman Ave., Baltimore, MD 21205 * Treasurer: Gene Shiflett*

International Brotherhood of Teamsters, DRIVE Chapter 238 (C00011957) *Phone: (319) 365-1461 * 5000 J St. S.W., Cedar Rapids, IA 52406 * Treasurer: Linda L. Frieden*

Local 500 Political Action Fund (C00094904) *Phone: (215) 288-6620 * 1100 E. Lycoming St., Philadelphia, PA 19124 * Treasurer: Edward F. Keyser Jr.*

Local Union DRIVE 25 (C00006759) *Phone: (617) 241-8705 * 544 Main St., Boston, MA 02129 * Treasurer: George W. Cashman*

Ohio DRIVE (Democratic Republican Independent Voter Education) (Teamsters) (C00008078) *Phone: (216) 881-0188 * 3150 Chester Ave., Cleveland, OH 44114 * Treasurer: Gary M. Tiboni*

Philadelphia Area Teamsters Political Action Committee (C00078675) *Phone: (215) 335-0100 * 2833 Cottman Ave., Philadelphia, PA 19149 * Treasurer: John P. Morris*

Teamsters Joint Council 10 DRIVE (C00010223) *Phone: (617) 262-2512 * 650 Beacon St., Boston, MA 02215 * Treasurer: George W. Cashman*

Teamsters Joint Council 53 Political Action Committee DRIVE (C00178541) *Phone: (215) 634-4567 * Fax: (215) 634-4556 * 3460 N. Delaware Ave., Suite 310, Philadelphia, PA 19134 * Treasurer: John Jackson*

Teamsters Local 115 Political Action Fund (also known as DRIVE Local 115) (C00010876) *Phone: (215) 335-0100 * Fax: (215) 333-4146 * 2833 Cottman Ave., Philadelphia, PA 19149 * Treasurer: John P. Morris*

Teamsters Local 20 - Pilot Federal (C00234377) *Phone: (419) 243-8800 * Fax: (419) 243-6270 * 435 S. Hawley, Toledo, OH 43609 * Treasurer: Lester A. Singer*

Teamsters Local 523 DRIVE Fund (C00138552) *Phone: (918) 587-3358 * Fax: (918) 587-3367 * P.O. Box 1836, Tulsa, OK 74101 * Treasurer: Roger L. Nelson*

Teamsters Local 623 Political Action Fund (C00118869) *Phone: (215) 289-0580 * 4369 Richmond St., Philadelphia, PA 19137 * Treasurer: James S. Merritt*

Teamsters Local 959 Alaska Labor Independent Voter Education (C00039164) *Phone: (907) 565-8252 * Fax: (907) 565-8196 * 520 E. 34th Ave., Anchorage, AK 99503 * Treasurer: Tracey L. Klee*

Teamsters Local Union 516 Democratic Republican Independent Voter Education (C00076778) *Phone: (918) 683-6587 * 1212 E. Okmulgee, Muskogee, OK 74403 * Treasurer: Kaye Rozelle*

Teamsters Local Union 688 PAC (C00282236) *Phone: (314) 658-5600 * Fax: (314) 658-5799 * 300 S. Grand Ave., St. Louis, MO 63103 * Treasurer: Joseph A. Galli*

Warehouse Employees Union Local 169 Political Action Committee (C00120253) *Phone: (215) 635-1696 * Fax: (215) 635-2441 * 1355 W. Cheltenham Ave., Elkins Park, PA 19027 * Treasurer: Andrew M. Montella*

Terminated PACs which contributed less than $5,000 during 1995-96 cycle:

Joint Council of Teamsters 37 DRIVE Fund (C00291492) *Phone: (503) 251-2337 * 1872 N.E. 162nd Ave., Portland, OR 97230 * Treasurer: Alfred O. Panek*

Washington Teamsters Legislative League - Fund A (C00231241) *553 John St., Seattle, WA 98109 * Treasurer: Jon L. Rabine*

Transport Workers Union

*Phone: (212) 873-6000 * Fax: (212) 721-1431*
80 West End Ave., New York, NY 10023
Web: www.twu.com

The Transport Workers Union represents more than 100,000 workers in the mass transportation, airline, railroad and utility industries. It also has members who work at universities and for municipal governments. The union represents flight attendants and ramp workers at Southwest and American airlines. Members of its largest local, in New York, operate the city's subway system and bus lines and make up more than one-third of the union's total membership.

TWU lobbies on many transportation issues, from federal funding for mass transit to legislation affecting airline personnel. It opposes changes to Occupational Safety and Health Administration regulations that it argues would endanger worker safety. It supports funding for Medicare and most positions taken by the AFL-CIO.

TWU was the leading PAC contributor to 1996 congressional candidates among transportation unions representing several industries. Although a union spokesperson says it has traditionally supported many Republican candidates, Democrats received more than 90 percent of TWU's contributions during the 1995-96 election cycle.

The top recipients were four Texas Democrats: Reps. Martin Frost, Ken Bentsen and Nick Lampson and 1996 House candidate Janet Carroll "Skeet" Richardson. The leading Republican recipient was Rep. Jack Quinn of New York.

Transport Workers Union Political Contributions Committee (C00008268) *Phone: (202) 638-6154 * Fax: (202) 638-6102 * 400 N. Capitol St., Washington, DC 20001 * E-mail: rtauss@worldnet.att.net * Treasurer: John J. Kerrigan * Contact: Roger Tauss, National Coordinator*

	1993-94	1995-96	1997	Totals
Receipts	$766,204	$937,718	$494,499	$2,198,421
Disburse	678,283	938,012	374,913	1,991,208
Cash	111,681	111,390	230,977	n/a
Contributions	510,760	703,263	231,750	1,445,773
Republicans	7,100	57,400	24,250	88,750
No. of Cand.	*6*	*23*	*20*	*49*
House	7,100	49,000	17,850	73,950
Senate	0	8,400	6,400	14,800
Democrats	493,660	643,363	202,500	1,339,523
No. of Cand.	*235*	*266*	*142*	*643*
House	389,350	530,663	162,000	1,082,013
Senate	104,310	112,700	40,500	257,510
Incumbents	397,260	418,300	202,250	1,017,810
Challengers	49,500	172,713	10,500	232,713
Open Seat	64,000	112,250	18,500	194,750
Winners	304,800	508,300	n/a	813,100
Losers	205,960	194,963	n/a	400,923

Transport Workers Union - Local 100 Political Contributions Committee (C00135475) *Phone: (212) 874-2500 * Fax: (212) 579-3381 * 80 West End Ave. (Sixth Floor), New York, NY 10023 * Web: www.twu-100.org * E-mail: ppi@bway.net * Treasurer: Dennis Calhoun*

Established in 1934, Transport Workers Union Local 100 represents the transit workers of New York City.

	1993-94	1995-96	1997	Totals
Receipts	$980,804	$1,121,688	$582,600	$2,685,092
Disburse	793,489	982,943	550,663	2,327,095
Cash	251,724	390,470	422,407	n/a
Contributions	4,490	6,300	0	10,790
Republicans	0	300	0	300
No. of Cand.	*0*	*1*	*0*	*1*
House	0	300	0	300
Senate	0	0	0	0
Democrats	4,490	6,000	0	10,490
No. of Cand.	*4*	*2*	*0*	*6*
House	1,990	6,000	0	7,990
Senate	2,500	0	0	2,500
Incumbents	4,000	2,300	0	6,300
Challengers	240	4,000	0	4,240
Open Seat	0	0	0	0
Winners	4,000	2,300	n/a	6,300
Losers	490	4,000	n/a	4,490

Transportation Communications International Union

*Phone: (301) 948-4910 * Fax: (301) 330-7673*
Three Research Pl., Rockville, MD 20850

The Transportation Communications International Union represents about 135,000 workers in a variety of industries, including railroads, computing, law enforcement and travel. Its members work in every state and throughout Canada. Many TCU members are railroad clerks and "carmen," although the union also represents hotel and motel clerks.

The union supports the Railroad Shippers Protection Act, which seeks to promote competition among railroad companies and reduce regulations for small shipping businesses. It opposes attempts to curtail the political use of union dues.

During the 1995-96 election cycle, TCU ranked third in congressional contributions among unions drawing from more than one transportation-related industry. The group contributed more than 79 percent of its money to winning candidates, one of the higher percentages among large labor PACs.

The top recipients were Reps. David E. Bonior, D-Mich., and Bob Wise, D-W.Va., who each received more at least $9,000. The leading Republican recipient was Sen. Alfonse M. D'Amato, R-N.Y., who received $4,000.

Responsible Citizens Political League - A Project of the Transportation Communication International Union (TCU) (formerly known as BRAC) (C00006338) *Address: same as sponsor * Treasurer: Frank Ferlin Jr. * Contact: Howard W. Randolph Jr., National Legislative Dir.*

	1993-94	1995-96	1997	Totals
Receipts	$582,665	$590,535	$267,205	$1,440,405
Disburse	545,077	610,458	177,034	1,332,569
Cash	63,436	43,556	133,730	n/a
Contributions	359,492	429,140	120,300	908,932
Republicans	7,500	48,250	16,000	71,750
No. of Cand.	*11*	*43*	*19*	*73*
House	6,500	35,750	14,000	56,250
Senate	1,000	12,500	2,000	15,500
Democrats	340,492	379,390	101,300	821,182
No. of Cand.	*293*	*300*	*123*	*716*
House	252,242	304,440	78,300	634,982
Senate	88,250	74,950	23,000	186,200
Incumbents	293,242	322,340	114,300	729,882
Challengers	25,250	49,300	1,000	75,550
Open Seat	40,650	57,500	4,500	102,650
Winners	231,500	339,640	n/a	571,140
Losers	127,992	89,500	n/a	217,492

United Transportation Union

*Phone: (216) 228-9400 * Fax: (216) 228-5755*
14600 Detroit Ave., Cleveland, OH 44107-4250
Web: www.utu.org

The United Transportation Union is the largest railroad operating union. It includes more than 700 locals in North America with about 75,000 active rail members and 150,000 total members. It represents engineers, conductors, brakeman, yardmasters and switchmen as well as bus drivers and transportation workers. The union is affiliated with the AFL-CIO.

The union is seeking to allow members of the Brotherhood of Locomotive Engineers to choose UTU as their union, a move other railroad unions oppose. UTU currently does not represent engineers. UTU lobbies for greater funding for Amtrak to pay for wage increases and capital improvements to the system. About 2,500 UTU members are Amtrak workers.

UTU ranked first among railroad unions in 1995-96 congressional contributions. It was the only railroad union to contribute more than $1 million to candidates. Like other AFL-CIO affiliates, UTU gives most of its PAC money — 83 percent — to Democratic candidates. Nineteen Republicans received $5,000 or more from UTU; 16 won their races.

Transportation Political Education League (C00001636) *Phone: (202) 347-0900 * Fax: (202) 347-0958 * 400 N. Capitol St. N.W., Suite 370, Washington, DC 20001 * E-mail: 110225.2747@compuserve.com * Treasurer: Roger D. Griffeth * Contact: James Brunkenhoefer, Legislative Dir.*

	1993-94	1995-96	1997	Totals
Receipts	$2,564,188	$2,532,859	$1,491,507	$6,588,554
Disburse	2,547,886	2,510,748	920,273	5,978,907
Cash	693,942	716,058	1,287,290	n/a
Contributions	1,233,555	1,260,600	462,650	2,956,805
Republicans	43,775	195,800	105,850	345,425
No. of Cand.	*21*	*58*	*51*	*130*
House	32,775	175,800	95,850	304,425
Senate	11,000	20,000	10,000	41,000
Democrats	1,163,280	1,055,800	346,300	2,565,380
No. of Cand.	*303*	*289*	*142*	*734*
House	942,300	819,300	271,000	2,032,600
Senate	220,980	236,500	75,300	532,780
Incumbents	929,055	748,750	397,650	2,075,455
Challengers	107,950	239,800	16,000	363,750
Open Seat	196,000	271,250	51,500	518,750
Winners	707,175	889,750	n/a	1,596,925
Losers	526,380	370,850	n/a	897,230

PAC UTU Carmen's Local 722 (C00236141) *Phone: (516) 887-2166 * 217 Earle Ave., Lynbrook, NY 11563 * Treasurer: Bruce F. Squeglia*

	1993-94	1995-96	1997	Totals
Receipts	$13,146	$13,480	$0	$26,626
Disburse	12,887	17,135	0	30,022
Cash	3,654	0	0	n/a
Contributions	2,500	5,900	0	8,400
Republicans	2,500	3,650	0	6,150
No. of Cand.	*1*	*2*	*0*	*3*
House	0	250	0	250
Senate	2,500	3,400	0	5,900
Democrats	0	0	0	0
No. of Cand.	*0*	*0*	*0*	*0*
House	0	ßΣ0	0	0
Senate	0	0	0	0
Incumbents	2,500	3,650	0	6,150
Challengers	0	0	0	0
Open Seat	0	0	0	0
Winners	2,500	3,650	n/a	6,150
Losers	0	2,250	n/a	2,250

Lawyers & Lobbyists

Lawyers/Law Firms

Adams & Reese

*Phone: (504) 581-3234 * Fax: (504) 566-0210*
4500 One Shell Square, New Orleans, LA 70139
*Web: www.arlaw.com * E-mail: info@arlaw.com*

Adams & Reese is a New Orleans-based legal and lobbying firm. Founded in 1951, the firm has about 160 lawyers, including 101 partners, who practice in six offices. Offices are in Baton Rouge, La.; Mobile, Ala.; Jackson, Miss.; Houston and Washington. The majority of the firm's attorneys work in Louisiana.

ARPAC, which is bipartisan, gives to federal candidates.

ARPAC (C00226472) *Phone: (504) 336-5200 * Fax: (504) 336-5220 * 451 Florida St., Bank One Centre N. Tower, 19th Floor, Baton Rouge, LA 70801 * Treasurer: Cheryl McCormick*

*Phone: (202) 737-3234 * Fax: (202) 737-0264 * 1455 Pennsylvania Ave. N.W., Suite 200, Washington, DC 20004*

*Contact: E. L. Henry, Partner * Phone: (504) 581-3234*

	1993-94	1995-96	1997	Totals
Receipts	$6,000	$9,000	$7,000	$22,000
Disburse	5,232	6,200	5,500	16,932
Cash	9,047	11,847	13,347	n/a
Contributions	4,000	6,200	5,500	15,700
Republicans	1,000	3,600	3,000	7,600
No. of Cand.	*1*	*4*	*4*	*9*
House	1,000	2,600	3,000	6,600
Senate	0	1,000	0	1,000
Democrats	3,000	2,600	2,500	8,100
No. of Cand.	*4*	*4*	*3*	*11*
House	1,500	1,600	1,000	4,100
Senate	1,500	1,000	1,500	4,000
Incumbents	3,500	2,500	5,500	11,500
Challengers	0	500	0	500
Open Seat	0	3,200	0	3,200
Winners	3,500	4,600	n/a	8,100
Losers	500	1,600	n/a	2,100

Akin, Gump, Strauss, Hauer & Feld

*Phone: (202) 887-4000 * Fax: (202) 659-9312*
1333 New Hampshire Ave. N.W., Suite 400, Washington, DC 20036
E-mail: csummers@akingump.com

Akin, Gump, Strauss, Hauer & Feld is a major law firm headquartered in Washington with four offices in Texas, three in Europe, and one each in Los Angeles and New York. The Washington office has more than 230 lawyers and practices in most major areas of the law, including government contracts, health care and tax. It was founded in Dallas in 1945.

The firm's partners include Michael Madigan, chief counsel of the Senate Governmental Affairs Committee's 1997 campaign finance investigation, and presidential adviser Vernon Jordan. Among its clients is agriculture giant Archer-Daniels-Midland Corp.

Akin Gump was the leading contributor among law firms to 1996 congressional candidates. It ranked fourth among the top 200 PACs in the percentage of money given to winning candidates — 91.7. Less than 5 percent of the firm's PAC contributions went to challengers and open seat races.

The leading recipients were Sen. Phil Gramm, R-Texas, and Rep. Martin Frost, D-Texas. Eight candidates received $5,000 or more. A majority of the firm's contributions went to Republican candidates.

Akin, Gump, Strauss, Hauer & Feld LLP Civic Action Committee (C00104901) *Address: same as sponsor * Treasurer: Joel Jankowsky * Contact: Connie R. Summers, Assistant Treasurer*

	1993-94	1995-96	1997	Totals
Receipts	$440,136	$458,741	$249,409	$1,148,286
Disburse	429,930	459,975	248,321	1,138,226
Cash	11,686	10,449	11,536	n/a
Contributions	325,687	366,833	188,109	880,629
Republicans	94,861	219,841	110,957	425,659
No. of Cand.	*72*	*149*	*109*	*330*
House	43,125	139,809	76,062	258,996
Senate	51,736	80,032	34,895	166,663
Democrats	229,826	146,992	77,152	453,970
No. of Cand.	*142*	*99*	*77*	*318*
House	183,473	117,819	49,026	350,318
Senate	46,353	29,173	28,126	103,652
Incumbents	312,687	347,626	186,609	846,922
Challengers	3,750	6,000	1,000	10,750
Open Seat	8,750	11,207	500	20,457
Winners	271,587	336,686	n/a	608,273
Losers	54,100	30,147	n/a	84,247

Arent Fox Kintner Plotkin & Kahn

*Phone: (202) 775-5736 * Fax: (202) 857-6395*
1050 Connecticut Ave. N.W., Washington, DC 20036-5339
Web: www.arentfox.com

Established in 1942, the law firm of Arent Fox Kintner Plotkin & Kahn has become involved in both national and international legal issues.

The firm has about 250 employees and five major departments: litigation, federal practice, general business, international, and EEHI (employment, ERISA, health and immigration). It also has a major environmental law practice and tracks related legislation in Congress and state legislatures.

In 1995 the firm provided legal and lobbying services to the government of the Republic of Haiti and then-President Jean-Bertrand Aristide.

Arent Fox Civic Participation Fund (C00241380) *Address: same as sponsor * Treasurer: Christopher Smith * Contact: Elliott I. Portnoy, Administrator*

	1993-94	1995-96	1997	Totals
Receipts	$48,350	$63,755	$29,727	$141,832
Disburse	49,907	64,143	27,766	141,816
Cash	1,821	1,433	3,394	n/a
Contributions	39,750	55,650	21,500	116,900
Republicans	3,100	22,650	7,500	33,250
No. of Cand.	*2*	*32*	*12*	*46*
House	100	12,150	6,000	18,250
Senate	3,000	10,500	1,500	15,000
Democrats	36,650	33,000	14,000	83,650
No. of Cand.	*41*	*42*	*14*	*97*
House	21,400	19,000	5,000	45,400
Senate	15,250	14,000	9,000	38,250
Incumbents	29,150	44,650	21,500	95,300
Challengers	1,100	4,550	0	5,650
Open Seat	9,500	6,450	0	15,950
Winners	29,750	46,850	n/a	76,600
Losers	10,000	8,800	n/a	18,800

Arnold & Porter

*Phone: (202) 942-5000 * Fax: (202) 942-5999*
Thurmond Arnold Building, 555 12th St. N.W., Washington, DC 20004

Arnold & Porter, with just more than 400 lawyers, is in the ranks of the top 50 largest firms in the United States. In 1996, the firm posted $175 million in revenues.

Arnold & Porter has 32 major practice groups, including government contracts, intellectual property and technology, international finance and litigation, product liability, real estate, tax, litigation, legislation and telecommunications. The bulk of its attorneys work in Washington, but the firm has offices in New York, Los Angeles, Denver and London.

The Washington law firm for Phillip Morris in the 1960s, Arnold & Porter is currently tied for 12th on the "most-used outside counsel" list of the Fortune 250. It has represented the governments of Panama, Turkey, Venezuela and Brazil.

Arnold & Porter Partners Political Action Committee (C00216895) *Address: same as sponsor * Treasurer: Martha L. Cochran*

	1993-94	1995-96	1997	Totals
Receipts	$149,434	$146,795	$74,218	$370,447
Disburse	133,806	157,943	57,539	349,288
Cash	18,722	7,575	24,255	n/a
Contributions	73,292	76,100	26,550	175,942
Republicans	11,800	35,850	10,550	58,200
No. of Cand.	*17*	*35*	*11*	*63*
House	5,100	21,250	6,050	32,400
Senate	6,700	14,600	4,500	25,800
Democrats	59,492	40,250	16,000	115,742
No. of Cand.	*53*	*45*	*12*	*110*
House	32,100	21,000	2,250	55,350
Senate	27,392	19,250	13,750	60,392
Incumbents	67,092	66,500	24,550	158,142
Challengers	2,000	1,500	1,000	4,500
Open Seat	4,200	8,100	0	12,300
Winners	59,452	67,250	n/a	126,702
Losers	13,840	8,850	n/a	22,690

Association of Trial Lawyers of America

*Phone: (202) 965-3500 * Fax: (202) 338-8709*
1050 31st St. N.W., Washington, DC 20007
*Web: www.atlanet.org * E-mail: barry.nace@atlahq.org*

The Association of Trial Lawyers of America began as a coalition of workers' compensation lawyers in 1946. Today it is the world's largest trial bar and has more than 60,000 members. The group and its members were one of the largest contributors to President Clinton's presidential campaigns.

The group lobbies against laws that limit product liability and damage payments to injured plaintiffs and their attorneys. In late 1997, the U.S. Chamber of Commerce announced plans to lobby for tort reform during 1998 and also to press for changes in judicial elections, two crucial issues with ATLA on the other side.

ATLA ranked first in contributions from lawyers' groups and businesses during the 1995-96 election cycle. Slightly less than 90 percent went to Democrats, mostly incumbents. Democratic candidates in Texas, California, New York and Illinois received the most money, while the leading Republican recipients included Sen. Alfonse M. D'Amato, R-N.Y., and Rep. Peter T. King, R-N.Y., both lawyers. More than 250 candidates received at least $5,000, including 128 Democrats who each received at least $10,000.

Association of Trial Lawyers of America Political Action Committee (C00024521) *Address: same as sponsor * Treasurer: Dan Cohen * Contact: Barry J. Nace, PAC Dir.*

	1993-94	1995-96	1997	Totals
Receipts	$4,540,066	$5,380,418	$2,761,007	$12,681,491
Disburse	4,572,423	5,084,785	2,820,099	12,477,307
Cash	333,257	628,889	584,797	n/a
Contributions	2,161,035	2,336,938	707,500	5,205,473
Republicans	132,500	239,500	67,500	439,500
No. of Cand.	*36*	*74*	*36*	*146*
House	92,000	148,500	50,500	291,000
Senate	40,500	91,000	17,000	148,500
Democrats	2,013,535	2,087,438	634,500	4,735,473
No. of Cand.	*337*	*324*	*195*	*856*
House	1,744,785	1,808,238	544,000	4,097,023
Senate	268,750	279,200	90,500	638,450
Incumbents	1,465,535	1,224,825	592,500	3,282,860
Challengers	259,000	592,500	36,000	887,500
Open Seat	436,500	518,613	75,500	1,030,613
Winners	1,239,180	1,536,200	n/a	2,775,380
Losers	921,855	800,738	n/a	1,722,593

Contributed less than $5,000 during 1995-96 cycle:

Consumer Attorneys Federal PAC (formerly known as California Trial Lawyers Association Federal PAC) (C00157412) *Phone: (916) 443-7621 * 980 Ninth St., Suite 200, Sacramento, CA 95814 * Treasurer: Josephine De Shiell*

Baker & Botts

*Phone: (713) 229-1234 * Fax: (713) 229-1522*
3000 One Shell Plaza, Houston, TX 77002
*Web: www.bakerbotts.com * E-mail: scott_rozzell@bakerbotts.com*

Houston-based civil law firm Baker & Botts has 521 lawyers in six cities — Austin, Dallas, Houston, New York, Washington and Moscow. Former Secretary of Treasury and State James A. Baker III is a prominent member of the firm, whose clients include more than half of the Fortune 100.

In late 1997, Baker & Botts merged with New York intellectual property boutique Brumbaugh, Graves, Donohue and Raymond to create the largest intellectual property practice in the nation among general law firms. More than 100 of Baker & Botts' lawyers are now dedicated to intellectual property law.

The Washington office, with about 60 lawyers, practices corporate, energy, international trade, environmental, finance, government contracts, intellectual property, litigation, real estate and tax law.

Founded in 1840, Baker & Botts is one of the oldest law firms in the United States. James A. Baker's great-grandfather was a firm leader.

Baker & Botts Bluebonnet Fund (C00077552) *Phone: (202) 639-7700 * Fax: (202) 639-7890 * 1299 Pennsylvania Ave. N.W., Washington, DC 20004-2400 * Treasurer: Scott E. Rozzell*

	1993-94	1995-96	1997	Totals
Receipts	$147,227	$90,355	$46,138	$283,720
Disburse	148,339	89,636	44,000	281,975
Cash	589	1,317	3,457	n/a
Contributions	105,447	53,500	34,000	192,947
Republicans	63,497	32,750	24,500	120,747
No. of Cand.	*27*	*28*	*13*	*68*
House	17,400	23,750	11,500	52,650
Senate	46,097	9,000	13,000	68,097

Democrats	41,950	20,750	9,500	72,200
No. of Cand.	*30*	*15*	*12*	*57*
House	23,500	12,750	5,500	41,750
Senate	18,450	8,000	4,000	30,450
Incumbents	75,350	39,750	33,000	148,100
Challengers	15,000	2,000	0	17,000
Open Seat	15,097	12,250	1,000	28,347
Winners	72,850	37,000	n/a	109,850
Losers	32,597	16,500	n/a	49,097

Baker & Hostetler

*Phone: (216) 621-0200 * Fax: (216) 696-0740*
1900 E. Ninth St., National City Center, Suite 3200, Cleveland, OH 44114

Baker & Hostetler is a general practice law firm with main offices in Cleveland. In 1997, it was ranked 34th in size by the National Law Journal. The firm has more than 470 lawyers in its 10 offices, located in Cleveland; Washington; Columbus, Ohio; Los Angeles; Orlando, Fla.; Houston; Denver; Long Beach, Calif.; Cincinnati; and Los Gatos, Calif.

Baker & Hostetler has played a role in reviving Cleveland as a cultural center, donating at least $50,000 per year to the city's arts program. It has also contributed to the Rock & Roll Hall of Fame, the Great Lakes Theatre Festival and the Cleveland Play House, as well as the Cleveland Center for Contemporary Art.

The firm was established in 1916. It posted $135 million in sales for 1996.

Baker & Hostetler Political Action Committee (C00174227)
*Phone: (202) 861-1500 * Fax: (202) 861-1783 * 1050 Connecticut Ave. N.W., Suite 1100, Washington, DC 20036-5304 * Treasurer: William H. Schweitzer * Contact: William H. Schweitzer*

	1993-94	1995-96	1997	Totals
Receipts	$55,918	$51,882	$2,685	$110,485
Disburse	63,580	39,126	17,481	120,187
Cash	2,092	14,854	58	n/a
Contributions	48,900	31,211	17,410	97,521
Republicans	23,250	16,037	9,595	48,882
No. of Cand.	*25*	*16*	*15*	*56*
House	9,250	9,037	7,000	25,287
Senate	14,000	7,000	2,595	23,595
Democrats	25,650	15,174	7,815	48,639
No. of Cand.	*33*	*14*	*9*	*56*
House	21,650	10,000	3,000	34,650
Senate	4,000	5,174	4,815	13,989
Incumbents	39,450	18,787	16,910	75,147
Challengers	3,000	8,000	500	11,500
Open Seat	7,450	4,424	0	11,874
Winners	33,950	17,500	n/a	51,450
Losers	14,950	13,711	n/a	28,661

Barrack, Rodos & Bacine

*Phone: (215) 963-0600 * Fax: (215) 230-1874*
7102 McCallum St., Philadelphia, PA 19119
*Web: www.barrack.com * E-mail: barrack@ix.netcom.com*

Barrack, Rodos & Bacine is a Philadelphia-based law firm with 16 lawyers in five offices.

Partners Leonard Barrack and Gerald J. Rodos were members of the 1996 Mother Jones 400, the magazine's list of the largest political donors between 1993 and June 1995. Both contributed primarily to Democratic candidates and committees.

The firm, which was founded in 1976, has offices in Philadelphia, San Diego, New York, Haddonfield, N.J. and Boston. It is a boutique law firm that specializes in complex litigation involving class action and bankruptcy proceedings.

Barrack, Rodos & Bacine Political Action Committee (C00258590)
*Address: same as sponsor * Treasurer: Daniel E. Bacine*

	1993-94	1995-96	1997	Totals
Receipts	$53,260	$25,383	$10,248	$88,891
Disburse	39,557	31,601	12,807	83,965
Cash	15,233	9,018	6,459	n/a
Contributions	35,700	18,500	4,250	58,450
Republicans	1,000	2,000	2,000	5,000
No. of Cand.	*1*	*2*	*2*	*5*
House	1,000	0	0	1,000
Senate	0	2,000	2,000	4,000
Democrats	34,700	16,500	2,250	53,450
No. of Cand.	*20*	*11*	*4*	*35*
House	8,000	4,000	250	12,250
Senate	26,700	12,500	2,000	41,200
Incumbents	28,200	11,000	4,250	43,450
Challengers	1,000	2,000	0	3,000
Open Seat	6,500	5,500	0	12,000
Winners	21,200	17,500	n/a	38,700
Losers	14,500	1,000	n/a	15,500

Berger & Montague

*Phone: (215) 875-3000 * Fax: (215) 875-4604*
1622 Locust St., Philadelphia, PA 19103
Web: www.bm.net/home

Berger & Montague is a Philadelphia-based law firm specializing in class action suits, particularly those involving securities and antitrust. It has been involved in class actions brought by Holocaust survivors against Swiss banks.

It was one of the principal counsel in the Drexel Burnham Lambert/Michael Milken securities and bankruptcy litigation after the collapse of the junk bond market and the bankruptcy of Drexel Burnham Lambert. It was also a principal counsel in the Exxon Valdez oil spill case.

Founded in 1970, the firm has 52 lawyers. Firm founder David Berger has contributed more than $100,000 to national and state Democratic Party committees since 1993.

Berger & Associates Public Interest PAC Inc. (formerly known as Shareholders of America PAC) (C00234716) *3220 N St. N.W., Suite 247, Washington, DC 20007 * Treasurer: Daniel Berger*

	1993-94	1995-96	1997	Totals
Receipts	$2,775	$31,520	$25,350	$59,645
Disburse	2,640	31,953	10,959	45,552
Cash	675	240	14,631	n/a
Contributions	2,000	15,000	10,750	27,750
Republicans	2,000	1,500	4,000	7,500
No. of Cand.	*1*	*2*	*3*	*6*
House	0	0	0	0
Senate	2,000	1,500	4,000	7,500
Democrats	0	13,500	6,750	20,250
No. of Cand.	*0*	*5*	*6*	*11*
House	0	0	500	500
Senate	0	13,500	6,250	19,750
Incumbents	2,000	4,000	10,250	16,250
Challengers	0	5,000	0	5,000
Open Seat	0	6,000	500	6,500
Winners	2,000	15,000	n/a	17,000
Losers	0	0	n/a	0

Bogle & Gates

*Phone: (206) 682-5151 * Fax: (206) 621-2660*
Two Union Square, 601 Union St., Suite 4700, Seattle, WA 98101-2346

Bogle & Gates is a law firm based in Seattle. The firm's PAC is bipartisan and generally gives to candidates who will represent Washington state or Alaska.

The firm's 200 lawyers also practice in Bellevue and Tacoma, Wash.; Anchorage, Alaska; Vancouver, Canada; Portland, Ore.; and Washington. Its clients have included Exxon Shipping Co. in the Exxon Valdez oil spill case and International Paper Co.

The firm was founded in the 1890s.

Bogle & Gates Political Action Committee (C00246512) *Phone: (202) 293-3600 * 1575 Eye St. N.W., Washington, DC 20005 * Treasurer: Charles R. Blumenfeld*

*Contact: Irwin Treiger, Partner * Phone: (206) 682-5151*

	1993-94	1995-96	1997	Totals
Receipts	$16,008	$27,000	$0	$43,008
Disburse	28,112	15,184	1,500	44,796
Cash	212	12,027	10,527	n/a
Contributions	28,100	13,650	1,500	43,250
Republicans	6,100	8,850	1,000	15,950
No. of Cand.	*4*	*13*	*1*	*18*
House	650	5,250	0	5,900
Senate	5,450	3,600	1,000	10,050
Democrats	22,000	4,800	500	27,300
No. of Cand.	*16*	*10*	*1*	*27*
House	20,500	3,050	500	24,050
Senate	1,500	1,750	0	3,250
Incumbents	23,850	10,500	1,500	35,850
Challengers	1,750	300	0	2,050
Open Seat	2,500	2,850	0	5,350
Winners	12,450	10,600	n/a	23,050
Losers	15,650	3,050	n/a	18,700

Bracewell & Patterson

*Phone: (713) 223-2900 * Fax: (713) 221-1212*
S. Tower Pennzoil Place, 711 Louisiana, Suite 2900, Houston, TX 77002-2781
*Web: www.bracepatt.com * E-mail: houston@bracepatt.com*

Law firm Bracewell & Patterson has more than 200 lawyers. Headquartered in Houston, the firm has offices in Dallas, Austin, Washington and London. It also has affiliations with firms in Mexico.

The firm is divided into the litigation group and the business group. More than half of the lawyers practice in the litigation group, which includes trial, labor, education, bankruptcy and appellate lawyers.

The business group includes corporate, energy, finance, banking, real estate, tax, employee benefits and estates lawyers. Clients of the company range from large public corporations and government entities to individuals and small, start-up businesses.

Bracewell & Patterson Political Action Committee (C00021295) *Phone: (202) 828-5800 * Fax: (202) 223-1225 * 2000 K St. N.W., Suite 500, Washington, DC 20006 * E-mail: ggodley@bracepatt.com * Treasurer: Gene E. Godley*

	1993-94	1995-96	1997	Totals
Receipts	$68,925	$75,462	$10,214	$154,601
Disburse	80,214	64,220	20,215	164,649
Cash	102	11,349	1,348	n/a
Contributions	77,099	52,129	20,136	149,364
Republicans	37,700	38,629	9,136	85,465
No. of Cand.	*23*	*35*	*11*	*69*
House	12,600	25,750	7,936	46,286
Senate	25,100	12,879	1,200	39,179
Democrats	39,399	13,500	11,000	63,899
No. of Cand.	*31*	*16*	*13*	*60*
House	29,899	9,500	7,000	46,399
Senate	9,500	4,000	4,000	17,500
Incumbents	67,999	45,300	19,136	132,435
Challengers	1,500	0	0	1,500
Open Seat	7,600	6,329	1,000	14,929
Winners	59,899	47,879	n/a	107,778
Losers	17,200	4,250	n/a	21,450

Buchanan Ingersoll

*Phone: (412) 562-8800 * Fax: (412) 562-1041*
One Oxford Centre, 301 Grant St., 20th Floor, Pittsburgh, PA 15219
Web: www.bipc.com

Buchanan Ingersoll is a Pennsylvania-based law firm with offices throughout the mid-Atlantic and Florida.

The firm, which has nearly 300 lawyers, deals in traditional legal areas but is expanding into developing areas such as trade secret protection, energy and health care restructuring and the Internet and security alarm industries. In 1996, the company handled more than 500 major transactions of business assets and financings valued at more than $32.5 billion.

Founded in 1850, Buchanan Ingersoll is today one of the hundred-largest law firms in the nation and the fourth-largest in Pennsylvania.

Buchanan Ingersoll Professional Corp. Committee for Effective Government (BIPC PAC) (C00195388) *Address: same as sponsor * Treasurer: Miles H. Simon * Contact: Mark R. Hornak, Chairman*

	1993-94	1995-96	1997	Totals
Receipts	$43,498	$46,075	$11,500	$101,073
Disburse	41,550	49,721	11,685	102,956
Cash	3,874	227	41	n/a
Contributions	19,000	25,750	4,600	49,350
Republicans	5,650	15,750	4,600	26,000
No. of Cand.	*4*	*6*	*4*	*14*
House	650	11,500	1,350	13,500
Senate	5,000	4,250	3,250	12,500
Democrats	13,350	10,000	0	23,350
No. of Cand.	*16*	*10*	*5*	*31*
House	12,350	8,000	0	20,350
Senate	1,000	2,000	0	3,000
Incumbents	6,700	12,750	3,250	22,700
Challengers	8,000	12,500	1,350	21,850
Open Seat	4,300	500	500	5,300
Winners	13,850	12,250	n/a	26,100
Losers	5,150	13,500	n/a	18,650

Climaco, Climaco, Lefkowitz & Garofoli

*Phone: (216) 621-8484 * Fax: (216) 771-1632*
1228 Euclid Ave., Suite 900, Cleveland, OH 44115

Climaco, Climaco, Lefkowitz & Garofoli is an Ohio-based law firm with offices in Cleveland, Columbus and Washington. It has 27 members and associates, many of whom specialize in civil rights, labor and personal injury law.

The firm also handles cases involving environmental law, bankruptcy, bond financing, intellectual property and public utilities.

Climaco, Climaco, Lefkowitz & Garofoli PAC (C00279489) *Address: same as sponsor * Treasurer: John Climaco*

	1993-94	1995-96	1997	Totals
Receipts	$125,661	$74,000	$32,500	$232,161
Disburse	83,803	107,980	33,735	225,518
Cash	41,857	7,877	6,642	n/a
Contributions	76,300	73,000	16,000	165,300
Republicans	39,500	24,500	6,000	70,000
No. of Cand.	*11*	*11*	*4*	*26*
House	24,000	10,000	250	34,250
Senate	15,500	14,500	5,750	35,750
Democrats	36,300	48,500	10,000	94,800
No. of Cand.	*33*	*23*	*2*	*58*
House	24,050	34,500	5,000	63,550
Senate	12,250	14,000	5,000	31,250
Incumbents	40,550	41,000	16,000	97,550
Challengers	15,000	26,000	0	41,000
Open Seat	20,750	6,000	0	26,750
Winners	59,550	45,000	n/a	104,550
Losers	16,750	28,000	n/a	44,750

Collier, Shannon, Rill & Scott

*Phone: (202) 342-8400 * Fax: (202) 342-8451*
3050 K St. N.W., Suite 400, Washington, DC 20007
*Web: www.colshan.com * E-mail: lawyers@colshan.com*

Collier, Shannon, Rill & Scott is a Washington-based law firm.

Founded in 1963, the firm originally focused on international trade, antitrust and trade regulation law. Today, the company has expanded to include 100 attorneys who practice law in the fields of consumer protection, advertising, energy, the environment, health and safety, government relations, intellectual property, international trade and labor.

The firm's clients include Fortune 500 corporations, smaller businesses in the manufacturing, agriculture, energy and service sectors, and more than 100 trade associations.

The firm also has an office in Sydney, Australia.

Collier, Shannon, Rill & Scott Political Action Committee (C00301929) *Address: same as sponsor * Treasurer: David A. Hartquist*

	1993-94	1995-96	1997	Totals
Receipts	$0	$67,500	$28,300	$95,800
Disburse	0	58,970	31,117	90,087
Cash	0	8,275	5,457	n/a
Contributions	0	52,824	26,500	79,324
Republicans	0	37,824	15,500	53,324
No. of Cand.	*0*	*42*	*21*	*63*
House	0	22,074	9,500	31,574
Senate	0	15,750	6,000	21,750
Democrats	0	15,000	11,000	26,000
No. of Cand.	*0*	*17*	*11*	*28*
House	0	10,000	8,000	18,000
Senate	0	5,000	3,000	8,000
Incumbents	0	44,074	25,500	69,574
Challengers	0	3,250	500	3,750
Open Seat	0	5,500	500	6,000
Winners	0	47,074	n/a	47,074
Losers	0	5,750	n/a	5,750

Commercial Law League of America

*Phone: (312) 781-2000 * Fax: (312) 781-2010*
150 N. Michigan Ave., Suite 600, Chicago, IL 60601
*Web: www.clla.org * E-mail: clla@clla.org*

The Commercial Law League of America is a national association of 5,000 collection lawyers, bankruptcy lawyers and collection agencies.

The league's bipartisan PAC gives to federal candidates across the nation. It is interested in general debt, bankruptcy and collection legislation as well as government debt collection.

The collection agency section of the league is located in New Jersey.

Commercial Law League of America Political Action Committee (C00234682) *Address: same as sponsor * Treasurer: Max G. Moses * Contact: Rick Johanson, President*

	1993-94	1995-96	1997	Totals
Receipts	$17,269	$14,847	$623	$32,739
Disburse	10,295	18,590	2,000	30,885
Cash	23,433	19,693	18,316	n/a
Contributions	8,490	13,500	2,000	23,990
Republicans	2,000	11,500	2,000	15,500
No. of Cand.	*2*	*8*	*3*	*13*
House	0	4,000	1,000	5,000
Senate	2,000	7,500	1,000	10,500
Democrats	6,490	2,000	0	8,490
No. of Cand.	*6*	*2*	*0*	*8*
House	3,250	0	0	3,250
Senate	3,240	2,000	0	5,240
Incumbents	8,490	11,500	2,000	21,990
Challengers	0	1,000	0	1,000
Open Seat	0	1,000	0	1,000
Winners	7,250	6,500	n/a	13,750
Losers	1,240	7,000	n/a	8,240

Crowell & Moring

*Phone: (202) 624-2680 * Fax: (202) 628-5116*
1001 Pennsylvania Ave. N.W., 11th Floor, Washington, DC 20004

Crowell & Moring is a general practice law firm with more than 220 lawyers at offices in Washington, Irvine, Calif. and London.

C&M belongs to the Environmental Law Institute Professional Program, a membership program for environmental law practices. Along with its environmental group, C&M has a large group of lawyers involved with torts, insurance practice and litigation.

Notable clients include CIGNA, Eli Lilly, The Product Liability Coordinating Committee and the American Tort Reform Association. The firm was founded in 1979.

Crowell & Moring PAC (C00199869) *Address: same as sponsor * Treasurer: Karen Hastie Williams*

	1993-94	1995-96	1997	Totals
Receipts	$42,050	$51,272	$12,275	$105,597
Disburse	52,125	55,150	22,125	129,400
Cash	15,758	11,880	2,030	n/a
Contributions	42,275	45,150	14,125	101,550
Republicans	14,525	29,900	9,875	54,300
No. of Cand.	*20*	*38*	*15*	*73*
House	5,225	12,000	2,625	19,850
Senate	9,300	17,900	7,250	34,450
Democrats	26,500	15,250	4,250	46,000
No. of Cand.	*36*	*20*	*7*	*63*
House	19,500	8,500	1,750	29,750
Senate	7,000	6,750	2,500	16,250
Incumbents	36,850	40,700	13,875	91,425
Challengers	2,300	700	0	3,000
Open Seat	2,625	3,750	250	6,625
Winners	32,225	37,200	n/a	69,425
Losers	10,050	7,950	n/a	18,000

Davis Wright Tremaine

*Phone: (206) 622-3150 * Fax: (206) 628-7040*
2600 Century Square, 1501 Fourth Ave., Seattle, WA 98101
Web: www.dwt.com

Davis Wright Tremaine is a Seattle-based law firm with more than 300 lawyers practicing in 11 offices around the world. The firm's PAC is bipartisan.

Its Washington office specializes in telecommunications, intellectual property and media law.

Davis Wright also has offices in the state of Washington; Los Angeles; Portland, Ore.; Boise, Idaho; Charlotte, N.C.; Anchorage, Alaska; Honolulu; and Shanghai, China.

Davis Wright Political Action Committee (C00163238) *Phone: (202) 508-6617 * Fax: (202) 508-6699 * 1155 Connecticut Ave. N.W., Suite 700, Washington, DC 20036 * Treasurer: Richard L. Cys*

	1993-94	1995-96	1997	Totals
Receipts	$12,469	$1,045	$540	$14,054
Disburse	13,430	12,755	2,240	28,425
Cash	10,158	1,448	1,448	n/a
Contributions	12,350	10,610	1,700	24,660
Republicans	3,000	8,310	700	12,010
No. of Cand.	*3*	*11*	*2*	*16*
House	500	5,310	500	6,310
Senate	2,500	3,000	200	5,700
Democrats	9,350	2,300	1,000	12,650
No. of Cand.	*12*	*4*	*2*	*18*
House	7,350	1,300	500	9,150
Senate	2,000	1,000	500	3,500
Incumbents	11,350	8,810	1,700	21,860
Challengers	1,000	300	0	1,300
Open Seat	0	1,500	0	1,500
Winners	7,100	8,310	n/a	15,410
Losers	5,250	2,300	n/a	7,550

Dickstein Shapiro Morin & Oshinsky

*Phone: (202) 785-9700 * Fax: (202) 887-0689*
2101 L St. N.W., Washington, DC 20037
Web: www.dsmo.com

Law and lobbying firm Dickstein Shapiro Morin & Oshinsky has 210 lawyers in Atlanta and Washington. Its practice areas include corporate, energy, environmental, health, international and technology law.

Founded in 1953 by Sidney Dickstein and David Shapiro, the original focus of the firm was civil liberties law, specifically defending targets of McCarthy-era loyalty and security investigations. Since then it has grown to become the 148th-largest law firm in the United States, according to the National Law Journal.

Dickstein's lobbying practice works on electrical utility restructuring, health care, financial services, and tobacco industry regulations. Clients include the Pipe Tobacco Council Inc., Home Box Office, the Exxon Valdez oil spill plaintiffs, FANNIE MAE, and the state governments of Georgia, Kansas, North Dakota, Pennsylvania and Rhode Island.

The firm's bipartisan PAC tends to favor incumbents. Leading recipients during the 1995-96 election cycle were Sens. Jesse Helms, R-N.C., and Pete V. Domenici, R-N.M., who received $3,000 each.

Dickstein Shapiro Morin & Oshinsky LLP Political Action Committee (DSMO PAC) (C00110197) *Address: same as sponsor * Treasurer: L. Andrew Zausner*

	1993-94	1995-96	1997	Totals
Receipts	$99,081	$79,888	$70,717	$249,686
Disburse	86,127	108,405	46,575	241,107
Cash	33,519	5,003	29,146	n/a
Contributions	75,290	87,650	35,000	197,940
Republicans	24,750	58,900	20,500	104,150
No. of Cand.	*27*	*66*	*23*	*116*
House	8,250	33,650	12,500	54,400
Senate	16,500	25,250	8,000	49,750
Democrats	50,540	28,750	14,500	93,790
No. of Cand.	*58*	*32*	*17*	*107*
House	32,050	17,750	7,500	57,300
Senate	18,490	11,000	7,000	36,490
Incumbents	61,890	72,400	33,000	167,290
Challengers	5,500	2,000	0	7,500
Open Seat	7,900	12,250	2,000	22,150
Winners	56,650	69,150	n/a	125,800
Losers	18,640	18,500	n/a	37,140

Dorsey & Whitney

*Phone: (612) 343-7900 * Fax: (612) 340-7834*
220 S. Sixth St., Minneapolis, MN 55402-1498
Web: www.dorseylaw.com

Minnesota-based international law firm Dorsey & Whitney practices in legal areas including corporate, banking, real estate, Indian laws and gaming, environmental, labor and employment law.

Established in 1912, the firm employs more than 400 attorneys and posted more than $130 million in sales in 1996. Dorsey & Whitney is one of the 50 largest law firms in the nation and was ranked first in the nation for mergers and acquisitions in 1997 by Securities Data Co.

In addition to its Minneapolis headquarters, the firm also maintains several offices throughout Minnesota and Montana and one each in New York and Washington. Dorsey & Whitney's international offices are located in Hong Kong, London and Brussels, Belgium.

Walter F. Mondale, former vice president of the United States and Ambassador to Japan, rejoined the firm as a partner in the international practice group in 1997.

Most of the committee's decisions are made by Warren Spannaus and Ed Pluimer, both of whom are partners with the firm.

Dorsey National Fund (C00018945) *Address: same as sponsor * Treasurer: Eugene S. Holderness*

	1993-94	1995-96	1997	Totals
Receipts	$87,286	$44,656	$38,599	$170,541
Disburse	91,867	45,308	20,700	157,875
Cash	2,399	1,748	19,648	n/a
Contributions	47,500	36,558	20,050	104,108
Republicans	14,900	10,958	4,650	30,508
No. of Cand.	*19*	*12*	*6*	*37*
House	9,025	5,600	3,750	18,375
Senate	5,875	5,358	900	12,133
Democrats	24,300	25,600	13,400	63,300
No. of Cand.	*26*	*26*	*15*	*67*
House	12,900	15,800	6,650	35,350
Senate	11,400	9,800	6,750	27,950
Incumbents	20,750	21,350	18,800	60,900
Challengers	6,425	12,258	950	19,633
Open Seat	20,325	2,850	300	23,475
Winners	22,600	26,600	n/a	49,200
Losers	24,900	9,958	n/a	34,858

Dyer Ellis & Joseph

*Phone: (202) 944-3000 * Fax: (202) 944-3068*
600 New Hampshire Ave. N.W., Suite 1000, Washington, DC 20037

Dyer Ellis & Joseph is a Washington law firm with about 35 lawyers who specialize in maritime, environmental, antitrust, securities, health care and aviation law. Its clients include national and international companies affected by federal regulation.

Dyer Ellis & Joseph PC PAC (C00295758) *Address: same as sponsor * Treasurer: Duncan C. Smith III*

	1993-94	1995-96	1997	Totals
Receipts	$18,000	$21,185	$14,670	$53,855
Disburse	16,714	20,700	13,000	50,414
Cash	1,285	1,531	3,201	n/a
Contributions	16,714	18,200	10,000	44,914
Republicans	8,989	15,800	6,500	31,289
No. of Cand.	*17*	*30*	*13*	*60*
House	2,500	9,300	6,000	17,800
Senate	6,489	6,500	500	13,489
Democrats	7,725	2,400	3,500	13,625
No. of Cand.	*21*	*8*	*7*	*36*
House	5,200	2,150	1,500	8,850
Senate	2,525	250	2,000	4,775
Incumbents	12,725	15,550	10,000	38,275
Challengers	500	1,150	0	1,650
Open Seat	3,489	1,000	0	4,489
Winners	12,714	13,850	n/a	26,564
Losers	4,000	4,350	n/a	8,350

Erickson & Sederstrom

*Phone: (402) 397-2200 * Fax: (402) 390-7137*
10330 Regency Pkwy. Dr., Omaha, NE 68114
*Web: www.eslaw.com * E-mail: mcw@eslaw.com*

Erickson & Sederstrom employs 30 lawyers in Omaha and Lincoln, Neb. It provides legal representation to individuals, businesses, health care institutions and governmental subdivisions in Nebraska and adjoining states.

Erickson & Sederstrom is a founding member of the State Capitol Law Firm Group, an association of law firms in the capitals of all 50 states.

Erickson & Sederstrom (E&S) Political Action Committee (C00183426) *Address: same as sponsor * Treasurer: Michael Washburn*

	1993-94	1995-96	1997	Totals
Receipts	$3,719	$5,933	$2,410	$12,062
Disburse	3,155	7,009	2,237	12,401
Cash	1,041	149	320	n/a
Contributions	3,000	4,935	300	8,235
Republicans	2,900	3,900	300	7,100
No. of Cand.	*5*	*4*	*2*	*11*
House	2,150	500	300	2,950
Senate	750	3,400	0	4,150
Democrats	100	1,035	0	1,135
No. of Cand.	*1*	*2*	*0*	*3*
House	0	35	0	35
Senate	100	1,000	0	1,100
Incumbents	300	500	0	800
Challengers	2,700	35	0	2,735
Open Seat	0	4,400	300	4,700
Winners	1,250	2,900	n/a	4,150
Losers	1,750	2,035	n/a	3,785

Faegre & Benson

*Phone: (612) 336-3000 * Fax: (612) 336-3026*
2200 Norwest Center, Minneapolis, MN 55402
Web: www.faegre.com

Minneapolis law firm Faegre & Benson, one of the 100 largest firms in the United States, has about 300 lawyers who practice in five offices. Its PAC is bipartisan.

The firm's other offices are in Denver; Des Moines, Iowa; London; and Frankfurt, Germany. It also has a multinational business-oriented practice in Almaty, Kazakhstan, that provides assistance to individuals and companies doing business or investing in the Republic of Kazakhstan and other central Asian republics of the former Soviet Union.

The firm was founded in 1886.

Faegre & Benson Professional Limited Liability Partnership (formerly known as Faegre & Benson) (C00215491) *Address: same as sponsor * Treasurer: John D. French*

	1993-94	1995-96	1997	Totals
Receipts	$19,500	$10,750	$2,500	$32,750
Disburse	17,666	11,615	3,668	32,949
Cash	2,322	1,455	286	n/a
Contributions	17,267	9,865	3,350	30,482
Republicans	3,500	2,000	1,100	6,600
No. of Cand.	*7*	*4*	*3*	*14*
House	2,000	1,500	600	4,100
Senate	1,500	500	500	2,500
Democrats	8,517	7,865	1,750	18,132
No. of Cand.	*12*	*13*	*4*	*29*
House	6,267	5,604	1,250	13,121
Senate	2,250	2,261	500	5,011
Incumbents	6,400	8,115	3,250	17,765
Challengers	500	1,750	100	2,350
Open Seat	10,367	0	0	10,367
Winners	9,792	8,615	n/a	18,407
Losers	7,475	1,250	n/a	8,725

Fulbright & Jaworski

*Phone: (713) 651-5151 * Fax: (713) 651-5246*
1301 McKinney St., Suite 1500, Houston, TX 77010-3031
*Web: www.fulbright.com * E-mail: info@fulbright.com*

Fulbright & Jaworski is the largest law firm in Texas, and the 11th-largest in the nation, with more than 650 lawyers. The firm offers a full range of legal services to its domestic and international clients, including individuals, public sector entities, charitable organizations and businesses.

For initial public offerings and venture capital, F&J leads law firms as both top issuer's and underwriter's counsel by number of offerings. In 1996, it was the sixth top issuer's counsel with 15 registrations valued at $661.6 million, and 13th for underwriter's counsel with 13 registrations valued at $522.7 million. Total firm sales in that year topped $243 million.

Founded in 1919 in Houston, Fulbright & Jaworski has other Texas offices in Austin, Dallas and San Antonio. It also has branches in Los Angeles, Washington, New York, London and Hong Kong.

Fulbright & Jaworski LLP Federal Committee (C00149013) *Address: same as sponsor * Treasurer: Richard D. Huff*

	1993-94	1995-96	1997	Totals
Receipts	$124,973	$140,623	$69,095	$334,691
Disburse	131,449	135,603	63,632	330,684
Cash	76,322	68,829	74,293	n/a
Contributions	98,650	89,812	44,262	232,724
Republicans	37,250	50,623	24,262	112,135
No. of Cand.	*15*	*40*	*26*	*81*
House	11,250	35,123	10,262	56,635
Senate	26,000	15,500	14,000	55,500
Democrats	61,400	39,189	20,000	120,589
No. of Cand.	*42*	*31*	*21*	*94*
House	41,150	33,939	15,000	90,089
Senate	20,250	5,250	5,000	30,500
Incumbents	64,550	62,823	35,012	162,385

Challengers	18,500	11,239	2,500	32,239
Open Seat	15,600	15,750	5,750	37,100
Winners	60,100	71,312	n/a	131,412
Losers	38,550	18,500	n/a	57,050

Garvey, Schubert & Barer

*Phone: (202) 965-7880 * Fax: (202) 965-1729*
1000 Potomac St. N.W., Fifth Floor, Washington, DC 20007-3501
Web: www.gsblaw.aa.psiweb.com

Garvey, Schubert & Barer has 88 lawyers in offices in Washington, Seattle and Portland, Ore.

The firm has expertise in antitrust and trade regulation, bankruptcy law, environmental law, estate planning, federal legislative and administrative representation, health care law, alternative dispute resolution and tax law.

Garvey, Schubert & Barer Political Action Committee (C00177550) *Address: same as sponsor * Treasurer: Alan A. Butchman*

	1993-94	1995-96	1997	Totals
Receipts	$53,511	$50,116	$25,290	$128,917
Disburse	52,250	45,850	27,189	125,289
Cash	5,277	7,449	5,549	n/a
Contributions	49,225	50,750	26,189	126,164
Republicans	12,500	28,000	10,000	50,500
No. of Cand.	*12*	*18*	*12*	*42*
House	7,000	22,000	9,000	38,000
Senate	5,500	6,000	1,000	12,500
Democrats	36,725	22,750	16,189	75,664
No. of Cand.	*31*	*17*	*16*	*64*
House	30,725	14,500	7,500	52,725
Senate	6,000	8,250	8,689	22,939
Incumbents	44,925	45,000	24,689	114,614
Challengers	500	1,000	0	1,500
Open Seat	3,800	5,750	1,500	11,050
Winners	28,925	45,500	n/a	74,425
Losers	20,300	5,250	n/a	25,550

Gray, Harris & Robinson

*Phone: (407) 843-8880 * Fax: (407) 244-5690*
201 E. Pine St., Suite 1200, Orlando, FL 32801-3068
E-mail: cgray@ghrlaw.com

Gray, Harris & Robinson is one of the largest law firms in Florida. Its areas of emphasis include corporate law, taxation, environmental and maritime law. It has Florida offices in Orlando, Melbourne and Tallahassee.

Among the firm's clients are First Union Bank, Southern States Utilities Inc., Ralston Purina, CNA Insurance Co. and the California Public Employees Retirement System.

Gray, Harris & Robinson PA Political Action Committee (C00224790) *Address: same as sponsor * Treasurer: John Charles Gray*

	1993-94	1995-96	1997	Totals
Receipts	$8,739	$13,429	$8,619	$30,787
Disburse	15,350	11,700	2,700	29,750
Cash	4,941	6,671	12,591	n/a
Contributions	6,500	9,200	2,700	18,400
Republicans	4,500	6,500	1,500	12,500
No. of Cand.	*4*	*6*	*2*	*12*
House	4,500	5,500	1,500	11,500
Senate	0	1,000	0	1,000
Democrats	2,000	2,700	1,200	5,900
No. of Cand.	*4*	*4*	*2*	*10*
House	2,000	1,700	200	3,900
Senate	0	1,000	1,000	2,000
Incumbents	6,000	7,200	2,700	15,900
Challengers	0	0	0	0
Open Seat	500	2,000	0	2,500
Winners	4,750	8,200	n/a	12,950
Losers	1,750	1,000	n/a	2,750

Gray, Plant, Mooty, Mooty & Bennett

*Phone: (612) 343-2800 * Fax: (612) 333-0066*
3400 City Center, 33 S. Sixth St., Minneapolis, MN 55402-3796
*Web: www.grayplantmooty.com * E-mail: tom.johnson@gpmlaw.com*

Gray, Plant, Mooty, Mooty & Bennett is a Minnesota-based law firm that practices in the areas of business, employee benefits, intellectual property, litigation, trusts and estates, real estate and taxes. The firm was established in 1866 and now employs more than 100 lawyers.

In 1992, the firm opened a consulting office in Beijing which serves both American and Japanese clients conducting business in China and Chinese clients conducting business in the United States.

The firm's clients have included Allstate Insurance Co., China National Aero-Technology Import & Export Corp., General Motors Corp., The Goodyear Tire & Rubber Co., MCI, Minnesota Vikings Football Club, R.J. Reynolds Tobacco Co. and St. Olaf College.

Gray, Plant, Mooty, Mooty & Bennett Public Affairs Committee (C00099473) *Address: same as sponsor * Treasurer: Thomas L. Johnson*

	1993-94	1995-96	1997	Totals
Receipts	$9,370	$7,993	$120	$17,483
Disburse	8,980	7,682	1,571	18,233
Cash	1,852	2,397	945	n/a
Contributions	2,339	4,717	500	7,556
Republicans	235	1,505	0	1,740
No. of Cand.	*2*	*3*	*0*	*5*
House	0	556	0	556
Senate	235	949	0	1,184
Democrats	1,704	3,212	500	5,416
No. of Cand.	*4*	*5*	*1*	*10*
House	1,304	2,326	500	4,130
Senate	400	886	0	1,286
Incumbents	750	3,718	500	4,968
Challengers	0	999	0	999
Open Seat	1,589	0	0	1,589
Winners	1,304	3,718	n/a	5,022
Losers	1,035	999	n/a	2,034

Greenberg, Traurig, Hoffman, Lipoff, Rosen & Quentel

*Phone: (305) 579-0500 * Fax: (305) 579-0717*
1221 Brickell Ave., Miami, FL 33121
*Web: www.gtlaw.com * E-mail: schulmanc@gtlaw.com*

Florida law and lobbying firm Greenberg Traurig has 340 lawyers in four Florida offices, Washington, New York, Philadelphia and Sao Paulo, Brazil.

The firm works with tax, litigation, finance, securities, capital markets, environmental, health care, intellectual property and other areas of business law. The Washington office also lobbies on transportation, international trade, immigration, housing and economic development.

Recent lobbying included negotiating a trade agreement between Mexican tomato growers and the United States, promoting funding for contracts with an Ingersoll Rand Corp. subsidiary and maintaining federal funding to North Miami Beach. Greenberg Traurig also is assisting The Viera Co. in seeking federal authorization for a new highway interchange in Jacksonville, Fla. and Trendstar Industries in the marketing and sale of its product, Dermax 2000, before the Department of Veterans Affairs.

Washington lawyers include Reta J. Lewis, who worked in the Office of Political Affairs in the Clinton White House, and James Miller, a Treasury Department official in the Bush administration.

Greenberg, Traurig, Hoffman, Lipoff, Rosen & Quentel PA Political Action Committee (C00266585) *Phone: (202) 331-3100 * Fax: (202) 331-3101 * 1300 Connecticut Ave. N.W., Suite 1000, Washington, DC 20036 * Treasurer: Fran M. Wylde*
*Contact: Cliff Schulman, Shareholder * Phone: (305) 579-0500*

	1993-94	1995-96	1997	Totals
Receipts	$69,045	$78,523	$101,483	$249,051
Disburse	71,488	77,092	61,530	210,110
Cash	85	1,514	41,469	n/a
Contributions	61,986	68,719	48,780	179,485
Republicans	9,098	19,181	18,280	46,559
No. of Cand.	*5*	*11*	*22*	*38*
House	4,000	7,250	10,930	22,180
Senate	5,098	11,931	7,350	24,379
Democrats	52,888	49,538	30,500	132,926
No. of Cand.	*31*	*39*	*27*	*97*
House	27,388	27,941	16,500	71,829
Senate	25,500	21,597	14,000	61,097
Incumbents	56,388	52,456	45,530	154,374
Challengers	0	2,000	2,000	4,000
Open Seat	5,500	13,697	1,250	20,447
Winners	52,818	64,153	n/a	116,971
Losers	9,168	4,566	n/a	13,734

Hannoch Weisman

*Phone: (973) 535-5326 * Fax: (973) 994-7198*
4 Becker Farm Rd., Roseland, NJ 07068
*Web: www.hannoch.com * E-mail: wrobertson@hannoch.com*

Hannoch Weisman is a New Jersey law firm specializing in representing family-owned businesses. Its other practice areas include white-collar crime, intellectual property law, planned charitable giving, real estate, securities and tax law and trusts and estates. The firm has about 80 lawyers.

Hannoch Weisman Political Action Committee (C00247635)
*Address: same as sponsor * Treasurer: William W. Robertson*

	1993-94	1995-96	1997	Totals
Receipts	$11,247	$6,682	$4,028	$21,957
Disburse	6,750	9,846	5,750	22,346
Cash	5,473	2,349	628	n/a
Contributions	4,750	8,500	1,000	14,250
Republicans	1,750	1,000	1,000	3,750
No. of Cand.	*3*	*1*	*1*	*5*
House	250	1,000	0	1,250
Senate	1,500	0	1,000	2,500
Democrats	3,000	7,500	0	10,500
No. of Cand.	*2*	*2*	*0*	*4*
House	2,000	0	0	2,000
Senate	1,000	7,500	0	8,500
Incumbents	3,150	3,500	1,000	7,650
Challengers	1,600	0	0	1,600
Open Seat	0	5,000	0	5,000
Winners	1,100	8,500	n/a	9,600
Losers	3,650	0	n/a	3,650

Harris Beach & Wilcox

*Phone: (716) 232-4440 * Fax: (716) 546-2571*
130 E. Main St., Rochester, NY 14604

Harris Beach & Wilcox is a Rochester, N.Y.-based firm that practices in all areas of law.

The firm, which was founded in 1856, has other New York offices in Ithaca, Albany, Hamburg, Syracuse and New York City. It also has offices in Hackensack, N.J., Milford, Conn. and Washington.

The firm has 180 lawyers.

Harris Beach & Wilcox LLP Political Committee - Federal (C00195891) *Phone: (202) 861-0001 * Fax: (202) 861-0011 * 1901 Pennsylvania Ave. N.W., Washington, DC 20006 * Treasurer: William H. Kedley*

	1993-94	1995-96	1997	Totals
Receipts	$3,175	$26,250	$3,610	$33,035
Disburse	3,338	24,304	5,715	33,357
Cash	449	2,374	268	n/a
Contributions	3,175	14,050	3,125	20,350
Republicans	1,625	9,300	3,125	14,050
No. of Cand.	*4*	*7*	*3*	*14*
House	1,625	2,800	1,625	6,050
Senate	0	6,500	1,500	8,000
Democrats	1,550	4,750	0	6,300
No. of Cand.	*2*	*3*	*0*	*5*
House	250	4,750	0	5,000
Senate	1,300	0	0	1,300
Incumbents	2,775	12,550	3,125	18,450
Challengers	400	1,000	0	1,400
Open Seat	0	500	0	500
Winners	2,775	12,550	n/a	15,325
Losers	400	1,500	n/a	1,900

Hogan & Hartson

*Phone: (202) 637-5600 * Fax: (202) 637-5910*
555 Thirteenth St. N.W., Eighth Floor, West Tower, Washington, DC 20004
E-mail: hhinfo@dc4.hhlaw.com

Hogan & Hartson is a full-service law and lobbying firm based in Washington. It has 523 lawyers and earned $165 million in sales during 1996. H&H is on the Legal Times' top 10 list of lobbying firms.

Roughly 175 H&H lawyers practice the full range of international, corporate, securities, financial, tax, real estate and other commercial matters. Another major division litigates commercial and other disputes before state, federal and international tribunals, and engages in international arbitration.

The firm's lobbying clients have included Mercedes-Benz, Hoffman-LaRoche, the Chickasaw Nation and U.S. Sugar Corp.

The firm has six domestic locations and offices in the European capitals of Paris; Brussels, Belgium; London; Moscow; Warsaw, Poland; and Prague, Czech Republic. It is also a member of the Pacific Rim Advisory Council, a strategic alliance of 27 major independent law firms that conduct substantial business in the Pacific Rim region.

Hogan & Hartson Political Action Committee (C00261339)
*Address: same as sponsor * Treasurer: W. Mike House*

	1993-94	1995-96	1997	Totals
Receipts	$136,702	$131,250	$63,540	$331,492
Disburse	136,389	128,335	64,000	328,724
Cash	5,362	8,280	7,824	n/a
Contributions	108,400	97,750	53,000	259,150
Republicans	32,850	60,750	29,500	123,100
No. of Cand.	*40*	*64*	*38*	*142*
House	14,350	31,750	16,500	62,600
Senate	18,500	29,000	13,000	60,500
Democrats	74,050	37,000	23,000	134,050
No. of Cand.	*74*	*45*	*30*	*149*
House	46,250	25,000	10,000	81,250
Senate	27,800	12,000	13,000	52,800
Incumbents	105,600	90,250	53,000	248,850
Challengers	0	500	0	500
Open Seat	2,300	7,000	0	9,300
Winners	92,500	86,750	n/a	179,250
Losers	15,900	11,000	n/a	26,900

Holland & Hart

*Phone: (303) 295-8000 * Fax: (303) 295-8261*
555 17th St., Suite 3200, Denver, CO 80202
*Web: www.hollandhart.com/law * E-mail: info@hollandhart.com*

Holland & Hart is a Denver-based law firm with 10 offices in Colorado, Wyoming, Idaho, Montana and Utah. Its 220 lawyers work in all areas of law.

The PAC is bipartisan and generally gives to candidates from the Rocky Mountain region.

Holland & Hart Federal PAC (C00137729) *Address: same as sponsor * Treasurer: James W. Davidson * Contact: H. Gregory Austin, Partner*

	1993-94	1995-96	1997	Totals
Receipts	$62,524	$45,834	$0	$108,358
Disburse	57,434	30,100	1,625	89,159
Cash	22,107	38,044	36,419	n/a
Contributions	50,425	25,600	125	76,150
Republicans	17,925	14,100	0	32,025
No. of Cand.	*17*	*17*	*0*	*34*
House	7,575	10,500	0	18,075
Senate	10,350	3,600	0	13,950
Democrats	32,500	11,500	125	44,125
No. of Cand.	*20*	*10*	*1*	*31*
House	18,500	10,500	125	29,125
Senate	14,000	1,000	0	15,000
Incumbents	40,625	19,500	125	60,250
Challengers	1,200	1,500	0	2,700
Open Seat	8,600	4,600	0	13,200
Winners	35,375	18,100	n/a	53,475
Losers	15,050	7,500	n/a	22,550

Holland & Knight

*Phone: (813) 227-8500 * Fax: (813) 229-0134*
400 N. Ashley Dr., Suite 2300, Tampa, FL 33602
Web: www.hklaw.com

Holland & Knight is the largest law firm in Florida with offices in 10 cities. The firm also maintains offices in New York City, Washington, Atlanta and San Francisco. It was formed in 1968 when two separate firms combined. One firm was founded in 1880 by Spessard Holland, former Florida governor and U.S. senator; the other was owned by Peter Knight, founder of Tampa Electric Co.

Holland & Knight employs about 600 lawyers who practice in more than 50 areas of general law.

Holland & Knight says it has a strong commitment to pro bono work and recommends its offices spend roughly 3 percent of their billable hours on public service.

Holland & Knight Committee for Effective Government (C00171330) *Phone: (202) 955-3000 * Fax: (202) 955-5564 * 2100 Pennsylvania Ave. N.W., Suite 400, Washington, DC 20037 * Treasurer: Stephen J. Powell*

	1993-94	1995-96	1997	Totals
Receipts	$95,870	$240,675	$143,152	$479,697
Disburse	104,343	222,819	130,479	457,641
Cash	4,454	22,312	34,986	n/a
Contributions	62,150	146,369	82,727	291,246
Republicans	27,450	77,545	40,500	145,495
No. of Cand.	*23*	*62*	*62*	*147*
House	19,450	38,045	28,250	85,745
Senate	8,000	39,500	12,250	59,750
Democrats	34,450	68,324	41,727	144,501
No. of Cand.	*33*	*71*	*42*	*146*
House	23,950	38,024	20,750	82,724
Senate	10,500	30,300	20,977	61,777
Incumbents	54,250	118,069	81,727	254,046
Challengers	700	4,500	500	5,700
Open Seat	6,700	22,800	500	30,000
Winners	52,200	128,619	n/a	180,819
Losers	9,950	17,750	n/a	27,700

Hopkins & Sutter

*Phone: (312) 558-6545 * Fax: (312) 558-6958*
Three First National Plaza, #4300, Chicago, IL 60602
Web: www.hopsut.com

Chicago-based Hopkins & Sutter is a general practice law and lobbying firm with about 150 lawyers. About 50 percent of its business is devoted to litigation, but it also has such diverse practice groups as airport services, energy and telecommunications and gaming law.

Established in 1921, the firm also maintains offices in Washington and Detroit. In 1995, it posted $156.5 million in revenues.

HS Political Fund (C00105338) *Address: same as sponsor * Treasurer: Gregory P. Marren*

	1993-94	1995-96	1997	Totals
Receipts	$114,830	$94,611	$39,515	$248,956
Disburse	117,554	99,561	38,720	255,835
Cash	5,162	212	1,007	n/a
Contributions	42,075	37,136	18,850	98,061
Republicans	18,325	24,800	14,350	57,475
No. of Cand.	*39*	*49*	*25*	*113*
House	7,325	17,950	8,350	33,625
Senate	11,000	6,850	6,000	23,850
Democrats	23,750	12,336	4,500	40,586
No. of Cand.	*32*	*22*	*10*	*64*
House	15,750	10,836	2,750	29,336
Senate	8,000	1,500	1,750	11,250
Incumbents	37,800	30,325	18,250	86,375
Challengers	500	2,100	0	2,600
Open Seat	4,000	1,650	600	6,250
Winners	34,050	29,725	n/a	63,775
Losers	8,025	7,411	n/a	15,436

Irell & Manella

*Phone: (310) 277-1010 * Fax: (310) 203-7199*
1800 Avenue Of The Stars, Suite 900, Los Angeles, CA 90067
Web: www.irell.com

Irell & Manella is a general practice law firm based in southern California. Established in 1941, the firm has more than 150 lawyers working out of its offices in Los Angeles and Newport Beach.

Irell & Manella's clients have included The Walt Disney Co., Intel Corp., and First Interstate Bancorp.

I & M PAC (C00215061) *Address: same as sponsor * Treasurer: Marvin S. Shapiro*

	1993-94	1995-96	1997	Totals
Receipts	$1,447	$763	$117	$2,327
Disburse	11,274	8,560	2,811	22,645
Cash	14,666	6,877	4,185	n/a
Contributions	6,500	5,400	2,754	14,654
Republicans	0	5,000	1,000	6,000
No. of Cand.	*0*	*1*	*1*	*2*
House	0	5,000	0	5,000
Senate	0	0	1,000	1,000
Democrats	6,500	400	1,754	8,654
No. of Cand.	*2*	*1*	*1*	*4*
House	500	400	1,754	2,654
Senate	6,000	0	0	6,000
Incumbents	6,500	5,000	1,754	13,254
Challengers	0	0	1,000	1,000
Open Seat	0	400	0	400
Winners	6,000	5,400	n/a	11,400
Losers	500	0	n/a	500

Jenkens & Gilchrist

*Phone: (214) 855-4301 * Fax: (214) 855-4300*
1445 Ross Ave., Suite 3200, Dallas, TX 75202-2799
*Web: www.jenkens.com * E-mail: jjenkens@ jenkens.com*

Jenkens & Gilchrist has more than 325 lawyers whose clients are primarily large companies and startup enterprises. It is headquartered in Dallas, with offices in Austin, Houston and San Antonio, Texas; Los Angeles; and Washington. The firm specializes in technology-related transactions and litigation, as well as intellectual property.

The Washington office has about 20 lawyers, several of whom work primarily on antitrust cases.

Jenkens & Gilchrist PC Political Action Committee (JGPAC) (C00232256) *Address: same as sponsor * Treasurer: Henry Gilchrist*

	1993-94	1995-96	1997	Totals
Receipts	$18,550	$20,851	$2,225	$41,626
Disburse	17,253	14,246	5,500	36,999
Cash	1,520	8,096	4,821	n/a
Contributions	14,900	10,000	3,500	28,400
Republicans	6,650	6,500	1,500	14,650
No. of Cand.	*5*	*4*	*2*	*11*
House	2,150	1,500	500	4,150
Senate	4,500	5,000	1,000	10,500
Democrats	8,250	3,500	2,000	13,750
No. of Cand.	*9*	*3*	*3*	*15*
House	5,750	3,500	500	9,750
Senate	2,500	0	1,500	4,000
Incumbents	10,150	8,500	3,000	21,650
Challengers	2,500	500	500	3,500
Open Seat	2,250	1,000	0	3,250
Winners	10,650	9,500	n/a	20,150
Losers	4,250	500	n/a	4,750

Jones, Walker, Waechter, Poitevent, Carrere & Denegre

*Phone: (504) 582-8194 * Fax: (504) 582-8011*
201 St. Charles Ave., 49th Floor, New Orleans, LA 70170
E-mail: marketing@jwlaw.com

Jones, Walker, Waechter, Poitevent, Carrere & Denegre is one of the largest law firms in the deep South. It has 98 partners and more than 160 lawyers who work in all areas of law.

The firm gives to Republican and Democratic federal candidates, usually Louisianans.

The firm is based in New Orleans and has two other state offices — in Baton Rouge and Lafayette — in addition to an office in Washington.

Jones, Walker, Waechter, Poitevent, Carrere & Denegre Political Action Committee (C00111534) *Phone: (202) 828-8363 * Fax: (202) 828-6907 * 1776 Eye St. N.W., Suite 245, Washington, DC * Treasurer: R. Patrick Vance*

	1993-94	1995-96	1997	Totals
Receipts	$9,022	$32,203	$28,004	$69,229
Disburse	13,750	31,000	25,000	69,750
Cash	3,466	4,669	7,673	n/a
Contributions	13,500	30,000	25,000	68,500
Republicans	3,500	14,500	11,000	29,000
No. of Cand.	*2*	*10*	*6*	*18*
House	3,500	10,000	10,000	23,500
Senate	0	4,500	1,000	5,500
Democrats	10,000	15,500	14,000	39,500
No. of Cand.	*7*	*3*	*3*	*13*
House	7,000	2,500	2,000	11,500
Senate	3,000	13,000	12,000	28,000
Incumbents	13,500	13,500	25,000	52,000
Challengers	0	0	0	0
Open Seat	0	16,500	0	16,500
Winners	13,500	21,000	n/a	34,500
Losers	0	9,000	n/a	9,000

Keck, Mahin & Cate

1201 New York Ave. N.W., Washington, DC 20005

KM&C PAC filed for termination in 1997.

KM&C PAC (C00303578) *Address: same as sponsor * Treasurer: Carl E. Zwisler*

	1993-94	1995-96	1997	Totals
Receipts	$0	$11,540	$0	$11,540
Disburse	0	11,411	71	11,482
Cash	0	83	12	n/a
Contributions	0	10,250	0	10,250
Republicans	0	6,250	0	6,250
No. of Cand.	*0*	*10*	*0*	*10*
House	0	4,250	0	4,250
Senate	0	2,000	0	2,000
Democrats	0	4,000	0	4,000
No. of Cand.	*0*	*8*	*0*	*8*
House	0	3,000	0	3,000
Senate	0	1,000	0	1,000
Incumbents	0	10,250	0	10,250
Challengers	0	0	0	0
Open Seat	0	0	0	0
Winners	0	10,250	n/a	10,250
Losers	0	0	n/a	0

King & Spalding

*Phone: (404) 572-4600 * Fax: (404) 572-5100*
191 Peachtree St., Atlanta, GA 30303-1763
Web: www.kslaw.com

King & Spalding is an Atlanta-based law firm with more than 400 lawyers, including former Sen. Sam Nunn, D-Ga., and former Carter administration Attorney General Griffin Bell.

It has a wide area of practice, including tax, real estate, banking and corporate law. The firm's government affairs lawyers are located in King & Spalding's Washington office. Other offices are in New York and Houston. King & Spalding ranked 14th among law firms in PAC contributions to congressional candidates during the 1995-96 election cycle.

King & Spalding Nonpartisan Committee for Good Government (C00204453) *Address: same as sponsor * Treasurer: Philip A. Theodore*

	1993-94	1995-96	1997	Totals
Receipts	$133,291	$79,211	$87,709	$300,211
Disburse	73,444	103,690	61,248	238,382
Cash	68,658	44,179	70,639	n/a
Contributions	61,500	92,290	54,596	208,386
Republicans	18,500	58,971	29,704	107,175
No. of Cand.	*18*	*48*	*31*	*97*
House	12,500	41,971	21,250	75,721
Senate	6,000	17,000	8,454	31,454
Democrats	43,000	33,319	24,892	101,211
No. of Cand.	*44*	*36*	*27*	*107*
House	32,500	23,319	15,000	70,819
Senate	10,500	10,000	9,892	30,392
Incumbents	58,500	90,540	54,596	203,636
Challengers	0	250	0	250
Open Seat	4,000	1,000	0	5,000
Winners	44,500	90,040	n/a	134,540
Losers	17,000	2,250	n/a	19,250

Kirkland & Ellis

*Phone: (312) 861-2000 * Fax: (312) 861-2200*
200 E. Randolph Dr., 59th Floor, Chicago, IL 60601
Web: www.kirkland.com

Based in Chicago, Kirkland & Ellis is a full-service firm of more than 500 lawyers. The National Law Journal ranks K&E as the 30th-largest firm in the country, and the firm is the second-most used outside counsel for Fortune 500 companies. K&E's corporate clients include General Motors Corp., Motorola Inc. and Dow Chemical Co.

Independent Counsel Kenneth Starr is one of Kirkland & Ellis' more famous members, practicing from its Washington and Chicago offices. He contributed $3,500 to K&E's PAC in 1994.

K&E was founded in 1908. It maintains additional offices in New York, Los Angeles and London.

Kirkland & Ellis PAC (formerly known as WSS PAC) (C00212142) *Phone: (202) 879-5000 * Fax: (202) 879-5200 * 655 15th St. N.W., Suite 1200, Washington, DC 20005 * Treasurer: William S. Singer*

	1993-94	1995-96	1997	Totals
Receipts	$184,475	$174,649	$66,915	$426,039
Disburse	184,322	163,882	74,605	422,809
Cash	265	11,032	3,343	n/a
Contributions	68,548	36,073	34,953	139,574
Republicans	9,900	7,292	3,500	20,692
No. of Cand.	*8*	*6*	*4*	*18*
House	1,500	475	500	2,475
Senate	8,400	6,817	3,000	18,217
Democrats	58,648	28,781	31,453	118,882
No. of Cand.	*38*	*19*	*15*	*72*
House	32,700	6,565	3,575	42,840
Senate	25,948	22,216	27,878	76,042
Incumbents	61,463	20,142	21,857	103,462
Challengers	900	5,315	2,896	9,111
Open Seat	6,185	10,616	10,000	26,801
Winners	47,213	26,467	n/a	73,680
Losers	21,335	9,606	n/a	30,941

Kirkpatrick & Lockhart

*Phone: (412) 355-6500 * Fax: (412) 355-6501*
1500 Oliver Building, Pittsburgh, PA 15222
*Web: www.kl.com * E-mail: info@kl.com*

Kirkpatrick & Lockhart is a general practice firm based in Pittsburgh.

The firm has one of the larger investment management practices in the United States, with more than 40 attorneys working exclusively or primarily on investment management matters. K&L has a strong background in environmental law, including nuclear power plant licensing, decommissioning and environmental projects.

K&L has more than 430 lawyers with offices in Boston, New York, Washington and Miami, as well as in Pittsburgh and Harrisburg, Pa. It was established in 1946.

Kirkpatrick & Lockhart Political Action Committee (C00199786) *Address: same as sponsor * Treasurer: John M. Sylvester * Contact: Walter A. Bunt Jr., Chairperson*

	1993-94	1995-96	1997	Totals
Receipts	$150,804	$147,522	$85,488	$383,814
Disburse	121,475	164,506	95,159	381,140
Cash	51,979	34,997	25,327	n/a
Contributions	37,300	56,279	29,950	123,529
Republicans	16,250	32,995	16,700	65,945
No. of Cand.	*10*	*32*	*19*	*61*
House	6,500	16,495	9,200	32,195
Senate	9,750	16,500	7,500	33,750
Democrats	21,050	23,284	13,250	57,584
No. of Cand.	*22*	*23*	*17*	*62*
House	18,050	19,534	12,250	49,834
Senate	3,000	3,750	1,000	7,750
Incumbents	21,300	41,045	29,950	92,295
Challengers	6,750	8,984	0	15,734
Open Seat	9,250	6,250	0	15,500
Winners	23,550	43,795	n/a	67,345
Losers	13,750	12,484	n/a	26,234

Kutak Rock

*Phone: (202) 828-2400 * Fax: (202) 828-2488*
1101 Connecticut Ave. N.W., Suite 1000, Washington, DC 20036-4374
Web: www.kutakrock.com

Kutak Rock is a nationwide law firm that practices in a wide range of legal areas.

Founded by three attorneys in Omaha, Neb. in 1965, the firm now employs more than 200 lawyers in offices throughout the United States and the world.

The firm practices in areas ranging from securities, health care, and real estate to insurance, environmental and technology law. Kutak Rock's clients include investment banking firms, as well as savings and loan associations, insurance companies, national real estate syndicators and developers, and several state and local governmental units.

Kutak Rock Political Action Committee (C00160986) *Address: same as sponsor * Treasurer: Gary J. Ceballos * Contact: Peter Mayberry, Gov. Affairs Dir.*

	1993-94	1995-96	1997	Totals
Receipts	$83,800	$88,700	$28,900	$201,400
Disburse	87,150	69,140	10,100	166,390
Cash	884	20,444	37,944	n/a
Contributions	25,450	27,150	3,500	56,100
Republicans	2,100	15,450	2,000	19,550
No. of Cand.	*4*	*13*	*3*	*20*
House	500	6,400	1,000	7,900
Senate	1,600	9,050	1,000	11,650
Democrats	23,550	11,700	1,500	36,750
No. of Cand.	*25*	*17*	*2*	*44*
House	17,050	5,250	1,500	23,800

Senate	6,500	6,450	0	12,950
Incumbents	21,800	12,350	3,500	37,650
Challengers	2,600	2,000	0	4,600
Open Seat	1,250	10,800	0	12,050
Winners	16,600	14,700	n/a	31,300
Losers	8,850	12,450	n/a	21,300

LeBoeuf, Lamb, Greene & MacRae

*Phone: (212) 424-8000 * Fax: (212) 424-8500*
125 W. 55th St., New York, NY 10019-5389
Web: www.llgm.com

LeBoeuf, Lamb, Greene & MacRae's main offices are in New York City. It practices on the national and international levels, with a range of clients in the areas of interactive media, entertainment, multimedia, telecommunications, banking, financial services, insurance, energy and transportation, as well as in fields of commercial activity, like manufacturing and real estate, trade associations and government agencies.

With 618 lawyers, LLG&M ranks 15th in total size. It maintains offices in London; Brussels, Belgium; Almaty, Kazakhstan; and Moscow. In addition, it has 14 domestic locations which include Washington, San Francisco, Denver and Pittsburgh. In 1996, the firm posted $195 million in sales.

LeBoeuf, Lamb, Greene & MacRae has been involved in preparing for legal issues arising from the year 2000 computer problem, such as software licensing agreement violations and jurisdictional conflicts. It has set up a subsidiary, LeBoeuf Computing Technologies, to handle "Y2K" risk management consulting.

LeBoeuf, Lamb, Greene & MacRae Political Action Committee (C00217885) *Address: same as sponsor * Treasurer: A. David Marshall*

	1993-94	1995-96	1997	Totals
Receipts	$123,385	$109,330	$90,750	$323,465
Disburse	106,537	125,067	68,947	300,551
Cash	20,248	4,510	26,313	n/a
Contributions	41,537	33,248	22,550	97,335
Republicans	19,212	26,100	16,500	61,812
No. of Cand.	*22*	*29*	*15*	*66*
House	7,850	13,600	7,500	28,950
Senate	11,362	12,500	9,000	32,862
Democrats	22,325	7,148	6,050	35,523
No. of Cand.	*24*	*14*	*7*	*45*
House	18,250	3,148	2,800	24,198
Senate	4,075	4,000	3,250	11,325
Incumbents	36,675	23,598	15,750	76,023
Challengers	1,612	2,300	3,000	6,912
Open Seat	3,250	7,850	3,800	14,900
Winners	34,925	31,448	n/a	66,373
Losers	6,612	1,800	n/a	8,412

Liddell, Sapp, Zivley, Hill & LaBoon

*Phone: (713) 226-1200 * Fax: (713) 223-3717*
3400 Texas Commerce Tower, Houston, TX 77002
Web: www.liddellsapp.com

Liddell, Sapp, Zivley, Hill & LaBoon PAC, formerly Concerned Texans in Action, is sponsored by that Houston-based law firm.

The firm previously had two PACs, the Democratic Concerned Texans in Action and the Republican League for Effective Government. In 1996 it terminated League for Effective Government and turned Concerned Texans in Action into the new, bipartisan PAC. The PAC generally gives to Texas candidates.

Partner John L. Hill was the chief justice of the state Supreme Court from 1984-89. He was secretary of state from 1966-68, state attorney general from 1972-79 and the Democratic nominee for governor in 1979.

Texas Gov. George W. Bush appointed Hill to the Texas Lottery Commission in January 1997.

Some of the firm's major clients are Texas Commerce Bank, El Paso Natural Gas, Kent Electronics, Service Corp. International and Baxter Health Care.

Liddell, Sapp, Zivley, Hill & LaBoon LLP PAC (formerly known as Concerned Texans in Action) (C00117861) *Address: same as sponsor * Treasurer: Robert D. Miller*

	1993-94	1995-96	1997	Totals
Receipts	$20,817	$31,369	$24,643	$76,829
Disburse	25,828	29,842	25,750	81,420
Cash	577	2,104	998	n/a
Contributions	22,750	10,600	11,750	45,100
Republicans	0	4,000	9,250	13,250
No. of Cand.	*0*	*5*	*2*	*7*
House	0	3,000	0	3,000
Senate	0	1,000	9,250	10,250
Democrats	22,750	6,600	2,250	31,600
No. of Cand.	*15*	*9*	*3*	*27*
House	10,750	5,600	2,250	18,600
Senate	12,000	1,000	0	13,000
Incumbents	12,250	5,500	11,500	29,250
Challengers	5,500	2,600	0	8,100
Open Seat	5,000	2,500	250	7,750
Winners	6,750	8,000	n/a	14,750
Losers	16,000	2,600	n/a	18,600

Terminated PACs which contributed less than $5,000 during 1995-96 cycle:

League for Effective Government (C00117879) *Address: Same as sponsor * Treasurer: Robert D. Miller*

Locke Purnell Rain Harrell

*Phone: (214) 740-8000 * Fax: (214) 740-8800*
2200 Ross Ave., Suite 2200, Dallas, TX 75201-6776
Web: www.lprh.com

Law firm Locke Purnell Rain Harrell has 170 lawyers in offices in Dallas and Austin, Texas and New Orleans.

Founded in 1891, the firm's practice areas include administrative, regulatory, bankruptcy, environmental and oil and gas law. The firm also has dealings with Mexican law.

Locke Purnell Rain Harrell Federal Political Action Committee (C00220483) *Address: same as sponsor * Treasurer: Robert Beatty*

	1993-94	1995-96	1997	Totals
Receipts	$4,859	$30,468	$15,066	$50,393
Disburse	29,500	24,960	7,500	61,960
Cash	2,891	8,404	15,970	n/a
Contributions	28,500	16,950	7,500	52,950
Republicans	19,000	7,200	3,000	29,200
No. of Cand.	*6*	*5*	*3*	*14*
House	2,000	1,200	500	3,700
Senate	17,000	6,000	2,500	25,500
Democrats	9,500	9,750	4,500	23,750
No. of Cand.	*10*	*5*	*4*	*19*
House	4,000	8,500	3,500	16,000
Senate	5,500	1,250	1,000	7,750
Incumbents	22,000	7,700	7,500	37,200
Challengers	6,000	750	0	6,750
Open Seat	500	8,500	0	9,000
Winners	22,500	14,200	n/a	36,700
Losers	6,000	2,750	n/a	8,750

Lockridge Grindal Nauen & Holstein

*Phone: (612) 339-6900 * Fax: (612) 339-0981*
100 Washington Ave. S., Suite 2200, Minneapolis, MN 55401
*Web: www.locklaw.com * E-mail: jmhubbell@locklaw.com*

Lockridge Grindal Nauen & Holstein practices in many different areas of law. Roughly 70 percent of its business deals with civil litigation in federal and state courts, but the firm also handles general corporate and commercial practice, antitrust, copyright and trademark, employment, environmental, health care, real estate, intellectual property and telecommunications law. The Washington office focuses almost exclusively on federal governmental relations.

The firm represents banks, trade and industry associations, real estate developers, health care professionals, telecommunications providers and casualty insurers. Some representative clients include Norwest Bank, Minnesota Mutual Life Insurance, West Information Publishing Group, the City of Minneapolis and Delta Dental.

Lockridge Grindal was founded in 1978 as Opperman & Paquin, and has changed its name four times since. The last change was from Schatz, Paquin, Lockridge, Grindal & Holstein, made on Jan. 1, 1997. The firm employs roughly 30 lawyers.

The Lockridge Grindal PAC is a bipartisan organization and consistently supports Minnesota candidates.

Lockridge Grindal Nauen & Holstein Political Fund (formerly known as Schatz Paquin Lockridge Grindal & Holstein PAC) (C00167916) *Address: same as sponsor * Treasurer: Christian M. Sande * Contact: Ted Grindal, Gov. Relations Dir.*

	1993-94	1995-96	1997	Totals
Receipts	$66,543	$37,789	$9,214	$113,546
Disburse	63,189	38,153	11,995	113,337
Cash	3,371	3,007	227	n/a
Contributions	42,981	30,786	11,006	84,773
Republicans	3,500	7,800	3,156	14,456
No. of Cand.	*3*	*7*	*4*	*14*
House	3,500	1,500	1,956	6,956
Senate	0	6,300	1,200	7,500
Democrats	34,006	22,986	4,500	61,492
No. of Cand.	*17*	*29*	*6*	*52*
House	7,771	15,500	4,000	27,271
Senate	26,235	7,486	500	34,221
Incumbents	39,281	23,929	11,006	74,216
Challengers	0	3,000	0	3,000
Open Seat	3,700	1,750	0	5,450
Winners	30,494	25,929	n/a	56,423
Losers	12,487	4,857	n/a	17,344

Manatt, Phelps & Phillips

*Phone: (310) 312-4249 * Fax: (310) 312-4224*
11355 W. Olympic Blvd., Eighth Floor, Los Angeles, CA 90064
*Web: www.manatt.com * E-mail: mpp@manatt.com*

Manatt, Phelps & Phillips has roughly 170 lawyers in Los Angeles, Washington, Nashville, Tenn., and Monterey, Mexico. Manatt specialties include financial services, health and entertainment law.

The firm's lobbying practice deals with issues of banking, customs, environment, health care, transportation and telecommunications. Clients include: BellSouth Corp., The Money Store Inc. and the Bay Area Rapid Transit District.

Manatt was established in 1965 by Charles T. Manatt and Thomas D. Phelps. Manatt is a former chairman of the Democratic National Committee and was co-chair of the 1992 Clinton/Gore Campaign. He has contributed more than $60,000 to national Democratic Party committees since 1993.

Leading PAC recipients during the 1995-96 election cycle included the Democratic Senatorial Campaign Committee; House Minority Leader Richard A. Gephardt, D-Mo.; Rep. Vic Fazio, D-Calif.; and Sen. John D. Rockefeller IV, D-W.Va.

Golden State Political Action Committee (formerly known as Manatt, Phelps, Rothenberg & Tunney PAC) (C00145342) *Address: same as sponsor * Treasurer: Ronald B. Turovsky*

	1993-94	1995-96	1997	Totals
Receipts	$74,965	$81,109	$56,221	$212,295
Disburse	74,454	81,783	42,681	198,918
Cash	2,042	1,366	14,904	n/a
Contributions	70,592	73,557	40,750	184,899
Republicans	18,500	30,000	14,500	63,000
No. of Cand.	*18*	*41*	*25*	*84*
House	6,500	27,000	11,500	45,000
Senate	12,000	3,000	3,000	18,000
Democrats	51,092	43,557	26,250	120,899
No. of Cand.	*52*	*50*	*35*	*137*
House	28,093	33,350	14,750	76,193
Senate	22,999	10,207	11,500	44,706
Incumbents	63,043	62,457	39,250	164,750
Challengers	800	1,300	1,500	3,600
Open Seat	6,500	9,800	0	16,300
Winners	49,599	66,207	n/a	115,806
Losers	20,993	7,350	n/a	28,343

Maynard, Cooper, Frierson & Gale

*Phone: (205) 254-1000 * Fax: (205) 254-1999*
1901 Sixth Ave. N., 2400 Amsouth/Harbert Plaza, Birmingham, AL 35203

Maynard, Cooper, Frierson & Gale is a general law firm with offices in Montgomery and Birmingham, Ala. The firm has 80 lawyers.

Clients include: AmSouth Bancorporation, Birmingham Airport Authority, Protective Life Corp., National Bank of Commerce of Birmingham and Sonat Inc.

Maynard, Cooper, Frierson & Gale PC Federal PAC (C00272724) *Address: same as sponsor * Treasurer: George G. Lynn * Contact: Fournier J. Gale III, Shareholder*

	1993-94	1995-96	1997	Totals
Receipts	$12,139	$12,537	$17,498	$42,174
Disburse	3,088	16,252	6,285	25,625
Cash	11,026	7,314	18,527	n/a
Contributions	2,500	10,000	3,250	15,750
Republicans	1,000	7,000	3,000	11,000
No. of Cand.	*1*	*4*	*3*	*8*
House	1,000	0	1,000	2,000
Senate	0	7,000	2,000	9,000
Democrats	1,500	3,000	250	4,750
No. of Cand.	*3*	*4*	*1*	*8*
House	500	1,000	0	1,500
Senate	1,000	2,000	250	3,250
Incumbents	2,500	1,500	3,000	7,000
Challengers	0	0	0	0
Open Seat	0	8,500	250	8,750
Winners	2,500	4,500	n/a	7,000
Losers	0	5,500	n/a	5,500

Mayor, Day, Caldwell & Keeton

*Phone: (713) 225-7000 * Fax: (713) 225-7047*
700 Louisiana, Suite 900, Houston, TX 77002

Mayor, Day, Caldwell & Keeton is a Houston-based civil law firm with more than 30 attorneys. The firm's PAC gives to both Republican and Democratic candidates, usually Texans. It has given to several city officials.

The firm, which was founded in the early 1980s, also has an office in Austin.

Mayor, Day, Caldwell & Keeton (C00178798) *Address: same as sponsor * Treasurer: Dawn A. Bebell * Contact: Jonathan Day, Managing Partner*

	1993-94	1995-96	1997	Totals
Receipts	$27,500	$32,200	$11,800	$71,500
Disburse	27,500	32,100	11,900	71,500
Cash	31	131	31	n/a
Contributions	13,250	15,500	6,000	34,750
Republicans	1,750	5,750	1,000	8,500
No. of Cand.	*3*	*6*	*1*	*10*
House	750	4,750	0	5,500
Senate	1,000	1,000	1,000	3,000
Democrats	11,500	9,750	5,000	26,250
No. of Cand.	*13*	*10*	*5*	*28*
House	8,000	8,750	5,000	21,750
Senate	3,500	1,000	0	4,500
Incumbents	8,250	11,000	5,000	24,250
Challengers	500	3,500	0	4,000
Open Seat	4,500	1,000	1,000	6,500
Winners	10,750	10,750	n/a	21,500
Losers	2,500	4,750	n/a	7,250

McDermott, Will & Emery

*Phone: (202) 756-8000 * Fax: (202) 756-8087*
600 13th St. N.W., Washington, DC 20005
*Web: www.mwe.com * E-mail: emigdail@mwe.com*

McDermott, Will & Emery is one of the 10 largest firms in the United States, with more than 700 lawyers in eight domestic and three international offices. It was also, according to the Center for Responsible Politics, the 23rd leading lobbying firm by income earned, with more than $1.6 million in fees collected during the first half of 1997.

In December 1997, former Massachusetts Gov. William Weld joined MW&E's Boston office to work with emerging markets in Latin America and Southeast Asia, and to serve as general counsel for domestic business interests.

Founded in 1934, the Chicago company's original tax law practice has grown into an established, full-service general practice. MW&E's clients range from large corporations to individuals, including 224 Fortune 500 companies.

McDermott, Will & Emery PAC (MW&E PAC) (C00299701) *Address: same as sponsor * Treasurer: Evan H. Migdail*

	1993-94	1995-96	1997	Totals
Receipts	$18,525	$219,758	$103,157	$341,440
Disburse	78	197,223	103,155	300,456
Cash	18,447	40,985	40,987	n/a
Contributions	0	147,453	77,400	224,853
Republicans	0	73,153	44,000	117,153
No. of Cand.	*0*	*64*	*40*	*104*
House	0	53,550	23,500	77,050

Senate	0	19,603	20,500	40,103
Democrats	0	74,300	33,400	107,700
No. of Cand.	*0*	*52*	*21*	*73*
House	0	50,800	15,400	66,200
Senate	0	23,500	18,000	41,500
Incumbents	0	121,953	75,000	196,953
Challengers	0	9,500	0	9,500
Open Seat	0	16,000	0	16,000
Winners	0	134,953	n/a	134,953
Losers	0	12,500	n/a	12,500

McGuire, Woods, Battle & Boothe

*Phone: (804) 775-1000 * Fax: (804) 775-1061*
One James Center, 901 E. Cary St., Richmond, VA 23219
*Web: www.mwbb.com * E-mail: info@mwbb.com*

McGuire, Woods, Battle & Boothe is a law firm with offices throughout the mid-Atlantic and Southeast. It has 377 members and associates and offices in Washington, Baltimore, Jacksonville, Fla. and five Virginia locations — Alexandria, Charlottesville, Norfolk, Richmond and Tysons Corner.

The firm specializes in securities, public finance, mergers and acquisitions, tax and real estate law. It also has a consulting arm, McGuire Woods Consulting, which provides professional services to corporate and government clients. Among the firm's clients are Bell Atlantic Corp., CSX Corp., General Motors and International Paper.

Two law firms, Mahoney Adams & Criser of Jacksonville, Fla. and Blakeney & Alexander of Charlotte, N.C., merged into McGuire Woods during 1998.

McGuire, Woods, Battle & Boothe Federal Political Action Committee (C00225342) *Address: same as sponsor * Treasurer: Marvin E. Jackson*

	1993-94	*1995-96*	*1997*	*Totals*
Receipts	$27,446	$40,859	$13,105	$81,410
Disburse	27,936	40,859	8,361	77,156
Cash	3,749	3,749	8,492	n/a
Contributions	19,650	16,177	6,250	42,077
Republicans	6,700	14,927	4,750	26,377
No. of Cand.	*7*	*7*	*4*	*18*
House	3,200	6,177	2,750	12,127
Senate	3,500	8,750	2,000	14,250
Democrats	10,450	1,250	1,500	13,200
No. of Cand.	*13*	*2*	*2*	*17*
House	7,700	1,250	1,000	9,950
Senate	2,750	0	500	3,250
Incumbents	13,150	15,177	6,250	34,577
Challengers	6,250	0	0	6,250
Open Seat	0	1,000	0	1,000
Winners	12,900	16,177	n/a	29,077
Losers	6,750	0	n/a	6,750

Meyer, Suozzi, English & Klein

*Phone: (516) 741-6565 * Fax: (516) 741-6706*
1505 Kellum Place, Mineola, NY 11501
*Web: www.msek.com * E-mail: info@msek.com*

General practice law firm Meyer, Suozzi, English & Klein has 39 lawyers in Mineola and Albany, N.Y. Founded in 1960, firm members include a former New York secretary of state and attorney general, as well as several former judges.

Meyer, Suozzi, English & Klein PC Federal PAC (also known as Suozzi, English & Klein PC Federal PAC) (C00152983) *Address: same as sponsor * Treasurer: Patricia Cairo*

	1993-94	*1995-96*	*1997*	*Totals*
Receipts	$12,276	$15,159	$10,260	$37,695
Disburse	12,735	12,745	6,050	31,530
Cash	744	3,161	7,371	n/a
Contributions	10,735	9,050	6,050	25,835
Republicans	2,035	1,050	2,000	5,085
No. of Cand.	*3*	*1*	*1*	*5*
House	1,000	1,050	0	2,050
Senate	1,035	0	2,000	3,035
Democrats	8,700	8,000	4,050	20,750
No. of Cand.	*7*	*8*	*6*	*21*
House	5,450	6,500	2,050	14,000
Senate	3,250	1,500	2,000	6,750
Incumbents	7,735	5,550	6,050	19,335
Challengers	2,000	2,500	0	4,500
Open Seat	1,000	1,000	0	2,000
Winners	8,735	7,550	n/a	16,285
Losers	2,000	1,500	n/a	3,500

Miller, Canfield, Paddock and Stone

*Phone: (313) 963-6420 * Fax: (313) 486-7600*
150 W. Jefferson, Suite 2500, Detroit, MI 48226-4415
Web: www.millercanfield.com

Miller, Canfield, Paddock and Stone is one of the largest law firms in Michigan. The firm practices general law and has offices in New York and Washington and affiliates in Pensacola, Fla., and Gdansk, Katowice and Warsaw, Poland. Established in 1852, the firm employs 250 attorneys.

The firm represents individuals in their personal and business concerns, trusts and estates, publicly traded and multinational companies and many start-up, small, and medium-sized businesses. Clients include the state of Michigan and many of its agencies, authorities and universities, cities, counties, townships, school and community college districts, and special authorities throughout the state.

The law firm's PAC, Michigan Independent PAC, was established in 1994. It is a nonpartisan PAC that provides contributions to federal political candidates.

Michigan Independent Political Action Committee (C00292367) *Address: same as sponsor * Treasurer: Daniel R. Hoin * Contact: William J. Danhof, Chairman*

	1993-94	*1995-96*	*1997*	*Totals*
Receipts	$10,882	$36,362	$13,500	$60,744
Disburse	10,501	34,389	2,413	47,303
Cash	379	2,349	13,435	n/a
Contributions	9,300	32,426	700	42,426
Republicans	7,800	26,202	450	34,452
No. of Cand.	*7*	*9*	*1*	*17*
House	3,300	16,550	450	20,300
Senate	4,500	9,652	0	14,152
Democrats	1,500	6,224	250	7,974
No. of Cand.	*2*	*7*	*2*	*11*
House	500	7,000	250	7,750
Senate	1,000	-776	0	224
Incumbents	1,300	18,576	700	20,576
Challengers	500	15,600	0	16,100
Open Seat	7,500	0	0	7,500
Winners	5,800	13,276	n/a	19,076
Losers	3,500	19,150	n/a	22,650

Morisset, Schlosser, Ayer & Jozwiak

*Phone: (206) 386-5200 * Fax: (206) 386-7322*
1115 Norton Bldg., 801 Second Ave., Seattle, WA 98104

The Seattle-based law firm of Morisset, Schlosser, Ayer & Jozwiak has represented several American Indian tribes in some high-profile cases against the federal government.

In 1995, the firm represented the Hoopa Valley American Indian tribe in a lawsuit with Interior Secretary Bruce Babbitt and the late Commerce Secretary Ron Brown over environmental regulations that restricted the tribe's territorial fishing rights. The tribe lost in the U.S. 9th Circuit Court of Appeals.

In August 1997, the firm represented the Skokomish American Indian Tribe in a case against the Federal Energy Regulatory Commission regarding the tribe's application for a preliminary permit to develop a hydropower facility on the North Fork of the Skokomish River in Mason County, Wash. After losing an earlier decision, the tribe won the appeal at the U.S. 9th Circuit Court of Appeals.

Morisset, Schlosser, Ayer & Jozwiak, A Professional Service Corp. PAC (C00277905) *Address: same as sponsor * Treasurer: Mason D. Morisset*

	1993-94	*1995-96*	*1997*	*Totals*
Receipts	$6,571	$6,168	$4,625	$17,364
Disburse	2,112	8,363	3,327	13,802
Cash	4,704	2,512	3,810	n/a
Contributions	2,000	6,850	2,950	11,800
Republicans	300	850	1,600	2,750
No. of Cand.	*2*	*3*	*3*	*8*
House	200	850	1,100	2,150
Senate	100	0	500	600
Democrats	1,400	6,000	1,350	8,750
No. of Cand.	*4*	*8*	*4*	*16*
House	1,150	4,000	1,100	6,250
Senate	250	2,000	250	2,500
Incumbents	1,650	4,350	2,950	8,950
Challengers	250	2,000	0	2,250
Open Seat	100	500	0	600
Winners	1,750	5,850	n/a	7,600
Losers	250	1,000	n/a	1,250

National Association of Securities and Commercial Law Attorneys

c/o Bernstein Litowitz Berger, 1285 Ave. of the Americas, 33rd Floor, New York, NY 10019

The National Association of Securities and Commercial Law Attorneys is a group of lawyers who represent clients involved in class action and fraud suits against the securities industry. The organization testifies before Congress and comments on proposed rules from the Securities and Exchange Commission.

National Association of Securities and Commercial Law Attorneys PAC (NASCAT PAC) (C00236687) *Phone: (202) 789-3963 * 317 Massachusetts Ave. N.E., Suite 300, Washington, DC 20002 * Treasurer: Jeffrey Klafter*

	1993-94	1995-96	1997	Totals
Receipts	$29,518	$10,311	$15,750	$55,579
Disburse	22,138	17,766	13,317	53,221
Cash	7,505	47	2,480	n/a
Contributions	16,000	15,500	9,000	40,500
Republicans	1,000	0	1,000	2,000
No. of Cand.	*1*	*0*	*1*	*2*
House	0	0	0	0
Senate	1,000	0	1,000	2,000
Democrats	15,000	15,500	8,000	38,500
No. of Cand.	*15*	*16*	*11*	*42*
House	7,000	9,000	5,500	21,500
Senate	8,000	6,500	2,500	17,000
Incumbents	14,000	12,000	8,000	34,000
Challengers	0	1,000	1,000	2,000
Open Seat	2,000	2,500	0	4,500
Winners	8,500	14,000	n/a	22,500
Losers	7,500	1,500	n/a	9,000

Nelson, Mullins, Riley & Scarborough

*Phone: (803) 799-2000 * Fax: (803) 256-7500*
1330 Lady St., Third Floor, P.O. Box 11070, Columbia, SC 29211
*Web: www.nmrs.com * E-mail: info@nmrs.com*

Nelson, Mullins, Riley & Scarborough is the largest law firm in South Carolina with more than 200 attorneys and seven offices.

The firm's main office is in Columbia, S.C. It has four other offices in the state, as well as one in Charlotte, N.C. and one in Atlanta.

The PAC gives to federal, state and local candidates, generally South Carolinians. It is bipartisan.

Nelson, Mullins, Riley & Scarborough Federal Political Committee (C00278895) *Address: same as sponsor * Treasurer: Kevin L. Bagwell * Contact: Ed Mullins, Partner*

	1993-94	1995-96	1997	Totals
Receipts	$20,210	$18,500	$9,000	$47,710
Disburse	18,650	24,500	2,524	45,674
Cash	6,160	160	6,636	n/a
Contributions	8,650	7,500	2,000	18,150
Republicans	1,150	4,500	0	5,650
No. of Cand.	*3*	*4*	*0*	*7*
House	1,150	500	0	1,650
Senate	0	4,000	0	4,000
Democrats	7,500	3,000	2,000	12,500
No. of Cand.	*8*	*4*	*2*	*14*
House	7,500	3,000	1,000	11,500
Senate	0	0	1,000	1,000
Incumbents	4,150	2,500	1,000	7,650
Challengers	0	1,500	0	1,500
Open Seat	4,500	1,500	0	6,000
Winners	3,150	3,000	n/a	6,150
Losers	5,500	4,500	n/a	10,000

O'Melveny & Myers

*Phone: (202) 383-5300 * Fax: (202) 383-5414*
555 13th St. N.W., Suite 500 W., Washington, DC 20004
Web: www.omm.com

O'Melveny & Myers ranks as the 19th largest law firm in the country, with 586 lawyers in Los Angeles, New York, Washington, San Francisco, Newport Beach and Century City, Calif., as well as in Shanghai, China, London, Hong Kong and Tokyo. The general practice law and lobbying firm is the oldest in Los Angeles, founded there in 1885.

Lawyers at O'Melveny practice in all areas, including public finance, financial institutions, corporate, securities, entertainment, real estate, bankruptcy, constitutional and tax law. The lobbying segment of the firm represents IBM as well as the Los Angeles Unified School System.

Warren Christopher, a former secretary of state, served as chairman of the firm prior to his appointment and is now back as a senior partner.

The O'Melveny & Myers PAC is a bipartisan group that supports federal and presidential candidates. During the 1995-96 election cycle, it contributed mostly to incumbents, although one of its leading recipients was Massachusetts Senate candidate Gov. William Weld, R, who received $4,000.

O'Melveny & Myers Political Action Committee (C00159954) *Address: same as sponsor * Treasurer: Donald T. Bliss*

	1993-94	1995-96	1997	Totals
Receipts	$155,035	$135,105	$38,246	$328,386
Disburse	139,897	111,503	61,076	312,476
Cash	60,104	62,021	55,645	n/a
Contributions	82,434	84,350	52,339	219,123
Republicans	18,100	53,500	36,089	107,689
No. of Cand.	*18*	*43*	*29*	*90*
House	8,100	22,000	17,465	47,565
Senate	10,000	31,500	18,624	60,124
Democrats	63,334	30,850	15,250	109,434
No. of Cand.	*38*	*29*	*14*	*81*
House	27,800	18,350	5,750	51,900
Senate	35,534	12,500	9,500	57,534
Incumbents	68,934	67,800	49,839	186,573
Challengers	7,500	7,000	2,500	17,000
Open Seat	6,000	10,050	0	16,050
Winners	62,334	68,350	n/a	130,684
Losers	20,100	16,000	n/a	36,100

Olsson, Frank and Weeda

*Phone: (202) 789-1212 * Fax: (202) 234-2686*
1400 16th St. N.W., Suite 400, Washington, DC 20036
*Web: www.ofwlaw.com * E-mail: info@ofwlaw.com*

Olsson, Frank and Weeda is a Washington law firm with 26 lawyers who specialize in food, drug, medical device and agricultural law, generally representing the food manufacturing industry. The firm was founded in 1979.

Olsson, Frank and Weeda PAC (C00273136) *Address: same as sponsor * Treasurer: John W. Bode*

	1993-94	1995-96	1997	Totals
Receipts	$10,150	$14,950	$7,250	$32,350
Disburse	9,884	16,301	5,350	31,535
Cash	1,482	130	2,030	n/a
Contributions	12,156	13,740	3,350	29,246
Republicans	3,806	6,790	2,250	12,846
No. of Cand.	*5*	*11*	*4*	*20*
House	1,306	4,790	1,750	7,846
Senate	2,500	2,000	500	5,000
Democrats	8,350	6,950	1,100	16,400
No. of Cand.	*10*	*11*	*4*	*25*
House	5,350	3,450	1,100	9,900
Senate	3,000	3,500	0	6,500
Incumbents	11,656	11,990	3,350	26,996
Challengers	0	1,000	0	1,000
Open Seat	500	750	0	1,250
Winners	10,656	13,240	n/a	23,896
Losers	1,500	500	n/a	2,000

Orrick, Herrington & Sutcliffe

*Phone: (415) 392-1122 * Fax: (415) 773-5759*
400 Sansome St., San Francisco, CA 94111
Web: www.orrick.com

Orrick, Herrington & Sutcliffe is a general practice law firm based in San Francisco. The 400-lawyer firm also maintains offices in Los Angeles, Sacramento and Menlo Park, Calif., as well as in New York City and Washington. It has international offices in Tokyo and Singapore.

The 20-lawyer Washington office mainly represents banks, financial institutions and securities firms in their dealings with the Securities and Exchange Commission and other government regulators.

Orrick, Herrington & Sutcliffe Political Action Committee (C00220558) *Phone: (916) 329-7901 * Fax: (916) 329-4900 * 400 Capitol Mall, Suite 3000, Sacramento, CA 95814 * Treasurer: James W. Bruner Jr.*

	1993-94	1995-96	1997	Totals
Receipts	$67,376	$30,186	$21,915	$119,477
Disburse	68,284	31,835	21,787	121,906
Cash	4,952	3,301	3,430	n/a
Contributions	23,150	12,700	10,500	46,350
Republicans	2,000	2,000	5,500	9,500
No. of Cand.	*1*	*2*	*2*	*5*
House	0	1,000	500	1,500
Senate	2,000	1,000	5,000	8,000
Democrats	21,150	10,700	5,000	36,850
No. of Cand.	*13*	*7*	*6*	*26*
House	15,650	11,200	4,000	30,850
Senate	5,500	-500	1,000	6,000
Incumbents	20,650	13,200	4,500	38,350
Challengers	500	0	5,000	5,500
Open Seat	2,000	500	1,000	3,500
Winners	20,150	13,700	n/a	33,850
Losers	3,000	-1000	n/a	2,000

Pepper, Hamilton & Scheetz

*Phone: (215) 981-4000 * Fax: (215) 981-4750*
3000 Two Logan Square, 18th & Arch Streets, Philadelphia, PA 19103
Web: www.constructlaw.com

Pepper, Hamilton & Scheetz is a general practice law firm based in Philadelphia. It has 10 additional offices in the United States (primarily in the Northeast), Moscow and London. Founded in 1890, PH&S now employs more than 250 lawyers.

The firm specializes in representing clients in the construction industry, from builders of power plants to railroad and highway contractors.

PH&S Federal PAC (C00279927) *Address: same as sponsor * Treasurer: John E. Pooler Jr.*

	1993-94	1995-96	1997	Totals
Receipts	$40,400	$168,325	$50,000	$258,725
Disburse	40,400	164,467	51,827	256,694
Cash	0	3,857	2,029	n/a
Contributions	34,900	64,175	15,300	114,375
Republicans	12,000	43,000	10,800	65,800
No. of Cand.	*8*	*29*	*11*	*48*
House	3,500	22,000	6,800	32,300
Senate	8,500	21,000	4,000	33,500
Democrats	22,900	21,175	4,500	48,575
No. of Cand.	*15*	*17*	*5*	*37*
House	7,150	15,175	3,500	25,825
Senate	15,750	6,000	1,000	22,750
Incumbents	22,150	57,925	15,300	95,375
Challengers	8,000	4,250	0	12,250
Open Seat	4,250	2,000	0	6,250
Winners	18,650	60,425	n/a	79,075
Losers	16,250	3,750	n/a	20,000

Perkins Coie

*Phone: (206) 583-8888 * Fax: (206) 583-8500*
1201 Third Ave., 40th Floor, Seattle, WA 98101-3099
Web: www.perkinscoie.com

Perkins Coie is the largest law firm in the Pacific Northwest with 350 lawyers in 12 offices. The firm represents nearly 100 Fortune 500 companies and 48 of their subsidiaries, privately held businesses, partnerships and other enterprises.

The firm's PAC is bipartisan and generally gives to federal candidates from Washington state, Oregon and Alaska.

Perkins Coie partner Tom Boeder was the lead attorney on the proposed merger between Boeing and McDonnell Douglas that was challenged by the European Union in July 1997. The EU eventually approved the deal.

In November 1997, partner Ronald M. Gould was nominated to an open seat on the 9th U.S. Circuit Court of Appeals.

Some of the firm's major clients are Delta Airlines, Northwest Airlines, Safeway Corp., General Electric, British Petroleum, AT&T, IBM and the state of Texas.

The firm has offices in the state of Washington as well as Anchorage, Alaska; Portland, Ore.; Denver; Los Angeles; Washington; London; Hong Kong; and Taipei, Taiwan. It was founded in 1912.

Perkins Coie Political Action Committee (C00199570) *Phone: (202) 628-6600 * Fax: (202) 434-1690 * 607 14th St. N.W., Suite 800, Washington, DC 20005 * Treasurer: Guy R. Martin*

	1993-94	1995-96	1997	Totals
Receipts	$16,988	$12,249	$10,013	$39,250
Disburse	13,122	14,115	4,055	31,292
Cash	12,962	11,097	17,056	n/a
Contributions	12,525	11,950	3,875	28,350
Republicans	3,700	5,850	2,375	11,925
No. of Cand.	*3*	*5*	*3*	*11*
House	3,000	3,750	2,000	8,750
Senate	700	2,100	375	3,175
Democrats	8,825	6,100	1,500	16,425
No. of Cand.	*9*	*8*	*4*	*21*
House	8,575	5,500	500	14,575
Senate	250	600	1,000	1,850
Incumbents	10,125	9,450	3,750	23,325
Challengers	2,000	2,000	0	4,000
Open Seat	400	500	125	1,025
Winners	6,850	9,950	n/a	16,800
Losers	5,675	2,000	n/a	7,675

Pillsbury Madison & Sutro

*Phone: (415) 983-1000 * Fax: (415) 983-1200*
225 Bush St., San Francisco, CA 94104
Web: www.pillsburylaw.com

Pillsbury Madison & Sutro is one of the largest law firms in the United States, employing almost 600 lawyers. It works in all areas of law.

The firm became involved in the Whitewater investigations when the Federal Deposit Insurance Corp. hired it as an outside counsel. In April 1996, Pillsbury Madison advised the FDIC not to sue the Rose Law Firm.

In August 1997, the firm settled for an undisclosed amount a lawsuit filed by seven legal secretaries and a human resources manager who claimed they were forced into retirement because of their age. The firm denied the charges.

The firm, which was founded in 1874 in San Francisco, also has offices in Los Angeles, Orange County, Sacramento, San Diego, Silicon Valley, New York, Washington, Hong Kong and Tokyo.

In June 1996, the firm's Washington office agreed to merge with the Washington-based firm Cushman Darby & Cushman, which specializes in intellectual property.

Pillsbury Madison & Sutro LLP Political Action Committee (C00177972) *Phone: (202) 861-3000 * Fax: (202) 822-0944 * 1100 New York Ave. N.W., Washington, DC 20005-3918 * Treasurer: Frederick K. Lowell*

*Contact: Frederick Lowell * Phone: (415) 983-1000*

	1993-94	1995-96	1997	Totals
Receipts	$62,262	$37,106	$0	$99,368
Disburse	64,526	37,973	2,575	105,074
Cash	5,880	5,009	2,433	n/a
Contributions	36,200	12,000	2,500	50,700
Republicans	7,500	11,000	1,500	20,000
No. of Cand.	*10*	*9*	*2*	*21*
House	4,000	9,500	500	14,000
Senate	3,500	1,500	1,000	6,000
Democrats	28,700	1,000	1,000	30,700
No. of Cand.	*24*	*3*	*1*	*28*
House	10,700	500	1,000	12,200
Senate	18,000	500	0	18,500
Incumbents	32,200	12,000	2,500	46,700
Challengers	2,500	0	0	2,500
Open Seat	1,500	0	0	1,500
Winners	30,700	9,500	n/a	40,200
Losers	5,500	2,500	n/a	8,000

Powell, Goldstein, Frazer & Murphy

*Phone: (404) 572-6600 * Fax: (404) 572-6999*
191 Peachtree St. N.E., Sixteenth Floor, Atlanta, GA 30303
Web: www.pgfm.com

Powell, Goldstein, Frazer & Murphy is one of Atlanta's oldest law firms, providing legal services in 27 practice areas, including corporate, international, health care, employment and technology law. Established in 1909, the firm now employs about 200 lawyers, a third of whom are in Washington. In 1997, the firm ranked No. 152 in size nationally, according to the National Law Journal.

Powell Goldstein lobbies on GATT implementation, health care, telecommunications and foreign investments. Lobbying clients include: America Online, the Ericsson Corp., IBM and British Air.

Under Secretary of State Stuart E. Eizenstat was formerly chairman of the Washington office.

The Powell, Goldstein, Frazer & Murphy PAC is a bipartisan contributor to federal candidates. In the 1995-96 election cycle, the PAC gave $8,000 to Georgia Senate candidate Guy Millner, R, and $5,000 to his opponent, now-Sen. Max Cleland, D-Ga.

Powell, Goldstein, Frazer & Murphy Political Action Committee (C00218891) *Phone: (202) 347-0066 * Fax: (202) 624-7222 * 1001 Pennsylvania Ave. N.W., Sixth Floor, Washington, DC 20004 * Treasurer: E. Penn Nicholson*

	1993-94	1995-96	1997	Totals
Receipts	$127,345	$127,357	$73,655	$328,357
Disburse	140,036	115,208	42,453	297,697
Cash	12,574	24,735	55,942	n/a
Contributions	59,821	64,415	19,902	144,138
Republicans	4,550	36,000	8,300	48,850
No. of Cand.	*5*	*33*	*10*	*48*
House	3,550	14,500	2,800	20,850
Senate	1,000	21,500	5,500	28,000
Democrats	55,271	28,415	11,602	95,288
No. of Cand.	*58*	*35*	*14*	*107*
House	21,600	14,165	2,750	38,515
Senate	33,671	14,250	8,852	56,773
Incumbents	50,496	40,665	17,402	108,563
Challengers	2,750	4,750	2,500	10,000
Open Seat	8,250	19,000	0	27,250
Winners	34,276	48,165	n/a	82,441
Losers	25,545	16,250	n/a	41,795

Powers, Pyles, Sutter & Verville

*Phone: (202) 466-6550 * Fax: (202) 785-1756*
1875 Eye St. N.W., 12th Floor, Washington, DC 20006-5409

Washington law firm Powers, Pyles, Sutter & Verville's 21 lawyers work on health law, which encompasses issues affecting hospitals, hospital associations, multi-hospital systems, provider associations, home health agencies, physicians and other health care professionals, alternative delivery systems, organ procurement organizations, purchasers of health care services and health-related businesses.

Clients include: the American Academy of Neurology, the American Psychoanalytic Association and the Coalition for Patient Rights.

Powers, Pyles, Sutter & Verville PC PAC (C00302687) *Address: same as sponsor * Treasurer: Peter W. Thomas * Contact: Richard Verville, Chairman of PAC*

	1993-94	1995-96	1997	Totals
Receipts	$0	$62,375	$20,000	$82,375
Disburse	0	54,272	13,500	67,772
Cash	0	8,107	14,607	n/a
Contributions	0	41,550	13,500	55,050
Republicans	0	16,500	6,000	22,500
No. of Cand.	*0*	*22*	*8*	*30*
House	0	13,750	4,500	18,250
Senate	0	2,750	1,500	4,250
Democrats	0	25,050	7,500	32,550
No. of Cand.	*0*	*32*	*8*	*40*
House	0	19,950	5,500	25,450
Senate	0	5,100	2,000	7,100
Incumbents	0	38,550	13,500	52,050
Challengers	0	0	0	0
Open Seat	0	2,500	0	2,500
Winners	0	39,050	n/a	39,050
Losers	0	2,500	n/a	2,500

Preston, Gates & Ellis

*Phone: (202) 628-1700 * Fax: (202) 331-1024*
1735 New York Ave. N.W., Suite 500, Washington, DC 20006-5209
Web: www.prestongates.com

Preston, Gates & Ellis is a full-service law firm that provides "counseling, litigation, legislative advocacy and transactional services in all areas of private and public sector law." In 1997, Preston Gates ranked as the 108th-largest firm in the United States, according to the National Law Journal.

The firm originated in Seattle in 1883 and its corporate clients include Starbucks, Burlington Northern Santa Fe, Delta Air Lines and PepsiCo Foods and Beverages International. Microsoft CEO Bill Gates was employed by the firm in 1964, and Preston Gates now serves as Microsoft's main outside counsel.

The Washington office of the firm, Preston, Gates, Ellis & Rouvelas, Meeds, earned more than $5.7 million in lobbying fees during 1996. Washingtonian magazine ranked firm partners former Rep. Lloyd Meeds, D-Wash., and Jack Abramoff 21st and 22nd among the 50 most powerful lobbyists. The ranking was "based on fees earned, power points won through legislative victories, and the opinions of their colleagues and of congressional and administrative officials."

The company has more than 275 attorneys in Seattle, San Francisco, Los Angeles, Orange County, Calif., Portland, Ore., Anchorage, Alaska, Spokane, Wash., and Coeur d'Alene, Idaho, as well as Hong Kong and Washington.

Preston, Gates, Ellis & Rouvelas, Meeds LLP PAC (C00213173)
*Address: same as sponsor * Treasurer: Rosanne Phillips*

	1993-94	1995-96	1997	Totals
Receipts	$127,982	$143,264	$82,494	$353,740
Disburse	121,506	149,384	78,696	349,586
Cash	10,093	3,969	7,767	n/a
Contributions	117,204	141,763	78,500	337,467
Republicans	37,690	95,765	50,000	183,455
No. of Cand.	*47*	*113*	*64*	*224*
House	30,690	71,765	35,500	137,955
Senate	7,000	24,000	14,500	45,500
Democrats	79,514	45,998	27,500	153,012
No. of Cand.	*91*	*63*	*41*	*195*
House	58,894	33,999	18,000	110,893
Senate	20,620	11,999	9,500	42,119
Incumbents	104,005	129,097	77,500	310,602
Challengers	5,000	2,000	0	7,000
Open Seat	8,199	10,666	1,000	19,865
Winners	90,654	124,513	n/a	215,167
Losers	26,550	17,250	n/a	43,800

Pullman & Comley

*Phone: (203) 330-2000 * Fax: (203) 576-8888*
850 Main St., Bridgeport, CT 06601

Pullman & Comley is a general practice law firm based in Bridgeport, Conn. It has 70 lawyers in five offices around the state.

The firm's federal PAC gives to Connecticut-based candidates, of any party, who partners think are supportive of the expansion and preservation of the Connecticut economy.

Pullman & Comley Political Action Committee (C00230201)
*Address: same as sponsor * Treasurer: John F. Stafstrom Jr.*

	1993-94	1995-96	1997	Totals
Receipts	$2,570	$6,501	$600	$9,671
Disburse	2,594	6,341	300	9,235
Cash	49	209	509	n/a
Contributions	1,100	5,250	0	6,350
Republicans	250	500	0	750
No. of Cand.	*2*	*2*	*0*	*4*
House	250	500	0	750
Senate	0	0	0	0
Democrats	850	4,750	0	5,600
No. of Cand.	*2*	*5*	*1*	*8*
House	0	2,750	0	2,750
Senate	850	2,000	0	2,850
Incumbents	1,100	4,000	0	5,100
Challengers	0	1,250	0	1,250
Open Seat	0	0	0	0
Winners	1,100	4,000	n/a	5,100
Losers	0	1,250	n/a	1,250

Reed Smith Shaw & McClay

*Phone: (412) 288-3131 * Fax: (412) 288-3063*
435 Sixth Ave., Pittsburgh, PA 15219
*Web: www.rssm.com * E-mail: rssm@rssm.com*

Pittsburgh-based law firm Reed Smith Shaw & McClay has more than 400 lawyers in eight offices. It works in all areas of law.

The firm's PAC, Reed Smith PAC, contributes to candidates of both parties and generally focuses on Pennsylvanian candidates.

The firm also has offices in Philadelphia and Harrisburg, Pa.; New York; Washington; McLean, Va.; and Newark and Princeton, N.J.

Reed Smith Political Action Committee (C00242057) *Phone: (202) 414-9200 * Fax: (202) 414-9299 * 1301 K St. N.W., Suite 1100 E. Tower, Washington, DC 20005 * Treasurer: J. Tomlinson Fort*

	1993-94	1995-96	1997	Totals
Receipts	$39,748	$23,158	$9,300	$72,206
Disburse	40,527	31,301	10,077	81,905
Cash	14,141	5,996	5,218	n/a
Contributions	33,900	21,825	8,840	64,565
Republicans	8,950	18,100	3,840	30,890
No. of Cand.	*10*	*15*	*7*	*32*
House	2,200	6,850	1,840	10,890
Senate	6,750	11,250	2,000	20,000
Democrats	24,950	3,725	5,000	33,675
No. of Cand.	*19*	*7*	*1*	*27*
House	13,950	3,725	5,000	22,675
Senate	11,000	0	0	11,000
Incumbents	26,950	17,075	7,840	51,865
Challengers	5,000	4,750	0	9,750
Open Seat	1,450	0	1,000	2,450
Winners	21,950	12,575	n/a	34,525
Losers	11,950	9,250	n/a	21,200

Reid & Priest

*Phone: (212) 603-2000 * Fax: (212) 603-2001*
40 W. 57th St., New York, NY 10019

Law firm Reid & Priest has roughly 160 lawyers in New York and Washington. It is affiliated with firms in China and India. The firm was established in 1935.

In February 1995, it merged with Sutton, Basseches, Magidoff & Amaral, a New York intellectual property boutique. Other major areas of practice include utilities, international trade, arbitration, corporate finance, tax, real estate and construction. Dawson Science Co., Carolina Power and Light Co. and Utility Decommissioning Tax Group are some of the firm's clients.

Reid & Priest Political Action Committee (C00248641) *Phone: (202) 508-4000 x140 * Fax: (202) 508-4321 * 701 Pennsylvania Ave. N.W., Suite 800, Washington, DC 20004 * Treasurer: Patricia M. Healy*

	1993-94	1995-96	1997	Totals
Receipts	$78,126	$77,250	$47,675	$203,051
Disburse	75,486	79,676	41,805	196,967
Cash	7,735	5,358	11,227	n/a
Contributions	62,950	70,976	38,305	172,231
Republicans	16,250	37,876	19,000	73,126
No. of Cand.	*18*	*43*	*18*	*79*
House	11,750	27,600	14,000	53,350
Senate	4,500	10,276	5,000	19,776
Democrats	46,700	33,100	18,305	98,105
No. of Cand.	*42*	*32*	*20*	*94*
House	37,700	31,500	14,305	83,505
Senate	9,000	1,600	4,000	14,600
Incumbents	57,700	61,526	37,805	157,031
Challengers	2,000	1,850	0	3,850
Open Seat	2,750	6,600	0	9,350
Winners	46,950	62,250	n/a	109,200
Losers	16,000	8,726	n/a	24,726

Robins, Kaplan, Miller & Ciresi

*Phone: (202) 775-0725 * Fax: (202) 223-8604*
1801 K St. N.W., Suite 1200, Washington, DC 20006

Established in 1938, the law firm of Robins, Kaplan, Miller & Ciresi practices general, commercial, employment and business litigation.

The firm's office in Washington maintains its PAC and provides representation in federal regulatory, legislative and international trade issues. Particular areas of emphasis include government contracts, environmental issues, corporate finance, military base closings and privatizations, maritime and transportation law as well as tax and real estate law.

The firm's California offices in Costa Mesa, Los Angeles and San Francisco concentrate on insurance, business and mass tort litigation. The Atlanta office focuses on business litigation, property insurance losses, intellectual property disputes and personal injury litigation.

The firm's other offices are in Minneapolis, Chicago and Boston.

Robins, Kaplan, Miller & Ciresi PAC (C00275909) *Address: same as sponsor * Treasurer: Harold E. Mesirow*

	1993-94	1995-96	1997	Totals
Receipts	$6,600	$72,250	$3,000	$81,850
Disburse	6,509	72,255	3,000	81,764
Cash	90	85	85	n/a
Contributions	4,500	15,250	3,000	22,750

Republicans	1,500	3,250	2,000	6,750
No. of Cand.	*1*	*4*	*2*	*7*
House	1,500	1,250	2,000	4,750
Senate	0	2,000	0	2,000
Democrats	2,000	11,000	1,000	14,000
No. of Cand.	*2*	*7*	*1*	*10*
House	2,000	5,500	1,000	8,500
Senate	0	5,500	0	5,500
Incumbents	3,500	11,250	3,000	17,750
Challengers	0	4,000	0	4,000
Open Seat	1,000	0	0	1,000
Winners	3,500	13,250	n/a	16,750
Losers	1,000	2,000	n/a	3,000

Roetzel & Andress

*Phone: (330) 849-6669 * Fax: (330) 376-4577*
75 E. Market St., Akron, OH 44308
Web: www.ralaw.com

With more than 100 attorneys, the law firm of Roetzel & Andress has offices in five Ohio cities and two locations in southwest Florida. It primarily practices business law. Some staffers will be brought to downtown Akron when a new office space is completed in late 1998.

Roetzel is trying to establish itself in the growing field of cyberspace law. The firm represented CompuServe in a case heard before the 6th U.S. Circuit Court of Appeals. In a July 1996 ruling on CompuServe v. Patterson, the court found that a Texas resident established, through the use of the Internet, a virtual presence in Ohio, subjecting him to the jurisdiction of the Ohio courts, even though he had never physically been in Ohio.

Roetzel & Andress Co. LPA FSL PAC (C00228379) *Address: same as sponsor * Treasurer: John M. Kelleher*

	1993-94	1995-96	1997	Totals
Receipts	$196,080	$260,655	$133,839	$590,574
Disburse	197,224	238,945	129,877	566,046
Cash	33	21,741	25,703	n/a
Contributions	9,142	10,520	8,300	27,962
Republicans	1,000	9,395	6,500	16,895
No. of Cand.	*2*	*6*	*1*	*9*
House	1,000	3,395	0	4,395
Senate	0	6,000	6,500	12,500
Democrats	8,142	1,125	1,800	11,067
No. of Cand.	*5*	*1*	*1*	*7*
House	7,142	1,125	1,800	10,067
Senate	1,000	0	0	1,000
Incumbents	6,492	4,450	8,300	19,242
Challengers	1,650	6,000	0	7,650
Open Seat	1,000	0	0	1,000
Winners	5,193	4,450	n/a	9,643
Losers	3,949	6,070	n/a	10,019

Shaw, Pittman, Potts & Trowbridge

*Phone: (202) 663-8000 * Fax: (202) 663-8007*
2300 N St. N.W., Washington, DC 20037
*Web: www.shawpittman.com * E-mail: info@shawpittman.com*

Washington law firm Shaw, Pittman, Potts & Trowbridge has experience in corporate finance and securities; information technology and telecommunications; intellectual property; financial institutions; energy and electric utility companies; government contracts and minority business; real estate and construction law; environmental law; and employment, diversity counseling and benefits law.

The firm's PAC is bipartisan and supports candidates for Congress and president.

Shaw Pittman employs about 270 lawyers, who are involved in civil and criminal litigation, federal agency proceedings, arbitration and bankruptcy cases, as well as administrative, legislative and regulatory advocacy before Congress and other governmental agencies.

Founded in 1954, Shaw Pittman maintains offices in Washington, New York City, McLean, Va., and Leesburg, Va.

Shaw, Pittman, Potts & Trowbridge Political Action Committee (C00244426) *Address: same as sponsor * Treasurer: J. E. Murdock III*

	1993-94	1995-96	1997	Totals
Receipts	$144,248	$153,833	$89,928	$388,009
Disburse	155,349	163,352	89,888	408,589
Cash	10,979	1,462	1,502	n/a
Contributions	113,614	105,067	68,500	287,181

(Data for Shaw, Pittman, Potts continued)

Republicans	30,700	57,167	31,000	118,867
No. of Cand.	*32*	*53*	*23*	*108*
House	11,700	30,500	18,500	60,700
Senate	19,000	26,667	12,500	58,167
Democrats	82,914	47,650	35,500	166,064
No. of Cand.	*71*	*49*	*33*	*153*
House	59,164	31,050	25,000	115,214
Senate	23,750	16,600	10,500	50,850
Incumbents	101,417	89,317	67,500	258,234
Challengers	5,047	4,250	500	9,797
Open Seat	6,650	11,500	0	18,150
Winners	92,649	90,067	n/a	182,716
Losers	20,965	15,000	n/a	35,965

Sher & Blackwell

*Phone: (202) 463-2500 * Fax: (202) 463-4950*
1850 M St. N.W., Suite 900, Washington, DC 20036

Sher & Blackwell is a Washington-based, boutique legal and lobbying firm that specializes in maritime law and labor issues.

The firm's bipartisan PAC assists candidates at all levels who are interested in maritime or labor issues.

Sixteen lawyers work out of the firm's Washington and San Francisco offices.

Sher & Blackwell Political Action Committee (C00301606)
*Address: same as sponsor * Treasurer: Marc J. Fink*

	1993-94	*1995-96*	*1997*	*Totals*
Receipts	$0	$12,300	$10,526	$22,826
Disburse	0	11,366	10,096	21,462
Cash	0	923	1,352	n/a
Contributions	0	6,950	9,000	15,950
Republicans	0	4,000	500	4,500
No. of Cand.	*0*	*4*	*1*	*5*
House	0	3,000	500	3,500
Senate	0	1,000	0	1,000
Democrats	0	2,950	8,500	11,450
No. of Cand.	*0*	*5*	*7*	*12*
House	0	2,200	4,500	6,700
Senate	0	750	4,000	4,750
Incumbents	0	4,500	9,000	13,500
Challengers	0	1,200	0	1,200
Open Seat	0	1,250	0	1,250
Winners	0	5,450	n/a	5,450
Losers	0	1,500	n/a	1,500

Sirote & Permutt

*Phone: (205) 933-7111 * Fax: (205) 930-5301*
2222 Arlington Ave. S., Birmingham, AL 35205

Alabama law firm Sirote & Permutt has about 100 lawyers in five offices who work on bankruptcy, corporate, securities, finance, environmental, small business, tax, real estate and intellectual property law.

Sirote & Permutt opened offices in Tuscaloosa in 1980, Huntsville in 1983, Mobile in 1986 and Montgomery in 1991.

Sirote & Permutt PC Lawyers for Good Government (C00229369)
*Address: same as sponsor * Treasurer: Jack E. Held*

	1993-94	*1995-96*	*1997*	*Totals*
Receipts	$11,448	$11,787	$10,150	$33,385
Disburse	11,520	7,936	7,714	27,170
Cash	1,122	4,005	6,440	n/a
Contributions	4,400	6,850	7,700	18,950
Republicans	2,000	5,250	5,200	12,450
No. of Cand.	*1*	*5*	*3*	*9*
House	2,000	2,750	1,000	5,750
Senate	0	2,500	4,200	6,700
Democrats	2,400	1,600	2,500	6,500
No. of Cand.	*3*	*3*	*3*	*9*
House	400	1,600	1,500	3,500
Senate	2,000	0	1,000	3,000
Incumbents	4,400	3,750	7,200	15,350
Challengers	0	0	500	500
Open Seat	0	3,100	0	3,100
Winners	3,400	4,500	n/a	7,900
Losers	1,000	2,350	n/a	3,350

Skadden, Arps, Slate, Meagher & Flom

*Phone: (202) 371-7000 * Fax: (202) 393-5760*
1440 New York Ave. N.W., Washington, DC 20005
Web: www.sasmf.com

Skadden, Arps, Slate, Meagher & Flom is the nation's third-largest law firm, according to the National Law Journal, as well as the most-used outside counsel for Fortune 500 companies. The firm's client list now includes about one-half of Fortune 250 companies and all 20 of the largest banks worldwide, Merrill Lynch & Co. Inc. and Travelers Group Inc. President Bill Clinton is also a client, represented by firm lawyer Robert S. Bennett.

Litigation accounts for roughly one-fifth of Skadden Arps' business, and corporate and securities practice about one-third. The firm posts leading figures in business mergers and acquisitions, and is ranked third for initial public offerings and venture capital by number of offerings. Skadden Arps represented Turner Broadcasting during its merger talks with Time Warner Inc.

Skadden Arps has 20 offices, with nine in the United States, plus one each in Beijing; Brussels, Belgium; Frankfurt, Germany; Hong Kong; London; Moscow; Paris; Singapore; Sydney, Australia; Tokyo; and Toronto. It employs more than 1,100 lawyers and posted $710 million in 1996 sales.

Skadden Arps PAC (C00232629) *Address: same as sponsor * Treasurer: Lynn R. Coleman*

	1993-94	*1995-96*	*1997*	*Totals*
Receipts	$156,561	$197,604	$112,789	$466,954
Disburse	157,006	152,900	91,550	401,456
Cash	165	44,870	66,709	n/a
Contributions	86,850	93,100	56,250	236,200
Republicans	28,500	46,000	22,750	97,250
No. of Cand.	*23*	*49*	*26*	*98*
House	6,000	23,750	6,500	36,250
Senate	22,500	22,250	16,250	61,000
Democrats	57,350	47,100	33,500	137,950
No. of Cand.	*50*	*45*	*31*	*126*
House	30,850	27,600	11,500	69,950
Senate	26,500	19,500	22,000	68,000
Incumbents	80,350	79,100	53,250	212,700
Challengers	2,000	2,000	0	4,000
Open Seat	4,500	12,000	3,000	19,500
Winners	65,850	79,100	n/a	144,950
Losers	21,000	14,000	n/a	35,000

Smith, Gambrell & Russell

*Phone: (404) 815-3500 * Fax: (404) 815-3509*
1230 Peachtree St. N.E., Atlanta, GA 30309-3592
Web: www.sgratl.com

Smith, Gambrell & Russell is a business law firm based in Atlanta. The firm's bipartisan PAC generally gives to candidates from Georgia.

The firm, which has more than 130 lawyers, is one of the oldest in the South. It celebrated its centennial in 1993.

The firm has formal and informal international connections, including affiliations with The Interlex Group, an international association of law firms; the Italian law firm Collodel, Leone, Ligi, Queirolo Studio Legale; and the British law firm Wragge & Co.

Smith, Gambrell & Russell Political Action Committee Trust - Federal (C00187112) *Address: same as sponsor * Treasurer: Robert Preston Brown*

	1993-94	*1995-96*	*1997*	*Totals*
Receipts	$4,999	$14,599	$9,600	$29,198
Disburse	2,700	11,400	1,500	15,600
Cash	3,126	6,326	14,426	n/a
Contributions	2,000	6,400	1,500	9,900
Republicans	1,150	3,900	1,500	6,550
No. of Cand.	*2*	*7*	*2*	*11*
House	1,150	1,400	1,000	3,550
Senate	0	2,500	500	3,000
Democrats	850	2,500	0	3,350
No. of Cand.	*3*	*3*	*0*	*6*
House	850	1,000	0	1,850
Senate	0	1,500	0	1,500
Incumbents	1,500	1,200	1,500	4,200
Challengers	500	1,700	0	2,200
Open Seat	0	3,500	0	3,500
Winners	1,500	2,700	n/a	4,200
Losers	500	3,700	n/a	4,200

Sonnenschein Nath & Rosenthal

*Phone: (312) 876-8000 * Fax: (312) 876-7934*
8000 Sears Tower, Chicago, IL 60606
Web: www.sonnenschein.com

Sonnenschein Nath & Rosenthal is a Chicago-based general practice law firm. It has more than 450 lawyers and is one of the 30 largest firms in the United States. The Washington office has 42 lawyers.

The firm has additional offices in New York, Los Angeles, San Francisco, St. Louis, Mo., Kansas City, Mo. and London.

Washington clients have included: McDonnell Douglas Corp., Bank of America, Prudential, the Canadian government, Hoover Group Inc., Northwest Broadcasting, NEXT USA and Riceland Foods Inc.

Sonnenschein Nath & Rosenthal Good Government Committee (C00216127) *Address: same as sponsor * Treasurer: David J. Schadler*

	1993-94	1995-96	1997	Totals
Receipts	$30,740	$36,776	$14,054	$81,570
Disburse	26,350	20,750	10,800	57,900
Cash	15,229	31,256	34,512	n/a
Contributions	7,750	4,450	500	12,700
Republicans	0	200	0	200
No. of Cand.	*0*	*2*	*0*	*2*
House	0	0	0	0
Senate	0	200	0	200
Democrats	7,750	4,250	500	12,500
No. of Cand.	*6*	*4*	*1*	*11*
House	6,750	4,250	0	11,000
Senate	1,000	0	500	1,500
Incumbents	6,750	4,000	0	10,750
Challengers	0	0	500	500
Open Seat	0	450	0	450
Winners	6,750	3,100	n/a	9,850
Losers	1,000	1,350	n/a	2,350

Sterns & Weinroth

Phone: (609) 392-2100
50 W. State St., P.O. Box 1298, Trenton, NJ 08607

New Jersey law firm Sterns & Weinroth has a large casino practice, with clients including Caesars World, ITB, The Trump Organization, Trump Plaza, Trump Taj Mahal and Trump's Castle, according to the Martindale-Hubbell directory.

The firm has roughly 35 lawyers at offices in Atlantic City and Trenton, N.J. and Washington.

Practice areas include: administrative, banking, bankruptcy, casino, civil and criminal litigation, commercial lending, corporate, creditor's rights, environmental, governmental finance, intellectual property, labor, land use, legislative, municipal, real estate, regulatory and technology law and white collar crime.

Sterns & Weinroth — A Professional Corp. Federal PAC (C00301218) *Address: same as sponsor * Treasurer: Richard K. Weinroth*

	1993-94	1995-96	1997	Totals
Receipts	$0	$14,981	$950	$15,931
Disburse	0	14,321	0	14,321
Cash	0	659	1,609	n/a
Contributions	0	13,300	0	13,300
Republicans	0	9,500	0	9,500
No. of Cand.	*0*	*7*	*0*	*7*
House	0	6,250	0	6,250
Senate	0	3,250	0	3,250
Democrats	0	3,800	0	3,800
No. of Cand.	*0*	*3*	*0*	*3*
House	0	800	0	800
Senate	0	3,000	0	3,000
Incumbents	0	5,550	0	5,550
Challengers	0	500	0	500
Open Seat	0	7,250	0	7,250
Winners	0	8,550	n/a	8,550
Losers	0	4,750	n/a	4,750

Stoel Rives

*Phone: (503) 224-3380 * Fax: (503) 220-2480*
900 S.W. Fifth Ave., Suite 2300, Portland, OR 97204
*Web: www.stoel.com * E-mail: rdvanbrocklin@stoel.com*

Stoel Rives is a Portland, Ore.-based law firm that specializes in general corporate and business practice. Its PAC is bipartisan.

The firm's major clients include Citicorp, Hollywood Entertainment Corp., PacifiCorp and Lewis & Clark College.

The 240-lawyer firm has other offices in Seattle; Boise, Idaho; Salt Lake City; Washington; and Vancouver, Wash.

Stoel Rives Political Action Committee (C00289165) *Phone: (202) 347-7744 * Fax: (202) 347-7750 * 1275 K St. N.W., Suite 810, Washington, DC 20005-4006 * Treasurer: Robert D. Van Brocklin*

	1993-94	1995-96	1997	Totals
Receipts	$10,000	$25,650	$3,875	$39,525
Disburse	7,850	27,800	3,875	39,525
Cash	2,150	500	500	n/a
Contributions	9,350	28,800	2,875	41,025
Republicans	5,000	12,400	1,500	18,900
No. of Cand.	*2*	*9*	*2*	*13*
House	0	3,400	0	3,400
Senate	5,000	9,000	1,500	15,500
Democrats	4,350	16,400	1,375	22,125
No. of Cand.	*5*	*5*	*2*	*12*
House	3,850	3,900	1,375	9,125
Senate	500	12,500	0	13,000
Incumbents	8,850	7,400	2,875	19,125
Challengers	500	3,900	0	4,400
Open Seat	0	17,500	0	17,500
Winners	7,500	19,900	n/a	27,400
Losers	1,850	8,900	n/a	10,750

Stoll, Keenon & Park

*Phone: (606) 231-3000 * Fax: (606) 253-1093*
201 E. Main St., Suite 1100, Lexington, KY 40507
Web: www.skp.com

Stoll, Keenon & Park is a Lexington, Ky.-based law firm that has two other offices in the state. The general practice firm has 82 lawyers.

The firm's federal PAC, which is bipartisan, gives to Kentucky candidates.

Stoll, Keenon & Park Federal PAC (C00212092) *Address: same as sponsor * Treasurer: Eileen M. O'Brien * Contact: Leslie W. Morris, Chairperson*

	1993-94	1995-96	1997	Totals
Receipts	$1,200	$7,600	$7,200	$16,000
Disburse	1,000	7,600	7,500	16,100
Cash	360	360	60	n/a
Contributions	1,000	6,900	7,500	15,400
Republicans	0	2,500	500	3,000
No. of Cand.	*0*	*2*	*1*	*3*
House	0	500	500	1,000
Senate	0	2,000	0	2,000
Democrats	1,000	4,400	7,000	12,400
No. of Cand.	*1*	*4*	*8*	*13*
House	1,000	2,400	5,500	8,900
Senate	0	2,000	1,500	3,500
Incumbents	1,000	3,000	500	4,500
Challengers	0	3,900	0	3,900
Open Seat	0	0	7,000	7,000
Winners	1,000	3,000	n/a	4,000
Losers	0	3,900	n/a	3,900

Stroock & Stroock & Lavan

*Phone: (212) 806-5851 * Fax: (212) 806-6006*
180 Maiden Ln., 34th Floor, New York, NY 10038
E-mail: jburns@stroock.com

New York City legal and lobbying firm Stroock & Stroock & Lavan has more than 200 lawyers who practice in all areas of law.

Founded in 1876, the firm also has offices in Boston, Los Angeles, Miami, Washington and Budapest, Hungary.

The Washington office has one registered lobbyist. Lobbying clients include American Home Products Corp., Major League Baseball and North General Hospital.

SSL Political Action Committee (C00297184) *Phone: (202) 452-9250 * Fax: (202) 293-2293 * 1150 17th St. N.W., Suite 600, Washington, DC 20036-4652 * Treasurer: James L. Burns*

	1993-94	1995-96	1997	Totals
Receipts	$10,000	$47,250	$9,462	$66,712
Disburse	5,000	32,088	12,030	49,118
Cash	6,000	21,162	18,579	n/a
Contributions	3,500	23,000	6,500	33,000
Republicans	1,000	13,500	4,500	19,000
No. of Cand.	*1*	*6*	*6*	*13*

(Data for SSL Political Action continued)

House	0	5,500	1,500	7,000
Senate	1,000	8,000	3,000	12,000
Democrats	2,500	9,500	2,000	14,000
No. of Cand.	*4*	*8*	*1*	*13*
House	1,500	7,500	2,000	11,000
Senate	1,000	2,000	0	3,000
Incumbents	2,500	21,000	6,500	30,000
Challengers	1,000	0	1,000	2,000
Open Seat	0	2,000	0	2,000
Winners	2,500	21,000	n/a	23,500
Losers	1,000	2,000	n/a	3,000

Stuzin & Camner

*Phone: (305) 442-4994 * Fax: (305) 442-2389*
550 Biltmore Way, Suite 700, Miami, FL 33134

Stuzin & Camner has about 12 lawyers in offices in Coral Gables and Miami, Fla., Columbus, Ohio and Houston. The firm mainly represents financial institutions.

Established in 1973, Stuzin & Camner's areas of practice include: regulatory, transactional and litigation matters for financial institutions, the FDIC and the RTC; civil trial and appellate practice; bankruptcy, creditors' rights and workouts; residential and commercial real estate matters; corporate law, securities regulation and mergers and acquisitions.

Excellence in Government Fund of Stuzin & Camner PA (C00225516) *Address: same as sponsor * Treasurer: Nikki Nedbor*

	1993-94	1995-96	1997	Totals
Receipts	$21,925	$21,605	$7,018	$50,548
Disburse	22,000	21,071	7,568	50,639
Cash	313	849	285	n/a
Contributions	12,500	12,000	2,000	26,500
Republicans	1,000	2,000	0	3,000
No. of Cand.	*1*	*1*	*0*	*2*
House	0	2,000	0	2,000
Senate	1,000	0	0	1,000
Democrats	11,500	10,000	2,000	23,500
No. of Cand.	*5*	*3*	*1*	*9*
House	3,500	5,000	2,000	10,500
Senate	8,000	5,000	0	13,000
Incumbents	12,500	12,000	2,000	26,500
Challengers	0	0	0	0
Open Seat	0	0	0	0
Winners	12,500	12,000	n/a	24,500
Losers	0	0	n/a	0

Swidler & Berlin

*Phone: (202) 424-7500 * Fax: (202) 424-7643*
3000 K St. N.W., Suite 300, Washington, DC 20007
Web: www.swidlaw.com

Swidler & Berlin is a Washington-based law firm that handles conflict resolution and corporate finance cases, as well as telecommunications, energy and environmental law.

The firm was established in 1982 with just 13 lawyers. It has grown to more than 160 lawyers and maintains such clients as US Airways, General Electric and the Chrysler Corp. In addition, Swidler & Berlin has registered to lobby for Philip Morris, Microsoft and Prudential.

Swidler & Berlin PAC (C00165621) *Address: same as sponsor * Treasurer: Brian W. Fitzgerald*

	1993-94	1995-96	1997	Totals
Receipts	$83,096	$94,347	$63,072	$240,515
Disburse	84,793	94,953	49,350	229,096
Cash	625	22	13,745	n/a
Contributions	66,870	64,889	41,600	173,359
Republicans	12,550	43,639	21,600	77,789
No. of Cand.	*17*	*43*	*21*	*81*
House	6,300	26,750	8,500	41,550
Senate	6,250	16,889	13,100	36,239
Democrats	52,070	21,250	20,000	93,320
No. of Cand.	*51*	*26*	*19*	*96*
House	26,450	11,750	7,500	45,700
Senate	25,620	9,500	12,500	47,620
Incumbents	55,420	56,139	39,600	151,159
Challengers	2,000	1,250	0	3,250
Open Seat	9,450	7,500	2,000	18,950
Winners	47,550	55,639	n/a	103,189
Losers	19,320	9,250	n/a	28,570

Thompson, Hine & Flory

*Phone: (216) 566-5500 * Fax: (216) 566-5800*
3900 Key Center, 127 Public Square, Cleveland, OH 44114
*Web: www.thf.com * E-mail: attorneys@thf.com*

Thompson, Hine & Flory is a Cleveland-based law firm. Founded in 1911, the firm has other offices in Cincinnati and Columbus, Ohio; Palm Beach, Fla.; Washington; and Brussels, Belgium. It has 334 lawyers worldwide.

The firm's PAC is bipartisan.

Thompson, Hine & Flory National Good Government Fund (C00163196) *Address: same as sponsor * Treasurer: Robert J. Taborn*

	1993-94	1995-96	1997	Totals
Receipts	$27,750	$22,000	$27,000	$76,750
Disburse	23,125	26,200	7,090	56,415
Cash	5,025	825	20,735	n/a
Contributions	20,800	12,000	5,590	38,390
Republicans	3,900	7,500	3,990	15,390
No. of Cand.	*4*	*5*	*4*	*13*
House	1,150	5,000	250	6,400
Senate	2,750	2,500	3,740	8,990
Democrats	16,900	4,500	1,600	23,000
No. of Cand.	*10*	*5*	*4*	*19*
House	12,400	4,500	1,350	18,250
Senate	4,500	0	250	4,750
Incumbents	14,250	8,750	3,850	26,850
Challengers	1,050	3,250	0	4,300
Open Seat	5,500	0	1,740	7,240
Winners	9,400	8,750	n/a	18,150
Losers	11,400	3,250	n/a	14,650

Troutman Sanders

*Phone: (404) 885-3000 * Fax: (404) 885-3900*
600 Peachtree St. N.E., Suite 5200, Atlanta, GA 30308

Troutman Sanders is an Atlanta-based law firm that specializes in the electric utilities industry. Its PAC is bipartisan.

The firm, which employs more than 200 lawyers, also has an office in Washington. Several of the firm's lawyers also are lobbyists.

Troutman Sanders LLP Political Action Committee Inc. (C00311142) *Phone: (202) 274-2951 * Fax: (202) 274-2994 * 1300 Eye St. N.W., Suite 500 E., Washington, DC 20005 * Treasurer: William B. Conway Jr.*

	1993-94	1995-96	1997	Totals
Receipts	$0	$20,030	$12,790	$32,820
Disburse	0	18,428	6,728	25,156
Cash	0	1,600	7,661	n/a
Contributions	0	17,233	6,700	23,933
Republicans	0	13,533	4,950	18,483
No. of Cand.	*0*	*18*	*9*	*27*
House	0	5,333	3,250	8,583
Senate	0	8,200	1,700	9,900
Democrats	0	3,700	1,750	5,450
No. of Cand.	*0*	*7*	*4*	*11*
House	0	1,700	500	2,200
Senate	0	2,000	1,250	3,250
Incumbents	0	6,400	6,700	13,100
Challengers	0	2,833	0	2,833
Open Seat	0	8,000	0	8,000
Winners	0	9,900	n/a	9,900
Losers	0	7,333	n/a	7,333

Ungaretti & Harris

*Phone: (312) 977-4400 * Fax: (312) 977-4405*
3500 Three First National Plaza, Chicago, IL 60602-4283
*Web: www.uhlaw.com * E-mail: info@uhlaw.com*

Ungaretti & Harris is a 70-attorney law firm with offices in Chicago and Washington. The firm changed its name from Coffield Ungaretti & Harris after partner Michael W. Coffield left in October 1996.

Practice areas include: bankruptcy and creditors' rights, corporate, securities and finance, employee benefits, environmental law, estate planning, health care, information technology, legislative and regulatory affairs, litigation, real estate and taxation.

The firm's four-person Washington office primarily works on local transportation issues, aviation regulations and employment law.

Ungaretti & Harris Political Action Committee (C00239012)
*Phone: (202) 872-4310 * Fax: (202) 331-1486 * 1747 Pennsylvania Ave. N.W., Suite 900, Washington, DC 20006-4604 * Treasurer: Judith Jacobson*

*Contact: Joseph Carey, Partner * Phone: (312) 977-4400*

	1993-94	1995-96	1997	Totals
Receipts	$82,490	$68,465	$13,933	$164,888
Disburse	61,715	70,850	32,580	165,145
Cash	21,031	18,647	0	n/a
Contributions	29,050	46,550	14,000	89,600
Republicans	0	0	3,000	3,000
No. of Cand.	*0*	*0*	*4*	*4*
House	0	0	1,500	1,500
Senate	0	0	1,500	1,500
Democrats	28,050	46,550	11,000	85,600
No. of Cand.	*29*	*33*	*9*	*71*
House	9,550	10,550	1,500	21,600
Senate	18,500	36,000	9,500	64,000
Incumbents	22,500	19,750	11,500	53,750
Challengers	2,000	10,350	0	12,350
Open Seat	4,450	16,000	2,000	22,450
Winners	16,500	32,350	n/a	48,850
Losers	12,550	14,200	n/a	26,750

Van Ness Feldman

*Phone: (202) 298-1800 * Fax: (202) 338-2416*
1050 Thomas Jefferson St. N.W., Suite 700, Washington, DC 20007-3877

Van Ness Feldman is a private law and lobbying firm based in Washington that specializes in legislative and regulatory issues related to environmental, energy and natural resources law. The firm was established in 1977 and today employs about 45 attorneys. The firm's second office is in Seattle.

Van Ness Feldman PC Political Action Committee (also known as Van Ness Feldman Political Action Committee) (C00205369)
*Address: same as sponsor * Treasurer: D. Eric Hultman * Contact: Richard A. Penna, Chairman*

	1993-94	1995-96	1997	Totals
Receipts	$45,558	$32,824	$20,190	$98,572
Disburse	33,634	41,454	22,150	97,238
Cash	13,106	4,476	2,516	n/a
Contributions	30,567	38,103	21,050	89,720
Republicans	9,817	24,078	8,300	42,195
No. of Cand.	*12*	*34*	*13*	*59*
House	4,750	15,350	4,800	24,900
Senate	5,067	8,728	3,500	17,295
Democrats	20,750	14,025	12,750	47,525
No. of Cand.	*28*	*20*	*17*	*65*
House	13,000	9,525	4,750	27,275
Senate	7,750	4,500	8,000	20,250
Incumbents	28,750	28,700	20,550	78,000
Challengers	817	2,175	0	2,992
Open Seat	1,000	7,228	500	8,728
Winners	24,250	30,854	n/a	55,104
Losers	6,317	7,249	n/a	13,566

Verner, Liipfert, Bernhard, McPherson & Hand

*Phone: (202) 371-6000 * Fax: (202) 371-6279*
901 15th St. N.W., Suite 700, Washington, DC 20005-2301
*Web: www.verner.com * E-mail: verner@verner.com*

A top Washington lobbying firm, Verner, Liipfert, Bernhard, McPherson & Hand counts among its employees former Senate Majority Leader and Republican presidential candidate Bob Dole. In 1997, the firm was paid $18.2 million to lobby the federal government, of which $10.3 million came from tobacco companies, according to lobbyist filings.

The firm's other clients include the Puerto Rico Economic Development Administration, General Motors, Kellogg, NBC and three major professional sports leagues: the NFL, NBA and NHL. The firm represents several foreign clients, including the governments of Oman and Uruguay. It has offices in Washington; McLean, Va.; Honolulu; Houston; and Austin, Texas; and employs more than 170 lawyers and consultants.

Verner Liipfert ranked second in 1996 congressional contributions among individual law firms. The firm donated money to more than 150 candidates in 1996, but just 13 received at least $5,000 (Dole's presidential campaign received the same amount). Verner Liipfert split its contributions almost equally between the parties; GOP candidates got slightly more. Sens. John Warner, R-Va., and Max Baucus, D-Mont., were the leading recipients.

Verner, Liipfert, Bernhard, McPherson & Hand PAC (C00151340)
*Address: same as sponsor * Treasurer: John A. Merrigan * Contact: Harry McPherson, Assistant Treasurer*

	1993-94	1995-96	1997	Totals
Receipts	$292,313	$321,137	$142,328	$755,778
Disburse	306,591	305,070	143,549	755,210
Cash	6,283	22,350	21,128	n/a
Contributions	245,335	251,941	135,041	632,317
Republicans	23,875	128,549	47,452	199,876
No. of Cand.	*21*	*92*	*51*	*164*
House	8,125	62,365	28,053	98,543
Senate	15,750	66,184	19,399	101,333
Democrats	218,960	123,392	83,589	425,941
No. of Cand.	*84*	*67*	*49*	*200*
House	100,771	64,799	24,249	189,819
Senate	118,189	58,593	59,340	236,122
Incumbents	213,577	217,837	130,291	561,705
Challengers	10,500	4,350	0	14,850
Open Seat	21,258	29,754	1,500	52,512
Winners	167,333	219,892	n/a	387,225
Losers	78,002	32,049	n/a	110,051

Vinson & Elkins

*Phone: (713) 758-2222 * Fax: (713) 758-2346*
2300 First City Tower, 1001 Fannin, Houston, TX 77002
Web: www.vinson-elkins.com

Texas-based law firm Vinson & Elkins handles nearly all areas of civil law and certain types of white-collar criminal law.

Established in 1917, the firm employs more than 535 attorneys and posted more than $230 million in earnings in 1996. Vinson & Elkins is consistently rated as one of the top 50 law firms in the United States. In 1996, the Petroleum Economist rated the firm as one of the best international energy law firms in the world.

Although based in Houston, Vinson & Elkins has close ties to Washington, and represented the Rose Law Firm in Whitewater investigations. The firm also maintains offices in Dallas and Austin, Texas; London; Moscow; and Singapore.

The National Good Government Fund (C00032797) *Phone: (202) 639-6500 * Fax: (202) 639-6604 * The Willard Office Building, 1455 Pennsylvania Ave. N.W., Washington, DC 20004-1008 * Treasurer: Joe B. Allen*

*Contact: Harry M. Reasoner, CEO * Phone: (713) 758-2222*

	1993-94	1995-96	1997	Totals
Receipts	$243,509	$277,707	$156,600	$677,816
Disburse	225,930	313,889	160,591	700,410
Cash	50,307	14,118	5,125	n/a
Contributions	169,500	181,187	99,357	450,044
Republicans	63,000	73,556	44,203	180,759
No. of Cand.	*25*	*48*	*34*	*107*
House	15,500	59,356	25,203	100,059
Senate	47,500	14,200	19,000	80,700
Democrats	106,500	107,631	54,654	268,785
No. of Cand.	*43*	*47*	*38*	*128*
House	72,000	81,051	28,154	181,205
Senate	34,500	26,580	26,500	87,580
Incumbents	113,500	108,387	94,857	316,744
Challengers	19,500	38,956	1,000	59,456
Open Seat	36,000	32,162	3,000	71,162
Winners	113,500	133,549	n/a	247,049
Losers	56,000	47,638	n/a	103,638

Vorys, Sater, Seymour & Pease

*Phone: (614) 464-6400 * Fax: (614) 464-6350*
P.O. Box 1008, Columbus, OH 43216-1008
Web: www.vssp.com

Vorys, Sater, Seymour & Pease is the largest and oldest law firm in central Ohio; it was founded in 1909. The firm has 285 attorneys in offices in Columbus, Cincinnati and Cleveland, Ohio and Washington.

Attorneys work on civil litigation, environmental, intellectual property, finance, securities, health care, international, labor and employee benefits, workers' compensation, real estate, financial institutions and banking law.

Clients include: The Limited Inc., Honda of America Mfg. Inc., Pitney Bowes Inc., General Electric, Bob Evans Farms and Worthington Industries.

VSS&P FedPAC (C00220764) *Address: same as sponsor * Treasurer: Williams S. Newcomb Jr.*

	1993-94	1995-96	1997	Totals
Receipts	$43,193	$94,578	$59,592	$197,363
Disburse	42,850	72,130	36,695	151,675
Cash	3,565	26,013	48,910	n/a
Contributions	42,850	52,450	34,100	129,400
Republicans	20,100	37,550	24,850	82,500
No. of Cand.	*23*	*23*	*22*	*68*
House	16,200	25,050	12,350	53,600
Senate	3,900	12,500	12,500	28,900
Democrats	22,750	14,900	9,250	46,900
No. of Cand.	*26*	*16*	*12*	*54*
House	13,750	12,900	7,250	33,900
Senate	9,000	2,000	2,000	13,000
Incumbents	36,300	48,050	28,850	113,200
Challengers	2,000	2,150	250	4,400
Open Seat	4,550	2,250	5,000	11,800
Winners	36,100	45,950	n/a	82,050
Losers	6,750	6,500	n/a	13,250

White & Case

*Phone: (212) 819-8200 * Fax: (212) 819-7604*
1155 Ave. of the Americas, New York, NY 10036-2787
Web: www.whitecase.com

White & Case, the seventh-largest law firm in the nation, has more than 752 lawyers in 28 offices in the United States, Latin America, Europe, the Middle East, Africa and Asia. Clients include public and privately held commercial businesses and financial institutions, as well as governments and state-owned entities.

The general practice firm specializes in international areas of law, including corporate and financial transactions and complex dispute resolution proceedings. It also is one of the most active law firms in the world in the restructuring and sale of state-owned entities.

Founded in New York in 1901, White & Case posted $282 million in sales for 1996.

White & Case Political Action Committee (C00302059) *Phone: (202) 626-3600 * Fax: (202) 639-9355 * 601 13th St. N.W., Suite 600 S., Washington, DC 20005 * Treasurer: William P. McClure*

	1993-94	1995-96	1997	Totals
Receipts	$0	$46,350	$19,550	$65,900
Disburse	0	41,257	17,000	58,257
Cash	0	5,091	7,641	n/a
Contributions	0	34,250	17,000	51,250
Republicans	0	19,250	11,000	30,250
No. of Cand.	*0*	*15*	*9*	*24*
House	0	15,250	6,500	21,750
Senate	0	4,000	4,500	8,500
Democrats	0	15,000	6,000	21,000
No. of Cand.	*0*	*12*	*6*	*18*
House	0	10,000	3,000	13,000
Senate	0	5,000	3,000	8,000
Incumbents	0	33,250	17,000	50,250
Challengers	0	1,000	0	1,000
Open Seat	0	0	0	0
Winners	0	31,250	n/a	31,250
Losers	0	3,000	n/a	3,000

Williams & Jensen

*Phone: (202) 659-8201 * Fax: (202) 659-5249*
1155 21st St. N.W., Suite 300, Washington, DC 20036

Williams & Jensen is a Washington law firm that specializes in federal policy law, including business, finance, tax, health, energy and international trade issues. Established in 1972, the firm employs 26 lawyers. For the first half of 1997, the firm earned almost $3.3 million in lobbying fees, the seventh highest amount during that period, according to the Center for Responsive Politics.

Former Rep. Butler C. Derrick Jr., D-S.C., is a partner.

Lobbying clients include: First Union Corp., Norfolk Southern Corp., Gateway 2000, JP Morgan & Co., Time Warner, America's Public Television Stations, Keystone Inc., Genzyme Corp., the Recording Industry Association of America, Oklahoma Gas & Electric, Continental Airlines, Glaxo Wellcome Inc., Credit Suisse First Boston and Church Alliance.

Williams & Jensen PC Political Action Committee (W&J PAC) (C00039206) *Address: same as sponsor * Treasurer: Barbara E. Wixon-Bonfiglio * Contact: J. Steven Hart, Chairman*

	1993-94	1995-96	1997	Totals
Receipts	$96,829	$104,540	$69,957	$271,326
Disburse	88,681	110,197	63,181	262,059
Cash	13,963	8,301	15,075	n/a
Contributions	84,533	103,994	59,517	248,044
Republicans	35,130	65,828	36,790	137,748
No. of Cand.	*55*	*108*	*58*	*221*
House	21,763	45,217	20,520	87,500
Senate	13,367	20,611	16,270	50,248
Democrats	48,903	38,166	22,227	109,296
No. of Cand.	*71*	*60*	*36*	*167*
House	31,305	30,625	10,345	72,275
Senate	17,598	7,541	11,882	37,021
Incumbents	75,935	89,936	58,517	224,388
Challengers	1,750	1,329	500	3,579
Open Seat	6,848	12,229	500	19,577
Winners	74,163	91,744	n/a	165,907
Losers	10,370	12,250	n/a	22,620

Winstead Sechrest & Minick

*Phone: (214) 743-3400 * Fax: (214) 743-3390*
5400 Renaissance Tower, 1201 Elm St., Dallas, TX 75270-2199
*Web: www.winstead.com * E-mail: gpryor@winstead.com*

Winstead Sechrest & Minick offers a wide array of legal services both nationally and internationally. Founded in 1973 with four attorneys, Winstead now has more than 200 practicing lawyers.

Winstead was No. 147 on National Law Journal's 1997 listing of the top 250 law firms in the United States.

The firm has four offices, with headquarters in Dallas. One hundred and thirty-nine attorneys practice at its headquarters, 50 practice at the firm's Houston office, 21 at the Austin, Texas office and four attorneys practice at Winstead's Mexico City office.

Winstead Sechrest & Minick P.C. Political Action Committee (C00194555) *Address: same as sponsor * Treasurer: Glen Charles Pryor*

	1993-94	1995-96	1997	Totals
Receipts	$41,225	$31,500	$41,600	$114,325
Disburse	41,400	40,750	8,400	90,550
Cash	31,454	22,204	55,404	n/a
Contributions	38,650	15,750	7,900	62,300
Republicans	16,750	2,500	3,400	22,650
No. of Cand.	*9*	*4*	*3*	*16*
House	5,750	2,500	3,400	11,650
Senate	11,000	0	0	11,000
Democrats	21,150	13,250	4,500	38,900
No. of Cand.	*18*	*17*	*5*	*40*
House	13,000	8,750	3,500	25,250
Senate	8,150	4,500	1,000	13,650
Incumbents	29,900	11,250	7,900	49,050
Challengers	2,250	750	0	3,000
Open Seat	6,500	3,750	0	10,250
Winners	26,400	13,000	n/a	39,400
Losers	12,250	2,750	n/a	15,000

Winston & Strawn

*Phone: (312) 588-5600 * Fax: (312) 588-5700*
35 W. Wacker Dr., Chicago, IL 60601
Web: www.winston.com

Winston & Strawn, founded in 1853, is one of the nation's oldest and largest law firms. It has nearly 525 attorneys and offices in New York, Chicago, Washington and overseas. Its main practice areas are litigation and corporate law, but the firm also has experience in international transactions, antitrust and trade regulations and bankruptcy.

Winston & Strawn's government affairs unit is headed by former Rep. Beryl F. Anthony Jr., D-Ark., Reagan administration Secretary of Transportation James H. Burnley IV and former Illinois Republican Gov. James R. Thompson, who is the firm's chairman.

Winston & Strawn Political Action Committee (C00282921) *Phone: (202) 371-5700 * Fax: (202) 371-5950 * 1400 L St. N.W., Washington, DC 20005-3502 * Treasurer: Former Rep. Beryl F. Anthony*

	1993-94	1995-96	1997	Totals
Receipts	$54,754	$100,571	$49,370	$204,695
Disburse	46,910	106,268	43,616	196,794
Cash	7,844	2,147	7,900	n/a
Contributions	33,400	72,086	38,750	144,236
Republicans	12,350	42,625	20,750	75,725
No. of Cand.	*17*	*50*	*26*	*93*
House	4,350	26,875	15,500	46,725
Senate	8,000	15,750	5,250	29,000
Democrats	20,050	29,461	18,000	67,511
No. of Cand.	*29*	*32*	*19*	*80*
House	14,050	15,950	5,500	35,500
Senate	6,000	13,511	12,500	32,011
Incumbents	22,600	58,425	37,750	118,775
Challengers	800	4,411	0	5,211
Open Seat	10,000	9,250	1,000	20,250
Winners	23,100	64,686	n/a	87,786
Losers	10,300	7,400	n/a	17,700

Wolf, Block, Schorr & Solis-Cohen

*Phone: (215) 977-2000 * Fax: (215) 977-2334*
111 S. 15th St., 12th Floor, Philadelphia, PA 19102
Web: www.wolfblock.com

Philadelphia-based law firm Wolf, Block, Schorr & Solis-Cohen works in all areas of law.

More than 200 lawyers work for the firm at offices in Philadelphia, Harrisburg, Blue Bell and Norristown, Pa.; Camden, N.J.; and Wilmington, Del. The firm was founded in 1903.

Tercentenary Fund (C00162719) *Address: same as sponsor * Treasurer: Gerald Gornish * Contact: Bernard Lee, Partner*

	1993-94	1995-96	1997	Totals
Receipts	$20,014	$26,950	$11,640	$58,604
Disburse	21,513	28,685	9,797	59,995
Cash	2,195	458	2,300	n/a
Contributions	15,825	18,900	9,300	44,025
Republicans	11,025	16,400	8,300	35,725
No. of Cand.	*8*	*14*	*5*	*27*
House	7,575	9,400	1,000	17,975
Senate	3,450	7,000	7,300	17,750
Democrats	4,800	2,500	1,000	8,300
No. of Cand.	*7*	*3*	*1*	*11*
House	2,250	1,500	0	3,750
Senate	2,550	1,000	1,000	4,550
Incumbents	7,300	8,650	9,300	25,250
Challengers	8,025	4,250	0	12,275
Open Seat	500	6,000	0	6,500
Winners	11,575	11,650	n/a	23,225
Losers	4,250	7,250	n/a	11,500

Lobbyists

Burson-Marsteller

*Phone: (202) 530-0400 * Fax: (202) 530-4500*
1801 K St. N.W., Suite 901-L, Washington, DC 20006
Web: www.bm.com

Burson-Marsteller is a global public relations and communications firm with more than 2,200 employees working in 30 countries. The firm's employees are specialists in media relations, event planning, publishing, communication training, research and advertising. A subsidiary of the privately held advertising firm Young & Rubicam, the company had sales of $211 million in 1995.

Other Young & Rubicam companies are: Y & R Advertising, Wunderman Cato Johnson, Landor Associates, Cohn and Wolfe, Sudler and Hennessey, Chapman Direct Advertising, Bravo Group, The Madison Group and Waring and LaRosa.

Burson-Marsteller subsidiaries include: Dentsu Burson-Marsteller, Black, Kelly, Scruggs and HealeyAdvocacy Communications Team, Marsteller Advertising, Gramercy Broadcast Center, Burson-Marsteller Productions and The Presentation Source.

U.S. locations include: New York, San Francisco, Sacramento and San Mateo, Calif., Los Angeles, Las Vegas, Chicago, Washington and Pittsburgh.

Burson-Marsteller Political Action Committee (C00201863)
*Address: same as sponsor * Treasurer: John F. Scruggs*

	1993-94	1995-96	1997	Totals
Receipts	$47,436	$53,412	$33,609	$134,457
Disburse	45,550	59,627	35,686	140,863
Cash	9,485	3,270	1,193	n/a
Contributions	38,650	54,077	31,928	124,655
Republicans	7,550	31,746	20,553	59,849
No. of Cand.	*14*	*43*	*28*	*85*
House	1,800	24,000	10,553	36,353
Senate	5,750	7,746	10,000	23,496
Democrats	31,100	22,331	11,375	64,806
No. of Cand.	*34*	*30*	*13*	*77*
House	15,850	15,781	5,625	37,256
Senate	15,250	6,550	5,750	27,550
Incumbents	27,150	46,077	30,228	103,455
Challengers	2,500	1,500	1,500	5,500
Open Seat	9,500	6,500	200	16,200
Winners	26,050	45,827	n/a	71,877
Losers	12,600	8,250	n/a	20,850

Fleishman-Hillard Inc.

*Phone: (314) 982-1700 * Fax: (314) 231-2313*
200 N. Broadway, St. Louis, MO 63102
Web: www.fleishman.com

Headquartered in St. Louis, Fleishman-Hillard is a public relations firm with offices throughout North America, Europe and Asia, as well as affiliates in Latin America. In North America it has offices in Kansas City, New York, Washington and other cities. It is a private, employee-owned company founded more than 50 years ago.

Anheuser-Busch has been a client of Fleishman-Hillard since 1959, and the company has other long-standing relationships with clients such as Emerson Electric.

Fleishman-Hillard Political Action Committee (C00200659) *Phone: (202) 828-8841 * Fax: (202) 223-8199 * 1615 L St. N.W., Suite 1000, Washington, DC 20036 * E-mail: dickerson@fleishman.com * Treasurer: Royce Rollins*

	1993-94	1995-96	1997	Totals
Receipts	$39,013	$55,776	$21,890	$116,679
Disburse	37,030	52,373	24,689	114,092
Cash	2,507	5,907	3,107	n/a
Contributions	28,300	39,750	15,750	83,800
Republicans	16,450	31,000	10,500	57,950
No. of Cand.	*14*	*31*	*12*	*57*
House	9,100	21,000	8,000	38,100
Senate	7,350	10,000	2,500	19,850
Democrats	11,850	8,750	5,250	25,850
No. of Cand.	*17*	*15*	*8*	*40*
House	8,600	6,500	3,750	18,850
Senate	3,250	2,250	1,500	7,000
Incumbents	18,950	31,000	15,000	64,950
Challengers	1,000	1,000	500	2,500
Open Seat	8,350	7,250	250	15,850
Winners	23,800	36,250	n/a	60,050
Losers	4,500	3,500	n/a	8,000

Hill & Knowlton Inc.

*Phone: (202) 333-7400 * Fax: (202) 944-1961*
600 New Hampshire Ave., Suite 601, Washington, DC 20037
Web: www.hillandknowlton.com

Hill & Knowlton is a worldwide public relations firm. Its services include corporate communications, media relations, financial relations, crisis communications, marketing communications and public affairs. The company is a wholly owned subsidiary of the WPP Group, the world's third-largest advertising firm.

Founded in 1927, Hill & Knowlton has 51 offices in 28 countries and employs more than 1,200 workers.

In December 1997, Hill & Knowlton entered into a joint venture agreement with China's International Business & Investment Consultant Corp.

Hill & Knowlton Inc. Political Action Committee (HillPAC) (formerly known as Gray & Co. PAC) (C00183087) *Address: Same as sponsor * Treasurer: Jeffrey B. Trammell*

	1993-94	1995-96	1997	Totals
Receipts	$20,528	$21,572	$31,992	$74,092
Disburse	15,798	21,434	26,646	63,878
Cash	6,546	0	9,922	n/a
Contributions	14,650	39,538	24,925	79,113
Republicans	3,300	22,038	15,000	40,338
No. of Cand.	*6*	*36*	*21*	*63*
House	3,300	16,250	10,000	29,550
Senate	0	5,788	5,000	10,788
Democrats	11,350	17,500	9,925	38,775
No. of Cand.	*21*	*27*	*15*	*63*
House	9,350	11,500	5,600	26,450
Senate	2,000	6,000	4,325	12,325
Incumbents	13,900	32,750	23,925	70,575
Challengers	250	1,500	1,000	2,750
Open Seat	500	4,000	0	4,500
Winners	11,650	34,750	n/a	46,400
Losers	3,000	4,788	n/a	7,788

The Wexler Group Political Action Committee (C00248195)
*Phone: (202) 638-2121 * Fax: (202) 638-7045 * 1317 F St. N.W., Suite 600, Washington, DC 20004 * Web: www.wexlergroup.com * E-mail: ingle@wexlergroup.com * Treasurer: R. Edward Ingle*

The 25-member government affairs firm The Wexler Group provides grass-roots development services in addition to direct lobbying and strategic planning. The firm is a wholly owned subsidiary of Hill & Knowlton.

Firm President Bob Walker was a Republican representative from Pennsylvania from 1977-96. Then-Minority Whip Newt Gingrich, R-Ga., brought him into the House Republican leadership in 1989.

Chairman Ann Wexler cultivated interest group support for President Jimmy Carter as his public liaison. She also served on the Clinton-Gore transition team. Her husband, Joseph Duffey, is director of the United States Information Agency.

Clients include: General Motors, Electric Fuel Ltd., the National Foreign Trade Council, the National Hydrogen Association, PacifiCare, American Airlines, CSX, Eastman Kodak, Lockheed Martin, Sallie Mae, UPS and Visa.

	1993-94	1995-96	1997	Totals
Receipts	$113,722	$113,618	$64,740	$292,080
Disburse	106,618	95,664	73,299	275,581
Cash	8,032	25,986	16,723	n/a
Contributions	92,755	79,270	58,498	230,523
Republicans	23,900	45,270	34,000	103,170
No. of Cand.	*37*	*60*	*42*	*139*
House	9,900	30,047	24,500	64,447
Senate	14,000	15,223	9,500	38,723
Democrats	66,355	34,000	24,498	124,853
No. of Cand.	*81*	*52*	*38*	*171*
House	41,691	25,500	15,532	82,723
Senate	24,664	8,500	8,966	42,130
Incumbents	76,955	75,770	57,998	210,723
Challengers	4,250	1,000	500	5,750
Open Seat	11,550	2,500	0	14,050
Winners	63,755	73,546	n/a	137,301
Losers	29,000	5,724	n/a	34,724

J. Roy Rowland PAC

P.O. Box 927, Dublin, GA 31040

The J. Roy Rowland PAC Account was the principal campaign committee for Rep. J. Roy Rowland Jr., D-Ga., who retired in 1993. The PAC was terminated after the 1996 election cycle.

Rowland is a lobbyist for several health care-related organizations, the National Restaurant Association and Coca-Cola Co., according to 1997 lobbyist filings.

J. Roy Rowland PAC Account (C00146142) *Address: same as sponsor * Treasurer: Ernest F. Jones Jr.*

	1993-94	1995-96	1997	Totals
Receipts	$0	$115,640	$0	$115,640
Disburse	0	139,043	0	139,043
Cash	0	0	0	n/a
Contributions	122,637	16,000	0	138,637
Republicans	0	7,500	0	7,500
No. of Cand.	*0*	*6*	*0*	*6*
House	0	5,500	0	5,500
Senate	0	2,000	0	2,000
Democrats	122,637	8,500	0	131,137
No. of Cand.	*10*	*11*	*0*	*21*
House	121,137	4,500	0	125,637
Senate	1,500	4,000	0	5,500
Incumbents	119,137	9,500	0	128,637
Challengers	0	1,500	0	1,500
Open Seat	3,500	5,000	0	8,500
Winners	2,000	12,500	n/a	14,500
Losers	120,637	3,500	n/a	124,137

Jefferson Group Inc.

*Phone: (202) 626-8500 * Fax: (202) 626-8585*
1341 G St. N.W., Suite 1100, Washington, DC 20005
*Web: www.jeffersongroup.com * E-mail: info@jeffersongroup.com*

Lobbying firm the Jefferson Group has clients in the business, information technologies and health care industries.

Clients include: Sandoz Corp., Pfizer Inc., Burlington Northern Santa Fe Corp., Amgen Inc., Hoffmann-La Roche, Dallas Area Rapid Transit Authority, Dow Chemical, Sallie Mae, Seminole Tribe of Florida, Hughes Data Systems and the city of Orlando, Fla.

Jefferson Group Inc. PAC (Jefferson PAC) (C00311530) *Address: same as sponsor * Treasurer: Patricia A. Ramsay * Contact: H. Bernard Schroeder, Chairman*

	1993-94	1995-96	1997	Totals
Receipts	$0	$14,004	$27,391	$41,395
Disburse	0	12,616	27,827	40,443
Cash	0	1,388	4,781	n/a
Contributions	0	13,250	27,400	40,650
Republicans	0	6,750	14,000	20,750
No. of Cand.	*0*	*14*	*19*	*33*
House	0	4,750	6,750	11,500
Senate	0	2,000	7,250	9,250
Democrats	0	6,500	12,400	18,900
No. of Cand.	*0*	*13*	*22*	*35*
House	0	4,500	10,400	14,900
Senate	0	2,000	2,000	4,000
Incumbents	0	10,250	27,400	37,650
Challengers	0	0	0	0
Open Seat	0	3,000	0	3,000
Winners	0	12,000	n/a	12,000
Losers	0	1,250	n/a	1,250

Kamber Group

*Phone: (202) 955-1225 * Fax: (202) 659-5559*
1920 L St. N.W., Washington, DC 20036
*Web: www.kamber.com * E-mail: jsandman@kamber.com*

The Kamber Group is a private public relations firm with offices in New York, Washington, Los Angeles and affiliates in Denver, London and Brussels, Belgium. The firm's services include image building, research, crisis communications, design, event management, fundraising, issues campaigns, media production, media relations and marketing and corporate products.

Established in 1980, the firm's clientele includes businesses, financial institutions and federal and state congressional candidates. The firm also represents the Miccosukee Tribe of Florida.

In 1997, The Kamber Group acquired The PR Consulting Group, a New York firm with specialties in business-to-business communications, issues-oriented publicity and litigation communications.

Kamber Group Political Action Fund (TKG PAC) (C00234708)
*Address: same as sponsor * Treasurer: Jeffrey Sandman*

	1993-94	1995-96	1997	Totals
Receipts	$21,208	$29,975	$12,907	$64,090
Disburse	24,451	22,050	16,175	62,676
Cash	5,247	13,172	9,904	n/a
Contributions	9,600	15,350	2,500	27,450
Republicans	500	0	0	500
No. of Cand.	*1*	*0*	*0*	*1*
House	500	0	0	500
Senate	0	0	0	0
Democrats	9,100	15,350	2,000	26,450
No. of Cand.	*15*	*24*	*2*	*41*
House	6,600	5,250	0	11,850
Senate	2,500	10,100	2,000	14,600
Incumbents	5,600	6,850	2,500	14,950
Challengers	1,000	4,500	0	5,500
Open Seat	3,000	4,000	0	7,000
Winners	6,600	9,350	n/a	15,950
Losers	3,000	6,000	n/a	9,000

Lent & Scrivner

*Phone: (202) 347-3030 * Fax: (202) 347-3133*
915 15th St. N.W., Suite 800, Washington, DC 20005
E-mail: lent@ix.netcom.net

Lent & Scrivner is a Washington lobbying firm, founded in 1994 by former Rep. Norman Lent, R-N.Y., and his chief of staff, Michael S. Scrivner. Lent was ranked among the top 50 most influential lobbyists by Washingtonian magazine. Lent's son, Norman Lent Jr., joined the firm in 1995.

Rep. Lent left office in 1993, before his party took over the House. Had he stayed, he would have become chairman of what was then the House Energy and Commerce Committee, since he had been the ranking member.

Lent's committee ties have shaped his client list. Major clients include a coalition of "Baby Bell" telephone firms affected by changes in telecommunications bills; Mobil; Florida Crystals, a major sugar producer; and Air Products and Chemicals.

In January 1998, Lent & Scrivner was awarded a $240,000 contract by the Tennessee Valley Authority to assist in dealings with an advisory committee studying deregulation for the Department of Energy.

The Lent & Scrivner PAC is supported mostly by Lent and his wife and son, and Scrivner. It mainly supports Republican candidates and members on relevant committees.

Lent & Scrivner PAC (C00000794) *P.O. Box 2301, Arlington, VA 22202 * Treasurer: Michael S. Scrivner*

	1993-94	1995-96	1997	Totals
Receipts	$4,910	$5,626	$20,000	$30,536
Disburse	656,891	40,122	11,179	708,192
Cash	41,300	6,803	15,623	n/a
Contributions	26,548	11,900	8,967	47,415
Republicans	18,794	11,650	8,717	39,161
No. of Cand.	*31*	*22*	*15*	*68*
House	14,450	8,250	5,217	27,917
Senate	4,344	3,400	3,500	11,244
Democrats	6,854	250	250	7,354
No. of Cand.	*11*	*1*	*1*	*13*
House	6,854	250	250	7,354
Senate	0	0	0	0
Incumbents	21,054	10,000	8,967	40,021
Challengers	2,294	1,400	0	3,694
Open Seat	3,700	500	0	4,200
Winners	21,754	9,250	n/a	31,004
Losers	4,794	2,650	n/a	7,444

Paul Magliocchetti Associates

*Phone: (703) 415-0344 * Fax: (703) 415-0182*
1755 Jefferson Davis Highway, Suite 1107, Arlington, VA 22202

Lobbying firm Paul Magliocchetti Associates employs about 13 lobbyists who are registered to lobby primarily on defense issues. Despite the low profile associates say the firm likes to keep, its PAC was the 14th-largest giver among lawyers and lobbyists during the 1995-96 election cycle.

Magliocchetti, a House Appropriations Committee aide when the Democrats controlled Congress, has recruited former military and civilian Department of Defense employees to his shop, according to a December 1996 Legal Times report. PAC Treasurer Joseph Littleton III was chief financial officer for naval aviation at the Pentagon.

Clients include: Lockheed Martin, Lucent Technologies, American Shipbuilding Association, BF Goodrich, Caterpillar, Diagnostic Retrieval Systems, Electronic Warfare Associates, General Atomics, General Dynamics, Schweizer Aircraft, Textron and VisiCom Laboratories.

Paul Magliocchetti Associates Inc. Political Action Committee (C00280321) *Address: same as sponsor * Treasurer: Joseph S. Littleton III*

	1993-94	1995-96	1997	Totals
Receipts	$61,991	$96,000	$40,700	$198,691
Disburse	60,751	78,386	46,510	185,647
Cash	1,237	18,851	13,041	n/a
Contributions	58,300	72,700	42,750	173,750
Republicans	23,800	44,250	25,000	93,050
No. of Cand.	*23*	*43*	*33*	*99*
House	18,800	37,250	17,000	73,050
Senate	5,000	7,000	8,000	20,000
Democrats	34,500	28,450	17,750	80,700
No. of Cand.	*33*	*27*	*27*	*87*
House	32,500	24,950	13,750	71,200
Senate	2,000	3,500	4,000	9,500
Incumbents	56,800	69,200	42,250	168,250
Challengers	500	0	0	500
Open Seat	1,000	3,500	500	5,000
Winners	48,800	65,700	n/a	114,500
Losers	9,500	7,000	n/a	16,500

R. Duffy Wall & Associates Inc.

*Phone: (202) 737-0100 * Fax: (202) 628-3965*
601 13th St. N.W., Suite 410 S., Washington, DC 20005

Lobbying firm R. Duffy Wall & Associates employs 10 lobbyists in Washington. According to the Center for Responsive Politics, during the first half of 1997 the firm earned more than $2.5 million in lobbying fees, making it the ninth largest firm by earnings.

Clients include: the Association of American Railroads, Bell Atlantic, ComSat Corp., The Betty Ford Center, Procter and Gamble and the states of California and North Carolina.

R. Duffy Wall & Associates Inc. Political Action Committee (C00201194) *Address: same as sponsor * Treasurer: Julia E. Chaney*

	1993-94	1995-96	1997	Totals
Receipts	$39,593	$65,892	$50,217	$155,702
Disburse	40,528	60,706	49,846	151,080
Cash	1,866	7,050	7,420	n/a
Contributions	35,527	52,587	42,906	131,020
Republicans	6,250	40,906	29,215	76,371
No. of Cand.	*11*	*50*	*41*	*102*
House	5,250	30,448	18,220	53,918
Senate	1,000	10,458	10,995	22,453
Democrats	29,277	11,681	13,191	54,149
No. of Cand.	*43*	*16*	*15*	*74*
House	20,777	5,303	6,000	32,080
Senate	8,500	6,378	7,191	22,069
Incumbents	31,727	45,245	41,906	118,878
Challengers	1,500	3,000	1,000	5,500
Open Seat	1,800	3,842	0	5,642
Winners	24,177	44,837	n/a	69,014
Losers	11,350	7,750	n/a	19,100

S-PAC

1820 Creek Crossing Rd., Vienna, VA 22182

S-PAC is a leadership PAC affiliated with former Rep. Dick Schulze, R-Pa. Schulze and his son, PAC Treasurer Richard T. Schulze Jr., were registered lobbyists during 1997, according to lobbyist filings. They represented clients such as Norfolk Southern Corp., the Nuclear Energy Institute, Koch Industries and Centeon.

During 1997, the PAC contributed to the Americans for a Republican Majority PAC.

S-PAC (C00281360) *Address: same as sponsor * Treasurer: Richard T. Schulze Jr.*

	1993-94	1995-96	1997	Totals
Receipts	$266,194	$24,792	$9,719	$300,705
Disburse	1,161	58,361	39,869	99,391
Cash	265,035	231,465	201,315	n/a
Contributions	0	23,750	8,600	32,350
Republicans	0	23,550	8,600	32,150
No. of Cand.	*0*	*38*	*22*	*60*
House	0	21,050	6,150	27,200
Senate	0	2,500	2,450	4,950
Democrats	0	200	0	200
No. of Cand.	*0*	*1*	*0*	*1*
House	0	200	0	200
Senate	0	0	0	0
Incumbents	0	16,350	6,200	22,550
Challengers	0	3,150	0	3,150
Open Seat	0	4,250	2,000	6,250
Winners	0	20,350	n/a	20,350
Losers	0	3,400	n/a	3,400

Symms, Lehn & Associates Inc.

*Phone: (703) 548-4205 * Fax: (703) 519-9212*
210 Cameron St., Alexandria, VA 22314

Symms PAC was listed in 1996 as the principal campaign committee for former Sen. Steve Symms, R-Idaho. Symms, a conservative who served in Congress for 19 years, decided not to seek reelection in 1992. He is now a registered lobbyist, and president of Symms, Lehn & Associates, whose clients include drug and mining companies, as well as the government of Nigeria.

Symms PAC disbursed more than $150,000 of leftover campaign funds during the 1995-96 election cycle, including $10,000 to the National Republican Congressional Committee. Other leading recipients included Reps. Michael D. Crapo, R-Idaho, and Philip Crane, R-Ill., chairman of the Ways and Means Trade Subcommittee.

Symms Political Action Committee (Symms PAC) (C00112359)

*Address: P.O. Box 1663, Alexandria, VA 22313 * Treasurer: Steve Symms*

	1993-94	*1995-96*	*1997*	*Totals*
Receipts	$36,000	$13,096	$3,412	$52,508
Disburse	136,992	153,103	20,980	311,075
Cash	259,962	119,954	102,386	n/a
Contributions	50,400	49,292	5,500	105,192
Republicans	49,900	49,292	5,500	104,692
No. of Cand.	*39*	*48*	*6*	*93*
House	27,650	22,100	4,000	53,750
Senate	22,250	27,192	1,500	50,942
Democrats	500	0	0	500
No. of Cand.	*1*	*0*	*0*	*1*
House	0	0	0	0
Senate	500	0	0	500
Incumbents	15,950	40,842	5,500	62,292
Challengers	25,450	6,500	0	31,950
Open Seat	9,000	1,950	0	10,950
Winners	29,700	42,142	n/a	71,842
Losers	20,700	7,150	n/a	27,850

Other

Education

Apollo Group Inc.

*Phone: (602) 966-5394 * Fax: (602) 968-1159*
4615 E. Elmwood St., Phoenix, AZ 85040
Web: www.apollogrp.com

Apollo Group offers higher-education programs to working adults. The public company offers computer, short-term night and weekend courses at 100 campuses and learning centers in 30 states and Puerto Rico. Sales totaled $283 million in 1997 and the company employs more than 6,000 workers. Apollo more than doubled its total enrollments and revenues between 1993 and 1997.

Subsidiary University of Phoenix has 60 campuses in 12 states, while Apollo's Institute for Professional Development provides program development and management services to nearly 40 campuses. Western International University, a third Apollo subsidiary, offers certificate, undergraduate and graduate degree programs on campuses in Arizona and the United Kingdom. The company also offers courses over the Internet.

Apollo Group Inc. Political Organization for Legislative Leadership (APOLLO-PAC) (C00309781) *Phone: (202) 546-5488 * 666 Pennsylvania Ave N.W., Suite 202, Washington, DC 20003 * Treasurer: Charles M. Seigel*

	1993-94	*1995-96*	*1997*	*Totals*
Receipts	$0	$67,255	$40,000	$107,255
Disburse	0	59,294	22,450	81,744
Cash	0	7,960	25,510	n/a
Contributions	0	53,043	21,950	74,993
Republicans	0	17,550	7,950	25,500
No. of Cand.	*0*	*13*	*3*	*16*
House	0	17,050	7,950	25,000
Senate	0	500	0	500
Democrats	0	35,493	14,000	49,493
No. of Cand.	*0*	*19*	*8*	*27*
House	0	16,493	7,000	23,493
Senate	0	19,000	7,000	26,000
Incumbents	0	39,043	21,450	60,493
Challengers	0	1,500	500	2,000
Open Seat	0	12,500	0	12,500
Winners	0	45,043	n/a	45,043
Losers	0	8,000	n/a	8,000

Career College Association

*Phone: (202) 336-6700 * Fax: (202) 336-6828*
750 First St. N.E., Suite 900, Washington, DC 20002
*Web: www.career.org * E-mail: cca@career.org*

The Career College Association represents 700 private and post-secondary career schools.

Private career colleges train those without a high school education in specific fields and provide workers an opportunity to upgrade their skills.

The association's Washington office promotes government legislation that will ensure access to quality career and skill education.

Career College Political Action Committee (formerly known as National Association of Trade and Technical Schools PAC) (C00213066) *Address: same as sponsor * Treasurer: R. Michael Harter * Contact: Tim Burga, PAC Dir.*

	1993-94	*1995-96*	*1997*	*Totals*
Receipts	$101,563	$98,930	$61,548	$262,041
Disburse	108,916	125,650	51,701	286,267
Cash	46,280	19,559	29,406	n/a
Contributions	100,668	116,208	44,014	260,890
Republicans	24,100	57,024	17,500	98,624
No. of Cand.	*25*	*36*	*16*	*77*
House	14,100	40,800	11,000	65,900
Senate	10,000	16,224	6,500	32,724
Democrats	76,568	59,184	26,514	162,266
No. of Cand.	*65*	*39*	*25*	*129*
House	60,224	46,184	19,350	125,758
Senate	16,344	13,000	7,164	36,508
Incumbents	82,418	92,466	44,014	218,898
Challengers	1,500	5,242	0	6,742
Open Seat	18,000	17,500	0	35,500
Winners	75,024	107,708	n/a	182,732
Losers	25,644	8,500	n/a	34,144

DeVry Inc.

*Phone: (630) 574-1906 * Fax: (630) 571-0317*
One Tower Lane, Suite 1000, Oakbrook Terrace, IL 60181-4624
Web: www.devry.com

DeVry owns and operates DeVry Institutes, Keller Graduate School of Management, Becker CPA Review and Corporate Educational Services, and is one of the largest publicly owned, international, higher-education companies in North America.

The institutes are located on 15 campuses with more than 30,000 full- and part-time students. Most courses educate students in business, computer and industrial applications. DeVry had $307 million in sales for 1997, and employs 2,500 workers.

DeVry Inc. Political Action Committee (C00198606) *Address: same as sponsor * Treasurer: Norman M. Levine*

	1993-94	1995-96	1997	Totals
Receipts	$5,563	$7,467	$3,575	$16,605
Disburse	7,895	7,525	1,325	16,745
Cash	1,824	1,772	4,023	n/a
Contributions	3,600	6,900	1,325	11,825
Republicans	750	1,800	800	3,350
No. of Cand.	*9*	*8*	*4*	*21*
House	600	1,800	300	2,700
Senate	150	0	500	650
Democrats	2,850	5,100	525	8,475
No. of Cand.	*19*	*15*	*5*	*39*
House	2,475	2,550	125	5,150
Senate	375	2,550	400	3,325
Incumbents	3,525	4,150	1,325	9,000
Challengers	75	400	0	475
Open Seat	200	2,350	0	2,550
Winners	2,925	6,250	n/a	9,175
Losers	675	650	n/a	1,325

Management and Training Corp.

*Phone: (801) 626-2033 * Fax: (801) 621-2685*
3293 Harrison Blvd., Ogden, UT 84403-1278

Management and Training operates private correctional facilities, with operations in Arizona, California, Texas and Utah. The private company also has 23 Job Corps centers and is the Department of Labor's biggest contractor. It contracts with the General Services Administration for maintenance of federal buildings, courthouses and post offices.

Based in Ogden, Utah, MTC has about 6,000 employees.

Management and Training Corp. Political Action Committee (C00208322) *Address: same as sponsor * Treasurer: Lyle Perry * Contact: Bernie Diamond, Chairperson*

	1993-94	1995-96	1997	Totals
Receipts	$15,599	$12,268	$812	$28,679
Disburse	11,320	10,378	3,500	25,198
Cash	9,307	11,199	13,604	n/a
Contributions	8,850	4,500	3,500	16,850
Republicans	4,000	2,750	3,500	10,250
No. of Cand.	*5*	*3*	*2*	*10*
House	1,250	250	0	1,500
Senate	2,750	2,500	3,500	8,750
Democrats	4,850	1,750	0	6,600
No. of Cand.	*10*	*5*	*0*	*15*
House	3,850	1,750	0	5,600
Senate	1,000	0	0	1,000
Incumbents	8,350	4,500	3,500	16,350
Challengers	0	0	0	0
Open Seat	500	0	0	500
Winners	5,850	4,500	n/a	10,350
Losers	3,000	0	n/a	3,000

Vocational PAC

1219 W. Gunn Rd., Rochester, MI 48306

Vocational Political Action Committee (V PAC Inc.) (C00235168) *Address: same as sponsor * Treasurer: James Hannemann*

	1993-94	1995-96	1997	Totals
Receipts	$13,154	$23,610	$9,811	$46,575
Disburse	10,477	15,196	8,171	33,844
Cash	8,761	17,450	20,266	n/a
Contributions	6,400	5,735	4,235	16,370
Republicans	800	1,450	1,500	3,750
No. of Cand.	*4*	*4*	*2*	*10*
House	300	1,450	1,500	3,250
Senate	500	0	0	500
Democrats	5,600	4,285	2,735	12,620
No. of Cand.	*14*	*6*	*3*	*23*
House	5,200	3,785	2,735	11,720
Senate	400	500	0	900
Incumbents	6,400	4,285	4,235	14,920
Challengers	0	500	0	500
Open Seat	0	950	0	950
Winners	4,400	4,535	n/a	8,935
Losers	2,000	1,200	n/a	3,200

Other

American School Food Service Association

*Phone: (703) 739-3900 * Fax: (703) 739-3915*
1600 Duke St., Seventh Floor, Alexandria, VA 22314-3436
Web: www.asfsa.org

The American School Food Service Association is a national association established to protect and enhance children's health and well-being by operating nutritious food service programs and providing proper nutrition education in public and nonprofit private schools.

Founded in 1946, the organization includes about 65,000 members comprised of state, city and district food service directors, managers and others involved in school food service and nutrition programs. More than 30,000 members are certified through ASFSA's certification program, indicating that they have completed formal training in areas of sanitation, safety, technical skills, management and nutrition.

American School Food Service Association Political Action Committee Inc. (C00166272) *Address: same as sponsor * Treasurer: Barbara S. Borschow*

	1993-94	1995-96	1997	Totals
Receipts	$0	$14,837	$5,391	$20,228
Disburse	0	15,174	3,938	19,112
Cash	0	901	2,353	n/a
Contributions	13,600	7,750	2,150	23,500
Republicans	2,000	750	750	3,500
No. of Cand.	*2*	*8*	*2*	*12*
House	1,000	1,000	250	2,250
Senate	1,000	-250	500	1,250
Democrats	11,600	7,000	1,400	20,000
No. of Cand.	*10*	*14*	*5*	*29*
House	8,350	4,750	650	13,750
Senate	3,250	2,250	750	6,250
Incumbents	13,350	6,000	2,150	21,500
Challengers	0	500	0	500
Open Seat	250	1,250	0	1,500
Winners	12,350	7,500	n/a	19,850
Losers	1,250	250	n/a	1,500

American Society of Association Executives

*Phone: (202) 626-2723 * Fax: (202) 371-8825*
1575 Eye St. N.W., Washington, DC 20005
Web: www.asaenet.org

Dedicated to promoting the value of associations, the American Society of Association Executives represents association management professionals. It promotes legislation and regulatory proposals affecting its more than 24,000 individual members.

American Society of Association Executives A-PAC (C00041566) *Address: same as sponsor * Treasurer: Malcolm Karl*

	1993-94	1995-96	1997	Totals
Receipts	$83,202	$84,704	$46,225	$214,131
Disburse	44,453	107,569	43,083	195,105
Cash	85,940	63,074	66,216	n/a
Contributions	41,999	105,500	42,555	190,054
Republicans	22,499	69,000	29,292	120,791
No. of Cand.	*25*	*73*	*45*	*143*
House	16,499	40,500	22,792	79,791
Senate	6,000	28,500	6,500	41,000
Democrats	19,500	36,500	13,263	69,263
No. of Cand.	*19*	*41*	*21*	*81*
House	14,000	31,500	10,513	56,013
Senate	5,500	5,000	2,750	13,250
Incumbents	33,250	86,750	40,055	160,055
Challengers	750	2,500	500	3,750
Open Seat	7,999	16,250	1,000	25,249
Winners	32,250	93,500	n/a	125,750
Losers	9,749	12,000	n/a	21,749

National Association of Social Workers

*Phone: (202) 408-8600 * Fax: (202) 336-8310*
750 First St. N.E., Suite 700, Washington, DC 20002
*Web: www.naswdc.org * E-mail: nasw@capcon.net*

The National Association of Social Workers is the largest organization of professional social workers with 155,000 members. It promotes, develops and protects the practice of social work and social workers.

A professional social worker has a degree in social work and meets state legal requirements. Professional social workers practice in family service agencies, community mental health centers, private practice, schools, hospitals, employee assistance programs and public and private agencies.

National Association of Social Workers Political Action for Candidate Election (C00060707) *Address: same as sponsor * Treasurer: Kathy Wood-Dobbins*

	1993-94	1995-96	1997	Totals
Receipts	$779,461	$1,026,184	$621,211	$2,426,856
Disburse	739,383	914,494	480,688	2,134,565
Cash	278,766	390,457	530,980	n/a
Contributions	164,870	171,550	57,100	393,520
Republicans	3,000	2,500	500	6,000
No. of Cand.	*3*	*3*	*1*	*7*
House	1,000	1,500	500	3,000
Senate	2,000	1,000	0	3,000
Democrats	156,770	168,550	56,600	381,920
No. of Cand.	*169*	*128*	*29*	*326*
House	119,650	124,400	38,600	282,650
Senate	37,120	44,150	18,000	99,270
Incumbents	86,070	45,400	28,100	159,570
Challengers	26,000	75,250	1,000	102,250
Open Seat	50,800	49,900	26,500	127,200
Winners	70,250	103,800	n/a	174,050
Losers	94,620	67,750	n/a	162,370

Unknown

American Free Enterprise PAC

Phone: (916) 446-9049

400 Capitol Mall, Suite 1560, Sacramento, CA 95814

American Free Enterprise PAC (C00305870) *Address: same as sponsor * Treasurer: David Bauer*

	1993-94	1995-96	1997	Totals
Receipts	$0	$42,660	$15,500	$58,160
Disburse	0	38,799	1,144	39,943
Cash	0	3,859	16,213	n/a
Contributions	0	40,500	0	40,500
Republicans	0	40,500	0	40,500
No. of Cand.	*0*	*26*	*0*	*26*
House	0	35,000	0	35,000
Senate	0	5,500	0	5,500
Democrats	0	0	0	0
No. of Cand.	*0*	*0*	*0*	*0*
House	0	0	0	0
Senate	0	0	0	0
Incumbents	0	14,000	0	14,000
Challengers	0	12,500	0	12,500
Open Seat	0	14,000	0	14,000
Winners	0	20,500	n/a	20,500
Losers	0	20,000	n/a	20,000

Lightfoot PAC

2020 K St. N.W., Suite 500, Washington, DC 20006

Lightfoot PAC filed for termination in 1997.

Lightfoot Political Action Committee (C00325068) *Address: same as sponsor * Treasurer: Victor E. Long*

	1993-94	1995-96	1997	Totals
Receipts	$0	$0	$4,500	$4,500
Disburse	0	15,766	9,575	25,341
Cash	0	106	0	n/a
Contributions	0	6,700	-4000	2,700
Republicans	0	0	0	0
No. of Cand.	*0*	*0*	*0*	*0*
House	0	0	0	0
Senate	0	0	0	0
Democrats	0	6,700	-4000	2,700
No. of Cand.	*0*	*5*	*1*	*6*
House	0	200	0	200
Senate	0	6,500	-4000	2,500
Incumbents	0	1,500	-4000	-2500
Challengers	0	5,000	0	5,000
Open Seat	0	200	0	200
Winners	0	6,700	n/a	6,700
Losers	0	0	n/a	0

North Texas Committee for Excellence in Government

2031 W. Colorado, Dallas, TX 75208

North Texas Committee for Excellence in Government (C00311621) *Address: same as sponsor * Treasurer: Michael L. Lunceford*

	1993-94	1995-96	1997	Totals
Receipts	$0	$23,676	$3,554	$27,230
Disburse	0	8,459	6,725	15,184
Cash	0	15,207	12,036	n/a
Contributions	0	6,250	3,000	9,250
Republicans	0	3,750	2,000	5,750
No. of Cand.	*0*	*5*	*2*	*7*
House	0	2,750	1,000	3,750
Senate	0	1,000	1,000	2,000
Democrats	0	2,500	1,000	3,500
No. of Cand.	*0*	*3*	*1*	*4*
House	0	1,500	1,000	2,500
Senate	0	1,000	0	1,000
Incumbents	0	5,000	3,000	8,000
Challengers	0	0	0	0
Open Seat	0	1,250	0	1,250
Winners	0	5,750	n/a	5,750
Losers	0	500	n/a	500

Superior California PAC

400 Capitol Mall, Suite 1560, Sacramento, CA 95814

Superior California Federal Leadership Fund (C00317511) *Address: same as sponsor * Treasurer: David Bauer*

	1993-94	1995-96	1997	Totals
Receipts	$0	$7,000	$1,500	$8,500
Disburse	0	6,191	2,230	8,421
Cash	0	807	77	n/a
Contributions	0	5,500	-1000	4,500
Republicans	0	5,500	-1000	4,500
No. of Cand.	*0*	*5*	*1*	*6*
House	0	2,500	0	2,500
Senate	0	3,000	-1000	2,000
Democrats	0	0	0	0
No. of Cand.	*0*	*0*	*0*	*0*
House	0	0	0	0
Senate	0	0	0	0
Incumbents	0	1,000	-1000	0
Challengers	0	1,500	0	1,500
Open Seat	0	3,000	0	3,000
Winners	0	3,000	n/a	3,000
Losers	0	2,500	n/a	2,500

Transportation

Air Transport

Air Transport Association of America

*Phone: (202) 626-4093 * Fax: (202) 626-7871*
1301 Pennsylvania Ave. N.W., Washington, DC 20004
Web: www.air-transport.org

The Air Transport Association of America represents 22 U.S. airlines and express delivery companies and has five foreign associate members. ATA airlines transport more than 95 percent of the passenger and cargo traffic in the United States.

The group studies safety issues, lobbies against aviation tax increases and reports on passenger and cargo industry trends. The ATA opposes lifting the $12 round-trip cap on fees that airports can charge each passenger.

Members include: Aeromexico, Air Canada, Alaska Airlines, Aloha Airlines, America West Airlines, American Airlines, American Trans Air, Canadian Airlines International, Continental Airlines, Delta Air Lines, DHL Airways, Emery Worldwide, Evergreen International Airlines, Federal Express, Hawaiian Airlines, KIWI International Air Lines, Mexicana Airlines, Midwest Express Airlines, Northwest Airlines, Polar Air Cargo, Reeve Aleutian Airways, Southwest Airlines, Trans World Airlines, United Airlines, United Parcel Service and US Airways.

Air Transportation Association of America PAC (C00114694)
*Address: same as sponsor * Treasurer: Richard T. Brandenburg*

	1993-94	1995-96	1997	Totals
Receipts	$3,411	$42,120	$8,096	$53,627
Disburse	7,410	33,083	14,402	54,895
Cash	2,010	11,047	4,741	n/a
Contributions	7,409	16,807	15,250	39,466
Republicans	1,386	12,307	11,750	25,443
No. of Cand.	*4*	*15*	*13*	*32*
House	1,206	9,307	7,500	18,013
Senate	180	3,000	4,250	7,430
Democrats	5,273	4,500	2,500	12,273
No. of Cand.	*14*	*5*	*3*	*22*
House	4,643	4,500	1,500	10,643
Senate	630	0	1,000	1,630
Incumbents	6,409	16,807	15,250	38,466
Challengers	0	0	0	0
Open Seat	1,000	0	0	1,000
Winners	4,016	14,307	n/a	18,323
Losers	3,393	2,500	n/a	5,893

Airborne Freight Corp.

*Phone: (937) 382-5591 * Fax: (937) 382-2452*
145 Hunter Dr., Wilmington, OH 45177
Web: www.airborne-express.com

Seattle-based Airborne Freight, commonly known as Airborne Express, offers overnight express delivery and other shipping services. The publicly owned company reported $2.9 billion in 1997 revenues and employs 20,700 people in more than 200 countries worldwide. Airborne owns and leases fleets of 114 airplanes and 13,265 delivery vehicles. It also owns an airport located in Wilmington, Ohio.

In 1997, it moved ahead with joint ventures in South Africa and the Netherlands and increased investment in its Middle Eastern operations.

Subsidiaries: ABX Air Inc., which operates and maintains the company's aircraft and package sorting facility in Wilmington; and Sky Courier, which offers air courier and express freight services.

Airborne Freight Corp. Political Action Committee (ABXPAC) (C00238311) *Address: same as sponsor * Treasurer: Joseph C. Hete*

	1993-94	1995-96	1997	Totals
Receipts	$74,460	$61,813	$29,568	$165,841
Disburse	37,439	33,889	8,841	80,169
Cash	83,638	111,565	132,292	n/a
Contributions	17,620	18,500	4,500	40,620
Republicans	13,620	15,500	2,000	31,120
No. of Cand.	*5*	*5*	*2*	*12*
House	6,620	15,500	1,000	23,120
Senate	7,000	0	1,000	8,000
Democrats	3,500	3,000	2,000	8,500
No. of Cand.	*1*	*1*	*1*	*3*
House	3,500	3,000	2,000	8,500
Senate	0	0	0	0
Incumbents	6,000	15,500	4,500	26,000
Challengers	5,620	3,000	0	8,620
Open Seat	6,000	0	0	6,000
Winners	14,120	10,000	n/a	24,120
Losers	3,500	8,500	n/a	12,000

Aircraft Owners and Pilots Association

*Phone: (301) 695-2000 * Fax: (301) 695-2357*
421 Aviation Way, Frederick, MD 21701-4798
Web: www.aopa.org

The Aircraft Owners and Pilots Association is a nonprofit organization dedicated to general aviation. AOPA has a membership base of more than 340,000, or half of all pilots in the United States.

Based on past experience, the group said it expects to provide about $300,000 in 1998 to help candidates for the House and Senate who support private aviation. Several candidates supported by the PAC are pilots and AOPA members.

AOPA opposes aviation "user fees" proposed by the Clinton Administration which would be collected during 2000-2003. It favors independent agency status for the Federal Aviation Administration and incremental modernization of the FAA's air traffic control system.

The only general aviation PAC to contribute at least $5,000 to 1996 congressional elections, AOPA favored Republican candidates. Sixteen candidates received $10,000 from the group, including Sens. John D. Rockefeller IV, D-W.Va., and Sam Brownback, R-Kan., and Reps. James L. Oberstar, D-Minn., and William O. Lipinski, D-Ill. All are members of aviation or transportation-related committees.

AOPA has another federal PAC which contributed $23,000 to congressional candidates during 1997.

Aircraft Owners and Pilots Association Political Action Committee (C00131185) *Phone: (202) 479-4050 * Fax: (202) 484-1312 * 500 E St. S.W., Suite 920, Washington, DC 20024 * E-mail: rick.hodges@aopa.org * Treasurer: Roger Myers * Contact: Rick Hodges, PAC Dir.*

	1993-94	1995-96	1997	Totals
Receipts	$1,419,776	$640,047	$7,313	$2,067,136
Disburse	1,283,336	892,545	66,993	2,242,874
Cash	306,159	53,663	26,207	n/a
Contributions	478,100	467,000	45,000	990,100
Republicans	227,000	332,000	42,000	601,000
No. of Cand.	*79*	*107*	*30*	*216*
House	145,000	214,000	26,500	385,500
Senate	82,000	118,000	15,500	215,500
Democrats	229,100	135,000	2,000	366,100
No. of Cand.	*82*	*61*	*2*	*145*
House	144,100	97,500	1,000	242,600
Senate	85,000	37,500	1,000	123,500
Incumbents	393,500	352,000	38,000	783,500
Challengers	17,000	41,000	5,000	63,000
Open Seat	67,500	72,000	0	139,500
Winners	401,000	360,750	n/a	761,750
Losers	77,100	106,250	n/a	183,350

Airport Systems International Inc.

*Phone: (913) 492-0861 * Fax: (913) 492-0870*
11300 W. 89th St., Overland Park, KS 66214

Formed in 1991, Airport Systems International is a publicly traded manufacturer of ground-based communication and navigational equipment for aircraft and a provider of ground-based navigational design services. Its products are in use in 40 countries and the company secured an $18 million contract with Indonesia in 1997.

Airport Systems International employs 129 people. Its sales in 1997 were about $20 million.

Its principal products are instrument landing systems, very high-frequency omni-range transmitters and distance-measuring equipment and airfield signs. Close to 90 percent of Airport Systems International's sales are to aviation authorities outside the United States.

Airport Systems International Inc. PAC (C00301226) *Address: same as sponsor * Treasurer: Thomas C. Cargin * Contact: Walter H. Stowell Jr., Chairman*

	1993-94	1995-96	1997	Totals
Receipts	$0	$12,799	$4,258	$17,057
Disburse	0	8,750	0	8,750
Cash	0	4,052	8,311	n/a
Contributions	0	8,250	0	8,250
Republicans	0	5,750	0	5,750
No. of Cand.	*0*	*12*	*2*	*14*
House	0	1,750	500	2,250
Senate	0	4,000	-500	3,500
Democrats	0	2,500	0	2,500
No. of Cand.	*0*	*5*	*0*	*5*
House	0	2,250	0	2,250
Senate	0	250	0	250
Incumbents	0	3,000	0	3,000
Challengers	0	1,500	0	1,500
Open Seat	0	3,750	0	3,750
Winners	0	5,500	n/a	5,500
Losers	0	2,750	n/a	2,750

Alaska Air Group Inc.

*Phone: (206) 431-3805 * Fax: (206) 433-3379*
P.O. Box 68900, Seattle, WA 98168
Web: www.alaskaair.com

Alaska Air Group is the publicly traded holding company for Alaska Airlines and Horizon Air Industries.

Founded in 1932, Alaska Airlines provides air service to 36 cities in Alaska, Arizona, California, Nevada, Oregon, Washington state, British Columbia, and eight destinations in Mexico and Russia. Its major hubs are in Anchorage, Alaska; Seattle; and Portland, Ore.

Horizon Air, established in 1981, provides air transportation to 40 destinations in Washington, Oregon, California, Idaho, Montana, Wyoming and Canada. Its major hubs are in Seattle, Portland, Spokane, Wash. and Boise, Idaho.

In December 1997, Alaska Air Group completed installation of "hush kits" on eight of its Boeing 737-200s, making it the first major U.S. airline to operate an all "Stage 3" fleet, two years ahead of the federal mandate. The mandate requires all commercial carriers to meet quieter Stage 3 noise standards by the year 2000.

Alaska Air Group Inc. Political Action Committee (C00024349) *Address: same as sponsor * Treasurer: Harry G. Lehr * Contact: William L. MacKay, Chairman*

	1993-94	1995-96	1997	Totals
Receipts	$28,650	$14,600	$13,900	$57,150
Disburse	21,000	25,587	9,032	55,619
Cash	12,085	1,098	5,958	n/a
Contributions	15,000	21,550	9,000	45,550
Republicans	6,250	16,000	5,000	27,250
No. of Cand.	*7*	*11*	*8*	*26*
House	3,000	8,500	2,500	14,000
Senate	3,250	7,500	2,500	13,250
Democrats	8,750	5,550	3,500	17,800
No. of Cand.	*10*	*7*	*4*	*21*
House	4,750	4,000	1,500	10,250
Senate	4,000	1,550	2,000	7,550
Incumbents	12,500	16,550	8,500	37,550
Challengers	2,500	1,000	0	3,500
Open Seat	0	4,000	0	4,000
Winners	10,750	16,050	n/a	26,800
Losers	4,250	5,500	n/a	9,750

Allison Engine Co.

*Phone: (317) 230-2000 * Fax: (317) 230-5100*
P.O. Box 420, Indianapolis, IN 46206
Web: www.allison.com

Allison Engine, a subsidiary of Rolls-Royce, is headquartered in Indianapolis and manufactures aerospace and aircraft equipment. The company employs 4,300 people.

Allison Engine provides aircraft parts to the Navy, Army and Air Force, as well as overseas companies.

A suit was filed in November 1997 against engine designers Allison Engine and Lockheed Martin by the families of five Air Force crew members who died in a crash. The crewmen were killed after the engines of their HC-130P rescue plane stopped running and repeated efforts to restart them failed.

Allison Engine Co. Political Action Committee (Allison Engine Co. PAC) (C00296822) *Address: same as sponsor * Treasurer: Beth Taylor*

	1993-94	1995-96	1997	Totals
Receipts	$10,898	$71,282	$36,328	$118,508
Disburse	3,446	46,929	26,419	76,794
Cash	7,452	31,810	41,720	n/a
Contributions	2,500	31,929	25,209	59,638
Republicans	1,000	19,679	18,709	39,388
No. of Cand.	*1*	*23*	*19*	*43*
House	1,000	16,567	14,709	32,276
Senate	0	3,112	4,000	7,112
Democrats	1,500	12,250	6,500	20,250
No. of Cand.	*2*	*11*	*9*	*22*
House	1,500	12,250	4,500	18,250
Senate	0	0	2,000	2,000
Incumbents	2,500	26,173	23,709	52,382
Challengers	0	1,250	0	1,250
Open Seat	0	4,500	1,500	6,000
Winners	1,000	28,673	n/a	29,673
Losers	1,500	3,256	n/a	4,756

America West Airlines Inc.

*Phone: (602) 693-5751 * Fax: (602) 693-5904*
4000 E. Sky Harbor Blvd., Phoenix, AZ 85034
Web: www.americawest.com

America West Airlines is the ninth-largest commercial airline carrier in the United States, operating through its principal hubs located in Phoenix and Las Vegas, and a mini-hub located in Columbus, Ohio. The airline's publicly traded holding company, America West Holding Corp., posted 1997 sales of $1.7 billion.

AWA is one of the lowest-cost full-service carriers in the United States. It serves 56 destinations, including six in Mexico and one in Canada, with a fleet of 101 aircraft. AWA offers service to an additional 18 destinations, through an alliance agreement with Continental Airlines, and 17 other commuter service and regional destinations.

America West Airlines Inc. Federal PAC (C00313650) *Address: same as sponsor * Treasurer: C. A. Howlett*

	1993-94	*1995-96*	*1997*	*Totals*
Receipts	$0	$24,771	$17,187	$41,958
Disburse	0	12,420	6,450	18,870
Cash	0	12,353	22,355	n/a
Contributions	0	11,850	5,450	17,300
Republicans	0	10,850	5,450	16,300
No. of Cand.	*0*	*12*	*7*	*19*
House	0	8,850	3,450	12,300
Senate	0	2,000	2,000	4,000
Democrats	0	1,000	0	1,000
No. of Cand.	*0*	*2*	*0*	*2*
House	0	500	0	500
Senate	0	500	0	500
Incumbents	0	9,850	5,450	15,300
Challengers	0	1,000	0	1,000
Open Seat	0	1,000	0	1,000
Winners	0	10,350	n/a	10,350
Losers	0	1,500	n/a	1,500

American Airlines

*Phone: (817) 963-1234 * Fax: (817) 967-9641*
4333 Amon Carter Blvd., Fort Worth, TX 76155
Web: www.amrcorp.com

American Airlines is the main subsidiary of AMR Corp., a public company headquartered in Fort Worth, Texas. The airline employs about 88,000 of AMR's 122,300 workers and set all-time company records for revenue passenger miles and load factor in 1997. It reported sales of $18.5 billion.

AMR operates American Eagle, a group of four small regional airlines. The company also owns more than 80 percent of the SABRE Group, operator of the travel reservation system SABRE.

It is one of four major airlines that has been the subject of federal regulators investigating price-cutting and anti-competitive practices at six "hub" airports. The investigation began in 1997 and expanded in February 1998. American and United Airlines together have 84 percent of the available passenger seats at Chicago's O'Hare International Airport.

AMR is concerned with most aviation-related legislation and particularly with proposals on competition within the industry. It generally opposes higher taxes on airline tickets.

The company ranked first among airline PACs in contributions to 1996 congressional elections. Republicans received slightly more money than Democrats. The top recipients were Rep. Martin Frost, D-Texas, and Sens. Richard J. Durbin, D-Ill., and James M. Inhofe, R-Okla.

American Airlines Political Action Committee (C00107300)
*Phone: (202) 496-5666 * Fax: (202) 496-5660 * 1101 17th St. N.W., Washington, DC 20036 * Treasurer: Julie L. Nichols * Contact: Shane Carr, Legislative Assistant*

	1993-94	*1995-96*	*1997*	*Totals*
Receipts	$391,908	$500,731	$258,533	$1,151,172
Disburse	426,852	475,808	289,125	1,191,785
Cash	20,996	45,928	15,746	n/a
Contributions	334,800	320,817	184,331	839,948
Republicans	124,300	182,938	92,919	400,157
No. of Cand.	*77*	*102*	*62*	*241*
House	71,300	123,939	71,419	266,658
Senate	53,000	58,999	21,500	133,499
Democrats	205,250	137,879	88,811	431,940
No. of Cand.	*127*	*86*	*46*	*259*
House	160,250	107,990	34,500	302,740
Senate	45,000	29,889	54,311	129,200
Incumbents	274,850	270,178	182,831	727,859
Challengers	8,150	5,500	1,500	15,150
Open Seat	50,800	45,139	0	95,939
Winners	266,300	275,568	n/a	541,868
Losers	68,500	45,249	n/a	113,749

American Association of Airport Executives

*Phone: (703) 824-0500 x145 * Fax: (703) 820-1385*
4212 King St., Alexandria, VA 22302
*Web: www.airportnet.org * E-mail: Todd.Hauptli@airportnet.org*

The American Association of Airport Executives is the largest professional organization for airport executives in the world. It represents airport management personnel at public-use airports nationwide.

Founded in 1928, the association's members consist of airport managers, superintendents, consultants, authorities and commissions, government officials and others interested in the construction, management and operation of airports. AAAE also awards the professional designation of Accredited Airport Executive.

American Association of Airport Executives Good Government Committee (C00176727) *Address: same as sponsor * Treasurer: Charles M. Barclay * Contact: Todd Hauptli, Senior V.P. of Federal Affairs*

	1993-94	*1995-96*	*1997*	*Totals*
Receipts	$47,157	$43,380	$19,025	$109,562
Disburse	32,897	33,655	29,126	95,678
Cash	18,191	27,925	17,828	n/a
Contributions	32,848	32,300	29,000	94,148
Republicans	12,350	22,300	17,000	51,650
No. of Cand.	*7*	*15*	*13*	*35*
House	4,350	13,800	12,000	30,150
Senate	8,000	8,500	5,000	21,500
Democrats	17,998	10,000	10,000	37,998
No. of Cand.	*19*	*5*	*6*	*30*
House	12,000	9,500	2,000	23,500
Senate	5,998	500	8,000	14,498
Incumbents	29,848	30,800	29,000	89,648
Challengers	0	1,000	0	1,000
Open Seat	3,000	500	0	3,500
Winners	27,848	23,500	n/a	51,348
Losers	5,000	8,800	n/a	13,800

Boeing Co.

*Phone: (206) 655-1968 * Fax: (206) 655-7004*
P.O. Box 3707, Mailstop 10-06, Seattle, WA 98124-2207
Web: www.boeing.com

Boeing manufactures jet airplanes, helicopters and systems for missile and aerospace programs. A public company based in Seattle, Boeing has more than 9,000 jetliners in service worldwide. The company's 1997 merger with McDonnell Douglas, the world's top military aircraft producer, makes Boeing the leading aerospace company in the world.

Boeing has 143,000 employees and operations in Washington state, California, Kansas, Pennsylvania, Missouri, Florida and Alabama. It reported 1997 sales of more than $45 billion.

Boeing's defense group is developing, with partners, the F-22 fighter, the V-22 tiltrotor aircraft and the RAH-66 Comanche helicopter. The addition of McDonnell Douglas gives the company the F/A-18 Hornet and F-15 Eagle fighters. The company has contracts for orders from Germany, Italy, Malaysia, Saudi Arabia and China, among other nations. The company also builds communication satellites and is developing a solar-powered payload transfer vehicle for the Air Force.

Boeing's PAC was the leading airplane manufacturing contributor to 1996 congressional candidates. It supported mostly Republican candidates and gave 97 percent of its money to incumbents. The top recipients were former Rep. Randy Tate, R-Wash., Rep. Rick White, R-Wash., Sen. Ted Stevens, R-Alaska, and Rep. Todd Tiahrt, R-Kan. Seven of the top 10 recipients were from Boeing's home state of Washington.

The McDonnell Douglas PAC contributed slightly more to congressional campaigns than did Boeing. Its contribution patterns were similar to Boeing's. The leading recipients were Rep. Jane Harman, D-Calif., Rep. James M. Talent, R-Mo., and Stevens.

Boeing Co. Political Action Committee (BPAC) (C00142711)
*Phone: (703) 558-9600 * Fax: (703) 558-9674 * 1700 N. Moore St., 21st Floor, Arlington, VA 22209 * E-mail: m.little@wdc.mdc.com * Treasurer: Michael N. Matton * Contact: Maria S. Little, PAC Administrator*

	1993-94	1995-96	1997	Totals
Receipts	$351,382	$384,902	$283,121	$1,019,405
Disburse	324,966	370,105	183,431	878,502
Cash	35,783	50,590	150,286	n/a
Contributions	286,521	341,105	179,619	807,245
Republicans	96,976	252,155	119,869	469,000
No. of Cand.	*58*	*120*	*105*	*283*
House	55,300	182,711	91,869	329,880
Senate	41,676	69,444	28,000	139,120
Democrats	187,545	88,950	59,250	335,745
No. of Cand.	*104*	*63*	*54*	*221*
House	146,675	80,500	45,500	272,675
Senate	40,870	8,450	13,750	63,070
Incumbents	267,021	314,088	179,619	760,728
Challengers	5,000	6,000	0	11,000
Open Seat	13,500	20,517	0	34,017
Winners	217,376	299,105	n/a	516,481
Losers	69,145	42,000	n/a	111,145

McDonnell Douglas Employees' Political Action Committee (C00040667) *Phone: (703) 558-3232 * Fax: (703) 558-9674 * 1700 N. Moore St., 20th Floor, Arlington, VA 22209 * E-mail: m.little@wdc.mdc.com * Treasurer: Michael N. Matton * Contact: Maria S. Little, PAC Administrator*

McDonnell Douglas had its roots as a producer of military and commercial airplanes and space vehicles before merging with Boeing in 1997. Before the merger, the company employed about 64,600 people.

	1993-94	1995-96	1997	Totals
Receipts	$234,927	$412,659	$232,528	$880,114
Disburse	247,901	389,367	228,745	866,013
Cash	23,331	40,105	43,894	n/a
Contributions	240,500	353,570	193,250	787,320
Republicans	80,150	230,570	124,000	434,720
No. of Cand.	*72*	*131*	*109*	*312*
House	56,150	164,549	98,000	318,699
Senate	24,000	66,021	26,000	116,021
Democrats	159,850	123,000	67,750	350,600
No. of Cand.	*110*	*76*	*76*	*262*
House	127,350	116,500	56,250	300,100
Senate	32,500	6,500	11,500	50,500
Incumbents	229,000	343,870	194,250	767,120
Challengers	1,000	2,200	0	3,200
Open Seat	10,500	7,000	0	17,500
Winners	206,750	317,370	n/a	524,120
Losers	33,750	36,200	n/a	69,950

Coltec Industries Inc.

*Phone: (704) 423-7101 * Fax: (704) 423-7011*
3 Coliseum Centre, 2550 W. Tyvola Rd., Charlotte, NC 28217
Web: www.coltec.com

Coltec Industries manufactures aerospace and industrial products in the United States and abroad. The publicly traded company, headquartered in North Carolina, employs 8,200 workers and reported sales of more than $1 billion in 1997.

In January 1998, Coltec purchased three Texas companies for $40 million. Tex-o-lon and Repro-lon are both involved in the semiconductor industry. Marine and Petroleum Mfg. Inc. manufactures products for the petrochemical industry. Coltec also purchased the sealing division of Carbone Lorraine for $47 million in February 1998.

Coltec Industries Voluntary Political Committee (formerly known as Colt Industries Voluntary Political Committee) (C00025205)
*Address: same as sponsor * Treasurer: John N. Maier*

	1993-94	1995-96	1997	Totals
Receipts	$66,224	$50,971	$20,361	$137,556
Disburse	61,770	67,538	16,597	145,905
Cash	73,158	56,597	60,362	n/a
Contributions	46,750	51,600	12,500	110,850
Republicans	28,500	38,000	9,000	75,500
No. of Cand.	*35*	*34*	*11*	*80*
House	11,500	18,000	4,000	33,500
Senate	17,000	20,000	5,000	42,000
Democrats	18,250	13,600	3,500	35,350
No. of Cand.	*17*	*9*	*6*	*32*
House	15,250	12,100	2,500	29,850
Senate	3,000	1,500	1,000	5,500
Incumbents	40,250	42,600	11,500	94,350
Challengers	1,500	3,000	1,000	5,500
Open Seat	5,000	6,000	0	11,000
Winners	38,750	45,600	n/a	84,350
Losers	8,000	6,000	n/a	14,000

Continental Airlines

*Phone: (713) 834-2950 * Fax: (713) 520-6329*
2929 Allen Pkwy., Suite 2010, Houston, TX 77019
Web: www.flycontinental.com

Continental Airlines is the fifth-largest airline in the United States, offering more than 2,000 departures daily to 132 domestic and 57 international destinations. Operating major hubs in Newark, N.J.; Houston; Cleveland; and Guam, Continental offers extensive service to North America, Latin America and Europe.

The Houston-based company recently joined other large airlines in lobbying successfully for an agreement with Japan that allows more nonstop flights per week into that country.

The publicly traded company reported 1997 revenues of $7.2 billion and was ranked the top airline in customer satisfaction among the nine major U.S. carriers on long-haul flights. About 92 percent of its revenue came from passenger services; the company also carries cargo and mail.

Continental distributed $105 million in profit-sharing payments to its employees in 1997. The figure represents 7 percent of annual wages.

Continental Airlines Inc. Employee Fund for a Better America (formerly known as Continental Holdings PAC) (C00101766)
*Phone: (202) 289-6060 * Fax: (202) 289-1546 * 1350 Eye St. N.W., Suite 1250, P.O. Box 12788, Washington, DC 20005 * Treasurer: Rebecca Cox * Contact: Nancy H. VanDuyne, Staff V.P.*

	1993-94	1995-96	1997	Totals
Receipts	$35,888	$155,713	$106,286	$297,887
Disburse	47,034	94,447	103,471	244,952
Cash	4,143	65,420	68,243	n/a
Contributions	44,500	62,250	49,500	156,250
Republicans	25,500	40,000	27,500	93,000
No. of Cand.	*14*	*28*	*21*	*63*
House	9,000	21,000	8,500	38,500
Senate	16,500	19,000	19,000	54,500
Democrats	19,000	22,250	21,000	62,250
No. of Cand.	*13*	*12*	*13*	*38*
House	10,000	12,250	13,000	35,250
Senate	9,000	10,000	8,000	27,000
Incumbents	40,500	41,250	44,500	126,250
Challengers	0	5,000	0	5,000
Open Seat	4,000	16,000	5,000	25,000
Winners	37,500	43,250	n/a	80,750
Losers	7,000	19,000	n/a	26,000

Delta Air Lines Inc.

*Phone: (404) 715-2455 * Fax: (404) 715-4779*
Hartsfield Atlanta International Airport,
Department 976, Atlanta, GA 30320-6001
Web: www.delta-air.com

Based on 1997 data, Delta is the largest U.S. airline as measured by aircraft departures and passengers carried and the third-largest U.S. airline as measured by operating revenues and revenue passenger miles flown. The publicly traded company posted $13.5 billion in 1997 sales.

Delta serves 149 cities in the United States, Puerto Rico and the Virgin Islands, as well as 41 cities in 25 foreign countries.

The company offers a frequent-flyer program called SkyMiles, SkyMiles credit cards through American Express and telecommunications products and services through DeltaTel, a wholly owned subsidiary.

Delta Air Lines Inc. Political Action Committee (C00076133)
*Phone: (202) 296-6464 * Fax: (202) 466-2610 * 1629 K St., Suite 501, Washington, DC 20006 * Treasurer: Delores Gallego*
*Contact: Harold L. Bevis, Chairman * Phone: (404) 715-2455*

	1993-94	1995-96	1997	Totals
Receipts	$153,353	$143,143	$89,286	$385,782
Disburse	161,770	145,844	96,000	403,614
Cash	15,888	13,187	6,479	n/a
Contributions	101,756	79,250	66,500	247,506

Republicans	46,800	63,750	51,000	161,550
No. of Cand.	*34*	*49*	*35*	*118*
House	21,800	48,250	32,000	102,050
Senate	25,000	15,500	19,000	59,500
Democrats	51,956	15,500	14,500	81,956
No. of Cand.	*43*	*21*	*16*	*80*
House	39,456	13,500	10,000	62,956
Senate	12,500	2,000	4,500	19,000
Incumbents	88,906	77,750	63,500	230,156
Challengers	3,500	500	0	4,000
Open Seat	8,350	1,000	3,000	12,350
Winners	80,800	68,250	n/a	149,050
Losers	20,956	11,000	n/a	31,956

Federal Express Corp.

*Phone: (901) 395-5171 * Fax: (901) 395-5172*
1980 Nonconnah Blvd., Memphis, TN 38132
Web: www.fedex.com

A leader in the overnight delivery business, Federal Express also offers freight shipping in more than 210 countries. The public company, based in Memphis, Tenn., has 126,000 employees. It reported 1997 sales of $11.5 billion.

FDX, the holding company for Federal Express, has five other units, including RPS, the second-largest domestic ground carrier of small packages; Roberts Express, the world's largest ground door-to-door, time-specific delivery service; and Viking Freight, a less-than-truckload carrier in the Western United States. FDX was formed in early 1998 after Federal Express acquired Caliber System Inc., an Ohio delivery company.

Federal Express follows legislation relating to transportation and aviation issues, including funding for ISTEA and the Federal Aviation Administration. It also lobbies on tax policy and trucking issues.

In 1996, Federal Express and its chairman contributed $275,000 to the Democratic National Committee and met with President Clinton to press for economic sanctions against Japan, which had refused to allow the company to deliver cargo from Japan to other Asian nations.

The company ranked second among express delivery businesses, behind United Parcel Service, in PAC contributions to 1996 congressional candidates. UPS contributed nearly twice as much money. About 70 percent of Federal Express' contributions went to Republican candidates. The leading recipients were Reps. Bob Clement, D-Tenn., John A. Boehner, R-Ohio, and Todd Tiahrt, R-Kan.

The Caliber System and Viking Freight PACs ranked fifth and eighth, respectively, among trucking companies in contributions to 1996 congressional elections. Neither PAC contributed more than $4,000 to any single congressional candidate.

Federal Express Corp. Political Action Committee (FEPAC) (C00068692) *Phone: (202) 546-1631 * Fax: (202) 546-3309 * 300 Maryland Ave. N.E., Washington, DC 20002 * Treasurer: A. Doyle Cloud Jr. * Contact: Marque Ledoux, Senior Federal Representative*

	1993-94	*1995-96*	*1997*	*Totals*
Receipts	$1,389,291	$1,725,213	$903,408	$4,017,912
Disburse	1,372,787	1,594,191	738,414	3,705,392
Cash	66,416	197,442	362,437	n/a
Contributions	816,600	943,000	379,250	2,138,850
Republicans	254,500	664,500	263,250	1,182,250
No. of Cand.	*81*	*211*	*133*	*425*
House	162,500	497,500	186,250	846,250
Senate	92,000	167,000	77,000	336,000
Democrats	552,100	277,500	113,000	942,600
No. of Cand.	*140*	*110*	*41*	*291*
House	413,500	218,000	61,500	693,000
Senate	138,600	59,500	51,500	249,600
Incumbents	706,100	745,500	354,250	1,805,850
Challengers	12,000	36,000	1,000	49,000
Open Seat	98,500	161,000	11,000	270,500
Winners	617,000	717,500	n/a	1,334,500
Losers	199,600	225,500	n/a	425,100

Caliber System Inc. (CalPAC) (C00106245) *Phone: (330) 665-8800 * Fax: (330) 665-8803 * P.O. Box 5459, Akron, OH 44334 * Treasurer: Kathryn W. Dindo*

*Phone: (703) 528-0233 * Fax: (703) 276-0594 * 1600 Wilson Blvd., Suite 807, Arlington, VA 22209 * Contact: Gerald Hughes, Gov. Affairs Dir.*

	1993-94	*1995-96*	*1997*	*Totals*
Receipts	$74,798	$169,245	$38,432	$282,475
Disburse	65,961	91,181	36,032	193,174
Cash	16,246	94,315	95,139	n/a
Contributions	57,800	67,300	26,750	151,850
Republicans	35,550	55,800	16,750	108,100
No. of Cand.	*45*	*63*	*24*	*132*
House	23,550	31,550	9,750	64,850
Senate	12,000	24,250	7,000	43,250
Democrats	21,000	11,500	10,000	42,500
No. of Cand.	*28*	*12*	*6*	*46*
House	17,000	9,000	4,000	30,000
Senate	4,000	2,500	6,000	12,500
Incumbents	48,300	56,000	23,250	127,550
Challengers	3,500	5,000	500	9,000
Open Seat	6,000	6,300	3,000	15,300
Winners	50,050	52,000	n/a	102,050
Losers	7,750	15,300	n/a	23,050

Viking Freight Inc. Political Action Committee (VikPAC) (C00213157) *411 E. Plumeria Dr., Suite 130, San Jose, CA 95134 * Treasurer: John B. Keen*

The Viking Freight PAC was terminated in 1996. The company was a subsidiary of Caliber System, which was purchased by Federal Express.

	1993-94	*1995-96*	*1997*	*Totals*
Receipts	$78,981	$55,854	$0	$134,835
Disburse	71,703	141,661	0	213,364
Cash	85,804	0	0	n/a
Contributions	22,495	19,000	0	41,495
Republicans	12,000	15,500	0	27,500
No. of Cand.	*20*	*19*	*0*	*39*
House	7,500	10,500	0	18,000
Senate	4,500	5,000	0	9,500
Democrats	10,495	3,500	0	13,995
No. of Cand.	*11*	*6*	*0*	*17*
House	8,995	3,500	0	12,495
Senate	1,500	0	0	1,500
Incumbents	17,345	15,000	0	32,345
Challengers	750	0	0	750
Open Seat	4,400	4,000	0	8,400
Winners	20,995	11,000	n/a	31,995
Losers	1,500	8,000	n/a	9,500

General Aviation Manufacturers Association

*Phone: (202) 393-1500 * Fax: (202) 842-4063*
1400 K St. N.W., Suite 801, Washington, DC 20005
Web: www.generalaviation.org

The General Aviation Manufacturers Association is a Washington-based national trade association representing manufacturers of aircraft components. It represents more than 54 manufacturers of fixed-wing aircraft, engines, avionics and components. Members include: Allied Signal, Boeing and Honeywell.

General Aviation Manufacturers Association Political Action Committee (GAMAPAC) (C00014878) *Address: same as sponsor * Treasurer: Jahan Ahmad*

	1993-94	*1995-96*	*1997*	*Totals*
Receipts	$53,573	$73,423	$21,325	$148,321
Disburse	41,036	50,882	34,996	126,914
Cash	26,971	49,516	35,845	n/a
Contributions	37,250	46,250	40,700	124,200
Republicans	12,700	37,250	26,500	76,450
No. of Cand.	*16*	*28*	*19*	*63*
House	7,950	18,750	12,500	39,200
Senate	4,750	18,500	14,000	37,250
Democrats	22,250	9,000	12,200	43,450
No. of Cand.	*33*	*9*	*10*	*52*
House	17,750	6,000	2,000	25,750
Senate	4,500	3,000	10,200	17,700
Incumbents	32,000	41,250	40,700	113,950
Challengers	500	2,500	0	3,000
Open Seat	4,750	1,500	0	6,250
Winners	28,150	33,750	n/a	61,900
Losers	9,100	12,500	n/a	21,600

Gulfstream Aerospace

*Phone: (912) 965-3000 * Fax: (912) 965-3775*
P.O. Box 2206, Savannah, GA 31402
Web: www.gulfstreamaircraft.com

Gulfstream Aerospace is the world's biggest maker of large business jet aircraft. The publicly traded company reported 1997 sales of $1.9 billion.

Gulfstream also offers aircraft services, including exterior painting and installation of customized interiors and optional avionics. It provides maintenance services and technical support for Gulfstream aircraft worldwide.

Founded in 1958, the company has about 5,000 employees. Private investment company Forstmann Little & Co. owns more than 40 percent of Gulfstream.

Gulfstream Aerospace Political Action Committee (C00158873)
*Phone: (703) 276-9500 * Fax: (703) 276-9516 * 1000 Wilson Blvd., Suite 2701, Arlington, VA 22209 * Treasurer: Edward W. Shaw*

*Contact: Helen Newman, Chairperson * Phone: (912) 965-3000*

	1993-94	1995-96	1997	Totals
Receipts	$25,572	$30,928	$19,286	$75,786
Disburse	24,898	27,523	8,500	60,921
Cash	2,106	5,516	16,304	n/a
Contributions	23,898	26,500	6,500	56,898
Republicans	6,198	21,500	4,000	31,698
No. of Cand.	7	15	4	26
House	3,948	11,000	2,000	16,948
Senate	2,250	10,500	2,000	14,750
Democrats	17,700	5,000	2,500	25,200
No. of Cand.	15	4	3	22
House	13,200	4,000	1,500	18,700
Senate	4,500	1,000	1,000	6,500
Incumbents	21,398	25,500	6,500	53,398
Challengers	0	0	0	0
Open Seat	2,500	1,000	0	3,500
Winners	17,698	25,000	n/a	42,698
Losers	6,200	1,500	n/a	7,700

Northwest Airlines Corp.

*Phone: (612) 726-2491 * Fax: (612) 726-3943*
5101 Northwest Dr., Department A1500, St. Paul, MN 55111-3035
Web: www.nwa.com

Northwest Airlines is the nation's fourth-largest passenger and air cargo carrier. It operates hubs in Minneapolis-St. Paul, Detroit, Memphis, Tenn. and Tokyo. Together with major airline alliances and Northwest Airlink partners, Northwest serves more than 390 cities in 80 countries on six continents. The airline has more destinations in Asia than any other U.S. airline, including the most nonstop flights between the United States and Japan.

A publicly traded company, Northwest has more than 47,000 employees and reported $10.2 billion in revenues during 1997.

Northwest's other interests include the WORLDSPAN computer reservation system and subsidiaries such as MLT Inc. and Northwest Aerospace Training Corp. Northwest has on order 115 aircraft, including Boeing 747-400s and 757-200s and Airbus A320s, A330s and A319s.

Northwest Airlines Political Action Committee (formerly known as Republic Airlines PAC) (C00104802) *Address: same as sponsor * Treasurer: J. O. Klinkenberg*

	1993-94	1995-96	1997	Totals
Receipts	$153,702	$222,997	$112,924	$489,623
Disburse	219,090	212,093	135,700	566,883
Cash	58,147	69,074	46,297	n/a
Contributions	161,541	144,730	102,390	408,661
Republicans	55,825	72,100	58,390	186,315
No. of Cand.	33	49	36	118
House	28,075	53,600	39,390	121,065
Senate	27,750	18,500	19,000	65,250
Democrats	88,216	72,630	38,500	199,346
No. of Cand.	47	41	26	114
House	58,096	46,500	15,500	120,096
Senate	30,120	26,130	23,000	79,250
Incumbents	134,341	128,350	103,390	366,081
Challengers	2,700	7,250	-500	9,450
Open Seat	22,500	8,630	0	31,130
Winners	117,225	124,850	n/a	242,075
Losers	44,316	19,880	n/a	64,196

Sabreliner Corp.

Phone: (314) 863-6880
7733 Forsyth Blvd., Suite 1500, Pierre Laclede Center, St. Louis, MO 63105

Sabreliner is a diversified aerospace company. The publicly held company provides services in airframe maintenance and modification, gas turbine engine overhaul and repair, aircraft systems upgrades and refurbishment, fleet logistics support and other aerospace products and services for aviation markets.

In 1997, Sabreliner and its wholly owned subsidiaries Midcoast Aviation Inc., SabreTech Inc., Dimension Aviation Inc. and Turbotech Repairs Inc. reported revenues of $260.9 million, of which 33 percent was provided by corporate aviation, 26 percent by commercial aviation and 41 percent by government aviation business.

SabrePAC Sabreliner Corp. Political Action Committee (C00178053) *Address: same as sponsor * Treasurer: Susan Seabury Aselage*

	1993-94	1995-96	1997	Totals
Receipts	$12,475	$20,825	$19,675	$52,975
Disburse	7,699	25,802	9,806	43,307
Cash	5,484	504	10,372	n/a
Contributions	5,500	16,300	9,450	31,250
Republicans	5,500	8,500	6,000	20,000
No. of Cand.	4	8	6	18
House	3,500	6,750	2,500	12,750
Senate	2,000	1,750	3,500	7,250
Democrats	0	7,800	3,450	11,250
No. of Cand.	0	6	3	9
House	0	7,300	3,450	10,750
Senate	0	500	0	500
Incumbents	3,000	11,550	9,450	24,000
Challengers	0	0	0	0
Open Seat	2,500	4,750	0	7,250
Winners	5,000	12,300	n/a	17,300
Losers	500	4,000	n/a	4,500

Sundstrand Corp.

*Phone: (815) 226-2136 * Fax: (815) 226-5399*
4949 Harrison Ave., P.O. Box 7003, Rockford, IL 61125-7003
Web: www.snds.com

Sundstrand designs and makes technology-based products for industrial and aerospace markets. Its electrical and mechanical products are used by most commercial airplanes and many military aircraft.

Sundstrand is a publicly held company with more than 10,000 employees. It reported 1997 sales of $1.75 billion. Sundstrand is based in Illinois, but maintains factories and offices throughout the United States, Asia, Europe and South America.

Subsidiaries include: Sundstrand Aerospace, which specializes in electric power generation and management and small engine turbine power; The Falk Co., which supplies small and large precision power transmission equipment; Milton Roy, which supplies metering pumps and systems to the water treatment industry; Hartell, which manufactures a line of small specialty pumps for consumer and commercial applications; Sullair, which provides compressed air solutions; and Sundstrand Fluid Handling, which manufactures engineered pumps and compressors.

In February 1997, Sundstrand established a new wholly owned subsidiary, Sundstrand Aerospace Germany, to manufacture solid state power controllers for aircraft electric power management systems.

Sundstrand Corp. Good Government Program (C00095422)
*Address: same as sponsor * Treasurer: Kenneth A. Bailey * Contact: Doug Smiley, PAC Dir.*

	1993-94	1995-96	1997	Totals
Receipts	$156,212	$147,615	$47,099	$350,926
Disburse	184,293	146,846	197,388	528,527
Cash	151,019	-2320	2,102	n/a
Contributions	14,526	16,064	4,691	35,281
Republicans	13,506	15,494	4,601	33,601
No. of Cand.	19	19	8	46
House	8,496	13,215	4,601	26,312
Senate	5,010	2,279	0	7,289
Democrats	1,020	570	90	1,680
No. of Cand.	6	3	1	10
House	1,020	570	90	1,680
Senate	0	0	0	0
Incumbents	11,221	13,165	4,691	29,077

Challengers	1,460	670	0	2,130
Open Seat	1,845	2,229	0	4,074
Winners	13,116	12,990	n/a	26,106
Losers	1,410	3,074	n/a	4,484

Sundstrand Corp. Good Government Support Fund (C00107169) *Phone: (703) 276-1626 * Fax: (703) 528-9415 * Two Colonial Pl., 2101 Wilson Blvd., Suite 1002, Arlington, VA 22201 * Treasurer: Kenneth A. Bailey * Contact: Ed Bullard, Washington Operations Dir.*

*Contact: Doug Smiley, PAC Dir. * Phone: (815) 226-2136*

	1993-94	1995-96	1997	Totals
Receipts	$16,982	$23,411	$15,169	$55,562
Disburse	9,345	29,630	8,129	47,104
Cash	7,640	580	8,452	n/a
Contributions	1,816	18,025	3,660	23,501
Republicans	1,000	18,025	2,750	21,775
No. of Cand.	*3*	*25*	*5*	*33*
House	1,000	12,025	2,750	15,775
Senate	0	6,000	0	6,000
Democrats	816	0	910	1,726
No. of Cand.	*3*	*0*	*2*	*5*
House	816	0	410	1,226
Senate	0	0	500	500
Incumbents	1,816	9,725	3,660	15,201
Challengers	0	2,300	0	2,300
Open Seat	0	6,000	0	6,000
Winners	1,816	14,225	n/a	16,041
Losers	0	3,800	n/a	3,800

UNC Inc.

Phone: (410) 266-7333
175 Admiral Cochran Dr., Annapolis, MD 21401

UNC's PAC filed for termination in September 1997.

UNC Inc. Public Responsibility Fund (C00167197) *Address: same as sponsor * Treasurer: Gregory M. Bubb*

	1993-94	1995-96	1997	Totals
Receipts	$49,097	$34,583	$3,771	$87,451
Disburse	36,054	46,946	14,613	97,613
Cash	23,204	10,841	0	n/a
Contributions	26,198	9,200	4,750	40,148
Republicans	16,498	5,500	2,250	24,248
No. of Cand.	*9*	*6*	*4*	*19*
House	5,100	5,500	2,250	12,850
Senate	11,398	0	0	11,398
Democrats	9,200	3,700	2,500	15,400
No. of Cand.	*8*	*4*	*3*	*15*
House	3,700	1,600	500	5,800
Senate	5,500	2,100	2,000	9,600
Incumbents	14,600	8,200	4,750	27,550
Challengers	9,998	0	0	9,998
Open Seat	1,600	0	0	1,600
Winners	15,200	7,700	n/a	22,900
Losers	10,998	1,500	n/a	12,498

US Airways

Phone: (703) 418-7411
Crystal Park Four, 2345 Crystal Drive, Arlington, VA 22227
Web: www.usairways.com

US Airways, formerly USAir, is the sixth-largest domestic airline. The public company has hubs in Pittsburgh, Baltimore, Philadelphia and Charlotte, N.C. It launched service to London and Paris in 1998.

US Airways, which employs about 42,000 workers, reported 1997 sales of $8.5 billion. The company discussed potential partnerships with United Airlines and American Airlines in early 1998, but those talks did not focus on mergers, according to The Wall Street Journal.

US Airways Political Action Committee (formerly known as USAir PAC) (C00040170) *Address: same as sponsor * Treasurer: Felicia J. Coffey*

	1993-94	1995-96	1997	Totals
Receipts	$31,314	$29,497	$14,849	$75,660
Disburse	42,034	29,604	19,965	91,603
Cash	15,469	13,872	8,757	n/a
Contributions	40,050	24,950	19,375	84,375
Republicans	21,850	17,300	14,475	53,625
No. of Cand.	*25*	*25*	*23*	*73*
House	8,850	9,350	8,475	26,675
Senate	13,000	7,950	6,000	26,950
Democrats	17,200	7,650	3,900	28,750
No. of Cand.	*25*	*15*	*7*	*47*
House	10,700	6,650	2,900	20,250
Senate	6,500	1,000	1,000	8,500
Incumbents	35,800	23,950	18,875	78,625
Challengers	3,750	500	0	4,250
Open Seat	500	500	500	1,500
Winners	32,700	21,450	n/a	54,150
Losers	7,350	3,500	n/a	10,850

United Airlines

*Phone: (847) 700-4000 * Fax: (847) 700-5229*
P.O. Box 66423, Chicago, IL 60666
Web: www.ual.com

United is a majority employee-owned airline which offers more than 2,200 flights a day to 136 destinations in 30 countries and two U.S. territories. It flies out of hubs in Chicago, Denver, San Francisco, Tokyo and Washington. United's publicly traded holding company, UAL Corp., reported 1997 sales of $17.3 billion. The company employs 91,000 workers.

The carrier has a partnership called the Star Alliance with Germany's Lufthansa and several other airlines. UAL's United Express feeds passengers from regional carriers into United's system. The company also operates Shuttle by United, offering more than 460 daily short-haul flights serving 20 western U.S. cities.

United Airlines Political Action Committee (C00078261) *Address: same as sponsor * Treasurer: Thomas A. Mutryn*

	1993-94	1995-96	1997	Totals
Receipts	$133,055	$202,695	$125,327	$461,077
Disburse	167,703	195,102	143,103	505,908
Cash	20,136	27,733	9,957	n/a
Contributions	139,500	181,550	114,350	435,400
Republicans	43,700	105,700	71,500	220,900
No. of Cand.	*34*	*67*	*57*	*158*
House	30,100	75,950	52,000	158,050
Senate	13,600	29,750	19,500	62,850
Democrats	92,800	75,850	40,350	209,000
No. of Cand.	*56*	*49*	*44*	*149*
House	55,300	53,150	18,000	126,450
Senate	37,500	22,700	22,350	82,550
Incumbents	130,300	169,100	111,850	411,250
Challengers	1,100	1,000	0	2,100
Open Seat	8,100	11,450	1,500	21,050
Winners	109,550	159,050	n/a	268,600
Losers	29,950	22,500	n/a	52,450

United Parcel Service of America Inc. (UPS)

*Phone: (404) 828-6000 * Fax: (404) 828-6593*
55 Glenlake Parkway N.E., Atlanta, GA 30328
Web: www.ups.com

UPS is the world's largest package delivery company and the nation's fifth-largest employer. It handled more than 3.1 billion packages and had $22 billion in revenues during 1996. Based in Atlanta, the company employs 338,000 people worldwide, including more than 300,000 in the United States. Many of its workers are represented by the Teamsters Union, which staged a 15-day strike in August 1997, the first in UPS's 90-year history. UPS is a private company; most company stock is owned by its employees.

Worker safety remains a large concern for the company. According to Occupational Safety and Health Administration statistics covering the past 12 years, more workers have filed complaints against UPS than against any other company. UPS is a founding member of the Welfare-to-Work Partnership, and the company announced in 1998 that it had hired 8,268 people who previously were on public assistance, including nearly 1,600 in the Chicago area.

UPS gave nearly $1.8 million to candidates during the 1995-96 election cycle, but that number was almost $1 million less than the company gave during the 1993-94 period, when it ranked first among PACs. Republican candidates received almost twice as much as Democrats during the 1996 cycle. UPS spent more than $100,000 on candidates in California, Texas and New York.

United Parcel Service of America Inc. Political Action Committee (UPSPAC) (C00064766) *Phone: (202) 675-4220 * 316 Pennsylvania Ave. S.E., Suite 300, Washington, DC 20003 * Treasurer: D. Scott Davis*

	1993-94	1995-96	1997	Totals
Receipts	$2,854,404	$2,967,944	$1,319,092	$7,141,440
Disburse	3,350,884	2,957,935	936,038	7,244,857
Cash	233,612	243,632	626,688	n/a
Contributions	2,646,113	1,788,147	572,683	5,006,943
Republicans	1,276,870	1,159,675	440,073	2,876,618
No. of Cand.	*266*	*282*	*160*	*708*
House	1,010,900	930,625	365,823	2,307,348
Senate	265,970	229,050	74,250	569,270
Democrats	1,340,043	628,472	131,210	2,099,725
No. of Cand.	*291*	*189*	*79*	*559*
House	1,176,623	581,347	115,710	1,873,680
Senate	163,420	47,125	15,500	226,045
Incumbents	2,243,048	1,507,672	542,433	4,293,153
Challengers	95,310	62,500	17,250	175,060
Open Seat	306,755	217,975	14,000	538,730
Winners	2,220,879	1,486,872	n/a	3,707,751
Losers	425,234	301,275	n/a	726,509

World Airways Inc.

*Phone: (703) 834-9200 * Fax: (703) 834-9211*
13873 Park Center Rd., Suite 490, Herndon, VA 20171
Web: www.worldair.com

World Airways provides air transportation for passengers and cargo under contracts with the U.S. military, airlines, tour operators and freight forwarders worldwide. The publicly traded Virginia company posted $309 million in 1997 sales. It is 51 percent held by WorldCorp, also a publicly traded company. A 17 percent bloc is controlled by MHS Berhad, a Malaysian strategic investor.

Founded in 1948, World Airways provides services to major international airlines, and provides administrative and maintenance support to commercial and military customers. Its passenger and freight operations employ 13 wide-body aircraft, operated under contracts primarily with Pacific Rim airlines.

World Airways has a significant customer relationship with the Air Force. The company leases office and warehouse space in Wilmington, Del.; Philadelphia; New York; Los Angeles; Kuala Lumpur, Malaysia; Yakota, Japan; and Frankfurt, Germany.

WorldCorp, which had its own PAC, filed a termination report with the FEC in April 1998. The company transferred its remaining PAC funds to its corporate treasury.

World Airways Inc. Political Action Committee (C00301804)
*Address: same as sponsor * Treasurer: Vance Fort*

	1993-94	1995-96	1997	Totals
Receipts	$0	$18,600	$2,350	$20,950
Disburse	0	12,299	3,000	15,299
Cash	0	10,444	9,794	n/a
Contributions	0	10,750	2,250	13,000
Republicans	0	9,000	2,000	11,000
No. of Cand.	*0*	*6*	*3*	*9*
House	0	8,000	1,500	9,500
Senate	0	1,000	500	1,500
Democrats	0	1,750	0	1,750
No. of Cand.	*0*	*1*	*0*	*1*
House	0	1,750	0	1,750
Senate	0	0	0	0
Incumbents	0	7,750	2,250	10,000
Challengers	0	0	0	0
Open Seat	0	0	0	0
Winners	0	7,750	n/a	7,750
Losers	0	3,000	n/a	3,000

WorldCorp Inc. Political Action Committee (C00226357) *Phone: (703) 834-9409 * Fax: (703) 834-9211 * 13873 Park Center Rd., Suite 490, Herndon, VA 20171 * E-mail: syarid@woa.com * Treasurer: Audrey S. Yarid * Contact: Coleman Andrews, Chairman of the Board*

	1993-94	1995-96	1997	Totals
Receipts	$1,000	$5,800	$0	$6,800
Disburse	1,000	5,305	0	6,305
Cash	0	525	525	n/a
Contributions	1,000	5,300	0	6,300
Republicans	1,000	5,300	0	6,300
No. of Cand.	*1*	*3*	*0*	*4*
House	1,000	5,300	0	6,300
Senate	0	0	0	0
Democrats	0	0	0	0
No. of Cand.	*0*	*0*	*0*	*0*
House	0	0	0	0
Senate	0	0	0	0
Incumbents	0	0	0	0
Challengers	1,000	0	0	1,000
Open Seat	0	2,000	0	2,000
Winners	1,000	0	n/a	1,000
Losers	0	5,300	n/a	5,300

Automotive

A.O. Smith Corp.

*Phone: (414) 359-4000 * Fax: (414) 359-4198*
P.O. Box 23966, 11270 W. Park Pl., Milwaukee, WI 53223
*Web: www.aosmith.com * E-mail: info@aosmith.com*

A.O. Smith makes electric motors, water heaters, wet and dry storage tanks and fiberglass piping systems for residential and commercial applications. Founded in 1874, the publicly traded company has 7,700 employees and had $832 million in 1997 sales.

A.O. Smith's 22 plants are located primarily in the South and Midwest, as well as in California and Washington state and in Canada, the Netherlands, China, Ireland and Mexico.

Subsidiaries: A.O. Smith Electrical Products Co., A.O. Smith Water Products Co., A.O. Smith Harvestore Products and Smith Fiberglass Products.

A.O. Smith Corp. Political Action Committee (AOSPAC) (C00104687) *Address: same as sponsor * Treasurer: Anthony J. Sevcik * Contact: Roger Smith, Manager of Advertising and Public Affairs*

	1993-94	1995-96	1997	Totals
Receipts	$12,168	$18,186	$6,555	$36,909
Disburse	10,781	18,270	500	29,551
Cash	2,904	2,343	8,399	n/a
Contributions	8,500	13,750	0	22,250
Republicans	8,500	13,750	0	22,250
No. of Cand.	*11*	*23*	*0*	*34*
House	3,500	7,750	0	11,250
Senate	5,000	6,000	0	11,000
Democrats	0	0	0	0
No. of Cand.	*0*	*0*	*0*	*0*
House	0	0	0	0
Senate	0	0	0	0
Incumbents	1,000	4,750	0	5,750
Challengers	4,000	3,000	0	7,000
Open Seat	3,500	6,000	0	9,500
Winners	6,000	7,250	n/a	13,250
Losers	2,500	6,500	n/a	9,000

Americans for Free International Trade

Phone: (703) 684-8880
112 S. West St., Suite 310, Alexandria, VA 22314

Americans for Free International Trade is an organization of imported car dealers. It formed in 1991 as an alternative to Auto PAC, another group of import dealers. According to Automotive News, the organization plans to raise and spend about $2.4 million during the 1997-98 election cycle.

The group was the leading import car dealer PAC in contributions to congressional candidates during the 1995-96 election cycle. It ranked among the top 15 PACs in total contributions to Republican candidates. Three-quarters of its contributions went to incumbent candidates.

AFIT contributed $10,000 to 24 candidates, including three Democrats. Among the recipients were Speaker Newt Gingrich, R-Ga., House Majority Leader Dick Armey, R-Texas, and Majority Whip Tom DeLay, R-Texas.

Americans for Free International Trade Political Action Committee Inc. (C00250399) *Address: same as sponsor * Treasurer: David Conant * Contact: Mary D. Hanagan, Executive Dir.*

	1993-94	1995-96	1997	Totals
Receipts	$1,397,604	$1,853,827	$1,059,971	$4,311,402
Disburse	1,596,302	1,851,113	686,065	4,133,480
Cash	85,238	113,044	486,951	n/a
Contributions	770,700	936,800	210,500	1,918,000
Republicans	595,700	829,800	165,000	1,590,500
No. of Cand.	*222*	*240*	*78*	*540*
House	421,200	617,800	121,000	1,160,000
Senate	174,500	212,000	44,000	430,500
Democrats	175,000	107,000	45,500	327,500
No. of Cand.	*49*	*30*	*17*	*96*
House	132,000	97,000	40,500	269,500
Senate	43,000	10,000	5,000	58,000
Incumbents	544,200	698,000	210,500	1,452,700
Challengers	101,000	61,500	-1000	161,500
Open Seat	125,500	168,300	1,000	294,800
Winners	672,200	749,300	n/a	1,421,500
Losers	98,500	187,500	n/a	286,000

Auto Dealers & Drivers for Free Trade

Phone: (718) 291-6900
153-12 Hillside Ave., Jamaica, NY 11432

The Auto Dealers & Drivers for Free Trade PAC, commonly referred to as Auto PAC, was sponsored by members of the Japanese Automobile Dealers' Association. In 1990, according to the PAC's director, Frank Glacken, 95 percent of the 1,500 contributors to the PAC were dealers of Japanese cars. The PAC aims to promote legislation that maintains favorable U.S.-Japanese trade relations.

The group's 1993-94, 1995-96 and 1997 filings with the FEC show a steady decline in contributions, either by other committees or individuals. Almost all incoming funds came from interest. After starting the 1993-94 cycle with more than $1 million, Auto PAC's coffers had $238,482 in cash on hand at the end of 1997. It continued to contribute to campaigns and to pay rent and consultants.

Auto Dealers & Drivers for Free Trade PAC (C00141903) *Address: same as sponsor * Treasurer: Edward G. Connelly*

	1993-94	1995-96	1997	Totals
Receipts	$37,527	$32,418	$9,211	$79,156
Disburse	512,785	252,220	83,650	848,655
Cash	532,645	312,842	238,482	n/a
Contributions	303,900	38,000	13,000	354,900
Republicans	159,125	15,500	7,000	181,625
No. of Cand.	*46*	*7*	*2*	*55*
House	128,875	2,000	0	130,875
Senate	30,250	13,500	7,000	50,750
Democrats	138,225	22,500	6,000	166,725
No. of Cand.	*39*	*9*	*2*	*50*
House	135,425	9,000	0	144,425
Senate	2,800	13,500	6,000	22,300
Incumbents	209,575	15,500	13,000	238,075
Challengers	25,100	2,000	0	27,100
Open Seat	69,225	18,000	0	87,225
Winners	209,125	22,500	n/a	231,625
Losers	94,775	15,500	n/a	110,275

AutoZone Inc.

*Phone: (901) 495-7962 * Fax: (901) 495-8303*
P.O. Box 2198, Memphis, TN 38101-9842
*Web: www.autozone.com * E-mail: ray.pohlman@autozone.com*

AutoZone is the nation's leading auto parts chain. The company sells auto parts, chemicals and accessories through its chain of 1,936 stores in 38 Southern and Midwestern states.

With more than 28,500 employees, the public company had 1997 sales of $2.7 billion and net income of $195 million. In addition to its stores, the company operates seven distribution centers located in Arizona, Georgia, Illinois, Louisiana, Ohio, Tennessee and Texas.

AutoZone Inc. Committee for Better Government (AutoZoners for Better Government) (C00233056) *Address: same as sponsor * Treasurer: John Pontius * Contact: Ray Pohlman, Dir. of Gov. Relations*

	1993-94	1995-96	1997	Totals
Receipts	$59,533	$92,385	$53,900	$205,818
Disburse	22,110	120,236	44,000	186,346
Cash	51,570	23,729	33,631	n/a
Contributions	14,750	40,350	17,000	72,100
Republicans	13,750	40,350	15,500	69,600
No. of Cand.	*8*	*37*	*18*	*63*
House	8,000	25,850	11,500	45,350
Senate	5,750	14,500	4,000	24,250
Democrats	1,000	0	1,500	2,500
No. of Cand.	*1*	*0*	*2*	*3*
House	1,000	0	500	1,500
Senate	0	0	1,000	1,000
Incumbents	6,750	27,850	17,500	52,100
Challengers	0	1,500	0	1,500
Open Seat	8,000	11,000	0	19,000
Winners	13,750	32,350	n/a	46,100
Losers	1,000	8,000	n/a	9,000

Automotive Service Industry Association

*Phone: (847) 228-1310 * Fax: (847) 228-1510*
25 N.W. Point Blvd., #425, Elk Grove Village, IL 60007-1035
Web: www.aftmkt.com/asia

The Automotive Service Industry Association is a 1,500-member international nonprofit trade association whose member companies manufacture, distribute and sell motor vehicle parts, accessories, tools, equipment, materials and supplies.

The Washington office handles federal and regulatory issues involving product liability reform, the EPA's national paint rule for automotive refinishing, on-board diagnostics, health insurance reform for small businesses and reform of overtime rules governing inside sales personnel.

ASIA publishes a quarterly magazine, Aftermarket Today, and two bi-monthly newsletters, Washington Insights and Hotline.

ASIA has an affiliated organization, the Heavy Duty Distribution Association.

Automotive/Aftermarket PAC of Automotive Service Industry Association (C00250753) *Phone: (202) 408-9550 * Fax: (202) 408-9553 * 805 15th St. N.W., Suite 240, Washington, DC 20005-2207 * E-mail: asiagovjma@aol.com * Treasurer: Gene A. Gardner * Contact: Tyler Wilson, Dir. of Gov. Relations*

	1993-94	1995-96	1997	Totals
Receipts	$7,495	$9,025	$0	$16,520
Disburse	5,275	15,450	1,300	22,025
Cash	12,549	6,124	4,824	n/a
Contributions	2,200	14,250	600	17,050
Republicans	1,100	13,050	500	14,650
No. of Cand.	*3*	*18*	*1*	*22*
House	350	10,050	500	10,900
Senate	750	3,000	0	3,750
Democrats	1,100	1,200	100	2,400
No. of Cand.	*3*	*2*	*1*	*6*
House	600	1,200	0	1,800
Senate	500	0	100	600
Incumbents	1,100	9,650	600	11,350
Challengers	0	2,000	0	2,000
Open Seat	1,100	2,600	0	3,700
Winners	1,700	9,450	n/a	11,150
Losers	500	4,800	n/a	5,300

Avis Inc.

*Phone: (516) 222-3000 * Fax: (516) 222-6677*
900 Old Country Rd., Garden City, NY 11530
Web: www.avis.com

Avis owns the brand name and reservation system for Avis Rent A Car, the second-largest car rental business in the world. Avis is a subsidiary of HFS Car Rental Inc., which is owned by Cendant Corp. Avis employs about 18,000 people and reported 1997 sales of $2 billion.

Avis Rent A Car has 193,000 vehicles and about 600 rental locations in the United States and 3,600 worldwide. It has international locations in Puerto Rico, the Virgin Islands, Canada, Argentina, Australia and New Zealand. Avis owns a 25 percent stake in Avis Rent A Car; the rest is publicly traded.

Cendant, which was created by the merger of HFS Inc. and CUC International Inc., is a global provider of hospitality and real estate services. Among its many subsidiaries: Days Inn, Howard Johnson, Coldwell Banker and PHH Corp. A public company, Cendant formed its own PAC in March 1998.

Avis Inc. Political Action Committee (Avis PAC) (C00199612)
*Address: same as sponsor * Treasurer: Vincent Manago*

	1993-94	1995-96	1997	Totals
Receipts	$3,057	$9,369	$1	$12,427
Disburse	5,015	11,788	126	16,929
Cash	2,538	124	0	n/a
Contributions	4,500	11,700	0	16,200
Republicans	500	9,700	0	10,200
No. of Cand.	*1*	*8*	*0*	*9*
House	500	8,450	0	8,950
Senate	0	1,250	0	1,250
Democrats	3,500	2,000	0	5,500
No. of Cand.	*3*	*3*	*0*	*6*
House	3,500	1,000	0	4,500
Senate	0	1,000	0	1,000
Incumbents	4,000	11,700	0	15,700
Challengers	500	0	0	500
Open Seat	0	0	0	0
Winners	4,000	4,450	n/a	8,450
Losers	500	7,250	n/a	7,750

PHH Corp. Employee Political Action Committee PHHPAC (C00160523) *Phone: (410) 771-1900 * Fax: (410) 771-2932 * 307 International Cir., Hunt Valley, MD 21030-1337 * Web: www.phh.com * Treasurer: Vacant*

PHH was purchased by HFS, which merged with CUC International Inc. in December 1997. The new company formed is Cendant. As of March 1998, a decision on the future of the PHH PAC had not yet been reached. PHH had $1.2 billion in 1996 sales.

PHH is the North American and European leader in leasing and management solutions for corporate, government and utility vehicle fleets. PHH manages 500,000 vehicles and more than 1 million fuel and service cards worldwide. The company purchases more than a billion gallons of fuel per year.

PHH also provides relocation services to individuals and companies and provides mortgage services for employees of corporations and credit unions.

PHH employs 1,700 workers worldwide. In addition to its headquarters in Hunt Valley, Md., PHH has branch offices in Irvine, Calif.; Oak Brook, Ill.; Manchester, N.H.; Irving, Texas; and New York City. Globally, PHH operates branches in Canada, the United Kingdom, France, Germany, Ireland and Italy.

	1993-94	1995-96	1997	Totals
Receipts	$10,731	$7,770	$2,632	$21,133
Disburse	4,376	8,927	8,757	22,060
Cash	39,098	37,945	31,821	n/a
Contributions	4,325	7,250	7,000	18,575
Republicans	1,500	5,750	3,000	10,250
No. of Cand.	*2*	*5*	*3*	*10*
House	1,500	4,250	3,000	8,750
Senate	0	1,500	0	1,500
Democrats	2,825	1,500	4,000	8,325
No. of Cand.	*3*	*2*	*3*	*8*
House	1,325	1,500	2,000	4,825
Senate	1,500	0	2,000	3,500
Incumbents	3,325	4,750	7,000	15,075
Challengers	0	0	0	0
Open Seat	1,000	2,500	0	3,500
Winners	3,825	5,750	n/a	9,575
Losers	500	1,500	n/a	2,000

Budd Co.

Phone: (248) 643-3500
P.O. Box 2601, Troy, MI 48007-2601
Web: www.buddcompany.com

Budd develops automotive body systems, chassis, suspensions and powertrains, as well as a wide variety of common automotive components and materials used in nearly 100 vehicle models produced in North America.

Budd employs more than 9,000 people at its 25 locations in Minnesota, Michigan, Wisconsin, Indiana, Ohio, Kentucky, Pennsylvania and in Canada. The company also has offices in Japan and Germany.

Budd is a wholly owned subsidiary of Thyssen Budd Automotive, which is itself a subsidiary of Thyssen AG, which had $25 billion in 1997 sales. The German industrial giant operates 330 businesses that produce pipes, ships, polymers, building products, steel, automotive parts and other trading, construction and telecommunication services.

Subsidiaries: Waupaca Foundry Inc., Milford Fabricating Co., Midland Design Service Inc., Phillips & Temro Industries and Greening Donald Co. Ltd.

Budd Co. Citizenship Committee (C00039404) *Address: same as sponsor * Treasurer: Mark A. Gordon * Contact: Paul Sichert, Chairman*

	1993-94	1995-96	1997	Totals
Receipts	$17,601	$16,052	$8,188	$41,841
Disburse	17,825	19,950	1,500	39,275
Cash	10,857	6,978	13,677	n/a
Contributions	14,825	19,950	1,500	36,275
Republicans	11,625	18,200	1,000	30,825
No. of Cand.	*17*	*25*	*3*	*45*
House	6,000	12,000	500	18,500
Senate	5,625	6,200	500	12,325
Democrats	3,200	1,750	500	5,450
No. of Cand.	*6*	*3*	*1*	*10*
House	2,700	1,250	500	4,450
Senate	500	500	0	1,000
Incumbents	8,700	10,250	750	19,700
Challengers	3,500	6,700	250	10,450
Open Seat	2,625	3,000	500	6,125
Winners	11,825	9,750	n/a	21,575
Losers	3,000	10,200	n/a	13,200

Chrysler Corp.

*Phone: (248) 576-5741 * Fax: (248) 556-3747*
1000 Chrysler Dr., Auburn Hills, MI 48326-2766
Web: www.chryslercorp.com

Chrysler is the nation's third-largest automaker, behind Ford and General Motors. A public company, it produces a wide range of vehicles under the Chrysler, Dodge, Eagle, Jeep and Plymouth brand names. Chrysler also offers a range of financing services to its dealers and customers. In 1997 it had 122,000 employees worldwide and total sales of $61.1 billion.

Though the company's cars and trucks are sold worldwide and it has manufacturing operations in Belgium, Singapore and South Africa, the vast majority of Chrysler's sales are made in the United States. It has 15 assembly plants, 11 powertrain plants, three stamping operations, eight component plants and five technical centers in North America.

Chrysler lobbies on trade, environmental and labor issues. It has lobbied against new regulatory mandates from Congress and emissions standards based on international treaties on global warming.

Chrysler's PAC spending during the 1995-96 election cycle tended to favor Republican candidates, although it gave more than $100,000 to candidates of both parties. The five leading recipients were Michigan incumbents: Sen. Carl Levin, D, and Reps. John D. Dingell, D, Dale E. Kildee, D, Sander M. Levin, D, and former Rep. Dick Chrysler, R. They were the only candidates to receive more than $5,000 from Chrysler.

Chrysler Technologies Corp., a defense electronics subsidiary, contributed nearly $20,000 to 1996 congressional candidates. Six of the 15 recipients were from Texas.

Chrysler Corp. Political Support Committee (also known as Chrysler Political Support Committee) (C00043687) *Phone: (202) 414-6700 * Fax: (202) 414-6743 * 1401 H St. N.W., Suite 700, Washington, DC 20005 * E-mail: btd2@chrysler.com * Treasurer: Thomas P. Capo * Contact: Brenda Day, Congressional Affairs Dir.*

	1993-94	1995-96	1997	Totals
Receipts	$439,892	$704,114	$496,852	$1,640,858
Disburse	417,015	659,369	377,407	1,453,791
Cash	55,384	100,142	219,593	n/a
Contributions	208,318	304,615	180,626	693,559
Republicans	69,800	188,250	113,050	371,100
No. of Cand.	*64*	*129*	*88*	*281*
House	48,300	125,750	64,050	238,100
Senate	21,500	62,500	49,000	133,000
Democrats	138,018	116,365	67,576	321,959
No. of Cand.	*102*	*77*	*53*	*232*
House	102,750	86,490	48,900	238,140
Senate	35,268	29,875	18,676	83,819
Incumbents	183,018	266,115	173,626	622,759
Challengers	500	12,000	1,000	13,500
Open Seat	25,300	27,500	6,000	58,800
Winners	171,050	270,615	n/a	441,665
Losers	37,268	34,000	n/a	71,268

Chrysler Technologies Corp. Political Support Committee (CTCPSC) (C00238261) *Phone: (703) 413-4416 * 1725 Jefferson Davis Hwy., Suite 500, Arlington, VA 22202 * Treasurer: Terrence R. Marcinko*

	1993-94	1995-96	1997	Totals
Receipts	$12,859	$13,677	$0	$26,536
Disburse	8,960	20,746	0	29,706
Cash	7,063	0	0	n/a
Contributions	8,500	19,666	0	28,166
Republicans	3,000	12,166	0	15,166
No. of Cand.	*4*	*11*	*0*	*15*
House	1,500	5,883	0	7,383
Senate	1,500	6,283	0	7,783
Democrats	5,500	7,500	0	13,000
No. of Cand.	*7*	*4*	*0*	*11*
House	5,000	6,500	0	11,500
Senate	500	1,000	0	1,500
Incumbents	8,500	17,100	0	25,600
Challengers	0	0	0	0
Open Seat	0	2,566	0	2,566
Winners	8,500	19,666	n/a	28,166
Losers	0	0	n/a	0

Dana Corp.

*Phone: (419) 535-4793 * Fax: (419) 535-4756*
4500 Dorr St., Toledo, OH 43615
Web: www.dana.com

Dana is a publicly traded $7.1 billion worldwide corporation that makes automotive/vehicular drivetrain systems, engine parts and other automotive products. Dana also owns Dana Credit Corp., a significant provider of lease financing services in certain markets.

Incorporated in 1905, Dana now has 181 locations in the United States and 329 locations worldwide. The company posted $8.8 billion in 1997 sales and has 50,000 employees in 30 countries. Dana's international sales were $2.3 billion, 26 percent of 1997 sales.

Dana has 296 subsidiaries in the United States, Canada, Europe, the Pacific Rim and Latin America.

Dana Corp. Political Action Committee (C00144816) *Address: same as sponsor * Treasurer: James E. Ayers * Contact: Carol Van Sickle, Manager of Gov. Relations*

	1993-94	1995-96	1997	Totals
Receipts	$9,852	$8,998	$3,384	$22,234
Disburse	11,500	12,000	0	23,500
Cash	5,801	2,954	6,343	n/a
Contributions	11,500	12,000	0	23,500
Republicans	11,500	11,500	0	23,000
No. of Cand.	*11*	*9*	*0*	*20*
House	4,500	3,500	0	8,000
Senate	7,000	8,000	0	15,000
Democrats	0	500	0	500
No. of Cand.	*0*	*1*	*0*	*1*
House	0	500	0	500
Senate	0	0	0	0
Incumbents	500	1,000	0	1,500
Challengers	3,500	3,500	0	7,000
Open Seat	6,500	7,500	0	14,000
Winners	9,500	5,500	n/a	15,000
Losers	2,000	6,500	n/a	8,500

Eaton Corp.

*Phone: (216) 523-4452 * Fax: (216) 479-7013*
1111 Superior Ave., Cleveland, OH 44114-2584
*Web: www.eaton.com * E-mail: jamesmason@eaton.com*

Cleveland-based Eaton nearly made Fortune's Top 200 in 1996, ranking No. 207. Its 49,000 employees work in 145 manufacturing sites in 26 countries around the world.

Eaton, which posted $7 billion in 1997 sales, operates three divisions: a vehicle components division, which makes transmissions and engine components; an electrical and electronic controls division, which manufactures components for the construction, aerospace and defense industries; and an ion implanters division.

In October 1997, publicly owned Eaton sold its AIL Systems division, which develops and produces high technology electronics for the U.S. military. Former astronaut Neil Armstrong is chairman of AIL's board of directors and continues to serve on Eaton's board of directors.

Eaton Corp. Public Policy Association (C00034827) *Address: same as sponsor * Treasurer: James L. Mason*

	1993-94	1995-96	1997	Totals
Receipts	$44,238	$43,648	$23,004	$110,890
Disburse	37,316	46,577	12,514	96,407
Cash	18,852	15,934	26,429	n/a
Contributions	22,000	18,250	5,000	45,250
Republicans	21,000	18,000	5,000	44,000
No. of Cand.	*8*	*12*	*5*	*25*
House	14,000	18,000	2,500	34,500
Senate	7,000	0	2,500	9,500
Democrats	1,000	250	0	1,250
No. of Cand.	*1*	*1*	*0*	*2*
House	1,000	250	0	1,250
Senate	0	0	0	0
Incumbents	4,000	18,250	3,000	25,250
Challengers	12,000	0	0	12,000
Open Seat	6,000	0	2,000	8,000
Winners	16,000	13,250	n/a	29,250
Losers	6,000	5,000	n/a	11,000

Enterprise Rent-A-Car Co.

*Phone: (314) 512-5000 * Fax: (314) 512-4202*
600 Corporate Park Dr., St. Louis, MO 63105
Web: www.pickenterprise.com

Enterprise Rent-A-Car is the largest rental car company in the United States in fleet size and number of locations. Enterprise operates more than 3,100 offices in the United States and more than 300 offices in Canada and the United Kingdom. Enterprise's revenues in 1997 were $3.6 billion. The privately held company employs 32,000 workers.

Enterprise Rent-A-Car Co. Political Action Committee (C00219642) *Address: same as sponsor * Treasurer: Andrew C. Taylor*

	1993-94	1995-96	1997	Totals
Receipts	$362,114	$514,702	$275,170	$1,151,986
Disburse	253,769	391,094	170,304	815,167
Cash	409,838	533,454	638,324	n/a
Contributions	13,000	32,400	31,450	76,850
Republicans	6,750	26,400	30,000	63,150
No. of Cand.	*3*	*16*	*11*	*30*
House	1,000	23,000	12,250	36,250
Senate	5,750	3,400	17,750	26,900
Democrats	6,250	6,000	1,450	13,700
No. of Cand.	*2*	*6*	*3*	*11*
House	6,250	2,500	450	9,200
Senate	0	3,500	1,000	4,500
Incumbents	8,250	13,250	31,250	52,750
Challengers	0	11,400	0	11,400
Open Seat	4,750	7,750	200	12,700
Winners	13,000	23,750	n/a	36,750
Losers	0	8,650	n/a	8,650

Ford Motor Co.

*Phone: (313) 322-3000 * Fax: (313) 323-2959*
The American Rd., Dearborn, MI 48121-1899
Web: www.ford.com

Ford, the world's largest truck maker and No. 2 producer of cars and trucks combined, employs 371,000 people worldwide. About one-third of the company's sales, which totaled $153 billion in 1997, come from outside the United States. A public company, Ford's several subsidiaries include Ford Motor Credit, the nation's largest automobile financing company. The company also has a majority interest in Hertz, the top rental car company in America.

Ford lobbies on dozens of issues, including labor-management relations, international trade and the environment. It opposes tight emissions controls on factories that release carbon dioxide and other greenhouse gases. The company also is a member of an industrial electricity customer group that opposes the repeal of the Public Utility Holding Company Act of 1935 because it fears higher electric rates.

Ford was the leading PAC contributor among automobile manufacturers to 1996 congressional campaigns. Still, it reduced its 1995-96 PAC contributions by more than 8 percent compared to the 1993-94 election cycle. Most of its contributions went to Republican candidates. The top recipients were Reps. John D. Dingell, D-Mich., Sander M. Levin, D-Mich., Tom Bliley, R-Va., and Charles B. Rangel, D-N.Y.

The Associates Corp. of America, a Ford affiliate, contributed $25,750 to congressional campaigns in 1996.

Ford Motor Co. Civic Action Fund (C00046474) *Phone: (202) 962-5369 * Fax: (202) 336-7226 * 1350 Eye St. N.W., Suite 1000, Washington, DC 20005 * Treasurer: Martha Hermance * Contact: Robert M. Howard, Legislative Manager*

	1993-94	1995-96	1997	Totals
Receipts	$842,139	$878,685	$443,106	$2,163,930
Disburse	645,801	884,214	414,076	1,944,091
Cash	344,489	338,973	368,008	n/a
Contributions	354,900	338,590	136,875	830,365
Republicans	158,720	244,790	100,700	504,210
No. of Cand.	*120*	*205*	*105*	*430*
House	97,620	176,040	65,950	339,610
Senate	61,100	68,750	34,750	164,600
Democrats	196,180	93,800	36,175	326,155
No. of Cand.	*145*	*78*	*37*	*260*
House	168,455	82,550	32,175	283,180
Senate	27,725	11,250	4,000	42,975
Incumbents	290,300	298,840	127,875	717,015
Challengers	11,250	7,250	1,000	19,500
Open Seat	53,350	33,500	8,000	94,850
Winners	280,350	302,940	n/a	583,290
Losers	74,550	35,650	n/a	110,200

Concerned Associates Employees (also known as Associates Corp. of North America PAC) (C00239400) *Phone: (248) 371-5562 * Fax: (248) 371-7272 * 250 E. Carpenter Fwy., Irving, TX 75062 * Treasurer: Martha Hermance * Contact: Chester D. Langamacker, Chairman*

	1993-94	1995-96	1997	Totals
Receipts	$277,126	$350,258	$244,968	$872,352
Disburse	297,487	342,269	146,336	786,092
Cash	8,652	16,644	115,281	n/a
Contributions	32,775	25,750	10,600	69,125
Republicans	18,375	16,500	3,500	38,375
No. of Cand.	*13*	*21*	*4*	*38*
House	3,125	13,000	1,500	17,625
Senate	15,250	3,500	2,000	20,750
Democrats	14,400	9,250	7,100	30,750
No. of Cand.	*18*	*11*	*6*	*35*
House	11,900	8,250	7,100	27,250
Senate	2,500	1,000	0	3,500
Incumbents	27,500	16,000	9,100	52,600
Challengers	1,000	2,750	0	3,750
Open Seat	4,275	7,000	1,500	12,775
Winners	28,000	17,250	n/a	45,250
Losers	4,775	8,500	n/a	13,275

General Motors Corp.

*Phone: (313) 556-5000 * Fax: (313) 556-5108*
3044 W. Grand Blvd., MC 482 111 139, Detroit, MI 48202
Web: www.gm.com

General Motors is the world's largest industrial corporation and full-line vehicle manufacturer. In 1996, the company employed more than 647,000 people and partnered with more than 30,000 supplier companies worldwide. As the largest U.S. exporter of cars and trucks, and having manufacturing, assembly, or component operations in 50 countries, General Motors has a presence in more than 190 nations. GM has more than 160 subsidiaries.

The company is interested in regulatory reform, fuel-economy standards and global warming. GM has lobbied against reductions of greenhouse gases said to cause global warming. The company has decided to stop giving "soft money" contributions.

Hughes Electronics, a subsidiary of General Motors Corp., is an umbrella company for several space and electronics businesses. Hughes' main defense business, Hughes Aircraft, merged into Raytheon in 1997, leaving Hughes Electronics with about 14,000 employees and 1996 revenues of $4.1 billion. Hughes will maintain its space and information systems operations, which supply satellite communications and weather observations to its contractors.

GM's PAC ranked second among automakers in contributions to 1996 congressional campaigns. It favored Republican candidates and incumbents. The leading recipients were Rep. Carolyn Cheeks Kilpatrick, D-Mich., Sen. Carl Levin, D-Mich., and former Rep. Dick Chrysler, R-Mich. Seven of the top 12 recipients were from Michigan.

The Hughes PAC has been terminated and a new committee, Hughes Electronics Fund, was formed in early 1998. The terminated PAC ranked first among defense electronics companies in 1996 congressional contributions, but the company said it expects its future PAC contributions to be much less.

Civic Involvement Program/General Motors Corp. (C00076810) *Phone: (202) 775-5057 * Fax: (202) 775-5023 * 1660 L St. N.W., Washington, DC 20036 * Treasurer: Martha Hermance * Contact: Tammy Hobby*

	1993-94	1995-96	1997	Totals
Receipts	$457,594	$872,627	$409,264	$1,739,485
Disburse	477,782	777,521	413,184	1,668,487
Cash	30,436	125,545	121,626	n/a
Contributions	196,015	305,475	155,540	657,030
Republicans	102,975	218,800	114,790	436,565
No. of Cand.	*57*	*134*	*79*	*270*
House	38,725	138,350	62,790	239,865
Senate	64,250	80,450	52,000	196,700
Democrats	92,540	86,675	40,750	219,965
No. of Cand.	*71*	*47*	*32*	*150*
House	75,800	71,675	31,250	178,725
Senate	16,740	15,000	9,500	41,240
Incumbents	140,515	269,025	145,040	554,580
Challengers	4,000	12,200	5,000	21,200
Open Seat	51,000	24,750	5,500	81,250
Winners	163,175	273,525	n/a	436,700
Losers	32,840	31,950	n/a	64,790

Hughes Defense Communications PAC (formerly known as MESC Electronic Systems Inc. PAC) (C00290353) *1010 Production Rd., Fort Wayne, IN 46808 * Treasurer: Tony P. Clouse*

In January 1997, the Hughes Defense Communications PAC, formerly known as the MESC Electronic Systems Inc. PAC, was terminated.

	1993-94	1995-96	1997	Totals
Receipts	$17,362	$59,622	$0	$76,984
Disburse	11,777	65,222	0	76,999
Cash	5,586	0	0	n/a
Contributions	11,500	50,200	0	61,700
Republicans	4,500	36,200	0	40,700
No. of Cand.	*5*	*21*	*0*	*26*
House	4,000	32,200	0	36,200
Senate	500	4,000	0	4,500
Democrats	7,000	14,000	0	21,000
No. of Cand.	*8*	*7*	*0*	*15*
House	5,000	14,000	0	19,000
Senate	2,000	0	0	2,000
Incumbents	11,000	43,500	0	54,500
Challengers	500	700	0	1,200
Open Seat	0	6,500	0	6,500
Winners	10,000	39,000	n/a	49,000
Losers	1,500	11,200	n/a	12,700

Goodyear Tire & Rubber Co.

*Phone: (330) 796-2121 * Fax: (330) 796-1021*
1144 E. Market St., Akron, OH 44316
Web: www.goodyear.com

Goodyear is the largest tire company in North America and a major competitor in the world market. The Akron, Ohio company has 36 plants in the United States that produce rubber and plastic products for automotive and industrial markets, in addition to Kelly-Springfield and Goodyear tires. About half of the company's tire sales are made in North America. The publicly traded company posted 1997 sales of $13 billion.

Celeron, a subsidiary, operates a 1,225-mile crude oil pipeline system, which reaches from California to central Texas.

Plant locations: Alabama, California, Georgia, Illinois, Iowa, Kansas, Maryland, Missouri, Nebraska, New York, North Carolina, Ohio, Oklahoma, South Carolina, Tennessee, Texas, Virginia and Wisconsin.

The company has 91,000 employees worldwide and 35,000 in the North American Tire unit.

Goodyear Tire & Rubber Co. Good Government Fund (Goodyear Good Government Fund) (C00100131) *Phone: (202) 682-9250 * Fax: (202) 682-1533 * 1420 New York Ave., Suite 200, Washington, DC 20005 * Treasurer: T. F. Lingo*

*Contact: Pat Kemph, Chairperson * Phone: (330) 796-2121*

	1993-94	1995-96	1997	Totals
Receipts	$54,504	$65,657	$86,365	$206,526
Disburse	25,700	87,700	37,113	150,513
Cash	42,437	20,397	69,648	n/a
Contributions	25,000	86,500	36,763	148,263
Republicans	19,000	79,000	30,263	128,263
No. of Cand.	*24*	*64*	*34*	*122*
House	3,500	36,500	16,250	56,250
Senate	15,500	42,500	14,013	72,013
Democrats	6,000	7,500	6,500	20,000
No. of Cand.	*9*	*7*	*8*	*24*
House	4,500	7,500	5,500	17,500
Senate	1,500	0	1,000	2,500

Incumbents	17,000	59,000	33,763	109,763
Challengers	2,500	8,500	0	11,000
Open Seat	5,500	19,000	3,000	27,500
Winners	20,500	69,500	n/a	90,000
Losers	4,500	17,000	n/a	21,500

JM Family Enterprises Inc.

*Phone: (954) 429-2182 * Fax: (954) 429-2677*
100 N.W. 12th Ave., P.O. Box 1160, Deerfield Beach, FL 33443
E-mail: apaulander@aol.com

JM Family Enterprises is a privately owned holding company for 25 automotive-related businesses. It is Florida's second-largest private company after Publix Supermarkets. It employs 3,000 workers and its 1997 sales were estimated at $5.4 billion.

Its primary subsidiary, Southeast Toyota Distributors Inc., is one of the world's largest Toyota distribution franchises, delivering cars, trucks and vans to more than 160 dealers in Alabama, Florida, Georgia, and North and South Carolina. In 1997, Southeast Toyota reported new annual sales records because of the introduction of the Camry and the Sienna models.

Other JM Enterprises divisions provide auto leasing, dealer financing and vehicle insurance.

JM Family Enterprises Inc. Political Action Committee (C00240911) *Address: same as sponsor * Treasurer: Paul Anderson*

	1993-94	1995-96	1997	Totals
Receipts	$51,270	$72,250	$52,100	$175,620
Disburse	55,647	70,300	37,750	163,697
Cash	3,167	5,117	19,467	n/a
Contributions	23,450	32,350	26,750	82,550
Republicans	13,600	20,600	20,750	54,950
No. of Cand.	*13*	*16*	*18*	*47*
House	8,850	13,600	7,250	29,700
Senate	4,750	7,000	13,500	25,250
Democrats	9,850	11,750	6,000	27,600
No. of Cand.	*13*	*13*	*5*	*31*
House	9,850	7,750	3,000	20,600
Senate	0	4,000	3,000	7,000
Incumbents	18,950	24,350	26,250	69,550
Challengers	1,500	1,000	0	2,500
Open Seat	3,000	6,500	500	10,000
Winners	19,950	27,350	n/a	47,300
Losers	3,500	5,000	n/a	8,500

Lear Corp.

*Phone: (248) 746-1500 * Fax: (248) 746-1593*
21557 Telegraph Rd., Southfield, MI 48034
Web: www.lear.com

Lear is one of the world's largest automotive suppliers, with 1997 sales of $7.3 billion. The publicly traded company's 50,000 employees design and manufacture seat systems, floor acoustic systems, door panels, headliners and instrument panels at 170 facilities located in 25 countries. The company's seat systems division accounted for 65 percent of the company's sales in 1997.

Lear sells to Ford, GM, Volvo, BMW, Chrysler, Fiat, Saab and Volkswagen, with 75 percent of sales going to Ford and GM. In December 1997, Lear's joint venture with Bing Manufacturing, Detroit Automotive Interiors, was chosen by Ford to build the rear seat assemblies for the Ford Explorer.

While the company's main focus is car interiors, it also manufactures a variety of blow-molded products and other automotive components such as fluid reservoirs, fuel tank shields and front grille assemblies.

Lear Corp. (also known as LearPAC) (C00297242) *Address: same as sponsor * Treasurer: Raymond F. Lowry*

	1993-94	1995-96	1997	Totals
Receipts	$33,830	$92,247	$59,118	$185,195
Disburse	28,900	66,950	58,925	154,775
Cash	4,930	30,231	30,425	n/a
Contributions	17,000	10,000	13,000	40,000
Republicans	16,000	8,000	13,000	37,000
No. of Cand.	*8*	*8*	*7*	*23*
House	14,000	6,000	10,500	30,500
Senate	2,000	2,000	2,500	6,500
Democrats	1,000	2,000	0	3,000
No. of Cand.	*1*	*1*	*0*	*2*
House	1,000	0	0	1,000
Senate	0	2,000	0	2,000
Incumbents	7,000	6,500	3,500	17,000
Challengers	4,000	3,500	10,000	17,500
Open Seat	6,000	0	500	6,500
Winners	11,000	4,000	n/a	15,000
Losers	6,000	6,000	n/a	12,000

National Association of Minority Automobile Dealers

Phone: (248) 557-2500
16000 W. Nine Mile Rd., Suite 603, Southfield, MI 48075

The National Association of Minority Automobile Dealers represents 425 minority-owned car and truck dealerships in the United States. The organization's purpose is to increase opportunities for minorities in the automobile industry.

During 1995, the top 100 black car dealers employed more than 8,600 people and generated sales of nearly $5.7 billion.

Ford Lincoln-Mercury Minority Dealers Association Political Action Committee (FLMMDA PAC) (C00324368) *Phone: (202) 789-3140 * Fax: (202) 789-3133 * 1111 14th St. N.W., Suite 720, Washington, DC 20005 * Treasurer: Laval Perry * Contact: Sheila Vaden-Williams, Executive Dir.*

	1993-94	1995-96	1997	Totals
Receipts	$0	$0	$15,500	$15,500
Disburse	0	0	3,510	3,510
Cash	0	0	15,928	n/a
Contributions	0	6,000	500	6,500
Republicans	0	0	0	0
No. of Cand.	*0*	*0*	*0*	*0*
House	0	0	0	0
Senate	0	0	0	0
Democrats	0	6,000	500	6,500
No. of Cand.	*0*	*2*	*4*	*6*
House	0	3,000	1,500	4,500
Senate	0	3,000	-1000	2,000
Incumbents	0	3,000	2,500	5,500
Challengers	0	3,000	0	3,000
Open Seat	0	0	0	0
Winners	0	3,000	n/a	3,000
Losers	0	3,000	n/a	3,000

National Automobile Dealers Association

*Phone: (703) 827-7407 * Fax: (703) 821-7075*
8400 Westpark Dr., McLean, VA 22102
Web: www.nada.org

The National Automobile Dealers Association represents nearly 20,000 new car and truck dealers in America. Its members operate about 40,000 individual franchises of domestic and imported vehicles. NADA's main goal is to preserve the franchise system. The group closely follows legislation relating to the environment, trade and the workplace.

NADA supports Superfund reform that would reduce the liability for businesses named as contributors to a hazardous waste site by placing greater burdens of proof on the EPA. It opposes an EPA air quality plan for ozone and particle matter and instead calls for further research. NADA favors national standards governing the process of selling rebuilt vehicles.

NADA was the leading automobile dealer contributor to 1996 congressional campaigns. It ranked second overall in total contributions given to incumbent candidates. It spent heavily on candidates in California and Texas — races in those two states accounted for nearly 25 percent of the $2.3 million it spent.

The group favored Republican candidates by a wide margin, and more than half of the 454 candidates who received money from NADA received at least $5,000. The leading recipients were Sen. Gordon H. Smith, R-Ore., and Reps. Greg Ganske, R-Iowa, Kevin Brady, R-Texas, and House Speaker Newt Gingrich, R-Ga. The top Democratic recipient was Rep. Ken Bentsen of Texas.

Dealers Election Action Committee of the National Automobile Dealers Association (NADA) (C00040998) *Phone: (202) 547-5500 * Fax: (202) 479-0168 * 412 First St. S.E., Washington, DC 20003 * E-mail: govaffs@nadanet.com * Treasurer: Leonard Fichtner * Contact: Gregory Knopp, PAC Dir. * Phone: (703) 827-7407*

	1993-94	1995-96	1997	Totals
Receipts	$2,925,513	$3,657,843	$2,109,781	$8,693,137
Disburse	2,751,789	3,248,147	1,244,237	7,244,173
Cash	2,188,350	2,599,195	3,469,580	n/a
Contributions	1,824,070	2,335,425	576,425	4,735,920
Republicans	1,276,300	1,906,925	366,025	3,549,250
No. of Cand.	*262*	*341*	*181*	*784*
House	1,099,550	1,580,875	300,275	2,980,700
Senate	176,750	326,050	65,750	568,550
Democrats	544,770	426,500	209,400	1,180,670
No. of Cand.	*168*	*114*	*89*	*371*
House	481,650	408,500	188,300	1,078,450
Senate	63,120	18,000	21,100	102,220
Incumbents	1,176,970	1,616,075	510,825	3,303,870
Challengers	306,000	263,500	18,500	588,000
Open Seat	341,100	454,500	45,500	841,100
Winners	1,464,050	1,771,675	n/a	3,235,725
Losers	360,020	563,750	n/a	923,770

New United Motor Manufacturing Inc.

*Phone: (510) 498-5646 * Fax: (510) 770-4010*
45500 Fremont Blvd., Fremont, CA 94538
Web: www.nummi.com

New United Motor Manufacturing manufactures select Geo and Toyota models through a joint venture with General Motors and Toyota. NUMMI builds 40 percent of its cars for General Motors and 60 percent for Toyota. All trucks built at NUMMI are sold to Toyota.

Founded in 1984, the company manufactures the Toyota Corolla, the Chevrolet Nova and the Toyota Tacoma. Its plant capacity is about 240,000 cars and 150,000 compact pickup trucks a year. NUMMI has fewer than 5,000 employees.

In 1996, NUMMI shipped $246 million worth of products to Japan, Australia and Canada, including 13,960 Toyota Corollas to Taiwan and 3,410 Toyota Tacomas to Canada, Puerto Rico, Guam, American Samoa and Saipan.

New United Motor Manufacturing Inc. Political Action Committee (C00205872) *Address: same as sponsor * Treasurer: D. William Childs * Contact: Patricia Pineda, Chairman*

	1993-94	1995-96	1997	Totals
Receipts	$26,478	$31,993	$13,934	$72,405
Disburse	34,225	25,900	4,108	64,233
Cash	5,241	11,334	21,160	n/a
Contributions	21,225	6,950	2,100	30,275
Republicans	3,200	3,900	100	7,200
No. of Cand.	*2*	*3*	*1*	*6*
House	3,200	3,900	100	7,200
Senate	0	0	0	0
Democrats	18,025	3,050	2,000	23,075
No. of Cand.	*14*	*5*	*1*	*20*
House	13,275	3,050	2,000	18,325
Senate	4,750	0	0	4,750
Incumbents	20,325	6,950	2,100	29,375
Challengers	100	0	0	100
Open Seat	800	0	0	800
Winners	20,575	4,950	n/a	25,525
Losers	650	2,000	n/a	2,650

Ryder System Inc.

Phone: (305) 500-3726
3600 N.W. 82nd Ave., Miami, FL 33166
Web: www.ryder.com

Ryder offers logistics, truck leasing and rental and public transportation services.

Ryder's global integrated logistics division coordinates goods transport for businesses. The company's truck leasing division has a fleet of more than 100,000 vehicles and more than 11,000 customers, making Ryder the largest full-service truck leasing company in the world. Ryder's public transportation division is the nation's leading provider of public transit contracting and management, serving more than 100 transit authorities, departments of transportation, federal agencies and private companies. This division is also responsible for transporting more than 500,000 students to and from school every day.

Founded in 1933, the publicly traded company had 1997 revenues of $4.9 billion and net earnings of $176 million. With more than 42,000 employees, Ryder operates throughout the United States and in Canada, the United Kingdom, Germany, Poland, the Netherlands, Mexico, Brazil and Argentina.

In September 1997, Ryder sold Ryder Automotive Carrier Services Inc. and RC Management Corp. to Allied Holdings Inc.

Ryder Employees Political Action Committee (formerly known as Ryder Committee Effective Government) (C00088435) *Phone: (202) 789-0062 * 1100 New York Ave. N.W., Suite 580, Washington, DC 20005 * Treasurer: George Scanlon * Contact: Linda Kelly, Manager of Federal Affairs*

	1993-94	1995-96	1997	Totals
Receipts	$102,640	$123,392	$37,468	$263,500
Disburse	74,903	142,129	53,272	270,304
Cash	39,332	24,711	8,914	n/a
Contributions	51,599	115,230	31,200	198,029
Republicans	21,250	81,000	20,950	123,200
No. of Cand.	*26*	*83*	*29*	*138*
House	9,750	52,750	13,950	76,450
Senate	11,500	28,250	7,000	46,750
Democrats	29,849	34,230	9,750	73,829
No. of Cand.	*36*	*37*	*13*	*86*
House	18,349	25,730	5,500	49,579
Senate	11,500	8,500	4,250	24,250
Incumbents	43,849	99,230	32,000	175,079
Challengers	1,750	1,750	0	3,500
Open Seat	6,500	14,250	0	20,750
Winners	42,349	95,000	n/a	137,349
Losers	9,250	20,230	n/a	29,480

Torrington Co.

*Phone: (860) 482-9511 * Fax: (860) 496-3601*
P.O. Box 1008, Torrington, CT 06790-1008
Web: www.torrington.com

Torrington, headquartered in Torrington, Conn., produces bearings, metal joints and precision metal parts and assemblies for automotive and industrial manufacturers. The company employs 12,000 people. Torrington is a subsidiary of Ingersoll-Rand, a major diversified industrial equipment and components manufacturer with more than 46,600 employees and 1997 sales of $7.1 billion.

Torrington operates a network of 27 manufacturing plants in North and South America, Europe and Asia. Its products serve a variety of industries, including transportation; metal and paper mills; oil, gas and mining; aerospace; industrial, construction and agricultural machinery; machine tools; defense; consumer products; and electronic and communication equipment.

Torrington Co. Political Action Committee (C00105247) *Address: same as sponsor * Treasurer: Lawrence M. Connors*

	1993-94	1995-96	1997	Totals
Receipts	$30,288	$41,604	$18,661	$90,553
Disburse	23,399	44,210	6,675	74,284
Cash	15,581	12,977	24,963	n/a
Contributions	23,200	37,947	6,500	67,647
Republicans	6,500	13,947	5,000	25,447
No. of Cand.	*6*	*10*	*5*	*21*
House	3,500	10,947	4,000	18,447
Senate	3,000	3,000	1,000	7,000
Democrats	16,700	24,000	1,500	42,200
No. of Cand.	*12*	*14*	*2*	*28*
House	11,200	18,000	1,500	30,700
Senate	5,500	6,000	0	11,500
Incumbents	19,500	35,947	6,500	61,947
Challengers	700	0	0	700
Open Seat	3,000	2,000	0	5,000
Winners	21,000	36,947	n/a	57,947
Losers	2,200	1,000	n/a	3,200

Misc. Transport

American Bus Association

*Phone: (202) 842-1645 * Fax: (202) 842-0850*
1100 New York Ave. N.W., Suite 1050, Washington, DC 20005
*Web: www.buses.org * E-mail: abainfo@buses.org*

The American Bus Association represents the interests of the North American motorcoach industry.

It consists of about 700 motorcoach and tour companies as well as 2,300 members of the tourism industry who work in partnership with these companies.

The motorcoach and tour companies operate charter, tour, regular-route and airport express services in the United States and Canada. They also operate commuter buses, school buses and transit services.

The association promotes motorcoach tourism and encourages a good relationship between motorcoach services and the travel industry.

BUSPAC-Political Action Committee of the American Bus Association (C00004879) *Address: same as sponsor * Treasurer: Kenneth Ryan*

	1993-94	1995-96	1997	Totals
Receipts	$72,690	$100,194	$46,910	$219,794
Disburse	76,187	86,877	48,187	211,251
Cash	1,496	14,812	13,535	n/a
Contributions	75,550	83,600	46,000	205,150
Republicans	25,550	49,750	26,000	101,300
No. of Cand.	*20*	*35*	*30*	*85*
House	21,550	40,750	20,500	82,800
Senate	4,000	9,000	5,500	18,500
Democrats	48,500	33,850	18,000	100,350
No. of Cand.	*47*	*31*	*24*	*102*
House	39,750	25,350	13,500	78,600
Senate	8,750	8,500	4,500	21,750
Incumbents	70,450	81,100	45,000	196,550
Challengers	500	500	0	1,000
Open Seat	4,600	2,000	1,000	7,600
Winners	63,700	66,600	n/a	130,300
Losers	11,850	17,000	n/a	28,850

American Motorcyclist Association

*Phone: (614) 891-2425 * Fax: (614) 891-5012*
33 Collegeview Rd., Westerville, OH 43081-1484
*Web: www.ama-cycle.org * E-mail: ama@ama-cycle.org*

The American Motorcyclist Association is a 220,000-member organization that furthers the interests of American motorcyclists. Founded in 1924, the group seeks to defend motorcyclists' rights in the United States.

It is the world's largest motorsports sanctioning body. Its pro racing division oversees more than 80 national-level racing events throughout the United States.

In February 1998, the group's board of trustees voted to oppose legislative initiatives that place further government restrictions on motorcyclists in exchange for lessening current state helmet-use requirements. The vote was in response to bills being considered in the state legislatures of Kentucky, Florida and California that would require motorcyclists to obtain health insurance in order to legally operate a motorcycle without a helmet.

American Motorcyclist Political Action Committee (C00120238) *Phone: (202) 682-4750 * Fax: (202) 789-0406 * 1225 Eye St. N.W., Suite 500, Washington, DC 20005 * Treasurer: Patricia S. DiPietro*

*Contact: Robert Rasor, Chairman * Phone: (614) 891-2425*

	1993-94	1995-96	1997	Totals
Receipts	$42,645	$58,960	$27,788	$129,393
Disburse	42,500	45,000	4,500	92,000
Cash	3,309	17,271	40,559	n/a
Contributions	41,000	47,000	4,500	92,500
Republicans	33,350	42,500	4,000	79,850
No. of Cand.	*54*	*57*	*7*	*118*
House	22,350	27,250	3,500	53,100
Senate	11,000	15,250	500	26,750
Democrats	7,650	4,500	500	12,650
No. of Cand.	*10*	*12*	*1*	*23*
House	3,500	3,750	500	7,750
Senate	4,150	750	0	4,900
Incumbents	24,150	28,250	4,500	56,900
Challengers	7,350	7,500	0	14,850
Open Seat	9,000	11,250	0	20,250
Winners	35,500	32,000	n/a	67,500
Losers	5,500	15,000	n/a	20,500

Boat Owners Association of the United States

*Phone: (703) 461-2864 * Fax: (703) 461-2845*
880 S. Pickett St., Alexandria, VA 22304-9834
Web: www.boatus.com

The Boat Owners Association of the United States represents the interests of owners of recreation boats, and also offers consumer protection and other services to its members. It has more than 500,000 members.

Founded in 1966, one of the association's primary missions has been to fight against "unfair" federal taxes, fees and regulations that single out boat owners. Its lobbying efforts have included the repeal of the federal boat "user fee" tax, the retention of interest deduction for boat loans and the creation of the Wallop-Breaux Trust Fund, which uses federal gas taxes to allow states to enact boating safety measures and the construction of launch ramps.

Boat Owners Association of the United States (BOAT/US) Political Action Committee (C00160812) *Address: same as sponsor * Treasurer: Michael Sciulla*

	1993-94	1995-96	1997	Totals
Receipts	$32,680	$11,584	$6,673	$50,937
Disburse	26,100	19,750	6,000	51,850
Cash	11,074	2,911	3,584	n/a
Contributions	25,100	18,500	6,000	49,600
Republicans	8,500	12,000	2,500	23,000
No. of Cand.	*11*	*9*	*3*	*23*
House	5,500	12,000	2,500	20,000
Senate	3,000	0	0	3,000
Democrats	16,600	6,500	3,500	26,600
No. of Cand.	*19*	*8*	*3*	*30*
House	14,600	6,000	500	21,100
Senate	2,000	500	3,000	5,500
Incumbents	23,600	18,000	6,000	47,600
Challengers	0	0	0	0
Open Seat	1,000	500	0	1,500
Winners	18,100	18,500	n/a	36,600
Losers	7,000	0	n/a	7,000

Brunswick Corp.

*Phone: (847) 735-4364 * Fax: (847) 735-4765*
1 N. Field Ct., Lake Forest, IL 60045-4811
E-mail: wmetzger@bruncorp.com

Brunswick, headquartered in Illinois, manufactures marine and recreation products and also operates a national bowling chain. Brunswick was No. 427 on Fortune 500's 1996 list with $3.16 billion in sales. It is a publicly held company and employs 22,800 people.

The marine division accounts for almost 75 percent of Brunswick's sales, selling fishing boats and related parts carrying the brand names of Astro, Bayliner, Boston Whaler and Starcraft. The recreation division sells bowling equipment, billiards accessories, golf equipment, bicycles, fishing gear and exercise equipment.

Brunswick Corp. Good Government Fund (C00110262) *Address: same as sponsor * Treasurer: Bill Metzger*

	1993-94	1995-96	1997	Totals
Receipts	$12,749	$19,627	$7,064	$39,440
Disburse	17,313	30,849	681	48,843
Cash	18,592	9,043	15,428	n/a
Contributions	16,900	30,148	500	47,548
Republicans	11,300	29,552	500	41,352
No. of Cand.	*22*	*32*	*1*	*55*
House	5,300	18,996	500	24,796
Senate	6,000	10,556	0	16,556
Democrats	5,100	596	0	5,696
No. of Cand.	*9*	*1*	*0*	*10*
House	4,600	596	0	5,196
Senate	500	0	0	500
Incumbents	10,400	19,996	500	30,896
Challengers	2,000	2,192	0	4,192
Open Seat	4,500	7,960	0	12,460
Winners	13,900	25,668	n/a	39,568
Losers	3,000	4,480	n/a	7,480

Greyhound Lines Inc.

*Phone: (972) 789-7026 * Fax: (972) 404-8739*
15110 N. Dallas Pkwy., Dallas, TX 75248
Web: www.greyhound.com

Greyhound Lines and its subsidiaries are the only nationwide providers of regular intercity bus transportation services in the United States.

During 1997, Greyhound operated 252 million miles of regularly scheduled service in the 48 contiguous states with 18,000 daily departures to more than 2,400 destinations with a fleet of about 2,100 buses. It reported $771 million in total sales for the year.

During 1995, the number of sales outlets increased by 50 to about 1,500. The company also provides package express delivery service and, in certain terminals, food service.

In February 1998, a lawsuit was filed in Topeka, Kan. federal district court against Greyhound regarding the bus accommodations for physically disabled passengers. The Topeka Independent Living Resource Center alleges that Greyhound buses are inaccessible to disabled passengers and the carrier has refused to "provide assistance, as needed ... in boarding and disembarking, including moving to and from the bus seat." The suit also alleges employees are not properly trained to assist disabled passengers. Action in that suit is pending.

Greyhound, a publicly held company, operates four subsidiary bus lines: Texas, New Mexico, and Oklahoma Coaches Inc. (TNM&O), serving the Southwest; Vermont Transit Co. Inc., serving the New England area; Carolina Trailways Inc., serving the mid-Atlantic states; and Valley Transit Company, serving South Texas and the Rio Grande Valley.

Greyhound Lines Political Action Committee (C00215129)
*Address: same as sponsor * Treasurer: Heidi R. Deen*

	1993-94	1995-96	1997	Totals
Receipts	$26,466	$27,542	$20,846	$74,854
Disburse	26,652	24,516	20,883	72,051
Cash	5,040	8,064	8,027	n/a
Contributions	25,500	24,000	18,500	68,000
Republicans	4,500	15,500	13,000	33,000
No. of Cand.	*3*	*12*	*10*	*25*
House	2,500	10,500	5,000	18,000
Senate	2,000	5,000	8,000	15,000
Democrats	21,000	8,500	4,000	33,500
No. of Cand.	*16*	*10*	*5*	*31*
House	16,500	7,500	4,000	28,000
Senate	4,500	1,000	0	5,500
Incumbents	24,000	23,000	16,500	63,500
Challengers	0	0	0	0
Open Seat	1,500	1,000	0	2,500
Winners	22,500	18,500	n/a	41,000
Losers	3,000	5,500	n/a	8,500

Harley-Davidson Inc.

*Phone: (414) 343-4411 * Fax: (414) 343-4806*
3700 W. Juneau Ave., P.O. Box 653, Milwaukee, WI 53208
Web: www.harley-davidson.com

Harley-Davidson is a publicly held motorcycle manufacturer and a leading global supplier of heavyweight motorcycles. Its product line includes 20 traditional, custom and touring motorcycles, including police and military models.

Founded in 1903, Harley-Davidson includes Harley-Davidson Motor Co., based in Milwaukee, Wis., and Eaglemark Financial Services Inc., based in Chicago, Ill. Harley-Davidson Motor Co. employs about 5,000 people and has nearly 600 dealerships throughout the United States. In 1996, net sales were $1.53 billion and net income was $166 million.

In November 1995, the company bought Eaglemark Financial Services Inc., which provides insurance, financing and credit card programs to customers and dealers.

Also in 1995, Harley-Davidson established its European headquarters in Windsor, England. The division is responsible for all of its European operations.

Harley-Davidson Inc. Political Action Committee (HarleyPAC) (C00224725) *Address: same as sponsor * Treasurer: Lisa Berman*

	1993-94	1995-96	1997	Totals
Receipts	$98	$252	$4,500	$4,850
Disburse	1,550	26,271	239	28,060
Cash	15,191	2,653	6,941	n/a
Contributions	1,500	7,500	0	9,000
Republicans	500	5,000	0	5,500
No. of Cand.	*1*	*6*	*0*	*7*
House	500	5,000	0	5,500
Senate	0	0	0	0
Democrats	1,000	2,500	0	3,500
No. of Cand.	*1*	*3*	*0*	*4*
House	1,000	2,500	0	3,500
Senate	0	0	0	0
Incumbents	1,500	7,500	0	9,000
Challengers	0	0	0	0
Open Seat	0	0	0	0
Winners	1,500	7,500	n/a	9,000
Losers	0	0	n/a	0

Huffy Corp.

*Phone: (937) 866-6251 * Fax: (937) 865-2857*
225 Byers Rd., Miamisburg, OH 45342
Web: www.huffysports.com

Huffy designs and makes bicycles, basketball backboards and lawn and garden tools. A retail services unit provides inventory, assembly, repair and merchandising services to customers. The publicly traded company reported $702 million in revenues in 1996.

The company's major brand names include Huffy Bicycles, Gerry, True Temper Hardware, Huffy Sports, Washington Inventory Services and Huffy Service First.

In 1997, Huffy acquired Royce Union Bicycle Co., based in Hauppauge, N.Y. Royce Union is part of the growing sporting goods distribution business and has revenues of about $35 million.

Formed in 1970, Huffy has more than 8,000 employees.

Huffy Corp. Political Action Committee (HuffyPAC) (C00135293)
*Address: same as sponsor * Treasurer: Jeffrey D. Bernhold * Contact: Stanley H. Davis, Chairman*

	1993-94	1995-96	1997	Totals
Receipts	$12,584	$21,130	$8,728	$42,442
Disburse	11,745	21,540	11,791	45,076
Cash	13,347	12,938	9,876	n/a
Contributions	11,045	7,700	4,700	23,445
Republicans	6,925	4,200	4,700	15,825
No. of Cand.	*8*	*5*	*6*	*19*
House	2,925	1,700	1,450	6,075
Senate	4,000	2,500	3,250	9,750
Democrats	4,120	3,500	0	7,620
No. of Cand.	*3*	*2*	*0*	*5*
House	4,000	3,500	0	7,500
Senate	120	0	0	120
Incumbents	5,395	5,000	2,450	12,845
Challengers	650	2,700	250	3,600
Open Seat	5,000	0	2,000	7,000
Winners	9,895	4,975	n/a	14,870
Losers	1,150	2,725	n/a	3,875

International Taxicab and Livery Association

*Phone: (301) 946-5700 * Fax: (301) 946-4641*
3849 Farragut Ave., Kensington, MD 20895
Web: www.ustaxi.com

The International Taxicab and Livery Association is a nonprofit organization that promotes quality service and management in the ground transportation industry. ITLA's mission is to enhance the ability of member organizations to serve effectively and profitably the local transportation needs of the public. It also publicly represents the for-hire-vehicle (taxicab, limousine, livery, van and minibus) industry.

ITLA's members and associations include more than 900 taxicab, livery and limousine companies across the United States and around the world.

International Taxicab and Livery Association Political Action Committee (C00132480) *Address: same as sponsor * Treasurer: Alfred B. Lagasse III * Contact: Anthony Palmeri, Chairman*

	1993-94	1995-96	1997	Totals
Receipts	$37,329	$36,600	$18,765	$92,694
Disburse	48,000	38,510	17,500	104,010
Cash	18,788	16,878	18,143	n/a
Contributions	48,000	38,500	17,500	104,000
Republicans	37,000	36,000	17,500	90,500
No. of Cand.	*16*	*17*	*9*	*42*
House	11,500	20,000	15,000	46,500
Senate	25,500	16,000	2,500	44,000
Democrats	11,000	2,500	0	13,500
No. of Cand.	*10*	*1*	*0*	*11*
House	7,000	0	0	7,000
Senate	4,000	2,500	0	6,500
Incumbents	27,000	23,500	14,500	65,000
Challengers	0	2,500	0	2,500
Open Seat	21,000	11,500	0	32,500
Winners	45,500	22,500	n/a	68,000
Losers	2,500	16,000	n/a	18,500

National Marine Manufacturers Association

*Phone: (202) 721-1608 * Fax: (202) 861-1181*
1819 L St. N.W., Suite 700, Washington, DC 20036
E-mail: boilman@nmma.org

The National Marine Manufacturers Association represents more than 1,500 recreational boat, marine engine and marine accessory manufacturers. The association is affiliated with the Marina Operators Association and the Personal Watercraft Industry Association.

It is interested in the reauthorization of aquatic resources, recreational issues, dredging and fishing regulations.

National Marine Manufacturers Association Political Action Committee (C00245548) *Address: same as sponsor * Treasurer: Mick Blackistone * Contact: Betsy Oilman, PAC Dir.*

	1993-94	*1995-96*	*1997*	*Totals*
Receipts	$35,696	$72,304	$34,160	$142,160
Disburse	34,539	64,250	3,500	102,289
Cash	3,471	11,529	42,190	n/a
Contributions	29,875	61,750	3,500	95,125
Republicans	17,600	50,250	2,500	70,350
No. of Cand.	*21*	*54*	*4*	*79*
House	11,100	37,250	2,500	50,850
Senate	6,500	13,000	0	19,500
Democrats	12,275	11,500	1,000	24,775
No. of Cand.	*14*	*12*	*1*	*27*
House	12,275	11,000	0	23,275
Senate	0	500	1,000	1,500
Incumbents	25,275	52,250	3,500	81,025
Challengers	1,000	2,000	0	3,000
Open Seat	3,600	7,500	0	11,100
Winners	25,425	54,250	n/a	79,675
Losers	4,450	7,500	n/a	11,950

National Moving and Storage Association

11150 Maine St., Suite 402, Fairfax, VA 22030

The National Moving and Storage Association PAC filed a termination report in July 1997.

National Moving and Storage Association Political Action Committee (C00136804) *Address: same as sponsor * Treasurer: Gary Frank Petty*

	1993-94	*1995-96*	*1997*	*Totals*
Receipts	$4,815	$10,614	$0	$15,429
Disburse	5,454	12,894	0	18,348
Cash	3,279	0	0	n/a
Contributions	5,000	12,750	0	17,750
Republicans	4,000	10,750	0	14,750
No. of Cand.	*4*	*10*	*0*	*14*
House	2,000	5,250	0	7,250
Senate	2,000	5,500	0	7,500
Democrats	1,000	2,000	0	3,000
No. of Cand.	*1*	*2*	*0*	*3*
House	1,000	1,000	0	2,000
Senate	0	1,000	0	1,000
Incumbents	2,000	7,750	0	9,750
Challengers	3,000	1,000	0	4,000
Open Seat	0	4,000	0	4,000
Winners	2,000	10,750	n/a	12,750
Losers	3,000	2,000	n/a	5,000

National School Transportation Association

*Phone: (703) 644-0700 * Fax: (703) 644-9385*
6213 Old Keene Mill Ct., P.O. Box 2639, Springfield, VA 22152-2639
Web: www.schooltrans.com

The National School Transportation Association is a group of private owners who operate school buses on contract, as well as bus manufacturers and allied companies. NSTA claims that since 1964, it has been the only industry voice in Washington.

In addition to its interest in school bus safety, the organization also works to reduce the regulatory burden faced by student transportation contractors.

National School Transportation Association Non-Partisan Transportation Action Committee (C00179275) *Address: same as sponsor * Treasurer: Karen Finkel*

	1993-94	*1995-96*	*1997*	*Totals*
Receipts	$11,455	$8,600	$5,050	$25,105
Disburse	11,841	6,880	3,088	21,809
Cash	4,753	6,472	8,433	n/a
Contributions	11,550	6,500	3,000	21,050
Republicans	3,500	5,000	2,000	10,500
No. of Cand.	*3*	*4*	*2*	*9*
House	3,500	4,000	2,000	9,500
Senate	0	1,000	0	1,000
Democrats	8,050	1,500	0	9,550
No. of Cand.	*9*	*2*	*0*	*11*
House	6,050	1,500	0	7,550
Senate	2,000	0	0	2,000
Incumbents	11,550	6,500	3,000	21,050
Challengers	0	0	0	0
Open Seat	0	0	0	0
Winners	10,000	6,500	n/a	16,500
Losers	1,550	0	n/a	1,550

Polaris Industries Inc.

*Phone: (612) 542-0500 * Fax: (612) 542-0599*
1225 Hwy. 169 N., Plymouth, MN 55441-5078
Web: www.polarisindustries.com

Publicly traded Polaris designs, engineers, manufactures and markets snowmobiles, all-terrain vehicles and personal watercraft for recreational and utility use. Polaris sells its products through 2,000 dealers in North America and 60 distributors in 118 countries. Polaris' 1997 sales were about $1 billion. The company employs 2,900 workers.

Polaris is the world's largest snowmobile manufacturer and one of the largest U.S. manufacturers of all-terrain vehicles and personal watercraft. Polaris also makes replacement parts, accessories (luggage, tow hitches and cargo racks) and clothing and gear such as snowsuits and helmets.

Polaris Industries Inc. Political Participation Program (C00279497) *Address: same as sponsor * Treasurer: Mary Zins * Contact: W. Hall Wendel Jr., Chairman and CEO*

	1993-94	*1995-96*	*1997*	*Totals*
Receipts	$18,767	$21,946	$11,192	$51,905
Disburse	7,148	9,020	0	16,168
Cash	11,619	24,548	35,742	n/a
Contributions	7,000	5,000	0	12,000
Republicans	4,500	3,000	0	7,500
No. of Cand.	*5*	*2*	*0*	*7*
House	2,500	0	0	2,500
Senate	2,000	3,000	0	5,000
Democrats	1,500	2,000	0	3,500
No. of Cand.	*2*	*1*	*0*	*3*
House	1,500	2,000	0	3,500
Senate	0	0	0	0
Incumbents	4,000	3,000	0	7,000
Challengers	0	2,000	0	2,000
Open Seat	3,000	0	0	3,000
Winners	5,500	3,000	n/a	8,500
Losers	1,500	2,000	n/a	3,500

Railroads

ABB Daimler-Benz Transportation

*Phone: (412) 655-5320 * Fax: (412) 655-5841*
1501 Lebanon Church Rd., L218, Pittsburgh, PA 15236-1491
Web: www.adtranz.com

ABB Daimler-Benz Transportation, known as Adtranz, is an international railway company.

Adtranz is the largest railcar maker in the world, with major offices in more than 50 countries, and branch offices or business partners in another 40. ABB Daimler-Benz Transportation (North America) is based in Pittsburgh and operates plants in Elmira Heights, N.Y. and Pittsburg, Calif.

Adtranz, a joint venture company, has a worldwide workforce of 22,000 people and reported $3 billion in 1996 revenues.

The company's products include electric and diesel locomotives, high-speed trains, inter-city and regional trains, underground trains, people movers, signal engineering and rail infrastructure systems.

ABB Daimler-Benz was formed by the 1996 merger of Daimler-Benz of Stuttgart, Germany and ABB, a Swiss-Swedish electrical engineering group, of Zurich, Switzerland.

ABB Daimler-Benz Transportation USA Employees' Political Fund (C00255356) *Address: same as sponsor * Treasurer: Rayna Scarlato * Contact: Peter Stetler, Chairman*

	1993-94	1995-96	1997	Totals
Receipts	$26,314	$23,122	$12,952	$62,388
Disburse	22,366	14,250	13,275	49,891
Cash	13,188	22,064	21,741	n/a
Contributions	15,061	13,000	7,275	35,336
Republicans	1,500	11,000	2,500	15,000
No. of Cand.	*2*	*4*	*3*	*9*
House	0	3,000	0	3,000
Senate	1,500	8,000	2,500	12,000
Democrats	13,561	2,000	4,775	20,336
No. of Cand.	*12*	*7*	*5*	*24*
House	9,061	500	4,275	13,836
Senate	4,500	1,500	500	6,500
Incumbents	12,567	12,500	7,275	32,342
Challengers	1,000	0	0	1,000
Open Seat	1,000	500	0	1,500
Winners	9,500	14,000	n/a	23,500
Losers	5,561	-1000	n/a	4,561

American Short Line and Regional Railroad Association

*Phone: (202) 628-4500 * Fax: (202) 628-6430*
1120 G St. N.W., Suite 520, Washington, DC 20005-3889
*Web: www.aslrra.org * E-mail: asaylor@aslrra.org*

The American Short Line and Regional Railroad Association represents the interests of small railroad companies in the United States. The organization changed its name from the American Short Line Railroad Association in 1998 after merging with the Regional Railroad Association.

The group represents small railroads in negotiations with larger rail companies and before the federal government. It also publishes a list of tariffs and contracts and manages an insurance fund.

PAC of the American Short Line and Regional Railroad Association (ASLRRA PAC) (C00298190) *Address: same as sponsor * Treasurer: Alice C. Saylor*

	1993-94	1995-96	1997	Totals
Receipts	$8,500	$19,915	$14,910	$43,325
Disburse	0	13,500	14,290	27,790
Cash	8,500	14,915	15,534	n/a
Contributions	0	13,500	14,290	27,790
Republicans	0	9,500	9,000	18,500
No. of Cand.	*0*	*10*	*14*	*24*
House	0	7,500	7,000	14,500
Senate	0	2,000	2,000	4,000
Democrats	0	4,000	4,790	8,790
No. of Cand.	*0*	*6*	*8*	*14*
House	0	3,500	4,290	7,790
Senate	0	500	500	1,000
Incumbents	0	13,500	14,290	27,790
Challengers	0	0	0	0
Open Seat	0	0	0	0
Winners	0	11,500	n/a	11,500
Losers	0	2,000	n/a	2,000

Association of American Railroads

*Phone: (202) 639-2537 * Fax: (202) 639-2526*
50 F St. N.W., Washington, DC 20001-1564
*Web: www.aar.org * E-mail: oobannon@lms.aar.org*

The Association of American Railroads collects information on railroad operations, safety and maintenance, economics and management. The group also conducts research and issues statistical reports.

AAR's members include: Amtrak, CSX Corp., Conrail, Kansas City Southern, Canadian National, Norfolk Southern, Burlington Northern Santa Fe, Union Pacific, Canadian Pacific Railway, Illinois Central, Ferrocarriles Nacionales de Mexico, Transportation Technology Center, Operation Lifesaver, American Short Line and Regional Railroad Association, Railway Progress Institute and Railway Association of Canada.

Association of American Railroads Political Action Committee (Rail PAC) (C00280743) *Address: same as sponsor * Treasurer: Cassandra Henry * Contact: Hubert O'Bannon, Assistant V.P.*

	1993-94	1995-96	1997	Totals
Receipts	$58,812	$85,651	$54,304	$198,767
Disburse	32,860	88,074	39,762	160,696
Cash	25,950	23,530	38,073	n/a
Contributions	32,166	86,500	39,250	157,916
Republicans	10,000	65,500	27,750	103,250
No. of Cand.	*13*	*50*	*34*	*97*
House	6,000	50,500	20,500	77,000
Senate	4,000	15,000	7,250	26,250
Democrats	22,166	21,000	9,500	52,666
No. of Cand.	*28*	*17*	*12*	*57*
House	16,166	16,000	7,500	39,666
Senate	6,000	5,000	2,000	13,000
Incumbents	31,166	84,000	39,250	154,416
Challengers	0	0	0	0
Open Seat	1,000	2,500	0	3,500
Winners	27,166	76,500	n/a	103,666
Losers	5,000	10,000	n/a	15,000

Burlington Northern Santa Fe Corp.

*Phone: (817) 333-2325 * Fax: (817) 352-2392*
P.O. Box 961039, 3017 Lou Menk Dr., Fort Worth, TX 76161
Web: www.bnsf.com

Burlington Northern Santa Fe is the second-largest railroad company in the United States. The company has about 35,000 miles of track located mostly west of the Mississippi River and extending from Canada to California to Texas.

BNSF was created on Sept. 22, 1995, from the merger of Burlington Northern Inc., the parent company of Burlington Northern Railroad, and Santa Fe Pacific Corp., parent company of the Atchison, Topeka and Santa Fe Railway. The publicly traded company employs more than 43,000 people and reported $8.4 billion in 1997 revenues.

About 25 percent of the company's business comes from hauling coal; it also carries automobile parts, chemicals and agricultural products. Among its subsidiaries is BN Leasing Corp., formed in 1989 to acquire railroad rolling stock and other equipment necessary for transportation and other business affairs of BN.

Burlington Northern Santa Fe Corp. RAILPAC (C00235739)
*Address: same as sponsor * Treasurer: Patricia Ann Tilson * Contact: Cathy Batky, Executive Dir.*

	1993-94	1995-96	1997	Totals
Receipts	$295,596	$317,491	$150,428	$763,515
Disburse	291,567	317,526	135,923	745,016
Cash	29,480	29,458	43,968	n/a
Contributions	203,741	223,982	102,850	530,573
Republicans	86,798	166,950	69,250	322,998
No. of Cand.	*64*	*123*	*59*	*246*
House	40,800	102,250	46,250	189,300
Senate	45,998	64,700	23,000	133,698
Democrats	115,193	57,032	31,100	203,325
No. of Cand.	*81*	*51*	*31*	*163*
House	79,323	40,532	16,100	135,955
Senate	35,870	16,500	15,000	67,370
Incumbents	176,142	180,282	102,850	459,274
Challengers	2,000	10,700	0	12,700
Open Seat	25,599	33,000	0	58,599
Winners	147,647	190,282	n/a	337,929
Losers	56,094	33,700	n/a	89,794

Santa Fe Pacific Gold Corp. Political Action Committee (GoldPAC) (C00298133) *6200 Uptown Blvd. N.E., Suite 400, Albuquerque, NM 87110 * Treasurer: Craig G. Pettit*

Santa Fe Pacific Gold PAC was terminated on July 24, 1997.

	1993-94	1995-96	1997	Totals
Receipts	$2,084	$31,940	$1,724	$35,748
Disburse	0	30,512	5,238	35,750
Cash	2,084	3,513	0	n/a
Contributions	0	29,500	5,184	34,684
Republicans	0	26,500	4,675	31,175
No. of Cand.	*0*	*23*	*9*	*32*
House	0	16,500	3,675	20,175
Senate	0	10,000	1,000	11,000
Democrats	0	3,000	509	3,509
No. of Cand.	*0*	*4*	*1*	*5*
House	0	1,000	0	1,000
Senate	0	2,000	509	2,509
Incumbents	0	27,000	5,184	32,184
Challengers	0	500	0	500
Open Seat	0	2,000	0	2,000
Winners	0	28,000	n/a	28,000
Losers	0	1,500	n/a	1,500

Santa Fe Pacific Corp. Political Action Committee (C00009902)
*Phone: (817) 333-2000 * 1700 E. Golf Rd., Schaumburg, IL 60173 * Treasurer: Kathleen M. Magiera*

Santa Fe Pacific Corp.'s PAC was dissolved in April 1996 because of the company's merger with Burlington Northern Inc. It now functions as a part of the Burlington Northern Santa Fe Corp. RAILPAC.

	1993-94	1995-96	1997	Totals
Receipts	$88,166	$45,702	$0	$133,868
Disburse	78,540	70,053	0	148,593
Cash	22,660	0	0	n/a
Contributions	51,300	8,500	0	59,800
Republicans	30,250	9,000	0	39,250
No. of Cand.	*36*	*14*	*0*	*50*
House	18,000	6,500	0	24,500
Senate	12,250	2,500	0	14,750
Democrats	21,050	-500	0	20,550
No. of Cand.	*27*	*2*	*0*	*29*
House	11,050	0	0	11,050
Senate	10,000	-500	0	9,500
Incumbents	43,450	9,000	0	52,450
Challengers	250	-500	0	-250
Open Seat	7,600	1,000	0	8,600
Winners	46,050	8,500	n/a	54,550
Losers	5,250	0	n/a	5,250

CSX Corp.

Phone: (804) 782-1561
901 E. Cary St., Richmond, VA 23219
Web: www.csx.com

CSX, headquartered in Richmond, Va., is a global transportation company offering a variety of rail, container-shipping, trucking and barge services.

Its rail system is the third-largest in the United States, linking 20 states in the East, the Midwest and the South, and Ontario, Canada. The rail system accounts for nearly half of the company's operating revenue and is a major carrier of paper, chemicals, coal and grain. CSX has 47,300 employees and posted 1997 sales of $10.6 billion.

After merger talks with Conrail in 1997, CSX will control half of Conrail's railroad system in the East — Norfolk Southern will run the other half. CSX had originally attempted to acquire Conrail's entire system but negotiations proved unsuccessful. With the addition of Conrail's lines, CSX will be able to reach every major market east of the Mississippi River. Conrail will maintain its federal PAC while the merger is being completed.

Among the company's subsidiaries is CSX Transportation, the largest coal hauler in the United States. CSX's Sea-Land Service, the biggest U.S. shipping company, has about 100 ships serving some 80 countries. CSX also operates American Commercial Barge Line, another ocean transport company. In addition, the company operates resorts in West Virginia and Wyoming, develops real estate and has a majority stake in Yukon Pacific, which promotes construction of the Trans-Alaska Gas System.

CSX has four federal PACs among its divisions. The main railroad PAC ranked second among all railroads in 1996 congressional contributions and favored Republican incumbents. Conrail ranked fifth and a second CSX PAC was eighth. Sea-Land Service and American Commercial Barge Line ranked first and ninth, respectively, among ocean transport companies.

CSX Transportation Inc. PAC (formerly known as Seaboard System Railroad PAC) (C00007831) *Phone: (202) 783-8124 * Fax: (202) 783-5929 * 1331 Pennsylvania Ave. N.W., Suite 560, Washington, DC 20004 * Treasurer: Alem Woldehawariat*

	1993-94	1995-96	1997	Totals
Receipts	$288,131	$273,752	$128,357	$690,240
Disburse	310,757	287,085	121,750	719,592
Cash	40,347	27,023	34,634	n/a
Contributions	279,233	242,600	101,500	623,333
Republicans	114,689	167,750	67,500	349,939
No. of Cand.	*99*	*118*	*83*	*300*
House	77,089	122,000	47,500	246,589
Senate	37,600	45,750	20,000	103,350
Democrats	164,544	74,850	33,000	272,394
No. of Cand.	*124*	*70*	*40*	*234*
House	118,442	58,850	22,500	199,792
Senate	46,102	16,000	10,500	72,602
Incumbents	229,225	213,500	98,500	541,225
Challengers	15,189	2,000	0	17,189
Open Seat	33,819	22,500	3,000	59,319
Winners	226,914	217,850	n/a	444,764
Losers	52,319	24,750	n/a	77,069

Sea-Land Service Inc. Associates Good Government Fund (C00100495) *Phone: (202) 783-8124 * Fax: (202) 783-5929 * 1331 Pennsylvania Ave. N.W., Suite 560, Washington, DC 20004 * Treasurer: Linda A. Mathis*

	1993-94	1995-96	1997	Totals
Receipts	$167,218	$181,896	$89,291	$438,405
Disburse	163,515	185,601	93,000	442,116
Cash	38,418	34,715	31,008	n/a
Contributions	153,950	170,000	90,000	413,950
Republicans	62,600	139,350	69,500	271,450
No. of Cand.	*41*	*87*	*65*	*193*
House	32,100	104,850	48,000	184,950
Senate	30,500	34,500	21,500	86,500
Democrats	91,350	30,650	19,500	141,500
No. of Cand.	*56*	*27*	*23*	*106*
House	52,850	26,150	12,500	91,500
Senate	38,500	4,500	7,000	50,000
Incumbents	144,950	157,000	90,000	391,950
Challengers	0	3,000	0	3,000
Open Seat	9,000	10,000	0	19,000
Winners	133,100	147,050	n/a	280,150
Losers	20,850	22,950	n/a	43,800

CSX Good Government Fund (C00163832) *Phone: (202) 783-8124 * Fax: (202) 783-5929 * 1331 Pennsylvania Ave. N.W., Suite 560, Washington, DC 20004 * Treasurer: Daniel S. Green * Contact: Alem Woldehawariat * Contact: Pat O'Grady * Phone: (804) 782-1561*

	1993-94	1995-96	1997	Totals
Receipts	$57,201	$66,789	$32,139	$156,129
Disburse	14,450	97,417	46,500	158,367
Cash	113,934	83,320	68,964	n/a
Contributions	13,850	53,250	37,000	104,100
Republicans	8,100	39,750	29,500	77,350
No. of Cand.	*5*	*35*	*29*	*69*
House	2,100	24,250	13,500	39,850
Senate	6,000	15,500	16,000	37,500
Democrats	5,750	13,500	7,500	26,750
No. of Cand.	*7*	*11*	*8*	*26*
House	5,500	7,500	1,500	14,500
Senate	250	6,000	6,000	12,250
Incumbents	8,350	43,750	35,000	87,100
Challengers	5,500	3,500	1,000	10,000
Open Seat	0	6,000	1,000	7,000
Winners	4,350	48,250	n/a	52,600
Losers	9,500	5,000	n/a	14,500

American Commercial Barge Line Inc. Effective Government Fund (C00077982) *Phone: (812) 288-0100 * Fax: (812) 288-0294 * 1701 E. Market St., P.O. Box 610, Jeffersonville, IN 47130-0610 * Web: www.aclines.com * Treasurer: David Meffert * Contact: Jim Adams, Asst. V.P. of Public and Regulatory Affairs*

	1993-94	1995-96	1997	Totals
Receipts	$55,435	$63,742	$34,733	$153,910
Disburse	58,600	49,601	33,630	141,831
Cash	23,218	37,370	38,479	n/a
Contributions	58,600	48,501	31,500	138,601
Republicans	38,350	38,750	26,500	103,600
No. of Cand.	*44*	*46*	*29*	*119*
House	33,850	31,750	17,000	82,600
Senate	4,500	7,000	9,500	21,000
Democrats	19,250	9,751	4,500	33,501
No. of Cand.	*21*	*9*	*6*	*36*
House	14,250	8,251	1,500	24,001
Senate	5,000	1,500	3,000	9,500
Incumbents	52,600	42,501	29,500	124,601
Challengers	1,000	3,000	0	4,000
Open Seat	5,000	3,000	2,000	10,000
Winners	53,600	43,001	n/a	96,601
Losers	5,000	5,500	n/a	10,500

Conrail Inc.

2001 Market St. -19 A, P.O. Box 41419, Philadelphia, PA 19101
*Web: www.conrail.com * E-mail: info@conrail.com*

Conrail was bought by CSX and Norfolk Southern railroad lines in 1997, and its PAC will be terminated in 1998.

Conrail operates the largest freight railroad in the northeast quarter of the United States, serving 12 states, the District of Columbia and the Canadian province of Quebec.

Conrail operates a railroad route network of about 11,000 miles, with a fleet of about 2,000 locomotives and more than 53,000 freight cars. Conrail is dedicated exclusively to freight transportation.

The railroad maintains access to the major ports of the region, including Baltimore, Boston, Cleveland, New York/New Jersey and Philadelphia. Conrail's connections with other railroads, barge operators, steamship lines, and trucking companies create access to markets throughout the United States and around the world.

Conrail's 1997 revenue totaled $3.7 billion. The company employs more than 23,510 workers.

Consolidated Rail Corp. Good Government Fund (Conrail Good Government Fund) (C00174185) *Address: same as sponsor * Treasurer: T. J. McFadden*

	1993-94	1995-96	1997	Totals
Receipts	$176,493	$161,464	$17,063	$355,020
Disburse	165,888	174,550	19,200	359,638
Cash	19,361	6,279	4,126	n/a
Contributions	119,768	127,424	13,250	260,442
Republicans	44,625	81,424	9,250	135,299
No. of Cand.	*51*	*72*	*12*	*135*
House	33,125	66,556	8,250	107,931
Senate	11,500	14,868	1,000	27,368
Democrats	74,393	46,000	3,000	123,393
No. of Cand.	*73*	*58*	*5*	*136*
House	51,800	37,500	3,000	92,300
Senate	22,593	8,500	0	31,093
Incumbents	110,343	117,174	13,250	240,767
Challengers	1,625	2,750	0	4,375
Open Seat	3,300	7,000	0	10,300
Winners	100,218	108,507	n/a	208,725
Losers	19,550	18,917	n/a	38,467

Delaware Otsego Corp.

*Phone: (607) 547-2555 x213 * Fax: (607) 547-9834*
One Railroad Ave., Cooperstown, NY 13326

Delaware Otsego is a private railroad holding company. It operates a 500-mile regional railroad in New York, New Jersey and Pennsylvania, of which 200 miles are owned by other railroads. It serves about 110 business customers. Otsego's railroad system is devoted principally to carrying freight, but it also generates revenue through the operation of passenger excursion trains.

Delaware Otsego's subsidiaries include Lackawaxen and Stourbridge Railroad, Cooperstown and Charlotte Valley Railroad and Staten Island Railway.

In 1996, sales were estimated at $32.3 million and the company had 172 employees.

Delaware Otsego Corp. Political Action Committee (C00192468) *Address: same as sponsor * Treasurer: William H. Matteson*

	1993-94	1995-96	1997	Totals
Receipts	$15,881	$28,189	$5,858	$49,928
Disburse	24,990	27,862	4,700	57,552
Cash	587	914	2,072	n/a
Contributions	20,229	27,001	1,950	49,180
Republicans	10,100	19,625	1,950	31,675
No. of Cand.	*9*	*13*	*9*	*31*
House	8,100	10,625	700	19,425
Senate	2,000	9,000	1,250	12,250
Democrats	10,129	7,376	0	17,505
No. of Cand.	*6*	*2*	*0*	*8*
House	1,629	0	0	1,629
Senate	8,500	7,376	0	15,876
Incumbents	17,950	20,325	2,250	40,525
Challengers	0	0	0	0
Open Seat	1,500	6,676	0	8,176
Winners	17,950	25,701	n/a	43,651
Losers	2,279	1,300	n/a	3,579

Duchossois Industries Inc.

*Phone: (630) 279-0486 * Fax: (630) 530-6057*
845 Larch Ave., Elmhurst, IL 60126-1114

Duchossois Industries has major operations in the manufacturing of railroad cars and transportation products. Organized in 1983, the company is a privately owned, diversified company with about 6,000 employees. It ranked No. 126 on the Forbes list of top private companies.

Duchossois also owns the now-closed Arlington International Racecourse near Chicago. In addition, the company maintains businesses in the manufacturing of garage door openers and ammunition and the operation of radio broadcasting stations.

Subsidiaries include: Chamberlain Group Inc., Thrall Car Manufacturing and Arlington International.

Duchossois Industries Inc. Political Action Committee (C00212308) *Address: same as sponsor * Treasurer: Robert L. Fealy*

	1993-94	1995-96	1997	Totals
Receipts	$62,303	$68,817	$50,350	$181,470
Disburse	26,683	114,733	31,765	173,181
Cash	65,094	19,189	37,781	n/a
Contributions	18,400	56,650	20,750	95,800
Republicans	14,400	47,650	19,500	81,550
No. of Cand.	*10*	*16*	*9*	*35*
House	9,700	32,150	11,500	53,350
Senate	4,700	15,500	8,000	28,200
Democrats	4,000	9,000	1,250	14,250
No. of Cand.	*4*	*5*	*2*	*11*
House	4,000	8,000	1,250	13,250
Senate	0	1,000	0	1,000
Incumbents	6,600	37,150	14,250	58,000
Challengers	100	3,500	6,500	10,100
Open Seat	11,200	16,000	0	27,200
Winners	14,800	29,500	n/a	44,300
Losers	3,600	27,150	n/a	30,750

GATX Corp.

*Phone: (312) 621-6200 * Fax: (312) 621-6645*
500 W. Monroe St., Chicago, IL 60661
Web: www.gatx.com

GATX is a publicly traded holding company that focuses on transportation and other services.

The company leases railroad cars and airplanes, operates pipeline terminals for oil and chemical companies and provides distribution and logistical services. It also has a fleet of vessels in the Great Lakes which help load and move construction materials and equipment. GATX owns no significant properties, and had 1997 revenues of $1.7 billion. The company has about 6,000 employees.

Subsidiaries: General American Transportation, GATX Capital, GATX Terminals, GATX Logistics and American Steamship.

GATX Corp. Good Government Program (C00118703) *Address: same as sponsor * Treasurer: Thomas W. Reedy * Contact: Joseph Lane, President and CEO*

	1993-94	1995-96	1997	Totals
Receipts	$3,236	$3,047	$1,253	$7,536
Disburse	4,456	13,105	4,531	22,092
Cash	74,581	64,527	61,249	n/a
Contributions	3,200	11,000	3,750	17,950
Republicans	500	8,000	2,750	11,250
No. of Cand.	*1*	*6*	*4*	*11*
House	500	6,500	3,000	10,000
Senate	0	1,500	-250	1,250
Democrats	2,700	3,000	0	5,700
No. of Cand.	*4*	*2*	*0*	*6*
House	1,700	0	0	1,700
Senate	1,000	3,000	0	4,000
Incumbents	2,200	9,000	3,750	14,950
Challengers	0	0	0	0
Open Seat	1,000	2,000	0	3,000
Winners	2,000	10,000	n/a	12,000
Losers	1,200	1,000	n/a	2,200

Genesee & Wyoming Inc.

Phone: (716) 382-3220
3 Parkway, P.O. Box 247, Leicester, NY 14481

Genesee & Wyoming is a public holding company operating shortline and regional freight railroads in western New York, Pennsylvania, Illinois, Texas, Louisiana and Oregon. The company also leases its cars and trucks to other rail shippers.

G&W, which has 12 railroads and about 700 employees, had estimated 1997 sales of $103 million.

Genesee & Wyoming Industries Inc. PAC (C00289058) *Address: same as sponsor * Treasurer: Alan R. Harris*

	1993-94	1995-96	1997	Totals
Receipts	$12,375	$26,675	$4,000	$43,050
Disburse	8,100	24,375	1,350	33,825
Cash	4,275	6,575	9,225	n/a
Contributions	1,000	9,750	1,000	11,750
Republicans	1,000	9,750	1,000	11,750
No. of Cand.	*1*	*9*	*1*	*11*
House	1,000	5,750	1,000	7,750
Senate	0	4,000	0	4,000
Democrats	0	0	0	0
No. of Cand.	*0*	*0*	*0*	*0*
House	0	0	0	0
Senate	0	0	0	0

Incumbents	1,000	7,250	1,000	9,250
Challengers	0	0	0	0
Open Seat	0	2,500	0	2,500
Winners	1,000	6,750	n/a	7,750
Losers	0	3,000	n/a	3,000

Grand Trunk Western Railroad Inc.

*Phone: (248) 740-6223 * Fax: (248) 740-6788*
800 Livernois, Suite 300, P.O. Box 5025, Troy, MI 48007

Grand Trunk Western Railroad is a railroad company operating in Michigan, Ohio, Illinois and Indiana and a subsidiary of the Canadian National Railway Co., a $4.6-billion, publicly owned company. Grand Trunk employs about 1,900 people, most of whom are union members.

Grand Trunk Rail PAC (C00095117) *Address: same as sponsor * Treasurer: Roger A. Cobb * Contact: Gloria Combe, Dir. of Public Relations*

	1993-94	*1995-96*	*1997*	*Totals*
Receipts	$9,775	$7,332	$3,036	$20,143
Disburse	12,800	11,160	6,113	30,073
Cash	19,511	15,686	12,610	n/a
Contributions	12,800	10,825	5,850	29,475
Republicans	4,750	5,850	2,500	13,100
No. of Cand.	*12*	*13*	*8*	*33*
House	3,250	5,100	1,500	9,850
Senate	1,500	750	1,000	3,250
Democrats	8,050	4,975	3,100	16,125
No. of Cand.	*12*	*10*	*7*	*29*
House	5,550	4,350	2,850	12,750
Senate	2,500	625	250	3,375
Incumbents	10,550	8,975	5,850	25,375
Challengers	0	1,350	0	1,350
Open Seat	2,250	500	0	2,750
Winners	8,550	8,975	n/a	17,525
Losers	4,250	1,850	n/a	6,100

Kansas City Southern Industries Inc.

*Phone: (816) 983-1523 * Fax: (816) 983-1375*
114 W. 11th St., Kansas City, MO 64105
Web: www.kcsi.com

Kansas City Southern Industries operates nearly 4,000 miles of railroad track in nine Midwestern and Southeastern states. The public company also owns controlling interests in Janus Capital and Berger Associates, which manage mutual funds totaling about $70 billion. The company reported $1 billion in 1997 revenues.

Kansas City Southern also has a 41 percent interest in DST Systems, which provides record-keeping services and software to the financial services industry. The company plans to split its Janus and Berger units from the railroad company.

Kansas City Southern Industries Inc. Employees Political Action Committee (KCSI PAC) (C00139451) *Address: same as sponsor * Treasurer: Linas Cesonis * Contact: Phil Brown, Chairman*

	1993-94	*1995-96*	*1997*	*Totals*
Receipts	$116,741	$95,824	$37,761	$250,326
Disburse	115,510	94,585	42,917	253,012
Cash	4,937	6,176	1,020	n/a
Contributions	101,409	70,450	39,417	211,276
Republicans	54,225	47,200	24,167	125,592
No. of Cand.	*51*	*47*	*20*	*118*
House	23,825	20,000	4,850	48,675
Senate	30,400	27,200	19,317	76,917
Democrats	47,184	23,250	14,750	85,184
No. of Cand.	*48*	*30*	*9*	*87*
House	33,100	15,250	2,250	50,600
Senate	14,084	8,000	12,500	34,584
Incumbents	71,284	48,250	39,317	158,851
Challengers	3,625	1,950	0	5,575
Open Seat	26,500	19,250	0	45,750
Winners	90,159	54,500	n/a	144,659
Losers	11,250	15,950	n/a	27,200

Norfolk Southern Corp.

*Phone: (757) 629-2380 * Fax: (757) 664-5137*
Three Commercial Pl., Norfolk, VA 23510-2191
Web: www.nscorp.com

Norfolk Southern is a Virginia-based holding company that owns Norfolk Southern Railway Co., a major freight railroad, and Pocahontas Land Corp., a natural resources company. The company sold North American Van Lines, a household moving and specialized freight handling subsidiary, in early 1998. A publicly traded company, Norfolk Southern posted 1997 sales of $4.2 billion.

The railroad system's lines extend across 14,400 miles of track in 20 states, primarily in the Southeast and Midwest, and in Ontario, Canada. Pocahontas Land manages about 900,000 acres of coal, natural gas and timber resources in Alabama, Illinois, Kentucky, Tennessee, Virginia and West Virginia.

Norfolk Southern and CSX purchased Conrail Inc. in 1997 under a joint ownership agreement. Norfolk Southern will control 58 percent of Conrail's 11,000 miles of routes, mainly into the New York City metropolitan area.

Norfolk Southern Corp. Good Government Fund (C00009282) *Address: same as sponsor * Treasurer: D. J. O'Brian * Contact: J. C. Bishop Jr., Chairman*

	1993-94	*1995-96*	*1997*	*Totals*
Receipts	$194,205	$223,694	$166,674	$584,573
Disburse	200,645	225,900	142,075	568,620
Cash	22,450	20,258	44,864	n/a
Contributions	177,270	195,600	119,000	491,870
Republicans	74,670	146,350	76,500	297,520
No. of Cand.	*71*	*101*	*92*	*264*
House	54,170	104,250	50,500	208,920
Senate	20,500	42,100	26,000	88,600
Democrats	100,600	49,250	41,500	191,350
No. of Cand.	*104*	*46*	*50*	*200*
House	78,700	36,250	28,500	143,450
Senate	21,900	13,000	13,000	47,900
Incumbents	161,650	169,600	111,500	442,750
Challengers	6,220	4,500	1,000	11,720
Open Seat	9,500	21,250	5,000	35,750
Winners	144,050	166,100	n/a	310,150
Losers	33,220	29,500	n/a	62,720

Terminated PACs which contributed less than $5,000 during 1995-96 cycle:

North American Van Lines Inc. PAC (NAPAC)/Norfolk Southern Corp. Good Government Fund (C00193581) *P.O. Box 13207, Fort Wayne, IN 46867 * Treasurer: Cynthia L. Thomas*

TTX Co.

*Phone: (312) 984-3835 * Fax: (312) 984-3790*
101 N. Wacker Dr., Chicago, IL 60606

TTX is a privately held railroad leasing company that leases railroad cars. The company owns 23 percent of the nation's freight cars. TTX's fleet includes cars that can carry trailers, containers and new automobiles, box cars, gondola cars and cars specially designed to carry commodities such as lumber and heavy machinery.

Formed in 1991, TTX has more than 1,900 employees. Its 1996 sales were estimated at $858 million.

TTX Co. Employees Political Action Committee (formerly known as Trailer Train Co.) (C00138974) *Address: same as sponsor * Treasurer: William F. Todd*

	1993-94	*1995-96*	*1997*	*Totals*
Receipts	$20,884	$21,848	$10,644	$53,376
Disburse	31,704	22,038	2,350	56,092
Cash	11,439	11,249	19,544	n/a
Contributions	28,750	18,319	2,250	49,319
Republicans	16,000	13,069	1,750	30,819
No. of Cand.	*17*	*18*	*3*	*38*
House	6,000	7,750	1,750	15,500
Senate	10,000	5,319	0	15,319
Democrats	12,750	5,250	0	18,000
No. of Cand.	*14*	*9*	*0*	*23*
House	9,250	3,250	0	12,500
Senate	3,500	2,000	0	5,500
Incumbents	19,250	16,250	2,250	37,750
Challengers	1,250	1,569	0	2,819
Open Seat	8,250	500	0	8,750
Winners	25,250	14,750	n/a	40,000
Losers	3,500	3,569	n/a	7,069

Transtar Inc.

*Phone: (412) 829-3475 * Fax: (412) 829-3448*
P.O. Box 68, 135 Jamison Ln., Monroeville, PA 15146

Transtar owns and operates seven railroads, a Great Lakes shipping fleet and an inland barge operation, all in the eastern United States. It is a transportation holding company primarily comprised of USX's former domestic transportation businesses. A private company, it is owned by Transtar Holdings, a limited partnership of Blackstone Transportation Partners, Blackstone Capital Partners and USX Corp. All of Transtar's subsidiaries are wholly owned by USX. Transtar subsidiaries carry raw materials, semi-finished products, and finished goods in Alabama, Illinois, Indiana, Minnesota, Ohio, Pennsylvania, Wisconsin and destinations on the Great Lakes.

Transtar provides the sole rail access to, as well as the primary water transport for, nearly all the steel making plants of USX Corp., servicing US Steel, USS Mining Co. and the USS/Kobe Steel Co. joint venture at Lorain, Ohio. Transtar derived 58 percent of its revenues in 1996 from serving these USX facilities. The steel industry accounted for 76 percent of Transtar's revenues in 1996.

Transtar owns Bessemer & Lake Erie Railroad, which is responsible for a $498 million antitrust judgment made against it in 1994.

Originally formed in 1988 as Blackstone Transportation Partners, it was renamed Transtar Holdings in 1993.

Subsidiaries: Transtar Capital Corp., Duluth, Missabe and Iron Range Railway Co., Elgin, Joliet and Eastern Railway Co., Bessemer and Lake Erie Railroad Co., Union Railroad Co., The Lake Terminal Railroad Co., McKeesport Connecting Railroad Co., Birmingham Southern Railroad Co., Pittsburgh & Conneaut Dock Co., Fairfield Southern Co. Inc., USS Great Lakes Fleet Inc. and Warrior & Gulf Navigation Co.

TransPAC Political Action Committee of Transtar Inc. (C00035048) *Address: same as sponsor * Treasurer: J. W. Schulte*

	1993-94	1995-96	1997	Totals
Receipts	$19,700	$22,107	$10,403	$52,210
Disburse	20,650	19,475	13,550	53,675
Cash	18,598	21,242	18,101	n/a
Contributions	9,550	11,025	6,850	27,425
Republicans	6,150	7,825	3,650	17,625
No. of Cand.	*6*	*14*	*9*	*29*
House	650	5,875	2,150	8,675
Senate	5,500	1,950	1,500	8,950
Democrats	3,400	3,200	3,200	9,800
No. of Cand.	*4*	*2*	*2*	*8*
House	3,000	3,200	3,200	9,400
Senate	400	0	0	400
Incumbents	5,300	7,575	6,350	19,225
Challengers	3,500	3,450	500	7,450
Open Seat	750	0	0	750
Winners	8,800	7,325	n/a	16,125
Losers	750	3,700	n/a	4,450

Trinity Industries

*Phone: (214) 631-4420 * Fax: (214) 589-8824*
2525 Stemmons Freeway, Dallas, TX 75207
Web: www.trin.net

Trinity Industries makes transportation, construction and industrial products including railcars, gondola cars, ready-mix concrete, highway guardrails, airport conveyers, barges and metal storage containers for liquid gas and chemicals. The publicly traded Dallas company reported $2.2 billion in 1997 revenues and has 12,700 employees.

In January 1998, Trinity sold its Stearns Airport Equipment Co. subsidiary. Stearns installed equipment at Washington National Airport and Baltimore Washington International during 1997.

Trinity has locations in: Alabama, Arkansas, Georgia, Indiana, Louisiana, Mississippi, Missouri, Montana, Nebraska, North Carolina, Ohio, Oklahoma, Pennsylvania, Tennessee, Texas, Utah and Wyoming.

Subsidiaries include: Syro in Dallas; Beaird Industries in Shreveport, La.; and Trinity Industries Leasing Co., which leases railcars.

Trinity Industries Employee Political Action Committee Inc. (C00268904) *Address: same as sponsor * Treasurer: Judy Arrington * Contact: Linda S. Sickels, Chairperson*

	1993-94	1995-96	1997	Totals
Receipts	$157,697	$154,587	$60,597	$372,881
Disburse	119,850	80,850	20,000	220,700
Cash	60,447	134,195	174,797	n/a
Contributions	92,500	60,850	10,500	163,850
Republicans	48,000	45,600	9,000	102,600
No. of Cand.	*12*	*21*	*8*	*41*
House	25,000	32,600	7,000	64,600
Senate	23,000	13,000	2,000	38,000
Democrats	44,500	15,250	1,500	61,250
No. of Cand.	*15*	*10*	*2*	*27*
House	36,500	11,000	1,500	49,000
Senate	8,000	4,250	0	12,250
Incumbents	92,000	51,600	10,500	154,100
Challengers	0	250	0	250
Open Seat	0	9,000	0	9,000
Winners	83,000	56,100	n/a	139,100
Losers	9,500	4,750	n/a	14,250

Union Pacific Corp.

*Phone: (214) 743-5600 * Fax: (214) 743-5656*
1717 Main St., Suite 5900, Dallas, TX 75201-4605
Web: www.up.com

Union Pacific is North America's biggest railroad company, having acquired rival Southern Pacific in 1996. The company has 36,000 route miles in 23 states, connecting nearly every major city between Chicago and the Pacific Ocean. UP also operates trucking and overnight delivery businesses in all 50 states.

UP has four operating companies: Union Pacific Railroad, Overnite Transportation, Skyway Freight Systems and Union Pacific Technologies. Overnite carries less-than-truckload shipments, while Skyway is a California company specializing in next-day delivery. UP's technology business provides support for the other units. The entire company has more than 65,000 employees. UP also owns Chicago & North Western Transport, which has its own PAC.

Following the Southern Pacific takeover, UP was hurt by repeated delays in shipping, especially along the Gulf Coast. As a result, the Railroad Commission of Texas recommended that the company transfer several Houston-area lines to other companies. In a rare partnership, UP agreed to share lines with competitor Burlington Northern.

Union Pacific was the leading railroad company contributor to 1996 congressional campaigns. Southern Pacific ranked ninth and Chicago & North Western Transport ranked 12th. Nearly 300 candidates received money from UP, but just nine of the top 100 recipients were Democrats. Former Rep. Susan Molinari, R-N.Y., who at the time headed a House subcommittee on railroads, was one of the leading recipients.

Union Pacific Fund for Effective Government (C00010470) *Phone: (202) 662-0140 * Fax: (202) 662-0199 * 600 13th St. N.W., Suite 340, Washington, DC 20005 * Treasurer: Mary E. McAuliffe * Contact: Katie Maness, Political Affairs Dir.*

	1993-94	1995-96	1997	Totals
Receipts	$1,161,214	$1,315,995	$560,408	$3,037,617
Disburse	1,299,256	1,335,754	398,893	3,033,903
Cash	73,714	53,964	215,482	n/a
Contributions	636,803	792,357	294,354	1,723,514
Republicans	446,558	693,558	239,455	1,379,571
No. of Cand.	*187*	*236*	*138*	*561*
House	271,461	427,790	161,358	860,609
Senate	175,097	265,768	78,097	518,962
Democrats	187,745	98,799	51,399	337,943
No. of Cand.	*109*	*60*	*37*	*206*
House	148,746	85,799	36,399	270,944
Senate	38,999	13,000	15,000	66,999
Incumbents	419,375	538,843	276,857	1,235,075
Challengers	77,987	75,747	9,998	163,732
Open Seat	139,822	178,267	6,999	325,088
Winners	525,195	625,359	n/a	1,150,554
Losers	111,608	166,998	n/a	278,606

Southern Pacific Transportation Co. Political Action Committee (C00009910) *816 Connecticut Ave. N.W., Washington, DC 20006 * Treasurer: Wiley N. Jones*

The Southern Pacific Transportation Co. PAC was terminated in October 1996.

	1993-94	1995-96	1997	Totals
Receipts	$82,710	$70,691	$0	$153,401
Disburse	77,331	78,729	0	156,060
Cash	8,030	0	0	n/a
Contributions	49,350	57,979	0	107,329
Republicans	24,100	43,229	0	67,329
No. of Cand.	*27*	*36*	*0*	*63*
House	8,850	25,000	0	33,850
Senate	15,250	18,229	0	33,479
Democrats	25,250	14,750	0	40,000
No. of Cand.	*28*	*20*	*0*	*48*
House	11,750	10,750	0	22,500
Senate	13,500	4,000	0	17,500
Incumbents	42,600	45,000	0	87,600
Challengers	1,750	1,000	0	2,750
Open Seat	5,000	11,479	0	16,479
Winners	44,350	40,479	n/a	84,829
Losers	5,000	17,500	n/a	22,500

North Western Officers Trust Account - Chicago & North Western Transportation Co. (C00040014) *165 N. Canal St., Eighth Floor, Chicago, IL 60606 * Treasurer: Robin Bourne-Caris*

	1993-94	1995-96	1997	Totals
Receipts	$92,708	$21,580	$0	$114,288
Disburse	90,041	27,505	0	117,546
Cash	6,515	0	0	n/a
Contributions	57,866	19,200	0	77,066
Republicans	32,600	12,200	0	44,800
No. of Cand.	*34*	*16*	*0*	*50*
House	25,100	9,000	0	34,100
Senate	7,500	3,200	0	10,700
Democrats	25,266	7,000	0	32,266
No. of Cand.	*27*	*4*	*0*	*31*
House	16,166	3,000	0	19,166
Senate	9,100	4,000	0	13,100
Incumbents	54,766	19,000	0	73,766
Challengers	1,000	200	0	1,200
Open Seat	1,100	0	0	1,100
Winners	47,866	17,000	n/a	64,866
Losers	10,000	2,200	n/a	12,200

Union Pacific Resources Group Inc. Political Action Committee (UPR PAC) (C00323196) *Phone: (202) 662-0125 * Fax: (202) 662-0199 * 600 13th St. N.W., Suite 340, Washington, DC 20005 * Web: www.upr.com * Treasurer: Prentiss W. Bolin Jr. * Contact: Jack Messman, Chairperson and CEO*

Union Pacific Resources Group, a spin-off of railroad giant Union Pacific, explores for and produces oil and natural gas in Colorado, Texas, Utah, Wyoming, the Gulf of Mexico and Canada.

The company is publicly traded and posted $1.9 billion in 1997 sales. It has 70 subsidiaries and 1,580 employees. Union Pacific Resources has interests in trona (a source of sodium compounds) and coal development, primarily in the form of royalties and joint ventures. Its Union Pacific Fuels marketing subsidiary sells gas directly to local distribution companies, power-generation facilities, pipelines, industrial plants and wholesale marketing companies.

Union Pacific Resources and Arco Pipeline are partners on a 270-mile natural gas pipeline in Louisiana.

	1993-94	1995-96	1997	Totals
Receipts	$0	$41,313	$173,317	$214,630
Disburse	0	12,607	63,450	76,057
Cash	0	28,707	138,578	n/a
Contributions	0	3,000	58,099	61,099
Republicans	0	0	42,599	42,599
No. of Cand.	*0*	*0*	*29*	*29*
House	0	0	24,599	24,599
Senate	0	0	18,000	18,000
Democrats	0	3,000	14,500	17,500
No. of Cand.	*0*	*3*	*11*	*14*
House	0	3,000	7,000	10,000
Senate	0	0	7,500	7,500
Incumbents	0	1,000	55,599	56,599
Challengers	0	0	1,500	1,500
Open Seat	0	2,000	1,000	3,000
Winners	0	3,000	n/a	3,000
Losers	0	0	n/a	0

Sea Transport

APL Limited

*Phone: (510) 272-8715 * Fax: (510) 272-8932*
1111 Broadway, Oakland, CA 94607
*Web: www.apl.com * E-mail: timothy_windle@ccgate.apl.com*

APL Limited, formerly known as American President Companies, operates one of the world's five largest container shipping lines. The Oakland, Calif. company uses ocean, rail and truck transportation to provide service in Asia, the Americas, Europe and the Middle East. APL also has a logistics service division that manages inventory for companies. APL reported $2.7 billion in 1996 revenues.

In late 1997, APL Limited was purchased by Neptune Orient Lines Ltd. of Singapore. As a result, APL will no longer be listed on the New York Stock Exchange or the Pacific Exchange. NOL's container business will be combined with APL's and will operate under the APL name. NOL, which has $1.3 billion in revenue, trades on the Singapore Stock Exchange. The combined company will have 8,800 employees.

APL has ocean shipping terminals in Los Angeles, Oakland, Calif. and Seattle and has 65 rail terminals in the United States, Canada and Mexico. Although APL owns 1,200 railcars and 20,000 containers, it contracts with major U.S. rail lines to do the actual rail shipping. The company also has 113 vessels including 76 container ships, 30 tankers and eight dry-bulk carriers.

Founded in 1848, APL is the oldest continuously operating shipping company in the United States. It was company tradition to name ships after U.S. presidents until 1995, when APL registered six ships abroad and began naming ships for ports they serve. APL later reflagged four of the six ships to U.S. registry in order to enter the Maritime Security Program, which makes them available to the Department of Defense during war.

Subsidiaries include: American Eagle Tankers Inc. Limited and American Ship Management.

APL Limited (formerly known as American President Companies Ltd Political Action Committee) (C00137828) *Address: same as sponsor * Treasurer: Tim J. Windle*

	1993-94	1995-96	1997	Totals
Receipts	$99,994	$76,123	$21,002	$197,119
Disburse	125,930	98,527	32,384	256,841
Cash	39,804	17,399	6,016	n/a
Contributions	115,680	87,527	30,633	233,840
Republicans	36,480	66,027	17,423	119,930
No. of Cand.	*22*	*44*	*12*	*78*
House	7,850	43,327	8,700	59,877
Senate	28,630	22,700	8,723	60,053
Democrats	79,200	21,500	12,210	112,910
No. of Cand.	*63*	*22*	*7*	*92*
House	42,450	16,500	2,750	61,700
Senate	36,750	5,000	9,460	51,210
Incumbents	108,030	81,850	30,633	220,513
Challengers	250	0	0	250
Open Seat	7,400	5,677	0	13,077
Winners	95,330	71,027	n/a	166,357
Losers	20,350	16,500	n/a	36,850

Alexander & Baldwin Inc.

*Phone: (808) 525-6669 * Fax: (808) 525-6677*
P.O. Box 3440, Honolulu, HI 96801-3440
Web: www.alexanderbaldwin.com

Alexander & Baldwin, founded in 1870 and incorporated in 1900, is a publicly traded company engaged principally in ocean transportation of goods from the West Coast, Hawaii and Marshall Islands.

The company also participates in real estate ownership, development, management, sale and leasing; agriculture and food production (growing of sugar cane, production of raw sugar and molasses); trucking; and investments, including equity positions in other companies.

Ocean transportation operations and related shoreside operations of A&B are conducted by a wholly owned subsidiary, Matson Navigation Co. Inc. and several Matson subsidiaries, all of which are headquartered in San Francisco. Matson has its own federal PAC.

Real property and food products operations are conducted by a wholly owned subsidiary of A&B, A&B-Hawaii Inc. and several ABHI subsidiaries, including California and Hawaiian Sugar Co. Inc., all of which are headquartered in Hawaii or California.

In 1997, the company reported revenues of $1.2 billion.

Alexander & Baldwin Inc. FEDPAC (A&B FEDPAC) (C00017681) *Address: same as sponsor * Treasurer: Scott A. Matsuura * Contact: Meredith Ching, Chairman*

	1993-94	1995-96	1997	Totals
Receipts	$40,744	$28,842	$1,500	$71,086
Disburse	18,950	26,000	4,500	49,450
Cash	39,905	42,748	39,748	n/a
Contributions	8,850	21,000	3,000	32,850
Republicans	250	5,500	500	6,250
No. of Cand.	*1*	*4*	*1*	*6*
House	250	5,500	500	6,250
Senate	0	0	0	0
Democrats	8,600	15,500	2,500	26,600
No. of Cand.	*5*	*8*	*4*	*17*
House	4,600	15,500	1,500	21,600
Senate	4,000	0	1,000	5,000
Incumbents	8,500	19,500	3,000	31,000
Challengers	350	1,500	0	1,850
Open Seat	0	0	0	0
Winners	8,500	16,500	n/a	25,000
Losers	350	4,500	n/a	4,850

Matson Navigation Co. Inc. Federal Election Committee (C00024752) *Phone: (415) 957-4768 * Fax: (415) 957-4076 * P.O. Box 7452, San Francisco, CA 94120 * Web: www.matson.com * Treasurer: Timothy H. Reid * Contact: D. Sloane White, Chairperson*

	1993-94	1995-96	1997	Totals
Receipts	$46,553	$58,287	$26,612	$131,452
Disburse	51,291	50,962	28,511	130,764
Cash	4,618	10,854	8,961	n/a
Contributions	49,700	49,200	27,500	126,400
Republicans	16,000	28,700	10,500	55,200
No. of Cand.	*12*	*24*	*16*	*52*
House	8,000	21,700	10,000	39,700
Senate	8,000	7,000	500	15,500
Democrats	33,700	20,500	16,500	70,700
No. of Cand.	*21*	*16*	*14*	*51*
House	20,700	17,000	7,000	44,700
Senate	13,000	3,500	9,500	26,000
Incumbents	46,700	45,700	27,500	119,900
Challengers	0	1,500	0	1,500
Open Seat	3,000	2,000	0	5,000
Winners	41,200	41,000	n/a	82,200
Losers	8,500	8,200	n/a	16,700

American Classic Voyages Co.

*Phone: (312) 466-6202 * Fax: (312) 466-6151*
Two N. Riverside Plaza, Suite 200, Chicago, IL 60606
*Web: www.classicruise.com * E-mail: allen@amcv.com*

American Classic Voyages is the holding company for American Hawaii Cruises and Delta Queen Steamboat Co., both of which operate cruise lines. In 1997, the company reported $177.9 million in sales. American Classic employs 1,470 people.

An investment group controlled by Chicago investor and Chairman Sam Zell owns about 53 percent of the company, which is publicly traded.

The company operates cruises on the Mississippi, Ohio, Arkansas, Atchafalaya, Cumberland, Tennessee and Illinois rivers, and its American Hawaii subsidiary operates cruises in the Hawaiian islands.

American Classic Voyages Co. PAC (formerly known as Delta Queen Steamboat Co. PAC) (C00286617) *Address: same as sponsor * Treasurer: John Rau * Contact: Jordan Allen, Assistant Treasurer*

	1993-94	1995-96	1997	Totals
Receipts	$36,269	$21,650	$18,000	$75,919
Disburse	17,000	38,032	14,500	69,532
Cash	19,269	2,887	6,387	n/a
Contributions	17,000	34,032	12,500	63,532
Republicans	4,500	16,532	4,000	25,032
No. of Cand.	*7*	*9*	*3*	*19*
House	3,500	12,000	4,000	19,500
Senate	1,000	4,532	0	5,532
Democrats	12,500	17,500	8,500	38,500
No. of Cand.	*15*	*7*	*5*	*27*
House	8,500	10,000	5,500	24,000
Senate	4,000	7,500	3,000	14,500
Incumbents	17,000	29,500	12,500	59,000
Challengers	0	0	0	0
Open Seat	0	4,532	0	4,532
Winners	17,000	31,500	n/a	48,500
Losers	0	2,532	n/a	2,532

American Pilots' Association Inc.

*Phone: (202) 484-0700 * Fax: (202) 484-9320*
499 S. Capitol St. S.W., Suite 409, Washington, DC 20003
E-mail: apaxdir@aol.com

The American Pilots' Association represents 1,200 state-licensed maritime pilots who operate different types of vessels in 22 coastal states and on three Great Lakes.

The association, which was founded in 1884, is interested in such legislative items as port regulations, Coast Guard issues, navigation matters, mapping and charting and port safety.

American Pilots' Association Political Action Committee (C00041061) *Address: same as sponsor * Treasurer: Captain Jack Sparks * Contact: Whit Smith, President*

	1993-94	1995-96	1997	Totals
Receipts	$94,421	$86,806	$52,860	$234,087
Disburse	100,412	77,873	35,500	213,785
Cash	2,347	11,278	28,638	n/a
Contributions	94,911	71,789	32,250	198,950
Republicans	36,392	44,641	18,250	99,283
No. of Cand.	*21*	*22*	*14*	*57*
House	34,892	41,641	18,250	94,783
Senate	1,500	3,000	0	4,500
Democrats	58,519	27,148	14,000	99,667
No. of Cand.	*35*	*18*	*10*	*63*
House	57,519	24,648	14,000	96,167
Senate	1,000	2,500	0	3,500
Incumbents	89,911	66,789	29,750	186,450
Challengers	1,000	0	0	1,000
Open Seat	4,000	5,000	2,500	11,500
Winners	76,911	62,289	n/a	139,200
Losers	18,000	9,500	n/a	27,500

American Waterways Operators

*Phone: (703) 841-9300 * Fax: (703) 841-0389*
1600 Wilson Blvd., Suite 1000, Arlington, VA 22209

American Waterways Operators is composed of commercial shipyard owners and operators of barges, tugboats and towboats on navigable coastal and inland waterways. Founded in 1944, the organization has more than 350 members.

The group monitors legislation and regulations and acts as a liaison with Congress, the Coast Guard, the Army Corps of Engineers and the Maritime Administration.

American Waterways Operators PAC (C00034678) *Address: same as sponsor * Treasurer: John A. Moran * Contact: Tom Allegretti, Chairman*

	1993-94	1995-96	1997	Totals
Receipts	$39,166	$69,696	$6,090	$114,952
Disburse	42,089	52,995	13,098	108,182
Cash	1,495	18,208	9,820	n/a
Contributions	41,267	52,410	14,094	107,771
Republicans	17,750	39,910	11,413	69,073
No. of Cand.	*26*	*52*	*11*	*89*
House	11,750	29,660	6,489	47,899
Senate	6,000	10,250	4,924	21,174
Democrats	23,517	12,500	1,804	37,821
No. of Cand.	*32*	*22*	*2*	*56*
House	19,200	10,000	1,804	31,004
Senate	4,317	2,500	0	6,817
Incumbents	34,967	48,910	14,094	97,971
Challengers	0	250	0	250
Open Seat	6,300	3,250	0	9,550
Winners	32,617	45,860	n/a	78,477
Losers	8,650	6,550	n/a	15,200

Atlantic Holding Co.

*Phone: (904) 251-1512 * Fax: (904) 251-3400*
8500 Heckscher Dr., Jacksonville, FL 32226
Web: www.atlanticmarine.com/eastcoast.html

Atlantic Marine Inc. and Atlantic Dry Dock Corp. build and repair marine vessels for domestic and international markets. Atlantic Marine posted 1997 sales of $41.8 million and employed 1,000 people; Atlantic Dry Dock reported $15.2 million in 1997 sales and employed 300 people.

Both companies are owned by Atlantic Holding, which operates construction and repair shipyards in Jacksonville, Fla., and Mobile, Ala. Atlantic Marine and Atlantic Dry Dock are based in Jacksonville, Fla.

Atlantic Marine Inc. & Atlantic Dry Dock Corp. Separate Segregated Fund (C00232264) *Address: same as sponsor * Treasurer: Byron Thompson*

	1993-94	1995-96	1997	Totals
Receipts	$29,859	$30,115	$12,284	$72,258
Disburse	31,990	34,744	9,596	76,330
Cash	6,656	2,027	4,715	n/a
Contributions	26,750	29,000	8,500	64,250
Republicans	25,500	28,000	6,000	59,500
No. of Cand.	*23*	*22*	*5*	*50*
House	25,500	20,000	2,500	48,000
Senate	0	8,000	3,500	11,500
Democrats	1,250	1,000	2,500	4,750
No. of Cand.	*2*	*1*	*2*	*5*
House	1,250	0	500	1,750
Senate	0	1,000	2,000	3,000
Incumbents	13,750	15,500	7,500	36,750
Challengers	6,000	2,500	1,000	9,500
Open Seat	7,000	11,000	0	18,000
Winners	20,500	24,500	n/a	45,000
Losers	6,250	4,500	n/a	10,750

Crescent River Port Pilots Association

*Phone: (504) 392-8001 * Fax: (504) 392-7598*
8712 Highway 23, Belle Chasse, LA 70037

The Crescent River Port Pilots Association is a group of 100 pilots who guide ocean-going vessels headed for the port of New Orleans along the Mississippi River. The group was founded in 1908.

The PAC's legislative issues include protection of the Jones Act, which gives special rights to American-flagged vessels traveling between American ports.

Crescent River Port Pilots Association Federal Political Action Committee/CRPPA Fed PAC (C00221077) *Address: same as sponsor * Treasurer: Ronald H. Blancq*

	1993-94	1995-96	1997	Totals
Receipts	$40,180	$37,814	$26,784	$104,778
Disburse	38,805	41,710	23,855	104,370
Cash	13,938	10,042	12,971	n/a
Contributions	11,000	11,500	5,800	28,300
Republicans	5,000	1,000	3,800	9,800
No. of Cand.	*4*	*1*	*2*	*7*
House	5,000	1,000	3,800	9,800
Senate	0	0	0	0
Democrats	6,000	10,500	2,000	18,500
No. of Cand.	*8*	*3*	*4*	*15*
House	4,000	4,000	1,000	9,000
Senate	2,000	6,500	1,000	9,500
Incumbents	9,500	5,000	5,800	20,300
Challengers	0	0	0	0
Open Seat	1,000	6,500	0	7,500
Winners	10,500	6,500	n/a	17,000
Losers	500	5,000	n/a	5,500

Crowley Maritime Corp.

*Phone: (510) 251-7500 * Fax: (510) 251-7625*
155 Grand Ave., 10th Floor, Oakland, CA 94612
Web: www.crowley.com

Crowley Maritime transports ocean freight cargo and petroleum products overseas through its fleet of 400 vessels. The California-based company is 90 percent owned by CEO Thomas Crowley, his family and the company's 5,000 employees. Crowley reported 1996 sales of $1.2 billion. It has offices in the United States, Latin America and the Caribbean.

Crowley supplied equipment and personnel for cleanup of the Exxon Valdez oil spill and chartered ships to the U.S. military for Operation Desert Storm.

In 1997, Crowley American Transport expanded its scope of services to include Chile as part of an enhanced U.S. East Coast-West Coast South America service.

Crowley Maritime Federal Political Action Committee (C00147231) *Phone: (202) 737-4728 * Fax: (202) 737-6045 * 1300 Pennsylvania Ave. N.W., Washington, DC 20004 * Treasurer: Gregory Keil * Contact: Michael Roberts, V.P. of Gov. Relations*

	1993-94	1995-96	1997	Totals
Receipts	$59,164	$59,244	$35,378	$153,786
Disburse	53,079	55,257	43,512	151,848
Cash	11,750	15,742	7,609	n/a
Contributions	48,523	55,250	35,500	139,273
Republicans	21,473	36,250	14,500	72,223
No. of Cand.	*21*	*31*	*19*	*71*
House	14,973	27,550	10,000	52,523
Senate	6,500	8,700	4,500	19,700
Democrats	27,050	19,000	20,000	66,050
No. of Cand.	*27*	*23*	*17*	*67*
House	16,550	13,500	6,500	36,550
Senate	10,500	5,500	13,500	29,500
Incumbents	43,023	50,750	35,000	128,773
Challengers	250	500	0	750
Open Seat	5,250	4,000	500	9,750
Winners	40,273	48,950	n/a	89,223
Losers	8,250	6,300	n/a	14,550

Cruise PAC

P.O. Box 18732, Washington, DC 20036

Cruise PAC filed for termination in 1996.

Cruise Political Action Committee (C00256040) *Address: same as sponsor * Treasurer: Cynthia A. Colenda*

	1993-94	1995-96	1997	Totals
Receipts	$106,680	$500	$0	$107,180
Disburse	94,177	25,209	0	119,386
Cash	24,710	0	0	n/a
Contributions	66,450	22,000	0	88,450
Republicans	30,200	17,500	0	47,700
No. of Cand.	*60*	*18*	*0*	*78*
House	22,700	11,500	0	34,200
Senate	7,500	6,000	0	13,500
Democrats	35,250	4,500	0	39,750
No. of Cand.	*39*	*6*	*0*	*45*
House	22,250	2,500	0	24,750
Senate	13,000	2,000	0	15,000
Incumbents	55,200	22,000	0	77,200
Challengers	2,000	0	0	2,000
Open Seat	9,250	0	0	9,250
Winners	57,450	19,000	n/a	76,450
Losers	9,000	3,000	n/a	12,000

Holland America Line Westours Inc.

*Phone: (206) 281-3535 * Fax: (206) 286-3936*
300 Elliott Ave. W., Seattle, WA 98119
Web: www.hollandamerica.com

Holland America Line Westours is the largest cruise tour company operating in Alaska. In 1995, the company recorded its eighth consecutive record season, with more than 178,000 passengers.

Holland America Line, marking its 125th year in business in 1998, and Holland America Westours, its Alaska and Canadian Rockies cruise tour subsidiary, have headquarters in Seattle. In 1989, Holland America Line became a wholly owned subsidiary of Carnival Corp., the largest cruise company in the world.

Holland America's fleet of seven luxury cruise ships offers cruises to Alaska, the Caribbean, Panama Canal, Hawaii, Eastern Canada and New England, Europe, the South Pacific, South America and around the world.

In addition, the company owns Westmark Hotels and Inns, the largest lodging group in Alaska and the Yukon Territory, with 16 hotels, as well as Gray Line of Alaska, Gray Line of Seattle and several other Gray Line franchises.

Holland America Line Westours Inc. PAC (HALPAC) (C00287714) *Address: same as sponsor * Treasurer: Larry Calkins*

	1993-94	1995-96	1997	Totals
Receipts	$50,617	$64,480	$47,267	$162,364
Disburse	35,053	67,756	16,900	119,709
Cash	15,565	12,290	42,658	n/a
Contributions	33,050	59,250	16,900	109,200
Republicans	17,250	43,000	12,400	72,650
No. of Cand.	*10*	*23*	*14*	*47*
House	8,250	29,000	9,400	46,650
Senate	9,000	14,000	3,000	26,000

(Data for Holland America continued)

Democrats	15,800	16,250	4,000	36,050
No. of Cand.	*14*	*14*	*6*	*34*
House	10,300	10,250	2,500	23,050
Senate	5,500	6,000	1,500	13,000
Incumbents	31,800	57,750	16,400	105,950
Challengers	0	1,000	0	1,000
Open Seat	1,250	500	500	2,250
Winners	29,300	52,750	n/a	82,050
Losers	3,750	6,500	n/a	10,250

Hollywood Marine Inc.

*Phone: (713) 868-1661 * Fax: (713) 868-6464*
P.O. Box 1343, Houston, TX 77251
*Web: www.hollywoodmarine.com * E-mail: stevev@hmi.net*

Hollywood Marine is one of the largest private tank barge companies on the Gulf Coast. Hollywood handles a broad range of petroleum products, including petrochemicals, pressurized gases and black oils. It also provides ship bunkering at major ports and stores petroleum products at its terminal facilities. Its ships travel the length of the Gulf Intracoastal Waterway, the Waterway's connecting tributaries, and the lower Mississippi River.

Hollywood Marine Inc. PAC (C00231134) *Address: same as sponsor * Treasurer: Steven P. Valerius*

	1993-94	1995-96	1997	Totals
Receipts	$71,825	$59,991	$29,998	$161,814
Disburse	102,213	62,074	26,136	190,423
Cash	4,579	2,501	6,363	n/a
Contributions	53,249	25,999	12,000	91,248
Republicans	30,999	21,499	8,000	60,498
No. of Cand.	*9*	*8*	*7*	*24*
House	5,250	17,499	4,000	26,749
Senate	25,749	4,000	4,000	33,749
Democrats	22,250	4,500	3,500	30,250
No. of Cand.	*15*	*3*	*4*	*22*
House	13,250	4,500	2,500	20,250
Senate	9,000	0	1,000	10,000
Incumbents	40,499	17,499	12,000	69,998
Challengers	5,000	0	0	5,000
Open Seat	7,250	8,500	0	15,750
Winners	41,249	17,000	n/a	58,249
Losers	12,000	8,999	n/a	20,999

International Council of Cruise Lines

*Phone: (202) 296-8463 * Fax: (202) 296-1676*
1211 Connecticut Ave. N.W., Suite 800, Washington, DC 20036
E-mail: overstr@iccl.org

The International Council of Cruise Lines was founded to represent 17 major U.S.-based cruise lines. The organization is interested in technology, safety and environmental issues. It was founded in 1996.

International Council of Cruise Lines Political Action Committee (ICCL-PAC) (C00303073) *Address: same as sponsor * Treasurer: Cynthia A. Colenda*

	1993-94	1995-96	1997	Totals
Receipts	$0	$177,365	$90,847	$268,212
Disburse	0	166,173	73,016	239,189
Cash	0	11,192	29,023	n/a
Contributions	0	129,500	70,250	199,750
Republicans	0	77,500	30,750	108,250
No. of Cand.	*0*	*52*	*27*	*79*
House	0	59,000	24,750	83,750
Senate	0	18,500	6,000	24,500
Democrats	0	52,000	37,500	89,500
No. of Cand.	*0*	*36*	*21*	*57*
House	0	32,000	12,500	44,500
Senate	0	20,000	25,000	45,000
Incumbents	0	113,250	69,250	182,500
Challengers	0	1,000	0	1,000
Open Seat	0	15,250	0	15,250
Winners	0	115,000	n/a	115,000
Losers	0	14,500	n/a	14,500

Kirby Corp.

*Phone: (713) 629-9370 * Fax: (713) 435-1149*
1775 St. James Pl., Suite 300, Houston, TX 77056-3453

Headquartered in Houston, Kirby conducts operations in two business segments: marine transportation and diesel engine repair. The company owns the nation's largest fleet of tank barges and posted 1997 sales of $335 million. It employs 1,850 people.

Kirby's marine transportation segment transports industrial chemicals, petrochemical feedstocks, agricultural chemicals, petroleum products and dry-bulk cargoes. Kirby's diesel repair segment is engaged in the sale, overhaul and repair of diesel engines and related parts sales.

Subsidiaries include: Chotin Carriers, Dixie Marine and TPT Transportation, all engaged in the transportation of chemicals and cargo, and Marine Systems and Rail Systems, which offer marine and rail diesel repair services.

Kirby Corp. Political Action Committee (C00250027) *Address: same as sponsor * Treasurer: Robert D. Guilbeau * Contact: Brian Harrington, PAC Dir.*

	1993-94	1995-96	1997	Totals
Receipts	$33,410	$54,391	$17,956	$105,757
Disburse	39,389	47,250	17,452	104,091
Cash	7,090	14,232	14,735	n/a
Contributions	30,538	38,500	9,500	78,538
Republicans	18,361	32,000	8,000	58,361
No. of Cand.	*7*	*19*	*9*	*35*
House	3,500	18,000	5,000	26,500
Senate	14,861	14,000	3,000	31,861
Democrats	12,177	6,500	1,000	19,677
No. of Cand.	*9*	*8*	*2*	*19*
House	9,177	2,500	1,000	12,677
Senate	3,000	4,000	0	7,000
Incumbents	25,177	34,000	9,500	68,677
Challengers	0	1,000	0	1,000
Open Seat	5,361	3,500	0	8,861
Winners	25,677	26,000	n/a	51,677
Losers	4,861	12,500	n/a	17,361

Maersk Inc.

*Phone: (973) 514-5000 * Fax: (973) 514-5410*
Madison Ave., P.O. Box 880, Madison, NJ 07940-0880
Web: www.maersk.com

Maersk drills oil and gas wells and is engaged in deep sea freight transportation. A privately held company, it employs 2,500 people and had estimated 1997 sales of about $236 million. It is headquartered in Madison, N.J.

Maersk Good Government Fund Maersk Inc. Political Action Committee (C00217471) *Phone: (202) 887-6770 * Fax: (202) 887-5014 * 1667 K St. N.W., Suite 350, Washington, DC 20006 * Treasurer: Mark R. Johnson*

	1993-94	1995-96	1997	Totals
Receipts	$42,917	$43,237	$21,341	$107,495
Disburse	55,608	37,730	17,500	110,838
Cash	10,543	16,055	19,896	n/a
Contributions	44,000	31,550	8,500	84,050
Republicans	12,500	27,800	4,500	44,800
No. of Cand.	*9*	*17*	*7*	*33*
House	7,500	14,800	4,500	26,800
Senate	5,000	13,000	0	18,000
Democrats	31,500	3,750	4,000	39,250
No. of Cand.	*15*	*4*	*3*	*22*
House	13,000	3,750	1,000	17,750
Senate	18,500	0	3,000	21,500
Incumbents	42,000	30,050	8,500	80,550
Challengers	0	500	0	500
Open Seat	2,000	1,000	0	3,000
Winners	38,000	24,550	n/a	62,550
Losers	6,000	7,000	n/a	13,000

Midland Enterprises Inc.

*Phone: (800) 950-4404 * Fax: (800) 950-2080*
300 Pike St., Second Floor, Cincinnati, OH 45202
Web: www.riverbarges.com

Midland Enterprises operates a fleet of 2,300 barges and 84 boats throughout the U.S. inland waterway system. Headquartered in Cincinnati, Midland is one of the largest barge companies in the United States.

In addition to its transportation subsidiaries, Midland operates several terminals, fleeting operations and a marine repair facility. Through a joint venture, the company also operates mooring and transfer facilities on the lower Mississippi River.

Midland had $375 million in sales in 1997. The company employs 956 workers. Midland Enterprises is a wholly owned subsidiary of publicly traded Eastern Enterprises.

Midland Enterprises Inc. Political Action Committee (C00040360) *Address: same as sponsor * Treasurer: Thomas J. Schmidt*

	1993-94	1995-96	1997	Totals
Receipts	$4,834	$7,793	$2,297	$14,924
Disburse	6,001	5,310	4,642	15,953
Cash	1,303	3,789	1,445	n/a
Contributions	5,450	5,300	3,500	14,250
Republicans	1,000	5,300	3,500	9,800
No. of Cand.	*2*	*9*	*7*	*18*
House	0	3,800	2,500	6,300
Senate	1,000	1,500	1,000	3,500
Democrats	4,450	0	0	4,450
No. of Cand.	*5*	*0*	*0*	*5*
House	3,450	0	0	3,450
Senate	1,000	0	0	1,000
Incumbents	4,950	4,800	3,500	13,250
Challengers	0	500	0	500
Open Seat	500	0	0	500
Winners	4,000	3,800	n/a	7,800
Losers	1,450	1,500	n/a	2,950

National Steel and Shipbuilding Co.

*Phone: (619) 544-3400 * Fax: (619) 544-3541*
Harbor Dr. and 28th St., P.O. Box 85278, San Diego, CA 92186
Web: www.nassco.com

National Steel and Shipbuilding is a ship design, construction and repair company located in San Diego. NASSCO is an employee-owned company, and was founded as a small machine shop in 1905. Its facility encompasses 147 acres and the company employs about 5,000 people.

Sales for 1996 were $503 million. In 1997, NASSCO's backlog stood at $1 trillion.

In May 1997, the company won a $227 million Navy contract to build a sixth strategic Sealift ship. In July of the same year, the company agreed to build a double-hull tanker for British Petroleum. NASSCO says it is the only West Coast shipyard capable of building and repairing large seagoing vessels.

National Steel and Shipbuilding Co. Political Action Committee (also known as NASSCO PAC) (C00237719) *Address: same as sponsor * Treasurer: Fred Hallett*

	1993-94	1995-96	1997	Totals
Receipts	$57,169	$64,859	$28,658	$150,686
Disburse	56,618	60,550	36,800	153,968
Cash	5,301	9,115	974	n/a
Contributions	56,118	53,050	33,000	142,168
Republicans	26,318	47,550	27,000	100,868
No. of Cand.	*11*	*12*	*8*	*31*
House	26,318	47,550	27,000	100,868
Senate	0	0	0	0
Democrats	29,800	5,500	6,000	41,300
No. of Cand.	*10*	*4*	*3*	*17*
House	17,800	3,500	5,000	26,300
Senate	12,000	2,000	1,000	15,000
Incumbents	53,096	51,300	33,000	137,396
Challengers	3,022	750	0	3,772
Open Seat	0	1,000	0	1,000
Winners	47,296	52,300	n/a	99,596
Losers	8,822	750	n/a	9,572

Outboard Marine Corp.

*Phone: (847) 689-5492 * Fax: (847) 689-5789*
100 Sea Horse Dr., Waukegan, IL 60085
Web: www.omc-online.com

Outboard Marine is a leading manufacturer and marketer of outboard engines, boats and accessories. The company markets Johnson Outboards' motors, Evinrude Outboards' motors and Ficht Engineering Company's fuel injection motors. Its own products include propellers, system check equipment, engine care kits and lubricants and oils.

In 1997, Outboard Marine merged with Greenmarine Acquisition. As a result of the merger, Greenmarine Holdings is now its sole stockholder.

Outboard Marine Corp. Political Action Committee (OMCPAC) (C00228809) *Address: same as sponsor * Treasurer: Michael Potter * Contact: Marlena Cannon, Chairperson*

	1993-94	1995-96	1997	Totals
Receipts	$29,614	$30,008	$13,211	$72,833
Disburse	31,715	27,049	6,750	65,514
Cash	2,880	5,845	12,307	n/a
Contributions	25,500	24,000	4,750	54,250
Republicans	24,000	23,500	4,750	52,250
No. of Cand.	*31*	*32*	*8*	*71*
House	13,000	20,500	2,250	35,750
Senate	11,000	3,000	2,500	16,500
Democrats	1,500	500	0	2,000
No. of Cand.	*3*	*1*	*0*	*4*
House	1,500	500	0	2,000
Senate	0	0	0	0
Incumbents	11,000	20,500	4,250	35,750
Challengers	3,500	1,500	500	5,500
Open Seat	11,000	2,000	0	13,000
Winners	24,000	20,000	n/a	44,000
Losers	1,500	4,000	n/a	5,500

Princess Cruises Inc.

*Phone: (310) 553-1770 * Fax: (310) 843-3811*
10100 Santa Monica Blvd., Los Angeles, CA 90067
Web: www.awcv.com/princess.html

Princess Cruises is a subsidiary of Peninsular and Oriental Inc. Headquartered in Los Angeles, the company offers Alaskan, European, Mediterranean, Caribbean and Panama Canal cruises. The company reported $484 million in 1997 sales and employs 5,000 people.

Princess Cruises Inc. PAC (Princess PAC) (C00301952) *Phone: (206) 728-3957 * Fax: (206) 728-3944 * 2815 Second Ave., Suite 400, Seattle, WA 98121-1299 * Treasurer: Anthony H. Kaufman * Contact: Tom Dow, V.P. of Public Affairs*

	1993-94	1995-96	1997	Totals
Receipts	$0	$42,269	$22,526	$64,795
Disburse	0	35,400	25,000	60,400
Cash	0	6,872	4,398	n/a
Contributions	0	28,400	24,000	52,400
Republicans	0	23,500	16,500	40,000
No. of Cand.	*0*	*11*	*17*	*28*
House	0	16,500	11,500	28,000
Senate	0	7,000	5,000	12,000
Democrats	0	4,900	7,000	11,900
No. of Cand.	*0*	*6*	*7*	*13*
House	0	3,400	2,000	5,400
Senate	0	1,500	5,000	6,500
Incumbents	0	27,900	24,000	51,900
Challengers	0	0	0	0
Open Seat	0	500	0	500
Winners	0	28,400	n/a	28,400
Losers	0	0	n/a	0

Royal Caribbean Cruises Ltd.

*Phone: (305) 539-6000 * Fax: (305) 539-6168*
1050 Caribbean Way, Miami, FL 33132
*Web: www.royalcaribbean.com * E-mail: wcomm@miamail01.rccl.com*

Royal Caribbean is a publicly held global cruise company that has almost 20 vessels. The cruise line, which also owns Celebrity Cruises, has regularly scheduled cruises to Alaska, the Bahamas, Bermuda, Canada, the Caribbean, Europe, the Far East, Hawaii, Mexico, New England, the Panama Canal and Scandinavia.

Miami Cruise PAC (C00191171) *Address: same as sponsor * Treasurer: John P. Fox*

	1993-94	1995-96	1997	Totals
Receipts	$12,880	$22,000	$0	$34,880
Disburse	33,750	21,880	250	55,880
Cash	169	289	39	n/a
Contributions	15,120	11,500	0	26,620
Republicans	4,250	4,500	0	8,750
No. of Cand.	*6*	*4*	*0*	*10*
House	2,000	1,500	0	3,500
Senate	2,250	3,000	0	5,250
Democrats	9,870	7,000	0	16,870
No. of Cand.	*17*	*8*	*0*	*25*

(Data for Royal Caribbean continued)

House	2,000	3,000	0	5,000
Senate	7,870	4,000	0	11,870
Incumbents	9,870	10,500	0	20,370
Challengers	1,000	0	0	1,000
Open Seat	4,250	1,000	0	5,250
Winners	10,250	9,500	n/a	19,750
Losers	4,870	2,000	n/a	6,870

Society for the Relief of Distressed Pilots

*Phone: (215) 979-1020 * Fax: (215) 979-1286*
One Liberty Pl., 42nd Floor, c/o Thomas J. Tumola Esq., Philadelphia, PA 19103

The Society for the Relief of Distressed and Decayed Pilots, Their Widows and Children is an organization of about 70 river pilots who work on the Delaware River and Bay.

The PAC was established in 1990.

Society for the Relief of Distressed and Decayed Pilots, Their Widows and Children PAC (C00240457) *Address: same as sponsor * Treasurer: Joseph W. Guilday * Contact: Michael J. Linton, Chairman*

	1993-94	1995-96	1997	Totals
Receipts	$6,350	$16,450	$9,910	$32,710
Disburse	6,634	16,411	6,690	29,735
Cash	167	206	3,426	n/a
Contributions	2,400	11,040	5,360	18,800
Republicans	900	6,540	3,360	10,800
No. of Cand.	*3*	*5*	*4*	*12*
House	150	5,290	2,860	8,300
Senate	750	1,250	500	2,500
Democrats	1,500	4,500	2,000	8,000
No. of Cand.	*1*	*1*	*1*	*3*
House	1,500	4,500	2,000	8,000
Senate	0	0	0	0
Incumbents	1,900	11,040	5,360	18,300
Challengers	500	0	0	500
Open Seat	0	0	0	0
Winners	2,400	11,040	n/a	13,440
Losers	0	0	n/a	0

Southwest Marine Inc.

*Phone: (619) 238-1000 x2661 * Fax: (619) 233-0218*
P.O. Box 13308, Foot of Sampson St., San Diego, CA 92170-3308

Southwest Marine is a privately held, San Diego company that builds, repairs, maintains and converts commercial and government boats. It was founded in 1977 by Art and Herb Engel and is reportedly one of the San Diego area's largest marine maintenance companies.

The company reports annual sales of about $100 million and employs 1,400 people in San Diego, San Pedro, Calif. and Ingleside, Texas. It has major contracts with the Navy, Military Sealift Command, the Maritime Administration, the Army and Coast Guard.

In October 1997, the company was acquired by the private merchant bank Carlyle Group of Washington for an undisclosed amount.

Southwest Marine Inc. PAC (C00140681) *Address: same as sponsor * Treasurer: Arthur E. Engel*

	1993-94	1995-96	1997	Totals
Receipts	$1,001	$25,000	$50,252	$76,253
Disburse	47,684	30,761	35,000	113,445
Cash	7,744	1,983	17,235	n/a
Contributions	31,672	16,200	35,000	82,872
Republicans	12,172	12,200	28,500	52,872
No. of Cand.	*7*	*7*	*7*	*21*
House	12,172	12,200	23,500	47,872
Senate	0	0	5,000	5,000
Democrats	19,500	4,000	6,500	30,000
No. of Cand.	*9*	*3*	*3*	*15*
House	13,000	4,000	6,000	23,000
Senate	6,500	0	500	7,000
Incumbents	27,672	12,950	30,000	70,622
Challengers	2,000	3,250	5,000	10,250
Open Seat	2,000	0	0	2,000
Winners	27,172	12,950	n/a	40,122
Losers	4,500	3,250	n/a	7,750

Totem Ocean Trailer Express Inc.

*Phone: (206) 628-4343 * Fax: (206) 628-9245*
1100 Olive Way, Suite 1100, Seattle, WA 98101
Web: www.totemocean.com

Totem Ocean Trailer Express is a privately owned Alaska corporation that operates cargo steamship service between Anchorage, Alaska and Tacoma, Wash. The firm is headquartered in Seattle and posted 1997 sales of about $130 million. Totem employs 150 people.

The company also provides highway trucking transport services and rail interconnections throughout greater Alaska, the lower 48 states and Canada.

Totem Ocean Trailer Express Inc./Foss Maritime Co. Political Action Committee (also known as Tote/Foss-PAC) (C00166512) *Address: same as sponsor * Treasurer: Robert B. McMillen*

	1993-94	1995-96	1997	Totals
Receipts	$39,968	$32,072	$15,700	$87,740
Disburse	38,900	37,700	10,875	87,475
Cash	7,271	1,648	6,897	n/a
Contributions	24,675	25,750	10,125	60,550
Republicans	8,600	19,750	4,000	32,350
No. of Cand.	*6*	*13*	*6*	*25*
House	4,300	8,800	2,600	15,700
Senate	4,300	10,950	1,400	16,650
Democrats	16,075	6,000	6,125	28,200
No. of Cand.	*11*	*7*	*7*	*25*
House	13,075	3,000	3,125	19,200
Senate	3,000	3,000	3,000	9,000
Incumbents	23,475	19,750	9,875	53,100
Challengers	500	1,000	250	1,750
Open Seat	700	5,000	0	5,700
Winners	14,900	21,700	n/a	36,600
Losers	9,775	4,050	n/a	13,825

Trucking

American Movers and Storage Association

*Phone: (703) 683-7410 * Fax: (703) 683-7527*
1611 Duke St., Alexandria, VA 22314
Web: www.amconf.org

The American Movers and Storage Association is composed of 3,000 professional moving companies. The association represents members' views before the Department of Transportation and other government agencies.

Its goals include keeping the public informed regarding the value of professional moving services; providing educational skills and training; improving members' businesses through information and technical assistance; providing advocacy for moving customers; and working for effective government regulations and policies which enable members to provide quality service and compensatory prices.

The association is affiliated with the American Trucking Associations.

American Movers and Storage Association (AM Moving PAC) (C00255257) *Address: same as sponsor * Treasurer: Jane Lind Downey*

	1993-94	1995-96	1997	Totals
Receipts	$47,146	$42,711	$16,770	$106,627
Disburse	40,694	50,851	14,350	105,895
Cash	11,616	3,477	5,909	n/a
Contributions	35,050	43,900	14,350	93,300
Republicans	14,350	30,450	9,350	54,150
No. of Cand.	*18*	*37*	*16*	*71*
House	6,200	23,950	7,850	38,000
Senate	8,150	6,500	1,500	16,150
Democrats	20,200	13,450	4,500	38,150
No. of Cand.	*22*	*19*	*9*	*50*
House	16,500	12,450	4,500	33,450
Senate	3,700	1,000	0	4,700
Incumbents	29,900	43,550	14,350	87,800
Challengers	500	0	0	500
Open Seat	4,650	350	0	5,000
Winners	29,850	35,650	n/a	65,500
Losers	5,200	8,250	n/a	13,450

American Trucking Associations

*Phone: (202) 544-7132 * Fax: (202) 675-6568*
430 First St. S.E., Washington, DC 20003
Web: www.trucking.org

The American Trucking Associations is the national trade association of the trucking industry. Its members include 4,500 trucking companies and related businesses. It has a network of affiliates that includes state trucking associations and specialty carriers which haul hazardous waste and cars. The ATA estimates that 9.3 million people are involved in the industry and truck companies buy more than 40 billion gallons of gasoline and diesel fuel each year.

The ATA lobbies on transportation issues such as ISTEA and gasoline taxes. The group favors more highway funding and opposes tolls on interstate highways and a ban on triple-trailers. The ATA also is seeking to lessen reporting requirements for trucking facilities under the Clean Water Act and to end a government freeze on Mexican trucks within states that border Mexico.

The ATA was the leading trucking PAC contributor to 1996 congressional candidates, and gave mostly to Republicans. The group's contributions increased more than 22 percent from 1994 to 1996. Leading recipients included transportation committee members Reps. Bud Shuster, R-Pa., and Nick J. Rahall II, D-W.Va., and former Sen. Larry Pressler, R-S.D.

Trucking Political Action Committee of the American Trucking Associations Inc. (C00002881) *Address: same as sponsor * Treasurer: Donna Weinrich * Contact: James R. Whittinghill, V.P. for Legislative Affairs*

	1993-94	1995-96	1997	Totals
Receipts	$365,321	$467,903	$156,301	$989,525
Disburse	366,311	464,369	148,927	979,607
Cash	24,703	28,448	35,828	n/a
Contributions	325,566	410,061	130,389	866,016
Republicans	143,581	318,161	92,905	554,647
No. of Cand.	*120*	*184*	*99*	*403*
House	85,496	225,761	68,655	379,912
Senate	58,085	92,400	24,250	174,735
Democrats	179,735	91,900	36,484	308,119
No. of Cand.	*144*	*72*	*43*	*259*
House	130,464	73,400	25,600	229,464
Senate	49,271	18,500	10,884	78,655
Incumbents	281,330	344,908	126,139	752,377
Challengers	5,500	7,050	750	13,300
Open Seat	40,236	58,103	2,500	100,839
Winners	266,910	342,986	n/a	609,896
Losers	58,656	67,075	n/a	125,731

Arkansas Best Corp.

*Phone: (501) 785-6000 * Fax: (501) 785-6124*
3801 Old Greenwood Rd., P.O. Box 10048, Fort Smith, AR 72903
*Web: www.arkbest.com * E-mail: info@arkbest.com*

Arkansas Best is a holding company with interests in international and intermodal freight transportation, truck tire retreading and sales, warehousing, logistics services and computer information services. The company posted $1.6 billion in 1997 sales.

Arkansas Best was ranked by Fortune as one of the top 10 revenue-generating trucking companies in the nation. The publicly traded company employs 16,000 workers across the nation.

Subsidiary ABF Freight Systems accounts for about 65 percent of revenues and focuses on long-haul shipments, offering direct service to almost every U.S. city with a population of 25,000 or more. ABF maintains 320 terminals, with operations in all 50 states, Puerto Rico and Canada. Arkansas Best also holds a 46 percent stake in Treadco, which is engaged in truck tire retreading and new truck tire sales.

Arkansas Best Corp. Political Action Committee (C00193383) *Address: same as sponsor * Treasurer: Richard F. Cooper*

	1993-94	1995-96	1997	Totals
Receipts	$18,154	$9,111	$0	$27,265
Disburse	17,750	8,500	0	26,250
Cash	417	1,029	1,029	n/a
Contributions	16,200	6,500	0	22,700
Republicans	2,200	2,500	0	4,700
No. of Cand.	*5*	*2*	*0*	*7*
House	1,200	2,500	0	3,700
Senate	1,000	0	0	1,000
Democrats	14,000	4,000	0	18,000
No. of Cand.	*14*	*6*	*0*	*20*
House	11,500	3,500	0	15,000
Senate	2,500	500	0	3,000
Incumbents	14,700	6,000	0	20,700
Challengers	0	0	0	0
Open Seat	1,500	500	0	2,000
Winners	12,700	3,500	n/a	16,200
Losers	3,500	3,000	n/a	6,500

CNF Transportation Inc.

*Phone: (650) 494-2900 * Fax: (650) 813-0164*
3240 Hillview Ave., Palo Alto, CA 94304
Web: www.cfwy.com

CNF Transportation is a diversified holding company with businesses in regional trucking, domestic and international air freight, global logistics management, trailer manufacturing and wholesale truck parts sales. The public company, which employs 25,000 people and reported 1997 revenues of $4.3 billion, operates primarily through its three main subsidiaries.

The company changed its name to CNF Transportation from Consolidated Freightways Inc. in 1996 when the company's former primary subsidiary spun off as Consolidated Freightways Corp. The new corporation has now created its own PAC, called Consolidated Freightways Corp. PAC.

Subsidiaries include: Emery Worldwide, which accounted for $2.3 billion of revenues and provides global air and ocean freight transportation and logistics management; Con-Way Transportation Services, a regional less-than-truckload (shipments of less than 10,000 pounds) carrier and truckload operator that generated $1.5 billion in revenues; and Menlo Logistics, which is a leading third-party logistics provider with clients like Nike, Hewlett-Packard, IBM, Sears, Dow Chemical and Coca-Cola.

CNF Transportation Inc. Political Action Committee (C00110759) *Address: same as sponsor * Treasurer: R. Guy Kraines * Contact: Robert D. Testa, V.P. of Gov. Relations*

	1993-94	1995-96	1997	Totals
Receipts	$128,457	$103,372	$21,039	$252,868
Disburse	119,006	118,356	22,366	259,728
Cash	68,788	46,555	49,042	n/a
Contributions	93,050	92,000	13,700	198,750
Republicans	55,250	78,500	7,700	141,450
No. of Cand.	*57*	*94*	*24*	*175*
House	30,250	61,500	7,200	98,950
Senate	25,000	17,000	500	42,500
Democrats	36,800	13,500	6,000	56,300
No. of Cand.	*33*	*16*	*9*	*58*
House	26,300	8,000	3,000	37,300
Senate	10,500	5,500	3,000	19,000
Incumbents	76,050	83,000	14,700	173,750
Challengers	1,000	4,000	-500	4,500
Open Seat	15,000	5,000	-500	19,500
Winners	83,050	73,000	n/a	156,050
Losers	10,000	19,000	n/a	29,000

National Tank Truck Carriers Inc.

*Phone: (703) 838-1960 * Fax: (703) 684-5753*
2200 Mill Rd., Alexandria, VA 22314

National Tank Truck Carriers represents about 200 trucking companies nationwide that haul commodities, such as gasoline and chemicals, in bulk. The organization was founded in 1945.

National Tank Truck Carriers Political Action Committee (C00188011) *Address: same as sponsor * Treasurer: John L. Conley*

	1993-94	1995-96	1997	Totals
Receipts	$17,400	$15,125	$7,575	$40,100
Disburse	16,492	20,920	6,100	43,512
Cash	14,949	9,154	10,629	n/a
Contributions	15,400	20,550	5,850	41,800
Republicans	7,100	15,050	4,850	27,000
No. of Cand.	*11*	*26*	*13*	*50*
House	5,350	12,500	3,350	21,200
Senate	1,750	2,550	1,500	5,800
Democrats	7,750	5,500	1,000	14,250
No. of Cand.	*13*	*9*	*2*	*24*
House	5,500	5,000	500	11,000
Senate	2,250	500	500	3,250
Incumbents	14,300	18,750	5,100	38,150
Challengers	0	250	500	750
Open Seat	1,100	1,550	0	2,650
Winners	11,600	15,300	n/a	26,900
Losers	3,800	5,250	n/a	9,050

Navistar International Transportation Corp.

*Phone: (312) 836-2605 * Fax: (312) 836-3982*
455 N. Cityfront Plaza Dr., Chicago, IL 60611
Web: www.navistar.com

Navistar International Transportation is a manufacturer and distributor of medium- and heavy-duty trucks, school buses and diesel engines in the United States and across the globe, under the brand name International. The company's trucks, engine parts and services are sold through a network of nearly 1,000 dealer outlets in the United States, Canada and nearly 80 dealers in 75 countries overseas. The publicly traded company reported 1997 sales of $6.4 billion and employed more than 16,000 workers.

In 1998, the company expanded its network of used truck dealerships to a total of 16 locations. An International Used Truck Center is open in Baltimore and another will open in Denver in the spring of 1998. Also, in early 1998, the company began building and selling commercial trucks in Brazil.

Navistar also provides financing for its customers and distributors through its wholly owned subsidiary Navistar Financial Corp.

Navistar International Transportation Corp. Good Government Committee (formerly known as International Harvester) (C00040840) *Address: same as sponsor * Treasurer: Sylvia Morrison * Contact: Thomas F. Luby, Chairman of PAC*

	1993-94	1995-96	1997	Totals
Receipts	$54,004	$44,677	$19,491	$118,172
Disburse	65,120	54,163	16,143	135,426
Cash	13,359	3,882	7,231	n/a
Contributions	35,250	30,550	11,000	76,800
Republicans	26,750	26,800	11,000	64,550
No. of Cand.	20	22	11	53
House	12,250	16,500	8,000	36,750
Senate	14,500	10,300	3,000	27,800
Democrats	8,500	3,750	0	12,250
No. of Cand.	5	6	0	11
House	7,000	2,750	0	9,750
Senate	1,500	1,000	0	2,500
Incumbents	23,750	15,500	8,500	47,750
Challengers	500	3,800	0	4,300
Open Seat	11,000	11,250	2,500	24,750
Winners	28,250	17,250	n/a	45,500
Losers	7,000	13,300	n/a	20,300

Oshkosh Truck Corp.

*Phone: (920) 235-9150 * Fax: (920) 233-9506*
P.O. Box 2566, Oshkosh, WI 54903-2566
Web: www.oshkoshtruck.com

Oshkosh Truck makes heavy-duty trucks in its fire and emergency, defense and commercial divisions. A public company, Oshkosh reported $683 million in 1997 sales.

Oshkosh employs 2,600 people at its headquarters in Oshkosh, Wis. and locations in Texas and Florida.

The company has added fire engine company Pierce Manufacturing Inc. and, in February 1998, Oshkosh Truck purchased McNeilus Companies, which has operations in the refuse truck body and concrete mixer industries, for $250 million.

Oshkosh Truck Corp. Employees Political Action Committee (OTCEPAC) (C00304477) *Address: same as sponsor * Treasurer: Russell L. Steinhorst * Contact: Fred Fielding, Chairperson*

	1993-94	1995-96	1997	Totals
Receipts	$0	$21,426	$28,190	$49,616
Disburse	0	18,010	16,263	34,273
Cash	0	3,919	9,563	n/a
Contributions	0	17,000	5,150	22,150
Republicans	0	14,000	3,150	17,150
No. of Cand.	0	11	6	17
House	0	11,500	1,500	13,000
Senate	0	2,500	1,650	4,150
Democrats	0	3,000	2,000	5,000
No. of Cand.	0	3	3	6
House	0	2,500	1,000	3,500
Senate	0	500	1,000	1,500
Incumbents	0	17,000	4,750	21,750
Challengers	0	0	400	400
Open Seat	0	0	0	0
Winners	0	17,000	n/a	17,000
Losers	0	0	n/a	0

Owner-Operator Independent Drivers Association Inc.

*Phone: (816) 229-5791 * Fax: (816) 229-0518*
311 R.D. Mize Rd., Grain Valley, MO 64029
*Web: www.ooida.com * E-mail: tspencer@ooida.com*

Headquartered in Grain Valley, Mo., the Owner-Operator Independent Drivers Association represents 39,000 professional truckers in all 50 states and Canada.

Founded in 1973, OOIDA is involved in the legislative process both on the federal and state level. The association tracks legislation affecting professional truckers, testifies at all major hearings on trucking issues and participates in industry-wide organizations and conferences. Issues of particular concern to the group include: speed limit laws, truck weight regulation and interstate highway tolls, as well as trucker safety and business issues.

Subsidiary Owner-Operator Services offers members benefit programs.

Owner-Operator Independent Drivers Association Inc. Political Action Committee (also known as OOIDA-PAC) (C00236778) *Phone: (202) 944-8600 * 1101 30th St. N.W., Suite 300, Washington, DC 20007 * Treasurer: K. Michael O'Connell*

*Contact: Todd Spencer, Chairman of PAC * Phone: (816) 229-5791*

	1993-94	1995-96	1997	Totals
Receipts	$26,722	$28,396	$13,587	$68,705
Disburse	4,760	17,775	26,144	48,679
Cash	39,127	49,748	37,052	n/a
Contributions	4,000	17,500	9,100	30,600
Republicans	500	16,000	8,000	24,500
No. of Cand.	1	4	5	10
House	500	16,000	7,000	23,500
Senate	0	0	1,000	1,000
Democrats	3,500	1,500	1,100	6,100
No. of Cand.	3	3	3	9
House	3,500	1,500	1,000	6,000
Senate	0	0	100	100
Incumbents	3,500	9,500	8,100	21,100
Challengers	0	0	0	0
Open Seat	500	8,000	0	8,500
Winners	3,500	15,500	n/a	19,000
Losers	500	2,000	n/a	2,500

PACCAR Inc.

*Phone: (425) 468-7885 * Fax: (425) 468-8216*
777 106th Ave. N.E., P.O. Box 1518, Bellevue, WA 98009

PACCAR is the world's second-largest heavy duty truck maker, manufacturing Kenworth, Peterbilt, DAF and Foden trucks worldwide. It also leases and finances trucks and sells automotive parts and accessories in the western United States through its 125 Al's Auto Supply and Grand Auto retailers.

With sales of $6.5 billion in 1997, the Bellevue, Wash.-based company is ranked No. 306 among Fortune 500 companies. It employs more than 17,000 workers.

In December 1997, PACCAR sold its Trico Industries operations, which make oilfield pumps, to EVI Inc. for $105 million.

Worldwide, PACCAR has operations in Australia, Belgium, Canada, China, Mexico, the Netherlands and the United Kingdom. Subsidiaries include: DAF Trucks, Kenworth Truck Co., PACCAR Automotive and Peterbilt Motors.

People PAC (PACCAR Inc. Employees Organized for Political Leadership and Education PAC) (C00034355) *Address: same as sponsor * Treasurer: Kirk Newman * Contact: Larry Young, Chairperson*

	1993-94	1995-96	1997	Totals
Receipts	$36,486	$62,718	$42,137	$141,341
Disburse	34,474	60,830	10,463	105,767
Cash	4,755	6,645	38,320	n/a
Contributions	31,875	54,725	10,397	96,997
Republicans	23,500	48,475	9,397	81,372
No. of Cand.	14	26	9	49
House	10,000	35,975	8,100	54,075
Senate	13,500	12,500	1,297	27,297
Democrats	8,375	6,250	1,000	15,625
No. of Cand.	7	6	1	14
House	7,875	6,250	1,000	15,125
Senate	500	0	0	500
Incumbents	21,875	51,225	10,397	83,497

Challengers	3,500	1,000	0	4,500
Open Seat	6,500	2,500	0	9,000
Winners	30,250	40,725	n/a	70,975
Losers	1,625	14,000	n/a	15,625

Ruan Corp.

*Phone: (515) 245-2675 * Fax: (515) 245-2556*
666 Grand Ave., P.O. Box 855, Des Moines, IA 50304

Contributors to PACEG are affiliated with the privately held Ruan Corp. of Des Moines. The PAC is bipartisan and supports Iowa candidates.

Founded in 1932, Ruan is made up of Ruan Transportation Management Systems (a trucking company), Bankers Trust of Des Moines and Ruan Properties.

PACEG Committee (C00074633) *Address: same as sponsor * Treasurer: Laverne C. Milbrandt * Contact: Garry Alvord, President*

	1993-94	1995-96	1997	Totals
Receipts	$16,539	$39,345	$34,769	$90,653
Disburse	17,928	37,269	8,000	63,197
Cash	2,027	4,106	30,875	n/a
Contributions	4,830	18,750	2,000	25,580
Republicans	3,830	17,250	1,000	22,080
No. of Cand.	*5*	*8*	*1*	*14*
House	2,830	9,000	1,000	12,830
Senate	1,000	8,250	0	9,250
Democrats	1,000	1,500	1,000	3,500
No. of Cand.	*1*	*2*	*1*	*4*
House	1,000	1,000	1,000	3,000
Senate	0	500	0	500
Incumbents	1,830	7,500	1,000	10,330
Challengers	1,000	8,000	1,000	10,000
Open Seat	2,000	3,250	0	5,250
Winners	3,830	8,750	n/a	12,580
Losers	1,000	10,000	n/a	11,000

Truckload Carriers Association

*Phone: (703) 838-1950 * Fax: (703) 836-6610*
2200 Mill Rd., Third Floor, Alexandria, VA 22314
*Web: www.truckload.org * E-mail: tca@truckload.org*

The Truckload Carriers Association is a national trade association with a focus on the common and contract truckload segment of the motor carrier industry. TCA represents dry van, refrigerated, flatbed, intermodal container and dump-trailer truckload carriers operating in 50 states, Mexico and Canada.

Established in 1983, TCA comprises about 1,000 members, including truckload carrier executives, industry suppliers, law firms and brokers.

The association is affiliated with the American Trucking Associations Inc. and is its largest conference.

Truckload Carriers Association PAC (C00168294) *Address: same as sponsor * Treasurer: Robert G. Rothstein * Contact: Wayne Tanverup, Chairman*

	1993-94	1995-96	1997	Totals
Receipts	$52,255	$61,849	$31,975	$146,079
Disburse	56,200	117,350	6,500	180,050
Cash	66,891	12,891	38,366	n/a
Contributions	56,700	113,600	5,500	175,800
Republicans	37,600	99,850	5,500	142,950
No. of Cand.	*44*	*96*	*7*	*147*
House	21,850	66,750	3,500	92,100
Senate	15,750	33,100	2,000	50,850
Democrats	18,350	13,750	0	32,100
No. of Cand.	*24*	*20*	*0*	*44*
House	14,350	10,250	0	24,600
Senate	4,000	3,500	0	7,500
Incumbents	40,850	81,100	5,500	127,450
Challengers	2,000	8,500	0	10,500
Open Seat	13,850	24,000	0	37,850
Winners	47,450	82,100	n/a	129,550
Losers	9,250	31,500	n/a	40,750

UniGroup Inc.

*Phone: (314) 349-2720 * Fax: (314) 349-8744*
One United Dr., Fenton, MO 63026
*Web: www.moovers.com * E-mail: ricks@moovers.com*

UniGroup is a privately owned, diversified moving and financial services company based in St. Louis. Its United Van Lines subsidiary is owned by its 123 agents and shareholders. United Van Lines is the principal operating company.

UniGroup has 1,600 employees and sales of $1.6 billion through its companies' operations in United Van Lines, Mayflower Transit, Vanliner Insurance and United Leasing.

UPAC (also known as UniGroup Inc. Political Action Committee) (C00108555) *Address: same as sponsor * Treasurer: Doug Wilton * Contact: Morton Golder, Executive V.P. of Financial Services*

	1993-94	1995-96	1997	Totals
Receipts	$16,122	$12,472	$70	$28,664
Disburse	26,951	11,419	15,134	53,504
Cash	20,928	19,368	4,304	n/a
Contributions	11,050	7,425	7,100	25,575
Republicans	8,550	5,425	6,100	20,075
No. of Cand.	*5*	*8*	*4*	*17*
House	2,050	3,000	600	5,650
Senate	6,500	2,425	5,500	14,425
Democrats	2,500	2,000	1,000	5,500
No. of Cand.	*2*	*1*	*1*	*4*
House	2,000	2,000	0	4,000
Senate	500	0	1,000	1,500
Incumbents	4,550	6,125	6,100	16,775
Challengers	0	800	1,000	1,800
Open Seat	6,500	500	0	7,000
Winners	11,050	6,625	n/a	17,675
Losers	0	800	n/a	800

Watkins Associated Industries

*Phone: (404) 872-3841 * Fax: (404) 872-2812*
P.O. Box 1738, Atlanta, GA 30301

Watkins Associated Industries is an Atlanta-based private holding company for Watkins Motor Lines, the Tree Communities apartment complexes and Tampa Maid Foods Inc., a seafood processing company. The company, which employs 8,000 workers, also builds and operates shopping centers. Watkins Motor Lines, a trucking company based in Florida, accounts for 75 percent of Watkins' revenue, which exceeded $600 million in 1996.

Watkins Associated Industries was ranked No. 360 among the Forbes 500 largest private companies in the United States in 1996. It was also ranked seventh among Georgia's top 100 private companies, according to the Atlanta Journal-Constitution.

Watkins expanded its trucking company to include carriers in Colorado and Delaware. In 1998, the company plans to add operations in Idaho, Nebraska, Virginia, New Mexico, California and West Virginia.

Watkins Associated Industries Inc. Employees for Good Government Committee (Watkins-PAC) (C00142307) *Address: same as sponsor * Treasurer: T. R. Wade * Contact: Bill Freeman, Chairperson*

	1993-94	1995-96	1997	Totals
Receipts	$200,211	$62,709	$35,734	$298,654
Disburse	158,245	63,787	19,333	241,365
Cash	95,041	93,966	110,368	n/a
Contributions	30,900	50,500	11,500	92,900
Republicans	24,400	47,500	10,500	82,400
No. of Cand.	*14*	*28*	*9*	*51*
House	20,400	32,000	6,500	58,900
Senate	4,000	15,500	4,000	23,500
Democrats	6,500	3,000	1,000	10,500
No. of Cand.	*6*	*2*	*1*	*9*
House	6,000	500	0	6,500
Senate	500	2,500	1,000	4,000
Incumbents	26,900	42,500	11,000	80,400
Challengers	2,000	3,500	0	5,500
Open Seat	2,000	4,500	0	6,500
Winners	28,900	46,000	n/a	74,900
Losers	2,000	4,500	n/a	6,500

Werner Enterprises Inc.

*Phone: (402) 895-6640 * Fax: (402) 894-3821*
P.O. Box 45308, Omaha, NE 68145-0308
*Web: www.werner.com * E-mail: werner@werner.com*

Werner Enterprises is a publicly owned trucking company providing interstate and intrastate transport. The company handles manufactured goods, retail store merchandise, food products and building materials for clients in 48 states and parts of Canada and Mexico.

Werner is headquartered in Omaha, Neb. It had 1996 sales of $643 million and 6,500 employees. Of the 11 trucking terminals Werner operates, it owns six.

Subsidiaries: Werner Leasing Inc., Werner Aire Inc., Gra-Gar Inc., Drivers Management Inc., Frontier Clinic Inc., Fleet Truck Sales Inc., Professional Truck Drivers School Inc., Werner Transportation Inc. and Worley Enterprises Inc.

Werner Enterprises Inc. Political Action Committee (C00236034) *Address: same as sponsor * Treasurer: Robert E. Synowicki * Contact: Curtis Werner, Vice Chairman of the Board*

	1993-94	1995-96	1997	Totals
Receipts	$14,168	$20,185	$877	$35,230
Disburse	22,250	16,950	2,500	41,700
Cash	1,386	4,622	3,000	n/a
Contributions	10,050	14,500	1,000	25,550
Republicans	9,050	9,500	1,000	19,550
No. of Cand.	*4*	*3*	*1*	*8*
House	7,500	5,000	0	12,500
Senate	1,550	4,500	1,000	7,050
Democrats	1,000	5,000	0	6,000
No. of Cand.	*1*	*1*	*0*	*2*
House	0	0	0	0
Senate	1,000	5,000	0	6,000
Incumbents	1,500	5,000	1,000	7,500
Challengers	8,550	1,000	0	9,550
Open Seat	0	8,500	0	8,500
Winners	8,000	8,500	n/a	16,500
Losers	2,050	6,000	n/a	8,050

Yellow Corp.

*Phone: (913) 696-6121 * Fax: (913) 696-6181*
10990 Roe Ave., Overland Park, KS 66211
Web: www.yellowcorp.com

Yellow provides freight transportation services primarily to the less-than-truckload market in North America. The publicly traded Kansas company reported 1997 revenues of more than $3 billion. Yellow has 34,400 employees in North America, Europe, Asia and the Caribbean.

Subsidiary Yellow Technology Services Inc. provides information technology services to the company and its subsidiaries.

Other subsidiaries include: Yellow Freight System Inc., Preston Trucking Co. Inc., Saia Motor Freight Line Inc. and WestEx Inc.

Yellow Corp. Political Action Committee (C00090209) *Address: same as sponsor * Treasurer: William F. Martin Jr.*

	1993-94	1995-96	1997	Totals
Receipts	$167,418	$120,585	$68,038	$356,041
Disburse	185,621	158,952	48,247	392,820
Cash	58,768	20,411	40,209	n/a
Contributions	142,803	106,793	28,500	278,096
Republicans	69,703	89,043	25,000	183,746
No. of Cand.	*78*	*82*	*34*	*194*
House	42,703	55,050	15,500	113,253
Senate	27,000	33,993	9,500	70,493
Democrats	71,850	17,750	3,500	93,100
No. of Cand.	*66*	*18*	*6*	*90*
House	47,350	13,250	1,500	62,100
Senate	24,500	4,500	2,000	31,000
Incumbents	120,303	86,800	29,500	236,603
Challengers	0	4,993	0	4,993
Open Seat	23,500	15,000	0	38,500
Winners	117,553	76,793	n/a	194,346
Losers	25,250	30,000	n/a	55,250

APPENDIX

Only PAC sponsors are listed in the following tables and some organizations may operate more than one PAC. For example, Lockheed Martin, BellSouth and the Marine Engineers Beneficial Union all have more than one affiliated PAC in the list of 200 PACs contributing the most money to congressional campaigns during the 1995–96 election cycle.

Top 35 PAC Contributors, 1997

Rank	PAC	1997 Total
1	AFSCME	$925,350
2	Association of Trial Lawyers of America	707,500
3	International Brotherhood of Electrical Workers (IBEW)	692,335
4	Teamsters Union	657,150
5	National Automobile Dealers Association	576,425
6	United Parcel Service of America Inc. (UPS)	572,683
7	National Association of Home Builders	533,250
8	Laborers' Union International of North America	524,250
9	United Food & Commercial Workers Union	523,941
10	Lockheed Martin	515,650
11	National Rifle Association	497,711
12	United Auto Workers	493,710
13	National Association of Realtors	491,238
14	American Bankers Association	472,100
15	Carpenters Union	471,068
16	United Transportation Union	462,650
17	AT&T Corp.	411,137
18	Philip Morris	408,026
19	Machinists and Aerospace Workers Union (IAM)	$405,150
20	Federal Express Corp.	379,250
21	Air Line Pilots Association	376,500
22	American Medical Association	367,650
23	American Dental Association	365,836
24	American Federation of Teachers (AFT)	362,550
25	National Education Association (NEA)	345,695
26	Ironworkers Union	341,450
27	National Association of Life Underwriters	341,000
28	National Beer Wholesalers' Association	340,219
29	Seafarers International Union	322,750
30	Communications Workers of America	322,160
31	American Hospital Association	321,557
32	Sheet Metal Workers International Association	319,900
33	International Association of Fire Fighters (IAFF)	312,450
34	General Electric Co.	307,950
35	National Association of Letter Carriers	307,646

Top 50 PAC Contributors to Republican Congressional Candidates, 1997

Rank	PAC	Republicans	% to Republicans	Democrats	% to Democrats	Total
1	United Parcel Service	$414,823	75.8	$132,610	24.2	$547,433
2	National Rifle Association	375,487	76.0	118,500	24.0	493,987
3	National Auto Dealers Association	351,525	66.7	175,400	33.3	526,925
4	Lockheed Martin	342,400	66.9	169,250	33.1	511,650
5	National Association of Home Builders	324,000	62.1	197,750	37.9	521,750
6	National Association of Realtors	274,738	58.7	193,500	41.3	468,238
7	Marine Engineers' Beneficial Association	269,000	58.2	193,500	41.8	462,500
8	Federal Express Corp.	254,250	68.9	115,000	31.1	369,250
9	Philip Morris	253,805	65.8	131,721	34.2	385,526
10	American Bankers Association	245,850	54.7	203,250	45.3	449,100
11	National Beer Wholesalers Association	241,750	79.1	64,000	20.9	305,750
12	American Medical Association	224,650	69.2	100,000	30.8	324,650
13	Union Pacific Corp.	214,458	79.6	54,899	20.4	269,357
14	AT&T	210,380	52.8	188,257	47.2	398,637
15	National Association of Life Underwriters	196,500	59.5	133,500	40.5	330,000
16	American Dental Association	177,214	53.2	156,203	46.8	333,417
17	MBNA America Bank	177,000	79.0	47,000	21.0	224,000
18	Northrop Grumman Corp.	175,725	63.8	99,850	36.2	275,575
19	General Electric	175,050	57.8	127,900	42.2	302,950
20	Banc One Corp.	168,211	65.3	89,500	34.7	257,711
21	Americans for Free International Trade	166,000	78.5	45,500	21.5	211,500
22	National Federation of Independent Business	163,413	84.7	29,500	15.3	192,913
23	National Restaurant Association	162,822	76.5	50,000	23.5	212,822
24	Associated General Contractors	160,500	86.5	25,000	13.5	185,500
25	Food Marketing Institute	156,152	80.4	38,000	19.6	194,152
26	Bell Atlantic	152,572	60.9	97,956	39.1	250,528
27	SBC Communications	151,200	63.7	86,000	36.3	237,200
28	American Hospital Association	149,640	49.2	154,417	50.8	304,057
29	BankAmerica Corp.	149,063	69.1	66,645	30.9	215,708
30	Ernst & Young LLP	148,499	52.2	135,999	47.8	284,498
31	AFLAC Inc.	146,500	58.6	103,500	41.4	250,000
32	RJR Nabisco	142,750	67.3	69,500	32.7	212,250
33	American Health Care Association	141,948	51.3	134,850	48.7	276,798
34	Ameritech Corp.	139,072	62.0	85,097	38.0	224,169
35	Deloitte & Touche LLP	138,575	59.1	95,741	40.9	234,316
36	Credit Union National Association	138,335	52.0	127,644	48.0	265,979
37	Action Committee for Rural Electrification	137,446	51.3	130,375	48.7	267,821
38	Dairy Farmers of America	137,000	54.3	115,500	45.7	252,500
39	Independent Insurance Agents of America	134,417	61.3	84,827	38.7	219,244
40	Coopers & Lybrand LLP	134,267	59.0	93,339	41.0	227,606
41	BellSouth Corp.	133,458	65.9	69,050	34.1	202,508
42	Investment Company Institute	130,902	65.3	69,445	34.7	200,347
43	Freedom Project	126,256	100.0	-	0.0	126,256
44	Mortgage Bankers Association of America	125,051	68.5	57,533	31.5	182,584
45	American Hotel & Motel Association	124,700	81.8	27,750	18.2	152,450
46	Boeing Co.	124,000	64.2	69,250	35.8	193,250
47	Glaxo Wellcome Inc.	122,627	65.0	66,125	35.0	188,752
48	Boeing Co.	119,869	66.7	59,750	33.3	179,619
49	National Association of Broadcasters	117,715	64.3	65,386	35.7	183,101
50	American Society of Anesthesiologists	115,750	51.5	109,219	48.5	224,969

Top 50 PAC Contributors to Democratic Congressional Candidates, 1997

Rank	UltOrg	Democrats	% to Democrats	Republicans	% to Republicans	Total
1	AFSCME	$814,350	95.7	$ 37,000	4.3	$851,350
2	International Brotherhood of Electrical Workers	604,225	97.6	15,160	2.4	619,385
3	Association of Trial Lawyers of America	559,000	89.2	67,500	10.8	626,500
4	International Brotherhood of Teamsters	547,150	91.6	50,000	8.4	597,150
5	Laborers' Union	437,250	88.4	57,500	11.6	494,750
6	United Food & Commercial Workers Union	436,391	96.6	15,300	3.4	451,691
7	United Auto Workers	421,210	99.6	1,500	0.4	422,710
8	Carpenters Union	390,750	92.6	31,318	7.4	422,068
9	Machinists & Aerospace Workers Union	356,650	100.0	-	0.0	356,650
10	American Federation of Teachers	321,350	97.7	7,700	2.3	329,050
11	United Transportation Union	312,300	74.7	105,850	25.3	418,150
12	National Education Association	286,595	95.5	13,600	4.5	300,195
13	Ironworkers Union	281,450	89.8	32,000	10.2	313,450
14	Air Line Pilots Association	272,500	73.0	101,000	27.0	373,500
15	Communications Workers of America	265,660	98.7	3,500	1.3	269,160
16	Sheet Metal Workers Union	263,500	92.5	21,500	7.5	285,000
17	National Association of Letter Carriers	249,646	85.6	42,000	14.4	291,646
18	Seafarers International Union	224,750	76.3	70,000	23.7	294,750
19	AFL-CIO	224,245	97.6	5,500	2.4	229,745
20	International Association of Fire Fighters	224,150	77.6	64,800	22.4	288,950
21	Service Employees International Union	221,750	93.1	16,500	6.9	238,250
22	Plumbers & Pipefitters Union	218,000	91.4	20,500	8.6	238,500
23	Boilermakers Union	206,250	93.0	15,500	7.0	221,750
24	American Bankers Association	203,250	45.3	245,850	54.7	449,100
25	National Association of Retired Federal Employees	203,000	84.7	36,750	15.3	239,750
26	National Association of Home Builders	197,750	37.9	324,000	62.1	521,750
27	National Association of Realtors	193,500	41.3	274,738	58.7	468,238
28	Marine Engineers' Beneficial Association	193,500	41.8	269,000	58.2	462,500
29	AT&T	188,257	47.2	210,380	52.8	398,637
30	Transport Workers Union	187,500	88.5	24,250	11.5	211,750
31	National Auto Dealers Association	175,400	33.3	351,525	66.7	526,925
32	Human Rights Campaign	173,775	83.1	35,229	16.9	209,004
33	American Postal Workers Union	172,470	96.0	7,200	4.0	179,670
34	Lockheed Martin	169,250	33.1	342,400	66.9	511,650
35	Amalgamated Transit Union	163,500	81.4	37,250	18.6	200,750
36	Operating Engineers Union	163,300	77.2	48,250	22.8	211,550
37	American Dental Association	156,203	46.8	177,214	53.2	333,417
38	American Hospital Association	154,417	50.8	149,640	49.2	304,057
39	National Air Traffic Controllers Association	142,500	80.4	34,650	19.6	177,150
40	National Committee to Preserve Social Security and Medicare	137,889	74.4	47,500	25.6	185,389
41	Ernst & Young LLP	135,999	47.8	148,499	52.2	284,498
42	American Health Care Association	134,850	48.7	141,948	51.3	276,798
43	National Association of Life Underwriters	133,500	40.5	196,500	59.5	330,000
44	United Parcel Service	132,610	24.2	414,823	75.8	547,433
45	Philip Morris	131,721	34.2	253,805	65.8	385,526
46	Action Committee for Rural Electrification	130,375	48.7	137,446	51.3	267,821
47	General Electric	127,900	42.2	175,050	57.8	302,950
48	Credit Union National Association	127,644	48.0	138,335	52.0	265,979
49	National Rural Letter Carriers Association	125,150	73.3	45,500	26.7	170,650
50	American Crystal Sugar Co.	124,500	54.4	104,500	45.6	229,000

Top 100 PAC Recipients, 1997

Rank	Candidate	Party	Office	State	1997 Total
1	Tom Daschle	D	Sen.	S.D.	$1,110,022
2	John B. Breaux	D	Sen.	La.	893,948
3	Richard C. Shelby	R	Sen.	Ala.	887,084
4	Christopher S. Bond	R	Sen.	Mo.	877,870
5	Alfonse M. D'Amato	R	Sen.	N.Y.	806,290
6	Richard A. Gephardt	D	Rep.	Mo.	771,741
7	Barbara Boxer	D	Sen.	Calif.	755,649
8	Arlen Specter	R	Sen.	Pa.	712,064
9	Christopher J. Dodd	D	Sen.	Conn.	683,020
10	Don Nickles	R	Sen.	Okla.	647,334
11	Byron L. Dorgan	D	Sen.	N.D.	644,108
12	Lauch Faircloth	R	Sen.	N.C.	591,000
13	Paul Coverdell	R	Sen.	Ga.	532,544
14	Charles E. Grassley	R	Sen.	Iowa	528,100
15	Bob Graham	D	Sen.	Fla.	511,766
16	Vito J. Fossella Jr.	R	Rep.	N.Y.	502,542
17	Michael D. Crapo	R	Sen.	Idaho	461,456
18	Ernest F. Hollings	D	Sen.	S.C.	450,926
19	Chuck Hagel	R	Sen.	Neb.	449,817
20	Ron Wyden	D	Sen.	Ore.	441,942
21	Martin Frost	D	Rep.	Texas	423,900
22	Harry Reid	D	Sen.	Nev.	421,128
23	Barbara A. Mikulski	D	Sen.	Md.	417,774
24	George V. Voinovich	R	Sen.	Ohio	415,865
25	Evan Bayh	D	Sen.	Ind.	413,090
26	John D. Dingell	D	Rep.	Mich.	411,622
27	Carol Moseley-Braun	D	Sen.	Ill.	404,235
28	Tom DeLay	R	Rep.	Texas	397,642
29	Robert F. Bennett	R	Sen.	Utah	391,580
30	Nancy Johnson	R	Rep.	Conn.	390,006
31	Ben Nighthorse Campbell	R	Sen.	Colo.	389,022
32	Newt Gingrich	R	Rep.	Ga.	378,003
33	Thomas J. Bliley Jr.	R	Rep.	Va.	372,173
34	Charles B. Rangel	D	Rep.	N.Y.	352,795
35	Sam Brownback	R	Sen.	Kan.	351,101
36	Ciro D. Rodriguez	D	Rep.	Texas	348,377
37	Eric Vitaliano	D	Rep.	N.Y.	346,410
38	John Ensign	R	Sen.	Nev.	342,120
39	Dick Armey	R	Rep.	Texas	335,034
40	Jim Bunning	R	Sen.	Ky.	334,881
41	Judd Gregg	R	Sen.	N.H.	328,371
42	Eric P. Serna	D	Rep.	N.M.	325,538
43	Bill Paxon	R	Rep.	N.Y.	319,390
44	Robert L. Livingston	R	Rep.	La.	315,955
45	Loretta Sanchez	D	Rep.	Calif.	314,485
46	Rick A. Lazio	R	Rep.	N.Y.	300,932
47	Joe L. Barton	R	Rep.	Texas	299,141
48	Bud Shuster	R	Rep.	Pa.	288,719
49	Jerry Weller	R	Rep.	Ill.	280,879
50	Bill Thomas	R	Rep.	Calif.	277,093
51	Gerald B. H. Solomon	R	Rep.	N.Y.	$276,652
52	Neil Abercrombie	D	Rep.	Hawaii	275,819
53	Vic Fazio	D	Rep.	Calif.	272,020
54	Sherrod Brown	D	Rep.	Ohio	271,033
55	Dirk Kempthorne	R	Sen.	Idaho	270,250
56	Bill Redmond	R	Rep.	N.M.	269,092
57	Charles W. Stenholm	D	Rep.	Texas	263,920
58	David E. Bonior	D	Rep.	Mich.	258,332
59	John M. Shimkus	R	Rep.	Ill.	257,633
60	Phil English	R	Rep.	Pa.	254,725
61	John McCain	R	Sen.	Ariz.	253,646
62	Bart Gordon	D	Rep.	Tenn.	251,510
63	Rick Santorum	R	Sen.	Pa.	248,956
64	John P. Murtha	D	Rep.	Pa.	243,800
65	Patty Murray	D	Sen.	Wash.	242,304
66	Tim Johnson	D	Sen.	S.D.	241,546
67	Lois Capps	D	Rep.	Calif.	241,286
68	Dan Schaefer	R	Rep.	Colo.	239,980
69	Kenny Hulshof	R	Rep.	Mo.	236,805
70	Kay Bailey Hutchison	R	Sen.	Texas	236,652
71	Don Young	R	Rep.	Alaska	235,626
72	Jennifer Dunn	R	Rep.	Wash.	233,872
73	Bob Riley	R	Rep.	Ala.	231,888
74	Steny H. Hoyer	D	Rep.	Md.	228,396
75	W. J. "Billy" Tauzin	R	Rep.	La.	226,641
76	Dennis Hastert	R	Rep.	Ill.	226,309
77	Charlie Norwood	R	Rep.	Ga.	225,654
78	Robert T. Matsui	D	Rep.	Calif.	224,992
79	Max Sandlin	D	Rep.	Texas	221,878
80	J. D. Hayworth	R	Rep.	Ariz.	219,612
81	John A. Boehner	R	Rep.	Ohio	218,430
82	John Linder	R	Rep.	Ga.	216,768
83	Michael G. Oxley	R	Rep.	Ohio	215,895
84	Jay Nixon	D	Sen.	Mo.	215,319
85	Gene Green	D	Rep.	Texas	214,496
86	James L. Oberstar	D	Rep.	Minn.	213,154
87	Wes Watkins	R	Rep.	Okla.	200,443
88	Bill Frist	R	Sen.	Tenn.	199,867
89	James E. Rogan	R	Rep.	Calif.	196,177
90	Thomas M. Davis III	R	Rep.	Va.	195,956
91	Bill McCollum	R	Rep.	Fla.	192,600
92	Edward M. Kennedy	D	Sen.	Ma.	191,400
93	Kay Granger	R	Rep.	Texas	191,399
94	Patrick J. Kennedy	D	Rep.	R.I.	191,295
95	Richard H. Baker	R	Rep.	La.	189,525
96	Robert Aderholt	R	Rep.	Ala.	188,541
97	David R. Obey	D	Rep.	Wis.	185,919
98	Philip M. Crane	R	Rep.	Ill.	185,184
99	Mary L. Landrieu	D	Sen.	La.	184,132
100	Debbie Stabenow	D	Rep.	Mich.	182,134

1997 PACs

These committees were formed in late 1996 or 1997 and have already begun to contribute thousands of dollars to congressional campaigns.

Newport News Shipbuilding Political Action Committee (SHIPPAC) (C00325092)
Phone: (202) 783-1400
801 Pennsylvania Ave. N.W., Suite 350
Washington, DC 20004
Web: www.nns.com
Contact: D. Rick Wyatt, Treasurer

Newport News Shipbuilding is the only company that builds new nuclear-powered aircraft carriers and one of two that builds nuclear-powered submarines. During 1997, the PAC raised $258,000 and contributed more than $88,000 to federal candidates and committees.

Campaign for Working Families (C00325076)
*Phone: (202) 479-9638 * Fax: (202) 488-3522*
499 S. Capitol St., Suite 410
Washington, DC 20003
Contact: Francis P. Cannon, Treasurer

The Campaign for Working Families is headed by conservative activist Gary L. Bauer, president of the Family Research Council. The PAC raised more than $2.1 million during 1997 and contributed about $91,000 to federal candidates and committees.

Lucent Technologies Inc. Political Action Committee (Lucent Technologies PAC) (C00321505)
*Phone: (202) 530-7060 * Fax: (202) 530-7067*
900 19th St. N.W., Suite 700
Washington, DC 20006
Web: www.lucent.com
Contact: Charles E. Crowder, Federal Public Affairs Director

Lucent Technologies is an AT&T spinoff company that makes communications hardware and microelectronics. The PAC contributed more than $100,000 to federal candidates and committees during 1997.

The Society of Thoracic Surgeons Political Action Committee (STS PAC) (C00325936)
*Phone: (202) 857-1100 * Fax: (202) 223-4579*
1200 19th St. N.W., Suite 300
Washington, DC 20036
Web: www.sts.org
Contact: Timothy J. Gardner, Treasurer

The Society of Thoracic Surgeons represents more than 4,000 specialists in the United States and Canada. The PAC contributed more than $35,000 to congressional candidates during 1997.

SABRE Group Inc. Political Action Committee (SABREPAC) (C00325811)
Phone: (202) 496-5666
1101 17th St. N.W., Suite 600
Washington, DC 20036
Web: www.sabre.com
Contact: Andrew B. Steinberg, Treasurer

The SABRE Group is a public company that provides computerized travel reservation services. The PAC, which is affiliated with the American Airlines Political Action Committee, contributed $18,500 to congressional candidates during 1997.

AirTran Airlines Inc. Political Action Committee (formerly known as ValuJet Airlines PAC) (C00325159)
Phone: (404) 233-2800
3490 Piedmont Rd., Suite 400
Atlanta, GA 30305
Web: www.airtran.com
Contact: Robert B. Goldberg, Treasurer

AirTran is the new name of ValuJet Airlines, a discount commercial airline. The PAC contributed $17,000 to congressional candidates during 1997.

CAT PAC (C00326439)
Phone: (916) 446-9049
400 Capitol Mall, Suite 1560
Sacramento, CA 95814
Contact: David Bauer, Treasurer

CAT PAC is the PAC of the Conservative Action Team, a group of 40 conservative members of Congress. Rep. David M. McIntosh, R-Ind., is the group's chairman. The PAC contributed $15,500 to Republican congressional candidates during 1997.

Pioneer Political Action Committee (C00325357)
Phone: (202) 484-5710
499 S. Capitol St. N.W., Suite 408
Washington, DC 20003
Contact: Karen Johnson, Executive Director

Pioneer PAC is the leadership PAC of Rep. John Kasich, R-Ohio, the chairman of the House Budget Committee and a potential presidential candidate in 2000. It contributed about $12,000 to congressional candidates in 1997, all of them Republicans.

American Neurological Surgery Political Action Committee (C00327171)
*Phone: (202) 628-1996 * Fax: (202) 628-5264*
P.O. Box 136
Washington, DC 20044-0136
Contact: Katherine O. Orrico, Assistant Treasurer

The American Neurological Surgery PAC is a group of physicians who are not associated with any organization. The PAC contributed $10,500 to congressional candidates during 1997.

Freedom and Free Enterprise PAC (C00326090)
1800 K St. N.W., Suite 714
Washington, DC 20006
Contact: Thomas P. Kemp, Treasurer

This non-connected PAC was formed in February 1997. It contributed $8,000 to Republican congressional candidates during 1997 and an additional $16,000 to other federal committees.

Top 200 Spending PACs, 1995–96

Rank	PAC Name	Contributions to Congressional Candidates	% to Republicans	% to Democrats
1	International Brotherhood of Teamsters	$2,606,140	3.9	95.7
2	AFSCME	2,504,021	1.6	98.0
3	United Auto Workers	2,467,319	0.4	99.1
4	Association of Trial Lawyers of America	2,336,938	10.2	89.3
5	National Auto Dealers Association	2,335,425	81.7	18.3
6	National Education Association	2,326,830	0.5	99.1
7	American Medical Association	2,321,197	81.0	19.0
8	National Association of Realtors	2,099,683	68.7	31.2
9	International Brotherhood of Electrical Workers	2,070,587	2.1	97.6
10	United Food & Commercial Workers Union	2,030,795	1.1	98.4
11	Machinists & Aerospace Workers Union	1,999,675	0.4	99.1
12	Laborers Union	1,917,800	8.7	90.9
13	United Parcel Service	1,788,147	64.9	35.1
14	National Association of Letter Carriers	1,706,564	12.1	87.4
15	American Institute of CPAs	1,690,925	67.7	32.0
16	American Federation of Teachers	1,614,833	1.2	98.5
17	National Rifle Association	1,560,871	83.4	16.6
18	United Steelworkers	1,523,650	0.0	100.0
19	Carpenters Union	1,464,606	4.5	94.9
20	National Association of Home Builders	1,442,849	82.0	18.0
21	National Association of Life Underwriters	1,426,750	69.0	31.0
22	National Beer Wholesalers Association	1,324,992	83.4	16.6
23	American Bankers Association	1,299,850	72.1	27.9
24	Communications Workers of America	1,297,286	0.1	99.3
25	American Dental Association	1,283,425	65.6	34.4
26	United Transportation Union	1,260,600	15.5	83.8
27	National Association of Retired Federal Employees	1,243,350	16.5	83.3
28	AT&T	1,239,046	63.2	36.8
29	AFL-CIO	1,190,514	0.8	98.9
30	National Committee for an Effective Congress	1,118,475	0.0	99.6
31	National Federation of Independent Business	1,070,543	93.6	6.4
32	Sheet Metal Workers Union	1,064,500	2.7	96.8
33	Lockheed Martin	1,013,850	70.0	30.0
34	Marine Engineers' Beneficial Association	973,960	56.8	43.1
35	Plumbers & Pipefitters Union	958,000	4.0	95.7
36	Federal Express Corp.	943,000	70.5	29.4
37	Americans for Free International Trade	936,800	88.6	11.4
38	Ernst & Young LLP	883,115	49.6	50.4
39	National Restaurant Association	880,119	88.6	11.4
40	American Hospital Association	879,863	51.3	48.6
41	Philip Morris	850,119	72.5	27.4
42	Campaign America	829,971	99.5	0.5
43	Ironworkers Union	828,615	5.1	94.5
44	Air Line Pilots Association	822,000	23.1	76.9
45	Service Employees International Union	820,950	0.3	99.6
46	Union Pacific Corp.	792,357	87.5	12.5
47	Associated General Contractors	791,050	93.9	6.1
48	American Nurses Association	788,508	10.5	88.8
49	Monday Morning PAC	766,500	100.0	0.0
50	Dairy Farmers of America	750,000	52.7	47.2
51	Majority Leader's Fund	737,558	100.0	0.0
52	Seafarers International Union	735,399	24.4	75.6
53	National Committee to Preserve Social Security and Medicare	709,426	21.3	78.2
54	International Association of Fire Fighters	703,875	10.1	89.8
55	Transport Workers Union	703,263	8.2	91.5
56	Human Rights Campaign	688,766	9.9	88.7

(Continued on next page)

Rank	PAC Name	Contributions to Congressional Candidates	% to Republicans	% to Democrats
57	Northrop Grumman Corp.	$681,675	72.2	27.8
58	Tenneco Inc.	658,725	69.7	30.3
59	American Postal Workers Union	657,110	3.7	95.8
60	Action Committee for Rural Electric	651,866	45.6	54.4
61	American Optometric Association	644,323	46.2	53.8
62	Credit Union National Association	642,688	57.7	42.2
63	RJR Nabisco	642,150	73.0	27.0
64	Ameritech Corp.	632,285	70.5	29.5
65	American Academy of Ophthalmology	606,975	45.6	54.4
66	American Council of Life Insurance	600,531	84.5	15.5
67	American Physical Therapy Association	593,737	47.7	52.3
68	Deloitte & Touche	588,402	67.8	32.2
69	Independent Insurance Agents of America	570,467	70.8	29.2
70	Amalgamated Transit Union	567,350	11.4	88.4
71	American Health Care Association	560,171	55.3	44.7
72	National PAC	560,000	53.8	46.2
73	International Longshoremen's Association	559,550	4.1	95.9
74	Exxon Corp.	556,950	97.0	3.0
75	American Crystal Sugar Co.	553,950	51.1	48.9
76	National Cable Television Association	547,346	68.1	31.9
77	General Electric Co.	546,550	63.9	36.0
78	BellSouth Corp.	545,867	60.9	38.8
79	National Rural Letter Carriers Association	541,800	24.2	74.9
80	American Society of Anesthesiologists	538,172	64.3	35.7
81	UST Inc.	528,000	79.6	20.4
82	Associated Builders and Contractors	524,600	99.8	0.2
83	J.P. Morgan & Co.	522,000	57.9	42.1
84	AFLAC Inc.	510,450	63.7	36.3
85	Operating Engineers Union	506,450	5.5	94.0
86	SBC Communications	504,333	71.2	28.8
87	Outback Steakhouse Inc.	493,950	94.7	5.3
88	Arthur Andersen LLP	480,301	57.6	42.4
89	Banc One Corp.	467,917	69.1	30.9
90	Aircraft Owners & Pilots Association	467,000	71.1	28.9
91	Harrah's Entertainment Inc.	462,115	68.4	31.6
92	Effective Government Committee	461,095	0.5	99.5
93	Dairy Farmers of America	457,500	57.5	42.5
94	American Podiatry Association	450,691	51.6	48.2
95	Food Marketing Institute	447,703	84.5	15.2
96	Investment Company Institute	444,014	61.0	39.0
97	NationsBank Corp.	442,285	51.2	48.6
98	GTE Corp.	435,691	76.2	23.8
99	National Association of Broadcasters	434,857	72.0	27.1
100	Transportation Communications International Union	429,140	11.2	88.4
101	American Association of Nurse Anesthetists	426,760	63.1	36.9
102	Boilermakers Union	422,350	3.4	95.8
103	Citicorp	418,800	62.6	37.4
104	United Mine Workers	414,200	1.0	98.9
105	Marine Engineers' Beneficial Association	411,905	45.1	54.9
106	Glaxo Wellcome Inc.	411,454	81.0	19.0
107	New Republican Majority Fund	410,142	100.0	0.0
108	American Trucking Associations	410,061	77.6	22.4
109	National Association of Postmasters	400,188	26.3	73.5
110	National Cattlemen's Beef Association	397,660	83.7	16.3
111	Coopers & Lybrand LLP	397,058	57.0	43.0
112	Republican Majority Fund	390,676	100.0	0.0
113	Morgan Stanley & Co.	384,000	58.3	41.7
114	Chicago Mercantile Exchange	377,000	58.0	42.0
115	Brown & Williamson Tobacco	375,000	80.9	19.1

(Continued on next page)

Rank	PAC Name	Contributions to Congressional Candidates	% to Republicans	% to Democrats
116	Chevron Corp.	$372,952	90.9	9.1
117	KidsPAC	372,000	0.5	99.2
118	Sierra Club	371,710	4.2	94.2
119	National Association of Convenience Stores	370,939	81.8	18.2
120	MBNA Corp.	367,904	86.3	13.7
121	Akin, Gump, Strauss, Hauer & Feld	366,833	59.9	40.1
122	Brotherhood of Locomotive Engineers	365,615	6.3	93.5
123	BankAmerica Corp.	362,651	63.2	36.8
124	Independent Bankers Association of America	358,500	66.9	32.9
125	National Air Traffic Controllers Association	356,990	23.7	76.3
126	Electronic Machine Furniture Workers	356,280	0.0	99.2
127	Boeing Co.	353,570	65.2	34.8
128	American Occupational Therapy Association	352,834	39.9	60.1
129	Boeing Co.	341,105	73.9	26.1
130	Ford Motor Co.	338,590	72.3	27.7
131	NationsBank Corp.	333,625	75.3	24.7
132	Price Waterhouse LLP	331,855	58.3	41.7
133	UNITE	324,629	1.4	98.5
134	Blue Cross and Blue Shield	322,221	69.0	31.0
135	Rockwell International	321,700	73.9	26.1
136	American Airlines	320,817	57.0	43.0
137	Adam Smith PAC	320,000	100.0	0.0
138	Waste Management Inc.	315,200	69.5	30.5
139	KPMG Peat Marwick LLP	314,750	62.3	37.7
140	Raytheon Co.	314,250	69.6	30.4
141	Chicago Board of Trade	308,893	60.1	39.9
142	BellSouth Corp.	308,250	75.8	24.2
143	Women's Campaign Fund	307,185	30.3	69.7
144	General Dynamics	306,062	64.3	35.7
145	General Motors	305,475	71.6	28.4
146	American Sugarbeet Growers Association	304,667	50.3	49.7
147	Chrysler Corp.	304,615	61.8	38.2
148	American College of Emergency Physicians	303,956	33.6	66.3
149	National Abortion Rights Action League	302,027	2.7	96.9
150	Bell Atlantic	300,550	68.7	31.3
151	Beneficial Management Corp.	299,819	67.8	32.2
152	Lockheed Martin	299,600	49.6	50.4
153	United Services Automobile Association Group	299,000	88.5	11.5
154	PepsiCo Inc.	297,489	83.0	17.0
155	Textron Inc.	295,800	64.0	36.0
156	Fluor Corp.	295,175	82.9	17.1
157	McDonald's Corp.	295,125	89.8	10.2
158	Koch Industries	294,500	95.6	4.4
159	Capitol Committee	292,000	100.0	0.0
160	American Veterinary Medical Association	291,500	63.6	36.4
161	Senate Victory Fund	283,711	100.0	0.0
162	America's Community Bankers	283,337	67.3	32.7
163	Time Warner	279,500	51.2	48.8
164	Bell Atlantic	275,998	65.6	34.4
165	Petroleum Marketers Association	275,888	87.1	12.9
166	Raytheon Co.	275,108	70.2	29.8
167	ConAgra Inc.	272,920	82.4	17.6
168	Massachusetts Mutual Life Insurance	267,178	70.5	29.5
169	United Technologies Corp.	266,874	69.9	30.1
170	US West Inc.	264,341	73.8	26.2
171	Pfizer Inc.	263,100	74.4	25.6
172	American Sugar Cane League	262,485	52.8	47.2
173	FMC Corp.	261,400	79.3	20.7
174	Merrill Lynch	254,427	74.6	25.4

(Continued on next page)

Rank	PAC Name	Contributions to Congressional Candidates	% to Republicans	% to Democrats
175	Brotherhood of Maintenance of Way Employees	$254,057	10.0	89.2
176	Emily's List	253,218	0.0	100.0
177	Bricklayers Union	252,300	2.0	98.0
178	Verner, Liipfert, Bernhard, McPherson & Hand	251,941	51.0	49.0
179	Mortgage Bankers Association of America	251,100	53.9	46.1
180	International Paper Co.	249,014	94.2	5.8
181	Chase Manhattan	247,625	71.6	28.4
182	Southern Minnesota Beet Sugar Co-Op	244,900	54.0	46.0
183	Farm Credit Council	244,602	61.4	38.6
184	General Atomics	244,250	74.0	25.8
185	National Association of Independent Insurers	244,215	95.4	4.6
186	JC Penney Co.	243,050	86.5	13.5
187	Eagle Forum	242,735	99.8	0.2
188	CSX Corp.	242,600	69.1	30.9
189	American Federation of Government Employees	241,200	2.4	97.4
190	TRW Inc.	241,061	80.2	19.8
191	Voters for Choice/Friends of Family Planning	240,432	2.5	96.2
192	EDS Corp.	237,749	53.8	46.2
193	Flowers Industries	237,500	100.0	0.0
194	Metropolitan Life	234,147	53.6	46.4
195	Southern California Edison	233,583	55.9	44.1
196	Cigna Corp.	230,300	90.0	10.0
197	Sprint Corp.	229,674	53.7	46.3
198	National Treasury Employees Union	229,429	9.9	89.8
199	Fight-PAC	227,500	100.0	0.0
200	College of American Pathologists	224,500	74.8	25.2

Top 50 PAC Contributors to Republican Congressional Candidates, 1995–96

Rank	PAC Name	Republicans	% to Republicans	Democrats	% to Democrats	Totals
1	National Auto Dealers Association	$1,906,925	81.7	$426,500	18.3	$2,335,425
2	American Medical Association	1,879,154	81.0	442,043	19.0	2,321,197
3	National Association of Realtors	1,441,448	68.7	655,235	31.2	2,099,683
4	National Rifle Association	1,301,771	83.4	259,100	16.6	1,560,871
5	National Association of Home Builders	1,183,849	82.0	259,000	18.0	1,442,849
6	United Parcel Service	1,159,675	64.9	628,472	35.1	1,788,147
7	American Institute of CPAs	1,145,425	67.7	540,500	32.0	1,690,925
8	National Beer Wholesalers Association	1,105,592	83.4	219,400	16.6	1,324,992
9	National Federation of Independent Business	1,001,851	93.6	68,692	6.4	1,070,543
10	National Association of Life Underwriters	984,750	69.0	442,000	31.0	1,426,750
11	American Bankers Association	937,650	72.1	362,200	27.9	1,299,850
12	American Dental Association	841,800	65.6	441,625	34.4	1,283,425
13	Americans for Free International Trade	829,800	88.6	107,000	11.4	936,800
14	Campaign America	825,971	99.5	4,000	0.5	829,971
15	AT&T	782,951	63.2	456,095	36.8	1,239,046
16	National Restaurant Association	780,069	88.6	100,050	11.4	880,119
17	Monday Morning PAC	766,500	100.0	-	0.0	766,500
18	Associated General Contractors	742,550	93.9	48,500	6.1	791,050
19	Majority Leader's Fund	737,558	100.0	-	0.0	737,558
20	Lockheed Martin	709,850	70.0	304,000	30.0	1,013,850
21	Union Pacific Corp.	693,558	87.5	98,799	12.5	792,357
22	Federal Express Corp.	664,500	70.5	277,500	29.4	943,000
23	Philip Morris Inc.	615,921	72.5	233,198	27.4	850,119
24	Marine Engineers' Beneficial Association	553,250	56.8	420,210	43.1	973,960
25	Exxon Corp.	540,450	97.0	16,500	3.0	556,950
26	Associated Builders and Contractors	523,600	99.8	1,000	0.2	524,600
27	American Council of Life Insurance	507,531	84.5	93,000	15.5	600,531
28	Northrop Grumman Corp.	492,325	72.2	189,350	27.8	681,675
29	RJR Nabisco	468,750	73.0	173,400	27.0	642,150
30	Outback Steakhouse Inc.	467,950	94.7	26,000	5.3	493,950
31	Tenneco Inc.	458,875	69.7	199,850	30.3	658,725
32	American Hospital Association	451,799	51.3	427,564	48.6	879,863
33	Ameritech Corp.	445,752	70.5	186,533	29.5	632,285
34	Ernst & Young LLP	438,075	49.6	445,040	50.4	883,115
35	U.S. Tobacco Co.	420,500	79.6	107,500	20.4	528,000
36	New Republican Majority Fund	410,142	100.0	-	0.0	410,142
37	Independent Insurance Agents of America	403,999	70.8	166,468	29.2	570,467
38	Deloitte & Touche LLP	399,089	67.8	189,313	32.2	588,402
39	Dairy Farmers of America	395,500	52.7	354,000	47.2	750,000
40	Republican Majority Fund	390,676	100.0	-	0.0	390,676
41	Food Marketing Institute	378,453	84.5	68,250	15.2	447,703
42	National Cable Television Association	372,976	68.1	174,370	31.9	547,346
43	Credit Union National Association	370,672	57.7	271,016	42.2	642,688
44	SBC Communications	359,133	71.2	145,200	28.8	504,333
45	General Electric	349,050	63.9	196,500	36.0	546,550
46	American Society of Anesthesiologists	346,312	64.3	191,860	35.7	538,172
47	Chevron Corp.	338,952	90.9	34,000	9.1	372,952
48	Glaxo Wellcome Inc.	333,129	81.0	78,325	19.0	411,454
49	National Cattlemen's Beef Association	333,007	83.7	64,653	16.3	397,660
50	BellSouth Telecommunications Inc.	332,367	60.9	212,000	38.8	545,867

Top 50 PAC Contributors to Democratic Congressional Candidates, 1995–96

Rank	PAC Name	Democrats	% to Democrats	Republicans	% to Republicans	Total
1	Teamsters Union	$2,495,330	95.7	$ 100,810	3.9	$2,606,140
2	AFSCME	2,453,096	98.0	40,925	1.6	2,504,021
3	United Auto Workers	2,446,344	99.1	10,975	0.4	2,467,319
4	National Education Association	2,304,980	99.1	11,850	0.5	2,326,830
5	Association of Trial Lawyers of America	2,087,438	89.3	239,500	10.2	2,336,938
6	International Brotherhood of Electrical Workers	2,020,450	97.6	43,637	2.1	2,070,587
7	United Food & Commercial Workers Union	1,998,745	98.4	23,050	1.1	2,030,795
8	Machinists & Aerospace Workers Union	1,981,925	99.1	7,750	0.4	1,999,675
9	Laborers' Political League	1,743,800	90.9	166,000	8.7	1,917,800
10	American Federation of Teachers	1,590,466	98.5	19,750	1.2	1,614,833
11	United Steelworkers	1,523,650	100.0	-	0.0	1,523,650
12	National Association of Letter Carriers	1,491,314	87.4	205,750	12.1	1,706,564
13	Carpenters & Joiners Union	1,390,606	94.9	66,500	4.5	1,464,606
14	Communications Workers of America	1,288,536	99.3	1,250	0.1	1,297,286
15	AFL-CIO	1,177,514	98.9	9,000	0.8	1,190,514
16	National Committee for an Effective Congress	1,113,475	99.6	-	0.0	1,118,475
17	United Transportation Union	1,055,800	83.8	195,800	15.5	1,260,600
18	National Association of Retired Federal Employees	1,035,950	83.3	205,400	16.5	1,243,350
19	Sheet Metal Workers Union	1,030,500	96.8	28,500	2.7	1,064,500
20	Plumbers & Pipefitters Union	916,500	95.7	38,500	4.0	958,000
21	Service Employees International Union	817,450	99.6	2,500	0.3	820,950
22	Ironworkers Union	783,045	94.5	42,070	5.1	828,615
23	American Nurses Association	700,259	88.8	82,695	10.5	788,508
24	National Association of Realtors	655,235	31.2	1,441,448	68.7	2,099,683
25	Transport Workers Union	643,363	91.5	57,400	8.2	703,263
26	Air Line Pilots Association	632,000	76.9	190,000	23.1	822,000
27	International Association of Fire Fighters	631,800	89.8	71,075	10.1	703,875
28	American Postal Workers Union	629,410	95.8	24,500	3.7	657,110
29	United Parcel Service	628,472	35.1	1,159,675	64.9	1,788,147
30	Human Rights Campaign	610,639	88.7	68,127	9.9	688,766
31	Seafarers International Union	556,300	75.6	179,099	24.4	735,399
32	National Committee to Preserve Social Security	555,044	78.2	151,382	21.3	709,426
33	American Institute of CPAs	540,500	32.0	1,145,425	67.7	1,690,925
34	International Longshoremen's Association	536,600	95.9	22,950	4.1	559,550
35	Amalgamated Transit Union	501,350	88.4	64,500	11.4	567,350
36	Operating Engineers Union	476,200	94.0	27,750	5.5	506,450
37	Effective Government Committee	458,905	99.5	2,190	0.5	461,095
38	AT&T	456,095	36.8	782,951	63.2	1,239,046
39	Ernst & Young LLP	445,040	50.4	438,075	49.6	883,115
40	American Medical Association	442,043	19.0	1,879,154	81.0	2,321,197
41	National Association of Life Underwriters	442,000	31.0	984,750	69.0	1,426,750
42	American Dental Association	441,625	34.4	841,800	65.6	1,283,425
43	American Hospital Association	427,564	48.6	451,799	51.3	879,863
44	National Auto Dealers Association	426,500	18.3	1,906,925	81.7	2,335,425
45	Marine Engineers' Beneficial Association	420,210	43.1	553,250	56.8	973,960
46	United Mine Workers	409,700	98.9	4,000	1.0	414,200
47	National Rural Letter Carriers Association	406,050	74.9	131,250	24.2	541,800
48	Boilermakers Union	404,600	95.8	14,250	3.4	422,350
49	Transportation Communications International Union	379,390	88.4	48,250	11.2	429,140
50	KidsPAC	369,000	99.2	2,000	0.5	372,000

Top 50 Industry Contributors to Republican Candidates, 1995–96

Rank	Industry	Republicans	% to Republicans	Democrats	% to Democrats	Total
1	Insurance	$7,593,809	73.3	$2,761,394	26.7	$10,356,203
2	Health Professionals	6,171,098	57.1	4,631,264	42.8	10,809,716
3	Leadership PACs	5,941,293	81.2	1,373,674	18.8	7,315,467
4	Commercial Banks	5,497,579	68.1	2,576,205	31.9	8,076,634
5	Oil & Gas	4,857,328	83.3	973,612	16.7	5,832,190
6	Telephone Utilities	3,873,176	66.2	1,974,811	33.8	5,849,487
7	Automotive	3,767,212	79.7	954,570	20.2	4,723,782
8	Air Transport	3,206,923	67.5	1,546,101	32.5	4,754,024
9	Electric Utilities	2,974,841	67.1	1,458,509	32.9	4,434,350
10	Accountants	2,916,849	61.7	1,809,170	38.2	4,731,019
11	Food Processing & Sales	2,611,042	85.5	440,067	14.4	3,052,109
12	Food & Beverage	2,575,631	86.8	390,758	13.2	2,966,889
13	Miscellaneous Manufacturing & Distributing	2,562,765	76.6	781,913	23.4	3,346,178
14	Lawyers/Law Firms	2,463,794	38.3	3,963,965	61.6	6,439,509
15	Pharmaceuticals/Health Products	2,456,474	73	910,055	27	3,366,529
16	Securities & Investment	2,454,928	63.4	1,414,773	36.6	3,869,701
17	Defense Aerospace	2,453,969	71.3	986,500	28.7	3,440,469
18	Crop Production & Basic Processing	2,197,341	57.7	1,610,231	42.3	3,808,072
19	Real Estate	2,130,903	68.8	963,006	31.1	3,096,909
20	General Contractors	2,064,075	89.7	236,541	10.3	2,300,616
21	Tobacco	2,056,421	75.5	666,098	24.5	2,723,519
22	Transportation Unions	2,044,429	18.3	9,085,975	81.4	11,165,704
23	Retail Sales	1,786,134	81	417,764	19	2,203,898
24	Agricultural Services/Products	1,782,623	66.3	906,063	33.7	2,688,686
25	Forestry & Forest Products	1,781,148	90.4	190,044	9.6	1,971,192
26	Beer, Wine & Liquor	1,717,500	75.6	553,923	24.4	2,271,423
27	Railroads	1,650,780	78.2	458,982	21.8	2,109,762
28	TV/Movies/Music	1,643,292	58.4	1,167,135	41.5	2,815,374
29	Defense Electronics	1,621,768	71.6	643,051	28.4	2,264,819
30	Home Builders	1,496,499	80.2	368,325	19.8	1,864,824
31	Gun Rights	1,494,442	84.2	280,140	15.8	1,774,582
32	Chemical & Related Manufacturing	1,469,522	78.5	401,500	21.5	1,871,022
33	Republican/Conservative PACs	1,366,117	99.7	3,021	0.2	1,370,338
34	Business Associations	1,270,843	87.8	177,137	12.2	1,447,980
35	Hospitals/Nursing Homes	1,215,599	52.4	1,099,422	47.4	2,320,521
36	Public Sector Unions	1,003,338	8	11,543,938	91.7	12,594,793
37	Dairy	993,787	60	661,750	40	1,656,037
38	Mining	977,177	82.5	206,970	17.5	1,184,147
39	Building Materials & Equipment	963,944	81.4	219,553	18.6	1,183,497
40	Pro-Israel	899,086	39.2	1,396,964	60.8	2,296,050
41	Trucking	889,804	81.6	200,850	18.4	1,090,654
42	Sea Transport	806,799	72.5	305,449	27.5	1,112,248
43	Finance/Credit Companies	750,185	72	292,238	28	1,042,423
44	Savings & Loans	652,035	72	252,483	27.9	905,518
45	Construction Services	650,361	67.8	308,502	32.2	958,963
46	Livestock	612,924	77.9	174,263	22.1	787,187
47	Business Services	531,374	69.1	237,605	30.9	768,979
48	Casinos/Gambling	524,590	63	307,506	37	832,096
49	Waste Management	521,639	72.1	201,975	27.9	723,614
50	Miscellaneous Issues	518,869	44.8	635,765	54.9	1,157,634

Top 50 Industry Contributors to Democratic Candidates, 1995–96

Rank	*Industry*	*Democrats*	*% to Democrats*	*Republicans*	*% to Republicans*	*Total*
1	Industrial Unions	$11,636,029	98.7	$ 102,362	0.9	$11,789,291
2	Public Sector Unions	11,543,938	91.7	1,003,338	8.0	12,594,793
3	Transportation Unions	9,085,975	81.4	2,044,429	18.3	11,165,704
4	Building Trade Unions	7,920,918	94.1	466,140	5.5	8,418,675
5	Miscellaneous Unions	4,784,655	98.2	72,061	1.5	4,870,966
6	Health Professionals	4,631,264	42.8	6,171,098	57.1	10,809,716
7	Lawyers/Law Firms	3,963,965	61.6	2,463,794	38.3	6,439,509
8	Insurance	2,761,394	26.7	7,593,809	73.3	10,356,203
9	Commercial Banks	2,576,205	31.9	5,497,579	68.1	8,076,634
10	Telephone Utilities	1,974,811	33.8	3,873,176	66.2	5,849,487
11	Democratic/Liberal	1,886,688	98.8	13,500	0.7	1,908,688
12	Accountants	1,809,170	38.2	2,916,849	61.7	4,731,019
13	Crop Production & Basic Processing	1,610,231	42.3	2,197,341	57.7	3,808,072
14	Air Transport	1,546,101	32.5	3,206,923	67.5	4,754,024
15	Electric Utilities	1,458,509	32.9	2,974,841	67.1	4,434,350
16	Securities & Investment	1,414,773	36.6	2,454,928	63.4	3,869,701
17	Pro-Israel	1,396,964	60.8	899,086	39.2	2,296,050
18	Leadership PACs	1,373,674	18.8	5,941,293	81.2	7,315,467
19	Human Rights	1,372,606	88.7	163,233	10.6	1,546,839
20	TV/Movies/Music	1,167,135	41.5	1,643,292	58.4	2,815,374
21	Hospitals/Nursing Homes	1,099,422	47.4	1,215,599	52.4	2,320,521
22	Defense Aerospace	986,500	28.7	2,453,969	71.3	3,440,469
23	Oil & Gas	973,612	16.7	4,857,328	83.3	5,832,190
24	Real Estate	963,006	31.1	2,130,903	68.8	3,096,909
25	Automotive	954,570	20.2	3,767,212	79.7	4,723,782
26	Pharmaceuticals/Health Products	910,055	27.0	2,456,474	73.0	3,366,529
27	Agricultural Services/Products	906,063	33.7	1,782,623	66.3	2,688,686
28	Miscellaneous Manufacturing & Distributing	781,913	23.4	2,562,765	76.6	3,346,178
29	Tobacco	666,098	24.5	2,056,421	75.5	2,723,519
30	Dairy	661,750	40.0	993,787	60.0	1,656,037
31	Defense Electronics	643,051	28.4	1,621,768	71.6	2,264,819
32	Miscellaneous Issues	635,765	54.9	518,869	44.8	1,157,634
33	Environment	626,529	93.6	34,906	5.2	669,163
34	Women's Issues	615,571	85.6	103,500	14.4	719,071
35	Abortion Policy/Pro-Choice	581,059	75.4	185,341	24.1	770,429
36	Beer, Wine & Liquor	553,923	24.4	1,717,500	75.6	2,271,423
37	Railroads	458,982	21.8	1,650,780	78.2	2,109,762
38	Food Processing & Sales	440,067	14.4	2,611,042	85.5	3,052,109
39	Retail Sales	417,764	19.0	1,786,134	81.0	2,203,898
40	Chemical & Related Manufacturing	401,500	21.5	1,469,522	78.5	1,871,022
41	Food & Beverage	390,758	13.2	2,575,631	86.8	2,966,889
42	Home Builders	368,325	19.8	1,496,499	80.2	1,864,824
43	Credit Unions	319,956	43.1	421,872	56.8	742,828
44	Construction Services	308,502	32.2	650,361	67.8	958,963
45	Casinos/Gambling	307,506	37.0	524,590	63.0	832,096
46	Sea Transport	305,449	27.5	806,799	72.5	1,112,248
47	Finance/Credit Companies	292,238	28.0	750,185	72.0	1,042,423
48	Health Services	288,013	47.7	315,349	52.3	603,362
49	Gun Rights	280,140	15.8	1,494,442	84.2	1,774,582
50	Foreign & Defense Policy	273,667	75.1	90,840	24.9	364,507

PAC Contributions to Banking Committee Members, 1995–96

This chart illustrates the ties between business PACs and congressional committees with jurisdiction over that industry. In this example, members of banking committees in the House and Senate are shown, along with the total amount of contributions from banking, savings & loan and credit union PACs during the 1995-96 election cycle.

Office	Committee Member	State	Party	Amount
Sen.	Alfonse M. D'Amato *	N.Y.	R	$223,378
Rep.	Bill McCollum #	Fla.	R	153,652
Sen.	Phil Gramm	Texas	R	132,206
Rep.	John J. LaFalce	N.Y.	D	117,699
Rep.	Frank A. Cremeans	Ohio	R	116,514
Rep.	Richard H. Baker	La.	R	113,605
Rep.	Rick A. Lazio	N.Y.	R	113,235
Rep.	Peter T. King	N.Y.	R	106,735
Sen.	Richard C. Shelby	Ala.	R	98,558
Rep.	Ken Bentsen	Texas	D	95,512
Rep.	Marge Roukema	N.J.	R	94,365
Sen.	Lauch Faircloth	N.C.	R	88,428
Rep.	Ed Royce	Calif.	R	87,551
Rep.	Bill Orton	Utah	D	82,722
Rep.	Bob Ney	Ohio	R	79,960
Rep.	Doug Bereuter	Neb.	R	79,541
Rep.	Bruce F. Vento	Minn.	D	77,605
Rep.	Dick Chrysler	Mich.	R	75,628
Rep.	Fred Heineman	N.C.	R	74,091
Rep.	Sonny Bono	Calif.	R	73,284
Sen.	Pete V. Domenici	N.M.	R	73,077
Rep.	Jon D. Fox	Pa.	R	69,434
Rep.	Bob Barr	Ga.	R	66,602
Rep.	Jerry Weller	Ill.	R	65,643
Rep.	Michael N. Castle	Del.	R	63,950
Rep.	Steve Stockman	Texas	R	63,800
Rep.	Spencer Bachus	Ala.	R	54,614
Rep.	Floyd H. Flake	N.Y.	D	49,638
Rep.	Jack Metcalf	Wash.	R	48,125
Rep.	Robert Ehrlich Jr.	Md.	R	47,962
Sen.	Christopher J. Dodd	Conn.	D	44,877
Rep.	J. C. Watts	Okla.	R	44,024
Sen.	Christopher S. Bond	Mo.	R	43,237
Rep.	Paul E. Kanjorski	Pa.	D	42,301
Rep.	Tom Campbell	Calif.	R	38,067
Rep.	Toby Roth	Wis.	R	37,314
Rep.	Sue W. Kelly	N.Y.	R	$36,946
Rep.	Frank D. Lucas	Okla.	R	36,734
Rep.	Charles E. Schumer	N.Y.	D	36,700
Sen.	Carol Moseley-Braun	Ill.	D	36,043
Rep.	Carolyn B. Maloney	N.Y.	D	33,900
Rep.	J. D. Hayworth	Ariz.	R	33,174
Rep.	Barney Frank	Mass.	D	33,100
Sen.	Robert F. Bennett	Utah	R	31,803
Rep.	Albert R. Wynn	Md.	D	28,085
Rep.	Gary L. Ackerman	N.Y.	D	26,250
Rep.	Thomas M. Barrett	Wis.	D	22,792
Rep.	Lucille Roybal-Allard	Calif.	D	21,200
Rep.	Frank A. LoBiondo	N.J.	R	19,694
Rep.	Luis V. Gutierrez	Ill.	D	17,400
Sen.	Connie Mack	Fla.	R	16,533
Rep.	Melvin Watt	N.C.	D	15,600
Sen.	Barbara Boxer	Calif.	D	14,354
Sen.	Rod Grams	Minn.	R	14,048
Rep.	Jesse Jackson Jr.	Ill.	D	13,389
Sen.	Patty Murray	Wash.	D	11,482
Rep.	Kweisi Mfume	Md.	D	7,000
Rep.	Maurice D. Hinchey	N.Y.	D	6,500
Rep.	Nydia M. Velazquez	N.Y.	D	5,500
Rep.	Joseph P. Kennedy II	Mass.	D	4,000
Rep.	Henry B. Gonzalez	Texas	D	3,000
Rep.	Bernard Sanders	Vt.	I	1,000
Rep.	Cleo Fields	La.	D	500
Sen.	Paul S. Sarbanes	Md.	D	300
Sen.	John Kerry	Mass.	D	250
Rep.	Maxine Waters	Calif.	D	-
Rep.	Jim Leach*	Iowa	R	-
Sen.	Richard H. Bryan	Nev.	D	(650)

* committee chairman
# committee vice-chairman

Top 100 PAC Contributors to Incumbents, 1995–96

Rank	PAC	Incumbents	% to Incumbents	Total
1	National Association of Realtors	$1,656,183	78.9	$2,099,683
2	National Auto Dealers Association	1,616,075	69.2	2,335,425
3	American Medical Association	1,572,358	67.7	2,321,197
4	United Parcel Service	1,507,672	84.3	1,788,147
5	American Institute of CPA's	1,404,725	83.1	1,690,925
6	AFSCME	1,245,074	49.7	2,504,021
7	Association of Trial Lawyers of America	1,224,825	52.4	2,336,938
8	Teamsters Union	1,192,140	45.7	2,606,140
9	Laborers' Political League	1,154,800	60.2	1,917,800
10	AT&T	1,099,181	88.7	1,239,046
11	National Association of Life Underwriters	1,087,750	76.2	1,426,750
12	National Association of Home Builders	1,087,349	75.4	1,442,849
13	National Rifle Association	1,053,675	67.5	1,560,871
14	United Auto Workers	1,049,269	42.5	2,467,319
15	National Education Association	1,035,380	44.5	2,326,830
16	American Bankers Association	1,027,850	79.1	1,299,850
17	American Dental Association	1,018,225	79.3	1,283,425
18	National Association of Letter Carriers	989,464	58.0	1,706,564
19	National Beer Wholesalers Association	948,742	71.6	1,324,992
20	United Food & Commercial Workers Union	948,351	46.7	2,030,795
21	Marine Engineers District 2 Maritime Officers	924,960	95.0	973,960
22	Machinists & Aerospace Workers Union	884,225	44.2	1,999,675
23	International Brotherhood of Electrical Workers	880,737	42.5	2,070,587
24	Lockheed Martin	869,050	85.7	1,013,850
25	National Association of Retired Federal Employees	799,850	64.3	1,243,350
26	American Federation of Teachers	750,436	46.5	1,614,833
27	United Transportation Union	748,750	59.4	1,260,600
28	Federal Express Corp.	745,500	79.1	943,000
29	Philip Morris Inc.	738,772	86.9	850,119
30	Carpenters & Joiners Union	721,756	49.3	1,464,606
31	Americans for Free International Trade	698,000	74.5	936,800
32	American Hospital Association	642,506	73.0	879,863
33	Air Line Pilots Association	625,000	76.0	822,000
34	Northrop Grumman Corp.	622,275	91.3	681,675
35	Ernst & Young LLP	610,815	69.2	883,115
36	United Steelworkers	575,150	37.7	1,523,650
37	Dairy Farmers of America	552,500	73.7	750,000
38	Tenneco Inc.	543,475	82.5	658,725
39	Union Pacific Corp.	538,843	68.0	792,357
40	National Federation of Independent Business	533,888	49.9	1,070,543
41	RJR Nabisco	521,650	81.2	642,150
42	Associated General Contractors	510,300	64.5	791,050
43	Communications Workers of America	506,020	39.0	1,297,286
44	American Crystal Sugar Co.	505,450	91.2	553,950
45	Deloitte & Touche LLP	501,973	85.3	588,402
46	Credit Union National Association	498,075	77.5	642,688
47	Seafarers International Union	497,599	67.7	735,399
48	National Restaurant Association	494,619	56.2	880,119
49	National Cable Television Association	493,846	90.2	547,346
50	ACRE (Action Committee for Rural Electricity)	487,966	74.9	651,866
51	General Electric	484,350	88.6	546,550
52	JP Morgan & Co.	484,000	92.7	522,000
53	Plumbers & Pipefitters Union	482,000	50.3	958,000
54	Ameritech Corp.	480,381	76.0	632,285
55	Sheet Metal Workers Union	473,750	44.5	1,064,500
56	Independent Insurance Agents of America	470,633	82.5	570,467

(Continued on next page)

Rank	PAC	Incumbents	% to Incumbents	Total
57	National Committee to Preserve Social Security	$468,724	66.1	$ 709,426
58	American Postal Workers Union	468,700	71.3	657,110
59	American Physical Therapy Association	458,212	77.2	593,737
60	AFLAC Inc.	449,250	88.0	510,450
61	American Optometric Association	441,073	68.5	644,323
62	Campaign America	440,175	53.0	829,971
63	Human Rights Campaign	432,065	62.7	688,766
64	US Tobacco Co.	426,000	80.7	528,000
65	American Health Care Association	424,362	75.8	560,171
66	National PAC	423,500	75.6	560,000
67	Transport Workers Union	418,300	59.5	703,263
68	American Society of Anesthesiologists	416,584	77.4	538,172
69	American Council of Life Insurance	416,031	69.3	600,531
70	BellSouth Telecommunications Inc.	414,217	75.9	545,867
71	American Nurses Association	405,684	51.4	788,508
72	Arthur Andersen LLP	404,551	84.2	480,301
73	Ironworkers Union	399,315	48.2	828,615
74	Banc One Corp.	395,167	84.5	467,917
75	Monday Morning PAC	392,000	51.1	766,500
76	National Committee for an Effective Congress	390,175	34.9	1,118,475
77	Investment Company Institute	385,514	86.8	444,014
78	Majority Leader's Fund	384,363	52.1	737,558
79	Morgan Stanley & Co.	380,000	99.0	384,000
80	Mid-America Dairymen	377,750	82.6	457,500
81	SBC Communications	376,179	74.6	504,333
82	American Academy of Ophthalmology	375,600	61.9	606,975
83	Amalgamated Transit Union	371,650	65.5	567,350
84	National Association of Broadcasters	371,160	85.4	434,857
85	AFL-CIO	366,220	30.8	1,190,514
86	Citicorp	365,320	87.2	418,800
87	NationsBank	364,285	82.4	442,285
88	Food Marketing Institute	361,774	80.8	447,703
89	American Podiatry Association	356,691	79.1	450,691
90	Aircraft Owners & Pilots Association	352,000	75.4	467,000
91	Service Employees Int'l Union	351,950	42.9	820,950
92	Coopers & Lybrand LLP	350,019	88.2	397,058
93	Akin, Gump et. al.	347,626	94.8	366,833
94	American Trucking Associations	344,908	84.1	410,061
95	McDonnell Douglas	343,870	97.3	353,570
96	Glaxo Wellcome Inc.	333,504	81.1	411,454
97	International Association of Fire Fighters	333,425	47.4	703,875
98	GTE Corp.	332,029	76.2	435,691
99	Marine Engineers District 1 (Pacific Coast District)	325,105	78.9	411,905
100	Transportation Communications International Union	322,340	75.1	429,140

Top PAC Independent Expenditures, 1995–96

Rank	PAC	Total	Candidate	Office	State	Party	Position	Amount
1	National Rifle Association	$1,723,823	J. D. Hayworth	Rep.	Ariz.	R	Support	$139,872
			Louis "Woody" Jenkins	Sen.	La.	R	Support	135,989
			Bob Smith	Sen.	N.H.	R	Support	76,174
			Randy Tate	Rep.	Wash.	R	Support	68,073
			Dick Chrysler	Rep.	Mich.	R	Support	61,291
2	National Right to Life Committee	1,543,935	Guy Millner	Sen.	Ga.	R	Support	118,012
			Albert Salvi	Sen.	Ill.	R	Support	70,744
			Jim Ross Lightfoot	Sen.	Iowa	R	Support	66,049
			Louis "Woody" Jenkins	Sen.	La.	R	Support	66,002
			Steve Stockman	Rep.	Texas	R	Support	62,134
3	League of Conservation Voters	1,213,687	Gordon H. Smith	Sen.	Ore.	R	Oppose	230,891
			Helen Chenoweth	Rep.	Idaho	R	Oppose	196,931
			Randy Tate	Rep.	Wash.	R	Oppose	196,028
			Larry Pressler	Sen.	S.D.	R	Oppose	140,350
			James B. Longley Jr.	Rep.	Maine	R	Oppose	110,859
4	American Medical Association	517,834	Susan M. Collins	Sen.	Maine	R	Support	129,697
			Randy Tate	Rep.	Wash.	R	Support	112,924
			Charlie Norwood	Rep.	Ga.	R	Support	109,695
			Anne M. Northrup	Rep.	Ky.	R	Support	80,307
			John Cooksey	Rep.	La.	R	Support	51,174
5	National Education Association	499,414	Frank A. Cremeans	Rep.	Ohio	R	Oppose	150,930
			Jim McGovern	Rep.	Mass.	D	Support	85,438
			David E. Price	Rep.	N.C.	D	Support	71,638
			Bob Ney	Rep.	Ohio	R	Support	45,204
			Peter I. Blute	Rep.	Mass.	R	Support	41,184

Top 100 PAC Recipients, 1995–96

Rank	Office	Candidate	State	Party	Total	Elected?
1	Sen.	Dick Zimmer	N.J.	R	$1,833,329	No
2	Sen.	John W. Warner	Va.	R	1,629,310	Yes
3	Sen.	Gordon Smith	Ore.	R	1,590,610	Yes
4	Sen.	Larry Pressler	S.D.	R	1,546,196	No
5	Sen.	Ron Wyden	Ore.	D	1,426,178	Yes
6	Sen.	Max Baucus	Mont.	D	1,376,718	Yes
7	Rep.	Vic Fazio	Calif.	D	1,355,985	Yes
8	Sen.	Mitch McConnell	Ky.	R	1,318,289	Yes
9	Sen.	Pat Roberts	Kan.	R	1,247,775	Yes
10	Rep.	Richard A. Gephardt	Mo.	D	1,242,070	Yes
11	Sen.	Ted Stevens	Alaska	R	1,225,547	Yes
12	Sen.	Richard J. Durbin	Ill.	D	1,211,094	Yes
13	Sen.	Pete V. Domenici	N.M.	R	1,175,829	Yes
14	Sen.	James M. Inhofe	Okla.	R	1,140,694	Yes
15	Rep.	Martin Frost	Texas	D	1,137,136	Yes
16	Sen.	Phil Gramm	Texas	R	1,131,711	Yes
17	Sen.	Tom Harkin	Iowa	D	1,118,602	Yes
18	Rep.	Newt Gingrich	Ga.	R	1,093,336	Yes
19	Sen.	Fred Thompson	Tenn.	R	1,091,345	Yes
20	Sen.	Alfonse M. D'Amato	N.Y.	R	1,083,571	Not Running
21	Sen.	Jack Reed	R.I.	D	1,079,503	Yes
22	Sen.	Wayne Allard	Colo.	R	1,078,775	Yes
23	Sen.	Jesse Helms	N.C.	R	1,069,969	Yes
24	Rep.	Tom DeLay	Texas	R	1,068,904	Yes
25	Sen.	Rudy Boschwitz	Minn.	R	1,066,652	Yes
26	Sen.	Larry E. Craig	Idaho	R	1,047,126	Yes
27	Rep.	Ken Bentsen	Texas	D	1,038,533	Yes
28	Sen.	John D. Rockefeller IV	W.Va.	D	1,001,599	Yes
29	Sen.	Robert G. Torricelli	N.J.	D	988,805	Yes
30	Sen.	Jeff Sessions	Ala.	R	969,673	Yes
31	Sen.	Ben Nelson	Neb.	D	935,746	No
32	Sen.	Carl Levin	Mich.	D	922,028	Yes
33	Sen.	Bob Smith	N.H.	R	900,839	Yes
34	Rep.	David E. Bonior	Mich.	D	890,704	Yes
35	Sen.	Tim Johnson	S.D.	D	889,621	Yes
36	Rep.	John D. Dingell	Mich.	D	883,439	Yes
37	Sen.	Sam Brownback	Kan.	R	843,519	Yes
38	Sen.	William F. Weld	Mass.	R	828,761	No
39	Sen.	Strom Thurmond	S.C.	R	802,106	Yes
40	Rep.	Bart Gordon	Tenn.	D	774,511	Yes
41	Rep.	Rick White	Wash.	R	755,804	Yes
42	Sen.	Max Cleland	Ga.	D	734,453	Yes
43	Rep.	Nick Lampson	Texas	D	721,145	Yes
44	Rep.	Randy Tate	Wash.	R	720,800	Yes
45	Rep.	John Ensign	Nev.	R	719,351	Yes
46	Rep.	Charles B. Rangel	N.Y.	D	719,332	Yes
47	Rep.	Greg Ganske	Iowa	R	709,951	Yes
48	Rep.	Steny H. Hoyer	Md.	D	702,467	Yes
49	Rep.	Phil English	Pa.	R	700,938	Yes
50	Rep.	Thomas J. Bliley Jr.	Va.	R	696,685	Yes
51	Rep.	Charlie Norwood	Ga.	R	691,151	Yes
52	Rep.	Bill Paxon	N.Y.	R	673,728	Yes
53	Rep.	Frank A. Cremeans	Ohio	R	668,865	Yes
54	Rep.	Jon Christensen	Neb.	R	650,908	Yes
55	Sen.	Tim Hutchinson	Ark.	R	649,775	Yes
56	Rep.	Tom Coburn	Okla.	R	647,932	Yes

(Continued on next page)

Rank	Office	Candidate	State	Party	Total	Elected?
57	Rep.	Bill Thomas	Calif.	R	$645,978	Yes
58	Sen.	Paul Wellstone	Minn.	D	642,824	Yes
59	Rep.	Robert L. Livingston	La.	R	639,295	Yes
60	Rep.	Greg Laughlin	Texas	R	637,489	No
61	Rep.	Steve Stockman	Texas	R	637,034	No
62	Rep.	Joe L. Barton	Texas	R	636,441	Yes
63	Sen.	Susan M. Collins	Maine	R	628,836	Yes
64	Rep.	Earl Pomeroy	N.D.	D	618,304	Yes
65	Sen.	Jim Ross Lightfoot	Iowa	R	614,686	No
66	Rep.	J. D. Hayworth	Ariz.	R	608,664	Yes
67	Rep.	Dick Armey	Texas	R	603,838	Yes
68	Sen.	Albert Salvi	Ill.	R	591,720	No
69	Rep.	Don Young	Alaska	R	589,043	Yes
70	Rep.	Tom Campbell	Calif.	R	587,969	Yes
71	Rep.	Sander M. Levin	Mich.	D	583,450	Yes
72	Sen.	Mary L. Landrieu	La.	D	583,008	Yes
73	Sen.	Guy Millner	Ga.	R	578,131	Yes
74	Rep.	John A. Boehner	Ohio	R	561,994	Yes
75	Sen.	Thad Cochran	Miss.	R	560,854	Yes
76	Rep.	W. J. "Billy" Tauzin	La.	R	556,866	Yes
77	Rep.	Dennis Hastert	Ill.	R	556,143	Yes
78	Rep.	Dan Schaefer	Colo.	R	554,751	Yes
79	Rep.	Daniel Frisa	N.Y.	R	551,967	No
80	Rep.	Frank Riggs	Calif.	R	550,739	Yes
81	Rep.	Bill Martini	N.J.	R	550,453	Yes
82	Rep.	Edward Whitfield	Ky.	R	550,148	Yes
83	Rep.	Bob Ney	Ohio	R	549,373	Yes
84	Rep.	Bud Shuster	Pa.	R	538,067	Yes
85	Rep.	Dick Chrysler	Mich.	R	535,281	Yes
86	Rep.	Jon D. Fox	Pa.	R	533,619	Yes
87	Rep.	Gerald D. Kleczka	Wis.	D	529,211	Yes
88	Rep.	Jane Harman	Calif.	D	518,569	Yes
89	Rep.	Bill Orton	Utah	D	515,296	Yes
90	Sen.	Louis "Woody" Jenkins	La.	R	513,249	No
91	Rep.	Sherrod Brown	Ohio	D	512,886	Yes
92	Sen.	Chuck Hagel	Neb.	R	511,634	Yes
93	Rep.	Brian P. Bilbray	Calif.	R	510,329	Yes
94	Rep.	Kevin Brady	Texas	R	508,782	Yes
95	Rep.	Gerald B. H. Solomon	N.Y.	R	507,450	Yes
96	Rep.	Bob Filner	Calif.	D	507,380	Yes
97	Sen.	Michael B. Enzi	Wyo.	R	501,535	Yes
98	Rep.	Susan Molinari	N.Y.	R	498,462	Yes
99	Rep.	Charles W. Stenholm	Texas	D	497,203	Yes
100	Rep.	Mike Ward	Ky.	D	495,887	No

Top 50 Agriculture PACs, 1995–96

Rank	*PAC*	*Contributions to Congressional Candidates*	*% to Democrats*	*% to Republicans*
1	Philip Morris	$850,119	27.4	72.5
2	RJR Nabisco	642,150	27.0	73.0
3	American Crystal Sugar Co.	553,950	48.9	51.1
4	UST Inc.	528,000	20.4	79.6
5	Dairy Farmers of America	457,500	42.5	57.5
6	Food Marketing Institute	447,703	15.2	84.5
7	National Cattlemen's Beef Association	397,660	16.3	83.7
8	Brown & Williamson Tobacco	375,000	19.1	80.9
9	American Sugarbeet Growers Association	304,667	49.7	50.3
10	PepsiCo Inc.	297,489	17.0	83.0
11	American Veterinary Medical Association	291,500	36.4	63.6
12	ConAgra Inc.	272,920	17.6	82.4
13	American Sugar Cane League	262,485	47.2	52.8
14	International Paper Co.	249,014	5.8	94.2
15	Southern Minnesota Beet Sugar Cooperative	244,900	46.0	54.0
16	Farm Credit Council	244,602	38.6	61.4
17	Flowers Industries	237,500	0.0	100.0
18	Alabama Farmers Federation	210,311	37.2	62.8
19	Archer-Daniels-Midland Co.	208,976	58.6	41.4
20	Champion International Corp.	205,235	20.1	79.9
21	Georgia-Pacific Corp.	187,076	12.8	87.2
22	International Dairy Foods Association	183,800	12.6	87.4
23	Westvaco Corp.	174,500	7.7	92.3
24	Georgia Peanut Producers Association	164,500	34.7	65.3
25	Stone Container Corp.	163,000	3.7	96.3
26	Cargill Inc.	162,500	12.3	87.7
27	National Cotton Council	159,226	32.4	67.3
28	American Meat Institute	158,729	16.4	83.6
29	Florida Sugar Cane League	153,873	48.4	51.6
30	Southwest Peanut Membership Organization	152,100	52.5	47.5
31	National Broiler Council	136,000	19.9	80.1
32	American Forest & Paper Association	133,800	8.2	91.8
33	Kellogg Co.	131,466	27.4	72.6
34	National Wholesale Grocers Association	122,986	2.0	98.0
35	Tyson Foods	122,700	41.8	58.2
36	National Council of Farmer Co-ops	119,062	46.9	53.1
37	Fleming Companies Inc.	116,750	5.1	94.9
38	Willamette Industries Inc.	116,000	5.4	94.6
39	Tobacco Institute	113,850	24.5	75.5
40	Grocery Manufacturers of America	113,500	10.1	89.9
41	Deere & Co.	111,500	10.1	89.9
42	United Egg Association	110,900	26.2	73.8
43	National Pork Producers Council	109,773	37.1	62.9
44	General Mills	106,887	18.7	81.3
45	Services Group of America	104,789	0.0	100.0
46	American Association of Crop Insurers	99,000	30.8	69.2
47	The Quaker Oats Co.	96,875	14.5	85.5
48	Texas Farm Bureau	93,429	24.4	75.6
49	American Bakers Association	91,400	0.5	99.5
50	Society of American Florists	89,602	9.7	90.3

Top 50 Agriculture PAC Recipients, 1995–96

Rank	Recipient	Party	State	Office	Total
1	Pat Roberts	R	Kan.	Sen.	$373,871
2	Gordon Smith	R	Ore.	Sen.	264,299
3	Larry E. Craig	R	Idaho	Sen.	230,891
4	Jesse Helms	R	N.C.	Sen.	200,031
5	Charles W. Stenholm	D	Texas	Rep.	176,537
6	Mitch McConnell	R	Ky.	Sen.	175,098
7	Wayne Allard	R	Colo.	Sen.	171,100
8	John W. Warner	R	Va.	Sen.	166,297
9	Rudy Boschwitz	R	Minn.	Sen.	161,229
10	Bob Smith	R	Ore.	Rep.	143,902
11	Thomas W. Ewing	R	Ill.	Rep.	143,093
12	Cal Dooley	D	Calif.	Rep.	141,247
13	Saxby Chambliss	R	Ga.	Rep.	138,980
14	Vic Fazio	D	Calif.	Rep.	136,150
15	Jeff Sessions	R	Ala.	Sen.	121,224
16	Tim Johnson	D	S.D.	Sen.	113,800
17	Tom Harkin	D	Iowa	Sen.	113,607
18	Fred Thompson	R	Tenn.	Sen.	113,550
19	Thad Cochran	R	Miss.	Sen.	107,563
20	Gary A. Condit	D	Calif.	Rep.	106,545
21	Tom Latham	R	Iowa	Rep.	103,050
22	Dick Zimmer	R	N.J.	Sen.	98,600
23	James M. Inhofe	R	Okla.	Sen.	97,540
24	Larry Combest	R	Texas	Rep.	96,900
25	Richard W. Pombo	R	Calif.	Rep.	96,575
26	Frank Riggs	R	Calif.	Rep.	$94,199
27	Newt Gingrich	R	Ga.	Rep.	94,100
28	Max Baucus	D	Mont.	Sen.	93,802
29	John A. Boehner	R	Ohio	Rep.	93,181
30	Charlie Norwood	R	Ga.	Rep.	91,823
31	Joe Skeen	R	N.M.	Rep.	91,800
32	Richard J. Durbin	D	Ill.	Sen.	91,280
33	Larry Pressler	R	S.D.	Sen.	90,352
34	Jim Ross Lightfoot	R	Iowa	Sen.	90,018
35	Ben Nelson	D	Neb.	Sen.	90,000
36	Collin C. Peterson	D	Minn.	Rep.	88,111
37	Michael D. Crapo	R	Idaho	Rep.	85,826
38	Phil Gramm	R	Texas	Sen.	83,600
39	Tom DeLay	R	Texas	Rep.	83,300
40	Helen Chenoweth	R	Idaho	Rep.	80,748
41	Bill Thomas	R	Calif.	Rep.	79,725
42	Guy Millner	R	Ga.	Sen.	79,600
43	Richard A. Gephardt	D	Mo.	Rep.	79,250
44	Edward Whitfield	R	Ky.	Rep.	78,639
45	Tim Hutchinson	R	Ark.	Sen.	78,500
46	Greg Ganske	R	Iowa	Rep.	77,979
47	David Funderburk	R	N.C.	Rep.	77,452
48	Sam Brownback	R	Kan.	Sen.	76,000
49	Bob Smith	R	N.H.	Sen.	75,606
50	William F. Weld	R	Mass.	Sen.	75,500

Top 50 Business PACs, 1995–96

Rank	*PAC*	*Contributions to Congressional Candidates*	*% to Democrats*	*% to Republicans*
1	National Beer Wholesalers' Association	$1,324,992	16.6	83.4
2	National Federation of Independent Business	1,070,543	6.4	93.6
3	National Restaurant Association	880,119	11.4	88.6
4	Tenneco Inc.	658,725	30.3	69.7
5	General Electric Co.	546,550	36.0	63.9
6	Outback Steakhouse Inc.	493,950	5.3	94.7
7	Harrah's Entertainment Inc.	462,115	31.6	68.4
8	National Association of Convenience Stores	370,939	18.2	81.8
9	McDonald's Corp.	295,125	10.2	89.8
10	FMC Corp.	261,400	20.7	79.3
11	J.C. Penney Co. Inc.	243,050	13.5	86.5
12	Cooper Industries Inc.	222,000	0.9	99.1
13	International Council of Shopping Centers	208,303	13.7	86.3
14	American Hotel & Motel Association	181,200	28.5	71.5
15	Corning Inc.	175,209	16.1	83.9
16	Wal-Mart Stores Inc.	166,100	1.7	98.3
17	Wine & Spirits Wholesalers of America	160,715	35.2	64.8
18	American Textile Manufacturers Institute	160,000	30.0	70.0
19	Brinker International Inc.	158,950	6.9	93.1
20	Coca-Cola Co.	153,400	31.8	68.2
21	Outdoor Advertising Association of America	144,022	35.8	64.2
22	Burlington Industries	143,915	31.7	68.3
23	Business Industry PAC	143,437	6.1	93.9
24	Zeneca Inc.	140,547	21.4	78.6
25	Pizza Hut Franchisees Association	138,250	2.5	97.5
26	American Furniture Manufacturers Association	137,700	8.4	91.6
27	Procter & Gamble Co.	136,125	20.7	79.3
28	E.I. du Pont de Nemours and Co.	133,700	14.6	85.4
29	Anheuser-Busch	126,450	40.3	59.7
30	Equipment Leasing Association of America	119,950	20.3	79.7
31	Limited Inc.	119,500	17.2	82.8
32	Professionals in Advertising PAC	111,750	31.1	68.9
33	May Department Stores Co.	110,250	11.8	88.2
34	Rite Aid Corp.	105,625	47.9	52.1
35	Darden Restaurants Inc.	104,800	20.0	80.0
36	National Soft Drink Association	102,526	26.4	73.6
37	Marriott International Inc.	101,200	4.9	95.1
38	National Retail Federation	100,374	14.2	85.8
39	Monsanto Co.	98,275	37.3	62.7
40	Dayton Hudson Corp.	94,200	29.1	70.9
41	National Association of Wholesale-Distributors	92,722	4.6	95.4
42	Eastman Kodak Co.	92,721	33.6	66.4
43	Greater Washington Board of Trade	92,500	45.4	54.6
44	Joseph E. Seagram & Sons Inc.	92,500	30.0	70.0
45	Wine Institute	89,349	66.2	33.8
46	Bureau of Wholesale Sales Representatives	86,300	14.4	85.6
47	BFGoodrich Co.	84,700	15.9	84.1
48	Direct Marketing Association	84,305	32.5	67.5
49	Association for Manufacturing Technology	83,050	16.3	83.7
50	Brown-Forman Corp.	83,000	15.1	84.9

Top 50 Business PAC Recipients, 1995–96

Rank	Recipient	Party	State	Office	Total
1	Gordon Smith	R	Ore.	Sen.	$235,436
2	Larry Pressler	R	S.D.	Sen.	218,807
3	Dick Zimmer	R	N.J.	Sen.	203,634
4	John W. Warner	R	Va.	Sen.	195,096
5	Rudy Boschwitz	R	Minn.	Sen.	192,130
6	Mitch McConnell	R	Ky.	Sen.	190,297
7	Wayne Allard	R	Colo.	Sen.	165,161
8	John Ensign	R	Nev.	Rep.	163,917
9	William F. Weld	R	Mass.	Sen.	161,848
10	Pat Roberts	R	Kan.	Sen.	151,539
11	Fred Thompson	R	Tenn.	Sen.	141,697
12	Newt Gingrich	R	Ga.	Rep.	138,426
13	Phil Gramm	R	Texas	Sen.	133,400
14	Tom DeLay	R	Texas	Rep.	131,790
15	Max Baucus	D	Mont.	Sen.	122,593
16	Phil English	R	Pa.	Rep.	118,319
17	Bob Smith	R	N.H.	Sen.	116,663
18	Jeff Sessions	R	Ala.	Sen.	116,272
19	Jesse Helms	R	N.C.	Sen.	115,848
20	Sam Brownback	R	Kan.	Sen.	103,622
21	James M. Inhofe	R	Okla.	Sen.	103,364
22	Strom Thurmond	R	S.C.	Sen.	97,200
23	Larry E. Craig	R	Idaho	Sen.	94,172
24	Pete V. Domenici	R	N.M.	Sen.	92,429
25	Jon Christensen	R	Neb.	Rep.	89,792
26	Susan M. Collins	R	Maine	Sen.	$89,547
27	Ted Stevens	R	Alaska	Sen.	88,000
28	Jim Ross Lightfoot	R	Iowa	Sen.	87,493
29	Tim Hutchinson	R	Ark.	Sen.	85,797
30	J. D. Hayworth	R	Ariz.	Rep.	84,398
31	David M. McIntosh	R	Ind.	Rep.	84,264
32	Albert Salvi	R	Ill.	Sen.	84,047
33	Guy Millner	R	Ga.	Sen.	83,750
34	Frank Riggs	R	Calif.	Rep.	80,926
35	John A. Boehner	R	Ohio	Rep.	79,634
36	John D. Rockefeller IV	D	W.Va.	Sen.	78,500
37	Robert W. Kustra	R	Ill.	Sen.	78,331
38	Richard A. Gephardt	D	Mo.	Rep.	78,007
39	Alfonse M. D'Amato	R	N.Y.	Sen.	76,150
40	Philip M. Crane	R	Ill.	Rep.	76,030
41	Edward Whitfield	R	Ky.	Rep.	74,748
42	Jim Gibbons	R	Nev.	Rep.	74,163
43	Greg Laughlin	R	Texas	Rep.	73,468
44	Rick White	R	Wash.	Rep.	72,342
45	Jim Bunning	R	Ky.	Rep.	72,234
46	Jo Ann Emerson	R	Mo.	Rep.	72,065
47	Steven C. LaTourette	R	Ohio	Rep.	72,047
48	Charlie Norwood	R	Ga.	Rep.	71,025
49	Frank A. Cremeans	R	Ohio	Rep.	71,023
50	Bob Ney	R	Ohio	Rep.	70,271

Top 50 Communications PACs, 1995–96

Rank	*PAC*	*Contributions to Congressional Candidates*	*% to Democrats*	*% to Republicans*
1	AT&T Corp.	$1,239,046	36.8	63.2
2	Ameritech Corp.	632,285	29.5	70.5
3	National Cable Television Association	547,346	31.9	68.1
4	BellSouth Corp.	545,867	38.8	60.9
5	SBC Communications Inc.	504,333	28.8	71.2
6	GTE Corp.	435,691	23.8	76.2
7	National Association of Broadcasters	434,857	27.1	72.0
8	Time Warner Inc.	279,500	48.8	51.2
9	Bell Atlantic Corp.	275,998	34.4	65.6
10	US West Inc.	264,341	26.2	73.8
11	EDS Corp.	237,749	46.2	53.8
12	Sprint Corp.	229,674	46.3	53.7
13	Printing Industries of America	221,275	0.5	99.3
14	MCI Communications Corp.	212,275	57.5	42.5
15	Viacom Inc.	181,757	45.9	54.1
16	Tele-Communications Inc.	163,650	41.2	58.8
17	ALLTEL Corp.	157,506	24.8	75.2
18	National Telephone Cooperative Association	141,848	39.9	60.1
19	American Society of Composers, Authors and Publishers	141,050	57.5	42.5
20	West Publishing Co.	140,928	55.7	44.3
21	Walt Disney Co.	139,949	54.3	45.7
22	United States Telephone Association	134,464	25.5	74.5
23	WorldCom Inc.	132,045	47.6	52.4
24	Motorola Inc.	114,508	32.6	67.4
25	Texas Instruments Inc.	100,500	29.4	70.6
26	Comcast Corp.	95,550	33.1	66.9
27	Sony Corp.	93,850	56.0	44.0
28	AMP Inc.	92,600	2.7	97.3
29	Cellular Telecom Industry Association	86,387	26.9	73.1
30	Hallmark Cards Inc.	80,250	21.2	78.8
31	Philips Electronics North America Corp.	76,646	8.4	91.6
32	Recording Industry Association of America	73,839	64.8	35.2
33	Computer Sciences Corp.	70,600	14.2	85.8
34	Hewlett-Packard Co.	66,000	18.2	81.8
35	Motion Picture Association of America	65,612	48.7	51.3
36	Phillips Publishing International Inc.	62,250	0.0	100.0
37	News Corp Ltd.	60,159	31.6	68.4
38	AirTouch Communications Inc.	60,131	27.1	72.9
39	Communications Satellite Corp.	58,400	25.7	74.3
40	Computing Devices International	54,669	31.5	68.5
41	General Instrument Corp.	54,250	12.9	87.1
42	Intergraph Corp.	45,750	26.2	73.8
43	Microsoft Corp.	43,500	40.2	59.8
44	Intel Corp.	41,950	19.3	80.7
45	R.R. Donnelley & Sons Co.	40,000	2.5	97.5
46	DSC Communications Corp.	38,545	22.7	77.3
47	Frontier Corp	36,000	28.1	71.9
48	American Public Communications Council	33,000	40.2	59.8
49	Storage Technology Corp.	32,750	16.0	84.0
50	Northern Telecom Inc.	30,591	40.3	59.7

Top 50 Communication PAC Recipients, 1995–96

Rank	Recipient	Party	State	Office	Total
1	Larry Pressler	R	S.D.	Sen.	$222,544
2	John D. Dingell	D	Mich.	Rep.	131,343
3	Rick White	R	Wash.	Rep.	126,499
4	Vic Fazio	D	Calif.	Rep.	124,767
5	Ted Stevens	R	Alaska	Sen.	117,400
6	Daniel Frisa	R	N.Y.	Rep.	113,149
7	John W. Warner	R	Va.	Sen.	108,091
8	Fred Thompson	R	Tenn.	Sen.	107,899
9	Charles "Chip" Pickering Jr.	R	Miss.	Rep.	93,750
10	Newt Gingrich	R	Ga.	Rep.	92,470
11	Thomas J. Bliley Jr.	R	Va.	Rep.	91,900
12	Rick Boucher	D	Va.	Rep.	84,783
13	Tom Coburn	R	Okla.	Rep.	83,066
14	Bill Paxon	R	N.Y.	Rep.	82,886
15	Dennis Hastert	R	Ill.	Rep.	81,401
16	Jack Reed	D	R.I.	Sen.	79,433
17	Richard A. Gephardt	D	Mo.	Rep.	77,828
18	Pete V. Domenici	R	N.M.	Sen.	77,599
19	Tom DeLay	R	Texas	Rep.	77,000
20	Gordon Smith	R	Ore.	Sen.	76,650
21	Max Baucus	D	Mont.	Sen.	74,556
22	Jack M. Fields Jr.	R	Texas	Rep.	73,842
23	W. J. "Billy" Tauzin	R	La.	Rep.	73,671
24	Michael G. Oxley	R	Ohio	Rep.	72,549
25	David E. Bonior	D	Mich.	Rep.	72,509
26	Bart Gordon	D	Tenn.	Rep.	$71,926
27	Henry J. Hyde	R	Ill.	Rep.	69,391
28	Joe L. Barton	R	Texas	Rep.	66,750
29	Phil Gramm	R	Texas	Sen.	65,499
30	Charlie Norwood	R	Ga.	Rep.	65,192
31	Martin Frost	D	Texas	Rep.	64,750
32	Mitch McConnell	R	Ky.	Sen.	64,174
33	John D. Rockefeller IV	D	W.Va.	Sen.	63,842
34	Scott L. Klug	R	Wis.	Rep.	63,263
35	Ernest F. Hollings	D	S.C.	Sen.	63,133
36	Ron Wyden	D	Ore.	Sen.	62,796
37	Greg Ganske	R	Iowa	Rep.	61,730
38	Strom Thurmond	R	S.C.	Sen.	60,700
39	Tom Harkin	D	Iowa	Sen.	60,000
40	Tom Campbell	R	Calif.	Rep.	58,500
41	Robert G. Torricelli	D	N.J.	Sen.	58,000
42	Larry E. Craig	R	Idaho	Sen.	57,294
43	Rudy Boschwitz	R	Minn.	Sen.	57,150
44	Dan Schaefer	R	Colo.	Rep.	56,925
45	Dick Armey	R	Texas	Rep.	56,728
46	John Linder	R	Ga.	Rep.	55,976
47	Jesse Helms	R	N.C.	Sen.	55,750
48	Dick Zimmer	R	N.J.	Sen.	54,450
49	Pat Roberts	R	Kan.	Sen.	53,340
50	Alfonse M. D'Amato	R	N.Y.	Sen.	53,159

Top 50 Construction PACs, 1995–96

Rank	PAC	Contributions to Congressional Candidates	% to Democrats	% to Republicans
1	National Association of Home Builders	$1,442,849	18.0	82.0
2	Associated General Contractors	791,050	6.1	93.9
3	Associated Builders and Contractors	524,600	0.2	99.8
4	Fluor Corp.	295,175	17.1	82.9
5	National Electrical Contractors Association	220,200	8.4	91.6
6	Caterpillar Inc.	197,000	3.3	96.7
7	National Utility Contractors Association	193,580	12.3	87.7
8	American Portland Cement Alliance	162,585	22.6	77.4
9	Bechtel Corp.	161,850	40.9	59.1
10	National Multi Housing Council	149,400	19.3	80.7
11	CH2M Hill	139,185	30.8	69.2
12	Sheet Metal and Air Conditioning Contractors National Association	136,800	15.5	84.5
13	Manufactured Housing Institute	131,000	31.8	68.2
14	National Roofing Contractors Association	129,000	1.2	98.8
15	American Consulting Engineers Council	94,420	18.5	81.5
16	Sverdrup Corp.	93,750	23.4	76.6
17	ICF Kaiser International Inc.	90,875	24.5	75.5
18	Jacobs Engineering Group	84,571	54.1	45.9
19	Owens Corning	82,975	33.1	66.9
20	National Stone Association	80,000	10.6	89.4
21	National Lumber & Building Material Dealers Association	77,002	13.0	87.0
22	American Supply Association	74,950	9.7	90.3
23	National Society of Professional Engineers	74,800	14.0	86.0
24	Parsons Brinckerhoff Inc.	73,847	47.6	52.4
25	Associated Equipment Distributors	73,200	13.0	87.0
26	Morrison-Knudsen	70,441	45.3	54.7
27	American Institute of Architects	63,625	64.0	36.0
28	Vulcan Materials Co.	59,500	22.2	77.8
29	Celotex Corp.	53,000	64.2	35.8
30	American Road & Transportation Builders Association	52,100	25.6	74.4
31	Stone & Webster Inc.	45,650	24.8	75.2
32	Walter Industries Inc.	43,650	41.9	58.1
33	National Concrete Masonry Association	39,100	11.4	88.6
34	Fleetwood Enterprises Inc.	35,450	12.7	87.3
35	Holnam Inc.	33,850	26.3	73.7
36	National Ready Mixed Concrete Association	33,500	3.0	97.0
37	Heavy Constructors Association	33,000	69.7	30.3
38	Blue Circle America Inc.	32,000	7.8	92.2
39	Parsons Corp.	31,800	37.4	62.6
40	Foster Wheeler Corp.	31,000	9.7	90.3
41	Johns Manville Corp.	31,000	17.7	82.3
42	Rural Builders of America PAC	30,500	31.1	68.9
43	HB Zachry Co.	29,250	30.8	69.2
44	Rogers Group Inc.	27,625	29.0	71.0
45	Ash Grove Cement Co.	27,250	11.0	89.0
46	Florida Rock Industries Inc.	26,000	60.6	39.4
47	Irby Construction Co.	24,500	0.0	100.0
48	Management Association for Private Photogrammetric Surveyors	22,243	2.2	97.8
49	Medusa Corp.	21,500	32.6	67.4
50	J.A. Jones Inc.	20,150	12.4	87.6

Top 50 Construction PAC Recipients, 1995–96

Rank	Recipient	Party	State	Office	Total
1	John W. Warner	R	Va.	Sen.	$90,093
2	Bud Shuster	R	Pa.	Rep.	85,125
3	Gordon Smith	R	Ore.	Sen.	72,750
4	Mitch McConnell	R	Ky.	Sen.	67,900
5	Dick Zimmer	R	N.J.	Sen.	67,000
6	Rudy Boschwitz	R	Minn.	Sen.	64,000
7	Wayne Allard	R	Colo.	Sen.	60,950
8	Jeff Sessions	R	Ala.	Sen.	58,000
9	Phil Gramm	R	Texas	Sen.	55,000
10	Ted Stevens	R	Alaska	Sen.	51,348
11	Bob Smith	R	N.H.	Sen.	50,500
12	Joe L. Barton	R	Texas	Rep.	50,450
13	Larry E. Craig	R	Idaho	Sen.	50,000
14	James M. Inhofe	R	Okla.	Sen.	49,594
15	William F. Weld	R	Mass.	Sen.	48,750
16	Fred Thompson	R	Tenn.	Sen.	45,606
17	Jimmy Hayes	R	La.	Sen.	45,500
18	Larry Pressler	R	S.D.	Sen.	45,500
19	Frank A. Cremeans	R	Ohio	Rep.	45,450
20	Newt Gingrich	R	Ga.	Rep.	45,250
21	Pete V. Domenici	R	N.M.	Sen.	44,750
22	Jim Ross Lightfoot	R	Iowa	Sen.	44,150
23	Strom Thurmond	R	S.C.	Sen.	42,800
24	Kevin Brady	R	Texas	Rep.	42,440
25	Sam Brownback	R	Kan.	Sen.	41,350
26	Pat Roberts	R	Kan.	Sen.	$40,750
27	Tom DeLay	R	Texas	Rep.	40,500
28	Rick A. Lazio	R	N.Y.	Rep.	39,000
29	Tom Petri	R	Wis.	Rep.	38,428
30	Randy Tate	R	Wash.	Rep.	36,750
31	Jesse Helms	R	N.C.	Sen.	35,500
32	Don Young	R	Alaska	Rep.	35,086
33	Robert L. Livingston	R	La.	Rep.	34,500
34	Bill Baker	R	Calif.	Rep.	34,175
35	Vic Fazio	D	Calif.	Rep.	34,050
36	Charlie Norwood	R	Ga.	Rep.	33,400
37	Thomas M. Davis III	R	Va.	Rep.	33,000
38	David M. McIntosh	R	Ind.	Rep.	32,250
39	Max Baucus	D	Mont.	Sen.	31,750
40	Rick White	R	Wash.	Rep.	31,250
41	Tim Hutchinson	R	Ark.	Sen.	31,000
42	Ron Packard	R	Calif.	Rep.	29,750
43	Ken Calvert	R	Calif.	Rep.	29,700
44	John A. Boehner	R	Ohio	Rep.	29,000
45	Guy Millner	R	Ga.	Sen.	28,750
46	Brian P. Bilbray	R	Calif.	Rep.	28,500
47	Chuck Hagel	R	Neb.	Sen.	28,500
48	Richard "Doc" Hastings	R	Wash.	Rep.	28,275
49	Greg Ganske	R	Iowa	Rep.	27,800
50	Jon Christensen	R	Neb.	Rep.	27,750

Top 40 Defense PACs, 1995–96

Rank	PAC	Contributions to Congressional Candidates	% to Democrats	% to Republicans
1	Lockheed Martin	$1,013,850	30.0	70.0
2	Northrop Grumman Corp.	681,675	27.8	72.2
3	Rockwell International Corp.	321,700	26.1	73.9
4	General Dynamics Corp.	306,062	35.7	64.3
5	Textron Inc.	295,800	36.0	64.0
6	Raytheon Co.	275,108	29.8	70.2
7	United Technologies Corp.	266,874	30.1	69.9
8	TRW Inc.	241,061	19.8	80.2
9	AlliedSignal Inc.	199,700	24.3	75.7
10	Tracor Inc.	167,865	28.1	71.9
11	Harris Corp.	156,133	0.3	99.7
12	Science Applications International Corp.	141,750	32.8	67.2
13	Litton Industries Inc.	126,299	23.4	76.6
14	Alliant Techsystems Inc.	93,450	31.4	68.6
15	GenCorp Inc.	73,650	32.9	67.1
16	DRS Technologies	64,250	45.1	54.9
17	ManTech International Corp.	58,675	31.9	68.1
18	Thiokol Corp.	53,800	32.7	67.3
19	DynCorp	50,950	18.1	81.9
20	ITT Industries	40,250	26.1	73.9
21	AAI Corp.	35,371	25.7	74.3
22	Marinette Marine Corp.	31,200	40.9	59.1
23	Sequa Corp.	30,465	24.6	75.4
24	Kaman Corp.	27,000	27.8	72.2
25	Cubic Corp.	26,000	1.9	98.1
26	Veda Inc.	26,000	3.8	96.2
27	AEL Industries Inc.	23,500	43.6	56.4
28	ESCO Electronics Corp.	23,450	12.8	87.2
29	Avondale Industries	23,425	19.2	80.8
30	GEC-Marconi Electronic Systems Corp.	22,550	15.5	84.5
31	Talley Industries Inc.	21,050	25.4	74.6
32	SPD Technologies Inc.	18,750	38.7	61.3
33	Norfolk Shipbuilding & Drydock Corp.	11,725	65.0	35.0
34	American Systems Corp.	10,300	0.0	100.0
35	FEL Corp.	10,193	24.5	75.5
36	Nichols Research Corp.	9,125	16.4	83.6
37	Mason & Hanger Corp.	8,500	20.6	79.4
38	Bird-Johnson Co.	8,300	39.8	60.2
39	Rotary Power International Inc.	7,000	64.3	35.7
40	Whittaker Corp.	5,550	0.0	100.0

Top 50 Defense PAC Recipients, 1995–96

Rank	Recipient	Party	State	Office	Total
1	John W. Warner	R	Va.	Sen.	$166,475
2	Ted Stevens	R	Alaska	Sen.	124,000
3	Robert L. Livingston	R	La.	Rep.	123,250
4	John P. Murtha	D	Pa.	Rep.	116,000
5	Duncan Hunter	R	Calif.	Rep.	92,546
6	James M. Inhofe	R	Okla.	Sen.	87,000
7	C. W. "Bill" Young	R	Fla.	Rep.	83,475
8	Strom Thurmond	R	S.C.	Sen.	79,500
9	Jerry Lewis	R	Calif.	Rep.	78,500
10	Randy "Duke" Cunningham	R	Calif.	Rep.	74,800
11	Jane Harman	D	Calif.	Rep.	70,750
12	Floyd D. Spence	R	S.C.	Rep.	67,000
13	Norm Dicks	D	Wash.	Rep.	67,000
14	Bob Smith	R	N.H.	Sen.	66,125
15	Chet Edwards	D	Texas	Rep.	64,749
16	Pete V. Domenici	R	N.M.	Sen.	63,975
17	Thomas M. Davis III	R	Va.	Rep.	62,350
18	Joseph M. McDade	R	Pa.	Rep.	61,849
19	Curt Weldon	R	Pa.	Rep.	61,000
20	Ike Skelton	D	Mo.	Rep.	56,000
21	Mitch McConnell	R	Ky.	Sen.	55,750
22	Martin Frost	D	Texas	Rep.	51,300
23	W. G. "Bill" Hefner	D	N.C.	Rep.	51,100
24	Vic Fazio	D	Calif.	Rep.	50,250
25	Larry Pressler	R	S.D.	Sen.	49,081
26	Newt Gingrich	R	Ga.	Rep.	$48,500
27	Thad Cochran	R	Miss.	Sen.	46,175
28	Fred Thompson	R	Tenn.	Sen.	45,675
29	Carl Levin	D	Mich.	Sen.	44,750
30	Henry Bonilla	R	Texas	Rep.	44,270
31	Jack Reed	D	R.I.	Sen.	43,315
32	Phil Gramm	R	Texas	Sen.	43,112
33	H. James Saxton	R	N.J.	Rep.	42,800
34	Howard P. "Buck" McKeon	R	Calif.	Rep.	42,350
35	William S. Cohen	R	Maine	Sen.	42,100
36	Jeff Sessions	R	Ala.	Sen.	40,533
37	Herbert H. Bateman	R	Va.	Rep.	39,750
38	Tom DeLay	R	Texas	Rep.	39,750
39	Dave Weldon	R	Fla.	Rep.	39,050
40	David L. Hobson	R	Ohio	Rep.	37,600
41	Saxby Chambliss	R	Ga.	Rep.	36,950
42	James B. Longley Jr.	R	Maine	Rep.	36,650
43	Richard C. Shelby	R	Ala.	Sen.	36,483
44	Steny H. Hoyer	D	Md.	Rep.	36,200
45	Charles Wilson	D	Texas	Rep.	36,000
46	John M. Spratt Jr.	D	S.C.	Rep.	35,500
47	Joe Skeen	R	N.M.	Rep.	34,500
48	Patrick J. Kennedy	D	R.I.	Rep.	34,500
49	Lee H. Hamilton	D	Ind.	Rep.	34,000
50	Ron Packard	R	Calif.	Rep.	33,750

Top 50 Energy PACs, 1995–96

Rank	*PAC*	*Contributions to Congressional Candidates*	*% to Democrats*	*% to Republicans*
1	Action Committee for Rural Electrification	$651,866	54.4	45.6
2	Exxon Corp.	556,950	3.0	97.0
3	Chevron Corp.	372,952	9.1	90.9
4	Waste Management Inc.	315,200	30.5	69.5
5	Koch Industries	294,500	4.4	95.6
6	Petroleum Marketers Association of America	275,888	12.9	87.1
7	General Atomics	244,250	25.8	74.0
8	Southern California Edison	233,583	44.1	55.9
9	Cyprus Amax Minerals Co.	222,595	12.3	87.7
10	CBS Corp.	218,855	32.3	67.7
11	National Mining Association	207,017	6.5	93.5
12	Amoco Corp.	202,550	17.0	83.0
13	Carolina Power & Light Co.	200,750	24.3	75.7
14	Coastal Corp.	190,700	33.8	66.2
15	Texaco Inc.	188,135	8.8	91.2
16	Atlantic Richfield Co.	176,650	13.0	87.0
17	Phillips Petroleum Co.	168,600	6.3	93.7
18	Ashland Inc.	165,475	16.7	83.3
19	Occidental Petroleum Corp.	164,500	33.7	66.3
20	Enron Corp.	154,171	18.0	82.0
21	Halliburton Co.	150,500	5.3	94.7
22	Detroit Edison	147,815	48.2	51.8
23	Pacific Gas & Electric Co.	143,402	32.5	67.5
24	Florida Power & Light Co.	143,250	17.1	82.9
25	Mobil Corp.	134,250	2.6	97.4
26	The Williams Companies	124,940	17.4	82.6
27	Houston Industries Inc.	119,490	37.2	62.8
28	CMS Energy Corp.	114,963	40.3	59.7
29	Drummond Co.	111,500	53.4	46.6
30	Shell Oil Co.	109,600	10.0	90.0
31	Browning-Ferris Industries	108,969	22.0	78.0
32	Columbia Energy Group	100,800	25.3	74.7
33	Public Service Electric & Gas Co.	99,432	34.3	65.7
34	OHM Corp.	98,645	23.9	76.1
35	Southern Co.	95,800	10.2	89.8
36	Interstate Natural Gas Association of America	94,317	25.1	74.9
37	GPU Inc.	94,043	33.0	67.0
38	Burlington Resources	91,400	20.2	79.8
39	MCN Energy Group	89,035	59.1	40.9
40	American Electric Power	87,000	24.1	75.9
41	Independent Petroleum Association of America	86,020	17.7	82.3
42	USX Corp.	83,669	40.1	59.9
43	Dominion Resources Inc.	83,600	20.8	79.2
44	MAPCO Inc.	82,450	3.0	97.0
45	Commonwealth Edison Co.	81,480	27.2	72.8
46	BP America	81,100	15.7	84.3
47	Edison Electric Institute	81,000	17.9	82.1
48	Phelps Dodge Corp.	79,740	7.8	92.2
49	Texas Utilities Co.	75,000	26.7	73.3
50	Unocal Corp.	75,000	11.3	88.7

Top 50 Energy PAC Recipients, 1995–96

Rank	Recipient	Party	State	Office	Total
1	Pete V. Domenici	R	N.M.	Sen.	$204,052
2	Larry E. Craig	R	Idaho	Sen.	180,862
3	John W. Warner	R	Va.	Sen.	164,100
4	Ted Stevens	R	Alaska	Sen.	158,805
5	Dan Schaefer	R	Colo.	Rep.	155,774
6	James M. Inhofe	R	Okla.	Sen.	144,950
7	Mitch McConnell	R	Ky.	Sen.	144,455
8	Tom DeLay	R	Texas	Rep.	131,885
9	Joe L. Barton	R	Texas	Rep.	127,065
10	John D. Dingell	D	Mich.	Rep.	124,850
11	Wayne Allard	R	Colo.	Sen.	124,513
12	Thomas J. Bliley Jr.	R	Va.	Rep.	111,305
13	Michael B. Enzi	R	Wyo.	Sen.	111,300
14	Phil Gramm	R	Texas	Sen.	110,850
15	Gordon Smith	R	Ore.	Sen.	110,000
16	Don Young	R	Alaska	Rep.	107,950
17	Larry Pressler	R	S.D.	Sen.	105,921
18	Bob Smith	R	N.H.	Sen.	105,050
19	Greg Laughlin	R	Texas	Rep.	96,126
20	W. J. "Billy" Tauzin	R	La.	Rep.	95,748
21	Kevin Brady	R	Texas	Rep.	83,064
22	Dick Zimmer	R	N.J.	Sen.	81,993
23	Rudy Boschwitz	R	Minn.	Sen.	81,950
24	Barbara Cubin	R	Wyo.	Rep.	80,126
25	Alfonse M. D'Amato	R	N.Y.	Sen.	78,500
26	Jeff Sessions	R	Ala.	Sen.	$77,750
27	William F. Weld	R	Mass.	Sen.	77,300
28	Tom Coburn	R	Okla.	Rep.	75,554
29	Pat Roberts	R	Kan.	Sen.	75,050
30	Jesse Helms	R	N.C.	Sen.	74,750
31	Robert L. Livingston	R	La.	Rep.	73,454
32	Michael G. Oxley	R	Ohio	Rep.	72,150
33	Jimmy Hayes	R	La.	Sen.	70,607
34	Michael D. Crapo	R	Idaho	Rep.	70,498
35	Vic Fazio	D	Calif.	Rep.	67,750
36	J. D. Hayworth	R	Ariz.	Rep.	67,581
37	Phil English	R	Pa.	Rep.	67,255
38	Dick Armey	R	Texas	Rep.	66,950
39	David M. McIntosh	R	Ind.	Rep.	63,288
40	Frank H. Murkowski	R	Alaska	Sen.	62,036
41	Ralph M. Hall	D	Texas	Rep.	61,500
42	Strom Thurmond	R	S.C.	Sen.	61,000
43	Edward Whitfield	R	Ky.	Rep.	59,881
44	John D. Rockefeller IV	D	W.Va.	Sen.	59,800
45	Brian P. Bilbray	R	Calif.	Rep.	59,250
46	John R. Kasich	R	Ohio	Rep.	58,800
47	Frank Pallone Jr.	D	N.J.	Rep.	57,214
48	Louis "Woody" Jenkins	R	La.	Sen.	57,000
49	Frank A. Cremeans	R	Ohio	Rep.	56,456
50	Charlie Norwood	R	Ga.	Rep.	55,617

Top 50 Financial, Real Estate and Insurance PACs, 1995–96

Rank	PAC	Contributions to Congressional Candidates	% to Democrats	% to Republicans
1	National Association of Realtors	$2,099,683	31.2	68.7
2	American Institute of CPAs	1,690,925	32.0	67.7
3	National Association of Life Underwriters	1,426,750	31.0	69.0
4	American Bankers Association	1,299,850	27.9	72.1
5	Ernst & Young LLP	883,115	50.4	49.6
6	Credit Union National Association	642,688	42.2	57.7
7	American Council of Life Insurance	600,531	15.5	84.5
8	Deloitte & Touche LLP	588,402	32.2	67.8
9	Independent Insurance Agents of America	570,467	29.2	70.8
10	J.P. Morgan & Co. Inc.	522,000	42.1	57.9
11	AFLAC Inc.	510,450	36.3	63.7
12	Arthur Andersen LLP	480,301	42.4	57.6
13	Banc One Corp.	467,917	30.9	69.1
14	Investment Company Institute	444,014	39.0	61.0
15	NationsBank Corp.	442,285	48.6	51.2
16	Citicorp	418,800	37.4	62.6
17	Coopers & Lybrand LLP	397,058	43.0	57.0
18	Morgan Stanley Dean Witter & Co.	384,000	41.7	58.3
19	Chicago Mercantile Exchange	377,000	42.0	58.0
20	MBNA Corp.	367,904	13.7	86.3
21	BankAmerica Corp.	362,651	36.8	63.2
22	Independent Bankers Association of America	358,500	32.9	66.9
23	Price Waterhouse	331,855	41.7	58.3
24	Blue Cross and Blue Shield	322,221	31.0	69.0
25	KPMG Peat Marwick LLP	314,750	37.7	62.3
26	Chicago Board of Trade	308,893	39.9	60.1
27	Beneficial Management Corp.	299,819	32.2	67.8
28	United Services Automobile Association Group	299,000	11.5	88.5
29	America's Community Bankers	283,337	32.7	67.3
30	Massachusetts Mutual Life Insurance Co.	267,178	29.5	70.5
31	Merrill Lynch & Co. Inc.	254,427	25.4	74.6
32	Mortgage Bankers Association of America	251,100	46.1	53.9
33	Chase Manhattan Corp.	247,625	28.4	71.6
34	National Association of Independent Insurers	244,215	4.6	95.4
35	Metropolitan Life Insurance Co.	234,147	46.4	53.6
36	Cigna Corp.	230,300	10.0	90.0
37	National Venture Capital Association	224,000	21.4	78.6
38	Prudential Insurance Co. of America	214,592	39.0	61.0
39	Council of Insurance Agents & Brokers	211,865	22.4	77.6
40	National Association of Professional Insurance Agents	205,050	13.2	86.8
41	Household International Inc.	198,625	29.0	71.0
42	Credit Suisse First Boston	195,500	32.2	67.8
43	Northwestern Mutual Life Insurance Co.	191,785	32.8	67.2
44	First Chicago NBD Corp.	189,650	39.9	60.1
45	Chubb Corp.	186,099	24.3	75.7
46	American Financial Services Association	183,653	10.0	90.0
47	New York Life Insurance Co.	180,300	38.2	61.8
48	Travelers Group Inc.	177,400	24.9	75.1
49	American Land Title Association	172,995	26.3	73.7
50	Mutual of Omaha Companies	170,029	27.0	72.7

Top 50 Finance, Real Estate and Insurance PAC Recipients, 1995–96

Rank	Recipient	Party	State	Office	Total
1	Alfonse M. D'Amato	R	N.Y.	Sen.	$535,376
2	Phil Gramm	R	Texas	Sen.	305,166
3	Max Baucus	D	Mont.	Sen.	281,926
4	Newt Gingrich	R	Ga.	Rep.	277,797
5	Dick Zimmer	R	N.J.	Sen.	275,895
6	Pete V. Domenici	R	N.M.	Sen.	271,425
7	Ben Nelson	D	Neb.	Sen.	266,346
8	Vic Fazio	D	Calif.	Rep.	265,263
9	Larry Pressler	R	S.D.	Sen.	254,033
10	John W. Warner	R	Va.	Sen.	234,626
11	Christopher J. Dodd	D	Conn.	Sen.	233,248
12	Rick A. Lazio	R	N.Y.	Rep.	231,553
13	Bill McCollum	R	Fla.	Rep.	229,397
14	Martin Frost	D	Texas	Rep.	229,200
15	Bill Paxon	R	N.Y.	Rep.	224,138
16	Mitch McConnell	R	Ky.	Sen.	221,061
17	Tom DeLay	R	Texas	Rep.	219,144
18	Jack Reed	D	R.I.	Sen.	209,767
19	Jon Christensen	R	Neb.	Rep.	207,321
20	Jeff Sessions	R	Ala.	Sen.	206,350
21	Gordon Smith	R	Ore.	Sen.	206,189
22	Ken Bentsen	D	Texas	Rep.	203,223
23	James M. Inhofe	R	Okla.	Sen.	200,814
24	Fred Thompson	R	Tenn.	Sen.	196,784
25	Charles B. Rangel	D	N.Y.	Rep.	192,569
26	Bob Smith	R	N.H.	Sen.	$190,187
27	Pat Roberts	R	Kan.	Sen.	188,289
28	Wayne Allard	R	Colo.	Sen.	187,556
29	Jesse Helms	R	N.C.	Sen.	186,750
30	Lauch Faircloth	R	N.C.	Sen.	183,077
31	Rudy Boschwitz	R	Minn.	Sen.	178,867
32	Thomas J. Bliley Jr.	R	Va.	Rep.	178,845
33	Earl Pomeroy	D	N.D.	Rep.	177,692
34	Richard A. Gephardt	D	Mo.	Rep.	177,168
35	Marge Roukema	R	N.J.	Rep.	172,325
36	Peter T. King	R	N.Y.	Rep.	170,135
37	Frank A. Cremeans	R	Ohio	Rep.	169,664
38	Bill Thomas	R	Calif.	Rep.	166,982
39	John J. LaFalce	D	N.Y.	Rep.	166,949
40	Richard J. Durbin	D	Ill.	Sen.	164,339
41	Richard H. Baker	R	La.	Rep.	163,553
42	William F. Weld	R	Mass.	Sen.	159,953
43	Christopher Cox	R	Calif.	Rep.	159,816
44	Jerry Weller	R	Ill.	Rep.	159,504
45	Bill Frist	R	Tenn.	Sen.	157,460
46	E. Clay Shaw Jr.	R	Fla.	Rep.	156,271
47	Rick White	R	Wash.	Rep.	156,097
48	Strom Thurmond	R	S.C.	Sen.	154,999
49	Dick Chrysler	R	Mich.	Rep.	154,827
50	John D. Rockefeller IV	D	W.Va.	Sen.	154,150

Top 50 Health and Medical PACs, 1995–96

Rank	PAC	Contributions to Congressional Candidates	% to Democrats	% to Republicans
1	American Medical Association	$2,321,197	19.0	81.0
2	American Dental Association	1,283,425	34.4	65.6
3	American Hospital Association	879,863	48.6	51.3
4	American Nurses Association	788,508	88.8	10.5
5	American Optometric Association	644,323	53.8	46.2
6	American Academy of Ophthalmology	606,975	54.4	45.6
7	American Physical Therapy Association	593,737	52.3	47.7
8	American Health Care Association	560,171	44.7	55.3
9	American Society of Anesthesiologists	538,172	35.7	64.3
10	American Podiatric Medical Association	450,691	48.2	51.6
11	American Association of Nurse Anesthetists	426,760	36.9	63.1
12	Glaxo Wellcome Inc.	411,454	19.0	81.0
13	American Occupational Therapy Association	352,834	60.1	39.9
14	American College of Emergency Physicians	303,956	66.3	33.6
15	Pfizer Inc.	263,100	25.6	74.4
16	College of American Pathologists	224,500	25.2	74.8
17	Merck & Co.	213,687	29.6	70.4
18	American Speech-Language-Hearing Association	213,249	74.0	26.0
19	American Chiropractic Association	191,410	48.9	51.1
20	Association for the Advancement of Psychology	190,789	56.2	43.8
21	Federation of American Health Systems	182,526	39.8	60.2
22	Eli Lilly and Co.	182,156	29.4	70.6
23	American Pharmaceutical Association	172,550	55.2	44.8
24	Bristol-Myers Squibb Co.	164,100	29.6	70.4
25	Abbott Laboratories	156,579	21.0	79.0
26	National Community Pharmacists Association	146,000	52.1	47.9
27	Schering-Plough Corp.	134,500	24.5	75.5
28	SmithKline Beecham	134,400	29.5	70.5
29	Novartis AG	132,746	20.7	79.3
30	Cooperative of American Physicians	120,239	30.5	69.5
31	Johnson & Johnson	117,350	31.6	68.4
32	American Psychiatric Association	108,944	59.9	40.1
33	American Association of Oral & Maxillofacial Surgeons	107,700	30.2	69.8
34	American Association of Orthodontists	107,000	20.6	79.4
35	National Association for Home Care	106,500	66.0	34.0
36	Pharmacia & Upjohn Inc.	106,000	26.4	73.6
37	Manor Care Inc.	105,600	60.2	39.8
38	Bayer Corp.	104,000	16.8	83.2
39	Committee for Quality Orthopaedic Health Care	102,578	29.9	70.1
40	Columbia/HCA Healthcare Corp.	99,700	38.7	61.3
41	Genentech Inc.	87,500	43.4	56.6
42	American Osteopathic Association	86,950	37.4	62.6
43	American Association of Clinical Urologists	74,000	23.6	76.4
44	American Home Products Corp.	70,000	30.7	69.3
45	American Society of Internal Medicine	68,100	40.4	59.6
46	Baxter Healthcare Corp.	67,849	33.2	66.8
47	American Society of Cataract & Refractive Surgery	67,430	45.2	54.8
48	Tenet Healthcare Corp.	66,446	44.0	56.0
49	Invacare Corp.	66,276	50.6	49.4
50	Transitional Hospitals Corp.	66,000	49.2	50.8

Top 50 Health and Medical PAC Recipients, 1995–96

Rank	Recipient	Party	State	Office	Total
1	Bill Thomas	R	Calif.	Rep.	$198,768
2	Greg Ganske	R	Iowa	Rep.	190,110
3	Tom Coburn	R	Okla.	Rep.	143,606
4	Richard A. Gephardt	D	Mo.	Rep.	139,362
5	Dick Zimmer	R	N.J.	Sen.	137,650
6	Max Baucus	D	Mont.	Sen.	135,251
7	Charlie Norwood	R	Ga.	Rep.	133,827
8	John D. Rockefeller IV	D	W.Va.	Sen.	133,700
9	Richard J. Durbin	D	Ill.	Sen.	131,850
10	John Ensign	R	Nev.	Rep.	129,379
11	Michael Bilirakis	R	Fla.	Rep.	124,150
12	Vic Fazio	D	Calif.	Rep.	123,234
13	Newt Gingrich	R	Ga.	Rep.	120,396
14	Ron Wyden	D	Ore.	Sen.	118,552
15	Pete V. Domenici	R	N.M.	Sen.	118,502
16	Ben Nelson	D	Neb.	Sen.	116,600
17	Tom Harkin	D	Iowa	Sen.	112,734
18	Frank Pallone Jr.	D	N.J.	Rep.	111,320
19	Tom DeLay	R	Texas	Rep.	108,550
20	Sherrod Brown	D	Ohio	Rep.	107,843
21	Jesse Helms	R	N.C.	Sen.	100,510
22	Tim Johnson	D	S.D.	Sen.	99,425
23	Jack Reed	D	R.I.	Sen.	97,808
24	Max Cleland	D	Ga.	Sen.	97,282
25	Benjamin L. Cardin	D	Md.	Rep.	93,916
26	Nancy Johnson	R	Conn.	Rep.	$93,279
27	Henry A. Waxman	D	Calif.	Rep.	93,000
28	John W. Warner	R	Va.	Sen.	92,400
29	Dennis Hastert	R	Ill.	Rep.	91,626
30	Bill Frist	R	Tenn.	Sen.	91,219
31	Phil Gramm	R	Texas	Sen.	90,500
32	Thomas J. Bliley Jr.	R	Va.	Rep.	89,751
33	Fred Thompson	R	Tenn.	Sen.	88,500
34	Jim McCrery	R	La.	Rep.	88,094
35	Charles B. Rangel	D	N.Y.	Rep.	87,156
36	Jeff Sessions	R	Ala.	Sen.	87,000
37	Martin Frost	D	Texas	Rep.	86,312
38	John Edward Porter	R	Ill.	Rep.	86,212
39	Gordon Smith	R	Ore.	Sen.	86,100
39	Phil English	R	Pa.	Rep.	86,100
41	Wayne Allard	R	Colo.	Sen.	85,250
42	Joe L. Barton	R	Texas	Rep.	84,750
43	Bart Gordon	D	Tenn.	Rep.	82,422
44	Sander M. Levin	D	Mich.	Rep.	82,279
45	John D. Dingell	D	Mich.	Rep.	81,100
46	Pat Roberts	R	Kan.	Sen.	80,186
47	Mitch McConnell	R	Ky.	Sen.	79,778
48	Brian P. Bilbray	R	Calif.	Rep.	77,550
49	Pete Stark	D	Calif.	Rep.	77,008
50	Scott L. Klug	R	Wis.	Rep.	75,674

Top 50 Ideological PACs, 1995–96

Rank	PAC	Contributions to Congressional Candidates	% to Democrats	% to Republicans
1	National Rifle Association	$1,560,871	16.6	83.4
2	National Committee for an Effective Congress	1,118,475	99.6	0.0
3	Campaign America	829,971	0.5	99.5
4	Monday Morning PAC	766,500	0.0	100.0
5	Majority Leader's Fund	737,558	0.0	100.0
6	National Committee to Preserve Social Security and Medicare	709,426	78.2	21.3
7	Human Rights Campaign	688,766	88.7	9.9
8	National PAC	560,000	46.2	53.8
9	Effective Government Committee	461,095	99.5	0.5
10	New Republican Majority Fund	410,142	0.0	100.0
11	Republican Majority Fund	390,676	0.0	100.0
12	KidsPAC	372,000	99.2	0.5
13	Sierra Club	371,710	94.2	4.2
14	Adam Smith PAC	320,000	0.0	100.0
15	Women's Campaign Fund	307,185	69.7	30.3
16	National Abortion and Reproductive Rights Action League (NARAL)	302,027	96.9	2.7
17	Capitol Committee	292,000	0.0	100.0
18	Senate Victory Fund	283,711	0.0	100.0
19	EMILY's List	253,218	100.0	0.0
20	Eagle Forum	242,735	0.2	99.8
21	Voters for Choice/Friends of Family Planning	240,432	96.2	2.5
22	Fight-PAC	227,500	0.0	100.0
23	Americans for a Republican Majority	222,059	0.0	100.0
24	Handgun Control Inc.	213,984	93.5	6.5
25	Freedom Project	210,221	0.0	100.0
26	Hollywood Women's Political Committee	197,500	98.7	0.0
27	Victory USA	166,550	99.4	0.6
28	National Right to Life Committee	155,577	8.5	91.5
29	Republican National Coalition for Life	151,570	0.0	100.0
30	Desert Caucus	147,750	60.2	39.8
31	Washington PAC	144,225	60.7	39.3
32	National Right to Work Committee	142,080	0.0	100.0
33	National Community Action Foundation	140,150	83.3	16.7
34	Safari Club International	135,500	14.4	85.6
35	Greenvote	129,400	100.0	0.0
36	Free Cuba PAC	126,550	47.2	52.8
37	Renew America PAC	125,500	0.0	100.0
38	Conservative Victory Fund	123,979	0.4	99.6
39	Re-Elect Freshmen of the Republican Majority	118,000	0.0	100.0
40	Fund for Democratic Leadership	113,000	99.1	0.9
41	Women's Alliance for Israel	113,000	59.7	40.3
42	Americans for Good Government Inc.	107,000	45.7	54.3
43	Blue Dog PAC	102,000	95.1	4.9
44	National Action Committee	101,050	65.8	34.2
45	Fund for a Responsible Future	97,224	0.0	100.0
46	AmeriPAC: The Fund for a Greater America	93,000	100.0	0.0
47	Citizens Organized PAC	93,000	68.3	31.7
48	St. Louisians for Better Government	93,000	79.6	20.4
49	Empire Majority Leadership Fund	92,500	0.0	100.0
50	Alliance for American Leadership	91,900	0.0	100.0

Top 50 Ideological PAC Recipients, 1995–96

Rank	Recipient	Party	State	Office	Total
1	Carl Levin	D	Mich.	Sen.	$196,332
2	Gordon Smith	R	Ore.	Sen.	182,810
3	Tom Harkin	D	Iowa	Sen.	178,909
4	Mitch McConnell	R	Ky.	Sen.	169,238
5	Louis "Woody" Jenkins	R	La.	Sen.	166,989
6	Ron Wyden	D	Ore.	Sen.	153,098
7	Richard J. Durbin	D	Ill.	Sen.	147,982
8	Steve Stockman	R	Texas	Rep.	146,457
9	Albert Salvi	R	Ill.	Sen.	141,815
10	Randy Tate	R	Wash.	Rep.	138,084
11	Dick Zimmer	R	N.J.	Sen.	135,224
12	Larry Pressler	R	S.D.	Sen.	134,300
13	Jesse Helms	R	N.C.	Sen.	130,871
14	Rudy Boschwitz	R	Minn.	Sen.	129,277
15	John W. Warner	R	Va.	Sen.	127,016
16	Max Baucus	D	Mont.	Sen.	126,627
17	Sam Brownback	R	Kan.	Sen.	125,978
18	Paul Wellstone	D	Minn.	Sen.	120,126
19	James M. Inhofe	R	Okla.	Sen.	117,708
20	Jack Reed	D	R.I.	Sen.	113,100
21	Robert G. Torricelli	D	N.J.	Sen.	109,723
22	Bob Smith	R	N.H.	Sen.	109,524
23	Cynthia A. McKinney	D	Ga.	Rep.	109,418
24	Elizabeth Furse	D	Ore.	Rep.	107,809
25	Andrea Seastrand	R	Calif.	Rep.	106,448
26	Susan M. Collins	R	Maine	Sen.	$104,703
27	Loretta Sanchez	D	Calif.	Rep.	104,639
28	Jim Ross Lightfoot	R	Iowa	Sen.	100,707
29	Ronna Romney	R	Mich.	Sen.	97,738
30	Jeff Sessions	R	Ala.	Sen.	97,724
31	Wayne Allard	R	Colo.	Sen.	96,979
32	Dick Swett	D	N.H.	Sen.	96,197
33	Fred Thompson	R	Tenn.	Sen.	95,310
34	Mary L. Landrieu	D	La.	Sen.	93,443
35	Ted Stevens	R	Alaska	Sen.	93,100
36	Pat Roberts	R	Kan.	Sen.	92,706
37	Lynn Rivers	D	Mich.	Rep.	89,510
38	Tim Johnson	D	S.D.	Sen.	88,910
39	Larry E. Craig	R	Idaho	Sen.	87,868
40	Helen Chenoweth	R	Idaho	Rep.	87,361
41	Darlene Hooley	D	Ore.	Rep.	87,008
42	Dennis Rehberg	R	Mont.	Sen.	86,370
43	Frank Riggs	R	Calif.	Rep.	85,776
44	Maurice D. Hinchey	D	N.Y.	Rep.	85,748
45	Michael B. Enzi	R	Wyo.	Sen.	84,155
46	Guy Millner	R	Ga.	Sen.	84,111
47	William F. Weld	R	Mass.	Sen.	84,035
48	Debbie Stabenow	D	Mich.	Rep.	83,861
49	Michela Alioto	D	Calif.	Rep.	83,310
50	John D. Rockefeller IV	D	W.Va.	Sen.	82,560

Top 50 Labor PACs, 1995–96

Rank	*PAC*	*Contributions to Congressional Candidates*	*% to Democrats*	*% to Republicans*
1	Teamsters Union	$2,606,140	95.7	3.9
2	AFSCME	2,504,021	98.0	1.6
3	United Auto Workers	2,467,319	99.1	0.4
4	National Education Association (NEA)	2,326,830	99.1	0.5
5	International Brotherhood of Electrical Workers (IBEW)	2,070,587	97.6	2.1
6	United Food & Commercial Workers Union	2,030,795	98.4	1.1
7	Machinists and Aerospace Workers Union (IAM)	1,999,675	99.1	0.4
8	Laborers' Union International of North America	1,917,800	90.9	8.7
9	National Association of Letter Carriers	1,706,564	87.4	12.1
10	American Federation of Teachers (AFT)	1,614,833	98.5	1.2
11	United Steelworkers of America	1,523,650	100.0	0.0
12	Carpenters Union	1,464,606	94.9	4.5
13	Communications Workers of America	1,297,286	99.3	0.1
14	United Transportation Union	1,260,600	83.8	15.5
15	National Association of Retired Federal Employees	1,243,350	83.3	16.5
16	AFL-CIO	1,190,514	98.9	0.8
17	Sheet Metal Workers International Association	1,064,500	96.8	2.7
18	Plumbers & Pipefitters Union (UA)	958,000	95.7	4.0
19	Ironworkers Union	828,615	94.5	5.1
20	Air Line Pilots Association	822,000	76.9	23.1
21	Service Employees International Union (SEIU)	820,950	99.6	0.3
22	Seafarers International Union	735,399	75.6	24.4
23	International Association of Fire Fighters (IAFF)	703,875	89.8	10.1
24	Transport Workers Union	703,263	91.5	8.2
25	American Postal Workers Union	657,110	95.8	3.7
26	Amalgamated Transit Union	567,350	88.4	11.4
27	International Longshoremen's Association	559,550	95.9	4.1
28	National Rural Letter Carriers' Association	541,800	74.9	24.2
29	International Union of Operating Engineers	506,450	94.0	5.5
30	Transportation Communications International Union	429,140	88.4	11.2
31	Boilermakers Union	422,350	95.8	3.4
32	United Mine Workers of America	414,200	98.9	1.0
33	Marine Engineers' Beneficial Association (MEBA)	411,905	54.9	45.1
34	National Association of Postmasters of the United States	400,188	73.5	26.3
35	Brotherhood of Locomotive Engineers	365,615	93.5	6.3
36	National Air Traffic Controllers Association	356,990	76.3	23.7
37	Electronic, Machine and Furniture Workers	356,280	99.2	0.0
38	UNITE	324,629	98.5	1.4
39	Brotherhood of Maintenance of Way Employees (BMWE)	254,057	89.2	10.0
40	Bricklayers Union	252,300	98.0	2.0
41	American Federation of Government Employees	241,200	97.4	2.4
42	National Treasury Employees Union	229,429	89.8	9.9
43	Hotel Employees & Restaurant Employees International Union (HEREIU)	215,915	84.3	15.7
44	Office & Professional Employees International Union (OPEIU)	212,825	100.0	0.0
45	Association of Flight Attendants	201,980	91.0	7.8
46	International Organization of Masters, Mates & Pilots	190,770	48.5	51.5
47	Painters & Allied Trades Union	185,620	97.0	3.0
48	National League of Postmasters	171,800	61.7	38.0
49	Oil, Chemical and Atomic Workers International Union (OCAW)	164,200	97.0	0.0
50	United Paperworkers International	162,400	97.9	0.0

Top 50 Labor PAC Recipients, 1995–96

Rank	Recipient	Party	State	Office	Total
1	David E. Bonior	D	Mich.	Rep.	$414,130
2	Martin Frost	D	Texas	Rep.	398,150
3	Robert G. Torricelli	D	N.J.	Sen.	396,200
4	Nick Lampson	D	Texas	Rep.	364,550
5	Richard J. Durbin	D	Ill.	Sen.	358,900
6	Ken Bentsen	D	Texas	Rep.	355,550
7	Richard A. Gephardt	D	Mo.	Rep.	339,500
8	Winston Bryant	D	Ark.	Sen.	329,700
9	Paul Wellstone	D	Minn.	Sen.	327,600
10	Tim Johnson	D	S.D.	Sen.	326,200
11	Carl Levin	D	Mich.	Sen.	320,596
12	Jack Reed	D	R.I.	Sen.	317,150
13	Vic Fazio	D	Calif.	Rep.	315,800
14	Tom Harkin	D	Iowa	Sen.	294,920
15	Roger Bedford	D	Ala.	Sen.	292,200
16	Neil Abercrombie	D	Hawaii	Rep.	292,100
17	Max Cleland	D	Ga.	Sen.	276,500
18	Max Baucus	D	Mont.	Sen.	270,750
19	Maurice D. Hinchey	D	N.Y.	Rep.	259,900
20	Bob Filner	D	Calif.	Rep.	253,850
21	Steny H. Hoyer	D	Md.	Rep.	253,400
22	Ron Wyden	D	Ore.	Sen.	250,600
23	John D. Rockefeller IV	D	W.Va.	Sen.	240,800
24	Frank R. Mascara	D	Pa.	Rep.	233,450
25	Ted Strickland	D	Ohio	Rep.	232,030
26	Harvey B. Gantt	D	N.C.	Sen.	$231,750
27	Sander M. Levin	D	Mich.	Rep.	231,732
28	Lane Evans	D	Ill.	Rep.	229,675
29	Jay C. Hoffman	D	Ill.	Rep.	228,050
30	Connie Galiazzo DeJuliis	D	Md.	Rep.	226,540
31	Louise M. Slaughter	D	N.Y.	Rep.	221,700
32	Mike Ward	D	Ky.	Rep.	221,050
33	Lynn Rivers	D	Mich.	Rep.	220,650
34	Dale E. Kildee	D	Mich.	Rep.	218,675
35	David R. Obey	D	Wis.	Rep.	218,500
36	Adam Smith	D	Wash.	Rep.	214,800
37	Joseph E. Brennan	D	Maine	Sen.	214,550
38	Debbie Stabenow	D	Mich.	Rep.	214,155
39	John F. Tierney	D	Mass.	Rep.	214,000
40	Mary L. Landrieu	D	La.	Sen.	213,050
41	Gene Green	D	Texas	Rep.	213,025
42	Tom Bruggere	D	Ore.	Sen.	212,150
43	John W. Olver	D	Mass.	Rep.	212,000
44	Gerald D. Kleczka	D	Wis.	Rep.	208,800
45	Sam Gejdenson	D	Conn.	Rep.	207,050
46	Dennis Kucinich	D	Ohio	Rep.	206,420
47	Bart Gordon	D	Tenn.	Rep.	205,450
48	Joseph P. Kennedy II	D	Mass.	Rep.	201,000
49	William P. "Bill" Luther	D	Minn.	Rep.	199,850
50	Rick Weiland	D	S.D.	Rep.	198,250

Top 50 Lawyer and Lobbyist PACs, 1995–96

Rank	*PAC*	*Contributions to Congressional Candidates*	*% to Democrats*	*% to Republicans*
1	Association of Trial Lawyers of America	$2,336,938	89.3	10.2
2	Akin, Gump, Strauss, Hauer & Feld	366,833	40.1	59.9
3	Verner, Liipfert, Bernhard, McPherson & Hand	251,941	49.0	51.0
4	Vinson & Elkins	181,187	59.4	40.6
5	McDermott, Will & Emery	147,453	50.4	49.6
6	Holland & Knight	146,369	46.7	53.0
7	Preston, Gates & Ellis	141,763	32.4	67.6
8	Shaw, Pittman, Potts & Trowbridge	105,067	45.4	54.4
9	Williams & Jensen	103,994	36.7	63.3
10	Hogan & Hartson	97,750	37.9	62.1
11	Skadden, Arps, Slate, Meagher & Flom	93,100	50.6	49.4
12	King & Spalding	92,290	36.1	63.9
13	Fulbright & Jaworski	89,812	43.6	56.4
14	Dickstein Shapiro Morin & Oshinsky	87,650	32.8	67.2
15	O'Melveny & Myers	84,350	36.6	63.4
16	Arnold & Porter	76,100	52.9	47.1
17	Manatt, Phelps & Phillips	73,557	59.2	40.8
18	Climaco, Climaco, Lefkowitz & Garofoli	73,000	66.4	33.6
19	Paul Magliocchetti Associates	72,700	39.1	60.9
20	Winston & Strawn	72,086	40.9	59.1
21	Reid & Priest	70,976	46.6	53.4
22	Greenberg, Traurig, Hoffman, Lipoff, Rosen & Quentel	68,719	72.1	27.9
23	Swidler & Berlin	64,889	32.7	67.3
24	Powell, Goldstein, Frazer & Murphy	64,415	44.1	55.9
25	Pepper, Hamilton & Scheetz	64,175	33.0	67.0
26	Kirkpatrick & Lockhart	56,279	41.4	58.6
27	Arent Fox Kintner Plotkin & Kahn	55,650	59.3	40.7
28	Burson-Marsteller	54,077	41.3	58.7
29	Baker & Botts	53,500	38.8	61.2
30	Collier, Shannon, Rill & Scott	52,824	28.4	71.6
31	R. Duffy Wall & Associates	52,587	22.2	77.8
32	Vorys, Sater, Seymour & Pease	52,450	28.4	71.6
33	Bracewell & Patterson	52,129	25.9	74.1
34	Garvey, Schubert & Barer	50,750	44.8	55.2
35	Symms, Lehn & Associates Inc.	49,292	0.0	100.0
36	Ungaretti & Harris	46,550	100.0	0.0
37	Crowell & Moring	45,150	33.8	66.2
38	Powers, Pyles, Sutter & Verville	41,550	60.3	39.7
39	Fleishman-Hillard Inc.	39,750	22.0	78.0
40	Hill & Knowlton	39,538	44.3	55.7
41	Van Ness Feldman	38,103	36.8	63.2
42	Hopkins & Sutter	37,136	33.2	66.8
43	Dorsey & Whitney	36,558	70.0	30.0
44	Kirkland & Ellis	36,073	79.8	20.2
45	White & Case	34,250	43.8	56.2
46	LeBoeuf, Lamb, Greene & MacRae	33,248	21.5	78.5
47	Miller, Canfield, Paddock and Stone	32,426	19.2	80.8
48	Baker & Hostetler	31,211	48.6	51.4
49	Lockridge Grindal Nauen & Holstein	30,786	74.7	25.3
50	Jones, Walker, Waechter, Poitevent, Carrere & Denegre	30,000	51.7	48.3

Top 50 Lawyer and Lobbyist PAC Recipients, 1995–96

Rank	Recipient	Party	State	Office	Total
1	Richard A. Gephardt	D	Mo.	Rep.	$70,058
2	Robert G. Torricelli	D	N.J.	Sen.	69,500
3	Alfonse M. D'Amato	R	N.Y.	Sen.	69,186
4	Max Baucus	D	Mont.	Sen.	69,136
5	John W. Warner	R	Va.	Sen.	67,566
6	Larry Pressler	R	S.D.	Sen.	64,275
7	Fred Thompson	R	Tenn.	Sen.	58,028
8	Ken Bentsen	D	Texas	Rep.	58,000
9	John D. Dingell	D	Mich.	Rep.	54,250
10	Ted Stevens	R	Alaska	Sen.	52,594
11	Martin Frost	D	Texas	Rep.	50,157
12	Tim Johnson	D	S.D.	Sen.	48,261
13	Richard J. Durbin	D	Ill.	Sen.	48,197
14	Pete V. Domenici	R	N.M.	Sen.	47,248
15	Tom Harkin	D	Iowa	Sen.	46,635
16	Tom DeLay	R	Texas	Rep.	45,496
17	Vic Fazio	D	Calif.	Rep.	44,931
18	Phil Gramm	R	Texas	Sen.	39,588
19	Charles B. Rangel	D	N.Y.	Rep.	39,350
20	John D. Rockefeller IV	D	W.Va.	Sen.	38,750
21	Newt Gingrich	R	Ga.	Rep.	37,499
22	Arlen Specter	R	Pa.	Sen.	36,750
23	Carl Levin	D	Mich.	Sen.	35,474
24	Tom Strickland	D	Colo.	Sen.	34,516
25	Richard C. Shelby	R	Ala.	Sen.	34,249
26	David E. Bonior	D	Mich.	Rep.	$34,125
27	Sander M. Levin	D	Mich.	Rep.	34,125
28	Don Young	R	Alaska	Rep.	34,074
29	Jack Reed	D	R.I.	Sen.	32,997
30	Christopher J. Dodd	D	Conn.	Sen.	32,500
31	Nick Lampson	D	Texas	Rep.	32,239
32	Mary L. Landrieu	D	La.	Sen.	30,793
33	Steny H. Hoyer	D	Md.	Rep.	29,950
34	Ron Wyden	D	Ore.	Sen.	29,550
35	Strom Thurmond	R	S.C.	Sen.	29,500
36	Max Cleland	D	Ga.	Sen.	29,000
37	Bud Shuster	R	Pa.	Rep.	28,950
38	Bill Thomas	R	Calif.	Rep.	28,000
38	Bob Graham	D	Fla.	Sen.	28,000
38	John P. Murtha	D	Pa.	Rep.	28,000
38	Tom Daschle	D	S.D.	Sen.	28,000
42	Robert L. Livingston	R	La.	Rep.	27,999
43	Robert T. Matsui	D	Calif.	Rep.	26,732
44	Barbara Boxer	D	Calif.	Sen.	26,500
45	Pat Roberts	R	Kan.	Sen.	26,083
46	William S. Cohen	R	Maine	Sen.	25,499
47	Mitch McConnell	R	Ky.	Sen.	25,000
48	Norm Dicks	D	Wash.	Rep.	24,350
49	Jesse Helms	R	N.C.	Sen.	24,000
50	Joe L. Barton	R	Texas	Rep.	23,500

Top 50 Transportation PACs, 1995–96

Rank	PAC	Contributions to Congressional Candidates	% to Democrats	% to Republicans
1	National Automobile Dealers Association	$2,335,425	18.3	81.7
2	United Parcel Service of America Inc. (UPS)	1,788,147	35.1	64.9
3	Federal Express Corp.	943,000	29.4	70.5
4	Americans for Free International Trade	936,800	11.4	88.6
5	Union Pacific Corp.	792,357	12.5	87.5
6	Aircraft Owners and Pilots Association	467,000	28.9	71.1
7	American Trucking Associations	410,061	22.4	77.6
8	Boeing Co.	341,105	26.1	73.9
9	Ford Motor Co.	338,590	27.7	72.3
10	American Airlines	320,817	43.0	57.0
11	General Motors Corp.	305,475	28.4	71.6
12	Chrysler Corp.	304,615	38.2	61.8
13	CSX Corp.	242,600	30.9	69.1
14	Burlington Northern Santa Fe Corp.	223,982	25.5	74.5
15	Norfolk Southern Corp.	195,600	25.2	74.8
16	UAL Corp.	181,550	41.8	58.2
17	Northwest Airlines Corp.	144,730	50.2	49.8
18	International Council of Cruise Lines	129,500	40.2	59.8
19	Conrail Inc.	127,424	36.1	63.9
20	Ryder System Inc.	115,230	29.7	70.3
21	Truckload Carriers Association	113,600	12.1	87.9
22	Yellow Corp.	106,793	16.6	83.4
23	CNF Transportation Inc.	92,000	14.7	85.3
24	APL Limited	87,527	24.6	75.4
25	Association of American Railroads	86,500	24.3	75.7
26	Goodyear Tire & Rubber Co.	86,500	8.7	91.3
27	American Bus Association	83,600	40.5	59.5
28	Delta Air Lines Inc.	79,250	19.6	80.4
29	American Pilots' Association Inc.	71,789	37.8	62.2
30	Kansas City Southern Industries Inc.	70,450	33.0	67.0
31	Continental Airlines	62,250	35.7	64.3
32	National Marine Manufacturers Association	61,750	18.6	81.4
33	Trinity Industries Inc.	60,850	25.1	74.9
34	Holland America Line Westours Inc.	59,250	27.4	72.6
35	Duchossois Industries Inc.	56,650	15.9	84.1
36	Crowley Maritime Corp.	55,250	34.4	65.6
37	PACCAR Inc.	54,725	11.4	88.6
38	National Steel and Shipbuilding Co.	53,050	10.4	89.6
39	American Waterways Operators	52,410	23.9	76.1
40	Coltec Industries Inc.	51,600	26.4	73.6
41	Watkins Associated Industries	50,500	5.9	94.1
42	American Motorcyclist Association	47,000	9.6	90.4
43	General Aviation Manufacturers Association	46,250	19.5	80.5
44	Orbital Sciences Corp.	44,100	4.5	95.5
45	American Movers and Storage Association	43,900	30.6	69.4
46	AutoZone Inc.	40,350	0.0	100.0
47	International Taxicab and Livery Association	38,500	6.5	93.5
48	Kirby Corp.	38,500	16.9	83.1
49	Auto Dealers & Drivers for Free Trade	38,000	59.2	40.8
50	Torrington Co.	37,947	63.2	36.8

Top 50 Transportation PAC Recipients, 1995–96

Rank	Recipient	Party	State	Office	Total
1	Larry Pressler	R	S.D.	Sen.	$208,298
2	Bud Shuster	R	Pa.	Rep.	178,557
3	Ted Stevens	R	Alaska	Sen.	151,000
4	James M. Inhofe	R	Okla.	Sen.	145,692
5	Tom DeLay	R	Texas	Rep.	132,500
6	Gordon Smith	R	Ore.	Sen.	116,767
7	John W. Warner	R	Va.	Sen.	114,650
8	Don Young	R	Alaska	Rep.	111,346
9	Randy Tate	R	Wash.	Rep.	109,350
10	Newt Gingrich	R	Ga.	Rep.	106,999
11	James L. Oberstar	D	Minn.	Rep.	98,000
12	Susan Molinari	R	N.Y.	Rep.	93,685
13	Mitch McConnell	R	Ky.	Sen.	91,000
14	Phil Gramm	R	Texas	Sen.	89,596
15	Jennifer Dunn	R	Wash.	Rep.	87,200
16	Robert L. Livingston	R	La.	Rep.	86,500
17	Pat Roberts	R	Kan.	Sen.	81,942
18	Fred Thompson	R	Tenn.	Sen.	81,596
19	Richard A. Gephardt	D	Mo.	Rep.	78,499
20	Tom Petri	R	Wis.	Rep.	77,496
21	Sam Brownback	R	Kan.	Sen.	75,089
22	Max Baucus	D	Mont.	Sen.	74,500
23	Rudy Boschwitz	R	Minn.	Sen.	74,365
24	Jim Ross Lightfoot	R	Iowa	Sen.	73,900
25	John J. "Jimmy" Duncan Jr.	R	Tenn.	Rep.	73,896
26	John D. Dingell	D	Mich.	Rep.	$73,850
27	Pete V. Domenici	R	N.M.	Sen.	71,875
28	Greg Laughlin	R	Texas	Rep.	70,500
29	Wayne Allard	R	Colo.	Sen.	70,370
30	Dick Zimmer	R	N.J.	Sen.	70,096
31	Larry E. Craig	R	Idaho	Sen.	67,050
32	Bill Baker	R	Calif.	Rep.	66,350
33	Ron Packard	R	Calif.	Rep.	66,000
34	E. Clay Shaw Jr.	R	Fla.	Rep.	65,596
35	Bob Smith	R	N.H.	Sen.	65,000
36	Jeff Sessions	R	Ala.	Sen.	63,500
37	Bob Clement	D	Tenn.	Rep.	62,251
38	Rick White	R	Wash.	Rep.	61,950
39	Dick Armey	R	Texas	Rep.	61,000
40	Nick J. Rahall II	D	W.Va.	Rep.	59,500
41	Mac Collins	R	Ga.	Rep.	59,000
42	Martin Frost	D	Texas	Rep.	59,000
43	Jerry Weller	R	Ill.	Rep.	58,300
44	Richard J. Durbin	D	Ill.	Sen.	56,700
45	Andrea Seastrand	R	Calif.	Rep.	56,050
46	Philip M. Crane	R	Ill.	Rep.	55,750
47	Guy Millner	R	Ga.	Sen.	53,500
48	Joe L. Barton	R	Texas	Rep.	53,100
49	Jon Christensen	R	Neb.	Rep.	53,000
50	Randy "Duke" Cunningham	R	Calif.	Rep.	52,676

Top 50 PAC Contributors to Republican Congressional Candidates, 1993–94

Rank	PAC Name	Republicans	% to Republicans	Democrats	% to Democrats	Totals
1	National Rifle Association	$1,442,519	77.8	$ 409,019	22.1	$1,853,038
2	American Medical Association	1,361,395	57.0	1,005,552	42.1	2,386,947
3	United Parcel Service	1,276,870	48.3	1,340,043	50.6	2,646,113
4	National Auto Dealers Association	1,276,300	70.0	544,770	29.9	1,824,070
5	National Beer Wholesalers Association	954,715	76.5	287,509	23.0	1,248,224
6	American Institute of CPAs	870,021	50.1	852,499	49.1	1,737,520
7	National Association of Realtors	856,845	46.3	970,633	52.4	1,851,478
8	National Association of Home Builders	836,800	62.9	488,799	36.8	1,329,599
9	American Bankers Association	704,100	52.4	632,050	47.1	1,343,150
10	National Association of Life Underwriters	696,750	52.0	636,140	47.5	1,338,890
11	Campaign America	598,910	98.9	1,000	0.2	605,759
12	Americans for Free International Trade	595,700	77.3	175,000	22.7	770,700
13	American Dental Association	569,584	48.4	604,613	51.4	1,177,197
14	Associated General Contractors	563,497	80.8	133,200	19.1	697,697
15	AT&T	528,631	41.0	757,003	58.6	1,290,884
16	National Restaurant Association	494,722	75.1	164,122	24.9	658,844
17	Exxon Corp.	465,425	93.8	30,350	6.1	496,275
18	Union Pacific Corp.	446,558	70.1	187,745	29.5	636,803
19	RJR Nabisco	417,650	53.2	366,000	46.7	784,400
20	Cooper Industries Inc.	402,000	98.0	8,000	2.0	410,000
21	American Academy of Ophthalmology	352,890	40.2	521,265	59.4	877,155
22	American Hospital Association	351,476	33.9	674,720	65.0	1,037,896
23	National Fedn of Independent Business	338,525	91.1	31,400	8.4	371,675
24	Marine Engineers' Beneficial Association	320,150	34.6	597,470	64.5	926,120
25	American Council of Life Insurance	317,152	53.3	278,263	46.7	595,415
26	Food Marketing Institute	309,661	68.4	142,054	31.4	452,465
27	Continue the Majority	295,653	98.8	2,585	0.9	299,238
28	National Cable Television Association	282,000	56.8	214,900	43.2	496,900
29	Philip Morris	268,849	39.9	402,317	59.7	673,666
30	Glaxo Wellcome Inc.	266,291	60.3	175,028	39.7	441,319
31	GTE Corp.	264,482	56.0	207,637	44.0	472,369
32	J.P. Morgan & Co.	260,000	48.9	271,550	51.1	531,550
33	Independent Insurance Agents of America	255,247	47.4	282,745	52.5	538,992
34	Federal Express Corp.	254,500	31.2	552,100	67.6	816,600
35	Lockheed Martin	254,401	42.9	337,160	56.9	592,611
36	Lockheed Martin	254,250	47.9	274,560	51.8	530,310
37	Chevron Corp.	254,049	75.3	83,449	24.7	337,498
38	National Cattlemen's Beef Association	246,374	67.8	115,450	31.8	363,324
39	McDonald's Corp.	246,250	75.5	80,500	24.7	326,250
40	National Association of Independent Insurers	242,070	89.1	29,500	10.9	271,570
41	NationsBank Corp.	235,950	37.6	390,850	62.4	626,800
42	Americans for a Republican Majority	227,601	100.0	20	0.0	227,627
43	PepsiCo Inc.	227,092	73.1	82,508	26.6	310,719
44	Aircraft Owners & Pilots Association	227,000	47.5	229,100	47.9	478,100
45	General Electric Co.	224,175	40.1	330,870	59.2	559,045
46	AFLAC Inc.	220,200	44.1	277,350	55.5	499,550
47	International Council of Shopping Centers	215,841	66.1	110,499	33.9	326,340
48	Credit Union National Association	213,423	40.6	308,173	58.6	526,096
49	American Society of Anesthesiologists	209,000	43.2	275,000	56.8	484,000
50	NationsBank Corp.	208,281	52.4	188,300	47.4	397,581

Top 50 PAC Contributors to Democratic Congressional Candidates, 1993–94

Rank	PAC Name	Democrats	% to Democrats	Republicans	% to Republicans	Total
1	AFSCME	$2,426,062	96.5	$ 40,120	1.6	$2,514,682
2	International Brotherhood of Teamsters	2,367,677	95.4	59,475	2.4	2,482,152
3	National Education Association	2,196,050	97.1	25,800	1.1	2,260,850
4	United Auto Workers	2,087,735	97.2	14,455	0.7	2,147,190
5	Association of Trial Lawyers of America	2,013,535	93.2	132,500	6.1	2,161,035
6	Machinists & Aerospace Workers Union	1,639,581	96.6	11,000	0.6	1,697,081
7	International Brotherhood of Electrical Workers	1,562,325	97.2	20,700	1.3	1,607,425
8	United Food & Commercial Workers Union	1,397,139	95.9	24,500	1.7	1,456,139
9	Carpenters Union	1,344,450	94.5	49,750	3.5	1,423,200
10	United Parcel Service	1,340,043	50.6	1,276,870	48.3	2,646,113
11	National Association of Letter Carriers	1,308,515	91.6	96,275	6.7	1,428,290
12	American Federation of Teachers	1,256,190	97.3	11,000	0.9	1,290,690
13	United Transportation Union	1,163,280	94.3	43,775	3.5	1,233,555
14	Laborers Union	1,114,617	92.8	60,750	5.1	1,201,367
15	Communications Workers of America	1,032,573	97.5	4,600	0.4	1,059,073
16	American Medical Association	1,005,552	42.1	1,361,395	57.0	2,386,947
17	United Steelworkers	1,004,262	96.6	2,000	0.2	1,039,762
18	American Nurses Association	973,483	89.8	92,025	8.5	1,084,508
19	National Association of Realtors	970,633	52.4	856,845	46.3	1,851,478
20	AFL-CIO	949,759	96.8	6,880	0.7	981,439
21	National of Association Retired Federal Employees	882,050	88.5	101,450	10.2	996,500
22	Service Employees International Union	866,694	96.7	14,000	1.6	896,194
23	American Institute of CPAs	852,499	49.1	870,021	50.1	1,737,520
24	Air Line Pilots Association	832,186	83.1	139,500	13.9	1,001,186
25	National Committee for an Effective Congress	765,999	98.1	-	0.0	780,499
26	AT&T	757,003	58.6	528,631	41.0	1,290,884
27	Sheet Metal Workers Union	744,050	95.3	10,000	1.3	781,050
28	League of Conservation Voters	725,301	93.4	34,949	4.5	776,559
29	American Postal Workers Union	702,235	94.4	28,500	3.8	744,235
30	Effective Government Committee	690,576	98.0	1,000	0.1	704,596
31	American Hospital Association	674,720	65.0	351,476	33.9	1,037,896
32	International Association of Fire Fighters	642,267	93.8	33,200	4.9	684,467
33	National Association of Life Underwriters	636,140	47.5	696,750	52.0	1,338,890
34	Seafarers International Union	633,444	89.3	75,100	10.6	709,544
35	American Bankers Association	632,050	47.1	704,100	52.4	1,343,150
36	American Dental Association	604,613	51.4	569,584	48.4	1,177,197
37	Plumbers & Pipefitters Union	603,850	94.9	18,500	2.9	636,350
38	Marine Engineers' Beneficial Association	597,470	64.5	320,150	34.6	926,120
39	Dairy Farmers of America	581,981	74.8	182,250	23.4	778,231
40	Human Rights Campaign	579,924	92.7	35,500	5.7	625,424
41	Federal Express Corp.	552,100	67.6	254,500	31.2	816,600
42	National Auto Dealers Association	544,770	29.9	1,276,300	70.0	1,824,070
43	American Academy of Ophthalmology	521,265	59.4	352,890	40.2	877,155
44	United Mine Workers	505,670	97.4	8,500	1.6	519,170
45	Transport Workers Union	493,660	96.7	7,100	1.4	510,760
46	National Association of Home Builders	488,799	36.8	836,800	62.9	1,329,599
47	Ironworkers Union	479,426	91.1	33,200	6.3	526,126
48	American Optometric Association	457,380	69.4	194,750	29.5	659,130
49	National Committee to Preserve Social Security and Medicare	441,705	81.3	90,806	16.7	543,511
50	American Chiropractic Association	441,328	77.2	124,300	21.7	571,628

Top 100 PAC Recipients, 1993–94

Rank	Office	Candidate	State	Party	Total	Elected?
1	Sen.	Kay Bailey Hutchison	Texas	R	$2,559,913	Yes
2	Sen.	Jim Sasser	Tenn.	D	1,755,944	No
3	Sen.	Dianne Feinstein	Calif.	D	1,626,962	Yes
4	Sen.	Mike DeWine	Ohio	R	1,482,247	Yes
5	Sen.	Kent Conrad	N.D.	D	1,445,441	Yes
6	Sen.	Rick Santorum	Pa.	R	1,368,686	Yes
7	Sen.	Conrad Burns	Mont.	R	1,349,348	Yes
8	Sen.	Bob Kerrey	Neb.	D	1,345,576	Yes
9	Sen.	Orrin G. Hatch	Utah	R	1,317,321	Yes
10	Sen.	Charles S. Robb	Va.	D	1,304,232	Yes
11	Sen.	Frank R. Lautenberg	N.J.	D	1,297,555	Yes
12	Sen.	Daniel Patrick Moynihan	N.Y.	D	1,280,476	Yes
13	Sen.	Richard H. Bryan	Nev.	D	1,276,509	Yes
14	Sen.	Slade Gorton	Wash.	R	1,195,185	Yes
15	Rep.	Thomas S. Foley	Wash.	D	1,187,154	No
16	Sen.	Joseph I. Lieberman	Conn.	D	1,147,050	Yes
17	Sen.	John Ashcroft	Mo.	R	1,119,356	Yes
18	Sen.	Jon Kyl	Ariz.	R	1,099,976	Yes
19	Rep.	Vic Fazio	Calif.	D	1,073,420	Yes
20	Sen.	Harris L. Wofford	Pa.	D	1,054,594	No
21	Sen.	Jeff Bingaman	N.M.	D	1,052,725	Yes
22	Sen.	Alan Wheat	Mo.	D	1,030,627	No
23	Sen.	Trent Lott	Miss.	R	1,022,850	Yes
24	Rep.	Richard A. Gephardt	Mo.	D	1,015,266	Yes
25	Sen.	John H. Chafee	R.I.	R	1,011,626	Yes
26	Sen.	Connie Mack	Fla.	R	1,006,075	Yes
27	Sen.	Bob Carr	Mich.	D	966,213	No
28	Sen.	Paul S. Sarbanes	Md.	D	958,266	Yes
29	Sen.	William V. Roth Jr.	Del.	R	934,579	Yes
30	Sen.	Robert "Bob" Krueger	Texas	D	905,681	No
31	Sen.	Olympia J. Snowe	Maine	R	865,572	Yes
32	Rep.	Steny H. Hoyer	Md.	D	862,226	Yes
33	Rep.	Sam M. Gibbons	Fla.	D	830,217	Yes
34	Rep.	Dan Rostenkowski	Ill.	D	809,119	No
35	Rep.	Peter Hoagland	Neb.	D	803,446	No
36	Rep.	David E. Bonior	Mich.	D	789,210	Yes
37	Rep.	Martin Frost	Texas	D	787,235	Yes
38	Sen.	Rod Grams	Minn.	R	775,375	Yes
39	Rep.	Charles B. Rangel	N.Y.	D	770,775	Yes
40	Rep.	Newt Gingrich	Ga.	R	766,993	Yes
41	Rep.	John D. Dingell	Mich.	D	762,610	Yes
42	Rep.	Peter William Barca	Wis.	D	758,906	No
43	Sen.	Craig Thomas	Wyo.	R	754,052	Yes
44	Sen.	Richard G. Lugar	Ind.	R	752,796	Yes
45	Sen.	Spencer Abraham	Mich.	R	699,747	Yes
46	Rep.	Sander M. Levin	Mich.	D	698,655	Yes
47	Rep.	Marjorie Margolies-Mezvinsky	Pa.	D	689,608	No
48	Rep.	Jack M. Fields Jr.	Texas	R	685,897	Yes
49	Rep.	Lynn Schenk	Calif.	D	674,108	No
50	Sen.	Fred Thompson	Tenn.	R	665,508	Yes
51	Rep.	Bill Brewster	Okla.	D	655,302	Yes
52	Rep.	Dale E. Kildee	Mich.	D	652,410	Yes
53	Rep.	Richard H. Lehman	Calif.	D	647,909	No
54	Sen.	Ann Louise Jobe Wynia	Minn.	D	640,515	No
55	Sen.	Dave McCurdy	Okla.	D	635,486	No
56	Rep.	Sherrod Brown	Ohio	D	635,153	Yes
57	Sen.	James M. Jeffords	Vt.	R	632,329	Yes

(Continued on next page)

Rank	Office	Candidate	State	Party	Total	Elected?
58	Sen.	Joel Hyatt	Ohio	D	$631,107	No
59	Rep.	Sam Farr	Calif.	D	627,950	Yes
60	Rep.	Bart Gordon	Tenn.	D	624,740	Yes
61	Rep.	L. F. Payne Jr.	Va.	D	621,668	Yes
62	Sen.	Michael Allen Andrews	Texas	D	587,122	No
63	Rep.	Robert T. Matsui	Calif.	D	584,594	Yes
64	Rep.	Charles Wilson	Texas	D	584,500	Yes
65	Sen.	James M. Inhofe	Okla.	R	581,909	Yes
66	Rep.	Norman Y. Mineta	Calif.	D	571,612	No
67	Sen.	Lauch Faircloth	N.C.	R	567,460	Yes
68	Rep.	Mike Kreidler	Wash.	D	549,480	No
69	Rep.	Larry Larocco	Idaho	D	539,416	No
70	Rep.	Earl Pomeroy	N.D.	D	534,815	Yes
71	Rep.	Jane Harman	Calif.	D	529,994	Yes
72	Rep.	Bart Stupak	Mich.	D	527,323	Yes
73	Rep.	Sam Gejdenson	Conn.	D	524,103	Yes
74	Rep.	John P. Murtha	Pa.	D	516,579	Yes
75	Rep.	W. J. "Billy" Tauzin	La.	R	516,089	Yes
76	Rep.	Jack Bascom Brooks	Texas	D	496,869	No
77	Rep.	Maria Cantwell	Wash.	D	491,053	No
78	Sen.	Garabed "Chuck" Haytaian	N.J.	R	483,346	No
79	Rep.	Richard J. Durbin	Ill.	D	481,866	Yes
80	Sen.	Charles M. Oberly III	Del.	D	481,479	No
81	Rep.	Frank Pallone Jr.	N.J.	D	479,660	Yes
82	Rep.	Leslie L. Byrne	Va.	D	478,810	No
83	Rep.	Carolyn B. Maloney	N.Y.	D	468,343	Yes
84	Rep.	Joe Moakley	Mass.	D	468,267	Yes
85	Rep.	Rick Boucher	Va.	D	468,038	Yes
86	Rep.	Karen L. Thurman	Fla.	D	463,860	Yes
87	Rep.	Tom Barlow	Ky.	D	460,552	No
88	Rep.	Gene Green	Texas	D	455,420	Yes
89	Rep.	Elizabeth Furse	Ore.	D	451,950	Yes
90	Rep.	Thomas J. Bliley Jr.	Va.	R	451,598	Yes
91	Rep.	Bob Filner	Calif.	D	451,300	Yes
92	Rep.	Jolene Unsoeld	Wash.	D	449,937	No
93	Sen.	Bill Frist	Tenn.	R	448,379	Yes
94	Rep.	Ronald D. Coleman	Texas	D	448,257	Yes
95	Rep.	John Lewis	Ga.	D	443,860	Yes
96	Rep.	Harold Martin Lancaster	N.C.	D	443,229	No
97	Rep.	Pete Stark	Calif.	D	442,075	Yes
98	Rep.	Louise M. Slaughter	N.Y.	D	440,739	Yes
99	Rep.	Bennie Thompson	Miss.	D	438,959	Yes
100	Rep.	Peter Deutsch	Fla.	D	438,635	Yes

Number of PACs, 1974–97

Date	Total	Date	Total	Date	Total
12/31/74	608	12/31/83	3,525	7/1/91	4,123
11/24/75	722	7/1/84	3,803	12/31/91	4,094
5/10/76	992	12/31/84	4,009	7/1/92	4,125
12/31/76	1,146	7/1/85	4,000	12/31/92	4,195
12/31/77	1,360	12/31/85	3,992	7/1/93	4,025
12/31/78	1,653	7/1/86	4,092	12/31/93	4,210
8/1/79	1,840	12/31/86	4,157	7/1/94	3,933
12/31/79	2,000	7/1/87	4,109	12/31/94	3,954
7/1/80	2,279	12/31/87	4,165	7/1/95	3,982
12/31/80	2,551	7/1/88	4,196	12/31/95	4,016
7/1/81	2,678	12/31/88	4,268	7/1/96	4,033
12/31/81	2,901	7/1/89	4,234	12/31/96	4,079
7/1/82	3,149	12/31/89	4,178	7/1/97	3,875
12/31/82	3,371	7/1/90	4,193	12/31/97	3,844
7/1/83	3,461	12/31/90	4,172		

PAC Financial Statistics, 1985–96

Election Cycle	Number of Committees	Total Receipts	Total Disbursements	Contributions to Candidates	Cash on Hand	Debts Owed By
1995–96	4,528	$437,372,321	$429,887,819	$217,830,619	$103,907,879	$13,111,507
1993–94	4,621	391,760,117	388,102,643	189,631,119	98,967,582	11,464,190
1991–92	4,727	385,530,507	394,785,896	188,927,768	95,155,888	11,957,810
1989–90	4,677	372,091,977	357,648,557	159,121,496	103,340,543	10,792,690
1987–88	4,832	384,617,093	364,201,275	159,243,241	88,963,751	12,009,463
1985–86	4,596	353,429,266	339,954,146	139,839,718	69,062,430	11,565,877

PAC Contributions by Candidate Type, 1992–96

Candidate Type	Cycle	Total
SENATE	1996	$45,641,623
	1994	47,196,702
	1992	51,205,020
Democrat	1996	$16,605,499
	1994	23,955,911
	1992	28,973,303
Incumbent	1996	$ 4,873,675
	1994	15,891,665
	1992	17,070,600
Challenger	1996	$2,670,502
	1994	2,474,486
	1992	6,227,442
Open Seat	1996	$9,061,322
	1994	5,589,760
	1992	5,675,261
Republican	1996	$29,033,095
	1994	23,211,875
	1992	22,219,967
Incumbent	1996	$14,485,778
	1994	10,457,836
	1992	14,810,622
Challenger	1996	$4,274,053
	1994	3,229,798
	1992	3,137,785
Open Seat	1996	$10,273,264
	1994	9,524,241
	1992	4,271,560
Other	1996	$ 3,029
	1994	28,916
	1992	11,750
HOUSE	1996	$155,805,330
	1994	132,395,687
	1992	127,439,240
Democrat	1996	$77,326,480
	1994	88,178,729
	1992	85,389,334
Incumbent	1996	$49,846,685
	1994	71,130,142
	1992	64,298,838
Challenger	1996	$16,547,676
	1994	6,201,368
	1992	7,697,603

Candidate Type	Cycle	Total
(HOUSE cont.)		
Open Seat	1996	$10,932,119
	1994	10,847,219
	1992	13,392,893
Republican	1996	$77,700,042
	1994	43,938,099
	1992	41,748,665
Incumbent	1996	$63,841,672
	1994	29,998,362
	1992	29,962,960
Challenger	1996	$4,722,724
	1994	6,503,329
	1992	4,395,283
Open Seat	1996	$9,135,646
	1994	7,436,408
	1992	7,390,422
Other	1996	$778,808
	1994	278,859
	1992	301,241
Incumbent	1996	$246,447
	1994	261,538
	1992	146,482
Challenger	1996	$118,120
	1994	6,847
	1992	144,923
Open Seat	1996	$414,241
	1994	10,474
	1992	9,836
PRESIDENT	1996	$2,441,970
	1994	0
	1992	816,563
Democrat	1996	$ 29,935
	1994	0
	1992	726,490
Republican	1996	$2,410,770
	1994	0
	1992	90,073
Other	1996	$1,265
	1994	0
	1992	0

(Continued on next page)

Candidate Type	Cycle	Total
SUMMARY		
Incumbent	1996	$133,324,192
	1994	127,739,543
	1992	126,289,502
Challenger	1996	$28,336,104
	1994	18,444,744
	1992	21,614,786
Open Seat	1996	$39,816,592
	1994	33,408,102
	1992	30,739,972
Democrat	1996	$ 93,961,914
	1994	112,134,640
	1992	115,089,127

Candidate Type	Cycle	Total
(SUMMARY cont.)		
Republican	1996	$109,143,907
	1994	67,149,974
	1992	64,058,705
Other	1996	$783,102
	1994	307,775
	1992	312,991
Total	1996	$203,888,923
	1994	179,592,389
	1992	179,460,823

Leadership PACs

Rank	PAC	Currently Affiliated with	1993–94 Total	1995–96 Total	1997 Total	Grand Total
1	Campaign America	Former Vice President Dan Quayle	$605,759	$829,971	$21,685	$1,457,415
2	Effective Government Committee	Rep. Richard A. Gephardt, D-Mo.	704,596	461,095	13,500	1,179,191
3	Monday Morning PAC	Rep. Newt Gingrich, R-Ga.	-	766,500	10,000	776,500
4	Majority Leader's Fund	Rep. Dick Armey, R-Texas	-	737,558	10,500	748,058
5	Americans for a Republican Majority	Rep. Tom DeLay, R-Texas	227,627	222,059	118,750	568,436
6	New Republican Majority Fund	Sen. Trent Lott, R-Miss.	-	410,142	107,499	517,641
7	Leadership America	Former Rep. Charlie Rose, D-N.C.	511,500	(11,000)	-	500,500
8	Republican Majority Fund	Sen. Don Nickles, R-Okla.	21,500	390,676	55,997	468,173
9	Adam Smith PAC	Sen. Connie Mack, R-Fla.	-	320,000	95,000	415,000
10	Senate Victory Fund	Sen. Thad Cochran, R-Miss.	98,655	283,711	5,000	387,366
11	Continue the Majority	Rep. Bill McCollum, R-Fla.	299,238	55,042	-	354,280
12	Freedom Project	Rep. John Boehner, R-Ohio	-	210,221	142,996	353,217
13	Victory USA	Rep. Vic Fazio, D-Calif.	134,000	166,550	13,500	314,050
14	Capitol Committee	Sen. Orrin Hatch, R-Utah	-	292,000	19,000	311,000
15	Alliance for American Leadership	Dick Cheney	178,250	91,900	-	270,150
16	Fund for Democratic Leadership	Rep. Bob Matsui, D-Calif.	126,000	113,000	-	239,000
17	Fight-PAC	Sen. Rick Santorum, R-Pa.	-	227,500	5,000	232,500
18	Renew America PAC	Sen. Alfonse M. D'Amato, R-N.Y.	48,500	125,500	17,500	191,500
19	Empire Majority Leadership Fund	Rep. Bill Paxon, R-N.Y. and former Rep. Susan Molinari, R-N.Y.	-	92,500	65,558	158,058
20	Republican Fund for the 90's	Lamar Alexander	78,649	79,250	-	157,899
21	Re-Elect Freshmen of the Republican Majority	Rep. Jerry Weller, R-Ill.	-	118,000	33,500	151,500
22	Committee for Responsible Government	Gov. Christine T. Whitman, R-N.J.	10,000	84,500	47,000	141,500
23	AmeriPAC: The Fund for a Greater America	Rep. Steny H. Hoyer, D-Md.	40,800	93,000	-	133,800
24	Chief Deputy Whip's Fund	Former Rep. Bill Richardson, D-N.M.	75,250	52,864	-	128,114
25	House Leadership Fund	Former Rep. Thomas Foley, D-Wash.	112,865	3,510	-	116,375
26	Victory America	Former Gov Carroll Campbell, R-S.C.	98,250	7,000	250	105,500
27	Fund for a Responsible Future	Rep. Thomas J. Bliley Jr., R-Va.	-	97,224	8,000	105,224
28	Committee for a Progressive Congress	Rep. David R. Obey, D-Wis.	62,693	25,500	10,000	98,193
29	Committee for a Democratic Majority	Sen. Edward M. Kennedy, D-Mass.	-	50,500	39,000	89,500
30	Faith, Family & Freedom PAC	Rep. David M. McIntosh, R-Ind.	-	85,250	-	85,250
31	Democrats for Economic Recovery	Lyndon LaRouche	-	82,100	-	82,100
32	Modern PAC	Former Rep. Bill Green, R-N.Y.	28,000	47,500	1,500	77,000
33	Leadership for America	Sen. Phil Gramm, R-Texas	33,166	39,500	918	73,584
34	Participation 2000	Former Gov. Richard Celeste, D-Ohio	23,949	39,650	2,811	66,410
35	GOPAC	Rep. John Shadegg, R-Ariz.	20,059	39,739	6,306	66,104
36	96 Leadership PAC	Rep. Michael G. Oxley, R-Ohio	-	57,000	8,000	65,000
37	Republican Leader's Fund	Former Rep. Bob Michel, R-Ill.	64,000	1,000	-	65,000
38	Rangel National Leadership PAC	Rep. Charles B. Rangel, D-N.Y.	-	62,805	2,000	64,805
39	Committee for a Democratic Consensus	Former Sen. Alan Cranston, D-Calif.	30,000	33,750	1,000	64,750
40	29th Congressional District of California PAC	Rep. Henry A. Waxman, D-Calif.	14,000	40,500	-	54,500
41	Congressional Black Caucus PAC	Rep. Chaka Fattah, D-Pa.	17,500	30,500	-	48,000
42	Washington Fund	Rep. Jennifer Dunn, R-Wash.	-	47,000	500	47,500
43	DiFrancesco 93		19,304	27,000	-	46,304
44	Committee for a Livable Future	Rep. Earl Blumenauer, D-Ore.	-	35,000	10,000	45,000
45	House Majority Fund	Rep. John Lewis, D-Ga.	-	43,000	-	43,000
46	People Helping People	Rep. Maxine Waters, D-Calif.	11,500	25,000	-	36,500
47	Oregon Smith Fund	Rep. Bob Smith, R-Ore.	2,408	31,000	-	33,408

(Continued on next page)

Rank	PAC	Currently Affiliated with	1993–94 Total	1995–96 Total	1997 Total	Grand Total
48	Rhode Island PAC	Rep. Patrick J. Kennedy, D-R.I.	-	$31,000	-	$31,000
49	Leadership for the Future	Former Sen. Jim Sasser, D-Tenn.	$24,000	5,000	-	29,000
50	Citizens for Gary J. LaPaille		6,600	19,000	$2,875	28,475
51	Committee for Democratic Action	Former Sen. Howard Metzenbaum, D-Ohio	11,500	13,650	2,750	27,900
52	America 2000 Fund	Former Gov. Jim Thompson, R-Ill.	9,500	14,250	2,500	26,250
53	Lone Star Fund	Rep. Martin Frost, D-Texas	2,000	18,000	5,250	25,250
54	Posthumus Victory Fund USA	Mich. state Sen. Dick Posthumus, R	7,000	17,000	-	24,000
55	Leadership for America Committee	Rep. Gerald B. H. Solomon, R-N.Y.	-	20,250	3,000	23,250
56	Leadership Council PAC	Former Rep. R. Lawrence Coughlin, R-Pa.	5,500	15,000	250	20,750
57	TR Fund	Sen. John I. Chafee, R-R.I./Rep. John A. Boehner, R-Ohio	-	15,650	625	16,275
58	Spirit of America	Sen. John Ashcroft, R-Mo.	-	15,000	322	15,322
59	Liberty PAC	Rep. Ron Paul, R-Texas	-	-	15,000	15,000
60	Grassroots Victory Fund	Former Sen. Larry Pressler, R-S.D.	2,300	10,960	1,000	14,260
61	Defend America PAC	Sen. Richard C. Shelby, R-Ala.	-	-	13,500	13,500
62	Time Future Inc	Former Sen. Bill Bradley, D-N.J.	-	14,000	(500)	13,500
63	Freedom Leadership PAC	Oliver North	12,020	1,250	-	13,270
64	Al Swift Congress PAC	Former Rep. Al Swift, D-Wash.	11,000	2,256	-	13,256
65	Pioneer PAC	Rep. John R. Kasich, R-Ohio	-	-	12,636	12,636
66	Acorn PAC	Former Rep. William Broomfield, R-Mich.	6,120	6,250	-	12,370
67	Campaign for a New American Century	Lamar Alexander	-	-	9,500	9,500
68	Citizens for a Competitive America	Sen. Ernest F. Hollings, D-S.C.	6,500	2,000	-	8,500
69	Freedom & Free Enterprise PAC	Former Rep. Jack Kemp, R-N.Y.	-	-	8,000	8,000
70	America First PAC	Pat Buchanan	100	7,500	-	7,600
71	ApplePAC	Former Rep. Douglas Applegate, D-Ohio	5,250	2,000	300	7,550
72	Leadership 21	Rep. John Tanner, D-Tenn.	-	-	5,500	5,500
73	Changing Tide Committee	Sen. Wayne Allard, R-Colo.	-	-	5,000	5,000
74	Fund to Keep America #1	Lewis Lehrman	-	5,000	-	5,000
75	HHH Fund	Hubert Humphrey III	2,750	2,000	-	4,750
76	Big Tent PAC	Sen. Arlen Specter, R-Pa.	1,500	3,000	-	4,500
77	Henry J. Nowak PAC	Former Rep. Henry J Nowak, D-N.Y.	1,350	2,200	-	3,550
78	Bluegrass Committee	Sen. Mitch McConnell, R-Ky.	1,055	2,000	-	3,055
79	Citizens for the Republic	Ronald Reagan	1,000	2,000	-	3,000
80	Committee for America's Future	Sen. Robert C. Byrd, D-W.Va.	-	-	2,883	2,883
81	97th Club Campaign Committee	Rep. David Dreier, R-Calif.	-	-	2,228	2,228
82	Progressive Politics Network	Sen. Paul Wellstone, D-Minn.	-	-	1,785	1,785
83	American Renewal PAC	Rep. J. C. Watts, R-Okla.	-	-	1,250	1,250
84	Catch the Spirit PAC	Former Sen. Bob Kasten, R-Wis.	-	-	1,000	1,000
85	Invest for America	Former Rep. Bill Baker, R-Calif.	-	-	1,000	1,000

Total PAC Contributions by Candidate Type, 1993–94 and 1995–96

	1993–94	*1995–96*
Incumbents	$136,564,075	$145,525,543
Challengers	17,803,243	28,527,304
Open Races	29,381,342	39,304,061

Business PAC Contributions by Party, 1993–94 and 1995–96

	1993–94	*1995–96*
Republicans	$61,898,072	$100,111,320
Democrats	64,095,923	43,570,056

Overall Contributions, 1993–94 and 1995–96

	1993–94	*1995–96*
Business	$126,775,785	$143,737,627
Labor	42,056,377	48,839,429
Ideological	14,960,175	20,564,299
Other	339,987	471,186
Unknown	2,971	169,147

GEOGRAPHIC INDEX

Colorado

Connecticut

Delaware

District of Columbia

Florida

Georgia

Hawaii

Idaho

Illinois

Indiana

Iowa

Michigan

Minnesota

Mississippi

Missouri

Montana

Nebraska

Nevada

New Hampshire

New Jersey

New Mexico

New York

North Carolina

North Dakota

Ohio

Rhode Island

South Carolina

South Dakota

Tennessee

Texas

Washington

West Virginia

Wisconsin

Wyoming

NAME INDEX

SPONSOR/PAC INDEX

Entries in **Bold** indicate the sponsoring organizations. Entries beginning with "The" are indexed under "T."